CONTENTS

DEDICATION

To Gregory Bateson
1904 - 1980

A pioneer in anthropology, psychology, cybernetics, and epistemology, he always called himself a biologist.

If I could count on Gregory's company in heaven, and I could get to heaven by being good, I'd be good.
— Stewart Brand

COVERS

"Got the Earth upside down, eh?" said astronaut Rusty Schweickart when he saw the front cover. "Worse than that," we replied. "Check the back cover. The Earth is sideways." Indeed, two conventions collide on the back cover. North is always supposed to be up, but the horizon is always supposed to be, aha, horizontal. Can't do both.

We inverted the front cover image so the titles would be more readable against the white dazzle of Antarctica, so a too-familiar image could be seen afresh, and so the viewer might be reminded that the Earth is not a map. Adrift in orbit, most of the time you would see Earth any old which way. This particular snapshot was taken by the Apollo 17 crew in December 1972 on their way back from the Moon.

The Moon photo on the back cover was taken earlier, July 1969, during Apollo II, the original Moon landing mission. Nowhere in the solar system is the contrast between a living and a dead planet so conspicuous as on the Moon at Earthrise. —SB

PURPOSE

WE ARE AS GODS and might as well get good at it. So far remotely done power and glory — as via government, big business, formal education, church — has succeeded to the point where gross defects obscure actual gains. In response to this dilemma and to these gains a realm of intimate, personal power is developing — the power of individuals to conduct their own education, find their own inspiration, shape their own environment, and share the adventure with whoever is interested. Tools that aid this process are sought and promoted by **The Next Whole Earth Catalog**.

FUNCTION

THE **Next Whole Earth Catalog** *is an evaluation and access device. With it, the user should know better what is worth getting and where and how to do the getting.*

An item is listed in the **Catalog** *if it is deemed:*

1. *Useful as a tool,*
2. *Relevant to independent education,*
3. *High quality or low cost,*
4. *Easily available by mail.*

The listings are continually revised according to the experience and suggestions of **Catalog** *users and staff.*

PROCEDURE

WE'RE HERE TO POINT, not to sell. We have no financial or other obligation to any of the suppliers listed. (No one's ever even tried to buy us, come to think of it.) We only review stuff we think is great. Why waste your time with anything less?

To the extent this is a book of things, you can buy them, get them mail order from anywhere in the world. To the extent this is a book of ideas, they come right off the page, yours as soon as you use them.

The Next Whole Earth Catalog *completely replaces* **The Last Whole Earth Catalog** *(1971) and the* **Whole Earth Epilog** *(1974), which are no longer in print.*

Left to Right, Top to Bottom:

Evelyn, Dianna, Nancy, Stephanie, Andrea, Lorrie, Dick

Kathleen, David W., Anne, Patricia, Susan, Sherry, Don

Stewart, Art, Mimi, Ben, David B., Angela

Editor
Stewart Brand

Research Editor
Art Kleiner

Research
Mimi Abrams, Ben Campbell, David Burnor, David Theis, Angela Gennino, Lynn Spigel, Jeanne Campbell, Liz Fial

Art Direction
Kathleen O'Neill, David Wills

Production Editor
Anne Herbert

Paste Up
Patricia Masters, Susan Crutchfield, John Prestianni, Sherry Bass, Tom Schneider

Camera
Don Ryan

Production Traffic
Jonathan Evelegh

Typesetting
Evelyn Eldridge-Diaz, Kara Adanalian, Dianna Rolfe

Proofreading
Nancy Dunn, Stephanie Mills, Jamie Nelson

Index
Betty Berenson

Soft Technology, Nomadics Evaluations
J. Baldwin

Land Use Evaluations
Richard Nilsen, Peter Warshall, Rosemary Menninger

Craft Evaluations
Diana Sloat, Marilyn Green

Stats
Marinstat

Office Manager
Andrea Sharp

Office
Lorrie Gallagher, Dick Fugett, Annette LaBette, Isabella Kirkland, Robert Brust

Whole Earth Household Store
Charles Cagnon

Agent
John Brockman

Random House
Rob Cowley, Jason Epstein, Anthony Schulte, Peter Mollman, Marilyn Doof, Sheryl Merser, Carolyn Reidy

Negatives
Warren's Waller Press, San Francisco

Printing and Binding
Rand McNally, Hammond, Indiana

1st Printing — Sept. 1980
140,000 — Rand McNally

Distributed in the United States by Random House, Inc., New York, and simultaneously in Canada by Random House of Canada Limited, Toronto.

Portions of this book appeared previously in **Quest/80** and **New Scientist**.

Library of Congress Cataloging in Publication Data.

The Next whole earth catalog.

Includes index.
1. Manufacturers — Catalogs. 2. Handicraft — Equipment and supplies — Catalogs. I. Brand, Stewart.
TS199.N56 1980 602'.9'473 80-5316
ISBN 394-73951-5 (Random House).

The CoEvolution Quarterly ▫ Issue No. 27 ▫ September 21, 1980. Publication number USPS 077-150. Published quarterly by POINT, a California nonprofit corporation. Office of publication (editorial and subscription): P.O. Box 428, Sausalito, CA 94966 (27 Gate 5 Road). Subscriptions: $14 per year. Inquire for international air rates. Second-class postage paid at Sausalito, CA, and at additional mailing office. Claims for missing issues will not be honored later than three months after publication; foreign claims, five months.

Subscription circulation: 25,000

POSTMASTER: Please send form 3547 or 3579.

MAIL ORDER

How to Order Items in This Catalog

Consider these points of mail-order etiquette essential. They'll make shopping by mail more pleasant for you, and they make work much lighter at the companies you're dealing with. This advice is distilled from the requests of hundreds of small firms we're listing, plus our own experience doing mail order for the past 12 years.

1. **Send payment.** *Most of the companies we list can't handle billing you later. Cash or stamps are no good. Checks or money orders made out to the company's name are best. If you're buying expensive products like music synthesizers or solar collectors, they usually come with catalogs which describe credit terms if there are any.*

2. **Say what you want on the outside of the envelope.** *Write "mail order" or "catalog request" or "subscription order" under the address. Why should several people have to look at a letter which only one person needs to see? That's how things get lost.*

3. **Expect prices to go up.** *The prices given in this first edition of the* **Next Catalog** *are accurate for summer 1980, and will doubtless climb in step with inflation. Most publishers and firms will write you back if you've sent too little money. Some will bill for the extra amount.*

4. **Expect prices to be higher if you live outside the U.S.** *A fair rule of thumb is to add a dollar or two if you live in Canada or Mexico, and add two or three dollars if you live outside North America. If you live overseas it's often best to write for the price. Enclose International Reply Coupons and a self-addressed envelope if you do.*

5. **Don't send U.S. checks or money overseas.** *It costs, for instance, a British firm $4 to cash a $2 U.S. check. Send International Reply Coupons, which you can buy at any post office. Since foreign exchange rates fluctuate, we've listed foreign prices in the foreign currencies, with an approximate U.S. equivalent for 1980.*

6. **Pay sales tax.** *It's only needed if you live in the same state as the firm you're ordering from. You should know what it is in your state. If you leave it out, some companies will fill the order anyway; others won't.*

7. **Use order numbers where we've listed them.** *For the Government Printing Office and the National Technical Information Service, for example, they're essential.*

8. **Be patient!** *It always takes at least a week or two for your goods to arrive; a month's wait is normal. You shouldn't worry unless it's taken more than two months. Keep a record of the date of purchase and a xerox or record of your check, so that if your order is lost, you can inquire with polite and detailed specifics. Include your full address and zip code every time you write.*

9. **Be gentle!** *Don't write to keep your mailbox full. Some businesses listed in the* **Last Whole Earth Catalog** *got swamped by curiosity mail and had to shut down. Write for information on the tools you think you'll use. If you write for free information, send a stamped self-addressed envelope or stamps to cover the return postage. When complaining about poor service, be aware that the person handling your complaint is almost never the same person who loused up your order, so wrath doesn't help.*

10. **Don't order from excerpts from catalogs that we review.** *When we are reviewing a catalog we often print excerpts from it. The prices in those excerpts are frequently out of date even as we print them. Unreasonable behavior around such orders has led several large firms we reviewed in the* **Last Whole Earth Catalog** *to refuse to participate in this one. Request a current catalog from suppliers before ordering.*

Information Currency

This first edition of **The Next Whole Earth Catalog** *was put together April — September, 1980. All price and access information was exhaustively checked. It will decay at the usual rate until next edition. The same goes for item evaluations.*

WHOLE EARTH HOUSEHOLD STORE

Founded along with the original **Whole Earth Catalog** *in 1968, in Menlo Park, California, it was then "The Whole Earth Truck Store." Now taken over and run by the San Francisco Zen Center, it has the new name and a splendid new location in the "arts park" of Fort Mason in San Francisco* *(see map, p. 594).*

Wherever you see the phrase

or Whole Earth
Household Store

under an item, that means you can mail order it from

Whole Earth Household Store
Fort Mason Center, Bldg. D
San Francisco, CA 94123

probably at the price indicated (allow for inflation). With each whole order add $2 for shipping and handling — same $2 whether you're getting 1 book or 20 (except for foreign orders).

The service is here strictly as a convenience. You can always get items from the original suppliers. With the Household Store you can group your orders, and you may well get faster and better service (we'll see). Almost certainly the Household Store will have books your local bookstore never stocks. **The Next Whole Earth Catalog** *has no more financial relation with the Household Store than with any other supplier — though Bookstore Charlie does keep us supplied with pastries from the Zen Center bakery, and we probably will share mailing list information. (Neither of us sells our lists.)*

An order form and envelope insert (blue) for the Whole Earth Household Store may be found in the back of the **Catalog**. *There is also more ordering information on p. 594.*

COEVOLUTION

"A regular periodical with **Whole Earth Catalog** *type information by the same people? Great! How often does* **CoEvolution Quarterly** *come out? Oh. Heh heh."*

Right, every three months, "quarterly," we do another 144-page issue, devoid of ads, full of review-and-access, articles, cartoons (R. Crumb and Dan O'Neill), and whatever else we find remarkable. Is there a unifying theme? No. I guess that's the unifying theme.

Over one third of what you see in this **Next Whole Earth Catalog** *first appeared in some form in* **CoEvolution**. *Circulation at present is about 40,000. If you want to make it about 40,001, here's how.*

CoEvolution Quarterly
Stewart Brand, Editor
$14 /year (4 issues) from:
CoEvolution Quarterly
Box 428
Sausalito, CA 94966

There is an order form (ivory) for **CoEvolution Quarterly** *and* **CQ** *maps, books, and products in the back of the* **Catalog**.

CONTRIBUTING TO COEVOLUTION AND LATER CATALOG EDITIONS

We pay for everything we print, including complaint letters. You get $15 apiece for any letter, review, or first suggestion of an item that is published. Cartoons and photographs get $25 and up. Articles get $150 to $300, depending on importance, illustrations, clarity, and ease of handling (length doesn't count particularly).

We're told by our famous contributors that they often prefer writing for **CoEvolution** *because their material is handled with more respect by us than other magazines. The un-famous contributors say that it's easier for an unknown to get into print with* **CQ** *than elsewhere. It may be that our lack of advertising or of foundation backing makes us more attentive to our contributors, on whom our existence depends.*

The evaluations in this **Catalog** *are in some cases no doubt inadequate. In any case they will date at the usual rate. When you're sure that something you know is better than what we've run, have at us, so that the next* **Next Catalog** *may be more comprehensively accurate in pointing at excellence.*

Our standard advice for writing a review goes like this. Give the information you would like to get. This should include what the item is good for, how it compares with others, and some clue of how competent you are to judge. Avoid comments like "This is a good book." Prove it.

Do not rave about an item which is merely good or the best of a bad lot. Also don't waste time picking nits with the author unless the matter is something the reader has to know about. Write as you would in a letter to some specific person you respect and like. Be succinct. Your function is to introduce item and reader to each other and get out of the way. Savvy readers will make most of their judgments on samples from the item — quotes, illustrations, etc. Select good ones — bits you didn't know before, bits that contain the item's essence, bits that pass on a whole useable idea. Study some reviews and excerptings in this **Catalog**. *Do better.*

Suppliers are invited to suggest their own goods. Samples or review copies are welcomed; response not predictable. We accept no payment for a listing and offer none. We owe accurate information exchange to suppliers, period.

Write to

CoEvolution Quarterly
Box 428
Sausalito, CA 94966

PREFACE

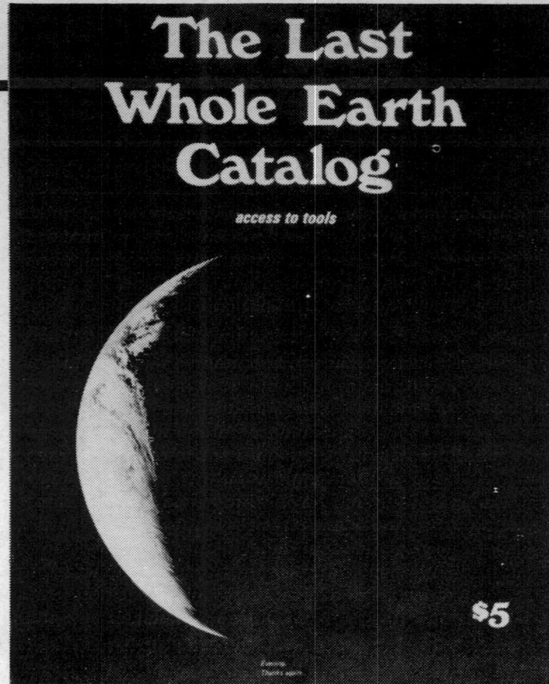

1971

THE INEVITABLE first question is always, "How much stuff from **The Last Whole Earth Catalog** is repeated in this **Next Whole Earth Catalog?**"

The answer is 11%. Of the approximately 2700 items in the **Next Catalog**, 300 are carryovers from the **Last Catalog** (1971).* That surprised us. We had expected there would be 30% repetition. The other surprise was how much is reviewed for the first time in the **Next Catalog** — not 10%, as we had predicted, but 36%, about 975 brand new items. From the **Whole Earth Epilog** (1974), 17% (450 items) are repeats. The remaining 36% (another 975) of items are updated from various issues of **CoEvolution Quarterly** since 1974. We do not regard "new" as necessarily "good," but it turned out to be better than we thought.

The inevitable second question is, "What's different?" (Why does anyone care? I guess because 1,600,000 copies of the **Last Whole Earth Catalog** sold, and "Whole Earth" became a generic name for a frame of mind and somewhat for a generation and historic time. Historic time now past. The hidden question is, "Is Whole Earth now a quaint anachronism, or is it once again a detailed sign of the times?")

Leaving the interpretation to you, here are some things that are different. In 1971 we listed (and could only list) 2 items on solar energy — the Solar Energy Society and Farrington Daniels' 1964 classic **Direct Use of the Sun's Energy**. In 1980 we're reviewing 63 solar items (pp. 182 - 195) — the cream of the cream of hundreds of solar goodies we've seen. [Good old Farrington Daniels (on p. 187) is still among the 63.]

The **Last Catalog** had 2 pages about computers. The **Next Catalog** has 12 pages (pp. 528 - 539) — calculators, home computers, computer networks, computer games, robotics, and computer futureness, all operable directly from the household. Computers and solar are only two of the domains that have taken off recently, with us flapping hard to fly in front of them. Others prominent in the **Next Catalog** include: space colonies (pp. 16 - 18), trees-as-solution-to-everything (pp. 77 - 89), wood heat (pp. 203 - 210) (there were half a dozen woodstove manufacturers in 1971; now there are over 400), underground architecture (pp. 240 - 241), old building preservation (pp. 235 - 236), urban homesteading (pp. 294 - 295), medical self-care and fitness (pp. 318 - 319, 321 - 324), care of the dying (pp. 330 - 332), hand gliding and wind-surfing (pp. 455 and 457), video (pp. 492 - 493), and the junior obsessive Role Playing Games such as "Dungeons & Dragons" (pp. 549 - 550).

There are even a couple of subjects where we got honest-to-God scoops — hot news not even we have printed before. One is our coverage of coppicing, a practice which is traditional all over Europe and completely unheard-of in America. It may be the most efficient producer of biomass alive. By taking advantage of certain species of trees that constantly re-sprout from the stump, says our author, a family of four can generate all the firewood it needs forever from a space 64 feet by 64 feet (p. 84). Then there's "amateur insemination," the rapidly growing practice among lesbians to make themselves pregnant without benefit of intercourse or M.D.s. As usual, we give the technical details of how to do it (p. 345).

Some subjects have diminished. Domes have practically disappeared. Though ingenious and efficient with materials, they proved quite difficult for amateur builders, and their notorious leaking taught a generation about redundancy. Any pinhole in the single skin of domes lets in rain, whereas the quadruple redundancy of shingles doesn't. As Steve Baer of Zomeworks (pp. 190 - 191) remarked about his much-photographed dome home in Albuquerque, New Mexico, "It came down to a question of blowing up our house or our marriage, or shingling." They shingled.

Free schools are mostly gone, replaced by more interest in home teaching and by conservatism generally. Neil Postman's **Teaching As a Subversive Activity** in the **Last Catalog** has been replaced by the same author's 1979 book **Teaching As a Conserving Activity** (p. 567). China, which had a whole 8-page section in the **Whole Earth Epilog**, is absent this time around, except as a goal for travel. After discussion with our Young China Hand Orville Schell (**Working in China**), we concluded that roles have reversed since Deng Xaoping supplanted Mao. Six years ago China was the model for radical America; now America is the model for technical and economic China. Another cultural survey that wasn't updated was our **Epilog** 4-page coverage of "Black Interest." For decades the tireless leader of the nation in civil rights and the arts, black culture seems to be getting a deserved rest these days.

The most conspicuous change to us in this **Catalog** is its very fabric. It is better designed and tighter in every respect, obviously in the layout of the pages, less obviously in the thoroughness of the research. Since I'm the same editor as before, all of that is clearly due to the skill and diligence of the people I'm privileged to work with (cliché but true). And though it's been more arduous, to put it mildly — five months for many of us without a day off — this has also been far the happiest of our productions. Another element, I realize, is the sheer accumulation of experience. **The Last Whole Earth Catalog** summarized three years. The **Whole Earth Epilog** was made in only nine months. This **Next Catalog** is the culmination of all twelve years of our evaluating and publishing.

Some of that span is visible even in conversation around the office. The **Next Catalog** project got going to a large degree because young (26) journalism graduate Art Kleiner wanted to work with **CoEvolution** and the only job I could think of was compiler of a new **Catalog**. One day early in production he approached typesetter Evelyn Eldridge-Diaz with some urgent advice on typing access. As Evelyn gazed at him patiently, Production Editor Anne Herbert observed drily, "Art, Evelyn was typesetting the **Whole Earth Catalog** when you were in tenth grade." Another typical exchange: Evelyn — ". . . She also advocates painting designs on your face with your menstrual blood and dancing around on moonlight nights with your friends. Hi, Art." Art — "I think I like it better on nights without a moon."

The Last Whole Earth Catalog was aimed at one audience, the menstrual blood painters of the late '60s and early '70s, though a lot of other people tuned in. This **Next Catalog** hopes it might be useful to three audiences. 1) Our contemporaries, who have aged into positions of responsibility (one of us governs California) with most of our generation's premises surprisingly intact and most of us still interested in acquiring more skills. 2) The new college age population, with its unusual ability (its artists, for example, routinely outclass the show-offs of the '60s) and its apparent lack of confidence to entrepreneur its own road. 3) The vast citizenry that has had it with inflation, people who are rapidly finding that when you fix or build your own house (car, education, body, community), you deal in uninflated coin, your time, and don't get taxed for the transaction.

Some among us foresee deep economic hardship soon. (I don't; Random House Editor-in-Chief Jason Epstein does; our tool and financial reviewer Paul Hawken says credit collapse in 1983 but we'll get over it.) I'm editing the **Next Catalog** because I think people have the affluence and time to use the book to refine their lives. Jason is distributing it because he thinks people will need it to save their lives. What's your excuse?

Put another way, "What's going on?" I like this note I got recently from our local Zen abbot, Richard Baker-roshi. "Japan is a 'thought' that provides for one hundred million people. The Victorian Age is a thought — reflected and reinforced in the first abundance of industrial goods. What is the thought of our age? Could an unthinkable age be a virtue?"

One thing that seems clear about our age is that the do-it-yourself approach to everything is still steadily increasing. Hardware stores and how-to book publishing are booming. In view of that growing market, there are some disturbing dysfunctions on the supply side. Excellent carpentry and gardening tools exist, for example, but it is nearly impossible for the amateur to get them. The reason apparently is this. There are so many sales steps between the manufacturer and the consumer that there is no evaluative feedback. Local keep-the-stock-turning hardware chains carry only cheap tools. If you ask for, say, an outstanding (though more expensive) Blue Grass hammer, the clerk has never heard of it and doesn't want to, and the question has no way to get through the clerk, manager, jobber, etc. to worry the manufacturer. Only professional carpenters can get Blue Grass hammers, usually only through wholesale dealers (p. 135). Though some beginnings are under way, mail order suppliers have yet to meet this market opportunity.

Something similar has gone wrong in book publishing. Every day of working on this **Catalog** we were maddened to learn that several invaluable books had been let go out of print. Many we dropped; many we ran anyway with the plea "Get this book back in print!" (Hm. A small publisher might do worse than republish just

*I hasten to footnote that the repeated items are thoroughly reworked to reflect recent editions or issues and any change in our evaluation of their standing amid the competition. As a result almost no review or set of excerpts is identical to what was in the **Last Catalog**.

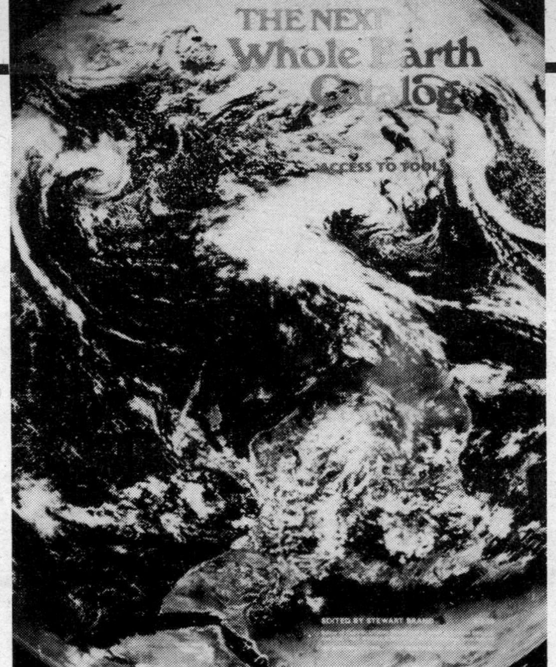

1980

those fifty or so books.) Again it's the fast-buck, quantity-kills-quality syndrome. Small publishing houses make their living by keeping slow-but-steady selling books on the market. The big houses make their killing by dropping a book as soon as its sales fall below a certain point. As a publicity lady at Crown put it, "Why are you reviewing our old books? Didn't you get the new ones we sent you?" Yes, lady, we did. They were inferior. Please keep the good ones in print, and revised, and promoted, and appreciated for the reputation they've made for your house.

*It's an idle sermon. Staff turnover is so rapid in big time publishing, continuity doesn't have a chance. In 1977 we made an elaborate contract for co-publishing with Penguin and put out two books with them (***Space Colonies** *and* **Soft Tech***). Two years later they had had so many new generations of senior people that no one even knew we had a contract. When shown the thing, they had zero interest in honoring it. (Apart from the decision-level discontinuity, our relationship with Penguin was an excellent one.)*

Large scale boom and bust. Small scale adaptability. From tool distribution to publishing to farming to neighborhood preservation, there is no doubt this is the major theme of the **Whole Earth Catalog***. It's in our own history. Though we are now distributed through New York, there's no way in hell we could have started in New York. Our first* **Catalogs** *(1968 - 1970) were made by three hippies in a garage and distributed by a local long-hair wholesaler (Bookpeople, Berkeley). We still are self-published. And New York tells us* **The Last Whole Earth Catalog** *invented the trade paperback. Interesting.*

The Last Catalog *enjoyed uniformly favorable notices, but, um (open wide, please, Gift Horse), their frequent superficiality is worth a look. We were touted as the voice of Back-to-the-Land and linked commonly with (the to us rather odious)* **Mother Earth News***. Back-to-Basics certainly is a major point we make, but so is Onward-and-Upward (space, computers, electronic music), and Outward-in-All-Directions-So-Long-As-It-Doesn't-Hurt-Anybody-Probably.*

*What I'm trying to get at is, the American reviewing apparatus is not good at reference books, which tend to be treated (as we were and probably will be) as news items, if at all. The sensational first two volumes (***Northwest** *and* **California***) of the Smithsonian's* **Handbook of North American Indians** *(p. 45) have been out since 1978 and reviewed nowhere. In the course of researching opinion on our favorite dictionary,* **The American Heritage Dictionary** *(p. 498), I had to rely on technical library publications from R.R. Bowker to find any insightful critique.*

I expect that many reviewers of **The Next Catalog** *will, as I probably would, settle for reviewing this preface, making a few observations about the passing and coming of decades, and letting it go at that. That's fine, and thank you, but it leaves unaddressed the question of whether the* **Next Catalog** *is any use as a tool. Actually that can be accomplished by two quick probes. Look up a subject area you know something about and see whether our reviewers know as much or more than you do or anyway enough. And look up a subject area unknown to you and see whether we can get you interested in it.*

I probably shouldn't knock American reviewing practice too much, because its failings are our stock in trade, but does anyone else think it odd that mail order suppliers are almost never critiqued in print? Or that magazines are noticed by other magazines only when they die? Or that the truly classic books in most fields don't have primary reviews to urge them on?

Consider the various experiences of three classic classics. Wolfgang Langewiesche's 1944 introduction to flying, **Stick and Rudder** *(p. 459), is so graceful and imaginative and fundamental that it has needed no revision to remain the leading text in its field. Because it lives robustly on unreviewed, people at large have no way of knowing that the wisdom of the book, like* **Zen and the Art of Archery***, reaches far outside its specialty.*

For contrast there's John Muir's **How to Keep Your Volkswagen Alive***. An intelligent, entertaining, amateur and self-published work, it got the* **Whole Earth Catalog** *treatment when it came out in 1969 — full page review in* **Life***, etc. As a result the book is in its 21st printing (p. 406), with sales over 1.3 million, and it has inspired a whole literature by now of imaginative how-to books.*

But then there's **A Pattern Language***, 1977, by Christopher Alexander (p. 217). It enjoys such biblical status among architects and designers that they refer to its rules by number. "15" means "Encourage the formation of a boundary around each neighborhood." "160" means "Treat the edge of a building as a 'thing,' a 'place,' a zone with volume to it." It's a book that should be in the hands of every citizen, city dweller, home builder, office worker. It's the only book in the* **Next Catalog** *that has a whole page all to itself. But since hardly anyone else is reviewing it to the general public, its best use (by amateurs) scarcely exists.*

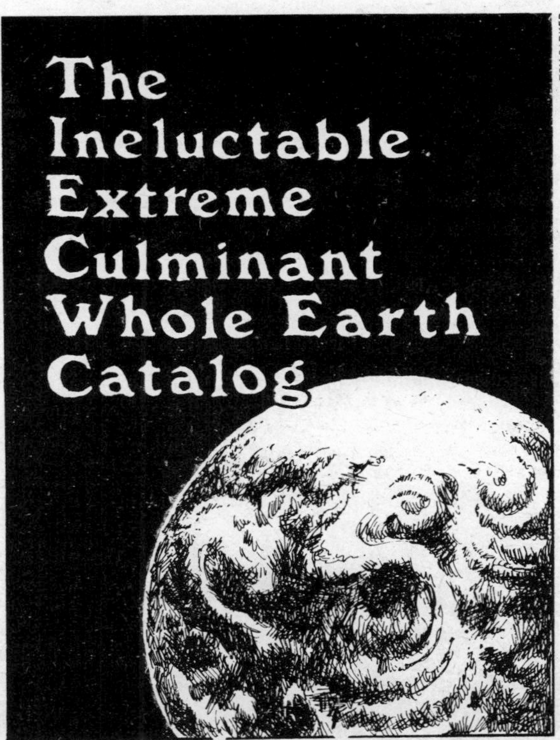

This may not seem like much right now . . . But wait 15 or 20 years, it might come in handy. —Tom Parker

Reviewing is not a particularly honored activity, for good reason, but it surely has its rewards, the most conspicuous of which is the gratitude you encounter when someone is glad you alerted them to something that made a big difference. Doug Roomian is one we read about in the newspapers. On the front page of the June 15, 1980 San Francisco **Examiner** *the "great guitar maker" told his origin story. Around 1970, while living with a group of anti-draft Americans in Canada, he "was reading the* **Whole Earth Catalog***, the magazine of the craft generation, and it had a way of making everything seem so integral — celestializing mundane jobs. Cherry picking was karmic." Our description of a book on guitar making got to him. After he returned to San Francisco he started a business where, for over $1000 an instrument, you can buy some of the best-sounding guitars anywhere. Research Editor Art Kleiner, with customary thoroughness, got in touch with the guy. You will find Doug Roomian's survey of instrument makers on pp. 474 - 475, come full circle. (Curious footnote — how come the common word for instrument maker, "luthier," is not in any dictionary?)*

We had two reporters visit at length during the assembling of the **Next Catalog***, and I watched with interest how they would be received by the overworked, overcrowded staff. Calvin Fentress, from* **Esquire** *and whom we liked a lot, always seemed to be asking each of us, "What does it all mean?" Linda Xiques, from the local weekly* **The Pacific Sun***, also had only one question, which she addressed in due course to each staff member — "What are you doing right now?" We felt that she got the better information.*

But then that's our style. We're generalists hopelessly in love with details. Fortunately for us it's also the national style, as American as cherry pie (how to cook it really well, where to find organically grown cherries, how to grow cherry trees, when to prune and pick . . .). It is karmic, isn't it?
—Stewart Brand (SB)

Rising Sun Neighborhood Newsletter

You will note that at the lower right hand corner of every spread (pair of facing pages) in this **Catalog** *there is something consistently peculiar going on. It is a gossip column. The items you see have been excerpted from two years or so of such* **Newsletters***, which are mustering toward a book. Most of the items are factual, really happened. Those in the whole latter part of the* **Catalog** *took place during the very making of the* **Catalog** *and star the makers, backstage. All part of our arch-mission to make all processes transparent.*

The author is Anne Herbert, Production Editor on this **Catalog** *and Assistant Editor of* **CoEvolution** *for several years. We got her by mail order. She wrote from Ohio, sent some writing, said we'd be glad if we hired her, so we did and we are.* *—SB*

THE RISING SUN
NEIGHBORHOOD NEWSLETTER

I was thinking that TV cameras are making us see only things kind of far away, and I was thinking that magazines are making us hear things only if they've been written down by someone we don't know, and I was thinking that newspapers are making us value only people we haven't met, so I started thinking we should start writing, drawing, painting, singing, shouting what we notice about the neighborhood right here to each other every day and maybe it will help us start to learn to treasure what we can also touch.

UNDERSTANDING WHOLE SYSTEMS means looking both larger and smaller than where our daily habits live and seeing clear through our cycles. The result is responsibility but the process is filled with the constant delight of surprise. Neither the Earth nor our lives are flat. What happened in the 20th century? The idea of self — the thing to be kept alive — expanded from the individual human to the whole Earth. —SB

Grand Design

The best book of aerial photographs ever (200 photos — half are in color). What is unique is the captioning — Gerster knows what he is floating over, or he studies it until he does. He knows the history of places, and why the farmers do odd things, and what the tribe is after, and how to keep sand dunes from covering the oasis. The book is a tour de force of form and content.

The range is so world-wide and culturally rich that no reader-flier can escape wanting to try things differently. That's the yield of perspective. I've seen no other book — not even the space satellite ones — with perspective like this.

Gerster's message comes across: if your place is beautiful from the air, it's beautiful to live in. If not, not. —SB

[Suggested by Wilson Clark and Allison Giballe]

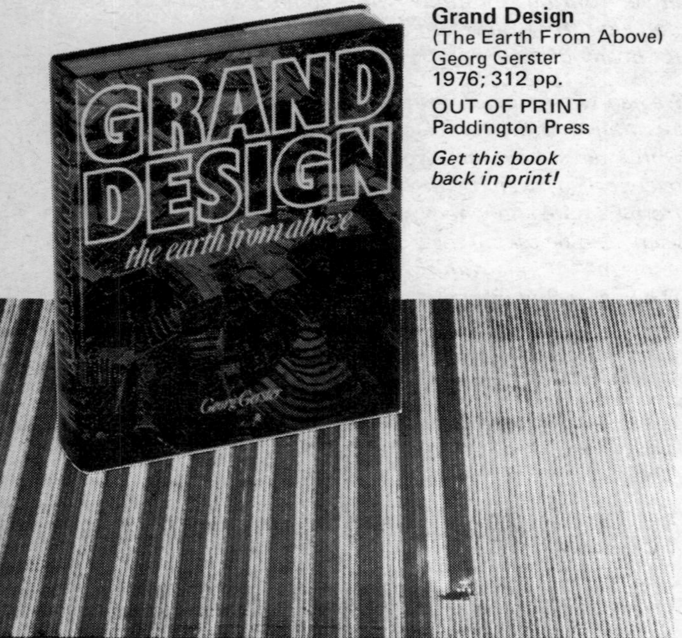

Grand Design
(The Earth From Above)
Georg Gerster
1976; 312 pp.
OUT OF PRINT
Paddington Press
Get this book back in print!

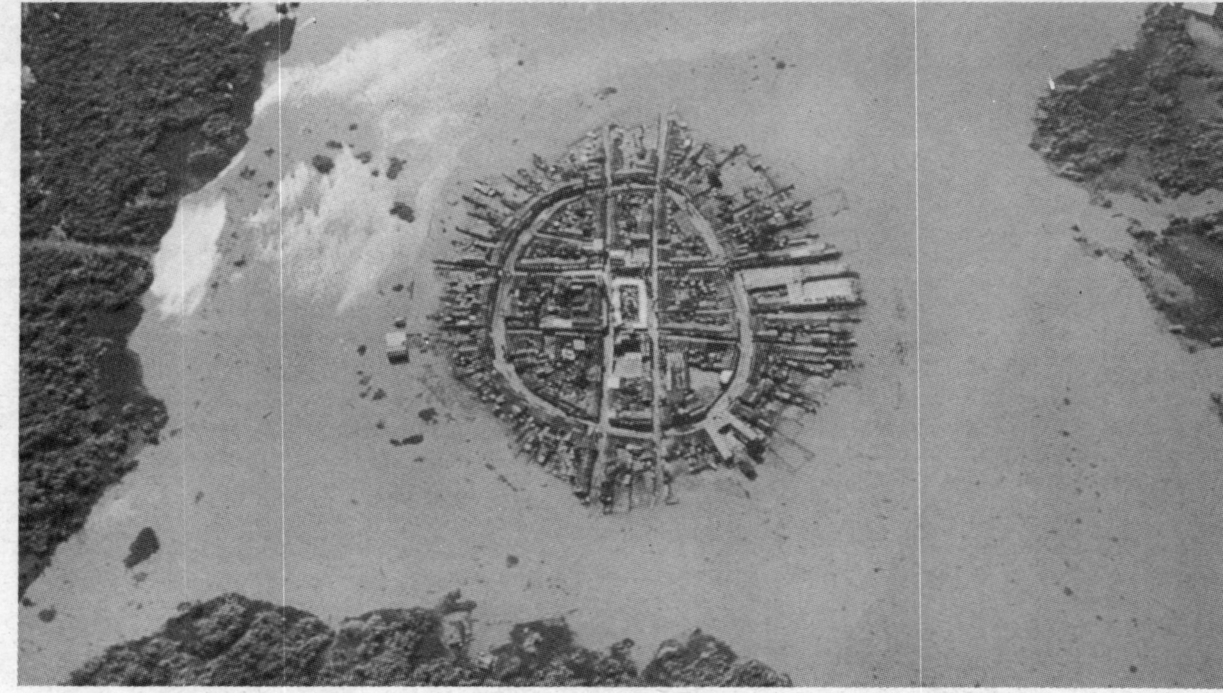

↑
Town and island of Mexcaltitán in the Mexican state of Nayarit. Mexcaltitán is situated in a lagoon on the Pacific coast, 155 miles northwest of Mexico's second largest town, Guadalajara. The shallow lagoon is alive with crabs, shrimps and fish, which are the population's main source of food and income. The settlement of the island dates back far into pre-colonial, pre-Spanish times. Some researchers even tend to equate Mexcaltitán with Aztlan, the original home of the Aztecs before they moved to their historical territories in the high valley of Mexico. Aztec legends about the origin and wandering of the tribe tell of an island in the middle of an inland lake, a paradise for fishermen and hunters of waterfowl. It is a fact that the memory of moon worship, Central America's oldest cult, lives on tenaciously in this village, and that its inhabitants are still quite convinced of the mystical-mythical significance of the circular settlement plan: for them, Mexcaltitán is the center of the universe. The cross formed by the four main streets inside the ring road that encloses the town mirrors the division of the heavens into the "world's four corners."

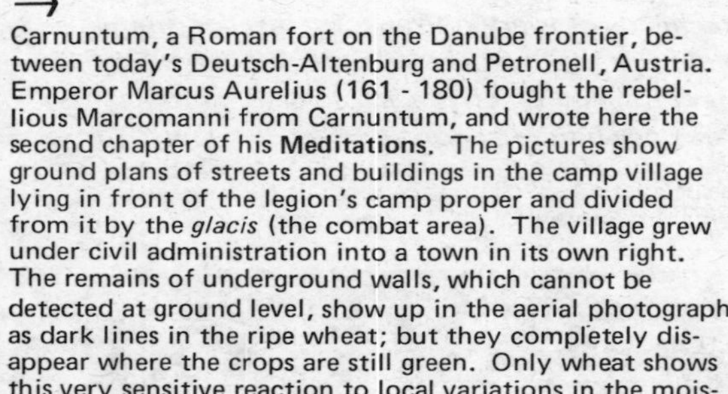

→
Carnuntum, a Roman fort on the Danube frontier, between today's Deutsch-Altenburg and Petronell, Austria. Emperor Marcus Aurelius (161 - 180) fought the rebellious Marcomanni from Carnuntum, and wrote here the second chapter of his **Meditations**. The pictures show ground plans of streets and buildings in the camp village lying in front of the legion's camp proper and divided from it by the *glacis* (the combat area). The village grew under civil administration into a town in its own right. The remains of underground walls, which cannot be detected at ground level, show up in the aerial photograph as dark lines in the ripe wheat; but they completely disappear where the crops are still green. Only wheat shows this very sensitive reaction to local variations in the moisture of the soil: the lime and mortar of the Roman walls extract moisture from the soil above them so that the plants grow less high and ripen earlier. The resolving power of this archaeological radiography is good enough to reveal underground walls only one foot thick.

↑
Vegetable growing in Imperial Valley, California, and in the New Territories, Hong Kong. Two types of fields, and two philosophies of life! In the first we see the dictate of the straight line, cultivation as subjugation, the conquest of nature by geometry. Imperial Valley as a whole is land wrested from the desert, a triumph of irrigation technology. In the second example: the Taoist philosophy of respecting and adapting oneself to the landscape, a tacit understanding with nature, agriculture as a way to cosmic harmony. Geomancy — *feng-shui* ("wind and water") — ensures that the homes of the living and the dead are in accord with the breath of the world that can be felt flowing through every landscape. A geomancer used to be called upon when a Chinese farmer wanted to fix the boundaries of new fields. The earth diviner rejected the straight line as soulless, and geometry as godless; in his opinion paths and watercourses should wind, fitting naturally into the landscape, for adaptation, not resistance, is the guarantor of good fortune.

Cosmic View

"The Universe in 40 Jumps" is the subtitle of the book. It delivers.

The man who conceived and rendered it, a Dutch schoolmaster named Kees Boeke, gave years of work to perfecting the information in his pictures. The result is one of the simplest, most thorough, inescapable mind blows ever printed. Your mind and you advance in and out through the universe, changing scale by a factor of ten. It very quickly becomes hard to breathe, and you realize how magnitude-bound we've been. —SB

Cosmic View
(The Universe in 40 Jumps)
Kees Boeke
1957; 48 pp.
$4.95 postpaid from:
The John Day Company
257 Park Avenue South
New York, NY 10010
or Whole Earth Household Store

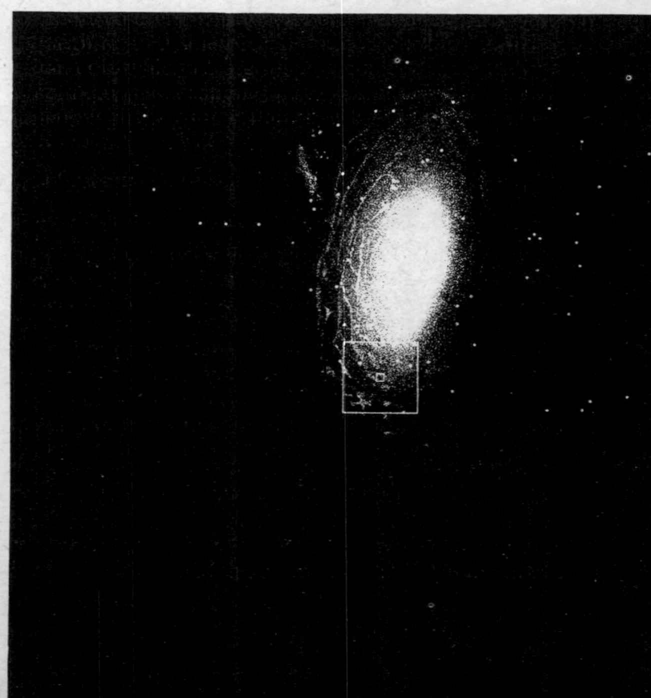

Gaia

This may turn out to be one of the epochal insights of this century: that the entire life of Earth, through its atmosphere and ocean, functions effectively as one self-regulated organism: Gaia (after the Greek Earth goddess).

Free-lance British scientist James Lovelock is the originator of the hypothesis (along with American microbiologist Lynn Margulis). As might be expected from a mind with the range to encompass the material requisite for the Gaian recognition, Lovelock writes a winning prose. This is a brief, personal, convincing performance. It even overcomes my lifelong aversion to chemistry, making fascinating sense of the difference between the chemical equilibrium of a dead planet and the chemical steady state of a live one.

Along the way Lovelock has astute criticism for some of the simplistic thinking that goes on in the environmental movement — as, for example, the premature hysteria over the effect of aerosol sprays on the ozone layer (a problem Lovelock helped discover). He notes that from Gaian perspective we are over-concerned with industrial pollution and under-concerned with protecting the integrity of the all-important tropical jungles and continental shelves of the sea. The health of Gaia is far more endangered by our agriculture than our industry.

As science and as poetry, Gaia (pronounced "gūy - a") is a major planetary self-discovery. It's likely that all our thinking will be re-oriented to accommodate the goddess.
—SB

Gaia
(A new look at life on Earth)
J.E. Lovelock
1979; 157 pp.

$11.95 postpaid from:
Oxford University Press
16 - 00 Pollitt Drive
Fair Lawn, NJ 07410
or Whole Earth Household Store

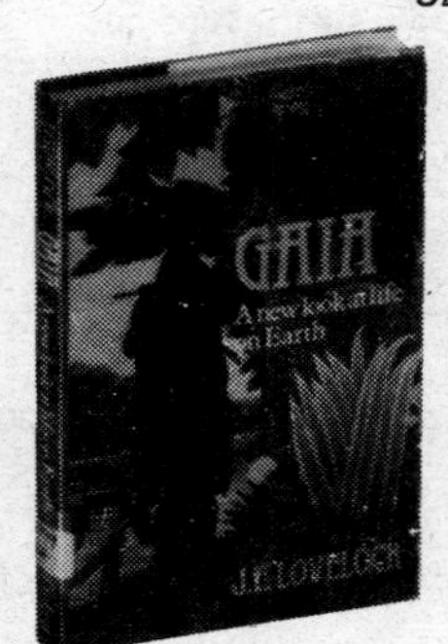

•

The start of the Gaia hypothesis was the view of the Earth from space, revealing the planet as a whole but not in detail. Ecology is rooted in down-to-Earth natural history and the detailed study of habitats and ecosystems without taking in the whole picture. The one cannot see the trees in the wood. The other cannot see the wood for the trees.

•

Considered solely as a life-detection experiment, atmospheric analysis was, if anything, too successful. Even then, enough was known about the Martian atmosphere to suggest that it consisted mostly of carbon dioxide and showed no signs of the exotic chemistry characteristic of Earth's atmosphere. The implication that Mars was probably a lifeless planet was unwelcome news to our sponsors in space research.

•

If we are a part of Gaia it becomes interesting to ask: "To what extent is our collective intelligence also a part of Gaia? Do we as a species constitute a Gaian nervous system and a brain which can consciously anticipate environmental changes?"

•

By now a planet-sized entity, albeit hypothetical, had been born, with properties which could not be predicted from the sum of its parts. It needed a name. Fortunately the author William Golding was a fellow-villager. Without hesitation he recommended that this creature be called Gaia, after the Greek Earth goddess also known as Ge, from which root the sciences of geography and geology derive their names. In spite of my ignorance of the classics, the suitability of this choice was obvious. It was a real four-lettered word and would thus forestall the creation of barbarous acronyms, such as Biocybernetic Universal System Tendency/Homeostasis. I felt also that in the days of Ancient Greece the concept itself was probably a familiar aspect of life, even if not formally expressed. Scientists are usually condemned to lead urban lives, but I find that country people still living close to the earth often seem puzzled that anyone should need to make a formal proposition of anything as obvious as the Gaia hypothesis. For them it is true and always has been.

Gas	Planet			
	Venus	Earth without life	Mars	Earth as it is
Carbon dioxide	98%	98%	95%	0.03%
Nitrogen	1.9%	1.9	2.7%	79%
Oxygen	trace	trace	0.13%	21%
Argon	0.1%	0.1%	2%	1%
Surface temperatures °C	477	290±50	−53	13
Total pressure bars	90	60	0064	1.0

Table 3. Some chemically reactive gases of the air

Gas	Abundance %	Flux in megatons per year	Extent of disequilibrium	Possible function under the Gaia hypothesis
Nitrogen	79	300	10^{10}	Pressure builder Fire extinguisher Alternative to nitrate in the sea
Oxygen	21	100,000	None. Taken as reference	Energy reference gas
Carbon dioxide	0.03	140,000	10	Photosynthesis Climate control
Methane	10^{-4}	1,000	Infinite	Oxygen regulation Ventilation of the anaerobic zone
Nitrous oxide	10^{-5}	100	10^{13}	Oxygen regulation Ozone regulation
Ammonia	10^{-6}	300	Infinite	pH control Climate control (formerly)
Sulphur gases	10^{-8}	100	Infinite	Transport gases of the sulphur cycle
Methyl chloride	10^{-7}	10	Infinite	Ozone regulation
Methyl iodide	10^{-10}	1	Infinite	Transport of iodine

Note: Infinite in column 4 means beyond limits of computation

•

Towards the end of 1975 the United States National Academy of Sciences issued a report prepared by an eight-man committee of their own distinguished members, assisted by forty-eight other scientists chosen from those expert in the effects of nuclear explosions and all things subsequent to them. The report suggested that if half of all of the nuclear weapons in the world's arsenals, about 10,000 megatons, were used in a nuclear war the effects on most of the human and man-made ecosystems of the world would be small at first and would become negligible within thirty years. Both aggressor and victim nations would of course suffer catastrophic local devastation, but areas remote from the battle and, especially important in the biosphere, marine and coastal ecosystems would be minimally disturbed.

To date, there seems to be only one serious scientific criticism of the report, namely, of the claim that the major global effect would be the partial destruction of the ozone layer by oxides of nitrogen generated in the heat of the nuclear explosions. We now suspect that this claim is false and that stratospheric ozone is not much disturbed by oxides of nitrogen. There was, of course, at the time of the report a strange and disproportionate concern in America about stratospheric ozone. It might in the end prove to be prescient, but then as now it was a speculation based on very tenuous evidence. In the nineteen-seventies it still seems that a nuclear war of major proportions, although no less horrific for the participants and their allies, would not be the global devastation so often portrayed. Certainly it would not much disturb Gaia.

The report itself was criticized then as now on political and moral grounds.

•

From a chemical viewpoint, although not in terms of abundance, the dominant gas of the air is oxygen. It establishes throughout our planet the reference level of chemical energy which makes it possible, given some combustible material, to light a fire anywhere on the Earth. It provides the chemical potential difference wide enough for birds to fly and for us to run and keep warm in winter; perhaps also to think. The present level of oxygen tension is to the contemporary biosphere what the high-voltage electricity supply is to our twentieth-century way of life. Things can go on without it, but the potentialities are substantially reduced. The comparison is a close one, since it is a convenience of chemistry to express the oxidizing power of an environment in terms of its reduction-oxidation (redox) potential, measured electrically and expressed in volts. It is in fact no more than the voltage of a hypothetical battery with one electrode in the oxygen and the other in the food.

Earth flag

The inspiration of a world saver named John McConnell, realized by an artist named Norman LaLiberte (working with an early Apollo photo), this is the only flag we've seen that excludes nobody. Looks nice, feels great. —SB

Earth Flags
$3 12" x 18"
$30 3' x 5'

from:
Earth Society Foundation
19 Troutmen Street
Brooklyn, NY 11206
or Whole Earth Household Store

Earth poster

Of the dozens of planetary posters we've seen I like this one best. Bright living blue and earthy brown, the ball shows a bit of its shadow of night against space's perpetual day.
—SB

Apollo View of the Earth
(poster)
29" x 22½"
$2.60 postpaid from:

Hanson Planetarium
Dept. A
15 South State Street
Salt Lake City, UT 84111

THE RISING SUN
NEIGHBORHOOD NEWSLETTER

I was born about ten thousand years ago and I know all the verses.

Jane's aunt became an aviator first because of getting to wear overalls and getting dirty. Had young girls been able to do this at home, as now, she is sure she would not have seen the midnight sun or the Nile.

Elizabeth the bus driver says she knows how to make crazy ladies. When a woman starts to talk a little strange or even friendly but too aggressive, don't answer her. She'll keep talking, you keep not answering and she's a crazy lady. Everyone in the bus agrees, you can feel them agreeing. Since she found this out, she has to answer everyone.

I took the ferry home from work. A drunk man sang with the foghorn, on key.

Star Maker

A man's consciousness unwillingly departs his body and his planet. Once in space he accomplishes willed travel in search of Star Maker. His journey takes him into the minds of other planetary beings; a company of these travel together and witness countless civilizations; eventually they participate in a combined consciousness of worlds that in time embraces the stars as well; this leads to galactic and cosmic consciousness and the culminating encounter with Star Maker.

Film-maker Jordan Belson, who I trust in these matters, asserts that it is a true vision, that Stapledon's whole life pointed at attaining it, and that the book will be used and discussed for centuries.

This Dover edition includes an earlier Stapledon story of similar scope, "Last and First Men." —SB

Last and First Men and Star Maker
Olaf Stapledon
1937; 188 pp.

$4 postpaid from:
Dover Books
180 Varick Street
New York, NY 10014
or Whole Earth
Household Store

•

The sheer beauty of our planet surprised me. It was a huge pearl, set in spangled ebony. It was nacreous, it was an opal. No, it was far more lovely than any jewel. Its patterned colouring was more subtle, more ethereal. It displayed the delicacy and brilliance, the intricacy and harmony of a live thing. Strange that in my remoteness I seemed to feel, as never before, the vital presence of Earth as of a creature alive but tranced and obscurely yearning to wake.

•

The sport of disembodied flight among the stars must surely be the most exhilarating of all athletic exercises. It was not without danger; but its danger, as we soon discovered, was psychological, not physical. In our bodiless state, collision with celestial objects mattered little. Sometimes, in the early stages of our adventure, we plunged by accident headlong into a star. Its interior would, of course, be inconceivably hot, but we experienced merely brilliance.

The psychological dangers of the sport were grave. We soon discovered that disheartenment, mental fatigue, fear, all tended to reduce our powers of movement. More than once we found ourselves immobile in space, like a derelict ship on the ocean; and such was the fear roused by this plight that there was no possibility of moving till, having experienced the whole gamut of despair, we passed through indifference and on into philosophic calm.

•

Though the pronoun "I" now applied to us all collectively, the pronoun "we" also applied to us. In one respect, namely unity of consciousness, we were indeed a single experiencing individual; yet at the same time we were in a very important and delightful manner distinct from one another.

•

With unreasoning passion we strove constantly to peer behind each minute particular event in the cosmos to see the very features of that infinity which, for lack of a truer name, we had called the Star Maker. But, peer as we might, we found nothing. Though in the whole and in each particular thing the dread presence indubitably confronted us, its very infinity prevented us from assigning to it any features whatever.

•

"When the cosmos wakes, if ever she does, she will find herself not the single beloved of her maker but merely a little bubble adrift on the boundless and bottomless ocean of being."

•

Almost certainly, the star's whole physical behaviour is normally experienced as a blissful, an ecstatic, an ever successful pursuit of formal beauty. This the minded worlds were able to discover through their own most formalistic aesthetic experience. In fact it was through this experience that they first made contact with stellar mind.

•

We, or rather I, now experienced the slow drift of the galaxies much as a man feels the swing of his own limbs. From my score of viewpoints I observed the great snowstorm of many million galaxies, streaming and circling, and ever withdrawing farther apart from one another with the relentless "expansion" of space. But though the vastness of space was increasing in relation to the size of galaxies and stars and worlds, to me, with my composite, scattered body, space seemed no bigger than a great vaulted hall.

•

From all the coincident and punctual centres of power, light leapt and blazed. The cosmos exploded, actualizing its potentiality of space and time. The centres of power, like fragments of a bursting bomb, were hurled apart. But each one retained in itself, as a memory and a longing, the single spirit of the whole; and each mirrored in itself aspects of all others throughout all the cosmical space and time.

•

I said, "It is enough, and far more than enough, to be the creature of so dread and lovely a spirit, whose potency is infinite, whose nature passes the comprehension even of a minded cosmos. It is enough to have been created, to have embodied for a moment the infinite and tumultuously creative spirit. It is infinitely more than enough to have been used, to have been the rough sketch for some perfected creation."

New Concise Atlas of the Universe

It's more important to have a recent atlas of the universe than a recent atlas of the Earth — the Earth is pretty well known and politically stable compared to the constant change of information coming in from astronomy and Space exploration. When you're very ignorant, as we are about the universe, a little information is a big change.

So, this is the most recent, comprehensive, and spectacular tome on what used to be called the heavens. I use it to cure confusion (where is the asteroid belt?), boredom ("Star Wars" is only a movie), and egotism (there are only 30 galaxies in the local galaxy group — a small group). —SB

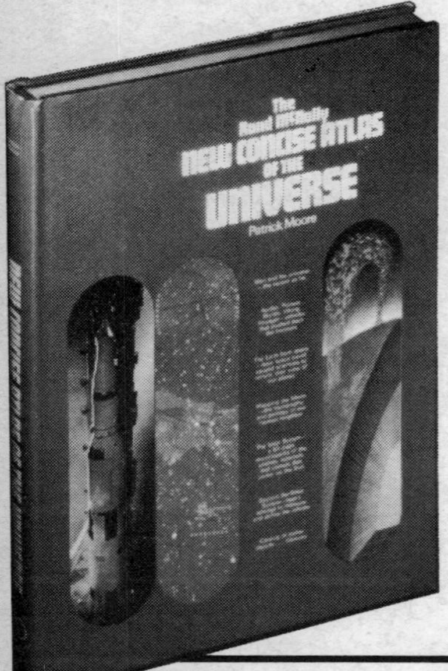

The Rand McNally New Concise Atlas of the Universe
Patrick Moore
1970, 1978; 190 pp.

$35 postpaid from:
Rand McNally & Co.
P.O. Box 7600
Chicago, IL 60680
or Whole Earth
Household Store

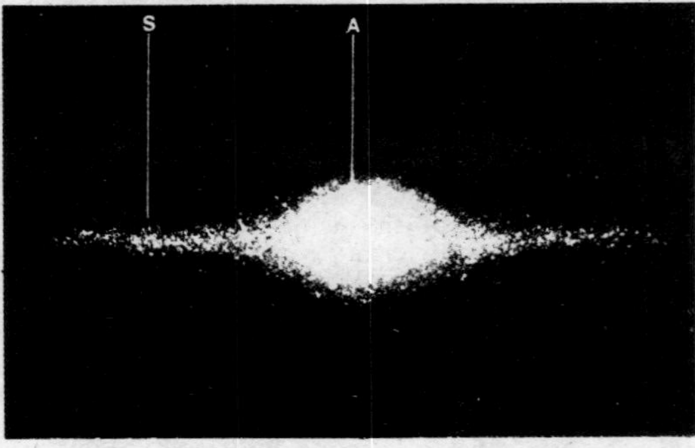

←
Our galaxy contains 100,000 million stars. It has an overall diameter of 100,000 light-years; the maximum breadth is 20,000 light-years, and the Sun, with its planets, lies close to the main plane, 32,000 light-years from the galactic centre.

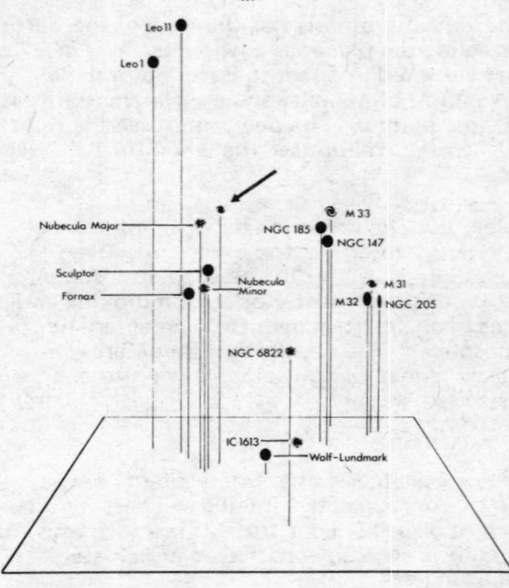

↑
Local Group of Galaxies
Our Local Group is a small cluster, having less than 30 known members: the spirals M31, M33 and our Galaxy; the Clouds of Magellan, and smaller elliptical and irregular systems. These galaxies are so close to us that their own peculiar motions mask the effect of the red shift/distance relation.

Intelligent Life in the Universe

There have been later, more specialized books on what has come to be called SETI — the Search for Extraterrestrial Intelligence — but this is the one that started it all and will start it best for you. Co-author Carl Sagan (whose fame began with this book) and the Russian Shklovskii never met in person while co-authoring. The text proceeds from superb introductions to evolutionary astronomy and biology, through a complete presentation of relevant recent discoveries (up to 1966), to brilliant speculation on the parameters of inter-civilization communication.
It's the best general astronomy book of recent years, but that's nothing next to its impact on all the biggest questions we know. —SB

Intelligent Life in the Universe
I.S. Shklovskii
and Carl Sagan
1966, 1978; 509 pp.

$3.95 postpaid from:
Delta Books
One Dag
Hammarskjold Plaza
245 East 47th St.
New York, NY 10017

•

The existence of more than one universe is impossible, by definition.

•

So, by an interesting coincidence, the distances between the stars in interstellar space, relative to their diameters, are just about the same as the distances between the atoms and molecules in interstellar space, relative to *their* diameters. Interstellar space is as empty as a cubical building, 60 miles long, 60 miles wide, and 60 miles high, containing a single grain of sand.

•

With 10^{11} stars in our Galaxy and 10^9 in other galaxies, there are at least 10^{20} stars in the universe. Most of them, as we shall see in subsequent chapters, may be accompanied by solar systems. If there are 10^{20} solar systems in the universe, and the universe is 10^{10} years old — and if, further, solar systems have formed roughly uniformly in time — then one solar system is formed every 10^{-10}yr = 3×10^{-3} seconds. On the average, a million solar systems are formed in the universe each hour.

•

Almost any other of the many accounts of alleged contacts of human beings with the crews of flying saucers — accounts which regale the flying saucer societies — follow the same pattern and stress the same points. The extraterrestrials are human, with few even minor physical differences from local cosmetic standards. (I know of no case of Negro saucerians, or Oriental saucerians, reported in the United States; but there are very few flying saucer reports made in this country by Negroes or by Orientals.)

•

Radio astronomers may be interested to know that the so-called "brightness temperature" of the Earth at television wavelengths is some hundreds of millions of degrees. This is 100 times greater than the radio brightness of the sun at comparable wavelengths, during a period of low sunspot activity.

•

"Well, ladies and gentlemen," Struve concluded, "it was pretty dull on Epsilon Eridani and Tau Ceti eleven years ago."

← Imaginary close-up of Cygnus X-1, showing intense flow of gas from supergiant star toward a dense star, possibly a black hole. Painting by Adolf Schaller.

Rings of Saturn. Painting by William K. Hartmann. ↓

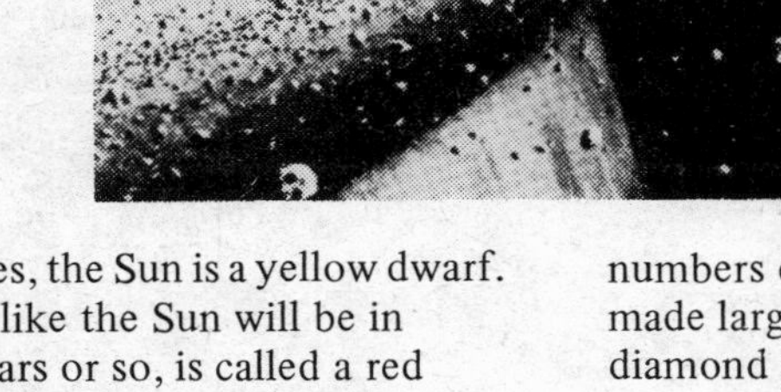

Illustrations from Astronomy: The Cosmic Journey, Wadsworth Publishing.

There is a place with four suns in the sky — red, white, blue, and yellow; two of them are so close together that they touch, and star-stuff flows between them.

I know of a world with a million moons.

I know of a sun the size of the Earth — and made of diamond.

There are atomic nuclei a few miles across which rotate thirty times a second.

There are tiny grains between the stars, with the size and atomic composition of bacteria.

There are stars leaving the Milky Way, and immense gas clouds falling into it.

There are turbulent plasmas writhing with X- and gamma-rays and mighty stellar explosions.

There are, perhaps, places which are outside our universe.

—Carl Sagan

Where, Carl?

Carl Sagan made these provocative statements in the introduction to his 1970 book, ***Planetary Exploration.*** *In 1973 we phoned him to ask, "Where are these wonders?" He said:*

The place with four suns in the sky . . . four different colors . . . and in touch . . . Well, first of all, most of the stars in the sky are not lone stars like the Sun but are binary or multiple star systems. A fair fraction of binary stars are called "contact binaries", in which the gravitational attraction of the more master star pulls matter out of the less master star — it flows from the donor to the receiver. Now, there are many cases where two binaries orbit each other. Two stars are revolving around a common center of mass. Another two stars are revolving around their center of mass, and the two centers of mass revolve around each other.

Now, as far as color goes, the Sun is a yellow dwarf. A highly evolved star, like the Sun will be in another five billion years or so, is called a red giant. A red giant usually winds up as a white dwarf. And a very hot star but still in middle age like the Sun is called a blue dwarf.

A world with a million moons . . . is Saturn. The Rings of Saturn are composed of snowballs which are certainly less than a meter across, perhaps ten centimeters across. There are millions of such snowballs making up the rings of Saturn.

A sun the size of the Earth and made of diamond . . . Many white dwarfs fit that description. Where hydrogen has been substantially lost they are crystals, stars which are crystals, and they're cold and cooling still more. So, for example, Sirius has a white dwarf companion. It was the first one discovered, but there are enormous numbers of such white dwarfs, many of which are made largely of carbon in crystal form. Therefore diamond is the correct description.

An atomic nucleus a mile across that rotates thirty times a second . . . is a neutron star, which is the end product of the evolution of a star more massive than the Sun. It becomes, not a white dwarf, but a neutron star. That is, it's composed entirely of nucleons — the elementary particles which make up the nucleus of atoms. Therefore they are atomic nuclei. And a mile across is how dense the thing shrinks to before the nuclear forces between particles pull the thing up against subsequent gravitational collapse. And they're rotating thirty times a second because of the conservation of angular momentum.

A star like the Sun spins once a month. When it contracts down to a mile across it's spinning something like thirty times a second. A specific example — the one that rotates thirty times a second — is the pulsar in the Crab Nebula, which is a neutron star.

OK, ***Tiny grains between the stars with the size and atomic composition of bacteria . . .*** Well, there's some absolutely tremendous number of them. If you take a look at a typical dark nebula, like say the Horsehead Nebula, the dark stuff is the kind of grains I'm talking about.

Hm, ***Stars leaving the Milky Way . . . Gas clouds falling into the Milky Way . . .*** Well, again it's quite common. We are a star which is in the plane, one of the spiral arms, of the Milky Way. But there are, for example, stars of a sort called "M dwarfs" which are oscillating out of the plane of the Milky Way — they spend most of their time out of it.

OK, ***Turbulent plasmas writhing with S- and gamma-rays and mighty stellar explosions . . .*** Again, the Crab Nebula. Not the star in the center of it, but the nebula itself, is a good example of this.

Places outside our universe . . . is a black hole. The nearest object which is thought by many astronomers to be a black is Cygnus X 1. I like to think of a black hole as a place where the gravity is so great that the fabric of space has become puckered — isolated from the rest of space so that light can't get out of it. ■

Horsehead Nebula.

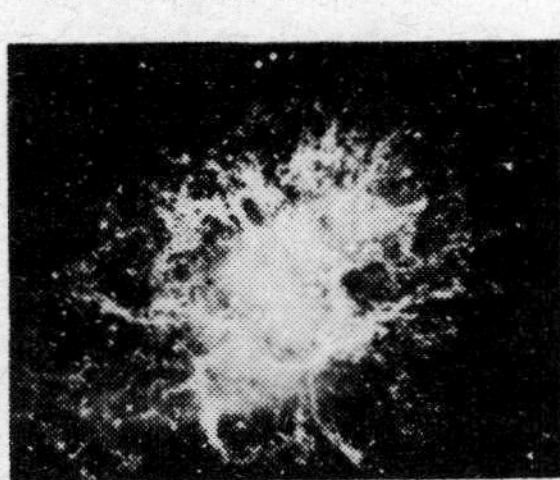

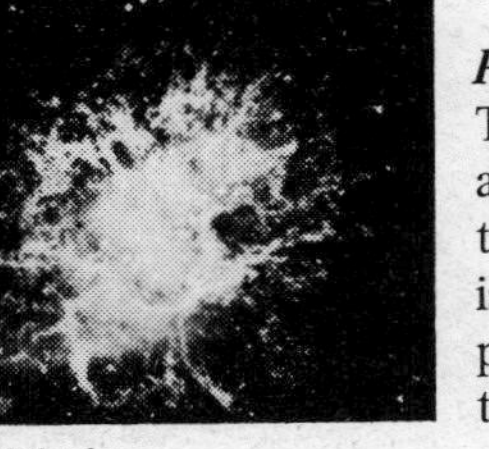

Crab Nebula.

EVOLUTION-COMPLETION IDEA *by Donald Burgy*

Each of the following sequences is an evolution. Complete each sequence according to the rules of change by which each example becomes the next.

1. TRANSPORTATION

A. walk	B. ride	C. fly	D.______

2. ECONOMICS

A. hunt gather	B. pasturage farm	C. industry commerce services	D.______

3. ABSTRACTION

A. words numbers	B. calendars maps	C. periodic table unified field theory	D.______

4. INFORMATION MEDIA

A. stone tablet carved bone	B. ink/paper paint/canvas	C. global TV telephone network	D.______

5. SELF-ORIENTATION IN UNIVERSE

A. egocentric	B. lococentric	C. geocentric	D. heliocentric	E.______

6. SOCIAL ORGANIZATION

A. individual	B. family tribe	C. city nation	D. empire united nations	E.______

7. SELF-REPRODUCTION

A. asexual replication of whole (single cell)	B. whole from part regeneration (annelids)	C. single organ regeneration (crustacea)	D. muscle nerve regeneration (mammals, man)	E.______

8. MATTER COMPLEXITY IN UNIVERSE

A. astronomical	B. geological	C. chemical	D. biological	E.______

THE RISING SUN
NEIGHBORHOOD NEWSLETTER

People in the depot after midnight must keep their feet on the floor.

The Astronomical Companion

We see from our position on Earth. The Sun travels east to west across the sky. The Milky Way makes a snow white bridge. But telescopes and space travel have given us a new view — the "real" view of how we are just a wee planet in a wee solar system in a wee galaxy. **The Astronomical Companion** *is an educational Atlas attempting to reconcile you to the differences between the "apparent" view of the heavens from Earth and the "real" image of the universe from outside our solar system. Ottewell is fully aware that the "real" view of the universe — the envelope of the cosmos — cannot be finalized and leaves us with quasars and redshifts and still further mysteries. Somewhat technical — in part because the vocabulary is so new — but by far the most mind-boggling atlas of what's out there.*

—Peter Warshall

Astronomical Companion
Guy Ottewell
1979; 73 pp.

$12 postpaid from:
Astronomical Calendar
Dept. of Physics
Furman University
Greenville, SC 29613

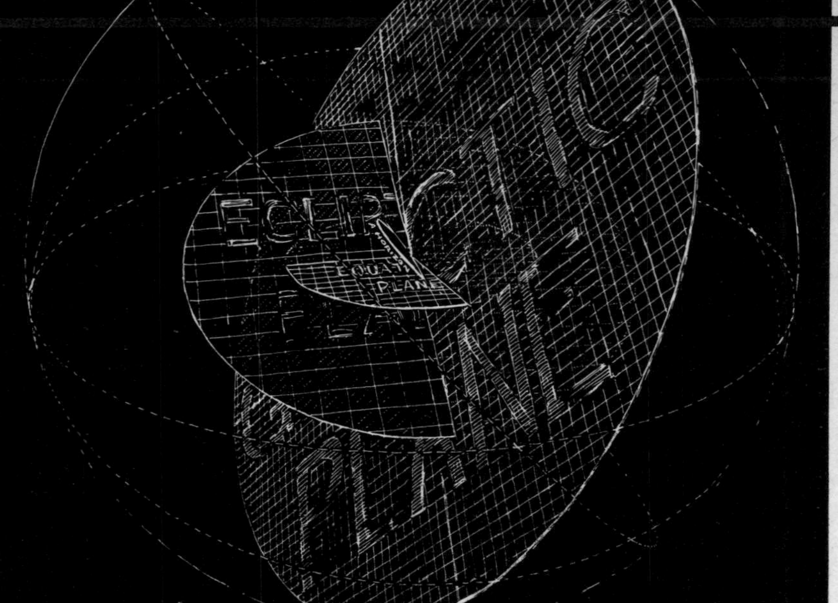

Equatorial, ecliptic and galactic planes

Look at the *last-quarter* moon. You are now looking *forward* along earth's orbit. You will be there — out in space at that point where the moon is now — in about 3½ hours.

The full moon: looking at it, you are looking out into territory beyond where the earth ventures, out into the colder wastes of the solar system.

Four Planes
The *horizon* system applies only to this place where we stand. Indeed there is a different horizon plane for each spot on earth at each time, so there is an infinity of horizons and the one shown is only an example. The other three systems are not multiple like this: each has only one fundamental plane.

The *equatorial* system applies only to the earth (as a whole), being the expression of its rotation. The *ecliptic* is solar-system-wide. (To be exact, it is the plane of the earth's orbit only; the true plane of the whole solar system is slightly different.) The *galactic* plane is of vastly wider importance, since it is that of (or, to be exact, parallel to that of) our Milky Way galaxy.

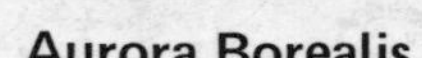

Aurora Borealis

Few phenomena give Earthlings as distinct and emotional a sense of their planet-as-astronomical-event as northern lights. Their awesome flickering silence has been even cited as close to the mystical event of facing Godhead, the Being of Being. How fine then to have a wonderful book full of color photographs and clear diagrams and the abundance of Alaskan experience to illuminate the subject.
—SB

Aurora Borealis
(The Amazing Northern Lights)
S.I. Akasofu
1979; 96 pp.

$7.95 postpaid from:
The Alaska Geographic Society
Box 4-EEE
Anchorage, AK 99509

•

We lay silent with upturned faces, watching this wonderful spectacle. Suddenly, the scattered lights ran together, as by a common impulse, joined their bright ends, twisted them through each other, and fell in a broad, luminous curtain straight downward through the air until its fringed hem swung apparently but a few yards over our heads. This phenomenon was so unexpected and startling, that for a moment I thought our faces would be touched by the skirts of the glorious drapery. It did not follow the spheric curve of the firmament, but hung plumb from the zenith, falling, apparently, millions of leagues through the air, its folds gathered together among the stars and its embroidery of flame sweeping the earth and shedding a pale, unearthly radiance over the wastes of snow. A moment afterwards and it was again drawn up, parted, waved its flambeaux and shot its lances hither and thither, advancing and retreating as before. Anything so strange, so capricious, so wonderful, so gloriously beautiful, I scarcely hope to see again.

—Prose Writings of Bayard Taylor, 1864

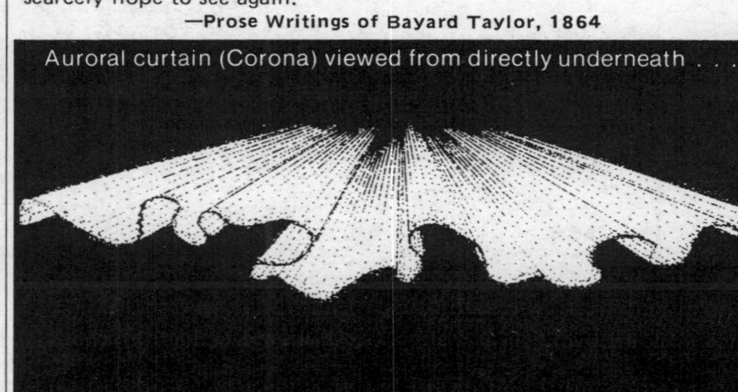

Auroral curtain (Corona) viewed from directly underneath . . .

Astronomical Calendar

I'm afraid that this is going to sound like one of those bar bets, but if one was asked to name the best annual astronomy guide it would have to be Guy Ottewell's **Astronomical Calendar.**

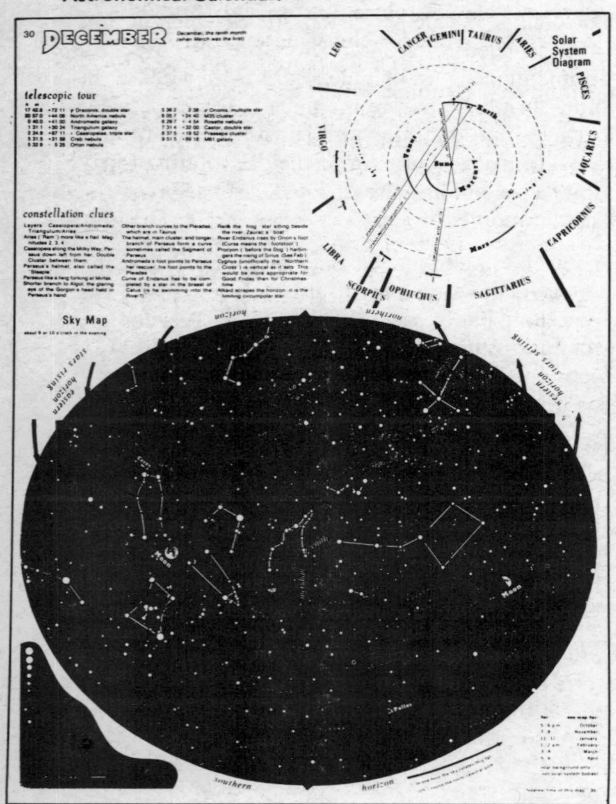

The **Calendar** *is published annually and contains all one wants to know and more about the coming events for the year. Guy himself does the cover illustration (15" x 11"), and produces, publishes and distributes the book himself. Somewhat like a Shakespearean play it seems to work on all levels: the casual amateur or the serious astronomer can read through it and find something to appreciate on every page.*

Guy has spent most of his life sleeping out of doors, and as a result the book lacks the cold detachment that turns one away from other similar books.

—Laurence Kent Sweeney

Each year's **Calendar** *is ready the previous October. A fine Christmas present.* *—SB*

Astronomical Calendar
Guy Ottewell
47 pp.

$8 postpaid from:
Astronomical Calendar
Dept. of Physics
Furman University
Greenville, SC 29613

Sky and Telescope

All good space cadets have first hand observational experience of the sun, moon, planets, and stars, and they use this magazine to keep up with new equipment, discoveries and gimcrackery such as meteorite rings ("the only rings on Earth with stones from outer space"), planet photos, etc.
—SB

Sky and Telescope
Joseph Ashbrook, Editor
$14 /year (12 issues)
$1.75 /single copy from:
Sky Publishing Corp.
49 Bay State Rd.
Cambridge, MA 02138

•

Points to Ponder for Astrophotographers

1. Spend the extra 30 minutes on polar alignment. It will be worth it later.
2. When near the telescope move head, hands, and feet at half normal speed.
3. When something works, make a note of it and standardize it.
4. Listen to others, but heed only yourself. Others may have yesterday's advice.
5. Focus on the faintest star possible, and take your time doing it.
6. Use off-axis guiding whenever possible. What you see is what you get.
7. When using a plug-type cold camera, dust everything at least twice.
8. Don't blame the telescope; you are the principal reason for success or failure.
9. Murphy's laws are merely a set of convenient excuses.
10. Good astrophotography techniques are poetry in motion.

John Dobson here places the 24-inch mirror on its flotation support, just before screwing shut the hinged "tailgate" of the telescope. The mirror is also cradled in a sling passing around the rim — an excellent support method that can only be adopted when the mounting is an altazimuth.

↑ The prominent cylindrical object in the lower right is a protective shroud that covered the surface sampler during transit to Mars.

The Martian Landscape

For the first time I got the feeling of actually being there, on Mars. The stereo viewer and stereo pictures, which give the illusion of three-dimensional pictures, must be seen by Earthlings. It will take you there.

I got a sense of the sun moving through the sky and the wind blowing hard. I kept seeing sagebrush in the long shots because some of the scenes resemble New Mexico. No sagebrush on Mars, folks. But you know it's real. It's a planet. Planet consciousness. Extra-planetary consciousness. —Michael O. Engle

The Martian Landscape
The Viking Lander Imaging Team
1978; 160pp.
(No. 033-000-00716-7)
$12 postpaid from:
Supt. of Documents
U.S. Govt. Printing Office
Washington, D.C. 20402
or Whole Earth Household Store

One Million Galaxies

See inside back cover.

Philip Morrison at **Scientific American** *wrote of the map, "No Tantric demon or benign celestial choir provides a more vivid symbol of the vastness of the universe in which we live."* —SB

One Million Galaxies
39" x 47"
$5 postpaid
(Continental U.S.;
all others $7.50) from:
CoEvolution Quarterly
Box 428
Sausalito, CA 94965

Detail of Galaxies Poster

Catalogs of astronomical photos

Maybe you want to watch a photograph of the Andromeda Galaxy, so similar to our own, and think about it. Maybe you want high quality illustrations for your cosmic ravings. Maybe you want to swirl in color with the bands of Jupiter or fix your mind on . . . (this could be a long list). Nice pix — $1.50 to $80 or so. —SB

Catalog
Astronomical Publications
free from:
Lick Observatory OP
University of California
Santa Cruz, CA 95064

Catalog
Astronomical Publications
free from:
Hansen Planetarium
15 South State Street
Salt Lake City, UT 84111

Catalog
of photographs and slides
free from:
Bookstore 1-51
California Institute of Technology
1201 East California Blvd.
Pasadena, CA 91109

Moon, Full Phase: age 14 days — Cal Tech

Head of Brooks' Comet, Oct. 21, 1911 — Lick Observatory

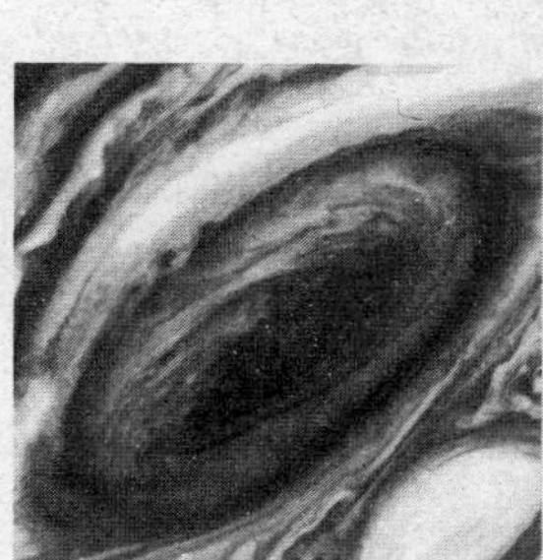

Red Spot & White Oval, Jupiter — Hansen Planetarium

Solar Eruption — Hansen Planetarium

Spaceflight

Far the most enjoyable and informative of all space magazines. It has three attributes conspicuously absent from American publications: articulate English, international perspective on diminishing U.S. efforts and everybody else's increasing space activity, and disciplined grand speculation —SB

Spaceflight
Kenneth W. Gatland, Editor
$27/year (12 issues)
from:
The British Interplanetary Society
27/29 South Lambeth Rd.
London SW8 1SZ
England

Vladimir Lyakhov and Valery Ryumin, after landing in the Soyuz 34 capsule, are taken from the cabin and placed in special chairs to ease their rehabilitation. In the background recovery teams have erected a double-walled inflatable tent for preliminary medical examinations. ↓

The Observer's Spaceflight Directory

A peerless reference book for all who deal with space. I wish to hell I'd had it when we were putting together our **Space Colonies** *book. Once again, the Brits are not ashamed to enthuse about space, to revel in the details of humanity's expanding edge. When I was on a tall square-rigged ship recently, I found myself thinking of it as an old spaceship, no more or less lively and fascinating than the new ones.* —SB

The Observer's Spaceflight Directory
Reginald Turnill
1978; 384 pp.
$15 postpaid from:
Frederick Warne and Co., Inc.
101 Fifth Avenue
New York, NY 10003

WORLD SPACE CENTRES

Successful Launch Total by Site 1957–1976

Place	Earth Orbit	Lunar or Escape	Total
Plesetsk, Russia	494		494
Tyuratam, Kazakhstan	370	49	419
Vandenberg AFB, California	395		395
Cape Canaveral, Florida	207	53	260
Kapustin Yar, Russia	64		64
Wallops Island, Virginia	16		16
Indian Ocean Platform, Kenya	8		8
Shuang Cheng-tzu, China	7		7
Uchinoura, Japan	6		6
Kourou, Guiana	6		6
Hammaguir, Algeria	4		4
Tanegashima, Japan	2		2
Woomera, Australia	2		2
Total	1581	102	1683

↓ 'Earthset' on Moon as seen on Aug 11 1969 by Soviet spacecraft Zond 7.

THE RISING SUN
NEIGHBORHOOD NEWSLETTER

This is why the first airplane flew at Kitty Hawk, North Carolina. Wilbur Wright and Orville Wright lived in Dayton, Ohio because their father and mother lived in Dayton, Ohio and they stayed there. (Their father and mother lived in Dayton, Ohio because their father was a minister and that's where his church told him to go once and he stayed even when his church later made him bishop of Oregon. Or his family stayed and he commuted, meaning Wilbur and Orville did not have a father breathing down their necks. He dropped in every few months and once gave them a toy propeller on a stick, which they liked.) In Dayton, Ohio, Wilbur and Orville sold bicycles in the summer and tried to invent the airplane in the winter. (Dayton, Ohio, was fairly far from Washington, D.C. where Professor Langley, head of the Smithsonian Institution had proven that it was not possible to build an airplane by using a large government grant and the resources of his position to build one that didn't work and sank into the Potomac. The government was not giving out more money but the Wright Brothers didn't need it as they had the bicycle shop. For credence and enthusiasm they had each other.) They flew kites and thought about them and then built gliders which they wanted to test more than they could in Dayton which isn't very windy as it isn't very anything else. They wrote to the Smithsonian Institution asking which were the places closest to Dayton, Ohio that had regular winds you could count on that were over 35 m.p.h. The first on the Smithsonian's list was Chicago which seemed to Wilbur and Orville not where they wanted to go in the winter. The second on the list was Kitty Hawk, North Carolina and they went there the next winter to test their glider. Kitty Hawk was nice. The winds were high; the dunes were soft to crash in; they made friends. When they ripped a wing, a daughter of a nearby family gave them her petticoat to fix it with. Their first glider did not do well because they had based it on the aerodynamic lift/velocity tables of their hero and mentor by letter, Otto Lillienthal, and the tables were completely wrong. They did not go to Kitty Hawk the next winter as they were home using a wind tunnel (the first, they invented it, a box about a yardstick long and half a ruler square) to make new tables. They did like Kitty Hawk and they went back the year after that with a glider that worked better and the year after that one with a glider with an engine that took off into the wind and stayed off the ground for 59 seconds and 852 feet. That's why the first airplane flew at Kitty Hawk, North Carolina. (The second one flew in Dayton a lot while they were learning to fly and when a visitor asked what it was overhead, a neighbor said, "Oh that's just one of the crazy Wright Brothers. They think they're going to invent a flying machine.)

The Right Stuff

Mind you, I've seen lots written about the astronauts, the program, the personalities, the challenge. Most of it bad and inaccurate, grinding some axe or other, some of it accurate and boring, and occasionally a good shot like Mike Collins' **Carrying the Fire.** *But nothing I've read paints the essential history as Tom Wolfe has done here.*

It's far from a complete history since the subject (except for Pete Conrad who is too juicy to pass up) is the fabulous First Seven and the Mercury Program. Missing from view are the thousands of characters whose brains and determination got the program off the ground. But that's classical history not Wolfeian. This is definitely written from the perspective of one "on the bus" — or "in the capsule" as it were. Wolfe has special prescription contact lenses that filter out the memoranda, meetings, reviews, milestones, simulators, procedures, checklists, protocols, etc., etc., and zoom in on Pete Conrad's enema and Al Shepard's enigmatic double personality.

My own delight with the book came not only from the Tom Wolfe which many (if not most) people appreciate, but from the Tom Wolfe whom only those on the inside can appreciate. The subtle groupings and relationships between the characters which are captured in a turn of phrase or literary glance brought many slow smiles of amazement to my face. How could he have picked up such valid subtleties without having lived it?

— Russell Schweickart (Apollo 9 Astronaut)

The Right Stuff
Tom Wolfe
1979; 436 pp.
$3.95 postpaid from:
Farrar, Strauss and Giroux
19 Union Square West
New York, NY 10003
or Whole Earth Household Store

•

So Conrad reports at seven one morning and gives himself the enema. He's supposed to undergo a lower gastrointestinal tract examination that morning. In the so-called lower G.I. examination, barium is pumped into the subject's bowels; then a little hose with a balloon on the end of it is inserted in the rectum, and the balloon is inflated, blocking the canal to keep the barium from forcing its way out before the radiologist can complete his examination. After the examination, like everyone who has ever been through the procedure, Conrad now feels as if there are eighty-five pounds of barium in his intestines and they are about to explode. The Smocks inform him that there is no john on this floor. He's supposed to pick up the tube that is coming out of his rectum and follow an orderly, who will lead him to a john two floors below. On the tube there is a clamp, and he can release the clamp, deflating the balloon, at the proper time. *It's unbelievable!* To try to walk, with this explosive load sloshing about in you pelvic saddle, is agony. Nevertheless, Conrad has on only the standard bed patient's tunic, the angel robes, open up the back. The tube leading out of his tail to the balloon gizmo is so short that he has to hunch over to about two feet off the floor to carry it in front of him. His tail is now, as the saying goes, flapping in the breeze, with a tube coming out of it. The orderly has on red cowboy boots. Conrad is intensely aware of that fact, because he is now hunched over so far that his eyes hit the orderly at about calf level. He's hunched over, with his tail in the breeze, scuttling like a crab after a pair of red cowboy boots. Out into a corridor they go, an ordinary public corridor, the full-moon hunchback and the red cowboy boots, amid men, women, children, nurses, nuns, the lot. The red cowboy boots are beginning to trot along like mad. The orderly is no fool. He's been through this before. He's been through the whole disaster. He's seen the explosions. Time is of the essence. There's a hunchback stick of dynamite behind him. To Conrad it becomes more incredible every step of the way. They actually have to go down an elevator — full of sane people — and do their crazy tango through another public hallway — agog with normal human beings — before finally reaching the goddamned john.

•

"God," he says, "you . . . look *awful!*" The Good Samaritan, A.A.D.! Also a Doctor! And he just gave his diagnosis! That's all a man needs . . . to be forty years old and to fall one hundred goddamned thousand feet in a flat spin and punch out and make a million-dollar hole in the ground and get half his head and his hand burned up and have his eye practically ripped out of his skull . . . and have the Good Samaritan, A.A.D., arrive as if sent by the spirit of Pancho Barnes herself to render a midnight verdict among the motherless Joshua trees while the screen doors bang and the pictures of a hundred dead pilots rattle in their frames: "My God! . . . you look awful."

A few minutes later the rescue helicopter arrived. The medics found Yeager standing out in the mesquite, him and some kid who had been passing by. Yeager was standing erect with his parachute rolled up and his helmet in the crook of his arm, right out of the manual, and staring at them quite levelly out of what was left of his face, as if they had had an appointment and he was on time.

•

Shepard waited for another stop in the countdown — this time it was to wait for some clouds to pass over the launch area — and he announced his problem over the closed radio circuit. He said he wanted to relieve his bladder. Finally they told him to go ahead and "do it in the suit." And he did. Because his seat, or couch, was angled back slightly, the flood headed north, toward his head, carrying consternation with it. The flood set off a suit thermometer, and the freon flow jumped from 30 to 45. On swept the flood until it hit his left lower chest sensor, which was being used to record his electrocardiogram, and it knocked that sensor out partially, and the doctors were nonplused. The news of the flood rushed through the worlds of the Life Science specialists and the suit technicians, like the destruction of Krakatoa, west of Java. There was no stopping it now. The wave rolled on, over rubber, wire, rib, flesh, and ten thousand baffled nerve endings, finally pooling in the valley up the middle of Shepard's back. Gradually it cooled, and he could feel a cool lake of urine in the valley. In any case, the discomfort in his bladder was gone and everything was still. They had not scratched the flight because of the dam break. He had not fucked up.

The next thing the medical team knew, a voice was coming over the closed loop, their private radio linkup with the Mercury capsule:

"Weh-ayl . . . I'm a wetback now."

If the Sun Dies

Philip Morrison, the peerless book reviewer for **Scientific American,** *suggested this book by handing his copy to me. "Read it."*

He's right. It's far the best book on space exploration, and I suspect it is Fallaci's best work. She addresses herself throughout to her father, who loathes Space, and reaches him through the experiences they shared in the Italian Resistance during the war. Unlike most American reporters she has an unashamed perception of heroism, and she is abundantly dubious of the freeze-dried delights of American culture.

It is thorough journalism. A year on the project (early, before the moon landing), she talked to the scientists, the engineers, the flacks, the astronauts especially, and to Ray Bradbury, who gave her the title. It's clear that the ones who weren't scared of her loved her and said unsayable things. (When I read Wally Schirra's remarks aloud to Rusty Schweickart, his response was "I don't believe it.") Fallaci finds herself liking Von Braun in spite of politics, and adoring Deke Slayton who personally bombed her in Florence and is stricken by that. Violating her every European instinct, Pete Conrad sells her on fast-food culture.

It's the chronicle of a conversion, reluctant, hard-fought, richly perceptive, convincing. —SB

[Suggested by Philip Morrison]

If the Sun Dies
Oriana Fallaci
1965; 400 pp.
from:
Atheneum Publishers
Out of Print
GET THIS BOOK BACK IN PRINT!

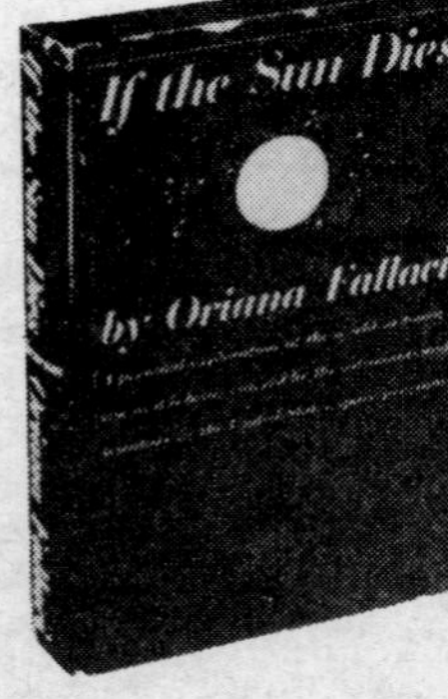

•

"I love the Earth, do you understand? I love the leaves and the birds, the fish and the sea, the snow and the wind! And I love green and blue and all the colors and the smells, and that's all there is, do you understand? That's all we have, and I don't want to lose it on account of your rockets, do you understand?"

You grew white with anger. And your every muscle warned me to be quiet, not to go on with my nonsense. But I couldn't keep quiet any longer: it was as if a war, a gulf, had opened up between us. And I told you, though I don't know if these were my words, that I love the Earth too, Father. It's my home and I love it. But a home you can never leave isn't a home at all, it's a prison, and you have always told me that man isn't made to stay in prison, he's made to escape from it and too bad if he risks getting killed escaping.

•

"Don't pay any attention to people who tell you they have such a wild look because of tension, of exhaustion, of joy at having made it. It's got nothing to do with these things. It's only rage at having come back to Earth. As if up there they're not only freed from weight, from the force of gravity, but from desires, affections, passions, ambitions, from the body. Do you know that for months John and Wally and Scott went around looking at the sky? You could speak to them and they didn't answer, you could touch them on the shoulder and they didn't notice: their only contact with the world was a dazed, absent, happy smile. They smiled at everything and everybody, and they were always tripping over things. They kept tripping over things because they never had their eyes on the ground."

"You seem to know them well," I exclaimed.

"Sure I know them well!" she said.

"What did you say your name was?" I persisted.

"I didn't say," she replied, amused. "My name's O'Hara. Dee O'Hara. I am the astronauts' nurse."

•

"We need art as we need dreams," Wally Schirra concluded.

"Dreams? Did you say dreams?"

"Without our dreams we wouldn't be where we are: dreaming of going to other planets, to other solar systems, and finding other Earths, our Earth, among billions of stars."

"Our Earth? Did you say our Earth?"

"Certainly. Because it's our Earth, it'll always be our Earth that we're looking for, it'll always be our Earth that we discover. I don't dream about the Moon. I know enough about the Moon to know how unpleasant and inhospitable it is. There's not one bit of Moon that's worth the Earth or that we could bring back to Earth as a trace of civilization. I don't dream about Mars. I know enough about Mars to know that you can't live there, you can't settle it. Mars and the Moon are two ugly islands. So then, you say, what's the point of going to them? The point is to be able to say I've been there, I've set foot on them and I can go further, to look for beautiful islands . . ."

•

Wally Shirra: "Feeling weightless . . . I don't know, it's so many things together. A feeling of pride, of healthy solitude, of dignified freedom from everything that's dirty, sticky. You feel exquisitely comfortable, that's the word for it, exquisitely . . . You feel comfortable and you feel you have so much energy, such an urge to do things, such ability to do things. And you work well, yes, you think well, you move well, without sweat, without difficulty, as if the biblical curse *In the sweat of thy face and in sorrow* no longer exists. As if you've been born again."

•

We must be ready to meet an intelligence and a justice that are the fruits of different evolutions. For example, we must forget our principle of "Don't treat others as you wouldn't like to be treated" and establish instead a principle that says "Treat them as they would like to be treated." The first thing they want, seeing that they're alive, is to live; so we mustn't kill them, we mustn't land on their territory in such a way as to damage it, we mustn't go there at all if we aren't invited.

•

"Don't you pray?"

Pete Conrad scratched his anchor, revealed his wide-spaced teeth.

"Well, not in swimming pools. Nor in churches either. I mean, I don't go to church and all that. But as for believing, I believe just the same, we all believe, more or less, even those who say: I don't believe in a thing, neither Heaven nor Hell nor anything. But I'd like to see them when . . Boy! At least three times I've nearly crashed and each time I commended myself to God like crazy. Those damn controls wouldn't be working one goddam bit and I'd pray to God, make them work, God! And you want to know something? I believe God helped me, that He made them work, those controls that weren't working: because I was really going to crash. It's the same, you see, with the Moon. You fool around, you joke about it, but when you think about actually going to the Moon the first thing you do is ask God's help. Then the second thing is you thank Him."

"But what if He doesn't help?"

"Dammit! You thank Him anyway. It's good manners. If I ask you for a match and you don't give it to me, I thank you anyway, don't I? It's good manners. So I ask myself, why should I be polite to you and not to God?"

Sunsets, and also sunrises, were accompanied by a vivid arc of colors like a rainbow stretching across the horizon.

A House in Space

No book, including the ones by astronauts, has given so compelling an account of life in Orbit. Henry Cooper, on assignment from **The New Yorker**, *talked to all the participants in the three Skylab missions which accumulated a total of 171 days — nearly six months — of constant weightlessness. What they found there were the kind of amazing occurrences that you will find yourself starting conversation with. The astronauts spent hours searching for lost objects that wandered off. Whenever they opened a drawer the stuff inside exploded out at them in slow motion. Whichever way they stood in a room was "local down." The third crew went on strike. Fascinating problems, ingenious solutions in a definitively exotic environment.* —SB

A House in Space
Henry S.F. Cooper, Jr.
1976; 184 pp.

$1.95 postpaid from:
Bantam Books
414 E. Golf Road
Des Plaines, IL 60016
or Whole Earth
Household Store

•

An astronaut could almost select, with his eyes, which vertical he wanted to follow, the room's or his own private one. "All one has to do is to rotate one's body to [a new] orientation and whammo! What one thinks is up is up," said Kerwin, the first crew's science pilot, who had discovered the phenomenon. "It's a feeling as though one could take this whole room and, by pushing a button, just rotate it around so that the ceiling up here would be the floor. It's a marvelous feeling of power over space — over the space around one. Closing one's eyes, of course, makes everything go away. And now one's body is like a planet all to itself, and one really doesn't know where the outside world is."

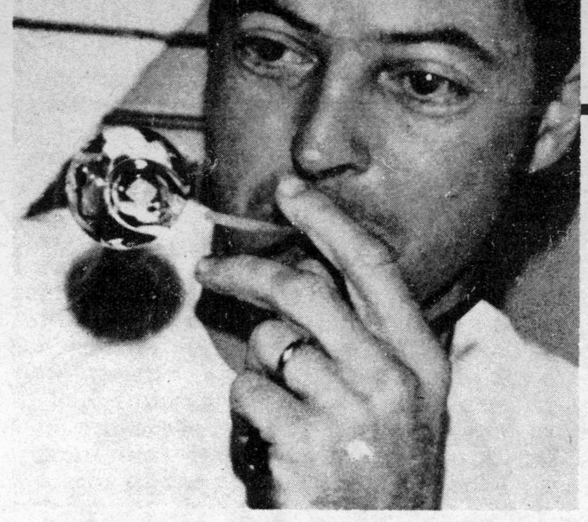

Kerwin, the first crew's science pilot, watches a ball of water, which he has just blown from a straw, as it floats away like a tiny planet.

•

The astronauts were continually surprised at how much time they spent looking not only at oceans and deserts but also at snowfields and mountainous areas, in none of which could they see any sign of life. In contrast to the Apollo astronauts who had looked back from the moon and described it as an oasis in space, the Skylab astronauts thought the earth a barren place. The toughest part of the earth to survive in that they passed over, the third crewmen thought, was the area from Tibet across Outer Mongolia. "There is nothing but a great big nothing out here now," Gibson said during the third mission. "Northern China, Outer Mongolia, and all that gold stuff: the Gobi Desert." Carr, especially, thought man had a tenuous foothold on his own planet, where the checkerboards of his cultivation seemed to be packed into the few temperate areas, or fringed the deserts and oceans like a green mold struggling for existence. "Not much of the earth is hospitable to man," he radioed down one day — as though Mission Control's presence there had somehow made it seem an alien place. "We don't occupy much of our world. We're crowded into small areas."

•

Lousma had said once, "A guy like me, who likes both sunsets and sunrises, mostly gets to see sunsets. But here, in space, every day we get sixteen of each." Whatever they were doing, the astronauts frequently crowded around the window at such times.

Lousma liked to leap from the workshop floor — just before he reached the center of the dome — to straighten out as cleanly as a diver hitting the water, in order to disappear through the hatch without touching its side.

Useful Attributes of Space

by Jesco von Puttkamer

- Easy gravity control from ambient zero-g (or micro-g) to any desired rotationally induced multi-g level
- Absence of atmosphere
  - unhampered viewing of space for astronomy, astrophysics, etc.
  - perfect vacuum and freedom from seismic, acoustic, and convection disturbances
- Comprehensive overview of Earth surface and atmosphere
- Isolation from Earth's biosphere (for hazardous processes)
- Freely available light, heat, and power
- Infinite natural reservoir for
  - unlimited disposal of waste products
  - safe storage of radioactive products
- Super-cold temperatures (heat sink)
- Large, three-dimensional volumes (storage, structures)
- Variety of non-diffuse (directed) radiation
- Magnetic field
- Extraterrestrial raw materials

Insight

Newsletter of the National Space Institute, a public lobby set up by Werner von Braun shortly before he died to help build a broad Space constituency and help keep Washington informed of what that constituency wants. Apparently it's pretty effective and is riding adroitly the new public interest in Space. —SB

Insight
Courtney A. Stadd,
Editor

$22/year (12 issues)
(includes membership)
postpaid from:
National Space Institute
P.O. Box 1420
933 North Kenmore
Arlington, VA 22210

•

The December issue of **The Sciences** (published by the New York Academy of Sciences) reports that America's civilian space program may be overshadowed by a 'man-in-space' capability for the Department of Defense.

Entitled "America's Other Space Program," by Trudy Bell, former NASA mission controller, the article claims that forty percent of the Space Shuttle flights in the initial years are dedicated to military purposes. These Shuttle missions will be piloted by military shuttle pilots, performed by military mission specialists and controlled from the ground by military mission controllers. . .

Bell also reports that the Defense Department's space budget of $4 billion is almost equal to NASA's $4.2 billion. In addition, while the civilian space budget is being steadily eroded by inflation, DOD's space spending has doubled since 1976.

Disturbing the Universe

A fascinating, ingenious, and moral physicist reflects on the science and bombs in his life and spins out some fascinating, ingenious, and moral speculation about the uses of space. —SB

Disturbing the Universe
(A Life in Science)
Freeman Dyson
1979; 283 pp.

$12.95 postpaid from:
Harper and Row, Publishers
Keystone Industrial Park
Scranton, PA 18512
or Whole Earth
Household Store

•

What are the exploitable resources of a galaxy? The raw materials are matter and energy — matter in the form of planets, comets or dust clouds, and energy in the form of starlight. To exploit these resources fully, a technological species must convert the available matter into biological living space and industrial machinery arranged in orbiting shells around the stars so as to utilize all the starlight. There is enough matter in a planet of the size and chemical composition of Jupiter to form an artificial biosphere exploiting fully the light from a star of the size of our sun.

•

The Mongolian nomads developed a tough skin and a slit-shaped eye to withstand the cold winds of Asia. If some of our grandchildren are born with an even tougher skin and an even narrower eye, they may walk bare-faced in the winds of Mars. The question that will decide our destiny is not whether we shall expand into space. It is: shall we be one species or a million? A million species will not exhaust the ecological niches that are awaiting the arrival of intelligence.

•

When we are a million species spreading through the galaxy, the question "Can man play God and still stay sane?" will lose some of its terrors. We shall be playing God, but only as local deities and not as lords of the universe. There is safety in numbers. Some of us will become insane, and rule over empires as crazy as Doctor Moreau's island. Some of us will shit on the morning star. There will be conflicts and tragedies. But in the long run, the sane will adapt and survive better than the insane. Nature's pruning of the unfit will limit the spread of insanity among species in the galaxy, as it does among individuals on earth. Sanity is, in its essence, nothing more than the ability to live in harmony with nature's laws.

Aviation Week and Space Technology

This is the magazine the space professionals use to stay current. —SB

Aviation Week and Space Technology
Robert Hutz, Editor

$45/year (12 issues)
("Qualified" aviation/ aerospace workers: $35/year.)
postpaid from:
McGraw Hill, Inc.
Fulfillment Manager
Aviation Week and
Space Technology
P.O. Box 430
Hightstown, NJ 08520

THE RISING SUN
NEIGHBORHOOD NEWSLETTER

The Giant 1978-1979 Edition of Movies on TV lists 47 movies that begin with the pronoun I. The last 26 are I Married a Monster from Outer Space, I Married a Witch, I Married a Woman, I Met a Murderer, I, Mobster, I Never Sang for My Father, I Passed for White, I Remember Mama, I Sailed to Tahiti with an All Girl Crew, I Saw What You Did, I Shot Jesse James, I Say, You Say, I Thank a Fool, I Wake Up Screaming, I Walk Alone, I Walk the Line, I Walked with a Zombie, I Want to Keep My Baby, I Want to Live, I Want You, I Wanted Wings, I Was a Communist for the F.B.I., I Was a Male War Bride, I Was a Parish Priest, I Was a Teenage Frankenstein, I Was Monty's Double, I Wonder Who's Kissing Her Now.

Rusty Schweickart was the first astronaut to go outside the space capsule without an umbilical (Apollo 9, 1969). He was working in the Applications department at NASA Headquarters in 1976 when our watershed editor Peter Warshall phoned him and asked about, uh, going to the bathroom in Space, where water does not shed. —SB

URINATION AND DEFECATION IN ZERO-G

There Ain't No Graceful Way

Astronaut **Russell Schweickart** *talking to Peter Warshall*

Peter Warshall: The thing that most people are really interested in, of course, is how you did it without gravity. That's what everyone asks: "Does it just float up?"

Russell Schweickart: Yeah, well it's kind of interesting Peter, because I just came back from a thing at Purdue University. I spent about two and a half days with a bunch of kids out there. It was a really nice program and I had four kids who were sort of my personal hosts and hostesses, and we really got into that line of material. You're right, everybody wants to know. That'd be kind of fun sometime, to just sit down and put together a whole article on how you do it in zero-g. Satisfy everybody's scatological curiosity.

It's something everybody's afraid to touch. Well, look if you've got a couple of minutes, I can describe a little bit of it to you. It's the end of the day, and why not.

Warshall: I'd love to hear it.

Schweickart: Well, of course there are basically two regimes. One is in the space suit and the other is out of the space suit. While you're in the space suit — which people always really mistake as a long period of time — we really wear the space suits relatively little. In Apollo and Skylab we wore the suits during launch and took them off shortly after getting into orbit, and put them on again only for EVA's (extra vehicle activities). So you can figure out how much time that is. And then again, depending on the mission, sometimes we wore them for entry and other times we did not. So you're basically talking about hours, maybe, depending again on the mission; anywhere from say, 4 to 20 hours, out of anything from 8 to 80 days.

Warshall: It's not really that much.

Schweickart: Yeah, it's not that much. But it's a fairly critical time, you know. When you're in there you don't have much choice, so you've got to design for it. Okay. So in the suit, for urine you use like a motorman's bag, which is basically composed of a bladder that holds about — boy, my numbers are really slipping Peter — but something between a liter and two liters, if I remember. A rubber bladder type of thing that sort of fits around your hips, and a roll-on cuff which is essentially a condom with the end cut out that's rolled over a flapper-type valve, you know, just a rubber flapper valve. It forms a one-way check valve.

Warshall: Oh, I see, so you don't have to do anything.

Schweickart: No, you don't do anything. You just roll it on as part of the suit-donning procedure, and then urinate into it through the one-way valve. There are lots of little cute problems and uncertainties. Unless you're an extremely unusual person, since the time you were about a year and a half old or so, you probably have not taken a leak laying flat on your back. And if you think that's easy, let me tell you, you've got some built-in psychological or survival programs, or something which you've got to overcome. So that's a tricky little thing. And then there's always the possibility that in maneuvering around in a suit you can end up pulling off the condom, and there's always — we have three sizes you know, small, medium and large — in diameter, and there's always this little ego thing about which one you do pick. Of course the smart guy picks the right size, because it's very important. But what happens is, if you get too small a size it effectively pinches off the flow and you just turn yellow because you can't go; and if, on the other hand you've got an ego problem and you decide on a large when you should have a medium, what happens is you take your first leak and you end up with half of the urine outside the bag on you. And that's the last time you make that mistake. So it's a cute little trick there.

In terms of defecation inside the suit, there ain't no graceful way to do it. So what we do is, we wear what's affectionately called a fecal containment system. The good old FCS is essentially like a pair of bermuda shorts with a hole for your penis to stick out of to roll on this other thing, but fairly well sealed around there.

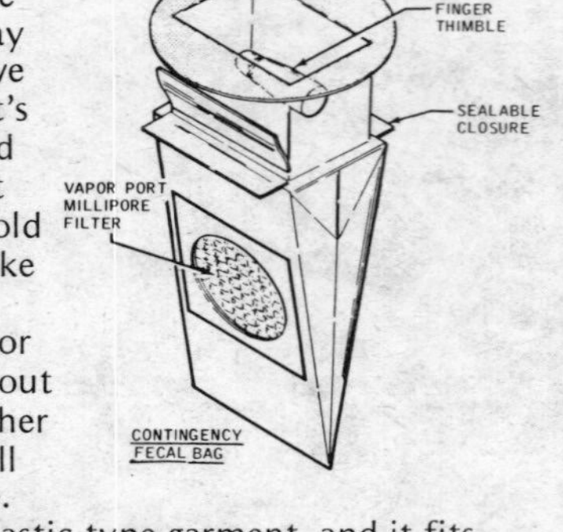

It's a tight fitting elastic type garment, and it fits especially tight around the thighs and around the waist. And it's just like a pair of diapers is what it is . . . made of material which obviously is non-permeable but still breathes and all it does is contain it. Now, to my knowledge, nobody's ever had to use that. But you wear it, because if you don't wear it, the consequences are rather drastic. Okay. So that sort of takes care of the in-the-suit situation.

Warshall: Then you would take off that bermuda short type thing when you got back into the spacecraft. . .

Schweickart: Yes, and you take off the transfer system, and if you'd used it, you transfer the urine into, well depending upon the policies on the particular mission, you either take a sample of it, for a scientific investigation, or you just dump it, one or the other.

In terms of not in the suit, and in the spacecraft, again that's varied. In Apollo, for feces you just stuck a plastic bag on your butt, which was 6 inches in diameter, something like that, maybe a little bit less, 12 inches or so long and the mouth of it had a flange at the top with an adhesive on it, and you'd peel the coating off the adhesive and literally stick it to your butt. Hopefully centrally located. And if you think you know where your rear end is, you really find out, because you'd paste it on very carefully! So, you stick that to your butt, and then you go ahead and take a crap. But then the problem comes, because there's no particular reason whatsoever for the feces to separate from your rear end. So as a result, the problem is left as an exercise to the student to peel the bag off and make sure everything stays within the bag, and get all wiped off. It's basically a one hour procedure.

Warshall: For each time?

Schweickart: Yeah, from the time you start to peel down to stick the bag on and all that, till the time you have finished cleaning up and have everything wrapped up and stowed and have your clothes back

Al Bean urinating in Skylab II. Just in front of his knee is the air-flushed fecal containment system, which you back up to. There's no particular "up" in this picture.

on and everything, it's damn near an hour. And at times it's taken longer. Because when you peel that bag off, you try to take a handful of paper, and you know, lead the way in with that, but by the time you get done, you've got stuff spread all over your backsides, and if you're not careful, your clothes, and everything else.

Warshall: Have you ever had an accident where the stuff got out of the bag?

Schweickart: No, because generally speaking it's fairly sticky, so once it's in the bag it doesn't come out, but the problem is making sure it's loose of <u>you</u> when you get the bag off. It just is not a simple procedure, no matter what you do. Well, in any case, that was in Apollo.

In terms of the urine system, that was simple in Apollo. It's just the same as a relief tube in airplanes. It's a tube with a funnel on the end that you urinate into. And at the other end of the tube is lower pressure than at the business end of it. So there's a differential pressure in the outward direction

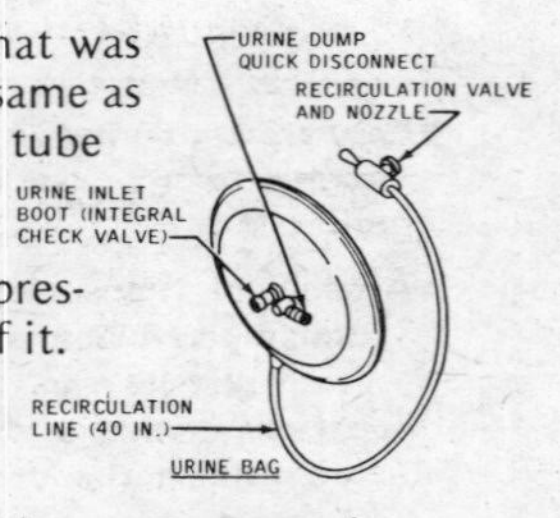

Well, we did exactly the same thing, except you know on the other end of the hose you've got a vacuum instead of a couple of psi down or something. So you just basically urinate into a relief tube. There have been various designs so you can use a roll-on cuff to do it or you can just hang it out there in the air and do it. There are a couple of different variations, but basically you urinated directly overboard through a relief tube. And of course, you didn't lose much cabin air, because while the liquid is in the tube, in the hose, no air is going down. It's differential pressure carrying the liquid. So it's only a matter of designing it for the right flow rate.

Warshall: They couldn't do that for feces, some kind of vacuum system?

Schweickart: Well, actually, in Skylab we did something similar to that. But on Apollo the urine then would go outside, and you'd have to heat the nozzle because, of course, it instantly flashes into ice crystals. And, in fact, I told Stewart this, the most beautiful sight in orbit, or one of the most beautiful sights, is a urine dump at sunset, because as the stuff comes out and as it hits the exit nozzle it instantly flashes into ten million little ice crystals which go out almost in a hemisphere, because, you know, you're exiting into

essentially a perfect vacuum, and so the stuff goes in every direction, and all radially out from the spacecraft at relatively high velocity. It's surprising, and it's an incredible stream of . . . just a spray of sparklers almost. It's really a spectacular sight. At any rate that's the urine system on Apollo.

Now, when you come to Skylab, it's a little more sophisticated. We tried to get sophisticated before that, but it never really worked. But on Skylab, the problem was that the medical experiments required that we sample all the urine and return all the feces because we were trying to make a total metabolic analysis. We could no longer dump the urine overboard because we had to measure the volume and take samples. What we did was to substitute a fan for the vacuum, and again use basically the same design, that is use a relief tube type of thing, except that the differential pressure was supplied by a fan which would decrease the pressure inside a bladder. You would pool 24 hours worth of urine. Then, after 24 hours, once a day, every morning, you would measure the volume, shake it up, get it nice and homogeneous and then take a 10 ml. sample, seal it up and throw the rest down the trash airlock.

Warshall: So each man had his own relief tube?

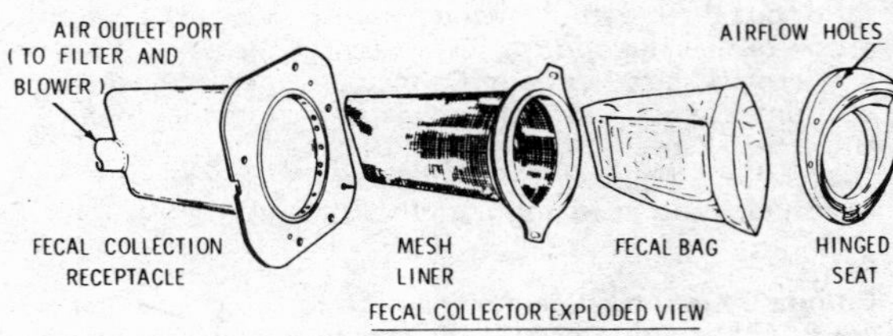

Schweickart: So each man had his own relief tube and his own collection system, right. On feces, we got very clever. Again we designed a plastic bag, but in this case, one side of the bag — now let me think if I can remember the words there —

Warshall: Was it like a stopper or something?

Schweickart: Well, one side of the bag had a material on it which would pass gas but not liquid. Oh yeah, a hydrophylic filter. And that bag, which again was something like 12 inches long and say 6 or 8 inches in diameter, got pushed down into a receptacle, and the receptacle was made of screen, and you drew a differential pressure across the bag with a fan so that the air flow was out through one side of the bag and of course sucked cabin air in through the top of the bag. Okay? Now, there was a little seat that folded down over the top of the bag and then you sat on that little seat. Well, sat . . . you floated. In fact, you strapped yourself to the seat to make a fairly good seal there. Then what happened, as you sealed the open part of the seat with your rear end, there were side vents, circumferential vents, just under the seat, which allowed air to flow in from the side, and all of these little orifices — circumferential orifices — were directed at the exit point of your anus. So the air flow now, if you can picture it when the guy was sitting on it, the air flow would be in around the periphery of the seat, but all directed in little streams, like little jets, and then down through the bag and out the side of the bottom of the bag, see. So what happened then, is you ended up with air flow substituting for gravity. And it would cause the bolus, so-called, to separate from your anus. Then the air flow would carry it down into the major volume of the bag.

Warshall: Kind of floating it in air down there.

Schweickart: Yeah. You just use air and air flow to substitute for gravity, and <u>that</u> worked very well.

Warshall: Really?

Schweickart: Surprisingly. And as a result you were able to take care of a defecation with relative ease and a lot shorter time. So the system worked well. But then after you did that, you sort of stuff the bag with wiping paper, seal it, then weigh it to get the mass, the wet mass, and then put it into a vacuum oven to bake, and evacuating all the water. Then you'd stick it in the stack with all the other cow pies and bring them all home for analysis. So all you got rid of was the water. You keep all the solid material.

Dr. Owen Garriott in "bed," lightly strapped into his sleeping bag. Since his exhaled breath has no reason to go anywhere, a fan is required near each sleeper's face to prevent CO_2 buildup.

Warshall: So you just kept it in the same bag and . . .

Schweickart: Yeah, you kept it in the same bag, and in fact, the vacuum system, the vacuum drying system, used the same port through the side of the bag to get rid of the water vapor.

Warshall: So then you needed only one for the crew, you didn't need one for each person?

Schweickart: Right; only one toilet to collect the solids, but each person had his own relief tube for urine.

Warshall: That's incredible.

Schweickart: It's really wild. And you know, people say, "Why don't you fly women?" Well, Jesus, I'd hate to think about the plumbing. You know, it's really funny, because a lot of the girls at Purdue asked that, "When are you going to take women in the program?" and I always throw that one out, the part about the plumbing requirement. We haven't had the proper plumbing in the past. Well, the fact of the matter is, we're designing it into shuttle. I don't know what it looks like, I haven't looked at any of the detailed design from Washington here, so I don't know what it looks like, but we are ready for women on this one.

Warshall: A lot of people were wondering what happens when you start dumping things into space. Like, what happens to the . . . do you use toilet paper, for instance?

Schweickart: Well, the only thing that gets dumped into space is the urine, and that no longer is dumped into space, or at least was not dumped during Skylab, but that was during the early, Mercury, Gemini and Apollo. The fecal matter has always been stored on board.

Warshall: Oh, I see. People have visions of fecal matter and urine ruining space.

Schweickart: No, no. The only thing that is left floating around out there is principally water which instantly flashes into ice crystals and then subsequently under the influence of solar radiation, sublimates and ends up in a purely gaseous state and my guess is then, I would suspect, I'm not sure the interaction of sunlight on the gases at that altitude, but they either decay down to the lower atmosphere, or they get blown off. I'm not sure which.

Warshall: So somewhere out in space is just some sublimated water crystals floating around.

Schweickart: Yeah.

Warshall: Well you can see what they were worried about. Some day the sun's rays . . . blocked out by . . .

Schweickart: It's all stored aboard, so they don't have to worry about it.

Warshall: Do you use any kind of special toilet paper?

Schweickart: No, not that I know of. There may be some flame retardant chemicals put into it just so you don't have any unnecessary flammable materials around, but I'm not sure whether that's the case or not.

Warshall: So it's just like any other toilet paper.

Schweickart: It's basically like any other toilet paper.

Warshall: Is it stuck in the bag and then burned, or . . .?

Schweickart: No, it is in the same bag with the fecal material, and in the early missions that was a plastic bag that you mixed in a disinfectant or actually an anti-gas, oh, what's the word I want, I guess disinfectant would be the best word, which holds down the generation of gas, and you mix that disinfectant liquid all through the fecal material. You mix it in, seal the plastic bag.

Warshall: How do you get it in there?

Schweickart: Well, it's in a small, like a ketchup, a little plastic container like you find ketchup in in restaurants, in a cafeteria or something, it's like that. You tear the slit across the top, being careful not to squeeze it so the stuff comes out, and then you drop that into the fecal container, and then seal the fecal container. Then you squeeze it through the, you know, externally, you know, which forces it out of the container, and then you mix it by massaging the fecal bag. It's really fun when it's still warm.

Warshall: The other thing that I've been asked about is how your diet affects everything; what you're actually eating; how that actually affects, you know, going to the bathroom, and do you do it once a day, since you said it took about an hour when you had . . .

Schweickart: Well, it's not at all clear how or whether the food really has any effect different from what you experience down here. The food does, I'm sure, have different preservatives and that kind of thing in it in order to be able to take it up there in the first place and be able to store it for long periods of time and that sort of thing. But I don't think there was any consistent observation, and there's no way to separate the effect of the weightless environment or other changes, physiological changes that are going on from the effect of the food.

Warshall: I mean, the image people have is you're mostly eating out of kind of toothpaste tubes or the food is being squeezed out, or something like that.

Schweickart: That's a pretty long conversation to try and get into, there are all different types, but the toothpaste-type tube has never been used in space. Well, it was used in early Mercury as a kind of test thing, but we have never in fact had toothpaste types of pastes or anything like it. It's always been freeze-dried food which you add water to to reconstitute, or what are called thermal-stabilized foods, almost exactly the same thing you would get in canned peaches or pears, that type of foods which you don't need to add water to, or in the case of Skylab, we also had about 10-15% of frozen foods, including filet mignon, and lobster and roast pork and vanilla ice cream for that matter.

Warshall: And you don't have to worry about that floating out into the space lab?

Schweickart: Well, if I could show you the movies, you'd see how we handle it. In some cases, like the filet for example, you cut a piece, and as you're taking it off of the fork the main piece of the filet may be floating up out of the plate, but you stab it with your fork and put it back down in, and if you do it carefully, the surface tension of the gravy will keep it in place. ■

THE RISING SUN
NEIGHBORHOOD NEWSLETTER

There isn't an unknown soldier from Vietnam because they identified them all.

David Frost talked to the priest in India who goes around all day feeding people and helping very sick people and Frost asked him what was the worst thing about it and he said the worst thing about it was that it was so boring.

The High Frontier

The one book you must have if you're interested in Space Colonies is this one by Gerard O'Neill. His scheme has aroused so much rabid support and rabid opposition that O'Neill's gentle voice and responsible perspective has a critical balancing influence. I have seen environmentalists who at first blush loathed the idea of Space Colonies come away from O'Neill's book impressed and interested.

Having one individual most strongly identified with a grand vision such as Space Colonies is the healthiest way to proceed, I'm convinced, and I'm glad Gerry has the job on this one. —SB

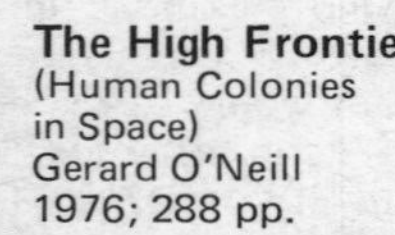

The High Frontier
(Human Colonies in Space)
Gerard O'Neill
1976; 288 pp.

$2.95 postpaid from:
Bantam Books, Inc.
414 E. Golf Road
Des Plaines, IL 60016
or Whole Earth Household Store

Stream of moon ore payloads leaving lunar mass driver for collection and possession in space. Thus the Space Colonies are built largely with extra-terrestrial material. ↓

•

When I have considered the effect of our discovering, one day, signals from a more advanced civilization (note that it would be, with almost 100 percent certainty, milennia more advanced than we are because of our own position at the threshold of communication) it has seemed to me overwhelmingly probable that the first effect of the discovery, as soon as the excitement and the novelty have worn off a little, would be to kill our science and our art. What purpose to study the natural sciences? We already know that they are universal, so if a civilization now radioing to us is 50,000 years ahead in its knowledge, why continue to study and search for scientific truth on our own? Gone then the possibility of new discovery, or surprise, and above all of pride and accomplishment; it seems to me horribly likely that as scientists we would become simply television addicts, contributing nothing of our own pain and work and effort to new discovery.

In the arts, music and literature, the case may be somewhat more unclear; yet on earth the almost invariable consequence of contact between a primitive civilization and one more advanced is the stagnation of the arts in the former. Only in the form of a "tourist trade" does art survive, in most cases.

If this sequence of effects is of more than local significance, as I think it is, it will be quite obvious to any civilization more advanced than our own. I would then add one more assumption: that the same characteristics which render a civilization immune to intellectual decay and stagnation, if there be such characteristics, are accompanied by a repugnance to inflict harm on others, in particular to other "emerging" civilizations more primitive than its own. In that case, "They may be out there, but they're kind enough to keep quiet."

•

I confess to a humanitarian bias in the design that I suggest. Technological revolution is a powerful force for social change, and in choosing among several technical possibilities I have been biased strongly toward those which seem to offer the greatest possibilities for enlarging human options, and for breaking through repressions which might otherwise be unbreakable. Yet I offer no Utopia; man changes only on a time scale of millennia, and he has always within him the capacity for evil as well as for good. Material well-being and freedom of choice do not guarantee happiness, and for some people choice can be threatening, even frightening. Though I acknowledge that my study will be of the physical environment, and only indirectly with the psychological, I will still try to describe an environment which combines with its efficiencies and its practicality opportunities for increasing the options, the pleasures, and the freedoms of individual human beings.

I have argued that there is only one way in which we can develop truly high-growth-rate industry, able to continue the course of its development for a very long time without environmental damage: to combine unlimited solar power, the virtually unlimited resources of the Moon and the asteroid belt, and locations near Earth but not on a planetary surface.

↑
A settlement built as a large spinning torus or doughnut (NASA painting) offers a compromise between the wish for spaciousness and the wish to keep something hidden beyond the horizon — even if the horizon curves upwards.

Spaceships of the Mind

If you're considering space as a realm of activity for yourself or Ourself, there's no point in thinking small. The old professional British explainer Calder does an admirable job of mustering all the relevant thought and experience that bears on the idea of space colonies and beyond. —SB

Spaceships of the Mind
Nigel Calder
1978; 144 pp.

$6.95 postpaid from:
Penguin Books
299 Murray Hill Pkwy.
East Rutherford, NJ 07073
or Whole Earth Household Store

•

To colonise space will be to take out insurance policies. With humans living in an immense variety of widely separated environments, whatever catastrophe might occur in one place, it surely will not occur in others. If the human species accepts the challenge, it has the opportunity to become perhaps immortal, for as long as the universe lasts. Smith found it hard to imagine anything other than an encounter with another civilisation that would stop the expansion of life filling the Galaxy.

•

The chief factor determining the rate of human expansion through the Galaxy will probably not be the speed of the ships, but the breath-catching period between the colonisation of one star and the departure for the next. Tom Kuiper and Mark Morris of Caltech assumed a 'regeneration time' of 500 years after each step of ten light-years, and a travel speed of ten per cent of the speed of light, to arrive at a figure of five million years for a technological civilisation to populate the Galaxy.

•

Compare the shoeshine man and the forester: the first works for a minute or two and gets prompt payment for a gleam that will not survive the next shower; the forester, on the other hand, plants trees that take so long to grow that he cannot live to harvest them. With the industrial revolution, forestry went out of fashion. Most of us, in the countries where it happened, began to live like shoeshine men. 'Better fifty years of Europe than a cycle of Cathay,' Tennyson declared. But people will have to learn patience again, if they are to take over the Solar System and then the Milky Way. It will mean planting many trees, both literally and figuratively.

Space Colonies

Like what's here, only more. Much more Gerard O'Neill, Rusty Schweickart, and spacy details. Much more discussion, including penetrating criticism of the whole idea by E.F. Schumacher, Ken Kesey, William Irwin Thompson, Garrett Hardin, Gary Snyder, and others. Wendell Berry says, "Humans are destructive in proportion to their supposition of abundance; if they are faced with infinite abundance, then they will become infinitely destructive." —SB

Space Colonies
Stewart Brand, Editor
1977, 160 pp.

$5 postpaid from:
CoEvolution Quarterly
Box 428
Sausalito, CA 94965

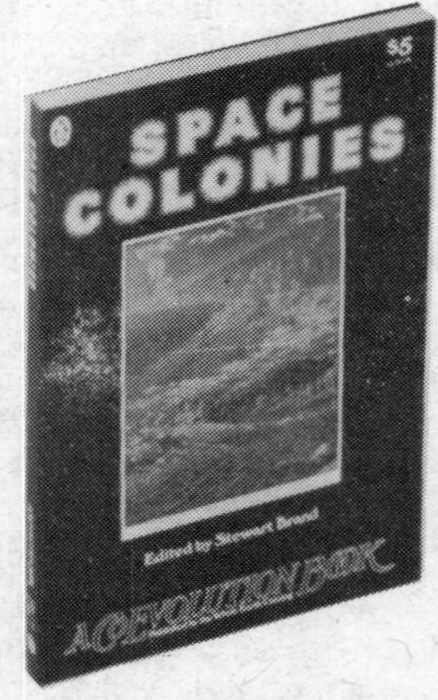

•

One can quite possibly turn a profit in supplying the surface of the earth with steel from the asteroid belt. The asteroids contain steel in chunks ranging from 100 kilometers in diameter down to dust. It is, in its native form, a strong, tough, ductile, and corrosion resistant material, and for engineering purposes, it is superior to most of the steel produced on the earth, because it contains about 5% nickel. —Eric Drexler

L-5 News

Much the best source of news on Space Colony matters, the **L-5 News** *is an enthusiast publication of admirable vigor, and it's no fanzine. The editors and contributors are in the thick of Space Colony design and speculation. They plan to live in Space.* —SB

L-5 News
Gerald B. Driggers, Editor

$20 /year (12 issues)
postpaid from:
L-5 Society
Membership Services
1620 N. Park Avenue
Tucson, AZ 85719

•

Space Tourism: As long as launch-to-orbit costs remain on the order of $150 to $300 per pound, there will be few tourists to orbit. For instance, a cost of $150 per pound gives a prohibitive per person cost of $26,250 (assuming 175 pounds per person). However, when cost of delivery to orbit reaches $25 per pound, that will mark the beginning of volume traffic. This would place the average ticket price at roughly $4000 — comparable to a present-day world cruise. This could occur between 1990 and 2000.

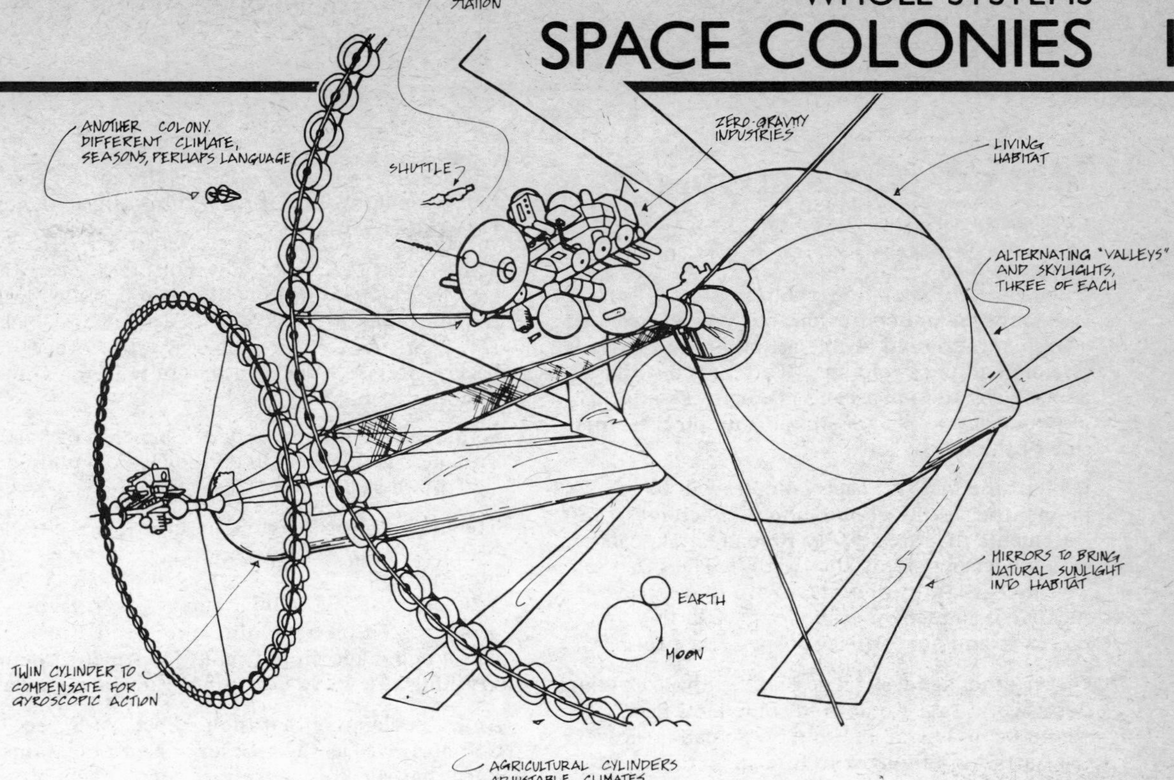

Education for space work

The following is reprinted (and updated) from the August '76 **Insight** *(formerly the* **National Space Institute Newsletter***; membership $22/year from* **Insight***, P.O. Box 1420, 933 N. Kenmore Station, Suite 221, Arlington, VA 22210).*

Many letters come to NSI asking what to study to break into a space-related career, and whether there will be more such work available in the future.

Comprehensive answers to the first question and implications for the second are contained in two volumes which NASA published in January, 1976, **Outlook for Space** and **A Forecast of Space Technology 1980-2000.** These present the careful, thorough conclusions of a two-year study conducted by a NASA team which conferred with many outsiders. The authors recognize two needs in a space program: to serve the physical requirements of humanity and immediate problems, and to challenge the mind. A zest for exploring the unknown is linked to national vitality. NSI members will cherish the latter point; letters reveal a straining toward the outer limits of space experience, but then NSI members are "the believers."

Outlook for Space urges that NASA, in its planning, be responsive to national needs. Future programs could elaborate on unique satellite services to the major concerns of food, energy, the understanding and protection of the environment, health care and such. Certainly the value of such programs can be generally appreciated, could bring NASA into more conversation with potential users of space, win support for more Earth-oriented programs . . . and so open more jobs.

According to NASA, the following five subjects will be at the heart of future technological developments, sure careers anywhere. (Incidentally, NASA is not the largest space employer; at the height of activity in the mid-1960s, 33,000 were on NASA payroll among the 500,000 believed involved in total space-related activity.)

1. Electromagnetic properties of solids
2. Integrated circuit technology
3. Cryogenics and superconductivity
4. Microstructures
5. Coherent radiation and integrated optics technology

Integrated optics is so new it is not even mentioned in **Physics in Perspective.** It means achieving in the optical region of the spectrum an analog of the present coherent microwave technology. According to Dr. John R. Pierce, Caltech, it offers the greatest advance in communications since the invention of the transistor.

The following organizations usually have career information to send:

American Institute of Aeronautics and Astronautics (AIAA)
1290 Ave. of the Americas
New York, NY 10104
(Send a self-addressed, self-stick label.)

American Society for Aerospace Education
1750 Pennsylvania Avenue N.W.
Suite 1303
Washington, D.C. 20006
(Write for free career information; they also publish a 48-page booklet about space careers and a 72-page Directory of Aviation and Space Education, at $5 each.)

Aerospace Industries Assn. of America, Inc.
1725 DeSales St. NW
Washington, DC 20036
Educational Director's Office. Ask for the reprint, "Career Opportunities in the Space Program."

Community and Education Services Branch, National Aeronautics and Space Administration (NASA) (LFG-9)
Washington, DC 20546

The Accreditation Board for Engineering and Technology
345 East 47th Street
New York, NY 10017
Sends lists of institutions for engineering or engineering technology study, those with aerospace departments noted. Price: $1 postpaid.

U.S. Government Printing Office
Washington, DC 20402
NASA Outlook for Space, 033-000-00140-3, $3.60; Forecast of Space Technology, 033-000-0064-1, $4.

Key Sciences for Space

Applied math (needed in more than half the following)

Thermodynamics
Atomic physics
Nuclear physics
Plasma physics
Fluid physics
Coherent radiation physics
Meteorology/atmospheric physics
Molecular physics
Solar physics
Geophysics
Low temperature physics
Biophysics
Elementary particles
Macromolecules and polymers
Colloids
Superfluids
Thin films and membranes
Superconductivity
Lattice dynamics
Structure of solids
Surfaces and interfaces
Metallurgy
Thermodyn phase phenomena
Transport phenomena
Catalysis
Reaction kinetics
Radiation effects in solids
Organic chemistry
High temperature chemistry
Solution chemistry
Electrochemistry
Photochemistry
Biochemistry
Biology
Exobiology
Space medicine
Optics EM
Particle optics
Optical properties
Magnetic properties
Electricity and magnetics
General relativity and gravity
Cosmic rays
X-rays
Gamma rays
Ultraviolet
Visible/near infrared
Radio
Celestial mechanics
Astronomy
Planetology
Metrology
Ecology
Computer science
Information theory
Artificial intelligence

The sky starts at your feet

by Stewart Brand

GERARD O'NEILL'S VISION of Space Colonies has turned the universe inside out for people. Instead of seeing the space program as just a "boondoggle for scientists", suddenly they can see Space as a path, or at least a metaphor, for their own liberation. And those who are critics of high technology can leverage their arguments from Space industrialization as the quintessence of what they are fighting. What's new is that people are extrapolating from the future and outside instead of just from the past and inside.

O'Neill's scheme invites you to give your imagination a Space Colony of one million inhabitants, each of whom has five acres of "land". Believe that it is readily possible by 2000 A.D. Have you any thoughts about how to organize its economy, politics, weather, land use, education, culture? Any thoughts about how to organize your life to get there?

O'Neill invites you to imagine an inside-out planet, cylindrical, with at the end caps mountain ranges which have the interesting property that as you climb higher your weight decreases. Near the top (center of rotation) at .1 g (1/10 Earth gravity) you can don wings and take flight. Or take a long slow dive into a swimming pool. Or watch someone else's slow-motion splash. At the foot of the mountain you might have a round river allowing you to canoe downstream several miles past the other two "valleys" and back to your home.

The details of the design and of the speculation change constantly, but O'Neill invites anyone to challenge the overall scale, engineering, budget, and schedule of the project. If you can find the fatal flaw you could bring this nonsense to a stop. Or, failing that, participate in the design and imagination of how Space Colonies might, in fact, work.

One thing that impresses me about the Space environment is that, hostile as it is to us pulpy organisms, it is wholly benign for electronic and mechanical machinery, much better for them than this corrosive, weighty Earth's surface. An engineering friend of mine, Michael Callahan, used to speculate that the machines have been longing for years to get into Space. They're using us to get there and when they've succeeded they'll throw us away. Or, maybe they'll give us something wonderful we don't even know we need. In whatever philosophical and technical configuration they are, we shall be obliged to rely upon machines to make Space habitable for us.

What got me interested in Space Colonies a few years ago was a chance remark by a grade school teacher. She said that most of her kids expected to live in Space. All their lives they'd been seeing "Star Trek" and American and Russian Space activities and drew the obvious conclusions. Suddenly I felt out-of-it. A generation that grew up with Space, I realized, was going to lead to another generation growing up in Space. Where did that leave me?

For these kids there's been a change in scope. They can hold the oceans of the world comfortably in their minds, like large lakes. Space is the ocean now. For those who long for the harshest freedoms, or who believe with Buckminster Fuller that a culture's creativity requires an Outlaw Area, Free Space becomes what the oceans have ceased to be – Outlaw Area too big and dilute for national control.

What's in it for Earth, then? Well, say the most dogmatic Space Colony proponents, you could solve, in order: the Energy Crisis, the Food Crisis, the Arms Race, the Population Problem, and maybe even the Climatic Shift.

Liberals and environmentalists hoot in derision. Then a year later some of them are back for a second look. And some of those, accurately perceiving possible benefits and possible frightful hazards of Space colonization, begin to participate in the debate and design.

Whenever the universe turns inside out, as happens

The sky starts at your feet. Think how brave you are to walk around. —*Anne Herbert*

THE RISING SUN
NEIGHBORHOOD NEWSLETTER

Did you ever notice that when newspapers, magazines and television decide to report on regular people, all they do is test them on whether they've been paying attention to newspapers, magazines and television? They go to some hog farmers in Indiana and quiz them to see if they know as much about the current media fad (Watergate, Korea, whatever) as the editorial writers for the New York Times and when they don't, that finishes them. I'd like to see some farmer interviewing Harrison Salisbury about weather or saving a sick piglet or anything.

The sky starts at your feet

(continued from p. 17)

from time to time in any civilization, you get a lot of disruption and confusion, but you also can get a fresh angle on old problems, public and personal. As a nomad once told me, "Think for a while about cows and fences and grazing. It's not just in your mind — the grass IS greener on the other side of the fence."

If built, the fact of Space Colonies will be as momentous as the atomic bomb. Each make statements that are equally fundamental. The one says, "We can destroy the Earth." The other says we can leave it, leave home. With that our perspective is suddenly cosmic, our Earth tiny and precious, and our motives properly suspect.

On the other hand, suppose that the Space Colonies don't work, that we do find some fatal flaw. It would be no less of an event. "We cannot leave the Earth" is a thought so foreign to the 20th Century that nothing would be unchanged by it.

Either way it goes the experiment should be made, because not knowing whether we can leave the planet begs all of our important questions. Either knowledge — knowing we can leave or knowing we can't — could make for more responsible habits. Either knowledge is a kind of growing up.

The same applies to the biology. If we can learn to successfully manage large complex ecosystems in the Space Colonies, that sophistication could help reverse our destructive practices on Earth. And if we fail, if our efforts to impersonate evolution in Space repeatedly runs amok, then we will have learned something as basic as Darwin about our biosphere — that we cannot manage it, that it manages us, that we are in the care of wisdom beyond our knowing (true anyway).

Is balance really possible where even the gravity is manufactured? It would be nice to know.

Space Colonies are distinguished from other high tech mischief such as nuclear energy, the SST, and the Arms Race by a major difference. They take place outside the Earth's atmosphere. They are separate whole systems. The experiment of Space Colonies endangers only the experimenters. When high tech goes wrong on Earth it is the innocent who get the consequences, down wind, downstream, and down the years. What Space Colonists use from Space — energy, materials, and location — is taken from no one else. They are out of the Earthly "zero sum game" where one group's gain is another's loss.

"North America all over again," is everyone's first response. "Now we'll pillage Space." Could be. But most of that thinking has scant comprehension of the nature of the Space environment. There's somewhat more than a lot of it. There is in fact no perceptible or theoretical end to it. Space is not like a continent, or the Pacific Ocean, or anything else we've experienced except possibly death and rebirth. It's more like a Buddhist chant: "No-air-no-gravity-no-night-no-day-no-up-no-down-no-motion-no-past-no-standing-still-no-life-also-no-death-no-thing-only-waves-of-star-star-star-star-star."

In de-emphasizing the exotic qualities of life in Space O'Neill is making a mistake I think. People want to go not because it may be nicer than what they have on Earth but because it will be harder. The harshness of Space will oblige a life-and-death reliance on each other which is the sort of thing that people romanticize and think about endlessly but seldom get to do.

This is where I look for new cultural ideas to emerge. There's nothing like an impossible task to pare things down to essentials — from which comes originality. You can only start over from basics, and, once there, never quite in the same direction as before.

So much for all the wonderful benefits of Space Colonies. Is there any likelihood we can politically get from here to there?

The most political argument against is the trade-off one — couldn't we spend $100 billion elsewhere more beneficially? I'm not so sure. The Apollo Program cost $25 billion, and as government projects go it probably did more good, did less harm, and made more friends for America than anything else we've done since the Marshall Plan.

And, I'm claiming that the prospect of Space Colonies gives us the best leverage on the Arms Race that we're ever likely to get this side of war. It employs the same nations, the same engineers, manufacturers, contractors, etc., and it's a more interesting story. The Arms Race is a big bore. Nothing ever happens.

Perhaps the leading U.S. and Russian Space planners should participate in the next round of SALT talks and turn them into Strategic Arms Conversion Talks. "We'll scrap the MX missile system and build a Model I Space Colony instead, if you'll do the equivalent." Conversion may be a great deal easier to monitor than Limitation — is the alternative project coming along or not? Look and see. It might even be that collaboration would have reason to replace competition — if only to check on each other's de-weaponization. Maybe Apollo-Soyuz was about something. America has better expertise in Space so far, but Russia has more imaginative long-range fantasies. And their astronauts sing better than ours.

Where mass support seems to be building is among college age and younger. Most science fiction readers — there are estimated to be two million avid ones in the U.S. — are between the ages of 12 and 26. The first printing for a set of Star Trek blueprints and space cadet manual was 450,000. A Star Trek convention in Chicago drew 15,000 people, and a second one a few weeks later in New York drew 30,000. They invited NASA officials and jammed their lectures.

Now is the time for NASA to encourage people besides engineers to get into the act. The program needs administrators who are not afraid of excellent artists, novelists, poets, film-makers, historians, anthropologists, and such who can speak to the full vision of what's going on. And their voice needs to be a design voice, not just advisory. America (and Russia) were in Space for ten years before they bothered to get a photograph of the Earth. That's pretty arid thinking. There's no reason it has to continue.

To be sure, if the soft sciences and arts are let into the Space Program there will be constant argument and much silliness. Good. One of the best points that O'Neill makes for Space Colonies is that they lead to divergence — many visions traveling in many directions. That could become their best real function.

Ten thousand or one million or many millions of people in Space is somewhat about engineering, but it's mostly about people.

Returning to the question of Artificial vs. Natural, my friend Dick Baker has his doubts. Some years before he became a Zen abbot he worked in the merchant marine and observed that too long on board in a totally man-made environment tended to make the seamen a bit crazy. The same, he's noticed, goes for cities.

It's true, we make ourselves dishonest in worlds we have had too much of the making of. Still, "Natural" has a way of getting through whatever barriers. As Baker said in another context, "From the Buddhist point of view everything is artificial."

The shocks of this Age are the shocks of pace. Change accelerates around us so rapidly that we are strangers to our own pasts and even more to our futures. Gregory Bateson comments, "I think we could have handled the industrial revolution, given 500 years."

In 100 years we have assuredly not handled it. We manufactured an "Age of Discontinuity" (Peter Drucker) whose time horizon forward is terrifyingly close — 4 years in politics, 10 years in major corporations. I feel serene when I can comfortably encompass two weeks ahead.

That's a pathological condition.

But I think it will pass, partly from its pure unworkability, partly from the move of some of humanity into space. The project of space exploration, industrialization, colonization, and migration is so big and so slow and so engrossing that I think it will bring the rest of human activity into its pace. If you want to inhabit a moon of Jupiter — that's a reasonable dream now— one of the skills you must cultivate is patience. It's not like a TV set or a better job — apparently cajolable from a quick politician. Your access to Jupiter has to be won — at its pace — from a difficult solar system.

With the first color photograph of the Earth from its Moon, the whole Earth became a political idea and ecology a political movement which has continued to strengthen in its 15 years so far. Though I have thought at times that the health of space perspective on Earthly activities has gone as far as it can, recently I'm not so sure.

The reach of human intelligence to the stars is an enormous undertaking. When I grasp the reality of that, not just the words, but the actual project, a religious scale of presence that spans centuries comforts me. Feeling comfortable and curious that far forward, and therefore that far backward, I begin to feel at home again. Interested in events longer than the ego's prison of "my lifetime", I'm free to care for other large continuities such as the life of the Earth and the drama of human culture. Previously overwhelming urgencies, like the deadline on this book for me, fall into microcosmic place — worth doing, connected, but not urgent.

Religious-scale projects — and their comforts — have often scourged humankind. I'm thinking of Egyptian dynasties, Moslem jihads, Mongol hordes, Christian crusades, the Third Reich, world Communism, maybe science itself. Part of their hazard is that they become their own universe — an infinite regress of self-reference grounded nowhere.

Space exploration is grounded firmly on the abyss. Space is so impossible an environment for us soft, moist creatures that even with our vaulting abstractions we will have to move carefully, ponderously into that dazzling vacuum.

The stars can't be rushed. Whew, that's a relief. ■

Earth and Moon, for once, drawn to scale. In this scale the nearest next item, Venus, would be fifty-eight yards away. Between, nothing. Except sunlight.

DON RYAN

Whose Earth?

by Russell Schweickart

PHOTOS BY NASA

→ March 1969, Earth-orbit, Apollo 9. Schweickart, pilot of the Lunar Module "Spider", goes outside to get a thermal sample. More "outside" than anyone had ever been. With him on the mission were James McDivitt and David Scott, who took the photograph.

UP THERE YOU GO AROUND every hour and a half, time after time after time. You wake up usually in the mornings. And just the way that the track of your orbits go, you wake up over the Mideast, over North Africa. As you eat breakfast you look out the window as you're going past and there's the Mediterranean area, and Greece, and Rome, and North Africa, and the Sinai, the whole area. And you realize that in one glance that what you're seeing is what was the whole history of man for years – the cradle of civilization. And you think of all that history that you can imagine, looking at that scene.

And you go around down across North Africa and out over the Indian Ocean, and look up at that great sub-continent of India pointed down toward you as you go past it. And Ceylon off to the side, Burma, Southeast Asia, out over the Philippines, and up across that monstrous Pacific Ocean, vast body of water – you've never realized how big that is before.

And you finally come up across the coast of California and look for those friendly things: Los Angeles, and Phoenix, and on across El Paso and there's Houston, there's home, and you look and sure enough there's the Astrodome. And you identify with that, you know – it's an attachment.

And down across New Orleans and then looking down to the south and there's the whole peninsula of Florida laid out. And all the hundreds of hours you spent flying across that route, down in the atmosphere, all that is friendly again. And you go out across the Atlantic Ocean and back across Africa.

And that identity – that you identify with Houston, and then you identify with Los Angeles, and Phoenix and New Orleans and everything. And the next thing you recognize in yourself, is you're identifying with North Africa. You look forward to that, you anticipate it. And there it is. That whole process begins to shift of what it is you identify with. When you go around it in an hour and a half you begin to recognize that your identity is with that whole thing. And that makes a change.

You look down there and you can't imagine how many borders and boundaries you crossed again and again and again. And you don't even see 'em. At that wake-up scene – the Mideast – you know there are hundreds of people killing each other over some imaginary line that you can't see. From where you see it, the thing is a whole, and it's so beautiful. And you wish you could take one from each side in hand and say, "Look at it from this perspective. Look at that. What's important?"

And so a little later on, your friend, again those same neighbors, another astronaut, the person next to you goes out to the Moon. And now he looks back and he sees the Earth not as something big, where he can see the beautiful details, but he sees the Earth as a small thing out there. And now that contrast between that bright blue and white Christmas tree ornament and that black sky, that infinite universe, really comes through.

The size of it, the significance of it – it becomes both things, it becomes so small and so fragile, and such a precious little spot in the universe, that you can block it out with your thumb, and you realize that on that small spot, that little blue and white thing is everything that means anything to you. All of history and music and poetry and art and war and death and birth and love, tears, joy, games, all of it is on that little spot out there that you can cover with your thumb.

And you realize that that perspective . . . that you've changed, that there's something new there. That relationship is no longer what it was. And then you look back on the time when you were outside on that EVA and those few moments that you had the time because the camera malfunctioned, that you had the time to think about what was happening. And you recall staring out there at the spectacle that went before your eyes. Because now you're no longer inside something with a window looking out at a picture, but now you're out there and what you've got around your head is a goldfish bowl and there are no limits here. There are no frames, there are no boundaries. You're really out there, over it, floating, going 25,000 mph, ripping through space, a vacuum, and there's not a sound. There's a silence the depth of which you've never experienced before, and that silence contrasts so markedly with the scenery, with what you're seeing, and the speed with which you know you're going. That contrast, the mix of those two things, really comes through.

And you think about what you're experiencing and why. Do you deserve this? This fantastic experience? Have you earned this in some way? Are you separated out to be touched by God to have some special experience here that other men cannot have? You know the answer to that is No. There's nothing that you've done that deserves that, that earned that. It's not a special thing for you. You know very well at that moment, and it comes through to you so powerfully, that you're the sensing element for man.

You look down and see the surface of that globe that you've lived on all this time and you know all those people down there. They are like you, they are you, and somehow you represent them when you are up there – a sensing element, that point out on the end, and that's a humbling feeling. It's a feeling that says you have a responsibility. It's not for yourself.

The eye that doesn't see does not do justice to the body. That's why it's there, that's why you're out there. And somehow you recognize that you're a piece of this total life. You're out on that forefront and you have to bring that back, somehow. And that becomes a rather special responsibility. It tells you something about your relationship with this thing we call life. And so that's a change, that's something new.

And when you come back, there's a difference in that world now, there's a difference in that relationship between you and that planet, and you and all those other forms of life on that planet, because you've had that kind of experience. It's a difference, and it's so precious. And all through this I've used the word *you* because it's not me, it's not Dave Scott, it's not Dick Gordon, Pete Conrad, John Glenn, it's you, it's us, it's we, it's life. It's had that experience. And it's not just *my* problem to integrate, it's not my challenge to integrate, my joy to integrate – it's yours, it's everybody's!

I guess that's really about all I'd like to say, except that – and I don't even know why, but to me it means a lot – I'd like to close this with a poem by e.e. cummings that has just become a part of me, somehow out of all this, and I'm not really sure how.

He says, that

> i thank You God for most this amazing
> day; for the leaping greenly spirits of trees
> and a blue true dream of sky; and for every-
> thing which is natural which is infinite
> which is yes.

Thank you. ■

Like a long pauseless chant, astronaut Russell Schweickart spoke these words in the summer of '74 before a brainy group meeting on "Planetary Culture" at the spiritual community of Lindisfarne, Long Island. Schweickart himself seemed amazed at what he was saying, amazed at the gathering he was attending, amazed – still – at the events which led him to drift bodily free between Earth and Universe. This is just the conclusion of his tape – $6.50 for the cassette from Lindisfarne Association, Box 1395, Southampton, NY 11968. In 1977 Schweickart became Science Advisor to California Governor Jerry Brown. In 1979 he was appointed Chairman of the California Energy Commission. —SB

The Mideast. "You realize that in one glance what you're seeing was the whole history of man for years — the cradle of civilization . . . You look down there and you can't imagine how many borders and boundaries you've crossed again and again and again. And you don't even see 'em."

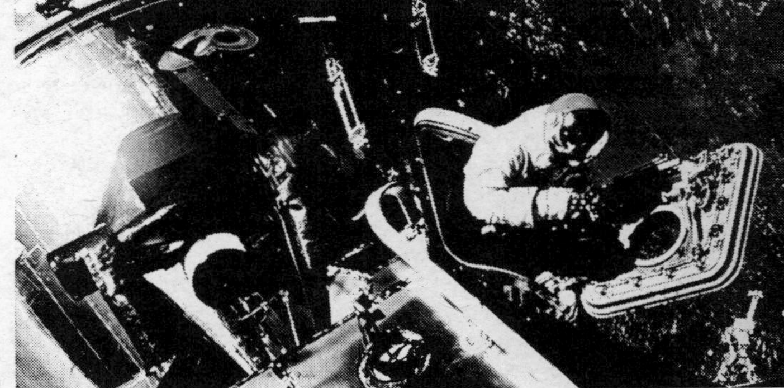

Photo by Russell Schweickart of David Scott standing out of the Apollo 9 Command Vehicle. "There are no frames, there are no boundaries. You're really out there, over it, floating, going 25,000 mph, ripping through space, a vacuum, and there's not a sound."

THE RISING SUN
NEIGHBORHOOD NEWSLETTER

General Washington does not like to be touched.

Basically, every movement with any good intentions that lasts becomes either the Rotary Club or the Spanish Inquisition and we were so afraid of being the Spanish Inquisition that we don't even have anyplace we can have lunch every Friday and tell each other how right we were about the FBI.

WE ALL JUST MAY BE NAVIGATORS amid the maps we make within our minds. When the maps "work" and the images of our world coincide with the pictures within our minds, it's clear sailing. When the maps don't work, we travel sorrowfully, blaming ourselves as inadequate navigators or blaming the map for providing such inadequate clues. Madness sometimes occurs: when we believe these mental maps are the world and forget how each of us must be a Columbus exploring unknown images, an Alan Shepard entering uncharted space.

Here is a guide to the images of the 1980s — images of our planet, our continent, our nation and the human settlement of the land and water surfaces. The 1980s will bring a new era of cartography — new geographical images of our environment. To old mapping techniques have been added photomaps from high-flying aircraft, satellites in false color infra-red, thermal infra-red, side-looking radar, and multiband overflight. We can now buy maps of the Moon, Mars and the galaxies, as well as maps of the ephemeral streams usually hidden by forests or hot discharges from nuclear power plants normally invisible to the human eye. We now have time-lapse maps like the speeded photomaps of weather fronts that appear each night on TV or computer maps like those of Star Wars. In New York the Maritime Union has a "movie map" of the entrance to the harbor which can be readjusted to show different storm conditions, maritime traffic, visibility and vessel speed for training tug boat operators. In short, here is access to the place you live — images called maps, simplified for special purposes, the prime tool to understanding the "where" of what we are.

—Peter Warshall

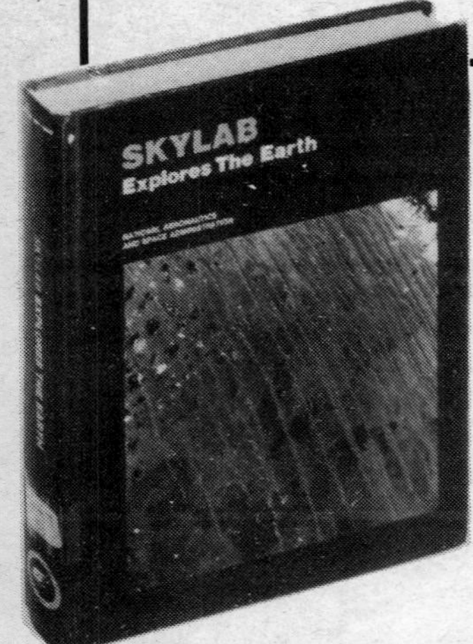

Skylab Explores the Earth

Photos of the Earth from space have always been grand, fascinating, lovely. This book makes them understandable. From innumerable color plates (the most informative yet from NASA), you learn to read the graphic news of geology, oceanography, meteorology, agriculture, development, pollution. This is the large-scale texture of the Earth. We are mites.

—SB

Skylab Explores the Earth
NASA Lyndon B. Johnson Space Center
1977; 517 pp.
(No. 033-000-00674-8)

$15 postpaid from:
Superintendent of Documents
U.S. Govt. Printing Office
Washington, D.C. 20402
or Whole Earth Household Store

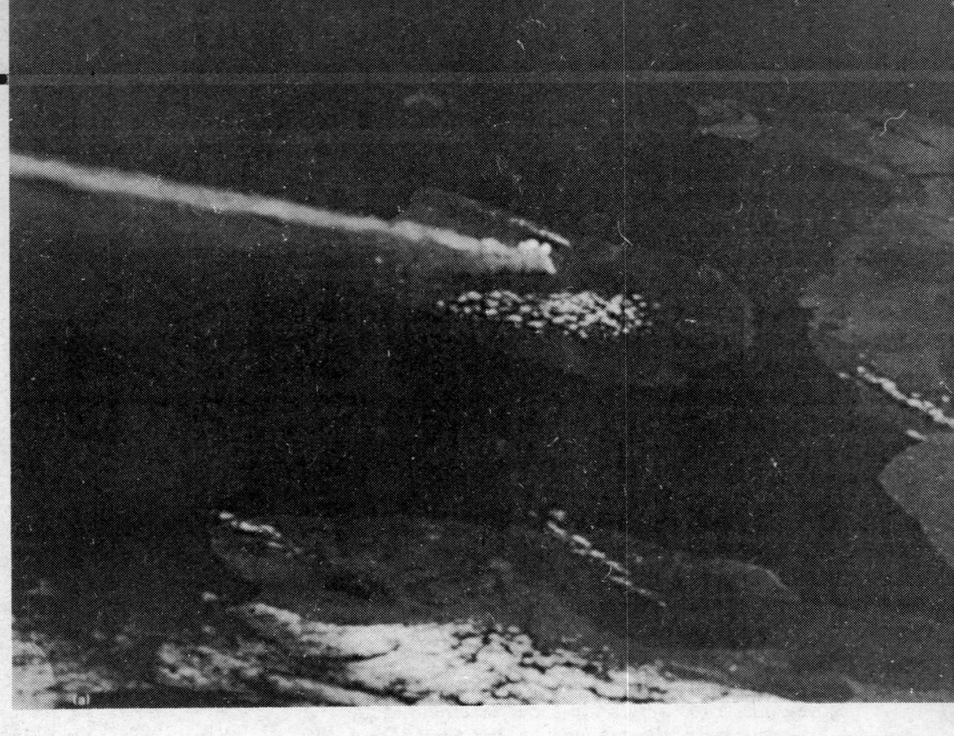

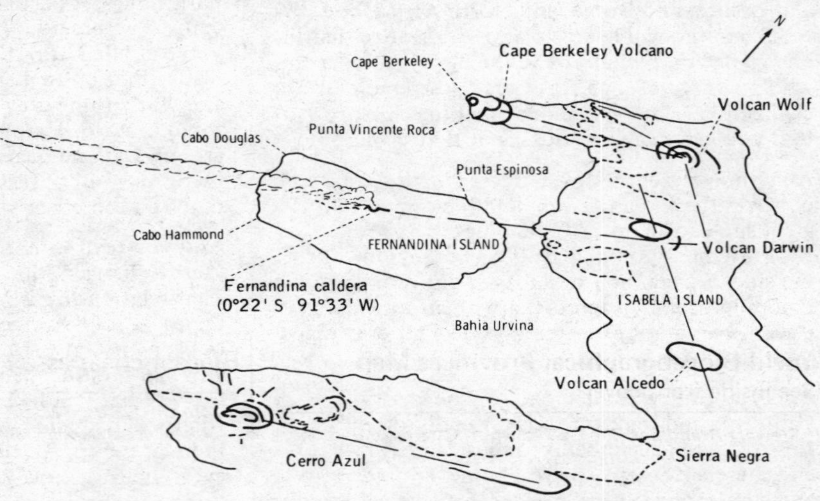

↑
Eruption cloud from Fernandina Volcano in the Galapagos Islands.

Mission to Earth: Landsat Views the World

While Skylab was an experiment, Landsat is the hard worker. Its satellite imagery is used for snow mapping mountain ranges, checking out surface water bodies, charting floods and large-scale watershed management. Landsat orbits further from Earth (570 miles) than Skylab. Photos cover 115 mile Earth pieces with clarity for objects 260 feet or larger.

The Skylab book resolves surface details as small as 33 feet wide, from 270 miles in space. The Skylab photos are in natural color, Landsat in computer-enhanced special filter color. The Landsat Atlas is pure coffee-table sumptuous detail of the textures of Mother Earth's remarkable skin. And the price is right.

—Peter Warshall

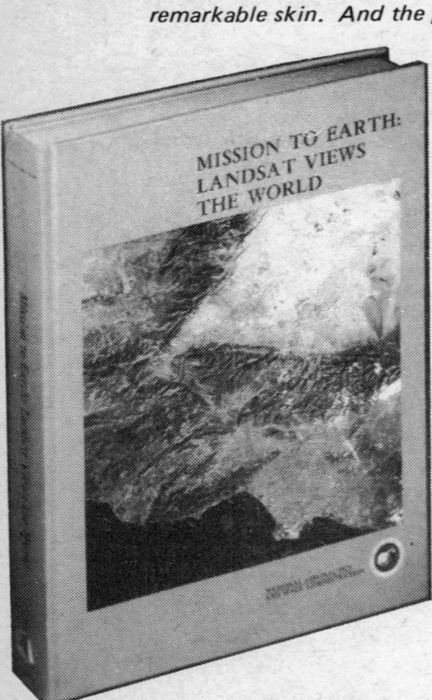

Mission to Earth: Landsat Views the World
Nicholas M. Short, Paul P. Lowman, Jr., Stanley C. Freden and William A. Finch, Jr.
1976; 459 pp.
(No. 033-000-00659-4)

$14 postpaid from:
Superintendent of Documents
U.S. Government Printing Office
Washington, D.C. 20402
or Whole Earth Household Store

↑

•
ARNHEM LAND, AUSTRALIA: One of the northernmost sections of continental Australia is the great aboriginal native preserve called Arnhem Land; it is part of the Northern Territory and stretches below the coastline of the Arafura Sea some 160 to 480 kilometers (100 to 300 miles) east of Darwin. The segment shown here is the Cobourg Peninsula (G–8) extending around Van Diemen Gulf (F-15). The peninsula consists mostly of Cretaceous rocks (C–8; H–9) with Pleistocene sediments further inland (O–11) and along the coasts (M–14; Q–10). The Wellington (R–14) and Spencer small hills (U–20) are outliers of Precambrian metamorphic rocks.

This scene, obtained during the dry season, shows most of the region to be covered by tall savanna grasses. Scattered rain forests (banyans, pandanus, and eucalypts) occur mainly along watercourses. Mangrove swamps develop around river estuaries (K–20). The nomadic aborigine tribes hunt plentiful game in this tropical zone. Kangaroo, bandicoots, wildcats, wild birds, waterfowl, and a wide variety of reptiles are typical inhabitants. The names of the two principal rivers, the East (O–19) and South (K–21) Alligator Rivers (actually populated by crocodiles), add to the junglelike flavor of the country. Domesticated animals are at a premium in Arnhem Land owing to the constant infestation by disease-bearing mosquitoes and flies.

Cloud patterns (G–13) mix with sediment patterns (C–13) in this scene. Coral islands (J–18) and reefs (B–5) are actively growing off the coast. 1069–00442; September 30, 1972.

Weather for the Mariner

I've been watching weather books since I was an obsessive teen. This one surpasses all the others as far as I'm concerned. It's sufficiently and fascinatingly technical without interrupting the comprehensive clarity that makes it so unique. It is a working text for people who live or die by the weather. No reason to limit its use to mariners.

—SB

Weather for the Mariner
William J. Kotsch,
Rear Admiral (Ret.)
1977; 272 pp.
2nd Edition

$16.95 postpaid from:
Naval Institute Press
Annapolis, MD 21402

•
Weather will generally change for the worse when:

Cirrus clouds change to cirrostratus and lower and thicken.

Rapidly moving clouds increase in number and lower in height.

Clouds move in different directions at different heights.

Clouds are moving from between NNE through east to south, and the wind speed increases with time.

Altocumulus or altostratus clouds darken the western horizon and the barometer begins to fall rapidly.

The wind shifts to the south or east. The greatest change occurs when the wind shifts from north through east to south.

The wind blows strongly in the early morning.

The temperature rises abnormally in the winter.

The temperature is far above or below "normal" for that time of year.

The barometer falls steadily.

There is a downpour at night.

A cold front, warm front, or occluded front approaches.

Wind at 60 knots. Entire sea takes on a whitish-green cast. ↓

Earth globe

This realistic globe from Rand McNally seems as good a deal as any. When looking up details I use an Atlas. But to check a time zone or remember where Rhodesia was, I give the old globe a spin. And there she sits, indubitably spherical, giving the proper lie to all those flat maps.
—SB

"The Admiral" Earth Globe
No. 86042-9
$21.95 postpaid from:
Rand McNally & Company
Box 7600
Chicago, IL 60680

Biggest cheapest world map ↑

From the Defense Mapping Agency comes this 7′ x 9½′ — when the six sheets are assembled — of beautiful color cartography. The sheets are equally enjoyable as separate sheets or as an entire wall, or, as J. Baldwin suggests, cover the whole with epoxy and make a wonderful floor. You make your check out to the the Treasurer of the United States.
—SB

(Note: These prices are approximations, which the Defense Mapping Agency may change when the map is finally released. In the meantime, you can take advantage of an even bigger bargain, Series 1142: nine 3′ x 4′ sheets which assemble into a 9′ x 12′ World Map, for only $10.00! The Agency does not guarantee the colors will match, and will not sell them after the 1150 series is released.)
—Art Kleiner

World Map Series 1150
(To be released sometime in late 1980.)
$2.50 each
3′ x 4′ sheets
$17.65 (all six)
7′ x 9½′ total
postpaid from:
Defense Mapping Agency
Office of
Distribution Services
Attn: DDCP
Washington, D.C. 20315

Two other World Map bargains from the same address:
$4.95 Series 1144
3 sheets, about 4½′ x 6′
$2.50 Series 1145
1 sheet, 42″ x 55″

World Biogeographical Provinces Map
(See inside front cover)

If Stewart Brand and the **CoEvolution Quarterly** *had only produced and distributed this one map, it would have been worth the whole 12 years of thought and work behind the* **Whole Earth Catalog**. *It is a map of the Earth's metabolic differences: how climate, soils, plants and animals create regions of similar life.. Besides being beautiful to look at, the map has immense information. For Ray Dasmann who helped design it and whose introductory pamphlet accompanies the map, it serves to guide us in creating reserves and parks to protect each kind of Earth bioregion. To me, it helped explain, for instance, why eucalyptus grow so well in California; why the southwest corners of each continent have parallel plant life; how these "mediterranean" bioregions have similar social and cultural heritages and can best be looked to for advice and contrast.*
—Peter Warshall

World Biogeographical Provinces Map
Miklos D.F. Udvardy, 1975
S. Brand and
T. Oberlander, 1976, 1978
↓

$3.50 postpaid from:
CoEvolution Quarterly
Box 428
Sausalito, CA 94965

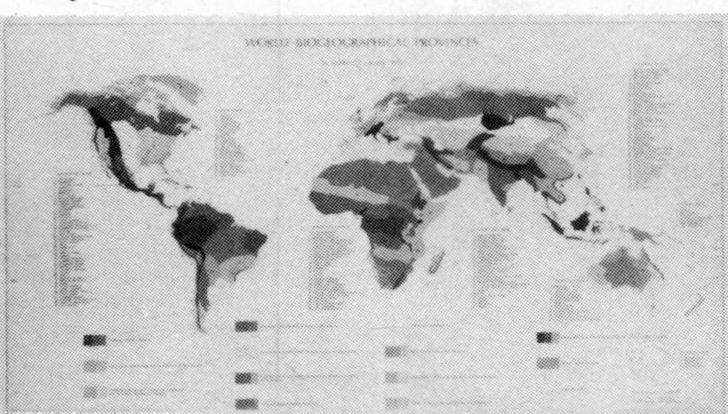

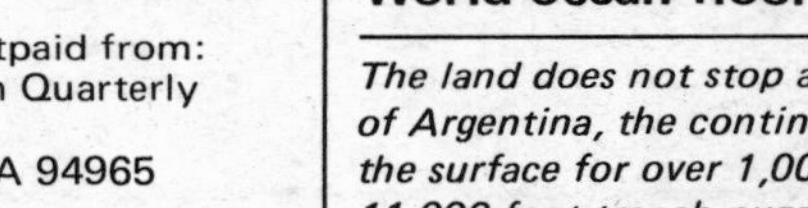

World ocean floor

The land does not stop at the water's edge. Off the coast of Argentina, the continent remains within 500 feet of the surface for over 1,000 miles. Off the coast of Peru, an 11,000 foot trench nuzzles the coastline. The great explorers of the twentieth century have been the oceanographers and their equipment. Their maps have confirmed the theory of floating continents, exposed mountain ranges taller than the Himalayas, located the last great caches of natural resources and made me feel even more reverent toward this birth-place of life. These maps are natural mandalas of whole Earth consciousness. They are accurate and beautiful.
—Peter Warshall

World Ocean Floor Panorama
Bruce C. Heezen and
Marie Tharp
1977
↓

$45 44″ x 76″
$18 24″ x 38″
both postpaid from:
Marie Tharp
1 Washington Avenue
South Nyack, NY 10960

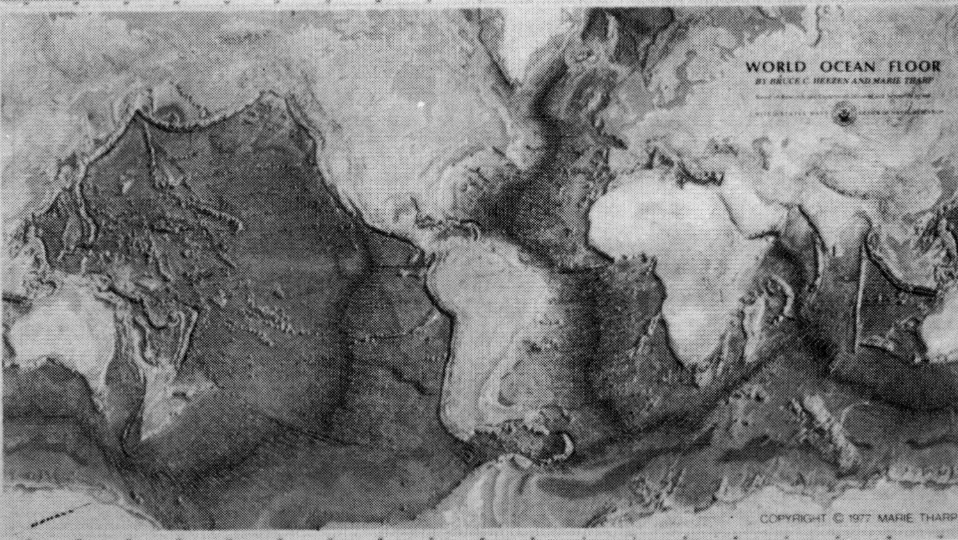

Weather imagery from space

22,300 miles over the equator a tiny satellite orbits at the exact speed the Earth turns. From Earth, the satellite appears not to move at all. It is this "geostationary" R2-D2 that beams TV weather images, ocean conditions and daily electromagnetic field status reports back to you. You can obtain images of the storm that wiped out last year's erosion control work or the County's expensive culvert or drove the snowy owl from the arctic to Massachusetts, or you can just track the major weather patterns over your watershed. Send inquiries to: NOAA ARCHIVE DIVISION, Space Science and Engineering Division, University of Wisconsin, Madison, WI 53706.
—Peter Warshall

THE RISING SUN
NEIGHBORHOOD NEWSLETTER

Whenever they ask I say, Date of Birth: 5/29/50, so the day before Memorial Day 1976 I'm turning 26 and remembering that every man my age had to go through one desert or another to reach this promised year of no more draft. They each lost something on the way: innocence, an arm, faith in whatever, freedom to flunk French, both legs, an entire country complete with relatives, a head that can hear backfires and not dive under the chair, friends, a certain natural honesty, the opportunity to cut college, the ability to do simple things like tie shoes and some just lost and aren't going into 26 with the rest of us. I glide to twenty-six with all of the above and the life of my choice since you knew on 5/29/50 that they weren't going to put my date of birth on any draft card or tombstone in Arlington at 3:01 p.m. when my vagina was born.

Goode's World Atlas →

Per buck, this atlas has the most and best — 372 pages of locational maps (from continent right down to city), landforms, climate, weather, vegetation, soil, population, agriculture, trade, language, resources, ocean floor, topped off with a fine pronouncing index. When something in the newspaper puzzles you, check here. Well, well, about 10 languages are spoken in different regions of the Soviet Union. —SB

[Suggested by David Brooks]

Goode's World Atlas
(15th Edition)
Edward B. Espenshade, Jr., Editor
1977; 372 pp.

$9.95 postpaid from:
Rand McNally & Co.
P.O. Box 7600
Chicago, IL 60680
or Whole Earth Household Store

•
112 Sausalito (sô-sá-lē'tô) CA. (San Francisco In.) 37-51 N 122-29 W

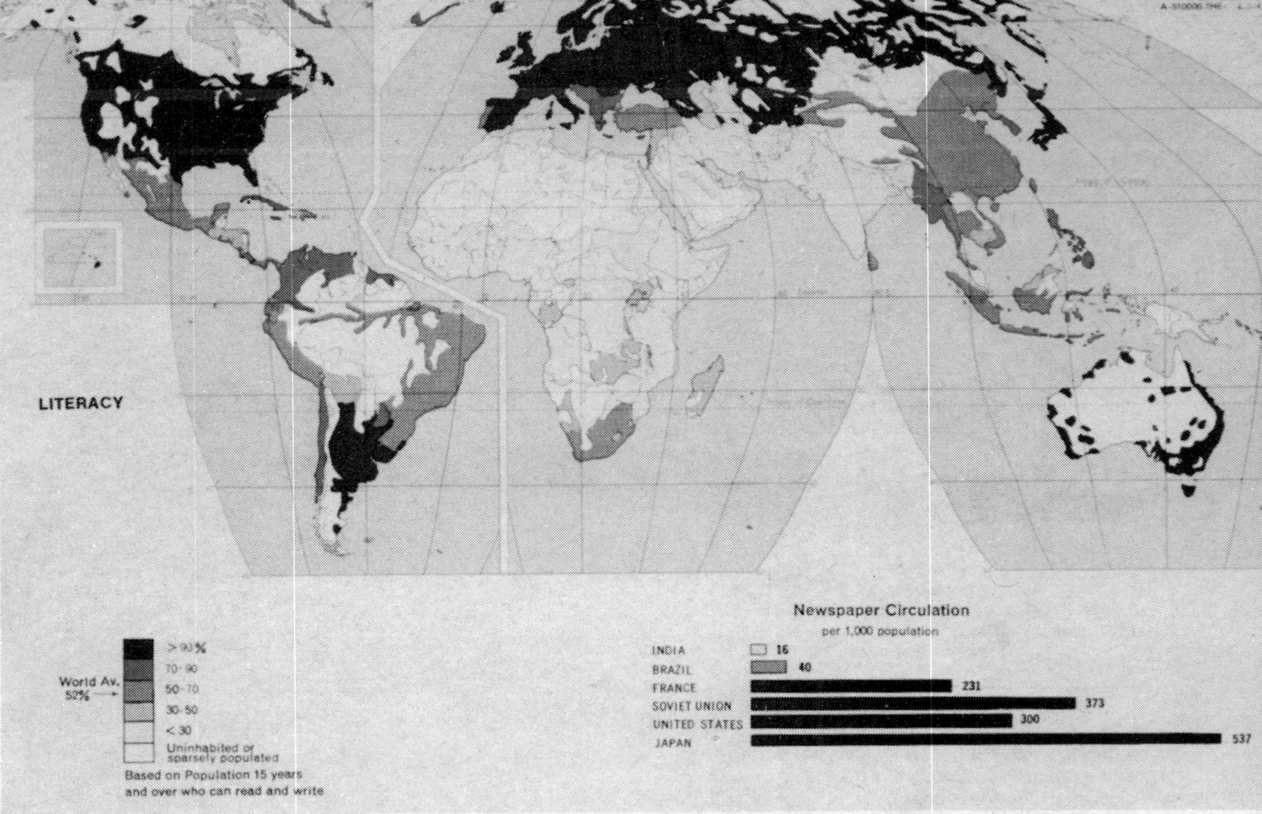

The Times Atlas of the World

'A world remade must be a world remapped.' That intelligent dictum was issued at the end of World War I by Lord Northcliffe, then proprietor of **The Times** *of London. He didn't wait for someone else to do the job;* **The Times Survey Atlas of the World,** *with cartography by John Bartholomew of Edinburgh, was issued in 1921, and was recognized immediately as one of the finest atlases ever printed. The tradition has been continued, and the latest* **Times Atlas** *is the best place for an English-reading person to find where in the world something is located. The book also has a unique ability to convey the feel of the world. It measures 18" x 12½" x 1-3/4", weighs 10 pounds, and contains 512 pages, of which 244 are double-page maps of superb accuracy and beauty — in 8 colors. The index-gazetteer includes more than 210,000 entries, incomparably more than any other atlas of the world, and the entries are keyed not only by individual map coordinates, but by latitude and longitude as well (a feature offered by no other atlas). Despite the huge number of place names the maps are extraordinarily legible, and they are mercifully free of the pink-purple-yellow political emphasis offered by lesser cartographers. Some of the place names may look strange to American readers, because the atlas follows the rules of the Permanent Committee of Geographical Names. This supra-political body sensibly believes that places should be called what their occupants call them. In cases where the generic name is unfamiliar, the traditional anglicized name is also given, in parentheses.*

This brand new Comprehensive Edition of **The Times Atlas of the World** *will make anything else on your coffee table seem puny, as the whole world should.*
—Morton Grosser

Times Atlas of the World
Comprehensive Edition
1980; 512 pp.

$125 postpaid from:
Times Books
3 Park Avenue
New York, NY 10016
or Whole Earth Household Store

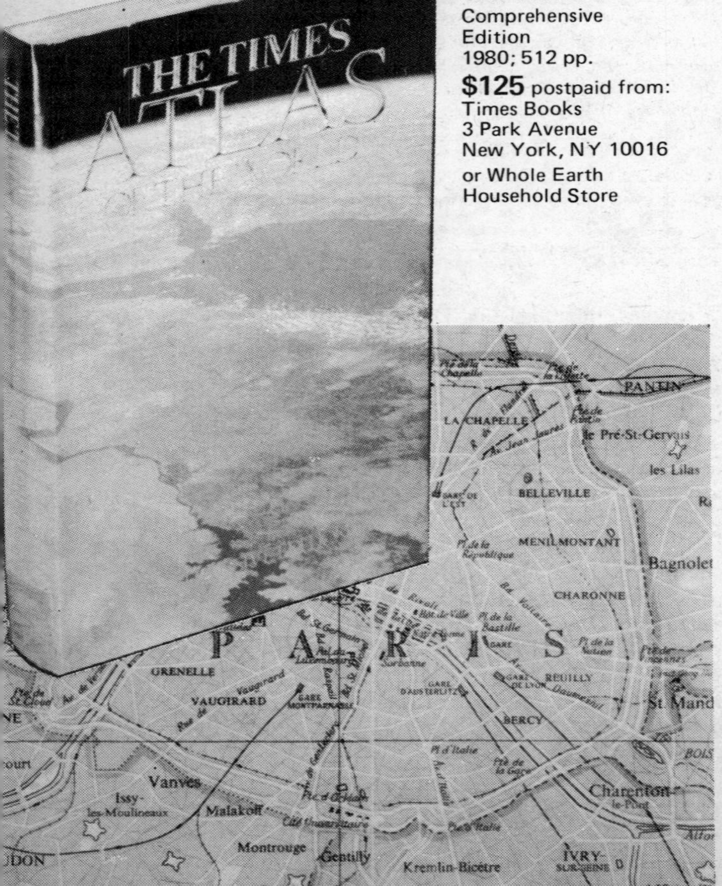

National Geographic maps

More than anyone's, National Geographic's are fantasy maps. Any region you care about, they have a gamut of maps of it, cheap, to place in your daily line of sight. Many of the sheets are highly annotated with points of interest to increase your hankering until you can stand it no longer, and go there. —SB

National Geographic maps
Price list

free from:
National Geographic Maps
P.O. Box 2806
Washington, D.C. 20013

PARTIAL LISTING

Africa, 47" x 61" (1980) $6

Asia, 43½"x61½" (1978) $6

Bible Lands Today, 67"x47" (1976) $6

Europe, 47"x61" (1977) $6

South America, 45"x60" (1980) $6

United States, 69½"x48½" (1976) $6
Index available $1.50 (02489)

World (political) 68"x47½" (1980) $6
Index available $1.50 (02495)

World (physical) 68"x47½" (1977) $6

Medieval England (1979) 23"x30", 1 in. = 20 mi. Historical, illustrations and descriptive notes. $3

Bird Migration in the Americas (1979) 23"x36" 1 in. = 316 mi. Illustrations, descriptive notes, migration routes. $3

Indians of North America (1979) 32½"x37½", 1 in. = 167 mi. Ethnological. Descriptive notes. $3

North America Before Columbus (1979) 32½"x37½", 1 in. = 167 mi. Archaeological. Inset chart highlighting North America prehistory. $3

Africa (1980) 23"x29", 1 in. = 227 mi. Printed both sides. $3

Antarctica (1975) 30"x23", 1 in. = 140 mi. $3

Asia (1978) 37½"x31½", 1 in. = 218 mi. $3

Australia (1979) 30"x23", 1 in. = 100 mi. $3

British Isles (1979) 23"x30", 1 in. = 31 mi. $3

Canada (1972) 31½"x23", 1 in. = 118 mi. $3

West Indies and Central America (1977) 38"x26½", 1 in. = 76 mi. $3

Europe (1977) Celtic Europe on reverse side 23"x30", 1 in. = 102 mi. $3

All prices postpaid.

CIA atlases

One of the things I learned while working on the **California Water Atlas** *is that it's hard to find cartographers: "They all work for the CIA." And their work, the CIA maps, is well-known and well-regarded. But I never knew the Agency did atlasses or that they are so fine. As suggestor Henricks says, "no fat, just good hard facts and figures that are interesting as hell." These three are all we've heard about (The Indian Ocean atlas has increased considerably in significance recently.) BARGAIN prices.* —SB

[Suggested by Ron Henricks]

Polar Regions Atlas
Central Intelligence Agency
1978; 66 pp.
No. 041-015-00094-2
$5 postpaid

Indian Ocean Atlas
Central Intelligence Agency
1976; 80 pp.
No. 041-015-00080-2
$7.50 postpaid

People's Republic of China Administrative Atlas
Central Intelligence Agency
1976; 66 pp.
No. 041-015-00076-4
$3.45 postpaid

all from:
Superintendent of Documents
U.S. Government Printing Office
Washington, DC 20402
or Whole Earth Household Store

•
Some authorities have estimated that reserves of 45 billion barrels of oil and 155 trillion cubic feet of natural may be in the Antartic, but these estimates are highly speculative . . . for a petroleum deposit to be economically exploitable in Antarctic conditions, it would probably have to rank in the giant or supergiant category (more than 500 million barrels of recoverable oil).
—**Polar Regions Atlas**

→
Ice is also a mineral, and Antarctic icebergs may eventually be a source of fresh water for the world's arid areas. Preliminary studies show that transportation costs will determine economic feasibility.
—Polar Regions Atlas

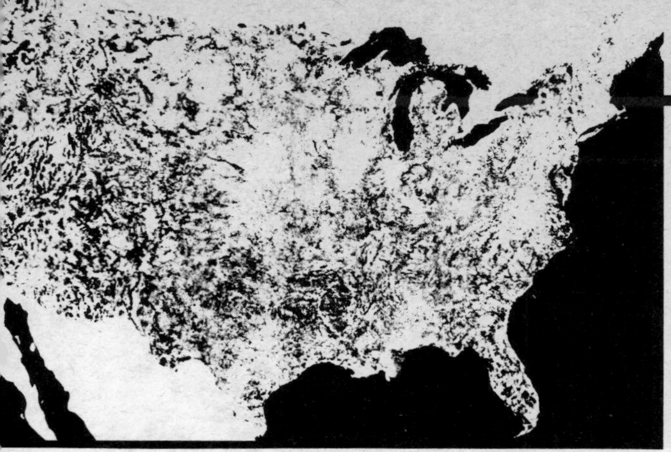

U.S. photo murals

Guaranteed fascination. Find the block you were born on, the stream you lost your virginity beside, your big town, your far peak — all in one picture for once. More detail per wall than anything comparable, and a bargain. Ask for Band 5, Conterminous U.S., Summer. They also have Alaska. —SB

[Suggested by Roger Critchlow]

U.S. Photo Murals
from:
Cartographic Division
Soil Conservation Service
Rm. G-110, Federal Bldg.
Hyattsville, MD 20782

Single print coverage:
14" x 21" $4
41" x 61" $17

6-print coverage:
20" x 24" $5/print ($30 total)
40" x 60" $17/print

17-print coverage:
40" x 48" $15/print

54-print coverage:
20" x 24" $5/print ($30 total)
40" x 60" $17/print

17-print coverage:
40" x 48" $15/print

State and regional atlases

Below are all the state atlases I could find of any here-and-now value. Historical atlases and specialty atlases are not included. Most are so-so — sloppy black-and-white sketchy maps. Only the great ones get a couple of words of praise. I am amazed how few good state atlases are in print. —Peter Warshall

Atlas of Alabama. Neal J. Lineback, editor, 1973. $8.75 from University of Alabama Press, Box 2877, University, AL 35486.

California Atlas (Patterns of the Land), 1976. $8.95 from Mayfield Publishing Company, 285 Hamilton Avenue, Palo Alto, CA 94301. *All kinds of information. Two color. Good, solid buy.*

Atlas of California. Michael Donley et. al., editors, 1979. $47.50 from Pacific Book Center, 9555 Washington Blvd., Culver City, CA 90230. *Brand new, brightly colored, not too bad.*

Atlas of Florida. Compiled by Erwin Raisz (see right). Originally published by the University of Florida Press, Gainesville, FL 32601. *Now out of print. The model for other state atlases. Old but wonderful.*

Atlas of Hawaii. Department of Geography, University of Hawaii, editors, 1973. $19.95 from University Press of Hawaii, 2840 Kolowalu Street, Honolulu, HI 96822. *One of the very best. Multicolor. Comprehensive.*

Atlas of Indiana. 1970. $2.17 from Occasional Pub. No. 3, Department of Geography, Indiana University, Bloomington, IN 47405. (Make your check payable to the Indiana University Foundation.)

Atlas of Kentucky. P.P. Karan and Cotton Mather, editors, 1977. $19.50 from University Press of Kentucky, Lexington, KY 40506.

Atlas of Maryland. 1977. $6.95 from Summer Programs, Turner Labs, College Park Campus, University of Maryland, College Park, MD 20742. Color. *Great!*

Atlas of Michigan. Laurence Sommers, 1977. $19.95 from Eerdmans Publishing Co., 255 Jefferson Ave. SE, Grand Rapids, MI 49503. Color. *Great!*

Atlas of Mississippi. Ralph D. Cross and Robert W. Wales, 1973. $15 from University Press of Mississippi, 3825 Ridgewood Road, Jackson, MS 39211. Color. *Good but not great.*

Montana in Maps. 1974. $7.50 from Big Sky Books, Montana State University, Bozeman, MT 59717. *Good but limited subjects.*

Two limited but great atlases of Nebraska are: **Economic Atlas of Nebraska,** Richard E. Lonsdale, 1977, $14.95; and **Agricultural Atlas of Nebraska,** James H. Williams and Doug Murfield, 1977, $12.95. Both from University of Nebraska Press, 901 N. 17th St., Lincoln, NE 68588.

North Carolina Atlas (Portrait of a Changing Southern State). James W. Clay et. al., editor, 1975. $17.95 from University of North Carolina Press, PO Box 2288, Chapel Hill, NC 27514. Color. *Great!*

Atlas of North Dakota. 1976. Write for the price from North Dakota Studies Inc., Box 612, Fargo, ND 58102.

Atlas of Oregon. William G.C. Loy, 1976. $29.95 from University of Oregon Books, University Publications, 139 Susan Campbell Hall, University of Oregon, Eugene, OR 97403. *Great! One of the best.*

Atlas of the Pacific Northwest (Washington, Oregon and Idaho). 5th Edition. Richard M. Highsmith, editor, 1973. $7.50 from Oregon State University Press, 101 Waldo Hall, Oregon State University, Corvallis, OR 97331. Blue overlay. *OK. Nice to see attempts to cover regions.*

Socioeconomic Patterns of Pennsylvania. A Department of Commerce Publication, State of Pennsylvania, 1975. $15 from Bureau of Management Services, State Book Store, PO Box 1365, Harrisburg, PA 17125. *Limited scope.*

Pennsylvania Atlas (A Thematic Atlas of the Keystone State). Paul Rizza, Alan Smith, et. al., 1976. $6.95 from Ptolemy Press, PO Box 243, Grove City, PA 16127. *I haven't seen it.*

Atlas of Texas. 1976. $20 from Bureau of Business Research, University of Texas, Box 7459, University Station, Austin, TX 78712. *Sumptuous. This edition has wonderful, entertaining cultural maps.*

Atlas of Wisconsin. Charles Collins, editor, 1972. $7.95 from University of Wisconsin Press, 114 N. Murray St., Madison, WI 53715.

Washington Environmental Atlas. Army Corps of Engineers, 1975. $48 from Government Printing Office, Washington, DC 20402. Stock number 008-020-00526-6. *Extravagant size and production.*

Geological highway maps

Incredible highway maps with more densely packed information than most textbooks. Each map has five maps: (1) a physiographic map of the major landforms and watersheds; (2) a tectonic map showing major uplifts, downwarps and fault lines; (3) a beautifully colored geology map showing highway routes so you can check out each rock formation you are driving past; (4) a geological cross section to show the structure of the rock formations below the surface; and (5) a chart to color co-ordinate the rock you're driving past with its age and mode of formation. In addition, there are special maps like the extent of glaciers in Alaska or a history of the ancient seas of Utah. —Peter Warshall

Geological Highway Maps
$4 postpaid (folded) from:
American Association of Petroleum Geologists
P.O. Box 979
Tulsa, OK 74101

Maps presently available:

1. Mid-Continent (KS, MO, OK, AK)
2. Southern Rockies (AZ, CO, NM, UT)
3. Pacific Southwest (CA, NV)
4. Mid-Atlantic Region (KY, WV, VA, MD, DL, TN, NC, SC)
5. Northern Rockies (ID, MT, WY)
6. Pacific Northwest (WA, OR)
7. Texas
8. Alaska and Hawaii
9. Southeast (AL, FL, GA, LA, MS)
10. Northeast (CT, ME, MA, NH, NJ, NY, PA, RI, VT)
11. Great Lakes Region (IL, IN, MI, OH, WI)
12. Northern Plains (MN, ND, SD, NB, IA)

↓

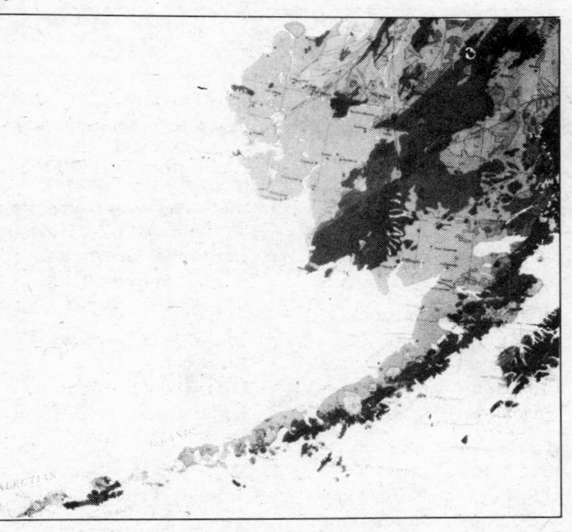

Raisz Landform Maps

Erwin Raisz was perhaps the last great artist-cartographer. He invented little images of all the Earth's landforms and then drew delicate lines with an understanding eye and a hand for utmost clarity. His big map of the United States (and **CQ***'s Biogeographical Map) are the two I keep up on the wall.* —Peter Warshall

↓

Raisz Landform Maps
Price sheet from:
Raisz Landform Maps
130 Charles Street
Boston, MA 02114

United States, $1.05, 42" x 27" black.

United States, $1.05 22" x 15", 3-color *Simplified version of of above*

Northwestern States, $1.05, 35" x 26" *Washington, Oregon, Idaho and parts of Montana*

Alaska, $1.05, 32" x 28" *Beautiful, in brown*

Mexico, $1.05, 41" x 28" *The best map for Mexico*

California and Nevada, $ .30, 17" x 11" *A must for Western watershed obsessives like myself*

Hudson Valley, $ .20, 11" x 18½" *With cross-sections, needed by every New York school kid*

Tennessee, $ .30, 11" x 18½" *With cross-sections*

North America, $ .20, 8½" x 11" *Small, but at least no borders*

Michigan, $ .20, 8½" x 11" *With cross-section and insets*

Utah, $ .20, 8½" x 11" *With cross-section*

. . . and many others.

You can get a complete set of 35 maps for $12! For mailing in a tube add $1 each. For mailing folded add $ .45 each.

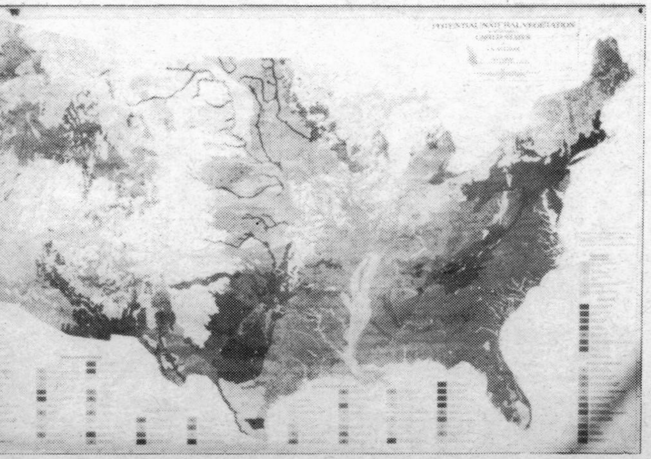

Potential Natural Vegetation of the United States

When you are despondent over the works of humans, hie yourself to the forested states and tall-grass prairies of this map of never-land, a USA gone native. It's not as pretty as our "Biogeographical Provinces Map" but it's considerably bigger and far more detailed and very much in the same spirit. Spirit of place. —SB

Potential Natural Vegetation of the Conterminous United States
A. W. Kuchler
revised edition, 1975

←

$14.50 postpaid from:
American Geographical Society
Broadway at 156th Street
New York, NY 10032

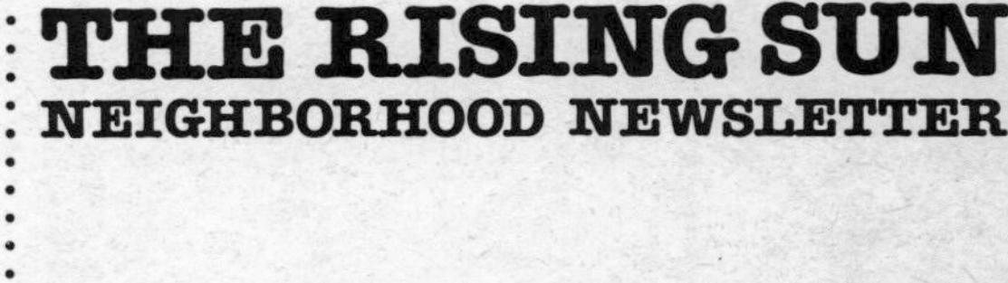

The lady who gave me a ride to work today had her front seat covered with about 200 packs of razor blades, 25 blades in each pack. She does paint and wallpaper for a living. She says the rich ladies she works for are jealous of her because she gets out and does things all the time and they can't think of anything to do.

Finding Maps

TART WITH A GOOD STORE. They will charge you a little more, but time is money. Map finding can take months. Then call the local county office and ask if they have a map room. Try the local library or, better still, a university library. If you're near a state capital you've got it easy, as they each have a staff cartographer. If still stuck, I find the United States Geological Survey (USGS) to be the friendliest and easiest big government office to work with. For ultimate scanning use the National Cartographic Information Center.
—Peter Warshall

National Cartographic Information Center

You want to know everything? All satellite images, all low altitude photomaps, all human-made maps and maybe some of the historical maps of where you live? The National Cartographic Information Center (NCIC) doesn't provide maps but coordinates for you all the major mapping agencies in the United States. It's the Super Geo-Search. It's free (subsidized by our taxes). It's thorough. It takes a long time to complete (up to three months). If you just want aerial or satellite, it's quicker to go direct to the EROS Data Center. If you just want low altitude photomaps, it's quicker through the USGS offices. If you just want a human-made map, it's quicker direct to the mapmaker agency if you know it.

HERE'S HOW: When writing NCIC, you should clearly state that you want it all or that you want all the maps for a particular purpose (all land use; all property owned by Federal agencies; all water-related maps; all historical maps, whatever). Carefully define geographic area of interest (the Eel River watershed, or Cincinnati or . . .). Make a sketch map and give latitudes and longitudes.

THIS WILL HAPPEN: NCIC sends you a postcard saying they have forwarded your request to a whole bunch of mapping agencies. (They say which.) Each mapping agency sends you a packet of info on how to get what you want. (Low altitude aerial photographs have an extra step; they send you a list of photo indexes and you order photo index which has snapshots of your watershed.) You find maps and/or find exact photo(s) from index and order on each separate agency's order forms. Mapping agency sends you maps and photos. You got it!
—Peter Warshall

National Cartographic Information Center
U.S. Geological Survey

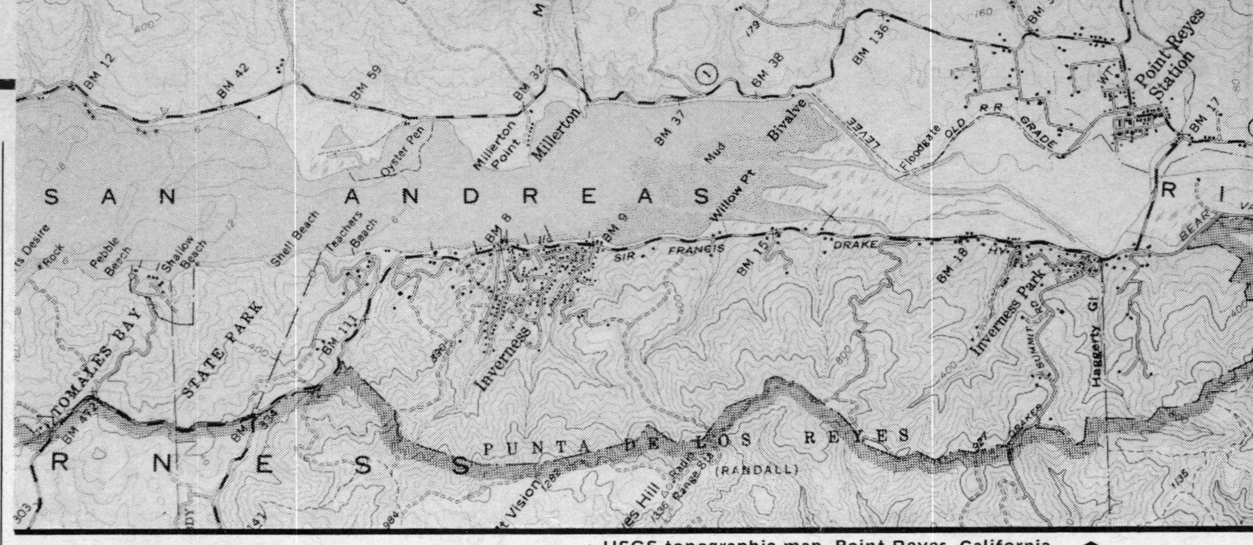

USGS topographic map, Point Reyes, California ↑

USGS topographic maps

THE basic maps. Start with these contour-lined topographic maps. You may want more detail later, but these are the only way to cut through the mental blocks of property-line thought. Streams, hillslopes and human settlement (roads, homes, airports, etc.). The detailed maps come in two basic scales — 1:24,000 (1" equals 2,000 feet) and 1:62,500 (1" equals about a mile). Usually available at local map stores or any of the USGS offices.
—Peter Warshall

Series	Scale	Cost	Area (square miles)	Map Size
7½ minute	1:24,000	$1.25	49 - 70	22" x 27"
15 minute	1:62,500	$1.25	197 - 282	17" x 21"
30 minute	1:100,000	$2.00	1,145 - 2,167	26" x 40"
1 degree	1:250,000	$2.00	4,580 - 8,669	22" x 31"

Distribution Offices:
For maps **by mail** (and over-the-counter) you can write to these offices.

Maps of areas east of the Mississippi River, including Minnesota, Puerto Rico, and the Virgin Islands, are distributed by mail from:

Washington Distribution Branch
U.S. Geological Survey
1200 South Eads Street
Arlington, VA 22202

Maps for areas west of the Mississippi River, including Alaska, Hawaii, Louisiana, Guam, and American Samoa, are distributed from:

Denver Distribution Branch
U.S. Geological Survey
Federal Center
Denver, CO 80225

Maps of Alaska may be ordered directly from:

Alaska Distribution Branch
U.S. Geological Survey
310 First Avenue
Fairbanks, AK 99701

United States Geological Survey (USGS)

This is my favorite government agency still bearing much of the honesty and tradition of its illustrious forefather John Wesley Powell. They are truly helpful to us, the citizens whose tax money supports their studies and mapping. Here's how to find them. —Peter Warshall

Regional Mapping Centers:
Over-the-counter sales of USGS maps. Orders quickly processed for aerial photographs. Locations as follows.

Eastern Mapping Center
U.S. Geological Survey
536 National Center
Reston, VA 22092

Rocky Mountain Mapping Center
U.S. Geological Survey
Box 25046
Federal Center
Denver, CO 80225

Mid-Continent Mapping Center
U.S. Geological Survey
Box 133
(or 900 Pine Street)
Rolla, MO 65401

Public Inquiries Offices:
Over-the-counter sales of local geologic, hydrologic and topographic maps and selected maps of general interest. Virginia and Washington offices have maps for entire nation. Anchorage, Spokane, Washington and Los Angeles also have satellite reference file on microfilm.

Public Inquiries Office
U.S. Geological Survey

108 Skyline Building
508 Second Avenue
Anchorage, AK 99501

7638 Federal Building
300 N. Los Angeles St.
Los Angeles, CA 90012

504 Custom House
555 Battery Street
San Francisco, CA 94111

1012 Federal Building
1961 Stout Street
Denver, CO 80202

1028 General Services Building
19th and F Sts, N.W.
Washington, D.C. 20244

1045 Federal Building
1100 Commerce Street
Dallas, TX 75202

8102 Federal Building
125 S. State Street
Salt Lake City, UT 84111

National Center
Room 1C402
Reston, VA 22092

678 U.S. Court House
West 920 Riverside Ave.
Spokane, WA 99201

USGS geology maps

Each USGS office has geology maps on a large scale (1:250,000 to 1:1,000,000). They have more detail than the Highway Geology Maps (p. 23). USGS also produces spectacular maps and folders with photos on earthquakes, volcanoes, minerals and the continental shelves.
—Peter Warshall

←

Plastic relief maps

Plastic relief maps of the continental United States and Hawaii on a scale of 1:250,000 made from Defense Department multi-color topographic maps. Great for kids and, of course, us lazy adults who get tired of squinting and tracing contour lines. —Peter Warshall

Plastic Relief Maps
$13.95 postpaid from:
T.N. Hubbard & Scientific Company
Northbrook, IL 60062

↓

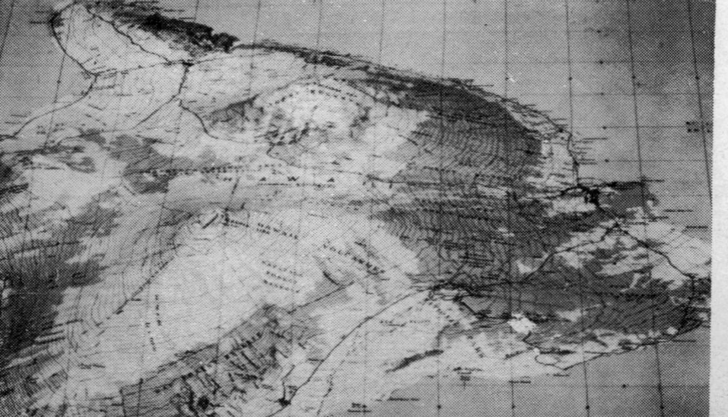

Maps for America

If you're using USGS maps a lot, this intriguing many-colored tome can deepen your use considerably. As a long time topo map lover, I revel in this stuff.
—SB

Maps for America
(Cartographic products of the U.S. Geological Survey and others)
Morris M. Thompson
(No. 024-001-03145-1)
1979; 265 pp.

$11 postpaid from:
Superintendent of Documents
U.S. Govt. Printing Office
Washington, D.C. 20402

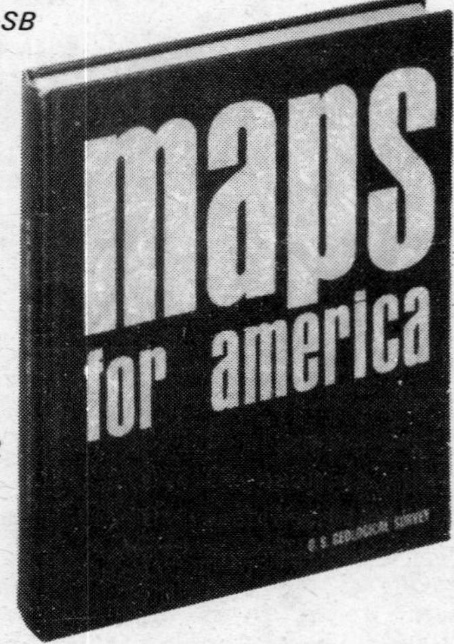

•
Woods, brushwood, and scrub are mapped if the growth is thick enough to provide cover for troops or to impede foot travel. This condition is considered to exist if density of the vegetative cover is 20 percent or more. Growth that meets the minimum density requirement is estimated as follows: if the average open-space distance between the crowns is equal to the average crown diameter, the density of the vegetative cover is 20 percent.

Soil maps

Valuable maps. They describe our most precious resource — the soil from which our food must come. These maps are definitely not detailed enough for some projects (like a house-to-house septic tank system survey or gardening problems), but for a grounded start at practical earthiness every citizen should be able to say: "I live on a sandy-clay-loam that is about ten feet deep and covers half my community." Scales vary from 1:24,000 (1" equals 2,000 feet) to 1:63,360 (1" equals a mile).

Maps are available from local Soil Conservation Districts — usually your county. They come ultimately from:

Soil Conservation Service
Department of Agriculture
Federal Building
6505 Belcrest Road
Hyattsville, MD 20782

Prices vary. So does quality. Much soil mapping is under way right now.
—Peter Warshall

↓

San Francisco Bay

Satellite photos of Earth from EROS Data Center

These images from space are not what the human eye can see. They are made with film specially sensitive to waves of the electromagnetic spectrum, such as infrared, that are invisible to us limited mammalian critters. For instance, computer enhanced false infrared (my favorite image) pops out healthy vegetation in bright red, makes clear water a glistening black, and asphalt or roof-tops are a soft blue to blue-gray.

Landsat satellite images (or "photomaps") of your home town are made every 18 days as this persevering satellite sticks tenaciously to its orbit. So, you can get (if the clouds are right) a complete calendar of your home or perhaps a photo of your birthplace on the day you were born.

ACCESS
As usual here on Earth, government-anything means lots of paperwork. Don't despair. It's absolutely interesting and worthwhile to view your home (or anywhere) from out there (and at many seasons and years). Just follow the procedures as if your taxes depended on it.

THE FOOL-PROOF METHOD
You get what you want, but it requires weeks to even months of patience. Simply write to:

Users Service Unit
EROS Data Center
Sioux Falls, SD 57198 or call
(605) 594-6511

Ask for "Geosearch Inquiry Form" and instructions. You fill it out for latitude/longitude, name or location of point of interest (the smaller the area, the quicker the results). They send you a computer printout (and cryptic decoder) of everything available in aerial photography. You choose the images and fill out an order form. Since you never see the images before buying them, this method is somewhat of a gamble.

THE SHORTCUT METHOD
Go directly to browse files set up for citizens. Go through the catalogs of available photos (a bunch of dates and codes) and, in many cases, look through the microfilm of actual photos. The person-in-charge will show you how to code your request to match the satellite path over your home and can give you the order forms. In the lingo, this is the "Quick Response System."

SOMEWHAT SHORTER METHOD IF YOU KNOW EXACTLY WHAT YOU WANT
If you don't live near a browse file, you might do this. Request: "Single ERTS Coverage" for one point on Earth. Single ERTS photomaps do not include Skylab, NASA aircraft, and low altitude flights. It's just Landsat satellites in b-and-w and false color. They send you a "Coverage Map" and you return a form which pinpoints the orbital path. —*Peter Warshall*

Prices for satellite photographs range from $8 to $50, depending on the size of the picture, whether it is black-and-white, color or color-infrared, and whether it is on film or paper. Prices for aircraft photographs range from $3 to $50, depending on the same criteria.

There are approximately 30 browse files in state capitals and other cities around the country, and the list is continually being expanded. The best way to find a browse file near you is to call or write one of the five following regional centers:

U.S. Geological Survey
National Cartographic
Information Center
507 National Center
Reston, VA 22092
(703) 860-6045

U.S.G.S., Mid-Continent
Mapping Center
N.C.I.C.
1400 Independence Road
Rolla, MO 65401
(314) 364-3680

U.S.G.S., Rocky Mountain
Mapping Center
N.C.I.C., Stop 504
Denver Federal Center
Denver CO 80225
(303) 234-2346

U.S.G.S., Western
Mapping Center
N.C.I.C., 345 Middlefield Rd.
Menlo Park, CA 94025
(415) 323-8111

U.S.G.S., N.C.I.C.
National Space
Technology Laboratories
NSTL Station, MS 39529
(Just east of New Orleans)
(601) 688-3544

The National Oceanographic and Atmospheric Administration (NOAA) also maintains archives of images from all meteorological satellites and a limited number of other research satellites. For information on imagery of a specific area, write:

The N.O.A.A. Satellite Data Service Division
World Weather Building, Room 100
Washington, DC 20233

Prices start at $3.00 (for photographs) and rise for film loops or microfiche. —*Art Kleiner*

Golden Gate Bridge, San Francisco ↑

Low-altitude aerial photomaps

Satellite photos are too far from everyday life on Earth. Low flying aircraft photos are closer to home. The U.S. Geological Survey (see "USGS," opposite page) has over 50,000 photo indexes to the aerial photos they use to make their maps. Request a photo index for your area first, then choose which photos to buy. Or go to a USGS office where photo indexes can be flipped through. Each 9" x 9" photo covers 3 to 7 miles on a side and costs only $3. Prints that are 36" x 36" cost $20. —*Peter Warshall*

Side looking radar

A ripoff of taxpayers' money. The U.S. Air Force makes these wonderful photos and deposits them with Goodyear which insists they cost $82 for a 5" x 15" photo. These are the best watershed photographs for landscape detail. The photos are not dependent on the Sun and make the only aerial photos possible in regions of long-term fog, clouds and smog. The photos show very subtle relief features especially stream patterns and faults — rarely visible by other aerial mapping methods. Not all of the U.S. has been photographed. Someone with influence in the Air Force should help correct this price outrage. —*Peter Warshall*

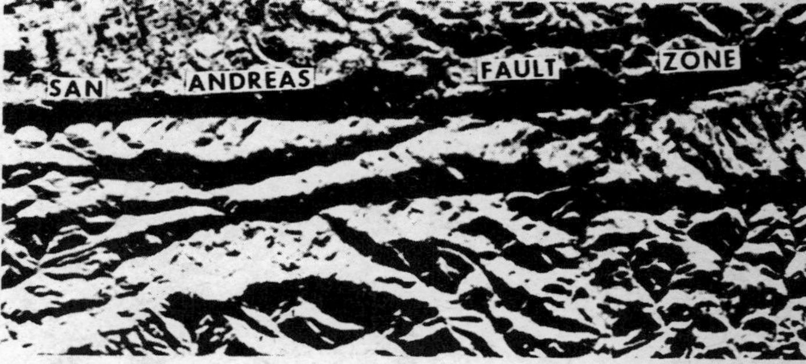

Interpretation of Aerial Photographs

Learn how to read aerial and satellite photos for tree species, geological trends, camouflaged missile sites, industrial pollution, and the peculiar configuration of your yard. The best book. —*SB*

Interpretation of Aerial Photographs
T. Eugene Avery
1962, 1977; 392 pp.

$16.95 postpaid from:
Burgess Publishing Co.
7108 Ohms Lane
Minneapolis, MN 55435

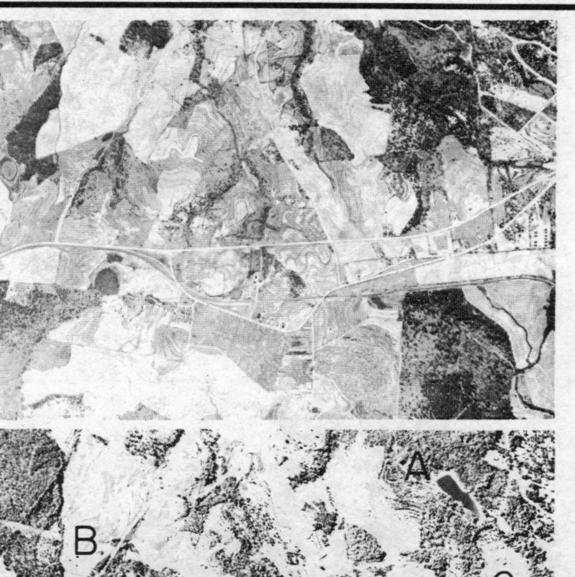

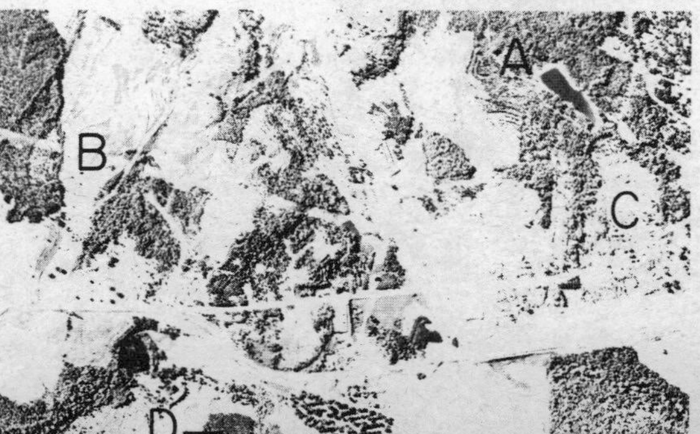

→ Rural area photographed before and after an interval of sixteen years. Among changes evident on the bottom exposure are: (A) a new pond; (B) a cleared right-of-way; (C) a new residential area; (D) a pine plantations.

Pilot Rock

Fine source of well-worked-out slide programs of high altitude pnotos on such subjects as "Trans-Alaska Pipeline," "California Coast," "Urban America," "Glaciology," "Midwest," etc. Prices for 10 to 40 slide sets range from $16.50 to $48.50. —*SB*

Pilot Rock
Price list

free from:
Pilot Rock
Arcata, CA 95501

THE RISING SUN
NEIGHBORHOOD NEWSLETTER

Some married people when they're cleaning up after a party and some of the guests are still there look at each other like they have a secret joke. Other married people act like they have a secret but it's not a joke.

If you have a fancy rubber stamp and you want it to stamp different colors at the same time, color it with water-soluble felt tip markers, spray it with Windex and stamp it.

Geology Illustrated

An artist of aerial photography, Shelton uses some 400 of his finest photos to illuminate a discussion of the whole-earth system. Not a traditional textbook, but a fascinating exploration of the problems posed by asking, "How did that come about?" Worth buying for the photos and book design alone, but you'll probably find yourself becoming interested in geology regardless of your original intentions. A masterpiece. —Larry McCombs

Geology Illustrated
John S. Shelton
1966; 434 pp.

$19.95 postpaid from:
W.H. Freeman and Co.
660 Market Street
San Francisco, CA 94104
or Whole Earth Household Store

↑ Part of a perennially snow-covered plateau and two of the valley glaciers that drain it, as seen from the air; about 125 miles southwest of Scoresby Sound at 69° N latitude near the east coast of Greenland.

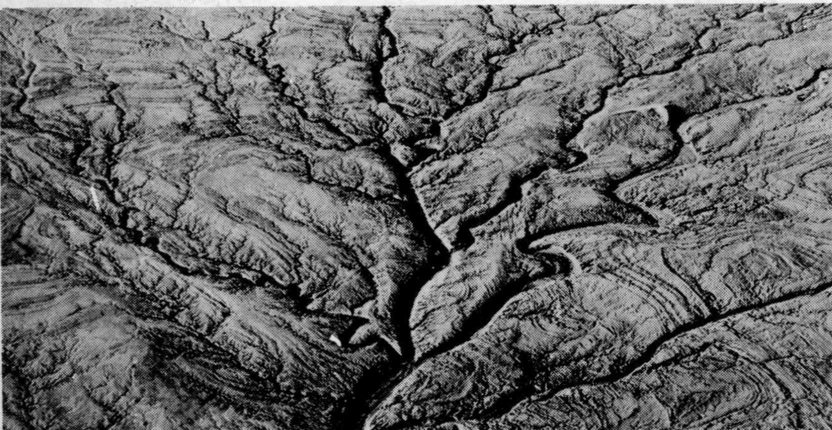

View upstream over upper Tule Wash, west of Salton Sea in southeastern California. Area, 6 square miles.

← Close-up of the two gullies offset by San Andreas earthquake fault 12 miles west of Taft, California.

Photographic Anatomy of the Human Body

As your home can never seem the same after looking down on it from the air, your physical self-image is due for changes on viewing these beautiful color photos of human organs, cross-sections, bone and muscle structures, an intricate universe within the skin. Hand the book to anyone; they become riveted. —SB
[Suggested by Tom Bender]

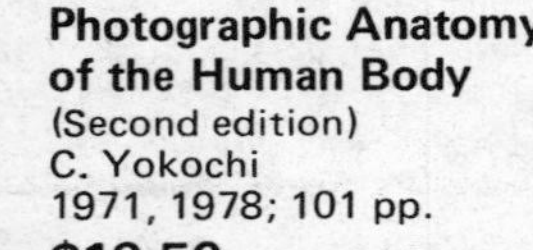

Photographic Anatomy of the Human Body
(Second edition)
C. Yokochi
1971, 1978; 101 pp.

$19.50 postpaid from:
University Park Press
233 East Redwood Street
Baltimore, MD 21202

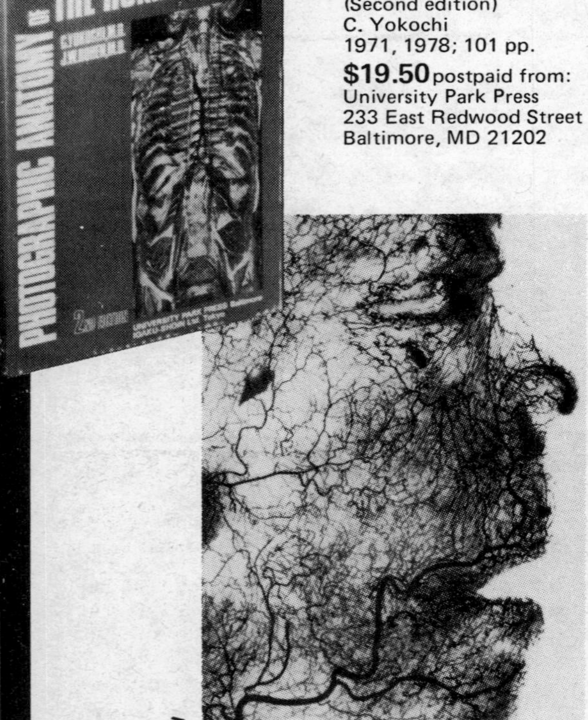

↗ The face has so many blood vessels that it can stand cold better than other areas of the body and excessive bleeding occurs when injured. However, the wound closes quickly and rarely suppurates.

← The small intestine starts from the duodenum (it derives its name from the fact that its length equals the width of twelve fingers) and runs down through the jejunum (meaning emptiness, which is in most cases the post-mortem state of this organ) and ileum (meaning an entangled or winding state) until it reaches the rectum. The large intestine starts from the cecum (meaning blind end), passes through the ascending, transverse, descending, and sigmoid colons into the rectum. The distended portion of the rectum slightly above the anus is referred to as the ampulla where the excreta are amassed.

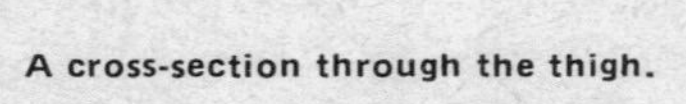

A cross-section through the thigh. →

Behold Man

If health is aided by a good mental image of the LIVING body, this book is the best medicine you can stock. Nilsson has gone beyond his famous embryo photographs to the entire human organism — cells, reproduction, blood vessels, lungs, intestines, skin, brain, eyes and ears and more — what a landscape. I wanted to put this book in our section on sex — it's that sensual. (*See Nilsson's* **A Child Is Born**, *p. 346.*) —SB

Behold Man
Lennart Nilsson
1974; 254 pp.

$9.95 postpaid from:
Little, Brown & Company
200 West Street
Waltham, MA 02154
or Whole Earth Household Store

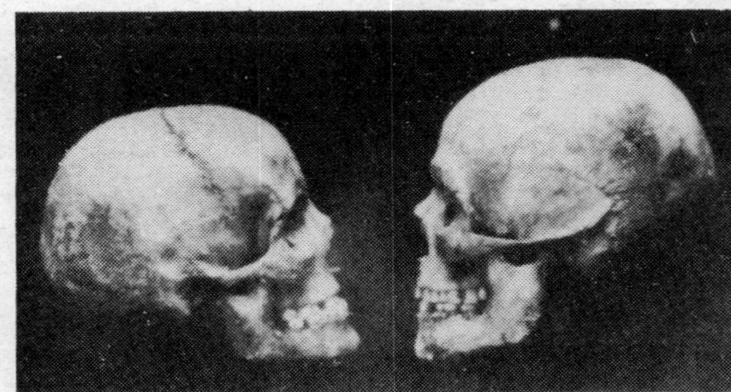

Skulls of an adult woman and man.

The woman's skull is on the left. The two skulls were found in a medieval graveyard on Froson near Ostersund, Sweden, buried in earth for almost a thousand years.

Male and female skulls differ in various ways. The male skull is often larger, has heavier brow ridges, a recessed root of the nose, and stronger muscular attachments.

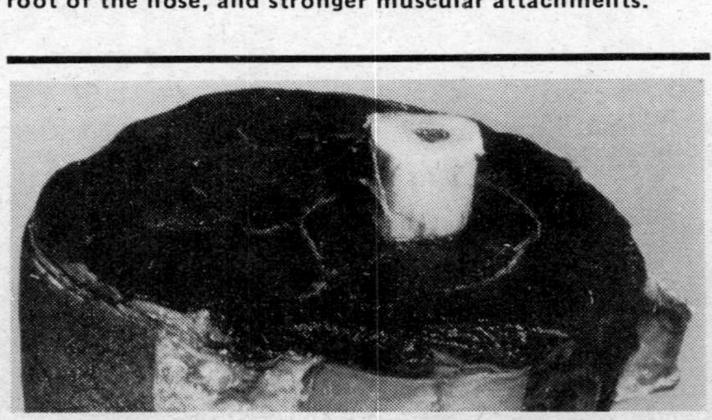

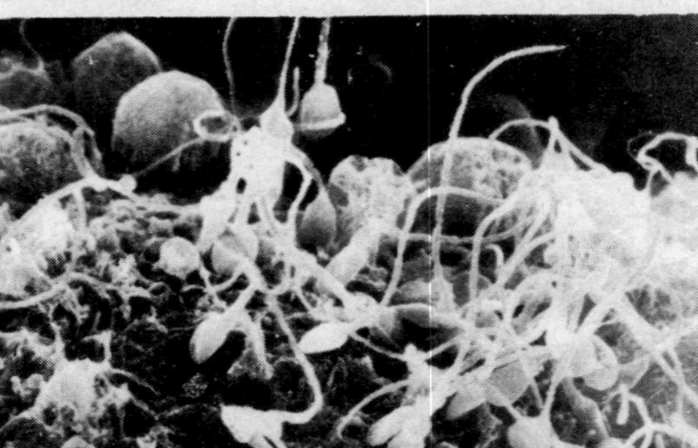

Spermatozoa with long tails swarm around the ovum's surface. Magnified about 2000 times.

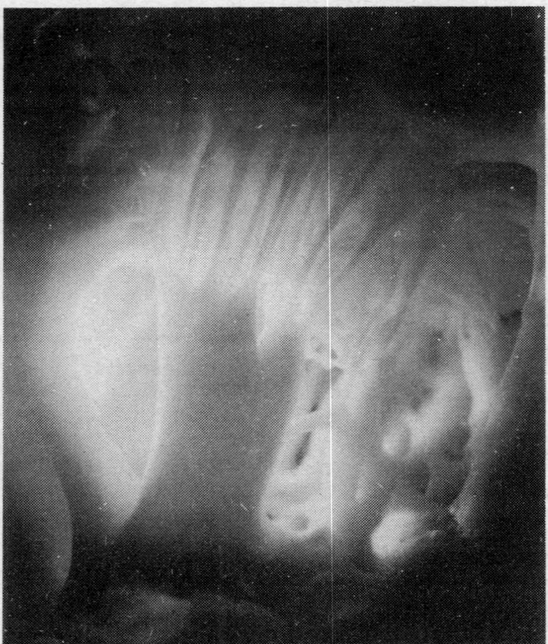

The interior part of the heart.

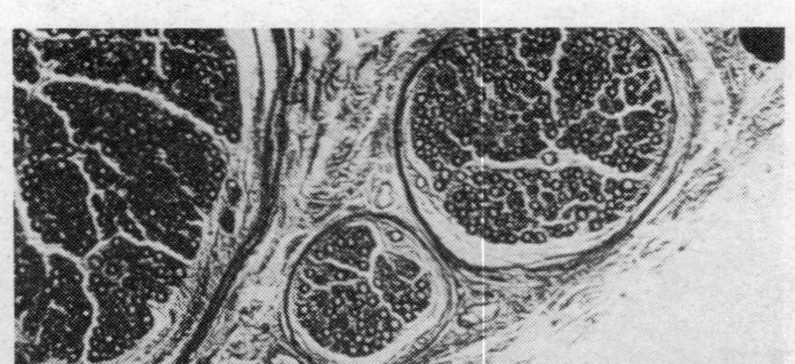

Cross section of a nerve.

On Growth and Form

A paradigm classic. Everyone dealing with growth or form in any manner can use the book. We've seen worn copies on the shelves of artists, inventors, engineers, computer systems designers, biologists. —SB

On Growth and Form
D'Arcy Wentworth Thompson
Two volume edition
1917, 1952; 1,116 pp.
$120 postpaid

Abridged paper edition
1917, 1961; 346 pp.
$11.95 postpaid from:
Cambridge University Press
510 North Avenue
New Rochelle, NY 10801
or Whole Earth Household Store

Diagrammatic construction of Callimitra. (a) A bubble suspended within a tetrahedral cage; (b) another bubble within a skeleton of the former bubble.

(a) (b)

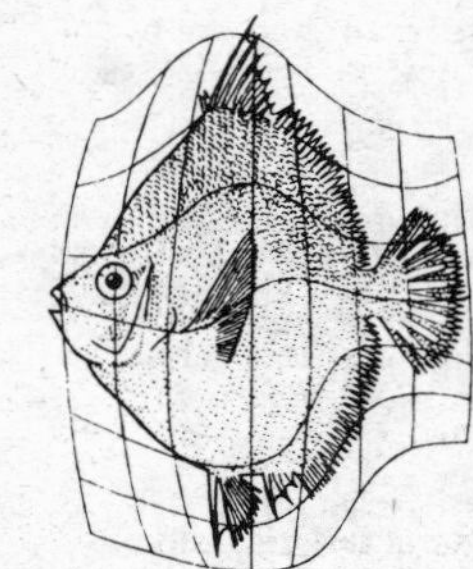
Antigonia capros.

Pseudopriacanthus altus.

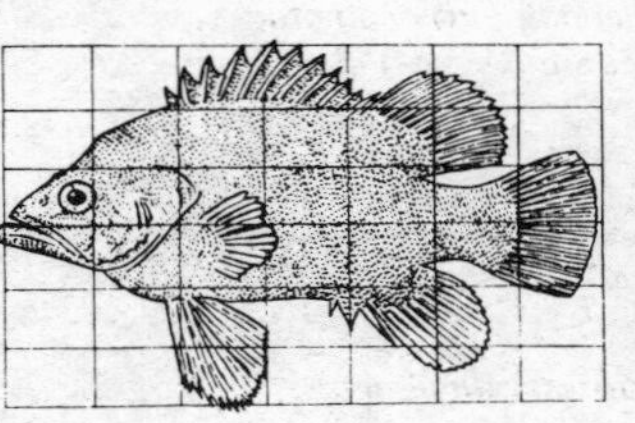
Polyprion.

The geometry of the little inner tetrahedron is not less simple and elegant. Its six edges and four faces are all equal. The films attaching it to the outer skeleton are all planes. Its faces are spherical, and each has its centre in the opposite corner. The edges are circular arcs, with cosine 1/3; each is in a plane perpendicular to the chord of the arc opposite, and each has its centre in the middle of that chord. Along each edge the two intersection spheres meet each other at an angle of 120°.

Patterns in Nature

This is a book in which, with a few photographs, some clear uncomplicated text and an occasional number, you are plunged into nature's mysteries. I suspect that the route to the frontier need never be more complicated than this, but there are so few guides who can show you the way.

I wish the book were five times as long as it is because reading it is such a pleasure. There are eight chapters:

1. *Space and Size*
2. *Basic Patterns*
3. *All Things Flow*
4. *Spirals, Meanders and Explosives*
5. *Models of Branching*
6. *Trees*
7. *Soap Bubbles*
8. *Packing and Cracking*

—*Steve Baer*

Patterns in Nature
Peter S. Stevens
1974; 240 pp.
$6.95 postpaid from:
Little, Brown and Co., Inc.
200 West Street
Waltham, MA 02154
or Whole Earth Household Store

•

In matters of visual form we sense that nature plays favorites. Among her darlings are spirals, meanders, branching patterns, and 120-degree joints. Those patterns occur again and again. Nature acts like a theatrical producer who brings on the same players each night in different costumes for different roles. The players perform a limited repertoire: pentagons make most of the flowers but none of the crystals; hexagons handle most of the repetitive two-dimensional patterns but never by themselves enclose three-dimensional space. On the other hand, the spiral is the height of versatility, playing roles in the replication of the smallest virus and in the arrangement of matter in the largest galaxy.

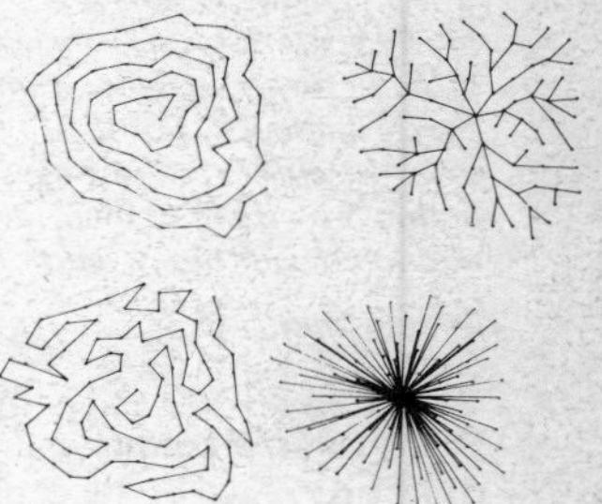

•

Another benefit of small leaves is that they enable the tree to adopt different patterns of growth in different environments. The giant fronds of the palm grow with a strict spiraling symmetry, the same on the north side as on the south, the same to windward as to leeward. Compare the palms, which have a strict geometrical leaf development, with the small leaves that the elm puts forth from freely flowing branches. The elm fills each chink of its environment with a specially tailored structure, while the palm builds the same edifice for every occasion.

•

The rule stands: cracking in elastic materials occurs suddenly, around 120° joints; cracking in inelastic material occurs sequentially, and new cracks join old ones at 90°. →

Consequently, films and cracks have a great deal in common. Films that are elastic, like films of soap and water, shift in relation to one another to meet at 120° — just like cracks; films that cannot deform their boundaries meet those boundaries at 90° — just like cracks.

•

Nature does not premeditate; she does not use mathematics; she does not deliberately produce whole patterns, she lets whole patterns produce themselves. Nature does what nature demands; she is beyond blame and responsibility.

Tissues and Organs

The poetry of the body — as seen by the scanning electron microscope. Taste buds like great leafy cabbages. The microstructure of the eye, tiny transparent cells dovetailed together as precisely as prisms. The delicate lacework of folded membranes within which the organelles of the cell hang like Christmas ornaments wrapped in swirls of gossamer. The macrophage cells like free-wandering dustmops, the street-cleaners of the lungs. And everywhere the delicately-sculptured complex of the blood vessels, reaching into the body's every corner.

Mostly pictures, as it should be. The captions and brief section introductions provide just the right amount of background information in a most readable form.
—*Tom Ferguson, M.D.*

Tissues and Organs
(A Text-Atlas of Scanning Electron Microscopy)
Richard G. Kessel and Randy H. Kardon
1979; 317 pp.
$12 postpaid from:
W.H. Freeman & Company
660 Market Street
San Francisco, CA 94104
or Whole Earth Household Store

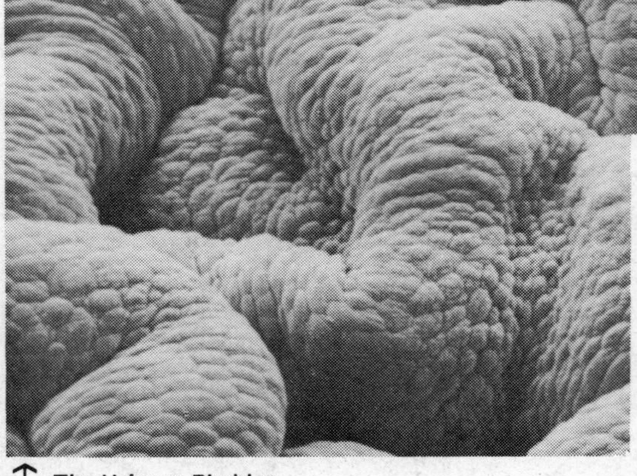
↑ The Urinary Bladder

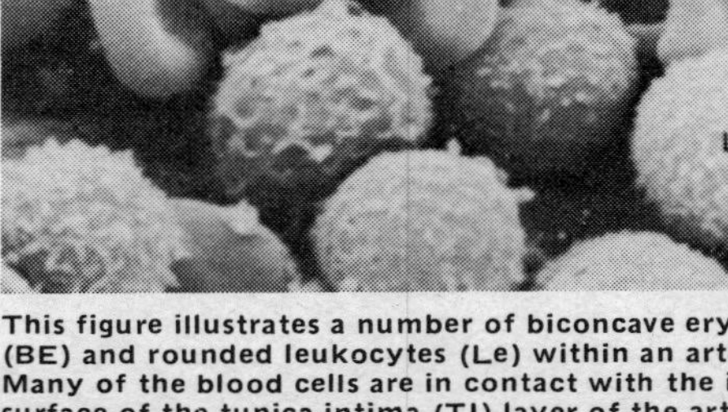
This figure illustrates a number of biconcave erythrocytes (BE) and rounded leukocytes (Le) within an arteriole. Many of the blood cells are in contact with the inner surface of the tunica intima (TI) layer of the arteriole.

← Eye Lens

THE RISING SUN
NEIGHBORHOOD NEWSLETTER

If you swish the dishwater and watch the reflection of the kitchen window in a bubble that was just made, you'll first see just the window color white, and then tiny swirls of red and green and then bigger, faster swirls of red and green and then bigger yet and faster swirls of purple and blue and then yellow swirls chasing them out and turning white. Then the white gets black dots in it, the black dots get bigger and bigger until it all looks like the night sky moving — tiny white dots in black, and then the bubble bursts. It always happens in roughly that order — red and green to start and black and white at the end for sure, and the other stuff in between is pretty much the same too. If you blow bubbles in the dark, they reflect more light than you thought was there. You can tell how far from the outside you are by blowing a bubble inside. If it falls straight to the ground, you're too far inside. If it blows around a little, you're ok.

Steps to an Ecology of Mind

Bateson has informed everything I've attempted since I read **Steps** *in 1972. Through him I became convinced that much more of whole systems could be understood than I thought, and that much more existed wholesomely beyond understanding than I thought — that mysticism, mood, ignorance, and paradox could be rigorous, for instance, and that the most potent tool for grasping these essences — these influence nets — is cybernetics.*

Bateson is responsible for a number of formal discoveries, most notably the "Double Bind" theory of schizophrenia. As an anthropologist he did pioneer work in New Guinea and (with Margaret Mead) in Bali. He participated in the Macy Foundation meetings that founded the science of cybernetics but kept a healthy distance from computers. He has wandered thornily in and out of various disciplines — biology, ethnology, linguistics, epistemology, psychotherapy — and left each of them altered with his passage.

This book chronicles the journey. It is a collection of all his major papers, 1935-1971. In recommending the book I've learned to suggest that it be read backwards. Read the recent broad analyses of mind and ecology at the end of the book and then work back to see where the premises come from.

In my view Bateson's special contribution to cybernetics is in exploring its second, more difficult realm (where the first is feedback, a process influencing itself, what Bateson calls "circuit"; and the second is the meta-realm of hierarchic levels, the domain of context, of paradox and abundant pathology, and of learning.)

Strong medicine. —*SB*

Steps to an Ecology of Mind
Gregory Bateson
1972; 517 pp.
$2.95 postpaid from:
Ballantine Books, Inc.
455 Hahn Road
Westminster, MD 24507
or Whole Earth Household Store

•

No organism can afford to be conscious of matters with which it could deal at unconscious levels.

•

Mere purposive rationality unaided by such phenomena as art, religion, dream, and the like, is necessarily pathogenic and destructive of life; its virulence springs specifically from the circumstance that life depends upon interlocking *circuits* of contingency, while consciousness can only see such short arcs as human purpose may direct.

•

The social scene is nowadays characterized by the existence of a large number of self-maximizing entities which, in law, have something like the status of 'persons' — trusts, companies, political parties, unions, commercial and financial agencies, nations, and the like. In biological fact, these entities are precisely *not* persons and are not even aggregates of whole persons. They are aggregates of *parts* of persons.

•

They say that power corrupts; but this, I suspect, is nonsense. What is true is that the *idea of power* corrupts.

•

My father, the geneticist William Bateson, used to read us passages of the Bible at breakfast — lest we grow up to be *empty-headed* athiests.

•

In no system which shows mental characteristics can any part have unilateral control over the whole. In other words, *the mental characteristics of the system are immanent, not in some part, but in the system as a whole.*

•

The Theology of Alcoholics Anonymous

Some outstanding points of the theology of AA are:

(1) *There is a Power greater than the self.* Cybernetics would go somewhat further and recognize that the "self" as ordinarily understood is only a small part of a much larger trial-and-error system which does the thinking, acting, and deciding. This system includes all the informational pathways which are relevant at any given moment to any given decision. The "self" is a false reification of an improperly delimited part of this much larger field of interlocking processes.

•

But what about "me"? Suppose I am a blind man, and I use a stick. I go tap, tap, tap. Where do *I* start? Is my mental system bounded at the handle of the stick? Is it bounded by my skin? Does it start halfway up the stick? Does it start at the tip of the stick? But these are nonsense questions. The stick is a pathway along which transforms of difference are being transmitted. The way to delineate the system is to draw the limiting line in such a way that you do not cut any of these pathways in ways which leave things inexplicable. If what you are trying to explain is a given piece of behavior, such as the locomotion of the blind man, then, for this purpose, you will need the street, the stick, the man; the street, the stick, and so on, round and round.

•

If you put God outside and set him vis-a-vis his creation and if you have the idea that you are created in his image, you will logically and naturally see yourself as outside and against the things around you. And as you arrogate all mind to yourself, you will see the world around you as mindless and therefore not entitled to moral or ethical consideration. The environment will seem to be yours to exploit. Your survival unit will be you and your folks or conspecifics against the environment of other social units, other races and the brutes and vegetables.

If this is your estimate of your relation to nature *and you have an advanced technology*, your likelihood of survival will be that of a snowball in hell. You will die either of the toxic by-products of your own hate, or simply, of overpopulation and overgrazing. The raw materials of the world are finite.

•

When you narrow down your epistemology and act on the premise "what interests me is me, or my organization, or my species," you chop off consideration of other loops of the loop structure. You decide that you want to get rid of the by-products of human life and that Lake Erie will be a good place to put them. You forget that the eco-mental system called Lake Erie is part of *your* wider eco-mental system — and that if Lake Erie is driven insane, its insanity is incorporated in the larger system of *your* thought and experience.

Mind and Nature: A Necessary Unity

The matter of the book is the hidden, though unoccult, dynamics of life — the misapprehension of which threatens to unhorse our civilization. There's lotsa books that attempt that; none I know of that succeed so comprehensively. Bateson doesn't have all the answers, he just has better questions — elegant, mature, embarrassing questions that tweak the quick of things.

One of the themes that emerges is the near identity between the process of evolving and the process of learning, and the on-going responsibility they have for each other which includes our responsibility, which we have shirked. We shirked it through ignorance. **Mind and Nature** *dispells that.*

All of Bateson's previous writing — **Steps to an Ecology of Mind, Naven, Communications: The Social Matrix of Psychiatry, Balinese Character** *— has been addressed to various audiences of specialists. Though this book has compelling news for his loyal audiences, it is addressed to a general readership. It is new thought in an old virtue — the use of fine original writing to express ideas whose excellence is embedded in the clarity of their expression.* —*SB*

Mind and Nature: A Necessary Unity
Gregory Bateson
1979; 277 pp.
$3.50 postpaid from:
Bantam Books, Inc.
414 E. Golf Road
Des Plaines, IL 60016
or Whole Earth Household Store

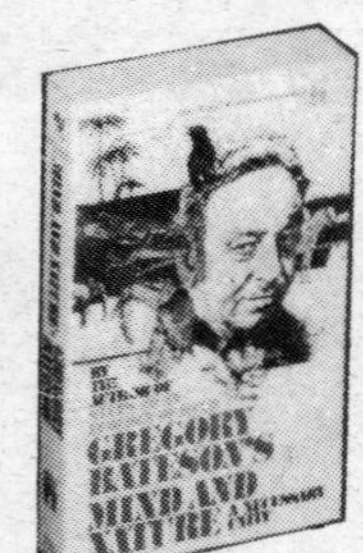

•

Human sense organs can receive *only* news of difference, and the differences must be coded into events in *time* (i.e., into *changes*) in order to be perceptible. Ordinary static differences that remain constant for more than a few seconds become perceptible only by scanning.

•

This analogy between the social system and the natural world is the religion that anthropologists call *totemism.* As an analogy, it is both more appropriate and more healthy than the analogy, familiar to us, which would liken people and society to nineteenth-century machines.

•

1. *A mind is an aggregate of interacting parts or components.*

2. *The interaction between parts of mind is triggered by difference,* and difference is a nonsubstantial phenomenon not located in space or time; difference is related to negentropy and entropy rather than to energy.

3. *Mental process requires collateral energy.*

4. *Mental process requires circular (or more complex) chains of determination.*

5. *In mental process, the effects of difference are to be regarded as transforms (i.e., coded versions) of events which preceded them.* The rules of such transformation must be comparatively stable (i.e., more stable than their content) but are themselves subject to transformation.

6. *The description and classification of these processes of transformation discloses a hierarchy of logical types immanent in the phenomena.*

I shall argue that the phenomena which we call *thought, evolution, ecology, life, learning,* and the like occur only in systems that satisfy these criteria.

•

It is a nontrivial matter that we are almost always unaware of trends in our changes of state. There is a quasi-scientific fable that if you can get a frog to sit quietly in a saucepan of cold water, and if you then raise the temperature of the water very slowly and smoothly so that there is no moment *marked* to be the moment at which the frog should jump, he will never jump. He will get boiled. Is the human species changing its own environment with slowly increasing pollution and rotting its mind with slowly deteriorating religion and education in such a saucepan?

•

We face, then, two great stochastic systems that are partly in interaction and partly isolated from each other. One system is within the individual and is called *learning*; the other is immanent in heredity and in populations and is called *evolution*. One is a matter of the single lifetime; the other is a matter of multiple generations of many individuals.

The task of this chapter is to show how these two stochastic systems, working at different levels of logical typing, fit together into a single ongoing biosphere that could not endure if either somatic or genetic change were fundamentally different from what it is.

The *unity* of the combined system is *necessary*.

•

It is very easy to fall into the notion that if the new is viable, then there must have been something wrong with the old. This view, to which organisms already suffering the pathologies of overrapid, frantic social change are inevitably prone, is, of course, mostly nonsense. What is *always* important is to be sure that the new is not *worse* than the old. It is still not certain that a society containing the internal combustion engine can be viable or that electronic communication devices such as television are compatible with the aggressive intraspecies competition generated by the Industrial Revolution. Other things being equal (which is not often the case), the old, which has been somewhat tested, is more likely to be viable than the new, which has not been tested at all.

•

Ross Ashby long ago pointed out that no system (neither computer nor organism) can produce anything *new* unless the system contains some source of the random. In the computer, this will be a random-number generator which will ensure that the "seeking," trial-and-error moves of the machine will ultimately cover all the possibilities of the set to be explored. . . .

This does not mean, by the way, that all divergent processes are stochastic. For that, the process requires not only access to the random but also a built-in comparator that in evolution is called "natural selection" and in thought "preference" or "reinforcement."

•

I do not believe that the original purpose of the rain dance was to make "it" rain. I suspect that that is a degenerate misunderstanding of a much more profound religious need: to affirm membership in what we may call the *ecological tautology*, the eternal verities of life and environment. There's always a tendency — almost a need — to vulgarize religion, to turn it into entertainment or politics or magic or "power."

•

Epistemology. A branch of science combined with a branch of philosophy. As science, epistemology is the study of how particular organisms or aggregates of organisms *know, think,* and *decide.* As philosophy, epistemology is the study of the necessary limits and other characteristics of the processes of knowing, thinking, and deciding.

•

Information. Any difference that makes a difference.

I and Thou

You can read **I and Thou** *in two hours and not get over it for the rest of your life. Buber tells you how you stand, either in a dialogical relationship with the Creative Force or in a position of "havingness" where you are a thing bounded by other things.* —Ken Kesey

A discovery more prime than Einstein's Relativity is Buber's distinction between the "experience" of I-It and the "relation" of I-You. It can cure at once the twin pathologies of Transcendent God and Controllable Nature. In "I-You" is the possibility of love that does not possess, as well as the realest perception of learning, which is coevolution. Martin Buber's original German torrent is well served by the translation and prologue by Walter Kaufmann. —SB

I and Thou
Martin Buber
1970; 185 pp.

$2.95 postpaid from:
Charles Scribner's Sons
Vreeland Avenue
Totowa, NJ 07512

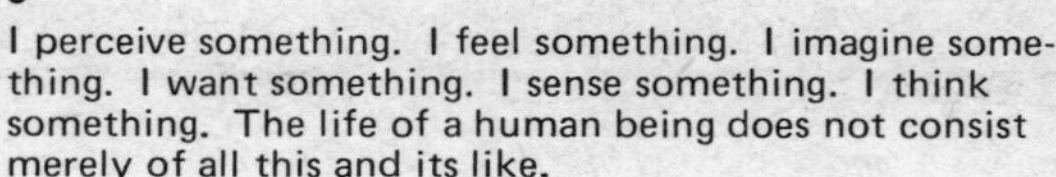

•

I perceive something. I feel something. I imagine something. I want something. I sense something. I think something. The life of a human being does not consist merely of all this and its like.

All this and its like is the basis of the realm of It.

But the realm of You has another basis.

•

When I confront a human being as my You and speak the basic word I-You to him, then he is no thing among things nor does he consist of things.

He is no longer He or She, limited by other Hes and Shes, a dot in the world grid of space and time, nor a condition that can be experienced and described, a loose bundle of named qualities. Neighborless and seamless, he is You and fills the firmament. Not as if there were nothing but he; but everything else lives in *his* light.

•

In truth language does not reside in man but man stands in language and speaks out of it.

•

Extended, the lines of relationships intersect in the eternal You. Every single You is a glimpse of that. Through every single You the basic word addresses the eternal You.

•

A man's relation to the "particular something" that arrogates the supreme throne of his life's values, pushing eternity aside, is always directed toward the experience and use of an It, a thing, an object of enjoyment. For only this kind of relation can bar the view to God, by interposing the impenetrable It-world; the relationship that says You always opens it up again.

•

Whoever says You does not have something for his object. For wherever there is something there is also another something; every It borders on other Its; It is only by virtue of bordering on others. But where You is said there is no something. You has no borders.

Whoever says You does not have something; he has nothing. But he stands in relation.

•

Throughout all of this the tree remains my object and has its place and its time span, its kind and condition.

But it can also happen, if will and grace are joined, that as I contemplate the tree I am drawn into a relation, and the tree ceases to be an It. The power of exclusiveness has seized me.

The Tao of Science

No high-minded bridging of East West, this. But a successful director of research showing how valuable an informed and experienced Taoist sense of harmony can be to the conduct of science. It can help balance the scientist, and it offers an avenue to balancing the application of what the scientist learns. Don't confuse this book with the more specialized (but also worthy) book by Fritjof Capra, **The Tao of Physics.** *For R.G.H. Siu on "power,"* *see page 397.* —SB

The Tao of Science
(An essay on Western knowledge and Eastern wisdom)
R.G.H. Siu
1957; 180 pp.

$4.95 postpaid from:
The M.I.T. Press
28 Carleton Street
Cambridge, Mass. 02142
or Whole Earth Household Store

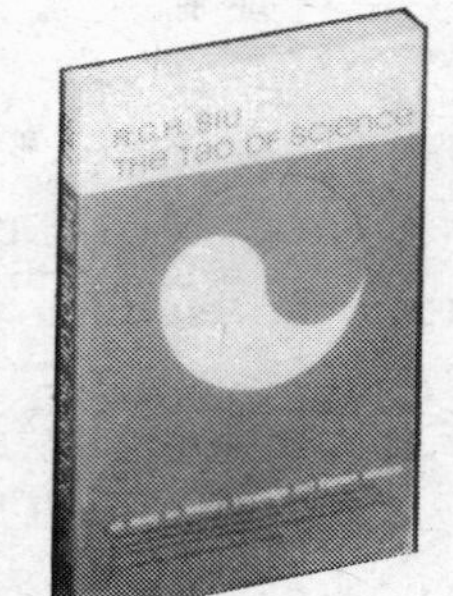

•

Ryle stresses the unreality of the dualistic mental-physical world of Descartes. Ryle claims it to be a category mistake, which is illustrated by the following story: A visitor to a university was shown the laboratories, the dormitories, the library, the classrooms, and the rest of the campus. Upon the completion of the tour, he appeared perplexed and inquired of his guide: "I've seen where the experiments are carried out, where the students live and study, where the bills are paid and all that. But where is the university?" The guide had to explain that the university is not another collateral institution. It is simply the coordinated working of all he saw. It does not belong in the same category as the constituent departments. Ryle goes on to show that it is a family of radical mistakes of this type that is responsible for the dualism of Descartes which envisions a mental ghost ensconced within a physical machine.

•

Let us distill the previous deliberations. We have touched upon the ancient roots of modern science. We have uncovered the shaky uncertainties on which her facts and methodologies are grounded. We have observed the pitfalls in the use of logic, especially when shrouded in the ambiguities of language. We have alluded to the inability of science to clarify the deeper significance of life. We have hinted at a deepening wedge that the abstractive domination of modern science is driving between herself and humanity. At the same time, we have searched encouraging avenues for a renaissance in science in devotion to the welfare of man. There is the negative method of education, imparting a deep awareness of nature without jeopardizing the development of specialists. There is the Median Way of leadership. There are the reassessed contributions of organized research. There is the expanded freedom of growth in social effort. There is no-knowledge.

•

An executive should develop the state of self-forgetfulness and purge away every taint of self-consciousness. This will enable him to let go of himself and latch on to the dreams of others. He should not emulate that self-oriented character in Hawthorne's story, *The Intelligence Office*, who is continually crying out, "I want my place, my own place, my proper sphere, my thing to do, which nature intended me to perform when she fashioned me thus awry and which I had vainly sought all my life."

Dreams fall upon the mind of the philosopher-executive like a scene upon a clear mirror. Only after they have been given the freedom of their full impact is his entire experience, including the dream, conjured forth in a novel totality. In this way the dream does not become merely an accretion to experience like a barnacle to a ship. It is assimilated in a recasting of the entirety into a fresh harmony.

Man and His Symbols

Carl Jung did a nice thing just before he died. He helped with a British effort to bring all of his work together in one richly illustrated introduction to the breadth of his realm. This book covers his concepts of the unconscious, myths, individuation, the visual arts, dreams, and analysis. Why aren't all psychology books illustrated? —SB

•

A still more subtle manifestation of a negative anima appears in some fairy tales in the form of a princess who asks her suitors to answer a series of riddles or, perhaps, to hide themselves under her nose. If they cannot give the answers, or if she can find them, they must die — and she invariably wins. The anima in this guise involves men in a destructive intellectual game. We can notice the effect of this anima trick in all those neurotic pseudo-intellectual dialogues that inhibit a man from getting into direct touch with life and its real decisions. He reflects about life so much that he cannot live it and loses all his spontaneity and outgoing feeling.

•

Oh, come, lonely hunter in the stillness of dusk.
Come, come! I miss you, I miss you!
Now I will embrace you, embrace you!

Come, come! My nest is near, my nest is near.
Come, come, lonely hunter, now in the stillness of dusk.

He throws off his clothes and swims across the river, but suddenly she flies away in the form of an owl, laughing mockingly at him. When he tries to swim back to find his clothes, he drowns in the cold river. ↓

Man and His Symbols
Carl G. Jung
1964; 320 pp.

$8.95 postpaid from:
Doubleday and Co.
501 Franklin Ave.
Garden City, NY 11530
or Whole Earth Household Store

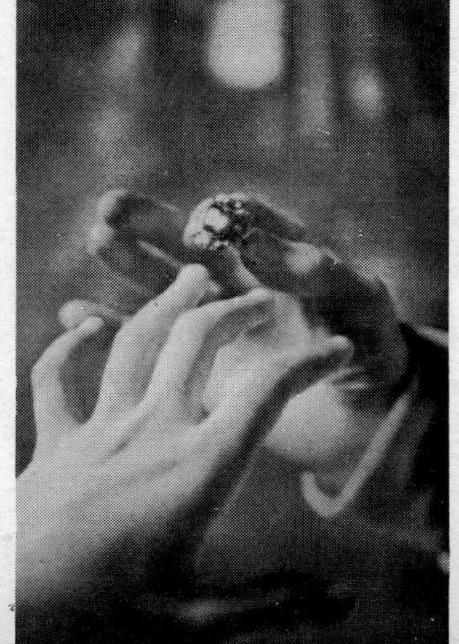

← The sign is always less than the concept it represents, while a symbol always stands for something more than its obvious and immediate meaning.

•

When an individual makes an attempt to see his shadow, he becomes aware of (and often ashamed of) those qualities and impulses he denies in himself but can plainly see in other people . . .

If you feel an overwhelming rage coming up in you when a friend reproaches you about a fault, you can be fairly sure that at this point you will find a part of your shadow, of which you are unconscious.

The archetypal sacred marriage (the union of opposites, of the male and female principles) represented here by a 19th-century Indian sculpture of the deities Siva and Parvati.

THE RISING SUN
NEIGHBORHOOD NEWSLETTER

John the minister noticed that "by the way" is a phrase that is almost always a lie. People stop by the office and talk trivia for an hour, get up to leave, stop by the door and say, "By the way, Elaine and I are thinking of getting a divorce."

CYBERNETICS IS THE DISCIPLINE *of whole systems thinking. For a field of such importance it is shocking there are so few introductory books. The ones here, like the Bateson books on* *p. 28**, introduce the cybernetic frame of mind and habits of mind that lead to on-going health effectiveness in all your dealings because they become self-adjusting. A whole system is a living system is a learning system. For more technical stuff proceed to* *p. 461.* *—SB*

An Introduction to General Systems Thinking

As one of those persons driven to try to "understand" things, I have been remotely fascinated by General Systems Theory for several years. It always seemed it would be too much work to approach any closer to this awesome-sounding subject via any of the "introductory" texts. When Weinberg's book was published last year, I took a chance and bought it immediately, based solely on the strength of his previous **The Psychology of Computer Programming.**

I haven't been disappointed. Viewed from just about any perspective this book is an exemplary introduction to a complex subject. The fascinating observations are well-organized and are stated in a consciously informal tone. Thoughtful questions for research and additional readings are provided for those who want to go beyond the scope of the book. Over a hundred wide-ranging quotes add to the fun. —William Courington

[Suggested by Dennis Geller]

An Introduction to General Systems Thinking
Gerald M. Weinberg
1975; 269 pp.

$24.50 postpaid from:
John Wiley & Sons, Inc.
One Wiley Drive
Somerset, NJ 08873
or Whole Earth Household Store

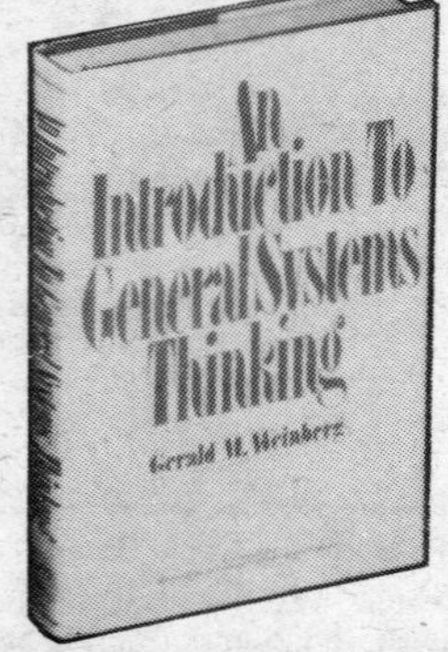

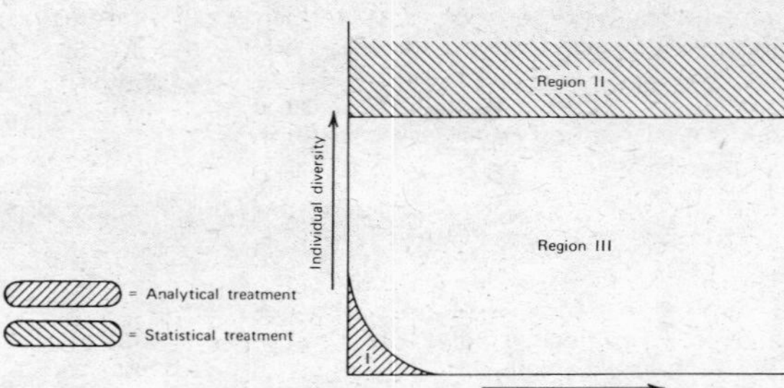

Types of populations in the prediction of epidemics.

•

Paradoxically, one way to master the power of a tool is to probe its weaknesses. Thus we offer the *Count-to-Three Principle:*

IF YOU CANNOT THINK OF THREE WAYS OF ABUSING A TOOL, YOU DO NOT UNDERSTAND HOW TO USE IT.

Faithful adherence to this principle would protect us from the enthusiasm of the optimizers, maximizers and other species of perfectionists — but mostly from ourselves.

•

Consider the following passage:

> General Motors exists to put out cars, not metal scraps, although it extrudes both. Universities exist to produce educated persons and scholars, not retired professors or academic failures.

That seems incontrovertible, but now consider what we should have thought had Miller written:

> Beavers exist to control floods, not to produce piles of wood chips. The oceans exist to produce fresh fish, not mud deposits or dead whales washed ashore.

With "man-made" systems, we talk about "purpose," whereas such language is forbidden for "natural" systems. Yet much of the dissatisfaction with our man-made systems stems precisely from disagreement about what the "purpose" of the system is: that is, what the system "really" is. The answer, of course, is that the system has not "purpose," for *"purpose" is a relation*, not a thing to "have." To the junk dealers, General Motors *does* exist to put out scrap metal, yet the stockholders probably couldn't care less whether General Motors is producing cars or string beans, as long as it is producing profits.

General Systemantics

You're heard of Parkinson's Law? Murphy's Law? The Peter Principle? Well this book is in the same spirit: a somewhat humorous presentation of some serious material. As I read along, I found myself being sensitized to some ideas that are all too often forgotten or overlooked; I saw disasters explained and potential disasters illuminated. I'll bet the book is making the rounds in many an engineering department. I like this book. —J. Baldwin

[Suggested by Dean Gengle]

General Systemantics
John Gall
1977; 144 pp.

$7.95 postpaid from:
Times Books
Harper & Row
Keystone Industrial Park
Scranton, PA 18512
or Whole Earth Household Store

•

A COMPLEX SYSTEM THAT WORKS IS INVARIABLY FOUND TO HAVE EVOLVED FROM A SIMPLE SYSTEM THAT WORKED.

The inverse proposition also appears to be true:

A COMPLEX SYSTEM DESIGNED FROM SCRATCH NEVER WORKS AND CANNOT BE MADE TO WORK. YOU HAVE TO START OVER , BEGINNING WITH A WORKING SIMPLE SYSTEM.

•

SYSTEMS DEVELOP GOALS OF THEIR OWN THE INSTANT THEY COME INTO BEING.

Furthermore, it seems axiomatically clear that:

INTRASYSTEM GOALS COME FIRST.

The reader who masters this powerful Axiom can readily comprehend why the United Nations recently suspended, for an entire day, its efforts at dealing with drought, detente, and desert oil, in order to debate whether UN employees should continue to ride first-class on airplanes.

The formulators of this Law failed to generalize to *systems as such*, thereby missing — by a whisker, so to speak — their chance of immortality: Not just animal behavior, but the behavior of complex systems generally, whether living or nonliving, is unpredictable.

•

SOLUTIONS USUALLY COME FROM PEOPLE WHO SEE IN THE PROBLEM ONLY AN INTERESTING PUZZLE, AND WHOSE QUALIFICATIONS WOULD NEVER SATISFY A SELECT COMMITTEE.

Item: When Pasteur accepted the challenge of the French silk producers to discover the cause of silk-worm disease, he had never seen, much less studied, a silkworm. He was not even a biologist.

Item: The Wright brothers, who built the first successful heavier-than-air machine, were bicycle makers.

•

27. "SUCCESS" OR "FUNCTION" IN ANY SYSTEM MAY BE FAILURE IN THE LARGER OR SMALLER SYSTEMS TO WHICH THE SYSTEM IS CONNECTED.

Corollary:

IN SETTING UP A NEW SYSTEM, TREAD SOFTLY. YOU MAY BE DISTURBING ANOTHER SYSTEM THAT IS ACTUALLY WORKING.

•

32. LOOSE SYSTEMS LAST LONGER AND WORK BETTER.

Corollary:

EFFICIENT SYSTEMS ARE DANGEROUS TO THEMSELVES AND TO OTHERS.

Cybernetics

McLuhan's assertion that computers constitute an extension of the human nervous system is an accurate historical statement. The research and speculation that led to computer design arose from investigation of healthy and pathological human response patterns embodied in the topological make-up of the nervous system. Insights here soon expanded into generalizations about communication that permitted the building of analogous electronic devices physically separate from the Central Nervous System. But they're just one artifact of these new understandings about communication. Society, from organism to community to civilization to universe, is the domain of cybernetics. Norbert Wiener has the story, and to some extent, is the story. —SB

Cybernetics
(Or Control and Communication in the Animal and the Machine)
Norbert Wiener
1948, 1961; 212 pp.

$4.95 postpaid from:
The M.I.T. Press
28 Carleton Street
Cambridge, MA 02142
or Whole Earth Household Store

•

To predict the future of a curve is to carry out a certain operation on its past.

•

The central nervous system no longer appears as a self-contained organ, receiving inputs from the senses and discharging into the muscles. On the contrary, some of its most characteristic activities are explicable only as circular processes, emerging from the nervous system into the muscles, and re-entering the nervous system through the sense organs, whether they be proprioceptors or organs of the special senses. This seemed to us to mark a new step in the study of that part of neurophysiology which concerns not solely the elementary processes of nerves and synapses but the performance of the nervous system as an integrated whole.

•

The feedback of voluntary activity is of this nature. We do not will the motions of certain muscles, and indeed we generally do not know which muscles are to be moved to accomplish a given task; we will, say, to pick up a cigarette. Our motion is regulated by some measure of the amount by which it has not yet been accomplished.

•

The mongoose begins with a feint, which provokes the snake to strike. The mongoose dodges and makes another such feint, so that we have a rhythmical pattern of activity on the part of the two animals. However, this dance is not static but develops progressively. As it goes on, the feints of the mongoose come earlier and earlier in phase with respect to the darts of the cobra, until finally the mongoose attacks when the cobra is extended and not in a position to move rapidly. This time the mongoose's attack is not a feint but a deadly accurate bite through the cobra's brain.

In other words, the snake's pattern of action is confined to single darts, each one for itself, while the pattern of the mongoose's action involves an appreciable, if not very long, segment of the whole past of the fight. To this extent the mongoose acts like a learning machine, and the real deadliness of its attack is dependent on a much more highly organized nervous system.

•

To use a biological analogy, the parallel system had a better homeostasis than the series system and therefore survived, while the series system eliminated itself by natural selection.

We thus see that a non-linear interaction causing the attraction of frequency can generate a self-organizing system . . .

The Human Use of Human Beings

A proper sequel to his **Cybernetics**, *this book is social, untechnical, ultimate in most of its considerations. Its domain is the whole earth of the mind. Norbert Wiener is one of the founders of an n-dimensional inhabited world whose nature we've yet to learn.* —SB

The Human Use of Human Beings
(Cybernetics and Society)
Norbert Wiener
1950, 1967; 288 pp.

$2.20 postpaid from:
Avon Books
Mail Order Dept.
250 West 55th Street
New York, NY 10019
or Whole Earth Household Store

•

It is the thesis of this book that society can only be understood through a study of the messages and the communication facilities which belong to it; and that in the future development of these messages and communication facilities, messages between man and machine and between machine and machine, are destined to play an ever-increasing part.

•

We are not stuff that abides, but patterns that perpetuate themselves. A pattern is a message, and may be transmitted as a message.

•

It is the great public which is demanding the utmost of secrecy for modern science in all things which may touch its military uses. This demand for secrecy is scarcely more than the wish of a sick civilization not to learn the progress of its own disease.

•

It is illuminating to know that the sort of phenomenon which is recorded subjectively as emotion may not be merely a useless epistage in learning, and in other similar processes.

Laws of Form

This epochal book has spawned whole disciplines, vast and surly arguments, and not a little mystical endeavor. Not bad for a rudimentary arithmetic book. In the beginning God said, "Draw a distinction." The primordial creative act. You can take it from there. —SB
[Suggested by Steve Baer]

Laws of Form
G. Spencer Brown
1969; 141 pp.
$4.95 postpaid from:
E.P. Dutton
2 Park Avenue
New York, NY 10016
or Whole Earth
Household Store

•

CONSTRUCTION
Draw a distinction.

CONTENT
Call it the first distinction.
Call the space in which it is drawn the space severed or cloven by the distinction.
Call the parts of the space shaped by the severance or cleft the sides of the distinction or, alternatively, the spaces, states, or contents distinguished by the distinction.

INTENT
Let any mark, token, or sign be taken in any way with or with regard to the distinction as a signal.
Call the use of any signal its intent.

•

In all mathematics it becomes apparent, at some stage, that we have for sometime been following a rule without being consciously aware of the fact. This might be described as the use of a *covert* convention. A recognizable aspect of the advancement of mathematics consists in the advancement of the consciousness of what we are doing, whereby the covert becomes overt. Mathematics is in this respect psychedelic.

•

The main difficulty in translating from the written to the verbal form comes from the fact that in mathematical writing we are free to mark the two dimensions of the plane, whereas in speech we can mark only the one dimension of time.

Much that is unnecessary and obstructive in mathematics today appears to be vestigial of this limitation of the spoken word.

•

Any evenly subverted equation of the second degree might be called, alternatively, evenly informed. We can see it over a subversion (turning under) of the surface upon which it is written, or alternatively, as an in-formation (formation within) of what it expresses.

Such an expression is thus informed in the sense of having its own form within it, and at the same time informed in the sense of remembering what has happened to it in the past.

We need not suppose that this is exactly how memory happens in an animal, but there are certainly memories, so-called, constructed this way in electronic computers, and engineers have constructed such in-formed memories with magnetic relays for the greater part of the present century.

We may perhaps look upon such memory, in this simplified information, as a precursor of the more complicated and varied forms of memory and information in man and the higher animals. We can also regard other manifestations of the classical forms of physical or biological science in the same spirit.

•

There is a tendency, especially today, to regard existence as the source of reality, and thus as a central concept. But as soon as it is formally examined, existence [*ex* = out, *stare* = stand. Thus to exist may be considered as to stand outside, to be exiled.] is seen to be highly peripheral and, as such, especially corrupt (in the formal sense) and vulnerable. The concept of truth is more central, although still recognizably peripheral. If the weakness of present-day science is that it centres round existence, the weakness of present-day logic is that it centres round truth.

Throughout the essay, we find no need of the concept of truth, apart from two avoidable appearances (true = open to proof) in the descriptive context. At no point, to say the least, is it a necessary inhabitant of the calculating forms. These forms are thus not only precursors of existence, they are also precursors of truth.

It is, I am afraid, the intellectual block which most of us come up against at the points where, to experience the world clearly, we must abandon existence to truth, truth to indication, indication to form, and form to void, that has so held up the development of logic and its mathematics.

Tools for Thought

The renowned biological philosopher C.H. Waddington did a generous and helpful thing shortly before he died. He assembled in one place with one sharp understanding all of the recent conceptual discoveries about the adroit handling of concepts. Browsing his book is like shopping in a fine hardware store. It is damn near sufficient for one to grasp the world's tail. —SB

Tools for Thought
C.H. Waddington
1977; 239 pp.
$12 postpaid from:
Basic Books, Inc.
10 East 53rd Street
New York, NY 10022
or Whole Earth
Household Store

•

Chreods and Epigenetic Landscapes
A phrase used to describe such systems, is to say that the pathway of change is canalized. For the pathway itself one can use the name *chreod*, a word derived from Greek, which means 'necessary path.' Many types of change going on in society have a more or less well-developed chreodic character; very difficult to divert them.

Different canalized pathways or chreods may have rather different types of stability built into them. These can be pictured in terms of the cross-section of the valley. You may, for instance, have a valley with a very narrow chasm running along the bottom, while the farther up the hillside you go, the less steep the slope; with such a configuration of the attractor surface, it needs a very stong push of some kind to divert a stream away from the bottom of the chasm (7b.2). If the system is acted on by only rather minor disturbances, it is likely always to stay very close to the bottom of the valley. If one can compare several examples of such a system, there will be very little difference between them, and they will look very invariable. In contrast, we have a valley which has a very flat bottom, and the hillside gets steeper and steeper as you go away from the central stream (7b.3). Then, minor disturbances can easily shunt the stream from one side of the flat valley bottom to the other; it would be rather a matter of chance where in the water-meadows in the valley bottom it flows. If one looks at a number of examples of a system with this type of stability, there will be a lot of small-scale variation between them.

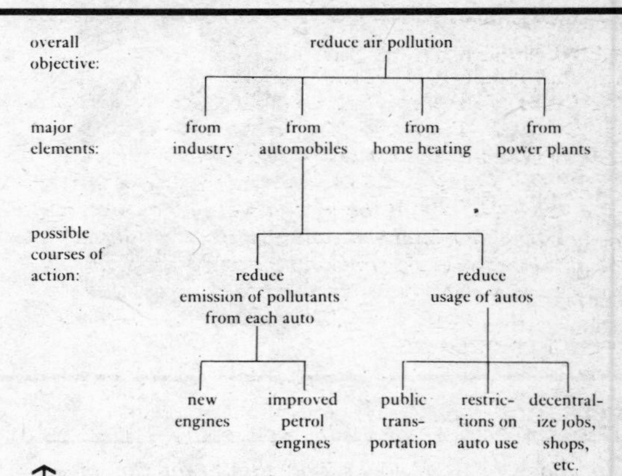

↑
The first step in the construction of a relevance tree is to identify a high-level objective that you wish to achieve at some time in the future — e.g. an overall objective may be to reduce air pollution levels.

The next step is to qualitatively relate the alternative courses of action (or the elements contributing towards the objective) to the overall objective using exploratory forecasting techniques when necessary. Above is a portion of a vertical relevance tree for air pollution.

Snake

By Anne Herbert

In the beginning God didn't make just one or two people; he made a bunch of us. Because he wanted us to have a lot of fun and he said you can't really have fun unless there's a whole gang of you. So he put us all in this sort of playground park place called Eden and told us to enjoy.

At first we did have fun just like he expected. We played all the time. We rolled down the hills, waded in the streams, climbed the trees, swung on the vines, ran in the meadows, frolicked in the woods, hid in the forest, and acted silly. We laughed a lot.

Then one day this snake told us that we weren't having real fun because we weren't keeping score. Back then, we didn't know what score was. When he explained it, we still couldn't see the fun. But he said that we should give an apple to the person who was best at playing and we'd never know who was best unless we kept score. We could all see the fun of that. We were all sure we were best.

It was different after that. We yelled a lot. We had to make up new scoring rules for most of the games we played. Other games, like frolicking, we stopped playing because they were too hard to score. By the time God found out about our new fun, we were spending about forty-five minutes a day in actual playing and the rest of the time working out the score. God was wroth about that – very, very wroth. He said we couldn't use his garden anymore because we weren't having any fun. We said we were having lots of fun and we were. He shouldn't have got upset just because it wasn't exactly the kind of fun he had in mind.

He wouldn't listen. He kicked us out and said we couldn't come back until we stopped keeping score. To rub it in (to get our attention, he said), he told us we were all going to die anyway and our scores wouldn't mean anything.

He was wrong. My cumulative all-game score is now 16,548 and that means a lot to me. If I can raise it to 20,000 before I die I'll know I've accomplished something. Even if I can't my life has a great deal of meaning because I've taught my children to score high and they'll all be able to reach 20,000 or even 30,000 I know.

Really, it was life in Eden that didn't mean anything. Fun is great in its place, but without scoring there's no reason for it. God has a very superficial view of life and I'm glad my children are being raised away from his influence. We were lucky to get out. We're all very grateful to the snake. ■

G. RUSS YOUNGREEN

THE RISING SUN
NEIGHBORHOOD NEWSLETTER

Remember when you could be a funeral connoisseur just watching TV? Churchill & Eisenhower & Adenauer & Kennedy & Kennedy & King all taking 1 or 2 or 3 days of live coverage of death rites and showing that some generations of leaders get to live longer than others and leading the fight against Nazis turned out to be safer than whatever the Kennedys and King were up to. I guess it's better to find your bad guys in other countries so people within shooting range don't get nervous.

BACK IN 1967 *the insights of Buckminster Fuller initiated the* **Whole Earth Catalog.** *The artists I hung out with in those days had all been electrified by Fuller's earliest, most radical book —* **Nine Chains to the Moon.** *Then I read the autobiographical* **Ideas and Integrities** *and picked up a number of rules I seldom break — go only where invited; don't show unfinished work; reflect the physical world's honesty and all will go well. Then I heard him lecture for a number of weeks at a nearby college — the amazingly rich material you can disappear into in the two* **Synergetics** *books. From all that came the ideas "access," "tools," and "whole systems." There's lots more in there.* —SB

Nine Chains to the Moon

Nine Chains to the Moon
R. Buckminster Fuller
1938, 1963; 375 pp.
$2.95 postpaid from:
Doubleday and Co., Inc.
501 Franklin Avenue
Garden City, NY 11530
or Whole Earth Household Store

•

Man?

A self-balancing, 28-jointed adapter-base biped; an electro-chemical reduction-plant, integral with segregated stowages of special energy extracts in storage batteries, for subsequent actuation of thousands of hydraulic and pneumatic pumps, with motors attached; 62,000 miles of capillaries; millions of warning signal, railroad and conveyor systems; crushers and cranes (of which the arms are magnificent 23-jointed affairs with self-surfacing and lubricating systems, and a universally distributed telephone system needing no service for 70 years if well managed); the whole, extraordinarily complex mechanism guided with exquisite precision from a turret in which are located telescopic and microscopic self-registering and recording range finders, a spectroscope, *et cetera,* the turret control being closely allied with an air conditioning intake-and-exhaust, and a main fuel intake.

Within the few cubic inches housing the turret mechanisms, there is room, also, for two sound-wave and sound-direction-finder recording diaphragms, a filing and instant reference system, and an expertly devised analytical laboratory large enough not only to contain minute records of every last and continual event of up to 70 years' experience, or more, but to extend, by computation and abstract fabrication, this experience with relative accuracy into all corners of the observed universe. There is, also, a forecasting and tactical plotting department for the reduction of future possibilities and probabilities to generally successful specific choice.

Finally, the whole structure is not only directly and simply mobile on land and in water, but, indirectly and by exquisite precision of complexity, mobile in air, and, even in the intangible, mathematically sensed electrical "world," by means of the extension of the primary integral mechanism to secondary mechanical compositions of its own devising, operable either by a direct mechanical hook-up with the device, or by indirect control through wired or wire-less electrical impulses.

"A man," indeed! Dismissed with the appellation Mr. "Jones"!

Common to all such "human" mechanisms — and without which they are imbecile contraptions — is their guidance by a phantom captain.

This phantom captain has neither weight nor sensorial tangibility, as has often been scientifically proven by careful weighing operations at the moment of abandonment of the ship by the phantom captain, i.e., at the instant of "death." He may be likened to the variant of polarity dominance in our bipolar electric world which, when balanced and unit, vanishes as abstract unity 1 or 0. With the phantom captain's departure, the mechanism becomes inoperative and very quickly disintegrates into basic chemical elements.

•

An illuminating rationalization indicated that *captains* — being phantom, abstract, infinite, and bound to other captains by a bond of understanding as proven by their recognition of each other's signals and the meaning thereof by reference to a common direction (toward "perfect") — *are not only all related, but are one and the same captain.* Mathematically, since characteristics of unity exist, they cannot be non-identical.

Ideas and Integrities

Ideas and Integrities
(A Spontaneous Autobiographical Disclosure)
R. Buckminster Fuller
1963; 318 pp.
$2.95 postpaid from:
Collier Books
The MacMillan Company
Order Department
Front and Brown Streets
Riverside, NJ 08075
or Whole Earth Household Store

•

Standing by the lake on a jump-or-think basis, the very first spontaneous question coming to mind was, "If you put aside everything you've ever been asked to believe and have recourse only to your own experiences do you have any conviction arising from those experiences which either discards or must assume an *a priori* greater intellect than the intellect of man?" The answer was swift and positive. Experience had clearly demonstrated an *a priori* anticipatory and only intellectually apprehendable orderliness of interactive principles operating in the universe into which we are born. These principles are discovered but are never invented by man. I said to myself, "I have faith in the integrity of the anticipatory intellectual wisdom which we may call 'God.'" My next question was, "Do I know best or does God know best whether I may be of any value to the integrity of universe?" The answer was, "You don't know and no man knows, but the faith you have just established out of experience imposes recognition of the *a priori* wisdom of the fact of your being." Apparently addressing myself, I said, "You do not have the right to eliminate yourself, you do not belong to you. You belong to the universe. The significance of you will forever remain obscure to you, but you may assume that you are fulfilling your significance if you apply yourself to converting all your experience to highest advantage of others. You and all men are here for the sake of other men."

•

I define "synergy" as follows: Synergy is the unique behavior of whole systems, unpredicted by behavior of their respective sub-systems' events.

Synergetics 1 & 2

This formidable pair of books is as close to the Compleat Bucky as you are likely to get. They benefit from the firm and empathetic editorial hand of E.J. Applewhite, who has adroitly disciplined the sometimes baffling complexity of Fuller's thought. The result is highly refined Bucky: elegant, clear, and upon occasion, outrageous. The geometric proofs are there of course, but I found the most exciting discussions to be those dealing with intuition, metaphysics, and the range of possibilities open to humanity.

The two books are intended to be read together and share a numbered paragraph system and a common index. This makes it possible to refer back to something that you remember reading but can't recall where, and makes it comparatively easy to dip back and forth between the books. There is work involved in reading them. I have found that the best way to get into reading them is to just pick one up and start prowling around. One thing soon leads to another (which is one of Bucky's main points) and soon you are immersed in a vision of Universe that seems much more substantially argued than in other Bucky writings. The approach is commendably cross-disciplinary, so it's easy to get involved. It's Bucky at his sharpest and most beautiful.

Friends will rejoice in what they find here. Foes will have to admit that Bucky has been proven right often enough to be disconcerting. History will likely regard these books as classic examples of the best of 20th century thought.
—J. Baldwin

Synergetics
(Explorations in the Geometry of Thinking)
R. Buckminster Fuller
1975; 876 pp.

Synergetics 2
(Further Explorations in the Geometry of Thinking)
R. Buckminster Fuller
1979; 592 pp.

$27.50 each
postpaid from:
MacMillan Publishing Company, Inc.
Order Department
Front and Brown Streets
Riverside, NJ 08075
or Whole Earth Household Store

1 mile + 1⅝ inches
1 mile
radius of earth 4000 miles
0.015°

Fig. 986.076 Diagram of Verrazano Bridge: The two towers are not parallel to each other.

•

1053.832 Radiation outcasts. Radiation does not broadcast; broadcast is a planar statement; there are no planes. *Out* is inherently omnidivergent. Radiation omnicasts but does not and cannot *in*cast; it can only go-in-to-go-out. *In* is gravity.

1053.833 If radiation "goes through" a system and comes out on the other side, it does so because (1) there was no frequency interference — it just occurred between the system's occurrence frequencies — or (2) there was tangential interference and deflection thereby of the angle of travel, wherefore it did not go through; it went by.

Fig. 1130.24 Reality is Spiro-orbital: All terrestrial critical path developments inherently orbit the Sun. No path can be linear. All paths are precessionally modulated by remotely operative forces producing spiralinear paths.

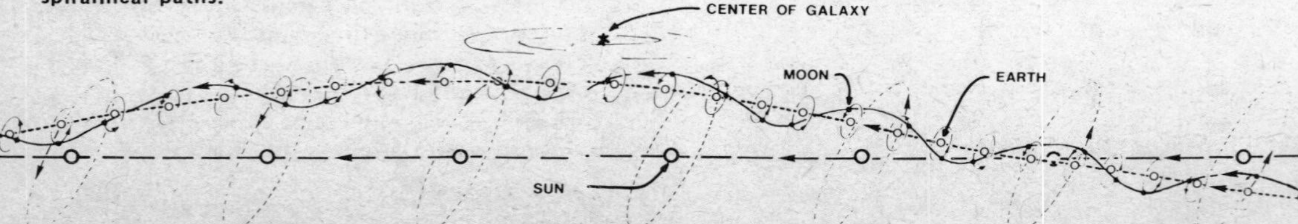

The Character of Physical Law

If you look larger or smaller than the skinny realm of life, all you see is physics. It is our substratum and superstratum. These famous Feynman lectures introduce the subject as no other book has. —SB
[Suggested by Lyle Burkhead]

The Character of Physical Law
Richard Feynman
1965; 173 pp.
$3.95 postpaid from:
M.I.T. Press
28 Carleton Street
Cambridge, MA 02142
or Whole Earth Household Store

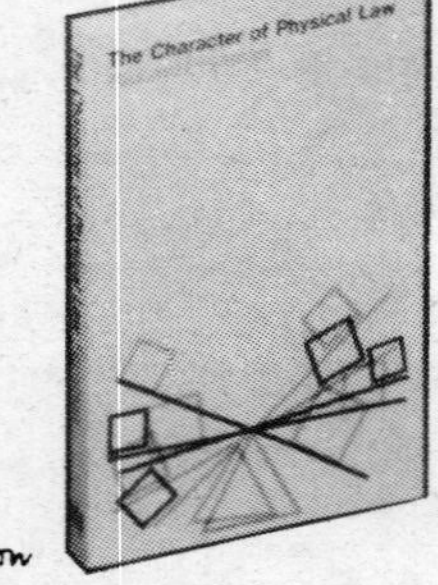

Moon
water pulled partly away from earth by moon

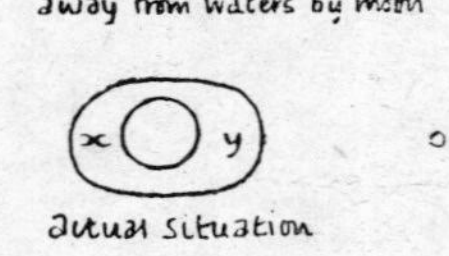

actual situation

The water at y is closer to the moon and the water at x is farther from the moon than the rigid earth. The water is pulled more towards the moon at y, and at x is less towards the moon than the earth, so there is a combination of those two pictures that makes a double tide.

Bucky tells all

Forty-three hours of good quality color video tapes (not all one lecture, despite his reputation) let R. Buckminster Fuller say the majority of what he has to say, but with a difference. In this format, he can make many of the intricate connections between concepts that cannot be made in a short one-shot lecture. Obviously he can go into things much more deeply than he does in his more-or-less standard beginner's lecture which is what most people are familiar with. Arrangements setting up a seminar featuring these tapes might be arranged by writing: —J. Baldwin

The Fuller Archives
3500 Market Street
Philadelphia, PA 19104

PRACTICALLY ALL OTHER NEWS — newspaper news, news in the arts, politics, economics, war, and social meanderings — is derivative from news in science. Therefore merely by watching these three splendid and quite different weeklies, you can stay six months to two years ahead of things. A useful advantage if you want to act rather than always be acted upon by events. —SB

Science News

Highly palatable digest of current top stories in science. The least demanding in terms of technical background. It's a quick read (only about 10 pages of editorial material per issue, with adequate pictures). Sometimes it has far the best coverage of fast-breaking stories such as the Viking lander tests for life on Mars. —SB

Science News
Robert J. Trotter, Editor
$15.50/year
(52 issues) from:
Science Service Inc.
Subscription Department
231 West Center Street
Marion, OH 43302

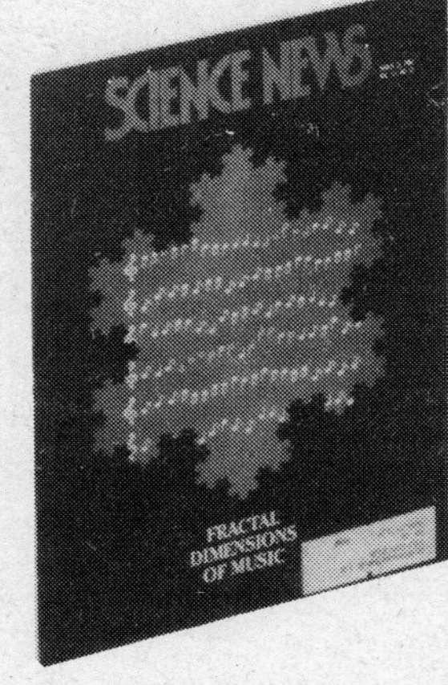

•

A certain professor of music, a specialist in the life and work of J.S. Bach, used to take pains to combat the notion that Bach and his contemporaries wrote "mathematicians' music," that you had to be a mathematician to appreciate a toccata or fugue. He insisted that there was an esthetic quality to a Bach fugue that was quite apart from any ability to analyze the numerical relations in the rhythmic and melodic progressions.

This professor's esthetic sense might have been gratified — or maybe not — to learn that the structure of music is based on fractals, those lacy, snowflaky figures with dimensions somewhere between one and two or two and three dimensions. He is likely to have been unhappy with the statement that the common element of all music is what physicists call 1/fnoise. To anyone who composes very dissonant modern music and has to contend with traditionalist critics "noise" is a touchy word indeed.

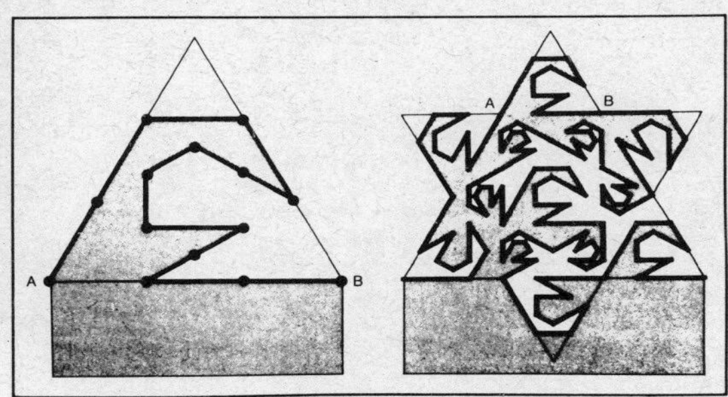

↑ The first steps in making the Peano curve. It gets rapidly more complicated.

Machine-made music based on random tone generation (top), $1/f^2$ noise and 1/f noise. 1/f seems most like real music. →

New Scientist

British, wide-ranging, quite readable, often critical, often humorous — this is the best vantage point for watching science go by. I'm honored to have a monthly column in it. —SB

New Scientist
Michael Kenward, Editor
$59 /year
(52 issues) from:
Publisher's Expediting, Inc.
200 Meacham Avenue
Elmont, NY 11003

•

Even after the Chinese had totally discarded the "small is beautiful" concept that Mao had introduced 30 years ago, India's Janata leaders continued under the illusion that Appropriate Technology (AT) would take care of all their country's ills. As it happened, after Mao's death the Chinese began to realise that AT could take them up to a point where they could feed themselves, and provide one change of garments a year and not an inch beyond. With the change of political guard in Peking, China felt that it had paid a heavy price for its blind, total dependence on "rural technology and agro-industries" to the exclusion of sophisticated technology. The current Chinese craze for "four modernisations" was propelled by the realisation that AT can play only a peripheral part in national development. And today Chinese leaders are scouting the world for the latest technology and are even prepared to allow 49 per cent foreign equity in joint ventures.

•

Part of the mythology of the new pastime of man-watching is that people exert an enormous degree of unconscious (yet precise) control over one another's movements in everyday interactions. We move in time to speech whether we are talking or listening, and the posture we adopt depends on to whom we are talking. →

Science

Top of the line. Possibly the best science magazine in the world (the major challenge would be from England's **Nature**). *This is where you can really watch news taking shape. Often pretty technical, but it's the real goods. —SB*

Science
Philip H. Abelson, Editor
$38 /year (51 issues)
includes membership in
American Association
for the Advancement
of Science

from:
Science
AAAS
1515 Massachusetts Avenue, NW
Washington, D.C. 20005

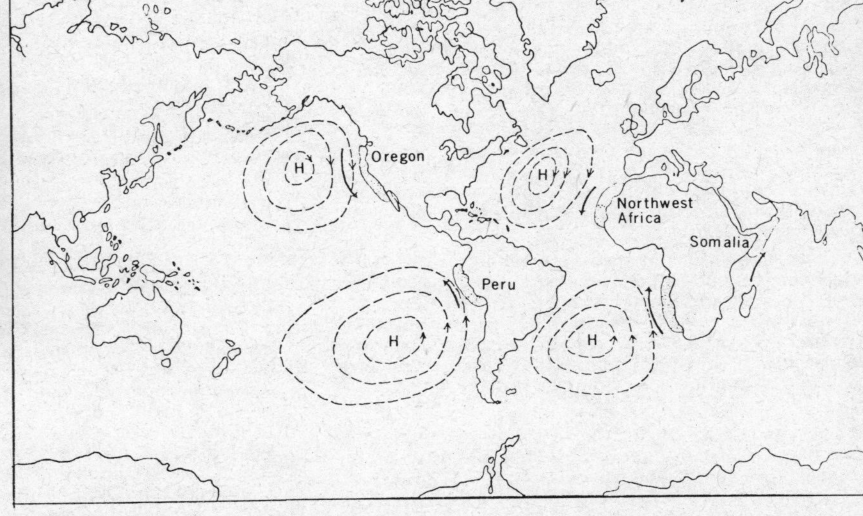

↗

Prime fishing grounds are so fertile that they supply more than half of the fish harvest although they comprise less than 1 percent of the sea. What distinguishes these areas is that they are close to shore, and nutrients in the surface water are replenished frequently from deeper in the ocean.

Recent studies reveal that each superb fishing system responds to its own balance of remote and local physical influences. Local winds, coastline shape, underwater topography, and nearshore currents are among the factors that govern the rate at which nutrients are brought to the surface. An 8-year interdisciplinary study that concludes this year made the exciting discovery that winds hundreds of thousands of kilometers away can disturb the local currents and affect the fertility of a coastal fishing ground ground. The results of this study, the Coastal Upwelling Ecosystems Analysis (CUEA), make it clear, says Richard Barber of Duke University, that "physical and biological processes are in a sequence, so understanding the ecosystem requires understanding the sequence. A [marine] biologist out there with no understanding of the meteorology or currents is just whistling in the dark."

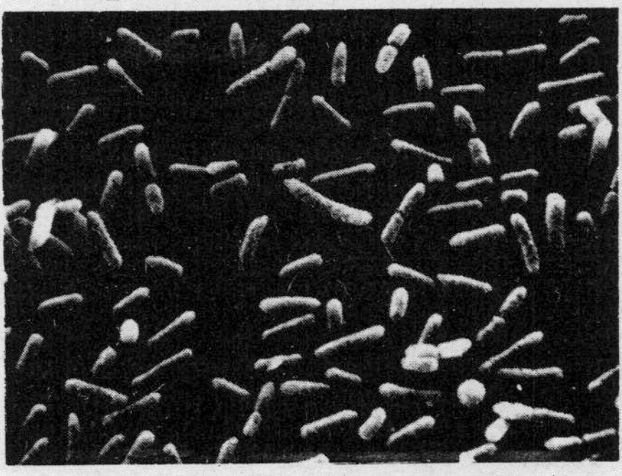

GE's oil-slick bugs: Are they patentable?

•

If a bacterium is patented, does it infringe the patent by reproducing? Does a person infected by it offend the patentee?

THE RISING SUN
NEIGHBORHOOD NEWSLETTER

A man on the BART train asked a woman on the BART train if she was done with her paper and she said yes, but she wanted to tear out a cartoon. So she tore out the cartoon and gave him the paper. The cartoon was a picture of a woman kneeling by a bed saying, "Dear Lord, was I put here on earth to cook, clean, sew, raise children, attend PTA meetings and be a loving wife, or was I put on earth to pull down $30,000 a year as an executive for a top New York-based firm? Send me a sign." The woman looked at that cartoon and smiled from the Oakland West station to the Financial District station, where she got off.

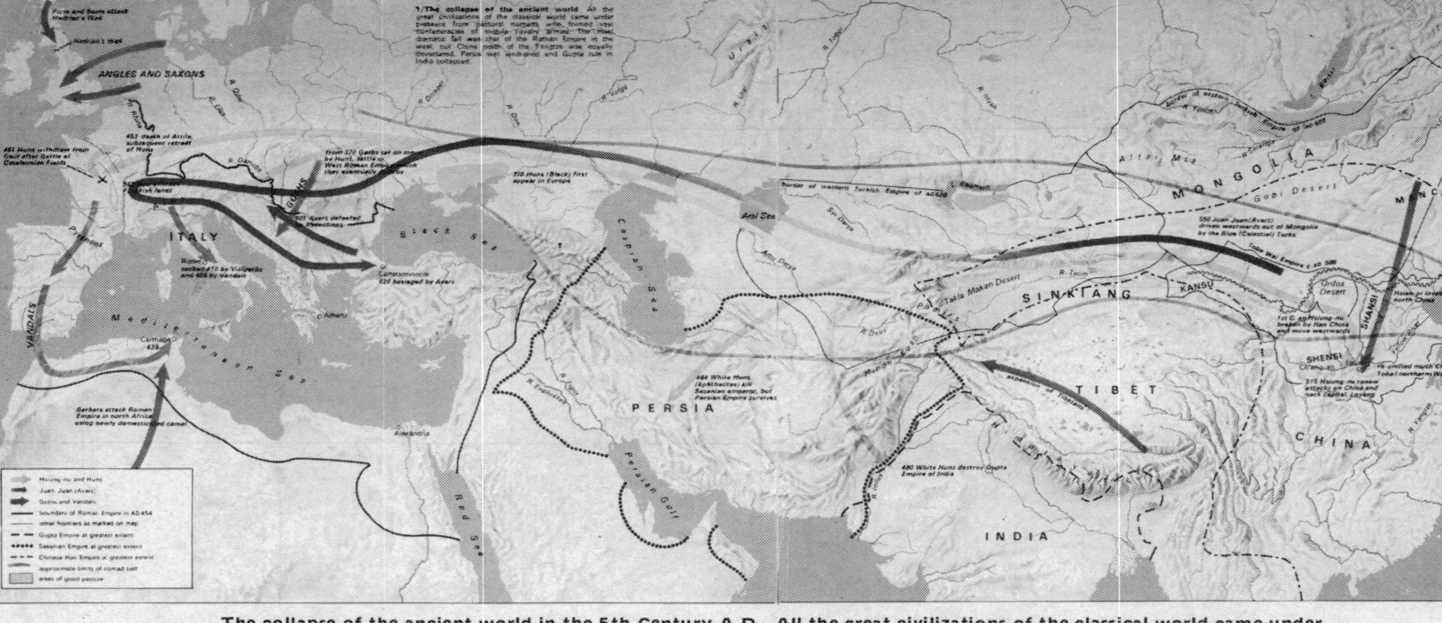

The collapse of the ancient world in the 5th Century A.D. All the great civilizations of the classical world came under pressure from pastoral nomads who formed vast confederacies of mobile cavalry armies. The most dramatic fall was that of the Roman Empire in the west, but China north of the Yangtze was equally devastated. Persia was weakened and Gupta rule in India collapsed.

The Times Atlas of World History

Most engrossing new reference book in decades.

It's a fine idea magnificently carried through. On planetary scale human history has a unity-within-boggling-variety, a headlong pace and sweep that puts our time in less frightening perspective. Praise be, the coverage of the volume corrects generations of Europe-centered versions of history. For example, Charlemagne's capital at Aix-la-Chapelle in 790 A.D. is shown in puny contrast to other capitals of the time — Ch'ang-an in China, Baghdad, Constantinople, and even Cordoba.

For me the volume is packed with news: complex fascinating sub-plots in regions I've scarcely thought of. The current uproar in the Mideast is minor compared to the centuries of surging conflict there. You can see the continent-changing impact of such social inventions as: plow agriculture; new cavalry and military intelligence tactics (Mongol tribesmen); aggressive religion (Christianity, Islam); ocean navigation (Spain and Portugal); joint-stock companies for foreign trade (Holland and England). There are recent re-interpretations of the familiar events (the Minoan civilization in Crete fell 50 years after the great earthquake of 1500 B.C., torched by conquerors from the mainland). Throughout, each map is ingeniously presented from the perspective of the time and people involved.

You read enough history in this dynamic a form and pretty soon you want to do some. —SB

The Times Atlas of World History
Geoffrey Barraclough, Editor
1978; 360 pp.

$70 postpaid from:
Hammond, Inc.
515 Valley Street
Maplewood, NJ 07040
or Whole Earth Household Store

•

The spread of food plants — almost all domesticated by prehistoric man in various parts of the world — had proceeded slowly until 1500, when they were transplanted to every continent. In addition, the American Indians were responsible for two major cash crops: tobacco and cotton (derived largely in its commercial form from varieties they had domesticated, though other species were known and used in the Orient before 1500). Cane sugar, introduced by Europeans into Brazil and the West Indies about 1640, also quickly became a staple of foreign trade.

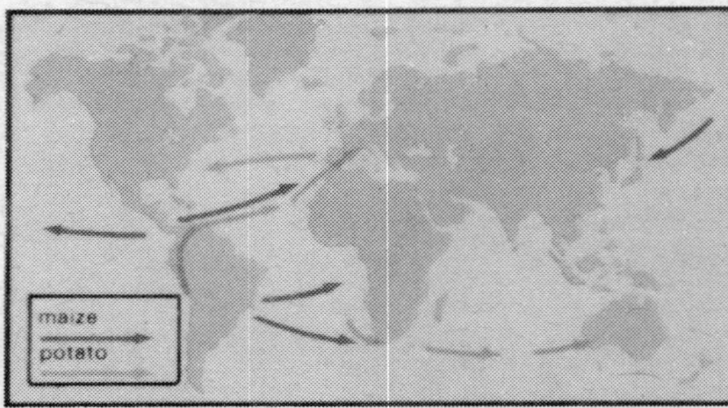

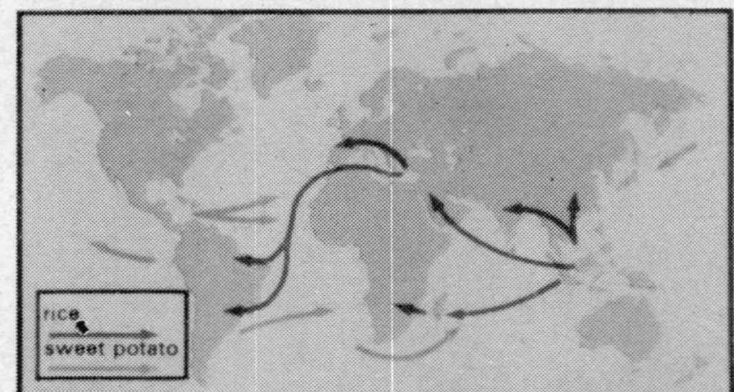

•

This interchange of plants produced an enormous increase in food supplies, which made possible the unprecedented increase of human populations in modern times. It also initiated a corresponding increase in intercontinental trade. Before 1500, this trade had been limited to Eurasia and Africa, and involved mostly luxury goods; after 1500, the combination of regional economic specialization and improvements in sea transport made possible the gradual transformation of the limited medieval luxury trade into the modern mass trade of new bulky necessities.

•

The conflict of Church and State is a capital fact in European history. Elsewhere kings and priests tended to work in harmony, and the result was a 'monolithic' society. In Europe, particularly in western Europe, the co-existence of two powers helped to promote the emergence of 'pluralistic' societies, in which the individual had to balance the different claims made on his allegiance. Here were the distant origins of modern individualism.

The Rise of the West

One humanity, one history, one fat little book. Some familiarity with world history will not help you to avoid mistakes, but it may help you recognize them and thus move on to more original ones. —SB
[Suggested by Jib Fowles]

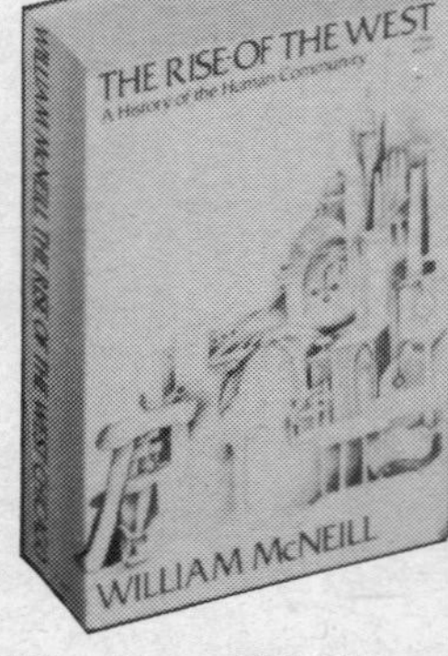

The Rise of The West
W.H. McNeil
1963; 896 pp.

$6.95 postpaid from:
University of Chicago Press
11030 South Langley Ave.
Chicago, IL 60628
or Whole Earth Household Store

↑

This seated diorite statue from Khafre's funerary temple in Giza shows the divine king both in his human form and as Falcon Horus. The sculptor overcame the inherent awkwardness of such an artistic undertaking magnificently, for the falcon's protecting wings bind the two figures indissolubly together; and the sublime severity of the Pharaoh's human face is reaffirmed by the aloof benevolence of the falcon's expression. Such sculpture symbolized, and in symbolizing perhaps helped also to strengthen and define, the all-important role of the god-king in ancient Egypt. This skilled and stylistically perfect work was executed under the Fourth Dynasty (2650–2500 B.C.), when the resources of all Egypt were drafted for the constuction of the great pyramids.

•

Men some centuries from now will surely look back upon our time as a golden age of unparalleled technical, intellectual, institutional, and perhaps even of artistic creativity. Life in Demosthenes' Athens, in Confucius' China, and in Mohammed's Arabia was violent, risky, and uncertain; hopes struggled with fears, greatness teetered perilously on the brim of disaster. We belong in this high company and should count ourselves fortunate to live in one of the great ages of the world.

Out of Revolution

Why is this unknown history of the West raved about by Martin Buber, W.H. Auden, Lewis Mumford, Reinhold Niebuhr, and Page Smith? The author Rosenstock-Huessy, writing in 1938, is personal, passionate, deeply unconventional, and, I'm convinced, deeply right. For him history proceeds by its national revolutions, its passionate self-encounters that bind past and future and startle the world system to renewed life.
I've never met a history book that was so biological, and biologically moral. —SB
[Suggested by Richard Baker]

Out of Revolution
(Autobiography of Western Man)
Eugen Rosenstock-Huessy
1938, 1966; 770 pp.

$9.35 postpaid from:
Argo Books, Inc.
Norwich, VT 05055
or Whole Earth Household Store

•

It is your own story that is told in this volume. That is to say: Any real man behaves in the volcanic hours of his own life as people behaved during revolutions. Those hours are extreme and terrible, yet they tell us more about the unity of human nature than soft days of peace from which behaviourists are apt to derive their political concepts . . .

It is not the boastful John Falstaff, but St. John lying on the ground like one dead, to whom we must compare a nation in the birth-throes of conversion to its eternal role. In every-day life the most similar event was perhaps the act of the bride who passed from her parents' house into that of her suitor by the one word "Yes." If she meant it, the full content of her life, her choice and her destination, was implied in this moment. That is why the word spoken at such an hour has little to do with the gabbling which is also called language, but which is only the rubbish and off-scourings of creative speech. The bride's single word of reply has a power as divine as the "Let there be light" of the world's first day. Like the cry in an hour of revolution, her "yes" carries a weight as heavy as the most heroic action. It is a revelation of the woman's whole future, a decision over her whole past. It is irrevocable, and it is true.

Such words and such moments are rare in the life of the individual, and in the life of mankind as well. Daily life prefers half measures and half lights. The pressure and danger must become tremendous, it must be a question of life and death, before our cold reason, our conventional language, and our fear of committing ourselves, will give way to the unmistakable and unique sounds of truth.

•

We sum up our statements thus: It is not valid to pretend that the workers are exploited by the capitalists because they get low wages. The real outcry of man's offended nature should be that he is degraded because his boss does not care for his past or his future, and because he, the worker, is deprived of the power to weave past or future into his own day of work.

The boss, by virtue of the privileges conferred upon him by liberalism, hires a man's force and skill and presence and brains as a ready-made product. All the traditions that were needed to concoct this man's talents, and all the props that are needed to keep up his character, are degraded into his own private affair.

•

The secret of the due process of revolution is a progressive change in vocabulary.

The Next 200 Years

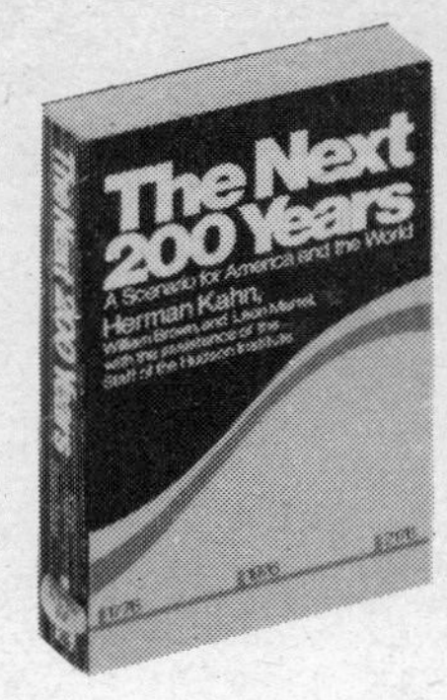

The Next 200 Years
(A Scenario for America and the World)
Herman Kahn, William Brown & Leon Martel
1976; 241 pp.

$4.50 postpaid from:
William Morrow and Co.
Wilmor Warehouse
6 Henderson Drive
West Caldwell, NJ 07006
or Whole Earth Household Store

By the year 2176, Kahn et al predict, the population of the world will be leveled at 15 billion souls, with a per capita economic activity of $20,000 (world per capita product now is $1500). The book proposes that the leveling off of population and economic growth will be based not on limitations of supply but limitations of demand. People will have enough.

That is diametric news, 180° out from most economic wisdom, which assumes always infinite demand meeting always finite supply. The authors make a persuasive case refuting **The Limits to Growth** *on the continuing availability of materials and energy. And they have paid close attention to the behavior of affluent groups such as the outlaw/citizens of the Counter Culture.*

In other words, they have an adaptive model, the only one I know of. It assumes that people learn. And interestingly it inverts the understandings of Marshall McCluhan, early Herman Kahn, and others who have said the technology determines values. Once the survival basics are covered, they suggest, then increasingly values determine technology.

Paul Ehrlich once commented that Kahn's first future book, **The Year 2000** *(1968), was fine as far as it went, except that it failed to even mention population, environment, or ecology, which practically from the date of publication became major determinants of events. That criticism won't hold for this book. Kahn is still an optimist, and still an economist, but his perspective is steadily more ecological. He's learned more than his critics (often from them), and has more of interest to say to me.*

A convert from my previous apocalyptic fervor, I now carry Kahn's as my working model of the future. After four years it's still holding up fine, which is unusual in the futures business. What I like best about Kahn is that he warns about the dangers of continuing affluence and peace, and how to withstand them. —SB

•

It is useful to distinguish four kinds of economic activities: primary, secondary, tertiary and quaternary.

Primary economic activities are extractive — principally agriculture, mining, forestry and fishing. One can think of the corresponding society and culture as being organized to "play games with and against nature" and for protection against "barbarian" invaders and raiders; in such a society the ratio of rural to urban dwellers is in the range of twenty to one, with the former supporting the latter by some kind of primary activity.

Secondary economic activities have to do with construction and manufacturing. The corresponding society and culture, primarily urban, are organized mainly to "play games with and against materials, as well as against nature," and the other major activity tends to be organized warfare, both offensive and defensive.

Initially the emerging postindustrial economy will be characterized by a service economy, emphasizing what are called *tertiary* economic activities — services that support primary and secondary activities, such as transportation, insurance, finance, management, many governmental activities, much education and training. Nature becomes a relatively controllable variable and constraints set by materials become less and less important as technology and affluence increase. This results in a society and culture, probably more suburban than urban, whose major activity is "games with and against organizations," and which is characterized by a structural society which emphasizes organizational and professional pluralism in the distribution of power and prestige. Knowledge rather than experience becomes the major asset and there is an increasing problem of "educated incapacity."* Wars no longer "pay" and the recourse to large-scale organized violence becomes restricted generally to defensive situations or attempts to preserve some aspect of the status quo.

Eventually, in the 21st century, we should expect a transition to a different kind of service economy, to what we term a *quaternary*, or truly postindustrial, economy. Here the primary, secondary and tertiary activities will constitute only a small part of human endeavors; more and more people will do things for their own sake, and even more than today ends will become more important than means.

*By "educated incapacity" we mean an **acquired or learned inability to understand or see a problem**, much less a solution. Increasingly, the more expert, or at least the more educated, a person is, the more likely he is to be affected by this.

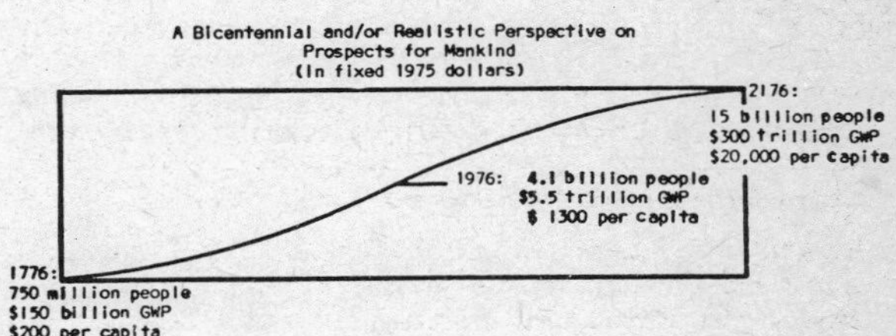

•

We would recommend the world-wide creation of a number of public and private institutions with various specific purposes, but all with an overall mission of the systematic and intense study of far-fetched and improbable phenomena, but phenomena which would be extremely important were they to occur. In effect, these institutions would together constitute an articulate lobby and an "early warning system" for long-term environmental problems. It is only fair to warn the public that anyone who studies such phenomena full time is almost certain to exaggerate their likelihood, impact and dangers. To do so is simply human nature. We do want the people making these studies to conduct them with an almost fanatic intensity, since such fanaticism can be very useful in sustaining interest, drive and even creativity. But we do not want this fanaticism to be carried over into judgments on public policy.

The Promise of the Coming Dark Age

The Promise of the Coming Dark Age
L.S. Stavrianos
1976; 211 pp.

$7.50 postpaid from:
W.H. Freeman & Co.
660 Market Street
San Francisco, CA 94104
or Whole Earth Household Store

This book is a rich work of contemporary scholarship — full of good stuff. In some ways, the flesh is better than the bones of it The Promise is: a diverse decentralist world humming with development at many levels, from the neighborhood to the nation. The tendencies which are leading us there are: "Demo-Technology," Worker Control, Participatory Democracy, and Self-Actualization: obvious, but nice bones.

Ah, but the pleasures of the flesh! Lots of his evidence is news; Stavrianos has admirable taste in information. There are sketches of rural industrialization in China, an experiment in "total systems" work enrichment at a Proctor and Gamble plant, McGovern's campaign and defeat, the successful revolution in Guineau-Bissau, the insights offered by Soviet dissidents, and the inequities underlying the Brazilian economic miracle, to give a few examples.

Being a responsible intellectual, Stavrianos balances things fairly. He admits the flaws in the exemplary systems — thus a nice comeuppance effect, which is the truth of an innovative situation. Just as you're beginning to think that Yugoslav experiments in worker control of factories spell the wave of the future, he tells you what the problems have been, then moves you on over to another drawing board.

Is it a curse or a blessing to live in interesting times? The latter if we can be wise enough to delight in the sight of grass sprouting up in the cracks of our cherished pavement. Stavrianos offers us a spectrum of developments that tend towards a liberation of humanity; that hope, arching in the noosphere, is a covenant to lighten up a present dark age. —Stephanie Mills

•

A reason for doubting the assumption that mankind cannot change its ways is indicated by the current paradoxical combination of global unity and global diversity. The unity is readily apparent in instant mass-communication media and the space voyages of astronauts and cosmonauts. Equally significant, however, although less obvious, is the unprecedented diversity in social philosophies and institutions. The variety in the Western world ranges from the United States to Sweden, in the Communist world from Yugoslavia to North Korea, and in the underdeveloped world from Bolivia to Tanzania. A significant new social mutation also appears to be emerging in China. In a shrinking world of such diversity, any creative achievement anywhere quickly becomes common knowledge. Sooner or later, enthusiastically, or grudgingly, it is studied and discussed and then imitated, adapted, or rejected. The net result is global interaction and cross-fertilization. The law of hybrid vigor operates in the cultural realm as well as the biological.

The View from the Barrio

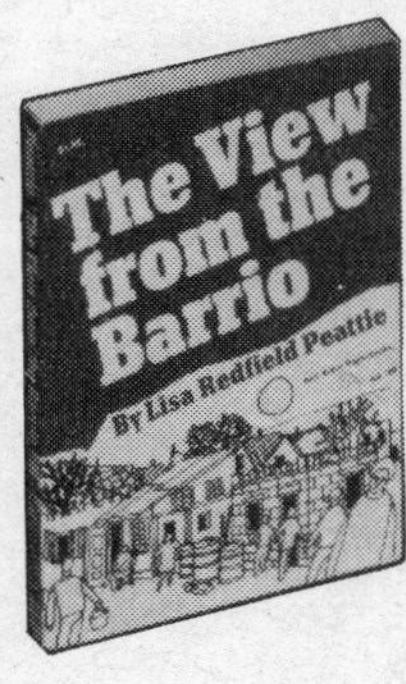

The View from the Barrio
Lisa Redfield Peattie
1968; 147 pp.

$2.95 postpaid from:
The University of Michigan Press
P.O. Box 1104
Ann Arbor, Michigan 48106

What a refreshment this book was after reading a handful of "future" books — scholarly radical technological inflated prophetic advice gas — which left me with a depressed feeling that the future is just words.

The real future will be made of much that is reported in this book (and approximately unknown to the scholars). Namely rural Third World people in newly rich economies and new planned cities, subverting the planners and transforming their own lives.

La Laja is a barrio in the planned Venezuelan city of Ciudad Guayana. Dr. Peattie was there for 2½ years with her family, taking part in barrio life and paying structured attention to what was going on. Social life around her was loose, fluid to a swiftly changing environment and economy. People were self-organizing only around critical community issues such as water or sewers. From the barrio it was a huge impassable distance to the planners, so when something came down that was intolerable they would beef futiley for a while and then plant dynamite under it. Nothing romantic. Just making do, getting by.

It dynamited my depression. —SB

•

Another part of La Laja's natural environment consists of the strip of unimproved land just beyond the Iron Mines fence. This land, covered with brush and cactus, is often used for toileting, especially by children; debris may be dumped there, and children collect certain wild fruits in the brush. Some medicinal plants (from an extensive fold pharmacopeia of herbal remedies) are collected there by adults. Some men of the barrio shoot birds in this piece of monte. Boys hunt birds and sometimes rats with stones, either thrown or projected with a sling shot; their accuracy is astonishing by American standards.

THE RISING SUN
NEIGHBORHOOD NEWSLETTER

Sometimes I wonder what Africans do with their time when they're not getting massacred or getting their leaders changed. I mean, if you only hear about folks when they suffer disasters, death looks natural on them.

And now, in memory of Pope Paul, who from a central location in the largest palace in the world bestowed on millions of Latin American women and children more birth and more death, who was the inspiration behind the successful movement to give black women back their coat hangers, who assured fag baiters that God is on their side, who was, within the limits of his changing time and his changing church, as anti-sex, anti-love and anti-life as he could possibly be, let us all spit three times toward Rome and vow that we will not let TV obituaries by Hallmark Cards make us forget who our real enemies are.

Science and Civilization in China

Joseph Needham is a renowned biologist who travelled into unexplored regions of Chinese technological history and became a yet more renowned historian and interpreter of what is for most of us the back of the planet. His series is awesome in size and depth; he's done the mining, but you've got to refine the ore to suit your own purposes. One purpose I might be learning about is Taoism and how its influence helped the Chinese discover and utilize some technology long before the West and also overlook or never utilize other stuff that the West seized on. Another purpose might be taking some of the mechanical inventions of old China — from man-kites to waterwheels — and applying them to your own hand technology of intentional communities. There's no source like the source in these matters.

You could acquire these wonderful volumes the way Needham and his collaborators are producing them — one every year or so. If you're timid, you could try the **Shorter Science and Civilization in China: 1** *(which condenses Volumes 1 & 2). Or you could blow $645, get 'em all, and then wait anxiously for the next one to rumble down the chute from Cambridge.*

Awesome books. —SB

Pictorial reconstruction of the astronomical clock-tower built by Su Sung and his collaborators at Khaifeng in Honan, then the capital of the empire, in + 1090. The clockwork, driven by a water-wheel, and fully enclosed within the tower, rotated an observational armillary sphere on the top platform and a celestial globe in the upper storey. Its time-announcing function was further fulfilled visually and audibly by the performances of numerous jacks mounted on the eight superimposed wheels of a time-keeping shaft and appearing at windows in the pagoda-like structure at the front of the tower. Within the building, some 40 ft. high, the driving wheel was provided with a special form of escapement, and the water was pumped back in the tanks periodically by manual means. The time annunciator must have included conversion gearing, since it gave 'unequal' as well as equal time signals, and the sphere probably also had this. Su Sung's treatise on the clock, the Hsin I Hsiang Fa Yao, constitutes a classic of horological engineering. Orig. drawing by John Christiansen. The staircase was actually inside the tower, as in the model of Wang Chen-To. The historical significance of the mechanical rotation of an astronomical instrument (a clock-drive) has already been discussed in Vol. 3, pp. 359 ff. —Vol. 4, Part 2

Science and Civilization in China
Joseph Needham

Volume I
(Introductory Orientations)
1954; 318 pp.
$35

Volume II
(History of Scientific Thought)
1956; 696 pp.
$75

Volume III
(Mathematics and Science of the Heavens and the Earth)
1959; 877 pp.
$90

Volume IV
(Physics and Physical Technology: Part I, Physics)
1962; 434 pp.
$45

(Physics and Physical Technology: Part 2, Mechanical Engineering)
1965; 759 pp.
$75

(Physics and Physical Technology: Part 3, Civil Engineering and Nautics)
1970; 990 pp.
$90

Volume V
(Chemistry and Chemical Technology: Part 2, Spagyrical Discovery and Invention: Magisteries of Gold and Immortality)
1974; 542 pp.
$65

(Chemistry and Chemical Technology: Part 3, Historical Survey, from Cinnabar Elixirs to Synthetic Insulin)
1976; 516 pp.
$65

(Chemistry and Chemical Technology: Part 4, Apparatus and Theory)
1980; 804 pp.
$105

The Shorter Science and Civilization in China, Vol. 1
Joseph Needham and Colin A. Ronan
1978; 326 pp.
$12.95

all from:
Cambridge University Press
510 North Avenue
New Rochelle, NY 10801

Typical Chinese horizontal windmill working a square-pallet chain-pump in the salterns at Taku, Hopei (King, 3). The fore-and-aft mat-and-batten type sails luff at a certain point in the cycle and oppose no resistance as they come back into the eye of the wind. —Vol. 4, Part 2

The Plan of St. Gall

The production of this book renews one's faith in universities as places devoted to the love of learning. The typography and design, the binding and the paper, the craftsmanly use of photo-offset to take in visual quotations from a wide range of medieval materials: all are brought together in a work that expresses a care for the infinite and the infinitesimal. This must certainly be the most beautiful book produced anywhere in a generation or two. As a study of the architecture and economy of a Carolingian monastery, **The Plan of St. Gall** *is really a research into the meaning of monasticism as a form of cultural preservation and creation. Now that we are once again in a period of rekindling of interest in monasticism, from Tassajara to Dharmadhatu to Benedictine Grange, we are perhaps in a better historical climate to appreciate that this research into the past is really a search into the future. For readers of* **CQ** *who are taken with the works of Brothers John Todd and Sim Van der Ryn, these three volumes provide another dimension to the design of "solar villages," a dimension in which technology is made appropriate to cosmology in a vision of the sacred. As all of us continue our work on the architecture and economy of a new way of life, whether in California, Colorado, or Massachusetts,* **The Plan of St. Gall** *should be a book to hold in the evening with clean hands after a day of work with compost and stones, windmills and solar collectors.*
—*William Irwin Thompson*

As **The Times Atlas of World History** *did, these big books have been leaving dents in my chest as I read them far into the night like detective stories, which they resemble. Within the account of how to build a ninth century A.D. space colony is considerable fascinating sleuth work. I was particularly taken by Volume II, which gives perhaps the first account of the brilliant vernacular northern European building, the three-aisled structure that you see alive and adapting in nearly every barn and cathedral. It dates back in unbroken lineage to several millenia B.C. It's pretty smart: no load-bearing walls, no ridge pole, rafters neatly balanced on posts that conveniently divide or impressively leave open the vast interior space. I want to build one.* —SB

•

The Plan of St. Gall gathers as in a lens an image of the whole of Carolingian life. Product of the first synthetic encounter between Antiquity and new civilization of the Barbarian north, it testifies the first pervasive alliance between Church and State in this nascent world, and the first successful integration into the fabric of the State, as a force at once spiritual, educational, and economic, of the ideal of monasticism which in Antiquity had taken its start as a counter culture.

The Plan of St. Gall
(A Study of the Architecture & Economy of, & Life in a Paradigmatic Carolingian Monastery)
Walter Horn and Ernest Born
1979; Vol I — 356 pp.; Vol II — 358 pp.; Vol III — 266 pp.
$325 postpaid from:
University of California Press
2223 Fulton Street
Berkeley, CA 94720

The men who conceived the Plan were of the intellectual elite of their time; they would have held striking presence among sagacious men of any age. They were expert in every facet of that microcosm of life compacted by history within the walls of a monastic enclosure: its spiritual and devotional aspirations, its educational endeavors, its medical and sanitary services, its industrial and technological facilities. Administrative and economic managers, they were accomplished in agriculture, viticulture, animal husbandry. Associated with them were the greatest scholars, illuminators, and metal workers of the time.

The makers of the Plan possessed consummate skill in architectural planning. They designed in a plot only 480 by 640 feet a self-sustaining community for some 270 souls. Each structure is scaled to a specific use, all are sited in relation to one another and to the whole so as to insure proximity among related and distance between disparate functions — a settlement of urban complexity, clustered around the imposing bulk of a basilica that, had it ever been built as conceived, would have been the most outstanding church of the Age of Charlemegne.

•

O quam gravis est scriptura: oculos gravat, renes frangit, simul et omnia membra contristat. Tria digit scribunt, totus corpul laborat.

Writing is excessive drudgery. It crooks your back, dims your sight, twists your stomach and your sides. Three fingers write, but the whole body labors.

Monk's cloister, cellar, kitchen, refectory, laundry & bath house, dormitory, latrine. Monastery, St. Gall.

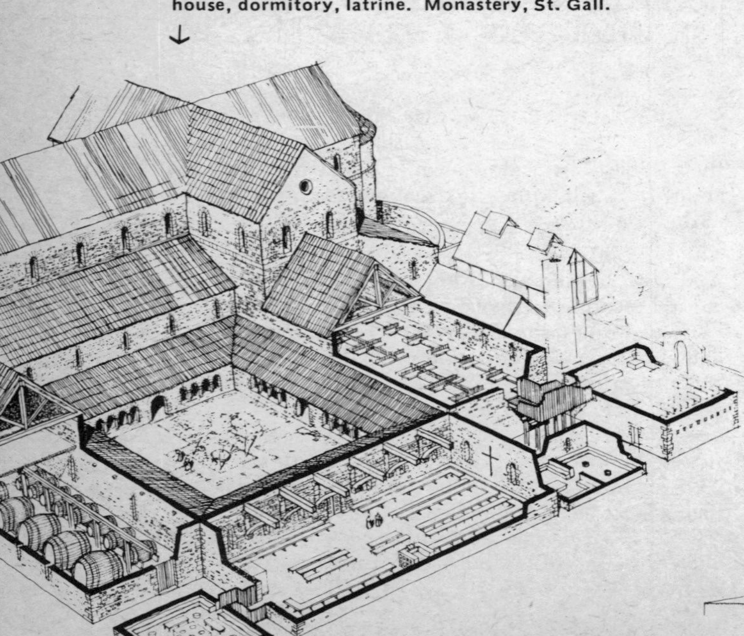

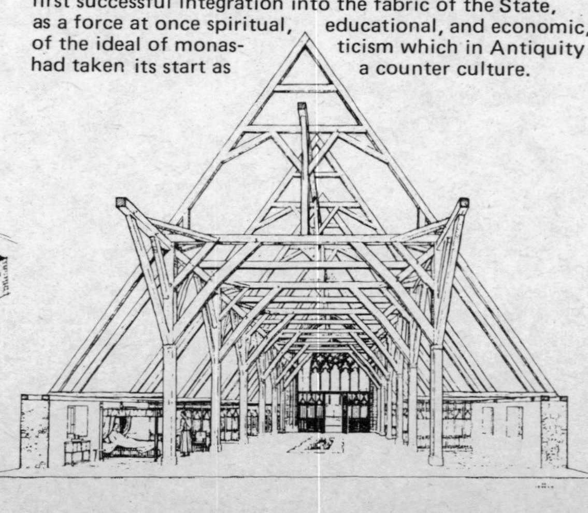

St. Mary's Hospital, Chicester, England, late 13th century

Capitalism and Material Life

The book is divided into sections, rice, corn, beer, furniture, alcohol, iron and many many others. I found that I paid close attention to Braudel; most history books make my mind wander. He turns the usual history upside down, details and more details of everyday life but perhaps no mention of the King. All his discussions are filled with quotes from first hand. On horses and urban transport in eighteenth century Paris —

At the end of the century two thousand seedy cabs plied for trade in the town; they were drawn by broken horses and driven by foul-mouthed coachmen who had to pay out twenty sous a day for 'the right to drive on the highway'. Congestion was notorious and we have many descriptions of it. 'When the cabs are empty,' said a Parisian, 'they are fairly docile; around midday they are more difficult, in the evening they are unmanageable.' And they were unobtainable at rush hours, for example at dinner time (for such it was) around two o'clock in the afternoon. 'You open the door of the cab, someone else does the same on the other side; he gets in, you get in. It is then necessary to go to the commissioner of police for him to decide who shall have it.' At such times a gilded carriage might be seen blocked by a cab crawling slowly along in front of it, at a slow and measured pace, 'all broken down, covered with burnt leather and with planks in place of glass.'

There are no chapters of theories concerning why this or that happened. Instead piece by piece you hear about furniture in China and Europe, alcohol in France, England and America. The details pour out of the book. Braudel has theories but they are stated succinctly and I felt that he would rather use a page to give you the essence of an age than any explanations of it.

Europe therefore neither discovered America and Africa, nor desecrated the mysterious continents. The nineteenth-century explorers of central Africa, so greatly admired in the past, travelled on the backs of the Black bearers. Their great mistake, Europe's mistake at that juncture, 'was to think they were discovering a sort of New World.' Similarly the discoverers of the South-American continent, even the *bandeirantes paulistas* who set off from the town of Sao Paulo, founded in 1554, for all their wonderful epics, merely rediscovered the old tracks and rivers, with canoes used by the Indians, during the sixteenth, seventeenth and eighteenth centuries. And they were generally guided by the Mamelucos (Portuguese and Indian halfbreeds).

The same adventure was repeated, to the profit of the French, from the Great Lakes to the Mississippi in the seventeenth and eighteenth centuries, thanks to Canadian halfbreeds, the *bois brules* as they were called. Europeans very often rediscovered the world with the eyes, legs and brains of others.

One of the nicest qualities of the book is that it can be opened anywhere and read for 20 minutes. Braudel has enough respect for life and the past to be immensely puzzled by it — so he never imposes some kind of false structure that you have to pay attention to.

—*Steve Baer*

Capitalism and Material Life, 1400 - 1800
Fernand Braudel
1967; 445 pp.

$5.50 postpaid from:
Harper Colophon Books
Harper & Row
Keystone Industrial Park
Scranton, PA 10022

or Whole Earth Household Store

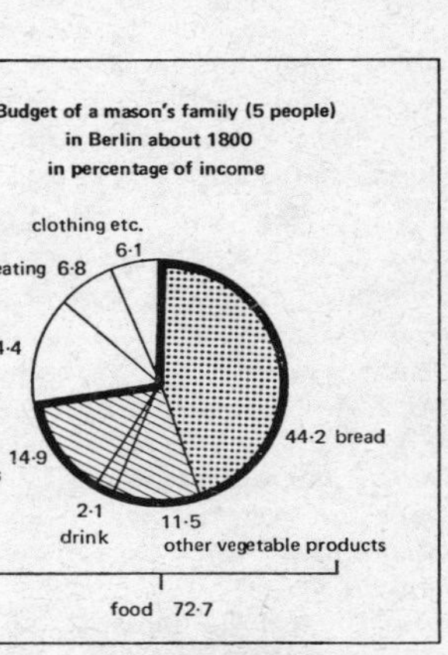

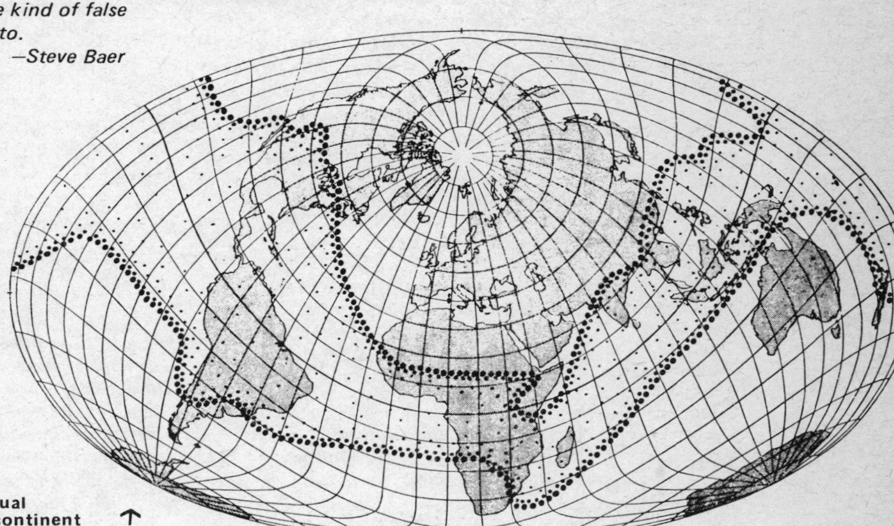

The belt of hoe-cultures. Note the unusual depth of the zone across the American continent and the islands of the Pacific. ↑

Technics and Civilization

I first read this book in 1957 then again in 1963 and then part of it in 1969.

Here is the first paragraph of the book.

During the last thousand years the material basis and the cultural forms of Western Civilization have been profoundly modified by the development of the machine. How did this come about? Where did it take place? What were the chief motives that encouraged this radical transformation of the environment and the routine of life: what were the ends in view: what were the means and methods: what unexpected values have arisen in the process? These are some of the questions that the present study seeks to answer.

Lewis Mumford is an unusual man. He is not an engineer or a scientist, he isn't an historian or sociologist, you can't identify him as a business man or a literary man or an academic. He seems beyond all those roles. This made him especially attractive to me when I was 19 because his style smelled of the place I wanted to go. He is profound, poetic, knowledgeable. He takes care of the large and small things in his books.

Technics and Civilization *is a good book to start with; if you like it, there are many others of his to turn to,* **Myth of the Machine, Arts and Technics, The City in History, Transformation of Man, The Pentagon of Power,** *etc.*

How I have used him: all through my twenties I used him as my guide.

—*Steve Baer*

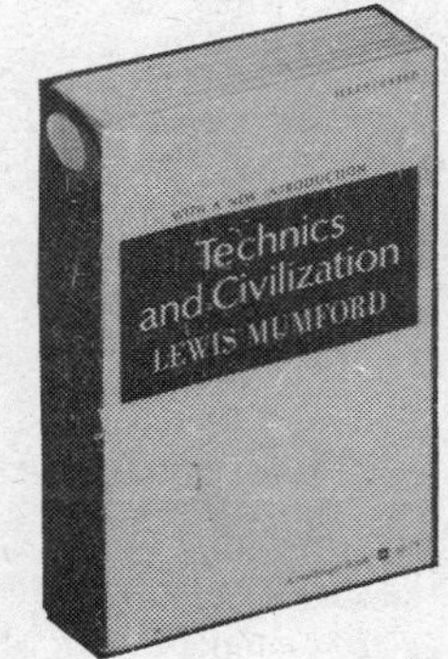

Technics and Civilization
Lewis Mumford
1934, 1963; 495 pp.

$4.75 postpaid from:
Harcourt, Brace & Jovanovich, Inc.
757 Third Avenue
New York, NY 10017

or Whole Earth Household Store

•

Most of the important inventions and discoveries that served as the nucleus for further mechanical development, did not arise, as Spengler would have it, out of some mystical inner drive of the Faustian soul: they were wind-blown seeds from other cultures. After the tenth century in Western Europe the ground was, as I have shown, well plowed and harrowed and dragged, ready to receive these seeds; and while the plants themselves were growing, the cultivators of art and science were busy keeping the soil friable. Taking root in medieval culture, in a different climate and soil, these seeds of the machine sprouted and took on new forms: perhaps, precisely because they had *not* originated in Western Europe and had no natural enemies there, they grew as rapidly and gigantically as the Canada thistle when it made its way onto the South American pampas. But at no point — and this is the important thing to remember — did the machine represent a complete break. So far from being unprepared for in human history, the modern machine age cannot be understood except in terms of a very long and diverse preparation. The notion that a handful of British inventors suddenly made the wheels hum in the eighteenth century is too crude even to dish up as a fairy tale to children.

The printing press was a powerful agent for producing uniformity in language and so, by degrees, in thought. Standardization, mass-production, and capitalistic enterprise came in with the printing press; and not without irony, the oldest known representation of the press, shown here, appeared in a Dance of Death printed at Lyons in 1499.
↓

Mechanization Takes Command

The swan song of complex and ingenious handicraft. The history of the door lock, the stove, the butcher's tools, agricultural plows and white bread. Watch the human hand shrivel and the machine take command. Finally, I could understand how floor mats turned to spring mattresses. A comprehensive look at what European and American humans believe is necessary for comfort.

—*Peter Warshall*

Mechanization Takes Command
(A Contribution to Anonymous History)
Siegfried Giedion
1948; 743 pp.

$7.45 postpaid from:
W.W. Norton & Co., Inc.
500 Fifth Avenue
New York, NY 10036

or Whole Earth Household Store

•

In the popular sense, 'streamline' is used interchangeably with the word 'modern.'

From the start, it was understood that the phrase was not to be taken literally. Today the layman, unfamiliar with aerodynamics, calls almost everything 'streamlined' when he really means 'graceful lines.' We have 'streamline' radio cabinets, toasters, cigarette lighters, and even gasoline with 'streamline' action. The development of the science of aerodynamics and its application to airships and airplanes has created in the public a sense for fleeting lines, and these lines, being recognized by designers as a decorative element, have been emphasized to give the impression of speed. The automobile manufacturer, to give the sales appeal of a visual impression of the speed that the engineer has built into his machine, has used and is using 'streamlining' extensively.

Streamlined Casing for Vacuum Cleaner, U.S. Patent Design, 1943. 'I have invented a new, original and ornamental Design for a Suction Cleaner Casing or the like.' U.S. Patent Design 135,974. →

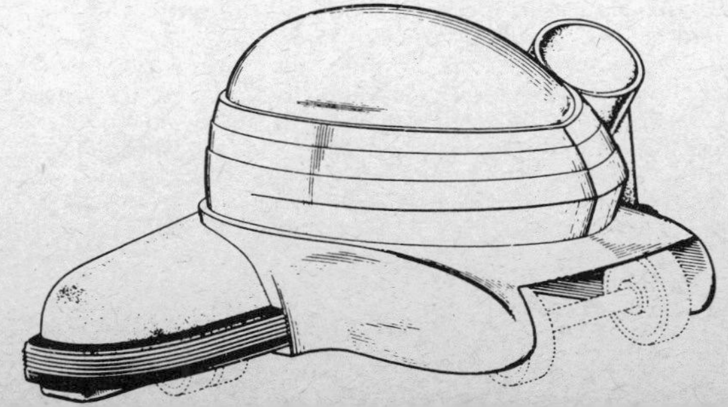

THE RISING SUN
NEIGHBORHOOD NEWSLETTER

I once burned off my eyelashes watching some toast toast on acid, Evelyn said when we were exchanging tales of the sixties.

Another tale of the sixties: Dick and Jane believed in open marriage. Jane started sleeping with Dick's best friend, an artist. When Dick found out he was very upset, he said, because it wasn't good for Jane to get involved with someone who wasn't political, it would hurt her political development. (That one from Susan.)

Muddling Toward Frugality

Mr. Johnson's thesis can be summarized without much difficulty: after generations of extravagant and reckless industrial expansion, we are clearly entering an age of economic scarcity. While human demands continue to rise, natural resources, especially the non-renewable kind, become harder to find and more expensive to extract, process, transport and distribute. This simple brute fact is the basic cause of inflation, despite the inability of most professional economists to see it. (The "dismal science" has never been more dismally obtuse than it is today.) The law of diminishing returns is coming into effect. Technological developments can delay the process but not halt or reverse it; nor can we rely on government or big business to save us. Planning for further growth delays the adjustments that must be made, makes a fair sharing of necessary sacrifices more troublesome, and if carried too far will make more severe and painful, because rapid, the inevitable decline of the international economic machine. The best way to deal with the end of affluence is to accept it — not fight it and to begin, here and now, the unavoidable adaptations, on an individual, family, and community basis. Piecemeal, experimental, and muddling.

This of course is the conservative approach to the future, conservative in the true, honest, root meaning of the word, and will be dismissed with impatience by those who still yearn for dramatic breakthroughs, global industrialism, a planetary state under the domination of Capitalism or Communism or some convergent combination of the two. We need heroes, the critics will cry, bold and giant figures — tragic heroes! — who will lead us on to ever grander adventures, up to the pyramids of power and beyond — ad astra. To the stars.

Anticipating this objection, Mr. Johnson offers us the comic hero. The tragic hero is always willing to risk everything (including our well-being) for his vision of the ideal. Modern history gives us numerous examples of the type. The comic hero, however, is more concerned with survival. Survival in comfort. Good food, adequate shelter, a decent wine, the love of wife and friends and neighbors, a satisfying job, a supportive community to live in, these comprise for the comic hero the essentials of a good life.

The comic hero is a muddler. He makes a science of muddling, that is, of feeling his way step by step through problems that allow no bypassing and cut off retreat. He is satisfied with small gains and willing to make small sacrifices. He distrusts abstractions, grand generalizations, all-embracing ideologies. When possible he dodges war, whether a war against another nation, another people, or against nature. He is ready to adapt and change when necessary rather than cling with loyal desperation to any cause, however traditional, that is clearly getting him into more and more trouble. He is ready, among other things, to give up his gas-hog pickup for a bicycle, his cross-country vacation tour for a walk in the hills, his color TV for a ballgame in the park, when the advantages of so doing become apparent. And he has enough foresight to surrender a job in a doomed industry — automobiles, for example — when a chance appears to make a living elsewhere.

Most good ideas are as old as humankind. The value of Mr. Johnson's book lies in his synthesis of several old ideas — voluntary simplicity, for example, and friendship, and community citizenship — in a sensible program for an entire nation. He does not propose to save the world. The rest of the world, as he makes clear, must save itself, and in this endeavor, as he points out, the so-called underdeveloped lands have in some respects a head start against the over-developed lands such as the United States. The majority of the people of Mexico, for instance, are well accustomed to poverty; if they can find a way to bring their population into balance with their land and its resources, and learn to share those resources in an equitable manner (through another revolution, if necessary), they will be better off than we North Americans, for whom frugality and commonwealth remain exotic, dangerous heresies.

Mr. Johnson shows in what I find a persuasive argument that if we have enough time, and if we begin to change our ways now, voluntarily, with patience, good humor and good will, we can not only avoid calamity but even regain a saner, easier, more rewarding way of life.

—Edward Abbey

Muddling Toward Frugality
Warren Johnson
1978; 252 pp.
$2.95 postpaid from:
Shambhala Publications
1123 Spruce Street
Boulder, CO 80302
or Whole Earth
Household Store

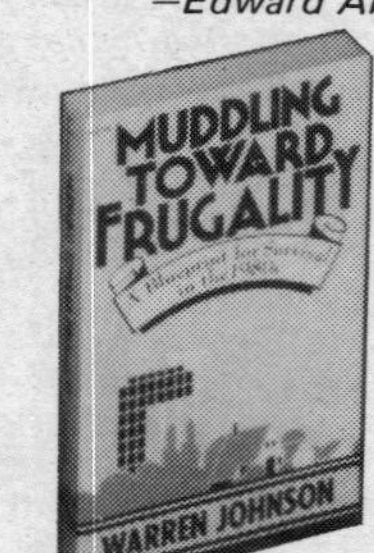

•

The process of muddling through is a gutsy, down-to-earth process full of inefficiencies and inconsistencies. It takes an inordinate amount of time to take modest incremental steps forward, and significant bold steps are clearly not in the cards. The process can be a lot of fun for those who enjoy it and do not take themselves too seriously — the politician who loves to talk to people, the lobbyist who thrives on finding ways to gain access to the influential, or the activist who enjoys organizing people. It keeps this country pretty close to the middle of the road, while still permitting slow, faltering adjustments to change. All the jibes about our political process seem pretty appropriate. Ralph Waldo Emerson said democracy was "a raft which would never sink, but then your feet are always in the water." E.B. White defined it as "the recurrent suspicion that more than half the people are right more than half the time." I rather like Plato's definition of democracy as "a charming form of government, full of variety and disorder, and dispensing a sort of equality to equals and unequals alike."

Steady-State Economics

Where **Toward a Steady-State Economy** *diagnoses the future selling ailment and inspires treatment, this subsequent and closely argued book by Daly prescribes specific medicine.*

The subject is balance.

—SB

Steady-State Economics
(The Economics of Biophysical Equilibrium and Moral Growth)
Herman E. Daly
1977; 185 pp.
$6.50 postpaid from:
W.H. Freeman and Co.
660 Market Street
San Francisco, CA 94104
or Whole Earth
Household Store

•

Once we have replaced the basic premise of "more is better" with the much sounder axiom that "enough is best," the social and technical problems of moving to a steady state become solvable, perhaps even trivial. But *unless* the underlying growth paradigm and its supporting values are altered, all the technical prowess and manipulative cleverness in the world will not solve our problems and, in fact, will make them worse.

•

The critical institution is likely to be the minimum and maximum limits on income and the maximum limit on wealth. Without some such limits, private property and the whole market economy lose their moral basis, and there would be no strong case for extending the market to cover birth quotas and depletion quotas as a means of institutionalizing environmental limits. Exchange relations are mutually beneficial among relative equals. Exchange between the powerful and the powerless is often only nominally voluntary and can easily be a mask for exploitation, especially in the labor market, as Marx has shown.

The Entropy Law and the Economic Process

Professor Georgescu, who has been a long time critic of mechanistic model builders within his discipline, demonstrates that the economic process is not circular and reversible as it is depicted in nearly every introductory economics textbook. It is linear and cannot be reversed. With impeccable logic and irrepressible wit Professor Georgescu lays bare the one-way nature of economic production; a process that starts with inputs of material "low entropy" upgraded by inputs of energy to produce an output which is degraded through use into waste after having provided the satisfaction for which it was made. Expanding economies process ever larger quantities of material and use greater amounts of energy thus depleting ever more quickly the remaining "low entropy" reserves of materials and energy while increasing the overall entropic flow in the environment. This lack of understanding the relationship between expanded economic activity and increased entropy has completely discounted any viewpoint not tightly focused on the short term. The consequence is that future generations, possibly not this one, will inherit a world whose dowry will have been squandered by men ignorant of the relationship between economics and entropy.

—Timothy Wessels

•

The common fact that heat always flows by itself from the hotter to the colder body, never in reverse, came to be generalized by the Entropy Law, which is the Second Law of Thermodynamics and which *is* in contradiction with the principles of Classical mechanics. Its complete enunciation is incredibly simple. All it says is that the entropy of the universe (or of an isolated structure) increases constantly and, I should like to add, irrevocably. We may say instead that in the universe there is

The Entropy Law and the Economic Process
Nicholas Georgescu-Roegen
1971; 457 pp.
$6.95 postpaid from:
Harvard University Press
79 Garden Street
Cambridge, MA 02138
or Whole Earth
Household Store

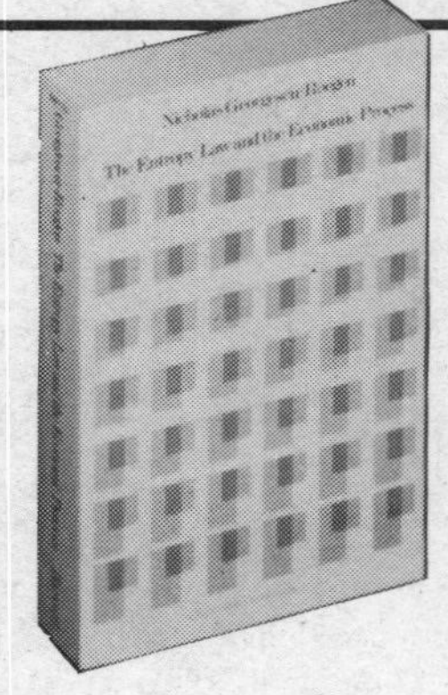

a *continuous* and *irrevocable* qualitative degradation of free into bound energy. . . .

There are some good reasons why I stress . . . the irrevocability of the entropic process. One reason interests the economist in particular. If the entropic process were not irrevocable, i.e., if the energy of a piece of coal or of uranium could be used over and over again ad infinitum, scarcity would hardly exist in man's life. Up to a certain level, even an increase in population would not create scarcity: mankind would simply have to use the existing stocks more frequently. Another reason is of more general interest. It concerns one of man's weaknesses, namely, our reluctance to recognize our limitations in relation to space, to time, and to matter and energy. It is because of this weakness that, even though no one would go so far as to maintain that it is possible to heat the boiler with some ashes, the idea that we may defeat the Entropy Law by bootlegging low entropy with the aid of some ingenious device has its periodical fits of fashion. Alternatively, man is prone to believe that there must exist some form of energy with a self-perpetuating power.

Economics, Ecology, Ethics

The Western Manifest Destiny of eternal growth is noisily convulsing its last. Meanwhile who is looking around for what's being born? Credit Daly with a sharp eye. In one comfortable book he has gathered the best essays, papers, analyses, speculations on the holy transition from self-exploitation to simple maintenance. Georgescu-Roegen, Ehrlich, Schumacher, Boulding, Hardin, Johnson, Ophuls, and C.S. Lewis. For a healthy world to be accomplished it must first be perceived. Start here. —SB

Economics, Ecology, Ethics
(Essays toward a steady-state economy)
Herman E. Daly, Editor
1973, 1980; 372 pp.
$7.95 postpaid from:
W.H. Freeman and Co.
660 Market Street
San Francisco, CA 94104
or Whole Earth
Household Store

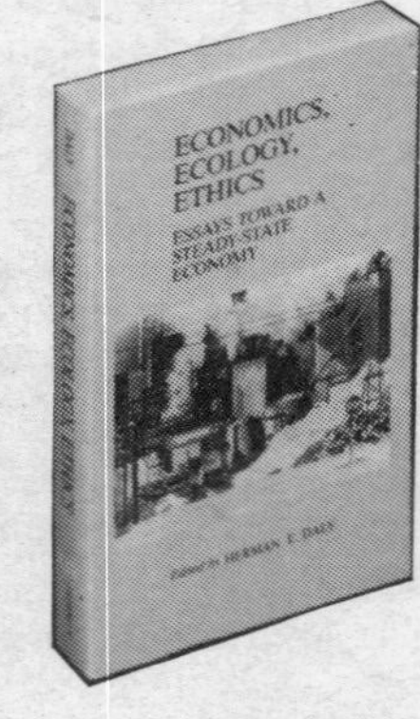

•

Behavior that is "rational" (consistent with profit maximization) over one time period is irrational over another. My favorite example is that of the village idiot who, when offered the choice between a nickel and a dime, always chose the nickel, much to the villagers' continuing amusement. Finally one day a villager said to him, "Look, I know you are not that stupid; you know a dime is worth more than a nickel — why do you always take the nickel?" To which the "idiot" replied "It's obvious — if I took the dime they would stop making the offer!" Idiocy on one time horizon is cleverness on another. But somehow we manage to choose an accounting period and muddle through, and so we could also in a steady state.

•

Like the aging of an organism, the working of the Entropy Law through the economic process is relatively slow but it never ceases. So, its effect makes itself visible only by accumulation over long periods. Thousands of years of sheep grazing elapsed before the exhaustion of the soil in the steppes of Eurasia led to the Great Migration. The Entropy Law enables us to perceive that a development of the same nature and of far greater consequences is running its full course now. Because of the pressure of population on agricultural land the area of which cannot be appreciably increased, man can no longer share the agricultural low entropy with his traditional companions of work, the beasts of burden. This fact is the most important reason why mechanization of agriculture must spread into one corner of the world after another, at least for a long time to come.

Free to Choose

The exquisite balance of nature, the complex ecology we admire, is based largely on competition expressed in constant individual deaths and sufferings and the survival of optimal genes. In a market economy, it is mostly prices that suffer, die, and converge to optimums. Centrally planned economies, by contrast, have all the elegance and self-regulating capabilities of cornfields.

Givens are seldom well-defended. Given a largely market economy, it is remarkable it has a defender as capable as Milton Friedman. He is an astute analyst, a highly efficient expounder, and, most amazing, has good ideas of his own — from the monetarism that got him his Nobel Prize to his voucher system for rejuvenating education.

The usual situation with such characters is that their wisdom is spread thin over dozens of books. Thanks to having his ideas star in a TV series on PBS in 1980, Milton and Rose Friedman put it all together in one accessible book. Whose price is right, a bargain for the value. —SB

Free to Choose
(A Personal Statement)
Milton and Rose Friedman
1980; 338 pp.
$9.95 postpaid from:
Harcourt Brace and Jovanovich
757 Third Avenue
New York, NY 10017
or Whole Earth Household Store

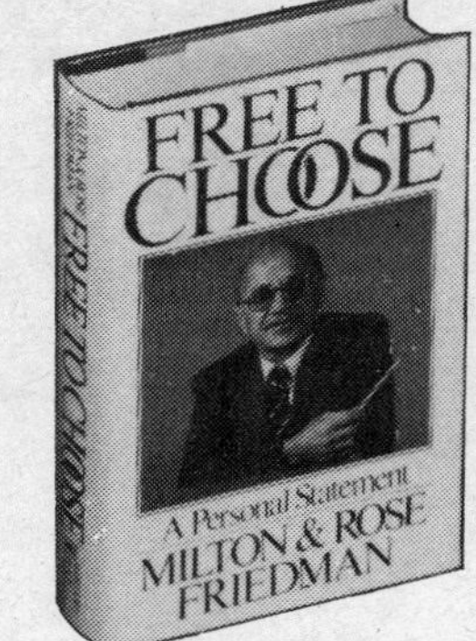

•

Economic freedom is an essential requisite for political freedom. By enabling people to cooperate with one another without coercion or central direction, it reduces the area over which political power is exercised. In addition, by dispersing power, the free market provides an offset to whatever concentration of political power may arise. The combination of economic and political *power* in the same hands is a sure recipe for tyranny.

•

Prices perform three functions in organizing economic activity: first, they transmit information; second, they provide an incentive to adopt those methods of production that are least costly and thereby use available resources for the most highly valued purposes; third, they determine who gets how much of the product — the distribution of income.

•

Most economists agree that a far better way to control pollution than the present method of specific regulation and supervision is to introduce market discipline by imposing effluent charges. For example, instead of requiring firms to erect specific kinds of waste disposal plants or to achieve a specified level of water quality in water discharged into a lake or river, impose a tax of a specified amount per unit of effluent discharged. That way, a firm would have an incentive to use the cheapest way to keep down the effluent. Equally important, that way there would be objective evidence of the costs of reducing pollution. If a small tax led to a large reduction, that would be a clear indication that there is little to gain from permitting the discharge. On the other hand, if even a high tax left much discharge, that would indicate the reverse, but also would provide substantial sums to compensate the losers or undo the damage. The tax rate itself could be varied as experience yielded information on costs and gains.

Like regulations, an effluent charge automatically puts the cost on the users of the products responsible for the pollution. Those products for which it is expensive to reduce pollution would go up in price compared to those for which it is cheap, just as now those products on which regulations impose heavy costs go up in price relative to others. The output of the former would go down, of the latter up. The difference between the effluent charge and the regulations is that the effluent charge would control pollution more effectively at lower cost, and impose fewer burdens on nonpolluting activities.

The Breakdown of Nations

A lovely, early book, now restored to print, about pathology and health in national scale. It merges very nicely with recent thought about bioregional politics. And, boy, does it explain handily the centuries and centuries of tribal stability in pre-white California, with its 26 language groups and innumerable tribelets. Herman Kahn likes to remark that the only discernible function of a nation state is to wage war. Small nations make small wars, Kohr would doubtless reply. —SB

The Breakdown of Nations
Leopold Kohr
1978; 250 pp.
$4.95 postpaid from:
E.P. Dutton and Company
Two Park Avenue
New York, NY 10016
or Whole Earth Household Store

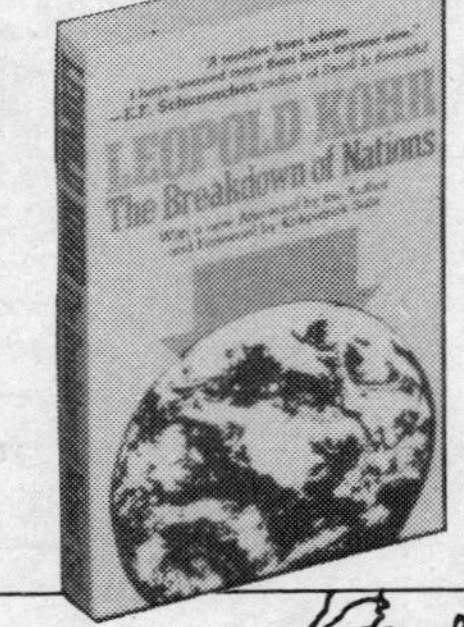

↑ **Unsuccessful federation. Were America organized as here, on the pattern of Europe's simplified, but unequally large blocks, Washington would be a purely decorative centre as Geneva was for the League of Nations. To enforce its authority it would have to ask the support of one or more of the powerful members. Wars would be as frequent as in Europe.**

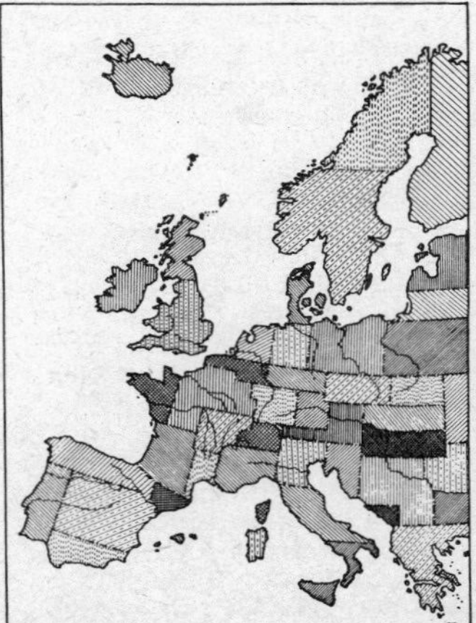

← **As on the preceding map America is shown 'simplified' in European style, the harmony and balance of its 48 states destroyed, this map shows Europe divided in American style. The arrogant, uncooperative, proud, self-glorifying nations (great powers) have given way to small states which could as easily be ruled by Geneva as the U.S. is ruled by Washington. A successful power maniac would be as harmless for the rest as Huey Long.**

→ **The purely geometrical division of America would, however, have to be modified in Europe along the traditional tribal frontiers. This map shows approximately the genuine component parts of Europe, historically subdividing the great powers, products not of nature but of force. Being all equal in size they are ideally fit to form a successful federation. Thus Europe's problem — as that of any federation — is one of division, not of union.**

The Overdeveloped Nations

Kohr's thesis is that when societies outgrow a certain critical size (15 million members), the problems they insurmount become inherent and insoluble consequences of that overgrowth. He deals with nations as having personality, and makes an excellent critique of Development in those terms. He argues frequently by analogy, and his theory stands up nicely throughout; it has the virtue of being the simplest possible explanation of the inability of mega-states to provide for the summum bonum of their members. It also explains the inexorable collectivization of even capitalist/individualist societies.

If, like me, you hope that nothing succeeds like secession, read **The Overdeveloped Nations.** *Then send a copy to your Congressman.* —Stephanie Mills

The Overdeveloped Nations
(The Diseconomies of Scale)
Leopold Kohr
1977; 185 pp.
$9.95 postpaid from:
Schocken Books
200 Madison Avenue
New York, NY 10016
or Whole Earth Household Store

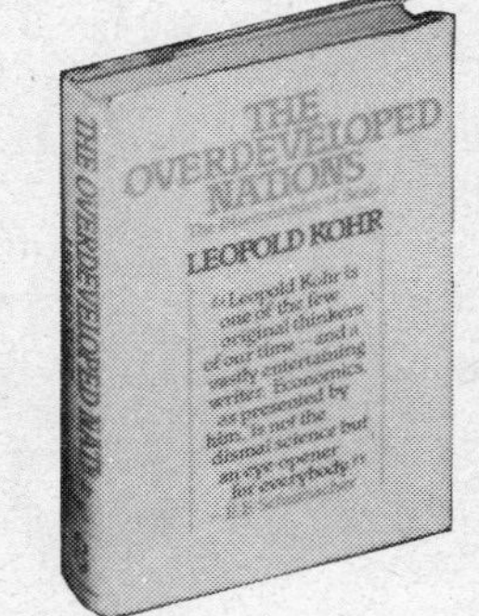

•

A change in the velocity of money has the same effect as if the quantity of money had changed. As an inflation may thus be caused quantitatively, by an increase in the supply of money, it may also be caused qualitatively, by an increase in the money's velocity.

•

The richest German regions are to this day those which until not so long ago were the small sovereign states of Hamburg, Bremen, Frankfort, Hesse, Wurtemberg, Bavaria Bavaria, Saxony rather than the large power of Prussia. Historically smallness, even in the absence of natural resources, can thus hardly be considered an obstacle preventing countries from getting rich. On the contrary.

•

Whatever the new nations are gaining in development, they seem to be losing in identity.

Development Without Aid

Development Without Aid *should be required reading for all the overpaid UN, USAID, and World Bank functionaries who seem to be hell bent on homogenizing the world's peoples through the sinister tactic of help. Leopold Kohr argues that a bootstrap approach is the only way to build authentic national identity and true prosperity; he proposes a lean "development" or "preventive" communism as the pull. Thus the why and how of saying no to international welfare statism. Cultural diversity and traditional approaches to subsistence are the happy outcomes.*

Like Kohr's **Overdeveloped Nations**, *it's a sensible book. Kohr's arguments against a multinational grants economy have sensual appeal. A courtly and charming man whose writing embodies his character, Kohr rightly delights in the beauties of medieval squares, the leisurely pace of underdevelopment, and the unenriched flavors of regional cuisine. Kohr's thinking on development proceeds from the known; it has human dimension and is humanly possible. He taught E.F. Schumacher a lot. Imagine what he has to offer the rest of us.*
—Stephanie Mills

Development Without Aid
(The Translucent Society)
Leopold Kohr
1973; 227 pp.
$12.95 postpaid from:
Schocken Books
200 Madison Avenue
New York, NY 10016
or Whole Earth Household Store

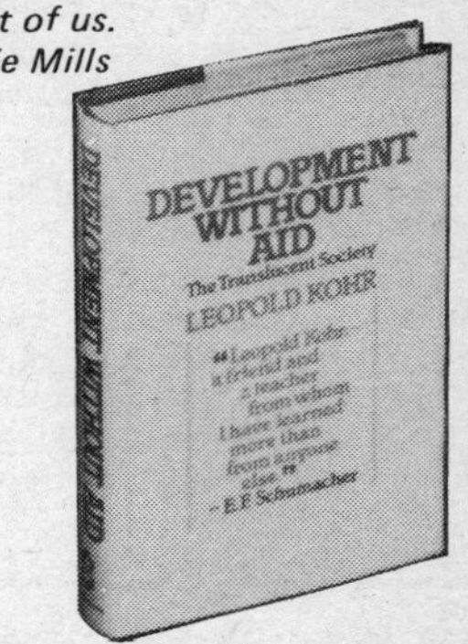

•

I have often been tempted to work out the comparative costs for a series of basic living standard items involving a slightly enlarged set of at least three regions: the Soviet Union, the United States, and a paradisiacal primitive village such as Loiza Aldea on the north coast of Puerto Rico, or any similar village you might think of in Bali, Ecuador, or Anguilla. Having not done so yet, I am lacking exact figures. Perhaps a sumptuous Ford grant can correct the situation. But, in the meantime, I feel confident that my findings would show approximately the following:

If it takes 15 years to acquire a unit of dwelling in the Soviet Union, and 5 in the United States, the cost in Loiza Aldea is probably in the neighbourhood of 2 weeks. Thus, if the American housing standard is 3 times higher than the Russian, the standard of Loiza Aldea is 140 times higher than the American, and 420 times higher than the Russian.

THE RISING SUN
NEIGHBORHOOD NEWSLETTER

Susan points out that another important lesson of being a preacher's kid is that whenever vacation is finally planned and definite, especially a good one like the eternally planned trip to the Smokies, someone will die and Dad will have to stay to do the funeral and that will be that.

Marvin Hatcher, the hardware store man, doesn't believe in sales tax, so he doesn't charge it, just pays it.

Small Is Beautiful

Few books have exerted such leverage on an Age as this one. I doubt if Americans have been so influenced by printed eloquence since Thomas Paine's **Common Sense** *helped focus our founding independence. Schumacher is fighting a similar oppression, only this time we colonized ourselves, as he reveals by sub-titling his book "Economics as if People Mattered."*

The wonder of Schumacher's work is his eminent practicality, based on his years with the British Coal Board (he predicted the 1973 Energy Crisis in 1958), and his effective proposals — most notably the re-invigoration of Intermediate Technology.

With good sense and a mature spirituality, Schumacher comes on like John Henry against the mega-machine, sure that he will win, and he is. —SB

Small is Beautiful
(Economics as if People Mattered)
E.F. Schumacher
1973; 290 pp.
$2.95 postpaid from:
Harper & Row
Keystone Industrial Park
Scranton, PA 18512
or Whole Earth
Household Store

•
Fossil fuels are merely a part of the "natural capital" which we steadfastly insist on treating as expendable, as if it were income, and by no means the most important part. If we squander our fossil fuels, we threaten civilisation; but if we squander the capital represented by living nature around us, we threaten life itself.

•
From an economic point of view, the central concept of wisdom is permanence. We must study the economics of permanence. Nothing makes economic sense unless its continuance for a long time can be projected without running into absurdities. There can be "growth" towards a limited objective, but there cannot be unlimited, generalised growth.

•
The cultivation and expansion of needs is the antithesis of wisdom. It is also the antithesis of freedom and peace. Every increase of needs tends to increase one's dependence on outside forces over which one cannot have control, and therefore increases existential fear.

•
As Gandhi said, the poor of the world cannot be helped by mass production, only by production by the masses. The system of *mass production*, based on sophisticated, highly capital-intensive, high energy-input dependent, and human labour-saving technology, presupposes that you are already rich, for a great deal of capital investment is needed to establish one single workplace. The system of *production by the masses* mobilises the priceless resources which are possessed by all human beings, their clever brains and skillful hands, *and supports them with first-class tools*. The technology of *mass production* is inherently violent, ecologically damaging, self-defeating in terms of non-renewable resources, and stultifying for the human person. The technology of *production by the masses*, making use of the best of modern knowledge and experience, is conducive to decentralisation, compatible with the laws of ecology, gentle in its use of scarce resources, and designed to serve the human person instead of making him the servant of machines. I have named it *intermediate technology* to signify that it is vastly superior to the primitive technology of bygone ages but at the same time much simpler, cheaper, and freer than the super-technology, or democratic or people's technology — a technology to which everybody can gain admittance and which is not reserved to those already rich and powerful.

E.F. Schumacher

•
I have no doubt that it is possible to give a new direction to technological development, a direction that shall lead it back to the real needs of man, and that also means: *to the actual size of man*. Man is small, and, therefore, small is beautiful. To go for giantism is to go for self-destruction. And what is the cost of a reorientation? We might remind ourselves that to calculate the cost of survival is perverse. No doubt, a price has to be paid for anything worth while: to redirect technology so that it serves man instead of destroying him requires primarily an effort of the imagination and an abandonment of fear.

Tools for Conviviality

What does Illich mean by "tool"? A car is a tool. So are the machines, the factory, the company, and the industry that make it. A scalpel is a tool — but so is a doctor, the AMA, a medical school, and the medical profession. Machines, corporations, institutions, professions, units of government — all are tools.

What is wrong now is that the tools are too big. They have turned us from tool-users into tool-tenders. The tools shape the product and the work.

A society of large tools cannot be democratic, egalitarian, socialistic, humane, and just. It must be hierarchical, exploitive, bureaucratic, and authoritarian. If the day comes when all of humanity's wants can be supplied by a few giant tools, the people who tend them will rule the world. (See Vonnegut's **Player Piano**.*) Illich wants us to make a society of tools to which we all may have access, and which we will direct and use to meet our own felt needs.* —John Holt

Tools for Conviviality
Ivan Illich
1973; 135 pp.
$1.50 postpaid from:
Harper & Row
Keystone Industrial Park
Scranton, PA 18512
or Whole Earth
Household Store

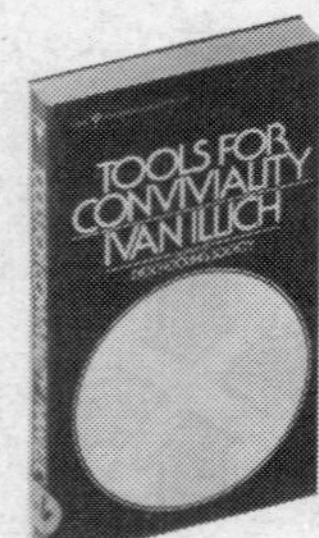

•
Convivial tools are those which give each person who uses them the greatest opportunity to enrich the environment with the fruits of his or her vision. Industrial tools deny this possibility to those who use them and they allow their designers to determine the meaning and expectations of others. Most tools today cannot be used in a convivial fashion.

•
Some institutions are structurally convivial tools. The telephone is an example. Anybody can dial the person of his choice if he can afford a coin. If untiring computers keep the lines occupied and thereby restrict the number of personal conversations, this is a misuse by the company of a license given so that persons can speak. The telephone lets anybody say what he wants to the person of his choice; he can conduct business, express love, or pick a quarrel. It is impossible for bureaucrats to define what people say to each other on the phone, even though they can interfere with — or protect — the privacy of their exchange.

•
Most hand tools lend themselves to convivial use unless they are artificially restricted through some institutional arrangements. They can be restricted by becoming the monopoly of one profession, as happens with dentist drills through the requirement of a license and with libraries or laboratories by placing them within schools. Also, tools can be purposely limited when simple pliers and screwdrivers are insufficient to repair modern cars.

•
I have identified five realms in each of which the efficiency of tools can upset the balance of life. Faulty technology can render the environment uninhabitable. Radical monopoly can force the demand for affluence to the point of paralyzing the ability to work. Overprogramming can transfer the world into a treatment ward in which people are constantly taught, socialized, normalized, tested, and reformed. Centralization and packaging of institutionally produced values can polarize society into irreversible structural despotism. And, finally, engineered obsolescence can break all bridges to a normative past.

•
Almost overnight people will lose confidence not only in the major institutions but also in the miracle prescriptions of the would-be crisis managers. The ability of present institutions to define values such as education, health, welfare, transportation, or news will suddenly be extinguished because it will be recognized as an illusion.

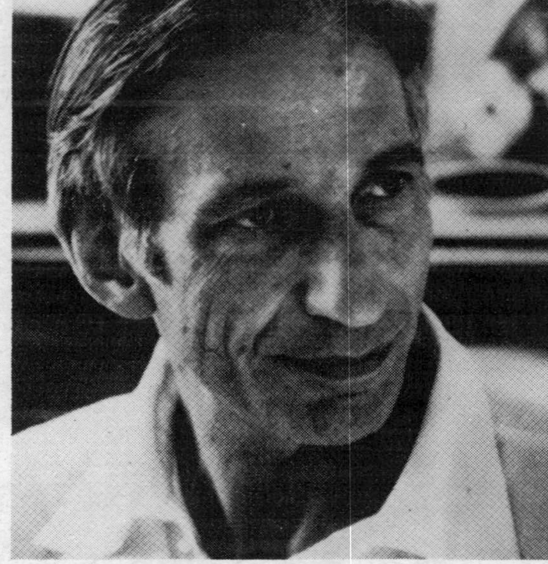

Ivan Illich

More Ivan Illich

See **Energy and Equity** *on p. 175;* **Medical Nemesis** *on p. 386.*

Toward a History of Needs

The penetrating mind and needle of Ivan Illich meets further bloated institutions of the world money made — all commodities and services which bulldoze culture flat. The enemies he identifies are everywhere, handy for your personal, local flanking moves. —SB

Toward a History of Needs
Ivan Illich
1977; 143 pp.
$3.50 postpaid from:
Bantam Books
414 East Golf Road
Des Plaines, Il 60016
or Whole Earth
Household Store

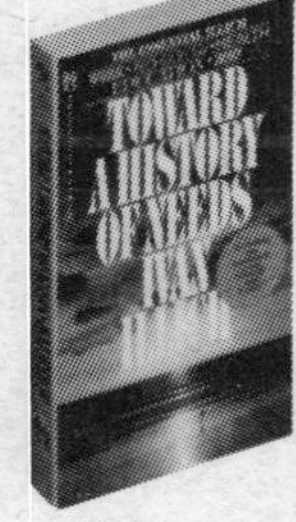

•
CONTENTS
Useful Unemployment and Its Professional Enemies
Outwitting Developed Nations
In Lieu of Education
Tantalizing Needs
Energy and Equity

•
Today, words that are directed to one person's attention have become rare.

•
For two decades now, about fifty languages have died each year; half of those still spoken in 1950 survive only as subjects for doctoral theses.

•
Beyond a certain threshold, the multiplication of commodities induces impotence, the incapacity to grow food, to sing, or to build. The toil and pleasure of the human condition become a faddish privilege restricted to some of the rich. When Kennedy launched the Alliance for Progress, Acatzingo, like most Mexican villages of its size, had four groups of musicians who played for a drink and served the population of eight hundred. Today, records and radios, hooked up to loudspeakers, drown out local talent.

•
Each car that Brazil puts on the road denies fifty people good transportation by bus. Each merchandised refrigerator reduces the chance of building a community freezer. Every dollar spent in Latin America on doctors and hospitals costs a hundred lives, to adopt a phrase of Jorge de Ahumada, the brilliant Chilean economist. Had each dollar been spent on providing safe drinking water, a hundred lives could have been saved. Each dollar spent on schooling means more privileges for the few at the cost of the many; at best it increases the number of those who, before dropping out, have been taught that those who stay longer have earned the right to more power, wealth, and prestige. What such schooling does is to teach the schooled the superiority of the better schooled.

The Household Economy

Whenever I'm asked what the **Whole Earth Catalog** *and my fundamental optimism are about, I invariably start quoting from* **The Household Economy.** *Author Scott Burns lives in the grip of an unusually dry humor which often expresses itself in appalling statistical anecdotes delivered deadpan. He finds appalling statistics because he investigates where economists fear to tread — the wilderness of non-monetary exchange, the household.*

By Burns' contention, the household is rapidly growing in economic significance as people give up on the public economy of accelerating inflation, taxes and energy costs and Do It Themselves. Where does the economic resilience of the culture reside? At home with the family, alive and learning fast. —SB

The Household Economy
Scott Burns
1975; 252 pp.

$4.95 postpaid from:
Beacon Press
c/o Harper & Row
Keystone Industrial Park
Scranton, PA 18512
or Whole Earth Household Store

•

Contents

Part One
THE INVISIBLE ECONOMY

1. The Revolution in Middle America
The household and its economy as an unrecognized instrument of change; the general size and shape of that economy; its immediate implications.

2. Workers Without Wages
The value of labor within the home; the value of a housewife, of a husband, of children. The volunteer economy and the co-operative economy.

The Changing Dominance in the Economic Triad

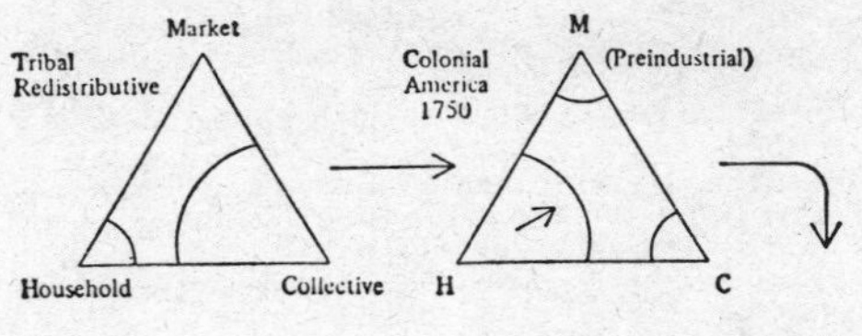

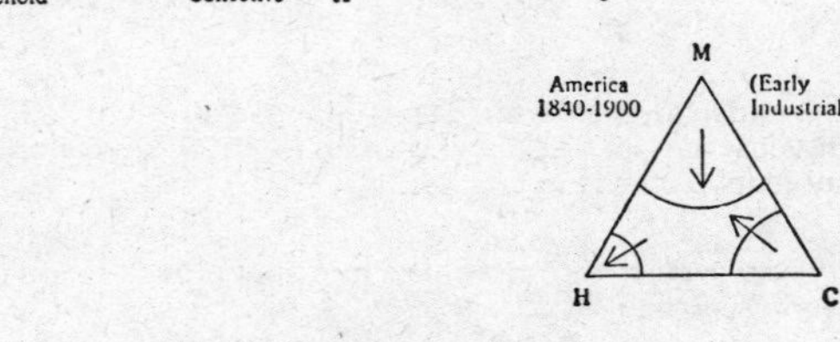

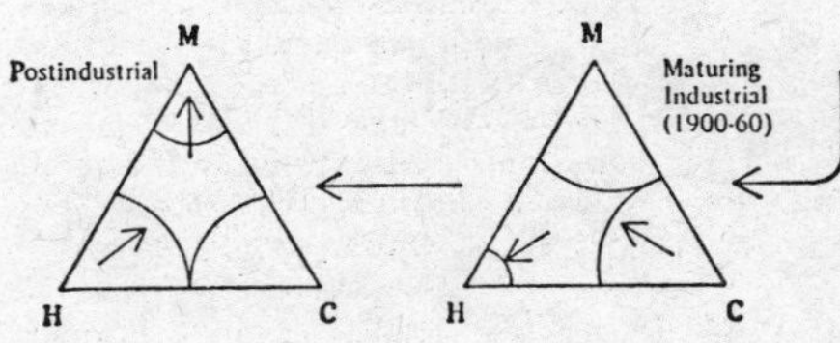

"Ask not what your country can do for you, do it yourself."
—Larry White
Pacific Sun

4. The Changing Balance of National Wealth
An examination of the national balance sheet and how it has shifted since 1929. The surprising news that corporate America, irrespective of ITT and other monsters, now owns less of the national wealth than it did at any time in the past fifty years. Why it will own even less in the future.

5. The Household Has No Bottom Line
The household as an economic operation, comparable to a business; why its activity is not included in conventional statistics.

3. The Rise of Household Capitalism
The storm window as blue chip and other anomalies; the rise of household investment and the logical incentives for same. The folk wisdom of the consumer and the rate of return on houses, cars, the homely washing machine, and the TV set; how they beat the market economy cold.

Part Two
THE PAST AND FUTURE OF THE HOUSEHOLD ECONOMY

6. The Natural Economy
An explanation of the three varieties of economic organization: the household, collective, and market economies. How our perception is obscured by money.

7. The Incredible Rise of the Market Economy
The American economic "take-off": the rise of the industrial system and the consequent decline of the houshold economy.

8. Critics of the Market, Defenders of the Household
How both capitalists and socialists each claim the other is destroying the family; the ideals of Jeffersonian democracy; ambivalence toward the rising market; Ralph Borsodi and the evils of the factory system; Paul Goodman and the logic of a subsistence economy. The powerlessness of these voices. The ebbing tide of consumer enthusiasm for the market economy.

9. Our Accidental Future . . . and How It Might Happen
How to stumble into the future; the creation of the Special Capital Bank; the nationalization of the railroads and Lockheed; the stock-market collapse of 1983-84; the government as investor of last resort; and the creation of the National Time Trust. The fifty-year revolution.

10. A Modest Utopia
The necessity of a stationary state; how the market is incompatible with stability, the household compatible. A consideration of the grimmest alternative.

11. The Dreary Alternative
The superstate, the knowledge society, and the guaranteed pecking order. Visions of bureaucracy unbound. The household economy as a vital buffer between the individual and powerful institutions.

Part Three
WHY THE MARKET ECONOMY MUST DECLINE

12. Inflation and the Dilemma of Investment Return
The dilemma of investment return: the anatomy of corporate returns on investment. Inflation and interest rates. Why the Coca-Cola Company is worth more than the entire industry. The inevitable nationalization of heavy industries.

13. Why Taxes Are Depressing
The increasing burden of taxation; the irrelevance of the public-versus-private-goods argument to the individual and household. How taxation works to force both labor and capital outside the market economy . . . and into the household economy.

14. The Scarcity of Time
The illusion of a leisure society; how material wealth and leisure are mutually exclusive; the effects of productivity in manufacturing, the economics of production, and a prediction (the eight-day week). More shifting of the balance between household and market.

15. The Very Lonely Crowd
The effect of productivity in services; the rising bulk of capital investment between buyer and seller; the depopulation of the services and how this will affect the emphasis on specialization.

16. The Age of Externality
What externalities are: the tiresome example of pollution. How all market organizations, by nature, create externalities. Increasing public consciousness of same. How shifting of labor from market to consumer works to increase the household economy.

17. Technology Comes Home
The technological counterwave and the rise of convenience. Problems with scale; the necessity of local production. How the market is becoming a subcontractor to the producing household. Borsodi's "institutional burden."

Part Four
AN EXPEDITION IN THE CURRENT MYTHOLOGY

18. The Narcissistic Vision
The limits of academia and the professional society. The aging of the new industrial state; its irrelevance to the future. The facts and figures of employment growth; the decline of corporate America.

Scott Burns and children

Epilogue
UN-MONEY
The making of a non-economic society, and a final note on the irrelevance of money.

•

Would you like some good investment advice? Go long on storm windows! Now and for the foreseeable future, the homely triple-channel aluminum storm window is probably the best investment any American can make. It offers a tax-free return on investment three or four times the interest rates on the highest-yield bonds and is likely to offer a better return, over a five to ten year period, than most of the hottest stocks of the sixties.

•

Few consumers see their household decisions as business or economic decisions; the household is perceived as a specialized consuming unit, never as a productive unit. *Yet a clear examination of consumer decisions indicates that families are increasingly opting to purchase the capital equipment necessary to obtain goods and services they would otherwise have to buy in the marketplace.* Implicitly, each decision for investment in household equipment and durables hints that household returns on investment are superior to marketplace returns. In fact, this is so.

•

While small colleges close their doors in bankruptcy and large universities announce rising deficits and curtail, at long last, the exponential growth of obscure deanships, new, ad-hoc institutions appear daily. Adult education, once limited to opportunities for teachers to exhibit slides taken on summer tours, is now booming, and the bankruptcy of conventional credentials is ever more evident. Course offerings include all the arts and crafts, home repair, automotive mechanics, financial management, cabinetry — just about anything, in short, that relates to producing for oneself and one's family. The publication of **The Whole Earth Catalog** was more than an instrument for the counterculture; it was the signal that a radically different concept of the use of knowledge was taking root, for the book attempts to offer relevant knowledge not for the competitive advantage of the consumer but for his *personal* use.

Barter

Barter and trade are a mainstay for living with less in Marin County. Carpenters trade shingling for new driveways; dentists barter lab work and inlays for roofing; roofers work on skylights and get plumbing in exchange. There are even complicated three- and four-way trades. Says hairdresser Cathy Simpson, owner of Cambiar in Mill Valley, "I look around my house and shop and almost every item and service has been a trade at one time or another. I trade my accountant, my photographer, my attorney. I've had massages, car repairs, blown glass and roller skates. People like to do it because it cuts down on their taxes. My dentist works on my teeth then we change places — *he* sits down and I cut his hair."

—**Pacific Sun**
March, 1980

THE RISING SUN
NEIGHBORHOOD NEWSLETTER

Did U know? in the 16th century the Pope after due consideration and talks with God reached the conclusion that Indians had souls, so good Catholics were instructed to convert them which they did by a variety of methods. Protestants, on the other hand, were left to their own consciences' conclusion that Indians weren't people and killed them outright en masse. I never got about how North Americans get off on being self-righteous about the Spanish invaders forcing conversions. At least the converts got to tell stories about Jesus as Coyote man and to live.

Patterns of Culture

Years go by and still no book replaces **Patterns of Culture**. *The graceful contrasts of human life. The reminder to reflect on our cultural prejudices before judging another tribe. Unique anthropology by a unique woman.*
—*Peter Warshall*

Patterns of Culture
Ruth Benedict
1934, 1959; 291 pp.

$3.95 postpaid from:
Houghton Mifflin Corp.
Wayside Road
Burlington, MA 01803
or Whole Earth Household Store

•

Later, traditionally when the boy is about fourteen and old enough to be responsible, he is whipped again by even stronger masked gods. It is at this initiation that the kachina mask is put upon his head, and it is revealed to him that the dancers, instead of being the supernaturals from the Sacred Lake, are in reality his neighbours and his relatives. After the final whipping, the four tallest boys are made to stand face to face with the scare kachinas who have whipped them. The priests lift the masks from their heads and place them upon the heads of the boys. It is the great revelation. The boys are terrified. The yucca whips are taken from the hands of the scare kachinas and put in the hands of the boys who face them, now with the masks upon their heads. They are commanded to whip the kachinas. It is their first object lesson in the truth that they, as mortals, must exercise all the functions which the uninitiated ascribe to the supernaturals themselves. The boys whip them, four times on the right arm, four on the left, four times on the right leg, four on the left. Afterward the kachinas are whipped in turn in the same way by all the boys, and the priests tell them the long myth of the boy who let fall the secret that the kachinas were merely impersonations and was killed by the masked gods. They cut his head from his body and kicked it all the way to the Sacred Lake. His body they left lying in the plaza. The boys must never, never tell. They are now members of the cult and may impersonate the masked gods.

•

It is difficult for us to lay aside our picture of the universe as a struggle between good and evil and see it as the Pueblos see it. They do not see the seasons, nor man's life, as a race run by life and death. Life is always present, death is always present. Death is no denial of life. The seasons unroll themselves before us, and man's life also. Their attitude involves 'no resignation, no subordination of desire to a stronger force, but the sense of man's oneness with the universe.' When they pray they say to their gods: We shall be one person.

Tristes Tropiques

This intimate account of Levi-Strauss' field work in Brazil galvanized budding anthropologists all over the world. Find here the intelligent roots of elegant sturcturalism.
—*SB*

•

The ensemble of a people's customs has always its particular style; they form into systems. I am convinced that the number of these systems is not unlimited and that human societies, like individual human beings (at play, in their dreams, or in moments of delirium), never create *absolutely*: all they can do is to choose certain combinations from a repertory of ideas which it should be possible to reconstitute.

•

When we make an effort to understand, we destroy the object of our attachment, substituting another whose nature is quite different. That other object requires of us another effort, which in its turn destroys the second object and substitutes a third — and so on until we reach the only enduring Presence, which is that in which all distinction between meaning and the absence of meaning disappears: and it is from that Presence that we started in the first place. It is now two thousand five hundred years since men discovered and formulated these truths. Since then we have discovered nothing new — unless it be that whenever we investigated what seemed to be a way out, we met with a further proof of the conclusions from which we had tried to escape.

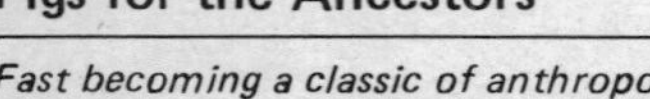

Tristes Tropiques
(An anthropological study of primitive societies in Brazil)
Claude Levi-Strauss
(John Weightman and Doreen Weightman, Translators)
1955, 1973; 403 pp.

$4.95 postpaid from:
Atheneum Publishers
c/o Book Warehouse, Inc.
Vreeland Avenue
Totowa, NJ 07512

The Last of the Nuba

With the impact of Ansel Adams' **This is the American Earth** *or Eliot Porter's* **In Wildness is the Preservation of the World**, *Leni Riefenstahl lovingly reveals what life in balance, a human culture in balance, might feel like. The Nuba is a remote East African tribe. Leni Riefenstahl is the lady who made the films "Triumph of the Will" and "Olympia". The book is almost all color photographs — sensuous, personal, charged.*

How it makes me feel is poverty-stricken. —*SB*

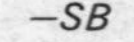

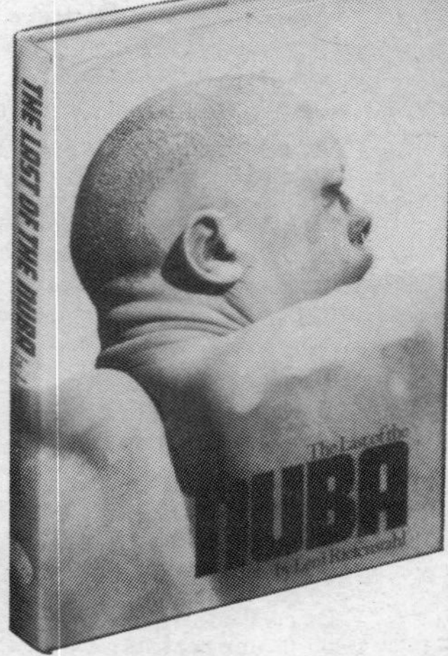

The Last of the Nuba
Leni Riefenstahl
1973; 208 pp.

$25 postpaid from:
Harper & Row
General Books
Keystone Industrial Park
Scranton, PA 18512

← **Generally well in control of their world, the Mesakin Nuba tend to be cheerful and friendly. Young people especially are conscious of and delight in their attractions even though they may, like Tutu, be rather shy. They are fond of ornament, decoration and jewelry and take great care with their appearance.**

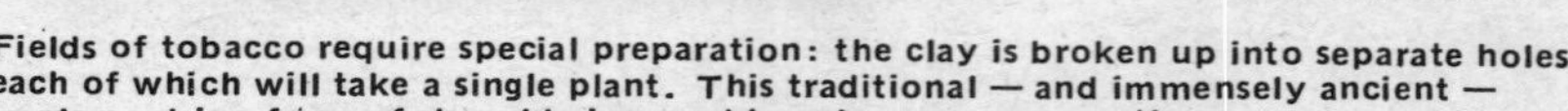

Fields of tobacco require special preparation: the clay is broken up into separate holes, each of which will take a single plant. This traditional — and immensely ancient — implement is a form of shovel being used here by a young wrestler. ↓

Pigs for the Ancestors

Fast becoming a classic of anthropological fieldwork, this study pioneers in the application of energetics (energy expenditure in gardening, for example) and of cybernetics (which shows how the Tsembaga's pig cycle, ritual cycle, and warfare cycle interact to accomplish ecological stability). We've carried two of Rappaport's papers in **The CoEvolution Quarterly** *— both of them based on this book's wild careful experience in New Guinea. Ideas here, I believe, are going to change how we think about our own culture and what we're going to do about it.*
—*SB*

•

Among the Tsembaga, and other Maring-speaking groups in New Guinea, through ritual the following are effected:

1. Relationships between people, pigs and gardens are regulated. This regulation operates directly to protect people from the possible parasitism and competition of their pigs and indirectly to protect the environment by helping to maintain extensive areas in virgin forest and assuring adequate cultivation-fallow ratios in secondary forest.
2. The slaughter, distribution, and consumption of pig is regulated and enhances the value of pork in the diet.
3. The consumption of nondomesticated animals is regulated in a way that tends to enhance their value to the population as a whole.
4. The marsupial fauna may be conserved.
5. The redispersal of people over land and the redistribution of land among territorial groups is accomplished.
6. The frequency of warfare is regulated.

Pigs for the Ancestors
(Ritual in the Ecology of a New Guinea People)
Roy A. Rappaport
1968; 311 pp.

$5.45 postpaid from:
Yale University Press
92A Yale Station
New Haven, CT 06520
or Whole Earth Household Store

← **A medium-sized pig is sacrificed to the Red Spirits. (Photo taken by Mrs. Cherry Vayda among the Fungai-Korama, a Maring group living east of the Tsembaga in the Simbai Valley.)**

The Lost World of the Kalahari

The magical account of a search and a brief time with a noble timeless people, the Bushmen of the Kalahari Desert in southwestern Africa. —SB

The Lost World of the Kalahari
Laurens van der Post
1958; 270 pp.

$3.95 postpaid from:
Harcourt Brace & Jovanovitch
757 Third Avenue
New York, NY 10017
or Whole Earth Household Store

•

Long before he saw us, we were able to identify the bare head of a young Bushman working energetically at something in the grass. When he heard us, he shot upright like an arrow out of the grass and grabbed his spear, but already Dabe was calling out loudly the ancient Bushman greeting, "Good day. I saw you from afar and I am dying of hunger."

The young man stuck his spear in the sand and with his right hand raised, palm open and fingers up, walked shyly toward us, saying in a tone I had never heard before before, "Good day! I have been dead, but now that you have come, I live again."

•

In the cool of the evening they and Xhooxham, "Lips of Finest Fat," led us some miles away to the deepest part of the old watercourse between dunes yellow in the sun. There we found several shallow excavations dug for water in ampler seasons, but the supply which never failed them was hidden, safe from evaporation of sun and wind, deep beneath the sand. Near the deepest excavation Bauxhau knelt down and dug into the sand to arm's length. Toward the end some moist sand but no water appeared. Then he took a tube almost five feet long made out of the stem of a bush with a soft core, wound about four inches of dry grass lightly around one end presumably to act as a kind of filter against the fine drift sand, inserted it into the hole and packed the sand back into it, stamping it down with his feet. He then took some empty ostrich-egg shells from Xhooxham and wedged them upright into the sand beside the tube, produced a little stick, one end of which he inserted into the opening in the shell and the other into the corner of his mouth. Then he put his lips to the tube. For about two minutes he sucked mightily without any result. His broad shoulders heaved with the immense effort and sweat began to run like water down his back. But at last the miracle happened and so suddenly that Jeremiah gasped and I had an impulse loudly to cheer. A bubble of pure bright water came out of the corner of Bauxhau's mouth, clung to the little stick and ran straight down its side into the shell without spilling one precious drop!

So it continued, faster and faster until shell after shell was filled, Bauxhau's whole being and strength joined in the single function of drawing water out of the sand and pumping it up into the light of day. Why he didn't fall down with exhaustion I don't know. I tried to do it, and though my shoulders are broad and my lungs good, I couldn't extract a single drop from the sand. We named that place, where we saw one of the oldest of legends about the Bushman become a miraculous twentieth-century fact, "the Sip-wells."

The Forest People

One of the most appealing peoples in the world, the BaMbuti pygmies of the African Congo are the subject of this classic account. Turnbull writes as effectively as he observes. —SB

The Forest People
Colin Turnbull
1968; 295 pp.

$2.95 postpaid from:
Simon and Schuster
Order Department
1230 Avenue of the Americas
New York, NY 10020
or Whole Earth Household Store

•

Whereas the other tribes are relatively recent arrivals, the Pygmies have been in the forest for many thousands of years. It is their world, and in return for their affection and trust it supplies them with all their needs. They do not have to cut the forest down to build plantations, for they know how to hunt the game of the region and gather the wild fruits that grow in abundance there, though hidden to outsiders. They know how to distinguish the innocent-looking *itaba* vine from the many others it resembles so closely, and they know how to follow it until it leads them to a cache of nutritious, sweet-tasting roots. They know the tiny sounds that tell where the bees have hidden their honey; they recognize the kind of weather that brings a multitude of different kinds of mushrooms springing to the surface; and they know what kinds of wood and leaves often disguise this food. The exact moment when termites swarm, at which they must be caught to provide an important delicacy, is a mystery to any but the people of the forest. They know the secret language that is denied all outsiders and without which life in the forest is an impossibility.

•

Co-operation is the key to Pygmy society; you can expect it and you can demand it, and you have to give it. If your wife nags you at night so that you cannot sleep, you merely have to raise your voice and call on your friends and relatives to help you. Your wife will do the same, so whether you like it or not the whole camp becomes involved. At this point someone — very often an older person with too many relatives and friends to be accused of being partisan — steps in with the familiar remark that everyone is making too much noise, or else diverts the issue onto a totally different track so that people forget the origin of the argument and give it up.

Issues other than disputes are settled the same way, without leadership appearing from any particular individual. If it is a matter involving the hunt, every adult male discusses it until there is agreement. The women can throw in their opinions, particularly if they know that the area the men have selected is barren of vegetable foods. But the men usually know this anyway.

The Mountain People

By the author of **The Forest People**, *this is a different story. Intellectual liberals have never quite recovered from it. Turnbull found that among the Ik of eastern Africa, family and altruism simply do not exist as values. A mother is glad when the leopard eats her baby, because she is released of the burden, and now the leopard will be sleepy enough to kill and eat, along with the remains of the child. How far can selfishness go? Read.* —SB

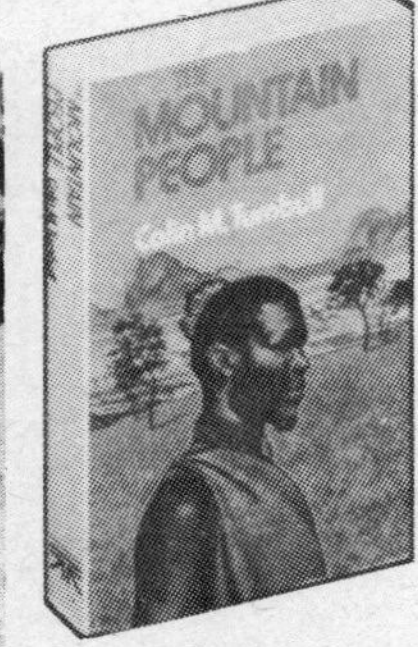

The Mountain People
Colin M. Turnbull
1978; 309 pp.

$2.95 postpaid from:
Simon and Schuster
Order Department
1230 Avenue of the Americas
New York, NY 10020
or Whole Earth Household Store

↑ **Lolim, the ritual priest, refused shelter by his son, staggers off to die on the barren, rocky mountainside. But he lay down to die so that the sun's first rays would strike his poor, dead eyes. He had hope, his son had none.**

•

It was *that* that killed her. She demanded that her parents love her. She kept going back to their compound, almost next to Atum's and the closest to my own. Finally they took her in, and Adupa was happy and stopped crying. She stopped crying forever, because her parents went away and closed the *asak* tight behind them, so tight that weak little Adupa could never have moved it if she had tried. But I doubt that she even thought of trying. She waited for them to come back with the food they promised her. When they came back she was still waiting for them. It was a week or ten days later, and her body was already almost too far gone to bury. In an Ik village who would notice the smell? And if she had cried, who would have noticed that? Her parents took what was left of her and threw it out, as one does the riper garbage, a good distance away. They even pulled some stones over it to stop the vultures and hyenas from scattering bits and pieces of their daughter in Atum's field; that would have been offensive, for they were good neighbors and shared the same *odok*.

•

The Ik teach us that our much vaunted human values are not inherent in humanity at all, but are associated only with a particular form of survival called society, and that all, even society itself, are luxuries that can be dispensed with. That does not make them any the less wonderful or desirable, and if man has any greatness it is surely in his ability to maintain these values, clinging to them to an often very bitter end, even shortening an already pitifully short life rather than sacrificing his humanity. But that too involves choice, and the Ik teach us that man can lose the will to make it. That is the point at which there is an end to truth, to goodness and to beauty; an end to the struggle for their achievement, which gives life to the individual while at the same time giving strength and meaning to society. The Ik have relinquished all luxury in the name of individual survival, and the result is that they live on as a people without life, without passion, beyond humanity.

Blind Logwara . . . when he tried to reach a dead hyena for a share of the putrid meat, his fellow Ik trampled him underfoot. He thought it quite funny. ↓

THE RISING SUN
NEIGHBORHOOD NEWSLETTER

The most insidious TV show going is "The Rep," mostly because it's as good as everyone says it is. It's a dramatic-with-some-comedy series about a young, good, college related performing company in the boondocks. For four weeks they rehearse a play, have love life problems, argue with professors, argue with mom and dad — generally high class soap opera with occasional intelligent discussions of how to perform George Bernard Shaw thrown in. And most actors I've talked to say the rehearsal scenes are good. Then on the fifth week, the show expands from one hour to two or two and a half hours and the company performs a play — a real play, the play they've been rehearsing. (The previous rehearsal scenes, like movie previews, have shown interesting moments of crisis but nothing about the ending.)

So what the series has going for it is the addictive power of any continuing story, the only real plays seen on TV in years, and the ultimate amazing trick — acting. The viewers get to see acting really happening by seeing the same people in different hard roles, and what it's like to prepare for them. But more than all that, the biggest reason why everyone has to watch the show is that when you watch it you get to watch a community of people working together to do a good thing. Hardly anyone gets to do that anymore; hardly anyone gets to do good work and those that do often have to work alone.

So who wouldn't want to watch people having fun and making something worthy at the same time? That's what's so insidious about it — it exploits the hole we're in but it doesn't do a thing to help us out of it. What are we supposed to do — become superb actors and get this fantasy job? Maybe television couldn't do anything to help us out of isolation, since it's essentially isolating, but maybe there is something it could do, like celebrating amateurism. Like showing an amateur theatre group that was truly uneven and letting people see how anyone can start a group to do anything if they don't expect slick perfection. The media render us more and more powerless by convincing us we shouldn't pay attention to or take part in anything that isn't glossy and error free — not necessarily good but flawless and not showing weakness, like the opening production number on a TV variety show.

The old rituals were nice because as long as you could walk in a straight line and follow simple directions, you could be part of something that was impressive — impressive because of the other people doing the same thing, or the clothes you had on or where you were doing it (Stonehenge, Chartres) but not because you were paid to practice until you did complicated things perfectly. But I guess if television tried to show us anything about stuff like that and how to do something like that today, we'd get bored.

The Sacred

I love this book. I read it like Jews and Christians read the Bible or Asian peoples read Lao Tzu or Confucius or Buddhists their sutras. Life may be complex, but the religious principles of traditional native peoples are simple, straightforward and clear. **The Sacred** *quietly, carefully and somewat bookishly lays out the morality of humans before the whiteman, as well as the growing bridge between modern Euro-American society and the strength, beauty and vitality of the American Indian People.*

Put this book with Carl Sauer's **Man In Nature: America Before the Days of the White Man**. *I cannot think of two more needed books to be read throughout America's educational system. Herein lie the roots of perhaps this continent's twenty-first century religious synthesis.*

—Peter Warshall

Note: This book was prepared for use by young Native Americans and largely put together by Native Americans. It's not academic or nostalgic. It's a spiritual field guide for North America. *—SB*

The Sacred
(Ways of Knowledge Sources of Life)
Peggy Beck and A.L. Walters
1977; 369 pp.

$9 postpaid from:
Navajo Community College Press
Curriculum Development Center
Navajo Community College
Tsaile RPO
Navajo Nation, AZ 86556

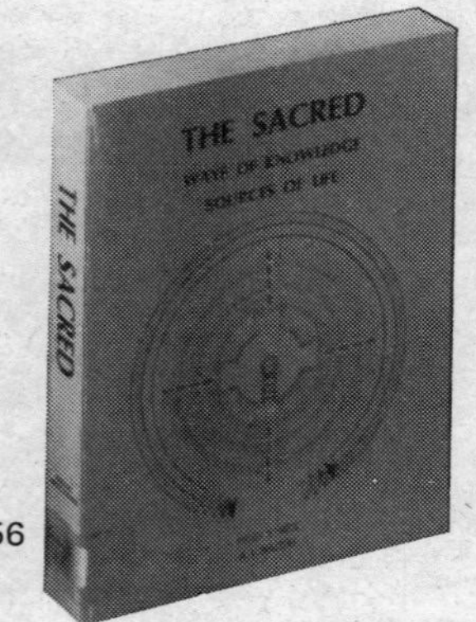

•

Another concept that North American sacred traditions have in common is that *all things in the universe are dependent on one another.* Everything, though having its own individuality and special place, is dependent on and shares in the growth and work of everything else. This means, for example, that if you take the life of an animal you have to let that animal know why you are doing so and that you are taking full responsibility for your act. Why? For one reason; because it is a way of showing that you understand the balances that exist in all natural systems, or *ecology*. For another reason (perhaps harder to see) because human beings and animals have a relationship to one another. Animals, for instance, know when they are in the presence of human beings, and they learn to avoid places where one of their own members has been killed. The elders and the oral histories tell us that long ago we once could speak the language of animals and that our survival depended on maintaining the relationships between animals, plants, rivers, feeding grounds, etc. Keeping this in mind, then, the concept of dependency and respect is not difficult to understand.

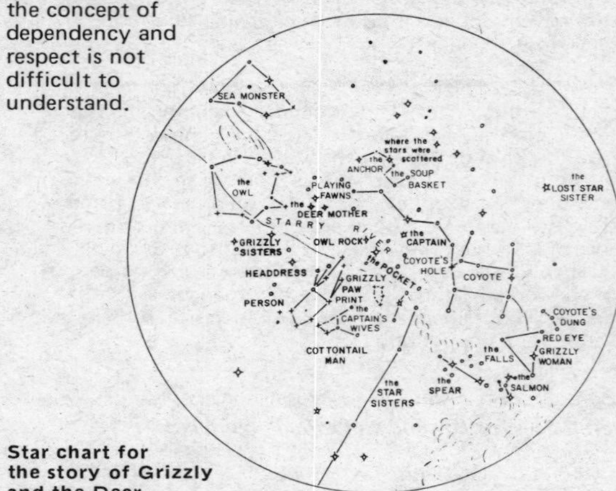

Star chart for the story of Grizzly and the Deer.

Entrance to Snake Kiva, Walpi.

Book of the Hopi

This book's business is the esoteric lore and historical drama which lives and protects the Hopi Indians in Arizona. They were possibly the farthest out of the American tribes (in present times they are not as together as Zuni, or Taos, but they are larger and so is what they attempted). This is the mysticism not of change but of stability, of the year cycle, of one more winter of food obtained by the hard knowledge from uncounted prior generations of winters and, they say, travels from world to world and place to place to arrive finally at the center, these bleak mesas, to here sustain forever responsiblity for the well-being of the world. Frank Waters was perhaps too eager to write a Bible, but I can't blame him. It's that kind of knowledge. *—SB*

Book of the Hopi
Frank Waters, Oswald White Bear Fredericks
1963; 423 pp.

$1.95 postpaid from:
Ballantine Books, Inc.
455 Hahn Road
Westminster, MD 21157
or Whole Earth Household Store

•

Over and over through the years one sees it, and it is never less beautiful: the still, flocculent dawn; the wonder and the mystery in the eyes of the villagers crowding the housetops; and, down below, the two spruce, male and female, standing in the empty plaza. Nothing breaks the silence save the great, proud bird tethered by one leg to his platform nearby. No living being has soared alone so high as this lord of the air. None is so proud — too proud to pick at the leash that tethers him. He simply flaps his great wings to soar aloft, only to be jerked down once more. One knows now again that this great proud eagle must die. And one knows why.

For suddenly, as the shafts of the sun are loosed from the horizon, the *kachinas* come in single file through the narrow streets into the plaza, the Powamu Chief, unmasked, wearing a single eagle feather and an embroidered kilt, leading the Kachina Father and his assistant, both members of the Powamu Society, wearing plain kilts, then some thirty *hemis kachinas* and eight or more *kachinamanas.*

Indian Tales

About twenty years ago a story went around that a beatnik girl in Sausalito wrote to Ezra Pound and asked him how to write poetry. Pound replied promptly, "Read **Indian Tales** *by Jaime de Angulo. It is how."*

De Angulo was a linguist at Berkeley, a bohemian personality in early Big Sur, and a good friend to the "primitive" Pit River Indians in Northern California. He wrote these stories for his children. They are made from odds and ends of his experiences with Indian stories, language, lore, and mysterious occasions. They are some of the best stories I know, and they are more simply Indian than anything else in print. The book is an American classic, like **Huckleberry Finn**. *—SB*

Indian Tales
Jaime de Angulo
1962; 246 pp.

$3.45 postpaid from:
Hill and Wang, Inc.
19 Union Square West
New York, NY 10003
or Whole Earth Household Store

•

Fox was laughing. He said, "Seriously, Oriole, why did we grow up so fast; Only yesterday, when we began our story and I started to see the world with my father, who was then a real Bear . . ."

Oriole interrupted. "No, you are mistaken, He was not a real Bear yet, he was only a beginning of a bear, he was a person-bear. Now he is a bearman — I mean a man-bear . . . I mean . . ."

"Oh, just keep quiet. You are getting me all mixed up again."

"No, Fox, listen to me; I will explain. The man who is telling our story, it's his fault, he has done something wrong with the machinery of time, he has let it go too fast. You see, he was supposed to take a million years to tell our story. The poor fellow, he is too old, he gets all mixed up. He should go and take a rest in the country for a while."

"Oh, my, my, my!" sighed the Fox, "the only thing to do is to start again RIGHT AT THE BEGINNING." Fox looked curiously at Oriole. "What do you mean, a MILLION years?"

"Why I mean an infinity of time, just as Tsimmu was telling in his story of the creation of the world, Don't you remember? Ten times ten times ten times ten years, *molossi molossi molossi tellim piduuwi.* When Cocoon Man was floating around in nothing but air and fog he waited a million years for that cloud to come near enough so he could jump on it."

"Yes," said Fox. "Yes, just like Marum'da, who made the world and then he went to sleep. That's an infinity of time, but it must stop somewhere — it can't go on forever. It must stop somewhere."

Oriole asked, "WHY?"

Fox thought a moment then he said, "I dunno. But listen, Oriole, what's time anyway?"

Oriole said, "Why, it's ten times ten times ten times ten years. What else do you want it to be?"

Fox said, "I dunno, I guess it's growing old."

Oriole said, "All right, then, some people grow old faster than others. You know that yourself. Just as some people walk faster than others. It all depends on who is looking at it."

"Why, Oriole, you are crazy. It depends on who is walking, not on the man who is looking at the fellow who is walking."

"No, certainly NOT. Look at that man over there walking. He seems to be just crawling along, but if you were closer to him, he would be going much faster. That's the way with the man who is telling this story. Sometimes he is closer and sometimes he is further away, so for him that makes us go faster or slower."

Fox said, "Oriole, you drive me crazy. Now I don't know whether I am standing on my head or my feet. It's like that time when we first met you and your father."

"Listen, Fox, it is not I who started this idea that there was a man telling this story, it was you. For all we know, there is no such man."

"Of course, there is not, I invented him."

Black Elk Speaks

The Pueblo tribes don't go in for visionary solitary mystical whizbangs. (Of all of them only Taos is into peyote very much.) The plains tribes are something else however. Their lives turned on their visions — solo manhood transports, dreams, name visions, sun dance ordeals, battle ecstasy, doctoring sessions . . . and later, ghost dance and peyote. This book is the power vision of one Oglala Sioux — and the extraordinary man it made. Black Elk's account, besides affording unusual insight into Sioux life and historical figures such as Crazy Horse, demonstrates the manner of recognizing a serious vision and being responsible for it, and the burden, joy and power of doing that. *—SB*

Black Elk Speaks
John G. Neihardt
1932, 1969; 280 pp.

$2.50 postpaid from:
Pocket Books
Order Department
1230 Avenue of the Americas
New York, NY 10020
or Whole Earth Household Store

•

. . . Then I was standing on the highest mountain of them all, and round about beneath me was the whole hoop of the world. And while I stood there I saw more than I can tell and I understood more than I saw; for I was seeing in a sacred manner the shapes of all things in the spirit, and the shape of all shapes as they must live together like one being. And I saw that the sacred hoop of my people was one of many hoops that made one circle, wide as daylight and as starlight, and in the center grew one mighty flowering tree to shelter all the children of one mother and one father. And I saw that it was holy.

Black Elk said the mountain he stood upon in his vision was Harney Peak, in the Black Hills. "But anywhere is the center of the world," he added.

•

When a vision comes from the thunder beings of the west, it comes with terror like a thunder storm; but when the storm of vision has passed, the world is greener and happier; for wherever the truth of vision comes upon the world, it is like rain. The world, you see, is happier after the terror of the storm.

•

I think I have told you, but if I have not, you must have understood, that a man who has a vision is not able to use the power of it until after he has performed the vision on earth for the people to see.

↑ Ishi

Ishi in Two Worlds

One August day in 1911 the last wild Indian in America, near gone with starvation, the rest of his tribe dead, walked into a northern California town. Adopted by the brilliant anthropologist, Alfred Kroeber, he lived his remaining years in a California museum. This book by Kroeber's wife reconstructs Ishi's wild years in the Deer Creek area and tells with affection of his civilized years in Berkeley. For now millions of readers, Ishi is our emotional link to native America. —SB

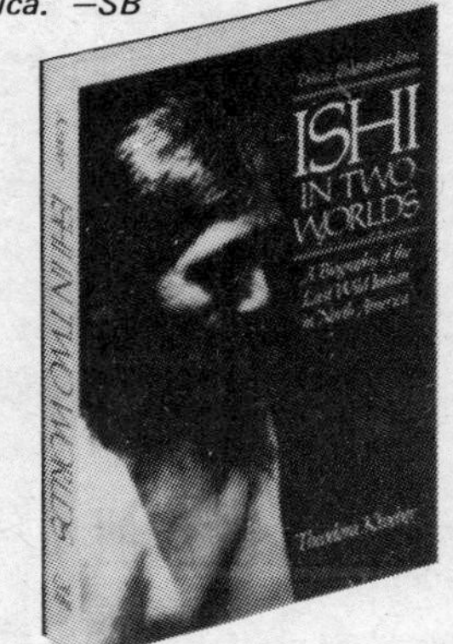

Ishi in Two Worlds
(A Biography of the Last Wild Indian in North America)
Theodora Kroeber
1961; 262 pp.

$3.95 postpaid from:
University of California Press
2223 Fulton Street
Berkeley, CA 94720
or Whole Earth Household Store

•

Reporters demanded to know his name, refusing to accept Kroeber's word that the question was in the circumstances unmannerly and futile. Batwi intervened, engaging to persuade the wild man to tell his name — a shocking gaucherie on Batwi's part. The wild man, saving his brother Yana's face, said that he had been alone so long that he had had no one to give him a name — a polite fiction, of course. A California Indian almost never speaks his own name, using it but rarely with those who already know it, and he would never tell it in reply to a direct question.

The reporters felt, not unnaturally, that they were being given the "runaround." Batwi lost caste with his fellow Yana without being of service to the whites; the museum people were themselves saying they must have something by which to call the Yahi, except just that. Kroeber felt more pushed than did his nameless friend who remained relatively detached not understanding most of what was said, and standing quietly by Indian custom so far as he did understand. Said Kroeber, "Very well. He shall be known as *Ishi*." He regretted that he was unable to think of a more distinctive name, but it was not inappropriate, meaning "man" in Yana, and hence not of the private or nickname category. Thus it was that the last of the Yahi was christened Ishi, and in historic fact, *became* Ishi.

The Ohlone Way

Margolin's book is in the grand tradition of American literary anthropology: the imaginative reconstruction of the by-gone days of this continent's tribal peoples. An admirable job of re-creation from the still surviving pieces of tattered information. His fine descriptions of pre-conquest California will hopefully make this book a regional best seller. —Peter Warshall

You know, such a book could be made for every region in the U.S., on the continent, on Earth. Without such felt history, respect is impossible. —SB

The Ohlone Way
(Indian life in the San Francisco - Monterey Bay Area)
Malcolm Margolin
1978; 182 pp.

$4.95 postpaid from:
Heyday Books
Box 9145
Berkeley, CA 94709
or Whole Earth Household Store

•

The men crowd together near the back wall of the sweat-house, and there is much joking and satisfaction among them. It is a good hot fire today; the older men feel a welcome looseness in their joints. Among them is a fourteen-year old youth, and they begin to tease him.

"Are you going to run out again today?" they ask.

"Make sure you run through the door and not through the wall," someone advises, and the other men laugh loud and long.

The young man does not answer. As the heat intensifies he feels the sweat ooze out of his pores and flow in rivulets down his body. Following the example of the others he runs a curved rib bone of a deer over his body to drain the sweat. He has been admitted to the sweat-house only a month before, yet (despite the teasing) he already feels a welcome easiness here, a sense of being at home. In fact, as he squats against the back wall he has the curious sense that he has been here a million times before. It is as if the closed sweat-house with its cluster of men is the real, eternal world, and the world of the village, the meadows, and the woods is merely a colorful but passing dream.

•

Today we are the heirs of that distance, and we take it entirely for granted that animals are naturally secretive and afraid of our presence. But for the Indians who lived here before us this was simply not the case. Animals and humans inhabited the very same world, and the distance between them was not very great.

Handbooks of North American Indians

These are the first two volumes in a twenty volume set of the Smithsonian's encyclopedia of what's known about the earliest peoples of North America, The people here at the time of European contact and the present-day descendants of these peoples. These volumes will be our basic references for all time and though cumbersome in approach and prose, they are filled with absorbing photos and information. A GREAT price for such a mountain range of historical reference. —Peter Warshall

Handbook of North American Indians, Vol. 15: Northeast
Bruce Trigger, Editor
1978; 924 pp.

$14.50

Vol. 8: California
Robert F. Heizer, Editor
1978; 800 pp.

$13.50

both postpaid from:
Smithsonian Press Distribution Center
1111 North Capitol Street
Washington, DC 20560
or Whole Earth Household Store

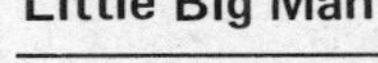

•

In northwestern California it was believed that everything humans did was derived from the way it was done in myth times. Originally the world was populated by a prehuman race of people who worked out how everything should be done. They waited until the present people appeared, taught them everything they knew, and then turned into animals, plants, rocks, and mountains (Harrington 1932:8). —**Vol. 8**

•

The research of Porter (1971), Aptheker (1939), and Woodson (1918) demonstrates the extent to which Negro slaves ran away, were sheltered by Indians, and intermarried with them. Furthermore, Indians themselves were often enslaved and held in bondage along with Blacks, with whom they mixed. Free Black ancestors are also demonstrable for some groups. However, the history of only a few mestizo communities has been the subject of scholarly research, and the origin and development of most of them remain undocumented. —**Vol. 15**

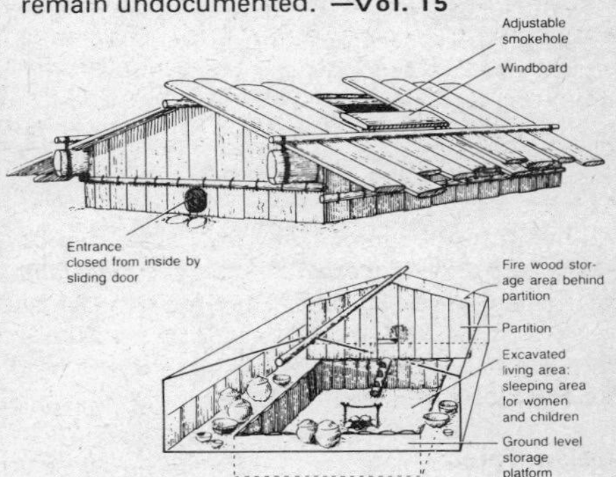

Reconstruction of Tolowa dwelling house. Exterior viewed from front, interior viewed from rear. —Vol. 8

Keepers of the Game

North American natives made a pact with the animal world — a pact of good manners, mutual courtesy and reasonable exploitation of each other's populations. When European diseases struck North American tribal peoples, the diseases were perceived as a vengeful, rude and unbalanced attack by wildlife. This disillusionment with animals allowed Christianity to replace native religions, allowed traders to persuade Indians to become avid exploiters of beaver, and ended the dialog between native humans and North America's living creatures.

Keepers of the Game *is the most interesting, recent academic history of the European conquest. It includes a thoughtful discussion, tinged with cynicism, about today's Christian-based conservationist attempt to resurrect the pre-Columbian Indian as the Noble Savage, guru to Whitey, and wise man of proper land and water use policies.* —Peter Warshall

Keepers of the Game
(Indian-Animal Relationships and the Fur Trade)
Calvin Martin
1978; 225 pp.

$10.95 postpaid from:
University of Calif. Press
2223 Fulton Street
Berkeley, CA 94720
or Whole Earth Household Store

Little Big Man

"There isn't a lie in it!" was the amazed response of the Ponca firebrand Clyde Warrior back when the book first came out. Arthur Penn later made a fine movie of it, starring Dustin Hoffman and Chief Dan George, but the book is better still. It's a tale of a fictional white boy adopted by the Cheyenne in the climax of their glory and dismemberment in the late 1800's. What's tragic and sacred and comic is as completely mixed as in real Indian life. —SB

Little Big Man
Thomas Berger
1964; 447 pp.

$2.50 postpaid from:
Fawcett Books
600 Third Avenue
New York, NY 10016

•

No, all seemed right to me at that moment. It was one of the few times I felt: this is the way things are and should be. I had medicine then, that's the only word for it. *I knew where the center of the world was.* A remarkable feeling, in which time turns in a circle, and he who stands at the core has power over everything that takes the form of line and angle and square. Like Old Lodge Skins drawing in them antelope within the little circle of his band, but concentric around them was all other Cheyenne, present and past, living and ghost, for the Mystery is continuous.

Sherman Red Eye driving a Packard preparatory to a feast for the False Face Society at the Allegheny Seneca community. Photograph by William N. Fenton, Aug. 1, 1934. —Vol. 15

THE RISING SUN
NEIGHBORHOOD NEWSLETTER

Aoki went to Idaho in 1960 to learn Nez Perce for the Idaho Historical Society and the UC Berkeley Linguistics Department. While there he met Joseph Watson, a white man who could speak Nez Perce. He had been traded to the Nez Perce for a milk cow when he was a baby and he'd lived with them all his life.

Walden

This edition is the one, I believe, that Thoreau would have bought. It costs a buck fifty. The prime document of America's 3rd Revolution, now in progress. —SB

Walden
(and "Civil Disobedience")
Henry David Thoreau
1854; 256 pp.

$1.50 postpaid from:
New American Library, Inc.
P.O. Box 120
120 Woodbine
Bergenfield, NJ 07621

•

Most of the luxuries, and many of the so-called comforts of life, are not only not indispensable, but positive hindrances to the elevation of mankind. With respect to luxuries and comforts, the wisest have ever lived a more simple and meagre life than the poor.

•

I learned this, at least, by my experiment: that if one advances confidently in the direction of his dreams, and endeavors to live the life which he has imagined, he will meet with a success unexpected in common hours. He will put some things behind, will pass an invisible boundary; new, universal, and more liberal laws will begin to establish themselves around and within him; or the old laws be expanded, and interpreted in his favor in a more liberal sense, and he will live with the license of a higher order of beings. In proportion as he simplifies his life, the laws of the universe will appear less complex, and solitude will not be solitude, nor poverty poverty, nor weakness weakness. If you have built castles in the air, your work need not be lost; that is where they should be. Now put the foundations under them.

•

Time is but the stream I go a-fishing in, I drink at it; but while I drink I see the sandy bottom and detect how shallow it is. Its thin current slides away, but eternity remains. I would drink deeper; fish in the sky, whose bottom is pebbly with stars.

•

After hoeing, or perhaps reading and writing, in the forenoon, I usually bathed again in the pond, swimming across one of its coves for a stint, and washed the dust of labor from my person, or smoothed out the last wrinkle which study had made, and for the afternoon was absolutely free. Every day or two I strolled to the village to hear some of the gossip which is incessantly going on there, circulating either from mouth, or from newspaper to newspaper, and which, taken in homeopathic doses, was really as refreshing in its way as the rustle of leaves and the peeping of frogs.

•

I heartily accept the motto, — "That government is best which governs least;" and I should like to see it acted up to more rapidly and systematically. Carried out, it finally amounts to this, which also I believe, — "That government is best which governs not at all," and when men are prepared for it, that will be the kind of government which they will have.

Sand County Almanac

"Classic" it's called now, because it was published in 1949 and still has bite. Wherever the ecologist looks the world weaves a wild story. This one looked at Sand County, Wisconsin, among other places, and was led to propose a Land Ethic. —SB

A Sand County Almanac
Aldo Leopold
1949; 295 pp.

$2.25 postpaid from:
Ballantine Books, Inc.
455 Hahn Road
Westminster, MD 21157
or Whole Earth
Household Store

•

American conservation is, I fear, still concerned for the most part with show pieces.

•

Perhaps the most serious obstacle impeding the evolution of a land ethic is the fact that our educational and economic system is headed away from, rather than toward, an intense consciousness of land. Your true modern is separated from the land by many middlemen, and by innumerable physical gadgets.

•

A thing is right when it tends to preserve the integrity, stability, and beauty of the biotic community. It is wrong when it tends otherwise.

•

In the beginning there was only the unity of the Ice Sheet. Then followed the unity of the March thaw, and the northward hegira of the international geese. Every March since the Pleistocene, the geese have honked unity from China Sea to Siberian Steppe, from Euphrates to Volga, from Nine to Murmansk, from Lincolnshire to Spitsbergen. Every March since the Pleistocene, the geese have honked unity from Currituck to Labrador, Matamuskeet to Ungava, Horseshoe Lake to Hudson's Bay, Avery Island to Baffin Land, Panhandle to Mackenzie, Sacramento to Yukon.

By this international commerce of geese, the waste corn of Illinois is carried through the clouds of the Arctic tundras, there to combine with the waste sunlight of a nightless June to grow goslings for all the lands between. And in this annual barter of food for light, and winter warmth for summer solitude, the whole continent receives as net profit a wild poem dropped from the murky skies upon the muds of March.

•

I was young then, and full of trigger-itch; I thought that because fewer wolves meant more deer, that no wolves would mean hunters' paradise.

•

We all strive for safety, prosperity, comfort, long life, and dullness.

Turtle Island

To understand whole evidently requires understanding with more than rational consciousness. I mean, with experience, with dreams, with art, with poetry — (not-quite synonyms for knowledge which is real but not nameable). Gary Snyder's poetry addresses the life-planet identification with unusual simplicity of style and complexity of effect. —SB

Turtle Island
Gary Snyder
1974; 114 pp.

$2.25 postpaid from:
New Directions
Publishing Corporation
c/o J.B. Lippincott Co.
East Washington Square
Philadelphia, PA 19105
or Whole Earth
Household Store

•

Stewardship means, for most of us, find your place on the planet, dig in, and take responsibility from there — the tiresome but tangible work of school boards, county supervisors, local foresters — local politics. Even while holding in mind the largest scale of potential change. Get a sense of workable territory, learn about it, and start acting point by point. On all levels from national to local the need to move toward steady state economy — equilibrium, dynamic balance, inner-growth stressed — must be taught. Maturity/diversity/climax/creativity.

•

"ONE SHOULD NOT TALK TO A SKILLED
HUNTER ABOUT WHAT IS FORBIDDEN
BY THE BUDDHA" —Hsiang-yen

A gray fox, female, nine pounds three ounces.
39 5/8" long with tail.
Peeling skin back (Kai
reminded us to chant the *Shingyo* first)
cold pelt. crinkle; and musky smell
mixed with dead-body odor starting.

Stomach content: a whole ground squirrel well chewed
plus one lizard foot
and somewhere from inside the ground squirrel
a bit of aluminum foil.

The secret.
and the secret hidden deep in that.

•

TOMORROW'S SONG

The USA slowly lost its mandate
in the middle and later twentieth century
it never gave the mountains and rivers,
  trees and animals,
    a vote.
all the people turned away from it
  myths die; even continents are impermanent

  Turtle Island returned.
  my friend broke open a dried coyote-scat
  removed a ground squirrel tooth
  pierced it, hung it
  from the gold ring
  in his ear.

We look to the future with pleasure
we need no fossil fuel
get power within
grow strong on less.

Grasp the tools and move in rhythm side by side
  flash gleams of wit and silent knowledge
    eye to eye
sit still like cats or snakes or stones
  as whole and holding as
    the blue black sky.
gentle and innocent as wolves
    as tricky as a prince

At work and in our place:
  in the service
  of the wilderness
  of life
  of death
  of the Mother's breasts!

The Unsettling of America

Our land is more undone by our agriculture than by any other mischief. Farmer, poet, essayist Wendell Berry speaks to the matter with plain speech — it rasps the brain, leaves a memory of the thought. Don't say it is no longer possible to do our farming right. Berry is. —SB

(See **The American Farm**, *p. 121, and Berry's novel* **The Memory of Old Jack**, *p. 75.)*

The Unsettling of America
(Culture & Agriculture)
Wendell Berry
1978; 228 pp.

$5.95 postpaid from:
Avon Books
250 W. 55th Street
New York, NY 10019
or Whole Earth
Household Store

•

We need wilderness as a standard of civilization and as a cultural model. Only by preserving areas where nature's processes are undisturbed can we preserve an accurate sense of the impact of civilization upon its natural sources. Only if we know how the land *was* can we tell how it *is*.

•

The Domestication of Absence

It is impossible to divorce the question of what we do from the question of where we are — or, where we think we are. That no sane creature befouls its own nest is accepted as generally true. What we conceive to be our nest, and where we think it is, are therefore questions of the greatest importance. Do we, for instance, carry on our work in our nest or do we only reside and get our mail there? Is our nest a place of consumption only or is it also a place of production? Is it the source of necessary goods, energies, and "services," or only their destination?

I have already spoken of the highly simplified role of the modern household with respect to the production and preparation of food: it has set itself increasingly aside from production and preparation and become more and more a place for the consumption of food produced and prepared elsewhere. But this setting aside of the nest or residence from the sources of life is more general and even more serious than that would indicate. The modern home, even more than the government and universities, has institutionalized the divisions and fragmentations of modern life.

•

A part of the health of a farm is the farmer's wish to remain there. His long-term good intention toward the place is signified by the presence of trees. A family is married to a farm more by their planting and protecting of trees than by their memories or their knowledge, for the trees stand for their fidelity and kindness to what they do not know. The most revealing sign of the ill health of industrial agriculture — its greed, its short-term ambitions — is its inclination to see trees as obstructions and to strip the land bare of them.

•

There are many people — ex-farmers, heirs of farmers, and would-be farmers — who want to farm but are prevented from doing so by high land costs, taxes, inheritance taxes, and interest rates. And these economic barriers, which exclude the small operator, directly favor not just the survival, but also the expansion, of the big operator. This is not a necessary result of "the way things are." It is the calculated effect of a deliberate policy to allow the big to grow bigger at the expense of the small. In addition, there are many farmers of the same kinds who are presently farming, but whose survival is in doubt for the same reasons.

•

As our present economy clearly shows, the small can survive only if the great are restrained. And there is nothing undemocratic or anti-libertarian about restraining them. To assume that ordinary citizens can compete successfully with people of wealth and with corporations, as our government presently tends to do, is simply to abandon the ordinary citizens. Restraint by taxation is the smallest, most obvious, simplest, and cheapest answer. This is not my idea. It is Thomas Jefferson's. Writing to Reverend James Madison on October 28, 1785, Jefferson spoke of the desirability of freehold tenure of property. And then he said: "Another means of silently lessening the inequality of property is to exempt all from taxation below a certain point, and to tax the higher portions of property in geometric progression as they rise. The earth is given as a common stock for man to labor and live on. If for the encouragement of industry [he means, of course, mainly agriculture] we allow it to be appropriated, we must take care that employment be provided to those excluded from the appropriation. If we do not, the fundamental right to labor the earth returns to the unemployed . . . it is not too soon to provide by every possible means that as few as possible shall be without a little portion of land. The small landholders are the most precious part of a state . . ." It would, of course, be necessary to consider how much land in any region ought to constitute a living for a family.

Man's Role in Changing the Face of the Earth

An unsurpassed achievement in assembling pertinent, insightful information of interest not only to serious students of the planet Earth, but to non-trained readers as well.

The three sections of the book are: I. "Retrospect", an historical background; II. "Process", methods and agencies involved in man's interactions with the land; and III. "Prospect", the effects and future implications of man's habitation of the Earth. Some typical subjects covered within these sections include: fire as the great force employed by man; origins and decline of woodlands; man and grass (sic); ecology of peasant life; harvests of the seas; ports channels and coastlines; the sewerage (don't belittle sewerage — society is structured around it).

This book rewards a reader like me because of its minimum of moralizing and its abundant substance. Edgar Anderson, former director of the Missouri Botanical Garden in St. Louis and without whom such a book as this would be certainly incomplete, pointed out that the average thoughtful person has little inkling of how man has reclothed the world. Even professional biologists have been tardy in recognizing that a significant portion of the plants and animals surrounding us are of our own making. For example, neither Kentucky bluegrass nor Canada bluegrass is native to those places, but came from Europe. The corn belt is a very obviously man-dominated landscape, but the casual observer might never realize that even the grass-covered and oak-dotted stretches of what looks like indigenous California vegetation came uninvited from the Old World along with the Spaniards.

—Richard Raymond

Man's Role In Changing the Face of the Earth, Volume 1
William L. Thomas, Jr., Editor (With the Collaboration of Carl Sauer, Marston Bates, and Lewis Mumford)
1956; 448 pp.
$4.75

Volume 2
1956; 1193 pp.
$6.95
both postpaid from:
University of Chicago Press
11030 South Langley Ave.
Chicago, IL 60628
or Whole Earth Household Store

Sudan, Bari Village. A closely knit social group occupies the compact and fenced-in space of this village. Here life is immediate, and the traditional huts are part of the landscape. The relationship between man and man and man and nature is intimate and direct. It is an "I-Thou" and reciprocal contact.

Belgian Congo, copper-miners' village. Unity through repetition is the characteristic note of this cantonment for the workers in the copper mines. The pathetic attempt to retain something of the indigenous style by putting thatched roofs on the standardized huts is an outward symbol of the helplessness and confusion of an atomized society which has spread its tentacles to this remote part of the world. The workers and their families living in these cells are uprooted and depersonalized beings and trained as human automata. They are estranged from nature and from each other. Life in this regimented agglomeration of huts has lost its immediacy and imposed all the prerequisites of an indirect and impersonal existence, of an "I-It" relationship.

•

Generally speaking, the plants which follow man around the world might be said to do so, not because they relish what man has done to the environment, but because they can stand it and most other plants cannot.

•

Almost every change in environmental conditions which man can make results in some change in the water economy or water budget at the earth's surface.

The grove of Cedrus libani at Les Cedres, Lebanon, protected remnant of a forest that once covered the intermediate slopes of the Lebanon Range.

Reinhabiting a Separate Country

In North America, the memory of the pre-humanized landscape is still close. Remnant primeval forests, patches of virgin prairies, maybe 50 significant stretches of untouched river, small herds of buffalo, an occasional grizzly all remind us of yesteryears. This memory (and an interest in the native peoples who lived in harmony with these creatures) has given birth to the "bioregionalists." They are a group of scientists, writers, actors, politicians and folk who would like to see the remnants of preEuro-American landscape preserved. They would like to see humans and modern governments adjusting themselves to what's left of Nature (rather than continually destroying Nature and then trying to adjust to the earthscape they have just destroyed).

The eloquent ideologue of the bioregional vision is Peter Berg. Whenever you get a feeling that you should slow down and talk to the old people, check out the magic mountains, settle in one watershed and become more intimate with the fabric of human settlement and water dynamics, then Peter's vocabulary coyotes into your speech. **Reinhabiting a Separate Country** *is the book he's edited. The "separate country" is defined by the mountain ranges that form the rim of the Great Valley of California plus some of the coastal ranges that drain into the Pacific ("northern" California). On Arthur Okamura's color map, the separate country appears as concentric circles with grassland in the middle, then a ring of oaks and another of conifers. Like the periodical* **Planet/Drum**, *the book is a collection — essays such as Albert Saijo's so gentle and intelligent, "Me, Muir and Sierra Nevada"; Joe Kim's personal telling of the Chinese along the Sacramento and the Yuba floods and the miraculous escape of the Bok I temple; science senses by Ray Dasmann, Bob Curry and Dennis Breedlove; poems, stories and pop economic theory. In the long-term theatre of Save-the-Planet, this is a heroic first step to stop time, take stock and give priority to local economy, watershed eco-systems and a "now primitive" culture.*

—Peter Warshall

Reinhabiting a Separate Country
(A Bioregional Anthology of Northern California)
Peter Berg, Editor
1978; 220 pp.

$8 postpaid from
Planet/Drum Foundation
Box 31251
San Francisco, CA 94131
or Whole Earth Household Store

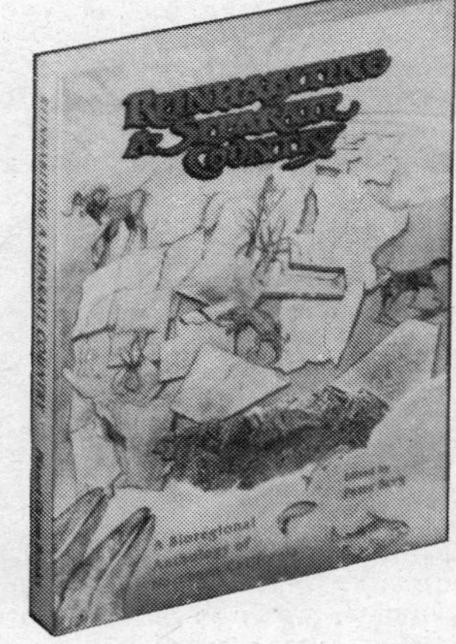

•

Muir the Preservationist added Guardian function to Thoreau's Witness function. Now through them we are to be the Guardian-Witness of Earth Sacrament.

•

Reinhabitation means learning to live-in-place in an area that has been disrupted and injured through past exploitation. It involves becoming native to a place through becoming aware of the particular ecological relationships that operate within and around it. It means understanding activities and evolving social behavior that will enrich the life of that place, restore its life-supporting systems, and establish an ecologically and socially sustainable pattern of existence within it. Simply stated it involves becoming fully alive in and with a place. It involves applying for membership in a biotic community and ceasing to be its exploiter.

•

We define *bioregion* in a sense different from the biotic province of Dasmann (1973) or the biogeographical province of Udvardy (1975). The term refers both to geographical terrain and a terrain of consciousness — to a place and the ideas that have developed about how to live in that place.

Planet/Drum

By the originators of **Reinhabiting a Separate Country** *and of the term "reinhabitation,"* **Planet/Drum** *is a sort of membership which gets you 4 newsletters annually, some privileged access to people and books, and a Bundle. Each year's Bundle is a selection of context-shifting oddments on such subjects as the Rockies, Watershed dwelling, etc. Exploratory thinking and publishing.*

—SB

Planet/Drum
$10 /year membership from:
Planet/Drum Foundation
P.O. Box 31251
San Francisco, CA 94131

•

Think of the Rocky Mountains as a sunburst or star — its rays are patterns of water and soil moving across North America. Soil fertility from the cornfields of Indiana to the delta of the Columbia in Oregon is owed to nutrients eroded from the Rockies by wind and water.

90% of all water in the major rivers west of the Mississippi (excluding Northern California) rises in the Rockies. Seventy-one cubic miles per year flows through the Columbia alone.

40% of the productivity of cereal grains in the Midwest and Plains is due to Rockies soil.

80% of vegetables grown west of the Mississippi (excluding California and Oregon) gain their nutrients from Rockies-derived soil.

Wild grasses and brush on 40% of all cattle lands in the continental United States grow in soil drifted from the Rockies.

People in the Rockies live in the heart of the star. People living in the Mississippi Delta, on the edges of the Bering Sea and the Gulf of California, around the Hudson Bay, people at the far reaches of the rays, all watch Rockies water go by.

THE RISING SUN
NEIGHBORHOOD NEWSLETTER

What happened was that there was this Depression and nobody had jobs so Roosevelt started the WPA to give people jobs even though giving jobs was more expensive than the dole and part of the WPA was arty and part of the arty part was the Federal Writers' Project. But it was hard to figure what to have the writers write because if they wrote what they wanted all Republican and most Democrat Congressmen would have heart attacks and withdraw funding because writers then were very political and very left. (Something about the Depression made them think capitalism didn't work and wasn't kind.) So someone came up with the idea (in those days there were many ideas in Washington and some of them worked) of having them write guidebooks — a guidebook for travelers for each state.

Interesting idea because Americans were just getting that there was a way to be about America besides H.L. Mencken cynicism and 4th of July babbling enthusiasm — looking at the folk and the land as they were and seeing something good. A Woody Guthrie way, in fact, and the Federal Writers' Project guidebooks are the encyclopedia to illustrate "This Land Is Your Land," and they're still a hell of a read. *continued on next spread*

Man and Earth's Ecosystems

I don't know that anyone has tried this before, a kind of regional culture history of the world in terms of environmental consequences of man's activities. Contemporary review of human-caused landscape modification from the first purposefully set fire (Peking Man was a charcoal-maker) right down to the latest oil spill or reactor leak. Some of these things are covered in the old-style economic and cultural geographies but they take on new and deeper meaning in this explicitly ecologic context. The real meat lies in the continent-by-continent surveys of human influences on the ecosystems of Subsaharan Africa, of Asia, of Europe and the Mediterranean, of Australia, of North America and of Latin America. To emphasize the time dimension each region is presented in the order in which the genus Homo *appears in the known fossil or cultural record. The concluding chapters are on islands (Hawaii, New Zealand, Madagascar) and on the oceans. Human influences on vegetation, on animal life, on surface and subsurface waters, on soils and geomorphology, on the atmosphere are discussed for each. Fire, agricultural systems, and the deliberate or accidental transfers of both wild and domestic plants and animals from one part of the world to another receive special emphasis. Carl Sauer would have approved. This is the basic text for a new ecosystems analysis major at UCLA. Photos are superb. It just might give you a new faith in what higher education is up to, and geographers.* —James J. Parsons

(See **Environmental Conservation**, *p. 50.)*

Man and Earth's Ecosystems
(An Introduction to the Geography of Human Modification of the Earth)
Charles F. Bennett, Jr.
1976; 331 pp.
$18.95 postpaid from:
John Wiley & Sons, Inc.
One Wiley Drive
Somerset, NJ 10873

Reforestation project in the People's Republic of China

HUMAN DISTURBANCE OF WILD VEGETATION OF SOUTH AMERICA

MAJOR DISTURBANCE: REMNANTS ONLY OF WILD VEGETATION
MODERATE TO HEAVY DISTURBANCE: SCATTERED LARGE AREAS OF WILD VEGETATION
SLIGHT DISTURBANCE: LARGE EXPANSES OF WILD VEGETATION
LITTLE OR NO DISTURBANCE: ESSENTIALLY "CLIMAX" VEGETATION

Terraced slopes in the Andes

← The development of irrigation systems in the Andean region is still the object of intensive study. The first known efforts of water control occurred in the oasis-like coastal valleys of Peru. They were later extended to the highland basins and valley slopes, where they underwent further development and modification. The irrigation works near the coast included great canals, sometimes extending for many kilometers, aqueducts, which carried water across valleys, and elaborate terrace systems, which may have been built partly to conserve water as well as soil. The earthworks associated with this water control may still be seen over thousands of square kilometers. They are evidence of the huge input of human labor extending over centuries since neither machines nor the wheel were available to these people. The water in the coastal valley streams and the limited runoff in parts of the central Andes were brought under the almost complete control of man.

How to Save the World

At last. A world conservation strategy. With the clout of major international organizations behind it — the International Union for Conservation of Nature and Natural Resources, the United Nations Environment Programme, and the World Wildlife Fund — here is a planet-scale priority list of where and how to proceed to save the most and best of the Earth's endangered diversity. This is a greatly needed perspective. It's all too easy to lose a continent while saving a species, and then lose the species too. —SB

How to Save the World
(Strategy for World Conservation)
Robert Allen
1980; 150 pp.
$12.95 postpaid from:
Unipub
P.O. Box 433
Murray Hill Station
New York, NY 10016

•

Irreversibility is the key criterion: highest priority is given to significant, urgent requirements to prevent further irreversible damage to living resources, notably the extinction of species, the extinction of varieties of useful plants and animals, the loss of essential life-support systems, and severe soil degradation.

If current rates of land degradation continue, close to one-third of the world's arable land (symbolized by the stalk of grain) will be destroyed in the next 20 years. Similarly, by the end of this century (at present rates of clearance), the remaining area of unlogged productive tropical forest will be halved. During this period the world population is expected to increase by almost half — from just over 4000 million to just under 6000 million.

The Sinking Ark

In the Bible, God tells man to take dominion over the species of the earth. Maybe that's too big a task so we're cutting the field down to a manageable size. **The Sinking Ark** *tells of the wondrous things we're beginning to learn from our fellow species. Lichens can monitor heavy metals pollution and black bear hormones revitalize human kidneys. What's needed to stop the assault before we wipe out nature's library of knowledge, the gene pool?*

Myers cites some political/economic measures for multinational corporations and governments to try, but his real hope is that the third world countries will develop and urbanize rapidly and leave the tropical rain forests alone.
—Rosemary Menninger

The Sinking Ark
Norman Myers
1979; 307 pp.
$8.95 postpaid from:
Pergamon Press
Maxwell House
Fairview Park
Elmsford, NY 10523
or Whole Earth
Household Store

•

The elimination of species would represent a distinct loss to society. Already tropical-forest species have made a major contribution to human welfare. They have supplied the origins of many staple foods, rice, millet, cassava, pigeon pea, mung bean, yam, taro, banana, pineapple and sugarcane, to name but the better known. A huge cornucopia of further foods waits to be investigated. In Indonesia alone, around 4000 plant species are thought to have proved useful to native peoples as food of one sort or another, yet less than one-tenth have come into wide use. At least 1650 plants of tropical forests offer highly nutritious leaves. In New Guinea, 251 tree species bear edible fruit, though only 43 have been brought into cultivation; a hitherto uncultivated fruit of Southeast Asia, the mangosteen, has been described as "perhaps the world's best tasting fruit." A vine from tropical forests of southern China, known as the Chinese gooseberry, bears fruit with juice 15 - 18 times richer in vitamin C than orange juice. Nor are all these foods limited to local consumption; high protein beans from Nigeria have found favor with Wisconsin farmers.

Earthbound

Park is one of the most distinguished geologists in the country, and a director of a mining company. He was David Brower's worthiest adversary in McPhee's **Encounters with the Archdruid**. *There he emerged as knowledgeable, resolutely practical, hard-thinking . . . compelling.*

Earthbound *is what you'd expect from such a man. Although it assumes that the status quo will likely be more persistent than many would wish (scoffs at windmills, hopes that we'll overcome our childish fears of nuclear reactors, sees very generous profits as vital to extractive industries), it isn't unsound. A certain disagreement with a good author can put a keen edge on one's appreciation of his/her work.*

The substance of Park's book is a quick and lucid introduction to mining — what is extracted from the earth, where it comes from, how it is mined, what it is used for, political situations affecting supplies — in short, a crash course in understanding the skeleton of our civilization. Amply illustrated with graphs, laden with facts, offering a different perspective, **Earthbound** *is a good solid reference book for the eco-catastrophobe.*
—Stephanie Mills

Earthbound
(Minerals, Energy, and Man's Future)
Charles F. Park, Jr.
1975; 279 pp.
$5.95 postpaid from:
Freeman, Cooper & Co.
1736 Stockton Street
San Francisco, CA 94133
or Whole Earth
Household Store

•

There has been, and still is, an unbelievable amount of searching for copper, and there are nations whose entire economies depend upon this metal. We note also that, although available quantities of most of the nonferrous metals have increased in the past few years, greater availability increased their usefulness. For that reason the demand has increased, so the metals remain in short supply. Substitutes for all uses of these metals have not been found; there is nothing at present that can for all needs take the place of copper or of mercury.

We note also in how many cases the manufacture of these metals requires large amounts of inexpensive energy.

Worldwatch Papers

What Amnesty International does for political imprisonment and torture, what the Council on Economic Priorities does for American business and government, Lester Brown's Worldwatch Institute does for environmental (and occasionally economic) problems worldwide. All three are private, highly respected, and widely used in the press.

In its five or so years Worldwatch has managed to become prolific in its output without sacrificing quality. The stuff is solidly researched, gently presented, and sometimes quite original — such as Erik Eckholm's celebrated report on the world firewood shortage. Even more remarkable, the work is politically astute and politically pointed without any limiting flavor of Leftness.

For outstanding (and frequent) environmental reporting, I can think of no better source. —SB

Worldwatch Institute
$25 /year
Worldwatch Papers
(back issues)
$2 each postpaid from:
Worldwatch Institute
1776 Massachusetts Ave., NW
Washington, D.C. 20036

The Worldwatch Paper Series

1. **The Other Energy Crisis: Firewood** by Erik Eckholm.
2. **The Politics and Responsibility of the North American Breadbasket** by Lester R. Brown.
3. **Women in Politics: A Global Review** by Kathleen Newland.
4. **Energy: The Case for Conservation** by Denis Hayes.
5. **Twenty-two Dimensions of the Population Problem** by Lester R. Brown, Patricia L. McGrath, and Bruce Stokes.
6. **Nuclear Power: The Fifth Horseman** by Denis Hayes.
7. **The Unfinished Assignment: Equal Education for Women** by Patricia L. McGrath.
8. **World Population Trends: Signs of Hope, Signs of Stress** by Lester R. Brown.
9. **The Two Faces of Malnutrition** by Erik Eckholm and Frank Record.
10. **Health: The Family Planning Factor** by Erik Eckholm and Frank Record.
11. **Energy: The Solar Prospect** by Denis Hayes.
12. **Filling the Family Planning Gap** by Bruce Stokes.
13. **Spreading Deserts — The Hand of Man** by Erik Eckholm and Lester R. Brown.
14. **Redefining National Security** by Lester R. Brown.
15. **Energy for Development: Third World Options** by Denis Hayes.
16. **Women and Population Growth: Choice Beyond Childbearing** by Kathleen Newland.
17. **Local Responses to Global Problems: A Key to Meeting Basic Human Needs** by Bruce Stokes.
18. **Cutting Tobacco's Toll** by Erik Eckholm.
19. **The Solar Energy Timetable** by Denis Hayes.
20. **The Global Economic Prospect: New Sources of Economic Stress** by Lester R. Brown.
21. **Soft Technologies, Hard Choices** by Colin Norman.
22. **Disappearing Species: The Social Challenge** by Erik Eckholm.
23. **Repairs Reuse, Recycling — First Steps Toward a Sustainable Society** by Denis Hayes.
24. **The Worldwide Loss of Cropland** by Lester R. Brown.
25. **Worker Participation — Productivity and the Quality of Work Life** by Bruce Stokes.
26. **Planting for the Future: Forestry for Human Needs** by Erik Eckholm
27. **Pollution: The Neglected Dimensions** by Denis Hayes.
28. **Global Employment and Economic Justice: The Policy Challenge** by Kathleen Newland.
29. **Resource Trends and Population Policy: A Time for Reassessment** by Lester R. Brown.
30. **The Dispossessed of the Earth: Land Reform and Sustainable Development** by Erik Eckholm.
31. **Knowledge and Power: The Global Research and Development Budget** by Colin Norman.
32. **The Future of the Automobile in an Oil-Short World** by Lester R. Brown, Christopher Flavin, and Colin Norman.
33. **International Migration: The Search for Work** by Kathleen Newland.
34. **Inflation: The Rising Cost of Living on a Small Planet** by Robert Fuller.
35. **Food or Fuel: New Competition for the World's Cropland** by Lester R. Brown.
36. **Synthetic Materials: The Shifting Balance** by Christopher Flavin.
37. **Women at Work** by Kathleen Newland.

•

The lack of a population policy is a national luxury that the world can ill afford. If population policies are to be intelligent, and if demographic projections are to be meaningful, most countries need far more information on the sustainable yields of their grasslands, forests, croplands, and fisheries. The scarcity of data in most areas points to the need for assessments of the carrying capacity of local biological systems under varying demand pressures and levels of management. . . .

—**Resource Trends and Population Policy: A Time for Reassessment**

Losing Ground

Desperate news. Firewood is disappearing in the world. So are mountain environments, irrigation systems, fisheries, rain forests, and soil. Chapters from this book have appeared as major articles in **Science, Natural History,** *and elsewhere because of Eckholm's uniquely detailed perspective on environmental degradation in the Third and "Fourth" (impoverished) World. From there the planetary picture is stark.* —SB

Losing Ground
(Environmental Stress and World Food Prospects)
Erik P. Eckholm
1976; 219 pp.
$3.95 postpaid from:
W.W. Norton & Co., Inc.
500 Fifth Avenue
New York, NY 10036
or Whole Earth Household Store

•

By the mid-twentieth century, said the Chinese minister of forestry in 1956, the country had "the greatest number of barren hills in the world." Throughout much of the country only temple groves remained as a reminder of the original tree-covered landscape.

•

Ecologically sound planning requires concern for the next decade, the next generation and beyond; only the strong and vocal support — or insistence — of an informed citizenry can allow — or force — leaders to depart from their usual fixation on the next month or year. A widespread public understanding of the ecological danger is ultimately the prime weapon for fighting any commercial interests — whether highly placed timber concessionaires in Indonesia or Pakistan or corporate farmers in Central America — threatened by environmental protection measures. If powerful economic and political interests oppose necessary reforms, then a stronger political force is necessary to override them, and information about the nature of the threats to well-being is essential for building such a coalition. This is broadly true of virtually all political systems — not just democracies.

•

Experience has proven that sound treatment of the land cannot be decreed by officials — particularly those viewed as alien or oppressive — and then forced upon people who do not understand why changes in their habits are necessary. Faced with serious soil erosion in their African colonies, the British in the 1940s and 1950s tried the coercive approach, and by any account the ultimate results were abysmal.

Soil and Civilization

Edward Hyams writes the first and best "watershed history" of ancient and present civilizations. Rather than focusing on the genius of Pericles or the naval talents of Themistocles, he focuses on the ultimate, long-term strength of Greece or any nation: its soil. He elegantly chronicles, for instance, how oak forest cutting led to topsoil erosion creating a subsoil economy (olives and vineyards) which made Athens dependent on naval trade to get topsoil crops (wheat). Includes the Euphrates and America's dustbowl. If one book on history should be read by everyone, I would choose **Soil and Civilization.**
—*Peter Warshall*

Soil and Civilization
Edward Hyams
1976; 315 pp.
$3.95 postpaid from:
Harper Colophon Books
Keystone Industrial Park
Scranton, PA 18512
or Whole Earth Household Store

•

The ecologists of America, and the practical men working to their plans, have found that they can restore dead soils to life by recreating upon them a "natural" and balanced soil community. They begin by introducing some undemanding weed which will colonize the most exhausted soils, they gradually introduce nobler vegetable species; they have to work with great care and great insight, balancing species against species, making sure that the trees they plant, when that becomes possible, will find themselves able to establish a mode of life with the ground plants. In the course of time species intrude of their own accord, and the ecologist has to decide whether these intruders shall or shall not be allowed to stay. Some of the artificially introduced species may grow too prosperous at the expense of others, and must be checked; others, too meek, encouraged. In time animal species are introduced, some living off the vegetation, and others, predatory on the former, to hold them in balance. The work must be like building a house of cards, excepting that when every single feat of delicate balance has been successfully accomplished, then the equilibrium of the finished artifact will be massive, not precarious. Now this creative ecology, if that will do as a name for it, is unquestionably an art: aesthetic insight, right feeling for the grain of life is what must animate it.

Map of World Distribution of Arid Regions

Not only an image to ponder on your wall, but nice details — where desert is encroaching and why, whether by human or animal pressure and what the local vulnerabilities are — salinization, alkalinisation, topsoil runoff, exposure of hardpan, etc. All put together, a big grim picture. —SB
[Suggested by Ron Hendricks]

Map of World Distribution of Arid Regions (UNESCO)
(2' x 3' map and 53-page booklet)
$16.50 postpaid from:
Unipub
345 Park Avenue South
New York, NY 10010

THE RISING SUN
NEIGHBORHOOD NEWSLETTER

continued from last spread

There are essays in the front of each of the 48 books about Agriculture and History and Labor and the like and they're pretty good, often written unsignedly by later famous writers and the labor part is more workery than anything you'd ever believe the Federal government would publish today, but the great part is the back. There are detailed tours which tell about the lay of the land in general and occasionally burst down into 6 point type and say something like:

*"Right on this road paralleling Dingman's Creek to the junction with a private dirt road (*open daily in summer months*) 0.4 miles; R. here, across the creek, to a parking space 1.1 m.; from which a footpath leads 400 yards to SILVER THREAD FALLS (adm. 25 cents), a giant step in the creek's 953-foot descent in a seven-mile course. The abundance of game is indicated by the signs requesting visitors not to take bear cubs or baby deer out of the woods. One third of a mile distant, on a similar path, is larger DINGMAN'S FALLS, 177 feet high; trees, ferns, and spray-drenched moss fringe the foaming white water."*

That's about Pennsylvania. I figure things aren't quite like that now, but you read that and if you're in Pennsylvania you notice how much it's changed or how much it's the same and either way you start paying attention, see a little depth in time around you. Whether this land is made for you and me or you and me were made for this land, reading a bunch of stuff like that couldn't hurt. If I said all libraries have all the guide books, I'd be lying, but not much. What was the place you live like in 1934? Even if you were there, I bet you don't remember. Look in the card catalog under Federal Writers' Project. (One way for us post-war babies to find out what we hath wrought.)

PEOPLE AND LAND: REGAINING THE BALANCE
Around the ancient neolithic rock circle at Avebury, England, a diversified pattern of field and village has persisted over centuries.

Environmental Conservation

Environmentally over-info'd out? I'd pretty much stopped reading. Just skimmed: field guides, "ecology" articles, and **CQ** *review books. THEN Environmental Conservation:*

— The ease of History. The old-fashioned insistence that we try to remember what was and learn by it. Carl Sauer. Lewis Mumford. Edgar Anderson. Now Dasmann's Fourth Edition of **Environmental Conservation** *(the first was seventeen years ago - 1959).*

— The thorough, intimate prose. Every "idea" is not an "idea," because it takes place in a habitat, in a town or desert, with humans trying but stumbling because their present desires have made them careless about mañana.

— The quiet passion. Never trying to say more than the "everyday" reality can hold. Simultaneously yearning for humans to change and to see and to gain loving guidance for the Planet.

To save wood pulp and forests, I hereby erase all recent college textbooks except Dasmann's **Environmental Conservation** *and its predecessor* **Man's Role in Changing the Face of the Earth** *(p. 47) and its pictorial cousin* **Man and the Earth's Ecosystems** *(p. 48).*

A heavy trio:
HUMANS, EARTH and TIME.
—Peter Warshall

Environmental Conservation
Raymond F. Dasmann
1959, 1976
(4th edition); 436 pp.
$12.50 postpaid from
John Wiley & Sons, Inc.
One Wiley Drive
Somerset, NJ 08873
or Whole Earth
Household Store

•

If the list of wildlife species now extinct or threatened with extinction is examined, it will be found that a high percentage of these species are like the mountain caribou. They are wilderness animals, dependent on the maintenance of climax or near-climax habitat conditions. The now-rare fur bearers of the United States, the marten, wolverine, and fisher, appear to be among these forms. They are now scarce in most areas of their former range, despite almost complete protection from hunting or trapping. . . .

The species of wildlife that form the bulk of our huntable game populations and those which have become pests of farmlands, forest lands, and rangelands are the successional forms. They have been favored by our use, and misuse, of the land and have exercised their biotic potentials in expanding into newly created habitats left by fire, loggers, or excessive numbers of sheep and cattle.

•

One of the characteristics of the human animal is a wide range of environmental tolerance, the ability to continue to exist under conditions from which most species would flee. A few other species — rats, mice, starlings, pigeons — seem able to tolerate the conditions under which people live, and they accompany mankind around the world. Fleas, lice, and house flies also qualify. This human trait, however, seems to be one which would actually permit people to destroy the biosphere.

Environmental Conservation Magazine

If, as Peter Berg avers, there are two fundamental impulses at war in the world these days — "global uniformity" versus "planetary diversity" — then this magazine qualifies as the single refereed journal most thoroughly in support of planetary diversity. Look at its subtitle (below). The contributors and stories cover the biosphere. And surprisingly, even when they are fairly technical, the articles are readily understandable, perhaps because so many people are politically active in these matters, perhaps because the science involved is human scale. *—SB*

*Best technical reviews in all areas of environmental conservation. Articles like effects of cement dust on growth and yield of olive trees; erosion rates and land-use history on an inland lake; marine parks needed and existing in Italy. International in scope. Better than all those others (***Ambio, Ecologist,** *etc.) for me — since I like the nitty-gritty and don't mind (too much) the scientific prose style.* *—Peter Warshall*

Environmental Conservation
(The international Journal devoted to maintaining global viability through exposing and countering environmental deterioration resulting from human population pressure and unwise technology)
Nicholas Polunin, Editor
$78.75/year (4 issues)
from:
Environmental Conservation
Elsevier Sequoia S.A.
P.O. Box 851
1001 Lausanne 1,
Switzerland

•

Deep ocean trenches are increasingly being proposed as ideal dumping-sites for highly toxic chemical and radioactive wastes. The assumption seems to be that the deeper these poisonous substances go, the less harmful they are likely to be. Yet our knowledge about the seabed below 2,000 m, and of the deep ocean trenches which run like canyons across it, is at best sketchy. Mankind may destroy this environment even before he has explored it.

Now the world's most influential conservation body — the International Union for Conservation of Nature and Natural Resources (IUCN) — has called upon governments to stop all dumping in these trenches, stating that the world's 22 ocean trenches constitute unique habitats, and that up to 60% of the life-forms in each separate trench are found nowhere else.

The Ecologist

Edited by the ebullient Teddy Goldsmith, this British mag is a nice mix of careful and radical. It has a strong point of view, lots of good ideas, and considerable effect.
—SB
[Suggested by Paul Ehrlich]

The Ecologist
Nicholas Hildyard,
Edward Goldsmith,
Editors
$28 /year (10 issues)
from:
The Ecologist
73 Molesworth Street
Wadebridge, Cornwall
PL27 7DS
United Kingdom

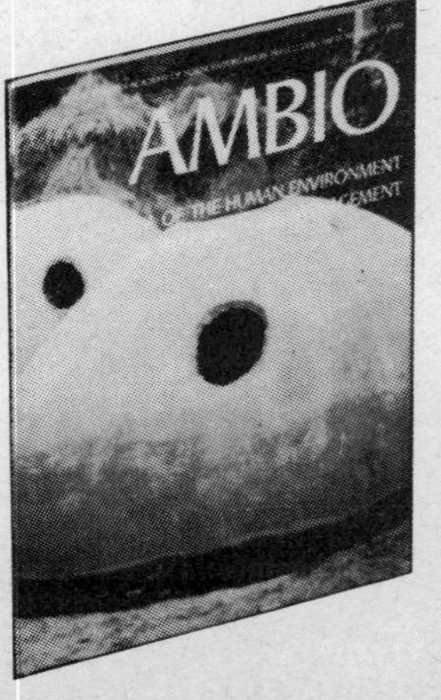

•

Will Deforestation Turn the Amazon into a Desert?

We normally associate deserts with dry areas, yet Harry Knowles, a former FAO ecologist who has spent 22 years in the Amazon region has predicted that: "If deforestation continues at the present rate, the Brazilians could very well end up creating another Sahara." But how could one of the wettest parts of the world become one of the driest? Surely the rich covering of vegetation must mean that the Amazon soils are very fertile and long lasting?

Nothing could be further from the truth. Soils beneath tropical rain forests are generally very poor, and heavy rainfall of up to 4000 mm (157 inches) has long ago washed most of the plant nutrients from the topsoil. Contrary to what is found in temperate areas, the fertility of an area of tropical rain forest is stored in the vegetation and not in the soil. Nutrients from dead organic matter are returned back to the vegetation as quickly as possible via the intermediaries of ants, termites and fungi, and if such a closed and rapid nutrient cycle was not in operation the nutrients would be leached down to the subsoil and as they would be lost to the surface plants so the overall fertility of the land would decrease.

The region of Bragantina around the eastern Amazon city of Bragantina was settled just before the end of the nineteenth century by European and Brazilian farmers. Year after year the fertility dropped until by the 1940s only coarse grass would grow there. Now all that is left is a ghost landscape with large areas of bare soil and rock. Crops gave high yields initially but as more and more of the finite fertility of the land was taken away to feed people, the soil became exhausted and a desert was formed.

Ambio

Authoritative and glossy. This Sweden-based magazine is the voice of establishment international environmentalism. When I was working a couple of years ago on an article about genotoxins — the flood of new chemicals that cause cancer and gene damage — **Ambio** *was my most indispensable source of up-to-date information.*
—SB

Ambio
Jeannie Peterson, Editor
$25 /year (6 issues) from:
Pergamon Press
Fairview Park
Elmsford, NY 10523
or:
Pergamon Press
Headington Hill Hall
Oxford OX3 OBW
United Kingdom
or
Ambio
Royal Swedish Academy
of Sciences
Box 50005
S-104 05
Stockholm, Sweden

Endangered Species, and WIN

We are at a point where Vigilance may be lost. The Furbish Lousewort and the Snail Darter seem so irrelevant to most humans that laws (desperately needed to preserve the gene pool of Earth) are being diluted. Saving cutesy baby seals and intelligent dolphins seems easy. But, the mysterious and unknown fish of the Little Tennessee called the Snail Darter . . . who cares?

Two bulletins are keeping the vigil. The **Endangered Species Technical Bulletin** *is published monthly by U.S. Fish and Wildlife Service, Dept. of Interior, Washington, D.C. 20240. It is available free to those organizations and individuals who show a direct involvement in the endangered species program. You must send a summary that clearly demonstrates need. It's a great stimulus to unceasing awareness.*

The action equivalent is **WIN** *($7/year to cover costs) from the Sierra Club Wildlife Involvement News, 800 Second Ave., New York, NY 10017. Wildlife ecology, political action, debates (should the California Condor be bred in captivity?) and news (the Red Wolf is currently the most endangered mammal in North America). Needs support. Does good work.*

—Peter Warshall
[Suggested by Dean Lyon]

Not Man Apart

Not Man Apart *from the Friends of the Earth, is not often very pleasant or optimistic reading. But it's the best straightforward tough politically active environmental periodical, and it does have a sense of humor.*
—Gary Snyder

More than any other environmentalist group, Dave Brower's Friends of the Earth initiate new subject areas. It was FOE who began the fight against nuclear power, employing Amory Lovins when he was unknown, and who raised doubts about recombinant DNA, and who early on took action against the dioxin-bearing herbicides 2,4,5-T and 2,4-D, and who even now are leading environmentalists into battle against nuclear weapons. Troops worth joining, with a fine periodical. *(See Friends of the Earth, p. 383.)*
—SB

Not Man Apart
Tom Turner, Editor
$15 /year (12 issues)
$25 /year (includes membership in Friends of the Earth)
from:
Friends of the Earth
124 Spear Street
San Francisco, CA 94105

•

The Canadians have come up with a novel solution to the problem of storing **banned hazardous chemicals:** Drop the ban. Saddled with 35,000 gallons of 2,4,5-T and 2,4,5-TP held in leaking containers, the Ontario Environment Ministry has decided that the best way to get rid of the toxic herbicides is to allow them to be sprayed along roadsides during the next year. Environment Minister Harry Parrott admitted that the proposal was not an ideal solution, but claimed that no safer means of disposing of the herbicide existed. Parrott also insisted that the Ministry's Pesticide Advisory Committee had concluded that lifting the ban for a year would not create any health or environmental hazard.

↓

In proposing the William O. Douglas Peace With the Earth Prizes (**NMA**, March 1980) we suggested five kinds of projects that might earn prizes. We proposed that the Douglas Prize jury might determine who had brought the most progress, globally, to:

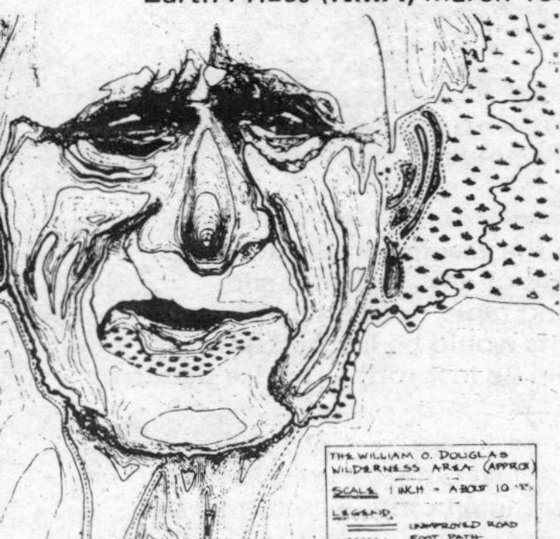

1. The economics of peaceful stability;
2. The advanced study of ecosystems;
3. The reinterpretation of nature;
4. Preserving the irreplaceables;
5. Building careers in preservation.

—David Brower

Environmental Action

Best way to stay abreast of legislative battles/opportunities in a broad spectrum of environmental issues, as they are coming up in Washington, as well as key stories from all over.
—Hazel Henderson

Environmental Action
Deborah Baldwin,
Janet Marinelli,
Gail Robinson, Editors
$15 /year (11 issues)
from:
Environmental Action, Inc.
Room 731
1346 Connecticut Ave. NW
Washington, D.C. 20036

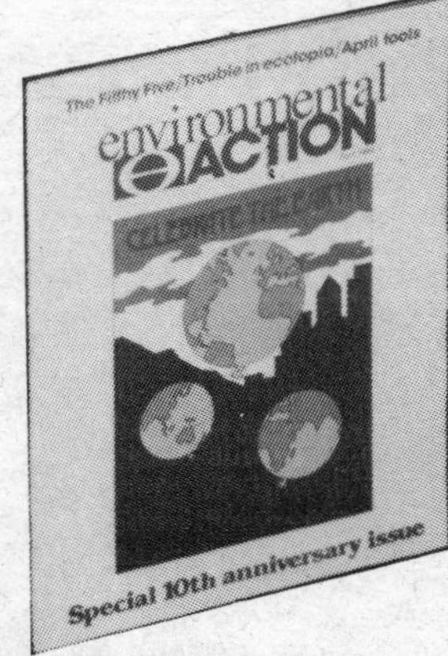

•

Months of research by Environmental Action have revealed a pattern of political donations by some of the nation's biggest polluters. Dubbed the Filthy Five, these companies and their top officials gave a total of $714,131 to congressional campaigns and candidates in 1978. The corporations — Dow Chemical, International Paper, Republic Steel, Occidental Petroleum and Amoco Oil — are polluting our democratic system of government as well as the nation's air and water.

The corporations are the target of Environmental Action's 1980 campaign to clean up government.

Massive erosion along the Gasquet-Orleans Road: Its completion will lay open the Blue Creek wilderness to shrieking saws.

Audubon

This is the strongest ecological-call-to-arms publication we've got. Its illustrations (both photographs and paintings) have visceral impact. The articles are thorough and authoritative. Audubon Society is no longer just birds but all life and it's into protection as much as appreciation. *(See National Audubon Society, p. 383.)*
—SB

Audubon
(The Magazine of the National Audubon Society)
Les Line, Editor
$13 /year (six issues)
from:
National Audubon Society
950 Third Avenue
New York, NY 10022

•

Teasel grows wild along road sides and in old fields and pastures throughout the country, flowering from July to September. Bees like its nectar, and teasel honey has a fine flavor. But woe to the tongue of a grazing cow that tries to lift a teasel leaf into its mouth. For everything about teasel is prickly — flowers, stems, leaves — and it is impossible to take hold of it anywhere without being stung by its spines. In its armored flower heads, however, we have a fascinating chapter from human history.

↑

I was looking at wild teasel *(Dipsacus sylvestris)*, a plant that grew in the hedges of England and in continental Europe before it came to America — perhaps, like many weeds, as seeds in the ballast of ships. But there is another kind of teasel, fuller's teasel *(Dipsacus fullonum)*, whose introduction on this side of the Atlantic was intentional. For the spines on its prickly heads have strongly developed hooks, and it was used for centuries in the gigging process by the woolen and worsted industry. It was called fuller's teasel because the fuller is the person in charge of the fulling or felting of the fabric.
—John K. Terres

•

In addition to its traditional role in Indian life, Blue Creek is a superb spawning stream for both steelhead and salmon — one of the finest in the Siskiyous, which are the most productive watershed in California — and the people know that logging will hasten the end of the dying salmon fishery so crucial to both whites and Indians in the depressed economy of this region. As Dick Myers says, "Poor logging practices make these creeks run too fast in winter and spring, so that they dry up much too soon during the summer. It spoils the rivers, and it spoils the fishing." Botanically, these mountains are one of the most various regions on the continent, and a reservoir of relict plants such as the Brewer's spruce, whose closest relation is found in northeast Asia, and such vanishing wild creatures as the wolverine and cougar. For all these reasons, very suddenly, this little-known wilderness has become one of the most controversial in the country.
—Peter Matthiessen

High Country News

This is the most informative news sheet on Rocky Mountain environmental affairs of anything published. Feature articles give facts, personalities, and history. Though mostly concerned with western states, has good articles on Alaska and elsewhere. Excellent analyses of government actions and their effects. Usually includes a long article on some individual person, especially persons concerned with conservation initiatives.
—Luna Leopold

For environmental news of the Rocky Mountain West, this small-town, shoe-string paper routinely scoops everybody else. Because they insist on balanced reporting and take the time to dig out details, **High Country News** *gets read by all interested parties — oil company executives, BLM bureaucrats, Senate Staffs and environmentalists. Increasingly, their turf is where the action is, and the blow by blow account gets reported here.*
—Richard Nilsen

High Country News
Geoffrey O'Gara, Editor
$15/year
(25 issues) from:
High Country News
331 Main
Lander, WY 82520

→

The cougar has a disturbing habit of following people. It will trail a person silently for miles without threatening or attacking, often making no effort at concealment. This audacious behavior is certainly nerve-racking, but there seems to be nothing sinister in its motive. The cougar is curious: that is all.

High Country News
New kind of 'public interest' group pushes growth

Natural Resources Defense Council

When the editorial page writers for the **Wall Street Journal** *start grousing about environmentalists, NRDC is who they point to. It's a deserved — if backhanded — compliment since NRDC continues to litigate, and win, major environmental battles. Issues like clean air, coal leasing, land and coastal use, nuclear power plant siting, safety and waste disposal, and timber management make an impressive list of achievements. They deserve support.* *(See Natural Resources Defense Council, p. 383.)*
—Richard Nilsen

Amicus
Peter Borrelli, Editor
$15 /year (4 issues; includes membership in Natural Resources Defense Council)
from:
N.R.D.C.
122 East 42nd Street
New York, NY 10168

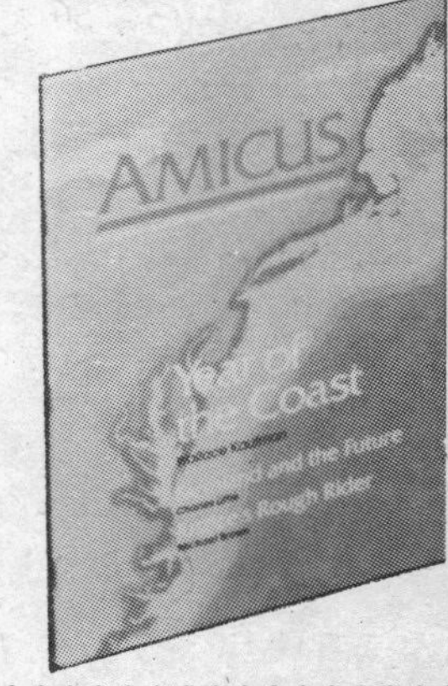

THE RISING SUN
NEIGHBORHOOD NEWSLETTER

"The way I see it you can treat your life like a fastball or a knuckleball, that's the choice. Now, a fastball pitcher grabs tight on the ball, throws it as hard as he can, it spins through the air in a straight line, the batter knows where it's heading and either he can hit it or he can't. A knuckleball pitcher just lets the ball go, holds it with his middle two knuckles like a claw and lets it go, no spin and no straight line. It floats toward the batter and any little breeze can make it do something else, and there's always a little breeze and the knuckleball surprises the catcher (who has to use a bigger glove and misses a lot anyway), the batter and the pitcher and the ball. Knuckleball pitchers can pitch a lot more years than fastball pitchers, but there aren't very many of them."

"**E**COLOGY" HAS COME TO MEAN JUST ABOUT ANYTHING. *Doom-gloom to the end-of-the-worlders. Mystical harmony to the religio-eco-freaks. Grants to the college crowd. The word comes from Greek: "Oikos" and "Logos". "Oikos" means house, or dwelling-place. "Logos" primarily means discourse, or "word, thought or speech". To the early Greeks, "logos" was the moving and regulating principle in things (associated with fire-energy), as well as the part of human nature that was able to see this ordering energy at work.*

Ecology, at its root and origin, means domestic chatter; talking about where-you-live; feeling out the household rules; remaining open and perceptive to the moving and regulating principle of your watershed and/or planet home.

We take three approaches to the subject:

- *Making the household part of everyday discourse. Become intimate with the household and all its*

An Ecological and Evolutionary Ethic

The subject is right. The essays are bite-size one-pagers full of anecdote and pith. The author must be young, though well field-experienced in ecology, and a classroom veteran, and, ye gods, a hippie scientist. I'm so happy with his book I want to argue with him about details.

Ethics used to be the <u>point</u> of philosophy and education. This unusual book can help restore that sensible practice.

—SB

[Suggested by Tom Pockat]

An Ecological and Evolutionary Ethic
Daniel G. Kozlovsky, Editor
1974; 116 pp.

$8.95 postpaid from:
Prentice-Hall, Inc.
Box 500
Englewood Cliffs, NJ 07632
or Whole Earth Household Store

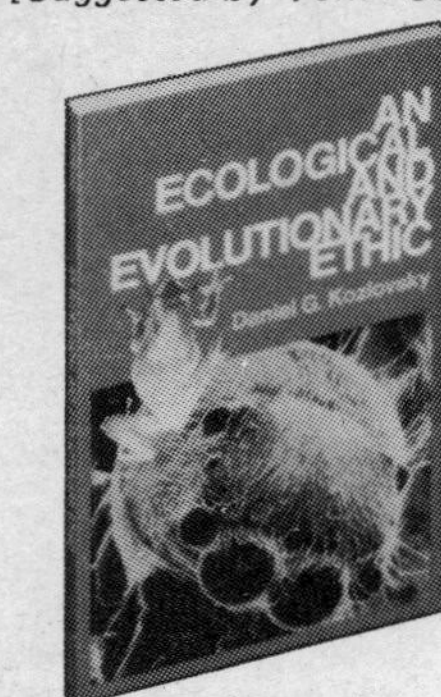

•

Nothing is as ridiculous, as pathetic, as obscene as an organism out of context.

•

There is no insurance so cheap and as easily drawn upon as human insurance, as the respect and concern and affection of your fellow man.

Each time you buy an insurance policy you add to the deterioration of the social organism.

•

A cock crows under my bedroom window, a wild jungle call. We never bred it out, probably because it doesn't affect laying capacity or meatiness. That crowing seems as wild and free and primitive as that of the northern Indian jungle fowl from which our domestic chickens are derived. Jungle under my window! . . .

For a thousand generations men woke to a crowing cock, had interjected into their subconscious lives that small part of jungle wildness. In a couple of generations we have excluded these cocks from town and barnyard, and even the farmer now wakes to an alarm clock. The human world is the poorer for it, but does not know that, *cannot* know that.

Can you regain what you do not know you should have?

•

A scientific animism would consider the phylogenetic possibilities of animal empathy (you can *stroke* a mammal), not ignoring a lady I know whose pet Great Horned Owl understands her moods, is happy when she is happy, is down when she is down, and who (I use *who* instead of *which;* you would too if you knew the owl) tries to cheer her up by getting into some ridiculous mischief when she's unhappy.

A scientific animism would consider the multitudinous ways in which animals train *you.*

•

It also becomes clear that the organism-environment dichotomy is nonsense; all living things are open systems, constantly exchanging atoms with other systems, living and nonliving — there are no impermeable boundaries. Don't be misled by that thick skin of yours; when you cease to exchange, eat, excrete, breathe, you're dead.

The organism-environment comparison is fundamentally meaningless. The atoms are transients; what is environment today is organism tomorrow, what is organism tomorrow is environment the next.

We should be careful of what we dump into the environment, because, physically and psychologically, tomorrow it's likely to be us.

•

I see that the elementary laws never apologize . . .

—Walt Whitman

Ecoscience

If you could save the world by throwing a book at it, this might be the book. (Actually the book that will do the saving will likely be called "Ecoreligion," and be derived in part from this book.) Meant to be as comprehensive an outline as possible (in a mere 1051 pages) of all that the young world-saver needs to know to find a worthy task and surround it, the book succeeds. —SB

Ecoscience
(Population, Resources, Environment)
Paul R. Ehrlich, Anne H. Ehrlich, John P. Holdren
1977; 1051 pp.

$22 postpaid from:
W.H. Freeman & Co.
660 Market Street
San Francisco, CA 94104
or Whole Earth Household Store

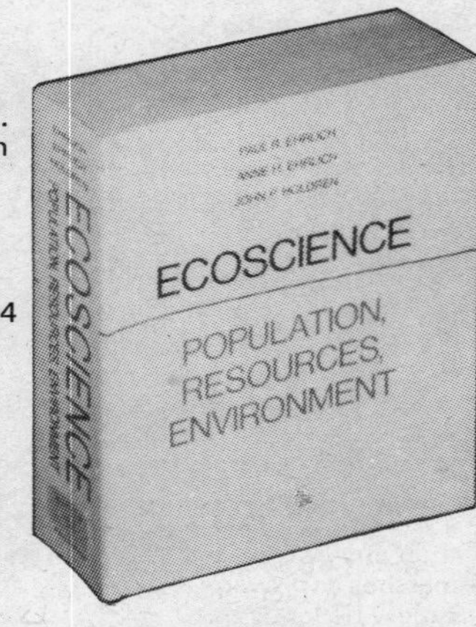

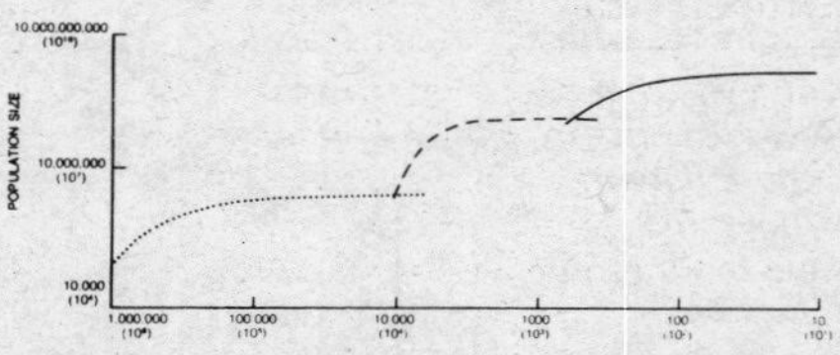

Human population growth plotted on a log-log scale. Plotted in this way, population growth is seen as occurring in three surges, associated with the cultural, agricultural, and industrial-medical revolutions.

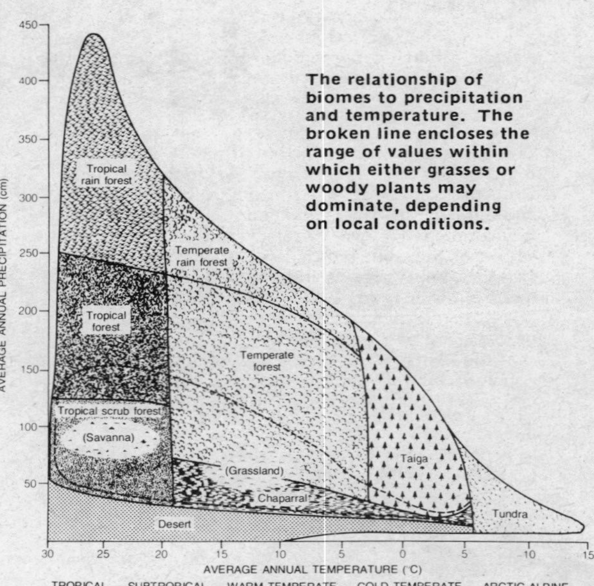

The relationship of biomes to precipitation and temperature. The broken line encloses the range of values within which either grasses or woody plants may dominate, depending on local conditions.

•

Of the defects in the cornucopian argument, the gravest are these:

1. The presumption that advanced technology will make energy very cheap;
2. The presumption that abundant, cheap energy — if available — would prove to be a sufficient condition for abundance of all kinds;
3. The serious underestimation of the degree of environmental degradation that would be generated by the proposed cornucopian technologies;
4. The even more serious underestimation of the impact on human well-being that major environmental disruption portends.

Stalking the Wild Taboo

Hardin has been stalking wild taboos for some time now. Abortion. Religion. Technology. Competition. The emphasis is on abortion and competition. Not your typical reading matter. Can make you angry at times. But that's what taboos are all about. Printed on easy-to-read tan paper with brown ink. —Graham Holmboe

[Suggested by Stephanie Mills]

Stalking the Wild Taboo
(Second Edition)
Garrett Hardin
1973, 1978; 284 pp.

$4.95 postpaid from:
William Kaufmann, Inc.
1 First Street
Los Altos, CA 94022
or Whole Earth Household Store

•

Society does not need more children; but it does need more loved children. Quite literally, we cannot afford unloved children — but we pay heavily for them every day. There should be not the slightest communal concern when a woman elects to destroy the life of her thousandth-of-an-ounce embryo. But all society should rise up in alarm when it hears that a baby that is not wanted is about to be born.

•

I refer to the principle by a name — the "competitive exclusion principle," or more briefly, the "exclusion principle." It may be briefly stated thus: *Complete competitors cannot coexist . . .* What does the exclusion principle mean? Roughly this: that (i) if two noninterbreeding populations "do the same thing" — that is, occupy precisely the same ecological niche in Elton's sense — and (ii) if they are "sympatric" — that is, if they occupy the same geographic territory — and (iii) if population *A* multiplies even the least bit faster than population *B*, then ultimately *A* will completely displace *B*, which will become extinct.

•

The General rule may be stated in either of two different ways: *Complete competitors cannot coexist* — as was said earlier; or, *Ecological differentiation is the necessary condition for coexistence.*

•

The Cybernetics of Monopoly

If a monopoly is produced, what then? Here is a question which Ricardo did not face. At first glance one might say that the monopoly price should be stable, because if it were to rise, new entrepreneurs would be attracted to the field and would lower the price. But this is a naive view. We know that it is more difficult to start a business than to continue one, and consequently a monopolist can maintain a price considerably above the "natural price." Furthermore, a realistic model must include much more than we have indicated so far. We must consider the whole complex of phenomena that we include under the word "power." *Social power is a process with positive feedback.* By innumerable strategems a monopolist will try to manipulate the machinery of society in such a way as to ward off all threats to re-establish negative feedback and a "natural" cybernetic equilibrium. And, as history shows, the monopolist in one field will seek to extend his power into others, without limit.

Should Trees Have Standing?

Yes.

Read why in this splendid essay that swayed the Supreme Court. Ecological health is (sequentially) a biological, spiritual, moral, ethical, and, now, legal matter. Economic is next.

—SB

[Suggested by Bob Ornstein]

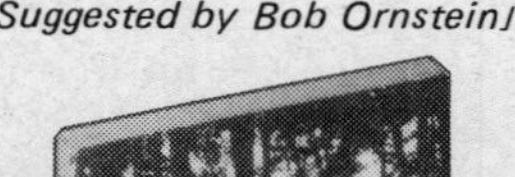

Should Trees Have Standing?
(Toward Legal Rights for Natural Objects)
Christopher D. Stone
1972; 102 pp.

$1.50 postpaid from:
Avon Books
Mail Order Department
250 W. 55th Street
New York, NY 10019

•

It is no answer to say that streams and forests cannot have standing because streams and forests cannot speak. Corporations cannot speak either; nor can states, estates, infants, incompetents, municipalities or universities. Lawyers speak for them, as they customarily do for the ordinary citizen with legal problems.

•

Wherever it carves out "property" rights, the legal system is engaged in the process of *creating* monetary worth.

•

"Rights" might well lie in unanticipated areas. It would seem, for example, that Chief Justice Warren was only stating the obvious when he observed in *Reynolds vs. Sims* that "legislators represent people, not trees or acres." Yet, could not a case be made for a system of apportionment which *did* take into account the wildlife of an area?

members; from raindrops to mushrooms, minerals to millipedes, hill slopes to higher plants. This is the naturalist end of the ecology spectra.

- *Learn the "logos" of the home: the words and thoughts of Western scientists who have attempted to make models to describe the moving and regulating energy of our Earth household. These are, in part, the mathematicians. Names like Odum or Margalef pop to mind.*

- *Defend the home. Applied ecology is entering politics armed by concern for an intimacy with our fellow house-holder; guided by Reason (the logos) understood from Nature — both human and otherwise.*

The slogan: "Nature to be commanded must be obeyed." —Francis Bacon, 1620.

—Peter Warshall

Fundamentals of Ecology

Here is the author who has done most to apply cybernetics and energy flow concepts to natural communities, yet he never forgets the fieldwork. Crisp reviews of habitat diversity (tundra, marsh, grasslands) complement a complete review of all ecological theory. This is the encyclopedia of ecology. It's the one academic reference to nature I keep on the nearby shelf. —Peter Warshall

Fundamentals of Ecology
(Third Edition)
Eugene P. Odum
1971; 574 pp.

$16.95 postpaid from:
W.B. Saunders Co.
West Washington Square
Philadelphia, PA 19105

Land types I and II comprise level areas with good agricultural soils that can be continuously cultivated with only simple precautions such as crop rotations and strip cropping, whereas land types III and IV (steeper slopes) require greater restrictions if cultivated, for example, periodic fallowing, perennial crops, or rotated pastures. Types V and VII are not suitable for cultivation and should be used for permanent pasture, tree crops, or retained in their natural state (for naturally developed forestry and wildlife, for example). Type VIII (steep slopes, thin soil) is productive only in its natural state, as habitat for game, furbearers, forest products, or is valued for recreational, scenic, watershed protection, or other uses; these latter uses are often more important than any "crop" the land may yield. In most cases, marshes and swamps should probably now be classified as type VIII lands because their value as water reservoirs and wildlife habitats outweighs their value as reclaimed farmland, since increased yields can now be obtained on existing farmland.

•

It is man the geological agent, not so much as man the animal, that is too much under the influence of positive feedback, and, therefore, must be subjected to negative feedback. Nature, with our intelligent help, can cope with man's physiological needs and wastes, but she has no homeostatic mechanisms to cope with bulldozers, concrete, and the kind of agroindustrial air, water, and soil pollution that will be hard to contain as long as the human population itself remains out of control.

Perspectives in Ecological Theory

High theoretics. The substantial hope that our myriad ecological observations might form a coherent perspective. Difficult to understand if you are unfamiliar with ecological jargon but, for those who wish to struggle through the prose, this book is totally mindbending. Margalef has a way of crystallizing whole books into one sentence.

—Peter Warshall

Perspectives in Ecological Theory
Ramón Margalef
1968; 111 pp.

$4.95 postpaid from:
University of Chicago Press
11030 South Langley Ave.
Chicago, IL 60628
or Whole Earth Household Store

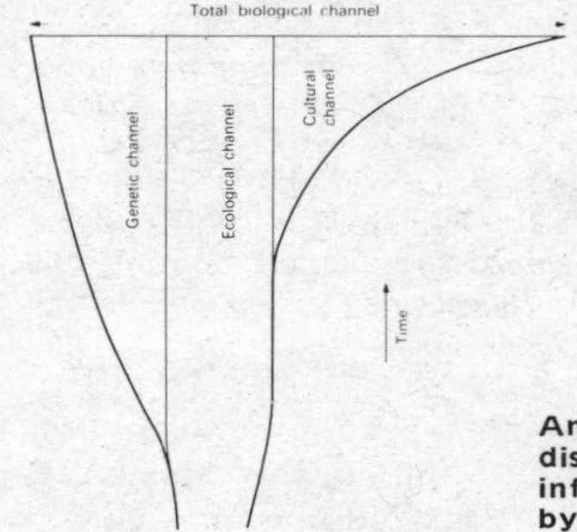

An idealized view of distribution along time of information forwarded by life, in three channels.

•

A measure of the organization of the ecosystem may be found in the average distance between the place of energy input and the energy sink. The distance can probably be measured either in terms of space or of time.

•

It is basic property of nature, from the point of view of cybernetics, that any exchange between two systems of different information content does not result in a partition or equalizing of the information, but increases the difference. The system with more accumulated information becomes still richer from the exchange. Broadly speaking, the same principle is valid for persons and human organizations: any exchange increases to a greater extent the information of the party already better informed.

•

The ecosystem may be considered as a channel which projects information into the future.

•

As books usually contain more information than tree trunks (or at least more readable information), it is clear that the conversion of trees into books will go on for some time.

•

It is a general property of many systems that acquired information is subsequently used to close the door to a further inflow of information. In general, the development of a personality involves the use of information to make oneself impermeable to new sources of information; this is, of course, regrettable, especially in the scientific personality.

•

During succession there is an increase in the proportion of inert or even dead matter with a low respiratory rate, such as wood, shells, and so on. The proportion of structures like burrows, paths, and territory markers, which may be considered as stores of information, also increases.

•

A more mature system always exploits a less mature system.

•

A strong exploitation of very mature ecosystems, like tropical forests or coral reefs, may produce a total collapse of a rich organization. In such stable biotopes, nature is not prepared for a step backward. Man has to be very careful in dealing with systems of high maturity.

•

Pumping more energy in and out of a system simplifies it; it becomes different and works differently.

•

Important evolutionary changes occur in areas of climatic fluctuation and then spread peripherally toward more stable climates where the lines are caught in the general trend of slow evolution. The tropical belt may not necessarily be a source of new lines but rather a refuge of types that have originated elsewhere and then migrated.

Ecology

For many years, scientists locked their perceptions into one telescope. Geneticists only looked at genes. Demographers only looked at birth rates and death rates. Evolutionary biologists only looked at "adaptions" and "natural selection". Behavioral psychologists only looked at sense perception and operant conditioning. Thank God, the telescope's disappeared, and Ricklef's is the first text to write clearly about the new synthesis.

Relatedness: a bee perceives ultra-violet, a flower evolves ultra-violet colors, the bee/flower complex co-evolves food gathering and mutually inter-dependent schemes for reproducing each other. Another one: the cryptic or advertising colors of fish relate to their predators or prey, which relate to their ups and downs in population size, which relates to the quality of their gene pool. The concepts of hip evolutionary theory and energy ecology flow fast and furious. The prose and math are academic.

—Peter Warshall

Ecology
Robert E. Ricklefs
1973, 1979; 966 pp.
2nd Edition

$18.95 postpaid from:
Chiron Press
Publisher's Storage and Shipping Corp.
2352 Main Street
Concord, MA 01742

Figure 29-8. An example of Williston's Law. The ancient trilobite (left) has many, similar segments and appendages. The modern crab (right) has relatively few, specialized segments and legs (after Simpson 1949).

Figure 14-6. Face views of an owl and a rabbit showing the forward placement of the eyes in a predator for binocular vision and depth perception, and placement of the eyes to the side of the head to maximize the visual field in a species that is often preyed upon.

Figure 16-3. Examples of crypsis achieved by disruptive coloration in the Jackknife-fish (left) and the Angelfish (right). If the contrast is strong enough, one tends to see the pattern rather than the fish itself (after Laglar, Bardach, and Miller 1962).

•

One of the reasons for man's astounding biological success is the extremely rapid rate of cultural evolution. Man's culture evolves too fast for organisms to keep pace with it genetically. The modes by which cultural information is transmitted produce more frequent mistakes than occur in genetic inheritance, thereby increasing the variability available for cultural evolution. It would indeed seem unlikely that cultural transmission by learning could match the precision of molecular application involved in the inheritance of genetic information.

THE RISING SUN
NEIGHBORHOOD NEWSLETTER

My sister visited me in California from Ohio and she said she got really tired to see all her house-plants outside being trees.

Joe is happy to have found out that pennecontemporaneously means at almost the same time. He works it into sentences frequently. "Am I late?" "No, we arrived pennecontemporaneously."

Nature and Man's Fate

THE introduction to theoretical and applied evolution. Hardin is further than anyone in blending the insights of evolution and cybernetics into what may be an embryonic science of general development. Still it's a completely earthly book. The specific history of Darwin and his idea. The specific application of evolutionary understanding to human survival now. —SB

Nature and Man's Fate
Garrett Hardin
1959; 320 pp.
$1.25 postpaid from:
The New American Library, Inc.
P.O. Box 120
120 Woodbine
Bergenfield, NJ 07621
or Whole Earth Household Store

•

As a species becomes increasingly "successful," its struggle for existence ceases to be one of struggle with the physical environment or with other species and comes to be almost exclusively competition with its own kind. *We call that species most successful that has made its own kind its worst enemy.* Man enjoys this kind of success.

•

It is one of the few rules of evolution that extreme specialization results in eventual extinction. Environmental changes are inevitable, and the specialist-species is too strongly committed to one way of life to be able rapidly enough to "back up" genetically and take off in another "direction." All the evidence of comparative morphology and paleontology, fragmentary though it is, indicates that each great new group of organisms arises from very unspecialized species of the group "below" it, not from the conspicuously specialized ones.

•

In order to make a perfect and beautiful machine, it is not requisite to know how to make it. Quite so.

. . . To Darwinians, Design emerges from blind Waste. "To be an Error and to be cast out is a part of God's Design," said William Blake.

•

The Competitive Exclusion Principle. No two organisms that compete in every activity can coexist indefinitely in the same environment. To coexist in time, organisms that are potentially completely competitive must be geographically isolated from each other. Otherwise, the one that is the less efficient yields to the more efficient, no matter how slight the difference. When two competing organisms coexist in the same geographical region, close examination always shows that they are not *complete* competitors, that one of them draws on a resource of the environment that is not available to the other. The corollary of the principle is that where there is no geographical isolation of genetically and reproductively isolated populations, there must be as many ecological niches as there are populations. The necessary condition for geographical coexistence is ecological specialization.

•

Darwin's life is symbolic. His **Autobiography** clearly and unconsciously reveals two elements that are needed to produce any creative genius: Irresponsibility and alienation.

He who is to see what other men have not seen must, in a real sense, become alienated from the crowd. The manner in which this alienation occurs is subject to an infinity of permutations. . . .

The wealthy eccentric is a nearly extinct dodo. The man of wealth is now an other-directed man. He may become a lawyer or a doctor. But not a scientist. He is too much a part of the world to achieve the alienation required to be creative. (What millionaire today would have the nerve to do what Darwin did — retire to a "non-productive" life in the country *to think?*)

. . . We can hardly expect a committee to acquiesce in the dethronement of tradition. Only an individual can do that, an individual who is not responsible to the mob. Now that the truly independent man of wealth has disappeared, now that the independence of the academic man is fast disappearing, where are we to find the conditions of partial alienation and irresponsibility needed for the highest creativity?

A large population, which is very sensitive to selection pressure, is narrowly confined to an adaptive peak (Mount Tory). A species broken up into many separate small breeding populations is much less responsive to selection pressures; its populations will wander widely from their adaptive peak (Mount Risky) — some to perish, some, perhaps, to find the way to new adaptive peaks like Mount Opportunity. As before, the water represents the threatening natural selection.

↓

The Illustrated Origin of Species

Darwin's epochal tract is long, wondrous, and rather inaccessible. By abridging and illustrating it, the field-born paleontologist Leakey (son of Louis and Mary Leakey) does a handy service. How was one man so right about so much so early? Darwin's scientific practice was the optimal blend of profound theory and relentless detail work. —SB

The Illustrated Origin of Species
(Abridged and Introduced by Richard E. Leakey)
Charles Darwin
1859, 1979; 240 pp.
$25 postpaid from:
Hill and Wang, Inc.
19 Union Square West
New York, NY 10003

•

In plants, the down on the fruit and the colour of the flesh are considered by botanists of trifling importance: yet in the United States, cultivated smooth-skinned fruits suffer far more from a beetle than those with down; purple plums suffer far more from a certain disease than yellow plums; whereas another disease attacks yellow-fleshed peaches far more than those with other coloured flesh. In a state of nature, such differences would effectually settle which variety should succeed. In looking at small points of difference between species which seem quite unimportant, it is necessary to bear in mind that, owing to the law of correlation, when one part varies, other modifications, often of the most unexpected nature, will ensue.

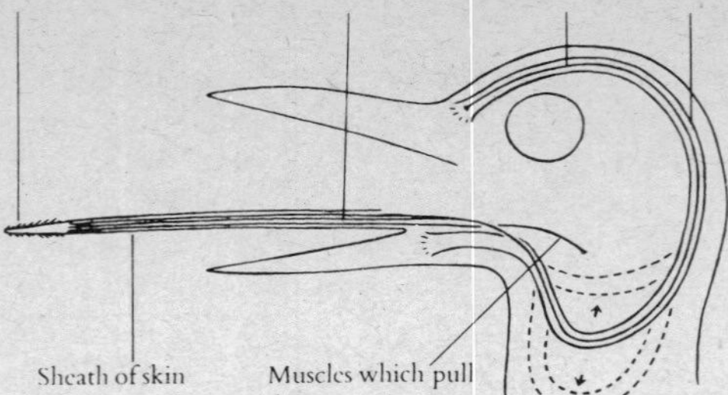

The woodpecker's skeleton shows several special adaptations. The skull is particularly sturdy to withstand the force of the blows as it hammers with its beak; the leg bones are large and strong; the end of the spine curves downwards to enable the tail feathers to act as a prop. One toe of the woodpecker's foot is reversed to give a stronger grip.

•

It is interesting to contemplate a tangled bank, clothed with many plants of many kinds, with birds singing on the bushes, with various insects flitting about, and with worms crawling through the damp earth, and to reflect that these elaborately constructed forms, so different from each other and dependent upon each other in so complex a manner, have all been produced by laws acting around us. These laws, taken in the largest sense, being Growth with Reproduction; Inheritance, which is almost implied by reproduction; Variability from the indirect and direct action of the conditions of life, and from use and disuse; a Ratio of Increase so high as to lead to a Struggle for Life, and as a consequence to Natural Selection, entailing Divergence of Character and the Extinction of less-improved forms. Thus, from the war of nature, from famine and death, the most exalted object which we are capable of conceiving, namely the production of the higher animals, directly follows. There is grandeur in this view of life, with its several powers, having been originally breathed by the Creator into a few forms or into one; and that, whilst this planet has gone cycling on according to the fixed law of gravity, from so simple a beginning endless forms most beautiful and most wonderful have been and are being evolved.

Darwinian terrorists and the Lamarckian puppies

I have a friend — my boss, in fact — named McElwain, who is a Lamarckian. I was sitting by the stove with Bill and a visitor, when Bill's dog Penrod walked through the kitchen.

"How did your dog lose its tail?" the man asked. "Was it hit by a car, or what?"

"No," says Bill, "but her grandmother was."

"What?" says the man. "Are you trying to tell me this dog *inherited* the missing tail from its grandmother, which was hit by a car?"

"Something like that," said Bill. He leaned back and took a puff on his cigar. "Penrod's grandmother was hit by a car — right out here in front of the house — and we had to have her tail amputated. About a year later she had puppies —"

"— And they were all born without tails!"

"Just so. But, word about this got around, and on one night a roving band of militant Darwinians broke into the house, and grafted tails onto all the puppies."

"But you cut the tails back off, and so the acquired trait was passed on."

"Why would I do a thing like that?" asked McElwain. "I let the tails stay. It was no skin off my ass.

"At any rate, we gave all the puppies away except Penrod's mother. In due time *she* had puppies —"

"And they all had tails."

"Yes."

"So the Darwinists were satisfied — things were back to normal."

"The Darwinians were fit to be tied: *They* grafted the tail onto Penrod's mother. They knew that. Thus, Penrod and her brothers and sisters had inherited an acquired characteristic. They should have been born *without* tails, as their mother was born. Those Darwinians were in a bad situation."

"So what did they do?"

"What Darwinians always do: they broke in again, and cut off the puppies' tails."

"And that's why Penrod doesn't have a tail."

"That's why Penrod has no tail — Darwinian terrorists cut it off."

The visitor, an intelligent and well-rounded local physician, looked thoughtful for a while. Finally he asked, "Did Penrod have puppies?"

"She did," answered Bill, much pleased.

"Tail-less, I presume."

"Of course."

"But the Darwinists found out."

"They always do."

"So they broke in again and — "

"Yeah but this time," said Bill, "I was waiting for them. I mean I don't really care about the tails, but I was tired of having my house broken into. So this time I stayed up with a shotgun, loaded with rock salt. And when those damned Darwinians broke in here, boy, I just let them have it. I hit one, too — I heard her yelp."

"Her?"

"Yeah, a lot of those Darwinians are women. I think it appeals to their mothering instincts. Anyway, I haven't had any more trouble with Darwinians around here — not with the dogs, or with my frogs, either."

The doctor didn't even bother to ask about the frogs — there was an excited light in his eyes.

"You know Bill," he said, "I think I may know who one of those Darwinists was."

"Really?" said Bill, quite surprised.

"Yes," said the doctor. "I delivered a baby for a young woman the other day — quite a fine girl — one of your students, in fact."

"I'm not surprised," said Bill. "Which one?"

"I won't say," said the doctor. "But I think she may have been the gal you hit."

"You saw —"

"Yes: there I was, you know, delivering her baby girl, and damned if she didn't have a tail full of rock salt."

"*She* did? Which one?"

The doctor smiled. "Both of them." ■

—Brian Donahue
Wayland, Massachusetts

Lupinus arcticus grown from a seed at least 10,000 years old. The seeds were found by a Yukon mining engineer in lemming burrows deeply buried in permanently frozen silt of the Pleistocene age.

Biology of Plants

I first heard of Peter Raven from a mind-blowing article about flower shapes, pollination and energy. Later, I met one of his students (Dennis Breedlove) whose intimacy with plant life floored all my previous vegetative understandings. This is Raven's textbook. Somewhat technical but so beautifully illustrated and so comprehensive: origins of life, DNA, cell life, the sun and its powers, water and soils and their powers, genetics, plant family groups, evolution and coevolution, plant growth and ecology. Most of the textbooky prose avoids irritating my more peyote sensibilities. —Peter Warshall

Biology of Plants
Peter Raven, Ray Evert, and Helena Curtis
1976; 685 pp.
$18.95 postpaid from:
Worth Publishers
444 Park Ave. South
New York, NY 10016

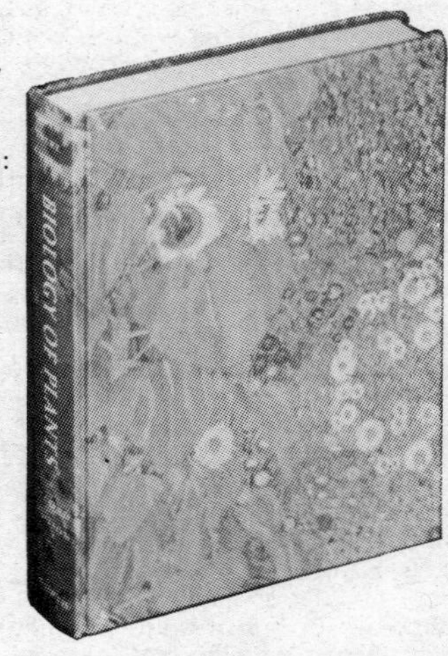

The Lives of a Cell

These "notes of a biology watcher" by the head of the Sloan-Kettering Cancer Center were a cult item in **The New England Journal of Medicine** *for years before they were assembled into this best-selling form. The title essay relates the symbiotic theory of Lynn Margulis that the organelles of higher cells used to be independent organisms which, in the course of deepening cooperation, joined inseparably and made possible the ever subtler complexity that has evolved since. Thomas makes you care about such things.* —SB

The Lives of a Cell
(Notes of a Biology Watcher)
Lewis Thomas
1974; 153 pp.
$2.25 postpaid from:
Bantam Books
414 E. Golf Road
Des Plaines, IL 60016
or Whole Earth Household Store

•

It is the protozoan *Myxotricha paradoxa*, which inhabits the inner reaches of the digestive tract of Australian termites. . . . At first glance, he appears to be an ordinary, motile protozoan, remarkable chiefly for the speed and directness with which he swims from place to place, engulfing fragments of wood finely chewed by his termite host. In the termite ecosystem, an arrangement of Byzantine complexity, he stands at the epicenter. . . . Without him there would be no termites, no farms of the fungi that are cultivated by the termites and will grow nowhere else, and no conversion of dead trees to loam.

The flagellae that beat in synchrony to propel myxotricha with such directness turn out, on closer scrutiny with the electron microscope, not to be flagellae at all. They are outsiders, in to help with the business: fully formed, perfect spirochetes that have attached themselves at regularly spaced intervals all over the surface of the protozoan.

Then there are oval organelles, embedded in the surface close to the point of attachment of the spirochetes, and other similar bodies drifting through the cytoplasm with the particles of still undigested wood. These, under high magnification, turn out to be bacteria, living in symbiosis with the spirochetes and the protozoan, probably contributing enzymes that break down cellulose.

The whole animal, or ecosystem, stuck for the time being halfway along in evolution, appears to be a model for the development of cells like our own.

Hugo de Vries, standing next to Amorphophallus titanum, a member of the same family as the calla lily. The plant, a native of the Sumatran jungles, has one of the most massive inflorescences of any of the angiosperms. This picture was taken in the arboretum of the Agricultural College at Wageningen, Holland in 1932.

The Ecological Theater and the Evolutionary Play

Once you're thoroughly confused by eco-jargon and once you've grasped eco-jargon, then try G.E. Hutchinson. A professor immersed in the eddy currents of eco-theory with the ability to pop the already initiated ecologist right back into the main stream of evolutionary thought. See also his **The Itinerant Ivory Tower** *and* **The Enchanted Voyage.** —Peter Warshall

The Ecological Theater and the Evolutionary Play
G. Evelyn Hutchinson
1965; 139 pp.
$10.50 postpaid from:
Yale University Press
92A Yale Street
New Haven, CT 06520
or Whole Earth Household Store

•

One way of avoiding being eaten is to be inconveniently large.

The Life Science

Biologists who deal with the public world are routinely appalled by the public ignorance of what biologists know and work with. People seem to know and care far more about physics or astronomy, sciences whose news affects them far less than do developments of understanding and technique in biology. Every so often a pissed-off biologist sets out to remedy the situation. The Medawars succeed. In personal, sometimes pungent prose here are your fundamentals, in a form the opposite of a textbook or a journalistic gloss. —SB

The Life Science
(Current Ideas of Biology)
P.B. Medawar and J.S. Medawar
1977; 196 pp.
$3.95 postpaid from:
Harper & Row General Books
Keystone Industrial Park
Scranton, PA 18512
or Whole Earth Household Store

•

This is a book about *ideas*, with no more factual information than is necessary to make the ideas intelligible. It is therefore in no sense a textbook: for one thing there are no diagrams of the insides of animals, and for another some of its content is too advanced for real beginners. Nevertheless, we think the book is a useful companion for genuine students of biology. It may also interest sociologists, anthropologists, philosophers, psychologists and literary folk who want to learn something of the conceptual framework of modern biology.

•

Being alive is a system property, i.e. a characteristic that can be attributed only to an organized system.

•

So far from being 'alive' a virus is simply a piece of bad news wrapped up in protein.

•

At a characteristically noisy cocktail party, people raise their voices in order to make themselves heard, and this adds to the prevailing din so that people must shout louder and louder in order to make themselves heard at all. This continues until eventually they say to themselves, 'I can't *bear* cocktail parties,' and take their leave. This is an example of positive feedback, a fundamentally unstable and in extreme cases self-destructive process.

THE RISING SUN
NEIGHBORHOOD NEWSLETTER

Tom decided to make his science project be instructions on how to live on a round Earth. Most people don't, he says. "They see globes and pictures from space and they believe them, but they don't believe that that round ball is where they live this minute, that that's where the sidewalk is and their bed." Here are his instructions:

1. First, turn your globe sideways. In your house or in your mind, there is a globe standing up and down, North Pole on top. Sometime, maybe when you were too young to remember, you tried to put yourself on the shiny cliff on the side of the globe where the name of where you lived was printed, but you fell off. You couldn't make yourself stick, and you haven't been able to believe you lived on a round thing since.

   So you need to give yourself a safe place on the globe you won't fall off of. And that's why you turn the globe sideways. Now it's standing on the end of a C-shaped thing – you need to turn it so it's standing on the middle of the C. Point the place where you live up. Try to believe there's a little you down there – it might work this time.

   Remember, since there's no up and down in space where the Earth lives, all this is as true as the North Pole up way. If the Earth is a top spinning through space, it's hard to understand how you stick to it. But if it's a ball rolling through space – and it might as well be – you might be able to believe now and then it's home.

2. After you've thought about living on a rolling globe ball for a while and seen on it a safe place to lie down, it's time to lie down on it.

   Go to a grassy place with nothing around it in the morning and lie down and point your feet to the sun. The Earth is rolling over toward the sun and taking you with it. Stay in that spot a few hours and you'll see yourself rolling under the sun a little and if you stay all day you'll feel yourself rolling down and under and away from the sun and into the shadow below. If you stayed all night rolling under the stars, your body on that piece of Earth would finally roll up to face the sun again. It happens every day, but running around in your own circles makes it hard to notice.

3. Believing the Earth is round when you're lying down is a lot easier than believing it's round when you're standing up and walking. That's because our eyes are usually looking in the wrong direction. The truth is that everyone on this round planet is facing out into space all the time. When you're lying down looking straight out with your eyes, you can remember that. When you're standing up, it's harder because even though your eyes are just grazing a bit of a very big ball on their way to staring into space, they feel like they're looking along a very big plate. It takes a lot of lying down on the rolling ball before you can know you're standing on it too. I don't really recommend it. Once you know you're standing on the round Earth, everything around you is falling away from your feet and you're alone and living in the sky.

Natural History Magazine

I use it two ways: The monthly column "This View of Life" by Stephen Jay Gould, who teaches Biology, Geology and History of Science at Harvard, regularly contributes to (or at least soundly reaffirms) my understanding of how the world works. He explains fundamental issues clearly and always sets them against a background of why anyone ever thought differently. Second, it is written and edited in such a way that my children (ages 10 and 12) seem to get as much out of it as we do. It is one of the few publications we've found that has this quality. A good magazine at a good price from a great institution. —George Putz

Natural History
Alan Ternes, Editor
$15 /year (12 issues)
from:
Natural History
Membership Services
Box 6000
Des Moines, IA 50340

At the approach of a western ribbon snake, a narrow-mouthed toad scuttles toward the safety of a female giant tarantula. Instead of a toad, the snake will get a faceful of spider feet and fangs.

•

As one male toad ducked under Ammonita and she touched him with a foot, I marveled at the interaction between these two dissimilar creatures. In its association with tarantulas, the narrow-mouthed toad has evolved an effective defense against the pressures of predation. The tarantula's fierce defensive behavior excludes most of those predators of a size dangerous to the diminutive toad, and the microhabitat of the burrow and overlying rock attracts small insects, providing a ready source of prey for the narrow-mouthed toads. And, with their appetite for ants, several toads per burrow can control these voracious invaders, which might otherwise harass adult tarantulas and consume eggs and spiderlings.

•

The observed equality of males and females, in the face of obvious advantages for female predominance if evolution worked upon groups, stands as one of our most elegant demonstrations that Darwin was right — natural selection works by the struggle of individuals to maximize their own reproductive success. The Darwinian argument was first framed by the great British mathematical biologist R.A. Fisher. Suppose, Fisher argued, that either sex began to predominate. Let us say, for example, that fewer males than females are born. Males now begin to leave more offspring than females since their opportunities for mating increase as they become rarer — that is, they impregnate more than one female on average. Thus, if any genetic factors influence the relative proportion of males born to a parent (and such factors do exist), then parents with a genetic inclination to produce males will gain a Darwinian advantage — they will produce more than an average number of grandchildren thanks to the superior reproductive success of their predominantly male offspring. Thus, genes that favor the production of males will spread and male births will rise in frequency. But this advantage for males fades out as male births increase and it disappears entirely when males equal females in number. Since the same argument works in reverse to favor female births when females are rare, the sex ratio is driven by Darwinian processes to its equilibrium value of one to one. —Stephen Jay Gould

The Wilderness World of John Muir

If you love running brooks and craggy cliffs, you'll love John Muir. If you love lush, energy-filled, exciting writing, you'll love John Muir. If you love adventure and vision quests, biographies of brave humans, he's just your man. A touchstone into the life of America's wildest human, watershed wizard, political savior, etc., etc., etc. —Peter Warshall

The Wilderness World of John Muir
Edwin Way Teale, Editor
1954; 332 pp.
$5.95 postpaid from:
Houghton-Mifflin
Wayside Road
Burlington, MA 01803
or Whole Earth
Household Store

•

The waterfalls of the Sierra are frequented by only one bird — the ouzel or water thrush *(Cinclus Mexicanus, Sw.)*. He is a singularly joyous and lovable little fellow, about the size of a robin, clad in a plain waterproof suit of bluish gray, with a tinge of chocolate on the head and shoulders. In form he is about as smoothly plump and compact as a pebble that had been whirled in a pot-hole, the flowing contour of his body being interrupted only by his strong feet and bill, the crisp wing-tips, and the up-slanted wren-like tail.

•

Only by going alone in silence, without baggage, can one truly get into the heart of the wilderness. All other travel is mere dust and hotels and baggage and chatter.

•

I have a low opinion of books; they are but piles of stones set up to show coming travelers where other minds have been, or at best signal smokes to call attention. Cadmus and all the other inventors of letters receive a thousand-fold more credit than they deserve. No amount of word-making will ever make a single soul to *know* these mountains. As well seek to warm the naked and frost-bitten by lectures on caloric and pictures of flame. One day's exposure to mountains is better than cartloads of books. See how willingly Nature poses herself upon photographer's plates. No earthly chemicals are so sensitive as those of the human soul. All that is required is exposure, and purity of material. "The pure in heart shall see God!"

A Species of Eternity

When Euro-Americans first hit the shores of Turtle Island, they saw this wilderness as alien — full of unfamiliar critters and non-useful plants. A small handful of men and women fell in love with North America — overjoyed with the mystery of new species lurking in streams and bushes. This is their story. The first half-crazed, half-scientist, half-artist, totally high naturalists in the "New World."

This is the story of my personal lineage of teachers of the 18th and early 19th centuries. Their kinship to each other and to the broadleaf woodlands has never been more humorously and accurately told. Many fine color reproductions of early drawings and engravings. —Peter Warshall

A Species of Eternity
Joseph Kastner
1977; 350 pp.
$8.95 postpaid from:
E.P. Dutton
2 Park Avenue
New York, NY 10016
or Whole Earth
Household Store

•

That night Audubon heard a great uproar from the naturalist's room "I opened his door and saw him running about naked in pursuit of bats. He had my favorite violin by the handle and proceeded to bash it against the wall in an attempt to kill the winged animals. He begged me to procure a bat for him — 'a new species.' I took the bow of my battered Cremona violin, and soon got specimens enough."

At Rafinesque's request, Audubon took him out into "one of those thickets or brakes in which the cane grows from twelve to thirty feet in height. A fallen tree obstructed our passage. We were about to go round it when out of the center of the tangled mass of branches sprang a bear with such force and snuffing the air in so frightful a way that Rafinesque was terrified. In his haste to escape he fell and was pinioned between the stalks. Despite his thorough fright, I could not refrain from laughing at the ridiculous exhibition he made. The way became more and more tangled. The thunder began to rumble. Heavy rain drenched us. Briars had scratched us, nettles stung us. Rafinesque threw away all his plants, emptied his pockets of fungi, lichens and mosses. I led him first one way, then another until I myself, though well acquainted with the brake, was all but lost in it. I kept him stumbling and crawling until long after midday."

Leading his guest through the canebrakes was cruel enough but even crueler was a scientific hoax Audubon played on him, describing and drawing a dozen local fish which never existed except in his own tall tales. Taking Audubon at his word, Rafinesque included ten of Audubon's imagined creatures in his pioneering work on western fishes.

"The Devil-Jack Diamond fish (Litholepsis admantinus) [Rafinesque wrote], the wonder of the Ohio. I have seen it but only at a distance and have been shown some of its singular scales. Wonderful stories are related concerning this fish but I have principally relied upon the description and figures given me by Mr. Audubon. Its length is 4 to 10 feet. The whole body is covered with large stone scales half an inch to one inch in diameter. They strike fire with steel! and are ballproof!"

It was perhaps inexcusable for Audubon to carry a joke so far. It was certainly inexcusable for a naturalist like Rafinesque to be gulled by such stuff. He was, after all, one of the most widely experienced scientists in America. "In knowledge," he wrote of himself, "I have been a botanist, naturalist, geologist, geographer, historian, poet, philosopher, economist, philanthropist. By profession, a traveler, merchant, draftsman, architect, engineer, author, editor. I hardly know what I may not become as yet." One of the most traveled men of his times, he covered "over 25,000 miles, half by sea, half by land. One-fourth pedestrian journeys . . . by mules, asses, litters, sedan chairs, chaises, men's backs, feluccas, tartans, boats, arks, scows, nearly all the possible manners except by camel and in balloons."

First Audubon bird painting published was female grackle in rear of this plate. Ironically it appeared in the Ornithology of his great rival, Alexander Wilson.

Basic Ecology

About as basic as you can get. So basic that I think this book is either for children or a solid reminder to specialists that have lost the forest for the trees. If you're tired of just talking "ecology" and "environment" and want to be introduced to the science, this is the easiest and simplest book. —Peter Warshall

Basic Ecology
Ralph and Mildred
Buchsbaum
1957, 195 pp.
$4.95 postpaid from:
The Boxwood Press
183 Ocean View Blvd.
Pacific Grove, CA 93950

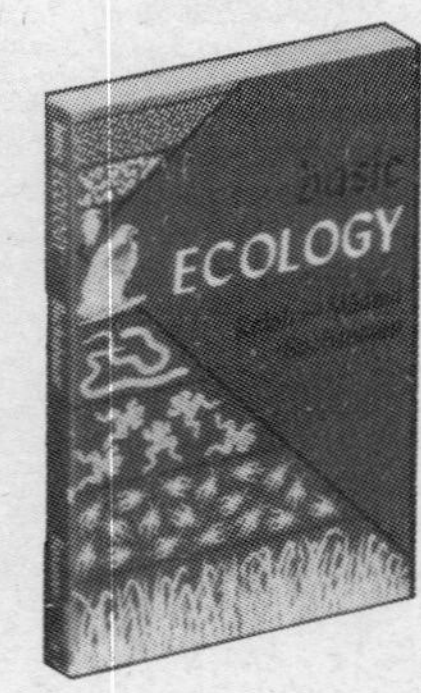

Hermit crab, Eupagurus bernhardus, has accepted a glass model of a snail shell for its house. This reveals the behavior of its annelid commensal (Nereis fucata), which here at rest occupies the smallest coils of the shell away from its host. As soon as the crab begins to eat, the commensal comes to the opening of the shell and snatches a morsel from its host.

Penguin rookery

Animal Ecology

Charles Elton invented the words "niche" and "food chain" and "pyramid of numbers." For 55 years he has been the untiring curious naturalist trying to understand how each thread of the ecologic fabric weaves and re-weaves. **Animal Ecology** *is his classic. Easy to read. Like Darwin in its unabashed straightforward love of natural history.*
—Peter Warshall

Animal Ecology
Charles Elton
1966; 206 pp.

$6.95 postpaid from:
Halsted Press
One Wiley Drive
Somerset, NJ 08873

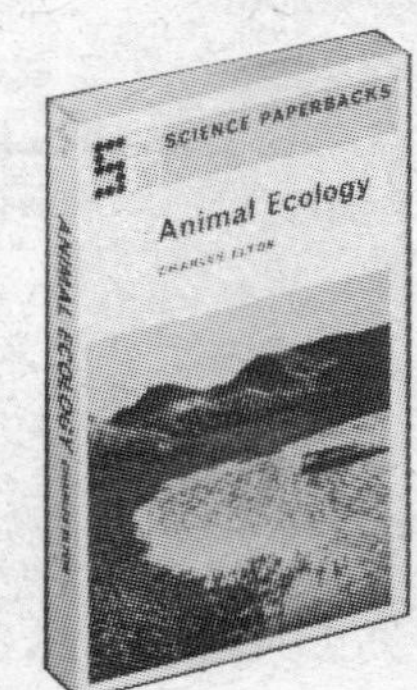

•

The general existence of this pyramid in numbers hardly requires proving, since it is a matter of common observation in the field. Actual figures for the relative numbers of different stages in a food-chain are very hard to obtain in the present state of our knowledge. But three examples will help to crystallise the idea of this "pyramid." Birge and Juday have calculated that the material which can be used as food by the plankton rotifers and crustacea of Lake Mendota in North America weighs twelve to eighteen times as much as they do. (The fish which eat the crustacea would weigh still less.) Again, Mawson estimated that one pair of skuas *(Megalestris)* on Haswell I. in the Antarctic regions, required about fifty to one hundred Adelie penguins to keep them supplied with food (in the form of eggs and young of the penguins); while Percival states that one lion will kill some fifty zebras per year, which gives us some idea of the large numbers of such a slow-breeding animal as the zebra which are required to produce this extra margin of numbers.

•

If one examines the photographs of Adelie penguin rookeries given in antarctic books of travel, one can get a vivid idea of the numbers of birds involved. Imagine several million short gentlemen in dress clothes (tails) standing about in a dense crowd covering several square miles of otherwise barren country. The birds represent the numbers from a very large feeding area concentrated in one place for breeding purposes; and to this extent they do not give a fair idea of the normal density of the population.

Predators that angle for their prey with dummy bait. The angling turtle Macroclemmys temmincki.

Mimicry in Plants and Animals

Mimicry will blow your mind. Beautiful illustrations of how two or three creatures have passed so much time together that they merge inextricably. Flowers mimic super-female wasps which the males fuck "mistakenly" and so fertilize the flower. One butterfly tastes bad and a dozen others evolve disguises so they appear to birds as a "bad taster." Spiders evolve to appear like ants so they can enter colonies for a meal. Hundreds of co-evolutionary mind-bogglers. *—Peter Warshall*

Mimicry in Plants and Animals
Wolfgang Wickler
1968; 249 pp.

$3.95 postpaid from:
McGraw-Hill Book Co.
Princeton Road
Hightstown, NJ 08520
or Whole Earth
Household Store

Butterflies of the genus Thecla **draw attention away from the true head and direct it to an imitation head at the hind end by means of converging colour stripes on the wings and antenna-like appendages on the wing tips. In addition,** Thecla togarna **on landing swings its hind end into the previous direction of flight and subsequently flies off in the opposite direction.**

Animal Forms and Patterns

No math. No schemata. Just a rambling discussion on how the appearance of animals gives clues to the internal mysteries. The best chapter covers molluscs and their shells — living molluscs, not Cartesian clams.
—Peter Warshall

Animal Forms and Patterns
(A Study of the Appearance of of Animals)
Adolf Portmann
1967; 257 pp.

$2.75 postpaid from:
Schocken Books Inc.
200 Madison Avenue
New York, NY 10016
or Whole Earth
Household Store

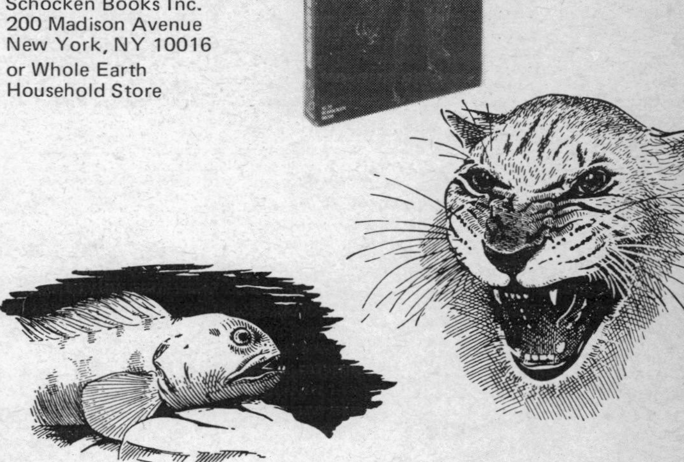
Formation of the face: almost expressionless or highly expressive, according to low or high level of differentiation (sea-cat and young lion).

The way the tail is held, raising the hair on the back or flattening it, the position of the ears, as well as the whole posture of the body, play a large part in the social life of wolves, and are understood by their companions to be a manifestation of internal conditions. The wolf to the left ranks high in the social structure of the group, the other ranks below it. (The illustration does not, however, represent a 'scene', but merely two postures.) At the same time the special form production at the anal pole is made clear.

Why Big Fierce Animals Are Rare

What does it all mean? Bigger creatures are rarer, smaller creatures more common. The more creatures living together means greater community stability. The fewer species, the greater the fluctuations. How do humans fit in? Colinvaux writes elegantly with a true philosopher's burning skepticism and passion for the Nature of Truth. No better introduction for those who just can't stand one more word of scientific, latinate, lingo-ese.
—Peter Warshall

Why Big Fierce Animals Are Rare
(An Ecologist's Perspective)
Paul Colinvaux
1978; 256 pp.

$4.95 postpaid from:
Princeton University Press
Order Department
Princeton, NJ 08540
or Whole Earth
Household Store

•

It thus seems very likely that the larger and fiercer predators are not nearly so important in regulating the numbers of animals in nature as common sense suggests. They are really to be looked upon as scavengers without the patience to wait for their meat to die. They cheat the bacteria who would have got the bodies otherwise. Two rather pleasing thoughts come from this discovery. One is that the lives of big game animals are lived in a large measure of freedom from the awful world of tooth and claw that we can conjure up by a careless reading of Darwin. Not only do these animals live in that peaceful coexistence with their neighbors, which the mathematical ecologists discovered, but they also may live with less fear of being killed than we had supposed, except as a sort of euthanasia. The second pleasing throught is that those who like to shoot big game themselves no longer have a pretext for killing off the wolves and cats before they start on the deer.

But if the firepower of a big cat is insufficient to devastate a herd of game, the firepower of the smaller predators may be truly awful. A spider or a wasp is a deadly efficient engine of destruction. Perhaps most of the species of hymenopteran insect that we loosely call wasps are in the business of hunting caterpillars and grubs of other insects, piercing them and laying their eggs under the skin, letting the maggots feed and grow on the living flesh of their victims, and eventually flying away from the empty carcass as mature wasps themselves. Although the victim thus takes long to die, the crucial predatory act is the initial attack by the female wasp on the caterpillar, and in this encounter the caterpillar stands no chance. When a wasp strikes, it is not like a tiger striking a buffalo; the issue is never in doubt; the chance of the wasp's being wounded is zero. The same must be true when a web-spider closes with a fly struggling in its meshes. It must also be true when a spider-hunting hornet plunges like a dive-bomber, with its armor-plated body and its poison-loaded stinger, on a spider sighted in the open. It must also be true when a tiger-beetle pounces, when a praying mantis reaches out with its dreadful arms, and when a large carnivorous diving beetle finds a small tadpole. In all these, the only hopes for the hunted are to escape detection or timely flight. We might expect, therefore, that small predators can have more potent effects on their prey than do large predators.

Natural history catalog

Lucas Book Company has the most extensive collection of records, folios, pamphlets and books on natural history, ecology, conservation and "outdoor life" of any store I've seen. Especially fine collection for flora & fauna west of the Rockies. Does mail order anywhere.
—Peter Warshall

Catalog free from:
Lucas Book Company
2430 Bancroft Way
Berkeley, CA 94704

THE RISING SUN
NEIGHBORHOOD NEWSLETTER

"My grandfather, who is 81, didn't have a telephone until 4 years ago. Since he and grandma live alone in a farmhouse several miles from the nearest neighbor, his grownup children worried about him a lot and argued a lot to get him to get a phone. He wouldn't because in 1932 when Morris Edwards brought telephones to town my grandfather was pissed at Morris Edwards about a church fight they were having. Edwards was only in the phone company for five years and it's changed hands a lot since then to being AT&T but grandfather wouldn't get a phone until he'd been in the hospital a couple of times and Uncle Luke came with the phone man and told him he was getting a phone like it or not. About the same time Grandpa got a phone he got an indoor bathroom, but when my mother and I were there to visit we noticed he never ever used it. Grandma did but he still used the place out back. The year before the bathroom he had gotten rid of the milk cow he milked for their own use and also got a propane heater to replace the coal stove. Milk prices went nuts that winter and the energy crisis happened and propane orders were based on last year's order and he didn't have a last year's order."

Natural Regions of the United States and Canada

Just open this book to an area you already know. Within pages, the land forms, soils, colors, plants, and importance of your watershed will intensify. An encyclopedia of physiography written in academic style. Lots of geologic history. The best book to practice mapping North America into your brain. Along with climate, this is the matrix for the continent life. —Peter Warshall

•

Between a third and a half of the combined area of Canada and the United States is forested and these forests constitute about 15 percent of the world's total. With only 6.5 percent of the world's population, North America is blessed with twice its share of forests.

Transect across the Sierra Nevada, illustrating contrast in vegetation on the wet windward slope (west) and the dry leeward slope. Low on the west side is grass with a belt of live oak and digger pine in the foothills.

Low on the dry east side is sagebrush with a belt of pinyon and juniper woodland in the foothills. Higher on the west side are belts of yellow pine, sequoia, and lodgepole pine; on the east slope is Jeffrey pine. At high altitudes on both sides is whitebark pine and alpine forms.

Natural Regions of the United States and Canada
Charles B. Hunt
1967, 1974; 725 pp.
$19.50 postpaid from:
W.H. Freeman & Co.
660 Market Street
San Francisco, CA 94104
or Whole Earth Household Store

Plants and Environment

My favorite recent discovery in ecology books. Plants are sensitive to all the strings in the ecological web, and Daubenmire pulls each one for the reader to see what happens. Strings with names like soil, water, temperature, fire, light, atmosphere, and other life forms. The non-linear approach. Academic prose. —Peter Warshall

Plants and Environment
(A Textbook of Plant Autecology)
R.F. Daubenmire
1974; 422 pp.
$18.95 postpaid from:
John Wiley & Sons
One Wiley Drive
Somerset, NJ 08873

←

Cupressus macrocarpa on the coast of California, showing the effects of landward winds. Xylem layers tend to be extremely thin except on the lee sides of the stems so that the trunk and branches become strongly flattened in a direction parallel to the wind.

How to Identify Plants

There is no easy road into plant architecture. Ovaries are superior or inferior; flower parts can be imbricate or valvate; surfaces can be scurfy, scabrous, comose, viscid, glaucous or otherwise. If you want to make the leap into botanical terms and use the more technical floras, then this book is the key to MONSTER VOCABULARY. Lists all the best technical floras by area. What a relief! —Peter Warshall

How to Identify Plants
H.D. Harrington and L.W. Durrell
1957; 203 pp.
$3.95 postpaid from:
Swallow Press, Inc.
811 West Junior Terrace
Chicago, IL 60613

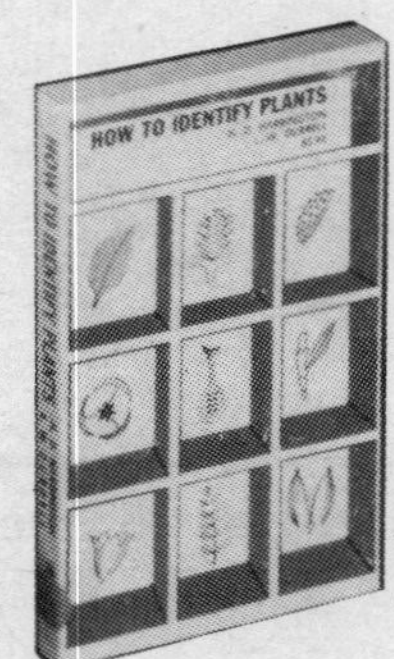

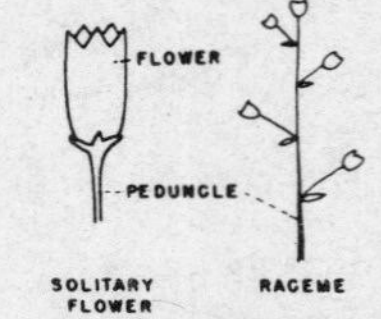

Fig. 421.

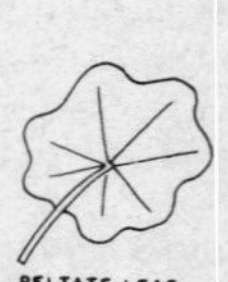

Fig. 422.

Fig. 423.

Evolution in Plant Design

Live dwellings — how soon? Houses of living vegetable tissue. The walls take up your CO_2 and return oxygen. They grow or diminish to accommodate your family changes. Add a piece of the kitchen wall to the stewpot. House as friend. Dweller and dwelling domesticate each other. Society for the Prevention of Cruelty to Structures.

Engineering lately has been inspired by bionics, the analysis of living systems for their technological accomplishments that might be borrowed by us. So far, plants have been overlooked.

Hey! Plants.

Start with this systemic lovely book and the nearest seed pod. —SB

Evolution in Plant Design
C.L. Duddington
1969; 258 pp.
$7.95 postpaid from:
Merrimack Book Service
22 South Broadway
Salem, NH 03079
or Whole Earth Household Store

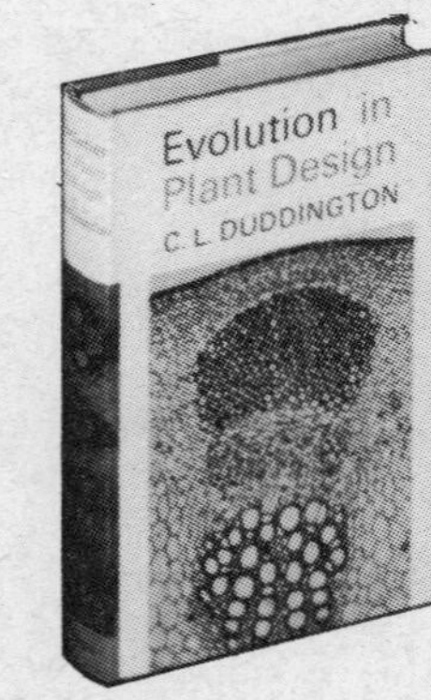

•

Water is not sucked up from the leaves, nor is it hoisted from below by root pressure, except, perhaps, in small plants. Our third possibility, that it is pumped up by some intermediate cell mechanism, also appears to be without foundation. One is tempted to say that it gets up by the grace of God, but scientists are chary about calling upon divine intervention in order to explain awkward facts. We must look again at our various possibilities (or impossibilities) and see whether we have missed something.

Turning once more to the theory that water is raised from above we can see at once that there is plenty of force available for the job, for transpiration sets up an osmotic gradient in the mesophyll of the leaf with pressures well above the ten or twelve atmospheres that we need for raising water even to the top of a *Sequoia*. The trouble begins when we try to see how it is applied. Suction just will not do, for we cannot get around the fact that the water barometer cannot exceed thirty-three feet. Some other phenomenon must be involved; something that can enable the pull in the leaves to reach right down into the roots and haul the water up. The answer to the problem seems to lie in a theory first put forward some time ago by Dixon and Joly, known as the 'cohesion theory'. A solid substance is held together by forces of cohesion between its molecules, which form a rigid crystal lattice that resists being broken. In a liquid the forces of cohesion do not hold so closely. The molecules can slide about over one another but they are still held by cohesive forces and prevented from escaping altogether. Only when a molecule gathers to itself sufficient kinetic energy (energy of movement) to overcome the force of cohesion does it fly away completely — in other words, vapourize. . . .

According to the Dixon cohesion theory, the water in the vessels forms an unbroken column from the roots up to the topmost leaves. The cohesive forces in this column of water resist breaking, so that when the osmotic gradient set up by transpiration exerts a pull on the top end of this column of water, the whole column moves upwards just as the oil dipstick of a motor car comes up when you pull the top end of it. Notice that we have now got rid of the idea of suction and the difficulty of the water barometer. The force that pulls the water up is an osmotic one, and it is transmitted down the stem by the cohesion between the water molecules.

Other plants, other pages

For **Trees,** see pp. 77-89.

For **Edible Wild Plants,** see p. 102.

For **Cannabis,** see p. 103.

For **Growing Plants,** see Land Use section, pp. 72-105.

How to Know the Lichens

Want a hobby all to yourself? Learn to recognize and collect lichens, the scaly or hairy stuff on rocks and trees, for a highly sophisticated appreciation of landscape detail. Inviting book. —SB

How to Know the Lichens
Mason E. Hale
1969, 1979; 246 pp.
$5.95 postpaid from:
Wm. C. Brown Company
2460 Karper Boulevard
Dubuque, IA 52001

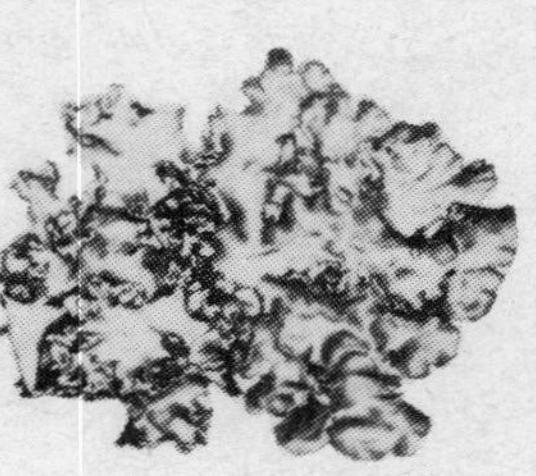

•

Everyone is familiar with plants as green chlorophyll-containing organisms that manufacture their own food. A lichen (pronounced "liken") is also a plant but a very special kind, for when we dissect and examine it under a microscope, we find that it is composed of two completely different organisms, microscopic green or blue-green **algae** that are related to free-living algae and colorless **fungal threads** called hyphae. These two components grow together in a harmonious association referred to as symbiosis, or more simply a "living together." Lichen symbiosis, however, differs basically from all other kinds in that a new plant body, the **thallus**, is formed, and this thallus has no resemblance to either a fungus or an alga growing alone. This new composite organism behaves as a single independent plant, the green alga manufacturing sugars by photosynthesis and the fungus living off these foodstuffs and making up the bulk of the plant body.

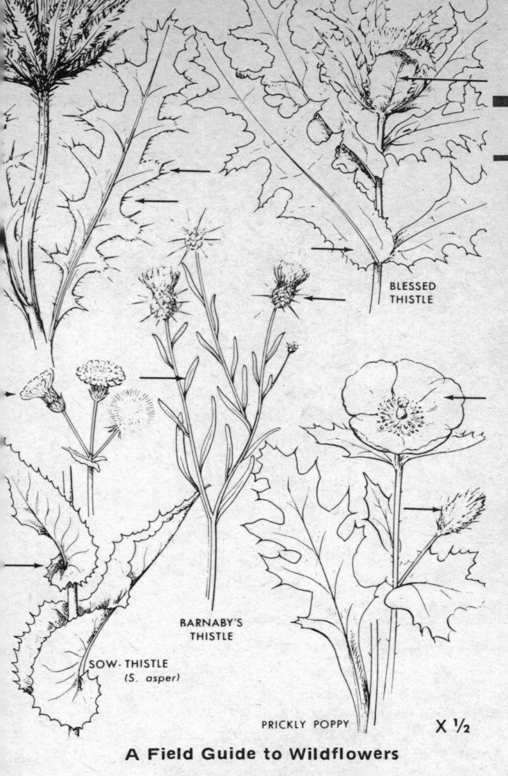

X ½

A Field Guide to Wildflowers

THISTLES AND OTHER PRICKLY PLANTS

See also Gorse, p. 154, and Prickly-pear, p. 100.

YELLOW THISTLE *Cirsium horridulum*
COMPOSITE FAMILY (Compositae)
Our native yellow thistle. Note the *deeply incised, extremely bristly leaves.* Flower head large (3 in.) supported by spiny bracts, sometimes purple or white. 1–3 ft. Sandy soil, fields, shores, salt marshes. Near coast from s. Maine south.
MAY–AUG.

BLESSED THISTLE Alien *Cnicus benedictus*
COMPOSITE FAMILY (Compositae)
A hairy, deep yellow thistle. Note the *large leafy bracts* that surround the flower head. Leaves not as spiny as in preceding species, broader at base. 10–30 in. Roadsides, waste places. Local, s. Canada, U.S. MAY–AUG.

BARNABY'S THISTLE Alien *Centaurea solstitialis*
COMPOSITE FAMILY (Compositae)
Note the *very long spines* at the base of the 1-in. flower head; no leafy bracts. Leaves woolly, *without spines.* 10–30 in. Fields, waste places, roadsides. Local, s. Ontario, New York, Massachusetts south. JULY–OCT.

SPINY-LEAVED SOW-THISTLE Alien *Sonchus asper*
COMPOSITE FAMILY (Compositae)
The sow-thistles have dandelionlike flowers and leaves edged with prickles. See p. 110 and accompanying color plate for further discussion and distinctions between 3 species of *Sonchus.*

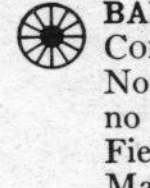
PRICKLY POPPY Alien *Argemone mexicana*
POPPY FAMILY (Papaveraceae)
POPPY SUBFAMILY (Papaveroideae)
The large *cuplike yellow flower* with 4 to 6 petals in conjunction with the somewhat *thistle-like leaves* identifies this species. Seedpod ovoid, prickly. Waste places. Escaped from cultivation locally. MAY–SEPT.

Wildflower guides by color

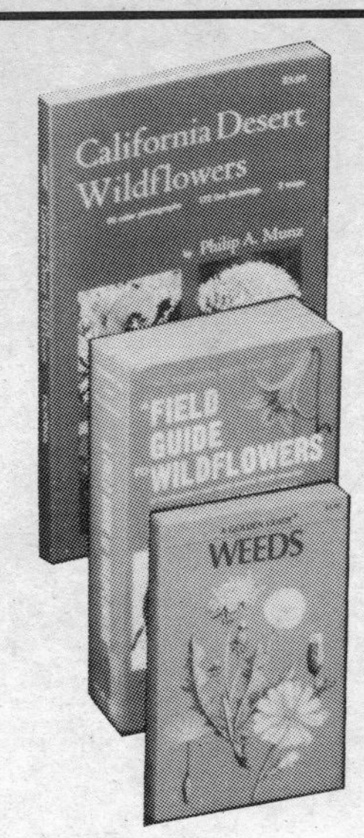

Can't stand learning tech words? These guides are arranged by flower color (sometimes fruit color) with more detail within each color section. North America only.
—Peter Warshall

A Golden Guide to Flowers (1950) and **A Golden Guide to Weeds** (1973), by H. Zim and A. Martin, $1.95 each from: Golden Press, P.O. Box 700, Racine, WI 53404.

East of the Rockies you need only one: **A Field Guide to the Wildflowers**, by Roger Tory Peterson and Margaret McKenny, 1977; $6.95 from: Houghton Mifflin Co., Wayside Road, Burlington, MA 01803.

West of the Rockies, the best series is by Philip A. Munz:

California Spring Wildflowers, 1961; $4.95.
California Desert Wildflowers, 1962; $3.95.
California Mountain Wildflowers, 1963; $3.95.
Shore Wildflowers of California, Oregon and Washington, 1965; $4.95.

All from: University of California Press, 2223 Fulton Street, Berkeley, CA 94720.

BUTTERCUPS There are about 40 species of Buttercups in the United States, distributed widely in low moist places, meadows, and marshes. A few even grow submerged in water. Some are creepers, but most are erect and branching. They all have shiny, "varnished," butter-yellow petals (occasionally white), enclosing numerous stamens. The Bulb Buttercup has adapted itself to lawns and meadows.—*Spring to fall. Crowfoot Family.*

40 species

—A Golden Guide to Flowers

Wildflowers and Weeds

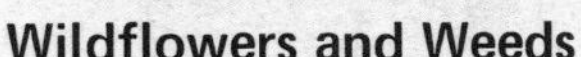

The best wildflower guide to date. Great key (using simplified taxonomy). 650 fine color photos. Accurate habitat notes. Pocket size. You couldn't ask for too much more.

Covers the Great Lakes Region of US/Canada. But, excellent for the Eastern Hardwood forest, the Great Lakes mixed Forest, the Northern Conifer Forest and the open prairies.
—Peter Warshall
[Suggested by David Mladenoff]

Wildflowers and Weeds
(A Guide in Full Color)
Booth Courtenay and James H. Zimmerman
1972, 1977; 144 pp.

$7.50 postpaid from:
Van Nostrand Reinhold Co.
Order Department
7625 Empire Drive
Florence, KY 41042
or Whole Earth Household Store

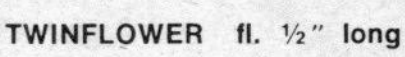
TWINFLOWER fl. ½" long

TINKER'S WEED fl. ½"

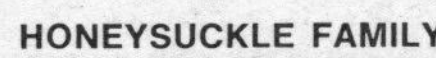
HONEYSUCKLE FAMILY

BUSH HONEYSUCKLE, ***Diervilla lonicera*** / June–July / ½'–3', erect to arching / Dry or rocky woods and forests, cliffs / Flowers yellow to red; leaves finely-toothed
(Other woody Honeysuckles, *Lonicera*, differ in having untoothed leaves.)

TINKER'S WEED, ***Triosteum perfoliatum*** / May–June / 2'–4' / Dry to medium woods / Leaves vary from slender-based to joining around stem; flowers red to greenish-yellow

TWINFLOWER, ***Linnaea borealis*** / June–Aug. / Flower stalks to 5" / Moist to dry forests / Flowers fragrant; plant creeping, evergreen

BUSH HONEYSUCKLE fl. ¾" long

MOCK CUCUMBER fl. ⅜"

•

A man must see before he can say. —*Thoreau*

This workbook is designed to help you *see* the wildflowers, those surviving without, or in spite of, man's hand.

Flowers of the Southwest (by ecological areas)

Flowers mean even more in the desert, and they are more specific to particular habitats. —*SB*

Flowers of the Southwest Mountains by Leslie P. Arnberger, 1952, 1974; $2.00.
Flowers of the Southwest Mesas by Pauline M. Patraw, 1952, 1977; $2.00.
Flowers of the Southwest Deserts by Natt N. Dodge, 1951, 1976; $2.00.

All from: Southwest Parks and Monuments Association, P.O. Box 1562, Globe, AZ 85501.

What Kinda Cactus Izzat?

Totally corny. Totally great. Yes, you can even learn dem cacti names. —*Peter Warshall*

What Kinda Cactus Izzat?
("Who's Who" in the Desert)
Reg Manning
1941; 107 pp.

$2.95 postpaid from:
Reganson Cartoon Books
Phoenix, AZ 85010

•

The jumping Cholla is covered with a mass of thistle-white needles that appear soft and harmless. But barely brush against 'em and they attach to you. The joints of the Cholla are so loosely attached that, in the resulting activity, a whole section may break loose and come with you. The victim of the jumping cactus may not realize that he has even touched the plant until he feels it take hold. When he comes to earth, he may be some distance from the offending plant — and, invariably, he will swear that the piece sticking to him JUMPED across the intervening space to make the attack.

Flower guides by simplified botany

No need for botanical lingo except words like "pistil" and "stamen." —*Peter Warshall*

Flower Finder (A Manual for Identifying Spring Wildflowers and Flower Families East of the Rockies) by Mary Watts, 1955; $1.25 from: Nature Study Guild, Box 972, Berkeley, CA 94701. *For spring flowers, east of the Rockies and north of the Smokies.*

New Field Book of American Wildflowers by Harold W. Rickett, 1963; $7.95 from: G.P. Putnam's Sons, 200 Madison Avenue, New York, NY 10016.

Notes on Making an Herbarium

Forget the museum stuffiness. Beautifully mounted flowers and grasses are works of art. This pamphlet is solid advice on collecting, drying, materials and mounting.
—Peter Warshall

Notes on Making an Herbarium
ARNOLDIA
Vol. 28, Nos. 8-9
1968; 42 pp.

$2 postpaid from:
The Arnold Arboretum
The Arborway
Jamaica Plain, MA 02130

THE RISING SUN
NEIGHBORHOOD NEWSLETTER

Fun Phrases to Sing Over and Over

1. "The Abraham Lincoln Memorial" (over and over) to the tune of The Mexican Hat Dance.
2. "Lloyd George knew my father, Father knew Lloyd George" (on and on) to the tune of Onward Christian Soldiers.
3. "Happy Anniversary" to the tune of the William Tell Overture.
4. "We gather together to gather together" to the tune of We Gather Together.
5. "George Washington Bridge" to the tune of that song they play at circuses while the trapeze show is on that may be called The Loveliest Night of the Year but I'm not sure because I always think of it as George Washington Bridge.
6. "Purple violets" to the tune of Purple Violets.

NOTE: Absolutely anything, no matter how mundane, obscene or nonsensical can be sung to the tune of Lead On, O King Eternal. At last week's party we sang The Declaration of Independence to that tune which is actually called Lancashire and next week we're starting on Das Kapital, in German.

7. "The Pentagon" to the tune of O Tannenbaum.

Insects of the World →

Of all the books I've seen while helping prepare this book, **Insects of the World** *is the most spectacular. Everybody's dream book (except for the price). Linsenmaier is artist, photographer, naturalist, ecologist, entomologist, writer, anatomist — just plain far out. All the usual book blurb adjectives go with this production — up-to-date, accurate, fascinating with awe-inspiring paintings, drawings, diagrams and photos. This man's totem love is not in doubt.* —Peter Warshall
[Suggested by John Todd]

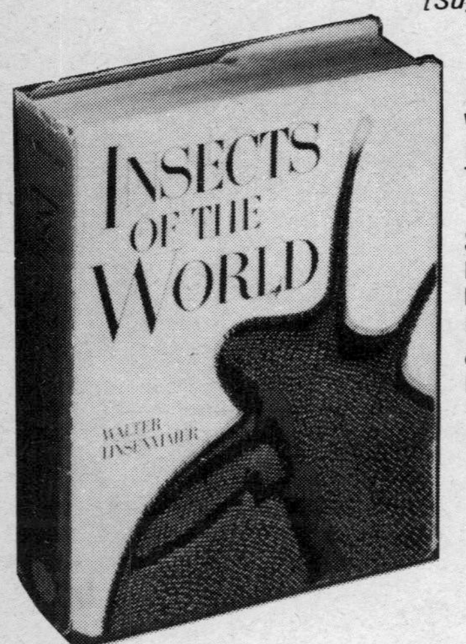

Insects of the World
Walter Linsenmaier
(Leigh E. Chadwick, Translator)
1972; 392 pp.
$25 postpaid from:
McGraw-Hill Book Co.
Princeton Road
Hightstown, NJ 08520
or Whole Earth
Household Store

•

WARNING COLORS

Many brightly colored insects, particularly larvae, show themselves openly and are conspicuous from afar. These insects do advertise their presence with warning colors, for they enjoy the protection of distasteful, even toxic, body fluids. There are many examples. Caterpillars that feed on poisonous herbs may carry the toxic effect through their development even to the mature form. The blister beetles *(meloidae)* contain canthardin, a toxin dangerous to man and beast. Many caterpillars are clothed with urticating (stinging) hairs or with thorns, some of which are filled with acid. Certain larval moths *(Dirphia)* imitate this kind of caterpillar not only in the coloration and specific hair pattern of the abdomen, but also in the contortions the body goes through.

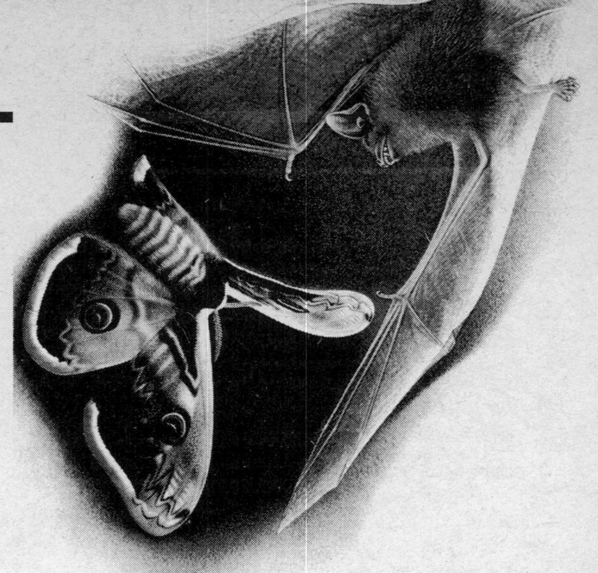

Blue underwing moth pursued by bat

Oleander hawk moth on woodbine

Insects In Flight

I look on insects as genius miniaturization. Like TV repairmen look at transistors. Remarkably small and intricate. Tiny, precise, almost jewels of mechanization. But, living and totally "pre"-occupied with sponging sweat from my palm's heart line.

This book is for the already converted. Unabashedly, Nachtigall is immersed in insect flight. How the fly lands on the ceiling. How the thrip swims through air. How the mosquito hums its wings in courtship. How the muscles rev up. It's just about the most irrelevant and interesting information I know. The photos and drawings cause a wondrous, dumbfounded stare. —Peter Warshall
[Suggested by Albert Saijo]

Insects In Flight
Werner Nachtigall
1968; 150 pp.
$17.95 postpaid from:
McGraw-Hill Book Co.
Princeton Road
Hightstown, NJ 08520

•

These minute insects cannot fall to the ground as quickly as can a shot bird, or a mayfly dying after its nuptial flight. Because of their small size and very small weight, they fall very, very slowly, somewhat like a small coin dropped into a pot of honey. Indeed to tiny insects the air is a viscous as honey is to a coin. To them the air is quite a different medium from the one we know, and they can propel themselves through it with much less trouble than we can, rowing themselves as an oarsman rows his boat, and as an *Acilius* swims through the water with its oarlike legs. All the factors concerned, the size and velocity of the moving bodies, and the density and viscosity of the surrounding medium, can be summarised by saying that for the tiniest insects the air behaves like a thick syrup, through which they can fly in the same way that a water-beetle can swim through water.

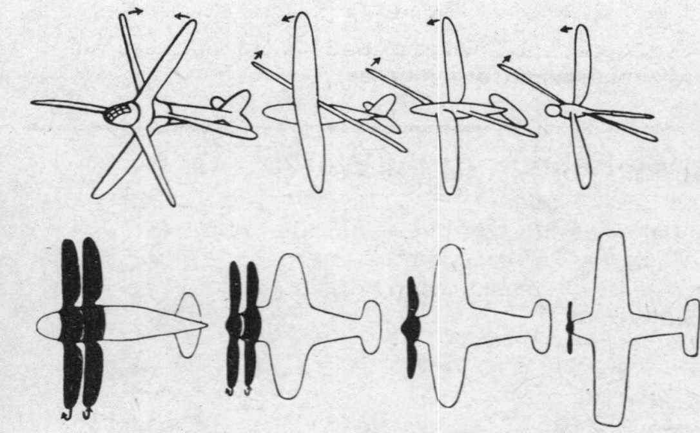

The sequence of ideas by which a biologist (above) and a technologist (below) might each arrive at the idea of a contrarotating propeller. Each sequence should be read from right to left, and is explained in the text.

A Field Guide to the Insects

90,000 species of insects inhabit North America: chewing lice, sucking lice, earwigs, stoneflies, springtails, twisted-winged parasites, butterflies, beetles, thrips and bugs. This guide covers 579 of the insect families and has at least one illustration for each. Amazing! I have rarely found the exact moth or water scorpion but always came close enough to feel good. Pretty easy to use considering the mind-boggling diversity.

Borror is also the author of the best textbook on insects — **An Introduction to the Study of Insects,** *3rd edition, Donald Borror and Dwight D. Long, 1970; $22.95 postpaid from Holt, Rinehart and Winston, 383 Madison Avenue, New York, NY 10017.* —Peter Warshall

A Field Guide to the Insects
(of America North of Mexico)
Donald J. Borror & Richard E. White
1974; 404 pp.
$6.95 postpaid from:
Houghton Mifflin Co.
Wayside Road
Burlington, MA 01803
or Whole Earth
Household Store

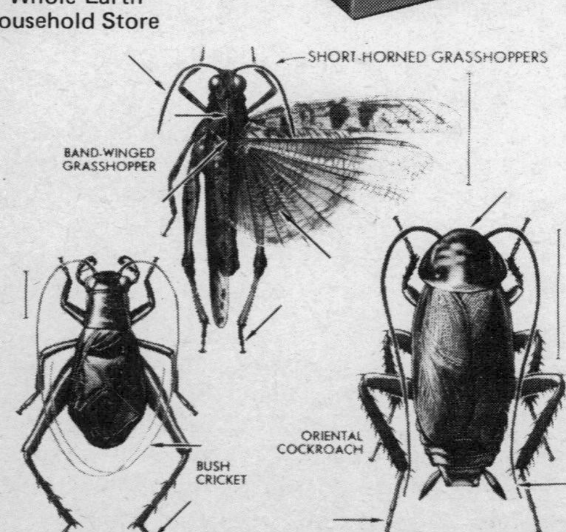

Butterflies and Moths

No book on moths and butterflies of North America has yet to knock me out. This little guide has about 3% of the 10,000 North American species. There is no real key but, by flipping through, I usually find the critter most like the one I saw. **The Moth Book** *by William Holland is more technical but also very complete (1968; $6 from Dover Press, 180 Varick Street, New York, NY 10014).* —Peter Warshall

Butterflies and Moths
(A Golden Nature Guide)
Robert T. Mitchell & Herbert Zim
1964; 160 pp.
$1.95 postpaid from:
Golden Press
P.O. Box 700
Racine, WI 53404
or Whole Earth
Household Store

BRUSH-FOOTED BUTTERFLIES are named for their tiny forelegs, hairy and useless for walking. Next to skippers they make up the largest butterfly family. Most are medium- to large-sized species.

THE GREATER FRITILLARIES are common in temperate regions. Males and females sometimes differ in color and markings. Caterpillars feed at night, mostly on violets. They remain hidden during the day. Most fritillaries raise a single brood and overwinter as larvae.

VARIEGATED FRITILLARY ranges over most of the U.S. except the Pacific Northwest. It lacks the typical silver spots on the underside of the wings. The Mexican Fritillary, similar in form but with plainer hindwings, is found from southern Texas to southern California.

REGAL FRITILLARY frequents roadsides and wet meadows, feeding on milkweed and thistle. Both rows of spots on the hindwing are creamy white on the female but only the inner row is on the male. Larva is like Great Spangled's but black, mottled with yellow.

Variegated Fritillary 2.3-2.5"

GREAT SPANGLED FRITILLARY is single-brooded in the North and double-brooded in the South. Larva hibernates soon after hatching and the following spring feeds at night on violets. The adults, in typical fritillary fashion, prefer marshes and damp meadows. This is one of the best known fritillaries.

APHRODITE FRITILLARY, similar to Great Spangled, is smaller and has a narrow, yellow marginal band under the hindwing. It prefers high elevations. Another species, the Mountain, resembles Aphrodite, but the hindwing beneath is darker and forewing has a dark margin. From so. Can. to the Rockies.

3.0-3.3"

Spiders and Their Kin

The most informative, accurate, entertaining and useful guide to spiders ever written. —Peter Warshall

Spiders and their Kin
(A Golden Nature Guide)
Herbert & Lorna Levi, and Herbert Zim
1968; 160 pp.
$1.95 postpaid from:
Golden Press
P.O. Box 700
Racine, WI 53404
or Whole Earth
Household Store

"How to Know" Series

Good technical illustrated keys for those naturalists that get heavily into knowing all that's happening. —Peter Warshall

Pictured Key Nature Series:
How to Know the Immature Insects ($3.95)
How to Know the Insects ($2.95)
How to Know the Butterflies ($5.95)
How to Know the Beetles ($7.95)
How to Know the Spiders ($6.95)

postpaid from:
William C. Brown & Co.
2460 Kerper Blvd.
Dubuque, IA 52001

Field guides to reptiles and amphibians

West: Better distribution maps, more illustrations of color variations (like the western garter snake group) and even pictures of tadpoles and salamander larvae — this guide is great for the southwest and area west of the Rockies. If you find something weird, it's probably a real discovery. Everything else Stebbins has covered.

East: Conant is older and less beautiful but equally useful for the eastern species. —Peter Warshall

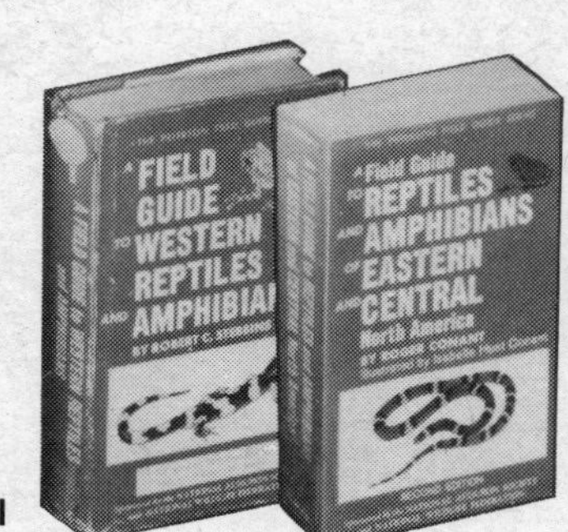

A Field Guide to Western Reptiles and Amphibians
(Peterson Field Guide No. 16)
Robert Stebbins
1966; 279 pp.
$7.95

A Field Guide to Reptiles and Amphibians of Eastern and Central North America
(Peterson Field Guide No. 12)
Roger Conant
1958; 429 pp.
$7.95

both postpaid from:
Houghton Mifflin Co.
Wayside Road
Burlington, MA 01803
or Whole Earth Household Store

•

HANDLING THE CATCH

1. **A Bullfrog**, like other amphibians, is slippery. Encircle its waist with your fingers so it won't kick itself free. Any large or medium-sized frogs may be held in the same way, but small frogs are best grasped by the hind legs.

2. **A Snapper's tail** makes a good handle, but keep the head aimed away from your leg.

↑

3. **Large salamanders** should be held firmly but gently with the entire hand. Let the head protrude. Small salamanders can be caged briefly within your clenched fist.

4. **Lizards** are best immobilized by holding their feet, but the body should also be gripped to prevent sudden lunges. Make it a practice *never* to grab or hold a lizard by the tail, for it may break right off in your hands.

5. **Softshell turtles** are difficult to hold. Pressing against the neck with your fingers will help keep the head from protruding far enough to turn around and bite at you. Also watch out for flailing legs with their sharp claws. *Large* snappers should be carried in this same fashion.

6. **Carrying a snake bag.** With your hand well above the knot and the bag held away from your leg, a venomous snake may be safely transported. In the case of a harmless species, the knot and the empty part of the bag may be thrust upward under your belt, letting the snake dangle there until you return to your car or base. This leaves both hands free.

7. **Glass jars** are safest for transporting small fragile specimens. They retain moisture and may save your catch from injury. More than one collector has sat or stepped on a collecting bag with fatal consequences to the specimens inside.

8. **A stevedore's hook** works well on logs, boards, and smaller rocks, but it requires stooping. An advantage is that it can be thrust under your belt when not in use.

9. **A potato rake** or similar tool is useful for overturning rocks. The long handle lets you stand erect and keeps you well away if by chance you should uncover a poisonous snake.

Living Reptiles of the World

Personally, I've had about as much joy from frog song as bird song, and a snake in the hand is as big a thrill as a chipmunk. This big picture book is a nice scan across the variety. —SB

Living Reptiles of the World
Karl Schmidt and Robert Inger
1957; 287 pp.

$19.95 postpaid from:
Doubleday & Co., Inc.
501 Franklin Avenue
Garden City, NY 11530

•

On account of our great familiarity with them, we are inclined to forget that turtles are really the oldest type of living reptiles, vastly more ancient in lineage than the fossil dinosaurs and most of the other extinct forms. The turtles really deserve the name of "living fossils" much more than do some of the creatures to which it is commonly applied.

Top Books in Reptiles and Amphibians

Gnomes of the Night: the Spadefoot Toads by Arthur Bragg, 1965; $7.00 from: University of Pennsylvania Press, 3933 Walnut Street, Philadelphia, PA 19104.

So Excellent a Fishe (A Natural History of Sea Turtles) by Archie Carr. Originally published 1973 by Doubleday; now out of print.

Turtles of the United States by Carl Ernst and Roger Barbour, 1972; $22.50 from: University Press of Kentucky, Lexington, KY 40506.

Snakes (The Keeper and the Kept) by Carl Kauffeld, 1969; $8.95 from: Doubleday Press, 501 Franklin Avenue, Garden City, NY 11530.

Rattlesnakes (Their habits, life histories, and influence on mankind — second edition) by Laurence Klauber, 2 volumes; 1533 pages, 1972; $50 from: University of California Press, 2223 Fulton Street, Berkeley, CA 94720.

The Last of the Ruling Reptiles (Alligators, Crocodiles and their Kin) by Wilfred T. Neill, 1971; $17.50 from: Columbia University Press, Stock Department, 136 South Broadway, Irvington-on-Hudson, NY 10533.

Herpetology by Kenneth Porter, 1972; $22.50 from: W.B. Saunders, West Washington Square, Philadelphia, PA 19105.

Of Scientists and Salamanders by Victor Chandler Twitty, 1966; $9.25 from: W.H. Freeman and Company, 660 Market Street, San Francisco, CA 94104.

—Joe Copp

A Field Guide to Rocks and Minerals

Don't just sit there. Go out and collect some rocks. Identify them and give them to your sweetie. "Here, hon, for you. It's kyanite. Matches your eyes. I found it in some mica schist." —SB

A Field Guide to Rocks and Minerals
(Fourth Edition; Peterson Field Guide No. 7)
Frederick H. Pough
1953, 1976; 315 pp.
$6.95 postpaid from:
Houghton Mifflin Co.
Wayside Road
Burlington, MA 01803
or Whole Earth Household Store

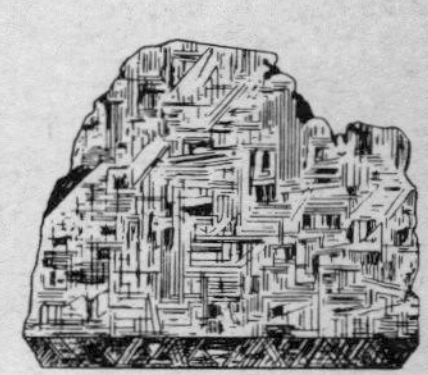

Meteorite

Minerals and Man

Get it straight. Organic means containing Carbon. Inorganic means no Carbon and usually a substance formed before life began on Earth. Oil and pearls are organic — and therefore not mineral. Asbestos (a "cloth") and brimstone (a rock that burns) are minerals. Any more questions? ***Minerals and Man*** *has sumptuous photographs, easy prose, and particularly excellent descriptions connecting man's use of and need for the inorganic world. There should be maps and maybe a section on "endangered" species of minerals. But this is the best expansive introduction.*

There is not a good field guide or easy path to identification of minerals. Hurlbut's edition of ***J.D. Dana's Manual of Minerology*** *(1971, 1977; $25.50 postpaid from: John Wiley and Sons, One Wiley Drive, Somerset, NJ 08873) is the best place to start.* —Peter Warshall

Minerals and Man
Cornelius S. Hurlbut
1970; 304 pp.

OUT OF PRINT
Random House

Get this book back in print!

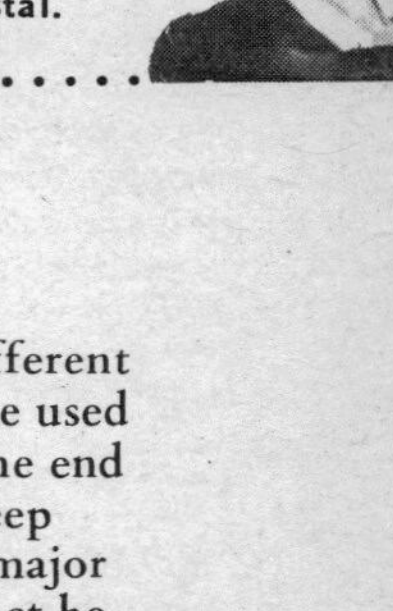

→ A transparent octahedral diamond crystal.

THE RISING SUN
NEIGHBORHOOD NEWSLETTER

Ray Jason juggles a knife, a sickle and a hatchet! Ray Jason juggles four torches! He juggles two hatchets and an apple while eating the apple while riding on a unicycle! Ray Jason juggles five balls and catches the last one without using his hands, elbows, armpits, knees, feet, or crotch! Sometimes he does all of the above and more looking directly into the late afternoon sun so the audience won't have to and sometimes he gets hurt — about every 2 months. I asked him if he had a funny line to reassure the audience when that happened and he said it depended; there isn't a lot to say if you're being carted off to the hospital.

Why does Ray Jason do these things? In 1968 he was supposed to enter Columbia law school, but the graduate student deferment was ended and he got drafted and went to Vietnam. When he came back he didn't feel much like contributing to the society. He was washing dishes and writing a book in San Francisco when he noticed some people were making good money as street performers even when they weren't good. He noticed there weren't any jugglers, and he had learned to juggle when he was a kid. He practiced a while and started juggling on the streets. He was a mute act at first; he was afraid to say anything even though he'd been a public speaking star in college — leader of his college debate team.

The hardest thing at the start was developing an audience. Recently, he performed at a shopping center in Castro Valley and doing his stuff all day he never had more than 8 people at a time. They just stared and kept walking. Too strange, too different than TV. That's what everyone was like at first, but now a lot of people are used to street performers and are willing to get involved. That's what makes street performance different than most of the entertainment people are used to — the audience is part of it. Toward the end of his torch juggling, Ray Jason says, "Keep those hands ready. We're approaching a major applause point." Toward the end of his act he says, "This is the last trick of the day so we're going to permit unrelenting applause." Sometimes on his cigar box trick, he has half of the audience ooh and the other half ahh. He's training his audience and they love it.

Now he wants to change other street performers. Ninety percent of them view the street as a step to the big time. He thinks they should think about street performing as medium manageable success. Street performing as a lifetime career. Work to make it respectable, work to make it a way to live. Learn to live and entertain and think on a neighborhood level.

Ray Jason told me these things at a craft fair on College Avenue where he was performing. He looked at some of the booths and said he'd been in on the beginning of the whole street fair movement and it had gotten commercial and out of hand in some ways, but he was really happy to see it happen. "These people are selling their stuff at 40% of what they'd have to sell it for in a store and that means for once they don't have to deal with the Pacific Heights matrons. I mean, that's where the money is, if you're making beautiful things that's who you have to deal with, but sometimes you get tired of those Pacific Heights ladies and want to sell things to your friends. And that's what fairs like this are about, dealing with people one to one, dealing with your friends."

Birds of North America

A good guide is portable, quickly gives you habitat, migration, locality, size, color patterns, and easily seen habits. No book guide has helped anyone to learn bird songs. I like a guide that coughs up the NAME of the bird without distracting me from the actual trip of being there with binoculars, my hearing, and flashing wings. In spite of problems with color reproduction and pages on the western flycatchers, Golden's little **Birds of North America** *provides the easiest access to bird identification. Drawings are conveniently opposite all the song, locality and comparative information. The book has summary pages of confusing groups like the sparrows, warblers and hawks. It also has accurate little vignettes on typical flight patterns and behavior like tail-wagging that makes it all the easier.* —Peter Warshall

Birds of North America
(A Golden Field Guide)
Robbins, Bruun, Zim, and Singer
1966; 340 pp.

$4.95 postpaid from:
Golden Press
P.O. Box 700
Racine, WI 53404
or Whole Earth Household Store

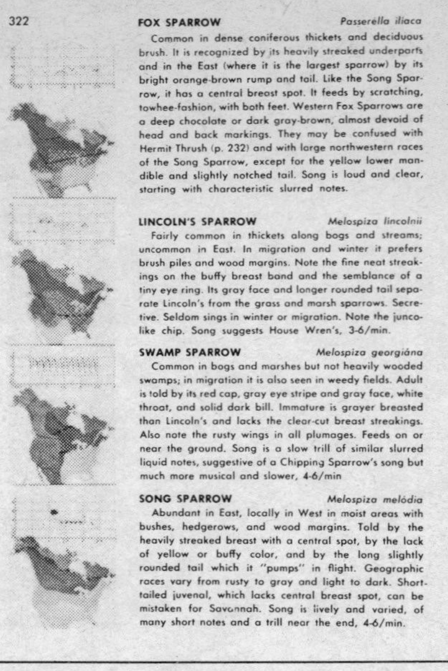

322

FOX SPARROW *Passerella iliaca*

Common in dense coniferous thickets and deciduous brush. It is recognized by its heavily streaked underparts and in the East (where it is the largest sparrow) by its bright orange-brown rump and tail. Like the Song Sparrow, it has a central breast spot. It feeds by scratching, towhee-fashion, with both feet. Western Fox Sparrows are a deep chocolate or dark gray-brown, almost devoid of head and back markings. They may be confused with Hermit Thrush (p. 232) and with large northwestern races of the Song Sparrow, except for the yellow lower mandible and slightly notched tail. Song is loud and clear, starting with characteristic slurred notes.

LINCOLN'S SPARROW *Melospiza lincolnii*

Fairly common in thickets along bogs and streams; uncommon in East. In migration and winter it prefers brush piles and wood margins. Note the fine neat streakings on the buffy breast band and the semblance of a tiny eye ring. Its gray face and longer rounded tail separate Lincoln's from the grass and marsh sparrows. Secretive. Seldom sings in winter or migration. Note the junco-like chip. Song suggests House Wren's, 3-6/min.

SWAMP SPARROW *Melospiza georgiána*

Common in bogs and marshes but not heavily wooded swamps; in migration it is also seen in weedy fields. Adult is told by its red cap, gray eye stripe and gray face, white throat, and solid dark bill. Immature is grayer breasted than Lincoln's and lacks the clear-cut breast streakings. Also note the rusty wings in all plumages. Feeds on or near the ground. Song is a slow trill of similar slurred liquid notes, suggestive of a Chipping Sparrow's song but much more musical and slower, 4-6/min

SONG SPARROW *Melospiza melódia*

Abundant in East, locally in West in moist areas with bushes, hedgerows, and wood margins. Told by the heavily streaked breast with a central spot, by the lack of yellow or buffy color, and by the long slightly rounded tail which it "pumps" in flight. Geographic races vary from rusty to gray and light to dark. Short-tailed juvenal, which lacks central breast spot, can be mistaken for Savannah. Song is lively and varied, of many short notes and a trill near the end, 4-6/min.

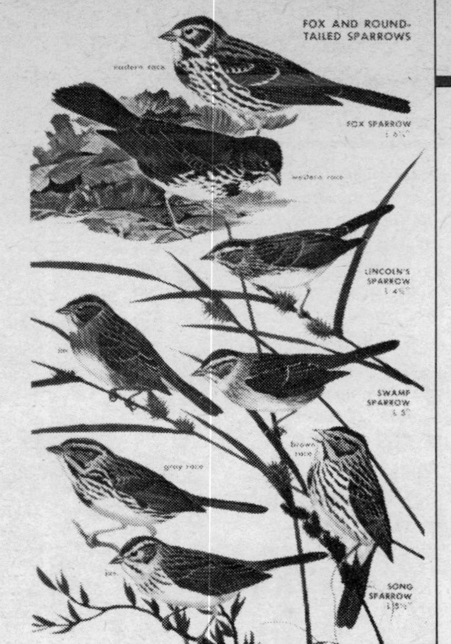

Peterson Field Guides

Peterson's guides run a close second to the Golden Guide but, except for his pointer technique, most important information is stashed on some other page than the one you're on. Migration dates and localities are difficult unless you can instantaneously conjure the map and seasons of North America. Peterson's still surpasses the new Audubon Society bird field guides. —Peter Warshall

Plate 27

LARGE SHORE-BIRDS

AVOCET Black and white back pattern, thin upturned bill.	p. 75
BLACK-NECKED STILT White below; black unpatterned wings.	p. 75
OYSTER-CATCHER (AMERICAN) White wing patches, black head, red bill.	p. 61
HUDSONIAN GODWIT Upturned bill, ringed tail.	p. 74
MARBLED GODWIT Long upturned bill, tawny brown color.	p. 74
HUDSONIAN CURLEW Decurved bill, brown color, striped crown.	p. 65

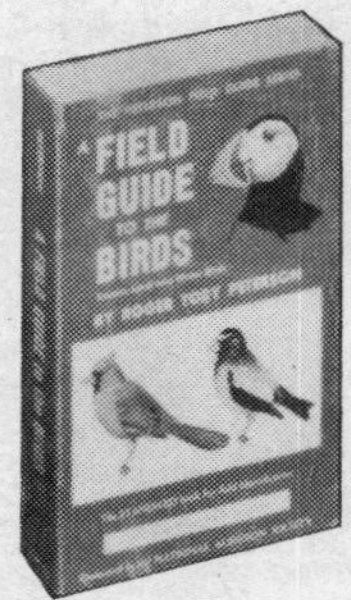

A Field Guide to the Birds
(Eastern North America — Eastern Land and Water Birds; Peterson Field Guide Number 1)
Roger Tory Peterson
1934, 1947; 230 pp.
$6.95

A Field Guide to Western Birds
(Peterson Field Guide Number 2)
Roger Tory Peterson
1961; 215 pp.
$7.95

A Field Guide to The Birds of Texas and Adjacent States
(Peterson Guide No. 13)
Roger Tory Peterson
1963; 304 pp.
$7.95
all postpaid from:
Houghton Mifflin Co.
Wayside Road
Burlington, MA 01803
or Whole Earth Household Store

A Field Guide to Mexican Birds

The most beautiful plates by Peterson I've seen. Synthesizes all previous bird books on Mexico. Carry this book and follow Peter Alden's advice in **Finding the Birds in Western Mexico** *(Sonora, Sinaloa & Nayarit, 1969; $5.95 from University of Arizona Press, Box 3398, Tucson, AZ 85722) and Ernest P. Edwards'* **Finding Birds in Mexico** *(all other Mexican states, 1968, 1976; $10.70 from E.P. Edwards, P.O. Box AQ, Sweet Briar, VA 24595). Edwards also has a field guide with Spanish bird name equivalents (***A Field Guide to the Birds in Mexico***, 1978; $10.70 from the same address).* —Peter Warshall

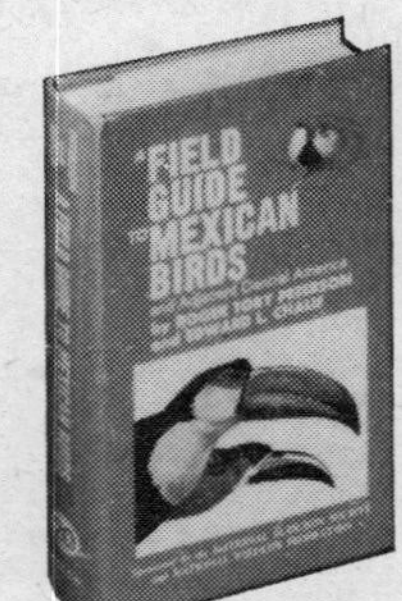

A Field Guide to Mexican Birds
Roger Tory Peterson and Edward Chalif
1973; 298 pp.

$10.95 postpaid from:
Houghton Mifflin Co.
Wayside Road
Burlington, MA 01803

Watching Birds

Fills the hole between "sport-birder" field guides and heavy-science ornithological textbooks. This delightful volume has abundant attractive drawings to illustrate its points. Current non-technical ornithological principles and concepts neatly embroidered with successful attempts to increase birders' effectiveness as biological interpreters. Concise summaries of giant notions. —Rich Stallcup

This Herring Gull is in the posture associated with the final stage of what behaviorists have named the "trumpeting call." It is a challenge that precedes — or prevents — aggressive encounters with other individuals.

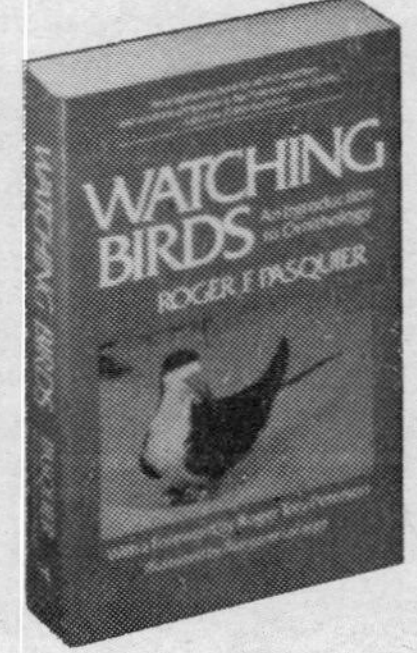

Watching Birds
(An Introduction to Ornithology)
Roger F. Pasquier
1977; 301 pp.

$11.95 postpaid from:
Houghton-Mifflin Co.
Wayside Road
Burlington, MA 01803
or Whole Earth Household Store

Best bird books

The Birds (Life Nature Library) by Roger T. Peterson, 1968; $7.95 from: Time-Life Books, 200 West Street, Waltham, MA 02154. *Best intro to all aspects of the Family of Birds.*

Families of Birds by Oliver Austin, 1971; $1.95 from: Golden Press, P.O. Box 700, Racine, WI 53404. *Best intro to whole Earth bird diversity.*

The Life of the Robin by David Lack, 1965; $1.50 from: Watts Publishing Co., 730 Fifth Avenue, New York, NY 10019. *The English robin by Britain's top birdman. There are many ways to view one bird.*

The Herring Gull's World by Niko Tinbergen, 1971; $3.95 from: Harper and Row, Keystone Industrial Park, Scranton, PA 18512. *He got a Nobel Prize for loving gulls. Pioneer in vertebrate perception.*

A Field Guide to the Nests, Eggs and Nestlings of North American Birds, by Colin Harrison, 1976; $12.50 from: Times Books, Harper and Row, Keystone Industrial Park, Scranton, PA 18512. *The darling baby birds, their beautiful eggs and diverse nests. A great gift for the newborn's mother.* —Peter Warshall

Regional bird guides and identification aids

WESTERN UNITED STATES

Birds of Idaho by T. Burleigh, 1958; $37.50 from: University of Oklahoma Press, 1005 Asp Avenue, Norman, OK 73019

Washington Birds by E. Larrison and John W. Weber, 1977; $1.75 from: University Press of Idaho, Idaho Research Foundation, Box 3368, Moscow, ID 83843.

EASTERN UNITED STATES

Alabama Birds (2nd edition), 1976; $22.50 from: University of Alabama Press, Box 2877, University, AL 35486.

Georgia Birds by T. Burleigh, 1958; $37.50 from: University of Oklahoma Press, 1005 Asp Avenue, Norman, OK 73019.

Kentucky Birds by R. Barbour et. al., 1973; $13.50 from: University Press of Kentucky, Lexington, KY 40506. *Great book.*

South Carolina Bird Life by A. Sprunt and E.C. Burnham, 1978; $19.50 from: University of South Carolina Press, Columbia, SC 29208.

A Guide to Bird Finding East of the Mississippi by O. Pettingill, 1977; $16.95 from: Oxford University Press. 200 Madison Avenue, New York, NY 10016. *Special on New York City and 147 other cities.*

A Guide to North American Hawk Watching by D. Heintzelman, 1979; $6.95 from: Pennsylvania State University Press, 215 Wagner Bldg., University Park, PA 16802.

OCEANS AND ISLANDS OFFSHORE NORTH AMERICA

Birds of the Ocean by Wilfrid B. Alexander, 1963; $6.95 from: G.P. Putnam and Sons, 200 Madison Avenue, New York, NY 10016.

COASTAL AND FRESH WATER BIRDS

Ducks, Geese and Swans of North America by Frank Bellrose, revised by E.H. Kortright, 1975; $15 from: Stackpole Books, Cameron and Keller Streets, P.O. Box 1831, Harrisburg, PA 17105. *Great for eclipse plumages and hybrids.*

Audubon Water Bird Guide (Water, Game and Large Land Birds) by Richard Pough, 1951; $9.95 from: Doubleday and Co., 501 Franklin Avenue, Garden City, NY 11530.

Water Birds of California by Howard L. Cogswell, 1977; $5.75 from: University of California Press, 2223 Fulton Street, Berkeley, CA 94720.

CANADA

The Birds of Canada by W. Godfrey, 1980; $27.50 from: University of Chicago Press, 5801 South Ellis Ave., Chicago, IL 60637. (Published in Canada by the National Museum of Canada, Ottawa.) —Peter Warshall

Our Magnificent Wildlife

An OUTSTANDING book, as we've come to expect from Reader's Digest. Not just a picture book, every page has some clearly presented new understanding, along with abundant encouragement for the reader to do something about it. The whole back end of the volume concerns making wildlife habitat in your backyard, photographing animals, and working with conservation organizations. This is the only book I've seen that tells preservation success stories.

Three cheers. —*SB*

Our Magnificent Wildlife
(How to Enjoy and Preserve It)
The Reader's Digest Association
1975; 352 pp.

$16.95 postpaid from:
Reader's Digest General Book Division
W.W. Norton and Co.
500 Fifth Avenue
New York, NY 10036
or Whole Earth Household Store

•

All wildlife, indeed all life, requires four basic elements to survive: Food; water; cover, as protection from natural enemies and the elements; and areas where it can reproduce and bear its young in safety. Combinations of these four elements differ for each species, but you can plan a habitat that offers enough combinations to attract the greatest number and variety of wildlife your area will support.

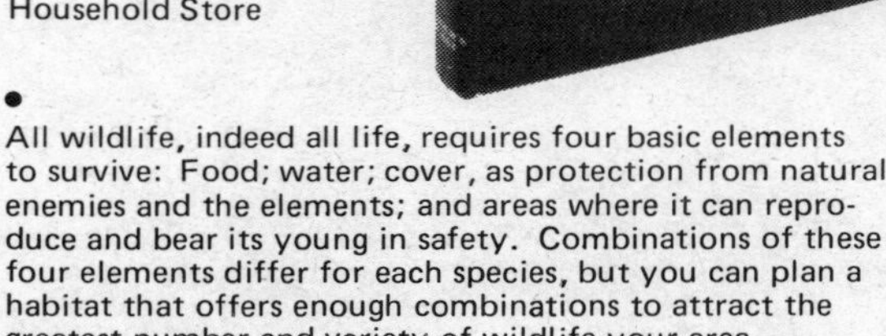

A well-chosen combination of plants provides food and cover for a variety of wildlife throughout the year, each plant filling a different need with the changing seasons. The plants have been positioned to create a "forest-edge" environment, which attracts the greatest variety of species. The plants shown here are some of those that grow well in the northeastern United States and southeastern Canada. →

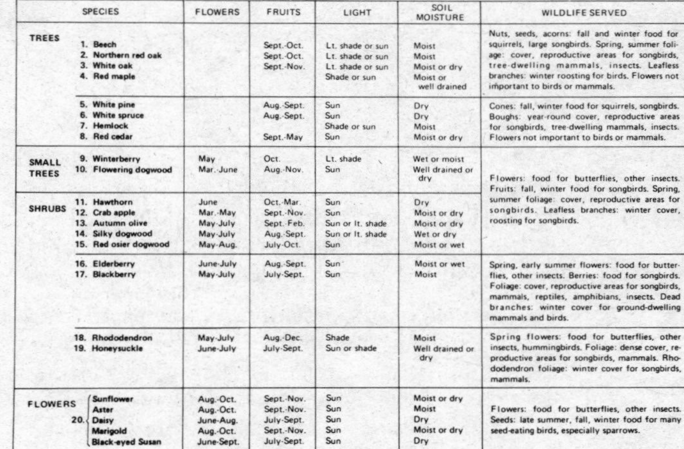

SPECIES		FLOWERS	FRUITS	LIGHT	SOIL MOISTURE	WILDLIFE SERVED
TREES	1. Beech		Sept.-Oct.	Lt. shade or sun	Moist	Nuts, seeds, acorns: fall and winter food for squirrels, large songbirds. Spring, summer foliage: cover, reproductive areas for songbirds, tree-dwelling mammals, insects. Leafless branches: winter roosting for birds. Flowers not important to birds or mammals.
	2. Northern red oak		Sept.-Oct.	Lt. shade or sun	Moist	
	3. White oak		Sept.-Nov.	Lt. shade or sun	Moist or dry	
	4. Red maple			Shade or sun	Moist or well drained	
	5. White pine		Aug.-Sept.	Sun	Dry	Cones: fall, winter food for squirrels, songbirds. Boughs: year-round cover, reproductive areas for songbirds, tree-dwelling mammals, insects. Flowers not important to birds or mammals.
	6. White spruce		Aug.-Sept.	Sun	Dry	
	7. Hemlock			Shade or sun	Moist	
	8. Red cedar		Sept.-May	Sun	Moist or dry	
SMALL TREES	9. Winterberry	May	Oct.	Lt. shade	Wet or moist	Flowers: food for butterflies, other insects. Fruits: fall, winter food for songbirds. Spring, summer foliage: cover, reproductive areas for songbirds. Leafless branches: winter cover, roosting for songbirds.
	10. Flowering dogwood	Mar.-June	Aug.-Nov.	Sun	Well drained or dry	
SHRUBS	11. Hawthorn	June	Oct.-Mar.	Sun	Dry	
	12. Crab apple	Mar.-May	Sept.-Nov.	Sun	Moist or dry	
	13. Autumn olive	May-July	Sept.-Feb.	Sun or lt. shade	Moist or dry	
	14. Silky dogwood	May-July	Aug.-Sept.	Sun or lt. shade	Wet or dry	
	15. Red osier dogwood	May-Aug.	July-Oct.	Sun	Moist or wet	
	16. Elderberry	June-July	Aug.-Sept.	Sun	Moist or wet	Spring, early summer flowers: food for butterflies, other insects. Berries: food for songbirds. Foliage: cover, reproductive areas for songbirds, mammals, reptiles, amphibians, insects. Dead branches: winter cover for ground-dwelling mammals and birds.
	17. Blackberry	May-July	July-Sept.	Sun	Moist	
	18. Rhododendron	May-July	Aug.-Dec.	Shade	Moist	Spring flowers: food for butterflies, other insects, hummingbirds. Foliage: dense cover, reproductive areas for songbirds, mammals. Rhododendron foliage: winter cover for songbirds, mammals.
	19. Honeysuckle	June-July	July-Sept.	Sun or shade	Well drained or dry	
FLOWERS	20. Sunflower	Aug.-Oct.	Sept.-Nov.	Sun	Moist or dry	Flowers: food for butterflies, other insects. Seeds: late summer, fall, winter food for many seed-eating birds, especially sparrows.
	Aster	Aug.-Oct.	Sept.-Nov.	Sun	Moist	
	Daisy	June-Aug.	July-Sept.	Sun	Dry	
	Marigold	Aug.-Oct.	Sept.-Nov.	Sun	Moist or dry	
	Black-eyed Susan	June-Sept.	July-Sept.	Sun	Dry	

Extinct Antlered Animals

Bush-antlered deer
The bush-antlered deer was an ice age European form.

Schomburgk's deer
The last of these deer was killed in Thailand in 1932.

Irish elk
The antlers of the giant deer spanned 12 feet.

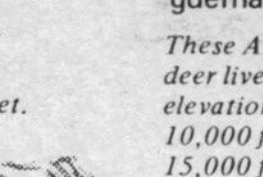

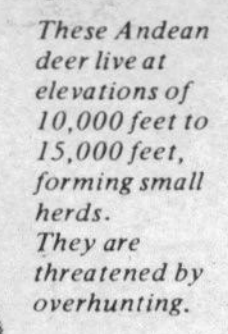

Threatened Antlered Animals

Peruvian guemal
These Andean deer live at elevations of 10,000 feet to 15,000 feet, forming small herds. They are threatened by overhunting.

Barasingha
Small numbers of the overhunted barasingha, or swamp deer, survive in India and Nepal.

Manipur brow-antlered deer
This deer lives in only one reserve in India, though a related race is found in Thailand.

Fea's muntjac
The muntjac, also called the barking deer because of its alarm call, is protected by law in Thailand and Burma but is killed illegally.

Persian fallow deer
Twice given up as extinct, this deer is losing out to domestic goats. Zoos are trying to establish breeding groups.

Key deer
Once numbering only 50, the smallest North American deer has been protected for several decades. The population is now about 600, but road accidents kill deer even in protected areas.

↑

Is There Room for the Horned and Antlered?

It is one of nature's paradoxes that the animals with the most conspicuous weapons are all vegetarians. No hoofed creature uses its horns or antlers to kill prey; they are used to threaten and, less often, to fight. But, except in defense against predators, the opponents are members of the same species, usually male, and the contest is generally over possession of space or of females. Why are so many of these creatures endangered? Man's hunting for food or sport has taken a toll. In addition, throughout the world man has occupied the habitats of many species, using the land for agriculture, cutting forests for lumber. Other hoofed animals have been eliminated because they competed with livestock for grazing.

A Field Guide to the Mammals

Although the drawings are mediocre (at least, the color plate reproductions), this is the best general guide to all of North America. I found difficulties with the subdivisions and descriptions of the Rocky Mountain chipmunks but, by using the annotated bibliography, you can get the needed details. Great section on skulls and many footprint diagrams.

For Mexico, use Aldo Starker Leopold's **Wildlife of Mexico** *(1959, $29.65 from: University of California Press, 2223 Fulton Street, Berkeley, CA 94720).*
—*Peter Warshall*

A Field Guide to the Mammals
(Peterson Field Guide Number 5)
William H. Burt and Richard Grossenheider
1952, 1964; 284 pp.

$5.95 postpaid from:
Houghton Mifflin Co.
Wayside Road
Burlington, MA 01803
or Whole Earth Household Store

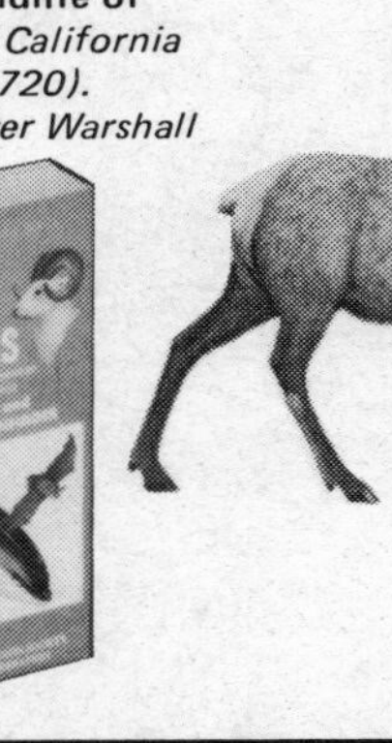

A Field Guide to Animal Tracks

Thanks to Murie, this is the only Peterson guide to sound human. Just good ol' backwoods details that tell you "The Animal's been here." Eaten branches, scratch marks, tracks and scats, sounds and smells.
—*Peter Warshall*

A Field Guide to Animal Tracks
(Peterson Field Guide Number 9)
Olaus Murie
1954; 374 pp.

$7.95 postpaid from:
Houghton Mifflin Co.
Wayside Road
Burlington, MA 01803
or Whole Earth Household Store

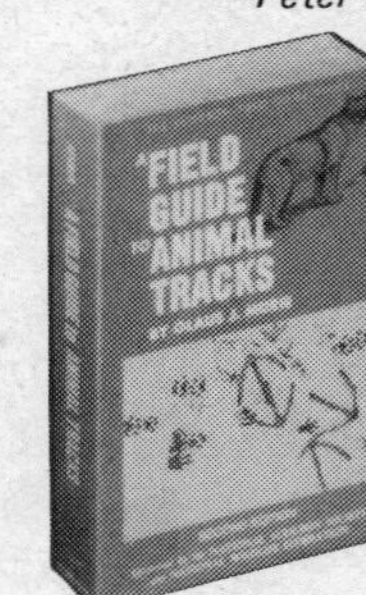

•

The shape of the track of the mule deer will vary somewhat with the type of ground on which the animal lives. On soft soil, as in some woodlands, the toes are likely to be relatively more pointed. On hard, rocky ground, found in some areas occupied by these deer, the hoofs are worn enough to produce tips.

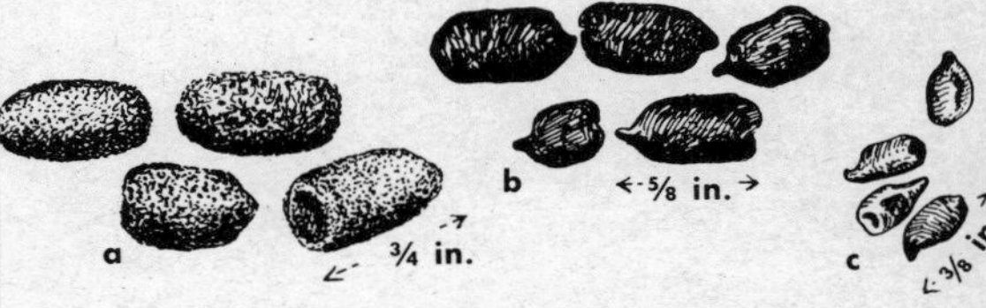

Mule deer droppings, about 2/3 natural size.

a. Winter droppings of adult male (Dinosaur National Monument, 1950).

b. Autumn droppings of adult male (Wyoming, November 8, 1938).

c. Fawn droppings (Wyoming).

Mammal books

GENERAL

Carnivores by R.F. Ewer, 1973; $29.50 from: Cornell University Press, 124 Roberts Place, P.O. Box 250, Ithaca, NY 14850.

Ethology of Mammals by R.F. Ewer, 1969; $32.50 from: Plenum Publishing Company, 227 West 17th Street, New York, NY 10011.

SPECIFIC SPECIES

Bats of America by Roger W. Barbour and Wayne H. Davis, 1969, 1979; $22.50 from: University Press of Kentucky, Lexington, KY 40506.

The Deer and the Tiger (A Study of Wildlife in India) by George B. Schaller, 1974; $6.95 from: University of Chicago Press, 11030 South Langley Avenue, Chicago, IL, 60628.

In the Shadow of Man (about chimpanzees) by Jane Van Lawick-Goodall, 1971; $10.00 from: Houghton-Mifflin, Wayside Road, Burlington, MA 01803.

The Serengeti Lion (A Study in Predator-Prey Relations) by George B. Schaller, 1972; $17.50 from: University of Chicago Press, 11030 South Langley Avenue, Chicago, IL 60628.

Voles, Mice and Lemmings by Charles Elton, 1942, 1971; $42 from: Lubrecht and Cramer, RFD 1, Box 227, Monticello, NY 12701.

ENDANGERED SPECIES

The Blue Whale by George L. Small, 1973; $3.95 from: Columbia University Press, Stock Department, 136 South Broadway, Irvington-on-Hudson, NY 10533.

The Buffalo Hunters by Mari Sandoz, 1954, 1975; $9.95 from: Hastings House, 10 East 40th Street, New York, NY 10016.

King of the Grizzlies (Originally titled **Biography of a Grizzly**) by Ernest T. Seton, 1910, 1970; $ .95 from: Scholastic Book Services, 906 Sylvan Avenue, Englewood Cliffs, NJ 07632.

Lives of the Hunted by Ernest T. Seton, 1901; $22.50 from: Norwood Editions, P.O. Box 38, Norwood, PA 19074.

Never Cry Wolf by Farley Mowat, 1963; $1.25 from: Dell Publishing Company, 1 Dag Hammarskjold Plaza, 245 East 47th Street, New York, NY 10017.

Whale for the Killing by Farley Mowat, 1972; $2.95 from: Penguin Books, 299 Murray Hill Parkway, East Rutherford, NJ 07073.

Wolf by L. David Mech, 1973; $9.95 from: Natural History Publishing Company, P.O. Box 962, La Jolla, CA 92038.
—*Peter Warshall*

THE RISING SUN
NEIGHBORHOOD NEWSLETTER

David looks in tide pools a lot. He says an unhealthy tidepool has a lot of a few species and a healthy tidepool has a few of a lot of species.

Streaming Wisdom

Watershed Consciousness in the Twentieth Century

by Peter Warshall

"Although the river and the hill-side do not resemble each other at first sight, they are only extreme members of a continuous series, and when this is appreciated, one may fairly extend the "river" all over the basin and up to its very divides. Ordinarily treated, the river is like the veins of a leaf; broadly viewed, it is like the entire leaf."
—W.M. Davis (1899)

There is a story in Brooklyn, where I spent much of my childhood, that has been repeated so many times (or happened so often) that I don't know if it's fact or legend. Two boys sit hunched at the curb. They watch with wonder a man flaking up pieces of asphalt with his pneumatic drill. One says to the other; "See, told you, that's where the city stores its dirt." I remembered this story years later while guiding some kids from the Oakland Panther School on a nature walk. We had to walk through the Green Gulch Zen Center vegetable garden and I casually picked a carrot. "Oh man, that's Bugs Bunny's carrot." Slowly, it dawned on me that most carrots come without tops, in plastic bags. Only on TV does the magic rabbit have a carrot with green leaves.

In our towns and cities, the essential sources of life — water to drink and soil to grow food — remain hidden from our eyes. The hills and valleys are coated in asphalt, ancient streams are buried beneath housing and soil is filler between gas, water, and electric piping. While we have touched the moon together through the amazing electronics of television, we have simultaneously lost touch with the most obvious questions of our everyday living:

- Where does the water come from when you turn on the faucet?
- Where does it go when you flush the toilet?
- What is the name of the land that channels rain and waterflow past your home and into a creek or lake?
- What kind of soils are you and your home sitting on?

Watershed consciousness is, in part, an invitation to peel off (not discard) the layer of industrial and technological activity that hides us from the water and soils of our communities. It is an invitation to reveal where you live.

As a child, my eyes had no ability to see waterflow and landscape. Land was blocks, read by street signs, gridded with no sense of shape or contour. Water has been the liberator. For water is both beautiful and ruthless. It flows from one piece of property to another without a thought. It erodes cracks in the New York City sidewalks or thousands of miles of badlands; carries nutrients down the whole Mississippi to the delta or down the White House roof to leaves caught in the gutter. It doesn't care if it's drunk or pissed, if it's shared by a thirsty family or hoarded by a cactus.

Because waterflow does not obey human desires, it forces humans to join together to control and to use and to re-use beneficially. Because waterflow does not follow human desires or subdivision maps, it creates the need for co-operation. What happens upstream changes life downstream, and the demands of downstream alter upstream activity. From the forested headwaters to the agricultural mid-stream valleys to the commercial and industrial centers at the river's mouth, good and bad news travels by way of water. Did my drinking water take a farmer's supply, cause his farm to close down and vegetables to be imported to the city from longer distances and at higher prices? Did my toilet flush give a downstream swimmer gastro-intestinal upset? Did my coastal car exhaust get carried back to the headwaters and fall on the forests as acid rain, killing trees and upping the price of lumber?

The mainstem of the river and the surrounding hill slopes enclose all these people — the upstream loggers and miners, the mid-stream farmers, the downstream office workers, fishermen, etc. — into one basin. The watershed is a hydraulic commons and a necessary community. Watershed consciousness is, in part, a little promotional campaign to advertise the mutual concerns and needs that bind upstream and downstream peoples and "life-styles" together.

My own sense of water's importance came from hitch-hiking to Los Angeles in 1965. The man who picked me up took me to his apartment to use his bathroom and call friends. I walked into the dark bathroom, unable to find the light switch. A turquoise glow came from the corner. The toilet bowl had an electric light inside the bowl. I pulled the little chromium lever and the toilet flushed absolutely silently. Eight years later, the town I lived in had to decide where their wastewater should go when they flushed their toilets. Should homes keep septic tank systems that returned treated sewage to backyard plantlife, or switch to centralized sewers that collected all the water and, after energy-expensive treatment, dumped it in the ocean? I wrote:

As industrialization intensified, Western civilization became more and more alienated from the body's plumbing and its connection to Nature's pathways. Instead of eating, defecating onto the ground, fertilizing plants with the feces, and eating again, we simply reach behind our backs and pull a little chromium lever. Instead of defecating into the earth, we sit on a toilet filled with good drinking water which comes from some unknown river and, after flushing, goes to some unknown destination. Instead of taking responsibility for our excrement, we are embarrassed by defecation and avoid direct discussion by substituting all kinds of diversionary vocabulary ("ca ca" and "poo poo" or abbreviations like "May I be excused.")

Four events created our alienation from the circle of feces-fertilizer-food-feces. Piped water eliminated the out-house and bedpan and led to the invention of the flush toilet. The flush toilet itself allowed the Victorian flush-and-forget mentality to flourish. Modern medicine, having conquered all the dangerous diseases caused by sewage, reduced the necessity to connect feces with the human body. Finally, the use of petroleum-based fertilizers temporarily broke the necessity of needing feces for growing food.

Helping the town led me to run for public office and wade through the turbulence of human self-interests, technological choices, cashflow, and personal vision. I emerged seeing the wounds all of us as recent inhabitants of this land have inflicted on the water and soils that sustain us. I became a "water-watcher," a consultant attempting to encourage humans to quickly diagnose watershed disease and to heal the polluted waters — the eroded clearcut slopes, the streams unnecessarily lined in concrete, the estuaries crudely drained and diked.

In summary, watershed consciousness focuses on place. It is not inner geography — the continuing attempt to feel better by mapping the mysterious meanderings of our minds; nor is it whole Earth geography — the struggle to gain some perspective of our place on the planet. We will not ask, When is my paranoia appropriate? nor, How long will the Earth's oil resources really last? The journey of this perspective is right out your window — the immediate valleys and hills that surround you, that channel rain and snowmelt into your nearest creeks and rivers and lakes. It is a first excursion of thought into the place you live. A Middle Way between Mind and Planet.

*Peter Warshall, 37, has been natural history editor with **CoEvolution Quarterly** since 1974. He got his Ph.D. in Biological Anthropology at Harvard after work in Africa and Puerto Rico and with Claude Levi-Strauss in France. For the last decade he has been a major water-public-servant for his town in Northern California. At present he is in Tucson, Arizona working on a major book called **Watersheds**. A less major previous book, **Septic Tank Practices** (p. 243), has a considerable following among the professionals and amateurs in that field.* —*SB*

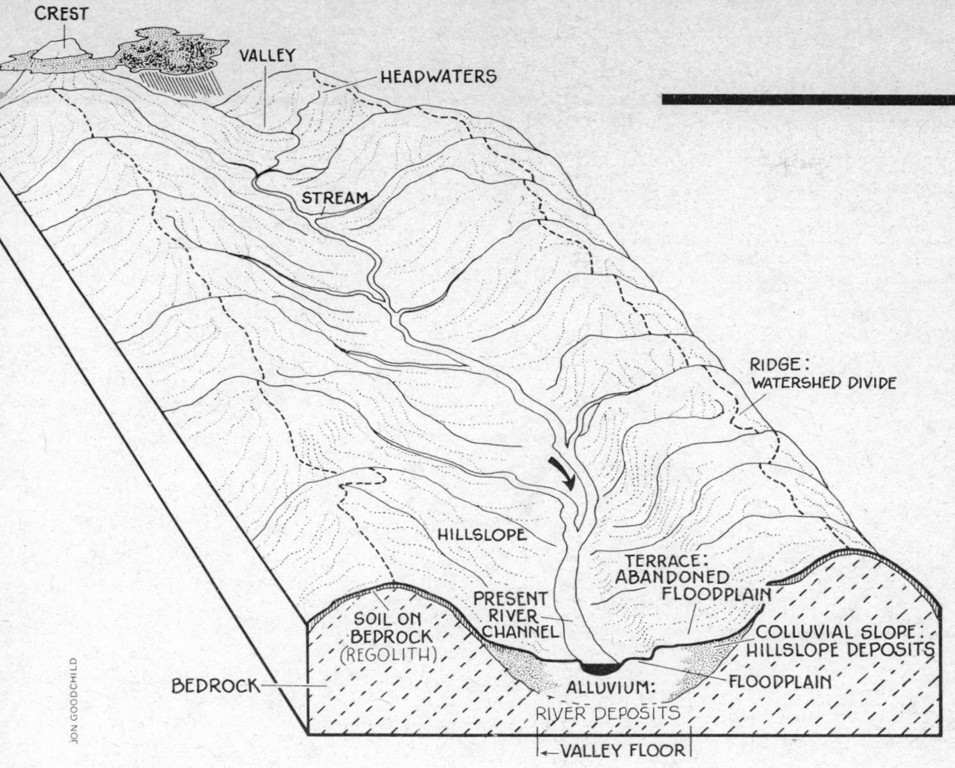

River: Headwaters to lower reaches with dominant resident fish. →

BASIC WATERSHED VOCABULARY

HEADWATER: The beginning of a stream or river. Its source or its upstream portion.

FLOODPLAIN: A strip of flat land bordering a stream or river, consisting of the sediment laid down over the centuries by the river when it overflowed during high floods.

TERRACE: A plateau on the side of a valley, representing an old floodplain no longer reached by the river below.

REGOLITH: The weathered surface. It may contain fine and coarse materials displaying various degrees of mineral alteration.

1. Head stream.

2. Shaded trout beck.

3. Upland trout beck.

4. Minnow reach.

5. Upper Salmonid zone of a large river.

6. Lowland river, upper zone (Chub or Barbel).

The Meaning of Watershed

"Shed" of watershed goes back to an ancient Anglo-Saxon word *(sceadu)* meaning: the parting of the hair, how it naturally separates and falls. As a verb, "shed" has evolved:

to shed tears
to shed the past
to shed skin
to shed water like a duck
to shed leaves
to shed the blood of thine enemy
to shed thy Light on me!

The 19th century sense of watershed *(wasserscheide)* as used by Lyle and Darwin came from the "parting" (of the rainfall) – its separation as it landed on one side of a mountain or the other. "Watershed" meant the boundary line that separated downward flow of rain or snow. In the U.S. we call this the DIVIDE, but in Europe and England watershed still means the line along the ridge which divides the waterflow.

The sense of separating a flow into two distinct directions has become intense among writers and journalists. Again and again, "watershed" is used to mean a crucially important or divisive moment or event in one's life. Meanwhile the Anglo-Saxon word for "shade" wandered around in history and wound up meaning "shed" – a lightly built structure like lean-tos, ramadas and arbors (parting the sunlight from the shade?). These slight buildings (woolsheds, wagonsheds, woodsheds) also included "watersheds" – housing for a well or pump. In the muddy cross-confluences of these two different Anglo-Saxon words, "shed" and "shed" changed hats and merged into one pun. "To shed blood" became "bloodshed" which is not the storage facility for the Red Cross.

In the United States, "to shed water" became WATERSHED – not a building, nor the line dividing rainfall along a ridge. In the U.S., watershed means the whole surface of the land, the area of waterflow over the land. The hill slopes are cheeks shedding tears into rivers that pour down the face of the land to the sea. As scientists say it: "An area of land which drains water, sediment and dissolved materials to a common point along a stream or river." Watershed is synonymous with DRAINAGE BASIN (following the French) or, in other countries, CATCHMENT AREA.

The size of the watershed can vary immensely. A little puddle forming on a sidewalk is a watershed. The Amazon River forms the Earth's largest watershed. In the U.S., a watershed is usually between a few hundred and a few thousand acres. Much more extensive drainage areas are called "river basins." But you can correctly say: the Mississippi River Basin contains thousands of watersheds; or, the Mississippi Watershed contains thousands of smaller basins.

The Watershed Way

While space physics has become super-sophisticated, the science of watersheds remains in its infancy. Most modern scientists have such compartmentalized points of view that those interested in watershed life (geologists, regional planners, meteorologists, foresters, public health officers . . .) must return to ancient China for a more wholistic vision. China was famous for a profession called "geomancer" – literally an Earth Diviner. The geomancer had a metal disc inscribed with astronomy and water signs. He placed the disc on a magnetic stone and from its orientation read the "lines of force" that stretched across a landscape. These lines were used to concentrate or disperse the energy of wind or water as it traversed the hills.

continued next page

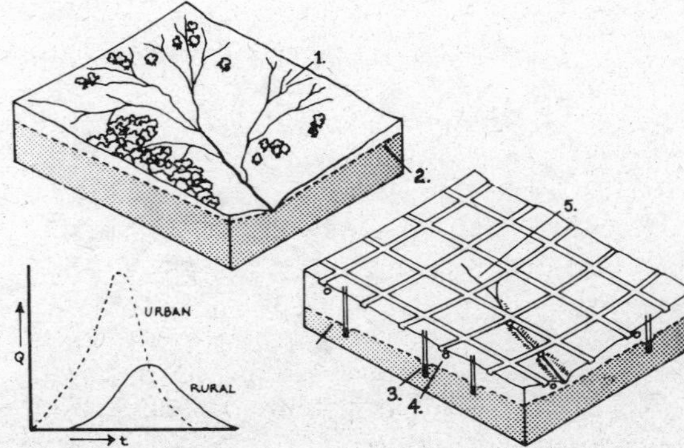

The urbanization of rural countryside leads to major watershed changes. First, watershed geometry changes. The stream network (1) is replaced by the storm sewer network (4). The streams are filled (5) as hills are cut and graded for home sites so that overland flow is completely different. The driveways, gutters and streetways usually doubles the number of channels which means water will concentrate faster (see hydro-graph). The new pavement means less water infiltrates so there is more runoff on the surface and less groundwater recharge (2). Rainstorms then not only concentrate runoff faster but there is also more of it. Downstream rivers (where the storm sewers empty) must readjust to this new volume and rhythm of stormflow. Erosion of channels and flooding are usual. Emergency or disaster expenses result.

THE RISING SUN
NEIGHBORHOOD NEWSLETTER

Don't tell them how to do it, show them how to do it and don't say a word. If you tell them, they'll watch your lips move, if you show them they'll want to do it themselves, and imitate you, said Marie Montessori, who thought she was talking about kids.

THE HYDROLOGIC CYCLE

During water's endless circulation from ocean to atmosphere to earth, it temporarily rests in place in the watershed. These temporary storage sites include the leaf canopy; the leaf litter and ground surface; the soil body plant and animal tissue; the groundwater basin beneath the watershed; and lakes and streams. Above the watershed in the ill-defined and fickle airshed, water is stored in clouds.

Between the resting places water flows. The pathway of water depends on the energy of the sun and wind. A raindrop can vaporize back into the atmosphere or be blown to the ground or flow down a plant stem by gravity. Each kind of flow has a name. *Throughfall* is the flow off the leaves, direct to the ground. *Stemfall* is water channeled by the shape of the tree down its branches and trunk. *Infiltration* is the flow of water through the soil surface. *Percolation* is the flow within the soil and deep within the bedrock. *Throughflow* is underground flow that more or less follows the surface contours towards a stream. It occurs in the most permeable layers of soil near the surface. The invisible water fluxes are *evaporation* (water turns to vapor from the surfaces of lakes, leaves, and the ground) and *transpiration* ("exhaled" water vapor from plants). Sometimes both occur at once (*evapotranspiration*).

→

Stored water is printed in this type face. *Flowing water (down or up) is printed in this type face.*

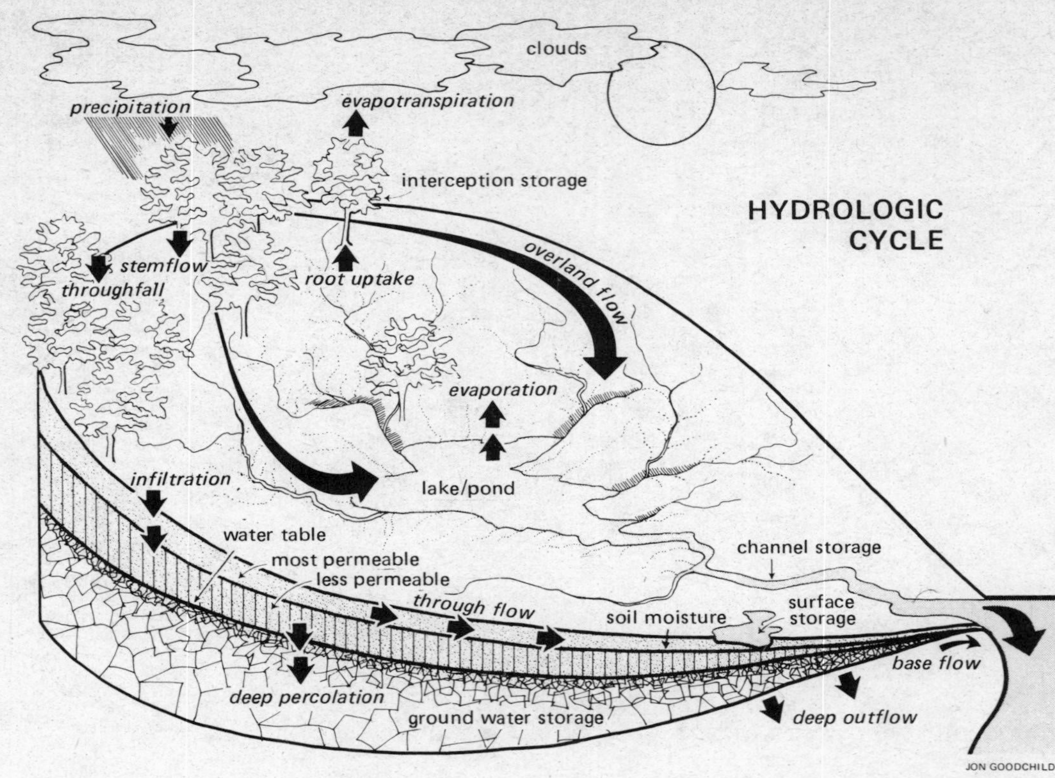

Some of the most beautiful Chinese villages and towns were designed by geomancers.

Today, we trace the lines of landscape force to two energies — the energy of gravity and the energy of the Sun. Water and land follow gravity to the sea. The Sun returns water to the sky by heating it up. Gravity returns it back to Earth. The spin of the Earth and its internal heat return land back from the sea uplifting and volcanoes. This is the Big Picture of watershed history.

Both water and soils are never lost as they follow the paths of gravity and the sun throughout the total biosphere of Earth. They only change position in a planetary closed system. But each watershed is an open system with imports of rain, dissolved gases, human-made molecules and dust; exports of streamflow, water vapor, sediment, nutrients and heat. Over time, each watershed evolves a special kinship to the passing storms and changing seasons of radiant energy. Each becomes a unique rain and sun collector; a unique processor and regulator of its imports and unique exporter of its products. The watershed accomplishes this by structuring its parts (especially the drainage pattern) to accommodate drought and flood, forest fire or windfall, a population explosion of deer, or any of the human influences that can upset the balance of hill slope and river.

River and hills send each other the news of recent upset. From the river's view, the news can be a change in the amount of water coming from the hills, soil eroded from the hillsides, or rock encountered by the river as it cuts deeper into the hillslopes' valley. The less the disruption — river cutting slices out of the hill, hill slope caving into the river, streams eroding topsoil, topsoil muddying rivers — the better the watershed can cradle its living plants and creatures, including us.

Think and see like water. The watershed is rain and solar collector. Pulses of water delivered by rainstorms fall into the complex folds of the watershed's outer skin. The hill slopes and rivers are just two kinds of pipe that convey water to the sea. The hill slope soils are a sieve. The river is an open channel. Plants, people, and ponds are just temporary and leaky canteens delaying water's downhill course. The Sun vaporizes moisture back to the sky, short-circuiting water's liquid journey, reducing its volume and power to sculpt and nourish the land.

Think and feel like soil. Water can take or make soils. Water makes soils by weathering rock (dissolving it and cracking it during freezing). Water takes whole hill slopes by slides, heaves, rock and earth flows. Moving the loosened soil and rock down the hill slopes to the streams and rivers is called erosion. Moving the floating soils and rocks downstream in the water is called sediment. Floodplains and lakes are just temporary storage, delaying soil's downhill course to the sea. When weathering and deposited sediment create a growing place for plantlife and the plants can hold the soil to the hills more than water erodes it off the slopes, the soil accumulates. The surface of the watershed builds and plantlife thrives.

Rainfall, Sun, plantlife and humans can alter this balance. They work together and encourage a watershed either to make or to sluff off its soil mantle.

Tying the water cycle and soils cycle to life and tying the physical landscape to the living ecosystem is the most intricate and complex cycle of them all — the BIO(life)-GEO(earth)-CHEMICAL (combined elements) cycle. Water makes soil; soils make trees; trees shed leaves into streams that fungi and bacteria decay; insect larvae and other

Geomancers

→

This airphoto view of stream channel form in the midwest illustrates how form reflects process and stability. The main trunk stream is meandering in a smooth sinusoidal pattern while flowing from left to right. Note that after the tributary stream discharges into the main stream, its meander wavelength and amplitude increase to accommodate the increased water and sediment. But also note that the tributary does not have a smooth equilibrium channel pattern. Close inspection reveals that it is dammed and water is taken out for irrigation. Further, at some point in time, the riparian vegetation of cottonwood trees was removed or partly cut, increasing sediment load. All of these assaults have created a non-equilibrium form that indicates that the channel will meander in an unpredictable way. This has been important in limiting the farm use of the lands adjacent to the side tributary. More land is not tilled next to the small tributary than next to the large stream. Disturbance of the watershed has cost in terms of stability and productivity of the side-stream tributary.

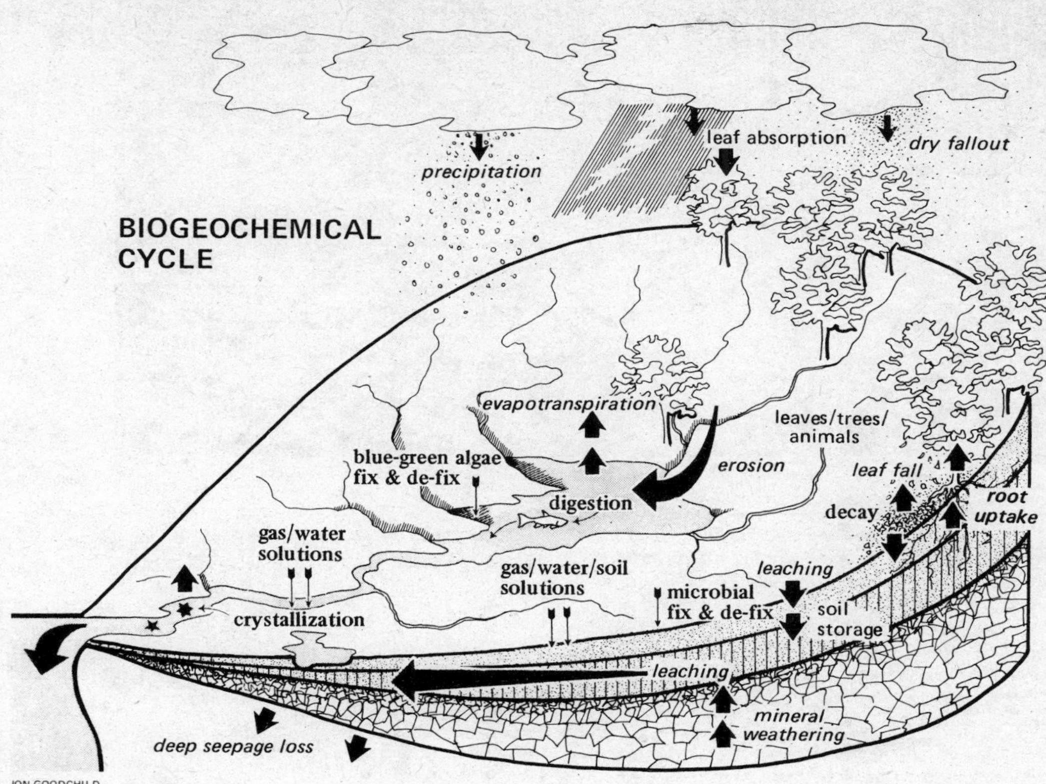

THE BIOGEOCHEMICAL CYCLE

If we could see atoms and molecules, each watershed would appear to be a huge biogeochemical bank. Some elements and compounds would be in safe deposit boxes; others would be free-floating currency. The Biogeochemical Cycle describes the changes in watershed accounting.

Major chemical withdrawals from the watershed occur by stream-flow, erosion, evaporation, deep percolation into the bedrock, animal migrations, and the wind. Funds "released" from the deposit boxes within the watershed include chemical compounds which are leached, weathered, and eroded by water from the mineral and soil storage sites; or which are released by animal excretion and microbes de-fixing trapped nitrogen compounds. Chemical compounds deposited into the watershed account come from precipitation (rain, snow, dust, fallout), photosynthesis by plants, fixing of atmospheric nitrogen by legumes, and in-migration of animals.

The fate of chemicals released within the watershed depends on what's happening. A nutrient molecule released by a microbe might be sucked up in a nearby root or, if it's raining, washed into a stream, or it might react with another chemical in the soil.

←

Stored chemicals are printed in this type face. **Compound Transformation is printed in this type face.** *Flowing chemicals are printed in this type face.*

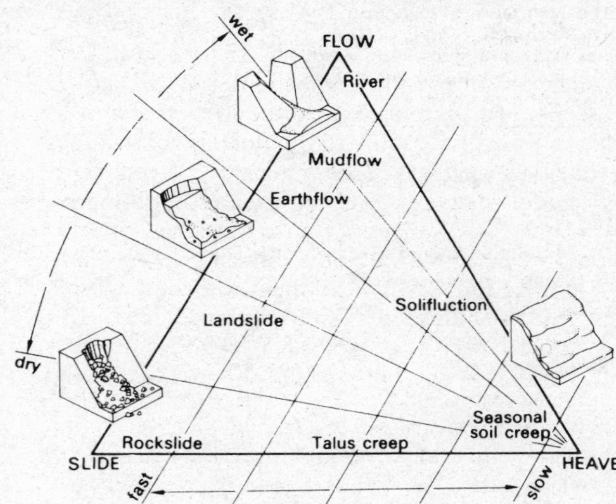

THE SLIDE, THE FLOW AND THE HEAVE

During mass movement of hill slopes, the particles of earth remain a coherent whole. The SLIDE moves like a brick down a chute. The FLOW moves like a liquid. During the HEAVE, soil expands and contracts perpendicular to the surface. Frost causes roads to heave. Not shown are particles (vs. mass) movements. Here individual particles move with little relation to their neighbors. Rain splash, surface wash and particles moving in solution (colloids) are examples of this smaller scale hill slope erosion process.

creatures eat bacteria which are, in turn, eaten by fish. The fish eventually die and decay, returning their body chemistry to the water which finds its way downstream to the flood plain where it may fertilize another tree. These bio-geo-chemical ties are so intimate we can think of some kinds of fish like the Coho salmon as part of the forest, as growing from the leaves on the trees.

As atoms and molecules journey from landscape to life by way of water, they are never lost from the Earth's biosphere.

Desirous Water

Armed with the tools of the modern geomancer – the Brunton compass and USGS topo map – Robert Curry, myself and others hiked a potential logging road along the Eel River in California. The Eel is the fastest eroding river in North America. I was particularly concerned about some summer-running steelhead trout that could lose their spawning grounds if road cutting de-stabilized the hill slope and further increased the sediment load. As we looked down from one of the ridges, we could see that its hillside had already naturally slumped and, in the crack behind the slump, small lakes had formed. The whole attitude of the watershed seemed to be: delay the water from flowing away. Store it. Make ponds to give water time to seep into the ground where it travels more slowly and arrives at the river in summer (long after the rains have ceased). Make it linger so it can nourish trees whose roots will hold the slopes. Slow its passage so the hill slope won't erode as quickly. All this so the steelhead will have a summer riverflow with clear water. In fact, slow the river by lengthening its channel, snaking its shape and providing a lazy twisting pipe instead of a straight chute.

Here at the headwaters, we were like the mind: at a subtle place high on the hill slope where the water tasted clear and pure almost like rain; where the hill slope suddenly opened up to start the river; where peace was needed among the timber because any change at the headwaters would be felt all the way downstream; and where the bare rock tributaries released minerals to be used and stored by plants and fish below. I thought that water somehow knew it was so desirous and beautiful – that the land and life clung to it, shaping itself to contain it. And the water just trickled past my shoes, doing what it does, paying no mind, streaming its course out to sea . . . (to sky to land to sea . . .) ■

WATERSHED SHAPE

If we consider watersheds from the Water Cycle view, hill slopes and rivers are simply two ways to move water (hill slope flow modified by soil and plants; river flow by channel shape and pattern). Watersheds from the Soil Cycle view consider hill slopes and rivers as two ways to remove debris (hill slope by erosion; rivers by sediment transport). From either point of view, the drainage network ties hill slope and river into an inseparable land/water togetherness.

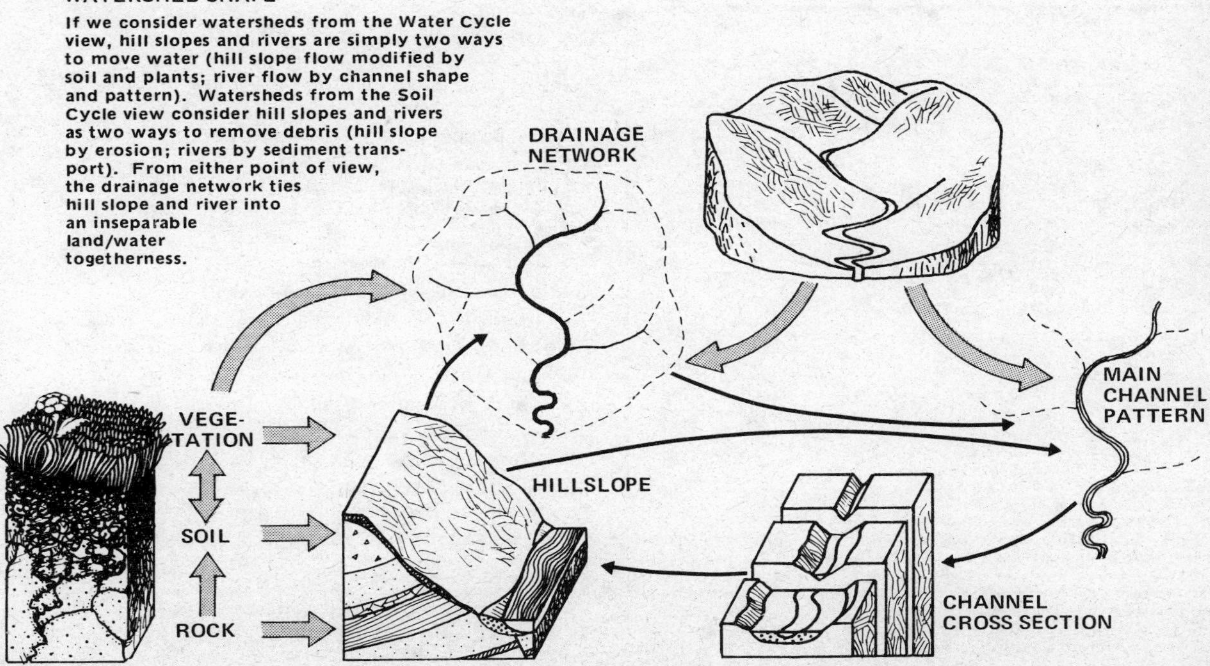

PIRKLE JONES, THIS IS THE AMERICAN EARTH

THE RISING SUN
NEIGHBORHOOD NEWSLETTER

David was on a ferry going up the coast and saw Northern Lights dancing in the sky and being flames in the sky and filling the whole sky and never standing still. He danced around himself, on deck till three-thirty, looking at the sky and the water shinier than with a full moon and being a little kid.

From Tao Te Ching

Sensitive Chaos

The ways that flowing forms our heart, cyclones, rivers and bird flight. How we flowed as embryos and our bones still spiral and loop with the markings of past eddy movements. Here is spiritual guidance in the greatest book of Jungian-Taoist natural history.
—Peter Warshall

Sensitive Chaos
Theodor Schwenk
1965; 147 pp.
$9.95 postpaid from:
Schocken Books
200 Madison Avenue
New York, NY 10016
or Whole Earth
Household Store

•

Together earth, plant world and atmosphere form a *single* great organism, in which water streams like living blood.

Rhythmical waves and flowing currents are two different elements of movement in water, but they can change over into one another or be superimposed one upon the other and work together. Fluid flow can arise through rhythms, and—— as we shall see later—— rhythms can also arise through flow movements. Here again is an important principle which nature applies in the creation of her living creatures out of the fluid medium. It has for instance been observed that in the hen's egg the inner formative processes in the embryo are accompanied by rhythmical wave movements. These run in a gentle wave of contractions over the amnion of the egg from one end to the other and back. It is a kind of rhythmical to and fro movement which continuously massages and moulds the content of the egg.

←
A photograph of a vortex taken under water reveals the spiralling surface between the water and the air which is being sucked in.

Veins in the sand on the beach. As the tide goes out, the ebbing water inscribes a whole network of intricate forms into the soft ground (aerial photograph).
↓

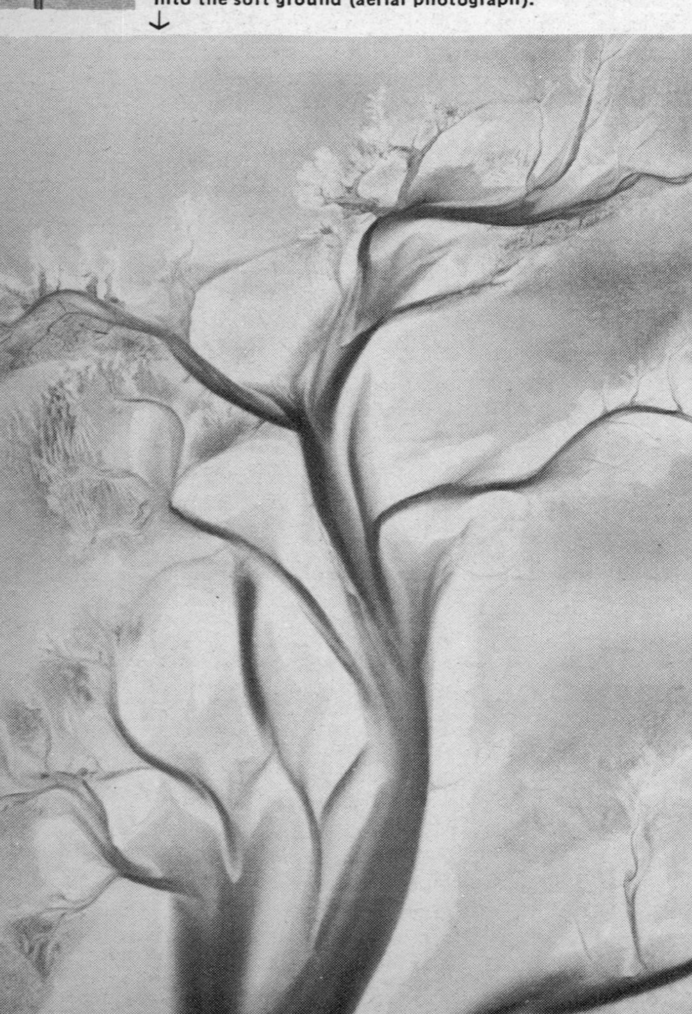

Tao Te Ching

Taoists watched water; opened their hearts and minds to water's teachings; took water as an ally in understanding. Their aqueous attitude washed out preconceived notions of religious righteousness; dissolved rigid ways of viewing the universe; liquefied frozen ambitions, social convictions, ideals and hopes. The elegance of Taoism was taking humans from their everydayness but not to "grace," being and nothingness, or samsara — simply to water, the liquid center of nature.

The **Tao Te Ching** *has many translators. Archie Bahm's is more fortune cookie than others. Witter Bynner's* **The Way of Life** *borders on turning Lao Tzu into a goodie-goodie, but feels more accurate. And is the best, in my opinion. Orville Schell who reads Chinese recommends Gia-Fu Feng's translation.* *—Peter Warshall*

Tao Teh King
Lao Tzu
Archie Bahm, Translator
1958; 126 pp.
$2.45 postpaid from:
Frederick Ungar Pub. Co.
250 Park Avenue South
New York, NY 10003
or Whole Earth
Household Store

The Way of Life According to Lao Tzu
Witter Bynner, Editor
1962; 162 pp.
$2.95 postpaid from:
Paragon Books
G.P. Putnam and Sons
200 Madison Avenue
New York, NY 10016

Tao Te Ching
Lao Tzu
(Jane English and Gia-Fu Feng, Translators)
1972; 160 pp.
$4.95 postpaid from:
Random House
455 Hahn Road
Westminster, MD 21157
or Whole Earth
Household Store

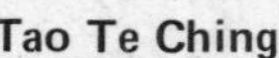

1. By its pulsating method of propulsion the jellyfish causes mirror images of itself to arise in the water

2. A small piece of wood circling in a vortex. It constantly points in the same direction

3. Water around a whirlpool moves in spirals

•

Once the whole is divided, the parts need names.
There are already enough names.
One must know when to stop.
Knowing when to stop averts trouble.
Tao in the world is like a river flowing home to the sea.
—Lao Tzu and Gia-Fu Feng

•

Man at his best, like water,
Serves as he goes along:
Like water he seeks his own level,
The common level of life,
Loves living close to the earth,
Living clear down in his heart,
Loves kinship with his neighbors,
The pick of words that tell the truth,
The even tenor of a well-run state,
The fair profit of able dealing,
The right timing of useful deeds,
And for blocking no one's way
No one blames him.
—Lao Tzu and Witter Bynner

•

The highest good is like water.
Water gives life to the ten thousand things and does not strive.
It flows in places men reject and so is like the Tao.
In dwelling, be close to the land.
In meditation, go deep in the heart.
In dealing with others, be gentle and kind.
In speech, be true.
In ruling, be just.
In business, be competent.
In action, watch the timing.
No fight: No blame.
—Lao Tzu and Gia-Fu Feng

•

The best way to conduct oneself may be observed in the behavior of water.

Water is useful to every living thing, yet it does not demand pay in return for its services; it does not even require that it be recognized, esteemed, or appreciated for its benefits.

This illustrates how intelligent behavior so closely approximates the behavior of Nature itself.

If experience teaches that houses should be built close to the ground,

That friendship should be based upon sympathy and good will,

That good government employs peaceful means of regulation,

That business is more successful it if employs efficient methods,

That wise behavior adapts itself appropriately to the particular circumstances,

All this is because these are the easiest ways.

If one proceeds naturally, without ambition or envy, everything works out for the best.
—Lao Tzu and Archie Bahm

•

Nothing is weaker than water;
Yet, for attacking what is hard and tough,
Nothing surpasses it, nothing equals it.
The principle, that what is weak overcomes what is strong,
And what is yielding conquers what is resistant,
Is known to everyone.
Yet few men utilize it profitably in practice.
But the intelligent man knows that:
He who willingly takes the blame for disgrace to his community is considered a responsible person,
And he who submissively accepts responsibility for the evils in his community naturally will be given enough authority for dealing with them.
These principles, no matter how paradoxical, are sound.
—Lao Tzu and Archie Bahm

Water

"Water. That's our life," a Navaho told me once. "Water's my favorite mineral," Phylis Morrison remarked.

By the formidable Luna Leopold, this book is the most accessible introduction to the sciences of water, illustrated with the customary plethora of photos by Time-Life.
—SB

Water
Luna B. Leopold
and Kenneth S. Davis
1970; 196 pp.

OUT OF PRINT
To be re-published by Life Science Library in 1981, but only in Europe

Get this book back in print in America!

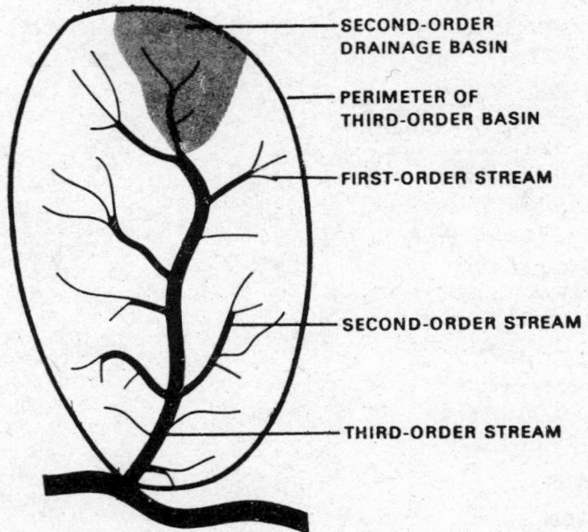

↑
A stream with no tributaries is designated as one of the first order. A river with one or more first-order tributaries is a stream of the second order. The river becomes third order only when it acquires at least one second-order tributary, and so on. The Mississippi is about 10th order, and the Amazon and Congo, largest rivers in the world, are variously classified as 12th or 13th order.

As might be expected, nearly every river system on earth includes fewer high-order than low-order streams. As the order increases, so does the length of the river, and so do both the total number of streams that feed into it and the area of the watershed that they drain. More surprising is the mathematical relationship that determines how many tributaries of each order a stream will possess. It turns out that the average stream has three or four tributaries of the next smaller order. That is, a second-order stream is fed by three or four first-order creeks, and a 10th-order river is fed by three or four ninth-order rivers. The Potomac is estimated to be seventh-order; its tributaries of approximately sixth order are the Shenandoah, the northern and southern branches of the Potomac, and the Monocacy.

Design with Nature

Ian McHarg is a landscape architect, and as a problem solver, he has taken on the huge challenge that ecology obviously represents to the land planner, making a positive constructive step towards a resolution. From his extensive knowledge of both landscape architecture and the biological science of ecology he has developed a methodology that no responsible land planner, city planner, or large land developer can overlook (nor any affected citizen allow to be overlooked). Through a systematic (and easily reproducible) method Mr. McHarg investigates the relevant ecological restraints inherent in any large planning area. Physiography, hydrology, geology, topology, flora and fauna ecologies, and other natural restraints are individually mapped for the area under consideration. These restrained portions of the area are mapped in varying transparent shades according to the degree of restraint the consideration warrants. By overlaying these numerous graded maps, a final map is evolved which designates where to not develop, where light development is compatible with the land, where specifically restrained development is permissible, and where other types of development (recreational, medium and high density) would be least objectionable.

Interspersed with chapters demonstrating the power of his method (including examples of projects his firm has done for clients and cities all over the county), the author describes his experiences and attitudes in moving chapters that express his love for Earth, and the profound reasons behind this love.
—Vic Conforti

Design with Nature
Ian L. McHarg
1969; 197 pp.

$7.95 postpaid from:
Doubleday and Company
501 Franklin Avenue
Garden City, NY 11530
or Whole Earth Household Store

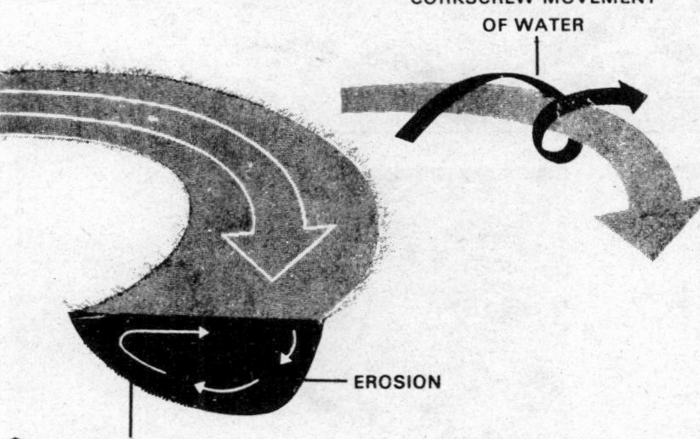

↑ NEW DEPOSITS

Shifting its course, a river moves sideways where it curves because of the way its water erodes and deposits bed material. Water rounding the curve is subjected to centrifugal force. The water at the bottom, retarded by friction, moves more slowly than the surface water. These influences combine to give a corkscrew movement to the water. As a result, silt picked up at the outer bank is deposited on the inner bank, slowly causing an increase in the curve's arc.

HISTORIC FEATURES VALUE

BEACH QUALITY

EXISTING FOREST QUALITY

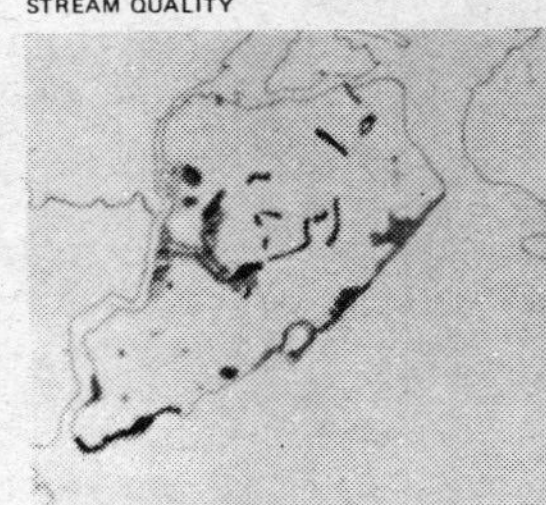

STREAM QUALITY

MARSH QUALITY

WATER WILDLIFE VALUE

INTERTIDAL HABITAT VALUE

SCENIC VALUE (LAND)

GEOLOGIC FEATURES VALUE

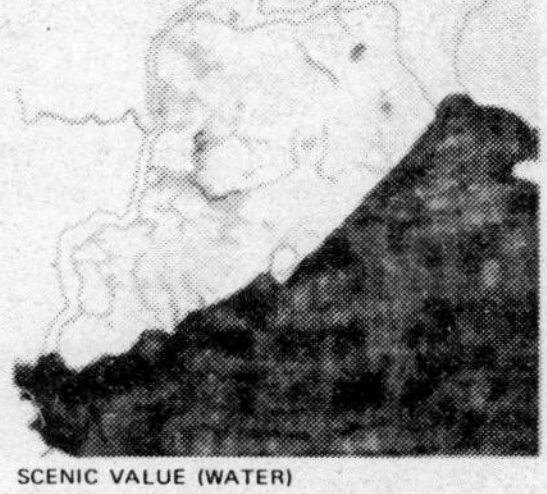

SCENIC VALUE (WATER)

PHYSIOGRAPHIC FEATURES VALUE

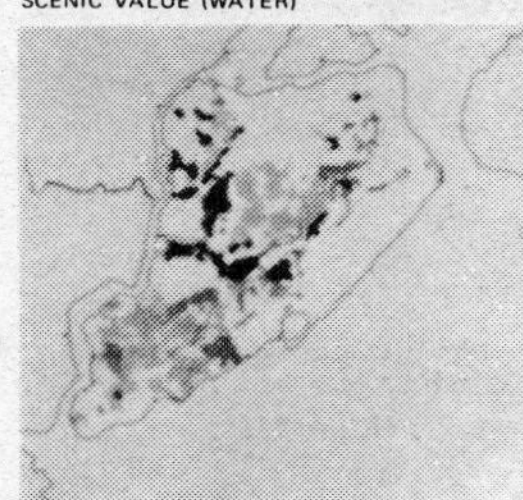

ECOLOGICAL ASSOCIATIONS VALUE

PHENOMENA	RECOMMENDED LAND USES
Surface water and riparian lands	Ports, harbors, marinas, water-treatment plants, water-related industry, open space for institutional and housing use, agriculture, forestry and recreation.
Marshes	Recreation
50-year floodplains	Ports, harbors, marinas, water-treatment plants, water-related industry, agriculture, forestry, recreation, institutional open space, open space for housing.
Aquifers	Agriculture, forestry, recreation, industries that do not produce toxic or offensive effluents. All land uses within limits set by percolation.
Aquifer recharge areas	As aquifers.
Prime agricultural lands	Agriculture, forestry, recreation, open space, housing at 1 house per 25 acres.
Steep lands	Forestry, recreation, housing at a maximum density of 1 house per 3 acres, where wooded.
Forests and woodlands	Forestry, recreation, housing at densities not higher than 1 house per acre.

Water in Environmental Planning

This is the watershed text. A diamond of the first water. Dunne and Leopold wield the swords of Reason and Science, insisting on Quantitative thought. Not just "It rained"; we must say: "A two-hour light rain (that's 1/10" per hour) that caused little overland flow." The book is required reading for those plunging into the nitty-gritty of Environmental Impact Reports; regional or local planning; fighting or supporting subdividers and developers; teaching about flood hazards, rotational slips, stormwater and groundwater overdraft. The writing is rationalist (citing sources, latinate, metrics and lotsa techno lingo). But, taking your time, eddying around in the paragraphs, is always instructive.
—Peter Warshall

Water in Environmental Planning
Thomas Dunne and Luna Leopold
1978; 818 pp.

$32 postpaid from:
W.H. Freeman & Co.
660 Market Street
San Francisco, CA 94104
or Whole Earth Household Store

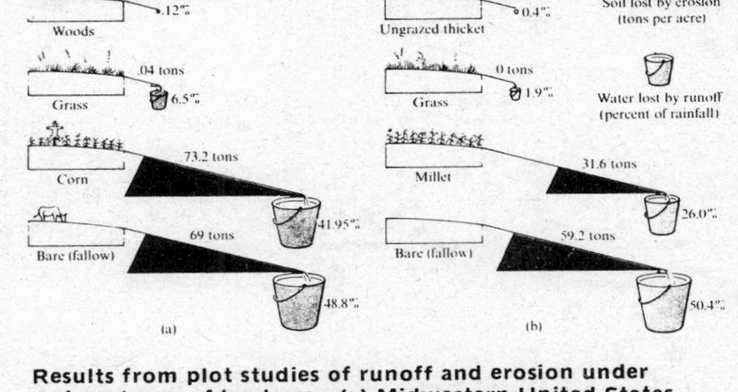

Results from plot studies of runoff and erosion under various types of land use. (a) Midwestern United States. (Soil Conservation Service.) (b) Mpwapwa, Tanzania.

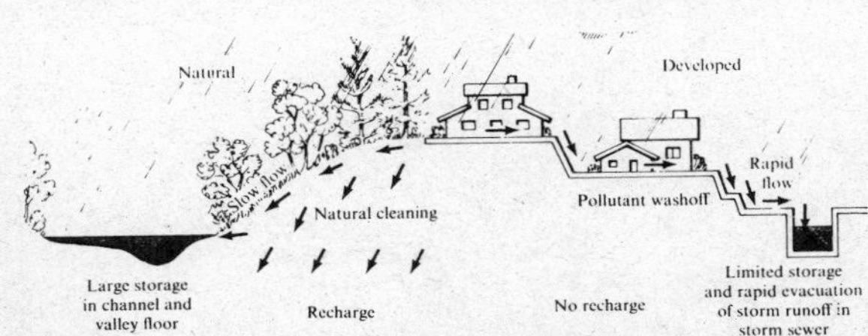

Schematic representation of problems to be managed in the control of urban storm runoff.

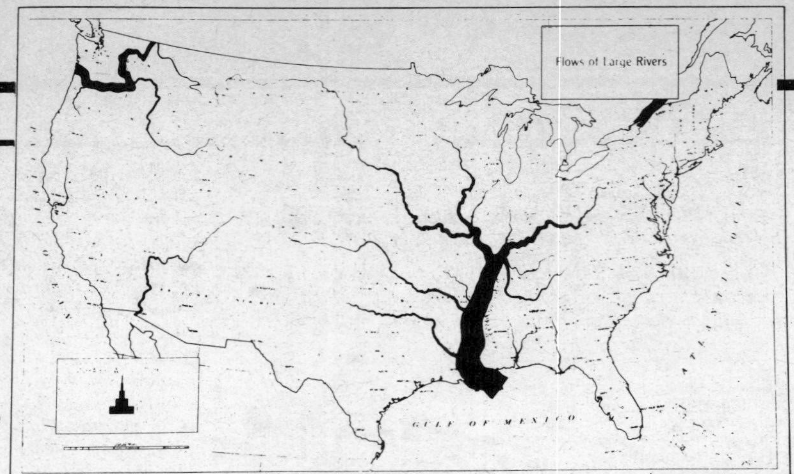

Water Atlas of the United States

A lovely way to spend cozy evenings, looking at the straightforward, easy-to-read maps on every aspect of water: Fishable Freshwater Areas; Withdrawal of Water for Air-Conditioning; Natural Flouride in Water Supplies; Depth of Frost Penetration, etc. — 122 maps. Gives a comforting or uncomfortable water cycle and how human tampering with water resources has changed the place where you live. (Ask for complete list of Water Center's publications when ordering.) —Peter Warshall

Water Atlas of the United States
(A Water Information Center Publication)
Geraghty, Miller, Van der Leeden, Troise
1973; 198 pp.

$40 postpaid from:
Water Information Center, Inc.
North Shore Atrium
6800 Jericho Turnpike
Syosset, NY 11791

The California Water Atlas

The realization that water is rapidly becoming a more critical resource than energy — and more explosive political issue — leads to recognition of the need for thorough collection and easily understandable presentation of all the fundamental water data. (The lack of such information in the energy field has caused much of our current hysterical energy policy.)

Here is a pioneering example of how best to present the big water picture for any area — in this case it's California, a state uniquely defined by its water situation. Happily, the book is a major success on several counts. It is a spectacular browse — dazzling full-page color maps and charts, needle-perfect resolution of highly-detailed satellite photos of river systems, intriguing historic photos — in all a piece of extremely fine bookmaking. The range of the contents approaches comprehensive — virgin flow, history of development, irrigation and crop use, water quality, ground water, snowpack, water treatment, dams, water law, water economics, the '76-'77 drought, etc., etc. And solid, well-researched text by sundry moist experts. It's big — 15½" x 18".

It's an important book. This is the mutual frame of reference, detailing the larger and smaller contexts that permit resolution of policy issues that otherwise might stalemate on for decades.

(Fortunately other reviewers are also raving about the book. If I were the only one, it would be suspect because several of us were involved in the project. I initiated it in the Governor's office. Don Ryan did some of the outstanding cartography. Peter Warshall advised and wrote some text.) —SB

The California Water Atlas
William L. Kahrl, et al.
1978, 1979; 118 pp.

$37.50 postpaid from:
William Kaufmann, Inc.
One First Street
Los Altos, CA 94022
or Whole Earth Household Store

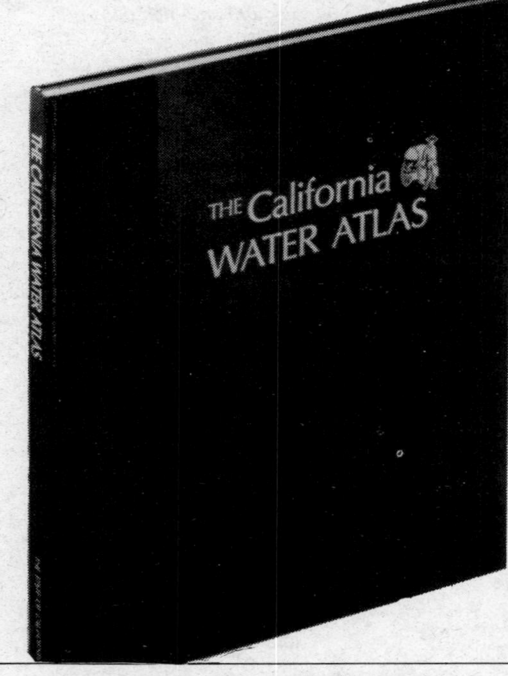

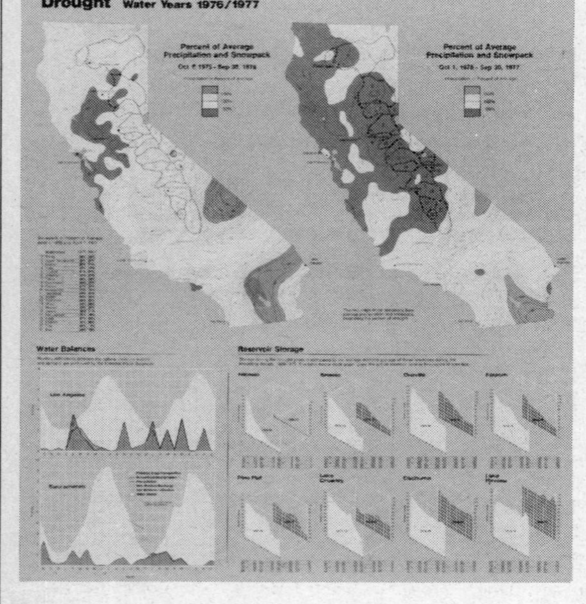

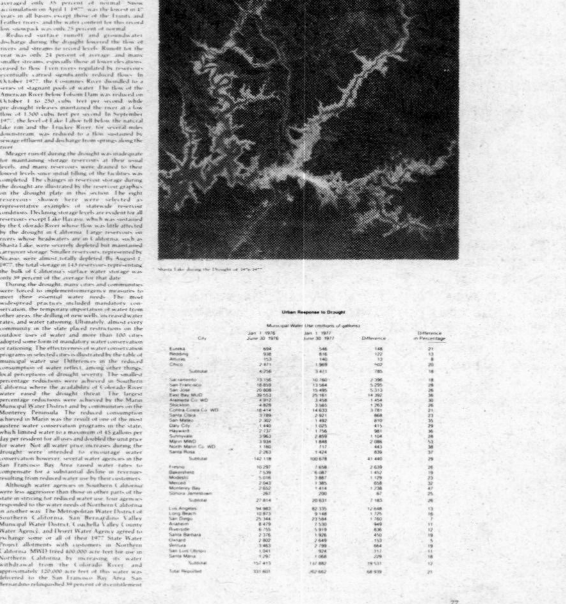

Nature To Be Commanded . . .

One of the great frustrations of trying to create an educational book about watersheds is mapping. For instance, in black-and-white, you can use stipples for sand, squares for bedrock, black for clastic dikes and then try to overlap these three textures with a ripple pattern for subterranean waterflow. The result: a difficult mish-mash of criss-crossed lines. One yearns for a blue overlay.

Well, one thing the government can do is print huge four-color maps and photos and sell them dirt cheap. **Nature To Be Commanded . . .** *(terrible title) is a best buy. Fine vignettes of land and water problems throughout the United States and how mapping and resource planning are essential tools to prevent disasters to both people and the place they inhabit. Vignettes include: Land-use Controls Arising from the Erosion of Seacliffs; Land-sliding and Fault Movement (California); Water Use in Long Island (New York); Gravel Mining and Resulting Ground Instability (Colorado); and Groundwater Resources and Housing Growth in Tucson. Boring prose style.* —Peter Warshall

Nature To Be Commanded . . .
(Earth-Science Maps Applied to Land and Water Management)
Geological Survey Professional Paper 950
G.D. Robinson and Andrew M. Spieker, Eds.
1978; 95 pp.

$7 postpaid from:
Supt. of Documents
U.S. Govt. Printing Office
Washington, D.C. 20402
or Whole Earth Household Store

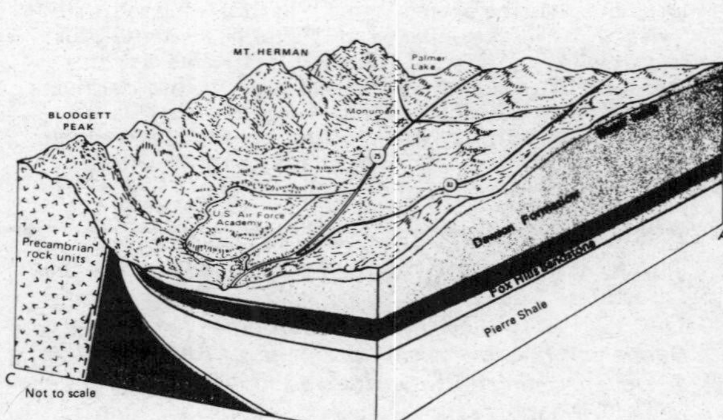

More Water for Arid Lands

Various techniques of saving water: including roof and hillside catchments, rainwater harvesting, saline water irrigation and other water conservation methods employed in deserts around the world. —Peter Warshall

More Water for Arid Lands
(Promising Technologies and Research Opportunities)
No. PB 239 472
1974; 153 pp.

$11 postpaid from:
NTIS
U.S. Dept. of Commerce
5285 Port Royal Road
Springfield, VA 22161

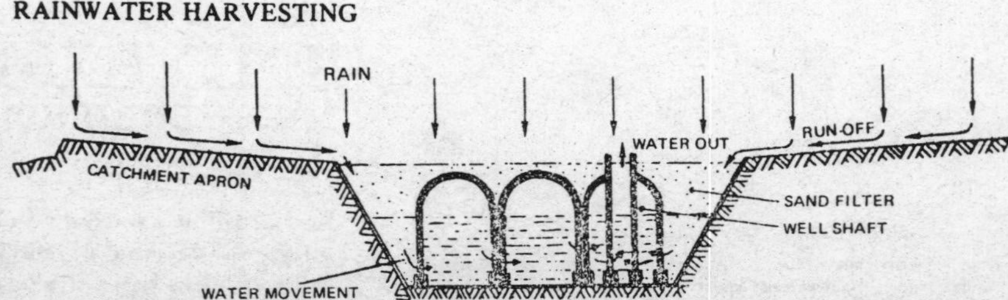

An experimental rainwater catchment with a sand-filled water-storage tank. The sand reduces evaporation and filters the water as it enters and is withdrawn, making water suitable for drinking. Tank is lined with thin plastic; storage capacity is increased by constructing beehive-shaped cells out of stacks of plastic sausages.

Protective covering of molded, lightweight, concrete slabs cut evaporation by an estimated 80 percent recently in full-scale tests on two reservoirs in Ovamboland, South-West Africa. Engineers cover reservoirs with 24-in^2, 2-in thick floating slabs of polystyrene, sand, and concrete. Exposed surface of each slab is painted white to reflect the intense sun rays, which hasten evaporation.

contour plowing minimizes erosion

temporary high water storage possible in creek corridor

livestock prevented from direct access to creek

water table

preserve all natural vegetation in creek corridor: retards erosion, preserves wildlife habitat

drain tile water infiltrates soil before reaching stream: filters nutrients, preserves water quality

creek corridor varies with conditions

creek

building set back from creek corridor

reserve parking area has permeable surface, allows infiltration

parking lot also stores excess storm water

roof runoff detained in retention pond

retention pond detains storm water runoff, settles solids

sewer line

sewage lift station

water table

creek corridor not developed

natural vegetation between building and creek

wildlife habitat

Protecting Creeksheds

Urban creeks are the proverbial third world of the Earth's water cycle. Creeks are either ignored until man needs a place to dump his old tires and mattresses, shoved out of his way into a concrete channel, or routed into a pipe and buried under his streets. Measures which allow a creek to become an asset to the community are reviewed in a useful little publication called **Protecting Creeksheds: Analysis and Action.** *It's geared for the community person who wants to do something about a creek rapidly being engulfed by urbanization. In non-technical language it briefly reviews the concept and elements of a "creekshed," a creekshed's potential benefits, the impact of urbanization, and land use management strategies to protect its quality and character. There's just enough information to get something started with city hall. For further battles, its big brother publication* **Protecting Creeksheds: Development and Evaluation of a Method to Manage Small, Urbanizing Watersheds Through Local Government Actions** *(E. Wayne Say and Allan Dines, 1974; 234 pp., $14 postpaid from National Technical Information Service) provides more detailed information including a useful literature review. The larger publication also reviews some enlightening case studies of creekshed protection which the authors performed in the Great Lakes region.* —*Joseph Alcamo*

Protecting Creeksheds
(Analysis and Action)
E. Wayne Say and
Allan Dines
(PB 239 140)
1974; 24 pp.

$6 postpaid from:
NTIS
U.S. Dept. of Commerce
5285 Port Royal Road
Springfield, VA 22161

AGRICULTURAL USE

In many areas land along a creek is being used for agricultural purposes. This kind of use can also affect the creek's quality both in the immediate area and downstream. The illustration above notes some of the land and water conservation practices which are appropriate for this land use. Some of these considerations have to do with physical changes: draintile which dissipates the water before it gets to the creek, contour plowing, preservation of a vegetated buffer strip along the creek corridor, fence lines along the creek corridor if the land is grazed. Other considerations have to do with treatment of the land: when and what kind of fertilizers are applied to fields, and what kind of crop (row crop or ground-covering crop) is grown near the creek.

INDUSTRIAL/COMMERCIAL USES

These uses can generate many adverse impacts on the creek at the point where they occur as well as downstream. Such uses often have large parking areas or roof surface areas. They may require a large volume of water for manufacturing products. This suggests a need for careful analysis of: wastewater disposal methods (domestic sewage or process water), quantity of runoff generated from buildings or parking lots, setback from creek corridor to preserve scenic or natural quality, and amount, kind and placement of vegetation elsewhere on the site.

Creekshed Scale

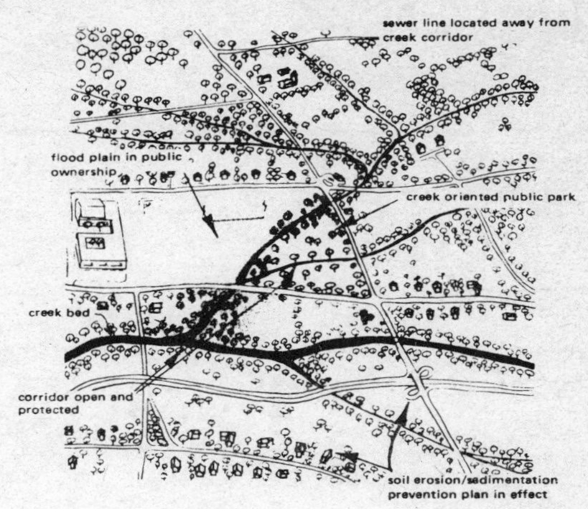

THE CREEKSHED SCALE

This scale is the entire creekshed. "Good" design or "wise" land use at this scale depends upon the implementation of the measures already mentioned for the site and project plus some assurance that expenditures for public services will not result in degradation of creek benefits. At this scale the benefit realized is a smoothly functioning, high quality creek system. The units of government and communities in the creekshed can enjoy many or all of the creek's benefits (drainage, wildlife, amenity, water supply, open space and local recreation). In addition, significant savings can be realized by *not* having to pay for pollution abatement or control, or installation and maintenance of drainage "improvements". Flooding will be minimized and private property values will be stablized or increased.

The Wetlands Project

The Wetlands Project exists to help townspeople protect their marshes, ponds, streams, swamps, floodplains — anything in Nature that holds water. Their written materials are a pleasure to read no matter where you live. If you dwell in the northeast forest bioregion, they can help with anything from wetland education to wetland government.

Wetlands and the Water Cycle (24 pp.; $.80 postpaid)
Clear thoughts and vision, as water when the brook runs deep.

Wetlands and Flood Plains On Paper (28 pp.; $.80 postpaid)
The process of flood plain and wetland mapping — all kinds.

Annotated Wetland Bibliography ($1.30 postpaid)
—*Peter Warshall*

all from:
The Wetlands Project
Massachusetts
Audubon Society
Lincoln, MA 01773

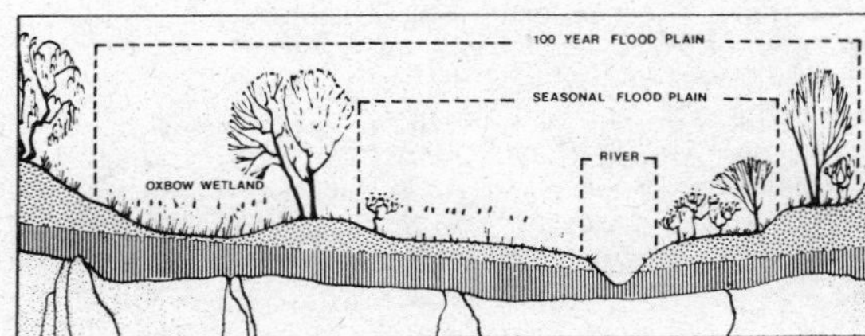

The undisturbed floodplain . . .

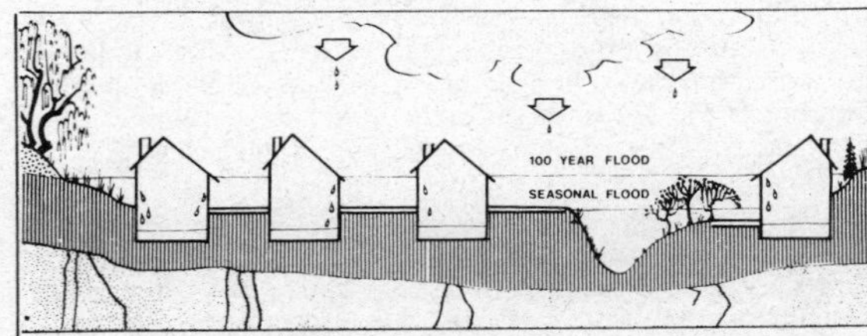

is filled and developed, but continues its natural flood.

Guidelines for Watershed Management No. 1

When you're down in the dirt and soiling your hands, this book is the best guide to watershed healing of erosion scars and gullied hill slope wounds. Fine technical essays with lots of equations and equipment by such watershed doctors as Thomas Dunne ("Evaluation of Erosion Conditions and Trends") and B.H. Heede ("Gully Control Structures and Systems"). For all those in forested watersheds that have been sloppily logged with thoughtless roads, this book is a must. For all those living in agricultural watersheds with problems of soil loss, this book will sparkle ideas. (Ask for complete list of related FAO publications when ordering.) —*Peter Warshall*

Guidelines for Watershed Management No. 1
Food and Agriculture Organization of the United Nations
1977; 293 pp.

$16.75 postpaid from:
Unipub
Box 433
Murray Hill Station
New York, NY 10016

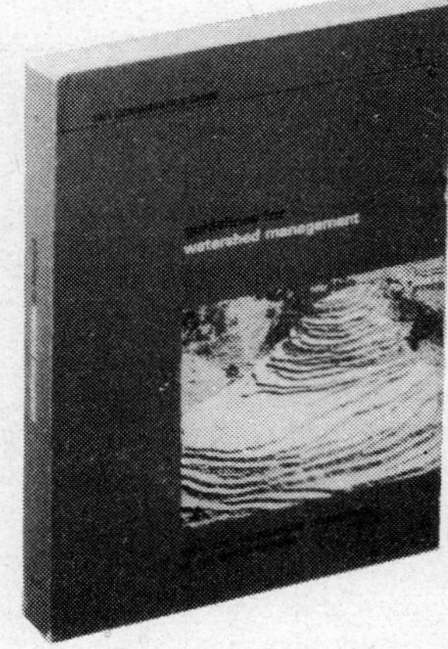

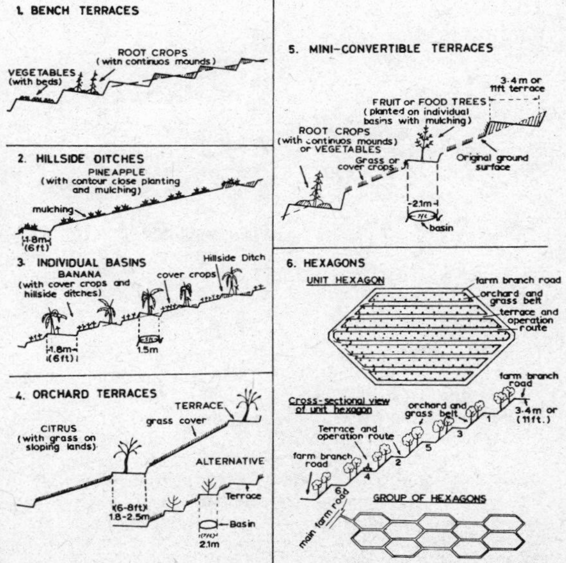

River Ecology and Man

A series of essays giving the sober, intimate judgments of scientists. Amazing, the number of ways a river can be fucked up. Technical writing but, if you have a river you want to protect, the vignettes on the Columbia, Delaware, Illinois, Nile, Thames and Danube will provide solid frames of reference. The chapters on politics are disappointing. —*Peter Warshall*

River Ecology and Man
Ray Oglesby, et al.
1972; 465 pp.

$32.50 postpaid from:
Academic Press, Inc.
111 Fifth Avenue
New York, NY 10003

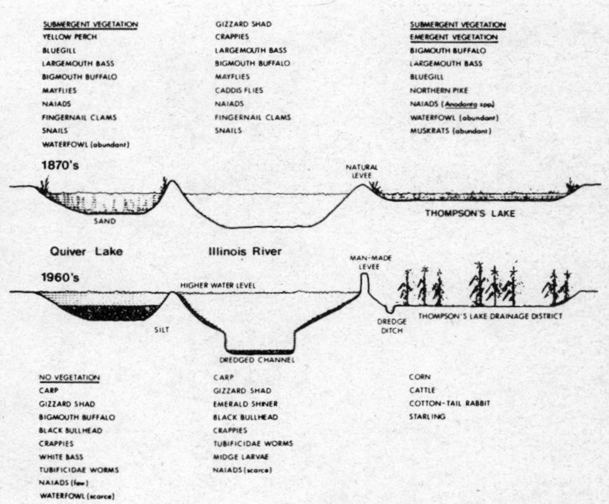

Figure 8. Schematic drawings demonstrating the impact man has had during the past century on the ecology of the Illinois River and two of its adjoining bottomland lakes near Havana (Figure 1)

More water care

For careful water use in the country see p. 245.

For careful water use around the house see p. 244.

For water politics see pp. 64-67.

THE RISING SUN
NEIGHBORHOOD NEWSLETTER

The lady at the bus stop said it rained more in Sausalito during the war, which made it even harder for the people from the shipyard who were always looking for a place to stay. She rented out her porch for $5 a week. There was so much demand for rooms that many landlords made everyone move after a week and then rented to someone new. I asked her why they did that, seemed like a hassle for the landlords and no more money, but she didn't know or couldn't explain it to a postwar mind.

BECAUSE "LAND USE" too often means "use up," there's considerable repair work to do. Usually it's a choice between soil and oil. Choose soil. It takes longer to make oil (about 40 million years longer). Oil was alive. Soil is alive.
—SB

The World of the Soil

An excursion through an amazing world by a scientist who explains the obvious with style and without condescension. The references are to English soils but the principles apply everywhere. Also see **Soil and Civilization** *(p. 49).*
—Richard Nilsen

The World of the Soil
Sir E. John Russell
1957; 237 pp.

$1.95 postpaid from:
Franklin Watts Inc.
730 Fifth Avenue
New York, NY 10019

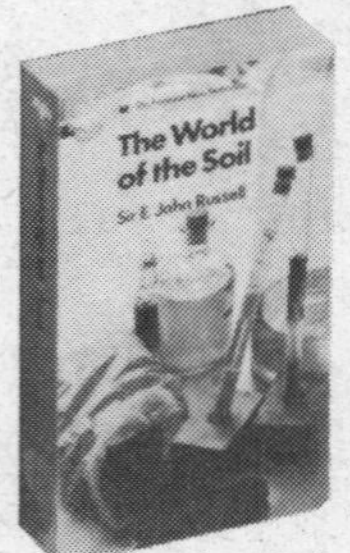

•

The chinks and crannies riddling the soil appear extremely minute to us and it seems incredible that any air could enter. But everything in Nature is relative: the molecules of oxygen are vastly smaller: crevices only 1/1000 of an inch wide, and far too small for us to see, are as large compared with an oxygen molecule as a valley about 120 miles wide in comparison with a man. For a proper appreciation of the soil one must try to see things as they would appear to its smallest inhabitants if they had the power of sight.

•

. . . during a year a bullock leaves in its faeces enough food to support an insect population of at least one fifth of its own weight, to say nothing of the bacteria, fungi, protozoa, nematodes and other organisms that also participate.

The Nature and Properties of Soils

A college text on soil science. The writing is clear, there is a glossary of terms, and the section headings make it easy to find the information you want quickly. More facts than most people need, but well worth consulting on specific subjects.
—Richard Nilsen

The Nature and Properties of Soils
Nyle C. Brady
8th Edition
1969; 653 pp.

$19.95 postpaid from:
The Macmillan Company
866 Third Avenue
New York, NY 10022
or Whole Earth Household Store

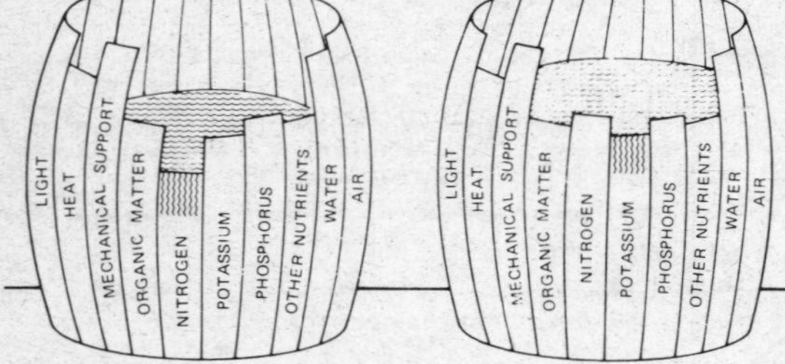

An illustration of the principle of limiting factors. The level of water in the barrels above represents the level of crop production. (Left) Nitrogen is represented as being the factor that is most limiting. Even though the other elements are present in more adequate amounts, crop production can be no higher than that allowed by the nitrogen. When nitrogen is added (right) the level of crop production is raised until it is controlled by the next most limiting factor, in this case, potassium.

↓ Puddled soil (left) and well-granulated soil (right). Plant roots and especially humus play the major role in soil granulation. For that reason a sod tends to encourage development of a granular structure in the surface horizon of cultivated land.

Approved Practices in Soil Conservation

How to control erosion from wind and water. Very complete — contouring, drainage, pond construction, shelterbelts, wildlife management. Many of the procedures assume you have access to a tractor and implements. Foster worked for the U.S. Soil Conservation Service, and much of the information is compiled from government pamphlets. They are usually referenced in the text, so you can use this book in a library to find which ones you want to send for.
—Richard Nilsen

Approved Practices in Soil Conservation
Albert B. Foster
1964; 497 pp.

$13 postpaid from:
The Interstate Printers & Publishers, Inc.
19-27 N. Jackson Street
Danville, IL 61832
or Whole Earth Household Store

•

The first step in contour farming is to establish a contour guide line that runs across the field almost at a constant level. All planting or farming operations will be done from this guide line. . . .Two people are needed—— one to use the level and one to be the target on which to take a sight and set the stakes. Equipment may consist of a hand level or a small carpenter's level mounted on a T-shaped stick of light weight. . . . In locating the first contour guide line on a slope, the usual practice is to go to the highest point in the field and then walk straight down the general slope from this point a distance of from 80 to 100 feet, depending on the steepness of the slope. . . .After the location of the first guide line has been selected, a stake is set and leveling is started from that position. With the levelman at the starting point, the helper paces 50 to 100 feet across the slope, staying approximately on the contour. The levelman directs the helper up or down the slope until he is on the same level or contour as the levelman. The helper sets a stake at this position and the levelman moves to the second stake, the helper moving another 50 to 100 feet across the slope. This procedure is continued until the line crosses the field.

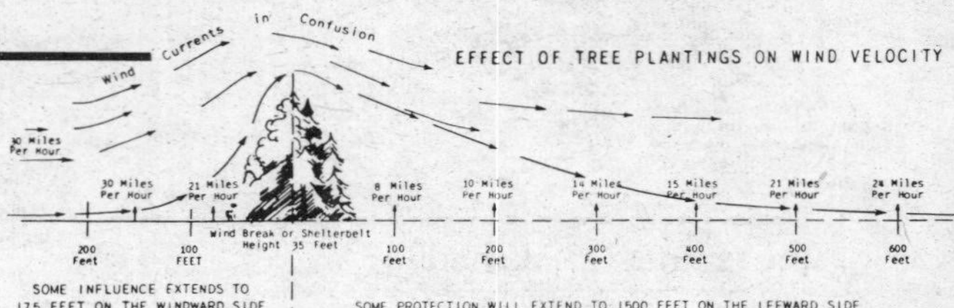

A pasture gully shaped and seeded to grass makes a useful waterway.

The Organic Method Primer

Within the organic gardening movement there are numerous schools of thought, and they are often contradictory. The advantage of **The Organic Method Primer** *is that the authors have made a compilation of the various beliefs and methods, and have added to them their own practical experience from years of teaching and gardening organically. You can learn what a BioDynamic farmer would do in a given situation, and then compare that with the advice of a mulch gardener. For its length, it is one of the most comprehensive gardening books I have read — relatively "far out" subjects like biomagnetics are covered, but there is also solid advice on what to look for when you buy a mechanical shredder. The section on organic pest control techniques is particularly complete; it would take a long time just to try all of the remedies that are described here. Note the quotation for instant soil technique.*
—Richard Nilsen

The Organic Method Primer
Bargyla and Gylver Rateaver
1973; 257 pp.

$11.50 postpaid from:
Bargyla Rateaver
Pauma Valley, CA 92061

•

Today the dirt in your garden is half mineral and the other half mostly air and water, with only 1% or so of it organic matter, maybe even as much as 5%. . . . Hardly anywhere can you find half the original layer of topsoil left; it is not only robbed of its organic content, but has been eroded away or blown away because it was no longer spongy enough to hold the water that fell on it. Your forefathers dug into that wonderful soil with destructive relish, and within a few years they had wrecked nearly all of it. Their sins are being visited on you. What can you do about it? . . .

If you have heavy clay, adobe, or caliche, you must take the preliminary step of fluffing it up. The best way to do this is by digging in rice hulls. You will need enough to cover the area 3 feet deep. They are slippery slivers which slide into any opening so easily that you may be able to do the job with a spading fork. If the ground is baked hard, you will need a tiller. First use a pick or the spading fork tines to nick little holes here and there, to give the tiller tines a toehold. Go over the bare ground 3 - 6 times to get a loose layer 3 inches or so thick. Then spread the hulls several inches deep and till 3 times. Add another layer of hulls and till again. Repeating this until the hulls are used up will give you a permanently good texture so that you never again have to worry about drainage or stickiness. Should the ground be too hard for even a pick, soak it first and watch it carefully for just the right stage of dryness before you till it. This is a nuisance, but it is a once-in-a-lifetime job and worth the fuss.

If you cannot get rice hulls, use buckwheat hulls, peanut shells or something similar. Should even these be unavailable, use sawdust mixed with something granular, like coffee grounds (get from an instant coffee factory, or restaurants). The important thing is to use enough so that instead of clay with hulls (or whatever) in it, you have hulls with bits of clay in it. . . .

From this point on, the procedure is the same as with sandy soil. ADD ORGANIC MATTER! Add enough so that half your soil is organic material and half the original sand or amended clay. Gather and store your amendments until you have enough, then take a day to spread it one layer at a time and till in. . . .

Texture has so much bearing on the ease with which you can garden, that the ideal loam should be your first goal.

Soil organisms will need nitrogen right away as they get to decomposing all this raw material, so spray the soil with fish emulsion and manure-weed-tea. Make the latter by soaking manure and weeds (especially stinging nettle) in unchlorinated water for days or weeks (the longer the better), and diluting it to a pale color. This is a good source of bacteria. . . .

If you do not supply the extra nitrogen, there will be competition beween the soil organisms and your crop roots for it, and the crops will lose out. After a time, when the organisms have died, the nitrogen they used will go back to the soil from their decaying bodies, but in the meantime it is up to you to supply the need.

THERE IS NO ONE BOOK on soils. Every author writes from their own niche. The engineer is concerned with foundations and soils; the farmer with fertility and soils; the sanitarian with the cleaning properties of soils; the ecologist with the life of soils; the geologist with the stability of hill slopes and their soils; the conservationist with erosion, soil destruction and the regeneration of soils. It's pitiful. Soil is the strength of any civilization. —Peter Warshall

Soil Test Kit

A soil kit enables you to test your garden soil for acidity/alkalinity, nitrogen, phosphorus, and potash. A test will show what is present and what is lacking. There are test tubes, chemicals, and a color chart to gauge results. Feed the soil, not the plant. —Lloyd Kahn

Soil Test Kit
Send for descriptive literature and current prices
$9.99 - $59.95 Kits postpaid from:
Sudbury Laboratory, Inc.
572 Dutton Road
Sudbury, MA 10776

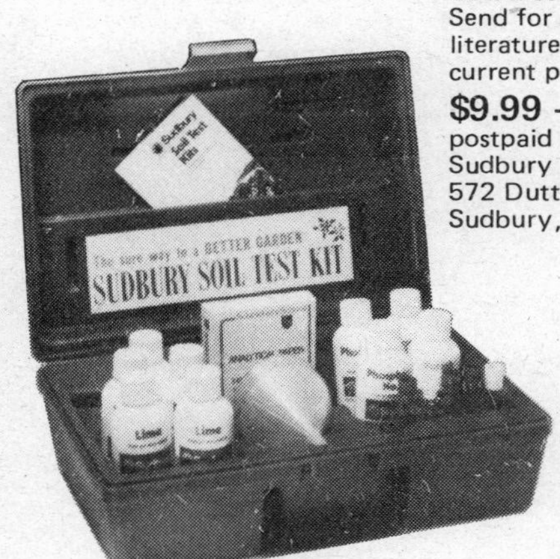

Soil test labs

If neither the small soil test kits nor information from the local agriculture department have given you the answers you're looking for, it may be time to try the pros. Here are 3 representative labs that can give you a thorough look into the composition and chemicals that make up Your Earth, at a cost of $15 to $20. The report you get back will give you pH, trace minerals, percent organic materials, available nutrient levels, cation exchange capacity, and more. If you're spending big bucks buying fertilizer, contemplating large scale gardening/farming, evaluating new land, or exploring the complexities of soil science to find out why the darn tomatoes died in August, this is money well spent. Write for info and prices. —Dick Fugett

Woods End Lab, RFD Box 65, Temple, ME 04984. *Different from most labs in that they'll make recommendations based on organic gardening principles.*

Harris Labs, Box 80837, Lincoln, NE 68501. *The standard soil tests are available, plus fertilizer, vitamin, pesticide & herbicide analysis.*

A & L Ag. Labs, 1010 Carver Rd., Modesto, CA 95350. *Same as Harris, but best of all is an 80 page booklet they sell for only $1, "Soil & Plant Analysis," technical but jammed with information.*

Ecology of Compost

Backyard composting, brief and simple. Composting is the most basic recycling there is, and, if you've priced fertilizers lately, one of the most sensible. —Richard Nilsen

Ecology of Compost
(A Public Involvement Project)
Daniel L. Dindal
1972; 12 pp.
$ .25 postpaid from:
Community Relations Office
State University of New York
College of Environmental Science and Forestry
Syracuse, NY 13210

ARRANGEMENT OF LAYERS FOR COMPOSTING

REPEAT THIS THREE LAYER SCHEME UNTIL PILE IS 3-5 FEET HIGH.

Harnessing the Earthworm

Darwin discovered that worms convert compost to humus within their digestive tract by the same chemical process which takes soil microbes months to perform. Barrett explains how farmers, gardeners and tree growers can cultivate earthworms on a large scale or small to replenish topsoil. Worms are an untapped natural resource, and anyone who reads this classic book will want to become a Johnny Appleseed of earthworms. —Rosemary Menninger

Harnessing the Earthworm
Thomas J. Barrett
1959, 1976; 192 pp.
$4.95 postpaid from:
Bookworm Publishing Co.
P.O. Box 3037
Ontario, CA 91761
or Whole Earth Household Store

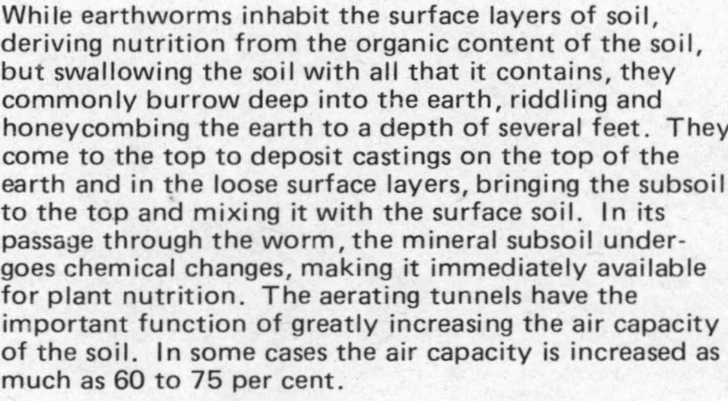

•

Where a rich compost is provided, a culture bed eight feet long, four feet wide and two feet deep will easily support a population of *fifty thousand* domesticated earthworms.

•

While earthworms inhabit the surface layers of soil, deriving nutrition from the organic content of the soil, but swallowing the soil with all that it contains, they commonly burrow deep into the earth, riddling and honeycombing the earth to a depth of several feet. They come to the top to deposit castings on the top of the earth and in the loose surface layers, bringing the subsoil to the top and mixing it with the surface soil. In its passage through the worm, the mineral subsoil undergoes chemical changes, making it immediately available for plant nutrition. The aerating tunnels have the important function of greatly increasing the air capacity of the soil. In some cases the air capacity is increased as much as 60 to 75 per cent.

Water penetration is improved where there is adequate earthworm population. Plough sole is eliminated. The rainfall is quickly absorbed, instead of running off or standing on the surface.

Wormcasts in acid soil are much less acid than the soil from which they are derived, the reduction in acidity in some instances amounting to as much as 75 per cent. In large numbers, the earthworms produce a topsoil that is practically a neutral humus. Also, earthworms reduce the alkalinity of the soil, so that alkaline soils are rendered less alkaline, while acid soils are rendered less acid. Wormcasts commonly contain a high percentage of carbonates as well as a high percentage of nitrogen. Earthworms increase the organic content of the surface soils by concentrating the organic content of the soil in the top layers. Colloid humus is increased in the topsoil.

Domesticated earthworm. Average life-size of mature worm is 4 inches long.

Compost

A small pamphlet, but it contains all you need to know in order to make and use good compost out of diverse materials and under a wide range of conditions. Koepf is one of the genuine experts in the fields of soil fertility and improvement via organic technique. Anything he writes is worth reading. —Steve Kaffka

Compost
(What it is, How it is made, What it does)
H.H. Koepf
1966; 18 pp.
$1.50 postpaid from:
Biodynamic Research Laboratory
Box 253
Wyoming, RI 02898
or Whole Earth Household Store

•

The Carbon:Nitrogen Ratio of the Compost Mixture

The most important information about just how rich or poor a compost mixture is, is indicated by the ratio of carbonaceous materials and nitrogen it contains. This is the so-called carbon:nitrogen ratio. Too little nitrogen causes a compost to work slowly. The product will be rather poor. More nitrogen than required for optimum fermentation is likely to cause nitrogen losses from the pile. It very likely also creates odor problems, since ammonia is the chemical compound by which nitrogen escapes into the atmosphere. The carbon:nitrogen ratio is expressed in a figure like 25:1 or simply 25. This means that the compound in question contains 25 times as much carbon as nitrogen. These are examples of the carbon:nitrogen ratio of materials or mixtures used for composting: sawdust 150; peat moss 50; straw, cornstalks, etc. 50-150; hay from legumes 15; leaves from alder and ash 20-30; leaves from oak, birch, maple, etc. 40-60; animal droppings 15; manure with bedding material 20-25.

The ideal initial mixture for composting 25-30
Finished compost of any kind 14-20
Stable humus in fertile soils 9-14

Earthworms: Buyer's Guide and Profitable Farming

The **Earthworm Buyer's Guide** *is a welcome sourcebook of worms. Lists the type of worm grown at each hatchery and whether they'll ship their worms. Pick a hatchery and call ahead to learn what growing medium they use. Worms transplanted into an alien environment will die; but wherever the new eggs hatch becomes their native turf.*

Profitable Earthworm Farming *is a complete manual of worm production, storage, selling and shipping geared to the live fishing bait market.* —Rosemary Menninger

Earthworm Buyer's Guide
(A Directory of Earthworm Hatcheries in the U.S.A. and Canada)
Robert F. Shields
1980; 78 pp.
$3 postpaid

Profitable Earth Worm Farming
Charlie Morgan
1957, 1978; 95 pp.
$3 postpaid
both from:
Shields Publications
P.O. Box 669
Eagle River, WI 54521

Weeds, Guardians of the Soil

Cocannouer explains how weeds help the soil and crops, when grown in a controlled way, by their deep roots which bring up minerals from the subsoil. They also help shallow-rooted crops (most cultivated crops are) get to deep water; and they conserve the soil, improve its texture, and are good to eat. Written in an anecdotal style containing much good information. —Stuart Ambler

Weeds, Guardians of the Soil
Joseph A. Cocannouer
1950; 179 pp.
$4.95 postpaid from:
The Devin-Adair Co., Inc.
143 Sound Beach Ave.
Old Greenwich, CT 06870
or Whole Earth Household Store

•

Near the top of the list I place pigweeds, two or three strains, and lamb's quarter, both familiar throughout the country in garden and field. Under most conditions these weeds are beneficial to the crop with which they may be growing. The same can be said for some of the nightshades, the ground cherry, and succulent purslane. Even some of the noxious weeds, like the cocklebur and bull nettle, are soil improvers where the individual plants have ample room for full root development.

THE RISING SUN
NEIGHBORHOOD NEWSLETTER

David showed me a pile of stones in Golden Gate Park that used to be a 14th century Spanish monastery. William Randolph Hearst bought it, dissassembled it with the stones numbered, brought it back and gave it to the City of San Francisco without giving them money to put it back together (very half-assed, Bill). So the city never had money to put it together, the crates rotted off and the numbers washed away and the monastery is now two piles of stones in Golden Gate Park.

Seeds, Spades, Hearths, and Herds

Those few gardeners and farmers left in this country who are not direct extensions of corporations eventually come to wonder where this agriculture business began and where they fit in. Supergeographer Sauer choreographs them through prehistory, all over the planet to trace the origins of crop cultivation and domestication of animals. He debunks the classical view of hungry hunters and gatherers inventing farming during bad years and suggests instead it began in cultures of plenty as an extension of leisure and even magic. —Malcolm Terence

Seeds, Spades, Hearths, and Herds
(The Domestication of Animals and Foodstuffs)
Carl O. Sauer
1969; 175 pp.
(2nd Edition)
$3.95 postpaid from:
The MIT Press
28 Carleton Street
Cambridge, MA 02142
or Whole Earth Household Store

•

The ancestors of most New World seed plants appear to have been attractive weeds. They were not tenacious intruders that the cultivator had difficulty in getting rid of, nor are they such as grow on trodden ground. They were gentle, well-behaved weeds that liked the sunshine, loose earth, and plant food of the tilled spaces, and had no great root system. Such volunteers, usable by man, were first tolerated, then protected, and finally planted. The tomato is in part still in the stage of becoming a cultivated plant. In many places in Mexico and Central America the little cherry tomato is the common form; it is not planted, but protected. It, in turn, derives from wild, inutile tomatoes of northwestern South America.

•

The dominant plants of North American agriculture were maize, beans, and squashes or pumpkins. These formed a symbiotic complex, without an equal elsewhere. The corn plants grow tall and have first claim on sunlight and moisture. The beans climb up the corn stalks for their share of light; their roots support colonies of nitrogen-fixing bacteria. The squashes or pumpkins grow mainly prone on the ground and complete the ground cover. . . with few exceptions, all three were grown together. By long cultivation varieties of all were selected, able to grow to the farthest climatic limits of Indian agriculture. Civilized man has not extended the limits of any of them and has introduced only a few crops that succeed under more extreme climates. . . The Hopi, living in a land of little and late rain, of short summers and cold nights, depend on them and by them have maintained themselves and their fine and gentle culture, our civilization lacking the skills to match theirs for this harsh environment.

Land & Life

The work of Carl O. Sauer is a rich guide, and a continual source of stimulation for Anyman's journey into the American Past. For over fifty years Dr. Sauer has been providing us with a series of incredibly compact and skillfully rendered 'portraits' of the forgotten peoples of the New World — Indians, proto-Indians and backwoods Whites — the people, it now seems, who have much to teach us about living here in balance with the American Earth. An historical geographer by training, and a man who has made many important contributions to the new social and environmental sciences — in short, a scholar's scholar — Dr. Sauer nonetheless writes clearly, and with great precision — a fact that has not been lost on some of the more important poets of our time. **Land & Life** *is a selection of Dr. Sauer's 'portraits', and can be easily slipped into your bookshelf right between the work of Basho & Lao Tsu.* —Robert Callahan

Land & Life
Carl O. Sauer
1963, 1974; 435 pp.
$3.95 postpaid from:
University of California Press
2223 Fulton Street
Berkeley, CA 94720
or Whole Earth Household Store

•

Dispersed living, the isolated family home, became most characteristic of the "Northern" folk on the frontier. In Europe nearly everyone had lived in a village or town; in this country the rural village disappeared or never existed. Our farmers lived in the "country" and went to "town" on business or pleasure. The word "village," like "brook," was one that poets might use; it was strange to even our western language. Land was available to the individual over here in tracts of a size beyond any holdings he might ever have had overseas. The village pattern was retained almost only where religious bonds or social planning prescribed living in close congregation.

•

Under natural conditions given a specific climate, vegetation, relief, and rock structure — there will be a characteristic soil as to depth and profile for any position on a slope. Soil and slope are in genetic relationship. Neither is static. Both naturally are changing very slowly. In the majority of cases the slope gradually grows less, and the soil on it weathers more deeply because it forms a bit more rapidly than it is removed at the surface. Soil formation and removal are either balanced, or formation exceeds removal; or, more rarely, removal exceeds formation. Soils develop slowly by weathering. The mechanically comminuted rock flour of our glacial lands has acquired approximately optimum characteristics in the course of about 25,000 years. This does not include weathering that starts from solid rock, but from the crushed materials of the glacial mill.

Plants, Man & Life

The classic on the domestication of plants, by a damned interesting man. Bless him, he annotates his bibliography. —SB

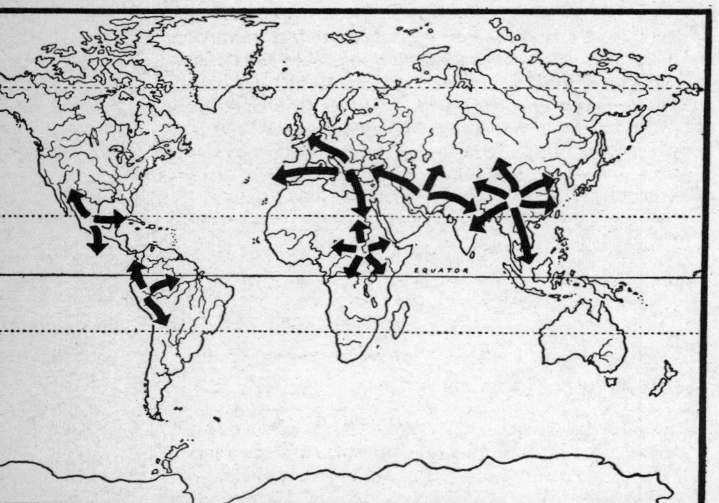

Centers of diversity for cultivated plants, according to Vavilov.

Plants, Man & Life
Edgar Anderson
1952, 1967; 251 pp.
$3.95 postpaid from:
University of California Press
2233 Fulton Street
Berkeley, CA 94720
or Whole Earth Household Store

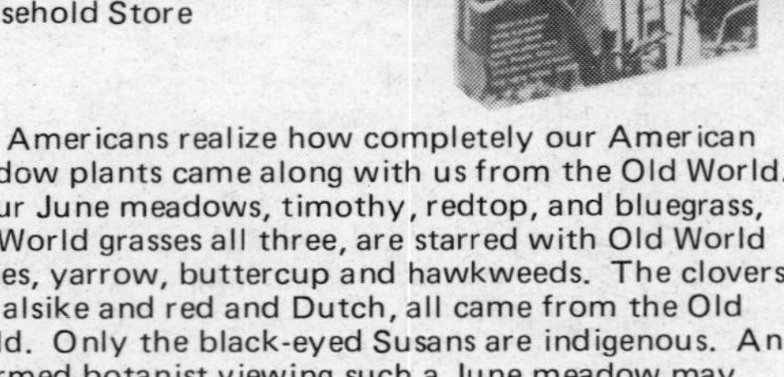

•

Few Americans realize how completely our American meadow plants came along with us from the Old World. In our June meadows, timothy, redtop, and bluegrass, Old World grasses all three, are starred with Old World daisies, yarrow, buttercup and hawkweeds. The clovers too, alsike and red and Dutch, all came from the Old World. Only the black-eyed Susans are indigenous. An informed botanist viewing such a June meadow may sometimes find it hard to point out a single species of plant which grew here in pre-Columbian times.

•

Amaranths are a dump-heap plant par excellence, and are common in barnyards, middens, and refuse dumps throughout the world. The ancient Aztecs in a sort of pagan communion ceremony mixed the popped seeds with human blood, molding the mess into the shape of a god which was sacrificed on the altars and then passed around to be eaten.

The One-Straw Revolution

By changing one of the grasses in his rice fields to another variety, Fukuoka started a process that brought his part of the ecosystem into a natural balance. On his farm he gets yields comparable to traditional farms but without plowing; he lets nature do the work. He simply plants and harvests — pretty revolutionary. The book describes his method. See also **Permaculture One** *and* **Permaculture Two**, *p. 83.* —Rosemary Menninger

The One-Straw Revolution
(An Introduction to Natural Farming)
Masanobu Fukuoka
1978; 224 pp.
$7.95 postpaid from:
Rodale Books
33 East Minor
Emmaus, PA 18049
or Whole Earth Household Store

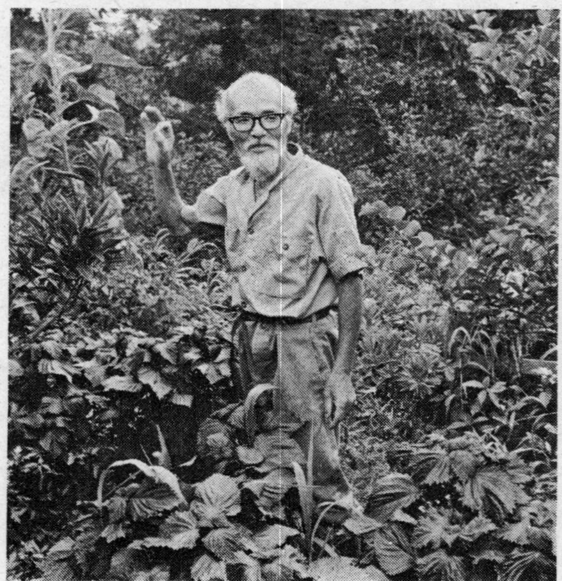

•

Near a small village on the island of Shikoku in southern Japan, Masanobu Fukuoka has been developing a method of natural farming which could help to reverse the degenerative momentum of modern agriculture. Natural farming requires no machines, no chemicals, and very little weeding. Mr. Fukuoka does not plow the soil or use prepared compost. He does not hold water in his rice fields throughout the growing season as farmers have done for centuries in the Orient and around the world. The soil of his fields has been left uncultivated for over twenty-five years, yet their yields compare favorably with those of the most productive Japanese farms. His method of farming requires less labor than any other. It creates no pollution and does not require the use of fossil fuels.

—Larry Korn, Introduction

•

In growing vegetables in a "semi-wild" way, making use of a vacant lot, riverbank or open wasteland, my idea is to just toss out the seeds and let the vegetables grow up with the weeds. I grow my vegetables on the mountainside in the spaces between the tangerine trees.

The important thing is knowing the right time to plant. For the spring vegetables the right time is when the winter weeds are dying back and just before the summer weeds have sprouted.* For the fall sowing, seeds should be tossed out when the summer grasses are fading away and the winter weeds have not yet appeared.

It is best to wait for a rain which is likely to last for several days. Cut a swath in the weed cover and put out the vegetable seeds. There is no need to cover them with soil; just lay the weeds you have cut back over the seeds to act as a mulch and to hide them from the birds and chickens until they can germinate. Of course the weeds will come right back, but by that time the vegetables will already have a head start.* Usually the weeds must be cut back once or twice, but sometimes even this is unnecessary.

Where the weeds and clover are not so thick, you can simply toss out the seeds. The chickens will eat some of them, but there are many which will germinate. If you plant in a row or furrow, there is a chance that beetles or other insects will devour many of the seeds. They walk in a straight line. Chickens also spot a patch which has been cleared and come to scratch around. It is my experience that it is best to scatter the seeds here and there.

* This method of growing vegetables has been developed by Mr. Fukuoka by trial and experiment according to his local conditions. Where he lives there are dependable spring rains, and a climate warm enough to grow vegetables in all seasons. Over the years he has come to know which vegetables can be grown among which weeds and the kind of care each requires.

In most parts of North America the specific method Mr. Fukuoka uses for growing vegetables would be impractical. It is up to each farmer who would grow vegetables in the semi-wild manner to develop a technique appropriate to the area from within his or her experience with the land and the natural vegetation.

Young peach orchard doing intense duty as a market garden, growing peas, cabbage and windsor beans.

Farmers of Forty Centuries
F.H. King
1911, 1973; 456 pp.
$8.95 postpaid from:
Rodale Books
33 East Minor
Emmaus, PA 18049
or Whole Earth Household Store

Farmers of Forty Centuries

I have come more and more strongly to believe that the ultimate moral goal, even the moral necessity, of the American people must be to become the aborigines of the American land. An aborigine, my dictionary says, is "an indigenous inhabitant . . . as contrasted with an invading or colonizing people." An indigenous people is one "living naturally in a particular region or environment." In general, aborigines are preservers of their land, whereas invaders or colonizers are the exploiters and destroyers of theirs. White Americans have for the most part remained the invaders and colonizers of the American continent; their relationship to the land has remained economic, exploitive, superficial, destructive. American history is to a fearful extent the history of a group of mercenary nomads, exhausting the land as they have moved over it.

A great mistake has been to assume that people could become American in any sense that would be meaningful and ennobling by means of the souped-up emotions of public patriotism, nationalism. The fact is that meaningful native Americanism would have to involve a complexly reverent and knowing and preserving attitude toward the land; it would manifest itself not only in public fervor but in private behavior; and it would be based on methods of land use. No matter how "sophisticated" and urban our society becomes, our basic relation to the land will continue to be agricultural. And if we are ever to have a decent relation to our land, we will probably have to begin by converting from agricultural methods that are exploitive and wasteful to methods that are preserving. For this we will need more than the scientific expertise that we have relied on so far; we will need models.

A great deal in the way of models and examples is to be learned from the American Indians, for their relation to this part of the earth seems to me to have been exemplary. Our assumption that we could learn to live here, ignoring their example, is a cultural disaster as well as an ecological one. But we have a great deal to learn from all truly indigenous peoples. The agricultural practices of primitives and peasants ought to be particularly instructive to us, for these people have farmed the land with a sense of profound unity with it; their ways, formed slowly over generations out of an intricate knowledge of the land and its needs, have tended to preserve it.

One of the richest sources of information about peasant agriculture is a book called **Farmers of Forty Centuries** *by an American professor of agriculture, F.H. King. In 1907 King traveled in Japan, Korea and China, looking closely at the local practices of agriculture and land management everywhere he went. He talked with experts and with peasants. He was full of interest in the knowledge and the life of farming. His book is loaded with details of the life of the people, observed sharply, and put down with delight and sympathy.*

The question that King bore in mind throughout his travels was how these people had preserved their land, which after thousands of years of intensive use was as fertile as ever. The answer involved a complexity of methods and practices and traditions, but what it amounted to was that the taking of produce from the land was always balanced by a return of organic matter. The sewage of towns and cities, instead of being flushed out to pollute the waterways as with us, was brought back to the fields; the mud dredged from the canals was carried to the fields; no organic waste of any kind was ever thrown away, but always worked back into the soil.

King has a lot to say about the methods of composting, intertillage, crop rotation, irrigation, green manuring, and so on. He has a scientist's respect for statistics and he supplies plenty of them. But he also gives the sort of lively information that he could only have got by talking, by "passing the time of day," with the people he met in the fields. He writes of practices, tools, materials, dimensions. His book is the best sort of manual; it is one of the pioneer books on organic farming. And for the same reasons it is the best sort of travel book; he talks occasionally about how the plants are cared for around some temple or shrine, but for the most part avoids "tourist attractions"; the life of the ordinary people, its sources and ways, was what fascinated him. There are more than two hundred photographs, not the work of a gifted photographer, certainly, but informative and useful.

This is a book that can suggest things for you to do, if you have a piece of ground to do them on. Whether or not you have a piece of ground, it is a book that can change your mind. —Wendell Berry

An Agricultural Testament

The first "organic gardener" I ever ran into was a man who ended all his sentences "thus saith the Lord." The Lord, it turned out, had been in the habit of speaking in a very conversational manner to this fellow, and had given him all manner of helpful hints on gardening — among other things, a recipe for fertilizer. I noticed that the Lord's side of the conversation tended to be most flattering to my new acquaintance, and most decidedly threatening to all the neighbors — a gang of villains, who were going to die of cancer because of such sins as listening to the wrong prophets, and cooking with aluminum pots.

Now I would be the last to deny the possibility that a man might receive the word from on high and speak beyond the usual powers of his head. But I am exceedingly mistrustful of a man who depends on divine revelation to show him what is obvious about the ground under his feet. This man deservedly belongs in "the lunatic fringe" of a discipline that demands respect and attention not because it is far out or esoteric or mystical, but because it makes good sense.

The principles of organic agriculture are not derived from mystical insight or revelation, but are based upon observation. They have been established in our part of the world in our time by men who were excellent observers, and who were moreover accomplished and respectable scientists. The scientific respectability of organic methods has been obscured for us both by those who have insisted upon making a cult of the obvious and by the affluence and glamor of the technological agriculture — the agriculture of chemicals and corporations.
Sir Albert Howard, in thirty years of research and experimentation, established scientifically the soundness of the ancient methods as seen in such books as **Farmers of Forty Centuries** *by F.H. King. Howard's work is based upon the premise that good agricultural practice is based upon the observation and the use of natural processes. King's book, Howard thought, demonstrated that an agriculture based upon natural processes could thrive for an unlimited time, whereas an agriculture that contradicts or ignores natural processes can only exhaust the land, and in its failure assures the failure of the society.*

Howard's thinking proceeds from one cardinal fact: "The forest manures itself." He later elaborates this observation in an agricultural metaphor:

The main characteristic of Nature's farming can therefore be summed up in a few words. Mother earth never attempts to farm without live stock; she always raises mixed crops; great pains are taken to preserve the soil and to prevent erosion; the mixed vegetable and animal wastes are converted into humus; there is no waste; the processes of growth and the processes of decay balance one another; ample provision is made to maintain large reserves of fertility; the greatest care is taken to store the rainfall; both plants and animals are left to protect themselves against disease.

And so the task Howard set himself was first to understand those processes and interrelationships by which the natural world sustains and renews itself, and then to work out methods by which people could use the land in cooperation with nature. He realized — and I think it would be hard to overestimate the importance of this — that the specialized analytical approach of "scientific" agriculture was creating more problems than it solved:

Instead of breaking up the subject into fragments and studying agriculture in piecemeal fashion by the analytical methods of science, appropriate only to the discovery of new facts, we must adopt a synthetic approach and look at the wheel of life as one great subject and not as if it were a patchwork of unrelated things.

He insisted that quality was a more important evaluative standard than quantity. He saw that the soil was more a process than a substance, that its life was more important than its analyzable contents, that its health was not a matter of inert proportions but a balance of live forces, and that therefore "the correct relation between the processes of growth and the processes of decay is the first principle of successful farming."

Howard's discoveries and methods and their implications are given in detail in **An Agricultural Testament**. *They are of enormous usefulness to gardeners and farmers, and to anyone else who may be interested in the history and the problems of land use. But aside from its practical worth, Howard's book is valuable for his ability to place his facts and insights within the perspectives of history. This book is a critique of civilizations, judging them not by their artifacts and victories but by their response to "the sacred duty of handing over unimpaired to the next generation the heritage of a fertile soil."*

A matter of considerable interest to me is that, written within the context of more knowledge and from the perspective of a more urgent time, **An Agricultural Testament** *can be read as a confirmation and elaboration of Jefferson's belief in the supreme importance of the small farmer — the man devoted in final terms to his own piece of his homeland, who makes of the life of the land a human way of life.* —Wendell Berry

An Agricultural Testament
Sir Albert Howard
1940, 1973; 272 pp.
$7.95 postpaid from:
Rodale Books
33 East Minor
Emmaus, PA 18049
or Whole Earth Household Store

The Memory of Old Jack

This fine novel established Wendell Berry as the preeminent voice of the culture in agriculture these years. For a strong sermon see **The Unsettling of America** *(p. 46). For a great read of the kind that might even take your own personal behavior to its depth, try this.*
—SB
[Suggested by Tom Macy]

The Memory of Old Jack
Wendell Berry
1974; 223 pp.
$3.50 postpaid from:
Harcourt Brace and Jovanich
757 Third Avenue
New York, NY 10017
or Whole Earth Household Store

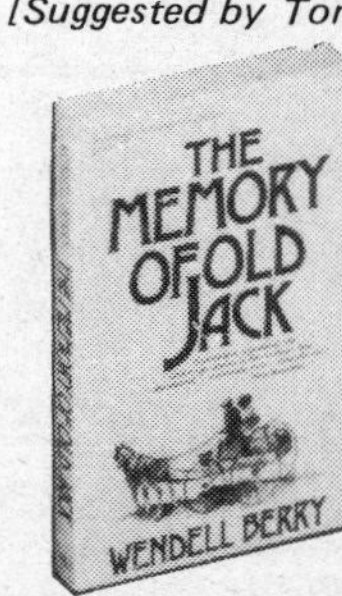

•

He was learning a new desire, the subtlety and power of which surprised him. Like the "strange woman" whose delights were so carefully understood by Solomon, this new place claimed an ample space in his mind, which it implanted with its impulse and will, and filled with visions. It possessed as much of his consciousness as might stray from his work; it kept him awake at night. He wanted to see that place respond to him. He wanted to see it dress itself in green and be fertile and abundant for his sake. Before long there was not a building or a field inside the Farrier line that was not invested with a plan or a vision that bore the by then unmistakable mark of the character and the ways of Jack Beechum. They were the good and saving ways that had doubled the health and the abundance of his own place in the years since his father's death.

THE RISING SUN
NEIGHBORHOOD NEWSLETTER

Pam went to Beloit College in Wisconsin. Daniel said that sounded like a frisbee landing on its side and Pam said they used to say it sounded like a marble dropping in a toilet.

Radical Agriculture

The range and quality of material assembled in this one book make it unique. Merrill, a west-coast New Alchemist, has a list of contributors that reads like a Who's Who of the alternative agriculture movement — Wendell Berry, John Todd, Jim Hightower, Michael Perelman, Peter Barnes — to name a few. The essays are well balanced between critiques of what's wrong with modern agriculture and explanations of what some of the possible alternatives are: self-sustaining agriculture, urban polyculture farming, aquaculture, community food organizing, biological pest control.

The buzz you can get reading here comes not from revelling in fantasies for romantic ex-urbanites, but from discovering chunks of an emerging, workable agricultural future.
—Richard Nilsen

Radical Agriculture
Richard Merrill, Editor
1976, 459 pp.
$6.95 postpaid from:
Harper and Row
General Books
Keystone Industrial Park
Scranton, PA 18512
or Whole Earth
Household Store

•

CONTENTS
Radical Agriculture *Murray Bookchin*
Where Cities and Farms Come Together *Wendell Berry*
Land Reform in America *Peter Barnes*
Agribusiness *Nick Kotz*
Corporate Accountability and the Family Farm *Sheldon L. Greene*
Efficiency in Agriculture: The Economics of Energy *Michael Perelman*
Hard Tomatoes, Hard Times: The Failure of the Land Grant College Complex *Jim Hightower*
The Green Revolution: American Agriculture in the Third World *Michael Perelman*
The National Sharecroppers Fund and the Farm Co-op Movement in the South *Robin Myers*
The Invisible Workers: Labor Organization on American Farms *George L. Baker*
Land Disputes at the Urban-Rural Border *Paul Relis*
Urban-Rural Food Alliances: A Perspective on Recent Community Food Organizing *Darryl McLeod*
Organic Force *Jerome Goldstein*
Polyculture Farming in the Cities *Warren Pierce*
A Modest Proposal: Science for the People *John Todd*
Toward a Self-Sustaining Agriculture *Richard Merrill*
Aquaculture: Toward an Ecological Approach *William O. McLarney*
Insect Population Management in Agro-Ecosystems *Helga and William Olkowski*
Small-Scale Utilization of Solar Energy *John F. Elter*
Local Energy Production for Rural Homesteads and Communities *Donald Marier and Ronald Weintraub*

Living the Good Life

Some decades ago Scott Nearing gave up an academic career and retreated to the Vermont woods with his wife Helen, where they promptly began to rediscover for themselves how to stay alive in the North Temperate Zone. Their advice is in this book. They perfected a way of living into the winter on crops taken in the summer from ingeniously constructed gardens and they relied — perhaps more than anyone today will care to rely — on a division of their labors between the hands and the head. They were a two person community. They never wasted anything (it will drive you mad to hear their paens of praise for used motor oil), they tried to ignore machines wherever possible, they tried to live on a cash-less basis (and largely succeeded), and they annoyed their old-timey Vermont neighbors by living in a more down-to-earth life than the Vermonters ever could and showing them how to maple sugar and farm. They beat them at their own game, and for thirty years it worked — until the ski crowds began to turn utopia into suburbia. The Nearings fled to Maine and started all over again.
—Stephan Chodorov

Living the Good Life
(How to Live Sanely and Simply in a Troubled World)
Helen and Scott Nearing
1954, 1970; 214 pp.
$4.95 postpaid from:
Schocken Books
200 Madison
New York, NY 10016
or Whole Earth
Household Store

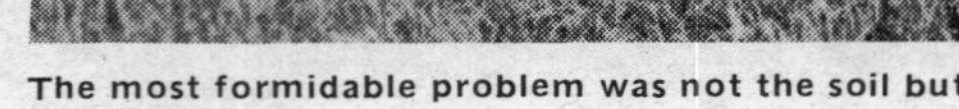

The most formidable problem was not the soil but the climate.

•

We would attempt to carry on this self-subsistent economy by the following steps: (1) Raising as much of our own food as local soil and climatic conditions would permit. (2) Bartering our products for those which we could not or did not produce. (3) Using wood for fuel and cutting it ourselves. (4) Putting up our own buildings with stone and wood from the place, doing the work ourselves. (5) Making such implements as sleds, drays, stoneboats, gravel screens, ladders. (6) Holding down to the barest minimum the number of implements, tools, gadgets and machines which we might buy from the assembly lines of big business. (7) If we had to have such machines for a few hours or days in a year (plough, tractor, rototiller, bull-dozer, chainsaw), we would rent or trade them from local people instead of buying and owning them.

•

We chose stone for several reasons. Stone buildings seem a natural out-cropping of the earth. They blend into the landscape and are a part of it. We like the varied color and character of the stones, which are lying around unused on most New England farms. Stone houses are poised, dignified and solid — sturdy in appearance and in fact, standing as they do for generations. They are cheaper to maintain, needing no paint, little or no upkeep or repair. They will not burn. They are cooler in summer and warmer in winter. If, combined with all these advantages, we could build them economically, we were convinced that stone was the right material for our needs.

Continuing the Good Life

A continuation of the saga begun in **Living the Good Life**, *this book chronicles the Nearings' move from Vermont to a "new" homestead in Maine, and the experiences they have gathered by living there since 1952. Few of us are as purposeful as the Nearings, but in an era of fads that last for 15 seconds, they are a tonic.* —Richard Nilsen

Continuing the Good Life
(Half a Century of Homesteading)
Helen and Scott Nearing
1979; 194 pp.
$4.95 postpaid from:
Schocken Books
200 Madison Avenue
New York, NY 10016
or Whole Earth
Household Store

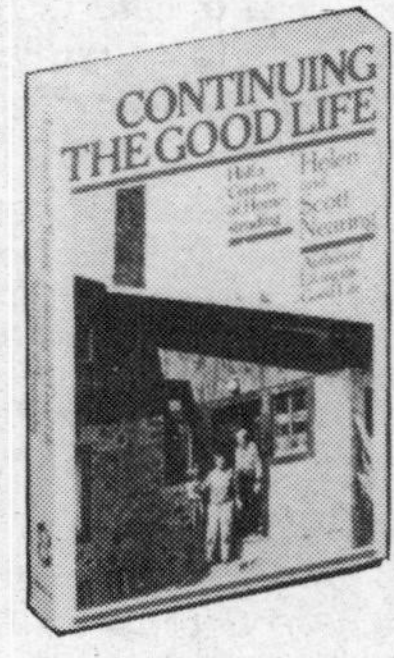

•

One of our first moves in Maine was to visit the local county agent and consult with him about the advisability of hybrid blueberries as a cash crop in Maine. His advice was brief and decisive: "Don't waste money or time planting them; they won't survive our cold winters." As we had grown them in the much colder Vermont climate, we thought they would survive in Maine, so we started with a few plants in our garden and then chose a quarter-acre plot of sandy loam, sloping to the south and west, lying to the east of our chosen pond site. The area had not been plowed or cultivated in recent years. Some of the white birch and spruce trees on the plot were a foot in diameter.

We cleared about a hundred feet square of this vigorous young forest. We cut all trees and brush as close as possible to the ground. We carted the brush away and piled it in a hollow along a small adjoining stream. The trees we cut up for firewood. In the autumn we mulched the entire patch with a layer of spruce sawdust and piled on as much spoiled hay as we could gather together. We did not plow, harrow or otherwise turn over the land. We dug no stumps. We merely planted around them. (In the early years the blueberry land was full of tree roots. As time passed and we continued mulching and weeding, the roots rotted out, enriching the land. After a dozen years the patch was virtually free of stumps and roots.)

•

How many hybrid blueberries do we pick each year? In 1957 we picked 5½ quarts; in 1958, 60 quarts; in 1960, 120 quarts. In a word, it was seven years before we had blueberries for sale. Thereafter the pick rose steadily to 655 quarts in 1965; 1034 quarts in 1970; and 1296 in 1971, which was our banner year. Since then we pick around 800 quarts.

Malabar Farm

Bromfield was a Pulitzer Prize-winning author who at the start of Hitler's war returned to his boyhood home in north central Ohio, bought several worn-out farms, established something which would probably be called a commune if it were done today (it wasn't called that as Bromfield and the people associated with him were ultra-respectable), and proceeded to use good conservation practices and numerous innovations to restore his land to fertility and health. —Pat Patterson

Malabar Farm
Louis Bromfield
1947, 1976; 470 pp.
$15.95 postpaid from:
Amereon Ltd.
P.O. Box 1200
Mattituck, NY 11952

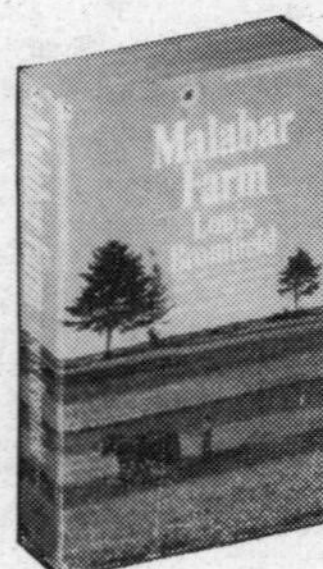

•

All our contour plowing, cover crops, and strip cropping have paid us great dividends. Throughout the drought when farms all over Ohio were hauling water, our springs kept up their flow, because the methods we took to stop erosion and the run-off of surface water had stored up great quantities of water underground. When we came here about 80 percent of the water in a heavy rainstorm ran off the place; today we keep on the place 80 to 90 percent of the rain that falls, trapped by sod, contours, and strips. It sinks deep into the earth to replenish the reservoirs in the great crevasses in the underlying sandstone rock.

•

The proper use of the land plus a simple program of game food and cover has certainly paid big dividends in fish, birds, and game. Everywhere at Malabar, since we established the farm as a game propagation area, the population of wild life has doubled and redoubled, again and again. Once the area becomes saturated, the excess population moves off into the neighboring territory where it provides sport for hunters. We do not shoot on the farm and allow no shooting but the sportsmen benefit enormously by the closed season on this large area. Big fox-squirrel, fox, raccoon and rabbits are especially abundant. Of course there is always plenty of quail (on which in Ohio there is no season) and some grouse and pheasant although the foxes kill off the latter pretty rapidly.

•

The whole theory of the ability of healthy plants grown in organically balanced and complete, mineralized soils to resist disease and even to some extent attacks by insects is not altogether new, either in the field of research among highly skilled market gardeners or among intelligent amateurs, but it is largely unknown in general agriculture. The theory of putting into the soil the means of resistance rather than applying it externally by dusts and sprays is much more revolutionary and comparatively little has been done along these lines.

Hard Tomatoes, Hard Times

America's Land Grant College system, potentially one of the greatest tools ever devised for the small farmer, no longer serves him. **Hard Tomatoes** *tells why. The system has become a corporate domain while farmers are going bankrupt by the thousands. This book was of interest to Congress and will be to anyone concerned about the future of small farming.* —Rosemary Menninger

Hard Tomatoes, Hard Times
Jim Hightower
1972; 268 pp.
$7.95 postpaid from:
Schenkman Publishing Co.
3 Mt. Auburn Place
Harvard Square
Cambridge, MA 02138

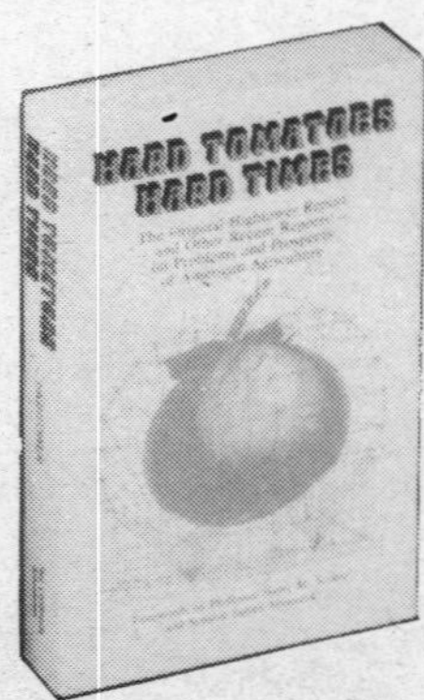

Plant a tree — is there any more certain an undubious good? Good for the soil, good for the watershed, good for the atmosphere (trees eat CO_2), good for the shade, good for the fruit, the firewood, the lumber, good for the aesthetics (Baker Roshi notes that nothing so affects people's opinion of a city neighborhood as the presence or absence of trees), good for the continuity, good for climbing and tree houses, a cheap, easy, enjoyable investment with non-stop rewards. —SB

The Oak Beams of New College, Oxford

by Gregory Bateson

I owe this story to a man who was I think a New College student and was head of the Department of Medicine at the University of Hawaii, where he told it to me.

New College, Oxford, is of rather late foundation, hence the name. It was probably founded around the late 16th century. It has, like other colleges, a great dining hall with big oak beams across the top, yes? These might be eighteen inches square, twenty feet long.

Some five to ten years ago, so I am told, some busy entomologist went up into the roof of the dining hall with a penknife and poked at the beams and found that they were full of beetles. This was reported to the College Council, who met in some dismay, because where would they get beams of that caliber nowadays?

One of the Junior Fellows stuck his neck out and suggested that there might be on College lands some oak. These colleges are endowed with pieces of land scattered across the country. So they called in the College Forester, who of course had not been near the college itself for some years, and asked him about oaks.

And he pulled his forelock and said, "Well sirs, we was wonderin' when you'd be askin'."

Upon further inquiry it was discovered that when the College was founded, a grove of oaks had been planted to replace the beams in the dining hall when they became beetly, because oak beams always become beetly in the end. This plan had been passed down from one Forester to the next for four hundred years. "You don't cut them oaks. Them's for the College Hall."

A nice story. That's the way to run a culture. ■

Tree of Life (Reprinted from *Manas*, 14 March 1979)

Twenty years ago an Englishwoman, Wendy Campbell-Purdy, having heard Richard St. Barbe Baker say that the spread of deserts could be stopped by a green wall of trees, bought a one-way ticket to North Africa and set to work planting trees. On forty-five acres of desert in Morocco (Tiznit), she planted 2,000 trees, and four years later they were twelve feet high. She proved that this manmade strip of oasis would change the climate (increase the surface humidity) by growing wheat and barley in the shelter the trees provided. Then she went to Algeria, where a reluctant Government gave her a 260-acre dump. The seedlings she set out there did so well that the astonished Algerian officials promised her help. She went home to England to raise some money, and eventually she formed the Bou Saada Trust to wage biological warfare against the Sahara. A few years later the 130,000 trees she had planted at Bou Saada (in Algeria) were flourishing and the fertile area they created was growing vegetables, citrus, and grain. Plans were then made to invade the great desert with the green things growing.

How urgent is this campaign against deserts? In 1977 a UN Conference on Desertification reported that the world's desert areas are rapidly spreading. One third of the land surface of the Earth is now desert, and every year the Sahara gains 250,000 acres of once-productive land. The lives of some 630 million people are threatened in the regions of the world now turning into desert wasteland.

Wendy Campbell-Purdy has recently formed a registered trust called Tree of Life to continue this project and undertake similar ones. The idea is to save "the vulnerable communities on the fringe of the Sahara and other world deserts by working with them to stop the deadly process of desertification, restore life to the land and protect the livelihood of the people." An explanatory booklet, **Tree of Life** (c/o Coutts & Co., Duncannon Branch, 440 Strand, London WC2R OQS, England), describes the program:

> The Tree of Life evolved directly from the work of the Bou Saada Trust in Algeria. This successful pilot reforestation scheme has now been incorporated in one of the world's most ambitious tree-planting programs — the thousand-mile protective "green wall" right across Algeria. The first task of the Tree of Life is to set up similar pilot projects, in cooperation with the Governments concerned, to continue the green wall along the entire northern edge of the Sahara desert. ■

Before and after tree planting at Bou Saada, Algeria.

THE RISING SUN
NEIGHBORHOOD NEWSLETTER

The only thing to teach is how to fall in love, how to be ready to fall in love, what to do then to make it last, make it a lifetime thing, to teach how to find out more about the beloved, to build something with the beloved, within the beloved, to teach all this perhaps before love ever happens so that when love comes be it of caterpillars or dead painters or wood and nails or computers that talk back, when it happens the feeling doesn't dissipate into a hopeless infatuation — "it must be wonderful to do that, to know about that, but I can't" — but is a release of power like real love that leads to knowing more because you know where to find it, to cherishing and building in this love because you know that someone can tell you how to do it and you keep looking until you find the one who can.

But teachers are afraid to teach love, and when they do, usually they teach "love what I love" (change your major) not the techniques and possibilities of taking something from the universe outside your skin, anything from the universe outside you and making it part of you and helping it be itself and helping it go on, not just be a spectator, but lover of the thing you were born to love. (Schools don't do that much, libraries probably do it more because they get out of the way and let it happen, remember the little kid who lived to look at Gauguin books in Goodbye, Columbus.)

The Man Who Planted Trees and Grew Happiness

by Jean Giono

FOR A HUMAN CHARACTER to reveal truly exceptional qualities, one must have the good fortune to be able to observe its performance over many years. If this performance is devoid of all egoism, if its guiding motive is unparalleled generosity, if it is absolutely certain that there is no thought of recompense and that, in addition, it has left its visible mark upon the earth, then there can be no mistake.

About forty years ago I was taking a long trip on foot over mountain heights quite unknown to tourists in that ancient region where the Alps thrust down into Provence. All this, at the time I embarked upon my long walk through these deserted regions, was barren and colorless land. Nothing grew there but wild lavender.

I was crossing the area at its widest point, and after three days' walking found myself in the midst of unparalleled desolation. I camped near the vestiges of an abandoned village. I had run out of water the day before, and had to find some. These clustered houses, although in ruins, like an old wasps' nest, suggested that there must once have been a spring or well here. There was, indeed, a spring, but it was dry. The five or six houses, roofless, gnawed by wind and rain, the tiny chapel with its crumbling steeple, stood about like the houses and chapels in living villages, but all life had vanished.

It was a fine June day, brilliant with sunlight, but over this unsheltered land, high in the sky, the wind blew with unendurable ferocity. It growled over the carcasses of the houses like a lion disturbed at its meal. I had to move my camp.

After five hours' walking I had still not found water, and there was nothing to give me any hope of finding any. All about me was the same dryness, the same coarse grasses. I thought I glimpsed in the distance a small black silhouette, upright, and took it for the trunk of a solitary tree. In any case I started towards it. It was a shepherd. Thirty sheep were lying about him on the baking earth.

He gave me a drink from his watergourd and, a little later, took me to his cottage in a fold of the plain. He drew his water – excellent water – from a very deep natural well above which he had constructed a primitive winch.

The man spoke little. This is the way of those who live alone, but one felt that he was sure of himself, and confident in his assurance. That was unexpected in this barren country. He lived, not in a cabin, but in a real house built of stone that bore plain evidence of how his own efforts had reclaimed the ruin he had found there on his arrival. His roof was strong and sound. The wind on its tiles made the sound of the sea upon its shores.

The place was in order, the dishes washed, the floor swept, his rifle oiled; his soup was boiling over the fire. I noticed then that he was cleanly shaved, that all his buttons were firmly sewed on, that his clothing had been mended with the meticulous care that makes the mending invisible. He shared his soup with me and afterwards, when I offered my tobacco pouch, he told me that he did not smoke. His dog, as silent as himself, was friendly without being servile.

It was understood from the first that I should spend the night there; the nearest village was still more than a day and a half away. And besides I was perfectly familiar with the nature of the rare villages in that region. There were four or five of them scattered well apart from each other on these mountain slopes, among white oak thickets, at the extreme end of the wagon roads. They were inhabited by charcoal-burners, and the living was bad. Families, crowded together in a climate that is excessively harsh both in winter and in summer found no escape from the unceasing conflict of personalities. Irrational ambition reached inordinate proportions in the continual desire for escape. The men took their wagonloads of charcoal to the town, then returned. The soundest characters broke under the perpetual grind. The women nursed their grievances. There was rivalry in everything, over the price of charcoal as over a pew in the church. And over all there was the wind, also ceaseless, to rasp upon the nerves. There were epidemics of suicide and frequent cases of insanity, usually homicidal.

The shepherd went to fetch a small sack and poured out a heap of acorns on the table. He began to inspect them, one by one, with great concentration, separating the good from the bad. I smoked my pipe. I did offer to help him. He told me that it was his job. And in fact, seeing the care he devoted to the task, I did not insist. That was the whole of our conversation. When he had set aside a large enough pile of good acorns he counted them out by tens, meanwhile eliminating the small ones or those which were slightly cracked, for now he examined them more closely. When he had thus selected one hundred perfect acorns he stopped and he went to bed.

There was peace in being with this man. The next day I asked if I might rest here for a day. He found it quite natural – or to be more exact, he gave me the impression that nothing could startle him. The rest was not absolutely necessary, but I was interested and wished to know more about him. He opened the pen and led his flocks to pasture. Before leaving, he plunged his sack of carefully selected and counted acorns into a pail of water.

I noticed that he carried for a stick an iron rod as thick as my thumb and about a yard and a half long. Resting myself by walking, I followed a path parallel to his. His pasture was in a valley. He left the little flock in charge of the dog and climbed towards where I stood. I was afraid that he was about to rebuke me for my indiscretion, but it was not that at all: this was the way he was going, and he invited me to go along if I had nothing better to do. He climbed to the top of the ridge about a hundred yards away.

There he began thrusting his iron rod into the earth, making a hole in which he planted an acorn; then he refilled the hole. He was planting an oak tree. I asked him if the land belonged to him. He answered no. Did he know whose it was? He did not. He supposed it was community property, or perhaps belonged to people who cared nothing about it. He was not interested in finding out whose it was. He planted his hundred acorns with the greatest care. After the midday meal he resumed his planting. I suppose I must have been fairly insistent in my questioning, for he answered me. For three years he had been planting trees in this wilderness. He had planted 100,000. Of these, 20,000 had sprouted. Of the 20,000 he still expected to lose about half to rodents or to the unpredictable designs of Providence. There remained 10,000 oak trees to grow where nothing had grown before.

That was when I began to wonder about the age of this man. He was obviously over fifty. Fifty-five, he told me. His name was Elzeard Bouffier. He had once had a farm in the lowlands. There he had had his life. He had lost his only son, then his wife. He had withdrawn into this solitude, where his pleasure was to live leisurely with his lambs and his dog. It was his opinion that this land was dying for want of trees. He added that, having no very pressing business of his own, he had resolved to remedy this state of affairs.

Since I was at that time, in spite of my youth, leading a solitary life, I understood how to deal gently with solitary spirits. But my very youth forced me to consider the future in relation to myself and to a certain quest for happiness. I told him that in thirty years his 10,000 oaks would be magnificent. He answered quite simply that if God granted him life, in thirty years he would have planted so many more that these 10,000 would be like a drop of water in the ocean.

Besides, he was now studying the reproduction of beech trees and had a nursery of seedlings grown from beechnuts near his cottage. The seedlings, which he protected from his sheep with a wire fence, were very beautiful. He was also considering birches for the valleys where, he told me, there was a certain amount of moisture a few yards below the surface of the soil.

The next day we parted.

The following year came the War of 1914, in which I was involved for the next five years. An infantryman hardly had time for reflecting upon trees. To tell the truth, the thing itself had made no impression upon me; I had considered it as a hobby, a stamp collection, and forgotten it.

The war over, I found myself possessed of a tiny demobilization bonus and a huge desire to breathe fresh air for a while. It was with no other objective that I again took the road to the barren lands.

The countryside had not changed. However, beyond the deserted village I glimpsed in the distance a sort of greyish mist that covered the mountaintops like a carpet. Since the day before, I had begun to think again of the shepherd tree-planter. "Ten thousand oaks," I reflected, "really take up quite a bit of space." I had seen too many men die during those five years not to imagine easily that Elzeard Bouffier was dead, especially since, at twenty, one regards men of fifty as old men with nothing left to do but die. He was not dead. As a matter of fact he was extremely spry. He had changed jobs. Now he had only four sheep but, instead, a hundred beehives. He had got rid of the sheep because they threatened his

A man plants trees and a region is changed. His story is told and a world is changed. I've no idea how many times this account has been reprinted. Our reprint is by kind permission of Mr. Martin R. Haase, Executive Secretary of The Friends of Nature. You can buy copies of the story for $1 from Friends of Nature, c/o D. Smith, Brooksville, ME 04617.

Illustrator Tom Parker, a former biologist, did the research to be sure he got the Provence landscape, barren and verdant, right.

Is the story true? I've heard vociferous denials and confident affirmations. If someone will do the proper research and report on the question, we'll gladly print it in **CoEvolution Quarterly.** *—SB*

TOM PARKER

young trees. For, he told me (and I saw for myself), the war had disturbed him not at all. He had imperturbably continued to plant.

The oaks of 1910 were then ten years old and taller than either of us. It was an impressive spectacle. I was literally speechless and, as he did not talk, we spent the whole day walking in silence through his forest. In three sections, it measured eleven kilometers in length and three kilometers at its greatest width. When you remembered that all this had sprung from the hands and the soul of this one man, without technical resources, you understand that men could be as effectual as God in realms other than that of destruction.

He had pursued his plan, and beech trees as high as my shoulder, spreading out as far as the eye could reach, confirmed it. He showed me handsome clumps of birch planted five years before – that is, in 1915, when I had been fighting at Verdun. He had set them out in all the valleys where he had guessed – and rightly – that there was moisture almost at the surface of the ground. They were as delicate as young girls, and very well established.

Creation seemed to come about in a sort of chain reaction. He did not worry about it; he was determinedly pursuing his task in all its simplicity; but as we went back towards the village I saw water flowing in brooks that had been dry since the memory of man. This was the most impressive result of chain reaction that I had seen. These dry streams had once, long ago, run with water. Some of the dreary villages I mentioned before had been built on the sites of ancient Roman settlements, traces of which still remained; and archaeologists, exploring there, had found fishhooks where, in the twentieth century, cisterns were needed to assure a small supply of water.

The wind, too, scattered seeds. As the water reappeared, so there reappeared willows, rushes, meadows, gardens, flowers, and a certain purpose in being alive. But the transformation took place so gradually that it became part of the pattern without causing any astonishment. Hunters, climbing into the wilderness in pursuit of hares or wild boar, had of course noticed the sudden growth of little trees, but had attributed it to some caprice of the earth. That is why no one meddled with Elzeard Bouffier's work. If he had been detected he would have had opposition. He was undetectable. Who in the villages or in the administration could have dreamed of such perseverance in a magnificent generosity?

To have anything like a precise idea of this exceptional character one must not forget that he worked in total solitude: so total that, towards the end of his life, he lost the habit of speech. Or perhaps it was that he saw no need for it.

In 1933 he received a visit from a forest ranger who notified him of an order against lighting fires out of doors for fear of endangering the growth of this *natural* forest. It was the first time, the man told him naively, that he had ever heard of a forest growing of its own accord. At that time Bouffier was about to plant beeches at a spot some twelve kilometers from his cottage. In order to avoid travelling back and forth – for he was then seventy-five – he planned to build a stone cabin right at the plantation. The next year he did so.

In 1935 a whole delegation came from the Government to examine the "natural forest." There was a high official from the Forest Service, a Deputy, technicians. There was a great deal of ineffectual talk. It was decided that something must be done and, fortunately, nothing was done except the only helpful thing: the whole forest was placed under the protection of the State, and charcoal burning prohibited. For it was impossible not to be captivated by the beauty of those young trees in the fullness of health, and they cast their spell over the Deputy himself.

A friend of mine was among the forestry officers of the delegation. To him I explained the mystery. One day the following week we went together to see Elzeard Bouffier. We found him hard at work, some ten kilometers from the spot where the inspection had taken place.

This forester was not my friend for nothing. He was aware of values. He knew how to keep silent. I delivered the eggs I had brought as a present. We shared our lunch among the three of us and spent several hours in wordless contemplation of the countryside.

In the direction from which we had come the slopes were covered with trees twenty to twenty-five feet tall. I remembered how the land had looked in 1913: a desert . . . Peaceful, regular toil, the vigorous mountain air, frugality and, above all, serenity in the spirit had endowed this old man with awe-inspiring health. He was one of God's athletes. I wondered how many more acres he was going to cover with trees.

Before leaving my friend simply made a brief suggestion about certain species of trees that the soil here seemed particularly suited for. He did not force the point, "for the very good reason," he told me later, "that Bouffier knows more about it than I do." At the end of an hour's walking – having turned it over in his mind – he added, "He knows a lot more about it than anybody. He's discovered a wonderful way to be happy!"

It was thanks to this officer that not only the forest but also the happiness of the man was protected. He delegated three rangers to the task, and so terrorized them that they remained proof against all the bottles of wine the charcoal-burners could offer.

The only serious danger to the work occurred during the War of 1939. As cars were being run on gazogenes (wood-burning generators), there was never enough wood. Cutting was started among the oaks of 1910, but the area was so far from any railway that the enterprise turned out to be financially unsound. It was abandoned. The shepherd had seen nothing of it. He was thirty kilometers away, peacefully continuing his work, ignoring the war of 1939 as he had ignored that of 1914.

I saw Elzeard Bouffier for the last time in June of 1945. He was then eighty-seven. I had started back along the route through the wastelands; but now, in spite of the disorder in which the war had left the country, there was a bus running between the Durance Valley and the mountain. I attributed the fact that I no longer recognized the scenes of my earlier journeys to this relatively speedy transportation. It took the name of a village to convince me that I was actually in that region that had been all ruins and desolation.

The bus put me down at Vergons. In 1913 this hamlet of ten or twelve houses had three inhabitants. They had been savage creatures, hating one another, living by trapping game, little removed, physically and morally, from the conditions of prehistoric man. All about them nettles were feeding upon the remains of abandoned houses. Their condition had been beyond hope. For them, nothing but to await death – a situation which rarely predisposes to virtue.

Everything was changed. Even the air. Instead of the harsh dry winds that used to attack me, a gentle breeze was blowing, laden with scents. A sound like water came from the mountains; it was the wind in the forest; most amazing of all, I heard the actual sound of water falling into a pool. I saw that a fountain had been built, that it flowed freely and – what touched me most – that someone had planted a linden beside it, a linden that must have been four years old, already in full leaf, the incontestable symbol of resurrection.

Besides, Vergons bore evidence of labor at the sort of undertaking for which hope is required. Hope, then, had returned. Ruins had been cleared away, dilapidated walls torn down and five houses restored. Now there were twenty-eight inhabitants, four of them young married couples. The new houses, freshly plastered, were surrounded by gardens where vegetables and flowers grew in orderly confusion, cabbages and roses, leeks and snapdragons, celery and anemones. It was now a village where one would like to live.

From that point I went on foot. The war just finished had not allowed the full blooming of life, but Lazarus was out of the tomb. On the lower slopes of the mountain I saw little fields of barley and rye; deep in that narrow valley the meadows were turning green.

It has taken only the eight years since then for the whole countryside to glow with health and prosperity. On the site of the ruins I had seen in 1913 now stand neat farms, cleanly plastered, testifying to a happy and comfortable life. The old streams, fed by the rains and snows that the forest conserves, are flowing again. Their waters have been channeled. On each farm, in groves of maples, fountain pools overflow on to carpets of fresh mint. Little by little the villages have been rebuilt. People from the plains, where land is costly, have settled here, bringing youth, motion, the spirit of adventure. Along the roads you meet hearty men and women, boys and girls who understand laughter and have recovered a taste for picnics. Counting the former population, unrecognizable now that they live in comfort, more than 10,000 people owe their happiness to Elzeard Bouffier.

When I reflect that one man, armed only with his own physical and moral resources, was able to cause this land of Canaan to spring from the wasteland, I am convinced that, in spite of everything, humanity is admirable. But when I compute the unfailing greatness of spirit and the tenacity of benevolence that it must have taken to achieve this result, I am taken with an immense respect for that old and unlearned peasant who was able to complete a work worthy of God.

Elzeard Bouffier died peacefully in 1947 at the hospice in Banon. ■

THE RISING SUN
NEIGHBORHOOD NEWSLETTER

Susan hasn't told her mother that she's very sick in the hospital. A nurse said, "Well, honey, you really should, even though I can understand how you want to protect her." And Susan said, "Her? I'm protecting myself. She'd fly out here and attack me while I'm defenseless."

Plant a Tree

Johnny Appleseed realized that planting trees is political. This book could create a tree planting movement simply by being such a good manual. It describes, state by state, city street tree planting programs; urban tree maintenance and the brand new practice of controlling street tree pests by releasing predator insects. There is equal discussion of planting and maintenance for various rural conditions, and a fine encyclopedia of many American, European and Oriental trees, with beautiful black and white photographs. These pictures for me are like fairy tales, recalling visions of trees in my childhood.

—Rosemary Menninger

Plant a Tree
(A Working Guide to Regreening America)
Michael Weiner
1975; 277 pp.

$6.95 postpaid from:
MacMillan Pub. Co.
Order Department
Front and Brown Streets
Riverside, NJ 08075
or Whole Earth
Household Store

•

Key Questions Important to the Survival of the Tree

1. Can the tree survive the minimum temperature of your locale for prolonged periods of time?
2. Can the tree tolerate the fumes, dust, smoke, and road salt it may be subject to?
3. Will it be able to thrive in the soil it is planted in?
4. Is the rainfall adequate for optimum growth, or will watering be required?
5. How resistant is the tree to diseases common to the area?

Seeds of Woody Plants in the United States

This government text is a treasury for anyone planting trees. It tells how to gather the seed of several thousand trees and shrubs, how to treat the seed if necessary, how to store it, and how to propagate the plants. This is all the information we need to reforest America.

—Rosemary Menninger
[Suggested by Charlie Mosher]

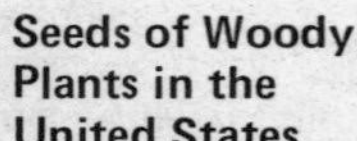

Seeds of Woody Plants in the United States
U.S. Forest Service
Agricultural Handbook
No. 001-000-02902-9
1974; 883 pp.

$15.75 postpaid from:
Supt. of Documents
U.S. Govt. Printing Office
Washington, D.C. 20402
or Whole Earth
Household Store

•

Growth habit, occurrence, and use. Maples are deciduous (rarely evergreen) trees comprising approximately 148 species in North America, Asia, Europe, and northern Africa. Some species of maple are sources of valuable lumber and veneer, and one *(A. saccharum)* is used for the production of maple sugar and maple syrup. Many of the maples have ornamental value because of their handsome foliage or their interesting crown shape, their flowers, or their fruit. Consequently, they are widely used for landscape planting. Several maples provide food and shelter for wildlife, and their occurrence on mountain slopes makes them useful in the protection of watersheds. The 15 maples considered here include 5 that are native to Europe and Asia, and have been used successfully in the United States in ornamental planting. Maples are only rarely used in reforestation plantings for the production of timber, but sugar maple *(A. saccharum)* has been planted for the production of syrup and sugar (sugarbush).

Key to seeds, fruits and nuts in border

1. Bur oak: 12-day-seedling.
2. Red maple: samara.
3. Common moonseed: seed.
4. Common buttonbush: fruits.
5. Cutleaf blackberry: seed.
6. American mountain-ash: seed.
7. Red pine: 1-day-old seedling.
8. Lodgepole pine: seed.
9. Pignut hickory: nut and husk.
10. European white birch: seed.
11. Thornless blackberry: fruit.
12. Red chokeberry: fruit cluster.
13. Fraser fir: seed.
14. White mulberry: fruit.
15. Black ash: 2, 1-day-old seedling.
16. Green ash: seed.
17. Chokecherry: 7-day-old seedling.
18. Abies fir: cones.
19. Red pine: 7-day-old seedling.
20. Ailanthus: seed.
21. Sawtooth oak: acorn.

Southern red oak

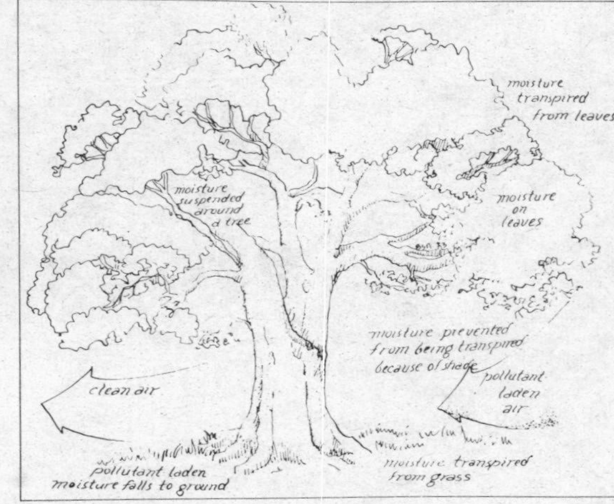

Air washer

The small conifer on the left is a Colorado Spruce (Picea pungens). **It was planted on the same day as the 12-foot Mondell pine (center).**

Mondell Pine

This fast-growing pine (P. eldarica) came to Arizona on a seed exchange from Pakistan several years ago. Extreme drought tolerance makes it ideally suited to regions in the southwest that don't usually get below 0° F in winter; but it is also being grown in the south for pulp and Christmas trees. These pines will grow more than 3 feet per year under good conditions, and can reach 70 feet when mature. One thing they can't stand is wet roots; in clay soils, care must be taken to let the root zone dry out between irrigations.

—Richard Nilsen
[Suggested by Jim Frazin]

Mondell Pine
12" tall trees in
6" long tubes

$11.95 for three from:
Shepard and Harris
Associates, Inc.
1481 East 9th Street
Pomona, CA 91766

Rescuing trees

After seven years of foot loose whimsy we shifted gears, got married, and began to look for land to grow on. Finding nine acres of overgrazed, heavily compacted clay underlaid by hardpan and well larded with gophers was like coming home. Not a tree on the place except a stunted oak discovered then lost for a year, and two straggly willow bushes.

Peter began drawing schemes for peculiar structures and I collected tree seeds. Empty milk cartons from school garbage cans held the seeds. Acquiring soil was a problem solved by dead-of-night digging.

In early spring a great many seeds hatched and grew. But in later spring came the amazing discovery of a flourishing seedling growing in an Insurance Company's token shrubbery. A sycamore, with all the vigor of a volunteer, brazenly shoving the privet aside. A week later it was gone . . . weeded.

I outfitted my bike with a small cardboard box, a trowel, and a half dozen large plastic "produce" bags each containing a handful of water. For the next month and a half, until the trees vanished, I scouted seedlings. Finding one, a circle of vertical stabs about 2" from the tree stem was made with the trowel, the plug of soil pried out, the tree slipped into its wet bag and the package set upright in the cardboard box. (Protection from sunlight is essential.) The trees waited patiently several hours for their semi-permanent home in a one-gallon can. (We had the incredible good fortune to stumble over a heap of cans being dumped after a landscaping project.)

Dear SB: Ask Governor Brown to let enthusiastic souls dig the volunteers out of the turf at Capitol Park. Sell them for $1 a tree (earnest money) to tourists or locals as a grand finale to the Tree Tour. It was painful to watch the mowers cut the seedlings down, but I caught sufficient hell for picking up fallen tree seeds in the park. After that I stuck to business-owned private property and was never hassled.

At the end of summer, when we relocated, we carted more than 500 trees to our place, setting them under an improvised lath shelter until they went dormant and could be planted out and mulched. Probably only about 50 were transplanted volunteers (I was working full time, going to school full time and got a late start on the season) but they were the hardiest individuals and the strongest species.

The following year grasshoppers whirred cackling over the tiny forest. The wind didn't blow and the windmill didn't turn for two solid summer months. Husband and I contracted a weird debilitating illness. At nadir, Husband ran away from home on his bicycle with a white hat and a salami. (He ran uphill however and was back, exhausted, by nightfall.) Autumn finally brought the rains and the wind. Three dozen trees had scraped through.

Now, seven years after becoming land owners, our nine acres have visible exclamation points of green. The tallest of those earliest survivors is nearly twenty feet, the shortest, six. The whole family, cats, chickens and kids (we conceived twins the year the earthquake failed to demolish our owner-built home) can lounge in the home-grown shade of a single maple tree.

The effort at reforestation continues. Annually I propagate eucalyptus and mulberry and grow oaks from available acorns, all trees that, heavily mulched, will survive the summer drought unwatered. A 100' roll of 36" screening converted into 50 magical tree envelopes foils everything but the gophers and provides a little shade for the first vulnerable years.

But I look forward to the time when we can journey again to Sacramento in the spring, armed with smiles and an air of bluff efficiency, to rescue more tiny trees. Sadly, this is strictly city sport. Anal retentive landscaping, automatic sprinklers, and large seed-bearing trees are required in reasonable proximity.

The free trees sprout every year. Rescue one from Limbo and the good feeling just grows.

Love,
Sylvia Meadowsong
Palermo, California

Where to buy cheap trees

The U.S. Forest Service does not sell trees, but any of their local offices can put you in touch with state and/or private nurseries or organizations that do sell them. Almost all of the states have their own forestry programs and departments — the names vary, but a look in your phone book will get you the information.

State Foresters furnish landowners with forest tree seedlings at moderate cost because these nurseries are subsidized by the government. There are some strings attached. Trees can be used for forest, windbarrier (also called shelterbelt), or watershed plantings. Often there are minimum orders. If you want a dozen trees to plant around your house, go to a private nursery. But if you need a dozen trees to keep your hillside from eroding, you can probably get them through the government.

The seedlings come either bareroot — packed in wet sawdust — or in thin cylindrical containers that get slipped right into the ground. It is amazingly easy to get carried away ordering trees on paper. Tree planting is hard work, and keeping them alive and seeing they survive is even harder. If it's your first time, talk to someone who has done it before you start.

The sources for trees from both public and private nurseries are listed in two booklets and your local Forest Service office has them. They are "A Directory of Forest Tree Nurseries in the United States" (U.S. Department of Agriculture, 1976), and "Seed and Planting Stock Dealers" (USDA No. FS-331, May, 1979). —Richard Nilsen

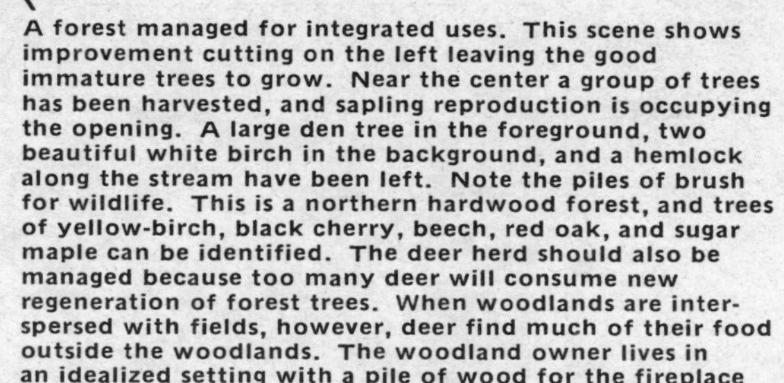

← A forest managed for integrated uses. This scene shows improvement cutting on the left leaving the good immature trees to grow. Near the center a group of trees has been harvested, and sapling reproduction is occupying the opening. A large den tree in the foreground, two beautiful white birch in the background, and a hemlock along the stream have been left. Note the piles of brush for wildlife. This is a northern hardwood forest, and trees of yellow-birch, black cherry, beech, red oak, and sugar maple can be identified. The deer herd should also be managed because too many deer will consume new regeneration of forest trees. When woodlands are interspersed with fields, however, deer find much of their food outside the woodlands. The woodland owner lives in an idealized setting with a pile of wood for the fireplace from the thinnings and the tops of sawlog trees.

A Tree Hurts, Too

The Life and Death of Trees. Their wounds and how they tend them. A story book in pictures of the hurts and healing powers of the plant kingdom's finest. —Peter Warshall

With this lovely color booklet and the tree surgery ones, instant Ecotopian. —SB

A Tree Hurts, Too
Forest Service USDA
1974; 28 pp.
No. 001-001-00388-7
$1.30 postpaid from:
Supt. of Documents
Govt. Printing Office
Washington, DC 20402

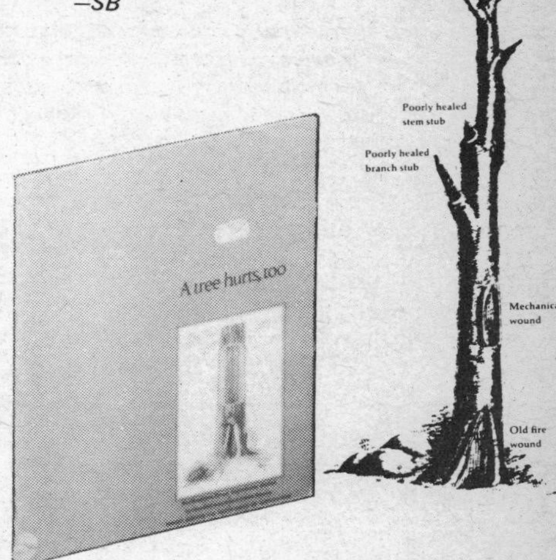

Woodland Ecology

73% of the forest land in the eastern United States is held by private, non-industrial owners, according to the author. He contends it is time these small owners realize their significance and begin to take better care of their woodlands. Mr. Minckler considers the eastern hardwood forest types, and in clear, non-technical language, he explains very basic woodland ecology and discusses the options a small owner has in deciding how to maintain and use his woods. The book includes an extensive appendix of references, well annotated. —Richard Nilsen

Woodland Ecology
(Environmental Forestry for the Small Owner)
Leon S. Minckler
1975, 1980; 229 pp.
$9.95 postpaid from:
Syracuse University Press
1011 East Water Street
Syracuse, NY 13210
or Whole Earth Household Store

Tree Surgery

If you want to learn about the business of doctoring trees, here is the book. Most of what a tree surgeon does is beyond the range of a weekend gardener, and a look here quickly shows why — special tools, ropes and safety harnesses — and the knowledge of how to use them. The text is aimed at on-the-job problem solving and the full page photographs and clear diagrams are excellent. —Richard Nilsen

Tree Surgery
(A Complete Guide)
P.H. Bridgeman
1976; 139 pp.
$16.95 postpaid from:
David & Charles
North Pomfret, VT 05053
or Whole Earth Household Store

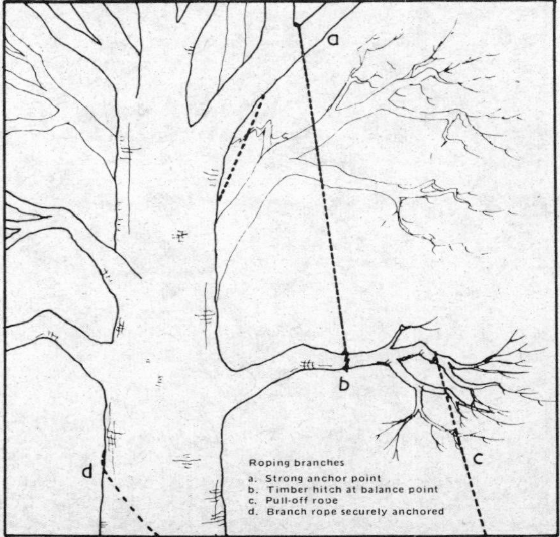

Forestry assistance programs

Three out of every five acres of America's commercial forest lands are owned by individuals — about 4 million separate ownerships. These lands supply more than half of the wood used by industry. The federal government, and many of the states, have programs to assist small owners, but you have to be willing to wade into and through the bureaucratic maze. Here is some deciphering.

All these aid programs use the carrot and stick approach. The government shares the cost of an improvement project on your land with you and provides free technical help (surveys, timber inventories, etc.), but you have to meet their specifications. This usually means there is an inspection before you collect any money.

Most of these programs are run by the Agricultural Stabilization and Conservation Service (ASCS), like the Forest Service in that it is a branch of the Department of Agriculture with local offices in almost every county. If you have no ASCS office near you, then contact your local State Forester or your County Extension Agent.

These bureaucracies overlap somewhat, and frequently you will find them all in the same government building. They're just sitting there drawing your salary; put them to work. They appreciate it too.

Money is currently available through the following alphabet soup programs:

Agricultural Conservation Program *(ACP): soil conservation, water management, pollution abatement and woodland preservation (ask for a pamphlet called "Solving Agricultural Conservation Problems," January, 1978).*

Forestry Incentives Program *(FIP): tree planting and timber stand improvement assistance for private forest landowners with less than 1,000 acres. Maximum annual federal cost-share limit of $10,000. (See "Forestry Incentives Program for the Forest Landowner," March, 1980).*

Rural Areas Development programs *(RAP): various forms of assistance and advice for small loggers and mill operators (see the Forest Service pamphlet "Forest Products Utilization and Marketing Assistance," No. PA-752).*

Urban Forestry Assistance*: the individual state comes up with the program and the federal government matches the funds 50-50. The point to note with this new program is that even if you live in a city (and nearly 80% of us do) you are no longer excluded from governmental arboreal largesse. Would your street look better with trees along it? (See the Forest Service pamphlet "Urban Forestry Assistance," August, 1979).* —Richard Nilsen

Tree Maintenance

This book is a classic. Its subject is the ornamental tree used in landscaping, parks and along streets. This is not the book if you want to learn how to prune a fruit tree. **Tree Maintenance** *is useful as a reference book, since common diseases of different tree species are discussed separately.* —Richard Nilsen

Tree Maintenance
P.P. Pirone
1954, 1978; 574 pp.
(5th Edition)
$27.50 postpaid from:
Oxford University Press
16-00 Pollitt Drive
Fair Lawn, NJ 07410
or Whole Earth Household Store

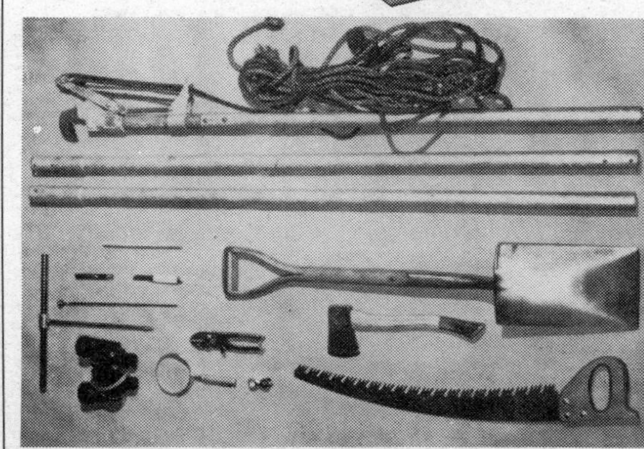

Some of the implements used by a tree disease diagnostician.

THE RISING SUN
NEIGHBORHOOD NEWSLETTER

What's happening to libraries lately is like they're shooting the stars out of the sky. Libraries are such unnatural, incredible incandescent miracles and it's so easy to take little chunks out of them, like nighttime hours when people stuck doing something they don't much like the rest of the day can spend a few hours checking out the rest of the universe. Emerson said that if the stars only shone once a century everyone would be out there in awe that whole night. Libraries to me are honest to God about that weird, but they're there all the time too, so chipping away at them don't seem much like amputating a unicorn but they are a wondrous beast.

You can take out expensive things that do not belong to you and keep them for a month, two weeks, just by proving you live where you live — just because you exist essentially. It's not a bookstore — you don't have to have any money. It's not a bookstore — you can get lots more than what's selling this month, you can get the wisdom of the ages and the crap of at least the last century and that's important too — if you feel suffocated by current touchy feely crap take a vacation in nineteenth century striving individualist crap.

Tree Crops

Smith sees trees as a cure for erosion from hillside farming and as a source of food. He has visited and photographed farmers around the world to demonstrate his argument. Many tree species are considered, including oak, chestnut, mulberry, honey locust, persimmon and mesquite. If you are involved with marginal farm land, there are food and livestock crops here you probably never thought of.

—Richard Nilsen

Now regarded as a classic, **Tree Crops** *set off a whole movement toward two-story agriculture. Where it will eventually lead is still unknown. As a research area it's as fertile and diverse as the technique itself.* *—SB*

Tree Crops
(A Permanent Agriculture)
J. Russell Smith
1950; 408 pp.

$5.95 postpaid from:
Harper and Row
Keystone Industrial Park
Scranton, PA 18512
or Whole Earth Household Store

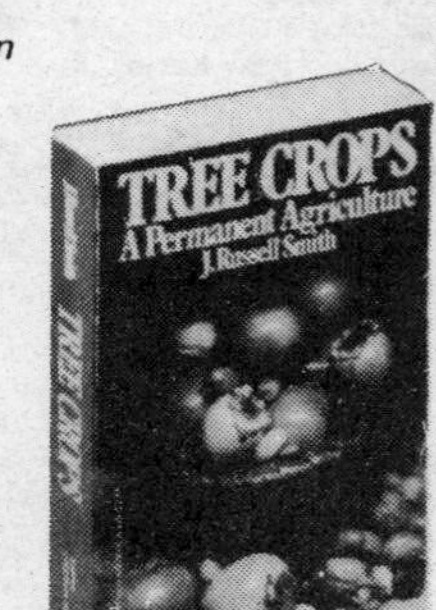

Limestone pasture in Portugal with scattered carobs. A good example of two-story agriculture.

Olive and fig trees on the hills of Kabylia, foothills of the Atlas Mountains, Algeria. Population twenty-five times as dense as on the same hills where there are no tree crops.

•

In place of the Appalachian corn bread, the Corsican has chestnut bread; in place of corn to feed the animals, the Corsican uses dried chestnuts. One of my informants — the mayor of the village — took me around to the barn and showed me how his horse relished a feed of dried chestnuts. She crunched them, shells and all, exactly as my horses crunched corn. . . .

Forest Farming

The essential tree library now includes **Tree Crops** *and* **Forest Farming**. *After these two books have been read, there is nothing to do but start working, experimenting, and writing your own local manual. A visionary integration of farming, animal husbandry, and horticulture with tree crops — fruit, nuts, oil, fodder. This is not a book on woodlots for maintaining firewood. Foreword by E.F. Schumacher.*

—Peter Warshall

Forest Farming
(Towards a Solution to Problems of World Hunger & Conservation)
J. Sholto Douglas & Robert A. de J. Hart
1976; 196 pp.

$8.95 postpaid from:
Rodale Books
33 East Minor
Emmaus, PA 18049
or Whole Earth Household Store

•

Jujube *(Zizyphus jujuba)*

This tree is suited to dry areas, and bears fruit profusely. The seeds are large and the pulp surrounding them becomes farinaceous on drying, being utilised in parts of Africa and China for making porridge and bread. There are several varieties and propagation is by grafting or layering. The plant also acts as a host for the scale insects producing lac. *Z. jujuba* yields a valuable cereal substitute and owing to its ability to thrive in rather arid regions is of considerable economic importance. It belongs to the family Rhamnaceae. The trees are small, of spreading habit and thorny, but it may be possible to select and multiply thornless stock.

•

Of the world's surface, only eight to ten per cent is at present used for food production. Pioneer agriculturists and scientists have demonstrated the feasibility of growing food-yielding trees in the most unlikely locations — rocky mountainsides and deserts with an annual rainfall of only two to four inches. With the aid of trees, at least three quarters of the earth could supply human needs, not only of food but of clothing, fuel, shelter and other basic products. At the same time wild-life could be conserved, pollution decreased, and the beauty of many landscapes enhanced, with consequent moral, spiritual and cultural benefits.

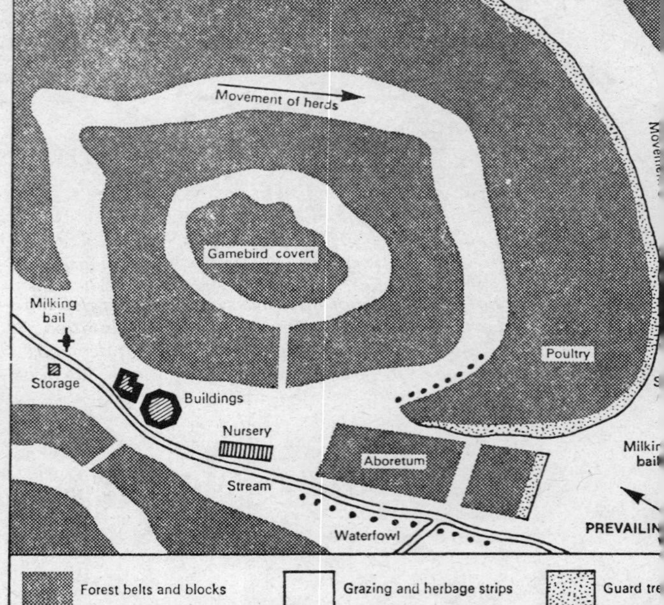

→ **A typical layout with supporting facilities.**

Dwarfed Fruit Trees

Tukey writes to make every reader an enthusiast and gives information that subsequent dwarf tree books have lacked. He discusses standard fruit trees and describes each type of dwarfing root stock with elegant graphics and charts, including his famous graphs showing what nutrients are taken up by a tree each month of the year. That enables a gardener to hand-feed the tree. The book is a classic.

—Rosemary Menninger

Dwarfed Fruit Trees
Harold Bradford Tukey
1964, 1978; 562 pp.

$32.50 postpaid from:
Cornell University Press
124 Roberts Place
Ithaca, NY 14850

•

One of the accepted features of the size-controlled tree is easier harvesting of the fruit. In fact, the expense and hazard of harvesting large trees from tall ladders has already demanded that such trees be brought down in height regardless of the crudeness and brutality of the method.

Much of the harvesting can be done from the ground by women and children, with less expense and less bruising. The growing interest in "pick-your-own" operations is accelerated by the small tree. Customers seemingly enjoy bringing their children to the orchard and picking the fruit themselves. Considerable emphasis has been placed on the possibility of "spot picking" from the small tree, in which trees are picked over more than once and only the properly matured fruit is harvested each time.

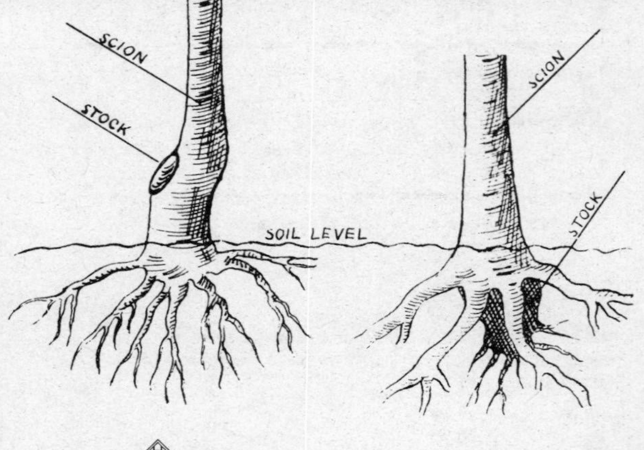

← **The graft union must be slightly above the soil level so as to avoid scion rooting, which destroys the effect of the rootstock. (Left) Graft union properly placed. (Right) Graft union placed too deep, with the result that scion has rooted and the effect of the dwarfing rootstock has been lost.**

← **Verrier palmettes used as a wall covering, consisting of a high-stemmed double palmette and two six-armed palmettes.**

Bending promotes fruiting and tends to dwarf the tree. Shoot bent down and fastened (festooned). A year later, bent shoots will carry flower buds and may be cut back as indicated. ↓

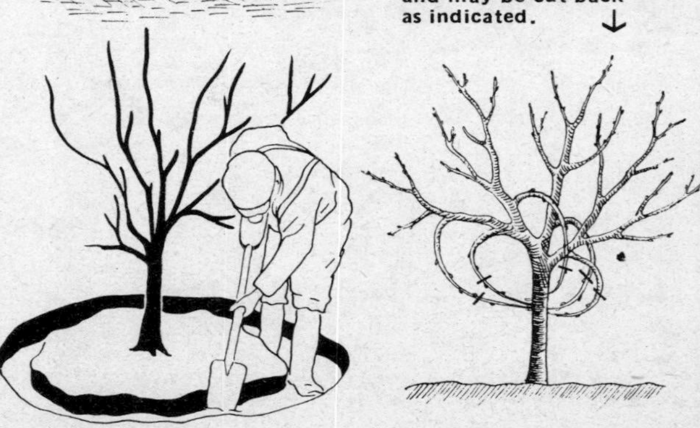

Root pruning induces early fruiting and also keeps a tree small. Courtesy of F.L.S. O'Rourke.

Dwarfed fruit trees are efficiently harvested. McIntosh/EM I, five years old.
↓

High Intensity Use
Dwelling
Herb garden
Glass house
Vegetable garden
Chicken forage system
Distance Increasing
Intensive fruit and nut system
Extensive food forest
Self-forage system for large animals
Low Intensity Use

Intensity of Use/Distance Relationship ↑

Permaculture One

Permaculture describes perennial-based low-maintenance gardening and farming. This book goes hand in hand with the Japanese edible wilderness gardening technique described in Rodale's **One Straw Revolution** *(p. 74). Together they conjure up the first whole-systems approach to agriculture, allowing nature to do most of the work and humans to do most of the harvesting.*

—Rosemary Menninger
[Suggested by Robert Kourik]

Permaculture One
(A Perennial Agriculture for Human Settlements)
Bill Mollison and David Holmgren
1978; 128 pp.

$8.95 postpaid from:
Transworld Publishers
3 Bowen Crescent
Melbourne Victoria 3004
Australia
(Note beginning Winter 1980-81, write for price from:
International Tree Crops Institute, Inc.
Box 888
Winters, CA 95694)

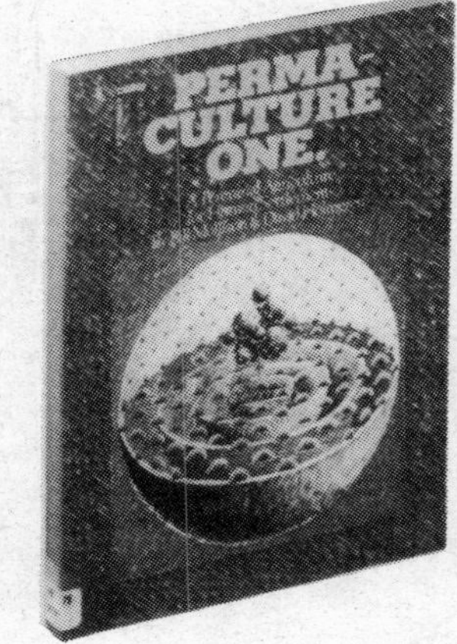

•

A few years ago, about 1974, we extracted from the world literature of plants 3,000 - 4,000 species useful to man — the peculiar thing about them is that most of them have quite specific niches which they like to fit.

•

You can construct, using these plants, a series of forests in which you start underground with tuberous species and with rhizomes and also there's a huge variety of fungi which live in the mulch leaf litter. You can come up, through short perennial herbs, through taller herbs, small bushes, small woody plants, medium-sized woody plants and so on up, and create, not so much a three-tier agriculture as a multi-tier agriculture which then forms a sort of a closed jungle system. If you stand off from that you can often see a place in it where you can put yet more species, for instance, even in a quite closed system, vines will emerge and thrive.

•

Even in a closed system, whether you introduce it or not, fungi will invade. In the same way a lot of the plants that we've used we've used for animal fodders. You can construct jungles quite specifically or forests or perennial plant assemblies, to feed pigs or poultry or other animals of use to man. So you can construct a food jungle, a medical jungle, a poultry jungle, a marine underwater jungle, a swamp jungle, all directly used by man and all perennial.

Permaculture Two

Permaculture Two *follows its innovative predecessor with further techniques in the fine art of sustaining the land's productivity through the use of trees and perennial plants. Crops that help shade and nourish each other are planted in patterns that catch water and sun and block the wind. Abundant drawings illustrate these systems for growing food, sheltering animals, and insulating a house behind earth mounds. Author Mollison is from Tasmania, Australia, where his Permaculture Association is pioneering research in arid land agriculture and getting people around the world excited about tree crops.*

—Rosemary Menninger

Permaculture Two
(Practical Design for Town and Country in Permanent Agriculture)
Bill Mollison
1979; 150 pp.

$10.95 postpaid from:
International Tree Crops Institute, Inc.
Box 888
Winters, CA 95694

•

The broad strategies of desert re-afforestation are now well tested. Hostile drying winds, rivers, and local oases are the focal points for expanding the vegetation: if we start from up-stream, securing the headwaters and catchments, from up-wind, and from oases, then plants generate moisture downstream, down-wind, and locally. . . .

The aim is to use many more deep-rooted and climatically-adjusted perennial plants for food and structural materials, in order that desert outstations may become more self-sufficient, and to devise low-maintenance systems of domestic agriculture. . . .

Not only will many important vegetables and tree crops grow in deserts, but the native vegetation, where not overburnt or overgrazed, is, in itself, a great resource.

Water lies close underground in many places. Mulch material, as plants or leaves, is abundant. Growth in desert soil is phenomenal if water is available. Modern drip-irrigation plus mulch will grow any domestic crop. While lawns, as such, are rather wasteful disasters, the potential is for a revolutionary forestry, and thus increased rainfall, and a reduction of dust and disease. China is planting 7,600 km of her desert fringe; Australia could do the same, but hasn't as yet started on the first 7 km, preferring to have an unemployment problem, dust, salted soils, and large profits for a few graziers! There has been little or no attempt to develop large desert water storages, or to encourage scour-hole lagoons, and no extensive use of keyline or Negev run-off techniques, although road graders are now available for such work.

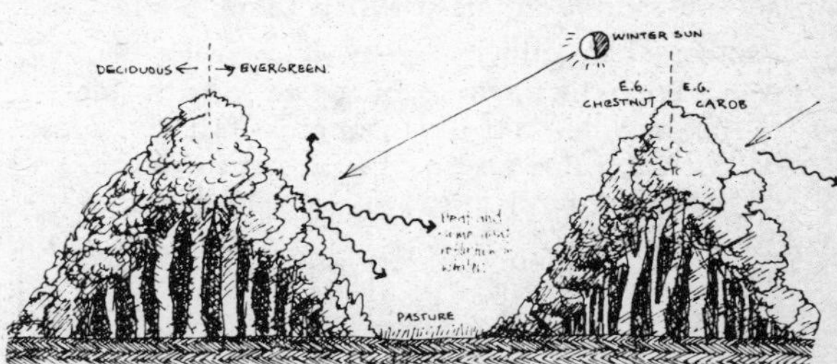

IDEAL-STRUCTURE OF TREE CROP SPECIES ON PLAINS. DECIDUOUS SPECIES TO SOUTH (N.), EVERGREEN SPECIES TO NORTH (S.). TREES ACT AS WINDBREAKS, HEAT REFLECTORS, STOCK PROTECTORS, CLIMATIC BUFFERS, CROP DIVERSIFICATION, POSSIBLE FUEL PRODUCERS, EROSION PROTECTORS, DROUGHT-PROOF STOCK FEED. FIG. 4.4.

Agricultural Involution

This tells the story of the decline of swidden — an ingenious but delicate, labor-intensive system of tree clearing and burning, then crop cultivation, then reforestation. It failed in Indonesia because the slow growth it demands was too slow for the flood of new population. The book could be used as a case either for the doom of or the promise of labor-intensive techniques in American forests.

—Rosemary Menninger

According to analysis by Roy Rappaport in the special **Scientific American** *issue on "Energy" a couple years ago, swidden agriculture is the most energy-efficient in the world.*

—SB

Agricultural Involution
(The Processes of Ecological Change in Indonesia)
Clifford Geertz
1963, 1977; 170 pp.

$4.25 postpaid from:
University of California Press
2223 Fulton Street
Berkeley, CA 94720
or Whole Earth Household Store

•

A significant proportion of the mineral energy upon which swidden crops, and especially the grains, draw for their growth comes from the ash remains of the fired forest, rather than from the soil as such, so that the completeness with which a plot is burnt is a crucial factor in determining its yield, a fact of which probably all swidden cultivators are aware.

•

In a swidden the jungle canopy is radically lowered, but much of its umbrella-like continuity is maintained, in part by planting cultigens not in an open field, crop-row manner, but helter-skelter in a tightly woven, dense botanical fabric, in part by planting shrub and tree crops of various sorts (coconuts, areca, jakfruit, banana, papaya, and today in more commercial areas rubber, pepper, abaca and coffee), and in part by leaving some trees standing. In such a way, excessive exposure of the soil to rain and sun is minimized and weeding, exhausting task in any case, is brought within reasonable proportions because light penetration to the floor is kept down to a much lower level than in an open-field system.

The Maple Sugar Book

My family had a sugar bush in Michigan, so we always had a cellar-room full of gallon cans of pure maple syrup, which solved most Christmas-giving problems and saddled me with an early addiction. This book by the Nearings (of **Living the Good Life**, *p. 76) continues their fine philosophical rap and lays out the definitive information of maple-sugaring. You don't have to have maple trees to enjoy it, but if you do . . .*

—SB

The Maple Sugar Book
(Together with Remarks on Pioneering as a Way of Living in the Twentieth Century)
Helen and Scott Nearing
1950, 1970; 273 pp.

$4.95 postpaid from:
Schocken Books
200 Madison Avenue
New York, NY 10016
or Whole Earth Household Store

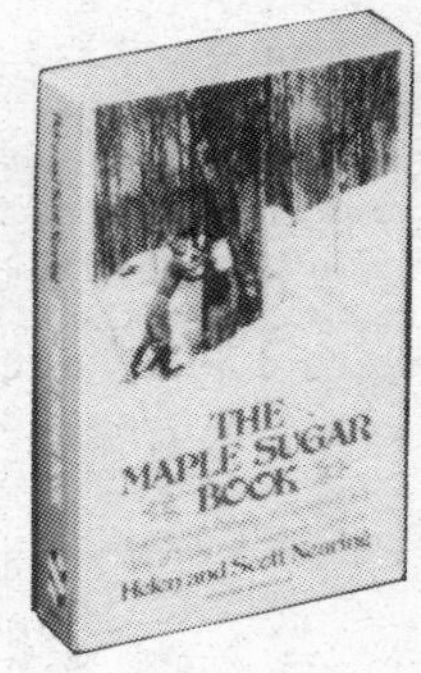

•

Here is a typical case in our neighborhood. The household is made up of a man, his wife, and five children, the oldest a boy of fifteen. Sugartime comes in late February or early March. The snow is so deep in the woods that logging and wood cutting (the usual winter occupations) are difficult or impossible. In the homestead there is little to do beside the regular chores. The family has a sugar bush, a sugarhouse, 1,500 buckets, covers, and spouts, an evaporator, a gathering tank, a team of horses standing idle in the barn, a supply of sugar wood. Not a single cash outlay is involved in the entire sugar operation.

Maple sugar equipment

The talented maple tree — source of leafy autumn fireworks, good furniture, good firewood, and a springly by-product of sweetness and something interesting to do during the maddening final snows of the year. For equipment, shop here for mailorder evaporators, tanks, pumps, buckets.

—SB

Maple Sugar Maker's Guide
Catalog

free from:
Leader Evaporator Company, Inc.
25 Stowell Street
St. Albans, VT 05478

This unit is designed as a Pleasure Model for the part time Sugar Maker or hobbyist. ↓

THE RISING SUN
NEIGHBORHOOD NEWSLETTER

Even a small branch library has a vast chunk of the whole world. To see how vast any library is, compare it to what you'd see on TV in a lifetime which is always going to be determined by attention grabbing, but a library has everything. And it has it for free in walking distance — knowledge really is power and the library has the only kind of power it's easy for poor people and children to get in this country — when there are branch libraries, when they are open late.

Omnipresent in Europe, the uses and techniques of coppicing are completely unknown in America. Dr. Geoffrey Stanford is director of the Greenhills Center for Studies at the Interface Between Town and Country (Rt. 1, Box 861, Cedar Hill, TX 75104, (214) 296-1955). He has been studying coppicing for over 10 years, and already has 15 species under trial at Greenhills. He has just completed an extensive literature review of coppicing and short-rotation harvesting (SRH) for the U.S. government's Solar Energy Research Institute. Copies may be available from SERI by early 1981. —Richard Nilsen

English oak coppice, with many stems arising from each stump. Used for firewood.
—Woodland Crafts in Britain

A hazel coppice in Kent, England, being harvested for split palings.
—Made in England

Coppicing Your Home Woodlot

Coppice: forest originating mainly from sprouts or root suckers rather than seed. (Webster's Dictionary)

by Geoffrey Stanford

YOU CAN DO ALL YOUR COOKING for a family of four forever with the wood you can cut from a tract of well-managed coppice that measures less than 65 ft. on the side (see Box 1). This is a rule-of thumb figure: the actual area of woodlot that you need depends on a large number of factors: how much cooking you actually do, how much heat you need for water and space heating, your local rainfall and water availability, whether you are taking over an abandoned woodland or planting a special energy plantation, whether your land is suited to trees. The figures in Box 2 give the range of some of these.

Harvesting

You can harvest your woodlot in three main ways: mature forestry, coppicing, and short-rotation harvesting. In mature forestry you cut down the largest, mature trees and let the younger ones grow up to take their place. In coppicing you preserve about ten large trees dotted on each acre of your land, and you cut all the others to a stump only an inch or two above ground level. New shoots will grow from the younger stumps, and you cut those when they are ready again – say in 5 - 20 years. People have been working coppiced woodlots like this in Europe for over 3,000 years. In short-rotation harvesting (SRH) you plant young cuttings or seedlings very closely – anything from 12 - 30 inches apart – and cut them to the ground every few years, or even every year. Pines and firs do not sprout again from the stump, so you cannot coppice or SRH them.

Factors That Influence Growth

Age: Trees, like people, have two growth stages: in the juvenile stage they can grow fast, but they do not form flowers or set seed. In the mature stage they grow more slowly.

Light: While there is plenty of light, trees can grow fast. Once their leaves cover the area completely, their growth rate slows down: the "canopy is closed." The closer they are spaced, the quicker the canopy is closed, and the shorter the harvest cycle. So it is likely that plants which normally grow well on the edge of a forest will be better for coppicing than deep-forest trees.

Nitrogen: Nitrogen supply is another limiting factor. Trees are unusual in that only the outer part of their stem and branches is truly alive; the bark and the wood are more-or-less dead. Since this outer ring contains most of the protein (which is rich in nitrogen) the smaller branches and twigs hold more nitrogen per pound of cut timber than does the thick stem. Put another way, SRH drains away more nitrogen than does coppicing.

Trace Essentials: Other essential and scarce materials are also removed with the nitrogen, notably trace minerals. So SRH can only be done successfully on acid soils (because the metals are in solution) and with trees that have the ability to fix atmospheric nitrogen: legumes, and alder, for example (see Box 3).

Exceptions: Osier (willow) is exceptional: it has always been harvested annually (SRH) for basket-making, but it is usually grown along stream banks, and probably gets ample nitrogen from the running water. Poplar is an exception to almost all these remarks, and may prove to outgrow all other species in some areas even though it has no apparent nitrogen-fixing mechanism.

Water: About 1000 pounds of water are need to make 1 pound of wood, and of course this is mostly needed during the growing season, so plants which grow naturally by a riverbank are more likely to have the in-built ability to grow fast than those which have adapted to dryer summers.

Shrubs: I assume that what you are probably looking for is the greatest annual yield of firewood that you can get from a small piece of land, so you don't need timber quality. Some shrubs can grow very fast, and you may find one that suits your land and will outproduce trees.

Exotics: A number of trees from other countries produce very large annual growth, but they mostly need hot moist weather, or are cut down or killed by cold wind and frost (see Box 3).

Summary: So if you are living in areas which have winter snow, you will be wise to investigate the coppicing value of your local trees and shrubs, and especially those which grow well on forest edge and riverbanks. If you are in a frost-free area then you can consider planting some of the special very fast-growing trees from the tropics.

Multiple purpose: Lastly, you may place as much value on flowering or nut-bearing as on fuel, and so select for multiple-purpose use; better still, you will plant several types of species.

Management

Planting: Planting a new coppice and replanting (infilling an existing rough woodlot) is best done in two rows, with the roots evenly spaced, sawtooth fashion. If you are planning for a five-year cycle, your roots should be 3 ft. apart, and each pair of rows spaced 4 ft. apart. These rows are all planted exactly on the contour-line, so that when you harvest you will be hauling comfortably on the level, between the paired rows.

Harvesting: You can harvest either with an axe or a chainsaw. Since your cut should be no more than 2 inches above ground-level, the stem is likely to be soiled and this will blunt your chain rapidly. With either tool you should make a slanting cut, or a "V" point. Take great care not to leave a split stump or torn bark. Harvest only during the dormant season – three weeks after leaf-fall until six weeks before bud-break is a good working practice.

Competition: Your most likely problem will be from browsing; the tender young regrowth being eaten by rabbits and deer. If you are planting a new coppice you will also have trouble from weeds, since you are attempting to introduce late members of the eco-succession into an area smothered with pioneers. (Historically, coppices were established within virgin forests, where the tree canopy shaded out weeds.) Since nobody has yet solved either of these difficulties, I cannot help you much. Of all the methods, weeds are best suppressed by planting through a hole in a sheet of black polyethylene. That's expensive, but so are all other methods if they are used effectively. On flat ground you can put the soil to tillage for row crops for a year, followed by a smother-crop of beans or clover, and then plant your trees among the debris in the fall; but that is difficult on the rocky, hilly slopes which are best put to coppicing.

Summary

A coppice provides a wonderful example of a mixed economy: it can flourish on otherwise unusable land, provide a beautiful vista, harbor birds and game, offer shady walks and (in the year following harvest) woodland flowers; it conserves rainfall and resists erosion; it can assimilate and cleanse sewage waters, and compost household garbage under its moist shade; and it will support and encourage nut trees; all this, and endless fuel too. Start your coppice now. ■

Box 1

WOOD NEEDED FOR FAMILY COOKING

A family of four needs about 5 million BTU each year for cooking food on a gas or electric stove. A wood stove is only about 1/3 as efficient as gas or electricity, so they will need 15 million BTU of wood. Dry wood has about 8000 BTU per pound.

$$\frac{15{,}000{,}000 \text{ BTU}}{8000 \frac{\text{BTU}}{\text{lb.}}} = 1875 \text{ lbs., or } 0.9375 \text{ tons of wood/yr.}$$

A well-managed coppice produces about 10 tons of dry wood per acre per year. An acre is 43,560 sq. ft. So they need:

$$\frac{0.9375 \text{ tons} \times 43{,}560 \text{ sq ft.}}{10 \text{ tons/acre/year}} = 4083 \text{ sq. ft.}$$

of space for a wood-lot, or an area a little less than 65 foot square.

Box 2

WOOD GROWTH	Woody growth (dry weight) in tons/acre/year
Scrubland	0.1 - 0.5
Rank mixed woodland	0.5 - 2.5
Natural forest regrowth	1.0 - 5.0
Selected forestry plantation	2.0 - 8.0
Natural mixed coppice	4.0 - 10.0
Hazel or chestnut, coppiced (England)	10.0 - 18.0
Poplar, short-rotation plantation	12.0 - 30.0
"Miracle-tree" plantation, coppiced (tropics)	15.0 - 40.0

WATER SUPPLY

Trees need at least 30 inches of rainfall equivalent per year; half or more of this should fall during the growth period. Trees use 500 - 1500 lbs. of water to make 1 lb. of wood (depending on species).

Box 3

SUITABLE SPECIES

TROPICAL & SUB-TROPICAL, exceptionally fast-growing (some species only).	Heat	High Humidity	Frost-Sensitive	Legume	Tree or Shrub	River Bank or Forest Edge	Flower, Fruit, Nut
Gmelina, "miracle-tree"	yes	yes	yes	no	tree	neither	no
Prosopis, mesquite	yes & no	yes & no	yes & no	yes	tree	neither	no
Leucaena, ipel-ipel	yes	yes & no	yes	yes	tree/shrub	neither	yes
Eucalyptus	yes	yes & no	yes & no	no	tree	neither	no
Gliricidium	yes	yes	yes	yes	tree	either	yes
TEMPERATE, respond well to coppicing.							
Hazel, lilac, dogwood	no	no	no	no	shrub	either	yes
Beech, chestnut	no	no	no	no	tree	neither	yes
Redbud	no	no	no	yes	tree	either	yes
Sequoia, redwood	no	yes	no	no	tree	neither	no
Robinia, locust	no	no	no	yes	tree	neither	yes

(See **Woodland Crafts in Britain** *review, p. 250.)*

SUPPLIERS

Prosopis seeds
Dr. Peter Felker, Dept. of Plant Protein Chemistry, University of California, Riverside, CA 92521

Leucaena seeds
Dr. James L. Brewbaker, University of Hawaii at Monoa, Dept. of Horticulture, St. John Plant Science Lab. 102, 3190 Maile Way, Honolulu, Hawaii 96822

Poplar stems
Tre-gro Inc., 13119 Westchester Trail, Chesterland, Ohio 44026

Windbreak trees
Forestry Service; ask your local Agricultural Extension Agent.

FURTHER READING

AFOCEL
Methode d'Exploitation d'une Coupe de Taillis (Procedures for Harvesting a Coppice) AFOCEL, 164 bd. Haussmann 75008 Paris
Splendid drawings easily understood by anyone: free.

COBBETT, William
The Woodlands: or, A Treatise on . . . the Cutting Down of Forest Trees & Underwoods . . . including those of America . . . published by the author, London, 1825.
Now rather rare, but well worth reading in public library. Precise instructions from an experienced nurseryman and landowner.

DEVEZE, Michel (1961)
La Vie de la Foret Francaise au XVIe Siecle S.E.V.P.E.N., Paris, 1961
A detailed account of the essential roles of the factories in the forest on which village life depended. Unfortunately, I know no English translation.

GOOR, A.Y., BARNEY, C.W.
Forest Tree Planting in Arid Zones, Ronald Press, N.Y. 1968
If you want to start coppicing in drylands, start here.

RACKHAM, Oliver
Hayley Wood: its history and ecology. Cambridgeshire Naturalists Trust Ltd. (England) 1975, 221 pp., index, illustrations, many references.
A comprehensive classic, covering many centuries of records, examined with modern insights.

SMITH, J. Russell
Tree Crops – a permanent agriculture. Devin Adair 1977
Not much on coppicing but essential for background understanding.

STANFORD, Geoffrey (1976)
Short-Rotation Forestry – Principles and Practices Greenhills Foundation, R1, B861, Cedar Hill, TX 75104. $5

STANFORD, Geoffrey (1980)
Coppicing: A Literature Review and Survey. SERI/DOE, Golden, CO 80401 (in preparation)

STANFORD, Geoffrey (1979)
The Home Woodlot for Managing Domestic Wastes Greenhills Foundation, R1, B861, Cedar Hill, TX 75104. $2.50

VIETMEYER, Noel (1980)
Firewood Crops: Shrub and Tree Species for Energy Production, National Academy of Sciences, Washington, D.C. 20418 (in preparation)

The Cheap Thrills Crew

The Hoedads

They have a legal, cooperative structure, their own credit union, a gypsy lifestyle, enough work to keep a little ways from foodstamps, no gurus, and a vision of a labor-intensive energy-efficient forest of the future.

by J.D. Smith

The Hoedads of Oregon were founded in 1973. **CoEvolution***'s resident cowboy J.D. Smith wrote this account of their success in 1976. Since then tree-planting cooperatives have sprung up absolutely everywhere in the American West. The longhairs of the '70s are reforesting this side of the continent, and within that little errand something even profounder may be going on.* —SB

Downswinging a hoedad

A CHINESE FELLOW ONCE SAID, IN translation, that one process of revolution is the dialectic progression from mutual aid societies (neighbors putting up hay together), through the cooperative movement, the worker's collectives, the commune, to the community, in all its full-blown national importance. When the wheat farmer figures out that he doesn't need a business agent, and his friends are too busy to help, he builds up a farm coop, a storage elevator, and goes to talk to the bigtime millers as a group. This is a producers' cooperative, a good cheap way to buy gearlube in bulk, but mostly a marketing device.

The Hoedads are a two-hundred person membership cooperative involved in the business of reforestation. They are legal, in the state of Oregon, bondable, mobile, and able to work thinning, planting, tubing, or slashpiling for the United States Department of Agriculture, (the Forest Service. . . . a bunch of inattentive tree farmers selling wood four or five generations of tree away from what is being planted). The Hoedads take their name from the basic tree planting tool, a long hoe affair with a curved handle like on a carpenter's adze. Doesn't take much of a linguist to figure out why it is called a hoedad.

I'm not a Hoedad. The only tree I have planted since gradeschool Arbor Days was a three foot redwood the day after my daughter was born. I planted it under a PG&E powerline. Before you run off to become a Hoedad be advised that two hundred treeplanters in a work cooperative have some trouble keeping each other in work west of the Rockies. They don't need the membership, even though it costs a thousand bucks to be a member, taken out of wages in a three year period. In April of this year, the Hoedads had five hundred thousand dollars worth of work under contract, most of it in planting. That sounds like a lot of money until you divide it by two hundred, six months, and the fact that climbing around the mess the loggers leave, poking in a tree every ten feet, can be shitty hard work.

I first met a Hoedad in Idaho about two years ago. Idaho is where the Sierra Club is considered to be a bunch of Californians who live in big redwood houses and think that a tree screams when the chainsaw bites the bark. I was holed up at a hotsprings and working in a sawmill. The Hoedad hopped the rocks up a washed-out road beside the River of No Return, in a Japanese pickup truck, first rig to make it up the road that year. I baked the Hoedad a loaf of bread and stole her heart for awhile.

This Spring I met her again, this time in the Mountain Tavern in Tiller, Oregon. She was late, so I had plenty of time to belly up to the beer, taste the jukebox, shoot pool with a helicopter pilot, and listen to the bartender's tales of twenty hungry Hoedads ordering burgers: "Heck, I just got to where I'd hold the sandwich up, call out what was on it, and give it to the first person with the money. That much long hair I just can't keep track of."

I was counting the beans in a half a bowl of chili when a pair of hands went over my eyes. Hoedad women are broad in the shoulder and hard of palm; I knew the lady I was waiting for was in the bar with me. We drank a few beers together, held hands, and tried to short circuit a few years with our eyes. More Hoedads started drifting in. Three crews were planting in that area. There was talk of hundred dollar days, sunny soft slopes where a planter could scalp away the overburden on the clearcut, poke the hoedad down into the dirt, fit in a young seedling (two or three years old), and toe the dirt back into place fast enough to make, by piecework, a hundred bucks a day. Fat city. I was buying drinks. We were in the Umpqua National Forest. They were camped six or eight miles up the creek. Did I want to go to camp?

THE CREW MEETING

A Hoedad camp smacks of the New Depression. This one belonging to the Cheap Thrills crew was on an old landing, where the trucks had come to get the butchered timber when it had been logged. There were a couple of nice big warm canvas and lath yurts, a smaller tent, a vintage house truck, and a few light travel trailers. We tiptoed across boards plunked down over the wet areas and snuggled into my Mama's quilts around the woodstove in the center of one of the yurts. Before sleep we talked of the dialectic, of the politics of doing what you mean to do, of the need for federations to supergroup the cooperatives in the northwestern part of Ecotopia, of the need for constant intention, which is to say: "Say what you mean, but mean what you say."

A little while before dawn I wandered outside to pee and waded into six inches of new wet snow. The Hoedads plant most of the winter in sloppy Oregon drizzle. Next to the hoedad and the tree sack, raingear is the important tool of a coastal reforester. You can't plant trees in snow, though, because you can't see where to put the trees. The Umpquas had

THE RISING SUN
NEIGHBORHOOD NEWSLETTER

Rightists and leftists gotta believe in libraries — for lefties they are the *only* property sharing thing, no qualifications, no strings, we've got going and it's a sin to let it die. (Nineteenth century anarchists pointed to free public libraries as the beginning of the revolution — and they were right, just because the rest of the revolution didn't happen doesn't mean that libraries aren't a little bit of workers' paradise now — when they're open nights, so workers and not just club ladies can go.) And if conservatives want to believe that Horatio Alger can still make the big jump, that everybody has a chance if they work hard, they better have a library open for Horatio to study up on the skills of his choice and it better be close to his house because he's tired and it better be open late.

Origin of the Hoedads

by Gary Rurkun

When Gary Rurkun wrote this in 1976, he was a 24-year-old biophysics grad student. His crew was the Natural Wonders.
—SB

A co-op of two hundred people doesn't just spring up from nothing, but like a crystal it grows from a nucleus of committed and seminal people.

My experience with the Hoedads began in the late summer and fall of 1973 in Eugene, Oregon. At the time I was looking for work, any work, as were many folks around Eugene. It turned out that every hitchhiker I picked up and asked about work (beats the want-ads) had heard something about an infinite fountain of work which began with the rains. There would be no bosses, you could smoke dope all day, make lots of money, "run by hippies, man." No one knew who or where or how it would come together, at least none of my sources. After hearing this same nebulous story from a number of different people, it became clear that this was no mass delusion and that perhaps there was such a thing as planting trees (images of huge tractors hefting Giant Sequoias) and that the hippie business existed.

Eventually with the help of several miracles I ended up at the pre-pre-pre general meeting of the primeval co-op on a piece of land outside of Eugene. We arrived on the scene to find vans, school buses, and assorted fifteen year old vehicles parked all around the small farm house. It was an assembly of perhaps 200 various Oregonites of every persuasion, from grizzled logger types to frizzled guru types, cork boots to thongs, Big Red to ginseng. All were looking as confused as the first day of high school because at that point for most of us Hoedads was a hum in the air more than a reality.

After a bit of moseying and a few rounds of rumoring, it turned out that someone was in control. A woodsy type character with a full beard, and huge build, and powerful voice called us all around him to chat. He was 25ish and articulate and had a very uneasy look on his face. We were probably 200 of the motliest, most disorganized folks he'd ever seen. But he and his friends were responsible for our being there that morning so he went on.

He explained the trip. He and his friends standing next to him had planted trees as a cooperative crew for a few years already and had really enjoyed working together, unlike commercial tree planting operations with a crew boss and hourly wage workers. They went on to explain the advantages of a cooperative tree planting for making money as well as for our souls.

But these boys didn't just want to enjoy their crew; being true new age entrepreneurs, they wanted to be the seed that creates a larger co-operative. They did not want to give the assembled crowd any work. They offered to get contracts for us, all of us, if we could organize ourselves into cohesive cooperative crews like their crew, the Cougar Mountain crew. They then went on to describe how to organize a crew; the necessity of some money, a crew crummy (the rig in which you ride to work), a treasurer, a crew ideology or by-laws, etc. A lot of information was passed on how they intended for us to get it together. Then a break.

The folks were left with their minds reeling. Is this for real? Could it possibly come together? What's their angle? Whose crew do I get on? How do you organize a group of undisciplined strangers into a work force?

The practicalities began to evolve that afternoon. The Cougar Mountain crew would put up their 300 acres of land as collateral to cover the bonding on the contracts for which we would bid. But we had to know how many crews in order to know how many contracts to bid on. It seemed that everyone there wanted to join a crew and was ready to plant. "Okay, then organize yourselves into crews of about twenty, right now," we were told. Now there was unspoken panic in the faces of many, shades of dances in junior high school and who will be picked to dance and who will stand by the wall. I wished my hair to grow and my voice to deepen. Somehow we all assembled ourselves into crews; some crews formed around existing collectives, a video group, a group who owned a commune out of town, some old friends. My housemate of one week knew a lot of people so I snuck into his crew.

The Cougar Mountain people then told each crew to go ahead and get organized, buy a crummy, train to plant with them. Any problems, just call CM for advice. The responsibility rested on the shoulders of each crew, but it might work. "It might work" was the thought of that day.

What followed was a period of disbelief and mistrust born from experiences with ripoffs and self-motivation. We had little experience with moral rather than monetary motivation. But discussion over these issues soon yielded to the trust and adventure of organizing the crew.

Our crew organized quickly and was ready to work. We were twenty people from varying backgrounds, a few woodsmen but mostly ex-college students, reformed surfers, and assorted followers of gurus. We collected a $20 membership fee to finance our 1953 Chevy crew carrier, the crew totem. We discussed the various forms our crew could take and agreement was reached to keep it loose at first until we understood the possible problems. We were then ready to report back to Central, as our headquarters became known.

Central was a committee composed of elected representatives from each crew

us snowed out. There was a big temptation to go back and wake up the bartender. The Cheap Thrills folks called for a crew meeting instead, to discuss the issues that would be brought up at the General Meeting in Eugene.

The crew is the basic Hoedad family unit. Groups of fifteen to twenty people, the majority being men, travel, work and camp together. There are twelve or so crews with proud names like Red Star, Mud Sharks, Cougar Mountain, Cheap Thrills, Different Strokes, and TNT (Tabasco 'n Tofu). The crew elects or appoints people to bid work through Hoedad Central (bondable), has its own treasurer, its own set of books, and is the initial resting place of the money from a contract. It pays, therefore, to have an interest in crew politics.

The meeting took place in the central yurt. We started by passing a long stemmed, heavy yet intricate pipe full of talk-and-stare weed. A chairperson was selected. Folks squatted in with their knees up around their ears and got down to business.

Did the Hoedads need a general store? There was a real need for a group-buying operation to supplement the existing quartermaster's function, but was a retail store worth the hassle? It was moved, seconded, and unanimously decided that should a Hoedad General Store ever come about, it would be a workers' collective within a membership cooperative. These folks were serious.

What should happen to the Hoedad General's $70,000 cash reserve fund which the membership fees and administrative withholding had created? This was a tough one. Should it be used for a treeplanters' retirement parcel, Hoedad Acres, or loaned out to movement folks with no cash funds? Nothing was decided. Well enough should be left alone. It was nice and warm in the yurt. Let the cash reserve fund grow.

What about a womens' crew? Was it separatist and away from the move toward federation? A group of woman Hoedads wanted to try planting together, without the sexual competition and "you are so cute when you plant trees" bullshit that comes with almost any American work situation. There are about sixty woman Hoedads, some of them loners, some of them coupled up with men, but most of them workers in their own right. I watched men's eyes drift out into the snow and imagined that I was losing my old lady to a new misunderstood power. Wasn't it sexist to split off like this? Couldn't more women become Hoedads and go for gradual change within the cooperative? It was the old rub: as a woman you couldn't vote against a notion like this, and as a man you could vote either way. There were mostly men in the yurt. It was decided that the Cheap Thrills crew would support the womens' crew at the general meeting in Eugene, in a week. Could I come?

THE GENERAL MEETING

The WOW hall used to be owned by the Woodmen of the World. It was built in a time when the prime timber was still in the stump, before yarders and balloons and helicopter logging, when it still took labor to harvest the tree crops. The Hoedads had slushed some money into the hall to save it from burger kingdom and were now renting it for their quarterly meeting. It was a nice place, in downtown Eugene, with a Grange hall feeling. Outside twenty folks cooled their Vibrams and watched the traffic. A Spanish Civil War veteran with bushy eyebrows taped political messages to the powerpoles. One of them read like this:

On Lonelyness

As an idle man
I find too many
things to do,
that I have no time
to be lonely.
Besides, it would be
deadly
boring to me.

Starting a meeting on a sunny Sunday isn't a cinch. There was an oval of stiff chairs on the meeting floor, a bunch of risers along the side, and people spilled here and there. The president acted as chairperson. Should we read the old minutes or rely on memory? The legalists prevailed. If the old minutes were going to be adopted then

BOB FOUS

Rainy day discussion. Raincoats can be tools.

Discussing the women's crew at the general meeting

DIANA FAIRBANKS

plus anyone else who knew what was going on. Thus Central was mostly Cougar Mountain in control because only they were informed. No votes were taken as decisions came forth in discussion. It was a primitive but effective governing body.

It turned out that seven crews organized like ours which meant there were eight crews including Cougar Mountain. After our first day of planting trees out in the rain and mud two weeks later, two of the crews disbanded. Only those crews which had formed with a solid foundation could survive the small money and wet feet of that day. So we were left with six crews ready to organize the cooperative. One hard core crew had within two months grown five more very fragile but ambitious crews.

The task at hand now for survival was to create a just system of representation for each crew in order to decide on business problems, dividing up contracts and income, etc. Being children of America, we chose a representative democracy with a temporary oligarchy by the Cougar Mountain crew since we were inexperienced.

After a few months of planting trees all became more familiar with the business and practicalities, and like a teenager growing up, we were ready to assume a more active role in the management of the co-op. A formal set of by-laws was adopted, the co-op was legally incorporated, and an elected council proceeded to usurp the power which Cougar Mountain had wielded. Their child had matured.

Once the organization was constructed the only worry was to keep it solvent which demanded both money and energy. The organization of the co-op was so enchanting that many just wanted to revel in its beauty and work on the business end of it. But our bread and butter was tree planting and that we did. By the end of our first season, we had done contracts all over Oregon, Washington, Idaho, Montana, and Alaska with the income coming into Central and dispersed to the crews.

At each step in the maturation of the co-op, the council made the decisions which improved our solvency, efficiency, and livability on the grand scale. But the unit of the co-op was the crew and the decisions at the crew level affected each of our lives more directly. While the council would affect how lucrative our contracts were, the crew would decide when to go to work, how long to work, who works, how to divide up the money, who cooks, who was in charge of keeping the Forest Service happy, etc. And each crew was autonomous. Some chose to organize even the meals on a communal level, with a dozen people planting and one person cooking and cleaning up camp, all for the same daily wage.

The crew is like a tribe, a mini-nation, and the method dispersing their income reflects the ideology of the crew. My crew began with the assumption that all were equal in ability or strength therefore our pay would be equal, i.e., divide up each day's crew earnings evenly among the day's workers. But it evolved that we were not equal, some could plant faster and longer, some were leaders. The obvious solution was to pay each according to the number of trees he or she planted. But that seemed too much like capitalism plus it bred competition among the crew members which has no place in a cooperative. So we tried a system based on attitude, each person received a full day's wage only if he or she felt that a hard day of work had been put in. If one didn't plant as hard as possible, he or she would then request less pay for the day. It was a system based on self-criticism and a minimum of peer pressure, and it did not work. No one ever felt that he or she had not put in a full day's effort, yet other crew members were quick to accuse others of laziness. We eventually, and most crews as well, divided up the income in the tried and true capitalist tradition of more output, more pay.

At the end of the first season of planting, the overwhelming feeling was of success. It had worked; details needed to be honed but by and large it had been an incredible lesson in self-organizing systems. The question which was on the mind of all was whether or not to continue to grow or not. It was well known that thousands in Oregon need the work but it was also felt that perhaps we were at the optimal size for a co-op, still personal but large enough to have some power. It was decided at a meeting of all Hoedads to add a few crews, and to help organize other co-ops in other areas.

The other direction which people in the co-op want to move is to diversify the business so that people can grow individually with varied work experiences as well as the communal growth which the co-op fosters. Tree planting is repetitive fairly unskilled work which lost its appeal to many members after a few years. The idea of a building and wrecking co-op was batted about and continues to be an issue. But the skills of the construction trade are not easily learned, plus the range of skills from foreman to shoveling involved contradictions to our ideas of equality on the crew. It is difficult to work in an egalitarian crew if everyone is doing jobs of varying skills. These are the problems with which the co-op is struggling today. It will be interesting to see the synergy of the people at work in their eventual solutions to them. . . .

The condition which allowed the birth of this large co-op does not, unfortunately, exist in many places. That condition is the availability of large quantities of labor intensive, semi-skilled work on a contractual basis. The reason the Hoedads were able to grow so quickly is that the main obstacle was organizing the crew into a workable unit, with the need for skill in tree planting not difficult to attain, and lots of work around.

But there are fountains of work just waiting for co-opertization in many agricultural areas, and the need for reforestation wherever logging is done. All that is a dozen people to organize themselves and then plant the seed. ■

BRUCE PIEPENBURG

Overlooking a planting unit

BRUCE PIEPENBURG

Two bundles of young trees with mudball roots. Three hundred of these in a tree sack is a good load uphill.

they damn well should be read. Someone was sent crosstown to get them. It was a slow beginning in the right direction. Meeting was part of work. Criticism and self-criticism are parts of the dialectic. I was beginning to learn about movement.

Over the course of the next two days it became evident that the Hoedads are, as a group, involved in all phases of reforestation, and are expanding the definition of their work to the benefit, perhaps the radicalization, of the industry. Take herbicides for instance. The Forest Service contracts out work to chopper companies to spray 2, 4-D and 2-4, 5-T on recently logged areas to limit the broadleaf growth. These chemicals are horribly close to Agent Orange, the defoliant used in Vietnam to uncover the Ho Chi Minh trail and ruin the agricultural base of the revolutionists. They cause birth defects. The Hoedads voted a thousand dollars for research into alternatives to spraying. They argue that with a little use of people the unwanted vegetation can be turned into energy, into wood alcohol or sheep fodder. Solve the problem with people, not poisons.

The tree crop has to be thinned, weeded, and the standard government method of doing this is to let a thinning contract, which is chainsaw work, just walking into the thick of it and knocking down everything but the strong plants, leaving the rest jackstrawed on the ground to rot into the forest floor. The Hoedads have begun to get thinning contracts. They talked of ways to utilize the slash, run portable stud mills, make two by fours out of the unwanted trees, and end up with a few houses out of each thinning contract.

The question of the womens' crew was brought to the floor. A woman read the title poem from **Monster** by Robin Morgan. The shuffling began; the "tee hee" jokes sprinkled through the crowd. Some things aren't meant to be decided by two hundred people. The Hoedads compromised: if there were ever to be a new crew added to Hoedad Central, then it would be the Women's Crew. Meanwhile a crew of women were going to plant together anyway, just to see how it worked.

You can judge a political movement by its parties. There were five kegs of beer and two bands that night at the tree planters' boogydown. Somebody asked me if I was a CIA agent. Somebody else said that by writing about Hoedads I would bring government attention. (He was legal but a little underground.) The dancefloor was getting muddied up from the wafflesole mountain boots tracking in that part of Oregon. I had the feeling that two hundred active members is about as big as a cooperative can get and still have fun at a party. Somehow the rain and the beer were getting me down.

On the train back to California we passed a big derailment, with boxcars strewn out in a riverbed like the Lord had dropped his Mahjong set. I envisioned five hundred people picking up the pieces. In the Sacramento Valley I wondered whether farm workers might not do better as cooperatives than as unions, and who was in charge of naming race horses. In all I was convinced that the Hoedads had their shit together. They had a legal, cooperative structure, their own credit union, a gypsy lifestyle, enough work to keep a little ways from foodstamps, no gurus, and a vision of a labor-intensive, energy-efficient forest of the future. I wondered if they would ever become a collective. ■

THE RISING SUN
NEIGHBORHOOD NEWSLETTER

Whatever your fantasy America, it needs libraries to ever be even a little bit true, but who really needs libraries are kids. Libraries are the only nice things most towns do for their smart kids. Being a smart kid is not exactly a burden in the category with not having enough to eat, but it's often difficult and usually boring, and if we're going to build a better space station or solar collector or have a better class of people to talk to at parties, it would be a good idea to not have being smart so unfun that smart kids start playing dumb so well that they stay dumb. (If you went to public school you saw that happen at least twice.) I remember about the second day of eighth grade history class our history teacher was bullshitting and asking a bunch of general knowledge questions to pass the time and I answered 12 and everyone else combined answered 2 and everyone looked at me real funny the rest of the day and I remember going over the recommended reading lists in reading class in junior high and the teacher asking who had read each title and me deciding how many to admit to (about half of how many I'd read seemed right). I'd learned then that the way or one way to be smart and not hated was to be bored and lie a lot, not raise your hand as soon as you knew the answer (if ever) and go to the library but not admit what you did there. (I sometimes wonder if tripping and being absent minded about practical things were another part of my way of making up for it but to be honest they seemed to come natural.)

Barnacle Parp's Chain Saw Guide

Barnacle Parp is Walter Hall's nickname in logging circles. Walter Hall is an editor of the Denver **Post**, *has written five books of poetry, and was recently Writer-in-Residence with the Iowa City Arts Council. Barnacle Parp loves chain saws, and seems to know everything about them. This is one of the few books since John Muir's* **How to Keep Your Volkswagen Alive** *that is really useable by the compleat idiot (beginner). This book is worth its price.*
—Drew Langsner

Barnacle Parp's Chain Saw Guide
(Buying, Using, and Maintaining Gas and Electric Chain Saws)
Walter Hall
1977; 288 pp.
$7.95 postpaid from:
Rodale Press, Inc.
33 E. Minor
Emmaus, PA 18049
or Whole Earth Household Store

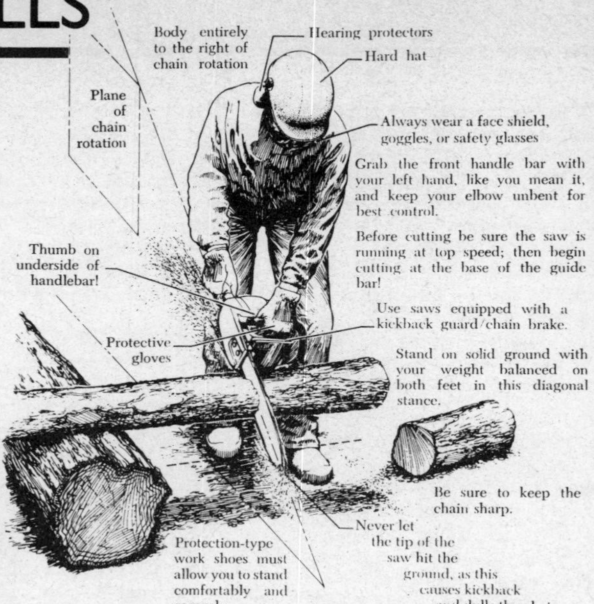
Body entirely to the right of chain rotation
Hearing protectors
Hard hat
Plane of chain rotation
Always wear a face shield, goggles, or safety glasses
Grab the front handle bar with your left hand, like you mean it, and keep your elbow unbent for best control.
Before cutting be sure the saw is running at top speed; then begin cutting at the base of the guide bar!
Thumb on underside of handlebar!
Use saws equipped with a kickback guard/chain brake.
Protective gloves
Stand on solid ground with your weight balanced on both feet in this diagonal stance.
Be sure to keep the chain sharp.
Never let the tip of the saw hit the ground, as this causes kickback and dulls the chain.
Protection-type work shoes must allow you to stand comfortably and securely

Husqvarna Chainsaw

480CD

Contrary to public belief, the Stihl 045 is not the best chainsaw going. At least according to those who make a living out of cutting wood in this part of the world (British Columbia). The saw that people are trading their Stihls in for? The Husqvarna 480 or 2100. Swedish made, Husqvarna is sturdy, dependable and QUIET. They pioneered the quiet chainsaw; it sounds like one of those two cycle motorbikes would, were it properly muffled. The best feature to my mind is the vibration damping. The three main parts of the saw (engine, front handle and rear handle) are joined together by special rubber mountings which wipe out engine and chain vibrations. The engine looks like it's floating on the rest of the framework. After 8 hours of cutting with the Husqvarna, you don't feel like you've been riding a horse with the gait of a jackrabbit. The Husqvarna outclasses the Stihl for chain oiling qualities as well. Mechanics tell me that you can't leave a Stihl 051 or 075 sitting around for any length of time (six months or more) without draining the chain oil because it leaks into the crankcase and then you have problems. Not so with the Husqvarna. What hasn't the Husqvarna got going for it? Well, around these parts it is a little more expensive than other comparably powered saws and a might bit heavier.
—Vic Marks

Husqvarna also makes the excellent Viking sewing machine, winning competition motorcycles, and firearms. Their rifles are highly regarded in Arctic climates.
—J. Baldwin

Husqvarna 480CD
$543.50 approx. with 24" blade from:
Husqvarna
224 Thorndale Ave.
Bensenville, IL 60106

Professional Timber Falling

This book is really good. I've been an amateur timber faller for about five years (cutting trees for lumber, two log buildings, craftswork, firewood, etc.) During this time I've picked up a number of bad habits that seemed to work. Dent explains the rules and why you should stick to them. He begins with the ideal tree, then goes on to explain safe and efficient falling techniques for all the different problem trees that anyone could come across. There are also chapters on bucking and limbing. **Professional Timber Falling** *is written for beginning and experienced woodsmen.*
—Drew Langsner

Professional Timber Falling
(A Procedural Approach)
D. Douglas Dent
1974; 181 pp.
$10.95 postpaid from:
D. Douglas Dent
P.O. Box 905
Beaverton, OR 97005

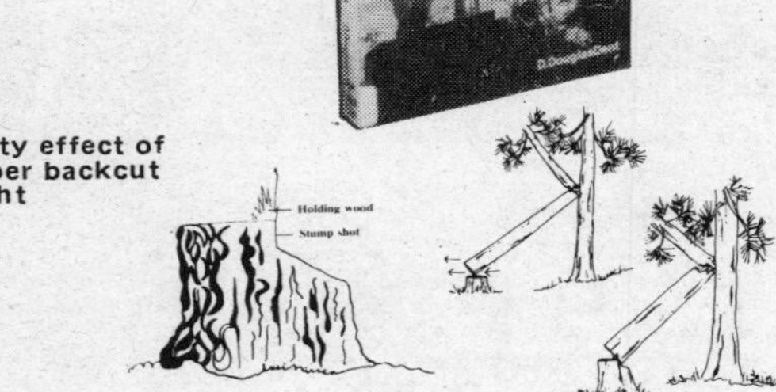
Holding wood
Stump shot
Safety effect of proper backcut height

Mobile Dimension Sawmill

Probably ranks as one of the most significant and revolutionary tools that exist today. As ingenious as the Model T Ford, it has the potential to have as profound an effect, for it makes it possible for more people to return to the land, to build their own structures, their own communities, and to get away from mass industrialized housing. Such small portable saws allow homesteaders to cut a few trees for their own needs, rather than participate in a system of lumber supply so wasteful and consumptive.

What makes the Mobile Dimension Saw so unique? First of all, the whole setup can be easily transported by a pickup or van, which makes it highly portable. Secondly, all the parts of the saw are pretty much standard machine shop parts, and available. A Volkswagen engine powers a four-foot main blade and edger blades, all of which is set on rollers and travels along a trellis or track. That track then is lifted up and into the log, which remains stationary. This way the saw can go to the log, rather than the log to the saw as in standard mill operations. And finally, the saw can cut any dimension lumber up to a 4 x 12 timber.

A professional forester, somewhat skeptical of what the saw could do, stood behind it and counted the boards as they came off. This he compared to the measurements of the log called scaling the log. (This is what the log was supposed to produce if it had been sent to the mill.) To the forester's amazement, the saw produced 50% over scale.
—Bill Wheeler

Mobile Dimension Sawmill
$8,000 (approx.) from:
Mobile Mfg. Co.
Rt. 2, Box 22A
Sundial Road
Troutdale, OR 97218

Mobile Dimension Sawmill

Chainsaw mills

Your chainsaw can make trees into roughcut boards. Along with the now-famous Alaska Mill thare are others as well. George's is a step more complicated, and it's easy to adjust. The Lumber/maker is about as simple as you can get. It works too. For heavier duty work, the Sperber Portable Chain Saw Mill represents a real professional production tool and is priced accordingly. The CLC is rail-mounted, which makes that first cut easier; it can even cut tapered siding. With a single lousy splitty bookshelf board bringing ten bucks, these machines are looking better and better. I should add that using them is not particularly relaxing; a whole day behind one is exhausting.
—J. Baldwin
[Suggested by Hap Heilman, Dan Gribi, and Stephen Anderson]

Haddon Lumber/maker
(includes book describing uses)
$39.95 from:
Haddon Tool
4719 West Route 120
McHenry, IL 60050

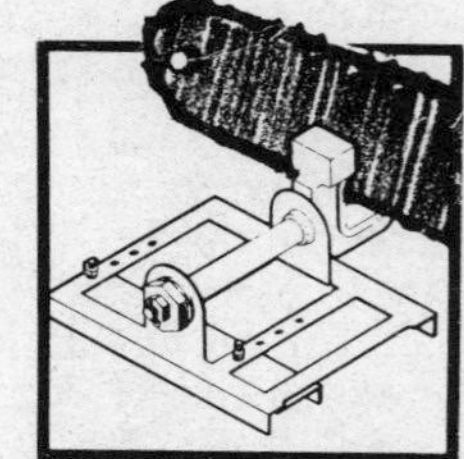
Haddon Lumber/maker

George's 36" Mill
$100 from:
George Grube
14135 Olde Hwy. 80
El Cajon, CA 92021

→

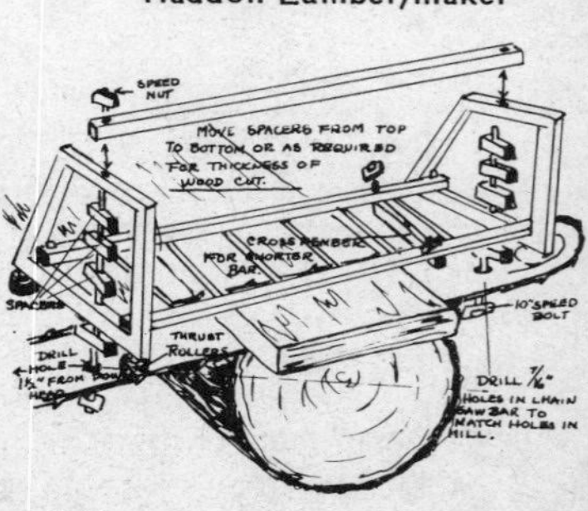

Mark III Alaskan Mill G776
24" to 56"
$109.95 to $467.50 from:
Granberg Industries, Inc.
200 S. Garrard Boulevard
Richmond, CA 94804

Alaska Mill

Sperber Portable Chain Saw Mill
$500 (average, depending on model) from:
Sperber Tool Works, Inc.
Box 1224
West Caldwell, N.J. 07006

Sperber Mill

CLC Nordic Prince Portable Sawmill
$975 from:
CLC Inc.
Box 189
LaGrande, OR 97850 ↓

Bailey's Catalog

Excellent woods tools at attractive prices. Getchyer corks, ear plugs, chainsaw bars, sharpeners, wedge pouches, gloves, branding hammers, carbide chain for cutting stumps, safety gear, and oh yes, first aid kits to mop up your gore.
—SB

Bailey's Bi-Centennial Free Enterprise Catalog
free from:
Bailey's
P.O. Box 550
Laytonville, CA 95454

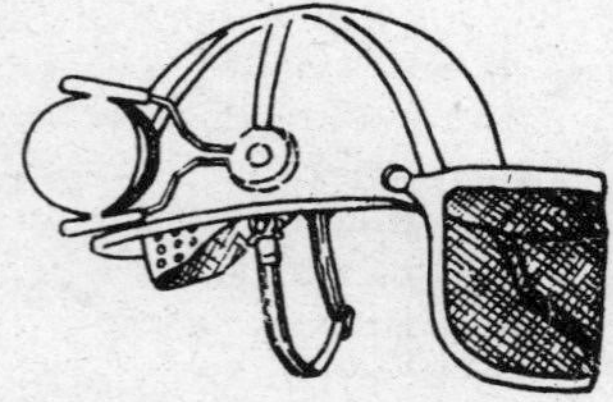
Complete helmet with ear protection, face screen, chin strap, $26.50.

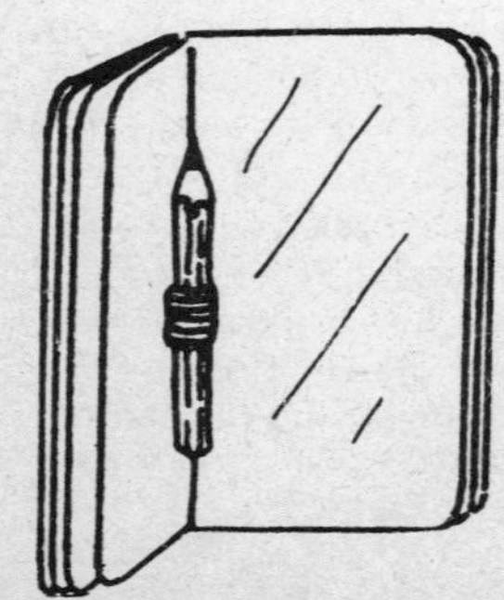
←
This 40 page waterproof notebook with handy pencil and holder is perfect for taking notes or jotting down your scale on rainy or hot, sweaty days. Created by Bailey's due to repeated customer request.

Rain-Write Notebook	
(ea.)	$1.50
By the doz.	$1.40
By the Gross	$1.30

Knowing Your Trees

The encyclopedia of trees in America, with descriptions and illustrations. There are photos of leaves, seed pods, bark, and the natural range of each type tree. Lovingly presented, in print for over 30 years. —Lloyd Kahn
[Suggested by Rodger Reid]

Knowing Your Trees
G.H. Collingwood and Warren D. Brush
Revised and edited by Devereux Butcher
1978; 389 pp.
$9.50 postpaid from:
The American Forestry Association
1319 - 18th Street N.W.
Washington, D.C. 20036
or Whole Earth Household Store

Eastern White Pine is typified by a straight trunk and a narrow, irregular crown supported by whorls of horizontal branches.

The sturdy, gradually tapering trunk and horizontal limbs of blue-green foliage of white pine are characteristic of our northern forests, where trees with trunks six feet in diameter and heights of 250 feet were reported by the early lumbermen.

It is the most rapid growing northern forest tree, occasionally averaging a yearly growth of one thousand board feet an acre over periods of forty to eighty years. It responds to silvicultural treatment and has been more widely planted than any other American tree.

The long tapering cones, slender bluish green needles in bunches of five, and clusters of yellow pollen-bearing blossoms of the Eastern White Pine

American Forests

Once the voice of the timber industry, now the voice of forest environmentalism, the small logger, the woodlot owner, the tree lover, and a bit still of the industry. A nice mix, making work more interesting for all of them. Now that I think of it, it's probably far more effective environmentally than the publications read only by environmentalists. —SB

American Forests
(The Magazine of Forests, Soil, Water, Wildlife, and Outdoor Recreation)
Bill Rooney, Editor
$15 /year (12 issues) from:
The American Forestry Association
1319- 18th Street N.W.
Washington, D.C. 20036

Tree Finder

For fast unromantic identification of trees, these shirt pocket books are excellent. —SB
[Suggested by Catherine Yronwode]

Master Tree Finder
(For area east of Rockies)
Winter Tree Finder
(East of Rockies)
Pacific Coast Tree Finder
Rocky Mountain Tree Finder
Desert Tree Finder

$1.50 each
postpaid from:
Nature Study Guild
Box 972
Berkeley, CA 94701
or Whole Earth Household Store

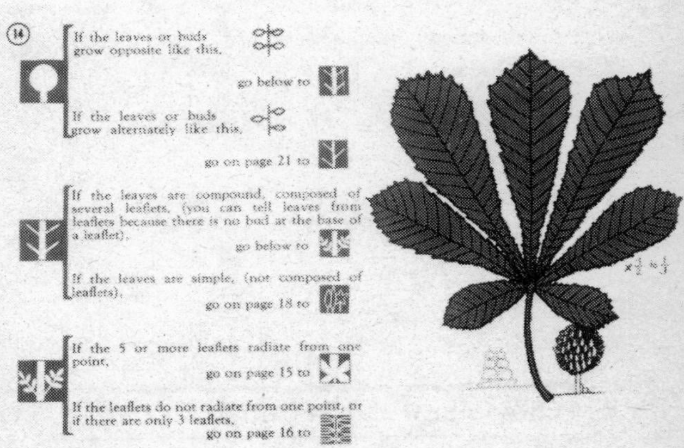

The International Book of Trees

Worth $30? Well, there's no other tree book that covers the whole Earth; no other tree book with such luscious photos; no other tree book arranged so clearly by Tree Families with such easy, accurate captions saying why this is a locust and that's a laburnum. English-oriented, so some fine planting suggestions must be tempered by earlier chapters on what grows where. —Peter Warshall

The International Book of Trees
Hugh Johnson
1973; 288 pp.
$29.95 postpaid from:
Simon & Schuster
Attn: Order Department
1230 Avenue of the Americas
New York, NY 10020
or Whole Earth Household Store

The ancient marriage of oil and wine; olive trees and vines grow together on the terraced hillsides of the island of Samos in the Aegean, punctuated with black spires of cypress.

The Illustrated Encyclopedia of Trees

The emphasis of the **Illustrated Encyclopedia** *is on forests and timber, with an interesting chapter on different logging methods world-wide; all the major families of trees are represented, illustrated with color photographs and paintings of typical and common trees of each family, including leaves, flowers, fruit and wood. This is an elegant book at an extraordinary price for such quality, produced with typically British love and respect for its subject.* —Carol Van Strum

The Illustrated Encyclopedia of Trees
(Timbers and Forests of the World)
Herbert Edlin, Maurice Nimmo, et al.
1978; 256 pp.
$15.95 postpaid from:
Crown Publishers
One Park Avenue
New York, NY 10016
or Whole Earth Household Store

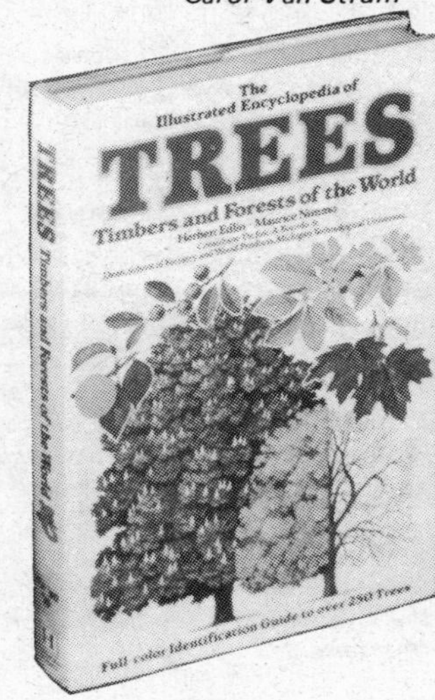

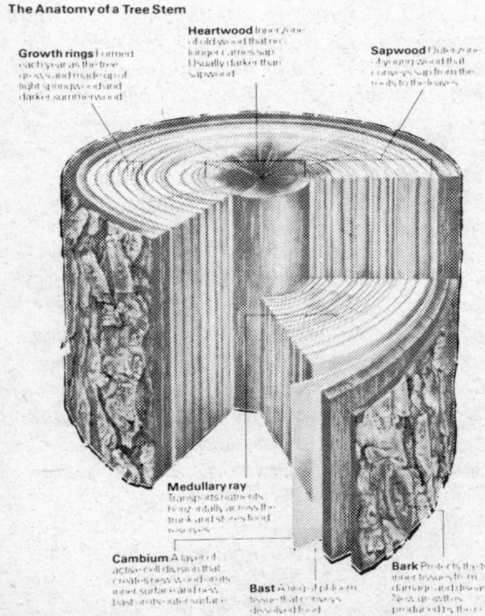

THE RISING SUN
NEIGHBORHOOD NEWSLETTER

If all you've got when you're a kid is heredity and environment and no choices, you can use a library to fake free will because enough books read one after the other day after day about everything you think you might be interested in become part of the environment, become part of you. It takes a lot of books before they're part of your world like your sisters and the trees and your friends and TV – it takes more books than you'd ever be able to buy. It takes more books than you would buy even if you were rich because it takes books you wouldn't be interested enough to buy, just to open up and leaf through and after leafing through a hundred slightly interesting books like that, you find another thing to love that you never would've met in your own world outside the library. Only the library has that many books and only a library on your block can show you that many books – it has to be no more than ten minutes to the rest of the universe or you can never really go often enough or stay long enough to believe the rest of the universe is there.

Finding and Buying Your Place in the Country

I'm glad somebody wrote this book, and did it so thoroughly. Scher is a lawyer who manages to wade with you through the waters of easements, zoning, taxes, contracts, deeds of trust, mortgages, and escrow without muddying them up. Also advice on evaluating property — soil, water, structures, and on bargaining strategies. If you study this book, there is no excuse for being "taken."
—Richard Nilsen

Finding and Buying Your Place In The Country
Les Scher
1974; 393 pp.

$7.95 postpaid from:
Macmillan Books
Order Department
Front and Brown Streets
Riverside, NJ 08075
or Whole Earth Household Store

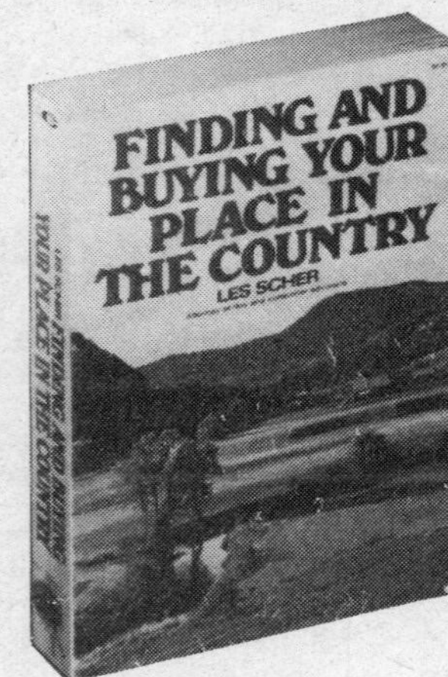

•

Work Out Everything Before the Deal Is Closed

Never buy land on the agent's promise or assurance that a problem can be worked out after the deal is closed. For example, if you are supposed to share a well with adjoining landowners but no agreement has been drawn up as to what the arrangement will be, the agent might tell you that your neighbors are great people and that you will have no problem working out an arrangement after you buy the land. This is a common and dangerous sales hustling technique. Once you pay your money and take title, the agent is out of the picture. If your neighbors don't turn out to be so nice, you can be in real trouble. Don't assume the agent is going to help you with problems once he gets his commission. If he can't arrange all the details in writing before you buy the land, he certainly won't do so afterwards.

•

These Lines Are Always Good for a Laugh

"I'll let you in on a secret about the seller."

"I'm going to show you something nobody else has seen."

"The land is really worth more than the seller is asking."

"So far, nobody else has seen this property."

"If I had the money, I'd buy this piece myself."

"Look, a lot of people are interested in this property, so you better make up your mind quickly."

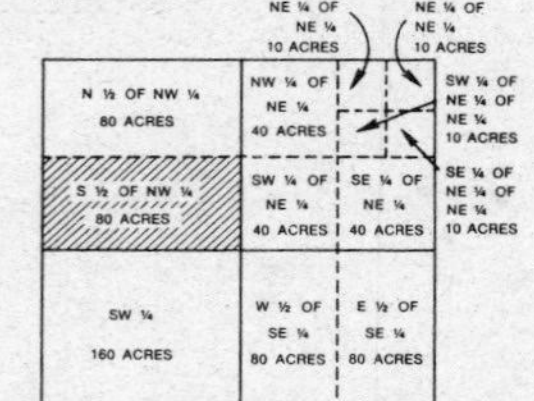

48. DIVIDING A SECTION INTO QUARTERS AND SMALLER PARCELS

United Farm and Strout

These catalogs will feed your land mania. —SB

United Farm
Catalog

free from:
United Farm Agency
612 West 47th Street
Kansas City, MO 64112
and the other local offices

Strout
Catalog

free from:
Strout Realty
Dept. WE
Plaza Towers
Springfield, MO 65804

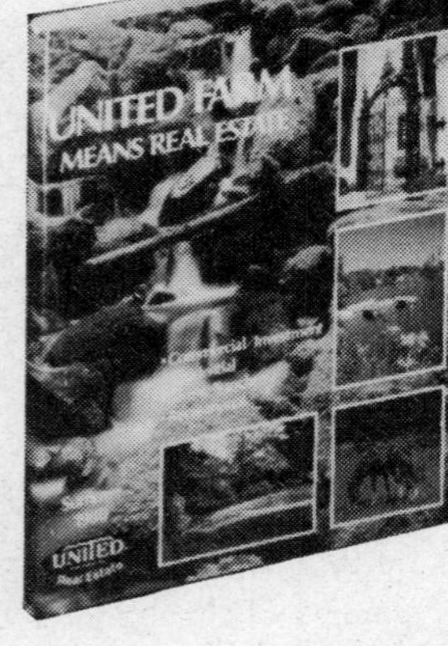

MOUNTAINS & MEADOWS

No. 1710—120 acres, $72,000. Beautiful mountain land in midst of good hunting area. Lots of deer, some elk, plenty of game birds. 120 acres, some pasture, lots of trees, springs and small creek. Plenty of perfect cabin sites. Electricity runs through, access to county road. Only $72,000, low down payment, owner financing. ***UNITED, Wheatland, Wyo.***

Finding and Buying Land

The trick is, helping the seller find you. The best way to do this is advertise. Find out what the land owners read, and advertise there. It may be the bulletin board at the general store or the six ranchers' journals of the northwestern states (find at libraries in the area).

Say in your ad what kind of land you're looking for and what you're willing to pay, e.g., "WANTED TO BUY, mountain land, south slope, timber, year-round flowing water, prefer no improvements and minimum roads; 200 - 600 acres, in northern Oregon or Washington state; will pay $200/acre if suitable, good cash terms. Mortimer Head, 1111 A St., Portland, OR, 16161, (007) 242-4242."

This procedure largely by-passes the real estate agents, and good riddance. Most are a foul breed, though one in twenty is all right and can help you.

To find out what land you want takes some research. Shop around locally and get a feel for the terminology and considerations of land buying (clear title, developed springs, pasture for 200 head, adjoining National Forest, county road, mineral rights, water rights, NE ¼ of section 28 R 17 T26, taxes last year, six-months option, etc.) Visit friends who have land and see what they like and don't like about it. Tell everybody you talk to that you're looking for land and let them rattle on.

Finding an area to suit you is partly a matter of maps and partly visits to see how the climate and vibrations are. Write for United Farm and Strout catalogs for rough (high) land values in various areas.

The most important source of information on a piece of land besides visiting it is the USGS (US Geological Survey) topographical map of the area. Order the index map for the state(s) you're interested in, have someone show you how to use Range and Township to locate yourself, and buy the appropriate maps. At $1.25 - $2.00 apiece they are an outstanding bargain. *See pp. 24 - 25 for USGS maps and aerial photos.*

Surveying

Surveying is the human way of pissing on all the corners of your property, so you know what's yours and what is theirs. It is also a way of leveling, finding corners, mapping, working out your water system. If you are going to use land, chances are you'll run into a survey. This book seems to cover the discipline and use of the surveyor's tools.
—J.D. Smith

Surveying
Charles B. Breed
1971; 445 pp.
Third Edition

$20.95 postpaid from:
John Wiley and Sons
One Wiley Drive
Somerset, NJ 08873
or Whole Earth Household Store

Rare Earth Report

Where Sealand specializes in cheap international properties, Rare Earth tends to go the other direction — castles, spas, towns, missile silos, whole islands, estates — exotic stuff, the stuff of dreams. Expensive dreams. —SB

Rare Earth Report
$36/year (6 issues)
$48 /year outside North America
from:
Rare Earth Real Estate, Inc.
Box 946
Sausalito, CA 94966

Wilderness trading post. Your Own Town!

Sealand

I would like to recommend **The Cheap Land Catalogue** and **Bulletins** from Sealand . . . it's how we found our haven/heaven here on Prince Edward Island, Canada, recently (10 acres of island with our own sandy beach for less than $5,000), and we could hardly be more satisfied.

Sealand don't sell land themselves but gather specific listings and news on seemingly all the cheaper than average land and housing still to be had in several different countries. Canadian and USA land listed is almost all under $250 per acre, Australian under $100 acre, South American under $50, etc.

They seem to cover most countries from time to time, but most listings are for Canada/USA. Owner financed (pay monthly) property is favored. In spite of the heavy American coverage, the catalogue and bulletins originate in England. Below average land there is expensive ($2,500 and up) but a few incredibly cheap town houses and country cottages are often listed, mostly under $8,000!

The catalogue is quarterly (and goes up and down in size a lot) the bulletins are issued in between. One current sample of catalog and bulletin are sent for $14.00, the full annual subscription is $50.00. Address is: Sealand, Ashenbottom Farm, Ewood Bridge, Rossendale, Lancashire, BB4 6JY, England.

—Evelyn Hayhurst
Prince Edward Island, Canada

Marshall and Swift: Residential Cost Handbook, and the Marshall Valuation Service

The appraisal publications of the Marshall and Swift Publication Company fall into the category of beautiful professional tools. In this instance, known to the appraisal profession and related fields but a mystery to everyone else. On the occasions I have asked appraisers if they were familiar with the Marshall and Swift **Residential Cost Handbook**, *the reply has always been, "Yes, it's the standard of the industry," or, "Certainly, it's the 'Appraisers' Bible'."*

Although I am not a professional appraiser, I have used these publications for many years. I find them of value in making real estate decisions of any kind in a rational manner instead of relying solely on the intuitive, seat-of-the-pants method or what the real estate agent, who is working for the seller, says is a great buy. I have an enterprising friend who met his college expenses doing appraisals for real estate agents and small savings and loan associations using only the **Residential Cost Handbook**, *a pad of appraisal forms and a calculator.*

The principal Marshall and Swift publications — the **Residential Cost Handbook** *and* **Marshall Valuation Service** *— come in a format that gives appraisal instructions and all of the necessary information to appraise a building. Descriptions of buildings with extensive photographic examples of type, quality and age are included. When a value for a building is arrived at, using the guides provided, you say O.K., so what is this building worth in Casper, Wyoming? or Montreal, Quebec? You turn to the section marked Local Multipliers and multiply your figure by the Current Cost Multiplier and then by the Local Multiplier (for Casper, Montreal or anywhere else) and you have the value of the building in question.*

The price for the publications, like all quality tools, may seem high, but the price of the **Residential Cost Handbook**, *at $33 for new subscribers and $29 for renewals, is about half the price of one appraisal. For a person doing something as basic as buying, remodeling and selling an occasional house this is a reasonable price to pay for the value received.*

The Residential Cost Handbook *provides a fast, accurate method to determine residential building cost. It fulfills, with equal effectiveness, the requirements of both the experienced appraiser and the occasional building cost estimator. Loose leaf quarterly supplements are provided to maintain up-to-date localized accuracy and reliability.*

The **Marshall Valuation Service** *provides accurate and authoritative methods for determining replacement costs, depreciated values and insurable values of all types of commercial, industrial, institutional and agricultural buildings, from simple sheds to large metropolitan buildings. Monthly supplements with updated cost and local multipliers, for over 550 locations in the United States and Canada, assure accurate results.*

Two other titles published by Marshall and Swift worth noting are the **Business Valuation Handbook** *and* **The Appraisal of Farm Real Estate.**

—*Joseph W. McShane*

The Residential Cost Handbook
(Rapid Method of Computing Residence Costs)

$33 /year (one book and four updates)

Marshall Valuation Service

$75 /year (one book and 12 updates)

both from:
Marshall and Swift Publication Company
1617 Beverly Boulevard
P.O. Box 26307
Los Angeles, CA 90026

Once you get to seriously considering a piece of land go to the County Assessor's office to find out what the County knows about it. They will have records showing what was paid the last time the property was bought and when the sale took place. They also will have maps showing who your neighbors are and where they can be reached. If you're trying to find the owner of a piece of land, that's the way. (Incidentally, wandering around in pretty country falling in love with various sites is no way to get land. It always either belongs to the government, who won't sell, or some guy who won't sell.)

Bear in mind there is a rural land boom going on. With prices to match. Stay away from developers and their prices. They buy a big hunk cheap and sell little hunks dear. They and the neighbors they'll get you are a pain in the ass.

When you buy land in a place and start living there, you become a citizen of the county and state. Don't be surprised if the other citizens are interested in you. Wouldn't you be? —SB

Brunton Pocket Transit

Great for rough topographical mapping necessary for planning and laying out water systems, roads, you name it.

Basically a high quality sighting compass with 1° graduations, it has an integral clinometer for vertical angles 1° to 90° with a vernier reading to 10 minutes. Very rugged.

Hand-held, it is hard to make use of its full capabilities, so there is a ball and socket head available for use with a tripod or Jacobs staff. The Brunton is available graduated in either quadrants or degrees, and with or without induction damping, and in waterproof and digital readout models. —Fred Richardson

Brunton Pocket Transit
$124.75 w/o damping
$128.75 with induction damping

Catalog or instruments from:
Brunton Company
620 East Monroe Ave.
Riverton, WY 82501

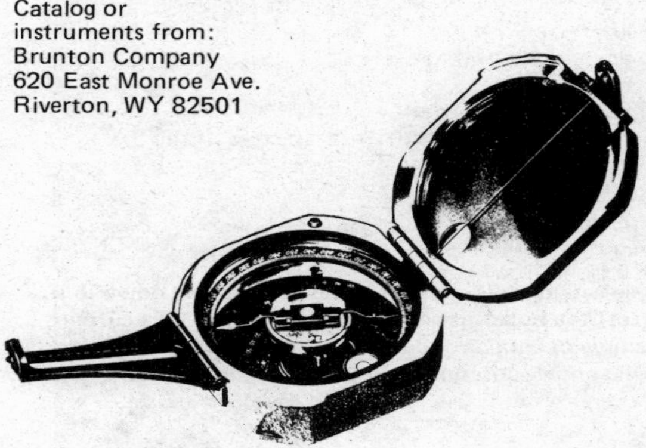

Building Stone Walls

There's a lot to be said for stone walls, but this modest book doesn't say it. Just good pictures explained by the terse, New England traditional few words. Especially good in that a wide variety of stones are utilized, not just flat ones. (More on stone walls, p. 230.) —J. Baldwin

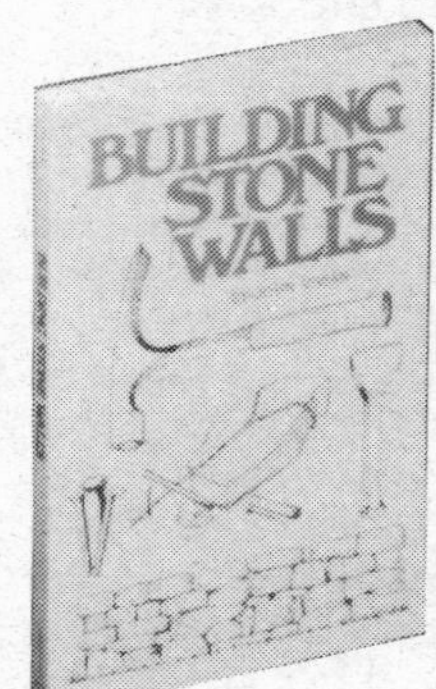

Building Stone Walls
John Vivian
1975, 1979; 112 pp.
$4.95 postpaid from:
Garden Way Publishing
Charlotte, VT 05445
or Whole Earth Household Store

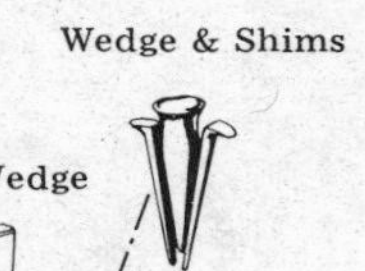

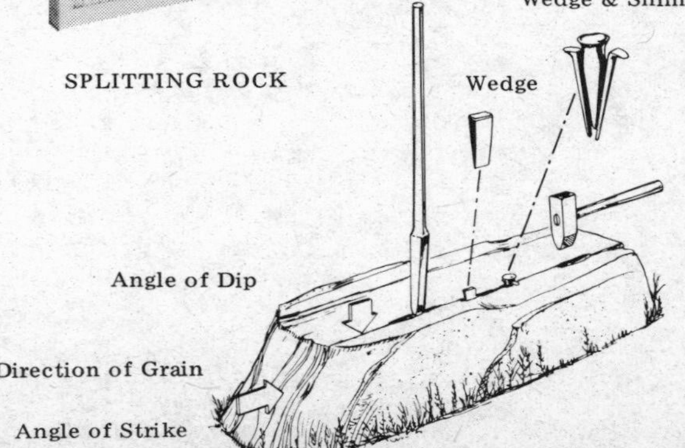

The Earth Manual

Just like the man says:

Between well-trimmed suburban lawns and the vast regions of mountain wilderness, there are millions of patches of land that are semi-wild. They may be wood lots, small forests, parks, a farm's "back forty," or even an unattended corner of a big back yard — land touched by civilization but far from conquered. This book is about how to take care of such land: how to stop its erosion, heal its scars, cure its injured trees, increase its wildlife, restock it with shrubs and wild flowers, and otherwise work with (rather than against) the wildness of the land.

A whole book of gentle advice and easily-absorbed wisdom. *—Peter Warshall*

The Earth Manual
Malcolm Margolin
1975; 190 pp.
$10 postpaid from:
Houghton Mifflin Co.
Wayside Road
Burlington, MA 01803
or Whole Earth Household Store

•

By slowing down the flow of water, you reduce the amount of damage it can do, and you very spectacularly reduce the amount of silt it can carry. If there is lots of silt suspended in the water, once you slow the water down, most of the silt will be dropped — thus building up the bottom of the gully again.

The principles of check dam architecture. There are many possible designs and materials for building check dams, but whichever one you choose must adhere to certain architectural principles of check dam construction.

HEAD-TO-TOE ALIGNMENT. The most effective way of building check dams is to build them in a series where the base of the upper dam is on a level with the top of the lower dam. This will eventually stabilize the whole gully bottom and will create a series of steps or terraces.

SMALLNESS. "The bigger they are, the harder they fall" applies particularly to check dams. For most gullies, the check dams should be no more than about two feet high. Anything much higher than two feet will necessitate anchors, *deadmen*, and other retaining-wall features. Several small dams are far more effective and easier to build than a few big dams.

DIGGING IT IN. The dam must be dug into the walls of the gully, not just laid genteelly up against them. Unless the dams are dug far enough in, water will sweep around them.

NOTCHING. A notch is a place where the water can flow over the dam. This is essential. Without one, the silt builds up behind the dam, the water flows on top of the silt, and instead of being led through the notch, it may start eating away at one of the slopes. Eventually, it may make a new channel around the dam. I've seen many erosion-control dams standing proudly and nobly on dry land while gullies flowed merrily around them.

APRON. Once the silt builds up behind the dam, the water flows through the notch like a waterfall. You'll need an apron to catch it before it digs out a pool and undermines the dam. The easiest apron is a bed of stones where the water can simply knock itself out and flow tamely to the next check dam.

Moving the Earth

The beauty of this tome is that it does not stop after postulating optimum conditions like a "long enough lever and a firm place to stand." After suggesting ways to clear land, remove tree stumps, or lay out an access road using rented machinery like dozers and dump trucks, it goes on to explain many other ways to get it done when the "proper" equipment is not available. Most conceivable snafus are dealt with. Not just how to use a dozer so it doesn't turn over, and rig a winch so it doesn't snarl; but how to get your dozer back on its treads without calling the AAA, and how to unsnarl your winch. All is explained in text and again in eminently understandable drawings. *—Alan Kalker*

Moving the Earth
(The Workbook of Excavation)
Herbert L. Nichols, Jr.
1955, 1976; 1760 pp.
$40 postpaid from:
North Castle Books
212 Bedford Road
Greenwich, CT 06830

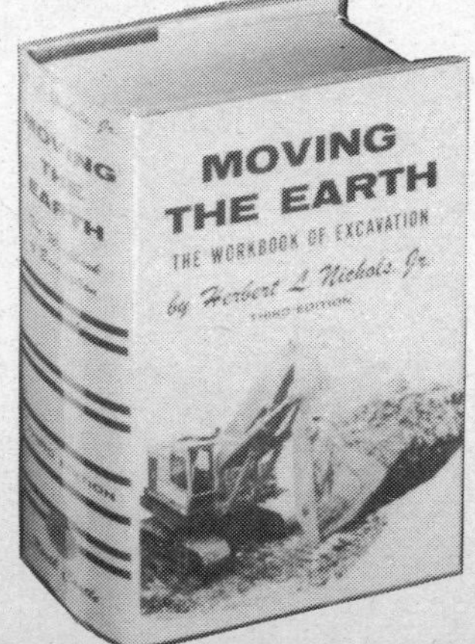

The simple life

I have this persistent fantasy of moving to a city, getting a small, white-walled studio apartment, and living with complete freedom. "The simple life" I call it, cutting down to essentials: a single bed, comfortable chair, desk, typewriter; a small kitchen, heat that just turns on, a toilet that flushes, hot running water, as much as I want. In my fantasy, I stride confidently down city streets, marveling at the pleasures of anonymity: thousands of people who don't know me and whom I'll never know. There's a library and bookstores with everything I've ever wanted to read; concerts, bars, and poetry readings. In my apartment, the phone never rings and for a few months, I don't go to any meetings at all.

Sitting in city apartments, picturing my bliss at such a life and jealously envying my friends, I tell them about my feelings. And they laugh or are shocked, because of course everyone knows the country is where you go for peace and freedom. And besides, I have left out earning a living, men on street corners, going nowhere alone at night, ever. I have forgotten I am a woman.

In the country, everything is personal; personalized. I am connected to all the life around me, and that's probably how things should be, but it asks more, takes more from me to live that way. I am responsible for my own survival, for heat, food, water, shelter. I have fifty-nine animals dependent on me for their survival too; and like a good pioneer woman I feed bottles to kids three times a day, five months out of every year. There's at least two meetings a week, and sometimes four. In a small community, there's only so many people to do what needs to be done. I don't pick who I'll work with, cause there's no choosing to do, and sometimes I am frustrated and lonely. The man at the post office, the woman at the store, my neighbor, a friend up the road, all know me and a good deal about my life, as I know about theirs. We have few secrets and a good deal of conversation. The price of land payments and taxes and animal feed and kerosene and truck parts comes to at least as much as a city life, and I've always worked another job off the farm to pay for it. For a sure laugh around here, all you have to say is "come to the country and lay back and relax."

I don't suppose I'd really trade, or not for long. I'm always saying I'll go to the city next month, when the kids are weaned, the sheep sheared, this issue of the magazine done . . . and I never get there. But once in a while the crazy writer in me gets desperate and even dreams nostalgically of cockroach-ridden, bath-down-the-hall, cheap downtown hotels — anyplace where I can be alone and responsible to no one and no thing but myself.

I guess I just want to say that, for me, the grass sometimes looks greener in Golden Gate Park.

—Sherry Thomas
Country Women, Dec. '76

THE RISING SUN
NEIGHBORHOOD NEWSLETTER

Some of us believe this is a free country and the rest of us believe it should be, but people without cars and without money, old people, poor people and children are prisoners of this town, whatever town they're living in, of whatever block they're on, and the only thing that frees them without trying to sell them something they can't buy is the library and if the library ain't close because the branch got closed or it ain't open because they cut back the hours, what you've got is a bunch of dreamers stuck with 4 walls and a TV set while high city officials who deferred the raise on their $40,000 a year salaries until next year for economy and closed branches of the dream and cut back hours of the dream for economy are going to the latest movies and the opening of the Civic Opera and cocktail parties with their friends for their entertainment and never dreaming of people who need dreams because they don't know what it's like to dream. There are always gonna be people who *know* that this block and this city aren't what they should be and if you don't let them have a library to see other ways that other places are and dream another way for this place, they are either gonna blow this way and this place to hell with righteous anger and dynamite or they are gonna give up and let it rot while they watch TV forever to see things they can't buy and don't want and you won't have nobody or nothing to collect your $50,000 a year from. But you can't believe that can you? You were never one for dreaming. You always just did the assignments and minded your own business and look how far it's got you. Well, seems like people who believe in doing something besides the assignment need to kick the asses of the opera goers to make them keep one of the few miracles we've got and cheap at twice the price.

The Postage Stamp Garden Book

This is the first pure and simple synthesis of what I would call the Urban Gardening Method: a lot of compost, a few containers, French Intensive beds planted closely without mulching and seeds started in milk carton halves.
—Rosemary Menninger

The Postage Stamp Garden Book
(How to Grow All the Food You Can Eat in Very Little Space)
Duane Newcomb
1975; 150 pp.

$5.95 postpaid from:
Houghton Mifflin Co.
Wayside Road
Burlington, NJ 01803
or Whole Earth Household Store

•

Cool season crops — adapted to 55° to 70° F:

Tolerant of some frost: asparagus, beets, broccoli, Brussels sprouts, cabbage, kale, mustard greens, New Zealand spinach, turnips and rutabagas.

Intolerant of frost at maturity: carrots, cauliflower, endive, lettuce, peas, rhubarb, Swiss chard.

Warm season crops — requiring 65° to 80° F. day and night (and readily damaged by frost): beans, corn, cucumbers, eggplant, melons, okra, peppers, squash, tomatoes.

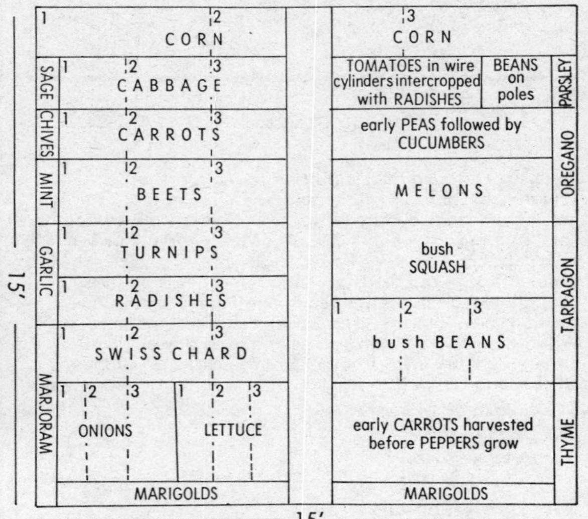

Garden 6. Here is the family food basket, large enough for a family of four (and some neighbors as well) and filled with most of the basic vegetables that anyone could want. Sections are planted in successive weeks and new seeds or seedlings are sown whenever spaces are harvested and become vacant.

How to Have a Green Thumb Without an Aching Back

This classic book simplifies the composting process to the laying down of mulch. Nothing more is needed, she says; just cover the soil with leaves and garbage and plant right in it. *—Rosemary Menninger*

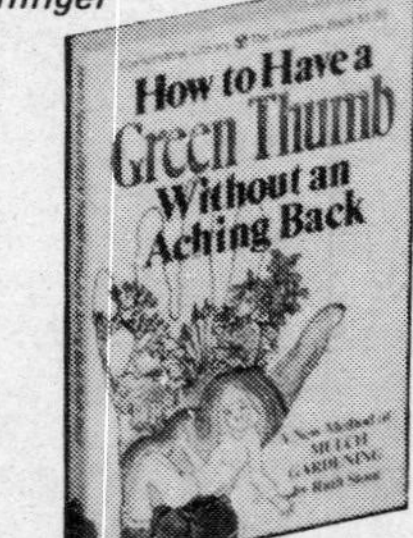

How to Have a Green Thumb Without an Aching Back
(A New Method of Mulch Gardening)
Ruth Stout
1973; 160 pp.

$3.50 postpaid from:
Simon & Schuster, Inc.
Attn: Order Department
1230 Avenue of the Americas
New York, NY 10020
or Whole Earth Household Store

•

My way is unscientific, but it has produced fine vegetables for eleven years. I simply spread mulch where I want the compost to be eventually. It rots and becomes rich dirt, with the valuable by-products of keeping down weeds, keeping the earth soft, holding moisture and eliminating plowing and spading, hoeing and cultivating.

I use lime, of course, to keep the soil from getting too acid and I put some cotton-seed meal on the strawberries, lettuce, spinach, corn and beets. This supplies the nitrogen they might otherwise lack.

•

Some people hesitate to adopt over-all mulching because they prefer the looks of a neatly cultivated garden. I used to, but now a garden with the earth exposed to the burning, baking sun looks helpless and pathetic to me. It looks fine if someone has just cultivated it after a good rain, but how often is that the case? At all other times an unmulched garden looks to me like some naked thing which, for one reason or another, would be better off with a few clothes on.

Good Food Naturally

A WONDERFUL BOOK! Harrison has been gardening one piece of land organically for 26 years and marketing his produce; so he knows feasibility — what works and what doesn't work. An apprenticeship with this book while gardening will make the most of what your garden and the book can teach. *—Rosemary Menninger*

Good Food Naturally
(How to Grow it, Cook it, Keep it)
John B. Harrison
1973; 111 pp.

$3.95 postpaid from:
Keats Publishing, Inc.
36 Grove Street
Box 876
New Canaan, CT 06840
or Whole Earth Household Store

•

Compacting of topsoil is never healthy or helpful for plant life so hoeing is required after any pounding downpour.

•

Even after the seed bed is sufficiently fine to begin planting, it will pay to wait a week or two to give weeds a chance to germinate. The tilling done to prepare the soil for seeding will have brought dormant weed seeds into germination, and even though these tiny seedlings are invisible they will be there. One fine raking before seeding will kill those weeds and save a great deal of effort later in the season thus validating the old adage that the time to kill weeds is before you see them.

•

The choice of plant variety poses a real problem for the organic grower. Many new varieties may be not satisfactory for organic culture. The reason is that the customers who buy the largest amounts of seed are the commercial growers who serve the processing factories or the retail trade, so that seed producers cater largely to their needs. Breeding plants with the characteristics that such customers require can result in the loss of vigor in variety and thus be of little use to the organic farmer whose aim is vigorous plants for maximum nutrition. . . .So stay with the tried and proven varieties unless you have information from an experienced person that a new variety has proven to be satisfactory over some years. . . Many of the newer varieties will have initials or numbers in the plant names indicating that they are newcomers and may have been bred for particular commercial qualities.

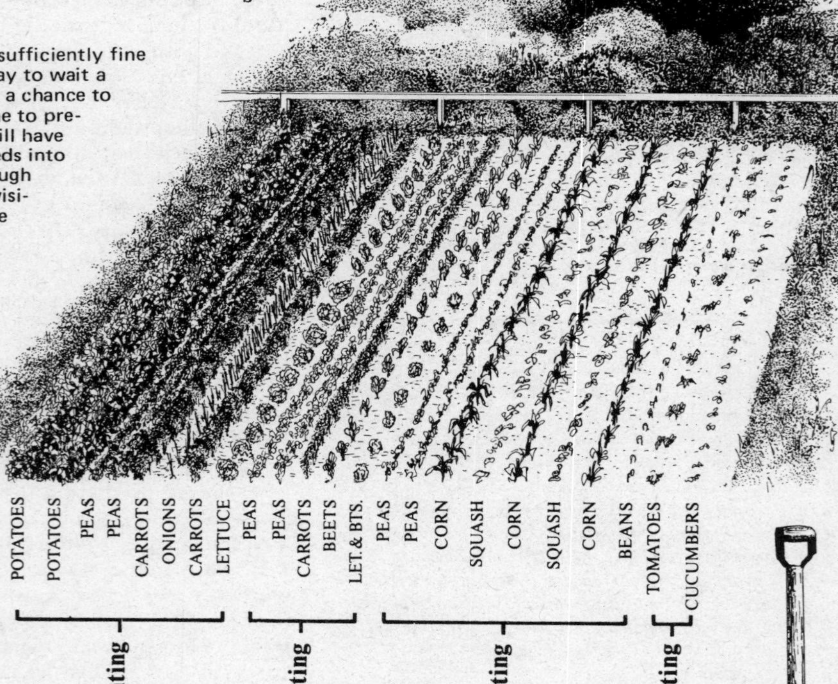

Sticks and string for marking

Pointed nose shovel

Planet Jr. wheel seeder with cultivating attachments

Wheelbarrow

Garden fork

The Organic Gardener

A comprehensive book for gardeners who really like to read. It covers more non-chemical tricks than I've seen in any gardening book. *—Rosemary Menninger*

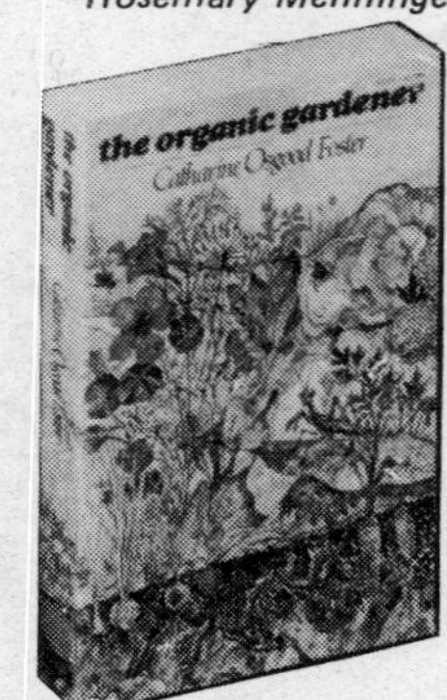

The Organic Gardener
Catherine Osgood Foster
1972; 234 pp.

$2.95 postpaid from:
Vintage Books
Random House
455 Hahn Road
Westminster, MD 21157
or Whole Earth Household Store

•

Many towns now have sewage treatment plants where the end product is activated sludge, which is germless, dry, and smells like the floor of the forest. It is a good source of nitrogen and minerals . . . By the time the organic gardener gets heated and bubbled activated sludge, the nitrogen content is about up to what it would be in cottonseed meal — that is, 5 to 6 percent — and its phosphorus up to 3 to 6 percent . . . For gardens and farmland, season it for six months and then put it on before rain, preferably in the autumn. Sludge will not only provide the major nutrients, it will also improve the physical properties of your soil and increase productivity of some if not all plants. Spinach is not much benefited by it; oats and beans are somewhat helped; and beets and turnips are very much helped from heavy applications.

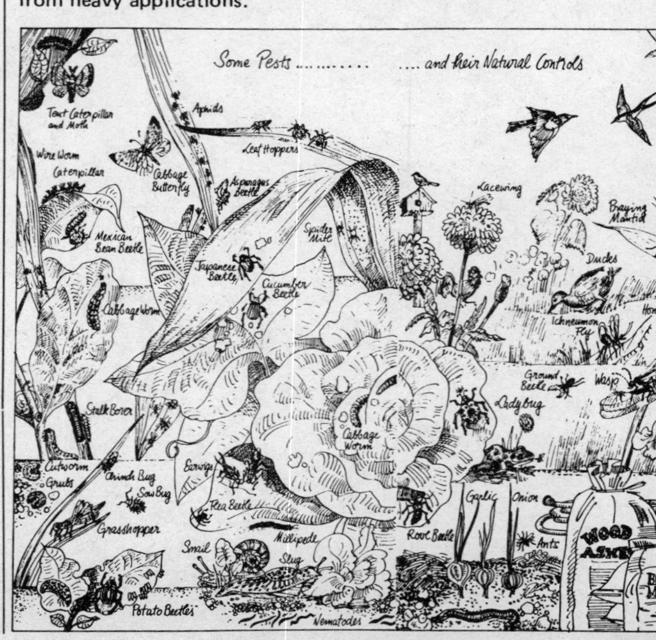

The Complete Vegetable Gardener's Sourcebook

Any beginning gardener will find this catalog/sourcebook useful, and more accomplished gardeners will probably be impressed with how complete it is. It's especially good on describing the different varieties of individual vegetables that are available, and listing the seeds houses that carry them — over 150 pages are devoted to this monster chapter. —Richard Nilsen

The Complete Vegetable Gardener's Sourcebook
Duane Newcomb
1980; 340 pp.
$10.20 postpaid from:
Avon Books
Mail Order Department
250 West 55th Street
New York, NY 10019
or Whole Earth Household Store

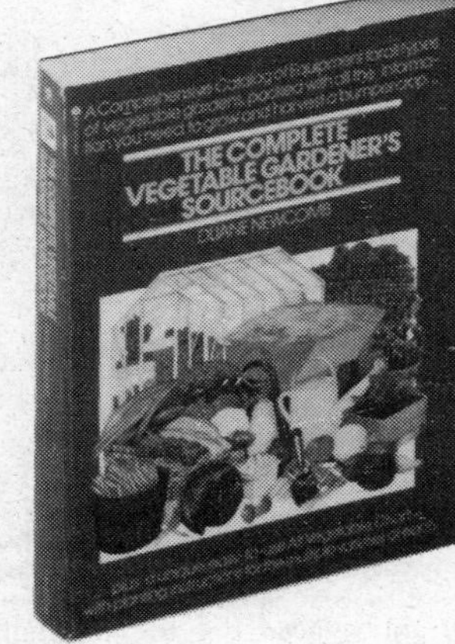

•

Garlic (Allium sativum)

Garlic is really strong medicine in any garden. Besides being an essential vegetable in the kitchen, many gardeners believe that it can be used to control a wide variety of insects. There are two basic types available — regular garlic bulbs, which contain a number of small cloves, and large garlic bulbs (elephant garlic), which have the flavor of regular garlic but none of its pungency.

HOW TO PLANT: In very early spring plant garlic cloves, or sets, 1-1½ inches deep, 2 inches apart, in rows 12-18 inches apart.

Harvesting: Dig up the roots when the tops fall over.

•

Jiffy Pots

These are fiber pots made of peat moss. Simply fill with synthetic soil. You can plant the entire pot directly in the garden. They come in several sizes.

Carefree Garden Products
P.O. Box 383
West Chicago, IL 60185

•

Solarvent

Solarvent operates using a heat-activated expanded chemical. It automatically begins to open the greenhouse window at 68° F. interior temperature. At 75° F. the window is wide open. When interior cools, the window closes automatically.

Dalen Products, Inc., 201 Sherlake Dr., Knoxville, TN 37922

Garlic

VARIETY	DAYS	REMARKS	SOURCES
California White Garlic	110	The best variety . . . stores like onions, or may be left in garden over winter	22 38
Extra Select		A pound of garlic sets plants about a 20-ft. row	10
Garlic Sets		Most pungent flavor of the onion family . . . use in soups, salad, stews	12 19 21 23 28 29 44 52 62 66 74 76 82 86 89
Mexican Garlic sets		An easy and interesting plant to grow	31
Oriental Garlic		18" Perineal	89
Rocambole (Spanish Garlic)		Makes cloves in small bulbs	44 81
Garlic Powder/Granular			90

Garlic — Large Bulbs

VARIETY	REMARKS	SOURCES
Bavarian Garlic	Bulbs are larger than those of common variety . . . keeps a very long time	14
Elephant Garlic	True garlic flavor, but more delicate . . . short growing season . . . often produces single, large, onionlike bulb . . . many bulbs weigh 1 lb., size 4-5"	21 27 28 43 46 50 61 62 89
Extra Large	Three bulbs will plant about a 10-15 ft. row	41
Jumbo Garlic	6" cloves. . . can be harvested in 18 mos.	68
Italian Garlic	Superior to standard . . . hotter than Elephant garlic	61
Silverskin	Very hardy . . .strong flavor. . .large bulbs	46 50

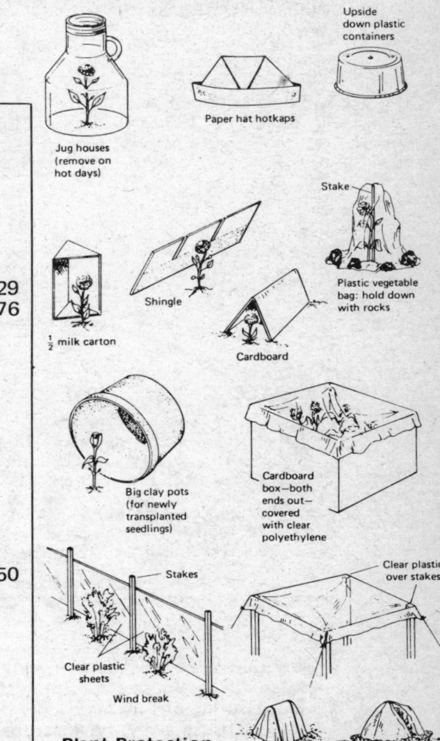

Plant Protection Devices.

Sunset New Western Garden Book

If you're gardening in the seven western states, this is a wonderful book to own. It has thorough and inviting basics for the beginning gardener. Nearly 350 pages of it is a "Western Plant Encyclopedia" including both common and scientific names. In addition, 24 climate zones are described. They are quite specific. Except for annuals and some house plants, each entry in the Encyclopedia includes the climate zones where the plant can be successfully grown. Sunset pulled out all the stops for this book, and it shows. —Richard Nilsen

Sunset New Western Garden Book
1967, 1979; 512 pp.
$9.95 postpaid from:
Lane Magazine and Book Company
Menlo Park, CA 94025
or Whole Earth Household Store

Winter sun
Warmest spot
Coldest spot
Cold air collects
Cold air drainage
S ⟷ N

Take advantage of garden microclimates to grow plants which require varying conditions. Hills and hollows, points of the compass, and structures influence microclimates.

•

Fire-retardant plants

No plant will completely stop a fire from advancing, but the plants listed here will certainly resist burning far better than most, and thereby may slow a fire's progress. Remember that if winds carry sparks from a fire even protective fire-retardant plantings can be breached.

Perennials, Vines

Achilia	Ice plants
Agave	Limonium peresii
Aloe	Portulacaria afra
Artemisia (low growing kinds)	Santolina virens
Atriplex (come)	Satureja montana
Campsis	Senecio cineraria
Convolvulus cneorum	Solanum jasminoides
Gazania	Yucca (trunkless kinds)

Down to Earth Vegetable Gardening Know-How

Raymond is the man quoted till Kingdom come in most Garden Way publications. His information here is excellent and the charts and graphics are some of the best I've seen anywhere. —Rosemary Menninger

Down to Earth Vegetable Gardening Know-How
Dick Raymond
1975; 156 pp.
$7.95 postpaid from:
Garden Way Publishing
Charlotte, VT 05445
or Whole Earth Household Store

•

If you plant a vegetable that matures before another in the same row, just harvest whatever is ripe and allow the other plants to take over the space that has just been vacated. This way, you can get more vegetables out of a restricted amount of space. There are a number of combinations that you can try: tomatoes with pepper plants, onions with cabbages, pole beans with corn.

VEGETABLES THAT CAN BE HARVESTED ALL OR MOST OF THE WINTER

Root Crops
Parsnips
Root Parsley
Salsify
Jerusalem Artichoke
Turnips*
Rutabagas*
Brussels Sprouts*

Greens
Kale
Collards*
Mustard*
Spinach*

(Root crops can be covered with straw to protect them from hard freezes.)

*In Southern gardens

To side dress crops, make a shallow furrow down both sides of the row and about 6 inches from it. Encircle hills or mounds with a furrow. Place fertilizer in furrows, then cover it.

Nearly indestructible pampas grass (Cortaderia selloana) takes wind in stride, as well as desert heat, coastal salt spray, poor soil, and drought.

THE RISING SUN
NEIGHBORHOOD NEWSLETTER

Stewart said that a good question to ask would be "What is the most interesting thing you ever saw that you weren't supposed to see?" so I asked him, what was the most interesting thing he ever saw that he wasn't supposed to see and he said, his brother-in-law the general almost let him see where all the Russian submarines in the Atlantic Ocean were. I said, "Why didn't he, did someone walk in the room?" Stewart said, "No, something walked from one part of his head to another and said, 'This is a man who is friends with Huey Newton and Abbie Hoffman.' So he didn't." What would Huey have done with or about Russian submarines? (The grownups in the sixties didn't know exactly what they were guarding against but killed and scared enough people that whatever it was didn't happen anyway.)

SOME PEOPLE IN THE ORGANIC MOVEMENT *today think of Rodale as an empire. They tend to forget all those years when J.I. Rodale ran a lonely outpost of common sense and got laughed at by the agricultural establishment for his trouble. I remember reading the* **Time** *magazine review of Rachel Carson's* **Silent Spring** *when it came out — a couple of quick, acerbic paragraphs and the reviewer had dismissed her as a little old lady quibbling about things the real world had neither the time nor the obligation to consider seriously.*

Neither J.I. Rodale or Rachel Carson are still around, but history has proved them both right, and what was once outlandish is now the mainstream. So the wheel turns. J.I.'s son Robert is continuing the good effort with distinction. If Rodale is an empire — **Organic Gardening, Prevention** *(p. 322), and* **The New Farm** *(p. 121) are three of their magazines; they publish a whole library of books; they have an experimental farm in Pennsylvania that tackles a lot of research problems the USDA should do but won't — then I wish we had more like them.*

The books and magazines on this page are small sample of what Rodale has available; write for their publication list to see it all.
—Richard Nilsen

Organic Gardening Magazine

The unending popularity of this magazine may be due to its being written largely by readers sharing their experiences with plants. It is folk-science and it is becoming ever more sophisticated. *—Rosemary Menninger*

Organic Gardening
Robert Rodale, Editor
$10/year (12 issues)
postpaid from:
Rodale Press
33 East Minor Street
Emmaus, PA 18049

●

More than once I've found myself on my back in the garden dirt, exhausted, imagining that the rivulets of hot sweat pouring off my face and chest are ice cold, and too weary to brush away the gnats that finally (ultimate gnat glee) bzz at will in my eyelashes. At such times I feel great peace, spent in a good cause. Once I caught myself saying, "This is fair dinkum."

Queer phrase to be served up by my mind. I hadn't used it in years. Learned it from an Australian soldier on a bus ride when I was 15. He said, "In Australia, we say fair dinkum for okay. It means something's all right." Years later I spotted the phrase, *"Vere dignum"* in a Latin prayerbook. It means, "Fitting indeed." Fair dinkum is obviously an anglicized, latter-day version of *vere dignum*. Pretty neat trick for the mind to come up with that phrase. Surprised me.

●

HERE ARE SOME important steps you can take to help preserve germ plasm resources:

1. Save your own open-pollinated variety seeds from one growing season to the next.
2. Maintain a special germ plasm conservation plot within your garden by planting heirloom varieties along with the latest vegetable selections.
3. Grow at least one new vegetable variety each year. Diversity is good for the diet as well as for the garden.
4. Spread your seed orders among more firms. Purchase seeds from alternative, smaller seed suppliers, as well as from big-name suppliers. You'll discover an exciting array of new vegetables you can enjoy.
5. Write your Representative and Senator and tell them how you feel about the Plant Variety Protection Act and H.R. 999 and S.B. 23. Ask them to keep you informed of any new developments in the pending legislation.

●

"Always keep your tool handles in good shape," they said. "Never leave a shovel or a pick out in the weather, where it can get rained on." In those days few people used work gloves. Even calloused hands soon became sore and blistered from a shovel handle that was rough and splintered from exposure to the weather. A good hickory handle, used often and kept dry, had a finish that was smooth and even shiny. The open wounds on my tender hands imprinted that lesson clearly on my mind.

"Work to a rhythm," I was told. "Don't jerk around or rush. And take rests. Lean on your shovel once in a while, like we do." There was a lot of snide joking in those days about WPA men who spent their days leaning on shovels at the government's expense, but I soon found that regular rest was an essential part of all-day digging. If you've ever tried to dig steadily for a few hours, you know how essential rest periods are.

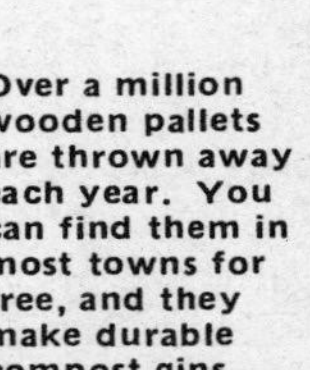

Over a million wooden pallets are thrown away each year. You can find them in most towns for free, and they make durable compost gins.

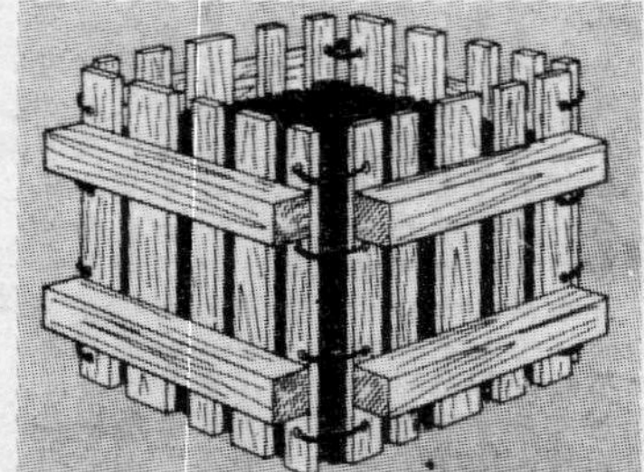

The Basic Book of Organic Gardening

More gardening know-how for less buck than anything else on the market. If you're thinking of growing vegetables to save money — a worthy reason — this book will meet your frame of mind. *—SB*

The Basic Book of Organic Gardening
Robert Rodale, Editor
1971; 377 pp.
$2.25 postpaid from:
Ballantine Books
455 Hahn Road
Westminster, MD 21157
or Whole Earth Household Store

●

My father first used the word *organic* to describe the natural method of gardening and farming, mainly because compost, humus and the organic fraction of the soil were emphasized so strongly. However, even in 1942, when **Organic Gardening and Farming** was born, J.I. Rodale saw that this method was more than just a way to husband the soil and grow plants and animals. He proclaimed that to be *organic* was to know and to understand the lessons of nature in all ways, and to use that knowledge to evaluate all of the "blessings" of science and technology. What good was it, he thought, to grow food without using chemical fertilizers or pesticides and then to process that food so that its content of vitamins and minerals would be depleted seriously? In fact, not caring whether he was called an extremist or a crackpot, J.I. Rodale created what might now be called a *strict constructionist* interpretation of natural life under the banner of organiculture.

If it is synthetic avoid it, he said. If it goes through a factory, examine it with special care. Follow the dictates of the cycle of life when growing things, he advised, and you will be blessed with foods of surpassing taste and quality that are less troubled by insects or disease.

●

There are 7 major sources of organic fertilizers, mulches and conditioners available in such profusion that the categories overlap — what you can't get in one, you can obtain in another. If animal manures are in short supply in your area, what about the blood meals, tankage, and fish scrap? If you can't get them, what about castor pomace, spent hops, cottonseed and soybean meal — all high in nitrogen? But the organic gardener is resourceful (he's got to be) and what he can't buy at the store or get from his local municipal composting plant or sawmill, he makes out of crop residues plus the contents of his garbage pail. Here are his almost never failing sources of supply:

1. *Animal manures;* cattle, livestock, poultry, rabbits.
2. *Animal tankage;* blood meal, dried blood, fish scrap.
3. *Vegetative manures;* the various bean and seed meals, spent hops, castor pomace.
4. *Minerals;* rock phosphate, colloidal phosphate, granite dust, greensand.
5. *Compost;* municipal, commercial and homemade.
6. *Soil conditioners and mulches;* leaves, hay, straw, crop residues, most vegetable fibrous materials, including wood chips and sawdust.
7. *Large-scale, commercial organic fertilizers,* mulches and soil conditioners.

Garden Way

Noting Richard's Rodale intro (above) there in fact is another such empire. Built on Lyman Wood's phenomenal mailorder success with Troy-bilt Rototillers (p. 127) and the Garden Way Cart (p. 131), Garden Way has a whole line of books, tools, periodicals and services for the organic way of life. As with Rodale, these are customarily of very high quality. *—SB*

Garden Way
Catalog
free from:
Garden Way Publishing
Charlotte, VT 05445

Gardens For All

This 5,000 member organization began in 1972 as a spin-off from Garden Way. They publish low-cost basic gardening information, and are helping to popularize the idea of edible landscapes for suburban houses. The **Gardens for All News** *keeps track of the growth of community and institutional gardens all around the country.* *—Richard Nilsen*

Gardens for All
(The National Association of Gardening News)
$10/year (4 issues; includes membership)
postpaid from:
Gardens for All
180 Flynn Avenue
Burlington, VT 05401

The Encyclopedia of Organic Gardening

Rodale's behemoth (1236 pages), new (1978 revision), comprehensive (2000-plus topics covered) one-volume reference to answer every organic gardening question that you can pose alphabetically. *—SB*

●

Charcoal

A black, porous form of carbon, charcoal is prepared from vegetable or animal substances, usually by charring wood in a kiln from which air is excluded.

Pieces of charcoal are often recommended as additions to potting soils, as they improve drainage.

Charcoal, and the ash left from burning charcoal in a stove or barbecue, contains valuable minerals and can be an excellent source of plant nutrients. Charcoal chunks make an unusual-appearing mulch in an ornamental garden.

→

To root hardwood cuttings, tie them in bundles and store them at 45°F. (7.22°C.) in a rooting medium of sand or peat moss.

The Encyclopedia of Organic Gardening
Staff of Organic Gardening Magazine
1959, 1978; 1236 pp.
$21.95 postpaid from:
Rodale Books
33 East Minor Street
Emmaus, PA 18049
or Whole Earth Household Store

Most herbs are best preserved by drying. Cut the stalks in early morning, gather them in small bunches and hang them in a cool, dry place for several weeks.

SUSAN EHMER, S.F. CHRONICLE

Clementina Garden in San Francisco adjoins a housing project for retired people. Chinese couples are especially active in the garden. Rosemary Menninger and Richard Nilsen helped start Clementina in 1973.

Community Gardening

by Rosemary Menninger

NEARLY 2/3 OF AMERICAN HOUSE-holds grow some of their own food, according to a 1980 Gallup Poll; and about 2 million people garden away from home in community gardens. Another 7 million people would like to join a community garden but don't yet have one in their neighborhood.

In the past decade community gardening programs have sprung up in cities across the country. Initial funds often came from city or county government. Now funding in health, education housing, crime prevention, and the arts, in both the public and private sector, is being broadened to include gardening. At the same time, the gardeners are doing much of the organizing and gathering of materials themselves, with money needed primarily for water hook-ups, insurance, and fencing.

Large tracts of land near public housing projects provide food for several hundred gardeners in Chicago and San Francisco. These are the new victory gardens. The plots are large, 25' x 50', and what isn't eaten by the gardeners' own family and friends is given away or traded or sold. The Frederick Douglass gardens in San Francisco include sixty large plots providing regular vegetables for more than 400 people. In the little town of Isla Vista, near Santa Barbara, California, a garden of Laotian and Hmong Chinese refugees have plots of only 10 feet x 20 feet. But through intensive gardening techniques, each plot provides daily food for 12 people.

In most American cities, community gardening programs have only scratched the surface of available vacant land. School grounds, hospital grounds, undeveloped park lands, vacant lots and even back yards that don't get used are suitable places to grow food, provided they're not facing a major street or highway. A 1980 survey conducted at food stamp distribution centers in Los Angeles showed that 86% of the people interviewed not only wanted to grow their own food but knew of vacant land within a block of their residence suitable for gardening. This indicates that the nudge of inflation is about to bring a lot of gardeners out of dormancy.

Even in rural areas, people who don't have land of their own are beginning to grow food together. Community gardens are springing up in migrant labor camps, for instance, and in several California towns, groups of farmworkers tend large community gardens on public land and market the produce collectively.

Prisons and state hospitals are re-discovering the logic of growing their own food. It's an old idea. Before World War II, many state hospitals were notorious for winning blue ribbons at the state fairs. They often had the best flowers, vegetables, livestock and fruit. But after the war came a great gush of equality, and America didn't want hospital patients doing "slave labor" in the fields.

For security reasons, prisons stopped having gardens until recently. Now a few, such as the Leavenworth State Penitentiary in Kansas, have begun to grow hundreds of pounds of vegetables. Gardening is a popular outdoor activity, the quality of the institution's diet is improved, and the staff often gets a chance to work side by side with the residents. Furthermore, the money saved in food and groundskeeping is considerable.

These are some of the reasons why horticultural therapy was listed by the **Wall Street Journal** as one of the 10 fastest growing careers for the '80s. A gardener can solicit work at hospitals, programs for the handicapped and half-way houses much as one solicits landscaping clients – except in this case it is people that are being cultivated as well as plants. At present, there are no basic horticultural therapy books in print. It's unfortunate, since gardening with the severely retarded or disabled requires special techniques, but other populations simply take care and common sense. Horticultural therapy is such a new field that academic credentials are not necessary. However, degree programs in horticultrual therapy are offered at state universities in Rhode Island, Delaware and Georgia; also at Texas Tech, Kansas State, Michigan State, University of Florida and Clemson College in South Carolina.

In both community gardens and institutional gardens, people do simple things, such as growing their own food and helping their neighbors, but the effect on those involved is often astonishing. A government study of school gardens found that children who gardened learned better in all of their subjects than those who didn't garden. The teachers said the gardening children gained a sense of power that made them feel more confident than before. Through gardening, people are able to effect a change in their environment and to effect a change in their lives; when they experience this together all kinds of barriers begin to disappear. ■

The Complete Book of Community Gardening

Community gardening's most interesting aspects are covered in this warm-hearted book – the wide variety of people involved, the nooks and crannies and open fields they find to grow their food in, and the techniques that evolve when people of different ethnic backgrounds garden together. Author Jamie Jobb documents community gardening by describing how people do it from coast to coast – including annotated lists of seed sources, organizations, publications, ect. Groups of plants and groups of people come together in community gardens.
—Rosemary Menninger

•

Guerilla Gardens

America has more vacant and abused lands than it has people who are willing or able to cultivate them. But there is one good way to put this land to use and make it productive. The secret is to broadcast-sow vacant lots with seeds of mother weeds and hearty cultivated plants so their dynamic qualities and aggressive root action can renew the land. Later these vacant lots could be used by neighborhood garden groups like yours or others. Or they can be left alone to grow and spread their wings as bona fide weed patches.

•

Seeds from any of these wild and cultivated plants can be used to start a guerilla garden. Simply break the soil a bit and then toss the seeds:

fava beans	vetch	goldenrod
clover	alfalfa	nasturtium
lupines	borage	flax
black nightshade	ground cherry	plantain
cherry tomato	cayenne pepper	shepherd's-purse
dandelion	sunflower	milkweed
cosmos	wild lettuce	lamb's quarters
marigold	Shasta daisy	stinging nettle
sow thistle	curly dock	burdock
sheep sorrel	cocklebur	amaranth
smartweed	mustard	rye

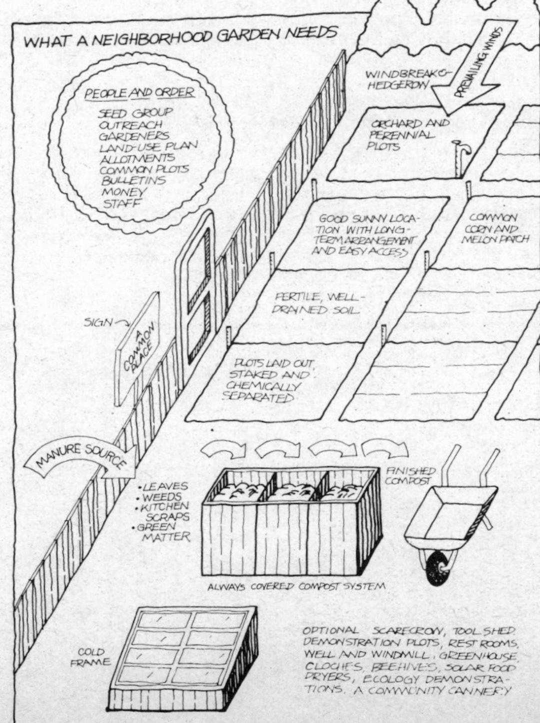

The Complete Book of Community Gardening
Jamie Jobb
1979; 185 pp.

$7.95 postpaid from:
William Morrow & Co., Inc.
Wilmor Warehouse
6 Henderson Drive
West Caldwell, NJ 07006
or Whole Earth Household Store

THE RISING SUN
NEIGHBORHOOD NEWSLETTER

People will usually tell you pretty directly what question they want to be asked. Usually they ask you. Watch for the slightly off the wall, somewhat left fieldish question from friends – "Do you like your job? Do your parents get along? What do you want to do the rest of your life?" Point the question toward them and they may take a chance they've been waiting for to work something out in words.

How to Grow More Vegetables

John Jeavons and his band at Ecology Action began nine years ago with good intentions, boundless energy, and a sun-baked clay strip of land slated for a parking lot. Along the way, careful records of the dramatic results were kept, enough so that nowadays Jeavons is explaining the idea to the UN and the World Bank, and setting up a demonstration project in Indonesia. Jeavons did not invent the bio-dynamic/French intensive method of gardening, but he clearly qualifies as its chief popularizer, and this book boils down the method to its simplest terms. It is organic gardening using hand labor, raised beds, close spacing between plants to eliminate weeds and conserve soil moisture, and heavy feeding and composting. It can produce very large yields in very small spaces, and is therefore applicable to many diverse situations. —Richard Nilsen

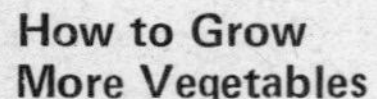

How to Grow More Vegetables
(Than you ever thought possible on less land than you can imagine)
John Jeavons
1974, 1979; 115 pp.
$5.95 postpaid

Como Cultivar Mas Hortalizas
(Spanish edition)
Rafael Siquieros, Translator
1974, 1979; 88 pp.
$5.50 postpaid

both from:
Ten Speed Press
900 Modoc Street
Berkeley, CA 94707
or Whole Earth Household Store
(English version only)

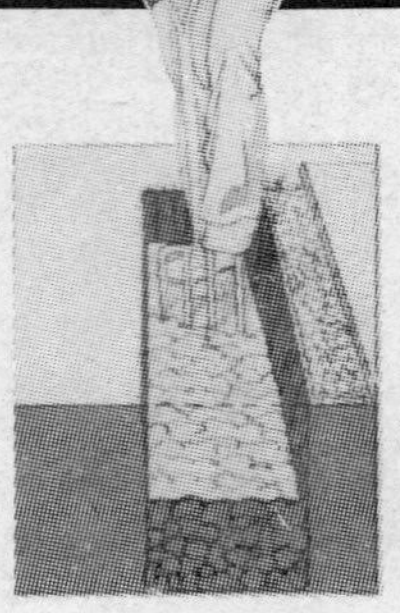

For moderately compacted soil: loosen soil an additional 12 inches with a spading fork by digging tool into its full depth and then pushing tool handle downward so fork tines will lever through soil, loosening and aerating it.

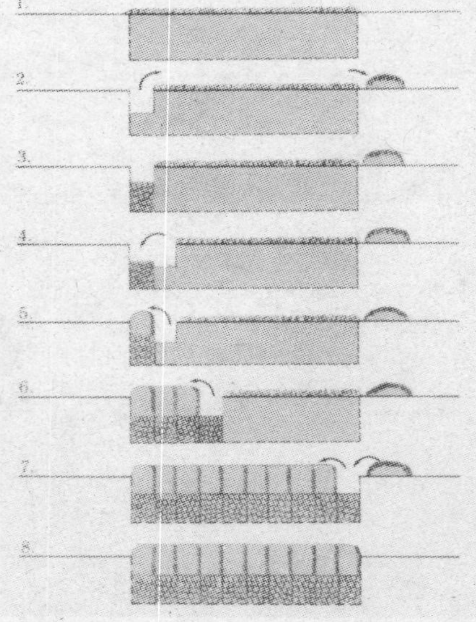

← The Double-Dig

1. Spread a layer of compost over entire area to be dug.
2. Remove soil from upper part of first trench and place at far end of bed.
3. Loosen soil an additional 12 inches.
4. Dig out upper part of second trench and throw forward into upper, open part of first trench.
5. Loosen lower part of second trench.
6. Continue "double-digging" process (repeating steps 4 and 5) for remaining trenches.
7. Place soil in mound at end of bed into open, upper part of last trench.
8. The completed "double-dig" bed.

Note that topsoil is moved forward and loosened trench by trench, while subsoil is loosened without being moved or turned.

(Left) Biodynamic/French intensive raised bed
(Right) traditional rows.

Bio-Dynamic Agriculture

Based on the techniques developed in the early part of this century by Rudolf Steiner, Bio-Dynamics is a well-researched attempt to orchestrate the relationships of plants, animals, microorganisms and the elements. The goal is to develop a natural harmony in the artificial situation of a farm or garden. Here are described the techniques used by the famous bio-dynamic farms of Europe to produce superior crops and livestock. While this may be an introduction, it is not for beginners.
—Rosemary Menninger
[Suggested by George de Alth]

Bio-Dynamic Agriculture
(An Introduction)
Herbert H. Koepf, Bo D. Pettersson, and Wolfgang Schaumann
1976; 416 pp.
$12 postpaid from:
Anthroposophic Press, Inc.
258 Hungry Hollow Road
Spring Valley, NY 10977
or Whole Earth Household Store

•

Experience gained over more than a decade has shown that the division of vegetables into roots, leaves and fruits is a good basis for establishing a crop rotation thus giving us a useful guideline when planning a vegetable garden. In successive years the soil is enabled to produce the different "organs" of the plant and in this way fertility is maintained instead of being weakened by, for instance, repeated demands to form leaf vegetables. In a four-year cycle each plot can produce first leaf vegetables, then roots, then fruits and seeds, and finally flowering plants.

Bio-Dynamic Literature

Nearly 40 titles of books, pamphlets, charts and back issues of the magazine **Bio-Dynamics** *are available in the current list. These are also the folks to write to for information about the Bio-Dynamic Farming and Gardening Association, which has regional groups various places around the country.* —Richard Nilsen

Bio-Dynamic Literature
price list

free from:
Bio-Dynamic Literature
P.O. Box 253
Wyoming, RI 02898

Secrets of Companion Planting

Companion planting is becoming a prime focus of non-chemical agricultural research because so little is known about what really works. This book is based on applied botanical knowledge, agricultural wisdom, and good sense. Good enough for now since the scientific results will be a long time coming. —Rosemary Menninger

Secrets of Companion Planting for Successful Gardening
Louise Riotte
1976; 219 pp.
$5.95 postpaid from:
Garden Way Publishing
Charlotte, VT 05445
or Whole Earth Household Store

•

LETTUCE *(Lactuca sativa)*. In spring I keep a supply of small lettuce plants growing in cold frames. When I pull every other green onion for table use I pop in lettuce plants. They will aid the onions, and the compost in the onion row will still be in good supply for the lettuce to feed on, while the onion will repel any rabbits.

Lettuce grows well with strawberries, cucumbers, carrots and it has long been considered good to team with carrots and radishes. Radishes grown with lettuce in summer are particularly succulent.

•

Garlic and onions are particularly beneficial to roses. In Bulgaria, where attar of roses is produced for perfumes, it is a common practice to interplant them with roses since they cause the roses to produce a stronger perfume in larger quantities.

If mice like your garden too well, repel them with bulb plantings of daffodils, narcissi, scilla or grape hyacinth.

The Adventurous Gardener

Anyone who relies on a garden for food is bound to get adventurous with unusual vegetables, medicinal plants, wildflowers and teas. This is one book that tells how to grow them all. —Rosemary Menninger

The Adventurous Gardener
Nancy Wilkes Bubel
1979; 231 pp.
$6.95 postpaid from:
David R. Godine, Publisher
306 Dartmouth Street
Boston, MA 02116
or Whole Earth Household Store

•

Learning to grow sweet potatoes is a new venture for many gardeners. Although sweets require no more care than tomatoes or lettuce, they are often overlooked when the garden plan is made out. I don't know why this should be so, for sweets are delicious, easy to grow, and widely enjoyed. If you want to find out what you've been missing, you can start by planting a summer crop of these heat-loving but trouble-free delicacies, progress to the point where you can store the sweets so that they will keep all winter, and achieve advanced standing by managing to start new plants in spring from sound roots you've kept over from the fall harvest.

Consider, first, what sweet potatoes require. An essentially undemanding plant, the sweet *(Ipomoea batatas)* is a member of the morning glory family. Its one absolute requirement is for a good 150 days of frost-free weather. A native of the tropics, the vine grows best at a temperature range of 70 to 85 degrees F. At 60 degrees F. it stops growing, and prolonged temperatures below 50 degrees F. retard the plant.

The Climate Near the Ground

This appears to be the definitive text on microclimatology: the climatic conditions within 6 feet or so of the earth's surface. The climate in this narrow stratum differs significantly from the overall climate, and the book analyzes, in some detail, the relation of soil, water, vegetation, topography, man and animals to the microclimate.
—Lloyd Kahn
[Suggested by Steve Baer]

The Climate Near the Ground
Rudolf Geiger
1966; 611 pp.
$25 postpaid from:
Harvard University Press
79 Garden Street
Cambridge, MA 02138
or Whole Earth Household Store

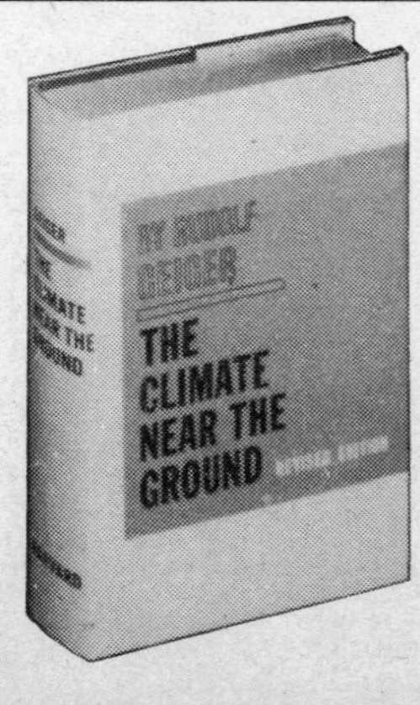

Amount of heat per hour derived from direct solar radiation on a standing tree trunk.

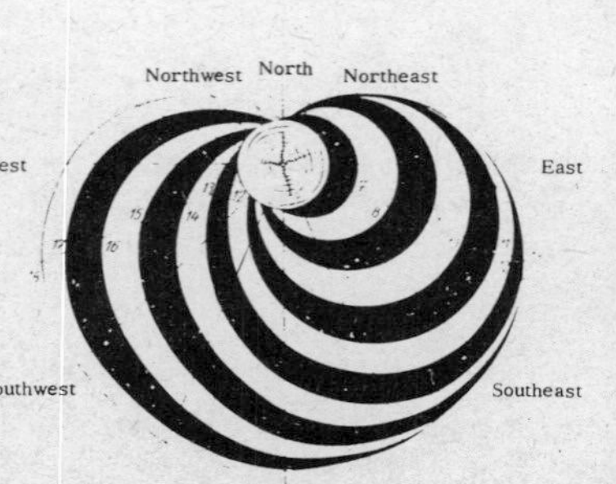

Fairview School gardens, summer of 1909 in Yonkers, N.Y.

Dump Heap

Boy, I like this little quarterly. It's tight, tidy, densely informative, innovative, elite, amateur — an enjoyable technical conversation among garden inventors. Makes you want to be one. —SB

Dump Heap
(The Journal of Diverse Unsung Miracle Plants for Healthy Evolution Among People)
Jamie Jobb, Editor
$6/year (4 issues)
postpaid from:
The Dump Heap
2950 Walnut Boulevard
Walnut Creek, CA 94598

•

TREE PEOPLE

International Dwarf Fruit Tree Association, Horticulture Department, Michigan State University, E. Lansing, MI 48824. Promotes research and education. Rootstock research. Founded in 1958. Publishes "Compact Fruit Tree."

Rare Fruit Council, Museum of Science, 3280 S. Miami Avenue, Miami, FL 33129. Aids those who raise tropical fruits. Aims for introduction of new species, varieties, mutations, clones of rare fruit trees. Publishes newsletter and yearbook.

American Pomological Society, 103 Tyson Building, University Park, PA 16802. Founded in 1848 to help amateurs and professionals improve fruit varieties. Publishes quarterly.

North American Fruit Explorers, 55 Madison Street, Hindsdale, IL 60521. Hobbyist growers and breeders working to develop new varieties and methods. Publishes quarterly "Pomona."

California Rare Fruit Growers, Star Route Box P, Bonsall, CA 92003. Gardeners working to increase use of less-common fruits and to upgrade familiar ones. Newsletter and yearbook.

Northern Nut Growers Association, 4518 Holston Hills Road, Knoxville, TN 37914. Founded 1910. Growers and amateurs interested in culture of hardy nut-bearing trees. "Nutshell" quarterly and "Handbook of North American Nut Trees."

Home Orchard Society, 6404 SE 40th Street, Portland, OR 97202. Educational group for amateurs. Breeding program, nursery, library. Publishes "Home News" quarterly.

International Association for Lesser Known Food Plants and Trees, P.O. Box 599, Lynwood, CA 90262. Dedicated to solving world hunger by helping people grow hardy types of uncommon food plants. Establishing growing ground in Mexico. Publishes "Good and Wild" quarterly.

Men of the Trees, Crawley Down, Crawley, Sussex, England. Conservation group which encourages tree plantings and forest preservation. Founded 1922. Publishes "Trees" semiannually.

Island Foundation Tree Crop Nursery, Route 1, Box 44B, Covelo, CA 95428. New project by innovative foundation. Seeks hardy fruit and nut varieties for local climate. Foundation also has reforestation project at same site. Staff people and apprentices dedicated to working and living in Round Valley area.

Brooklyn Botanic Garden

This is an outstanding source of information on nearly everything useful relating to plants, greenhouse, vines, bonsai, pruning, the lot. And a fine periodical, **Plants and Gardens.** —SB

Plants and Gardens
(Brooklyn Botanic Garden Record)
Frederick McGourty, Editor
$5 /year (4 issues)

Brooklyn Botanic Garden Publications
List
free
both from:
Brooklyn Botanic Garden
1000 Washington Avenue
Brooklyn, NY 11225

Simon & Schuster's Complete Guide to Plants and Flowers

A flower gardener's encyclopedia, a seed catalogue's companion, and a visual delight. Five hundred half-page color photos with graphic cultivation tips for common varieties of flowers, cactus, houseplants, and other ornamentals.
—Rosemary Menninger

Simon & Schuster's Complete Guide to Plants and Flowers
Frances Perry, Editor
1974; 522 pp.
$7.95 postpaid from:
Simon & Schuster
Attn: Mail Order Dept.
1230 Avenue of the Americas
New York, NY 10020
or Whole Earth Household Store

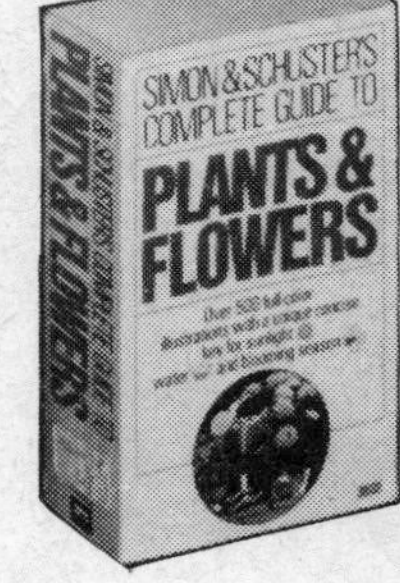

← 281 **BELLADONNA LILY**
Amaryllis belladonna:

FULL SUN
Summer Autumn Winter Spring
FLOWERING PERIOD
SPARINGLY
⑨

Family: Amaryllidaceae. Named after the shepherd, Amaryllis, in classical poetry.
Place of origin: South Africa.
Description: a monotypic genus, the species a showy, late-flowering bulb. Leaves strap-shaped, channelled, appearing in winter or early spring. Flowers large, funnel-shaped, 6 parted, rose-red or paler, sweet-scented, on stout 18–30 in. (45–75 cm) stems, before the foliage in autumn.
Flowering time: early autumn.
Use: in temperate climates, against sunny walls or as pot plants; in climates with mild winters, in small flower beds or borders.
Propagation: by division of the bulbs at the base of the mother plant.
Environment and light: full sun.
Type of soil: plant bulbs 6–9 in. (15–23 cm) deep. Equal parts good fibrous loam, leaf-mould and sand.
Soil moisture: water quite sparingly, only as required.
Remarks: hardy. Cover with 1–2 in. (2–5 cm) soil. Reasonably hardy zones 5–8. Cover 9 in. (22 cm) of soil and give plenty of sun and shelter.

The Vegetable Garden

This reprint of the 1885 English translation of Vilmorin's classic from the 1860s is a monumental work. The format is cold and temperate climate vegetables from A to Z (in this case, Alexanders to Yams), complete with engraved illustrations, descriptions, and extensive cultural information. The detail is astounding, and can only have come from a vast personal experience. Not everyone may want or need 56 pages devoted to peas (for example), but for the serious or inquisitive gardener, this book is a treasure. —Richard Nilsen

•

It may be said that the cultivation of the Cauliflower is one of the most simple processes, and, at the same time, one of the most difficult to carry out well. In fact, with the exception of the spring Cauliflowers, which are sown in autumn and wintered under frames, it is grown as an annual, which is sown in the spring in the open ground and yields a crop in the course of the same year, without requiring any attention whatever except frequent waterings. But, on the other hand, it is certain that, in order to obtain a fine crop, the cultivation of the cauliflower requires a certain amount of skill and tact which no mere cultural directions can supply. The "head" will not be regularly formed unless the growth of the plant proceeds rapidly and without any check from beginning to end, and the greatest watchfulness and most assiduous care sometimes fail to insure this.

The Vegetable Garden
Mm. Vilmorin-Andrieux
1978; 620 pp.
$13 postpaid from:
The Jeavons-Leler Press
855 Clara Drive
Palo Alto, CA 94303
or Whole Earth Household Store

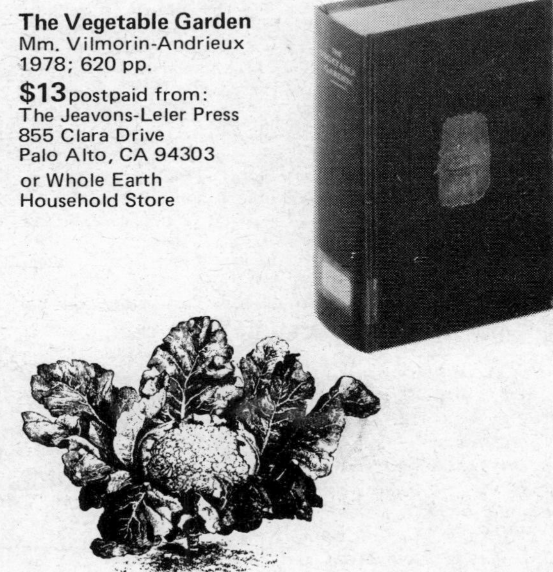

The Mulch Book

The Mulch Book *answers dozens of questions about mulching and suggests specific mulches for each vegetable. It's the most complete book available on the subject.*
—Rosemary Menninger

The Mulch Book
(A Guide for the Family Food Gardener)
Stu Campbell
1973; 131 pp.
$4.95 postpaid from:
Garden Way Publishing
Charlotte, VT 05445

BLACK POLYETHYLENE MULCH. Lay the plastic before you plant, being sure the soil is fairly moist first. Be certain that it is weighted down properly and that all edges are covered with dirt so the wind can't get under it and blow it away. Cut round, X-shaped or T-shaped holes in the film so plants can grow up and water can go down.

THE RISING SUN
NEIGHBORHOOD NEWSLETTER

I sure hope Lee Butler, the rather touchy solar inventor, can write, because he does say interesting things on the phone. He said, the goal of solar heating is not to recreate a regular house, with all its drafts and flaws, but to recreate the tropical climate that people evolved in and that they would be most comfortable in now. Tom Smith, the guy who lives in the Tahoe house Butler designed, noticed that the climate in his house was exactly like the climate of Honolulu in January. That reminded Lee that what he wanted when he started solar designing was to live on the coast of Nova Scotia and be absolutely comfortable — not to gather wood, or to burn oil, but live in a natural climate that was designed for a human body. But he'd gotten involved with numbers and equations and ventilation systems and forgotten that.

What he designed with his numbers was a pocket of air that circulates all around the perimeter of a house — an air wall inside the regular walls that isolates the air inside the house from the air outside. The air inside doesn't know what the outside climate is, and develops its own climate which is warm and free of the drafts that are caused by the outside cold sneaking in. A semi-tropical climate in fact, the climate Lee dreamed of before he started engineering.

Maybe that's 21st century engineering. 19th century engineering was beating nature awkwardly and slowly with gears and joints and hot pistons. 20th century engineering is beating nature fast, instantly, the minute you think of it with electronics and explosives. Maybe in the 21st century we'll stop fucking with nature and start making love, ask her nicely if she'll make our dreams come true.

Growing Unusual Fruit

An illustrated reference work aimed at the home gardener rather than botanists. Close to 100 varieties from around the world are covered. The plant history and cultivation instructions are generally better than the information on cooking and eating. Since one man's rarity is another's common-place, the varieties covered are a bit surprising — "common" fruits like oranges, bananas, almonds and olives, along with "rare" species like buffalo berry, manzanita, prickly pear and water chestnut. Directions on greenhouse cultivation for tropical fruits are included, which is a help.
—Richard Nilsen

Growing Unusual Fruit
Alan H. Simmons
1972; 354 pp.

OUT OF PRINT
Walker and Company

Get this book back in print!

Akebia fruit
Almond
Alpine strawberry
Appleberry
Applerose
Apricot
Avocado pear
Banana
Barbados cherry
Barberry
Bilberry
Blueberry
Brambleberry
Brazilian cherry
Buffalo berry
Cape gooseberry
Carambola
Casimiroa
Checkerberry
Chequers
Cherry plum
Chinese gooseberry
Cloudberry
Coffee bean
Cornelian cherry
Cranberry
Crowberry
Custard apple
Custard banana
Desert plum
Elderberry
Eve's date
Feijoa
Fig
Fuchsia berry
Goumi
Grape
Guava
Guelderberry
Holboella
Hottentot fig
Huckleberry
Japanese quince
Jujube
Juneberry
Kilarney strawberry
Kumquat
Lemon
Lime
Litchee
Loquat
Mandarin
Mango
Manzanita
Marmelos
Mediterranean medlar
Medlar
Mombin fruit
Monstera
Mulberry
Nectarine
Olive
Orange
Oregon grape
Passion fruit
Paw Paw
Persimmon
Pineapple
Pomegranate
Poncirus
Prickly pear
Pummelo
Quince
Raspberry — black, purple, yellow
Rowanberry
Sea Berry
Snowberry
Strawberry-raspberry
Sugarberry
Tree tomato
Twinberry
Ugni
Umbinza
Water chestnut; Singara nut
Wineberry
Worcesterberry
Zabala fruit

Small-Scale Grain Raising

Our household consumes 2 - 3 bushels of wheat per year. We buy this wheat at a local mill which charged $4.20 for a 60 pound bushel sack last time around. At seven cents/pound why bother to raise your own? In this very basic book, Gene Logsdon tells why, and then how.

Grains can be easily fitted into all but the smallest garden schemes. The yield per acre requires very little space for the needs of an average family. A fair yield of wheat would provide three bushels from 1/10 acre. This can be worked into a rotation with row crops and as a cover crop to build soil and give protection from erosion during wintertime. Grain straw makes superb, clean mulch. Some grains, such as oats, make excellent hay, especially for horses. There is a certain security in providing for one's family and animals. It's possible to grow your own roofing (thatching, see **The Thatcher's Craft**, *p. 233). And grains are beautiful.*
—Drew Langsner

Small-Scale Grain Raising
Gene Logsdon
1977; 305 pp.

$5.95 postpaid from:
Rodale Books
33 East Minor
Emmaus, PA 18049
or Whole Earth Household Store

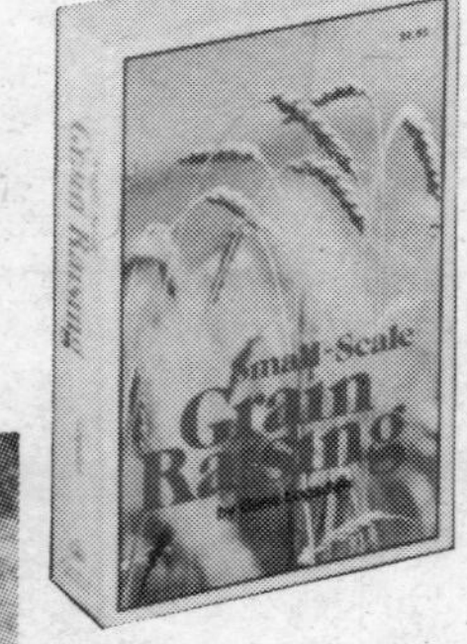

Sorghum is excellent feed for chickens, if only because there's a minimum of processing necessary. The birds will peck the grains from the unthreshed heads.

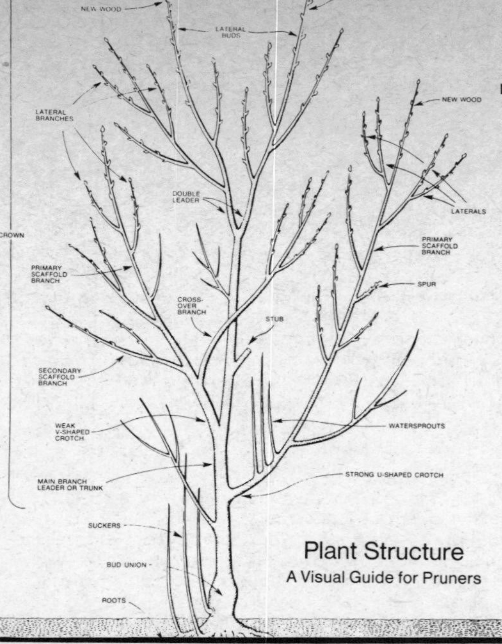

Plant Structure
A Visual Guide for Pruners

Pruning Handbook

It starts with a basic description of the way plants grow, lists pruning tools and their uses, and describes pruning systems for ornamental and fruit trees, berries and grapes, roses and vines.
—SB
[Suggested by Fred Richardson]

Pruning Handbook
Sunset Editors
1972; 96 pp.

$2.95 postpaid from:
Lane Publishing Co.
Menlo Park, CA 94025
or Whole Earth Household Store

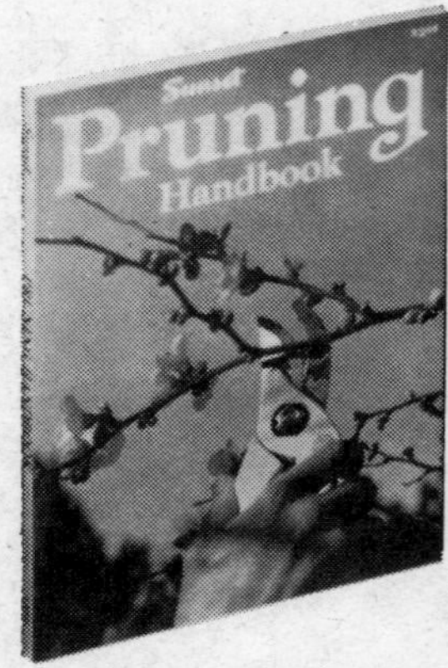

Save Your Own Seed

Hills is one of the greatest horticultural writers in the world. Here he concentrates plant by plant on a topic most gardening books leave out.
—Rosemary Menninger

Save Your Own Seed
Lawrence D. Hills
1975; 46 pp.

50 p. (about $1.50)
postpaid from:
The Henry Doubleday Research Association
Bocking, Braintree
Essex, England

•

The kale problem is that these are now as rare as the oryx or the Hawaiian goose and many have joined the dodo in extinction. The world's gene pool has lost the qualities that it may well need to breed a "superkale," which would blend attractive flavour with high Vitamin A and Vitamin C, plus resistance to both clubroot and to wood pigeons. We need a campaign by Friends of the Earth to "Save the Kale," for this could be more important to a vegetarian world than either whales, or lost botanical treasures.

Low Maintenance Perennials

I can't keep this book in my hands; everyone who sees it wants to borrow it. A discussion of several hundred hardy flowers and ornamental grasses, many of them drought-resistant. Their cultivation is primarily a head-trip: first studying the requirements of the plants and the conditions of the garden; then matching a plant to a suitable spot. If the plant is well-situated, nature will do the gardening. The illustrations are good and the suggested designs for trellises and staking are superb.
—Rosemary Menninger

Low Maintenance Perennials
Robert S. Hebb
1975; 216 pp.

$9 postpaid from:
Times Books
Keystone Industrial Park
Scranton, PA 18512

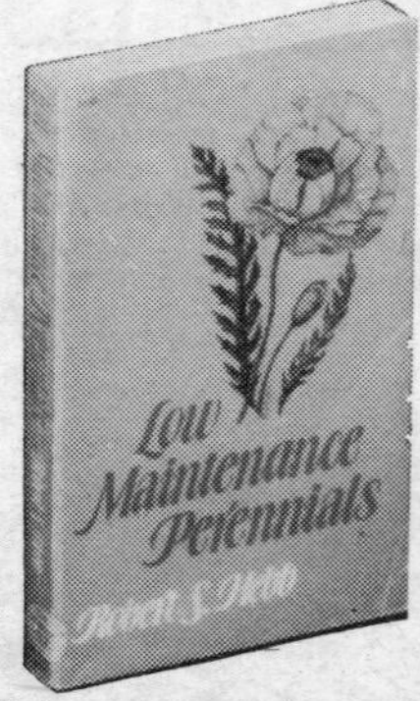

•

Many plants that produce multiple stems may be staked with small twiggy branches set in the ground just as, or even before, plants commence growth in the spring. This is an old European method, particularly favored with Asters. Seldom used in this country, it is most effective.

Strawberries should be planted in wide, shallow holes with their roots spread down the sides of a mount in the middle, so their growing-points are well above soil level.

Grow Your Own Fruit and Vegetables

Excellent organic advice from a British master on vegetables, fruit and berries. He not only shares his techniques, he also lets you know the people and vegetables share a long and endlessly intertwined history.
—Richard Nilsen

Grow Your Own Fruit and Vegetables
Lawrence D. Hills
1971, 1973; 328 pp.

$6.95 postpaid from:
Merrimack Book Service
99 Main Street
Salem, NH 03079

Mushroom Growing for Everyone

Apparently the main effort in growing mushrooms is having, or making, marvelous compost to grow them on. Beyond that they're a low-maintenance grow-em-in-corners item. This British book has the details. *—SB*
(See mushroom kits, p. 356, and also p. 418.)

Mushroom Growing for Everyone
Roy Genders
1970; 216 pp.

$11.50 postpaid from:
Transatlantic Arts, Inc.
Trade Department
North Village Green
Levittown, NY 11756
or Whole Earth Household Store

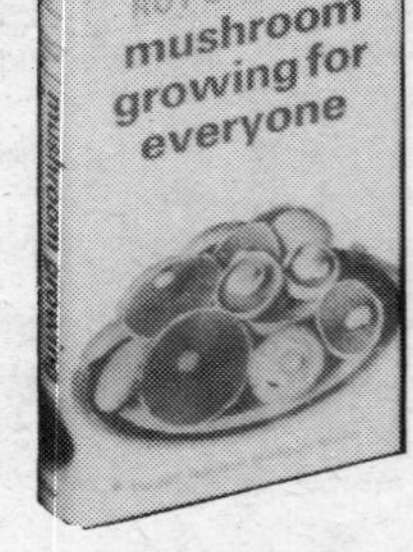

•

A crop of mushrooms may be produced in boxes beneath the kitchen sink, in a cellar or in a garden shed. They may be grown in a cupboard beneath the stairs, or in an attic room, where perhaps no more than two or three boxes may be planted with spawn; these would take the minimum amount of time to care for, just a few minutes each day. When the crop came into bearing and, provided the temperature did not fall below 45°F (7°C) there would be a few mushrooms each week for possibly three months or more. Artificial heat is not necessary for mushrooms, but the beds (or boxes) will not bear if the temperature falls below 40°F (4°C). Though the beds may become completely frozen, no harm will be done, and the crop will begin again as soon as the air temperature rises. This is another advantage in growing mushrooms in comparison with plants which may be damaged by hard frosts. Indeed, the best quality mushrooms will be obtained where the temperature does not rise above 55°F (13°C), and a cool place is better than one which is too warm, when pest and disease will be at a minimum.

Comfrey Report

Dr. Rateaver has edited for Americans the many years of research reports on comfrey done by Lawrence Hills and the Henry Doubleday Research Association. Comfrey can, under optimum conditions, produce more protein per acre than soybeans. It is also the only land plant known to extract vitamin B12 from the soil. One section of the book explains its use as a healing herb for people, but it also cures several ailments in livestock. The leaves are rich enough in NPK to use as fertilizer without even bothering to compost them first. Sounds remarkable, but there's plenty of data to back up these claims.
—Richard Nilsen

Comfrey Report
Lawrence D. Hills
1975; 139 pp.

$5.50 postpaid from:
Bargyla Rateaver
Pauma Valley, CA 92061

•

Comfrey was a "health food" for horses traditionally used by gypsies to put a gloss on the coats of bad bargains.

1 Prune a plant in the dormant season to induce stems with a high capacity to produce roots.

2 Cultivate some soil the following spring. Add peat and grit if necessary. Dig a very large hole.

3 Lift the plant with as complete a root ball as possible. Place it in the hole.

4 Leave only 1in of the stem tips exposed when covering the plant with soil. Firm it in and label.

5 Water during the growing season if the soil dries.

6 Lift the plant in autumn. Cut away each rooted stem and plant it out or pot it up. Label clearly.

Plant Propagation

Leave it to the Royal Horticultural Society to bring us a book that exhibits the same meticulous care as an English garden. **Plant Propagation** *clearly presents the tricks of the trade that make the difference between success and frustration. It is my basic reference for "how to" horticultural questions. Straightforward, non-technical text and very helpful illustrations dispel the mystique surrounding plant propagation. The various propagation techniques are categorized according to whether they involve seeds, roots, modified stems, stems, or leaves. Each procedure occupies facing pages. This allows the spiral-bound paperback to be folded and placed inside its see-through, plastic envelope so it may be used in the field without damage. Also included are special sections covering equipment, grafting and budding, a glossary, and an index referencing the best propagation procedures for over 700 genera of plants.*

I qualify my praise with a caution against the book's excessive recommendations of fungicide use. Many commercial growers face serious problems with resistant strains of fungi that have developed from just such practices. A concerted sanitation program and observation schedule are better strategies for many reasons besides being ultimately more effective. Otherwise, this is the best practical guide to plant propagation available.

—Edward Goodell
New Alchemy Institute

Plant Propagation
(Seeds, Roots, Bulbs and Corms, Layering, Stem Cuttings, Leaf Cuttings, Budding and Grafting)
Philip McMillan Browse
1979; 96 pp.

$7.95 postpaid from:
Simon and Schuster
Attn: Order Dept.
1230 Avenue of the Americas
New York, NY 10020
or Whole Earth Household Store

The Nursery-Manual

This is an old book, first published in 1896, revised the last time in 1922. Its age is an advantage to the organic gardener. When Bailey wrote, there were no sure-fire fungicides and herbicides, no rooting hormones, no mist systems. To be successful, you had to watch your plants closely, be careful and systematic, and have an intuitive, practical understanding of how plants grow. So often modern technology is offered as a substitute for observation and sensitivity to the growth processes of plants. Much is lost when that is the case. Bailey leads you into a world where there is no technological substitute for care and active involvement.

Some of the material is a bit out of date or peculiar. But it doesn't matter. **The Nursery-Manual** *is loaded with information, illustrations and pictures of how to do all kinds of plant propagation. The sections on cuttings and on layering are particularly useful. There is a good index (223 pp.) of plants and how they are propagated, that answers the question: How and when do I propagate this? You can have fun with this book.* *—Steve Kaffka*

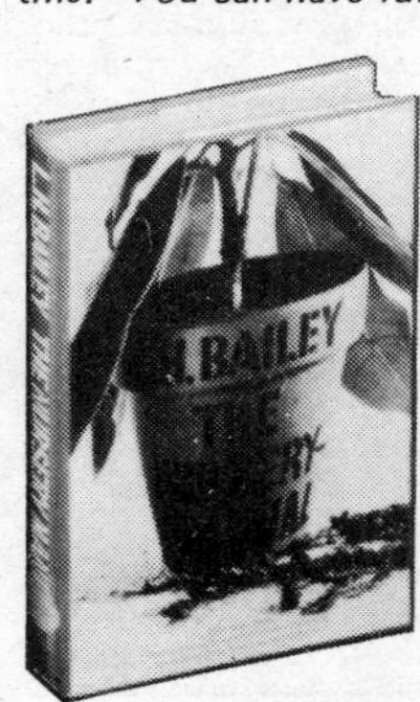

The Nursery-Manual
L.H. Bailey
1896, 1967; 456 pp.
18th Printing

$9.95 postpaid from:
The Macmillan Co.
Order Department
Front & Brown Streets
Riverside, NJ 08075

In making *softwood cuttings*, the first thing to learn is the proper texture or age of shoot. A very soft and flabby cutting does not grow readily, or if it does it is particularly liable to damp-off, and it usually makes a weak plant. Too old wood is slow to root, makes a poor stunted plant and is handled with difficulty in many species. The ordinary test for beginners is the way in which the shoot breaks. If, on being bent, the shoot snaps off squarely so as to hang together with only a bit of bark, as in the upper break in Fig. 115, it is in the proper condition for cuttings; but if it bends or crushes, as in the lower part of the figure, it is either too old or too young for good results. The tips of the shoots of soft-wooded plants are usually employed, and all or some of the leaves are allowed to remain.

Fig. 115. Tough and brittle wood.

The cuttings are inserted in sharp sand to a sufficient depth to hold them in place, and the atmosphere and soil must be kept moist to prevent wilting or "flagging." The cuttings should also be shaded for the first week or two. It is a common practice to cover newly set cuttings with newspapers in the heat of the day. A propagating-frame is often employed.

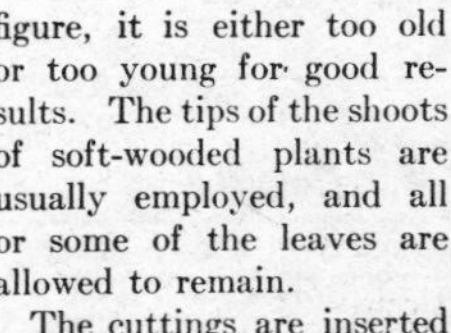

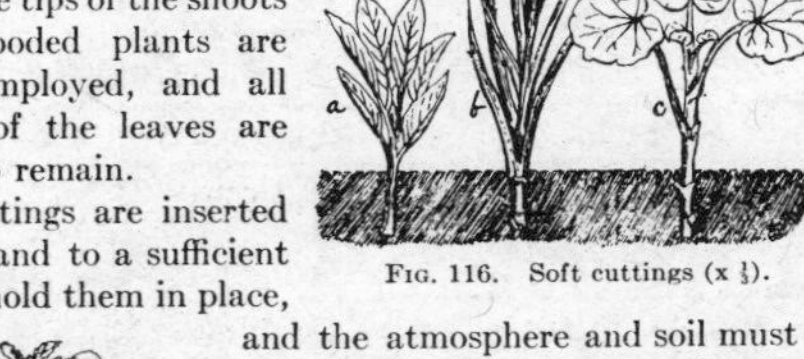

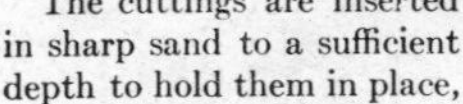

Fig. 116. Soft cuttings (x ½).

Fig. 117. Coleus cutting (x ½).

Plant Propagation: Principles and Practices

This is a very current, comprehensive and technical book. Many of the techniques and methods described are appropriate to the horticultural industry and the professional technician, but there is a good deal of information that is simple and straightforward. Anybody who is seriously interested in plants — in what goes on inside them and what measurable influences control their growth — will find this book extremely valuable.

Start with **The Nursery Manual** *and work up to* **Plant Propagation.** *Absorbing too much scientific and technical information before you have any personal experience can often hinder your ability to learn from plants directly.*

—Steve Kaffka
[Suggested by Ed Clinker]

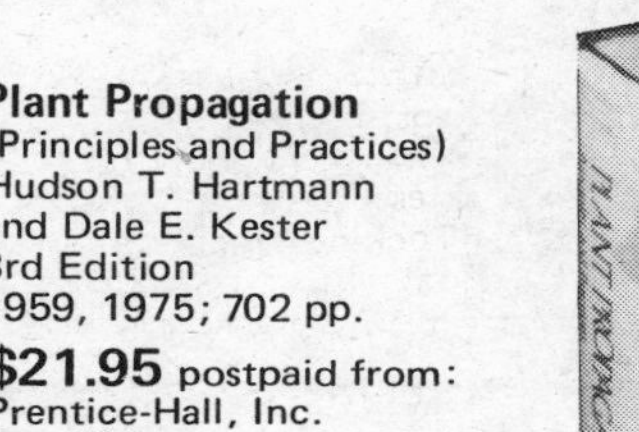

Plant Propagation
(Principles and Practices)
Hudson T. Hartmann and Dale E. Kester
3rd Edition
1959, 1975; 702 pp.

$21.95 postpaid from:
Prentice-Hall, Inc.
Box 500
Englewood Cliffs, NJ 07632
or Whole Earth Household Store

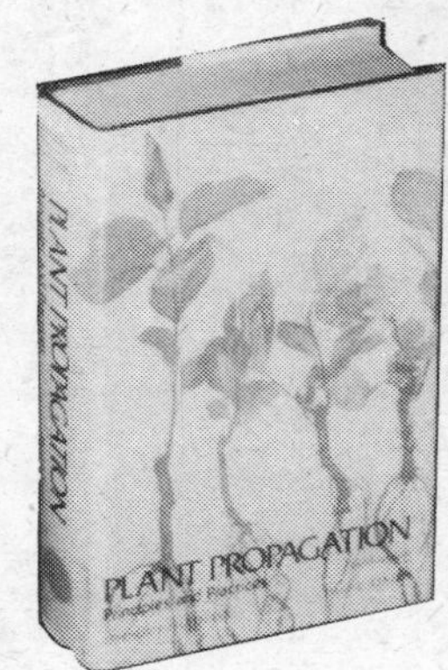

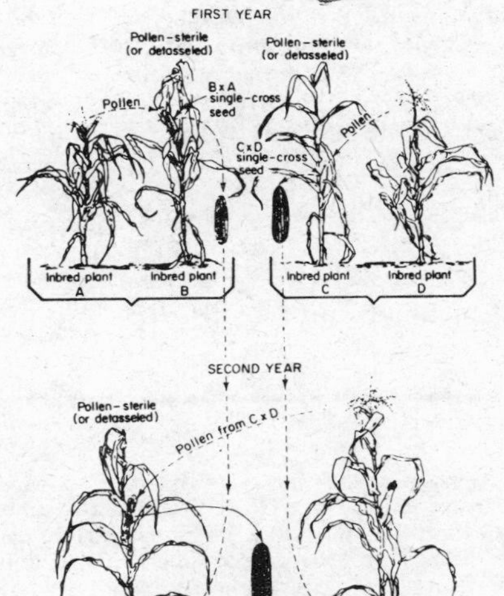

Hybrid varieties have become an increasingly important category of cultivated plants within recent years. These are the progeny produced by the repetitive crossing of two or more parental lines that are maintained either (a) by seed, such as inbred lines, or (b) asexually, such as clones. To produce commercial hybrid seed, the parental lines must be grown side by side so that cross-pollination takes place between them. The seed produced (the F_1 progeny of the cross) is the seed used to grow commercial crops. This cross must be repeated every time the seeds are produced.

Pasture and Range Plants

If you buy this book, it will be because it is surely the handsomest picture book of grasses in existence. Instead of the ubiquitous black and white line drawings (with their own spare sort of good looks) this is a collection of lush watercolor in greens, yellows and lavenders on black backgrounds. There's a remarkable amount of personality in all that wavy stuff out there. And good to use for identification: major range grasses, legumes and shrubs, a modest poison plant section.

Prose is just enough, chatty and informative with a Rombauer-like browseability: tumblegrass is also called ticklegrass, geese graze crabgrass out of crops, stinkgrass seeds are two million to the pound, Sand lovegrass is the ice-cream grass of the prairie. Also common names, scientific names, soil types, seeding suggestions, translation of interesting scientific names, palatability, range, etc.

Designed for lay use, and thus one of the few in the usually encapsulated realms of agrostology and range management. Language is delightfully normal, descriptive English words, and sensual too.

A very pretty book. Creamy.

—Melissa Savage
[Suggested by Debbie Oakes]

Pasture and Range Plants
Phillips Petroleum Co.
1963, 1980; 175 pp.

$9.50 postpaid from:
Phillips Petroleum Co.
4A1 Phillips Bldg.
Bartlesville, OK 74004

Tall fescue (Festúca arundinácea)

Herb Growing

Sixty plus herbs and aromatic plants: how to identify, propagate, harvest and use them. This is a hardback British import, which has something to do with its high price, but it is nicely laid out and easy to use.

—Richard Nilsen

Herb Growing
(A Visual Guide)
The Diagram Group;
Bernard Cleves, Editor
1978; 144 pp.

$12.50 postpaid from:
International Scholarly Book Service
P.O. Box 555
Forest Grove, OR 97116
or Whole Earth Household Store

•

The resentment that gardeners tend to have against the dandelion is by no means shared by everyone. Statistically it contains 12 times the Vitamin A of a lettuce and about three times its Vitamin C. Its young leaves — the bigger leaves are bitter — can be used in salads and may be cooked, like spinach, as a green vegetable. Its flowers are used to make dandelion wine.

THE RISING SUN
NEIGHBORHOOD NEWSLETTER

Sylvia Weinstein's poster for the Board of Education says, "It will be a great day when the schools have all the money they need and the Navy has to hold a bake sale to buy a ship."

BUYING SEED IS A GREAT INVESTMENT; if it is planted and cared for, the return can be a hundred-fold in just a few short months. A tiny living plant is contained in every seed, and within it is the summation of all the environments that affected its predecessors. Seeds are beginnings; they come from a long line of beginnings. Maybe that's why reading seed catalogs on winter nights is so satisfying.
—Rosemary Menninger

ORGANICALLY GROWN SEED

Johnny's Selected Seeds
(Organic Seed and Crop Research)
Catalog

free from:
Johnny's Selected Seeds
Albion, ME 04910

The most complete catalog of organic seed, with many unusual varieties and cool season crops. Primarily vegetables; highly recommended.

Vita Green Farms
(Seed Listing)

free from:
Vita Green Farms
P.O. Box 878
Vista, CA 92803

Organic vegetable and herb seed; fairly wide selection. Also untreated beans and seed potatoes.

Abundant Life Seed Foundation
Catalog

$1 from:
Abundant Life Seed Foundation
Box 772
Port Townsend, WA 98638

A wide selection of organic seed adapted to the Pacific Northwest. Includes vegetables, herbs, wildflowers, flowers and trees.

Self Reliance Seeds
Catalog

$2 from:
Self Reliance Seeds
Box 44 W
Guilderland, NY 12084

Crop seeds for organic farmers. Genetically diverse, old strains of corn, beans and grains.

SEED SWAPPING

Seed Saver's Exchange
Catalog

$3 from:
Seed Saver's Exchange
Kent Whealy
Rural Route 2
Princeton, MO 64673

The Seed Saver's Exchange (formerly the True Seed Exchange) offers home gardeners an opportunity to play around in their back yard gene pool in hopes of expanding its diversity. Members of the Exchange, hundreds of them from North America and several foreign countries, offer seed to each other of rare or old-fashioned fruit and vegetable varieties they have grown.

Both members and non-members can participate in the seed exchange, but members trade seed to cover the postage costs, while non-members must include $1.00 for each seed variety requested.

To become a member you must have something (seeds or cuttings) to offer. The Seed Saver's Exchange Yearbook lists the members with their offers and includes seed saving information and a smattering of plant breeding news from around the world.

Redwood City Seed Company
Catalog

$ .25 from:
Redwood City Seed Co.
P.O. Box 361
Redwood City, CA 94064

Redwood has a seed exchange program; they will swap you some of their seed in exchange for seed you either grow or collect. They are particularly interested in dye plants, wildflowers, herbs and edible plants not available commercially.

HERB CATALOGS

Otto Richter & Sons Ltd.
Catalog

$ .75 from:
Otto Richter & Sons
Herb Catalogue
Goodwood, Ontario
LOC 1AO
Canada

Otto Richter has the largest herb seed catalog, with ancient and common herbs, 10 varieties of basil, carob, belladonna, and even seed for dye plants.

Meadowbrook Herb Garden
Catalog

$ .50 from:
Meadowbrook
Herb Garden
Greene, RI 02827

Meadowbrook carries organically grown herbs and seeds and seaweed.

Greene Herb Gardens
Catalog

free from:
Greene Herb Gardens
Wyoming, RI 02898

Greene's Herbs has a small selection but several hard-to-find herbs are offered. Reasonable prices, and their "catalog" is a charming newsletter.

(See herb suppliers, p. 373.)

3625 ENGLISH LAVENDER/P
L. angustifolia *hicm* 13
Typical form. Compact, narrow foliage; flowers lavender-blue. **Pkt./75¢**
Otto Richter

4040 SPEARMINT/P
M. spicata *tcmi* 135
Best cooking mint. Excellent with carrots, peas and potatoes, and for making mint sauce for roast lamb. **Pkt./75¢**
See also #4460 Pennyroyal (M. pulegium).
Otto Richter

202 YELLOW GLOBE DANVERS: 106 days. Mid-early maturing, slightly flattened, extra hard onions for storage. The bulbs are smaller than Early Yellow Globe, about 2½" (6 cm.) in diameter, with very heavy copper colored skin. Suited to long storage well into spring. Minipack 55¢; PKT. 75¢; Oz. $2.35; ¼ Lb. $5.85; ½ Lb. $9.60; Lb. $16.00; 5 Lbs. @ $15.20.

GROWING SCHEDULE (Key on pg. 46)	MAR	APR	MAY	JUN	JUL	AUG	SEP	OCT	NOV
EARLY YELLOW GLOBE									
YELLOW SWEET SPANISH									
EXTRA EARLY KAIZUKA									

184 KING CROWN: 64 days. A new variety of the Great Lakes group, but over a week earlier in heading. Not only is the lettuce early, the heads are very large, - 7-8" across, and very firm. Sweetness, juicyness, and flavor are among the best, and King Crown grows well despite adverse weather and in a wide range of soil conditions. Resists tipburn and bottom rot.
Minipack 60¢; PKT. 85¢; ½ Oz. $2.15; Oz. $3.60; ¼ Lb. $9.00; ½ Lb. $15.00; Lb. $25.00; 5 Lbs. @ $23.75.

GROWING SCHEDULE (Key on pg. 46)	MAR	APR	MAY	JUN	JUL	AUG	SEP	OCT	NOV
LOOSELEAF LETTUCES									
BIBB LETTUCES									
ROMAINE & CRISPHEAD									

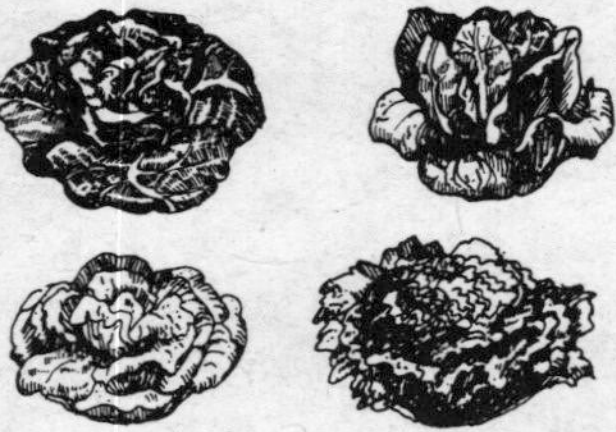

Johnny's Selected Seeds

●

Some Recent North American Seed Company Takeovers

NEW OWNER	SEED COMPANY
Anderson Clayton	Paymaster Farms Tomco-Genetic Giant
Cargill	Dorman Seeds Kroeker Seeds PAG
Celanese	Cepril Inc. Moran Seeds Joseph Harris
Central Soya	O's Gold Seed Co.
Ciba-Geigy	Funk Seeds Int'l. Stewart Seeds Louisiana Seed Co.
FMC Corp.	Seed Research Assoc.
Garden Products	Gurney Seeds
Hilleshoeg/Cardo	Int'l. Forest Seeds Co.
Int'l. Multifoods	Baird Inc. Lynk Bros.
I.T.T.	Burpee Seeds O.M. Scott & Sons
Kent Food Co.	L. Teweles Seed Co.
Kleinwanzieberer Swatzucht AG	Coker's Pedigreed Seed Co.
NAPB (Olin & Royal Dutch Shell)	Agripro, Inc. Tekseed Hybrid
Occidental Petroleum	Ring Around Products
Pioneer Hi-bred	Lankhart Lockett Arnold Thomas Seed Co. Peterson
Pfizer	Clemens Seed Farms Jordan Wholesale Co. Trojan Seed Co. Warwick Seeds
Purex	Advanced Seeds Ferry-Morse Seeds Hulting Hybrids
Rorer-Amchem	Jacques Seed Co.
Sandoz	National-NK Northrup-King Rogers Brothers
Southwide, Inc.	Delta & Pine Land Greenfield Seed
Tate & Lyle	Berger & Plate
Tejon Ranch Co.	Waterman-Loomis Co.
Union Carbide	Keystone Seed Co.
Upjohn	Asgrow Seeds Associated Seeds

Seeds of the Earth

The plant patenting issue, as it is commonly known, seems to be just one stripe on the zebra. **Seeds of the Earth** *reveals a more complex controversy of corporate seed control, third world exploitation, the extinction of our major crops' genetic bases, a possible dependency on a chemically oriented agriculture and other dismal tidings. On the positive side, it offers some excellent recommendations for action regarding each area of controversy.*

There isn't much arm-twisting needed to gain your concern; the facts do the convincing. It will be interesting to watch the battle lines form, but, the corporate viewpoint isn't on the defensive . . . yet.

—Shane Smith
[Suggested by Judy Clark]

Seeds of the Earth
(A Private or Public Resource?)
1979; 120 pp.

$7.50 (U.S. dollars)
(specify English, French, or Spanish edition)
postpaid from:
Inter Pares
205 Pretoria Avenue
Ottawa, KIS 1X1
Canada

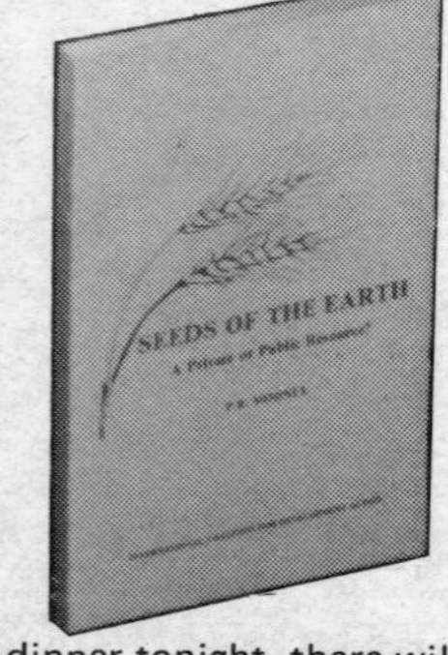

●

When you settle down to dinner tonight, there will be nothing on your plate that does not come to you directly, and/or indirectly, from the Third World. Our food system is vastly more interdependent than most of us would have imagined. Should anything happen to severely reduce the genetic diversity of the Third World, or make it impossible for the First World to obtain vital germ plasm, the potential for a world-wide food crisis would be very real.

Graham Center Seed Directory →

This booklet is a collection of access to small seed companies that offer many of the older, forgotten and traditional seed varieties. It also includes a brief but thorough discussion of the seed patenting issue.

The Graham Center is a non-profit organization dedicated to the preservation and promotion of the small family farm. They are also a clearinghouse for information dealing with the fight against plant seed patenting in the U.S. The **Seed Directory** *is a dollar well spent.*

—Shane Smith

Graham Center Seed Directory
Cary Fowler
1979; 16 pp.

$1 postpaid from:
Frank Porter
Graham Center
Rt. 3, Box 95
Wadesboro, NC 28170

●

Genetic 'erosion' means far more than a theoretical loss for future scientists: "Quite literally, the genetic diversity of a millennium in a particular variety can disappear in a single bowl of porridge . . . Suddenly in the 1970s, we are discovering Mexican farmers growing hybrid corn seed from a midwestern seed firm, Tibetan farmers planting barley from a Scandinavian plant breeding station, and Turkish farmers planting wheat from the Mexican programme. Each of these classic areas of crop-specific genetic diversity is rapidly becoming an area of seed uniformity."

—*Dr. Garrison Wilkes, Boston, Mass, USA, 1977.*

●

We have noted that the Green Revolution was also a fertilizer or agrichemical revolution; therefore, seeds and chemicals are already linked in farming practices. Now that biocide firms are also seed companies, however, there is more to understand about their interests in the seed industry.

GENERAL GARDEN CATALOGS

All are free.

W. Atlee Burpee Co.
P.O. Box 748
Riverside, CA 92502

Burpee is the biggest, fastest and most efficient of the seed catalogs, but they run out of their catalogs by April so order it in January.

Joseph Harris & Co.
Moreton Farm
Rochester, NY 14624

Harris Seeds is a classy commercial vegetable growers catalog with the best descriptions of different varieties of any of the companies listed here. No minimum order even though they primarily sell bulk seed.

Butterbrooke Farm
87 Barry Road
Oxford, CT 06483

Butterbrooke has the lowest prices — $.25 per packet of 100 seeds, for 50 basic vegetable varieties.

Henry Field Seed and Nursery
Shenandoah, IA 51602

Henry Field's has a full catalog of vegetables, flowers and fruit trees at low prices. Since 1892.

Stokes Seeds, Inc.
737 Main Street
Box 548
Buffalo, NY 14240

Stokes has bulk seed for all vegetables and more varieties per vegetable than any other company.

R.H. Shumway Seedsman
628 Cedar Street
Rockford, IL 61101

Shumway, after 110 years, is one of the few large seed companies that is still locally owned. Specializing in vegetables and flowers at prices slightly lower than Stokes' but higher than Field's — an attractive catalog.

Geo. W. Park Seed Co., Inc.
P.O. Box 31
Greenwood, SC 29447

One of the best. Flower and vegetable seed in abundant variety.

Internode Seed Co.
Box 2011, Dept. L
So. San Francisco, CA 94080

A smaller seed company, with excellent vegetable and herb seed and the prettiest packets in the business. Low prices, too.

Gurney Seed & Nursery Co.
Yankton, SD 57079

Gurney is the most complete northern climate catalog, with the best guarantee in the business. At least a few varieties of everything — even blue potatoes.

J.E. Miller Nurseries
Canadaigna, NY 14424

Miller's specializes in a wide selection of semi-dwarf apples in addition to berries, standard fruits and nuts.

Stark Brothers' Nurseries and Orchards
Louisiana, MO 63353

Stark Brothers' is one of the oldest and largest fruit nurseries in the country. Many semi-dwarf varieties.

Thompson and Morgan
P.O. Box 24
401 Kennedy Blvd.
Somerdale, NJ 08083

Thompson and Morgan is the catalog for hard to find seed, including loofah, passion fruits, Chinese and other exotic vegetables, as well as common vegetables, herbs and flowers.

Sanctuary Seeds
1913 Yew Street
Vancouver, B.C.
Canada V6K 3G3

Sanctuary Seeds has a lovely little catalog with a complete vegetable and herb listing, including some oriental varieties. All seed is untreated, but not all is organically grown. Special discount for food co-ops.

Musser Forests
Box 340
Indiana, PA 15701

Musser Forests handles tree seedlings and some shrubs. The largest nursery of its kind in the U.S.

UNUSUAL SEED CATALOGS

Exotica Seeds Co.
Catalog
$1 from:
Exotica Seeds Co.
1742 Laurel Canyon Rd.
Los Angeles, CA 90046

Exotica Seeds is a small Los Angeles outfit involved in enlarging the tropics. Founder Steven Spangler takes yearly trips to the Pacific, Mexico, and South America looking for high-altitude, cold-adapted forms of tropical fruits and vegetables. No North Dakota papayas yet — but try the Andean tree tomatoes, from 8000 feet in Ecuador.

Kitazawa Seed Co.
Catalog
free from:
Kitazawa Seed Co.
A 356 W. Taylor St.
San Jose, CA 95110

Kitazawa is a supplier of oriental seeds such as Chinese cabbage, Japanese onion, edible burdock, etc.

Horticultural Enterprises
Catalog
free from:
Horticultural Enterprises
P.O. Box 340082
Dallas, TX 75234

29 varieties of chili peppers and a handful of Mexican vegetables in a catalog that's really a poster.

Vermont Bean Seed Company
Catalog
free from:
Vermont Bean Seed Co.
Garden Lane
Bomoseen, VT 05732

This company ran some ads last year in large circulation gardening magazines and got swamped. One result is that this year they have discontinued selling packets of seed (see your local nursery, or another catalog, for these). Minimum orders are now ½ lb. of seed, plus postage and handling.

Nichols Garden Nursery
Catalog
free from:
Nichols Garden Nursery
1190 NW Pacific Hwy.
Albany, OR 97321

Nichols' sells rare seeds and herbs and plants, plus beer and wine-making supplies.

NATIVE PLANTS

Environmental Seed Producers, Inc.
Price list
free from:
Environmental Seed Producers, Inc.
P.O. Box 5904
El Monte, CA 91734

E.S.P. has a unique wildflower seed "catalog" that's actually a stack of 64 file cards in a zip-open plastic pouch. Each card duplicates the seed packet, with color photo on one side, full info on the back. By combining short sentences with a hole punch system, the card gives the plant's basic statistics, health requirements, native territory, etc. Their seed isn't cheap but it's reliable. Sold in bulk only.

Soil Conservation Society of America
Catalog
$2 from:
Soil Conservation Society of America
7515 Northeast Ankeny Road
Ankeny, IA 50021

Soil Conservation Society of America gives sources of native seeds and plants and identifies local native plant nurseries. Listings from every region in the U.S. except the Southeast.

Gardens of the Blue Ridge
Catalog
free from:
Gardens of the Blue Ridge
Ashford, NC 28603

Gardens of the Blue Ridge is a pretty catalog of wildflowers, trees, shrubs and bulbs from the East and South.

Larner Seeds
Pricelist
free from:
Larner Seeds
P.O. Box 11143
Palo Alto, CA 94305

Larner carries hand-gathered seed of native plants and wildflowers.

Woodland Acres Nursery
Catalog
$ .25 from:
Woodland Acres Nursery
Rt. 2
Crivitz, WI 54114

Woodland Acres Nursery specializes in wildflowers and ferns; they sell mostly live plants which they can ship successfully.

Grass Land
Jim and Alice Wilson, text
Steven C. Wilson, photography
1967; 30 pp.
$3.25 postpaid

Catalog and price list
free
all from:
Stock Seed Farms, Inc.
Box 112
Murdock, NB 68407

Grass Land specializes in native American prairie grass seed for farmers, conservation plantings and landscaping. They also handle non-native species, legumes and prairie flower seed. They also have a wealth of how-to information on grasses, lawns and pastures which they sell as mimeographed handouts for $ .30 each. **Grass Land** *is a booklet of color photography celebrating the prairie; it shows that these folks love the product they sell.*

★ **Dwarf Telephone or Daisy Pea - 70 days.** Our improved strain is a very vigorous grower standing about 2' high. Because of its hardy upright growth some people grow the Dwarf Telephone without any support. The pods are round and fat, filled with 9 or 10 large, lush green peas. The Dwarf Telephone is very popular with our farmers and market gardeners here in Vermont. It will grow very well in cooler climates.

Vermont Bean

HUSTLER
EARLY FREEZER

★ **Hustler - 57 days.** A super early new variety just developed for fresh table use and freezing. A lush garden-green 28" vigorous plant that "hustles" along the vine producing exceptionally fine quality sweet, deep green peas. Early enough for all gardens, in all climates. Always a heavy cropper and reliable! We have found no better freezing peas on the market. We guarantee the Hustler will be the pride of your garden.

Vermont Bean

CHINESE GIANT PEPPER

653 Chinese Giant

For size this pepper is unequalled. Fruits are large, with moderately thick meat. Tender and sweet flavored. Rich green color turns a brilliant cherry red at maturity. Slice it or use as a stuffed pepper for excellent results. **Pkt. $.90; ½ oz. $1.40; oz. $2.50; ¼ lb. $7.50; ½ lb. $13.50; 1 lb. $24.00.**

Shumway's

569 Southport White Globe

65 days for spring onions and 120 days for large round onions with pure paper white skin. The flesh is also pure white, sweet, juicy and mild flavored. Often grown as a spring onion. Stores well for winter consumption. A great early market onion and a big money maker for large commercial growers. **Pkt. $.70; oz. $2.50; ¼ lb. $7.50; ½ lb. $13.50; 1 lb. $24.00.**

Shumway's

116 QUICKSILVER White Sweet Corn

An Earlier Silver Queen Type

Bred for early planting and ready *nearly three weeks* ahead of Silver Queen. This is a Harris development that everyone who enjoys the real corn taste of white sweet corn should try. Its ears are most attractive, 7–7½ inches long and filled right to the tips with kernels of glistening white. Quicksilver sprouts and grows quickly even in chilly soil, and will provide you with big yields of particularly delicious white corn in the second-early season.
Pkt. 75c; ½ Lb. $2.10; Lb. $3.50; 5 Lbs. $14.00; 10 Lbs. $25.00.

Harris

SMALL RED CHILI PEPPER

660 Small Red Chili

80 days. One of the hottest peppers for making pickles and tabasco sauce. Small, deep red, cone shaped peppers about 2 inches long. Can be dried for winter use. **Pkt. $.90; ½ oz. $1.40; oz. $2.50; ¼ lb. $7.50; ½ lb. $13.50; 1 lb. $24.00.**

Shumway's

8934 Sungold. Dozens of big, full-double blooms of brilliant golden-yellow. 5 ft. Pkt. (100 seeds) 50c; 2 Pkts. 90c; 4 Pkts. $1.60.

Harris

Picotee Marginata

Want the finest for your garden, patio, porch or greenhouse? This beautiful form of the ruffled Begonia is one of the most spectacular of all! Each full, double flower has heavily ruffled and fluted petals, their edges in a contrasting color to the rest of the flower.

7141—APRICOT WITH SCARLET EDGE
7142—WHITE WITH PINK EDGE
7143—WHITE WITH RED EDGE
7147—PICOTEE MARGINATA MIXED

$1.85 each; 3 (one item) **$4.70;** 5 (one item) **$7.75**

Park Seed

THE RISING SUN
NEIGHBORHOOD NEWSLETTER

Rectangles do not occur in nature but are frequent where people live.

Hop

The Oxford Book of Food Plants

A beautiful book, for looking and for reference. Color plates as illustration of every plant, emphasizing the part which supplies food. Arranged in a practical way — plants are grouped according to the kind of food they produce: fruits, herbs, leaf vegetables, oil crops, sugar crops, root vegetables, etc. Common and botanical name included, and an index which lists both, plus a glossary of descriptive botanical words. Description of each plant tells its use, history, countries of origin and regions where it grows, along with a physical description accompanied by a drawing, food value, and economic value. —D. Smith

The Oxford Book of Food Plants
G.B. Masefield, M. Wallis, S.G. Harrison, and B.E. Nicholson
1969; 205 pp.
$17.95 postpaid from:
Oxford University Press
16-00 Pollitt Drive
Fair Lawn, NJ 07140
or Whole Earth Household Store

↑

Hop *(Humulus lupulus)* is a native of Europe (including the British Isles), and western Asia. It does not seem to have been widely used for brewing beer before the Middle Ages, although ale was flavoured with various bitter herbs in early times. Hopped ale was introduced from the Continent and later brewed in Britain from imported hops during the 15th century. Hops did not become a commercial crop in this country until about 1520. Today, they are grown in many parts of the world, where conditions are suitable, e.g. in Australia, New Zealand, and North America, as well as in Europe. The part used in brewing is the female 'cone', which consists of a cluster of pale, yellowish-green bracts and bracteoles, enclosing the small flowers and later the fruits. Resin glands, at the base of the bracteoles, produce glistening yellow spots of lupulin — the substance containing the essential oils and soft resins which give the hop its aroma and beer its flavour. The small male flowers (1A) are normally borne on separate plants and are quite different in appearance.

The hop is a perennial vine belonging to the Hemp family (Cannabiaceae). It dies down to near ground level at the end of the season and produces new shoots each spring. The shoots, or 'bines', grow rapidly, reaching a length of 18 to 25 feet (1B). In cultivation, they are trained up a framework of poles, wires and strings. Before World War II, hops were traditionally picked by hand. Now, about 90 percent of the English crop is picked by machine.

The young shoots, which are thinned out in spring, are used as a boiled vegetable in some countries but have never become popular in Britain.

Winged Bean Flyer

A newsletter of research on the tropical winged bean, a high-protein legume that can grow in North America. —Rosemary Menninger

The Winged Bean Flyer
$2/year (2 issues)
postpaid from:
International Council for the Development of Underutilized Plants
18 Meadow Park Court
Orinda, CA 94563
or The Winged Bean Flyer
c/o Ms. J.C. Sison
Searca College, Laguna,
Phillipines 3720

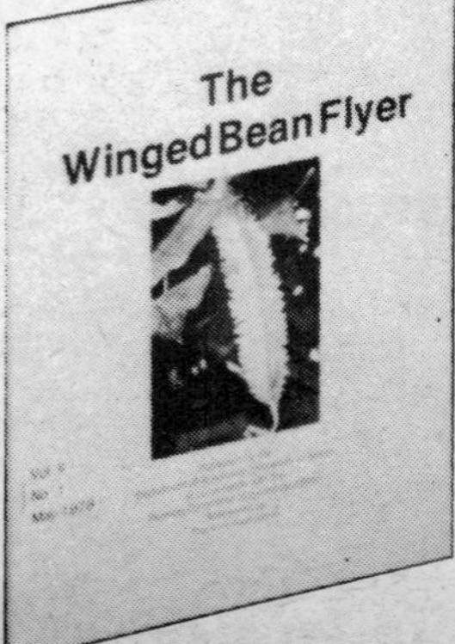

Amaranth

To the Aztecs, amaranth was like buffalo — a food of many uses and part of sacrificial rites. Rodale Press encourages its readers to try it in their gardens. The results of the amateurs' efforts combined with those of scientists make this an interesting and useful book. Chickens love the grain of amaranth, and the leaves are high in protein. —Rosemary Menninger

Amaranth
(From the Past for the Future)
John N. Cole
1979; 300 pp.
$8.95 postpaid from:
Rodale Books
33 East Minor
Emmaus, PA 18049
or Whole Earth Household Store

•

Wherever you look for information about the amaranth's times past, you find that this modest plant which evolved from one of the planet's most ubiquitous weeds is endowed with more than merely nutritive assets. . . .

Its flowers are still placed on the altars of cathedrals in Spain. English colonists sailing for America carried amulets of the seed with them; later, Victorian Americans would claim that the plant attracted lightning. Mexicans of ancient times made idols from amaranth seed for their religious ceremonies; after those ancient deities had been replaced, they molded rosary beads from amaranth dough. Hopi Indians in North America have a centuries-old tradition of using amaranth dough as a traditional food for ritual celebrations. Hondurans grow the plant as a magic medicine, Inca cultures used it in their complex religious pageants. The Chinese call it millet from heaven, and in India it is known as the immortal grain. . . .

Are you aware of any other foodstuff that is known by its metaphysical as well as its physical dimensions around the world, across time and through cultures as diverse as the Hopi Indian and the Szechwan Chinese?

Seeds of an improved selection of A. hypochondriacus are available from Gurney Seed and Nursery Co., Yankton, SD 55078; and Johnny's Selected Seeds, Albion, ME 04910.

Underexploited Tropical Plants with Promising Economic Value

The modern classic of new crops research. Thirty-six plants are discussed: their crop potential, limitations and specific research needs. This book has its own fan club — people who go on to subscribe to "Winged Bean Flyer," reviewed below. —Rosemary Menninger

Underexploited Tropical Plants with Promising Economic Value
(Order No. PB 251 656)
National Academy of Sciences
1975; 186 pp.
$12 postpaid from:
NTIS
U.S. Department of Commerce
5285 Port Royal Road
Springfield, VA 22161

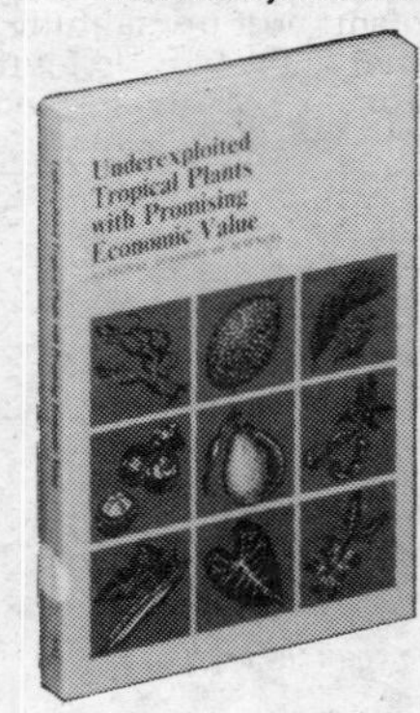

Making Aquatic Weeds Useful

Includes uses of water plants for methane production and for extraction of heavy metals from the water. —Rosemary Menninger

Making Aquatic Weeds Useful
(Some Perspectives for Developing Countries)
No. PB 265 161
1976; 175 pp.

$12 postpaid from:
NTIS
U.S. Dept. of Commerce
5285 Port Royal Road
Springfield, VA 22161

Wild Rice

Lord god, imagine having enough wild rice.

I always thought that Indians had some kind of legal monopoly on this expensive staple-delicacy. Maybe not. Maybe you can grow the expensive staple-delicacy in your own fresh-water shallows. —SB
[Suggested by Ron O'dor]

Wild Rice
William G. Dore
1975; 84 pp.
$3.60 postpaid from:
Information Canada
Ottowa, Ontario
Canada K14 0S9

Wild rice

Grain

Hulled

•

All the wild-rice sold today comes from untended stands that grow in streams and other waterways. There have been attempts to control the supply and level of the water, or to create new impoundments in localities where this is possible, but cultivation in a paddy has been done only on an experimental scale. Most of the grain is still harvested by hand from canoes. The operation of harvesting, however, is conducted on a much larger scale than formerly, and, in some regions, it follows a well-organized plan.

Jojoba Happenings

The desert shrub jojoba (ho-hó-ba) produces a finer oil than even the sperm whale — which might be protected by widespread jojoba cultivation — and shows promise as a highly economic arid land crop. The field is developing rapidly. Stay current with **Jojoba Happenings.** —SB

Jojoba Happenings
$10/year (4 issues)
postpaid from:
Jojoba Happenings
845 N. Park Avenue
Tucson, AZ 85719

General Viticulture

This book includes everything needed to know by anyone really interested in grapes. It is mainly concerned with vineyard production but it contains valuable information for small arbors and home gardening as well. Winkler deals with soils, propagation, pruning, irrigation, diseases, pests, raisins, wine grapes, table grapes and even includes a detailed appendix of costs involved. This book is the only complete work on grape production. Make your own raisins, too. —Ron Pietrowski

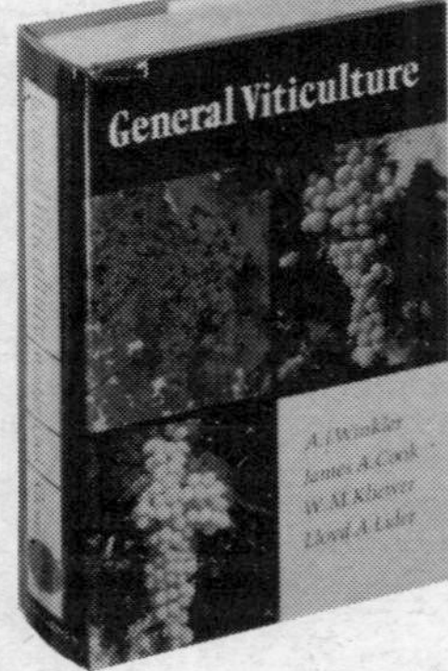

General Viticulture
A.J. Winkler, et al.
1974; 710 pp.
$27.50 postpaid from:
University of California Press
2223 Fulton Street
Berkeley, CA 94720
or Whole Earth Household Store

A wine grape in region 1 of the North Coastal area of California in spring. →

•

For best development the *vinifera* grape requires long, warm-to-hot, dry summers and cool winters. It is not suited to humid summers, owing to its susceptibility to certain fungus diseases and insect pests that flourish under humid conditions. Neither will it withstand intense winter cold. A long growing season is required to mature the fruit, and, since the green parts of growing vines are likely to be frozen at temperatures below 30°F., areas subject to late spring and early fall frosts must be avoided. Rain is desirable during the winter, but deficiencies in rainfall can be made up by irrigation. Rains early in the growing season make disease and pest control difficult, but are otherwise not detrimental to the growth of the vine. Rains or cloudy weather during the blooming period may result in a poor set of the berries, especially in some varieties, and rains during ripening and harvest permit much damage through fruit rot. Where raisins are to be produced by sun-drying between the vine-rows, as in California, a month of clear, warm, rainless weather is essential after the grapes are mature. Higher humidity can be tolerated in cool regions than in warm regions.

GROWING YOUR OWN MARIJUANA SAVES A LOT OF MONEY; *you get better product than you can buy; there's no question of paraquat poisoning in the weed; you're not involved in enriching the mafia, a few families in Colombia, or anti-smuggling bureaucracies; and it's a gorgeous plant. Tens of thousands of Americans have been introduced to the joys of gardening by first growing their own dope. Later they diversified to food.* —SB

Marijuana Grower's Guide

If you are only going to buy one book on the subject, this is the choice. How to grow it indoors and out, how to harvest, dry and store. There is an index, and the chapters are broken down into sections, so a beginner can navigate easily. For the serious grower or breeder, there is enough information on cannabinoids — the stuff that produces the high — to bring back memories of college organic chemistry.
—Richard Nilsen

% THC: 1.0, 2.0, 3.0, 4.0
AGE IN WEEKS: 0 2 4 6 8 10 12 14 16 18 20 22 24 26 28 30
germination · seedling · vegetative · preflowering · flowering · seed set
number of blades increases; number of blades decreases; phyllotaxy changes to alternate; growth slows; full bloom; pollen released; full bloom; seeds matured
male: ♂♂♂♂ female: ++++ juveniles; ♂♂♂♂ ♀♀♀♀ adults (flowering)

THC graph.

Marijuana Grower's Guide
(Deluxe edition)
Mel Frank and
Ed Rosenthal
1978; 330 pp.
$9.95 postpaid from:
And/Or Press
P.O. Box 2246
Berkeley, CA 94702

•

The life cycle of *Cannabis* is usually complete in four to nine months. The actual time depends on variety, but it is regulated by local growing conditions, specifically the photoperiod (length of day vs. night). *Cannabis* is a long-night (or short-day) plant. When exposed to a period of two weeks of long nights — that is, 13 or more hours of continuous darkness each night — the plants respond by flowering. This has important implications, for it allows the grower to control the life cycle of the plant and adapt it to local growing conditions or unique situations. Since you can control flowering, you control maturation and, hence, the age of the plants at harvest.

•

A small but well-cultivated garden, say, ten by ten feet, can yield over four pounds of grass each crop. By planning realistically, you'll harvest a good stash of potent grass rather than a lot of disappointment.

Most people who grow marijuana plant it in their backyards. They hide the plants from curious neighbors and passers-by with walls, fences, arbors, or similar enclosures. Some people plant *Cannibis* as part of their vegetable garden, pruning the plants to make them less conspicuous.

Gardeners often use ingenious ideas to keep their gardens secret. A woman on Long Island grows over thirty large plants in containers in her drained swimming pool. Although some of the plants reach a height of 12 feet, they can't be seen over the enclosing fence.

A couple living near Nashville, Tennessee, took the roof off their three-car garage and painted the walls white to create a high-walled garden. Other growers use sheds with translucent roofs.

•

Cannabis can be detected from both the ground and the air. From the ground, marijuana is revealed by its familiar shape, unmistakeable leaves, and odor. Tall plants are usually more conspicuous than shorter ones. From the air, stands may have a different color than the surrounding vegetation, especially where natural vegetation is not as lush as marijuana. Individual plants usually have a circular profile when viewed from above; this can be altered by bending or pruning the plant. Varieties which are naturally tall-growing may need to be cut several times during the season to keep them hidden.

Sinsemilla

Best coffee table dope book. But also the book most likely to have mud-smudged pages, since it is the easiest one to use for sexing plants. For these reasons it is a book for beginners, although the kind of dope this book shows you how to grow — seedless female flower buds, full of resin — is anything but elementary.
—Richard Nilsen

Sinsemilla
(Marijuana Flowers)
Jim Richardson
photographs by
Arik Woods
1976; 96 pp.
$11.95 postpaid from:
And/Or Press
P.O. Box 2246
Berkeley, CA 94702

→

We must look very closely to see where the hemp first shows gender. We look near the top of the plant, on the main stalk or on the large branches, usually at the second or third crotch below the growing tip. At the crotch, large fan leaves and branch systems shoot out from the trunk. Here on the face of the stalk occurs a swelling called a node. From the nodes grow spearlike protrusions one-fourth to one-half inch long. Where the branches grow opposite, these leaf spurs cross their tips, forming a tipi pattern against the trunk. Nestled behind the spur, in the crotch formed by the leaf stem and the main stalk, appear the first sexual organs. These single, isolated flowers can usually be seen several weeks before the true flower clusters become visible on the branches. Their cycle is identical to that of the later flowers.

•

If the flowers are to be harvested properly, the rhythm of each plant must be carefully observed during florescence. The scent of the blossoms is the best indication of maturity. The aroma is the quintessence of the herb. Ripe blossoms have an electric sweetness and an ethereal penetrating quality. After the peak of bloom, the aroma becomes more earthy and begins to acquire more body. It gradually loses its lightness and takes on a heavier aspect.

The Primo Plant

What a lovely pleasure. Quiet writing with ease and charm. You hardly notice all the attentive experience behind the advice. Very good advice. My one hesitancy — the drawings don't help.
—Peter Warshall

The Primo Plant
(Growing Sinsemilla
Marijuana)
Mountain Girl
1977; 100 pp.
$4.50 postpaid from:
Wingbow Press
c/o Bookpeople
2940 Seventh Street
Berkeley, CA 94710

•

All pot fans have heard of sinsemilla. This translates to "seedless." Sinsemilla is a female plant grown to full blossoming maturity without any male pollen reaching it. No pollen, no seeds. Why is this desirable? Seeds are the final, ultimate purpose of marijuana life, so the strong female plant will make as many as it can (if you let it). Pot seeds are high in proteins, fats, and stored sugars to start that baby plant. The plant will spend its entire store of nutrients and energy making pounds of seeds, not resin.

Seedless or very slightly seeded plants make many more flowers, with a much stronger high and a sweeter taste. Plants grown this way will continue to produce new flowers every day at the tops of each flower cluster until the tops are huge. Plants that have been heavily pollinated seem to stop growing new flowers right away, and throw all their energy into seed making.

A few seeds are a good idea, two or three per top. It helps the plant remain convinced of its femininity, assuring next year's crop in case the plant is "The One." It is truly entertaining to begin crossing favorite types and this is where the labels pay off.

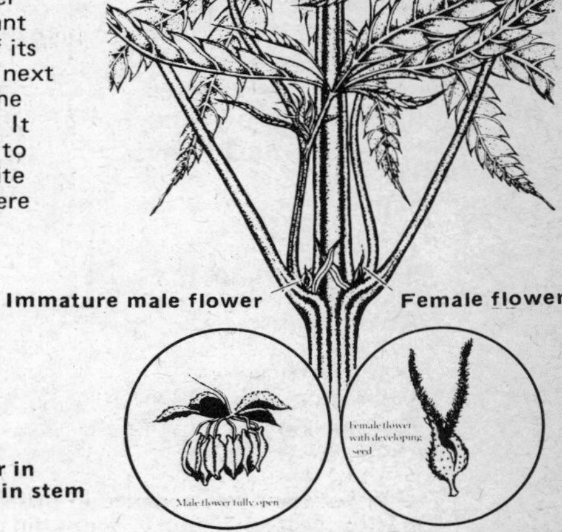

Immature male flower **Female flower**

→ **Early flowers appear in the joints on the main stem**

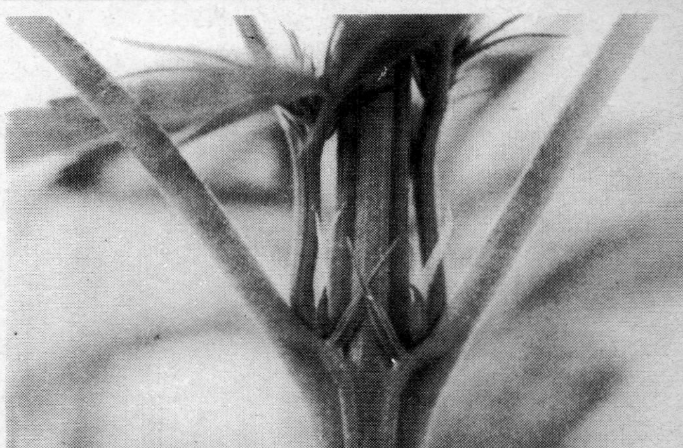

The classic female form

The Marijuana Farmers

This book veers between being a political tract and a very readable brief history of the economic and spiritual uses of marijuana. Frazier, who has "decided to donate a portion of the profits from this book toward reestablishing the hemp industry in North America," emphasizes the origins and movement of the plant throughout the world and its uses as hemp — in rope, clothing and paper. An Appendix reprints a growers guide from 1765.
—Richard Nilsen

The Marijuana Farmers
(Hemp cults
and cultures)
Jack Frazier
1974; 133 pp.
$4.95 postpaid from:
Solar Age Press
Indian Mills, WV 24949

A
TREATISE
OF
Hemp-Hufbandry;

Being a Collection of approved Inftructions, as to the Choice and Preparation of the Soils, moft proper for the *Growth* of that ufeful and valuable material, and alfo as to the fubfequent Management thereof, agreable to the Experience of feveralCountries wherein it has been produced, both in *Europe* and *America*.

With fome introductory Obfervations, upon the Neceffity which the *American Britifh* Colonies are under, generally to engage in the faid Production; and upon the extenfive Ufefulnefs, and great Utility of the faid material.

By EDMUND QUINCY, *Efq*;

Lucem redde tuae--------Patriae. Hor.

BOSTON:

Printed by *Green* & *Ruffell*, by Order of the Honorable Houfe of REPRESENTATIVES. MDCCLXV.

THE RISING SUN
NEIGHBORHOOD NEWSLETTER

Young Charles Darwin thought you shouldn't address the question of "Why Are There Species?" Why, for example, aren't we all worms or elephants or snail darters, until you had studied particular species for a while, like years. His species were barnacles; he discovered a new kind of barnacle but found out he couldn't honestly say shit about it until he rethought and reobserved barnacledom as a whole, so he did, in his handy home lab, for a decade or two, while also thinking about the origin of all the species. When Darwin's son was visiting a neighbor's house he seemed puzzled and asked later, "But where does he do his barnacles?"

Information from *Apes, Angels and Victorians*.

Planning for an Individual Water System

The no-fooling-around American-style do-it-yourself manual. High tech. The best for electric pumps and wiring your water supply system. Gorgeously illustrated with lots of great safety tips. —Peter Warshall

Planning for an Individual Water System
American Association for Vocational Instructional Materials
1973; 156 pp.

$6.95 postpaid from:
American Association for Vocational Instructional Materials
Engineering Center
Athens, GA 30602
or Whole Earth Household Store

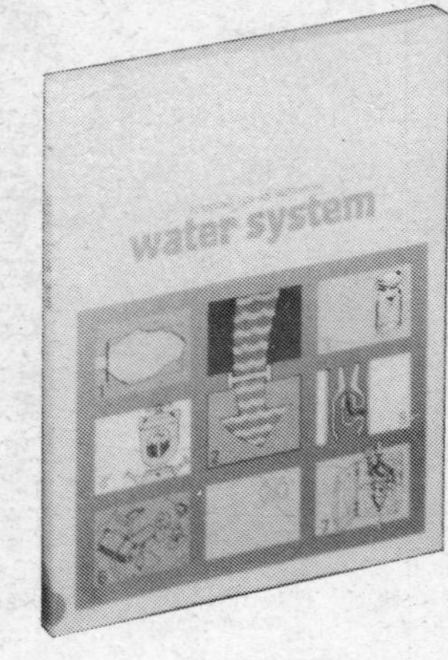

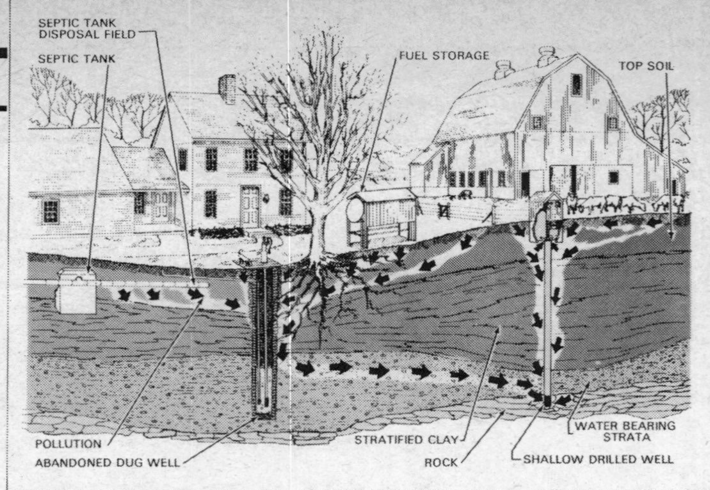

Shallow wells can become polluted more readily than deep wells. Note that pollution can come from underground sources as well as from surface sources.

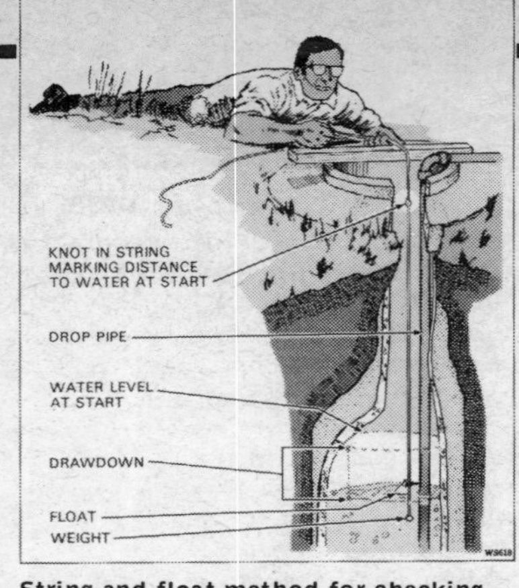

String-and-float method for checking draw-down in wells of large diameter.

Methods of roof washing for cistern water. (a) Hand-operated diversion valve used to waste first rainfall. After roof is washed, the valve is changed so water will enter the cistern. (b) Automatic roofwash. The first rainfall flows into the drum. After the drum is filled, the remaining water flows into the cistern. During a period without rainfall, water dripping from the opening in the waste line empties the drum. →

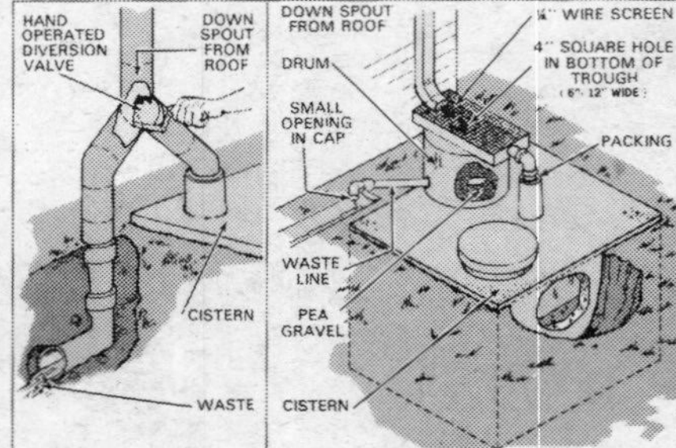

Manual of Individual Water Supply Systems

Duplicates most of the material in **Planning for an Individual Water System** *for less money. Published by the Environmental Protection Agency, it has more information on preventing possible health problems, understanding water quality, and techniques like well disinfection.*

Gives a good feel for the present tone of government attitudes (interference?) toward single household water supply (yuk! so much chlorine!). —Peter Warshall

Manual of Individual Water Supply Systems
Environmental Protection Agency
#055-001-00626-8

$3 postpaid from:
Superintendent of Documents
Government Printing Office
Washington, DC 20402
or Whole Earth Household Store

•

TYPES OF WELLS

Wells may be classified with respect to construction methods as dug, bored, driven, drilled, and jetted.

Drilled wells may be drilled by either the rotary or percussion method.

Each type of well has distinguishing physical characteristics and is best adapted to meet particular water-development requirements.

The following factors should be considered when choosing the type of well to be constructed in a given situation.

1. Characteristics of the subsurface strata to be penetrated and their influence upon the methods of construction.
2. Hydrology of the specific situation and hydraulic properties of the aquifer; seasonal fluctuations of water levels.
3. Degree of sanitary protection desired, particularly as this is affected by well depth.
4. Cost of construction work and materials.

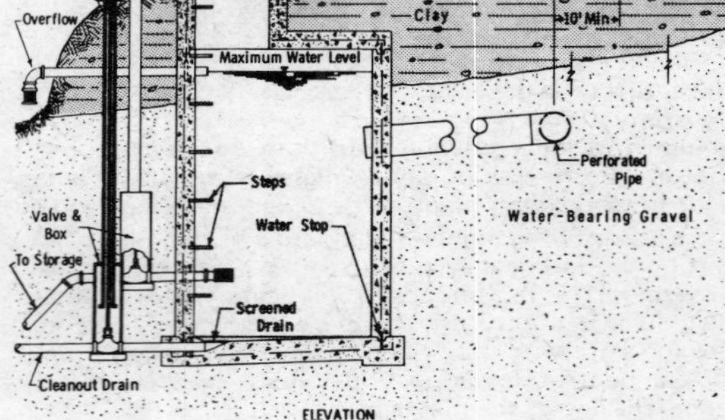

Spring protection.

Drip irrigation

Drip irrigation puts water where the plant roots are, at a controlled rate that discourages waterlogging of the soil — allowing a healthy moisture/air/soil ratio to exist in the ground. It can be used in any climate where supplemental irrigation is required, but it is especially beneficial in areas of relatively low rainfall (because it conserves water) and where the growing season is dry. Another benefit is reduced cultivation requirements; few weeds grow in the unwatered spaces between the irrigated crops. Harvests are not dependent on watering schedules, since the rows between the crops stay dry. Drip irrigation is unsurpassed for vineyards, bushes, and young trees. —David Batts

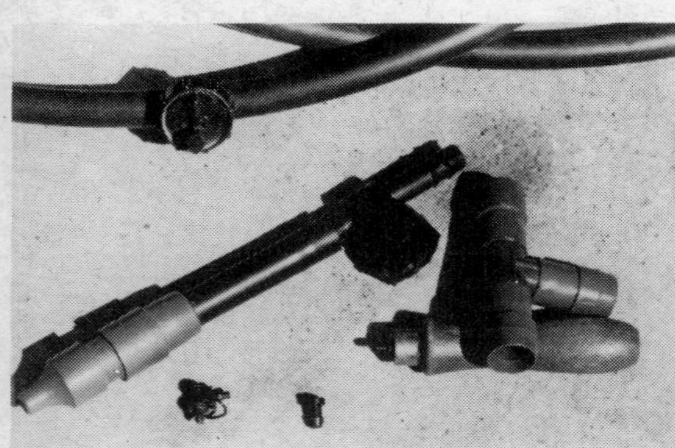

↑

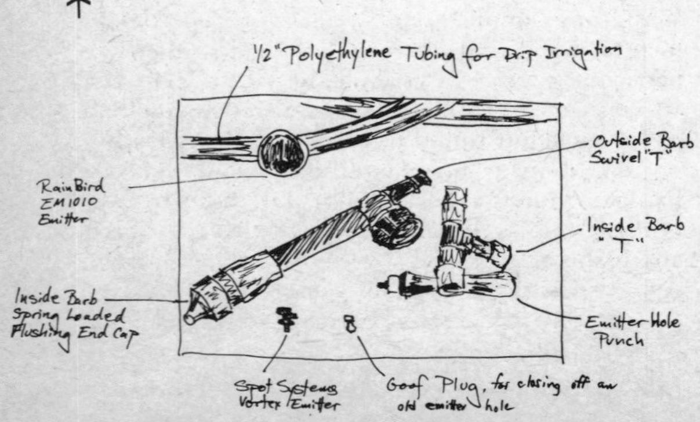

Drip Irrigation & Low Volume Sprinkler Suppliers

Aquatic Irrigation Systems, Inc.
619e E. Gutierrez
Santa Barbara, CA 93103
(805) 965-5125

Bowsmith
P.O. Box 428
Exeter, CA 93221
(209) 592-9485

Chapin Watermatics, Inc.
740 Water Street
Watertown, NY 13601
(315) 782-1170

DICOA Irrigation Systems, Inc.
14675 Titus Street
Panorama City, CA 91402

PEPCO
10030 S. Greenleaf Ave.
Santa Fe Springs, CA 90670
(213) 944-6171

Rain Bird
7045 North Grand Ave.
Glendora, CA 91740

Reed Irrigation Systems
1588 N. Marshall Street
P.O. Box X
El Cajon, CA 92022
(714) 440-2100
Telex 695411

Spot Systems
div. of Wisdom Industries
1559 Sunland Way
Costa Mesa, CA 92626
(714) 957-8071

Submatic Irrigation Systems
P.O. Box 246
Lubbock, TX 79408
(806) 747-9000

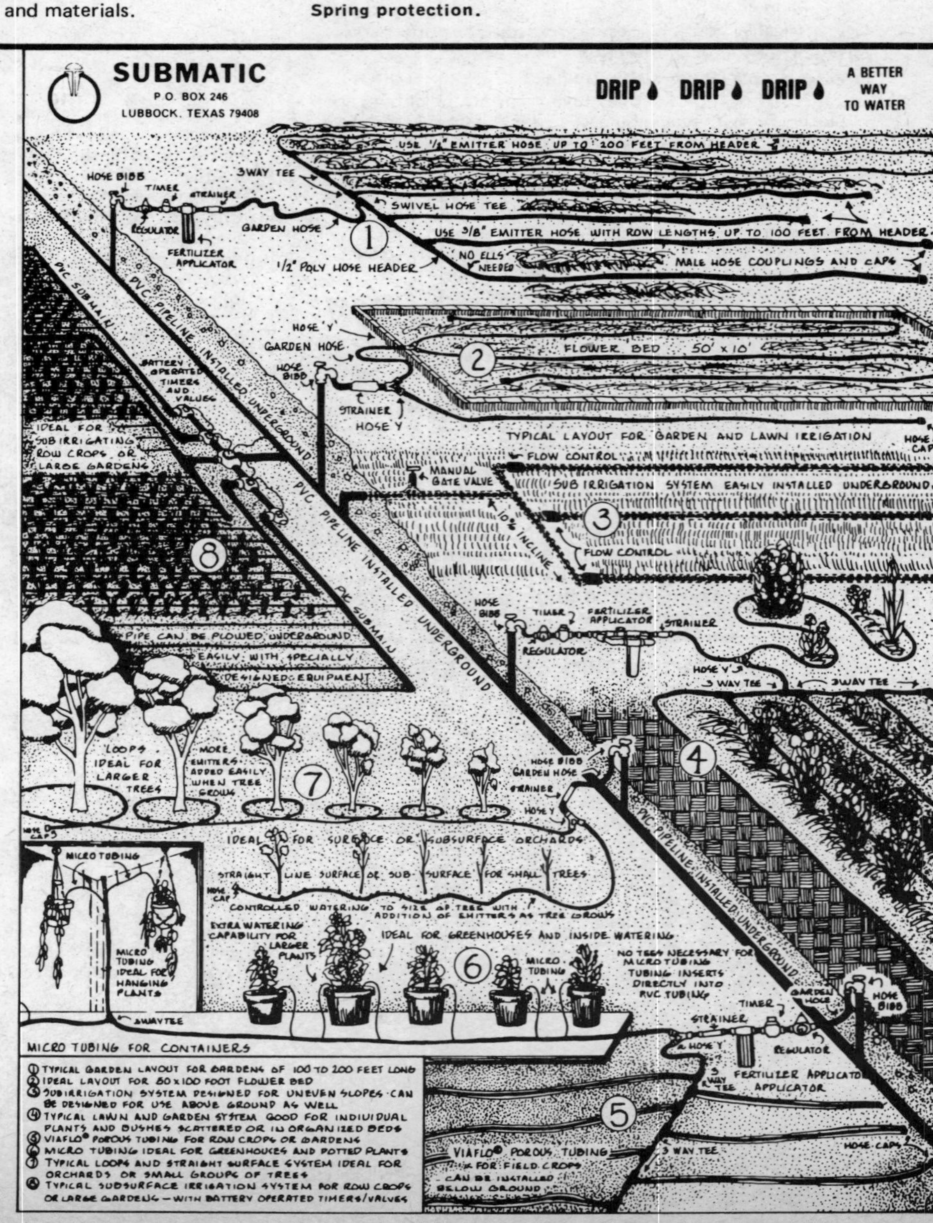

Beginner's Guide to Hydroponics

Sholto Douglas is an authority on hydroponics — growing plants without soil and feeding them water and fertilizer regularly. His introduction to the subject is a good place to start. The pros and cons of hydroponics versus growing plants in dirt will never be settled, but two advantages of hydroponics are clear: it can be done virtually anywhere, and once set up, it does require regular attentiveness, but it takes very little time.

—Richard Nilsen

Beginner's Guide to Hydroponics
James Sholto Douglas
1972; 156 pp.

$4.95 postpaid from:
Sterling Publishing Co.
Two Park Avenue
New York, NY 10016
or Whole Earth Household Store

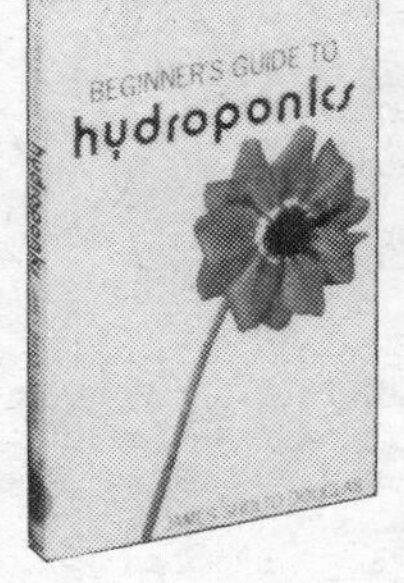

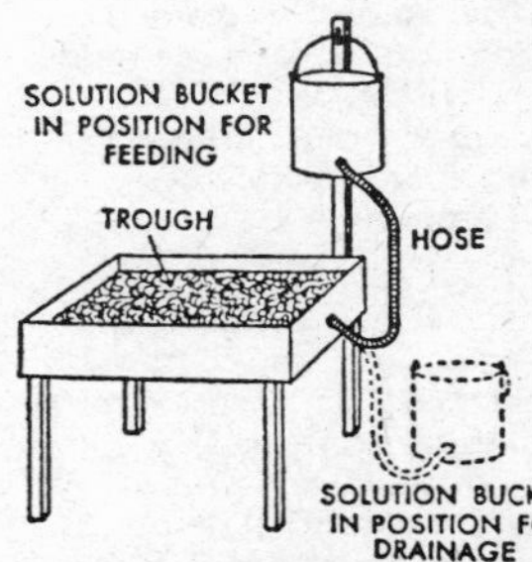

A portable household trough with semi-automatic feeding and drainage. This is useful for moving from place to place as required.

Hydroponic Food Production

This book describes hydroponics of the scale some oil-rich Mideast countries like to buy, "Uhh, yes, we'll take 5 acres of salad greens and put them on that sand dune over there . . ." Any small scale commercial grower will find it useful also; and with the rising cost of transportation pushing fresh vegetables prices ever upwards, truck garden hydroponics is looking better all the time.

—Richard Nilsen

Hydroponic Food Production
(A Definitive Guidebook for the Advanced Home Gardener and the Commercial Hydroponic Grower)
Howard M. Resh, Ph.D.
1978; 287 pp.

$14.95 postpaid from:
Woodbridge Press Publishing Company
P.O. Box 6189
Santa Barbara, CA 93111
or Whole Earth Household Store

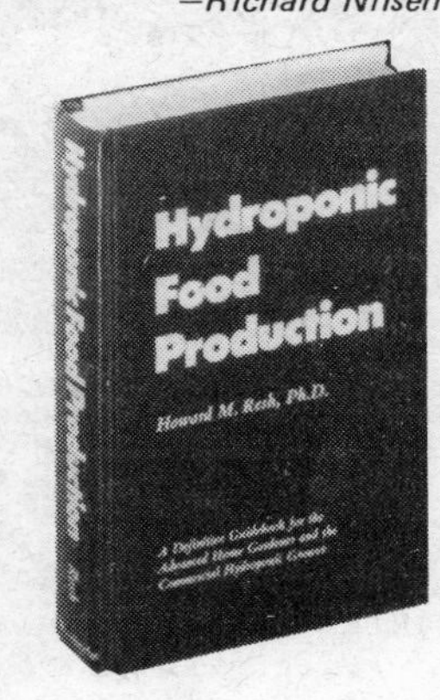

Air-inflated greenhouses are especially suited to low-growing crops such as turnips. (Courtesy of the government of Abu Dhabi, The Environmental Research Laboratory and Manley, Inc., Tucson, Arizona.)

•

Most publications on greenhouse tomato production suggest space allowances of 3 to 4 square feet per plant under soil culture. This is a population of 14,520 or 10,890 plants per acre, respectively. Plantings as dense as 18,500 per acre (about 2 square feet per plant) have been used in hydroponic culture in California and Arizona with good yields and quality. Plants are placed in double rows per bed. Plant rows should be 16 to 18 inches apart and plants 12 to 14 inches apart within each row. Plants may be placed in staggered positions in adjacent rows, in order to maximize the exposure of the leaves to sunlight, and to minimize physical interference ot the leaves between adjacent plants.

Hydro-Story

A hippie-dip introduction to home-scale hydroponics, though not the final word by any means. There is useful information about "organic hydroponics" — nutrient solutions made from locally available natural and organic substances instead of store-bought chemicals.

—Richard Nilsen

Hydro-Story
(The Complete Manual of Hydroponic Gardening at Home)
Charles E. Sherman and Hap Brenizer
1976; 95 pp.

$4.95 postpaid from:
Nolo Press
P.O. Box 544
Occidental, CA 95465

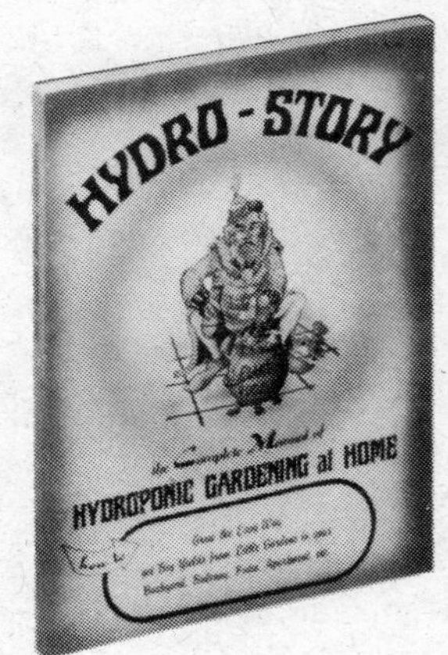

•

Set into the beds at 2 to 3 foot intervals are sludge-pots — any kind of covered vessel which will hold about two pounds of sludge, lined with a screen and pierced with numerous little holes in the bottom. Here is one recipe for nutrient sludge:

Natural Sauce
organic hydroponic plant food

Some Source Materials

per cent.:	n	p	k
Dried blood meal	13	1-5	1
Cottonseed meal	7	2-3	1+
Sewage, activated	5	3	
" digested	2		
Bone meal, raw	3	23	
" " steamed	2	30	
Manure, dried	1-2	1-2	3
" fresh	2	1	1
Grass clippings	1+	2	
Colloidal phosphate		20	
Shrimp waste		10	
Raw sugar waste		8	
Wool waste		3	3
Wood ash		1+	8
Greensand marl			7
Tobacco stems			7
Seaweed			5
Straw, millet			2+

The Complete Book of Gardening Under Lights

All the specifics of how different types of plants perform under lights. McDonald is an expert writer and gardener.

—Rosemary Menninger

The Complete Book of Gardening Under Lights
Elvin McDonald
1965; 220 pp.

$1.50 postpaid from:
Popular Library
600 Third Avenue
New York, NY 10016
or Whole Earth Household Store

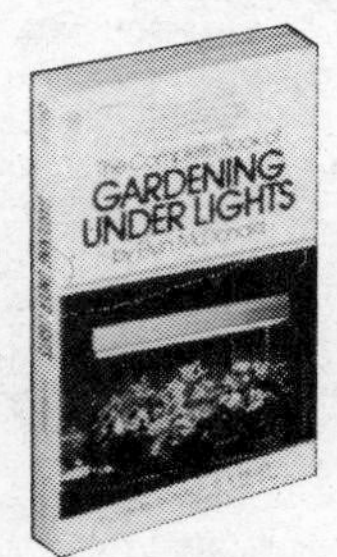

Organic Gardening Under Glass

This is the best book yet on food crops from greenhouses. More detailed than most outdoor gardening books on cultivation of specific plants. Good herb section, and general information on growing plants in containers.

—Rosemary Menninger

Organic Gardening Under Glass
(Fruits, Vegetables, and Ornamentals in the Greenhouse)
George and Katy Abraham
1975; 320 pp.

$10.95 postpaid from:
Rodale Books
33 East Minor
Emmaus, PA 18049
or Whole Earth Household Store

•

There are pros and cons to mulching in the greenhouse. Some people feel mulches bring rodents and snails. We feel if your greenhouse is tightly sealed you won't have this problem. Ground benches have deep soil and thus tend to hold moisture well without mulching, but because raised benches are generally 8 inches deep at most, they tend to dry out quicker during hot weather, and could benefit from a layer of mulch.

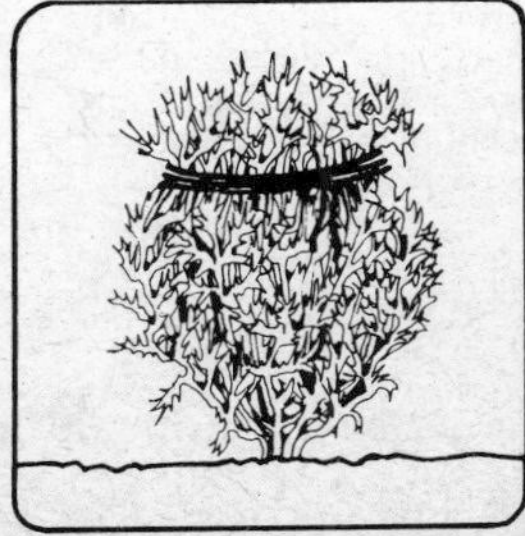

To make endive more tender, blanch the inner leaves by pulling and tying the outer ones up and over the heart. Leave the head tied for about two weeks, then harvest.

Gardening Under Artificial Light

According to this book, there are two types of artificial lighting for plants, both done best by fluorescent lamps. Photosynthetic lighting supplements natural light in rooms and greenhouses, especially during fall and winter months. Photoperiodic lighting can create day and night for flowers, houseplants, and a few kinds of vegetables. Flowers can be forced into bloom, seeds or bulbs germinated, and strawberries brought to fruit with careful lighting. Many plants, given a brief light bath during the night, require less intense light during the day. **Gardening Under Artificial Light** *provides the uncomplicated facts, but not the detail of* **The Complete Book of Gardening Under Lights.**

—Rosemary Menninger

Gardening Under Artificial Light
(A Handbook)
Brooklyn Botanic Gardens
1970; 65 pp.

$1.95 postpaid from:
Brooklyn Botanic Gardens
1000 Washington Avenue
Brooklyn, NY 11225
or Whole Earth Household Store

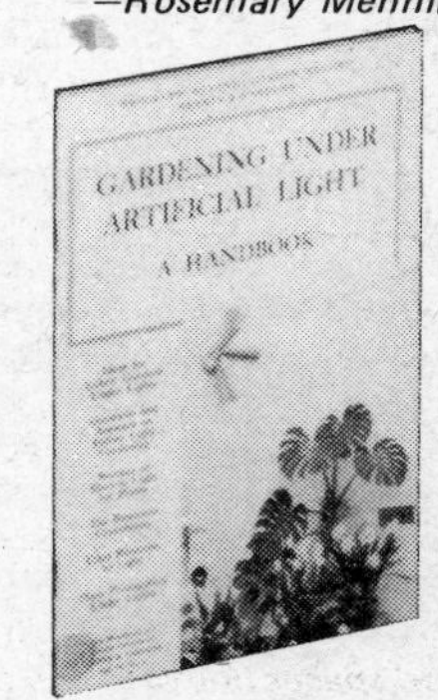

•

Frequent temperature check-ups may be required when tubes are close together as too much heat results for the plant's welfare.

THE RISING SUN
NEIGHBORHOOD NEWSLETTER

The Moon hasn't changed much in the last four billion years since many, many large and small meteorites hit it at once. Many of them are exactly where they were. They are being looked at and appreciated by the new Moon Lovers Club at the high school. Jane and Michael, who started the club, think that the Moon is going to change very much before they die and they want to slow down the process and to remember what the moon was like in the billions of years before people. "Neil Armstrong was like Lewis and Clark," Jane says, "and it's not far from Lewis and Clark to parking lots and strip mines. The main delay in both cases is developing the travel machines and the destruction machines that make far-away places convenient. We want to slow that down, but first mostly we want to be good Moon lovers." They look at the Moon frequently from different angles, in their telescope and in their minds. "The picture to remember hasn't been taken yet. From Mars, we look like a double planet, because we are. The little one is a fourth as big as the big one, and they're very close. You can tell they're in it together."

The Pesticide Conspiracy

You plant a crop, you know it must be bug-free or it will ultimately be rejected by the food processor. This is not because the bugs are dangerous, but rather because federal cosmetic laws on produce require ridiculously low bug counts and because consumers have been taught to be squeamish about the little multi-legged creatures. The answer is to spray and over-spray for insurance.

The result is that you kill off the good bugs that eat the bad bugs; then the fittest bad bugs survive the spray and become pesticide-resistant. The bug problem gets worse, spray dosage increases, becomes economically unfeasible, and a new improved product is introduced to repeat the cycle.

Who wins? The companies that make and sell pesticides. Who loses? The farmer who spends more per acre, the farm and factory workers who suffer from pesticide poisoning (sterility, nerve disorders, cancer), and the consumers who buy contaminated food and thus jeopardize their health.

A walk through the field of biological control in agriculture, guided by an insect-loving University of California professor, whose experiences with the pesticide mafia have metamorphosed him into an eco-radical.
—*Ruthanne Cecil*

The Pesticide Conspiracy
(An alarming look at pest control and the people who keep us "hooked" on deadly chemicals)
Robert van den Bosch
1978; 224 pp.

$4.95 postpaid from:
Doubleday and Company
501 Franklin Avenue
Garden City, NY 11530
or Whole Earth Household Store

•

Perhaps the greatest absurdity in contemporary pest control is the dominant role of the pesticide salesman, who simultaneously acts as diagnostician, therapist, nostrum prescriber, and pill peddler. It is difficult to imagine a situation in which society entrusts so great a responsibility to such poorly qualified persons. Pesticides rank with the most dangerous and ecologically disruptive materials known to science, yet under the prevailing system these biocides are scattered like dust in the environment by persons often utterly unqualified to prescribe and supervise their use.

Pest-control advisement should be a high-grade technology conducted by thoroughly qualified technicians. Instead it is overwhelmingly in the hands of skilled merchandise hucksters employed by the agri-chemical industry. Little wonder that contemporary pest control is characterized by economic, ecological, and social chaos.

•

Thirty years ago, at the outset of the synthetic-insecticide era, when the nation used roughly 50 million pounds of insecticides, the insects destroyed about 7 per cent of our preharvest crops; today, under a 600-million-pound insecticide load, we are losing 13 per cent of our preharvest yield to the rampaging insects. In other words, a major "reward" of our eleven-fold increase in insecticide use has been a doubling of the bug problem.

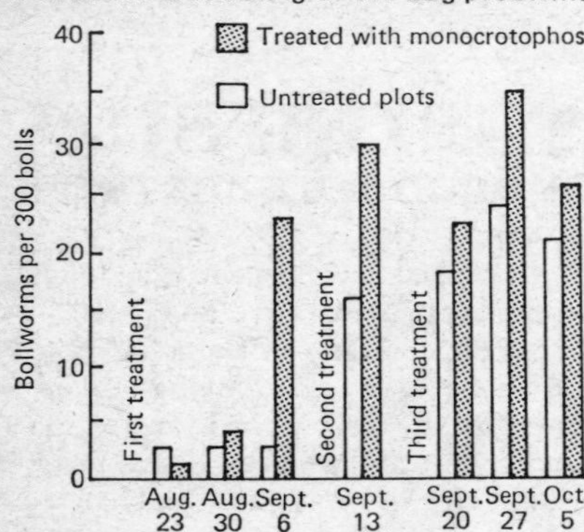

↑ **Target-pest resurgence following applications of a "control" insecticide. In this experiment, plots treated with monocrotophos, an insecticide federally registered for bollworm control, suffered heavier infestations than untreated plots. Note particularly the strong bollworm resurgence following the initial treatment. Simultaneous samplings of predators revealed that the insecticide destroyed bollworm predators and thus permitted resurgence of the pest.**

Pest-control costs in approximately one thousand acres of apple in Washington prior to and following adoption of an integrated control program for spider mites. ↓

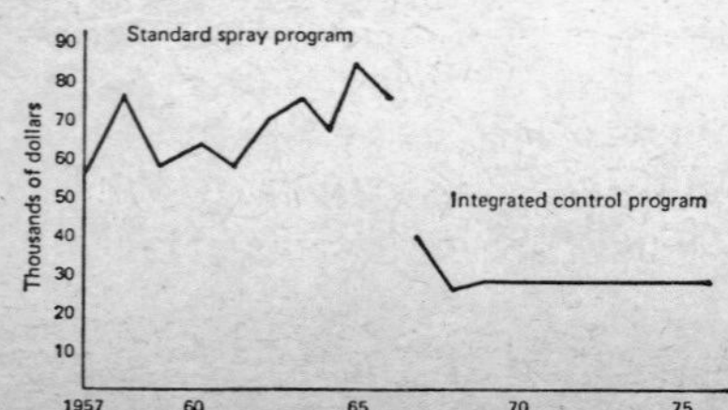

The small capillary tube hanging from the center of this insect trap releases a controlled amount of a sex attractant blend which permeates the orchard and confuses the males so they cannot find females for mating.

The Least Is Best Pesticide Strategy

This book is not essential to any gardener who knows when to go out and pick the horn-worms off the tomatoes. But as the scale increases, so do the pest problems, especially with mono-cultures. Integrated pest management is the best available solution; and Goldstein's book is a useful layman's survey of the state of the art, and not a how-to manual. One great feature is 26 pages of access to 41 U.S. and Canadian institutions that offer college-level instruction in IPM and related fields. IPM means being able to think through a pest problem to a solution, instead of running for the spray gun. People with those skills are going to be in demand. —*Richard Nilsen*

The Least Is Best Pesticide Strategy
(A Guide for Putting Integrated Pest Management into Action)
Jerome Goldstein, Editor
1978; 205 pp.

$8.95 postpaid from:
The J.G. Press, Inc.
Box 351
Emmaus, PA 18049

•

In the 30 years following World War II, the number of pounds of pesticide used has increased by more than tenfold. But in that same period, losses to pests remained about the same — about one-third of all crops in the field. Of the 25 most serious agricultural insect pests in California, nearly 75 percent are resistant to one or more insecticides — and 95 percent are either insecticide-aggravated or insecticide-induced pests.

•

For pesticide makers — though sales figures are ever-increasing, pressures from EPA regulations, the costs and red tape of obtaining official clearance for marketing new pesticides, the problems with pollution controls and worker safety at the manufacturing site all add up to major headaches for pesticide manufacturers. The costs of developing a new pesticide are in the range of $15 to $20 million.

The IPM Practitioner

This newsletter is an excellent way to stay on top of a fast-moving and technical field. Integrated pest management is the closest thing on the horizon to a cure for the agricultural addiction to synthetic pesticides. IPM is a highly sophisticated management strategy — a systemic approach — to controlling pest damage. It includes biological control (e.g., introduction of natural enemies of a pest), crop rotation, cultural control, but also, and only when absolutely necessary, the use of synthetic pesticides. The trick is to look at all the factors that relate to any pest problem, and not just to spray every two weeks because it says so on the can of pesticide.

The **IPM Practitioner** *contains news briefs, access to products and services, abstracts of current technical articles, book reviews, and a calendar of events.* —*Richard Nilsen*

The IPM Practitioner
(The Newsletter of Integrated Pest Management)
Joanna Graham, Editor

$10 /year (12 issues) from:
Bio-Integral Resource Center
P.O. Box 7242
Berkeley, CA 94707

•

BTI, a new strain of *Bacillus thuringiensis* with a high degree of lethal activity against mosquito larvae, shows excellent potential as a biological control agent in mosquito control programs. Named *Bacillus thuringiensis* var. *israelensis* (BTI) after the location where it was discovered, the pathogen, like other strains of *B.t.*, acts initially and perhaps primarily as a stomach poison, damaging cells of the midgut epithelium of infected mosquito larvae, according to recent studies.

•

Chickens were used successfully as biological controls against grasshoppers in the Siskiyou National Forest in Oregon, where forest officials, rather than applying insecticide against an unusually large hatch of grasshoppers, fenced in a five-acre area containing valuable tree seedlings, and stocked it with 175 chickens. At the start of the project, 200 to 600 grasshoppers per square yard were counted, but within a short time, the chickens had so reduced the grasshopper population that chicken feed had to be purchased.

•

For the Home Gardener

Wheast, a high-protein by-product of the cheese industry, commonly used to feed honeybees during the winter, can be used to sustain beneficial insects in home greenhouses. Lacewings and ladybeetles, both general predators, have been used to control a variety of pests such as aphids and mealybugs on greenhouse plants. Once such beneficial insects have been introduced, their populations can be successfully maintained by screening all openings to the outside and setting out wheast feeding stations to carry over the predators when pest populations are low. Wheast can be obtained from: CRS Food Service and Supply Company, 6043 Hudson Road, St. Paul, MN 55119 (ask for CRS formula No. 57) *or* Rincon Vitova Insectaries, Inc., Box 45, Oak View, CA 93022. A picture and description of the simple construction of such a feeding station (built to exclude ants) can be found on p. 411 of **The Integral Urban House** (1979), Sierra Club Books, 530 Bush, San Francisco, CA 94108.

Sources of beneficial insects for biological control

Biological control is applied ecology. The term normally applies to the control of insect pests through the manipulation of their natural enemies — predators, parasites or diseases. Raising these beneficial insects (natural enemies) is often a tricky business in the lab, but mass-rearing millions of them, and shipping them all over the country, and making a profit at it is even harder. Not many companies have succeeded.

The best at it is Rincon-Vitova Insectaries. Beneficial insects are tiny livestock — they have to be fed and watered and kept at the right temperature and humidity or they don't make it. Rincon-Vitova has pioneered many of the techniques and offers more insects to control more different pests, than anyone else. —*Richard Nilsen*

Rincon-Vitova Insectaries, Inc.
P.O. Box 95
Oak View, CA 93022

Bio-Control Co.
13451 Highway 174
P.O. Box 247
Cedar Ridge, CA 95924
Ladybug beetles, praying mantis eggs, and lacewings.

Gothard, Inc.
P.O. Box 370
Canutillo, TX 79835
Specializes in trichogramma wasps.

Mincemoyer's Nursery
R.D. 5, Box 379
New Prospect Road
Jackson, NJ 08527
Mantis egg cases, both native and Chinese.

Praying Mantis from Mincemoyer.

Fountain's Sierra Bug Company
P.O. Box 114
Rough and Ready, CA 95975
Ladybugs only. They ship from early March to late September.

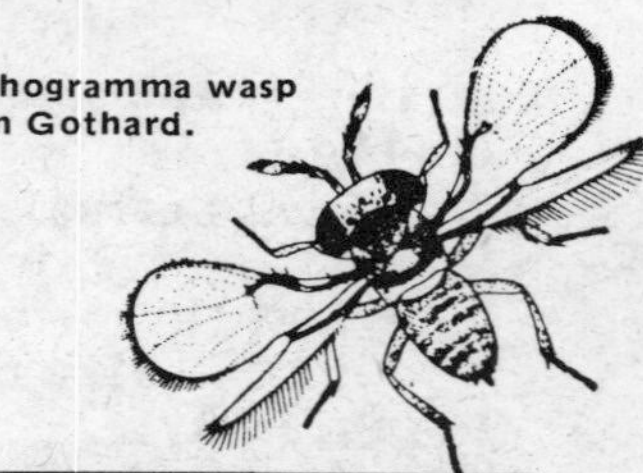

Trichogramma wasp from Gothard.

Pests in the city

Urban pests include rats, roaches, mosquitoes, fleas, flies, yellow jackets and termites. If you think you have a problem, but don't want to hire the man to come and spray poison around where you live, write these folks with your questions. They can probably help.
—*Richard Nilsen*

Technical Assistance Center for Urban Integrated Pest Management
John Muir Institute
P.O. Box 7162
Berkeley, CA 94707

Rodale's Color Handbook of Garden Insects

↑ Sphinx Moth and Caterpillar

More than 300 pests and beneficial insects leap from these pages in close-up color photographs. While your own worst enemy may not appear (because the insect world is far more varied than a single book can cover), a similar species is probably listed — along with organic controls, geographic range and life cycle data.

—Rosemary Menninger

Rodale's Color Handbook of Garden Insects
Anna Carr
1979; 256 pp.

$12.95 postpaid from:
Rodale Books
33 East Minor
Emmaus, PA 18049
or Whole Earth Household Store

↑ **CATERPILLAR**
Whitelined Sphinx Moth
Hyles lineata

Range: United States and southern Canada.

Description: Greenish yellow with a yellow horn and head and pale spots outlined in black; 2½ to 3 inches long. ADULT: Brown moth with white stripes running diagonally across the wings and a broad, buff-colored band; thick antennae; resembles a small hummingbird; 3-inch wingspan. EGGS: Laid on the underside of leaves.

Life Cycle: Two generations per year. Winter is passed in the pupal stage.

Host Plants: Beet, currant, grape, melon, pear, plum, tomato.

Feeding Habits: Hornworms feed on leaves and fruits, but they are easily controlled by handpicking.

Animal traps

If you're getting rid of a pest without being too mean about it, or if you're after a wild pet, these traps will catch sundry small animals alive. Raccoons, possums, mice, turtles, sparrows, quail, fish, rabbits, crabs, rats, pigeons. Havahart is the best known. —SB

Havahart
Catalog
$1 postpaid from:
Woodstream Corporation
Front and Locust Streets
Lititz, PA 17543

Tomahawk Live Traps
Catalog
free from:
Tomahawk Live Traps
Box 323
Tomahawk, WI 54487

Havahart

Tomahawk

Owl holes in English barns

Many large barns in the country have a small round hole at the end just below the angle of the gable. This is to allow the entrance of owls. Great mischief is done to the grain or other food stored in barns by the rats and the farmers suffer considerable loss from the raids of these pesky creatures but, as owls live largely on rats and mice, it is to great advantage to the farmer if an owl makes a nest in her barn. The birds pounce down upon the rodents at night when they are at their damaging work and so keep down the number of these pests. **(The Children's Treasure House/Arthur Mee).**

Lots of Love 'n all,

David Wills
(sojourning in native Great Britain)

The Bug Book

A useful compilation of imaginative methods used by practicing bio-dynamic gardeners to combat insect and animal pests. The bugs are arranged alphabetically with accompanying sketches and descriptions for easy identification. Remedies are suggested, and in the back is a listing of effective brews and potions. An invasion of blister beetles can be checked, say the authors, by calling in the neighbors and tromping through the garden beating the bushes and waving sticks and scaring them off.

—Richard Nilsen

The Bug Book
(Harmless Insect Controls)
Helen and John Philbrick
1974; 124 pp.

$3.95 postpaid from:
Garden Way Publishing Co.
Charlotte, VT 05545
or Whole Earth Household Store

•

Fruit Flies

Many insect books rather pompously declare that this tiny fly must be controlled with fly sprays, but we have experimented and found a safer method for home use, a method that is much cheaper and easier. All flies are attracted to light. Pull the shades over all but one window. Pull even that shade down until there is about a two inch crack to admit the light. The fruit flies will fly every time to that one light crack. To reinforce the effect of the light, leave a dish of overripe fruit near the window and the fruit flies will gather there by the dozens. Next, pick up the dish of fruit with its covering of flies and rush it out the door while the flies are busy eating the fruit. Once outdoors, the flies will disappear in search of more decaying fruit on vines and trees. They will not return to the house — but there may be more to replace them!

Living Off the Country for Fun and Profit

There have been so many books on this subject by now that it is a bit surprising when a good one comes along. Well-seasoned experience, and a perspective that considers rural livelihood in the context of an inflationary economy are what make this one worth reading. Anyone with sheep or cattle should take a look at the chapter on raising and training three breeds of European livestock guard dogs.

—Richard Nilsen

Living Off the Country for Fun and Profit
John L. Parker
1978; 193 pp.

$4.95 postpaid from:
Bookworm Publishing Company
Box 3037
Ontario, CA 91761
or Whole Earth Household Store

•

The natural instinct of any guard dog is to protect against the wild predators, wild dogs and two-legged vandals. Predators are wary of the dogs and are often warned off by traces the dogs leave along the way. Stray or wild dogs are usually unwilling to cross the lines set up by the guards even when running in packs, and the guards will attack wild dogs as quickly as they go after any other predator. This is important because livestock raisers say that in many areas wild dog packs are becoming a greater menace than coyotes.

The Komondor ↓

The *Komondor* is the first of the imported European livestock guard dogs to be used for guarding in this country. A native of Hungary, the word means *Lord of the Dogs* and the plural is Komondorok. The Magyars brought these big husky dogs with them to Hungary more than a thousand years ago as they seized land and protected their livestock in this wolf-infested region with their dogs.

Japanese Ama (sea woman) diving for awabi. Human forms are always surrounded by an infrared aura, as are night-flying moths.

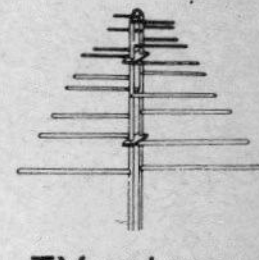
TV antenna

Cabbage Looper sex-scent antenna

Tuning in to Nature

This book is causing considerable controversy in scientific circles. Some entomologists believe the discoveries documented here will do for our understanding of insect communication what the plate theory has done for geology. Others think Callahan is barking up the wrong tree. Maybe it's just that the critics don't like a scientist who uses exclamation marks in his writing.

Callahan believes insect antennae work like radio antennae, except that insects are sensitive to infrared radiations instead of radio waves. Insects navigate and communicate by using these radiations. If Callahan is right, the most important future spin-off from this would be to learn to mimic these frequencies, and then either lure pests into traps or jam their communications to prevent mating. This novel alternative to chemical pesticides comes from a self-confessed mystic with a prose style at times reminiscent of Loren Eiseley. Callahan has been working as an insect morphologist for the past 20 years for the USDA in Florida.

—Richard Nilsen

Tuning in to Nature
(Solar Energy, Infrared Radiation and the Insect Communication System)
Philip S. Callahan
1975; 240 pp.

$10 postpaid from:
The Devin-Adair Co.
143 Sound Beach Ave.
Old Greenwich, CT 06870
or Whole Earth Household Store

•

Infrared frequencies are the natural frequencies in which we are bathed all our lives. Inasmuch as the attractant, or jamming, frequencies would be narrowband, they would be of extremely low energy. In fact, the radiated molecules from innumerable scents floating under your local mercury-vapor streetlamps are, no doubt, putting out hundreds of such frequencies at every street corner in America. It is these lamp-radiated scent molecules that attract and confuse so many night-flying insects swarming around in the radiated vapors under the lamp.

There is one final practical advantage to such an insect control device, in addition to its ability to attract only the selected species to which it is tuned: It can be turned off when not in use. That is precisely what is wrong with insecticides — they cannot be turned off.

Antenna of the male cecropia moth. The family of saturnid moths contains the largest members of night-flying moths. The photograph clearly shows the lateral arms extending from the antenna in pairs. The arms support thousands of sensilla that are arranged in arrays along the arms and detect scent molecules. The sex life of the moth is complicated beyond imagination, and these flying, egg-laying machines seem to exist as if directed by some incomprehensible force; as if some huge impersonal computer were feeding signals from a controlling transmitter into the moth's antenna-detector.

THE RISING SUN
NEIGHBORHOOD NEWSLETTER

The rich are very clean. It's all they have to do. When they need mud, they have to steal it from us.

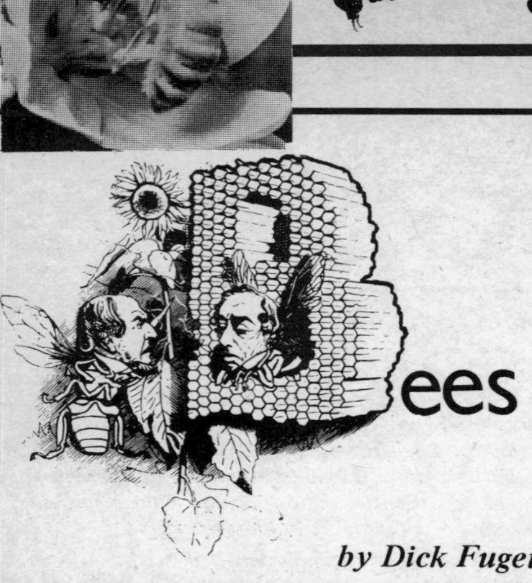

Bees

by Dick Fugett

Combs built irregularly outside on the branches of a tree.
—ABC and XYZ of Bee Culture

First Lessons in Beekeeping

If you're starting from a condition of total ignorance there's no better book to be first on your list than this old classic. Definitions of the terms, basic equipment needs, plenty of pictures, techniques for installing package bees, and as much wisdom as the printed page can transmit to assist you with the actual arrival of bees in your life.

First Lessons in Beekeeping
C.P. Dadant, et al.
1917, 1976; 127 pp.
$1 postpaid from:
Dadant and Sons
51 South Second Street
Hamilton, IL 62341

•

Smoking the bees subdues them in that at the first sign of smoke, the bees go to the unsealed cells and fill their abdomens with honey. They are then much easier to handle as they tend to be much quieter on the combs. Perhaps they are merely more docile with a stomach full of honey; perhaps they find it slightly more difficult to curve the abdomen into a stinging position with a full stomach. No one knows the exact reasoning or reactions of the bees but they are easier to handle and much quieter if the smoker is used with care. The smoke should be a cool smoke and the minimum amount necessary to calm the bees should be used.

This hobby kit contains everything that the beginner will need with the exception of the bees.

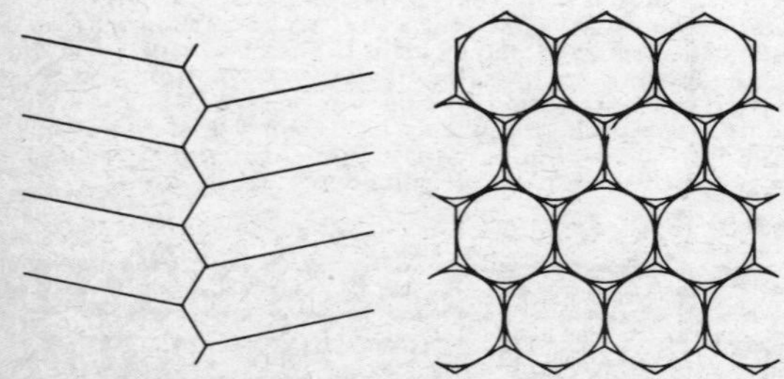

Diagrams showing slope of cells from front to middle of comb and the economy of the hexagonal shape for making honeycomb cells.

The Hive and the Honeybee
ABC and XYZ of Bee Culture

Since the major technical breakthroughs in beekeeping — moveable frames, wax foundations and the honey extractor — were all made over 100 years ago, beekeepers today can devote their efforts to improving technique rather than trying to keep up with state-of-the-art equipment advances. So when it comes to bee books, it follows that the old can be as useful as the new, and sometimes more so.

Beekeeping starts with knowing the rules, and here are two books that can do it for you, to the extent that a book can substitute for experience. Neither of them conveys any Feel, but the dry mechanical aspects of First Principles must be understood, and here they are.

Hive *is still going strong after 35 years, now in a 5th printing of a 3rd edition which was in fact inspired by a book published in 1853. It's passed the test of time — if any single volume could be said to present the topic this would be it.*

ABC *is the other standard, a 700 page giant that's equally revered after 37 editions and jammed with even more information, but whose encyclopedic arrangement makes it a reference book for the dedicated more than a book to be read cover to cover.*

The Hive and the Honey Bee
Charles Dadant, Roy A. Grout, et al.
1946, 1973; 556 pp.
$10.95 postpaid from:
Dadant and Sons
51 South Second Street
Hamilton, IL 62341

ABC and XYZ of Bee Culture
A.I. Root, E.R. Root, et al.
1877, 1970; 726 pp.
(37th Edition)
$12.98 postpaid from:
A.I. Root Company
Medina, OH 44256

•

The first consideration in choosing the location of an apiary is whether or not there are sufficient sources of nectar and pollen near. Bear in mind that honey bees obtain most of their nectar and pollen within a half-mile radius, but can gather at distances of 1 to 2 miles, depending on the ruggedness of the country and to some extent on the prevailing winds. Even in the heart of large cities, there are often sufficient sources of nectar and pollen to provide for a limited number of colonies, and even to produce surplus honey. A city lawn, a back yard, a flat roof, a pasture on a farm, a grove of trees — all will be satisfactory locations as the occasion demands.
—The Hive and the Honey Bee

•

Many beekeepers are overly anxious to determine whether or not the queens have been accepted after their introduction. Frequent examination of the colony, or examination in inclement weather, may result in the loss of the new queen through being balled by the worker bees. Balling occurs when the worker bees cluster tightly about the queen and pull at her legs and wings until she is badly injured and frequently killed. When a colony is examined to make sure the new queen has been accepted, if eggs are seen, the queen is there. The hive should be closed and the colony left alone.
—The Hive and the Honey Bee

Drone

Queen

Worker

—The Hive and the Honey Bee

The Joys of Beekeeping

Now what if you haven't decided whether you want any bees in your life? Here's the book to browse through if you're still contemplating beekeeping or just wondering why anyone would want to hang out with a bunch of little bugs when they could be inside watching TV.

"My book is a rejoicing and I have no other objective in writing it," begins Taylor, who then takes us through the annual cycle of the bees. Spring swarms and swarm capturing are followed by summer honeyflows, then the fall harvest brings honey extracting, to be replaced at last by wintering procedures and snow. The day to day pleasures, as well as the efforts, are described. As opposed to the Rules, here's some of the Feel. Other books tell you How To; this one illustrates Why.

Bees have a unique fascination when you get to know them, for they represent a tiny facet of the magic of our existence. It's hard to put into words, but this book can pass a little of it on.

The Joys of Beekeeping
Richard Taylor
1974; 166 pp.
$4.95 postpaid from:
St. Martin's Press
175 Fifth Avenue
New York, NY 10010
or Whole Earth Household Store

•

One of the joys of a woodlot yard is to look skyward in the spring, through a break in the foliage, to see the thousands of bees cascading in like a waterfall and rising in equal numbers to scatter over the countryside for miles around. How they do this without constant collision I cannot imagine. They stream upward and downward without any interference whatever, threading their individual irregular paths with such speed that it would be difficult to follow them if there were not such numbers. They are oblivious to me, even though I may be standing directly beneath the break in the foliage that is their entrance to the yard. They swoop past me on every side, then each to its own hive, which is indelibly fixed in its memory from among the twenty or more hives that are there.

Gleanings in Bee Culture

Gleanings in Bee Culture *is a monthly which has been published for 107 years and appears to be here to stay. It has current info on everything of interest to the hobbyist from techniques, research, and disease to meetings, books and equipment.*

Gleanings in Bee Culture
Lawrence Goltz, Editor
$8.75 /year (12 issues) from:
The A.I. Root Co.
P.O. Box 706
Medina, OH 44256

CLUBS

There's a number of beekeeping clubs around, but they keep a low profile and you may have to work to find one. If you succeed you'll be rewarded by the company of experienced beekeepers. In a hobby that is very much "hands-on," you can be sure that learning from others sure beats hell out of do-it-yourself. After one field trip all your book learning suddenly makes sense! Check with your county agriculture department bee inspector.

SWARMS

With the price of a two-pound package of bees nearing $30 there's economic incentive to eliminate the middleman. So as soon as you possess the basic skills, why not bring some adventure into your life by capturing swarms? The real-life challenges met during the hiving of a swarm of bees from someone's tree or attic will advance your skills and broaden your horizons. Contact your county Ag. Dept. or local Fire Dept. to be put on the list of people called when panicky citizens overreact to masses of bees coming to visit.

The Art and Adventure of Beekeeping
Mastering the Art of Beekeeping

Ormond and Harry Aebi are a father and son team in Santa Cruz, California, with an incredible 1½ centuries of beekeeping experience between them. In 1974 they made a splash in the normally calm waters of beekeeping with a world record harvest of 404 pounds of honey from a single hive. Needless to say, people wanted to know how they did it, so the book **The Art & Adventure of Beekeeping** *came into being to give us a look at their methods and a feel for their philosophy. Both are unique. Now they've followed up with Vol. II,* **Mastering the Art of Beekeeping**, *which deserves the attention of anyone serious about bees. The two books complement each other without overlapping, but* **Art & Adventure** *is a better introduction.*

Each book is essentially a record of the Aebis' day to day experiences as they ply their trade. They employ the same approach that a race mechanic uses to squeeze the last erg out of a turbo Porsche — Fine Tuning. The Aebis concern themselves with details as minute as thermal loss caused by handhold indents, and preheating of supers before they are put on the hive. Their techniques range from counting individual bees alighting on the landing board to predicting honey production by listening to the hives. The Aebis work with a style so fine that some of us may feel like oafs in comparison, but their example gives us a goal to aim for if we're willing to put out the effort.

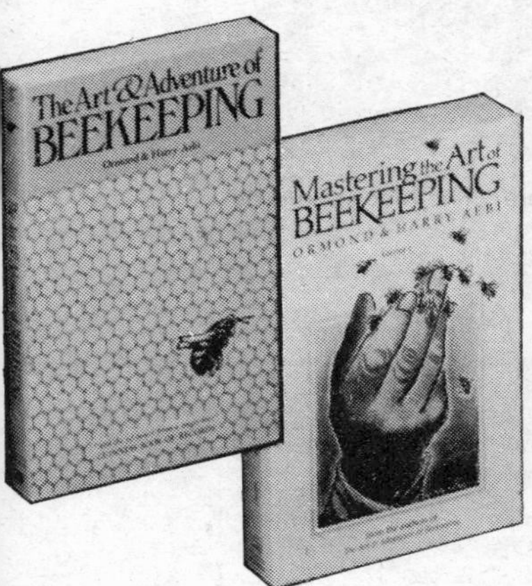

The Art and Adventure of Beekeeping
Ormond and Harry Aebi
1975, 1980; 184 pp.
$5.95 postpaid

Mastering the Art of Beekeeping
Ormond and Harry Aebi
1979; 283 pp.
$7.95 postpaid
both from:
Unity Press
P.O. Box 1037
Santa Cruz, CA 95061
or Whole Earth Household Store

•

Always scrape the stinger off the flesh with a fingernail, knife, or even a scissors blade. *Never* pull out the stinger with a tweezers! That is the worst possible thing that one can do for it squeezes the poison sac forcing all of the venom out through the stinger and into the wound. Scraping off the stinger stops the flow of poison while the stinger is being pulled out.

—Mastering the Art of Beekeeping

•

The rule is that bees do not sting during swarming and may be hived easily. There are exceptions to this rule. If a swarm has been unable to find a new home, it may remain clustered on a post or among vines for as long as two weeks. Cold or rainy weather also causes bees to remain clustered until they become hungry; they are cross when disturbed, so play it safe. As time goes by, many folk will learn to hive bees without veil or gloves as some of us do, but always have the veil and gloves handy.

—The Art and Adventure of Beekeeping

Supers Added & date

January 30	Queen Excluder & first super		
February 20	Replaced old excluder with new one & added super		
March 12	One Super	June 6	One Super
March 13	One Super	June 7	One Super
March 20	One Super	June 13	One Super
April 4	One Super	July 1	Two Supers
April 12	One Super	July 17	One Super
May 27	Two Supers		

—Art and Adventure of Beekeeping

Bless Those Eager Beekeepers

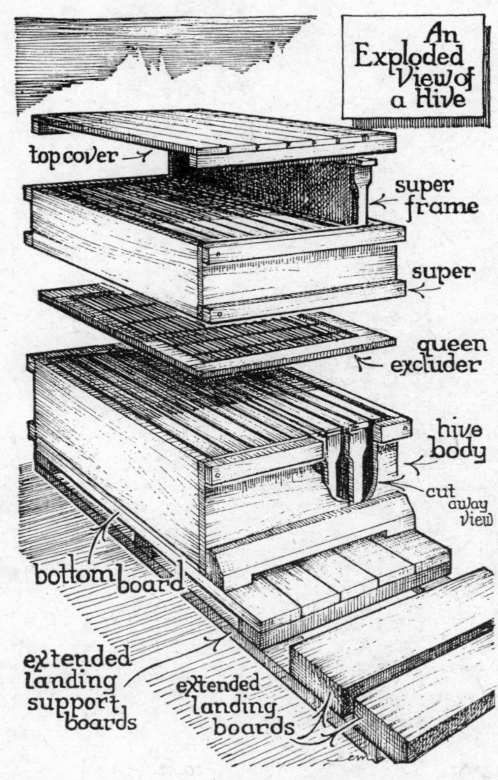

—Mastering the Art of Beekeeping

•

We can learn a great deal about each hive of bees by getting up at night and listening to what the bees are doing. I press my ear against the side of each hive body and listen, then listen to each super in turn until I get to the top super. Then I go to the next hive and listen in the same way, listening to each hive we own. In this way I am able to tell by the voices, noises, rustlings and fanning roar inside the hives what the bees are doing at present and what they are likely to do in the near future. I am also able to tell a few days in advance which hive is going to swarm by the "squeaks" the young queens make in their cells while they are still sealed in. They give these sounds most often just at or after dusk.

—The Art and Adventure of Beekeeping

HONEY EXTRACTOR

The single most expensive item to buy (they can also be borrowed or rented) is a honey extractor, and sooner or later you'll want your own. If money is a factor, then consider building one. Buying all the parts new at 1980 prices is a $60 investment, or about 1/3 the cost of a store bought. If you follow the plans you'll get a 2-frame model, but with a little creativity you can jiggle the measurements to produce a full 4 framer.

Make Your Own Honey Extractor
1977; 8 pp.

$3.95 postpaid from:
Garden Way Publishing
Charlotte, VT 05445
or Whole Earth Household Store

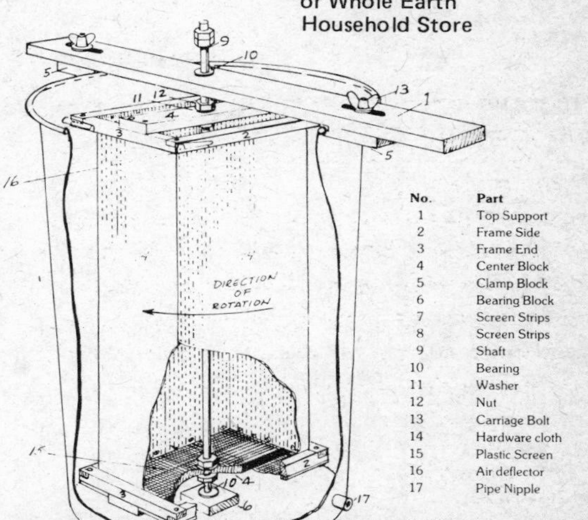

No.	Part
1	Top Support
2	Frame Side
3	Frame End
4	Center Block
5	Clamp Block
6	Bearing Block
7	Screen Strips
8	Screen Strips
9	Shaft
10	Bearing
11	Washer
12	Nut
13	Carriage Bolt
14	Hardware cloth
15	Plastic Screen
16	Air deflector
17	Pipe Nipple

American Honey Plants

Flowers claim much of the bees attention, and after you begin to see the world from their point of view, you'll get the same way. When that happens here's the book for you; it lists over one hundred plants and trees that attract bees.

American Honey Plants
Frank C. Pellett
1947, 1976; 467 pp.
$8.25 postpaid from:
Dadant and Sons
51 South Second Street
Hamilton, IL 62341

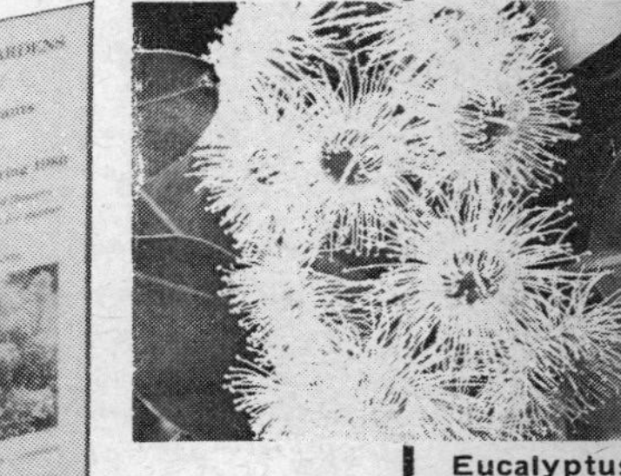

Eucalyptus globulus

SOWING SEEDS

If you reach the last stage in this regenerative disease known as Bee Fever, you'll end up in your own garden, making life easier for your bug buddies. When you decide to start planting for their benefit, the best source is Pellett Gardens. For 40 years they've been selling seeds and plants of various species favored by bees as pollen and nectar sources. Whether it's a matter of remedying an early spring or late fall nectar drought or just doing some gardening that will put a few more pounds of honey in the hive, here's the place to go.

Pellett Gardens
Catalog

free from:
Pellett Gardens
Atlantic, IA 50022

MAIL ORDER SUPPLIES

Since bee supply stores are few and far between, mail order becomes a necessity. Each of the following dealers will send a free catalog on request:

Diamond International
Apiary Department
Box 1070
Chico, CA 95927

A.I. Root
P.O. Box 706
Medina, OH 44256

Walter Kelly
Clarkson, KY 42726
(Kelly puts out a beginner's book for $1.50)

Dadant & Sons
51 South Second Street
Hamilton, IL 62341

and a new, small outfit for the East:

Betterbee
Box 37, Rt. 29
Greenwich, NY 12834

[Suggested by Kevin Kelly]

BEES
ITALIAN
(Non Taxable)

Quality Bees and Queens from experienced Bee Breeder Shippers. Shipped via Parcel Post. Depending on weather conditions, shipments will begin about April 15. Avoid Rush Orders; Order and Prepay Now. Both 2 and 3 pound packages include Queens, ALL POSTAGE PREPAID.

Queens Only	2 lb. Pkg. (Including Queen) Ship. Wt. 7 lbs.	3 lb. Pkg. (Including Queen) Ship. Wt. 8 lbs.
$9.00	$29.95	$36.00

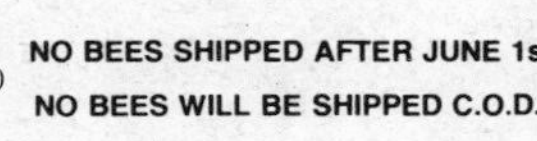

NO BEES SHIPPED AFTER JUNE 1st
NO BEES WILL BE SHIPPED C.O.D.

(Above includes all postage charges within continental U.S.)

10% VALUE OF GOODS CHARGED UPON RETURN, UNLESS PERMISSION IS GRANTED OTHERWISE.

—Diamond International

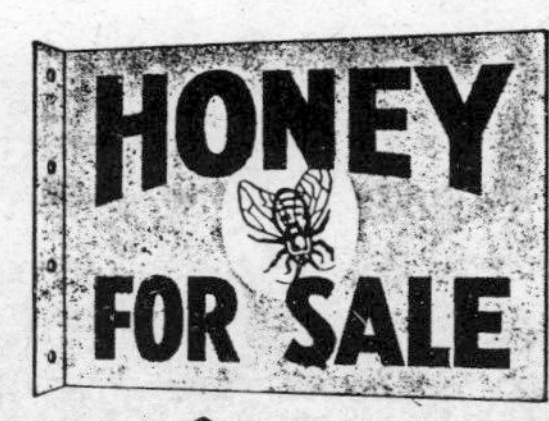

↑ **Walter Kelly Co.**
← **Dadant & Sons**

EUCALYPTUS

No single tree can keep bees happier for months at a time than the eucalyptus, which can be grown in areas where minimum temps stay in the 20° F range. The tree grows from seed without undue difficulty, and different types range from 10 to 100 feet in height, so you can put one in your front yard and plant a dozen down by the river bed. For seed varieties of 40 different eucalypts and notes on their merits for the bees, write to the following address mentioning that you are a beekeeper:

The Secretary
Forestry Commission of NSW
GPO Box 2667
Sydney, NSW 2001 Australia ■

THE RISING SUN
NEIGHBORHOOD NEWSLETTER

Every soap opera has one male and one female Catholic (never married to each other) so they can tie everyone else up by refusing to get divorced, she can refuse to get an abortion, he can refuse to let his girlfriend get an abortion and the plot can march on, Susan says.

Recipe for Raising Chickens

Unlike bees, chickens are not something I'd want to spend my evenings reading about. A "recipe" is really what this is. She gives the basics plus the tender love and care and tricks it might take years to discover. Tells how to learn from your chickens, and except for the omission of butchering, it's the best beginning chicken book I've seen.
—Rosemary Menninger

Minnie Rose Lovgreen's Recipe for Raising Chickens
Nancy Rekow and Claire Frost, Editors
1975; 31 pp.

$2 postpaid from:
Pacific Search
222 Dexter Avenue N.
Seattle, WA 98109
or Whole Earth Household Store

•
You can test a hen to see if she's laying. There are two bones either side of a hen's rectum. You see, a hen only has one vent for everything. If you can fit two of your folded knuckles between those two bones, then the hen is laying. Otherwise not. The technique takes a bit of practice, but it's worth it. The longest it pays to keep a hen is about 2½ to 3 years.

•
In the bug line, they like beetles and earwigs and small worms. Earwigs especially. They help keep your garden free of bugs. I had an apple tree with a crotch in it, and at night I used to take an old newspaper and roll it up and put it in that crotch. In the morning it'd be full of earwigs because the earwigs like to crawl in the newspaper at night. I'd take that out and shake it, and every time the chickens saw I was about to take that paper out, they'd come running right away.

Crested Roman geese. $75 pair, trio $100.

Black Spanish. $85 pair, 15 eggs $30.

Stromberg's Chicks & Pets Unlimited

For non-killed protein nothing beats milk and eggs. For ordinary chickens go to local sources. For particular chickens, fancy ones, and geese, ducks, pigeons, turkeys, partridges, peacocks — plus all MANNER of exotic animals — Stromberg's. More on pets, p. 354 - 355.
—SB

Stromberg's Chicks and Pets Unlimited
Catalog

$1 from:
Stromberg's
Pine River, MN 56474

Otter, "Clowns of the Wilds." $750, adults $475.

American giant homer. $20 pair, choice $30 pair.

Silver pencilled wyandotte. $25 pair, 15 hatching eggs $9.95.

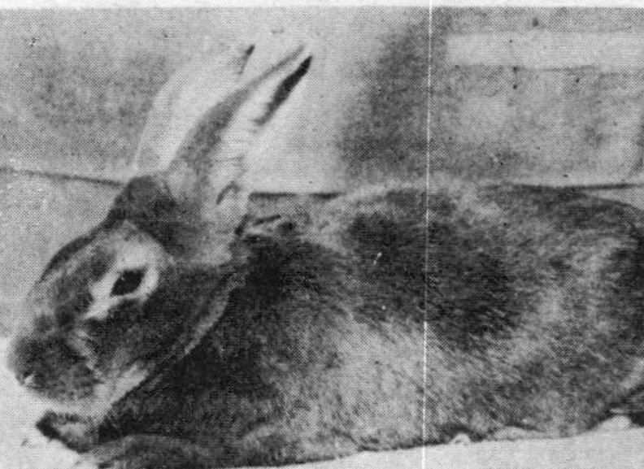
New Zealand red. $35 pair.

Murray McMurray Hatchery

Many kinds of chicks both plain and fancy, great service, a catalog that's an education in itself, good prices (it was cheaper for us here in N. Idaho to pay air mail postage than to order locally and selection is so much better), and fine chickens. We ordered a bar-b-que special that grew so fast we butchered at 8½ weeks and had chickens (dressed) average 3-3/4 lbs. each! They also respond quickly to questions — we got an individual reply to ours in less than a week.
—Daryl Ann Kyle

Murray McMurray Hatchery
Catalog

free from:
Murray McMurray Hatchery
Webster City, IA 50595

Fish Farming in Your Solar Greenhouse

This is a fascinating book that will provide those aspiring to self-sufficiency with a solid start in integrating aquaculture into their greenhouse systems. Applying the principles of solar energy and aquaculture to produce both fish and vegetables in abundance, the authors provide a readable analysis of relevant fish biology and environmental requirements. This book is an excellent "how to" guide for beginning a home-size aquaculture system.
—Richard Wilen

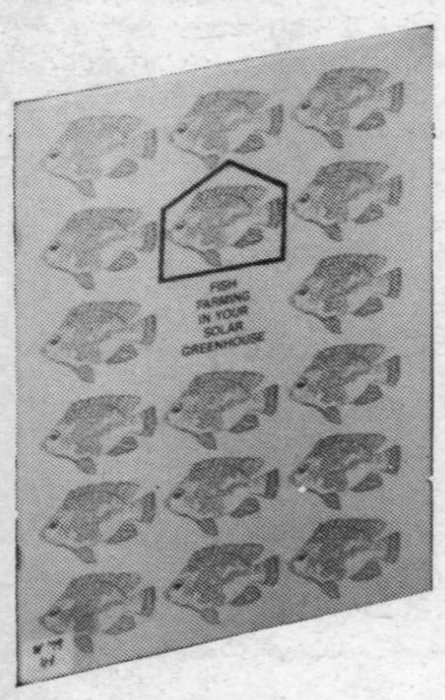

Fish Farming in Your Solar Greenhouse
William Head,
Jon Splane
1979; 43 pp.

$5 postpaid from:
Amity Foundation
P.O. Box 7066
Eugene, OR 97401

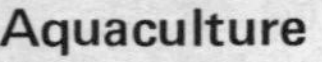

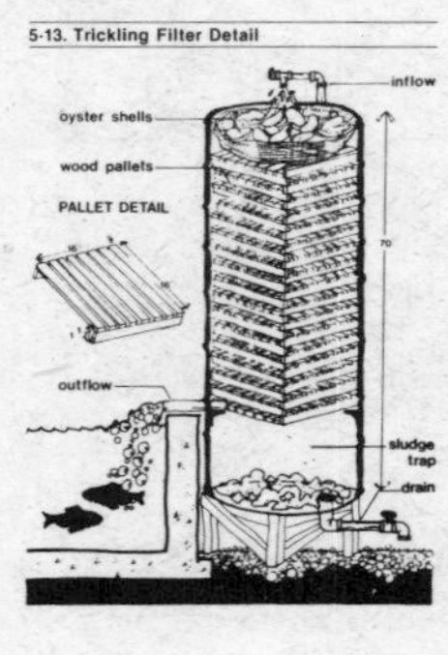

DRAIN OUTFLOW
FILTER TOWERS
INFLOW WATER INTO FILTERS
OUTFLOW WATER FROM FILTERS
INTERMEDIATE WATER RELEASE VALVES
3/4" PVC PIPE
INFLOW WATER PUMPED TO FILTER SUBMERSIBLE PUMP
HOSE

TRICKLING FILTER SYSTEM
NORTH TANK

•

Advantages of small ponds

1. Easier and quicker to harvest.
2. Can be drained and refilled more quickly.
3. Easier to treat disease and parasites.
4. If for any reason all or part of the stock in one pond is lost, it represents less of a financial loss.
5. Less subject to dam and levee erosion by wind.

Advantages of large ponds

1. Less construction cost per acre of water.
2. Take up less space per acre of water.
3. More subject to wind action, therefore less susceptible to oxygen deficiency.
4. More conducive to rotation with rice or terrestrial crops.

The Will-O'-the-Wisp Bug Light Fish Feeder

Ordinary commercial fish feed contains a lot of ingredients, but the key one is fish meal. If the economic and ecological implications of that bother you, here is an alternative. The Will-O'-the-Wisp feeder attracts insects with U-V light and blows them down into the water for fish to eat. Insects are better than a good substitute for fish meal. The amino acid balance is better for at least some fish (including trout) than that of fish meal or "complete" commercial diets and the quality of the resulting fish may be superior. There are only a few sites "buggy" enough for this tool to supply the entire diet of cultured fish, but it can significantly enhance growth and/or cut down on commercial feed use in most situations.

As compared to other devices of this type, the Will-O'-the-Wisp is better built and safer. One of manufacturer Elmer Hedlund's prototypes has run every night, winter and summer, for five years with no maintenance other than replacement of the bulb; our experience with three of the lights at New Alchemy parallels this. The original unit draws one kilowatt hour of electricity per ten hours of operation, and improvements in the motor and fan may have reduced this. It may make some potential purchasers feel better to know that Hedlund's purpose in marketing the light is to help finance his personal pet project, a 370-acre wildlife preserve he manages in northern Wisconsin.
—Bill McLarney

Will-O'-the-Wisp Bug Light Fish Feeder

$144.95 postpaid from:
Hedlunds of Medford, Inc.
P.O. Box 305
Medford, WI 54451

Aquaculture

If you're interested in vastly increasing your protein production, this is the Bible. Every kind of fish, lobsters, shrimps, seaweeds. If it can be grown in water, there's a chapter. Plus, a great appendix on pond siting and construction. Co-author McLarney is one of the Cape Cod New Alchemists (p. 177).
—Peter Warshall
[Suggested by John Todd]

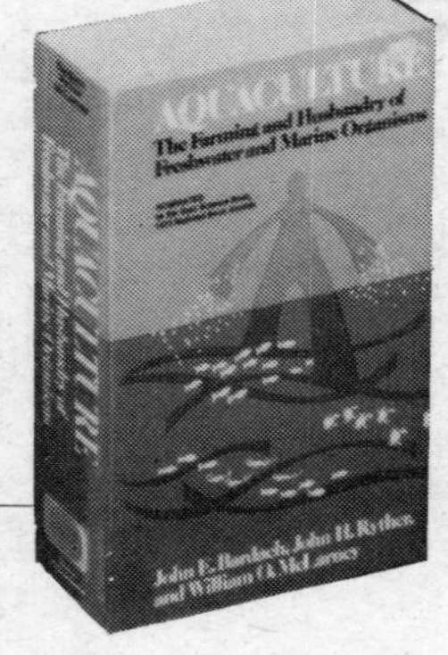

Aquaculture
(The Farming and Husbandry of Freshwater and Marine Organisms)
John E. Bardach,
John H. Ryther, and
William O. McLarney
1972; 868 pp.

$21.95 postpaid from:
John Wiley and Sons
One Wiley Drive
Somerset, NJ 08873

←

Habitat and feeding niches of the principal species in classical Chinese carp culture. (1) Grass carp (Ctenopharyngodon idellus) **feeding on vegetable tops. (2) Big head** (Aristichtys nobilis) **feeding on zooplankton in midwater. (3) Silver carp** (Hypophthalmichtys molitrix) **feeding on phytoplankton in midwater. (4) Mud carp** (Cirrhinus molitorella) **feeding on benthic animals and detritus, including grass carp feces. (5) Common carp** (Cyprinus carpio) **feeding on benthic animals and detritus, including grass carp feces. (6) Black carp** (Mylopharyngodon piceus) **feeding on mollusks.**

Backyard Livestock

Backyard in this sense does not mean city. At least, this book does not deal with zoning ordinances or soundproofing chickens. In fact, what orients the book to homes as well as homesteads is its simplicity. Even backyard veal now seems feasible. —*Rosemary Menninger*

Backyard Livestock
Steven Thomas
1976; 288 pp.

$5.95 postpaid from:
Charles Scribner's Sons
Vreeland Avenue
Totowa, NJ 07512

Veal calf pen

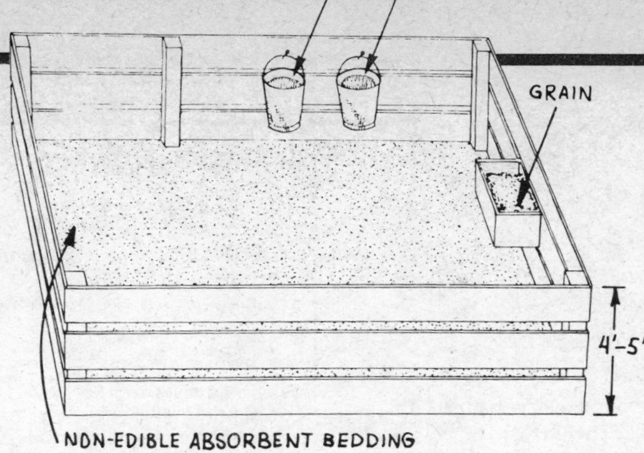

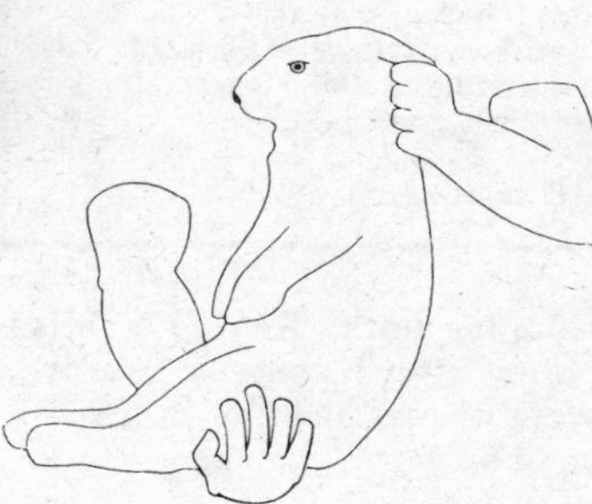

← The correct way to pick up and carry a rabbit is by grabbing the skin of one shoulder in one hand and placing the other hand under the rump for support. The feet should always be pointed away from the body to prevent scratching.

•

In the case of orphaned litters or when a doe won't nurse, you can foist some on another doe if they were born within three days of hers. To prevent her from rejecting them, put some Vaseline on her nose. In cases where you have no other doe to pass orphans or "extras" from a large litter on to, you *can* raise them yourself but, please, think twice. Raising any animal from birth is a taxing job, and rabbits are among the most demanding. They must be fed with an eyedropper or doll bottle at least four times a day (and at night). If you're not sure you'll stick with it, drown them and dispose of them. (You can feed them to your pig if you're up to it.) This is preferable to stringing them along for a few days slowly starving, and then deciding the drudgery is no longer worth it.

Approximate Time Per Day To Care For Livestock

Animal	Time/Day (Minutes) Summer	Winter
Poultry	5	7
Sheep	5*	10
Milk Goat	15-30	15-30
Pig	5	7
Rabbit	5	7
Veal Calf	7	10

*If you raise grass lambs that are contained by fencing you will have practically no time investment (except to check for their general well-being) other than to bring water. If you grain them in the summer figure an additional few minutes.

Raising Small Meat Animals

If your average country vet doesn't know too much about sick rabbits and chickens, that's because he spends most of his time doctoring horses and cattle. Dr. Giammattei helps fill the void with this excellent book. There are 39 pages of diagnostic keys for various animal diseases, plus instructions on how to doctor your own flocks. Details on nutrition, housing, breeding, management and butchering are equally well presented.
—*Richard Nilsen*

Raising Small Meat Animals
Victor M. Giammattei
1976; 433 pp.

$12.35 postpaid from:
The Interstate Publishers, Inc.
19-27 N. Jackson Street
Danville, IL 61832

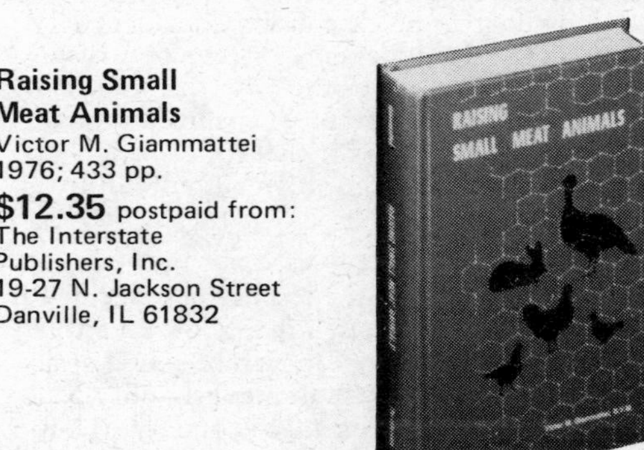

Table 1-1. Analysis of Savings on Home-Grown Small Meat Animals

Type of Small Meat Animal	Approx. Cost of Home Production for One Lb. of Dressed Carcass	Approx. Retail Price per Lb. of Dressed Carcass (California grown)	Retail Price Saved on Home-Grown Carcasses
	($)	($)	(%)
Chicken broiler	.45	.55	18.4
Turkey roaster	.56	.61	8.2
Cornish game hen[1]	.70	.89	19.2
Rabbit fryer	.75	1.60	53.0
Squab	1.00	2.35	57.5

1. Arkansas grown.

•

Anytime an odd number of birds or unpaired birds are left in a pen with mated birds, there'll be trouble. The odd bird or unpaired birds will intervene between a working pair. A male may attempt to mate with a female and end up fighting her mate. Or a singleton of either sex may try and take over a nesting area, fighting the occupants.

Regardless of the situation, remember that just one extra adult bird can cause unbelievable havoc. If you have a number of extras in a pen, your squabbers may become nearly functionless. Never let this situation arise; remove all extras immediately. If, for example, a member of a pair dies, the survivor should be removed. If a member of a pair gets sick and you remove it, also remove its mate and the nest box.

↑ Debeak only when you see one or several birds under constant attack to the point where they're left bleeding. You generally have plenty of time; your birds aren't going to turn into killers overnight. To debeak, use an ordinary pair of sharp side cutters (wire cutters), large fingernail clippers, or dog toenail clippers and clip the upper beak off squarely, about halfway from the tip to its base. This position is critical, because if you cut too close to the base you'll cause excessive bleeding and the bird will have a difficult time eating. After cutting off the upper beak, snip off just the very tip of the bottom.

•

If you want to produce 20 pounds of rabbit fryer meat per month, you must maintain one buck rabbit and five does the year around. Routine care for this number will take only minutes per day and will require very little work. It will require more work and be more time-consuming, however, than producing an equivalent amount of broiler chicken meat, but probably less than for producing an equivalent amount of squab meat.

Countryside

The concerns and thousand odd questions of homesteaders and small livestock farmers get better regular treatment in **Countryside** *than anywhere else. Separate columns for rabbits, pigs, goats, cows, woodlots, bees, feeds, marketing and more make it easy to zero in on your interests. It is also a good place to shop — there are lots of farm-related supplies advertised, many available by mail-order.* —*Richard Nilsen*

Countryside
(The Magazine for Serious Homesteaders)
Jerome Belanger, Editor

$12 /year (12 issues)
from:
Countryside Small Stock Journal
312 Portland Road
Waterloo, WI 53594

•

Electric fencing can work quite well for goats, but they must be trained to respect it. Start out with some electric fencing in a small area that's clear of weeds or tall grass so the goats can see the fencing easily and learn that it "stings."

Electric fence is a low-cost way to fence pasture or subdivide it, but I suggest wovenwire fence for the barnyard and exercise pens. The wovenwire is more secure, will confine the animals without any training, and keeps out dogs. Dogs can kill goats, and often you put up fencing to protect the goats as much as to confine them.

•

A recent article about chicken houses suggested dirt floors are satisfactory for light soil areas. They aren't satisfactory if you have predator problems! We live in a wooded hill area on a river and there is no way our hens would last very long with a dirt floor in the house.

Even a large knothole can let in a snake large enough to eat eggs and newly hatched chicks.

Chickens absolutely do fight over the highest roost. Folks should remember that the birds will roost on the highest *anything*. Make sure the nests are lower than the roosts or you will have hens roosting in the nests and lots of dirty eggs.

Rabbit hutch with metal self-feeder for commercial pelleted feed. Notice inside the hutch, the aluminum beer can for the rabbit to kick around for amusement.

Weeder geese

White Chinese Geese are a variety of domestic geese that are excellent grass eaters in row crops, orchards and vineyards. Before the eightfold increase in the last ten years of herbicides on California farms this species of geese played an integral part in the production of a variety of crops. They will control and eliminate Johnson, Bermuda, and Nut grass. They are still used in cotton (mainly), citrus, nuts, stonefruit, grapes, raisins, and tomatoes. Besides being effective in weed control, costs for using geese run about $20 - $30 an acre as compared to $100 - $200 an acre for the same kind of control using herbicides.

John Mason, a greenhouse tomato grower in Barstow, CA finds 2 - 3 geese per acre will do the weeding job of one full-time person. Shipped one day old, 10 or more only, $35 for 10, $3 each for 100 or more geese from:

Fruit's Weeder Geese
19459 Avenue 144
Porterville, CA 93257

—Rich Purvis

THE RISING SUN
NEIGHBORHOOD NEWSLETTER

Postcard from East Tennessee — If I lay me down between the mountains in the deep green furry valleys, will I slide into a hole as soft as mine that gentles you?

Domestic Rabbit Production

Rabbits are an ideal source of meat for urban dwellers — they mature rapidly, take up little space, and make no noise to bother neighbors. This book will provide answers for a person with 4 or 400 rabbits. —Richard Nilsen

11-pound doe and her annual production of four litters, totaling 120 pounds, over 1000 percent of her live weight.

Domestic Rabbit Production
George S. Templeton
1955, 1968; 213 pp.

$7.95 postpaid from:
The Interstate Printers and Publishers, Inc.
19-27 North Jackson St.
Danville, IL 61832

Commercial Rabbit Raising

This is a good cheap booklet. It covers all the basics like how to select a breed, feed and manage the herd etc. It also tells how to use the manure (as if you didn't know) and cure rabbit skins. —Martin K. Rorapaugh

•

Earthworms in the Rabbitry

Where earthworms are active throughout the year as in warm climates, they may be used to advantage under rabbit hutches to save labor in removing fertilizer. Make bins for confining the worms the same length and width as the hutch and 1 foot deep. Place bins on the ground, not on solid floors, and keep the fertilizer moist to insure the worms working throughout the bin.

Earthworms convert the rabbit droppings into casts — a convenient form of fertilizer for use with flowers, lawns, shrubs, trees, and other foliage. If you keep a large population of worms, there will be no objectionable odor. Very few flies will breed in the bins. It is necessary to remove the manure only at 5- to 6-month intervals.

Commercial Rabbit Raising
(Agriculture Handbook No. 309)
R.B. Casady et al.
#001-000-01376-9
1966, 1971; 69 pp.

$1.60 postpaid from:
Superintendent of Documents
U.S. Government Printing Office
Washington, DC 20402

Rambling Rabbit Rap

by Gurney Norman

I spent most of this past summer with a farmer friend of mine who raises rabbits as a main source of table meat for his family. Six does and a buck kept in hutches at the edge of the garden provide regular meat for his family of four. Other than the heavy work of removing the manure as it accumulates, the rabbits are in the care of my friend's twelve-year-old daughter, who feeds and waters them as part of her daily chores. Her father does the slaughtering as the young rabbits mature. The meat is kept in the freezer, and eaten at the rate of about one, sometimes two, a week.

I'd tasted wild rabbit before, but I didn't remember much about it, except that the occasion was loaded with an atmosphere of muted guilt, or at least an uncomfortable degree of self-consciousness. I was a kid at the time and I don't remember who the adults were, cooking and serving the meat. But I do remember the almost compulsive talk that went on among them about how wild rabbits were sometimes dangerous to eat, about how we probably ought not be eating this one, but let's just take a bit of him anyway, and see. I took my bite, but what I tasted was the general misgivings about the whole thing. And those misgivings stayed in my head for 25 years, until this very summer when we were eating rabbit as a regular staple.

And it was great! It was at least as good as fried chicken, and maybe even a little better, depending on whose chicken you've been eating. My friend said that as far as the work of meat-production is concerned, rabbits are far less trouble to keep than chickens. He keeps chickens, but mainly for the eggs. (He raises beef and pork too, as well as a fantastic organic garden, all on twelve rather hilly acres. Working together, he and his wife and their two children come as close as anyone I know to total organic self-sufficiency.)

We talked some about the question of animal slaughter, of killing other creatures to feed on them. He said that in the beginning he had some trouble killing his rabbits, but that he finally overcame it when he quit thinking of them as "bunnies" and looked upon them as simply a source of protein. That attitude will no doubt trouble the more committed vegetarians; but not many farmers putting in 10 and 12 hours work a day are vegetarians. If a rabbit is a fellow being, so is a corn stalk. Creatures eat creatures. Some day worms will eat us all, and whatever debt we may owe the carbon-nitrogen cycle will no doubt then be paid in full.

So went our dialogue. Or one chapter of it, anyway. One of the great things about the summer on the farm was the kind of running conversation we had, picking up hours and even days later where the talk left off before. Farmers certainly work a good deal more than they talk, but when they do talk, it's grand to listen in. The language of men working together in a field is a rare and special thing. Men who work together, summer after summer, for years, have a common body of lore, a mutual frame of reference that underlies everything they say. When it's best is when the words begin from a concrete subject, rise into a grand abstraction, convolute a time or two then return to earth again. Our talk about rabbits was like that. We talked about them as "bunnies," against rabbits as food to eat. That got us into talk about the esoteric loveliness of a wagon wheel as a thing you paint and display in your front yard, against the loveliness of a wheel on an actual wagon that's helping you do the work necessary to your livelihood. Then we got into the difference between vocation and avocation, of the unhappiness that comes when a person's play is too far removed from his work. Raising rabbits is play, it's fun, a hobby. But it can also be work, good, productive work of the kind that contributes to health and vigor by getting good home-grown food on the table.

And so we got into the organic life as an ideal, a life in which opposites like "work" and "play" are reconciled. When your life is one of daily, personal "creation," of work that satisfies like play does, you're less in need of purchased, artificial re-creation. The average industrial worker does a job he hates in order to buy the things he loves, like food, and entertainment. His vocation is one thing, his avocation another, and never the twain shall meet. This split ultimately leads to the deadly division between city and country. And in the same way the modern vocation, or industrial job, is deadly to the individual worker's creative spirit, the city has become the deadly enemy of the countryside. To satisfy the appetites of the city, the countryside is pillaged by industrial, mechanized farms for food and strip mines for fuel for electric power. How neurotic, how divided our culture against itself!

And thus we came to the question, can the lowly rabbit possibly come to the rescue? We decided it could. Rabbits can be raised in any back yard, as food, primarily; but they can also be raised as a metaphor of a new and simultaneously old possibility, the possibility of cottage economy. They can be raised as a metaphor of opposites reconciled, of cultural schizophrenia overcome. They can stand as an image of country stuff happening in town, of town style stretched to embrace country substance, of work become play and play become work, which, after all, is not far from Adam and Eve's set-up in the Original Garden. I don't plan to hold my breath till the Golden Age arrives. But I do plan to raise some rabbits in my suburban backyard this year, and to eat the little morsels one by one when they are grown. ■

Raising Milk Goats the Modern Way

Belanger's book is a good jumping off point for the first-time goat owner. Goats are to homesteads what cows are to dairies. And the taste of goat's milk is purely a matter of conditioning — children raised on goat's milk will think cow's milk tastes funny the first time they try it. —Richard Nilsen

Goats can be trained to pull small carts — to the delight of youngsters or to the relief of homesteaders who want to move compost and other materials. Almost any book on dog training can be used to train goats.

Raising Milk Goats The Modern Way
Jerry Belanger
1975, 1980; 152 pp.

$4.95 postpaid from:
Garden Way Publishing Co.
Charlotte, VT 05545
or Whole Earth Household Store

Dairy Goats

This book bridges the gap between a 4-H pamphlet and the $17 goat book. It covers everything you should know before and when you get into goats. You can skip the analysis/amplification (if you want) of how a goat's stomach works, the manufacture of proteins, etc. and just discover that one half pound of good dairy mix grain for each pound of milk produced is what you want.
—Steve Katona
[Suggested by Al Ames]

•

The small flat globules and the soft curd of goat's milk contribute to its ease of digestibility. Some persons who are allergic to cow's milk can consume goat's milk readily, due largely perhaps to its easier digestibility. In a great many cases goat's milk has proved especially valuable for infants and invalids.

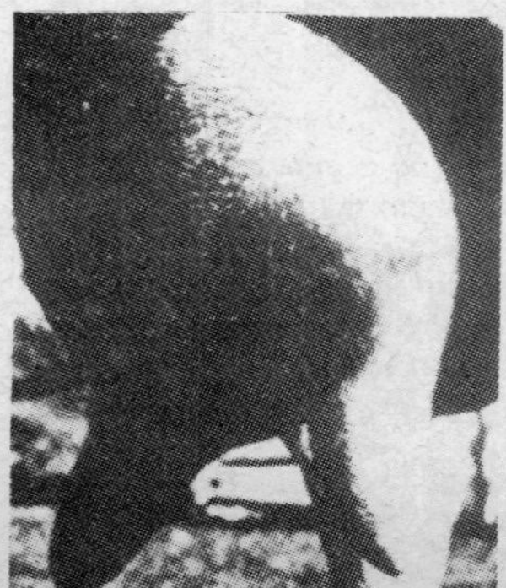

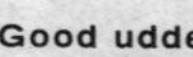

Good udder

Dairy Goats
(Breeding/ Feeding/ Management)
Byron E. Colby
1966, 1972; 77 pp.

$2 postpaid from:
The American Dairy Goat Association
P.O. Box 865
Spindale, NC 28160

The Family Cow

This book is for beginners interested in keeping one milk cow, and it is a joy to read — combining the best information, old and new, with long personal experience, and a clear, light-hearted style. Although for many a milk goat may be a better choice — they eat less and give less milk than cows — this book is well worth reading if you are trying to decide which is best suited to your scale of farming. Lots of detailed information, including feed rations.
—Richard Nilsen

The Family Cow
Dirk van Loon
1976; 257 pp.
$5.95 postpaid from:
Garden Way Publishing
Charlotte, VT 05445
or Whole Earth
Household Store

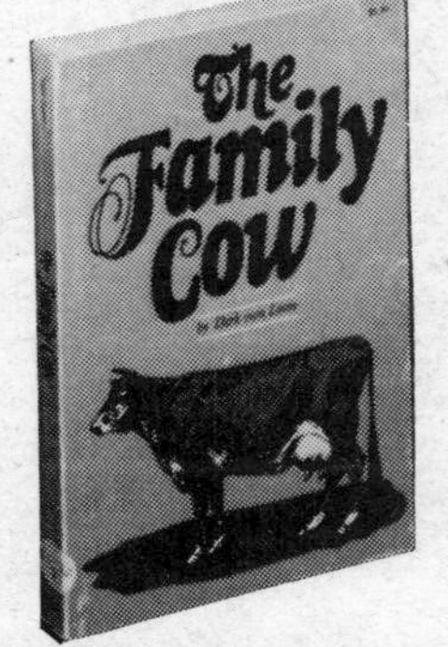

← The Brown Swiss cow. Average weight, 1200 to 1400 pounds. Light gray to almost black, with a lighter streak down the center of the back. Muzzle light, nose and switch black. A white udder and white extending forward under the belly and as far as the navel is acceptable. The breed averages 11,000 pounds of milk a year, 4 percent butterfat. Originated in Switzerland. The Brown Swiss Cattle Breeders' Association of America was founded in 1880. Brown Swiss cows are the largest of the dairy breeds. They are fleshier and less angular than the others.

•

I don't believe anyone with no domestic animals and the responsibilities that go with them should jump into owning a cow. It's not that they take so much time, but that in most cases they are an everyday, two-or-three-times-a-day obligation, especially when they are in milk.

Also, the cow makes the most sense when she is able to play at the hub of a coordinated whole that includes a garden — whose scraps she eats — and chickens and pigs that are able to make the most out of excess milk or milk by-products the family can't use.

•

I had thought of calling this book **The Neighborhood Cow**, for the reason that we have become a society of people who hate to be tied down. And unless there is at least one other person to step in on occasion to milk, feed and clean up after the cow, the idea of a day or weekend off can become an obsession.

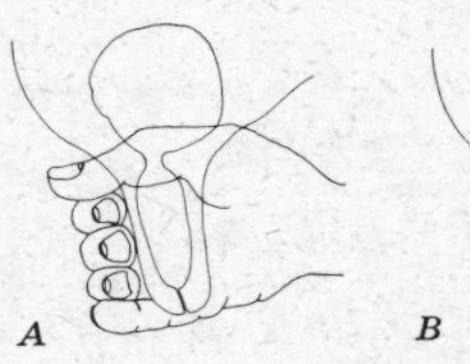

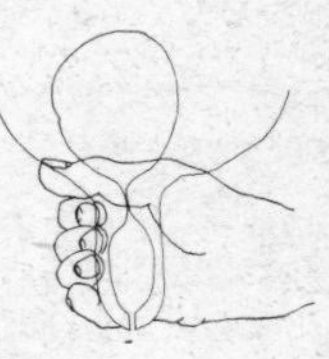

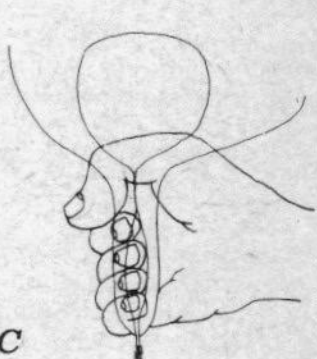

↑ In hand milking, (A) Grasp the teat high so that the thumb and index finger are able to circle the teat where it meets the body of the udder. (B) Close off the top of the teat cistern by squeezing thumb and index finger together over the annular fold. (C) Close rest of fist so that the milk trapped within the teat cistern is forced through the streak canal.

Small-Scale Pig Raising

Most all livestock books deal with pigs, but it is nice to be able to reach for one volume that has everything a beginner will likely need. Excellent illustrations throughout. The photo sequence on butchering is particularly well done.
—Richard Nilsen

Small-Scale Pig Raising
Dirk van Loon
1978; 263 pp.
$5.95 postpaid from:
Garden Way Publishing
Charlotte, VT 05445

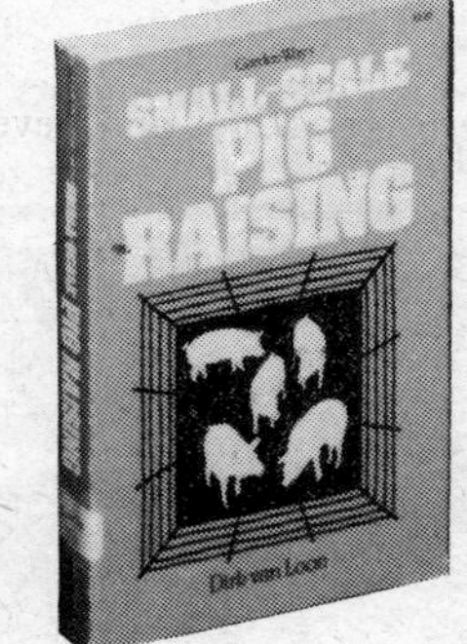

•

Clearing Land with Pigs
Far from discouraging rooting, many people do everything they can to encourage the practice in the course of using pigs to clear out and plow land. A thorough job can be done on thicketed scrub land or on old fields that are returning to second growth.

The pigs should be confined so that they will root the enclosed area completely. Moveable electric fences are ideal on the roughest, brushiest and rockiest land. On more open ground portable huts with attached exercise yards may be better.

After two or three weeks pigs will have all but the largest shrubs uprooted. Rocks will be tossed on end where they're easy to roll onto a stoneboat. The larger trees may be uneaithed as well, if you "plant" cracked corn, apples or other goodies in crowbar holes poked amongst their roots.

A combination of hogs and sheep may be used to establish pasture on shrubby barrens or reverted crop lands. I've not tried it, but the system sounds reasonable and is sworn to by the person who worked it out in New Brunswick.

•

He first ran hogs on the barrens (rough, sour and rocky land covered with waist-high shrubs). Once most of the vegetation was dead or well beaten down, lime was spread casually with a shovel. It did not matter if the lime was not well scattered. The pigs finished the spreading.

When winter came and snow covered the area, bales of hay were broken and fed to sheep over the same ground. Hay seed, direct from the bales, or passed through the sheep, sprouted over the rich bed, found once the snows melted in spring.

Raising Sheep the Modern Way

There's something special about lambing season; even the toughest ranch hands show some tender love and care. This book reflects that gentle thoroughness. It quietly tells you everything about sheep, though it omits specifics on grazing in mountains, deserts and other marginally productive land.
—Rosemary Menninger

(See Simmons' yarn, p. 279.)

Raising Sheep the Modern Way
Paula Simmons
1976; 234 pp.
$5.95 postpaid from:
Garden Way Publishing Co.
Charlotte, VT 05545

•

If you have a ram who already butts at you, try the water cure: a half pail of water in his face when he comes at you. After that, a water pistol or dose syringe of water in his face usually suffices to reinforce the training.

Goat Husbandry

The definitive goat book.
—SB
[Suggested by Steve Durkee]

Goat Husbandry
David Mackenzie
1967; 368 pp.
OUT OF PRINT
Revised edition will appear in 1981 from:
Faber and Faber
99 Main Street
Salem, NH 03079

•

The goatherd who knows his flock and range can lead on the first stage or two of their wanderings and as soon as they are all busy at a popular stop he can quietly slip away. The flock queen will call him when she is ready to move on, but if he has disappeared she will take the lead herself. This tactic works well in broken wooded country; but in open country the delinquent leader is caught in the act of escape and the whole flock comes scampering after him.

Under such conditions the goatherd must use plain language to tell his flock when he has ceased to be their king billy. Mere rudeness won't suffice; king billy's manners are not of the best; a push and a grunt and a show of displeasure convey his warning to the flock to obey and follow him more closely. But king billy doesn't throw sticks or stones; the performance of such an act is a special characteristic of man and monkey which is peculiarly repulsive to all other species. So long as it is carried out calmly and ceremonially, so as not to be mistaken for mere rudeness, the flock will turn their backs on the goatherd, will go their way and leave him go to his. The popular use of effeminate males has produced flocks of half-witted goats which may be incapable of finding amongst themselves a flock queen of sufficient independence of character to accept even so broad a hint as the thrown stick. If such a flock refuses to be content without a king billy to lead them, the only cure is to give them a real one.

Dairy Goat Journal

Monthly goat gab, latest in goat gear, goats for sale, goat cheese recipes, goatkeepers' classifieds. Get your goat.
—J.D. Smith

Dairy Goat Journal
Kent Leach, Editor
$11/year (12 issues)
postpaid from:
Dairy Goat Journal
P.O. Box 1808
Scottsdale, AZ 85252

•

To keep your goats from eating the bark off your favorite trees, bushes, etc., gather a good-sized pail full of goat droppings, add water and mix until it reaches the consistency of paint. Then paint the trunks of the trees high enough so the goats can't reach past when standing. Same mixture can be thinned and sprayed on bushes, shrubs, etc. or wherever you don't want the goats to eat. The mixture is harmless and will also act as a fertilizer. May have to be repeated after a rain.
—Mrs. Frances Fleck
Bernardsville, NJ

For Better Health
DRINK GOAT MILK

←

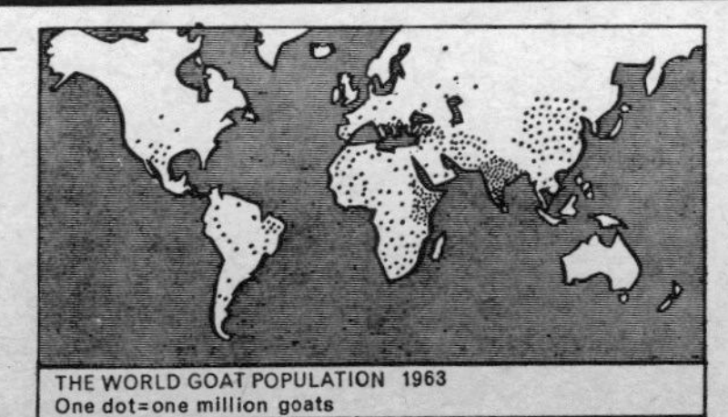

Targhee ewe with newborn lamb.

THE RISING SUN
NEIGHBORHOOD NEWSLETTER

People are tired of explaining the Amanda Madison Memorial Nonsense Box at Smitty's Bar to out-of-towners, and some people in town don't know the whole story. So I'm going to explain it all because I knew her and I like to explain things and everybody else who knew her would rather write postcards than explain. Amanda died in 1969 and was old and everyone loved her. She started her unusual career by not marrying which was quite unusual at the time. Some people like to tell Delta Dawn stories about that, but Amanda said, when I asked her about it once, "I never had a beau who surprised me once as much as I surprise myself 8 or 9 times daily. I see no reason to marry into boredom when the streets are littered with it." So she lived on almost no money in her father's house and did typical small town things in weird ways. *continued*

Livestock Supplies

I work with sheep and goats a lot. Often farmer's co-ops don't have supplies for small livestock — they're geared towards beef agribusiness. ***Mid-States Wool Grower's Co-op*** *handles everything from antibiotics to sheep clippers. My friend, a state fair sheep judge with a fine flock of his own swears by them. Good service.*

—*John Benecki*

Livestock Supplies
Catalog
free from:
Mid-States Wool
Growers Cooperative
8270 Nieman Road
Shawnee Mission, KS 66214

HOOF TRIMMING KNIVES

No. 110–114 Right Hand
No. 111–115 Left Hand

$ 4.99

Sheep and Cow bells. Rectangular type, tapering toward top. Made from one piece of metal. No rivets. Smooth and mellow tone.

No.	Size	ea.	Per Doz.
8	⅓"x1½" (Sh. Wt. 3 lbs.)	75¢	$8.55
9	2⅝"x1½" (Sh. Wt. 4 lbs.)	95¢	10.85
10	3x2¼" (Sh. Wt. 5 lbs.)	1.10	12.55

Plastic Sheep Bell Strap 80¢ ea. or 8.55 doz. (Sh. Wt. 14 oz.)

Fertility Pastures and Cover Crops

If you graze livestock, are planning a pasture, or can't afford the cost of concentrated feed, this book is worth the money. Turner was a gentleman farmer who had the time and curiosity to plant identically sized patches of 35 different grasses and herbs, and then turn his dairy cows loose and observe the order in which they were grazed off. He believed in a balanced diet for his stock, and that meant diversity. Included are 21 different pasture mixes, for different soil types, for early and late season grazing, even ones for chickens and pigs. Several of these mixes contain 20 or more different varieties of grasses and herbs. One of the finer how-to farming books I've come across.

—*Richard Nilsen*

Fertility Pastures and Cover Crops
Newman Turner
1974; 202 pp.

$11.50 postpaid from:
Bargyla Rateaver
Pauma Valley, CA 92061

As much as they like up to 130 lb. a day; lot wasted this way

About 100 lb. a day, no waste

About 80 lb. a day; no waste

60 lb. a day; no waste

Cross sections of the silage clamp showing how the quantity of silage a cow can take varies with the angle of the feeding face.

Feeds and Feeding

A comprehensive textbook worth consulting to learn more about what is in the feeds you buy, and what should be in the livestock rations you raise yourself. It is about feeds for cattle, sheep, swine and horses kept in confinement — there is very little here about pasturage. The emphasis is on modern methods, with chapters on growth hormones and the feeding of animal wastes; what's most useful is the wealth of nutritional details.

—*Richard Nilsen*

Feeds and Feeding
(Second edition)
Arthur E. Cullison
1979; 595 pp.

$15.95 postpaid from:
Reston Publishing Co.
Prentice-Hall, Inc.
Box 500
Englewood Cliffs,
NJ 07632

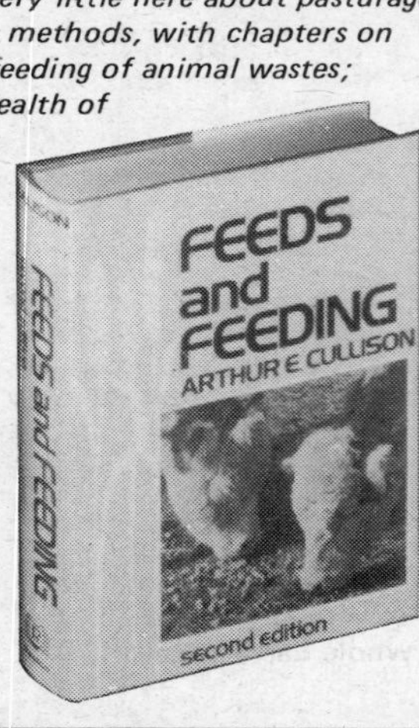

The four major feed grains.

The National Stock Dog Magazine

A small quarterly composed partly of letters from readers. The "Breeders Directory" includes listings from coast to coast (but not Canada) for Australian and English Shepherds, Australian Cattle Dogs (Queensland Blue Heelers), and Border Collies — all working dogs. —*Richard Nilsen*

The National Stock Dog Magazine
Jerry Belanger and
Dave Skeloda, Editors

$5/year (4 issues)
postpaid from:
Countryside
Publications, Ltd.
312 Portland Road
Waterloo, WI 53594

Jeteye Alice, C.W., about to meet an irate cow head-on. Alice readily grips either end of a cow.

A Veterinary Guide for Animal Owners

Spaulding sounds like the kind of vet I'd want to trust. His style is clear and readable, and often even entertaining. Much of the book focuses on preventive medicine, and if you have cattle, goats, sheep, horses, pigs, poultry, rabbits, or just a dog or cat, spending thirteen bucks on this book might save you a lot more later on.

One of the interesting things I learned from this book is that it's okay for rabbits to eat their own droppings; it's how they get their vitamin B. Imagine my relief.

—*John Vara*

A Veterinary Guide for Animal Owners
(Cattle, Goats, Sheep, Horses, Pigs, Poultry, Rabbits, Dogs, Cats)
C.E. Spaulding, D.V.M.
1976; 432 pp.

$12.95 postpaid from:
Rodale Press
33 East Minor
Emmaus, PA 18049
or Whole Earth
Household Store

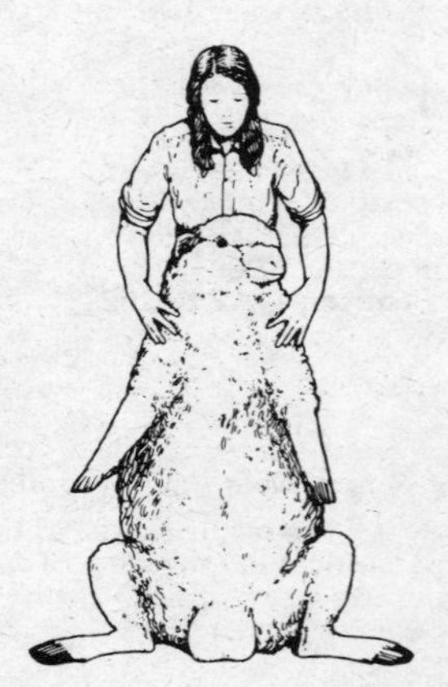

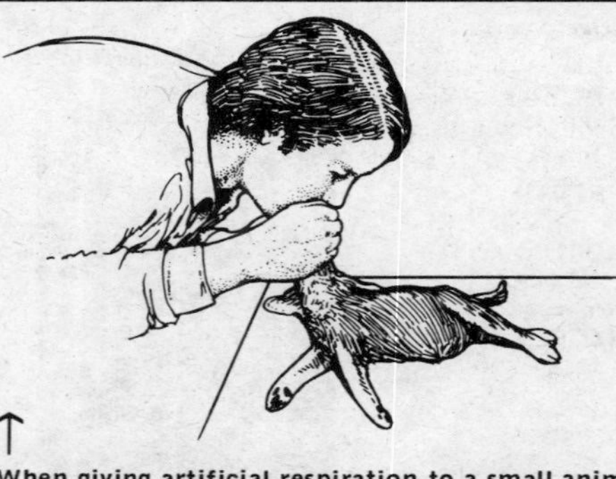

↑ **When giving artificial respiration to a small animal, cup your hands to prevent air from escaping when you blow.**

← **Sheep restraint achieved by it sitting down with its back on assistant's legs.**

Veterinary Guide for Farmers

Specifically for farm animals, this is fine, graphic how-to text. Its clarity imparts confidence, which I can see is often needed.

I didn't know cows had clitorises. —*SB*

Veterinary Guide for Farmers
(Popular Mechanics Revised Edition)
G.W. Stamm
1961, 1975; 303 pp.

$9.95 postpaid from:
E.P. Dutton and Company
Two Park Avenue
New York, NY 10016
or Whole Earth
Household Store

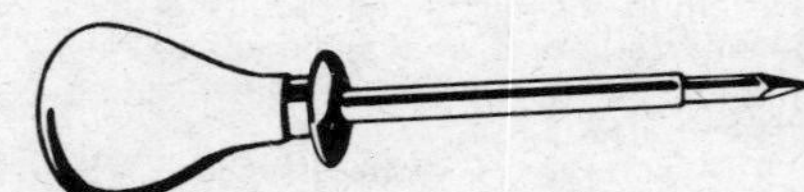

↑ **The trocar is used to relieve cattle bloat. This one is shown encased in its cannula. This is the part that remains in the cow's loin to allow gas to escape after the trocar is withdrawn.**

↗ **Arrow shows approximate position where cow with bloat should be tapped. A knife can be used for this purpose but it's better to use a trocar.**

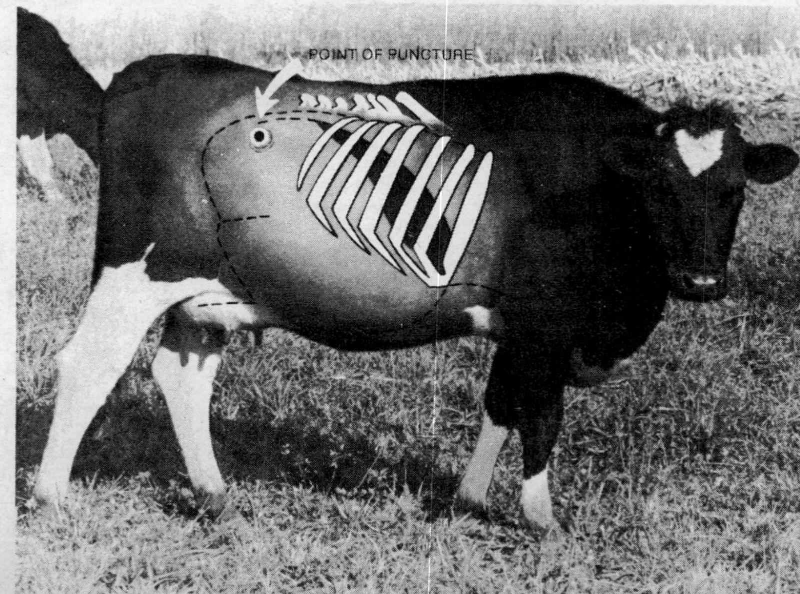

The Soay resembles more closely than any other existing breed the early domesticated neolithic sheep, which reached Britain about 5,000 years ago. Trials in England have shown that a Soay ewe rearing twin lambs will yield 1.57 times her own body weight of milk in one lactation, compared with one of the most popular ewes in Great Britain, the Scotch Halfbred, which yields only 1.21 times her own body weight of milk.

←

The Chance to Survive

This is a visually beautiful book on a seemingly incredible subject: the extinction of domesticated breeds of cattle, sheep, goats, horses and pigs in the British Isles. Domesticated breeds — many with thousands of years of careful breeding behind them — should be prime candidates for preservation, but this is not the case. Britain has lost close to 25 native breeds this century; 110 breeds remain today, and over half of them are in danger of extinction. And this is not a unique situation: In 1947 there were 42 Italian breeds of cattle. By 1974 only 22 breeds remained, and of these 13 were gravely endangered.

The author is an advisor to the Rare Breeds Survival Trust in Britain. His book is a sensitive tour through a barnyard of chilling memories. —Richard Nilsen

The Chance to Survive
(Rare Breeds in a Changing World)
Lawrence Alderson
1978; 192 pp.

$19.95 postpaid from:
The Stephen Greene Press
P.O. Box 1000
Fessenden Road
Brattleboro, VT 05301

or **£7.50** (about $18) from:
Cameron and Taylor Books Ltd.
25 Lloyd Baker Street
London WC1X 9AT
England

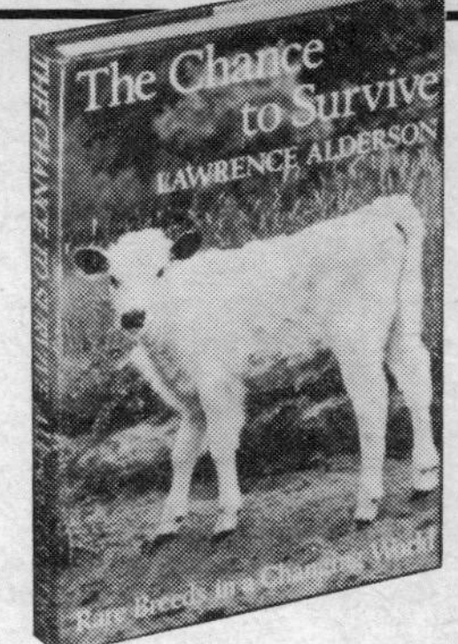

The Moral Status of Animals

If anybody needs a philosophical justification for vegetarianism, here it is. Clark is a British moral philosopher "strongly influenced by Mahayana Buddhism", and his prose is dry and his argument relentless. He could easily qualify for the post of chief theoretician to the growing animal rights movement. —Richard Nilsen

The Moral Status of Animals
Stephen R.L. Clark
1977; 221 pp.

$26.50 postpaid from:
Oxford University Press
16-00 Pollitt Drive
Fair Lawn, NJ 07410
or Whole Earth Household Store

•

Lest the central issue of my discourse be lost in the tangle of a hundred codicils, I therefore state it here: whatever else be true, whether there be gods or only atoms, whether men are significantly superior to non-human animals or no, whether there be a life to come or this poor accident be all, this at least cannot be true, that it is proper to be the cause of avoidable ill. There may be other moral principles than this, but this at least is dogma. And if this minimal principle be accepted, there is no other honest course than the immediate rejection of all flesh-foods and most bio-medical research.

The point, whatever its later complications, is a simple one, and the attempts of our hypocrisy to evade the issue provide a fascinating case-history of the corruption of our moral and philosophical sense.

The Merck Veterinary Manual

Very technical descriptions of diseases and injuries in animals; diagnoses and treatments. Written for vets, probably useful for anyone caring for animals. —Diana Barich

The Merck Veterinary Manual
(A Handbook of Diagnoses and Therapy for the Veterinarian)
5th Edition
1953, 1979; 1700 pp.

$17.75 postpaid from:
Dairy Goat Journal
P.O. Box 1808
Scottsdale, AZ 85252

Veterinary supplies

Two companies selling serums, vaccines, instruments, and drugs, by mail. —J.D. Smith

PetCo Animal Supplies
Catalog
free from:
PetCo Animal Supplies
P.O. Box 1076
8693 La Mesa Boulevard
La Mesa, CA 92041

Kansas City Vaccine Company
Catalog
free from:
Kansas City Vaccine Company
Stock Yards
Kansas City, MO 64102

•

Galvanized pail with built-in nipple for feed milk replacer to calves, foals.

	Retail	Wholesale
Each	9.95	6.78
Nipple only	1.29	.97
Valve only	2.40	1.84

—PetCo Animal Supplies

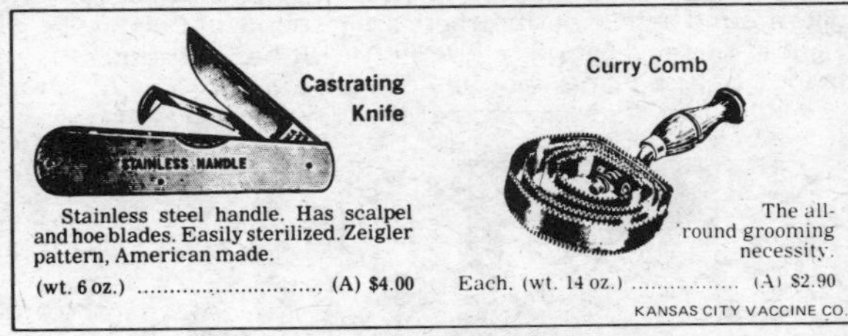

Castrating Knife
STAINLESS HANDLE
Stainless steel handle. Has scalpel and hoe blades. Easily sterilized. Zeigler pattern, American made.
(wt. 6 oz.) .... (A) $4.00
Curry Comb
The all-'round grooming necessity.
Each. (wt. 14 oz.) .... (A) $2.90
KANSAS CITY VACCINE CO.

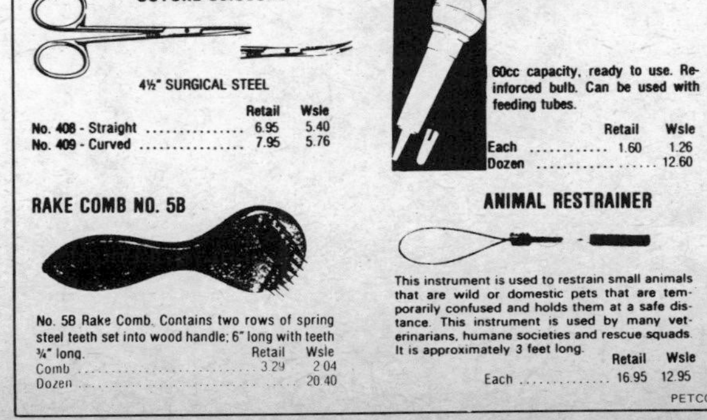

SUTURE SCISSORS
4½" SURGICAL STEEL
Retail Wsle
No. 408 - Straight 6.95 5.40
No. 409 - Curved 7.95 5.76
BULB DOSE SYRINGE
60cc capacity, ready to use. Reinforced bulb. Can be used with feeding tubes.
Retail Wsle
Each 1.60 1.26
Dozen 12.60
RAKE COMB NO. 5B
No. 5B Rake Comb. Contains two rows of spring steel teeth set into wood handle; 6" long with teeth ¾" long.
Retail Wsle
Comb 3.29 2.04
Dozen 20.40
ANIMAL RESTRAINER
This instrument is used to restrain small animals that are wild or domestic pets that are temporarily confused and holds them at a safe distance. This instrument is used by many veterinarians, humane societies and rescue squads. It is approximately 3 feet long.
Retail Wsle
Each 16.95 12.95
PETCO

The Buffalo Book

It was the U.S. strategy of killing off the buffalo that made possible the conquest of Indian civilization. This buffalo history dates mostly from the white man's contact with the beast, but that alone is a dramatic chunk. For guilt-free animal interest, it scores with the better chimp and dolphin books. Some details for raising your own buffalo herd. —Rosemary Menninger

The Buffalo Book
David A. Dary
1974; 361 pp.

$2.75 postpaid from:
Avon Books
Mail Order Department
250 West 55th Street
New York, NY 10019
or Whole Earth Household Store

•

Houck spoke of another advantage buffalo have over cattle: "They don't take as much feed to put on weight, as they forage some weeds that cattle pass up. That's why three buffalo can live on range that would support only two cows."

•

Buffalo, like most other big-game animals, thrive best where not closely confined. Large, open, grass pastures with a plentiful supply of clean, fresh water are best adapted to their needs. Although shade may not be an absolute survival requirement, herds may spend many mid-summer hours in the shade where available. Also, the presence of trees or large rocks adds to their well-being by providing rubbing sites.

Fences for confining buffalo should be strongly constructed. Minimum recommended fencing consists of 47" (Style No. 1047-6-11 or No. 1047-6-9) woven wire set about 10" above ground level extending to the top of 7' heavy duty posts spaced not more than 1 rod apart. Under normal conditions, buffalo are not likely to test the fence very severely, but when excited they may charge blindly into it, and then even the strongest fences may fail.

Corrals and chutes should be made of planks or heavy poles so the animals can readily see them and tend to avoid them. Such fences also obscure the view of activities outside the corral and thus reduce disturbance within. Plank corrals are easy for a man to climb, a distinct advantage when he is seeking escape from excited animals.

Barbed wire should not be used in buffalo fences. The barbs are ineffective in deterring the animals from attempting to escape and are a source of injury and infection. The range should be kept free of all loose wire, nails, etc. to prevent injury or infection.

Regardless of the extent of handling and of apparent domestication, buffalo are *dangerous wild animals* of uncertain temperament and should never be trusted. Supposedly tame animals have attacked owners caught off guard. *Buffalo are not suitable for pets or mascots.*

Ropes should not be used around the neck of the buffalo because the windpipe is easily crushed by such a form of restraint.

Buffalo bones stacked at the Michigan Carbon Works in Detroit, 1880s.

THE RISING SUN
NEIGHBORHOOD NEWSLETTER

continued from last spread

She taught Sunday School, for example, and one time had her 8th graders read the story in Matthew where Jesus curses the fig tree for no apparent reason and it dies. She asked each member of the class if they understood why Jesus did that and if they thought it was nice. After they all said no to both, she said, "You don't understand Jesus and he wasn't nice. Remember that. Now let's go play volleyball until it's time for church." She took unexpected gifts to people, like the time she took Lisa who had been a girls' basketball star and then got laid up with leukemia a purple baseball cap with yellow foam wings sticking out on the side and said, "I know you are tired of people looking at you with mushy eyes like you really are a sick person. Wear this and for one moment when they walk in they will forget that you are a sick person and remember you are a weirdo." Amanda did lots of other stuff, but the relevant thing here is that she wrote notes. She attended everything in town, and wrote alert thank you notes to participants. One time she wrote Tommy Wills, "Dear Tommy, I know it was difficult to keep a straight face in the Christmas program when Amy was having such unfortunate difficulties with her undergear, but I appreciate your making the effort. Many others would have laughed out loud and yet you said your lines exactly as you were supposed to. This denotes a level of self-control and consideration for others that will no doubt be of use to you in many endeavours throughout your life. Your Admirer, Amanda." She always wrote to the assistant of the person who got all the glory, the last person on the cleanup committee to leave and also wrote to people who quit something or other, city council, the Fourth of July parade committee, in disgust with bad feelings all around and thanked them for their past efforts. *continued on next spread*

A PASTURED HORSE IS A LITTLE LIKE A PARKED CAR, except the car isn't grazing and the horse doesn't need tires.

The side saddle was invented when it was determined that women could derive pleasure from straddling a horse.

Horse pictures play an important part in American adolescent development.

On Horseshoeing: You are never going to be stronger than the horse. You can be smarter most of the time. If you are going to try to shoe just any old horse, it would help to know how to throw the horse.

There was a sign at the Methodist Church in Alliance, Nebraska that said: "Horse sense is what keeps horses from betting on people."

If you are not strong in the arm, it doesn't hurt to knee a horse a little when you are cinching up.

Horses are like slaves in a way. Folks trade them for real high prices, and figure on making a profit most of the time.

Horses reproduce easier than tractors do.

Horses are, per capita, photographed more often than cattle.

Horses are like dogs. We don't eat them very often, but if they don't get along with us, we stop feeding them.

If people in cities who are worrying about continued food supplies would in some way support the use of horses for work, there would be fewer people and horses standing around hungry. —J.D. Smith

The Western Horseman

This is THE horse magazine of the American Cowboy, probably second only to **Reader's Digest** *for subscriptions in ranchland. Includes a little of everything from rodeo fashions and twelve year old horsegirls looking for penpals, to new product evaluations (kickbacks?) and general coverage of all important national horse shows. It is quarter horse biased, the cattle industry is too, but every October it prints a special "All Breeds Issue" in which access information is published for all the various registries in this country. If you own a pleasure horse, here is your mag. If you plan on getting a horse when you get the rest of your shit together, you can do some nice picture-shopping while you wait. If you are scared of horses but like boots and hats, here is your mail-order marketplace. Not terribly organic in its philosophies, but might change with its readership.* —J.D. Smith

The Western Horseman
Chan Bergen, Editor

$10 /year (12 issues)
from:
Western Horseman, Inc.
Box 7980
Colorado Springs, CO 80933

•

She was never hauled to any horse shows or race meets, but proved to be sure-footed and quick, and possessed enough cow savvy to make her a natural candidate as a broodmare. She was turned into the broodmare band at age three, and doubled as a working ranch horse for the following five years; she was last ridden in 1970.

Jennie led an idle life after that, wandering the lush mountain pastures during the summers to prepare for each winter. And when the snows did come and the temperatures hit 30 below zero, she continued to do well on the hay that was thrown from the horse-drawn sled every morning. Jennie had learned from the beginning to be aggressive enough to insure herself and the unborn foal an adequate supply of feed. A horse at the bottom of the herd's order of dominance finds itself at the end of the hay line.

Jennie, with foal in tow, in her old home country near Steamboat Springs, Colorado. ↓

The Draft Horse Journal

One good thing about the energy crunch is that it might take the generation that is going to have to live with it back into an examination of the use of horses as working, pulling machines. **The Draft Horse Journal** *devotes more space to the country fair pulling contests than it does to the actual logistics of getting work out of a horse, but if you are thinking about harnessing up ol' Dobbin, then get ahold of a copy of this quarterly journal. Their advertising rates are cheap enough so many folks with used harness and equipment run little ads about their goods, and though their emphasis runs a little to the purebred side, they do provide access to mules, multi-team hitches, and horsedrawn equipment. You might want to get their book,* **The Draft Horse Primer** *(edited by Maurice Telleen, 1977, $10.95 postpaid from Rodale Books, 33 East Minor, Emmaus, PA 18049).*
—J.D. Smith
[Suggested by Wendell Berry]

The Draft Horse Journal
Maurice Telleen, Editor
$10 /year (4 issues)
from:
The Draft Horse Journal
Route 3
Waverly, IA 60577

When the snow gets deep enough, Jim puts a couple extra horses on the spreader. ↓

Small Farmer's Journal

A quarterly for those who are serious about farming on a small scale. The editor, Lynn R. Miller, farms 80 acres with Belgian draft horses. The slant features "practical horse farming," and other solid information that can be put to use. —Drew Langsner

This is a big magazine with big beautiful pictures of horses working. —SB

Small Farmer's Journal
Lynn R. Miller, Editor
$10 /year (4 issues)
from:
Small Farmer's Journal
P.O. Box 197
Junction City, OR 97448

•

It requires on the average, 4 acres to feed a horse. You can operate a quarter-section farm, efficiently, with 6 horses.

•

Dale: I baby my horses. If you're going to go get out a load of logs a day you got to take care of them.

Christene: About how many thousand board feet are in a load?

Dale: They'll average 3000'.

Christene: That's a day's work?

Dale: That's a good day's work if you don't have any breakdown time or till you have to skid too far. We try to run 50 to 60 logs which is a load. 'Course the bigger the logs the less it takes. This stuff here runs 60 to 70 logs per load. That's about 30 - 35 trips. When the sun gets around a little better, there are a couple of big ones right in there. That one's just a little bit husky for nice going. I like big ones, but you can get too big. You're using your horses every inch of the way to get it.

Dale Greenough taking a log down the hill with his team.

Veterinary Notes for Horse Owners

An old standard. Semi-technical, exhaustive, reference guide. I can't see much application for the book if you don't own a horse, but if you do, it could save you a few hundred dollars in vet bills. —J.D. Smith
[Suggested by Peter Ratner]

Veterinary Notes for Horse Owners
M. Horace Hayes
1877, 1964; 656 pp.
$15 postpaid from:
Arco Publishing Company
219 Park Avenue South
New York, NY 10003
or Whole Earth Household Store

Normal parturition.

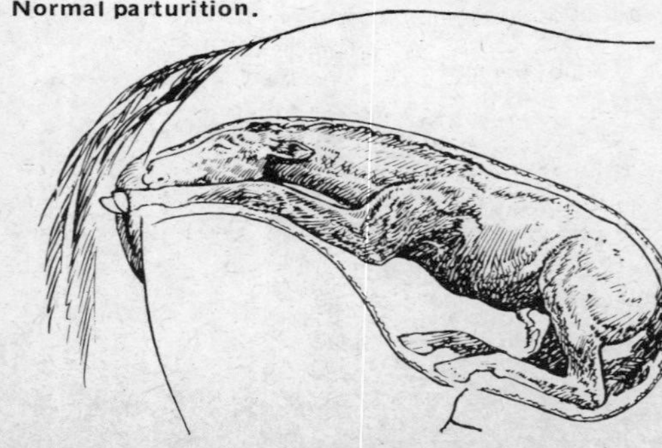

Horsecare & Horseshoeing

by Jeb Barton

Lameness in Horses *is my personal education source when dealing with my own horses, buying horses, or shoeing. It is direct, clearly written, very well illustrated with drawings and photographs, and written in language that is easy to follow — both common and Latin names usually occurring side by side. Every lameness is accompanied by a section on; Definition, Etiology (theory of the causes), Signs, Diagnosis and Differential Diagnosis, Treatment, and Prognosis (expected future course of the disease). Virtually all horse lameness of any significance are included and every common lameness is thoroughly covered.*

If you know nothing of horses and are thinking of buying one, the first 50 pages of the book (including 32 drawings and photos) offer an excellent introduction to conformation guidelines — what a horse should and should not look like to the untrained eye. Very informative. There are also 10 additional pages explaining how to determine whether or not the horse you are looking at is "sound" — "Examination for Soundness."

The book includes a section on horseshoeing and trimming, 25 pages. The information is good and well illustrated. I regard it as helpful to the unfamiliar but not to be used as a sole guide to someone who has never trimmed a horse's foot, let alone shod one. There is a limit to the do-it-yourself-from-a-book and I feel it stops abruptly with living things. No one should attempt to trim (certainly not shoe) a horse until they have had some first hand instruction from a reliable teacher. 90% of horse lameness occurs from the knee down!

Lameness in Horses
O.R. Adams
1962, 1966; 563 pp.
$12.50 postpaid from:
Lea & Febiger
600 Washington Square
Philadelphia, PA 19106

← Normal position of forelimb

The best book on horseshoeing that I have ever seen is **Horseshoeing**, *by A. Lungwitz.*

I received my Farrier's Certificate Degree from Oregon State University and this was one of our primary texts. I have studied this book in depth. The illustrations are excellent and the chronology of information is easy to follow.

If you own a horse you should at least know the basic anatomy and pathology of the animal's foot. If you want to learn to trim/shoe your horse then this is the book to have. However, any book should be regarded as a supplement to first hand instruction from a reliable teacher, not a substitute for it.

Horseshoeing
(A Textbook of Horseshoeing for Horseshoers and Veterinarians)
A. Lungwitz and John W. Adams
1966; 216 pp.
$6 postpaid from:
Oregon State University Press
University Press
101 Waldo Hall
Oregon State University
Corvallis, OR 97331

HORSESHOEING AND FARRIER'S TOOLS

The best Farrier's tools made in this country are made by G.E. Forge and Tool works. G.E. stands for George Earnest, and as their catalog says, "George Earnest spent a lifetime of work at the hoseshoeing and blacksmith trades and as a result of his many years of experience and understanding for the need of a good quality tool, he designed the G.E. set of tools." They claim, "Our tools are made from the very best quality refined tool steel on the market today." I think it's true. With the recent addition of new tempering ovens their tool quality is even better now than in the past. This attitude of constant improvement is certainly commendable.

The G.E. saddle horse clinchers and gooseneck clinchers are two of the best designed tools that I have ever held in my hand. Most of their tools cost between $25 - $55. That is more expensive than most other tool makers but G.E. tools are worth the additional cost. Even with frequent use they should outlast the owner if given proper care. They will even rebuild tools that begin to show wear. "For a fraction of the original cost, worn nippers can usually be rebuilt. Since metal is removed from the cutting edge to form the new blade, (happens every time you sharpen your nippers) the head will be slightly smaller each time it is reworked."

G.E. makes nippers, clinchers, pull offs, crease nail pullers, hoof testers, fire tongs and rounding hammers.

G.E. Forge and Tool Works
Catalog

free from:
G.E. Forge and Tool Works
P.O. Box 369
Arroyo Grande, CA 93420

If you can't afford G.E. tools then the next best name is Diamond. (I prefer Diamond fire tongs rather than the G.E.'s.) Diamond tools are well designed, the steel quality is adequate, they are about half as expensive as G.E. tools, and they can be ordered through most feed stores or saddle shops. Example, 15" Diamond nippers are about $35. 15" G.E. nippers are about $54.

Unless you simply have no other choice, avoid tools made by S.S.S., Multi-Products, Enderes or Heller. Nicholson makes the best horse rasp, but only leads Willie-Charlie by a nose, while Heller and the rest trail far behind. The best hoof knife is made by Erik Frost of Sweden. Well designed. Their wide blade knife is more useful than their narrow blade knife. Both right and left handed knives are available. Can be found at most feed stores or saddle shops. Bordizzo of Italy is a poorly designed hoof knife, but they do make the only extra thin blade knife that I have seen. It is quite useful for scouring out abscesses.

Farrier's Anvils: The two most important aspects of an anvil are its steel quality and its conformation. (A farrier's anvil is different in design from a blacksmith's anvil.) A farrier's anvil should weigh between 100 and 125 lbs. Of those readily available, the G.E. ($350) and the Centaur ($325) are the best. G.E. also has a new "Bruce Daniels Design" anvil that is an excellent professional anvil. $375. I use a G.E. I have never used a Centaur but it has been highly recommended by a seasoned farrier who knows what he's looking at. I have seen the complete specifications on the Centaur anvil and it does look every bit as good as a G.E.

Centaur Company
(Blacksmiths' and Horseshoers' Supplies)
Catalog

free from:
Centaur Company
P.O. Box 239
Burlington, WI 53105

(The Centaur Co. does carry D.S. Handmade horseshoeing tools. D.S. tools are comparable to G.E. tools but usually not as available.)

Horsehoeing Nails: The best nails are made by Capewell. The standard saddle horse size is City Head 5. They are expensive. About $2 per lb. Do not use Multi-Products Co. nails. They are only $1.10 per lb, but are so thick that they almost always split the hoof wall — even with careful nailing on a thick-walled foot! You are also liable to cause undue and unseen pressure on the sensitive laminae. ■

Detweiler's Harness Shop

Lotta harness has gone bad from lack of use over the past thirty years. These folks are still building new harness the old way. Looks to be a complete line of draft horse paraphernalia right down to the tools you need for harness repair.
—*J.D. Smith*

Detweiler's Harness Supplies
Catalog
$7 postpaid from:
Lester Detweiler
Box 237
Albany, WI 53502

Big Sky Leatherworks

A propitious sign of the times — more suppliers of working harness coming on. Get some sleigh bells — put a team, bob sled, and snowy road under them. —*SB*
[Suggested by Jeb Barton]

Big Sky Leatherworks
Catalog
$2 from:
Big Sky Leatherworks
Route 3
Billings, MT 59101

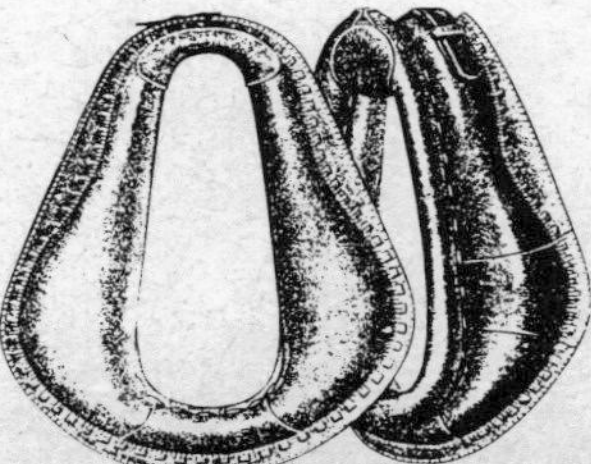

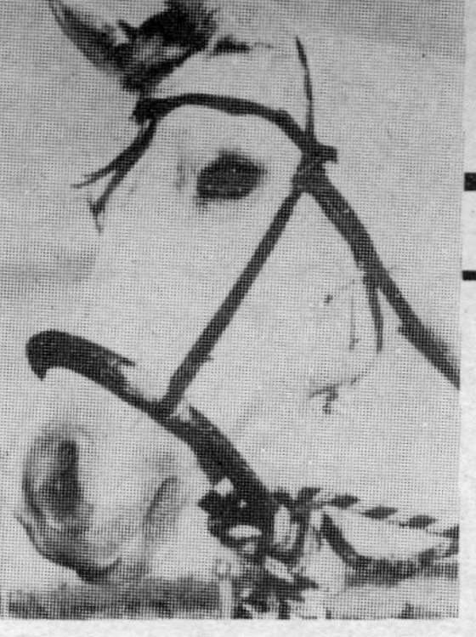

No metal is used in the traditional California hackamore outfit illustrated, only latigo leather rawhide, horsehair and as a bow to technological advances, nylon for the fiadore. Rawhide-cored bosal is laced with soft latigo as colts are tender-skinned. Browband is adjustable to keep pressure on poll in leading or doubling and hold bosal in correct position. Mecate is tied in, of genuine horsehair for "affinity" horsemen claim is calming agent in first hackamores. Half-hitches ahead of hackamore knot, made by lead rope, adjust bosal size. Outfit is shipped assembled, ready to use. $75.

Carroll Saddle Company

These folks are exponents of the hackamore, snaffle, spade progression in the training of a saddle horse. Their saddles and gear are designed by some of the top trainers in America, Ed Connell, Lee Wood, and Dave Jones among others. Their saddle designs reflect their interests in horses that rein easily, like cow ponies and cutting horses. The weight of the rider is distributed more over the withers, more forward than in the conventional Sears saddle. The catalog is not nearly so nicely crafted as their saddles, which is a good sign to me that they aren't pouring a load of time and money into advertising. Jack Carroll could make a living by word of mouth.
—*J.D. Smith*
[Suggested by Marcia Anderson]

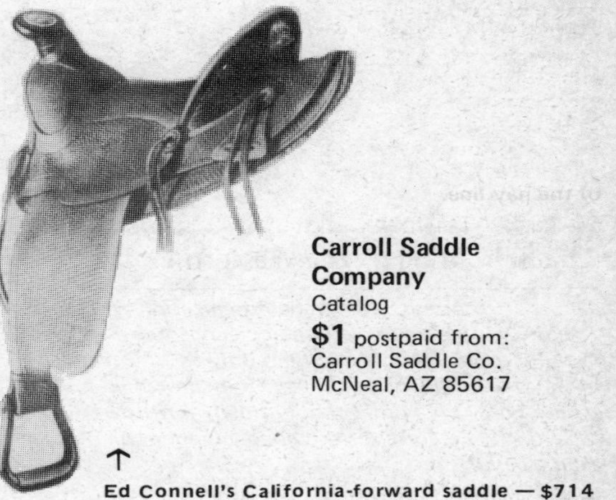

Carroll Saddle Company
Catalog
$1 postpaid from:
Carroll Saddle Co.
McNeal, AZ 85617

↑
Ed Connell's California-forward saddle — $714

THE RISING SUN
NEIGHBORHOOD NEWSLETTER

continued from last spread

She and LuAnn Sellers, who was 8 at the time, carried on a long correspondence as if they were both going around the world, one west to east and one east to west. Even though Amanda and LuAnn saw each other at least once a week at church, they never talked about it. Just kept writing. LuAnn was one of the most crushed people when we met at Smitty's after Amanda's funeral to get wasted. "I'm only in Bengali," she said, "I never got to tell her how much I liked her card about the organ grinders' convention in Kansas City, Kansas. I thought we'd talk about our trips when they were over, but now we never can." I said write about the rest of your trip to me and that's when we all realized that Amanda could live forever in the mail. We could send her postcards to people who hadn't seen them and we could write to each other in the spirit of Amanda — write about the dog shit in the backyard or the grocery prices on Mars and we do, and we usually sign them Amanda or Rose or Trailler, never with our own names. Rose and Trailler were these friends of Amanda who had the most incredible adventures around the world as Missionaries for Not Just the Acceptance but the Love of the Law of Gravity and we always thought she made them up until she died and we found piles of letters from them in her bureau. ("This little urchin took gravity into her heart tonight, Amanda; I wish you'd been here.") The nice thing about everyone using the same names is that you're never totally sure who sent you any given postcard. Amanda may write you asking for advice about treating her turtle's acne and you may send your reply as Rose to the wrong person who may reply to you or to someone else. People around here know each other's handwriting pretty well, but it does get interesting.

continued on next spread

Breaking and Training the Stock Horse

Most books on, and methods of, training the western type riding horse are a collection of anecdotal tricks and clever gimmicks with which you may force or frighten the horse into doing what you have in mind. Mr. Williamson's is not. It is a concise, orderly, and complete explanation of how, with minimum paraphernalia, to condition the horse to interpret the most subtle movements and pressures of the legs, hands, and entire body and to turn these commands into movement with the freedom and ease of an un-mounted horse. A horse well trained by this method can easily be ridden without a bridle. Williamson's method develops discipline and sensitivity in the trainer as well as in the horse.

Breaking and Training the Stock Horse
Charles O. Williamson
1950,1968; 123 pp.
$12.50 postpaid from:
Williamson School of Horsemanship
P.O. Box 506
Hamilton, MT 59840

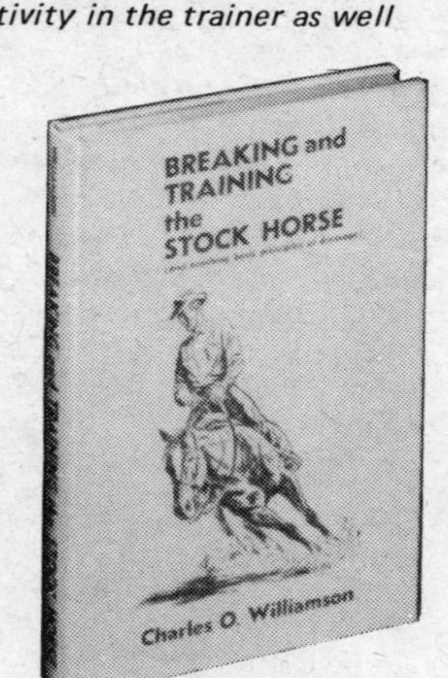

Stopping properly on hind feet; done chiefly with rider's legs and shifting of weight. Reins slack, nose down, horse relaxed.

Although intended primarily for the stock horse, its basic training principles can be applied to the training of any type of riding horse, including hunter, jumper, gaited, and high school dressage. There are also chapters on horsemanship, riding, and riding a bucking horse.
—Paul Bandy

•

Contrary to the usual idea *little* equipment is necessary in the proper training of saddle horses.

•

A horse responds to training to relieve pressure on some part of his body. He follows you when you are leading him to relieve pressure on his poll. He goes forward when the legs are used to relieve pressure on his sides. He stops or slows when the reins are pulled backward to relieve pressure on his mouth. When he does what you want, if you do not slack and relieve pressure, he has no incentive to do the same thing again for you and finally gives up in disgust and carries you about in a listless or even defiant manner because he must.

The Western Horse: Advice and Training

This book supersedes **Practical Western Training** *by the same author. As well as dealing effectively with all the subjects carried in* **PWT**, *this new book represents new insights and learnings by a fellow who has spent most of his life learning about horses. Best parts are his dedication to the hackamore, his discussion of the use of blindfolds, and the special section on ground handling, including how to rope, hobble, and throw a horse, trim hooves, use bowlines. All in all, this is a nice uncluttered piece of advice on breaking and training a horse to the cow business.*
—J.D. Smith

The Western Horse
(Advice and Training)
Dave Jones
1974; 175 pp.
$9.95 postpaid from:
Univ. of Oklahoma Press
1005 Asp Avenue
Norman, OK 73069
or Whole Earth Household Store

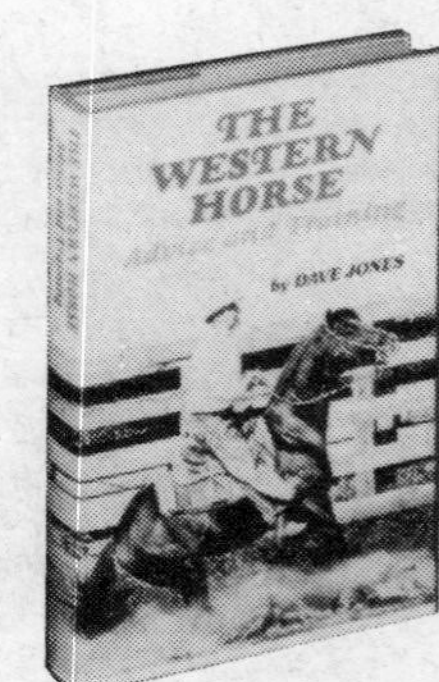

•

Horsemanship is controlling your temper.

↑

I don't believe I would have thought of using the blindfold if I hadn't seen it so widely used in South America. We soon were blindfolding mares for shots, hoof trimming, doctoring, and the like and almost completely discarded the twitch.

One time we had a filly to doctor. She was a four-year-old with a hormone imbalance. I took a twitch with me, roped the filly, and screwed the twitch on her nose. Then the vet brought the shot. Popping the needle in her vein produced quick results. She reared and struck, hitting me in the shoulder before I could blink.

Now, you don't fight these Pasos. You try to get along with them, as you should with any horse. I knew that I might have to throw her and tie her down, but I tried the blindfold first. She stood, never moving at all, had her shot, and was released with no trouble.

From all this I found the blindfold to be a very useful tool in horse handling. Nothing could be simpler to make. Cut a slit for the ears in a thirty-by-thirty-inch cheap cotton saddle blanket. A hole to tie a string in and another hole opposite can secure the blindfold under the jaw.

If you want a blindfold on your hackamore, soft latigo makes a good one. It's rigged right under the browband, on the headstall. The slits should be small so it will stay in place until you want to pull it down.

The Schooling of the Western Horse

This is an inspiring book on communication with horses. It explains at length how a rider can become a teacher to every horse he mounts, and that only as a teacher can he begin to learn from horses. Carefully described is a method of training that should finally obsolete any idea of "breaking a horse." Also good argument on proper saddle design.

—Rosemary Menninger
[Suggested by Bob Roessel]

The Schooling of the Western Horse
John Richard Young
1954; 322 pp.
$12.50 postpaid from:
Univ. of Oklahoma Press
1005 Asp Avenue
Norman, OK 73019
or Whole Earth Household Store

•

Mental laziness and a love of routine are dominant characteristics of the horse. A creature of strong habit, he tends to dislike change and to look with suspicion on anything new. But get him accustomed to a regular schedule and he will follow it as unquestioningly as a milkman's horse follows a regular route. A trainer can use this liking for routine to make many lessons easier for a green horse to catch onto, as well as easily to win the horse's co-operation.

If, for example, we are teaching a colt to stop when we feel the reins, he will get the idea more quickly if we give him the signal each time he reaches the same spot in the training ring. The same idea can be applied in teaching turns, offsets, changing from one gait to another, etc.

Ride 'em! Bill Coleman wishes he'd left the hobbles on the bronc. ↓

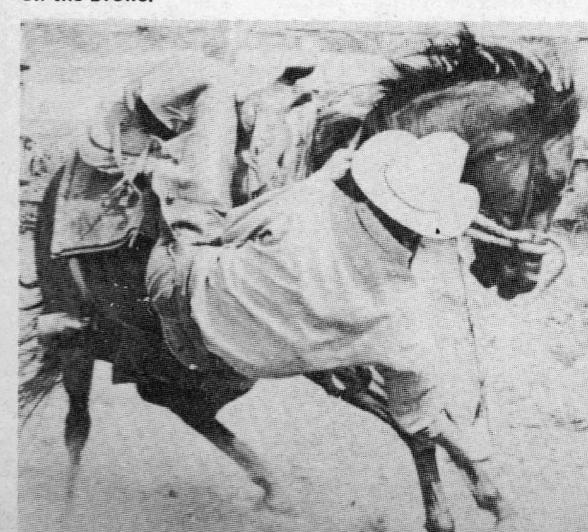

After a few trials, as he approaches that certain spot the colt will anticipate the signal; all we need do is give it and he will respond almost automatically.

Later, of course, after we know that he understands and can execute the order, we'll have to check his anticipation, not permitting him to stop or turn or change gaits, or whatever the lesson is, when reaching that certain spot; but while the colt is learning we can make good use of routine in all our schooling.

Almost all troubles that one is likely to encounter in schooling a horse stem from four principal errors commonly committed by a majority of horsemen. These errors are:

1. Lack of a definite plan, method, or system of procedure, with a clearly conceived objective in view, *before* the training is begun.
2. Inconsistency by the trainer in applying cues or aids to which he expects the horse to respond.
3. Demanding too much of a horse at one time.
4. "Rushing" a young horse's progress, demanding not only too much but demanding it too soon.

Horses

When handling horses there is no substitute for experience, but this book is as close as you can get. In the first 115 pages the author presents encyclopedic information on all phases of horse management. The last fifty pages are devoted to a brief discussion of eastern riding and showing.
—Michael S. Kaye

Simple, thorough; a classic.
—Rosemary Menninger

Horses
(Their Selection, Care and Handling)
Margaret Cabell Self
1943, 1977; 170 pp.
$3.50 postpaid from:
Wilshire Book Company
12015 Sherman Road
North Hollywood, CA 91605
or Whole Earth Household Store

•

I. SELECTION OF THE HORSE
Familiar breeds of horses, how they came to be developed and for what purposes they may be used — Where to buy your horse — Tests for soundness.

II. SELECTION AND CARE OF EQUIPMENT
Types of saddles and bridles — Grooming tools and other stable equipment needed — Harness — Types of vehicles — Care of tack.

III. THE STABLE
Location — Materials — Dimension of stalls — Flooring — Stable accessories — Ventilation and lighting — The tack room — The hay loft — Paddocks and pastures — Converting a garage.

IV. GENERAL CARE
Principles of feeding and watering — Amounts and kinds of food necessary — Cost — Amount of time needed — Bedding — Grooming — Shoeing — Clipping — Vanning — Methods of tieing.

V. FIRST AID
Accidents and injuries — Treatment of lameness due to injury — Lameness due to wounds or infections — Lameness due to chronic condition or disease — Wounds — Treatment of common illnesses — For the medicine chest.

VI. HANDLING THE HORSE
General characteristics and temperament — Fundamental rules for handling and controlling in the stable — How to lead — How to back out of a stall — Working around a kicker — Catching a horse in pasture — Bridling and saddling.

VII. CAUSE AND CONTROL OF VICES
Stable vices: Cribbing — Tearing the blanket — Weaving — Crowding — Kicking in the stall — Backing out of the stall suddenly.

Other vices: Kicking while under the saddle — Kicking while being mounted — Biting another horse — Charging in the pasture — Rearing under the saddle — Bolting — Shying — Refusing to leave his companions, or to leave the stable alone — Eating grass while under the saddle — Shying out at jumps — Getting overexcited at jumps.

Horses, Hitches and Rocky Trails

Right. You got your land fifteen miles into nowhere from the nearest roadhead. You deplore noisy trail bikes and you can't afford a helicopter. Then you're into packing. Joe Back is a packer, and talker, and illustrator, and he can help you.
—SB

Horses, Hitches and Rocky Trails
Joe Back
1959; 117 pp.

$8 postpaid from:
Johnson Publishing
1880 South 57th Court
Book Division
Boulder, CO 80301
or Whole Earth
Household Store

•

If you can, pick a good short-backed horse, thick in the body, with strong sturdy legs. A long-pasterned horse cripples up faster than one with short pasterns. You'll find a lot of thin, spindly-legged ponies that'll pack OK but they don't stand up well. Too heavy and too big horses slow you down and are not agile. About a 1200 lb. horse is just right for weight, although lots of smaller horses are used and stay right in the ring. The Morgan type is the boy if you can pick and choose, but don't get too choosey or we'll never get to camp.

•

If you don't balance each load, it's your hard luck. The handiest and cheapest tool you can buy is a fairly accurate spring or other scale that will take weights up to 100 or 150 pounds. It will last for years and you'll always use it. Some people like the style with a hook at the bottom and a ring or handle at the top. Seven or eight bucks for one will save you and your outfit a million dollars worth of grief.

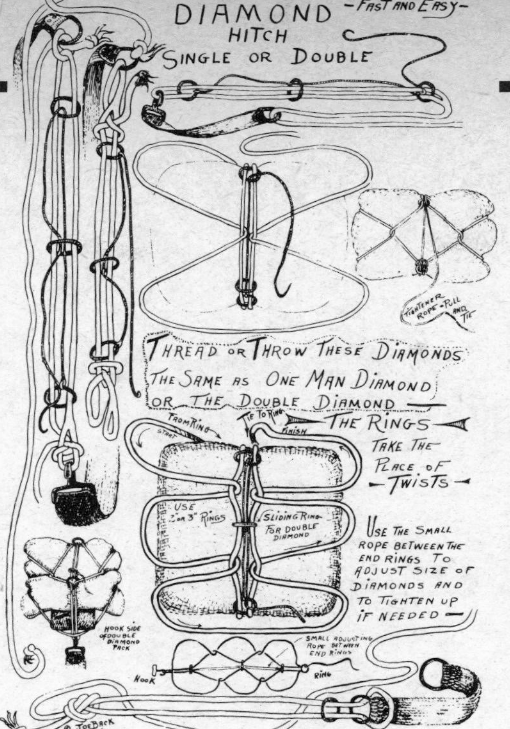

Balance the two sides of each pack, being sure they weigh the same, whether they're panniers, side packs of any kind, mantied cargo, bedrolls, tents, or any daggoned ordinary pack you load.

Wilshire Horse Lovers' Library

One good thing about this series of books is that they are cheap, (from two to ten bucks) at a time when the publishing industry seems to be going for all the bread they can get. I have only looked at a half a dozen of the titles, and am recommending the entire series because those I did see were of good quality. There are quite a few reprints in the series: the horseshoeing guide is a 1941 War Department Manual, one of the vet books is from the early forties, the **Illustrated Book of the Horse** *was originally published in 1875. Most of the time old books about horses are a little better than new ones because horses used to be more widely used as tools than they are now. There are 70 books in the series.*

Of particular interest to me in this series are the two books on harness or driving horses. Horsepower as an energy concept has been bastardized by the automobile industry. One good horse will pull you and your family just as well as two hundred mechanical horsepower concepts will pull you and your family and your new 1980 Chrysler subsidy.

Pick a title of interest from the list and see for yourself.
—J.D. Smith

Wilshire Horse Lover's Library
Melvin Powers, Editor
Catalog

$ .25 postpaid from:
Wilshire Book Company
12015 Sherman Road
North Hollywood, CA
91605

Amateur Horse Breeder A.C. Leighton Hardman $3
American Quarter Horse in Pictures Margaret Cabell Self $3
Appaloosa Horse Donna & Bill Richardson $3
Arabian Horse Reginald S. Summerhays $2
Art of Western Riding Suzanne Norton Jones $3
At the Horse Show Margaret Cabell Self $3
Back-yard Foal Peggy Jett Pittinger $3
Back-yard Horse Peggy Jett Pittinger $3
Basic Dressage Jean Froissard $2
Beginner's Guide to Horseback Riding Sheila Wall $2
Beginner's Guide to the Western Horse Natlee Kenoyer $2
Bits — Their History, Use and Misuse Louis Taylor $3
Breaking & Training the Driving Horse Doris Ganton $2
Breaking Your Horse's Bad Habits W. Dayton Sumner $3
Cavalry Manual of Horsemanship Gordon Wright $3
Complete Training of Horse and Rider Colonel Alois Podhajsky $4
Disorders of the Horse & What To Do About Them E. Hanauer $3
Dog Training Made Easy & Fun John W. Kellogg $3
Dressage — A Study of the Finer Points in Riding Henry Wynmalen $4
Driving Horses Sallie Walrond $3
Endurance Riding Ann Hyland $2
Equitation Jean Froissard $4
First Aid for Horses Dr. Charles H. Denning, Jr. $2
Fun of Raising a Colt Rubye & Frank Griffith $3
Fun on Horseback Margaret Cabell Self
Gymkhana Games Natlee Kenoyer
Horse Diseases — Causes, Symptoms & Treatment Dr. H.G. Belschner
Fun of Raising a Colt Rubye & Frank Griffith $3
Fun on Horseback Margaret Cabell Self $4
Gymkhana Games Natlee Kenoyer $2
Horse Diseases — Causes, Symptoms & Treatment Dr. H. G. Belschner $4
Horse Owner's Concise Guide Elsie V. Hanauer $2
Horse Selection & Care for Beginners George H. Conn $3
Horse Sense — A complete guide to riding and care Alan Deacon $4
Horseback Riding for Beginners Louis Taylor $4
Horseback Riding Made Easy & Fun Sue Henderson Coen $3
How to Buy a Better Horse & Sell the Horse You Own $3
How to Enjoy Your Quarter Horse Williard H. Porter $3
Hunter in Pictures Margaret Cabell Self $2
Illustrated Book of the Horse S. Sidney (8½" x 11") $10
Illustrated Horse Management — 400 illustrations, Dr. E. Mayhew $6
Illustrated Horse Training Captain M.H. Hayes $5
Illustrated Horseback Riding for Beginners Jeanne Mellin $2
Jumping — Learning & Teaching Jean Froissard $3
Know All About Horses Harry Disston $3
Lame Horse — Causes, Symptoms & Treatment Dr. James R. Rooney $4
Law & Your Horse Edward H. Greene $5
Lipizzaners & the Spanish Riding School W. Reuter (4¼" x 6") $2.50
Manual of Horsemanship Harold Black $5
Morgan Horse in Pictures Margaret Cabell Self $2
Movie Horses — The Fascinating Techniques of Training Anthony Amaral $2
Police Horses Judith Campbell $2
Practical Guide to Horseshoeing $3
Practical Guide to Owning Your Own Horse Steven D. Price $2
Practical Horse Psychology Moyra Williams $3
Problem Horses — Guide for Curing Serious Behavior Habits Summerhays $2
Reinsman of the West — Bridles & Bits Ed Connell $4
Reschooling the Thoroughbred Peggy Jett Pittenger $3
Ride Western Louis Taylor $3
Schooling Your Young Horse George Wheatley $2
Stable Management For the Owner-Groom George Wheatley $4
Stallion Management — A Guide for Stud Owners A.C. Hardman $3
Teaching Your Horse to Jump W.J. Froud $2
Trail Horses & Trail Riding Anne & Perry Westbrook $2
Training Your Horse to Show Neale Haley $3
Treating Common Diseases of Your Horse Dr. George H. Conn $3
Treating Horse Ailments G.W. Serth $2
Western Horseback Riding Glen Balch $3
You and Your Pony Pepper Mainwaring Healey (8½" x 11") $6
Your First Horse George C. Saunders, M.D. $3
Your Pony Book Hermann Wiederhold $2
Your Western Horse Nelson C. Nye $2

The Mule

If every freed slave had gotten forty acres and a mule, we might still appreciate this animal. In the mountains they are far more surefooted than horses. Overall, they're smarter than horses, and for plowing fields they are cheaper to buy and feed than draft horses. **The Mule** *was written in 1867, about the rearing, breeding, training, breaking, uses, abuses, character and ailments of the mule.*
—Rosemary Menninger

The Mule
(A Treatise on the Breeding, Training, and Uses, to Which He May Be Put)
Harvey Riley
1867; 107 pp.
(reprinted)

$5.60 postpaid from:
Hee Haw Book Service
Paul and Betsy Hutchins
Rt. 5, Box 65
Denton, TX 76201

Barb — Locality: North Africa — Algeria, Morocco. Colour and characteristics: Generally dark bay, brown, chestnut, black and grey. Characteristically flat shoulders, sloping quarters, with low-set tail; head and face straight. Height: 14 to 15 h.h.

Horses of the World

Most books on horse breeds list so few "recognized breeds" as to make most horseflesh seem like scum. Some breeds evolve with nature; many are bred. This book lists 188, with sensational photographs of each.
—Rosemary Menninger

Horses of the World
(An Illustrated Survey)
Daphne Machin Goodall
1965, 1974; 272 pp.

$12.95 postpaid from:
Macmillan Publishing Company
Order Department
Front & Brown Streets
Riverside, NJ 08075

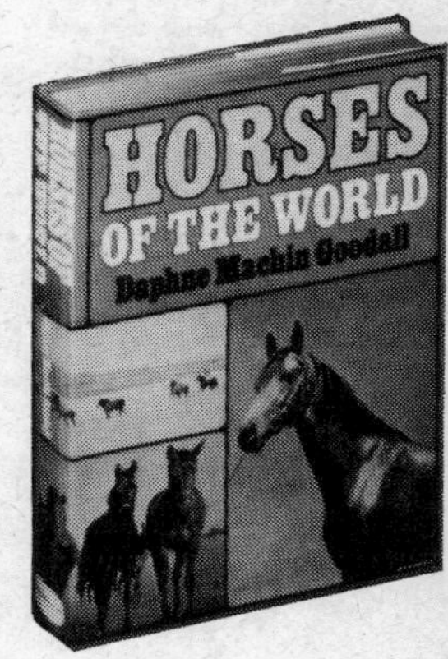

↑

The native home of the *Barb* is Algeria — where there is a large stud in Constantine — and Morocco. There were several strains varying a little one from the other. From about 800 A.D. Oriental horses including *Barbs* were imported in great numbers into Spain, considerably influencing the *Andalusian* and *Spanish* horse, and through them most of the other breeds of horses in Europe. Today the *Barb* possesses a certain amount of *Arab* blood, although attention is paid to keeping the type to the ancient *Barb*. It is extraordinarily hard, docile, and can live on small quantities of poor fare. It has a relatively long head, flat shoulders and the tail is set fairly low. It is essentially a riding horse and of an older breed than the *Arab*; it therefore seems a pity that breeding is confined almost exclusively to the north coast of Africa.

THE RISING SUN
NEIGHBORHOOD NEWSLETTER

continued from last spread

But as time went on, she started writing other things. People say she got crazy when she got old, but I say she went from not caring much about what people thought to not caring at all. She started writing postcards to everyone, to people she saw every day, that had nothing to do with anything. Postcards of Miami Beach written as if she were an antarctic explorer — "Took this in my gear to remind me of warm weather. We'll meet on the beach soon, love. Progress is good, but we had to put down a penguin rebellion last night. It was rough but we're safe now. Think of you always. Norbert." Once you stopped worrying about senility, they were great, and people started writing back. Especially the young men going into the service who stopped by Amanda's house to say goodbye. She always said, "If you don't want to write me about what you're doing, write me about what you'd rather be doing," and they did. She got cards about preparing and serving a gourmet dinner from Anzio, about sitting in front of the fireplace drinking a case of wine from Korea and about planning and financing and building and using the perfect doll house factory from Vietnam.

continued on next spread

Grow It!

Far more useful than **Five Acres and Independence** *(a book that took many people back to the land in the 30's),* **Grow It!** *thoroughly covers the operations of any small organic farm from pruning to goat cheese making to pond stocking. No subject is glossed over, and there's more help on gardening than in many gardening books. With it, a first time farmer can start farming, or anyone thinking of buying a farm can get excited.* —Rosemary Menninger

(See Langer's **Grow It Indoors**, *p. 356.)*

Grow It!
Richard W. Langer
1972; 365 pp.
$4.95 postpaid from:
Avon Books
Mail Order Department
250 W. 55th Street
New York, NY 10019
or Whole Earth Household Store

•

Gathering Your Own Seed

Hybrid plants often do not breed true from seed. But with non-hybrid plants, instead of buying seeds every year, collect and save seeds from the best vegetables you've grown in your garden to plant. You may well develop a breed particularly suited to your region. Sometimes you'll have to buy seeds the second year, even if you decide to grow your own, simply because your plants won't produce seed till their second year. But be patient.

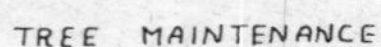

TREE MAINTENANCE

1. CUT AWAY ROOT SUCKERS.
2. PRUNE CROSSED BRANCHES.
3. CUT AWAY WATER SPROUTS.
4. PRUNE UNDER BRANCHES.
5. FILL DEEP CUTS WITH PITCH TO PREVENT ROT FROM SETTING IN.
6. TO MINIMIZE INSECTS, USE A TANGLEFOOT BAND (A STICKY NO MAN'S LAND THAT KEEPS DESTRUCTIVE BUGS FROM CLIMBING TRUNK).
7. FOR BEST GROWTH, MAKE A MULCH RING AROUND THE TREE, EXTENDING IT AT LEAST AS FAR OUT AS THE LONGEST BRANCH.

Always pick the best overall plants as your seeders. With crops such as spinach or leaf lettuce, where it's the leaves you want to harvest, select a plant that takes a long time to go to seed. With root crops such as radishes and carrots, use those plants that go to seed first, since this will mean earlier roots in your new plants.

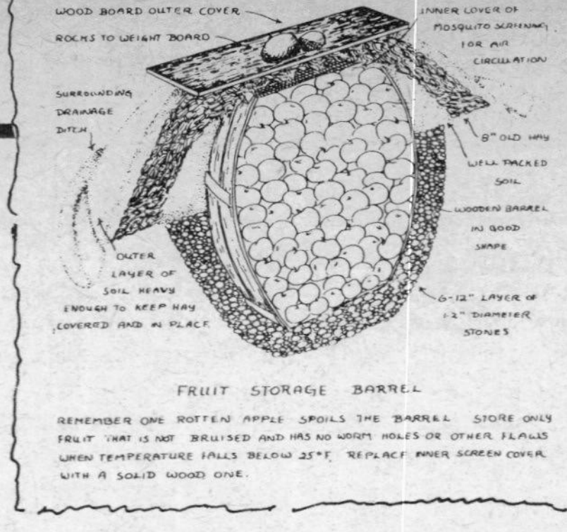

FRUIT STORAGE BARREL

REMEMBER ONE ROTTEN APPLE SPOILS THE BARREL. STORE ONLY FRUIT THAT IS NOT BRUISED AND HAS NO WORM HOLES OR OTHER FLAWS. WHEN TEMPERATURE FALLS BELOW 25°F, REPLACE INNER SCREEN COVER WITH A SOLID WOOD ONE.

•

The fundamentals of crop rotation can be listed quite simply, as follows:

1. The area for each crop should be about the same and the demarcation of the fields should remain constant over the years.
2. The whole cycle should contain at least one legume, one deeprooted crop such as alfalfa, and one sod-building crop.
3. When possible, have an extra field in your rotation, or on the sidelines, so to speak. Keep this field in a pasture crop for two to four years, then reenter it into rotation with the grain crop. The field most recently used for the grain crop is then given over to the pasture crop for the same number of years.
4. By using one field for pasture, rather than cutting all the forage and hauling it to the barn, manure will be delivered directly to the field by the grazing livestock. This will assure maximum utilization of the manure, particularly the urine.

Strip farming and contour plowing may not be necessary on your field. Crop rotation always is. And although the lay of your land might not permit you to follow the above plan exactly, the closer you come to the ideal, the better your results. Sit down and plan your crops before you plow and plant.

The Guide to Self Sufficiency

Englishman John Seymour's vast personal experience and wry wit are interspersed with excellent illustrations covering more farm chores than you'll probably have time for — from ploughing, slaughtering pigs and snaring hares to making cheese, beer and chutney. The techniques are traditional, small-scale, and labor-intensive. —Richard Nilsen

The Guide to Self-Sufficiency
John Seymour
1976; 251 pp.
$10 postpaid from:
Hearst Books
P.O. Box 1406
Radio City Station
New York, NY 10019
or Whole Earth Household Store

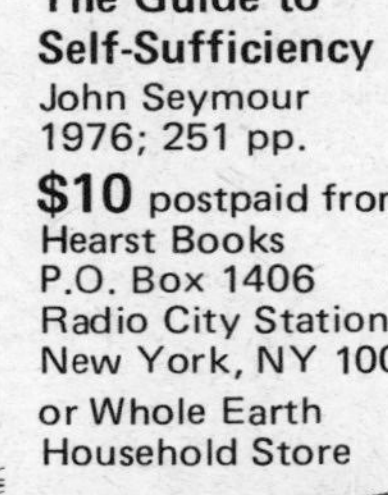

↑ **Building or repairing a hedge**

Cut stakes out of your hedge so as to leave strong bushes at intervals of about a foot. Wear a leather hedging glove on your left hand. Bend each trunk over and half-cut through it near the base with a bill-hook.

Force the half-cut trunk down to nearly horizontal and try to push the end under its neighbor so as to hold it in position. Be sure not to break it off. Take the stakes you have just cut and drive them in roughly at right angles to, and interwoven with the trunks. Weave tops of stakes together with some pliable growth such as hazel or willow. By the time the stakes have rotted the living hedge will be secure.

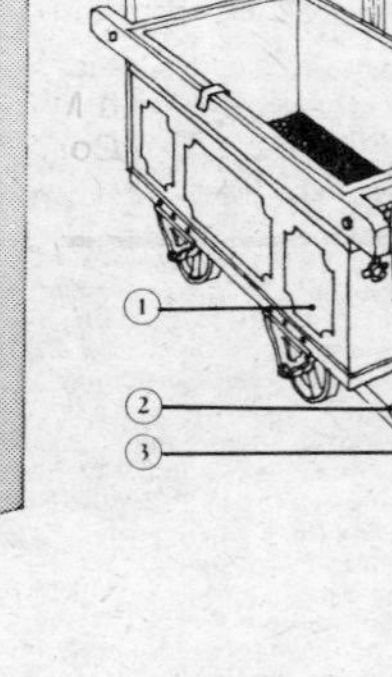

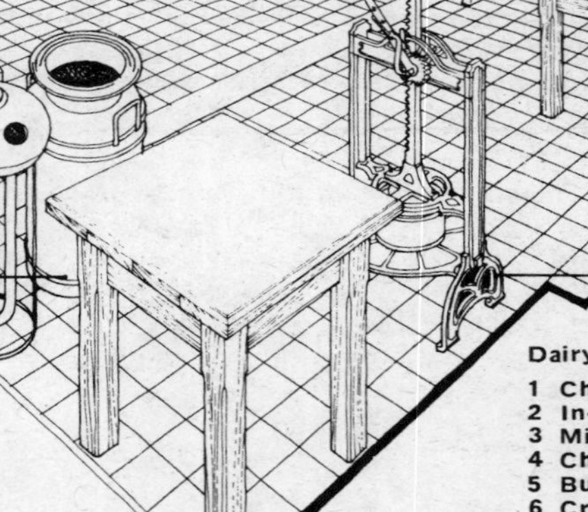

The dairy ⟶

Butter and cheese can be made in the kitchen, but if you have a room or outbuilding you don't know what to do with, it is well worth equipping it as a dairy. If possible the floor should be made of tiles, or concrete with a drain. Install plenty of faucets for hot and cold water, a large sink and draining boards made of spaced dowels.

Dairy equipment
1 Cheese vat
2 In-churn cooler
3 Milk churn
4 Cheese press
5 Butter churn
6 Cream separator
7 Butter-worker
8 Vertical curd knife
9 Horizontal curd knife.

↓ **Early Summer — Successional planting must go on unabated with many crops during April, May, and June.**

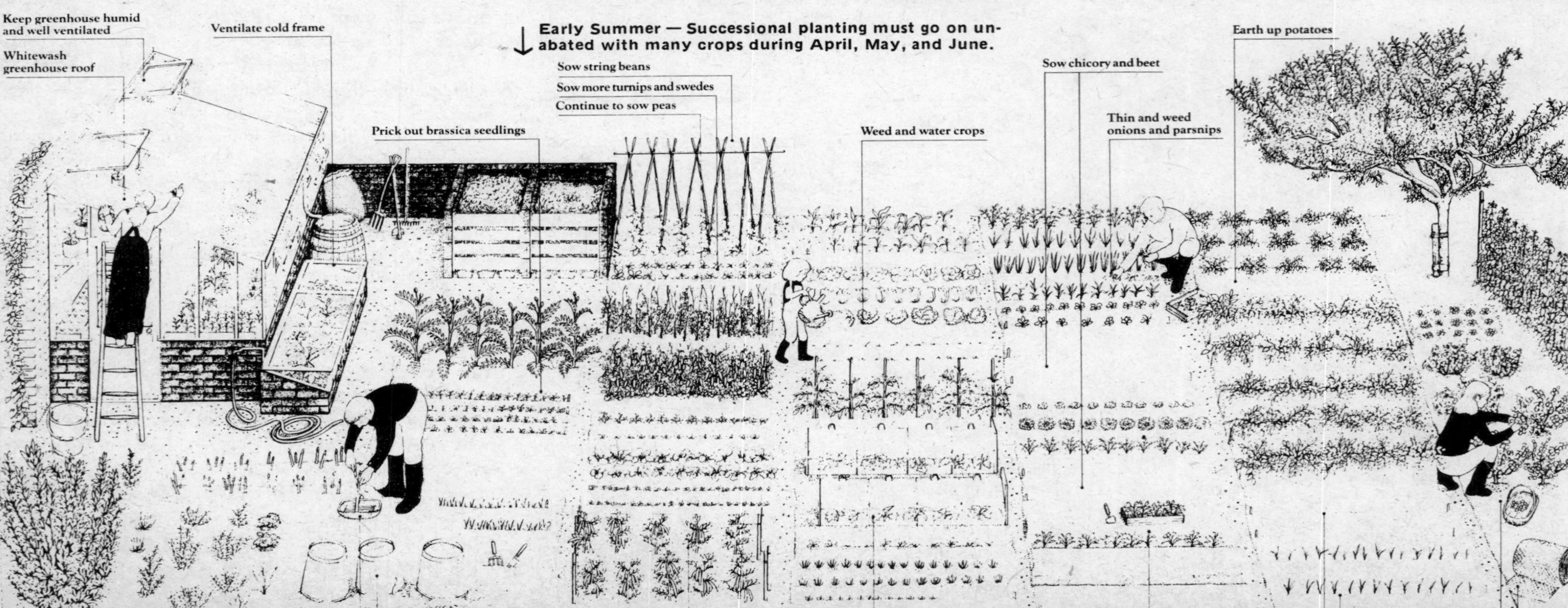

Need Help In Locating Used Equipment?
For farmers living in parts of the country not well served by regional newspapers or farm-related "want-ads," finding that single-row combine, 40 HP tractor or ground-driven manure spreader can be like seeking the needle in the haystack.

As a service to readers in search of older, hard-to-find tractors and implements, THE NEW FARM maintains a Used Equipment Clearinghouse. If you have used equipment you'd like to sell or trade, send us a clear description of it, including condition and asking price. Please limit listings to models no longer on the market.

If you are searching for a particular model of tractor or implement, let us know. We'll try to match up buyer and seller.

Submit all items to THE NEW FARM, C/O "Equipment Clearinghouse," Box 96, Maxatawny, Pennsylvania 19538.

The New Farm

The several-decade push for farm "efficiency" has left only two ways to do many jobs — by hand, or with an $80,000 machine. This leaves empty a huge middle ground, and it is being filled, slowly but surely, by Rodale's **The New Farm**. *The articles are well-researched, the point of view is organic, and Wendell Berry and Gene Logsdon contribute regularly. When the words of advice on where to find old farm equipment turn into manufacturer's advertisements for new versions of the same small-scale gear, this magazine will have succeeded. See* **Organic Gardening**, *p. 94.* —*Richard Nilsen*

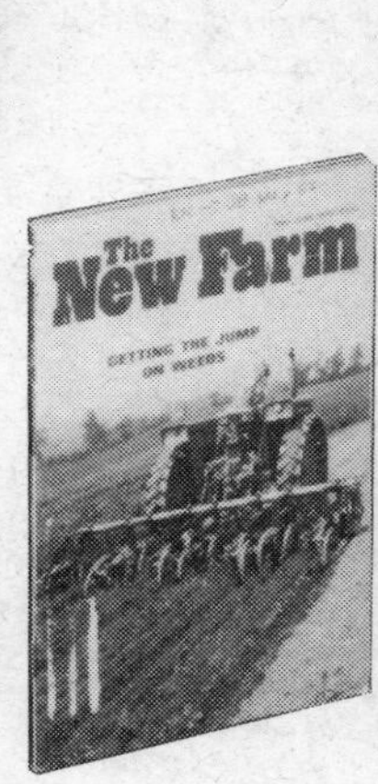

The New Farm
Robert Rodale, Editor
$10/year (7 issues)
postpaid from:

Rodale Press
33 East Minor
Emmaus, PA 18049

I was much interested to learn of the availability in this country of the so-called New Zealand electric fence equipment. I wrote for information to various suppliers. What I read, and what I saw when I went to see some of this fence in use, convinced me that it was worth a try. Last summer, I purchased the necessary materials, and built thirty-one rod of this fence.

I wanted to enclose a small pasture in a corner of my place, which was already fenced along the road and the property line with woven wire. The new fence had to be sheep-tight, and it would go over very steep, uneven ground through the woods. I found the New Zealand fence to be satisfactory on all counts: it goes up quick, with far less trouble than woven wire; it makes a good fence; and it is comparatively cheap. —*Wendell Berry*

Wire strainers at the end posts are a permanent part of the New Zealand fence. Small ratchets are turned with a wrench until uniformly tight.

Suppliers of New Zealand Fencing Materials

Kiwi Fence Systems, Inc., RD 5, Box 122, Waynesburg, PA 15370

Koppers Co., Inc., Koppers Building, Pittsburgh, PA 15219

Live Wire Products, P.O. Box 150, Grass Valley, CA 95945

Snell Systems, Inc., 10910 Wye Drive, San Antonio, TX 78217

Henry and Cornelia Swayze, Brookside Farm, Tunbridge, VT 05077

Waterford Corporation, P.O. Box 1513, 1449 Riverside, Fort Collins, CO 80522

Acres, U.S.A.

This newspaper provides a unique perspective on the transformation Midwest farmers are increasingly making away from chemical fertilizers and synthetic biocides toward organic methods, or what **Acres** *calls "eco-agriculture." As editor/publisher Charles Walters makes very clear, it is a change prompted by economics more than anything else. This is very much a one-man paper, and Walters has the stridency and condescension of a long-time outcast whose ideas have only recently been acknowledged as true by the ag-biz forces.*

The paper merely comments on hard news stories and concentrates instead on the details of how farmers are making organic methods work in their own fields — there is a lot of soil science here, and much of it is the kind of thing you won't find anyplace else. —*Richard Nilsen*

Acres, U.S.A.
(A Voice for Eco-Agriculture)
Charles Walters, Jr., Editor
$8/year (12 issues)
postpaid from:

Acres, U.S.A.
Box 9547
Raytown, MO 64133

•

Scientists at Penn State and Cornell universities have discovered a grasshopper which is secreting a protective froth of spray that contains man-made chemicals.

Dr. Lawrence Hendry of Penn State said the grasshopper has managed to incorporate the powerful new ingredient into its own defense mechanism. . . "It's a little like equipping a skunk with Mace," said Hendry . . . he and three colleagues from Cornell made the discovery while studying the defensive froth of a 4 to 5 inch long lightless grasshopper, *Romanica microptera*. The froth's odor drives away enemies.

"We found the usual range of gaseous components common to froths, clouds and other defensive sprays.

"But when we isolated 2,5 dichlorophenol we were astounded.

"That compound is not found in nature. We could only speculate that the grasshopper gleaned it from fields by chemically processing another man-made compound, 2,4-D, a common commercial herbicide.

Hendry said grasshoppers taken from fields where no 2,4-D had been sprayed showed no 2,5 dichlorophenol. . . . He added, "over a short time period, the grasshopper has managed to latch on to a man-made chemical for its own purpose. It is not very pleasant to speculate what might happen after a wide variety of hard chemicals have been in common use for 100 years."

The American Farm

The text and photographs in this beautiful book have a cumulative effect. The weathered faces, filled with the harshness and loneliness of farm life, belong to our recent ancestors. We have been freed from ever having to live like they did by a host of puffing machines, and most of us now live in cities. Between these two places, the farm and the new city, a lot of unsettled questions still linger. See also **The Unsettling of America**, *reviewed on p. 46.* —*Richard Nilsen*

•

During the second half of the nineteenth century, American production of food and feed crops rose at an almost unbelievable rate. Corn production increased by four and a half times, hay by five times, oats and wheat by seven times . . . it was the onset of the Civil War that provided the great stimulus for the mechanization of northern agriculture. With sons and hired laborers inducted into the army and grain prices on the rise, northern farmers rushed to avail themselves of the new labor-saving equipment. In 1860, there were approximately 80,000 reapers in the country; five years later there were 350,000.

The American Farm
(A Photographic History)
Maisie Conrat and
Richard Conrat
1977; 256 pp.

$9.95 postpaid from:
Houghton Mifflin Co.
Wayside Road
Burlington, MA 01803
or Whole Earth
Household Store

Combines at work in Washington wheat fields, c. 1900.

THE RISING SUN
NEIGHBORHOOD NEWSLETTER

continued from last spread

Amanda liked things interesting. I remember once we were half-way through a bottle of wine and she said, "Life is alternately boring and horrifying and we are all quite unreasonably lonely and I see no reason to treat dreams as some unmentionable head disease like lice. We all have them and might as well mail them to each other until we learn to talk." So that is why, Stranger, Smitty's has the largest selection of postcards you ever seen jumbled together in a box (people bring back dozens from vacation) and why some of them are used — those are Amanda's, that she wrote herself, and we keep them moving, some have 25 stamps and addresses layered on by now.)

This doesn't, however, explain why the sign over the bar says, "Invest in it!" That's there because whenever you'd ask Amanda if one of her fantastic stories was true, she'd say, "Are you planning to invest in it?" One time I was fed up with her and I said, "What the hell do you mean by that?" and she said, "Well, if you thought it was true, you'd invest in it, wouldn't you? You'd make something else be true because this was true. If you thought the true thing was bad, you'd try to stop it and if you thought it was good you'd try to spread it, but why do you need to know if it's true? If it hits your heart close enough that you care if it's true, you should invest in it anyway." So if you like Amanda enough to care if she's true, invest in her. Send a dream postcard to a friend and she's true for you too.

— This item written with the help of Andrea Sharp who surprised me when I sent her a strange postcard signed Amanda by sending back an even stranger one signed Trailler and never saying a word about it.

Practical Farm Buildings

If you're just trying to build a shed for your goats, this is not the book. But if you need to know how to build a loft so it can hold up 50 bushels of corn, or how much insulation you'll need in a wall to keep your cows warm at −40°, this book will tell you. It defines terms and explains the mathematical formulas necessary for designing farm buildings. Lots of invaluable tables and charts; nothing on plumbing or wiring. —Richard Nilsen

Practical Farm Buildings
(A Text and Handbook)
2nd Edition
James S. Boyd
1973, 1979; 292 pp.

$10.60 postpaid from:
The Interstate Printers & Publishers, Inc.
19-27 N. Jackson St.
Danville, IL 61832
or Whole Earth Household Store

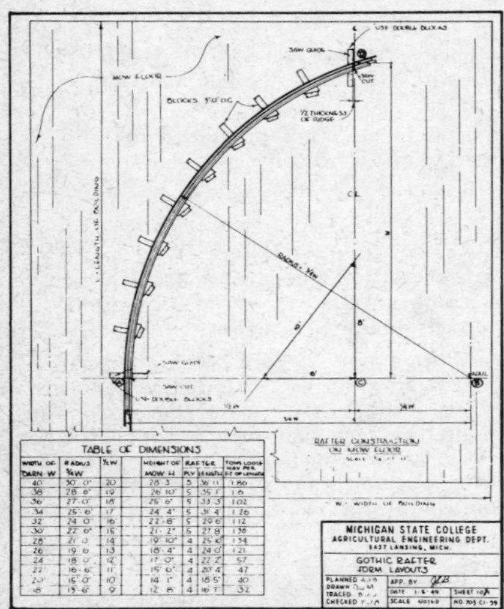

↑ In states where supplies of low-grade wood are available, laminated rafters for gothic roofs can be made of 1" x 4" boards bent into a form and nailed as shown. The curve on the rafter is three-fourths the width of the building. The laminations should be nailed every 8 inches from both sides so there will be a nail every 4 inches in the rafter. These rafters should be spaced 2 feet O.C. and every sixth rafter braced similar to a gambrel rafter.

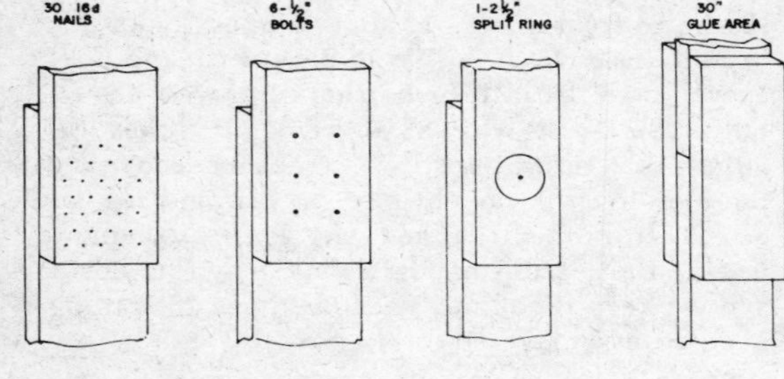

Joints of equal strength

Building plans for farmers

The U.S. Department of Agriculture, working through the state agricultural schools, makes a vast amount of low-cost information available to farmers. Some of these plans are full-sized prints, some are reductions. They have barns, livestock housing, hay, grain and machinery storage facilities, and also plans for houses. —Richard Nilsen
[Suggested by Henry Esbenshade and John Benecki]

USDA Plans List
free from:
Western Regional Agricultural Engineering Service
Agricultural Engineering Department
Oregon State University
Corvallis, OR 97331

Midwest Plan Service
Catalog
free from:
Midwest Plan Service
122 Davidson
Iowa State University
Ames, IA 50011

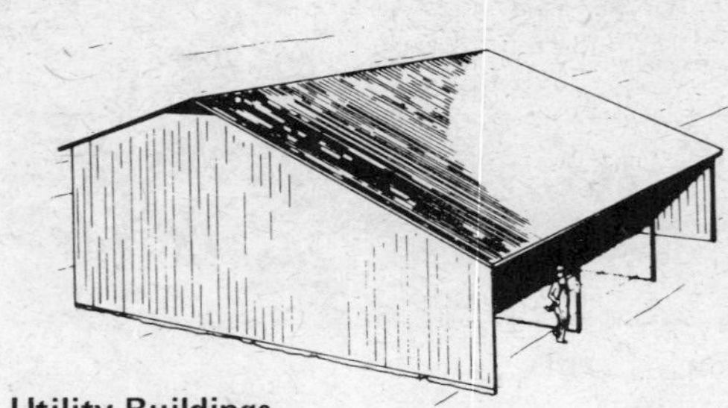

Utility Buildings

Pole Utility Buildings **mwps-72050 $1.00**
The basic pole frame adapts to building widths in 14' increments and lengths of 14' increments. A 28' truss is included so one of the poles may be omitted.

SWINE HANDBOOK — Housing and Equipment
MWP-8 $2.50

One of the most popular MWPS handbooks, MWPS-8 has 84 pages on building systems, ventilation, waste management and equipment. From selecting a layout to building feeders and fences, this book has the how-to details for improving your swine operation.
ISBN 0-89373-005-X 3rd Ed. 1972

Production Alternatives	Waste Disposal
Building Selection	Fencing
Ventilation	Handling Equipment

FARMSTEAD PLANNING HANDBOOK
MWP-2 $2.50

This book leads the reader through the planning process for a successful farmstead. Detailed information is included on site, building separation, drainage and space. Requirements for each activity center are included: family living; machinery storage, repair, and services; fuel, chemical, and fertilizer storage; grain storage and processing; and livestock production. ISBN 0-89373-001-7 1974

500 More Things to Make for Farm and Home
600 More Things to Make for Farm and Home

American Ingenuity of fabled quality may not be found in everybody. Moreover, if you have to make a feed hopper, just how far apart do you make the boards so that the feed comes out like it's supposed to? These books are just solid packed with drawings, photos and diagrams of construction you'll doubtless need sooner or later around the farm. Most of the stuff is pretty crude, which is in keeping with what's really needed, usually. The authors assume a certain expertise with farm shop tools, but as with most farm equipment, common sense prevails. They were written just before everything went crazy with fancy hardware at great expense. Should be truly useful to the back-to-the-landers. —J. Baldwin
[Suggested by George de Alth]

500 More Things to Make
(For Farm and Home)
Glen Charles Cook
1944; 471 pp.
$13.35 postpaid

600 More Things to Make
(For Farm and Home)
Glen Charles Cook and Lloyd Phipps
1952; 599 pp.
$10.35 postpaid

both from:
The Interstate Printers and Publishers, Inc.
19-27 North Jackson St.
Danville, IL 61832
or Whole Earth Household Store

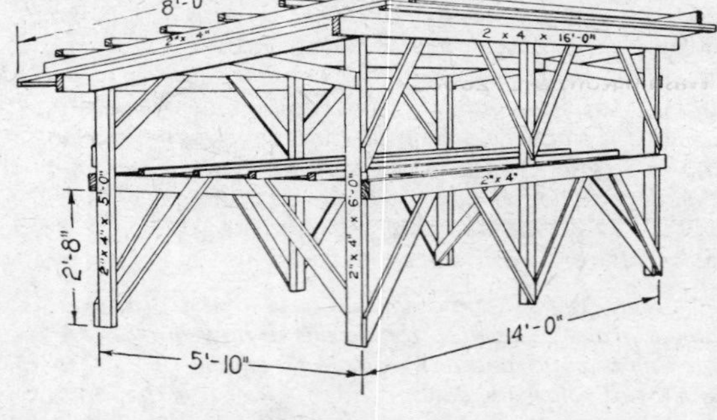

Plan of turkey range shelter.

"There is a solid roof on this shelter with additional roosts set on 2 x 4s. Birds will take to the roof in good weather so one might as well provide something for them to sit on. Many growers build this shelter on skids for easy moving. In a large flock, these shelters may be set back to back."
—500 More Things to Make

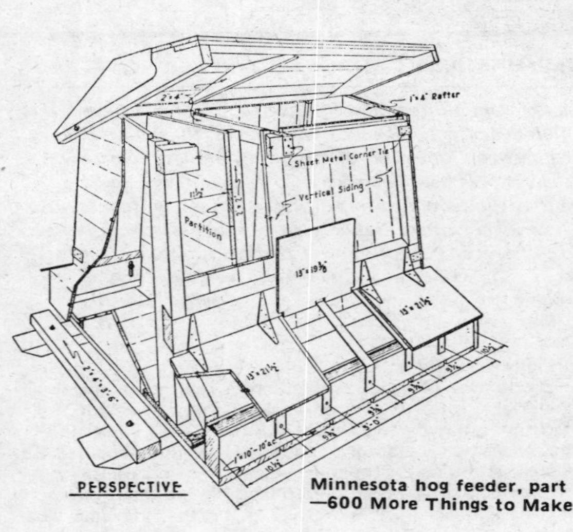

Minnesota hog feeder, part B.
—600 More Things to Make

Small Farm Energy Project Newsletter

The nice thing about this newsletter is that it is down-home America working out the energy options, change from the inside out. Each issue features specific energy projects that farmers are doing with the encouragement of the Small Farm Energy Project, along with farm-energy news, publications, and events. It is a newsletter for farmers who still love the family farm and would like to keep it that way; consequently the discussion and projects tend to be of hard-nosed practicality. —Rho Weber Mack

Small Farm Energy Project Newsletter
Dennis Demmel, Editor

$5 /year (6 issues)
from:
Small Farm Energy Project
P.O. Box 736
Hartington, NE 68739

•

Some researchers, like Loyd Fischer, ag economist at the U. of Nebr., think that the reins ought to be pulled on the alcohol momentum. He hasn't found farm alcohol production, or even large scale production, to be cost effective, even though energy will at least double in three years. . . .

Fischer figures a farm plant producing in the range of 6000 gal. of ethanol per year, which would approach the annual needs of the average Energy Project farm, would require an investment of over $73,000 based mostly on ag. engineering studies at Iowa State U. $30,000 of the cost would be for the actual plant components, with the balance required for a building and assembly of the system. Cost of the ethanol produced would be over $4 per gallon. . . .

Construction work underway on the Pinkleman solar farrowing barn. Fiberglass was placed over 2 x 2 purlins, which were mounted to the original sheet metal roof. The roof was painted black. Holes at either end of the roof are used to move air between the barn and the collector. Heat storage is located in the loft of the barn, which has a capacity for farrowing 22 sows at a time. →

Fischer notes that very few completed plants are operating successfully and that owners of some are more successful "at sending tourists through at $100 per head."

A few strands of barbed wire will keep stock out of this old gully, preventing washing and permitting wildlife cover to grow.

The small owls are almost universally beneficial. The farmer will do well to protect them.

The farmer who owns this marsh derives 25 percent of his income from pelts. Muskrats also help to keep marshes open, thus maintaining their value for waterfowl.

The Farmer and Wildlife

A farm that encourages wildlife is much more of a self-balancing low-maintenance system than one without. Also it's less boring. Encouraging wildlife mostly consists of not discouraging it so much, like leaving your brush-piles instead of burning them, damming the gully instead of letting it erode, leaving a bit of woodlot instead of stripping the land. —SB

The Farmer and Wildlife
Durward L. Allen
1949, 1977; 63 pp.

$1 postpaid from:
Wildlife Management Institute
Wire Building
1000 Vermont Ave. NW
Washington, D.C. 20005

•

A grazed woodlot is neither a good woodlot nor a good pasture. The farmer will profit by making it one or the other.

•

On many farms the muskrat population represents the greatest cash value of any kind of wildlife. This animal can live in practically any spot where there is water the year around and enough fertility to grow marsh plants.

Average muskrat yields for Michigan are 2 or 3 per acre of suitable marsh. Maryland production is much the same. These averages for large areas mean that high quality local tracts will do considerably better — possibly up to 10 or 11 pelts per acre. An Ohio investigator estimated that a good marsh should yield 15. Frequently, unpolluted streams are productive also.

↑

Formerly it was assumed that brushy fence lines might harbor crop pests. More recently we have learned that they are much more likely to serve as cover for birds, predaceous and parasitic insects, and insect-eating small mammals. An Ohio biologist whose work was mentioned before showed that there were 32 times as many song-birds in brushy fencerows as in open cropfields. Such field borders also contained 60 times as many aphid-destroying lady beetles as sodded fence lines.

In addition to songbirds, a strip of brush between fields is attractive to skunks, weasels, and birds of prey which feed upon the meadow mice in hay and grain fields. The small animals that live in shrubby fencerows are for the most part either beneficial, like the shrews, or of kinds like the woodmouse which do not commonly destroy crops. Sodded field borders are likely to harbor heavy populations of destructive meadow mice, which spread into cropfields. These animals do not live in thick brush.

Climates of the United States

Except for soil here's all the basics for agriculture (and many other activities) — sun, rain, cold, wind, seasons. Northern Minnesota routinely ranges 65° F between its coldest and warmest months. Maximum sunlight? Death Valley. —SB

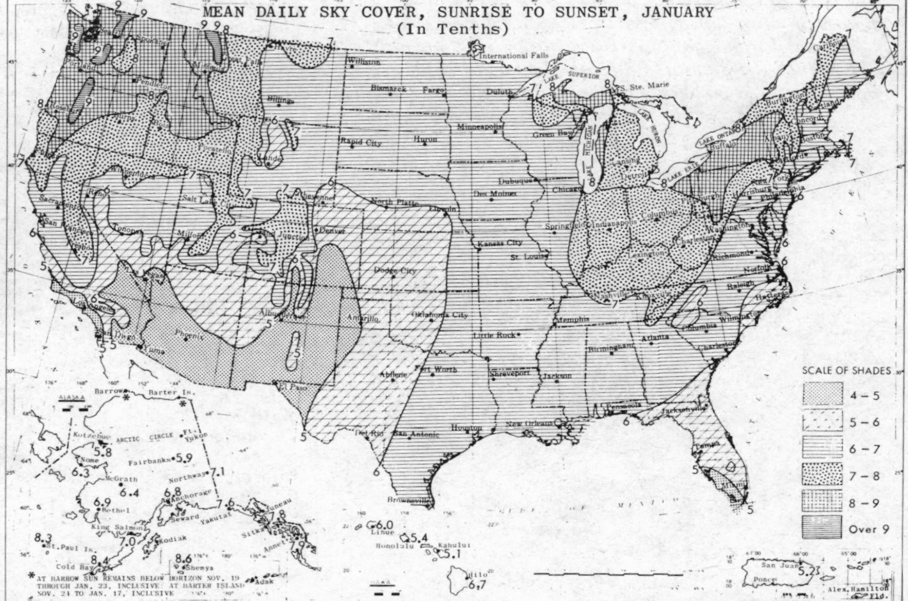

Climates of the United States
John L. Baldwin
1973; 113 pp.
No. 003-017-00211-0

$2.50 postpaid from:
Superintendent of Documents
U.S. Govt. Printing Office
Washington, D.C. 20402

Agricultural Extension Services

Each of the 50 states provides agricultural advice and services through county or area offices of their Agricultural Extension Service. These services are twofold:

1. Farm Advisors, extension agents, or county agents — depending on which state you live in, staff personnel under one of the above names are available for consultation or house calls in any area or agriculture or related fields such as turf care, home gardening, livestock, pest or rodent control and soil and water conservation to name a few. Most staffs usually also have a home economist.

2. Publications — a wide range of publications are also available through the AES or the U.S. Department of Agriculture. Some are for sale, but most are free. They are non-scientific and are written for the lay person. These publications cover a wide range of subjects of interest in commercial agriculture, home gardening or homemaking. Most states will have a catalog of their publications. If you have specific questions, it is often best to pick up brochures at the county office so that you may consult the farm adviser at the same time. Agricultural Extension Offices are normally listed in the phone book under the county listings. —Ed Johnson

Earthwork/Center for Rural Studies

Earthwork/Center for Rural Studies serves as a grassroots information center for a wide variety of issues dealing with alternative agriculture and food distribution and farmworkers. Several of their books and pamphlets are available nowhere else. Some movies are also in Spanish.

One current project is linking producers with consumers through direct marketing and food co-ops. They also keep tabs on the world-wide doings in the various ag-biz empires — Del Monte, Tenneco, etc. Good folks working on a very slim budget; they deserve your support. —Richard Nilsen

Earthwork
Catalog of books about food and land, and information about food buying clubs
free

How to Use Audiovisuals as Educational Tools
$1 postpaid

Directory of Films, Videotapes and Slide Shows
(Films on Food and Land)
$1 postpaid

all from:
Earthwork
3410 19th Street
San Francisco, CA 94110

National Climatic Center

Climatological data from weather stations in all the states is for sale here, either as summaries or by subscription. There is a $3 minimum charge for each publication order. If you are seeking climatic data for a given place, its usefulness will depend on how close you live to the nearest station. —Richard Nilsen

National Climatic Center
Information
free from:
National Climatic Center
Federal Building
Asheville, NC 28801

THE RISING SUN
NEIGHBORHOOD NEWSLETTER

American Association for Vocational Instructional Materials

The mechanical side of farming as seen through nearly 30 different titles mostly designed for high school agriculture courses. They are low cost ($3-10), well illustrated and especially good at explaining why and how things work — which makes this series ideal for first-time farmers.
—*Richard Nilsen*

American Association for Vocational Instructional Materials
Catalog and price list

free from:
AAVIM
Engineering Center
Athens, GA 30602

•

PUBLICATIONS

Spec. for Tune-Up Service of Farm Tractors	$5.95
Selecting & Storing Fuels and Lub.	3.45
Tractor Maintenance — Prin. & Procedures	7.95
Tractor Transmissions	1.75
Tractor Electrical System	3.25
Small Engines, Vol. I	6.95
Small Engines, Vol. II	8.95
Hydraulics, Vol. I	3.95
Hydraulics, Vol. II	4.95
Operating Grounds Keeping Tractors	3.95
Applying Pesticides	5.95
How Electric Motors Start & Run	2.75
Maintaining the Lighting & Wiring System	5.50
Electric Motors — Sel., Prot., Drives	3.95
Understanding Elec. & Electrical Terms	3.95
Electric Energy	2.95
Electrical Wiring	9.95
Shop Planning	3.95
Planning Machinery Protection	2.95
Utility buildings	3.95
Building Fences	3.95
Planning for an Irrigation System	7.95
Planning for an Indiv. Water System	6.95
Ball & Roller Bearings	1.50
Understanding & Measuring Power	4.50
Shop Safety Skills	6.75

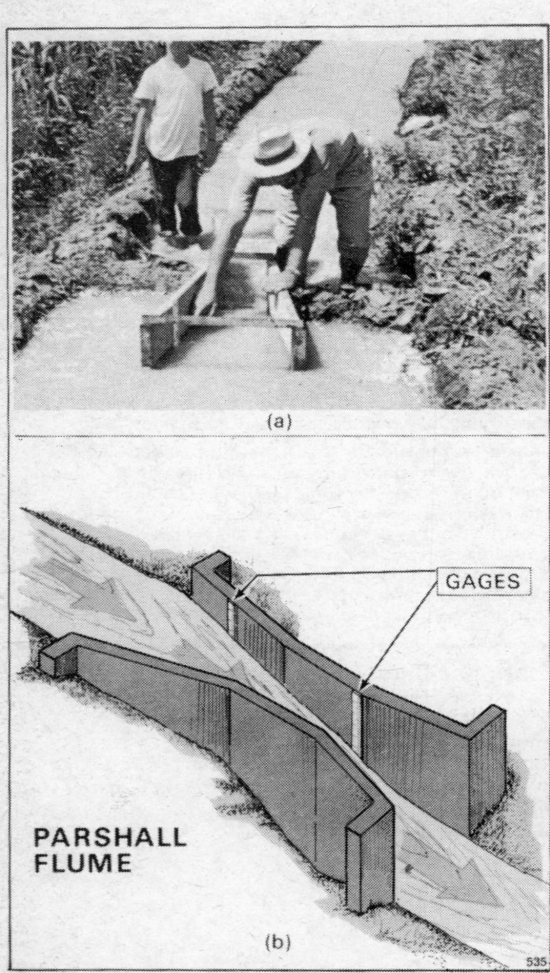

Parshall flume in an irrigation ditch for measuring the water flow. The depth of the water is measured at two points in the flume by gages. Then the quantity of flow is determined from a table of values perpared for that particular size Parshall flume.

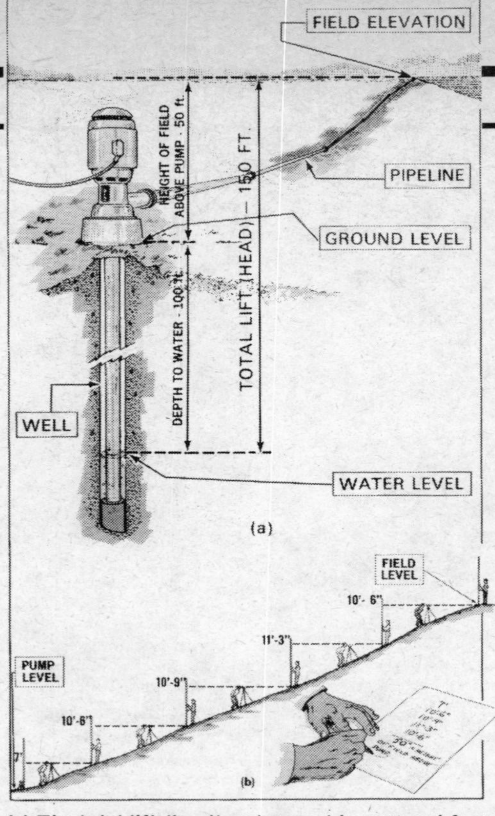

(a) The total lift (head) water must be pumped from wells is from the water level in the well to the elevation of your field. (b) Determining the elevation between the pump and the field.

Ideas for All Around the Farm

What American farmers tinker with when they're not busy feeding the world. **Successful Farming** *magazine collected these suggestions from farmers over the years. 1250 handy ideas and 540 illustrations showing down home engineering and "making it work right" creativity.*
—*Paul Kokesch*

Ideas for All Around the Farm
Editors of Successful Farming
1974; 98 pp.
2nd Edition

$2 postpaid from:
Successful Farming
Box 384
Des Moines, IA 50336

I make bale stacks stronger by using different lengths of pipe with holes drilled at intervals and long ¼" bolts fastened in them. With these pipes at different levels in the stack, I can make bigger stacks. Bales are held tightly together keeping out rain and snow and there is less spoilage.

Farm Show

This nifty little newspaper has something in common with our magazine, the **CoEvolution Quarterly** *— it contains no advertising. Focusing exclusively on new products and product evaluations, it is like having the information from a yearly farm equipment show mailed to your house — with one important difference. Because there are no ads, tips on poor products and bad buys are included too. Editor-publisher Harold Johnson lets his readers handle this chore in a regular write-in feature.*

Farm Show *is a good place to follow the incredible amount of tinkering going on as American farmers look for alternatives to expensive or scarce gas and diesel fuel. You won't find any horse-drawn plows here, or any discussion of the moral or ecological consequences of large-scale grain-alcohol fuel production, but there are farmers out there running their tractors and trucks on wood chips, old crankcase oil, and hydrogen.*
—*Richard Nilsen*
[Suggested by J.D. Smith]

Farm Show
Harold M. Johnson, Editor

$9/year (6 issues)
postpaid from:
Farm Show Publishing, Inc.
P.O. Box 704
Lakeville, MN
55044

In bright sunshine, the solar pump can lift almost as much water in an hour as any similar-sized windmill would in a good stiff breeze. It cannot rival the windmill for its maximum performance. But DeBeer claims that, in the longer term — like several months — his device "outperforms a windmill by far."
↓

Technical Publications Shop Manuals

If it runs on a gasoline engine and isn't a car, truck or industrial engine, then chances are very good that Technical Publications can sell you a shop manual for repair and maintenance. The list includes chain saws, walking and riding lawnmowers, snowmobiles, motorcycles, small tractors, inboard and outboard motors for boats, and wheel-type tractors. The tractor manuals generally cover both diesel and gas models.

The real tractor-saving jewels are the shop manuals for older tractors. The chances of buying a used farm tractor and getting the shop manual with it are remote at best, but fortunately this outfit stocks manuals for the older makes of Allis-Chalmers, Case, Deere, Ford, International Harvester, Massey-Ferguson, Minneapolis-Moline and Oliver.
—*Richard Nilsen*

Technical Publications Shop Manuals
catalog
free

Chain Saw Service Manual
1980; 320 pp.
6th Edition

Small Tractor Service Manual, Vol. 1
1972, 1975; 259 pp.
4th Edition

all from:
Technical Publications Division
Intertec Publishing Corp.
P.O. Box 12901
Overland Park, KS 66212

Plans for the solar pump are available for $24.00 (American dollars) from: Invent-A-Plan, 76 Montpelier Rise, Wembley, Middlesex HA9 8 RQ, England

•

Melvin Frueh, Donnelson, Iowa: 'It was a lemon from the first hour on, with bolts falling out, power steering locking up and the transmission oil filter plugging every five hours," says Melvin about his "worst buy" 2390 Case tractor. "When they tore it down after 60 hours, they found that some wear washers in the rear end had been left out at the factory. The dealer was helpful in getting things right, but the tractor I traded in — a 1370 — was nearly the same way. In 800 hours, it was down at least six times."

On the plus side, Melvin salutes his International 820 grain platform. "You can get nearer to the ground to get those low-standing soybean pods and make the field look as if you cut it with a lawn mower. Also, the cutting knife is faster so you can drive up to 4.5 mph and not strip the stems off. I've even been in a field with a John Deere row crop head and done just as good a job, yet can still use my head for small grain and drilled soybeans, which you can't with the Deere model."

Satoh Beaver, about $4,250 in California. Prices elsewhere will vary due to additional freight charges.

Central Tractor Farm and Family Center

A mail-order supply house for farm machinery and parts that also sells used tractor engine parts for all major makes of American tractors. They offer a 30 day guarantee on used parts, and the listings are quite extensive. So if you have an old but reliable tractor that will run fine if only that part that's been back-ordered for 10 months ever arrives, you might do better checking here.
—Richard Nilsen

Central Tractor Farm and Family Center
Catalog

free from:
Central Tractor Farm
and Family Center
1515 East Euclid Avenue
Des Moines, IA 50316

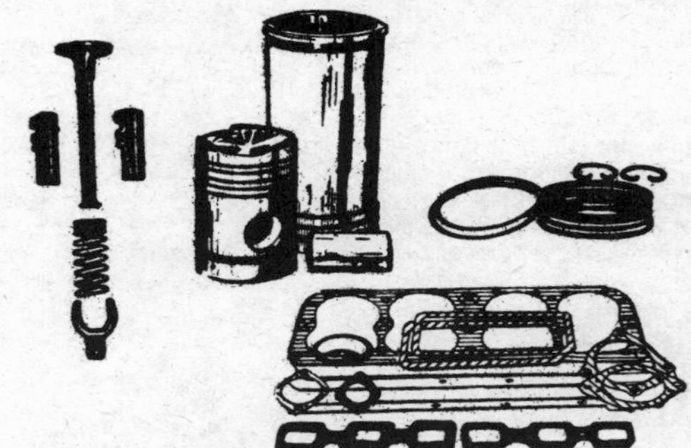

•

Overhaul Sets

All of the following overhaul sets contain the major components needed for complete engine overhaul. You also save 10% when purchasing the complete overhaul set. All components must be ordered in order to take this 10% discount. The bearings in these overhaul sets are all either standard or .002 oversize. We do stock a large number of the oversize bearings in our Des Moines Warehouse. If you need a different oversize, please specify the size you need on your order.

•

STARTER SWITCH FOR JOHN DEERE
A, B, G, 50, 60, 70, (Mfg. No. 820052). Wt. 5 oz.
2397-020. . . . . 4.50

FOR ALLIS CHALMERS (foot type)
B, C, CA, RC, WC, WD. (Replaces No. 1925781). Wt. ½ lb.
2386-020. . . . . 5.75

FOR CASE AND IHC (foot type)
D, DC, L, R, V, VC, series, IRC models H and M. Wt. ½ lb.
2381-020. . . . . 4.99

Hay Baling Hooks

Made of high quality steel rod and is designed for better grip on bales yet is easily released. Well constructed. Wood handle reinforced with steel.

11" long, 1 lb. 12940-048 **2.45**
17" long, 1¼ lbs. 12941-048 **2.65**

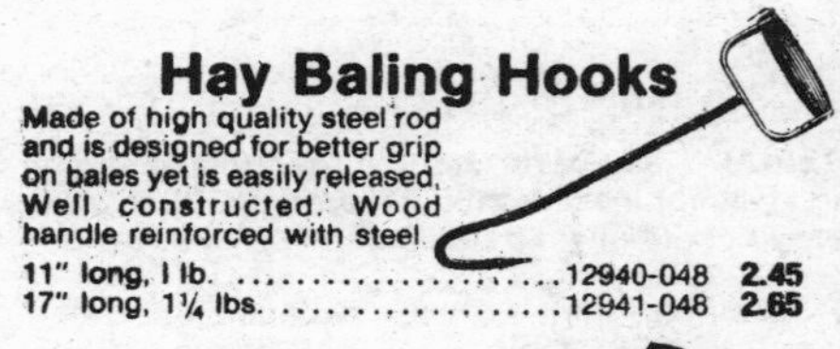

STARTER SWITCH FOR JOHN DEERE

A, B, G, 50, 60, 70 (Mfg. No. 820052). Wt. 5 oz.
2397-020 . . . . 4.50

FOR ALLIS CHALMERS (foot type)

B, C, CA, RC, WC, WD. (Replaces No. 1925781). Wt. ½.
2386-020 . . . . 5.75

FOR CASE and IHC (foot type)

D, DC, L, R, V, VC, series, IRC models H and M. Wt. ½ lb.
2381-020 . . . . 4.99

Rock and Dirt

Getchyer D-8 cat, your 6 x 6 2-1/2 ton truck, your surplus half-track, your 1800 x 24 tires, your tower crane your 8 pound sledge, your 80 ton diesel locomotive. Snort.
—SB

Rock and Dirt
$9.50 /year (36 issues)
postpaid from:
Rock and Dirt
Crossville, TN 38555

SPRING SPECIALS DOZERS

CASE 580B, ROPS encl., heater, wiper, new rubber, excellent **$14,500**

CASE W24, fully encl. cab, new center pin, new rubber, -0- hrs. on engine overhaul, excellent **$26,000**

PONDMASTER

Keeps any area 12 feet in diameter open at 3° below zero with normal winds. 3 wing twin blade model. Free-proof lever drive shaft. Brings warm water to surface in winter, cool water to surface in the summer. Hardware package sold separately. Wt. 25 lbs.
. . . . 20209-156 **116.50**

Economy Unit 2 wing model, lighter in con-struction. Wt. 16 lbs. 20212-156 **69.50**

Hardware Package includes cross bars and two angle brackets as pictured.
. . . . .20210-156 **30.50**

Flotation Assembly includes Hardware Package plus three floats to allow the entire Pondmaster to float in the water.
. . . . .20213-156 **72.99**

For Ford

9N, 2N, 8N to Serial #433578 3$3/_{16}$" Bore

Sleeve Assy.	2209-020	109.99
Valve Train Set	12179-133	54.50
Rod Bearing Set . . .	12375-052	8.99
Complete Gasket Set	3813-007	13.79
	TOTAL	187.27
	Less 10%	18.73
	You Pay ONLY	**168.54**

8N, after Serial #433578 with .090 thick-wall sleeves

Sleeve Assy.	1131-023	119.99
Valve Train Set	12181-133	80.25
Rod Bearing Set . . .	12375-052	8.99
Complete Gasket Set	3813-007	13.79
	TOTAL	223.02
	Less 10%	22.30
	You Pay ONLY	**200.72**

NAA, 600, 700, 2000, 134 Engine

Sleeve Assy.	1234-023	131.75
Valve Train Set	12183-133	69.25
Rod Bearing Set . . .	12387-052	13.39
Head Gasket Set	3978-007	15.39
Oil Pan Gasket Set . .	3979-007	3.10
	TOTAL	232.88
	Less 10%	23.29
	You Pay ONLY	**209.59**

FOR JOHN DEERE B

Ser # is found on right hand side of main case at front. Please write for free parts & price list below Ser #96,000.

MAIN CASE

Description	Part No.	Price ea
Trans. Case B1840R Ser. #96,000-200,999	AB2741R	79.95
Trans. case B2840R #201,000 & up	AB3518R	94.95
FRONT FRAME		
Front Support AB4247R #201,000 & up		109.95
ENGINE PARTS		
Manifold B1786R, #96,000 -183, 971	AB2846R	24.95
Manifold #183, 972-200, 999	B2179R	27.95
Manifold B2803R #96,000-200,999	AB3980R	27.95
Manifold #201,000 & up . .	B2282R	27.95
Manifold #201,000 & up . .	B2472R	29.95
Crankshaft B1847R #96,000 to 200,999	AB2752R	109.95
Crankshaft B2460R #201,000 & up	AB3509R	109.95
pistons Specify ser #		24.95

Satoh Small Tractors ↑

A Japanese water-cooled diesel tractor with several models in the 15-18 horse-power range. The 15 hp Beaver is competitively priced, and offers a wide range of features and attachments.
—Richard Nilsen

Satoh Small Tractors
Information and location of nearest dealer

free from:
Satoh
P.O. Box 5020
New York, NY 10022

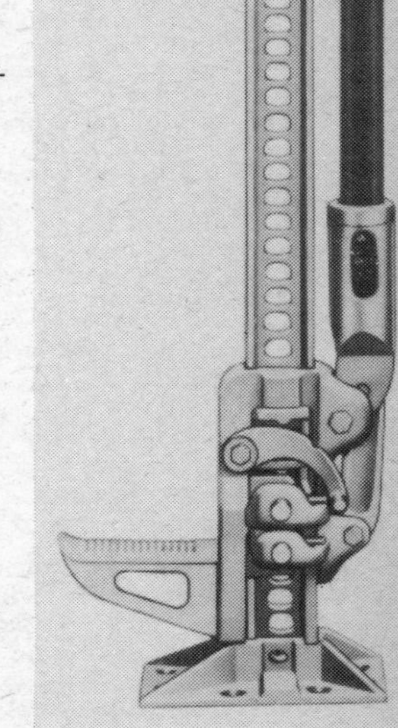

Handyman Jack

Basically the Handyman Jack is a super heavy duty bumper jack but it bears no resemblance to the inadequate things that Detroit supplies with their inadequate automobiles. It weighs 29 pounds, has a capacity of 3½ tons, is four feet tall, and has a lift of three feet. The jack is guaranteed for 18 months, and complete repair parts are available should they ever be required.

I've used mine for lifting my truck, stretching shrunken plastic water pipe, and a number of odd lifting and spreading jobs, and wouldn't part with it for anything.

WARNING: Beware of handle, or EAT TEETH. —Douglas Canning

Handyman Jack ⟶
29 pounds
$41 (approx.) from:
Harrah Manufacturing Co.
46 West Spring Street
Bloomfield, IN 47424

THE RISING SUN
NEIGHBORHOOD NEWSLETTER

We all have two poems – the only answer for someone else's question and the only question for someone else's answer.

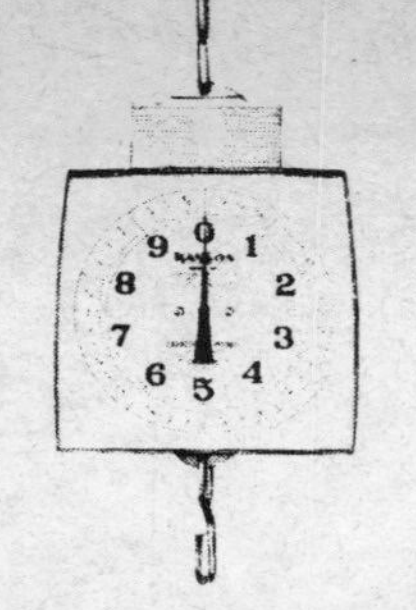

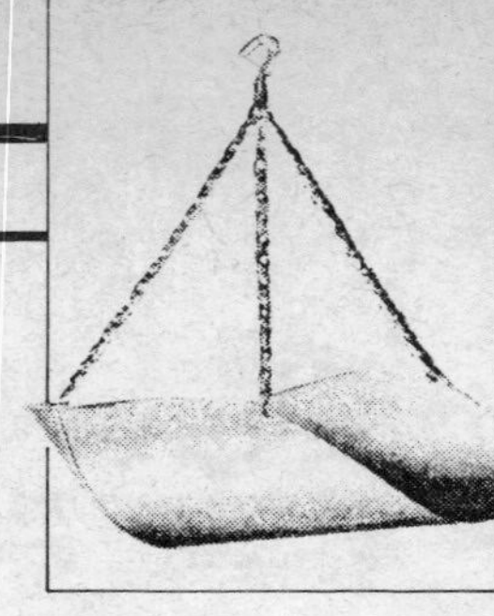

Nasco Farm and Ranch Catalog

Part of the trouble with going back to the farm, just like going into a new job or hobby, is that the technology of gadgets must be looked into, so the new farmer will be able to tell whether he really needs a master artificial vagina, liquid semen refrigerator, and trans-jector electronic ejaculator, or whether he is going to believe in a little more organic process.

The Nasco catalog sits smack in the middle of farmy equipment consciousness, and carries all of the above mentioned goodies. But, Nasco also carries the more staple farm tools, like crank forges, seed sowers, cant hooks, load binders, pulaskis, lopping shears, and post hole diggers.

If you are a windowshopping farmer, or farmy window-shopper, write for the catalog. —J.D. Smith

Nasco Farm and Ranch Catalog
322 pp.

free from:
Nasco
901 Janesville Avenue
Fort Atkinson, WI 53538

10 **TUNED IN HARMONY — SWISS COW BELLS**
Very best Swiss bell metal. The kind of pleasure they give is what makes farm life really worthwhile. You can afford their small luxury. Bells measure 4", 5", and 6¼". Straps not included.
C7084N-A Set of 3 bells. Sh. wt. 7 lbs. **$48.00**
C7085N Set of 3 straps. Sh. wt. 1 lb. 25.35 ~~**$21.95**~~

4 **HANSON HANGING SCALE**
Constructed and tested according to specifications, tolerances, and regulations of the National Bureau of Standards for commercial weighing devices. Legal for sale of fruit and vegetables. Has screw adjustment pointer. Two, tempered steel, precision check springs and extra heavy gravity milled rack. Size 8" x 2" x 16". Graduated in ounces. Capacity 20 lbs. in two revolutions. Large dial, easy to read. Ideal for scoop and steel pan. Order Scoop C6370. Sh. wt. 3 lbs. 7 oz.
C6369N-842 **$14.95**

5 **SCOOP WITH CHAIN**
For Hanson Hanging Scales. Galvanized steel. 17" x 11-5/8" x 5-7/16". Sh. wt. 2 lbs. 8 oz.
C6370N-8 **$8.65**

1 **GALVANIZED FEED PAIL**
Holds about half a bushel. It is 14-9/16" in diameter by 8¼" in height. Sturdy construction. Heavy wire bail handle. Fine for show animals. Capacity 4 gallons. Sh. wt. 3 lbs.
C112N-4AS **$3.95**

2 **EXTRA HEAVY STOCK PAILS**
Hot-dip galvanized after forming. Four rivet, heavy butterfly ears, with heavy galvanized iron bail.
15 QT. PAIL. Top dia. 12½", bottom dia. 9¼", height 10¼". Sh. wt. 4 lbs. 8 oz.
C4440N-1515 **$5.95**
18 QT. PAIL. Top dia. 13¼", bottom dia. 9¾", height 11½". Sh. wt. 5 lbs.
C4441N-1518 **$6.95**

Domestic Growers Supply Catalog

Mail-order catalog from a young company specializing in water storage and delivery systems. Redwood tanks, solid or collapsible plastic tanks, drip irrigation hardware, portable water pumps, hose couplings. —Richard Nilsen

Domestic Growers Supply
Catalog

$1 postpaid from:
Domestic Growers Supply, Inc.
P.O. Box 809
Cave Junction, OR 97523

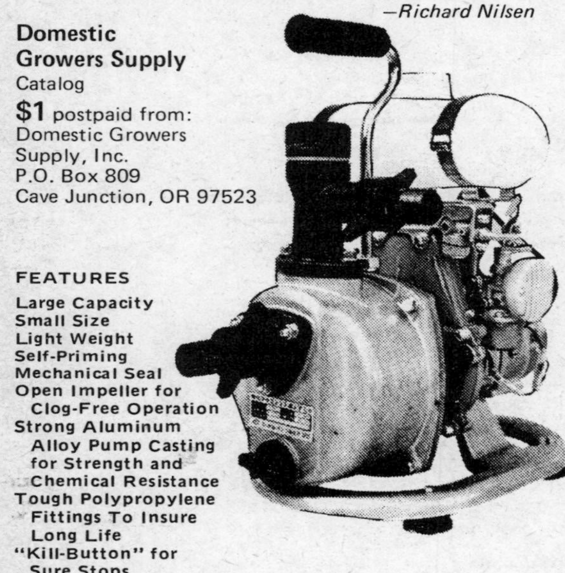

FEATURES
Large Capacity
Small Size
Light Weight
Self-Priming
Mechanical Seal
Open Impeller for Clog-Free Operation
Strong Aluminum Alloy Pump Casting for Strength and Chemical Resistance
Tough Polypropylene Fittings To Insure Long Life
"Kill-Button" for Sure Stops

An exceptional pump, small on the outside, but with a big heart . . . that won't let you down . . . Model E-ON $279 delivered.

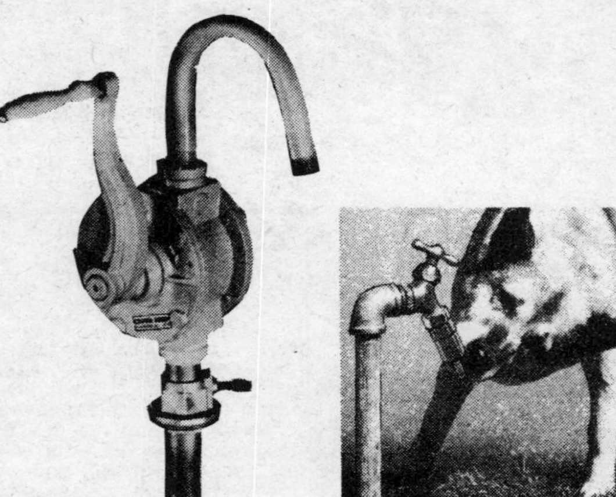

2 **ROTARY BARREL PUMP**
Extremely fast manual pumping, rated at 7.0 gallons per minute. Suitable for two viscosity oils such as gasoline, kerosene, diesel fuels, light oils, waxes, antifreeze, etc. Not recommended for acids, alkalies, and other chemicals. Cast-iron body. Brass blades. Steel suction pipe. Sh. wt. 14 lbs. 8 oz.
C7200N-RP90 **$48.80**

6 **LIXIT — Drinker Valve for Dogs**
The animal simply licks or nudges the lever control, and clean, fresh water flows directly into its mouth. Shuts off automatically. LIXIT attaches by hand, direct to outside faucets or to end of garden hose. Eliminates scrubbing and sanitizing of "contaminated" water pans and the never ending, daily watering chore. Sh. wt. 7 oz.
C2609N-L100 Each **$5.62;** 10 or more, each **$4.87**

Stockman's National Supply Company

If you need a serious quantity of stock fence or irrigation pipe, check Stockman's prices. Their current prices on field fence are similar to Sears and on farm gates 25% less. Since Stockman's prices include prepaid freight, while Sears do not, Stockman's is 10 to 35% cheaper. They carry a variety of other heavy duty items such as cattle guards, large stock tanks, windmills, hog feeders, and squeeze chutes. Some of their fabricated steel items are surprisingly cheap; less than what it would cost you to build it of wood or steel. —Alan Kalker

Stockman's National Supply Company
(Formerly Bernstein Brothers)
Catalog

free from:
Stockman's National Supply Company
P.O. Box 917
Pueblo, CO 81002

WALNUT AND CORN SHELLER ↑
Easily operated by hand crank. Made of quality cast iron and painted with non-toxic finish. Attaches to barrel or box by clamps designed into the unit. Cob ejector and tipping attachment included. Spring adjusts to fit all size ears. Capacity 10 to 15 bushels per hour. 8¼-in. picker wheel.

TIE DOWN
Ratchet Strap →
A rugged, light-weight tool for use on the farm or ranch or wherever it is needed. 1½ inch wide rugged nylon webbing. A 9 to 1 mechanical advantage lets you really cinch down loads to prevent damage or shifting. Double ratchet keeps strap pull centered and straight. Frame is all steel with special plating. Hooks at each end of webbing. Strap is 15 feet long. Entire unit weighs less than 2 pounds.

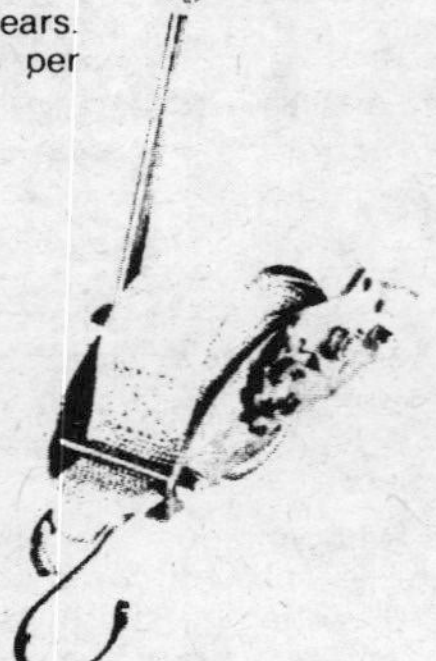

Fully Hardened, Galvanized, High-Carbon Spring Steel 5-Panel Farm Gates

ALL GATES 52 INCHES HIGH

PANEL MATERIAL: Full hard, hot-dip galvanized, high carbon spring steel, for maximum tensil strength. Built light enough for easy handling, yet gauge of steel is heaviest on the market.
CONSTRUCTION: Four-point aircraft type aluminum riveting at every joint. (NO SPOT WELDS in entire assembly to pull loose or break). All gates are 52 inches high.
HARDWARE: Hinges of 12-gauge steel, galvanized. Screw hooks, for wooden posts, are ⅝-inch diameter, 6 inches long with 1½-inch pintle, hot rolled and formed, galvanized. Slide latch with handle and matching receiver for post.

Opening	Height	Internal Braces	Zone 1	Zone 2	Zone 3
4 Ft.	52"	0	$17.25	$17.75	$18.75
6 Ft.	52"	1	$24.50	$25.00	$26.50
8 Ft.	52"	2	$33.25	$34.00	$34.50
10 Ft.	52"	3	$38.00	$39.00	$40.00
12 Ft.	52"	3	$42.75	$43.50	$45.75
14 Ft.	52"	5	$51.50	$52.75	$57.75
16 Ft.	52"	5	$54.50	$56.00	$59.75
18 Ft.	52"	5	$60.00	$61.50	$67.00

Ben Meadows Company

The Ben Meadows Company informed us they did not want to be listed in our ***Catalog****, and refused to send us their excellent catalog of forestry and engineering supplies. They said they would sell to individuals, but made it very clear they prefer selling multi-thousand dollar orders to Weyhauser and the U.S. Forest Service. That's either a pain in the ass or an opportunity for some new company serving small customers to fill an empty niche, depending on how you look at it.* —Richard Nilsen

The Ben Meadows Company
(Forestry and Engineering Supplies)
Catalog

$3 postpaid from:
The Ben Meadows Co.
P.O. Box 80549
Atlanta, GA 30366

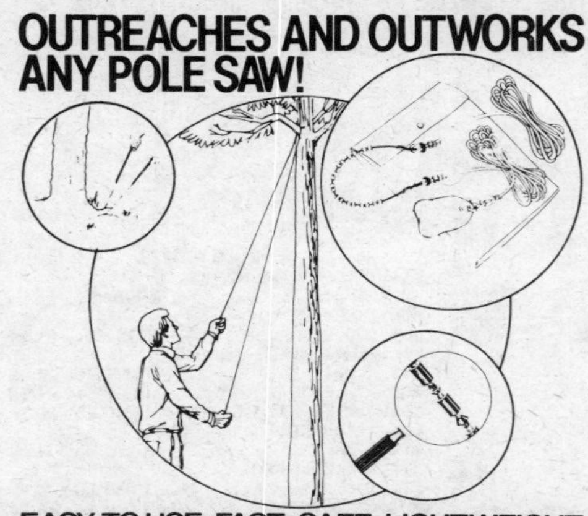

The Troybilt Horse (available in 6, 7, or 8 hp).

Gravely tractors, left to right: Model 8183T — 18 hp riding tractor with 3 blade center mount rotary mower, Model 5200 — 8 hp convertible (walking or riding) tractor with 30 inch mower, Model 5460 — 10 hp convertible tractor with snow dozer, Model 8183T — riding tractor with 40 inch 2 blade mower, Model 5660 — 12 hp convertible tractor with 50 inch blade rotary mower, Model 5260 — 8 hp convertible tractor with rotary plow, Model 8123 — 12 hp riding tractor with 3 blade center mount rotary mower.

Troybilt Tillers ↑

A new owner discovers that Troybilt tillers have a personality all their own. First there's the construction — they're built solid as a Russian dumptruck, with an engineering approach that stresses ease of maintenance and durability rather than the latest in convenience features. When all the other tillers come equipped with Dynaflow, Troybilt won't.

Then there's the owner's manual, 200 pages loaded with pictures of how to use and maintain the tiller, covering everything from green manuring and sheet composting to shimming the drive shaft and replacing the transmission. The manual stirs memories of John Muir's **Idiot Book** *for VW's, for it tells you how to do the tune up or repair, instead of confusing you with 4 pages of fluff and leaving you with a trip to some $25/hr. 'expert'. For good measure Troybilt's service department has a toll free 800 phone number.*

If your long term goal is self sufficiency, the Troybilt is not only a tool to help you grow your own food but also a chance to take responsibility for your own machinery. In the process, the mystification that alienates most people from understanding machines can be overcome.

Troybilt tillers range from 5 to 8 hp, and in price from $585 to $1047. There's also a unique pricing scheme in which off-season prices are discounted — for example you get 20% off by ordering in the fall. —Dick Fugett

Troybilt Tillers
Information and price list

free from:
Troybilt
102nd St. & 9th Ave.
Troy, NY 12180

Sickle bar mowers

Both these companies manufacture sickle bar mowers. The Jari has bar widths that range from 16 to 60 inches. Kinco also makes an 18 inch walk-behind thatcher, which cuts the runners on St. Augustine grass and is popular in Florida. —Richard Nilsen

Jari Sickle Mowing Machines
$500 - $700
Information and nearest dealer location

free from:
Jari Division
P.O. Box 2075
Mankato, MN 56001

Self Propelled Sickle Bar
(About $600)
Information and nearest dealer location

free from:
Kinco Manufacturing
168 North Pascal Street
St. Paul, MN 55104

Gravely Tractor ↑

I own an old one — and my 5 acres is more like 35. We mow, plow, cultivate, cut brush, saw wood, pump water, plow and blow deep snow, clear ice, haul, etc., with it. No belts and plenty of power. (Don't try to help it — it's stronger than you are.) Rotary plow turns organic debris under and leaves a ready-to-plant seed bed in one operation. —George D. James, Jr.

Gravely Tractors
(2-wheel tractors about $2,000; 4-wheel tractors range from about $2,500 to $4,500)
Brochure and price list

free from:
Clarke-Gravely Lane
Clemmons, NC 27012
or check your local farm equipment supplier.

←
The Jari Monarch (5 hp) — Designed for both the occasional user and every day commercial application.

Roto-Hoe Shredders

Roto-Hoe makes one of the finest compost shredders for home gardeners. They have four models, which range from a 3 or 5 hp model with a 10 inch hopper, to an 8 hp double belt drive model with a 20 inch hopper. Any brand of compost shredder is designed to handle green, succulent plant material only. If you want to shred a pile of tree limbs and branches that have sat out for two years, you don't want a compost shredder. What you'll need is called a chipper, and for such occasional use, the best thing to do is rent one. —Richard Nilsen

Roto-Hoe Shredders
$249 - $549
Brochure, price list and nearest dealer location

free from:
The Roto-Hoe Company
Newbury, OH 44065

The Roto-Hoe 8hp Model 2000 Shredder, about $750

Mainline Rotary Tiller

Don't be thrown by the name "rotary tiller." Mainline actually makes a rugged and versatile line of walking tractor power plants and implements, among which are rotary tillers. Some of these Italian machines are pretty specialized and only have a few attachments listed. Others can take a very wide range of attachments. Some attachments are not interchangeable between certain models. The majority of models come as rotary tillers, but those can be ordered without the tiller attachment, if desired. Only two bolts need be removed to take the tiller off the power unit and expose the splined power take-off (PTO). A throttle lock and mechanical governor maintain constant speed for attachable pumps, generators, and the like. Mainline attachments include various sickle bar mowers (and optional swathboard ends to lay the cut material in windows), potato digger, hydraulic log splitter, dump cart, sprayer, disc, plow, sheaf binder, and so on. To attach the sickle bar mower to a power unit, the rear mounted tiller is first removed. Then the tractor handles are pivoted to 180°, and the transmission is put in reverse, putting the PTO at what is now the front of the tractor. Then the sickle bar cutting unit is put on. The whole operation takes about 15 minutes with the model 715.

All the #715 models have three speeds forward and one in reverse. The #725 and #735 models have five speeds forward and two in reverse. Engine sizes are 5, 8, and 10 hp air-cooled gasoline, and 8 and 15 hp air-cooled diesel. Choice of Lombardini or ACME engines on the 8 hp diesel; most other models ACME. The ACME engines have been built since 1947 and have lots of nice features like hardened valve seats, externally accessible points and condenser, replacable valve guides, fuel tank shut-off, replaceable connecting rod, and ball bearings at both ends of the crankshaft. Adjustable tilling widths are in steps from 8" to 27" depending on the tiller (except the

↑
Mainline Model 715
8 hp diesel on left, with tiller unit attached. On right with handlebars reversed and sickle bar mower attached. The power unit with tiller costs about $1600.

Model 705 has adjustable tilling widths of 22" - 27"). Offset wheel rims and optional narrow wheels allow coordination of wheel width with tilling width. One model has extended axles for stability on slopes. —David Batts

Mainline Rotary Tillers
$919 - $3889
Brochures, price and nearest dealer information

free from:
Central States Mainline
Box 348
London, OH 43140

The Garden Way Gardener's Catalog

Jess Clarke and Dick Raymond have put together as yet another Garden Way company, this time a mail order tool catalog featuring lightweight tools aimed at the older gardener. Raymond's philosophy is if it isn't light, you won't use it, so most of the garden tools concentrate on weight rather than durability. More important than weight is that Raymond has used most of the tools in the catalog and the descriptions are written by someone who sounds like he knows his business. Somebody there has thought long and hard about the backyard gardener, and this is the result. I haven't ordered from this company, it is so new, but if it is like the other Garden Way companies, you can expect fast service and a no questions return policy if you aren't satisfied. —Paul Hawken

The Garden Way Gardener's Catalog

free from:
Garden Way
Charlotte, VT 05445

#9610 Small Cell Seed Starter Flat: For lettuce, parsley, onions, herbs, flowers. 128 cells, each cell 1½ x 1½ x 2½" deep. Overall flat size is 26 3/8 l x 13½ w x 2½" deep **$5.25**

#9612 Medium Cell Seed Starter Flat A most popular size! 72 cells, each cell 1¾ x 1¾ x 2½" deep. For flowers, cabbage, smaller transplants of peppers, tomatoes, eggplant and more! Overall flat size 26 3/8 l x 13½ w x 2½ deep **$5.45**

#9614 Large Cell Seed Starter Flat: 32 cells, each cell 3 x 3 x 3" deep. For larger transplants of peppers, tomatoes, eggplants. Also squash, melons, cucumbers and more! Overall size is 26 3/8 l x 13½ w x 3" deep . **$5.95**

•

Here's why the TODD Planter Flat System is superior to all other methods of seed starting and plant propagation. Inverted pyramid and bottom opening encourage downward root growth and create natural "air-pruning." There's less chance of bound root problems, transplant shock is eliminated!

SAVE $1
#942A Set of 2 Picker-Pockets, 1 Small, 1 Large
ONLY $9.90

↑

Your hand was not created to hold fruit and pick at the same time! The Garden Way PICKER-POCKET makes picking berries, fruits, nuts and vegetables a JOY...**No more** berry cans dangling from you neck! **No more** juggling containers in one hand while you pick with the other! **No more** extra trips to empty pint-sized berry boxes. **And, thankfully, no more backache from constantly bending** to drop berries and fruits—one at a time—into boxes on the ground!

ACTUALLY CUTS PICKING TIME BY 30% OR MORE

Garden Way's **Picker-Pocket™ Bag** fits on your arm like a big stocking. Simply slide your fingers through the calf leather hand patch and easily flick every berry, nut, cherry tomato or pole bean into the pouch. And, with **just one hand picking,** the other hand is alway free to push aside thick bushes to pick clean and quick—without thorn scratches!

Made of 4 oz. waterproof "tent" nylon, the PICKER-POCKET is tough enough for seasons of use. Flexible wire rim opens wide or small to make picking easier from any position. In bright "day-glo" orange, it's hard to lose, even in the thickest bushes!

#939 Small (1¼ qt.) Picker-Pocket $4.95
#940 Large (3 qt.) Picker-Pocket $5.95
#941 Giant (10 qt.) Open Chute Picker-Pocket $8.95
#942 All 3 (Small, Large and Giant) $17.00

A.M. Leonard, Inc.

For the serious gardener, or plant propagator, Leonard's has the most complete line of pruning shears, grafting and budding knives, nursery hoes, planting tools, and watering accessories available by mail order. Most horticultural supply companies demand professional credentials before they will sell to you — Leonard doesn't. Prices are retail, but if you order more than one of most items, there are discounts. On some items, 25% is discounted if you order in half dozen amounts. Leonard has been around for a long time, and most of the products have withstood the test of their professional users over time. Other useful items are tagging and marking equipment, Wilkinson Sword Garden Tools, Arkansas Oilstones, and Leonard's own full steel strap nursery spades. —Paul Hawken

Horticultural Tool and Supply Catalogue
76 pp.

free from:
A.M. Leonard, Inc.
6665 Spiker Road
Piqua, OH 45356

•

B-95 EARTH AUGER →
.... **ea. $25**
For tree feeding and soil testing, 2 in. in diameter, 40 in. long with 6 in. twist, wood handle. Weight, 6 lbs.

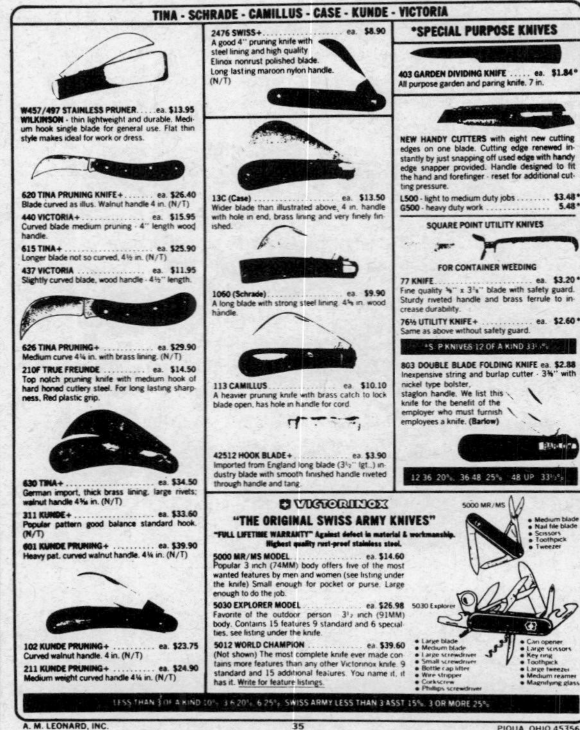

TINA - SCHRADE - CAMILLUS - CASE - KUNDE - VICTORIA

W457/497 STAINLESS PRUNER.....ea. $13.95
WILKINSON - thin lightweight and durable. Medium hook single blade for general use. Flat thin style makes ideal for work or dress.

620 TINA PRUNING KNIFE+ .... ea. $26.40
Blade curved as illus. Walnut handle 4 in. (N/T)

440 VICTORIA+ .... ea. $15.95
Curved blade medium pruning - 4" length wood handle.

615 TINA+ .... ea. $25.90
Longer blade not so curved, 4½ in. (N/T)

437 VICTORIA .... ea. $11.95
Slightly curved blade, wood handle - 4½" length.

626 TINA PRUNING+ .... ea. $29.90
Medium curve 4¼ in. with brass lining. (N/T)

210F TRUE FREUNDE .... ea. $14.50
Top notch pruning knife with medium hook of hard honed cutlery steel. For long lasting sharpness. Red plastic grip.

630 TINA+ .... ea. $34.50
German import, thick brass lining, large rivets; walnut handle 4⅜ in. (N/T)

311 KUNDE+ .... ea. $33.60
Popular pattern good balance standard hook. (N/T)

601 KUNDE PRUNING+ .... ea. $39.90
Heavy pat. curved walnut handle. 4¼ in. (N/T)

102 KUNDE PRUNING+ .... ea. $23.75
Curved walnut handle. 4 in. (N/T)

211 KUNDE PRUNING+ .... ea. $24.90
Medium weight curved handle 4¼ in. (N/T)

2476 SWISS+ .... ea. $8.90
A good 4" pruning knife with steel lining and high quality Elinox nonrust polished blade. Long lasting maroon nylon handle. (N/T)

13C (Case) .... ea. $13.50
Wider blade than illustrated above, 4 in. handle with hole in end, brass lining and very finely finished.

1060 (Schrade) .... ea. $9.90
A long blade with strong steel lining. 4⅝ in. wood handle.

113 CAMILLUS .... ea. $10.10
A heavier pruning knife with brass catch to lock blade open, has hole in handle for cord.

42512 HOOK BLADE+ .... ea. $3.90
Imported from England long blade (3½" lgt.) industry blade with smooth finished handle riveted through handle and tang.

***SPECIAL PURPOSE KNIVES**

403 GARDEN DIVIDING KNIFE ..... ea. $1.84*
All purpose garden and paring knife. 7 in.

NEW HANDY CUTTERS with eight new cutting edges on one blade. Cutting edge renewed instantly by just snapping off used edge with handy edge snapper provided. Handle designed to fit the hand and forefinger - reset for additional cutting pressure.
L500 - light to medium duty jobs $3.48*
G500 - heavy duty work 5.48*

SQUARE POINT UTILITY KNIVES
FOR CONTAINER WEEDING

77 KNIFE .... ea. $3.20*
Fine quality ⅝" x 3¼" blade with safety guard. Sturdy riveted handle and brass ferrule to increase durability.

76½ UTILITY KNIFE+ .... ea. $2.60*
Same as above without safety guard.

*S. P. KNIVES 12 OF A KIND 33⅓%

803 DOUBLE BLADE FOLDING KNIFE ea. $2.88
Inexpensive string and burlap cutter - 3⅜" with nickel type bolster, stagion handle. We list this knife for the benefit of the employer who must furnish employees a knife. (Barlow)

12-36 20%, 36-48 25%, 48 UP 33⅓%

VICTORINOX

"THE ORIGINAL SWISS ARMY KNIVES"
"FULL LIFETIME WARRANTY" Against defect in material & workmanship. Highest quality rust-proof stainless steel.

5000 MR/MS MODEL .... ea. $14.60
Popular 3 inch (74MM) body offers five of the most wanted features by men and women (see listing under the knife) Small enough for pocket or purse. Large enough to do the job.

5030 EXPLORER MODEL .... ea. $26.98
Favorite of the outdoor person 3½ inch (91MM) body. Contains 15 features 9 standard and 6 specialties, see listing under the knife.

5012 WORLD CHAMPION .... ea. $39.60
(Not shown) The most complete knife ever made contains more features than any other Victorinox knife. 9 standard and 15 additional features. You name it, it has it. Write for feature listings.

5000 MR/MS
• Medium blade
• Nail file blade
• Scissors
• Toothpick
• Tweezer

5030 Explorer
• Large blade
• Medium blade
• Large screwdriver
• Small screwdriver
• Bottle cap lifter
• Wire stripper
• Corkscrew
• Phillips screwdriver
• Can opener
• Large scissors
• Key ring
• Toothpick
• Large tweezer
• Medium reamer
• Magnifying glass

LESS THAN 3 OF A KIND 10%, 3-6 20%, 6 25%, SWISS ARMY LESS THAN 3 ASST 15%, 3 OR MORE 25%

A. M. LEONARD, INC. 35 PIQUA, OHIO 45356

Walt Nicke's

Nicke's, like Leonard's, has been around long enough to know what a useful tool is and isn't. Although the catalog tends towards the cutesy, the items are good quality, many imported. Nicke imports John Guy trowels and shears, the unsurpassable Haws watering can, Solo Sprayers and Rolcut secauteurs. Nicke is the only company I know of that sells the glass cloches first used by the Parisienne marchiers at the turn of the century. The glass cloches act as greenhouses and will give the northern gardner a few extra weeks at the beginning of the season. Nicke's is not the fastest mail order company, so be patient after you send your money. —Paul Hawken

Walt Nicke's Garden Talk
Catalog

$.25 postpaid from:
Walter F. Nicke
Box 667G
Hudson, NY 12534

↑
NO. 170:
HAWS POLYTHENE
From genuine Haw's range of famous watering cans, made from high density polythene. Extra light and extremely hard wearing. Perfect balance. Supplied with Haws non-drip brass oval rose. Attractive red colour.
4 quart size **$16.95**
6 quart size **$22.95**

←
LONG HANDLED TROWEL
Finest Sheffield Steel. Blade shank is wrapped around the hardwood handle and riveted for extra strength. The overall length is 17".
No. 20 ..... **$6.95**

SLIMLINE HEDGESHEAR

↑
Notched 8½" finest Sheffield Steel blades. Hollow ground, electronically hardened, Teflon coated. Distinctive black blades with chrome fittings and attractive orange handles. Handles pegged through ferule and shank. Instructions for care and use included. A London Design Center selection.
No. 80 .... **$9.95** each

•

Rolcut Secateurs are British excellence. All blades are sharp Sheffield Steel. All pruners have a two-position catch for easy light work. Pruning hints and instructions are sent with each. All parts are replaceable. In all, we give you a selection of Rolcut models and since we sell so many, we can keep prices low. Great for you and a fine gift for a friend.

↓

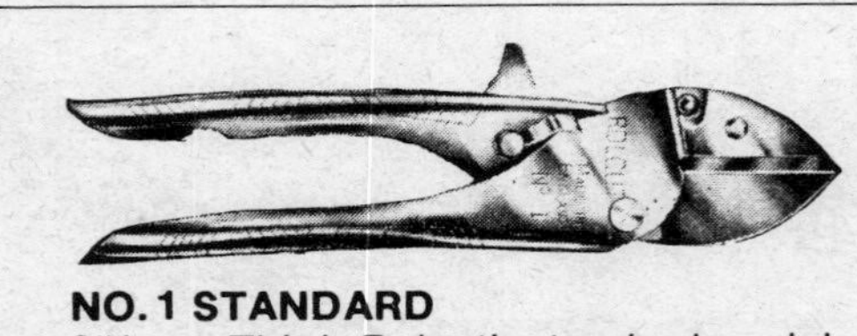

NO. 1 STANDARD
8" long. This is Rolcut's standard model for general pruning.........**$6.75**

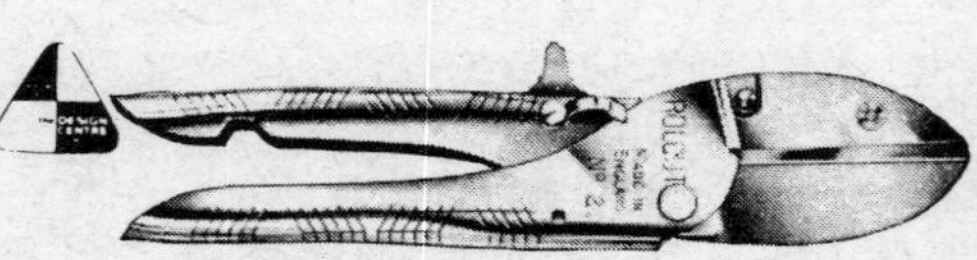

NO. 2 MAJOR
8½" long. A larger and heavier model with a longer blade. For heavy duty work ...about as far as you can go with a one hand operated pruner....... **$6.95**

For an early garden, the glass tent — A sturdy aluminum clip holds two panes of glass (up to 12" x 18") to form a glass tent section. Placed end to end, these sections can cover your garden row like a miniature greenhouse. This makes protection, helps seed germination, and produces early crops. $1.50 each; 5 for $4.95, 10 for $8.95

↓

915 PLANTING BAG →

Convenient for hand field planting. Made of heavy olive green ducking, reinforced strap, 1¼" wide and 40" long with buckle to hold bag to waist; bags have leg tie grommet holes. Bags are 9" in. diameter, approximately 15" deep.
EACH.. NET $7.90

↑

Haws (of England) manufacturer of world famous professional watering cans for over a hundred years (many of the original time consuming techniques and detailed hand work is still being employed today) **Haws** cans are made of galvanized heavy gauge steel lead coated and then finally coated with zinc chromate. **Haws** cans are perfectly balanced and handle well full or empty. Equipped with **Haws** pure brass rose perforated with tiny holes for fine soft spray.

190 - 1 gallon capacity **$40.98**
Traditional design with cross-piece which adds rigidity and doubles as a carrying handle. 27 in. spout including rose.

190 - 2 gallon capacity **$46.98**
Same as 1 gallon design with twice the capacity, a better buy where additional capacity is required.

→

37 PULASKI MATTOCK-AXE .... ea. **$34.39**
A general forestry tool, especially good for cutting large tree roots. 36 in. straight handle.

5610 Medium Garden Spade	5615 Heavyduty Garden Spade	5609 Border Spade	5676 All Metal Spade (Professional)	4504 Tree Planting Tool	4612 Irish Garden Spade
$28.50	$35.50	$24	$34	$39.50	$31

Smith & Hawken Tool Company

Bulldog Tools of England, a 200-year-old company with a high-quality line of hand gardening tools, now has an American distributor. They are built to last, and the prices reflect this — most of the spades, forks and hoes are in the $20 - $40 range. Most come with the all-wood durable D-style handles, and many have specialized uses. Smith and Hawken also carries Haws watering cans; Chillington "Crocodile" hoes; Spear & Jackson axes, hammers, saws and files; Martindale machetes; Scovill hoes; Austrian scythes; Wolf & Bangert cross-cut saws; plus assorted pruning and grafting knives, books, and secauteurs. ("Hawken" is the Paul Hawken who founded Erewhon, wrote **The Magic of Findhorn** *and has contributed reviews of items on these gardening pages and elsewhere in* **the Next Whole Earth Catalog***).*

—Richard Nilsen

Smith & Hawken Tool Company
Catalog & price list
free from:
Smith & Hawken
Tool Company
68 Homer Street
Palo Alto, CA 94301

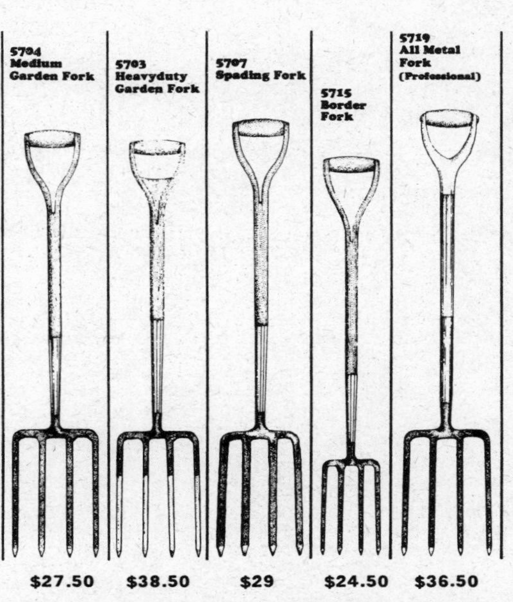

$27.50 $38.50 $29 $24.50 $36.50

$32 $36.50

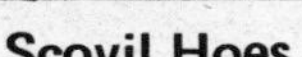

Scovil Hoes

Scovil is one of the oldest tool companies in the United States and it still makes the best domestic hoes . . . although now they're made in Japan. The eye hoe will outlast a tang and ferrule draw hoe and is the only kind to use in heavy soils and clay. Scovil hoes are made from single sheet carbon steel, which means the hoes are uniform in thickness and relatively light in wieght when compared to roll-forged hoes like Chillington. The eye hoe uses a handle that is flared on the end like a mattock — in other words, the head won't come off. I like the Italian grape hoe for hacking through the summer clay.

Available from Leonard's, Walter Nicke and most good gardening outlets.

—Paul Hawken

Scovil Hoes
$7.99 to $8.49
each (approx.)
information and nearest dealer location

free from:
Scovil Hoe Company
Higganum, CT 06441

FG6

FG7

A

S

← FIELD AND GARDEN PATTERN

No.	Width of Blade	Depth of Blade	Weight per Dozen
FG 6	6″	4½″	26 lbs.
FG 6½	6½″	5″	27 lbs.
FG 7	7″	3½″	28 lbs.
AMERICAN PATTERN			
A	6″	4½″	24 lbs.
SOUTHERN BELLE			
The finest all purpose gardening cultivator and hoe ever designed. Available with a 4½′ or 15″ handle.			
S	3½″	10½″	25 lbs.
S-15 As above, but with a 15″ handle.			

1 Solid Socket
The blade forging processes shown below are followed by hardening and tempering. ↓

T-section

socket rolled and sheared

socket formed

blade rolled and sheared

socket cranked and blade dished

Spear & Jackson, England

Shovels and spades

When buying a shovel or spade, try to avoid anything that is sold in a regular nursery or hardware store. Although American tool companies do make some fairly strong and reliable tools, they are rarely sold through consumer outlets. Go to landscape supply companies that sell sand, compost, and soil conditioners to gardeners. They will generally carry a manufacturer's higher quality tools. These cost more but will last longer.

When buying a shovel, look at the head and determine whether it is a (1) **solid shank or socket,** *(2)* **solid strapped** *or (3)* **open socket tool.** *Except for snow shovels and grain shovels, avoid tools that have open socket or hollow back construction. They are lighter but they will not hold up under regular use. To determine whether a tool is open socket, look at the back of the head. If the metal on the shovel looks as though it has been bent around to form a socket for the handle and the handle protrudes or is visible at the base of the crank, it is open socket construction.*

Solid socket *or* **solid strapped** *tools are forged from a solid bar of steel, usually high carbon for hardness and are tempered to give them proper resilience and ductility. The socket gives a stronger purchase to the handle and can stand up to harder use in the field.*

There are virtually only four shovel companies left in the United States: Ames, Tru-Temper, Union Fork and Hoe, and John Houchins & Sons. To find your nearest dealer that will carry a solid socket or strapped tool, write to the addresses below and inquire after the brand names listed with the company. These are the brands that are sold to contractors and industry, and these are the tools that will give you the longest run for your money. They are slightly heavier, but the extra weight is worth it.

Of the four companies, I'd probably rank the smallest, John Houchins & Sons, as the best and certainly the most interesting. Overseas in England and Germany, the spades and shovels are vastly superior to American, but they are largely unavailable in this country. —Paul Hawken

2 Solid Neck Strapped ↓

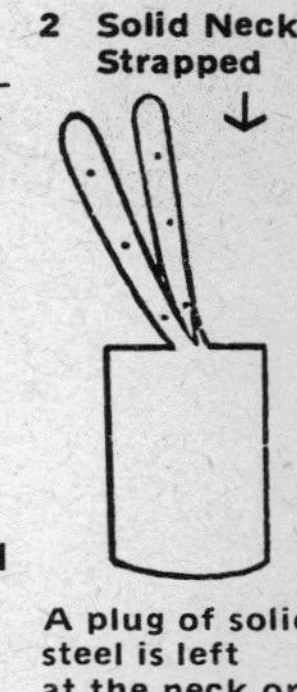

A plug of solid steel is left at the neck or root, hence the name solid neck.

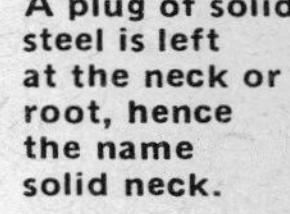

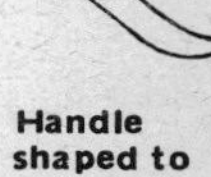

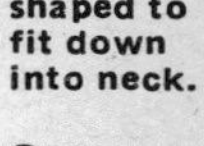

Handle shaped to fit down into neck.

3 Open Socket ↓

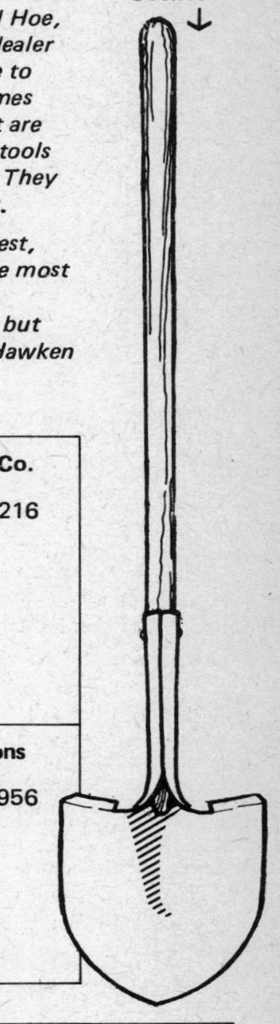

MANUFACTURERS AND THEIR BRANDS

Ames Box 1774 Parkersburg, WV 26101 *Brands to buy:* Husky Bronco, Pony *Brands to avoid:* American Made, Dig-Ezy, Peerless Ram	**Union Fork & Hoe Co.** 500 Dublin Avenue Columbus, Ohio 43216 *Brand to buy:* Atlas Deluxe *Brands to avoid:* Green Thumb, "Made in America"
Tru-Temper Corporation Hardware Division 1623 Euclid Avenue Cleveland, OH 44115 *Brands to buy:* Fox, Bantam *Brands to avoid:* Tru-Temper "Finest Quality," Little Giant	**John Houchins & Sons** 801 North Main Schulenberg, TX 78956 *Brands to buy:* Hi Quality, Hi Temper *Brand to avoid:* All American

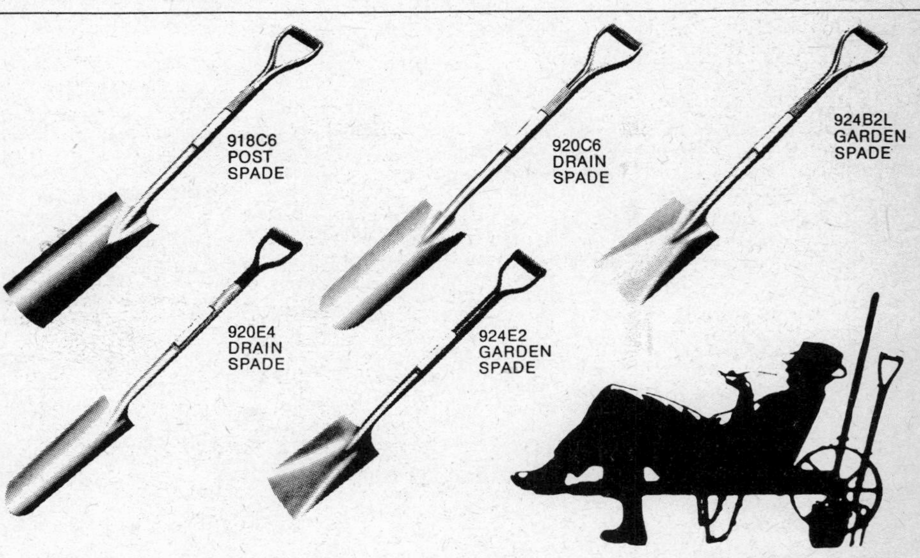

—John Houchins & Sons

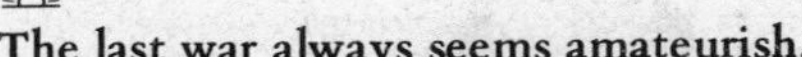

The last war always seems amateurish.

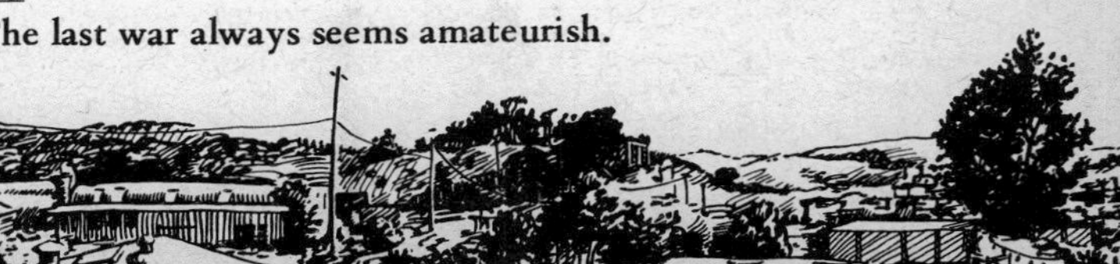

Scythes

by David Tresemer
(By Hand and Foot, Ltd.)
PHOTOGRAPHS BY
JOSEPH DeCARLO

There are several tasks which a scythe can perform for a homeowner, a gardener, and a farmer:

1. **Mowing hay**: in small fields at the average rate of 1 acre per person per day (up to four for a skilled mower) to produce hay for animals and for mulching. Even for mowing lawns, the traditional method of scything is economically competitive with a gas-powered mower for areas up to 4000 sq. ft.

2. **Cutting weeds**: to keep them from going to seed and to destroy nesting sites of insect pests. This approach is called "clean culture" and begins to show dramatically positive effects in the next season. A scythe can cut around trees in corners where machines cannot go.

3. **Harvesting small grains**: for small patches of homegrown wheat, barley, oats . . . One quarter of an acre provides a year's bread (and waffles) for a family of four; a reaper can harvest nearly an acre in a day.

In each case, for a certain range of areas the scythe is as good economically as any gasoline-powered alternative, and is healthier.

We have tested many scythe systems in the last three years, and are offering the very best. European farmers impressed upon us that it is the very best tool one should have to labor in the fields, a tool that will be passed on to the next generation.

There are several parts of the scythe system:

Blade: Unlike most hardware store scythe blades which are stamped and ground, this Austrian blade is made by hand in 26 separate steps of hammering and tempering. No machine is capable of the artistry and judgment required to produce a blade so light; it is soft enough to bend instead of break if a stone is accidentally hit, hard enough to keep a razor-sharp edge. The 26" (65 cm) length is the best for the tasks demanded of the scythe.

$26 plus mailing

Blade cover: to protect the blade — and people — from nicks in transit. Made from heavy canvas hemmed with safety stitch.

$5.60 plus mailing

Metal snath: This light tubular steel (not aluminum!) snath sets the scythe blade at exactly the right angle in relationship to the ground. Handle adjusts to accommodate everyone. This is what we recommend for beginners and occasional users. Requires little care or adjustment.

$19 plus mailing

Wooden snath: Straight snath of air-dried ash made in Vermont; unique offset handle is adjustable within a mortised channel so a person of any size can use comfortably. Like a wooden boat, a wooden snath requires extra care: if it gets too wet, it can warp slightly and need adjustment. The advantage is the ability to tinker with it to perfect a tool uniquely fitted to you; but without some experience these adjustments are hard to make. We do not recommend this for the beginner. The serious mower will find it light, sturdy, and graceful.

$24 plus mailing

SHARPENING

These blades are made of a somewhat softer steel than stainless to permit a much keener edge. However, they dull more quickly than stainless and must be resharpened in a two-stage process: first, peening with small hammer and anvil; second, fine honing with a whetstone. Complete instructions are given in the manual, "Mowing Hay, Cutting Weeds, and Harvesting Grain with the Scythe."

Hammer and anvil: Every other day under constant use, the blade is lightly hammered on a small anvil to draw out the metal into a thin edge and to harden it.

Hammer **$9.10** plus mailing
Anvil **$8.80** plus mailing

Whetstone: For final honing and retouching in the field. You mow once around the field and pause for a minute to sharpen the blade.

$5.20 plus mailing

Whetstone holder: The holder is partly filled with water to rinse the metal grits from the pores of the stone after sharpening. Made of hard yellow plastic, this stone holder is less cumbersome than the traditional wooden holder and can be more easily seen in the field. Belt clip for carrying with stone.

$5.30 plus mailing

ACCESSORIES

Grain cradle: Four wooden tines follow the curve of the scythe blade and catch the stalks of grain as they are cut. Traditionally a separate tool, modern methods permit us to manufacture a detachable grain cradle for our scythe. Put it on for assistance in harvesting wheat, barley, oats, and other small grains.

$24 plus mailing

Wooden hay fork: Superior to a metal tine fork for cleaning the field of hay and straw. Made from a single ash pole, this fork is expensive but will last for many years.

$22 plus mailing

More than any written accounts, the grass will teach you how to use the scythe. Further instruction is available at several summer workshops sponsored by By Hand & Foot, Ltd.: schedule is included with brochure. ■

all from:
By Hand & Foot, Ltd.
P.O. Box 611
Brattleboro, VT 05301

(These folks also devised a woodsplitting system, p. 210.)

Tools for Homesteaders, Gardeners, and Small-Scale Farmers

If you live in the country and raise food, get your hands on this catalog. No rural town or county library should be without it. Rodale has taken John Boyd's work for Intermediate Technology Publications on appropriate agricultural tools for the third world, and added a very comprehensive listing for American-made tools, old and new. Access to dealers, foreign and domestic, is included. Chapters on hand tools, tractors, tillers, cultivating implements, planting and harvesting equipment, threshers, and more, all illustrated. A healthy respect for the farmer as tinkerer and recycler of old machinery is shown throughout.

Before you go out and reinvent the wheel, flip through these pages; somebody may have beat you to it.
—Richard Nilsen

Tools for Homesteaders, Gardeners, and Small-Scale Farmers
(A Catalog of Hard-to-Find Implements and Equipment)
Diana S. Branch, Editor
1978; 528 pp.

$12.95 postpaid from
Rodale Books
33 East Minor
Emmaus, PA 18049
or Whole Earth Household Store

•

Throughout the compilation of this book, we have selected the tool over the machine . . . Tools humanize; machines dehumanize. Tools make unique products — each a little different from the other, each speaking eloquently of the tool's user. A machine deals in multiplied sameness no matter who or what operates it. The best machine operators are other machines . . .

•

A large percentage of our inventors came from rural communities, and virtually all of the industries which grew up in the United States in the 1800s started on a very small scale, often as one-man operations. Cyrus McCormick, Oliver Evans, Eli Whitney, even Henry Ford — each grew up on a farm. The inventors of tools we still need will most likely come from the ranks of today's small farmers — and their children.

Eric Brunet and his U-Bar Digger. ↑

↑
Cage Culture

There are many advantages to raising fish in cages. Cage confinement means fish can be grown in streams and rapidly moving water without any fear of losing them to the natural environment. Feed waste is greatly reduced since the feeding is concentrated in a very small area. Because the movement of the fish is restricted, they do not need much feed to survive. They just eat and grow! Monitoring fish growth and health is greatly simplified, and the threat of predators is reduced. For a 100-percent harvest, the cages are simply lifted from the water — no fishing, draining, or seining (harvesting with a drag net) is necessary.

Double-Q Fish Cages, Inqua Corp., P.O. Box 1325, Homestead, FL 33036.

Mini Nibex Planter

The Mini Nibex hand planter is for growers with up to 10 acres and will sow up to 2 acres in a day. The Nibex cup system includes 25 types of cups for different seeds — both natural and pelleted. This wide range makes it possible to be able to choose the most suitable cup for the desired drilling method. The seeding rate can be varied from 4 to almost 2,000 seeds per running yard — either thin-line or band-drilled in widths of 2, 2.5 or 4 inches (50, 65, or 105 millimeters). The cup system is largely unaffected by variations in seed size. To reduce the amount of seed required when sowing small and expensive seeds, a regulator-economizer insert is available for use in the seed-housing unit.

Nibe-Verken AB, S-285 00 Markaryd, Sweden.

Planet Jr. Seeder and Wheel Hoe

I am a market gardener in Southern Vermont, going on my tenth season. The **Planet Jr. Seeder** is the best seeder I have run across in its price range. It has 40 different settings for rate of seeding, 7 settings for depth. With careful experimentation, you can get it to sow a stand of carrots that will need no thinning. You can plant as fast as you can walk, though it does require a well-prepared, trash-free seedbed. It currently costs $205 plus shipping. I got mine from Johnny's Seeds, Box 22, Albion, Maine 04910 (great seeds, great people to deal with).

The ultimate in seeders is the Stanhey, made in England. It is super accurate and requires the use of sized seeds. You have to either be a large grower or a co-op to afford it ($1300). But I have a friend who plants 40 acres with his **Planet Jr.**

Next suggestion: the **Planet Jr. Wheel Hoe**. You can sometimes find these in junk sales and auctions; snap them up if you do. They allow you to cultivate both sides of a row simultaneously, by off-setting the wheel, or to cultivate completely between two rows. For the small, low tech grower, this is where it's at for cultivation. You run this thing thru your rows when the weeds are just germinating (on a hot sunny day), and you have saved yourself hours of hoeing, or worse, hand weeding. The next step up is a Lilleston, but you have to be doing a fairly large acreage for it to be worth it to you. The **Planet Jr. Wheel Hoe** is also available from Johnny's, for about $75 plus shipping.

—Joseph Klein
West Brattleboro, Vermont

Note: Planet Junior tools are distributed by: Planet Junior Division, Piper Industries, Box 1188, Freeport Center, VT 84106. —SB

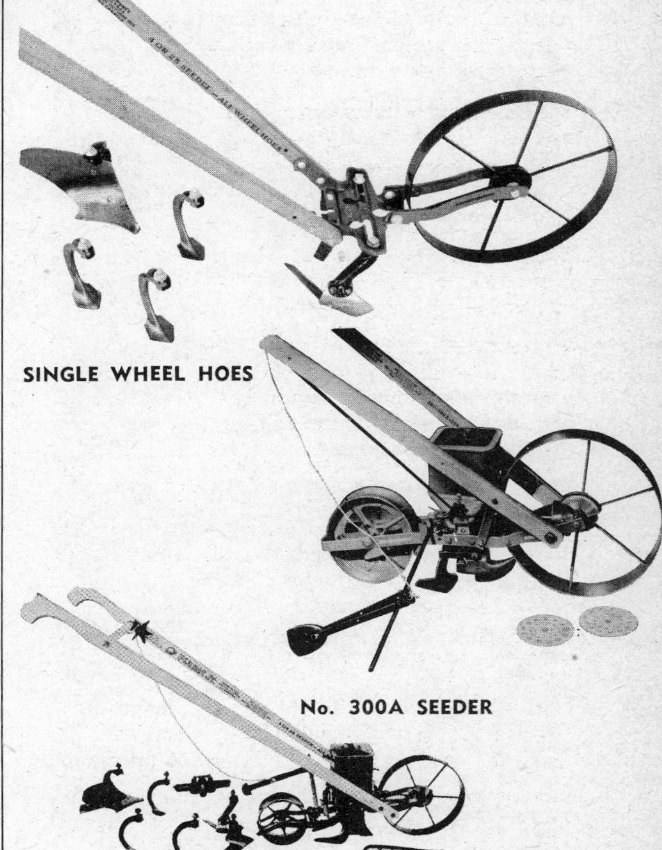

SINGLE WHEEL HOES

No. 300A SEEDER

No. 4 SEEDER & WHEEL HOE

Yorkshire bill hook

Looking like something you'd use to remove the head of a Saxon Churl, this formidable weapon really does the deed in brush and heavy undergrowth. Its weight and nasty shape make it remarkably effective, obsolescing the "Woodman's Pal." It's built stronger than you are. I'd add a wrist strap to the thing, especially if it was in use nearby by someone else. —J. Baldwin

Yorkshire Bill Hook
$35.50 postpaid from:
Smith & Hawken Tool Co.
68 Homer Street
Palo Alto, CA 94301

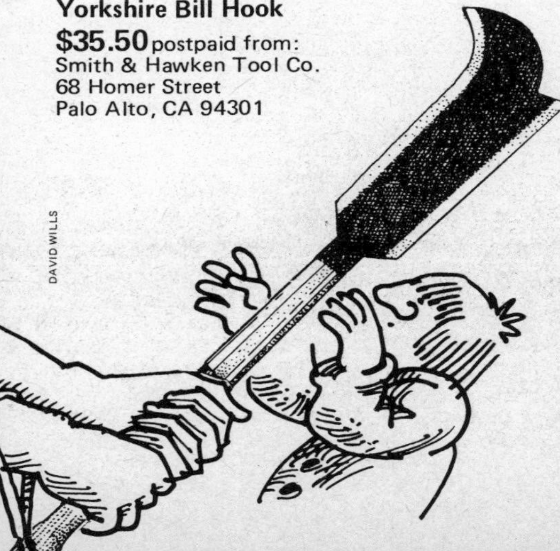

Garden Way cart

As gardens get bigger so does the demand for a bigger wheelbarrow. The Garden Way Cart, Model 26, has an international reputation, but for anyone who hasn't heard of it, the cart is lightweight and balanced so that a bulky, heavy load can be carried with ease. It's the same principle as a horse-drawn sulky in a trotting race, which enables the horse to run with the least possible drag. Comes with a try-it-you'll-like-it-or-your-money-back guarantee.
—Rosemary Menninger

Garden Way Cart
(Model 26)
$149.50 + shipping
(Also available in other models and kit form.

Write for price list. from:
Garden Way
Charlotte, VT 05445

THE RISING SUN
NEIGHBORHOOD NEWSLETTER

When I was a kid I kept three scrap books, my world hunger scrapbook, my Adolph Eichmann's trial scrapbook and my What is Amanda Madison up to scrapbook. I was that kind of kid, trying for existential despair at ten. Fortunately Amanda gave me something to be positively curious about — I thought if I wrote down what she did at different specific times I would begin to figure out what she was up to in general and have a better idea what to be when I grew up. Here's an entry from when Amanda was a counselor and song leader and general oddness maker at church camp for junior highs: *continued on next spread*

THIS CATALOG IS METAPHORICALLY ABOUT TOOLS, but it is also about tools. A tool consists of a use on one end and a grasp on the other. Tools, uses, and grasps — and ultimately users — all co-evolve with each other. A tool, or a technology, that doesn't push its user around qualifies as "soft." The difference between Hard and Soft Technology is the difference between a command and an understanding.
—SB

Swiss Army Officers' Knife

The most useful tool any of us have every owned. Mine is employed at least 6 times a day, and I'm a wimpy office worker. It's an "Explorer"; every one of its 11 blades gets used at least once a month. Most minor repair jobs — on a house, a 30 foot boat, a typewriter, or my shoes — are well within its scope. When Amory Lovins got married in the woods with 50 revelers, he and his bride Hunter gave each other beautiful hunting knives that could gut a bear but could not open their wedding wine — my Swiss Army knife did that. My favorite conceptual blade is the magnifying glass, which allows microsurgery when using the tweezers on an elusive splinter.

Get only Victorinox — they're available in most good hardware stores. All other similarly red multi-bladed knives, including Wenger (L.L. Bean and R.E.I. should know better than to a carry Wengers), are shoddy imitations. The Victorinox knives come with a lifetime warranty and act like it.

If you wear a belt, I strongly recommend getting a sheath (sometimes called pouch) for your knife — note that the supplier we're giving here because of their fair range and good prices, EMS, has three different sized sheaths. With a sheath you don't lose the knife, and it's one quick move to get the tool in your hand. If ever I lose my "Explorer," I am gonna get the "Champion" — 15 blades. —SB

Victorinox Swiss Army Officers' Knives
$9.95 — $34.95
postpaid

Swiss Army Officers' Knife Sheaths
$5.50 postpaid

both from:
Eastern Mountain Sports, Inc.
Vose Farm Road
Peterborough, NH 03458

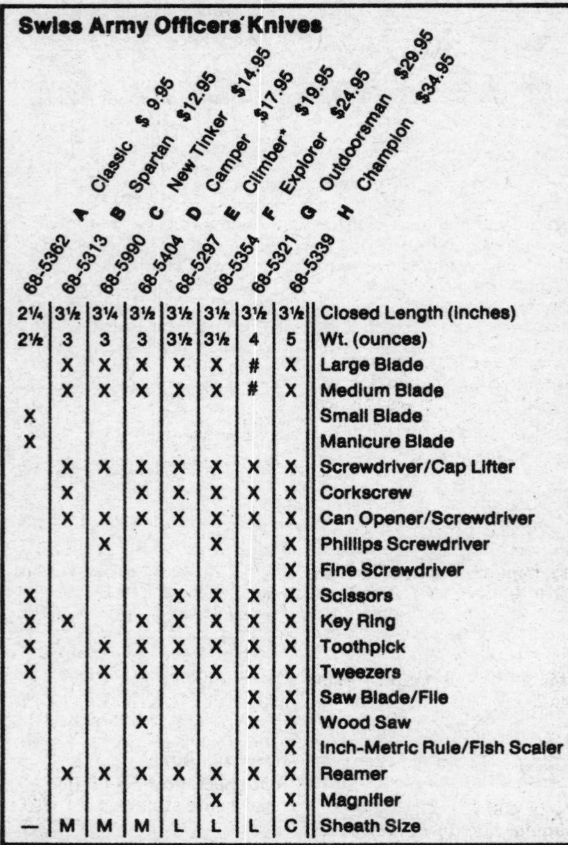

Swiss Army Officers' Knives

A Classic $9.95 68-5362	B Spartan $12.95 68-5313	C New Tinker $14.95 68-5990	D Camper $17.95 68-5404	E Climber* $19.95 68-5297	F Explorer $24.95 68-5354	G Outdoorsman $29.95 68-5321	H Champion $34.95 68-5339	
2¼	3½	3¼	3½	3½	3½	3½	3½	Closed Length (inches)
2½	3	3	3	3½	3½	4	5	Wt. (ounces)
	X	X	X	X	X	#	X	Large Blade
	X	X	X	X	X	#	X	Medium Blade
X								Small Blade
X								Manicure Blade
	X	X	X	X	X	X	X	Screwdriver/Cap Lifter
	X		X	X	X	X	X	Corkscrew
	X	X	X	X	X	X	X	Can Opener/Screwdriver
		X			X		X	Phillips Screwdriver
							X	Fine Screwdriver
X				X	X	X	X	Scissors
X	X		X	X	X	X	X	Key Ring
X		X	X	X	X	X	X	Toothpick
X		X	X	X	X	X	X	Tweezers
						X	X	Saw Blade/File
			X			X	X	Wood Saw
							X	Inch-Metric Rule/Fish Scaler
	X	X	X	X	X	X	X	Reamer
					X		X	Magnifier
—	M	M	M	L	L	L	C	Sheath Size

* Formerly the Backpacker
# Two special blades: serrated, which cuts anything; and a hooked pruning blade.

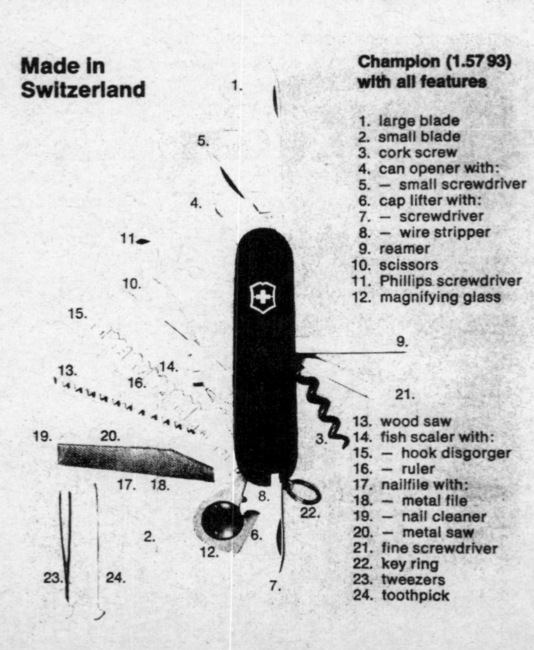

A roll each of Arno Tape and Stagestik holding themselves up on a window. ↑

Duct tape

Miraculous all-purpose fix-it material. It's two inches wide, waterproof, leakproof, grey usually, very sticky but easily removed, strong but you can tear off a hunk with your fingers. It began its saga of usefulness as a joint sealer for air conditioning ducts. It's known widely as "duck tape," as "silver tape," and as "gaffer's tape" — this last because sound gaffers in show biz use it constantly — to attach microphones to anything, to temporarily cover lines on the floor, to hold up scenery. No cruising sailor would risk leaving port without the stuff because most boat emergencies respond quickest to duct tape treatment. You find it at most good hardware stores. If you need to get it by mail, U.S. General (p. 145) is a good source.
—SB

Duct Tape
#521-908 Cloth,
2" x 180 ft.

$7 (approx.)
postpaid from:
U.S. General
Supply Corporation
(p. 145)
or check your local
hardware store.

WD 40

The universal lubricant. If something is stuck, or squeaking, or rusting, you point this spray can at it, go pshhht, and the problem disappears. It even drives water out of electrical circuits. (There I was, dependent at sea on a two-cylinder gas engine perpetually re-drenched with sea water and laboring hideously on one cylinder. I pointed the WD-40 can in the general direction of the spark plugs, went pshhht, and the engine purred into robust life and threatened me with that particular problem never again.) It's especially good at freeing stuck bolts and such. No one knows what the secret ingredient is, but WD-40 can be used nearly anywhere without fear of it attacking rubber, paint, fabric, etc.

For around the house, office, or car a can is fine. If you're using a lot of the stuff it's decidedly worth it to buy in gallon bulk. Brookstone (p. 143) has a nice spray pump (#F-7382, about $19 postpaid). Most places that sell tools sell WD-40 for about $1.50 per can. —SB

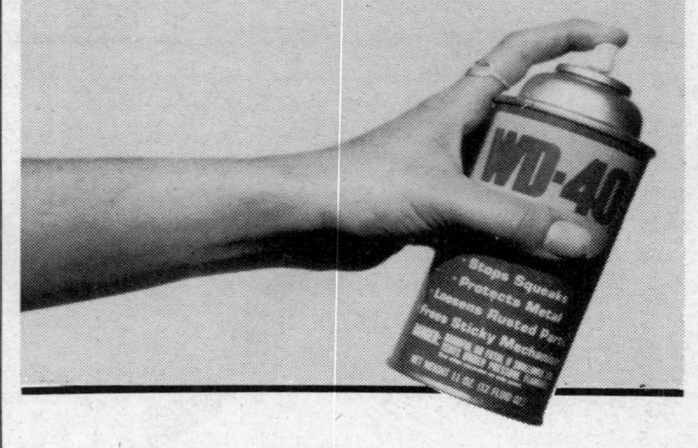

Before ↓ After ↓

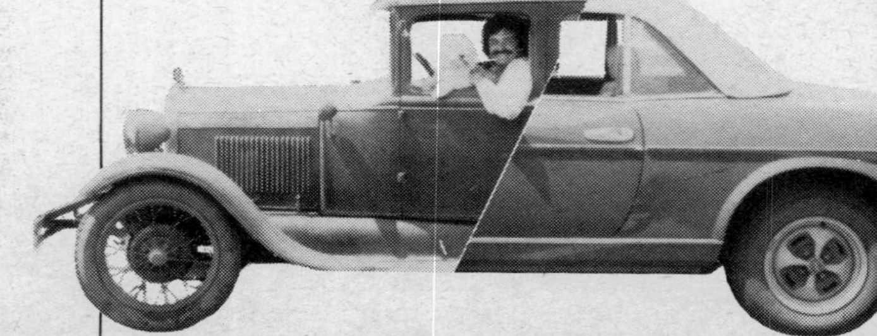

How to borrow tools and keep friendship

If people can trust you with their tools, there isn't a hell of a lot more they need to know about you. How trust is made:

- **When you borrow the tool, have the owner check you out on it, even if you know it cold. This encourages the owner and insures you.**
- **Agree on a time it will be returned by. Return it by then.**
- **Return it either to the owner's hand or to the exact place you picked it up from.**
- **Use it carefully. If you break it, replace it immediately, preferably with a better one.**
- **When you're finished, service it. Clean it, sharpen it, oil it, fuel it, fix it. If you return someone's tools improved, they'll let you have anything they've got.**
- **If you make anyone loan you something out of guilt, you'll be sorry.** —SB

Vise-Grip

A locking plier wrench which grips and holds, with the size of the grip adjustable. Hold things hard without muscle, hold things together, hold things with just the right pressure. Many's the busted faucet you see with a vise-grip biting it as temporary handle. Get Vise-Grip brand — the others aren't as good. Available everywhere for about $5. —SB

Vise-Grip Straight Jaws
#10R-P3, 10" long
#7R-P3, 7" long

$5.50 (approx.)
postpaid from:
Silvo Hardware Co.
(p. 144)
or check your local hardware store

Shoe Rasp

These 4 way rasps are just the ticket for solving most household needs for taking off a bit of wood here and there. Each rasp has a rough "shark teeth" section and a medium rough file section flat and half-round. I wear out one a year. —J. Baldwin

Nicholson Shoe Rasp
#18924-N2 8"
#18962-N2 10"

$4.50 (approx.)
postpaid from:
Silvo Hardware Company
(p. 144)
or check your local hardware store

Nail puller

With lumber prices what they are and wood eminently re-usable, this old time tool is enjoying a well-deserved comeback. To use it, apply the open jaws to both sides of the nailhead and slam the built-in slide handle. The jaws will burrow into the wood (leaving a repairable scar), grabbing the head or even a broken-off shank. A fast levering motion of the whole tool extracts the nail neatly, usually in one try. It can be used in any position. This tool is best used with heavy gloves, as the slamming motion tends to bruise your hand, and the shape of it invites your unsuspecting palm to the blood blister of a lifetime. —J. Baldwin

Greenlee Nail Puller
#515-G12

$18 (approx.)
postpaid from:
Silvo Hardware Co.
(see p. 144)
or check your local hardware store.

Christy Knives

Did you know that the good old Christy Knife is still available? They've been Good Stuff for 85 years now! —J. Baldwin

Genuine Christy Knife
$5.50 postpaid from:
The Christy Company
905E Dickinson Street
Fremont, OH 43420
or check your local dealer

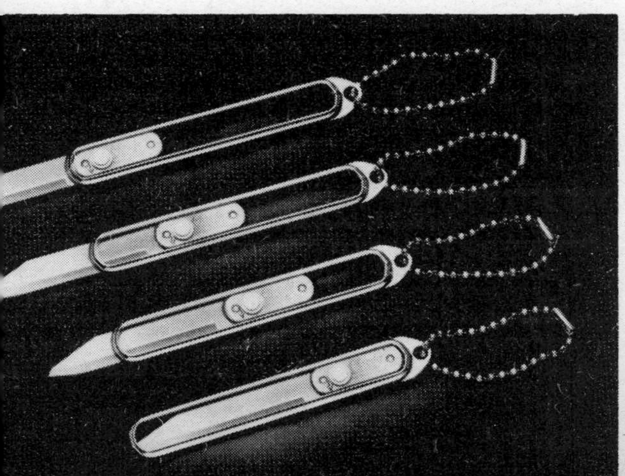

Osmundson's Wizard Bar

An enlightened modification of a basic tool. Not just a doodad — this thing really works. Gets into corners a regular wrecking bar is useless in. I used a 3/4" x 30" model to pull 50d nails after getting them started with a cat's paw. Didn't have to use any blocks. Cost $7 instead of the $5 a regular bar the same size cost. I don't know how easy the Osmundson's Bar is to get nation wide. If you have trouble finding or ordering one at a local hardware store, write the manufacturer or check to see if you can order one from a True-Value hardware store (the local T.V. had the one I got in stock). —David Batts

Osmundson's Wizard Bar

Information and local dealer location
$.50 from:
Osmundson's Forge Company, Inc.
Webster City, IA 50595

Workmate

At first I thought this portable workbench/giant vise from Black & Decker was a homeowner's gadget. But now that I have one I find I use it all the time as a portable workstation next to me while I work under the car hood, fix a damaged shutter, hand a door, etc. and etc. I'm actually wearing the thing out! —J. Baldwin

Black & Decker Bench-top Workmate
#101-79020W3449
$38 (approx.)

Black & Decker Dual Height Workmate
#8101-79001
$80 (approx.)

both from:
U.S. General Supply Corporation
(see p. 145)
or check your local hardware store.

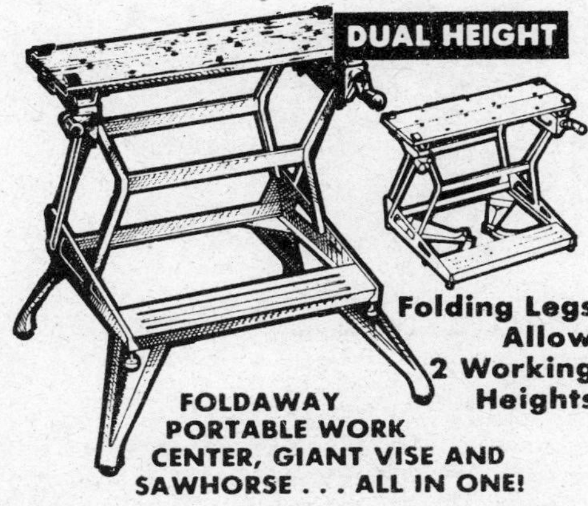

DUAL HEIGHT
Folding Legs Allow 2 Working Heights
FOLDAWAY PORTABLE WORK CENTER, GIANT VISE AND SAWHORSE . . . ALL IN ONE!

Features a vise-grip top, holds work of almost any shape up to 12"W, up to 21" diag. Grooved jaws let you tackle boards, pipes, machinery, odd-shaped pieces. Solid plywood table top (19¾ x 29" open) has holes designed to accept swivel grip pegs that grasp any object and hold it rigidly. Feet adjust to uneven floors. Folding legs allow two working heights 31⅞ and 23¾". Extra strong steel frame.

B101-79001W6880 .... ~~$79.99~~

THE RISING SUN
NEIGHBORHOOD NEWSLETTER

July 28, 1964

Aside from the songs Amanda makes up, she explains them a lot. Take Camptown Ladies which goes, "Camptown ladies sing this song, doo dah, doo dah, Camptown races five miles long, o doo dah day. Gwana run all night, gwana run all day, bet my money on a bob tail nag, somebody bet on the bay." Amanda played the tune over and over on the piano and told us that the Camptown Ladies were radical abolitionists and all around right thinkers and wierdos and they thought their husbands were not nice people for making money off of slavery and gambling. The ladies encouraged the men to go to the track all they wanted because then the ladies had free, unobserved time to help slaves escape and collect anti-slavery petitions to send to congress and whenever their husbands would ask what they did all day they would say, "O honey, I swept the rug and burped the babes and gossiped with the girls," or to put it another way, (and she'd be at the right point in her piano playing) "Doodah, doodah," and whenever their husbands would wonder how so many slaves were being able to escape, they'd just say they were simple homebodies and didn't understand such matters, "O doo dah day," and then she asked us all what we'd say if we were trying to change things and somebody asked us what we were doing, and we all sang "Doo dah, doo dah" and if somebody asked us why things aren't as nice and quiet as they used to be, we don't show them our noisemaker, we just say, "O doo dah day." *continued on next spread*

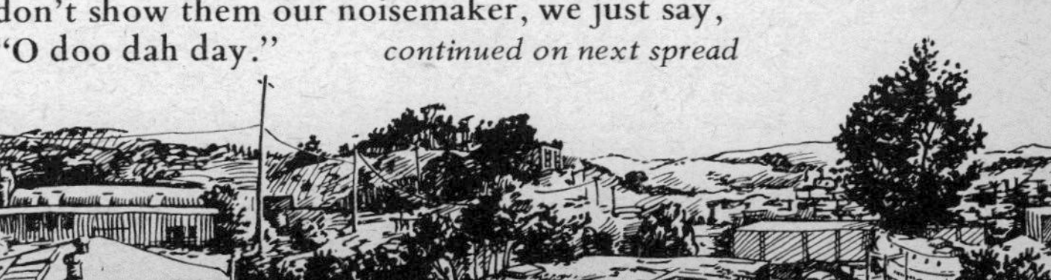

by J. Baldwin

For that one-shot job requiring expensive and/or uncommon tools, renting is often the way to go. A rented tool will let you do a job yourself instead of hiring a contractor or other worker whose only real attribute is ownership of a tool you don't have. Pouring concrete is a good example: assuming that there will be one person present who knows about concrete, a crew of friends with rented concrete tools can pour that garage floor at a fraction of the cost of a contractor. Engines can be overhauled, buildings spray-painted, pipe laid, floors refinished . . . a good rental store stocks a surprising array of equipment and associated supplies. These are often biased towards local needs; mud country rentals will include all manner of jacks and come-alongs for instance. Areas where there is a lot of gardening will have manure-carrying trailers. You might be surprised what they have.

You should shop around. I have often found that competing rent-its have very different prices and policies. One may have a better selection than another, or maybe their brand of tool is better or in better condition. Always check a tool for condition, not only to save yourself a drive back to get another if the one you rent fails on the job, but to make sure that the renter won't try and stick you for your damage deposit. Make sure damage is noted on the sales slip. Certain machines like ditch-diggers and floor-sanders should be inspected with extra care. I personally run them before acceptance if there is any question. To "get a good one," it is a good idea to shop early in the morning. Some stores will allow you to take the machine the night before with no extra charge. Don't be afraid to ask. Sometimes one clerk will be more enlightened than another, and it will pay you to bufter up such a person for future use. Get their name. Ask them to save you the good cement mixer for next Sunday. Sometimes you can even talk them into adding a tool you need to their stock. A friendly clerk can also give you invaluable information on using the tool. You should be sure that the directions are complete and that you understand them, but the directions for a floor sander rarely include the advice necessary to prevent the fatal WHAP! flup-flup-flup of the sandpaper breaking that costs you a buck each time it happens. (Pound in all the nail heads first, or they catch the paper.) In the case of a sander, the paper costs can far exceed the rental fee, so watch out when figuring the savings of do-it-yourself.

If you'll be needing the tool often, it will probably pay to buy it. This would be true for car tuning equipment. For the cost of one professional tune-up you can purchase a set of reasonably good tuning instruments and the instruction book. Have a friend supervise the first time you use 'em and from then on you're saving money. Even in this example, though, it may pay to rent the equipment first time around. That way you can try out different brand names without actually buying, and you can also sample the idea of whether you really want to be your own mechanic. Renting also allows you to use a tool of better quality than you could otherwise afford.

If renting is still more costly than you'd like, consider sharing the rental with a neighbor; schedule your jobs together. (But bear in mind that your name on the contract makes you liable for damage if your neighbor blows it.) Renting together can also save money by reducing the time a tool sleeps while nonetheless being charged for. For instance, you sand your kitchen counter and while the first coat of varnish dries, your friends sand their boat deck. By the time you are ready for the second coat, the sander is back to you again. Like that. It is well to overestimate the time jobs take, especially if you are not adept. Your rental store can usually give you a good estimate of time, assuming they are honest. They've had many customers like yourself. They are in business to serve you and can't take the chance of getting a bad reputation. Usually. With a bit of good sense you should be able to do well, save yourself some money, and be just a bit more independent. ■

Milwaukee Power Tools

If you're a serious user of drills, saws and grinders or any of a host of other electric hand tools, Milwaukee is a good way to go. Everything they make is heavy duty, and some of their offerings have achieved the enviable ultimate accolade: their names have become THE name for the tool. Hole Hawg and Sawzall are two that come to mind. Many of their tools have a nifty cord that snaps out of the handle so you can put the drill to bed without having to roll the cord around it into the inevitable snake tangle. Much of their line is double-insulated making it safer to use under poor conditions. There are other worthy domestic brands but Milwaukee is my favorite. Expensive and worth every penny. —J. Baldwin

Milwaukee Electric Tools
Manufactured by:
Milwaukee Electric Tool Corporation
Brookfield, WI 53005

Not available by mail order. Check your local electric tools supplier or Silvo & U.S. General, pp. 144 - 145.

Heavy-duty Hole Hawgs

Heavy-Duty Saw

Cutawl

Virtually every display and exhibit shop has one of these precision woodpeckers and I have used mine for all manner of wonderful and occasionally bizarre purposes. The thing can be guided so accurately that it is actually reasonable to cut lacework out of Masonite or thin metal. They come with a grand assortment of blades: the knife blades can be used to cut cloth patterns, tiny saws will deal with all cuttable metals, chisels cut cardboard (leaving a beveled edge!) for gaskets and display work, leather, plexiglas, formica, contour models, etc. It's sort of like a sabresaw in its uses, but much easier to control. The edge it leaves usually requires no finishing — it's that good. —J. Baldwin

Cutawl
(About $400)
Information, price list and nearest dealer location

free from:
The Cutawl Company
Route 6
Bethel, CT 06801

ORBITAL ACTION JIG SAW—VARIABLE SPEED, MODEL 1578
- THE TOP OF THE LINE!
- Speed Control—Solid-State Electronics maintain full power output even at low speeds required for very hard materials 1000-3000 strokes per minute
- Unique blade motion control and blade speed control provides the right combination for all your cutting requirements
- Top Handle Design puts your hand over the work for extra control under heavy loads
- Light—5.5 lbs. Compact—9⅝" long 115V AC

Bosch Power Tools

The ultimate in heavy duty electric hand tools. Many rental stores rent Bosch for good reason: they last. Some of their tools are the very best available anywhere, the orbital-action jigsaw being a famous example. Costing up to three times more than a domestic industrial saw, it can do things, easily, that no other can. For instance, I once cut an 8 inch round hole in the side of a huge ¼" thick steel tank in a location that made a cutting torch too dangerous. It only took about 15 minutes! My Bosch drills have been in hard use for ten years without trouble. Don't be fooled by horsepower or ampere ratings of Bosch versus other brands. Bosch has a good electrical design that uses less juice but puts out more power — their smallest ¼" drill will wind your arm off at the root if you aren't careful! All of my own hand electric tools are Bosch. —J. Baldwin

Bosch Power Tools
Manufactured by:
Robert Bosch Corporation
Broadview, IL 60153

Not available by mail order. Check your local electric tools supplier.

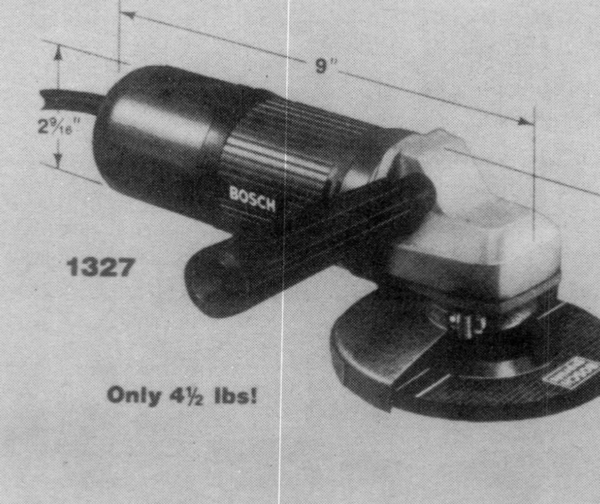

4-1/2" "MINIMAX" GRINDER, MODEL 1327
- 11,000 RPM = fast stock removal.
- Perfect maintenance tool for grinding, cutting, brushing, sanding, etc.
- Uses standard 4½" dia. wheel with ⅞" arbor hole.
- Side handle can be installed on either side.
- Ball and needle bearings throughout.
- Thumb controlled switch with "lock-on" feature.
- Only 4½ lbs.! 9" long! Get into places that no full-size grinder can handle.
- 115V—AC/DC, UL listed.

Portalign

Control. Until this tool, the only things I had found to give precise control to using a hand drill were those small drill-press type mounts. There isn't much that those devices can do that this can't do just as easily. I leave mine permanently attached to my drill. In nearly a year, I haven't had any job for my drill that this didn't make easier and more accurate. —August Mohr

Portalign Precision Drill Guide
No. 199-110
$20 (approx.)
from:
U.S. General Supply Corporation
(p. 145)
or check your local hardware store.

ANGLE DRILLING

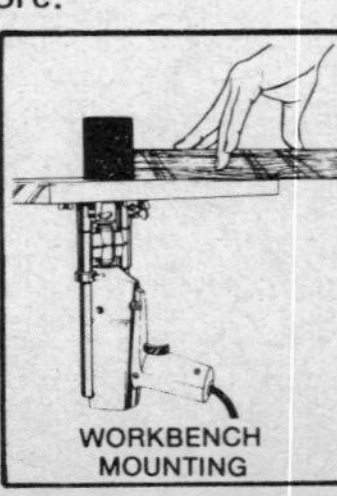
WORKBENCH MOUNTING

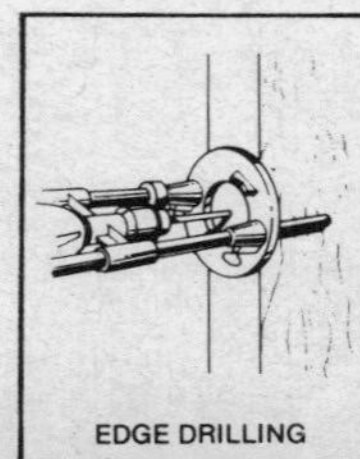
EDGE DRILLING

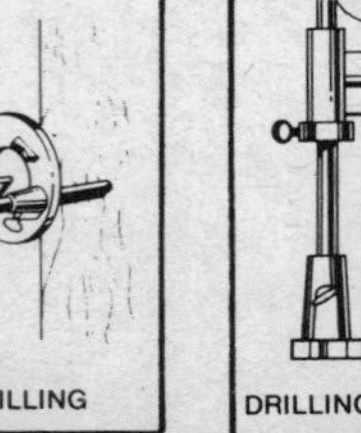
DRILLING

MOST OF THE TOOL REVIEWS in Soft Technology and Land Use are by J. Baldwin and Richard Nilsen.

Baldwin is a professional project and product developer, a teacher, and a wide-travelling bricoleur. He has worked with most of the pioneer soft technology groups — Farallones, Integrated Living Systems, Zomeworks, and currently the New Alchemists. He's worked for Moss Tents and Buckminster Fuller. He's taught design at Southern Illinois University, San Francisco State College, and University of California, Davis. He's been reviewing for **Whole Earth** *since 1968.*

Richard Nilsen is a serious farmer (Colorado, summers) and a professional building carpenter (California, winters). He's reviewed for **Whole Earth** *since 1973.*

Both are appalled at how hard it is for the layman to get decent tools. Stores can get them easily from wholesalers but won't carry them. Lots of the best stuff seems to be available from NOWHERE by mail order.

A scandal. And an opportunity for intelligent business. Meanwhile, see "Breaking the Wholesale Barrier" on p. 148. —SB

Fas Set sawhorses

These versatile 12 gauge steel sawhorses cost less than the labor and materials you'd need to make your own from wood. Two styles — the Step-Bench, designed for indoor scaffolding, and the Industrial Sawhorse, which has the great feature of self-stabilizing on uneven ground. Just lean on it, and all four legs are on the ground. Both models come apart for compact storage or transport. Fas Set also makes the Easy Buck, a pair of metal jaws that clamp onto the Industrial Sawhorse and turn it into a buck sawhorse for sawing logs. —Richard Nilsen
[Suggested by J.D. Smith]

Fas Set Sawhorses
Prices range from about $11 to $17
Price list and information

$ .25 postpaid from:
Fas Set Manufacturing, Inc.
P.O. Box 798
Sebastopol, CA 95472
or, in Western states, check your local lumberyard or hardware store.

← Easy Buck, about $11

Industrial Sawhorse, about $16 (For a pair of legs to make one horse; wood not included.)

Step-Bench, about $17

Pro Level

This dial level has a wide range of uses ranging from setting the true angle of a solar collector to accurately measuring the angle of an existing roof so the addition will match perfectly. It's useful to half a degree, and has a table of rise-and-run on the back. Some models have a magnet so you can stick the level to a pipe or other metal you are bending to a desired angle. You can get one incorporated into a standard carpenter's level, and in several sizes. I've found that the large size is easiest to read and use. You'll have to make a box for yours; they're easily munched in a toolbox. —J. Baldwin

Pro Level
No. 509-200
$7.50 (approx.)
postpaid from:
U.S. General
Supply Corporation
(p. 145)
or check your local hardware store.

Squangle

There are a lot of giant protractors and angle sawing guides on the market, but the Squangle seems to be the most useful. I'm sure many of you carpenters already know it, but I'll bet many of you are unfamiliar with the clever device. It makes easy work of cutting roof rafter angles, especially the must-be-accurate "birdsmouth" cuts. When used with the companion Rafterule there's no faster or more accurate way to make the complex cuts that defeat so many amateur builders. They're sturdily made with etched numbers that won't wear off, and plated against rust. —J. Baldwin

Squangle
No. 202-45
$7.50 (approx.)
postpaid from:
U.S. General
Supply Corporation
(p. 145)
or check your local hardware store.

Xtenda-Leg

Tired of antzy tilting ladders? These legs really do the deed! You can even put a ladder sideways on a flight of stairs safely with 'em, and that 's saying a lot. I've been using them for a couple of years now, and can truly say "I wouldn't be without them." Sure does beat the hell out of balancing on wobbly half bricks . . . —J. Baldwin

Xtenda-Leg
Ladder Levelers
and Extenders
No. K243-600
$17 (approx.)

postpaid from:
U.S. General
Supply Corporation
(p. 145)
or check your local hardware store.

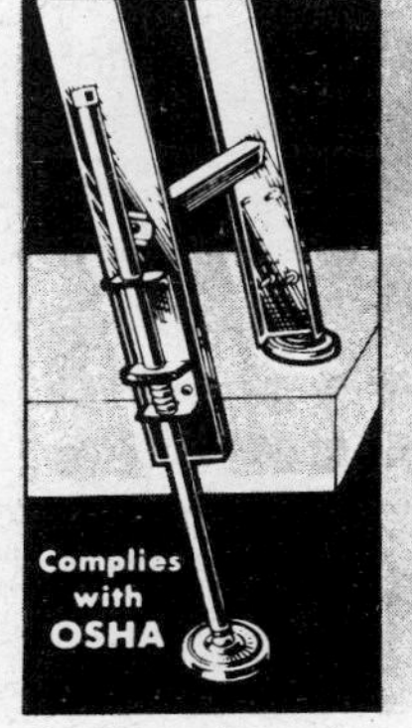

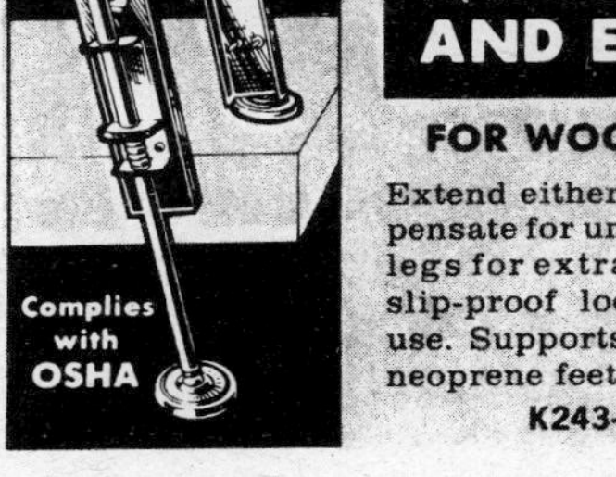

Blue Grass Tools

Blue Grass Tools have been made at one factory in Louisville, Kentucky since 1840. Their quality is hard to beat and their line of hand tools is very complete. In addition to hammers, saws and screwdrivers, they make tool boxes, cement finishing trowels, cotton and hay hooks, leather nail pouches, grinding wheels, adzes and soldering guns.

I have used a 16 oz. Blue Grass claw hammer with a hickory handle for 6 years. It's the best balanced hammer I have ever swung and I have yet to break the handle. The claw is so finely made that even though the hammer is really beat up, I can still pull nails with it that other hammers won't get. —Richard Nilsen

Correctly shaped and balanced head gives maximum driving power.

Crowned face prevents scarring of wood. Chamfered edge minimizes chipping. Claw bite pulls headless pins or 20D nails. Long curve of claws affords greatest leverage. Eyes of hammer are forged with double taper on all four sides so that heads when driven have a positive grip on the handle at the center of the eye. The taper of the handle matches the taper of the eye, ensuring a very tight fit on all surfaces of the eye when the end of the handle is wedged.

Straight grain full octagon white hickory handles are put through a special treatment before driving which prevents any shrinkage of the wood in the eye, thus preventing the handles from becoming loose. Spring neck handle absorbs shock. Swell end grip insures perfect hand hold.

Blue Grass Tools
Manufactured by:
Balknap, Inc.
Louisville, KY 40232
Not available by mail order, but at hardware stores and lumber yards in 28 states in the east and south (and parts of Kansas and New Mexico.) Check your local hardware store.

THE RISING SUN
NEIGHBORHOOD NEWSLETTER

continued from last spread

And then we sang the whole thing through again, and it sounded different and we did the other verses, that Amanda had printed up with her throwing in commentary. "Old muley cow come onto the track, doo dah, doo dah, the bob tail fly her over her back, o etc." was a distracting plot by the Camptown ladies to cover a slave escape. Promises tomorrow to tell us how "I've Been Working on the Railroad" is a song of women plotting for freedom as their men work for multinational corporations ("Who's in the kitchen with Dinah? We won't know until she blows her horn and ITT comes tumbling down!")

It was the straightest explanation I'd ever heard Amanda give of herself — of her non-explanation of herself. It is truly true that if you ask Amanda what's she doing she will always say "doo dah doo dah" one way or another and I'd really like to know, but I guess if she doesn't want me to it's her right. She sure seems a lot more part of some revolution at camp than it would do for people in Rising Sun to find out about.

Style W62
Walnut Chest
$270

Gerstner Tool Chests

If you enjoy reading this **Catalog** *you are probably the kind of person that is seized by an irresistible urge to open all those beautifully fitted little drawers in antique cabinets. You can satisfy the urge in your own home thanks to H. Gerstner & Sons, Inc.*

They make superb wood cases that will hold small interesting things of almost any size and shape: machinist's chests, medical instrument cases, boxes for artists, photographers, dental hygienists, and so on, ad infinitum. The thing that sets Gerstner apart from their competitors is their concern with quality. You can buy a box from them that will stand with perfect aplomb on your Chippendale end table. Their cases are made of polished quartersawed oak, American black walnut, or can be covered with black leather or vinyl. Prices range from $115 to $269 and one look will convince you that their products are a rare bargain in an injection-molded age. Their service is personal and quick; illustrated literature is available. You can get factory seconds at reduced prices (less 20%) too.
—Morton Grosser

Gerstner Tool Chests
Information

free from:
H. Gerstner & Sons, Inc.
P.O. Box 517
Dayton, OH 45402

Style W41C
Walnut Chest
$180

Enduring, distinctive styling is inherent in the classic Apprentice Series of fine tool chests. Gerstner set the standard for tool chests in the early 1900's and it still holds true today. Built for use by professionals with the normal number of precision tools, the Apprentice chest has seven hand fitted, smooth sliding long and short drawers to accomodate all sizes of tools or instruments . . . as well as an extra deep top compartment for oversize tools and equipment.

All interiors are felt-lined — — steel plated drawer bottoms provide extra strength. Exacting preciseness goes into the hand crafting of tongue and groove joinery. This is necessary to assure a perfect fit thus resisting temperature changes and protection from dust, moisture and condensation.

Style No.	Wood Finish	Overall Size L x H x D	No. Drws.	Ship. Wt.
O41C	Oak	20 x 12¼ x 9½	7	26 Lbs.
W41C	Walnut	20 x 12¼ x 9½	7	26 Lbs.
O41A	Oak	18 x 12¼ x8½	7	22 Lbs.
W41A	Walnut	18 x 12¼ x 8½	7	22 Lbs.
O41	Oak	16 x 12¼ x 8½	7	20 Lbs.
W41	Walnut	16 x 12¼ x 8½	7	20 Lbs.

Tool chests

A note on the Gerstner tool chests. In the old days, craftsmen made their own tools and tool chests. When they went for a job, they didn't turn in a resumé, they hauled their tool chests in and the boss looked them over. On the basis of the quality of the work, he was hired or not. Tools and tool chests were very personal things.
—Max Pepke
New York, New York

Snap-On Tools

Outstanding very expensive mechanics tools. Considered the best. If you're professional they're worth it. Otherwise no. Check the phone book, call, and they'll send delivery truck of samples. *—SB*
[Suggested by Morton Grosser]

Snap-On Tools Corporation
Kenosha, WI 53140

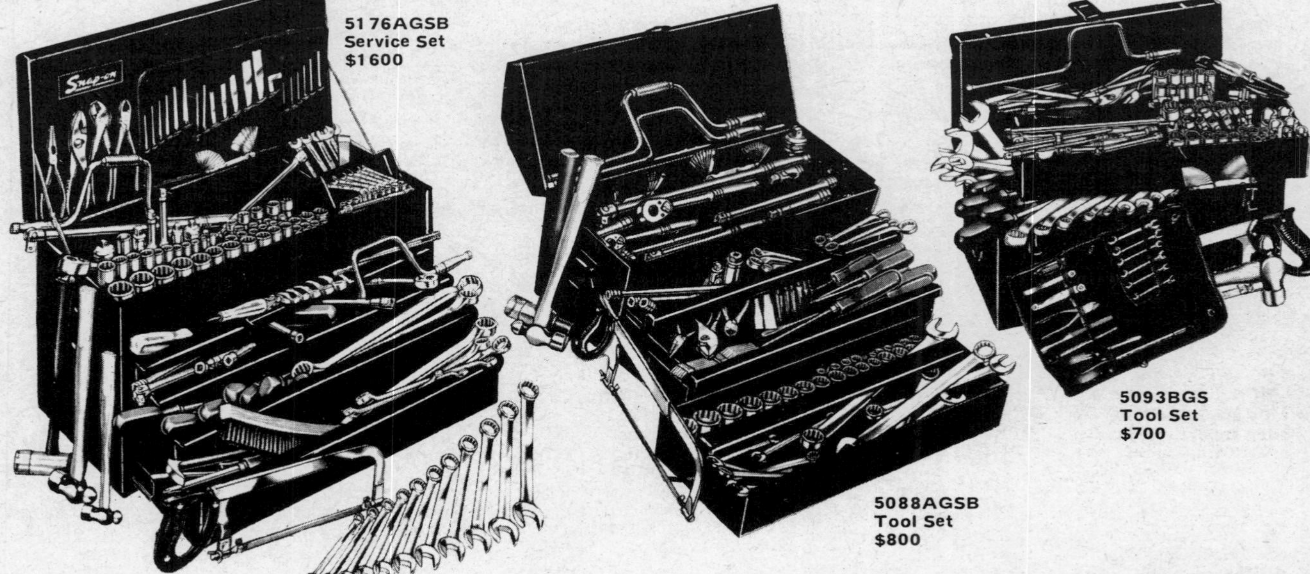

5176AGSB
Service Set
$1600

5088AGSB
Tool Set
$800

5093BGS
Tool Set
$700

Solidox Welding Torch

A medium lightweight welding torch that uses pellets for oxygen. Very portable. The Solidox torch is available in hardware stores, home-improvement centers and do-it-yourself stores across the country. The whole kit only costs about $30 from say, Silvo (p. 144). 5000° hot.
—SB

Solidox Welding Torch Kit
$26.95 postpaid from:

Cleanweld Products
P.O. Box 2184
Irwindale, CA 91706
or check your local hardware store.

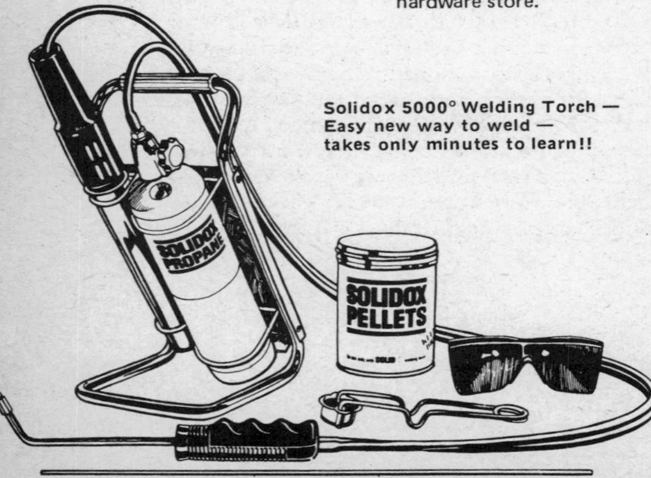

Solidox 5000° Welding Torch — Easy new way to weld — takes only minutes to learn!!

AMPCO Safety Tools

A good tool kit on board a boat is, in effect, a gland full of antibodies the boat uses to fight infection. The problem is that a boat tool kit is the second most infection-liable organ aboard (the first is the bloody electrical system). Tool steel rusts horribly. Of the several manufacturers of nonferrous, nonsparking, nonmagnetic (don't have to worry about setting them near the compass), and corrosion-resistant tools, here's AMPCO. No sparks means no unscheduled explosions. *—George Putz*

AMPCO Safety Tools
Information and nearest distributor location

free from:
AMPCO Metal
P.O. Box 2004
Milwaukee, WI 53201

AMPCO kit M-47 — Combination pliers, screwdriver, adjustable wrench, hammer and claw crate opener, groove joint pliers

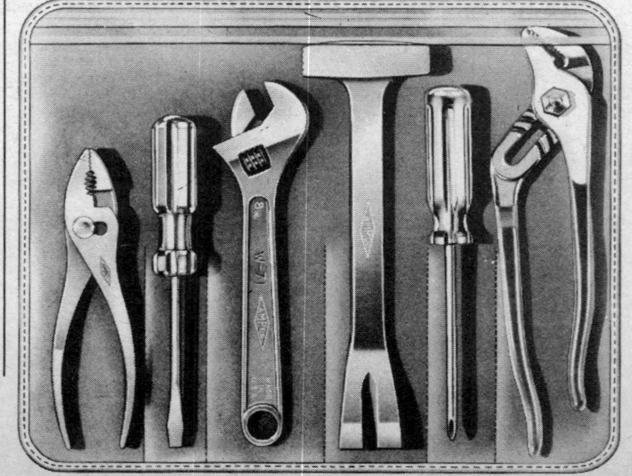

LeverSnips

Taking my prize for the Tool Most Improved Over The Traditional Type, these "tin snips" are so much better than others that it's hard to believe that the old kind still sells at all. The secret is in a weird twist in the blade that lets you slide the tool along under the metal without contorting the work and marring it with wrinkles (and your hand with the Dreaded Sharp Edges). They come in lefts and rights as do other snips. Ballbearing action takes less pressure too. *—J. Baldwin*

LeverSnips
#343-9L (Left and Straight Cuts)
#343-9R (Right and Straight Cuts)

$12.50 (approx.)
postpaid from:
U.S. General Supply Corp.
(p. 141)
or check your local hardware store.

OFFSET CUTTING TOOLS
Compound Leverage

Cuts sheet metal, carpet, linoleum, Formica, rubber, cardboard. Offset blades allow cut material to flow unobstructed past blades. Special heat-treated alloy steel blades. Compound leverage with roller bearing action greatly increases cutting power. Serrated blade cuts quicker and easier. Cushion grip vinyl covered handles. 9" long.
343-9LW1180 (For Left and Straight Cuts).... ~~$12.98~~
343-9RW1180 (For Right and Straight Cuts)..., ~~12.98~~

Aushalser

Uh, for those of you that don't know what an Aushalser is, it's a device that makes holes in the sides of tubes so you can attach other tubes there without T fittings. It's too expensive for the average toolbox, but if you have to make a bunch of manifold type flat plate collectors it could save you money. The joints are more reliable and cheaper than T fittings. The tool is made with typical German precision. They also make a nifty small tubing bender. The tool can also be purchased separately for less.
—J. Baldwin

Aushalser Kit
$350 and up (approx.)
from:
Rothenberger
981 Lunt Avenue
Schaumberg, IL 60193

or check your local industrial supply distributor.

Aushalser making a hole in tubing — better than T fittings

Loctite Technology

Mechanics, especially those working on old, frapped-out machinery, will dig Loctite. Anything threaded will stay together and not vibrate loose if you use the stuff. This is God's gift to the motorcycle fixer. The same company also makes a glop that you can use to make gaskets with right on the part; and for those engaged in putting new bearings in VW transmissions, they make a bearing seating compound that enables you to use wobbly old transmission cases instead of throwing them away. It works.
—J. Baldwin

Loctite Technology
Catalog

free from:
Loctite Corporation
North Mountain Road
Newington, CT 06111

Locking pulley socket screw with Threadlocker 242

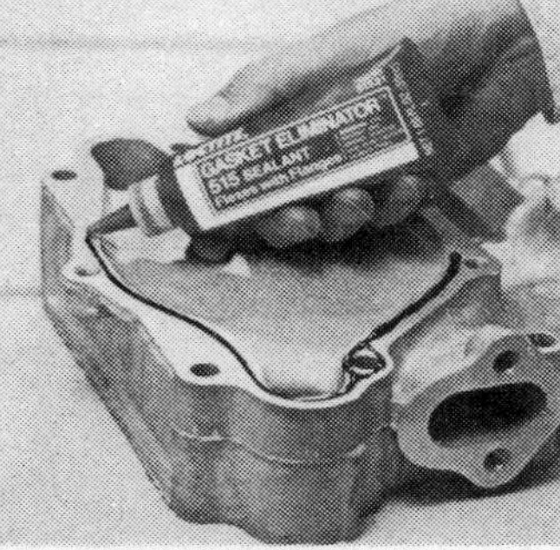

Water pump gasket

← Locking carburetor screw

Aerolite Glue

Aerolite glues are well regarded, and come formulated for a wide range of uses, including sailplane construction, skis, and boats.
—J. Baldwin

Aerolite Glue
Catalog

free from:
Leavens Bros. Ltd.
2555 Derry Road E.
Mississauga, Ont.
Canada L4T 1A1

Aerolite Glue used in airplane construction

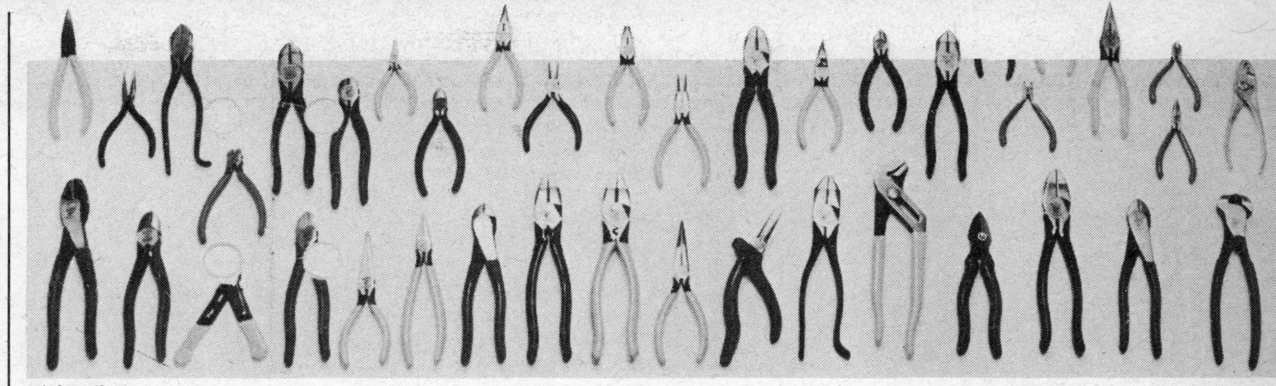

Klein pliers

Klein Tools ↑

Klein is famous for their pliers and lineman's tools, belts and safety harnesses. They make close to 80 different kinds of pliers for all kinds of applications. Pliers definitely fit in that category of hand tool where spending a few dollars more gets you a tool that not only lasts longer and is easier to use but can also do more things than a cheapo model. —Richard Nilsen

Klein Tools
Manufactured by
Klein Tools, Inc.
Chicago, IL

Not available by mail order.
Check your local hardware store.

Pyramid Foundry Sets

I haven't actually seen one of these outfits, but they appear to be typical of the breed. This one seems to have a better-than-average blower system. Sets range from 3 lbs. to 53 lbs. and they claim iron, bronze and aluminum can all be easily handled. The ability to make castings adds an interesting capability to any shop or studio. For instance, you can cast duplicates or missing parts of old wind generators . . . —J. Baldwin

Pyramid Foundry Sets
Catalog

free from:
Pyramid Products
3736 South 7th Avenue
Phoenix, AZ 85041

Metal Capacity	Model Number	Shipping Weight	Price Of Set	Price Of Short Set
3 lbs.	1	65 lbs.	$155	$143
10 lbs.	4	100 lbs.	$180	$166
20 lbs.	8	140 lbs.	$230	$210
36 lbs.	10	210 lbs.	$270	$247
53 lbs.	16	265 lbs.	$285	$260

(Short set comes minus sand, flask, and compound.)

Regular Pyramid foundry set

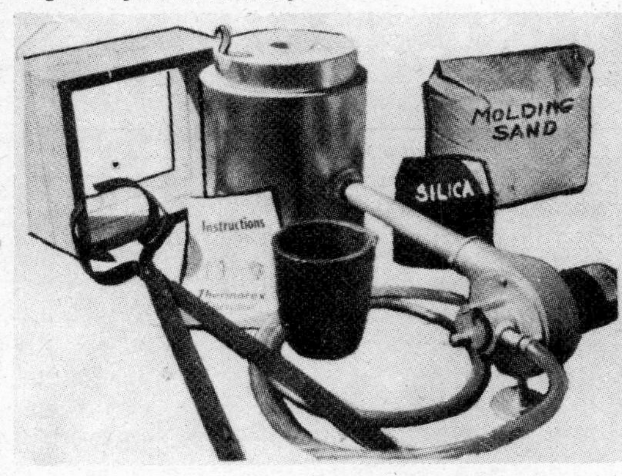

Pouring the casting with the No. 4 crucible

Vaco Products Company ↓

A professional quality line with national distribution, Vaco specializes in screw and nut drivers, solderless connectors for wiring, and other electrical hand tools. Their tools are designed for the person who is going to be using them all day, every day. I like their magnetic screwdriver with interchangeable bits (No. 70035). Spare bits store inside the hollow handle, and they are magnetized, which means you spend less time on the floor on your hands and knees looking for that tiny screw that got away.

A variation on this is the No. 70427 — the same idea, but with four of the new TORX bits. These are the new 6 pointed screws — also called Star fasteners — that hold together parts of many new cars and appliances.
—Richard Nilsen

Vaco Tools
$8 (approx.)
Manufactured by
The Vaco Products Co.
Northbrook, IL

Not available by mail order.
Check your local hardware store.

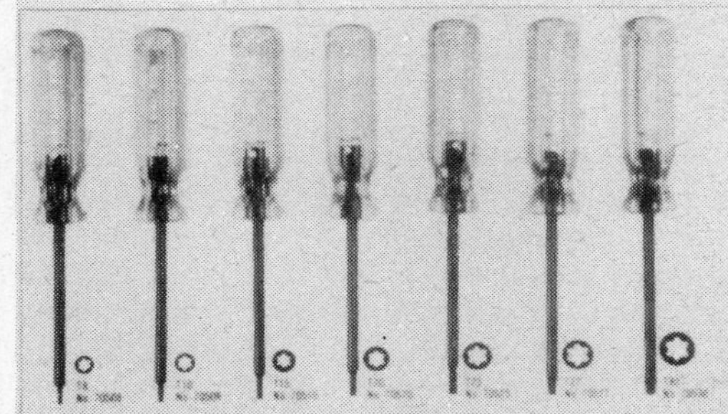

Stock No.	TORX® Size	Handle Size Dia. x Length	Blade Length	Overall Length	Std. Pkg.	Wt. Per Std. Pkg.
70508	T8	1-3/16" x 4-1/2"	4"	8-1/2"	6	1-1/2 Lbs.
70509	T10	1-3/16" x 4-1/2"	4"	8-1/2"	6	1-1/2 Lbs.
70515	T15	1-3/16" x 4-1/2"	4"	8-1/2"	6	1-1/2 Lbs.
70520	T20	1-3/16" x 4-1/2"	4"	8-1/2"	6	1-1/2 Lbs.
70525	T25	1-3/16" x 4-1/2"	4"	8-1/2"	6	1-1/2 Lbs.
70527	T27	1-3/16" x 4-1/2"	4"	8-1/2"	6	1-1/2 Lbs.
70530	T30	1-3/16" x 4-1/2"	4"	8-1/2"	6	1-1/2 Lbs.

8 inch Torx Bulldriver screwdrivers with a variety of Torx sizes

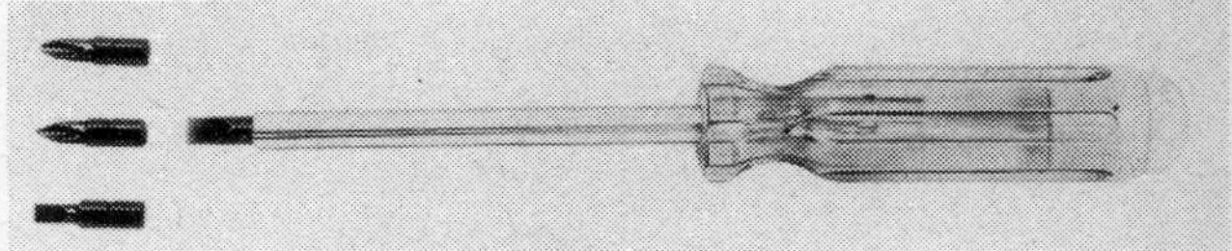

3-in-1 Torx magnetic screwdriver. Shaft length — 4½ inches. Overall length — 9 inches

THE RISING SUN
NEIGHBORHOOD NEWSLETTER

Every Sunday morning on KPFA they play Bach for two hours and a couple of Sundays ago I was listening and they went right from a Brandenburg Concerto to a really down home, sounded like it was recorded in church "Ezekiel Saw the Wheel," and then two more real soulful numbers, "Swing Low" and "He's Got the Whole World," and then the announcer Bill Sokol said, "That is in memory of all the sweet sad brothers and sisters who died in Guyana last week who were, as you may have forgotten, mostly poor, mostly black, mostly middle aged or old people who were trying to find an alternative to the mass urban poverty that trapped them in this dreamy wonderland you and I live in." Then he played four more gospel songs including "Jesus is my only friend. When my neighbors all betray me, Jesus is my only friend. When my pastor will not help me, Jesus is my only friend." And I said 912 dead people is a lot if they're all real.

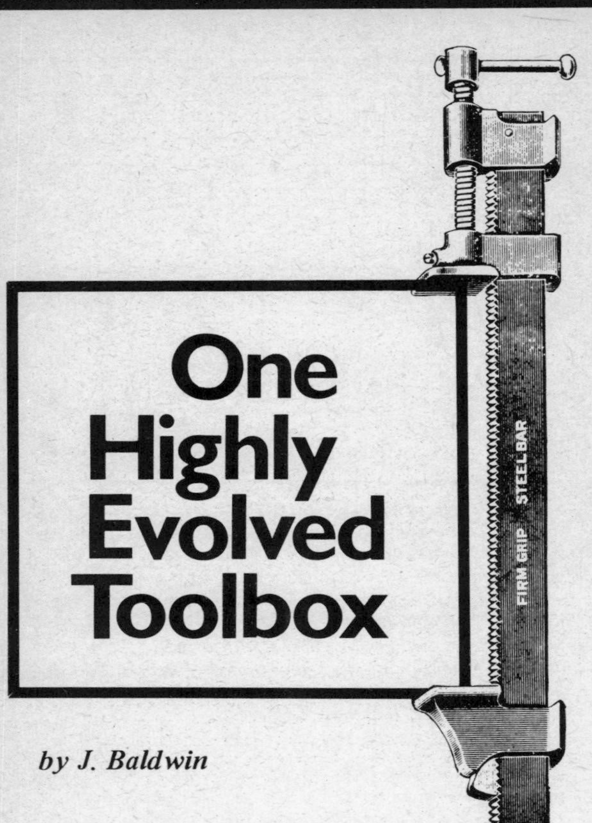

One Highly Evolved Toolbox

by J. Baldwin

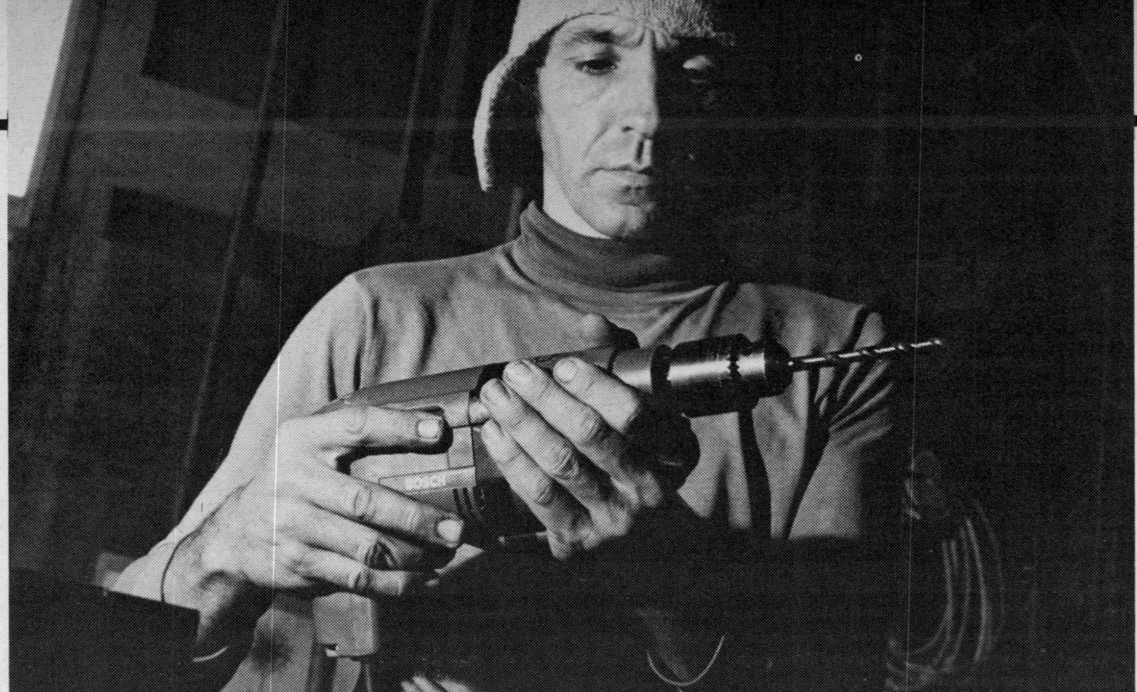

BOSCH TOOLS — Note how this drill fits my hand, putting my weight directly behind the bit. It's the only drill we've seen where your hand doesn't cover cooling slots. Smooth and super powerful, these drills last a long time. They are also double insulated which makes them a lot safer, particularly outdoors. The Bosch jig-saw is merely the best there is. Ask anyone who has used one. My only regret is that I waited 5 years to get one, and made do with a poorly designed domestic commercial grade machine whose bearings failed regularly and whose handle soon got too hot to hold. (Sears best grade jig-saw is more versatile but not as high quality.)

Not pictured. GLOVES & GOGGLES — The goggles save your eyes. The gloves (leather) save your hands and let you add double power to screwdrivers and snips. (I should be wearing goggles in these posed photographs.)

Our portable shop has been evolving for about 20 years now. There's nothing really very special about it except that a continuing process of removing obsolete or inadequate tools and replacing them with more suitable ones has resulted in a collection that has become a thing-making system rather than a pile of hardware. It's a generalist's shop; we're not equipped to produce fine cabinetry or precision machine work. We can manipulate all common materials. It's orderly enough to permit strangers to find things, but it stops short of compulsive anal neatness. It enables things to get done with less hassle and so things GET done with less hassle. We use it as a three-dimensional sketchpad.

People keep asking us what tools to get, where to get them, and how to keep them ready to use. Here's the story:

STAND IN SEARS Tool Dept, and it'll soon be obvious that you don't need one-of-each even if you have the money. Ask a craftsman what to buy, and you'll get as many answers as people you ask, for each has his own favorites and specialized needs. They'll all agree on one thing though: BUY THE BEST YOU CAN. And the more a tool will be used, the better the quality should be. Tools used every day, especially electric tools, should be of commercial or production line grade. You usually can't find these at hardware stores. Industrial supply houses are where to go. Take a friend who can buy wholesale. These tools will be expensive, so we'd better justify the cost.

For many, the best reason to go first class is that good tools are a real pleasure to use and handle. This helps make work less labor. The heavy duty stuff looks brutal. It wasn't made to look good in the box, it was made to do the job and has been perfected over many years. The tough ones have their own kind of beauty that you'll see better as your viewpoint gets aligned with reality. Such tools, of course, last longer and are repairable when they finally do wear. They can take a lot more abuse, especially the inevitable overload. They can handle the bigger jobs and poor working conditions that would soon trash cheap versions. And after a few years in your hand, they often get to be old friends.

For tools that get used now and then, middle quality will do. By that I mean Sears better grades and no lower. Really cheapo tools are of no use at all, can be dangerous, and often break the first time you use them. They are also discouraging to use, which might even cause a beginner to give up. Our only regrets have been not buying the best when we could have. Tools that receive great strain, such as gear pullers, should be super top quality only. If you only need one every five years, rent it.

OK so what tools do you need? How do you start the stash? There are a few basic tools that everyone should have available: Hammer, crosscut saw, adjustable wrench, pliers, screwdrivers (get a set), tape measure, hand drill and bits. Beyond these, you'd best gather tools as you need them. Auto work will require a rather complete set of wrenches and a whole boxfull of special tools, some of which are for particular vehicles. Carpentry will require another whole group: planes, chisels, etc. Electrical and plumbing still more. Our rule of thumb is if we need to borrow a common tool more than once, we buy one.

Fleamarkets are a good place to look for expensive items like vises or anvils. Absolutely the best place to get a whole mess of tools at once is to keep alert for a widow selling off her deceased husband's retirement shop. Another place to look is auctions, but you'd better know what you're doing. You should shop around. Recently in the Bay Area, we were quoted prices varying 50% on a tool we wanted! If you want to buy a bunch all at once, (which makes sense these days of inflation — tools are a good savings account), some stores will make you a 20% deal. Even Sears can be dealt with, as the sales people work on commission. They and other stores also have unadvertised freight-damaged goods hidden away. These can be good deals, as the damage is often merely cosmetic. You can give a salesman your name (and take his card) and have him call you when a certain tool is on sale or arrives damaged.

Whether in a Big Store or private sale, you should critically inspect each tool for condition. These days, many new tools by reputable (?) manufacturers are faulty. Used ones may be worn beyond repair. Anyway, be nitpicky about it; you'll be living with it in your hand. And beware of package deals claimed to be a great saving. The "complete mechanics tool set for $450.00" often includes tools you don't need, and may force you to take inferior items that you would be better off picking up individually.

What do you do about that little voice that whispers, "Buy one, you might need it someday!" Well, it's *possible* you'll be needing them *all* someday, but Sears is only the tip of the iceberg. Have you ever seen a *real* hardware catalog? 2000 pages? On the other hand it often does pay to get a set of tools that greatly increases your capability, such as a welding rig. Another way to go is for a group to buy a set of tools for working on one particular item, such as old Chevy 6 engines, and then everyone in the group that needs a vehicle gets one that uses that engine and hence those tools, and the consequent parts pile. (That's being done around here. There must be *dozens* of 56 Chevy pickups and flatbeds within 30 miles.) Some groups get known for specialties: "the Butterfly Mountain people fix tractors." Those communities and families pool their resources and buy a set of expensive heavy duty tools maybe for tractor repair. You have to be pretty mellow to make this work, especially if there is a high turnover of people. But this is a growing trend, and we think a good one. It leads to barter and lessens the need for duplicate sets of specialty equipment.

Our shop is known for its versatility. It's portable — we've installed the entire thing in a recycled 20-year-old, 2½ ton bookmobile née breadtruck. Some tools like the radial arm saw deploy through hatches in the side of the truck to be used outdoors. Others fold under the workbenches (which are all the same height to facilitate handling large projects). Windows are strategically placed to permit long items to be handled in the drillpress and bandsaw. Sixty drawers from an old post office hold a host of small commonly used items and 500 babyfood jars are pregnant with various sizes of fasteners. An assortment of scrap metal rides in lockers under the chassis along with a 4000 watt slow-running gasoline generator and the welding rig. The curbside body wall unfolds like a camping tent trailer to raise the floor area to 12 x 13 feet with a folding 6 x 7 workbench in the middle augmenting the ones along the walls. It's been set up in 12 locations in 10 years. It also pulls the 20-foot Airstream Trailer (The Silver Turd) I live in.

The tools were chosen for quality and versatility. With versatility goes a handy ability to work in harmony with other tools, enhancing all. For example, with the drills and vises we have, we can drill a hole at any angle in just about anything. The combinations allow us to easily mass-produce parts like dome struts or Inkle-loom frames. This gives a nice potential for making money as well as greatly easing tasks that might be as bad as working in Detroit. Versatility also means needing fewer tools which means less money out, less space for storage, and less tools to keep track of.

Mail Order Tool Supplies
For more, see pp. 142-154.

Brookstone Tools
Catalog
free from:
Brookstone Company
127 Vose Farm Road
Peterborough, NH 03458

Garrett Wade Co.
Catalog
$1 from:
Garrett Wade Co., Inc.
161 Ave. of the Americas
New York, NY 10013

W.W. Grainger, Inc.
Catalog
free from:
W.W. Grainger, Inc.
5959 West Howard St.
Chicago, IL 60648

Silvo Hardware Co.
Catalog
$1 from:
Silvo Hardware Co.
c/o Advertising Dept.
2205 Richmond Street
Philadelphia, PA 19125

U.S. General Supply Company
Catalog
$1 from:
U.S. General
Supply Company
100 General Place
Department WE
Jericho, NY 11753

Woodcraft Supply Company
Catalog
$1 from:
Woodcraft Supply Co.
313 Montvale Avenue
Woburn, MA 01888

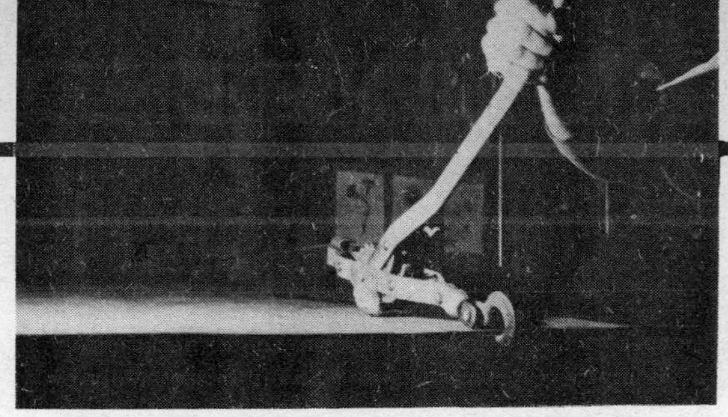

COME-ALONG — It's surprising how often this thing gets used if you're living in the country. Lifting engines, "battening down," unsticking cars in the mud, dragging loads into trucks, straightening sagging sheds, stretching fence, moving things over just a little . . .

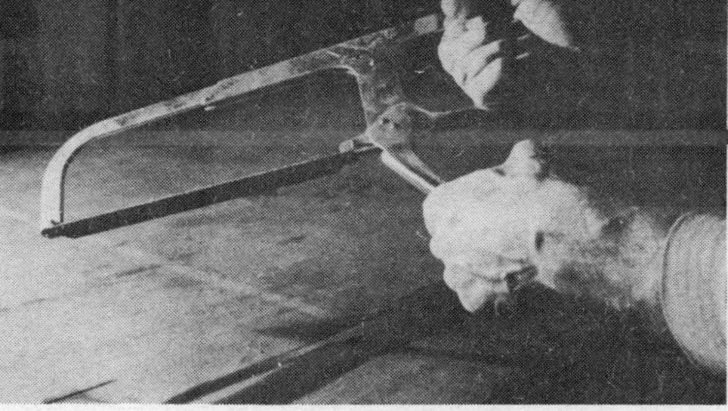

MILLERS FALLS HACKSAW No. 300 — Lever makes blades super-tight in seconds without diddling little wing-nuts. Blades last longer, and you can change blade type and position easily too (and thus do) and things go much better. (Silvo No. 300-M18)

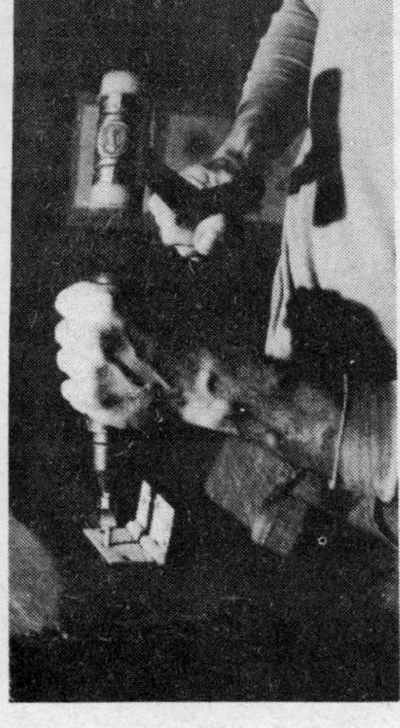

NEEDLENOSE PLIERS WITH SPRING (left) — the spring and delicate jaw shape permits very delicate nabbing. You can actually pick up a live ant without damaging it (physically, anyway). (Klein, p. 137)

IMPACT DRIVER (right) — This works like those air operated tire wrenches in garages except the power in this case is your hand. This tool is often the only practical way to loosen rusted screws and bolts on older machines. Wear goggles and gloves while using. Comes with several different bits and can be used with air drive socket wrench sockets too. (Craftsman No. 9 GT 47634)

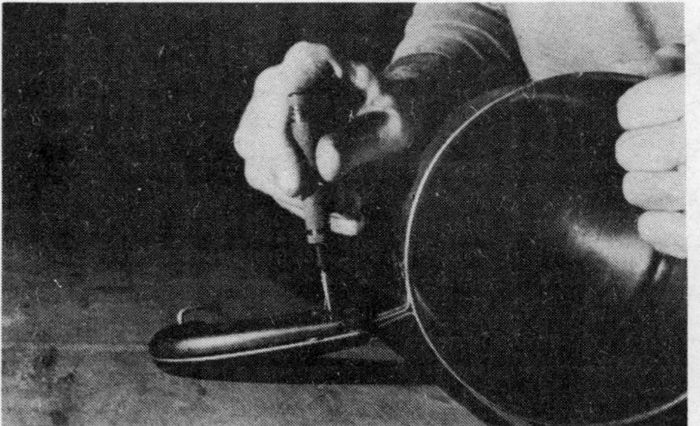

AUTO-PUNCH — Instead of having to beat on this punch with a hammer, you just press it. The smite is adjustable, making it ideal for fine work and sheet metal layout. (Brookstone)

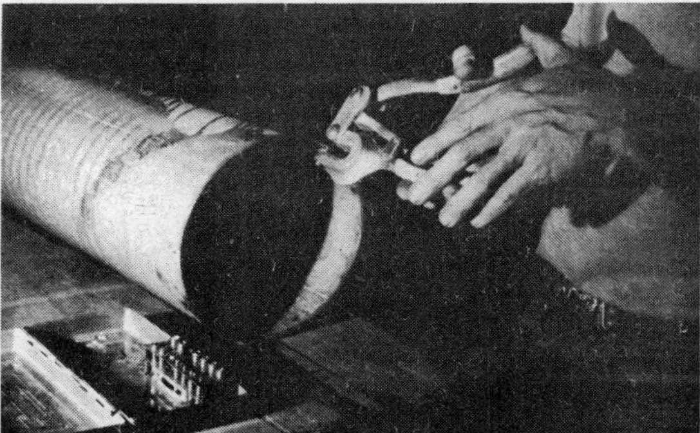

WHITNEY PUNCH — A fine punch set that can handle heavy leather and sheetmetal. We use it a lot in conjunction with the Popriveter. (U.S. General No. 600-8500)

For many people, the biggest problem with tools is keeping them together. That was our problem too for awhile, especially at an alternative high school where there were always a number of young people who didn't yet see that tools are in a different category than other possessions. Our answer has been to take the time to try and give people a good feeling about tools being extensions of their own hands, and that tools are the means to getting good shelter and other desirable results. A French poet (whose name I regrettably can't remember) said, "Hammers spend a lot of time sleeping. . ." We like to see the tools at work. We show people how to use the tools and encourage them to in turn show still others how. Having good tools in the hand, together with that tasty feeling that comes from teaching somebody else, gives the tool borrowers a respect for the whole bit.

We also have all the tools marked with a colored stripe. This not only reduces arguments on job sites where lots of people's tools are at work, but it makes it easy for people of good heart to return strays. We put out the word: "Bring a blue stripe tool to breakfast" and we round 'em up. We also ask that tools be brought back at sundown unless needed that night. There's a place to bring them back to. This is essential. A casual pig-pen shop just can't keep its tools because there "isn't any there, there." As an experiment, we abandoned our collapsed old bureau toolbox and bought a (freight damaged) Sears (the best for the money) rolling mechanics tool chest like you see in big auto shops. We segregated the tools by function and labeled the drawers. The result is that tools are easily looked over and selected and just as easily put to bed. To our great surprise, we found that this chest caused a drastic increase in the number of tools being used and a similar increase in action. We even found that we were using our own tools more! The neat storage made it easy to see who was missing, but people brought them back much more reliably than before anyway. The chest can be locked to control unannounced borrowing which is always a disaster. The overall effect has been that under very poor risk conditions, both sociological and physical, we've only lost about $50.00 worth of tools in 7 years! And this without having to get too heavy or "high school shoppish" about things. In case you wondered, we did try the toolboard-on-the-wall. It didn't work, and nobody we know that's tried it has made it work either, though it is nice to see all those tools hangin'. It has not been necessary to sentence anyone to being tool crib librarian either. We'll admit that it takes some time to develop tool-consciousness in a crew, but it can be done, and peaceably. The tools spend a lot less time sleeping too.

Making a deliberate effort to raise your own tool consciousness can result in some interesting new possibilities in your life. As with most mysterious-appearing phenomena, a bit of learning soon clears things up and you wonder what had been previously keeping you from doing your own repairs and thing-making. Sometimes all it takes is a different point of view.

I've remarked that tools are extensions of your hands. No mystery there; a hammer is just a hard fist; a screwdriver, a tough fingernail. But hands usually operate according to instructions from head, so it can also be said that tools are an extension of your mind. Looked at this way, the big (expensive) mechanic's cabinet with all the tools of similar function stored together with high visibility becomes even easier to justify. I find it is effective to store the tools by function rather than by name because this is the most useful way to think of the best tool when you are selecting. Hitters, grabbers, slashers, abraders — regardless of what they are called, are there in their places. You take your pick. Often, just looking at them will give you a better idea not only of what tool to use, but how to do the job or how to design the object. That's a big advantage of the neat toolbox. If the tools are "somewhere out on the back porch or maybe in the back seat of the VW" then your mind is deflected from creative thinking into a hunting mode, and the aggravation can easily cause you to lose your ability to get things done.

Easily accessible, functionally sorted tools also give you a ready familiarity with the tools you have. This has two effects. First is that as you get to know your tools, you gain the easy fluid motions that go with using them. You're not afraid of them any more, though respect is increased. This makes you able to work faster with less fatigue just as good form in sports often makes a big difference. It makes you safer too. Safety is also enhanced by having the tools where you can easily inspect them for condition, sharpness and rust. We have found that safety is largely a matter of attitude. The closer tools are to being a working extension of your mind, the safer you'll be. Self-preservation.

The second effect is that you get to "know" all the tools you own without having to consciously think about it. This makes it simple to round up strays, of course, and it's easier to see where there are annoying gaps in your capabilities ("we don't have a lightweight mallet"). More importantly, you begin to think in terms of the tools you have. The eventual result is that you and your entire toolbox and shop become a big, complex tool with many possibilities. You begin to sense what you can do together. Buying tools with overall flexibility of purpose in mind keeps you from falling into the trap of building a one-function capability with accompanying tendency to conservatively fossilize your creativity. This tendency is strengthened as the value of the tools rises, which is the main reason society doesn't get fast response to its changing needs from large corporations who have sunk enormous capital into shops that make that only. Like fat cars. Once in that position, it's difficult to evolve at all, let alone without damage or drastic change of form.

So you begin to build your tool capability into the way you think about making things. As anyone who makes lots of stuff will tell you, the tools soon become sort of an automatic part of the design process. Beginners worry too much about skill and safety, rather like new drivers worry most about jerking the clutch when learning to drive a stick shift. It doesn't take long before more serious aspects take over, and the manipulation problems fade out. But tools can't become part of your design process if you don't know what is available and what the various tools do. In addition to buying tools that I find useful, I spend some time reading catalogs so as to become familiar with tools that I can't afford or don't need at the time. Tool catalogs such as Silvo (p. 144) are rather like my cabinet in appearance so I find it painless to sort of automatically file the information away in the back room somewhere. Tool dictionaries, especially of older tools, are helpful too.

Some of you are saying about now, "Who wants to get into it that far anyway?" Friends, there are advantages. Obviously, making or repairing things yourself can save you money and time. Well, maybe it isn't so obvious. Example: next time your car breaks down, find out how many hours it will likely take to fix it. You don't have the time, right? OK, how many hours will you have to work at some job so you can pay that mechanic? For many of you, the hours you have to work to pay the mechanic will be more than the job would take if you did it yourself. Moreover, you don't have to pay yourself, and the job can be done to your standards and at your convenience. If you don't have the skills or the tools, that's what we're talking about! Doing it

THE RISING SUN
NEIGHBORHOOD NEWSLETTER

A friend of mine was sitting at the kitchen table one day thinking about how all cocks are different and they're all the same when suddenly she was someplace else and could see everything and knew everything and it was very fine. (This was before she'd taken acid and when she took acid later she was disappointed because she thought it would be like that and it wasn't.) She didn't know how long she was gone but it seemed like forever. Since then, when she starts to think about how things are the same and things are different at the same time, sometimes she feels that it might happen again and stops thinking because she thinks she might not come back.

She hardly ever talks to people about it because either they haven't had the experience and they don't believe her or they have had the experience "and all we can do is smile at each other and say 'when you know, you know.' "

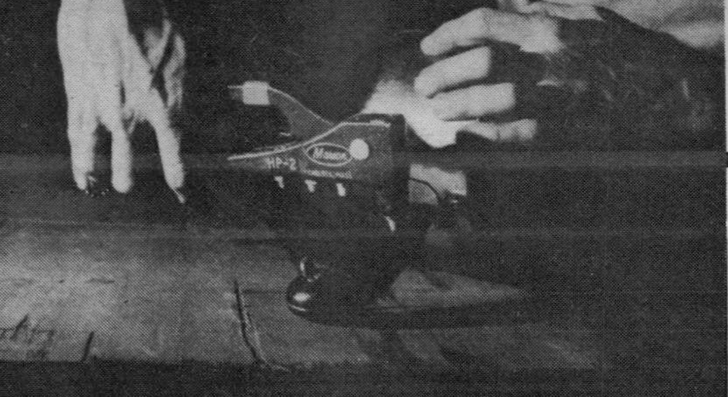

POPRIVETS — We use Poprivets for lots of things. Especially good for repairing sheet metal (as in car bodies) where welding isn't practical. They'll work in leather, Masonite, plastic, too.

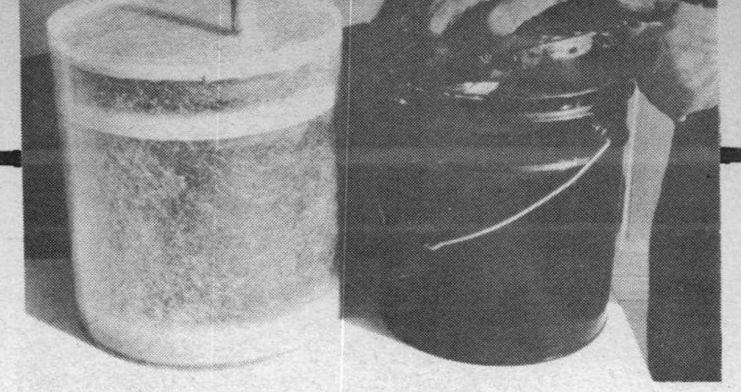

To test several schemes for a SOLAR HOT WATER HEATER, we're making up a number of identical new 5-gallon cans and covering them with a variety of heat-retaining skins. Then we'll race them. To have these made for us would not only be horrifyingly expensive, but we'd lose the experience gained by actually working with the various materials that we will be specifying eventually.

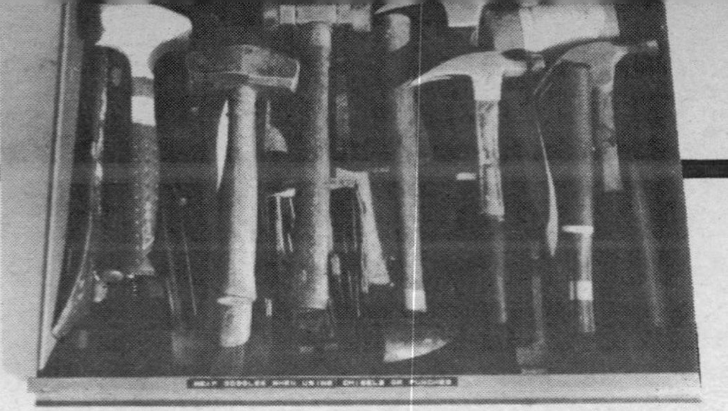

HITTERS — Wood handled hand sledge has been replaced by more reliable and better-balanced Estwing model. I'll give the old one away to a friend who has none and doesn't mind replacing the handle again. Our big sledgehammer lives with "outdoor" tools hanging on the wall. Third hammer from left is a BB-filled "no-bounce," really great for sheet metal and chisel work. (U.S. General No. 433-1)

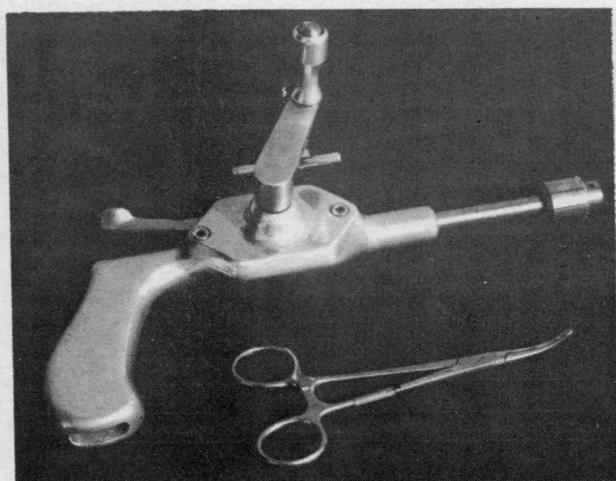

SURPLUS SURGICAL TOOLS are often ergonomically excellent and are useful for precise work. Bone surgeon's drill and this hemostat aren't really absolutely necessary in your shop, but are very satisfying to use. (Hemostat from Brookstone, p. 143)

SIMPLE JIG holds each 2 x 4 inserted for drilling in the same relative grip, and so each will have its hold in the same place. Be sure and blow out chips so part will fit snugly, and always mark jigs so you can detect if they are slowly moving as parts thump into place. CLAMPS are a good thing to have lots of.

ABRADER DEPARTMENT — Spring keeps files separate so you can see them, and also keeps files from filing each other. Drawer lining is indoor-outdoor carpet.

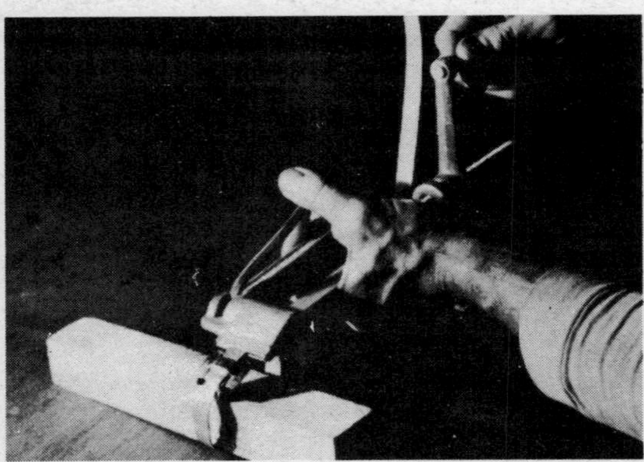

BANDIT — Designed for making hose clamps on the job, this tool can be used for banding just about anything with a variety of band sizes and metals. This was used to make dome hubs, band concrete forms, secure crates, make barrels, extend tipi poles, repair broken spars on sailboats, reinforce porch railings, etc., etc.

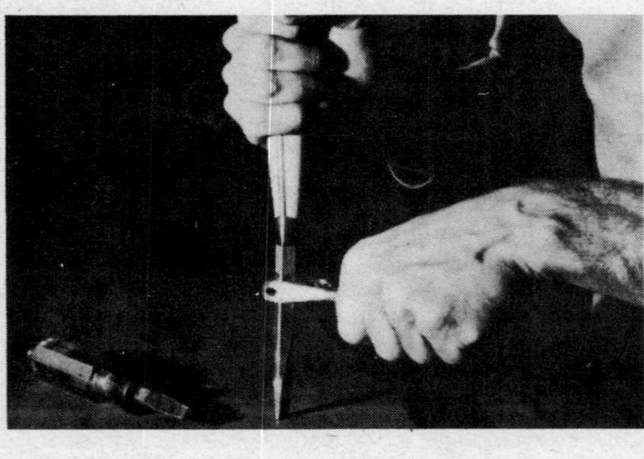

FAT SCREWDRIVERS — Big handles, heavy blade, compact size, make Sears No. 41586 and Irwin our favorite screwdrivers. Square shank allows help with wrench. You can't own too many screwdrivers, as they grow legs easily, and there are so many screw sizes.

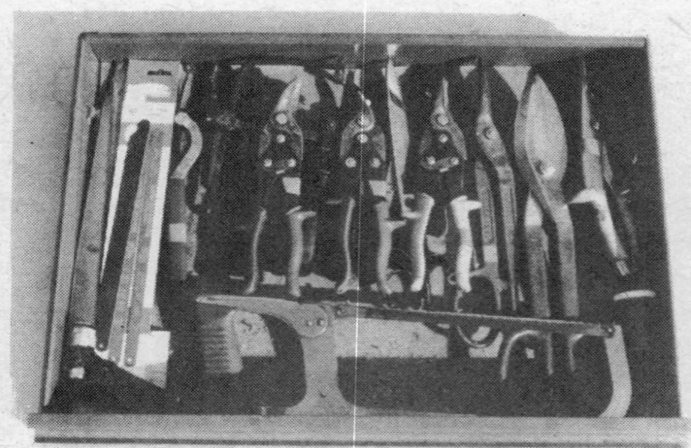

SAWS AND SNIPS DEPARTMENT — Don't get hung up on tool names. "Tin snips" can cut lots of other things such as leather. The three identical-looking guys are "aircraft snips" and they aren't identical at all. The yellow handled ones cut straight; the green handled ones cut righthanded circles or curves and are just the thing for lefthanded people; the redhandled ones cut left as you might expect.

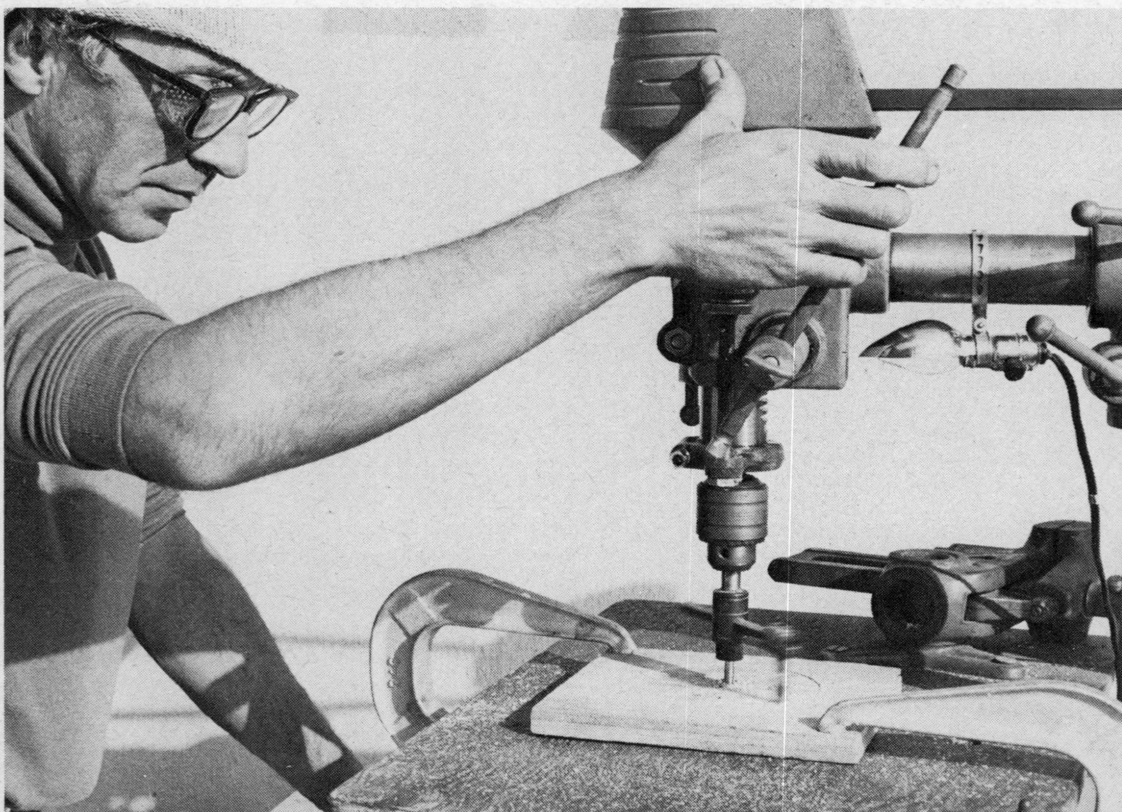

HOLE CUTTER making discs. I have a small town phonebook in my shirt just in case something lets go. I've picked metal out of it twice. It doesn't take a Ph.D. thesis to tell you that certain tools require a certain caution. Be extra careful as you go through the super-cool, smarty-pants phase of tool familiarity. Except for rare freak accidents, few tools will cut things that you don't deliberately feed them.

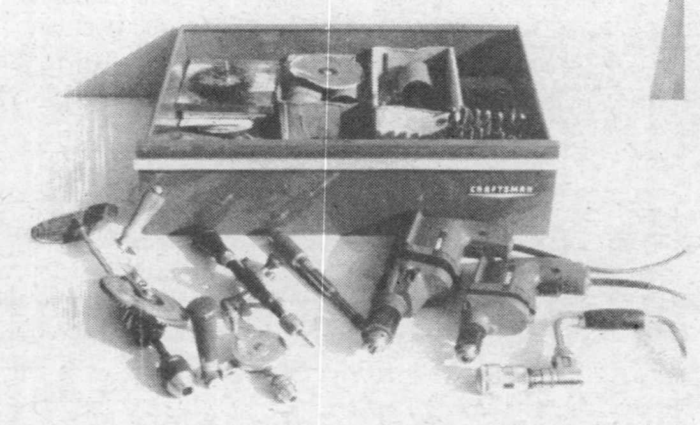

HOLE-MAKING DEPARTMENT gets heaviest use, partly because the rotary devices are so versatile in other modes. Assortment of hand drills is because we often work where there is no power available. Their lair is rather deep for a photo, so I've had them sit on the step for a class portrait.

ASSORTED UNSORTABLE DEPARTMENT — You didn't really think that there was a way around having one of these did you? Nobody, including me, knows what's in here.

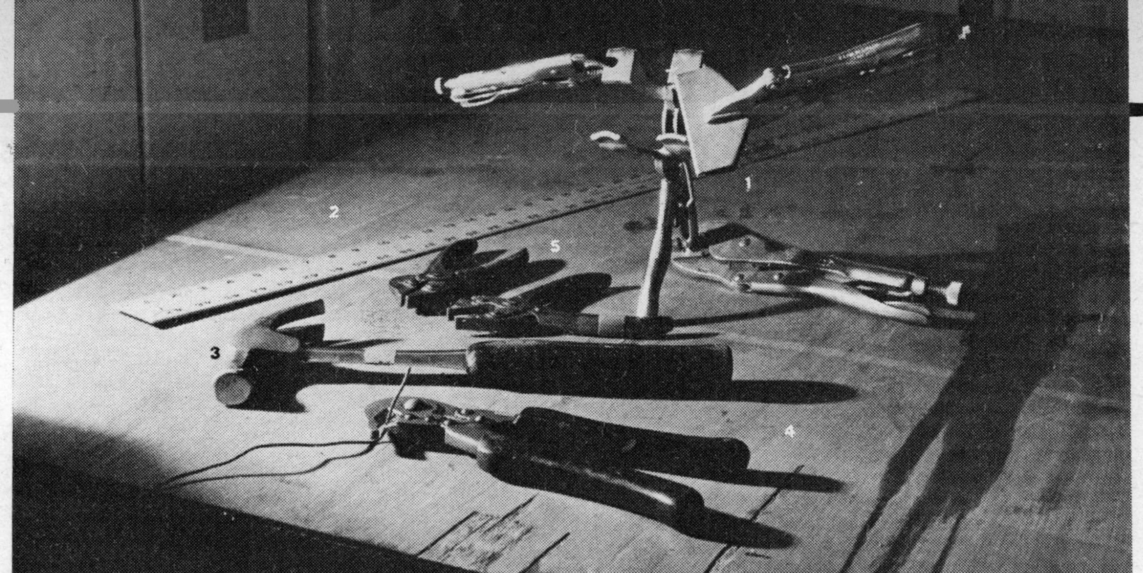

1 **BIRDHEADS (Sometimes called "Parrot") — If you do a lot of work with heavy wire, these are just the thing. Compound levers let you snip through most wire like it wasn't there. Nose makes working overhead easy. (Silvo No. 690C - P14)**

2 **FOUR-FOOT RULER — If you work with plywood or 4 x 8 anything, one of these will save you lots of time and grief. NB. Some new plywood isn't 90° square!! Check it always. Best rulers have etched numbers.**

3 **STEEL-HANDLED HAMMERS — Steel or fiberglas may not be as aesthetic as wood, but the heads don't fly off when dry weather shrinks the handle. Violent nail pulling won't break them either. Pro carpenters don't like them, claiming that they eventually injure elbows if used every day.**

4 **VISEGRIPS — Buy these by the genuine name Visegrip. They come in an array of sizes and jaw shapes, allowing you to grab what you see with a grip strong enough to crush things. Handy for undoing old rusty machines, and as a portable vise for welding, etc.**

5 **"BERNARDS" — Pliers whose jaws work parallel (there's a nifty wire cutter too). We often use these in pairs for twisting and shaping small parts, and glass breaking. Our most pilfered item too; we've lost a dozen pairs. I can see why. (U.S. General No. 348-1022)**

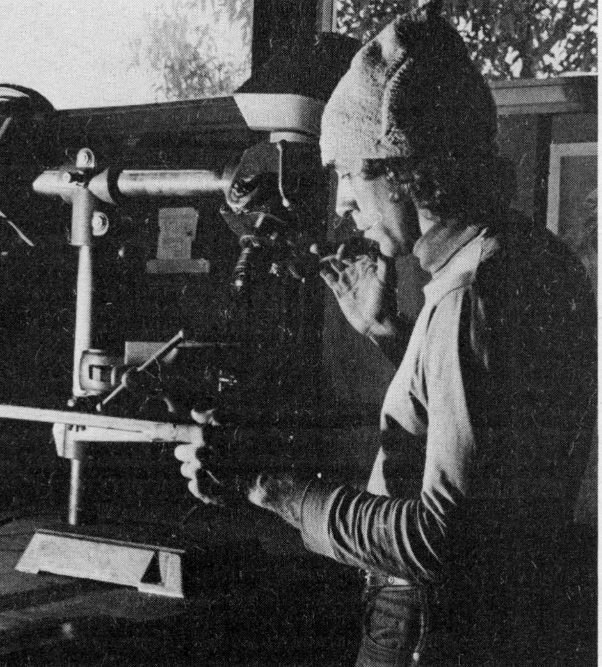

ROCKWELL RADIAL DRILL PRESS — Our most-used tool, bar none. This ½-inch drill can extend to drill a hole in the center of a 32" circle, and can swivel out to drill big things sitting on the floor. It can drill at any angle, including horizontal. Though not of machine shop accuracy, it will do 99% of the work most people will ask of it. Radial feature costs extra and is worth every penny. You clamp the work down (we use a Versa Vise) and bring the drill to it at the desired angle. We have it mounted on a box that holds accessories and brings typical drill table height to that of other shop benches so we can support long objects being drilled. Dependable too: no repairs in 14 years. It's light enough to carry to a big job.

VERSA VISE — These wonderful vises can stand up, lay down, swivel, and come with a clamp base that you can take to the job on the third floor. We have two, and a number of bases (one on the drill press table), allowing us to grip just about anything you could name short of a dead sheep in any position. They can be used as clamps when removed from base, a 1-second operation. Come with pipe jaws, too. Not for heavy metal work or heavy pounding. (Silvo No. 73½-C15)

yourself can free you from certain dependencies that you may find smothering. What if the $20.00/hour plumber can't come until next Friday? Repairing pipes is relatively easy. Once you learn how, you not only avoid being at someone's mercy, you have a skill that can help friends or make money for you. How-to books are tools, in case you haven't guessed.

Another advantage of having some tools that you know how to use, is that as you get an easy, facile familiarity using them, you begin to get a better feel of the ergonomics of other techno-hardware that you use or make. (Ergonomics is the man-machine interface; how the steering wheel feels in the hand and how it tells you what's happening to the wheels; the wrist-breaking poor feel of eggbeaters; the built-into-you feel of a good rifle). Poor ergonomics is one of the main reasons behind the recent public disenchantment with technology. Things are made with the convenience of the machine in mind instead of the human user. The result is hardware that is hard to hold, too cold or too hot, difficult to repair, easy to lose or lose control of, easily broken, etc., etc., etc. The machine is in control of you instead of the other way around. You can do better, yes? Most highly evolved good quality tools are ergonomically good. (Rifles are tools. You peaceable types can put down your neck hairs, it was only an example.) So without having to take a course in the subject, you can gain an informed feel of what is satisfying. As with most problems brought to us by technology, ergonomic problems are often best solved not with more technology but with clear thought and a better-informed intuition.

An informed tool intuition works best if it's augmented by an informed materials and processes intuition. For instance, if you don't know anything about foundry work (casting), it's unlikely that you will come up with ideas that require it. Often, this ignorance (ignore-ance) is easily remedied. A bit of inquiry may well show that what you had considered a black art is actually not one at all. Bronze and aluminum castings, for instance, are made every day in high school art departments by unskilled students using scrap metals from auto wrecking yards. Anyway, things take a form dictated by the possibilities inherent in the material to be used and the tools that can shape it, and the ideas in the head of the worker. It follows that the more you read, and snoop around and experiment and practice, the easier it will all come and the more independent you can be. Freedom rising.

The ultimate is to make your own tools. Tools fitted intimately to you by you. What could be niftier? Blacksmiths are really into that. A good example is found in the books by Alexander Weygers (p. 160). But tools need not be limited to the shop. How about making your own personal canoe paddle? Or your own left-handed kitchen equipment? You can modify existing tools too. For instance, when we needed to make 7-inch diameter pistons for a small production run of giant raft-inflating hand pumps, we reversed the bit in a hole cutter so it made discs instead. The pistons were then easily and accurately cut from heavy plywood with a great saving in time and material compared to turning them on a lathe that we would have had to borrow. Making the big pump's leather "piston ring" seals proved to be easy after we spent some time talking to craftsmen in a sandal shop. With their advice, we soaked heavy leather discs in Mink Oil and then pressed them into the desired shape with a matched male and female die rammed by our vise. The dies were made on a bandsaw modified with a simple homemade attachment that enabled us to cut bevelled round holes with good accuracy. That attachment was also used to make the next batch of pistons, as it proved faster than the disc-maker on the drill press. Tools making tools making tools.

I can hear some of you saying "small production run! Yuk. . ." Unless you are an artist, and maybe even then, you will sooner or later need a bunch of things all alike. Even with only the most basic tools, you can mass-produce things. The precision and complexity of the produced parts is somewhat dependent upon the adaptability and quality of your tool bank, another reason to intelligently gather good stuff. Large scale mass-production tends to enslave both the workers and the customers. The workers are used as if they were machines. The huge capital outlay for the factory means that there must be a huge and relatively steady demand. This in turn means heavy manipulation of public "desires" and almost always involves politics and coercion.

Small scale production, though, can mean a great reduction in drudgery as well as interesting possibilities in barter. By means of jigs and other simple fixtures that you can figure out yourself, you can be freed from having to measure each part. Hold the piece of wood against the jig and hit it with the drill and all the holes will be in exactly the same place in each part. (See *Jigs and Fixtures,* p. 163).
We've mass-produced thousands of dome struts and parts for conventional construction. We've also produced simple looms and the aforementioned pumps (which we bartered for a fleet of rafts and got into the whitewater river running business), solar collector parts, signs (during an anti-freeway fight), toys, boxes, electronic parts, concrete forms, fence rails, adobe blocks, tents, shelving, lighting systems, and model parts, to name but a few. The ability to get on a small production run frees you from dependence on larger less efficient manufacturers, their prices, specifications and schedules. It can be rather fun, too, if it doesn't go on for too long. "Shop Yoga," we sometimes call it.

And it can be done without sophisticated expensive equipment if you take the time to think it all out first. The thinking is the most powerful part. You can actually <u>change</u> some things out there! Maybe not in a big way, but certainly at a scale that you can understand. You will find that as you work, your understanding of technology will increase a bit, and your fears based on ignorance will decrease. (Your fears based on newfound understanding might well increase, but that's another paper.) In a modest way, you can combat the "machines taking over" by having better control of the technology you live with. It's a good feeling. ■

THE RISING SUN
NEIGHBORHOOD NEWSLETTER

Mystics seem to do the creation story backwards — God goes from light to people, they go from people to light.

Garrett Wade Company

For the livin' end in catalogs of expensive professional woodworking tools take a look at this! The studio color photographs give a good feel of the high quality (though I admit that even Globemaster tools would look good shown in this context). The contrast with your Local Hardware Store is obvious and deadly. I hold such catalogs in high regard not only for their yummy contents, but for their educational value; the accurate descriptions together with the sharp illustrations show what's available and what the tools do, and thus can inspire the craftsperson to assume new responsibilities. For further guidance, see **The Garrett Wade Book of Woodworking Tools** *(p. 162).* —*J. Baldwin*

(More woodcarving tools, p. 249.)

Garret Wade Company, Inc.
Catalog

$1 postpaid from:
Garrett Wade Co., Inc.
161 Avenue of the Americas
New York, NY 10014

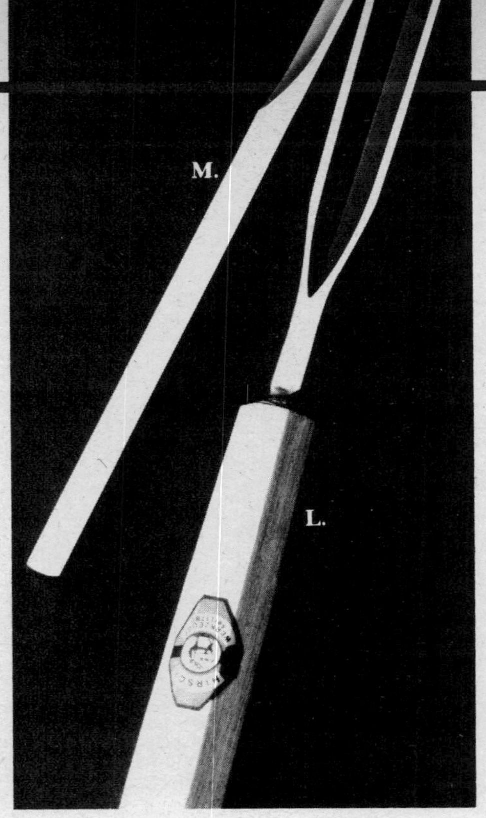

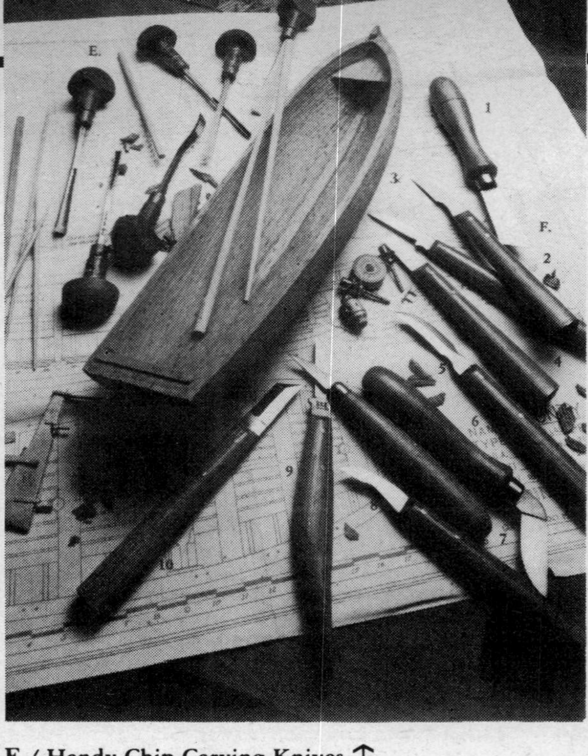

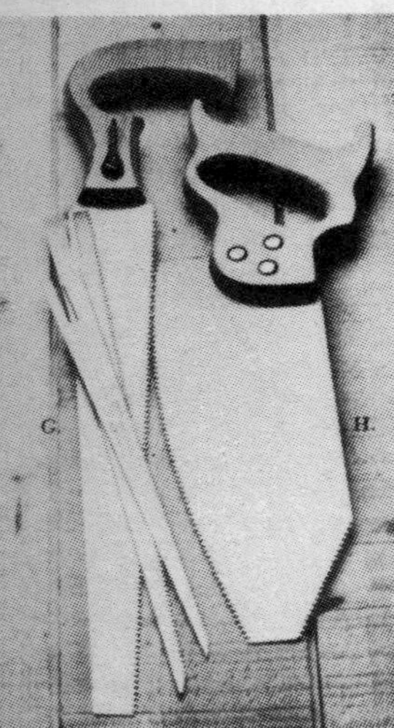

G / Nest of Saws ←
Same fine Sheffield steel as used in the Compass Saw. The polished Beech handle has a lever fitting for quick blade removal. Supplied with two "keyhole" blades (10" and 12"—10 and 8 teeth per inch respectively) and a 15½" squared off blade (7 teeth per inch) for more general cutting. A very versatile tool for home and shop.

87I02.01 Nest of Saws **$12.80**

H / Flooring Saw ←
Polished Beech handle. Hardened and tempered Sheffield steel. Blade is 13" long. Designed to cut into boards and panels without using a drilled hole to start. 7 teeth per inch. The angle of the saw edge on the upper side allows you to cut to the bottom of a panel or board working in an upright position. This is a very useful tool for those who do construction and framing work.

87I04.01 Flooring Saw **$17.90**

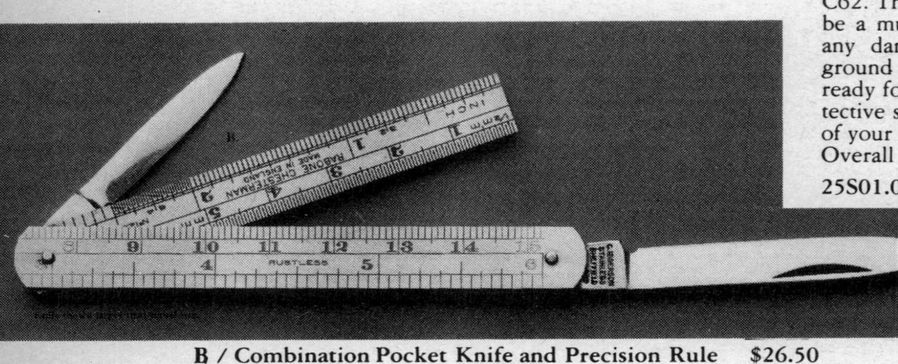

B / Combination Pocket Knife and Precision Rule $26.50

L / Large Corner Chisel ↑
For those craftsmen who need a corner chisel larger than the ⅜" size, this new mortising tool is fitted with a White Beech handle. For mortises 9/16" wide and larger. The bevel is ground on the inside so you can cut absolutely square clean corners. The edge is ground to shape, but may require some honing to achieve a final working edge. 10" long overall.

70S01.01 Large Corner Chisel **$26.20**

M / Cabinetmaker's Corner Chisel ↑
Hand-made to very precise standards for Garrett Wade by a small American firm, these all steel chisels are designed with a cabinetmaker's needs in mind. ⅜" on a side, the cutting end is hardened to a very hard Rockwell C62. The striking end is tempered separately to be a much milder Rockwell C54 to eliminate any danger of chipping. Precision in-cannel ground to exactly 90° and honed very sharp ready for use, each chisel comes in its own protective sheath. This will ensure that the corners of your mortises will be clean, crisp and square. Overall length 7½".

25S01.01 Corner Chisel **$23.80**

F / Handy Chip Carving Knives ↑
It's surprising how much easier it is to do the work you want with the right tools. These very attractive, splendid knives are for chip carving or whittling. Conveniently shaped and comfortable to use. Fine German steel will give years of satisfying use. Polished White Beech handles. Overall length about 6".

1.) 06D01.01—10.) 06D01.10		**$ 4.90 each**
06C01.10	10 Knife Set	**$46.10**
06C02.05	5 Knife Set (#3, 5, 7, 8 & 10)	**$23.00**

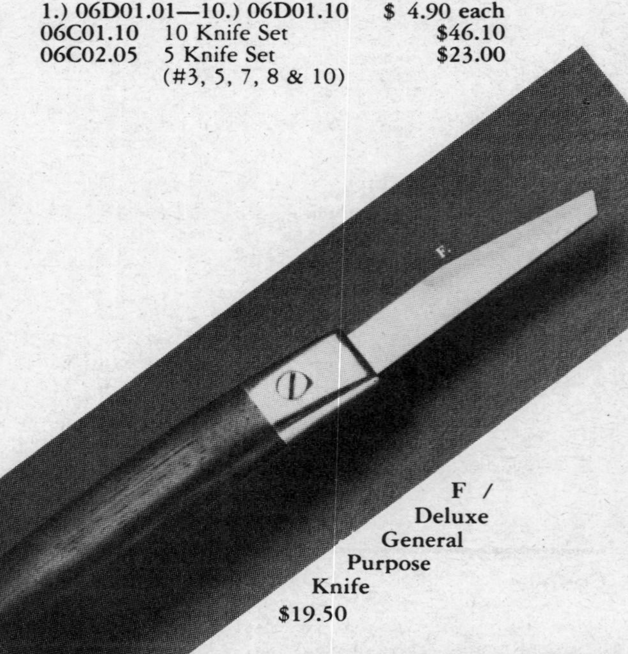

F / Deluxe General Purpose Knife $19.50

Frog Tools

Typical of an increasing number of small specialty shops that feature the finest tools available. Their selection is wider in some areas than the larger outfits. We've had good reader reports on these people. —*J. Baldwin*

Frog Tools
Catalog

$1 postpaid from:
Frog Tool Co. Ltd.
700 W. Jackson Blvd.
Chicago, IL 60606

↑ DEBARKING TOOL
Large blade takes off bark FAST. Flat blade 5½" wide, forged German steel with socket for handle. Less handle.

882A28 **$17.50 ppd.**

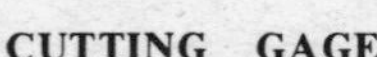

CUTTING GAGE
Made of beechwood with a cutting knife held in place by a small brass chuck . Plastic tightening screw.

650G3 ↓ **$6.50 ppd.**

BRASS FINGER PLANES
Solid brass instrument makers planes can be used wherever wood needs to be shaped. Such as with stringed musical instruments, wood carvings and sculptured furniture. They are not toys and remove a surprising amount of wood in a short time. The planes in the whale series have slightly convex bottoms - their blade angles are about 40 degrees for normal planing. The fish series have very low angles, about 12 degrees, and flat bottoms for smooth cuts on end grain. Each piece is well constructed with a brushed brass finish and ebony wedges to hold tool steel blades in place. They are well worth the money.

SALE Buy any three planes and give yourself a 10% discount.

WHALE SERIES

Cat. No.	Length	Blade Width	Price
5W5	1⅜"	⅜"	$23.20 ppd.
5W6	1¾"	½"	$24.40 ppd.
5W7	2⅛"	⅝"	$27.00 ppd.

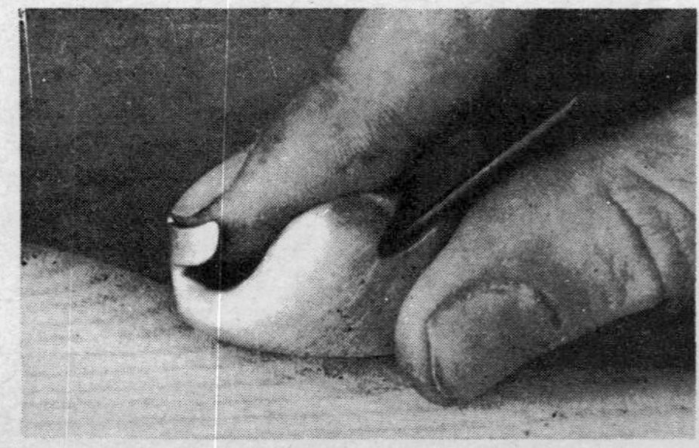

ADZ ↑
For hewing timber surfaces such as heavy posts and beams or ships' keels and timbers. Eye tapered so handle may be removed for sharpening. Has pin on poll for driving leftover nails or screws, saving sharp edge. Forged German tool steel blade 3¾" wide. Supplied with 32" handle.

882E4 **$37.40 ppd.**

REAMER AWL →
A four sided shaft 1¾" long x ⅛" with a beechwood handle and solid brass ferrule. Used for starting holes for screws and for drilling and making holes larger.

655N3 **$3.60 ppd.**

ADJUSTABLE MOUTH SPOKESHAVE
Mouth is adjustable to plane against the grain or to produce very fine work. Cast iron body. 10" length, 2 1/16" cutter.

808H22 **$9.20 ppd.**
808B22 Spare blade for 53H5 **$2.30 ppd.**

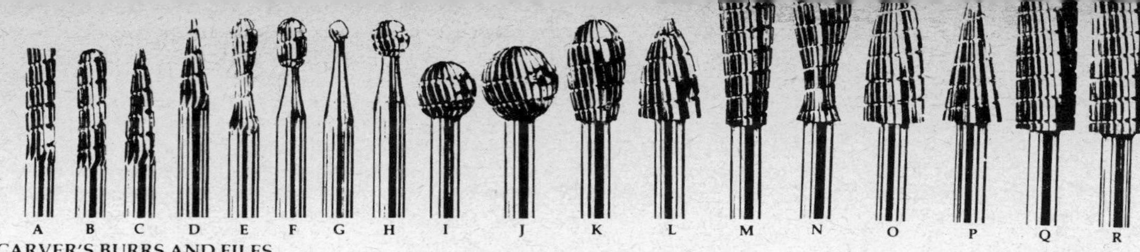

CARVER'S BURRS AND FILES
Set of 18 pieces, mounted in a wooden base, especially for use with the Foredom Flexible Shaft Tool. Carbon steel. Shank diameter 6mm (¼").
09V30-BR Set of 18 **$86.20 ppd.**

Burrs also available individually. Specify stock number. 09V30-BR and style, e.g., A, B, etc.
Styles A-G **$3.80 each ppd.**
Styles H-R **$6.80 each ppd.**

Woodcraft Supply

Though this catalog looks rather like that of rival Garrett Wade, Woodcraft stocks a number of items found no place else. We've heard a few reader complaints about their service recently, but not of their quality. I shop both catalogs when I need high quality woodworking tools.
—J. Baldwin

Woodcraft Supply
Catalog
$1 postpaid from:
Woodcraft Supply Corp.
313 Montvale Avenue
Woburn, MA 01801

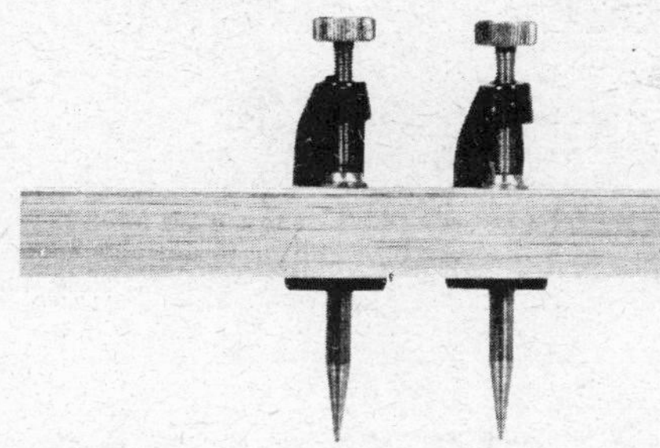

TRAMMEL HEADS
A useful tool for scribing circles or arcs which are beyond the capacity of dividers. They are very easy to control because of the short (35mm) points, and because of the automatic perpendicular setting in relation to the workpiece. A pencil may be inserted in place of one of the points. Will take a wood beam up to (33mm) 1⁵⁄₁₆" in thickness. Japanned finish.
16O31-EG **$10.10 ppd.**

← SLICK
When a large area must be pared down, nothing is more efficient than a slick. The long, hardwood handle affords a variety of grips for power as one hand guides the cut. Blade width 48mm (1⅞"); Length of blade and socket 250mm (10").
06V61-X **$42.75 ppd.**

KENT HEWING AXE
The blade of this general purpose axe is sharpened on both sides, like a knife edge, and evenly tapered. It is equipped with a heavy square poll, and the handle is generally, but not always, set straight. Widely used for rough shaping of all kinds by carpenters, shipbuilders, ← wheelwrights, and others. Weight 5 lbs., with a 152mm (6") cutting edge. Unhandled.
11W41-FE **$24.30 ppd.**

Straight handle (34") for 11W41-FE.
15F31-CA **$7.80 ppd.**

↓ CROOKED KNIFE
A traditional finishing instrument, used to shape and to carve wood which has been rough cut by an axe or froe. Many craftspeople find it easier to work with than a drawknife because it is held by one hand and, like a whittling knife in the hands of a woodcarver, it becomes an extension of the arm and hand. Blade is 16mm (⅝") wide and 123mm (8") in overall length. Supplied unhandled with instructions for fashioning a wooden handle to suit the user's need.
04R51-IJ **$4.95 ppd.**

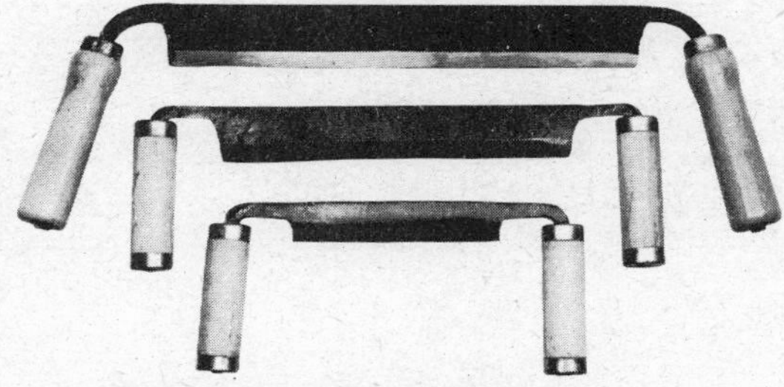

AMERICAN DRAWKNIVES
Hand-made of high quality carbon steel, the blade is ground straight across and tapered from the back to the edge. The tang ends extend completely through the handle and peened over for a tight fit and durability. This is a heavy-duty drawknife and a favorite among post and beam builders and loggers.

	Blade dimensions	
11A02-SN	6" x 1¼"	**$21.50 ppd.**
11A03-SN	10" x 1½"	**$23.75 ppd.**
11A04-SN	13¼" x 2"	**$31.65 ppd.**

Brookstone

Long a source of unusual and hard to find tools, Brookstone is famous for impeccable service and the best guarantee around: if you don't like the item, send it back. I've bought many things from them and have nothing but praise for the hardware and the service. Before buying, you should check one of the big hardware catalogs such as Silvo or U.S. General — Brookstone prices are highish. Their recent stocking of "gift items" sort of stuff doesn't seem to have hurt anything.
—J. Baldwin

Brookstone
Catalog
free from:
Brookstone Company
127 Vose Farm Road
Peterborough, NH 03458

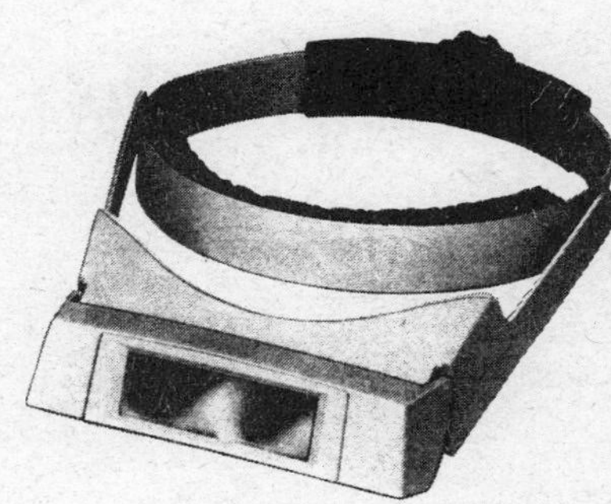

Lightweight Headband Magnifier Concentrates Your Vision On Tiny Details

Fits comfortably over your head, enlarges miniature or detailed work 1¾ times so it's easily visible. Lens holder adjusts to any position, swings up and out of the way when not needed. Even works with eyeglasses. Working distance about 8" to 14".
Used extensively by modelmakers, jewelers, tool and die makers, dentists, hobbyists, repairmen.
Single-lens design eliminates the distracting centerpost found in other models, means clearer vision with less strain. Of optical quality, shatter resistant acrylic. ABS plastic headband with comfort cushion adjusts to any size.
F-3510 Headband magnifier **$14.95**

Breast Drill L-e-a-n-s Into The Hardest Work

For *tough* drilling jobs, the breast drill lets you provide needed *extra* pressure with your chest. It's a favorite of mechanics and craftsmen for drilling into plate steel or the hardest woods.
A novel feature of this English-made drill is that its round wooden handle is interchangeable with the flat metal breast plate. Merely loosen a set screw, remove the wooden handle, and fit the breast plate in its place. Reverse the process when you wish to use it as a hand drill.
All moving parts are precision machined; the body is die cast for extra strength. Double pinion gears provide rigidity and smoothness of action. A ⅜" Jacobs chuck assures dead-center drilling. About 13¾" overall. Chuch key and hex wrench provided.
A beautifully made drill, carefully engineered for maximum utility and years of service.
F-7387 Breast drill **$29.95**

One-Hand "C" Clamps Adjust Automatically →

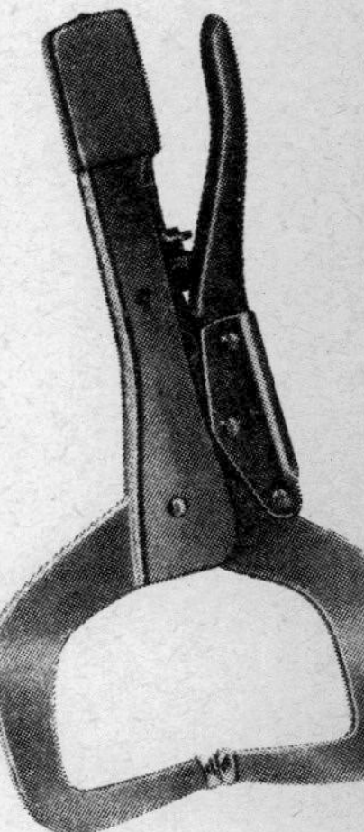

The only clamp we know that needs but one hand for size adjustment and pressure. Merely position it around the work and squeeze handles shut. Automatically "sizes" and locks itself in place. The amount of tension applied is adjusted by a small thumbscrew.
The 8" model is about 7⅝" long with a jaw opening of 1¼"; the 12" model is about 11¾" long with an opening of 2½". All steel parts are nickel-plated; the handles have comfortable vinyl grips.
F-7166 One-hand clamp, 8" **$8.75**
F-7167 One-hand clamp, 12" **$11.95**

Conover

This modest collection of woodworker's tools features heavy duty industrial grade wood shop machinery of the sort not often seen these days. One table saw has a gas engine option!
—J. Baldwin

Conover
Catalog
free from:
Conover Woodcraft Specialties, Inc.
18125 Madison Road
Parkman, Ohio 44080

Twelve inch Long Bed Industrial Joiner
A Joiner your grandchildren will rave about

• →

Battleship gray in color, it is easy to mistake this Joiner for an aircraft carrier. Heavy, rugged constuction and the finest of quality and workmanship, make this machine a real buy. The cutterhead is fully 12" long, and incorporates three high speed steel knives as standard equipment. The knives are also 1/8" wider than standard. This extra grind stock allows for more sharpenings. Also included is a jig for aligning the blades to uniform height. The cutterhead turns at 5000 RPMs and is powered by a 2 H.P. single phase motor.

Both the infeed and outfeed tables on this Joiner are surface ground and adjustable. Adjustable outfeed table makes blade setting simpler and accommodates unusual joinery such as tapers. Surface grinding means that this machine will turn out work which is really flat. With a 58" overall length, long lumber can be accommodated. The cast iron fence is also surface ground and is adjustable three ways.

Specifications
Twelve Inch Long Bed Industrial Joiner,
Construction: Solid cast iron throughout.
Motor: 2 H.P. Single Phase 110/220 Volts with full electrics.
Infeed Table: Surface ground 28⅜" x 12⅝".
Outfeed Table: Surface ground 28½" x 12".
Overall Length: 58".
Fence: Surface ground 35½" x 4".
Height of Table: 29".
Cutterhead: 12", high speed with three knives.
Blades: High speed steel.
Weight: 550 pounds.
Shipping Weight: 726 pounds.
Twelve Inch Long Bed Joiner with full electrics and knife adjusting jig **$2100.00** FOB Parkman, Ohio.

THE RISING SUN
NEIGHBORHOOD NEWSLETTER

An orchestra is deceptive. It doesn't sound like elbows and ties. Maybe an ecstatic furry dinosaur humming to itself or an overgrown garden hooked up to an amp.

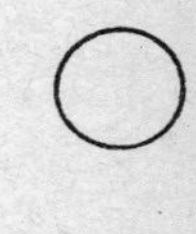

Silvo Hardware

Tools tools tools tools. Brand names. Mostly good stuff. Several quality levels on almost all items. If you know what you want, it is probably here. Prices good, sometimes better than U.S. General these days. I have been pleased by their service on returned items. —Fred Richardson

Silvo Hardware
Catalog

$1 postpaid from:
Silvo Hardware Company
Department WEC
2205 Richmond Street
Philadelphia, PA 19125

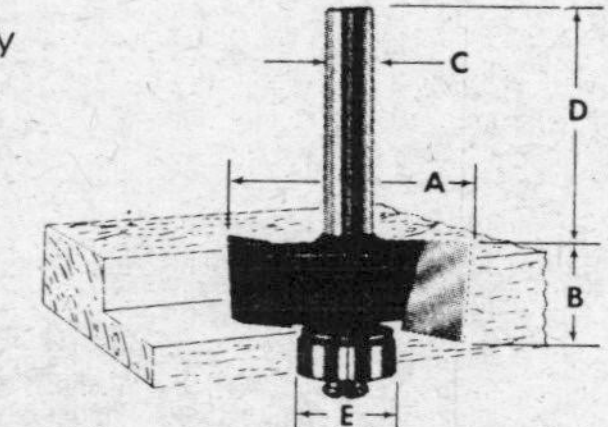

Stanley Forming Rabbeting Bit—Two flutes for fast, smooth rabbeting cuts without use of router guide.
85218M-S20 A=1¼, B=½ **Rabbet width ⅜"** **$20.59**

Carpenters Adze — Another traditional craftsmen's tool with many applications in shaping and finishing wood. Forged from tool steel in Europe, our adze is further enhanced by the fitted 32" white, bowed ash handle.
83B-70-K1 P—8 lbs. **$36.90**

No. 450 Speedy Sprayer Mobile Tank Outfit — Automatic, with motor. Twin diaphragm compressor is mounted on 12 gal. tank for constant air supply. Rubber tired wheels; sturdy handle is quickly removable. Diaphragms and bearings need no lubrication, assuring oil-free air. Complete with air shut-off cock, pressure gauge, pressure switch set at 30-45 PSI, 15 ft. air hose and tire chuck; No. 331 multi-purpose spray gun uses 1 qt. cup or 2½ gal. paint tank. Air delivery 4 CFM at 35 PSI, 6.8 CFM air displacement, 50 PSI safety valve setting. ¼ in. IPS thread. ½ HP, 110V. 60 cy. AC capacitor motor.
450-M17 H—100 lbs. **$231.25**

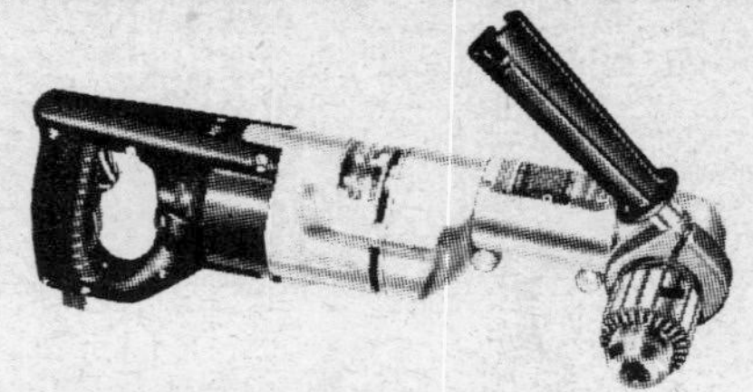

Milwaukee Right Angle Drill Kits—No. 3102-1 Plumbers Kit Contains: No. 1101-1, **500 RPM—Heavy Duty** ½" reversing drill, No. 48-06-2871 reversing Angle Drive, wrench, chuck remover bar, side handle and No. 48-55-0085 steel carrying case. RPM of Drill only 600—RPM with right angle drive—low side 335—high side 750 RPM.
3102-1-M9 P—22 lbs. . . **(APL) Tool—$180.00**

Nicholas Carpenter's Waist Apron—Deluxe Extra H. D. — 10 pocket 2 Bag Split leg canvas and leather — Canvas web belt and buckle adjusts to 46" waist — Leather hammer loops on both sides — All pockets double stitched and copper riveted at stress points
C26-M4 P—1 lb. **$5.89**

No. 90098 Stanley 1 H.P. Shop Router—Heavy Duty—Minimum size and weight for one-hand operation (Motor dia. 3⁹⁄₁₆"). 25,000 RPMs for fast, clean cutting (laminate trimming). ¼" collet. All sealed Ball Bearing, Flat top housing for fast, easy bit setting. Recessed toggle switch. Two-wrench bit changing. Universal A.C. Motor, 120V, 6 Amps. Net weight 5⅞ lbs. **Note:** 90098 Router accepts same router accessories as 90088 Router (templet and router guides, plane attachments etc.).
90098-S20 P—7 lbs. .... **(APL) Tool—$87.50**

Maza Small Bench Anvil — So useful you'll wonder how you managed without! Comes with 4 base holes for mounting on work bench/table. Made from cast iron, it has great strength for bending, flattening, straightening, forming etc. Indispensable for the model maker and home workshop. Measures 5¼ x 1¾ with height of 2½".
111-M6A P—3 lbs. **$4.98**

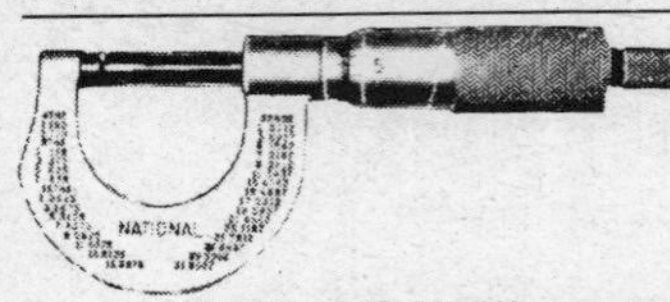

National O-1" Micrometer — Full finished frame with decimal equivalents. Satin finish thruout with easy to read black graduations. Friction thimble for more sensitive pressure. Fully adjustable for wear. 1/1000 readings. With instructions.
102-G5 P—1 lb. **$8.98**

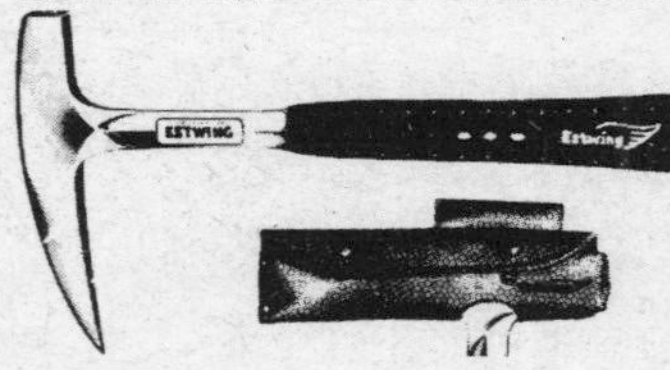

Estwing Rock Pick — Solid Steel — **Nylon Grip — Pointed Tip** —
E3-22P-E6 22 oz. **$12.39**

Leather Belt Sheath — for above Pointed Tip Rock Pick.
LBS-E6 Sheath **$2.65**

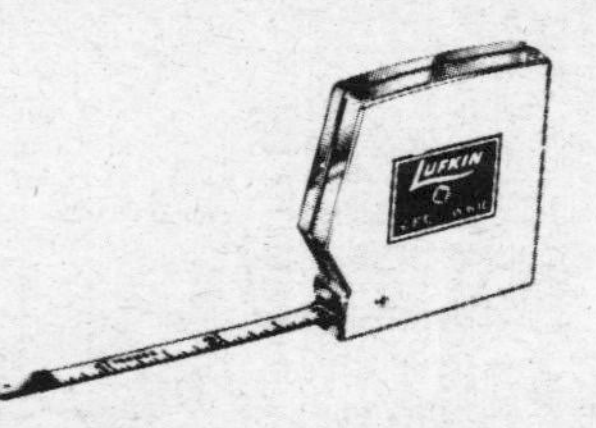

Lufkin Pee Wee Tape — White clad —for the pocket, purse, sewing basket or desk drawer. Case is chrome plated and measures only 1¾-inches square. Blade is only ¼-inch wide, black graduations on white background. Graduated consecutively inches to 16ths — first 12-inches to 32nds. Foot figures are in red and 16-inch stud centers are indicated. Graduations last longer due to tough, transparent epoxy coating covering entire blade.
W616-L7 ¼" x 6 ft. **$1.59**
W6110-L7 ¼" x 10 ft. **$2.29**

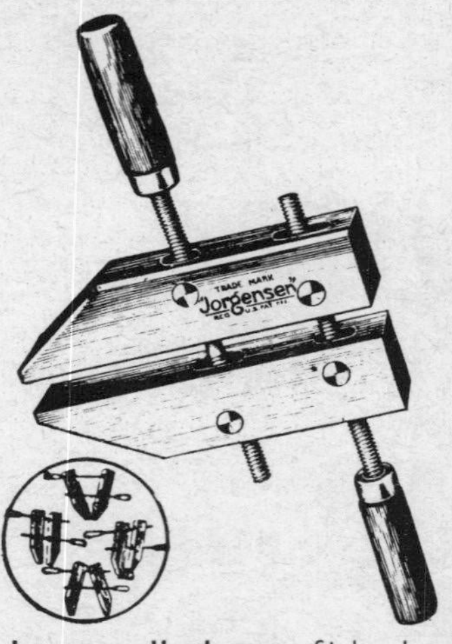

Jorgensen Handscrews—Style J—adjustable to any angle—Jaws of carefully selected and seasoned hard maple, perfect grain, oil finished and tested. Spindles and nuts are special analysis cold drawn steel with special rapid type threads. Hard maple handles with extra heavy steel ferrules.
J=length of jaws. O = Opening between jaws.

5/0 A2	1 lb.	J—4"	O—2"	$6.69
4/0-A2	1 lb.	J—5"	O-2½"	$7.19
3/0-A2	2 lbs.	J—6"	O—3"	$7.69
2/0-A2	2 lbs.	J—7"	O-3½	$8.29
0-A2	2 lbs.	J—8"	O—4½"	$8.89
1-A2	3 lbs.	J—10"	O—6"	$10.12
2-A2	4 lbs.	J—12"	O—8½	$11.69
3-A2	6 lbs.	J—14"	0-10"	$14.79

Stanley Bevels — Hardwood handle with handy grip, brass tips and locking device. Black finish on blade.
25TB-S19 8" Blade **$5.59**

No. 7554 Rockwell X.H.D. Drill—½" "D" handle Reversing. 920 Watts. 8 Amp Motor. S 500 RPM. ½" chuck with Capacity of ½ steel and 1¾" in wood. 3 stage Gear re tion. Net weight 7½ lbs. 15¾" long.
7554-R7 P—11 lbs. .... **(APL) Tool—$16**

An exceptionally well made gauge consisting of 51 pitches; V, American National and U.S. Standard. 60° threads, pitches 4 to 84.

General Screw Pitch Gauge
251-G5 has 51 pitches **$11.25**

Milwaukee H.D. Polisher—Ball and Roller bearings—wih exclusive spring loaded drive mechanism—Prevents harmful backlash shock of unbalanced pads to drive mechanism—won't slip under load—greatly extends gear life. **7" Dia. Cat. No. 5450** Lightweight polisher, 1750 RPM used with standard liquid polishes. Standard equipment includes rubber backing pad, disc nut and polish pad. 120 Volts, 9 Amps, 14½" long, Net wt. 9¼ lbs.
5450-M9 P—16 lbs. ... **(APL) Tool—$169.00**

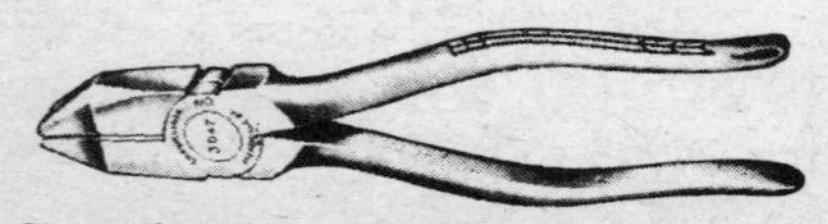

Channellock Linemen's Pliers—Bevel nose, side cutters—with **Plastic Grips.**
3046G-C6 6" long **$6.49**
3047G-C6 7" long **$6.79**
3048½G-C6 8½" long **$7.98**

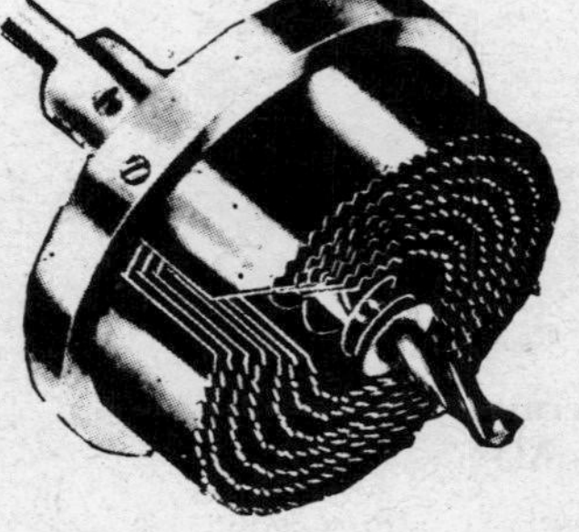

"ARCO HOLE-SAW" (7 Hole Saws In One)—Has new Automatic "Slug-Ejector" for faster work than any other hole saw. Cuts 1", 1¼", 1½", 1¾", 2", 2¼" & 2½" holes thru any ¾" stock. Zips thru wood, plastics, metals, formica, etc. 7 Circular blades slip into grooves in Tool Head and are easily exchanged. Safety-lock screw prevents blades from "jumping-out". Consists of Alloy Tool Head, 7 quality shatter-proof blades, "Slug-Ejector" and ¼" drill bit.
650-S6 P—1 lb. **$9.95**

Kennedy Tool Box — Lift-out tray with middle compartment 18½ x 7⅝ in. Two small compartments, one each end, 2½ x 7⅝ in. Will handle long screw drivers, pipe wrenches, saws, ripping chisels, wrecking bars, masonry drills, extension bars, levels and special tools. Piano type continuous hinge; draw bolt hasp and staple for padlock. Dark brown ripple baked enamel finish; tray in smooth green enamel.
K24-K3 P—17 lbs. 24" long **$26.69**

Miller Falls Mitre Box — with 4" x 16" back saw. Adjustable. Sturdy steel and wood construction. Heavy pressed steel back ribbed for extra strength. Die cast guide post holds steel saw guides. Positive depth lock, adjustable 0" to 3". Accurate angle cuts 0° to 50° with graduated index plate and quick-acting lock. Lacquered hardwood bed. Holes in steel legs for bench fastening. Front legs "lipped" for bench stops when sawing. Accommodates standard hand or back saw.
1816-M18 P—8 lbs. **$29.98**

BEAR MULTI-OILSTONE is the most popular choice of hotel and motel kitchens, restaurants, markets and hospitals for complete sharpening of all cutlery. This combination of three oil-filled reversible stones includes sharp CRYSTOLON Coarse, CRYSTOLON Medium and precision-cutting INDIA Fine. The two stones not in use are immersed in oil. Heavy non-skid base. Lubricate with BEAR Oil. Price includes pint can of Bear Oil.
1M313-B5 P—16 lbs. Stone size is 11½ x 2½ x ½" **$67.98**

Diamond Glass Cutter — This truly professional tool embraces polished rosewood handle, brass stem head, breaker rack for 4 thicknesses of glass and finest industrial cutting diamond. Ideal for mirrors up to ¼" thick, plate glass, antique, stained and very hard glass. The swivel head facilitates curved, template or free hand cutting and the handle has a ball end for tapping. The additional cost of this polished diamond cutter is quickly recovered by savings of broken glass and the longer life than wheel cutters. You will quickly recognize the value of razor sharp cutting action too!
1002-T4 .... **$17.50**

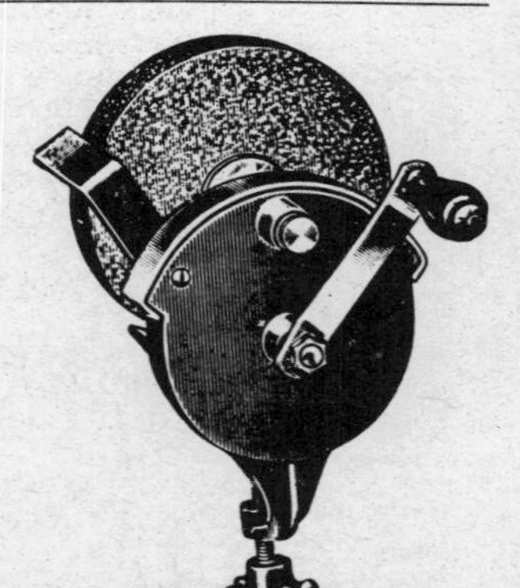

Hand Grinder — Heavy Duty Cast Iron, extra long bearings, machine cut gears wheel size 6" x 1".
U6-P15 P—7 lbs. **$13.98**

U.S. General Supply Corporation

A fabulous array of tools, arranged in a way that is easy to peruse, graded by "homeowner", "mechanic", and "industrial" quality, fairly priced, and delivered by mail without hassle. I shop here a lot and have never been unsatisfied. As with Silvo, their arch-rival, you should compare prices locally so you don't feel silly seeing the thing you just ordered offered for twenty bucks less at the spring True Value sale downtown. The General has a little tricky price thing in the catalog: the "price" isn't. The number after the W in the stock number, is.

—J. Baldwin

U.S. General Supply Corporation
Catalog

$1 postpaid from:
U.S. General
Supply Corporation
100 General Place
Department WE
Jericho, NY 11753

QUICK-CLIP SPEED CUTTER

Cuts Thread, Cloth, Paper, Flowers Tapes

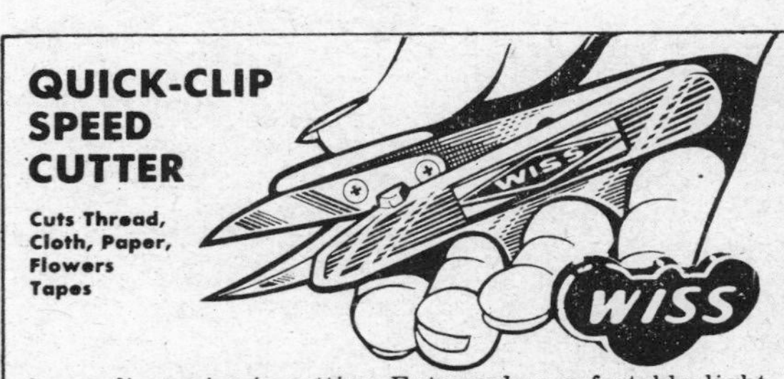

A new dimension in cutting. Extremely comfortable; lightweight. Sturdy Delrin frame. Stainless steel blades with extra sharp points. Hidden spring reopens blades after each cut.
314-1573W470 .... $6.25

NEW! OSBORNE CANVAS & LEATHER STRETCHING TOOL

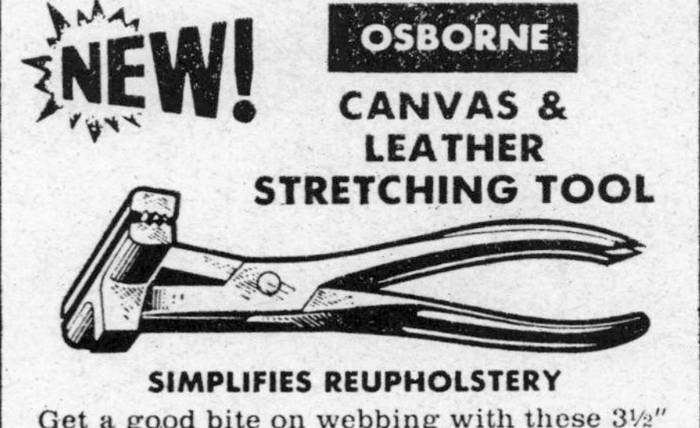

SIMPLIFIES REUPHOLSTERY
Get a good bite on webbing with these 3½" jaws! Also useful for stretching canvas, leather and other fabrics. Hammer jaw and tack puller in handle make this a great all-around tool for upholsterers. Length 8¾". Weighs 1 lb. 2 oz.
226-250W899 .... $10.91

NAIL HAMMERS One Piece Solid Steel Head, Handle

LEATHER HANDLE GRIP

STRAIGHT CLAW
215-16SW1265 (16-oz.) $13.98
215-20SW1380 (20-oz.) 15.50

CURVED CLAW
215-16CW1265 (16-oz.) $13.98
215-20CW1380 (20-oz.) 15.50

16" RAFTER/FRAMING

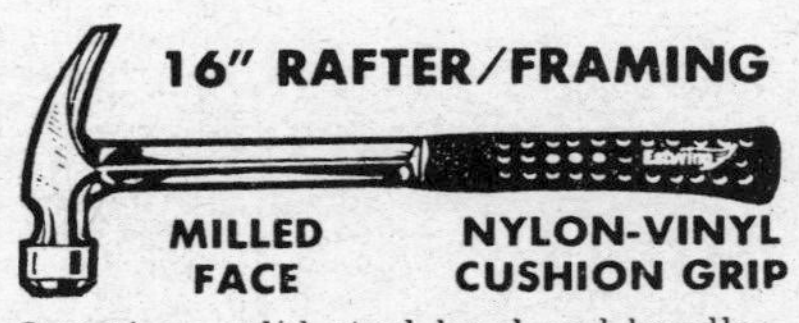

MILLED FACE **NYLON-VINYL CUSHION GRIP**
One-piece solid steel head and handle—strongest construction ever! Milled face resists slipping on impact; nail goes in straight. Straight claw. Fully polished.
215-322SMW1649 (22-oz.) $18.30
215-328SMW1749 (28-oz.) 19.44

MASON/TILE SETTER **20 Oz.**

NYLON-VINYL CUSHION GRIP
The perfect masonry tool. One-piece solid steel head and handle—the strongest construction known.
215-320BLW1380 .... $15.40

Milwaukee RIGHT-ANGLE DRIVE KITS INDUSTRIAL QUALITY Ball & Roller Bearings

½" DRILL

2 SPEEDS
- **HIGH (Small Holes)**
- **LOW (Large Holes)**

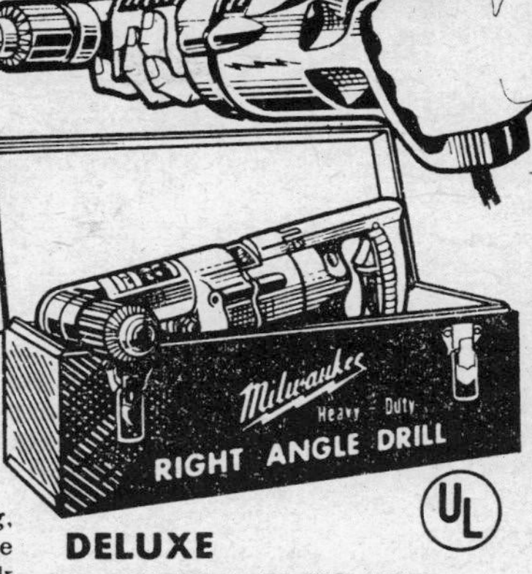

Designed to use as a straight drill or with the right-angle drive to drill between joists and other hard-to-reach areas. With right-angle drive, drills have two speeds—high for small holes, low for large ones.

PROFESSIONAL PLUMBER'S KIT
Kit contains 500 RPM reversing, heavy-duty ½" drill, right angle drive, wrench, side handle, chuck remover bar and steel carrying case.
B107-31021W16275 (Complete Kit) $175.00
Same as above with **350 RPM Reversing** Heavy Duty ½" Drill
B107-32021W16275 (Complete Kit) $175.00

DELUXE ELECTRICIAN'S KIT
Kit contains 600 RPM reversing heavy-duty ½" drill, right angle drive, wrench, chuck remover bar, side handle and steel carrying case.
B107-30021W15255 (Complete Kit) $164.00

NEW! GREENLEE CARVER'S MALLET ENGLISH BEECH HEAD

HEFTY 1-Lb.
FOCUSES ITS WEIGHT BEHIND THE STRIKING SURFACE
Comfortable hardwood handle. 3¾" head dia., 8¼" long. Made in England.
245-3540W1180 .... $13.80

"GUILDMASTER" Imported from Sweden **SANDVIK**

Professional quality, made of Swedish charcoal alloy steel, fully taper-ground. Ship-point. High-crown tooth line. Extra polished blade. Laminated plywood handle.
219-271W1525 (26"—8 or 10 Pt.) $16.95

SAVE ELECTRICITY, MONEY AND TIME

PUT A "BULB MISER" IN EVERY SOCKET

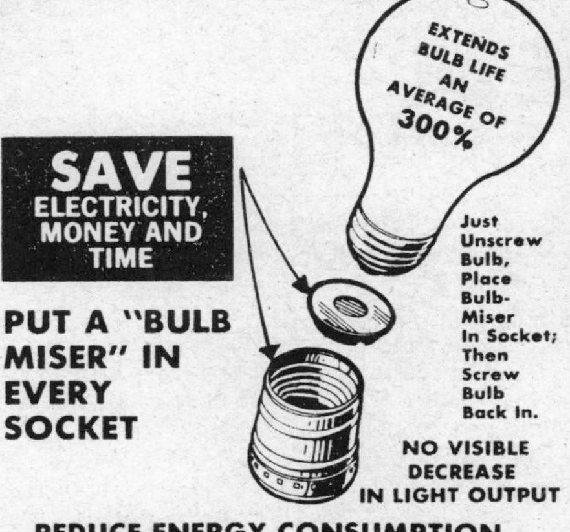

REDUCE ENERGY CONSUMPTION
Bulb-Misers act as thermal shock absorbers to let the filament heat up slowly . . . and thus prevent burnout. They actually extend the life of incandescent bulbs an average of 300%. And they reduce the consumption of electricity without any visible decrease in light. Easy to install . . . never wear out. Developed during NASA's Apollo Moon Program.
539-3W549 (Pkg. of 3) $6.20

MECHANICS QUALITY 5" 2.6 Amps **INDUSTRIAL QUALITY 6"** 4.4 Amps

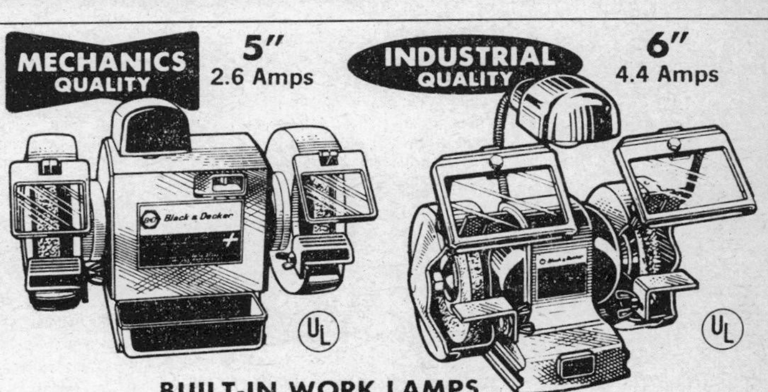

BUILT-IN WORK LAMPS
Grind . . . polish . . . clean . . . sharpen . . . these are the tools for the job! Adjustable lamps put light right on your workpiece. Tool rests adjust for angle. Positive clamps; removable end covers. ON-OFF switch. 3600 RPM, 120V, AC. Grinding wheel and wirewheel brush included.

5" 1/4 HP BENCH GRINDER . . . SLEEVE BEARINGS
2.6 Amps. ¾" wheel width. Sleeve bearings. Adjustable eye shields. 6-ft. cord, water tray.
B101-7912W4480 (¼ HP Grinder) $48.07

6" 1/2 HP BENCH GRINDER . . . BALL BEARINGS
4.4 Amps. ⅝" wheel width. Ball bearings. Individual eye shields. Two adjustable spark shields. 6-ft. cord.
B101-7917W13275 (½ HP Grinder) $156.03

THE RISING SUN
NEIGHBORHOOD NEWSLETTER

The nice thing about the way they make bombs is disarmament can be an issue of local interest for almost everyone. It goes like this:

All nuclear bombs and the nuclear parts of nuclear bombs are designed in
Livermore, California and Los Alamos, New Mexico

The plutonium that would explode comes from reactors in
Hanford, Washington and Savannah River, South Carolina

The plutonium parts of nuclear bombs are put together at
Rocky Flats, Colorado upwind of Denver

Non-nuclear parts of nuclear bombs are designed at
Livermore, California and Albuquerque, New Mexico by Sandia Corp., part of Western Electric, part of AT&T

Electric and electro magnetic parts of nuclear bombs are made in
Kansas City, Missouri by Bendix Corporation

Detonators are made in
Miamisburg, Ohio by Monsanto Corporation and Miamisburg Mound Space Laboratory

Neutron generators are made in
Pinellas, Florida

Bombs are made from all these parts being put together in
Pantex, Texas and Burlington, Iowa by Mason and Hanger-Silas Mason, Inc.

Old bombs do not die. When outdated by new bombs they are stored in
Manano Mountain, New Mexico near Albuquerque

or taken apart in
Pantex, Texas or Burlington, Iowa

The plutonium taken out of dismantled bombs goes back to
Rocky Flats, Colorado

Isn't it exciting to think of all those nuclear parts of nuclear bombs going on planes and trucks and trains all over the country?

The really neat chart I don't think exists is of all these places and the accidents that have happened there — the big fire at Rocky Flats, the earthquake at Livermore — and the health record of employees and people who live nearby and the local groups organizing against, if any, and the number of direct and indirect jobs provided and a map of the commonly used transportation routes for radioactive stuff between the sites and stuff like that.

— All information about where it's all made from *Local Hazard: Global Threat: Rocky Flats Nuclear Weapons Plant*, available for $1 from Rocky Flats Action Group, 1428 Lafayette Street, Denver, Colorado 80218

Woodline: The Japan Woodworker

For exquisite woodworking with exquisite tools, you can do no better than with Japanese techniques and implements, the product of centuries of carefulness. Woodline has the best such tools available in America, many of them far finer than our skills can make use of yet. It's an interesting experience to be shamed by a tool. The catalog includes a number of high quality non-exotic items such as bow saws, good Arkansas sharpening stones, etc. —SB

Woodline
(The Japan Woodworker)
Catalog

$1 postpaid from:
Woodline Tool
and Supply Corporation
1004 Central Avenue
Alameda, CA 94501

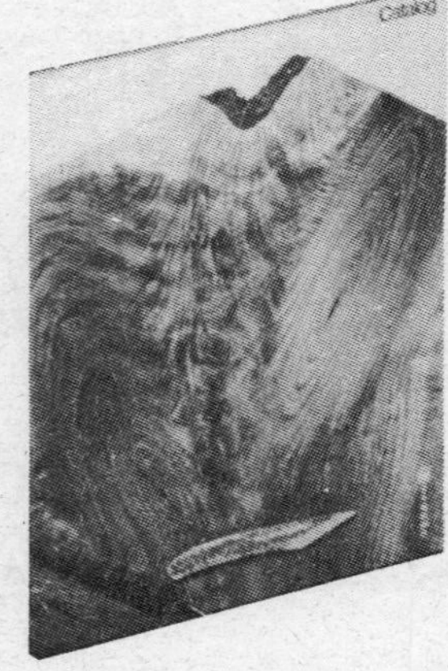

↓

Japanese saws are unlike Western saws in several respects. They cut on the pull stroke, which gives greater control and accuracy. Since the saw is in tension when cutting, the blade can be much thinner and tempered to a greater hardness. All of our professional Japanese saws test between 52 - 54 on the Rockwell C Scale. These saws can be given a razor-like edge.

Because of the thinness and brittleness of the blade, extreme care should be exercised when using these saws. *Due to the Westerner's experience with saws that cut on the push stroke, he will have to retrain himself to successfully use Japanese saws and avoid damaging the blade.* The saws are so sharp that little force is required to keep them cutting rapidly and smoothly, and therefore only a light touch is required. Care should be taken not to bind the saw on the push stroke or attempt to force it in a kerf that is binding. It is good practice when first using the saw to hold the handle between thumb and forefinger until feel and rhythm are established. The results obtained with our professional grade Japanese saws can be described with one word: spectacular.

A final note: it is a common misconception among those with little or no experience with Japanese tools that Japanese saws do not have any set to their teeth. By holding the saw up to light and sighting across the saw, the set will be readily apparent. It is true, however, that the set is very small in relation to Western saws. This, combined with the thinness of the blade, allows a precise cut to be made. The teeth of each saw are cut, set, and sharpened by hand. If the user does not feel confident to resharpen his saw, he should take the saw, with one of our saw files, to a hand filer of Western saws. The user is encouraged to keep his saws well oiled.

Timberman's Saw
A Order No.: 01.117.01 $35.55

Mortise Saws
B Order No.: 15.121.05 $16.75
C Order No.: 15.121.90 $15.45

Curved Edge Saw
D Order No.: 15.112.10 $46.90
E Order No.: 15.112.40 $48.10

Carpenter's Saw
This is the standard saw of the Japanese carpenter. With crosscut teeth on one side and rip teeth on the other, this saw can be used either to crosscut or to rip. The size of the teeth varies with the length of the saw. The longer the saw, the larger the teeth. In each size of saw, the teeth are smaller nearer the handle and increase in size toward the opposite end.

In use, the cut is started near the handle and the larger teeth come into play as the cut deepens. It is normal practice to use a specific size saw for the thickness of stock being cut:

F Order No.: 01.111.70 $48.10
G Order No.: 01.111.40 $46.90
H Order No.: 01.111.10 $46.90

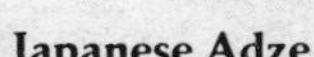

↑

Japanese Adze
The Japanese Adze is dissimilar to its Western counterpart in shape, however, it is used for the same purpose. Manufactured of laminated steel, providing a superior cutting edge.

Width of cutting edge: 3 7/8"
B *Order #*: 01.601 *Price*: $39.95

Adze Handle ⟶
While the Kununge sapling is still growing, it is bent and tied to the shape pictured at left. After cutting and drying, the handle maintains this shape, offering tremendous flexibility and resistance to breaking or splitting. The carpenter fits the handle to his adze.

Length: Approx. 23"
C *Order #*: 01.601 *Price*: $16.80

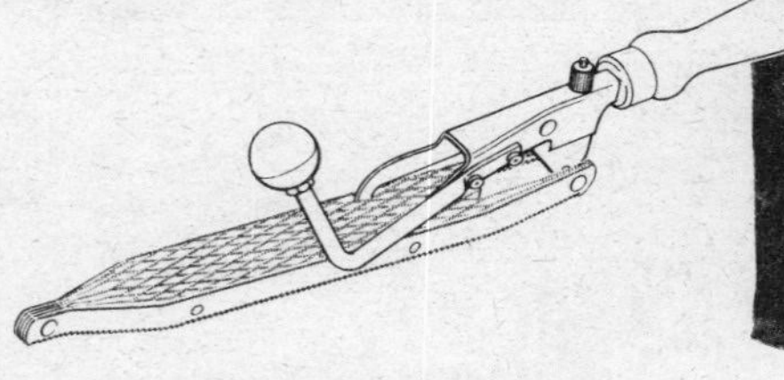

→

Saw rasps are one of the finest tools to come along in some time.

Invented several years ago by the Shinto Saw Works in Japan, they are manufactured from the highest quality hacksaw blades with coarse teeth (11 teeth per inch) on one side and fine teeth (25 teeth per inch) on the other. Because of the open design clogging is eliminated.

With the coarse side, very rapid removal of material is possible while the fine side will give a smooth finish cut. Saw rasps are also suitable for soft metals, formicas, plastics, etc.

The sander type saw rasp shown comes with a removable blade. The advantage of this type of saw rasp is that it can be easily used over a large surface. Saw rasps also come with fixed handles. $11.95

Shears ⟶
Japanese Professional
Garden Shears
(Mikan Hasami)
Order No. Length Price
A 01.917 7¼" $23.15

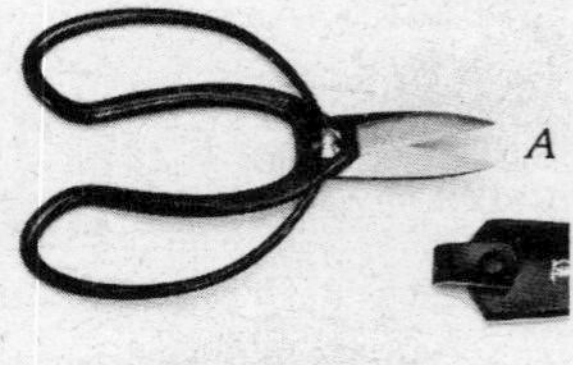

Tashiro Hardware

More limited range of Japanese tools than Woodline, more medium quality, and lower prices. I would shop both. —SB

Tashiro Hardware
Information

free from:
Tashiro Hardware Co.
109 Prefontaine Place
Seattle, WA 98104

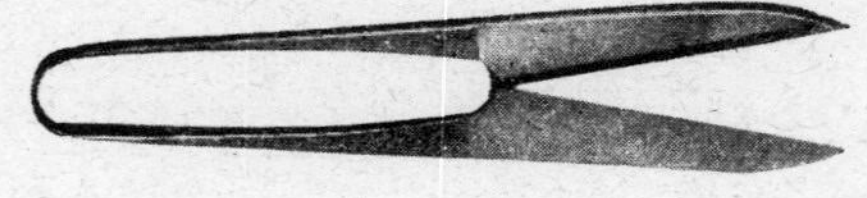

Bow Scissors

Used by the millions by seamstresses for cutting threads and ripping seams. Handy leader snippers for fishermen. Ideal for fine pruning of Bonsai trees. Properly used by palming scissor and operating between the thumb and the forefinger. Hold close to the blade points for accuracy and leverage. Inlaid steel blades for superior performance. $2.25

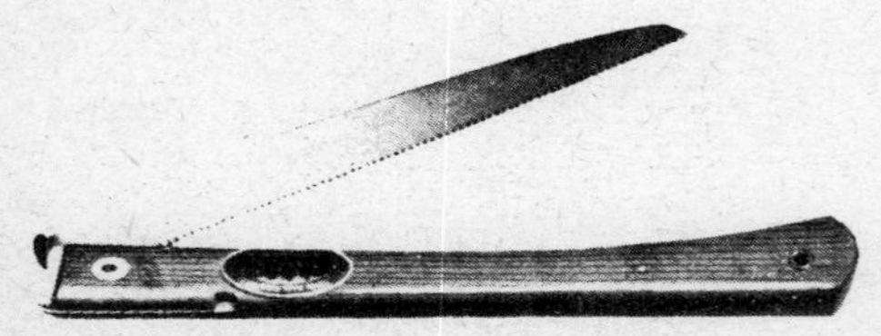

Folding Tension Saw

Handy folding saw with general purpose teeth for wood. The blade automatically locks open for safe use. $3.25

Lee Valley Tools

The Canadian Counterpart of Garrett Wade (they even share some of the catalog photos) this outfit carries a remarkable stock of tools for log building building. As there is duty to be paid (at the post office upon receipt of the order) Lee Valley will tell you where to get the same tools in the U.S. if possible rather than taking advantage of your order. The log stuff is mostly not available in the U.S., though, so Lee Valley is good to know about. —J. Baldwin

Lee Valley
Catalog

$1 postpaid from:
Lee Valley Tools Ltd.
P.O. Box 6295
Ottawa, Ontario
Canada K2A 1T4

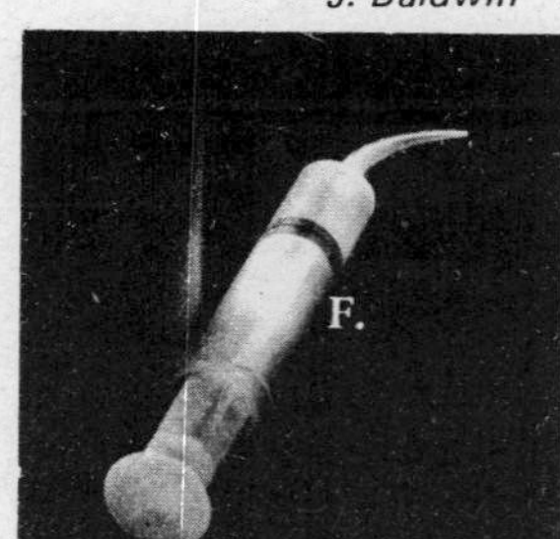

Glue Syringe
Have you ever had to apply a little bit of glue in a very narrow place or awkward location and made a mess of it? Here's a solution: Unbreakable plastic syringe which holds about one-half ounce. Any glue will work fine in it. You'll use it all the time. They do wear out eventually, so we're making them available in lots of three.

63J01.01 3 Glue Syringes **$2.25**

Log Scribe (Log Race)
A different sort of scribe, this is used to permanently mark logs by making a "U"-shaped groove in the wood. Very handy for numbering logs on a building to be disassembled for moving, or for marking matching mortise and tenon joints, etc. It has two cutting edges, one for linear cuts and one for circular cuts. 8" overall. Swedish chrome vanadium steel.

64U93.02 Log scribe **$18.75**

↓

Carpenter's Broad Hatchet

A traditional carpenter's broad hatchet with an offset handle, this is really a smaller version of a broad-axe. The face is beveled only on the right hand side with the other side being ground flat. This is an ideal tool for facing timbers for lintels, sills, cripple studs, etc. It is equally useful for rough shaping smaller tenons and lap joints in log building. The Austrian design includes a nail-notch on the inside blade edge and pulling claws on the poll. The blade is 4½" wide; the weight is 2¼ lbs. and the handle length is 14½".

64D01.01 Broad Hatchet ↓ $30.25

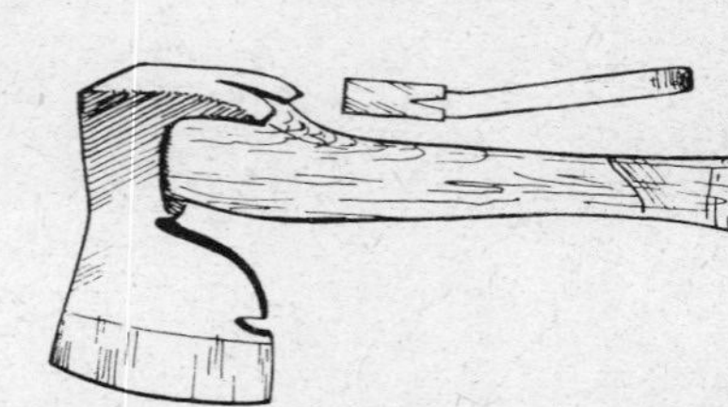

The Blairhampton Alternative

This unique catalog/newspaper combines tools for the log builder with anti-nuke comments, advice on logmanship in its various forms, a bibliography, and general Log House chat. Looks from here like a fine and friendly outfit. —J. Baldwin

The Blairhampton Alternative
Catalog

free from:
The Blairhampton
Alternative
Resourcery, Inc.
P.O. Box 748
Haliburton, Ontario
Canada K0M 1S0

PSSST!
A CANT HOOK CAN TOO. PASS IT ON.

Cant Hook $34 →

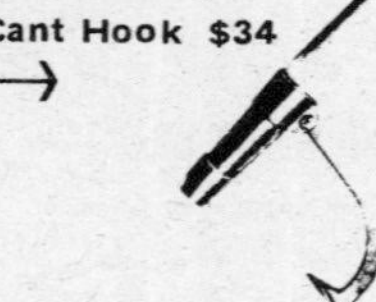

Timber Tote $44 ⟶
Consists of a 60" hardwood handle and a swivel mounted set of 'dogs' that allow two people to drag around poles, or move logs and timbers if another set of totes are used as well. Very simple and very effective - be sure to keep the 'dogs' well sharpened.

Builder's Knife $95 →

A knife figures prominently in the daily activities of a log building site. Anything and everything from pencil sharpening to etching the scribe lines of a notch prior to chainsaw use. Last year we met Joe Cebek, Knifemaker, at the OLBA exhibit of the Toronto Sportsmens Show. We designed a model we thought would cater to the peculiarities of log building and used it for the past year. We like it a lot, and offer it in the catalog. Overall, it's 7½" long, and weighs a solid-feeling 8 ounces. The handle is 4½" x 1-3/16" x 5/8", thick enough that you can get two hands around it when steering the tip along a notch scribe, and keep it under full control. The handle is bone or white "micarda" depending on what Joe has around his shop at the time. In either case, they are fitted to last a lifetime.

Sears Catalog (for tools)

Besides being useful for raising small children to table level at Thanksgiving, the mighty Sears Catalog brings Big City shopping to those of us who don't live near Big Cities. I've personally had varying luck with these people lately. They'll send the next size if they're out of your size, hoping you'll keep it anyway and make do. Quality also seems to have slipped even in the otherwise excellent tool department. Blister packing some items has made Sears less of a good deal than in the past. But all things considered, Sears is still the meaning of "typical" in assortment, prices and quality, and it must be said that they still back their guarantees. I recently broke a 30 year old Craftsman wrench and they gave me a new one! (These days it's a good idea to inspect each item you buy to make sure you get a good one. If you get a reject, use that guarantee, it'll help keep them honest!) You can sometimes make extra good deals watching Sears sales, and you should remember that Sears stores have freight damaged merchandise if you ask. Their repair shops also have secondhand tools and other items returned on warranty and subsequently repaired. I shop Sears a lot. Their non-electric hand tools are the best available for the money.

—J. Baldwin

Sears Roebuck and Company
Catalog
free

Check your phone book under Sears or write for location of nearest mail order plant from:
Sears Roebuck & Company
925 South Homan Avenue
Chicago, IL 60607

406-pc. Mechanic's Tool Set (1/4, 3/8, 1/2-inch square drive)
Save $300.83 $839.99

Gilliom Power Tool Kits

Gilliom is a company which sells and manufactures plans, kits and parts for power tools. They carry a 12 inch and 18 inch Band Saw, a Belt Sander, a 9" tilt table bench saw, a shaper, a 10" tilting arbor floor saw, and a combination drill press-lathe. Can buy either the plans or the kit. The plans and kit make it possible to build your own power tools with Gilliom parts at a fraction of what a pre-assembled tool would cost. The metal parts are included in the kit and you can build the housings out of 3/4" plywood. The plans are simple to follow.

—Marc Lerner

Gilliom Power Tool Kits
Information
$.50 from:
Gilliam Manufacturing Inc.
1109 N. 2nd Street
St. Charles, Missouri 63301

12-inch band saw, $3 for plans alone; $82.49 kit with plans

Drill Stand with Vise gives your hand drill the versatility of a drill press
Save $10
$32.98
Separate prices total $42.98

For 1/4 or 3/8-in. pistol grip drills; drill in vertical position, sand and grind in horizontal. 18 in. high tubular steel column; locking depth gauge from 0 to 2½ in. with automatic return. Throat depth 4½ in. Protective grinding guard. Swing-away table tilts, locks at any point. 6x6 in. cast aluminum base. 4 in. long aluminum base vise with 2 in. opening bolts to drill stand. Unassembled; drill, bolts not included. *Separate prices from our 1979-80 Tool Book, page 58.*
9 R 25933—Shpg. wt. 9 lbs. 8 oz. **$32.98**

AMT Power Tools

AMT makes and sells direct by mail order a line of low cost simple power tools, primarily for woodworking.

Included in the line are an 8-inch table saw, a jointer planer, belt and disc sander, drill press, wood lathe and wood shaper kit. All the tools are simple "stripped down" versions, but they work effectively. They are generally relatively small, but instructions are furnished for making larger tables, etc. Be sure to read the catalog sheets carefully, as almost all accessories are available only at extra cost (low, however) and also some good features can be specified, such as ball bearings in the table saw for a nominal extra price. Request their accessory sheet, as it contains some useful extras, and also good prices on saw blades, etc. The accessory sheet includes a motor base adaptor which allows easy use of an old washing machine motor for powering the tools.

AMT has been forthright and honest in mail order dealings. Their factory at Royersford is near Valley Forge, and if you are in the area you can stop in and see the real thing(s) on display.

—Karl C. Thomas

AMT Power Tools
Brochure and specifications

free from:
American Machine and Tool Co.
Fourth and Spring Streets
Royersford, PA 19468

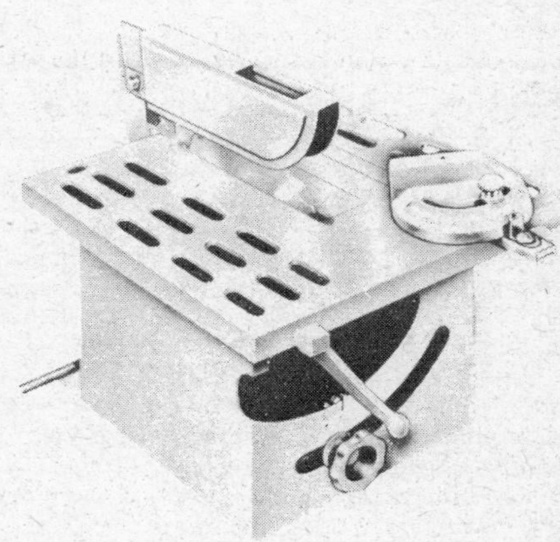

Power saw model no. 21655, $44.60 less blade

Iron Horse Antiques

Iron Horse Antiques primarily serves as a mail-order outlet for books on traditional tools and crafts. You will find titles on woodturning, leatherworking, blacksmithing, the history of tools, and industrial archaeology. In addition to the mail-order service, Iron Horse also deals in antique tools, and from time to time holds auctions. Subscribers to the tool catalog also receive the auction catalog. Mail bids are accepted if accompanied with a deposit.

—Pete Hartman

Iron Horse Antiques, Inc.
Catalog

$6 /year (2 issues)
postpaid from:
Iron Horse Antiques
RD No. 2
Poultney, VT 05764

FIGURE 29 -

20-29-1... PAIR of gun metal calipers. Heavy iron riveted joint. Ca. 1850. 16½ inch straight hinge from joint to tip. Handmade. Polished up, will knock your eyes out. (773AD) $75.00

20-29-2... Very interesting calking mallet. Iron bands on each end with 2 inch wide copper band in center. Handle is a replacement, but not easy to tell. Mallet in very good condition. Showy. Head is 10 3/4 inches long. (673AD) $60.00

20-29-3... All brass egg beater drill. Ca. 1840. Crank handle in steel. Chuck cover is missing, otherwise in fine condition. I can just imagine what this will look like after it is polished. Owners stamp, "W. J. COMSTOCK" (could be the maker). 11 inches tall. (3973AD) $250.00

20-29-4... Very heavy, brass and ebony, adjustable mortise gauge. Heavy brass wear plate on ebony fence and shaft of very heavy brass. No maker. 6½ inches long. Ca. 1830-40. English. (623AD) $65.00

20-29-5... Violin-makers thickness gage. A most intriguing example, as it is all hand forged. The graduated scale is hand stamped brass. Two owners names stamped on wooden handle, "R. BLACK" and "G. TEACH". 14 inches overall length. Excellent condition. (423AD) $45.00

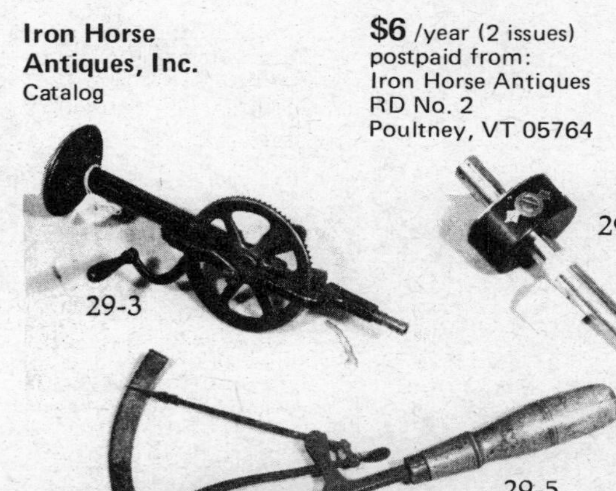

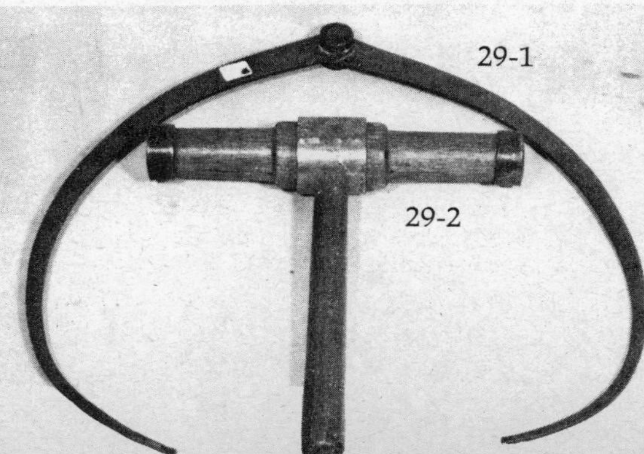

THE RISING SUN
NEIGHBORHOOD NEWSLETTER

"I used to throw the I Ching every morning."
"Was that when you were a hippy?"
"No, that's when I was an unhappy."
— Evelyn and me

Breaking the Wholesale Barrier

by J. Baldwin

Fury! Recently I wanted to buy a vise. The downtown hardware store had it for $59.95. Last year the same vise was $25 in the same store, and the year before it was $13. Other vises, even by the same authors, only became a bit more expensive, so increased material costs couldn't be the explanation. I looked for it in U.S. General and found them asking about $45. Silvo had the same vise for ten bucks less. A moment on the phone to a friend with a wholesale catalog said it was $25 there. The wholesaler had probably paid about $15 or so, though that is a hard fact to find out. Well . . . either the thing is worth $59.95 or $25 but not both! Isn't that maddening? Few things horn me off more!

The retailer will claim that his overhead makes it necessary to have the high price, and that is what you must pay for the privilege of being able to see it, fondle it, and take it with you right then. Don't let 'em fool you. Just down the street at the wholesaler's store, you can do the same thing, only without fancy graphics and a flashy pot-and-pan department. What it comes down to is that except in relatively remote areas where there are no wholesalers, the retail store is basically a rip. The question then becomes, how do you get into the wholesale store?

I use several tricks to accomplish this noble aim. Best and easiest is to make a deal with someone you know with a "resale number." In most states, this number is furnished for tax reasons; the person with the number doesn't have to pay tax on something that will be later sold to someone else. It is assumed by wholesalers that the holder of a resale number is in effect a retailer and thus eligible for the retailers' discount — typically 40%. Who has such a number? Contractors do. Architects do. Repair shops do. Tradesmen do. Does your uncle have a plumbing business? Ask him if you can use his number to get into Grainger's. I recently used the number of a solar home contractor and nabbed an air compressor for exactly half the Sears (sale) price for the same rig. It is considered good etiquette to offer the contractor friend maybe ten bucks for the paperwork time. It is also a good idea to order in quantity and not bother people for a discount on a single two-dollar item. Don't press your luck. Under some circumstances, it may be reasonable for you to incorporate and get your own number. It's worth considering. *(I did it once. Sure was worth it. Best technique, I think. —SB)*

Another ploy that sometimes works when all else fails is to dress like a carpenter or whatever trade is appropriate and brazen it out. Walk right in and say, "We need another 500 feet of Romex . . . I have the cash!" If you look the part, you may make it. I've done that plenty, but only since I've deployed a few grey hairs in my old age. Do not try this bit if you only need small stuff, they won't be interested. But a hundred buck order may tempt them into not being so stuffy about it, especially at a wholesale counter (that's what it is called) where the people behind it work on commission. I have many times buttered up a certain clerk who looks friendly. Use his name. Or you can call up first and say "Schwartz Plumbing is sending someone down to pick up 65 feet of 2 inch pipe." (If you are male, have a female play "secretary" for this play.) A pet clerk makes this especially easy. It's illegal too, for you are avoiding tax payments in such activities. Be cool. If they ask for a tax number, say "Shit, Mr. Schwartz didn't give it to me and I forget it," and see what happens. You may get away with it, especially if this comes up, as it often does, after your order has been delivered to the counter and the paper is all made out. Have cash on hand, in about the right change if you want to be asked back. Just pay the tax and shut up.

Another play is to confer a bottle of Cutty Sark or perhaps a sixpack on the clerk of your choice at a suitable time. I've done this too. It works.

A trifle more complex deal can sometimes be worked out by approaching a contractor who is obviously pricing out a job and have him add your order to his. This is an effective way to buy lumber and other building supplies, because your order makes his order bigger and may get him (and you) an even bigger discount at the lumber yard. That'll typically save you about 25%. A similar play can sometimes be made if your own order is big enough. If you are buying $5,000 worth of plywood, you can wheel and deal yourself. Ask to see the boss and make an offer. Hem and haw. They want your business. Different houses have different straightness of policy, so shop around, and tell 'em you're going to do that. Be hard. And remember even your local True Value store may give you 10% if you're a regular customer or buy in quantity. Ask!

Never, never go into a wholesale deal not knowing the terminology, model numbers, etc. You have to know what you want. You have to act like a pro to be treated like one. With a bit of practice you should be able to buy nearly anything wholesale with the exception of small quantities of low-priced items. It's satisfying to break the wholesale barrier. Ego satisfying too — a tribute to your acting ability. Good Luck! ■

Chilton's Hardware Age Buyer's Guide

Though you can't order direct from here (it's intended for "the trade") you can get a good idea of who makes what, and more importantly IF something is made. Catalogs such as this can save you a lot of trouble making something that can actually be better bought — sort of a Poor Man's Thomas Register. You can get addresses here.
—J. Baldwin
[Suggested by Roger Knights]

•
FIREPLACE BELLOWS
Building Products Mfg. Co.
Christen Inc.
Hart Fireplace Furnishings
Marian Hearthside Products
Ongard — See
  Vogelzang Brothers Inc.
Portland Willamette Co.
Seymour Mfg. Co.
Vogelzang Brothers Inc.

•
TRACTOR TIRE PUMPS
Deming Div. Crane Co.
Flexroller — See Hypro
Flexrotor — See Hypro

•
TREE WOUND SEALERS
Seymour Smith & Son Inc. & Son Inc.
J & L Adikes Inc.
Dynatron/Bondo
  Corp (Spray)
John H. Graham Co. Inc.
Gro-Well — See
  J & L Adikes Inc.
Heal-Rite — See
Nott Mfg. Co. Inc.
Snap-Cut — See Seymour Smith & Son Inc.
The Tanglefoot Co.

Hardware Age Buyer's Guide
(The "Who Makes It" Buyer's Guide issue of Hardware Age Magazine)
Published every December
$10 postpaid from:
Hardware Age
Chilton Company
Chilton Way
Radnor, PA 19087

Thomas Register of American Manufacturers

Let it all hang out: 16 volumes, 20,000 pages, 100,000 product ads, 140,000 classifications. It's the great American industrial yellow pages — and like the yellow pages, an education. If the Sears Catalog will tell you where American consumption is at TR tells you what's happening in production. And if you're trying to make the switch toward production, TR can help you find what you need.
—SB

Thomas Register can often be gotten FREE (also last year's) by approaching industrial libraries, or even the local Public Library, who generally get swamped by everybody's old edition. Big businesses make a real thing out of keeping up to date and Thomas doesn't update with supplements — new 16 volumes every year.
—Peter Heinlein

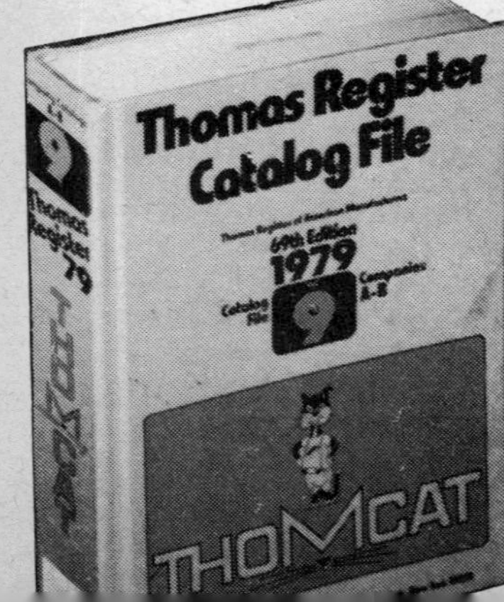

Thomas Register
$120 (16 volumes)
from:
Thomas Register
Sales Division
310 E. 44th St.
New York, NY 10017

Thomas' and Sweet's are also most useful if you need to know where the manufacturer of that hard-to-find tool lives.
—Art Kleiner

NEO-SPONGE COMFORT MATS (NS-900)

Sweet's Files

It's a shame some of the best tools are the hardest to get to. Though Sweet's are free, they are given only to public libraries in cities of more than 250,000 people and to the 10,000 most active architectural firms in the U.S. It's often possible to talk a local architect out of last year's edition if you speak for it early. They do not become obsolete just because they are a year or two old.

Sweet's is essentially a catalog of catalogs, a filing system in a yard of volumes which binds, lists and cross-references catalogs of manufacturers. It covers six areas that I know of: Industrial, Residential and Commercial Construction and Product, Interior and Plant Design. Each file in these areas is a separate entity. The commercial construction file is the one most architects have and for any one building, it is the most useful. It is very helpful when improvising details for it provides a full spectrum of what is already available for the ready made answers to most problems. Manufacturers usually do a pretty good job with the material they include in the files so there's not much left to question as to how their product works. If there is any question, the manufacturer's representative is usually listed, with his phone number and address. He'll usually bend over backwards to help you if you say you saw it in Sweet's.
—Onyx

There is one thing that you should keep in mind when using Sweet's Files: What is shown there is not all that is available. In fact, much of what's there is pretty mundane and tends to be the lowest price in order to attract the eye of the cost estimator who is making out the company bid on a job. "Sweet's File Architecture" — what you see in the sleaziest developments — is all too often the result. Watch it.
—J. Baldwin

Sweet's Files
Distributed by Sweet's Construction Division
McGraw-Hill Information Systems Company
1221 Avenue of the Americas, 21st floor
New York, NY 10020
Not for sale. Check your public library.

Translucent Spires ⟶
Wiedemann Translucent Spires are designed to be lighted internally. The dignity of the church edifice can be emphasized by the warm, even glow of the translucent spire, as it quietly points the way to the church by day and by night. The designs shown in this brochure will enable you to select a style compatible with your building. Constructed of anodized aluminum ribbing and translucent plastic panels.

Material Flow

Industrial supplies of all sorts. Especially good selection of racks and handling equipment such as tote pans. Many items can be useful around the home, ship and farm, and are not easily obtained at ordinary retail outlets. High Tech enthusiasts (see p. 297) could outfit their entire house or apartment here.
—*J. Baldwin*

Material Flow, Inc.
Catalog and nearest dealer location

free from:
Material Flow, Inc.
835 North Wood Street
Chicago, IL 60622

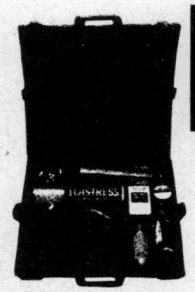

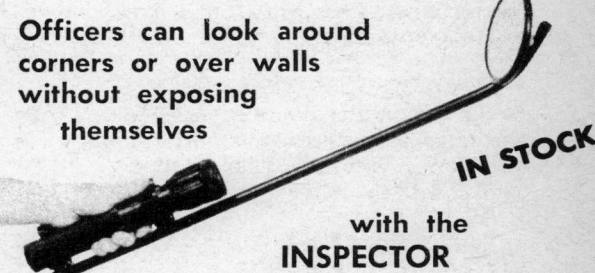

Sa-So

One big fat catalog of general supplies available by mail. The variety is just plain astounding! Bike racks, fire equipment, all manner of signs, janitor stuff, park benches, handcuffs, uniforms, body armor (!), narc kits, office gear, safety things . . . Often looking through such a catalog will give you ideas for using what's shown in imaginative ways.
—*J. Baldwin*

Sa-So
General Catalog

$5 postpaid from:
Sargent-Sowell, Inc.
1185 108th Street
Grand Prairie, TX 75050

New Equipment Digest

To technofreaks, this big mag is a mother lode fairly stuffed with the gizmos and whatnots of production. The very tone will be a turn-off to those interested in a humane world less marred by industrialism, but open-minded snooping will often turn up procedures and devices with interesting possibilities. Some are the result of OSHA safety standards and many are intended for something else than what you might have in mind. You have to be imaginative. You'll also have to be imaginative getting ahold of most of what's shown, as it's behind "whole-sale curtain."
—*J. Baldwin*
[Suggested by Ken Shepard]

New Equipment Digest
$24/year (12 issues)
Penton/IPC, Inc.
Penton Plaza
1111 Chester Avenue
Cleveland, OH 44114

THE RISING SUN
NEIGHBORHOOD NEWSLETTER

A high school in Phillipsburg, Indiana is using soap opera plots as a way of teaching foreign languages. "It's important for the students to want the information they are reading, and soap operas are inherently interesting," says Jennie Whalen who thought of the program. "We tried using real French conversation I transcribed in Paris and using real English conversation translated into French, but it didn't work. Real sentences uttered in conversation are just the tip of an iceberg of meaning inherent both in the culture and in the situation. You really do have to be there. If someone is actually in a situation that demands that they say, 'My aunt's fountain pen is on the table' they don't say it that way. It's always something more interesting or at least more cryptic like 'Just like her to leave it on the white tablecloth' or 'Use your eyes, stupid.'

"So we decided to go for plot instead of conversation because it can be both straightforward and interesting. The kids in the program are junior high age, and fascinated by sex. We use the soap opera plot summary magazine they sell at super markets and sort of mix and match plots. The students can submit proposed plots, in French or Spanish, and if they're good enough, dramatically and grammatically, we use them. We have installments every day and plot breaks every two weeks where the students argue about what could and should and would happen and submit proposals. They do get involved."

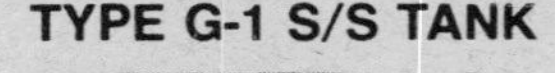

Holds 9 liquid gallons (2100 cu/in) and has a 400 PSI rating. Ribbed exterior — measures 12" dia. x 24" long. Has ¼" pipe port on each end. Good surplus condition in stainless steel. **USED $52.50**
NEW $75.00

Palley's

There are many so-called "surplus" stores, most with some sort of specialty. They usually have started as war surplus, but now include all manner of industrial surplus, some of which is surplus for good reason. Some stores also carry cheap shoddy junk and "seconds" that are not at all bargains. Shopping for surplus can be tricky, but if you know what you are doing you can often do very well. It is helpful to know something about the merchandise in question and what it would cost at a straight supplier. It is better to shop in person rather than by mail because some examples are in better condition than others, and the catalog descriptions are often incomplete. It is also easier to haggle. You should keep in mind that there may be repair parts problems with surplus machines, and that it is unwise to depend upon a certain item being always available. Some otherwise succulent tidbits may turn out to work only on 27 volts DC; a bummer. Keep in mind that the "it may not be here tomorrow" feeling in a surplus store can hypnotically lead the unwary to bringing home a bunch of junk that "may come in handy later." Ingenious persons can often work wonders with aerospace stuff.

Palley's is known as the largest surplus house in the country. The most recent catalog lists mostly industrial surplus. Pumps, generator sets, storage tanks, fans, switches, power tools, vehicle winches, and gasoline engine powered carpenter saws and drills are among the items useful to the commune. They can get you specific stuff; and will haggle quantity prices. —J. Baldwin

Palley Supply Co.
Catalog

free from:
Palley Supply Co.
11630 Burke Street
Los Nietos, CA 90606

Airborne Sales

Airborne Sales Company is not the usual surplus melange. Emphasis seems to be on electrical, electronic, pneumatic, hydraulic and mechanical systems and attendant parts and pieces. Their stock includes both new and used, marine specialties, tool room items and "hard-to-find" things and stuff. Pumps and motors for a variety of applications and power sources are available. Gauges, tools and fittings are available for much of the pneumatic, electronic, hydraulic and mechanical systems common to aeronautic and space programs.
—C.P. Christianson

I shop here a lot and have enjoyed good service.
—J. Baldwin

Airborne Sales
Catalog

$ .35 from:
Airborne Sales Company
8501 Stellar Drive
Culver City, CA 90230

**DON'T WAIT FOR ANOTHER NUCLEAR SCARE . . .
KEEP ONE ON HAND — YOUR LIFE COULD DEPEND ON IT!**

U.S. ARMY RADIAC SET

This is a self-contained nuclear radiation survey meter that can instantaneously detect gamma radiations of strength up to 50,000 milliroetgens per hour and can be used: to localize areas of radio-activity either to warn people of possible overexposure to radiation or to locate radioactive objects. Can also determine the degree of radio-active contamination of clothing and equipment. Also to localize areas of radioactive fallout and determine if areas are radiologically safe for human beings. Unit has 5 different sensitivity scales which are easily selected by the turn of a switch (5-50-500-5K-50K) also battery condition switch meter zero adjustor, and on and off switch are contained in the controls. Dial may be illuminated at night by use of pushbutton switch in the handle. Operates from self-contained batteries (not supplied with unit).

Dim. 6¼" W x 10¼" L x 7½" H. In excellent condition. Tested prior to shipment. Ship. wt. 8 lbs. Gov't. cost in quantity $119.00 ea. (Complete with operating instructions.)
No. 4207 . . . . **$29.95**

Surplus Center Equipment Catalogs

Not only are these catalogs handy to whomever may need such parts, but they can also serve as idea-generators for solving certain mechanical problems — thumb through the pages. Some of the parts are better hunted locally where you can see, try, discuss with salesmen and haggle. Some are rare and good deals. Best suited to the mechanically hip, especially away from big city sources. All "surplus" is risky stuff unless you're familiar with it.
—J. Baldwin

Surplus Center
Catalog

$ .25 from:
Surplus Center
Box 82209
Lincoln, NB 68501

115-VAC Centrifugal Blower

(ITEM #16-922)
$13.95
F.O.B. Lincoln

• (ITEM #16-922) - - Excellent for trailers, campers, bathroom, kitchen, darkroom ventilation. 115-volt, 60-cycle, AC. 200 CFM. Intake 3" diameter. Rectangular discharge 3" x 3-1/4". Overall size 8-1/4" x 8-1/4" x 7-1/4". Shipping wt. 8 lbs.

Grainger's

Grainger's is behind the wholesale barrier, but if you can crack it, they are a good outfit to do business with. I have found that the barrier is pretty easy to crack (see "Breaking the Wholesale Barrier," p. 148) and very much worth cracking. They carry all sorts of industrial hardware, parts and tools, but are at their best with air compressors, fans, motors, and the heavier stuff. I recently purchased an air compressor set from them — it cost me about half what Sears was asking for a lesser machine. Like that. There's a Grainger's in most larger American cities. Find them in the phonebook. —J. Baldwin

Grainger's
Wholesale Net Price
Motorbook Catalog

free from:
W.W. Grainger, Inc.
5760 Commerce Blvd.
Rohnert Park, CA 94928

40 and 56" 3-SPEED EXTRA-QUIET CEILING FANS

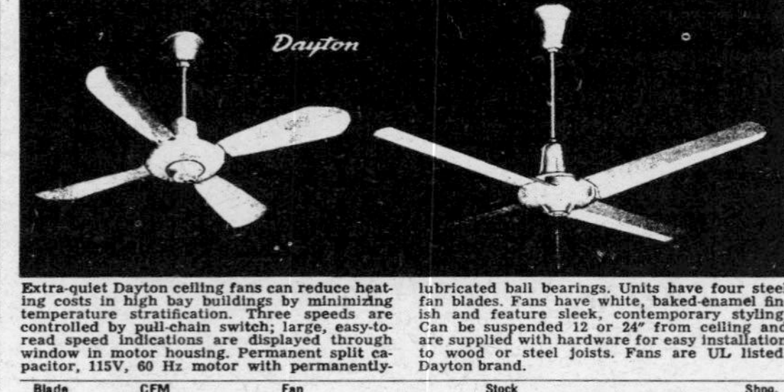

Extra-quiet Dayton ceiling fans can reduce heating costs in high bay buildings by minimizing temperature stratification. Three speeds are controlled by pull-chain switch; large, easy-to-read speed indications are displayed through window in motor housing. Permanent split capacitor, 115V, 60 Hz motor with permanently-lubricated ball bearings. Units have four steel fan blades. Fans have white, baked-enamel finish and feature sleek, contemporary styling. Can be suspended 12 or 24" from ceiling and are supplied with hardware for easy installation to wood or steel joists. Fans are UL listed. Dayton brand.

Blade Dia.	CFM Air Delivery	Fan RPM	Watts	Stock No.	Retail	Each	Shpg. Wt.
40"	5700/3600/2200	240/162/103	67/51/36	4C598	$126.85	$84.55	15
56	8800/6100/3900	210/155/100	82/63/42	4C569	170.40	113.61	20

SEE WARRANTY INFORMATION ON PAGE BEFORE INDEX 859

HIGGINS Bronze Centrifugal Pump
• (ITEM #254) - - Brand new, gov't surplus, genuine HIGGINS, all bronze, turbine-centrifugal pump. Unique turbine impeller design gives this unit more capacity than other pumps 3 or 4 times its size.
• Will handle over 14,000 g.p.h. An ideal unit for bilge pumping on large boats, for irrigation, pool and excavation draining, liquid transfer, etc. Farmers, contractors, marine services, etc., will find dozens of applications for this excellent unit.
SPECIFICATIONS
• Capacity over 14,000 g.p.h.
• Total head over 60 ft.
• Required driving power 1/4 to 6 h.p.
• Suction port 2" p.t.
• Discharge port 2-7/8" i.d. hose
• Monel shaft 1/2" diam. x 1-7/8"
• Rotation clockwise facing shaft
• Sealed ball-bearings
• Overall size, 12" x 12" x 10"
• Shipping weight 35 lbs.
Cut-away view shows unique turbine-type impeller
TABLE OF CAPACITIES AT VARIOUS HEADS AND HORSEPOWER
H.P. | G.P.M. | HEAD/FT. | R.P.M.
1/4 | 70 | 14 | 1400
1.0 | 105 | 15 | 2550
2.0 | 95 | 45 | 3350
4.0 | 210 | 4 | 3950
4.0 | 232 | 4 | 4550
6.0 | 180 | 60 | 4550
(ITEM #254)
$97.85
F.O.B. Lincoln

Why govt. surplus is cheap

This is irrelevant, but good: friend of a friend in San Diego bought a big steel cabinet-machine at a government surplus place, ($50). Took it home & tried all the knobs & switches; nothing worked. Pried open the back, and saw some connectors out of their sockets. Plugged them in. Tried a switch. Machine whined and began to clang — loud. Tried more switches. It wouldn't shut off. After ten minutes, a siren started — deafening. Tried all the knobs & switches. Wouldn't stop wailing. He got scared, and ran out. His house blew up. It was a U.S. Navy self-destruct bomb designed to destroy captain's cabin & all papers, in case of capture.

Will Baker
Davis, California

SURPLUS PROPERTY FROM UNCLE SAM

by Alan Kalker

LAND AND BUILDINGS FOR NON-PROFIT GROUPS

If your group has an educational or health purpose (including research), you may be able to get a surplus government office building or missile silo at a discount before it is offered for public sale. To qualify you discuss your needs with one of the regional HEW/ROFEC/Real Estate Planning and Management branches. These folks seem willing to discuss unconventional programs that are serious and well thought out. When you are qualified you are notified of all relevant surplus real property. If you convince them a particular offering fits your program, you can get a discount from the fair market value of up to 100%.

How to Acquire Federal Surplus Real Property for Health and Educational Purposes

free from:
U.S. Dept. of Health, Education, & Welfare
Office of Facilities Engineering
Division of Realty
Washington, D.C. 20201

SURPLUS GOVERNMENT LAND

A number of other programs have a priority claim on surplus federal real property — historical monuments, low income housing, parks, airports, wildlife conservation, state and local public entities, etc. These are outlined in the "Disposal of Surplus Real Property" booklet. If not claimed under these programs, surplus land and buildings are offered for public sale. To learn of these sales you get a "Real Property Mailing List Application Card" from the relevant regional office of the General Services Administration (GSA). Before bidding be sure to carefully check access to the land and for other claimants. At a minimum check the local tax assessor to see if someone has been paying taxes on the land. On occasion others may have come to believe they own the land the government is selling. In addition to GSA's surplus land program, land and building sale programs are administered by the Department of Housing and Urban Development, Tennessee Valley Authority, and the Department of Agriculture. If you already own land adjacent to unused federal land you may be allowed to negotiate purchase directly with the federal agency holding title, e.g., the Bureau of Land Management.

Disposal of Surplus Real Property
and
Real Property Mailing List Application Card

free from:
U.S. General Services Administration
Federal Property Resources Service
Real Property Division
(Use regional office address from list below)

SPECIAL DEAL FOR THE FEDERALLY FUNDED

If you have managed to get a federal appropriate technology, research, or other federal funding, or Uncle Sam employs you to watch for forest fires, tornados, or hostile forces, you can really stretch your budget by trying the excess property utilization program. The procedure is simple: draw up a specific list of your needs and send a copy of your list to each of the regional GSA offices, marked to the attention of Federal Utilization Branch, Federal Property Resources Service. The Utilization Branch receives reports of most all civil and military

TEMS 365 THRU 379 ARE LOCATED AT NORTH ISLAND, CA.

55. CAMERA, STILL PICTURE, HAND HELD: J. A. Maurer, P/N KE28B, with the following accessories: Lens, Leitz P/N 301-105-000-1, 6" F/2.8, lens core, P/N 301-104-000, lens cover, P/N 301-105-000-4; filter, P/N 301-105-000-2(G); filter P/N 301-105-000-3-(2B); and case P/N 301-162-000. NSN 6720-00-909-4331.
Inside - Can M Row 04 - In Boxes, Cans, Cartons and Cases - Used - Good Condition
Total Cost $16,640
Est. Total Wt. 300 lbs. 20 EACH

The Following Articles apply:
AI: Military/Munitions List Items
AP: Tie-in or All-or-None Bids

56. CAMERA, STILL PICTURE, HAND HELD: Same description and contract provisions as Item 365. 20 EACH

57. CAMERA, STILL PICTURE, HAND HELD: Same description and contract provisions as Item 365. 20 EACH

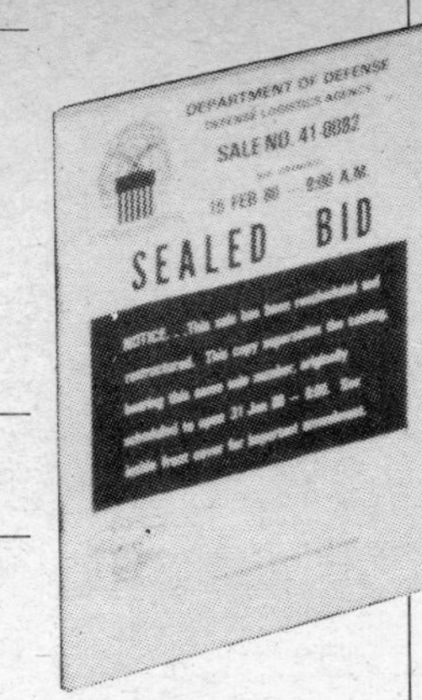

excess property in their region. If they notify you they have found a match to your needs lists, you then put a request for approval through normal channels. In most cases the only GSA charge to your budget is the cost of transportation, though some agencies add further charges if you are a government contractor rather than a government employee. You may want to try this program even though you qualify under other programs (e.g. you do federally funded research at a state university). Under the federal utilization program your request has a higher priority and usually lower cost than under the state donation program. The major disadvantage to the federal utilization program is that you may have to return the property when the federal contract expires.

SPECIAL DEAL FOR NON-PROFIT GROUPS

Each state has an agency for distributing donated federal surplus personal property to non-profit groups within their borders. Eligible recipients include some Indian groups, local and state entities, educational and health activities (e.g., child care centers, PBS TV stations, schools) and educational activities of special interest to the armed services (e.g., the Camp Fire Girls). The state agency charges only what it costs them to handle it. Usually you get a very good price, but on occasion you may do better by buying from the public sale auction and sealed bid sales. Naturally each state has a slightly different title for the agency responsible. Try writing "State Agency for Federal Property Assistance" at your state capitol for information on how to qualify. If that doesn't work, request:

Federal Surplus Personal Property Donation Programs

free from:
Office of Personal Property Disposal (FW)
Federal Property Resources Service
U.S. General Services Administration
Washington, D.C. 20406

GENERAL INFO ON SURPLUS SALES

The following pamphlet is a bit sketchy and overpriced, but it seems to be the only general guide around. It will at least give you current addresses for further information on special programs: sales to fire fighting agencies, law enforcement, local sales, etc. It is worth noting their comments on the rumored $50 jeeps:

Jeeps are limited in quantity and the possibility of jeeps in operable condition being offered for sale is very remote. Additionally, the M151 series vehicles have been determined to be unsafe for public highway use by the National Highway Traffic Safety Administration. Accordingly, these vehicles must be mutilated by cutting the three rear differential mounting pads out of the body frame and the body completely cut and severed at a point near the center of the vehicle. This is a safety requirement. Generally, jeeps sold by the Department of Defense are used, no longer meet military standards because of age and/or condition and in most cases are missing various components. They are sold at location by competitive bid.

From time to time stories or rumors are circulated advising the public that jeeps are available for unusually low prices if bought in quantity or disassembled in crates. Such stories are unfounded and should be brought to the attention of the DOD Bidders Control Office, P.O. Box 1370, Battle Creek, Michigan 49016.

I once saw a DOD Jeep sold for about fifty bucks, but it had suffered extensive "air drop damage" (military parlance for what happens when a parachute fails to open). Note that if what you want is a four wheel drive vehicle, and a station wagon or truck rather than a jeep will do, a fair supply in good condition are sold by GSA as surplus from civilian agencies — Immigration, USGS, and the Forest Service.

How to Buy Surplus Personal Property From The Department of Defense
No. 008-007-02939-8

$1 postpaid from:
Superintendent of Documents
U.S. Govt. Printing Office
Washington, D.C. 20402

DEFENSE SURPLUS

Much of the surplus you see in your neighborhood Army and Navy store may have come from a nearby Department of Defense retail store where you can buy small quantities from Uncle exactly as the store owner did. While intended to be open to all, the retail stores are becoming more difficult to find and visit. Your neighborhood store owner probably will not help. Many Defense Surplus Sales Offices (a list of these come when you request a Department of Defense Surplus Bidder application [below]) have retail stores, and each will send a list of those in your area on request. Competitive bid bulk lot sales are basically simple once you get into them, but none of the information the Government sends you will allow you to believe a non professional can figure it out. "Sale by Reference," a Department of Defense term for non retail sales, includes methods no more esoteric than an auction. The only way to find out easily about these non retail sales is to put your name on the DOD mailing list for sale announcements. For the DOD there is one central address for the continental United States. You must ask specifically if you also want announcements of sales in Alaska, Morocco, etc. In exchange for your name and address to the below central office, you will get a bidder's application form asking which kinds of things you are interested in purchasing and which geographic regions you will purchase from. Check every type of thing you conceivably may need, since adding another category will take at least six weeks. Check at least two nearby geographic regions, and all geographical regions if you are interested in vehicles, boats, aircraft. When your "bidder's application" is returned you will receive a pamphlet entitled "Sale by Reference" containing page after page of impenetrable small print, DO NOT CHUCK IT OUT, save it for ye shall need it. Also, save the sale catalogs for "sealed bid" sales for about 6 months. Get in the habit of looking at the mailing label on your sales announcements. Every two months or so the numeral 2 will appear in the middle of the first line, and you must send back a post card saying you are still interested in receiving the announcements. If you forget, it will again take at least six weeks to get back on the mailing list.

A recent convenience from the DOD: Customer Service on Small Parcel Post Shipments. If your bid wins on items marked "mailable" in the sale catalog, DOD will pack and mail it to you for a small service charge (typically $4) plus postage. Be sure to note special conditions and loading legends. A 60 foot landing craft may seem ideal for a house boat until you notice the loading legend requires you remove it by truck rather than the nearby water way. You might want to consider this an indirect warning that DOD is afraid a dry docked vessel may sink in their harbor.

Bidders List Application

free from:
Department of Defense Surplus Sales
P.O. Box 1370
Battle Creek, MI 49016

GSA (CIVILIAN) SURPLUS

The General Services Administration has charge of disposing of a large variety of non-military stuff — office and lab equipment, tools, furniture, vehicles, vessels, and aircraft (including those seized from incompetent smugglers). Their most common method of sale is the sealed bid. With some vehicle sales GSA uses the spot bid method. For this type of sale written bids are collected for each item in the sale, and the winning bid is announced before you must submit your written bid for the next item in the sale. This can give you a guide if a number of almost identical vehicles are offered in the same spot bid sale. You will know the winning bid on the first item before you must submit your written bid on the second. On occasion GSA sells some items at auction.

There is no single central office for GSA sale information. You must request that each regional office put your name on their sale announcement mailing list. COMMENT: Neither DOD nor GSA would seem to have much incentive to maximize revenue from surplus sales by making it easier for more people, including the inexperienced purchaser, to participate. While the expenses related to surplus sales come from their budgets, most revenues go directly back to the U.S. Treasury. Efforts to increase participation should only provide indirect general government benefit: increased general revenue and better public relations. The costs of such efforts are direct. I found it interesting that DOD nevertheless seems willing to make the effort to experiment with means for making participation easier — e.g. with retail stores, by providing packing and shipping for a nominal charge on mailable items, and by full descriptions of sale items including estimated weight and acquisition cost. GSA has no retail stores, no mailing service, and some recent sale catalogs omit all mention of weight and cost. For example a recent GSA catalog describes the quantity of fasteners offered as ". . . a large lot. . ." (7DPS-80-35, item 89).

The basis for GSA's approach is unclear. I attempted to discuss possible means of increasing participation and revenue with San Francisco GSA sales officials. I was only allowed to speak with the sales officials in the presence of a GSA Business Service Center functionary. This functionary facilitated my discussion with sales officials until I attempted to discuss with them possible means of increasing revenue and participation. Then the functionary terminated my discussion with the GSA sales officials. Such questions, it seems, are "vague, meandering, hypothetical, and a waste of the time of GSA sales officials."

Buying Government Personal Property
and
Surplus Personal Property Mailing List Application

free from:
U.S. General Services Administration
Business Services Center
(Use regional office address from list below)

BIDDING AIDS FOR DOD AND GSA SALES

For vehicle sales look up the "blue book" value (typically government vehicles are sold after 60,000 miles). If the vehicle sale is at a motor pool, mechanics who serviced the vehicles may know of problems. Some bidders bring a spark plug wrench and compression tester to the "motor starting" that often preceeds vehicle sales.

Sealed bid sales are the most difficult for the inexperienced purchaser. If you save old sale catalogs for about the last six months you may find a clue from the successful bid for a similar item in a completed sale. If you have the old sale number and item number you can find the amount of the successful bid from DOD or GSA by phone or letter. Warning: on occasion the successful bid for a used item may be more than the current retail price for the same item new. Always check the acquisition cost, if given, in the sale catalog. Find the current price your local scrap yard will pay for various metals. This plus the weight, if given, and rough transportation costs can give you a rough idea of a minimum bid for things like steel pipe or stainless steel tables. It is really important to inspect items carefully, many DOD electrical items work on weird voltages and frequencies.

OTHER GOVERNMENT SURPLUS

The Post Office now handles sales of all surplus it obtained after becoming independent — contact your local postmaster for details. The Tennessee Valley Authority has a sales office, write them at: Chattanooga, TN 37401. Small craft and other maritime type property are sold by the Maritime Administration's Eastern and Central Regional offices (the Western Region uses GSA) write to the Administrative Services Officer, Maritime Administration at: 26 Federal Plaza, New York, NY 10007; and, International Trade Mart Bldg., No. 2 Canal Street, New Orleans, LA 70130. If you want to start your own navy with vessels over 1500 gross tons, contact: The Chief, Fleet Disposal Branch, Division of Reserve Fleet, Maritime Administration, Washington, D.C. 20230.

GSA OFFICE ADDRESSES

Post Office and Courthouse
Boston, MA 02109
(CT, ME, MA, NH, RI, VT)

26 Federal Plaza
New York, NY 10007
(NJ, NY, PR, VI)

7th & D Streets, S.W.
Washington, D.C. 20407
(DE, DC, MD, PA, VA, WV)

75 Spring Street, S.W.
Atlanta, GA 30303
(AL, FL, GA, KY, MI, NC, SC, TN)

230 S. Dearborn Street
Chicago, IL 60604
(IL, IN, MI, MN, OH, WI)

1500 E. Bannister Rd.
Kansas City, MO 64131
(IA, KS, MO, NB)

819 Taylor Street
Fort Worth, TX 76102
(AR, LA, NM, OK, TX)

Denver Federal Center
Building 41
Denver, CO 80225
(CO, MT, ND, SD, UT, WY)

525 Market Street
San Francisco, CA 94105
(AZ, CA, NV)

Federal Building
300 Ala Moana Blvd.
Honolulu, HI 96850
(HI)

GSA Center
Auburn, WA 98002
(ID, OR, WA)

P.O. Box 1632
Anchorage, AK 99510
(AK)

THE RISING SUN
NEIGHBORHOOD NEWSLETTER

"Once an angry man dragged his father along the ground through his own orchard. 'Stop' cried the groaning old man at last. 'Stop! I did not drag my father beyond this tree.' "

—Gertrude Stein *The Making of Americans*

Jet Tools

Mention the word "lathe" to a thingmaker and the glitter of desire flickers in the eye. But who can afford one? Jet Tools has a line of unusually fine lathes and milling/drilling machines that are not exactly cheap, but are excellent value for the money. That's about as good as you can do these days. They also sell a beautiful vise and many other tools. Someday . . . —J. Baldwin

Jet Tools
Catalog
free from:
Jet Equipment and Tools
1901 Jefferson Avenue
Tacoma, WA 98402

JET-1024P Bench Lathe — $2,250.

Jensen Tools

Primarily stuff for electronics and precision assembly. Very, very nice kits. The prices seem unduly high, but they are postpaid. —SB

Jensen
Catalog
free from:
Jensen Tools and Alloys
P.O. Box 22030
Phoenix, AZ 85266

Vertical Pipe Wrench
Ideal for use in hard-to-get-at locations. Attaches at right angles to ½" square rod or socket wrench extension handle by means of ½" hole and set screw. Jaw capacity 2".
482B016 Pipe Wrench . . . $12.95

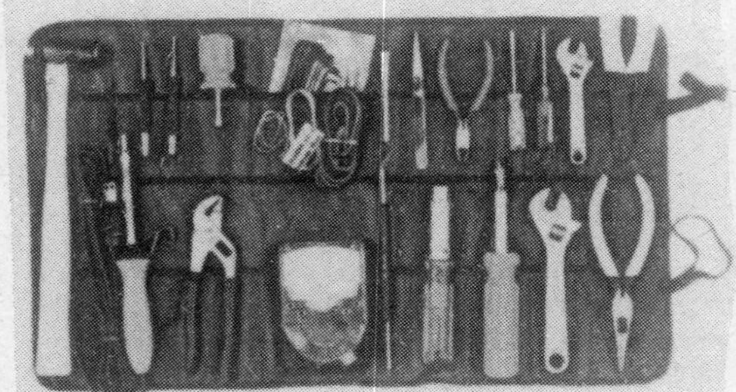

A handy vinyl-coated roll pouch containing a select complement of tools for troubleshooting, servicing, repairing most electronic-electrical equipment. Includes pliers, screwdrivers, nutdrivers, tweezers, wrenches, hex and spline keys, soldering iron, hammer and more. See complete listing at right. All tools fit snugly in a 12 x 21" roll pouch. A Triplett 310 VOM test meter is an optional accessory. A good looking kit at an attractive price.
JTK-84L Without Meter . . .$99.00
(6-10, $91.10 ea.; 11-24, $84.15 ea.; 25-49, $79.20 ea.)
JTK-84W With Triplett 310 VOM Meter . . .$163.00
(6-10, $154.10 ea.; 11-24, $146.15 ea.; 25-49, $140.20 ea.)
286B477 Pouch only . . . $10.50

Troubleshooter's Roll Pouch Kit
★ 25 essential tools

These fine tools included in JTK-84*

- Hammer, 4-oz. ball pein
- Hex key set
- Knife
- Nutdriver, self-adjusting, ¼ to 7/16"
- Plier, chain nose with cutter, 6½"
- Plier, diagonal cutter, 4-1/8"
- Plier, groove joint, 6"
- Punch, center, 3/32"
- Pin punch, pin, 1/8"
- Punch, pin, 1/16"
- Rule, 6"
- Screwdriver, 2-in-l stubby
- Screwdriver, 4-in-1
- Screwdriver, pocket, Phillips
- Screwdriver, pocket, slotted
- Solder aid
- Solder brush
- Soldering iron
- Solder sample
- Solder wick sample
- Spline key set
- Tweezers, cross locking
- Wire stripper
- Wrench, adjustable, 4"
- Wrench, adjustable, 6"
- Roll pouch, 12 x 21"

Stortz Tools

One of the most interesting tool distributors in the country. Stortz carries specialized tools of certain trades (they are strong on masonry and roofing) and is a place always to check before abandoning hope or seeking the conversational "guess what this is." —George Putz

Stortz Tools
Catalog
$2 postpaid from:
John Stortz & Sons
210 Vine Street
Philadelphia, PA 19106

OYSTER OR CRACK KNIFE
Square, All Steel—Seaboard Style

Square carbon tool steel stock, forged to thin tapering blade, which is fully polished and tempered specially; for prying or cracking oysters. Handle finished in black.

Item Number	108-A	108-B	108-C
Blade Length	3"	3"	3"
Stock Size	½"	⅝"	¾"
Length Overall	7½"	8"	8¼"

STORTZ X. L. CASE HOOK
(Excel)

EXTRA POPULAR WITH LONGSHOREMEN, TEAMSTERS, LUMBER AND FREIGHT HANDLERS

Forged of high quality carbon tool steel. Steel Hook is made with enough weight, properly distributed in the swelled curve of the hook to give it hammer-like weight when swinging it into heavy cases, thereby preventing hook from coming loose from case when it is pulled from truck or platform to floor. Steel is fully and finely polished, shank is riveted through large size, shellac finished, hardwood handle.

ITEM NUMBER	LENGTH UNDER HANDLE	THICKNESS OF STEEL
128-A	7"	¾"
128-B	8"	¾"
128-C	9"	¾"
128-D	10"	⅞"
128-E	12"	⅞"

A TOUGH, SERVICEABLE, TOP QUALITY HOOK

SLATER'S HAMMER

Forged of high quality carbon tool steel. Point, claw and hammer face especially heat treated to stand hard usage. Claw at center for pulling nails. Steel part of handle has beveled edge at top for cutting slates; balance of handle has grip of leather, smoothly finished and polished to fit hand, and for ease in using.

Note: This hammer is fully and finely polished overall as illustrated. A top quality and finely finished hammer.

Item Number	83-B	83-C
Type	Right-hand	Left-hand
Size Head Face	⅝"	⅝"
Length Overall	12"	12"
Weight Complete, approx.	1 lb. 4 oz.	1 lb. 4 oz.

NOTE: HAMMER ILLUSTRATED IS FOR RIGHT-HAND PERSON. LEFT-HAND HAMMER HAS CLAW ON REVERSE SIDE OF HEAD.

OTHER WEIGHTS AND DESIGNS MADE TO ORDER—SUBMIT DETAILS

Goldblatt Tools

An amazing catalog of specialized masonry and builders' tools. All manner of trowels and concrete tools, stilts, brick hammers and chisels, concrete saws, scaffolds, knee pads, wheelbarrows, hods, tool pouches. Good prices. See also masonry, p. 230. —SB
[Suggested by Robert McElroy]

Goldblatt Trowel Trades Tools
Catalog
free from:
Goldblatt Tool Co.
511 Osage
Kansas City, KS 66110

• BRICK, STONE & TILE CUTTER — A solid whack with a 2-lb. hammer (or heavier) cuts brick, block or stone up to 8" wide, 4" high. Entire tool is carefully machined steel, painted with rust resistant paint. Blades of tempered steel, height, 8¾". Base, 11" x 4" x ½". Wt. 15 lbs.
11 313 E5....$37.90

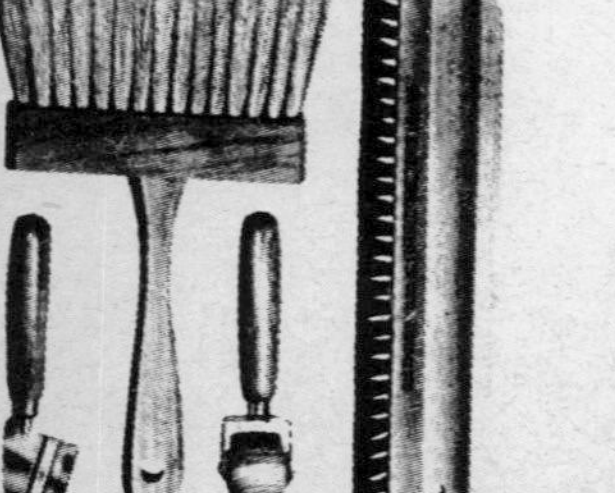

• VINYL WALLCOVERING KIT — Includes a compact kit of all the tools needed for hanging vinyl wallcoverings. Comes complete with a trimming knife, smoothing brush, seam roller, paste brush and instruction sheet. Packed in a polyethylene bag with hanging display header. Portable and easy to use. Shipping weight 12 lbs.
07 963 H7....$6.05

C & H Sales

A good source of small motors, relays, instruments, etc. The selection is similar to Airborne (p. 150). It's a good idea to look at several sources of this sort of equipment so you can compare specifications and prices. $20 minimum order. —J. Baldwin
[Suggested by David Friedman]

C & H Sales
Catalog
free from:
C & H Sales Co.
2176 East Colorado Blvd.
Pasadena, CA 91107

CHART RECORDER, ESTERLINE-ANGUS Model AW 0-1 MA, DC millimeter, permanent magnet moving coil type. Dual speed drive (hour and minute). Spring wound or 110 VAC motor driven. Portable case. Specify choice.
Stock #CR1101 .... **$200.00**

ASTRO COMPASS. Gives absolute heading, determines bearings and compass errors, enables identification of stars. Also serves as a starlight pelorus. A precision instrument with extremely fast and simple operation. One of the most important navigation developments of the past century. Ideal for yachtsmen, airmen, boat owners, maritime service or airline operations. Complete with instructions.
Stock #OL7802 .... **$39.95**

Nat Cam

Originally oriented to camera repair, they now have all manner of tools for fine work. —SB

Nat Cam
Catalog
$1/year (4 issues)

Sample catalog
free from:
Nat Cam
1835 West Union Avenue
Englewood, CO 80110

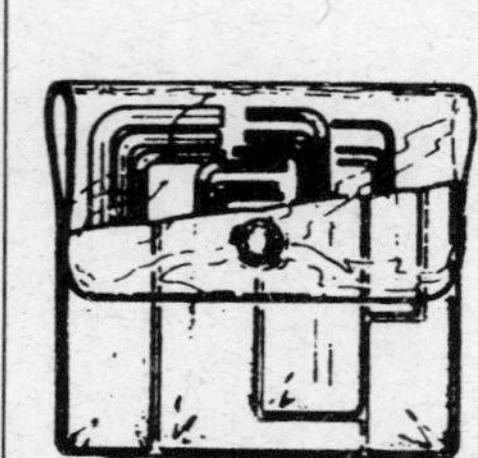

TINY SPLINE AND HEX SET

Twelve most popular hex and spline sizes in a plastic pouch. Six hex keys with fine plated finish sizes .050, 1/16, 5/64, 3/32, 1/8 and 5/32. Six spline keys with black finish in sizes .033-4, .048-4, .060, .076-4, .072 and .096. $3.95

ECONOMY COLLIMATOR

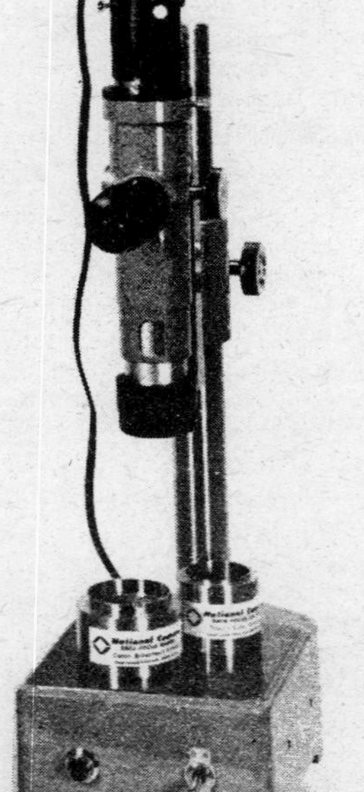

Autocollimator **$1493.00**

Wreckers' close-out sales

If you are interested in high quality lumber and other materials, and age is not a deterrent, and perhaps is even an attraction, then look for wrecked buildings.

Don't buy at first visit unless you see something you really want. These materials get cheaper as the job goes on — and in the end are free. The wrecker's situation is generally this: The wrecker contracts not only to clear a site, but to do it by a certain date. Material salvaged and sold at the site is added income and saves hauling and storage or disposal expense. Another basic expense is the removal of salvageable material from the building itself. You can save if you bargain to tear the item or the material out yourself. This can be tricky, so watch the wrecker a while.

As the contract date nears, the wrecker will cut prices to enlist your help in clearing the site. The price reaches zero as the date arrives. The wrecker gives the material away to clear the site and avoid paying a penalty or sacrificing a deposit. At this point, you won't get the pick of the lot, but you will get dimension lumber, flooring, sills, bricks and some glass and fixtures that haven't sold.

The "Wait til they're desperate" approach works well with the small wrecker. The big ones do little salvaging and are primarily trash haulers. Again though, if you come around late in the day and ask for something they really have no use for, you're helping them move their trash, and it's yours free.

H.C. Clark
Houston, Texas

American Plywood Association

What makes plywood such a desirable building material is its extremely favorable cost/strength ratio. Also, it's quick to install, as each piece you nail down covers 32 square feet.

The American Plywood Association has hundreds of pamphlets available on different uses of plywood. For a complete listing, write for the Plywood Publications Index.

—Lloyd Kahn

You should keep in mind that plywood these days is a sorry imitation of what it once was. The quality codes are broken as a matter of course. Huge structurally weak voids abound even in the quality grades (except for the $100 a sheet marine stuff), glue failures, ratty surfaces, and (maddening!) out-of-squareness is the rule rather than the exception. This is too bad, especially in the light of the high prices being asked. It's especially too bad because good quality plywood is mighty useful.

—J. Baldwin

Typical grade-trademark backstamp

Grade of veneer on panel face
Grade of veneer on panel back
A-C
Species Group number — GROUP 2 (APA)
Designates the type of plywood Exterior or Interior — EXTERIOR
Product Standard governing manufacture — PS 1-74 000
Mill number

Typical edgemark

A-B · G-1 · EXT-APA · PS 1-74 · 000

Grade of veneer on panel face; Grade of veneer on panel back; Species Group number; Designates the type of plywood Exterior or Interior; Product Standard governing manufacture; Mill number

Plywood Encyclopedia
Form No. X505

Plywood How-To Book
Form No. V605

Plywood Construction Basics
Form No. A100

House Building Basics
Form No. X461

Plywood Specification & Grade Guide
Form No. C20

Stains & Paints On Plywood
Form No. B407

Introducing the Non-Basement Basement
Form No. D415

$1 each

Plywood Publications Index
Form No. B300

free from:
American Plywood Association
P.O. Box 11700
Tacoma, WA 98411

Slotted angle

Very handy stuff for making racks, partitions, workbenches etc. There are several brands, and most are compatible with one another. The stuff can be re-used over and over, so buying it second hand can mean significant savings. I use it a lot fabricating camper interiors in busses and trucks. Two of the most common brands are AIM and Dexion. Look under Slotted angle or Rack in the Yellow Pages of a fair sized city. *—J. Baldwin*

AIM
Manufactured by:
Interlake Inc.
Chicago, IL

Dexion
Manufactured by:
Pacific Shelving
Compton, CA

Not available by mail order. Check your local industrial supply store.

AIM.

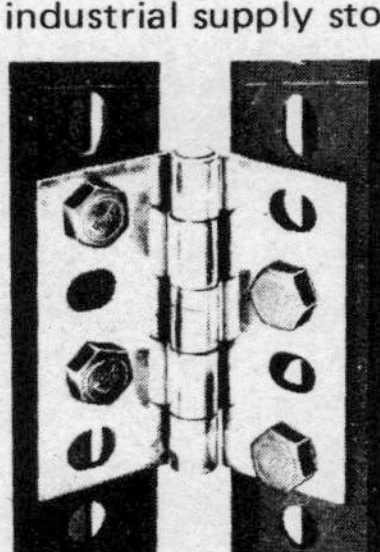

Dexion.

Unistrut

Unistrut is great stuff. You can make houses, furniture, partitions, stage sets, boat trailers and just about all sorts of things out of it, and can take them apart later and use the Unistrut again. It comes in several sizes, in several metals and finishes, and is completely adjustable. I've used it for such diverse things as tables, store interiors, pack frames, animation stands and camera dollies, telescopes. Unistrut is distributed nationwide, but locally there may be competitors that offer cheaper prices and different finishes. Good for space frames such as Fuller's octet truss.

—J. Baldwin

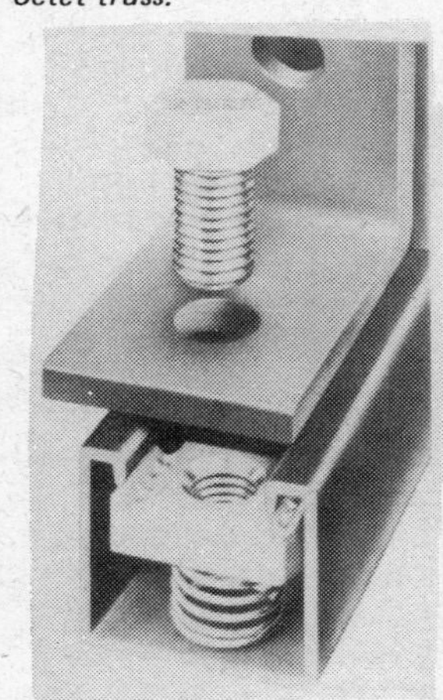

METAL FRAMING SYSTEMS

LOOK FOR THESE FEATURES:

Large chamfer in nut eases starting of bolt.

Special shaped clamping ridges and tapered, serrated grooves produce strong vise-like grip between channel and nut.

- Channel and nut are aligned since the special shaped clamping ridges and the nut's tapered grooves act as guides.
- Nut grooves grip clamping ridges tying channel sides together as bolt is tightened.
- Longitudinal movement of nut is resisted as hardened teeth dig into the clamping ridges.

Spring holds nut in place — the workman's "third hand".

Unistrut
General Engineering Catalog

free from:
Unistrut Corporation
World Headquarters
Wayne, MI 48184

Nichols Net & Twine Co. Inc.

Commercial fishing supplies, mostly nets, floats, weights, and associated gear. There are a lot of uses for netting other than for fish.

—J. Baldwin

Nichols Net & Twine Company Inc.
Catalog

$.50 postpaid from:
Nichols Net & Twine Co. Inc.
RR 3, Bend Road
East St. Louis, IL 62201

NYLON CAST NETS

100% Nylon excellent nets for bait catching, Minnows, Shad, Crayfish, etc. Thrown and operated by one man. Whole schools of bait fish may be captured at one throw. Natural bait caught alive on the spot is always best.

Mesh Sq.	Dia.	Weight	Price
3/8"	6 ft.	4.0 lbs.	$20.00
3/8"	7 ft.	4.0 lbs.	$21.00
3/8"	8 ft.	4.7 lbs.	$22.00

Screw appreciation

The subject of this letter is screws. Since this is probably too commonplace a title to attract much attention let's call them fastening devices. This particular device is a combination of so many improvements on the standard wood screw that I'll be surprised if someone else hasn't brought it to your attention. In case no one has, here goes.

It's a Sheet Rock Screw. They are made to attach sheet rock to metal studs. They are designed to be driven with a power screw gun. They can be driven by hand, of course, and in fact are easier to drive than ordinary screws. Ideally, however, one should use a good quality variable speed and reversible drill. In the hands of the woodworker the applications are unlimited.

To appreciate the screw, one must break it down to its components:

1. It has a self tap point. No awl is required to mark the location and keep it there. It zips into wood or thin metal.

2. There are two threads. The hi thread is at 30 degrees instead of the normal 60 for faster penetration. The lo thread reduces wobble and provides lateral pressure.

3. The shank is reduced in size giving greater thread exposure and gripping power. I'm told that it holds better alone than the same number of regular screws and glue. My experience with them seems to verify this, but I can't prove it. The narrow shank also eliminates the need to pre-drill in all but the hardest woods and thicker metal. There are minimum splitting problems.

4. The finish is an attractive gray created by a zinc phosphate coating with baked-on linseed oil. It is supposed to be corrosion resistant.

5. The head is a patented shape called "Bugle" head. For the woodworker, the advantage is no countersinking. It pulls down flush with little or no surface damage.

6. The slot is a No. 2 Phillips, the advantages of which are well known. The pros use magnetic bits and don't even hold the screw to guide it as it's being started. The steel they are made of is so tough it's almost impossible to damage even the appearance of the slot with a spinning power bit.

7. Since the awl, drill and countersink have been eliminated, the speed in driving with power or by hand is obvious. They are equally easy to extract if you make a mistake, want to dissassemble your work and/or salvage the screws.

If the above sounds like the manufacturer's sales pitch, it is. I copied most of it from the specifications, omitting the many other advantages that are probably only of interest to the sheet rock people. They are made by U.S. Gypsum Company, 101 S. Wacker Drive, Chicago, IL 60606. They come in various lengths and styles. There are variations for plastic, trim, sheet rock to wood, and a plain point for wood only, to mention a few.

After using them, their superiority is so apparent that one feels cheated if he has to use the old kind again. If all this is so, why isn't everybody using them? Why can't you buy them in the neighborhood hardware store? I don't really know. Anyway, I get mine at a building materials supply house that specializes in sheet rock, lath and plastering supplies, etc. I don't recommend them for the novice or occasional do-it-yourselfer. But for the guy who is "always building one thing or another" they are fabulous and worth obtaining. Instead of being the specialized fastening device they were designed to be, they are damn near universal. The only place I would hesitate to use them would be on a job where shear was important, such as a gate hinge.

Fred Barrett
Portland, Oregon

THE RISING SUN
NEIGHBORHOOD NEWSLETTER

One time these neighbors of mine across the street with 2 kids went to a college area movie theatre to see a Peter Sellers movie which included Peter Sellers trying to put the make on this woman in a field and them being all the time interrupted by a curious cow. They noticed they were laughing *much* harder than anyone else and figured out that was because that's what it's like to try to make love when you have kids.

VW prime mover

This company can help you put that old bug engine to work as a reliable and efficient stationary power source for driving irrigation pumps, compressors or a host of equipment. Upon request, they will send product data sheets for conversion accessories such as a universal bell housing, direct drive, pump drives, T-box (on special request), a universal clutch housing, double or single shaft reduction gears, drive plates, spline shafts, etc. They also sell 40 and 53 hp VW engines modified slightly for stationary use. Ask for a price sheet.

They provide specifications and also graphs of power output versus RPM, torque versus RPM and fuel consumption versus RPM for both engines (handy to have).

You might want to consider using methane or fuel/alcohol as an alternative or backup to gasoline.
—Bill Hutchinson

Type 122 and 126A VW Industrial Engine and Accessories
Information

free from:
Industrial Engine Division
Volkswagen of America, Inc.
3737 Lake Cook Road
Deerfield, IL 60015

Type 122 Volkswagon industrial engine

Devcon

One way to conserve energy and resources is to fix things that break rather than throwing them away. The Devcon Corporation makes a wide variety of products that can solve some very nasty repair problems as well as increasing the life of various hardware. Typical is Plastic Steel and Plastic Aluminum. A far cry from their sissy hardware store counterparts, they are super strong and you can (for instance) repair engine blocks. They make a paint called "Z" that actually outperforms hot dip galvanizing (Milspec no less). Their Devcon Rubber repairs split rubber boots better than anything else I've seen. They make a wear resistant self-lubricating epoxy compound that can be used to make long wearing bearing surfaces in wood. (It can also be used to build up worn shafts.) The list goes on. I've used all this stuff and find it to be at least as good as they say. Not many companies are worthy these days. This one is. You'll probably have to get their products from an industrial supply house. The catalog is available there too.
—J. Baldwin

Devcon
Catalog and nearest dealer location

free from:
Devcon Corporation
Danvers, MA 01923
or check your local industrial supply dealer.

Devcon cleaners and repair compounds

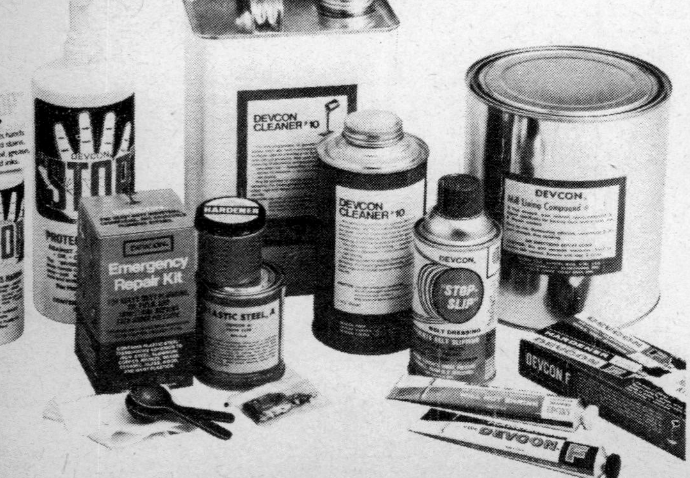

CeCoCo Guide Book

This guide catalogs several hundred tools, all manufactured or distributed by CeCoCo (Central Commercial Co.), and all applicable to what they term "cottage industry."

One spends hours studying specifications, diagrams, and photos of CeCoCo "making" machines. In the wire products section, for instance, one finds paper pin making machine, staple pin making machine, hair pin making machine, safety pin making machine, snap button making machine, nail making machine, barbed wire making machine, chain making machine, zip-fastener making machine, etc.
—Ken Kern

Guide Book for Rural Cottage and Small and Medium Scale Industries
158 pp.

$14 postpaid from:
CeCoCo
Exhibition
Demonstration Center
Ibaraki City
Osaki Pref.
Japan

"CeCoCo" Bird and Animal Scarer Bang

Care should be taken to scare the bird when the seedling is being nursed in bed and when the rice is becoming matured in the paddy field to prevent a great damage caused by ravages. Acetylene gas with air mixture is automatically ignited at short intervals in 't'-type explosion pipe which goes with a 'Bang'.

"CeCoCo" Bird and Animal Scarer is equally effective against sparrow or any other birds, rodent rabbit, wild boar, monkey, bear and other ravages of paddy field, orchard and field crops of food such as rice, wheat, fruits, radish, sweet potatoes, vegetable, nuts etc. It is a most ingenious apparatus, producing reports at intervals of 3, 5, 10 and 20 minutes which can easily be adjusted and operated with low operational cost of 120 times of explosions with one pound of carbite. It is reliable in operation and is not dangerous to handle even by young folks, and is strongly recommended to adapt during the night for animal.

Adhesive Engineering Company

These guys are doing what construction people never figured could be done. They take structures like collapsed concrete bridges, jack them back into place, inject some adhesive, and the bridge is stronger than before it collapsed. They print a pamphlet called Construction Adhesives Coatings and Sealants, and they provide information and survey to about every possible application of industrial gluing. Alan Kalker suggested it, through Herb Grubb. Alan's idea was that there might be an application here for prepoured concrete dome sections. Just pour the sections, hoist them in place, and stick them together.
—J. D. Smith

Adhesive Engineering Company
Information

free from:
Adhesive Engineering Co.
1411 Industrial Road
San Carlos, CA 94070

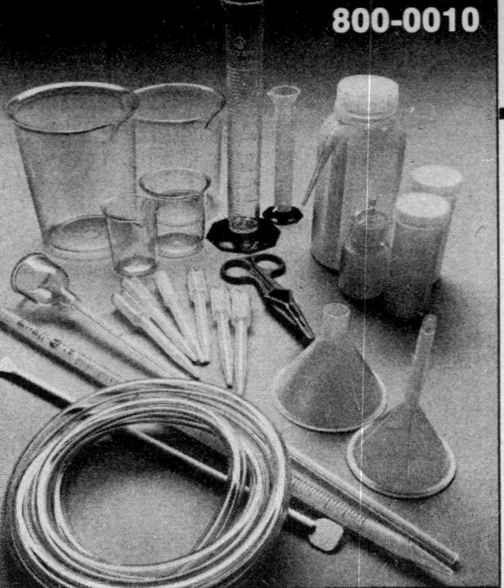

Labware student kit for high schools and colleges.

Nalgene Labware

Plastic lab equipment of unusually good design and utility presented in a catalog that makes one wish one had a spare $300 to spend. They'd prefer you'd attend your local dealer. Send for the catalog only if you're serious.
—J. Baldwin

Nalgene Labware
Nearest dealer location

free from:
Nalgene Company
Division of Sybron Corp.
Rochester, NY 14602
or check your local industrial supply dealer.

Hardware Products Springs

Hardware Products two-page catalog of springs contains more useful data than a dozen handbooks. It lists actual, stock springs of varying wire diameters, outside diameters, and lengths, with spring rate (the increase in pressure per inch of squeeze or extension) and the price per spring, postpaid! The charts make it easy to select the right size spring, compression or extension, for whatever job you have.
—Stephen P. Baldwin

Stock Springs
Information and price list

free from:
Hardware Products Co.
84 Fulton Street
Boston, MA 02113

SPECIFY HOOKS OR LOOPS

Magnets

Magnets have many more uses when they come in a variety of styles. These folks stock many types, including strips, at good prices.
—J. Baldwin

Permanent Magnets
Catalog

free from:
Maryland Magnet Co.
8825 Allenswood Road
Randallstown, MD 21133

MAGNETIC TOOL HOLDER

KEEP YOUR MOST-USED TOOLS AT YOUR FINGER TIPS!

This ingenious new MAGNETIC TOOL HOLDER solves the problem of holding various shaped tools on ONE rack. Designed to hold securely—tools, knives, scissors, utensils, instruments—in fact any implement made of Steel!

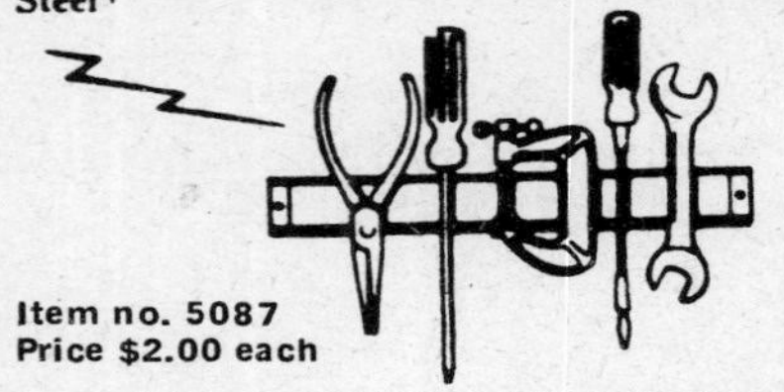

Item no. 5087
Price $2.00 each

Cadco Plastics

Sheet, rod, pipe, tape, rod, film, adhesives. Vinyl, polyethylene, nylon, mylar polypropylene, ABS, PVC. Comprehensive stock, offices nearly everywhere.
—SB
[Suggested by Fred Borcherdt]

Cadillac Plastic and Safety Buyers Guide

free from:
Cadillac Plastic and Chemical Company
Corporate Headquarters
P.O. Box 810
Detroit, MI 48232

FLARED TIP

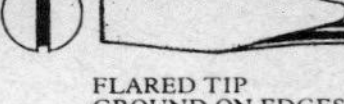

Care of screwdrivers
Choose a screwdriver which is correctly ground and the right size to fit snugly in the screw head. A rounded, chipped or undersized tip will slip and damage either the screw slot or the work itself. Similarly avoid using a tip that is too large and projects from either side of a countersunk screw. This will damage the work as the screw is driven home.

Use the correct cross head driver to fit the screw. Using a straight tip or another make of cross head can damage the screw, and once a cross head screw has been damaged it is very difficult to remove.

Make sure that driver tips fit properly into screw heads, as shown above.

A tip that is too large (above left) will damage surrounding work; a tip that is too small will not grip the screw correctly.

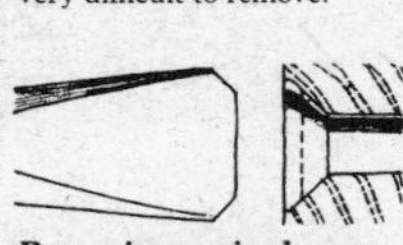

Removing a seized screw
To do this you may need a large powerful screwdriver. If the blade is too large to fit the screw head, grind the corners until the blade fits the slot.

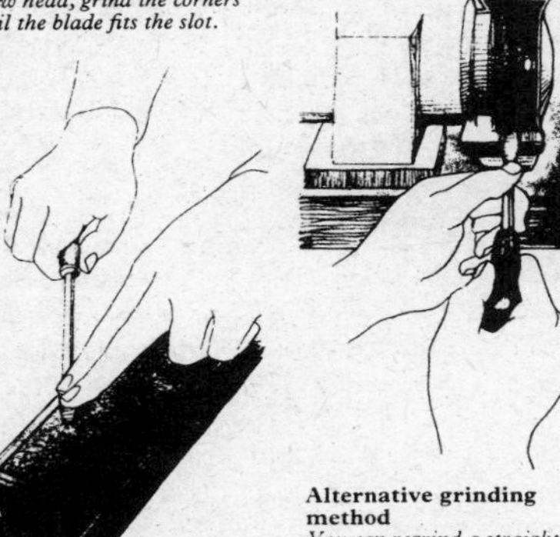

Repairing a straight edged screwdriver
Grind the side of the tip on an oilstone, keeping the blade at the correct angle.

Alternative grinding method
You can regrind a straight tipped screwdriver on an emery wheel, although this is not recommended by every manufacturer.

Tools and How to Use Them

The best guide to the range of tools a householder or homesteader might need to know and use. There are fifteen hundred drawings of common items as well as forgotten tools. Descriptions include the alternative generic names the tools have been known by, usage, sizes, and care of the tool. The section on brushes alone is worth the price of the book. Even though I trained as an apprentice house painter, not until Jackson and Day's book did I hear of a washing down brush, a mottler, a flogger, softener, a pencil overgrainer, or a fitch.

—Paul Hawken

[Suggested by Lloyd Kahn]

Tools and How to Use Them
Albert Jackson and David Day
1978; 352 pp.
$8.95 postpaid from:
Alfred A. Knopf, Inc.
Random House
455 Hahn Road
Westminster, MD 21157
or Whole Earth Household Store

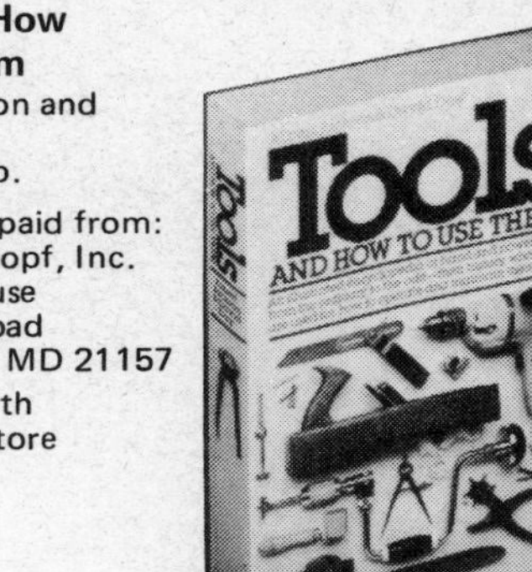

De Cristoforo's Complete Book of Power Tools

The author has been writing on tools and shop projects for 20 years. This book amasses a comprehensive collection of techniques and instructions for the use of power tools. It is without a doubt the best single volume I have ever encountered for the amateur. It is especially good at showing how to overcome the frustrations of the inexperienced user in obtaining the precision results he knows are obtained by the professional, using the same tools. The author shows how to make numerous jigs and fixtures that make difficult jobs easy. By far the greatest emphasis is on the table saw and the radial saw. Since these are usually the first stationary power tools purchased, the book is eminently practical.

De Cristoforo's style is very readable, and the illustrations and photographs are numerous and of excellent quality. Whenever one reads the De Cristoforo method for accomplishing an action he has attempted previously himself, it is immediately apparent that De Cristoforo "has been there before" and has developed a superior and probably safer method.

—Karl C. Thomas

De Cristoforo's Complete Book of Power Tools
(Both Stationary and Portable)
R.J. De Cristoforo
1972; 434 pp.
$16.95 postpaid from:
Harper and Row
Keystone Industrial Park
Scranton, PA 18512
or Whole Earth Household Store

→
Basic parts of a woodworking lathe

Get a true cove by setting the blade at right-angles to the work centerline. Tilt the blade toward the direction from which you will be feeding the stock. The radius of the arc will be determined by the size of the saw blade.
↓

Serrated Edge Trowel

OTHER NAMES: Mastic trowel, adhesive trowel, notched trowel
SIZE: Blade length: 4½ × 11in.
MATERIAL: *Blade:* steel; *Handle:* hardwood
USE: To spread ceramic tile adhesive

The serrated edge trowel is used to spread adhesive over large areas for operations such as covering a floor with ceramic tiles. There are two types of blades for the trowel which can be bolted to the frame. One blade has small "V" serrations all around, while the other is deeply notched on one side and end, leaving the other edges straight for normal troweling operations.

Cover about 1 square yard of the floor with adhesive at a time. Holding the blade of the trowel at an angle to the floor, drag it through the adhesive to spread it across the floor to the stipulated thickness.

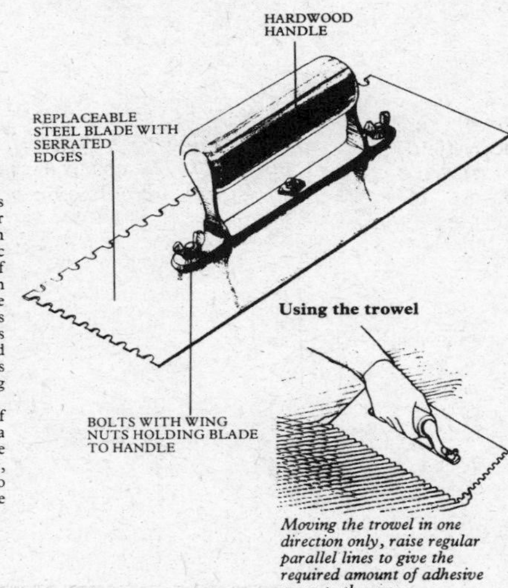

Using the trowel
Moving the trowel in one direction only, raise regular parallel lines to give the required amount of adhesive cover to the area.

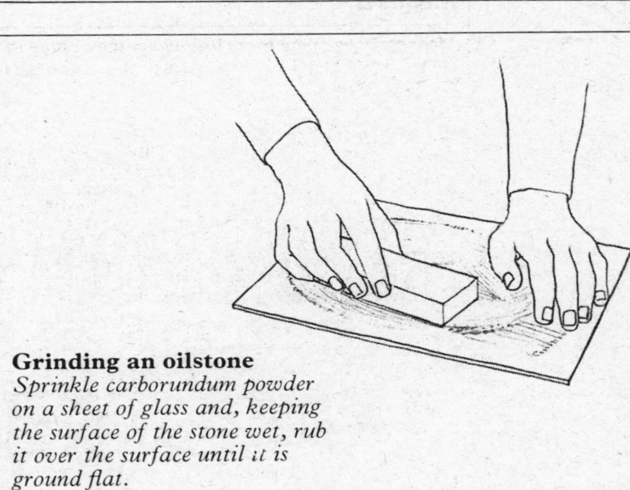

Grinding an oilstone
Sprinkle carborundum powder on a sheet of glass and, keeping the surface of the stone wet, rub it over the surface until it is ground flat.

Drawer Lock Chisel

OTHER NAMES: Bolt chisel, bolting iron, lock bolt chisel
SIZE: 6in.
MATERIAL: Steel
USE: To cut lock recesses

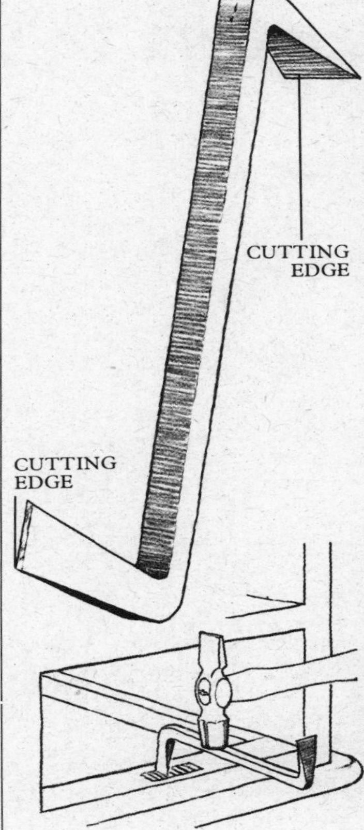

The drawer lock chisel is used for cutting housings or mortises for locks where there is not enough room to use a conventional chisel. It is a square sectioned steel bar, cranked at right angles at both ends. Each end is tapered and ground to a sharp edge. One cutting edge is set parallel with the long axis of the tool, the other is set at right angles to it.

The cutting edge is positioned on the work and its back is struck with a hammer. In a confined space the side of the hammer may have to be used.

Hanging a strip of wallpaper
When cutting wallpaper to wall lengths, allow an extra 2in. top and bottom for trimming to fit.

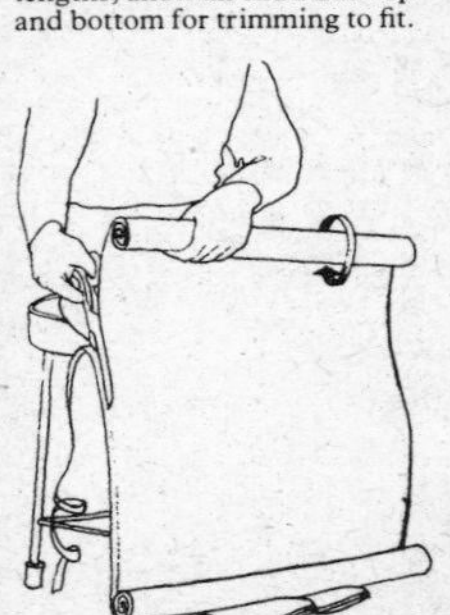

Very expensive or traditionally made wallpapers may need to have the selvedge trimmed in the old-fashioned way.

Gently mark the ceiling or baseboard line on the paper with the point of the scissors.

Peel back the paper, trim off the excess and brush back into place.

"Nibbling" pieces of glass

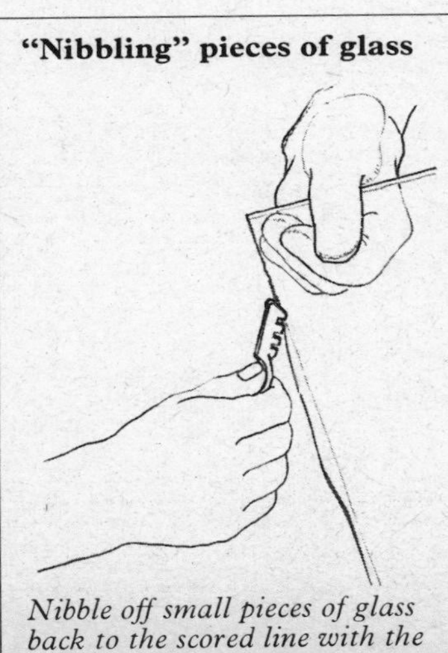

Nibble off small pieces of glass back to the scored line with the notches on the cutter.

THE RISING SUN
NEIGHBORHOOD NEWSLETTER

"I guess this has been pretty hard on you."
"Yeah, I feel like someone has taken the corks out of my feet and I'm running out."

Reader's Digest Complete Do-It-Yourself Manual

Jack up that sagging house, recane that worn-through chair, replace that rotten window sill. It's all here, in the most complete home repair book in print. 600 pages of clear instructions on building, mending, maintaining, carpentry, plumbing, wiring, tools, furniture, climate control, metalwork, brick laying, concrete, heating, and so forth. Good index. Reader's Digest has got it together.

—*Lloyd Kahn*
[Suggested by Al Perrin]

Reader's Digest Complete Do-It-Yourself Manual
1973; 600 pp.

$19.95 postpaid from:
W.W. Norton & Co.
500 Fifth Avenue
New York, NY 10036
or Whole Earth Household Store

A slate cutter, which you can rent, is used to cut down tiles to fit odd spaces.

Reader's Digest Fix-It-Yourself Manual

Say what you will about the **Reader's Digest**, *you're going to have to admit that they do a great manual. Their* **Complete Do-it-yourself Manual**, *which dealt mostly with the house itself and its various components, set a standard for such books that has not been surpassed in seven years, and I expect that this one will do the same. With it at your side, nearly anyone can undertake the repair of just about any object found in a typical USA household. If you don't know about tools, the book tells you what they are and how to use them, and does it without a trace of male chauvinism. The range of subjects covered is remarkable — everything from tightening loose rungs in the kitchen stool to whipping that rusty Coleman Stove back into shape. Only in a very few places (Auto Repair) does the dreaded oversimplification appear, and then only briefly. The text is terse and the illustrations are superior in every way. In fact, the entire book is superior in every way; it's by far the best available.*

—*J. Baldwin*

Reader's Digest Fix-It-Yourself Manual
1977; 480 pp.

$19.95 postpaid from:
W.W. Norton & Co.
500 Fifth Avenue
New York, NY 10036
or Whole Earth Household Store

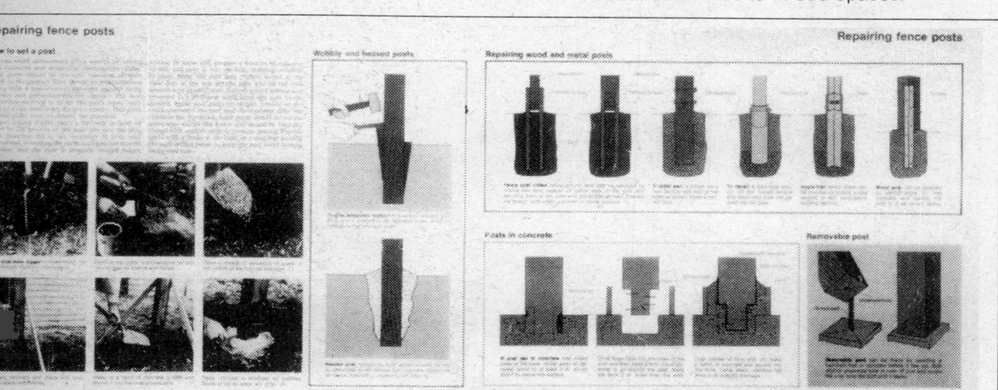

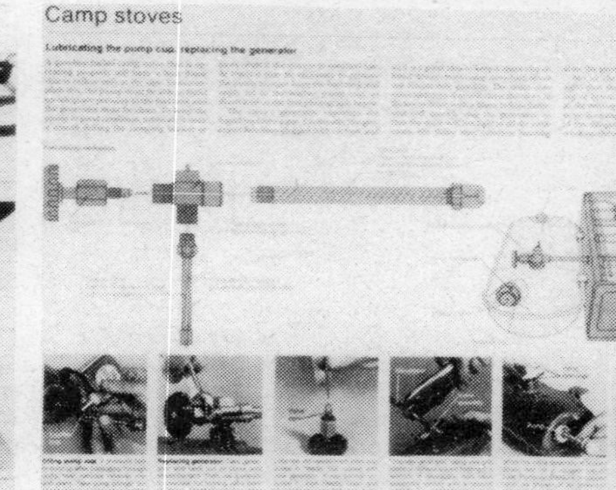

Replacing wood shingles

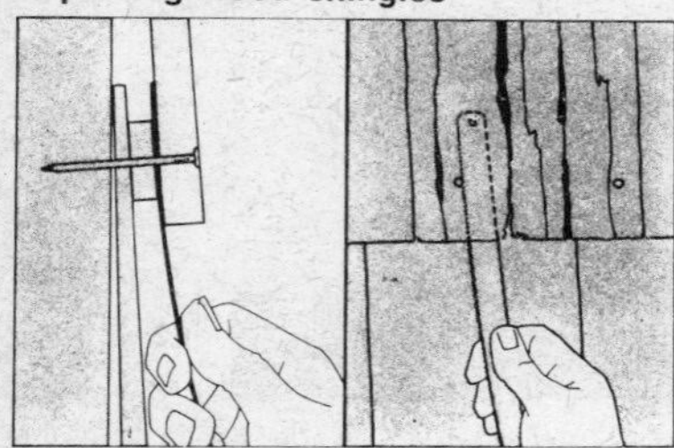

Slip a hacksaw blade under the bottom of the good shingle and cut the nails that hold the top of the damaged shingle. In the same way, cut nails at bottom of the damaged shingle.

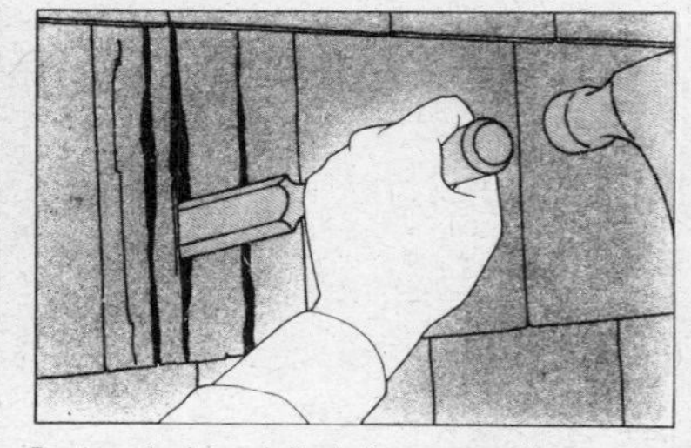

To remove the damaged shingle, it is necessary, first, to splinter it. Then remove stubs of previously cut nails with a claw hammer or with pincers.

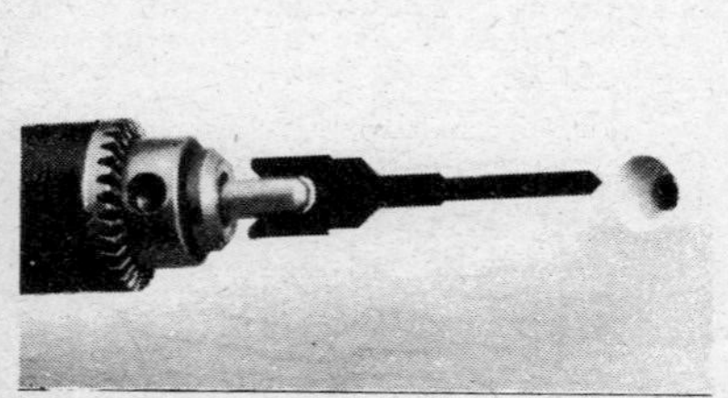

Screw-mate device enables you to drill pilot hole, shank clearance hole, and countersink all in one operation.

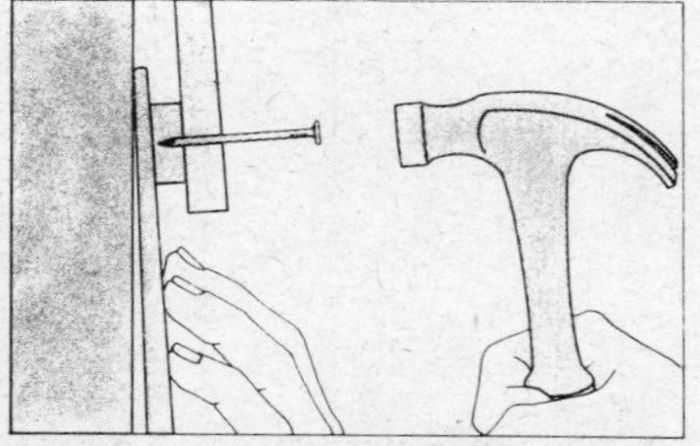

Slip a new shingle, the same size and thickness as the old one, into the open cavity. Top of new shingle is overlapped by upper shingle course; bottom overlaps lower shingle course.

Methods of nailing wood to wood

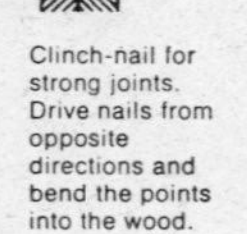
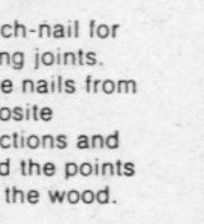
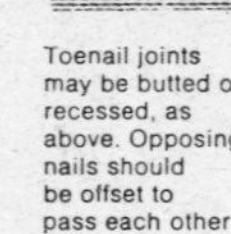

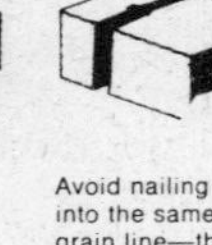

Use nails 2½ to 3 times longer than the thickness of the wood they must hold. Always nail light work to heavy.

Clinch-nail for strong joints. Drive nails from opposite directions and bend the points into the wood.

Toenail joints may be butted or recessed, as above. Opposing nails should be offset to pass each other.

Use a clamp and a block of wood to steady a frame when toenailing. First nail will hold while the second is driven.

Dovetail nailing is done by driving nails at angles for better grip. Slant nails have hook effect.

Avoid nailing into the same grain line—this will split the wood. Use blunt nails near the ends.

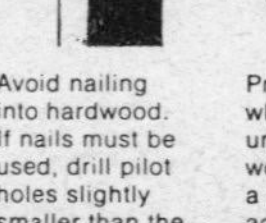
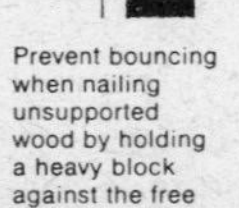
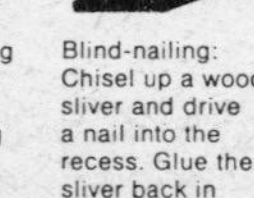

Split ends can be minimized by cutting wood overlength. Nail it in place before sawing off the excess.

Avoid nailing into hardwood. If nails must be used, drill pilot holes slightly smaller than the nail shank.

Prevent bouncing when nailing unsupported wood by holding a heavy block against the free side of the work.

Blind-nailing: Chisel up a wood sliver and drive a nail into the recess. Glue the sliver back in position.

Blind-nail into floorboards by driving through tongue and shoulder. Drive at slight angle as shown.

Push small nails and tacks through a thin cardboard holder so that fingers can be kept clear of the hammer.

Hidden screws and trick connections

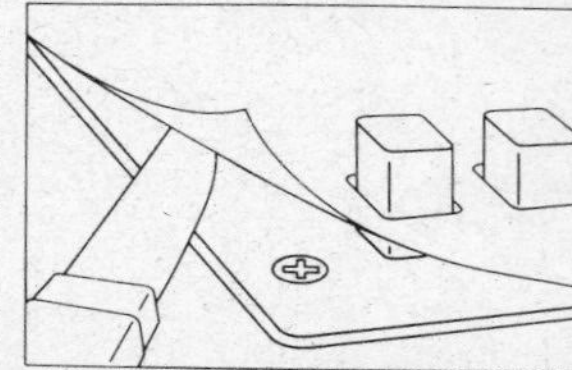

Screws are often concealed under decorative metal facings. Press facing with finger to locate screws, then pry facing up with knife. Work carefully to minimize creasing. Use strong contact cement to reglue.

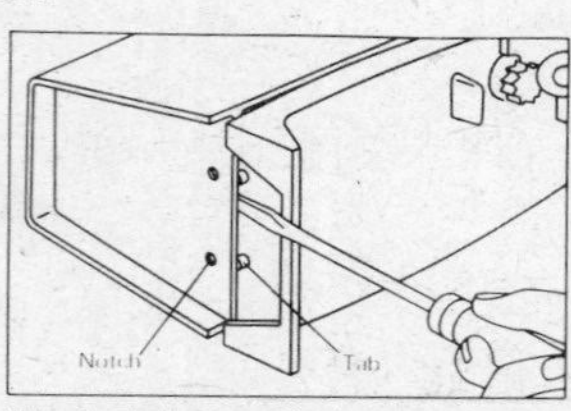

Natural springiness permits plastic parts to be connected by simple tab and notch arrangements. Illustration shows housing of can opener. Posts on one half of housing are being pried from holes in other half.

To separate parts held together by keyhole and bolt method, slide one part horizontally with respect to the other, then pull the two apart. Sharp rap may help if parts are stuck. Bolts are adjustable for tighter fit.

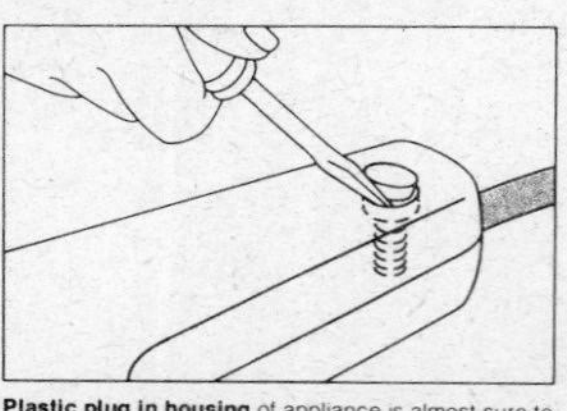

Plastic plug in housing of appliance is almost sure to have assembly screw beneath it. Pry plug out with strong, sharp instrument. Some marring of finish is inevitable no matter how carefully you work.

Top of clothes dryer may be held by hidden spring clips. To release top, insert putty knife under it, push knife against clip, and pull up on top. Pair of clips 2 in. from each end are usually used.

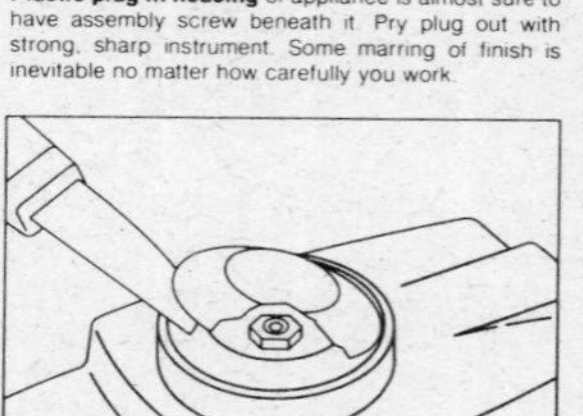

Metal cap must be pried off to reach both main assembly nut and thermostat adjustment screw of this fryer control. Nut can be removed with hollow shank nut driver. Adjustment screw is in center of control shaft.

How to fix a broken handle

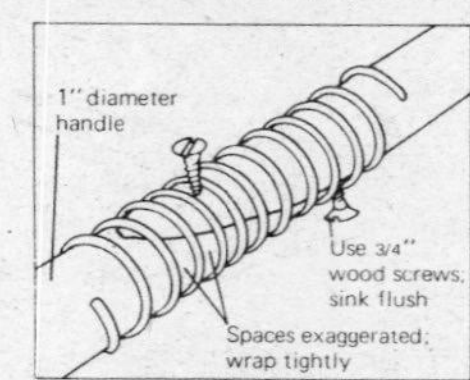

Glue a long split with epoxy adhesive. Add short wood screws to thick handles, as shown. Soak heavy twine in adhesive and wrap it around handle for added strength.

Eight tools in one

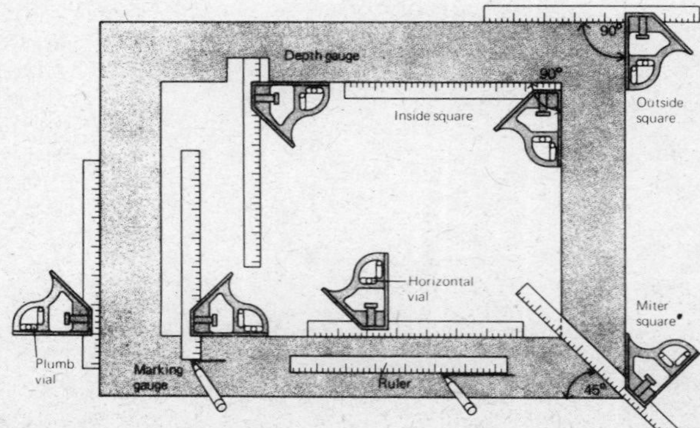

Combination square contains a ruler, 45° and 90° angles, and two levels. The ruler can be separated from the remainder of the tool. In various configurations, this square can be used as eight different tools, including a vertical (plumb) or horizontal level, a depth gauge, and a marking gauge for cutting lumber.

↑
Repairing a Windsor armchair. Interlocking joints must be kept tight to keep entire structure together.

using the friction of misaligned rollers to slow progress

braking

Moving Heavy Things

I remember once watching in wonder as a lone man carried a full size upright piano up a flight of stairs! 600 lbs. How did he do it? This marvelous little primer by the inimitable Jan Adkins (world's youngest Old Salt) brings to us mere mortals the secrets of manipulating weighty objects. Not only are the secrets well explained and illustrated, the essential spirit is properly attended. The book encourages independence. Every household should have one. —J. Baldwin

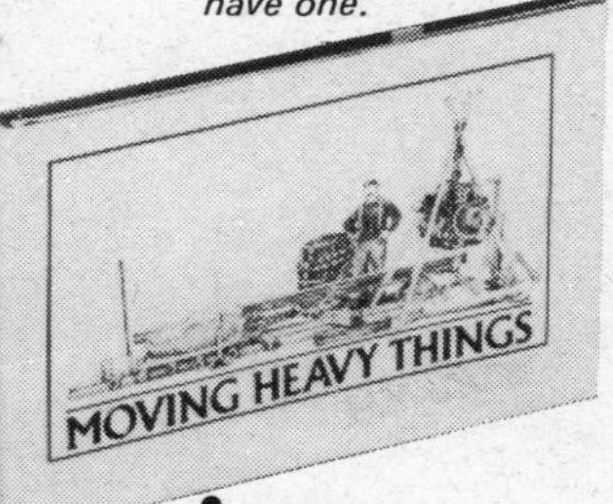

Moving Heavy Things
Jan Adkins
1980; 48 pp.
$6.95 postpaid from:
Houghton Mifflin Co.
Wayside Road
Burlington, MA 01803
or Whole Earth
Household Store

•

Precept Five:
Applied Sloth
As stated in the stagehand's axiom: "Never lift what you can drag, never drag what you can roll, never roll what you can leave." Creativity germinates in indolence, and the cleverest people are often the laziest: they are always looking for an easier way. The easiest way is often the simplest, most direct, and the best way.

•

There is always one more way to skin a cat. Jay Baldwin, technical editor of **CoEvolution Quarterly**, tells of a boat-builder who proudly announced to Jay that he had *not* built his boat too big to bring out of his garage; he had allowed a full ½" top and sides. Jay could not imagine how they could put wheels or rollers under the boat in half an inch. Oh. The boat came smoothly out . . . on bacon rinds. It was so well lubricated that it slid down the driveway and into the street.

Using two fulcrums to continue a lift: as the lever is rocked additional blocking is slipped under the angle of the lever.

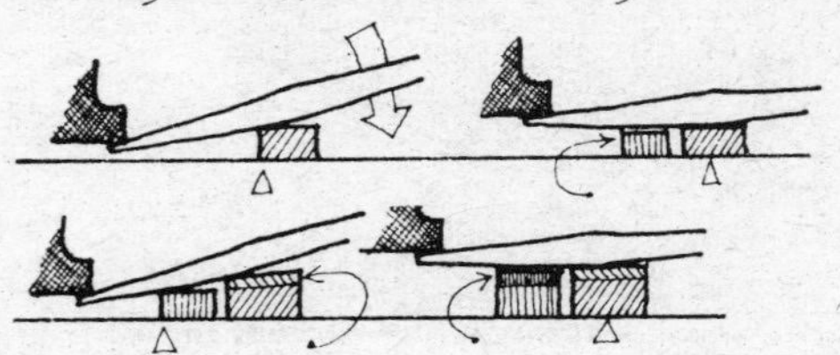

The porter's knot is a head cushion. Sling a trunk to a pole and share the load.

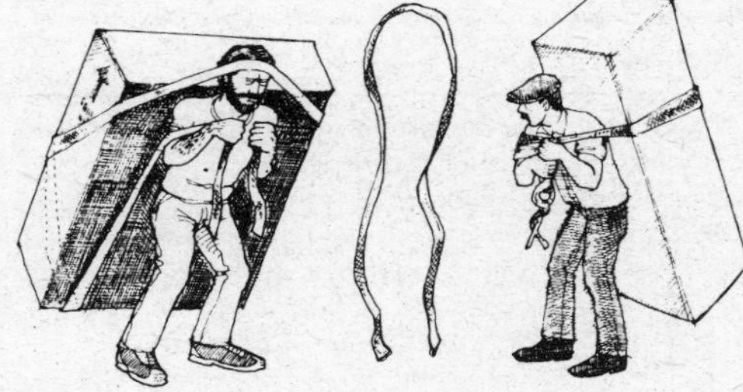

The lineman's loop is a secure, nonjamming loop ideal for a shoulder harness along a long line.

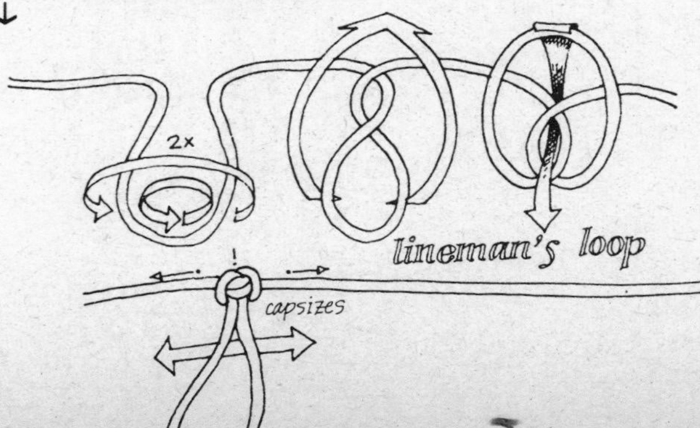

Do-It-Yourself Plumbing

There are many books that adequately handle this subject, but this one is special: In addition to being commendably clear on repairs, both graphically and in the text, it has a really fine section on designing your own plumbing system. I especially like the author's insistence on explaining the basic reasons underlying his instructions and also building codes. That way you really learn something. This is another of the excellent Popular Science books. —J. Baldwin

Do-It-Yourself Plumbing
Max Alth
1975; 301 pp.
$12.95 postpaid from:
Harper and Row
Keystone Industrial Park
Scranton, PA 18512
or Whole Earth
Household Store

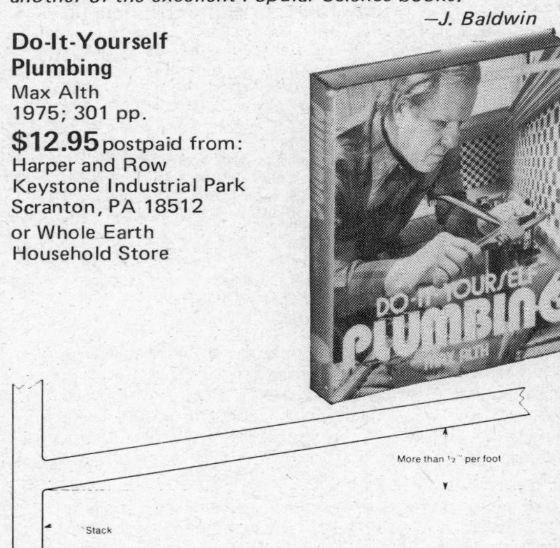

More than ½ per foot
Stack
45
¼ per foot

If you have to pitch any drainpipe more than ½ inch to the foot to reach a stack, run a section of the pipe at 45 or more degrees and the balance at ½ or ¼ inch to the foot.

Wiring Simplified

Other than that this book is a most useful tool for the home electrician, the thing I like about it is that it has a hole punched all the way through it, for hanging over a nail. That is a kind of practicality that all American publishers should learn. Everything you'll need to wire your home yourself. —J.D. Smith

Wiring Simplified
(32nd Edition)
H.P. Richter
1978; 160 pp.
$2.80 postpaid from:
Park Publishing
1999 Shepard Road
St. Paul, MN 55116
or Whole Earth
Household Store

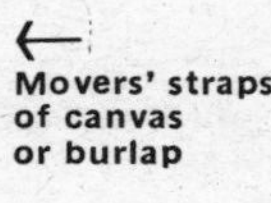

Movers' straps of canvas or burlap

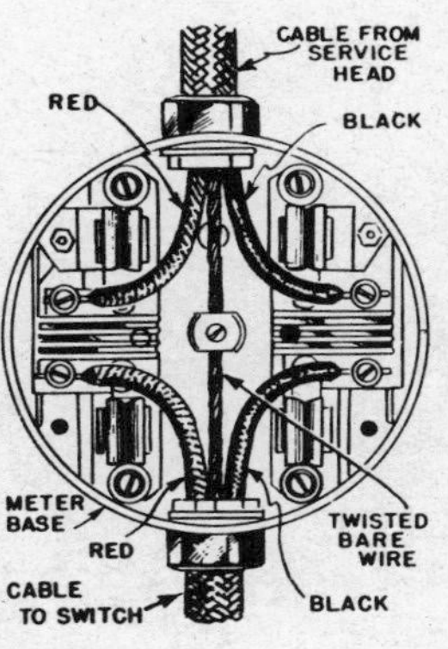

Fig. 8-20. How wires are connected to the meter base or socket. The bare, uninsulated wire is always connected to the neutral center contact of the socket.

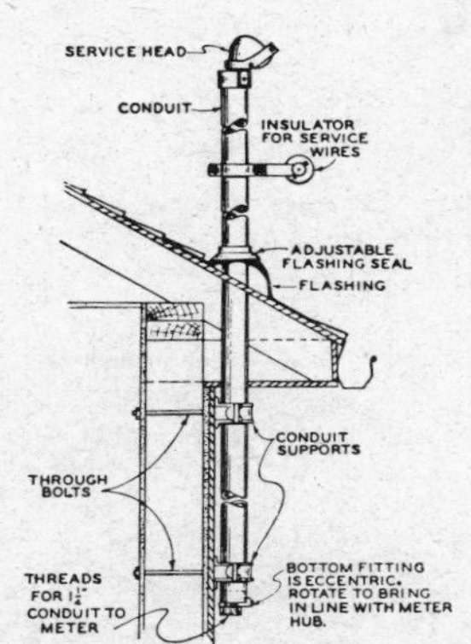

Fig. 8-11. On rambler or ranch-house type of construction, use a mast to give the service wires the necessary clearance above ground.

Cutting and Joining Plastic Pipe

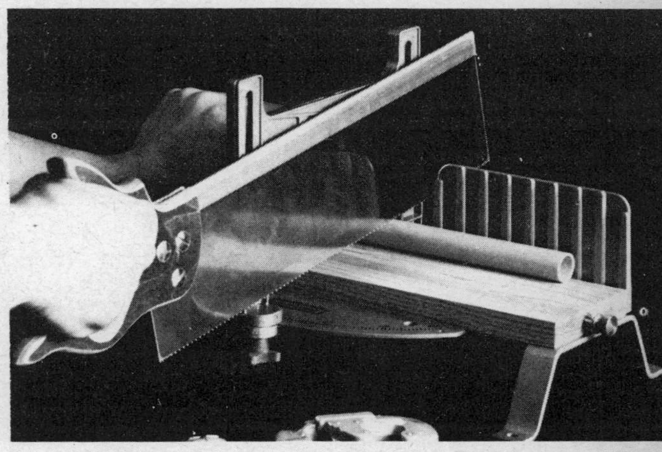

1. Cut the pipe end as squarely as possible, preferably with the aid of a miter box. Any saw can be used.

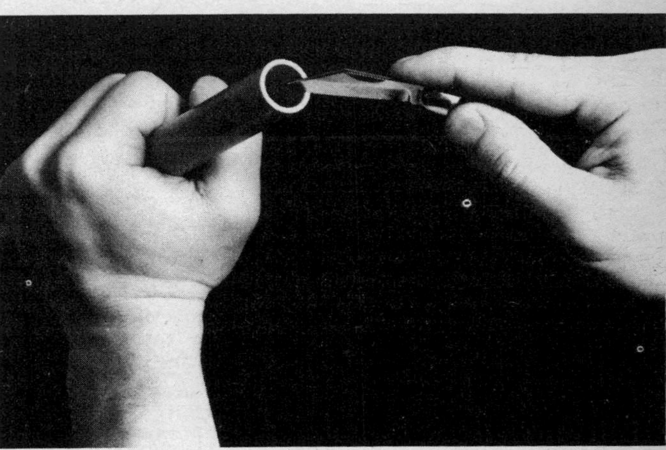

2. The inside end of the pipe is either reamed with a standard reamer or deburred with a penknife.

3. Coat the end of the pipe and the inside surface of the fitting with pipe cement.

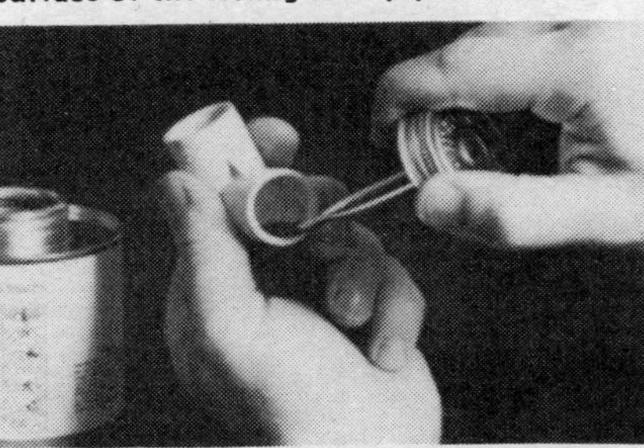

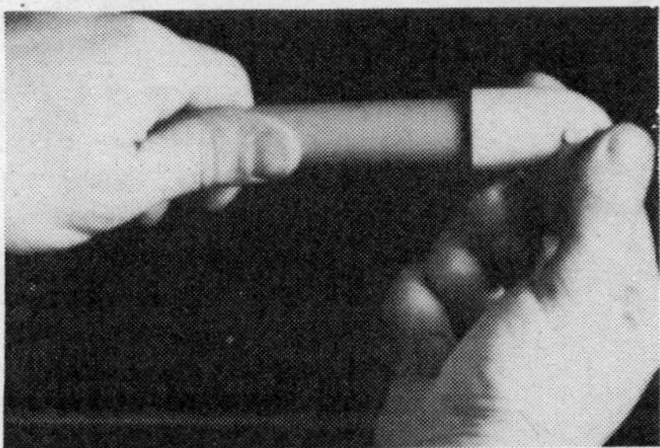

4. Assemble the joint and give the fitting a fraction of a turn to make certain the cement has been evenly distributed. Allow to harden in correct position. Courtesy B.F. Goodrich Chemical Co.

THE RISING SUN
NEIGHBORHOOD NEWSLETTER

"The law, in its majestic equality, forbids the rich as well as the poor to sleep under bridges, to pee in the streets and to steal bread."

— Anatole France

Shop Tactics

This is a truly useful book for those who make things or who would like to be able to make things. After years of being a professional thing-maker I find much I didn't know here. Better, it's a good reference in case you need to solder something but have forgotten how, for instance. But best of all the book is written in an encouraging, friendly way so that the Mysteries of the Shop are revealed about as much as they can be short of lousing up some material practicing. Virtually all common shop practices are shown, explained, and illustrated. Many of the basic principles involved in various shop tactics are explained so that you learn in depth. My only regrets arise from a basic philosophy he holds: "Overbuild everything." This is how a lot of American waste gets generated, as that attitude tends to discourage sharp thought. Bill Abler wants you to make things as easily as he does. With this book and a few brains, you probably can.

—J. Baldwin

Shop Tactics
(The Common-Sense Way of Using Tools and Working with Woods, Metals, Plastics and Glass)
William Abler
1976; 117 pp.

$3.95 postpaid from:
Running Press
38 South 19th Street
Philadelphia, PA 19103

or Whole Earth Household Store

Solder
hot iron
Hold iron beneath the joint
Good Solder Joint (shiny)

Hold the hot iron beneath the mechanically joined wires, pressing it firmly against the joint, and press the solder between the wires and the iron. The object of these procedures is to heat the wires as quickly as possible. The advantage of this is that the shorter the time that the wires are hot, the less time the heat will have to be conducted along them and ruin electrical components, and the less time the metal will have to oxidize. As the solder begins to melt it will conduct heat to the wires and further increase the speed of their heating. The solder will flow by capillarity into the narrow crack between the joined pieces of wire. After the solder has flowed you may want to touch the solder to the top of the wire joint to add a bit of solder there. Usually this is not necessary.

•

The finished product is only the garbage of the work. It is the making of it that must be enjoyed. Then the excellent product will take care of itself.

•

Don't worry if you never made things before. Remember that Ben Franklin was a pretty fair violinist, and he prescribed this formula for learning: "Begin young, as I did, at age fifty-five. Practice regularly, as I do, while waiting for other people to keep appointments, and you are sure to succeed."

One last word. Making of gadgets and machines is a skill indispensable in art and science. Every sculptor is a gadgeteer, and many scientists have been gadgeteers, among them Newton (the reflecting telescope), Galileo (the refracting lens telescope), and Archimedes (the toothed wheel). I would even say that the genius of these men was a measure not of their IQ but of their feel for the way objects and materials behave, and a measure of the delight they took in exercising that feeling.

Popular Mechanics
Popular Science

Take your choice, the difference between them is about as important as the difference between a Ford and a Chevy — largely in your head. Both offer fast looks at what's coming, what's here, and how to use what's here. Both present their information in a way that makes picking it up fast and painless, but of course at the expense of detail. (This may well be a boon in an age of media overload.) These magazines are to me the best way to keep up with technological developments at a consumer level. My subscription is to **Popular Science**, *but I can't defend that choice in any logical way. Habit, I guess.*

—J. Baldwin

Popular Science
(The What's New Magazine)
Hubert P. Luckett, Editor

$9.94 /year (12 issues)
from:
Popular Science
Subscription Department
Boulder, CO 80302

Popular Mechanics
John A. Linkletter, Editor

$8.97 /year (12 issues)
from:
Popular Mechanics
P.O. Box 10064
Des Moines, IA 50350

Sharpening

I like this sharpening book the best of any I've seen because it tells you why you're doing it the way they suggest, so you really learn something, and it only costs a buck twenty-five.

—J. Baldwin

A Manual on Sharpening Hand Woodworking Tools
J.K. Coggin,
L.O. Armstrong,
G.W. Giles
1943; 48 pp.

$1.25 postpaid from:
The Interstate Printers and Publishers, Inc.
19-27 North Jackson St.
Danville, IL 61832

or Whole Earth Household Store

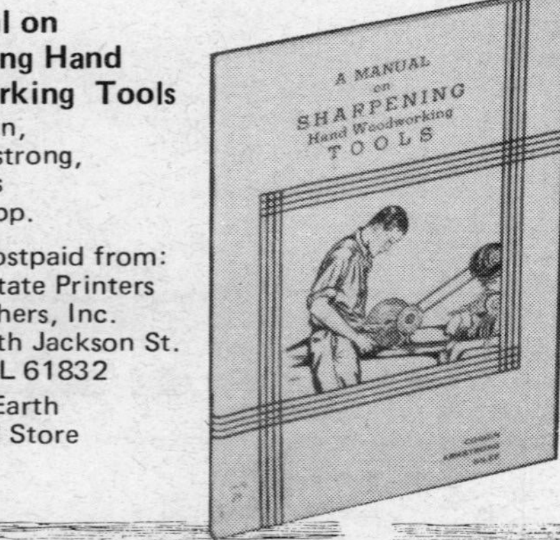

UNTIL EDGE DOES NOT REFLECT LIGHT—
(10)

OR UNTIL EDGE FEELS SMOOTH AND KEEN UNDER THUMB TEST.
(11)

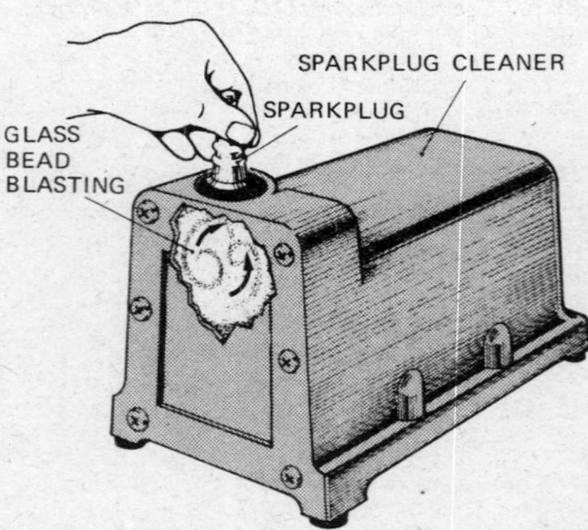

Portable sparkplug cleaner is the best way to clean electrodes and restore plugs.

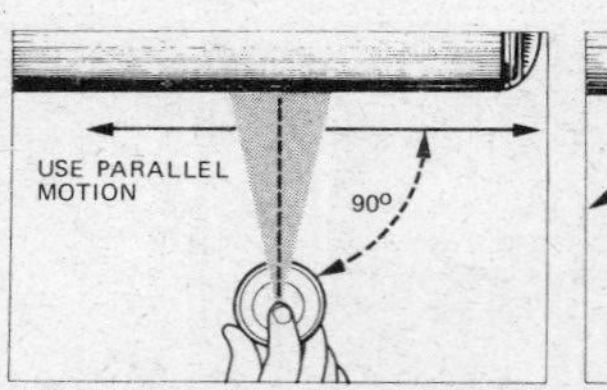

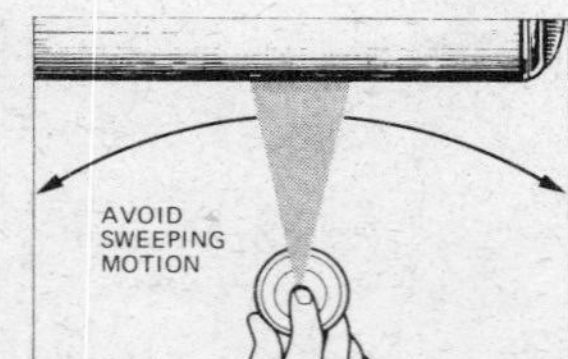

Use even rapid strokes in applying the paint. Keep the can parallel to the surface you are painting and apply the spray in light coats to avoid runs. —Popular Mechanics

Kerodex Barrier Cream

I have been using Kerodex Barrier Creams by Ayerst Laboratories, Inc., New York, NY, for years with excellent results. These creams are applied to the hands *before* you start working with irritating chemicals. I find them especially useful when working with paints and concrete. With paints the solvents don't hurt my hands and paint does not stick to them as much as it does without. With concrete I can work the concrete with my bare hands (being less than expert with trowels) without having the skin dry out and shrink.

They are also supposed to be very good for protection when working with resins or liquid plastics. I've never used them for these substances. I have used them when working fiberglass insulation with good results. Also have pulled poison oak with only the cream as protection.

Comes in two types: No. 51 for dry work; if you get it wet you must reapply at once. No. 71 for wet work like concrete.

Available in most drugstores. There is a complete list of things it protects against included in the box.

Glen A. Twombly
Pomona, New York

Bag Balm

Check into Bag Balm, an antiseptic medication for cows' udders, teats, whatever, which happens to be the most fantastic hand lotion ever made by anybody anywhere. Used by dishwashers, clam diggers, and lobstermen up here to change cracked callused skin into beautiful soft flesh overnight! No shit. 10 oz. can for $2.50 plus $.50 handling charge. Contact:

Dairy Association Co., Inc.
Lyndonville, Vermont

Charles Miller
Monhegan Island
Maine

Lineman's gloves

Until a pair of these landed on my hands I had about given up on ever finding decent workgloves. These beauties are about the best I've ever seen. Soft, sturdy and with a trick thumb contour that lets you do fairly delicate nabbing, they really protect your hands and wrists. Send a draw-around of your hand to get the right size. They come with winter liners.

—J. "50-fingers" Baldwin

Lineman's Gloves

$20 (approx.) from:
Technical Fix Inc.
Box 233
Chelsea, VT 05038

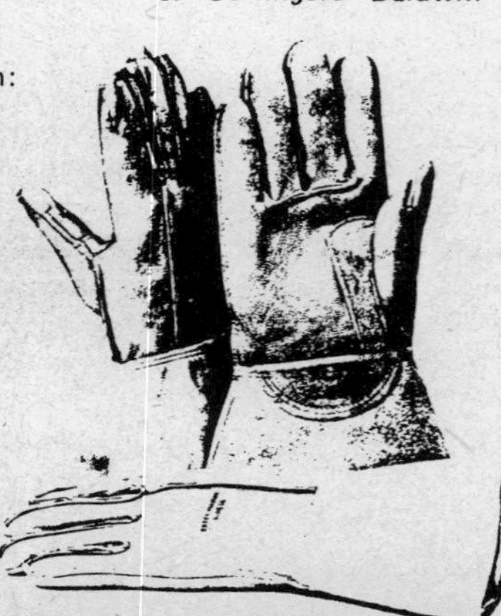

Safety Equipment

Critical information (these days)
which is very hard to find

by Richard Nilsen

THE BACK OF THE CAN SAYS "Use with adequate ventilation," but you are scrunched up in the crawl space under the house gluing plastic pipe together. Or laying tile in the corner of a windowless bathroom where the exhaust fan isn't hooked up yet. Actual working conditions are almost never "ideal".

Remedies like respirators, goggles, ear muffs and hard hats are often marketed mainly to factory and construction workers. The two manufacturers whose products you see here, American Optical Corporation of Southbridge, Massachusetts, and Norton Company of Worcester, Massachusetts, are by no means the only companies making this kind of equipment. These two do have complete lines, and offer high quality at competitive prices. And equally important, each is out to attract the growing do-it-yourself market, which means you can find their products at your local hardware or paint supply store. If you strike out there, the yellow pages of a big city phone book, under Safety Equipment, will sometimes put you in touch with someone who can tell you where to go. Neither of these companies sells mail order. Prices are "suggested retail."

Norton Spray Paint Respirator (7531P), this one fitted with cartridges and pre-filters for paint spray mists. $18.50.

American Optical R5000/6000 Dual-Element Respirators.

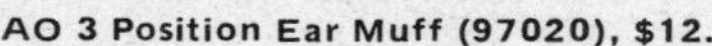

AO 3 Position Ear Muff (97020), $12.

EYE, HEARING AND HEAD PROTECTION

The American Optical Head of the House Protection Kit (99510, $40) is a hard hat with attached hearing protectors and face shield. Also included are impact goggles. Ideal for protection when using chainsaws, or any power saw.

If goggles bother you because they sometimes fog up, American Optical also makes protective eyewear with side shields (91011, $8). And if you wear glasses to begin with, the AO Liteliner Eyeguards (9111, $2) will fit over your own glasses. They are great if you are painting, and also protect against minor impact from flying chips and particles.

American Optical also makes an inexpensive goggle for gas welding. It's the Weld-View Vision (91225, $9.20). And for hearing protection, their three position ear muff (97020, $12) can be worn over the top of the head, around the back of the neck, or under the chin. ■

AO Safety Glasses with sideshields (91011), $8.

AO Liteliner eyeguards (91111), $2.

AO Weld-View Welders goggle (91225), $9.20.

DUST MASKS

The American Optical Dust Demon (R1050, $1.29 each) is a throw-away mask, but it has the great advantage of folding flat and sliding into your pocket when not in use. Weighs only .4 ounces and is for use against pneumoconiosis and fibrosis-producing dusts, including — but not limited to — aluminum, asbestos, coal, flour, iron ore and free silica. It is also easy to talk while wearing one. AO has been selling quite a few to winter joggers, who use the them to help warm icy winter air.

Norton's Dust Mask (GB50, $2.85) has a replaceable filter element (GB001, a pack of 5 filters for $1.89). But before you do that, you can simply wash the filter in warm sudsy water, dry it out, and stick it back in. This mask is only for non-toxic dusts and pollen — hay-fever sufferers take note — and unlike the AO Dust Demon, does not work for pneumoconiosis-producing dusts. Neither companies' dust mask will protect you against toxic vapors or gases, and of course neither will supply oxygen in a space where there is not enough, or protect against carbon monoxide.

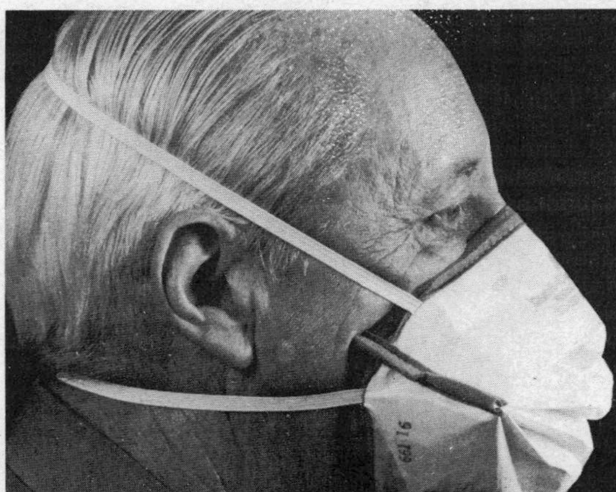

American Optical Dust Demon (R1050), $1.70.

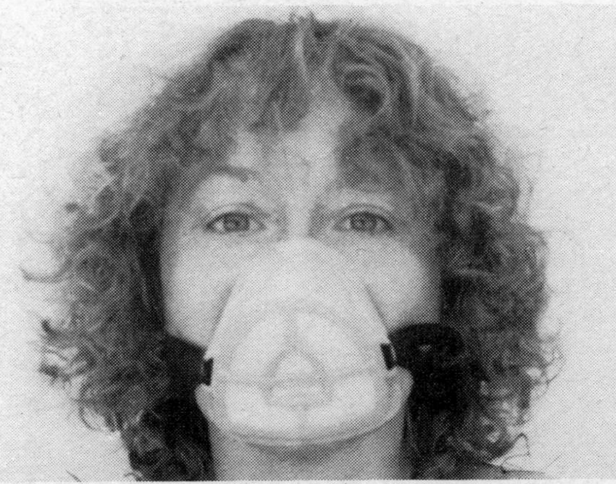

Norton Spray Paint Respirator (7531P), $18.50, this one fitted with cartridges and pre-filters for paint spray mists.

RESPIRATORS

Both Norton and American Optical have full lines of dual cartridge respirators. You buy one face piece (and there are different sizes in each line, so if you have a small face or a big nose, get the one that fits best), and into it you screw pairs of cartridges for a wide assortment of different toxic materials. You have to have the correct cartridges for the material you are working with; otherwise you will not be protected. For example, the cartridges for chlorine gas won't work if you are spraying lacquer, and the ones for ammonia won't work if you are spraying pesticides.

When breathing becomes difficult, or when you start to smell the substance you are working with through the mask, the cartridges are filled up, and they should be discarded and new ones screwed on. No respirator supplies oxygen; equipment that does — with tanks, air hoses and masks — is not reviewed here. And none of them is any good against carbon monoxide gas.

Organic vapor cartridges are for things like plastic cements for pipe and tile, epoxy resins, and paint. However if you are spraying paint, you also need a pre-filter on each cartridge to capture the larger particles. These are held in place by round louvers. I have used my Norton respirator for various jobs over the years. It has two head straps, so the mask stays put and keeps a nice positive seal around your mouth and nose.

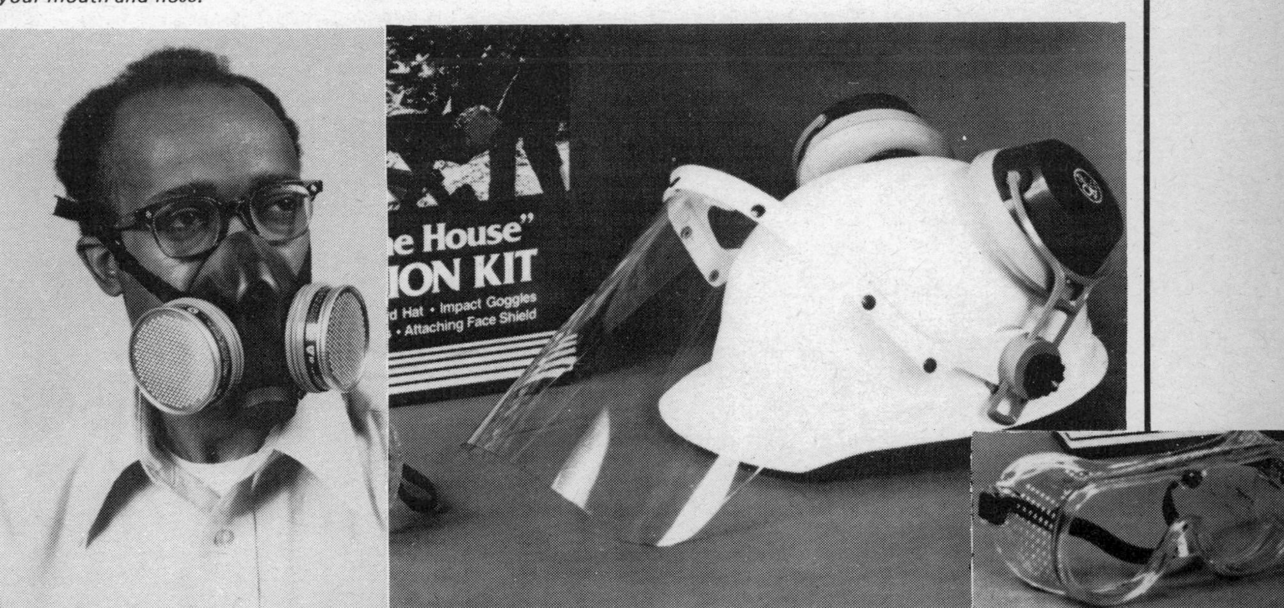

Respirator with cartridges for fumes from welding, $22.

American Optical Head of the House Protection Kit (99510), $40; flexible mask impact goggle with clear anti-fog lens.

More safety

For further safety information see Occupational Hazards of Construction *(p. 225) and* Health Hazards for Artists *(p. 248).*

THE RISING SUN
NEIGHBORHOOD NEWSLETTER

A village is made of stories about itself.

The Making of Tools

Using tools to make tools is as high a craft and calling as they come. Get your forge, anvil, drill-press, and this well-made book. Start with screwdrivers. Work up to shears. With the sequel below, move on to chisels, shovels, and tools of your own invention. —SB

The Making of Tools
Alexander G. Weygers
1973; 93 pp.

$6.95 postpaid from:
Van Nostrand
Reinhold Company
Order Department
7625 Empire Drive
Florence, KY 41042
or Whole Earth
Household Store

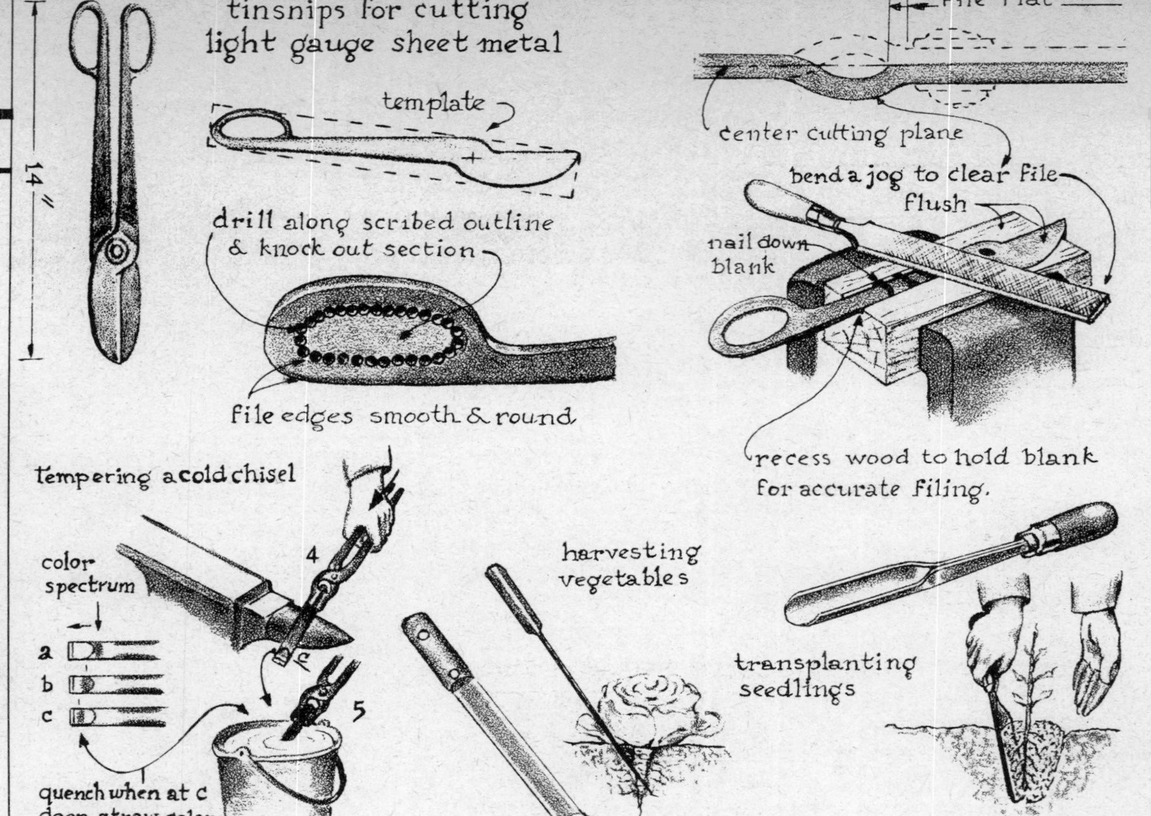

•

Most tools are made of high-carbon steel. This is *temperable* steel. It can be bought cheaply at steel scrap-yards and automobile junkyards. And, once you develop an eye for it, great amounts are found strewn along highways and in vacant lots to add to your own scrap pile. No matter how beat-up or rusty a piece of discarded scrap may be, add it to your own supply. Scrap is cheap, and as rusty, corroded surfaces are usually only skin deep, they can easily be ground clean.

•

Files will often remove steel as efficiently as grindstones — generally as quickly, and with greater control. Don't neglect learning how to file accurately. Make yourself carry out, at least once, the excercises recommended in dealing with hinged tools like tinsnips, shears, pliers, etc. Try to master the filing technique, for it will benefit all you plan to accomplish in toolmaking.

•

You will sometimes find yourself tempted to whip out a needed, easy-to-make tool that you have lost or mislaid. I have often made a duplicate wrench, screwdriver, hammer, garden tool, rather than spend the time searching for it. The happy result is that wherever I happen to be working — in the shop, studio, house, or garden — there is always a spare one nearby.

The Modern Blacksmith

If you've ever considered learning the Blacksmith trade, you're no longer safe. If you think that blacksmithing means making horseshoes and little else, you might investigate further. Mr. Weygers' beautiful book stresses making your own tools and the clever utilization of scrap metal. Starting with a few wise words concerning attitude, he goes on to explain the possibilities that a skill in blacksmithing opens for the craftsman. He continues with explanations of the tools, shop space, materials and basic techniques. He then clearly shows the more advanced tricks of the trade. Every important point is illustrated (by him) with lucid drawings. But the best thing about this book is that it makes you want to go out and Do it. This book is unusually well done, and the author's spirit of quiet joy and competence shines through in a way that is rare these days. Now to find a used anvil . . .
—J. Baldwin

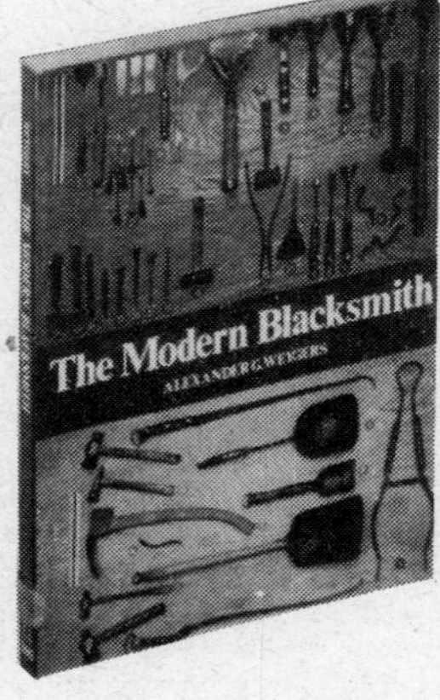

The Modern Blacksmith
Alexander G. Weygers
1974; 96 pp.

$6.95 postpaid from:
Van Nostrand
Reinhold Company
Order Department
7625 Empire Drive
Florence, KY 41042
or Whole Earth
Household Store

principles in use of
hammer & body motions,

shoulder is down & stationary
all muscles & joints are at
maximum use.

The Recycling, Use, & Repair of Tools

Even if you are an experienced smith, the most recent Weygers book will probably have some things you don't know; it speaks extensively of recycling old metalworking machines such as lathes and even a trip-hammer. There is a nifty chapter on making bearings, and another on making a good wood lathe from scrap metal. The index shows a diversity stemming from his almost unbelievably varied experience.
—J. Baldwin

The Recycling, Use, & Repair of Tools
Alexander G. Weygers
1978; 112 pp.

$6.95 postpaid from:
Van Nostrand
Reinhold Company
Order Department
7625 Empire Drive
Florence, KY 41042
or Whole Earth
Household Store

•

If the file teeth are not too worn, they can be sharpened somewhat by immersing the files in a bath of acid. The acid seems to bite into the walls of the tooth serration, rather than into its edge, and thus sharpens that edge to some degree. I have successfully used the acid from old car batteries for this purpose.

•

A Modern Method of "Stropping" Tool Edges ⟶

In the shop, a cotton buffing wheel replaces the strop. The rim of the buffer is rubbed with a tripoli abrasive compound and the final burr of the tool edge is cleanly removed by it. It does what the barber's strop did, but better and a thousand times faster.

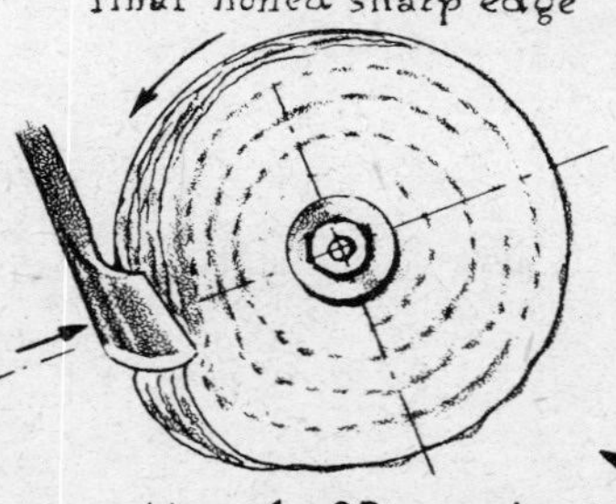

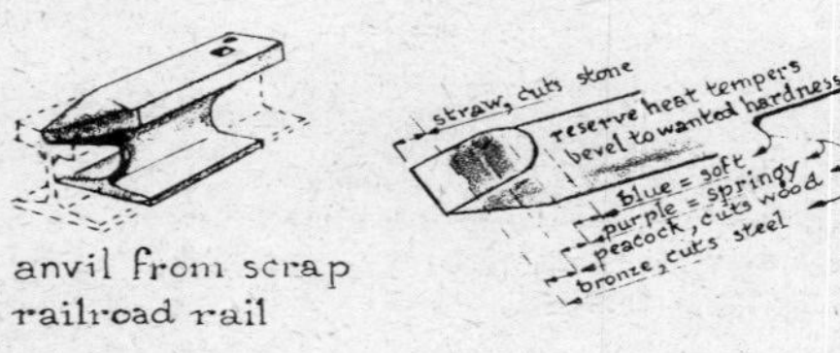

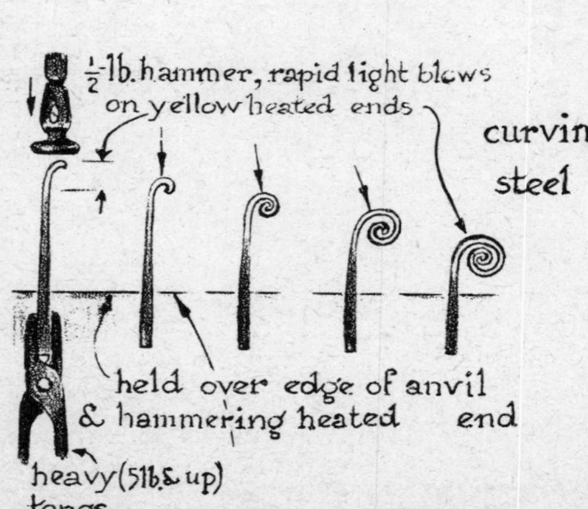

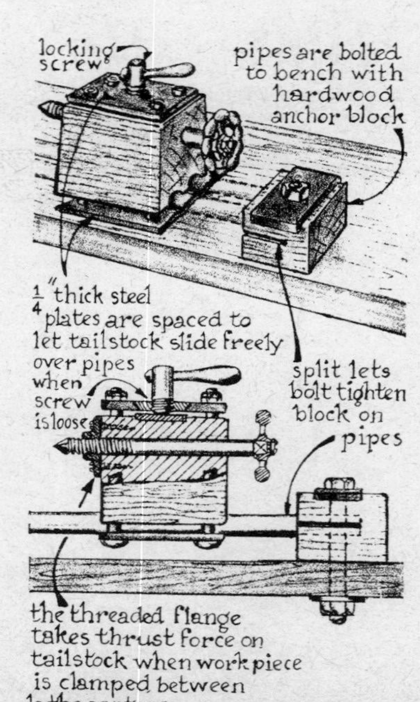

SOFT-HEAD HAMMER

FAUCET HANDLE FOR HEAD

Hand Made Hand Tools

This nostalgic array of shop tricks and other examples of making-do is a monument to American Ingenuity, and is still mighty useful too. It's all too easy to forget what one did before there was a local True Value store. The book is valuable for the home made tools it shows, of course, but its main value may well be the attitude it encourages. It should see considerable use around a shop or farm. I'm glad I have a copy. —J. Baldwin

Hand Made Hand Tools
Keith W. Daniels, Editor
1978; 289 pp.

$8.95 postpaid from:
Lost Data Press
P.O. Box 4889
Austin, TX 78765

FAUCET HANDLE MAKES SMALL "SOFT HAMMER"

A SMALL hammer made of brass, copper, or lead is of great value in assembling or adjusting fine machinery. A hammer of this sort, small enough to be used for such delicate work as gun repairing, can be obtained without cost by fitting a suitable wooden handle to a brass T-handle taken from an old household water faucet.—V. A. L.

Handy Midget Jack Made From Bolt and Nut

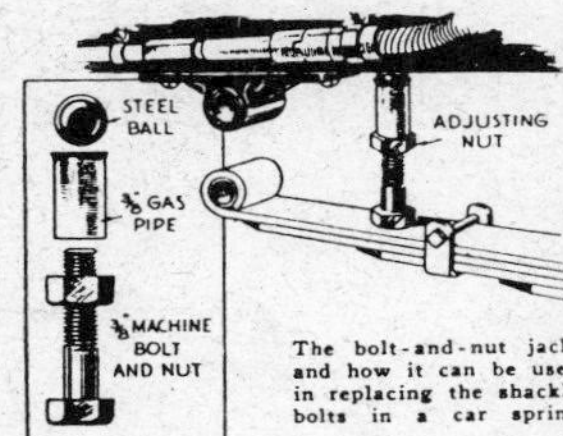

The bolt-and-nut jack, and how it can be used in replacing the shackle bolts in a car spring

FROM an ordinary machine bolt and nut, a scrap of gas pipe, and a steel ball bearing, the amateur mechanic can provide himself with a powerful midget jack that will prove valuable for many types of repair jobs. As shown in the drawing, the jack is assembled by slipping the pipe over the end of the bolt and placing the ball bearing in the upper end of the pipe. To adjust the jack, it is necessary only to turn the nut with a wrench. A considerable amount of lifting power is obtained.—F. C.

A Skimming Spoon

A handy skimming spoon can be made very quickly of an ordinary spoon of any size desired. Slits are sawn across the bowl in the manner shown, using a hacksaw. The illustration is self-explanatory.—Contributed by G. H. Holter, Jasper, Minn.

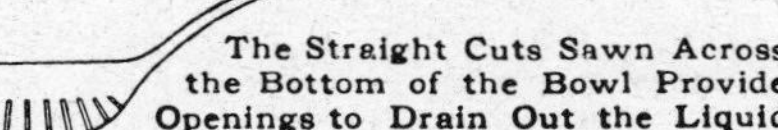

The Straight Cuts Sawn Across the Bottom of the Bowl Provide Openings to Drain Out the Liquid

Recycling & Repairing

Similar to **Hand Made Hand Tools** *in character and intent, this book is a mostly-still-useful collection of down home ingenuity applied to a large variety of situations likely to be found around the homestead. Many of the tricks of the trade are of the sort us moderns are not used to seeing, but with a tightening economy the sort of thinking demonstrated here has renewed validity.* —J. Baldwin

Recycling & Repairing
Keith Daniels, Editor
1978; 290 pp.

$8.95 postpaid from:
Lost Data Press
P.O. Box 4889
Austin, TX 78765

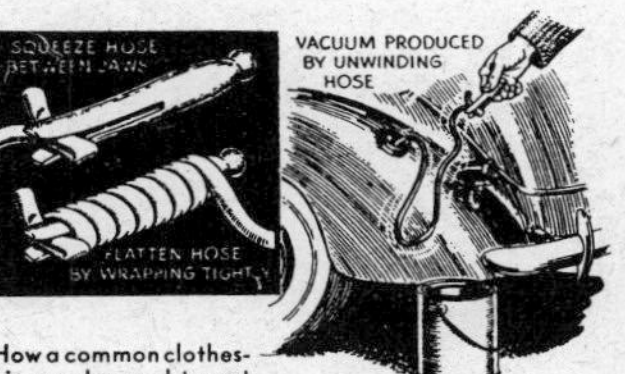

How a common clothes-pin can be used to get siphon action started

Clothespin Starts Siphon

YOU can use a clothespin to start siphoning gasoline from a car tank, avoiding the danger of sucking poisonous chemicals into your mouth. Pinch one end of a rubber tube between the jaws of the pin, and wrap the tube tightly over the whole pin. Place the other end in the liquid and unwind the tube. It will quickly fill with gas.—L. W.

Carbon Paper Is Aid in Cutting Wall Board

WHEN you are ready to cut the wallboard or plywood panels for a new attic room, a closet, or the like that has switch and receptacle boxes already in place on the studs, it's not always easy to locate just where to cut the holes for these outlets. I found in building a darkroom recently that the large number of electrical fittings made this job extra difficult. So I took pieces of carbon paper and taped them, face out, over the receptacle boxes. Then I set the plywood sheet in place and tapped it with a mallet. The outlines of the holes to be cut were then shown clearly on the back of the panel.—LEONARD C. CROWTON.

Country Craft Tools

How did pre-industrial craftsmen make tapered holes for ladder rungs? How did they make round things? In a just-the-facts, ma'am manner, Mr. Blandford shows us the tools and how they were made. Clear drawings show enough so you could do it too. Explanations of how to use the tools are regrettably too brief, but you still get a good idea of how they did it then. —J. Baldwin

Country Craft Tools
Percy W. Blandford
1974; 240 pp.

$23 postpaid from:
Gale Research Co.
Book Tower
Detroit, MI 48226

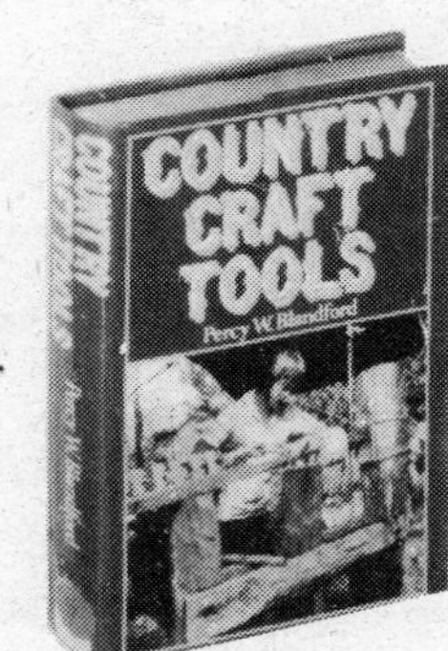

•
An ice axe also had a straight blade. The value of ice for preserving food was known from at least the early nineteenth century, when country estates had ice houses (favoured in America) or pits or caves (more usual in Britain). Winter ice from rivers and lakes was used for as long as it would last into the summer. The tool that was used to trim blocks of ice was two-handed, with a long thin blade and a pick at the other side.

•
An ice saw was used with the ice axe for cutting blocks of ice for preserving food in an ice house. This was something like a small pit saw, but with very large spiked teeth.

HACK SAW FISH SCRAPER

By Harry G. Yocum

A good fish scraper, which will work better than many bought articles, can be made from three hack saw blades and a handle. Holes should be punched in the blades at different distances from the end, as in the illustration, and the blades fastened to the handle with a thumb nut.

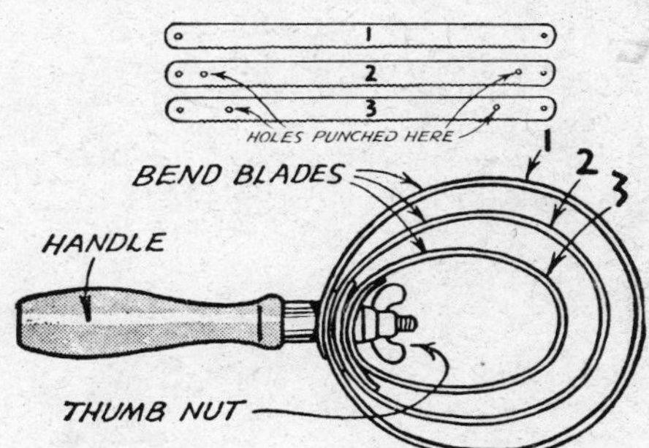

Antique Woodworking Tools

Restaurant owners and suburbanites of the world, take those antique tools off the wall and use them for real work. Here's how to purchase, restore, and use. And antiquers, classic work demands classic tools. Nice book. —Peter Spectre

Antique Woodworking Tools
(A Guide to the Purchase, Restoration and Use of Old Tools for Today's Shop)
Michael Dunbar
1977; 192 pp.

$12.50 postpaid from:
Hastings House
10 East 40th Street
New York, NY 10016

•
Before a piece of wood could be shaped it had to be made uniform. The gashes left by the saw while cutting the board from the log were quite deep. It was a waste of time to remove only a thin shaving with each pass of the plane and obviously something dramatic was called for. The plane which was used for this purpose had been developed well before the birth of Christ. In fact, if Jesus was indeed a carpenter, he was also faced with the need to remove a thick chip from the surface of rough lumber. The tool which was used was called alternately a jack or a fore plane.

English saws. Left — Tillotson of Sheffield. Right — Ibbotson Peace & Co. Eagle Works. Most comfortable. →

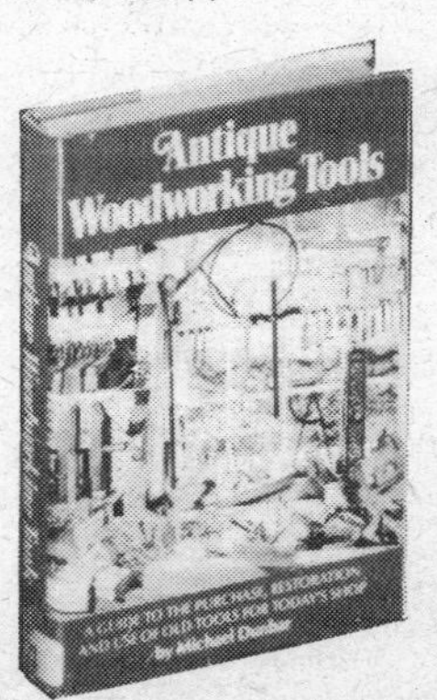

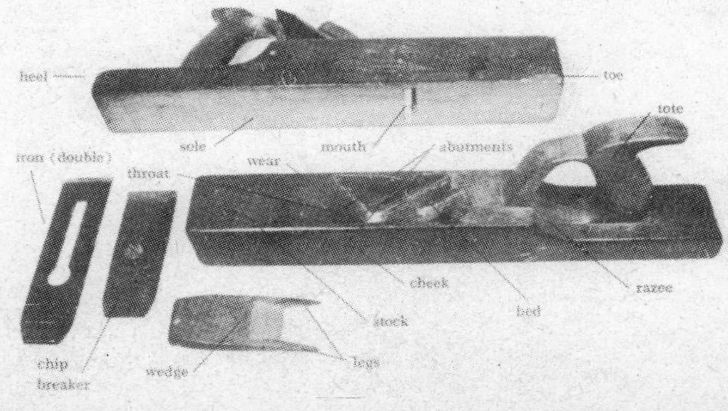

→
A wooden plane has many parts whose names are unfamiliar to the modern woodworker.

THE RISING SUN
NEIGHBORHOOD NEWSLETTER

"The most amazing thing happened. I'd been planning a trip to India next year to get something in the way of enlightenment, but we took a vacation in Mexico and it happened there."

I told Susan he said that and she said, "It happens to Americans when they visit countries of very poor people."

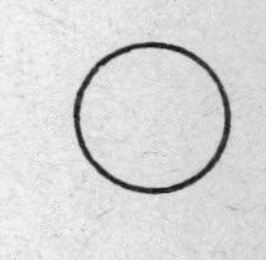

Handtool Handbook for Woodworking

Tool-use books must be among the most deadly boring literature available in our society, probably because they are written for retarded seventh-graders. The few books that avoid such an accusation tend to be written in the imperious tone of a retired Master Sergeant shop teacher. I for one simply can't read them. An exception is available. R.J. DeCristoforo, who brought us his excellent **Complete Book of Power Tools** *(p. 155) has done it again for common woodworking hand tools. The first page I opened to showed me something I didn't know (the dowel trick, right).* —J. Baldwin

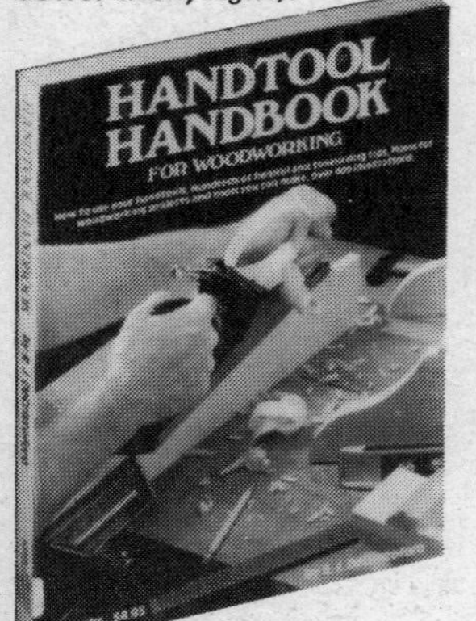

Handtool Handbook for Woodworking
R.J. DeCristoforo
1977; 184 pp.
$5.95 postpaid from:
HP Books
P.O. Box 5367
Tucson, AZ 85703
or Whole Earth Household Store

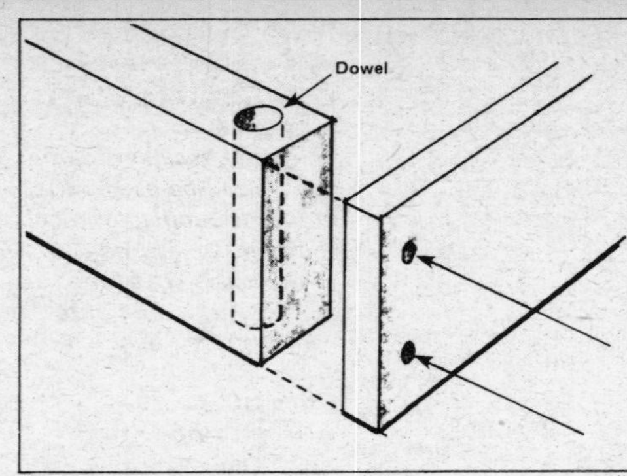

↑ A dowel can be placed in a drilled hole to help hold screws driven into weak end grain.

A piece of the molding you are working on can make a sanding block that fits exactly. Here the edges of the block have been sawed off so it will fit the major contours better. ↑

Nails driven at a slight angle will provide a better grip than nails that are driven straight. ↓

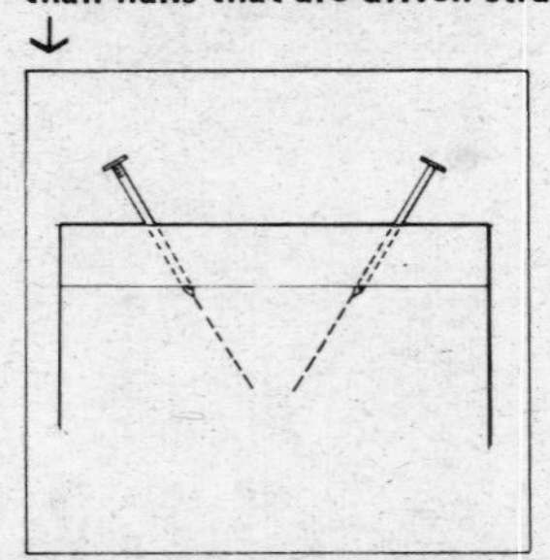

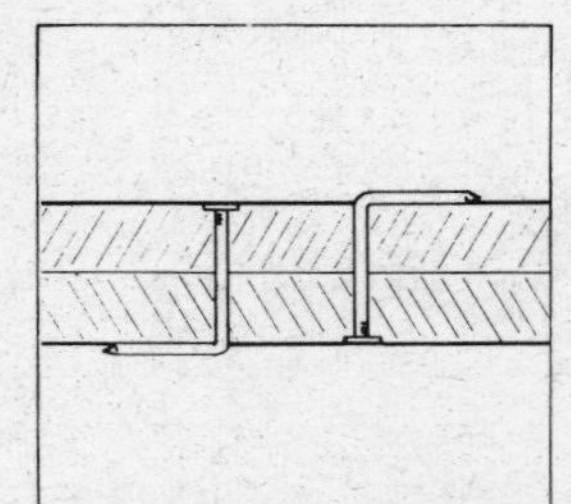

Nails that are clinched from both sides of an assembly make a very strong joint. ↙

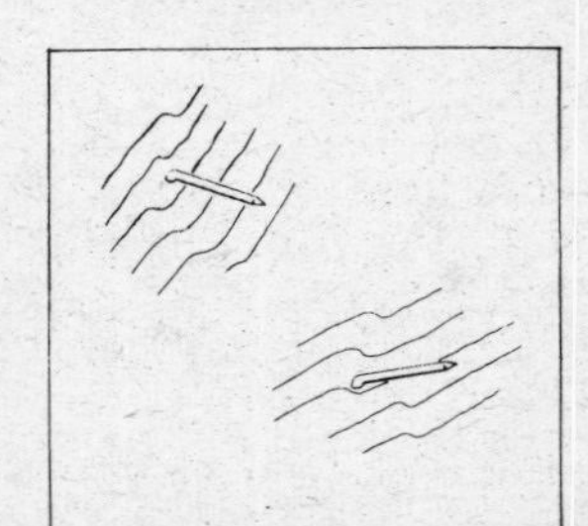

← Nails that are clinched across the grain are much stronger than nails that are clinched with the grain.

The Garrett Wade Book of Woodworking Tools

The impressive Garrett Wade catalog (p. 142) comes to life with detailed instructions and comments on the use and care of the several tools they carry in stock. A look at this will help you decide what to buy — not always an easy task when dealing with a catalog offering so many choices. Delightful! Inciting! Yummy! —J. Baldwin

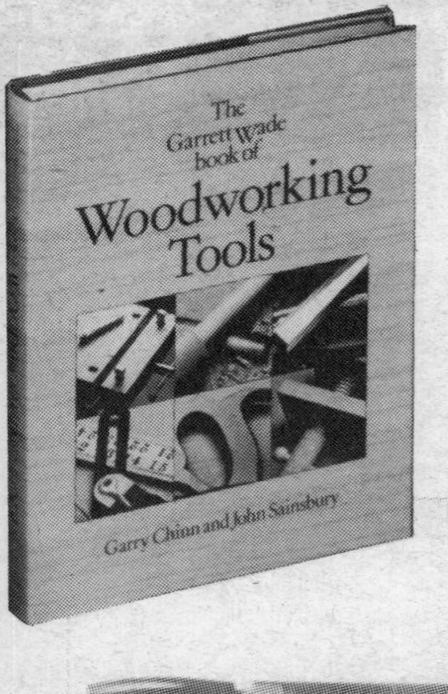

The Garrett Wade Book of Woodworking Tools
Gary Chinn and John Sains
1979; 191 pp.
$17.50 postpaid from:
T.Y. Crowell and Co.
Harper and Row
Keystone Industrial Park
Scranton, PA 18512
or Whole Earth Household Store

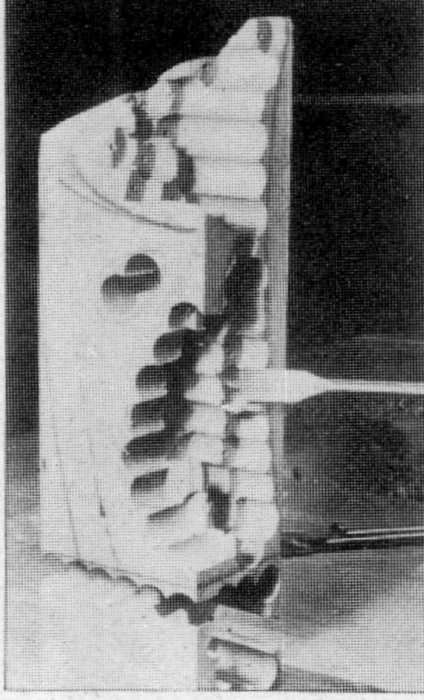

↑ A quick way to rough down and remove waste is to use a flatbit attached to a power drill.

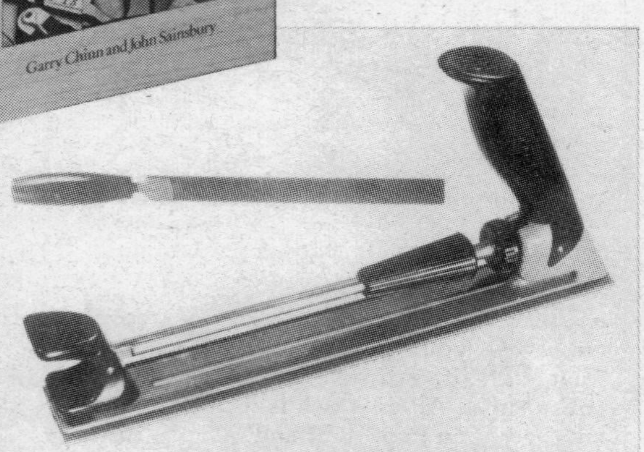

← The Aven Filemaster (top) has one surface of cross-filed teeth for rough work and one of curved teeth, which gives an extra-smooth finish. The Trimmatool (bottom) offers the special facility of an adjustable curved blade for concave cuts. The curved teeth of these tools are virtually self-cleaning.

The Care and Use of Japanese Woodworking Tools

Those beautiful, light Japanese woodworking tools are fully explained and illustrated in this modest manual. Both the drawings and text are in the same quiet spirit of competence appropriate to the tools. (I almost said instruments.) Yum. For the purchase of such tools, see p. 146. —J. Baldwin

The Care and Use of Japanese Woodworking Tools
Kip Mesirow and Ron Herman
1975; 95 pp.
$8 postpaid from:
Woodcraft Supply Corp.
313 Montvale Avenue
Woburn, MA 01888

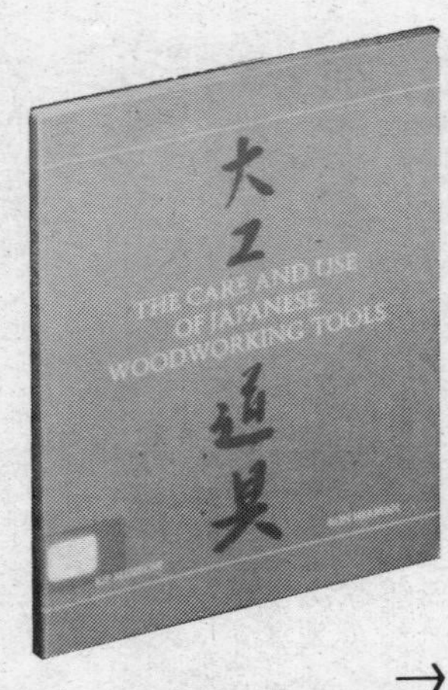

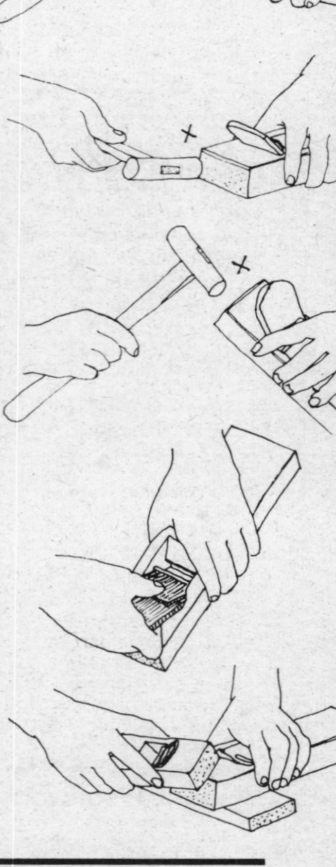

Shown here is the most natural way of holding kanna and a mallet (in front of chest). In grasping kanna hold blade with thumb and index finger, while the other fingers hold the body. Strike the body with the mallet parallel with blade until blade loosens, also listen to the sound change when the blade becomes loose. →

After tapping in the correct way and the blade has become loose, hold kanna head side down and pull out the blade with the other hand.

The edge of body which is tapped to remove blade may wear with repeated use. To prevent this from occurring chamfer the edge of the head.

Dictionary of Tools

Tool freaks, this is the ultimate tool book! Not only an incredible array of woodworking tools from past and present shown, but plenty of special purpose (e.g., wheelwrighting) ones, too. The extra clear illustrations often show the tool in action, which should enable you let's-do-it-the-old-way people to get at it. There are diagrams of such things as coaches, barrels, farm wagon undercarriages, Dutch windmills, and the like. All wood. This adds up to a book that is much more than a museum display of artifacts. It is, in my opinion, worth the money which is a special deal by the importer. Perhaps you can talk your library into it, but serious workers will want one of their own. —J. Baldwin

[Suggested by Jonathan Katz]

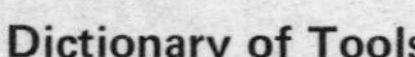

Dictionary of Tools
(Used in the woodworking and allied trades c. 1700-1970)
R.A. Salaman
1975; 545 pp.
No. 10S31-DM
$48.75 postpaid from:
Woodcraft Supply Corp.
313 Montvale Avenue
Woburn, MA 01888

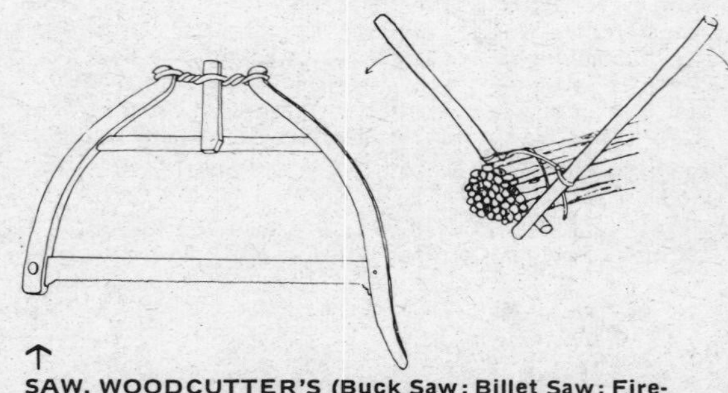

↑ SAW, WOODCUTTER'S (Buck Saw; Billet Saw; Firewood Saw) — A bow-type Saw with a saw blade 24 - 30 in. long, held in a wooden frame with one side-piece extended to form the handle. It differs from the usual Bow Saw in having a rigid blade which cannot be turned, for it is intended for cross-cutting firewood, etc. Mercer (U.S.A., 1929) writes that "it is still used among farmers etc. who grease the blade with a piece of hog fat, kept hung on a nail in the wood shed."

← WOODMAN'S GRIP — Two strong poles, about 3 ft. 6 in. long, connected by a length of rope at a point about a foot from the lower end. Its purpose is to compress rods and stakes into bundles for tying up before carting away.

THE BREAST BIB — A piece of hardwood shaped to the chest and secured by a light leather harness. It has a recess on the front surface in which the head of the Brace is held. Its purpose was to distribute the pressure exerted by the head of the Brace over the area of the chest; and by locating the head of the Brace, it helped to steer it accurately at the right angle. Sometimes Breast Bibs are found with a groove across the recess on the front. This is where the Chairmaker used his chest, protected by the Bib, as a cramp to force parts of a chair together. ↓

CARRYING STICK (Carrying Cane; Frail Stick) — A crooked or S-shaped stick, often cut from the hedge. One end of the crook lies on the shoulder, the other forms a handle. It is used for carrying a bag of tools, and a wooden pin is set near the end to prevent the bag from slipping off. →

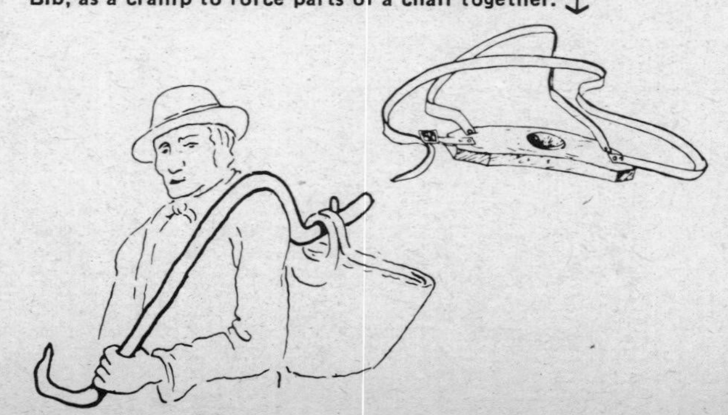

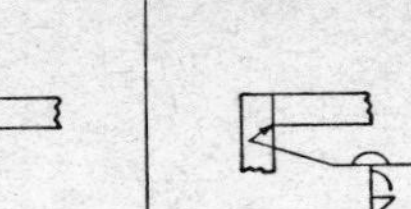

Symbol indicates a built-up surface ⅛ inch thick.

Symbol indicates a bead-type back weld on the *other side* of joint, and a J-groove grooved horizontal member (shown by break in arrow) and fillet weld on *arrow side* of the joint.

Machinery's Handbook

If you make things out of metal you need **Machinery's Handbook**. *This thick, comprehensive guide to shop and engineering practice was originally designed to fit in the tall center drawer of a machinist's chest. Machinist's chests have stayed the same size, but the shaping of metal has become more and more complicated.* **Machinery's** *has coped with the squeeze heroically; the current (21st) edition contains 2420 pages printed on fine India paper, and it still fits the drawer. You can find in it things like tap drill sizes for S.A.E., metric, and Whitworth threads, what welding rod to use for which metal, and how much weight you can hang on a rope if it goes around a fat (or thin) barrel. You can also look up logarithms, area, volumes, and centers of gravity, and learn how to design helical gears, replace bearings, grind a lathe bit, and do many other useful and not-so-obvious things. The book is divided into thirteen main sections, indexed, thumb-indexed, and bound in tough, satisfyingly archaic industrial green with gold stamping.*

—Morton Grosser

Machinery's Handbook
Paul B. Schubert, Editor
1914, 1975; 2420 pp.
21st Edition
$32 postpaid from:
Industrial Press, Inc.
T.D.S. Building 424
Raritan Center
Edison, NJ 08817

The Starrett Book for Student Machinists

This is an excellent reference and introduction to machining. It can be used in place of the **Machinery's Handbook** *by many people, although it does not pretend to replace it. Chapters like: reading Working Drawings; Facts About Fits; Drills and How to Use Them; Jigs and Fixtures; and Lathe Work. The book is well bound and small, making it an easy volume to keep.* —Fred Richardson

The Starrett Book for Student Machinists
The L.S. Starrett Co.
1941, 1975; 159 pp.
16th Edition
$4.75 postpaid from:
The L.S. Starrett Co.
Athol, MA 01330

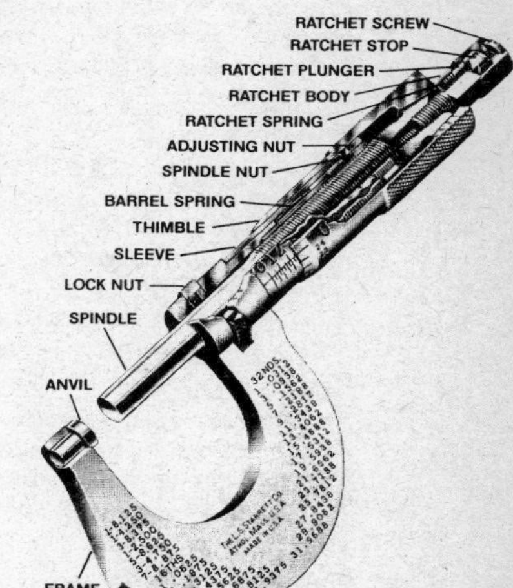

→
The great accuracy of the micrometer screw becomes evident when the extreme accuracy of manufacture of threaded spindles is realized. Micrometers are designed for either inside or outside measurements and are available in a variety of shapes and sizes.

Jigs & Fixtures for Limited Production

This book is a manual of tactics for making inexpensive jigs. It's intended mainly for machine shops, but it can be quite handy for anyone who has to make a number of similar parts, such as for a dome. Jigs are also handy when a single part has to be done with high accuracy. Anyone who is into making things or repairing various artifacts could learn a bag of tricks from the book. The author shows how to convert commonly available objects such as a vise into a drilling jig. There's a chapter on making epoxy tooling. The language is non-technical, with most of the terms being defined. For most makers it won't be bedtime reading, but will be a good reference when the problems get tough. —J. Baldwin

Jigs & Fixtures for Limited Production
Harold Sedlik
1970; 136 pp.
$11 postpaid from:
Society of Manufacturing Engineers
P.O. Box 930
One SME Drive
Dearborn, MI 48128

↓
If an item does not warrant special tooling, there may be an economic advantage in using the master part system. The system, as the name implies, uses a simulated or actual part fabricated to slightly closer tolerances than the intended product and used as a template or jig.

When a master part is used as a jig for locating holes, the master and the part to be worked are clamped together as shown, and the hole locations are transferred from the master to the part with a duplicating punch. If possible, hardened bushings are inserted into the master part, making it possible to transfer holes directly by drilling. The addition of drill bushings improves accuracy and increases tool life.

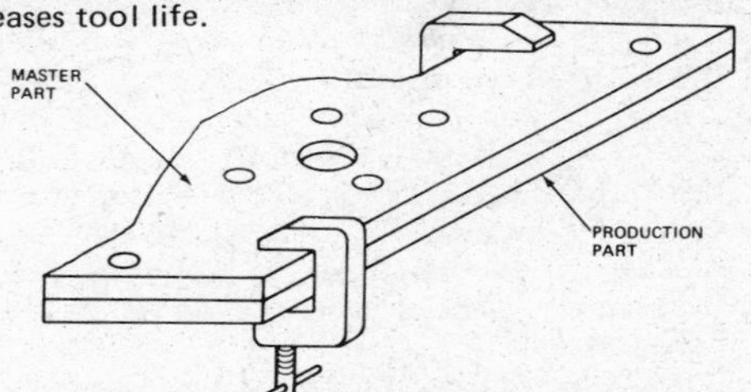

Master part method of transferring hole locations.

How to Run a Lathe

Lathes are great. I've got one made about 1910. Cost a couple hundred and took a week of work cleaning it up and rebuilding it. It's at least as good as a new one costing $6000.

I've looked at a lot of books on lathes and this one covers all of it. I've been reading it for a year now and there are still things in it I haven't learned. Oil and clean your lathe a lot. Lots of lathes get ruined by not being oiled.

—Fred Richardson

How to Run a Lathe
(The Care and Operation of a Screw Cutting Lathe)
Available in English, Spanish, Portuguese.
South Bend Lathe
1914, 1966; 128 pp.
$2 postpaid from:
South Bend Lathe
400 W. Sample Street
South Bend, IN 46625

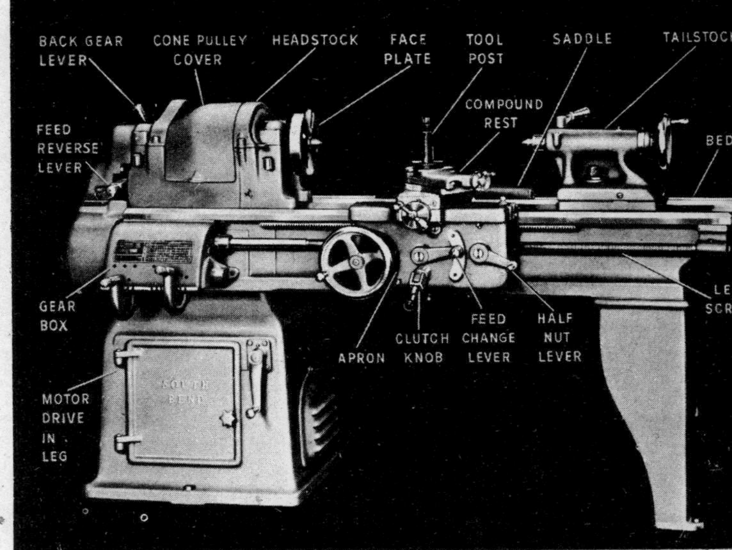

Creative Woodturning

Most wood lathe books are recycled high school texts, full of stale projects — primarily gavels and candlesticks. Finally here is a book that does justice to the elegant beauty of wood-turning. Literally hundreds of detailed photographs and a concise text. Chapters of special interest include: unusual mounting devices, laminated constructions, working with unseasoned wood, and inspiring photos of finished pieces done by the author and other wood-turners. Quite a bargain. —Doug Dylla

Creative Woodturning
Dale L. Nish
1975, 1977; 248 pp.
$9.95 postpaid from:
Brigham Young University Press
205 University Press Building
Provo, UT 84602
or Whole Earth Household Store

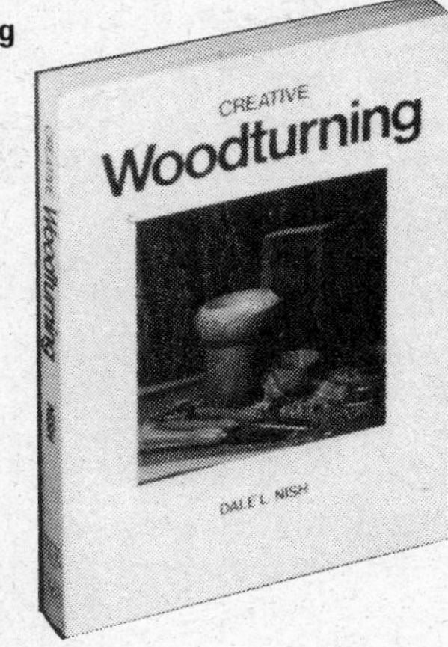

←
For cutting a bead, the skew should be held at an angle of 25° to 30° to the stock.

THE RISING SUN
NEIGHBORHOOD NEWSLETTER

The difference between the sound of b and the sound of p, is for b your vocal cords are making noise and for p they ain't. Make those sounds by themselves with your hands on your throat and you will observe that the throat vibrations are the only difference. That is also the only difference between f and v and between s and z and d and t. Otherwise, your mouth is doing the same tricks. That's the difference between voiced and voiceless consonants. All of which is to tell you in Hungarian there is an important and meaningful difference between the voiced and voiceless k sound — a difference that English speakers can neither hear nor reproduce. Between that and the fact that nodding and shaking your head mean the opposite thing, you'd look like a real idiot in Budapest, and they say it's pretty there.

Another difference between kinds of consonants is between stops and fricatives. Stops like b and p and d and t you can only say once and it's over. Fricatives like f and v and s you can say for as long as your lungs are big. So you can say that f is a voiceless fricative and v is a voiced fricative and d is a voiced stop and stuff like that. I don't know why you'd want to, but I rather enjoy it. Some people like pistachio nuts, others like whips and chains, me, I enjoy knowing that b is a bilabial voiced stop. The bilabial means you make it with two lips. D is a dental voiced stop because you make it with your teeth. So about every consonant you can say what part of your mouth you make it with, whether it's voiced or voiceless and whether it stops or fricatives on and when you say those three things each consonant is unique. V is the only voiced labial-dental fricative there is in English. Ok, I'll quit.

The Procedure Handbook of Arc Welding

As a welder in a large plant using many different welding processes every day, I have found this to be the most comprehensive and current book on arc welding going.

Reliable information on all arc processes (stick, inner-shield, submerged, electro-slag, MIG, TIG), weldability of metals (carbon and stainless steels, aluminum, cast iron, copper) including sheet metals, with special sections on design, machinery, testing and qualification procedures, pipe and out-of-position techniques, distortion control, underwater welding, arc-gouging, galvanized and concrete re-bar welding, and hardsurfacing. All clearly explained with plenty of photos and diagrams, tables and graphs.

Really an eye-opener into the welding field; information valuable to the worker in a large metal fabrication plant as well as the farm welder and small shop. First printed in 1933, it is currently in its 12th edition, updated last in 1973.

Their mail service is prompt (I received my copy in about 2 weeks, their catalog arrived within 4 days) and at a fair price too. They also have learning manuals available plus some excellent volumes on welded structures throughout the world. —Steve Keleher

The Procedure Handbook of Arc Welding
1933, 1973; 700 pp.
$5 postpaid from:
The Lincoln Electric Co.
22801 St. Clair Avenue
Cleveland, OH 44117

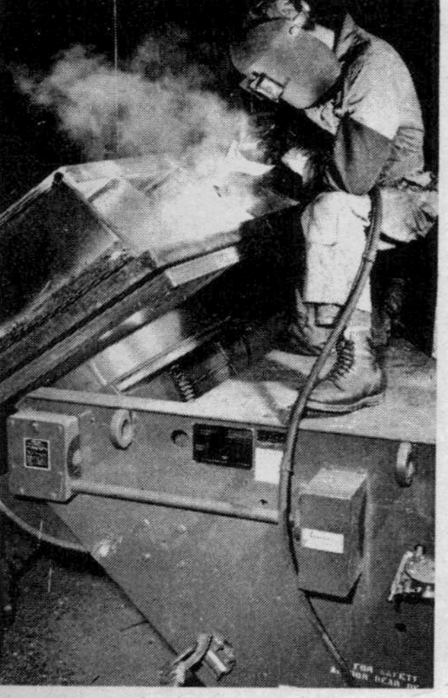

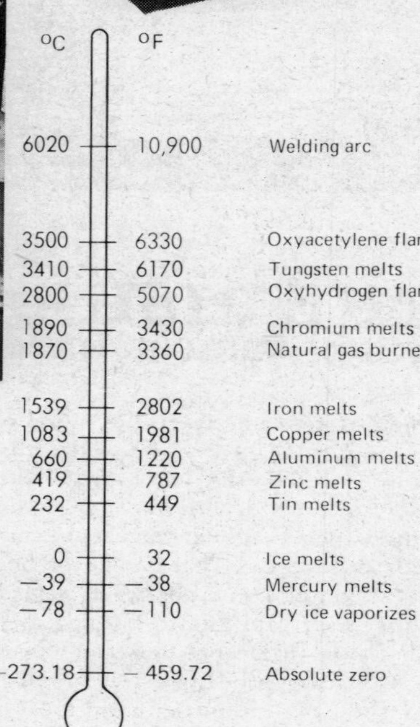

Audel

Long a tradition in professional manuals, Audel offers books for home owners and do-it-yourselfers too. They're generally well turned out and reliable. Subjects range from oil burner overhaul and earthmover hydraulics to bicycle maintenance. I've used many Audel books over the years and have few complaints. —J. Baldwin

Audel
Catalog
free from:
Howard W. Sams & Co.
Audel Division
4300 West 62nd Street
P.O. Box 558
Indianapolis, IN 46206

Foundrywork for the Amateur

A foundry need not be a huge industrial complex or even a purchased kit. You can start with your kitchen stove, an old pot, some sand, scrap aluminum, and this book. Such a kitchen foundry would give you an immediate source of emergency replacements for a broken pulley or small bracket on that old "patented 1892" water pump. Recycling a scrap auto into cast bridge washers and boot scrapers takes a bit more. Directions for construction of the requisite backyard blast furnace, patterns, and molds are provided. —Alan Kalker

Foundrywork for the Amateur
B. Terry Aspin
1972, 1975; 108 pp.

£1.25 (about $2.75)
postpaid from:
Model & Allied Publications
Argus Books Ltd.
Station Road
Kings Langley, Herts
HP1 1EE England

Small Gas Engines

A non-intimidating book commendably designed so the mechanical dumb-dumb can keep the little guy running. For the amateur, it's the best we've seen. For major work, you'll also need a shop manual for the engine you have. —J. Baldwin

Small Gas Engines
James A. Gray and Richard W. Barlow
1976; 248 pp.
$12.95 postpaid from:
Prentice-Hall, Inc.
Box 500
Englewood Cliffs, NJ 07632
or Whole Earth Household Store

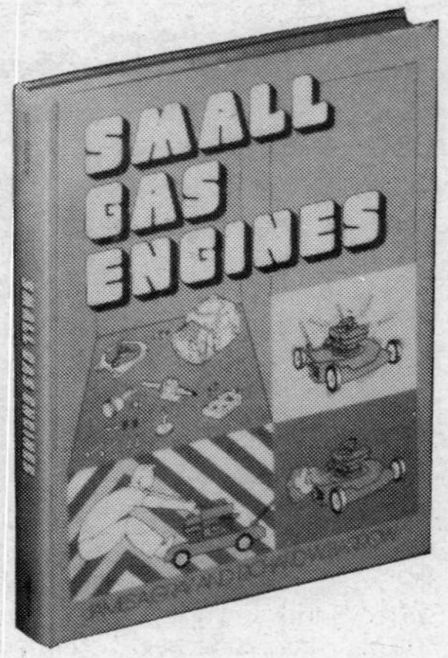

Chart 43 — HEAD GASKET REPLACEMENT

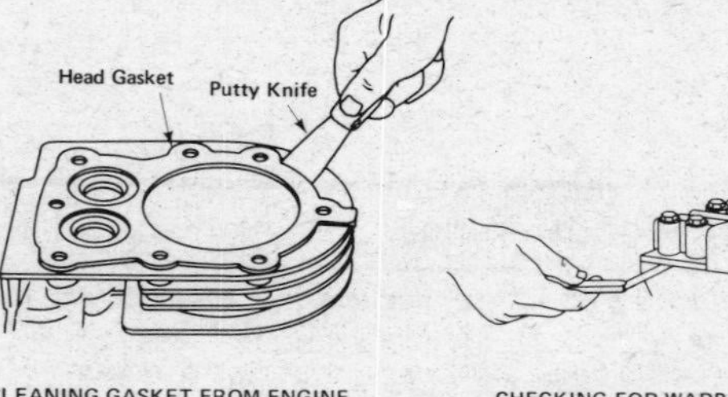

Glues and Adhesives

The proliferation of types of adhesives has made choosing the best one a chancy business (I was about to say a sticky business) these days, particularly when modern high-tech materials are what is being glued. This timely book should be a big help. It's done up in the usual impeccable Popular Science manner too, and part of a wide-ranging series of skill books. —J. Baldwin

Home and Workshop Guide to Glues and Adhesives
(Popular Science Skill Book)
George Daniels
1979; 120 pp.
$4.95 postpaid from:
Harper and Row
Keystone Industrial Park
Scranton, PA 18512
or Whole Earth Household Store

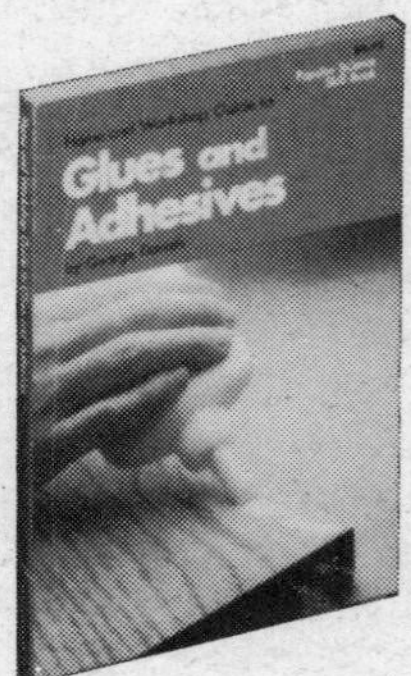

Parts of this ornamental dog are held in position with wire solder while the adhesive hardens. Bend the solder before applying adhesive. The solder forms a cradle and positions the dog's limbs.

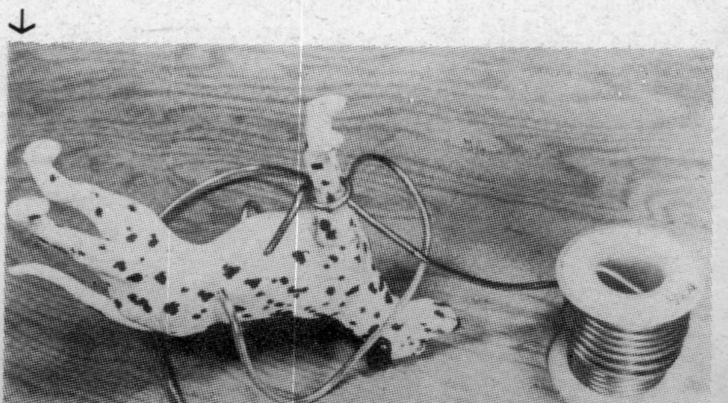

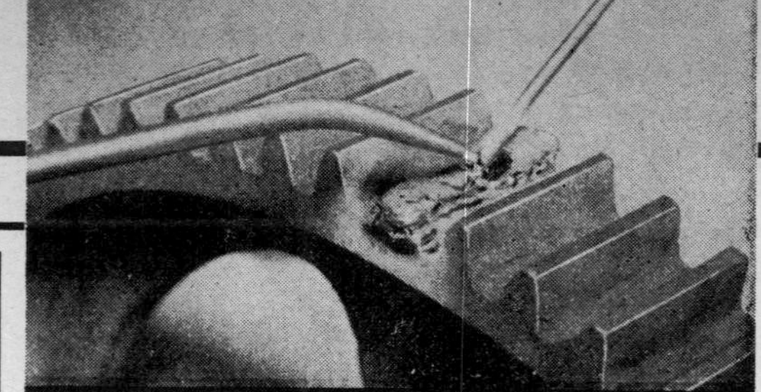

Broken parts and worn surfaces are quickly and efficiently repaired by the braze-welding or bronze-surfacing operation. Such parts frequently give longer and better service than the original.

The Oxy- Acetylene Handbook

The corporations that make the product often publish the best manuals on how to use it well, in the hopes of encouraging further sales. So it is that Union Carbide brings us this authoritative textbook at a very fair price. (You'll still need an experienced instructor though.) Comprehensive, to say the least. —J. Baldwin

The Oxy-Acetylene Handbook
1943, 1976; 300 pp.
$9 postpaid from:
Union Carbide Corp.
Linde Reference Library
47-36 36th Street
Long Island City, NY 11101

Hardness is usually defined as the resistance a material has to forcible penetration by another material. That is why a hard substance resists scratching or wear. It takes a combination of hardness and toughness to withstand heavy pounding.

A brittle substance is one that fails without appreciable permanent deformation. A brittle substance also has low resistance to shock, or loads rapidly applied.

A ductile substance is one that can be permanently deformed without failure. In other words, it can be stretched, bent, or twisted and, after the force is removed, it remains deformed.

Malleability is defined as "that property of a material by virtue of which it can be rolled or hammered into thinner sheets."

TAB Books

This is a publisher you should know about. They have titles on an absolutely amazing number of subjects; **How to Build Doll Houses, How to Repair Fork Lift Trucks, Modern Diesel Cars . . .** *you name it. I've found TAB quality to be highly variable. Some of their books seem to be offered merely so they can say that they offer them. Their books on alternative energy, for instance, are inferior in my opinion. On the other hand, a TAB book is often the only book available on the subject, or is by far the first one available. Such books are then quite valuable, though printing errors and typos abound in many of them. Balancing that, TAB books are usually cheap. My advice is, that if you need a book on an unusual subject and can't find it in your bookstore, send for TAB's catalog. They currently offer 650 titles!* —J. Baldwin

TAB Books
Title list

free from:
TAB Books
Blue Ridge Summit, PA 17214

Materials Handbook

Specifications, uses, handling techniques and other data on some 13,000 materials and substances likely to be encountered in manufacturing or other aspects of your life and work. Included are chemicals, industrial materials, fuels, plastics, rubbers, textiles, chemicals, finishes, pharmaceuticals, foodstuffs and natural plant materials. Now in its eleventh edition (proof enough of its usefulness), this mighty wad of information has been where you go to find out about it for a long time now.
—J. Baldwin

Materials Handbook
(An Encyclopedia for Managers, Technical Professionals, Purchasing and Production Managers, Technicians, Supervisors and Foremen)
George S. Brady and Henry R. Clauser
1929, 1977; 1011 pp.
11th Edition
$39.50 postpaid from:
McGraw-Hill Book Co.
Princeton Road
Hightstown, NJ 08520
or Whole Earth Household Store

•

Gutta Percha. A gum obtained by boiling the sap of species of trees of the order *Sapotaceae,* chiefly *Palaquium gutta* and *P. oblongifolia,* native to Borneo, New Guinea, and Malaya. It is grayish white, very pliable, but not elastic like rubber. It is harder and a better insulator than rubber. Gutta percha, like rubber, will vulcanize with sulfur and form a hard material. It is used for mixing with rubber, but its chief use was in the covering of electric cables. It has a greater pliability than rubber for the given hardness required in cable insulation. This property with its greater resistance to water makes it valuable for golf balls and dental fillings. It molds easily at 180° F. It is also employed like balata for impregnating driving belts, and for washers and valve seats, and in adhesives. Gutta percha is often imported as mixtures with inferior guttas from other trees. **Gutta soh**, for example, is a mixture from Singapore often colored red artificially. **Gutta siak** is a low-grade gutta from Sumatra. It has a reddish color, and is lightly elastic. **Gutta sundik** is from the tree *Payena leerii* of Malaya and Indonesia. It is white in color, and is mixed with gutta percha. Another gutta used to adulterate gutta percha is **gutta hangkang**, from the *Palaquium leiocarpum* of Borneo. It is slightly reddish. **Gutta jangkar** is a low-grade red gutta from Sarawak. **Gutta susu** of Indonesia is a gray-colored material, slightly elastic. With increasing use of synthetic resin insulating materials, gutta percha has become of only secondary importance.

Design for the Real World

Industrial design is in deservedly bad odor lately, and this book will give you many of the reasons — most of them having to do with pandering to self-exaggerating marketplace fashion, the disposable environment.

Victor Papanek is a Bush Designer. He prefers to hang out in Third World places, where the problems are physical and serious, and where native design genius can be learned and applied to them using industrial materials. This book works on distinguishing between real and phoney design problems, and their solutions. —SB

Design for the Real World
Victor Papanek
1971; 378 pp.
$8.95 postpaid from:
Pantheon Books
Random House
455 Hahn Road
Westminster, MD 21157
or Whole Earth Household Store

Artificial burrs, 40cm long, made of bio-degradable plastic and coated with plant seeds and a growth-boosting solution. To reverse erosion cycles in arid regions. Student designed by James Herold and Jolan Truan, Purdue University.
↓

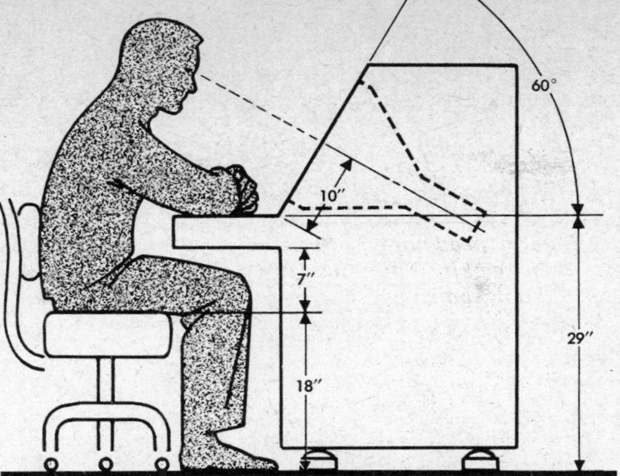

Illustration of angular mounting of visual display.

Human Engineering Guide

↑

Buy this book and keep it at hand at all times if you design or build anything that will be used by, for, or come in contact with people. Concise statement of ideas both through the informative writing and clear illustrations. The authors have followed their own guidelines and produced a device (this book) which will do well what it was designed to do, transfer a large amount of information between people. If you want information on human engineering, design of equipment and work space, vision, audition and body measurement, it's all in this book chapter by chapter. This book should be used by all design engineers, but it is not necessary to be a design engineer or even an engineer to use it. Really fundamental ideas clearly stated can be understood by anyone. —M. Le Brun

Human Engineering Guide
(For Equipment Designers)
Wesley E. Woodson and Donald W. Conover
1954, 1965; 486 pp.
Second Edition
$20 postpaid from:
University of California Press
2223 Fulton Street
Berkeley, CA 94720
or Whole Earth Household Store

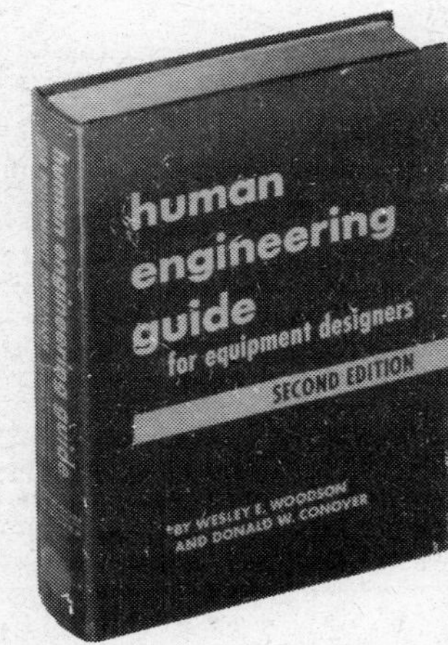

"Stacked" knobs should be designed so as to minimize interferences as shown below. Although three stacked knobs are possible, only two are recommended.
↓

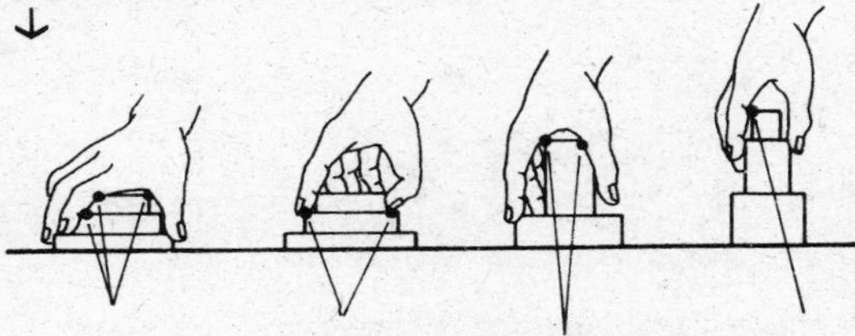

NOTE UNINTENTIONAL CONTACT POINTS

Handbook of Chemistry and Physics

Among handbooks, this "Rubber Bible" is prodigiously wealthy in basic information. Its 6-figure math tables are the standard. Its chemistry and physics tables constitute a comprehensive inventory of invisible effects. It doesn't teach you how to use or even read the inventory, but if you know how, here's the know-what tool chest. —SB
[Suggested by Lloyd Martin]

Handbook of Chemistry and Physics
Robert C. Weast, Editor
1918, 1976; 2436 pp.
60th Edition
$49.95 postpaid from:
CRC Press
18901 Cranwood Parkway
Cleveland, OH 44128
or check the Chemistry Department bulletin boards at a local college for occasional great promotional offers.

Noyes Data on Industrial Equipment

When you're shopping for big industrial goodies like Waste Water Cleanup Equipment, Desalinization Plants, Artificial Kidneys, Superconducting Materials, Freeze-Drying processes, Air Pollution Devices, Soundproof Building Materials, Solar Cells, etc. these big books ($30 - $55 for each subject) will give you the technological specs, operating principles, etc. for comparison shopping. —SB

Noyes Data Corporation
Publications list
free from:
Noyes Data Corporation
Noyes Building
Park Ridge, NJ 07656

Mark's Standard Handbook for Mechanical Engineers

For 52 years this has been where engineers, inventors and the curious have looked it up. It's sort of a huge review book of the math, formulas, and principles of the various fields of mechanical engineering. This includes, in addition to the expected thermodynamics, piping, hydraulics, etc. chapters on pollution control, cost accounting, and safety. As an example of using the book, I recently had to determine how far away from our house I could erect a wind machine without getting an unacceptable voltage drop in the wire I had available. A few minutes in the index and about 5 minutes on a cheap calculator and I had a drop of half a volt at 200 feet, which is OK. Like that. The book has been in print a long time, so there are certain out-of-date items. But the hard number stuff is right there where you need it, and the bibliography tells where to find more details. —J. Baldwin

Mark's Standard Handbook for Mechanical Engineers
Theodore Baumeister, Editor
1916, 1978; 2456 pp.
8th Edition
$44.50 postpaid from:
McGraw-Hill Book Co.
Princeton Road
Hightstown, NJ 08520

Introduction to Engineering Design

Out of a whole section of books on design in a university engineering library this book looked far the best. Steve Baer, solar designer at Zomeworks, came across it in the office, sat down and paged, then got up and wrote a letter to a friend about the book and its author. I asked Steve to pick out some useful quotes and pictures and he wouldn't. "Look anywhere you open it," he advised, then ordered a copy.

Contents of the book include: The Engineering Problem Situation, Design Project Organization, Information and the Need Analysis, Identification of the Problems, Information Sources, Synthesis of Alternatives, Estimation and Order-of-Magnitude Analysis, Engineering and Money, Preliminary Design, Engineering Problem Modeling, The Iconic Model, Conceptual Representation, Expansion of the Criterion Function, Checking in Engineering Design, Optimization, etc., etc. —SB

Introduction to Engineering Design
Thomas T. Woodson
1966; 434 pp.
$17 postpaid from:
McGraw-Hill Book Co.
Princeton Road
Hightstown, NJ 08520
or Whole Earth Household Store

THE RISING SUN
NEIGHBORHOOD NEWSLETTER

Why it's supposed to be bad to split infinitives — Renaissance English intellectuals thought the classics were neatest and Latin was best and in Latin, like several other languages, you can't split infinitives because they are one word— *esse:* to be and *habere:* to have — and like that. Therefore in order to snottily and pointlessly bring their language into false similarity with Latin they tried to greatly limit its flexibility by imposing the no split infinitives rule. Obviously, this is cultural imperialism to be resisted by all right-minded people.

Same thing with ending sentences with prepositions. In Latin, you can't, no matter how hard you try, so we heirs to grunting German tribes shouldn't be able to. Or so said 16th century assimilationists, and some still listen. Death to tyrants! Split to infinitives!

Nest of a harvest mouse in an oat field. An oat stem nearby has been bent and incorporated into the nest for extra support.

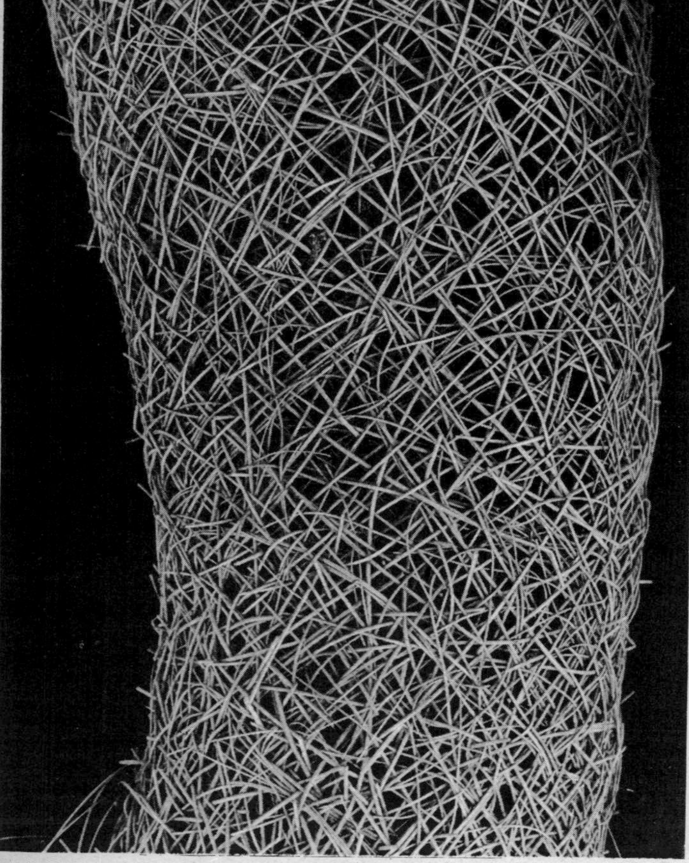

Detail of a weaverbird's nest.

Nature As Designer

THESE BOOKS TAKE A FASCINATED AND FASCINATING look at The Way Things Work in nature. I find that the more I attend such matters, the better my design work tends to be. This sort of knowledge is part of the path to that essential respect for universe that is so lacking in technosociety.

—J. Baldwin

Animal Architecture

*A sensitive and wonder-filled look at how animals shelter themselves and their young. This is one of those books that has you continually jumping up to show someone what you've just learned. It also could cause you to reinspect your attitudes towards "house" and two-by-fours. The author is the same man who gave us those amazing dance-language-of-bees books. (***The Dancing Bees: An Account of the Life and Senses of the Honey Bee***, 1961. Harcourt Brace Jovanich, Inc.) This book is in the same spirit and of the same high intellectual and artistic quality.*

—J. Baldwin

Animal Architecture
Karl von Frisch
1974, 1976; 306 pp.

$12.95 postpaid from:
Harcourt Brace
and Jovanovich
757 Third Avenue
New York, NY 10017
or Whole Earth
Household Store

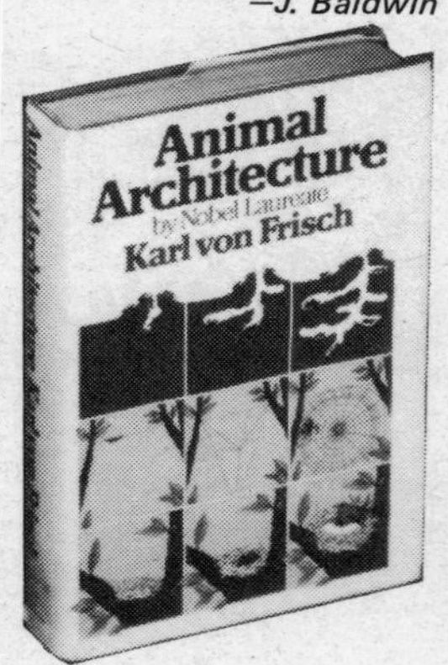

•

The ventilation system of the termitary is completely automatic. This is how it functions. The air in the fungus chambers is heated by the fermentation processes taking place there. Like any tightly packed group of breathing animals, the termites themselves cause a rise in temperature. This hot air rises and is forced by the pressure of the continuous stream of hot air into the duct system of the ridges. The exterior and interior walls of these ridges are so porous that they enable a gas exchange to take place. Carbon dioxide escapes and oxygen penetrates from outside. The ridges with their system of ducts might be called the lungs of the colony. As has been experimentally confirmed, the air is cooled during its passage through the ridges; this cooler, regenerated air now flows into the cellar by way of the lower system of wide ducts. From there it returns to the nest via the surrounding air space, replacing the rising warm air. ↓

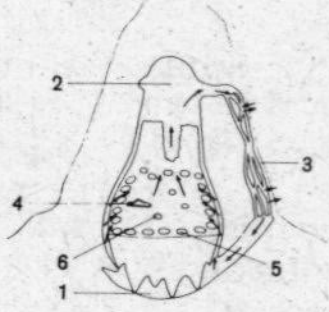

Diagram of the circulation of air in nests of Macrotermes bellicosus (natalensis): right, in a nest from the Ivory Coast; left, in a nest from Uganda. The arrows indicate the direction in which the air moves. (1) Cellar; (2) upper air space; (3) ducts in the ridges; (4) royal cell; (5) fungus chambers; (6) brood chambers.

↑

The structures of compass termites in the Australian steppe. Their broad sides face east and west.

←

Bower of the orange-crested gardener in the rain forest of New Guinea. The two openings in front of the hut are connected inside by a semicircular passage. The bird has covered column between the two openings with dark moss. It is decorated on one side with blue iridescent beetles, in the middle with yellow flowers, and on the other side with broken shells. In front of the bower is a fence plaited from twigs and decorated with brightly colored fruits (sometimes with flowers as well), which forms boundary of the "garden." The male (left) has just rushed out of the tunnel and greets the female by displaying his nuchal crest.

Cross section through part of a badger's burrow. ↓

Analysis of Vertebrate Structure

It isn't often we champion a college textbook, but this one is just plain fascinating. It tells how vertebrate animals work. Of course the usual zoology information is there, but the emphasis is on mechanism. The mechanisms are admirably illustrated and the illustrations are backed by a text that assumes an intelligent but not highly experienced reader. (The author himself says, ". . . I will be pleased if the reader occasionally forgets the forthcoming examination and reads on thinking. 'Wow, that's really something!' "). Just as a hill is more than just a hill after you get into geology, a dog is going to be more than just a dog after you read this. Real education. The book also is a rarity in the textbook field; it is written in a way that reveals the mysteries. Most textbooks subtly hide what they purport to teach, apparently because the authors subconsciously don't want their expert status diluted. Not so here. It could scarcely be more clear.

—J. Baldwin

[Suggested by Kathleen Whitacre]

Analysis of Vertebrate Structure
Milton Hildebrand
1974; 710 pp.

$25.50 postpaid from:
John Wiley & Sons, Inc.
One Wiley Drive
Somerset, NJ 08873

Hand wing turned to establish positive angle of attack
Wrist flexed
Individual primary feathers rotated thus opening spaces between them

Backstroke of wings in ascending flight of a medium-sized bird shown by a gull, Larus.

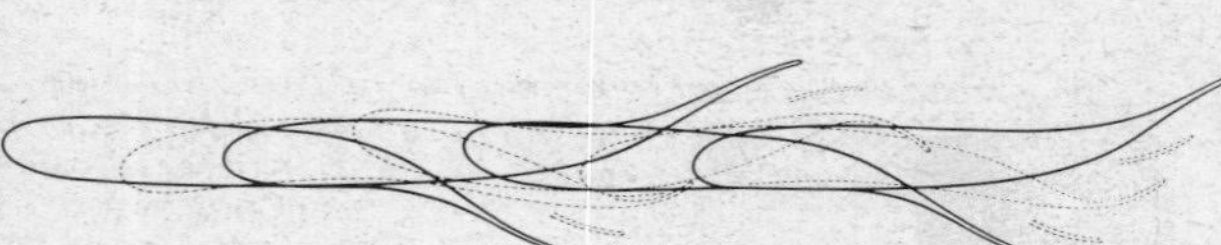

Path of a swimming trout as seen from above.

Horizontal tail flukes supported by connective tissue, not bone
Centra deeper than broad benefiting lateral flection of body
Centra broader than deep benefiting vertical flection of tail
Dolphin, *Delphinus*

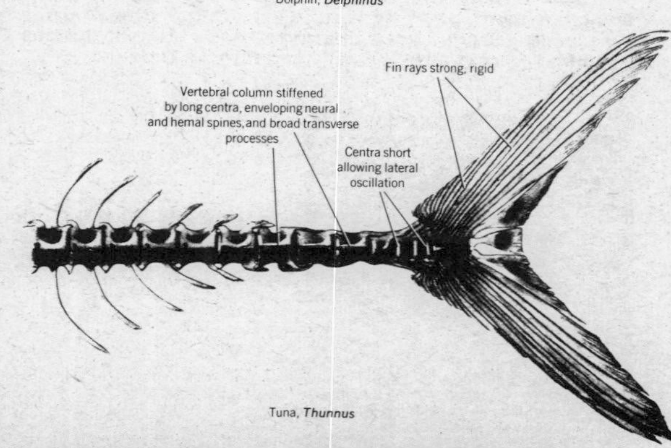

Caudal skeletons of two very different fast swimmers.

You may buy this eternally contemporary piece of design in any authentic Chinese hardware shop.

The Ganges Shark (Platypodon gangeticus).

McDonnell Voodoo F-101A (1954).

•

Burn your idols once in a while, and start all over again.

Structure, Form and Movement

The usual procedure is that R&D comes up with a new process, it's implemented for several years, and then some biologist says Hey did you know porpoises did that? (or snakes did that, or bees or elm seeds). And everybody says My, my, ain't Nature smart.

Herr Hertel and colleagues are trying to reverse the order, learn from nature first, save time and stay humble. This book thoroughly displays the approach that research may take to bugs, birds, fish, etc. for yield in navigation, flight, streamlining, etc. —SB

Structure, Form and Movement
Heinrich Hertel
1963, 1966; 251 pp.

$21.50 postpaid from:
Robert E. Krieger Publishing Company
645 New York Avenue
Huntington, NY 11743

•

Beginning of take-off = wing stroke forward and down
Incident flow - downwash - forces.
Below: stagnation point; flow around the leading edge.

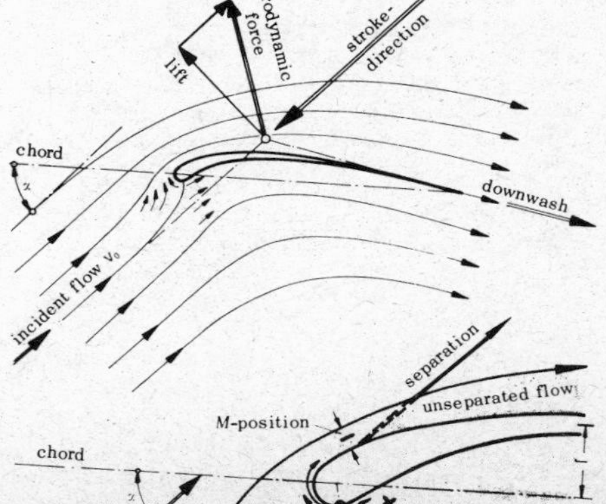

Form, Function & Design

The book is wonderful. Here is a man trying to tell the truth about design and about our lives and civilization. I never heard of him, when I read his book I can't understand why. —Steve Baer

There really is no better introduction to all that is admirable in design. Baer had to remind me of the book: I had forgotten how much I owe to it. It is full of the kind of lore and wisdom that you immediately take for your own. —SB

Form, Function and Design
(Formerly **What is Design?**)
Paul Jacques Grillo
1960, 1975; 238 pp.

$6 postpaid from
Dover Publications
180 Varick Street
New York, NY 10014
or Whole Earth Household Store

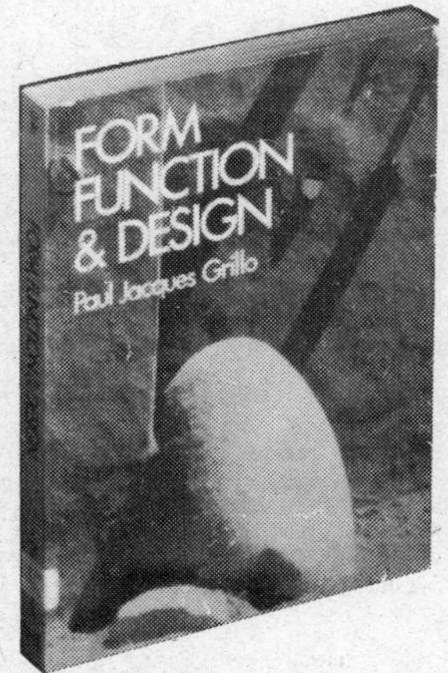

•

The general adoption of the metric system by all but English speaking countries has promoted a new standard of proportions and dimensions that cannot satisfy the designer . . . We are beginning to judge the results of the *exclusive* use of the meter and the decimal arithmetic proportions of the metric system in the poor proportion of the majority of designs in countries that have adopted this system, since the time they put it into practice, while the uncanny persistency of good proportion in countries that still ignore the metric system may often be a source of astonishment to any visitor gifted with a sense of proportion. The reason is not that the designers of these countries have a better sense of proportion than the others: it is that, without their even knowing it, they are tuned to the scale range of human activity, exactly as a radio set can only make a certain station heard if it is tuned to this particular wave length.

•

IN DESIGN, THE SHORTEST DISTANCE BETWEEN TWO POINTS IS NOT THE STRAIGHT LINE, BUT THE SLALOM.

Slaloms are curves of natural acceleration and deceleration that represent trajectories *constantly controlled by man.*

A ballistic missile obeying only initial thrust and gravity will describe an orbit mathematically perfect of the conic section family. But as soon as man sits at the controls, he will make his own orbit, his *slalom.*

Curves described by a man in movement — a car, a bicycle — on a flat surface, are two dimension slaloms, or curves of the second order that may be approximately analyzed in quadratic equations.

A mountain climber, an airplane, a submarine — as well as a skier — describe third order slaloms that may be analyzed in cubic equations.

The interest of slalom curves for the designer lies in the fact that they are all *curves of least effort,* and thus represent the most *economical* pattern of flow.

•

The hand remiges of birds are masterfully perfected to obviate flutter:

- The hollow cross section of the supporting frame consisting of the feather quill is continuous over the entire length and approximates a cylinder, which resists torsion well. This cross section also improves resistance to bending.
- The ultralight construction of the vanes ensures minimum moment of mass about the quill axis.
- Variations in aerodynamic forces during oscillation affect 25% of the remiges, with narrower anterior vane sections and broader posterior vane sections, is appropriate for aeroelastic reasons.

Golden eagle. Leaping off. Legs flexed at left, extended at right.

How Animals Work

This book explains how kangaroo rats live in the hot desert where there is no water. It discusses how animals utilize heat exchangers to conserve body heat and moisture. I found it a useful book, because it discusses questions I have pondered and never seen mentioned elsewhere. Why do dogs pant? Why do they pant so rapidly? This is one of a number of everyday questions answered to my satisfaction. It is also a great pleasure to read a book by a well known professor and have him say that it was a student who solved an intriguing puzzle. Too often a professor later becomes confused and believes he was the one who solved the puzzle or the good idea is successfully ignored. This book should be required reading for architecture students in dry climates. These are the subjects to explore, these are the lessons to learn. —Steve Baer

How Animals Work
Kurt Schmidt-Nielsen
1972; 114 pp.

$4.95 postpaid from:
Cambridge University Press
510 North Avenue
New Rochelle, NY 10801
or Whole Earth Household Store

•

About ten years ago it was suggested by Eugene Crawford, then a student at Duke University, that dogs seem to pant at a resonant frequency (Crawford, 1962). Due to its elastic properties, the entire respiratory system has a natural frequency of oscillation, and to keep the system oscillating at this frequency requires the expenditure of only minimal muscular effort. As a consequence, the heat production by the respiratory muscles is at a minimum, thus adding only little to the heat load. Crawford estimated that if panting were to take place without the benefit of a resonant system, the increased muscular effort would generate more heat than the total amount the panting process can dissipate.

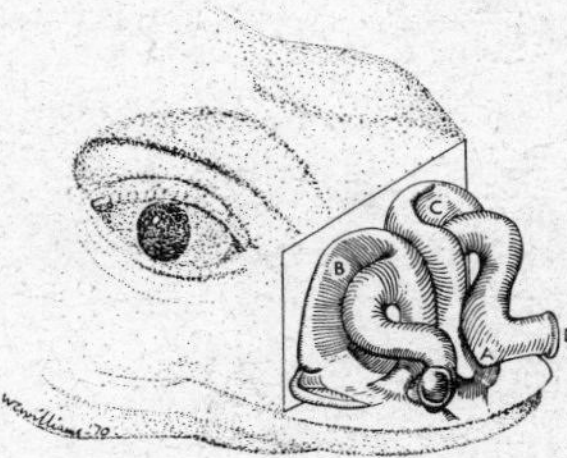

The nasal passage of the desert iguana forms a slight depression (A), just inside the external nares (D). Fluid from the nasal salt-excreting glands (located at B and C) accumulates in this depression and contributes moisture to the humidification of the respiratory air.

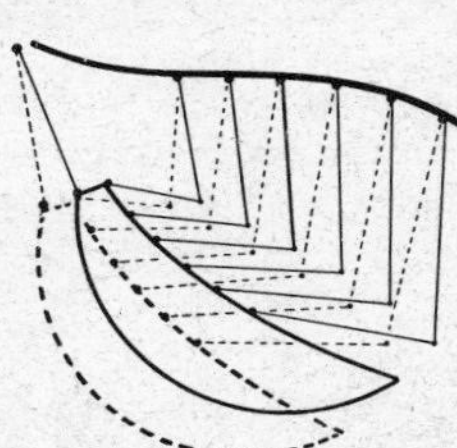

The arrangement of the hinged ribs and the sternum of birds permits large volume changes of the thorax, in which the lungs and some of the air-sacs are located.

THE RISING SUN
NEIGHBORHOOD NEWSLETTER

Don's master's thesis was about how to portray mountains on maps — different ways it's been done at different times and could be done and all. Mountains are often not represented on maps at all because they are hard to do, or many cartographers think they are. Lawrence of Arabia, before being famous, supervised a map making project in Cairo that was mapping parts of Turkey. One of his cartographers asked if he could not draw the mountains. Lawrence said, "Oh, do let us have hills! It would be such fun to have hills!" Don would like to turn his master's thesis into a book about showing mountains on maps, telling how the earliest maps known, which were done by Babylonians, had mountains and how Leonardo da Vinci drew mountains and many other facts and many drawings and maps. He would like to call his book one or the other of the sentences Lawrence of Arabia said, or maybe both.

The Design of Design

It's superficially a book for design engineers, but should be useful to anyone engaged in the design of physical objects or strategies. Simple and basic. More advanced treatment of design techniques gets you into computers and very sophisticated decision making theory. The main trip is concentrated on getting your head straight so that design decisions of any sort can be made intelligently. There's a good bit of practical advice concealed in a slurry of English Humour. The only book of its type that we know of. Among the better points:

Concentration and then relaxation is the common pattern behind most creative thinking.

Beware of intrinsic impossibilities.

Beware of pseudo-technical words.
[He means words like "sturdy," "big," "beautiful," etc.]

Define problems in figures or configurations.

Aim at continuity of energy.

He really gets to the center of the modern-technology-versus New-Mexico-Funk argument:

If the design of a particular machine or production line is based on the way the process was originally done by hand, it is unlikely to be the final form. The feeding forward by mechanizing a style that was handy when only hands were available is doomed, in the long run, to be superseded by the feeding back of ideas and materials from the physical sciences. Beware of well-dressed arts and crafts. —*J. Baldwin*

•

Suspension bridge designers thought at first that the major problem would be the load, and learned by spectacular experience that it was really the stability.

The Design of Design
Gordon L. Glegg
1969; 93 pp.

$11.95 postpaid from:
Cambridge University Press
510 North Avenue
New Rochelle, NY 10801
or Whole Earth
Household Store

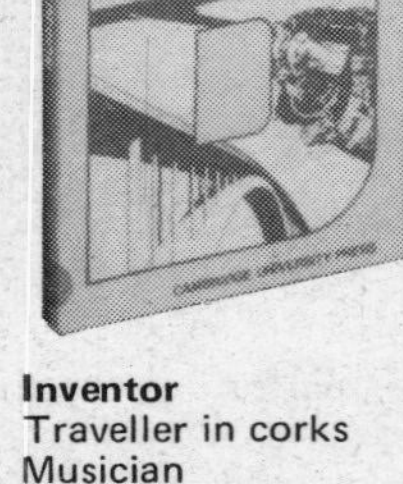

•

Invention	Inventor
Safety razor	Traveller in corks
Kodachrome films	Musician
Ballpoint pen	Sculptor
Automatic telephone	Undertaker
Parking meter	Journalist
Pneumatic tyre	Veterinary surgeon
Long-playing record	Television engineer

The contrast of style between the bicycle and the cart-wheel can be seen in the Forth railway bridge and the Severn road bridge.

The Science of Design

Mr. Glegg continues his useful thoughts with special emphasis on helping the designer/engineer handle scientific research. The author contends that most designers are not competent to set up and interpret experiments, and he illustrates this point (as usual) with horrifying examples and considerable wit. He then goes on to show how experiments can be done and their results put to use. The subject is not at all an easy one, as I can attest from experience. The book will be useful to non-professional designers too, as it is actually a treatise encouraging clear thinking set apart from ego-pitfalls. The small number of pages per dollar is deceiving. All meat, and good reading too. —*J. Baldwin*

The Science of Design
Gordon L. Glegg
1973; 94 pp.

$13.95 postpaid from:
Cambridge University Press
510 North Avenue
New Rochelle, NY 10801
or Whole Earth
Household Store

•

(1) You can define exactly a two dimensional figure.
(2) You cannot define exactly a three-dimensional figure.
(3) With (2) what you will see will be dictated by what you want or expect to see. In other words you are believing yourself, not believing the object. From this follows:
(4) A two-dimensional figure tells you nothing about itself in three dimensions.

Design Methods

The discipline of design is misunderstood by many people. This book helps explain things. The author briefly presents some of the obvious design failures in our industrial society, such as traffic congestion, noise pollution, etc., and says . . .

These need not be regarded as accidents of nature or as acts of God, to be passively accepted: they can instead be thought of as human failures to design for conditions brought about by the products of designing. Many will resist this view because it places too much responsibility on designers and too little upon everyone else. If such is the case then it is high time that everyone who is affected by the oversights and limitations of designers got in on the design act.

The book outlines traditional approaches. It then goes ahead and gives a really useful review of thirty five recently developed strategies, a brief description of each, and a way of determining which will likely be most useful to you. Many of the strategies are ways of organizing your information so that your intuition can be well enough informed to act. Several of the strategies are mainly concerned with preparing your head so that it may intuit effectively. Methods of analyzing the results are also presented.

As far as I know, this book is the only overall collection and review of strategies. I see it as a truly useful tool. I've ordered one myself. —*J. Baldwin*

Design Methods
(Seeds of Human Futures)
J. Christopher Jones
1970; 407 pp.

$25.75 postpaid from:
John Wiley & Sons
One Wiley Drive
Somerset, NJ 08873
or Whole Earth
Household Store

The complicated pattern of the network on the left can be transformed into the simple pattern on the right by re-arranging the nodes. This is analogous to the "change of set" which can enable one to solve a previously insoluble problem.

The Nature & Aesthetics of Design

David Pye seeks a basic theory of design and disputes much current jargon. Form follows a lot more than function. —*Lloyd Kahn*
[Suggested by Bob Brooks]

The Nature & Aesthetics of Design
(Formerly **The Nature of Design**)
David Pye
1964, 1978; 159 pp.

$12.95 postpaid from:
Van Nostrand Reinhold
Order Department
7625 Empire Drive
Florence, KY 41042
or Whole Earth
Household Store

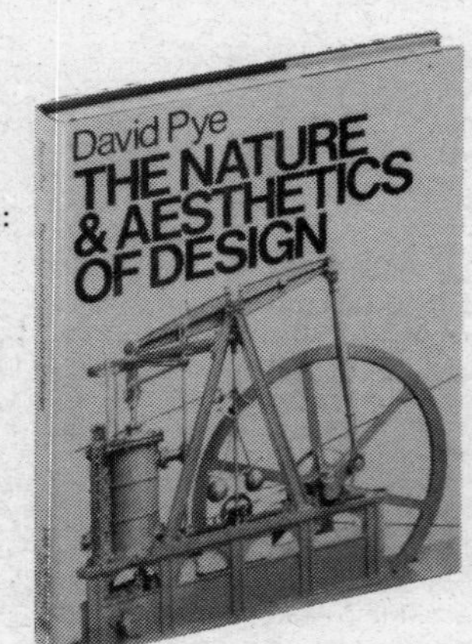

•

It is a most diverting spectacle to see the experts in work study exercising their considerable ingenuity to find the one cheapest way of doing operations which could perfectly well be dispensed with; for example, getting shiny surfaces on furniture. The 'one best way' of doing things like that is not to do them.

•

Because there has not been any coherent theory of the nature of design, and because it is evident that what a thing does has some bearing on what it looks like, 'function' has been loosely used to cover any or all the factors which limit preference. It has diverted attention from the fact that those influences are many, disparate, and of various effect, and particularly from the fact that economy, not physics, is always the predominant influence because directly and indirectly it sets the most limits. 'Function' apparently covers economy as well as anything else you please. It is a wonderful hindrance to any understanding of design and will die hard, for it makes a fairly intricate subject look simple.

The Art and Science of Inventing

This is the first book I've encountered on this subject that matches my actual field experience. The author wishes to prevent the inexperienced innovator from following "pre-doomed paths." For a good start he introduces things with "Some Fundamental Principles of Technology"; one of the best expositions I've seen. That chapter alone should be required reading for the wind and solar experimenters. Equally nifty chapters on model making, prototyping, testing, patents, and design procedure add up to a book that is actually useful! There is a particularly good section on avoiding dead-ends and self-defeating activities. Many of the professional hassles of my life could have been avoided if this book had been available years ago. Ah well . . . —*J. Baldwin*

The Art and Science of Inventing
Gilbert Kivenson
1977; 195 pp.

$11.95 postpaid from:
Van Nostrand Reinhold
Order Department
7625 Empire Drive
Florence, KY 41042
or Whole Earth
Household Store

•

Sometimes unusually high accuracy or efficiency can be obtained by clever utilization of system characteristics.

At other times, a system can be so coupled as to aid in its own operation. The self-generating principle may be defined as the art of utilizing part of the forces already present in a device for its overall guidance or for an improvement in its performance. It is a kind of feedback without the use of discrete amplifying elements . . . A difficult military problem before the days of air transport was the moving of men and equipment across wide and fast flowing streams. An ancient but elegant solution makes use of the river's force.

The first step is getting a strong swimmer across the stream with one end of a light cord. When this has been done, several strong "pendulum" lines are brought across and anchored firmly to a large tree or rock at point A. A raft is then constructed and lashed to the pendulum lines. A control line is tied to the raft and snubbed around a tree at point B; the raft is now loaded. The control line is carefully paid out; the force of the flow will move the raft and its load across the river. When unloaded, the empty raft is easily returned for another load by use of the control line. Employing a long control line, the last man (or team) can use the raft to cross the river. All lines and the raft are then recovered and stored for later use.

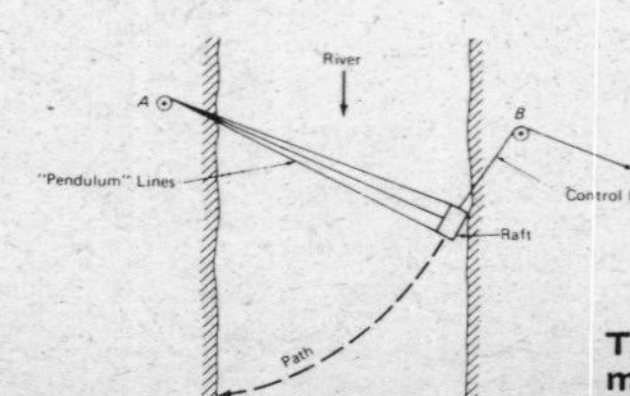

The "pendulum" method for harnessing river power.

Inventors' Services: Some Really Work

by Alan Kalker

What started as a quest of interest mainly to aspiring inventors turned up some new information of interest to university treasurers and business theologians. University treasurers can skip to the section on "university innovation centers" for news of a challenge for students and faculty that can produce a new source of revenue. Business theologians may wish to ponder the indications in the section on "reputable invention managers" that the "nice guy" style of business might produce more income than the ordinary big business style.

Working with the Innovation Center at the University of Utah, Robert Williams fabricated the prototype of this automatic transmission for bicycles. Mr. Williams has now formed his own company to pursue commercialization of the device.

Source: Innovation Center, University of Oregon, Eugene, OR 97403

My quest was to find a way to get some inventions I had lying around out into the market place. One approach, suggested by J.D. Smith, was to make them freely available by publishing them, perhaps with a moral obligation on those who profited to return part of the profit to a foundation. To some, publishing a socially desirable invention is one way of keeping big companies from monopolizing and making a huge profit at the expense of the public. J. Baldwin recalled this was one of the motives for publishing the Domebook series. In retrospect he now feels this may not have been such a good idea. One reason why domes are not too common today may be that by putting most of the ideas in the public domain they removed much of the incentive for many to invest in mass production of domes and dome components. (Another reason, suggested by Stewart, may be that they are uncomfortable.)

J. now thinks the best way to get socially desirable inventions broadly available is to patent them. This is the approach used by Buckminster Fuller, J. noted, and Fuller has never had to sue for patent infringement. The problem with the patent approach is cost. A preliminary patent search costs more than $125. Even if you learn to do the search by yourself at a regional patent library[1] a patent attorney or agent will probably set you back a minimum of $250. If a patent infringement suit is necessary, budget an additional $50,000. A growing alternative is the trade secret approach. While cheaper, it offers long-term protection only in fields like chemical processes and electronics where it is difficult to determine from the finished product the secret method used. Most famous example of a trade secret: the formula for Coca-Cola.

Which of the mutually exclusive methods of patents or trade secrets is best is, unfortunately, a complex technical-legal question.[2] Before spending money for a professional answer to that question, it would be nice to find out if you have any chance of recovering the cost of such professional advice.

Industry submissions

A positive response from industry could justify laying out some money for advice. Unfortunately for most inventors this should be the last step rather than the first. A survey of industry's response to unsolicited new product ideas indicates little uniformity — most common was a reluctant review to maintain good will. Many require the inventor to sign a waiver form before considering the idea. The only saving grace of many of these forms is that they are ". . . so blatant in their attempts to remove all rights from the inventor that they probably would not stand up in court."[3] The usual way around the waiver forms is to know somebody who knows somebody. That somebody could be a patent attorney, banker, university innovation center, reputable invention manager, or merely your neighbor.

Since hope blooms eternal and many attempt industry submissions without professional help, I'll outline the steps that will help minimize the damage. First, before any outside submission, document the date of invention. At a minimum you need a complete description of every known and speculated aspect of the invention, dated and signed by the inventor. The complete description must be shown to someone who is not a co-inventor who can understand the invention. That person must sign and date a notation at the end of each page "understood and witnessed by . . .". Optional at additional cost is notarizing the complete description. An alternate or additional documentation of date of invention is the Patent Office disclosure document filing program. For this you need two copies of the complete disclosure signed and dated by the inventor, a self-addressed stamped envelope, and a check for $10 payable to "Commissioner of Patents." Send the lot to the Commissioner, Washington, D.C. 20231. The Commissioner will stamp both copies, retain one for two years and return the other to you in about a month.

Second, prepare an abstract of the invention containing no proprietary information. ("Proprietary" is the polite business equivalent of "confidential"). Tell generally the type of invention and its expected advantages — how it is better, cheaper, or different than the competition. Omit all specifics and the secret of how such wondrous advantages are obtained. Exactly how much to disclose is a problem. You will not get far with the classic South Sea Bubble disclosure: "For an Undertaking which shall in due time be revealed." The abstract must be sufficient to disclose any potential conflict of interest. The recipient firm should be able to be sure that they are not already working on something similar to your invention. Receiving proprietary information from an outside source on a problem they are working on puts them in the difficult position of disputing a claim for payment for information they had already independently developed. Near simultaneous independent discovery or invention is remarkably common in science and industry. At any one time many are aware of current needs and current methods. It is not unusual for the connection between a particular need and particular method to become apparent to more than one. Industry's interest in the nonproprietary abstract of an unpatented invention may justify the cost of professional aid in negotiating the next phase: a confidential disclosure agreement. Even between corporate giants a complex ritual is required, with several layers of commitment matched with layers of disclosure.

One method of contacting industry is advertising your invention in a computerized technology transfer data bank. Dr. Dvorkovitz lists only market-ready inventions and trade secrets that they think are of interest to industry. They charge the inventor nothing. Industry pays the freight in access fees or commissions. Inventions need not be new; old technology appropriate to developing countries is OK. Technotec will carry any inventor's message, but charges $100 a year minimum rent for memory space that holds a 1,000-character message. For a limited time inventors with solar energy, agriculture, and food processing patents get a one year listing for free.

Request forms from:

Dr. Dvorkovitz & Associates
P.O. Box 1748
Ormond Beach, FL 32074

Control Data Technotec
P.O. Box O
Minneapolis, MN 55440

Energy related inventions

If an invention can save energy you can get a free evaluation of its technical and economic feasibility from the government. You need no special format, nor know if it is an invention or trade secret. If clearly marked "confidential," it will be evaluated in secret, protected from disclosure or conflict of interest by contract and criminal sanction. To obtain this free service simply dispatch a complete description of your invention to: Office of Energy-Related Inventions, National Bureau of Standards, Washington, D.C. 20234. They will send you an Evaluation Request form which you sign and return to start the evaluation. Then, you wait.

One invention I submitted was rejected in 5 weeks, another was rejected after six months. Had my inventions been in the select 2% recommended to the Department of Energy for support, another delay for their independent evaluation would be required. The remote possibility of DOE support some time far in the future is not the only reason for sending an invention to the OERI. The rejections are reasoned in summary form in the letter you receive. If you make a follow-up phone call to the OERI evaluator, you can obtain a wealth of insight into the questions you must consider before sinking more effort or money into the invention. Similar useful feedback can be obtained on the phone if you submit your invention to the DOE Small-Scale Appropriate Energy Technology Grants Program by requesting a "de-briefing."

Useful information from government experts can easily be obtained for free in person or on the phone if you sound half-way reasonable. In letters the reasons for rejections are usually terse and opaque. This state of affairs is based on time, effort, and an instinct for bureaucratic survival. Some inventors are emotionally involved with their inventions. One OERI rejection gave as a reason that the invention violated the Second Law of Thermodynamics. The response of the irate inventor, relayed through his Congressman, was: "I don't have to obey all the idiotic laws you guys in Washington pass."[4]

The major problem with the OERI/DOE program is the time delay. I have found two shortcuts. One is limited geographically, the other by type of invention. Both require preparing 200-word typewritten abstracts of features, advantages, and applications of the invention. One program is open only to those living in Oregon, Washington, Idaho, Northern California, and Nevada. An abstract sent to Energy Related Invention, 131 Gilbert Hall, Univ. of Oregon, Eugene, OR 97403 will, if deemed of high potential, be forwarded by them to OERI on a priority basis for special attention.

The second method is to send an "unsolicited preproposal" to the government office evaluating your specific type of invention.[5] This is the route used often by industry and university researchers. In one case funding was provided six months before OERI approval. This route should only be used by those sure of their technical basis and recent academic literature. To keep this route open, limit your submission to a typewritten 200-word technical abstract (nonconfidential preferred). Limited facilities will probably permit a reply ONLY if their impression is favorable. Please, no phone calls. If you get no response, submit your invention to OERI to get feedback. Do not expect this program to supply a reasoned rejection or explanation.

If you do get a favorable response from any of these, it is usually better to have filed your patent application before accepting government funding.

University Innovation Centers

The bright new hope for the independent inventor, and possibly the university treasurer. Five years in the making, the innovation center experiment drew favorable reactions at a University of California Santa Cruz conference in November '78. Produced by the U.S. Congress, directed by the National Science Foundation, the experiment stars a bevy of prominent universities.

I found the main advertised plot of the experiment not terribly exciting: ". . . to determine if combining formal classroom training in engineering and business theory and hands-on clinical experience in generating new ideas, developing and evaluating new products, and initiating new ventures can increase the . . . probability of the . . . participants becoming successful entrepreneurs."[6] Even assuming the aim is "good," good for the students and good for the productivity of the nation, the experiment would be just very interesting.

More noteworthy is the way R. Colton and A. Ezra of NSF structured the experiment. Normally the approach would be for the government to fund the courses, evaluate the students after five years, then use the results to determine if continued funding was desirable. Instead, they took as their unstated premise: you cannot do good for long if the process of doing good does not of itself generate sufficient revenues to continue the good work. One source of revenue is the "hands-on clinical experience." Since the students and faculty were to attempt to solve real world business problems, a successful solution could generate real world revenue. It was reasonable for the students and university to be repaid for the value of the services rendered, if the venture was successful, through notes, equity, and royalties. If the service seemed valuable to business

THE RISING SUN
NEIGHBORHOOD NEWSLETTER

The creatures who live at the bottom of earth's sky are much like the creatures who live at the bottom of earth's sea — pale and oddly shaped with eyes bulging out of their heads to try and see earth's other dim figures by what's left of the sunlight after it's filtered through the miles of swirling slime above them, long appendages to drag them along the bottom and hold them up against the fierce gravity. They cannot imagine the world outside the odd substance, filled with invisible life, that they breathe through them at every moment. They can't imagine that much light.

—Press release from the Moon Club

and government, they might contract for work to be done. Alumni might wish to support the program. Government funds were only seed money. Each innovation center should try to prove its utility by becoming self-sufficient within the grant period of five years. As new businesses take some time to produce enough revenue to repay notes and provide royalties, and even longer before paying dividends, this is a tough test. Surprisingly one of the innovation centers has already become more than self-sufficient. The center at the Massachusetts Institute of Technology budgeted for fiscal year 1978 over $150,000 in income from royalties and $350,000 in contracts.

Also noteworthy is the underlying attempt at fiscal responsibility. A continuing part of the project is an attempt to measure new tax monies generated against the tax monies expended to seed the centers. Interim figures are impressive. ". . . in 1977 alone the federal taxes collected as a result of the profits and wages attributed to the new ventures initiated by the Innovation Centers exceeded $2,500,000, approximately four times the annual federal investment of $670,000. . . ."[7] It is hoped the final report takes at least a stab at the most difficult task of separating truly new tax revenues from merely relocated tax revenues.

Pennsylvania: Center for Entrepreneurial Development, Carnegie-Mellon Univ., 4516 Henry St., Pittsburgh, PA 15213. Dr. Dwight Baumann, Director. New company focus, provides a "maternity ward" for new business startups. An inventor/entrepreneur can obtain up to $40,000 worth of engineering and management expertise on a continuing basis against notes and equity in the new company. Assurance of CED management assistance allowed one company to obtain $150,000 startup capital. Substantial assistance has been provided inventors of a microcomputer energy management and security systems, a blood test serum for gonorrhea, a blood oximeter, and a remote control unit for locomotives and cranes. CED has aided community needs by devising a method of providing cheap taxi service and a method of subsistence for out-of-work actors. Local inventor's submissions seem mostly to require market potential evaluation, capital, and an entrepreneur to reduce the idea to practice. They note ". . . the shortage is in technological entrepreneurs rather than in inventors."

Access: Stop by the CED office (phone first). A continuing assistance approach requires that the inventor/entrepreneur reside or relocate nearby. Comment: Day to day involvement in the operation of a new business is an arduous and controversial role for a university. It holds promise of providing the most realistic education for students and greatest financial rewards for the university.

National & Oregon: Innovation Center, College of Business Administration, University of Oregon, Eugene, OR 47405. Dr. Gerald Udell, Director. Inventor and new product focus. Attempts to provide a badly needed nationwide business oriented evaluation service to inventors of new products and services. For the neophyte inventor, desperate for impartial advice, it provides for a computerized indication of whether further effort and expense is justified. Evaluation is directed toward the sad plight of the amateur inventor who spends thousands of hours and dollars achieving a product that works well, has full patent protection . . . and no economic viability. About 1% of inventions evaluated are deemed worthy enough to receive center assistance in reaching the marketplace. Distant inventors are referred to SBA's Small Business Institute program which uses college students to aid the inventor. Local inventors may receive marketing aid from the Center. Successfully marketed products seem mostly to fall in the categories of appropriate technology (wood stoves, low fuel consumption vehicles) or cottage industry (etched glass, wood frames). Only invention refused evaluation: a marijuana gin.

Access: Mail request for "Innovation Registration and Disclosure" form to Center.

Comment: For the first time inventor desperate for inexpensive independent guidance by mail this seems the only game around. As with the dog who could play the piano, the amazing thing is that it is done at all. The quality of the performance need not be perfect. The computerized evaluation process is itself under continuing evaluation.

The main qualm I have is the minimal level of protection guaranteed the inventor in the waiver the inventor must sign. The evaluation form requests details on information not protected under copyright or patent laws — test results, market information, and product cost details. Yet the inventor is required to sign a waiver acknowledging: "For protection of my idea, I rely solely upon existing or future copyrights or patents which will be obtained at my sole expense."

On the other hand, the waiver indicates the disclosure will be treated "with care" and the brochure supplied to applicants promises one of the features of the program is "confidentiality, that is, only individuals who have signed nondisclosure agreements will see an idea without written authorization from the inventor."[8]

The problem is that many first time inventors suffer from "inventor's paranoia" and will be dissuaded from using the service by the wording of the waiver they must sign. The waiver form fails to provide for the growing use of trade secrets in fields like electronics. Some in the electronics field note that "black boxing" — sealing components in epoxy or sanding off part numbers, rather than using patents — is their usual method of protection. One government aide observed: ". . . it's pretty commonly known that there's an increasing reliance on trade secrets instead of patents. . . ."[9] A potential licensee of a trade secret might note the terms of the waiver in determining that the scope of possible trade secret protection has been lessened. A court may cite the terms of the brochure in determining that the Center is liable to the inventor for breach of a confidence. As it stands the waiver seems to offer unpleasant consequences for both possible interpretations, but if currently contemplated changes are satisfactory, it may be of use to even the most prudent inventor.

Massachusetts (maybe): MIT Innovation center, Massachusetts Institute of Technology, Room 33-111, Cambridge, MA 02139. Dr. Yao Tzu Li, Director. "Inventing done, on contract, while you wait" might be the slogan of the Center. A majority of current income seems to come from inventing on contract. Industry — need a TV game or precious metal forgery detector? Government — need a method of evaluating and marketing energy efficient inventions? MIT Innovation Center will invent one, provided you supply the necessary funds. Add to this a startling array of student, faculty and outside inventions and you have a more than self-sufficient innovation center. Some of the 1975-76 projects — wide-band electronic guitar, wheel torque feedback controlled front brake, thermally controlled liquid gas, small molecule detector, pulse-width-modulated amplifier and communications link, high efficiency bow, dynamic paper making process, desalination process, bicycle frameset, and an automatic banana peeler. Inventor is given a flat 35% of income from patents or licensing agreements.

Access: In November 1978 the Center director indicated they are currently unable to handle submissions from outside inventors. In the past, and hopefully in the future, an outside invention program provides access.

Utah: Utah Innovation Center, University of Utah, Merrill Engineering Building, Salt Lake City, UT 84112. Dr. Wayne S. Brown, Director. Newest NSF center funded in 1977, four years after the others, ". . . to replicate the concept based on the experiences of the originally funded Innovation Centers." First outside inventor project is an infinitely variable bicycle transmission which automatically varies gear ratios to fit road gradients. Has R & D prototype shops with facilities for injection molding, heat treating, etc. Has previous experience in successfully marketing faculty inventions (e.g., portable dialysis machines) by cooperating with industry in latter stages of development to insure rapid commercialization. Has a tradition of faculty entrepreneurship — several faculty members have founded their own businesses located in a nearby university research park.

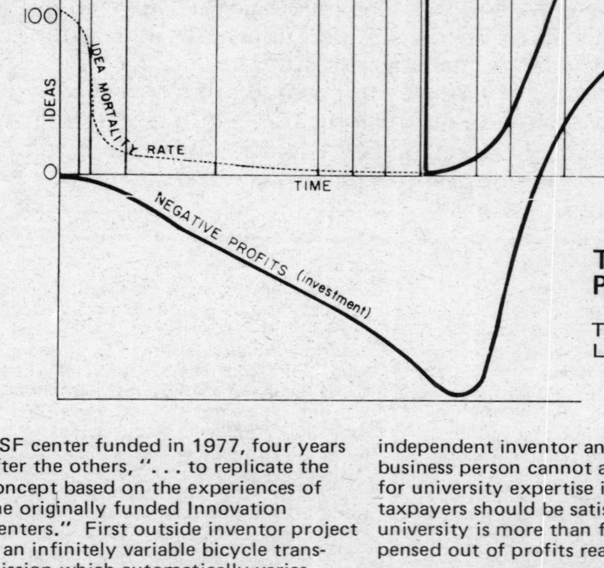

THE INNOVATION PROCESS

THE PRODUCT LIFE CYCLE

Access: 200-word typewritten non-proprietary abstract of the invention. Inventor should reside or be willing to relocate nearby so the Center can give assistance on a continuing basis. Possible exception for bio-medical inventions, an area of particular interest to this Center.

Comment: Looks like a winner. Open enthusiasm of the staff of this Center at the Santa Cruz conference impressed me. Indicates that a public university faculty can openly be involved in commerce without public outcry or befouling its reputation. Indicates a public university that allows faculty entrepreneurship can attract and hold exceptionally qualified faculty even though they cannot match salary offers of private universities or industry.

OTHER: Many other universities in the U.S. and Canada have or are planning innovation center activities. If you live near a university check the business administration and engineering school catalogs — 138 schools now offer entrepreneurship or small business courses. Many of these courses ask students to solve real life new business problems; the professor for the course may allow them to attempt to solve yours. Some faculty of public universities covertly aid budding inventors. Try to find someone teaching a course in your area of interest. Likely sources of information — the dean's secretary, university patent attorney, and professors of aeronautical engineering.

Aid from public university faculty has been covert or ad hoc because they fear criticism from the taxpayers for using public facilities for private gain. The fear of this criticism is commonly expressed by university and government officials. At the Santa Cruz conference innovation center staff members agreed the feared criticism never came from taxpayers. Indeed, one endowment officer remembered that when he mentioned the innovation center to an alumnus he received a substantial contribution, the alumnus commenting, "That's the first thing I've seen the university do for the small businessman." In reality, the expertise of the university can be said to have always been available to big business, whose needs are frequently reflected in government grants made available to universities for research. Big business can afford to hire faculty as consultants. Even though the independent inventor and small business person cannot afford to pay for university expertise in advance, taxpayers should be satisfied if the university is more than fully recompensed out of profits realized.

Out of pocket expense for the university is small. The requisite expertise and laboratories are already "purchased" for another purpose, teaching. One of the big problems of the innovation centers has been faculty resistance to sharing their expertise with the center for what they feel is an unprofessional activity. Ironically, some of the same faculty members feel no such qualms when they share their expertise with an outside company as a paid consultant. Sharing expertise with independent inventors for the eventual financial benefit of the university may seem less unprofessional if viewed as a means of survival for universities.

The demographic, taxpayer, stock-market and inflationary squeeze on the university is fierce. A source of funds to continue the "good" work of education other than the public purse should be welcomed. The NSF experiment indicates that at least some universities can benefit. One conference participant, noting the poor stock market performance of the schools endowment, was considering suggesting that the trustees invest some of the school's endowment in innovation center activities. He felt the combined expertise of the business and engineering faculty could pick a winner as accurately as a venture capital company. Venture capital returns when they pick a winner are huge — 30% compounded a year on invested capital. If he convinces the trustees we may see proof or disproof of the old adage that "people who can't make a living at something end up teaching it."

Less venturesome university officials may wish to participate in the drafting of legislation to provide funds to seed new innovation centers by contacting Professor Wayne S. Brown at the University of Utah.

Advertised idea brokers

Market demand for university innovation centers is indicated by the unworthy success of a group of charming charlatans, the widely advertised idea brokers. They take in some $100 million each year from some 100,000 hopeful inventors,[10] providing a great deal of ego gratification and an occasional handsome patent certificate suitable for framing. Those who expect to receive more for their fees are usually disappointed. One firm seems to have "assisted" some 30,000 aspiring inventors. Only three of these received income greater than the fees paid.[11] Another, the SEC charged, received some $4 million in fees from some 4,000 inventors. None received income greater than the fees paid.[12]

Remember, a patent is no guarantee of economic viability. It can cost as much to search and patent an invention that is viable as one that is not. Patent

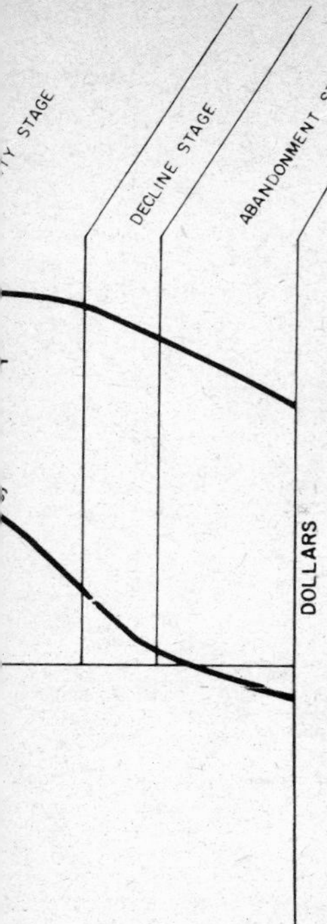

Two seniors at the University of Utah (John DeJong and Douglas Kihm) worked with its Innovation Center in their patent and feasibility study of their microcircuit-controlled programmable breadboard device.

JERRY BYBEE

protection can vary from broad protection to extremely narrow. At the bottom is the design patent. This can almost always be obtained, but only protects you from a product whose appearance is almost identical to yours.

Reputable Invention Managers

Not all invention managers are charlatans. Some have a proven record of returning more than they take. Two available to the independent inventor are Battelle Development Co. (BDC) and Arthur D. Little, Inc. (ADL). As the two giants in this backwater of industry who are quite similar in some respects, they offer a provocative contrast of business styles and results of interest to business theologians.

Unlike the charlatans, neither advertises or charges the inventor a fee. Evaluation, patents, development, and marketing costs the inventor nothing unless the invention is successfully marketed. If it is, they get a portion of royalties received. Both invention management groups were formed originally to market the inventions of employees of a large company providing independent science and engineering consulting services to governments and industry worldwide. Inventions of outside inventors usually are considered only if the invention manager's expertise will help make the invention market ready for license to unaffiliated manufacturers, though both recently have added a very limited venture capital capacity.

Though little known to the general public, the parent consulting companies are prominent in their field, and hardly small potatoes. Together, in 1976, they had more employees and revenue than the brokerage firm of Dean Witter, Inc. Battelle's four facilities had reimbursable costs and fees earned of $185 million, 6,000 employees, and technology licensing revenues of $656,000.[13] Arthur D. Little had gross sales of $86 million, 2,000 employees, and technology licensing revenues of $2 million.[14] (Rough 1976 data.)

Both companies have broad technical expertise of the highest caliber, and could handle almost any conceivable invention. They differ in their likes and dislikes, but both can be said to have very high standards. They want only substantial improvements, not mere minor modifications of existing devices. ADL puts it this way: "The submitted invention should stimulate the enthusiasm of the staff. . . . Since ADL's staff members deal largely with advanced technology, it is not probable — although it is possible — that they would be interested in such items as household devices, automobile accessories, toys, games, and wearing apparel." Both companies have considerable expertise and interest in alternative energy, especially solar. Areas of invention disliked by BDC — liquor or tobacco industry, nuclear, large-scale chemical or heavy industry, auto engines or original equipment, games, sporting goods, weapons, building systems, products requiring governmental action before acceptance by industry.

The packets sent by each company to an aspiring outside inventor have one common element. Neither, initially at least, wants a confidential relationship (as between attorney and client) with the inventor. Such a relationship might require the company to avoid all possible conflict of interest by turning down future paid research contracts in the area of the submitted invention even though they had decided not to develop it with their own funds. It might also require the company to reveal past or present independent or sponsored similar research. Fair enough.

The packets do seem to differ in their initial submission requirements.
BDC: Duty of care: ". . . no obligation, either expressed or implied. . . . $1,000 . . . shall be the maximum damages for any and all liability of BDC with respect to such information or unpatented idea, including, but not limited to, BDC's disclosure thereof." Waiver form: full page of legalese. Submission: full and complete details. Time for evaluation: 6 to 10 months (if rejected on initial screening: two weeks).
ADL: Duty of care: ". . . exercises due care to prevent submitted material from being communicated to others outside of the company and treats such material in accordance with [its] established professional standards." No dollar limitation of liability. Waiver form: four simple lines. Submission: brief description. Time for evaluation: three weeks (may then request confidential information).

Comment: Just because BDC might not seem obligated to treat an unsolicited idea with much more care than an unsolicited bag of excrement does not mean they might even consider doing so. What we have here is a difference of business style. BDC's waiver is written in normal big business style —protect the company and let the inventor take care of herself.
ADL uses the nice style — protect the company and the inventor. BDC's waiver has about the same one-sided approach used in waivers required for many industrial submissions, but when coupled with the request for full and complete details it can put the inventor in an unfair predicament. The problem here is similar to the problem discussed above in the section about the Oregon Innovation Center waiver. Here, however, the problem is worse since BDC's form is more unequivocal. A potential licensee of a trade secret might feel the terms of BDC's waiver lessens the scope of possible trade secret protection. A very prudent inventor who has not sought professional advice probably will use the procedure outlined in the "industry submissions" section for both firms.

The packets sent the outside inventor seem to differ also in the terms of the "typical" agreement offered the inventor.
BDC: Depending on stage of development, 30% to 60% of "net" income (license fees minus administrative, development, licensing, and all other BDC expenses) to inventor. Inventor grants all rights and title to patent to BDC. BDC is obliged to return patent if it fails to use reasonable diligence to negotiate licenses and promote commercial use. If returned, and BDC's R & D and patent expenses exceed $1,000, inventor pays 30% of future net income until BDC gets double its expenses.

ADL: Royalties usually split 50/50. Inventor grants one year exclusive right to license. If ADL fails to find licensee within year, all patent rights and applications, models and data produced given without obligation or cost to inventor.[15]

Comment: BDC seems obliged to a reasonably diligent effort, ADL to a specific result by a specific date. In my experience in dealing with big business (not BDC or ADL) this distinction, not dishonesty, is the real problem. Exclusive rights to an invention should either be paid for (even while being evaluated) or have a specific deadline. The problem is one of priorities. I have received many good honest reasons for delayed decisions or actions — "Joe was called out of town, next week for sure," or "We just got a new section leader, it is right on the top of the pile." Each time I felt the speaker honestly intended to do what was promised, but something with a higher priority came up. In every big business there are many important projects competing for limited time and funds. Unless delay costs the company money, or there is an external deadline, even with the best corporate intentions your invention may not be commercialized.

ADL's 'nice' approach insures the inventor can look elsewhere if, for whatever good reason, results are not obtained by a certain date. Generally this approach can aid rapid commercialization by giving the invention management officer a justification for insisting that corporate management provide requisite funds this month rather than next. BDC uses the normal big business style: make a reasonable offer that protects the company and let the inventor bargain for the terms she feels necessary to protect herself. Some people love big business bargaining; I don't. Sometimes it's just silly: the need for terms that protect both parties is obvious from the start. Then, any accompanying hassle, aggravation, and mutual suspicion is needless. The normal big business style is common, despite the aggravation, because it is thought more businesslike, paying dividends on the balance sheet. Nice guys finish last . . . or do they?

It is probably misleading to compare the technology licensing revenues of these two companies. No doubt it is probably a reflection of much more than business style. On the basis of clearly inadequate information I can prove or imply nothing. Still, I find it interesting (and only interesting) to compare the results adjusted by number of employees. Since technology licensing revenues include both employee and outside inventions, this seems a possible basis for comparison. Adjusted for number of employees, ADL beat BDC by about 2 to 1 in 1975, about 7 to 1 in '76, and about 7 to 1 in '77.[16]

Perhaps ADL's use of the nice business style may signal a trend. A substantial portion of ADL's income comes from providing business management consulting services. Each year big business pays them millions for advice on how to become more profitable. Free advice for big business from ADL vice president Walter Cairns: ". . . Some companies behave as though hard-nosed bargaining is essential in doing business with technology sources, even though such an attitude may result in lost opportunities, poor relations with the party from whom technology has been acquired, and a reputation for being tough to deal with. While the management of a company must naturally protect the interests of its stockholders and employees . . . remember that adherence to fairness . . . may frequently produce unexpected dividends in the continuing development of improvements by the technology source, as well as disclosures of other opportunities the source may develop in the future."[17]

Access: request invention submission forms from: Battelle Development Co., 505 King Avenue, Columbus, OH 43201 and Arthur D. Little Enterprises, 20 Acorn Park, Cambridge, MA 02140. ■

1979

REFERENCES

1. Univ. of State of N.Y., Albany; Georgia Tech, Atlanta; Boston Public Library [PL]; Buffalo & Erie County PL; Chicago PL; Cincinnatti PL; Cleveland PL; Ohio State Univ., Columbus; Detroit PL; Linda Hall Library, Kansas City, MO; Los Angeles PL; State Historical Society of Wisconsin, Madison; Milwaukee PL; Newark, NJ PL; New York PL; Franklin Institute, Philadelphia; Carnegie Library, Pittsburgh; Providence PL; St. Louis PL; Oklahoma A & M College, Stillwater; Sunnyvale PL, CA; Toledo PL.

2. Brosnahan, ed., **Attorney's Guide to Trade Secrets,** 1971.

3. Hawkins, **Corporate Policy and Unsolicited New Product Ideas,** 1976, 15.

4. Paraphrase of anecdote related by Jacob Rabinow, unofficial NBS raconteur.

5. Propose research evaluating your invention. Energy efficient (e.g., solar) inventions ONLY. Crop drying: W.R. Fox, Mississippi State Univ., Mississippi St., MS 39762, Livestock production: J.P. Mason, Jr., Virginia Polytechnic, Blacksburg, VA 24061. Greenhouses & rural residences: L.D. Albright, Riley-Robb Hall, Cornell Univ., Ithaca, NY 14853. Windows & Lighting: S. Selkowitz, Bldg. 90, Rm. 3111, LBL, UC, Berkeley, CA 94720. For others, contact the Department of Energy, Unsolicited Research Proposal Branch, Procurement & Contracts Management Directorate, Washington, D.C. 20545; or try phoning a government scientist with published work similar to yours.

6. Colton, "Technological Innovation Through Entrepreneurship," **Engineering Education,** Nov. 1978, 193.

7. Ibid., 194.

8. Udell & Baker, **Exploring New Ideas,** 1978, 5.

9. Aide to head of President's innovation study due April 1979 quoted in: Shapley, "Electronics Industry Takes to 'Potting' Its Products for Market," **Science, 202,** 849 (1978).

10. Udell quoted in: "For the Independent Inventor, Assistance or Abuse," (panel), 1976 **Bul. Am. Patent L. Assoc. 109,** 110.

11. **J. Assoc. for Advancement of Invention & Innovation,** 82 (1977).

12. Ibid., 84.

13. Battelle Memorial Institute [BMI], President's Report and Annual Review, 1976, 20, 25, 28. For Consolidated Balance Sheet purposes accountants deduct from the category "reimburseable costs and fees earned" $57 million (costs directly reimbursed by ERDA) and $23 million (costs and fees earned by Battelle-Institute, accounts examined by other auditors). BMI, 1976, 23, 27, 28.

14. "O-P-S Survey," **Invention Management,** Oct. 1977.

15. ADL sometimes requires some cost reimbursement before split, e.g., if extraordinary out-of-pocket expenses are anticipated.

16. "Technology licensing revenues" does not include all intellectual property income, e.g., income from sales of intellectual property. Battelle: employees, 6000 in '75, 6100 in '76, 6300 in '77; technology licensing revenues, $2,099,000 in '75, $656,000 in '76, $707,000 in '77. Fn. 13, BMI, 1977, 18, 25, 28. ADL: employees, 1800 in '75, 2000 in '76 and '77; technology licensing revenues, $1.5 to $2 million in '75, '76, and '77. Unpublished source.

17. "Product Opportunities: Fact and Fable," Industry, Assoc. Industries of Massachusetts, April, 1978.

THE RISING SUN
NEIGHBORHOOD NEWSLETTER

You can sing Stopping by the Woods on a Snowy Evening all the way through to the tune of Hernando's Hideaway. "Whose woods! These are! I think I know!" —Courtesy Stewart

Explaining Energy

Just that, and very well done, too. I recommend it highly not only to the outsider, but to the insider as well. The various controversies seem to be fairly dealt with despite the publisher being the Berkeley "Rad Lab." I'll nominate this paper as the best introduction to the subject I've seen so far. Lee Schipper is a man to watch; his work is seen more and more often where people are trying to find the facts needed for good decisions.
—J. Baldwin

Explaining Energy
(A Manual of Non-Style for the Energy Outsider Who Wants In!)
Lee Schipper
Lawrence Berkeley Laboratory
1976; 72 pp.
(No. LBL 4458 ERG 76-04)

$8 postpaid from:
NTIS
U.S. Department of Commerce
5285 Port Royal Road
Springfield, VA 22161

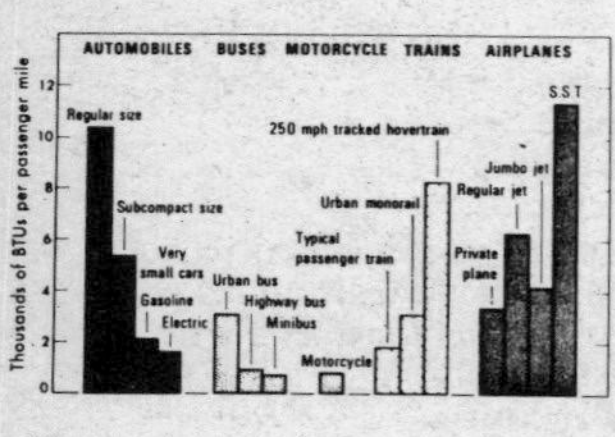

← **Energy consumption of various transportation modes.**

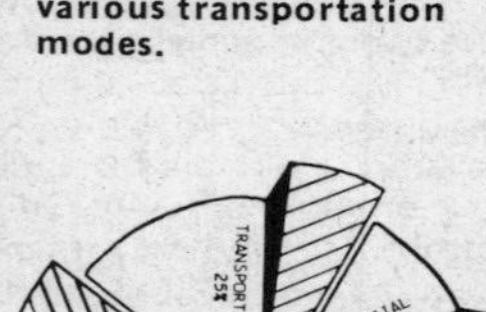

→ **United States energy use potential savings.**

Energy Basis for Man and Nature

The Odums' great contribution has been "net energy accounting," called "energetics." The idea is, you check how much energy goes into mining oil shale or into making a solar collector and compare that with the energy output. Many such energy "sources" turn out to be energy losers rather than gainers. (By such accounting the most efficient solar collectors by far turn out to be plants.)

Using their elegant notation for energy cycles, you can convince even politicians of the hidden wisdom or unwisdom of various energy paths. Since 1973 we have been given an energy X-ray of our economy by the historic events around oil pricing. This book and Howard Odum's more technical and earlier **Environment, Power, and Society** *are the kindly doctor showing what the X-ray means and what to do about it.*

In the world of energy, this book is about how to think. (The Odums' ideas about information — "high quality energy" — are not as convincing.)
—SB

Energy Basis for Man and Nature
Howard T. Odum and Elizabeth C. Odum
1976; 297 pp.

$12.95 postpaid from:
McGraw-Hill Book Co.
Princeton Road
Hightstown, NJ 08520
or Whole Earth Household Store

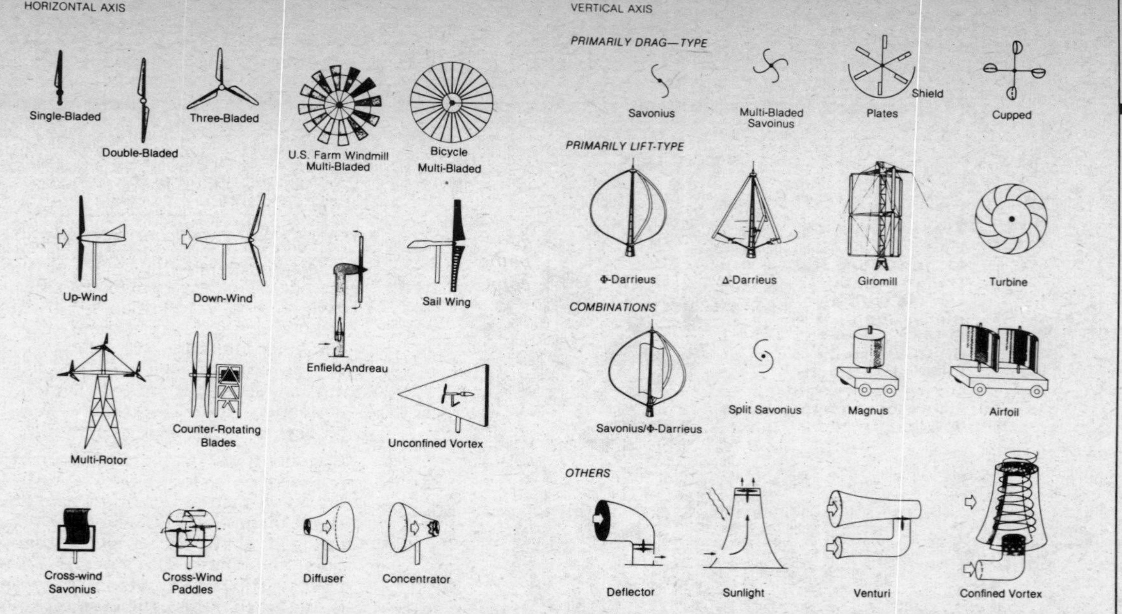

Wind Machines Taxonomy ↑

Energy Earth and Everyone

This book is very different from any other energy book we know of, in that it not only explains, but quantifies and prescribes. If energy is your interest, you really should have one of these at hand. The new 1980 edition brings the contents up to date.
—J. Baldwin

Energy Earth and Everyone
(Energy Strategies for Spaceship Earth)
Medard Gabel and the World Game Laboratory
1975, 1980; 264 pp.

$6.95 postpaid from:
Doubleday and Company
501 Franklin Avenue
Garden City, NY 11530

or Whole Earth Household Store

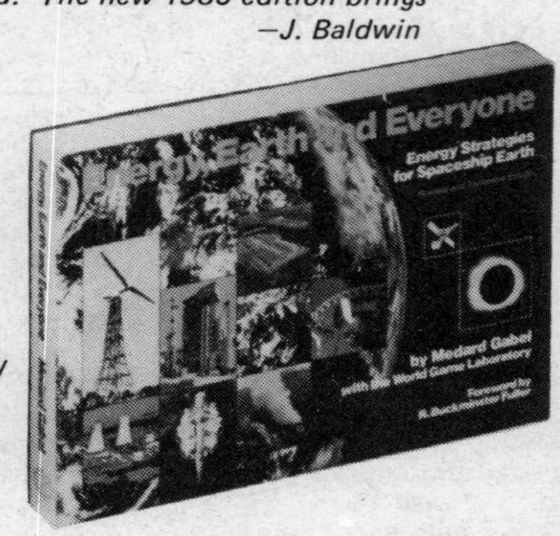

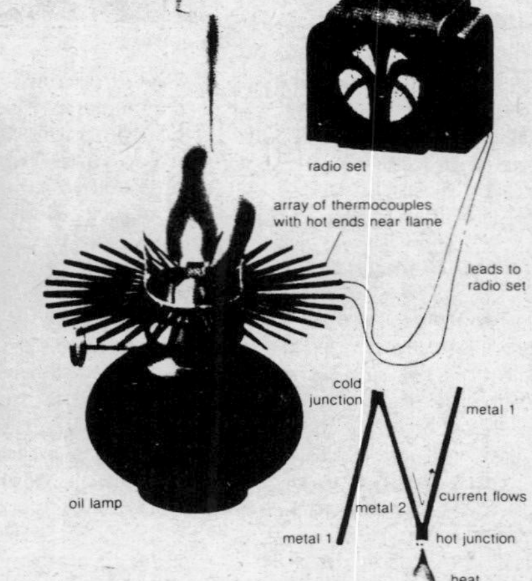

↑ **A simple Russian thermoelectric device was used during the 1930s and 1940s to power radios. It was a thermopile — thermocouples connected in series to give the necessary voltage — with the hot junctions heated by an ordinary oil lamp.**

↘ Nitinol has a seemingly unique property for a solid metal: it bends easily when cooled and springs back to its original shape when warmed. This "shape memory," or ability to resume an original shape after being deformed, can potentially be harnessed for power. One scheme for such a purpose developed by Ridgeway Banks at Lawrence Radiation Laboratory in Berkeley, uses the unique physical characteristics of nitinol in an engine. The engine is a spoked wheel with 20 u-shaped stripes of nitinol hanging from individual spokes. When the wheel is lowered into a round pan divided into semi-circles of hot and cold water, it begins rotating because one set of wires are cold and go limp, while the others — those passing through the hot water — "fire" with a piston-like motion, thereby driving the wheel around. Power output of this first prototype has been measured at .23 watts. This type of engine could make use of numerous sources of waste heat, as in nearly all current power production plants and other natural sources that previously have been unsuitable for tapping.

Advantages
1. There is no direct fuel consumption with a nitinol engine (though heat is "consumed").
2. There are no by-products from the power production — such as air or water emisisions.

Disadvantages
1. Current nitinol engines have low power output.
2. Engines are only at prototype stage; there is as yet no information on size limitations and capabilities.

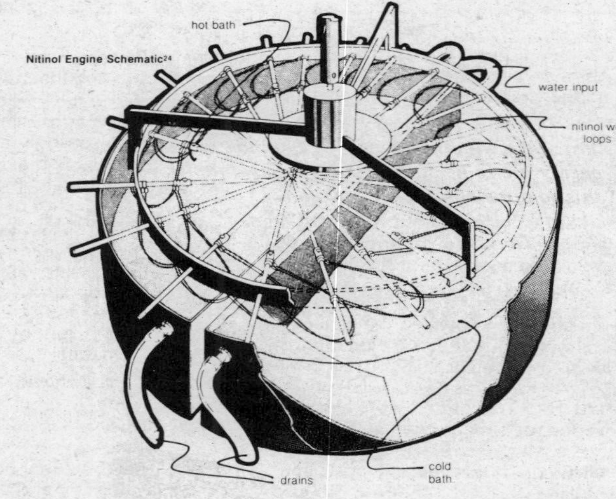

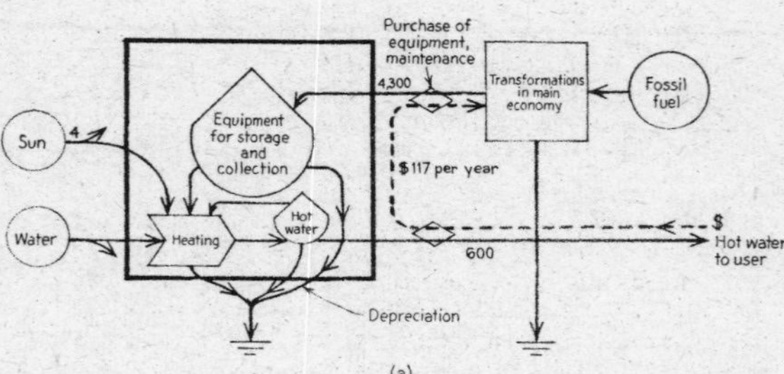

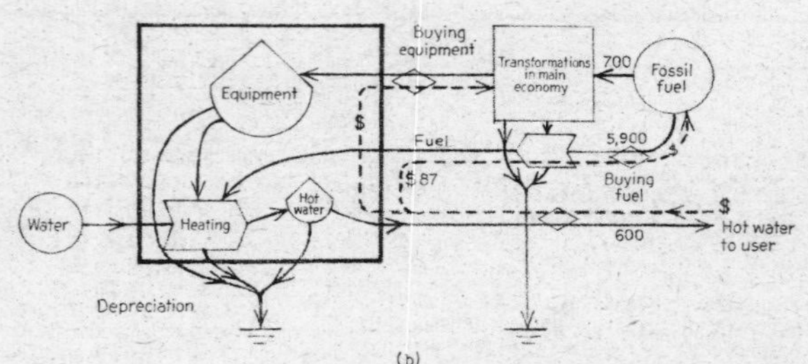

● Solar heating of houses and water uses much fossil fuel indirectly in the installations. Solar heaters have been used for a long time in sunny climates. Figure *a* and *b* compares a solar water heater and a fossil-fuel water heater. In this case solar energy is being used to make low-quality heat energy. In sunny climates, using some sunlight along with fossil fuels, energy is saved by solar heaters as compared with electric and gas water heaters. However, solar heaters use much more fossil fuels than solar energy when they are compared on an equal-quality basis (fossil-fuel equivalents). No net energy is yielded. Capital costs at the start are high in terms of money and energy; savings are obtained later, after the heater has run for several years. One unanswered question is this: Would more energy have been saved if fossil fuels had been put into something else rather than into solar water heaters? As the energy for required materials becomes more costly, technology for solar heating will also become more costly. One concludes that there are ways to conserve energy using solar technology, but solar technology is not a source of energy for running our economy generally.

↑ **Energy flows in solar technology: comparison of (a) solar water heater and (b) fossil-fuel (gas) water heater. Numbers are thousands of Calories per year (fossil-fuel equivalents). (Zuchetto and Brown, 1975.) Both systems use fossil fuel indirectly to supply and maintain equipment. The solar heater takes more equipment but uses less fuel directly. The fossil-fuel heater involves less equipment and storage and less depreciation but requires the purchase of fuel.**

An Alternate Illustrative Future for U.S. Gross Primary Energy Use

QUADRILLION (10^{15}) BTU PER YEAR
250 200 150 100 50
COAL
OIL AND GAS
SOFT TECHNOLOGIES
1975 2000 2025
* OR QUINTILLION (10^{18}) JOULES PER YEAR

Soft Energy Paths

Amory Lovins is one of the good guys if you happen to be anti-nuclear and pro-environment. But to many economists and other conventional wisdom freaks, he is a pie-in-the-sky type given to utopian, emotional over-simplifications. I find his simplifications to be the result of crap-removal, and his arguments to be essentially reasonable if humanity is to last much longer. His discussion of nuclear matters is particularly enlightening. I've noticed that his noisiest foes are the emotionalists these days; Mr. Lovins is the one with the documentation.
—J. Baldwin

Soft Energy Paths
(Toward a Durable Peace)
Amory B. Lovins
1979; 231 pp.
$3.95 postpaid from:
Harper & Row
Keystone Industrial Park
Scranton, PA 18512
or Whole Earth
Household Store

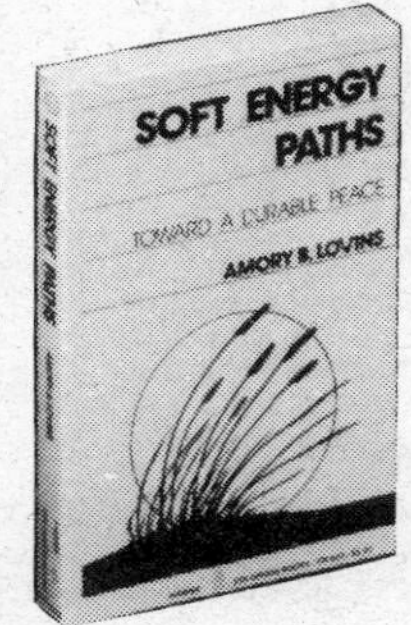

•

People do not want electricity or oil, nor such economic abstractions as "residential services," but rather comfortable rooms, light, vehicular motion, food, tables, and other real things. Such end-use needs can be classified by the physical nature of the task to be done. In the United States today, about 58 percent of all energy at the point of end use is required as heat, split roughly 23-35 between temperatures above and below the boiling point of water. (In Western Europe the low temperature heat alone is often a half of all end-use energy.) Another 38 percent of all U.S. end use energy provides mechanical motion: 31 percent in vehicles, 3 percent in pipelines, 4 percent in industrial electric motors. The rest, a mere 4 percent of delivered energy, represents *all* lighting, electronics, tele-communications, electrometallurgy, electrochemistry, arc welding, electric motors in home appliances and in railways, and similar end uses that now *require* electricity.

Energy for Survival

Just about the first analysis of Big Industrial Society energy use to be noticed by the conventional institutions, this comprehensive overview remains one of the best and most useful. Starting with basic thermodynamic principle, Wilson proceeds to explain what part energy plays in our society, and what the probable result will be if we continue our wastrel ways. He concludes with a look at probable and possible ways of producing and conserving power. This book was an eye-opener when it first appeared and it still is if you are not well versed in these matters. The documentation is formidable.
—J. Baldwin

Energy for Survival
(The Alternative
to Extinction)
Wilson Clark
1975; 652 pp.
$5.95 postpaid from:
Doubleday and Company
501 Franklin Avenue
Garden City, NY 11530
or Whole Earth
Household Store

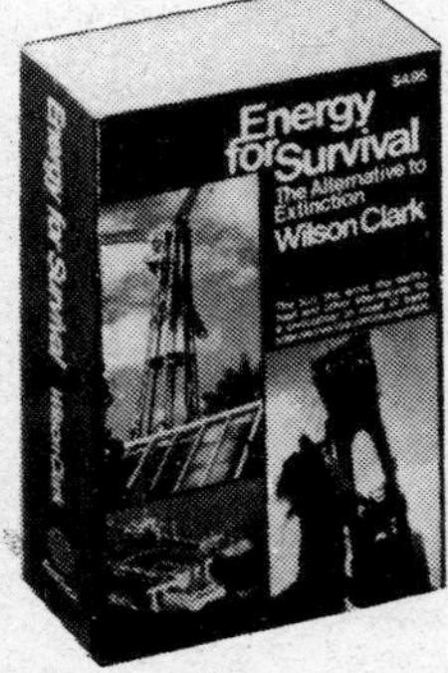

•

The reason heat pumps are not in wider use today is two-fold: First, the reputation of unreliability has haunted the electric heat pump since its premature introduction on the commercial market in the 1950s. Additionally, since the improved heat pumps have become available, virtually no attempts have been made nationally by electric utilities, manufacturers, or retail outlets to inform the public of their superiority — or even of their existence. This blackout of advertising is astounding in the light of the heat pump's remarkable efficiency and the fact that the initial cost of central home heat pump installations are rarely more than 10 to 20 percent more expensive than those of conventional central air-conditioning systems. Assuming the higher operating expense of home electric heating equipment, it is quite possible that heat pumps are cheaper in most areas than the combined cost of a central air-conditioning and heating system; and the operating costs of the heat pump will save an average of two thirds of the yearly electric power bill — while using one third the energy of the common electrical resistance heating system.

The Energy Controversy

Amory Lovins wasn't the first to advocate "soft energy paths" but he certainly was first to do it in a way that commanded the attention of the hard-path people and their friends. They have tried just about every ploy imaginable to refute his carefully documented analytic papers. This book presents the arguments of his more vocal critics and congruently presents Amory at his formidable best as he cuts his august detractors down to size. But the book can be more than that; many of us on the side of the good and the true also have doubts that we can't readily express in the present atmosphere of politicized side-choosing without risking reputation. Often such doubts turn out to be the very ones brought up by the critics here. Thus these debates can be instructive to all of us, and a study of them can affirm our soft energy stance by furnishing us with further ammunition for local argument. And once again, not only has Amory Lovins done our homework for us, he serves as a fine example of what can be done by one person in a situation that so often seems hopeless. The widely-hailed **Energy Future** *from Harvard Business School is essentially Amory's findings checked out and dully presented.*
—J. Baldwin

The Energy Controversy
(Soft Path Questions
and Answers)
Amory Lovins et al;
Hugh Nash, Editor
1979; 450 pp.
$6.95 postpaid from:
Friends Of The Earth
124 Spear Street
San Francisco, CA 94105
or Whole Earth
Household Store

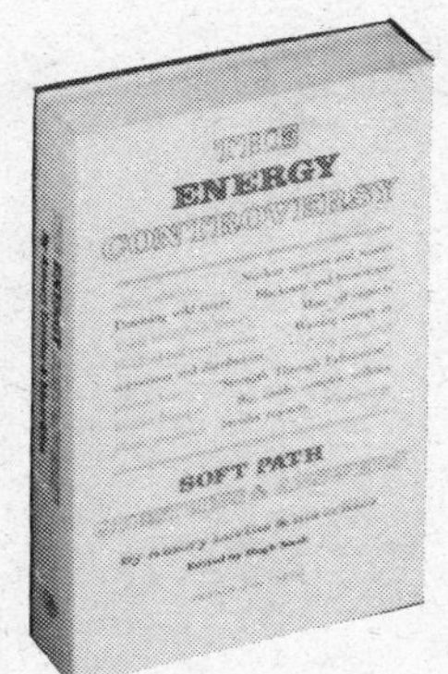

Energy Future

The prestigious Harvard Business School adds its establishment voice to the call for an energy conserving solar society. A perfectly straightforward cold-blooded economic case is made in support of this view, using the accepted form but not (surprise) the expected conventional wisdom information sources. The arrival of this book has lent a certain credence to the work of other authors such as Amory Lovins whose work has not necessarily been accepted in high places. It's a good job. It even reads pretty well. It is a big help to those attempting to convince the powers that be.
—J. Baldwin

Energy Future
(Report of the Energy
Project at the Harvard
Business School)
Robert Stobaugh and
Daniel Yergin, Editors
1979; 353 pp.
$2.95 postpaid from:
Random House
455 Hahn Road
Westminster, MD 21157
or Whole Earth
Household Store

•

Already by mid-1977 there was a national de facto moratorium on the purchase of nuclear generating equipment in the United States. As a consequence, the 1979 outlook for nuclear power in the United States is much different from what it seemed to be in the wake of the 1973-74 OPEC actions. Actually, since the early 1970s there have been successive downward revisions in projections of future installed capacity in all of the Western oil-importing countries.

•

At an energy conference in Los Angeles, the oil people told the heroic story of tapping Alaska's North Slope; the nuclear people talked about advanced nuclear technology; the coal people discussed synthetic fuels and slurry pipelines. The engineer from Los Angeles' Department of Water and Power then stood up to explain how it got the residents of Los Angeles to go along with an effort that substantially reduced consumption of electricity: "We advised citizens to do such things as shut their curtains at night." Here was a conference devoted to the great energy crisis, the moral equivalent of war, and here was a man who was saying that the solution is for people to do such bold things as close their curtains at night.

This is why, when an aide to one of the most powerful senators on energy issues was asked why the distinguished legislator has never given a speech on conservation, the aide replied, "It would either be filled with platitudes or so specific that everybody's nose would fall into his Rice Krispies."

Soft Energy Notes

Friends Of The Earth (FOE) has, among its many enterprises, a division called International Project For Soft Energy Paths. Among the names on the masthead is Amory Lovins, as you might expect from the name of this newsletter. **Soft Energy Notes** *started as a Xerox stack of interesting papers but has now graduated to being a real magazine. It's one of the most informative around, and because of the considerable travels of Mr. Lovins and the network connections of the other editors and contributors, the contents reflect the forefront of current thought, analysis, and even hardware upon occasion. Many's the time I've added luster to my reputation by quoting from this worthy paper. Your subscription helps finance FOE too.*
—J. Baldwin

Soft Energy Notes
Charles Drucker, Editor
$25/year (6 issues)
(make your check payable to
Friends of the Earth)
postpaid from:
International Project for
Soft Energy Paths
124 Spear Street
San Francisco CA 94105

One principal work makes conventional wisdom out-of-date. That is the normal looking, cheap, even frumpy house built by Eugene Leger in north-central Massachusetts. Based on a computer-generated, Lo-Cal design, Leger's house demonstrates that a low cost residence, with no striking design constraints, can operate in Massachusetts' severe climate with a winter heating bill of less than $10 per month ($38.50 for January through April, or 11.5 GJ over 2.144 Celsius degree days). This performance level sets a high standard for other designers to match in economics, comfort, design flexibility, and environmental side effects.

What is remarkable about Leger's house is that there is nothing solar about it: it has windows on the north, east, and west sides, and no huge expanse on the south side. It does not contain tons of concrete, piles of rock, or walls of water as "thermal mass." So how does Leger perform his low-energy trick? With a superb building "envelope": extra-thick insulation combined with painstaking efforts to reduce air leaks. Leger placed a continuous overlapping sheet of polyethylene on the exterior walls and ceiling. To avoid breaking this air and vapor seal with electrical outlets and plumbing, he installed a newly developed surface-mounted electrical system called the "Gould Electrostrip". This device is an important part of Leger's energy-tight design, demonstrating how innovations in one sector can spur advances in another.

Eugene Leger's house in East Pepperell, Massachusetts hides extraordinary energy efficiency behind a plain exterior. Its price, like its appearance, raises no eyebrows in the neighborhood.

THE RISING SUN
NEIGHBORHOOD NEWSLETTER

When they used to march soldiers to within a mile of bomb tests to watch and show soldiers could function under post bomb conditions, guys would hold their hands over their eyes and see every single bone.

Energy Primer

The original **Energy Primer** *arrived in 1975, filling the need for an "alternative energy" workbook that was a step above the generalized overviews for beginners, yet not requiring a Ph.D. to understand. It replaced and obsoleted a whole shelfload of scientifically loose energy books that didn't offer much useful to people actually involved in developing hardware.* **Energy Primer** *was remarkably successful, and rightly so. It was so well done that no other book offered it serious competition. On the other hand, energy matters are subject to rapid changes, and the* **Primer** *was getting a bit long in the tooth. Hence this 1978 edition. As with the first one, the new* **Primer** *has a very strong bibliography that contains even more specialized bibliographies.* —J. Baldwin

Energy Primer
(Revised and Updated)
Richard Merrill and
Tom Gage
1974, 1978; 256 pp.
$7.95 postpaid from:
Delta Books
c/o Montville
Warehousing Company
Change Bridge Road
Pine Brook, NJ 07058
or Whole Earth
Household Store

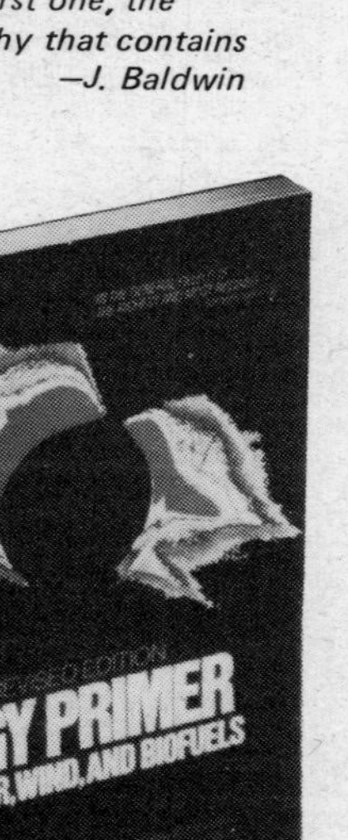

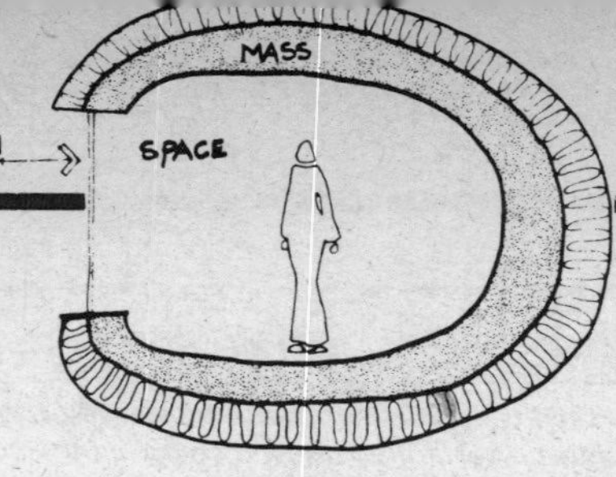

SUN-SPACE-MASS
(DIRECT)

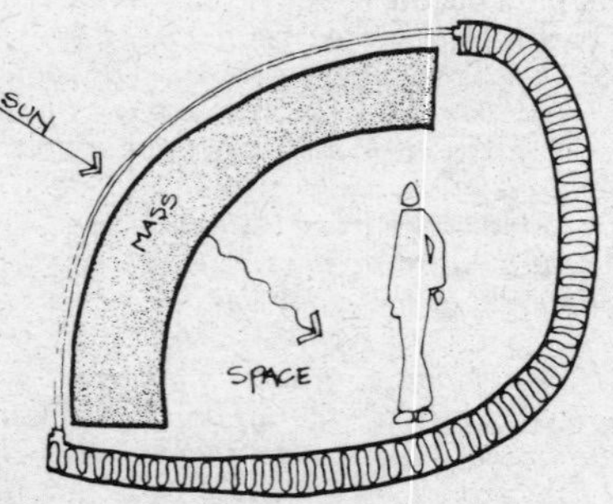

SUN-MASS-SPACE
(INTEGRATED)

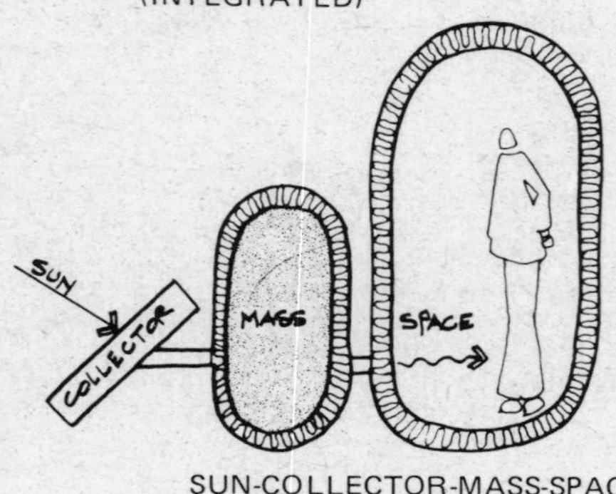

SUN-COLLECTOR-MASS-SPACE
(INDIRECT)

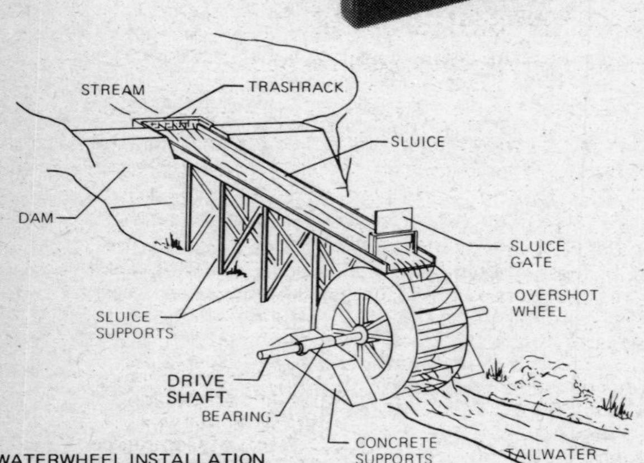

WATERWHEEL INSTALLATION

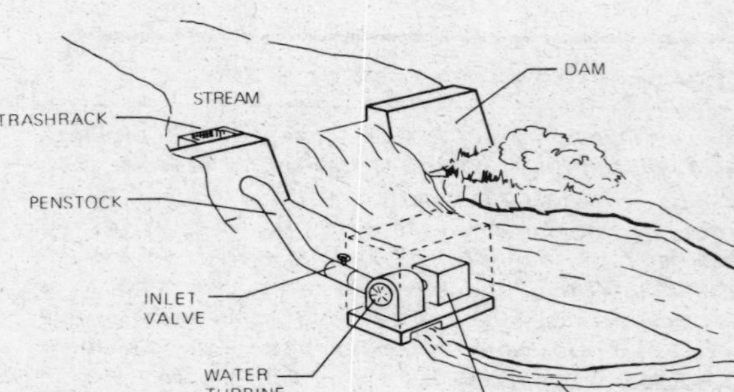

WATER TURBINE INSTALLATION

Small and efficient, FTM of St. Louis, Inc.'s electric tram; one of a fleet of six used in a thirty-three month community shuttle experiment in St. Louis' Central West End. It carried 100,000 passengers while revitalizing the neighborhood business district.

Alternative Sources of Energy

For a good overview of what's going on in all departments of "alternative" energy, **ASE** *remains a good magazine to have coming in six times a year. There has been a steady improvement in quality of reporting, especially in the articles concerned with experimental projects. They are often just plain exciting, and they've been on the case since 1973.* —J. Baldwin

Alternative Sources of Energy
Donald Marier, Editor
$15 /year (6 issues)
from:
Alternative Sources
of Energy
107 S. Central Ave.
Milaca, MN 56353

•

Although simple photovoltaic cells using selenium were first assembled nearly a century ago, it wasn't until the early 1950s that much practical use was made of the concept for power production. With prices at that time running in the neighborhood of $2000 per peak watt ("peak" watts are a cell's output in full sunlight), about the only uses made of the technology was for spacecraft and very remote terrestrial applications. Prices have fallen drastically since those early days of the industry, however, with $175 per watt as an average 1961 price and $8 to $15 per peak watt being a typical quantity price today. The current goal, set for the industry by the Department of Energy, is to have photovoltaic cells that will produce power for 70 cents per watt of generating capacity (in 1980 dollars) by 1986. If this goal is achieved, photoelectric power would be competitive with line power in most parts of the country. Even at $1 per watt, the economics of solar electricity will be attractive in many locales. Obviously this is a technology with a promising future.

Energybook 2

The first **Energybook** *didn't stand up too well against its competition, but this one does. You'll find many sophisticated discussions of things in here that have not been discussed elsewhere. They've tightened up the technical bits too. That's about all you can ask. Nice printing job makes it a pleasure to read.* —J. Baldwin

Energybook
(More Natural Sources &
Backyard Applications)
John Prenis, Editor
1977; 125 pp.
$5.25 postpaid from:
Running Press
38 South 19th Street
Philadelphia, PA 19103
or Whole Earth
Household Store

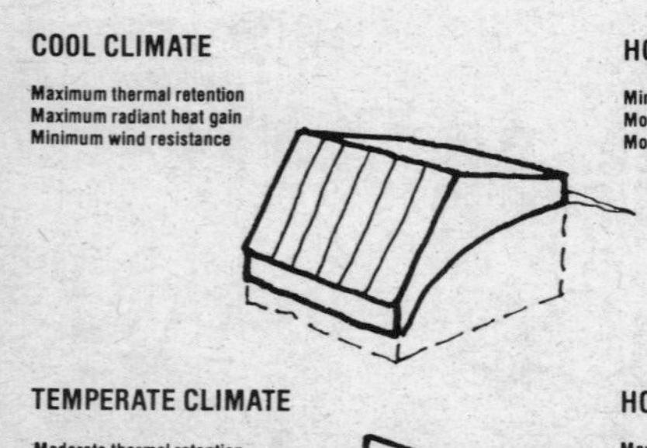

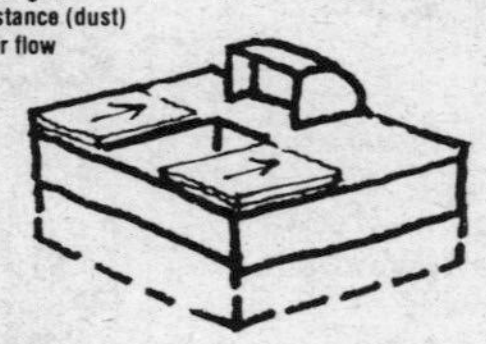

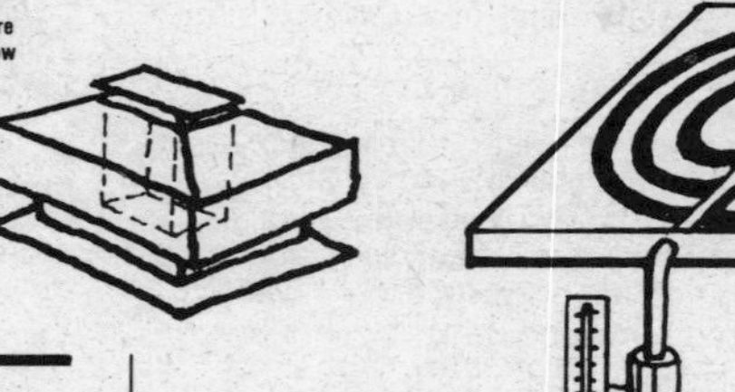

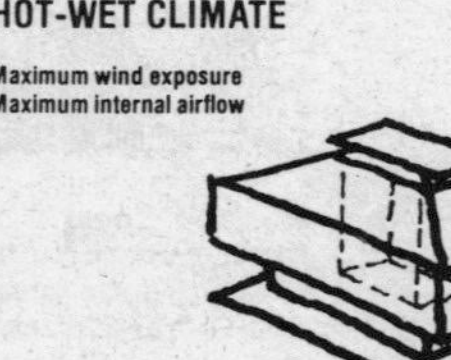

Energy Review

Competent abstract of papers pertaining to energy. No apparent political or group bias. Includes much-needed computerized access. —J. Baldwin

Energy Review
$55 /year (6 issues)
from:
International Academy
2074 Alameda
Padre Serra
Santa Barbara, CA 93103

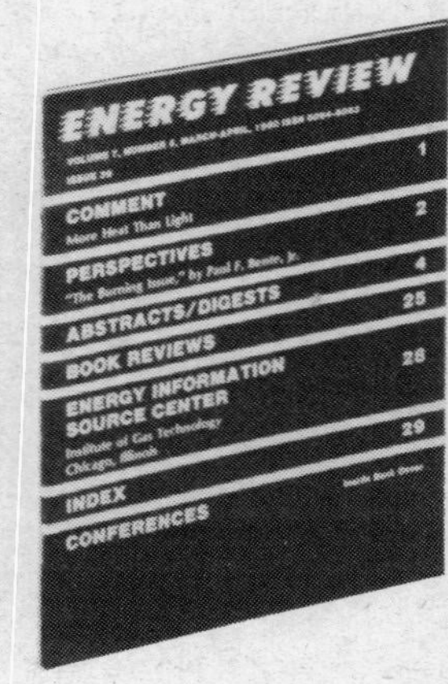

•

CONSERVATION, ENERGY — RESIDENTIAL

"How to Cut Fat Out of Your Home Energy Budget," Jan Adkins, Illus., **Smithsonian**, March 1974, p. 54-64.

•

The lawn is an energy sink. To grow grass is to engage in a vast struggle against nature. It is fine in damp England, but grass was simply not supposed to grow in many parts of the United States. Except for the cooling effect of grass as opposed to concrete, a lawn is a classic model of the negative energy system. It takes 162,000 BTUs worth of natural gas to produce the nitrogen in a 50-pound bag of fertilizer. A 10,000 square foot lawn requires as much as five bags a season. It then takes half a million or more BTUs worth of gasoline to mow that much lawn, and the only product of all this input energy — the grass clippings — is usually thrown away instead of being put to use. . . ARTICLE DEMONSTRATES IN FINE DETAIL AMERICANS EXCESSIVE USE OF LOW BUILDING AND PRODUCTION COSTS AT THE EXPENSE OF OPERATING EFFICIENCY.

EARS

Environmental Action Reprint Service has a nice catalog of books, films, plans, even bumper stickers, having to do with "alternative" energy and related subjects. Especially good selection of anti-nuclear power literature. There's a fresh one every nine months. —J. Baldwin

EARS Catalog
free from:
EARS
Box 545
La Veta, CO 81055

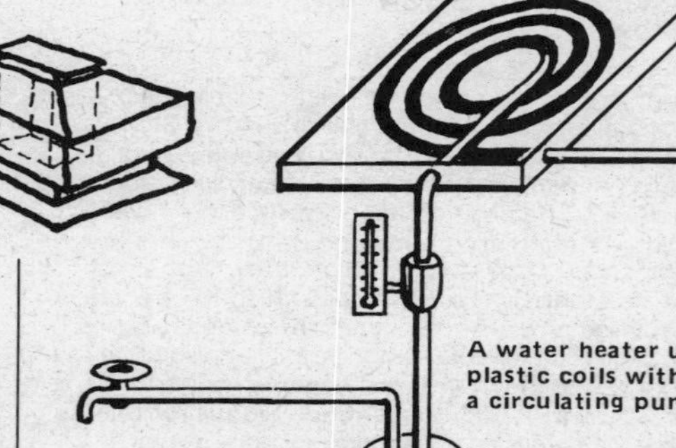

A water heater using plastic coils without a circulating pump.

Energy and Equity

One hell of a book. Half the reason I like it is format. Here are author and publisher working to extend developing ideas to critics. The address of the author is included, invitation to criticize is extended, and opportunity for corrections is allowed by the promise of future editions. The book is 84 pages — pamphlet length — concisely phrased, with a spine so you can read its title on the bookshelf. Other half the reason I like it: Whenever a society runs its vehicles faster than 15 miles an hour, the distribution of power gets loopy; and the culture goes BANANAS. (More on Illich, p. 40.)

—Jim Harding

Energy and Equity
Ivan Illich
1974; 84 pp.
OUT OF PRINT
Harper & Row
Get this book back in print!

•

The typical American male devotes more than 1,600 hours a year to his car. He sits in it while it goes and while it stands idling. He parks it and searches for it. And this figure does not take into account the time consumed by other activities dictated by transport: time spent in hospitals, traffic courts and garages; time spent watching automobile commercials or attending consumer education meetings to improve the quality of the next buy. The model American puts in 1,600 hours to get 7,500 miles: less than five miles per hour. In countries deprived of a transportation industry, people manage to do the same, walking wherever they want to go, and they allocate only three to eight per cent of their society's time budget to traffic instead of 28 per cent. What distinguishes the traffic in rich countries from the traffic in poor countries is not more mileage per hour of life-time for the majority, but more hours of compulsory consumption of high doses of energy, packaged and unequally distributed by the transportation industry.

Energy, Jobs and the Economy

This deadly book brilliantly illuminates (by natural means, of course) the realities underlying the conventional wisdom excuse that a clean healthy environment means loss of jobs. This is the stuff of the Next American Revolution, I'll bet, and ought to be required reading for just about anyone older than 12. The rapier of Hazel Henderson is involved here too; she's one of the directors of this outfit.

—J. Baldwin

[Suggested by James Edison Notestein]

Energy, Jobs and the Economy
Richard Grossman and Gail Daneker
1977, 1979; 124 pp.
$3.45 individual
$15 institutional
from:
Environmentalists for Full Employment
1536 16th St. N.W.
First Floor
Washington, D.C. 20036
or Whole Earth Household Store

•

The report stressed that employment associated with energy conservation techniques is local, low- to moderately-skilled, and concentrated in or near urbanized areas which are experiencing the most acute unemployment problems. In contrast, centralized, expensive energy production complexes usually have to bring in highly-skilled labor from outside the construction area. (These transients create a large amount of disruption: temporary housing and many services must be supplied to meet the problems temporary workers create. In many of the energy "boom towns" of the western United States, crime, alcoholism, family break-ups are well above average. Serving the needs of transient labor ends up being a drain on the local economies the transients were supposed to be stimulating.)

County Energy Plan Guidebook

While it is easy to see the merit in individual energy conservation efforts, it is less obvious what to do at larger scale — city and county. This guide is intended to help county officials and citizens organize a study of energy conservation and the county's potential for renewable energy resources. It is hoped that such studies will enable a county to shift much of its energy needs to renewable forms by the turn of the century. The authors of this guide intend that all of the nation's 3000 counties will complete such work, thereby encouraging decentralized energy planning with democratic control. This guidebook looks pretty good to me; it should be a big help in achieving those goals.

—J. Baldwin

County Energy Plan Guidebook
Alan Okagaki and Jim Benson
1979; 200 pp.

$7.50 postpaid from:
Institute for Ecological Policies
9208 Christopher Street
Fairfax, VA 22031
or Whole Earth Household Store

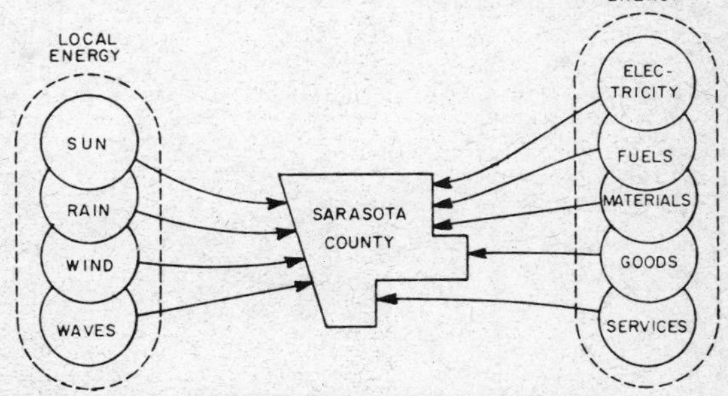

↑ **Diagram showing types of energy available in Sarasota County**

Energy Self-Sufficiency in Northampton, Massachusetts

The same sort of approach as in the **County Energy Plan Guidebook** *is taken at city level in this model study of an actual city. Though there are necessarily large differences between cities, this study provides a good example of how such an enterprise is carried out. Many cities are undertaking such studies. It will be interesting to see if such a plan can actually be implemented.* *—J. Baldwin*
(For more local energy models, see **Shining Examples***, p. 378.)*

Energy Self-Sufficiency in Northampton, Massachusetts
Hampshire College
No. DOE/PE/4706
1979; 222 pp.

$16 postpaid from:
National Technical Information Service
U.S. Dept. of Commerce
5285 Port Royal Road
Springfield, VA 22161

Summary of Energy End Use
Northampton, Massachusetts — 1977

	BTU x 10^{11}	MW	% of Total
Low Temperature Heat	24.0	80.2	71.6
Cooking, Laundry and Miscellaneous Heating	1.2	4.0	3.5
Industrial Process Heat	.49	1.6	1.4
Transportation	2.4	8.0	7.2
Lighting, Appliances, Machinery and Air Conditioning	5.4	18.1	16.1
TOTAL	33.5	111.9	99.8%

Energy and Form

This is not a casual environmentalist's workbook. Problems such as "how are we going to house our doubled population due in 35 years?" are dealt with. Mr. Knowles performs a remarkable analysis of the solar energy flows in Pueblos as a demonstration of what might be expected if such factors were considered in the design of buildings. He suggests that if the energy flows of an entire area were known, then it would be possible to design structures and urban layouts that would take advantage of them. He presents a detailed study of California's Owens Valley as an example. This amounts to a wider view of architecture and planning than has usually been the case. It seems to me that it is also a necessary view. Mr. Knowles is one of the forces pushing architecture into new territory.

—J. Baldwin

Energy and Form
(An Ecological Approach to Urban Growth)
Ralph L. Knowles
1978; 198 pp.
$8.95 postpaid from:
The MIT Press
28 Carleton Street
Cambridge, MA 02142
or Whole Earth Household Store

•

Both Old and New Bonito operate efficiently as energy systems that mitigate seasonal variation in insolation. Each has a higher efficiency curve in winter than summer. The truly remarkable fact about New Bonito is the precision of the curves. From sunrise to sunset during the winter solstice, the efficiency profile is absolutely flat, suggesting that the greatest advantage possible is being taken by the system to receive and store energy during the daylight hours to carry through the cold winter night. During the summer solstice, not only is the efficiency profile lower, as it should be to mitigate seasonal variation but the curve is higher in the morning when ambient air temperatures are high. New Bonito mitigates daily as well as seasonal variations in insolation.

Pueblo Bonito in Chaco Canyon, New Mexico, as it was unearthed by N.M. Judd during seven National Geographic Society expeditions, 1921 - 1927. ↓

Canadian Renewable Energy News

Canada has a newspaper covering the energy front. It seems to be getting better and better with each issue.

—J. Baldwin

[Suggested by John Meissner]

Canadian Renewable Energy News
$10 /year (12 issues)
from:
C.R.E.N.
P.O. Box 4869
Station E
Ottawa, Ontario
Canada K1S 5B4

THE RISING SUN
NEIGHBORHOOD NEWSLETTER

Freeman Dyson, a nuclear scientist, was against the above ground nuclear test ban treaty until he was assigned to do a statistical analysis of all the bomb tests since it was invented. Every test was done to answer some question, and every test generated at least two more really valid important questions. So the number of tests had been doubling every year since the first one and there was no intrascience, search-for-knowledge reason for it to ever stop doubling. So Dyson thought about that and changed to pro treaty.

—From his autobiography
Disturbing the Universe

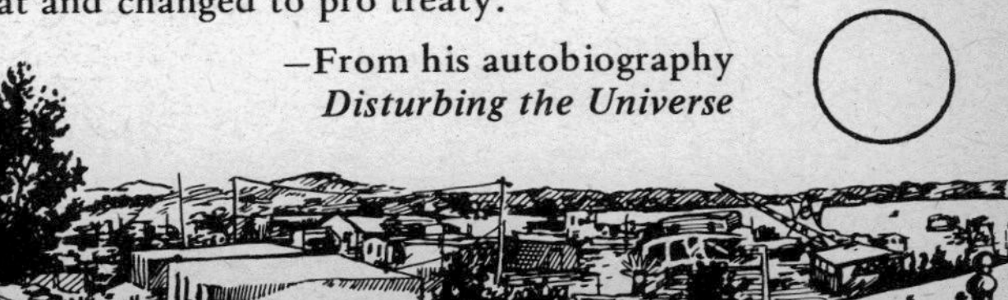

Radical Technology

Ah yes. Wind machines, poorly detailed solar collectors, goats, pyramids, and typical bourgeois schemes masquerading as environmentally OK because they are wearing the less-embarrassing pre-washed Levis which make them look like they've been working. You can find lots of books that look like this one in any "organic bookshop." But this book is different. It has sharp criticism of society and just about everything else you might think of (done in that sly British manner) and this is coupled with the best presentation of "Visions" of what may be done that I've seen. The emphasis is on changing social order by taking responsibility for your actions into your own hands. The publisher's blurb calls it "the encyclopedia of a multifaceted quest." The only book in this part of the culture that I have personally found exciting and excited. It's by the **Undercurrents** *people.* —J. Baldwin

Radical Technology
Godfrey Boyle and
Peter Harper, Editors
1976; 304 pp.

$5.95 postpaid from:
Pantheon Books
Random House
455 Hahn Road
Westminster, MD 21157

(Possibly out of print)

Where rows of houses share back-yards, the land can be shared for better use and co-operative food production. The idea suggested here is to divide the area into that which remains private and that which is worked collectively. Other pooled yards could have different functions — for kids, light industry, etc.

With such intensive cultivation, more food can be grown per acre in the towns than on farms.

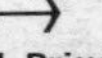

1 Private space
2 Espalier fruit trees
3 Solar water heaters
4 Solar clothes drier
5 Vertical growing on nets
6 Shed
7 Chicken house
8 Compost heap
9 Pit greenhouse
10 Beehive
11 Cold frames
12 Glass cloches

Some Utopian Characteristics of Soft Technology

by Robin Clarke

	"HARD" technology society	"SOFT" technology society
1	ecologically unsound	ecologically sound
2	large energy input	small energy input
3	high pollution rate	low or no pollution rate
4	non-reversible use of materials and energy sources	reversible materials and energy sources only
5	functional for limited time only	functional for all time
6	mass production	craft industry
7	high specialization	low specialization
8	nuclear family	communal units
9	city emphasis	village emphasis
10	alienation from nature	integration with nature
11	consensus politics	democratic politics
12	technical boundaries	technical boundaries set by nature
13	world-wide trade	local bartering
14	destructive of local culture	compatible with local culture
15	technology liable to misuse	safeguards against misuse
16	highly destructive to other species	dependent on well-being of other species
17	innovation regulated by profit and war	innovation regulated by need
18	growth-oriented economy	steady-state economy
19	capital intensive	labour intensive
20	alienates young and old	integrates young and old
21	centralist	decentralist
22	general efficiency increases with size	general efficiency increases with smallness
23	operating modes too complicated for general comprehension	operating modes understandable by all
24	technological accidents frequent and serious	technological accidents few and unimportant
25	singular solutions to technical and social problems	diverse solutions to technical and social problems
26	agricultural emphasis on mono-culture	agricultural emphasis on diversity
27	quantity criteria highly valued	quality criteria highly valued
28	food production specialized industry	food production shared by all
29	work undertaken primarily for income	work underaken primarily for satisfaction
30	small units totally dependent on others	small units self-sufficient
31	science and technology alienated from culture	science and technology integrated with culture
32	science and technology performed by specialist elites	science and technology performed by all
33	strong work/leisure distinction	weak or non-existent work/leisure distinction
34	high unemployment	(concept not valid)
35	technical goals valid for only a small proportion of the globe for a finite time	technical goals valid 'for all men for all time'

Undercurrents

Any anarchist technology bi-monthly that lasts 12 years, keeping the heat on everybody's assumptions the while, has got something more lively than idealism in its plucky heart. —SB

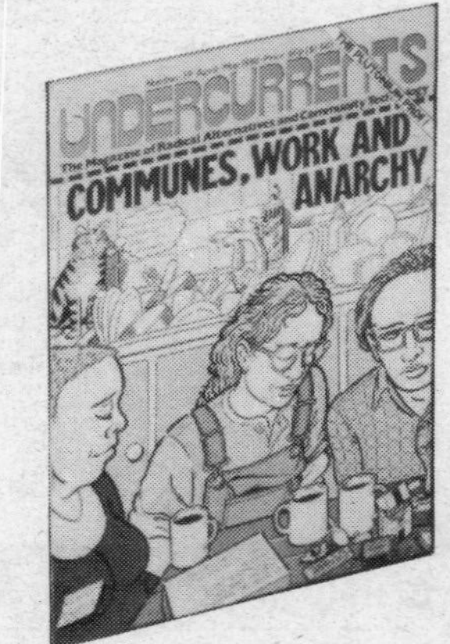

Undercurrents
(The Magazine of
Radical Alternatives and
Community Technology)

$11/year (6 issues)
postpaid from:
Undercurrents Ltd.
27 Clerkenwell Close
London EC1R 0AT
England

•

Seven Illusions of Idealism (as seen by the "small is beautiful" true believer), by Jim Sullivan.

- Ideological purity is more important than effective action.
- No matter if the machinery collapses, as long as the intentions are good.
- Any sophistication is suspect.
- Making money is beyond the pale.
- Politics should be left to the politicians.
- Inspiration can take the place of perspiration.
- A vision of the perfect future is more important than a better plan for next year.

•

Good Work, E.F. Schumacher, Jonathan Cape. £4.95.

'There's something wrong in having a census which treats people as if they were units, whereas they're not. Each is a universe'. The speaker is E.F. Schumacher, who, as is plain from these lectures (delivered to American audiences shortly before his death), was developing new thoughts up to the very end of his life. There's more original thinking here than all 635 MPs together will ever produce. The main theme is work.

Building for Self-Sufficiency

Robin Clarke has been one of England's more noticeable "self-sufficiency" advocates. In 1973, he and friends commenced to build a self-sufficient commune complete with most of the ecologically acceptable attributes that one could hope for. As a commune, the attempt failed. As a learning bit, it seems to have been a success. He Tells All here in a droll British Wit manner that is at times painfully frank. Those of us who've tried such an experiment will see our own failures and triumphs again. Those who haven't taken the plunge will find plenty to think about. For anyone, a personal account such as this one makes a lot more interesting reading than the usual "observations" of academic visitors to the scene.
—J. Baldwin

Building for Self-Sufficiency
(Tools, Materials, Building, Heat, Insulation, Solar Energy, Wind Power, Water & Plumbing, Waste & Compost, Methane, Transport, Food)
Robin Clarke
1976; 296 pp.

$5.95 postpaid from:
Universe Books
381 Park Ave. South
New York, NY 10016
or Whole Earth
Household Store

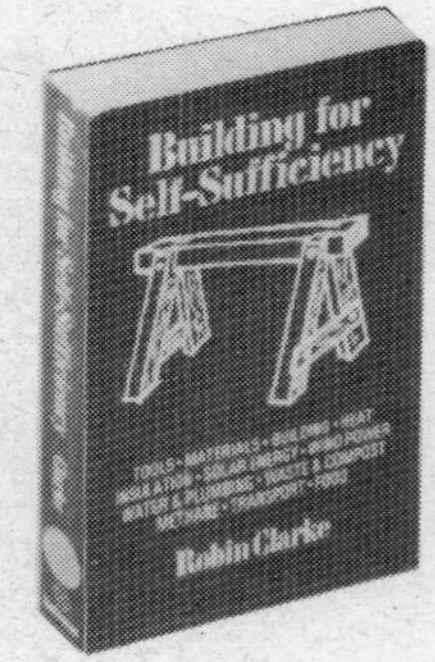

•

Never join a community because you want to live in a community, or think you do. Do so only if you discover a group of people, or even one or two, with whom you positively think a shared life would be a turn for the better. I've met a good few such people — and some of them were at Eithin. Some of them visited Eithin but left before they decided to join. Those people are the only reason for living in a community. The economic ones, or whatever other justifications you care to discover for yourself, are secondary. They are the spin-offs, the trade-ins which pay you their interest for sharing your life.

But never make the mistake of thinking them to be the reason. All such communities are bound to fail.

And, second, how do you know whether you really want to live in a community with someone? I'm quite sure there's no easy answer — in the positive sense. But there is one negative test, in which I'd put quite a lot of faith. Take your prospective communard, and get stoned, or drunk, or whatever your thing is, with him for a whole evening. If the evening's a success, it just might work. If it isn't, it certainly won't.

Autonomous Technology

It's a true pleasure to see the less pleasant aspects of technology illuminated in an unemotional erudite manner! The subject is uncontrolled technology — whether in fact it can be controlled once things get developed beyond a certain point. Mr. Winner offers a scholarly, enthusiastically documented analysis of the relationship of society and technology, with particular emphasis on the forces that tend to put society in the service of technology rather than the other way around. I found this book to be a useful thought-provoker. Tangles of complex interactions are nicely unsnarled, allowing you the opportunity of understanding and hopefully doing something about our most serious problem. Mr. Winner deserves some sort of Gold Palm for bringing us this in a form that is not only readable but fascinating. —J. Baldwin

Autonomous Technology
(Technics-out-of-Control as a Theme in Political Thought)
Langdon Winner
1977; 386 pp.

$6.95 postpaid from:
The M.I.T. Press
28 Carleton Street
Cambridge MA 02142
or Whole Earth
Household Store

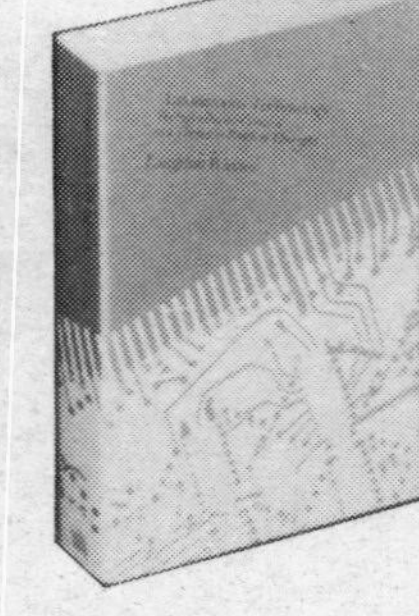

•

In the American model of pluralism founded by Madison and perfected in our time by David Truman, Robert Dahl, and others, the life of the polity rests in the many interest groups that serve as guardians of the welfare of their constituencies. The theory is based on the idea that individuals perceive their own interests, organize around concerns that affect their well-being, voice their desires through these organizations, and battle other similarly organized interests for scarce resources. Certain aspects of theories of technological change articulated in recent years fly directly in the face of this mode. Social scientists have become aware of the fact that many of the changes that affect people are truly "unanticipated" or "unforeseen." Very often these technology-associated alterations take place with remarkable speed and are, in some cases, "irreversible." What this means is that possible interest groups which could form around an issue concerning the effects of technological change will in many cases simply come too late. The effects will have already taken hold. The business of voicing one's interest at this point can have little significance other than as a plea for redistribution of benefits or for reparations on the injuries suffered. A new class of "losers" is born into the political system.

New Alchemy Institute

Many an outfit has been founded to do research aimed at environmentally benign ways of food raising, providing shelter, and dealing with energy needs. Few have come up with much that works and keeps working in a convincing way, and none but the New Alchemists, as far as I know, have managed to combine food production, energy making, and shelter into an integrated "ecosystem." It has taken more than ten years of experimenting, hard work, and fundraising (perhaps the toughest part) to accomplish this, and the work is only now beginning to yield results that permit some cautious talk of its potential.

Much of the research of the past ten years has come together in unique buildings named Arks. There are two — one on Cape Cod and the other much further north on Prince Edward Island, Canada, running mostly solar even in that tough climate, and probably able to run 100% solar with a bit of tuning. Arks raise fish and vegetables, can process sewage, and require no fossil fuel for operation. They could be used as neighborhood food raising facilities, as hospitals, old folks' homes, or schools. Big ones could BE neighborhoods . . . The Arks are discussed in detail in John and Nancy Jack Todd's **Tomorrow Is Our Permanent Address,** *a book that also gives a very personal account of the reasoning underlying all the New Alchemist work.*

The Book of the New Alchemists *gives a rather more detailed overall view of work that has been going on at the institute for many years — the parts that came together to make up the Ark as well as the garden experiments and other projects. The annual* **Journal of the New Alchemists** *presents what has been learned during the past year. The most recent, #6, features articles on: The Alkies' increasing emphasis on tree crops; innovative windmill designs; a definitive water pumping windmill discussion; solar aquaculture; news from the Alchemist division in Costa Rica; a variety of articles on philosophies germane to New Alchemy work; and a free-swinging critique of three years of Ark experience. Late news is carried by the* **New Alchemy Newsletter,** *a quarterly that comes with your membership (as does the Journal). A number of how-to books based on New Alchemy research is planned for the near future. You can visit New Alchemy too, on Saturdays May through September. Apprenticeships are available and volunteers are usually welcome. There are also workshops, classes, tours, and people who will give lectures.*

I think highly enough of the work of the New Alchemists that I accepted (flattered) an invitation to join the fray. It's not a commune. We live in the surrounding community and are active in civic affairs. There is a tendency to live near the farm, and I suspect a wonderful neighborhood may be a-building. Though I haven't been there even a year yet, I think it's clear that one of the reasons that so much has been accomplished is that this group works together unusually well. I think that a common goal has helped smooth over the bumps a bit, and a commendable scientific rigor has given the results a credibility not often seen outside of universities. We hope to be an inspiration to others. There's plenty left to do.

—J. Baldwin

New Alchemy Institute
Memberships:
$25 /year
(Associate)
$100 /year
(Sustaining)
$1000 /year
(Patron)
(Membership includes the Journal, the newsletter, other mailings and certain privileges)

The Journal of the New Alchemists
(Number 6)
Nancy Jack Todd, Editor
1980; 184 pp.
$9.95 postpaid
(Inquire for prices of available back issues)

New Alchemy Newsletter
$1 each

Information brochure

all from:
The New Alchemy Institute
237 Hatchville Road
East Falmouth, MA 02536

Tomorrow Is Our Permanent Address
John Todd and Nancy Jack Todd
1980; 156 pp.
$4.95 postpaid from:
Harper & Row
Keystone Industrial Park
Scranton, PA 18512
or Whole Earth Household Store

The Book of the New Alchemists
Nancy Jack Todd, Editor
1977; 174 pp.
$6.95 postpaid from:
E.P. Dutton & Co.
Two Park Avenue
New York, NY 10016
or Whole Earth Household Store

Inside the Cape Cod ark.

Woven basket-like cage allows poultry to eat the growing tips of the comfrey leaves.

Basket is woven of basket willow (Salix purpurea). Comfrey (Symphytum officinale) is a high-protein perennial herb, eagerly eaten by chickens and geese.

•

Most agricultural environments are intrinsically unstable because the crops are planted, removed, and altered from season to season. This instability can lead to pest outbreaks because biological regulatory mechanisms do not have time to become well established. In the Arks we have increased the ecological diversity and biological stability through the creation of aquatic and terrestrial "islands" throughout the interiors. These "islands" include stable perennial plants such as herbs, flowers, and grasses, like bamboo, that are not cropped. These provide stable habitats for pollinators, predators, and the parasites of pest organisms. Among the predators are wasps, flies, predatory mites, spiders, frogs, and lizards. The aquatic "islands" have a special function in that they offer a habitat for damsel flies that prey on whiteflies *(Trialeurodes vaporium)* and other pests. The entire network of undisturbed islands is located in growing areas that are less than optimal for crop plants.

—Tomorrow Is Our Permanent Address

•

Although feeding a dog from a can or watering a plant is hardly tending a complex ecosystem, there are people who maintain vegetable gardens or tropical fish aquaria, and in so doing are, in a simplified form, caring for ecosystems. The step from a garden or aquarium to a bioshelter is one of degree, not kind. In 1978 over half of the householders in North America had some kind of food garden. There are many million tropical-fish hobbyists. Both these facts suggest that people are willing to work with ecologies based on the same principles as exist with the Ark. These people represent a broad cross section of society.

—Tomorrow Is Our Permanent Address

Looking through the southern facade into the interior of the Cape Cod Ark.

← Windbreak succession/diversification. As early suntolerant pioneer trees grow, resulting shade and wind protection provides microclimates for less hardy plants.

↑ Coppiced willow as living fence, with live posts woven with trimmed shoots.

•

Insulation of Building with Planted Windbreaks

Windbreaks of living plants have been well documented for their beneficial effect of reducing heat loss from buildings. The effect is due to reduced infiltration through cracks, reduced exterior convection loss, and in some cases reduced radiant heat loss. The net result is that a house with good wind protection on three sides (north/west/east) can reduce fuel use up to 30% in comparison to a similar house exposed to full wind. Windbreaks perform as insulation, just as other more familiar methods such as double glazing, materials in wall cavities and weatherstripping do. Like these other methods, establishing a windbreak has a capital investment cost, a maintenance cost, an expected working lifetime and a payback period that can be evaluated economically.

Unlike these other methods, windbreaks are biological and appreciate in value rather than depreciate. They improve their performance automatically, using available sunlight rather than an initial input of fuel energy of manufacture. It is thus a unique insulation technique which requires a relatively small investment in order ultimately to obtain large benefits.

The benefits of growing external insulation will be particularly useful to older homes which often have high infiltration rates and walls too thin for adequate amounts of wall insulation: both of these difficulties are amenable to the effects of a good windbreak. The strategy of growing insulation is an example of applying biological solutions to what is normally conceived as a technological problem. The concept involved is that biological systems (in this case, plants) maintain and perpetuate themselves using solar energy, while technological systems usually require energy of manufacture, maintenance, repair and disposal in the form of fossil fuels under the attention of people. In addition, while protecting from wind the plants can:

—produce food,
—preserve soil,
—control and purify water,
—filter air of dust, smoke, odors, and
—provide comfortable and pleasant living conditions.

Each of these services has values that become apparent when a community must construct substitutes.

—Journal of the New Alchemists, #6

THE RISING SUN
NEIGHBORHOOD NEWSLETTER

Maybe it's a good flag for right now because the stars and stripes and the general feel are based on quilt work and quilt work is based on scarcity — not having much material but making the most of what you've got. The flag actually looks like it was made from an odd bunch of scraps — quilt together a life that'll make it past 2000.

Harrowsmith

Canada's answer to **Mother Earth News** *has matured into the best magazine of its type around. Real people doing real things, sometimes successfully and sometimes not, tell what they know without propaganda or speculative hype. The whole magazine is less gentleman farmer oriented than its U.S.A. counterparts such as* **Country Journal**, *feels friendly, and promotes competence in homesteading matters.* —*Peter Warshall*

Harrowsmith
James I. Lawrence,
Editor
$12/year (8 issues)
from:
Camden House
Publishing
Camden East
Queen Victoria Road
Ontario K0K 1J0
Canada

Although the furnace is turning out huge amounts of heat, above its smokestack there is only the shimmering distortion of heat waves similar to the mirage visible above a blacktop road on a hot summer's day. There is no smoke, just clean, intense heat . . . →

Now being produced by Hampton Technologies Corporation of Charlottetown, Prince Edward Island, the Jetstream design is based on a concept of Professor Richard C. Hill of the University of Maine. It represents a complete rejection of the current movement toward airtight wood-burning devices and draws heavily on a fact that oldtime wood burners have known for years: a fast, hot fire burns cleanly and prevents creosote build-up in chimneys. . .

Hill's design works to trap the heat produced by the furnace — at full tilt it blasts out energy at the rate of 120,000 Btu's per hour — and stores it in a separate, unpressurized water tank . . .

Combustion in the Jetstream is virtually complete, with 0.2 per cent of the wood, by weight, left behind as white ash. Some heat does escape up the chimney, however, and the overall efficiency of the furnace computed by applying the standard stack-loss method, has been estimated to be between 75 and 80 per cent. . . .

Fan motor for combustion air and exhaust draft
A 3' by 12" diameter vertical loading fuel chamber for large load capacity. Water jacketed to inhibit burning outside of combustion chamber
A 50-gallon water jacket, vented to atmosphere
Temperature and pressure safety valve
Hot water out to hea storage medium (hot water, rock storage)
Fire tube heat exchangers
Cold water in
Wood burns in refractory combustion chamber where high temperatures (1200-2000 degrees F) and turbulent, forced draft air produce optimum combustion characteristics
High temperature tunnel provides ignition of any unburned residues
High temperature refractory and vermicu concrete base for maximum strength, hea retention and insulating characteristics

Alone, the furnace is now selling for $2,000. With the added costs of the storage tank set at about $1.00 per gallon of water capacity and the installation charge, the price tag for a ready-to-burn Jetstream system would fall between $3,000 and $4,000. Using recycled storage tanks and doing the installation oneself would reduce the price substantially. (Some Jetstream users have improvised their own storage systems by linking in a series three or more discarded 250-gallon oil tanks.)

The Harrowsmith Sourcebook

Billed as "A Consumer Guide to the Conserver Society" this collection has many items familiar to readers of the **Next Whole Earth Catalog** *but also a host of Canadian specialties and many more specific products than we list — woodstoves and such. A good bit of the information given is by persons actually using or otherwise familiar with what's being talked about, which can be a big help in making up your own mind. (But some items, solar collectors and wind machines, for instance, are presented mostly with uncritical manufacturer's briefs.) Many lively articles comment upon such subjects as buying solar equipment, wood stoves, reforestation and a cow. The whole book is done up with the friendly good spirit one would expect of the editors of* **Harrowsmith** *magazine. I recommend it highly. One flaw: no index.*
—*J. Baldwin*

The Harrowsmith Sourcebook
(Canada's National Compendium of Alternative Tools, Goods, & Services)
James Lawrence,
Editor
1979; 320 pp.
$7.95 postpaid from:
Camden House
Publishing Company
Queen Victoria Road
Camden East
Ontario K0K 1J0
Canada

or Whole Earth
Household Store

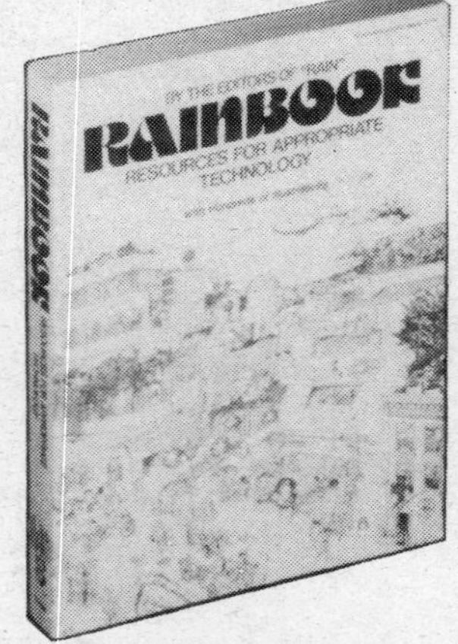

•

Replacement Mica

When I bought my pretty little cast-iron parlour stove, it was missing the mica 'windows' that fold open at the front, allowing either the wood or coal to be inserted; closed, the flickers of flame could be seen. But where to find mica sheets in this day and age?

Fortunately I discovered Y. Franks' store in Vancouver, where all sorts of spare parts for cast-iron stoves are available — including 4" by 6" mica sheets for $3 each.

Now the stove not only looks pretty but is functional, living up to the name emblazoned on the front — "Good Cheer"!

Y. Franks Limited
1490 Kingsway
Vancouver, B.C.
Phone (604) 879-9407

—Paula Gustafson,
Yarrow, British Columbia

Page from the Harrowsmith Sourcebook ↓

Description: Box stove with air circulator on inside of door. Front-end combustion.
Airtight
Made in Denmark
$495
Smaller model: Morso 2B $365

FINDLAY COMFORT SYSTEMS
60 Otonabee Drive
Kitchener, Ont. N2C 1L6
(519) 893-6531
(Manufacturer)

MODEL: Findlay Conestogo
Material: Steel, cast-iron doors, firebrick lined
Description: Stepstove design. Horizontal baffle. Twin draft control.
Airtight
Made in Canada
For price: contact local Findlay dealer.

FRECO LIMITED
1408, 13th Avenue Ouest
Charny, Cté Levis, P.Q
G6W 3Z2
(418) 832-4605
(Manufacturer)

MODEL: Turtle
Material: Steel
Description: Cylindrical stove with one cooking lid. For cottages, garages, camping.
Not airtight
Made in Canada
$125

RAINBOOK

The editors of **RAIN** *bring you a finely sifted collection of what has proven to be good and useful in the baffling tangle of what's available. The sifting is done (as usual) by persons who are actually working with the subject of the review, giving a quiet honesty that permeates the entire* **RAINBOOK.** *There's also a refreshing emphasis on a sense of community development rather than the lone-homesteader-against-the-world; "let's work together" instead of "screw you." Makes you feel good just to open* **RAINBOOK** *anywhere and snoop around.*

In the time **RAINBOOK** *has been with us, I have used it a lot. Most of the contents are still usable and at least informative. My copy, my third (the first two grew legs), is dog-eared beyond belief, a sure sign of a truly useful and successful book.* —*J. Baldwin*

RAINBOOK
(Resources for Appropriate Technology)
Editors of Rain
1977; 256 pp.
$7.95 postpaid from:
Schocken Books
200 Madison Avenue
New York, NY 10016
or Whole Earth
Household Store

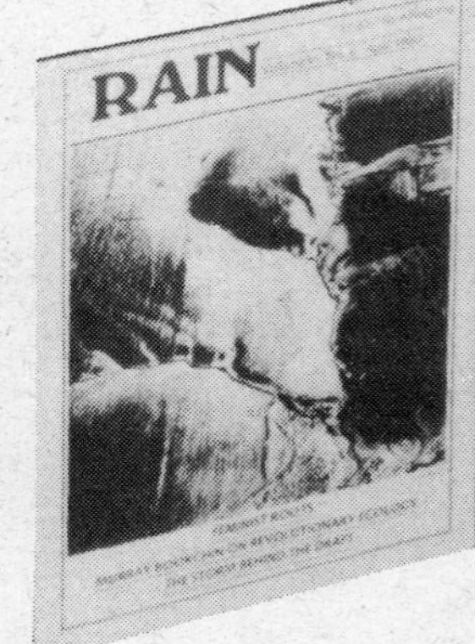

•

The best technologies are often the invisible ones — where people have figured out how to avoid problems rather than to solve them. Often all that is required is a perceptual change such as seeing grasshoppers as an airborne mobile protein harvesting and conversion unit — a food source — rather than a destructive pest. Or living near where we work rather than building better transportation technologies. Or eating lower on the food chain so you don't have to pay for or grow food for the conversion losses of meat animals. Or planting trees rather than air conditioners.

The second-best technologies are also invisible. They're based on people's skills and relationships rather than machines — the skilled calligrapher drawing a line or carpenter cutting a line rather than needing a jig or machine; good neighbors rather than locks on doors; caring for the ill or elderly at home rather than in a Home; hiking rather than mini-biking; an auto mechanic or piano tuner's ear rather than a tuning machine.

RAIN

One of the few magazines I actually look forward to receiving is **RAIN.** *The several crewmembers seem to come and go but the quality of the reporting remains lively, accurate, and current. (I'll admit that I often can't wait to see what* **RAIN** *has said about a book that I also have reviewed.) I find myself being informed by* **RAIN**: *many times it's where I first hear of things.* —*J. Baldwin*

RAIN
(Journal of Appropriate Technology)
$15 /year (10 issues)
from:
Rain Magazine
2270 N.W. Irving
Portland, OR 97210

•

Build a Drain-Back Solar Water Heater, 1980, $4.25, 57 pages, by/from: Chris Fried, Rt. 3, Box 229 G, Catawissa, PA 17820.

This is a good build-your-own book from a group in Pennsylvania which has constructed over 50 units in workshops. The system detailed is a drain down (where the water drains back into the storage tank when the collector is not being used). The book shows good construction details and step-by-step assembly procedures. There are useful lists of specific products which are suitable for solar application. —Gail Katz

Guide To Convivial Tools

Have you noticed that your local library doesn't seem to carry the books that you want to see for your work in alternative technologies? Your bookstore is little, if any, better unless you live in one of the few places where people are hip to such matters. If you were a friendly librarian who wanted to install a good radical technology reference section, where would you start? You start with this remarkable bibliography of sources, references, books, other bibliographies, and general information. Better yet, it's useful in any country, and offers many information sources in a variety of languages. (The capsule reviews are in English for all references.) Altogether a superior effort, and badly needed too. The compiler is a cohort of Ivan Illich. —*J. Baldwin*

Guide To Convivial Tools
(LJ Special Report #13)
Valentina Borremans
1979; 112 pp.
$7 postpaid from:
R.R. Bowker Co.
Fulfillment Department
P.O. Box 1807
Ann Arbor, MI 48106
or Whole Earth
Household Store

Appropriate Technology Sourcebook

"The idea behind the Sourcebook is to provide access to practical plans and books on village technology, small community technology, and alternative technology — materials currently in print only. We wanted to enable a reader in Indonesia, for example, to find material of value and relevance, and know something about what he/she was going to get before laying out the rupiahs to get the pubs. In that country, for example, $10 represents a month's salary for a field worker. You're careful what books you buy under the circumstances! Well, the book has been well received — it is being used in more than 80 countries and every state in the U.S." —Ken Darrow

This is the best AT bibliography for those who are actually getting their hands dirty, and it's a fine bargain at the price, too. —J. Baldwin

Appropriate Technology Sourcebook
Ken Darrow and Rick Pam
1976, 1978; 318 pp.

$4.50 postpaid from:
Volunteers In Asia
Box 4543
Stanford, CA 94305

or Whole Earth Household Store

•

Slow Sand Filtration, book. 115 pages, L. Huisman and W. Wood, 1974, $7.40 from WHO regional distributors; or from WHO Distribution and Sales Service, 1211 Geneva 27, Switzerland.

Several scales of design are discussed and illustrated, although knowledge of basic engineering mathematics would be helpful. The last part of the book discusses the use of sand filters for recharging ground water, an important consideration for arid areas. In areas of known biological contamination, however, the use of chemical treatment (chlorine or preferably iodine) along with sand filtration would provide a very safe water supply.

Slow sand filtration methods are also very simple to operate: "Provided that a plant has been well designed and constructed there is little that can go wrong as long as the simple routine of operation is carried out."

A very valuable book for those involved with planning water supplies for small to medium size communities.

The slow sand filter is one of the best means of treating a raw water supply where specialized chemical technology is not available. Far from being an old-fashioned technology, the authors feel that the slow-sand method can be the cheapest, simplest and most efficient method of water treatment.

FIG. 1. DIAGRAM OF A SLOW SAND FILTER

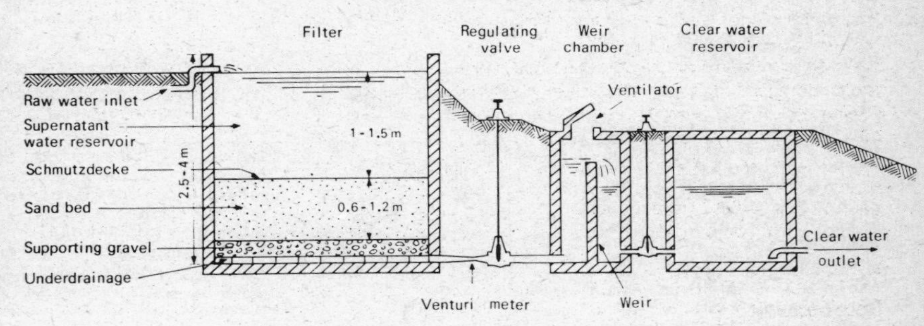

Country Comforts

"Designs for the Homestead" is the subtitle of this very fine presentation of designs for a wide variety of homestead needs as diverse as outdoor hotweather cook stoves and augers for making wooden waterpipes from logs. The designs are exceptionally well described with text, clear drawings and (a flourish of French horns please) photographs! This means, folks, that we have here real live designs actually done and proven. Not only that, but the work has obviously been done by people that it would be nice to know. The book has been done by them too. It would be possible to pick a nit here and there, but on the whole this book sets a high standard for its breed. (See also the book by the same people on log houses, **In Harmony With Nature**, *p. 228.)*
—J. Baldwin

Country Comforts
(Designs for the Homestead)
Christian Bruyère and Robert Inwood
1976, 1979; 237 pp.

$6.95 postpaid from:
Sterling Publishing Co.
Two Park Avenue
New York, NY 10016

or Whole Earth Household Store

China at Work

This was originally published in 1937 by a man with good eyes. It's an amazing array of pre-industrual Chinese tools for making what is needed for feeding, clothing, sheltering and transporting a people who were and are necessarily adept at survival. Everything is illustrated with photographs (sometimes fuzzy but always readable) that include a scale rule so that you can get a good idea of sizes and proportions. Tool-making tools are included too. The text clearly describes how to make and use them all. The tools shown are crude, but nonetheless highly refined as the result of thousands of years of development. They didn't waste anything, especially metal; methods of using scrap are stressed. The book not only shows enough detail to permit the reader to make similar tools for himself, it also transmits an attitude towards tools and their use that helps explain events in China today. I felt indicted as a wastrel as I read and learned.

I'd like to make clear that this book is quite extraordinary, especially at the low price. It's one of those you keep jumping up and showing to bystanders as you find yet another beautiful item. —J. Baldwin

China at Work
Rudolf P. Hommel
1937, 1970; 366 pp.

$9.95 postpaid from:
MIT Press
28 Carleton Street
Cambridge, MA 02142

or Whole Earth Household Store

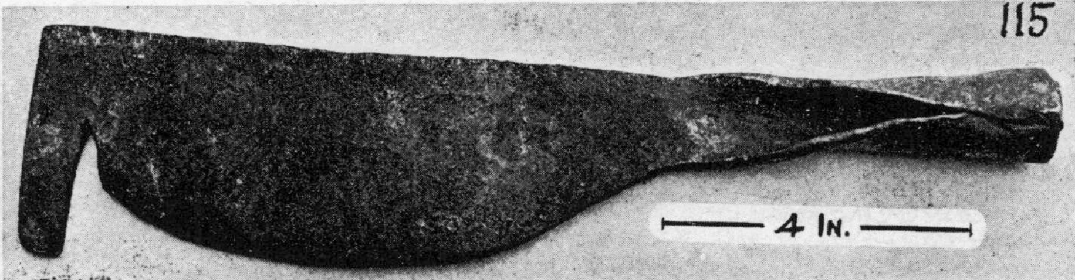

Firewood cleaver. Projection prevents blade from striking ground, making chopping block unnecessary.

Box bellows with top lid removed, showing feathers that seal piston.

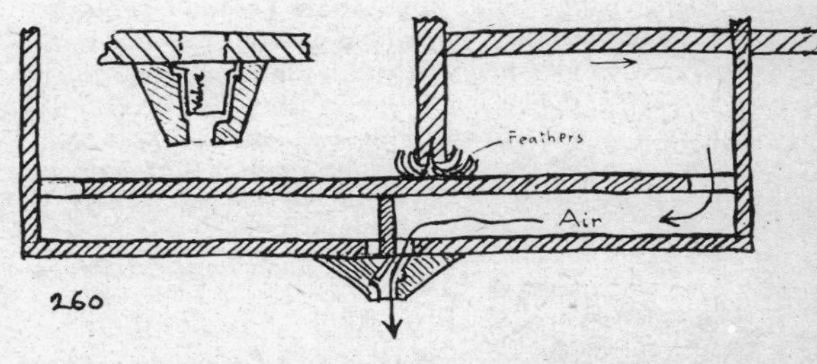

Section through box bellows, with top cover not shown. Note feathers used as gasket. It pumps on both push and pull strokes, producing a nearly constant air output.

THE RISING SUN NEIGHBORHOOD NEWSLETTER

"Achieve Immortality. Instructions $1.00. Divinamics, Box 1867 (McN), Covina, CA 91722."
—Real ad in *McCall's Needlework* magazine found by Evelyn

VITA

Volunteers in Technical Assistance is one of the small number of outfits providing specific practical information on small group technology and non-industrial farming we've found. They sponsor many programs throughout the world, and publish a host of useful books and pamphlets on such diverse subjects as well digging, bat control, glue, water wheels, plows, stoves and fly traps; more than 60! Their information on developing water sources is particularly good.

Their best known book is the incomparable **Village Technology Handbook**. *It concentrates on water resources, sanitation, food raising and shelter — all accomplished with simple technology well suited to rural low-income areas.* **VITA News** *is a quarterly with the latest news of the group's activities and research findings. You can join VITA too, as a volunteer with recompense to be worked out. You'd be one of about 4500. And of course your contributions of money and expert information are most welcome. VITA is one of the very few places where our wastrel society pays its dues to the rest of the world.*

—J. Baldwin

VITA
Information and publications list
(Many publications are in several languages)
$1

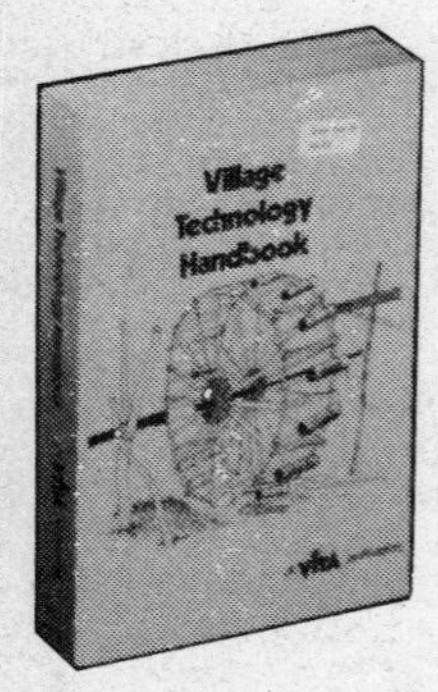

Village Technology Handbook
Volunteers in Technical Assistance, Editors
1963, 1978; 387 pp.
$9.95
or Whole Earth Household Store (Handbook only)

VITA News
$10/year (4 issues)

all postpaid from:
VITA
3706 Rhode Island Ave.
Mt. Rainier, MD 20822

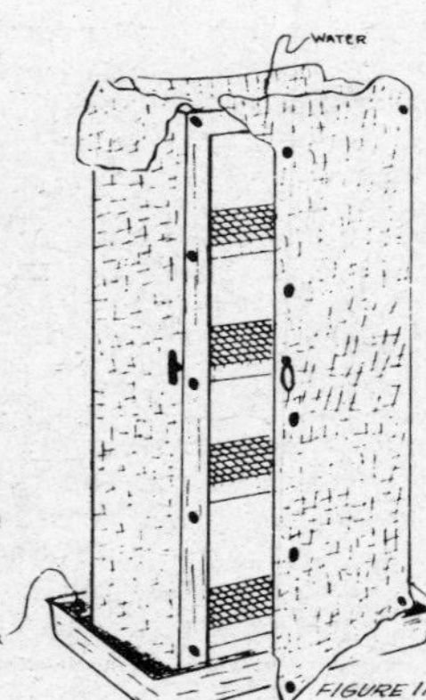

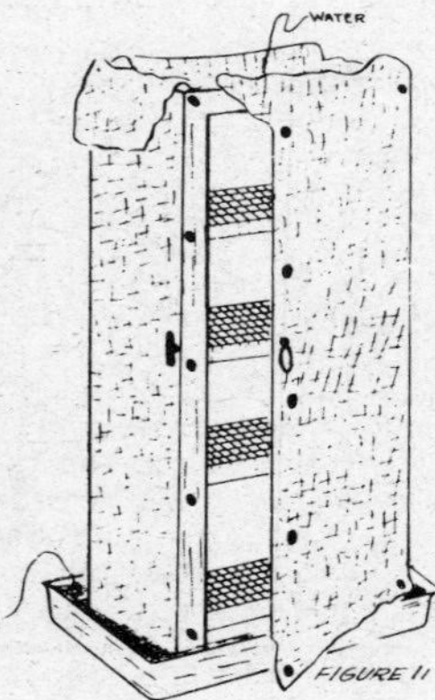

EVAPORATIVE FOOD COOLER — The evaporative food cooler is cooled by the evaporation of water from its cloth cover. The cloth is moistened as capillary action moves water from the pans through it.

If the climate is dry and the cooler is kept in a breezy spot in the shade, it will cool food considerably below the prevailing temperature. To be safe, the cooler must be kept clean. The cooler's cloth cover keeps flying insects out. The water-filled lower pan discourages roaches and other crawling insects. (Village Technology Handbook)

Design Manual for Water Wheels, VITA 1975; 80 pp., English, $4.50.

Construct an overshot water wheel to provide power for grinding grain, pumping water. Requires no added devices. Includes plan for attaching simple pump.

How to Get Waterproofing Substances from Plants by Joseph Boatwright, VITA 1973; 14 pp., English, French, $2.25.

Tap local trees and other plant materials to provide substances for waterproofing. Particularly effective for use on constructions made of earth.

Design Guide for Light Aircraft Airport by VITA/ Lockheed-Georgia, VITA 1970; 50 pp., English $2.95.

How to build an airstrip in remote areas. Complete instructions.

Equipment for Rural Workshops by John Boyd, IT Pub., 1978; 93 pp., English, $9.95.

Guide for anyone who wishes to equip workshop — from basic tools for a one or two person carpentry workshop without power to more sophisticated establishment requiring power equipment for both wood and metal working.

—VITA Catalog

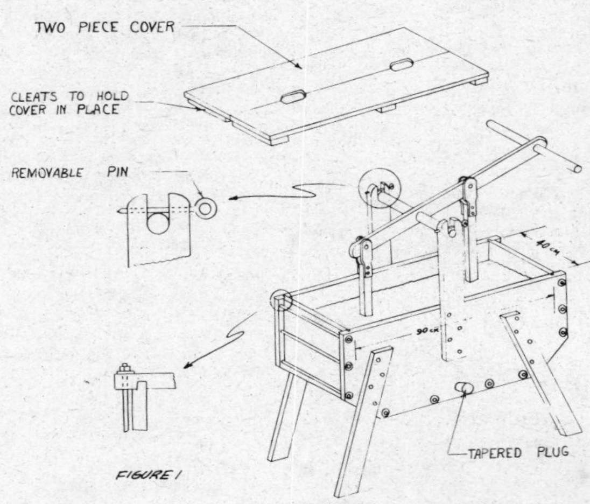

HAND-OPERATED WASHING MACHINE — This easily-operated washing machine can be built by a good carpenter from materials easily found in most countries. It is easy on clothes, effective and sanitary. The machine, which can take 3-kilogram (6-pound) load of clothes, can be shared by several families.

Clothes will last much longer if they are washed in this washing machine rather than beaten or scrubbed on rocks. Washing with the machine is also much less work. A pilot model of the machine was made by the U.S. Department of Agriculture and tested in the U.S.D.A. Home Economics Laboratory, Beltsville, Maryland. Under test conditions, a comparison with standard electric commercial washers was very favorable. If the cost of the machine is too much for one family, it can be used by several. However, if there are too many users, competition for times of use will become keen and the machine will wear faster. (Village Technology Handbook)

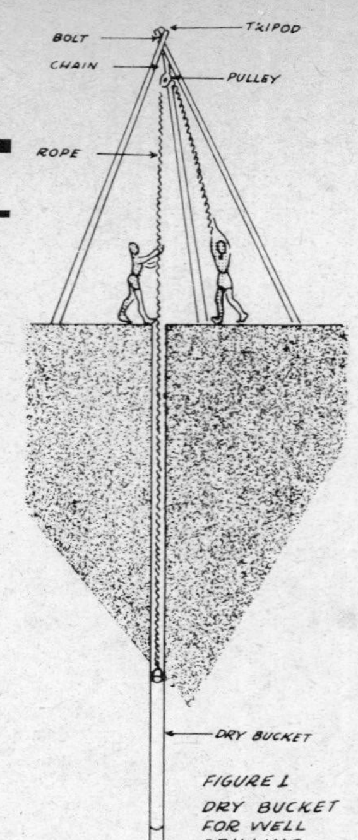

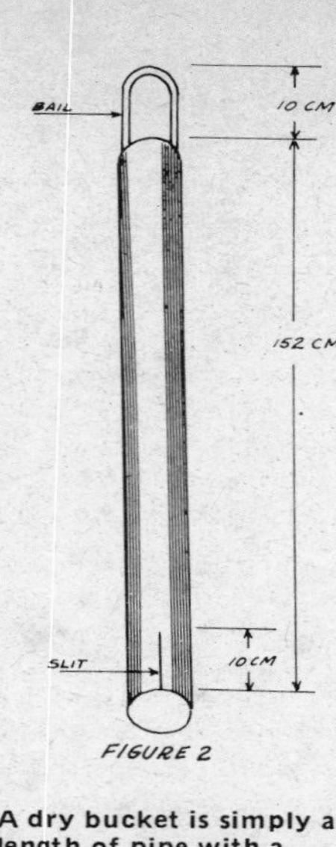

A dry bucket is simply a length of pipe with a bail or handle welded to one end and a slit cut in the other.

DRY BUCKET WELL DRILLING — The dry bucket is a simple and quick method of drilling wells in dry soil which is free of rocks. It can be used for 5cm to 7.5cm (2" to 3") diameter wells in which steel pipe is to be installed. For wells which are wider in diameter, it is a quick method of removing dry soil before completing the bore with a wet bucket, tubewell sand bailer or tubewell sand auger.

The dry bucket is held about 10 cm (several inches) above the ground, centered above the hole location and then dropped (see Figure 1). This drives a small amount of soil up into the bucket. After this is repeated two or three times, the bucket is removed, held to one side and tapped with a hammer or a piece of iron to dislodge the soil. The process is repeated until damp soil is reached and the bucket will no longer remove soil.

—Village Technology Handbook

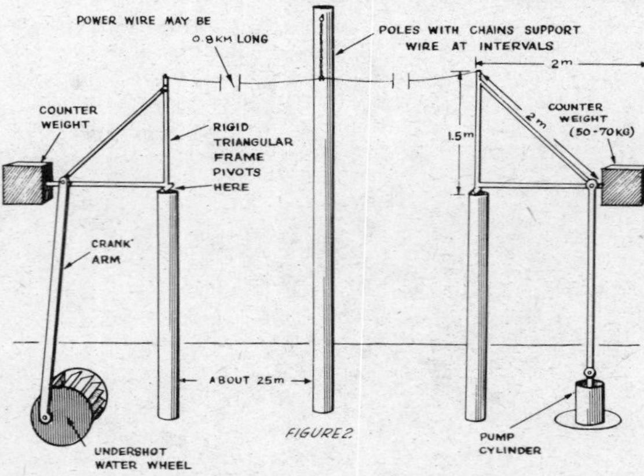

RECIPROCATING WIRE POWER TRANSMISSION FOR SMALL WATER WHEELS — A reciprocating wire can transmit power from a water wheel to a point up to 0.8km (½ mile) away where it is usually used to pump well water. These devices have been used for many years by the Amish people of Pennsylvania. If they are properly installed, they give long, trouble-free service.

—Village Technology Handbook

Intermediate Technology Publications

Though sharing the same concerns as VITA, these people publish a wider range of books and technical bulletins for use in less developed areas of the world. Obviously much of the information available could be adapted for use in rural USA. I have found that this list does not really compete with that of VITA. As there is so much diversity, it is advantageous to read all you can on a given subject.

Intermediate Technology Publications also puts out the excellent, highly useful **Appropriate Technology** *quarterly. In it, the very latest findings and reports from the field are presented in a manner that makes the information easy to use and hence likely to BE used. It's probably the best place to keep up with developments in simple technology, and there is a pleasing feeling of lots of people in remote places working hard to make things a bit better. If such things interest you, a subscription is indispensible.*

—J. Baldwin

Intermediate Technology Publications Catalog
free

Appropriate Technology
Frank Solomon, Editor
£5 (about $12.50)/year (4 issues)
postpaid from:
Intermediate Technology Development Group
9 King Street
London WC2E 8HN, England

North American publications list
free from:
I.T.D.G.-North America
P.O. Box 337
Croton-on-Hudson, NY 10520

Fig.1 Folding type solar cooker.

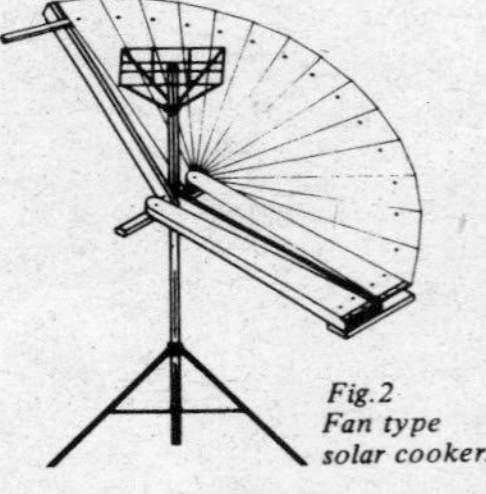

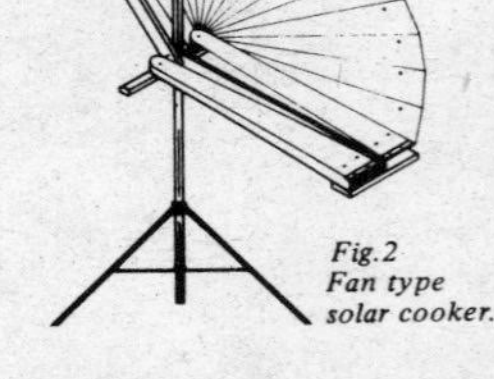

Fig.2 Fan type solar cooker.

Fig.1 Where to place your fingers.

Fig.3 Box solar stove.

↑
Solar cookers represent the most visible impact of solar energy in China today. Here are three common types in use.
—Appropriate Technology

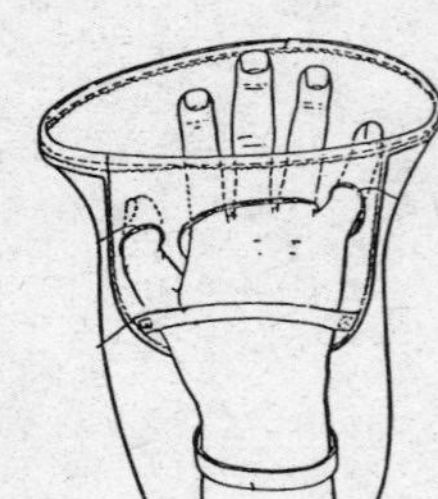

The Dixie Bag Hand Harvesting Aid ↑

The Dixie Bag is a simple hand harvesting aid designed to increase the speed and effectiveness of hand harvesting. Any producer of a crop which must be hand-picked, be it fruit, nuts or coffee beans, faces certain basic problems, namely the low output per picker and the associated costs of hand harvesting.

For further information contact: The Dixie Bag Company Ltd., 10 Islington High Street, London N1 8EQ, England.
—Appropriate Technology

Introduction to Appropriate Technology

Though most of the ideas will be familiar to followers of the Intermediate Technology Development Group, this is the first collection I've seen of such variety and documentation. It's a real kick to see "Small Is Beautiful" in action. Real people doing real things! I recommend this set of papers highly to anyone who has in mind taking Appropriate Soft Technology beyond mere talk.

—J. Baldwin

Introduction to Appropriate Technology
(formerly Lectures on Socially Appropriate Technology)
R.J. Congdon
1975, 1977; 235 pp.

$6.95 postpaid from:
Rodale Books
33 East Minor
Emmaus, PA 18049
or Whole Earth Household Store

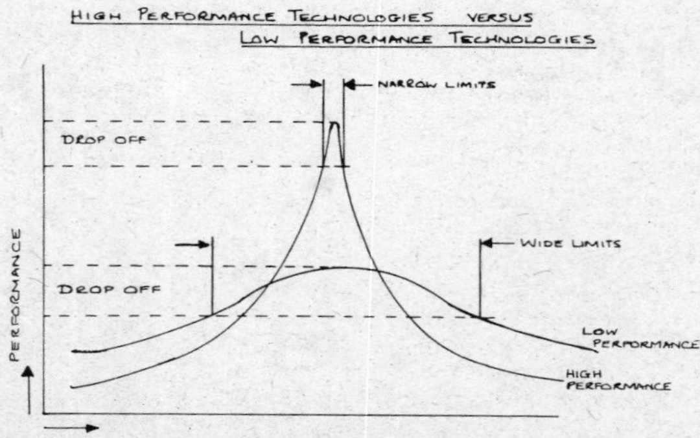

High performance technologies tend to fall drastically away from peak conditions.

The Poor Man's Wisdom
Small Enterprises In Developing Countries

These books are typical of a new and hopefully more enlightened approach to the bringing of an improved standard of living to developing countries. All of these books make use of case histories. Comparing them with my own experience, I find the analysis accompanying the case histories to be quite good.

The Poor Man's Wisdom *stresses small businesses in general, and particularly those which can be operated and controlled (most important!) by the very poorest people you might imagine. OXFAM, the publisher, is one of the most effective outfits working with appropriate technology and the very poor.* **Small Enterprises In Developing Countries** *is personal accounts, and thus a more intimate look at the successes and problems involved.*

Both of these books should be useful to anyone contemplating working in a less developed country, or to anyone who must introduce an unfamiliar technology to any local society. The message is clear: Not only must the technology be right and the hardware adequate, the method of integrating it into the lives of the people who must use it has to be worked out as well. —J. Baldwin

The Poor Man's Wisdom
(Technology and the Very Poor)
Adrian Moyes
1979; 40 pp.
70 p. (about $1.60)
postpaid from:
OXFAM
274 Banbury Road
Oxford OX2 7DZ
England

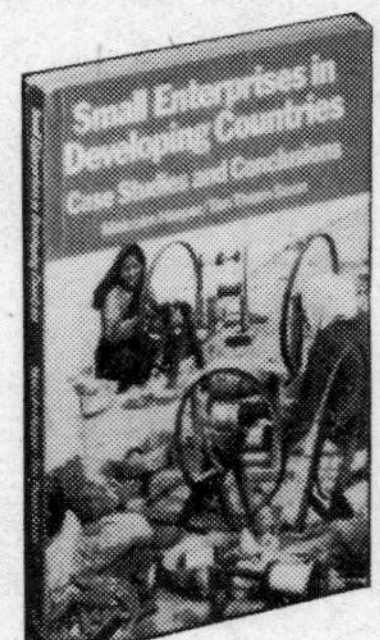

Small Enterprises in Developing Countries
(Case Studies and Conclusions)
Malcolm Harper and
Tan Thiam Soon
1979; 115 pp.
$7.50 postpaid from:
Intermediate Technology
Development Group of
North America
P.O. Box 337
Croton-on-Hudson, NY 10520

or Whole Earth
Household Store

or **£2.95** postpaid from:
Intermediate Technology
Development Group
9 King Street
London, WC2E 8HN

•

Talk of the Town Beer Parlour (Nigeria)

Local currency: Naira (₦) = 100 Kobo = U.S. $0.75

John Okafor is the type who has an eye for business. He is full of energy and has a great deal of confidence in his ability to succeed in any small-scale business venture. One evening he talked to his friend who was a salesman for a brewery about the feasibility of his opening a beer parlour. His friend assured him that adequate supplies of beer would be available at a good price.

John, therefore, decided to open a beer parlour and started to look for a strategic location. He was determined to have a considerably higher class beer parlour than the other bars. In January 1974 he found a site in a perfect location on the corner of Liberty Road and Trans-Ekulu Avenue quite near the bus turnaround. The rent for the special building was rather high (₦80.00 a month) but John was confident he could still make it. Besides, he thought, he could always close down if something went wrong. After all, to make it one must take a small risk.

He proceeded to furnish the place putting in cushioned chairs and centre tables and building an imposing drinking counter with high bar stools. By the time he had finished decorating the place, he found out, to his amazement, that he had spent about ₦3,000.00 which was all the money he had. He still had to get the place licensed by having it inspected by the Ministry of Health and the Police. By the time everything was ready, he was so completely out of money that he did not bother to have the opening ceremony which would have involved a big fanfare with free drinks for everybody passing by. He simply started selling beer.

The response was tremendous. He attracted many customers from the first day. He realised that an opening ceremony was not really necessary. People were attracted by the good facilities and more especially by the low price. He was selling beer at 55 Kobo a bottle while the other beer parlours were selling at 65 Kobo a bottle. His customers increased day by day and at times his three helpers were completely overwhelmed. People were sitting on the counter, on the window ledge and even on the floor. Some even brought their own chairs and sat outside. The place became the talk of the town and that is how it got its name — The Talk of the Town Bar.

This dramatic success, however, was a mixed blessing, and the business was almost out of control. His three employees could not cope with the situation and he hired a fourth. He increased the price to 65 Kobo a bottle in a vain attempt to limit the number of customers, but without success. People kept coming. With people standing outside and drinking beer like a street party, his neighbours became alarmed and on several occasions called in the police. Fortunately the police came from the local post whose staff were regular customers of the bar and so did nothing. His biggest problem, however, came from the landlord who also owned a hotel about two hundred metres from the bar. This hotel had lost most of its custom to the Talk of the Town, and the landlord retaliated by sending John a notice to quit six months after his opening. John pleaded with the landlord and asked his friends to talk to him but the landlord was adamant. John braced himself for a fight and contacted his lawyer. A threatening letter from the lawyer brought the landlord back to his senses, and he stopped harassing John.

The boom continued. The bar was netting an average of ₦500.00 a month. John's friend from the brewery arranged a direct allocation from the factory for him and he also put him in touch with the other breweries' salesmen who gave him direct allocations from their breweries. Under normal circumstances the beer supplies would have been more than enough but there were still too many customers.

John put one of his boys in charge of the sales and devoted his entire time to collecting more beer. He arranged for a dealer to deliver a large quantity of fried meat, a delicacy which increased the thirst of his drinking customers, and this increased his profit to ₦650.00 a month. After nine months of operation he was doing so well that he started thinking of finding a bigger place, but before he could do anything real trouble started.

A price control edict was enacted setting the wholesale price of beer at ₦5.00 per carton of 12 bottles and the retail price at 50 Kobo per bottle. This meant that John's profit was now only ₦1.00 per carton which made little difference so long as he was getting enough beer. However, almost simultaneously with the promulgation of the edict, his salesman friend was transferred to Lagos, a distance of some 350 miles. Although his official allocations were the same he was unable to procure additional supplies since the beer distributors started evading the edict by selling on the black market. For the first time he was unable to satisfy the demands of his ever thirsty customers. At first John refused to buy on the black market but when he started to have problems even with his official allocations he entered the black market. He knew this was very dangerous because the price control inspectors were always on the look out. Sometimes his beer parlour had to be closed for a whole day when his informants reported the presence of price control officials in the neighbourhood. His business went from poor to dismal, and he did not even make enough sales to pay for the rental. He hung on for a while hoping that business would improve but instead things got worse and in frustration he simply closed down, disregarding the advice of his friends. After auctioning his old furniture and fittings he had saved ₦6,000 after a year and a half of operation.

Three months later an amendment to the edict came out imposing mandatory prison terms for violators. One morning he read in the papers that two of his former competitors had received six month's jail terms for selling beer above the controlled price; John celebrated his foresight with a bottle of beer which he bought for ₦1.00.

Comment

This case study describes one venture of a typical entrepreneur, who seized an opportunity when he saw it, took a calculated risk by going into the business and then withdrew from the market when the prospects declined. Entrepreneurs of this type will continue to seek out opportunities regardless of whether or not they receive support from the government and it may be argued that a beer parlour is not a suitable industry for government support. Nevertheless, economic activity of any sort which is not illegal all contributes to development and employment, and governments should avoid rapid price changes such as occurred in this situation when these are likely to cause major problems to indigenous small-scale entrepreneurs who distribute the product.

It may be possible for breweries and other suppliers of staples to promote and train indigenous distributors since this increases their own sales. Many of the best small business assistance programmes are in fact run by manufacturers of shoes, beer, fats and other staple products. It should also be noted that entrepreneurs of this type are perhaps the scarcest commodity of all in most developing countries, and it may be possible through judicious advice and encouragement to turn their attention towards industries which are more directly beneficial to the economy in terms of the product they produce and the numbers they employ. All too often, entrepreneurs of this type are regarded as 'cowboys' or quasi-criminals rather than as partners in the process of economic development.

—**Small Enterprises in Developing Countries**

Economically Appropriate Technologies for Developing Countries

Bibliographies usually don't make Book-of-the Month, but this one is so well annotated I read it from cover to cover! The subject matter is one of those "coming things" that isn't quite in the everyday public eye yet. Dr. Carr's fine work should help. —J. Baldwin

Economically Appropriate Technologies for Developing Countries
(An Annotated Bibliography)
Dr. Marilyn Carr, Compiler
1976; 101 pp.

$8.25 postpaid from:
Intermediate Technology
Development Group
of North America
P.O. Box 337
Croton-on-Hudson,
NY 10520

or Whole Earth
Household Store

or **£2.75** postpaid from:
Intermediate Technology
Development Group
9 King Street
Cornwall, London
WC2E 8HN
England

•

Cabanos, P., **Jeepney Manufacturing in the Philippines: A Model for Developing the Agricultural Machinery Industry**, Agricultural Mechanization in Asia, Autumn, 1971.

Describes how the 'jeepney' industry started in the Philippines after World War II, based on a preponderance of cheap surplus material and a great need for public conveyance. The jeepney is low cost, simple vehicle based on a re-conditioned engine (in 1971, a jeepney capable of carrying 12 persons cost $1,600). As soon as the concept was developed, small shops producing crude versions cropped up almost overnight, and the industry has flourished to such an extent that annual sales in 1971 had reached 17 million dollars. Gives details of two large companies which started from scratch in the 1950s using simple tools.

Rural Home Techniques

Ingenious living basics from the U.N. It's amazing what you can do with clear drawing, describing, and thinking. —SB
[Suggested by Thomas Laughlin]

Rural Home Techniques
Food and Agriculture Organization of the United Nations
Volume:
1. Food Preservation (FPR) - Series 1
2. Labour Saving Ideas (LSI) - Series 1
3. Food Preparation (FPP) - Series 1
4. Labour Saving Ideas - Series 2
5. Food Preservation - Series 2
6. Labour Saving Ideas - Series 3
7. Household Furnishing & Equipment (HFE) - Series 1

$8.50 each postpaid from:
UNIPUB
345 Park Avenue South
New York, NY 10010

Hanging Clothes
Twisted rope method. Twist two pieces of clothesline. Place one end of a piece of clothing through one of the loops that have been formed by the twisted clothesline, and the other end of the clothing through another of the loops. The rope will tighten and hold the piece of clothing in place.

Labour Saving Ideas — Series 1 — Volume II

THE RISING SUN
NEIGHBORHOOD NEWSLETTER

Walking down an urban street since the large scale release of mental patients, you can feel that you are really really together and the most apart you've ever been in your life has been a model of reality touching, or you can feel like you're walking down the streets of some mental Calcutta, stepping on the faces of people who didn't get your breaks and broke. What exactly is the appropriate response to someone who in these days of inflation asks you for a nickle and asks you so slowly and painstakingly that you know this is one of the two or three sentences the guy has in the world? How much money would Thomas Szasz give him? What would the Good Samaritan do?

SOLAR ENERGY HAS AT LAST HIT THE BIG TIME with subsidies, code requirements, bank terms, and fancy color catalogs. There's a growing solar hardware industry too, and like most new industries it is a strange mixture of dedicated ineptitude, cool professionalism, and fraud. Right now it's pretty hard to sort it all out — so many of the companies involved are small and local that investigating each one is virtually impossible. For this reason we are not presenting collectors and other devices except where we personally know the people, or the idea is clearly one to watch.

Hardware is not where it's at anyway. The focus (heh heh) of much household scale solar work is on "passive" design — the building itself is the collector and storage. This isn't so flashy and doesn't appeal so readily to those who like to show off things they've bought, but it works, and there is an increasingly competent literature based on field experience. Passive designs tend to be more modest too, a welcome turn away from what I have called "solar Buicks" — large houses that are essentially energy hogs made "energy efficient" by the addition of expensive devices.

In any case, it's buyer beware. You can get a good idea of what is available by attending to the several publications dedicated to that worthy goal, and you can educate yourself pretty well from a few definitive books. You should remember that the ultimate goal is for all of us to live on renewable energy. That means sleazy workmanship, poor design, short-lived materials, and the usual build-it-as-tacky-as-you-can-and-still-sell-it attitude are not appropriate. Unfortunately, many manufacturers have not agreed, nor have many do-it-yourselfers whose only idea is to save money. Oh, there's money to be saved alright, but it takes a while to show. It is unlikely that there will be any solar strategy that will make a big, sudden dramatic difference. We got into our energy-wasting mess in small steps, and it is by careful attention to doing the small things right that we will get out.

—J. Baldwin

The Solar Home Book

Most of the basic information on solar energy has been established and published in every imaginable nuance, but application of the basics surges ahead so fast that usually only the journals can keep up. Unfortunately, the journals can't afford to be highly detailed, and the hardcover publishers can't afford to bring out new titles. Once again Bruce Anderson and friends come to the rescue, and once again they are in front of the pack. There's a lot in the book about passive systems. The whole book is rich in what-we-have-learned-by-trying-it and gives examples from many different parts of the U.S.A. This is in marked contrast to most others. If you are dealing sun these days, the book is essential reading. Incidentally, Bruce Anderson is also executive editor of the ever-better **Solar Age** *magazine (opposite page).*

—J. Baldwin

The Solar Home Book
Bruce Anderson with Michael Riordan
1976; 298 pp.
$9.50 postpaid from:
Brick House Publishing
3 Main Street
Andover, MA 01810
or Whole Earth Household Store

SUMMER COOLING

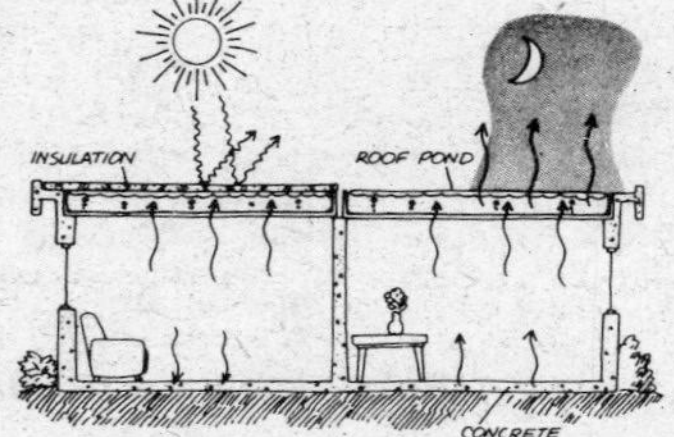

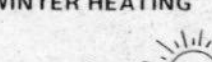

WINTER HEATING

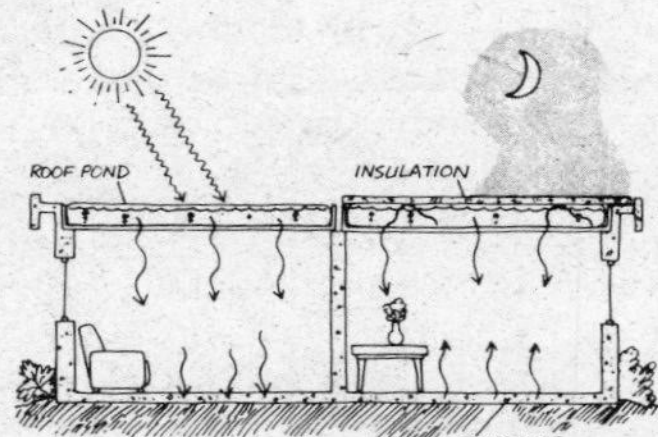

← **Roof pond collectors — summer and winter operation.**

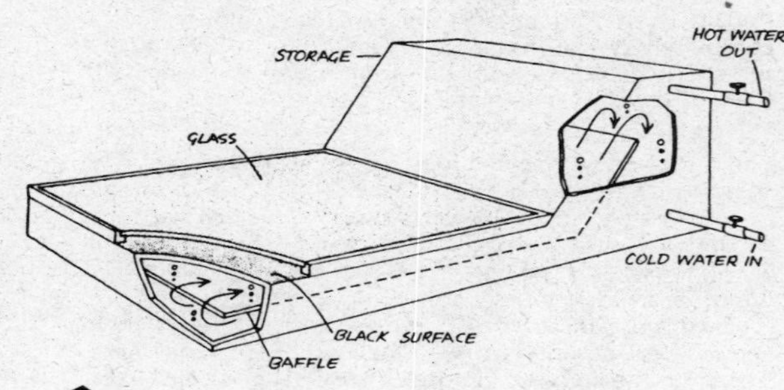

↑ **Thermosiphoning solar water heater developed in the West Indies.**

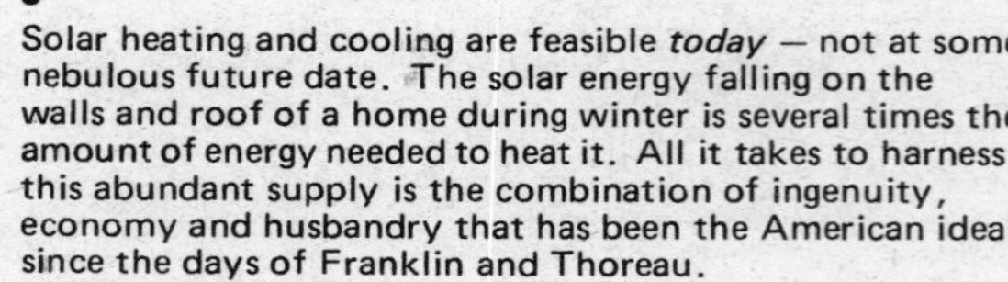

•

Solar heating and cooling are feasible *today* — not at some nebulous future date. The solar energy falling on the walls and roof of a home during winter is several times the amount of energy needed to heat it. All it takes to harness this abundant supply is the combination of ingenuity, economy and husbandry that has been the American ideal since the days of Franklin and Thoreau.

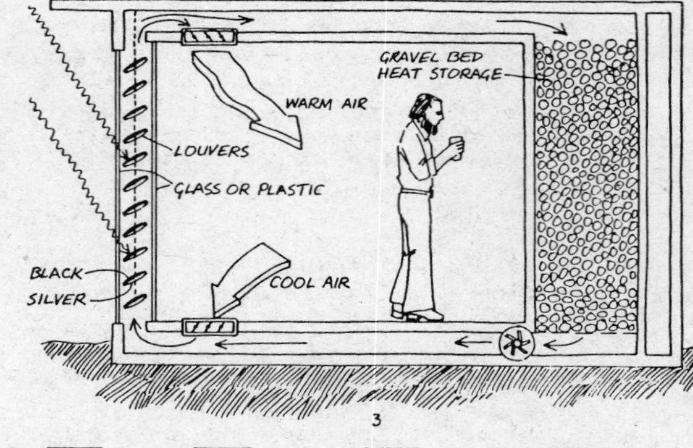

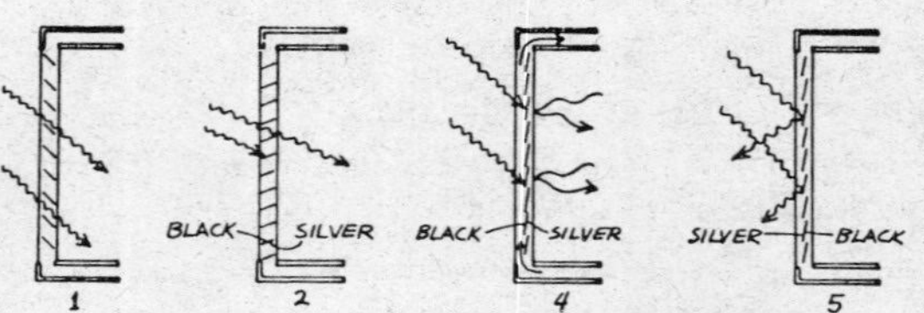

A "Venetian blind" solar collector and heat control device — various operating modes.

The Passive Solar Energy Book

I have come to regard new solar energy books almost as a personal assault. The majority are the same old stuff with a new title, are dull, and are maddening to review. Once in a while, though, a really fine useful book comes by that makes up for the others. This is one of those books. It has all the attributes that one could reasonably demand: basic principles are explained with unusual brilliance (the best I've seen), the principles are reduced to "rules of thumb," examples are given, and a workbook format makes it easy to apply what you've learned. This expanded professional edition has massive references and charts of such essentials as Time Lag Of Heat Flow Through Walls and Roofs. The latest numbers are from field work (in contrast to many other books) and give the designer the tools to calculate passive details with confidence. Also included are transparent overlays that enable the figures to be applied to your particular geographical area. The charts (along with the photos and illustrations) are mercifully large and well printed. The whole thing has a friendly tone to it instead of the more common preaching-to-the-dumb-dumbs. What more could one ask? Incidentally, this is the book that government officials are using as a reference when making the solar tax rebate laws for passive buildings. It's already regarded as a classic, for good reason.

—J. Baldwin

The Passive Solar Energy Book
(Expanded Professional Edition)
Edward Mazria
1979; 704 pp.
$24.95 postpaid from:
Rodale Books
33 East Minor
Emmaus, PA 18049
or Whole Earth Household Store

•

The most common definition of a passive solar-heating and cooling system is that it is a system in which the thermal energy flows in the system are by natural means such as radiation, conduction and natural convection. In essence, the building structure or some element of it *is* the system. There are no separate collectors, storage units or mechanical elements. The most striking difference between the systems is that the passive system operates on the energy available in its immediate environment and the active system imports energy, such as electricity, to power the fans and pumps which make the system work.

•

There are two basic elements in every passive solar-heating system: south-facing glass (or transparent plastic) for solar collection, and thermal mass for heat absorption, storage and distribution. Popular belief has it that a passive building must incorporate large quantities of these two elements. Our studies show, however, that while there must be some thermal mass and glazing in each space, when properly designed they are not necessarily excessive.

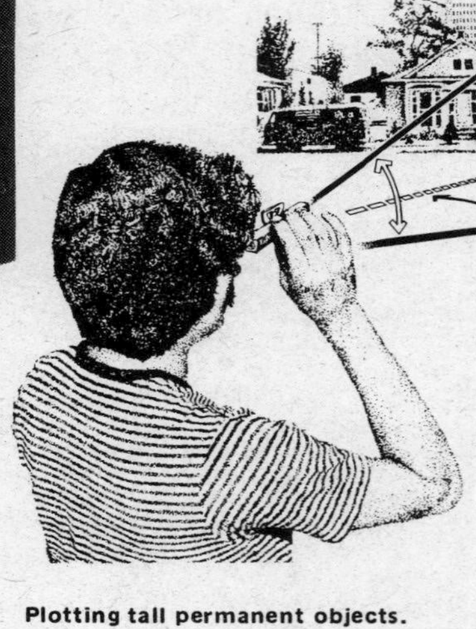

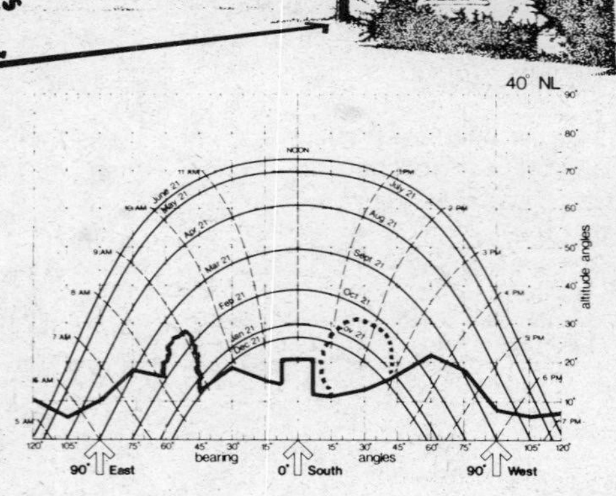

Plotting tall permanent objects.

•

While good at storing heat, a masonry exterior wall used as a heat storage medium within a space will also readily pass this heat to the outside. Masonry materials such as brick, stone, concrete and adobe can store large amounts of heat. A masonry wall by itself, though, does not provide good insulation. For example, 3½ inches of fiberglass insulation has the insulating properties of 12 feet of concrete or 4 feet of adobe. In a Direct Gain System a large portion of the heat stored in an exposed masonry wall will be lost to the exterior.

The Recommendation

When using a masonry wall (exposed to the exterior) for heat storage, place insulation on the outside of the wall. Also, at the perimeter of foundation walls, apply approximately 1½ to 2 feet of 2-inch rigid waterproof insulation below grade. This will prevent any heat stored in the walls and floor from being conducted rapidly to the outside.

square inch

square inch

← **Energy density is determined by the angle of incidence.**

Sloping Roof

Figure 1. No Pitch Adjustment Required.

Figure 2. Pitch Adjustment Required.

Flat Roof

Figure 3.

A. Collectors mounted directly to roof

Advantages over B
- Simplest and least expensive mounting method;
- Lightest mounting method;
- Collectors need not be mounted at roof peak (except in regions where ice damming is prevalent).

Note: If roofing is more permanent than asphalt shingles, re-roofing will be less of a concern.

B. Collectors mounted to weatherproofed platform

Advantages over A
- Simplifies re-roofing task (collectors need not be removed to replace surrounding roof);
- Since water cannot course under the array, elaborate flashings of roof penetrations required in A is not necessary (provided spaces between collectors are weatherproofed);
- Distributes weight more evenly over roof surface.

C. Collectors Mounted to Rack

Advantages over D
- Simpler & less expensive than dormer mount;
- Lighter than dormer;
- If adequate working space is provided, re-roofing may take place without necessitating removal of rack;
- Collectors need not be mounted at peak.

D. Collectors Mounted to Dormer

Advantages over C
- Simplifies re-roofing task (Collectors need not be removed to replace surrounding roof);
- Since water cannot course under the array, elaborate flashing of roof penetrations required in C is not necessary (provided spaces between collectors are weatherproof);
- Distributes weight more evenly over roof surface.

E. Collectors mounted to Rack

Advantages over F
- Simpler and less expensive than dormer mount;
- Lighter than dormer.
- If adequate working space is provided, re-roofing may take place without necessitating removal of rack.

F. Collectors Mounted to Dormer

Advantages over E
- Simplifies re-roofing task (collectors need not be removed to replace surrounding roof);
- Since water cannot course under the array, elaborate flashing of roof penetrations required in E is not necessary (provided spaces between collectors are weatherproofed);
- Distributes weight more evenly over roof surface.

Solar Age

This magazine is now the official publication of the American Section of the International Solar Energy Society. The editor is Bruce Andersen, who is one of the authors of the excellent **Solar Home Book** *(opposite page). In the four years it has been with us,* **Solar Age** *has developed into a truly useful tool. It's where you look for the latest results from the field, professional controversies being worked upon, and detailed discussions of news items briefly covered in various media. Many of the articles are of a caliber one expects to see in a formal book, but in* **Solar Age** *you get it about two years sooner. You can subscribe in the normal way, or get it as a part of your membership in the Solar Energy Society (p. 194).*

—J. Baldwin

Solar Age
Bruce Anderson, Editor
$20/year (12 issues)

from:
Solar Age
P.O. Box 4934
Manchester, NH 03108

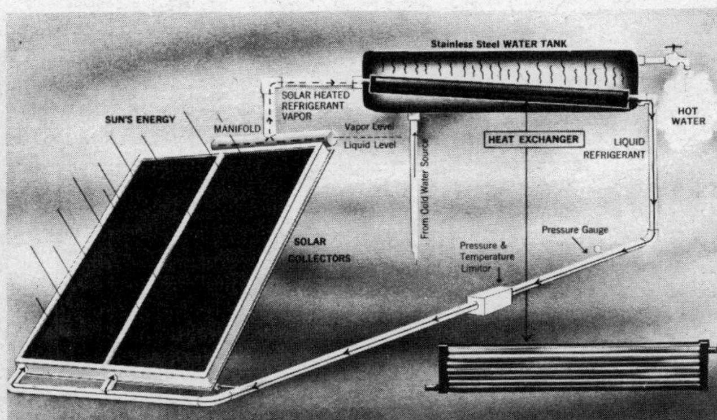

•

Koldwave, Div. Heat Exchangers, Inc.
8100 N. Monticello Avenue, Skokie, IL 60076
Lloyd L. Ludkey (312) 267-8282

Koldwave Heat Pumps - 5K9 - 90CMHT, 5KC19 - 204DHT

Koldwave water-to-air heat pumps, used in residential and commercial applications, convert solar energy, collected by plate collectors, to space heating and cooling. Cooling capacities range from 9,500-228,000 Btu/hr. Heating capacities range from 11,500-268,000 Btu/hr. **Features:** Self-contained, pre-charged units. **Options:** Heat pump water regulating valve. Cupro/Nickel condensor. **Installation Requirements:** On heating cycle, minimum entering water temperature required is 50°F.

Guarantee/Warranty: 1st year - furnish replacement for any defective part; 2nd-5th year - furnish replacement for any defective part in the sealed refrigeration system.

THE RISING SUN
NEIGHBORHOOD NEWSLETTER

The churches in the city run a place where foreign visitors in town can stay. The churches started it because Africans visiting in the '50s could only stay in the ghetto. One African doctor visiting the medical center killed himself in his motel room which seemed like it might have something to do with living in a motel room in a foreign city for 3 months. So the churches built this nice place for foreign visitors to stay together, and Elizabeth's husband is the director of it. She told me various things about living there.

1. She never did like small talk, and it's worse when much of it consists of saying, "How are you/I am fine" slowly.

2. Her husband can translate from English into English better than anyone. Any English as a second language person can say to him things that they think are English and very few native speakers of English can understand, and he can translate into intelligible English.

3. The people who stay there are either aristocrats or radicals. The radicals talk about the CIA ruining their country. The aristocrats kiss your hand a lot and tell you you're beautiful.

4. Some Egyptians told a lot of Anwar Sadat stories. They amounted to saying he's a good boss, pleasant, cheerful even right after he wakes up.

5. One night at midnight people were laughing so loud it woke up the whole floor. They went to see what it was and the man from Uganda was telling Idi Amin jokes.

6. The aristocrats and the radicals fight a lot, loudly. They haven't yet had aristocrats and radicals from the same country at the same time, but it's not necessary for them to be from the same country to fight.

7. A doctor from a straight churchy background gave a speech about his trip to China. He said when he compared the health care in the sticks of China to the health care in American ghettos, he decided freedom isn't worth it if that's the price we pay, the price we make poor people pay.

8. A Russian emigrant family stayed for a while. The husband had a bad cold the first day and the director looked in the phone book for a doctor. The Russian said, I'll just go to the doctor for this district and he was very upset to discover there wasn't just one doctor for this district. They also had mini-nervous breakdowns in supermarket aisles because of the choices.

Sun Up to Sun Down

This welcome new book makes the many ways of utilizing the Sun easy to understand even if you have no background in math or physics. In contrast to the usual math-heavy technical books and the lightweight poorly explained popularizers, this commendable effort teaches by analogy. It's the best introduction I've seen. The book has an outstanding discussion of the Thermic Diode Solar Panel, which isn't surprising since the author invented it. This nifty idea is a marvellously simple valve that prevents the solar heated water from back-siphoning at night and losing its hard-won BTUs. This scheme also has the advantage of being self-contained — it serves as its own heat storage tank. No pumps either. I regard this invention as important because it offers a real hope of reducing the complexity and cost of active solar systems.

—J. Baldwin

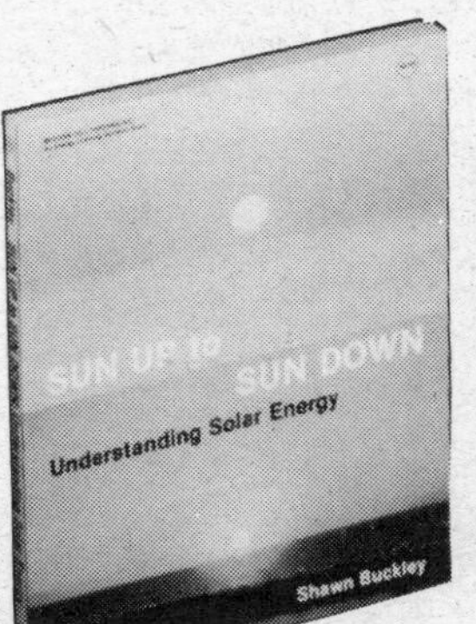

Sun Up to Sun Down
(Understanding Solar Energy)
Shawn Buckley
1979; 166 pp.

$6.95 postpaid from:
McGraw-Hill Book Company
Princeton Road
Hightstown, NJ 08520
or Whole Earth Household Store

Thermic Diode Water Heating

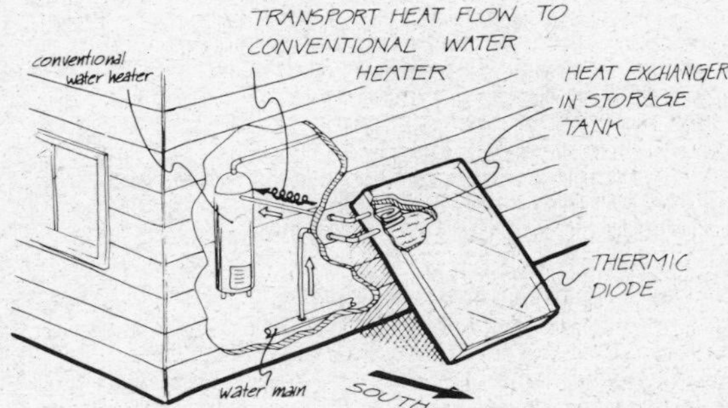

Water Flows One Way Through Oil Valve

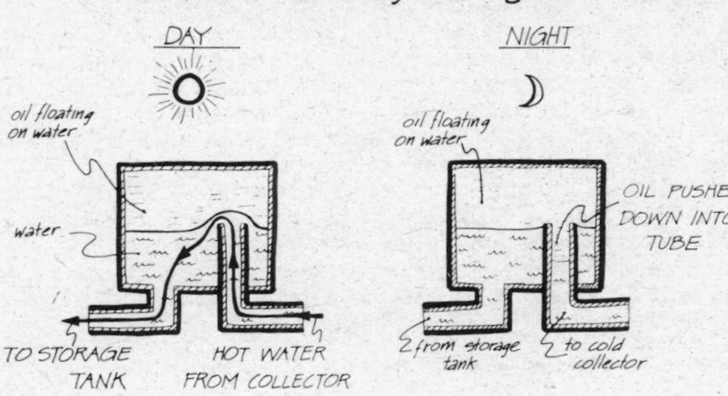

High Efficiency Collection with Empty Pipe

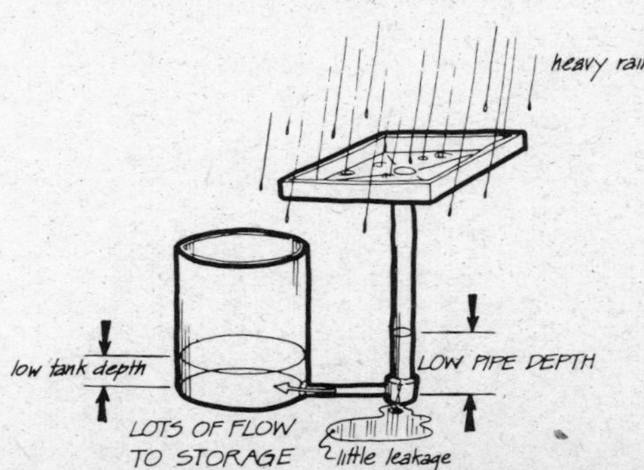

High Collection Efficiency with Cool Collector

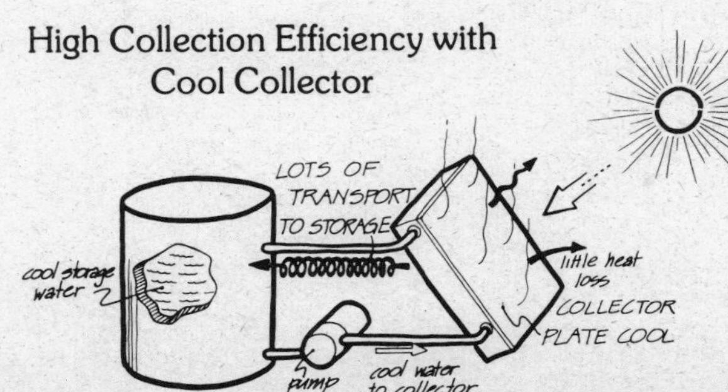

Solar Heating & Cooling

If you need to familiarize yourself or someone else with the many options available to those who would go solar, this book offers one of the very best overviews. The schemes are shown and explained with **Sunset**'*s usual high standard of publishing and writing, but many of the drawings are so small that it is difficult to tell one from another after looking at them for awhile. For this reason I have been reluctant to review it, but so many readers have recommended it that I hereby relent. In most ways it is one of the very best places to start your solar education. At the price, it is an unusual bargain.* —J. Baldwin

Sunset Homeowner's Guide to Solar Heating and Cooling
(Active & Passive Systems, Hot Water Heaters, Pools, Spas & Tubs)
Holly Lyman Antolini, Editor
1978; 96 pp.

$3.95 postpaid from:
Lane Publishing Company
Menlo Park, CA 94025
or Whole Earth Household Store

Five possible collector locations:

Mounted on freestanding shed in garden, facing south

Mounted on east or west-facing roof; turned to face south

Mounted on shed against south-facing wall (or, with reflectors, on wall itself)

Mounted on south-facing garage roof

Mounted atop freestanding trellis in garden

W N S E

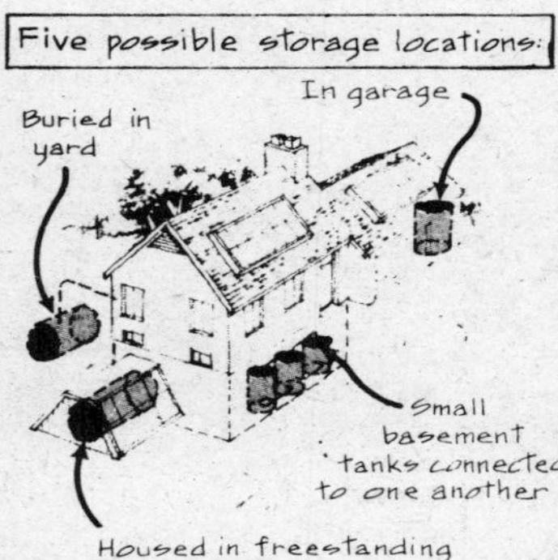

To evaluate your home's solar potential, seven major factors must be weighed in considerable detail.

1. Its existing heating system.
2. Its heat loss.
3. Its orientation and available sunlight.
4. Its roof slope.
5. Its exposure to sunlight.
6. Its indoor installation restrictions. And . . .
7. Its outdoor installation restrictions.

At Home in the Sun

Real people living in real solar houses tell what it's like, both good and bad. Though many readers will have fun trying to imagine living in these houses, to me the usefulness of this book stems from its effect as a myth-reducer. The mindless pro-solar crazies get brought back to day-to-day realities such as leaks and overdesign, and the solar-doesn't-work people must admit that it does indeed work for quite ordinary families. Lots of good photographs and diagrams lend an air of truth to the book. Refreshing. —J. Baldwin

At Home in the Sun
(An Open House Tour of Solar Homes in the United States)
Norah Deakin Davis and Linda Lindsey
1979; 236 pp.

$9.95 postpaid from:
Garden Way Publishing Company
Charlotte, VT 05545
or Whole Earth Household Store

Shutters · Insulative Curtains · Vents · Thermal Storage · Adobe Wall · Filon · Concrete Piers · Adobe · Flagstone · Banco

The adobe living room wall accumulates heat from the greenhouse and radiates it to the inside.

No fans are used in this entirely passive system. Air circulates between the greenhouse and the living area through vents at the top and bottom of the south adobe wall. Hot air flows from the greenhouse into the living area through the top vent, and as it cools it descends and is drawn back into the greenhouse. At night the vents are closed manually so that heat is not lost. The only auxiliary heating comes from a wood stove in the bedroom and an adobe fireplace which is not particularly energy-efficient. Last winter the interior stayed at 65°F. during the day; the greenhouse, at 90°F. On really cold nights Kathie and Al stoked the stove, but in March Al noticed that the woodpile had hardly gone down at all, so they started using the fireplace in the evenings for enjoyment. Half a cord would have carried them through.

Solar Heated Buildings of North America

Each building is described, diagrammed and photographed, specifications and costs are given, and (important) actual experience with the solar heating systems is noted, including failures. This is as good a place as any to get an idea of what is going on these days. It is exciting to see so many things being tried. There are signs of struggle. —J. Baldwin

Solar Heated Buildings of North America
(120 Outstanding Examples)
William A. Shurcliff
1978; 298 pp.

$8.95 postpaid from:
Brick House Publishing Company
3 Main Street
Andover, MA 01810
or Whole Earth Household Store

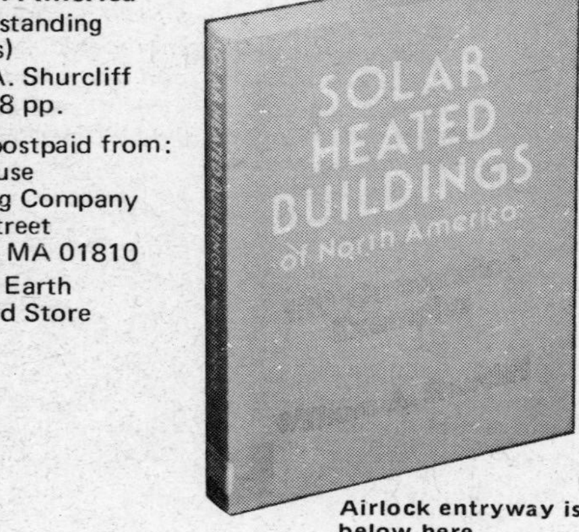

MIT Solar Building V

Building This one-room, 40-by-22-foot experimental building, with 10-foot inside height, is used as a classroom and drafting room. Because the lot was small and was oriented 20 degrees east of south, the designer was forced to orient the building similarly. Yet by providing four 20-degree-slanted bays be was able to have the four main window areas face exactly south. Each bay is 8 feet long and is displaced 3 feet with respect to the next bay. The windows on the east, north, and west sides of the building are of negligible area and are double-glazed. At the north corner of the building there is an air-lock entryway.
The floor is a 4-inch concrete slab resting on gravel. The slab perimeter is insulated by the 4-inch layer of Styrofoam SM which extends 18 inches downward and then runs 36 inches outward. The walls include 6-inch fiberglass batts confined between gypsum boards. Because the 6-inch studs are of steel (to conform to the building code applicable to classrooms) and could constitute a major path for conductive loss of heat, a 1-inch sheet of Styrofoam board, protected by 1/8 inch of stucco cement, has been applied to the exterior of the wall.

Comment on General Performance The system operates with no moving parts, no noise, no adjustments (except adjustment of the venetian blinds every few weeks), and no dependence on electricity. It avoids several drawbacks of earlier types of passive solar heating systems employing large window-walls: near the window-walls of such systems the occupants may find the glare to be excessive by day and may feel cold at night; also, much heat is lost through those walls at night. In the present system, the venetian blinds and dark-colored window seats greatly reduce glare (but without sacrifice of view, because the slats are nearly horizontal); the warm window-seats eliminate chill; and the third glazing sheet, with its infrared-reflecting coatings, greatly reduces heat loss.
The durability of the present system has not been fully demonstrated, but thermal cycling tests of the PCM-filled pouches have been encouraging: by the end of February 1978 several such pouches had been heated and cooled two thousand times, melting and refreezing the 3/8-inch layers of PCM each time, with no detectable change in performance.

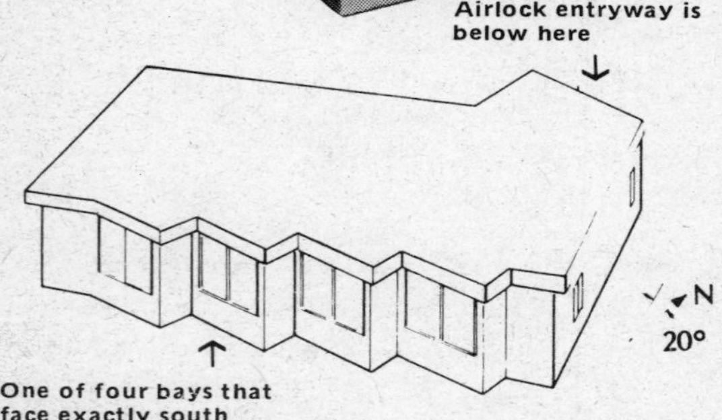

Solar Energy, Fundamentals in Building Design

This is the professional architect's version of the **Solar Home Book** *(p. 182). Fortunately, Bruce Anderson makes the principles useable and clear without the discouragingly complex math found in the typical engineering treatise. A very complete bibliography and index adds the final touch of excellence.* —J. Baldwin

Solar Energy: Fundamentals in Building Design
Bruce Anderson
1977; 374 pp.

$26.50 postpaid from:
McGraw-Hill Book Co.
Princeton Road
Hightstown, NJ 08520
or Whole Earth Household Store

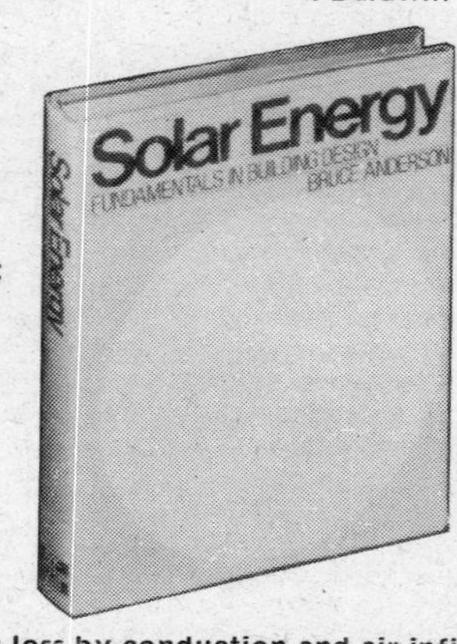

Relative amounts of heat loss by conduction and air infiltration for various combinations of window sash and glass.

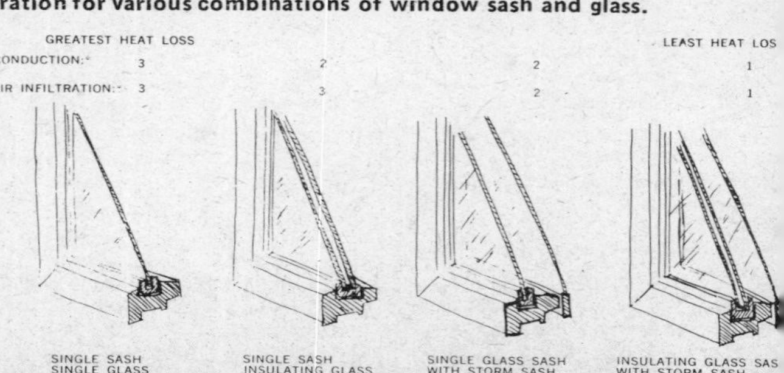

Your Home's Solar Potential

If you already have a house, how do you go about figuring out if there is any sense in retrofitting a solar heating system? Hiring somebody to check out your place can be expensive, and doing it yourself is likely to prove difficult unless you have training. But with the help of this book, you don't need the training. What it amounts to is a list of things to check; things like roof angles, compass orientation, and local climate. By using an evaluation system given, you score the various categories. A final overall score is compared with a rating scale that tells you whether it makes sense to go solar with your house. This is a nifty way of getting at this sort of work, but I do wish the book had been published a little less slick at a little less price. Even so, it's a lot less than hiring someone, even assuming there is someone competent nearby to hire. —J. Baldwin

Your Home's Solar Potential
Irwin Spetgang and Malcolm Wells
1976; 60 pp.
No. 9515

$11.25 postpaid from:
Edmund Scientific Corp.
2255-7082 Edscorp Bldg.
Barrington, NJ 08007
or Whole Earth Household Store

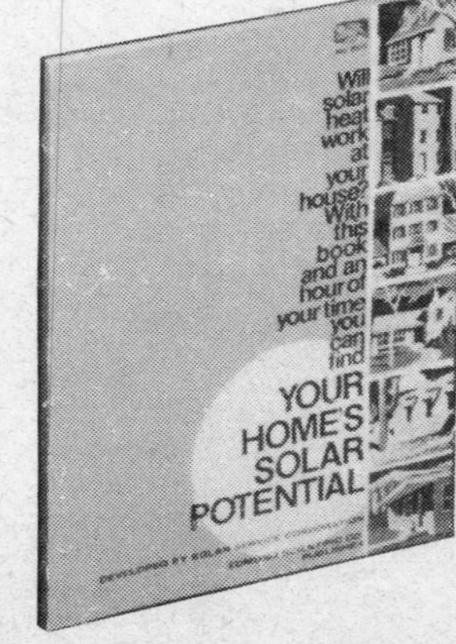

The Solar Room

The Food and Heat Producing Solar Greenhouse

In the four years this book has been available, it has become the one where you look first. For good reason too — somebody or other has actually done what's shown, and there's a lot shown. More than shown, really, because there's also lots of how and why too. And a good bibliography with comment. And good photographs of proven details. And step-by-step instruction on both building and operating. In fact, the book is a marvel. Lots of love in it. —J. Baldwin

The 1980 revised edition deepens the marvel. For most homes solar greenhouses are the way to go. With Steve Baer's Big Fin (p. 190) you even get hot water easy. —SB

The Food and Heat Producing Solar Greenhouse
(Design, Construction & Operation)
Rick Fisher and Bill Yanda
1976, 1980; 208 pp.

$8 postpaid from:
John Muir Publications
P.O. Box 613
Santa Fe, NM 87501
or Whole Earth Household Store

↑

Since the first edition of this book, the Solar Room has proven itself to be one of the best buys in "BTUs for the buck". Literally millions of American homes could save heating dollars immediately by the installation of a Solar Room.

Here is Steve Kenin's explanation of his product:

"The Solar Room is a device that turns the southern side of a home into a solar heater. Made of a special plastic, a Solar Room can supply 35% to 65% of home space heating needs. With heat storage and insulation options, its heating capacity is greatly increased. The Solar Room is available in kit form and is designed to be an exterior room, seven feet wide and as long as space permits; 20, 30 or 40 feet. The longer the Solar Room, the more heat is collected.

"Not only a heat collector, the Solar Room is a versatile, inexpensive addition to the home, costing $3.50 to $4.50 per square foot of floor space. It is an airtight, thermally efficient space, and can serve as a greenhouse, a winter playroom for children or as a foyer to the house where coats, boots and bicycles can be stored out of the winter weather. As a greenhouse, the Solar Room is an especially efficient space, providing warmth for the household and fresh vegetables for the dinner table. In the spring the garden can be started early in the greenhouse and transplanted outside when danger of frost is past.

•

The Solar Fan made by the William Lamb Co. is a high quality air mover powered by a small photovoltaic array. The company sells it primarily as an attic ventilator, but it is perfect for a small greenhouse. The 12-volt D.C. unit can push over 600 cfm quietly and dependably. In the exhaust mode, it is moving air out of the greenhouse in the summer. Come fall, when heat is needed by the office, the fan is pivoted 90° to blow apex greenhouse air to the back room fifteen feet away. The third mode is a switch that directs the power down a line to charge a 12-volt battery. The attribute I enjoy most about the fan is its high quality. There's nothing second rate about it. The heavy little motor runs without a sound and must have sealed bearings because I can't find anywhere to oil it. (I don't anticipate the need, either.) The photovoltaic array is totally sealed against weathering.

Finally, a built-in feature makes the unit unique. Because it is linked directly to the sun, the Solar Fan regulates itself. The fan works the hardest when the sun is brightest. So it's going full tilt on a bright day to charge an adjoining room or exhaust outdoors. When it gets cloudy, the Solar Fan slows down or stops completely. It's like having a tiny little brain linking the power of the sun to the spinning of a fan blade — for your benefit. Both of these products demonstrate remarkable and totally beneficial use of technology.

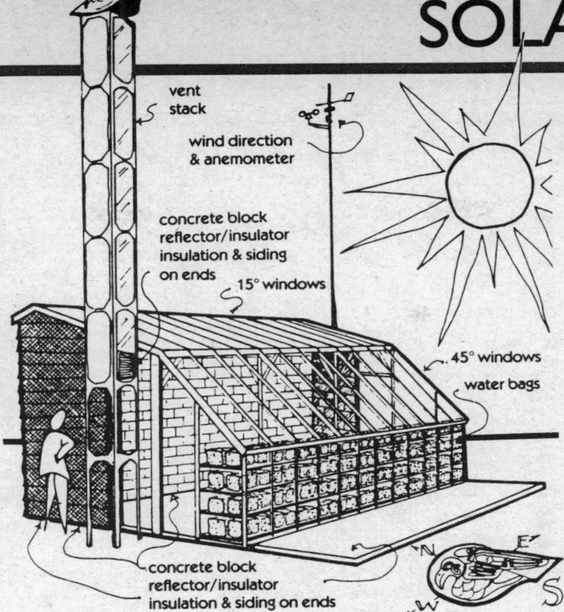

Illustrated is the solar chimney of the Ecotope group. Only the south side of the twelve-foot stack is glazed, with the rest sheathed solidly. It is designed to provide ventilation of 900 cubic feet per minute on a summer day — the equivalent of a sizeable greenhouse fan — without using any electrical power. ↑

The Complete Greenhouse Book

Much more of an overall look at greenhouse operation than **The Food and Heat Producing Solar Greenhouse.** *Virtually everything is looked at — the building (including solar aspects), plants, pest management. It's one of the several new books pointing the way towards a more useful concept of "greenhouse." Handsome and well done in every way.* —J. Baldwin

The Complete Greenhouse Book
(Building and Using Greenhouses from Cold Frames to Solar Structures)
Peter Clegg and Derry Watkins
1978; 280 pp.

$9.95 postpaid from:
Garden Way Publishing Company
Charlotte, VT 05545
or Whole Earth Household Store

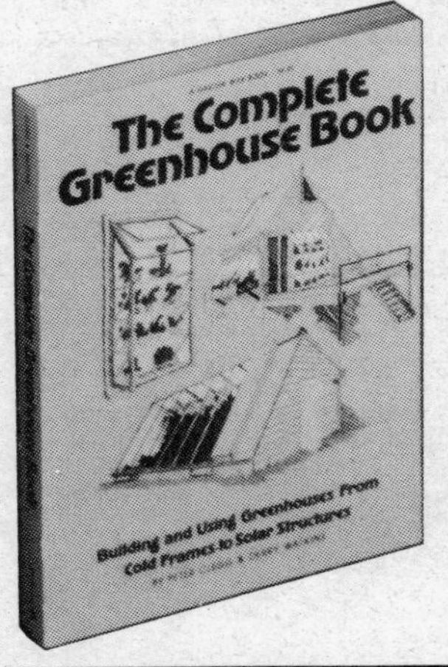

The Solar Greenhouse Book

Every gardener dreams of a year-round harvest, and the best way to get it without moving to Hawaii is with a solar greenhouse. This book has good technical data for the early stages of planning, including assessment of glazing materials, estimating heat loss, and sun path diagrams, as well as construction details and plenty of pictures of completed greenhouses that can't help but give you some new ideas no matter how long you've been designing the project. And when the building is done, there's advice that will reduce considerably your first year trial and error agonies — everything from when seed should be sown to the particular requirements each crop has when it's grown under glass. —Dick Fugett

The Solar Greenhouse Book
James C. McCullagh, Editor
1978; 328 pp.

$9.95 postpaid from:
Rodale Books
33 East Minor
Emmaus, PA 18049
or Whole Earth Household Store

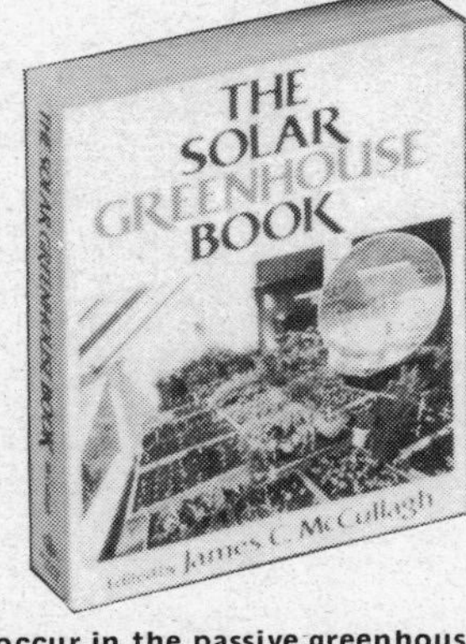

Microclimatic zones can occur in the passive greenhouse. They will change slightly with the seasons: the rear is shaded in the summer and the area near the glazing can become quite cold on winter nights. Circulating the air will reduce temperature differences between regions.

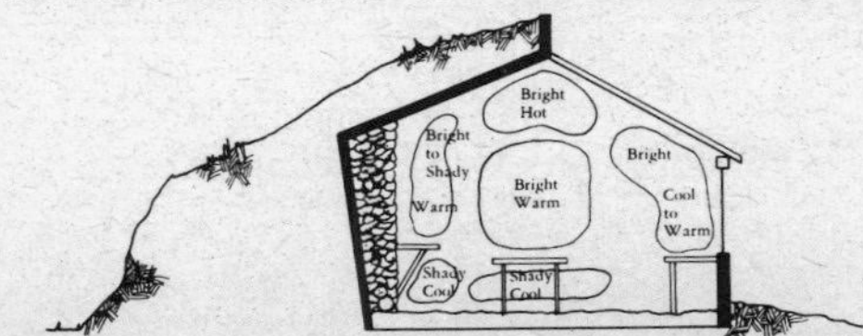

Solar Living and Solar Greenhouse Digest

Any idea whose time has come needs a forum where the latest information can be shared and discussed, and here it is. Early issues are chatty, knowledgeable, useful, and getting better. Bill Yanda is involved, along with many others who have been doing the solar greenhouse bit for some time now. —J. Baldwin
[Suggested by Chris Winne]

Solar Living and Solar Greenhouse Digest
Twila de Vries, Editor

$10/year (6 issues)
from:
Solar Greenhouse Digest
P.O. Box 2626
Flagstaff, AZ 86003

•

Why must ducts always be opaque? Let's treat ourselves to the fun of seeing air zipping along the duct — visually verifying the whole solar heating system is working by the use of transparent ducts.

• Transparent ducts should be used in a greenhouse or living room of a house that has a big, integral south-facing greenhouse and a big thermal mass in the basement.

• Transport hot air from the top of the greenhouse to the thermal mass via a vertical or near vertical transparent duct which contains ribbons, paper streamers, rotable pinwheel whorls or other mobile ornaments.

• As the air travels, the ribbons dance in a colorful manner.

The Glass House

"Greenhouse," that is. Plants generally require much more sophisticated control of their environment than do humans, and so it isn't surprising that horticulturists know more about artificial climate than do architects. This elegant book reveals that much of the knowledge needed for the design of solar houses and "biospheres" has been known for more than 100 years! I was also quite surprised to find out how large some of the indoor agricultural projects were and are; for instance there are more than 17,000 acres of greenhouse in use today in the Netherlands. Mr. Hix doesn't furnish us with thermal performance figures, but he includes a juicy bibliography and a glittering collection of sharp photographs and drawings. A real find for indoor food-raisers and solar house designers. —J. Baldwin
[Suggested by Day Charoudi]

The Glass House
John Hix
1974; 208 pp.

$25 postpaid from:
The MIT Press
28 Carleton Street
Cambridge, MA 02142
or Whole Earth Household Store

Palms in the dome of the winter garden, Laeken Palace, Brussels (1876).

THE RISING SUN
NEIGHBORHOOD NEWSLETTER

If you notice that all the leaders who might make things better get shot you can:

1. Assume their deaths were no coincidence and give up;
2. Spend years proving their deaths were no coincidence and trying to convince others of same;
3. Need leaders less.

Superinsulated Houses and Double-Envelope Houses

William A. Shurcliff is one of those people who does homework for the rest of us, and I'm always glad to see his latest efforts. In this case, he has tackled a controversial subject: do these houses work OK, and also, how do they work? As is his custom, he surveys a number of houses and elicits comments from the owners. Tentative conclusions in this first edition are that superinsulated houses are very fine if designed well, and double-envelope houses are also fine but may work for reasons as yet unproven. For this reason, he is rather reserved in his enthusiasm for double-envelope construction. But draw your own conclusions; the latest facts and figures are there, with his analysis, for you to read all in one place. Many thanks, sir! (Mr. Shurcliff asks that owners of such houses write him of their experiences for future editions.)

—J. Baldwin

Superinsulated Houses and Double-Envelope Houses
(A Preliminary Survey of Principles and Practices)
William A. Shurcliff
1980; 147 pp.

$14 first class postpaid from:
William A. Shurcliff
19 Appleton Street
Cambridge, MA 02138
or Whole Earth Household Store

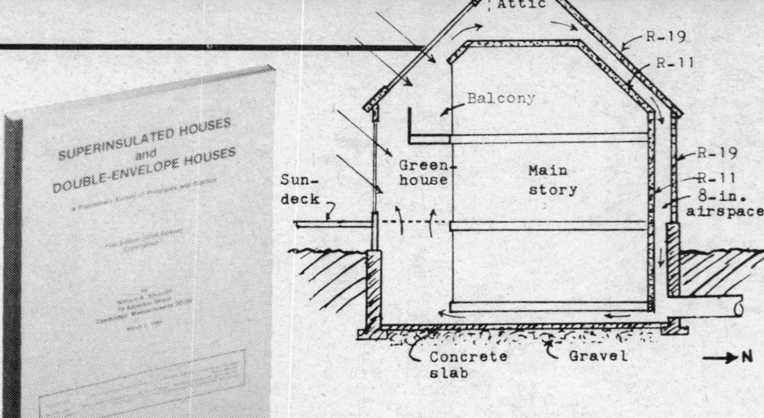

Three-story double-envelope building with 2100 sq. ft. of living area, or 2600 sq. ft. including greenhouse and space below it. Plan dimensions: 33 ft. (E-W) x 22 ft., or 33 ft. x 30 ft. including greenhouse. There are four bedrooms and two bathrooms.

Gutter
Fiberglass (12 in.)
Vent in soffit
Drywall
Vapor barrier
½-in.Thermax between 2x6's
Triple-glazed south window
N
Drywall
Siding
Fiberglass (8½ in.)
Sheathing
Wires
Vapor barrier
Floor
Pipes
Earth
5½ in. fiberglass insulation
Foundation wall (concrete blocks)
2 in. of Styrofoam

Vertical section of south wall

•

HALLMARKS OF A SUPERINSULATED HOUSE

The main distinguishing characteristics, or hallmarks, of a superinsulated house are:

Truly superb insulation. Even at the sills, headers, eaves, window frames, door frames, and electric outlet boxes at least a moderate amount of insulation is provided. In summary, the insulation is thick and thorough.

An almost airtight envelope. Even on windy days the rate of air change is low.

No added thermal mass. No Trombe wall, no water-filled drums, no concrete floors (except basement floor).

No very large south-window area. The amount of direct-gain passive solar heating is modest.

The combined area of windows on west, north, and east is less than the area of south windows. Perhaps only half.

No furnace. There may be some electric heaters or a wood-burning stove, but these are used only rarely.

No large system for distributing heat among the rooms.

No distorted shape of house.

Some corollaries:

There is no big added expense. The costs of the extra insulation and extra care in construction are largely offset by the savings from having no huge area of Thermopane, no huge expensive thermal shutters for huge south windows, no furnace, no big heat distribution system.

The passive solar heating system is almost incidental.

Room humidity remains at least fairly high throughout the winter. Sometimes it may be too high! There is no need for humidifiers (but there may be a need for a dehumidifier or an air-to-air heat-exchanger).

In summer the house usually stays cool automatically, if windows are opened wide each night. Even the south rooms usually stay cool: the area of south windows is small and, in summer, these windows are shaded by the wide eaves.

How to Save Money by Insulating Your Home

In the Bank . . . or Up the Chimney

Lotta books on this subject these days, many overpriced. Here's two priced fairly. The pamphlet will get you started; the fat one will tell you enough to actually do the deed or hire a contractor confidently. It's prepared by the Office of Policy Development and Research, Division of Energy, Building Technology, and Standards, U.S. Department of Housing and Urban Development, better known as HUD. How's that for bureaucracy? Though this book is OK, I personally find the compartmentalization of knowledge and responsibility (response-ability) by our government rather creepy. It makes it virtually impossible for citizens to get into the act at a level below large corporate.

—J. Baldwin

(More on insulation, p. 234.)

How to Save Money by Insulating Your Home
(Practical Instructions and Advice on Doing It Yourself or Hiring a Contractor)
1980; 23 pp.

$.40 postpaid from:
Mineral Insulation Manufacturers Association
328 Springfield Avenue
Summit, NJ 07901

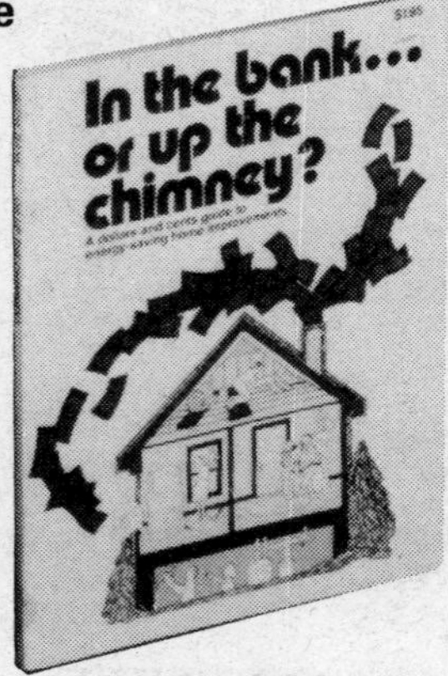

In the Bank . . . or Up the Chimney?
(A Dollars and Cents Guide to Energy-Saving Home Improvements)
HUD
1976, 1980; 73 pp.

$3.95 postpaid from:
Chilton Book Company
Sales Services Department
Chilton Way
Radnor, PA 19089
or Whole Earth Household Store

•

To insulate floors above cold spaces, push the batts or blankets between the floor joists from below, vapor barriers up. To support the insulation, lace wire back and forth among nails spaced about 2 feet apart in the bottoms of the joists. Pieces of blanket cut to size should be fitted, vapor barriers in, along the sill at the ends of the floor area.

—How to Save Money by Insulating Your Home

•

Once or twice a year, drain a bucket of water out of the bottom of the heater tank — sometimes it's full of sediment. The sediment *insulates* the water in the tank from the burner flame — *that* wastes energy.

—In the Bank . . . or Up the Chimney

Windows

A new approach to technology transfer. An attractive irregular periodical intended to bring together all aspects of energy efficient windows: products and inventions available or needed, research opportunities and results, codes and legislation. Another purpose: "bringing 'grass roots' communications to the attention of those in the complex structure of federal, state, and local energy programs." If it works, and it will only if people interact with the publication (as they do with **CoEvolution***) it could do more to facilitate energy saving than a myriad of R&D or demonstrating projects. Government money well spent. Good going, LBL & DOE.*

—Alan Kalker

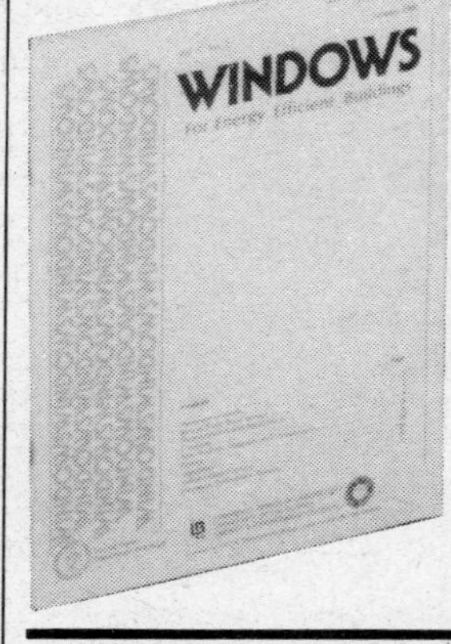

Windows for Energy Efficient Buildings

free from:
Energy Efficient Window Program
c/o Stephen Selkowitz
Bldg. 90 Rm. 3111
Lawrence Berkeley Lab.
1 Cyclotron Road
Berkeley, CA 94720

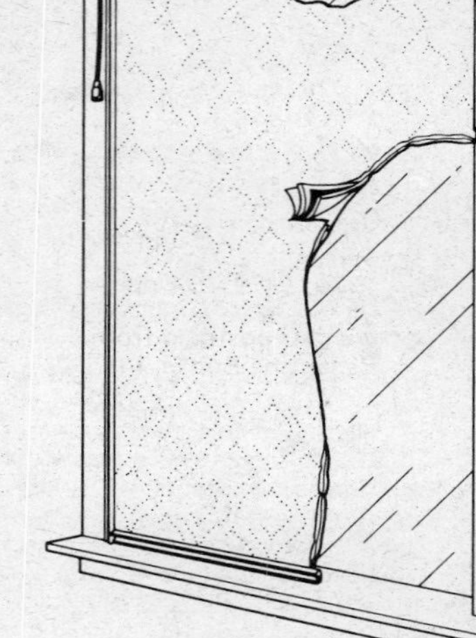

Window Quilt, Appropriate Technology Corporation, P.O. Box 975, Brattleboro, VT 05301, 802/257-1773.

Improving Energy Efficiency In Buildings

Proper management of a building can greatly reduce its energy needs. This book is a manager's guide to auditing the building's energy use, its leaks, and its energy-eating flaws. A good bit of the book is devoted to what to do about what the audit finds. Though intended more for factories and large structures than houses, the same principles apply. If you have a big building in your life, a look at this professional text will probably save you lots of money.

—J. Baldwin

Improving Energy Efficiency in Buildings
Dennis Landsberg and Ronald Stewart
1980; 321 pp.

$9.95 postpaid from:
State University of New York Press
State University Plaza
Albany, NY 12246
or Whole Earth Household Store

Distribution Of Electric Energy In A Typical Office Building

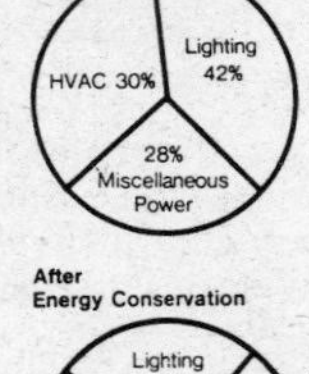

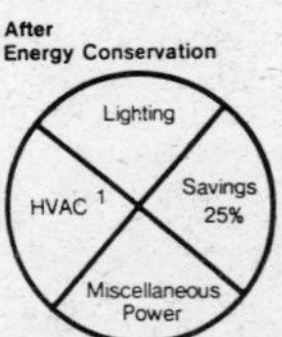

(HVAC is Heating Ventilating and Air Conditioning.)

Advertisement for the Climax solar water heater, 1892. The price of this, Kemp's smallest unit, had just dropped from $25 to $15.

A Golden Thread

The past gives permission to the future, vaulting hysterias of Nowness. It's the difference between some kid intoning solar slogans and granddad remarking that yeah, well, why in hell do you think he built the family's Cape Cod salt box with the main rooms on the south side?

***CoEvolution** has been party to the making of this book — we ran Butti & Perlin's surprising history of solar water heaters in California around 1900 in Fall '77, solar water heaters in Florida around 1930 in Spring '78, and a stroll past 2500 years of solar invention in Winter '79. It's wonderful stuff, not only for the permission and fascination in it, but also as a peerless source of design ideas.*
—SB

A Golden Thread
(2500 Years of Solar Architecture and Technology)
Ken Butti and John Perlin
1980; 304 pp.

$15.95 postpaid from:
Cheshire Books
514 Bryant Street
Palo Alto, CA 94301
or Whole Earth Household Store

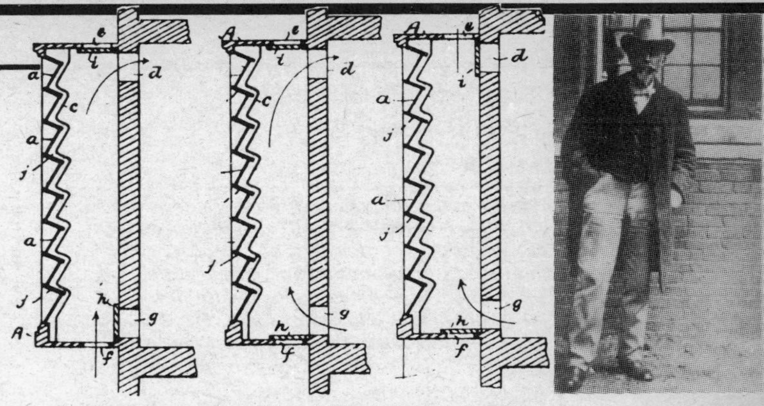

Professor Edward S. Morse (right). Patent drawings of his first solar heater, 1881 (left), showing three different modes of operation.

•

Some of the technical lessons of solar energy found in **A Golden Thread** are still being relearned today. The drawbacks of high-temperature solar concentrators for driving heat engines were discovered almost a century ago. These same drawbacks are today leading many of our best analysts to turn from solar "power towers" to low-technology, low-temperature systems like solar ponds with Rankine cycle engines. Likewise, it is today the conventional wisdom to advocate extensive use of some of the more expensive solar technologies in remote rural areas and in the Third World — where conventional energy costs are prohibitively high. Exactly the same logic led to the pioneering early work in solar irrigation pumping in the American Southwest and in the French and British colonies of North Africa. Once again we have come full circle.
—Amory Lovins (introduction)

Direct Use of the Sun's Energy

The best book on Solar Energy that I know of.

Any curious and intelligent person can learn a great deal about our planet and ourselves by reading this book about ways of using sunlight. There are many numbers in the book but the math never goes beyond 8th grade arithmetic. The book is clear and simple whether talking about heating water —

For general domestic use of hot water for bathing and washing dishes a temperature of 135°F (57°C) is considered adequate and 20 gal per person per day is a reasonable consumption. In many sunny climates these requirements can be met with an insulated storage tank and solar radiation absorber which has an area of 0.75 ft^2 gal^{-1} of hot water. A family of four would need a tank of 80 gal and a solar absorber of 60 ft^2.

or photochemical reactions —

The photo dissociation of iodine (I_2) molecules into atoms absorbs most of the visible light of the sun with a considerable amount of energy which cannot be retained. It is immediately evolved as heat during the exposure to light.

I read the book on a Greyhound bus in Texas in 1966 and it has changed my life and my way of thinking.
—Steve Baer

Direct Use of the Sun's Energy
Farrington Daniels
1964, 1979; 271 pp.

$2.50 postpaid from:
Ballantine Books, Inc.
414 East Golf
Des Plaines, IL 60016
or Whole Earth Household Store

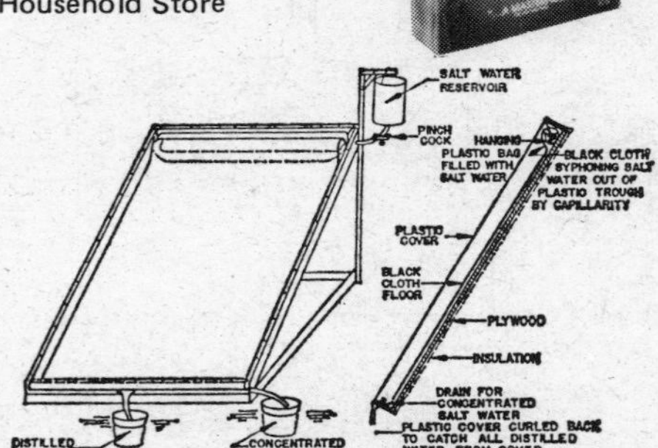

32. Tilted plastic still of simple construction.

Thermal Shutters & Shades
Movable Insulation

When the energy crunch came in the early seventies, and people began to realize how much heat can leak out a window on a cold night, one quick solution was to build houses with fewer windows. Like many instant answers it was a bad choice, because windows also let heat and light into a house, and are a big part of what makes a house livable or not.

A better solution can be found in either of these new books. They are now the state of the art in a rapidly evolving field. Shutters, curtains, hinged or movable panels, interior or exterior installation — the range of choices is large, and the energy saved can easily pay for the cost of either book.
—Richard Nilsen

Thermal Shutters & Shades
(Over 100 Schemes for Reducing Heat Loss Through Windows)
William A. Shurcliff
1980; 238 pp.

$12.95 postpaid from:
Brick House Publishing Company
3 Main Street
Andover, MA 01810
or Whole Earth Household Store

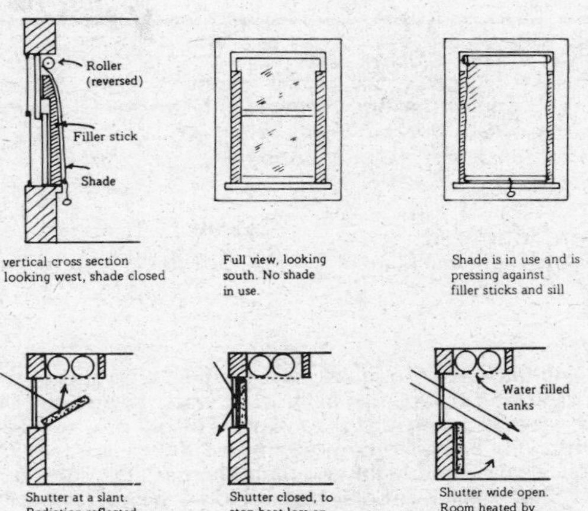

—Thermal Shutters & Shades

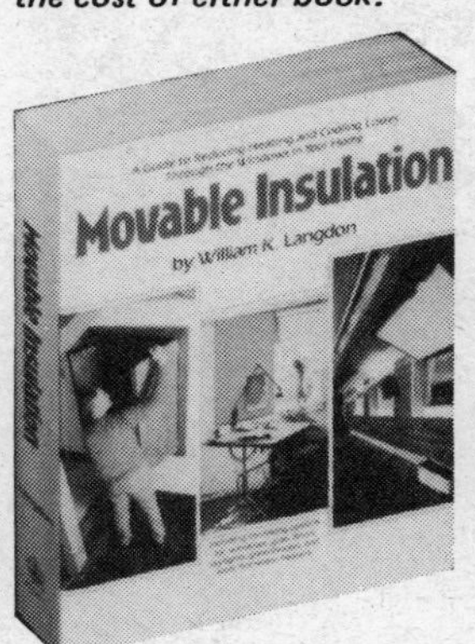

Movable Insulation
(A Guide to Reducing Heating and Cooling Losses Through the Windows in Your Home)
William K. Langdon
1980; 379 pp.

$9.95 postpaid from:
Rodale Books
33 East Minor
Emmaus, PA 18049
or Whole Earth Household Store

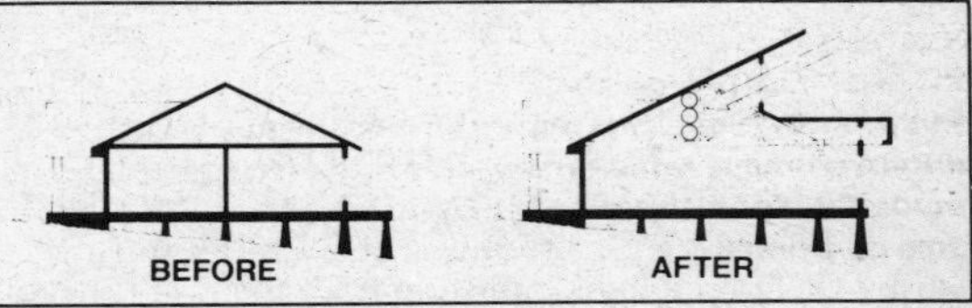

Solar clerestory retrofit.

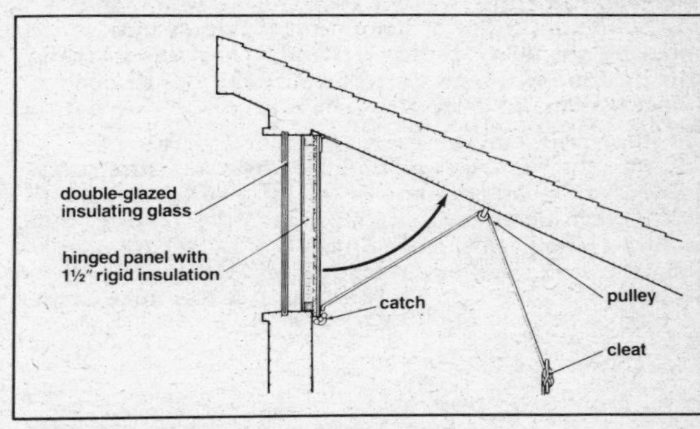

A top-hinged clerestory shutter.
—Movable Insulation

Solar Energy Digest

Though I still consider this newsletter to be a bit skinny for the money, it is where you often hear of new developments first. Also, the editor puts the money to good use in his research and lobbying efforts. It's been coming our way since 1973, and I always look forward to the new issue. I must have sent away for dozens of things I first saw here.
—J. Baldwin

Solar Energy Digest
$35 /year (12 issues)
from:
Solar Energy Digest
P.O. Box 17776
San Diego, CA 92117

•

A solar refrigerator with no moving parts is now available from The Zeopower Company, 75 Middlesex Avenue, Natick, MA 01760, (617) 655-4125.

The 8-square-foot solar collector of the unit is filled with zeolite, a silicon mineral, which performs the same function as the compressor in an electric refrigerator. When the zeolite is heated by the sun, water vapor is driven out of the collector, condensing in an outside finned cooling coil and falling as a liquid into the storage tank evaporator inside the refrigerator. At night, the zeolite in the solar collector cools to the temperature of the outside air and is ready to absorb the water that was driven off during the day. At the same time, water in the storage tank inside the refrigerator absorbs heat from the interior of the refrigerator and any food therein, turning the water to vapor again. At the low pressure in the system, the water boils below 32°F. and freezes itself.

The zeolite absorbs the water vapor from the storage tank-evaporator and is ready to repeat the day-time part of the cycle again. During the day, slowly melting ice in the storage tank-evaporator provides continuous cooling inside the refrigerator.

Since the hermetically sealed cooling system has no moving parts, it will operate trouble-free for years, using only the power of the sun.

The refrigerator has a capacity of four cubic feet and has an ice-making capacity of 15 pounds per day. It will continue cooling during three days of bad weather after a series of three or more sunny days.

THE RISING SUN
NEIGHBORHOOD NEWSLETTER

How I Became a Good Listener

The year after I graduated from high school, I didn't go to college and I didn't get a job. Naturally people kindly or cattily wondered what I was doing. Since all I was doing was hanging around my parents' house feeling bad about myself, I didn't want to talk about it. So I got good at thinking of leading questions and follow up questions to ask people what they were doing.

The best defense is a good offense and sometimes I would have whole conversations with people without them asking what my plans were. Coincidentally, I found out that most people have something interesting about them and not what you would have expected and if you listen long enough and ask enough questions, they'll tell you.

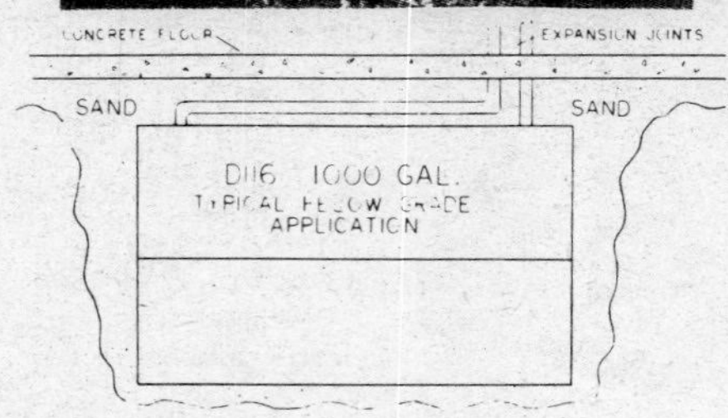

The Solar Age Resource Book
Solar Age Catalog
The Guide

All from the outstanding **Solar Age** *magazine people (p. 183), the* **Resource Book** *(1979) and the* **Catalog** *(1977) are anthologies of articles on solar savvy and well-annotated (though not comparatively evaluated) solar products. Very fine work, highly useful for intelligent shopping in a booming field.* **The Guide** *we haven't seen, but it is described as a Solar Products Specifications Guide for solar professionals, listing 500 products in 35 categories. For your $165 you also get a year of bi-monthly updates.* —SB

The Solar Age Resource Book
(The Complete Guidebook to the Dramatic Power of Solar Energy)
Martin McPhillips, Editor
1979; 242 pp.

$9.95 postpaid from:
Everest House
Box 978
Edison, NJ 08817

Solar Age Catalog
(A Guide to Solar Energy Knowledge and Materials)
The Staff of Solar Age Magazine
1977; 232 pp.

$8.50 postpaid

The Guide
(Solar Products Specifications Guide)
The Staff of Solar Age Magazine
1980; 500 pp.
(2 volumes, plus 6 updates /yr.)

$165 postpaid both from:
Solar Age
Church Hill
Harrisville, NH 03450

•

Solar Vent, Model 11706 — Revere Chemical Corp., 30887 Carter Street, Solon, OH 44139; Mal Hansen (216) 248-0606. Solar Vent

Solar Vent is a one-way roof vent that utilizes solar energy to pump trapped moisture from the roof assembly and eject it into the atmosphere. The one-way, elastomeric inlet valve inside Solar Vent's insulated stem sucks roof moisture into the vent's transparent solar dome. An aluminum collector plate turns the dome into a high-pressure chamber, absorbing the sun's heat and increasing the pressure within to force the moist air out through a one-way exhaust valve.

Features: one-way valves will not allow moisture to re-enter the roofing assembly. Removes moisture many times faster than ordinary vents. Installation requirements/considerations: area must get at least 6-hr of direct sunlight a day. Install one SolarVent/1,000 sq. ft. Availability: 3-wk. Suggested retail price: $49.76.

—**The Solar Age Resource Book**

↑

Thermal Storage Vaults — Manufactured by: American Solarize Inc., 19 Vandeventer Ave., Princeton, NJ 08540; Joe Beudis; phone: (609) 924-5645.

Vaults are made of lightweight cellular aggregates, vermiculite cement, and other additives. Can be used for rock storage or liquid tubes or be filled directly with liquid. Needs no other insulation. Features and options: standard sizes or custom made. Installation requirements/considerations: suitable for above or below ground applications. Guarantee/warranty: on manufacturing defects and failure to meet warranty specifications. Manufacturer's technical services: design service available, field supervision when necessary. Availability: f.o.b. from factory. Price: $250 to $6,000.

—**Solar Age Catalog**

•

One square foot of sunlight must be spread over several square feet of masonry if you want to be able to remain in the room while it is being charged with heat.
Some methods:

1. Have the wall at a very oblique angle to the sun.
2. Bounce the sun off a white wall first and spread it out over a wider area.
3. Admit the sun in patches that sweep the floor and walls as the sun moves — no one area is then exposed for any great length of time.

Of course, one needn't take these precautions too seriously. There may well be parts of a room where it is fine to let a slab floor climb in temperature to 110°F during a winter day.

—Steve Baer, **Solar Age Catalog**

•

A solar heating system can only be judged on its cost-effectiveness, and cost-effectiveness is a function of an immense number of variables. There are four component areas that decide the eventual performance of the system. Any mistake within one of these will cause the economic failure or premature aging of the system. *Collectors, heat exchangers, heat transfer fluids,* and *insulation* are the critical components.

—**The Solar Age Resource Book**

People's Solar Sourcebook

Starts with an unusually clear and comprehensive scan of all the kinds of solar systems now available. Then a 1979 roster of solar tax benefits listed by state. The rest is full-page reproductions of manufacturers' literature on their solar products — no annotation. —SB

People's Solar Sourcebook
(Buyer's Catalogue of Solar Energy Products)
1980; 352 pp.

$5 postpaid from:
Solar Usage Now
450 East Tiffin Street
Bascom, OH 44809
or Whole Earth Household Store

HOT WATER ROOM HEATER

FOR LOW TEMP. WATER

Magnetic Drive Coupling Between Pump and Motor - No Water Seals or Packing Connections to Leak - No Belts on Gears to Wear Out.

Cross Section of Unit

CABINET SIZE

NEW
$342.00
#6110

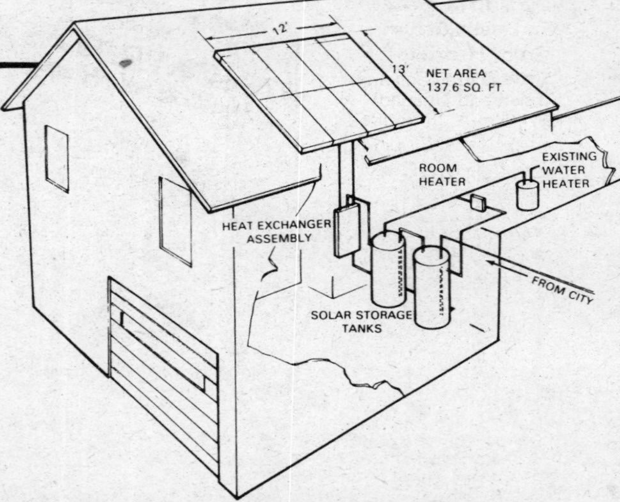

Solar Unlimited

Typical of a trend towards solar supply stores, this one stocks a wide variety. Not so typical is that the quality appears to be first class. (Another supplier is Solar Components, p. 193). —J. Baldwin

Solar Unlimited
Catalog/Technical Manual

$2.50 postpaid from:
Solar Unlimited
Box 337
Clay, KY 42404

→

Heating Capacity: In many parts of the country, the Model 8DSSZ will heat the domestic water and up to 500 square feet of living area the majority of the time in traditionally insulated homes: up to 1000 square feet in "passive solar" and highly insulated homes. Consult your Solar Shop Dealer or Solar Unlimited for heating capacity and energy savings specifics for your home and location.

The First and Second Passive Solar Catalogs

David Bainbridge, highly active in the Davis, California solar enterprises, is assembling a sequence of catalogs collecting the gathering wisdom and products of passive solar goodness. Sort of uncritical. —SB

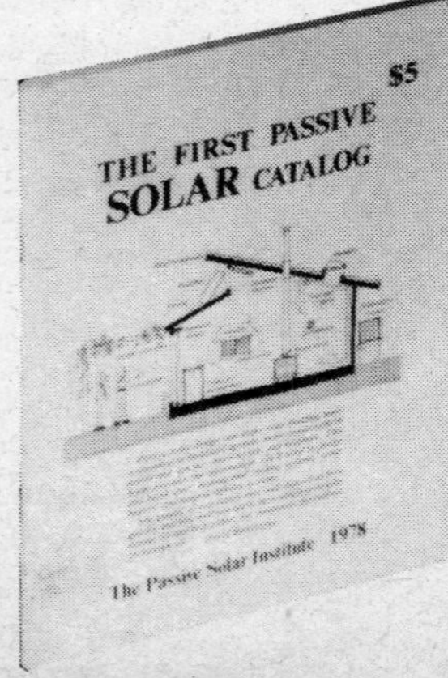

The First Passive Solar Catalog
David Bainbridge
1978; 72 pp.

$5 postpaid

The Second Passive Solar Catalog
David Bainbridge
1980; 112 pp.

$12.50 postpaid both from:
The Passive Solar Institute
P.O. Box 722
Davis, CA 95616

This efficiency is reflected in reduced costs of lighting using skylights rather than artificial lights, Table 6. This is particularly important in this era of rising energy prices. A life cycle comparison of lighting cost makes natural lighting look even better.

TABLE 6: COMPARATIVE COSTS OF SKYLIGHTS AND FLOURESCENT LIGHTS

	Source of Illumination	
Cost Consideration	Skylights[1]	Fluorescent Light Units[2]
First cost of lighting installation (less lamps)	$480.00	$657.00
Uniform annual cost of recovering first cost at 3% for an operating period of 25 years	27.50	37.75
Annual cost for insurance at 1.2% of first cost	5.76	7.89
Annual cost for lamps	- - -	8.72
Annual labor costs for cleaning and relamping	3.00	10.80
Annual power cost	- - -	59.24
Total annual lighting cost	$ 36.72	$124.40
Annual cost per foot-candle	.74	2.43

[1]Six skylights, 38 x 36 in., 43% transmission with louver shade; average lighting level: 49 foot-candles.

[2]Eighteen fluorescent units, two 40-watt lamps, 45 degree louvers; average lighting level: 51 foot-candles.

The additional weight of collector panels.

How to Buy Solar Heating without Getting Burnt

The inimitable Malcolm Wells (of building underground fame, p. 218 - 219 and p. 240) takes us through a solar basic training course that includes debunking, dejargoning, demystifying and delight. His office conducted a poll of 100 solar homeowners to see what their experience has been. The results show up the joys and the things that failed in detail. The authors go so far as to present model contracts in case you wish solar equipment built. All this has been sorely needed for a long time, and I am happy to say that it has been done right. If you intend to buy or build solar hardware, this is necessary reading if only for the discussion of things to avoid — information not easily available anyplace else at this time! Presented with usual Rodale quality too.

—J. Baldwin

How to Buy Solar Heating Without Getting Burnt
(A Consumer's Guide to Choosing, Financing, and Installing Solar House Heating Equipment)
Malcolm Wells and Irwin Spetgang
1978; 272 pp.

$6.95 postpaid from:
Rodale Books
33 East Minor
Emmaus, PA 18049
or Whole Earth Household Store

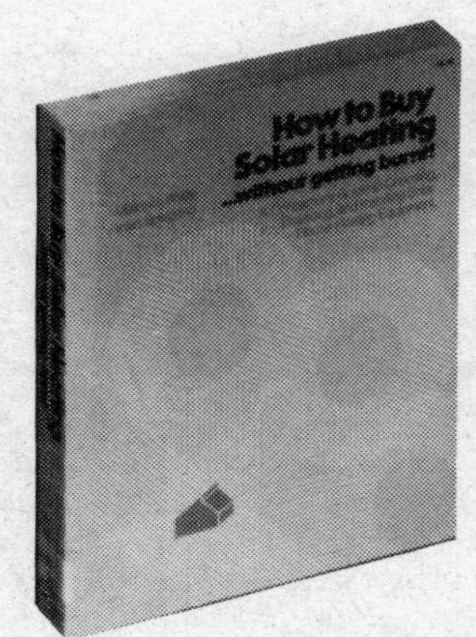

Build Your Own Solar Water Heater

Um hm, another one. I commend this to you prospective water heater builders because it's written with experience, not just theory, as the basis for the text. As such, it is typical of a second generation of books about solar thingamajigs. However, it is better than typical in quality and usefulness. Many little essentials you don't see discussed in the older books are discussed in detail. For instance, do you know how to load the pipes for the first time? A few years ago, it took me many hours of cussing to find that one out. Here, a paragraph tells how. So. Another good (or at least better) one from Garden Way.

—J. Baldwin

Build Your Own Solar Water Heater
Stu Campbell with Doug Taff
1978; 109 pp.

$7.95 postpaid from:
Garden Way Publishing Company
Charlotte, VT 05545
or Whole Earth Household Store

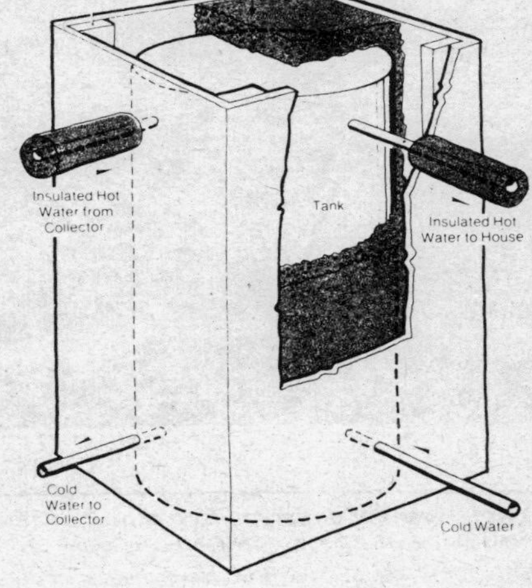

One of the best ways to insulate a solar hot water tank is to build a plywood insulation bin around it. This can be filled with styrofoam beads, sheets of urethane foam, blown cellulose insulation, or foamed-in-place insulation.

5 Water leaks (or leaks of antifreeze-treated water). "Hoses leaked at panel couplings on roof." "Ice formed between panels because covers weren't installed over joints. Ice pressure broke fittings." "They've got to solve the expansion problems. The collectors can go from 0° in the morning to boiling by noon." "The collector-cover caulking got hard and leaked." "Trickle systems are notorious leakers." "Plastic gallon jugs (for heat storage in air systems) will leak if stacked. You've got to stand them on individual shelves."

New Inventions in Low-Cost Solar Heating

No less than a hundred unusual designs, mostly unproven, but all with considerable potential, are presented with wit and skill by the now famous Dr. Shurcliff. I won't presume to describe anything; you'll be wanting to buy this book anyway if solar tinkering is your game. Of all the solar books I've looked at in the past few years, this is the most exciting by far; actually hard to put down once you start reading. Highly recommended.

—J. Baldwin

New Inventions in Low-Cost Solar Heating
(100 Daring Schemes Tried and Untried)
William A. Shurcliff
1979; 293 pp.

$12 postpaid from:
Brick House Publishing Company
Three Main Street
Andover, MA 01810
or Whole Earth Household Store

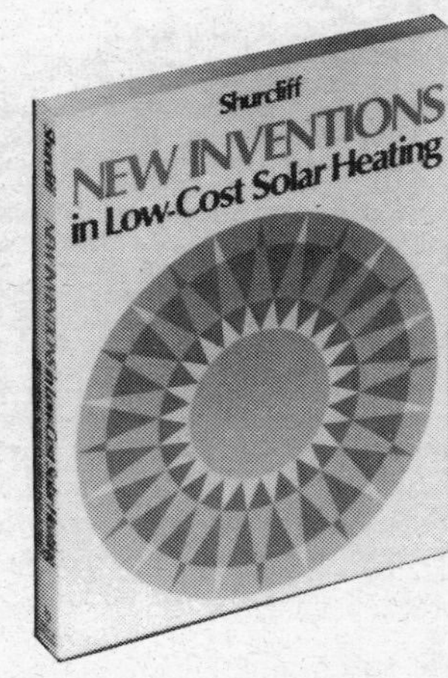

•

Bin-of-Stones Employing Three Sizes of Stones in Three Zones to Increase Thermal Capacity and Pneumatic Conductance

Proposed Scheme

Divide the bin-of-stones into three zones and use different size stones in each. In the top, middle, and bottom zones, use stones having average diameters of 1 in., 3 in., and 5 in., respectively. The hot air from the collector is blower-driven *downward* through the bin; thus, passing first through the quantity of small stones and last through the large stones. Thermal performance is improved and the requirement on blower power is reduced. . . .

The top zone sees most of the action — it plays the most important role. In midwinter, when the amount of energy in the bin is small, the solar energy collected in a period of bright sunshine is delivered to the top zone of the bin, and when the rooms next need heat, heat is extracted from this top zone. Again and again it is the top zone that is active.

The bottom zone is seldom active. Usually it takes up energy only when the two superior zones are already fairly full of energy, which occurs mainly in fall and spring. The bottom zone may be regarded as a kind of stand-by component, storing energy only when there is near-surplus.

Yet the pneumatic conductance of the bottom zone is no greater than that of the top zone.

In summary, the bottom zone is much less useful, yet imposes the *same* burden on the blower.

ASHRAE

When you hear someone say "ash-ree," they're talking about the American Society of Heating, Refrigeration, and Air Conditioning Engineers, Inc., an outfit that publishes a number of handbooks and engineering references as well as establishing industry standards. (Whew!) Well, ASHRAE has long been where you look it up when you are dealing with heating and cooling, including solar. Two of their books may prove useful to you if you are designing solar hardware: **ASHRAE Handbook Fundamentals** *(1977) contains data and theory needed to design systems and hardware to heat and cool buildings. One chapter, for instance, deals with calculating heat transfer through windows. Others give you the numbers for mass flow, rates of flow, etc. All stuff for engineers and rather difficult to use if you do not have the math background.*

Applications of Solar Energy for Heating and Cooling of Buildings *offers the technical background necessary for the development of low temperature solar energy applications. This is for "active systems." Both of these books are highly technical, but also are the most authoritative. When you "need the numbers", here they are.*

—J. Baldwin

ASHRAE Handbook
(1977 Fundamentals)
ASHRAE Staff
1977; 748 pp.

$42 postpaid

Applications of Solar Energy for Heating and Cooling of Buildings
Richard C. Jordan and Benjamin Y.H. Liu, Editors
1977; 206 pp.

$9 postpaid
both from:
ASHRAE
Publication Sales Dept.
345 East 47th Street
New York, NY 10017

N

Three-function multi-layer quilt assembly that can be (1) rolled up to allow passive solar heating of the room, (2) rolled down and expanded to constitute an indoor air-type collector, or (3) pressed against the adjacent window at night to insulate it.

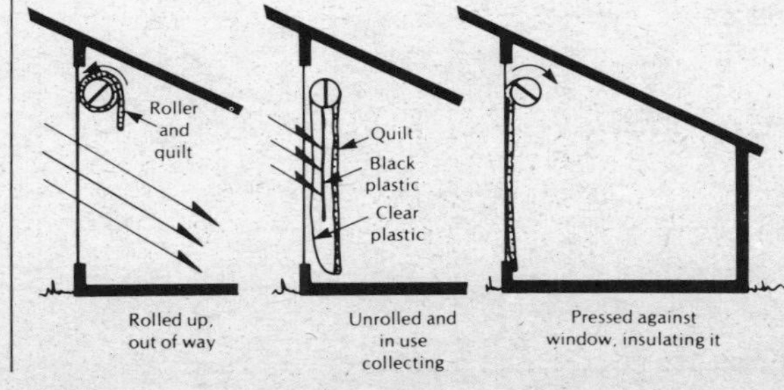

Sun Angles for Design

There are a number of charts and devices available for easing the often maddening task of finding where the shadows will fall on March 3 at 10 a.m. This chart set appears to be one of the easiest to use; the consequence of being set up in a way that is basically intuitive instead of requiring mental knot-tying. The book is printed a bit too small for my eyes, but enlarged charts for your area are available at reasonable cost. Of all the boo-boos I've witnessed amongst the solar builders, improperly guessed orientation is the most common. No excuse now, though a prudent builder might benefit from testing a model too. From the equator to 60° North Latitude.

—J. Baldwin

Sun Angles for Design
Robert Bennett
1978; 77 pp.

$5 postpaid

Enlarged charts

$2.50 each
both from:
Robert Bennett
6 Snowden Road
Bala Cynwyd, PA 19004

37°N to 39°N LATITUDE

Athens, Greece
Carbondale, Illinois
Cedar City, Utah
Charlottesville, Virginia
Colorado Springs, Colorado
Dodge City, Kansas
Evansville, Indiana
Izmir, Turkey
Jefferson City, Missouri
Lexington, Kentucky
Lisbon, Portugal
Livermore, California
Louisville, Kentucky
Oakland, California
Petaluma, California
Ponta Delgada, Azores
Portsmouth, Ohio
Pueblo, Colorado
Rezaiyeh, Iran
Richmond, Virginia
Sacramento, California
Salisbury, Maryland
San Francisco, California
San Jose, California
Seoul, Korea
Sevilla, Spain
Sicily, Italy
St. Louis, Missouri
Tonopah, Nevada
Washington, D.C.
Wichita, Kansas

BENNETT SUN ANGLE CHART

North 0 — East 90 — South 180 — West 270 — North 360

SOLAR ALTITUDE (Degrees) — Zenith — Horizon

SOLAR AZIMUTH (Degrees)

38° NORTH LATITUDE

THE RISING SUN
NEIGHBORHOOD NEWSLETTER

When Kathy was with draft avoiders in Canada, they all got sure the horrible repression and falling apart was coming and they bought guns and went out to a field to practice. Kathy was the only one who had ever shot a gun before and she wouldn't. She was from Wisconsin. They were from the East Coast.

ZOMEWORKS

WHILE THE GOVERNMENT IN ITS WISDOM lays multimillion dollar contracts on space hardware firms to try to create good solar ideas, Steve Baer and his innovative Zomeworkers manage to come up with the good ideas that actually work. They do it without government largesse (though not without interference). I think that the attitude exemplified by these people is as important as the products they come up with. They currently offer a selection of proven hardware and plans. I'm personally familiar with much of this stuff and hold Zomeworks in the highest esteem. Here's what they're up to:
—J. Baldwin

Big Fin (TM)

The most hot water per dollar, midst a chorus of argh, why-didn't-I-think-of-that-myself from the solar proletariat. With commercial solar hot water heaters costing around $2000, the Big Fin looks good at about $125 per person in the family or $600, let's say. There is, of course, a catch: you have to already have a greenhouse attached to your house. If you do, you've already furnished the glazing and the case, which is a large part of the cost of a conventional design. Simple, huh? Maddening, even. *—J. Baldwin*

(More on greenhouses, p. 185.)

Big Fin Greenhouse Collectors
8' x 8"
$26 each plus crating and shipping

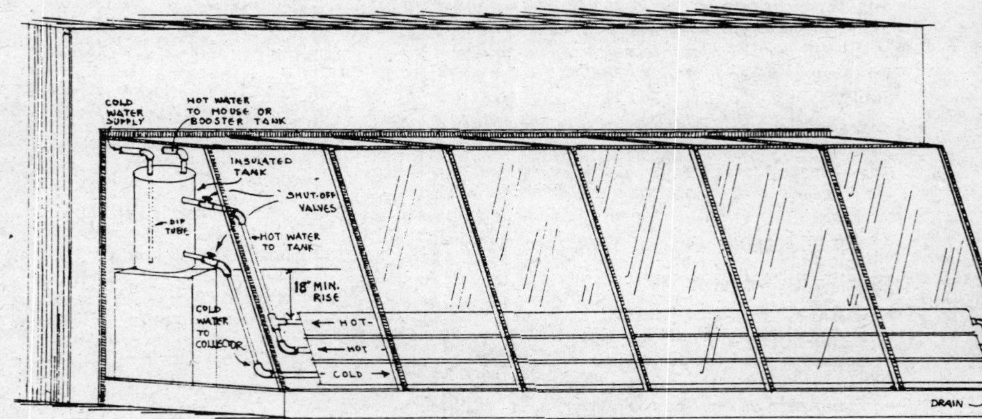

Beadwall® self-insulating window panels

Insulating foam beads are blown into the cavity between two window panels to insulate it at night or whenever it is desired to block heat escape through the glass. You can buy the complete system, or you can build it yourself (see plans). Not only do Beadwall window panels work well, they are fascinating to watch. I once observed about 100 people transfixed by the windows filling at the airport in Aspen, Colorado. *—J. Baldwin*

Beadwall
(Self-insulating window panels and components)
$15 - $25/ sq. ft.
plus shipping

Skylid® louvers

"Giant Venetian blinds" might be a useful way to imagine these shutters that open or close according to the sunlight falling on the operating cylinders that subtly shift their balance. Better than double glazed windows, the Skylid louvers let in more winter sun and keep out the unwanted summer sun (by reflecting it). *—J. Baldwin*

$14 - $30/sq. ft.
plus shipping

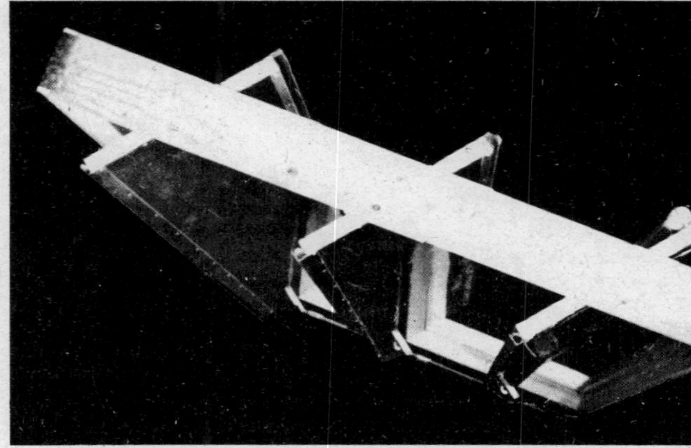

Information on any of the Zomeworks products shown on these pages
free from:
Zomeworks
P.O. Box 712
Albuquerque, NM 87103

PLANS

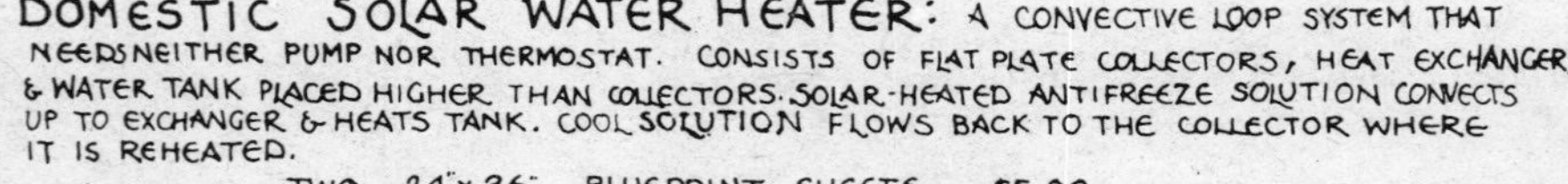

DOMESTIC SOLAR WATER HEATER: A CONVECTIVE LOOP SYSTEM THAT NEEDS NEITHER PUMP NOR THERMOSTAT. CONSISTS OF FLAT PLATE COLLECTORS, HEAT EXCHANGER, & WATER TANK PLACED HIGHER THAN COLLECTORS. SOLAR-HEATED ANTIFREEZE SOLUTION CONVECTS UP TO EXCHANGER & HEATS TANK. COOL SOLUTION FLOWS BACK TO THE COLLECTOR WHERE IT IS REHEATED.

TWO 24"×36" BLUEPRINT SHEETS, $5.00

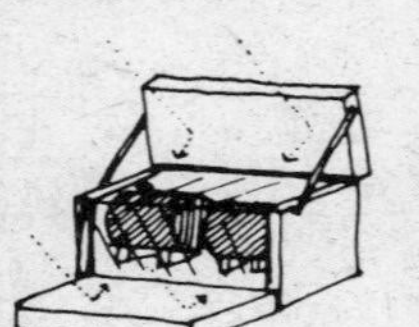

BREADBOX & PRO HEATER PLANS

THE BREADBOX WATER HEATER CONSISTS OF 2 HORIZONTAL TANKS IN A DOUBLE-GLAZED BOX WHOSE LID & FRONT OPEN AS REFLECTORS DURING THE DAY & CLOSE AS INSULATION AT NIGHT. IT CAN SIT ON A ROOF; PLANS INCLUDE A REMOTE-CONTROL DEVICE.
THE PRO HEATER IS AN UPRIGHT TANK INSIDE A GLAZED COVER WITH AN INSULATED COVER WHICH IS PUT ON AT NIGHT AND REMOVED IN THE MORNING. SIMPLE REFLECTORS INCREASE THE HEAT GAIN. MUCH GENERAL INFORMATION ABOUT SIMPLE WATER HEATING METHODS IS ALSO INCLUDED.

TWO 24" × 36" BLUEPRINT SHEETS, $5.00

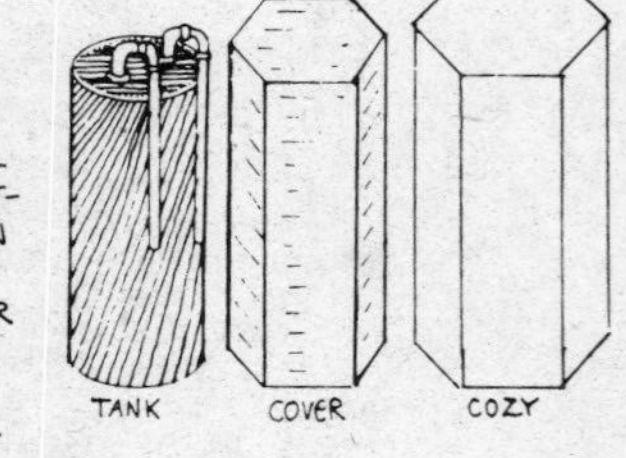

DRUMWALL: A DIRECT GAIN SOLAR HEATING SYSTEM USING WATER-FILLED 55 GAL. DRUMS FOR HEAT STORAGE. PLANS SHOW METHODS FOR STACKING DRUMS & BUILDING INSULATED REFLECTOR DOORS & INCLUDE A DETAILED DISCUSSION OF METHODS FOR CALCULATING THE SYSTEM'S EFFICIENCY.

TWO 24" × 36" BLUEPRINT SHEETS, $5.00

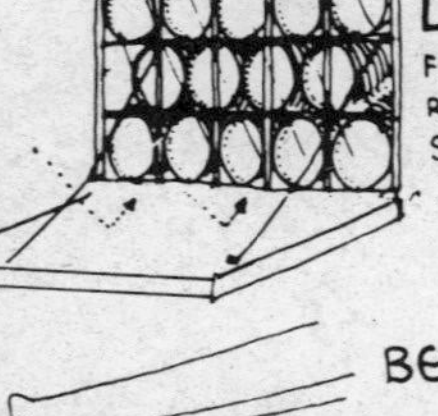

BEADWALL® SELF-INSULATING WINDOWS:

AN INSULATING SYSTEM IN WHICH A MOTOR-STORAGE UNIT CHARGED WITH EXPANDED POLYSTYRENE BEADS FILLS & EMPTIES THE SPACE BETWEEN TWO LAYERS OF GLASS.

SEVEN 18" × 24" SHEETS, $15.00

Desk-top sun-angle calculator

"Shows sun paths and altitude/azimuth for any day and hour at any latitude. Mirror in base permits calculation of shading patterns. Solid mahogany, brass fittings."
—J. Baldwin

Desk-top Sun-angle Calculator
$63.50 postpaid

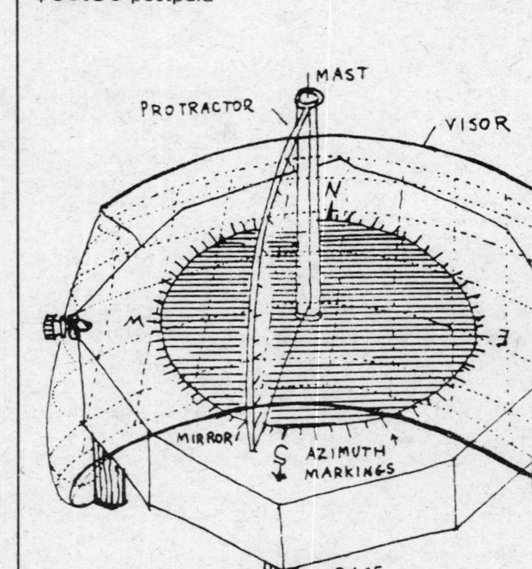

66 Gallon glass-lined water tank

42" × 80" double glazed acrylic dome skylight.

Adjustable aluminum reflector wit. mahogany struts + aluminum & stainless steel fittings

Add $150 crating charge per complete unit if you want the skylight water heater shipped.

Skylight pre-heater

Transform a skylight into a hot water pre-heater for your existing hot water heater. This is done with an adjustable reflector over the skylight, and a black tank under the skylight as the pre-heater. You still get skylight from the skylight too. —J. Baldwin

Skylight Pre-heater
$835 plus shipping

Domestic solar heater

A convective loop (no pumps) hot water heater system similar to the one they sell plans for. This system will work where temperatures go below freezing. —J. Baldwin

Domestic Solar Heater
(passive)
$900 plus shipping
(active)
$1125 plus shipping

THE DOMESTIC SOLAR WATER HEATER

66 gallon glass-lined tank with integral heat exchanger:		$300.
2 17 ft.^{2} collectors glazed with iron-free glass @ $230.	:	460.
Expansion tank @ $25 + pressure valve @ $10	:	35.
TOTAL	:	795. + tax

Non-toxic Antifreeze : $7.00/gallon
Optional electric back up element + thermostat $20.

If collectors are to be shipped, add $100. per pair crating charge.

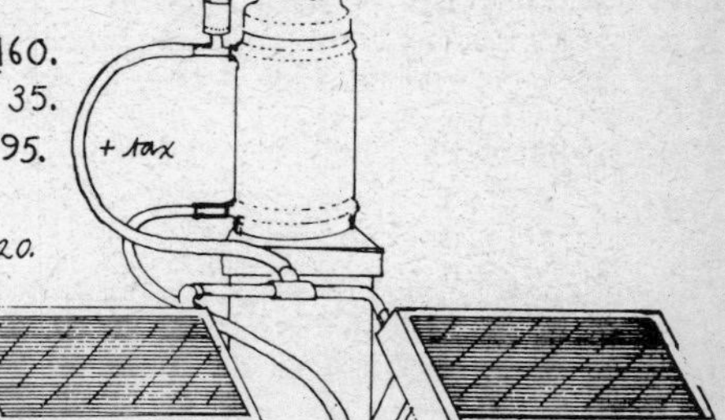

Nightwall® Clips and Nightwall® Spring Clips

Little stick-on magnetic clips and spring clips that enable you to affix foam boards equipped with matching clips directly to the glass. Cheap, simple and effective, especially for retrofit. —J. Baldwin

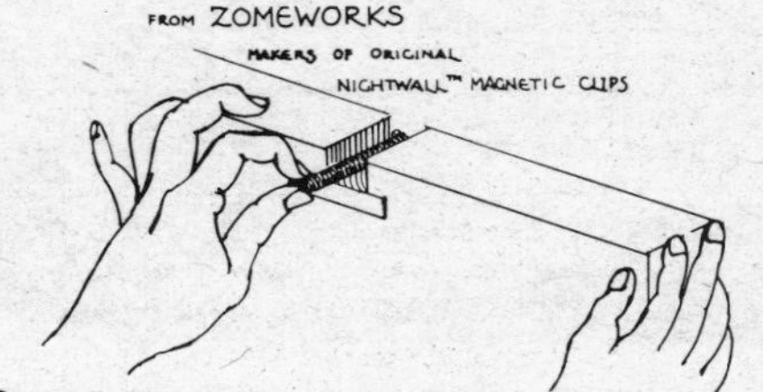

•

1½" Nightwall(TM) Spring Clips (for 1" insulating board) @ $ .50 ea.
2½" Spring Clips (5 lb. full) (for 2" insulating board) @ $ .70 ea.
Minimum order 10 clips.
Include $2.50 postage and handling — $3.50 if ordering over 100.

•

Nightwall® Clips are ½" wide and come in 3" and 6" lengths. The 3" length, placed every 18" - 24" of perimeter, is adequate for 1" beadboard; for heavier insulation, use the 6" length. Installation instructions are included with orders. Prices are as follows:

	3"	6"
20 clips min. order	$7.00	$10.00
20 - 39 clips	.35 ea.	.50
40 - 99	.33	.48
100 - 999	.30	.46
1000+	.28	.44

Shipping & handling charges:

	3"	6"	
1 - 100 clips	$2.00	$ 3.00	
101 - 200	3.00	4.00	
201 - 300	4.00	5.00	etc.

(NM residents: please add 4% sales tax; Canadian residents: please pay in U.S. dollars.)

Nightwall Clips
(One clip needed for every 2' of window perimeter)
20 3" clips for small panels
$9 postpaid
20 6" clips for big panels
$13 postpaid
10 1½" spring clips for warped, thick, sloped or exterior panels
$7.50 postpaid
10 2½" spring clips
$9.50 postpaid

Sunspots

This is the deepest of Steve Baer's works and also the most crisply presented. Here is accummulated the experience of Zomeworks' 15 years of successful experimentation, design, and delivery of solar energy systems. All that richly blended with Steve's J.G. Ballard-type fantasies and his acerbic criticism of federal energy studies, modern engineering text literary style, and the like.

If a real philosopher were a real engineer, he would write like this. —SB

Sunspots
(An Exploration of Solar Energy through Fact and Fiction)
Steve Baer
1975, 1979; 127 pp.

$5.95 postpaid from:
Cloudburst Press
1716 North 45th Street
Seattle, WA 98103
or Whole Earth Household Store

•

The Sun Riots

The lower floor offices of city hall and the police department have been gutted by fire. Black streaks surround the windows which are now shiny with aluminum foil. The police are still unable to confiscate mirrors; the matter is in the courts.

A week earlier at a demonstration a large van was driven next to the crowd. The driver, a swarthy man of about 40, opened the back doors and began passing out foot square mirrors. "Give 'em some sunshine."

A few dozen mirrors began playing beams of sunlight on a police car that had been dogging the rear end of the demonstration. The officers were caught by surprise. The driver managed to back the car down the street, but not before his partner, panicked by the glare and the rapidly rising temperature, had jumped out and run. More and more mirrors were out in the crowd now. The crowd glinted like a bank of crystals.

The mirrors couldn't reach the police car, which had found protection behind a drive-up liquor store. The man with the van now stood on top of the store. "Let's burn it up, yeh — this!"

His voice is hoarse and breaking. A few mirrors flit across the van and the man on top. More focus on the tin side. The man climbs off. People are pulling the last mirrors from inside the van as the others begin to focus on it. There are 800 mirrors out in the street.

The crowd is silent. The blob of brilliant light on the side of the truck is fringed with trembling squares of light flitting in and out of target. You can hardly hear a noise. Then the sheet metal side of the van "oil cans" as the van swells. A few more moments and smoke appears. The crowd has results. That was at 11:00 a.m. — by dark there have been 100 fires.

The police appear with arc welders' masks. They fire on the demonstrators. The demonstrators disperse, but the light keeps coming. More mirrors appear on the street. Funny shaped mirrors — mirrors with ornamental frames, tiny pocket mirrors in the hands of children.

Smoke is seen from another part of town. Television crews arrive. The footage in the evening news across the nation is over-exposed — an occasional clear image and then the picture goes white and over-exposed.

The mirror crowds are completely silent. They move everywhere on foot. A secretary at City Hall says, "They just looked so funny — a whole crowd of them standing just as still as could be holding onto those mirrors and then pretty soon the store across the street was burning."

"Get those damned kids with the mirrors off the street."

"But officers, I'm just usin' this mirror 'cause I'm combin' my hair — no law against combin' your hair, is there?"

Dozens of youths in the street combing their hair peering into gigantic foot square mirrors.

•

If you take down your clothesline and buy an electric clothes dryer the electric consumption of the nation rises slightly. If you go in the other direction and remove the electric clothes dryer and install a clothesline the consumption of electricity drops slightly, but there is no credit given anywhere on the charts and graphs to solar energy which is now drying the clothes.

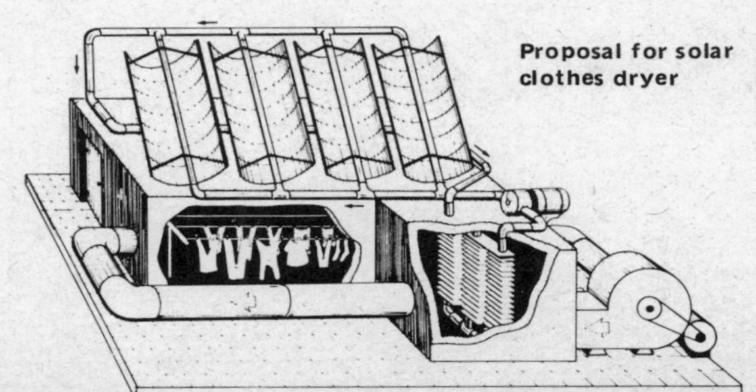
Proposal for solar clothes dryer

Solar beanie and music box

Far more effective than a T-shirt, more fun than a solar collector, these toys demonstrate your solar obsession to your public. The propeller on the beanie spins when you stand in sunlight (varying sensitively with angle, partial shade, etc. — interesting); the music box tinkles to the sunshine, "You Are My Sunshine," and other tunes. These novelties are available from other sources, but Zomeworks has easily the best prices. —SB

Solar Music Box
$21 postpaid

Solar Beanie
$13 postpaid

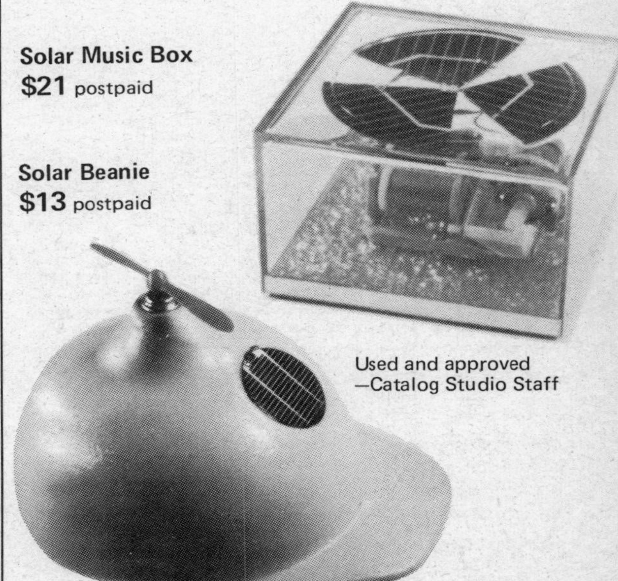
Used and approved
—Catalog Studio Staff

THE RISING SUN
NEIGHBORHOOD NEWSLETTER

Kathy blanched at the party when the speakers went off and said, "Whenever the lights go out or music stops suddenly, I think for a second it's the end of everything."

SolaRoll →

I just have to mention this unusual idea because it works so well, and it is so readily adapted to do-it-yourself. Made of weatherproof synthetic rubber, SolaRoll's inherent floppiness makes it easy to install under conditions where rigidity would be a hassle. The stuff can be bent, trimmed to size, and buried in concrete to make radiant floors. It's light, nice to work with, ships small. Nothing to break either. Best of all is the dramatically low price compared with most other systems. If I needed an active collector, this is what I'd look at first.
—*J. Baldwin*

SolaRoll
Catalog
free postpaid from:
Bio-Energy
Systems, Inc.
Box 87
Ellenville, NY 12428

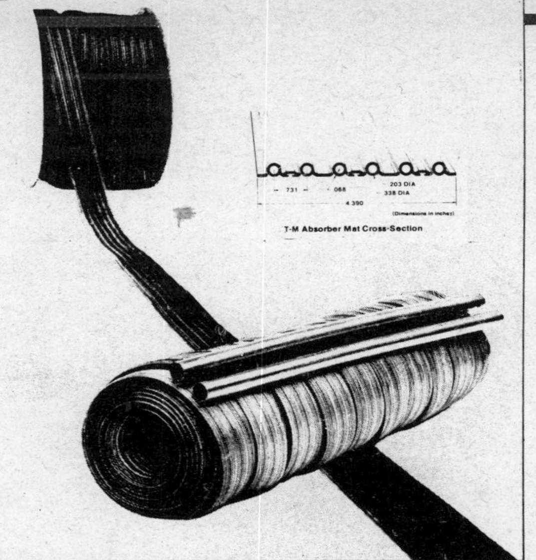

Tranter Platecoil

A number of companies are manufacturing tube-in-sheet and other types of heat exchangers suitable for use as solar collectors. Tranter, Inc., is one, and they make some panels that are especially intended for this use, called Econocoil. Their catalog is an education in itself, as it contains all the formulas you need for calculating heat transfer and pressure drops. The panels are of very high quality and not especially cheap, but they are also very efficient and easy to handle.
—*J. Baldwin*

Tranter, Inc.
Catalog

free from:
Tranter, Inc.
Platecoil Division
735 Hazel Street
Lansing, MI 48909

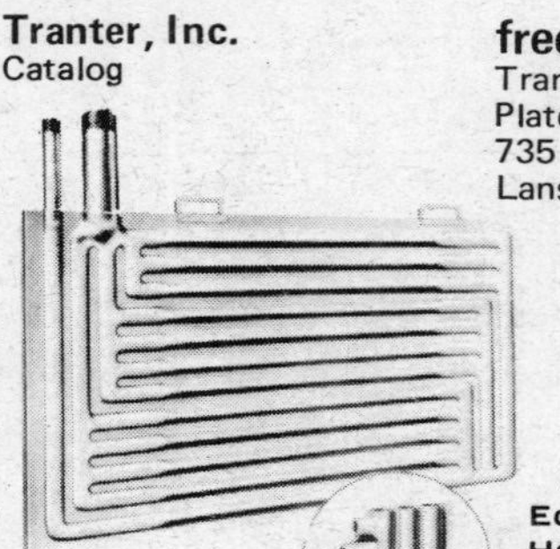

Econocoil Solar Water Heater Collector Plates

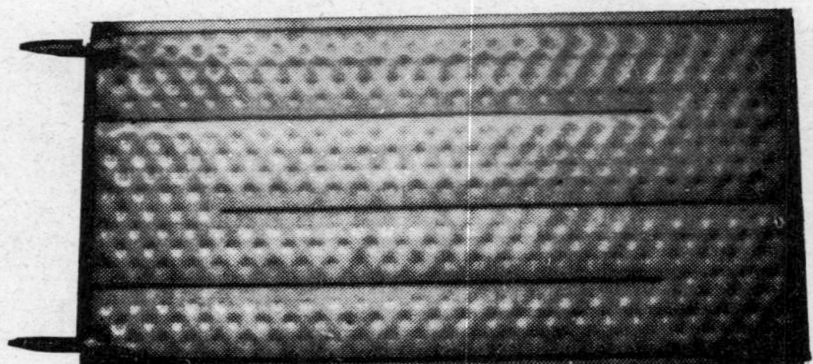

A highly efficient flat plate solar collector, having about 90% internally wetted surfaces.

Easco Aluminum

Tight, sturdy, lasting, light, non-warping, no-maintenance solar collector frames are easily made from aluminum extrusions from this company. They also make extruded flat plate collector clamp-to-the-tube fins. They do custom extrusions too. Despite the high energy cost of making aluminum, it is easily recycled later because it doesn't rust (unless under salt water), and it is reliable. Collectors have to last at least 20 years to be truly useful from a net energy standpoint, so I think that aluminum is appropriately used in this way. At least it's better than beer cans. Anyway, Easco has been at the forefront of the more responsible and responsive companies bringing in reliable solar equipment.
—*J. Baldwin*

Easco Aluminum
Information
←

free from:
New Jersey
Aluminum Company
P.O. Box 73
North Brunswick, NJ 08902

Solar hardware

"Inevitably the fields of Solar Energy and Refrigeration and Air Conditioning will become intertwined . . ." says this catalog of heat exchangers, collector plates and other goodies (including the new 4 Mil Tedlar glazing). This is typical of a growing number of companies that see what's coming. *(More solar catalogs, p. 188.)*
—*J. Baldwin*

Components for Solar Energy Systems
Catalog
$1 from:
Refrigeration
Research, Inc.
Solar Research Div.
525 N. Fifth Street
Brighton, MI 48116

Type II: The No. 5840 heat exchanger is for various liquid to liquid applications. It may be used to provide heat interchange between liquid circulating from a solar collector and water to be heated in a water heater or pre-storage tank for the water heater. Depending upon the application, a circulating pump will be required in one or both of the water circuits. Larger heat exchangers of this type are available upon special order. Capacity of the No. 5840 is indicated by the following curve:

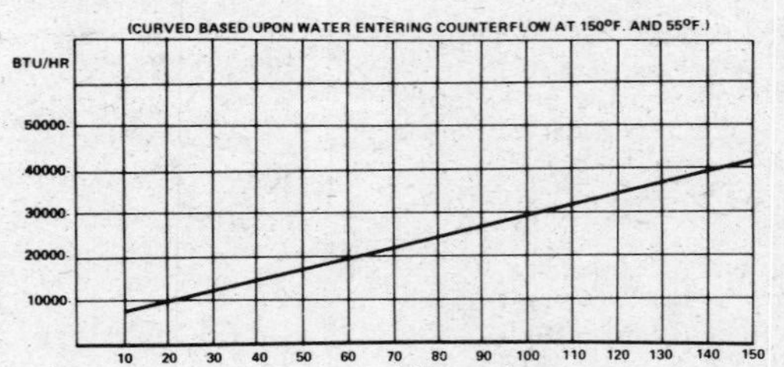

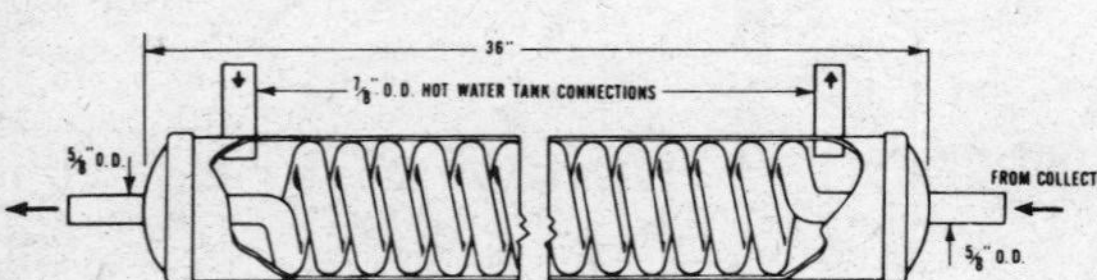

PART NO. 5840, Type III: Special heat exchangers can be made to special order. This includes special heat exchangers made for interchange between a solar collector system and absorption air conditioning system.

Grumman Sunstream solar hotwater system

The biggies get into the act with all the goods and bads such attention implies. The collector is a more-or-less conventional flat plate affair used primarily as a hot water heater booster. What's new is having a huge corporation making and marketing it. That in itself together with a typically competent big-corporation product finish, should generally upgrade public confidence in the entire industry. Not so good is that many small entrepreneurs who brought in that industry will now be driven out by it, thus suppressing innovation at a time when it is needed most.

It will be interesting to see how this and other expensive solar hardware fares. How many thousand-dollar water heaters can you sell? There are many, many manufacturers of similar equipment. We're showing this as a typical big-corporation offering.
—*J. Baldwin*

Grumman Sunstream
Information
free from:
Sunstream
4175 Veterans
Memorial Highway
Ronkonkoma
Long Island, NY 11779

Tuffak-Twinwall

Rohm & Haas, makers of Plexiglas, have developed this double walled sheet material. It looks like transparent square tubes lined up side by side and is an easy way to double glaze, say, a greenhouse. It's much stronger than glass, though it will scratch. Sunlight will not harm it.
—*J. Baldwin*

Tuffak-Twinwall
Brochure and nearest
dealer location
free from:
Rohm and Haas
Plastics Department
Independence Mall West
Philadelphia, PA 19105
Or check your local
plastics dealer

Heat Mirror

Heat Mirror (TM) is very thin plastic carrying a special coating that is transparent to light and short wave infrared (that's what you want to come in through the windows to help heat the house) and opaque to longwave infra-red (that's the heat you don't want to escape). It is, in effect, transparent insulation. Because heat mirror is not particularly durable when exposed to weather, it is available only as an inner layer in commercially available multipane windows. It works well, as I can attest from personal experience.
—*J. Baldwin*

Heat Mirror
Brochure and nearest
dealer location

free from:
The Southwall Corp.
3961 East Bayshore Rd.
Palo Alto, CA 94303

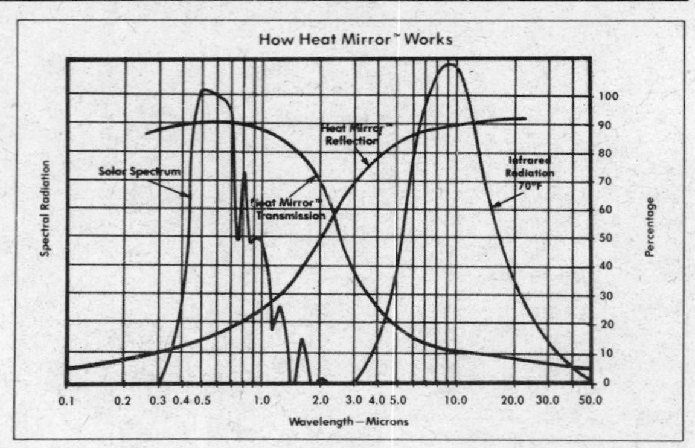

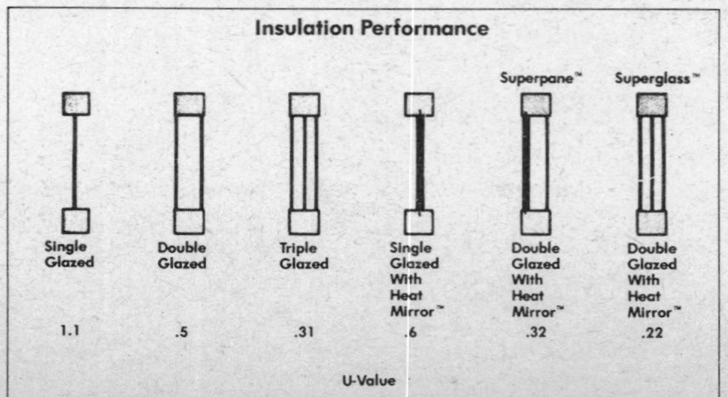

Right: Relative heat loss of various windows. Above: Radiation measurements show how Heat Mirror (TM) transparent insulation transmits short-wave sunlight (the solar spectrum, 0.3 - 2.0 microns) but reflects long-wave infrared (heat) radiation (2.0 - 50 microns).

Solar components

The Kalwall Corporation has a store, claimed to be the "largest solar mail order house in the U.S.A." The catalog is downright fascinating, and shows many devices I've needed but never seen before. Their best item is the heat-storing solar tubes. —J. Baldwin

Solar Components
Catalog
free from:
Solar Components Division
P.O. Box 237
Manchester, NH 03105

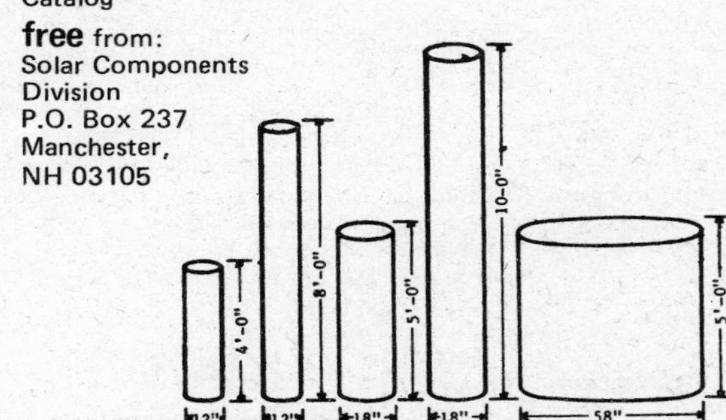

22 gal. 45 gal. 64 gal. 128 gal. 725 gal.
$34 $47 $60 $80 $195

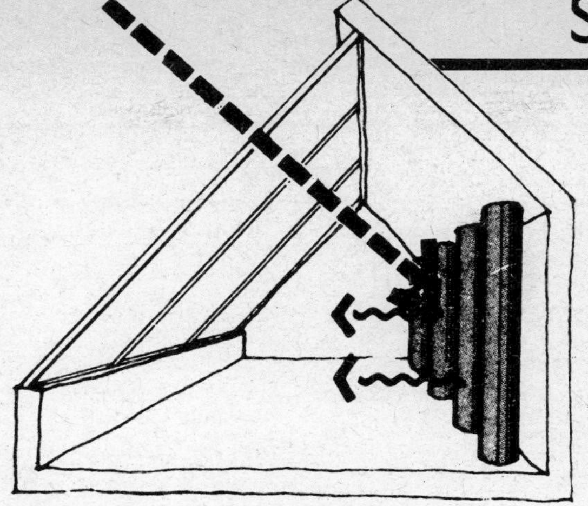

Direct Gain Sloped Wall

Sun-Lite Tubes and Tanks have been utilized by a number of research groups and colleges experimenting in the field of aquaculture. When ordering tubes or tanks, please specify the use, such as "heat storage" or "aquaculture."

Armaflex flexible pipe insulation is available in 6' lengths in tubular form. Ideal for easy installation on new or existing pipe. Use 5/8" Armaflex for 1/2" I.D. pipe and 7/8" Armaflex for 3/4" I.D. pipe. Use Armaflex to eliminate condensation on cold lines or to prevent heat transfer on either hot or cold lines. 3/4" sidewall R = 2.96.

Openers

There is considerable advantage in automatic control of vents and other openings and devices that must respond to temperature changes. There are several devices on the market that extend a control rod from a cylinder in proportion to temperature rise of the cylinder. They work by means of the expansion of a substance in the cylinder, rather like some automobile thermostats. They can typically lift 15 - 50 lbs. depending on the model. They work fine and require no power input. The temperature sensitivity can be adjusted to suit your needs. —J. Baldwin

Two brands, differing in capacity and detail are:

Heat Motors
$74.50 postpaid
Information
free from
John Michael Gendron
P.O. Box 411
Fair Oaks, CA 95628

and

Thermofor Solar Powered Automatic Ventilator Controllers
$49.50 postpaid
Information
free from:
Bramen Company, Inc.
P.O. Box 70
Salem, MA 01970

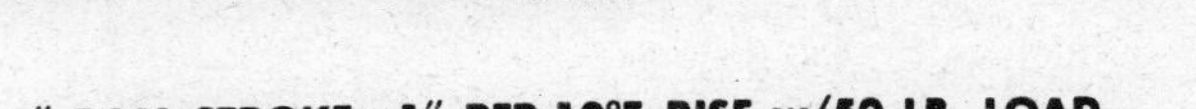

6" RAM STROKE – 1" PER 10°F RISE w/50-LB. LOAD –
(15.24 cm RAM STROKE — 4.58 cm PER 10°C RISE WITH 22.68 KILO LOAD.)

Heat Motor

Thermofor

- Uses no electricity — needs no wiring
- Fits any greenhouse ventilating sash — any cold frame
- Holds vent where needed to maintain desired temperature — up to 12-inch opening
- Step-by-step instructions for easy installation
- Adjustable to start opening vent between 55-85 F

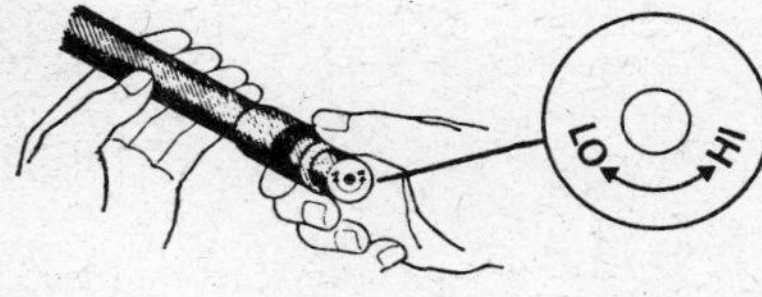

Pocket solar meter

In the past, if you wanted to actually measure the "power" in the sunlight falling on a site or collector, you had to use a very expensive instrument called a pyranometer. Now you can do it much cheaper with this ingenious meter which is calibrated for direct readings in BTUs per square foot per hour; Langleys per hour, and mW/cm². It's solar powered too; no batteries. Diffuse radiation can also be measured, as can losses through transparent materials. Looks good to me, especially at the price. —J. Baldwin

Pocket Solar Meter
$57 postpaid
$6.50 case
both from:
Dodge Products
Box 19781
Houston, TX 77024

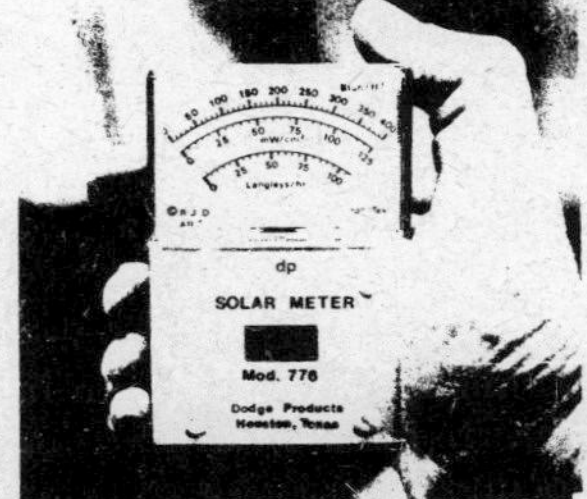

Solar Pathfinder

A gadget came into my hands a few days ago that **Whole Earth** *readers who do any amount of solar work might want to know about. In designing houses and evaluating the potential of a site for solar, you need to know how much sun is available. This simple gadget displays daily sun paths and shading from surrounding objects directly on its transparent dome. Usually, to get the same information, you'd have to coordinate the sun chart with a hand level to plot obstructions such as trees. It's a nicely designed tool for designers.* —Sim Van der Ryn

Solar Pathfinder
$124 postpaid from:
Solar Pathways, Inc.
Valley Commercial Plaza
3710 Highway 82
Glenwood Springs, CO 81601

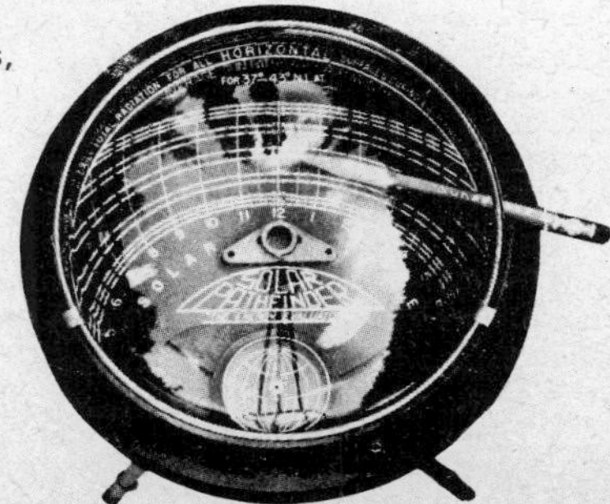

Sorod Roof De-Icer

In those places in the country where people are in danger of freezing to death in the dark, there can be a problem with ice building up under the shingles of a building. You can buy electric heaters to prevent the problem, or you could try some of these solar powered heaters. I'm not sure how well they work, but the idea seems good. Let us know if you've tried 'em. —J. Baldwin

Sorod Solar Powered Roof De-Icer
$10 (approx.)
Catalog
free from:
Tindev Inc.
RFD No. 1 Box 325B
Lincoln, MA 01773

The SOROD ice dam lancer absorbs free energy from the sun and conducts it into the ice dams which form at building eaves. A small tunnel is melted through the ice and the dammed water flows harmlessly away. If not released this water can find its way through the shingles and into the house where it may do considerable damage.

Alten Solar/Ground to Air Heat Pump Systems

The heat pump principle is not new, but most you see are air-to-air jobs that roar, ice up, and don't work all that well in winter when they're needed most. This one uses the ground as the heat source and by so doing gets heat from rain soaking into the ground as well. If you live where it gets really cold, a solar booster is easily added. The system works very well, even in the drizzly Pacific Northwest where it is claimed it has saved up to 80% of the heating bills of the homes where it has been installed. I have no experience with all this, but it looks as if it is an idea whose time has come. —J. Baldwin

Alten Solar/Ground to Air Heat Pump System SG-12
Information
free from:
Alten Northwest
1134 Poplar Place South
Seattle, WA 98144

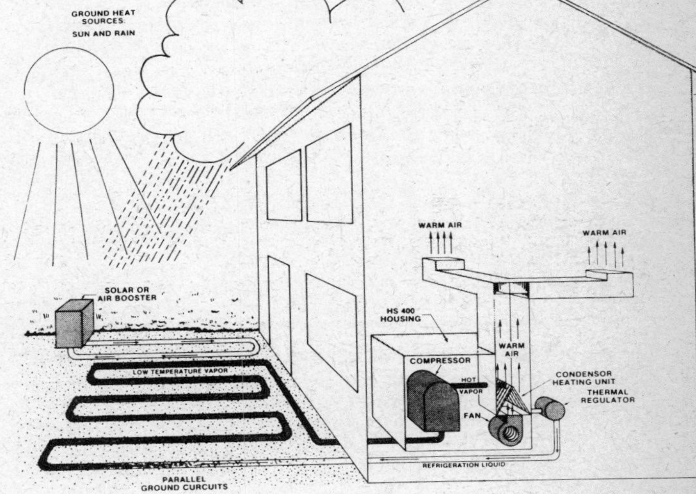

THE RISING SUN
NEIGHBORHOOD NEWSLETTER

Thinking the world should entertain you leads to boredom and sloth. Thinking you should entertain the world leads to bright clothes, odd graffiti and amazing grace in running for the bus.

Solar Energy Society

The American Section of the International Solar Energy Society Inc. sounds pretty stuffy, but it's the official name for the organization dedicated to making solar energy an increasingly important part of our lives. Most solar experimenters and others involved in encouraging the use of solar energy are members of local chapters as well as the International Solar Energy Society (ISES) itself, which is a separate organization. If you are interested in getting together with sun workers, the local chapter is your best bet.

I'm finding that much of the solar information that I need and use has come to me through the very lively New Mexico Solar Energy Association. As with other chapters, their newsletters are full of the very latest experimental data, much of it regionally appropriate. The chapter publications often bring you information years ahead of formal books. Here's a list of existing chapters and those in the making:

Alabama Solar Energy Association
P.O. Box 1247
Huntsville, AL 35807
(205) 895-6323
Bernard Levine, Chairman
7105 Hickory Hill Lane
Huntsville, AL 35802
(205) 881-9174, 889-6257

Arizona Solar Energy Association
Don Osborn, Chairman
Arizona Solar Energy Commission
Capital Tower Room 502
1700 W. Washington
Phoenix, AZ 85007
(602) 255-3682
Jeffrey Cook, Sec.-Treas.
c/o Dept. of Planning
College of Architecture
Arizona State University
Tempe, AZ 85281
(602) 965-6210

Colorado Solar Energy Association
P.O. Box 5272-TA
Denver, CO 80217
(303) 231-1192
Arne Ekstrom, Coordinator
CSEA Bookstore
2139 E. Colfax Avenue
Denver, CO 80206

Eastern New York Solar Energy Association
P.O. Box 5181
Albany, NY 12205
(518) 457-7584
William Rogers, President
Jim Healy (contact)
(518) 457-4930

Georgia Solar Energy Association
Tom McGowan, Pres.
Engineering Experiment Station
Energy Research Lab
Georgia Institute of Technology
Atlanta, GA 30332
(404) 894-3448

Hoosier Solar Energy Assn., Inc.
Gordon Clark, Chairman
6523 Carrolton Avenue
Indianapolis, IN 46204
(317) 259-7711
Keith Fisher, Sec.-Treas.
Box 44443
Indianapolis, IN 46204

Kansas Solar Energy Assn.
Donald E. Stewart
1102 South Washington
Wichita, Kansas 67211
(316) 262-7427

Metropolitan New York Solar Energy Association
Phil Bobenhausen
2465 Palisade Avenue
Riverdale, NY 10463
(313) 663-7799

Michigan Solar Energy Association
Karen Kanniainen, Coordinator
201 E. Liberty Street
Suite 15
Ann Arbor, MI 48104
(313) 663-7799

Mid-Atlantic Solar Energy Association
Linda Knapp, Director
2233 Grays Ferry Ave.
Philadelphia, PA 19146
(215) 963-0880
Peter Hollander, Chairman
1911 Arch Street
Philadelphia, PA 19103
(215) 299-2517

Minnesota Solar Energy Association, Inc.
Larry Opseth
Myers-Bennet Architecture
2829 University Ave., SE
Minneapolis, MN 55414
(612) 379-7878

Mississippi Solar Energy Association
Dr. Pablo Okhuysen
225 West Lampkin Road
Starkville, MS 39759
(601) 323-7246

Nebraska Solar Energy Association
Dr. Bing Chen
University of Nebraska
Department of Electrical Technology
60th & Dodge Streets
Omaha, NE 68182
(402) 554-2769
(402) 554 3104 (home)

New England Solar Energy Association
Tom Minnon, Exec. Dir.
P.O. Box 541
Brattleboro, VT 05301
(802) 254-2386

New Mexico Solar Energy Association
Steve Meilleur, Exec. Dir.
P.O. Box 2004
Santa Fe, NM 87501
(505) 983-1006
Jane Napier, Assistant
(505) 983-1006

North Carolina Solar Energy Association
Ben T. Gravely, Chairman
7001 Buckhead Drive
Raleigh, NC 27609
(919) 566-3111
Leon Neal, Vice-Chairman
NC/STRC
P.O. Box 12235
Research Triangle Park, NC 27709
(919) 549-0671

Northern California Solar Energy Association
Harry Miller, President
808 Cerrito Street
Albany, CA 94706
(415) 526-4594

Northern Illinois Solar Energy Association
James A. Hartley, Chairman
6 N. 201 Denker Road
St. Charles, IL 60174
(312) 377-1509

Ohio Solar Energy Assn.
Dr. Bruce T. Austin, Chairman
Environmental Studies Program, Secretariat
Wright State University
Dayton, OH 45435
(513) 767-7324, Ext. 78
(513) 873-2169
(513) 767-5341 (home)

Oklahoma Solar Energy Association
Dr. Bruce V. Ketcham
Solar Energy Laboratory
University of Tulsa
Tulsa, OK 74104
(918) 592-6000

Pacific Northwest Solar Energy Association
2332 E. Madison
Seattle, WA 98112
Dr. Douglas R. Boleyn, Chairman
17610 Spring Hill Place
Gladstone, Oregon 97027
(503) 226-8478

South Central Illinois Solar Energy Association
B. McFadden (contact)
2801 Rochester Road
Springfield, IL 62703
(217) 523-0423

Tennessee Solar Energy Association
Mr. Joe Hultquist, Executive Director
P.O. Box 127
Kodak, TN 37764

Texas Solar Energy Society
Russell E. Smith, Executive Director
1007 South Congress, Suite 359
Austin, TX 78704
(512) 443-2528

Virginia Solar Energy Association
Lawrence C. Perry
P.O. Box 12365
Roanoke, VA 24025
(703) 342-1816
Craig Crawford, Sec.
P.O. Box 11084
Richmond, VA 23230
(804) 358-9111

Wisconsin Solar Energy Association
Ernest Rogers, Chairman
Windworks
Rt. 3, Box 44A
Mukwonago, WI 53149
(608) 831-4446 (home)
(414) 363-4088

American Section of the International Solar Energy Society
Membership
$30/yr (ISES only)
$25/yr (American Section only)
$50/yr (combined)
Membership forms and catalog
free from:
International Solar Energy Society
American Section
Research Institute for Advanced Technology
U.S. Highway 190 West
Kileen, TX 76541

Southwest Bulletin
(Journal of the New Mexico Solar Energy Association)
Michael Shepard, Mark Lee, Editors
$15/yr (12 issues)
from:
New Mexico Solar Energy Association
P.O. Box 2004
Santa Fe, NM 87501

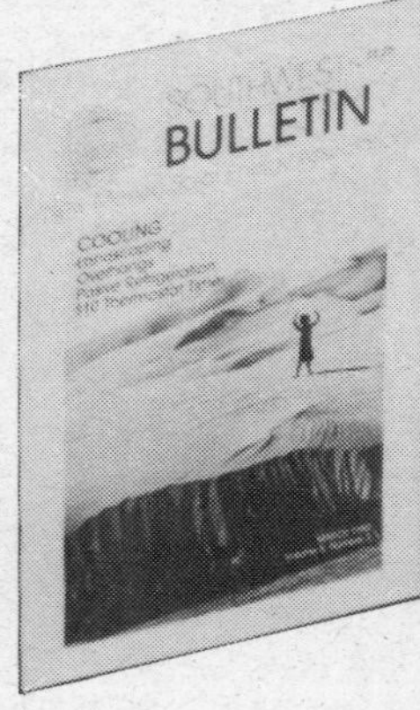

Membership in the American Section gets you a subscription to the excellent **Solar Age** *magazine (p. 183) as well as an annual membership directory, proceedings from the annual meeting, and several other publications. Membership in ISES also includes the bi-monthly* **Technical Journal**, *a quarterly called* **Sunworld**, *and the* **International Newsletter**, *also published quarterly. Members also receive discounts on a variety of books, kits, and reprints. Most sun workers I know are members of both groups. In addition to all this, the American Section also offers affiliations with the special interest groups listed below.*
—*J. Baldwin*

DIFFERENT FROM OLD-FASHIONED ICE HOUSE

The design is different from the ice house of 75 years ago in four respects. Because I freeze the water right in place, I don't have to cut ice in the winter. Therefore it's a much simpler operation. Second, I bring the food to the ice, rather than bringing the ice to the food. Thus I never have to open up the ice house in the warm months, letting warm air in. Third, because the ice is contained in a lined waterproof tank the melted ice does not soak the insulation or rot the building. Fourth, we have the advantage of all the advances in insulation materials.

SOUTHWEST BULLETIN

AGRICULTURE
Includes the areas of greenhouses, drying, crop improvements, energy plantations, animals, irrigation, and desalinization. Contact: Dr. C. Direlle Baird, Department of Agricultural Sciences, University of Florida, Gainesville, FL 32611.

BIOLOGY AND CHEMISTRY
Includes the areas of bioconversion, photobiology, photochemistry, chemical storage, photoelectrolysis, photogalvanics, bio-medical and bio-engineering. Contact: Dr. C. James R. Bolton, Department of Chemistry, University of Western Ontario, London, Ontario, Canada N6A3K7.

ENGINEERING
Includes areas of solar thermal applications, heating and cooling, system modeling, thermal storage, heat transfer, thermodynamics, engineering, process heat, and ocean thermal. Contact: Dr. J. Richard Williams, Associate Dean of Engineering, Georgia Institute of Technology, Atlanta, GA 30332

PASSIVE SYSTEMS
Includes the areas of architecture, energy conservation, natural cooling, heat storage, thermal flow control, siting and microclimate, daylighting and thermal comfort criteria. Contact: Dr. J. Douglas Balcomb, M.S. 571, Los Alamos Scientific Laboratory, P.O. Box 1663, Los Alamos, NM 87548.

PHYSICS
Includes the areas of photovoltaics, optics (coatings), solid state physics, and material sciences. Contact: Dr. Karl W. Boer, College of Engineering, University of Delaware, Newark, DE 19711.

SOCIO-ECONOMICS
Includes the areas of commerce, the law, communications, economics, education, institutions, and legislation. Contact: Mr. Keith Haggard, P.O. Box 2004, Santa Fe, NM 87501.

RADIATION
Includes the areas of climatology, solar energy data, atmospheric physics and meteorological optics, instrumentation and radiometry and radiation transfer. Contact: Dr. Kinsell L. Coulson, Department of Land, Air and Water Resources, University of California, Davis, CA 95616.

WIND POWER
Includes the areas of meteorology and climatology, aerodynamics, ocean waves, and engineering of wind power systems. Contact: Dr. C G. Justus, School of Aerospace Engineering, Georgia Institute of Technology, Atlanta, GA 30332.

The Chapters of the Section provide information and participatory opportunities for interested laypersons. Chapter activities include technical, educational, social and publications programs and opportunities to assist legislators in their actions. Members are encouraged to participate and to join their colleagues in forming new chapters.

Assistance in organizing Chapters and Chapter Formation Packets are available from the Section's National Coordinator and the Headquarters staff.

SERI

The Solar Energy Research Institute publishes all manner of bulletins, papers, and news of how the solar game is being played. Since SERI was taken over by Dennis Hayes, a man on Our Side, things are looking up and we are beginning to see some worthwhile enterprises and publications from this outfit at last. I find myself looking forward to mail with their logo. You can get on their mailing list by writing.
—*J. Baldwin*

SERI
Information
free from:
Document Distribution Center
1617 Cole Boulevard
Golden, CO 80401

National Solar Energy Education Directory

We get a lot of mail asking where does one get an education in matters solar. Here's where you find out. It's arranged by states and gives full information as to course content, program, degree, etc. Just about what you'd expect.
—*J. Baldwin*

National Solar Energy Education Directory
George Corcoleotes, Stephen Cronin, et al.
1980; 198 pp.
No. 061-000-00368-1
$5.50 postpaid from:
Superintendent of Documents
U.S. Govt. Printing Office
Washington, D.C. 20402
or Whole Earth Household Store

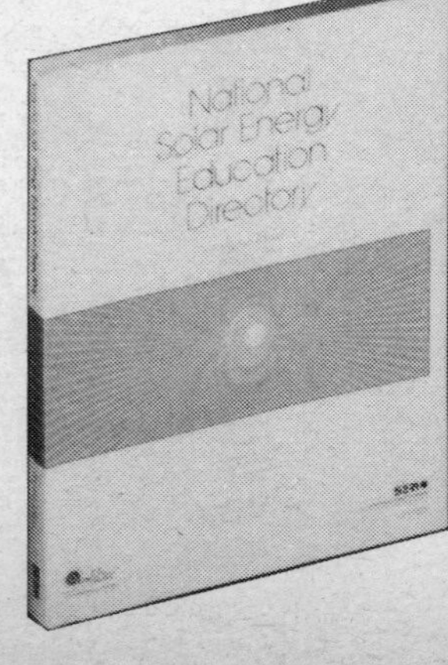

Brace Research Institute Plans

A better grade of plans than most. Crude, aimed at underdeveloped countries and people adjusted to a less technical life.
—*J. Baldwin*

Brace Research Institute
Publications list
free from:
Publication Department
Brace Research Institute
MacDonald College of McGill University
Ste. Anne De Bellevue 800
Quebec, Canada
H9X 1C0

How to Make a Solar Still (Plastic Covered), by A. Whillier and G.T. Ward, 9 pp., January 1965, Revised February 1973. $1.50.

How to Make a Solar Steam Cooker, by A. Whillier, 6 pp., January 1965. Revised October 1972. $1.50.

How to Heat Your Swimming Pool Using Solar Energy, by A. Whillier, 2 pp., January 1965. Revised February 1973. $1.00.

How to Construct a Cheap Wind Machine for Pumping Water, by A. Bodek, 12 pp., February 1965. Revised February 1973. $1.50.

How to Make a Solar Cabinet Dryer for Agricultural Produce, by T.A. Lawand, 9 pp., March 1966. Revised March 1973, $1.50.

Instructions for Constructing a Simple 8 sq. ft. Solar Still for Domestic Use and Gas Stations, by T.A. Lawand, 6 pp. Revised September 1967. $1.50.

Plans for a Glass and Concrete Solar Still, by T.A. Lawand and R. Alward, 9 pp., December 1968. Revised October 1972. $1.50.

Production Drawing for Solar Cabinet Dryer, by O. Goldstein, June 1973. $2.50.

All orders subject to a $1.50 handling charge.

Solar Law Reporter

What do you do if that new apartment next door shades the solar water heater you just installed for $564.23? What can you do if that new collector panel falls apart two weeks after you get it? How do the various states compare in tax rebates for solar? How are the federal energy laws being interpreted? What are the legal implications of large corporations getting into solar energy? You can bet it's complicated! This publication will help you keep up with how such questions are being answered in the courts, and what may reasonably be expected. This is a "professional journal" in every way and should be very helpful in reducing the inevitable hassles that accompany any new ideas. Sharp editing makes it easy for the layman to understand the issues presented. Fresh ammunition for fighting city hall!
—*J. Baldwin*

Solar Law Reporter
Dale Saunders, Editor
$12 /year (6 issues)
from:
Superintendent of Documents
U.S. Govt. Printing Office
Washington, D.C. 20402

Living Systems

Living Systems, the folks who started the solar awareness program that resulted in the Davis Solar Code, have a collection of short papers on their latest efforts. There are four papers: **The Suncatcher Tour House** *(it's a demonstrator); a design that quite literally "catches" the sun.* **The Thermosiphoning Cool Pool - a Natural Cooling System** *uses a north-facing evaporative roof pond to thermosiphon cooler water into heat absorbing water filled cylinders in the building.* **Cooling From An Evaporating Thermosiphoning Roof Pond** *discusses a computer program that accurately simulates the Cool Pool performance, allowing it to be easily designed for a variety of climates.* **Planning Solar Neighborhoods** *— How to go about it.* —J. Baldwin

Collected Short Papers
(Passive Solar Design Advancements)
1978, 1979; 20 pp.

$4 /four papers
$1.25 each
postpaid from:
Living Systems
Route 1, Box 170
Winters, CA 95694

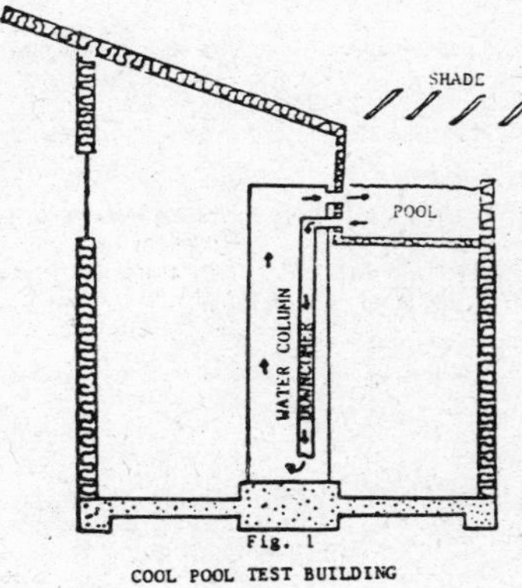

→

The Cool Pool, a passive cooling system, is an evaporating, shaded roof pond which thermosiphons cool water into water filled columns within a building. The system requires no moveable insulation or supplementary energy to function. Experimental data on air and water temperatures, cooling performance and net radiation from the roof pond is presented. The theoretical contributions of convection, evaporation and radiation to the cooling of the roof pond are also discussed.

DECEMBER 21, 12:00 · 26° SUN ANGLE
WINTER RADIANT GAINS CAN BE INCREASED 50% THROUGH THE "SUNCATCHER" SCOOP BY THE USE OF REFLECTIVE SURFACES ON THE ROOF BELOW AND THE EAVE ABOVE THE WINDOW. THE WINDOW IS SHUTTERED TO PREVENT NIGHT HEAT LOSS.

AUGUST 21, 12:00 · 62° SUN ANGLE
SUMMER HEAT GAINS ARE MINIMICED. THE OVERHANG SHADES THE WINDOW FROM DIRECT SOLAR RADIATION, AND THE GEOMETRY OF THE "SUNCATCHER" PREVENTS SUNLIGHT REFLECTED OFF OF THE ROOF FROM ENTERING THE WINDOWS. IN ADDITION, THE WINDOW IS SHUTTERED TO REDUCE CONCUCTED HEAT GAIN.

Sun Times

Now with 30,000 members, the Solar Lobby is gathering enough clout to make things happen in Washington. Their work already has resulted in solar and conservation tax credits and new building energy performance standards. If that sounds good to you, they can use your help. They publish **Sun Times.** *It comes with your membership.* —J. Baldwin

SUN TIMES
In Review: A Sampling of the Latest Solar Literature

Sun Times
$15 /year (12 issues)
includes membership
from:
Solar Lobby
1001 Connecticut Ave. NW
Fifth Floor
Washington, D.C. 20036

Convection Loops

This monthly "magazine" (it's a stack of poorly reproduced papers) has much exciting news and — amazing! — controversy having to do with double-envelope houses and other uses of natural and forced convection. I find it one of the more interesting and alive periodicals in the field of solar energy. It's very fine to hear those who are actually doing the deed having at one another learning as they go. —J. Baldwin

Convection Loops
Jim Berk, Editor

$7.50 /year (12 issues)
from:
Convection Loops
Box AF
Stanford, CA 94305

•

One of the most archaic (out-of-date) and outrageous parts of the building code is the 5% of floor space ventilation requirement. This apparently was written into the code on the assumption that openable windows were the only source of ventilation. Windows are terrible ventilators unless there is a wind blowing at them. Windows are generally in the middle of the wall for "seeing" purposes. If you want to ventilate one space to another, then you will arrange for high/low vents, or in other words, provide a loop.

Solar Distillation

A typical, competent UN paper. Conclusions are that though solar stills are capital intensive, they may be the most economical way to get water where seawater and sun are in good supply. They cite that 25 gallons per square foot of collector per year may be expected under average circumstances. Very comprehensive. Has graphs, formulas, drawings — everything you likely need to know. The economics of various schemes are examined more thoroughly than you'll likely read. —J. Baldwin
[Suggested by Joseph LoMonaco]

Solar Distillation As A Means of Meeting Small-Scale Water Demands
United Nations
Department of Economic and Social Affairs
1970; 86 pp.

$6 postpaid from:
United Nations
Publications
Room A-3315
United Nations
New York, NY 10017

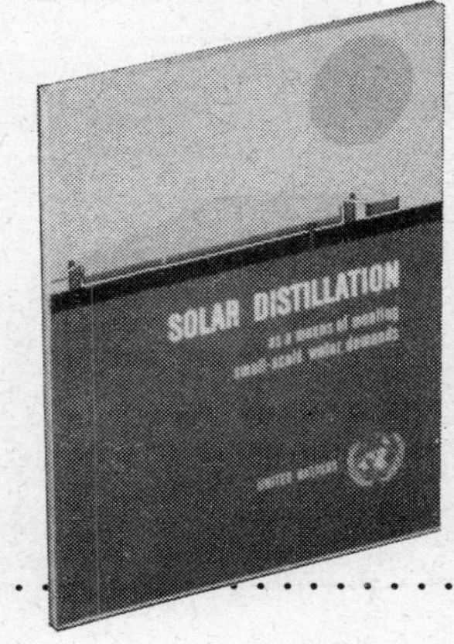

Davis Energy Conservation Report

This is what was proposed in energy-famous Davis, California, and how the program was implemented. It's more than a solar building code, and, as this report shows so nicely, a real savings of energy — 50% for the entire town, — can be realized with virtually no reduction of the standard of living. I show this paper because it can be used as an example to your own situation. Many times city fathers will see better in the light of city fathers who saw better. —J. Baldwin

Davis Energy Conservation Report
1977; 129 pp.

$10 postpaid from:
Living Systems
Route 1, Box 170
Winters, CA 95694

or Whole Earth Household Store

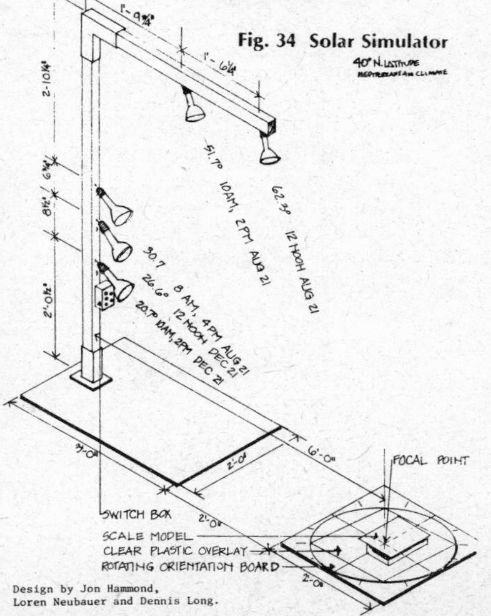

Fig. 34 Solar Simulator

Design by Jon Hammond, Loren Neubauer and Dennis Long.

THE RISING SUN
NEIGHBORHOOD NEWSLETTER

Around 1920, astronomers weren't sure whether or not the Milky Way galaxy and the universe were the same thing. They didn't know if the Milky Way was everything there was or if there was other stuff outside it. (Not only did they not know there were a million galaxies, they didn't know there were two.) Some astronomers thought the spiral nebulae were made up of stars and were like the Milky Way and were very far away. Others thought the spiral nebulae were made up of gases and were inside the Milky Way. So along came this guy Van Maanen who was comparing photographs of the sky taken at different times, and he found that the arms of the spiral nebulae were moving. The amount they were moving was ok if they were inside the Milky Way and fairly close — just an average rotation. However, if the nebulae were as far away as the people who thought they were galaxies said, they would have to be moving much faster to look like that in photos. In fact, they would have to be rotating, at the edges, at one third the speed of light, which isn't possible (even now, we still think it isn't possible.)

So most astronomers took Van Maanen's work as proof that the spiral nebulae were close and the Milky Way Galaxy was about all there was.

The interesting thing about Van Maanen is that he was just wrong, measured wrong, screwed up, kept the millions of galaxies from being believed in for about 4 more years, which they didn't mind I'm sure. The distances he was measuring on his photos were unbelievably small and at the edge of what the available technology could measure, but no one questioned his work because he had previously been very good at measuring incredibly small distances. And no one ever exactly proved him wrong; they just found other evidence that showed that he *had* to be wrong.

What happened was Edwin Hubble was able to use the Mount Wilson telescope to resolve the edges of two spiral nebula into regular old stars, and was able to use a generally accepted technique to measure the distance of those stars from Earth and they were far, far away. He discovered this in 1923 but didn't publish until 1924 because he knew he was saying Van Maanen was wrong wrong wrong, and he felt kind of bad about that. Many scientists accepted Hubble's results right away, but others stood by Van Maanen's results, so as late as 1930 it was still a live issue in some astronomical circles whether the spiral nebulae were island universes or not. (When the spiral nebulae being galaxies was a theory it was called the "island universe" theory, but when it became a fact they just called the nebulae galaxies. I kind of like Island Universe, but I guess once they found out a galaxy and a universe weren't the same thing, they had to decide which word to use for which.)

— Information from *Man Discovers the Galaxies*, by Berenzer, Hart and Seeley

IT'S DIFFICULT TO BE ENTIRELY rational about windpower; the machines are so dramatic and the fact that something real is happening is so irrefutable. But making a good wind turbine powered device has proven to be a challenge that few can meet. Even well-known manufacturers sell hardware that is far from reliable, though one would never guess that from the literature. In fact some of the least worthy machines are the best known (Wincharger, Elektro), and are used as shining examples of "free power from the wind" by a largely uncritical press. Home-builts, though instructive, are often short on reliability too. The big problem is the cost of constructing devices that can withstand the continuous beating of the weather: ice buildup, dust, rust, hail, gusts, lightning, vibration and metal fatigue, not to mention bullets and deliberate sabotage by dealers of rival makes (a problem in the '30s and rumored to be making a comeback).

Lack of system reliability has been discouraging prospective buyers for some time now, and for good reason. Fortunately there is now a government sponsored test facility at Rocky Flats, Colorado, where manufacturers' claims are called out under vicious weather conditions. (Test results are not available as this is written, but should be in late 1980.) My experience in the field with 25 types of machines or so is that useful reliable wind-electric systems are not yet available in a form whose performance can be predicted with confidence. Most wind-electric systems do not live up to catalog claims. Most do not have good output at low wind speeds; performance-minded Americans apparently cannot resist boasts of high outputs in high winds despite the fact that there are few sites with high average winds in this country. And there has been a distressing lack of heavy-duty quality; many manufacturers seem to think automobile-grade quality will do. It won't. I'd say offhand that if a machine can't run for 20 years or more without major maintenance, then it probably will never pay off in net energy and probably won't pay off in dollars either.

The above remarks are discouraging to someone who wants to put the wind to work right now. What to do? First is to be brutally honest about your needs, desires, and money matters. It is unlikely that a windmill will pay its way (except possibly for water pumping) if city power is already at the scene. In all but a few cases, a small wind-electric system will not pay, especially if there are storage batteries in the system. Those systems you read about are mostly for symbolic value; their owners don't really care very much about payoff or net energy. The records of most of the highly publicized rigs show a very poor return on investment as well as questionable reliability. If you live beyond city power and/or where there is a lot of

Harnessing the Wind for Home Energy

When people ask me "where do I find out about wind energy," I tell them to buy this modest book. Wind experimenters will wish for a more technical treatise, but for the uninitiated the book is complete, the bibliography respectable, and the selection of hardware typical of what's available. —J. Baldwin

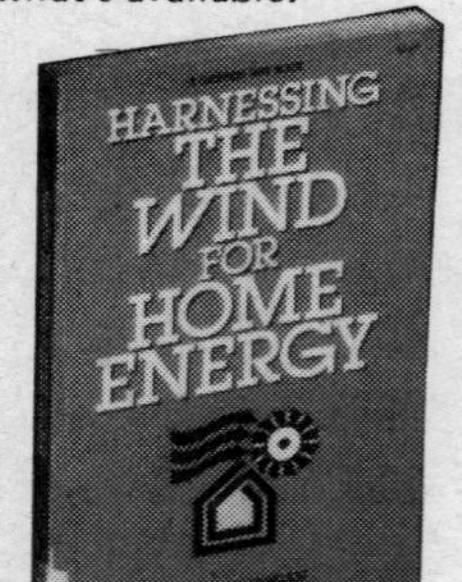

Harnessing the Wind for Home Energy
Dermot McGuigan
1978; 134 pp.
$4.95 postpaid from:
Garden Way Publishing Co.
Charlotte, VT 05545
or Whole Earth Household Store

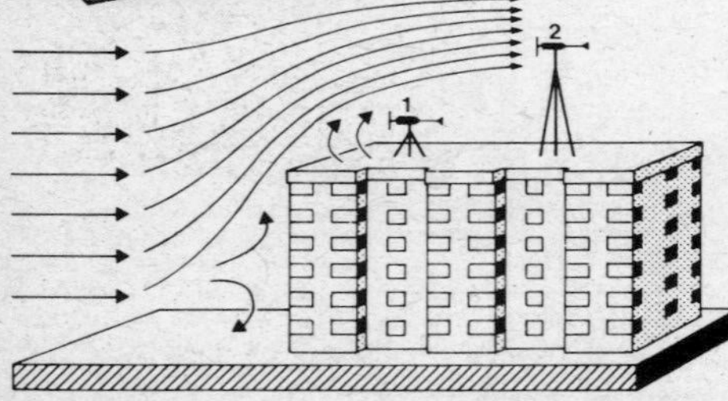

The building is diverting the wind stream from generator 1, but actually increases the windspeed for generator 2.

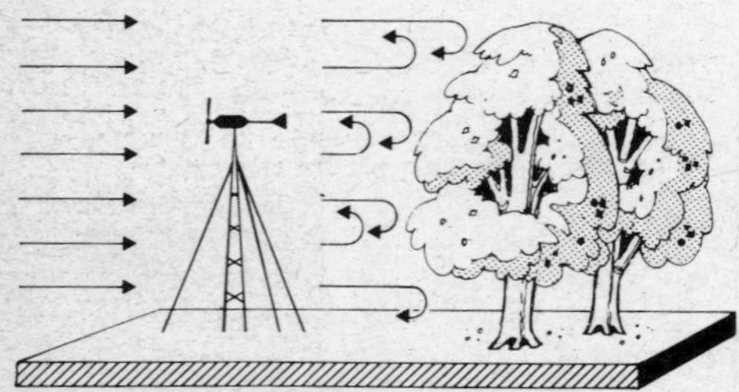

Obstructions cause wind turbulence whether they are in front of or behind the generator, as here. The mast should be extended 20 - 30 feet above the trees or sited 300 - 500 feet away from them.

← **An example of the cheapest type of tower or mast — a telephone pole is used to support an old and heavy Jacobs mill.. The 70-ft. pole is tied with guy wires and hinged at the bottom to a concrete base. As a result of the hinge the whole tower, with the Jacobs on top, may be lowered and raised by means of a winch for servicing. It is also good to know that should a hurricane threaten, the mill can "lie low" in safety. The main difficulty with wooden poles is that the portion left underground eventually rots, but with this system that need never happen.**

•

Coulson Wind Electric
RFD 1 Box 225
Polk City, IA 50226
Phone: (515) 984-6038

Roland Coulson sells a wide range of reconditioned wind generators originally manufactured back in the Thirties and Forties, such as the Air Electric, Delco, Parris-Dunn, Wincharger and Windpower. . . .

Coulson powers his workshop with a 1.2 kw Wincharger on an 80-foot tower and a 2.5 kw Windpower on a 65-foot tower. All the workshop equipment is run on 32 volts DC: a lathe, valve and bench grinders, drills, air compressor, vacuum cleaner, radio and lights.

•

Elektro G.m.b.H.
St. Gallerstrasse 27,
Winterthur, Switzerland

Elektro, a tiny outfit, has been quietly manufacturing wind generators in Switzerland for the past 36 years and all went well until about 1969 when suddenly everybody wanted to buy Elektros. Reeling under a deluge of mail and orders, the small workshop where Elektros are hand-built became hurried and cluttered. New people were employed who did not understand the fine art of wind-craft, and so quality control slipped. About the same time Elektro allowed itself to be pushed into premature manufacture of a 10 kw generator by an English company. The result was that the blades on the first batch of 10 kw mills broke, and Elektro's reputation suffered badly as a result.

It must be said, however, that a company expert subsequently personally visted and de-bugged most of the faulty Elektros in Europe. Having recently met Mr. Kern and Mr. Schaufelberger of Elektro, I'm personally satisfied that they have matters back in hand again and are intent upon improving their quality control.

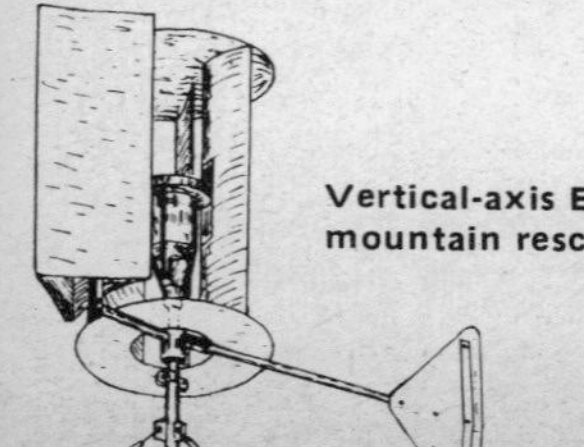

Vertical-axis Elektro shown powering a mountain rescue post in the Alps.

Simplified Wind Power Systems for Experimenters

Here's a how-to-design-it book for wind machine neophytes that looks like it's organized logically and not too heavy mathematically. Written by an engineer accustomed to teaching inexperienced aerospace technicians, it relies heavily on simple graphs and example problems. In addition to the usual power required/power available calculations, it covers airfoil, mechanical, and structural design, the latter particularly well. Battery storage technology and electronic controls are not treated well.

This is not a design cook book full of plans, but rather a simple, graphic engineering text for those thinking about building their first windplant.
—Chuck Missar

Simplified Wind Power Systems for Experimenters
Jack Park
1974; 72 pp.
$9 postpaid from:
Jack Park
Box 445
Brownsville, CA 95919
or Whole Earth Household Store

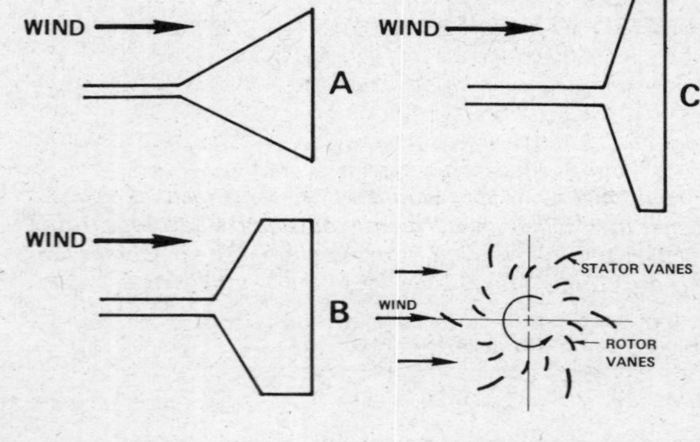

Types of vanes used are illustrated in Figures A, B, and C. Design A is a bit of nostalgia, but it works. Design B is a great improvement, and C is the best. The reason is simple. You want the tail vane which is most sensitive and responsive to changes in wind direction. Design C has the highest ratio of vane span, which is the distance from top to bottom on the vane, to vane chord, the distance from leading edge to trailing edge. Such vanes are like glider wings which are designed to make the most use of light up-drafts to support these craft aloft without benefit of a motor. Practical ratios of span divided by chord for the vane might be between two and ten. In other words, a typical vane might be five times as tall as it is wide.

Homemade Windmills of Nebraska

Handcarved blades tipped with stainless steel? Ball bearings? Gears? Feathering mechanisms? Nope. A few boards and lots of "American Ingenuity" (for which this country is justly famed) make practical working machines that pump, saw, and in later times generate electricity. This paper was originally published in the 1890s and it's a real eye-opener. Funky, yes. Down-home, for sure. And it may well cause more people to make working machines than any windpower book yet published. Interesting sociologically, too. —J. Baldwin

Homemade Windmills of Nebraska
Erwin Barbour
1898; 78 pp.
$3.50 postpaid from:
Farallones Institute
15290 Coleman Valley Rd.
Occidental, CA 95465

or Whole Earth Household Store

→
A six fan Jumbo windmill on the farm of W. W. Goodrich, Bethany, Nebraska, used in watering a six acre patch of eggplants for the Lincoln market. The fans are each nine feet long with arms five and one-half feet long. Jumbo box nine by eleven by six feet high, with door below for the escape of dead air. Extra well built. Axis of Damascus steel. Total cost, $8.00.

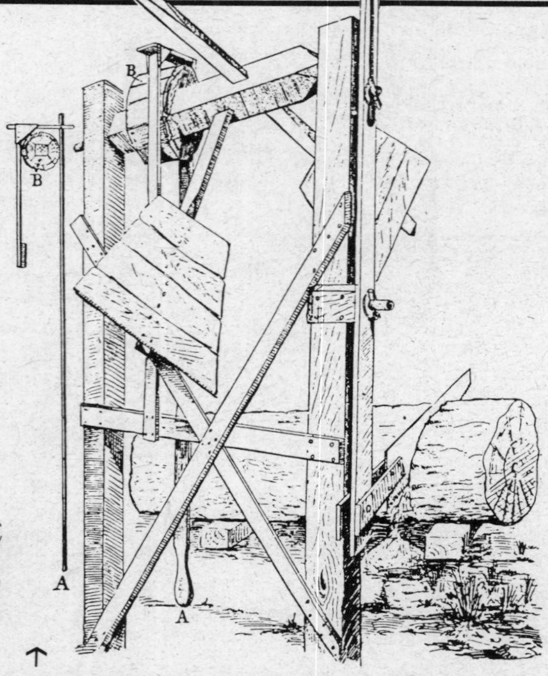

↑
The Battle-ax windmill of Mr. A.G. Tingley, Verdon, Nebraska, as seen sawing a thirty-inch log. Diameter of wheel ten feet. The wooden drum and brake is self-explanatory. This mill saws the wood for the family, and requires but little superintendence. To the left is seen a plan of the brake. The handle A cramps upon the wooden drum B. It is a cheap, simple, and satisfactory device.

wind, a small wind-electric system might pay, but you'd better figure it with a very sharp pencil before you buy. Good home-builts are another matter. The better ones have been among the very best, but note that while they may be homemade, they are designed to meet rigorous standards. (My house, a 21-foot Airstream trailer, has been mostly windpowered for the past 7 years by a 250 watt Paris-Dunn on a 33-foot folding pole. I use two 190 amp-hour golf cart batteries. They last about three years. This works out to about $5.00/month.)

Another problem has been a tendency to concentrate on "making a windmill" while ignoring the inefficiency of the intended end use. It is folly, for instance, to attempt to power a commercial freezer with a wind-electric system. The wind system would have to be too big and the costs would be ridiculous because the freezer was never designed to be energy efficient. Complete wind systems including end-use hardware are just now being designed. It's going to be a while before they are available, and you can bet they will be expensive to buy, though not necessarily to operate. Water pumpers are a much more developed breed. Their makers furnish reliable tables of pumping ability, and the hardware is well proven and long-lived.

What I think will probably happen commercially is that there will be a few reputable, tested systems available soon and they will not be cheap. They will be of a size (2 - 10 KW) that can be mass produced in quantities sufficient to bring down the current prices which are very high considering what you get. (A typical small wind machine costs as much as a highly complex automobile and all its thousands of high precision parts.) Machines of this size can be ganged together to obtain higher output without the necessity of developing very expensive specially designed larger ones and the required capital. This strategy also has the effect of increasing the sales of the more modest size machine and further lowering its asking price.*

Something else to consider is that the steady reduction in the price of photovoltaics may make small wind-electric systems uneconomical for most users, particularly in mountain locations where weather is harsh but sun is bright. (It is easy to make photovoltaics weather resistant.) In any case, it should not be long before things are more clear. The usual media such as **Popular Science** *(p. 158) will keep you informed on developments in huge commercial wind electric enterprises, some of which may prove to be economically and energetically acceptable. The following are sources of general wind information and where to keep up with developments. Bear in mind that depending on wind for other than water pumping and sailboats is still very much a pioneer endeavor.*

—J. Baldwin

*KW = Kilowatt = 1,000 watts. A kilowatt-hour (kwh) is ten 100-watt bulbs burning an hour.

Wind Power Digest

This quarterly just gets better and better as time goes by. It has acquired a good "professional" tone to its articles without being out of reach of the newcomer. The magazine's annual Wind Energy Directory is a model of what such things should be and is certainly the best single source of wind hardware information. Performance figures not available anywhere else are included in the presentations. The advertisements offer a good look at what's available too. Good job. —J. Baldwin

Wind Power Digest
Michael Evans, Editor

$8 /yr. (4 issues) from:
Wind Power Digest
109 E. Lexington
Elkhart, IN 46514

Example 2: A 4 KW wind system costs $5,000. Electricity costs 5 cents/KWH. The system produces 6,000 KWH/yr, and will be bought with cash from a savings account earning 6% annually. Electricity costs rise annually at 13%. What is the Payback?

Solution:

$$AV = \frac{\$0.05}{KWH} \times \frac{6{,}000\ KWH}{yr} = \$300/yr$$

$$C = \$5{,}000$$

$$i_1 = 15\%\ \text{from Table 1}$$

$$i_1 - i_2 = 2\%$$

$$CRF = \frac{AV}{C} = \frac{\$300}{\$6{,}000} = 0.05$$

Years to Payback: 26

Enertech 1500 atop Mt. Washington, New Hampshire ↓

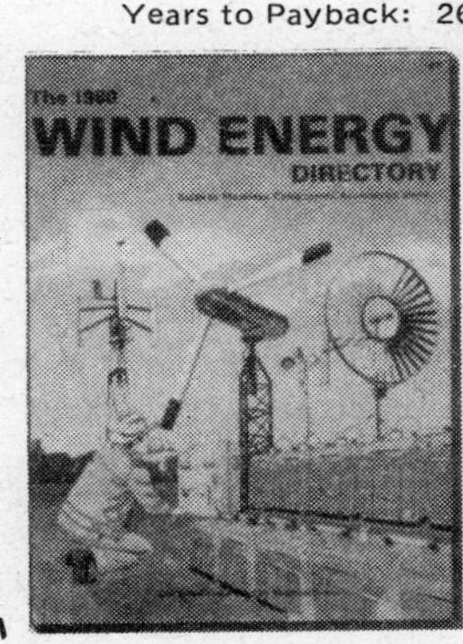

↗ Again this year, as last, the editors of **Wind Power Digest** have compiled the most comprehensive listing of wind energy resources available anywhere. **The 1980 Wind Energy Directory** is an all-in-one resource guide to wind machine specifications, wind system components and accessories, manufacturers, distributors, and researchers in the wind energy field.

In an important departure from our previous Wind Access Catalogs, we have independently analyzed each of the nearly fifty commercially available wind machines and provide a computer-generated graph for each machine that estimates yearly power output (in kilowatt-hours) plotted against average wind speeds. This comparative analysis is designed to give the consumer a handy tool with which to assess the relative value of different wind machine designs. In all the over 100 pages of wind energy information provide a comprehensive guide to the wind-powered electrification of homes, business and local communities *($4.95 postpaid)*.

Food From Windmills

ITDG (Intermediate Technology Development Group) has published an exciting book describing how a program of simple sailwing windmill waterpumps has considerably raised the food production of a bit of Ethiopia. Though no actual dimensioned plans are given, enough details of the laboriously evolved machines are given so that you could make one that would work. Mr. Fraenkel claims that their sailwings will greatly outpump a Savonius Rotor, especially in low wind. Cost less too. The machines look pretty funky, but those of you that actually have made windmills will appreciate the excellence of the work done by Mr. Fraenkel and his associates. It is often more difficult to develop a reliable simple machine than to do it super-slick with an NSF grant.

And for the sailwing or other simple machinery, you can make bearings from wood. This is a skill well worth learning, as it enables you to make and service equipment that would otherwise be entirely dependent upon the supply of industrial bearings. I can think of circumstances where this could be critical. How to do it is nicely shown in the Feb. '76 issue of the ITDG quarterly **Appropriate Technology.** *—J. Baldwin*

Food From Windmills
Peter Fraenkel
1977; 75 pp.

$7.95 postpaid from:
Intermediate Technology Development Group of North America
P.O. Box 337
Croton-On-Hudson
New York, NY 10520

or

£3.25 postpaid
($7.50 approx.) from:
I. T. D. G.
9 King Street
London WCZE 8HN
England

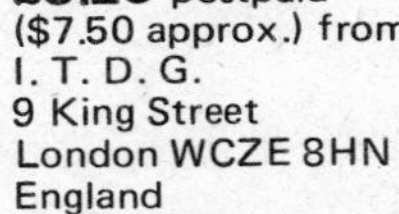

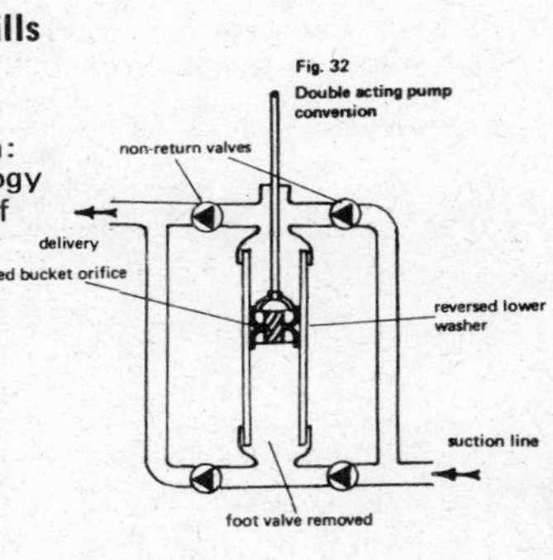

A 16-foot sailwing machine constructed by students at Farallones Institute using ideas from this book.

Wind and Windspinners

This was one of the first books to show amateurs how to make a working wind machine, and it remains one of the best introductions to home-builts. Even if the featured split oil drum Savonius type rotor doesn't interest you, the discussion of wiring, batteries, wind calculations and other general information is valuable. —J. Baldwin

Wind and Windspinners
Michael Hackelman, et al.
1974; 140 pp.

$8.95 postpaid from:
Peace Press
3828 Willat Avenue
Culver City, CA 90034
or Whole Earth Household Store

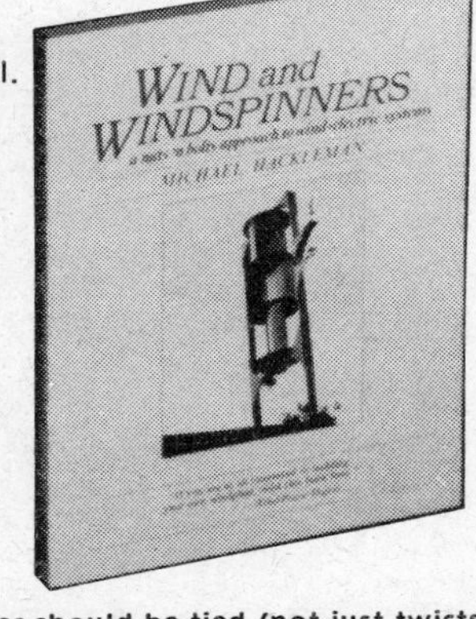

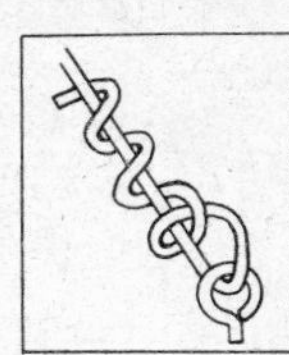

Guy wires should be tied (not just twisted); falling S-rotors are rude awakeners.

Homebuilt Wind-Generated Electricity

The same people who brought us **Wind and Windspinners** *now offer this book to those considering restoration of an old machine. (The title is a bit misleading; there is little about building your own.) The chapters on towers and raising machines, electronics, and why, are extensive and well illustrated with diagrams and good photos. The chapter on finding that old machine will probably result in there not being any more findable machines. But the book is marred by shallow research that shows up in the sketchy restoration chapter and a lack of critical details such as how to size tower fasteners. The breezy conversational style makes the book easy to read but not easy to peruse for quick facts when you need to know something. Nevertheless, it'll do until somebody writes that much-needed Compleat Manual of Antique Wind Machines, and it should help many who are struggling with the complexities of getting some power from wind. —J. Baldwin*

The Homebuilt Wind-Generated Electricity Handbook
Michael A. Hackleman
1975; 195 pp.

$7.95 postpaid from:
Peace Press, Inc.
3828 Willat Avenue
Culver City, CA 90230
or Whole Earth Household Store

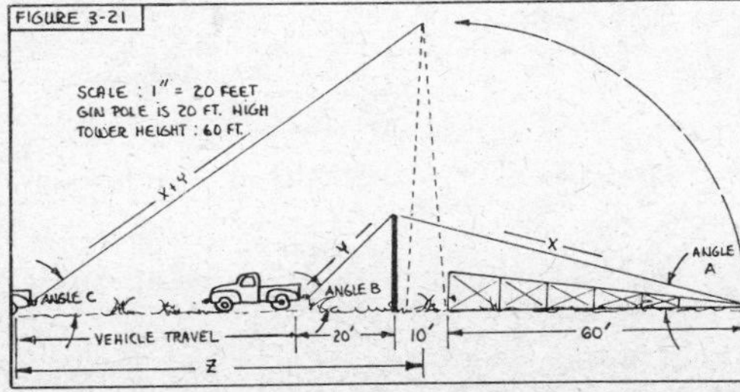

THE RISING SUN
NEIGHBORHOOD NEWSLETTER

She was too old to care and probably never had and she told anyone who asked and some who didn't, "I've had five husbands, left two, outlived three and what I say is, have you ever seen them put up a fence post? They get out there and dig the hole and pound the post down in and in a few years the post rots or rusts and they have to go back and put another one in and they may have to do that a dozen times, but the hole's always there, just as good as new."

Kathy said anything you've done more times than you can count on your fingers and toes, you should stop counting.

Wind Power For Farms, Homes and Small Industry

Much more detailed than **Harness the Wind for Home Energy** *(p. 196), this poorly Xeroxed book is probably the all-around most useful to a person seriously interested in installing wind hardware. Virtually every aspect of small-scale wind power is considered, including such concerns as insurance liability, wind rights, lightning protection and economic analysis. If this book was rounded out with a good printing job and fancy graphics there would be little need for most of the others. It's the one I use.*

—J. Baldwin

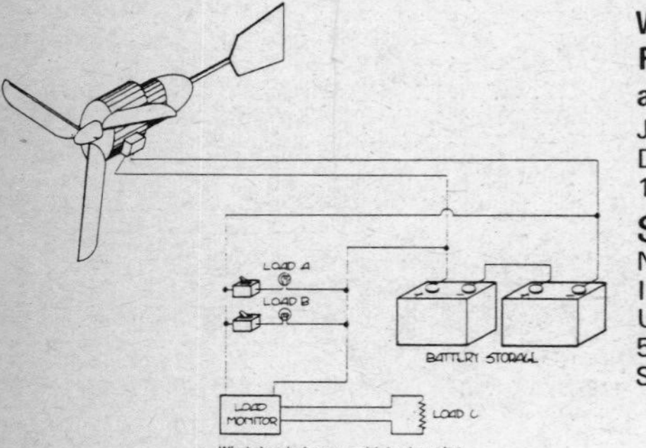

Wind electrical system with load monitor.

Wind Power for Farms, Homes and Small Industry
Jack Park and
Dick Schwind
1978; 232 pp.

$14 postpaid from:
National Technical Information Service
U.S. Dept. of Commerce
5285 Port Royal Road
Springfield, VA 22161

•

Suppose that the wind turbine generator supplies more kilowatt-hours than are needed. The batteries would be overcharged. Energy would be wasted. To preclude this situation, a load monitor is used. The load monitor senses situations when the wind generator creates more power than the electric system needs, and reacts by switching on load C. Load C might be a resistance electric heater immersed in a water heater tank. It may be another battery bank, or any other load that will use the excess power. The load monitor thus prevents energy waste, and in so doing improves the energy utilization of the simple battery system.

Load monitors can be used another way. Suppose that the wind turbine generator does not supply the required energy. Perhaps a week of no wind occurs, and the batteries are nearly discharged. A load monitor can be used to sense this condition and activate a backup system.

The backup system could be a gasoline powered generator, another set of batteries, or an extension cord to your neighbor's house. In any case, the load monitor can control the source. In the case of the gasoline powered generator, the load monitor can flash a light, ring a bell, or otherwise warn you of the situation, or it can energize the starter circuit on the auxiliary generator to bring it on-line.

•

From a historical standpoint, you might purchase a good automobile and drive it an average of 50 mph for 100,000 miles. This translates to 2000 hours of operation. You likely would have the car serviced every 5000 miles, or 100 hours. Sales brochures for small WECS, on the other hand, sometimes speak of 20 years of trouble-free operation. Factory representatives talk of customers asking how long their wind turbine will last before it needs fixing.

There are 8760 hours in a year. If your wind turbine operates just one-fourth of the hours in one year — a reasonable number — it will have as many hours on it in one year as your automobile does when you trade it in. It is also reasonable to expect to change the oil, grease a bearing, or change the brushes just once a year to get long-life performance out of a machine. Here are some of the factors you should consider before making the final selection of your system:

- Maintenance history of WECS components
- Can routine maintenance be easily performed up on a tower, or must the machine be lowered?
- Frequency of expected routine maintenance
- Nature of monthly, or yearly, expected routine maintenance: lubrication, component replacement, and inspection
- Number of different tools required to perform maintenance tasks
- Availability and cost of spare parts
- Completeness of owner's manual/maintenance documentation
- Relative safety: can machine be shut off, is there sufficient blade clearance from maintenance personnel, and are there exposed shafts, wires, and potential hazards?
- Is a factory-trained, experienced installation/maintenance organization available?

Wind Technology Journal

The official publication of the American Wind Energy Association (AWEA) presents technical articles of interest to the serious wind experimenter/developer. No fluff at all.

—J. Baldwin

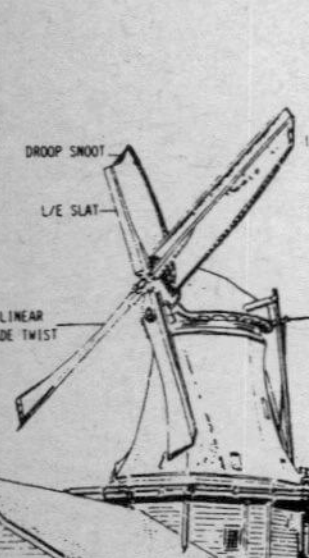
A typical Dutch windmill as developed by the end of the 17th century

Wind Technology Journal
Herman Meijer Drees, Ed.

$20 /year (quarterly)
postpaid from:
P.O. Box 7
Marstons Mills, MA 02648

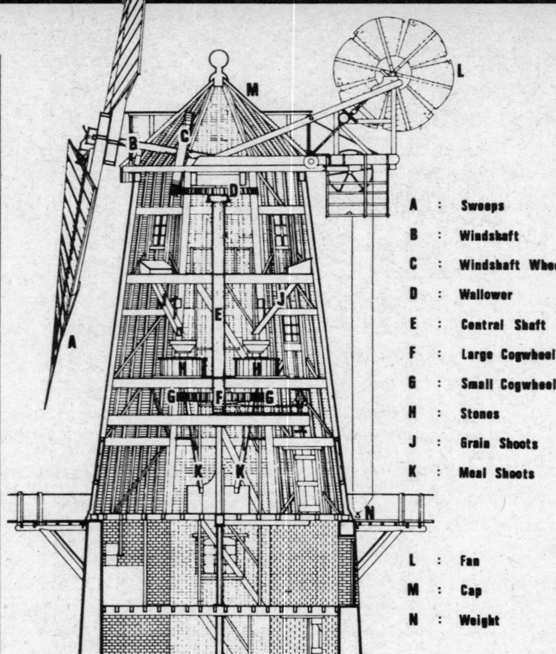

Windmills

People have asked me if Stewart lets the reviewer/evaluators take the books as payment for their work. He doesn't, dammit, or this book would for sure be one I'd cop. It's just beautiful, and it goes way beyond the usual historical-esthetic presentation typical of expensive coffee table pretties. You actually get the complete explanation of how they work! Complete enough, in fact, to make one . . . (guess I'll just borrow it awhile, heh heh) and I'd like to extend a sincere compliment for the reasonable price too,

—J. Baldwin

Windmills
Suzanne Beedell
1975; 143 pp.

$9.95 postpaid from:
Charles Scribner's Sons
Vreeland Ave.
Totowa, NJ 07512
or Whole Earth Household Store

•

There are tales that, in areas where smuggling went on, windmills were frequently used to convey warning signals. On a prearranged code, the sails would quietly be turned to a certain position at the approach of the revenue men, for instance, thus passing a message very quickly over miles of countryside.

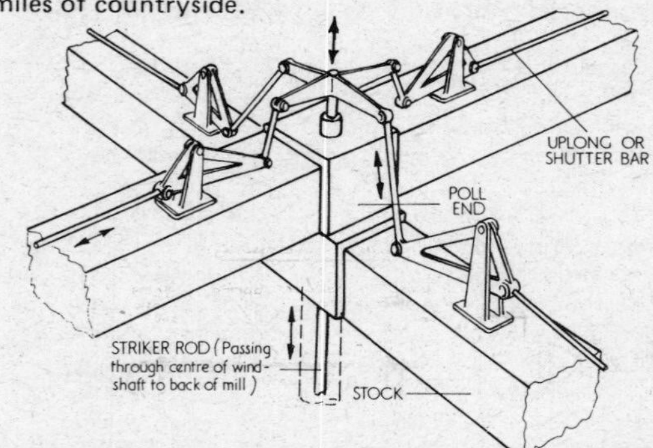

Energy from the Wind (Annotated Bibliography)

This hefty number is just what you'd expect: complete right down to the last zephyr. "Annotated" means you get a very brief whiff of what the paper is about. The latest supplement is as up to date as you're likely to get unless you're writing it up this afternoon.

—J. Baldwin

Energy from the Wind
(Annotated Bibliography)
Barbara L. Burke and
Robert N. Meroney
(About 3 inches thick total)
1975, 1977, 1979

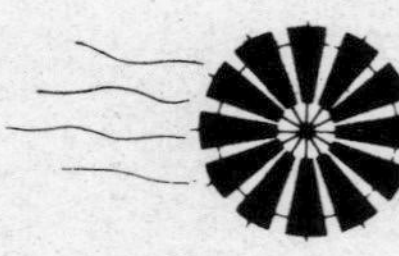

Basic volume
$7.50 ($8.00 foreign)
First supplement
$10.00 ($11.00 foreign)
Second supplement
$15.00 ($16.00 foreign)

All three
$25.00 ($27.00 foreign)
postpaid from:
Publications
Engineering Research Center
Foothills Campus
Colorado State University
Fort Collins, CO 80523

Gemini Synchronous Inverter Systems

The Gemini takes power from a varying, intermittent DC power source such as a wind generator, and inverts it into household 120/240 volts AC. A Gemini system has no batteries. If the wind machine is making more power than you need, the Gemini feeds the excess back into the power company's "grid" (the network of wires). The power company sees this as a reduced demand on their generators, but it is not necessarily true that energy is saved. This is because the huge commercial equipment can't respond quickly to small load differences. Also, the extra power sent to them by your Gemini system may arrive at a time when it is not needed.

If the wind machine isn't making enough electricity for your needs, the Gemini automatically switches on commercial power to make up the difference. The power company sees this as an intermittent load that may occur at a time when demand is already high, so they must build and maintain equipment ready to deliver that power if required. They must also build and maintain the grid. For these reasons, the power companies are not anxious to pay Gemini owners for the power fed back into the grid; certainly not at the rates that you pay them for their power. Nonetheless, Hans Meyer and the crew at Windworks report that power companies have on the whole been cooperative in arranging for the installation of Gemini units (including suitable rates) in their territories.

There is a precedent for this cooperation. For many years there has been what is termed "regeneration". An example of this is an elevator that requires a large surge of power to rise, and by means of a relatively simple circuit, returns power to the grid as it descends. There are many instances where it is reasonable to regenerate, though the practice is not widespread. With cheap energy, it has been cheaper to ignore the possibilities of savings. For example, manufacturers of large diesel engines commonly run them for many hours as a test. The power is dumped without use! With a Gemini, this power could be used to run machinery and lights in the factory as well as feeding surrounding homes. A Gemini system also can be used in "co-generation" schemes where waste process heat is used to run generators that can power other industries or homes. (That steam you see rising from factories is often usable energy being dumped.)

Windworks now has more than 250 Gemini systems on line, including several interfacing with solar cells and hydro turbines. Gemini units can also be used to interface an intermittent power source with an auxiliary; a wind machine with a diesel generator, for instance. Gemini systems are available in large sizes and 3 phase too.

—J. Baldwin

Gemini Synchronous Inverter Systems
PCU 40-11 **$1290**
PCU 80-11 **$1825**
(write for prices of bigger ones, 3 phase equipment, and quantity discounts)

Technical information package
$3 postpaid
all from:
Windworks, Inc.
Route 3, Box 44A
Mukwonago, WI 53149
(414) 363-4088

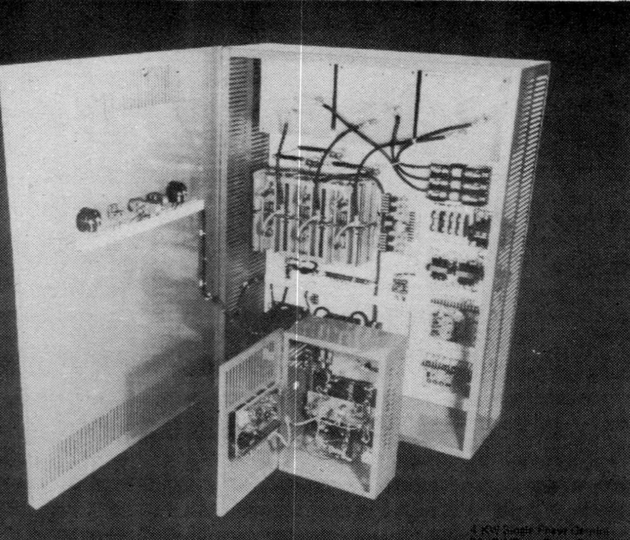

Other good sources of wind energy info

Alternative Sources of Energy *magazine (ASE) which has regular features on wind hardware design and a famous regular column in which wind energy pioneer Martin Jopp answers questions and generally holds forth (p. 174).*

The Energy Primer *(revised and updated) which has an extensive section on wind machines and associated equipment (p. 174).*

The Power Guide *has a good section on internationally available wind machines (p. 200).* *—J. Baldwin*

Harnessing Water Power for Home Energy

Got some flow and head? (so many cubic feet/minute of water dropping so many feet). Plug into it with a wheel for direct olde-timey mechanical energy or with a turbine or geared-up wheel for day-and-night electricity. This fine little book from Garden Way is the only decent one on the subject. It tells you how to hook up to plowing water — lots of different ways — and where to get the gear. For visual delight, nothing beats the overshot wheel, and it's 65% efficient. —SB

Harnessing Water Power for Home Energy
Dermot McGuigan
1978; 101 pp.

$4.95 postpaid from:
Garden Way Publishing Company
Charlotte, VT 05545
or Whole Earth Household Store

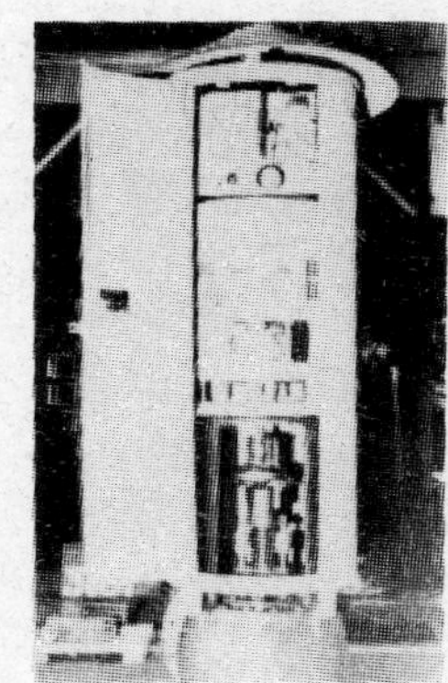

Leffel & Company's Hoppes unit designed to produce 5 kw at 120 volts; 60 hertz on a 25 foot head.

Chinese Hydro-electric Generator Sets

There's a lot of talk about exploiting many small existing dams, but there hasn't been much action because the small scale hardware has not been readily available at a decent price. Now it is. Fully proven (80,000 in use!) these 5 kw (kilowatt) sets come in two forms: a high head model needing a water source about 130 feet higher, and low head job that needs a dam only 16 feet high. They make bigger sets too. Rumour has it that these machines are of very high quality and hence satisfyingly reliable.
—J. Baldwin
[Suggested by Wilson Clark]

Chinese Hydro-electric Generator Sets
Information

free from:
Oriental Engineering and Supply Company
1485 Bayshore Blvd.
Suite 368
San Francisco, CA 94124

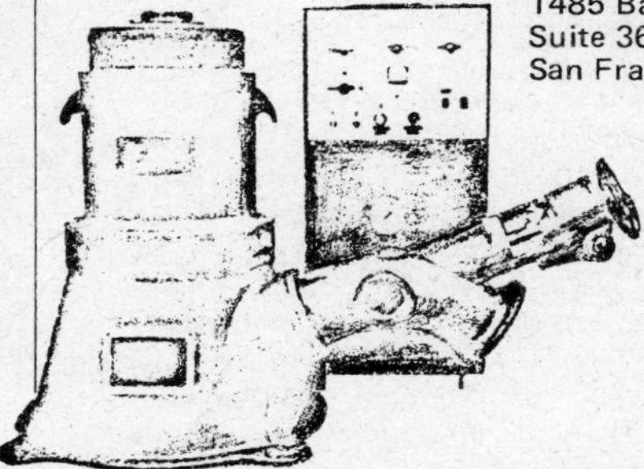

Windmills

If you're pumping water where the wind comes sweepin' 'cross the plain, these two companies have lots of experience with a well-proven never-lapsed wind technology. —SB

The Heller-Aller Company
Information

free from:
The Heller-Aller Company
Corner Perry and Oakwood
Napoleon, OH 43545

Dempster Pumps and Windmills
Information

free from:
Dempster Industries, Inc.
Box 848
Beatrice, NB 68310

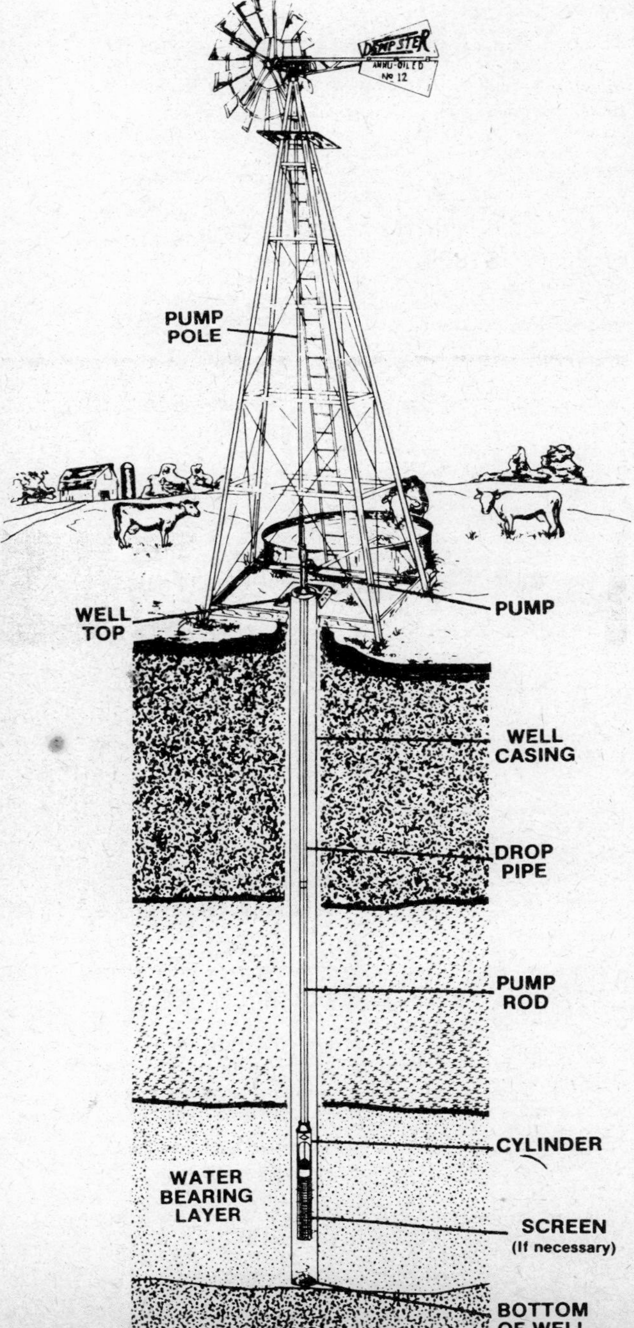

A Manual of Information on the Automatic Hydraulic Ram Pump

Excellent, extra-clear plans for making your own hydraulic ram water pump from standard pipe fittings. This paper is good news indeed, as commerically available rams are expensive (though more efficient). In case you just came in, a hydraulic ram is a motorless water pump that can raise water much higher than the source by sort of bouncing it up the pipe on a cushion of air, a fine idea that works well. You have to have a source of at least 1½ gallons/minute to make this one work. It'll ram best to a weight about 3 times higher than the source head, but it can pump much higher; as high as 450 feet from a 9 foot head! If you need more water delivery, you can make a row of rams working side by side. VITA (p. 180) has a similar paper available too, though for smaller water systems. —J. Baldwin

A Manual of Information on the Automatic Hydraulic Ram Pump
S.B. Watt
1975; 38 pp.

£1.50 postpaid from:
Intermediate Technology Development Group
9 King Street
London WC2E 8HN
England

or

$5.25 postpaid from:
I.T.D.G.
North America
P.O. Box 337
Croton-on-Hudson, NY 10520
or Whole Earth Household Store

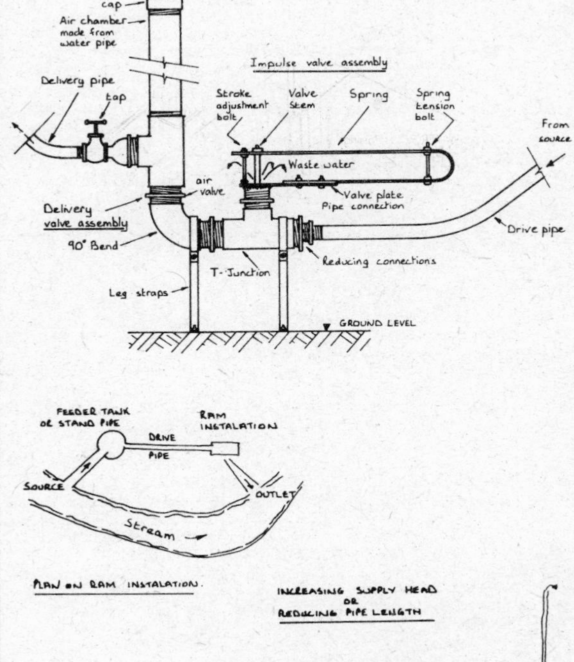

Leffel Hydraulic Turbines

If you have a good head of water nearby, a creek, river, reservoir, or dam, then you can build an electrical system powered by the water. There are homemade methods, and used turbines, but it helps if you understand what it takes to change the creek into a lightbulb. Leffel has been doing this industrially for a hundred or so years, but they also have single family systems. Ask for Pamphlet A and Bulletin H-49. —J.D. Smith
[Suggested by Pete Schermerhorn]

Leffel Hydraulic Turbines
Information

free from:
The James Leffel Co.
426 East Street
Springfield, OH 45501

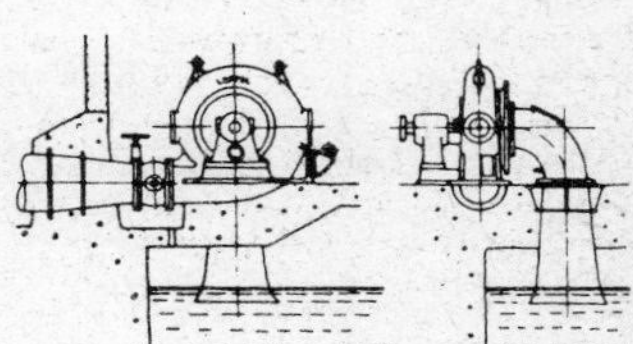

Rife Hydraulic Rams

A good tailormade hydraulic ram pump. Size and price run from one for $398 that takes a maximum 15 ft. fall and pumps it up to 150 ft. (2 - 13 gallon-per-minute) to a $7,500 job that rams a maximum 50 ft. fall up to 500 ft. (150 - 750 gallon-per-minute). —SB

Rife Hydraulic Water Rams
(Manual of Information)

$.25 postpaid from:
Rife Hydraulic Engine Manufacturing Company
132 Main Street
Andover, NJ 07821

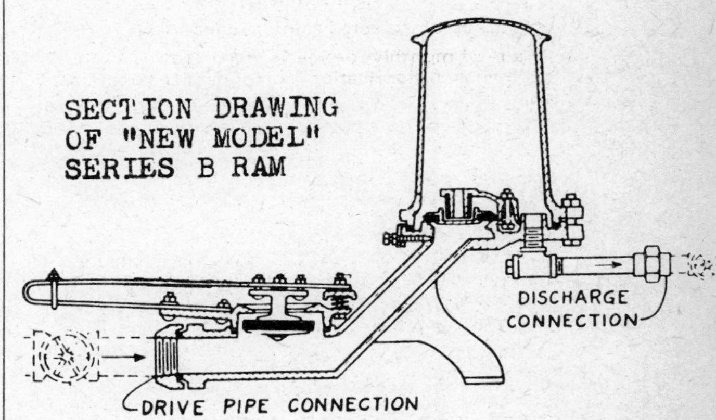

THE RISING SUN
NEIGHBORHOOD NEWSLETTER

The woman asked the gallery guard if he liked the exhibit and he said he'd been working there a year and had gallery white out. It happens to pilots in snow storms and means you can't see anything.

Fiat's TOTEM (Total Energy Module)

Well we've seen a lot of writing about saving energy by being more efficient, but we haven't seen much hardware to back up the talk. Here's an idea that I believe needs to at least be tried. It has some good things going for it: it permits decentralized electric power, it can be financed a bit at a time by private parties (or more accurately, neighborhoods), it can greatly reduce the need for expensive standby peak-load power stations and their distribution networks, it eliminates the possibility of wide power outage, and it is a commendable 90% efficient! (That's compared with about 55% efficient for municipal power.) So how does it work?

A small auto engine (Fiat, of course) runs an electric generator. The generator is already quite efficient, but auto engines are notoriously inefficient. Many are 10% as installed in cars. What is inefficient about them is that they turn most of the power available in the fuel into heat instead of work. TOTEM catches this heat and uses it to make hot water, for space heating, and to run heat pumps. The heat-catcher housing also stops noise from escaping. The whole thing makes less pollution than a common oil burner furnace. It can be rigged to run on methane. One hundred cows can power a small neighborhood. System costs, including running, fuel and overhaul every 3,000 hours are less than for typical municipal power. So TOTEM could save 70% on fossil fuel in addition to the above advantages. Sounds good doesn't it? Fiat thinks a TOTEM unit could sell for about $3,000.

—J. Baldwin
[Suggested by Eric MacKnight]

Fiat TOTEM
Information
free from:
Fiat Motors of
North America, Inc.
155 Chestnut Ridge Rd.
Montvale, NJ 07645

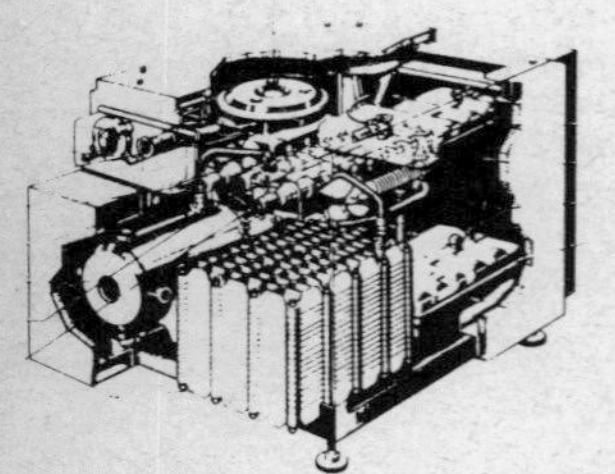

1. 127 Engine
2. Water tank
3. Gas/water heat exchanger
4. Oil/water heat exchanger
5. Oil/tank
6. Water/water heat exchanger
7. Hot water output
8. Gas exhaust
9. Electric motor
10. Cold water input
11. Connection to network
12. Air intake
13. Methane supply

Electric vehicles

When considering the idea of electric vehicles, it is well to remember that in many locations "electric car" means in reality "nuclear car." A widespread, sudden demand for electric vehicles would almost certainly require environmentally disastrous increases in the demand for electric generating plants and the consequent fuels thereof. I see electric vehicles, at least in their present state of development, to be potentially the biggest problem facing the anti-nuke movement and the environmentally concerned citizen. Nonetheless, you might have some reason to be interested in where things are these days. —J. Baldwin

World Guide to Battery-Powered Road Transportation
Jeffrey M. Christian, Editor
1980; 392 pp.
$49.50 postpaid from:
McGraw-Hill Book Co.
Princeton Road
Hightstown, NJ 08520
or Whole Earth
Household Store

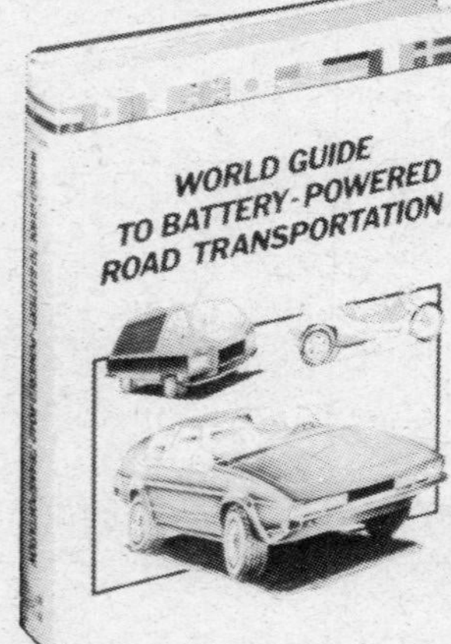

World Guide to Battery Powered Road Transportation *is a straight listing of descriptions and technical specifications of all electric road vehicles existing at the time of publication.*

•

Yare, Electric passenger car, U.S.
T.P. Laboratories
Box 73
La Porte, IN 46350

Base price, single unit: $20,000

The Power Guide

This catalog of small scale power equipment is by far the most comprehensive and useful I have seen. Mr. Fraenkel, who brought us the excellent **Food From Windmills** *has outdone himself. Included are not only the expected windmills etc., but steam engines, diesel generating sets, and that relic that you thought nobody was making anymore, the slow-revving, big-flywheel, last-forever donkey engine. A very complete world list of manufacturers brings up the rear. This is where you look first.*

—J. Baldwin

The Power Guide
(A Catalogue of Small Scale Power Equipment)
Peter Fraenkel
1979; 240 pp.
£7.50 postpaid from:
Intermediate Technology Development Group
9 King Street
London WC2E 8HN
England
or
$16.50 postpaid from:
I.T.D.G.
North America
P.O. Box 337
Croton-on-Hudson
New York, NY 10520

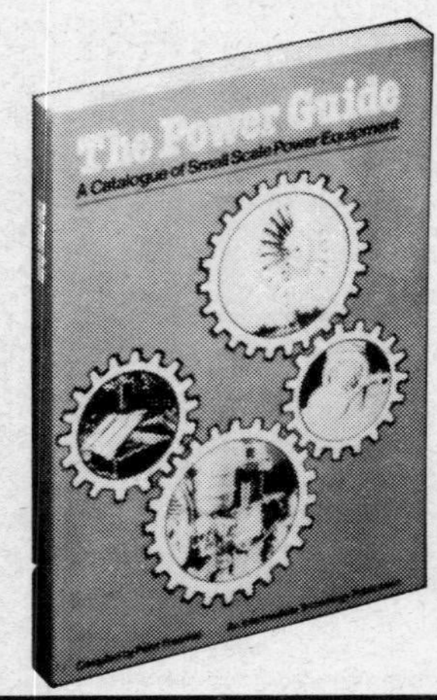

The Storage Battery

The men who make 'em give what you need to know about choosing, using and caring for batteries, in simple language (thank goodness). Yet there are so many variables, that batteries are still a bit of a black art even in this high tech age. You'll get a good start understanding them here.

—J. Baldwin

The Storage Battery
(lead-acid types)
1969; 34 pp.

$1 postpaid from:
Exide Power Systems Division
ESB Inc.
Rising Sun and Adams Avenues
Box 5723
Philadelphia, PA 19120

Storage Batteries

This highly technical text is the complete Word on batteries. Though not directly aimed at wind generator system storage problems, you can find the information you need by combining information from various chapters. Considering the subject matter, it's surprisingly easy to understand. One of the oldies-but-goodies.

—J. Baldwin
[Suggested by Jim Bukey]

Storage Batteries
George Wood Vinal
1924, 1955; 446 pp.

$29.50 postpaid from:
John Wiley & Sons
One Wiley Drive
Somerset, NJ 08873

•

WESTWARD MOULDINGS, LTD.
Greenhill Works
Delaware Road
Gunnislake
Cornwall
England
Phone: Gunnislake (0822) 832120

16ft Wheel Producing 20 b.h.p.

Manufacturers of fibreglass water wheels to order. Units can be overshot or breast wheels with diameters of 8 ft., 16 ft., and 20 ft. Wheels can be built to any width and can be shipped in sections and erected on site. Typical power outputs as follows:

Diameter	Width	Nominal power (max)
8 ft. (2.4 m)	2.5 ft. (0.76 m)	6 b.h.p.
16 ft. (4.8 m)	3.0 ft. (0.91 m)	25 b.h.p.
20 ft. (6.0 m)	4.5 ft. (1.4 m)	35 b.h.p.

DP-60 Engine

•

A range of heavy duty, low-speed, horizontal, two-stroke engines, developed for pumping oil in oilfields but well-suited for driving reciprocating water pumps. Very little maintenance required — engines have particularly long operational life.

•

STIRLING ENGINES
Harwell TMG
AGA Navigation Aids
77 High Street
Brentford
Middlesex, U.K.
Telex: 935956
Cables: Agafaros, Hounslow
Phone: 01-950-6465

Aga Harwell Thermo Mechanical Generat

The Aga Harwell Thermo Mechanical Generator is an unconventional device invented at the Harwell nuclear research center. It works on the Stirling engine principle, but has no rotating parts. The output is via a linear, oscillating electric generator that produces a 25 watt, 100Hz AC electrical primary output which is then rectified to maintain 10 12V nickel cadmium cells capable of sustaining a 36 watt electrical load for a mean duty of 14 hours in each 24.

Its function is to produce a reliable electrical output from a propane (or other heat) energy input source, consumption being 200kg of propane per year. The device is intended to run for ten years without maintenance other than cleaning the propane burner annually when the fuel supply is replenished. Typical applications are remote unattended low power electrical devices such as marine buoys, microwave repeaters.

It is likely that further, higher powered models of this device will become available later.

The Complete Book of Electric Vehicles
Sheldon R. Shacket
1979; 168 pp.
$7.95 postpaid from:
Domus Books
Quality Books, Inc.
400 Anthony Trail
Northbrook, IL 60062

The Complete Book of Electric Vehicles *is a good look at what has been done, and includes many weird experimental machines as well as "hybrids" (gasoline/electric) and a pretty good discussion of theory.*

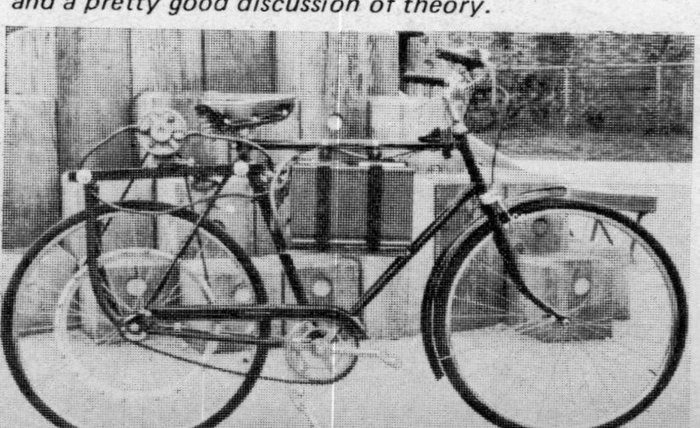

•

Sheldon Shacket, the author of this book, has built over 15 two- and three-wheeled electric vehicle prototypes.

The Model Three is a lightweight electric bicycle built on a Raleigh three-speed frame. Power from the type 27 marine battery, rated at 95 amp hours, is directed through a single-speed on/off switch. The motor is a 1/2 hp, permanent magnet type with vee-belt drive to the rear wheel. Range is 20 miles (32 km) at 16 mph (26 km). Top speed is 18 mph (29 km).

Electric Vehicles
(Design and Build Your Own)
Michael Hackleman
1980; 214 pp.
2nd Edition
$8.95 postpaid from:
Peace Press
3828 Willat Avenue
Culver City, CA 90230
or Whole Earth
Household Store

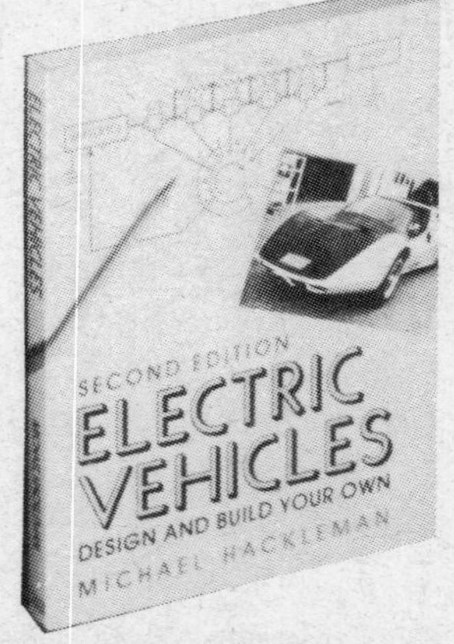

Electric Vehicles *gives sufficient information to allow you to at least get a handle on building your own. The numbers are all there and the attitude is right for the experimenter.*

Steamboat

Live Steam

*Initially oriented to building working replicas of steam locomotives and traction engines (steam tractors) due to the technical background of many of **Live Steam**'s readers, the magazine now is branching out to steamboats, stationary power, and automobiles. And it's really good on machine shop techniques. Coupled with more modern materials for bearings and sealants, reliability engineering, and electronic control, more efficient prime movers could be developed to utilize coal or wood. With GM and GE in control of the loco industry, GM in control of the bus and much of the truck industry, they won't change. As fuel oil goes up, the field will be open.* —J. Garwood

Live Steam
William C. Fitt, Editor
$20 /year (12 issues)
from:
Live Steam Magazine
P.O. Box 581
Traverse City, MI 49684

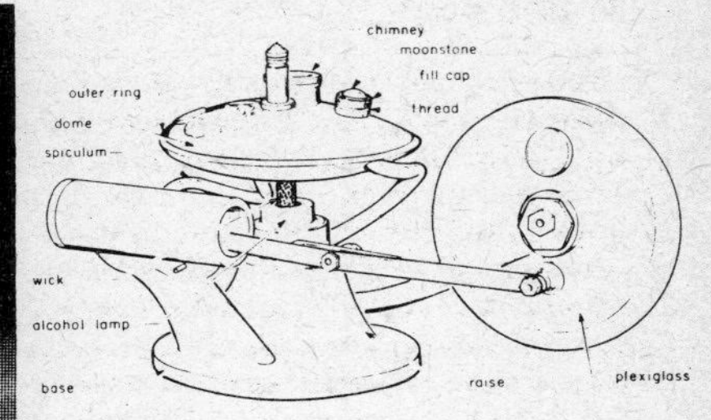

John Quick's Silver Engine

Day-Land steam engines

In case any of you would like to make a 20 horsepower steam engine, Mr. Moore sells plans and castings ready to machine. It's an old proven design similar to the one used in Stanley Steamer automobiles, but it has been updated with more modern materials and details. He also sent us the following steam power source list. Lotsa people talkin' about it but few doin' it. Now there's no excuse.
—J. Baldwin

Day-Land Steam Engine
Brochure, price information and source list

$2 postpaid from:
C. William Moore, ME
P.O. Box 756
Pleasanton, CA 94566

•

Sources for Steam Engines & Supplies

Cole's Power Models
Box 788
Ventura, CA 93002
Model engines, boilers, etc.

Light Steam Power
Kirk Michael
Isle of Man, U.K.
Engine castings, plans for engines, boilers, and books on steam.

Paul R. Breisch
187 Ridge Pike
Royersford, PA 19468
Model engine, pump, etc., castings

William T. Blake
Box 54
Canandaigua, NY 14424
Model supplies.

Geothermal scam

Friends:

This Geothermal scam is very serious and is getting out of hand.

Steam from the earth as an energy source sounds good, but to see it at work a la P.G.&E. is another story.

The air around here in Lake County, California, is getting thick with poisonous gases, and huge trucks drive on the local roads with loads of toxic sludge which gets taken to the local dump.

The whole trip is dangerous and expensive. It is more centralized, corporate-owned electricity; "mined," here in rural Lake County and pumped to the Bay Area. It gets good press though, down in the city. Even from the anti-nuke folks, and usual foes of P.G.&E. They call it "alternative energy" and say it's clean. Can you give us some help on this? Please see enclosed flyer for hard facts.

Sincerely,
Herb Gura
Lake County, California

The Geysers 11 Geothermal power plants emit an estimated 1,790 pounds of toxic chemical gases into our atmosphere hourly. These poisons include hydrogen sulphide, boron, arsenic, and radon. The air quality in our county has dipped below the legal standard while the construction and planning of new geothermal projects continue with the blessings of our local officials.

Despite complaints of nausea, dizziness, loss of sleep, stillbirths, and lung problems, no extensive studies have been made to determine the possible hazards of geothermal pollution to our health.
Other problems such as noise, road damage, water pollution, damage to wildlife, and increased earthquake danger, need more serious study. These issues have not been addressed satisfactorily.

—**"Geothermal power poisoning you?"** leaflet
Clearlake Highlands, California

Hot Air Engine Primer

The "hot air" engine has been a matter of renewed interest lately, as the type can be raised to a useful efficiency while making less pollution. They are powered by an external heat source, solar being one possibility. Information about all the different types that have been tried and proposed has been difficult to find except in bits and pieces. Mr. Aun has done considerable legwork getting this booklet together, hence the price. If you desire an education in hot air machines, this is where to start. Lots of diagrams make it all easier to understand. —SB

Hot Air Engine Primer
Tonu O. Aun
1978; 52 pp.

$6 postpaid from:
Tonu O. Aun
P.O. Box 515
Adelaide Street
Postal Station
Toronto, Ontario
Canada M5C 2J6

How to Be Your Own Power Company

You can equip a home to use 12 volt DC power. I've lived that way for more than 5 years with no serious problems (and no washing machine or freezer), so I can vouch that it can be done without having to live like a swine. The basic idea is that you power your household needs with a 12 volt battery which is recharged by your car (it can be done as you drive if you wish) or other source of power such as a small gasoline generator set or a wind machine. These books (for some reason there are three) tell you what you need to know to rig the hardware for safe efficient use. It can be done to meet code. Everything is explained by big clear diagrams and a text that assumes that you know nothing about electricity. The publishers also sell an assortment of necessary hardware, though some of their selections might be the subject of controversy. The books are intended for beginners. Experienced 12-volters will not find much new.
—J. Baldwin

How to Be Your Own Power Company
(The Low-Voltage, Direct Current, Power-Generating System)
Jim Cullen
1978, 1980; 142 pp.

$11.95 postpaid from:
Van Nostrand
Reinhold Company
Order Department
7625 Empire Drive
Florence, KY 41042

Incongruous Technology

by Witold Rybczynski

Some years ago, studies of urban slums uncovered a startling fact — very poor people often drive Cadillacs. This was disturbing not only because it depreciated the value of the status symbol, but also because it attacked an important American belief — that technology should be congruous. According to this belief technological development occurs on a step-by-step, across-the-board basis; hence a poor person ought to drive a "poor" car. A poor person driving an expensive car was considered inefficient, and in some vague way immoral. This (Protestant) belief has colored our view of technology and technological development for the last fifty years, and whether we are Buck Rogers technologists or Appropriate Technologists, we inevitably take technological congruity for granted. We have come to believe that we must have all or nothing.

A view of other cultures, particularly ones which are just now beginning their industrial development, gives rise to the possibility that perhaps technological congruity is not inevitable.

I recently did some work for a Cree Indian community in northern Canada. The daily life of the 500 or so people who live in Big Trout Lake is a strange mixture of the old and the new, and illustrates what I mean by technological incongruity.

The Cree are trappers who spend extended periods in the bush, in the winter, relying on ageless woodcraft for survival; yet to reach their trap-lines, a 30-mile trip, they charter a plane. Domestic life is largely unaffected by modern gadgets. The toilet is an outhouse, cooking and heating are done with wood, there is no running water — it is brought from the lake in buckets — but outside many of the houses stand washing machines, powered by small gas motors. Likewise, though there is no electricity, most of the homes have inexpensive portable radios. Some even have small Honda generators which are cranked up periodically so that colour television, via satellite, can be watched.

It would be a mistake to conclude that the Cree are being overtaken by white man's technology. They are not trapped by our vision of technological congruity, and hence see nothing wrong in letting the new and the old evolve side by side.

Another brief example.

In the Philippines I had been asked to give a talk to a group of students in a squatter settlement in Manila. I had planned to show slides, but 10 minutes before the start there was still no projector. I assumed we would have to forego the slides, but I was mistaken. My friend there said he was sure he could *make* a slide projector — after all wasn't it just a lens and a light bulb?

My point is that this reaction — if your shoelace breaks, look for a piece of string — has become increasingly rare in America. Unlike people who live with technological incongruities we have become intimidated by our machines and no longer control them. The first step away from this unhappy situation is not to look for moral consistency in our technologies but to cultivate technological incongruities.

Perhaps the first Chinese astronaut will use an abacus? ■

THE RISING SUN
NEIGHBORHOOD NEWSLETTER

57 Bumblebees alighting on my left arm for a moment and leaving without a sting were definitely a sign, but of what?

Biogas

AS FAR AS I KNOW, nobody in continental U.S.A. has made a domestic (family) size methane generator that works in a reliable, useful, year-round manner with an operating routine that everyday people can accept. All these references then, are either for outfits larger than family size, or are presumably useful for experimenters. Good luck! —J. Baldwin

A Chinese Biogas Manual

With seven million biogas generators working in China today, it seems safe to say that they know how to do it. The book is a direct translation from the Chinese and consequently gives a feeling of the culture that actually uses it as an instruction book. A wide variety of soil types and climates are considered, along with the various materials that can be digested. Successful operation methods are emphasized. Readers of more familiar biogas texts will be pleased at the absence of grandiose claims and self-righteous hype: It's just plain folks, making it work. —J. Baldwin

A Chinese Biogas Manual
(Popularising Technology in the Countryside)
Ariane van Buren, Editor
1979; 135 pp.

£4.55 postpaid from:
Intermediate Technology Development Group
9 King Street
London WC2E 8HN
England

or

$8.75 postpaid from:
I.T.D.G.
North America
P.O. Box 337
Croton-on-Hudson
NY 10520

or Whole Earth Household Store

gas inlet
air inlet hole
air and gas mixing channel
clay head
gauze mantle

The quantity of liquid material should never exceed ¾ of the pit volume

When removing slurry for fertilizer, do not let the level fall below the upper edge of the passage to the fermentation compartment

↑ Right beside this concave concrete dish, a hole is dug for the pit, filled with water until the concave dish beside it floats and can then be floated over until positioned above the hole. The water is then pumped out, bringing the dish to rest in place at the bottom of the hole. A cork is then removed from the centre of the dish, so that it will not float upwards as the water seeps back into the hole. With the concrete dish as a firm base to stand on, workers can then proceed to build up the brick walls of the pit along the rim of the dish. Heavy clay is packed over the top of the completed fermentation tank to increase the downward pressure on the pit. Enough water is also kept in the pit at all times to prevent flotation.

The Compleat Biogas Handbook

Hoo BOY, is it compleat! The author recognizes that a practical long-lasting everyday use biogas plant hasn't really been done yet, but he doesn't concede that it can't be. So lots of the numbers you need are here, and many hard-won tips are shown from often bitter experience. This book fills a real need, and I am happy to say that it seems to be well executed. Directions for making that mythical generator aren't here, but a good proven learning one is shown. The book's main value is in showing how to do things that have been glossed over or ignored in other books. Such as burning methane in a gasoline engine. If biogas interests you enough to consider making a generator, this book is your next assignment. —J. Baldwin

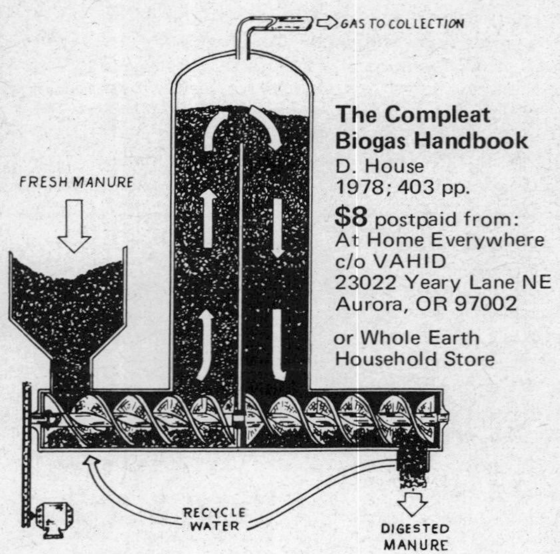

The Compleat Biogas Handbook
D. House
1978; 403 pp.

$8 postpaid from:
At Home Everywhere
c/o VAHID
23022 Yeary Lane NE
Aurora, OR 97002

or Whole Earth Household Store

•

Heavy metals, which are often the consequence of industrial pollution, harm the biogas bacteria. The principal culprits are Cr (chromium), Cu (copper), Ni (nickel), Zn (zinc), and Hg (mercury). Of these, copper is commonly used in compounds to combat fungus, for example on grapes. Zinc is of course used in galvanizing buckets, pipes and other metal devices exposed to weather or water. Probably the zinc would not appear in the generator unless a galvanized surface were directly exposed to organic matter, as with galvanized slurry pipes. Use plastic or clay pipe. Anything acidic, next to a galvanized surface, will "leach" the zinc into itself. Dilution or avoidance.

Synthetic detergents have also proven harmful. If you plan to use a biogas generator as your sewage disposal system, there are several ways to approach this. If the house to which this biogas "septic tank" is to be attached is as yet unbuilt, consider installing several drainage systems for various water-using appliances. The hot water from the bath or shower, which, as water, adds nothing to the actual production of biogas except the increased cost which results from the larger volume needed, may serve to *heat* the generator. On the other hand, toilet water should go into the generator. A sink might be hooked up to drain dish water to the "heating" system, but allow disposal wastes to go into the generator. Many good publications are available on these and related ideas. See for example, McGill University's **Stop the Five Gallon Flush**, or publications and magazine articles on "grey water." In any case, with reference to toxins, make sure to watch your use of toxic cleansers (new Comet with Clorinal), chemicalized soaps, detergents, shampoos, toilet bowl cleaners, caustic drain cleaners, and so on. If codes will not allow above ground disposal of sewage, consider installing the generator where it can be easily heated and serviced (in a basement?) and run the effluent out through an ordinary leach line system or into your septic tank.

Practical methane

Here is a cold blooded, well executed study of a practical methane plant. The net energy aspects of this real life hardware test are well attended, an absolute necessity if one is to avoid kidding oneself. Not only that, but the investigators also examine the operation for ways to maximize the economic advantage to the farmer through various financing schemes and careful attention to idealizing the size. This study is certainly one of the most useful yet done and completely avoids the (cow)pie-in-the-sky sort of reporting more often found. You'll need at least 200 cows to make it pay. —J. Baldwin

Report on the Design and Operation of a Full-scale Anaerobic Dairy Manure Digester
Elizabeth Coppinger, et al.
1979; 78 pp.

$10.65 postpaid from:
Ecotope Groupe
2332 East Madison
Seattle, WA 98112

•

The following is concluded after two years of digester operation:

1. A full-scale dairy manure digester is capable of providing a consistent and reliable source of fuel.

2. Dairy manure digesters develop stable microbiological populations, and no alteration of naturally occurring biological parameters is required.

3. In-tank mixing is not necessary for full-scale, rigid tank, dairy manure digesters. Natural mixing from convection currents and gas bubbling is adequate, provided the %TS in the tank remains above the point at which scum formation ceases to be a problem.

4. Influent/effluent shell and tube heat exchangers are not a good prospect for efficient effluent heat recovery with dairy manure digesters.

5. Energy produced by farmer-financed dairy manure digesters is competitive in cost with other energy sources, especially propane and fuel oil.

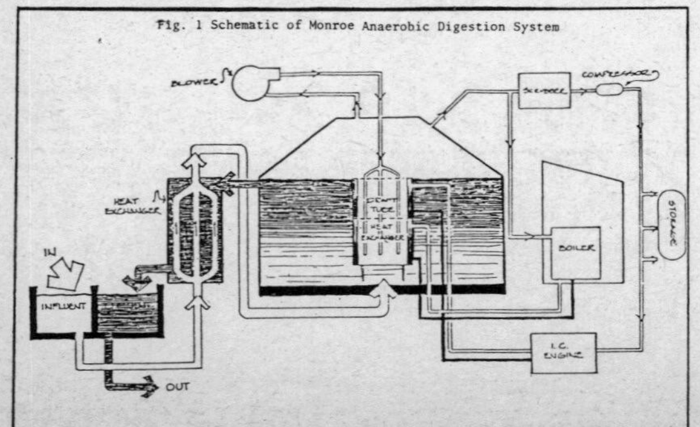

The Do's and Don't's of Methane

Al Rutan, the Methane Man has been counselling us on biogas matters for some time now in the pages of **ASE** *magazine (***Alternative Sources of Energy***, p. 174). This book is an update of an earlier edition in 1975 and contains a great deal of field experience and experimentation with methane production. Mr. Rutan makes a good case for methane, but he stops short of claiming that small methane generators are working on a practical day-to-day basis with a regimen that one would care to include in one's daily life. Nonetheless methane holds great promise, particularly for farmers and perhaps neighborhoods, and this book certainly will help bring practical methane to general use. If Al Rutan can get it to cook in chilly Minnesota, that's good news indeed.* —J. Baldwin

The Do's & Don't's of Methane
Al Rutan
1975, 1979; 160 pp.

$15 postpaid from:
Rutan Publishing
P.O. Box 3585
Minneapolis, MN 55403

or Whole Earth Household Store

•

Well, after a few days I started to get methane and then I lost it. The tank was still producing a lot of gas, but it was carbon dioxide. The pig manure I had begun to feed the digester along with the slurry from the St. Cloud plant was just too much raw material for the process. So there was lots of carbon dioxide and acid. The acid forming bacteria were having a field day.

I mentioned this problem to a friend with whom I was working at the time. He said, "I make a lot of wine at home. And every once in a while I have the same problem. And when I do I add a little baking soda. It straightens out the condition right away. And the nice thing is that it doesn't leave an aftertaste. But in your case that isn't a problem!"

So I tried the baking soda. It worked like a charm. Within three days I had methane on the way. At a seminar I was presenting a few weeks later I mentioned this to the group. Baking soda was my "discovery" for straightening out the pH in the digester.

The Anaerobic Digestion of Livestock Wastes to Produce Methane

A very fine annotated bibliography of methane papers, compiled by men who know what's what. —J. Baldwin

The Anaerobic Digestion of Livestock Wastes to Produce Methane
(1946-June 1975: A Bibliography With Abstracts)
Gregg Shadduck and James A. Moore
1975; 103 pp.

$2.50 postpaid from:
Dr. James A. Moore
Department of Agricultural Engineering
University of Minnesota
1390 Eckles Avenue
St. Paul, MN 55108

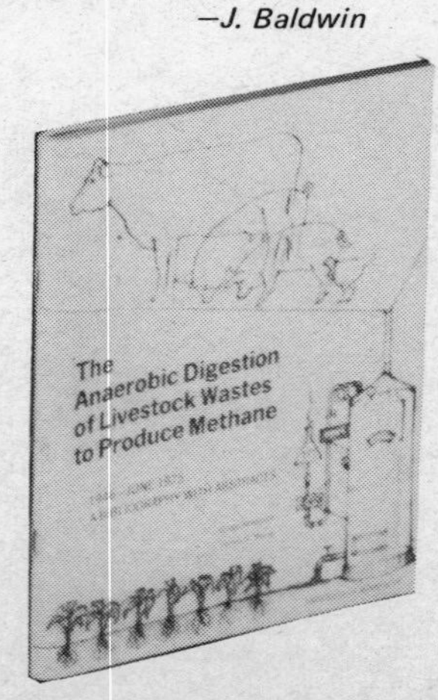

The Art and Ingenuity of the Woodstove

Easily the most esthetic of the "stove books," this friendly look at the phenomenon ranges through history to the present, all illustrated with Mr. Adkins' incomparable drawings. There's lots of good advice too, explained so you'll have some idea of why you're expected to do things a certain way. You can tell he's done more than read catalogs. My favorite chapter is on how stoves are made. —J. Baldwin

(See **Woodstove Cookery**, *p. 370.)*

The Art and Ingenuity of the Woodstove
Jan Adkins
1978; 137 pp.
$7.95 postpaid from:
Everest House
1133 Avenue of the Americas
New York, NY 10036
or Whole Earth Household Store

Some equipment for home woodburning

← The best wood is dry wood. How dry your wood will be depends on how you store it. Stored outside its moisture content may wither to 14 - 25 percent. Under cover without heat it can dip to 10 - 15 percent and in the heated house, 5 - 12 percent. Curing usually takes more than a year, but wood stacked in the sun under a vented clear plastic shelter can be ready for good burning in three to four months. Storing wood in the house or garage could be disappointing; trees are homes for a nation of wood eating insects that think of a frame house as dessert. A woodshed, even a simple structure, will shelter and cure stovewood almost as well.

↑
In thinking of stove placement, turn your house upside down in your mind's eye. See the stove as a spigot of running heat, splashing first on the ceiling below it and starting to fill up the ceiling pan until it runs over the door headers and begins to fill up the ceilings of the adjacent rooms or cascades down the ceiling of the stairs and flows into the second floor. There will be convective currents that run against this upside-down scenario, but the bulk of warm air will stay pooled at the ceiling. Plan a space for a fan — wall, pedestal or table model — to roil those air pools and get them moving around. Consider rooms that can and should be cold. Don't squander heat on closets and cupboards that don't need it. Get it working to warm bodies.

Wood Heat →

All those little things that other books assume you know, but probably don't, are worked at here, and probably illustrated too. There's a particularly good section on wood range cooking. Also very good is the discussion of procedures such as lighting up. There's even a plan for a flue fire alarm! I learned more from this very personal account than from anything else I've read on the subject. —J. Baldwin

Wood Heat
(New, Improved)
John Vivian
1978; 428 pp.
$7.95 postpaid from:
Rodale Books
33 East Minor
Emmaus, PA 18049
or Whole Earth Household Store

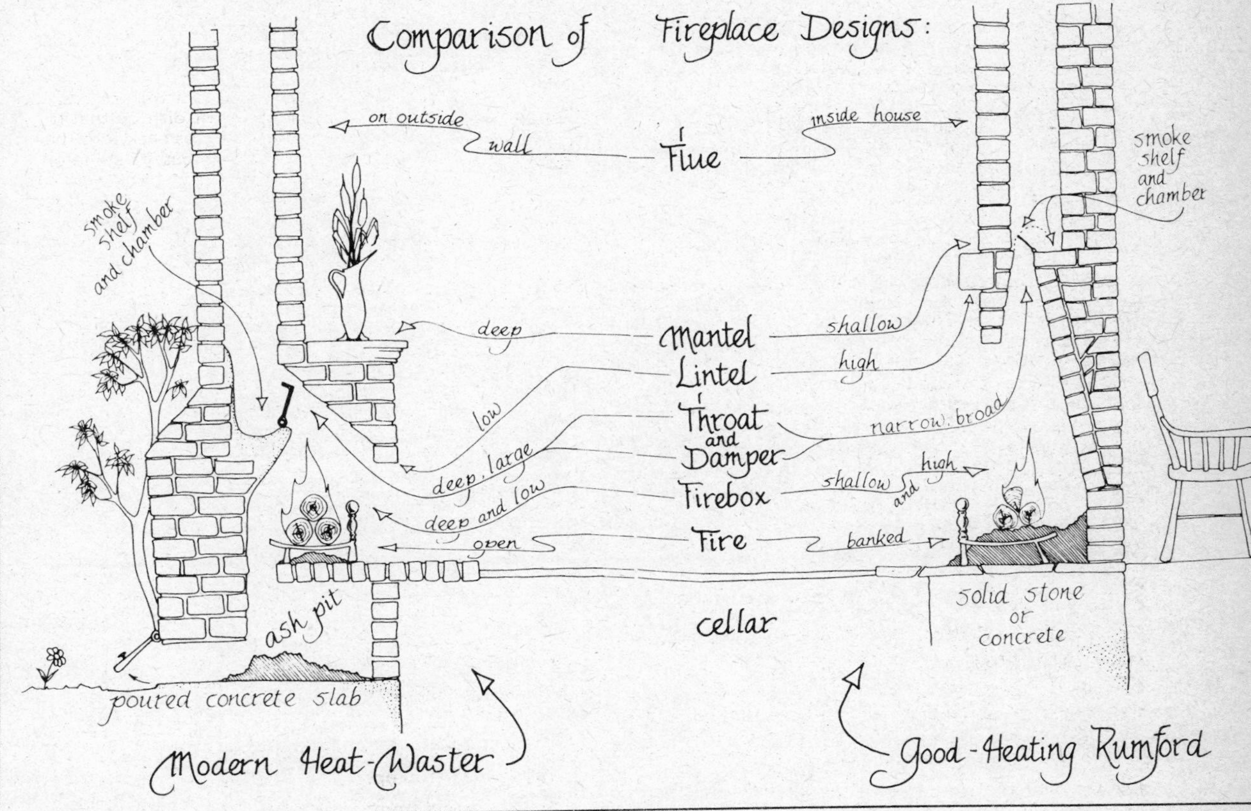

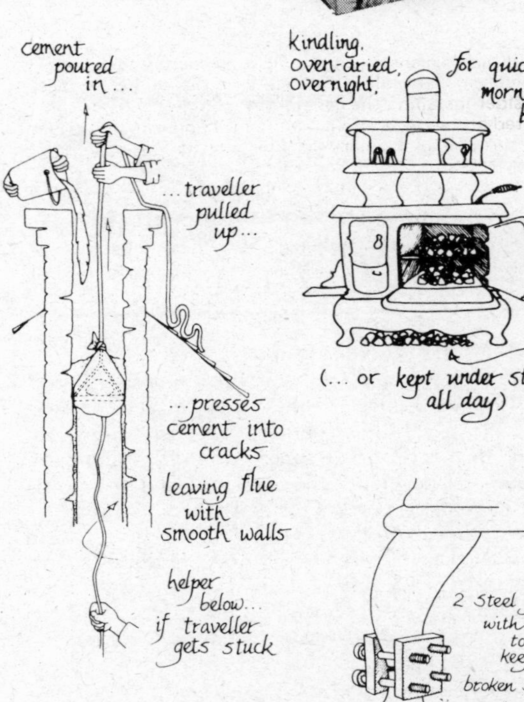

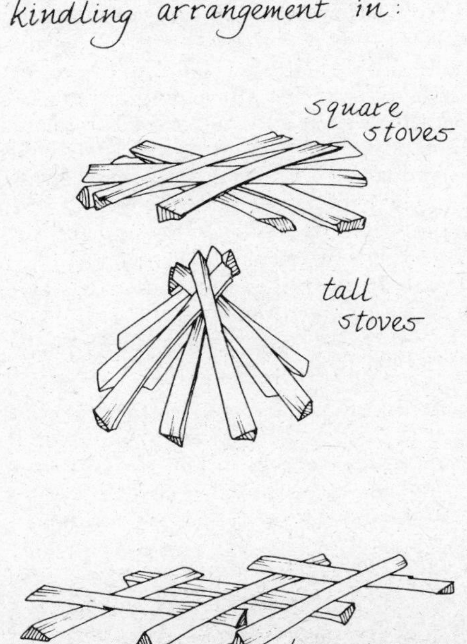

THE RISING SUN
NEIGHBORHOOD NEWSLETTER

The women's john in the Fruitvale BART station has a large triangular window (8 feet long, 1 foot to 6 feet high) that lets in the sky and the sun and nothing else and shocked me into thinking how beautiful the sky and the sun are (especially when they sneak up on you like that) and how rarely public restrooms are beautiful. One is excessively thankful for not repulsive and not scary.

Wood Heat Safety

Jay Shelton was among the first to do comparative testing of wood stoves and must be considered an expert of experts. In this detailed, very specific book, he considers virtually every detail (including water heating). It's a good thing he does too; the attitude of energy independence that has grown along with the increasing popularity of wood heat has also brought forth a disregard for hazard that often approaches the foolhardy. I've been in homes recently that had installations so flagrantly unsafe that I wouldn't spend the night. An added bonus to Mr. Shelton's recommendations is that he mostly refrains from scary war stories and guilt-inducing admonitions. It's just the facts you need to know, and no more or less. A commendably good job in every way: you needn't wait for a better one to come along. —J. Baldwin

Wood Heat Safety
Jay W. Shelton
1979; 165 pp.

$8.95 postpaid from:
Garden Way Publishing Company
Charlotte, VT 05545
or Whole Earth Household Store

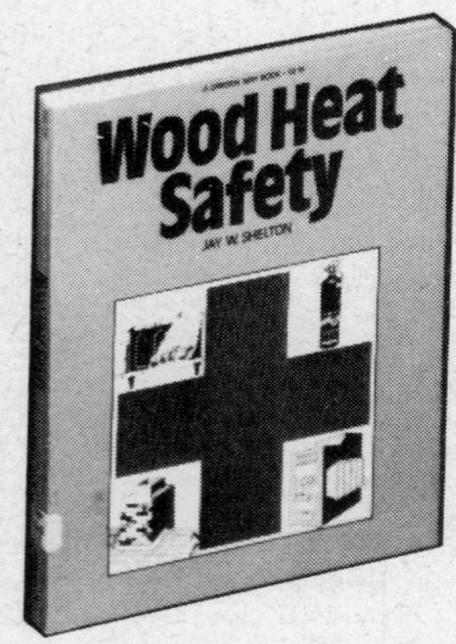

•

My personal preference, not considering cost or convenience of installation in an existing house, is an interior masonry chimney with all its walls exposed to the living spaces. By trying to avoid smoldering fires I manage to avoid much creosote buildup, and the exposed masonry contributes considerable heat. However I have installed some prefabricated metal chimneys in my homes because of the ease of installation.

•

There is an unusual kind of chimney damper available for masonry chimneys serving fireplaces. The damper is at the top of the chimney and the damper's position is controlled from the fireplace inside the house. Such dampers have the potential advantage of preventing cold outdoor air from descending into and cooling the chimney and then the house when the fireplace is not in use. It is absolutely critical that the damper never shut due to heat, breakage, or wind, when there is a fire in the fireplace. As a practical matter, such dampers should also not be damaged by chimney fires. The dampers should probably also be designed so they cannot freeze shut; people often light fires before remembering to open the damper. Until both the safety of such devices is clear and the possible beneficial effects are quantified, I would be hesitant about using them.

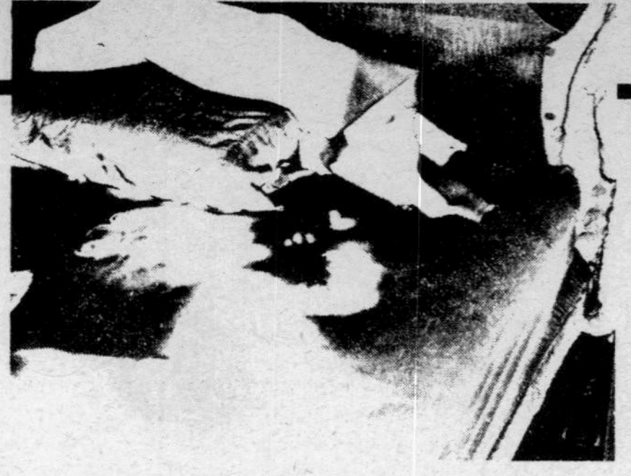

The "smoke-shadow" of a small girl who died of asphyxiation along with two sisters, a brother and her mother. Such accidents are much less likely in homes with smoke detectors.

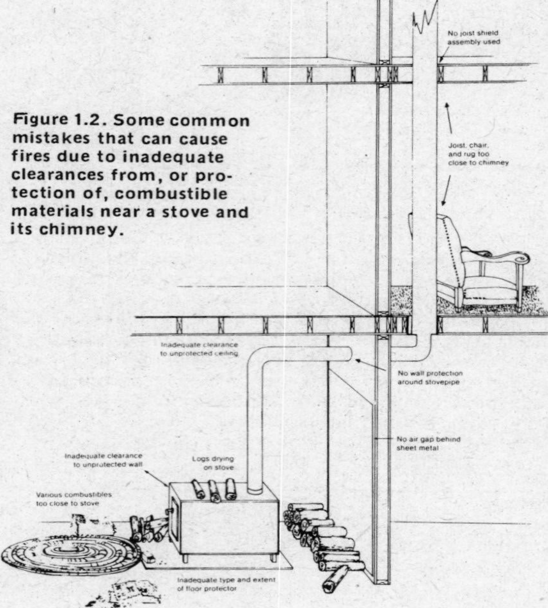

Figure 1.2. Some common mistakes that can cause fires due to inadequate clearances from, or protection of, combustible materials near a stove and its chimney.

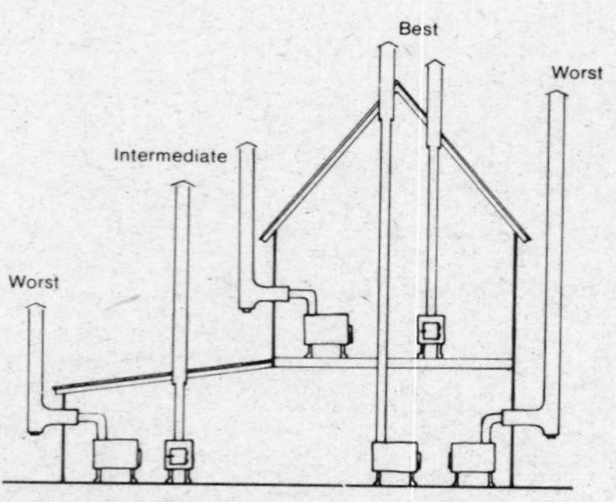

Figure 2-5. Chimney location and draft. Various chimney locations are marked in the figure with respect to draft quality and freedom from flow reversal and non-self-starting problems.

Home Energy Digest (Wood Burning Quarterly)

The advertising manager of this magazine told me that 400 new manufacturers of wood stoves have started business in the U.S. since 1970 (without word-one or dollar-one of encouragement from the government, it should be gladly noted). If you're shopping for wood heat equipment, this is the place to do it — 224 pages in a recent issue. Only drawback; perhaps because it is such an advertising medium, the product reviews are not critical. In all other respects the magazine has a fine, useful currency in a field that's moving pretty rapidly considering how traditional it is. —SB

Home Energy Digest (Wood Burning Quarterly)

$9.95/year (4 issues)
from:
Home Energy Digest
8009 34th Avenue South
Minneapolis, MN 55420

This cute little manually controlled, procelain enamelled, cast iron stove from Denmark is designed to burn pea coal, coke, or charcoal. Its firebox is firebrick lined and has a removable ringed lid on top for cooking. Although it measures only 31¾ high, 15¼ in. wide and 17 in. deep (including ash lip), this 154 lb. (shipping weight) unit has a claimed heating capacity of 3000-5000 cu. ft. It accepts 5 in. flue pipe and is available in various colors. Lange also makes a beautiful little coal burning ship's stove complete with rings on top for various size pots and a brass rail (optional) to complete the nautical motif. It's designed to heat a medium sized boat or 1-2 average sized rooms. A large capacity wood-or-coal unit, the 6302 RA, is also in the works. (From the Svendborg Co., P.O. Box 5, Hanover, NH 03755)

•

As a home heating fuel, wood has rekindled its popularity to near-recordsetting proportions: over one million people now heat their home with wood; by 1985, the figure's expected to climb to 15 million. But it will certainly be up to all of us to assure that the forest lands we now have in abundance are not mismanaged.

Burning Wood

by J. Baldwin

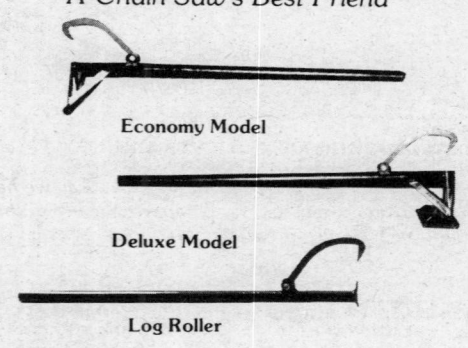

Shortages and high cost of conventional fuels have encouraged many people to turn to wood. Too many, probably, for this country's wood supply to service over the long haul unless disciplined forest management is practiced. This seems to be an unlikely prospect until there are shortages of wood too; cord-cutting is a quick profit business. It obviously takes a lot less time to cut and burn a tree than it takes to grow one. How many of you who burn wood plant trees? Of course, you can justify using "downed wood," but that is taking needed soil nutrients and it deprives certain wildlife of necessary shelter and food. You can burn "slash" cuttings and stumps left over from lumbering – but this is definitely a limited resource and it smacks a bit of secretly condoning the awful lumbering methods that result in slash. Rather like not thinking about where your hamburger really comes from. A great many woodburning civilizations have completely destroyed their forests (old China, for example) and many others are well on the way (India and many South American countries.) In this country we plant approximately one tree for each ten cut, so we aren't safe either. Wood may be renewable but it isn't inexhaustible unless managed. Even that holds a possibility of soil depletion over a long period of time.

Whether you are going to be honest about it and manage a woodlot (or buy from a managed lot), or whether you are going to transfer a fossil fuel attitude to wood burning and ignore the real issues as long as you are warm today, it will pay to use as little wood as possible. This means good insulation and a weather-tight building (rarely seen in a rural setting) and good equipment. Tradition isn't always a good indicator of efficiency either. Our forefathers saw the forests as inexhaustible and if their high-ceilinged houses leaked a lot of heat, they just put on another log. Look at the gigantic size of many colonial fireplaces! Even the famous "Franklin Stove" is an energy hog. (Though Ben Franklin's original was not. What we have today are cheap imitations of the cheap imitations of his day.) In any case, an increased use of wood as fuel is going to add pressure to an already overloaded environment as the demand for trees increases and as air pollution is increased from burning a not-quite-simple fire in the fireplace on a rainy night.

In the hardware department also there is controversy. "My Ashley is better than your Trolla!" and every other possible combination of brand loyalty, myth, and unfounded claim is heard these days. Professor Jay Shelton, (of **Wood Heat Safety**, above) has actually run tests on many stoves under laboratory conditions in an effort to settle some of the arguments. I don't know whether he has settled them or not. Now I hear, "Yes, but his lab is different from my adobe," and like that. It's clear that there will have to be a lot more research if we are really going to know what we are doing. I'll guess that certain stoves are best for certain structures, weather, and wood type. Best is probably to ask around, as there are many local problems. For instance, did you know that burning driftwood just eats the hell out of steel stoves? The salt. (I can hear it now . . . "But our stove has been fed driftwood right here in Coos Bay for 35 years and it's just like new!") Ah well. Here are some books on the subject, and some stoves that our readers seem to like. We haven't had any letters on what readers dislike, probably because it's too embarrassing to spend $300 on a turkey. For sure you should shop around. Many stoves are heavily discounted. And keep in mind what you're doing to our trees . . . ■

Defiant parlor stove.

Vigilant parlor stove.

Defiant and Vigilant parlor stoves

I've lived with an Ashley Thermostatic. I've lived with the spiffy airtight European enameled lovelies (Jotul and Lange). Now my cottage has a Vigilant, the junior of the two parlor stoves from Vermont Castings, and I expect never to find a better.

First of all, it opens up so you can bask your mind in firelight and be right there with it while it starts to warm the room. It's better than a TV to watch. Second, it has the best burning design in the business (with two distributive air entries, one with a thermostat, an excellent long flamepath when operating closed, good airtight construction). Third, it has the best looking design (to my conservative New England tastes). Fourth, it has the best service (cheery and quick response, intelligent instructions, a feeling of a solid company behind it).

Quality. The kind that makes you think about lifetimes.
—SB

[Suggested by Jan Adkins]

The Defiant
Height 32", length 36", depth 22", weight 340 lbs., heats 8,000 to 10,000 cubic feet, woodlength 24"

$575 plus shipping

both from:
Vermont Castings, Inc.
3762 Prince Street
Randolph, VT 05060

The Vigilant
Height 30", length 32", depth 24", weight 245 lbs., heats 6,500 to 8,500 cubic feet, woodlength, 18"

$470 plus shipping

Operators manual and literature
$1 postpaid

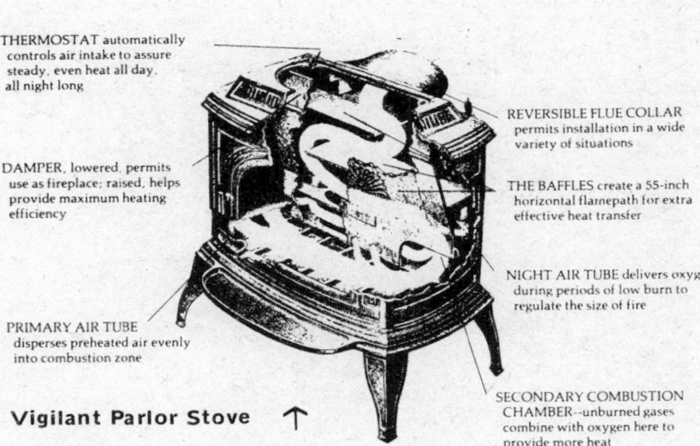

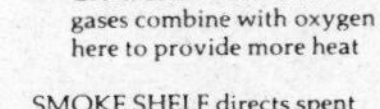

Vigilant Parlor Stove ↑

DEFIANT® Parlor Stove

Top or Rear flue exit models are available for installation in a wide variety of situations.

THERMOSTAT automatically controls air intake to assure steady, even heat all day, all night long

DAMPER, lowered, permits use as fireplace; raised, helps provide maximum heating efficiency

DAMPER CONTROL HANDLE, as all handles and accent hardware, are nickle plated

SECONDARY AIR ENTRANCE PORT

PRIMARY AIR ENTRY PORTS disperse preheated air evenly into combustion zone

SECONDARY COMBUSTION CHAMBER—unburned gases combine with oxygen here to provide more heat

SMOKE SHELF directs spent gases into upper chamber, where they release additional heat before rising up flue

THE BAFFLE creates a 60-inch horizontal flame path for extra effective heat transfer

SECONDARY AIR TUBE feeds preheated oxygen to secondary combustion chamber

The Woodburner's Encyclopedia

Technical, thorough, and fascinating, here's all we have in the way of wood heat science. Shop with higher sophistication. Watch your fire with closer understanding. —SB

The Woodburner's Encyclopedia
(Wood as Energy)
Jay Shelton and Andrew B. Shapiro
1976; 155 pp.

$8.95 postpaid from:
Vermont Crossroads Press
Box 30
Waitsfield, VT 05673

or Whole Earth Household Store

Effect of a cold surface on a flame

Be Your Own Chimney Sweep

Few enterprises are so ripe for disaster as sweeping the potential fire hazard out of a dirty chimney. This well-illustrated book tells how to do it right and appears to be realistic about the difficulties. The usual Garden Way publication quality includes a source list for necessary supplies. —J. Baldwin

Be Your Own Chimney Sweep
Christopher Curtis and Donald Post
1979; 101 pp.

$4.95 postpaid from:
Garden Way Publishing Company
Charlotte, VT 05545

or Whole Earth Household Store

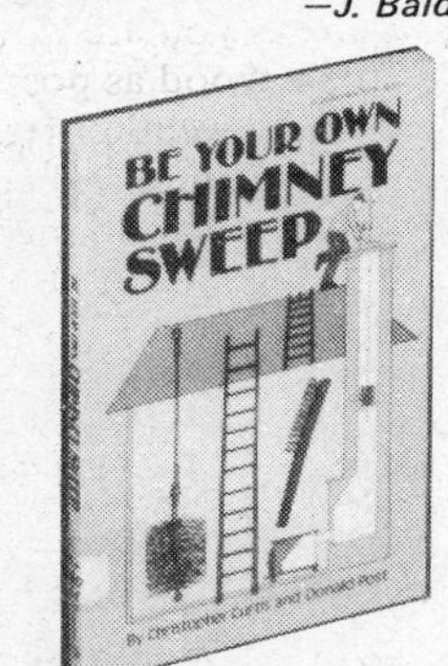

Horizontal cross sections through fireplaces, illustrating the importance of angled sides for efficient indirect radiation. For clarity, the indirect radiation is shown coming from only one point; in reality it comes from all the fireplace's surfaces. The angled sides not only can radiate and reflect to a larger part of the room, but, being closer to the fire, they are hotter and thus emit more intense radiation.

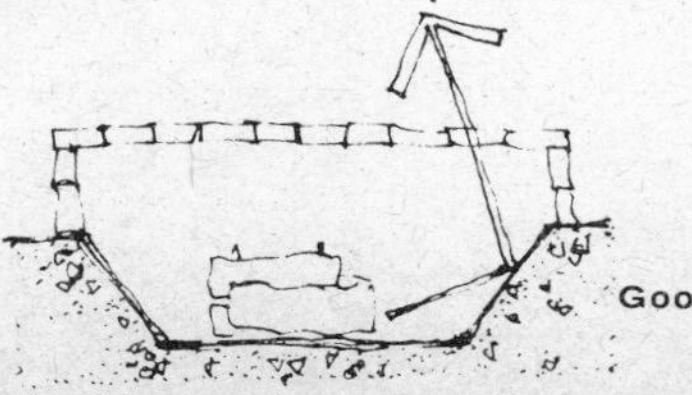

Good

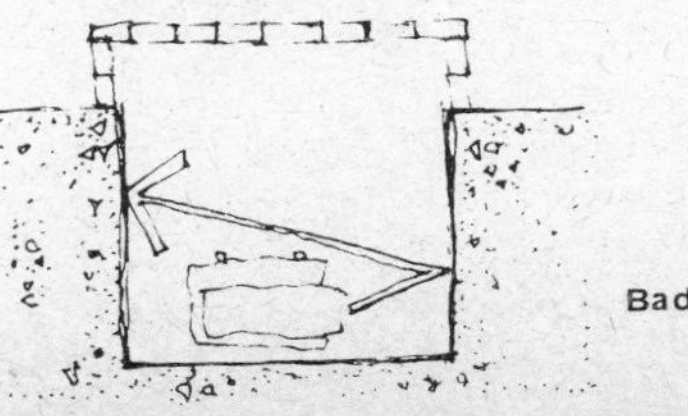

Bad

Stanley wood cookstove

Testimony to the Stanley. It will hold a fire all night, because it's airtight and has a cavernous firebox — you can put whole rounds of Oregon alder in it. The oven will get up to 350°F. within half an hour of lighting the kindling. It heats evenly, will get up to 600°F. very rapidly, and can broil things on the highest rack. (The temperature gauge is set high on the oven door, though, so if you want an accurate reading for the oven floor, where you'd bake cakes, pies, bread, etc., you need to stick one of those oven thermometers in there.) The stove is designed to burn wood, peat, or coal. We've only used wood — hardwoods like alder, holly, cascara, cherry and maple — and so long as the wood is dry and you keep the oven door closed (to prevent the oven walls cooling and trapping soot) the fire produces only the smallest quantity of fine ash and only needs cleaning every six weeks or so. The stove comes with a set of cleaning and adjusting tools. We paid $600 for it in 1978, but with the waterfont it would be considerably more. It's very efficient, burns large hunks of wood (important for a compulsive baker who can devote only minimal time to cutting, splitting and hauling wood), and can brew a pot of coffee on 2 sheets of the **Wall St. Journal** *and a few sticks of kindling faster than a hotplate. One medium dog fits comfortably underneath it, and the warming bar across the front accommodates three shivering adults easily.*
—Carol Van Strum

Stanley Woodburning Range
Width 16", Height 13", Depth 15 - 3/4"
Distributed wholesale by
Waterford Ironfounders Export Ltd.,
P.O. Box 2407
Grand Central Station
New York, NY 10017

$1225 plus shipping from:
Lehman Hardware and Appliances
(p. 206).

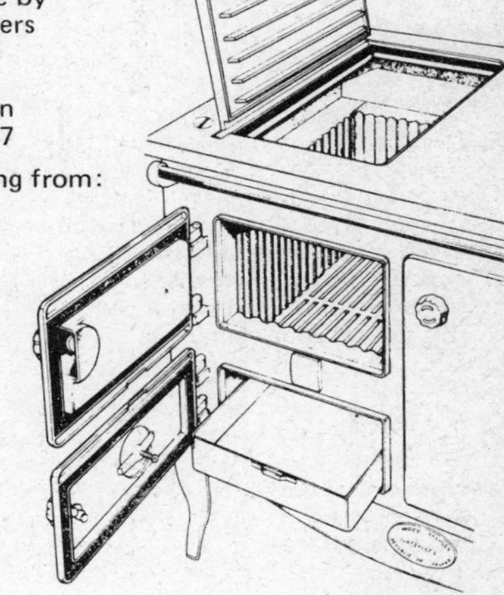

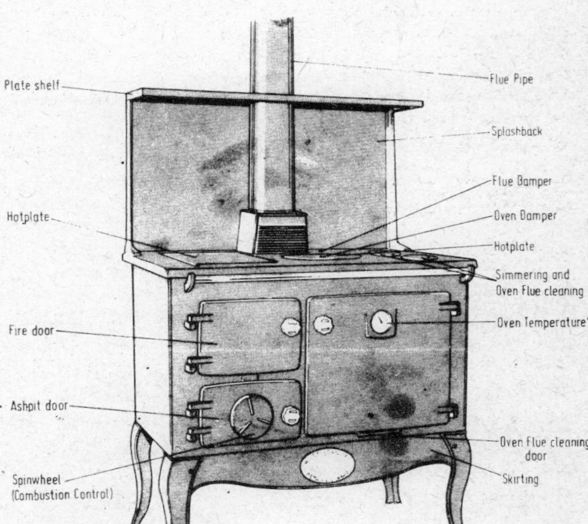

THE RISING SUN
NEIGHBORHOOD NEWSLETTER

I am not familiar with the theories of modern architecture but what it looks like from the outside is that architects noticed they were designing for the masses and decided the masses didn't deserve to have any fun. Old architecture, Victorian, Gothic, you can play all kinds of games with — treasure hunt, hide and seek — because the builders left curlycues and knickknacks around for you to discover but about all you can say to the maker of a glass skyscraper is You win. (You don't win fair but you win.)

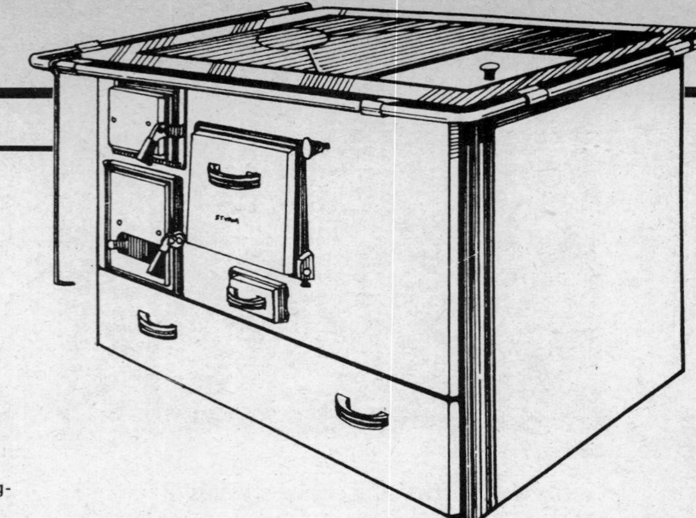

Quality Wood Cookstove Catalogue and Review

It's the "and Review" that makes this paper so interesting — they've actually road tested many wood cookstoves. The results and specifications are published right out where you can see them, making this catalog much more useful than any other we've seen. Where to buy 'em is there too. A low bow, friends; a new day is dawning when we don't have to depend on manufacturers' grandiose claims! —J. Baldwin

Quality Wood Cookstove Catalogue and Review

$1.50 postpaid from:
Maine Wood Heat Co.
R.F.D. 1 Box 38
Norridgewock, ME 04957

→
Styria 130, $2000 plus.

Manufacturer:
Merry Music
10 McKown Street
Boothbay Harbor, ME 04538

Special feature: Heat-accumulating firebrick mass used liberally throughout the stove.

Built like a Rolls Royce of very heavy, high quality materials, this stove is a lifetime investment. The stove has a water reservoir but does not come with either a domestic water jacket or a central heating hot water jacket, which limits its flexibility, we think. As a cooking-baking stove, however, it has to be ranked among the very best ever.

Woodstove Directory 1980

A wide variety of wood heating equipment, well illustrated and described, but (too bad) not critically evaluated. In short, this'll let you avoid writing away for all the catalogs. —J. Baldwin

Woodstove Directory
(Fireplace and Equipment — The International Sourcebook of Woodheat Equipment)
1980; 208 pp.

$2.50 postpaid from:
Energy Communications Press
P.O. Box 4474
Manchester, NH 03108
or Whole Earth Household Store

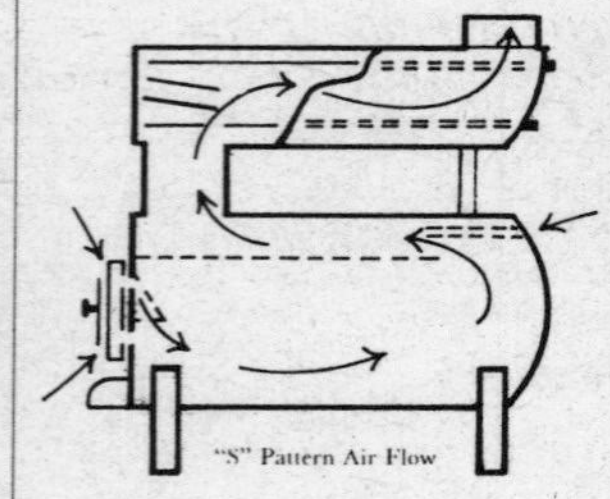

↑
The Sevca

The double-barrel Sevca design is considered by most experts as the most energy-efficient design available. Test results confirm that these stoves can deliver 65 - 72% efficiency.

Green Mountain
Stove Works, Inc.
Route 121
P.O. Box 477
Saxtons River, VT 05154
802-869-2772

↑
Hearthstone Soapstone Stove

Soapstone is the heart of the stove. Its marble-like hue, accented by the sculptured cast iron framework, gives the Hearthstone its elegant appearance. Since the 18th century, soapstone has been used in furnaces and kilns, in griddles, boot warmers, bed warmers and in wood stoves. Once heated, this natural stone can retain and radiate heat hours longer than most substances, either natural or man-made.

Hearthstone Corporation
Northgate Plaza,
Dept. WD
Morrisville, VT 05661
802-888-4586

Wood Furnaces & Boilers

A brief overview of the breed, done in the expected competent Garden Way style. Remember, please, that these beasts must be fed. —J. Baldwin

Wood Furnaces & Boilers
(Garden Way Bulletin A-25)
Larry Gay
1978; 32 pp.

$1 postpaid from:
Garden Way
Publishing Company
Charlotte, VT 05545

•

Sawdust furnaces are still made in the United States, mostly for the West Coast market. The Conifer was produced in great numbers in the thirties and forties by the Western Foundry Co., Portland, OR. Some of the manufacturing and all of the distribution are now in the hands of the American Fyr-Feeder Engineers of Des Plaines, IL. The good thing about burning sawdust is that it can be handled automatically. A truck dumps sawdust through a chute into a bin in the basement every five weeks or so. The bad thing about it is that the sawdust packs together, especially if it is wet, when it reaches the combustion chamber. This prevents air from getting into the burning zone, causing the fire to smolder. To take care of this a terraced grate is used which can be shaken once or twice a day to fluff up the sawdust and stimulate combustion. Fyr-Feeder is producing several household models as well as industrial sizes, up to eight million BTUs per hour. Conveyors to move sawdust from the storage bin to the hopper are available.

↓

GREEN WOOD FUEL
SECONDARY AIR
COMBUSTION CHAMBER
PRIMARY AIR
CARBONIZED BED

The Conifer sawdust burner.

The "Good Neighbor" Heritage Catalog

A cookstove catalog and an old-time general store type catalog, both full of satisfyingly durable goods. They carry the Stanley cookstove, and Aladdin lamps, and other delights. —SB

The "Good Neighbor" Heritage Catalog
$2

The "Good Neighbor" Cooking Range Catalog
$1

from:
Lehman Hardware and Appliances, Inc.
Box 41
Kidron, OH 44636

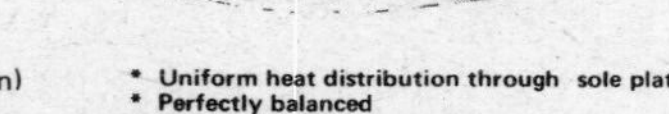

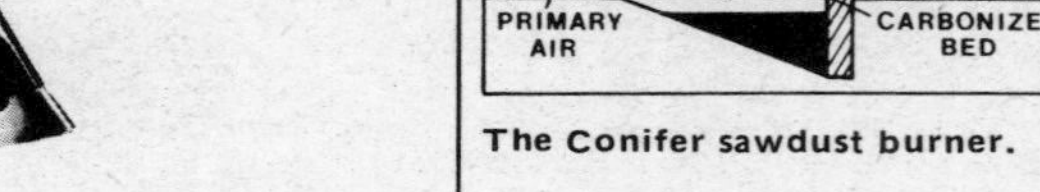

Kerosene (Paraffin)
Coleman

Preheats Quickly With Alcohol (Meth. Spirits)

Light Weight Aluminum Sole Plate

- Uniform heat distribution through sole plate
- Perfectly balanced
- Modern design
- Cool, comfortable handle
- Tapered ironing edge
- Iron in comfort; no muscular fatigue.
- No wires or connections can be used anywhere
- Sturdy, long-life generator
- Built-in pump
- Large opening for refilling or fuel tank
- Generator and tank assembly easily removed for service
- Burns for approximately 2 hours on one tank of fuel

WOODEN BUTTER CHURN

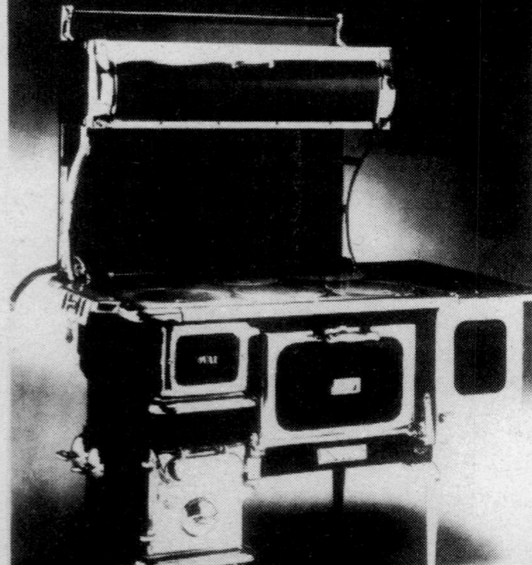

←
$1845 Findlay Oval

Pioneer Lamps and Stoves Co.

This is to me the most fascinating stove catalog available. They also have restored, incredibly beautiful stoves at museum prices. (Well at least you can drool.) Their production stoves cover a wide range (so to speak) of types and sizes not often seen. —J. Baldwin

Pioneer Lamps and Stoves
Catalog

$3 postpaid from:
Pioneer Lamps and
and Stoves
71A Yesler Way
Seattle, WA 98104

New Pacific Princess $985 (add $75 for reservoir).

THE FREE FLOW STOVES

$470 $600 $740 $885

	THE GEM heats cabins and vacation homes	THE CIRCULATOR heats small dwellings	THE WONDER heats the average size house	THE FURNACE meets the heating demands of large dwellings
Height	26"	33"	35"	37"
Width	22"	23"	25"	28"
Weight	150 lbs.	200 lbs.	260 lbs.	325 lbs.
Heating capacity*	VT: 5,000 cu' PA: 10,000 cu'	VT: 8,000 cu' PA: 16,000 cu'	VT: 12,000 cu' PA: 24,000 cu'	VT: 25,000 cu' PA: 38,000 cu'
Loading capacity	1.7 cu'	3.5 cu'	5 cu'	7 cu'
Length of logs	16"	22"	27"	30"
Diameter of door	11"	13"	14"	15"
Flue height	23"	28"	30"	32"

*Varies according to harshness of climate. Figures above give approximate heating capacity in Vermont and in Pennsylvania.

Free Flow

My own stove is a Free Flow, so I can report from experience that it works as claimed. That is, it "pumps" hot air around the house without a fan. (It also pumps dust if you don't keep the area around the base clean.) I find that it heats the house from cold much faster than any other stove I've tried, and that stratification (hot head with cold feet) is much less. The surface of the stove is cooler than others which means less chance of accidental burns but no stovetop cooking. The Free Flow seems to like running hard, so don't buy one that's too big.

—J. Baldwin

Free Flow Stoves
Catalog
free from:
Free Flow Stove Works
South Stratford, VT
05070

Greenwood Eagle

This stove apparently actually does burn green unsplit logs! I haven't seen one yet, but the mail is good. They claim that creosote is no problem. How does it work? The stove is lined with "refractory material" which is another way of saying it's a very high grade of firebrick-like material only better. The refractory enables the stove to get so hot that it'll burn most anything, yet not burn itself out in the process. Sounds like a good idea. I suspect that we'll be seeing more stoves like this one as pollution standards are raised.

—J. Baldwin

Greenwood Eagle
Information
free from:
Greenwood Energy Corp.
Executive Drive
Hudson, NH 03051

Kero-Sun Portable Heaters

In Japan, where wasteful central heating is rare, portable kerosene heaters like these are the primary source of heat. Seven models are available, ranging from 7200 to 18,000 BTU/hour. Fuel consumption at full output ranges from over 22 hours/gallon with the smallest heater to over 9 hours/gallon with the largest. The longest burning model will burn at maximum output for over 30 hours. Because of their super-efficiency, there is no odor and no need for chimney venting. All have battery-powered igniters and automatic shutoff in case of tip-over. Either kerosene or No. 1 fuel oil may be used.

Portable heat makes a lot of sense, and besides that these heaters are just plain fun to have around. I've become quite attached to mine and regard it as a cheerful and ever-faithful friend.

—Gary Beaver

Kero-Sun Portable Heaters
$140 - $240 (approx.)
Information
free from:
Innovations in Depth
222 West 1st Street
Duluth, MN 55802

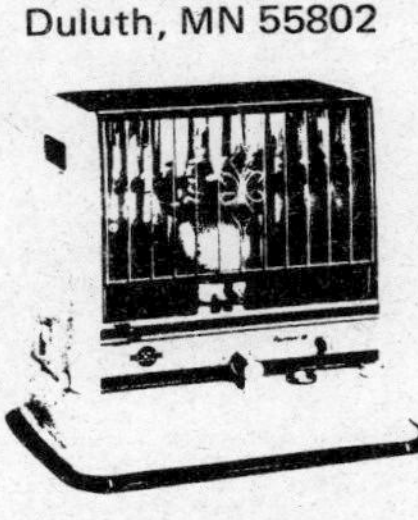

Omni 15

Radiant 10

Moonlighter

The newest and brightest idea in Kero-Sun portable heaters because it gives both heat and light wherever you need them! (With a cooktop you can heat a pot on it.) Lightweight to go anywhere! Rich brown enamel with a clear pyrex combustion chamber. Clear View fuel guage. Maximum output: 340 lumens, 9,000 BTU/hour.

Aito Sauna Stoves

For those who are pickynit about having their sauna just right, a stove made for the purpose is indispensible. This one is from Finland and appears to be very well made. (See Nippa sauna heater, p. 320.)

—J. Baldwin

Aito Sauna Stove
$430 - $680 (approx.)
Information

free from:
Solar Sauna
Hollis, NH 03049

Kutrieb Waste Oil Heater

Claimed to be "smokeless and odorless," these space heaters use old crankcase oil for fuel. It can also use other waste lubricants. It's only a matter of time before "waste lubricants" will be recycled extensively, but meantime, this is a lot better use for them than pouring them into the ditch or down the drain. It'll provide 87,000 BTU/hour from .62 gallon of oil with heat distribution by radiant/convection. It might be an interim answer for your heating problems.

—J. Baldwin

Kutrieb Waste Oil Heater
Information
free from:
Lenan Enterprises, Inc.
P.O. Box 94
Milton, WI 53563

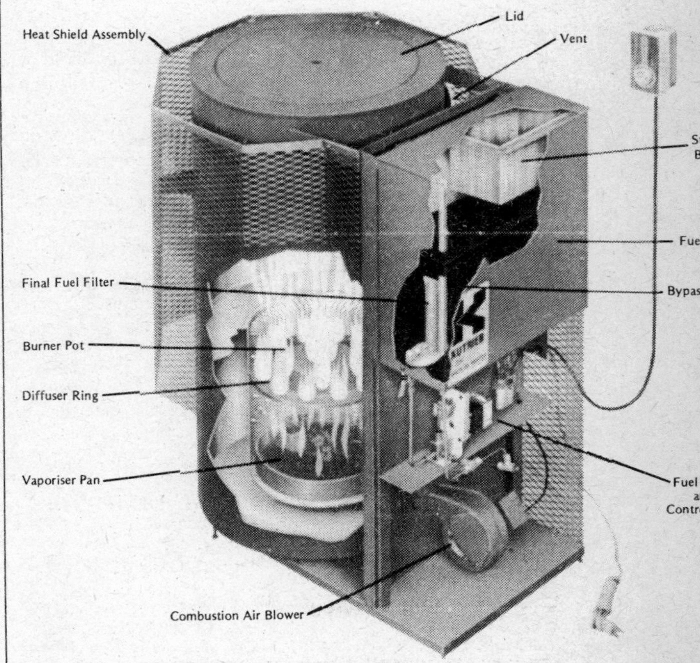

Woodburning water heater

This is the heater you see in Latin America. Rugged, simple and not very expensive, these heat up 14 gallons of water in about 15 minutes using a few pieces of kindling or the optional fuel-oil conversion. They keep delivering hot water as long as you stoke 'em, so don't be dismayed by the rather small 14 gallon tank. They're designed to be used on normal household water pressure, and obviously could be incorporated into a solar rig. Hecho en Mexico. I don't know what codes say about it (if you care). Very hard water may make trouble.

—J. Baldwin

Woodburning Water Heater
$119.50 wood only
$144.50 with quick switchover to fuel oil
Information
free from:
Appropriate Technology Importers, Inc.
P.O. Box 5
El Rito, NM 87530

Handmade Hot Water Systems

The best text on stove-made hot water. The chapters on solar water heaters are nothing new, but the woodstove water heaters are treated in great detail that is not available elsewhere. Most of what is shown has been field tested, and the diagrams are among the most clear I've ever seen in any book, anywhere, on any subject.

The same people operate an outfit called "Blazing Showers," manufacturers of hot water heating systems to fit your stove or fireplace (Box 327, Point Arena, CA 95468).

—J. Baldwin

Handmade Hot Water Systems
Art Sussman and Richard Frazier
1978; 91 pp.

$5.95 postpaid from:
Garcia River Press
P.O. Box 527
Point Arena, CA 95468
or Whole Earth Household Store

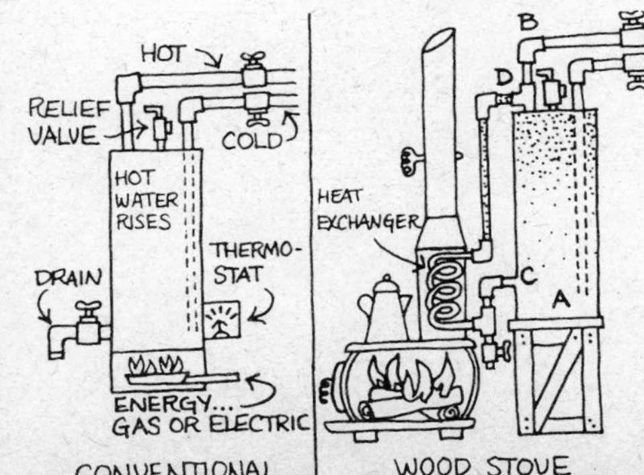

THE RISING SUN
NEIGHBORHOOD NEWSLETTER

"A quirk of populist history has fixed the Victorian in the modern mind as inflexibly reactionary and insufferably dowdy. But the Victorian mind provided the greatest burst of scientific invention this globe has seen. . . . Victorians, proper or otherwise, delighted in new gadgets and new machines as well as in archaeology and maintaining colorful ceremonies from the past. They were curious and excitable. . . . After all, the Victorians created American California."

— Caption to a doorway to a Victorian house at the Oakland Museum

Fireplaces

Ken Kern adds a worthy addition to his Owner Builder series with this excellent manual on building a successful fireplace. (If you think a good fireplace is easy to build, just consider how many awful, smoky recalcitrant black holes you've had to contend with.) As expected, the authors patiently go over the theory, and follow up with an unprecedented presentation of the tiniest details and tricks of the trade so necessary to good performance. They are particularly excellent when explaining how to do hot water systems and heater arrangements, including integrated solar. This is by far the best book on the subject.
—*J. Baldwin*

Fireplaces
Ken Kern and
Steve Magers
1978; 192 pp.

$7.95 postpaid from:
Owner Builder Publications
Box 817
North Fork, CA 93643
or Whole Earth
Household Store

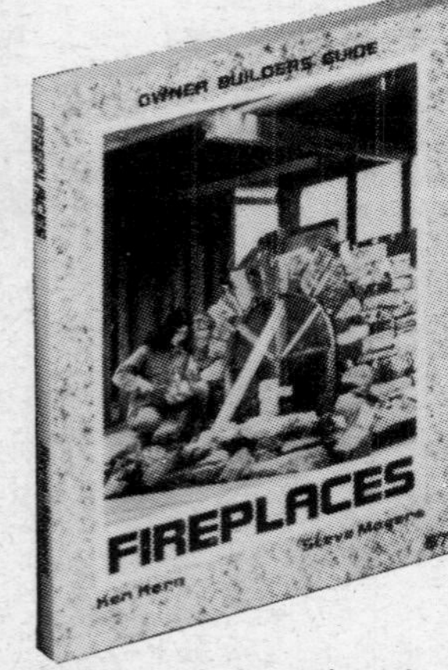

←
The throat, with its thin slit opening, works in conjunction with the more voluminous expansion chamber to promote a rapid flow of hot gases upward from the firebox, much as the Venturi principle increases lift on an air foil or carburetor flow in a gasoline engine. At the time this is happening, cold air from above is arrested by the throat in its fall down the chimney. It accumulates in the larger expansion chamber, where it is warmed and its flow is reversed. Hot air rushing upward through the throat impedes the entrance of these downdrafts into the firebox. It has been determined that the cross-sectional area of the throat must be approximately equal to the cross-sectional area of the flue. The placement of the throat should be toward the front of the firebox, considerably above the breast. Thus, smoke will not be able to find its way into the room.

Ironically, the same principle that causes the chimney to function well is also the force that must be overcome to maintain the heat efficiency of the firebox. If the chimney flue draws too well, the effect will be counter-productive. A large firebox opening and flue can easily draw more heated room air than they contribute in radiant heat to the house. Therefore, we do not recommend that fireplace openings be larger than 42 inches in width. Beyond this opening width, a fireplace gives diminishing returns unless an inordinate amount of wood is wastefully burned to rectify heat losses.

↑
This cantilevered design dispenses with the necessity to use metal support posts, which are unattractive and block one's view of the fire. This modified firebox will radiate slightly more heat than one with full covings. Although it reacts temperamentally when a fire is first lit, it draws well once the chimney is hot. Occasionally, it will smoke when a breeze from an opening blows across the fire.

Curing Smoky Fireplaces

First aid for that most obnoxious of fireplace flaws.
—*J. Baldwin*

Curing Smoky Fireplaces
(Garden Way Bulletin A-41)
1980; 32 pp.

$1 postpaid from:
Garden Way
Publishing Company
Charlotte, VT 05545

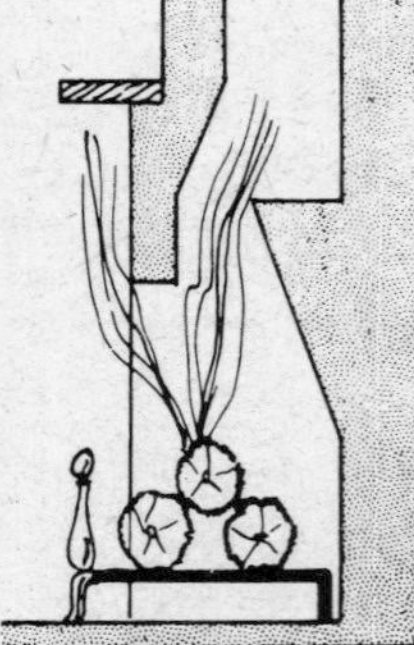

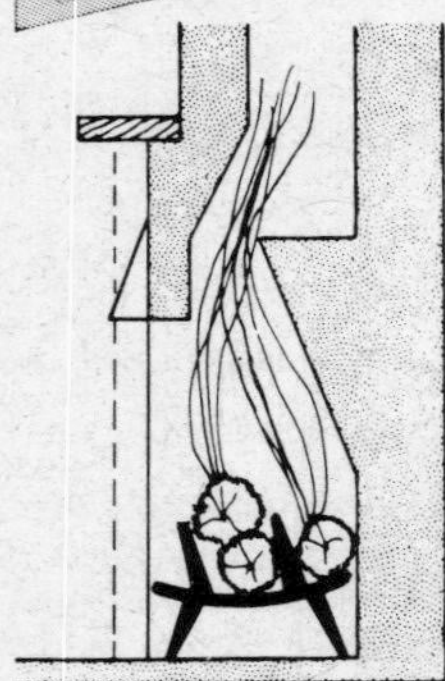

In the first illustration, smoke flows out of the fireplace. This flow is directed up the chimney when a log holder holds the fire higher off the hearth and close to the fireplace back, and when a hood is added to the front of the fireplace.

Adobe Fireplaces

Plans for the traditional corner adobe fireplace.
—*Lloyd Kahn*

Adobe Fireplaces
Myrtle Stedman
1977; 16 pp.

$2.50 postpaid from:
The Sunstone Press
P.O. Box 2321
Santa Fe, NM 87501
or Whole Earth
Household Store

Cooking on a large Lorena stove in Guatemala.

Lorena Owner-Built Stoves

Our book details the design and construction of an innovative highly efficient cookstove, originally developed in highland Guatemala (and taught in stove building workshops in California and Oregon). The stove costs almost nothing to make, yet saves half or more of the firewood normally used in cooking. Some 80 percent of the energy consumption in rural areas of the Third World is for cooking, and many of these same areas are suffering from major deforestation problems. Lorena stoves thus appear to offer a very important tool in fighting deforestation, extending traditional fuel supplies, and easing the burden of long-distance hauling of wood by millions of people. Another low technology 'plug' as energy 'resource.'

Curiously, by relying on easily learned skills brought into communities via footpaths, these stoves seem likely to have much greater impact than the kind of high-tech integrated solar photovoltaic/windgenerator/biogas systems being proposed by some international agencies, among the villages of the world. (Having bought into the 'Biogas Bonanza' ourselves 5½ years ago, we are surprised at the advantages offered by simple improved stoves.)
—*Ken Darrow, Volunteers in Asia*

Lorena Owner-Built Stoves
Ianto Evans
1979; 80 pp.

$3.59 postpaid from:
Volunteers in Asia
Box 4543
Stanford, CA 94305
or Whole Earth
Household Store

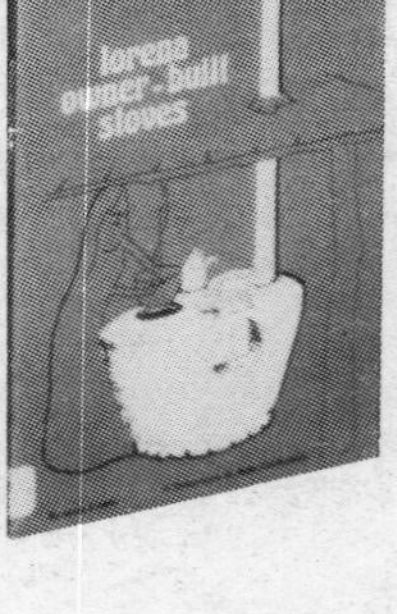

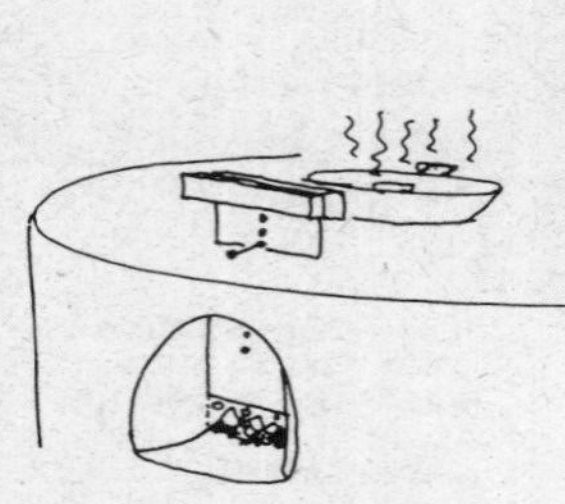

Make a row of small holes in the damper. A thin nail placed through one of these holes will allow you to adjust the depth of the damper in the stove tunnel.

Masonry Stove Guild Newsletter

Joining the Masonry Guild gets you this newsletter, which — though skinny — is all we have. It is the beginning of a gathering of information on masonry stoves, ovens and heaters, and the people who know how to make them. Eventually there will be a definitive book. These big, heavy structures are perhaps the most efficient way to burn wood. A clever design can cook, bake, heat water, and heat the house. The huge thermal mass keeps the heat for a long time. They've been doing it in Europe (including Russia and Finland) for a long long time. If masonry stoves interest you, then your support and/or information contribution would be most welcome. In case you wondered, a masonry stove can be wedded to a solar collector. It's being tried now. —*J. Baldwin*

Masonry Stove Guild Newsletter

$5 with Guild membership from:
Maine Wood Heat Co.
R.F.D. 1 Box 38
Norridgewock, ME 04957

R.F. in progress showing four of the five arches used in its construction. At left front is firebox followed by oven door. Around corner out of sight is warming oven, then cleanout access and at rear is arch reducing heat transfer wall to single brick thickness. Slot on left side will receive boiler pipes.

Masonry Stove Plans

Complete plans and instructions for construction and operation of a masonry stove. The plans look easy enough to use, but it's gonna take patience as there is a lot to it.
—*J. Baldwin*
[Suggested by Thomas A. McCarey]

Masonry Stove Plans
(An original design adapting the masonry stove for American materials)
Basilio Lepuschenko

$10 postpaid from:
Basilio Lepuschenko
Alexandra Road
Richmond, ME 04357

Heat with flowerpots

I know a few things that might be of interest to other CQ readers (old-world-hints). Maybe you know them already, but what the hell! First, the flowerpot-heater (an old trick from my mother from World War II when coal was scarce) for people with freezing kitchens and gas stoves (like me). Instead of turning on an electrical heater, light the burner and place a big empty unglazed clay flowerpot (the red kind with a hole in the bottom that sell for a few pennies at garden supplies stores) upside-down over the flame. The pot will get hot very fast and reflect the heat much more efficiently than the flame alone. (Don't touch the pot, it might get red-hot!) In a short time your kitchen will be warm and cozy.

—Barbara Besser
Munster, W. Germany

(Make sure pot is dry or it'll explode. —J. Baldwin)

Wood Stoves

Yes, you can make a stove if you're reasonably adept with tools. You'll likely save quite a bit of money, too, considering the inflated price of the better grade of commercial jobs. Stovemaking might also be a good way for woodbutchers to get into metalworking, as the proper attitude will be familiar even if the materials are not. Very fine diagrams and photographs back a chatty, experienced text in this comprehensive manual. Many proven designs are shown, including cookstoves. The author is a warm Alaskan. —J. Baldwin

Wood Stoves
(How to Make and Use Them)
Ole Wik
1977; 194 pp.
$5.95 postpaid from:
Alaska Northwest Publishing Co.
Box 4-EEE
Anchorage, AK 99509
or Whole Earth Household Store

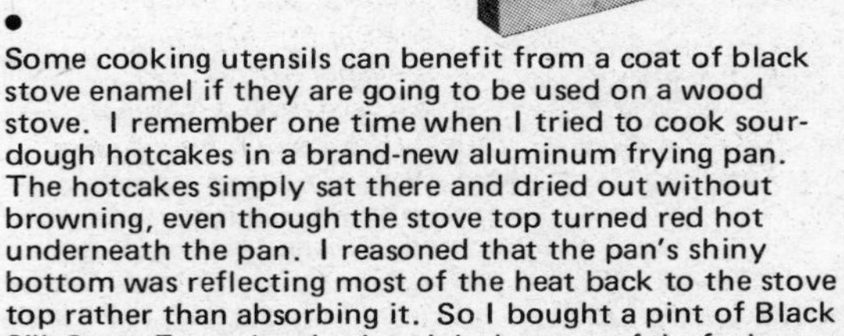

•

Some cooking utensils can benefit from a coat of black stove enamel if they are going to be used on a wood stove. I remember one time when I tried to cook sourdough hotcakes in a brand-new aluminum frying pan. The hotcakes simply sat there and dried out without browning, even though the stove top turned red hot underneath the pan. I reasoned that the pan's shiny bottom was reflecting most of the heat back to the stove top rather than absorbing it. So I bought a pint of Black Silk Stove Enamel and painted the bottom of the frying pan.

The next time I used the pan, the results were perfect: golden-brown hotcakes, no red-hot stove top. The blackened pan absorbed the heat rather than reflecting it. Encouraged by this success, I painted the bottom of every vessel that ever touched the stove — the pots, pans, kettles, dishpans, wash basins and snow-melting buckets. The trick is well worth remembering. Roughen the bottom of the vessel with sandpaper before painting it, use two coats, and let it dry for 24 hours in a warm place before using. And be sure to use the stove *enamel*, not the *polish*.

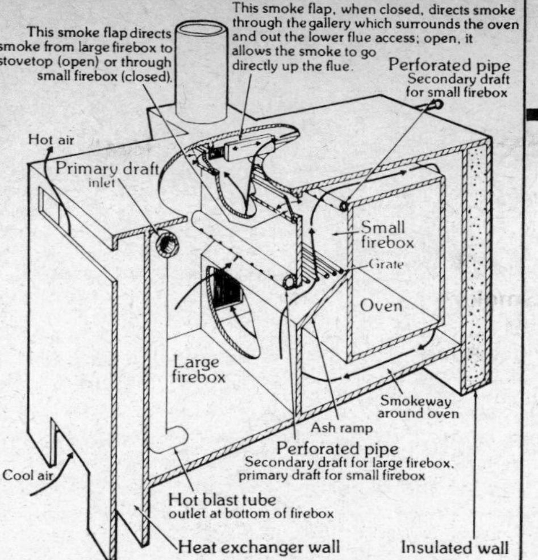

Hypothetical dual-fire range

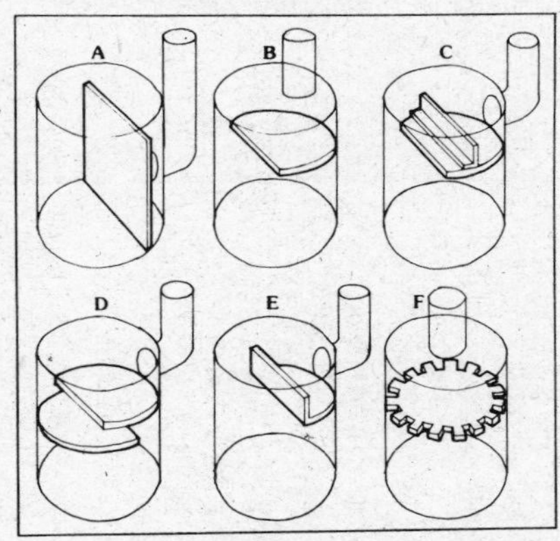

Various baffle arrangements for vertical drum stoves

Madawaska Wood Furnace

Hill's stick wood furnaces (see below left) are beginning to be available from commercial manufacturers. One whose literature we've seen — it looks promising — lists wood and wood/oil boilers at about $2500, storage tanks with heat exchanger about $300. How about somebody who's lived with one of these devices letting us know about their practicality? —SB

Madawaska Wood Furnace
Information
free from:
Dumont Industries
Main Street
Monmouth, ME 04259

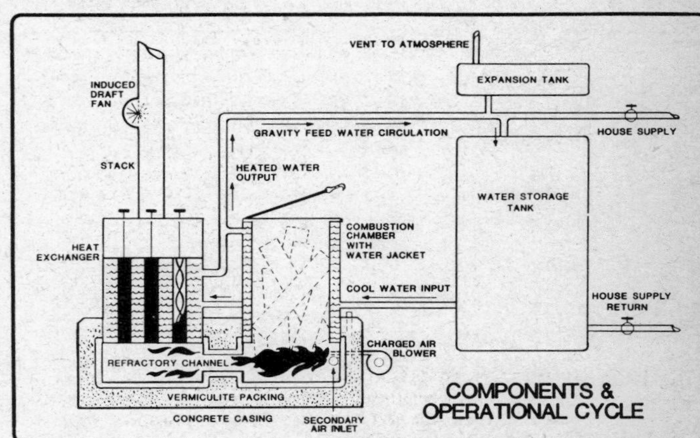

The Madawaska Wood Furnace uses logs up to 36 inches, of any wood species, and will accommodate scrap or junk wood, seasoned or new. 70 pounds of wood can be loaded at once. Additional wood can be added at any time without affecting furnace performance.

Barrel stove conversion

Typical of a number of similar kits available, this box of parts converts a 55 gallon drum into a reasonably decent stove. I don't know if this kit is any better or worse than others — they all seem about the same. But the idea works well enough if you're not handy enough with tools to make your own. —Richard Nilsen

Enderes Wood Burning Barrel Stove Assembly
$54 postpaid
Information and nearest dealer location
free from:
Enderes Tools
Albert Lea, MN 56007

DEAR OPEC: Keep your oil, send us the barrels.

Sawdust stove

If you have access to free sawdust, you can build a stove to use it from a 55-gallon drum. —SB
[Suggested by Christopher Caldwell at **Workbench Magazine***]*

Double-Drum Sawdust Stove
(USDA Forest Service Research Note NE-208)
1975; 4 pp.
free

Sawdust Stove
(A Natural for Heating Cabins and Cutting Fuel Costs)
1975; 4 pp.
Photo Story No. 30
free
both from:
Northeastern Forest Experiment Station
370 Reed Road
Broomall, PA 19008

Filling the inner barrel with sawdust. Note the wooden insert in the center. To pack sawdust in the barrel tightly enough, it should be tamped down.

Design, Construction and Performance of Stick-Wood Fired Furnace for Residential and Small Commercial Application

Professor Richard Hill has designed a state-of-the-art wood furnace that solves the major problems associated with burning wood. In conventional wood burning central heating furnaces where the thermostat in the living area controls the amount of air reaching the fire, the furnace is often burning wood in an air-starved condition, producing creosote buildup in the flue and air pollution (a very real problem usually ignored by wood burning advocates). Hill has separated the combustion and heat exchange areas of the furnace, as conditions favoring one process are detrimental to the other. The wood is burned in a refractory chamber with a forced air supply. This high temperature burn gives complete combustion so there is virtually no creosote or air pollution (some smoke is produced at the start of the burning cycle). Heat in the stack gases is extracted by a heat exchanger and stored in a 500-gallon water tank. The thermostat then controls the circulation, via a pump, of the heated water thru baseboard radiators. Normally the furnace is fired once a day, but the storage capacity is sufficient to keep a tight, well-insulated home above freezing for several days. A patent has been applied for and currently three companies (names and addresses in booklet) are producing the furnace. The cost is comparable with conventional systems. —Jim Buttitta

Design, Construction and Performance of Stick-Wood Fired Furnace for Residential and Small Commercial Application
Richard C. Hill
1979; 26 pp.
$2 postpaid from:
Richard C. Hill
109 Boardman Hall
University of Maine
Orono, ME 04469

Woodstove Construction

Detailed instructions for making two stoves, a "double drum" type and a rectangular box. The cost of either should be about $100, which is not bad these days. Both require considerable welding. Both are well-proven, efficient designs. The instructions are well detailed and should enable anyone with the necessary skills to produce a good house heater. —J. Baldwin

Woodstove Construction
(How to Build Excellent Wood Heaters)
Al Ulmer
1979; 46 pp.
$3.50 postpaid from:
Small Farm Energy Conservation Project
Federation of Southern Cooperatives
P.O. Box 95
Epes, AL 35460

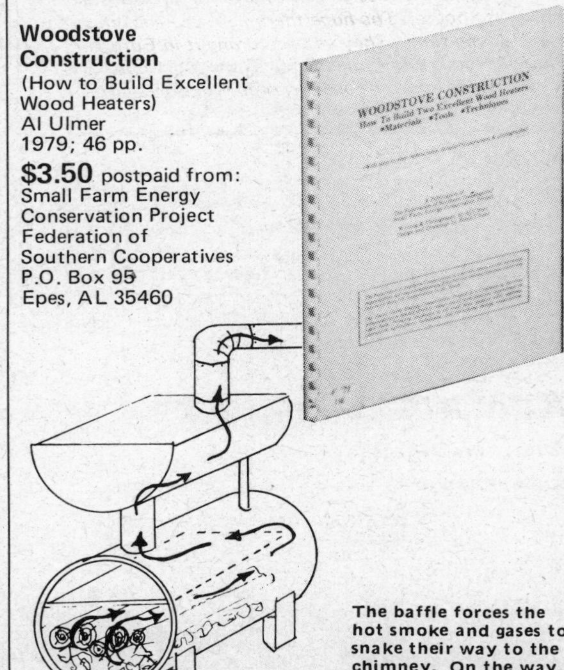

The baffle forces the hot smoke and gases to snake their way to the chimney. On the way, they give more of their heat to your house.

THE RISING SUN
NEIGHBORHOOD NEWSLETTER

continued from last spread

The last sentence is worth thinking about. 1849, when the goldrush started, was in the middle of Victoria's reign and the earthquake a few years after her death. As soon as the golddiggers made their money they spent it in Victorian ways and on Victorian houses. Nowadays, one of our favorite ways of expressing our free spirits is to paint their houses bright colors — but the colors wouldn't go so well if there weren't so many nooks and crannies to put them in and if the buildings and the times hadn't been crazier than they were stodgy to start with.

"There simply is no Victorian style of furniture. Designers, heady with the opportunities given by mechanical advances, copied, adapted, and mixed styles from all ages and areas."

—Caption to some fairly strange chairs at the Oakland Museum

From left to right, the Sotz Monster Maul, the Chopper 1 Axe, and the winnah the Snow & Neally maul.

The Woodsplitting Tool System

A fatally curious fellow named David Tresemer decided to settle the constant dispute about wood-splitting by racing the relevant tools. (I don't know if that included an auger-type splitter.) He quickly narrowed the field from 20 to 4 — a Sotz Monster Maul, a Chopper 1 Axe (has levered spreaders in the head), a Snow & Neally standard maul, and a 10 horsepower hydraulic splitter. The average of three tries at a fifth of a cord each time came out: hydraulic splitter, 37 minutes, 17 seconds; Snow & Neally Maul, 39:26; Sotz Monster Maul, 41:44; Chopper 1 Axe, 43:40. Comparing the pleasantness of the experience, the Snow & Neally Maul came out ahead. (The Monster Maul was unwieldy, the Chopper 1 was finicky, and the hydraulic splitter was noisy and boring.)

Accordingly (yuk yuk) the same By Hand & Foot people who purvey the nifty scythe system on our p. 130 have assembled for sale a nifty woodsplitting system. As follows. —SB

The Woodsplitting Tool System

We have tested twenty separate hand and gasoline-powered methods for splitting firewood and have found this system to be as fast, more economical, and healthier than any other system. Request the report of our research ($1.50 postpaid).

As a result of this work, we decided to make the Snow & Nealley maul and accessories available as an integrated woodsplitting system.

Our complete brochure for the tools in this system is available for $1 (postpaid). The manual, **Remembering How to Split Firewood**, free with the purchase of a splitting maul, is also available for $1 (postpaid).

I. MOST SPLITTING:

Splitting maul, by Snow & Nealley of Bangor, Maine, makers of axes and forestry tools for many years. The temper of this steel is perfect — not as brittle as an axe so it will not chip, not so soft it will dull. Developed by Maine loggers who have achieved the right weight and shape of head. Handle of straight-grain hickory (not fiberglass!) is light and smooth and is easily replaced if it is accidentally broken. $24 plus mailing.

Replacement handle — Have one just in case. Making your own is described in **Remembering How to Split Firewood.** $8 plus mailing.

Handle guard — We recommend a guard for beginners and infrequent users to protect the handle from breaking because of a near miss. $2.90 plus mailing.

II. HARDER SPLITTING

Occasionally the maul is not enough and a tough piece requires a wedge or two wedges. However, the collision of the metal maul and the metal wedge risks the chipping of either, endangering the eye. We offer two methods for reducing this danger.

Safety glasses — We have found that plastic safety *goggles* scratch easily and fog up when we exert energy. Industrial safety spectacles made of high-impact proof glass are comfortable and perfectly clear. In other words, you will wear them when you need to. Small, medium, and large sizes. $9 plus mailing.

Wood-and-steel wedge — These wedges have edges of steel and heads of hardwood. There is no steel head to mushroom and send chips flying, eventually needing replacement. The grain of the wood head, held together by a steel ring, is bent over. When the wooden insert is completely pounded down (a long time!), it can be replaced inexpensively — perhaps with a piece of the wood you are splitting. $10.50 plus mailing.

The Woodsplitting Tool System
Tool price list
free on request
Brochure on wood-splitting research
$1.50 postpaid

"Remembering How to Split Firewood"
$1 postpaid
all from:
By Hand & Foot, Ltd.
P.O. Box 611
Brattleboro, VT 05301

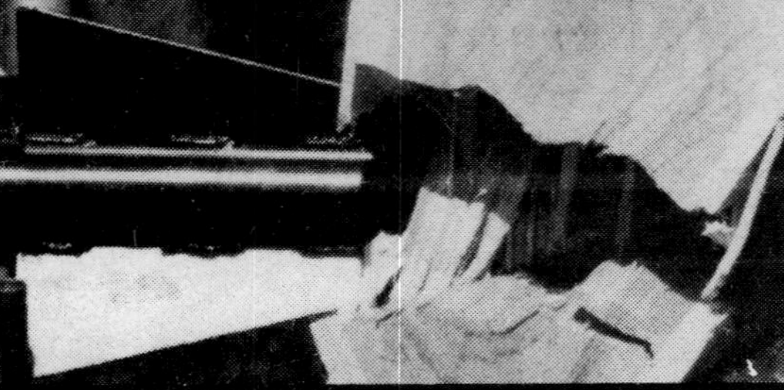

Bark-Buster

It all started with the Stickler Woodsplitter a couple years back. You attached an auger looking thing to a vehicle's drive hub, jacked it up, set it going, and watched it obsolesce all hydraulic splitters by tearing through a cord of wood an hour — even stumps! The idea was widely copied, the original company seems to have vanished, and here we are recommending one of the surviving competitors, who offer devices that run off your tractor, off a 5-horse engine, or off your car (simpler system — you just drive on to it). Beware of long hair or other entanglements around the turning auger. —SB

Bark-Buster
$375 - $485 (approx.)
Information
free from:
Bark-Buster, Inc.
14508 21st St. N.
Minneapolis, MN 55441

Firewood

Nifty idea: a book that helps you identify the best firewoods, summer or winter. Good illustrations and photos together with brief descriptions make it a lot easier for those unfamiliar with the woods to nab that cord. —J. Baldwin

Firewood
(A Woodcutter's Field-guide to Trees in Summer and Winter)
M. Michaelson
1979; 159 pp.
$2.95 postpaid from:
Gabriel Books
Minnesota Scholarly Press
P.O. Box 224
Mankato, MN 56001

•

If you cut your own firewood, use this guide to distinguish between inferior and valuable species of trees. The proverb that the woodcutter is warmed twice by firewood — once when cutting it and again when burning it — is true enough regardless of the wood. But it also is true that a cord of hickory, the queen of fire wood, delivers about 25 million BTUs compared to the same amount of American elm with only 17 million BTUs and that a cord of white oak has 23 million BTUs compared to aspen's 13 million.

Crosscut Saw Manual

This manual of big-saw sharpening and care is unusual for a government document; it names brand names and has a lot of rather personalized detail. Perhaps that's because it is published for the use of Forest Service employees. I recently hand sharpened a tired saw using the techniques shown, and enjoyed dramatically improved cutting. Nice. —J. Baldwin
[Suggested by David Nimick]

Crosscut Saw Manual
Warren Miller
1977; 27 pp.
No. 001-001-00434-1
$1.50 postpaid from:
Superintendent of Documents
U.S. Government Printing Office
Washington, DC 20402

•

Now, I know of only one company manufacturing crosscut saws in the United States: Jemco Tool Corp., Saw Division, 60 State Street, Seneca Falls, NY 13148. The company distributes a catalog of its saws.

A toolkit for crosscut saw reconditioning is available from Century Tool Co., Inc., Ginkgo Industrial Park, 102 Richard Road, Ivyland, PA 18974.

Crosscut

And, of course, you can cut it by hand. I do. Hand cutting is quiet, and tends to keep one realistic about being a wood hog. Tends to keep your canoe arm in shape over winter, too. It's also cheap. (And reliable, though I'll admit occasionally hard to start in the cold.) —J. Baldwin

Two-man crosscut saw
$62.65 postpaid

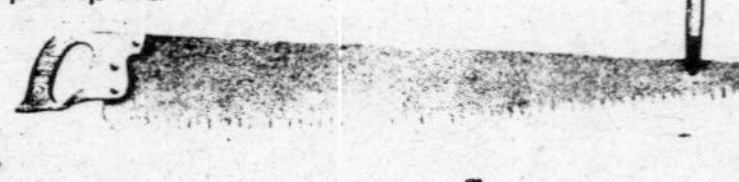

One-man crosscut saw
$36.60 postpaid

Bucksaw
$18.80 postpaid
all from:
Woodcraft Supply Corp.
313 Montvale Avenue
Woburn, MA 01801

Master Builders of the Middle Ages

The story of what happened in Europe after the Crusaders (early missionaries) discovered the dazzling architecture of the Middle East: the Gothic cathedrals, the masons who built them, the secrets of building kept in masonic lodges, a period in history when the church and monarchs could not control their builders, and the early seeds of architecture. —Lloyd Kahn

Master Builders of the Middle Ages
David Jacobs
1969; 153 pp.
$9.95 postpaid from:
Harper & Row
Keystone Industrial Park
Scranton, PA 18512
or Whole Earth Household Store

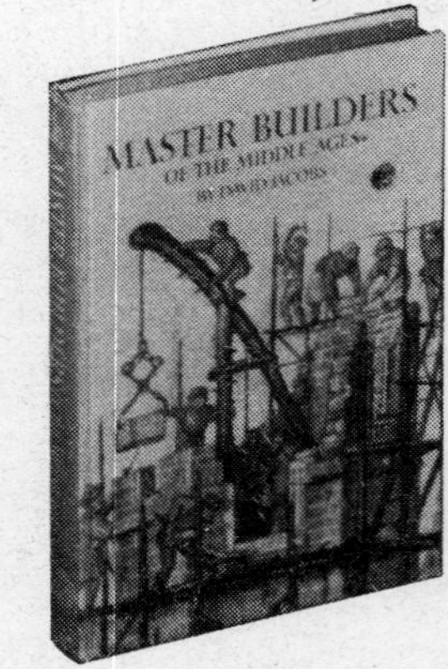

•

As soon as he realized how important he was becoming, the mason quickly asserted and flaunted his independence. He asked for higher pay, and he got it. He dressed garishly, favoring showy silks and satins and huge capes of bright solid colors, lined with gaily patterned prints. He let his hair grow long and cultivated an unruly beard — at a time when short-cropped hair and a clean-shaven face were signs of piety and self-sacrifice.

In 1230 the Church decided that it had had enough. The bishops realized that they had allowed things to go so far because of their own competitiveness; thus divided, they had been powerless. Now they were determined to put aside their rivalries and unite. Only through a show of unity could they shake the masons of their worldly ways and force them to end their defiance of the Church. An order went out from every abbey and cathedral: the masons (for a start) were to shave off their beards and cut their hair short. The masons refused . . . The order would not be obeyed. In fact, it must be rescinded. If it were not, the brotherhood of masons would systematically burn to the ground every last church, monastery, and cathedral in France.

Considering the enormous power of the Church, this was an incredible ultimatum. Nevertheless, the bishops backed down. Still long-haired and bearded, the masons gave the word to resume work, and the cathedral crusade continued.

Self portrait, Adam Krafft sculptor, 1455-1508 →

Shelter, Sign & Symbol

At first glance, this book resembles **The Prodigious Builders**, *but the resemblance is only superficial. Here, we get an astute analysis of why people have built their cities and buildings the way they do. The incomprehensible (to Western eyes) patterns begin to take on some meaning. I find this sort of thing absolutely fascinating because such learning tends to open up completely new areas to my mind. Our own building looks different too. Hmmm. Anyway, this is one of those books I actually "couldn't put down" and I recommend it to the hungry.* —J. Baldwin

Shelter, Sign & Symbol
Paul Oliver
1977; 228 pp.
$8.95 (paperback price)
postpaid from:
The Overlook Press
The Viking Press
299 Murray Hill Pkwy.
East Rutherford, NJ 07073
or WholeEarth Household Store

Examples of calligraphy from various Pakistani trucks, with their translations.

ت کے منہ میں بیٹھ کر خوشیاں
منانے والے حافظ خدا تمہارا راکٹ
چلانے والے

THOSE WHO SIT IN THE JAWS OF DEATH AND REJOICE, MAY GOD PROTECT YOU — YOU WHO DRIVE THE ROCKET.

ہیں جنت کے قابل ہوں
دوزق میرے قابل ہے۔ تیری
رضا جو ہو چاہے ادھر کردے چاہے
ادھر کردے

I AM NOT WORTHY OF HEAVEN, NOR IS HELL WORTHY OF ME. I COULD BE PLACED IN EITHER AT THY WISH.

↑Cupola of a Turkish bathhouse — a whirlpool of bright stars, arrested, as it were, in its movement. The luminous disks embedded in the dome are thick, lens-like glass blocks. Iznic, Turkey. Othmanli period.

Architecture Without Architects

If I were to name a single book that utterly changed the way I think about a considerable body of information, it would be this one. My whole idea of shelter, architecture and building in general was completely dismantled by the sudden realization that people did their best work without restrictions and much of the time (but not all of the time) without anyone acting as "architect." The book hasn't lost any of its abilities in the years it's been with us. When I teach design, it is the first and usually only book I assign. And it is one of the very few books about anything I read over and over. Yup . . . that good.
—J. Baldwin

Architecture Without Architects
(A Short Introduction to Non-Pedigreed Architecture)
Bernard Rudofsky
1964, 1969; 160 pp.

$5.95 postpaid from:
Doubleday & Company
501 Franklin Avenue
Garden City, NY 11531
or Whole Earth Household Store

←
Many so-called primitive peoples deplore our habit of moving (with all our belongings) from one house, or apartment, to another. Moreover, the thought of having to live in rooms that have been inhabited by strangers seems to them as humiliating as buying second hand old clothes for one's wardrobe. When they move, they prefer to build new houses or to take their old ones along.

→
A street at the oasis Kharga, in the Libyan Desert. Such pictures may strike terror into the heart of the urbanite because he automatically associates them with unspeakable crimes. In underdeveloped countries, however, such streets are usually as safe as a church at high mass. Still, although they are taken for granted by the natives, to us they seem unreal, devoid as they are of sidewalks, traffic lights, parked cars, and batteries of garbage cans, all of which we have come to accept as the attributes of higher civilization. Photographs can only hint at the actual experience of traversing passages through complicated space that plays on all senses: sheafs of light piercing darkness; waves of coolness and warmth; the echo of one's own footsteps; the odor of sun-baked stones.

The Prodigious Builders

The **Prodigious Builders** *considers an even wider selection of vernacular building than* **Architecture Without Architects**, *and adds erudite commentary based on insights gained by Mr. Rudofsky as he traveled many years observing and photographing. His ideas seem to be even more relevant when compared with the limp proposals offered by so many contemporary architects. Exciting stuff!*
—J. Baldwin

The Prodigious Builders
Bernard Rudofsky
1977; 383 pp.

$7.95 postpaid from:
Harcourt Brace Jovanovich,
757 Third Avenue
New York, NY 10017
or Whole Earth Household Store

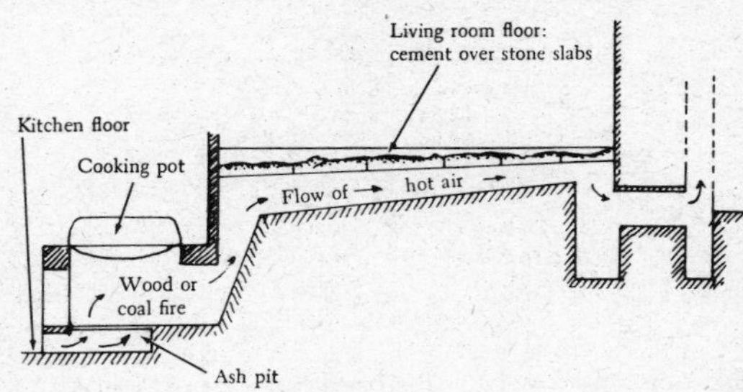

Floor heating, considered a luxury in our part of the world, has been a long-standing commodity in the peasant houses of Korea and northern China, where it is called a k'ang.

Door and window of this house in the oasis of Walata in Mauretania are typical of the traditional way for improving the looks of the austere architecture.

•
Even though Simopetra ranks as one of Athos's most sturdy buildings, a visit to it is not recommended to anyone unpracticed on the flying trapeze. A close brush with eternity awaits one at the guest quarters, located on the top floor of the outermost wing. The sagging wooden galleries that gird the cyclopean walls, which in places provide the only communication between the rooms, do not just look fragile; they are. A single misstep will cut short your journey. The floorboards, as thin as shingles, curl up under one's weight, while the *trompe-l'oeil* railings stand upright by sheer inertia. Self-preservation has taught the monks a way of floating angel-like over these aerial corridors — no doubt a matter of faith rather than gravity, like walking over glowing coals. Seeing you blanch, your guide hastens to tell you by way of encouragement the story of a fellow monk who, while carrying a tray with coffee cups along the very gallery you are standing on, broke through the treacherous planks and fell several hundred feet to his death. And here one might suppose the story ends. But no; the doomed monk shortly emerged from a crack in the rocks, hale and unperturbed, the glasses on his tray in place and not a drop of coffee spilled. At Simopetra it pays to take out afterlife insurance.
↓

Tomb of a sixteenth-century Muslim ruler of the Songhai Empire, West Africa, the present Mali. A stairway leads to the top of the truncated pyramid, whence one enjoys a view of the countryside. The sticks serve as permanent scaffolding.

THE RISING SUN
NEIGHBORHOOD NEWSLETTER

I used to live right on the water and now I live right on a busy street. Some effects:

1. I am happy to see people moving like people outside my window. Seeing waves moving like waves was sometimes oppressive. (Maybe because, not being a sailor or a swimmer, I couldn't join in.)

2. I leave the windows open unless it's very cold because the air used to be alive.

3. I notice that distant, or windows-shut traffic noise is not as different from distant, or windows-shut, water noise as good taste dictates it should be. (The water in waves goes round and round, the arms on pistons go round and round.) As Ngaio Marsh once asked, with almost no context at all, why is the spot of red in the forest so beautiful when we think it's a flower and so horrible when we find it's a candy wrapper?

Dwelling near Kudan, Tokyo

Japanese Homes and Their Surroundings

One of the most wonderful books in print. In 1877 the American, Morse (he was curator of the Peabody Museum in Salem, Massachusetts and an early solar inventor — see p. 187) travelled to Japan, fell in love with the culture, and opened the West to it (Fenollosa and Ezra Pound followed his lead). Lovingly perceived, understood, and illustrated, the detailed genius of Japanese home life comes across intact. —SB

Japanese Homes & Their Surroundings
Edward S. Morse
1886, 1961; 372 pp.
$4.50 postpaid from:
Dover Publications
180 Varick Street
New York, NY 10014
or Whole Earth Household Store

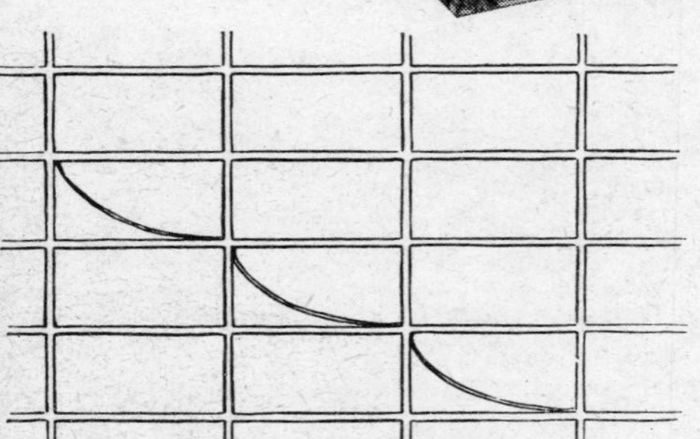

STRAIGHTENING SHŌJI FRAME.

Sometimes the frame of a *shōji* gets sprung or thrown out of its true rectangular shape; this is remedied by inserting at intervals in the meshes of the frame-work elastic strips of bamboo, and the constant pressure of these strips in one direction tends to bring the frame straight again.

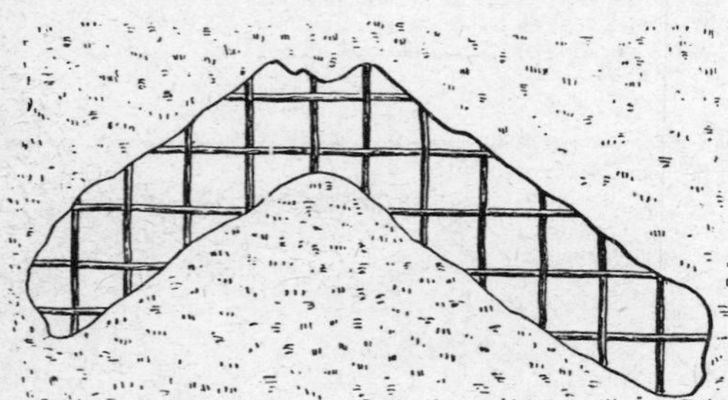

RUSTIC OPENING IN SUMMER-HOUSE, OKAZAKI.

•

In certain areas of the kitchen floor the planks are removable, the edges of special planks being notched to admit the finger, so that they can be lifted up one by one; and beneath them a large space is revealed, in which wood and charcoal are kept.

•

It may be well to say here that the wood composing the staircase, as well as certain floors, is highly finished, often with a surface like polished ivory. I have frequently examined the wood for evidences of wax or polish applied to its surface, but found none. Inquiry brought out the curious information that the water from the bath is often used to moisten the cloth with which the wood is wiped; and evidently the sebaceous secretions of the skin had much to do with the beautiful polish often attained.

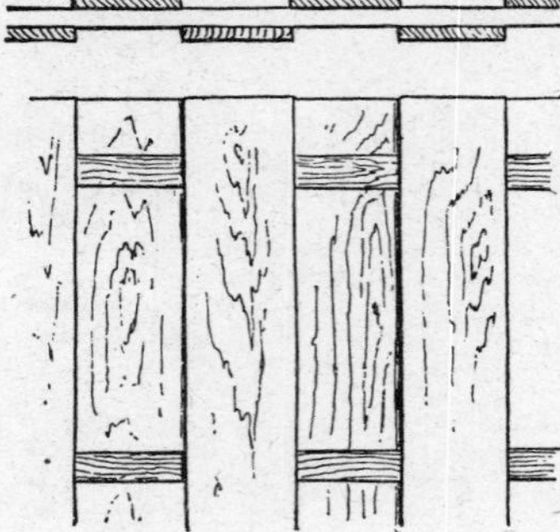

ORDINARY WOODEN FENCE.

A useful modification of the ordinary board-fence consists in having the upper and lower rails of thick board, three or four inches wide, and nailed sideways to the fenceposts. The fence-boards are nailed to these rails alternately on one side and on the other. A pretty effect is produced by the interrupted appearance of the rails, and a useful purpose also is subserved by lessening the pressure of the wind which so often blows with great violence, since by securing the boards in this way interspaces occur between the boards the width of the rails.

BALCONY RAIL.

Generally a narrow bar runs from post to post close to the platform, so that any object dropped may not roll out; between the end posts of the rail this piece is often removable, to allow dust and dirt to be more easily swept away. (The piece marked *A* is removable.)

Illustrated Handbook of Vernacular Architecture

A concise review, with many good drawings and photos of cottages, farm buildings, mills, inns and manor houses of England. Heavy timber framing, thatch, wattle and daub, tile and stone work. Windows, doors, staircases, design and plans. Excellent for building ideas as well as vernacular history, useful in building restoration. —Lloyd Kahn

Illustrated Handbook of Vernacular Architecture
R.W. Brunskill
1970, 1979; 230 pp.
$7.95 postpaid from:
Merrimack Book Service
99 Main Street
Salem, NH 03029
or Whole Earth Household Store

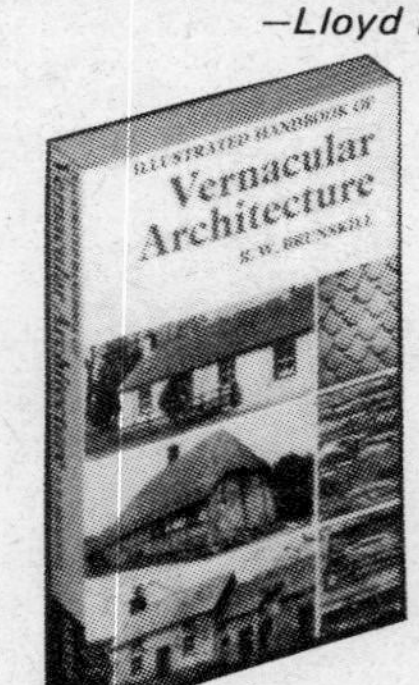

Timber Walling: Wattle and Daub Infill

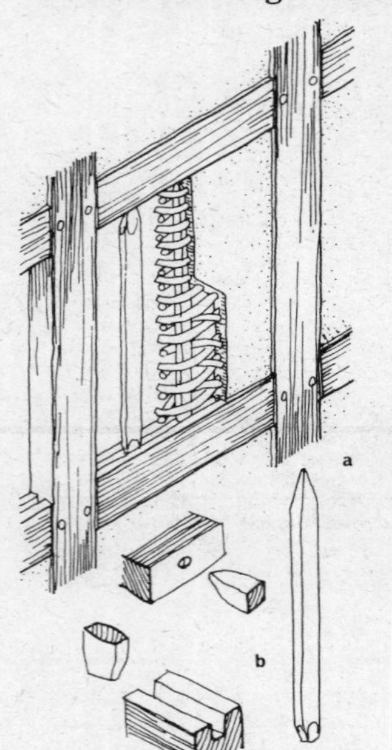

a. The cutaway isometric shows, diagrammatically, the vertical studs and horizontal rails joined to make a square panel. Staves sprung into the underside of one rail and slotted into the top of another form a base for woven wattles. The daub on both sides is finished with a thin plaster coating.
b. Here the shape of the staves, and details at top and bottom are indicated.
c. An undaubed panel is illustrated, typical of the ventilator panels used in the wall of timber-framed barns in Hereford and Shropshire. There are many local variations of size and weave used in such panels.

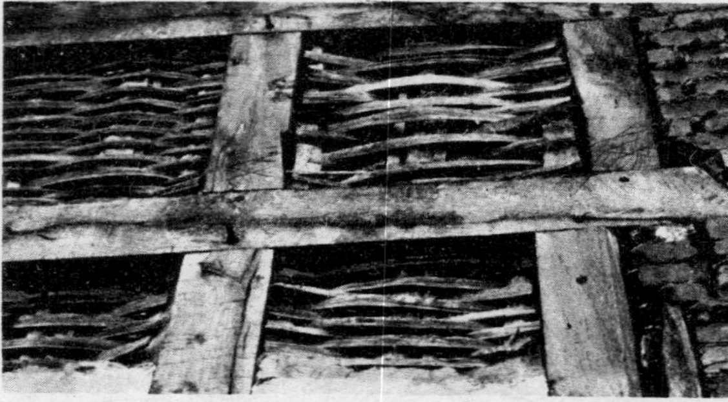

The Japanese House

Without getting all sentimental and exotic, we're still going to agree that Japanese make better houses than anybody else. If you're going to build your own house and don't mind some inspiration on the subject, this book was laboriously made for you. It's a great big Christmas present of a book full of yummy photos and diagrams and details of technique, all of which seems right within reach: I-can-do-it. Nice cure for nothing-can-be-done-because-it's-too-damned-big industrial blues.

$57.50 may choke you up, in which case get **Japanese Homes and Their Surroundings**, *$4.50 from Dover Publications — straight information on how to hand-make a lovable environment. (See above).* —SB

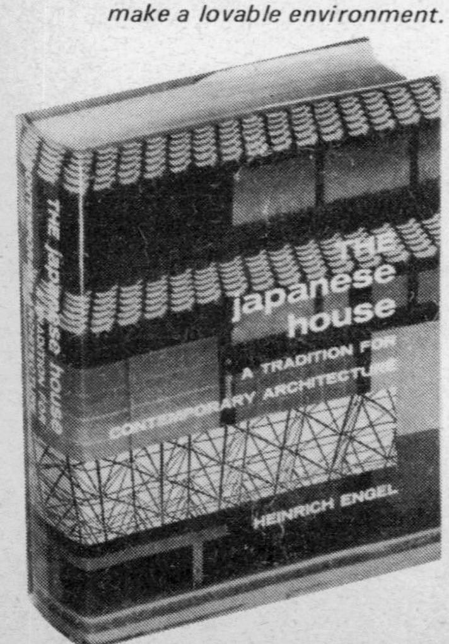

The Japanese House
(A Tradition for Contemporary Architecture)
Heinrich Engel
1964; 495 pp.
$57.50 postpaid from:
Charles E. Tuttle Co., Inc.
Rutland, VT 05701
or Whole Earth Household Store

•

Shōji paper is the "glass" of the Japanese house. Its qualities, however, are of a different nature, and, thus, also are its effects. The light, broken already by the broad overhang of the eaves, is diffused by the paper and creates a characteristic light condition comparable to twilight. This situation does not change basically even if the evening or winter sun hits the paper directly. No glare, no shadows; a general gloom creates a soft, emotional atmosphere. With artificial light in use, the *shoji* paper shows its reflective-diffusing ability, and at night with lights turned out, might even offer an interesting shadow play the moon has staged with the old weather-worn pine tree. As time passes, the paper darkens. Here and there, a torn piece is carefully cut out and replaced by new, lighter paper. The paper pattern becomes, though irregular, more interesting and lively. The paper ages, as does man.

The veranda of the warrior residence. It served both domestic and official functions.

Translucent paper panel. The shoji is the sliding screen that admits light and serves as door, window, or space enclosure.

↑
This is a two-poled Turkish oval tent pitched in the Wae Wawel Museum in Poland. It was taken as war booty in the seventeenth century by Polish armies. It measures 44 x 10½ feet. Although the exterior is plain, the interior is blue canvas decorated with a mosaic of multicolored satin, canvas, and leather appliques.

The Tent Book

A detailed and well-illustrated history of tents is contrasted with the very latest tension structures and camping equipment in the nicest tent book I've had the pleasure to see. There's a good discussion of camp tents, and a not especially comprehensive buyer's guide to get you started. I like books such as this one because there isn't any cause being pushed, yet there is a certain hard-to-resist insistence that the reader accept the basic ideas. In this case you are asked to agree that a tent can be a good home. In a day when a "low-cost" house is $150,000 by the time the mortgage is paid, there will be more and more interest in tension structures. This is a good place to start getting used to the idea. —J. Baldwin

The Tent Book
E.M. Hatton
1979; 244 pp.
$9.95 postpaid from:
Houghton Mifflin Co.
Wayside Road
Burlington, MA 01803
or Whole Earth
Household Store

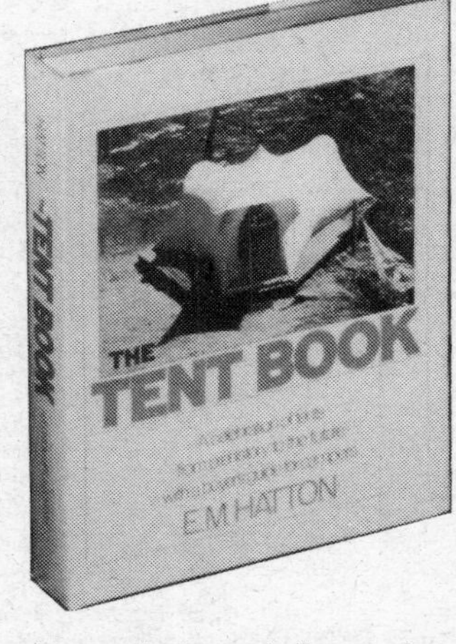

←
These tents of the Tibetan nomads are made from yak hair which is pulled, not shorn, from the bellies of the yak. This tent is supported by six poles (as opposed to the customary nine of the Bedouin) and, unlike the desert tent, has a central vent in the roof.

The Barn

If you're on property with a fine old barn, or if you're interested in the techniques and history of North America's finest (grandest) framing system (inherited from 3,000 years of practical northern Europeans), **The Barn** *is worth maybe having and certainly viewing.*

The book is excellent on the matter of taxonomy: Dutch barns, English barns, Pennsylvania barns, Connected barns, Polygonal barns, etc. Excellent also on history: barn design is traceable to upturned Iron Age ships and to ancient Basilican churches. The authors are "architectural" in their aesthetic appreciation; they pay due attention to the agricultural functioning and design innovations of various barns; they are less instructive about the dynamics of evolution in this splendidly vernacular and diverse medium. Happily, they cover the extraordinary barns of eastern Canada as well as northeastern U.S. The barns of the Deep South and Western States are not well explored.

The major resource in the book is scads of glorious photographs, many in color, many of fine structural detail.
—SB

The Barn
(A Vanishing Landmark in North America)
Eric Arthur and Dudley Whitney
1975; 256 pp.
$10.95 postpaid from:
A & W Publishers, Inc.
95 Madison Avenue
New York, NY 10016
or Whole Earth
Household Store

→
How indebted we are to the farmer who saw his sheepcote silhouetted against the sky as more than a shelter for sheep. He kept hay in the loft and legend has it that he could watch over his flocks in the fields through a dormer on all four faces. This wonderful little building is near Millpoint in New York State.

The interior of the ring barn at Shelburne, Vermont, looking toward the silos.
↓

The Log Cabin

A historical look at North American log buildings, profusely illustrated with nifty photographs, many in color. Though you might think that a whole book of log cabin pictures might be dull going, I note that visitors who start casually leafing through it are soon unavailable for conversation. —J. Baldwin

The Log Cabin
Alex W. Bealer and John O. Ellis
1978; 192 pp.
$9.45 postpaid from:
Barre Publishing
Crown Publishers
One Park Avenue
New York, NY 10016
or Whole Earth
Household Store

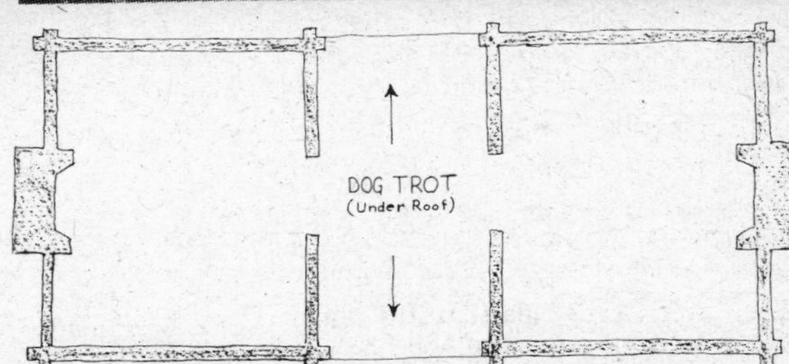

The town of Lumpkin, Georgia, uses a beautifully crafted restored dogtrot cabin for its library.

•
Another design for a log house, which also followed traditional English patterns of house building, was the dogtrot cabin, its colloquial-sounding name belying its potential for elegance. Like the double-pen house it consisted of two rooms, but the rooms were separated, not by a wall but by an open hallway, or dogtrot. Rooms and hallway shared a common floor and were covered by a common roof. Each room generally had a fireplace in its end wall and each had a door opening on the dogtrot.

One can easily imagine how such a floor plan could be altered to fit a large and busy family. Each room, for instance, could be divided into two with two doors to the open hallway and with corner fireplaces in each, using a common flue. The dogtrot could be covered at each end, making it into an interior hall. Then if the walls were raised higher, one could have a two-story, eight-room house of exactly the same basic plan as Washington's beloved and beautiful Mount Vernon.

Arts and Crafts of Hawaii — Section II, Houses

The art of Hawaiian lashing. Details on gable and hip-roofed buildings lashed together with a three-ply braid of 'uki'uki grass. —Lloyd Kahn

Arts and Crafts of Hawaii
(Section II — Houses)
Te Rangi Hiroa
(Peter H. Buck)
1964; 39 pp.
$2.50 postpaid from:
Bishop Museum Press
P.O. Box 19000-A
Honolulu, HI 96819

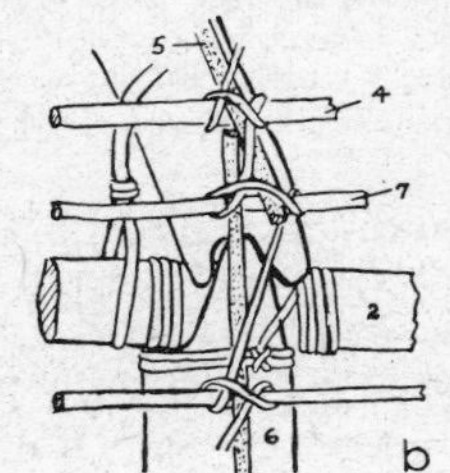

Junction of roof and wall rods: a, side view of junction between roof rod (5) and wall rod (6) with extra purlin (7); b, continuation of clove-hitch lashing down over extra purlin (7); c, close-up of junction join with wall rod (6) on right; d, junction join with wall rod (6) on left.

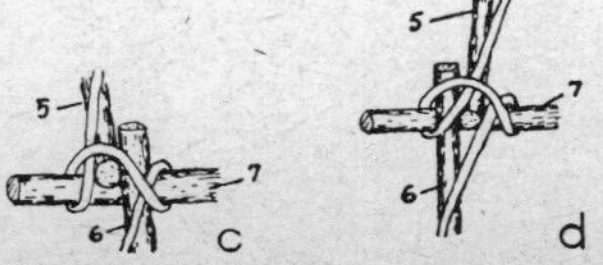

THE RISING SUN
NEIGHBORHOOD NEWSLETTER

I was reading the list of movies to be shown at this old movie place in Berkeley and noticed *The Lion Hunters and Margaret Mead* and loved it until I found out it was two movies, both pretty predictable. There for a minute I thought I could see everybody's favorite wise short anthropologist observing a bunch of studs out of Ernest Hemingway.

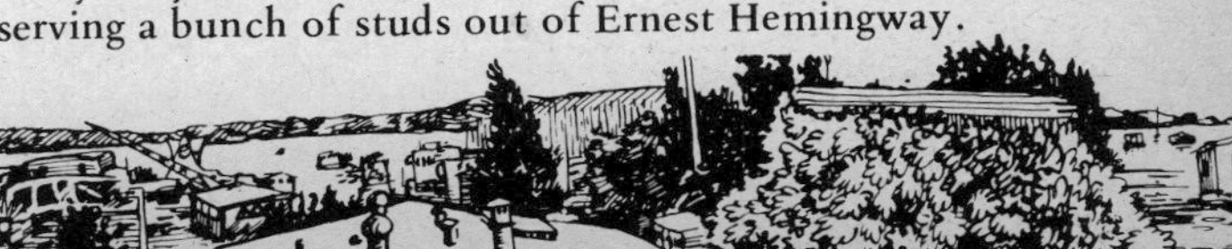

Frame walls full height for maximum strength. Add bevelled nailing plate to top plate on high wall.

Minimum 4:12 roof pitch for installation of asphalt shingles.

Fire-block

Seat rafters with birds-mouth on low wall plate.

Walls framed higher than 8'-0" must be fireblocked horizontally at 8'-0" high.

Studs and rafters at 24" on center. Rafters must align directly over studs.

Shelter and Shelter II

Lloyd Kahn, who wrote many of the nearby reviews, puts his publishing where his reviewing is in these two books of vernacular architectural technique. They rely heavily on voluminous mail as well as Kahn's own travels, so the range is considerable. Huts, caves, tipis, heavy timber, barns, conventional frame primer, salvaging, house cars, domes, yurts, foundation techniques, bamboo, sod roofs, and termite inhibition — to skip lightly across the contents. Gives you sharp, eclectic eyes and an itch to busy your hands. —SB

Shelter
Lloyd Kahn, Editor
1973; 176 pp.
$10 postpaid

Shelter II
Lloyd Kahn, Editor
1978; 224 pp.
$10 postpaid
both from:
Home Book Service
Box 650
Bolinas, CA 94924
or Whole Earth
Household Store
(**Shelter II** only)

•

A builder can take two very important steps to save energy: build small and insulate well. **—Shelter**

•

Tips on building with used wood:

Always look for the shortest length piece; this is a discipline you follow throughout the building process. It's a good feeling to cut a 10¼" block from an 11" piece of scrap.

Look at both ends of the board to be used. If one end is chewed up, make that the waste end.

Bevelling edges with small block plane makes used wood look good.

Remove all nails when dismantling. It will save your saw blades later on.

Discard any wood that has powder post beetle holes or dry rot (or cut off the rotted portion). **—Shelter II**

•

Building small to start will give you basic experience. A small shed can be a place to live in or store things while you study the land and decide what to do next. You can watch the rising and setting of sun and moon, study outlook and orientation, learn about seasonal temperatures and wind direction, vegetation, rainfall: the many considerations that should help you decide what kind of house will suit your needs and fit the site.

The small building can then be expanded as needed. *You* will change during the building process, and building in increments gives you flexibility and adaptability as you go.

Building is hard work, costly and relatively permanent. Unlike a painter or potter, the builder cannot throw away an unsatisfactory result. There it stands, for all to see, for many years. Thus there is wisdom, especially for a new builder, in starting small, simply, and heeding local advice. **—Shelter**

•

What's good about 90° walls: they don't catch dust, rain doesn't sit on them, easy to add to; gravity, not tension, holds them in place. It's easy to build in counters, shelves, arrange furniture, bathtubs, beds. *We* are 90° to the earth. Not important how much a building weighs. It *is* important how much a bird weighs, but a building doesn't have to move or fly. Certainly an adobe house weighs tremendously. So? Would it be better if it were built of plastic of 1/100th the weight and 10,000 times as polluting in its manufacture? **—Shelter**

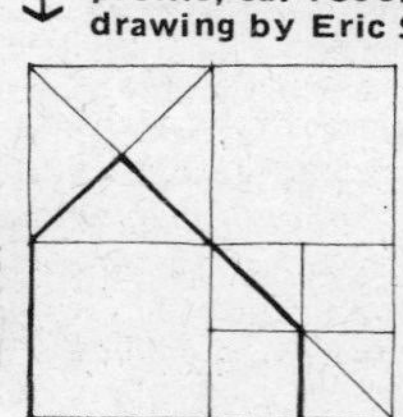

Classic New England saltbox ↓ profile, ca. 1690. After drawing by Eric Sloane.

↑

The saltbox shape is generally associated with the New England states and severe winters. They are often oriented with the high side to the south, the low side to the north. This allows winter sun to hit the high side, and snow (a good insulator) to accumulate on the lower, shallower roof to the north. Snow or bales of hay are often banked against the north side in winter for insulation. **—Shelter II**

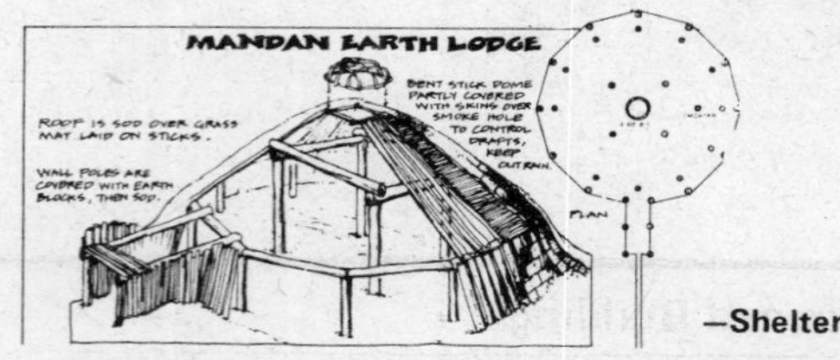

—Shelter

Handmade Houses

Architects, look out. Funky cottage builders are out there solving building and design problems once thought to be only in your domain. The saw mightier than the pencil? The case is presented here with the finest quality color prints, small owner-built houses presented in a manner usually reserved for Palladian mansions. A small yet valuable book. —Bob Easton

Handmade Houses
(A Guide to the Woodbutcher's Art)
Art Boericke and Barry Shapiro
1973; 87 pp.
$6.95 postpaid from:
A & W Publishers
95 Madison Avenue
New York, NY 10016
or Whole Earth
Household Store

Looking down from logging cables, a new-world tea house hovers over a swiftly-flowing stream.

House Boats

Who hasn't dreamt of living on a houseboat? If you have haven't, this photo essay will likely prove provocative. If you have, it may be more than you can stand. Houseboats from all over the world are shown in beautiful color photographs that capture the romance of life afloat. Not shown are the problems of leaks, rats, dampness, toilet failure, the law — but so what?! Feast your mind and eat your heat out at the same time. —J. Baldwin

An acknowledgment. Without the fine free creativity of the Sausalito houseboat community surrounding our office, the **Whole Earth Catalog** *and* **CoEvolution Quarterly** *could never have grown as they have. As always, the community is threatened by civic narrow-minded short-sighted block-headedness. And as always neighborhood preservation is an ecological issue, deserving eternal vigilance.* —SB

House Boats
(Living on the Water around the World)
Mark Gabor
1979; 128 pp.
$17.95 postpaid from:
Ballantine Books
455 Hahn Road
Westminster, MD 21157
or Whole Earth
Household Store

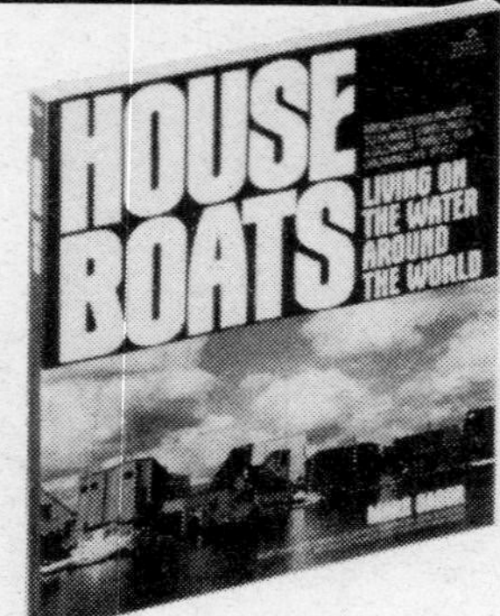

•

The largest, most famous, and now most controversial houseboat area in California is in Sausalito. There one finds a series of docks containing hundreds of houseboats of every size, shape, and description. Each dock, referred to as a "gate" in Sausalito, has its own distinct personality. Houseboats range from the expensive, elegant, floating-home type, to medium-sized hand-crafted boats that look like floating sculpture, and to unique water-shanties simply thrown together, such as the VW microbus sitting in the middle of a small open dinghy. Nowhere else is there such a concentration of different, if not disparate, houseboats as in Sausalito.

The rise in houseboat living came to this town following World War II. At that time Sausalito began attracting many writers, painters, and craftspeople, whose creativity was applied to the challenge of living cheaply on water. The artists did not confine themselves to a particular type of houseboat construction. They used whatever resources were available, including abandoned ferries and military hulls, scraps of metal and wood gathered inland, and flotsam and jetsam. Ignoring building codes and most rules and regulations, the artists wound up creating an impressive conglomeration of live-in sculpture — patched, fantasy structures, vividly colored in an endless variety of paints and other materials. Most have no electricity, phones, or running water. These houseboats reside at several docks, known collectively as Waldo Point.

Through recent decades Waldo Point has been a haven for the poor artist, with moorage fees as low as $25 per month for a small houseboat. To the inexperienced eye, the maze of docks and gangplanks, the random positioning of the 203 houseboats, and the accumulation of apparent junk lying about lead one to believe it is an area characterized by squalor and chaos. But that is far from the truth. Each dock is its own neighborhood, with names like "Muck and Mire Boulevard" and "Sleazie's." Everyone knows where everyone else lives. The positioning of the boats is not so much random as it is complex, differing at each bend and turn along the dockways as an expression of the artists' desires to be unregimented, improvisational. The so-called junk lying about is a colossal stockpile of building and sculptural materials — essentially an effort to recycle what middle-class society would casually discard as obsolete.

As the Seine wanders through the wealthy Paris suburb of Neuilly, there is a row of thirty-four higher-class houseboats. Some are large floating homes, others are converted barges and luxury cruisers. All are permanently and legally moored along a thickly treed bank. The moorage includes the adjacent land, on which most of the well-to-do owners grow lush flower gardens.

An immaculately kept all-teak Thai houseboat on the bank of the Chao Phraya River, near Bangkok. Its hull empty, this typical cargo boat, with its corrugated tin roof, sits quite high on the water.

Iron grating of the chamfered corner of the Casa Mila from the interior.

Gaudi

Expensive coffee table books don't interest us very often because they tend to be mostly fluff. This one is mostly rock. Gaudi is being "rediscovered" by many persons who are fed up with glittery aluminum and glass modern styles. His work shows a bold imagination and a remarkable variety of form and color. Yet he based his designs on meticulous discipline and structural analysis. Gaudi didn't write much, but the author spent many years in his studio, so there is ample anecdote and discussion of theories. The book is well illustrated, complete, and annotated to a fare-thee-well. All his work is displayed, much of it for the first time in print, so even Gaudi lovers will find a lot here. —J. Baldwin

May God damn architects who bore and stifle and preen their chickenyard feathers. Give us more jungle birds like Gaudi. Last winter I spent an afternoon soaring through the towers of his Sagrada Familia cathedral in Barcelona. Spain can spend 200 years finishing that building and it will still be ahead of its time. No one can reveal the shallowness of one's aesthetic habits as devastatingly as Gaudi. —SB

Gaudi
(His Life, His Theories, His Work)
Cesar Martinell
1975; 486 pp.
$55 postpaid from:
The M.I.T. Press
28 Carleton Street
Cambridge, MA 02142

←
The Towers of the Sagrada Familia. 1901-1926

The temple of the Sagrada Familia was the master's work of fulfillment, and at each stage it reveals his current architectural preoccupations.

Above the vertical walls of the twelve tall openings, the world-famous parabolic structures begin. This is the most architecturally interesting part of the temple, for it summarizes the new structural theory which he was never able to apply to more complex structures. In his enthusiastic search for antecedents for his works, Gaudi said that these towers were the perfection of the Gothic campaniles with set-back floors. In reality, however, he had developed a new clearly defined system of structural equilibrium which the Gothic architects could never have achieved except by trial and error or by accident. Twelve vertical structural elements resting on the pillars between the tall slender openings rise uninterruptedly upward as they converge slowly together at the top; they are united by stone plaques which slant downward and serve as sounding boards for the bells. These plaques follow a helicoidal distribution which parallels the interior staircase.

Protective screen of a patio skylight at the Casa Battló.→

Writings and Buildings

I read this while I was in the Army, where our bugle calls came on scratchy records.

Frank Lloyd Wright's reveille is still ringing. —SB

Writings and Buildings
Frank Lloyd Wright
Edgar Kaufman,
Ben Raeburn, Editors
1960; 346 pp.
$7.95 postpaid from:
Horizon Press
156 Fifth Avenue
New York, NY 10010
or Whole Earth
Household Store

•

Style is a free product but, still, a by-product: the result of the organic working in, and out of, a project entirely in character, altogether and in one state of feeling.

•

Beware of the architectural school except as the exponent on engineering.

Go into the field where you can see the machines and methods at work that make the modern buildings, or stay in construction direct and simple until you can work naturally into building-design from the nature of construction.

Immediately begin to form the habit of thinking "why" concerning any effects that please or displease you.

Take nothing for granted as beautiful or ugly, but take every building to pieces, and challenge every feature. Learn to distinguish the curious from the beautiful.

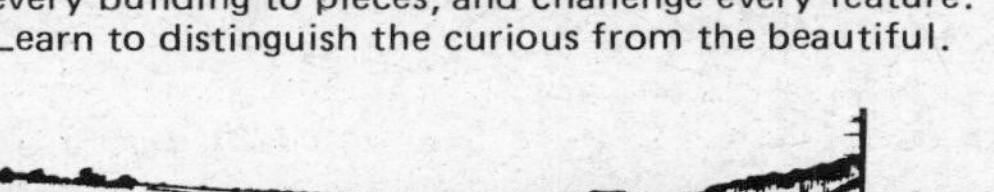

1949 The San Francisco Bay Crossing project

The Natural House

It is always good to review one's premises before starting a project. This collection is a tight presentation of most of our tacit assumptions about home design and construction by their author. Honesty in materials, simple space use, straightforward construction and a realistic attempt at low cost housing are presented here. It is a chance to review popular styles and attitudes, as well as a source of specific ideas and techniques. Using many pictures and plans of well designed homes these collected writings bring all the abstract philosophy down to a personal and specific level. Design for the site and the owner, with simplicity and beauty. —Peter Calthorpe

The Natural House
Frank Lloyd Wright
1970; 224 pp.
$11.95 postpaid from:
Horizon Press
156 Fifth Avenue
New York, NY 10010
or Whole Earth
Household Store

•

A stone building will no more *be* nor will it *look* like a steel building. A pottery, or terra cotta building, will not be nor should it look like a stone building. A wood building will look like none other, for it will glorify the stick. A steel-and-glass building could not possibly look like anything but itself. It will glorify steel and glass. And so on all the way down the long list of available riches in materials: stone, wood, concrete, metals, glass, textiles, pulp, and plastics; riches so great to our hand today that no comparison with ancient architecture is at all sensible or anything but obstruction to our modern architecture.

In this particular, as you may see, architecture is going back to learn from the natural source of all natural things.

•

To me air conditioning is a dangerous circumstance. The extreme changes in temperature that tear down a building also tear down the human body.

Arcology

If I get it right (and getting it at all is someting: it takes either lots of work or none at all) Soleri sees the next step in evolution as humanity's job. He sees that step manifested in an organism and that organism is the city. Soleri says that the first part of his book is the most important. But on seeing the second part it's very difficult to muster much time for the first part. It pays, though, nicely. Soleri refers to Teilhard de Chardin in approaching the understanding of man as a cosmic problem by ascending from physics, chemistry, biology and geology, Western man must rise from his technology and one (I think) way is by being aware (of it) but ignoring it at the same time. The manifestation of a process like this is, I think, a series of drawings like that of the second part of the book. These drawings are like doorways, they're of fantastic cities, wholly improbable but obviously, cosmically, possible. In fact, they are made real just by their presence in one place (the book) and by the interrelatedness of one project to the next, page to page, with seminal sketches appearing in the corners here and there. What's most fascinating are the next obvious steps: the Cosanti and Arcosanti buildings in Arizona. He's not starting all at once, big money style, but the way cities have always started: little by little. Like Nieuw Amsterdam on the tip of Manhattan Island or whatever city began at whatever river crossing or natural harbor, Soleri is beginning at a crossing of cosmic consciousness. —Ron Williams

Arcology
(The City in the Image of Man)
Paolo Soleri
1969; 121 pp.

$14.95 postpaid from:
The MIT Press
28 Carleton Street
Cambridge, MA 02142
or Whole Earth
Household Store

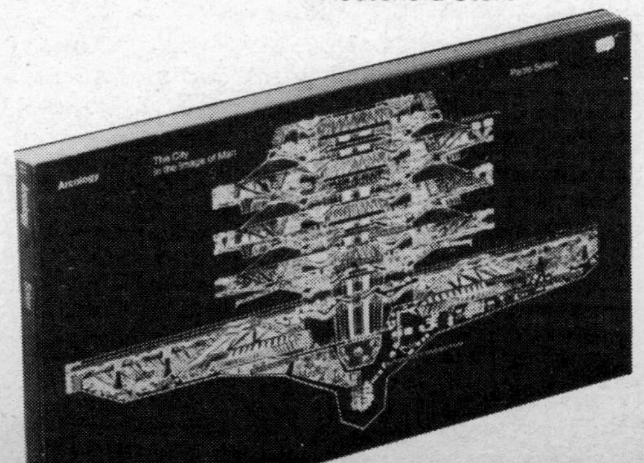

Paolo Soleri and the Arcosanti project

Not a man who is satisfied with mere talk, Paolo Soleri has developed the organization to actually build his bold ideas. There are many who are excited by his Arcosanti project near Prescott, Arizona (I among them), and the building continues apace with a host of apprentices mixing the cement. You can join the fray by attending one of the five week workshops ($300.00). From what I have seen, you'll work hard there, getting dirty and learning a lot. —J. Baldwin

You can find out about the workshops and other Cosanti Foundation activities by writing:

Cosanti Foundation
6433 Doubletree Road
Scottsdale, AZ 85253

THE RISING SUN
NEIGHBORHOOD NEWSLETTER

"I feel very lonely without a war. Do you feel that way?"

— Winston Churchill to his doctor, June, 1945

House Form and Culture

A relatively unknown and thought-provoking book on primitive and vernacular forces, culture and materials that bring (brought) about their designs. Valuable and instructive for that critical factor in house design: approach.
—*Lloyd Kahn*
[Suggested by Sim Van der Ryn]

House Form and Culture
Amos Rapaport
1969; 146 pp.
$5.95 postpaid from:
Prentice-Hall, Inc.
Box 500
Englewood Cliffs, NJ 07632
or Whole Earth Household Store

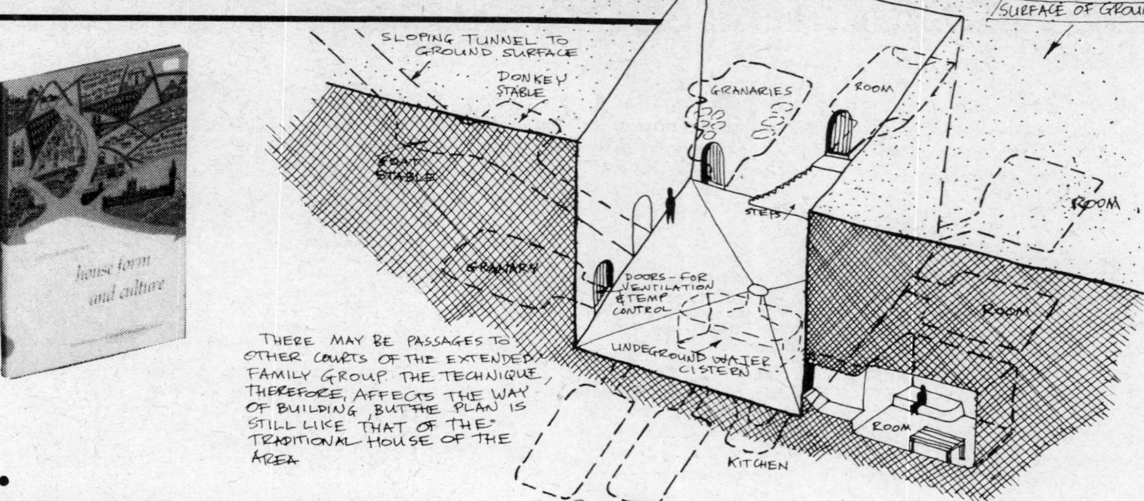

Cutaway view of Matmata dwelling, Sahara. (Adapted from a number of sources, primarily Haan in Architects' Yearbook 11 **and** New Frontiers in Architecture.**)**

•

The pueblo looks like a land form because the close relation of house form and landscape reflects the harmony of man and nature. The whole landscape is sacred, as is the house, and the whole environment influences all of Pueblo life. In fact, Pueblo Indians beg forgiveness every time they fell a tree or kill a jack rabbit. Corn growing is for them a religious act and an essential part of the total spiritual life. It is this attitude which affects the house, its form, siting, and relation to the land, and helps explain why such buildings enhance rather than damage the landscape.

•

It could be argued that, if we consider hostility of environment and available resources, the problems faced by the Eskimo are not unlike those involved in the design of a space capsule. The difference is less than one would imagine.

American Building

Fitch criticizes architects for not dealing with environmental forces. He finds that our highly developed technology and equipment for manipulating the natural environment have led architects to ignore natural forces as a factor in design. Air conditioning has allowed gigantic buildings of glass facing summer sun, etc. This is an important study of what has gone wrong, why, and what can be done about creating a more human architecture, a more harmonious relationship between buildings and their environment.
—*Lloyd Kahn*
[Suggested by Bob Brooks]

American Building
(The Environmental Forces That Shape It)
James Marston Fitch
1972; 349 pp.
$20 postpaid from:
Houghton Mifflin Company
Wayside Road
Burlington, MA 01803
or Whole Earth Household Store

Rooftop wind scoops, Hyderabad, Sind. A rare climatic paradox — high humidities superimposed on Arabian desert temperatures — makes ventilation mandatory. These wind scoops are oriented to prevailing breezes.

The Healthy House

*One of my respected friends has called this book "strange." Yup, and I strongly disagree with some of the not-very-rigorously-proven assertions. But. But it's that Old Master of Philosophy of Building Ken Kern speaking, and we know from all the good things he's brought out in the past (**The Owner Built Home**, p. 223, for instance) that Ken is worth listening to. I find the proposals refreshingly annoying, exciting, and I happily admit that reading **The Healthy House** has started me thinking more carefully about a number of aspects of building. Typical of Ken is that he has built a house incorporating his philosophy: it's underground, compound-curved, bamboo-reinforced stabilized clay. Egad! Living in it helps protect you from a variety of assaults (some of which you may not have heard of) and augments natural forces that tend to promote good health. Definitely worth a look, especially for the very different point of view.*
—*J. Baldwin*

The Healthy House
Ken Kern
1978; 152 pp.
$5.75 postpaid from:
Owner-Builder Publications
Box 817
North Fork, CA 93643
or Whole Earth Household Store

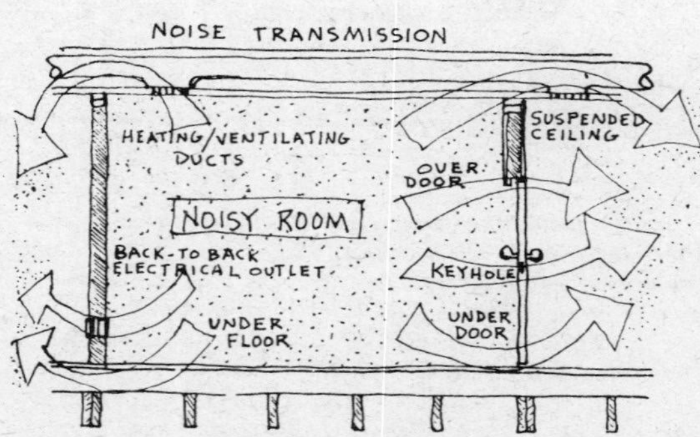

The Poetics of Space

There's been so much written in the last few years about the external construction of shelters. This book is about the house as interior construct, the house of dreams, the "dream house" that we're always building until the day we die, and the house of reverie which is the house we were born in, our first earthly home where "a lamp is always waiting in the window, and through it the house too is waiting" for each of us to come in, curl up, and dream. The external metaphor Bachelard uses for the house is the nest that the bird constructs with his own body, using his breast for a tool. He (the bird) suggests that a house is built by and for the body, that it takes form from the inside. "This being the case," writes Bachelard, "if I were asked to name the chief benefit of the house, I should say: the house shelters day-dreaming, the house protects the dreamer, the house allows one to dream in peace." The county ought to write that into its building code.
—*Lewis MacAdams, Jr.*

The Poetics of Space
Gaston Bachelard
1964; 241 pp.
$5.95 postpaid from:
Beacon Press
c/o Harper and Row
Keystone Industrial Park
Scranton, PA 18512
or Whole Earth Household Store

•

Housed everywhere but nowhere shut in, this is the motto of the dreamer of dwellings.

•

To begin with, the corner is a haven that ensures us one of the things we prize most highly — immobility.

•

If a poet looks through a microscope or a telescope, he always sees the same thing.

Distance, too, creates miniatures at all points on the horizon, and the dreamer, faced with these spectacles of distant nature, picks out these miniatures as so many nests of solitude in which he dreams of living.

Learning Architecture *by Lloyd Kahn*

Once I did a slide show at a nearby college. A student came up afterwards and asked if I knew of any good architecture schools in the country. I didn't.

We went across the street for some coffee and as we sat I told him what I'd do if I were him and wanted to learn building design: spend some months reading high-quality books on vernacular building as well as the world's great architecture. Then set off with sleeping bag, backpack, camera and notebook for a year or two of travel — studying, sketching, recording, listening, learning. Shelter being so basic, people of all lands seem willing to talk about it. They are proud of handwork (where it still exists), eager to show an interested visitor buildings, local ingenuity. Study humble, indigenous buildings as well as some monumental feats, letting circumstance and intuition guide the way. Sooner or later return home, put notes together, develop film, ponder what has been learned. In between travel and study — preferably before — work for a builder; and learn to draw.

To learn building you'll probably have to search around to find someone to take you on. Start as a laborer if need be; you'll pick up the skills as you go. Keep working on and off until you know something about building. It's a skill useful for a lifetime.

Draw as much as possible. Books can be helpful, but nothing is better than a compatible teacher. There might be someone at a college (this could mean a trek from school to school) who would be the right one. Or you might find a job working for an architect: he'd teach you drawing, you'd help him do drafting and get a salary that increased along with your proficiency.

Study, travel, building, drawing — not in any particular order — could make you into a fine architect, although without the credentials. It could also make you a misfit in today's western world of building and design, but who knows how long it will all last.

I didn't have all this together as we sat there on our second cup of coffee, but I've been thinking about it since. Because with what architecture has become, it's hard to learn the skills on a human scale, and most colleges are of little help.

I guess what I've done is outlined an alternative (that word again) course in architecture. For those who can't afford a good school or find one, it would be a vital way to learn the art and science of building. ■

A Pattern Language

This thick little book is so excitingly full of delights that it's hard to put down long enough to review. No possible doubt: it's simply a great book — a bracing adventure in architectural thought, a lift for the spirit, an inspiration for practical work!

The project is overwhelmingly ambitious — to establish a language for talking about what people really need from buildings and communities, drawing from many epochs and cultures but focusing on our own. Astonishingly, Alexander and his colleagues bring it off, and with calm, assured brilliance. Their 253 "patterns" range from general items like "the shape of indoor space" or "promenade" to extremely particular items like "built-in seats." Some patterns, like the "raised walks" recommended to insulate pedestrians from auto traffic, are virtually unknown in the U.S.; others, like "car connections," are omnipresent but ill-planned. The genius of Alexander et al. is that they simply ignore the stylistic fad-mongering that passes for architectural thought, and get on with sensible, useful, highly distilled wisdom about what works and what doesn't. They're not shy about laying down rules of thumb ("Balconies and porches which are less than six feet deep are hardly ever used") — often with research citations to back them up, and charming, pointed illustrations.

The most important book in architecture and planning for many decades, a landmark whose clarity and humanity give hope that our private and public spaces can yet be made gracefully habitable.

—Ernest Callenbach

(For more on urban patterns, see p. 300.)

I suspect this is the best and most useful book in the **Catalog.** *—SB*

A Pattern Language
(Towns, Buildings, Construction)
Christopher Alexander, Sara Ishikawa and Murray Silverstein
1977; 1169 pp.

$39.50 postpaid from:
Oxford University Press
16-00 Pollitt Drive
Fair Lawn, NJ 07410
or Whole Earth Household Store

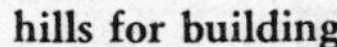

Preserve all agricultural valleys as farmland and protect this land from any development which would destroy or lock up the unique fertility of the soil. Even when valleys are not cultivated now, protect them: keep them for farms and parks and wilds.

•

People feel comfortable when they have access to the countryside, experience of open fields, and agriculture; access to wild plants and birds and animals. For this access, cities must have boundaries with the countryside near every point. At the same time, a city becomes good for life only when it contains a great density of interactions among people and work, and different ways of life. For the sake of this interaction, the city must be continuous — not broken up. In this pattern we shall try to bring these two facts to balance.

•

Parks are dead and artificial. Farms, when treated as private property, rob the people of their natural biological heritage — the countryside from which they came.

In Norway, England, Austria, it is commonly understood that people have a right to picnic in farmland, and walk and play — provided they respect the animals and crops. And the reverse is also true — there is no wilderness which is abandoned to its own processes — even the mountainsides are terraced, mown, and graced and cared for.

We may summarize these ideas by saying that there is only one kind of nonurban land — *the countryside*. There are no parks; no farms; no uncharted wilderness. Every piece of countryside has keepers who have the right to farm it, if it is arable; or the obligation to look after it, if it is wild; and every piece of land is open to the people at large, provided they respect the organic processes which are going on there.

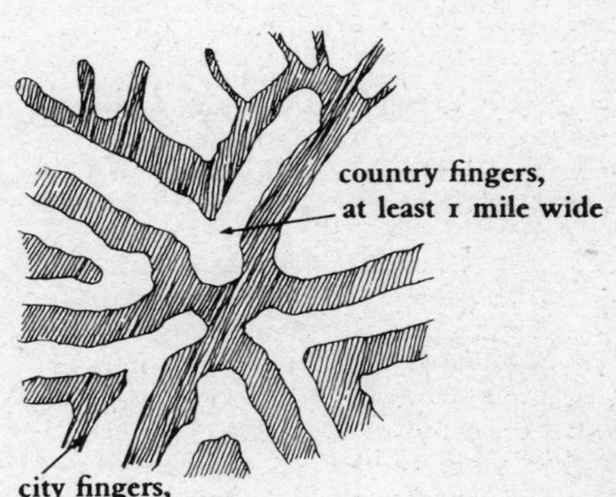

Keep interlocking fingers of farmland and urban land, even at the center of the metropolis. The urban fingers should never be more than 1 mile wide, while the farmland fingers should never be less than 1 mile wide.

•

Encourage the formation of a boundary around each neighborhood, to separate it from the next door neighborhoods. Form this boundary by closing down streets and limiting access to the neighborhood — cut the normal number of streets at least in half. Place gateways at those points where the restricted access paths cross the boundary; and make the boundary zone wide enough to contain meeting places for the common functions shared by several neighborhoods.

six passenger buses

telephone-radio dispatch

bus stops every 600 feet

Establish a system of small taxi-like buses, carrying up to six people each, radio-controlled, on call by telephone, able to provide point-to-point service according to the passengers' needs, and supplemented by a computer system which guarantees minimum detours, and minimum waiting times. Make bus stops for the mini-buses every 600 feet in each direction, and equip these bus stops with a phone for dialing a bus.

125'. minimum

Sixteen collision points. . . . Three collision points.

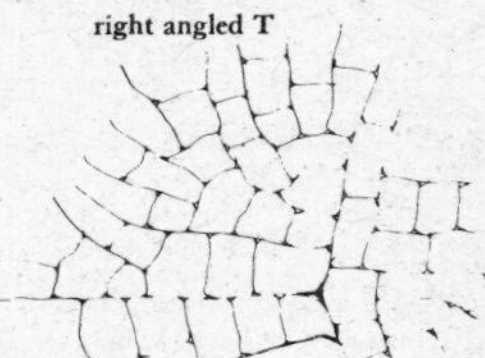

Lay out the road system so that any two roads which meet at a grade, meet in three-way T junctions as near 90 degrees as possible. Avoid four-way intersections and crossing movements.

•

Do what you can to encourage the development of individually owned shops. Approve applications for business licenses only if the business is owned by those people who actually work and manage the store. Approve new commercial building permits only if the proposed structure includes many very very small rental spaces.

Shop run as a way of life

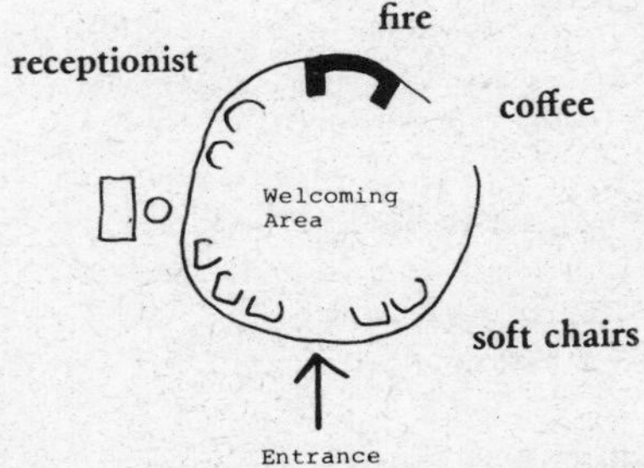

Arrange a series of welcoming things immediately inside the entrance — soft chairs, a fireplace, food, coffee. Place the reception desk so that it is not between the receptionist and the welcoming area, but to one side at an angle — so that she, or he, can get up and walk toward the people who come in, greet them, and then invite them to sit down.

Connect buildings with arcades, and outdoor rooms, and courtyards where they cannot be connected physically, wall to wall —

•

Connect your building up, wherever possible, to the existing buildings round about. Do not keep set backs between buildings; instead, try to form new buildings as continuations of the older buildings.

Where buildings run alongside busy streets, build windows with window seats, looking out onto the street. Place them in bedrooms or at some point on a passage or stair, where people keep passing by. On the first floor, keep these windows high enough to be private.

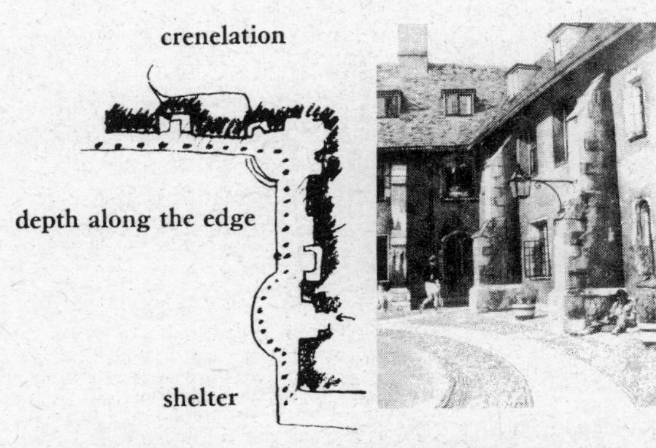

Make sure that you treat the edge of the building as a "thing," a "place," a zone with volume to it, not a line or interface which has no thickness. Crenelate the edge of buildings with places that invite people to stop. Make places that have depth and a covering, places to sit, lean, and walk, especially at those points along the perimeter which look onto interesting outdoor life.

•

When plate glass windows became possible, people thought that they would put us more directly in touch with nature. In fact, they do the opposite.

THE RISING SUN
NEIGHBORHOOD NEWSLETTER

Mir, the Russian word for peace, also means community, so the book is called *War and Community* as well as *War and Peace*. Everyone who lives gets married and has kids (except Sonya, who's a good aunt.)

—Information from John Bayley's introduction to the Signet edition of *W & P*

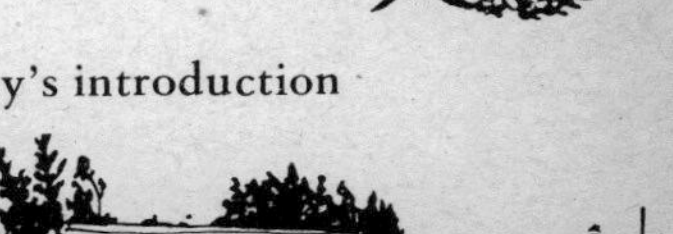

THE ABSOLUTELY CONSTANT INCONTESTABLY STABLE ARCHITECTURAL VALUE SYSTEM*

	−100 always	−75 usually	−50 sometimes	−25 seldom	+25 seldom	+50 sometimes	+75 usually	+100 always	
destroys pure air									creates pure air
destroys pure water									creates pure water
wastes rainwater									stores rainwater
produces no food									produces its own food
destroys rich soil									creates rich soil
wastes solar energy									uses solar energy
stores no solar energy									stores solar energy
destroys silence									creates silence
dumps its wastes unused									consumes its own wastes
needs cleaning and repair									maintains itself
disregards nature's cycles									matches nature's cycles
destroys wildlife habitat									provides wildlife habitat
destroys human habitat									provides human habitat
intensifies local weather									moderates local weather
is ugly									is beautiful

negative score, out of a possible 1500	positive score, out of a possible 1500

final score:

Please feel free to use, reproduce, and/or modify this scale in any way. No permission is needed.

by Malcolm Wells

Malcolm Wells is the leading light at the end of the underground architecture tunnel, which itself is a hot topic among innovative energy-saving designers. Wells was talking to a bunch of them on April 18, 1980, at the National Technical Conference, Earth Sheltered Building Design Innovations, Oklahoma State University, Oklahoma City. As follows. (See also Wells' book, ***Underground Designs****, p. 240, and* ***How to Buy Solar Heating without Getting Burnt****, p. 189.)* —SB

It's pretty satisfying to cover a building with earth and then watch the utility bills shrink. If the roof doesn't leak — or collapse — the temptation to congratulate oneself is at times almost irresistible. Just think: natural shelter from all extremes of heat and cold, shelter made of ordinary on-site subsoil, a material not yet thought to be in very short supply.

It's satisfying to live and work underground, too, satisfying in more ways than that of energy saving. There's the silence, the security, the in-tune-ness you feel, not to mention the reduced outdoor maintenance costs, so those of us in the earth-shelter business tend to lose our perspectives just as easily as anyone else. We get smug. We think we have found The Solution. The fact that earth-shelter has almost no measurable effect upon The Problem is swept away by our own self-satisfaction.

The Problem is something a bit wider than anything earth-sheltered buildings alone can hope to solve. Most descriptions of it go something like this:

- nuclear war,
- nuclear accidents,
- starvation/overpopulation
- the growth of deserts,
- toxic materials in the environment,
- loss of topsoil,
- the proliferation of pesticides, herbicides, and chemical fertilizers,
- destruction of the ozone layer,
- increasing concentrations of atmospheric CO_2,
- overpaving,
- the depletion of natural resources,
- genetic manipulation,
- the extinction of species,
- habitat destruction, etc., etc., all the way down to an
- exploding crime rate, and
- inflation.

We are, in other words, in a colossal mess, the scale of which is so vast there appears, in statistical terms, to be little hope of our correcting it before life itself — certainly every higher form of life — disappears.

And yet there *is* hope. Every day we hear of changes that can move us in the direction of the life priorities; little things, sometimes, but important ones, sometimes nothing more than talk, but the direction is there . . .

- arms limitation,
- a moratorium on nuclear power,
- the widening use of birth control devices,
- soil conservation practices,
- waste management,
- reforestation,
- world conferences on the destruction of the atmosphere and the extinction of endangered species,
- recycling,
- water conservation,
- gasoline rationing,
- solar heating,
- protected wilderness areas . . .

things that must soon begin to happen on a planetary scale if they are to have any impact upon our current slide toward oblivion.

Seen in that light, the piling of dirt on buildings seems pitifully naive, even trivial. So what, if we build half a million earth-sheltered buildings by the year 2000? How many of the other kind will we have built during the same period? So what, if we built *ten million* earth-sheltered buildings? Or a hundred million? If the world situation is 80% hopeless right now, all our underground efforts during the next generation could at best improve it to, say, 79.6% hopeless, *unless* we can take some sort of giant leap forward.

This is not meant to be discouraging. My intention is to make us see our work in proper perspective, to show us how terribly important it is that we commit ourselves to doing our best — *and then some* — not only in earth shelter and solar heating but in the way we practice every facet of architecture and in the way we live each moment of our lives. Each of us will talk to hundreds of other persons this year. If what we say to them is, in effect, nothing more than an earth-covered version of what we've always said we'll get nowhere. To build underground simply to save fuel in order to go on living just as we did before is a perversion of a potentially good idea.

We've got to catch fire with a dream.

We've got to see, and tell others about, a future world almost as beautiful and as timeless as the one we just destroyed. (Two hundred years to erase a continent-wide wilderness was not a very long time.) We've got to practice sky-mining instead of earth-mining. And we've got to get back in tune with the nature song, the one that goes something like this . . .

Wilderness was not just one of, say, a dozen wholly different responses to the physical environment and resources here on earth. The silent green world from which we so recently evolved was a precisely-balanced organism making the fullest use of the available resources *compatible with long-term existence*. It was a stable solar economy, in other words. It was *the* answer, no matter how many other variations on its basic theme different mutations might have produced. It was a green, solar, recycling, soil-enriching, clean, efficient, complex community, and we must get back in step with it if *we* are to have a long-term existence as well. It seems virtually certain that no other response to the earth environment can last very long. Whatever we do, it's got to be pretty much like what natural systems are. For proof of this, look around you; everything out of step with those systems is already in trouble.

Shoveling dirt onto a building is not exactly what I mean by getting back into step with natural systems. They're so complex that billions of observers over thousands of years have so far failed to understand them all. Shoveling dirt onto a building is but one tiny step toward a whole earth architecture no one has yet even begun to conceive. A lot more of those tiny steps have got to be taken before we can say we've taken one big one. And the steps must be danced to the nature tune or they will continue to be nothing more than steps taken backward. The natural world *is* the way. All we can do is mimic it, use it, grope for its principles, and hope there's still time.

I don't have the slightest idea what happens to make an egg turn into a man, or a man into compost, or compost into plant substance, or plant substance turn into an egg, but I do know that that's the way this particular world happens to work. I have a superficial view of such metamorphoses but as to what really goes on I haven't a clue. All I know is that a miracle is at work all around me, and inside of me, every minute of the day. All I can hope to do for it is to stay out of its way, to let it happen with as little interference as possible, and to try to do better each time I fall.

---

*This title, the scale to which it refers, and another article of mine describing them, were first published by **Progressive Architecture** in 1971.

	−100 always	−75 usually	−50 sometimes	−25 seldom	+25 seldom	+50 sometimes	+75 usually	+100 always	
destroys pure air									creates pure air
destroys pure water									creates pure water
wastes rainwater									stores rainwater
produces no food									produces its own food
destroys rich soil									creates rich soil
wastes solar energy									uses solar energy
stores no solar energy									stores solar energy
destroys silence									creates silence
dumps its wastes unused									consumes its own wastes
needs cleaning and repair									maintains itself
disregards nature's cycles									matches nature's cycles
destroys wildlife habitat									provides wildlife habitat
destroys human habitat									provides human habitat
intensifies local weather									moderates local weather
is ugly									is beautiful

negative score, out of a possible 1500	positive score, out of a possible 1500
0	+1500

final score: +1500

WILDERNESS

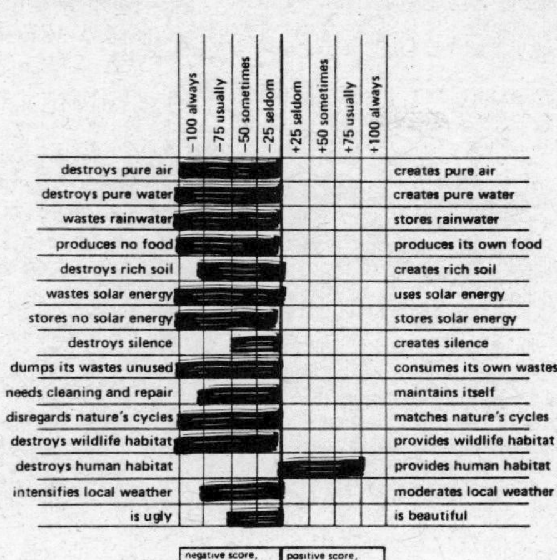

TYPICAL MODERN BUILDING

. . . nothing more than an earth-covered version of what we've always had.

ANOTHER KIND OF MEGALOPOLIS (PROPOSAL)

Sun-terrace housing, a garden outside every door, cars and warehouses tucked away inside the hill where they belong. Powered by the sun and wind, recycling their wastes, such cities will give us brilliant skies and sparkling rivers again.

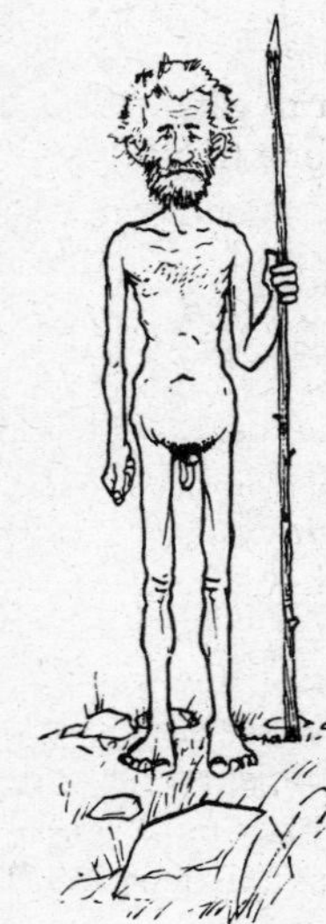

The only way I could live in perfect harmony with the natural world would be to throw away my credit cards, my clothes, my toothbrush, my Blue Cross, my vitamins, my house, my car — everything — and walk off into the bush, naked, ready to win or lose on my cunning alone. With luck, I might last as long as two days, so I've got to find another way to live successfully, and that's what architecture should be all about: trying to compromise with nature, trying to find alternative ways of life compatible with the right way, the naked-in-the-wilderness way. If we still had a wild instinct we might find them a lot faster, but we traded that instinct for a brain, and so must *think* our way along, step by step.

I have neither the time nor the inclination to study natural systems in any detail. I'm nowhere near smart enough anyway. I've got to keep it simple. That's why I developed the diagram above.

It's my simplified version of all the things natural systems always do, arranged in such a way that I can rate the things *I* do in contrast to them. Admittedly, it's highly subjective and very unscientific, but even when I cheat badly in favor of myself the damning message is still there. If the score comes out plus, I'm going forward; negative, back.

It's not as easy as it sounds; almost every building that you and I have ever seen earns a negative score on this scale. The exceptions: a few — an extremely few — really well thought out solar and wind-powered buildings, some wilderness shelters, and perhaps the huts of primitive people far from civilization. Your house, my house, New York City, your favorite building — all are deep in the red; disasters.

Think about Oklahoma State University for a moment. What was the land like before the buildings and lawns covered it? Was it healthier then? Where does all the rainwater go now? Where does the food come from? Is sunlight used to run the university? Then where does its energy come from? At what cost? Where do all the wastes go? Do these buildings respond to natural cycles, to the seasons? Where is all the wildlife? Would you want to live here all your life? Is a bitter windy day — or a blazing hot one — tempered or intensified by the architecture of this campus? Is OSU beautiful? Does it please the eye the way a natural landscape does? Or is it simply a collection of architectural ego trips?

Here's Oklahoma State University on the wilderness values scale:

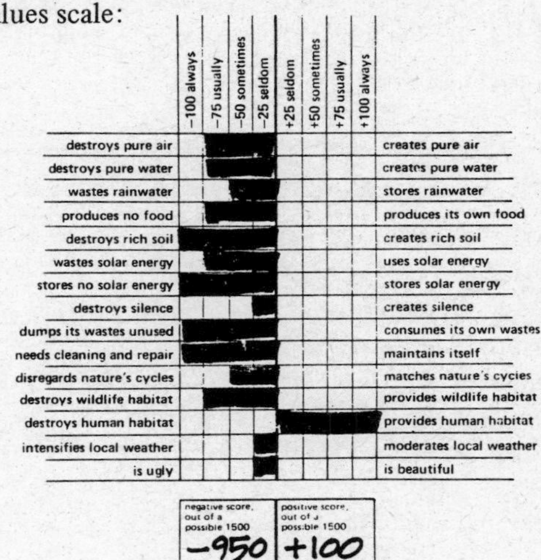

Imagine: *a large and well-endowed seat of learning in a state which depends upon healthy land for much of its income, earning a destructively negative score on a scale of life values any eighth grader could understand!*

That score, that minus-850 score, is the central, overriding fact about OSU. It is the grinding truth about all the OSUs in America, and about the civilization that continues to produce them. But what do we see, most of us, when we visit this campus? We don't see disaster. We see the home of a big football team, or we see wide lawns, brick buildings, and another generation of young Americans being educated. How can we dare call ourselves expert at anything until we can see the central truth about what it is we're all doing?

Where land is healthy and all creatures are in tune with it, plants — living green plants — cover almost every inch. They do everything that architecture — even earth-sheltered architecture — does not do. Plants manage the soil resource, giving us food and fuel and oxygen, collecting rainwater for earth storage, preventing erosion, reusing all wastes, providing wildlife habitat, responding to the seasons, offering us shelter, and creating the stunning panoramas we flee cities to enjoy.

Architects are professional destroyers of plants. We're taught to be. We set aside green areas only grudgingly, after all building requirements have been met, when in any but a sick society architecture would start with plants, if only out of enlightened self-interest, start with concern for their health and the health of the land, *and then* see if a building or a road or a bit of mowed lawn would cause an unacceptable level of damage.

If we ever manage to get ourselves around to that way of thinking we may even begin to have some impact upon The Problem itself. The big one.

There is an important message, to all who pass, from any truly appropriate architectural response to a site, not so much from the actual, physical good being done by the building as from the signals it broadcasts. When a building is appropriate *and beautiful* we don't even need wilderness scales to tell us it's right. It can show us — and say to the hungry world all around — that those wasteful, unthinking Americans have finally begun to change. That's when we can start to have real hope for the future again, for once a good idea is set loose in the world its power can be greater than that of a thermonuclear bomb.

Windows in the hillsides will signal the reemergence of both a healthy land and a healthy people — *if* the buildings behind those windows are truly in tune with the nature song. What could be better for us than to work toward the dream of flowering cities, of orchard towns, of villages in the wildflowers? What could be better than an architecture that did all that, and more?

If we push earth-shelter hard, push it far beyond itself, make it climb far up the charts of the wilderness values scale, then and only then will we have begun to discharge our responsibilities as earthpeople, and to help get the world out of its mess. ■

THE RISING SUN
NEIGHBORHOOD NEWSLETTER

"Once you turn it off, there are an infinite number of channels to choose from.

— Another bus voice

Housing By People

Quite simply, each and every Planner still at large in the several societies of this world should be made to sit out in the weather until he or she has read and acknowledged understanding the principles outlined in this little rapier of a book. The ideas are well illustrated with devastating examples of governmental inadequacy and beautiful examples of ordinary people at work on their own living accommodations. Mr. Turner is not alone in his views, and with more support such ideas will gain enough momentum to make a real difference for a lot of people.
—J. Baldwin
[Suggested by Ian Hogan]

Housing By People
(Towards Autonomy in Building Environments)
John F.C. Turner
1976; 162 pp.
$3.95 postpaid from:
Pantheon Books
455 Hahn Road
Westminster, MD 21157
or Whole Earth Household Store

•

Turner is not a great believer in the value of books, (the present work was wrung out of him by Ivan Illich's admonition that he was burying his ideas under a lot of Peruvian mud bricks), but out of his past writings and speeches I have, without any authorization from him, distilled Turner's three laws of housing. Turner's Second Law says that the important thing about housing is not what it *is*, but what it *does* in people's lives, in other words that dweller satisfaction is not necessarily related to the imposition of standards. Turner's Third Law says that deficiencies and imperfections in *your* housing are infinitely more tolerable if they are your responsibility than if they are *somebody else's*. But beyond the psychological truths of the second and third laws, are the social and economic truths of Turner's First Law, which I take from the book *Freedom to Build:*

"When dwellers control the major decisions and are free to make their own contribution to the design, construction or management of their housing, both the process and the environment produced stimulate individual and social well-being. When people have no control over, nor responsibility for key decisions in the housing process, on the other hand, dwelling environments may instead become a barrier to personal fulfillment and a burden on the economy."

The block of flats above is a few hundred feet away from the houses below. This example from Las Palmas, Canary Islands, supports the proposition that aesthetically hideous, socially alienating and technically incompetent architecture is bound to replace that with traditional values when fossil-fuelled heteronomy takes over.

•

In the Mexican context anyway, the demand and will to invest in housing at lower income levels is far greater than that of the substantially higher, moderate income sector. It may even be that the prospects of fulfilling housing demands are generally greater for lower income households, because they are able and willing to build for themselves while moderate income households are not, even though they may earn two to three times as much.

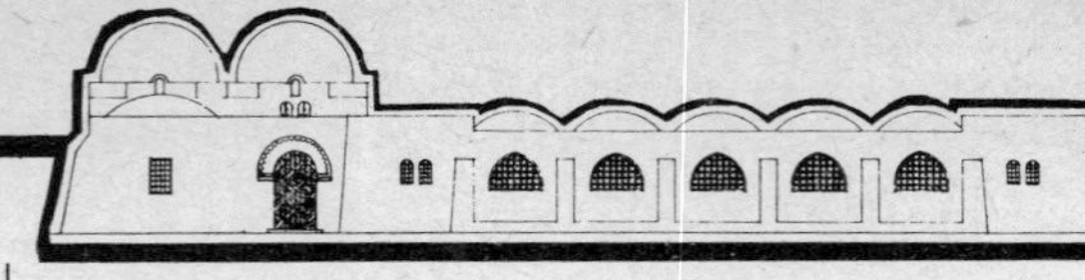

Mushrabiya **(oriel window with latticework screen) at Sehem House.**

Architecture for the Poor

Egyptian architect Hassan Fathy calls for architects to work with poor people, helping them design and build their own homes with local techniques and materials. Mud brick in the desert, wood where it grows, rock where fields must be cleared of it. In an inspiring personal history, Fathy describes the thought, planning and construction of a Moslem village in the upper Nile in the 1940s. Families were consulted individually and their needs incorporated into design of their homes. Craftsmen, trained on the site, built a series of handsome mud brick buildings: homes, schools, theater, marketplace and mosque. Though the project was not completed, it generated much useful information on adobe, dome and vault construction and natural cooling techniques. Moreover, it demonstrated Fathy's vision that the poor of the earth, with architectural help and crafts training, can build housing they can afford, and that is aesthetically satisfying. *—Lloyd Kahn*
[Suggested by Art Boericke]

Architecture for the Poor
Hassan Fathy
1973; 233 pp.
$6.50 postpaid from:
University of Chicago Press
Department PK
5801 South Ellis Avenue
Chicago, IL 60637
or Whole Earth Household Store

•

One interesting technical discovery emerged from the Mitel-Nasara project, and that was how to make bricks quickly. Because of the acute distress of the villagers we had to build the village as quickly as possible, and so I was ready to use any means of saving time. Dr. Ytzhar, a coil mechanics consultant to the Baum-Marpin Company, came to help us, and he suggested speeding up brick manufacture by mixing the dry constituents — earth and sand — in a mechanical cement mixer with a carefully controlled quantity of steam. The steam would penetrate the lumps of earth much better than water could, and would envelop each particle in a film of water, thus achieving instant and complete amalgamation of earth and water in exactly the right proportions without the need to make excessively wet mud and then leave it for days to dry.

•

Foundations and roofing are the two biggest technical and economic problems in cheap rural housing.

Design with Climate

Indian desert pueblos were built of massive adobe roofs and walls that afforded good insulation and delayed heat impact. Windows were small and orientation was such that summer sun was minimized, winter sun (when it was welcome) maximized. Today's buildings — whether high rise or tract house — tend to ignore climatic factors and orientation, depend upon prodigious amounts of fuel for cooling and heating. In this valuable, sensitive book, Victor Olgyay discusses the dwellings and responsiveness to climate of various peoples of the past, presents a thorough and readable survey of biology, meteorology and engineering as an approach to rational architectural design and practice. A blending of past solutions and current knowledge and technology to assist architects in tuning their buildings into natural forces.
—Lloyd Kahn

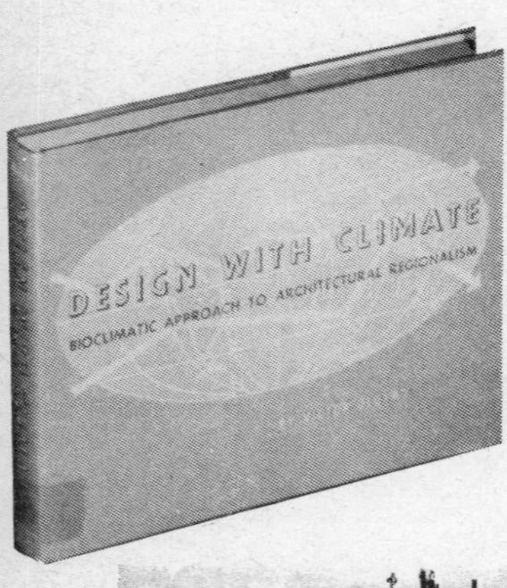

Design With Climate
(Bioclimatic Approach to Architectural Regionalism)
Victor Olgyay
1963, 190 pp.
$32.50 postpaid from:
Princeton University Press
Princeton, NJ 08540
or Whole Earth Household Store

Hot-arid area. ↑

↓ **Hot-humid area.**

Plants/People/And Environmental Quality

How to use plants to dampen sound, purify the atmosphere, articulate space, provide privacy, and control sun, wind, rain, and temperature. Important for architects, designers, owner-builders. Important concepts to know before designing a structure. *—Lloyd Kahn*
[Suggested by Bob Brooks]

Plants/People/And Environmental Quality
Gary O. Robinette
1972; 140 pp.
No. 024-005-00479-3

$4.35 postpaid from:
Superintendent of Documents
U.S. Government Printing Office
Washington, DC 20402
or Whole Earth Household Store

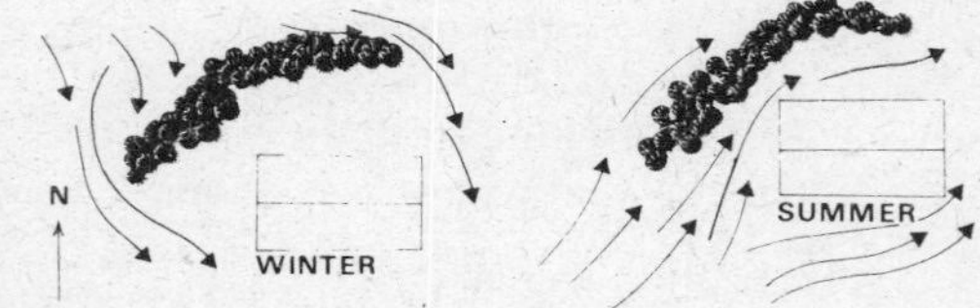

•

In the daytime, the ground temperature in a forest may be as much as 25° cooler than the top of the tree canopy. A vinecovered wall is cooler than a bare wall. Evergreen trees planted close to a wall of a building will create a dead-air space, and insulate the building from abrupt temperature changes. Plants at the base of slopes create a cold air or frost pocket.

The Elements of Structure

*Lots of sketches (usually 2 per page) and not many numbers. Almost as if Ken Kern (***The Owner Built Home***, p. 223) had written a book on structural engineering.*
—Bob Cunningham

The Elements of Structure
W. Morgan
1973 296 pp.
$18.50 postpaid from:
Sportshelf Soccer Associates
P.O. Box 634
New Rochelle, NY 10802

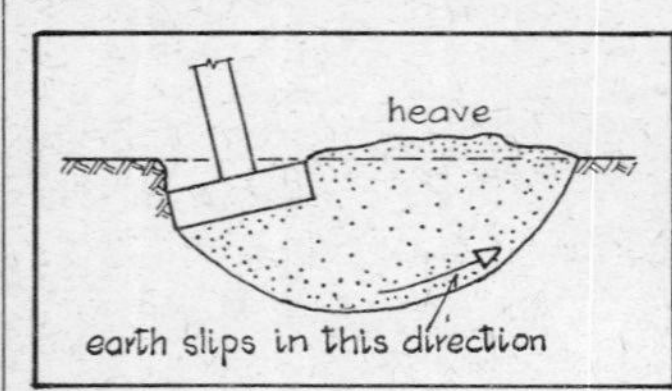

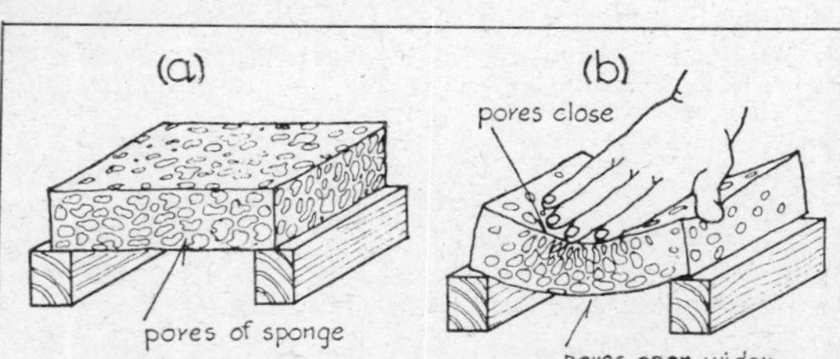

Aircraft hangar at Orbetello, Italy ↓

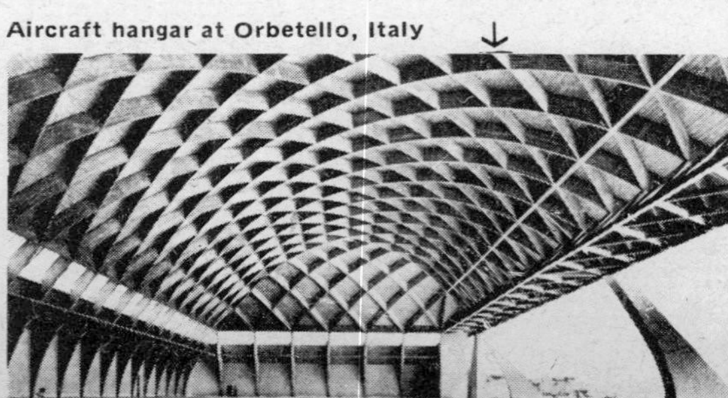

Figure 15

Figure 16

Structures

Guess who stayed up all night reading a structure book? That's extreme behavior even for a technotwit! What fascinates me about this book is the way it illuminates a traditionally difficult subject. Most other books challenge the reader not so much with the task of understanding the subject matter, as with comprehending the writing. No problem here; this must be one of the all-time great examples of clear presentation combined with an interest-holding writing style. (What good are clear explanations if you fall out of your chair from boredom?) Such matters as stress, strain, Young's Modulus, cantilevers, shear, and torsion are discussed as theory nicely tied to real-life examples. Simple illustrations and competent photographs reinforce the often witty text. The Secrets Are Revealed. Now if Mr. Gordon would only write on elementary physics and chemistry. In these days when an exclusive knowledge of technology can be used to exploit a populace, such books as this one have a particular importance. I recommend it highly both as a means of understanding the structures around you and as an example of how good a technical book can be.
—J. Baldwin

Structures
(or Why things don't fall down)
J. E. Gordon
1978; 395 pp.
$17.95 postpaid from:
Plenum Publishing Co.
227 W. 17th Street
New York, NY 10011
or Whole Earth Household Store

•

What makes the arch dramatically different from a mere plebeian wall is that, whereas the wall falls down (with a severe crack), the arch does not. From Figure 15 it can be seen that no fewer than *three* hingepoints can develop in an arch without anything very dramatic happening. In fact a good many modern arch bridges are deliberately built with three hinged joints so as to allow for thermal expansion.

If we really want the bridge to fall down then we shall need *four* hinge-points so that the arch can become in effect a three-linked chain or "mechanism" which is now at liberty to fold itself up and collapse (Figure 16). Incidentally, this is why, if you want to demolish a bridge — for good or bad reasons — it is best to put the explosive charge somewhere near the "thirds point" of the arch. This generally involves digging down through the roadway so as to reach the top of the arch ring. Since this takes time, the demolition of bridges behind a retreating army is often ineffectual.

All this means that arches are extraordinarily stable and are not unduly sensitive to the movements of their foundations. If there is any appreciable movement in the foundation a wall will probably collapse*; arches do not much mind, and some sort of distortion is quite common.

*This is the rationale of mining or sapping under fortress walls during siege warfare. When the end of the tunnel was beneath the foundations of the wall its roof was supported by wooden props. At an appropriate moment a fire was lit so as to burn through the props, when it was hoped that the wall would collapse. The function of both wet and dry moats was chiefly to prevent sapping.

•

It will be seen that there is a large premium on low density, thus steel comes out rather badly, even compared with bricks and concrete. Furthermore, for many light-weight applications — such as airships or artificial limbs — wood is even better than carbon-fibre materials, besides being much cheaper.

In Table 8 these virtues are expressed in terms of energy cost.

The structural efficiency of various materials in terms of the energy needed to make them

Material	Energy needed to ensure a given stiffness in the structure as a whole	Energy needed to produce a panel of given compressive strength
Steel	1	1
Titanium	13	9
Aluminum	4	2
Brick	0.4	0.1
Concrete	0.3	0.05
Wood	0.02	0.002
Carbon-fibre composite	17	17.0

These figures are based on mild steel as unity. They are only very approximate.

Here the advantage of the traditional materials — wood, brick and concrete — is overwhelming. This table makes one wonder whether the pursuit of materials based on exotic fibres is really justified. What really pays off for most of the common purposes of life is not carbon fibres, but holes. Nature tumbled to this a long time ago when she invented wood; and so did the Romans when they started to build churches from empty wine bottles. Holes are enormously cheaper, both in money and in energy, than any conceivable form of high-stiffness material. It would probably be better to spend more time and money on developing cellular or porous materials and less on boron or carbon fibres.

Design Drawing Experiences

A good workbook on learning to draw. The author did all the drawings (many) with a $1 Schaeffer cartridge fountain pen. Drawing as an aid to design rather than grand architectural renderings.
—Lloyd Kahn
[Suggested by Bob Brooks]

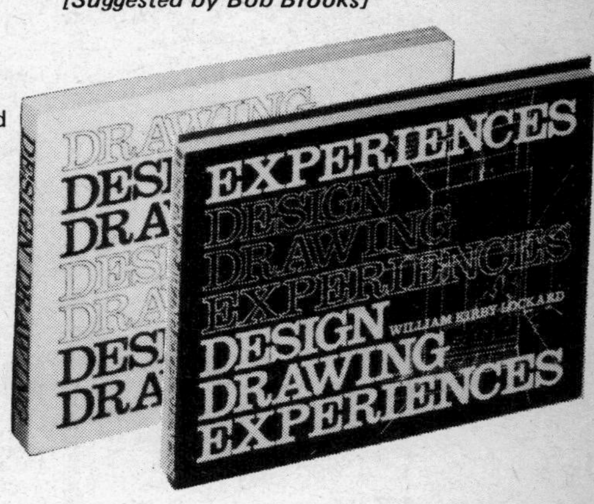

Design Drawing Experiences
William Kirby Lockard
1973, 1979; 111 pp.
4th Edition
$10 postpaid

Design Drawing
(Companion to Design Drawing Experiences)
1974, 1980; 267 pp.
$12.50 postpaid
both from:
Pepper Publishing
2901 East Mabel
Tucson, AZ 85716
or Whole Earth Household Store

LINE SPATIALLY PROFILED

- spatial edges and planar corners defined with lines.
- spatial edges should be profiled.
- the more an edge would move visually against its background as the observer moves toward it, the heavier the line should be.

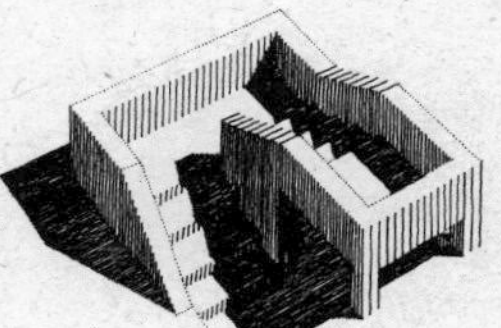

TONE OF LINES

- spatial edges and planar corners defined by a change in line spacing
- tones made by evenly spaced lines.
- stroking direction should respond to vertical or horizontal orientation of the surfaces.

TONE

- spatial edges and planar corners defined by a change in tone - no lines.
- stroking direction should respond to vertical or horizontal orientation of the surfaces.

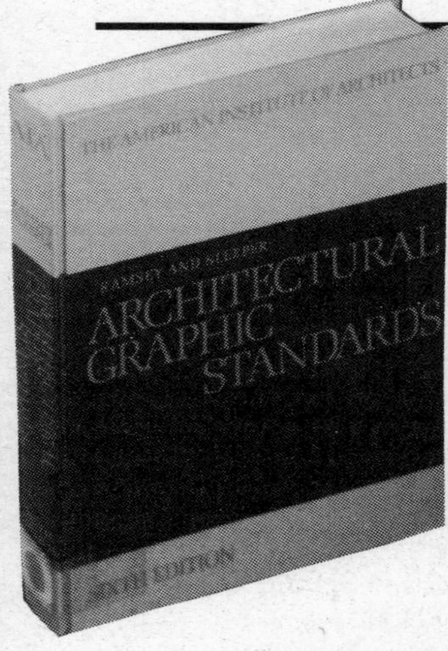

Architectural Graphic Standards

If Sweet's (p. 148) is a kind of magic lamp in many architects' and builders' libraries, the genie might well be **Graphic Standards.** *This volume has been around for years; its latest edition is its sixth. Whenever the office expert hasn't got the answer,* **Graphic Standards** *usually does. It is* the *how-to-do-it book of construction. It doesn't cover domes, but if there's anything else you have in mind, it's probably in there. Older construction techniques (stone masonry, etc.) are covered as well as relatively newer techniques; it's very useful in remodeling and repair work. Everything is done with a minimum of verbiage and a maximum of illustrations and very useable charts and graphs.* **Graphic Standards** *is so taken for granted by any architecture student or office that it's almost become a challenge to stay away from it; ultimately, however, there's seldom a building built without reference to it in the U.S. today. TOOL.*
—Onyx

Architectural Graphic Standards for Architects, Engineers, Decorators, Builders, Draftsmen and Students
Charles G. Ramsey and Harold R. Sleeper
1970; 695 pp.
6th Edition

$65 postpaid from:
John Wiley and Sons
One Wiley Drive
Somerset, NJ 08873

(A new edition will appear in 1981.)

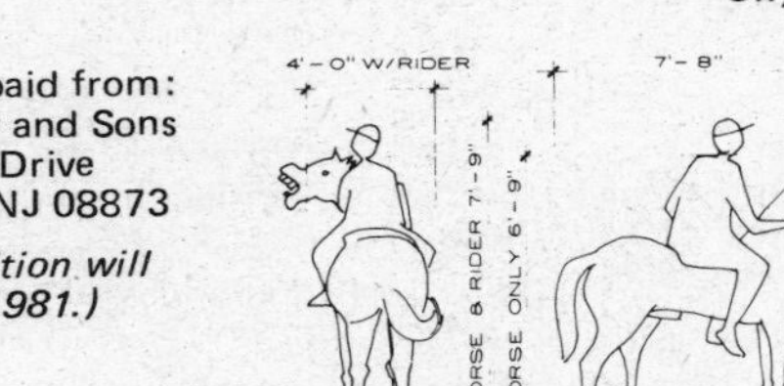

CLEARANCES FOR HORSE AND RIDER

NAIL TYPE **		SIZE		MATERIAL
NCSF 1 1/8" NEEDLE; #15 GAUGE	PARQUET FLOORING NAIL OR BRAD	1", 1 1/8", 1 1/4"		SMOOTH OR BARBED
	FLOORING NAILS	4d TO 10d		IRON OR STEEL (CUT)
OVAL, - ALSO CS HEAD; 1/4" HEAVY CHISEL	HINGE NAILS	HEAVY: 1/4" TO 3/8" DIA. / LIGHT-3/16" TO 1/4" DIA	1 1/2" TO 4" LONG	SMOOTH, BRIGHT OR ANNEALED
OVAL LONG D; 3/16" LIGHT	HINGE NAILS	HEAVY-1/4" DIA. / LIGHT - 3/16" DIA.	1 1/2" TO 3" ALSO TO *4"	SMOOTH, BRIGHT OR ANNEALED
F 3d - 1 1/8" D; #15 GAUGE	LATH NAILS (WOOD)	2d, 2d LIGHT 3d 3d, LIGHT, 3d HEAVY 4d.		BRIGHT (NOT RECOMMENDED) BLU CEMENT COATED
F CHECKERED, OVAL CHISEL OR D; 3/16" - 1 1/4" GAUGE	GUTTER SPIKES	6" TO 10"		STEEL, ZINC COATED
O R	HINGE NAILS	1 1/2" TO 3"		STEEL, ZINC COATED

Building Construction Illustrated

A drafting instructor I know calls this "the poor man's **Architectural Graphic Standards.**" *The emphasis in this book is on the "illustrated." Virtually every significant (and insignificant) feature of small-and-medium-size wood, steel, or concrete building construction is covered, usually with several different views — especially axonometrics and plan obliques. You name it — it's here: site, foundation, structure, materials, environmental controls, mechanical/electrical. Even nail sizes, the composition of different paint types, and a list of trade associations (information sources). If you're designing or remodeling room-size or bigger, you need this book.*
—Larry Phalan
[Suggested by Lonny J. Brown]

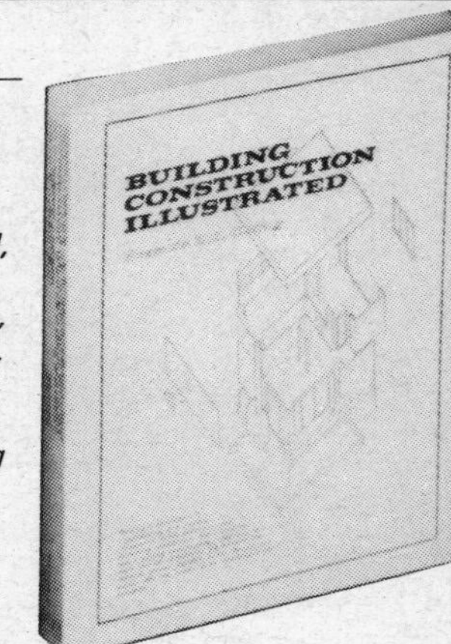

Building Construction Illustrated
Francis D. K. Ching
1975; 314 pp.
$11.95 postpaid from:
Van Nostrand Reinhold Company
Order Department
7625 Empire Drive
Florence, KY 41042
or Whole Earth Household Store

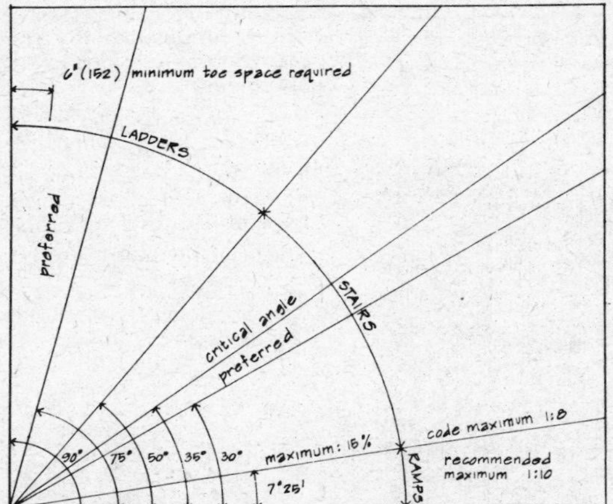

Stair, ramp, ladder ratios — stairs can be physically tiring as well as psychologically forbidding. They should be neither too steep nor too shallow.

David says there's a plant in Death Valley that has a root structure that's two inches deep and eighteen feet in diameter.

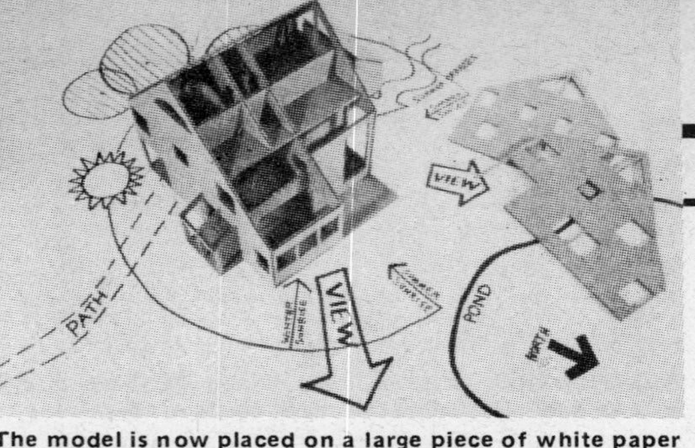

The model is now placed on a large piece of white paper and the size is sketched at an appropriate size so that views, sun, shade, and breezes can be checked. Necessary changes are made.

don't like painted wood on outside of house. would rather have natural weathered wood

AESTHETIC of farmhouses with big porches

like vines growing over house and lots of plants and flowers

don't like shutters unless they're necessary

Designing Houses

Though not billed as such, **Designing Houses** *is a thing-maker's dream book! Even if designing and building your own "big house" is not within your current reach, you cannot help being caught up in the enthusiasm generated within. Model making is stressed throughout, starting with the setting up of your own "architect's office," obtaining the instruments and tools of the trade and quite an ample course on cardboard construction. Best of all are the drawings: neat, simple, funky, their inevitable influence on your own sketches makes this handsome volume underpriced . . . now where did I lay my X-acto . . .*
—Joe Eddy Brown

I agree with Joe Eddy Brown that this is an exceptionally fine book. My only reservation is that the presentation subtly tends to keep you traditional, which for many will do just fine anyway.
—J. Baldwin

Designing Houses
(An Illustrated Guide)
Les Walker and
Jeff Milstein
1976; 153 pp.

$5.95 (paperback price)
postpaid from:
The Overlook Press
Viking Press
299 Murray Hill Parkway
East Rutherford, NJ 07073

or Whole Earth
Household Store

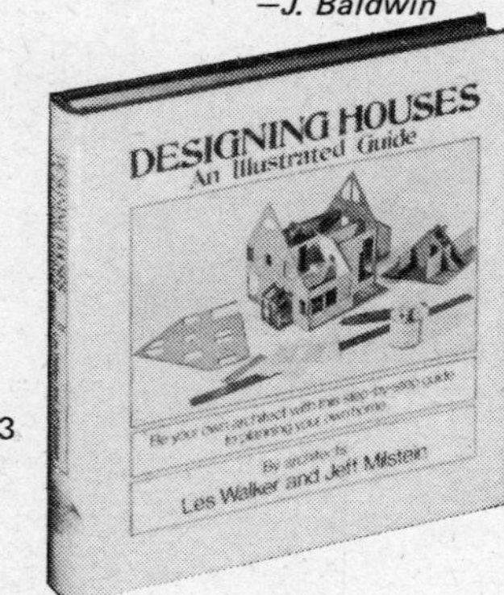

The Owner-Builder and The Code

When push comes to shove, the Big Problem with building your own home is usually something to do with getting the abode of your desires past the building inspector. This is even more of a problem if you are not quite the sort of folks the local folks are used to. What do you do? This handbook of case histories and strategy is by none other than that old master Ken Kern and friends. It's about as good a source of information as one could hope for. Whether your inclination is compliance or defiance, you'd best give this a look. See also **Building Regulations**, *p. 225.*
—J. Baldwin

The Owner-Builder and The Code
(Politics of Building Your Home)
Ken Kern, Ted Kogon, and Rob Thallon
1976; 182 pp.

$5 postpaid from:
Owner-Builder
Publications
P.O. Box 817
North Fork, CA 93643

or Whole Earth
Household Store

•

An example comes to mind of three owner-builders in a rural, Northern California county who were ordered to tear down their "substandard" homes. They had been cited for typical housing code violations — lack of proper water closet, lack of adequate heating facilities, room dimensions less than those required by the code, etc. Rather than pay the expense of having the county do it, they dismantled the homes themselves. The three, knowing that demolition of their homes was inevitable, had lived under psychological duress during the year-long abatement proceedings against them. Even the local building inspector conceded that the houses, though tacky in appearance, were warm and cozy quarters inside. The destruction of their homes put an end to their homestead development and virtually ruined them economically. Ultimately, they were forced to move into a rat-infested apartment building in the city. The rent was exorbitant, as city rates often are, and the creaky building was a far cry from the comfort they had known in their former homes, which were vermin-free. The letter of the code had been served, but had justice?

→

A poorly designed bedroom with the minimum "superficial floor area" allowed by the code compared to a bedroom with one sixth the allowable area.

From the Ground Up

After the first wave of books on a given subject a host of imitators usually appears offering little improvement other than an occasional gimmick. The gimmick in this book on post-industrial home-building is worth checking out: the authors have included a quickie course in structural principles. They are also good on frost heaving, selection of wood, and other arcana that is very good to know but that is usually left out of similar books. They want you to know why you're being told to do it that way. Nice drawings, too.
—J. Baldwin

From the Ground Up
John N. Cole and
Charles Wing
1976; 244 pp.

$7.95 postpaid from:
Little, Brown & Co., Inc.
200 West Street
Waltham, MA 02154

or Whole Earth
Household Store

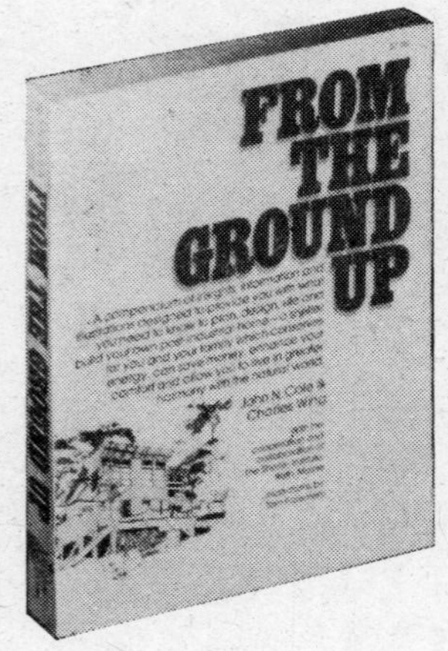

•

You have two choices: Build a practice house and make all of your mistakes before you start your own; or "build it" on paper with a sharp pencil and architect's scale. I recommend the latter. If the house doesn't work out all you've wasted is a piece of paper and a few evenings of fun.

Here is what a set of drawings, done carefully with a minimum number of drafting tools, will do for you:

(1) As you develop the details of the drawings, you will be forced to make design decisions that you otherwise could put off until actually confronted with the physical reality. A scale drawing would have shown an acquaintance of mine that his window glass was larger than the window frame opening and that the windowsill wasn't wide enough to extend beyond the wall sheathing, with the result that rainwater flowed into the wall space.

(2) Because you are actually building the house on paper, fastening problems become immediately apparent. How will the Sheetrock be nailed at the room corners? How will the wiring be concealed?

(3) Your material list will be precise because the number and dimensions of all framing members are easily calculated from the drawing.

(4) Angle cuts such as are required for rafters can be measured on paper instead of by intricate trigonometric calculations or by seat-of-the-pants guesswork.

(5) You will better know how the house will finally look on its site.

(6) You will have an efficient means of communication with:

(a) the banker, who will be more willing to loan money. A picture may be worth a thousand words but it's also worth several thousand dollars.

(b) subcontractors, who will dare to give tighter bids if they know precisely what is involved.
(c) your workers, who won't require your presence at every turn. The amount of time your workers will not be sitting under a tree drinking beer while you fret over an unexpected problem will alone pay for your initial effort.
(d) yourself. When everything seems to be going wrong and three people are bugging you over details any fool should understand, your blueprints will remain unperturbed.

(7) Last and most important, drafting will teach you a self-discipline that is required in efficient and low-cost housebuilding.

In summary, a month of evenings at the drafting board will save weeks of labor, as much as 25 percent of the cost.

Your Engineered House

A real good book for goosing your thinking about house design. Some wisdom, some good ideas, and some bad ideas, just like you'll have. Rex Roberts' book has primed a lot of mental pumps.
—SB

Your Engineered House
Rex Roberts
1964; 237 pp.

$5.95 postpaid from:
M. Evans and Company
216 East 49th Street
New York, NY 10017

or Whole Earth
Household Store

←
First, the built-in, slightly slanted windowpanes. I don't mean the heavily slanted windows used by some architects in an attempt to be different. For years I've been building all my glass with the top leaning out at an angle of about one inch in twenty. I've never happened to run across this detail in any other house, or in a book or magazine. Yet at one look the benefits of this detail are there to see.

The glare is strikingly less than from a vertical pane. This is the first thing you notice.

The glass stays clean longer on the outside, which collects more dirt and is less convenient to clean. The dirt it does have, either inside or out is less noticeable.

The acoustic improvement is tremendous.

Tipping the panes slightly, not in itself noticeable unless your attention is called to it, removes what some people feel is the glacial unfriendliness of large expanses of glass.

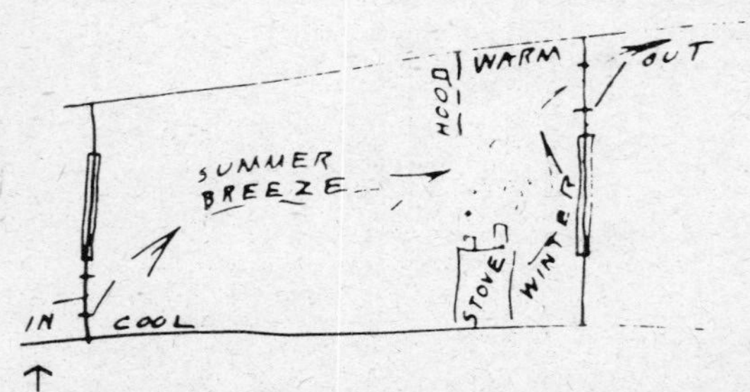

↑
Second and very very important, are the manifold virtues of a single-slope roof with its long dimension and high side toward the south, or ideally, south by southeast.

This one structural detail contributes to more of our housing goals than any other single thing I can think of.

It invites heat in winter, keeps it out in summer.

It invites winter light, controls summer light.

It provides a roofed, sunny outside area at no extra charge.

Its acoustics are superb. No charge.

Ventilation works perfectly without further effort or expense.

It confines the water run-off problem to one side only, the least useful side, at that.

It contributes to a feeling of spaciousness, but the actual cubic content to be heated is the same as with an A-frame, or a little less.

Its interior shape is friendly, varied, inviting, pleasantly unsymmetrical.

Its outside weather surface is cheap to build and easy to maintain. All parts of its roof structure involve a minimum of cutting and fitting.

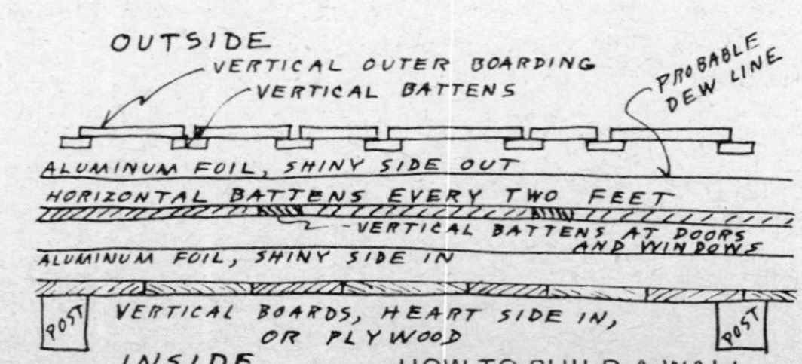

HOW TO BUILD A WALL

2 RAFTERS BOLTED TO POLE
1" DIAGIONAL SHEATHING OR PLYWOOD
2x4 OR 2x6 PURLINS 24" O.C.
6" TOP DIA. PRESSURE TREATED POLE
BAY LENGTH 8' TO 14'
WALL GIRT 2x6 OR 2x8 NOTCH TO FIT 4x4
1x12 BOARD SIDING OR 5/8" PLYWOOD
2x4 WINDOW FRAME
2 - 1/2" BOLTS
END DETAIL
WALL GIRT
POLE
MAX. 4 FT CANTILEVER
2x4 OR 2x6 FLOOR JOISTS 24" O.C.
2x12 SPLATTER BOARD
3" CONCRETE
4x4 POST
4" GRAVEL FILL
2 JOISTS BOLTED TO POLE
TAMPED BACKFILL
SEE 26.2 TO DETERMINE WIDTH AND DEPTH OF HOLE
CONC. PIER
1/2" DOWEL
8" CONC.

26.3 POLE FRAME DETAILS

26.2 POLE EMBEDMENT

NOTE: HOLE DEPTH IS FIGURED FOR 8-FT POLE SPACINGS. ADD 6" DEPTH FOR EACH 2 FT. INCREASE IN SPACING.

HOLE DEPTH – FEET; HOLE DIAMETER – INCHES

POOR: SILT, SOFT CLAY, SOFT WET SAND — FAIR: FIRM CLAY, FIRM SAND, SAND & CLAY — GOOD: HARD CLAY, COURSE SAND, SAND & GRAVEL — EXCELLENT: COARSE GRAVEL, COMPACTED CLAY, COMPACTED GRAVEL

Good dope on concrete-proportions, additives such as sawdust or emulsified asphalt for "comfort cushion" floor. Details on wood framing, how stud wall houses are overbuilt, the strength of threaded nails.

There is much good data on building with rock and earth, how to make a sliding form for rammed earth and a discussion of the strength of rammed earth and soil cement. Why don't you hear anything these days about earth wall buildings?

Kern says: Inasmuch as there is nothing in bare earth to sell, no commercial group can be found to extol its merits. *(See Kern's* **Stone Masonry**, *p. 231.)* —*Lloyd Kahn*

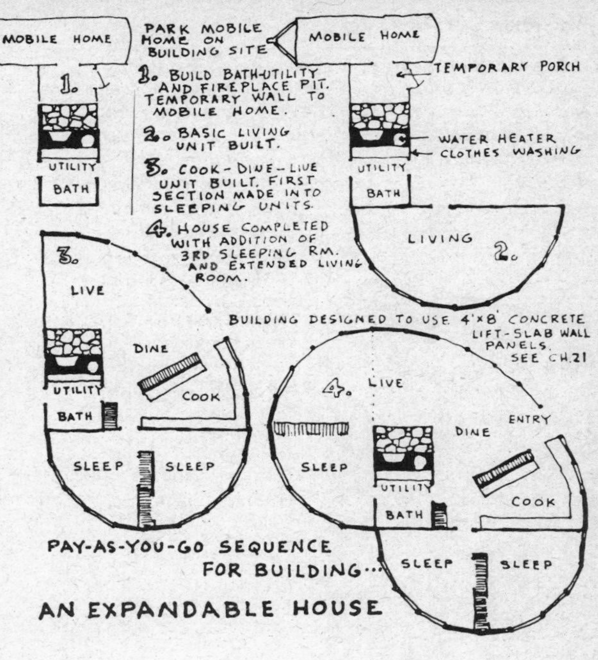

The Owner-Built Home

This book is sound advice on the best low-cost building techniques from around the world — Africa, India, Israel — countries that cannot afford U.S. style waste. Much of it is not in print elsewhere.

A 1" concrete floor with loading stresses of 450 lbs. per sq. ft.; houses built of earth, woven bamboo and bottles, as well as of conventional materials. How to hook up your plumbing in a simple central core.

The Owner-Built Home
(A How-to-do-it Book)
Ken Kern
1972, 1975; 374 pp.

$9.20 postpaid from:
Charles Scribner's Sons
Vreeland Avenue
Totowa, NJ 07512
or Whole Earth
Household Store

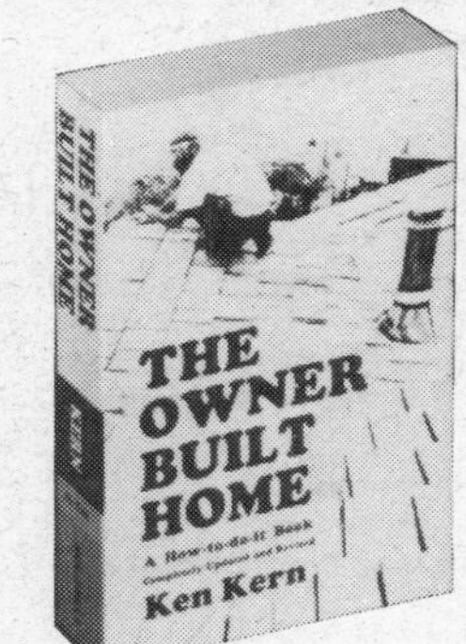

The Owner-Built Homestead

Not only is this good, clear (and the best) single source of information for the homestead builder, but it's good reading. As in his immensely useful **The Owner-Built Home**, *Ken Kern has digested, selected and condensed from a huge amount of material, and presents his findings in an attempt to show people how to "bridge the gap between primitive inability and a wholesome use of science, technique, and civilization."* —*Lloyd Kahn*

The Owner-Built Homestead
Ken Kern
1974; 210 pp.

$9.20 postpaid from:
Charles Scribner's Sons
Vreeland Avenue
Totowa, NJ 07512
or Whole Earth
Household Store

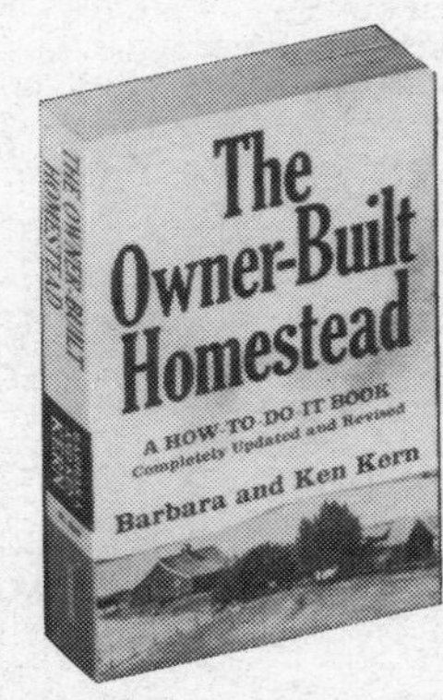

•

The model hillside homestead, is divided into six equal fields, each under an acre in size. Here, at all times, livestock have access to at least a single grazing field; one parcel is allocated, for example, as an irrigated hayfield. One of two fields combining sod and row crops produces silage crops. As crop areas advance downhill, part of the receding section is fallowed or hogged down during the appropriate season. A fish pond is located at the lowest point of the land, where it receives used irrigation and "clean" waste water by gravity.

1. TRASH BARRELS
2. WOOD HEATER
3. RADIAL ARM SAW
4. PIPE VISE
5. PLUMBING TOOLS
6. PAINT BENCH
7. PAINT STORAGE
8. HARDWARE BIN
9. ELECTRICAL TOOLS
10. WORKBENCH
11. POWER TOOLS
12. WOOD VISE
13. HAND TOOL RACK
14. MASONRY TOOLS
15. DESK-STOOL
16. IMPLEMENTS
17. BINS
18. ARC WELDER
19. WELDING TABLE
20. OXYACETYLENE
21. WELDER TOOLS
22. SINK
23. BATTERY EQUIP.
24. PORTABLE BENCH
25. WORKBENCH
26. VISE
27. GRINDER
28. DRILL PRESS
29. TOOL DRAWER
30. TOOL RACK
31. AUTO REPAIR TOOLS
32. LUBE CENTER
33. AIR COMPRESSOR
34. TUBE REPAIR
35. TIRE REPAIR TOOLS
36. STORAGE BIN
37. FIRE EXTINGUISHERS
38. FIRST-AID KIT

GASOLINE, DEISEL, OIL, HOIST RAIL, WOOD, GENERAL, METAL, LOADING PLATFORM, RECOILING DROP LITE, GREASE PIT, STORAGE, FLOOR DRAIN, OVERHEAD DOOR, SCALE, FLOOR PLAN, CROSS SECTION, SOD ROOF

17.1 HOMESTEAD SHOP

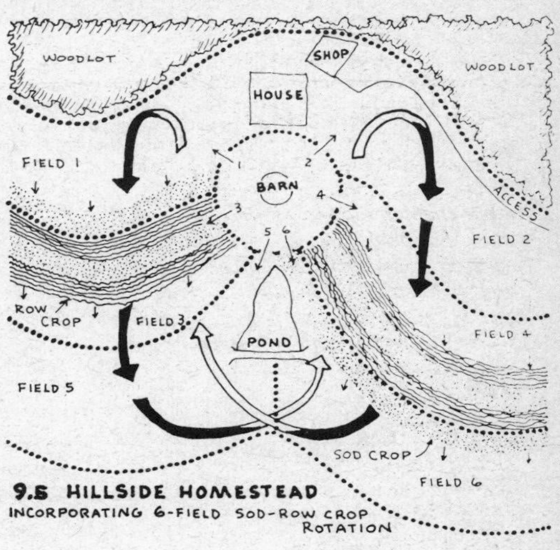

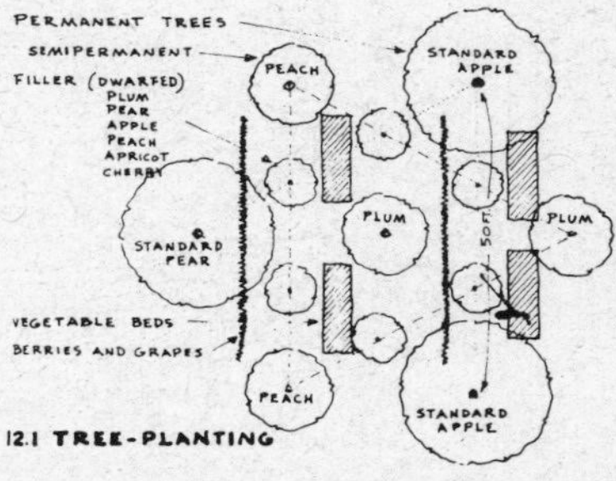

The Work Book

Many books have been written about how to build houses (your own or someone else's). None of them begins to suggest the impact of the owner-building process on personal life. Ken Kern has now teamed up with his sister — psychologist Evelyn Turner — to describe what it feels like to build your own house.

The Work Book *explores the personal politics and psychology of homebuilding through a collection of very real case studies representing a range of "successes" and "failures." Few books intended to encourage self-help construction have dared tell readers of the tremendous emotional investment and costs involved. I applaud the addition of this reality therapy to the literature available on owner-building.* —*Hal Levin*

Hal reports that in his own work as an owner-builder consultant he spends more time doing marriage counselling than giving advice on buildings. —*Richard Nilsen*

About 80 percent of the couples I know who have built a house or a boat, they build it, then they split up. Happened to me too. —*SB*

•

"Mike thought I was being argumentive," Sharon writes, "just for the sake of doing it my way, and I felt that he did not appreciate or even want my input." Fighting between them began with their house plans and continued as building progressed and changes had to be made.

The Work Book
(Personal Politics of Building Your Home)
Ken Kern and
Evelyn Turner
1979; 316 pp.

$7.95 postpaid from:
Owner-Builder
Publications
P.O. Box 817
North Fork, CA 93643
or Whole Earth
Household Store

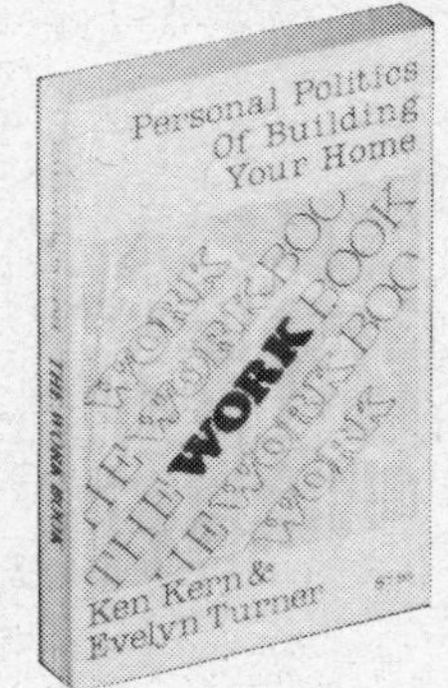

Sharon says they grossly underestimated both the length of time it would take to build and the burden of psychological stress that accompanied the work. They were aware that they were taking on a tremendous work load. There were times when they were frightened by the task and longed to abandon it totally. In addition, they were naive about many things, such as the cost of materials. "If we had known all the pitfalls before we began," Sharon says, "we might have decided not to build." Learning to live with the hassles, to come to terms with their differing ideas, to constantly work out minor disagreements and irritations, brought Sharon and Mike closer as a family unit. "However," Sharon says, "I would not recommend it for everyone, because it does create a considerable strain on the family and on personal relationships."

Other than money, the two most constant sources of frustration were time and weather. Every step took at least twice as long as they anticipated. "We never completed a project by the time we had set," Sharon remarks, "and so we were putting ourselves under the constant pressure of time. We finally realized that this was not really necessary as the pressure was self-created. You have to be able to relax a little bit and enjoy the work while doing it or end up as a bundle of frayed nerve endings looking for a place to explode!"

THE RISING SUN
NEIGHBORHOOD NEWSLETTER

When she left at the height of the London season to join him at his tropical plantation she neither went crazy nor slept with the foreman as had been predicted by her acquaintances, but started a missionary school where the native children taught her to observe the unfolding, growth and withering of the kakoah leaf which she now does all afternoon on the veranda, drinking tea and giving every appearance of being the perfect colonial wife. He now finds her more exciting in bed than his native girl, a fact which appalls him by day.

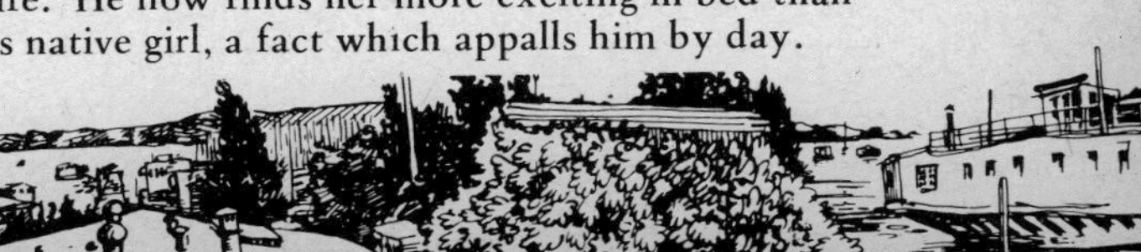

Modern Carpentry

If I had to choose just one house carpentry book, this would be it. Carpenter unions use it to teach apprentices, and it gets updated frequently. It contains a wealth of information well presented — the pictures and illustrations are understandable and are nicely integrated into the text. —Richard Nilsen

Modern Carpentry
(Building Construction Details in Easy-to-Understand Form)
Willis H. Wagner
1969, 1979; 480 pp.

$13.28 postpaid from:
The Goodheart Wilcox Company, Inc.
123 West Taft Drive
South Holland, IL 60473
or Whole Earth Household Store

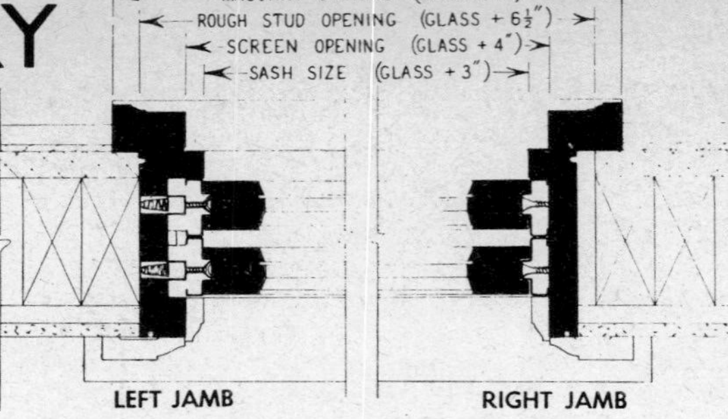

Besides the type and position of the window, the carpenter should know the size of each unit or combination of units. Window sizes may include several or all of the following: (1) glass size, (2) sash size, (3) rough frame opening, and (4) masonry or unit opening. The figure shows the position of these measurements and approximately how they are figured from the glass size. They will vary slightly from one manufacturer to another.

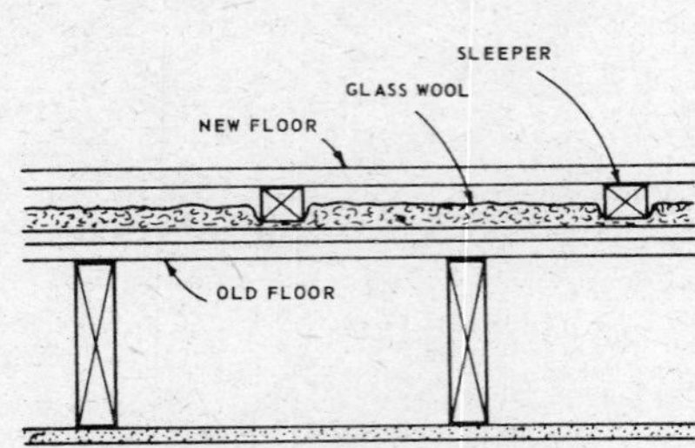

Soundproofing an existing floor.

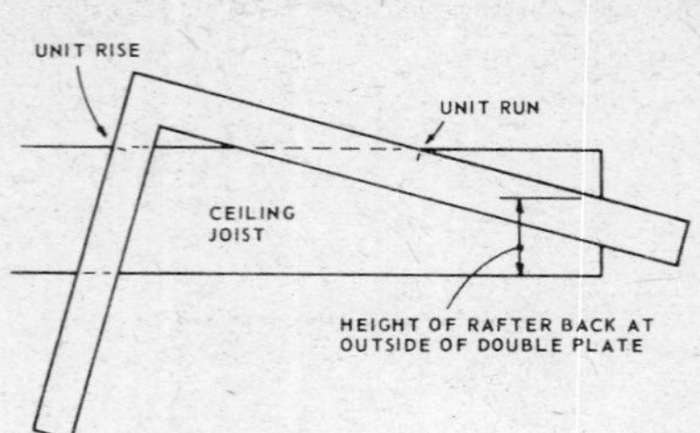

Laying out the trim cut on the end of a ceiling joist to match the slope of the roof.

Preventing drip from gable. A length of beveled siding gives an inward tilt to the shingles.

Anti nail-in-foot

A good way to prevent the dreaded Nail-In-The-Foot when working around old used lumber is to cut insoles out of sheet metal to wear under your sox. With heavy sox you'll never feel the metal in there, but you won't feel the nails either. It works better than you'd think. —J. Baldwin

In Germany, it was traditional to nail "a roof tree" (an evergreen branch) to the first pair of rafters completed while the house is being built. It was originally done to propitiate the gods for approaching too close.
—**Illustrated Housebuilding**

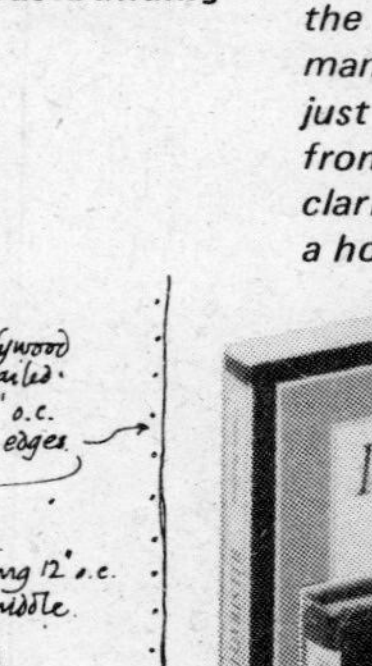

Plywood sheathing
—**Illustrated Housebuilding**

Illustrated Housebuilding
Illustrated Interior Carpentry

Housebuilding books usually are either so simplified that the necessary small details aren't there or there are so many details that you drown in them. These books are just right. A novice could actually build a good house from them. The illustrations deserve special mention for clarity. These are the books I'd use myself if I had to do a house. —J. Baldwin

Illustrated Housebuilding
Graham Blackburn
1974; 156 pp.

$4.95 postpaid from:

Illustrated Interior Carpentry
Graham Blackburn
1979; 191 pp.

$5.95 postpaid

both from:
The Overlook Press
c/o The Viking Press
299 Murray Hill Parkway
East Rutherford, NJ 07073
or Whole Earth Household Store

•

As well as customs and ceremonies associated with housebuilding, there are also many time-honored tricks played by tradesmen to ensure payment. One such trick was the mason's habit of building a pane of glass across the chimney, high up in the flue. The glass being clear, no obstruction could be seen, but the fire would not draw until the mason was paid — when he would then simply drop a brick down the chimney.
—**Illustrated Housebuilding**

Installing plywood sheathing. Provide 1/8 in. space along edge joints. Corner bracing is not required.
—**Illustrated Housebuilding**

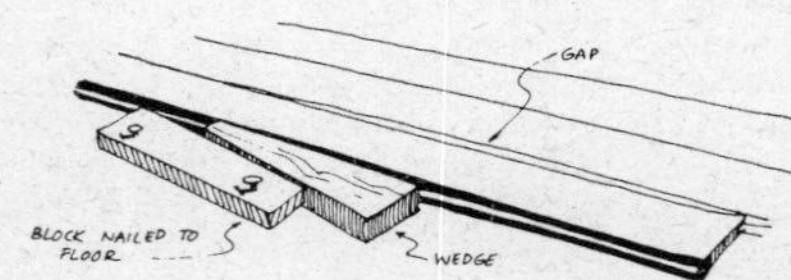

How to close gap
—**Illustrated Interior Carpentry**

The secret of getting the last few boards down tightly lies in not nailing them! Fit them together, buckled, and then press them into place by standing on them.
—**Illustrated Interior Carpentry**

Wood-frame House Construction

Construction details for a wood framed house that can be easily understood. Chapters on floor and wall framing are especially simple and clear. Plans and designs are beyond the scope of the book but what's presented are a good use of materials and the simplest methods of standard house construction. —John Bradbury
[Suggested by Bob Easton]

Wood-frame House Construction
L.O. Anderson
1971, 1976; 235 pp.

$5 postpaid from:
Craftsman Book Company of America
542 Stevens Avenue
Solana Beach, CA 92075
or Whole Earth Household Store

Floor framing: (1) Nailing bridging to joists; (2) nailing board subfloor to joists; (3) nailing header to joists; (4) toenailing header to sill.

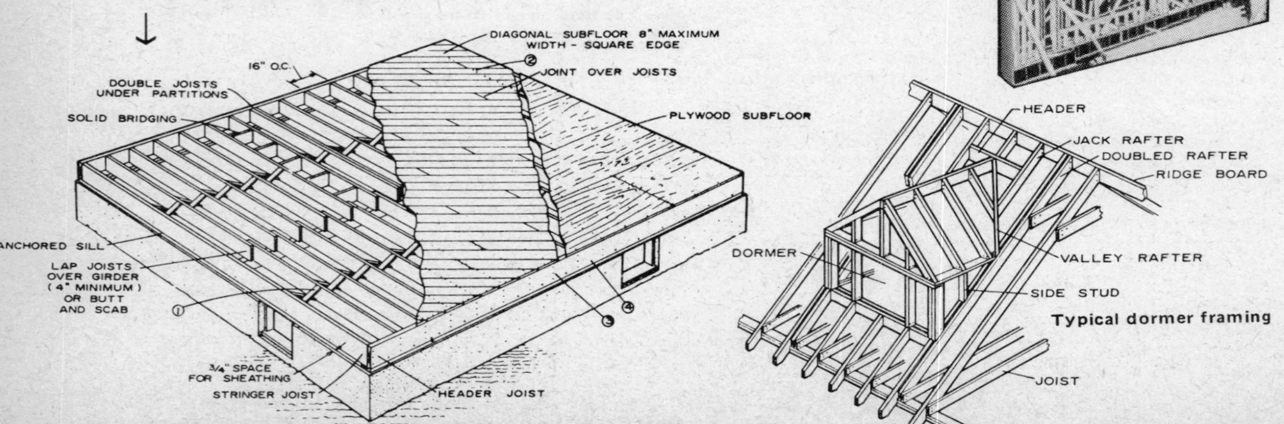

Typical dormer framing

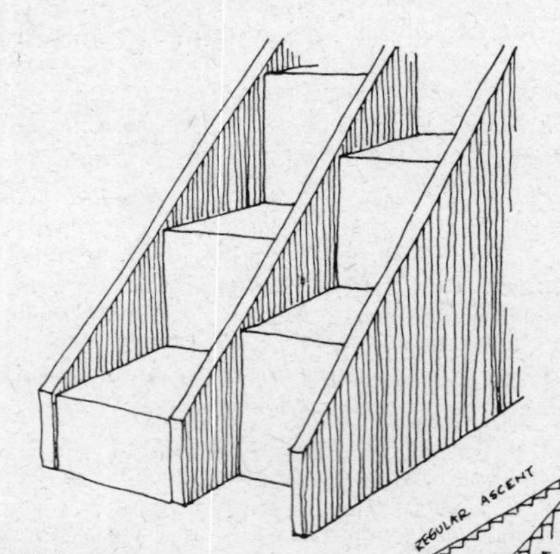

Double-step Staircase
For use where the ascent would be too steep for a regular stair.
—**Illustrated Interior Carpentry**

National Construction Estimator

The 1980 edition is $7.50, and is well worth every penny to the owner-builder or carpenter/free-lance builder. The information provided allows estimating materials and labor costs. By using the wage rates table, labor costs can be converted to time estimates for skilled labor, thus, the owner-builder can calculate average time required for a specific job, he can use the information to decide whether to do the job himself or hire someone based on time/skill/cost/job desirability considerations. The materials list also provides a good survey of available alternatives. Information of this type is quite valuable to owner-builders as well as professionals. Quick cost comparisons of alternatives are quite easy. —Hal Levin

National Construction Estimator
Gary Moselle, Editor
1952, 1980; 286 pp.
8th Edition
$7.50 postpaid from:
Craftsman Book Co. of America
542 Stevens Avenue
Solana Beach, CA 92075
or Whole Earth Household Store

•

The percent saving in heat loss is five times greater if glass areas are reduced than would be achieved by increasing wall insulation.

Item	Unit	Material	Labor	Total
Asphalt shingles				
Thick butt, 235 lb., 12" x 36", three tab	Sq	37.90	27.30	65.20
Self-sealing tab, 235 lb., 12" x 36"	Sq	38.30	27.30	65.60
Square butt (2 or 3 tab), 300 lb., 12" x 36"	Sq	47.60	29.10	76.70
Self-sealing tab, 300 lb., 12" x 36"	Sq	48.00	29.10	77.10
Architect mark 25, 12" x 36", 290 lb	Sq	43.00	29.10	72.10
Wind seal jet, 12" x 36", 238 lb	Sq	34.90	27.30	62.20

Building Regulations

They ain't no hassle like a building inspector hassle, as many persons of good intent have discovered to their sorrow. Ken Kern's ***The Owner-Builder and the Code*** *(p. 223) is good on strategy, but this is the first book that helps you to understand the codes yourself. With it in one hand and the code in the other (and a firm grip on your blood pressure) you should be able to determine what your chances are for getting a new idea passed. Mr. Vitale explains the codes section by section and then inserts lucid paragraphs labelled "Code Reading Technique" to help you untangle your own local situation. He also makes the best case I've seen for code reform, and does it in a way that will help you present your views to your congressman or board of supervisors. Massive references to state codes finish up this most excellent and useful book. I don't envy Mr. Vitale for reading all those codes, but I'm glad he did. —J. Baldwin*

Building Regulations
(A Self-Help Guide for the Owner-Builder)
Edmund Vitale
1979; 212 pp.
$12.95 postpaid from:
Charles Scribner's Sons
Vreeland Avenue
Totowa, NJ 07512
or Whole Earth Household Store

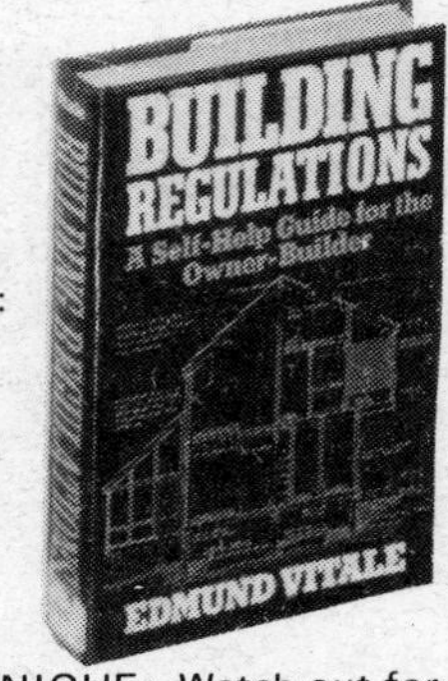

•

CODE-READING TECHNIQUE: Watch out for explanatory and other (sometimes self-serving) statements found in prefaces or introductions to a code. These kinds of remarks may not be part of the code's binding regulations. And if there is an inconsistency between the intent of a particular regulation as expressed in the introduction and the language of the code section itself, the code provision always prevails. The courts (and therefore administrative agencies and, sometimes, building inspectors) would only consult the intent expressed in the preface if there was an ambiguity in the text of the code requirement itself. If there is no ambiguity (which of course is different from an inconsistency), the code provision prevails — even if the text contradicts the intent expressed in the introduction. So don't, if you can help it, base any of your arguments to the building inspector on statements made in prefatory comments; use those statements only to back up what is already apparent in the text of the code. If there are no other sections you can use, refer to the introduction, preface, or anything else you can find to make your argument.

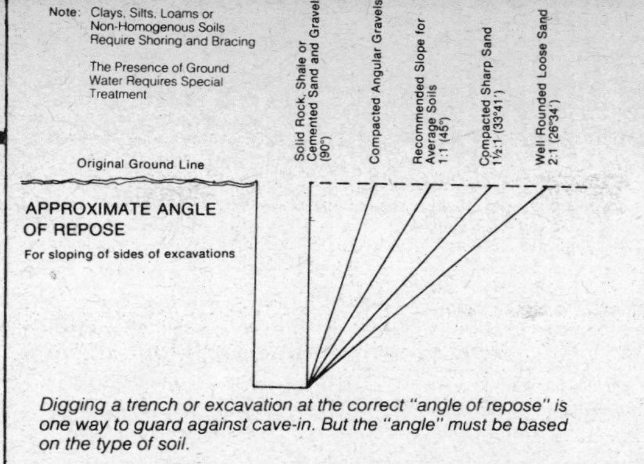

Digging a trench or excavation at the correct "angle of repose" is one way to guard against cave-in. But the "angle" must be based on the type of soil.

Occupational Hazards of Construction

The Department of Labor's Occupational Safety and Health Administration (OSHA) has raised a lot of hackles — and several lawsuits — but their grant money for this book was taxpayers' dollars well spent.

If you work construction for your trade this is an obvious book to own, and at a bargain price. If you do your own repairs and remodelling, you can check here to find what safety and health hazards are connected with what jobs -- and how to prevent them. It is particularly good on comes into contact with at some point nowadays. Grandpa may have never worn a respirator and lived to be 80, but then he probably never had to inhale methyl ethyl ketone fumes either. See "Safety Equipment," pp. 158-159.
—Richard Nilsen
[Suggested by Hal Levin]

Occupational Hazards of Construction
Janet Bertunison and Sidney Weinstein
1978; 212 pp.
$3.50 postpaid from:
Labor Occupational Health Program
Institute of Industrial Relations
University of California
Berkeley, CA 94720
(Make checks payable to: Regents of U.C.)

•

Pure asbestos is no longer used as an insulation material in many states. However, building trades workers, especially asbestos workers, laborers, and carpenters, may still be exposed to some asbestos insulation, and large amounts during demolition or remodel jobs. In addition asbestos may still be found in some taping compounds, asbestos cements, pipes, and floor tiles. Vinyl asbestos floor tiles may be as much as 15 to 20 percent asbestos, which is released when old flooring is sanded.

Asbestos can cause a number of very harmful, chronic diseases. These diseases take a long time to develop, sometimes 40 years. And once they've appeared, they are **irreversible.**

Asbestos can cause asbestosis and various cancers. **Cigarette smoking definitely increases the risk of asbestosis and lung cancer.** In fact, asbestos workers who smoke have a 92 times greater risk of developing lung cancer than nonsmokers who are not exposed to asbestos.

Full Length Roof Framer
Simplified Stair Building

Many an amateur carpenter has crashed and burned when it came time to figure the roof rafter lengths and angles. Since 1917 there has been no excuse: this little book has all the numbers and how to use them. It's skinny and has armored covers so it can live a long useful life in the pocket of your overalls or on the radial arm saw bench. Wish someone had told me about this a long time ago.

The stair book is big and floppy so it'll lie flat on your desk while you figure things out, and also to allow big clear diagrams. —J. Baldwin

Full Length Roof Framer
A.F.J. Riechers
1917; 118 pp.
$5 postpaid

Simplified Stair Building
A.F.J. Riechers
1947; 16 pp.

$3 postpaid
both from:
A. Riechers
P.O. Box 405
Palo Alto, CA 94302
or Whole Earth Household Store

Simplified Engineering for Architects and Builders

Back around the turn of the last decade, a lot of us headed into the hinterlands and among other things we built houses — some of them still standing. We probably over-built in most cases, intuiting beam, joist, and rafter sizes with a conservative margin of error. With a roof over our heads, some time to read — and maybe another building in the offing — Parker will earn the stiff cost of this book, saving materials, at least, if not lives. This isn't "Engineering for the Compleat Idiot" — it's a sound explanation of the principles of structural mechanics, covering steel, wood, and concrete construction and roof trusses. Includes an index, table of units and abbreviations, clear explanation of forces, stress, compression, shear, bending moment, modulus of elasticity, etc. — enough theory and nomenclature to understand and converse with engineers, or to build a shed or a house that won't fall with the first wet snow. Full of handy tables, clear diagrams, and numerous sample problems (the real life kind), with answers. I've found it equally useful in a structures course and on the job site; sure, I hate math too — but it's fun to understand how and why to build, for which this is as useful and necessary as a square or level. Unfortunately, engineers went decimal quite while ago, but there's a convenient table on the inside cover that can be used to convert back to the fractions you're reading on your tape measure. —Tom Keefe

Simplified Engineering for Architects and Builders
Harry Parker
1975; 411 pp.
5th Edition
$22.95 postpaid from:
John Wiley and Sons
One Wiley Drive
Somerset, NJ 08873

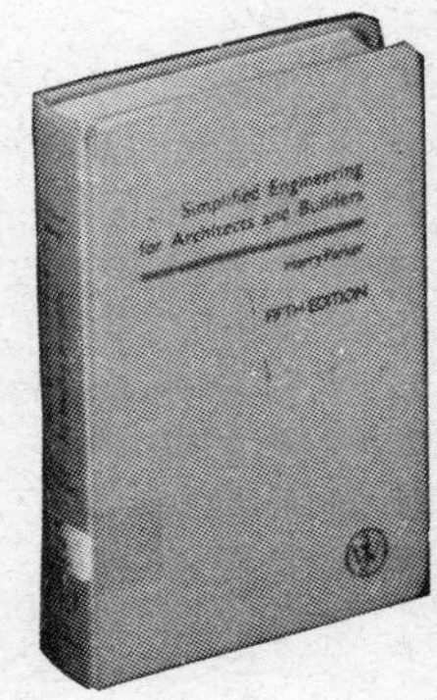

Floors	Pounds per square foot
Board flooring, per inch of thickness	3
Granolithic flooring, per inch of thickness	12
Floor tile, per inch of thickness	10
Asphalt mastic, per inch of thickness	12
Wood block, per inch of thickness	4
Cinder-concrete fill, per inch of thickness	8
Stone-concrete slab, per inch of thickness	12
Slag-concrete slab, per inch of thickness	10
Ceiling, suspended, metal lath and plaster	10
Ceiling, pressed steel	2

TABLE 19-4. Snow Loads for Roof Trusses in Pounds per Square Foot of Roof Surface

Locality	Slope of roof				
	45°	30°	25°	20°	Flat
Northwestern and New England states	15	20	30	35	40
Western and Central states	10	15	25	30	35
Pacific and Southern states	0	5	10	10	10

THE RISING SUN
NEIGHBORHOOD NEWSLETTER

What is a pilot hole? If you want to cut a hole in the middle of a piece of wood without sawing in from the edge, first you drill a little hole in the middle of where you want the big hole to be and then you can put your pointy saw in the little hole and cut the big hole from the inside out and the little hole is the pilot hole.

I had minutes of fun, over the years, making up what Ducks Unlimited, an organization listed in the *World Almanac*, might be until someone told me it was an organization of hunters who want to protect the breeding grounds of ducks, so they can be shot later. My life has been the poorer since, though knowing what a pilot hole actually is doesn't stop me from thinking of the first star to turn itself inside out and go black and the room behind a local bar where RAF flyers hide from their commander when they're about to go crazy. He knows about it but does nothing because they always come back and they *are* saving England.

The Green Wood House

Unseasoned rough cut wood is available almost everywhere with a bit of searching, it is dirt cheap, and because you lose nothing to the planer it is stronger than dimensional lumber from the retail yard. This book tells you how to build with green oak for much less than you would ordinarily pay for spruce or fir. It contains specially formulated joist tables for hardwood, and clearly describes framing and construction techniques, which take advantage of oak's strength. Larry Hackenberg has also devised nailing methods and schedules that accommodate the natural shrinkage of unseasoned wood so that the lumber does not split or crack while drying and the wood draws together as it contracts.

Although some of the architectural drawings are not as clear as they might be (particularly the floor plans) the general approach to design seems to have been influenced by Ken Kern and features an open use of space with good convective patterns. The photographs illustrate an imaginative use of the texture and solidity of the building material. This is the only book I know of that even mentions the peculiarities of building with rough sawn green lumber. The perfect companion for a chainsaw mill (p. 88).

—Len Gilday

The Green Wood House
(How to Build and Own a Beautiful, Inexpensive House)
Larry Michael Hackenberg
1976, 1978; 139 pp.

$9.75 postpaid from:
University Press of Virginia
Box 3608
University Station
Charlottesville, VA 22903

or Whole Earth Household Store

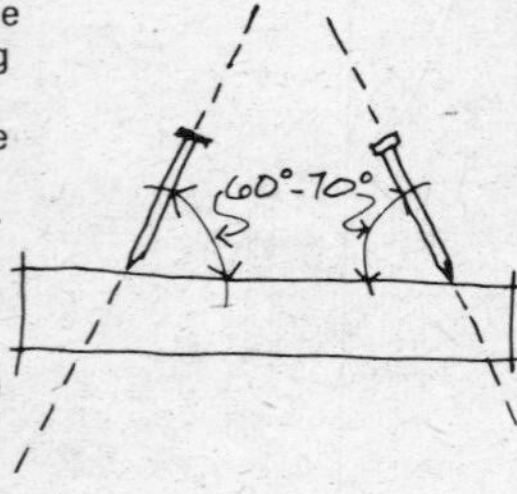

•

Each nail must be driven at an angle of 60° to 70° up from the face of the board and pointing toward the edge of the board. This is very important because it allows the board to shrink and pull the nail slightly without splitting the board in the center. If the nail is perpendicular to the face, the nail will hold so tightly that as the board shrinks it will pull itself apart in the middle and leave big ugly cracks.

•

A house should be designed not for what your life is but, rather, for what you want it to become.

•

Golden Rule Number 1: Never use lumber that is wider than 6 inches. Obviously, the narrower the piece of wood, the less likelihood of finding extreme mixed graining. However, never use less than 1"-thick lumber.

Building the Timber Frame House

A wood house of post and beams held together by wooden pegs is what this book is about. 2 x 4 stud framing has made timber joinery something of a lost art, and its revival today is based on more than sentiment and aesthetics. The houses are very strong and the timbers remain visible inside the structure. As long as the protective and insulating skin stays intact, timber frame houses can easily last hundreds of years. More skill is required to build this way, but the author claims his costs are comparable to conventional methods.

Raising a timber frame house requires many hands. Each house stands as a symbol of the neighbors and community that raised it. How many stud frame houses can you say that about? A beautiful book. *—Richard Nilsen*

Building the Timber Frame House
(A Revival of the Forgotten Craft)
Tedd Benson and James Gruber
1980; 211 pp.

$17.95 postpaid from:
Charles Scribner's Sons
Vreeland Avenue
Totowa, NJ 07512

or Whole Earth Household Store

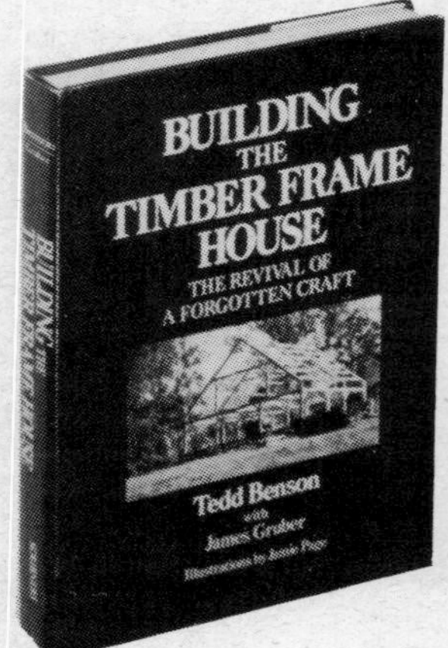

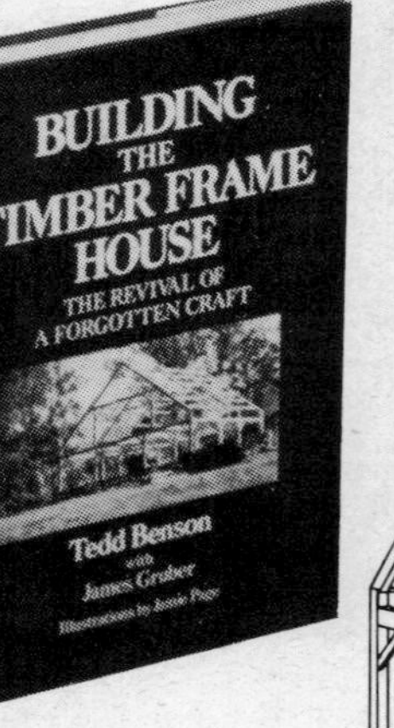

Ed Levin of Canaan, New Hampshire, constructed this inspiring hammer-beam truss roof for Dimitri Gerakaris's blacksmith shop.

TIMBERS OF THE FRAME

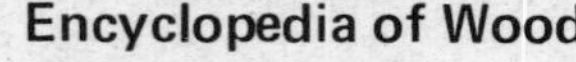

IN DRAW-BORING, HOLES ARE OFFSET TO FORCE A TIGHT FIT WHEN THE PIN IS DRIVEN.

•

With the use of rigid foam panels, we can now completely wrap our framework with a blanket of insulation, instead of interrupting the insulation with the frame as we do in stud construction. By separating a rigid frame from the insulating skin, each becomes as effective as it can be without needing to compensate for the other.

Encyclopedia of Wood

Do you really know the best way to "toenail"? (I didn't either.) What formula do you use to calculate the load-carrying ability of a stressed skin plywood floor? Is it safe to use dead wood for structural parts? Do you think you know it all? Well a quick look in this authoritative handbook will illuminate your ignorance and show you the stuff you need to know about wood and how to use it. Not an ego-book either; there's 60 years of Forest Service laboratory tests behind the recommendations. Everything, and I mean everything, is covered right down to the last splinter.

—J. Baldwin
[Suggested by Carl Zipper]

The Encyclopedia of Wood
(Formerly Wood Handbook)
Forest Products Laboratory,
U.S. Department of Agriculture
1974, 1980; 376 pp.

$12.95 postpaid from:
Sterling Publishing Co.
Two Park Avenue
New York, NY 10016

or Whole Earth Household Store

Recommended nailing methods for various types of wood siding.

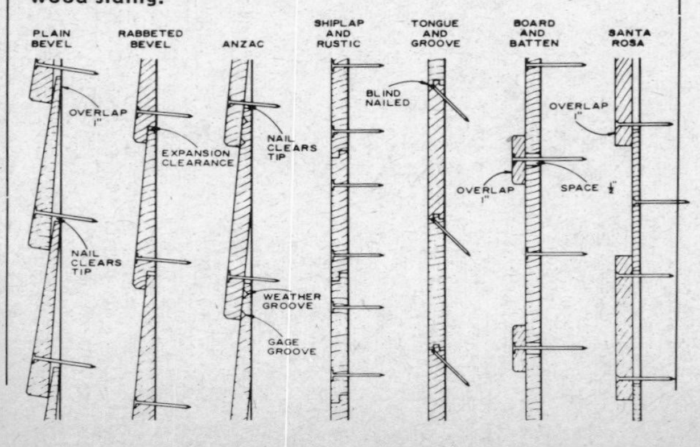

A Manual on Building Construction

A useful, sensible book on building prepared by a missionary to Sudan in 1948 and just now reprinted. Building with earth, concrete and brick (including making a kiln for wood-fired burned brick), making clay roofing tiles, construction of a dirt roof, sanitation systems that won't pass the building codes but will work fine in sparsely populated, dry areas. Two annoying aspects of the book are the missionary attitude (what horrors they have wrought) and poor perspective in many of the drawings. Yet much of the hard building information is not to be found elsewhere.

—Lloyd Kahn

A Manual of Building Construction
Reverend Harold K. Dancy
1948, 1975; 362 pp.

£5 postpaid from:
Intermediate Technology Development Group
9 King Street
London, WC2E 8HN
England

or

$8.75 postpaid from:
I.T.D.G.
North America
P.O. Box 337
Croton-on-Hudson, NY 10520

or Whole Earth Household Store

If the four foot stick has not enough weight in itself to hold the work, have a stone or another piece of wood handy and place it on the end of the holder at 'S'.

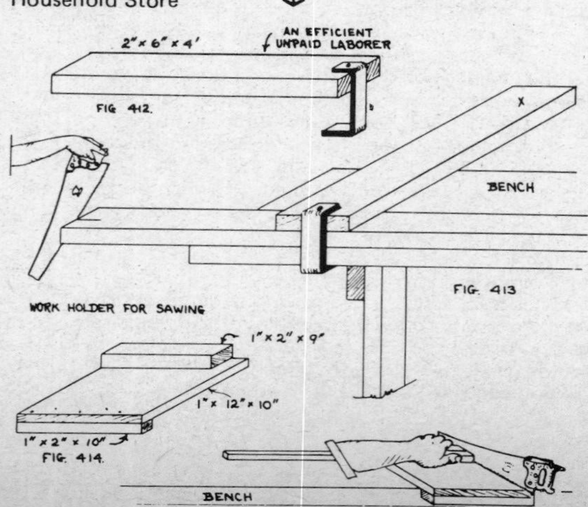

Low-Cost Pole Building Construction

An old Japanese building technique born out of the need for a structure to withstand earthquakes, pole framing contains many diverse advantages over standard construction. Instead of separate roof, wall and foundation elements, pole construction integrates those elements with the structural simplicity of a tree. Here are some of the advantages:

1. Simple foundation excavation — drilling holes is much simpler and less expensive than trenching and forming standard foundations.
2. Uses less cement, often back-filled with earth — a big saving.
3. Eliminates step foundations on a steep site and most under-floor cross bracing.
4. Will support floor and roof, eliminating load bearing walls. This means no headers, bracing in walls, 16" centers and special joists for interior load bearing walls.
5. Roof can be put up quickly after the poles are set if rain is a problem.
6. Simplifies construction for the owner builder by providing a stable structure with less parts.

Not only are pole houses good for earthquake conditions, a feature based on their relative flexibility, but since the poles are set much deeper (4' to 8') than standard foundation they are more stable in flood, slide and weak soil conditions.

The main disadvantage is the large timbers needed to span the longer distance between supports. This can be dealt with in some cases by added intermediary post and pier supports for floors.

The poles, as cantilevered members from the ground, serve the multiple purpose of foundation, lateral bracing and framework. The walls, roof and floor are all load free and are merely fastened to the pole frame. Also, the round pole is 18% stronger in bending than a comparably sized and graded skilled timber. Wood is stronger in its natural form because the grain rings are not broken.

There are painfully few sources of information on pole construction. **Low Cost Pole Building Construction,** *while extensively unimaginative, outlines the basic principles and techniques involved. It adheres to standard construction, not taking full advantage of the forms and details made possible by the poles. This new construction becomes an exciting opportunity for innovation as well as savings for the owner-builder.*

—Peter Calthorpe

Low-Cost Pole Building Construction
Ralph Wolfe,
Doug Merrilees,
Evelyn Loveday
1973, 1980; 176 pp.

$9.95 postpaid from:
Garden Way
Publishing Company
Charlotte, VT 05445
or Whole Earth
Household Store

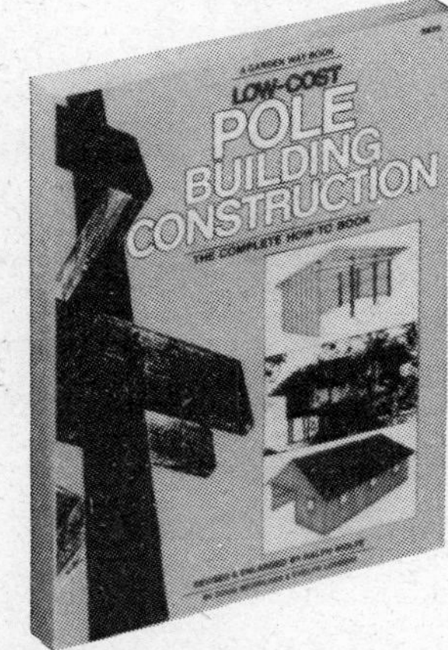

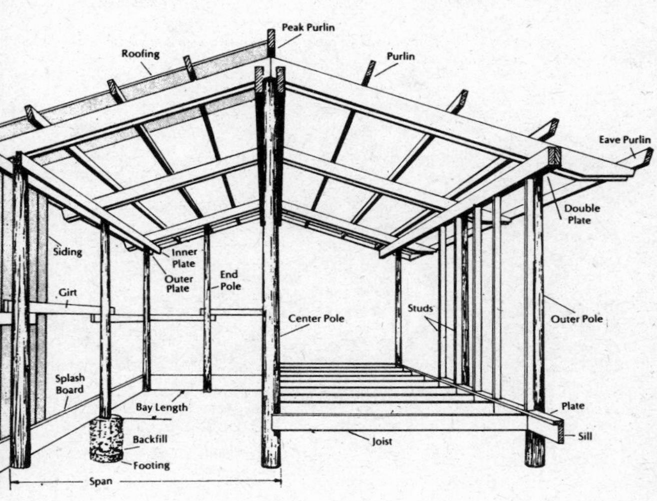

•

One firm which manufactures treated poles says: "In the Thirties a well-treated pole was supposed to last 30 years. Now this estimate has risen to 45 to 50 years, since anticipated failures did not occur. The length of service has been achieved under the most severe conditions. Of course, any pole which you use inside your building will be protected, and an even longer life can be expected."

Old Ways of Working Wood

Chopping, splitting, sawing, boring, chiseling, shaping, planing and turning wood, the old way. Purely hand woodwork: taking down the trees in the woods (including extensive axe info), squaring them into timbers, splitting them into shingles, shakes or posts, and performing a variety of operations without a lumber mill, skillsaw, powerdrill, or Stanley Sureform. —Lloyd Kahn

Old Ways of Working Wood
Alex W. Bealer
1972, 1980; 256 pp.

$12.50 postpaid from:
Barre Books
Crown Publishers
One Park Avenue
New York, NY 10016
or Whole Earth
Household Store

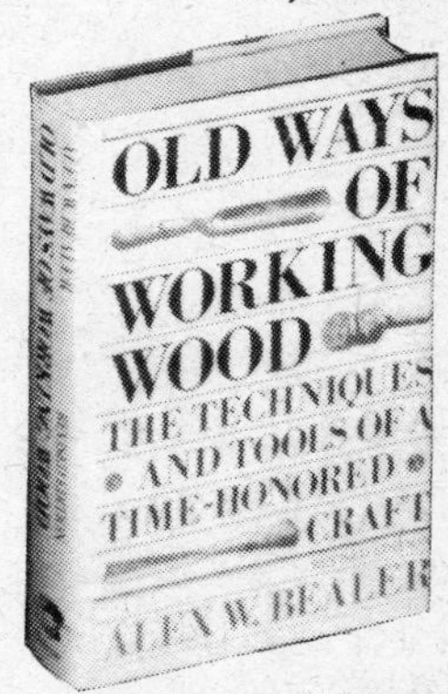

•

The earliest form of lathe, still being used in many parts of the world including the United States is no more than two logs, or heavy beams stuck in the ground with a pointed pin in one and a pointed screw at the same level in the other. Stuff being turned is fixed in its longitudinal center between these points and held there by the tightening of the screw. Before the use of screws, one of the points was probably held in place by a small wedge after being driven into the center of the stuff.

Power to turn the stuff comes from a long primitive treadle and springy pole, or lath, attached to the ceiling joists above the lathe or, for outdoor installations, from a springy, growing limb of a tree, with a strap stretched between the two. The strap wraps once around the stuff and is held taut by the spring of the lath. When the treadle is depressed the strap rotates the stuff rapidly; when the treadle is released the spring of the lath rotates the stuff in the opposite direction, returning it to its original position, a matter of simplicity itself. Shaping is done by holding a turning chisel against the stuff on the downward stroke of the treadle, removing it on the reciprocal motion, and repeating the process until the stuff is formed. During turning, the chisel rests on a small board fastened between the two parts, its top edge slightly above the center axis of the stuff.

↓

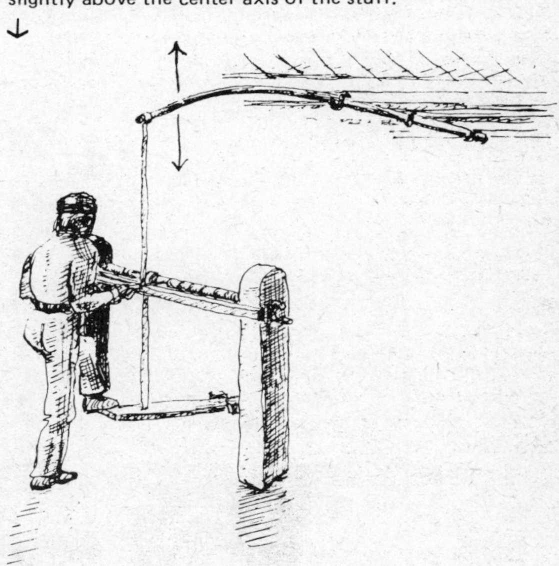

Use of spring pole — when the trunk of the tree is nearly severed, the spring of the pole will push it in the desired direction of fall.

→

Barns, Sheds and Outbuildings

Old-timers to learn from are getting hard to find but they're not all dead. This old time book knows about how to build an ice-house, a cool-room, and a Swiss birdhouse, among other things. Root cellars too. Though it is intended as an instruction manual of basic designs, I found it reasonable to sit right down and read the whole thing through as if it were a novel, which it sort of is. The pay scales are a little off for today's labor market, though, a dollar a day is what they paid then.

—J. Baldwin

Barns, Sheds and Outbuildings
Byron D. Halsted, Editor
1881, 1977; 240 pp.

$7.95 postpaid from:
The Stephen Greene Press
P.O. Box 1000
Fessenden Road
Brattleboro, VT 05301
or Whole Earth
Household Store

•

With winter come the piercing winds, the intense cold, and, unless well protected, the greatest suffering that the farm animals experience during the whole year. It is the season when to keep the stock warm is no less a matter of economy than to keep them well fed; in fact, they are fed in a great measure to keep up the animal heat, the food serving much the same end that coal does to the furnace.

Farm Builder's Handbook

How far is it safe to span with 2 X 10 floor joists? Where do you find out stuff like that? Here. But be warned that this is not a build-your-own barn book. The author assumes that you already know how to build. This book sets safe standards for farm structures where usual city codes don't apply. Even if you don't follow his advice, his numbers will be an indicator of how far you can stray and still be safe. The book is particularly good for figuring pole type buildings. —J. Baldwin

Farm Builder's Handbook
R.J. Lyle et al.
1973, 1978; 264 pp.
3rd Edition

$24.95 postpaid from:
Structures Publishing Co.
Box 1002
Farmington, MI 48024
or Whole Earth
Household Store

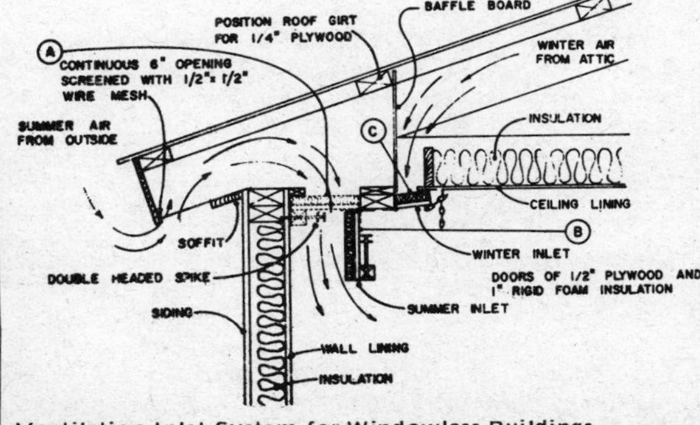

Ventilation Inlet System for Windowless Buildings.

THE RISING SUN
NEIGHBORHOOD NEWSLETTER

Kathy and I had run out of the weather and office gossip and were talking about the difference between art and craft. Kathy said that art had a definite personality left in it — the artist had started a conversation that someone else could pick up whenever they saw the art.

Building With Logs
Notches of All Kinds
Log House Plans

B. Allan Mackie spent a good part of his life studying different methods of log house construction throughout Canada, evolved his own organic Canadian style, and now teaches it at his own school. His goal is to convince people that in the forested parts of Canada, log houses are viable. He detests the term log cabin (the dictionary says "a small house . . . rudely constructed"). His houses are built of perfectly notched and fitted logs (careful scribing is the secret) with no need for chinking. They are strikingly handsome and will last for centuries.

Log houses are labor-intensive shelters, but if you have the logs and the time and the bodies, but don't have money, they can be built for a fraction of the materials cost of a conventional house. You don't need to buy insulation, paneling, siding, nails or dimensional lumber.

Mr. Mackie and his wife Mary write and publish their own books, run the school and put out a journal called **Canadian Log House. Building With Logs** *is the book to get first, it includes step-by-step building instructions with clear pictures and wonderfully detailed and understandable illustrations.* **Notches of All Kinds** *is a companion advanced textbook.* **Log House Plans** *contains complete plans for 37 different Mackie houses which, along with photographs of almost every model, make it a real snow country dream book. (For inspiring pictures of American log houses, see* **The Log Cabin**, *p. 213.)*

—Richard Nilsen

Design #776 — 1744 feet. This design has a central fireplace, exposed stairway, lofty living room, extra bedrooms upstairs and exposed timber framing.
—Log House Plans

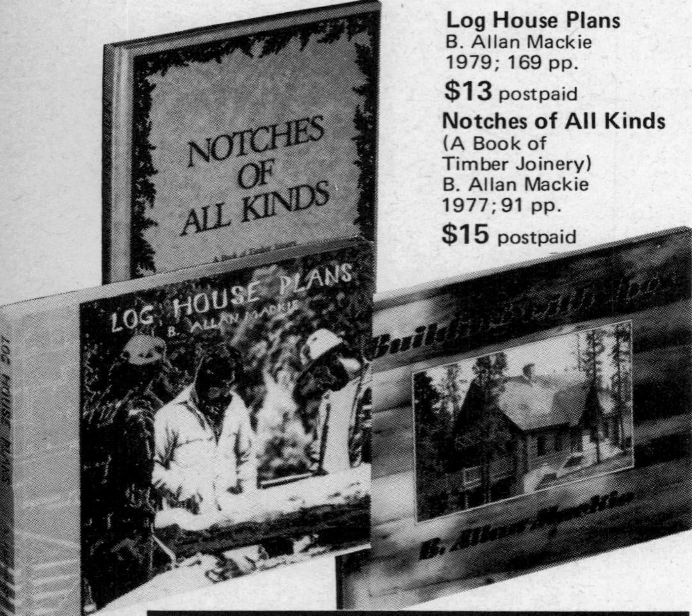

Log House Plans
B. Allan Mackie
1979; 169 pp.
$13 postpaid

Notches of All Kinds
(A Book of Timber Joinery)
B. Allan Mackie
1977; 91 pp.
$15 postpaid

Building With Logs
B. Allan Mackie
1974, 1979; 91 pp.
$13 postpaid

all from:
Log House Publishing Company, Ltd.
P.O. Box 1205
Prince George, BC
Canada V2L 4V3
or Whole Earth Household Store

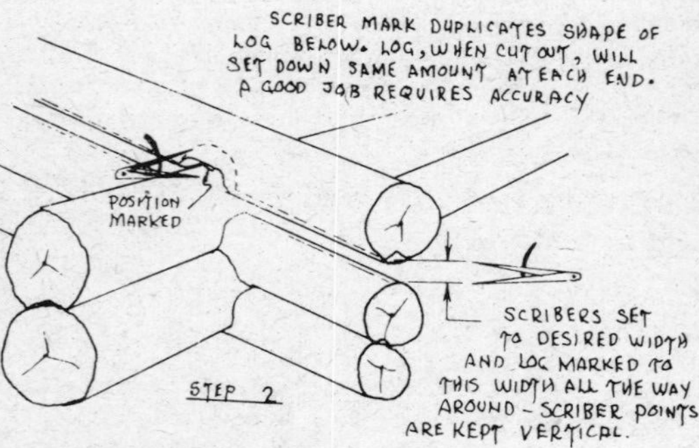

— Building with Logs

The above photograph shows a mitered joint where the King Post and the Collar Tie cross. A mortise and tenon join would have served as well, but the visual effect would have been less striking.
— Notches of All Kinds

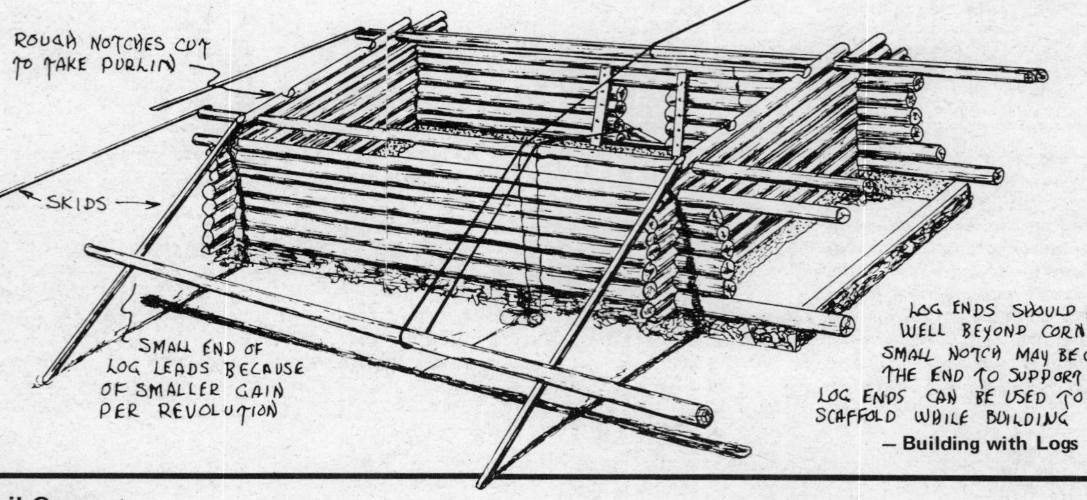

— Building with Logs

In Harmony with Nature

A fine book on log house construction. It is new, long haired, beautifully detailed in its illustration, and applies both the use of the traditional tools (adze, axe, broad-axe, chisel) and the ever lovin' chainsaw (p. 88). If you have a piece of land with some trees on it, I strongly recommend this book. The same craftsmen did **Country Comforts** *on p. 179.*
—J.D. Smith

In Harmony with Nature
(Creative Country Construction)
Christian Bruyére and Robert Inwood
1975, 1979; 213 pp.
$6.95 postpaid from:
Sterling Publishing Co.
Two Park Avenue
New York, NY 10016
or Whole Earth Household Store

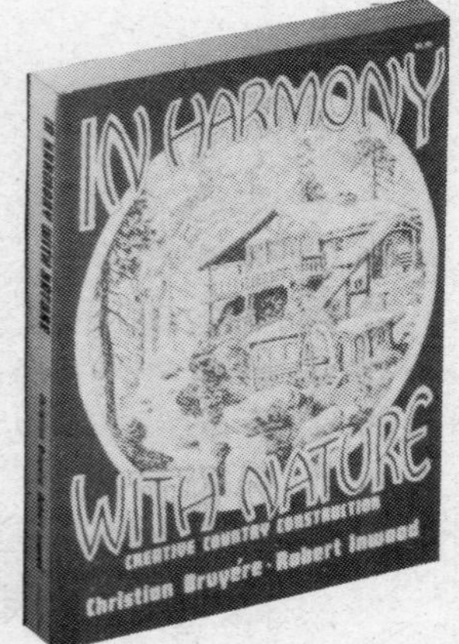

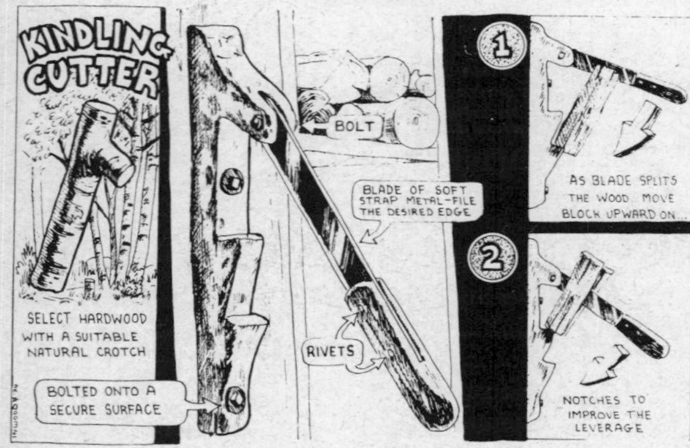

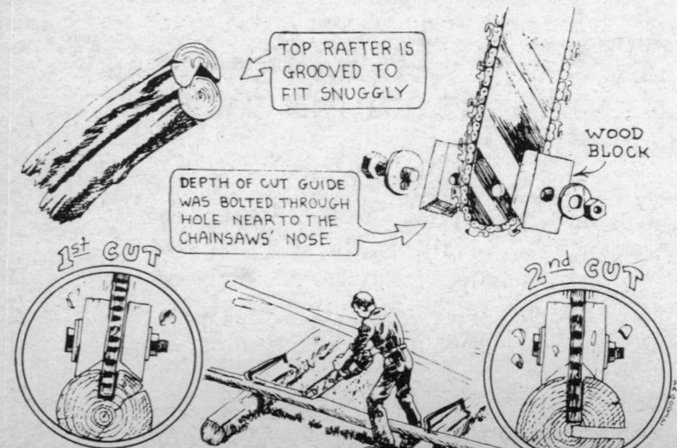

Soil-Cement

A well-detailed booklet on the stabilization of earth with cement, and describes all aspects of using the Cinva-Ram earth moulder.
—Lloyd Kahn

•

FORMS IN WHICH SOIL IS USED:

Soil is used in construction in the following forms:
(a) In the form of rubble, cut from the surface of the earth, in pieces or blocks of soil.
(b) As bricks, made in wooden forms or molds with soil moistened to the required degree.
(c) Moistened soil compacted *in situ* in suitable rigid frames to form monolithic walling (rammed earth).
(d) As stabilized soil, by combining it with an agent in order to improve its constructive properties.

Soil-Cement
(Its Use in Building)
1964; 87 pp.
93 illustrations
$7 postpaid from:
United Nations Publications
Room A-3315
New York, NY 10017
or Whole Earth Household Store

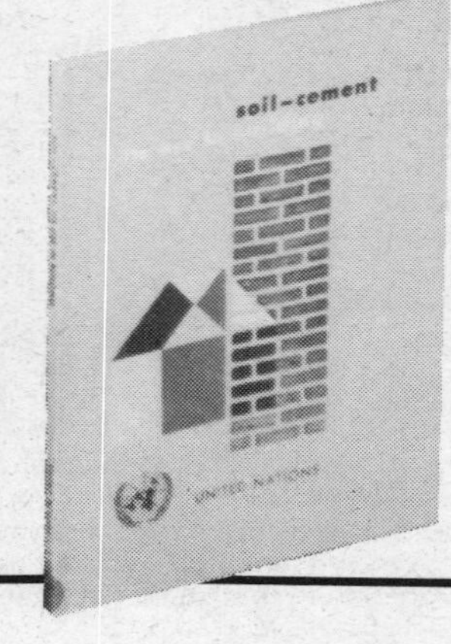

Cinva-Ram Block Press

As you probably know, this machine is manufactured in Bogota, Columbia, by Metalibec Ltda. We are handling the complete importation of this unit into the United States and pay all the importation charges, such as customs duties, ocean freight and marine insurance, plus forwarding fees and handling charges.

Our selling price for this CINVA-RAM press is $300 (U.S.) F.O.B. our warehouse, Akron, Ohio. The freight charges from our warehouse to ultimate destination will be on a "freight collect" basis. The press comes equipped with three wooden inserts to produce different types of blocks and tiles, plus an operations manual. The unit weighs 140 lbs. net, 155 lbs. gross (crated for shipment) and has a gross cubic measurement of 3.05 cubic feet each. With the cost of importation, freight, insurance, customs duties and handling charges which we must pay in bringing these presses into the United States, we are unable to extend any discounts of any kind for the CINVA-RAM block press.

Shipment can be made immediately upon receipt of your Purchase Order, together with your check or money order payable to Schrader Bellows Division.

Sincerely
(Miss) K. Easterling

Cinva-Ram Block Press
$330 plus shipping

Information
$1 postpaid from:
Schrader Bellows Division
200 West Exchange Street
Akron, OH 44309

Mud Space & Spirit

A book of adobe houses and the people who build and live in them. Ideas and inspiration that flow from a reverence for the high desert of the American southwest.
—Richard Nilsen

Mud, Space & Spirit
Virginia Gray, Alan Macrae, and Wayne McCall
1976; 95 pp.

$7.95 postpaid from:
Capra Press
631 State Street
Santa Barbara, CA 93101
or Whole Earth Household Store

•

Certain processes and stages of adobe work have become associated exclusively with women. To the *enjarradora*, broadly "plasteress" in English, belong the final phases of construction, the finishing. The *enjarradora* gives the whole architecture its final shape, color and detail.

Adobe

A very thorough book on many aspects of adobe construction. Mientras que descansas has adobes. *(While you're resting, make some adobes.)*
—Lloyd Kahn

↑ **Ranchos de Taos Church, Ranchos de Taos, New Mexico. Masses of heavy masonry help support a corner which has started to tip, from either lack of a bond beam or weakened foundations.**

Adobe
(Build It Yourself)
Paul Graham McHenry, Jr.
1973; 157 pp.

$9.95 postpaid from:
The University of Arizona Press
Box 3398
Tucson, AZ 85722
or Whole Earth Household Store

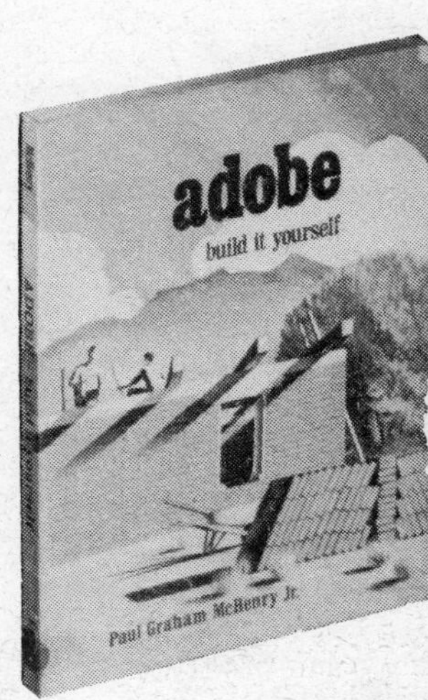

Adobe Today

Adobe is one of the best ways to build if you live where it is practical to do so. Not only is it esthetically pleasing, it makes use of local materials and is thus a fine example of resource-conservation. There's a bonus too: adobe lends itself well to "passive" solar heating and cooling schemes. (You use the house as both collector and storage instead of a mess of hardware.) The best way I know of to get a feel for the possibilities is to read this nifty paper. The articles treat both tradition and the experimental new with some of the most friendly real-people reporting I've seen.
—J. Baldwin
[Suggested by Jon Davis]

Adobe Today
$10 /year (6 issues)
from:
Adobe News
P.O. Box 1178
Belen, NM 87002

Making the Adobe Brick

Eugene Boudreau shows a good structural system that passes the Uniform Building Code and makes sense in earthquake country: ½" steel rebars connect concrete foundation to bond beam for structural strength inside the adobe walls. He and his wife made 120 tons of adobe bricks, did their own engineering, built the house, and wrote this book when they finished. Not a thorough analysis of adobe construction but a good account of building one type house.
—Lloyd Kahn

Making the Adobe Brick
Eugene H. Boudreau
1971; 88 pp.

$4.95 postpaid from:
Random House
455 Hahn Road
Westminster, MD 21157
or Whole Earth Household Store

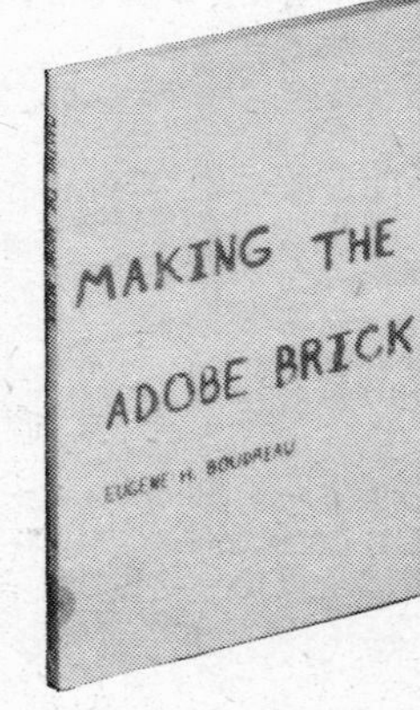

•

Personal experience with daily rates of adobe production showed that I could make a maximum of about 70 of the 4x7½x16 inch adobes, or 35 of the 4x12x18 inch adobes in 8 or 9 hours of continuous hard work. Often I could not achieve this level of production because there were bricks to be stacked, dirt to be excavated, etc. My maximum level of production added up to about one ton of adobes per man per day, and this weight had to be handled several times in the process of turning undisturbed soil into a stack of cured bricks.

↓ **Working the mud into the corners of the mold**

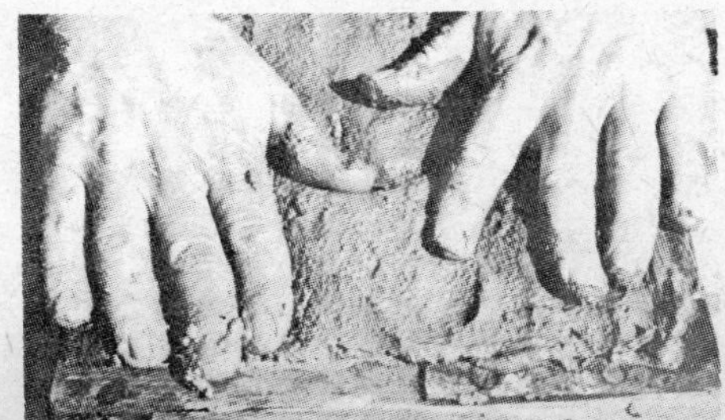

Adobe Craft

Technical manual on small-scale adobe construction, including landscaping and adobe sculpture. Plans for home-built electric soil sifter and adobe mixer powered by heavy duty drill motor.
—Lloyd Kahn

Adobe Craft
Karl V. Schultz, Ph.D.
1972; 71 pp.

$6.59 postpaid from:
Adobe-Craft
18322 Carlwyn Drive
Castro Valley, CA 94546
or Whole Earth Household Store

•

Adobe has a number of characteristics which make it attractive for construction and craft-related applications: 1) Virtually waterproof when clay/sand proportions are maintained and thorough mixing is carried out; 2) Good insulation to sound, heat, and cold; 3) Termite proof; 4) Fireproof; 5) Resistant to wind and sandstorm erosion; 6) High crushing strength (varies with soil, reported to be approximately 450 to 800 p.s.i. Uniform Building Code requirement is 300 p.s.i.); 7) Material is easily molded, molds may be removed immediately for air and sun drying; 8) Cured adobe is less dense than fired brick or concrete blocks, hence, can be readily cracked, sawed, or drilled using masonry tools; 9) Interior and exterior surface finishing are not necessary but may be applied.

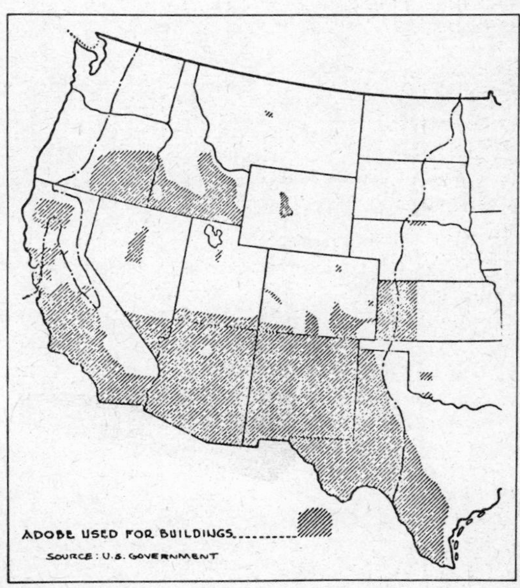

THE RISING SUN
NEIGHBORHOOD NEWSLETTER

Hey, ya know why Plutonium is called Plutonium? Well, the planets go like this, Uranus, Neptune, Pluto, and for a while there Uranium was the heaviest element and then they discovered one heavier and called it Neptunium and then one heavier still and called it Plutonium. This may not be obvious to your unscientific mind, but two separate semi-secret laboratories in the U.S. and Britain discovered the same elements at about the same time and called them the same thing, without talking it over.

—Info from *Lawrence and Oppenheimer* by Nuel Pharr Davis

Spacing is being checked by lining up the corners with a straightedge.

Modern Masonry

Brick and stone have always been charming because of their beauty. With today's construction prices they are expensive, but the cost of heating a house has added a new factor into the equation. Both these materials are excellent ways to store heat inside a passive solar structure; the extra initial cost may well be offset by savings in heating bills over the life of the house.

Modern Masonry *covers brick, stone and concrete block. It is designed as a trade-school text, which means it is very complete. The how-to steps here are accessible to anyone, but if you have ever watched the speed at which a skilled mason can work, you may rightly conclude that masonry is one part of house building where hiring out the work may be cost-effective. Like adobe, it is hard work. (For good masonry tools, check Goldblatt's Catalog, p. 152.)* —Richard Nilsen

Modern Masonry
Clois E. Kicklighter
1977; 256 pp.
$10.64 postpaid from:
The Goodheart-Wilcox Company
123 West Taft Drive
South Holland, IL 60473
or Whole Earth Household Store

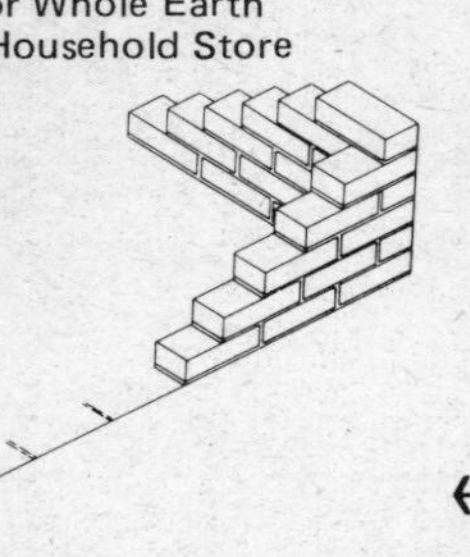

← Leads are the built-up sections of wall at each corner. This is done to establish proper height for each course and provide a place to attach the mason's line. It is important that these corners be as near perfect as possible.

Bricklaying Simplified

The subtitle of this book is "Outdoor Barbecues," and while it is aimed at the backyard adventurer, there are enough details for lots of simpler projects, like laying a brick patio. —Richard Nilsen

Bricklaying Simplified
Donald R. Brann
1979; 146 pp.
$5.95 postpaid from:
East-Bild
P.O. Box 215
Briarcliff Manor, NY 10510
or Whole Earth Household Store

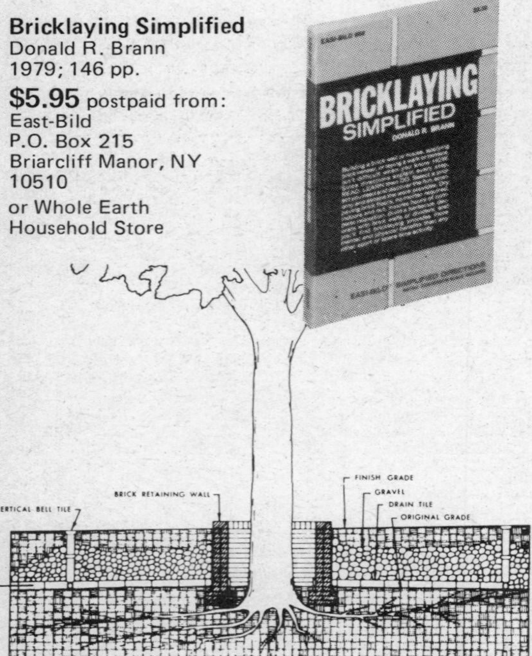

•

Always cut surplus mortar away from joint. Throw it back into the mortar on board. Before taking another full trowel, work the glob thrown back into the mortar so it doesn't become a dry, hardened orphan. Always cut away mortar as quickly as it is squeezed out. This prevents staining face of brick.

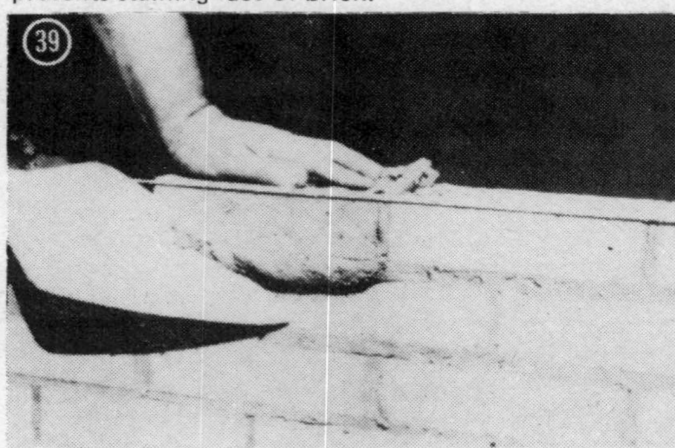

•

Brick Tree Wells

Tree roots require air, water and minerals. When a grade is changed and the depth of soil over the roots is increased or decreased, the roots have difficulty attaining a normal amount of air, water and minerals.

If you raise a grade 6" or less, and the soil is high in organic matter, the change won't affect most trees. When making a drastic change, you can supply what the tree needs by constructing a brick well in position shown.

Vertical bell tiles, placed in position shown, provide air and water to roots.

The Forgotten Art of Building a Stone Wall

How to build mortarless flat-stone walls. Instructions on splitting mica schist and granite, on building new walls and repairing old ones. Of use where this type of stone is available (as in New England). Also see the excellent **Building Stone Walls** *on p. 91.* —Lloyd Kahn

The Forgotten Art of Building a Stone Wall
Curtis P. Fields
1971; 64 pp.
$4.70 postpaid from:
Yankee, Inc.
Dublin, NH 03444
or Whole Earth Household Store

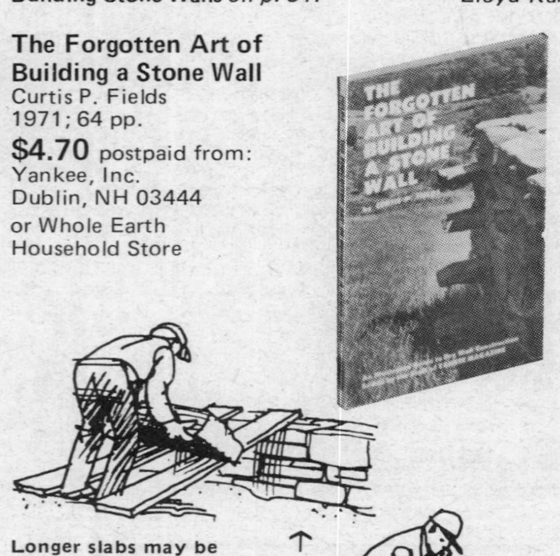

Longer slabs may be more easily lifted in place by the use of two planks. →

← Pounding the bevel-edged hammer with the sledge concentrates the blow to points along the line of the intended split scratched on the stone.

•

Before long I learned by trial and error how to split smaller pieces of mica schist— say, 6" x 12" x 24"— without drilling holes. This was done by using two heavy hand hammers one of which was flattened on both faces and was used to pound. The other, which received the blows, was squared on one of its faces and beveled to a splitting edge on the other.

This beveled edge was moved back and forth along the grain of the stone which stood upright on its narrow 6" side and at right angles to the body. It was pounded in three positions: middle, near end and far end — over and over until a crevice began to show. Then a few blows on the middle of the longest side finished the job.

Construction Manual: Concrete and Formwork

For 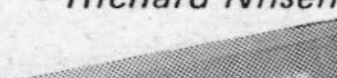many owner-builder applications, concrete block is a better choice than concrete — quicker and easier, since you don't have to build forms. But even concrete block needs to sit on a poured concrete footing, which gets you involved with this book at least to that extent. The information here is aimed at someone building a house, not a high-rise, and is adequate. The diagrams are well done with one exception — they show you how to build wall forms out of one by sixes. Unless you wanted the pattern of the wood forms to show on the exposed wall, you'd never do that (use plywood instead). —Richard Nilsen

Construction Manual: Concrete and Formwork
T.W. Love
1973; 176 pp.
$4.25 postpaid from:
Craftsman Book Company of America
542 Stevens Avenue
Solana Beach, CA 92075
or Whole Earth Household Store

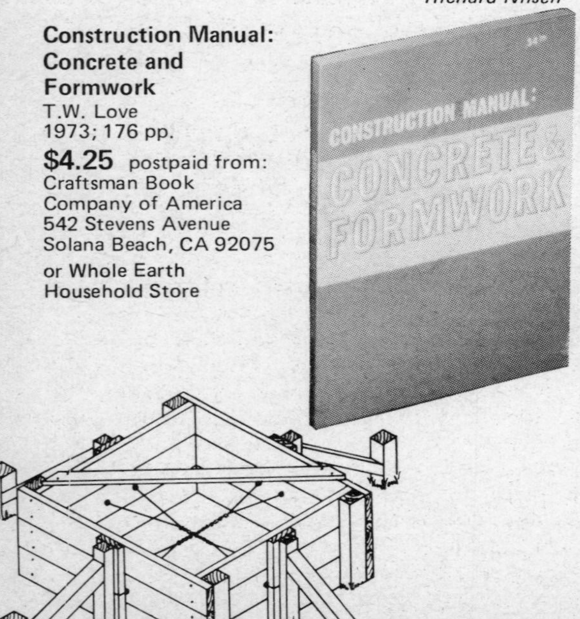

Ferrocement: Applications in Developing Countries

Some of the most difficult technical problems for developing countries (or homesteaders) are solved using ferrocement technology. That technology is within the reach of many, as it is labor rather than capital intensive. The book is not a manual, but shows the possibilities as applied to food and water storage, boats and roofing. The food storage bins, for instance, can radically cut the 25% loss to rodents that is the general rule in many countries. Hollow ferrocement walls might be good solar storage? —J. Baldwin
[Suggested by Meredith Foyle]

Ferrocement: Applications in Developing Countries
National Academy of Sciences
1973; 89 pp.
free (to researchers or universities working with developing countries or to people living in the developing world.)
from:
Board on Science and Technology for International Development
Office of the Foreign Secretary
National Academy of Sciences
2101 Constitution Avenue NW
Washington, D.C. 20418

•

In an airtight ferrocement bin, respiration of grain, or similar products, quickly removes oxygen from the atmosphere inside and replaces it with carbon dioxide. Any insects (adults, larvae, pupae, or eggs) or aerobic microorganisms present cannot survive to damage the stored product.

Severe floods on a village farm in Thailand floated this silo off its earth foundation, but it was reset, still dry inside and undamaged, when the floods subsided. This ability to resist vagaries of foundation conditions is an important characteristic. →

creek stone

field stone

quarried stone

cobble stone

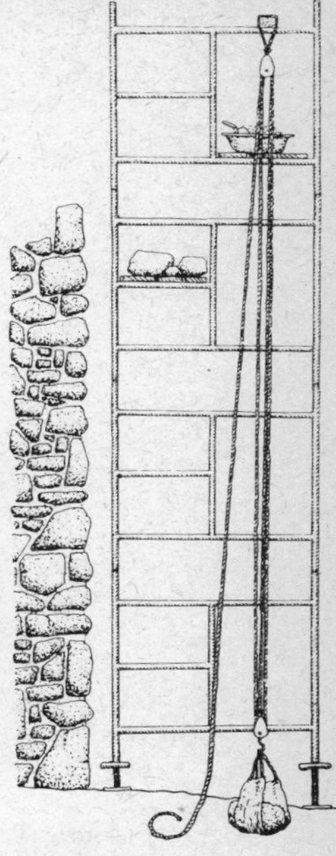

Stone Masonry

Would you believe that the best most comprehensive book on building with stone would have Ken Kern (of **The Owner-Built Home**, *p. 223) involved in there someplace? Well, the old master is at it again (with worthy friends) and the result is a joy to behold. As you might expect, esthetics are held to be as important as structure. Also expected and delivered are chapters on both dry and mortared technique, facings, and formed work. With the renewed interest in building with natural materials, this is all just in time. With photographs of everything.*

—J. Baldwin

Stone Masonry
Ken Kern, Steve Magers, Lou Penfield
1976, 1977; 192 pp.

$12.20 postpaid from:
Charles Scribner's Sons
Vreeland Avenue
Totowa, NJ 07512
or Whole Earth Household Store

•

Sometimes one happens to find an old foundation or a chimney of stone. What a prize! Not only is the material stacked in one place but each stone has already proven useful. Most old foundations or chimneys are built dry (without mortar) or merely with mud, so dissembling them is not difficult. . . .

If permission to dissemble one of these structures is obtained, much can be learned about masonry while you take it down. As each stone is removed, pay close attention to how it was bedded in relation to other stones around it. The mere fact that this structure is still standing shows it was well built. Or if it is in partial ruin perhaps the reason will be indicated through your observation.

How to Build a Low-Cost House of Stone

*The Watson family (Lewis, Sharon, two girls) built a handsome low-cost 1100 sq. ft. stone house, moved in and wrote this fine booklet on their experiences. It's the Flagg technique, as used by Helen and Scott Nearing (***Living the Good Life***, p. 76), using wooden forms to hold the stone and concrete until it sets. Amateurs can build straight walls this way. Rassle with rocks, not mortgage payments.*

—Lloyd Kahn

How to Build a Low-Cost House of Stone
Lewis & Sharon Watson
1980; 96 pp.
6th Edition

$6 postpaid from:
Stonehouse Publications
Box 500
Sweet, ID 83670
or Whole Earth Household Store

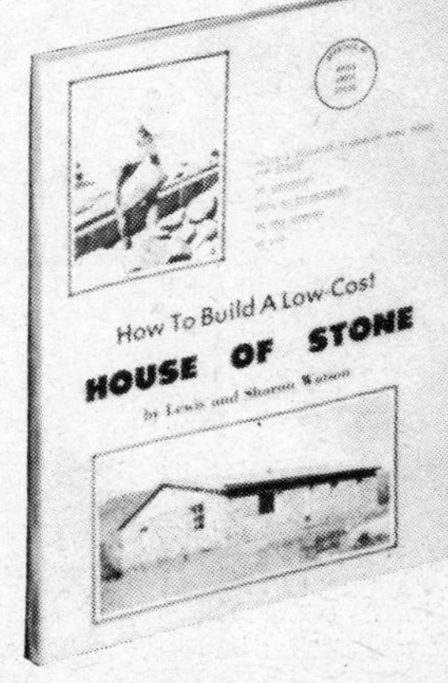

•

The slab floor was prepared and completed in about four days, the roof in about ten days, the wiring in a week, and the doors, windows, and miscellaneous basic finishing in about two weeks. With many other assorted jobs (trips to town, reading "how-to" books, asking questions, etc.), we were actively building the house for about five months, May-September, 1973.

•

Decide how thick you want your walls. (We used 10" for 8' walls and wouldn't recommend smaller diameters for this kind of construction.) Make sure all stones you gather have at least one axis that size or smaller. A rock with even 1/4" extra must either be chipped off or discarded, for it simply will not fit between the rigid forms you'll be using.

Stone Shelters

This is an utterly beautiful book, a study of the people, history, geography, and vernacular architecture in a small area in southern Italy known as the Murgia of Trulli.

The several different types of stone shelters of the region are covered extensively, including cave dwellings hewn from solid stone, unmortared stone domes called trulli, *and arches and vaults built with "ragbag patchwork technique" by the masons of Cisternino.*

The book is primarily concerned with how the architectural forms came into being and how the building techniques derived from the needs of the builders.

Descriptions and text are clear, photos superb.

—Lloyd Kahn

Stone Shelters
Edward Allen
1969; 199 pp.

$7.95 postpaid from:
The MIT Press
28 Carleton Street
Cambridge, MA 02142
or Whole Earth Household Store

•

The masons of Cisternino were men of exceptional ingenuity. They sometimes laid up walls of regular stone blocks, but in other cases made walls by compacting irregular stones and mortar between wood forms. Their combinations of arches and vaults were often graceful and correct, but more often were brutally expedient, and were most often full-blooded, lusty, folk-art inventions that made some charmingly naive concessions to grace and correctness. Nothing was sacred to the masons but the sheer physical stability of what they built. A half-arch could support a stair, a tilted barrel vault could cover it. A round barrel vault could be intersected by pointed-vault dormers. A triangular piece of vaulting could support a diagonal balcony front if held at its vertex on a projecting stone bracket. A buttress to a building across the street could resist the excessive thrust of a roof vault, or of a too-ambitiously cantilevered balcony. An irregular room shape was easily covered with a skewed vault. Almost anything could be supported or spanned by cutting, twisting, tilting, truncating, or combining the standard forms of vaulting in non-standard ways.

A transitional form of trullo field shelter, nonrectilinear in plan. A main space is joined to a smaller one housing a fireplace. Such shelters are often found with two or three smaller spaces attached to the main space, as illustrated in the small sketches. (Plan and section courtesy Byggekunst, redrawn by the author.)

•

The making of a cave is the antithesis of the usual construction process. A cave is space produced directly by the subtraction of a relatively small amount of solid material from a very large mass. A more conventional shelter, whether it be a *trullo*, a vaulted stone townhouse, or the reader's own dwelling, is space produced indirectly by its enclosure with pieces of solid material added together.

THE RISING SUN
NEIGHBORHOOD NEWSLETTER

The Moon Club had a subtlety battle over the Widmanstatten pattern T-shirt. If you take an iron meteorite (one of the three kinds) and cut it and polish it with acid (it's not clear why this was done the first time, except presumably nineteenth century German Scientists have as many dull days as anyone else, maybe more), then these marks called Widmanstatten patterns appear and they appear on no other rock or substance, no matter what you do, unless you draw it. They look like a drunk has been repeatedly trying to draw a stop sign, but hasn't been able to make the lines connect even once, though the lines from different attempts sometimes cross each other. Well, the proposed T-shirt has marks like that and the question is should they say nothing and be explained on request, should they say the sky is falling, or should they say the sky *is* falling. It was an interesting discussion with a boring outcome — no italics and a split run with and without printing.

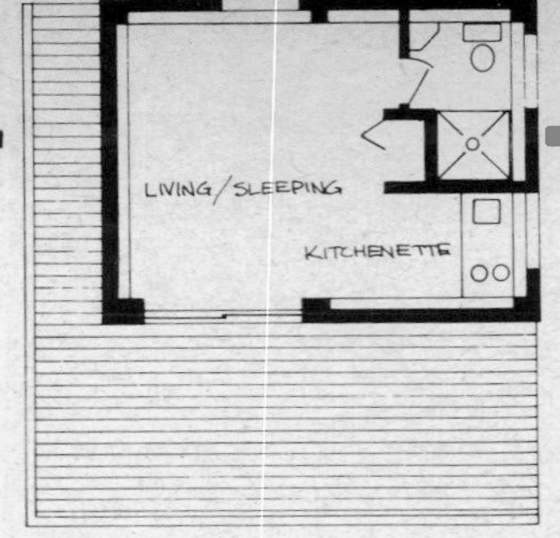

Kit Houses By Mail
Brad McDole and
Chris Jerome
1979; 206 pp.
$14.95 postpaid from:
The Stonesong Press
Grosset & Dunlap, Inc.
51 Madison Avenue
New York, NY 10010
or Whole Earth
Household Store

Kit Houses By Mail

Somewhere between the unaffordable dream and the entirely self-built abode there's a middle ground: the kit. There are a lot of different kinds. Some are simple and some are complex. Some come with instructions and some come with instructors. This book doesn't pretend to present all available kits, but rather shows a selection. The text is unusually free of catalog purple prose and seems to be acceptably realistic about the money involved. (There is money involved; more than you might hope.) I found the book to be the best overall introduction to kit houses I've seen. It covers the field well — floor plans, prices, photos and descriptions of log cabins, domes, shacks (oops, cabins), all the way through $100,000 palaces. Easily read too. It would be more useful in paperback at less cost though. —J. Baldwin

•

The appeal of a kit to most buyers is that it might save them money. Just looking at the price lists for the kits can create euphoric expectations. You see an elaborate 2,000-square-foot barn for $20,000 and you figure $10 a square foot, a number that has not been heard around construction sites since the late 1950s. Labor won't add much to that, especially if you bring in the family, friends, and neighbors. The rest of the materials you can get on sale or at the salvage yard. The finished house shouldn't cost more than $30,000, or $35,000 at the most. At today's prices that's a house at a 50% discount.

Such calculations are as common as they are improbable. You can save money with house kits, but it is unlikely that you will save anywhere near 50%. The cost of the kit itself, appealing as it looks alone in a booklet, represents only 25% to 50% of the cost of the finished house. How carefully you can estimate that final cost will determine the extent of your pleasure of your dismay.

•

Type of Structure: One-story post-and-beam shell package

Manufacturer: Cluster Shed, Inc., Twistback Road, Claremont, NH 03743, (603) 542-7762

Materials Provided: Eastern white pine timbers with interlocking mortise-and-tenon joints, pegged with square oak trunnels for frame. Exterior walls resawn pine board-and-batten; interior white vinyl-faced Homasote. Roof and wall systems of tongue-and-groove kiln-dried pine, 2" rigid isocyanurate insulation with both sides foil-faced, strapping. Felt, shingle ribs, hand-split Western red cedar shakes for roofing. Double-pane insulated windows, pine doors, patio doors of tempered insulating glass. Hardware and trim included.

Exterior Dimensions: 16' x 12'

Living Area: 192 sq. ft.

Price: $3,790 FOB Claremont, NH. Includes shell only, no interior finish.

Price/sq. ft.: $19.73

Warranty: 60 days for materials and workmanship

Special Features: This is the simplest of four basic Cluster Sheds designed to be combined with each other or larger models. Cluster Shed prices range from $3,790 to $9,950 for single units and up to $25,957 for combinations. Highly adaptable to sloping sites.

Energy Features: System includes layer of tongue-and-groove and layer 2" insulation board separated by strapping to create air space. Insulation values said to be R-22 for walls and R-23 for roof.

Notes: Timberpeg materials are good quality, details are attractive, and simpler designs are possible for do-it-yourselfers. Network of dealer-contractors or consultation with manufacturer suggested. Shipped on 40' flatbed trucks.

Price of Information Kit: $4

Miller Solsearch house plans

House plans for a plain-looking energy efficient dwelling designed to meet Canadian government specifications. Super-insulated, carefully detailed, low-cost housing that has been tested and uses only 100 gallons of heating oil per year. Finding out what works in energy conserving housing is one thing. Getting the costs down to where people on average incomes can afford it is quite another. These plans are a step in that direction. —Richard Nilsen

Conserver One
(Split entry wood frame house)
Set of house plans
$50 postpaid
Brochure
free

Conserver Two
(Cape Cod style home)
Set of house plans
$50 postpaid
Brochure
free

all from:
Miller Solsearch
49 Pownal Street
P.O. Box 2320
Charlottetown, Prince Edward Island
Canada C1A 1H9

Acadia House

Fed up with the ridiculous cost of new houses, architect Charles Haynes and 20 students from University of British Columbia Centre for Continuing Education designed and built a 1000 sq. ft. house for about half the accepted expense. The building crew consisted of inexperienced people and included six women. They came up with a house that many people would consider to be nice and energy-efficient at that. Now there is an introductory booklet, a set of plans, and an instruction book (and by now more houses) all well adapted to the Canadian climate, and all assuming that inexperienced people working together can make good houses for themselves. That's the sort of news we like to hear, isn't it? Wonder how we came to forget that this is how we used to do it. Some of you may be especially interested in the treated wood foundation. No concrete. The plans are among the clearest I've ever seen; about as close to no-particular-skill-required as one could hope. —J. Baldwin

The Acadia House Story
1978; 12 pp.
free

Self-Help Housing
(Acadia House Design and Construction Manual)
1979, 300 pp.
$12.95 postpaid

Acadia House Plans
33 pp.
$.50 postpaid

all from:
The Architecture Shop
1114 West Broadway
Vancouver, BC
V5Z 1J1 Canada

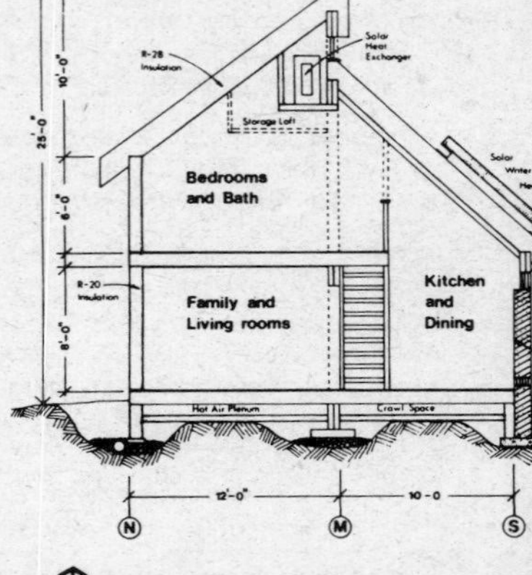

↑ Typical section — Acadia House

Construction Bargaineer

As with Rock and Dirt *(p. 125), this is one of those bargain-yellow tabloids where your cat-skinner tank driver tattooed roughneck soul can revel in visions of big tough tools — backhoes, loaders, scrapers, cherry pickers, grapple rakes, and their kind. Things a community might buy, or a rich eccentric, or an entrepreneur looking to rent themselves with the tool. New, used and surplus. (Spanish edition also available.)* —SB

Construction Bargaineer
$9/year (24 issues)
from:
The Construction Bargaineer
P.O. Box 16365
St. Paul, MN 55116

Peace of Mind in Earthquake Country

Fascinating. There's no better book on earthquakes and no other book at all that tells you what to do about them: where to locate, evaluating sites and buildings, insurance, design, and where to run. —SB

Peace of Mind in Earthquake Country
(How to Save Your Home and Life)
Peter Yanev
1974; 304 pp.
$5.95 postpaid from:
Chronicle Books
870 Market Street
San Francisco, CA 94102
or Whole Earth
Household Store

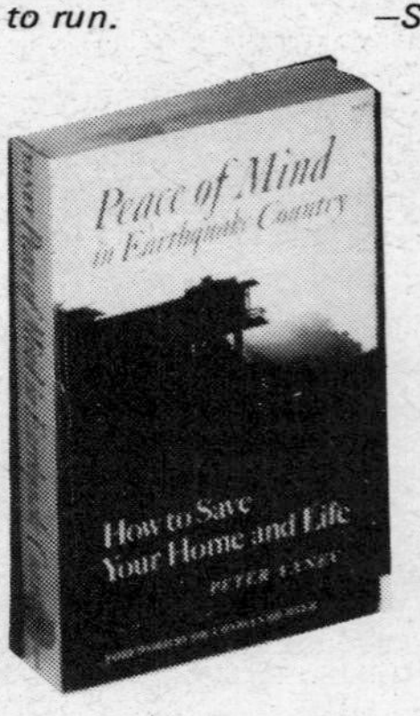

Of all utility components, water heaters are most susceptible to being knocked over by a quake. The heater is almost always ruined by a fall, but the real hazard is the likely rupture of the gas feeder line. All gas heating components, water heaters, furnaces and free-standing room heaters, should be anchored to the floor or to the studs of a solid wall. →

Here, naturally stable ground has been disrupted by improperly graded or compacted landfill. New hillside developments are frequently stacked in a parallel series of cuts into the slope and landfills below the cuts to provide flat building sites. If the fill is not carefully engineered, it will be very subject to settlement or sliding during an earthquake. →

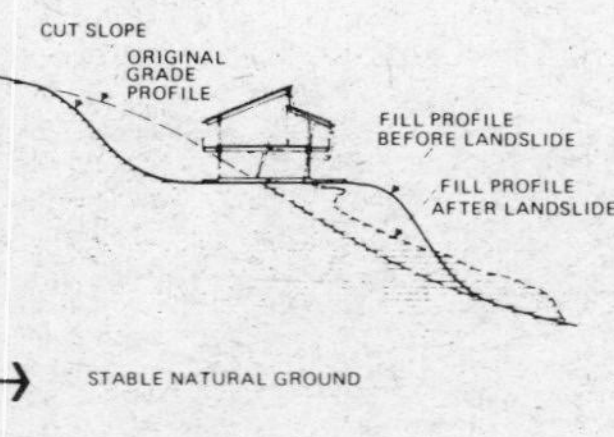

The exceptionally strong and durable plywood sheathing kept this building intact despite the blows it suffered both from the huge Alaska earthquake and the landsliding that destroyed its foundation and knocked it down the hill. The building was severely damaged, but it presented little threat to the occupants at the time of the quake and slide. →

Roofing Simplified

Basic application procedures for roll roofing, asphalt shingles, wood shingles, slate, metal, canvas and fiberglass roofs. Includes uses of flashing, gutters, skylights, dormers, simple scaffolds, a safety harness and more. Clear basic techniques for a weather tight roof and also building procedures which will make your work safe and efficient. —John Bradbury

Roofing Simplified
Donald R. Brann
1972, 1979; 130 pp.
$3.50 postpaid from:
Easi-Bild
P.O. Box 215
Briarcliff Manor, NY 10510
or Whole Earth
Household Store

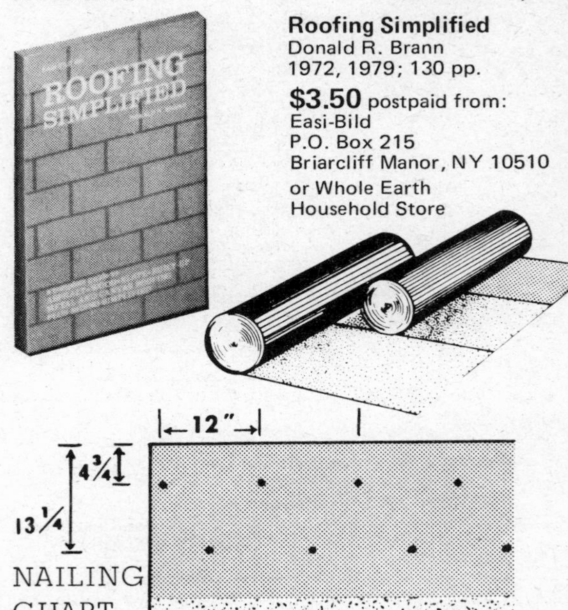

One of the easiest, quickest, and least complicated methods of applying a good roof fast is with mineral faced, double coverage, roll roofing. Each course laps 19". This mineral faced roofing comes 36" wide. The lower half of the surface is covered with mineral coated pellets, the upper half is smooth. Each roll covers 51 sq. ft.

Double coverage roll roofing may be applied when pitch is as low as 1" per foot. Always use the size, kind, quantity and space nails manufacturer recommends. The entire first course is embedded in asphalt cement and nailed or stapled every 4 feet, or space manufacturer recommends. Roll roofing with a roofer's roller to bond course to roof. Allow first course to project 1" over edge of eave or keep it flush with starter strip.

A 19" wide starting strip (use width roofing manufacturer recommends) can be cut to length needed. This is embedded in asphalt cement with mineral face down. The starter strip is nailed every 12" with big head 1" roofing nails, and rolled to bind it securely in position.

The width of the starter strip is determined by slope of roof. If roof pitches 4" or more per foot, the starter strip should extend up roof to a point approximately 12" from interior wall. Where the slope is less than 4" per foot, follow directions as outlined for built-up roofing on page 62.

The first 36" wide strip of roofing should be embedded in asphalt cement, rolled, and nailed in place.

Asphalt cement is applied to the upper half. The next course is rolled into position. Always lap each course amount roofing manufacturer recommends.

Insect-proof door

Item: I think it's from the *American Legion Magazine.* "Insect-proof door has been designed by Alvin Stewart of Sanford, N.C. He takes a sheet of clear plastic slightly wider and longer than the door space, shreds it into 3/4-inch ribbons starting at the bottom and reaching almost to the top, hangs it over the door opening. It's easy to walk through and, he claims, its fluttering keeps out more bugs than a screen door."

Curiously yours,
J. Feiman, Canton, Ohio

This works surprisingly well. —J. Baldwin

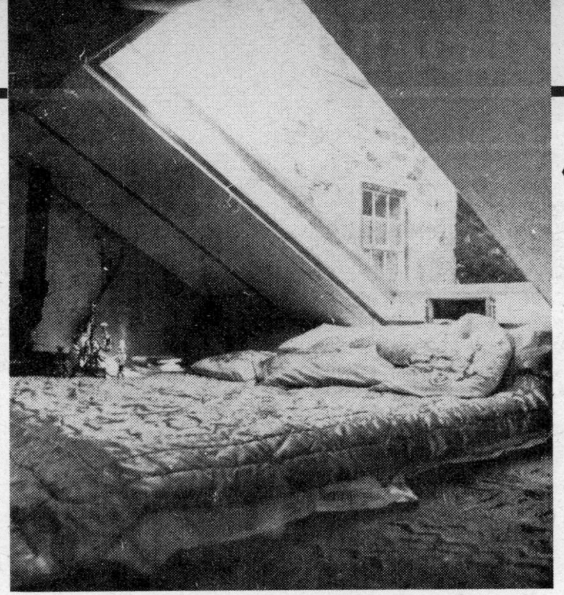

← Domed skylight in Pennsylvania farmhouse

Slate Roofs

My dad's house had a slate roof that weighed 12 tons. In the 30 years we lived in that house, there was not one leak. This was in a part of New Jersey where the weather was just plain nasty, including such assaults as hurricanes and deep snow. The only damage we ever had to repair was a few slates busted by high fly balls from nearby baseball games. What other roof gives that kind of performance, is a beautiful natural material, and is fireproof? Not cheap, of course, but sometimes you can strip an old house back east. Anyway . . . this is the complete slate bit, reprinted from a 1926 edition. As such, the booklet is history as well as a handbook. You probably won't want to know more than they show. —J. Baldwin

Slate Roofs
National Slate Association
1926; 84 pp.
$7.25 postpaid from:
Vermont Structural
Slate Company, Inc.
P.O. Box 98
Fair Haven, VT 05743

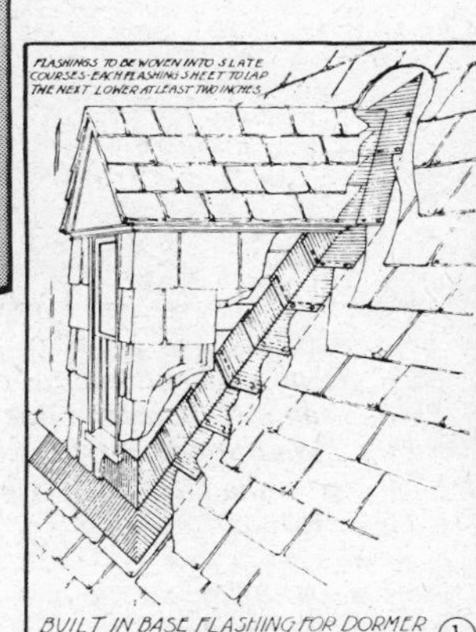

BUILT IN BASE FLASHING FOR DORMER WINDOW ON SLATE ROOF
1

The Skylight Book

There are a lot of nifty things you can do with a skylight, buy if you don't want to get wet, you'd better know what you are doing before you make the gaping hole in the roof. Absolutely everything you need to know is shown here, and very nicely too. Pass the saw, it's time we got some light into this dump! —J. Baldwin

The Skylight Book
(Capturing the Sun and the Moon, A Guide to Creating Natural Light)
Al Burns
1976; 111 pp.

Running Press
38 South 19th Street
Philadelphia, PA 19103
OUT OF PRINT
Revision forthcoming

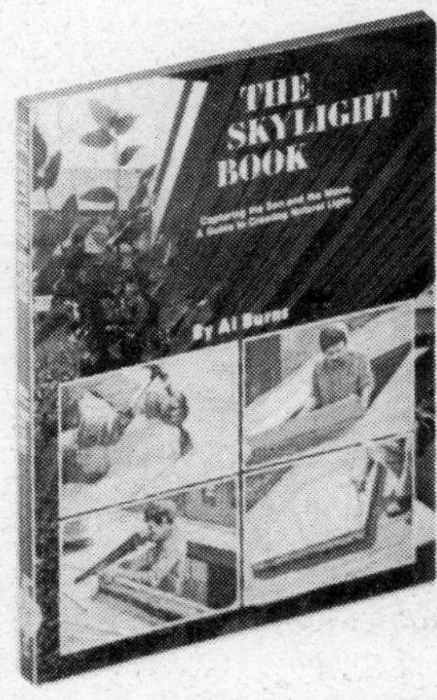

The Thatcher's Craft

There are several hundred thatchers still at work in England. This is a highly detailed book, with over 500 photos, on their sophisticated craft. It covers three types of thatch: Norfolk reed, which lasts 50 - 60 years; combed wheat reed, 25 - 40 years, and long straw thatch, 10 - 20 years. How to gather, prepare and apply. With growing scarcity and expense of processed materials, thatching could become an increasingly useful craft. See **Small Scale Grain Raising**, *p. 98.* —Lloyd Kahn

The Thatcher's Craft
Rural Industries Bureau
1961; 225 pp.
£4.20 (about $10)
postpaid from:
Council for Small
Industries in Rural Areas
141 Castle Street
Salisbury, Wiltshire
England SP1 3TP

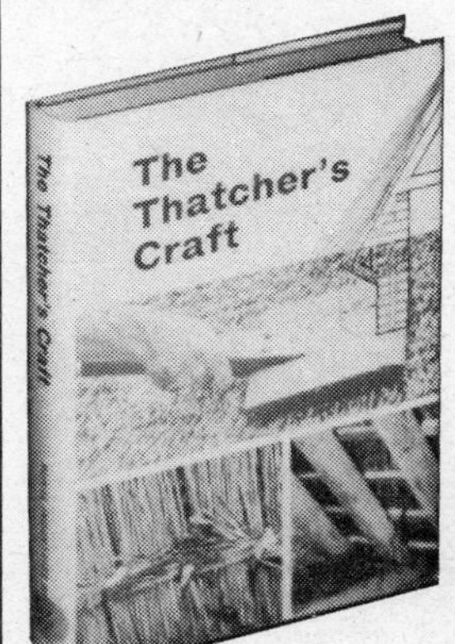

→ Eaves window built into the roof

•

The older varieties of wheat all produced good long straw, which not only provided ample bedding material for cattle, but also material for the form of thatch known as long straw thatch. These older varieties suffered however from various defects. The plants themselves were vulnerable to wind and rain, were easily beaten down, and were subsequently difficult to harvest. Scientific plant selection and breeding has now produced varieties which are available to the farmer, and which serve the dual purpose of providing both a good yield of grain, and straw suitable for thatching.

Laying the ridge and thatched roof

The Lightning Book

What it is, what it does, and how to protect yourself and your possessions from it. For all the wonderful stories ("didn't hurt him much, just came down the drain pipe, through the window, popped the buttons off his shirt, and blew up the TV"), lightning is scary. —Richard Nilsen

The Lightning Book
(The nature of lightning and how to protect yourself from it)
Peter E. Viemeister
1972; 316 pp.
$3.95 postpaid from:
The MIT Press
28 Carleton Street
Cambridge, MA 02142
or Whole Earth
Household Store

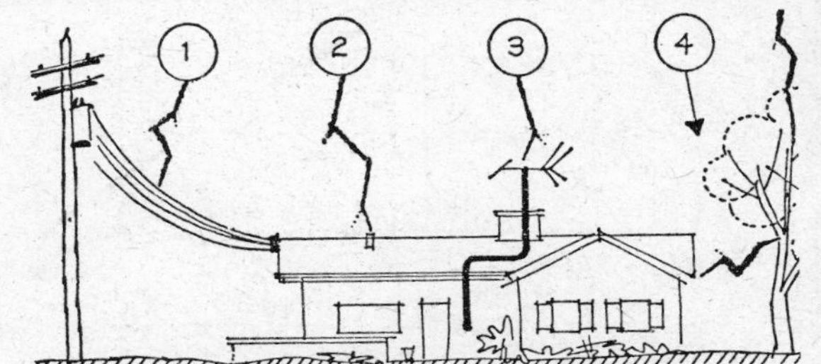

How lightning could enter your home. (1) Strike or induced surge may follow utility lines into building. Arresters can divert these. (2) Direct stroke to building. Lightning rods can intercept these and lead them to ground. (3) Strike to TV or radio antenna. Good ground connection on mast and arrester on lead-in will keep these strokes out. (4) Side flash from nearby tree struck by lightning. Keep trees away from house or install conductors on house and trees.

THE RISING SUN
NEIGHBORHOOD NEWSLETTER

It's only because of the accident of time that history is in the past. Nothing intends to have, or deserves, such a fate.

— Spoofy Dorf in the first issue of *Place* magazine

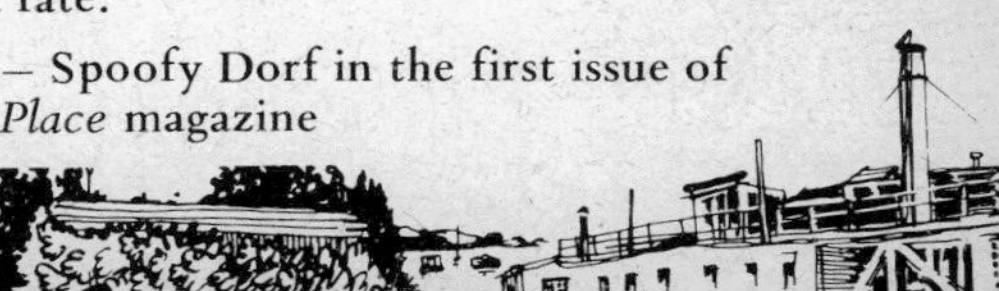

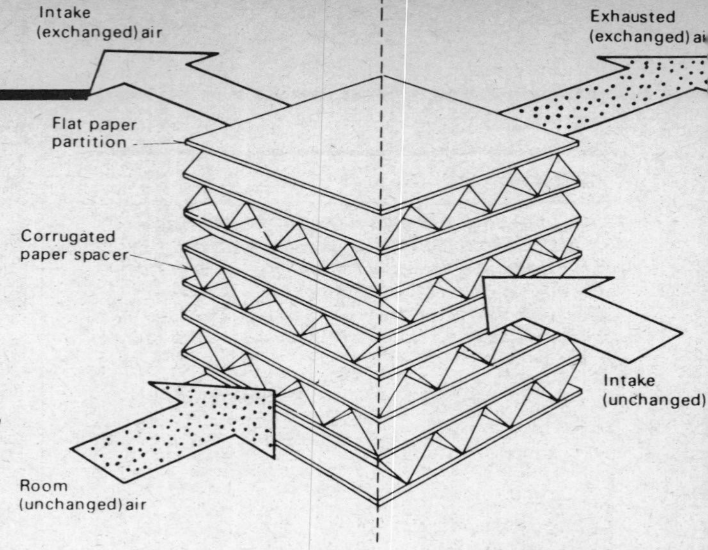

↑ A Lossnay element showing air passage and heat exchange.

Lossnay heat exchange ventilators

When Amory Lovins first told me about this air-to-air heat exchanger, I found its claimed performance hard to believe — it'll retrieve about 75% of the heat from stale air on the way out of your building! In superinsulated low-infiltration homes, stale air can be a serious problem. In some construction such as brick, there can even be a buildup of mildly radioactive gases inherent in many building materials unless there is a considerable air change rate. But high change rates meant high heat losses until this simple and surprisingly cheap device came along. It'll work backwards too, keeping in the cool air in summer and reducing air conditioner loads. In either case, the interior humidity is more or less unaffected.

Amazing! Lossnays come in many sizes ranging from a bathroom window unit to a huge industrial monster. By Mitsubishi.
—J. Baldwin
[Suggested by Amory Lovins]

Lossnay
$104 - $18,000

Catalog
$1 from:
Melco Sales Inc.
3030 E. Victoria Street
Compton, CA 90221

How to Build a Superinsulated House

Not really how-to, but a chatty selection of things to think about when planning a building in very cold climates. Most of the tips come from hard experience in Fairbanks, and represent the beginning of a documentation of proven cold weather building strategies. It's worth a look. The bibliography includes specialized papers from U. Alaska on such subjects as floors for arctic shelters. —J. Baldwin

How To Build a Superinsulated House
(Cold Weather Edition Project 2020)
Ed McGrath and Friends
1978; 37 pp.

$7 postpaid from:
Project 2020
Box 80707
Fairbanks, AK 99708

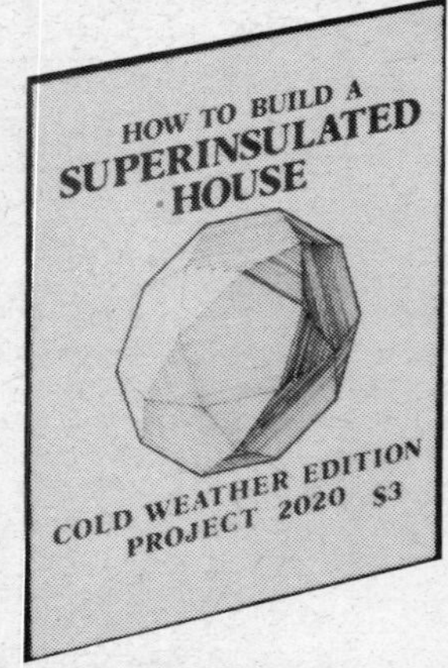

•

VB vs Ventilation

The colder your outside design temperature, the more important a leakfree vapor barrier becomes, and the less you can rely on ventilation. If the temperature stays under 32 degrees for an extended period of time, any moisture which gets into the insulation will freeze there, melting only when the temperature warms up.

In milder climates you can get away with a less than perfect vapor barrier, provided you have plenty of ventilation.

But any moisture in the insulation makes it much less effective (R19 fiberglass performs as R9.5 when 3% of the weight of the insulation is water), so if you can arrange it, a good VB is desirable, even in comparatively mild climates.

WINTER — Heater | SUMMER — Cooler

Fresh warm air
Stale warm air
Fresh cool air
Stale cool air

Insulation

The real name of the game for saving energy in dwellings is insulation. This is particularly true of existing structures that may not be easily adapted to solar or other fom forms of "alternative" energy. These two booklets give very useful information. **Insulation Manual** *shows clearly how to figure insulation needs for heating and air conditioning with a large variety of materials and construction methods. Intended for contractors, it has tables for computing the needs in all 50 states.* **Optimum Insulation Thickness in Wood-Framed Homes** *shows how to figure cost versus thickness, cost being both insulation costs and energy costs saved over the life of the building. This book covers fiberglass only, but their methodology could easily be adapted to other materials. The two books together should enable you to do a pretty rational job.*

For handy techniques of "movable insulation," see pp. 186-187. —J. Baldwin

Insulation Manual
NAHB Research Foundation
1971; 44 pp.

$10 postpaid from:
National Association of Home Builders Research Foundation
P.O. Box 1627
Rockville, MD 20850

Optimum Insulation Thickness in Wood-Framed Homes
(USDA Forest Service General Technical Report)
A.E. Oviatt
1975; 37 pp.
No. 001-001-00394-8

$ .85 postpaid from:
Superintendent of Documents
U.S. Govt. Printing Office
Washington, D.C. 20402

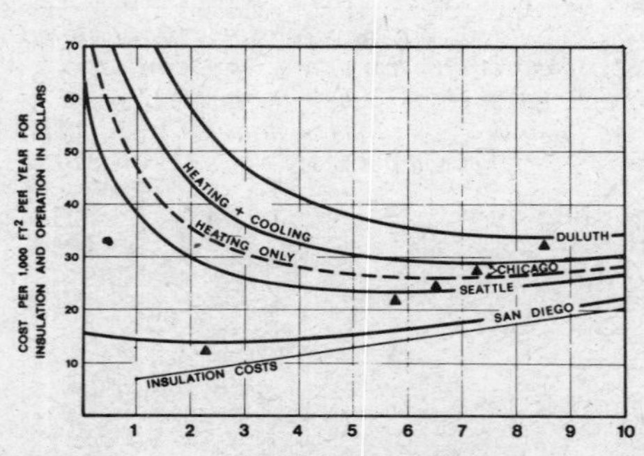

Optimum roof-ceiling insulation thickness.

Room air circulator

A vertical temperature difference of 15°F in rooms with 8-foot ceilings is not uncommon. Hot air rises: to maintain a 70° temperature near the floor of such a house requires at least 85° of unusuable heat at the ceiling. Recycling the hot air with a circulator makes room air temperature more uniform, resulting in less work for the furnace.

An air circulator is a hollow vertical tube sitting on top of a squirrel cage blower that is mounted in a box. The fan sucks hot air down the tube and blows it out at the floor.

To build one yourself requires not much time or cost. All you need is a 6-inch diameter tube that extends to 6 inches below the ceiling. Plastic pipe, cardboard, or wood (four 1 X 6s to make a square tube) work equally well. Sheet fiberglass, held in a tube shape by wooden collars, also does the trick.

Below the tube the fan sits in a box with a vent in one side. The whole unit is light enough to pick up and move from room to room.

For remodeling or new construction, consider building a circulator into the wall as a permanent fixture, similar to a wall-mounted gas furnace. One fan could then service two rooms simultaneously. This is also an effective way of transferring warm air from a heated room to an adjoining room that has no heat source, as long as you provide for a return of cool air to the heated room. A door or a connecting hallway will do; the point is to equalize the pressure between the two rooms so the blower doesn't work so hard.

Electric blowers are rated by cubic feet of air moved per minute. Air conditioning or electrical supply houses sell them. Size the motor so that the blower is able to cycle a room's volume of air 3 times each hour (1/20th of a volume change per minute). With this air flow rate, you can get your floor and ceiling air temperatures to within 2-3° of each other.

—Richard Nilsen
[Suggested by Jay McGrew and Don Frey]

DON RYAN

The Handbook of Moving Air

The ventilation professionals show how to control the air circulation in your humble abode. They cover both nature-powered methods and equipment as well as mechanical. An architect's office would probably wish for more engineering features, but this paper will do just fine for most of us. The material is not copyrighted; a commendable attitude. —J. Baldwin

The Handbook of Moving Air
(A Compilation by The American Ventilation Association)
Harrison A. Dunlavy, Editor
1976; 55 pp.

$2 postpaid from:
American Ventilation Association
P.O. Box 7464
Houston, TX 77008

NOT VENTILATED: 160° 145° 85° 82° 80°
VENTILATED AND INSULATED: 120° 115° 105° 75° 72° 70°

The important part of this sketch is that it shows a hot attic causes a hot ceiling which causes a hot living area.

•

The every day process of living in the home generates surprising quantities of water vapor. Cooking, bathing, washing clothes or dishes, all add water vapor to the air. Each member of the family contributes from 1-1/2 to 2 lbs. of water vapor each day. The total water vapor by a family of 4 living in a modern home adds up to 150 lbs. or 18 gallons per week.

From the Walls In

This is a book for those of us living in this country's 80,000,000 existing dwellings who can't afford or don't want to build new houses and who don't want to work for the utility company or shiver either. It is about remodeling old houses to conserve energy — the space-age word is retrofit. *This is a how-to book worth curling up with on a cold evening and actually reading sequentially — in this genre, a rare thing indeed.*

—Richard Nilsen

From the Walls In
Charles Wing
1979; 226 pp.
$9.95 postpaid from:
Little, Brown and Co.
200 West Street
Waltham, MA 02154
or Whole Earth Household Store

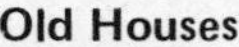

•

Preservation means vigilant maintenance of a building in its original form.
Reconstruction means duplication of an old building, using either new or used materials.
Restoration means undoing all changes made after original construction.
Renovation means changing in any way to make more useful.
Retrofit means improving the energy efficiency of a building.

•

Suppose you have an older structure that never reached the finished wall stage. The boards and framing of such buildings are often quite attractive in a rustic sort of way. Not only would it be an aesthetic loss to install fiberglass and drywall, but an economic loss in terms of living space. In fact, a strict economic analysis shows it to be cheaper in terms of life-cycle cost to insulate on the outside of such buildings. The illustration shows how to add 3½" of rigid foam to an unfinished cottage without in any way changing its inside appearance. Other thicknesses can be accommodated by simply changing the dimensions of the framing. R factors can be traded for dollars by substituting beadboard for Styrofoam. Check prior to the work with the local building inspector. He may insist on 5/8" Sheetrock between the foam and the interior.

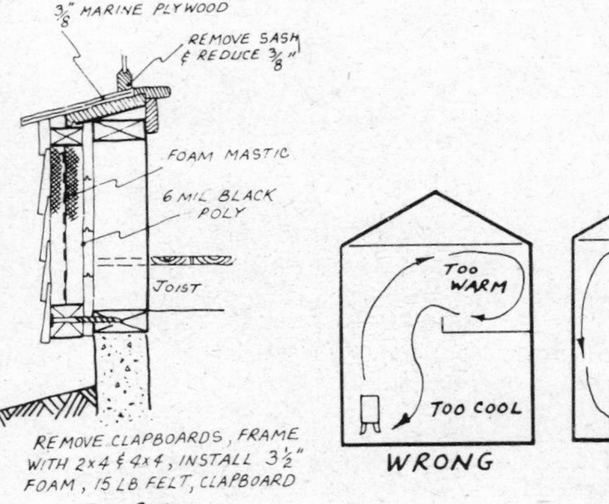

TOO WARM
TOO COOL
WARM
WARM
WRONG
RIGHT

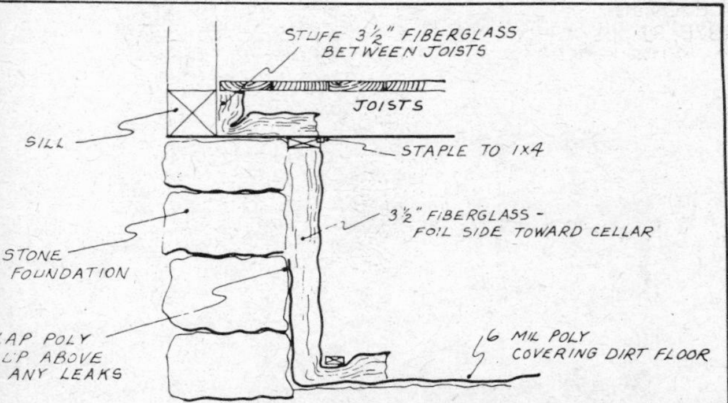

Turbine ventilators

Motorless air conditioning. Here's one supplier.

—Lloyd Kahn

Lomanco Turbine Ventilators
Brochure and nearest dealer location
free from:
Lomanco, Inc.
P.O. Box 519
Jacksonville, AR 72076

Anatomy of window troubles

Old Houses

At times it seems the author of this book has missed his calling — he should have been a country preacher. But when the advice is this detailed and the technical information so well presented, the moralistic tone is no intrusion — in fact it adds to the richness. There is advice on country etiquette, how to pace a project so you don't burn out, and sexual politics, all with a nice Vermont flavor from an author who has been there himself.

If the illustrations and photos were as good as the text, this would be a great book. The photos are, with a single exception, uncaptioned and only fair. The line illustrations are plentiful and detailed and terrible — I suspect they were drawn by someone who has not remodelled. If you were to stack the cribbing as it is drawn in the chapter on foundations, the house you are jacking up could come crashing down on top of you. Fair warning.

After an excellent list of things to look out for in an old rural house, Nash assumes you end up buying the old junker anyway. Often, as in the author's case, it is all that can be afforded. He explains how to remodel an old house from foundation to roof, without glossing over details or ignoring the tremendous amount of hard work involved. Here you can find the remodelling how-to that most carpentry books about new construction leave out. It includes a fine annotated bibliography.

—Richard Nilsen

Old Houses
(A Rebuilder's Manual)
George Nash
1980; 366 pp.
$12.95 postpaid from:
Prentice-Hall, Inc.
Box 500
Englewood Cliffs, NJ 07632
or Whole Earth Household Store

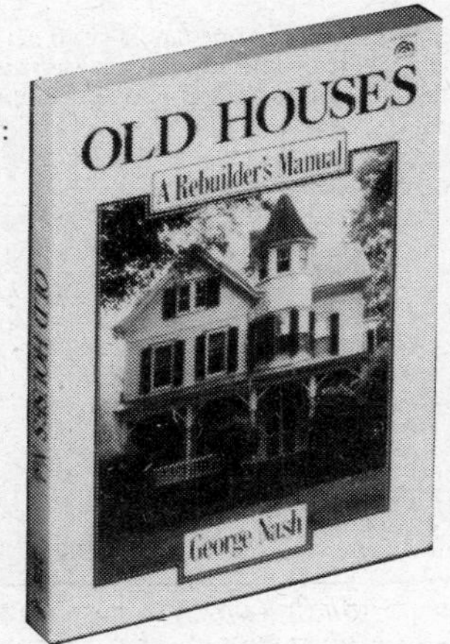

•

. . . a house without tight walls is little better than an open shed. You may as well insulate the walls with dollar bills to save on heat.

•

Try to avoid passing out the beer before the work is well advanced however. The results might not shed water.

•

Many a marriage, many a self-image, have run aground on the rocks of rebuilding. All too often the rebuilder is caught in a whirlpool of obsession, the work at hand becomes more important than the reason it is being done.

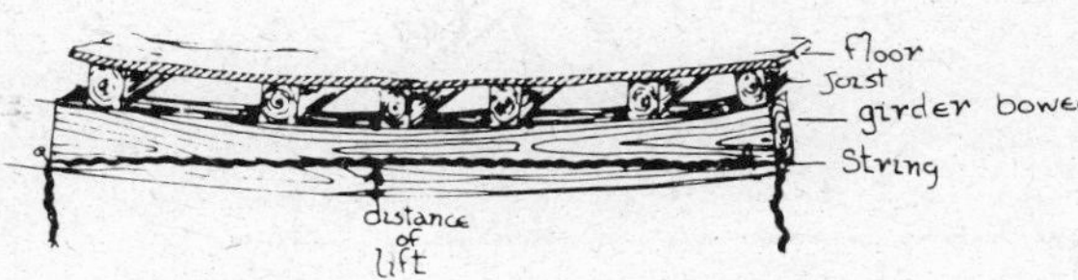

Finding the sag

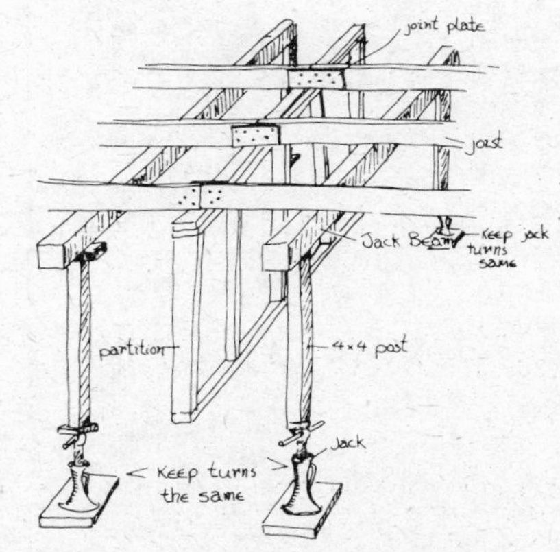

Supporting the floor when removing a load-bearing partition wall.

How to Remodel Buildings

Where the other two books on this page are aimed accurately at the home owner, this one is for the urban sweat-equity types. It's how to turn all or part of a run-down city building into pleasant living again (and pleasant selling, come to that). As the cost of commuting is revaluing urban dwelling, these techniques are getting exercise. It's a big improvement over wreck-and-develop.

—SB

How to Remodel Buildings
Donald R. Brann
1974, 1978; 258 pp.
$5.95 postpaid from:
Easi-Bild
P.O. Box 215
Briarcliff Manor, NY 10510
or Whole Earth Household Store

•

Don't allow piles of garbage, abandoned furniture, cracked plaster or obsolete plumbing to discourage you. In most houses all lead and copper piping has been ripped out. What you see is what you get. Sound floor joists and framing, resting on a solid foundation wall is what you want.

•

Many well-fed cats will eat a poisoned rat. Always drop dead rats in a polyethylene bag. Tie the bag tight before dropping it into a covered garbage container. Many people love cats so don't alienate your new neighbors by destroying their loved ones.

•

Always use exterior grade plywood for subflooring in a bathroom or kitchen. Exterior grade provides an ideal base for ceramic or asphalt tile, linoleum or carpeting. The plywood eliminates movement while it provides a smooth and solid base for floor covering. The addition of plywood subflooring frequently necessitates removing all doors and sawing these 1/2 to 3/4" less across the bottom.

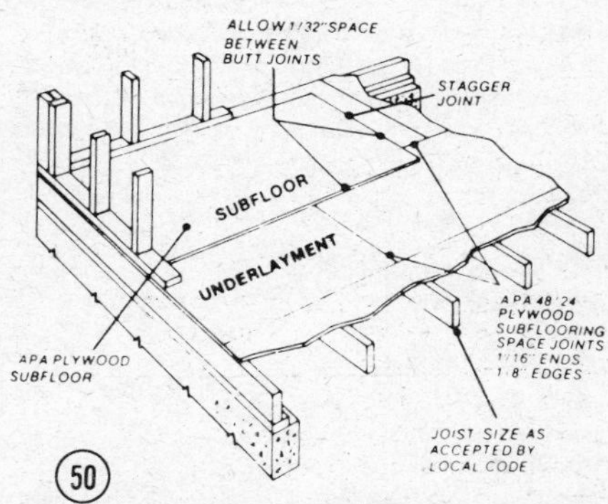

DOUBLE PLYWOOD INSTALLATION
RECOMMENDED FOR TILE, CARPET, LINOLEUM, OR OTHER NONSTRUCTURAL FLOORING

Ceiling fans

Slow turning and quiet, paddle bladed ceiling fans gently stir air to better distribute heat and cool and keep things just moving a bit. They're nice to watch and to sit near too. Here are two sources.

—J. Baldwin

Old-Time Ceiling Fan
$119 plus shipping from:
Delaware Electric Imports
111 S. Delaware Avenue
Yardley, PA 19067

Sears
Paddle Ceiling Fan
$65 plus shipping
(see our p. 348 for address)

•

Costs no more to operate than a light bulb (far less than the smallest air conditioner).

To be hung only on 9' or taller ceilings.

56" diamter 5 speed, white enamel. Spray any color you like!

No oiling ever (maintenance-free sealed bearings).

Great for places that can't be air-conditioned such as laundries and bakeries. —**Old-Time Ceiling Fan brochure**

THE RISING SUN
NEIGHBORHOOD NEWSLETTER

David said he decided a long time ago not to be a revolutionary because no revolutionaries could destroy the bad things about this country as fast as this country will destroy itself because of its bad things.

The Old-House Journal

Preserving restoring old houses is a Good. This loving monthly has the loving details — where to get wood gutters, reactivating old gaslights, slate roof repair, color-matching wood filler, et cetera. —SB
(See **Return to the City**, *p. 313.)*

The Old-House Journal
Clem Lebine, Editor

$16/year (12 issues)
from:
The Old-House Journal Corporation
69 A Seventh Avenue
Brooklyn, NY 11217

•

The government's emphasis on "insulate everything" has led countless thousands to blow sidewall insulation into their old houses. It will be a decade or more before the folly of this step shows up fully in rotted sills and clapboards.

Making Babies

FIRST REMOVE any broken slate, with the Ripper **1** . Slip the pointed end under the broken slate, and hook it over the nail. By hammering downward on the other end of the tool, you'll cut the nail shaft **2**. (You can pry up the surrounding slates by gently driving nails in sideways. Or use the ripper like a shoehorn.) Replace the broken slate

TECHNOLOGICAL TRASHING: The facade of this handsome house has been hidden behind an ugly glass wall that is supposed to act as a solar heat collector.

An 1880 home in Jacksonville, Oregon

American Preservation
Historic Preservation
Preservation News

The attitude and practice of preservation — of whole communities as well as buildings — is getting pretty sophisticated. You can catch up and keep up with these snazzy magazines. **American Preservation** *has the sexiest pictures.* **Historic Preservation** *and* **Preservation News** *are the 4-color bimonthly and newsprint monthly that come with membership in the official National Trust for Historic Preservation.* —SB

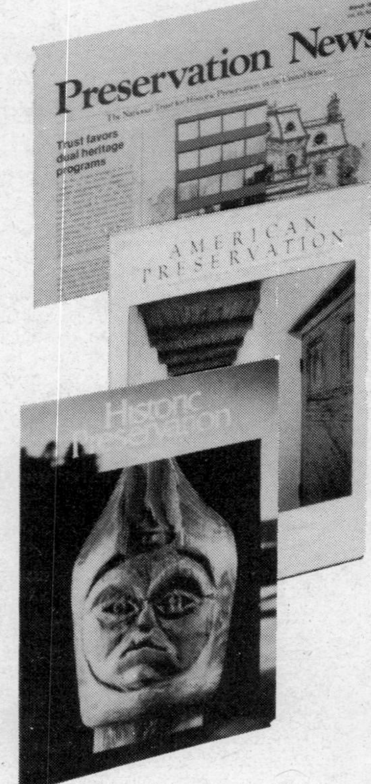

Preservation News
Carleton Knight III, Editor
12 issues/year

Historic Preservation
Thomas J. Colin, Editor
6 issues/year

$15/year for both (includes membership)
from:
National Trust for Historic Preservation
1785 Massachusetts Avenue NW
Washington, DC 20036

American Preservation
(The Magazine for Historic and Neighborhood Preservation)
Porter Briggs, Editor

$15/year (6 issues)
from:
American Preservation
Bracy House
620 East Sixth
Little Rock, AR 72203

The Old-House Journal Catalog

Restoration, not remodelling, is the name of the game here, and when they say old, they mean it — all of the items listed are for houses built before 1920. That gets broken down into 3 categories: Early American — 1700-1840, Victorian — 1840-1900, and Turn-Of-Century — 1900-20.

This book is an outgrowth of **The Old-House Journal,** *and if these folks restore their houses as well as they make catalogs, I'd love to see one someday. 830 companies are listed, 8717 different products and services, all well indexed and cross-referenced. Before saying "They don't make 'em like that any more," look here — you may be pleasantly surprised.* —Richard Nilsen

The Old-House Journal Catalog
Carolyn Flaherty, Mike Carew, et al., Editors
1980; 112 pp.

$8.95 postpaid from:
The Old-House Journal Corporation
69 A Seventh Avenue
Brooklyn, NY 11217

↑ From Beveled Glass Industries, 900 North La Cienega Blvd., Los Angeles, CA 90069.

Tin Ceilings. Especially appropriate for Victorian houses. Send for free brochure. AA Abbingdon Ceiling Co., 2149 Utica Ave., Brooklyn, NY 11234. Tel. (212) BE 6-3251.

RITTER & SON
HARDWARE
SOLID BRASS
DRESSER PULLS
DP-5 $2.95
K-1 K-2 K-3
$1.05 $1.15 $1.15
BIN PULLS
BP-2 $2.25
KEY HOLES
E-1 $1.10
E-6 $1.45
E-8 $1.15
ICEBOX HARDWARE
IB-1 3/8" OFFSET $4.95
HAT HOOKS
HH-2 $2.10
RITTER & SON HARDWARE
DEPT. 990, GUALALA, CA 95445
Send $1.00 for catalog of 100 solid brass 19th Century furniture hardware replicas.
TO ORDER CALL TOLL FREE 800-358-9120
CALIFORNIA CALL—707-884-3363
VISA

•

The Old-House Journal Catalog is your road map to the complex world of old-house supplies. In this Catalog, you'll find 830 companies who sell authentic products and services for houses built before 1920. The Catalog is extensively indexed to make it easy to find what you're looking for.

Porch Parts—Stock Items

(1) Balusters
(2) Posts
(3) Columns
(4) Capitals
(5) Spindlework
(6) Other

By Gone Era (GA)
C—E Morgan (WI) *(2,3,5,5)*
Cumberland Woodcraft Co., Inc. (PA) *(2)*
Hallelujah Redwood Products (CA)
House of Moulding (CA) *(1,2,5)*
E.A. Nord Company, Inc. (WA) *(1,2,3,5)*
Turncraft (OR) *(1,2,3,5)*
Verine Products & Co. (UK) *(3)*
Victorian Reproduction Enterprises (MN)
Vintage Wood Works (TX) *(5)*

● **Renovator's Supply**
71-A Northfield Rd.
Millers Falls, MA 01349
(413) 659-3542
RS/O MO
A wide selection of fine quality items for restoration, renovation and decoration of the Antique Home. Comprehensive 48-page catalog of old style Brass and Wrought Iron hardware, specialty lighting, building supplies, tools, plumbing fixtures, fireplace equipment, pewter and brass accessories, garden supplies and other miscellaneous items suited to restoration work. Illustrated catalog $2.00 refundable with purchase.

PULL CHAIN TOILET

•Handcrafted oak tank with durable stainless steel liner, brass pipe and fittings
•Designed by licensed plumber and craftsman

Also available copper kitchen sink, oak bath sink, and copper bathtub

Send $1.00 for brochure

S. Chris Rheinschild
2220 Carlton Way
Santa Barbara
California 93109
(805) 962-8598

•

We would like to expose the logs on the historic log house we have purchased, but we have heard that it is not a good idea to remove the clapboard siding and the interior plaster. Why? C. M. Johnson, Cleveland, Ohio

Removal of the siding and plaster may be historically incorrect and also physically detrimental to the structure. Even if you accept the maintenance problem of patching the mud mortar, the logs are still exposed to the weather. Modern water repellants or "water-proof" coatings have generally proved to be ineffective, lasting only two to three years, often trapping moisture and darkening the logs or giving them a glossy unnatural appearance. (David W. Look, AIA, HCRS)

—Historic Preservation

"We like to think of it as a partial victory for the forces of historic preservation."

—Preservation News

The Dome Builder's Handbook

After the spate of domes and dome books of the 60's — following Buckminster Fuller's lead — the practice has dwindled in enthusiasm and gained in precision and practicality. This book has both, along with sundry construction dramas and the fair warning, "If you want to build a full-fledged dome house, it should be because you want to live in that kind of space and are willing to go to a little extra trouble to have a house that is unique."
—SB

The Dome Builder's Handbook
John Prenis, Editor
1973; 107 pp.

$5.60 postpaid from:
Running Press
38 South 19th Street
Philadelphia, PA 19103
or Whole Earth
Household Store

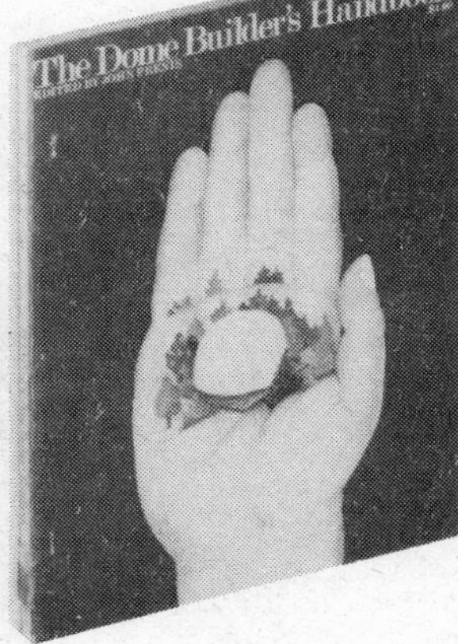

•

Another time, my helpers and I had the dome about three quarters complete when it became obvious that something was badly wrong. Struts refused to stay in place, hubs pushed outwards, while others pressed inwards. I pushed and pulled at base hubs, and shifted leveling blocks from one spot to another, to no avail. Naturally this was just the time when a crowd of curious bystanders gathered to ask foolish questions about the dome and why it wasn't working. Finally we found the trouble—— someone had put a short strut where a long one should have been. When that was corrected, the distortion disappeared, and so did all our problems. With proper color coding, the mistake would have been obvious at once, or more likely, would not have happened at all.
Be sure tools and materials will be available when needed, and don't skimp on things like ladders and scaffolding. Trying to make do with makeshifts can get somebody hurt.

•

After the dome was completed and all seemed fine because of the low cost, the happy sightseers, the attention and discussion, it was distressing to find that it was almost impossible to seal weather tight. Apparently others have had the same problem, but I didn't know that or how to profit from their experience, so it took at least three attempts to get favorable results. Metal strips and caulking worked for about a month, until the differences in expansion rates allowed the seams to pop open again. Resealing with heavier roofing compounds had the same dismal effect. Aluminum sheets from the Twin Falls newspaper printing department applied with staples worked much better. The most positive way to roof a dome that I have found is shingling. Asphalt shingles are easier to apply than cedar shingles, also the former cost less.

A fifty-foot full oblate spheroid (2v with a 14" hub and 6 x 8 struts on the lower hemisphere and 4 x 8 struts on the upper) with windows of smoked Plexiglas and eleven pie-shaped decks inside. Completing this ship took several years out of Alan Hart and Robert Good's lives.

Dome Builder's Handbook No. 2

The best book for deciding if you want to live in a dome. It has a wealth of color pix of various domes and a good rundown on all the major dome manufacturers. —SB

Dome Builder's Handbook No. 2
William Yarnall
1978; 126 pp.

$6.95 postpaid from:
Running Press
38 South 19th Street
Philadelphia, PA 19103
or Whole Earth
Household Store

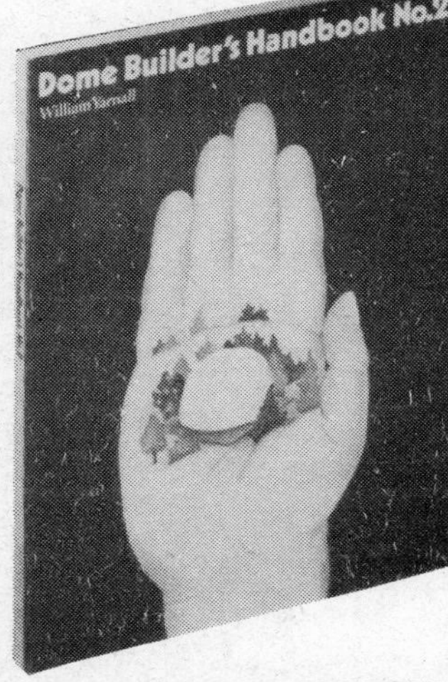

Space Structures

One of the very few outfits to get away from building domes that are mere shingled blobs on the landscape, Space Structures offers a wide variety of stock and custom mass-producible types and sizes. —J. Baldwin

Space Structures
Catalogs

free from:
Space Structures
155 DuPont Street
Plainview, NY 11803

↑
International Exhibit Center, Jeddah, Saudi Arabia. Client: Al-Harithy Establishment

Dome Notes

Many leaky domes have pretty well removed such construction from faddishness. Yet there are still very good reasons for making a dome. Extraordinarily good thermal performance is probably the most important. Regrettably, most available dome books concentrate on esthetics, grooviness or economics (usually unrealistically), leaving waterproofing and other real-world details to the builder's guess. Now there are some real workbooks beginning to appear. This is one. It concentrates mostly on clearly explaining the geometry, tensegrity structures, the design and testing of hubs, and fire safety. The fire section is most detailed; the author actually deliberately burned down an instrumented dome to get the facts! If domes are part of your life, you might be interested.
—J. Baldwin

Dome Notes
Peter Hjersman
1975; 201 pp.

$7.50 postpaid from:
Bookpeople
2940 Seventh Street
Berkeley, CA 94710
or Whole Earth
Household Store

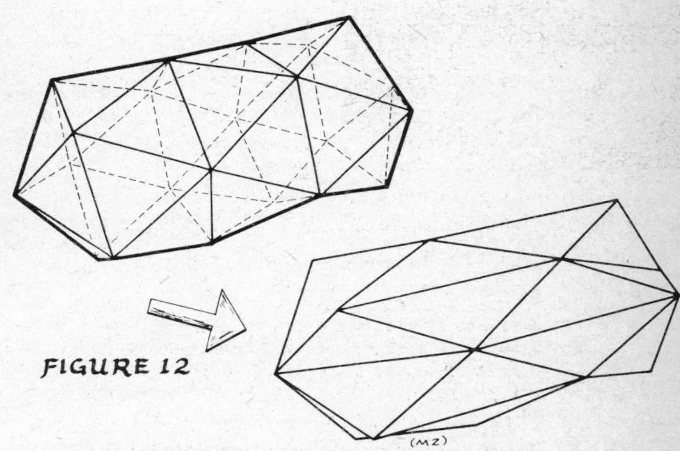

Aggregates: Icosahedra can be aggregated and diamond solids can be generated from some of them.

FRAME AND PANEL ASSEMBLY

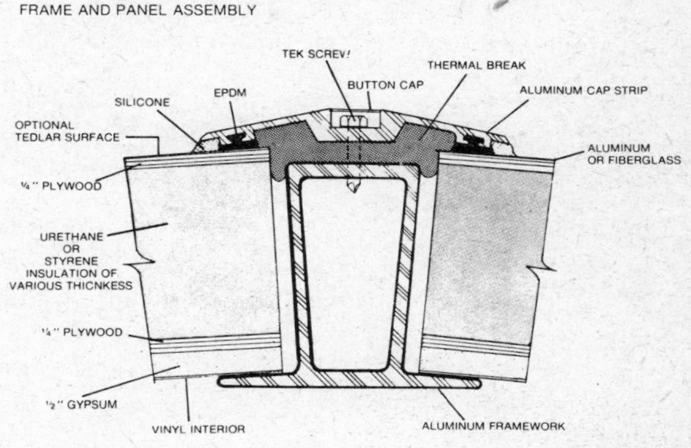

THE ARCHIMEDEAN OR SEMI-REGULAR SOLIDS ANALYSED BY NUMBER AND SHAPE OF FACES

THE POLYGONS OF THE SEMI-REGULAR SOLID FACES

truncated icosahedron
truncated octahedron
icosidodecahedron
THE NUCLEAR TRUNCATED TETRAHEDRON
cuboctahedron
rhombicosidodecahedron
truncated cuboctahedron
snub dodecahedron
snub cube
small rhombicosidodecahedron
small rhombicuboctahedron
truncated dodecahedron
truncated cube

ALTERNATIVE DODECAHEDRAL FACE
ALTERNATIVE CUBIC FACE
FACE NODE EDGE
EDGE NODE FACE
ICOSAHEDRON
OCTAHEDRON

RELATIONSHIP OF FACES TO PARENT SOLIDS

Order in Space

A book by an experimental mathematician on order in space. ". . . space defining, distribution patterns, space filling properties, packing & stacking, economy grids and communication linkages." There are exciting insights into structure in nature, and exploratory diagrams of the functions possible in space. —Lloyd Kahn

Order in Space
(A design source book)
Keith Critchlow
1970; 120 pp.

$9.95 postpaid from:
The Viking Press
299 Murray Hill Parkway
East Rutherford, NJ 07073
or Whole Earth
Household Store

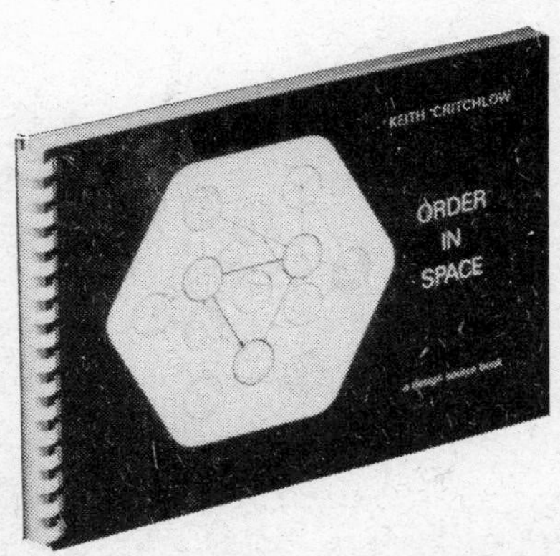

THE RISING SUN
NEIGHBORHOOD NEWSLETTER

Peter Spectre went to a Frank Zappa concert in Amherst, and in the middle of it, someone in the balcony threw a whiskey bottle at Frank Zappa and hit him in the arm. Zappa instantly stopped the music, called for the houselights, hauled his stool to the middle of the stage and said, "I'm not playing another note till the cocksucker who threw that bottle is in jail." Peter thought, "There goes the concert." But as soon as Zappa spoke, the people in front started looking back because they knew that was generally where it had come from and of course the closer people were sitting to the thrower the more specifically they knew where he was and they looked in that specific direction and the people next to him and in back of him looked right at him and within 4 or 5 seconds everyone in the whole place was looking at one guy, and the cops went over, picked him up and took him away. He didn't say a word. Zappa ordered the houselights down, went back to his guitar, and finished the concert.

Frei Otto and Institute for Lightweight Structures

Tension structures are one of the better ways to cover a space with minimum material. Such structures are not the floppy, buffeting, awkward canvas shapes we recognize in revival meeting tents. Rather, they are tough, semi-rigid membranes of startling grace that can withstand weather extremes without failure. The technique invites lightness and portability. Smaller scale structures can be executed by individuals at a technical level that results in useful performance.

Tensile Structures *is devoted to pneumatic structures and tent and cable-net structures, both amazingly explored.*

IL 1 *— Deals with determination of minimal net structures by use of soap film analysis and other methods.*

IL 2 *— Explores "The City in the Arctic." The covering of a large area which would be maintained as an artificial climate in a location otherwise not easily inhabited. Not exactly back to the land, but there are many exciting ideas presented in the form of feasibility studies.*

IL 6 *— Covers an array of subjects including more biology, spiderwebs, structural analysis of plants, some more soap film work, and a presentation of computer-drawn structures that can be viewed in 3D using special goggles provided with the book.*

IL 7 *— A comprehensive report on studies made for shade roofs made from plastic nets in a hot dry climate. Includes climate studies, various proposals, and a discussion of the economics involved.*

IL 8 *— This one includes every kind of net you can think of, including anti-submarine nets and spiderwebs, with the theory, construction techniques, and architectural possibilities of nets. Otto's Montreal and Munich structures are shown in detail.*

The other Tensile Structure books include: **Nets in Nature and Technics, Pneumatics in Nature and Technics, Lightweight and Energy Technics, Convertible Pneumatics, Tents** *and a forthcoming volume called the* **Air Hall Handbook.**

The entire group of IL books will noticeably dent your savings account, as well as feed and inspire your mind. Your local library might go for the whole set.

—J. Baldwin

Tensile Structures
Frei Otto, Editor
1962, 1973; 171 pp.
$19.95 postpaid from:
The M.I.T. Press
28 Carleton Street
Cambridge, MA 02142
or Whole Earth Household Store

These are the books from the Institute for Lightweight Structures:

IL 1: The Experimental Determination of Minimal Nets
1971; 56 pp.
$7.50 postpaid

IL 2: Project Study City in the Arctic
1971; 56 pp.
$10 postpaid

IL 6: Biology and Building, Part Three
1973; 86 pp.
$15 postpaid

IL 7: Shadow in the Desert
1972; 88 pp.
$10 postpaid

IL 8: Nets in Nature and Technics
1975; 430 pp.
$34.50 postpaid

IL 9: Pneumatics in Nature and Technics
1977; 336 pp.
$28.50 postpaid

IL 11: Lightweight and Energy Technics
1978; 256 pp;
$32.50 postpaid

IL 12: Convertible Pneumatics
1976; 211 pp.
$17.50 postpaid

IL 16: Tents One
1976; 160 pp.
$20 postpaid

all from:
Wittenborn Art Books
1018 Madison Avenue
New York, 10022

Model for Otto's West German Pavillion at Expo 67, Montreal. —Tensile Structures

Stable edge knot with fitting for textile net cables; specific hole for fixing the net cable termination; IL model (1973). —IL 8

Olympic Roofs Munich 1972 —IL 8

Pneumatic Structures

The modern Big Bad Wolf doesn't huff and puff, he pulls the plug on your blower or maybe takes a bite out of your dining room wall. It wouldn't be the house coming down that would get you, though. Pneumatic structures have advanced far beyond being threatened by simple failures. They've gone beyond the pool-cover shape too, as this exciting presentation shows. And the presentation goes beyond photographs (707 of them) by including pattern theory and an explanation of how to calculate stresses. This is the most thorough book on the subject I've seen. (Something pneu on every page, har har.)

—J. Baldwin

A star-shaped plan with widened ends makes the constrictions and saddle surfaces appear clearly. The membrane is higher at the center than at the lateral domes. Even if the surface areas were equal, the curvature of the membrane, due to the constrictions, would cause the central dome to rise above the lateral domes. This experiment also revealed that pneumatic structures are unrivaled in adaptability. Any plan shape can be spanned by a pneumatically tensed membrane. However, the resulting shapes frequently differ in usefulness and structural efficiency. —Tensile Structures

Pneumatic Structures
(A Handbook of Inflatable Architecture)
Thomas Herzog
1976; 192 pp.
OUT OF PRINT
Oxford University Press

Get this book back in print!

BLASTING

by Keith Britton
Blast Masters, Inc.
San Leandro, California

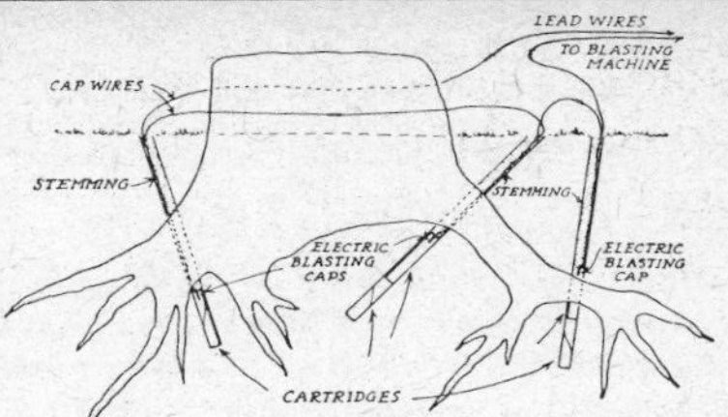

IN THE DRAWING BELOW, WE ILLUSTRATE THE LOADING OF A LARGE, HEAVILY-ROOTED STUMP WITH A NUMBER OF DISTRIBUTED CHARGES. NOTE THAT ELECTRIC FIRING HAS BEEN USED, TO ACHIEVE INSTANTANEOUS DETONATION OF ALL CHARGES. AND, WHEN PLACING MULTIPLE CHARGES, ONE CHARGE IS OFTEN PLACED DIRECTLY UI DER THE TRUNK AREA TO SPLIT AND LIFT IT, AND THE OTHER CHARGES PLACED UNDER THE HEAVIEST ROOTS.

—**Blaster's Handbook**

BLASTING is rapidly changing from an undesirable laborer's job to a skilled profession with good pay and status. Smart employers are learning that good people cost much less than bad blasting, and in many states employers are required to hire only licensed blasters. Professional blasting has never looked better as a career or an important extension of marketable skills. Amateur blasting has lost ground. Though in some states only blasters qualified by experience and examination may use explosives, in most it is still fairly easy to obtain explosives and blast legally on your own or a neighbour's property, so long as it is rural and not a site of employment.

The amateur or small user has made some gains, the most important being two part explosives. One part is a powder, mostly ammonium nitrate, a strong oxidiser, and good garden fertiliser. The other is a liquid, mostly a nitroparaffin widely used as a paint stripper. Combine the two parts by pouring the liquid into the powder and you have manufactured an excellent high explosive, an act which requires a manufacturer-limited permit from the ATF (Alcohol, Tobacco and Firearms), $10. Unmixed, no magazine is required for storage — though anyone not totally irresponsible will store the components separately and under lock and key. Blasting caps are necessary and require proper storage, but it is not difficult to meet ATF Class II indoor storage requirements for quantities of 100 caps or less. Two part explosives are available as KINEPAK from Atlas distributors and, in a superior formulation, as NIPAK from other distributors (information on the latter from: Nipak Energy Corporation, 13601 Preston Road, Suite 1007-W, Dallas, Texas 75240).

While on the subject of blasting caps, it may be worth noting that recent studies have proved what many blasters have felt for years — Hercules lousy, Du Pont fair, Atlas noticeably better, Ensign Bickford non-electrics clear best. I can add my personal observation that British ICI caps were even worse than Hercules. The ranking is liable to change, of course, as future and even some present products differ from those tested.

An intelligent, careful individual, with the self discipline to rigidly follow safety rules to the letter can learn blasting entirely from books and with hazards no greater than those involved in becoming a self taught electrician. But it is far preferable to obtain help and guidance from someone experienced. Ask your local explosives distributor — under "explosives" in the yellow pages — for the name of someone who may help. And ask your local sheriff too. Rural policemen are almost invariably knowledgeable and outstandingly helpful, and you will be starting a relationship you may later find invaluable for crowd or traffic control. Both the sheriff and the experienced blaster will be able to help with the maze of regulations, and in some states you need all the help you can get, but the latter can also teach you his craft.

If you have to go it alone, it may be worth buying **Explosive Training Manual** by R.C. Friend. The book is unattractively written and even less attractively produced, but is the only book available which is organised to teach. For the modern professional blaster it is simplified to the point of oversimplification and much, particularly the explosive material featured, is obsolescent or obsolete. But for that reason the book is valuable in that it contains much "that it was once needful for the wise to know" — particularly regarding the tools, methods and uses for explosives in a low technology agricultural environment, material otherwise out of print.

Be warned, however, that some of the advice is lethally unsound on page 33 of the **Explosive Training Manual** regarding use of a carbide lamp for lighting fuse. First, naked flames are NEVER safe in the vicinity of explosives. Second, a carbide cap lamp is positioned where an inadvertent movement of the head may light one fuse while the blaster is working on another. Third and most important, a large hot flame tends to melt the tarry coating of the fuse which burns and drips, masking the "spit" which is the indication that the fuse is burning, and which is rendered even more difficult to see against the brilliant glare of the carbide flame. It's not good to be still doggedly frying one end of a fuse when the flame reaches the other . . .

Use electric caps for safety, fired by a purpose-designed exploder, never batteries. Low voltage circuit design and testing is generally well beyond the skill and equipment of even experienced professionals, which is why a practice like lighting fuse with a carbide lamp is forbidden in most blasting regulations. Because of such defects in the book, it should not be bought unless there is available a cross check of unimpeachable soundness — such as the **Du Pont Blasters Handbook**. ■

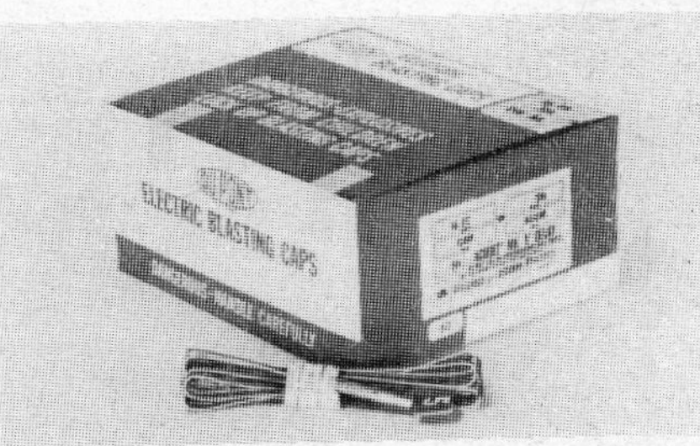

Explosives Training Manual
(A complete illustrated course dealing with the safe handling and effective use of explosives)
Robert C. Friend
1975; 212 pp.
$10 postpaid

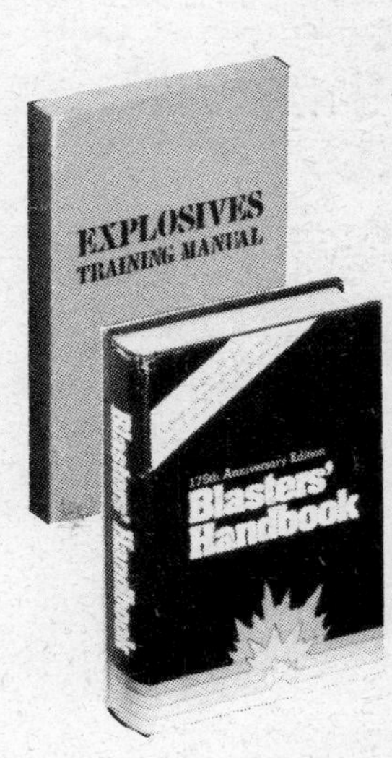

Blaster's Handbook
(175th Anniversary Edition Edition)
E.I. du Pont de Nemours Company
1802, 1977; 494 pp.
$18 postpaid

both from:
ABA Publishing Company
406 West 32nd Street
Wilmington, DE 19802

Yurts

The traditional yurt in modern dress is a rather nice place to live. Tighter and more solid (but more complex and heavier) than a tipi, a yurt might make a good vacation home or place to stay while you're building a house. When you're done with it, take it down. There is also a yurt-like building available that is not portable. These are easy ways to make a round simple house, if that's what you want. The outfits listed below are related in some way I can't figure out. I'd deal with the nearest one.

—J. Baldwin

Yurts Plans
$10 - $20 (approx.)

Yurts Information
free

both from:
Centering Shelterworks
84065 N. Pacific Highway
Creswell, OR 97426

or Vital Designs
P.O. Box 18
Talmage, CA 95481

or The Yurt Foundation
Bucks Harbor, ME 04618

•

Complete Yurt — Consists of our standard yurt frame: Center ring, rafters, lattice wall and door frame with . . .
- Octagonal skylight
- Trimmed door and latch
- Canvas top and sidecover, including 2 Velcro-framed windows and screens

Yurts Diameters and Costs: 14' is $1720, 16' is $1860, 20' is $2430, 24' is $3145.

Kit Yurt — Kit form of Complete Yurt. Includes the standard yurt frame — cut, drilled and ready to assemble with . . .
- Octagonal skylight, ready to assemble
- Trimmed door and latch
- Sewn canvas top and sidecover with 2 Velcro-framed windows and screens
- Completed center ring
- Complete set of instructions for assembly

Yurts Diameters and Costs: 14' is $1400, 16' is $1500, 20' is $2075, 24' is $2645.

—**Shelterworks**

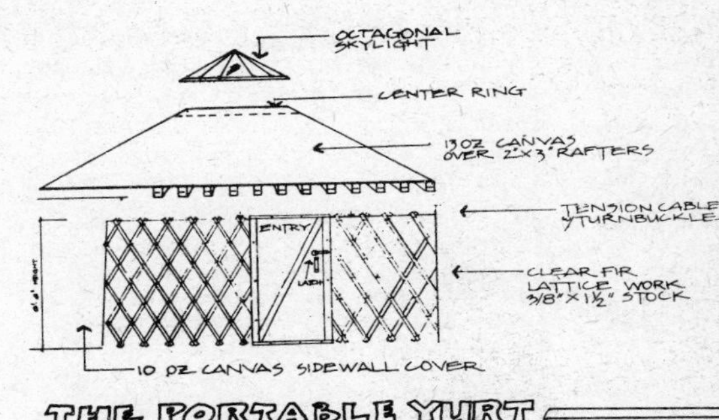

THE PORTABLE YURT

Lo Tech Air Domes

Puffed-up temporary structures. Inflatables ARE fun.

—SB

Lo Tech Air Domes
Poor Willie Productions
1973; 74 pp.
$5 postpaid from:
Poor Willie Productions
Boston Center for the Arts
539 Tremont Street
Boston, MA 02116

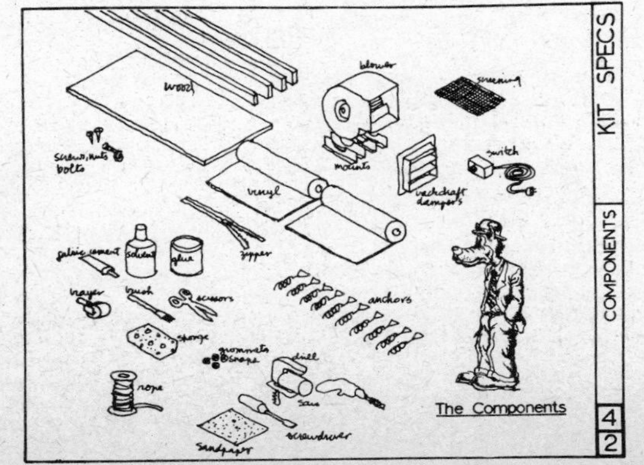

THE RISING SUN
NEIGHBORHOOD NEWSLETTER

The first day of the BART shutdown, when the buses were such a mess, TV news showed interviews with the people waiting in line for hours at the Transbay Terminal. Andrea noticed that all the people who were good-natured about it ("Oh, it's not so bad.") were men and all the people who were angry ("This is a disgrace!") were women. She figured out it was because the women had to go home and make dinner and the men would find dinner waiting whenever they got there.

The Underground House Book

What domes were to the '60s-with-a-capital-6, underground houses appear to be to the '80s (no capital 8 yet). Hopefully, they will fare better than domes did. One excellent reason they might is that they often make the best use of the best habitat for homes — on hillsides, out of the agriculturally valuable, flood-prone valleys. Dug into south-facing slopes in cold climes and north-facing slopes in hot climes (vice-versa south of equator), the cozy buildings are earth-tempered solariums.

This book from always-competent Garden Way is a highly inviting survey of most of what's been tried (3000 by 1979) and imagined so far. —SB

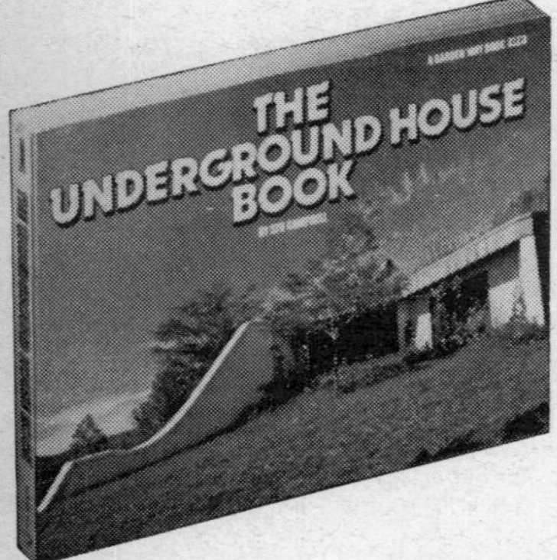

The Underground House Book
Stu Campbell
1980; 210 pp.
$9.95 postpaid from:
Garden Way Publishing Company
Charlotte, VT 05545
or Whole Earth Household Store

Underground Designs

Malcolm Wells, the bearded prophet of underground dwelling (see his article on our pp. 218-219), lets his imagination burrow rampant in this collection of home designs and practical details. Some of the designs are already working, quietly (boy, are they) saving on energy and maintenance. Dig in. —SB

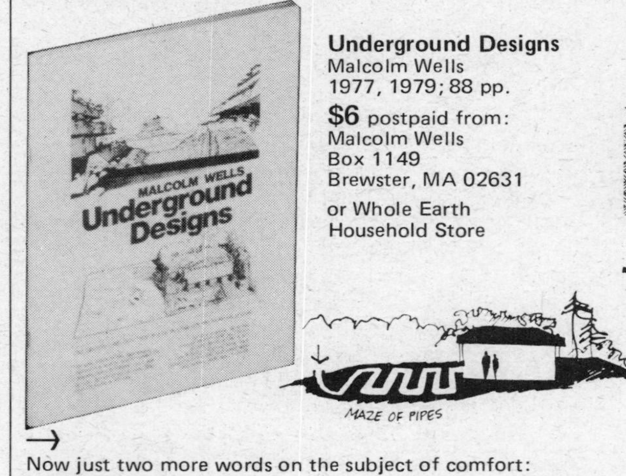

Underground Designs
Malcolm Wells
1977, 1979; 88 pp.
$6 postpaid from:
Malcolm Wells
Box 1149
Brewster, MA 02631
or Whole Earth Household Store

→
Now just two more words on the subject of comfort: *earth pipes*.

You're going to hear a lot about them in the next few years. So far, they seem to exist mainly in the imaginations of underground architects, but they have great potential. The earth pipes, that is, not the imaginations of underground architects. We hear about hotels built above caves being cooled all summer by air drawn from the caverns below. We enter an unheated subway station in January and notice the delightful warmth. And we think about earth pipes, about drawing fresh air into buildings — above-ground or below-ground buildings — through long, buried pipes that would warm the icy winds of winter and cool the hot air of summer, making air conditioning and heating far less expensive. But strangely, very little work appears to be under way in this field.

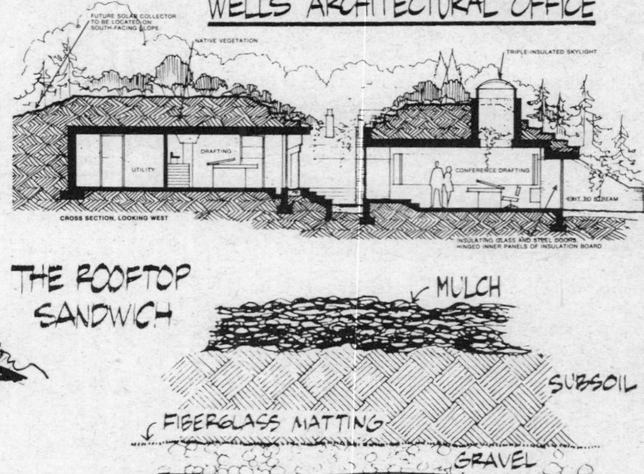

•
Native plants provide not only ecological appropriateness, but also greater drought-resistance and economy. Shallow earth-covered roofs are sometimes very dry during hot, rainless weather. Hardy natives are the best candidates to pull through. In a natural wildgarden only the fittest plants will survive. They will choose from among themselves each year the species best suited for your roof. It's an everchanging, ever-better extravaganza. It's usually best to start by planting a few key shrubs and small trees (if desired), but, given the time, the remaining areas will seed themselves. What about the roots? The plant experts say that roots tend only to go where water goes. Plants have no motive to disturb structures kept dry by waterproofing.

Frank Lloyd Wright's Solar Hemicycle was designed in 1943, but the concept was borrowed from a similar Wright building — a boathouse in Madison, Wisconsin built before the turn of the century. With its earth berm, passive solar heating and cantilevered roof, it's not far from state-of-the-art underground homes of the 1980s.

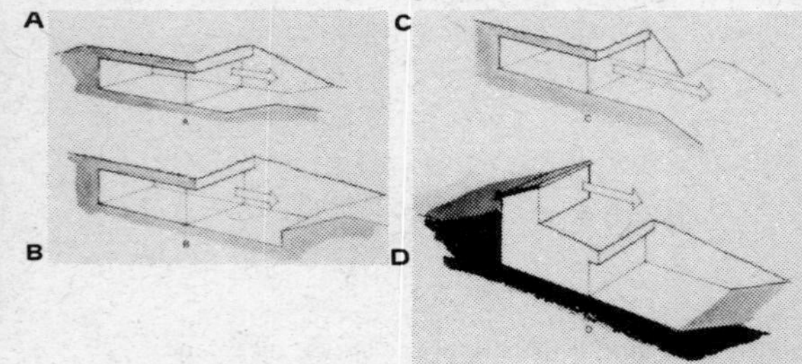

A "bermed" house has earth piled behind it (A). A house that's recessed (B) can have open walls, but the view may be obstructed. A house that's backed into a hillside has an open view (C), while a combination above- and below-grade building might have the best of both worlds (D).

Underground Houses

Another in the growing number of "underground" books, this one is worth a look for its attention to details that only the hard lessons of experience can provide. As with most underground designs unbuilt or built, this one can't be vouched for when it comes to longevity. It's pioneer territory. Exciting and a little maddening. But one thing you won't go wrong on here is attitude. The tips on how to select an excavating contractor, how to pour concrete and how to choose lumber are just right, and are all too often left out of building manuals. If I were considering building an underground house, I'd certainly have this book on hand whether I agreed with all its details or not. —J. Baldwin

Underground Houses
(How to Build a Low-cost Home)
Robert L. Roy
1979; 128 pp.
$5.95 postpaid from:
Sterling Publishing
2 Park Avenue
New York, NY 10016
or Whole Earth Household Store

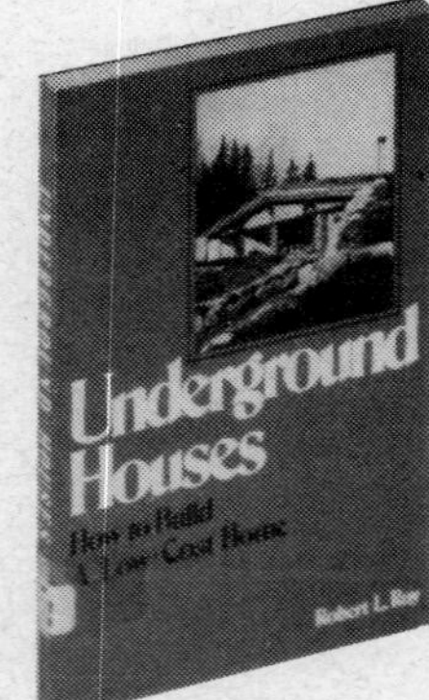

•
Leaks in Skylights

Proper flashing of skylights is tricky business. Our primary mistake, as we learned, was to use soil with poor drainage near the skylights. Drainage is of paramount importance in taking the pressure off any waterproofing system. We cured the problem by digging up all the earth within a foot of the skylights and the main stovepipe. We then cleaned and dried the area thoroughly and applied plenty of roofing cement and 6-mil black polyethylene, well lapped. Finally, we used sand to backfill the skylights and spread wood chips over the sand for the sake of appearance. The sandy area around the large living-room skylight is connected to the bathroom skylight area by a 4-inch non-perforated flexible drain pipe imbedded in the intermediate topsoil. I carefully placed loose hay over both ends of this pipe to prevent infiltration of sand and soil. The bathroom and office skylight areas are similarly drained to the sand-backfilled area adjacent to the east and west walls. The sandy areas around the skylights, then, are finally drained to the primary footing drain system. The 4-inch pipes are sod-covered and invisible. ↓

Skylight of underground house

Earth Sheltered Housing Design

In contrast with previous underground building books however good (Malcolm Wells), this one is a manual of proven procedures; what to do. It's a good one too, though obviously not the last word. More like the second word. It's enough, though, to let you actually design an underground structure with a degree of confidence. That's saying a lot. It is commendably comprehensive and a good value for the money. Astoundingly, over 80,000 copies of the book have been bought. Something's going on. —J. Baldwin

Earth Sheltered Housing Design
(Guidelines, Examples, and References)
The Underground Space Center
University of Minnesota
1979; 318 pp.
$10.95 postpaid from:
Van Nostrand Reinhold
Order Department
7625 Empire Drive
Florence, KY 41042
or Whole Earth Household Store

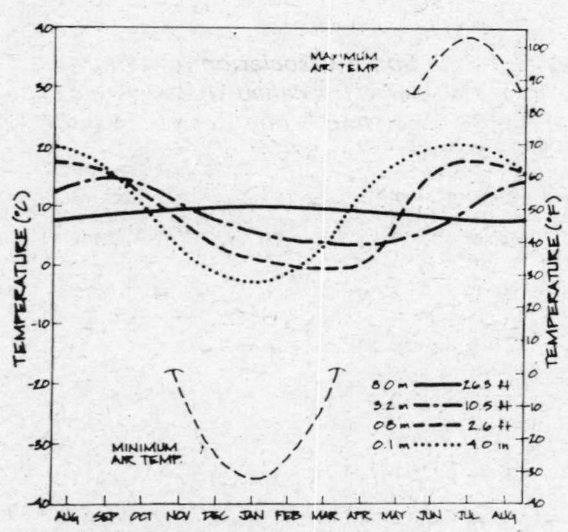

3-2 soil temperature distribution

↑
The great recent interest in earth sheltered housing has resulted primarily from anticipation of substantial energy savings. In typical above ground construction energy is wasted by unwanted heating or cooling of the surroundings. By reducing heat transfer to and from the surroundings less energy is required to maintain desired conditions. Heat loss (or gain) from a structure principally depends on two factors: the ventilation load for heating or cooling intake air, and the heat transmission through the building envelope. In most residences the ventilation load consists of uncontrolled air infiltrating through cracks and holes. These infiltration losses are reduced greatly or eliminated by earth covered construction. Ventilation air then can be controlled so that heat recovery systems can be used effectively.

Dune house, Atlantic Beach, Florida, by William Morgan Architects

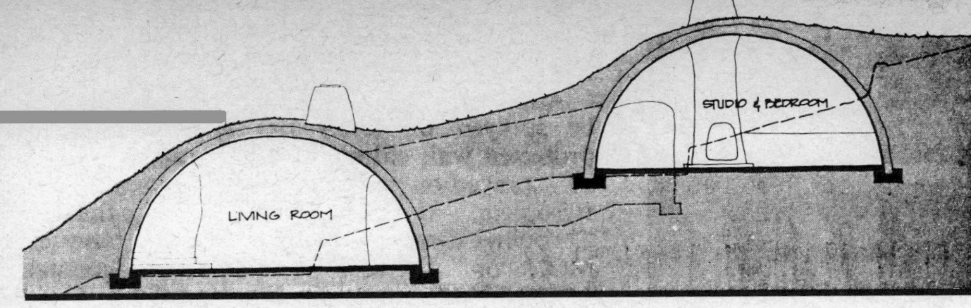

← Each room in the tube home has a fireplace, masonry covered with plaster then blown over with foam.

Earthshelter Digest

As national energy problems (and perhaps cumulative paranoia) loom larger on the near horizon, interest in underground building is picking up steadily. **Earthshelter Digest** *has brief-but-competent presentations of several innovative sub-surface structures, reports on assorted institutional/governmental carryings-on, upcoming conferences, underground waterproofing, what it's like living below surface, landscape architecture, tax benefits on underground shelters, etc. Future issues will contain stuff on financing sub-surface homes, zoning problems, underground recreation, insulating below ground, sub-surface lighting, a regular special section on alternative energy and its applications vis-a-vis underground structures, and like that. A clean editing job by responsible, concerned folks. Support your local underground by subscribing.* —Lewis Watson

Earthshelter Digest
(& Energy Report)
Herb Oviatt, Editor
$15 /year (6 issues)
from:
Earth Shelter Digest
479 Fort Road
St. Paul, MN 55102

The Use of Earth Covered Buildings

This 1975 conference report is still the most comprehensive look at "underground" architecture. The various papers cover everything from history to legal aspects and insurance. There's a fine bibliography with a list of people working on underground structures. This and Malcolm Wells' book are required reading if you're tempted by the advantages of going below the surface.
—J. Baldwin

The Use of Earth Covered Buildings
(Proceedings and Notes of a Conference Held in Ft. Worth, Texas, July 9-12, 1975)
1976; 353 pp.
No. 038-000-00286-4
$5.25 postpaid from:
Superintendent of Documents
U.S. Govt. Printing Office
Washington, D.C. 20402

or Whole Earth Household Store

•

The list of the advantages of earth covered communities over suburbia is compelling: increased housing density (say 3 to 5 times most suburbian developments), increased open space, increased green space, increased acoustic privacy, increased visual privacy, public facilities closer to most dwellings, shopping facilities closer to most dwellings, better opportunities for fully supported and convenient public transit, minimum maintenance to individuals and community, minimum operating expenses, conservation of resources, positive environmental impact relative to alternatives. I have learned that one always needs to add that one can also "see outside" of earth covered dwellings, indeed, such dwellings need not even be below grade. —Frank Moreland

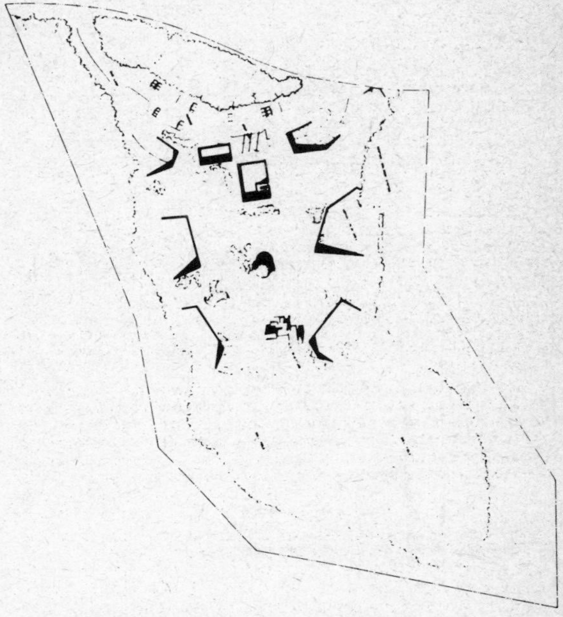

Terraset Elementary School — Reston, Virginia.

The $50 & Up Underground House Book

A boom in private underground shelter construction is clearly trying to happen, and still none of the major publishers have come up with a comprehensive how-to guide for the do-it-yourselfer. Oehler flatly doesn't like concrete, and at the structural core of his sub-surface dwellings is what he calls the "PSP system" (post-shoring-polyethylene), which admittedly flunks most Code requirements. Nevertheless, it sounds like the very best low-cost outlaw home going. Even if you're holding out for a guide on concrete underground construction, Oehler's book provides many times its cost in perceptive tips on sub-surface design, philosophy, living, and underground building in general. —Lewis Watson

The $50 & Up Underground House Book
Mike Oehler
1978; 112 pp.
$7 postpaid from:
Mole Publishing Company
Rt. 1, Box 618
Bonners Ferry, ID 83805

or Whole Earth Household Store

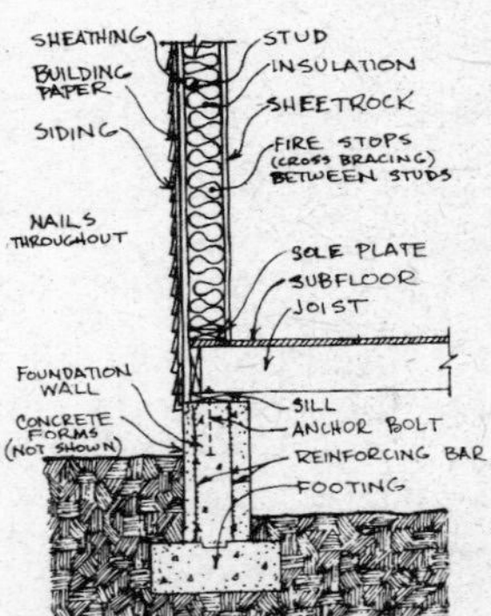

•

While wood is the basic component of the PSP system, polyethylene is the secret of its success. Polyethylene is inexpensive, easy to work with, and readily available. It is an absolute moisture barrier and is what keeps the wooden walls from rotting. While it is true that this plastic deteriorates quickly when exposed to the ultraviolet rays of sunlight, it lasts indefinitely underground.

Cross-section of $500 house

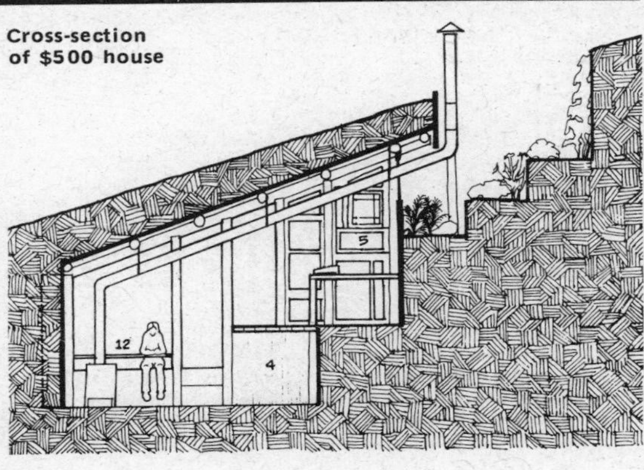

•

We will be dealing primarily with underground houses on hillsides. Hillsides are preferred building sites for a number of reasons. For one, the drainage is better. For another, you stand a better chance of getting a sweeping view. Still another is that hilly land is traditionally less expensive than flat land, and it is what most back-to-the-landers usually wind up with. Sewage disposal is greatly simplified when there is indoor plumbing. Then there are the terrain advantages of building on the warm, sunny south slopes in cold climates and on the cooler northern slopes in hot climates. Finally, and perhaps most importantly, flat land is usually prime agricultural land and should be left as such.

Underground building

There are two organizations concerned with "underground" building. If you are interested in keeping up with the latest developments and/or contributing your findings to the general knowledge, it might pay you to get involved.

American Underground Space Association puts out a publication for its members. It's called **Underground Space**, *runs about 50 pages, and is published bi-monthly. Membership and subscription is $75 a year from:*

Underground Space
Pergamon Press, Inc.
Maxwell House
Fairview Park
Elmsford, NY 10523

And there's the Clearinghouse for Earth Covered Buildings, an information exchange that publishes articles and books and promotes underground building. (Funded by the National Science Foundation [NSF].) You can get information from:

Frank Moreland
The Clearinghouse for Earth-Covered Buildings
P.O. Box 9428
Fort Worth, TX 76107

—J. Baldwin

Design of underground school building

THE RISING SUN
NEIGHBORHOOD NEWSLETTER

When Jesus healed Peter's mother-in-law, who is not identified by name, she immediately got up and made him and the disciples supper.

— Mark 1:30

Homesite Sewage Treatment

SINCE THE FIRST **Whole Earth Catalog**, *consciousness has changed. Most public health officials still have their heads in energy-intensive, high cost, out-of-sight-out-of-mind sewage systems. BUT, the warriors for recycling and returning our feces to fertilizers can be flushed with pride. Laws have begun to change. Grant proposals must include recycling possibilities. The five gallon toilet will be an antique in ten years. Waterless toilets, new types of septic tank system drainfields, greywater recycling systems, bio-gas plants are "experimentally" acceptable. Here's access to a group of people that proved perseverance furthers.* *(For the big picture on water, see pp. 64 - 71.)* *—Peter Warshall*

Goodbye to the Flush Toilet

The best introductory catalog for waterless toilets. Love of composting comes to you and your plumbing. Joel Tarr's essay, "How We Got Where We Are, or the Why and Wherefrom of Sewers" wins the Grammy for top bathroom reading. *—Peter Warshall*

Goodbye to the Flush Toilet
(Water-Saving Alternatives to Cesspools, Septic Tanks, and Sewers)
Carol Hupping Stoner, Editor
1977; 285 pp.

$6.95 postpaid from:
Rodale Books
33 East Minor
Emmaus, PA 18049
or Whole Earth Household Store

•

Science knows now that the most fertilizing and effective manure is the human manure. . . . Do you know what these piles of ordure are, those carts of mud carried off at night from the streets, the frightful barrels of the nightman, and the fetid streams of subterranean mud which the pavement conceals from you? All this is a flowering field, it is green grass, it is the mint and thyme and sage, it is game, it is cattle, it is the satisfied lowing of heavy kine, it is perfumed hay, it is gilded wheat, it is bread on your table, it is warm blood in your veins.
—Victor Hugo, **Les Miserables**, 1862

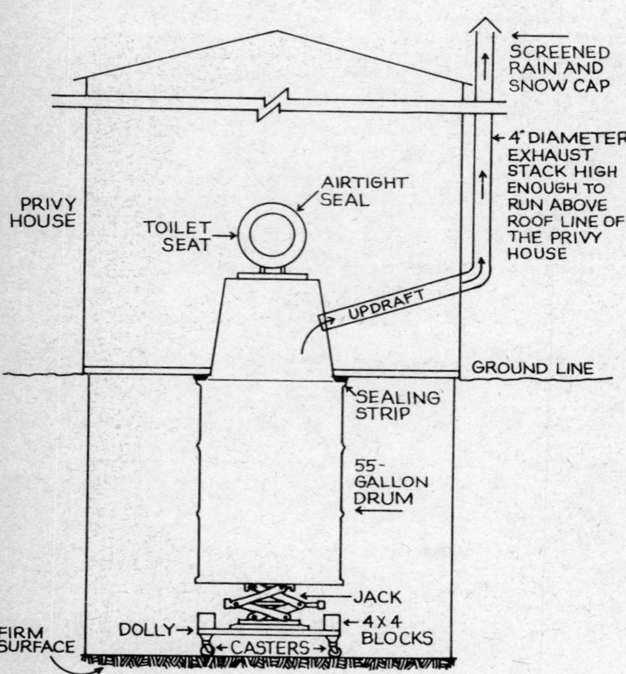

↑

A drum privy can be held tightly against the privy house floor by a small scissors jack dolly.

A heat exchanger built into the ventilation stack of the Clivus Multrum, as shown here, enables cold outside air entering the house to be tempered first by the rising warm air inside the decomposition tank.

↓

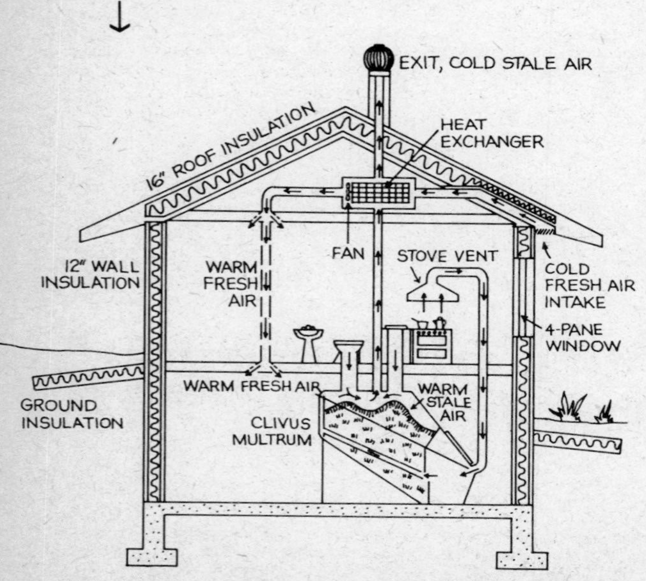

The Toilet Book

If only every fix-it book was as good as this one! Written for the utter dumb-dumb, it explains that porcelain throne in more detail (and with more humor) than most people will believe possible. *—J. Baldwin*

The Toilet Book
(Knowing Your Toilet and How to Fix It — Sometimes)
Helen McKenna
1975; 80 pp.

$3 postpaid from:
Bookpeople
2940 Seventh Street
Berkeley, CA 94710
or Whole Earth Household Store

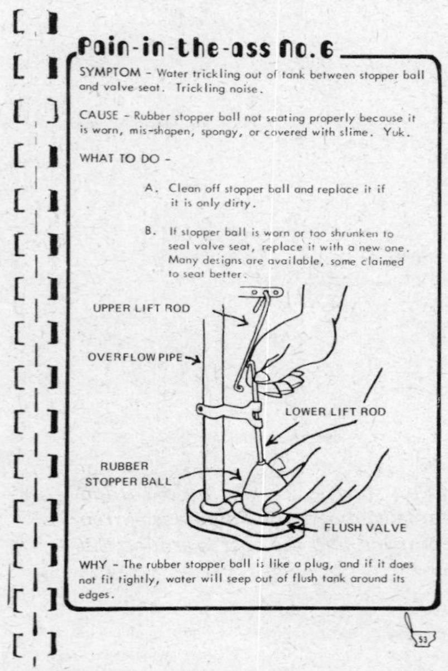

Pain-in-the-ass No. 6

SYMPTOM – Water trickling out of tank between stopper ball and valve seat. Trickling noise.

CAUSE – Rubber stopper ball not seating properly because it is worn, mis-shapen, spongy, or covered with slime. Yuk.

WHAT TO DO –

A. Clean off stopper ball and replace it if it is only dirty.

B. If stopper ball is worn or too shrunken to seal valve seat, replace it with a new one. Many designs are available, some claimed to seat better.

WHY – The rubber stopper ball is like a plug, and if it does not fit tightly, water will seep out of flush tank around its edges.

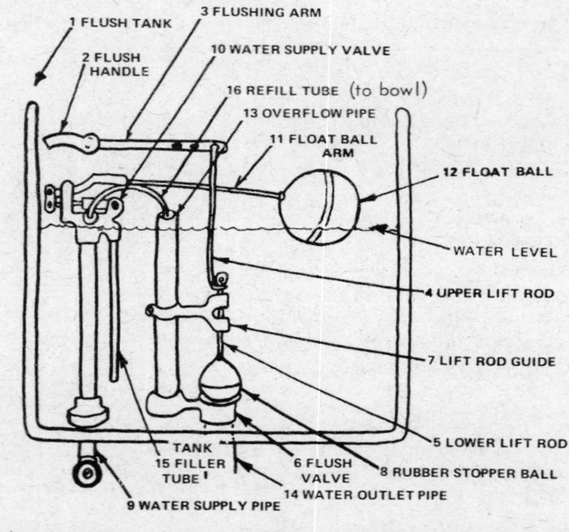

The Toilet Papers

When I first met Sim, the town I lived in was embroiled in Sewage Kung-Fu. State agencies, federal agencies, county agencies and a split electorate all battling about what should be done with the town's "wastes." I was a crazed evangelist for putting our wastes back on the land. Sim asked what was happening. The town summarized: "Shit's the truth."

Soon Sim was State Architect of California, an elegant statesman and educator. He tried to bring to public consciousness the need and delight in recycling feces, urine and water. **The Toilet Papers** *is his book: a compilation of history, dry toilets, greywater designs and philosophical musings on sewage.*
—Peter Warshall

The Toilet Papers
(Designs to Recycle Human Waste and Water: Dry Toilets, Greywater Systems, and Urban Sewage)
Sim Van der Ryn
1978; 124 pp.

$4.95 postpaid from:
Capra Press
631 State Street
Santa Barbara, CA 93101
or Whole Earth Household Store

•

Cities with millions of people living on coastal desert plains using water pumped in from six hundred miles away hang on a very slender thread. As the city devoted to the care and feeding of the automobile fades, streets will be torn up and gardens planted. The soil, now compressed and lifeless dirt, will be restored to life with our composted wastes and greywater. Like the hill towns of Italy which for centuries perched themselves on the rocky unproductive hills, reserving the rich bottom lands for food, the pattern can be reversed so that the ruined agricultural valleys can bloom again, and the hills will be terraced with gardens and houses. In the cities, wind-powered solar heated aquacultural greenhouses will grow fish and shrimp on wastewaters and return purified water for use in the home. The soft edges of wetlands and marshes, cushions against flood and superb biological filters of impurities, can be restored.

•

There is no easy answer to the code dilemma facing the person who wants to build a composting toilet. As is true of building codes, health codes give discretion to the local health officer (usually a medical doctor) to accept alternative systems. But, again, few local officials choose to use the authority they have. Proprietary and generic types of composting toilets and greywater systems are now being tested in Oregon, California, and elsewhere. One approach is to request an experimental permit and agree to submit to regular laboratory tests that measure the fecal coliform present in greywater effluent or compost containing human fecal matter. If you are remodeling your existing house, you may not need to apply for a permit at all. Or you can call your concrete block compost privy a "root cellar."

Astro-Pure

An Astro-Pure rig on your faucet will remove virtually all the coliform bacteria, chloroform traces, bacteria causing diseases such as typhoid and cholera, dysentery, and the several bad tastes like plastic and chlorine. All this for about 4 cents a gallon. Astro-Pure devices come in a number of sizes to fit your needs. *—J. Baldwin*

Astro-Pure
Catalog

free from:
Supermarine
Box 619
Sausalito, CA 94966

AT YOUR GALLEY SINK

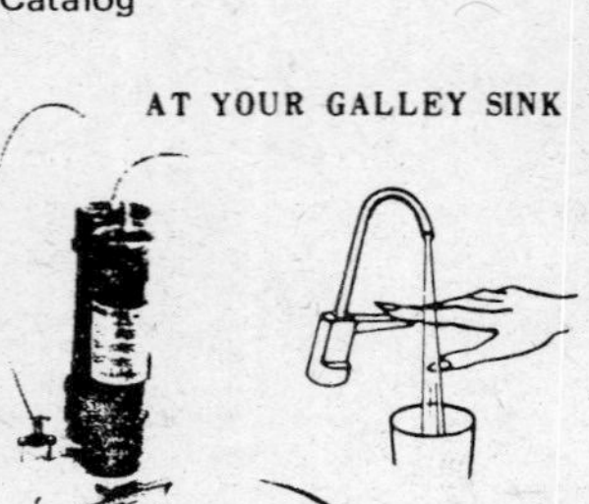

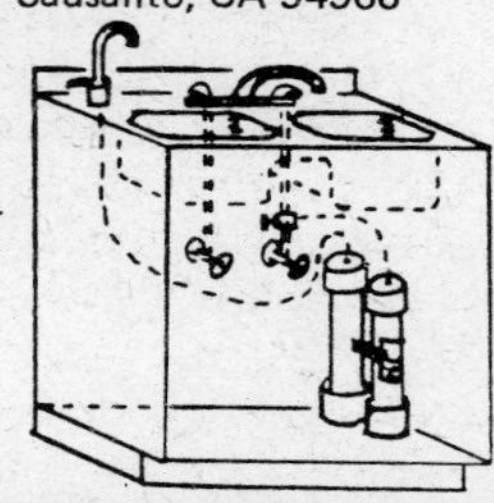

The brick

An American toilet uses between 3 to 6 gallons of good, fresh drinking water with every flush. The most direct way to save water is to stop flushing it away. One brick in the tank above your toilet will displace the water and save you up to a quart on each flush. Two bricks — if this doesn't interfere with flushing power — will save you more. Cherry Hill, New Jersey spent $2,000 on 27,000 bricks. In one year, the council estimated a saving of 34 million gallons. Cherry Hill has 17,000 homes.
—Peter Warshall

Carousel Composting Toilet

The Carousel Composting Toilet has been in use in Norway for six years and is now being manufactured in the United States by Enviroscope, Inc. in Southern California. It is the only composting toilet sold in this country at this time that has the National Sanitation Foundation seal of acceptance.

The Carousel is an aerobic composting toilet that will process both kitchen and body wastes. The composting chamber is divided into four rotating sections. You use one section for six months then rotate to the next one. After all chambers have been used, you return to the first and remove the compost from that chamber and start the process again. This insures that when you remove compost it has not come in contact with fresh wastes for a period of one and a half years.

Small Carousel — for use in a summer cabin or for 2 adults year around, $1,195.

Large Carousel — for year around family use, $1,598.

This is a substantial investment but when you deduct the savings in plumbing lines, vents and connections, the 40% reduction in household water use and the subsequent reduction in leach field size if using a septic tank (where allowed, substitution with a greywater system to recycle bath, dish and wash water), the Carousel becomes a practical alternative to wasting so precious a resource as water and the energy used to transport it to a home and then remove and process the wastes.

—Joseph W. McShane

Carousel Composting Toilet
Information
free from:
Enviroscope, Inc.
2400 West Coast Hwy.
Suite D, Box 2933
Newport Beach, CA
92663

INSTALLATION

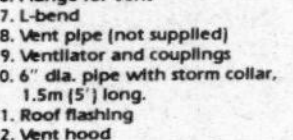

The CAROUSEL consists of:
1. Outer container
2. Inner container
3. Cover
4. Connecting pipe, length 1m (3′ 4″)
5. Commode
6. Flange for vent
7. L-bend
8. Vent pipe (not supplied)
9. Ventilator and couplings
10. 6″ dia. pipe with storm collar, 1.5m (5′) long.
11. Roof flashing
12. Vent hood

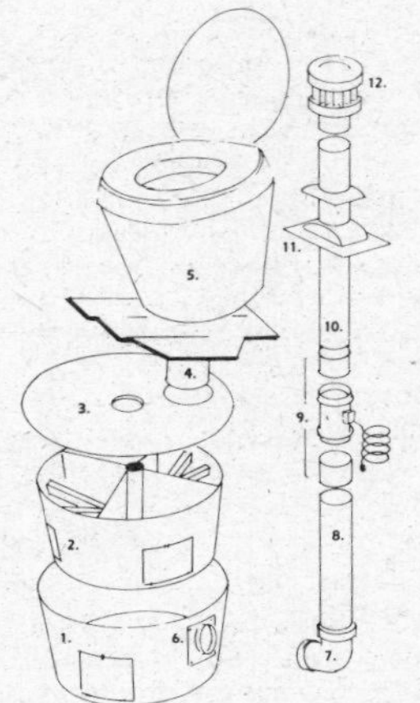

IFO Cascade
Information
$3 from:
Western Builders Co-op
2150 Pine Drive
Prescott AZ 86301

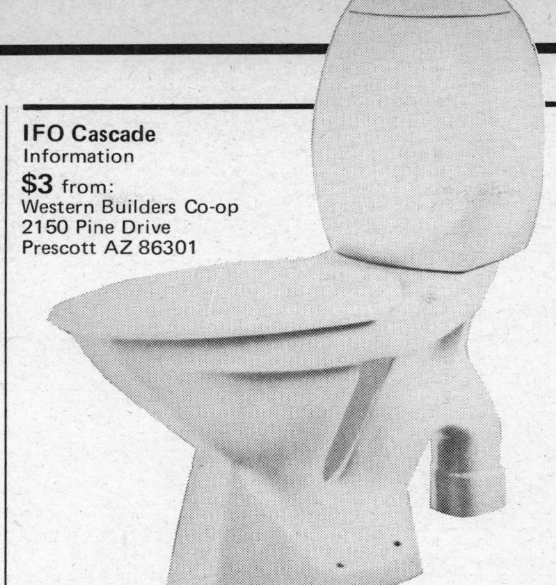

IFO Cascade Toilet

The IFO Cascade 3 liter toilet has to be high on the list of the most efficient water saving devices ever created. Manufactured in Sweden by IFO Sanitar AB, the 3 liter toilet is 77% more efficient than a typical 3.5 gallon American water saving toilet. It uses a very efficient flushing cycle and flushes in only 3 seconds as compared to 10 seconds for American toilets. The 3 liter IFO Cascade toilet is made of vitreous china, with a visible trap and is available in a variety of colors.

The 3 liter toilet should be used with 3 inch pipe wherever possible. The line from toilet to sewer main or septic tank should not exceed 100 feet and there should be a minimum slope of ¼ inch per foot with 30 degree bends.

The price of an IFO Cascade 3 liter toilet, in white, is $290 at this time. Colors are an additional $44.

—Joseph W. McShane
[Suggested by Sim Van der Ryn]

Paloma Demand Water Heater

Many years ago a plumber convinced me to tear out a wonderful old Ruud demand water heater that had been in service some fifty years in my house. I gave the heater to Sandy Jacobs who built what may have been Marin's first hot tub and as far as I know the thing is still going strong. The principle of the demand water heater is simple: water is heated as you need it by passing the pipe coil directly through the gas flame. Turning on the hot water activates the burner and the water is heated to almost boiling instantaneously. The advantage of the demand type water heater is that it only uses gas when hot water is required and this saves up to 50% of your water heating bill. Besides requiring much less space (since there is no storage tank), it provides an unlimited supply of hot water. I have been using two of the Japanese-made Palomas for three years now and they have provided faultless service. Unlike my old Ruud which took four people to move, the Paloma is extremely lightweight and compact, and the cost is around $200. They are equipped with electric ignition.

—Sim Van der Ryn

•

Model		Weight	BTU Input	List
PH-4*	-	12 lbs	30,000	$ 189
PH-5*	-	12 ″	38,000	235
PH-6	AGA	20 ″	43,880	330
PH-12	AGA	40 ″	89,300	618
PH-16	AGA	70 ″	121,500	908
PH-24	AGA	82 ″	178,500	1,017

*Venting should be according to local codes. Always vent to the outdoors where units are installed in a closed or confined area. A MUST IN SLEEPING AREAS.

Paloma Water Heaters
Information and nearest dealer location
free from:
Paloma Company
241 James Street
Bensenville, IL 60106

Paloma Instant Gas Water Heater Model PH5-2F ↓

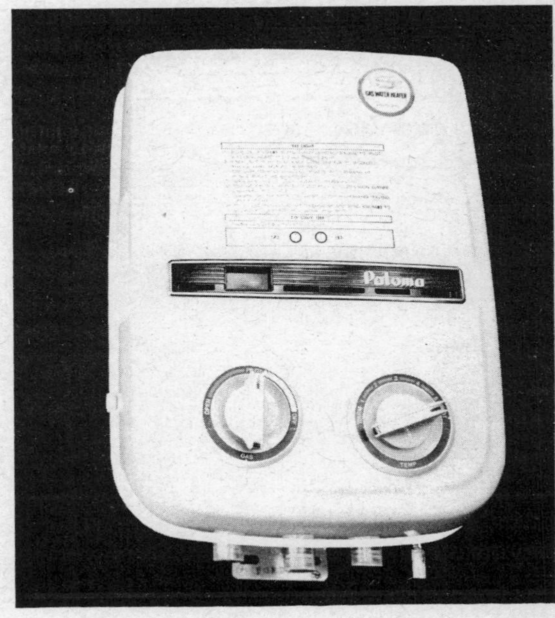

Septic Tanks

ONE-QUARTER OF AMERICA'S homes (20+ million homes or 50+ million citizens) have home-site sewage systems, mostly septic tank systems. Americans have been forced to install mechanically baroque systems in order to meet the demands of paranoid health officials. Sometimes so much hardware is required that it appears cheaper to install huge, centralized sewer systems. Yet, septic tank systems are fine sub-irrigation systems that recycle water and nutrients to your backyard plantlife.

—Peter Warshall

Septic Tank Practices

A lively discourse (by one of our editors) on the theory, construction, care and feeding of septic tank systems as well as suggestions for conserving and reusing household waste water ("grey water"). The complete poop, so to speak. Many diagrams and drawings, lots of authoritative facts, and good arguments for fighting the "big sewer."

—J. Baldwin

Weird mutual editorial modesty going on here. The book is wonderful — outrageous and authoritative simultaneously.

—SB

Septic Tank Practices
(A Primer in the Conservation and Re-use of Household Wastewaters)
Peter Warshall
1975, 1979; 177 pp.
$3.95 postpaid from:
Doubleday and Company
501 Franklin Avenue
Garden City, NY 11530
or Whole Earth Household Store

•

Finally, the Big Sewer works against American freedom of choice. If a sewer runs by your house, you *must* hook up to it and pay the costs. In other words, you are not allowed to keep your home-site system with all its advantages — even if it's working beautifully. This loss of option is killing the old American sense of self-reliance and responsibility. Undoubtedly, some backwoods Benjamin Franklin, unimpressed by the language of city-educated sewage experts, will soon stand up and say: "I won't." It will be a fine American court battle.

Home-site sewage treatment is cheaper, pollutes less, recycles more, slows or controls suburban sprawl, has fewer health hazards, and remains personal and intimate with the necessities of water, nutrients, and the lives of other creatures. Centralized sewage disposal, shielded by public authorities, has kept citizens unaware of sewage costs, inadequate treatment and disposal as well as their own natural responsibility for recyling their own wastes and keeping other plants and animals productive and healthy.

•

Drainfield Construction

WARNING: Trenches should be dug with a back-hoe or by hand tools. Seepage pits can be dug with a back-hoe, bucket auger or hand tools. Do not use spiral augers or trenchers. This equipment will compact the sidewalls and smear the infiltration surface — totally ruining the treatment process.

THE RISING SUN
NEIGHBORHOOD NEWSLETTER

Which do you think is more important to career development — not being able to type or not being able to cook? Which do you think is more important to revolution development — men typing or men cooking?

Residential Water Conservation

You need no other book.

You can conserve by changing habits. Milne describes changing habits. You can conserve by installing water-saving devices. They're all here. You can conserve by recycling. Most of it's here. Great bibliography. Great access list to all manufacturers of needed appliances.
—Peter Warshall

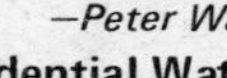

Residential Water Conservation
(California Water Resources Center Report No. 35)
Murray Milne
No. PB-288-157
1975; 468 pp.

$14 postpaid from:
NTIS
U.S. Dept. of Commerce
5285 Port Royal Road
Springfield, VA 22161

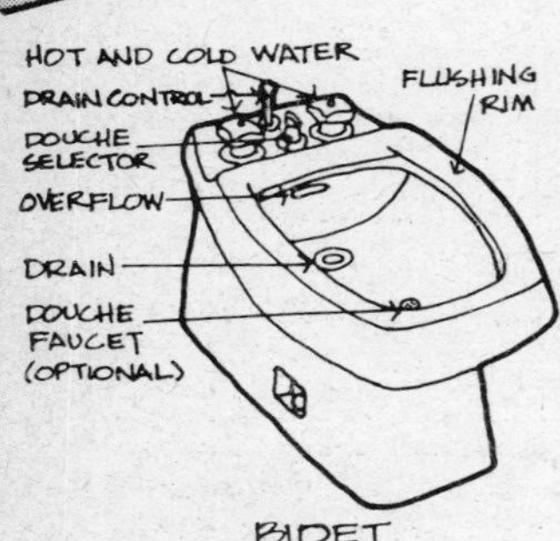

• Water Consumption: The bidet holds only a gallon or two of water. When it is not necessary to wash one's entire body, the bidet offers significant water savings compared to filling a bathtub or running a shower.

Water Conservation and the Mist Experience

An eccentric and delightful pamphlet on the water savings achieved by washing with water mists and sprays. All you want to know about nozzles and hygiene.
—Peter Warshall

Water Conservation and the Mist Experience
Alex Morse, Vikram Bhatt and Witold Rybczynski
1978; 59 pp.

$4 postpaid from:
Minimum Cost Housing Group
School of Architecture
McGill University
3480 University Street
Montreal, Quebec
Canada H3A 2A7

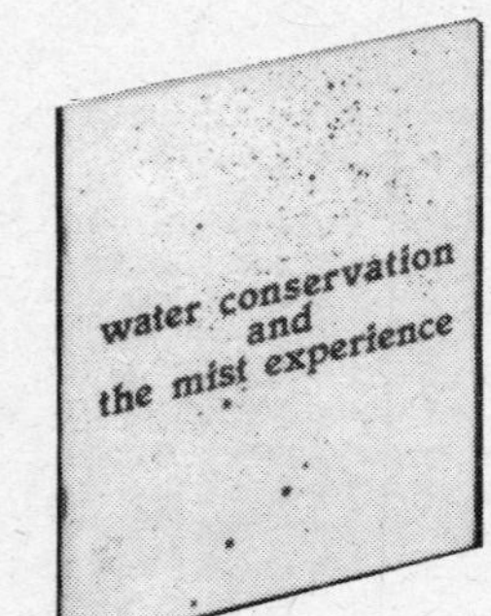

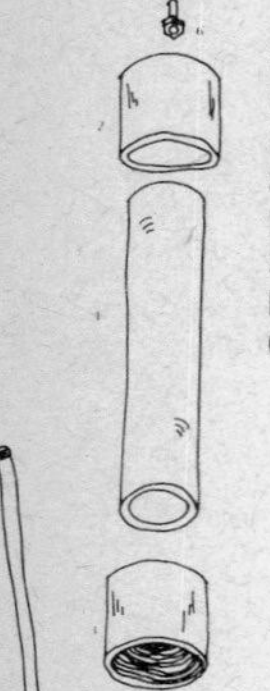

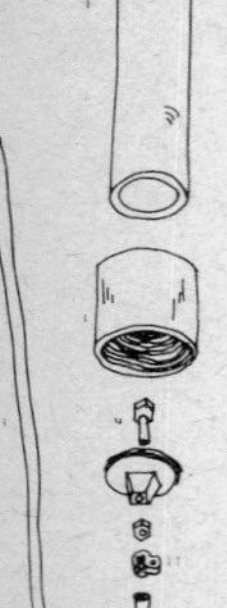

↑ How does it feel to use an atomized shower?

The atomized shower produces a different sensation from the normal shower. Although the device is similar to the telephone shower which can reach close to all parts of the body, the spray impact is much less, so the needle-like massage is missing and a softer flow of water is felt since the droplet size is finer. During rinsing, the soap comes off more slowly and sometimes must be wiped off with the help of a cloth or sponge since the weaker impact spray does not move the suds as fast as with the normal shower. But on completion, one has the same exhilaration and clean feeling as after the normal shower.

Perhaps it could best be compared to a gentle rain in contrast to a driving rain.

Mini-Mister

PARTS LIST

1. TUBE, ABS
   75 mm(3") diameter
   Length as required (approx. 50 cm, 20")
2. THREADED CAP, ABS
3. THREADED CAP, ABS
4. CLEAN-OUT, ABS
5. CLEAN-OUT, ABS
6. INSERT, COPPER OR BRASS
7. NUT, COPPER OR BRASS
8. BICYCLE VALVE
9. INSERT, COPPER OR BRASS
10. NUT, COPPER OR BRASS
11. HOSE CLAMP
12. HOSE CLAMP
13. HOSE, VINYL
    6.3 mm (1/4") diameter
    Length as required (approx. 1.8m, 6')
14. CHAPIN CONTROL VALVE
15. ADAPTER ASSEMBLY, COPPER OR BRASS
16. ADAPTER ASSEMBLY, COPPER OR BRASS
17. ATOMIZER NOZZLE, BRASS

Almost all of these parts are available from plumbing suppliers. The ABS parts are for water drains and could be of PVC plastic as well, though ABS is cheaper. The hose and control valve could be common garden variety... depending on the ingenuity of the builder.

A SEWERLESS SOCIETY
48% REDUCTION

PER CAPITA CONSUMPTION 73 GCD
INDOOR 49 GCD
COOKING & DRINKING 3 GCD
CONSUMED
BATHING 21 GCD
TREATMENT
TOILET 32 GCD
LAUNDRY 14 GCD
TREATMENT
IRRIGATION
WATER TABLE
OUTDOOR 24 GCD
CAR WASHING
SWIMMING POOLS
EVAPORATION

A PICTURE OF RESIDENTIAL CONSUMPTION

DAILY PER CAPITA WATER CONSUMPTION 140 GALLONS
INDOOR CONSUMPTION- 70 GALLONS
TOILETS 45%-32 GAL
BATHING & PERSONAL 30%-21 GAL
LAUNDRY & DISHES 20%-14 GAL
DRINKING & COOKING 5%-3 GAL
OUTDOOR CONSUMPTION- 70 GALLONS
IRRIGATION VARIABLE
SWIMMING POOLS VARIABLE
CAR WASHING VARIABLE
LEAKAGE VARIABLE

FRESH WATER
SHOWER
SINK
TOILET

REUSE SYSTEM (STAN. PROD., 1971)

SIPHON TANK (ROOSA, 1972)

Feasibility of Rainwater Collection Systems in California

A technical report on rainwater water supply systems. For nitty-gritty calculations, especially balancing water flow demand with rainfall supply. That is, making sure there's water after the rains stop.
—Peter Warshall

Feasibility of Rainwater Collection Systems in California
(California Water Resources Center Contribution No. 173)
David Jenkins, Frank Pearson, et al.
1978; 55 pp.

free from:
Water Resources Center
University of California
475 Kerr Hall
Davis, CA 95616

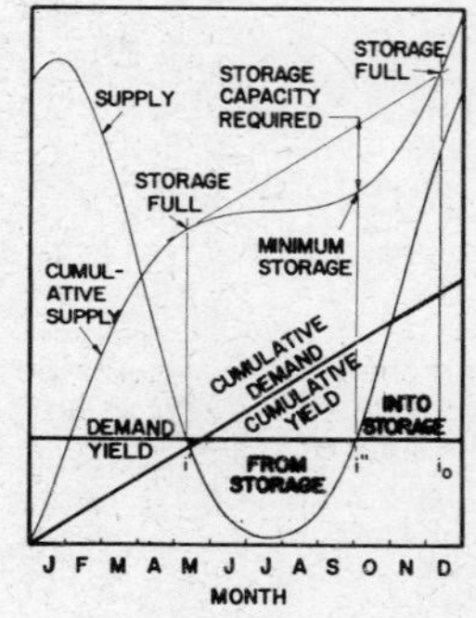

Supply-demand-storage relationships for a 100% reliable system

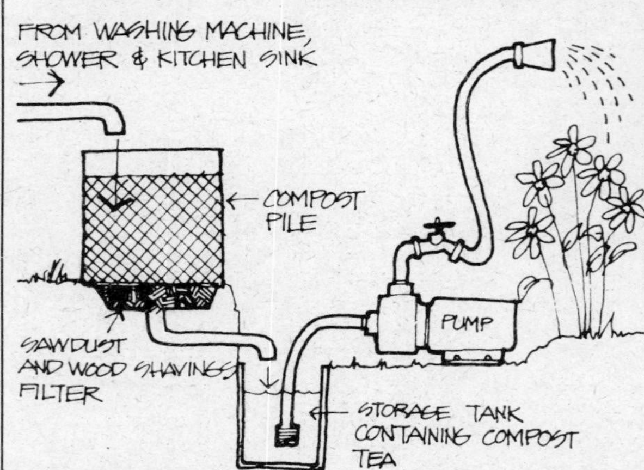

Dan Clancy converted an old barn in Olga, Washington into a 3-bedroom house with a complete on-site waste recycling system which filters greywater through a compost pile in order to help biodegrade detergents and make a nutrient-rich liquid fertilizer.

Residential Water Re-Use

Every greywater (water re-use) system around from the Rube Goldberg junkyard extravaganzas to the space age chromium plated cadillacs. Like a fashion show. Detailed chapter on components (filters, backflow prevention devices, piping, etc.). Most greywater systems have been used only one to three years so the final judgment can't be made. Includes other re-use possibilities such as groundwater and rainfall.
—Peter Warshall

Residential Water Re-Use
(California Water Resources Center Report No. 46)
Murray Milne
1979; 553 pp.

$10 postpaid from:
California Water Resources Center
University of California
Davis, CA 95616

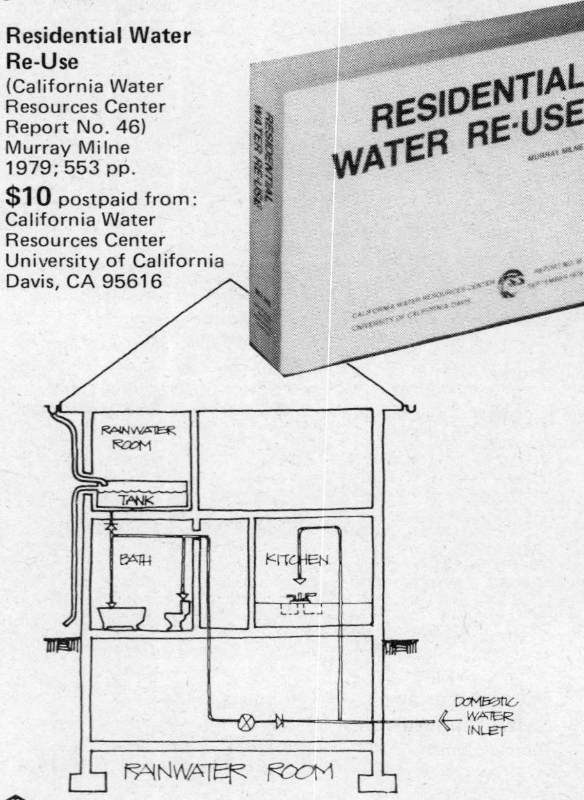

↑ Monica Brandies had a surprise when her family moved into an old home in Wilton, Iowa. Little did they realize when they purchased the house, they had a rainwater cistern tank in an empty room above the bathroom. They were later assured that tanks such as theirs were common occurrences in such old Victorian houses. For years in this part of Iowa no one would have considered building a house without a cistern. Such a system made much more sense than an open rain barrel at the end of a gutter because gravity alone can supply water to all the indoor fixtures.

Water flows by gravity from the cistern through a 3/4" pipe, welded to the bottom of the tank, to a valve in the basement marked "gravity feed." This valve connects the cistern to the "regular system," which is supplied by a well pump, and feeds all the faucets except the cold (drinking) water in the kitchen.

Ms. Brandies does not mention any check valves at this location, although two would probably be required; one to prevent any possible backflow into the part of the system supplying the kitchen sink, and the other to prevent the well pump from forcing water back up to the rainwater room, possibly overflowing the tank. Another alternative might be to replace the "gravity feed" valve with a standard pressure reducing valve, which if carefully adjusted would automatically pass "regular" water only when the cistern was empty. A potential inconvenience will always be the low pressure in the cistern-fed system, although it can be improved by maximizing the height of the cistern above the fixtures and reducing the friction loss in the piping (by minimizing length and number of fittings or maximizing diameter and smoothness).

• **Cloth Bag Filter**

The cheapest and easiest way to remove large particles, lint and hair from household greywater is with a cloth bag or an old stocking tied on the end of the outlet pipe.

Operation — Nothing could be simpler; the greywater flows out of the pipe and seeps through the cloth. Everything that is left behind is gradually pushed down to the far end of the cloth bag. The bag can be held in place with a spring, wire, rubber band, or hose clamp.

Maintenance — Cleanable bags are turned inside out, hosed off, and left to dry in the sun, or perhaps even laundered. If old stockings are used they can simply be removed, discarded, and replaced with another old stocking.

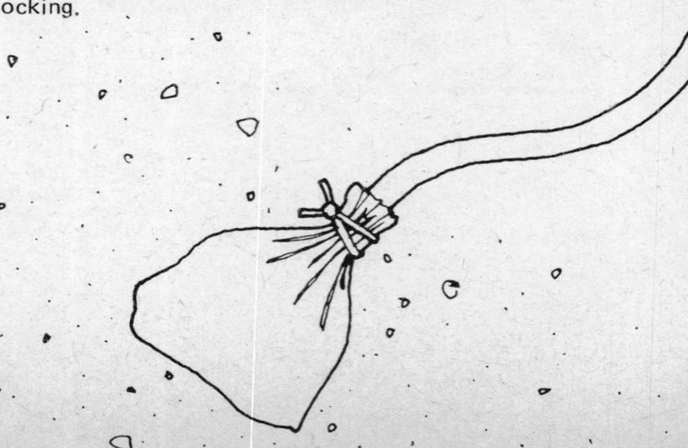

Homesite Water Supply

THE BOOK YOU WANT will depend on the volume of water you need (enough for washing dishes or for fire protection), the possible source (well, pond, or roof collector), the quality of the water (potable or possibly polluted), the conveyance mechanism (electricity or gravity feed and trade-offs between how much money you have and how much time you can spend operating and maintaining your water supply (hand pumps, backwash filter or automatic chlorinator). You'll most likely end up with more than one book. (More on rural water, see p. 104.)

—Peter Warshall

Water Supply for Rural Areas and Small Communities

The most interesting guide — especially for daydreams of when you own God's special acre. Designed for "underdeveloped" nations, so the book lets you live with the least technology. Not as fussy as American books about health and water treatment but totally reliable for achieving delicious, healthful water. Great on spring boxes and shallowish wells. —Peter Warshall

Water Supply for Rural Areas and Small Communities
(World Health Organization Monograph Series No. 42)
Edmund G. Wagner and J.N. Lanoix
1959; 340 pp.

$27.65 postpaid from:
World Health Organization
Q Corporation
49 Sheridan Avenue
Albany, NY 12210

or Whole Earth Household Store

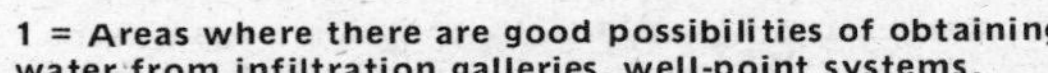

1 = Areas where there are good possibilities of obtaining water from infiltration galleries, well-point systems.

2 = Ground water is outcropping at this point, so that a flowing spring is formed. At the foot of river banks and hills other springs may possibly be found.

3 = Top of ground-water table.

4 = Area of infiltration to supply formation B.

A = Non-confined (non-artesian), water-bearing formation covered with top soil.

B = Confined (artesian), water-bearing formation.

C = Impervious rock, or hard-pan formation.

To supply a village situated along the banks of the main river in this rolling country with a good ground water table, the first thing to look for is a spring above the town that could be developed and would flow by gravity. If no springs were found within a reasonable distance above the point of consumption, some might be found outcropping near the stream bed. If no springs were found within a reasonable distance, any well penetrating formation A would produce water. If large quantities were required, a well-point system or a gallery at points indicated would probably work. A deep well, properly constructed and developed, penetrating formation B would probably produce considerable water.

↓

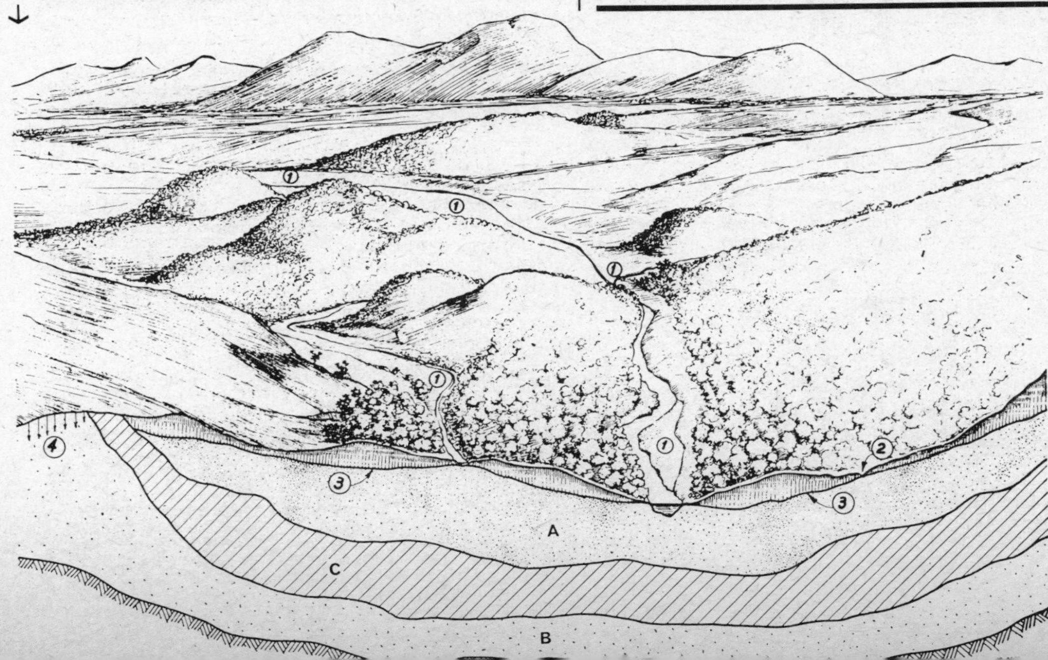

Hydra-Drill

↑

A handy rig for drilling your own well — up to 3½ inches diameter and 200 feet deep. Won't tear up your garden like the driller in the phone book with his pick-up mounted rig. Also can drill blasting holes. Neighbors might share the $500 cost. —SB

Hydra Drill
Information

free from:
Deeprock Manufacturing Company
Box 1
Opelika, AL 36802

Chinese Chain and Washer Pumps

These simple pumps may be just what is needed for low-lift water pumping not only in less developed countries but for the homesteader. They can be ganged together to produce the volume needed for irrigation; difficult to do with most other designs. Presented in the usual ITDG competent manner. —J. Baldwin

Chinese Chain and Washer Pumps
Simon Watt, Editor
1976; 49 pp.

£1.81 postpaid from:
Intermediate Technology Development Group
9 King Street
London WC2E 8HN
England

or

$3.75 postpaid from:
I.T.D.G.
North America
P.O. Box 337
Croton-on-Hudson
NY 10520

or Whole Earth Household Store

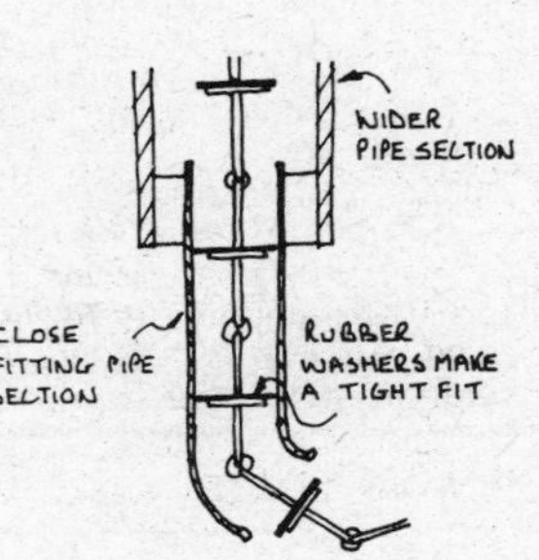

→

The accurately cut or rubber sealed washers make a tight fit in this section of pipe (which may be steel or plastic), and fit only loosely in the wider section of pipe above. The washers do the work of lifting in the close fitting section, reducing leakage to a minimum; in the looser and cheaper section of pipe above, they do no lifting work, but they also do not wear themselves out against the sides of the pipe in friction.

This is a most useful innovation. It might be possible to manufacture the washers and the lower pipe section in a workshop, then distribute them to local areas to be built into the locally made body of the pump. Other innovations include a bell mouth entry at the bottom of the pipe to guide the washers into the pipe, and a non-return ratchet on the chain wheel to prevent the chain from running backwards under the weight of water in the pipe.

Excreta Disposal for Rural Areas and Small Communities

The classic. Sensible because it's for societies not yet addicted to the techno-fix. This book started the waterless toilet crusade in North America. Still has some of the best designs for bored-hole latrines, etc.

—Peter Warshall
[Suggested by Craige Schensted]

Excreta Disposal for Rural Areas and Small Communities
(World Health Organization Monograph Series No. 39)
Edmund G. Wagner and J.N. Lanoix
1958; 187 pp.

$18.05 postpaid from:
World Health Organization
Q Corporation
49 Sheridan Avenue
Albany, NY 12210

or Whole Earth Household Store

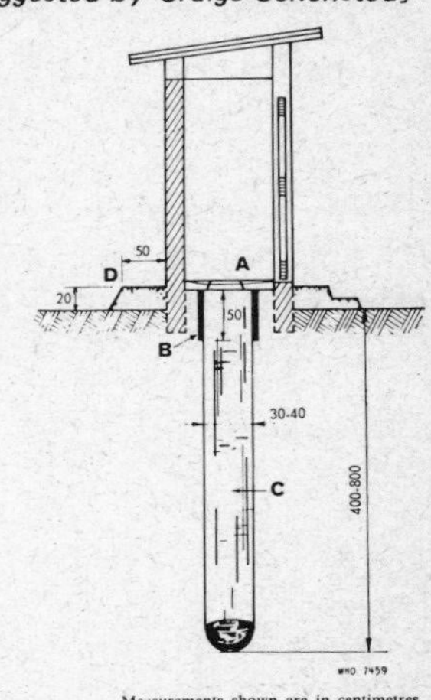

→

Typical Bored-hole Latrine

A = Squatting slab. Note sides sloping towards hole. B = Impervious clay-tile lining. C = Woven-bamboo lining. D = Earth mound, well tamped.

Air powered pump systems

Before city power and water, one of the ways to have a pressurized water system was to have an air compressor run by whatever machine (tractor?) you had around to charge a compressed air tank. Air from that was piped to the airdriven pumps submerged in the well or cistern. The result was pressure at the faucet on demand without the necessity of a water storage tank. These systems were well adapted to intermittent power sources and might be useful for some "alternative" energy powered outfits. You can still get the hardware! Their information uses some material from the original 1923 catalog. —J. Baldwin

Air Operated Fresh Water Pumps
$315 - $415 (approx.)

Information
$ .50 from:
Stauffer's Machine Shop
RD3
Pleasant Valley Road
Ephrata, PA 17522

Hand water pumps

A real good one for deep well hand pumping is model 23F from Dempster. Monitor also has quality, including one with a drinking fountain (costs $290 — Monitor's cheapest pump is $80). —SB

Dempster Pumps
Information

free from:
Dempster Pumps
Box 648
Beatrice, NE 68310

Monitor Pumps
Information

free from:
Baker
Monitor Division
133 Enterprise Street
Evansville, WI 53536

Monitor drinking fountain pump

THE RISING SUN
NEIGHBORHOOD NEWSLETTER

When Jesus visited his friends Mary and Martha, Martha got angry because Mary was listening to Jesus instead of helping in the kitchen. She said, "Lord, do you not care that my sister has left me to serve alone. Tell her then to help me." And Jesus said, "Martha, Martha, you are anxious and troubled about so many things, but only one thing is needful. Mary has chosen the good portion, which shall not be taken away from her." Which is fairly typical of men — not only is the cook supposed to make 247 variables reach a crescendo on the same table at the same moment — she's supposed to be calm about it and take time to talk about great issues.

— Quotes from Luke 10:40 (King James)

Wyatt frydenland,
a student of mine,
once said

"Do it right the first time."

Now, that's a little bit tightass when applied to homedone things.

Maybe it should read "Practice until you can do it right the first time."

or "A thing worth doing is worth doing."

or "Just go ahead and do it, whatever it is, and learn from your mistakes."

or "Find somebody who knows something and learn it from them."

or "Through industry we prosper," and all that craft.

—J.D. Smith

The type face of the headline above, set in Gill Sans Bold 72 pt, was designed in 1928-30 by Eric Gill (1887-1940), British artist-craftsman who also did this wood-engraving 'The Thorn in the Flesh.' From Craft Magazine. **See page 249 for wood engraving tools.**

SCOTTISH ARTS COUNCIL

Crafts

The showcase for the best in British crafts, and one of the most beautifully produced and designed crafts magazines around. Regularly features (in glowing four-color) the work of the brightest new stars among weavers, jewelers, glassblowers and potters. Feature articles on trends, opportunities and problems in crafts. Includes a complete calendar and directory of craft galleries and shops, and runs a large classified advertising section of jobs, business opportunities and full- and part-time course listings. Reviews exhibitions and books (and prints a list of all books received.) What excites me so much about this magazine is the superb color photography and layout which translates the work and its essence so effectively and sensitively.

—J. Prestianni

Crafts
Martina Margetts, Editor
$18 /year (6 issues)
from:
Expediters of the Printed Word, Ltd.
527 Madison Avenue
Suite 1217
New York, NY 10022
or
£9.20 /year (6 issues)
from:
Crafts Magazine
28 Haymarket
London SW1Y 4SU
England

Domino set in box by Desmond Ryan, 1975-77

Front of a drawer, Early Eighteenth century

Back of the same drawer

The Nature and Art of Workmanship

An attempt to define the aesthetics of craftsmanship in a classical scholarly mode. It has clear insight and sound criteria for judging the quality of the objects that surround us without the blanket rejection of technology that is trapping many people in an alternative lifestyle of shoddy creativity.

—Terry Gunesch

The Nature and Art of Workmanship
David Pye
1968, 1979; 101 pp.
$7.95 postpaid from:
Cambridge University Press
510 North Avenue
New Rochelle, NY 10801
or Whole Earth Household Store

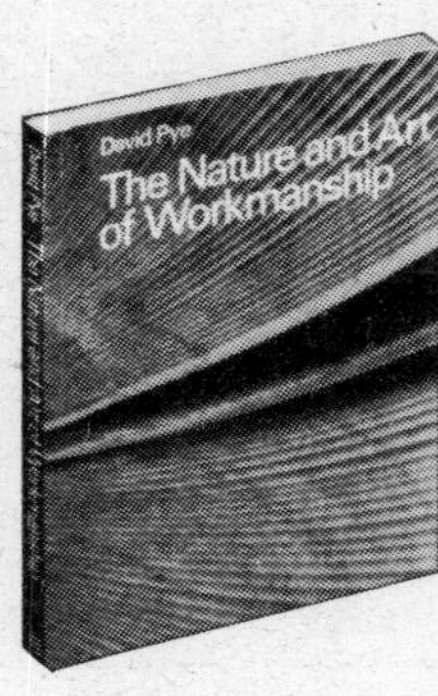

↑ It must be said at once that much furniture of this date was better made than this contemptible example, but really bad workmanship was not uncommon and it may be that the best was rarer than is generally supposed. Much of what survives is quite well made, but that perhaps merely confirms that quality is a good preservative. Things that are well made and well designed tend to survive and things like this drawer tend to perish; which indeed it would probably have done but for the walnut veneering on the front, of which the workmanship is quite fair, and to which age has given a pleasant quality.

At the back of it the point of the hand-forged nail has been shamelessly airing itself for two hundred and fifty years or so, but the slip of wood below the bottom at the corner, and the slobber of glue above it, are more recent embellishments.

It is of very bad workmanship indeed, but that has not prevented it from serving its purpose all those years. The nail with its point in the air has undeniably kept the bottom on the drawer. Workmanship is not to be judged on a merely utilitarian footing.

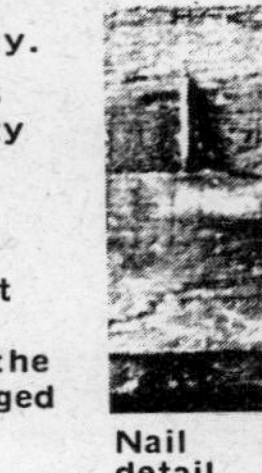

Nail detail

•

For the crafts, in the modern world, there can be no half measures. There can be no reason for them to continue unless they produce only the best possible workmanship, free or regulated, allied to the best possible design: in other words, unless they produce only the very best quality. That quality is never got so quickly as more ordinary qualities are.

•

The crafts will survive as a means of livelihood only where there is a sufficient demand for the *very best quality at any price.*

•

Free workmanship is one of the main sources of diversity. To achieve diversity in all its possible manifestations is the chief reason for continuing the workmanship of risk as a productive undertaking: in other words for perpetuating craftsmanship.

•

There is a very present danger that, as the kinds of medium-scale diversity which free workmanship used to impart to building become less readily available, what little can be had in that way will be over-played and in the end travestied. We do not want every piece of concrete to show board-marks, every piece of paving to be cobbled, every piece of masonry to be random rubble, every piece of brickwork to be left unplastered. There is a place for all those things, but such elephantine capers unaccompanied by diversity at smaller scales become merely ludicrous. What we want is diversity which begins at the smallest visible scale and develops continuously upwards from that; and even then we do not want it always and everywhere. Vitamins are necessary to life, but only in small amounts. Take them in large amounts and they make you ill. So I believe it is with diversification in workmanship. I do not suggest it is more — or less — than a vitamin: not a diet: not a panacea: merely something which, though we may not take much notice of it, we need to have.

Ruskin said, "If we build, let us think that we build forever." Shall we say, "If we build, let us remember to build for the scrapheap?" Shall we make everything so that it goes wrong or breaks pretty quickly? I think not. Men do not live by economics alone. There is a question of morale involved. A world in which everything was ephemeral would not be worth working for. There are overwhelming social and aesthetic arguments for durability in certain things even if, as we are told, there are no economic ones. These are:

First of all, the things we inherit from the past remind us that the men who made them were like us and give us a tangible link with them. This is a thought to set off against the knowledge that life is short. Hitherto it has been inconceivable that any one generation should discard all the equipment it has inherited and replace it completely. That may yet become possible. Even if it does, it will still be imperative for each generation deliberately to make some of its equipment so that it lasts and survives its makers.

Secondly, if you are making a thing so that it goes wrong or breaks, then, however honestly you state the fact, two other facts remain. One is that you are putting as little into the job as you decently can. The other is that you are in a fair way to force its user to spend his money on replacing that thing instead of for some other purpose. He may be glad to replace it, in an age of materialism and the passion for novelty. But why should we all be compelled to keep spending money on renewing our car, our cooker and our refrigerator? These things for some people are merely means to other ends in life. Why should we not save the money so as to pursue those ends the better: altruistic, learned or artistic, say? Things which are made to fall early should be made maintainable and repairable, so that a man who cares for something other than novelty and status-symbols can make them last his time respectably while he gets on with his life. Optional durability is what we want.

The Book of Country Crafts

Most craft books, I've noticed, either treat you as a retarded fifth grader or as an ambitious acolyte to The Craft of whatever. This book is by a man who enjoys doing his own stuff at his own place, and he makes you feel the same and shortens the route into doing it. He has range as well as depth: sections include Working with Wood, with Clay, with Metals, with Stone, and with Color.

—SB

[Suggested by Jude Harris]

The Book of Country Crafts
Randolph Wardell Johnston
1964; 211 pp.
$5.95 postpaid from:
A.S. Barnes and Company
P.O. Box 421
Cranbury, NJ 08512
or Whole Earth Household Store

The wheel shown is made of odds and ends. The shaft is an old Ford axle. At top and bottom are the original ball bearings of the car. The flywheel is from an old circular saw and is filled with cement. The wheel head is a clutch plate fitted tightly on the shaft end, and filled with plaster. The plaster was next turned true and recessed to hold bats of a certain size, by nailing a temporary tool rest across and turning the plaster as if it were wood on a lathe. The rounded front guard is half of an old paint pail. And the seat is one of the older style, made of cast iron, from a hay rake. The cast iron ones are much superior to the pressed steel variety. I show this wheel because it has proven very handy.

↓

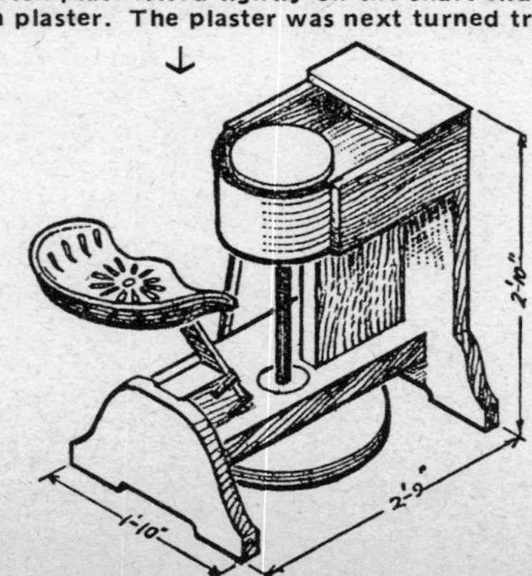

•

Kinds of Stone

Of all the stones used by the colonists for grave markers none has better resisted the weather than slate. The neat inscriptions on slabs of polished slate show even the light scratches that served as guides to the letterers. Artists should consider this when selecting stones on which to work. Slate is a pleasant material to carve. I have carved a full-size portrait relief in gray slate, direct from life, and I found it possible to use a wooden mallet and wood-carving chisels on the stone. To be sure it took the finest edge off the chisels, but not much more than this. A fine toothed claw chisel is good for roughing out. One soon becomes accustomed to the grain. Files, rifflers, sandpaper, and pumice all help in finishing.

•

Your blows should be light but plentiful, rather than strong and few, and this applies to any kind of metal shaping.

•

Throughout the Scottish Highlands they clean wool with stale human urine, one part urine to four parts water. The bath is no hotter than the hand can bear — about 101°F. The wool is squeezed and worked about by hand until it is clean, then thoroughly rinsed. Although nothing leaves the wool softer than urine, many people will prefer to wash it in a solution of ammonia or soft soap and hot water. Do not use washing soda, it makes the wool harsh. The wool loses about 20% of its weight.

↓ Shaping by hammering in a hollow block

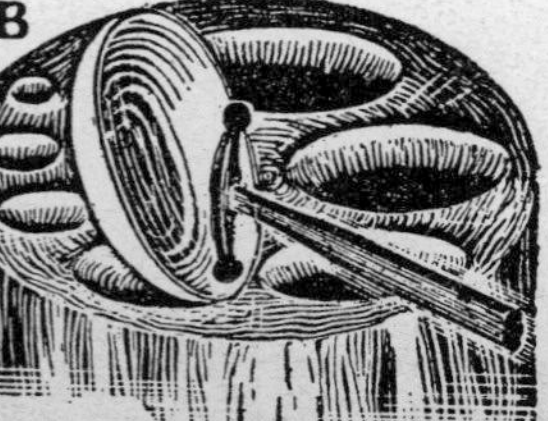

Brass
all lamp

The Goodfellow Catalog of Wonderful Things

The Goodfellow Catalog *is a direct mail order catalog of hand-crafted items available directly from the craftspeople. The publishers juried each craftsperson included in the catalog, but the craftspeople get all the profits. The quality of the crafts is high and prices are, for the most part, very reasonable. The catalog also includes listings of major crafts fairs held in the U.S. each year, reviews of books on various crafts, and listings of crafts organizations, schools, and publications.*

—Marilyn Green

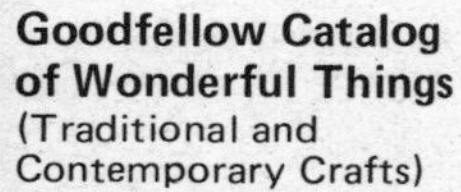

Goodfellow Catalog of Wonderful Things
(Traditional and Contemporary Crafts)
Christopher Weills, Editor
1977; 418 pp.

$8.95 postpaid from:
Goodfellow Catalog
P.O. Box 4520
Berkeley, CA 94704
or Whole Earth Household Store

stic-roll
all lamp

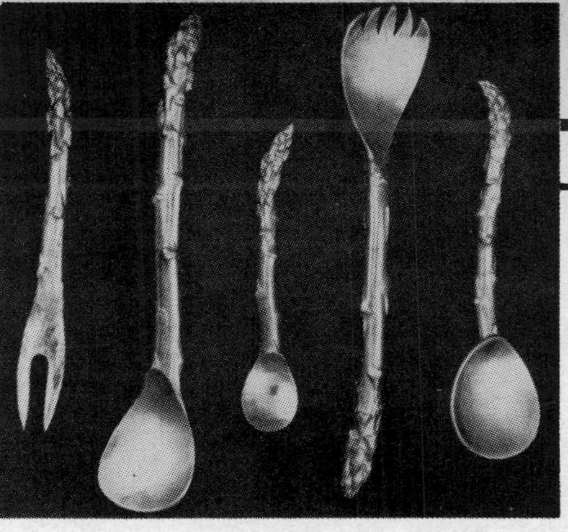

←
Pewter Dining Ware These serving pieces are made in lead-free pewter from life-castings of real asparagus. They weigh from 4 to 14 oz. and are 94% tin and 6% copper. They have an exceptionally high finish for pewter and are often mistaken for silver. Each is hand-finished. Pieces come gift-boxed. Relish spoon, $12; salad spoon and salad fork (sold only as set), $30; jam spoon, $7.50; two-tine fork; $12.

All prices postpaid.
Walter White
5024 North Frace Street
Tacoma, WA 98407

←
Country Store Hanging Lamp — The standard lamp used in the churches and meeting halls of yesteryear. Brass lamp has iron shade and brass hanging yoke. Oil-burning model lifts out of the center hanging ring for easy refueling. The electrified model comes with concealed wires and 12′ transparent cord.

Height: 28″. Diameter: 15″. $62, with brass shade, $77, shipping not included.

Bob Stokes
c/o Carriage Trade of Tahoe
P.O. Box 2011
Olympic Valley, CA 95730

How to Start Your Own Craft Business

Remarkably clear, comprehensive book. By simply stating how to do it, why, and including a copy of the completed form, it leads you painlessly through the paperwork of getting licensed, financed, legally-covered, and taxed. Equally fine sections demonstrate streamlined systems for bookkeeping, inventorying, shipping, using the U.P.S., selling an area (wholesale, consignment, direct), doing fairs and shows, collecting bills, and once launched, how to analyze your progress, and where to expand or cut. To echo those who know, "Wish I'd read it when I started!"

—Diana Sloat

How to Start Your Own Craft Business
Herb Genfan and Lyn Taetzsch
1974; 203 pp.

$10.95 postpaid from:
Watson-Guptill Publications
2160 Patterson Street
Cincinnati, OH 45214
or Whole Earth Household Store

•

If you are selling to retail stores who like the way your work sells, their customers expect a ready supply of your work. Store owners, you'll find, want your goods on their shelves within a week or two after they order. Your success at this stage depends almost entirely on how quickly you deliver.

The nature of a good system allows you to see exactly what you have and need at a glance. It's a powerful planning tool for all the materials, tools, labor, and stock you'll need to have to fill orders quickly. When selling in volume, your reputation depends upon delivering on time, particularly during holidays. You'll notice that many orders have a cancellation date written in. If the stores don't receive their orders by a certain date, they have the right to send all your goods back. It's even possible that they'll give up on you and choose another craftsperson who can supply them as they need it.

Production and inventory systems are well worth the time in planning and in keeping them up to date. If you've heard of a business failing because of "poor management," lack of organization is one of the factors that cause such failure. With other craftspeople competing for customers you can, by using control systems, be the one that makes it and stays in business.

•

Your own business, as you can see, will be quite a challenge. It lives, and you live with it; in a fairly short time you can see the results of actions, your decisions. If you buy a new tool either it works or it doesn't. If you design a new vase, it sells or it doesn't. In any case, you learn something, you change and grow.

If you want to expand and take out a loan, you work it out on paper, scrape together as many numbers and quantifiable facts as possible, throw in a dash of pure intuition and hope, and plunge ahead. What you accomplish lifts you right off the ground. And your failures provide useful feedback for the next decision, the next risk.

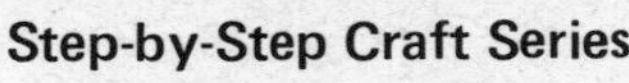

Scribing a guide line for sawing.

awing ring
to halves

Design achieved by filing.

Halves bound with wire ready for soldering.

Filed areas oxidized then buffed.

Step-by-Step Craft Series

A remarkably fine, low-priced series of introductory craft books. Each one has a thorough list of relevant periodicals, books, material suppliers, and schools which give courses in the subject. It's an intelligent way to begin — light, quick, and real.

—SB
[Suggested by Jan McClain]

Step-by-Step Jewelry
Thomas Gentille
1968; 96 pp.
$2.95 postpaid

Step-by-Step Weaving
Nell Znamierowski
1967; 96 pp.
$2.95 postpaid

Step-by-Step Macrame
Mary Walker Phillips
1970; 80 pp.
$2.95 postpaid

Step-by-Step Printmaking
Erwin Schachner
1970; 80 pp.
$2.95 postpaid

All from:
Golden Press Division
Western Publishing Company, Inc.
1220 Mound Avenue
Racine, WI 53404
or Whole Earth Household Store

•

↑ The split ring will enable you to make a three dimensional design within the band.

—Step-by-Step Jewelry

←
The knotting board is the working surface; the one shown is a piece of Celotex, an insulating material, covered with brown wrapping paper. Celotex can be cut into various sizes; a good selection to have would be sizes 12″ x 24″, 20″ x 36″, and 24″ x 48″, or whatever other size suits the piece you plan to make. In place of Celotex, padded cardboard may be used or cork covered with paper. The important thing is that the board be lightweight, rigid, yet pliable enough so that pins can be easily inserted.

—Step-by-Step Macrame

Goodfellow Review of Crafts

Goodfellow Review of Crafts *is aimed at craftspeople interested in marketing their goods. Each issue contains a nationwide listing of craft fairs with information on how to participate in each. I also found the column called "For Immediate Release" quite useful. It's full of information on everything from health hazards of various materials to information on insurance for artists. The periodical also offers reasonable classified advertising space to craftspeople—20 cents per word.* —Marilyn Green

Goodfellow Review of Crafts
$10 /2 years (12 issues) from:
Goodfellow Catalog
P.O. Box 4520
Berkeley, CA 94704

Calligraphy by Judy Foss

SELLING laziness! Selling laziness!/Just before the New Year's Eve./Selling dog fleas, selling wood termites,/Just before the New Year's Day. In the streets of Chinese villages over 50 years ago, this song was a playful gesture on parents' parts to rid themselves of their offsprings' bad habits before the lunar new year began. Major housecleaning, the purchase of new clothes, visits to family and the exchange of gifts; firecrackers, fancy foods, money tucked in bright red envelopes—these are still part of a traditional Chinese New Year.

Here in San Francisco, the Year of the Monkey was ushered in with its own Spring Festival, held February 23 & 24 at the Chinese Culture Foundation. As part of the Festival, eight craftspeople, housed in bamboo booths festooned with sprightly spring bunting, designed by Maizie Ung, demonstrated to hundreds of visitors the ancient crafts of a venerable people.

節
慶
會

THE RISING SUN
NEIGHBORHOOD NEWSLETTER

In some churches, the women's group is called The Mary and Martha Society, to show that both the spiritual and busy approach are necessary, which isn't what Jesus said, though I assume he ate the food. When I was growing up, the name was wrong because all the women in such groups were Marthas and they crowded into the church kitchen together, making great meals and having bitter battles about where to store the pie plates. Now churches have fewer church dinners and kitchen fights than they used to because the new generation of Marthas has gone to work for money.

The Crafts Business Encyclopedia

Its big advantage over the other crafts business guides is that entries are organized in convenient dictionary form. It's a good general reference guide which will either tell you what you want to know about the crafts business or, if not, where to find out. —*Marilyn Green*

•

Depreciation

Two methods of calculating depreciation are most commonly used:

1. *Straight Line.* The total cost is divided into equal parts over the expected number of years the item will last. If a kiln costs $600 and is expected to last ten years, it will be depreciated by $60 every year. After one year, then, the kiln has a book value of $540, after two years $480, until at last, ten years later, it theoretically has no further value at all.

2. *Declining Balance.* The value of the item is reduced by a specified percentage each year. If the amount is, for example, 10 percent of the balance each year, then the $600 kiln would be depreciated $60 the first year (to $540), $54 the second year (to $486), $48.60 the third year, and so on.

When a fixed asset has both a business use and a personal use — a building which houses both your home and your shop, or a car which is used for family as well as business purposes — only that portion of the depreciation which applies to the business purpose can be deducted as a business expense.

Depreciation not only helps you calculate your cost of doing business more accurately, but also establishes the value of your fixed assets at any given time.

The Crafts Business Encyclopedia
(Marketing, Management and Money)
Michael Scott
1977, 1979; 286 pp.
$3.95 postpaid from:
Harcourt Brace & Jovanovitch
757 Third Avenue
New York, NY 10017
or Whole Earth Household Store

The Crafts Fair Guide

Funky and useful: ratings and comments on western crafts fairs (mainly California) by crafts people who've participated. Covers fees, attendance, promotion, site conditions, etc. Costs $20 (with 10-day money-back guarantee) for 10 issues, but could easily save you a few issues' cost on an entrance fee and a dog of a weekend. Good idea getting organized. I just like the crazy thing after sitting through some awful times doing fairs.
—*Diana Sloat*

```
July 18-22, 1979
BAKERSFIELD:  Valley Plaza
   Inside.  Typical mall.  Very hot weather.
   75 Stores.  5000 PS.  EACM.  RC.
COST:  $25 & 10%
ATTENDANCE:  High
WOULD YOU RETURN?:  Yes-1   No-1
0 1 2 3 4 5 6 7 8 9 10      RATING:  4.8
P                 X         S/E:     5.0/4.5
                            1978:    5.5
COMMENTS ABOUT THE FAIR:  "Security:  lots
ripped off at night.  People very friendly.
Good down home town, appreciated arts and
crafts -- have aesthetic values!  If they
liked, they bought.  Instant buying, not wishy-
washy.  Price didn't really matter." (10/8/9)
..."Absolute bust.  Too hot, average 106 degrees.
Got stuck in Brach's Dept. Store aisle.  Dead."
(0/0)
COMMENTS ABOUT THE PROMOTER:  (Lee Gilpin, see
Promoter's List):  "Typical Lee." (10/8/9)...
"Gilpin came by with more shit again.  Always
a hassle to have to talk to." (0/0)
```

Crafts Fair Guide
Lee Spiegel, Editor
$20 /year (10 issues)
from:
Crafts Fair Guide
P.O. Box 262
Mill Valley, CA 94941

Health Hazards Manual for Artists

In a previous incarnation, I taught art at a state college. I was alarmed at the number of students that ran into trouble with various substances but I didn't know where to look for information. (I got epoxy poisoning myself.) This pamphlet spells it out clear and simple. It is appalling. You don't necessarily have to be an artist to get poisoned by the materials mentioned, of course. Wintergreen flavored library paste is not listed. I suppose if it were toxic, we'd have lost an entire generation.
—*J. Baldwin*

•

In general, solvents are one of the most underrated hazards in art. They are used for a million purposes: to dissolve and mix with oils, resins, varnishes, inks; to remove paint, varnish, lacquers; to clean brushes, tools, silk screens, and even hands. As a result, artists are continually being exposed to solvents.

Almost all organic solvents are poisonous if swallowed or inhaled in sufficient quantity, and most cause dermatitis after sufficient skin contact. High concentrations of most solvents can cause narcosis (dizziness, nausea, fatigue, loss of coordination, coma, etc.). This can increase the chances for mistakes and accidents. Some solvents — for example, benzol (benzene) and carbon tetrachloride — are so toxic that they shouldn't be used. Other solvents — for example, acetone and ethanol (ethyl or grain alcohol) — are reasonably safe.

Solvents fall into several classes with similar properties. If one member of a class of solvents is toxic, usually another safer member can be chosen. . . .

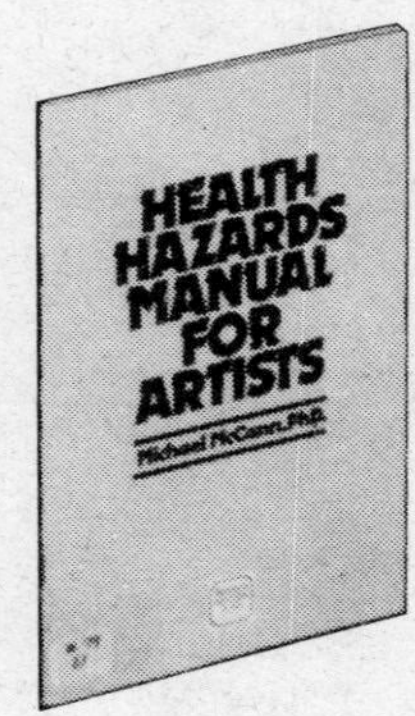

Health Hazards Manual for Artists
Michael McCann, Ph.D.
1975; 28 pp.
$2.75 postpaid from:
Foundation for the Community of Artists
Art Hazards Resource Center
220 Fifth Avenue
New York, NY 10001

The Crafts Report

This periodical — edited by the author of **The Crafts Business Encyclopedia** *— is a must for keeping up on the latest developments in the crafts business. Articles on marketing, safety in the workplace, legislation of interest to craftspersons and the like.*
—*Marilyn Green*

•

Jewelry — Refinement and simplicity are the key words. We're seeing less interest in stones and more interest in what the metal is doing. Tac pins and bar pins have replaced stick pins. Gold sales continue to climb despite the price. We would like to see more jewelry for men, particularly bracelets.

•

Free Listings for Architectural Crafts — A reference book for architects that will list craftspeople who make exterior architectural ornaments is being compiled by Brent C. Bolin for publication by Van Nostrand Reinhold. "The Handbook of Architectural Ornament" will be marketed to 80,000 design professionals, according to Mr. Bolin. Craftspeople will be listed free of charge. To be considered for a listing, send information and illustrative material to Brent C. Bolin, 25 Washington Square North, New York, NY 10011.

The Crafts Report
(The Newsmonthly of Marketing, Management and Money for Crafts Professionals)
Michael Scott, Editor
$13.50 /year (12 issues)
from:
The Crafts Report
700 Orange Street
P.O. Box 1992
Wilmington, DE 19899

Safe Practices in the Arts and Crafts

This book should be in every artist/craftsperson's library. It is a guide to intelligent handling of hazardous materials and processes. The basic OSHA guidelines — ventilation, protective clothing, and housekeeping and storage are presented then hazards related to various crafts are listed by craft (ceramics, glassmaking, etc.). The format is straightforward and easy to read. Substances and processes are presented in graph form along with what sort of contact could be harmful and the possible effects of overexposure. At the end of each section is a simple list of what to do to keep your craft work area safe. Appendices list poison control centers, sources for protective respiratory devices and additional sources of information. The back cover is a fold-out health and work history chart which the owner of the book can use.
—*Marilyn Green*

(See "Safety Equipment," pp. 158 - 159.)

Safe Practices in the Arts and Crafts
(A Studio Guide)
Gail Coningsby Barzaghi
1978; 73 pp.
$3.75 postpaid from:
College Art Association of America
16 East 52nd Street
New York, NY 10022

Metals: Foundry

Contact	Substances and Processes	Effects of Overexposure
Inhalation	Dusts:	
	Asbestos in fillers, gloves, insulating materials	Can cause cancer. *No exposure to asbestos fibers is tolerable*
	Silica sand, silica flour (mold release), French chalk (talc)	Air-borne "free silica" can cause silicosis, see Glassmaking. First symptoms: shortness of breath, loss of appetite, dry cough, and increasing fatigue appearing anywhere from 6 months to 20 years after initial exposure. The only cure for silicosis is prevention
	Any dusts in abrasive grinding operations	Lung injury
	Fumes occurring at melting or vaporization point of each metal:	
	Copper, zinc, iron, bronze alloys	Cause flu-like symptoms 6 or more hours after exposure. Fever, head- and muscle aches; "bronze fever" or "zinc shakes" last about 24 hours
	Cadmium	*Highly toxic.* Can be fatal after a few hours of exposure. *Avoid any exposure* Note: If what seems to be a metal fume fever lasts for more than 24 hours after working with unknown alloys, cadmium poisoning should be suspected and medical treatment sought at once
	Beryllium	*Highly toxic.* Cause disabling and ultimately fatal berylliosis. *Avoid any exposure*
	Lead	*Highly toxic.* Continuous exposure results in systemic poisoning
	Manganese	May cause pneumonia, other lung diseases
	Resins and solvents used in mold and core making:	
	Isocyanates (in resins) and their thermal decomposition products such as ammonia	Irritation and sensitization of lungs, asthma
	Formaldehyde in resins used to bind sand molds can ignite when hot metal strikes mold and combine with hydrochloric acid to form bis-chloromethylether	Bis-chloromethylether is a potent carcinogen
	Nickel carbonyl used in mold making	*Carcinogen*
	Carbon monoxide	Replaces oxygen in blood at low levels, causes headaches, weakness, dizziness. *Increased levels may cause death*
	Acid vapors from finishing and etching operations	Irritate mucous membranes, lungs
	Smoke of burning or heated wax in model work or lost wax processes	Irritates mucous membranes, lungs
	Thermal decomposition products of styrofoam molds, burnout	Irritate skin; cause fatigue, nausea, headache, possibly other systemic damage
Skin contact, ingestion	Oils, grease, acid compounds	Dermatitis, ulcerations; can be ingested while eating or smoking
	Solvents:	See Solvents
	Benzene, carbon tetrachloride, trichlorethylene	Blood disorders, leukemias, and other cancers. *They should not be used*
	Methyl n-butyl ketone	Industrial exposure is known to cause peripheral nerve damage and other nervous system disturbances

Wood for Wood-Carvers and Craftsmen

"Wood is where you find it," and how you handle it. An inveterate wood scrounge, this man knows his stuff and says it clearly, albeit a little dryly. A valuable tool.
—*Diana Sloat*

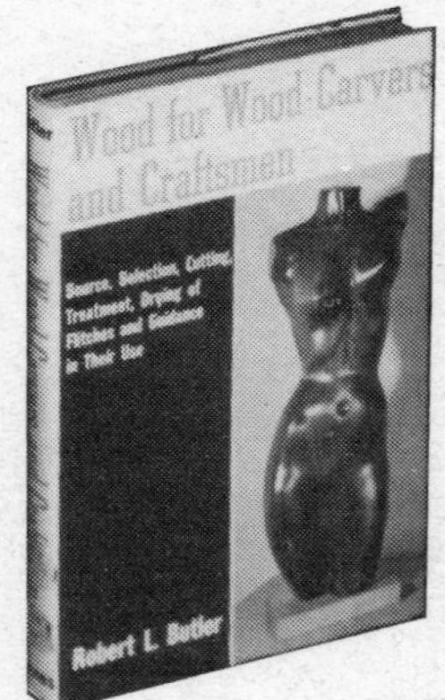

Wood for Wood-Carvers and Craftsmen
(Source, Selection, Cutting, Treatment, Drying of Flitches and Guidance in Their Use)
Robert L. Butler
1974; 122 pp.
$4.95 postpaid from:
A.S. Barnes & Co.
Box 421
Cranbury, NJ 08512
or Whole Earth Household Store

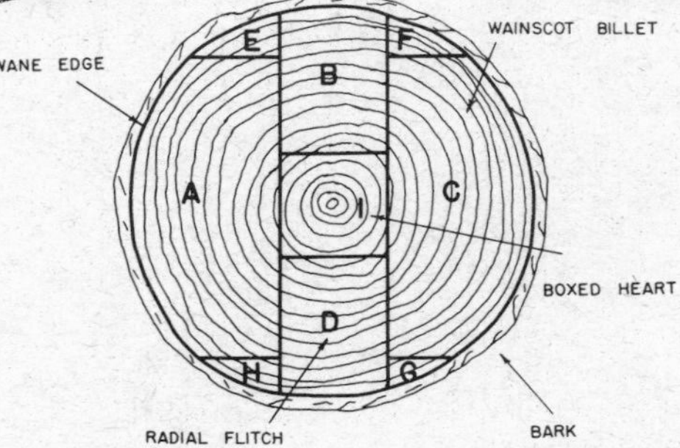

Diagram of flitches (A through H) that should be cut from a log without defects. Wainscot billets (A and C) are for large carvings; flitches B and D are radially sawed but smaller flitches; and E through H are of least value. The heart with pith (1) should be "boxed out" (discarded). It is a section highly susceptible to checking.

•

The most important item is some type of temperature control unit which will contain paraffin or candle wax. A deep-fat fryer is excellent if temperatures below 212°F can be maintained. A double cooker does this inexpensively and it can be assembled from the kitchen without so much as a raised eyebrow from your spouse. . . The paraffin can be purchased in pound blocks at the grocery store from the canning supplies section. This is paraffin used for sealing preserves and jellies. I have found Gulf-wax 33 manufactured by the Gulf Oil Company the best. It has a melting point of 133°F and spreads as lightly as water when heated to 170-180°F. It comes in 55-pound cases at almost one-third the cost of paraffin purchased at the grocery store. . . Be sure the largest end of the flitch is squared. During the drying and storage period it will stand on end so that the air can circulate to all unparaffined surfaces. Brush both ends clean and apply hot paraffin in a thin and penetrating coat. Penetration of the paraffin is assured only if the surface is dry and warm. A test of the correct technique is to observe whether or not the applied paraffin is transparent, that is, the annual rings and the wood structure are readily observed through the coat. If, however, the application is opaque, one or two or both requirements have not been met. If the surface is wet, paraffin cannot fill the excised cells. An opaque layer is an indication that there is an air space between the paraffin and the wood structure. In time it will chip off, moisture will be lost too rapidly from the ends of the flitch, and checking will follow.

The author's lode of flitches, representing many domestic species in a great variety of shapes and sizes

•

Wood is where you find it. Neatly stacked piles of hardwood often contain species of unusual color and grain. The tree-top left following the removal of veneer or peeler logs, or an old orchard that has finished its days of bearing fruit or nuts contains a gold mine for the carver. Clearings made by a bulldozer for roads and building sites often contain many worthwhile logs that the construction boss is happy to have removed.

Fine Hardwoods Selectorama

The title sounds corny as hell, but the book packs a whale of a lot of information. The book has a three-page graph illustrating the "comparative physical properties of some popular species." The graph deals mainly with domestics (alder, hackberry, osage orange, willow, etc.) and includes some exotics. Specific gravity, lbs./ft.³, strength, stiffness, hardness, shock resisting ability, bending strength, and shrinkage from green to dry states are the categories covered. The book then lists nearly every wood of any commercial importance (domestic and foreign) conveying unusual characteristics, availability, relative cost, source, and Latin names (interesting to see who's in the same family). The soft cover book has 58 pages, 189 photographs, and 75 different woods are shown.
—*Thomas Rein*

Fine Hardwoods Selectorama
(A Guide to the Selection and Use of the World's Most Popular Species)
1978; 57 pp.
$5 postpaid from:
Fine Hardwoods/ American Walnut Assn.
666 North Lake Shore Drive, Suite 1730
Chicago, IL 60611

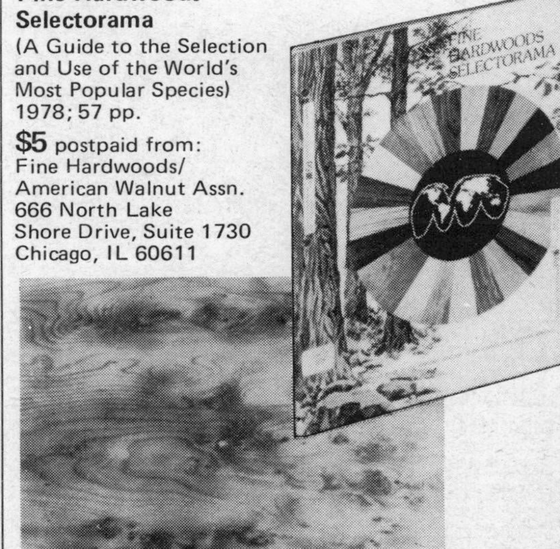

Yew, English (Taxus baccata) European, Caucasian. Source: England. Color: White to pale lemon to pale pink, sometimes orange to reddish-brown to rose red. Pattern: Smooth, lustrous grain frequently made distinctive and attractive with tiny black burls or pips, straight grained to wavy. Characteristics: Fine textured, strong, elastic. Availability: Limited. Price Range: Valuable.

Whittling and Woodcarving

Remember sitting by the monkeycage at the Alliance Zoo (two male spidermonkeys with piles), and watching a gandydancer (must have been a gandy . . . wasn't an Indian. It was the middle of the day, and he wasn't at work) whittling on a chunk of two by four. It took him about two hours to carve it down into a cage with three balls locked inside. I've tried whittling away Montana nights. Turned out a double-ended wooden spoon and made the bandaid people thirty cents richer. Should've read the book. A classic.
—*J.D. Smith*

Whittling and Woodcarving
E.J. Tangerman
1936, 1962; 293 pp.
$3.50 postpaid from:
Dover Publications Inc.
180 Varick Street
New York, NY 10014
or Whole Earth Household Store

How to Carve Totem Poles

I can report from experience that there are few things more satisfying than carving a totem pole. Don't knock it until you've tried it. The author has been carving for 20 years. He's good at it, and his book is good too. I might also add that totem carving is a great family enterprise; your pole can accommodate everyone's personal ideas and yet be one thing. Think of how our cities would look if the power companies let us decorate their poles. The book is one of those rare labors of love.
—*J. Baldwin*
[Suggested by Meryl & Mike Domina]

How to Carve Totem Poles
Paul N. Luvera, Sr.
1977; 160 pp.
$11.95 postpaid from:
Paul N. Luvera, Sr.
2102 9th Street
Anacortes, WA 98221

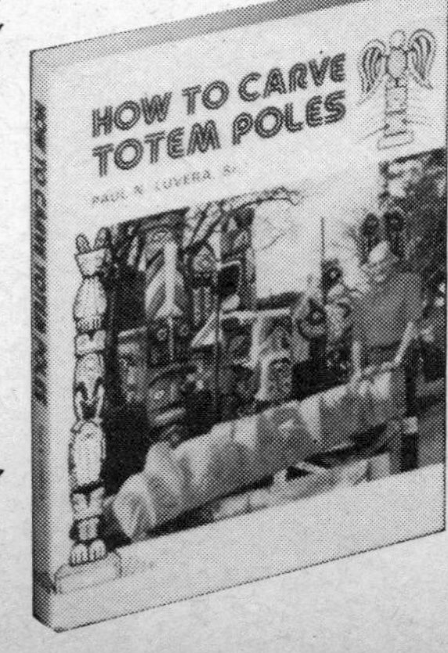

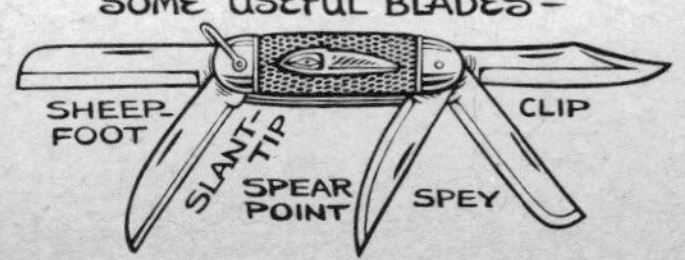
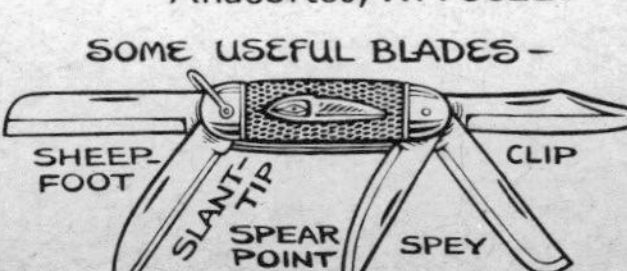
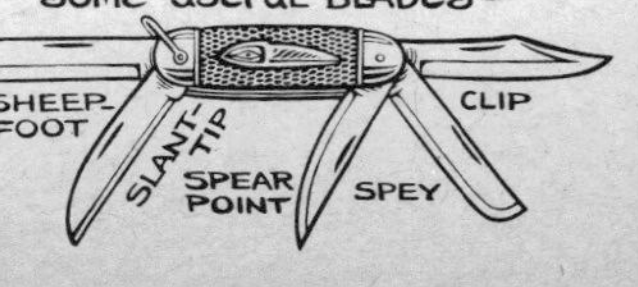

Woodcarvers tools

Three sources of high quality carving tools. (Besides Garrett Wade and Woodcraft Supply, pp. 142-143.) As Bruce Erman suggests, why not carve up your bed a bit, the doors in your life, the kitchen table, a redwood stump, or that attractive slab of firewood that became a suggestive flitch precisely as you hefted it toward the flames (don't carve by firelight).
—*SB*
[Suggested by Bruce Erman and James Jones]

Frank Mittermeier
Catalog
free from:
Frank Mittermeier, Inc.
3577 East Tremont Ave.
Bronx, NY 10465

Imported Wood Carving Tools
Brochures
free from:
Sculpture Associates, Ltd.
114 East 25th Street
New York, NY 10010

Carl Heidtmann
Information
Send 3 International Reply Coupons (about $1.20) to:
Carl Heidtmann
5630 Remscheid-Hasten
Unterholter Strasse 46
Postfach 140245
West Germany

Consists of 3 tools, 2 bench knives and 1 gouge 4 mm wide, with easy to use palm handle. It is the perfect set for whittling and chip carving and useful on many odd cutting jobs. Complete set, in plastic bag, $15.95.
—**Frank Mittermeier**

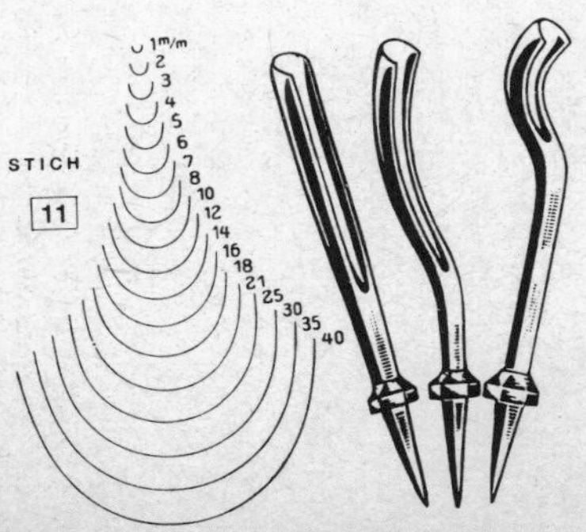

Shapes for sculpture tools. Handles separate.
—**Sculpture Associates, Ltd.**

What Wood is That?

Forty actual wafer-thin samples of wood are contained in the fold-out frontispiece to this book, from afromosia to zebrawood. The samples and a unique classification system using 14 characteristics (rings, pores, weight, smell, leaf shape, etc.) are used to identify the woods most widely used in the U.S.
—*Lloyd Kahn*
[Suggested by Ann Rockler]

What Wood is That?
(A Manual of Wood Identification)
Herbert L. Edlin
1969; 160 pp.
$16.50 postpaid from:
The Viking Press
299 Murray Hill Parkway
East Rutherford, NJ 07073
or Whole Earth Household Store

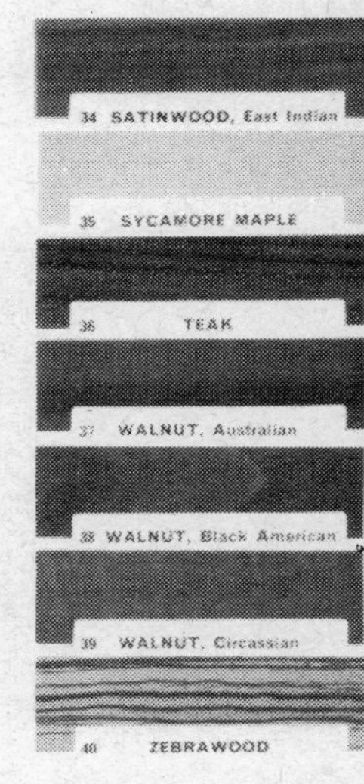

THE RISING SUN
NEIGHBORHOOD NEWSLETTER

In Sunday School literature, there will sometimes be a lesson entitled "Are you a Mary or a Martha?" They never ask, "Are you a Jesus?" — calm about buses and condescending toward women who fuss. I tend to be like that. I have solved my own cooking problem by waiting till the urge for hot, complexly mixed food becomes unbearable and going to a medium priced restaurant and letting underpaid people of darker skin than mine cook for me and clean up after me.

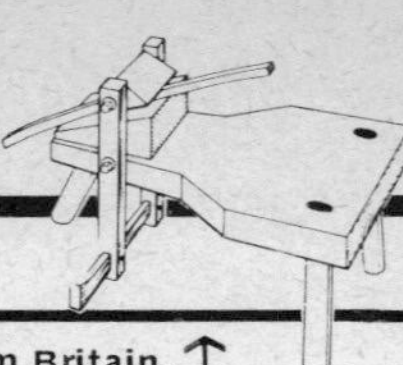

A wee, three-legged shaving horse from Britain. ↑

Country Woodcraft

Once in a while a book crosses my desk that is so impeccable that I find myself grinning from ear to ear as I read it. I had seen early rough drafts of this and knew it would be a good one, but it's better than I could have dreamed; damn near perfect. Drew Langsner and his wife Louise give more than the usually dry history of old-time woodworking techniques; they've become masters of the art. They want you to be too, and give all the information you'll need for making a wide variety of objects ranging from plows to baskets. The photographs are unusually clear. The text is spare, competent, and loving. I'm sure that this will be a classic. Get one for yourself and give one to someone you like a lot. —J. Baldwin

Country Woodcraft
Drew Langsner
1978; 320 pp.

$9.95 postpaid from:
Rodale Books
33 East Minor
Emmaus, PA 18049
or Whole Earth
Household Store

CONTENTS

1. The Basic Tools
2. Materials
3. Felling
4. The Woodshed
5. Sawbuck
6. Shaving Horses
7. Clubs, Mauls, and Mallets
8. Bow Saws
9. Tool Handles
10. Wedges
11. The Workbench
12. A Spring-Pole Lathe
13. Hay Rakes
14. Pitchforks
15. The Wheelbarrow
16. Swiss Milking Stool
17. A Hauling Yoke
18. Sleds
19. Bull Tongue Plow
20. Spike-Tooth A-Harrow
21. Drags
22. Poke
23. Broom Tying
24. Bark Boxes — Louise Langsner
25. White Oak Basketry — Louise Langsner
26. Spoons
27. Dough Troughs
28. A Farmhouse Table
29. A Dining Bench
30. Pine Whisks

Appendix I. Mortise and Tenon Joinery
Appendix II. Wood Finishes
Appendix III. Uses of Usually Useless Woods
Appendix IV. Tool Suppliers
Annotated Bibliography
Index

A pitchfork

A shaving or drawing horse.

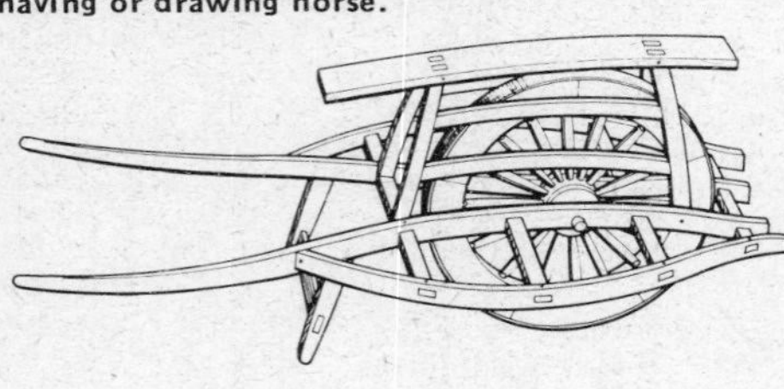

↑
The ideal solution would locate the load over the wheel itself, so that the operator can concentrate his energy on forward movement, not lifting. The genius of this is fully realized in traditional Chinese wheelbarrows. In the Chinese design, a framework is placed around and above the wheel, which is very large (fully 3 feet in diameter), so that it's comparatively easy to negotiate the rough roads or paths around farm plots. Very heavy loads — several persons, huge bundles of produce, wood, or goods — can be carried. But the load has to be tied on as there is no handy compartment to dump stuff into.

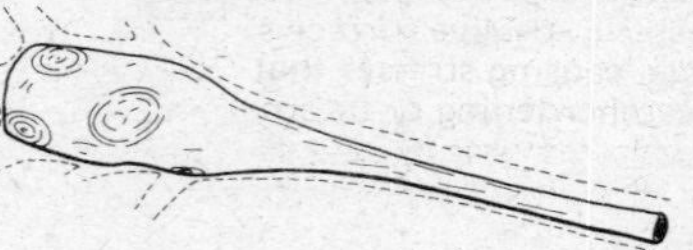

Cudgel. Carved from root and butt of a dogwood or hickory sapling. Length 28 to 36 inches, approximately 10 pounds.

Country Furniture

I began building furniture without hardware partly as a discipline and partly because I lived thirty miles away from the nearest hardware store, and was surrounded by a forest of nice round lodgepole pine with no electric wires strung between them. I began with a pretty good load of hand tools, and a couple of picture books, built a shaving horse from the pictures in Eric Sloane's **Museum of Early American Tools**, *and then went to drawknifing and drilling and pegging wood to wood.*

One thing for sure: **Country Furniture** *is a good picture book, mainly because its author is a book illustrator, but also because there is a lot of interest shown in the working procedures and tools of early American furniture makers. This is not a step-by-step manual, more of a collection of lost knowledge which can be put to good use by the crafts person who is having a little trouble finding someone to whom to apprentice nowadays. If only I could build furniture as precisely as Aldren Watson can illustrate.* —J.D. Smith

Country Furniture
Aldren A. Watson
1974; 274 pp.

$4.95 postpaid from:
Plume Books
New American Library
P.O. Box 120
Woodbine, NJ 07621
or Whole Earth
Household Store

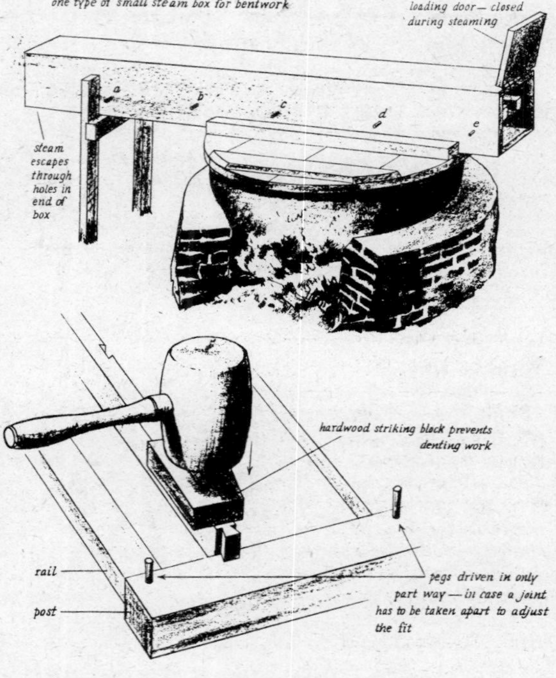

A Museum of Early American Tools

Behind making your own stuff there's another level: making your own tools to make your own stuff. This book gives detailed design information and fine illustration of America's pre-industrial tools, plus how to use them. Tell the twentieth century to go jump. —SB
[Suggested by Robert V. Allen]

A Museum of Early American Tools
Eric Sloane
1973; 108 pp.

$3.95 postpaid from:
Ballantine Books
455 Hahn Road
Westminster, MD 21157
or Whole Earth
Household Store

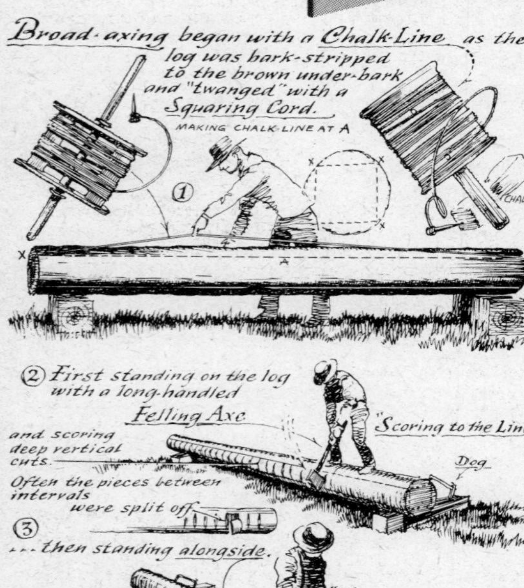

Broad-axing began with a Chalk-Line as the log was bark-stripped to the brown under-bark and "twanged" with a Squaring Cord.
MAKING CHALK-LINE AT A
①
② First standing on the log with a long-handled Felling Axe
and scoring deep vertical cuts.
"Scoring to the Line"
Dog
Often the pieces between intervals were split off
③
... then standing alongside.
"Hewing to the Line."
Holding the Broad axe with two hands, right hand foremost and left knee close to the log, the final smooth hewing was done

Woodland Crafts in Britain

Mr. Edlin is a forester, so his approach to country crafts comes through his interest in trees and wood. The work is authoritative and has much information available nowhere else. Chapters are divided by tree species; individual crafts and cross references are contained within. Much of the woodworking here uses coppice wood — see **Catalog** *p. 84 for how to grow it.* —Drew Langsner

Woodland Crafts in Britain
(An Account of the Traditional Uses of Trees and Timbers in the British Countryside)
Herbert L. Edlin
1949, 1973; 182 pp.

$15 postpaid from:
David & Charles Inc.
North Pomfret, VT 05053
or Whole Earth
Household Store

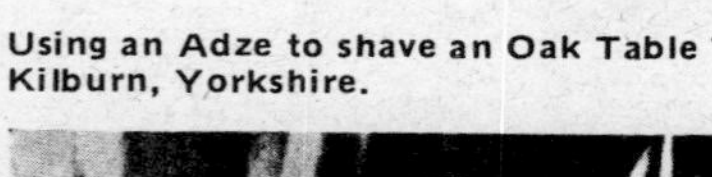

Using an Adze to shave an Oak Table Top; Kilburn, Yorkshire.

DETAILS OF WATTLE HURDLE MAKING. Twisting a rod at the end of the hurdle and weaving it between the upright sails.

Fine Woodworking Magazine

Journals give you more information for your money than most books, and this one's a fine example — fascinating, informative, and handsome, too. Articles are precise, clearly diagrammed and photographed, with sources listed throughout. Well worth the money.
—Diana Sloat

Damn fine magazine making I call it.
—SB

Fine Woodworking
Paul Roman, Editor
$14 /year (6 issues)
from:
The Taunton Press
P.O. Box 355
Newton, CT 06470

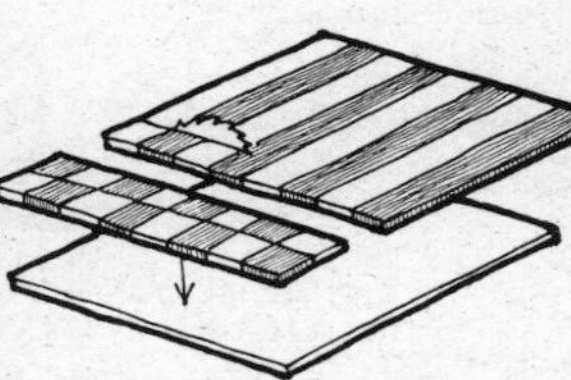

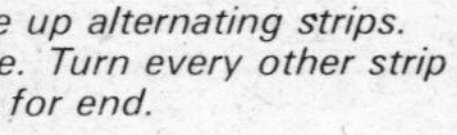

...ue up alternating strips. ...ce. Turn every other strip ...d for end.

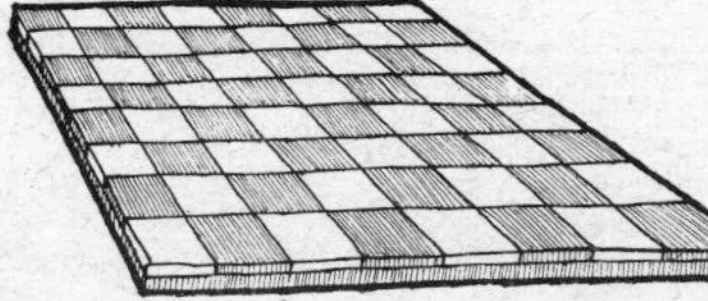

Laminate to plywood for extra strength.

Here's how I build a 16-in. checkerboard with a tenth of the work and time of the individual-square method.

Tackle box by Doug Cranmer was bent as shown in sketch below.

Although the art of the Pacific Northwest Coast Indians has long been recognized, little attention has been given to how they actually made things. Most people will think of their massive totem poles, dugout canoes and sculptural masks, but the kerf-bent wooden box is the more ingenious example of a woodworking technology developed through eons of practice. It consists of just two planks of cedar. One is the flat bottom, rabbeted all around to receive the sides. The other is a single plank that has been deeply kerfed in three places, plasticized by controlled steam and bent at right angles to form four sides. The last corner is sewn or pegged together. The result will hold water.

↓

Two-thirds of the energy used to manufacture lumber goes into drying it. Burning mill residue supplies only part of the energy used by conventional kilns; most of it is fossil fuel and electrical energy. In the United States, we use more than 10^{13} BTUs of fuel each year to dry lumber. Energy-efficient solar and dehumidifier kilns are important alternatives both to industry and to the individual woodworker.

Drying green wood involves removing both free water and some bound water. Free water is water in the cell cavities, and it evaporates relatively quickly and easily. But at the fiber saturation point (30% for most species) bound water must be extracted from within the cell walls, and shrinkage begins. If a board is dried too quickly, the moisture gradient between the surface and the core becomes too steep. Excessive surface shrinkage precedes internal shrinkage, causing stresses that can result in surface checks, casehardening or internal collapse (honeycomb). Proper drying requires careful pacing and close control of both temperature and humidity throughout the process.

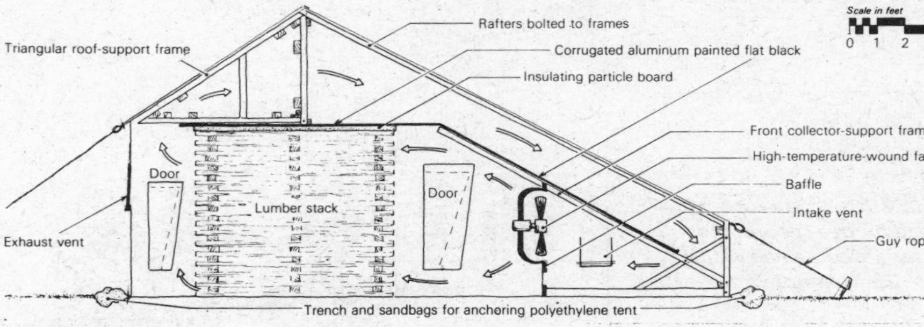

Oxford kiln

Fine Woodworking Biennial Design Book and Design Book Two

Ain't nothin' like some good examples to inspire the continuing rise of handmade crafts. These nicely produced books show the best work of about 1000 artists. I have greatly admired the attitude shown in these books and their parent magazine. The remarkably high quality displayed and the absence of artzy-fartzy "projects," is rare these days. Looking at these wonderful objects is pure pleasure. Too bad you can't meet the people too.
—J. Baldwin

Fine Woodworking Biennial Design Book
Editors of Fine Woodworking Magazine
1977; 175 pp.
$10 postpaid

Fine Woodworking Design Book Two
Editors of Fine Woodworking Magazine
1979; 288 pp.
$12 postpaid
both from:
The Taunton Press
P.O. Box 355
Newton, CT 06470
or Whole Earth Household Store

Don Kenyon, Naples, NY. Rocker with cradle. Pine, cherry, birch, maple, ash, 38 x 20 x 49; $595.

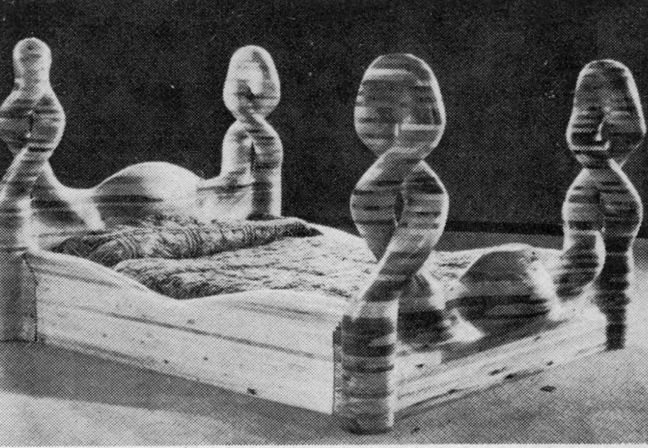

Larry Davis, Salem, Ohio. Sculptural Bed; pine, poplar; interior, 72 x 60; exterior, 96 x 84 x 60, $4,000. Laminated wood curved with a Craftsman 7-in. grinder and sanded with a Rockwell block sander.

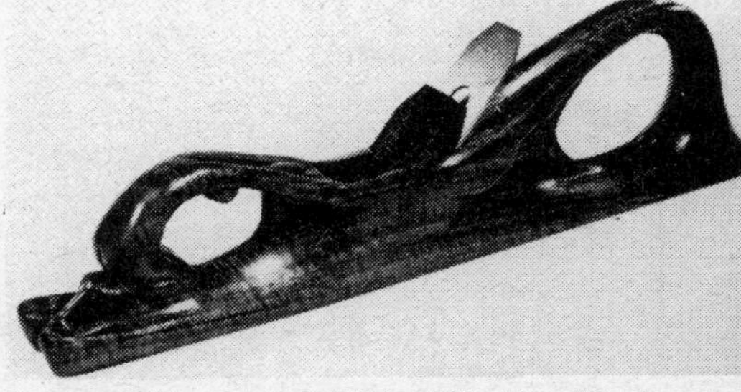

Cary Childress, Santa Monica, Calif. Two Figures on a Plane; shedua; 21 x 2½ x 6. **"I did it the hard way, no power tools. The design evolved from clay models that fit my hands. It feels comfortable no matter where I hold it. I purposely tried to make it look and feel light. But I found the weight was needed for function."**

Fine Woodworking Techniques 1 and 2

Almost 100 articles reprinted from **Fine Woodworking** *magazine make up these handsome books. Many of the subject headings deal with uncommon information. There is, for instance, an extensive article on making furniture that will not shrink apart in a desert climate. Master's secrets such as the art of French Polish are shown in detail. All by pros, for pros, and presented in a first-class manner befitting a tradition of meticulous craftsmanship.*
—J. Baldwin

Fine Woodworking Techniques One
Editors of Fine Woodworking Magazine
1978; 189 pp.
$15 postpaid

Fine Woodworking Techniques Two
Editors of Fine Woodworking Magazine
1980; 208 pp.
$15 postpaid
both from:
The Taunton Press
Box 355
Newtown, CT 06470
or Whole Earth Household Store

← The expansion bit is the wooden screwmaker's cup of tea. It's an inexpensive tool that is continuously adjustable from an inch to more than three inches in diameter. Normal auger bits come in 1/16-inch increments and aren't commonly available larger than an inch and a half. Expansion bits are made for use in the drill press or the hand brace.

The most popular bits for hand use are the Irwin "Microdial" and "Lockhead." The adjustment on the "Lockhead" cannot be tightened enough to hold its setting in hardwood; the more expensive "Microdial" locks more securely. Even so, it sometimes slips to a larger size. I find it necessary to grip the drill head in a vise and bear down hard on the screwdriver.

These drills have a spur that tends to bend outward as the drilling progresses. This enlarges the hole and makes it hard to turn the brace. The cure is to file the spur to about half its original length. After the spur has been shortened it must be filed on the inside surface to reduce its thickness and to re-establish a sharp cutting edge at the top. Auger bits seldom arrive sharp enough to make a clean cut in hardwood. It pays to dress the cutter edges with a fine India stone, then an Arkansas slip.

The little scale printed on the drill is much too coarse for accuracy. I always test the setting in scrap wood, and may adjust it four or five times before arriving at the exact setting.

Auger bits will leave a rough exit hole unless you clamp a piece of scrap behind the stock and drill through onto it. I like to clamp a piece of paper between the woods. When paper shavings emerge, the hole is through the stock.

THE RISING SUN
NEIGHBORHOOD NEWSLETTER

"That's the American dream — a covered wagon that will go 95 miles an hour all day long."
— David

Tage Frid Teaches Woodworking

This is destined to become a classic work, a book that serious amateurs and professionals will want to own and consult. It is a practical, well illustrated —both with photography and drawings — woodworking book. It covers both hand and power tool techniques concisely and thoughtfully. If a book warrants space on a craft person's shelf, this is one. —Rafael Diaz Guerrero

Tage Frid Teaches Woodworking
(Joinery: Tools and Techniques)
Tage Frid
1979; 206 pp.
$16 postpaid from:
The Taunton Press
P.O. Box 355
Newton, CT 06470
or Whole Earth Household Store

On a new marking gauge the steel pin that scribes the line into the wood is rounded down to a point. When scribing across the grain, the rounded point scratches the fibers and makes a fuzzy line. Therefore the pin of every new marking gauge must be refiled.

If you are right-handed, the edge that will face you when you pull the tool should be filed as sharp as a knife. If you are left-handed, you can reverse the filing to make the gauge easier for you to use.

The difference that refiling makes is easy to see. The round point makes a fuzzy line (top), while the refiled point makes a crisp, clear line (bottom) with no tendency to wander with the grain.

1

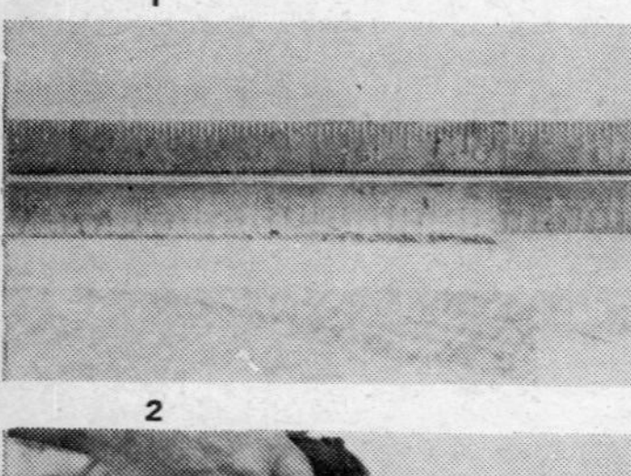

2

3

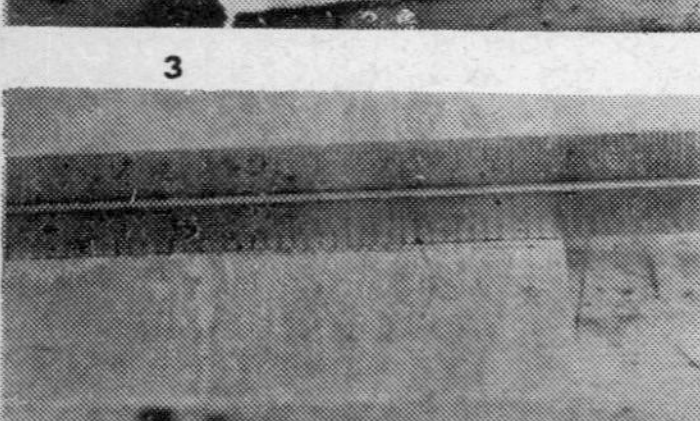

Straightening Warped Wood

If a board warps before the joint is cut, and the joints are cut while the board is still warped, the joints will never fit correctly. (1) In this picture, the convex side is up to show how warped the board is. To straighten out the board so the joints can be cut, wet a cloth and place it on the concave side of the board.

Using a hot iron (2), steam the board until it is straight. (3) The board will straighten out very fast. Then hurry up and cut cut your joints while the board is straight. Even if the board warps again, the pieces will go back together straight because the joints were cut when the boards were straight.

The Woodworker's Bible

Disregarding its pretentious title, **The Woodworker's Bible** *is a valuable reference book. It covers every facet of woodshop production, offering excellent information for any craftsman considering production. The emphasis is on large-scale power tools. If you're considering more elaborate shop tools, the book is useful for thinking about that.* —Rafael Diaz Guerrero

The Woodworker's Bible
Alf Martensson
1979; 288 pp.
$15.95 postpaid from:
Bobbs-Merrill Company
4300 West 62nd Street
Indianapolis, IN 46268
or Whole Earth Household Store

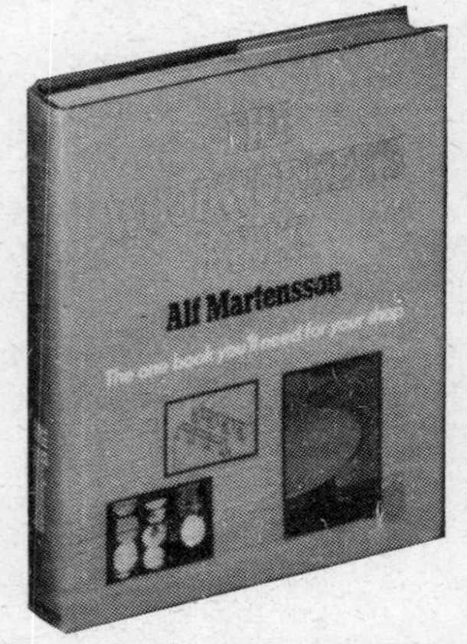

•

The simplest knock-down fitting of all is the screwed joint with washers fitted under the head. These can be surface fitting (screw cups) or flush fitting (screw sockets), but the former are much easier to fix and do not require any countersinking.

Various devices for screws.

A simple knock-down device: screws with washers. Left: screw sockets. Right: screw cups.

One method I have often used and found very satisfactory is to insert a wall plug into the second piece of wood. This can be the plastic or fiber type used for screwing into masonry walls. It holds by friction rather than mechanically by the threads, so it can be used in end grain and plywood, making it particularly suitable for screwing the ends to the shelves on bookcases.

Craftsman Wood Service

Much the same stuff as Constantine's Wood Catalog. Some things cost less, others more. Craftsman has some things Constantine doesn't, and vice versa. If you use one of them, you really need both. Craftsman has almost anything you could think of for fine woodworking, from the wood itself to books telling you how, and including tools, cabinet hardware (more kinds of hinges, for example, than you could imagine), and upholstery supplies. If you would like to try your hand at making a violin, they can provide you with an instruction book and all the materials (no ready-to-assemble kit, praises be). —Edwin L. Powers

Craftsman Wood Service
Catalog
$.50 from:
Craftsman Wood Service Company
1735 W. Cortland Court
Addison, IL 60101

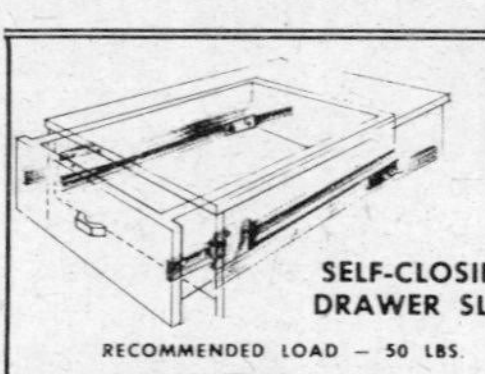

SELF-CLOSING DRAWER SLIDE

RECOMMENDED LOAD — 50 LBS.

Closes automatically when drawer is within 4½" of closing—glides shut easily, smoothly, noiselessly on ball-bearing nylon rollers. Allow ½" on each side and for length measure from back of drawer front to rear of drawer. 10% discount on 10 pair or more of one size.

Number	Length	Travel	Shpg. Wt.	
H8407	18"	12½"	Wt. 2½ lbs.	$5.20
H8408	20"	14½"	Wt. 2¾ lbs.	5.40
H8409	22"	16½"	Wt. 3 lbs.	5.59
H8410	24"	18½"	Wt. 3¼ lbs.	5.75

CRAFTSMAN WHERE QUALITY IS IMPORTANT

CRAFTSMAN'S TRIPLE A (AAA) GRADE LUMBER
SUPPLIED FLAT—SANDED TOP AND BOTTOM—SIDES CUT PARALLEL
Cherry Walnut Mahogany

These boards are SOMETHING special. We select only top quality lumber from which to make them. They are all clear one side—no knots, cracks or twist, a small percentage having occasional minor defects on the other side. Surfaced smooth both sides with edges cut with parallel surfaces ready for gluing. Sizes are nominal, pieces usually overcut to some extent.

Thickness x Width x Length	Cherry Item No.	Cherry Price per Piece	Walnut Item No.	Walnut Price per Piece	Mahogany Item No.	Mahogany Price per Piece	Length	Cherry Item No.	Cherry Price per Piece	Walnut Item No.	Walnut Price per Piece	Mahogany Item No.	Mahogany Price per Piece
⅛ x 5½ x 18"	W4501	$1.33	W4601	$1.78	W4701	$1.57	36"	W4556	$2.92	W4656	$3.75	W4756	$3.30
¼ x 5½ x 18"	W4502	1.77	W4602	2.41	W4702	2.12	36"	W4557	3.94	W4657	5.13	W4757	4.53

Wood Finishing and Refinishing

Wood Finishing and Refinishing *is a complete text on the subject. It is concise, answering any question on wood finishing one might have. An excellent and needed sourcebook.* —Rafael Diaz Guerrero

Wood Finishing and Refinishing
S.W. Gibbia
1954, 1971; 271 pp.
$6.95 postpaid from:
Van Nostrand Reinhold Company
Order Department
7625 Empire Drive
Florence, KY 41042
or Whole Earth Household Store

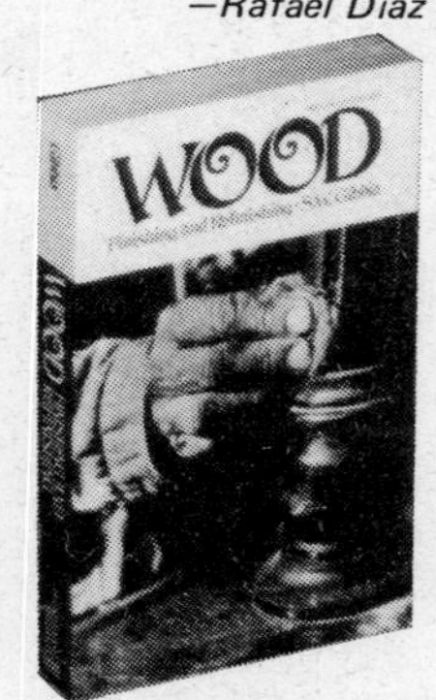

Varnish is flowed on the surface across the grain. When the surface is covered, the brush is dried over the edge of the varnish can, and the dry brush is used with the grain. Then the brush is dried again and just the tip of it is used to make long even strokes with the grain.

↓

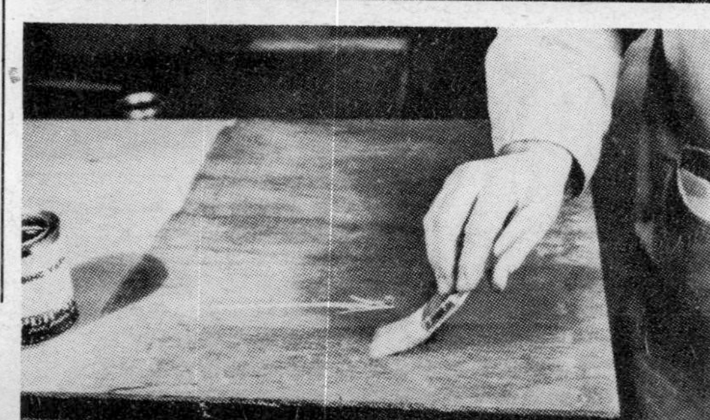

Constantine's Woodworker's Catalog

Lots of things for woodworking. Prices are high, but if you can't get it anywhere else. . . Lots of fancy woods and finishes. Guitar materials. Fancy cabinet hardware. —Fred Richardson

Constantine's Woodworker's Catalog
Catalog
$.50 from:
Albert Constantine and Son, Inc.
2050 Eastchester Road
Bronx, NY 10461

SIZE	THICK-NESS	SH. WT. LB.	CHERRY	MAHOGANY	MAPLE	OAK	POPLAR
7½ x 24	¼	2	$ 4.25	$ 3.80	$ 2.80	$ 4.40	$ 2.60
	½	2	6.50	5.90	4.60	7.10	3.60
	¾	3	7.50	6.90	5.60	8.10	4.60
	1¼	6	10.40	8.90	6.60	10.90	6.80
	1¾	7	13.90	11.80	10.40	18.00	7.40
7½ x 36	¼	2	6.00	5.50	4.20	6.60	3.90
	½	4	9.50	9.20	6.70	10.50	5.40
	¾	4	10.50	10.20	7.70	11.50	6.40
	1¼	8	14.70	13.80	9.90	16.90	8.80
	1¾	10	20.50	18.40	14.60	26.00	11.10

WHITTLER'S KNIFE

This knife was selected as being the most useful for size and shape for most kinds of whittling. Made of the finest quality steel and will give many years of service. Further your enjoyment and increase your ability in carving. Also very handy to have for all types of craft work.
No. 170K9—Blade 1½". Sh. wt. 3 oz.
Price ea. **$2.50**

By Shaker Hands

I have been an admirer and kindergarten student of Shaker furniture for several years, trying somehow to make my hands perform acts of simple beauty while my head was still in the catacombs of California. I have built several pieces of furniture and have read most of the literature on the subject, but this work, by a young woman of extraordinary graphic expertise, comes closer to teaching me about the hand-eye-God connections than anything else has to this point in my education. June Sprigg worked with what Shakers are left (celibacy is one means of zero population growth), and has created a great book, full of detailed drawings, good prose, and a love of labor. Did you know that the circular saw was invented by a spinner, Sister Tabitha Babbit?

—J.D. Smith

By Shaker Hands
June Sprigg
1975; 208 pp.

$9.95 postpaid from:
Alfred A. Knopf
Random House
455 Hahn Road
Westminster, MD 21157
or Whole Earth
Household Store

Double calipers saved time for the carpenter because he could record two different measurements at once.

↑ **Space was at a premium in Shaker Dwellinghouses, since a Shaker Family often numbered over a hundred. They made the most of limited space by furnishing very simply. Ideally, a Shaker dwellingroom for Brother or Sister was to contain little more than (clockwise from upper left):**

one candlestand
two beds on rollers, easily movable
several large windows for light and ventilation
two straight chairs
one lamp
one table
one broom and several clothesbrushes
one small iron woodburning stove for heating
one or more built-in cupboards and sets of drawers
one woodbox with dustbrush
one small hanging mirror
one simple carpet
. . . and of course wall pegs.

•

My Mother is a carpenter
She hews the crooked stick
And she will have it strait and squair
Altho it cuts the quick.

How to Build Your Own Furniture

Unlike most books on do-it-yourself furniture, **How to Build Your Own Furniture** *by R.J. DeCristoforo contains no plans on how to build your own furniture. What it does contain is information on what should go into the design of a given piece of furniture to make it function properly. If you have ever built a table that wobbled or a drawer that wouldn't open, you will appreciate this book.*

The book gives a wealth of information and illustrations on techniques and methods of quality furniture craftsmanship. There are chapters on materials and general design and construction with separate chapters on each of the different categories of furniture (such as tables, chairs, desks, chests, etc.). The book is very concise and the instructions and illustrations are easily understandable. This is definitely a standard work for the designer-craftsman.

—Lloyd Martin

How to Build Your Own Furniture
R.J. DeCristoforo
1976; 176 pp.

$3.95 postpaid from:
Barnes and Noble Books
Keystone Industrial Bldg.
Scranton, PA 18512
or Whole Earth
Household Books

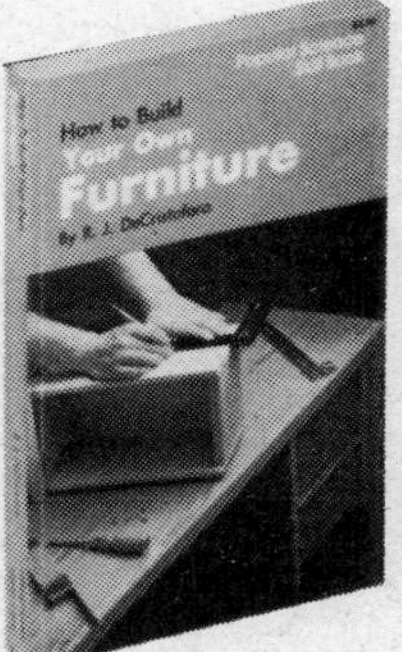

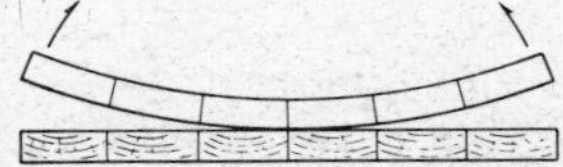
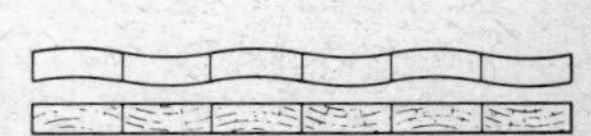

↑ **When gluing up boards to make a slab, alternate end grain of each board (right) so warping is confined to individual boards. (Warping is exaggerated in drawing.) After finishing with sander or planer, slab will be flat and smooth. If end grain of each board faces in same direction (left), warping is cumulative and affects the entire slab.**

Seat Weaving

This little book is a jewel. It was first printed in 1917 to be used as a text for industrial art workshops in schools. The only thing out of date is the prices one should charge for caning (he says $2.00 maximum for an average size chair). Here in western North Carolina I get about $15.00. The photographs are great, especially the close-ups of ten different designs to use on flat reed and split seats. The book also tells you how to gather, prepare and use rush (cat-tails) for seat bottoming. You can order it and all kinds of high quality seat materials from:

H.H. Perkins Co.
10 South Bradley Road
Woodbridge, CT 06525

I've been dealing with them for five years, they are a very reliable company. *—Deborah Shell*

Seat Weaving
L. Day Perry
1917, 1940; 94 pp.

$2.60 postpaid from:
Charles A. Bennett Company
809 West Detweiller Dr.
Peoria, IL 61614

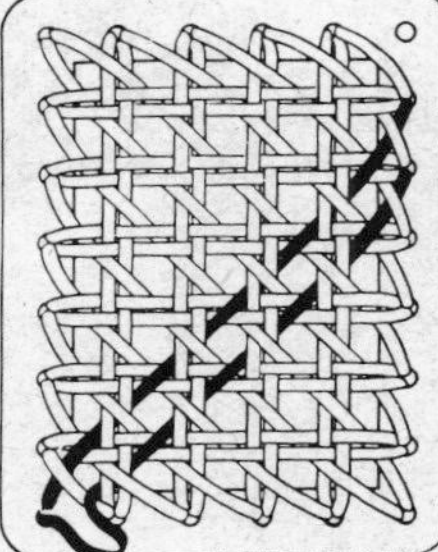

Weaving the second diagonal strands

Make a Chair from a Tree

Loving, detailed instructions (and thoughts) on making a traditional slat back chair. Using hand tools, Alexander first shows how to make a low work bench and a shaving horse, then goes into the many elements involved in making a chair — design considerations (looks, strength, comfortable fit), properties of working wood (especially green hardwood), with detailed chapters on the rungs, posts, slats and woven seating.

John Alexander is a Baltimore lawyer who has been making chairs with a passion for 13 years. He has evolved a personal style, and it is his hope that the reader/craftsman will do likewise. A beautiful book.

—Drew Langsner

Make a Chair from a Tree
(An Introduction to Working Green Wood)
John D. Alexander, Jr.
1978; 125 pp.

$7.95 postpaid from:
The Taunton Press
P.O. Box 355
Newtown, CT 06470

or Whole Earth
Household Store

•

Chairs are for people to sit on. They should be built for individual bodies, not on the basis of arbitrary measurements. Don't copy the dimensions of an existing chair unless the intended user has sat upon it and found it fits. A quick sit isn't enough — spend some time in a chair before you declare it comfortable.

The shape of shaved rungs follows the long fibers, which aren't always straight. Shaving keeps the long fibers intact — these rungs are strong and flexible. ↓

The Encyclopedia of Furniture Making

Joyce is British; his approach to wood is that of a "machine-assisted" hand craftsman soaked in the rich tradition of English joinery. He has high standards and a wealth of knowledge to offer the craftsman interested in making top quality furniture. His book is lavishly illustrated, fun to read and savor. *—Norman Potter*

The Encyclopedia of Furniture Making
Ernest Joyce
1979, 494 pp.

$14.95 postpaid from:
Sterling Publishing Co.
Two Park Avenue
New York, NY 10016
or Whole Earth
Household Store

Victorian rocking-chair in steam-bent beech

Cohasset Colonial furniture kits

If you're not going to make your own furniture, you can at least assemble it. These are well-crafted antique reproductions with a clean spare quality to them. *—SB*

Cohasset Colonials
Catalog

$1.00 from:
Cohasset Colonials
Cohasset, MA 02025

Large Shaker dining table. Spacious ¾" pine top measures 82" long and 30" wide. Height 30". Seats eight comfortably. Kit $197.00 — wt. 80 lbs.

THE RISING SUN
NEIGHBORHOOD NEWSLETTER

It was really important to Freud that oceanic experience be really sexual. Oceanic experiences are characteristically had by children 7 to 9 who are walking around outside and suddenly feel that they are part of it all and it all is part of them and there are no lines between any of it. Time stops and the kid feels good. Freud said this was because children have an overdeveloped ego that feels it actually can encompass everything and also because they really want to have a little sex with someone but they repress that desire and it comes out as this false feeling of oneness.

It was really important to Freud that oceanic experience be really sexual because he didn't want there to be an ocean. You could think there is an ocean and sex is one of the beaches and there are other beaches, but it wasn't Freud's kind of thought.

Entering Ceramics

by Mary Law

Japanese Stoneware Dish — 18th century. Horse-eye pattern.

In attempting an overview of ceramics, I feel the most important thing to discuss is its diversity – in approach and in result. Clay has been used for thousands of years, and one of the reasons for its use is its very nature. It is plastic and flexible, and then upon drying (and, usually, firing) it becomes hard, durable and permanent; it is thus a very adaptable, multi-purpose material. Those same characteristics contribute to its widely varying usage today.

As one travels around this country (and certainly, the world), it seems that people are approaching clay in every conceivable way. Some choose clay for its malleable and receptive nature, working spontaneously and quickly; others plan and execute exact, sometimes very complex forms from the same material. Some people rejoice in the lack of control over the clay in certain types of firing, while others opt for a more controlled approach with quite predictable results, sometimes even firing with the aid of a computer. A person's approach to clay is at times a part of a whole lifestyle: people interested in a self-sufficient existence may place importance on digging their own clay and using local renewable fuels (for example wood) for firing their work. Probably the majority of people using clay rely on the permanence achieved by firing the piece, but others make statements of their own by leaving the clay unfired and therefore fragile and impermanent. Some people use clay solely to make an artistic statement, and others feel that function is the main impetus in their work. Some are self-taught, others have years of training behind them. Of course, these diverse positions are not mutually exclusive, but are rather interrelated aspects of the whole.

Work situations too vary widely. They can range from a small room or even a tabletop in someone's house, to a large studio designed to accommodate a particular person's work needs. Some people choose to work in a cooperative group studio, which could range from two or more people sharing a single space to perhaps twenty or more separate studios in the same building. Some people enroll in classes and do most of their work in the ceramics department. An apprenticeship, though rare, sometimes provides a person with the space in which to work. Studios seem to exist in every possible location – they can be found right in the heart of the city as well as in remote, rural areas.

A word should be said, I think, about occupational or professional avenues open to people who work in clay. Making a living by selling one's work is a →

Finding One's Way With Clay

One of the best books for beginners I know of, because it doesn't intimidate but rather encourages one to try and see. Excellent photographs. It shows a nice approach to working in general – enough technique (and clearly explained) for control, accompanied by the important message that mistakes and surprises are alright. Many good suggestions for next steps and for how to move in new directions in general. I cherish this book.

—*Mary Law*

•

This exercise came about when I needed to develop a way of practice to help counteract two traits I experience in myself and observe in some of my students as well. The first trait I would liken to a form of addiction. I come to a way of working that I like and enjoy and find important for a time, and find myself continuing with it well past the time that the light and life in this way have gone out of it. . . .

The second trait is one that I believe I share with many students of pottery. It has to do with a quality of willfulness. Often I work with a predetermined vision of what I would like to make, and while this, in many instances, seems to work fine for me, there are many other instances when this way of working produces a kind of deafness and sightlessness and lack of sensitivity to what is actually happening. . . .

So I set myself this task: to take a small amount of clay and wrap it freely and simply with soft yarn and then to pinch out the clay, moving only where the yarn allowed me to move. I would follow what the yarn design established. If there were an open area the clay would move out; it if were a bound area the clay would have to move up or down. I didn't seem to have to make any decisions. What resulted were forms unlike any I had ever made or seen before. ↓

Finding One's Way With Clay
Paulus Berensohn
1972; 158 pp.

$7.95 postpaid from:
Simon & Schuster
Rockefeller Center
630 Fifth Avenue
New York, NY 10020
or Whole Earth
Household Store

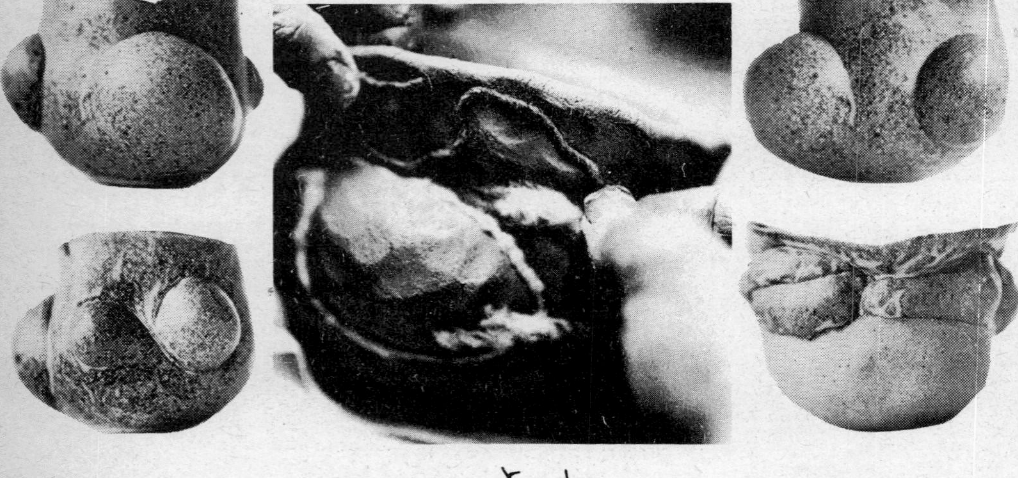

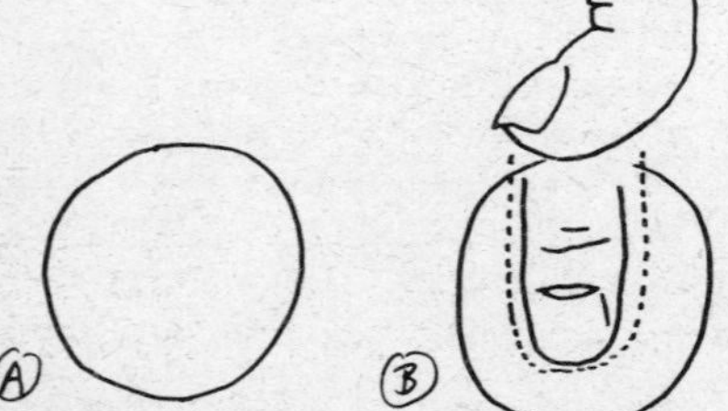

Lifted Bowl: A) Starting with a round ball B) Thumb starts flat and ends straight C) Stroking up with even pressure

Ceramics

This book contains a very brief coverage of technical information about clay, then more detailed sections on building, throwing and decorating techniques. There is an especially good section on glazes and glaze calculation, also a detailed chapter on the professional potter, including much about industrial methods, and a section about studio equipment. There is a sampling of recipes in the back, and a really good variety of photographs throughout. This book provides a good way for a beginner to get a sense of how many possibilities there are.

—*Mary Law*
[Suggested by Jon Kaplan]

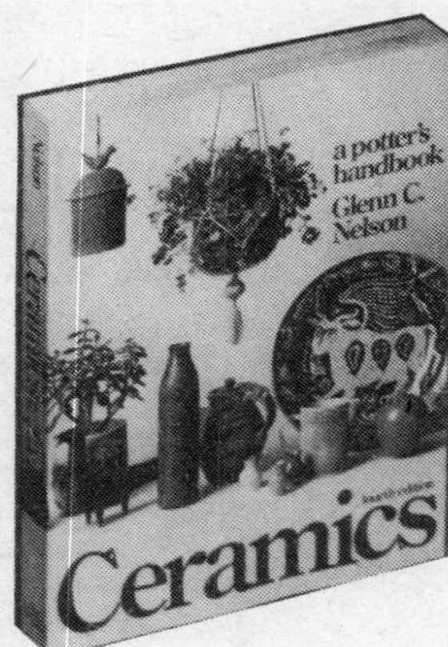

Ceramics
(A Potter's Handbook)
Glenn C. Nelson
1960, 1978; 339 pp.

$15.95 postpaid from:
Holt, Rinehart
and Winston
383 Madison Avenue
New York, NY 10017
or Whole Earth
Household Store

↑
Stem cup. Chinese (Hsuan-Te period). 1426-1435. Porcelain with fish design in copper-red, height 3-5/8" (8.5 cm). Victoria & Albert Museum, London (Crown Copyright). A pedestal foot is usually thrown separately.

Pablo Picasso, France. Centaur. 1950. Terra cotta, with painted design, height 17" (42.5 cm). Courtesy the Arts Council of Great Britain, London. →

Rolf Overberg, Germany. Fruit. Wheel-thrown and altered spheres with green and rust ash glazes on a dark manganese body, wood-fired to cone 6; height 6" (15 cm). The slabs with type set in relief increase the tactile quality of these objects.
↓

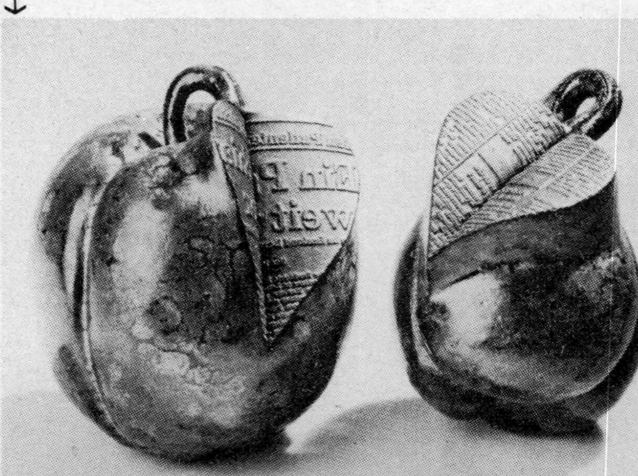

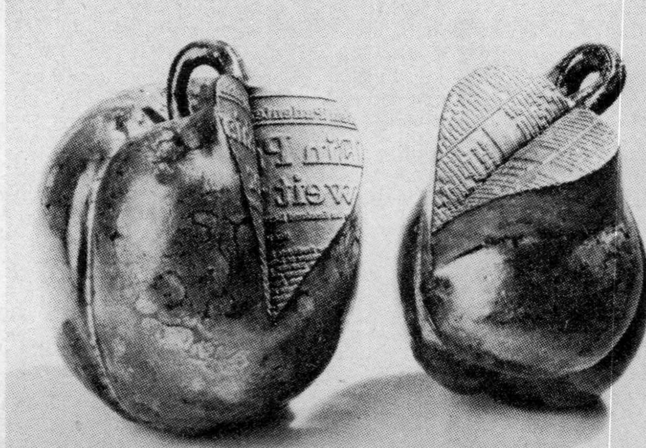

English 18th century trailed Slipware Dish.

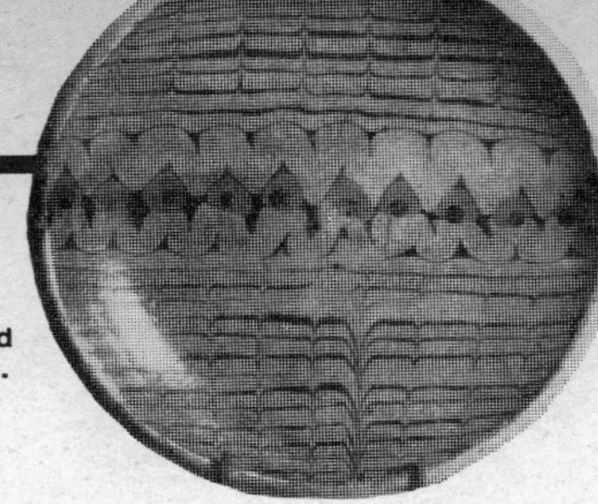

Combed Slipware Oven Dish.

Spanish Peasant-ware plate 16th century.

All plates from A Potter's Book

difficult, although possible, endeavor. There are other alternatives, too. Some people work as consultants to industry or as designers of machine-made wares. Teaching positions are scarce, but do exist, and at many different levels, including more accessible programs such as adult education or recreational classes. Many people work part-time at a salaried job in order to be able to support their work in clay. I think the fact that people continue to stay involved with clay even when it is quite difficult for them to do so financially is a tribute to what a fascinating and rewarding field it is.

After working with clay steadily for twelve years, I continue to find the daily processes involved in my work very satisfying. It's wonderful to step back and realize how smoothly things work when each part of the process is done at the right time, by paying attention to the clay itself. I enjoy noticing specific qualities of different clays and trying to put a particular clay's characteristics to work in the best way. I am constantly recharged by the immediacy inherent in the clay, its ability to freeze a moment in time. It's exciting to keep learning new things about the material, and to realize that this learning doesn't stop.

So, where does a person go who wants to begin working with clay? Here are several suggestions.

First, find someone whose work you respect and like. Look in museums, galleries and stores, and when you see something you like, find out who made it and how you can contact the artist. Some of the books mentioned below could be good starting places for locating work you enjoy. Then try asking the person if you can work for her or him. If not, the person might be able to give you advice on where you can study or how you can begin, where you can obtain materials, etc.

Look into the ceramics departments at local schools – you may be able to audit classes, or receive good advice about materials suppliers, local people working in clay, other places to learn by asking the students and faculty there.

Word-of-mouth is one of the best ways to find out about a new field. Ask local potters/artists the same questions; they can be especially helpful about sources for local materials.

In this country there are several schools known for their ceramics departments that offer full-time courses, summer sessions, or both. Some of the summer sessions are tailored to fit two- or three-week vacation times. Here is a small selection:

Penland School
of Crafts
Penland, NC 28765

Haystack Mountain
School of Crafts
Deer Isle, ME 04627

N.Y. State College
of Ceramics
Alfred University
Alfred, NY 14802

Big Creek Pottery
Davenport, CA 95017

These are popular places and do fill up quickly – write for catalogs and respond as early as possible. There are many other summer courses available; the spring issue of **Ceramics Monthly** (see below) lists them each year.

If all else fails to give you the necessary information for obtaining materials, peruse the yellow pages for ceramic suppliers (use the phone book for the nearest big city) and investigate ads in ceramics magazines (listed below).

Following are some of the best books and periodicals in the field. I use some for factual information and others for inspiration. Also included are a (very) few reliable suppliers' catalogs. ■

Pioneer Pottery

A good book for those wanting to "pioneer" in the sense of digging their own clay, making their own kiln bricks, etc. – or for those who simply want to know more about the basic materials involved. Also some beautiful African pots included in the photographs. There's lots of information on geology for potters – if the first few chapters are too technical, skip to the 7th, "Making Pots," for some interesting techniques. —Mary Law

•

We saw that bodies are heterogeneous both in the raw and in the fired state. To this there is added the further complication that they carry a coat, or rather a skin, of yet another material – glass. The potter thus has to steer clear of the Scylla of crazing and the Charybdis of its opposite, which is given various names according to its severity, 'edge-chipping' is the mild form of the disease, 'shivering' or 'spiral-cracking' is the typical manifestation (the spiral cracks follow the alignment of clay particles caused by throwing); 'shattering' is the most acute form.

Pioneer Pottery
Michael Cardew
1971; 327 pp.
$6.95 postpaid from:
St. Martin's Press, Inc.
175 Fifth Avenue
New York, NY 10010
or Whole Earth
Household Store

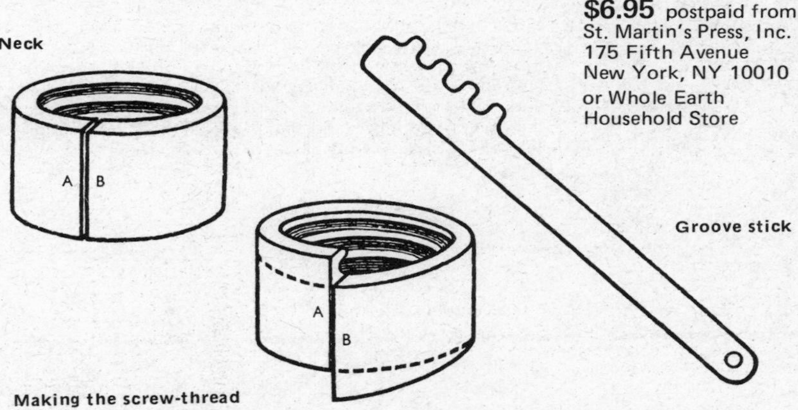

Making the screw-thread

Ceramic Art: Comment and Review 1882-1977

An anthology of writings on ceramics over the past century. Worth it for the introduction alone, a brief overview of modern ceramic history. Thought provoking to almost anyone working in clay. I especially enjoyed John Coplans' "Abstract Expressionist Ceramics." —Mary Law

•

"It is indeed an exciting moment when the work is taken from the oven. You have pictured, for instance, a splendid combination of colours for your amphora; you wished the *coulee* of the glazing on your vase to stop at two-thirds of its height; or on another piece you wanted to see a coating of rich enamel. But in one case it has all gone black; in another the drops have flowed too low; in a third the bottom has blistered, and is all over dull pustules; or all the materials have run into one another in the fusion; all is incoherence and disorder; the vitrified matter has distributed itself badly, and the earthenware reappears in patches!

"But, on the other hand, how boundless the domain of the process! What miracles these twelve hundred degrees of heat can perform! And what joy, what triumph, when one succeeds in bringing to perfection a beautiful piece of pottery, complete and satisfactory in its smallest details as in its entirety! I can assure you one's trouble is fully repaid, for the tints of the finest colourists can never equal the splendour, the brilliant variety, the deep, rich sumptuousness of some of these enamels."

Ceramic Art: Comment and Review 1882-1977
(An Anthology of Writings on Modern Ceramic Art)
Garth Clark, Editor
1978; 197 pp.
$9.95 postpaid from:
E.P. Dutton and Co.
Two Park Avenue
New York, NY 10016
or Whole Earth
Household Store

Judy Chicago: Gaea, china painted plate for The Dinner Party. Los Angeles, 1975. D. 13 13/16" (35 cm). Photograph: Diane Gelon →

A Potter's Book

The handbook for many potters. It contains many good descriptions of tools and processes. Leach imparts practical technique but combines it with his beliefs about pottery. A nice mix of hard fact and philosophy. —Mary Law

A Potter's Book
Bernard Leach
1967, 1976; 296 pp.
$10 postpaid from:
Transatlantic Arts
Trade Department
88 Bridge Road
Central Islip, NY 11722
or Whole Earth
Household Store

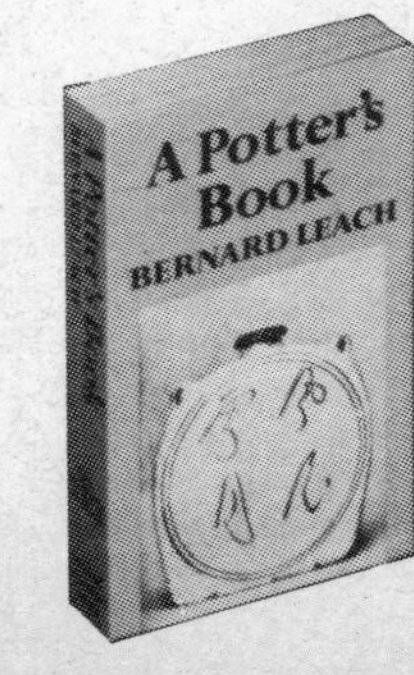

•

I cannot do better than give a more or less condensed and paraphrased extract from an essay on popular, or folk, arts and crafts by Soetsu Yanagi, the intellectual leader of the Japanese craft movement of today:

'I have many occasions to call at the residences of well-known art collectors, but I find too often that the articles of everyday use in their homes are far from being artistic, to say the least. They often leave me with a sad suspicion as to how much these collectors really appreciate beauty.

'To me the greatest thing is to live beauty in our daily life and to crowd every moment with things of beauty. It is then, and then only, that the art of the people as a whole is endowed with its richest significance. For its products are those made by a great many craftsmen for the mass of the people, and the moment this art declines the life of the nation is removed far away from beauty. So long as beauty abides in only a few articles created by a few geniuses, the Kingdom of Beauty is nowhere near realization.'

THE RISING SUN
NEIGHBORHOOD NEWSLETTER

Gandhi said that the ally you must always seek is the part of your enemy that knows what is right.

The Kiln Book

The best book on kiln building I've ever seen. A true handbook: well designed, clear, easy to locate information — chock-full of it, too! If you are building a kiln, this is THE book to consult. —Mary Law

The Kiln Book
Frederick L. Olsen
1978; 146 pp.
$9.50 postpaid from:
Keramos Books
Westwood Ceramic Supply
14400 Lomitas Avenue
City of Industry, CA 91744
or Whole Earth Household Store

•

The electric kiln is a product of the Twentieth Century and could prove to be the fourth most important innovation in kiln building history. The first was the building of the fundamental kiln container in which pots were placed. The second was the development of high temperature refractories both in the Orient and Europe, along with the introduction of fossil fuels in Europe. The third was the development of light-weight insulation bricks and related refractory materials which started during the 1930s. The fourth was the electric kiln, a totally original conception in the firing of ceramic ware using completely different principles in design, involving the laws of electricity and electrical wire technology with the lightweight insulation refractories.

Inside the Tamba Tube Kiln

Big Creek pottery wheel plans

This is a good way to get yourself a fine wheel at a low price — if you are willing to put some time and energy into the project by building it yourself. With the soaring prices of good ready-made wheels, and kits too, this build-your-own approach makes better and better sense.

The prototype for this wheel is excellent: I used one for six weeks at a Big Creek workshop and can report all good things about it. The design is good, the construction is simple and solid, it is comfortable to use, easy to clean: in short, it works well. It should be fairly easy to put together, and, if you follow the directions right and use good quality materials, you should end up with a wheel as good as those at Big Creek.
—Elina Holst Levy

Big Creek Pottery Wheel
Plans

$2.50 postpaid from:
Bruce A. McDougal
Big Creek Pottery
Davenport, CA 95017

Kiln Building With Space-Age Materials

Those of us involved in high energy high temperature crafts (I'm working in bronze casting as well as pottery) are severely affected by fuel shortages and costs. Since alternative sources of energy don't meet the temperature or aesthetic requirements of high temperature reduction firing (except wood firing which many rural potters are returning to) a more efficient method of using the fuel we have needs to be found. Colson introduced the ceramic-fiber insulations in an article in **Craft Horizons** *about ten years ago. Now his book gives methods, sources of supply and proven designs that will allow us to continue to work with greatly reduced consumption of fuel.* —Lee Ferber

Kiln Building with Space-Age Materials
Frank A. Colson
1975; 127 pp.
$7.95 postpaid from:
Van Nostrand Reinhold
Order Department
7625 Empire Drive
Florence, KY 41042
or Whole Earth Household Store

•

In the developmental stage of the United States space program, it was evident that it would be virtually impossible for a rocket to be launched off its pad if its firebox was lined with conventional firebricks. Materials had to be developed with extremely high heat insulating qualities combined with practically no weight. . . .

Among the most available and diversified of the materials are the alumina-silica ceramic fibers. Although there are several other types of ceramic fibers made from zirconium, quartz, and other minerals tolerant to high temperatures, the alumina-silica fibers are the most easily available and reasonably priced. Weighing one-fortieth the equivalent volume of firebrick, these materials have a normal heat exposure range of 2300°F. Quite recently, new fibers containing 20 percent more alumina have been developed which have a working temperature of 2600°F., well within the potter's heat range for stoneware temperatures. One manufacturer is presently developing an alumina-silica fiber with a heat tolerance above 2600°F. . . .

Since ceramic-fiber thermal materials became available, I have been using them as an integrated part of many kilns both for myself and other craftsmen. First I used the alumina-silica "blanket" as a partial replacement for bricks, and this alone cut fuel costs to one-fourth, firing time to one-third, and labor and materials to one-half for high-temperature reduction kilns.

← The portable raku kiln

Ceramic Science for the Potter

If you sit down to read this cover to cover, don't be put off by the heavy emphasis on chemistry in the first two chapters — it gets easier. This book is more technical than many potters I know will tolerate, but if it's solid information you want, I recommend as especially helpful chapters 5 (clay slips), 9 (firing), and 11 (glaze fit). I found myself ready for this information after making pots for several years without really understanding many of the reasons why things worked. Not essential information to doing good work, of course, but very satisfying to some. —Mary Law

Ceramic Science for the Potter
W.G. Lawrence
1972; 239 pp.
$12.95 postpaid from:
Chilton Book Company
Attn: Sales Service Dept.
Chilton Way
Radnor, PA 19089

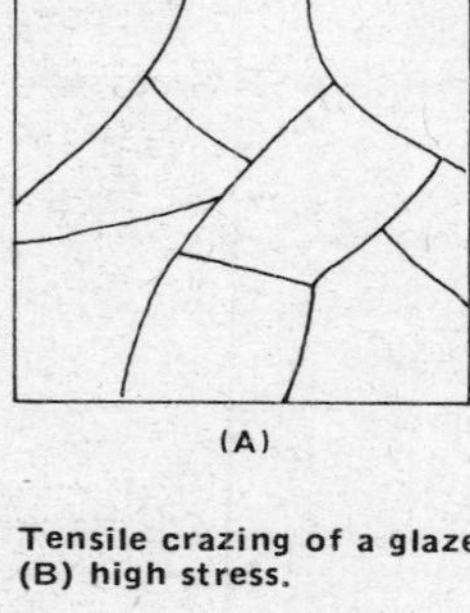
(A)

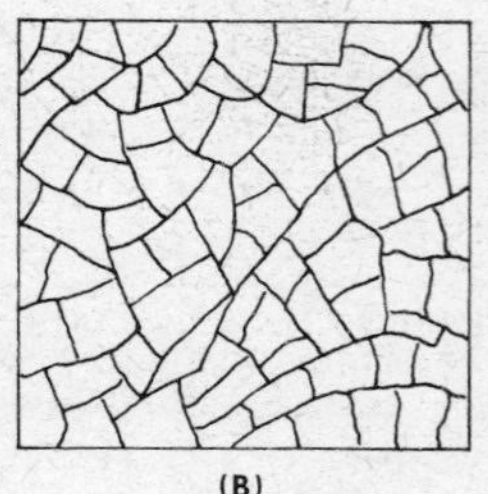
(B)

Tensile crazing of a glaze. (A) low stress, (B) high stress. ↑

Compression defects in glazes. (A) shivering, (B) peeling, (C) fracture of body in tension, usually at its thinnest or weakest point. ↓

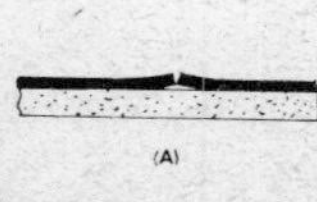
(A)

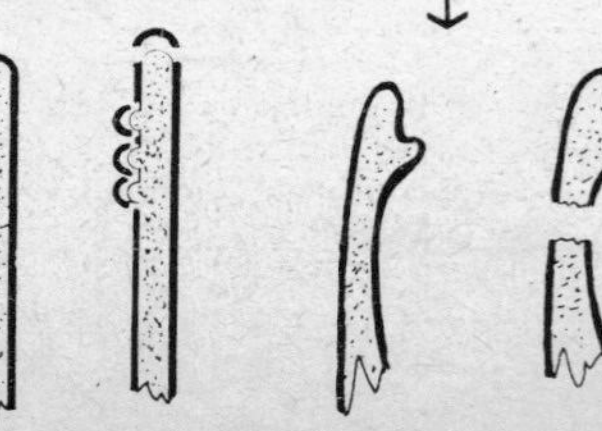
(B) (C)

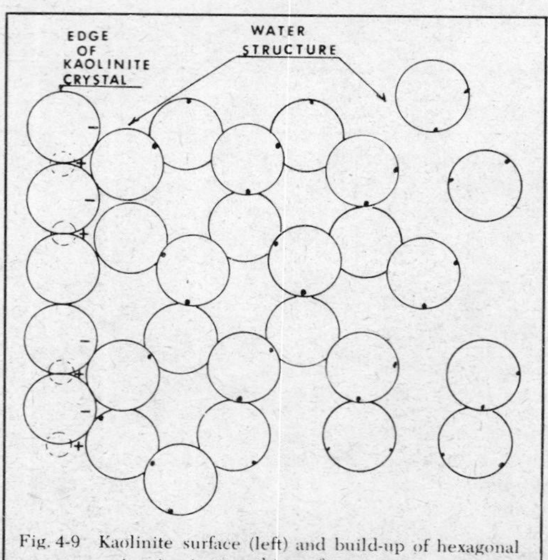

Fig. 4-9 Kaolinite surface (left) and build-up of hexagonal water structure on this surface.

Studio Potter Book ↑

The best of the first twelve issues of **Studio Potter** *magazine — if you're a recent subscriber it would be well worth having.* —Mary Law

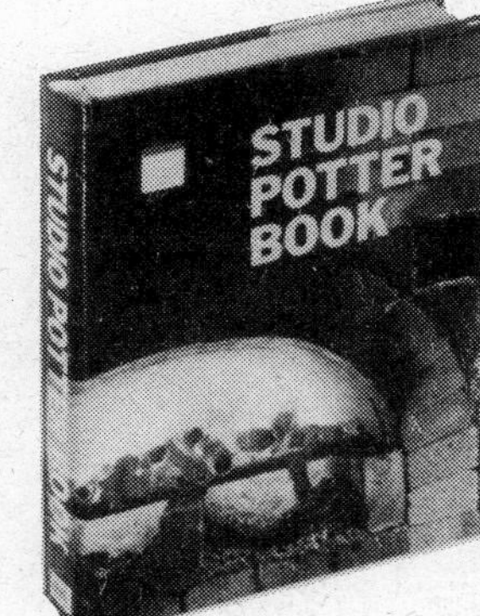

The Studio Potter Book
Gerry Williams, et al.
1978; 304 pp.
$22.50 postpaid from:
Van Nostrand Reinhold
Order Department
7625 Empire Drive
Florence, KY 41042
or Whole Earth Household Store

●

The Mark of This Fire

I am not interested in how fast I can reach temperature. If rapid firing were my goal, wood surely would not be my choice of fuel. It is the oneness with the kiln — the exhilaration — the awe of firing. Both of these emotions are heightened by the physical effort involved.

From dull red to bright yellow a quiet strength is gathering in the kiln. During the glaze reduction there is a "voice" in the stack — I usually reply.

All firing alters the ware, but my pots, fired unsaggered in this wood-burning kiln, have an additional alteration. During the firing, wood ash is deposited on the ware throughout the pot chamber; when high temperatures are reached the ash melts and fuses with the glaze, engobe, or with the clay of the pot.

Over the years that I have fired with wood these variable effects of the wood ash have become more and more predictable and thus planned for. It is this variable and unique quality — the mark inherent to this fire — that continues to hold my interest, is often my delight, and that always demands my respect.

—Ruth Gowdy McKinley

Studio Potter

Truly a magazine written by potters for potters (and glassworkers). Each issue is jam-packed with information about how other potters operate. Frequently you will find alternative solutions, especially concerning energy, and ways to make traditional methods more efficient. A fantastic magazine! —Mary Law

Studio Potter
Peter Sabin and
Gerry Williams, Editors
$8.50 /year (2 issues)
from:
Studio Potter
Box 172
Warner, NH 03278

●

Porcelain is a kind of in-word among potters and those who buy pots. Everyone talks about P*O*R*C*E*-L*A*I*N. It has become P*O*P*U*L*A*R. As frequently happens, this enlarges the definitions, which sounds grand but frequently means only the removal of standards. This has certainly happened with and to porcelain, and almost any clay which fires white is now called porcelain and takes advantage of the fashion.

Porcelain is white and translucent, clay-becoming-glass, a transition between the opaque and the transparent, between earth and air. Difficult enough to work, with little of the fluid plasticity of stoneware, in the kiln it will warp, stick down, distort, destruct unless it is treated with a special respect and consideration.

●

I Like Porcelain Because Blood Shows Up Better On It.

John Knapp's woodfired climbing kiln 1978.

The Potter's Dictionary

A thick glossy technical manual, full of lucid and comprehensive answers to all manner of questions about potting. Organized as a dictionary, it has very complete and detailed essays on glazing, clay, and firing chemistry and processes, e.g., "crack" — 8 pages!

My only criticisms are that it has little to say on design or throwing problems, and, written for a British audience, gives a fair amount of space to British potting terms, pictures and historical descriptions of British wares. For advanced potters concerned with solving many of the complex problems often left untouched and unanswered in the flood of how-to books of recent years.
—Elina Holst Levy

The Potter's Dictionary of Materials and Techniques
Frank Hamer
1975; 349 pp.
$30 postpaid from:
Watson-Guptil
2160 Patterson Street
Cincinnati, OH 45214

↓

In throwing, the hands describe a slow spiral up a pot in a clockwise direction — clockwise seen from above on an anti-clockwise wheel. The particles will follow this course which coincides with the throwing rings. The line of greatest shrinkage therefore becomes a steep twist at right angles to the throwing rings. A quickly thrown pot will have more twist shrinkage than one thrown slowly with very close throwing rings.

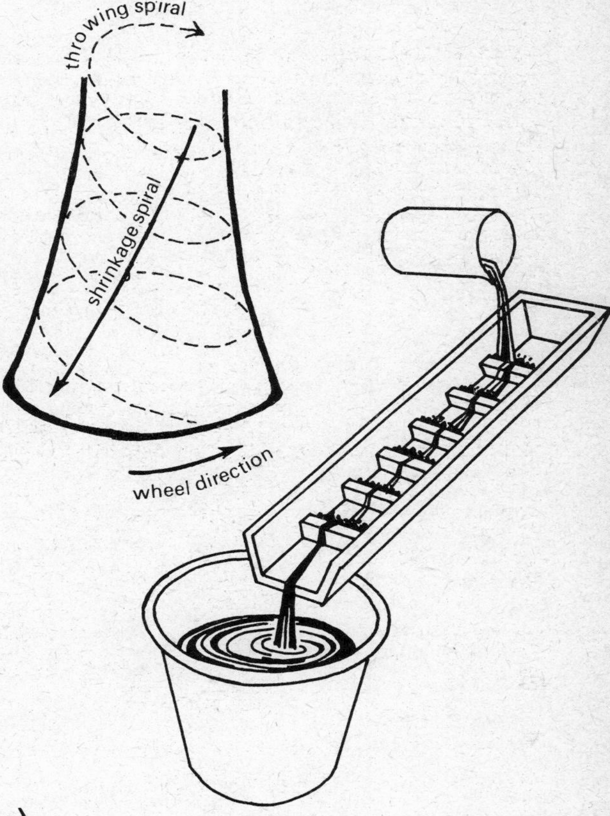

→

Levigation. The process of passing a thin slurry through a series of traps where the heavier particles settle and finer particles overflow. The process is used for clays which contain unwanted material like sand which is too fine to be caught in a mesh.

Ceramics Monthly

Informative and newsy (enables you to keep up on who's showing where and what work they're doing). **CM** *is much improved over the past several years. (It used to feel more like a hobbyist's magazine.) Every issue contains: notice of upcoming exhibitions, fairs and sales; reviews of exhibitions; specific technical information, such as glaze recipes; picture-laden articles on individual artist/potters; a wonderful array of ads for suppliers of materials, equipment, tools and books.* —Mary Law

Ceramics Monthly
Spencer L. Davis, Editor
$12 /year (10 issues)
from:
Circulation Department
Ceramics Monthly
Box 12448
Columbus, OH 43212

●

Representing explorations of surface treatment, a one-man show of salt-glazed stoneware by Jeff Procter, Salem, Oregon, was presented at Bush Barn Art Center, Salem, through March. Having employed salt-glazing for the past ten years, Jeff continues that tradition, combining it with local clay glazes, iron oxide slips and Barnard clay washes; rutile slip patterns are sponge-stamped for additional detailing.

THE RISING SUN
NEIGHBORHOOD NEWSLETTER

David was wondering how long people will keep saying they are dialing the phone when they're really punching the phone. Dial could go into the 2000s as one of those common words that seems mysterious when you think about it or it could be replaced by punch soon when everyone's punching computers and makes the transfer.

CERAMIC SUPPLIERS

by Mary Law

Leslie Ceramics Supply Company
1212 San Pablo Avenue
Berkeley, CA 94706

A reliable, friendly supply house, doing local and mail order business. Also a treat to visit, as the owners have a wonderful collection of Bay Area ceramics, crowded into display cases in their store. It's a gold mine — old and new pots by some very famous (and not so famous) artists/potters. The free catalog is functional rather than glamorous.

Wenger's Limited
Etruria Stoke-on-Trent
Staffordshire ST4 7BQ
England

A beautiful glossy catalog with photos of many of the tools and equipment available. Good brush selection. Payment should be made in pounds sterling — send £1 (about $2.30) for their catalog.

These other supply houses are ones I have heard recommended but do not know first-hand:

Eagle Ceramics
1226-A Wilkins Avenue
Rockville, MD 20852
Catalog $1

Kickwheel Pottery Supply
1428 Mayson Street NE
Atlanta, GA 30324
Catalog $1

Minnesota Clay
8001 Grand Avenue So.
Bloomington, MN 55420
Catalog $2

Rovin Ceramics
6912 Schaefer Road
Dearborn, MI 48216
Catalog $1

Standard Ceramic Supply Company
Box 1435
Pittsburgh, PA 15205
Catalog $1 ■

TS1 Throwing Stick $2.95 from Standard Ceramic Supply Company

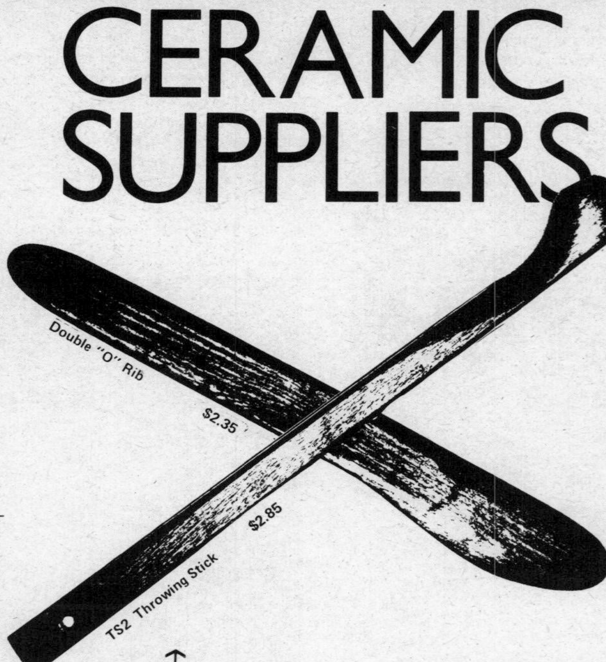

Throwing Sticks
This rib is hand formed and finished from imported hardwood and is used for cutting, slicing, shaping and smoothing soft clay. Approximately 12" long.

Patterned from the ancient Japanese egote, these throwing sticks aid in shaping and compressing deep and narrow necked wheel-thrown pieces. These throwing sticks are made in two sizes of fine imported hardwood and are polished to a satin-smooth finish. Approximately 12½" long. **—Standard Ceramic Supply Company**

•

Saviac 110D Kick Wheel
The Saviac 110D, developed and designed for Wenger by David Ballantyne FSD-C, is of the traditional direct-drive type but the characteristics distinguishing it from other models are a combination of ergonomic planning with a geometric layout carefully coordinated to exploit the high efficiency of the 50 kg flywheel. It incorporates a novel reverse-thrust bracket which contributes to a performance of exceptional smoothness and eliminates all trace of "jerk" in the left foot movement.

The 110D is not a wheel to be flung into violent action but a sensitive instrument which can and should, strongly influence the form of the thrower's work. The natural rhythm of the foot motion and the one-to-one ratio between lever and shaft cycles, results in a relatively low head speed, affording the opportunity to achieve close harmony between hands, foot and vision.

The framework is of timber construction with a removable wooden sink. The drive-pedal is on the left-hand side of the wheel and is suspended, independently of its lever, by a chain from a point just in front of and below the knee. The design allows the foot to swing in a pendulum arc and is adjustable to accommodate throwers of any stature, from long-legged adults to small children. Properly adjusted, the system ensures freedom from fatigue due to spinal torque. **—Wegner's**

Soldner Clay Mixer
Model #311

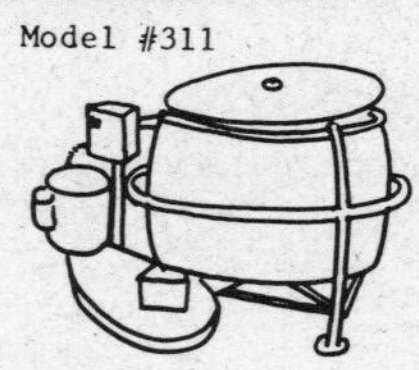

Soldner Clay Mixer Model No. 311
The Soldner Clay Mixer is the fastest, safest and most convenient way of mixing clay to throwing consistency.

Rotating tub type. 3 hp motor. Rugged steel frame. Overside bearings. Non rusting, 30" x 16" tub. Magnet starter. Capacity: 300 lbs. wet.

Standard No. 310 — $1965
Model No. 311, stainless shaft and blades — $2090

Prices: FOB Silt, Colorado
—Leslie Ceramics Supply

Brent Slab Rollers

SR-14 Table model 14" bed	210#	**$480**
Leg set for SR-14	50#	**75**
SR-20 20" bed	487#	**740**
SR-36 36" bed	706#	**935**

A rugged, reliable heavy duty slab rolling machine with rollers that move across the stationary bed. Slabs possible from 1/8" to 1-1/4" thicknesses. Adjustable in 1/8" increments with the use of masonite boards. Quality cast iron mounted ball bearings used throughout. Maximum slab size = roller width by 5 ft. long bed.
—Minnesota Clay

by Bruce McDougal

The enclosed is a list of suppliers that I am more or less familiar with, some of whom I do business with regularly, others I just know about. There are many more good ones I am sure, and if I've missed any that's because I don't know about them.

Bruce McDougal runs Big Creek Pottery, Davenport, CA 95017. His studio looks like a fine place to learn and work pottery.
—J.D. Smith

Westwood Ceramic Supply
14400 Lomitas Avenue
City of Industry,
CA 91744

Complete line of clay, glazes, glaze materials, chemicals, tools, wheels, kilns, etc. Good service and prices. Write for catalog $1.

Western Ceramic Supply
1601 Howard Street
San Francisco, CA 94103

Complete line of materials, clay, wheels, etc. Prepared glazes. Excellent source of enamels at good prices. They have a good kick wheel. Write for free catalog. Also, new cone 10 lead-free glazes.

Ceramics & Crafts Supply Company
490 5th Street
San Francisco, CA 94107

Clays and glazes — at better small lot prices than you can get from Westwood. Materials of all kinds. Lockerbie wheels. Reliable supplier. Write for free catalog.

Leslie Ceramics Supply
1212 San Pablo Avenue
Berkeley, CA 94706

Clays, glazes, kilns, wheels, chemical materials, tools. An excellent all-around source in the East Bay. More of everything than anybody.

Thorley Pottery Supply
1183 Industrial Avenue
South Gate, CA 90280

Kiln shelves and stilts. An excellent source for fired clay shelves in large sizes that will take cone 10-11 reduction firing without trouble at about 1/3 the cost of silicon carbide. Price break for orders of 25 shelves at a time. They aren't set up to handle orders for 1 or 2 shelves at a time, so get together and order a bunch. Free catalog.

Robert Brent Company
128 Mill Street
Healdsburg, CA 95448

Wheels, clay, slab rollers. Probably the best power wheel on the market: their "C" model is standard, and they go up and down from there. Sold direct or through local dealers (see yellow pages). Good service. Catalog free.

American Art Clay Company
4717 West 16th Street
Indianapolis, IN 46200

An old company, making kilns, wheels, and selling all kinds of supplies. Oriented toward schools, their kilns are built massively and with all kinds of safety controls available to satisfy the most picky fire marshal. More expensive than some. Write for free catalog.

Kemper Manufacturing Company
P.O. Box 545
Chino, CA 91710

Kemper specializes in making hand tools for the potter and sculptor. They do a good job, have a wide selection, and offer quantity discounts for direct sale. Write for free catalog.

A.D. Alpine, Inc.
3051 Fujita Street
Torrance, CA 90505

Kilns, mainly — also wheels and other ceramic gear. Top drawer but expensive. Their kilns have for many years been the poor potter's friend, because they have sold so many that they are easier to find second hand than almost any other (at least in the west). They take a little experience to fire, are excellent, reliable and long-lived. Free catalog.

Duncan Ceramic Supply
5649 East Shields
Fresno, CA 93727

This is a remarkable place, well worth visiting if you are in Fresno. They have an excellent line of low fire glazes, and other supplies. They come highly recommended, and have a free catalog.

Quyle Kilns
3353 East Highway Four
Murphys, CA 95247

A variety of excellent clay bodies. Sold in small quantities through Leslie and Western. Larger quantities (a ton or more) sold direct. Free catalog.

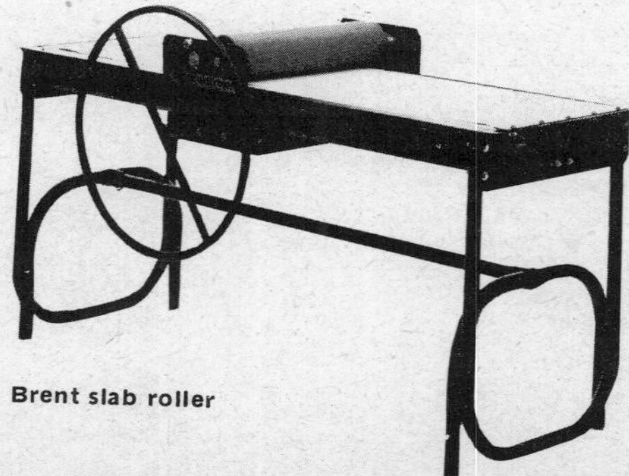

Brent slab roller

Carborundum Company
Refractories and Electronics Division
Keasbey, NJ 08832

Silicon carbide shelves; excellent shelves for any use, but the ONLY shelves we know of that are impervious to salt and can be used in salt kilns. (Other silicon carbide shelves are NOT, they bubble and melt and clay shelves soon collapse.) Note: This has to do with the BINDER used in the manufacture of the $SiCO_3$ shelves. Free catalog.

Industrial Minerals Company
1057 Commercial Street
San Carlos, CA 94070

Clay bodies and clay materials. A very good supplier. Information free.

Minnesota Clay Company
8001 Grand Avenue So.
Bloomington, MN 55420

Clay, materials, equipment. Highly recommended: "They care." Catalog $2.

Bluebird Manufacturing Company
100 Gregory Road
Fort Collins, CO 80521

They make machinery for potters: pug mills, mixers, blungers. Their catalog is part catalog, part philosophy, and part how-to-do-it. The firm is also well-known as the Judson Pottery. They are the only people who make a tap and die set for screw-on lids. Catalog $2.

Aardvark Clay and Supplies
1400 East Pomona Street
Santa Ana, CA 92705

A complete collection of supplies. Roughly comparable to Westwood. Free catalog.

Also recommended for sources of all kinds of stuff: the **Ceramic Data Book**, *published annually; $6 postpaid from Cahners Publishing Company, 270 Saint Paul Street, Denver, CO 80206. It lists sources for every conceivable ceramic product you can think of. In addition,* **Ceramics Monthly**'s *advertisements are the place to look for ceramics suppliers.* ■

The Great Wax Wonder

Candles coming alive! Abounds with information about every aspect of candlemaking and its history. Written in a warm, chatty style with drawings and/or vivid photographs on every page. Well worth the extra time needed to read the many varied irregular scripts. Contains a good number of sources for materials. —Barbara Erfani

The Great Wax Wonder
Book Two
Cherie Hooper
1972; 148 pp.

$2.25 postpaid from:
Hidden House Press
81 Encina
Palo Alto, CA 94301

the GREAT WAX WONDER BOOK TWO by cherie hooper

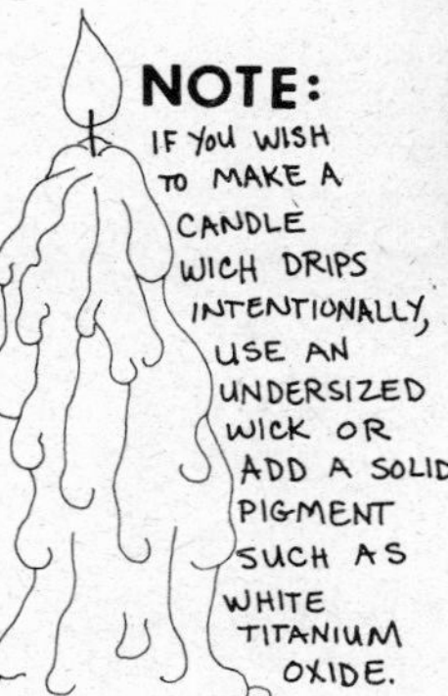

NOTE:
IF YOU WISH TO MAKE A CANDLE WICH DRIPS INTENTIONALLY, USE AN UNDERSIZED WICK OR ADD A SOLID PIGMENT SUCH AS WHITE TITANIUM OXIDE.

SPICES

VARIETY

A CANDLE CAN BE MADE TO HAVE A MARVELOUS MARBLEIZED PATTERN IN IT BY SHAVING LITTLE PIECES OF CONCENTRATED DYE CHIPS (DARK COLORS) AND DROPPING THEM INTO AN ALREADY POURED (LIGHT COLORS) MOLD.

BEEKEEPERS USE PRE-FAB HONEYCOMB SHEETS OF BEES WAX TO SAVE BEES THE WORK OF WAX PRODUCTION AND CELL-BUILDING SO THE BEES WILL STOCK THEIR HIVES WITH HONEY. THESE HONEYCOMB SHEETS CAN ALSO BE MADE INTO CANDLES. THEY CAN BE OBTAINED AT HOBBY SHOPS, CANDLE SUPPLIERS, BEEKEEPERS, AND HONEY WHOLESALERS. THEY ARE SOLD NOW IN BRIGHT COLORS AS WELL AS THE NATURAL BEESWAX COLOR.

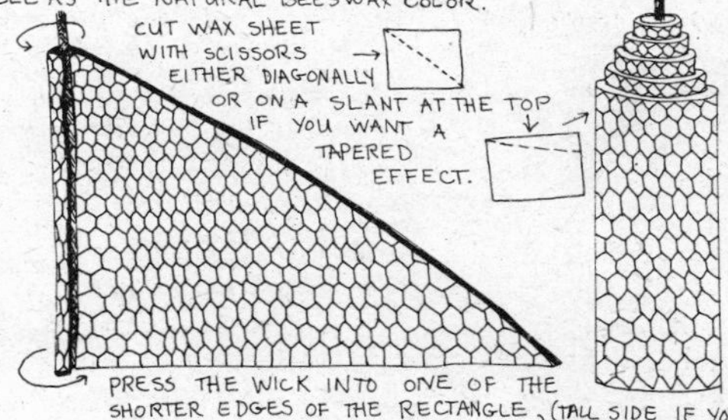

CUT WAX SHEET WITH SCISSORS EITHER DIAGONALLY OR ON A SLANT AT THE TOP IF YOU WANT A TAPERED EFFECT.
PRESS THE WICK INTO ONE OF THE SHORTER EDGES OF THE RECTANGLE, (TALL SIDE IF YOU TAPER-CUT IT) AND ROLL UP.

Honeycomb beeswax can also be wrapped around the outside of other candles: BLOCK, TAPER, HURRICANE, OR SHAPES CAN BE CUT OUT OF IT AND PRESSED ON OTHER CANDLES AS DECORATION.

Sculpture suppliers

For shaping wax, clay, plaster, stone, wood. —SB

Sculpture House
Catalog

$1 from:
Sculpture House
38 East 30th Street
New York, NY 10016

Art Consultants
Catalog

$1 from:
Art Consultants
Box 476
Brooklyn, NY 11230

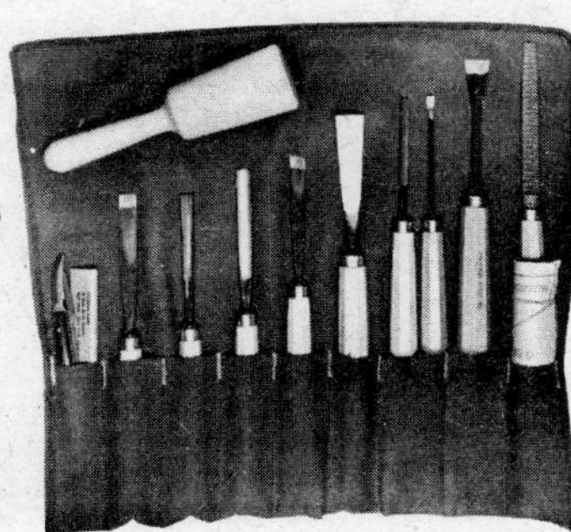

→
Woodcarving Kit — One 1" chisel; one 5/8" chisel; one skew; one 1" gouge; one shallow gouge; one medium gouge; one short bent; one parting tool; one riffler; one carving knife; one cabinet rasp; one sharpening stone; one mallet; sandpaper. $74.

—**Sculpture House**

Adhesive Products

Silicone molding rubber (cast anything!) at low prices and Monzini epoxy based casting compounds. Twentieth century materials. —Jeff Schlanger

Adhesive Products
Brochure and price list

free from:
Adhesive Products Corporation
1660 Boone Avenue
Bronx, NY 10460

HOW TO USE MONZINI® LIQUID Casting Compound

To get the best results with MONZINI first learn to understand the material. Do NOT think of it as a replacement for plaster. Do NOT use it to make cheap reproductions. Think of MONZINI as an improvement over marble or ivory. With MONZINI it is possible to reproduce fine details which cannot be had in plaster. If cast on glass, it will reproduce the polish and luster of glass.
—**Adhesive Products**

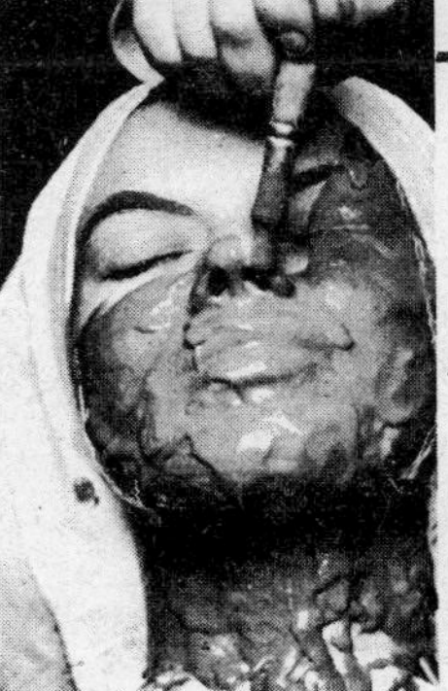

Moulage $12.95 — Sculpture House

A mold material for taking impressions from life—for reproducing valued antiques when an ancient patina must be preserved, too delicate to submit to being molded in plaster, rubber or gelatine. Applied warm with brush and palette knife, captures minutest details, complete instructions. Wax base Posmoulage produces lifelike casts.

Sax Art Supplies

Big catalog, sort of school oriented, widest range of art and craft supplies of any we've seen. —SB

Sax Art Supplies
Catalog

$3 from:
Sax Arts & Crafts
P.O. Box 2002
Milwaukee, WI 53201

Scratchboard Scratcher™

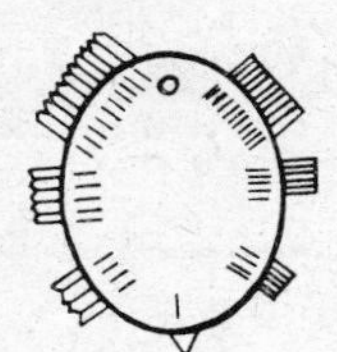

For Sgraffito; Scratchboard; Dry-Point Etching;
Practical steel tool that replaces more costly scratch pens, knives, and tools. Scratcher produces a variety of single or multi-grooved parallel scratched lines — up to 10 individual lines with one stroke. Hints and instructions included.

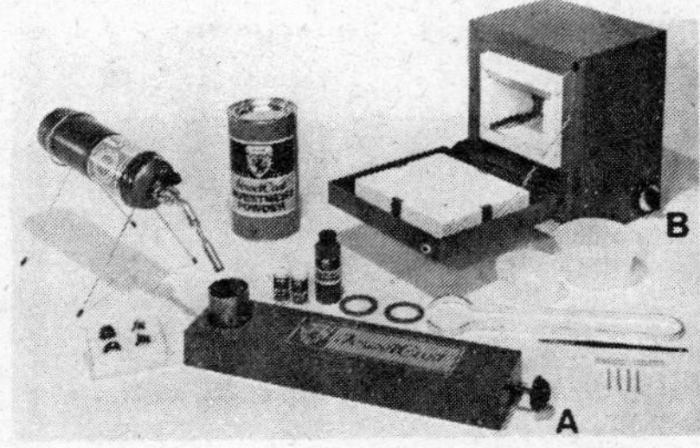

Jewel Cast Metal Casting Kit

The safest and most dependable vacuum casting jewelry kit available. Includes: a 2000° F temp. controlled 110V kiln, 4" deep x 4-1/4" wide x 3-3/8" high, heavy duty vacuum caster, jeweler's torch with stand, 2" dia. flask, casting metal, tongs — all necessary accessories.
510-2405 **$220.00**

Fezandie and Sperrle

Colors. Aniline colors, artists colors, batik colors, cement, even concrete colors.

Tie dye your sidewalks.
—J.D. Smith

Fezandie and Sperrle
Brochure and price list

free from:
Fezandie and Sperrle, Inc.
111 Eighth Avenue
New York, NY 10011

Fezan lime-proof colors for cement, concrete, mortar and stucco

Shade	Price per pound
Black	2.25
Brilliant Turquoise	3.50
	4.75
Red Mahogany	2.25
Brown Mahogany	2.25
Chocolate	2.25
Sage	3.40
Sea	4.60
Grass	4.75
Brick	2.25
Crimson	2.25
Rose	2.25
Maroon	2.25
Light ochre	2.25
Medium ochre	2.25
Deep ochre	2.25
Golden	2.25

Candle making suppliers

Two good sources. Pourette is high quality and range, high cost. North Penn is lower cost. —SB

Pourette Candle Making Supplies
Catalog

$.50 from:
Pourette
Box 15220
Seattle, WA 98115

North Penn Forms
Price list

$.50 from:
North Penn Forms
P.O. Box 99
Hatfield, PA 19440

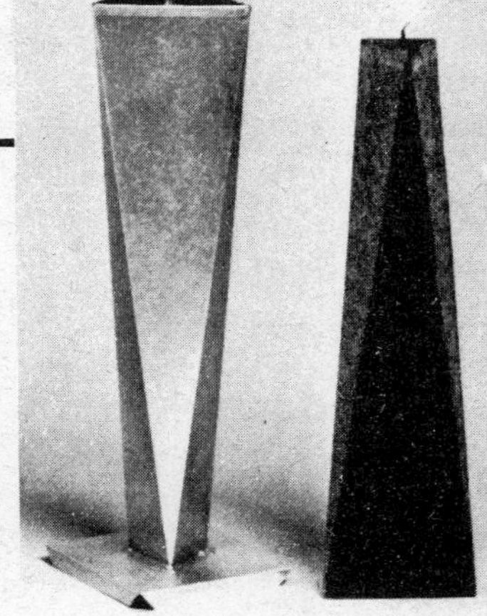

→
Triangle Oblique
B613A - 12½" tall
B614B - 9½" tall
Base - 3½"
Wax - 1 lb. 8 oz.
Wick Recom: S.B.
—**Pourette**

THE RISING SUN
NEIGHBORHOOD NEWSLETTER

Lillie didn't marry because she was taking care of her mother and father and then her two aunts and then her sister as they aged and died. She's old now, and people don't do that anymore.

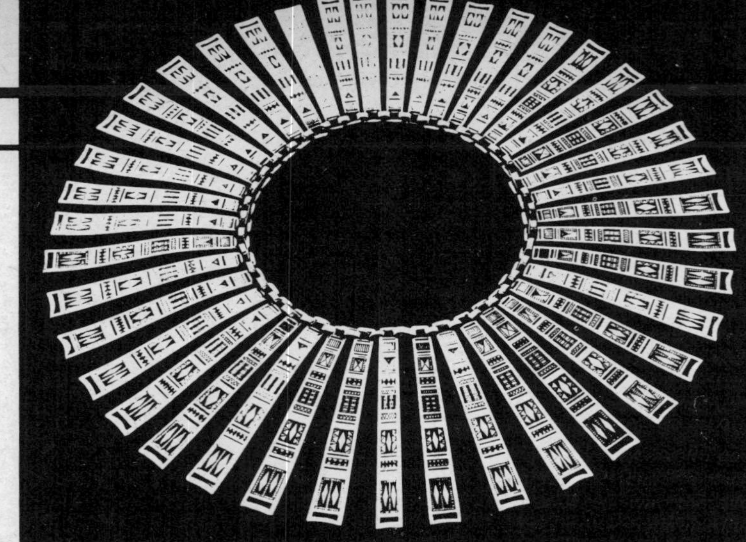

Design stamps

Metal Techniques for Craftsmen

If you read this book, you'll know more about metalworking than just about anybody you know. International in scope, it covers an incredible collection of techniques from many countries and cultures. The various techniques are presented with a complete set of instructions for each one and are illustrated by excellent photographs, often of native craftsmen doing their thing. Tools are described and illustrated in detail. Everything is described in detail. Reading this book will take you right up to that point where you'll have to do it awhile yourself to get into it any further. This is a real assembly of diverse information, some of it hard to find, and a metal-crafter-jeweler should be into new things within an hour of getting his hands on it. This is one of those rare and super books written by someone that wanted to lay his trip on others. Well worth the money. The "definitive text," as they say. —J. Baldwin

Metal Techniques for Craftsmen
Oppi Untracht
1968; 509 pp.

$19.95 postpaid from:
Doubleday & Company
501 Franklin Avenue
Garden City, NY 11531
or Whole Earth Household Store

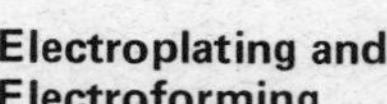

↑ Sterling silver necklace utilizing 18-guage metal, by Mary Ann Scherr. Length: 16½ inches; each unit: 3½ inches by ½ inch. The intaglio pattern was created with an etching solution of half nitric acid and half water and was then oxidized.

← Repousse or chasing hammers are made with steel heads of various diameters with polished faces up to 1¼ inches across, and have thinly tapered wood handles ten inches long, ending with oval, pistol, or round grip. The face is hardened so that when properly used with tools, being hit lightly and squarely at the repousse or chasing tool end, it should not become dented. The tapered wood handle is designed to give the tool spring, and its light weight and form allow the tool to be applied rapidly. The broad face of the hammer is designed to provide a relatively large striking area, so that this part of the work need not be watched. Vision is concentrated on the action of the tool on the metal.

Tools are generally extensions of the functions of the hands, but in some cultures, of the feet as well. We in the West deprive ourselves of the use of our feet in work for the sake of comfort, immobilizing them in stockings and shoes. Wherever metalsmiths work in India, they use their feet to hold, guide, manipulate, and support large objects under work, as naturally as they use their feet for standing and walking. Shown here is a brass worker (thathera) from Pemberti, Andhra Pradesh, in South India, planishing a brass water pot with hand and hammer, at the same time using one foot to guide its movement over the earth-anchored anvil, and the other to help keep it in position to receive the regular rain of blows over its surface. →

Electroplating and Electroforming

Thought by many to be restricted to chroming bumpers and making cheap forks look like they were swiped from the royal table, electroplating is now available for use at home. If you plate something a lot, you can actually build it up into a substantial object — that's electroforming. Jewelers will be most intrigued, but model makers and heirloom restorers will also be interested.

This book is easily understood, gives supply sources, takes care to attend to safety matters, and is generally a very useful handbook of procedure. —J. Baldwin

Electroplating and Electroforming
(For Artists and Craftsmen)
Lee Scott Newman and Jay Hartley Newman
1979; 96 pp.

$6.95 postpaid from:
Crown Publishers
One Park Avenue South
New York, NY 10016
or Whole Earth Household Store

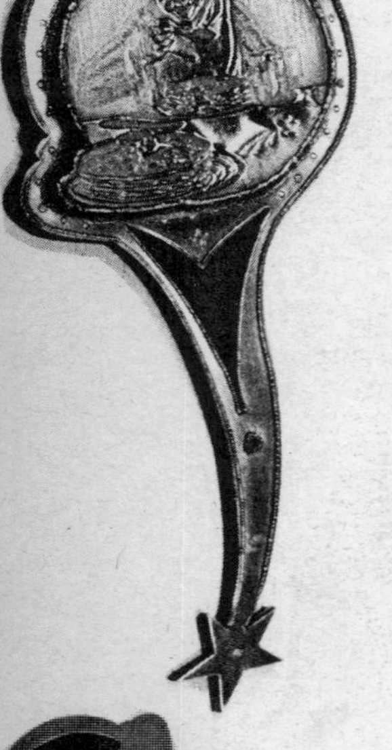

← This hand mirror by Tim Glotzbach will be constructed of brass, Plexiglas, plate-glass mirror, and copper electroformed over a wax matrix. Electroformed copper plates will decorate the front and back of the hand mirror. Each will be formed over a wax matrix that will be removed after forming. Here a printing plate will be used to impart a pattern to wax that will become the base object. It has been covered with plastic wrap to prevent it from sticking to the wax.

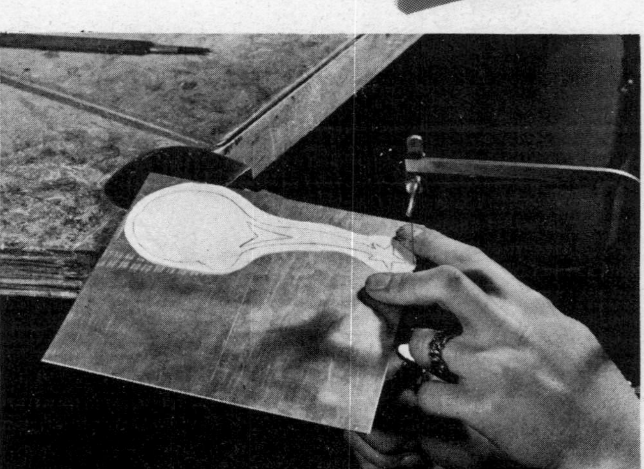

The template for the body of the hand mirror is dry mounted to a sheet of brass, and the shape is cut using a jeweler's saw. Two sections like this one will become the body of the mirror. →

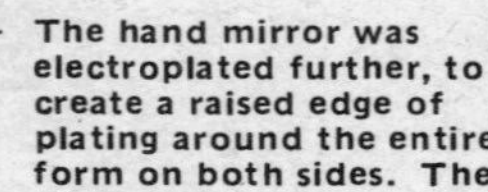

A hole is cut in one of the brass sections. This will accommodate a piece of plate-glass mirror. ←

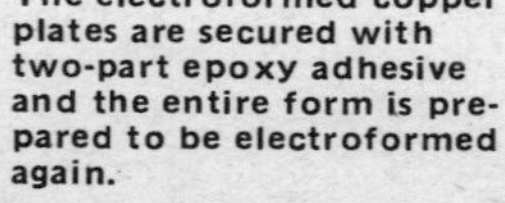

← The hand mirror was electroplated further, to create a raised edge of plating around the entire form on both sides. The piece was finished with a soft patina.

The electroformed copper plates are secured with two-part epoxy adhesive and the entire form is prepared to be electroformed again. →

Tuck-ni-sala woodburning equipment

Pyrography is not arson but rather the delicate art of burning designs in wood using a special heated pen. The pyrography machine sold by the Tuck-ni-sala Company looks like a good one. The tool has a heat control knob and one can add various shaped tips to the pen for different effects. The machine can be used to decorate wood leather and plastic and reportedly "cuts through styrofoam like a knife through butter." —Marilyn Green

Pyrography Machines
Information

free from:
Tuck-ni-sala Company
P.O. Box 2066
Hobbs, NM 88240

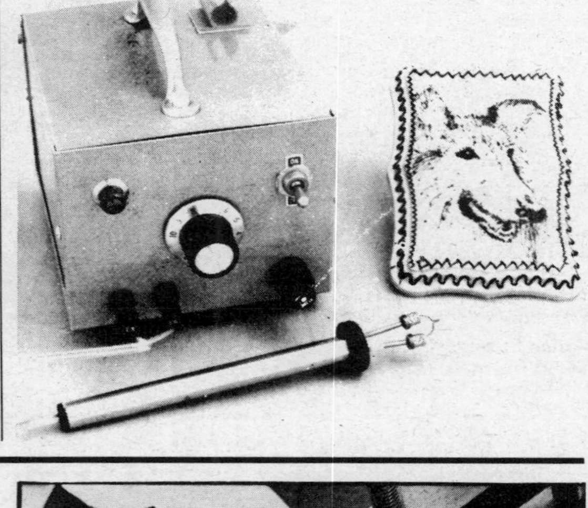

Lewis Pyro-loop Machine with pen. $68.95.

The Art of Engraving

The only book available which will actually show you how to engrave. Fortunately, it was written by a man who cares about the beginner. No mysteries or secrets here. Beautifully illustrated, by the author, of course. A bargain. —David L. Kitterman

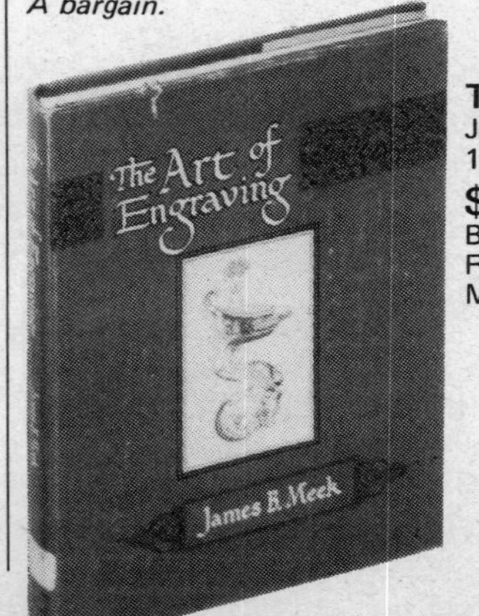

The Art of Engraving
James B. Meek
1973, 1977; 196 pp.

$19.95 postpaid from:
Brownell's, Inc.
Route 2, Box 1
Montezuma, Iowa 50171

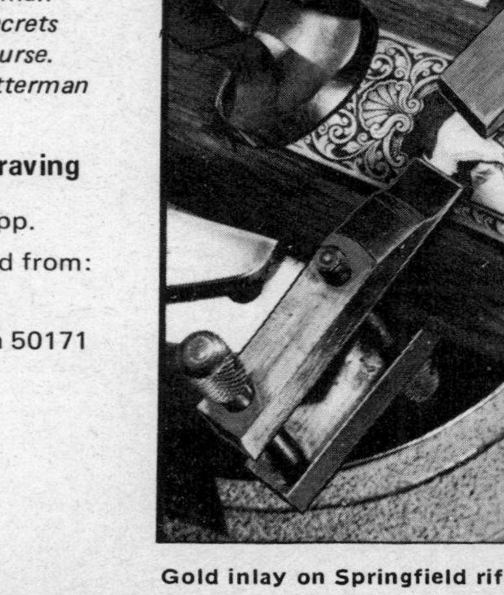

Gold inlay on Springfield rifle floor plate

Lapidary Journal

I get an itch in my fingers and groin looking at the pictures in this magazine. More beguiling than jewelry-store jewelry, this solid journal has the really fascinating stuff — the finding and working of the GEMS! Gorgeous, tiny, perfect . . . (This isn't gonna translate into black & white pictures.) Look at that sapphire! —SB

Lapidary Journal
(for Gem Cutters, Gem Collectors, and Jewelry Craftsmen)
Pansy Kraus, Editor
$12/year (12 issues)
from:
Lapidary Journal
P.O. Box 80937
San Diego, CA 92138

The discovery of the golden amethyst: just when you thought you'd seen it all they discover a new gem!

Bushy formations as well as delicate line patterns are found in dedritic deposits of pyrolusite in limestone or shale. Beginners often mistake them for fossilized remains of plant growth. Rather, they are crystalline deposits of pyrolusite resulting from a solution which crept into the rock matrix.

•

The birthstone for April is *diamond,* and thanks to the state of Arkansas, every collector who wishes to pay the modest fee may dig for diamonds at Crater of Diamonds State Park near Murfreesboro. Many precious diamonds are found each year in this old location which was never commercially successful. The collecting fee is $2.00 a day. Finders are keepers here. Besides the occasional diamond, there are garnets, amethyst, peridots and other gemstones. The park is open all year, and a campsite, also with moderate fees, is nearby.

Alluvial diamonds have been found at various places in the Midwest, including Ohio, Michigan, Indiana, Wisconsin and Illinois, as well as in some of the Appalachian states, but such finds are rare and largely a matter of luck.

The Design and Creation of Jewelry

From brooch to buckle, from lapidary to enameling, filigree, cloisonne, forging, casting, Japanese **kasane uchi**, *Renaissance* **niello**, *twentieth century photo etching . . . this is your guide to a craft with but one aim: decorative, personal adornment.* —Don Lohr

The Design and Creation of Jewelry
(Revised Edition)
Robert von Neumann
1961, 1972; 271 pp.
$8.95 postpaid from:
Chilton Book Company
Sales Service Department
Chilton Way
Radnor, PA 19089
or Whole Earth Household Store

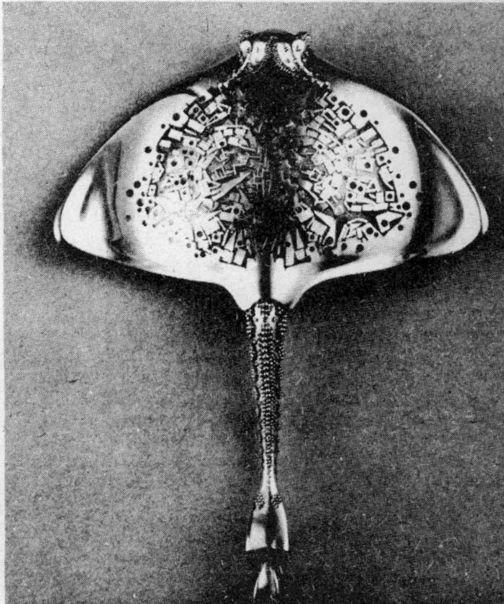

"Skate," pendant, gold and enamel

Jewelry books

Once you've begun to delight in creating jewelry, you'll probably solder your soul to one particular technique. Here's the best for specialized detail. Remember, each author has his/her eye for decorative design. You'll probably want a few books. Some of the metal techniques go back four thousand or more years. —Don Lohr

Silversmithing and Art Metal (for Schools, Tradesmen, Craftsmen) by Murray Bovin, 1971, 1980, 287 pp.; $10.95 from: Bovin Publishing, 68-36 108th Street, Forest Hills, NY 11375, or Whole Earth Household Store.

The Jewelry Engraver's Manual by R. Allen Hardy, 1976, 143 pp.; $6.95 from: Van Nostrand Reinhold Company, Order Department, 7625 Empire Drive, Florence, KY 41042, or Whole Earth Household Store. *American style. Up-to-date.*

Engraving on Precious Metals by A. Brittain, et. al., 1977, 179 pp.; $7.95 from: Wehman Brothers, Inc., Ridgedale Avenue, Morris County Mall, Cedar Knolls, NJ 07927. *Classic. English. Elegant.*

Metalwork and Enamelling (A Practical Treatise on Gold and Silversmiths' Work and Their Allied Crafts) by Herbert Maryon, 1955, 1971, 237 pp.; $7 from: Peter Smith, 6 Lexington Avenue, Magnolia, MA 01930, or Whole Earth Household Store. *When you want to make* **everything**, *use this classic. Written before you could buy solder, it tells you how to make your own. You get to control every step.*

Creative Casting (Arts and Crafts Series) by Sharr Choate, 1966, 224 pp.; $9.95 from: Crown Publishers, One Park Avenue South, New York, NY 10016, or Whole Earth Household Store. *The new school of casting.*

Indian Silver Smithing by W. Ben Hunt, 1971, 158 pp.; $4.50 from: Macmillan Publishing Company, Order Department, Front and Brown Streets, Riverside, NJ 08075, or Whole Earth Household Store. *Native American silverwork alive and well.*

Hanneman Lapidary Specialties

No, you don't have to scratch your most beautiful gem with a steel pencil to make sure it's diamond and not quartz. All you have to do to learn how to identify gems and precious stones is write to Dr. Hanneman. Besides having the best equipment (e.g., Rayner products) and having invented others (e.g., the specific gravity Hanneman Balance), this mail order house costs about half the others. The best in home-grown cottage industries. The best for a complete gemological home-based laboratory. —Don Lohr

Hanneman Lapidary Specialties
Catalog
free from:
Hanneman Lapidary Specialties
P.O. Box 2453
Castro Valley, CA 94546

Hanneman Portable Gemological Laboratory, professional model: lab bench and mirror, 10x magnifier, 50x microscope, specific gravity fluids, refractive index fluids, viewing bench, polariscope, dichroscope, examination cells, "strainless" glass sphere, hollow glass sphere, selected gem specimens, instructions for use. $60.

Allcraft

Excellent catalog of tools and materials for jewelry work, enameling, metalsmithing, silversmithing, and casting. —SB

Allcraft
Catalog
$2.50 from:
Allcraft Tool and Supply Company
100 Frank Road
Hicksvill, NY 11801

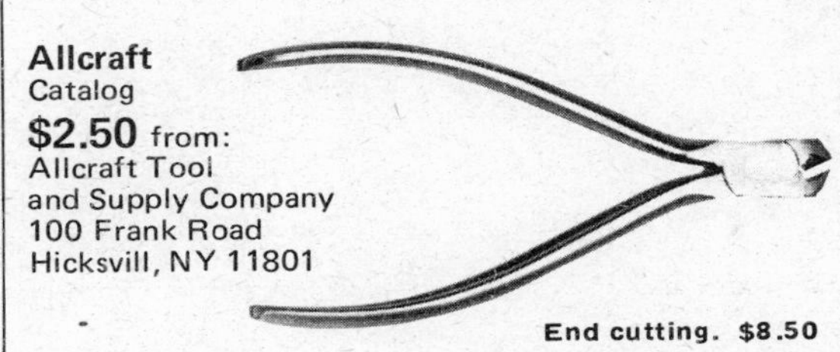

End cutting. $8.50

T-stake, 17" long, 1 7/8" wide, 20½ lbs. $90

A rugged little mill which would complement any jewelry or school shop. Model makers should find this mill indispensible. Specifications: Rolls: 2 3/4" wide x 1 3/4". Unit: 8" wide x 8" deep x 14" high with handles in place 17" wide. Gears: A large gear for easy turning. Wgt: 25 lbs. $230. ↓

Dixon tools & supplies

Precision tools. And not a sloppy catalog either. —SB

Precision Tools and Equipment
Catalog and price list
free from:
William Dixon, Inc.
Carlstadt, NJ 07072

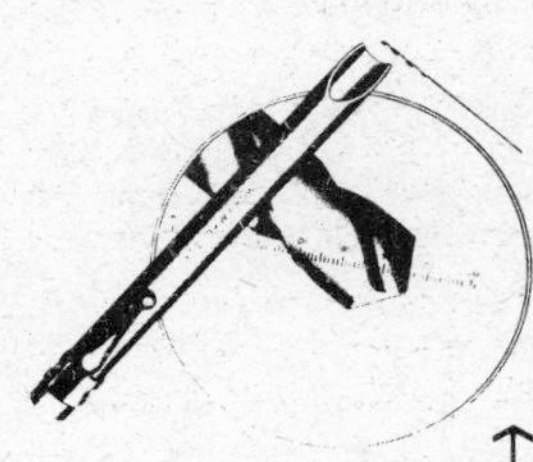

↑ These unique, extremely useful, and very popular microscopes, about the size of a pen and equipped with a pocket clip, are available in either twenty or forty power without any markings or with inch-decimal or metric scales inscribed on the lens.

→ Although primarily for use with chasing tools, these fine hammers have been adapted for many other purposes at the jeweler's bench and elsewhere.

↑ Although designed originally for the jewelry industry, Dixon work benches have found extensive use in almost every type of shop. The front edge of the two inch hardwood top is provided with removable bench pin and arm rest. An ample tool drawer slides easily between the top and lap tray designed to catch precious filings. Well supported steel legs can be bolted to the floor.

THE RISING SUN
NEIGHBORHOOD NEWSLETTER

The day after big news, the bus sounds like someone trying to get to sleep in a newspaper sleeping bag.

Glass Magazine
Glass Studio Magazine

Two fine magazines from the same people in Portland, Oregon. **Glass** *is mostly inspirational — mostly color, more expensive — for customers you might say.* **Glass Studio** *is mostly informative — only a little color, cheaper — for makers. It's a dazzling craft, one of the few that really tempts me.*
—SB

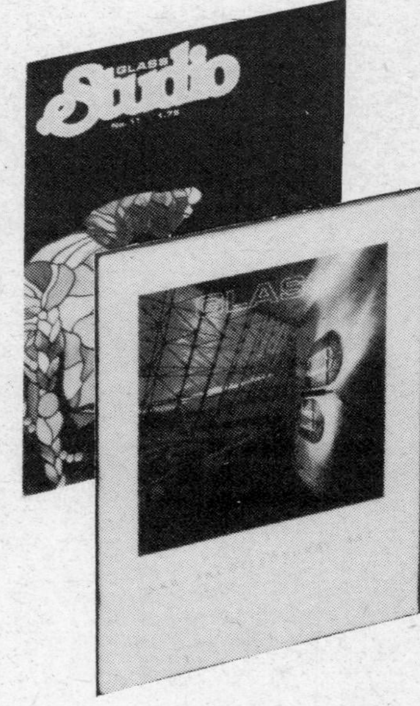

Glass Studio
Maureen Michelson, Editor
$9 /year (6 issues)

Glass
Jim Wilson, Editor
$24 /year (6 issues)
both from:
Glass Studio
P.O. Box 23383
Portland, OR 97223

•
Stained glass, far more than a host of fixtures, upon which considerable amounts of money are almost routinely spent, is the most spectacularly visible design element with which the architect can possibly work.
—Glass

•
Asbestos materials and clothing (gloves, sleeves, etc.) should be eliminated from the studio and replaced by glass fiber materials or firebrick for insulation purposes. Welders' leather gloves, and gloves made of new materials for potters and others who work with hot materials can be used in place of those containing asbestos. *No exposure to asbestos fibers is considered safe.*

Warning: removal of asbestos insulating materials must be done with extreme caution. The asbestos must be wetted down to prevent fibers from becoming airborne, and then stored in sealed plastic bags for removal.
—Glass Studio

Marbles by Dick Marquis at Elements Gallery.
—Glass Studio

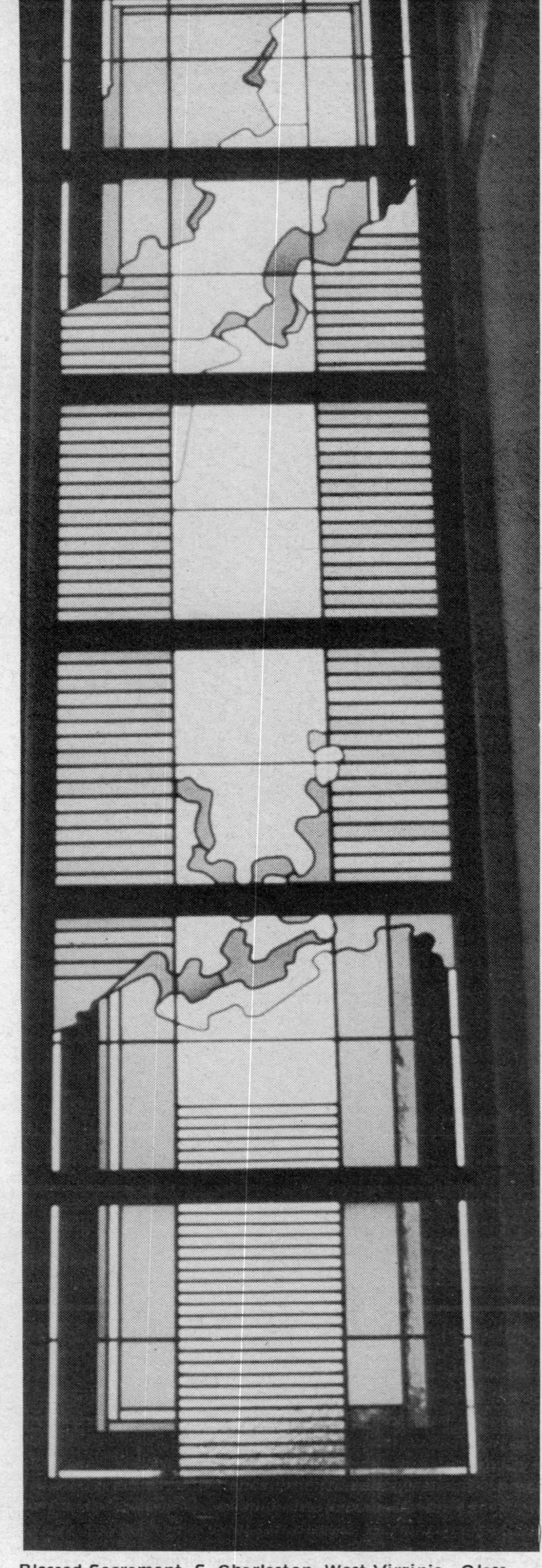

Blessed Sacrament, S. Charleston, West Virginia. Glass Design: David Wilson (S. New Berlin, New York), 1978. Architect: Clinton Beyan.
—Glass

BORING HOLES IN GLASS

Spiral was cut from a bulb with a sandblast gun. ↑

The Encyclopedia of Working with Glass

Not at all hip, contemporary, or — um — cutting edge, but there's a wealth of well-illustrated information in this stodgy volume — the usually unstated basic kind of lore that can set you off in a different direction from the contemporary crowd. The book makes no great distinction between working glass (labware, fiberglass, etc.) and art glass.
—SB
[Suggested by A.W. Griffin]

The Encyclopedia of Working with Glass
Milton K. Berlye
1968; 270 pp.
$20 postpaid from:
Oceana Publications
75 Main Street
Dobbs Ferry, NY 10522

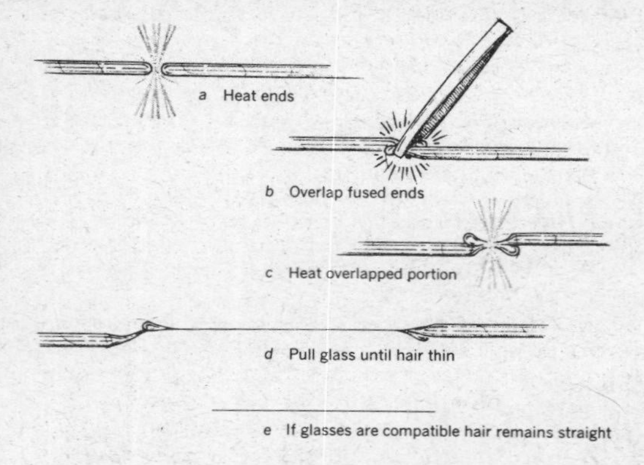
a Heat ends
b Overlap fused ends
c Heat overlapped portion
d Pull glass until hair thin
e If glasses are compatible hair remains straight
f If glasses are incompatible hair will curl

↑
Testing to see if two different glasses will form solid seals

Making a tortoise
↓

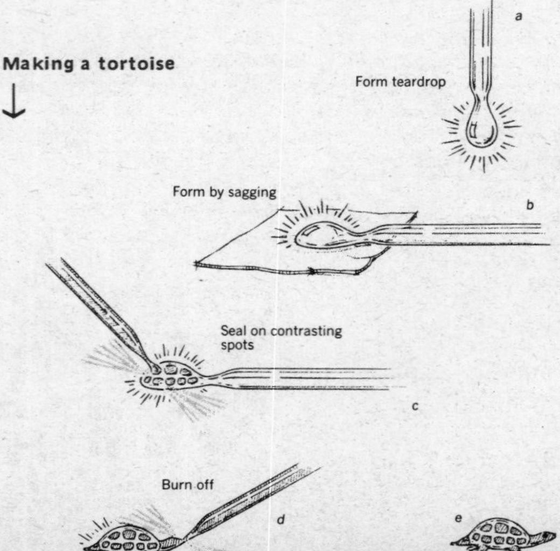
a
Form teardrop
Form by sagging
b
Seal on contrasting spots
c
Burn off
d
e

Glass story

"Show you something," said Dick Marquis the master glasscrafter of Berkeley. "Watch." He reached a metal rod into the glory hole, glommed a dollop of molten glass, held it on by rotating the rod, then let a long tear drop of glass ooze down. It dropped slowly off into a bucket of water with a big sizzle. He picked it out almost immediately with his bare hand, palped the still-soft fat part of the tear drop in his fingers. Once it was hard, he placed it on an anvil and beat on it with a hammer. No effect. Then he handed it to me. "Close your fist around it."

I enclosed the bulb of glass firmly in my hand. Marquis took the end of the long skinny tail of glass and snapped it off. BAM! went the glass in my fist. I opened my fingers gingerly, expecting gore. All there was was fine white sand.

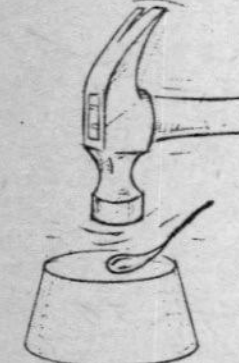

"Surface tension," explained Marquis. "When I disrupted its continuity, the whole thing went. At the studio in Italy when I worked, the guys would come up behind you and pop 'em in the crack of your ass."
—SB

Creative Glass Blowing

This well-illustrated and carefully written book begins with the statement "Anyone can learn to blow glass." To a large extent, the authors, one of whom is a professional glass blower, succeed in making that statement believable. However, the first 50 pages are concerned with the tools of the glass blower and I found myself wondering, "Yes, but can anyone learn to be a pipe-fitter, metal worker, carpenter, and electrician?" If you can do those things, there is little doubt that this book (and several hundred dollars worth of tools and related supplies) will enable you to blow glass — probably creatively.
—Richard Raymond

Creative Glass Blowing
(Scientific and Ornamental)
James E. Hammesfahr, Clair L. Stong
1968, 1978; 196 pp.
$10.95 postpaid from:
W.H. Freeman & Company
660 Market Street
San Francisco, CA 94104
or Whole Earth Household Store

Creative Glass blowing

James Hubbell. Shower skylight and wall (partial view). 1976. Hubbell residence.

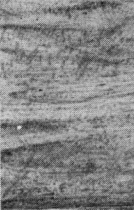

New Glass

A sampling of West Coast stained glass with statements from each artist. A particularly valuable book in a field hoary with centuries-old tradition, where examples don't travel well. Seeing the new work is a bit difficult. Much of it is intimate, its magic tied up with its surroundings and light source. Hard to roll all that up for shipping to a local museum, but it publishes nicely.

—Diana Sloat

New Glass
Otto B. Rigan
1976, 1977; 117 pp.
$7.95 postpaid from:
Ballantine Books, Inc.
455 Hahn Road
Westminster, MD 21157
or Whole Earth Household Store

STREAKY

SEEDY

GLUE CHIP

HAMMERED

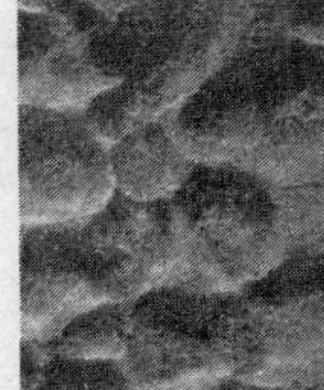

CREPE

CATS PAW

FLEMISH

Envisioning a Marriage, 1975.
Kathie Stockpole Bunnell — New Glass

Stained glass suppliers

Stained glass supplies,
everything you need
to change your view of
the neighbors
into a flyeye leaded
splendor.
I met a fellow on a
train,
once,
who paid for his bumdom,
by packing around two
suitcases
full of glassworkers tools,
fixing leaded windows,
here and there.

—J.D. Smith
[Suggested by Renee Gallery and Randy Street]

Whittemore and Durgin
Catalog
$ .25 from:
Whittemore Durgin Glass Company
Box 2065
Hanover, MA 02339

S.A. Bendheim
Catalog
$ .25 from:
S.A. Bendheim Company, Inc.
122 Hudson Street
New York, NY 10013

Ed Hoy's Stained Glass
Catalog
free from:
Ed Hoy's Stained Glass
999 East Chicago Ave.
Naperville, IL 60540

No. 5001 Deluxe Tool Kit for Stained Glass, includes.
No. 7000 Soldering Iron
No. 7072 Tip
No. 6860 Lead Knife
No. 6851 Horseshoe Nails
No. 6853 Glass Pliers
No. 6801, No. 6803, and No. 6805 Cutters
No. 7800 Solder
No. 7354 Flux Brush
No. 7343 2 oz. Flux
No. 5003 Tool Box
No. 7300 Copper Foil (36 yards)
No. 7074, No. 7070 Tips for No. 7000 Iron
No. 7078 Wattage Controller
No. 6845 Pattern Shears
No. 7342 Hanging Wire
No. 7350 Solder Black
No. 7341 Glass Handler's Gloves
No. 7345 Lead Straightener
No. 6847 Grazing Pliers

$105 from Whittemore-Durgin

—Ed Hoy's Stained Glass

Stained Glass Primer 1 & 2

The beauty is in the instruction: basic (Vol. 1) and advanced (Vol. 2) techniques in simple, straightforward language for the artist-student. Covers making easels and easel waxes, painting and surface abrading techniques, reinforcing and installing stained glass, and includes a short chapter on kilns and firing. Next best thing to an apprenticeship. But the prize is the annotated bibliography in Volume 2. It's his extensive glass library categorized and commented on both informatively and with feeling — lively reading and an invaluable resource.

—Diana Sloat

Stained Glass Primer, Vol. 1
Peter Mollica
1971, 1973; 87 pp.
$4.55 postpaid

Volume 2
Peter Mollica
1977; 207 pp.
$5.55 postpaid
both from:
Mollica Stained Glass Press
10033 Broadway Terrace
Oakland, CA 94611
or Whole Earth Household Store

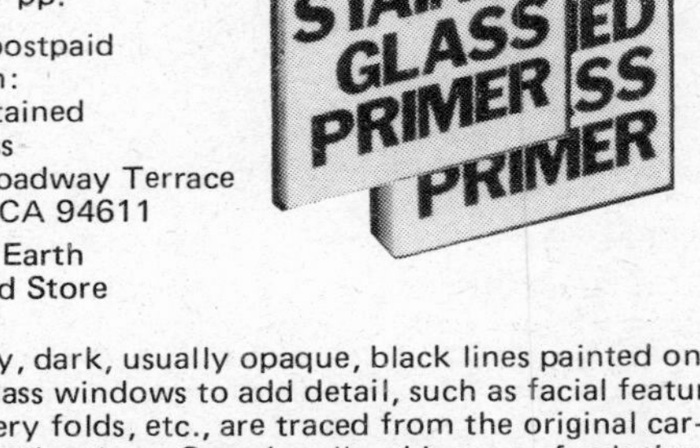

•

The heavy, dark, usually opaque, black lines painted on stained glass windows to add detail, such as facial features and drapery folds, etc., are traced from the original cartoon onto the glass. Occasionally, this type of painting is done free-hand while the glass is stuck up on the easel, but usually it is done by laying the glass on the cartoon and tracing. A simple light box is very handy for tracing, especially when the glass is dark. —Vol. 2

A simple light box is very handy for tracing, especially when the glass is dark.

•

Duval, Jean-Jacques, **Working With Stained Glass**, Thomas Crowell Company, New York, 1972.

This book introduces the novice to the essentials of making leaded glass window panels. It also describes techniques for laminating glass to glass, building a slab- glass panel, and construction of a lampshade using copper foil. The photographs and drawings are very good. The photographs are taken as you would view the action while doing it and as though the camera were mounted on your forehead. There are also many photographs of unusual hobby work. A good first book.

•

Reyntiens, Patrick, **The Technique of Stained Glass**, Watson-Guptill Publishers, New York City, 1967.

This book led the way for all the recent technique books. It is still among the best and most comprehensive. It covers Dalle-de-Verre, fused glass, epoxy glass on glass, as well as the traditional techniques of leaded glass. The section on painting on glass is thorough and offers methods of applying and manipulating the paint that go beyond the traditional techniques. Photographs of the many effects possible using expressionistic techniques to apply and texture the paint before firing.

My other favorite chapter is that which describes the ideal studio, from tea-making equipment to insurance. Although much of this advice is beyond the reach of most artists just starting out, the theory behind suggesting a separate room for each operation is sound. Having an ideal in mind can be very helpful when you go to make up your own studio. But don't get discouraged if you can't have it all at once.

Chapters proceed in a logical sequence as the steps in making a window: cutting, painting, firing, glazing, installing with additional sections on packing, exhibiting, and other techniques.

I understand that a revised and expanded edition is soon to appear.

It is often convenient to make the most difficult score first. If it fails to break correctly the pattern can be moved and the cut again attempted. Here the first score would be the concave one.

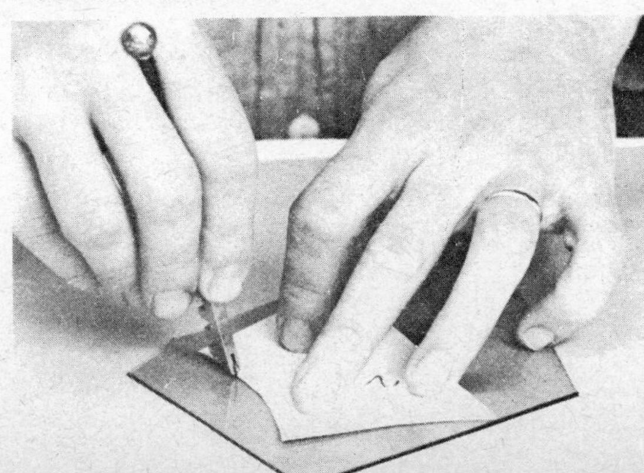

THE RISING SUN
NEIGHBORHOOD NEWSLETTER

Usually analyses of revivalism begin with the wealth of evangelists, but I think it's better to begin with life is a crock. Life is a crock or often feels like it as you keep trying to climb up the sides and sliding down into the same old shit. I certainly wouldn't begrudge giving 20% of my income to anyone who could fly me out the top and give me a bath and clean clothes and permanent sunshine and the fact that a whole bunch of other people were giving 20% of their income and it was buying cars and mansions wouldn't really have anything to do with it. A small price to pay if it works.

Unfortunately, it never worked for me, which is why everything I've ever said about revivals has been nasty. Jealous, you know.

Modern Leather Design

Beginning leatherworkers who consider leather a serious design medium will especially appreciate this comprehensive introductory text. Willcox's fine-art approach to leatherworking makes for inspiring reading and promotes a sophisticated sense of contemporary leather design, from functional accessories and clothing to sculpture and furniture. But despite the lofty approach, there's no sacrifice of hands-on technical information and expertise. Well-organized chapters define and explore the history of leatherworking, the nature, characteristics, and behavior of the medium, and the tools and techniques involved in working with it. If you're strictly in the market for a how-to manual, you may be disappointed; use Willcox's book as a general introduction and reference and follow his recommendations for more detailed instruction sources. When you finish this book you will no longer consider yourself a beginner, and will be well on your way to making well-designed, high quality leather creations.

—Mimi Abrams

Modern Leather Design
Donald Willcox
1969; 160 pp.
$16.50 postpaid from:
Watson-Guptill Publications
2160 Patterson Street
Cincinnati, OH 45214
or Whole Earth Household Store

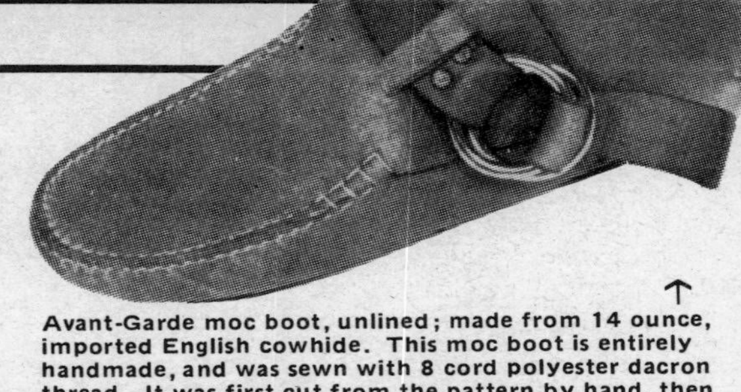

Avant-Garde moc boot, unlined; made from 14 ounce, imported English cowhide. This moc boot is entirely handmade, and was sewn with 8 cord polyester dacron thread. It was first cut from the pattern by hand, then tacked to a last and sewn with a locking stitch, using two needles and two lengths of thread. Notice that the heel seam is raised up enough to prevent the wearer from walking on it. (I have a pair of these moc boots and can honestly say that they're the most comfortable things I've ever worn on my feet.) Made by Walter Dyer, Rockport, Mass.

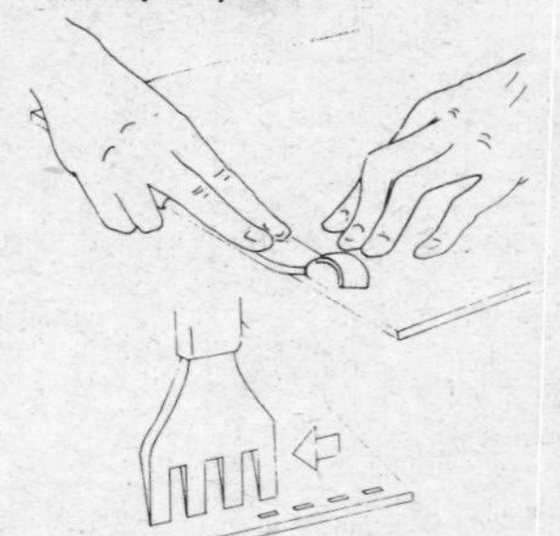

Position of the hands while skiving

A 4-prong thronging chisel in use (arrow shows direction of movement), with last prong using last hole on previous punch as a spacing guide

•

If you decided to earn a living as a leather craftsman, you could set yourself up in business with an initial investment in tools of about $150, exclusive of any electrical machinery. With this initial $150 investment in tools and supplies, you would be fully equipped to make every item covered in this book.

•

While reducing thickness, the process of skiving also makes leather more flexible. Skiving is therefore used whenever you run up against any thickness problem in folding, creasing, flexing, or edge turning.

Brendan's Leather Book

Brendan's yankee practicality will launch you into heavier leathers, belts, bags, sandals. His chatter's funny. His information on basics is often excellent, as in sections on buying cowhide, setting up a workshop, dyeing leather well (mixing, thinning and correcting mistakes). He even shows how to put that razor edge on a knife that'll have you cutting leather like cheese. Be aware that his price quotes are from 1972. Since leather workers have been such a close-mouthed lot, it's a pleasure to see his obviously hardwon design ideas and shortcuts so generously shared.

—Diana Sloat

Brendan's Leather Book
1972; 162 pp.
$4.50 postpaid from:
Outer Straubville Press
P.O. Box 612
Cotati, CA 94928
or Whole Earth Household Store

•

THE SADDLER'S STITCH

For sewing thick leather, unroll a length of thread 3½ times the length of your seam. Be generous. There is nothing more annoying than running out of thread in mid-seam. You can become more exact with practice. Now thread a needle onto each end of the thread. That's right, each end. Take the leather you're going to be sewing and hold it, seam up, between your knees. Find your first hole; it should be nearest your body. Shove one of the needles through and pull until you have an equal amount of thread on both sides, like this:

Now, take a needle in each hand and push it into the next hole away from your body. *Don't* cross over the top of the seam, just follow them dotted lines. A close-up at this time would look like this:

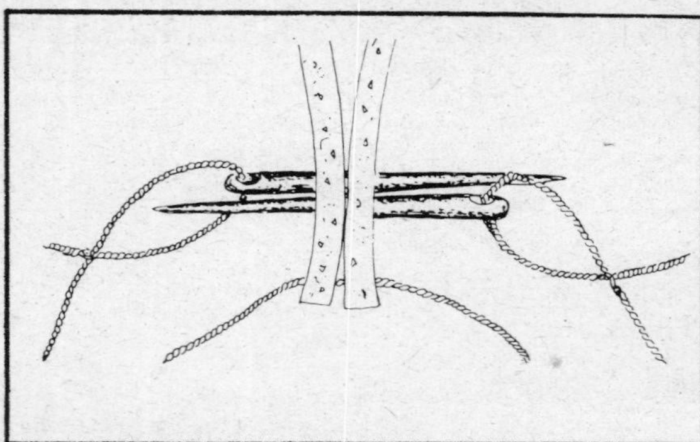

See how one needle is placed "in front" of the other? In this case it's the one on the left. Well, if you start with that left hand needle in front, all the other stitches should be the same way — that is, the left hand needle should always be in front. It doesn't matter which side you choose, just as long as you stick to it. Your sewing will be ragged and uneven if you aren't consistent.

Leathercrafting

Raymond Cherry's leathercraft manual emphasizes good basic construction of functional leather items and offers the detailed, step-by-step instructions necessary for making them. As a high school industrial arts instructor, Cherry has tested and proven his procedures over years of working with students, and the training you'll get with his manual is top-rate. This book begins with a short illustrated encyclopedia of tools and materials used in leatherworking, followed by a comprehensive section on the "fundamental operations" involved. In the back of the manual, patterns and detailed instructions are provided for 31 different leather projects, both basic and complex, mostly calling for stiffer leathers (bags, belts, cases) rather than supple ones (clothing).

—Mimi Abrams

Leathercrafting
(Procedures and Projects)
5th Edition
Raymond Cherry
1940; 128 pp.
$4.54 postpaid from:
McKnight Publications
Taplinger Publishing Co.
200 Park Avenue South
New York, NY 10003
or Whole Earth Household Store

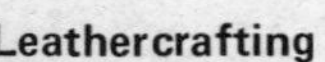

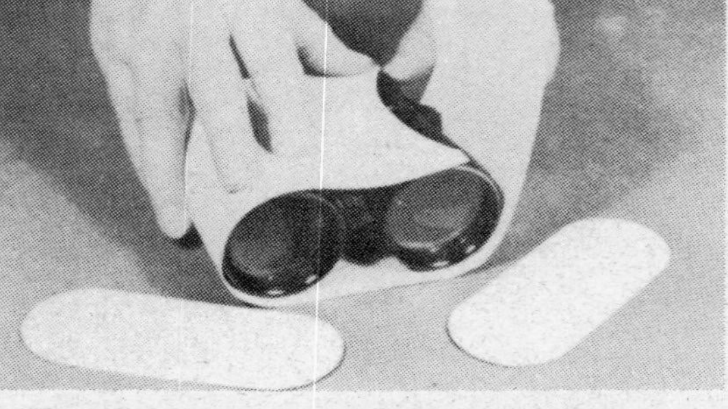

In designing a pattern for a case for something like field glasses, place heavy paper around the object. Make the cover approximately ¼" wider than the object to allow for the gussets or end pieces.

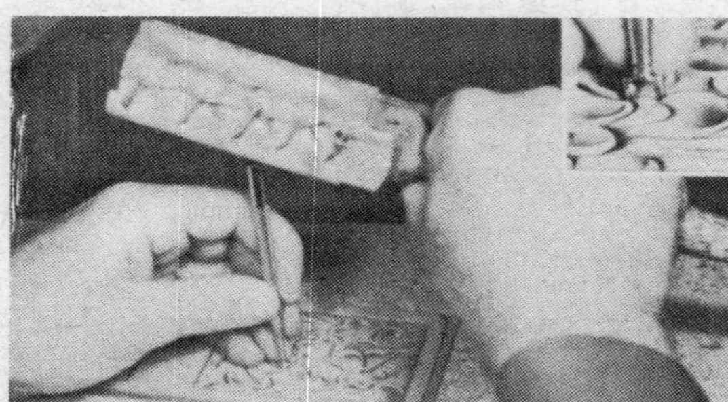

Holding a background tool

Blue Mountain Buckskin

A thoroughly native low-cost method of tanning deer hides to make buckskin. The process is slow and arduous. This manual explains it well. A small buckskin sample is included in each book.

—Marilyn Green
[Suggested by Stephen Anderson]

Blue Mountain Buckskin
(A Working Manual)
Jim Riggs
1979; 63 pp.
$6 postpaid from:
Blue Mountain Buckskin
P.O. Box 35
Lostine, OR 97857

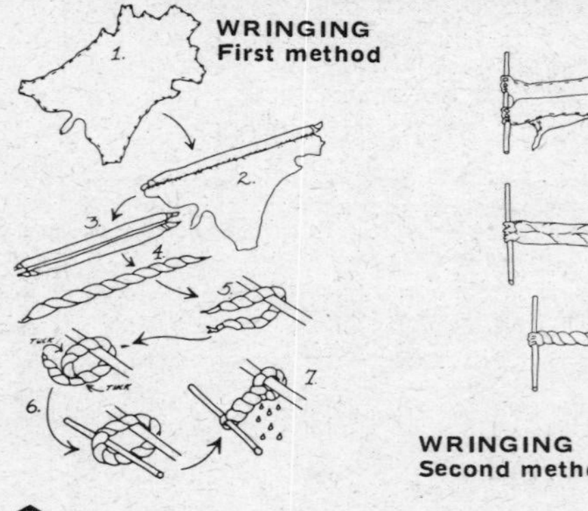

Wringing is the important preparatory step to working a brained hide dry and soft. Wringing serves two main functions: 1) It removes excess moisture from the skin, thus reducing the length of time needed to work it dry, and 2) It begins to stretch the hide.

Home Tanning and Leather Making Guide

Best information on tanning we've seen. If you're eating deer or calf or dog or whatever and throwing the skin away, you don't need this book. Meathead.

—SB

Home Tanning and Leather Making Guide
A.B. Farnham
1950; 176 pp.
$3 postpaid from:
Harding's Books
2878 East Main Street
Columbus, Ohio 43209

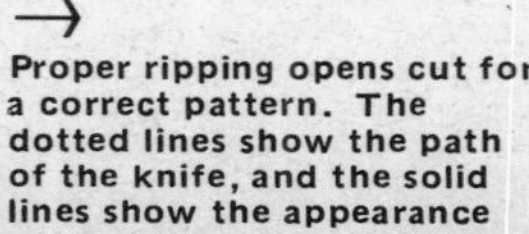

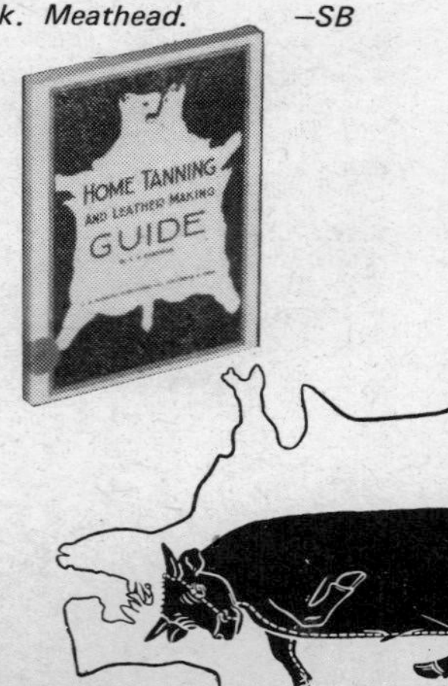

Proper ripping opens cut for a correct pattern. The dotted lines show the path of the knife, and the solid lines show the appearance of the hide when spread out.

Osborne tools

Always wanted to be a saddlemaker.
Closest I've come so far is drugstore cowboy sandalmaker.
Try cutting a sole bend with a pocketknife,
or punching holes with a screwdriver,
and you begin to appreciate good leatherworking tools.
Osborne is the best. —*J.D. Smith*
[Suggested by Michael J. Green]

Osborne Tools
Catalog and list of distributors

free from:
C.S. Osborne and Company
125 Jersey Street
Harrison, NJ 07029

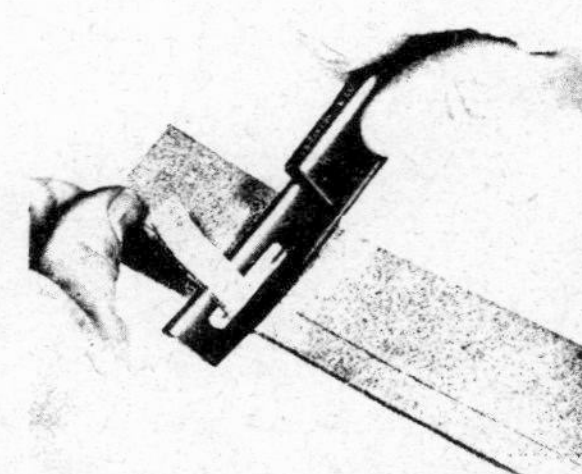

← **The Skife — $1.30 Makes remarkably easy job of skiving. Increases both speed and accuracy. This essential tool is fitted with a Schick razor blade.**

↑ **Revolving Punch for professional and industrial use — $34.**

This Punch has been known for many years as the best Revolving Punch ever made. The frame is made of forged steel, highly polished. The cutting tubes are hand turned from high carbon tool steel and threaded to allow easy replacement. These tubes are individually tempered.

Saddlery and Harnessmaking

Professional saddlers and harness makers are often very expensive and tend, in this country at least (Great Britain), to be a tight lipped bunch who don't want to tell you things that they had to serve a five year apprenticeship to learn.

This book is unique (I think) and tells it all. It's a straight reprint of the edition written in 1904, when these trades were as commonplace as motor mechanics is now, by one Paul Hasluck, who was then Master of the Worshipfull Company of Saddlers. This is the complete (300 tightly printed pages with 300 drawings) textbook of the trade. It covers all the common repairs as well as manufacture. All hand work, no machines.

If you want to make an English side saddle or a complete set of plough gear or waggon harness, or just repair a broken trace or whip or reline a collar, this book tells you exactly how, which knife and leather to use — precise shapes and sizes to cut — where and how to sew and with what thread, etc., etc. —*Anonymous*
Argyll, Scotland

Saddlery and Harness-Making
Paul N. Hasluck
1904, 1975; 156 pp.

$9 postpaid from:
J.A. Allen and Company, Ltd.
Sporting Book Center
Canaan, NY 12029

→ Holding and gripping tools include the clamp, known also as the pair of clams. Held between the knees in a slightly slanting position, the clamp keeps the work firmly in position while the stitching is being done; it lies against the left knee, and by throwing the right leg over it the work is held fast between the gripping points. Note that the saddler has the clamp between his legs in a slanting direction, and not as the shoemaker, who has them straight up, almost against his nose, when bending over the work. One reason for this is that the work done by the saddler with the clamp requires more force to press the awl through than the work done by the shoemaker; consequently the saddler must set his clamp against some firm object (his left knee) so that it will not yield under the pressure.

Berman Leathercraft

Berman Leather has a fine mail order catalog. Prices on leather, buckles, tools, cements, Fiebling's dyes and finishes considerably lower than MacPherson's, enough to justify shipping costs to the West Coast. Selection of tools by manufacturer is not so extensive, but tool pictures are up to date — what you see is what you get, and you won't have to eat your heart out for a handsome old Osborne punch that's not been made for years.

For sandalmakers there are 3/8 brass and iron clinching nails unavailable at shoe findings suppliers on the West Coast. Since I've never tried it, can't vouch for mail-ordering leather, but the selection, prices and pictures look downright tempting. In fact, so does the whole catalog. —*Diana Sloat*

Berman Leathercraft
Catalog

$1 postpaid from:
Berman Leathercraft
147 South Street
Boston, MA 02111

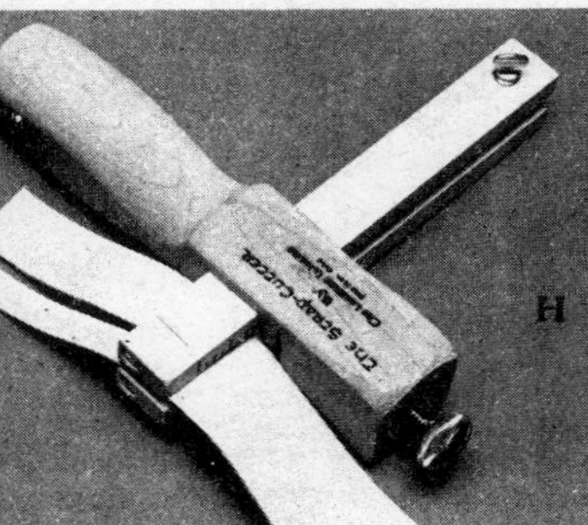

← **Wooden Strap Cutter — $8.95. Cuts straps for belts, bags, etc. Wood construction compliments the finest design we've ever used.**

How to Make Cowboy Horse Gear

A highly practical book on the uses of rawhide. Included is a section on how to cure "green leather" and make your own rawhide. When braided, leather is strong and durable. This book illustrates the use of rawhide for "horse gear"; there are certainly other situations where leather braiding can be used to advantage.
—*Mary McCabe*
[Suggested by Gary Snyder]

How to Make Cowboy Horse Gear
Bruce Grant
1953; 186 pp.

$6 postpaid from:
Cornell Maritime Press
Box 456
Centerville, MD 21617
or Whole Earth Household Store

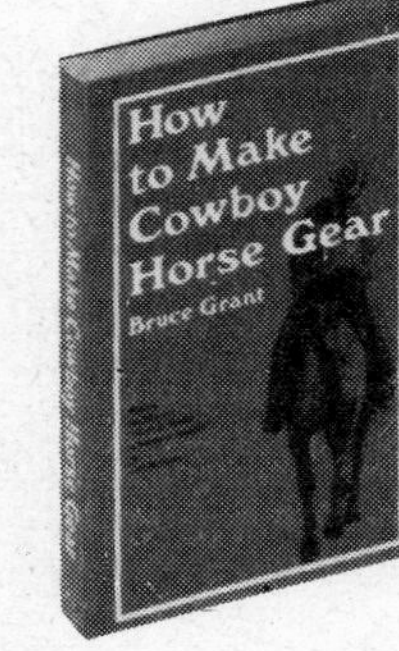

•

Sonny Strong has passed over the Great Divide, but his way of making rawhide lives on.

This is it: When the hide or skin is taken off the carcass and while the body heat is still in it, spread it out flat with the flesh side up and salt it down with 40 or 50 pounds of fine stock salt. This is for a mature hide. For a yearling or calf skin use half the amount of salt. Spread the salt evenly and fold the hide over so the hair side is out and the flesh sides are together.

Leave the hide in a shady, dry place for from a week to ten days. It is important to salt the hide while the body heat is still in it, Rickman emphasizes. So if you do not actually remove the hide yourself, get the person who does to salt it down for you. The salt runs the blood and glue out of the hide before it congeals and Rickman feels this is important in keeping the hide pliable.

Encyclopedia of Rawhide and Leather Braiding

A major reference work — undisputedly excellent. Its main drawback is FRUSTRATION. No one wants to start simply and learn slowly, when right there's this 5-part Inside Trick Braid. ". . . Uh, well, . . . it looked so so logical and easy!"

But in case you've secretly hankered to try a bola, attach a stone to a hatchet handle, or do any of a thousand other fancy braids, buttons, knots, applique lacings, suspenders, whips, dog collars and horse gear . . . you know where to go.
—*Diana Sloat*

Encyclopedia of Rawhide and Leather Braiding
Bruce Grant
1972; 528 pp.

$15 postpaid from:
Cornell Maritime Press
P.O. Box 456
Centerville, MD 21617
or Whole Earth Household Store

•

Milton F. Farley, an old-time buckaroo of Crawfordsville, Oregon, wrote me recently that, after years of trying to find some easy and satisfactory method of thinning and evening rawhide strings, he had learned from an old fellow how to skive them by a very simple and homey way.

"Now, here's what I want you to do," he wrote. "Go to a hardware store and tell the salesman you want a good joiner's plane. When you get it in your hands it explains itself. You turn the screw behind the bit clockwise to close the gap behind the bit. When you turn the screw anticlockwise it opens the gap. If the strings are one inch or smaller I hold the plane in my left hand, pull the string with my right. When the strings are wider, I fasten the plane in a vise. Darn it, Bruce, it's so simple it's silly!"

Handle of Argentine rebenque **covered with rawhide multiple Conquistador braid** ↓

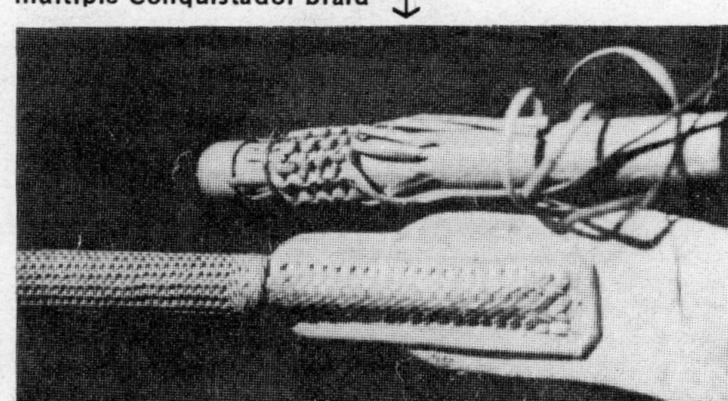

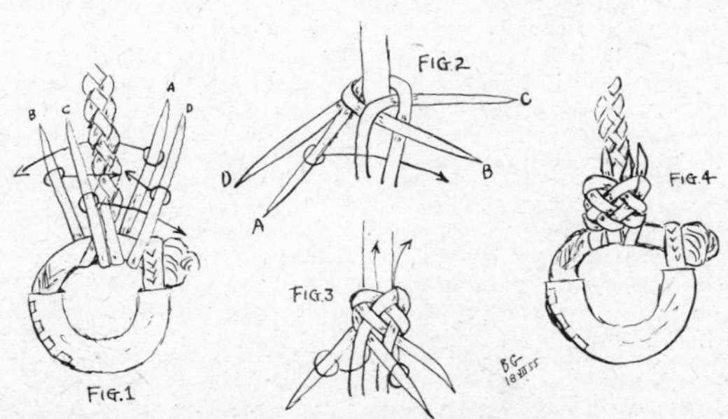

How to tie the reata to the honda ↑

MacPherson Leathercraft Supplies

Some all-in-one do-it-yourself quicky professional type leathercraft kits, and some professional quality tools. They mail order good leathers at decent prices. (Ask for leather price lists.) If nothing else, you can get an idea of what you will need. —*J. D. Smith*
[Suggested by Jack de Swart]

MacPherson Leathercraft
Catalog

free from:
MacPherson Brothers
730 Polk Street
San Francisco, CA 94109

← **Handy Last Patented two-sided unbreakable last**

THE RISING SUN NEIGHBORHOOD NEWSLETTER

A nineteenth century Hasidic rabbi told a story about a house burning in a forest and someone cries within but no one hears and the owner is gone and no one knows where and the house burns down. He admitted he didn't know what it was about, but twentieth century Hasids found out it was about the Holocaust. (The owner was God.) If we were allowed to think like that, the Hindenberg in the late '30s would do ok as a preview and warning of the '40s, you just think you're on vacation living your life, then the half you're not in catches on fire and scares you and then the half you're in catches on fire and kills you and you fall into the ocean and all that's left is a stupid announcer crying to people who aren't there and can't do anything anyway.

Reader's Digest Complete Guide to Sewing

Easily the one book I would recommend for any home sewer, whether beginner or accomplished old-timer. It's much better than the previous champion, the **Vogue Sewing Book**. *Tools, methods, and techniques are covered with thorough and easy-to-follow instructions and every option and variation imaginable. The sewing machine section, compiled with the aid of Singer, is a comprehensive overview of electric sewing machines, how to use, maintain, and understand them. Sections on special techniques for men's and children's clothing, and sewing for the home, are included.* —Evelyn Eldridge-Diaz

Reader's Digest Complete Guide to Sewing
1976; 528 pp.

$18.95 postpaid from:
W.W. Norton and Company
500 Fifth Avenue
New York, NY 10036
or Whole Earth Household Store

Gathering foot gathers up a length of fabric as it is being stitched. Some gathering feet will simultaneously gather one layer of fabric while stitching it to another flat piece of fabric.

Overedge foot is designed to be placed along a fabric edge so that the stitches will fall over the edge of the fabric. A metal bar holds edge in place so stitches will set properly.

Shears and scissors

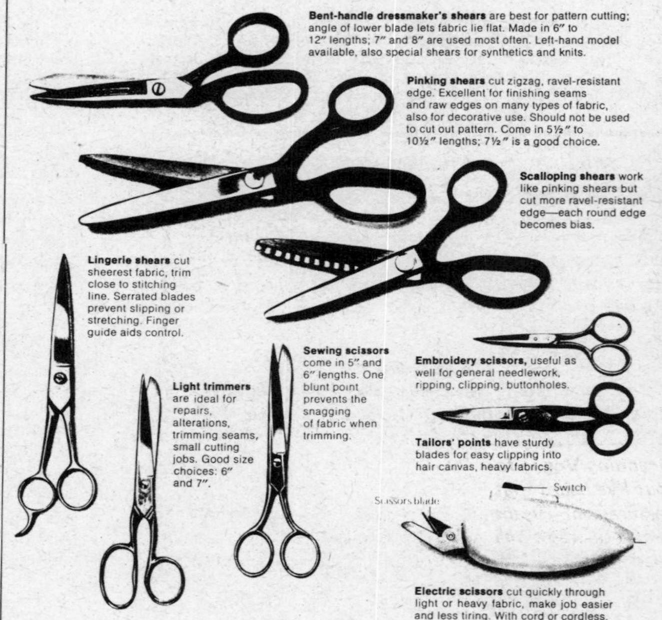

Bent-handle dressmaker's shears are best for pattern cutting; angle of lower blade lets fabric lie flat. Made in 6″ to 12″ lengths; 7″ and 8″ are used most often. Left-hand model available, also special shears for synthetics and knits.
Pinking shears cut zigzag, ravel-resistant edge. Excellent for finishing seams and raw edges on many types of fabric, also for decorative use. Should not be used to cut out pattern. Come in 5½″ to 10½″ lengths; 7½″ is a good choice.
Scalloping shears work like pinking shears but cut more ravel-resistant edge—each round edge becomes bias.
Lingerie shears cut sheerest fabric, trim close to stitching line. Serrated blades prevent slipping or stretching. Finger guide aids control.
Light trimmers are ideal for repairs, alterations, trimming seams, small cutting jobs. Good size choices: 6″ and 7″.
Sewing scissors come in 5″ and 6″ lengths. One blunt point prevents the snagging of fabric when trimming.
Embroidery scissors, useful as well for general needlework, ripping, clipping, buttonholes.
Tailors' points have sturdy blades for easy clipping into hair canvas, heavy fabrics.
Switch
Scissors blade
Electric scissors cut quickly through light or heavy fabric, make job easier and less tiring. With cord or cordless.

Making garments easy to put on and take off

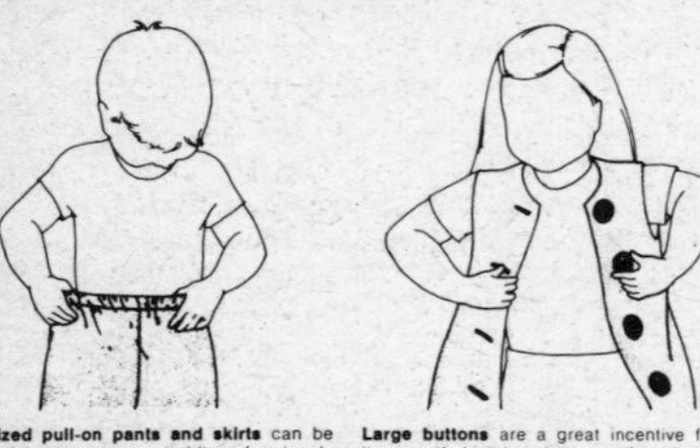

Elasticized pull-on pants and skirts can be managed by even young toddlers (sewing is easy, too). If garment front and back are different, mark back with ribbon or tape.

Large buttons are a great incentive for do-it-yourself dressing, because they don't take much dexterity and are easy for little fingers to grasp. Sew buttons very securely.

A zipper with a large pull is best for first attempts at zipping up. Buy a decorative zipper with a fancy pull, or add a ring to any type. Install zipper in garment front.

No-sew snaps are the easiest type for small fingers to cope with, and they have good holding power. Use single snaps for spot closings and snap tape for longer plackets.

Timed sequence in stitch formation

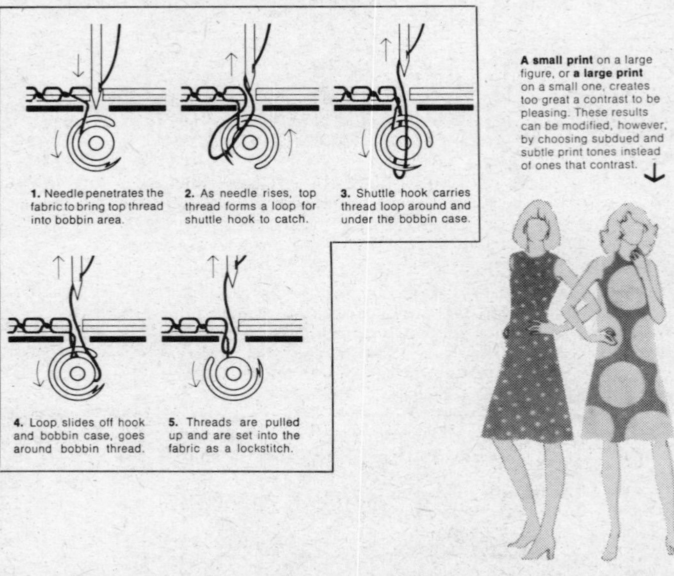

1. Needle penetrates the fabric to bring top thread into bobbin area.

2. As needle rises, top thread forms a loop for shuttle hook to catch.

3. Shuttle hook carries thread loop around and under the bobbin case.

4. Loop slides off hook and bobbin case, goes around bobbin thread.

5. Threads are pulled up and are set into the fabric as a lockstitch.

A small print on a large figure, or **a large print** on a small one, creates too great a contrast to be pleasing. These results can be modified, however, by choosing subdued and subtle print tones instead of ones that contrast. ↓

Gingher scissors

How often have you tried to cut something out of a heavy fabric such as corduroy, and had your hand be partially paralyzed because the scissors you used just weren't up to the job, or been frustrated because your shears wouldn't cut all the way to the tip of the blade? Gingher knife edge shears and scissors can cut through more layers of fabric with less effort than any other scissors I've ever used. And they cut through those masses of material all the way to the tips of the blades. They come in sizes and for purposes for nearly every sewer or stitcher: scissors, trimmers, shears, leather shears, applique scissors, kitchen shears, etc. All are sold in their own protective box, with instructions for sharpening and general care. They are not cheap (about $10 - $30), but good tools seldom are. —Evelyn Eldridge-Diaz

Gingher scissors
Information and price list

free from:
Gingher, Inc.
P.O. Box 8865
Greensboro, NC 27410

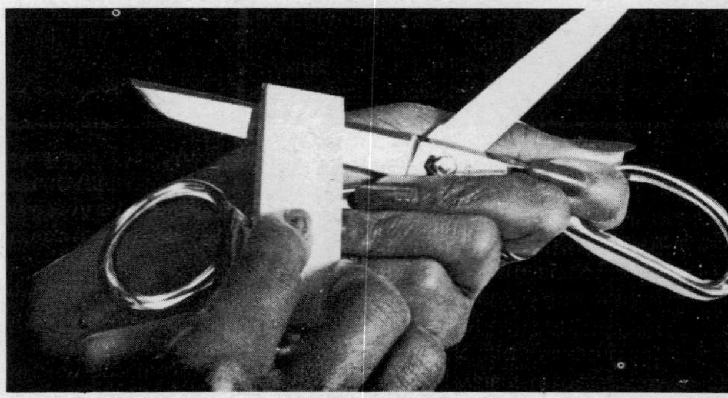

Keeping the knife edge sharp is vital to its effective performance and long life. Only the blade adjacent to the lock-nut is ground with a knife edge (learn to recognize it and respect it). This blade can be resharpened in seconds by honing firmly with a fine-grit whetstone or sharpening stone in the manner shown.

CAUTION: All honing must be done on the outside bevel surface of the knife edge (the inside surface must not be disturbed). Grasp shears firmly as illustrated, avoiding finger contact with the knife edge. Hold sharpening stone against the outside bevel surface of the knife edge at the steepest angle which will permit contact with the extreme edge. With firm upward strokes hone the edge, working from the tip of the blade to the shank with overlapping strokes. Proper honing will create a continuous burr along the inside cutting edge which can be removed simply by closing the sharpened shears. It is important that both cutting edges then be wiped clean before further use.

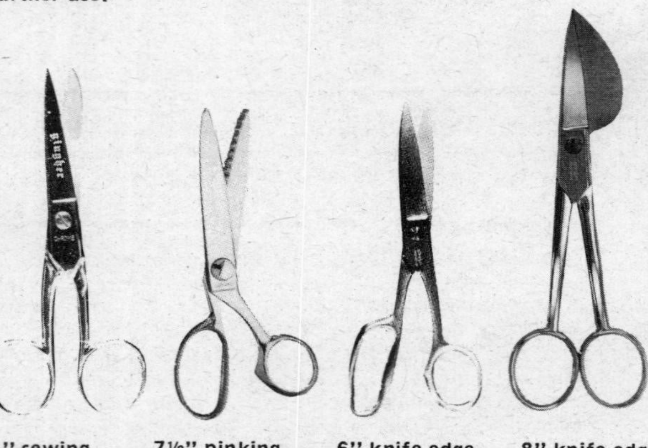

5" sewing scissors — $12.50 · **7½" pinking shears — $26.50** · **6" knife edge applique scissors — $18.50** · **8" knife edge leather shears — $16.95**

The Sewing Corner

The twice-yearly catalogs from the Sewing Corner in Lake Park, Florida are worth a look. The company publishes two separate editions. One is full of hundreds of wonderful thimbles. Ranging from "earthly character" thimbles carved by Parson Hayes, "noted American wood sculptor" to a set of "Austrial Finger Huts." The catalog also includes a chart on how to determine your personal thimble size. Catalog number 2 offers every Geegaw a seamstress might desire. Catalogs are only two bits and they even gift wrap. —Marilyn Green

The Sewing Corner
Catalog

$.25 postpaid from:
The Sewing Corner
1313 South Killian
Lake Park, FL 33403

FANTASTIC FIT®

Pants Former—A flexible, hinged ruler to help fit any pants pattern to your body contour, from front to back through crotch. Easy How-To instructions included.**9896:$2.95**

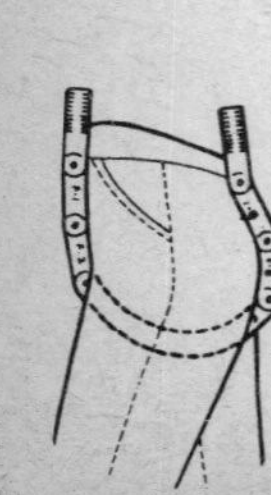

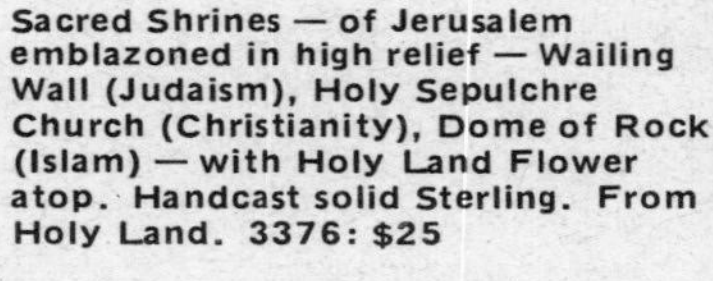

Sacred Shrines — of Jerusalem emblazoned in high relief — Wailing Wall (Judaism), Holy Sepulchre Church (Christianity), Dome of Rock (Islam) — with Holy Land Flower atop. Handcast solid Sterling. From Holy Land. 3376: $25

Holy City — revered panorama of Jerusalem in sculptured high relief, encircles solid Sterling Thimble, topped by Peace Sign. Handcrafted in Jerusalem. 3377: $25 ⟶

"Big Eye" Needle. ↑
Hand-sewing, embroidery, crewel, Rya knots, tie quilting — you name it — is done easily and quickly with our new BIG EYE — EASY THREADING NEEDLE. Just tug it slightly, thread or yarn is locked or unlocked, eye closes automatically when needle is pulled through fabric. Truly a blessing for anyone who loves to sew but dreads threading. Goldplated nickel. Comes with how-to-use instructions. 9810: $.79; 2 for only $1.50

Mini Snips

Carry them in your pocket, in a purse. Easy on the fingers. Sharp little rascals. Indispensable. (Made of surgical steel with chromed handles.) —Diana Sloat

Mini Snips
No. C343-3W

$3.65 postpaid from:
U.S. General Tools and Hardware (p. 145)
or check your local variety store.

Made in U.S.A.
3¼" Folded
CARRY THESE FOLDING SCISSORS IN YOUR POCKET
Mini Snips offer folding convenience and protection from accidental injuries. Stainless steel blades keep their super-sharp cutting edge. To open—just pull handles apart. Will fit in any pocket or purse.
C343-3W365 .... $4.02

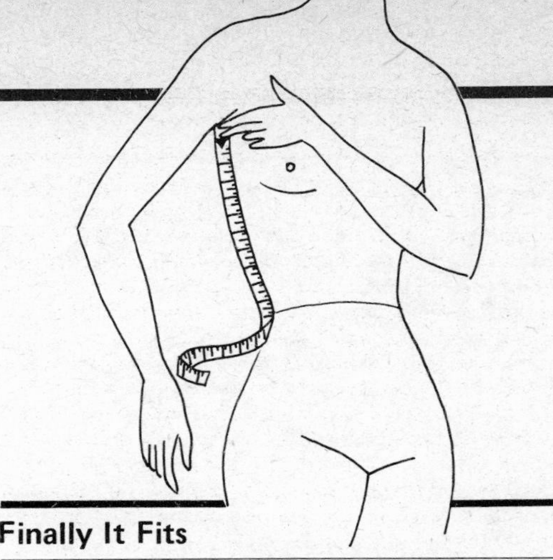

Finally It Fits

There comes a time for most sewers when what you have in mind to make simply is not available in commercial pattern books. If the frustration leads to determination not to be thwarted, this book will be a natural to turn to. In it are complete instructions for making your own personalized "slopers." Slopers are the basic pattern pieces that most manufacturers start from and from which all patterns are derived. Once you have made your slopers, you should be able to design for yourself or whomever you sew for, anything from an Elizabethan wardrobe to a Devo jumpsuit. A word of caution, however, it takes precise measuring, and a helper for the initial measurements is almost a must. —Evelyn Eldridge-Diaz

Finally It Fits
(The no-scare Home Patternmaking System for everyone, every size)
Ruth Amiel and Happy Gerhard
1973; 235 pp.

$6.95 postpaid from:
Times Books
Harper and Row
Keystone Industrial Park
Scranton, PA 18512
or Whole Earth Household Store

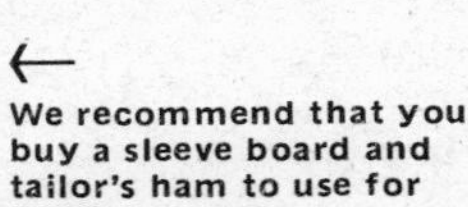

← We recommend that you buy a sleeve board and tailor's ham to use for pressing curves.

Pattern Making by the Flat Pattern Method

Excellent instructions and technique. —Judy Sears

Pattern Making by the Flat Pattern Method
Norma R. Hollen
1972, 1975; 219 pp.

$10.95 postpaid from:
Burgess Publishing Co.
7108 Ohms Lane
Minneapolis, MN 55435

•

FLAT-PATTERN work starts with a commercial basic pattern that has previously been altered to fit the individual. The pattern work consists of changing this altered basic pattern to make a pattern for a chosen design. The work is done in paper on a flat surface.

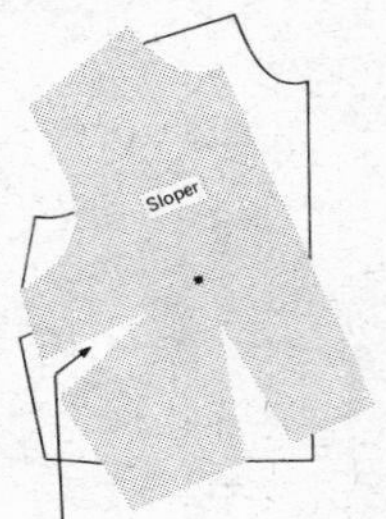

STEP I

Thumbtack the sloper to the paper pattern at the bust point. Pivot the sloper until the bust-fitting dart of the sloper is moved down to the place where the new dart should be (see arrow). Trace the dart. Remove the sloper.

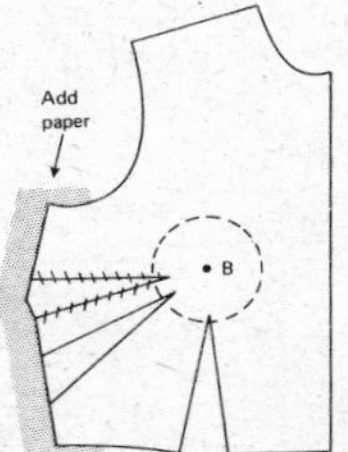

STEP II

Add some paper. Extend the new dart lines to the underarm seamline. Cross out the original dart. Fold the new dart on the lower line and perfect the underarm seamline.

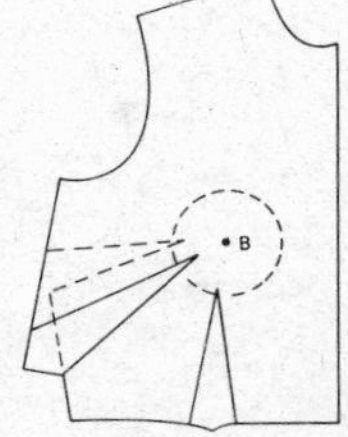

STEP III

Cut off excess paper to shape the dart. Notice that the new dart "looks" larger, but that is only because it is longer. The size is the same as the original. Dotted lines show the original pattern lines.

Tailoring Suits the Professional Way

This is the finest book I've read on tailoring in 13 years of self-taught sewing. Most books I've read deal only with women's clothes constructed in the air of rapidly changing fashion and intense commercial manufacturing, so a great deal of attention is not given to fit or technique — just the quickest, easiest way of getting it together. This book deals concisely, yet simply with the steps of tailoring men's and women's coats, pants, vests and skirts. It also provides formulas for drafting patterns of each and is a bountiful source of "tricks" of the tailoring trade, like how to get rid of a scorch. If you're really interested in tailoring as a craft, you can read this book like a novel. —Judy Sears

Tailoring Suits the Professional Way
Clarence Poulin
1973; 213 pp.

$8.20 postpaid from:
Charles A. Bennett Co.
809 W. Detweller Drive
Peoria, IL 61614

•

If the coat is properly drafted and the balance right, its fronts will hang side by side almost perpendicularly when it is tried on. It is to be expected that the space between them will be a trifle wider at the waist than at the chest, because of the unfinished condition of the edges; but the fronts will neither gape wide open at the bottom nor criss-cross there. If they show a tendency to do either, the balance of the garment is faulty.

Fig. 36. The extent of the defect determined by pinning out a fold across the front shoulder. This lifts up the fronts to their normal position by shortening them from the top.
Fig. 37. One method of altering for the defect. Lower the shoulder seam from A-B to C-D, removing the shaded portion. To the same extent lower the top of the revers, as from E-F to G-H; and deepen the armhole from I-J.

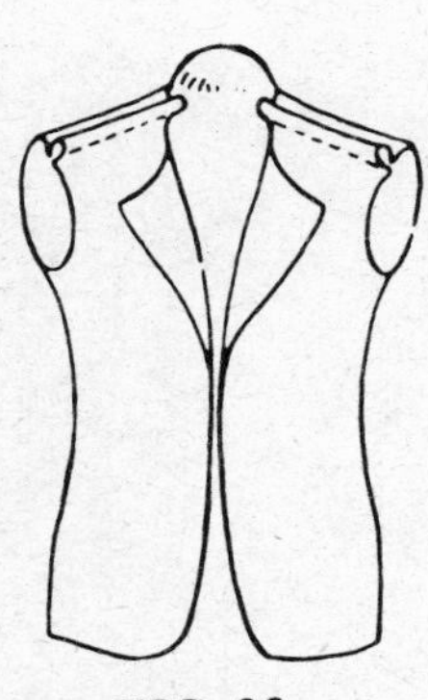

FIG. 36.

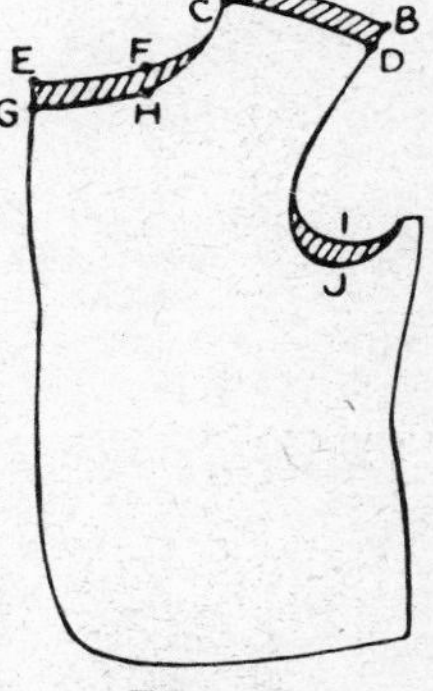

FIG. 37.

Costume Patterns and Designs

Scanning **Vogue** *for sewing ideas can be demoralizing. But I've heard that famous designers rely on this book for inspiration. Essentially no text; several hundred color plates of traditional garments from all over the world, drawn so that their construction can be understood.*

To translate the ideas into clothes, a basic ability in pattern drafting is needed. Then get a bunch of muslin or old sheets; open the book and consider your experiments an education in design. —Rosemary Menninger

I'm no clothes-horse, but this book makes me gasp and covet. —SB

Costume Patterns and Designs
Max Tilke
1956, 1974; 158 pp.

OUT OF PRINT
Hastings House
Get this book back in print!

•

In examining a garment one should first note those seams which are in any way emphasized or stressed by ornamental decoration, disregarding those which have arisen accidentally or through lack of material. Then the shape of the sleeves should be observed, the kind of neck opening, the fastenings, trimmings and colour. The garments of the earliest epochs are the most simply cut and show the fewest seams. Complicated garments may be reduced to a characteristic core which remains when all decoration, indicated by seams, is removed.

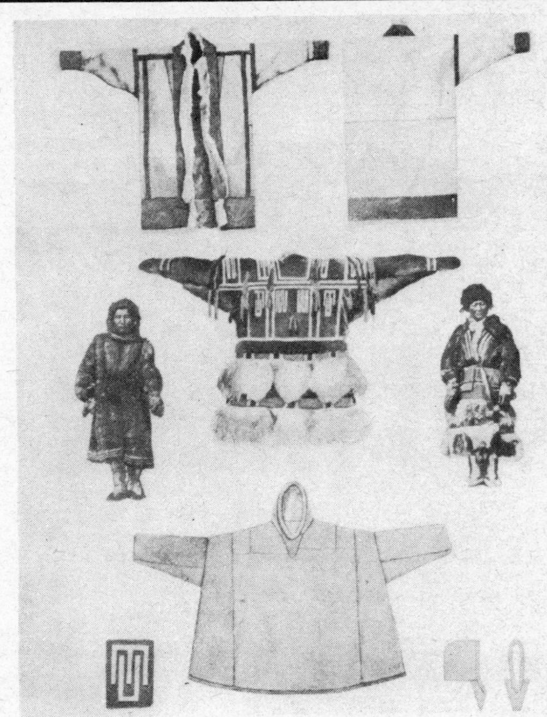

Western Siberia: Ostyaks and Samoyedes

Tibet

Rumanian influence on South-Slavonic costume

THE RISING SUN
NEIGHBORHOOD NEWSLETTER

As a mother and daughter walked into the gas chamber, the child was heard to say, "It's dark, Mother, it's so dark and I've been so good."

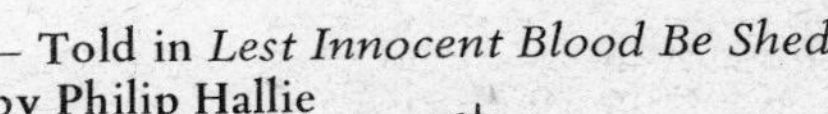

— Told in *Lest Innocent Blood Be Shed* by Philip Hallie

Mexican Indian Costumes

FRONT a

FRONT b(1)
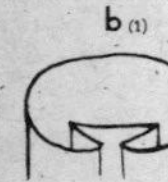
FRONT b(2)
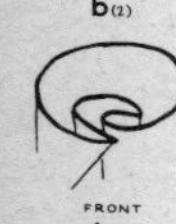
FRONT b(3)
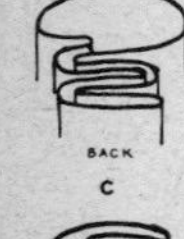
BACK c

FRONT d(1)

FRONT d(2)

FRONT d(3)

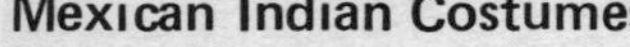
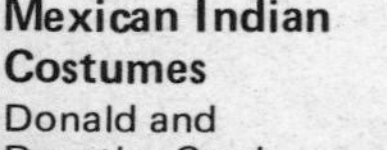

← Various methods of assembling wrap-around skirts.

A powerful and compelling book. The photographs capture the beauty of the textiles and the dignity of the people who make and wear them. The text provides a loving and careful treatment of the textile arts and their place in the lives of 24 separate Indian cultures, some already vanished and others fast dying. Interlaced with mythology and history it encompasses tools and their use, materials and how they are gathered, and the infinite variations in design and function of the finished pieces across all of the cultures.

A book I go back to for peace of soul, for design inspiration, for technical information, and to experience kinship with those for whom weaving is viewed not as technique but quite literally as part of the fabric of life.

—Diana Sloat

Mexican Indian Costumes
Donald and Dorothy Cordry
1968; 373 pp.

$35 postpaid from:
University of Texas Press
P.O. Box 7819
U.T. Station
Austin, TX 78712
or Whole Earth Household Store

A girl of Xochistlahuaca, Guerrero, showing the old manner of wearing the skirt in this village. (Amusgo). 1965.

This excellently woven red and white Mixe huipil from San Juan Mazatlān, Oaxaca, is similar to those woven and worn in San Pedro Acatlān. →

Celtic Art

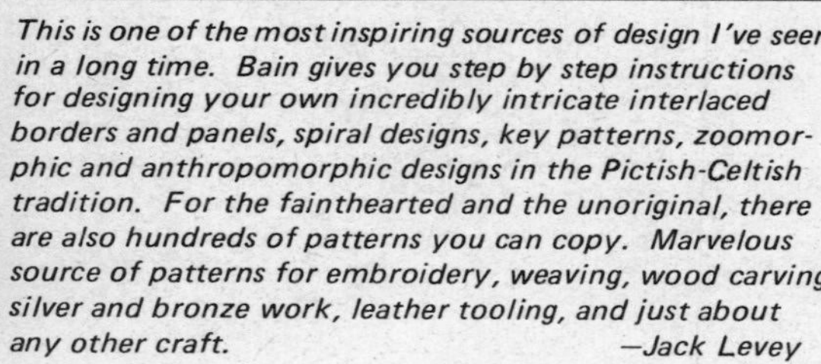

A, Book of Kells.

This is one of the most inspiring sources of design I've seen in a long time. Bain gives you step by step instructions for designing your own incredibly intricate interlaced borders and panels, spiral designs, key patterns, zoomorphic and anthropomorphic designs in the Pictish-Celtish tradition. For the fainthearted and the unoriginal, there are also hundreds of patterns you can copy. Marvelous source of patterns for embroidery, weaving, wood carving, silver and bronze work, leather tooling, and just about any other craft.

—Jack Levey

Celtic Art
(The Methods of Construction)
George Bain
1973; 159 pp.

$5 postpaid from:
Dover Publications
180 Varick Street
New York, NY 10014
or Whole Earth Household Store

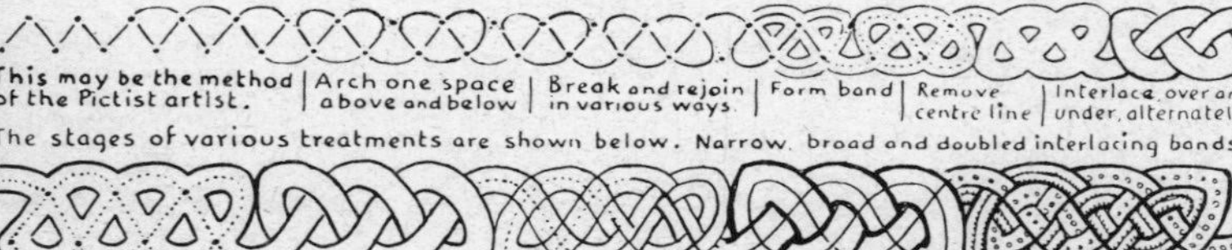

Folkwear Patterns

Evolution of man-made design, as in nature, seeks elegant and effective solutions. Ethnic clothing with its strict parameters of comfort and economy gives us samples of simple elegant beauty. Folkwear, Inc., with a broad and exciting selection of clothing patterns based on traditional folk garments, provides the home sewer an opportunity to create beautiful, comfortable, individual, and long lasting garments. Over thirty patterns are currently available — from Afghani Nomad Dresses to Japanese Field Garments to Victorian shirts and Edwardian under things. Two new patterns are introduced every year. The patterns, carefully derived from folk garments, are simple and easily made, with clear instructions, and where appropriate, detailed descriptions of finishing touches such as traditional embroidery designs.

—Rafael Diaz Guerrero

FRENCH CHEESEMAKER'S SMOCK: A traditional men's smock — now styled by Folkwear for women too.

ROUMANIAN BLOUSE: A very simple drawstring blouse, with optional smocking, embroidery and crochet techniques.

Folkwear Patterns
$3.50 - $5.50
(approx.)
Brochure and price list
free from:
Folkwear, Inc.
Box 3798
San Rafael, CA 94902

Cut My Cote

Small beautiful pamphlet on the development of sewn garments, Europe thru the Far East, both history and how to make them.

—Diana Sloat

Cut My Cote
Dorothy K. Burnham
1973; 36 pp.

$2.50 postpaid from:
Royal Ontario Museum
Information Services
100 Queens Park
Toronto, Ontario
Canada M5S 2C6

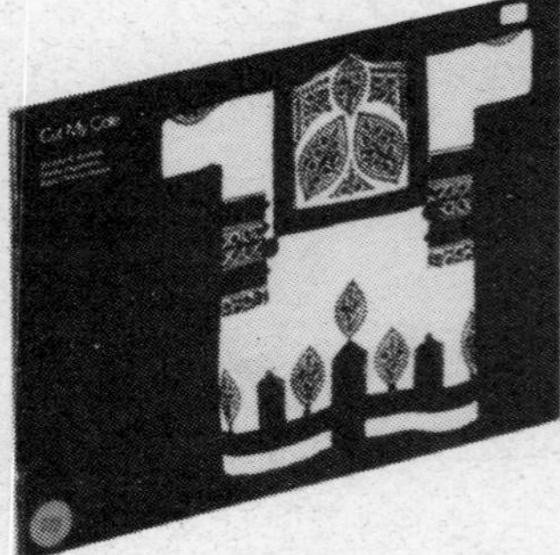

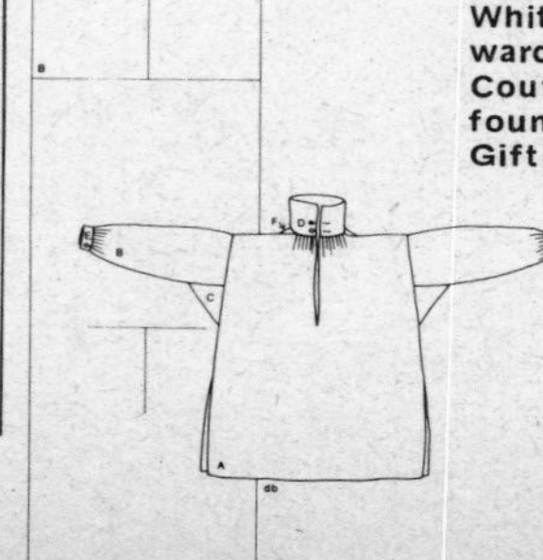

Man's shirt. English. Early 19th century. White cotton. Part of the wardrobe of Thomas Coutts (died 1822), founder of Coutts Bank. Gift of Mr. Francis Coutts.

QUILTING AND PATCHWORK

by Marilyn Green

PATCHWORK AND QUILTING ARE TWO different things. Patchwork is the process of sewing several pieces of fabric together in a pleasing pattern and quilting is the stitching (also often done in a pattern) that holds together the sandwich made of the sewn together pieces of fabric, a quilt batt and a piece of backing fabric.

You can make a quilt using these two processes. A quilt can be made from scraps of fabric you have lying around the house or from a selection of fabrics bought specifically for the quilt. It's a good idea to use fabrics of the same ilk together in a quilt rather than mixing cottons, wools, polyesters, etc. together. This way your quilt will be easier to clean and care for. I'd recommend starting with a simple pattern that looks like one you can master easily. A first success will insure that you'll want to go on to bigger and more beautiful things — and you won't end up with a mass of partially patchworked fabric in the corner of your closet rather than on the bed or wall to enjoy.

There are relatively few supplies you'll need for quilting. You probably already have some of them in your sewing kit. Basically, all you need are scraps of fabric, thread, scissors, needles, thimble, and a quilt batt.

NEEDLES

The quilters I talked to all agree that needles are pretty much the same. The best size for quilting are No. 8 or No. 9 betweens. These are short, sharp needles which are easy to handle when making short quilting stitches. Longer needles are harder for beginners to handle and often bend (something you may or may not mind). An accomplished English quilter friend swears by the needles manufactured by the Boye Needle Company in England. They are available in some American stores. Boye needles stay sharper longer and seem to have stronger eyes than other needles.

THREAD

Good strong quilting thread is manufactured by the J. and P. Coats Company and it's being sold in many fabric stores these days. This thread is a bit heavier than regular sewing thread; it doesn't knot up and doesn't have to be waxed before quilting. At this time, it's only available in fourteen colors. If the color you need isn't among them, you can quilt with regular sewing thread if you wax it first (except if you're quilting by machine). Waxing the thread before quilting helps it pull through the quilt more easily plus the wax adds strength to the thread. Wax the thread with paraffin, wax from a white candle or with the special beeswax that's sold in fabric stores.

J. and P. Coats Dual Duty Plus Extra Strong Hand Quilting Cotton-covered Polyester Thread

$1 /spool (250 yards)
Manufactured by Coats and Clark. Check your local sewing shop or variety store.

THIMBLE

A thimble is a must for quilting; it will keep your fingers from getting pricked by the needle and the hard surface is handy to help push the needle through the layers of fabric. Many quilters wear two thimbles (one on the index finger of the left hand and the other on the middle finger of the right hand — and just the opposite if you're left-handed). I had a hard time getting used to a thimble as I like to be able to feel what I'm doing. I use a soft leather thimble, like the Finger Guard.

The Finger Guard is made of soft leather which conforms to the size of your finger. It lets you feel what you're doing and even has a slit in the top so your fingernail can stick out.

Leather Finger Guard
$1.25 postpaid from:
Needleart Guild
2729 Oakwood, NE
Grand Rapids, MI 49505

QUILT BATTING

The quilt batt is what goes between the quilt top and backing; it adds warmth and body to your quilt. An old woolen blanket is a great quilt batt. You can also buy commercial batts in fabric stores or through the mail.

Cotton batts are usually not recommended as they tend to shift and bunch over time. The best commercial batts are dacron/polyester. They launder well, don't tend to bunch up and are light weight while adding warmth to the quilt. Dacron/polyester batts vary in quality from brand to brand. "Yours Truly" brand and "Poly-Fil" are two good ones. The main thing to remember is to get a batt that is bonded — treated to make the surface of the batt slightly stiff to the touch and to prevent the dacron/polyester fibers from penetrating the surface of your quilt top. Non-bonded batts can poke through the quilt top making it look (as one friend puts it) "like it needs a shave." I've heard some bad reports about "Mountain Mist" brand quilt batts lately. Friends have said that even the "Mountain Mist" bonded batts have poked through their quilt tops.

Polyfil Quilt and Comforter Battings
$3 and up (approx.)
Information
free from:
Fairfield Processing Corporation
88 Rose Hill Avenue
P.O. Drawer 1157
Danbury, CT 06810

Yours Truly Quilt Battings
$3 and up (approx.)
Catalog
free from:
Yours Truly, Inc.
Atlanta, GA 30366

QUILTING FRAME

A quilting frame is great to have for quilting larger quilts. The frame holds the quilt taut and makes it much easier to handle the massive amount of fabric. A great quilting frame is available from the Sears Roebuck & Co. catalog. It comes unassembled (even a child can put it together) with a metal braced stand. Once assembled, it will adjust to any angle and fabric thickness; the hoop part is removable for small quilting. The price is right, too — $12. Many of the quilting books have patterns and instructions for building larger more traditional "church basement" type frames. You could do this, if you prefer. I like the portability of the smaller Sears' frame.

Oval Needlework Frame
No. 24 K 4809C

$11.99 plus shipping from:
Sears Roebuck and Co.
(see our page 348)

Patchwork Patterns

Once you've gotten hooked on patchwork, you'll find Beyer's book a fascinating discovery. The appeal of the book is her innovative system for drafting geometric patchwork patterns. She uses paperfolding and makes drafting seem easy even to math klutzes like me. Her methods could be used for any craft requiring a geometric design — not just for quiltmaking. Beyer's quilts are breathtaking in their use of color and intricate technical perfection. Now you can do it, too.

x Quilt

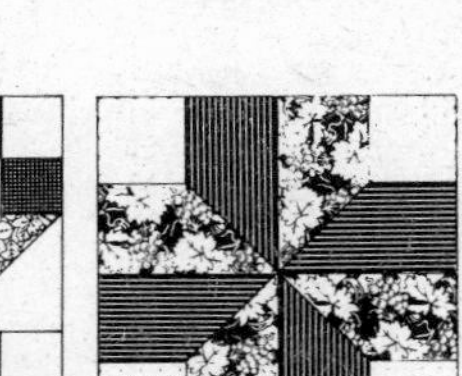

hoo-Fly

Patchwork Patterns
Jinny Beyer
1979; 200 pp.
$15.95 postpaid from:
EPM Publications
P.O. Box 490
McLean, VA 22101

Ladder Nelson's Victory

Necker's Cube Quilt. Hand-pieced, hand-quilted cotton; polyester batting, 76" x 76" (Michael James, 1977).
—The Quiltmaker's Handbook

The Quiltmaker's Handbook

A very complete, well-written instruction book for quilters. A beginner could start with this book and follow it to go on to bigger, more intricate projects. James explains things better than nearly any craft author I've come across. Appended sections on English paper patchwork (a method for achieving precision in pieced work), pressed piecing, seminole patchwork and color. If I were to buy just one book on quiltmaking, this would be it.

The Quiltmaker's Handbook
(A Guide to Design and Construction)
Michael James
1978; 143 pp.
$6.95 postpaid from:
Prentice-Hall
Box 500
Englewood Cliffs, NJ 07632

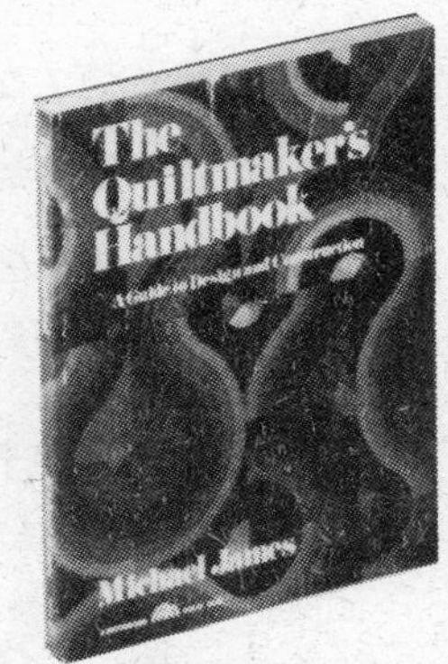

The Complete Book of Machine Quilting

Most books on quilting don't go into much (if any) detail on quilting with a sewing machine. **The Complete Book of Machine Quilting** *makes up for what the other books have skipped. This book has everything — including a very clear and complete explanation of how a sewing machine does what it does, and instructions for projects and cautions/directions for working with unusual materials on the sewing machine. The discussion of finishing the edges of a quilt is the best I have seen. In a section entitled "How NOT to Machine Quilt a Sheet," The Fannings follow someone else's instructions and the project doesn't work. They explain what's going wrong as they work on it so the same won't happen to us. The book is clever, comprehensive and useful. It's a good buy for traditional quilters as well as for the busy person who wants to make a quilt in one day.*

The Complete Book of Machine Quilting
Robbie Fanning and Tony Fanning
1980; 334 pp.

$9.95 postpaid from:
Chilton Book Company
Sales Service Department
Chilton Way
Radnor, PA 19089

If the fabric is not flat against the needle plate, the loop lifts out of reach of the bobbin and a stitch is skipped.

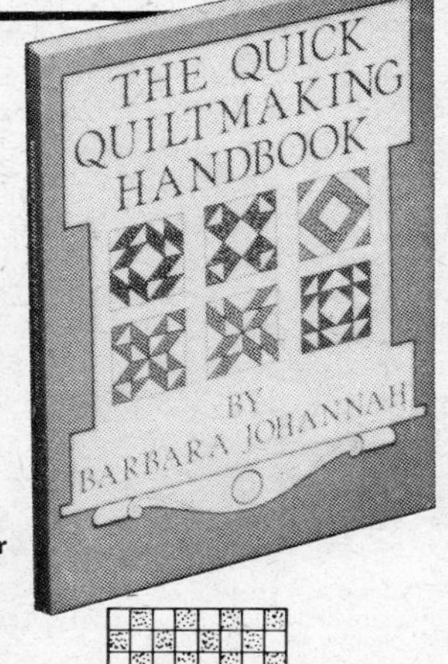

Quilter's Newsletter Magazine

Quilter's Newsletter *remains the quilting periodical. They do a good job providing information on current news, shows, materials, books, etc. The classified ads offer various quilting supplies and aids as well as folks who will quilt your quilt for a fee. The format is getting a bit more contemporary — less dowdy. Each issue includes several patterns and you can send for other patterns and quilting aids available from the publisher.*

•

Lancaster, Ohio . . . All the world loves brides, but nowhere are they more smiled upon than at Betty Bishop's "A Stitch in Time Quilt Shop" at 221 E. Sixth Avenue, Lancaster, Ohio. Betty and her staff of 25 feel that "Brides are beautiful, so let's make the weddings as beautiful as possible, too." And that they do — with quilted finery and fabulous bridal quilts. Each June the shop presents a wedding party, complete with an original bridal gown and other quilted and patchwork accessories for members of the wedding.

Quilter's Newsletter Magazine
Bonnie Leman, Editor
$8 year (10 issues) from:
Leman Publications
Box 394
Wheatridge, CO 80033

—Quilter's Newsletter Magazine

Quilting

Minimal text but pages and pages of design inspiration for quilts and quilting. This book would also be handy to have for identifying an old quilt pattern. Diagrams and instructions for building your own quilting frame and a section on color.

Quilting
Averil Colby
1971; 212 pp.

$8.95 postpaid from:
Charles Scribner's Sons
Vreeland Avenue
Totowa, NY 07512

Man's cord-quilted linen cap, lined with cotton. The crown is in four sections with an additional piece for the brim. English, early eighteenth century.

The Quick Quiltmaking Handbook

Many would-be quilters are stymied before they even get started at the prospect of cutting all those little patches and sewing thousands of tiny seams. Barbara Johannah presents a method which is so simple and logical I wondered why someone hadn't come up with it before. Using this method of marking and cutting or ripping, then assembling the pieces, you can literally start and complete a quilt top in a weekend. A liberation of a book. —Evelyn Eldridge-Diaz

The Quick Quiltmaking Handbook
Barbara Johannah
1979; 128 pp.
$9.45 postpaid from:
Pride of the Forest Press
P.O. Box 7266
Menlo Park, CA 94025

4. Put the strata on the cutting board wrong side up. Mark every 5". Cut on the lines marked.

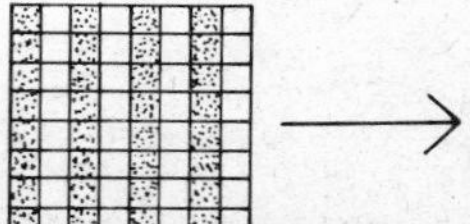

5. Alternate the rows. Sew the rows together to complete the top.

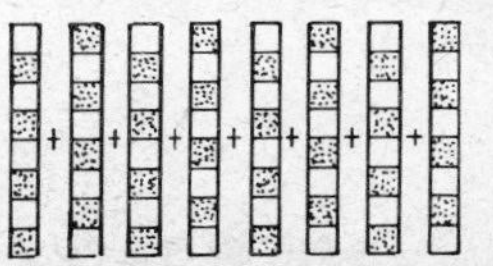

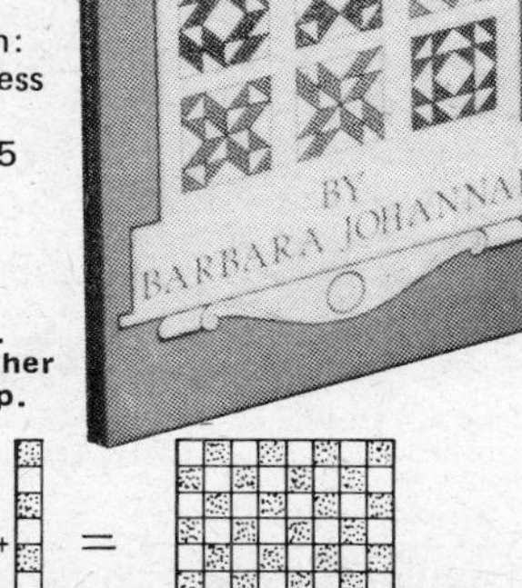

THE RISING SUN NEIGHBORHOOD NEWSLETTER

The Hasids thought that praying was a real activity, like sending in troops or building buildings, only realler, so they had a bitter debate about whether to pray for Napoleon when he was invading Russia. It was agreed that Napoleon was a horrible, godless destroyer. The question was whether one could ask, or demand, that God use him to destroy the Czar, who was even worse. After much argument, the two most important Hasidic rebs couldn't agree, so one prayed for him and one prayed against him. It is said that if they had both prayed for him he would have won.

— This is the subject of a whole book by Martin Buber, called *For the Sake of Heaven.*

The Reader's Digest Complete Guide to Needlework

The title of this book should be changed to the **Reader's Digest GOOD Guide to Needlework.** *Though it is not complete, the skills are covered with an excellence I've come to expect from Reader's Digest how-to books. Tools, basic techniques, and materials are covered thoroughly, with sample projects suggested at the end of each section. All illustrations and instructions are exceptionally clear and easy to follow. A good companion to the* **Complete Encyclopedia of Needlework** *(below) and recommended jumping-off point for a beginning needle worker.* —Evelyn Eldridge-Diaz

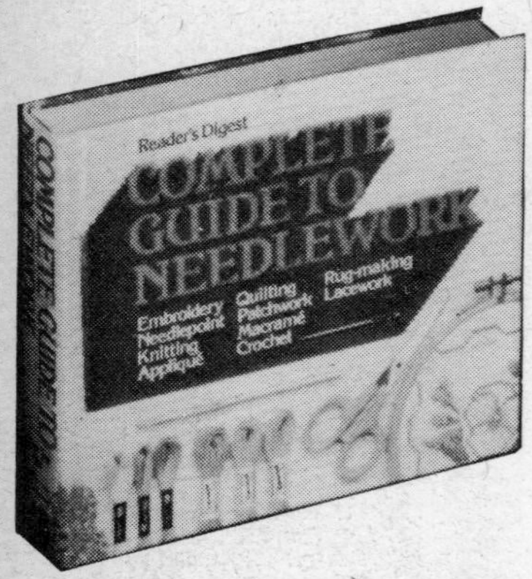

Reader's Digest Complete Guide to Needlework
Virginia Colton, Editor
1979; 504 pp.
$18.95 postpaid from:
W.W. Norton & Company
500 Fifth Avenue
New York, NY 10036
or Whole Earth Household Store

↑ **Sampler can serve as a "dictionary" of stitches.**

Fern stitches: Start at upper left and work all rows down the canvas.

If left-handed, turn canvas, start in lower right corner and work all rows up the canvas.

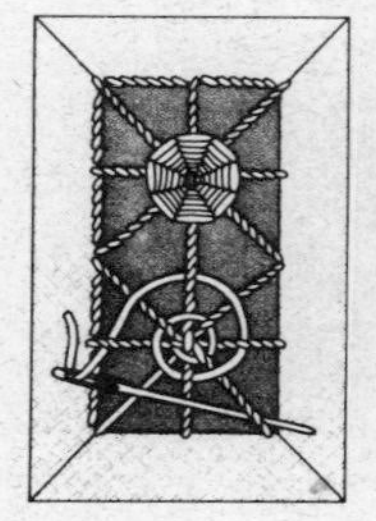

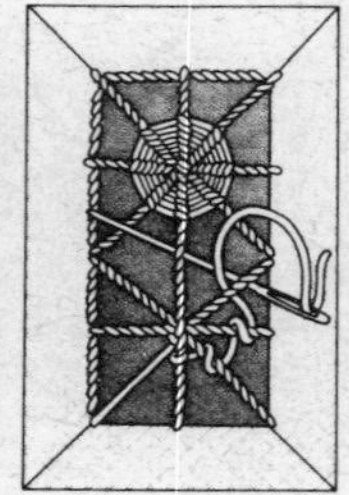

Spider webs (#28A, #28B): This stitch is good for filling small spaces. First make 4 twisted bars, 2 across the center in both directions, and 2 diagonally between corners. Twist the fourth bar only to the center, work spider web, then complete the bar.
Woven web (#28A): Working from the center out, weave a wheel, skipping 1 bar at the end of each round so threads will alternate on each row.
Ridged web (#28B): Starting at the center, take thread under 2 bars, then weave in a circle, going back over 1 bar, forward under 2 bars.

Braid is shown at left being made with braiding cones that automatically fold the fabric strips; one cone has a reel attachment to prevent the strip from tangling. A clothespin holds the end of the braid. A blunt-edged lacer and heavy thread are used to lace the braids together.

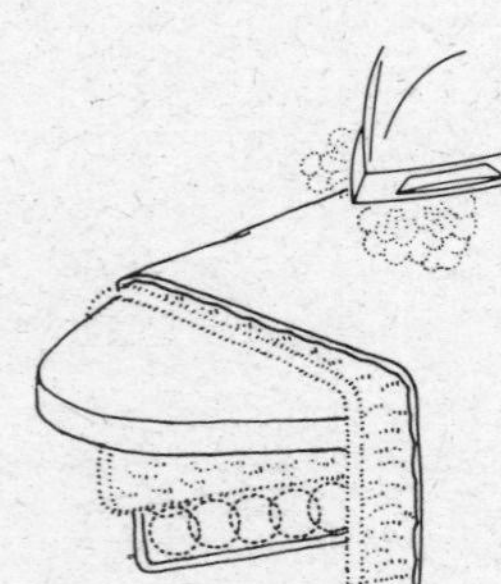

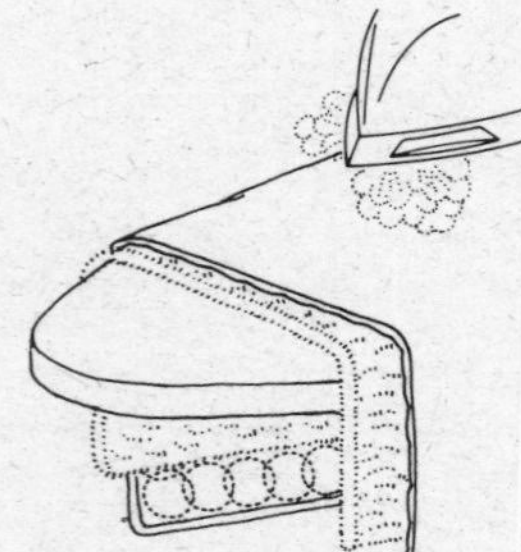

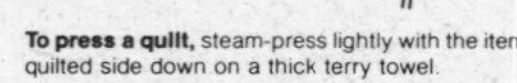

To press a quilt, steam-press lightly with the item quilted side down on a thick terry towel.

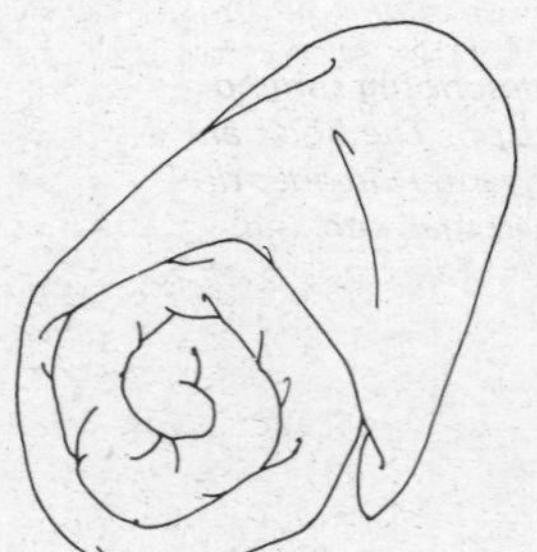

Store a quilt by rolling it up in a clean sheet. Do not use plastic; it does not breathe.

A Tatted Doily or Centerpiece of Unusual and Lovely Design

Designs and Patterns ↑

Many authentic, old-time patterns for dolls, quilts, tatting, crochet and the like are available for $ .50 per booklet from Original Tower Press, Seabrook, New Hampshire. Each booklet, printed on newsprint, contains from 20 - 50 patterns. While the booklets won't hold up for years, for the price and quality of design, they are a real deal. It's well worth sending for a list of their available booklets. —Marilyn Green

Designs and Patterns
List of booklets
$ .50 postpaid from:
The Original Tower Press, Inc.
P.O. Box 428
Seabrook, NY 03874

The Complete Encyclopedia of Needlework

France's needlework "bible." Believe the title; it has it all, *carefully written, with clear precise diagramming and instructions even to needle size, thread weight, and how to modify designs. It's old-fashioned and pretty and it* works. —Diana Sloat

The Complete Encyclopedia of Needlework
Th. de Dillmont
1972, 1978; 700 pp.
$8.70 postpaid from:
The Running Press
38 South 19th Street
Philadelphia, PA 19103
or Whole Earth Household Store

← **Pompon with crochet sheath**

Square in Teneriffe lace. How to work the embroidered embroidered motifs.

Section of Braid Trimming for Cloth Coat

• **Stroking the gathers.** When the gathering thread has been run in, draw up the gather almost tight and twist the thread round a pin put upright at the end. Holding the work between the thumb and forefinger of the left hand, take a strong needle and stroke it down vertically between the gathers so as to fix them evenly side by side. In doing this, push each gather under the left thumb to keep it in place, while the other fingers support the stuff at the back. ↓

Macrame braid with corner ↓

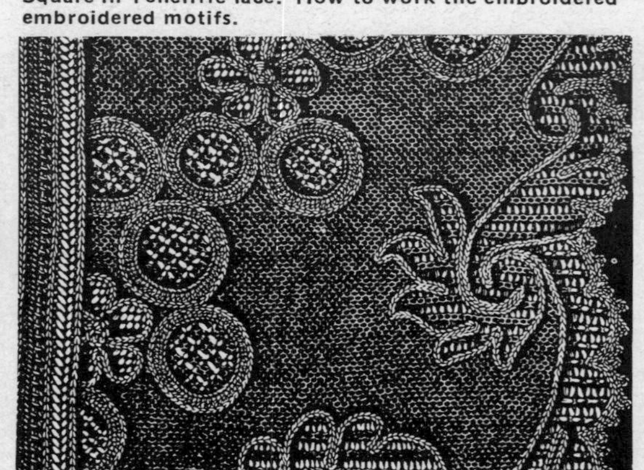

Wide lace embroidered on net with various filling stitches and outlines in crochet braid. Second part.

Pillowlace, 17th century Flemish style ↓

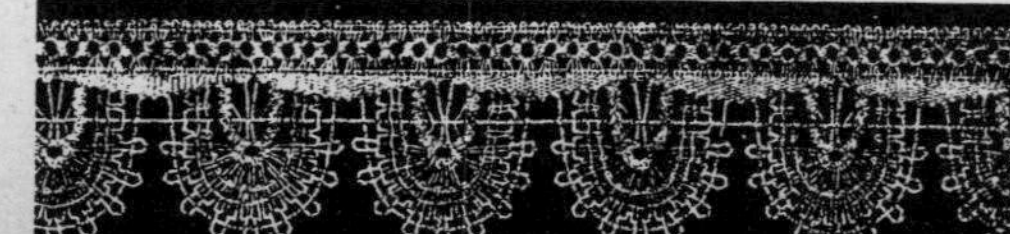

One Hundred Embroidery Stitches

For those of you who want to learn how to do embroidery rather than gaze upon lovely and expensive color photographs of how someone else did it this is the best and only necessary booklet. It contains schematic diagrams of the most popular and useful stitches with short suggestions for their application to various embroidery situations. We've "taught" several people embroidery and our first lesson is "buy this book." With the lowest price-per-stitch rate of any text on the subject it is invaluable. —Peter and Catherin Yronwode

One Hundred Embroidery Stitches
(Coats & Clark's Book No. 150-B)
1964; 34 pp.
$ .60 postpaid from:
Coats & Clark's Sales Corporation
75 Rockefeller Plaza
New York, NY 10019

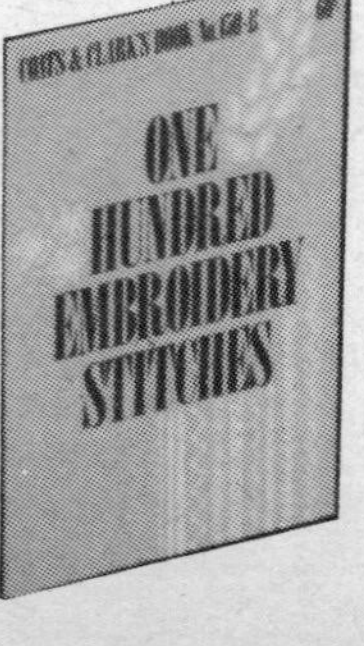

Faggoting

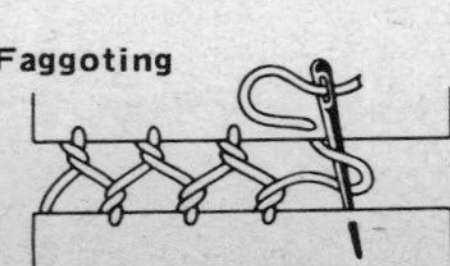

The Complete Book of Knitting

A great source of help and information. Guides the beginner in the selection of equipment and the right yarn to go along with it. The instructions and sketches carefully cover everything from casting on, several ways to increase, decrease, to the common problems beginning knitters face. The advanced knitter will enjoy the many varied methods discussed, the interpretations of foreign language patterns and the fine notes on how to measure and tailor-finish your articles. To put all you will learn to good use the author adds a great number of unusual pattern stitches with instructions.
—Barbara Erfani

The Complete Book of Knitting
Barbara Abbey
1971; 239 pp.
$12.95 postpaid from:
The Viking Press,
625 Madison Avenue
New York, NY 10022
or Whole Earth
Household Store

•

For working out the *shape* of a large article, graph paper is almost indispensible. Each square on the paper represents one single stitch or row, and the outline of the work can be drawn on the paper, square by square. The knitter will then be able to see at a glance the form the piece of knitting under consideration will take. Colored pencils can be used to plot multicolor designs. Each stitch will stand out clearly and the graph will be easy to follow.

Patterns for Guernseys, Jerseys & Arans

An obscure book on knitting I use often, and which seems to be borrowed from me frequently. These sweaters take a long time to make, but one should be sufficient for most of a lifetime. Owning one gives you an incredible sense of security.
—Gail Temple

Full knitting instructions are given for some of the sweaters but only for the pattern blocks for some of the more complex types, such as the arans.
—Diana Sloat

Patterns for Guernseys, Jerseys & Arans
Gladys Thompson
1971; 162 pp.
$3.50 postpaid from:
Dover Publications,
180 Varick Street
New York, NY 10014

A fisherman's guernsey in cable and cross-over patterns

Harry Freeman, only survivor of Whitby lifeboat disaster 1881

•

One day I found myself in Queen Street in the old town, and I called at a whitewashed stone cottage with walls at least a foot thick. An old lady opened the door, and when she heard I wanted guernsey patterns she asked me into the kitchen. A tortoiseshell cat sat by the fire, and an old man lay asleep on his side on a horsehair sofa. She asked me to sit down and went to fetch some guernseys from up the yard. She showed me one or two, and then pointing to the sofa said, 'Tak a Leeak at yon gansey he's wearing; yer can tun him over and see t'pattern!"

A Treasury of Knitting Patterns

Page after page of exquisite, unusual patterns. The patterns are grouped into several categories and are preceded by a general description of the patterns and how to knit them. Instructions deal with the usual knitting terms and abbreviations, and include a short paragraph describing some of the pattern's possible uses. The book also contains a short chapter on adapting the patterns to circular knitting. To fully enjoy and use this book basic knitting skills are definitely needed.
—Barbara Erfani

A Treasury of Knitting Patterns
Barbara G. Walker
1968; 301 pp.
$10 postpaid from:
Charles Scribner's & Sons
Vreeland Avenue
Totowa, NJ 07512

Lattice Cable

The Last Word on North American Magazines of Interest to Thread Benders

by Robbie Fanning

Small press publishing flourishes in the craft field, especially in needlework (including knit and crochet). This list focuses on small press, a qualification difficult to define. It has more to do with the vision and bankroll of the originator(s) than with circulation size. **Needlecraft for Today**, *then, with 500,000 subscribers is in because of the close involvement of the editor and publishers, while* **Quilt!** *is out because it is backed by a large disinterested corporation.* ♦*means I have not examined a copy.*

STITCHERY

Embroiderers' Association of Canada Magazine. Helen Russell, Editor, 441 Avalon Road, Winnipeg, MN, Canada, R2M 2L4, $10/year (includes membership), quarterly. *Just coming into its own as a full-fledged magazine, reporting the doings of the Canadian Embroiderers' Association.*

Embroidery. Embroiderers' Guild of London, Nora Jones, Lynette de Denne, Editors, c/o de Denne Ltd., Kenton, Harrow, Middlesex HA 3 OEU, England, $14 /year, quarterly. *In England, embroidery is a four-year art school discipline and the high quality work is regularly featured in this inspiring magazine — highly recommended.*

The Flying Needle. National Standards Council of American Embroiderers (NSC), Mary Ann Butterfield, Editor, 6290 E. Pinchot, Scottsdale, AZ 85251, $15 /year (includes membership), quarterly. *Reports on groups, correspondence school, conventions; features more contemporary work than* **NeedleArts**. *Both NSC and EGA suffer the highs and lows in quality common to all-volunteer publications.*

Hands On! Box 198 Osgood Road, Milford, NH 03055, $50/year, monthly. *A monthly packet of unusual fabric and thread, with instructions for a small learning project. They also publish* **The World In Stitches**, *the best mail order embroidery catalog in the U.S., for $1.*

♦ **International Old Lacers Newsletter.** Mrs. Caroline E. Pierce, Editor, 5206 Olley Lane, Burke, VA 22015, $6 /year.

Needle Arts. Embroiderers' Guild of America (EGA), Judith Leibman, Editor, 6 E. 45th Street, Room 1501, New York, NY 10017, $17 /year (includes membership), quarterly. *Reports on regional activities, conventions, Master Craftsman and correspondence courses. About four times bigger than NSC. Reflects the more traditional approach to needlework, with heavy emphasis on technique and less on experimentation and original design.*

Treadleart. Janet Stocker, Editor/publisher, 2458 W. Lomita Blvd., Lomita, CA 90717, $6/year, $1 single, bimonthly. *Subtitled "For sewing machine art enthusiasts," the approach is folksy, with patterns for machine embroidery, recipes for the microwave (to save time for more sewing), news on classes. Improving with each issue.*

QUILTING

Canada Quilts. Mary Conroy, Editor/publisher, 360 Stewart Drive, Sudbury, Ontario, Canada P3E 2R8, $6 /5 times a year ($6.50 in U.S.A.). *A friendly and ambitious one-woman attempt to be the* **Quilters' Newsletter Magazine** *for Canada — includes patterns, games, guild news, how-to's, book reviews.*

♦ **Clearinghouse Newsletter.** North American Quilt Guild, P.O. Box 1195, Shepherdstown, WV 25443, $15/year (includes membership), quarterly.

♦ **The Patchword.** Hearthside Crafts Quilter's Club, P.O. Box 305, Westview Station, Binghamton, NY 13905, $8 /year (includes membership).

Patchwork Patter. National Quilting Association, P.O. Box 62, Greenbelt, MD 20770, $5 /year (includes membership), quarterly. *Down-home news of quilters with pictures of their quilts.*

Quilters' Journal. Joyce Gross, Editor/publisher, P.O. Box 270, Mill Valley, CA 94941, $7.50 /year, quarterly. *Scholarly studies of historic quilts and quilters.*

Quilting and Related Needle Arts. Ruth Briggs, Editor/publisher, P.O. Box 403, Rancho Santa Fe, CA 92067, $5/year, quarterly. *Patterns for traditional quilting, applique, and piecing; first issue (Feb '79) reprinted 1934* **Sears Quilt Book.**

♦ **Tumbling Alley.** Evelyn Brown, Editor/publisher, 425 NE 6th Street, Gainesville, FL 32601.

COUNTED THREAD (needlepoint, cross stitch, etc.)

Counted Thread. Counted Thread Society of America, Elizabeth Stears, Editor/publisher, 3305 S. Newport Street, Denver, CO 80224, $5/year, quarterly. *A sensible and interesting publication delving into the international history and techniques of counted thread (cross stitch, darning, Hardanger, canvas work, etc.).*

National Needlepoint News. Sherry Baker, Editor/publisher, 171 Guadalupe Drive, Sonoma, CA 95476, $4.50/year, three times a year. *A trade newspaper for small yarn shop owners; reports on kit companies, business trends, convention news.*

Needlepoint Bulletin. Sharlene Weldon Krenkel, Editor/publisher, 50 South U.S. 1, Suite 200, Jupiter, FL 33458, $12 /year, bimonthly. *Patterns, designs, and news for needlepointers — almost all material generated by editor/publisher, who oddly remains invisible, not even putting her name on masthead.*

Needlepoint News. Carol LaBranche, Editor/publisher, Box 668, Evanston, IL 60204, $9 /year, bimonthly. *The editor's highly personal writing style with strong opinions on everything makes this how-to a favorite of needlepointers — patterns, techniques, book reviews, show coverage.*

♦ **Smocking Arts Guild Newsletter.** Vicky Alexander, Editor, 824 Eden Court, Alexandria, VA 22308.

Stitches Count. Suzanne Weyer, Editor/publisher, 8991 Jane Road North, Lake Elmo, MN 55042, $3 /year, quarterly. *Many patterns for small cross stitch and other counted thread projects.*

CROSS-FIELD

Center for the History of American Needlework Newsletter (CHAN). Rachel Maines, Editor, Old Economy Village, 14th and Church Street, Ambridge, Pa 15003, $10/year (includes membership). *Feminist historian Maines has kept* **CHAN** *in touch with all levels of needlework — from factory workers through doily makers to the fine artists — an organization worth supporting.*

Craftsman and Craft News. Elizabeth Dingman, Editor, Ontario Crafts Council, 346 Dundas Street West, Toronto, Ontario, Canada M5T 1G5, $15/year (includes membership). *Well-written features on Ontario craftspeople, from an area of outstanding international talent.*

Interweave. Linda Ligon, Editor/publisher, 306 N. Washington, Loveland, CO 80537, $10 /year, quarterly. *Originally published to cover weaving and fiber arts in the Rocky Mountain states but expanded to national in response to enthusiastic readers. Bears the stamp of honesty, integrity, and sound journalistic background of editor/publisher.* *(See p. 273.)*

Needlecraft for Today. Fredrica Daugherty, Editor, P.O. Box 10142, Des Moines, IA 50340, $7.95 /year, bimonthly. *Instructions for quilted, stitched, knitted, and crocheted items for the home — what distinguishes this from the usual ladies' magazines is no ads and the sincerity of the editorial staff, which leads to sharing information freely with a loyal readership of over 500,000.*

The Needlework Times. Elaine Coorens and T. Devon Wray, Editors/publishers, P.O. Box 87263, Chicago, IL 60680, $9 /year, bimonthly. *News on products and stitchers with a new Home Study Course feature.*

Silhouette. Valentine Museum, 1015 E. Clay Street, Richmond, VA 23219. *Interesting historical articles on American techniques and on museum pieces.*

Textile Museum Newsletter. 2320 S St., NW, Washington, D.C. 20008, quarterly. *Reports on conferences, classes, shows, and academic conferences at the museum.*

♦ **Weaving and Fiber News.** P.O. Box 259, Homer, NY 13077.

♦ **Interloop, the Knitters' and Crocheters' Art.** 1636 N. Twin Oaks Road, San Marcos, CA 92069, $12/year, quarterly.

♦ **The Needle's Eye.** 1801 Whitney, Idaho Falls, ID 83401.

The Platypus Newsletter. Colette Wolff, Editor/publisher, Box 396, Planetarium Station, New York, NY 10024. *Not available by subscription but free with orders and well worth buying one pattern merely to receive the newsletter — well-written comments on stuffing toys, the right and wrong way of embroidering features, teaching, etc.*

Textile Artists' Newsletter. Susan C. Druding, Editor/publisher, 5533 College Avenue, Oakland, CA 94618, $6 /year, quarterly. *Druding, owner of Straw Into Gold, a mail order fiber and dye supply store, publishes valuable technical articles on yarn and dyeing.*

Wool Gathering. Elizabeth Zimmerman, Editor/publisher, Box 57, Babcock, WI 54413, $5 /3 years or free with $10 purchase. *The piquant wit of the editor comes through on every page, even in the directions for knit sweaters, vests, hats, and socks, which are often designed for circular needles — a must-read.* ■

Thunderbird. Twelve full size quilt patterns of authentic American Indian designs by sandpainter David Villasenor. $3 plus $1 handling.
—Quilting and Related Needlecraft

THE RISING SUN
NEIGHBORHOOD NEWSLETTER

Isn't it funny that not only marching band members but also creative types such as ballerinas and first violins and piano virtuosos spend every minute of their creative life counting. You listen or look at soaring and they're both soaring and "1, 2, 3, 4 . . ."

TEXTILE QUARTERLIES

THE QUARTERLIES ARE WHERE TO find what's new, who's doing it, and what they think about it. Information's a year or so ahead of the books. More varied and cheaper, too.

Shuttle, Spindle & Dyepot *("S.S.&D.") is the old, solid standby, guild-based with articles for weavers, spinners, and dyers.* **Interweave**, *with* **Handwoven** *(its offshoot for starting weavers, as its title implies), is a weaving journal with specific focus in each issue on a particular area of weaving — e.g., Early American, tapestry, etc. (***Spinoff** *is their annual for spinners.)* **Fiberarts** *concentrates on the art-aspect of the field, with coverage of major shows and articles on particular artists and their work. Then there's the youngest, the* **Textile Artists' Newsletter** *(T.A.N.), which is quite technical with emphasis on fibers and dyes (structure and chemistry), textile tools, books, and little known areas of weaving, all in newsprint. Lively fantasy-tickling or technical stuff for anyone with a weaving, spinning, dyeing or soft-sculpting bent.*

—Diana Sloat

•

"Now this is how it works," she said. She wiggled her legs through the hole in the box, her toes extending out the other end. The weight of her body rested on the extending board. Placing some wool on the carding cloth, she took the small board and with the cards face to face, began pulling the board toward her. At the end of the stroke she lifted it and repeated the process until the wool was satisfactorily carded. To return the wool to the bottom card she reversed her stroke.

I was amazed. This simple wooden box allowed her to card much more and much faster than I had ever seen anyone do with hand cards. The weight of her body held the bottom card steady and allowed her to use two hands to pull the top card across it. It seemed a far more efficient way to use the human body, as any weak-wristed hand carder would appreciate.

—Shuttle Spindle & Dyepot

←

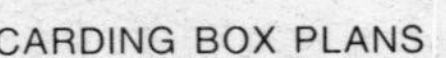

CARDING BOX PLANS

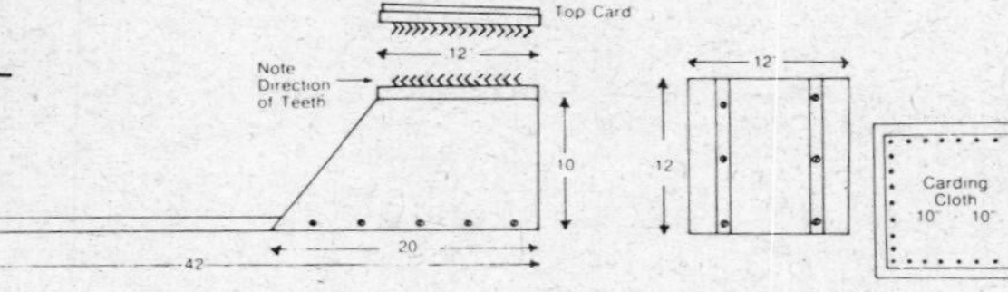

Lifting technique for rotating the strands in Kumi Himo
—Textile Artists' Newsletter

Shuttle, Spindle and Dyepot
Kevin Chase, Editor-in-Chief
$15/year (4 issues)
from:
The Handweavers Guild of America
P.O. Box 3-374
65 La Salle Road
West Hartford, CT 06107

Interweave
Linda C. Ligon, Editor
$10/year (4 issues)

Handwoven
Linda C. Ligon, Editor
$7/year (2 issues)

Spin-Off
Linda C. Ligon, Editor
$5/year (1 issue)
all from:
Interweave Press
306 North Washington Avenue
Loveland, CO 80537

Fiberarts
Jane Luddecke, Editor
$12/year (6 issues)
from:
Fiberarts Magazine
50 College Street
Asheville, NC 28801

Textile Artists' Newsletter
(A Quarterly Review of the Fiber Arts)
Susan C. Druding, Editor
$6/year (4 issues)
from:
Textile Artists' Newsletter
5533 College Avenue
Oakland, CA 94618

A miniature "Lee's Surrender" coverlet on brass bed 6½" long
—Interweave

Quilted Vest — Satin fabric, silk and metallic threads, sequins, rhinestones —Fiberarts

•

Kumi Himo, the most delicate of braiding techniques, was developed in Japan over a one thousand year period where it has gone beyond mere technique, becoming twined with the social and cultural traditions of this culture.

The traditional silk cords of *Kumi Himo* are found on armour and illuminated sutra scrolls dating back to the 8th Century. In more recent times they have served as a functional, as well as decorative, element as ties for the traditional *obie* and *kimono*. Today, these cords have adapted to the contemporary materials and less formal uses that we now seek. Contemporary textile artists are finding the *Kumi Himo* technique a wonderful tool for creative expression in jewelry, garment trim and sculptural pieces.

The basic braiding concept involves weighted cords plaited around each other in a repetitive sequence. In addition to texture, color and pattern, the plaiting sequence also determines the shape of the braid: flat, square, round and multi-sided braids all possible. The free ends of the weighted cords make it a simple matter to change braid designs and patterns within an initial set-up.

—Textile Artists' Newsletter

•

On cold days like today, when my cat curls up in a nearby armchair and sleeps peacefully despite the sputter of a woodfire, there's satisfaction in knowing that I can dress in comfortable clothes, brew a pot of tea and sit in a favorite corner to work. At such times, I sympathize with those who must brave bad weather and highway traffic to reach their jobs, who must conform to other's schedules, and priorities in order to pay their bills. On these days, when I like my home and my subject and my own company, working at home is a fundamental source of pleasure.

But not every day is like today, and when I quit a regular job to work for myself, I wasn't prepared for the many problems that I would face. I didn't realize that I would have to create a spacious yet private work area in my home, that I would struggle to find the discipline to establish goals and meet deadlines, or that family and friends would have to be persuaded to respect my work schedule and refrain from calling or visiting during the day. And I failed to foresee that I would sometimes be lonely because I no longer work with colleagues.

—Fiberarts

All undulating, slub, knopped, beaded, flake, cloud, or Scandia yarns should have a uniform base thread. The undulations or flecks can be scattered, uniformly spaced, or vary in diameter, but the base thread must be constant. This will give a uniform stitch gauge in knitting or crocheting, and an overall texture to weaving. —Spin-Off →

Slub spiral
Base Thread
Slub to slub in ply
Undulating slub thread
Taut base thread and slub
Base thread

Textile books suppliers

Buying a book you've never seen is chancy. These two annotated mail order sources will ease the strain.

The Unicorn has an excellent textile book selection. Send $2.00 for 4 editions of catalog/year, or a large stamped self-addressed envelope per specified area of interest: batik, leather, textile, etc.

K.R. Drummond has an incredible textile book selection; haven't seen the other areas. Many small publishers. Long wait for books but no duty. Send one international reply coupon per each specified area of interest, or 2 coupons for 3 areas. (5 pence = 1 coupon)

—Diana Sloat

The Unicorn
Catalog
free from:
The Unicorn
Box 645
Rockville, MD 20851

K.R. Drummond
Catalog
3 international reply coupons
($1.20 approx.)
from:
K.R. Drummond Bookseller
30 Hart Grove
Ealing Common
London WS, England

•

Animal Coat by Charlotte Attig. The author and her husband raise a large variety of animals, 10 of which are illustrated here, each with a brief description of the fiber obtained from it and an actual sample of that fiber. Included is the Angora goat from which we obtain Mohair, the Samoyed dog, the Llama, Alpaca, Angora rabbit, the Reindeer, sheep, cow, sheepdog, and finally the camel. This book would make a nice gift for a spinner.

•

Art of Taaniko Weaving by S.M. Mead. A study of the culture, technique, style and development. Taaniko is part of the traditional Maori costume. Examples of ancient and modern styles in clothing and in the patterns. Includes cloaks, piupiu, bodices, headbands, belts, table mats, and much more. Fully, beautifully illustrated, including clear diagrams of techniques and directions. The patterns can easily be adapted to other items also. The Maori are the native people of New Zealand.

—The Unicorn

The Weaving, Spinning and Dyeing Book

For a beginning weaver, this is a meaty, provocative, well-formatted, non-intimidating introduction to a variety of weaving techniques — card, inkle, backstrap, Navajo, all covered well enough to get you started and keep you inspired with endless project ideas. Its sections on buying a floor loom, beginning acid dyeing (synthetic) and extensive annotated supplier's list are superb.
—Diana Sloat

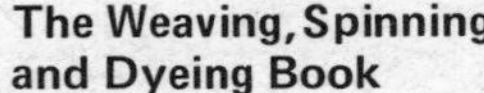

The Weaving, Spinning and Dyeing Book
Rachel Brown
1979; 366 pp.
$12.95 postpaid from:
Alfred A. Knopt
455 Hahn Road
Westminster, MD 21157
or Whole Earth
Household Store

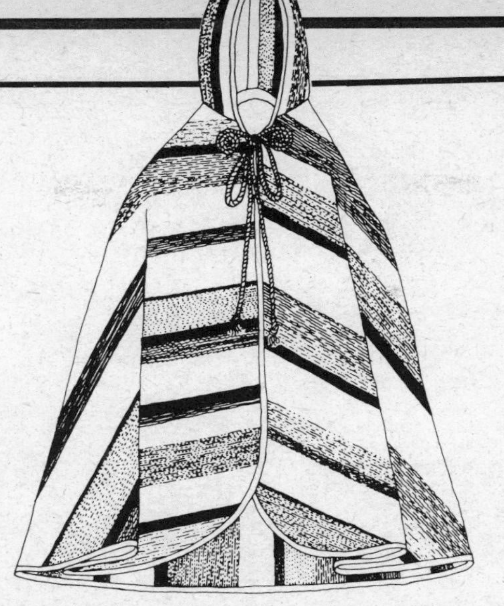

The authentic North African burnoose is a simple hooded cape, cut from a single rectangular piece of material: a very simple design and yet an extremely striking garment. Our burnoose is modeled directly on the authentic ones, woven in horizontal stripes with two different-weight yarns — one fairly heavy and textured to add interest.

Method 1

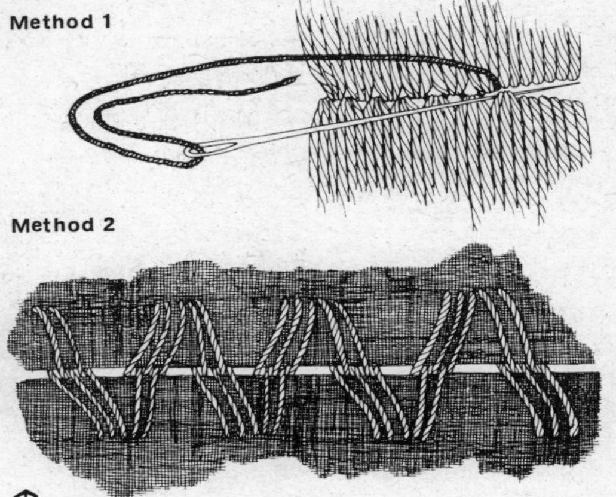

Method 2

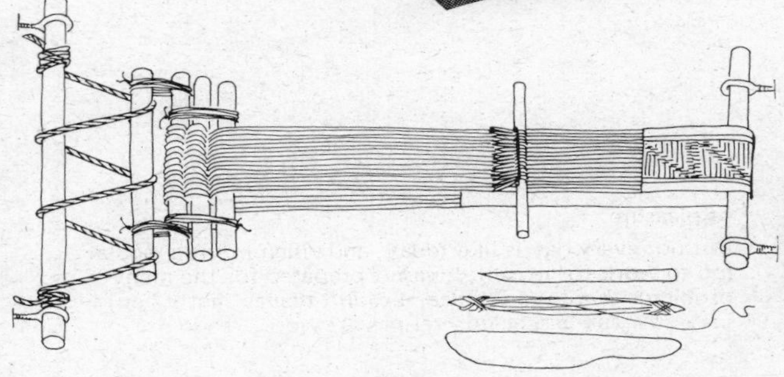

↑

The Hopi belt loom is a beautifully simple weaving device that happens to be my favorite belt loom, mainly because the warp is stretched in a vertical position (as it is on the Navajo loom) — the most convenient position, in my opinion, for weaving with primitive tools.

This is not a loom you can buy; you will simply set it up when you are ready to weave, using dowels or old broom handles.

Sometimes you can't weave a fabric as wide as you want all in one piece. For such cases here are two professional-looking ways of joining two pieces of weaving.

Method 1. The two pieces of fabric are laid side by side on a flat surface, making sure ends match (check this often as you sew, because they tend to get out of line).

↑

With a large needle and the same thread as the warp, you sew up through a few weft threads on one edge and then up through the same number on the other. This method is mainly useful for weft-face fabrics.

Method 2. Using a large needle and yarn to match the weft (or any color if you want a decorative effect, even changing the color every time the needle runs out), sew from the under side of one piece to the top surface of the other piece at a diagonal. In other words, your needle enters one side from the top (about one-quarter inch in from the edge), comes up in between the two fabrics, and enters again from the top side of the second piece (about one-quarter inch in from the edge). This is a nice joining for poncho widths: they use it a lot in South America.

Spider's Games

This is one of the better beginning weaving books I've seen. Morrison begins with VERY basic things like how to wind a ball of yarn and progresses gradually to twill, brocade and more advanced techniques. She gets you into weaving using things you might have around the house (a picture frame for a loom and spokes from an old umbrella for needles) and even tells how to make a simple scale for weighing yarn. The beginning projects are attractive, useful and manageable. They won't turn out looking like Bozo made them. The illustrations are very nice and instructions clear. Approach to weaving is creative — I like the section on cat's cradles as an introduction to the craft. Nice title too.
—Marilyn Green

Spider's Games
(A Book for Beginning Weavers)
Phylis Morrison
1979; 128 pp.

$14.95 postpaid from
Univ. of Washington Press
Seattle, WA 98105
or Whole Earth
Household Store

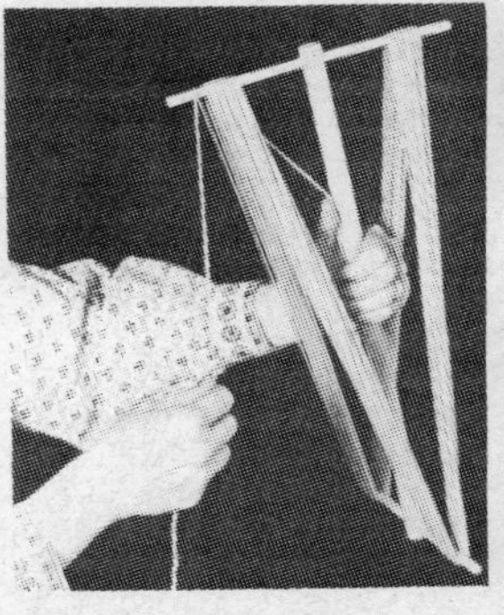

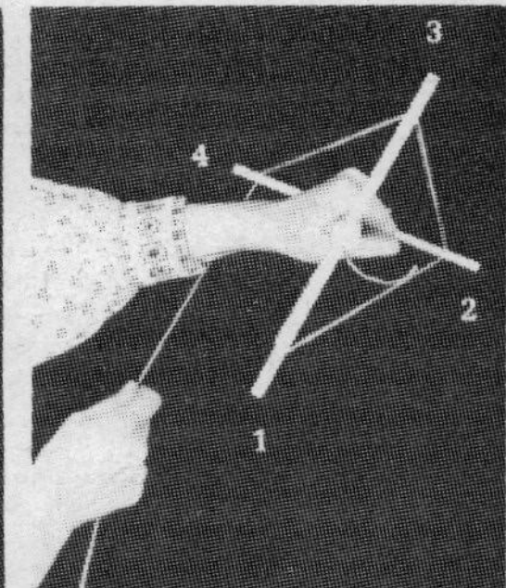

To start winding on a niddy-noddy, grasp it at its middle, holding the yarn's end in that grasp as well. Think of the four ends of the crossbars as being numbered in turn, as in the photo. Wind your yarn over 1, under 2, over 3, and under 4, then back over the first bar again.

As you fall into the rhythm of the winding, the tool will begin to nod. "Niddy-noddy, niddy-noddy, All head and no body." (Old rhyme)

Three ribbons, all woven by machine. They are warp-faced. →

This Nigerian cloth has been set up and woven to produce rectangles of narrow stripes. While the optical effect is that of striped ribbons interwoven, careful examination shows it to be constructed of perfectly regular plain weave with two colors of yarn.

Step-By-Step Tablet Weaving

The perfect cardweaving (or tablet weaving) book is in the future, but here's a very good start. Advantages for beginners: clearly explains how the shedding process works, gives two of several methods of warping and threading cards, demonstrates how threading direction affects the texture of the piece, and gives thorough weaving, joining and end finishing instructions. Drawbacks are hurriedly finished sample pieces and incomplete remedies for common problems like "Argh, my warp thread broke!" and "How do they keep the edges so straight?" The section on the complex double-turn techniques is exceptional.
—Diana Sloat

Step-By-Step Tablet Weaving
Marjorie and William Snow
1973; 80 pp.
$2.95 postpaid from:
Golden Press
P.O. Box 700
Racine, WI 53404

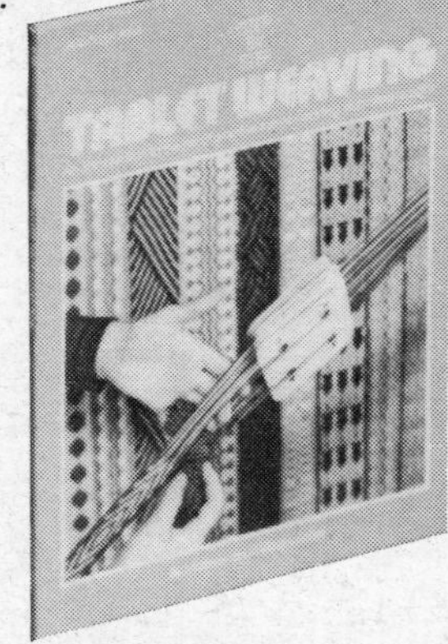

Cardweaving cards

Nice ones designed by Mary Meigs Atwater. —SB

Cardweaving Cards
$5.85/100 cards from:
Belding Lily Co.
P.O. Box 88
Shelby, NC 28150

Cardweaving

A more exciting book with a better history and list of suppliers and more tips on the weaving process itself. Occasional omissions of basics like "put your knots at the ends of the warp, never in the center" make it tough on beginners. But if you already know them, the book moves easily through a number of techniques encouraging you to explore the practically open-ended variations and sculptural possibilities in cardweaving. —Diana Sloat

Cardweaving
Candace Crockett
1973; 144 pp.
$12.95 postpaid from:
Watson-Guptill Publications
2160 Patterson Street
Cincinnati, OH 45214

Cards are shifted laterally to move warp threads, create texture, and shift color. The cards to be shifted are actually picked up and moved to a new position, then tucked back into the pack of cards. ↓

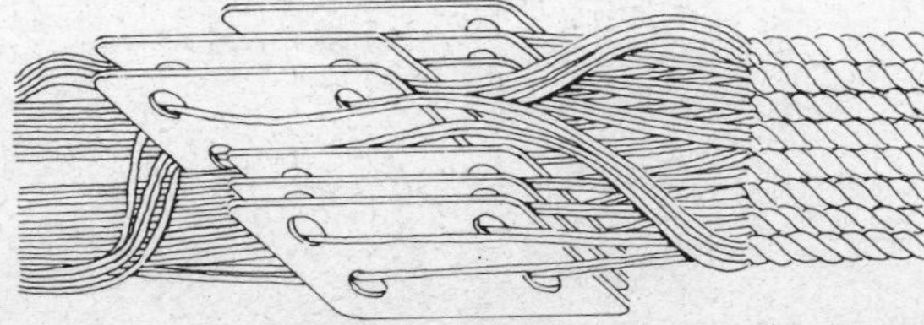

THE RISING SUN
NEIGHBORHOOD NEWSLETTER

Earlier I was trying to figure out why every time I typed balloon, I'd type bal and do a short but total freeze. Yes, I know I'm not the world's greatest typist, but I'm usually fast and unhesitant which is part of the problem. Anyway, I finally remembered that when I was in second grade, my teacher was in the hospital for a really long time (and eventually died), and one day the substitute told us if we all got perfect spelling tests, she'd send them to Mrs. Robinson and make her feel better and I was the only in the class who made a mistake, I spelled balloon baloon. The substitute said that meant we couldn't send them because it wasn't a perfect set. As I cried (in public, and at that point in my life I scarcely talked in public), my best friend looked at my Wednesday practice test of the same words and I had spelled it baloon and the substitute hadn't marked it wrong. So then the sub said it was OK to send all the ones but mine and it wasn't my fault. She didn't say she was sorry, but if you ever want to know that saloon has one l and balloon has two, you can ask me and after I think a minute, I'll know.

The Techniques of Rug Weaving

Here at last and it's ALL here! Like some fantastic teacher — gives you just what you need to know — being thorough, comprehensive, scholarly, inspiring (I'M GOING TO WEAVE A RUG!) Over 400 lucid diagrams, 174 illustrations, only four in color but how much can one ask? Detailed coverage of every aspect of rug weaving from fundamentals to most advanced and formerly obscure techniques; from ancient methods to Collingwood's own inventive technical developments. As further application beyond rugs can be made for most of the weaves, this is a book for all weavers. Formidable! —Sarah Kahn

The Techniques of Rug Weaving
Peter Collingwood
1968; 480 pp.
$35 postpaid from:
Watson-Guptill Publications
2160 Patterson Street
Cincinnati, OH 45214
or Whole Earth Household Store

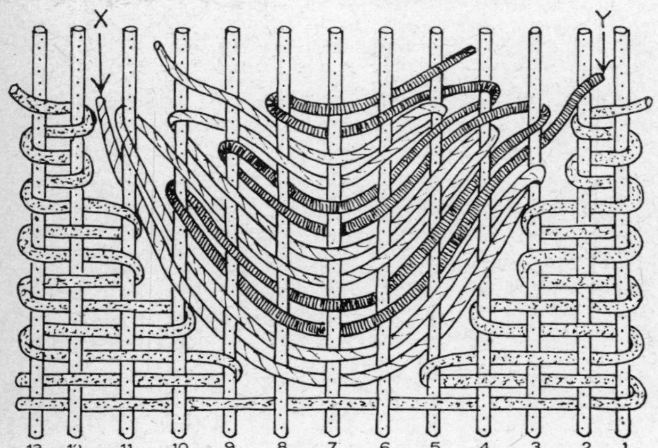

↑ **Kilim. Weaving an oval with two wefts, detailed view.**

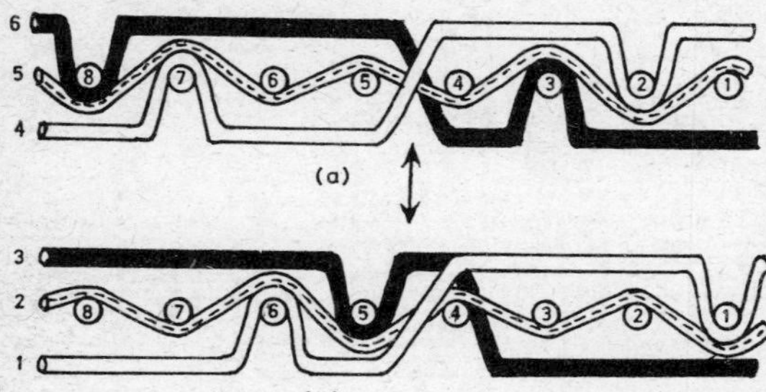

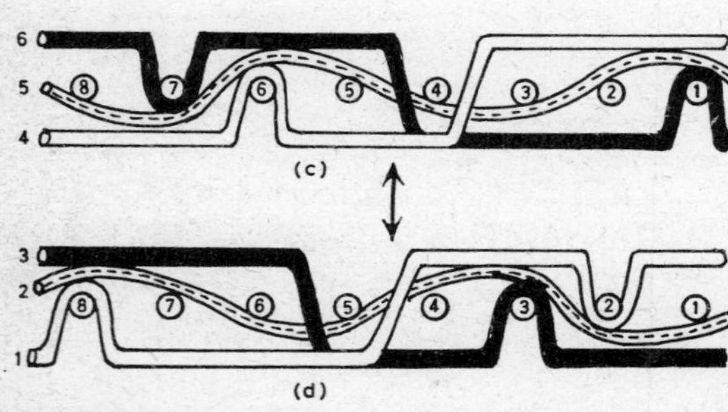

↑ **Block Weaves based on Three-Weft Double-Faced Weaves. (a) and (b) Cross-sections o picks in Fig. 292(a) (c) and (d) Cross-sections o picks in Fig. 292(c)**

Weft twining. Part of rug in twined tapestry, from Abyssinia. ↓

New Key to Weaving

A one-book weaver's library. A comprehensive textbook covering all aspects of loom weaving. Incredibly packed. Section on tapestry weaving alone is worth the cost of the book. —Sarah Kahn
[Suggested by Victoria Becker]

New Key to Weaving
Mary Black
1945, 1980; 573 pp.
$19.95 postpaid from:
Macmillan
Publishing Company
Order Department
Front and Brown Streets
Riverside, NJ 08075
or Whole Earth Household Store

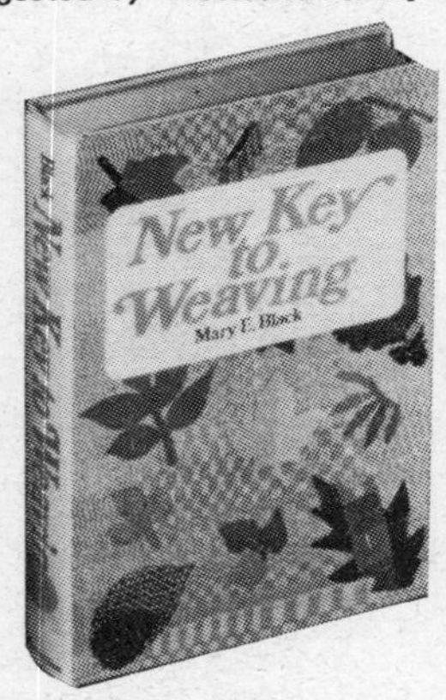

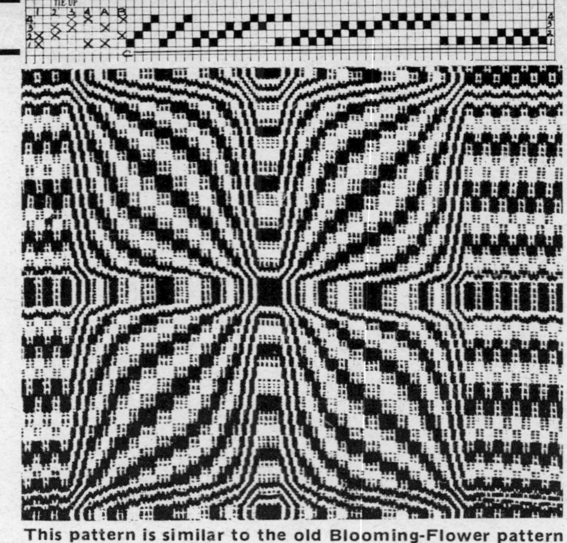

This pattern is similar to the old Blooming-Flower pattern but is more interesting because of the addition of a table motif. The result is more pleasing and, when used for large objects such as bedspreads and drapes, the threading produces a better design, lacking the monotony of the Blooming-Flower pattern.

Hand Weaving and Cloth Design

Years of teaching and industrial experience distilled into one deceptively modest and simple-looking small book. The only book organized and clear enough to give separate threading and treadling drafts for each type of harness-raising system: rising shed, sinking shed, countermarch, table loom and dobby pegging. Should be a cornerstone of every intelligent weaver's library. —Diana Sloat

Hand Weaving and Cloth Design
Marianne Straub
1977; 152 pp.
$14.95 postpaid from:
The Viking Press
299 Murray Hill Parkway
East Rutherford, NJ 07073
or Whole Earth Household Store

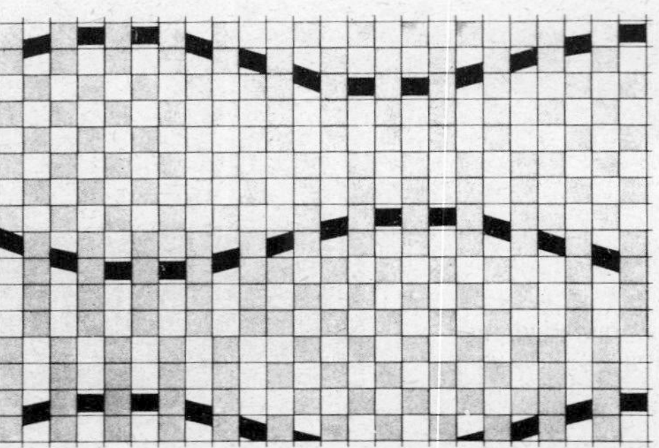

Single picks of a contrasting yarn introduced between the alternating densely woven areas emphasize the distortion.

A Handweaver's Pattern Book

Enough traditional patterns for a chunk of a lifetime — threading, tie-up, and treadling drafts with photos of woven samples. —Diana Sloat

A Handweaver's Pattern Book
(Revised Edition)
Marguerite Porter Davison
1944, 1950; 217 pp.
$15 postpaid from:
M.P. Davison, Publishers
Box 263
Swarthmore, PA 19081

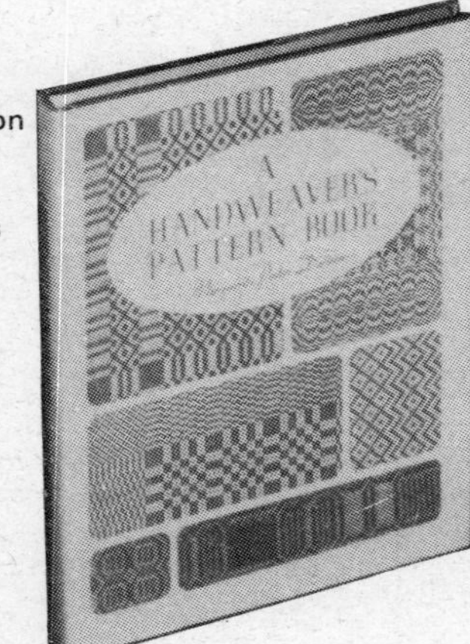

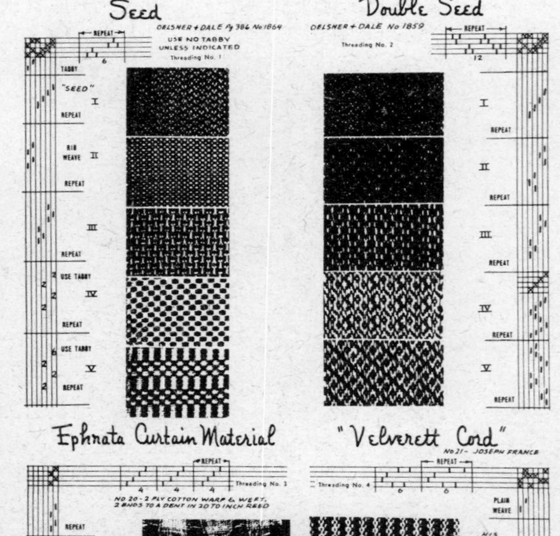

More Than Four

For weavers with "more than 4-harness" looms who want to design their own patterns, it's an excellent self-teaching tool. Her system for diagramming threading and treadling drafts, explanation of the theory and structure and weaves, and the language in general is the clearest I've seen. Excellent coverage of satins, overshot, multi-layers, M's and O's, summer and winter, and superbly — twills.

Physically, the book is a pleasure to use. Set up as a spiral bound "workbook," it lies flat, with each diagram and bibliographical reference located right beside the text in wide margins. No page flipping necessary; plenty of room for notes. Nice to see design and function work so well. —Diana Sloat
[Suggested by Janice Martin]

More Than Four
(A book for multiple harness weavers)
Mary Elizabeth Laughlin
1976; 179 pp.
$11.95 postpaid from:
Laughlin Enterprises
1845 Oak Terrace
Newcastle, CA 95658

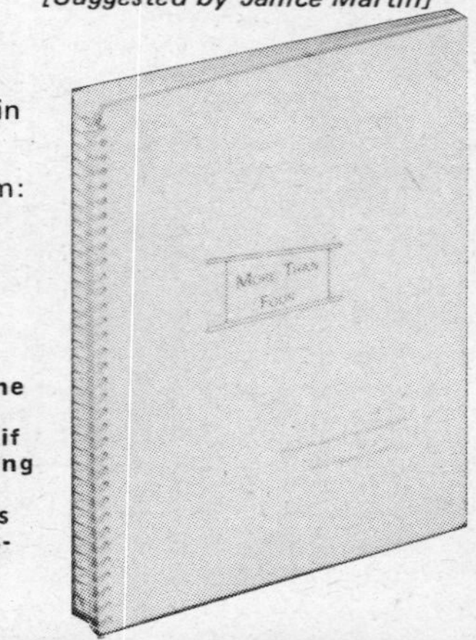

The figure illustrates one possible combination that could be designed if a twelve harness threading were used, i.e., if the direct twill four harness threading and the transposed twill draft were used, three times. ↓

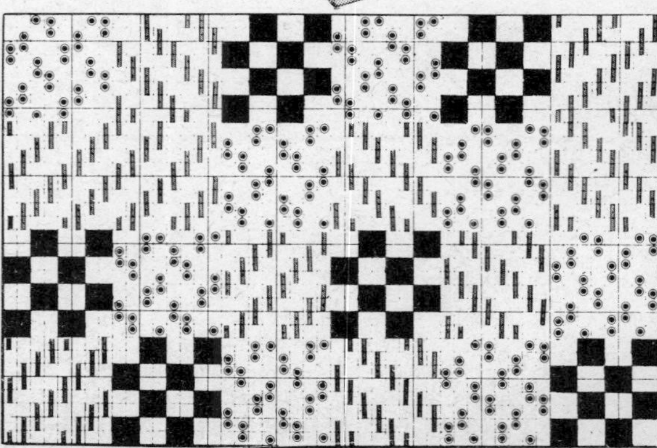

Richly attired personage with halo. In his right hand he holds a sceptre ornamented with four serpents, in his left hand are five darts.

Bonnet wig of network made in peruke stitch.

Textiles of Ancient Peru and their Techniques

An extraordinary book on an extraordinary subject. Divided into three sections: Woven Fabrics, Non-woven Fabrics (such as plaiting, network, felt) and Ornamentation and Trimming of Fabrics (includes embroideries). Clear diagrams and explanation of techniques of pre-Columbian weaving, and a multitude of exciting photographs of Peruvian textiles. All depth, richness, inspiration! If I could have but one book on textile arts, this would be it.

—Sarah Kahn

Textiles of Ancient Peru and their Techniques
Raoul d'Harcourt
1974; 309 pp.
$14.95 postpaid from:
The University of Washington Press
Seattle, WA 98105
or Whole Earth Household Store

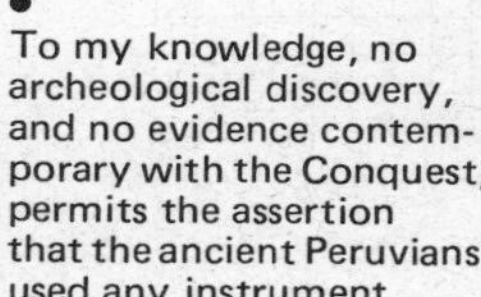

•

To my knowledge, no archeological discovery, and no evidence contemporary with the Conquest, permits the assertion that the ancient Peruvians used any instrument other than a needle with an eye for joining yarns to each other or to a fabric. Crochet hooks and knitting needles seem to have been unknown. There were needles with eyes in both curved and straight shapes, of metal, of fishbone, of wood, and of thorns. Some of them must have been very fine, suitable for the close work that still arouses our admiration today.

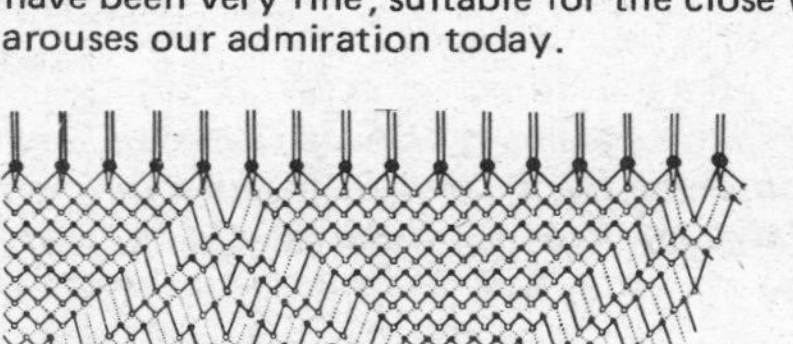

← Arrangement of meshes of the network of the cap shown in here. The meshes of this network are not uniform and were executed in square knot. ↓

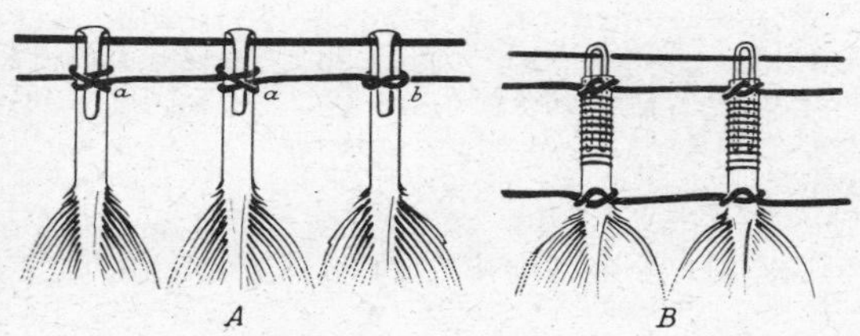

Methods of fastening feathers for imbricating on cloth in overlapping rows. A: fine feathers with folded quills, a) knot with two loops, b) simple knot; B: coarse feathers with tapered quills provided with a small terminal loop; two small cords fasten the quills and keep them separate.

←

1. White cotton fabric of two yarn and three-yarn gauze.
2. In the method of weaving shown here, the fabric has yarns twisted in pairs.
3. Network of agave fiber, made in square knotting.
4. Network of agave fiber, made with a simple knot, painted in blackish and red brown colors forming step motives.

All are same size as original

Keep Me Warm One Night

A big wonderful weaving book. The detailed study of the handweaving in Eastern Canada up to 1900 with notes on the period, equipment, materials and styles. The bulk of the book is a richly illustrated discussion of early styles and techniques. Each coverlet is described, analyzed and the threading draft given: an amazing slice of textile history and a work of love. Worth saving for.

—Daphne Stewart

Keep Me Warm One Night
H.B. Burnham and D.K. Burnham
1972; 387 pp.
$35 postpaid from:
University of Toronto Press
33 E. Tupper Street
Buffalo, NY 14203
or Whole Earth Household Store

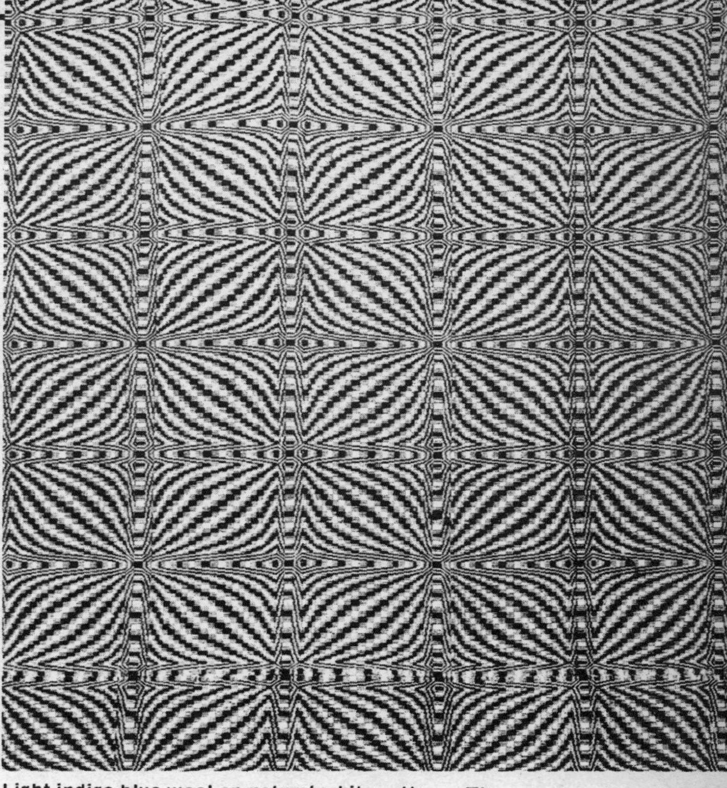

Light indigo blue wool on natural white cotton. The design is similar to the preceding ones, but is without a 'table.' In eastern Ontario it is known as 'Turkey Tracks.'

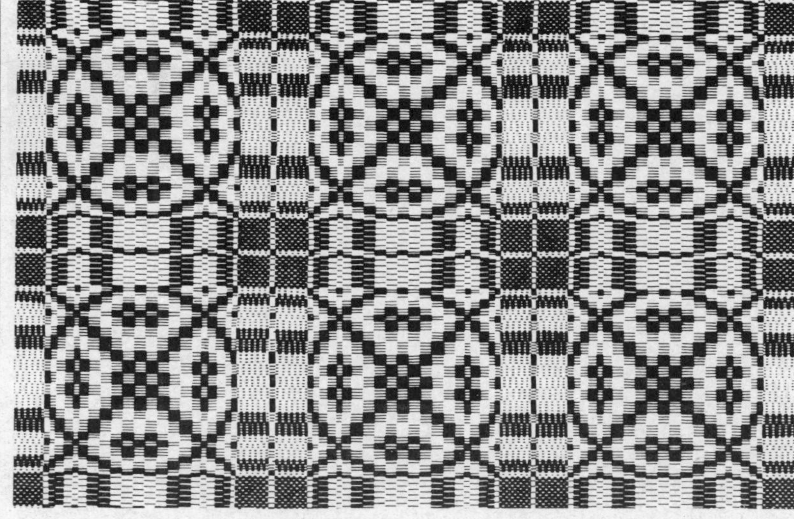

← Nova Scotia. Cape Breton. 19th century. Gift of Mrs. F.M. Mackley. Fourshaft overshot pattern draft: 'Keep Me Warm One Night'

This draft from Cape Breton is the source of the title of this book and is one of the loveliest pattern names that has been found in Canada. The design is similar to another with a wide distribution and a constant name: 'Chariot Wheels and Church Windows' (Nos. 66,347). This draft has a larger nine-part table.

The Art of Bolivian Highland Weaving

A monumental and challenging work covering a particularly beautiful and little known area of weaving. Comparable in scope to d'Harcourt's Textiles of Ancient Peru *for contemporary Bolivian weaving, it is by contrast set up to teach, with a rare combination of careful research, competence in textile analysis,* and *the experience of having searched out, lived and worked with weavers of particular regions of Bolivia, learning their techniques.*

The pebble and twill weaves and the complex structures which produce them as well as the animal and geometric figures are presented as weavers there learn them, by developing the necessary dexterity through doing a series of bands, each increasingly intricate in structure but more and more exciting to learn. The text and diagrams are extremely clear and the color plates downright inspiring. Instructions culminate in how to weave the small "chuspa" (coca leaf bag), the awayo (carrying cloth), and how to adapt traditional methods and equipment for use on inkle and floor looms. The appendix includes an extensive bibliography, supplier's list, glossary and instructions with grids and examples for planning and diagramming contemporary and traditional designs.

It's an exceptional book.

—Diana Sloat

The Art of Bolivian Highland Weaving
(Unique, Traditional Techniques for the Modern Weaver)
Marjorie Cason and Adele Cahlander
1976; 216 pp.
$24.50 postpaid from:
Watson-Guptill Publications
2160 Patterson Street
Cincinnati, OH 45214
or Whole Earth Household Store

Beads are attached to the edges of winchas in various arrangements. →

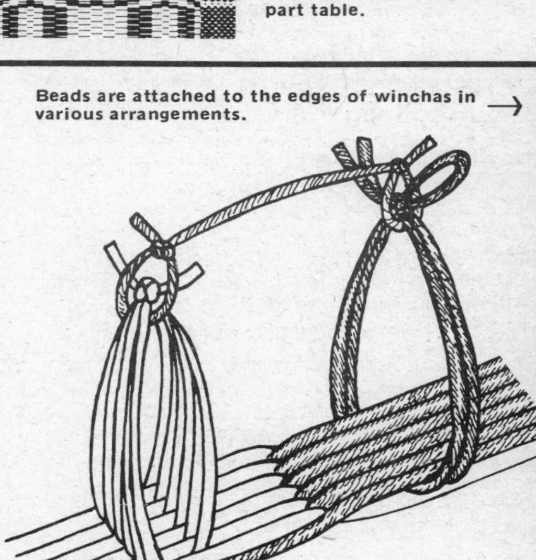

↑ A cord connecting two heddles makes it easier to lift them together.

THE RISING SUN
NEIGHBORHOOD NEWSLETTER

Nobody but the Chinese knew how to make porcelain until this German king who was an art collector spent all his money and raised taxes and spent them and sold family heirlooms to buy porcelain and then told his court alchemist that he had to learn to turn lead into gold to buy porcelain or he would be beheaded. So the alchemist figured out how to make porcelain.

— TV show on "Splendours of Dresden"

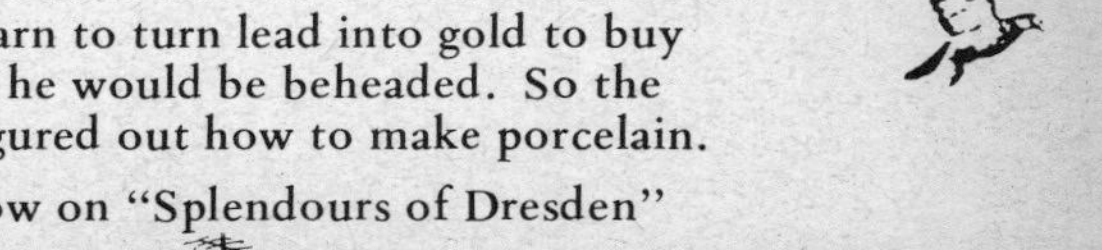

Navajo and Hopi Weaving Techniques

Technically, though not in beauty of spirit, Mary Pendleton's book replaces **Working with the Wool** *as the best beginning Navajo rug weaving book. Years of teaching experience back the clearly-stated, efficient instructions for carding, spinning, dyeing yarns and warping, weaving and correcting common mistakes. Each step is photographed clearly. Also included are sections on loom building, Hopi methods of belt weaving, sash weaving and spinning, and suppliers' lists. So, experienced or no, buy the materials and you're into it!* —Diana Sloat

Navajo and Hopi Weaving Techniques
Mary Pendleton
1974; 158 pp.

$5.95 postpaid from:
Macmillan Publishing Co.
Order Department
Front & Brown Streets
Riverside, NJ 08075
or Whole Earth Household Store

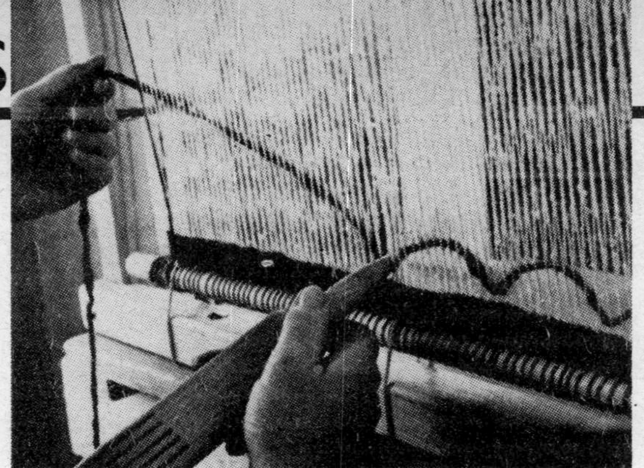

Correct way to hold comb — beating from bound end of weft.

•

Warp tension has but one rule. It should be very tight. Many of your problems can be avoided if you remember this. Your warp yarn may stretch as you weave and beat so keep adjusting tension. If the warp is not tight, it will feel spongy when you beat. Too loose a tension in the warp can cause problems such as:

Weft does not beat down as easily.

Warp ends separate more readily where colors join.

Side edges bulge out.

Side edges draw in.

Batten keeps turning vertically in shed.

Straw Into Gold

An institution and an exceptional mail order house: their selection of fibers, yarns, spinning equipment, dye supplies and books is mind-boggling, and they even offer a full range of dyepots. The catalog's throwaway lines are stuff whole books will be written about. An absolute fountain of information and new ideas. —Diana Sloat

Straw Into Gold
Catalog

$1 from:
Straw Into Gold
5533 College Avenue
Oakland, CA 94618

•

Alpaca

The Alpaca is a relative of the camel and closely related to the llama. They live at high altitudes (above 10,000 ft.) in Peru, Bolivia and elsewhere in So. America. The fiber has become scarcer (and of course more expensive in recent years.) We no longer carry alpaca top, but you will find the LLAMA TOP almost identical in softness. We do have scoured, uncarded alpaca in mixed colors. Buy it uncarded and sort and card it yourself, or buy it carded by us on our sample card. The uncarded mix is brown, blonde, black which you can hand sort. We often have "odd lot" alpaca laps (pieces of combed alpaca top 4 - 12" long). We notify envelope people, or send a SASE with 22 cents postage and we will send you a fat sample.

1043-1. Scoured, uncarded alpaca, mixed colors.
1 lb. $9.95.
1043-5. Scoured, uncarded alpaca, mixed colors.
5 lbs. $44.
1043C-H. Scoured, Carded Alpaca, blended.
8 oz. $13.95.
1043C-3. Scoured, Carded Alpaca, blended colors.
3 lbs. $37.65.

•

USA-Corriedale fleece, raw. A white wool of about 56's count. Soft and nice to spin. The staple is sometimes as long as the NZ wools, but averages a little shorter (3"). Our Corriedale is raised by a large-scale prize-winning Corriedale ranch in California and is quite clean and free of tags. It is usually a little dirtier than the average NZ fleece, however. A good, all-purpose fleece for weaving, knitting, etc.

1003 - 1. Corriedale, raw. 1 lb. bag, $2.95.
1003 - F. Corriedale, whole fleece. Usually about 6 - 8 lbs., $2.70/lb.

Ikat: An Introduction

A thorough, well-written instruction manual for Japanese ikat, the ancient technique of resist dyeing warp, weft threads or both, before weaving to create ghostly luminescent patterns in the woven fabric. All four basic types of ikat are covered, weft, warp, double, and weft figure. An excellent brief history and bibliography are included. Be forewarned: the booklet presupposes knowledge of basic weaving and dyeing techniques and terminology.

Instructions for calculating, warping and binding the pattern bundles are simple and clear. The special illustrated is dynamite: speedy and tight, yet unties easily with a sharp yank (a slip of the scissors in the center of your carefully bound, dipped and dried-8-times pattern is disastrous!). There are directions for a *cold-water* *indigo dye process which once it's made up, can stand in the vat and be roused over a two-month span. It produces dark, rich fast color on cotton or silk, a bit lighter on wool, and dyes up to 20 lbs. of material. A note on materials: 1) The special nylon tape recommended for the bindings is faster and more convenient to use than other materials like raffia or string. It's about two inches wide, can readily be split into narrower strips, and shrinks with heat to even further tighten the resist areas. Results in sharper patterns. 2) The dye vat proportions are set for the Kasuri Dye Works indigo. (Straw Into Gold's is similar and can be interchanged with it.) Since indigos do vary in strength depending on how much and what they're cut with, you may have to adjust the dye vat proportions to suit the indigo from your usual source.* —Diana Sloat

Ikat: An Introduction
Diane Ritch and Yoshiko Wada
1975; 26 pp.

$3.20 postpaid from:
Kasuri Dye Works
1959 Shattuck Avenue
Berkeley, CA 94704

Adding an extra amount of width to the weft skeins allows the weaver to invent different patterns. Illustrated are some of the variations which can be achieved with the skeins tied in only two places. ↓

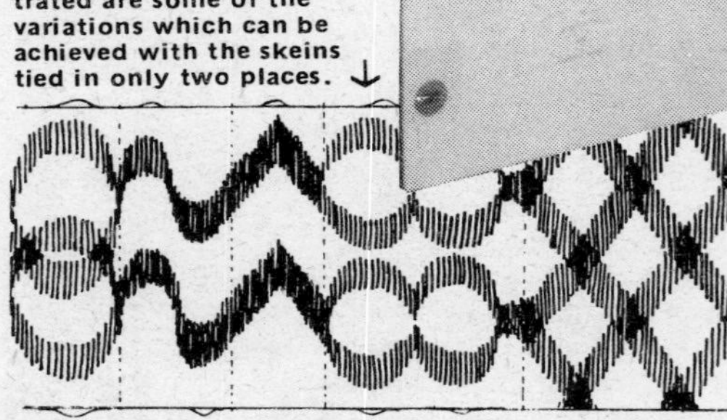

Textile suppliers

Three good sources. Backings, yarns, dyes, looms, frames, hookers, books, etc. —SB

The Mannings
Catalog
$ .50 from:
The Mannings
RD 2
East Berlin, PA 17316

Some Place
Catalog
$ .50 from:
Some Place
2990 Adeline Street
Berkeley, CA 94703

The Ruggery
Catalog
$ .50 from:
The Ruggery
Glen Head
Long Island, NY 11545

Buying a Floor Loom

by Diana Sloat

A floor loom is a big investment. It is a tool for making a living, or at least for clothing the family and decorating and insulating the house. People frequently and mistakenly buy highly advertised and widely distributed looms that are flimsy and poorly made, simply because they are available and familiar. In fact, most buy the same loom they learned on whether or not they are appropriate to their needs. To make an informed choice consider these things:

• **Is it a good tool?** It should have:

1. A strong, rigid frame – If it moves or shimmies when you shake or tug it, it'll walk (move across the floor) as you beat heavier textiles.
2. Harnesses that are easy to raise and smooth treadle action.
3. Treadles that are easy for the feet to find.
4. Good shed – just enough height for the shuttle to run cleanly on the race.
5. Ease of access to the interior for threading – removable or fold up breast and back beams.
6. An easy tie-up system – does it snap in, button, slide into a slot, or whatever?
7. Friction, tension or cable brake on warp beam. These are convenient, not necessary.

• **Does it fit physically?**

1. Taller people prefer larger looms; shorter people smaller ones, for a reason. At a long-legged 5'9" I have to duck-walk the treadles of the Gilmore and Schacht looms or my knees stretch the cloth. Raise the bench height and I have to bend over to weave. Beater and treadles should be within easy reach with a *straight back*.
2. Beginners often overbuy; the biggest and best can be intimidating. "Most people *comfortably* (without stretching) weave, i.e., throw and catch a shuttle, about 30 - 36 inches depending on arm span. Beyond that a fly shuttle is required." (Inger Jensen of Pacific Basin Textiles.)

• **Is it well-crafted? Does it feel good to hand and eye?**

• **If your lifestyle is mobile, is your loom also?**

The Scandinavian looms dismantle and reassemble completely in 10 - 15 minutes, some jack looms don't dismantle at all.

• **Is it designed for the kind of weaving you intend to do?**

This is hard for a beginner to know, so a detailed discussion follows. Of the two main approaches to weaving, the "One-on-one-off" is most common in my area. This way is often more art-oriented, the weaver designs a single piece, warps it, weaves it, and goes on to a different project. This demands a versatile, easily-set-up loom with excellent shed and maximum patterning possibility. The weaving process can be slow; experimentation with the design often takes place as the weaving progresses. The jack-type or rising shed looms (Macomber, Gilmore, Schacht, Fireside and Storz) fit this approach. They allow you to lift a single harness or three, as well as pairs; they are low swing, compact and look somewhat like a small piano. With a space problem they are a must. Many fold up to some degree for storing when not in use. Their tie-up systems are easy and quick. Most have friction brakes. Disadvantages: their metal heddles make the harnesses heavy and slow to lift, particularly on the 8-harness models, throw more strain on the back, and make a metallic racket when used. The amount of warp tension necessary for rugs interferes with the lifting mechanism and makes a good shed difficult; additionally, the small looms aren't stable enough for the heavy beating rugs require.

MORE LOOMS NEXT PAGE →

In the other approach, production weaving, weavers make their living weaving. They put on long warps for yardage or a series of the same thing, and weave for long hours regularly. The pleasure is in the physical process, in the rhythmical, repetitive motions. Speed, stability, efficiency, harness weight, noise level, and above all, *ease* of operating the loom (ease of treadling, beating, lifting the harnesses, releasing warp tension and advancing the warp) count most over an 8-hour day. Design is a relatively small portion of the process; it is usually loom-determined in threading, color and treadling sequence.

The Scandinavian looms with their solid, strong, rigid frames, overhead beaters and light harnesses with string or polyester heddles take up more room but better suit production weaving. They are quieter, faster, easier to operate and capable of handling the widest range of textiles from rugs to lace weaves. The counterbalance looms (with rollers) are the simplest, easiest to learn on and use, but lose patterning possibilities because they are a *balanced* system – the harnesses are attached in pairs so in order to raise one harness, its corresponding harness must sink.

The countermarch looms are more complex (they combine rising and sinking shed action), match the counterbalance's ease of action *and* the jack's ability to lift odd numbers of harnesses, but have been *the devil* to set up. On the old ones you took a thermos of whatever and crawled under the loom for the day tying up and adjusting multiple sets of everything. They are tall looms; the jacks operate from overhead, and their two sets of lams require double operating space under the loom. Once set up, they're magnificently efficient, handsome and worth the effort. Glimakra uses the new "Texsolv" polyester loop and button system on its looms which reduces tie-up time to 45 minutes and makes the countermarch system attractive again. (You *can* buy the button tie-ups independently of buying the loom.)

By far the best standard treadling system production loom is not currently being manufactured because of low demand – it's the Ahrens and Violette 45" 10-harness, *side* tie-up loom with the lightest harnesses, sandpaper breast/cloth beam combined (yes!), friction brake, and counterweight system which *automatically* tensions and rolls the woven cloth onto the cloth beam at the back of the loom when the brake is released. Jim Ahrens, production weaver, mechanical engineer and designer of the loom, knows what he is doing. Hopefully increased demand will bring it back into production; they keep a list of names of those who would order if they eventually do so.

What Ahrens and Violette have in production are their Dobby looms, in speed closest to the power loom. Small and compact for Dobbys, they allow the weaver to peg the tie-up and treadling sequence into the Dobby chain, a mechanism reminiscent of a player piano's connected to the harnesses at the side of the loom. Treadling the two treadles then moves the Dobby through repeats of the sequence, a very fast, sweet and efficient system for lifting the harnesses. Making a living at weaving extremely complex and beautiful textiles is being done on these looms. Additionally with the optional fly shutter, their ease of operation has allowed people with a variety of handicaps to weave.

To speak to the "hardwood" vs. "softwood" controversy, "judicious selection of stock, adherence to a good design, proper joinery techniques and careful workmanship have a great deal more to do with building satisfactory textile tools than the mere choice of hardwood over softwood. And always remember that a hard wood can be a softwood and a soft wood a hardwood." For history of the controversy and further technical details of comparison of wood qualities (shear value, shrinkage, rupture value, hardness, etc.) see the rest of Alden Amos' article "Wood Used for Textile Tools" in **Textile Artist's Newsletter**, Vol. II No. 2. Suffice it to say that the Scandinavian looms in use for generations and the original Ahrens are of "softwood." So are the Nagy and most Canadian spinning wheels. They are all excellent tools.

Where to begin with all this information?

- Buy used – want ads, notices on church, supermarket and laundromat bulletin boards often turn up surprisingly good equipment. Then trade up to what you find you need.
- Copy a good loom.
- If buying new try to attend a handweaver's conference or as many handweaving stores in your area as possible to try out a wide range of looms. The good ones stand out.
- The looms reviewed here have proven themselves over time. Good luck! ■

← **Production Dobby: $2,770. 16-harness, 48" weaving width, fly shuttle beater, rigid overhead frame, sandpaper roller and automatic advance of the woven cloth onto a storage roller at the back of the loom. The lightest, fanciest textiles to rugs can be woven on this loom — the answer to a true production weaver's prayer.**

Ahrens and Violette Dobby looms

Unsurpassed as "appropriate technology," these are unique in the field of specialized, serious looms, the fastest, most efficient tools designed (60 picks per minute). They both have automatic systems for warp advance and constant, consistent tensioning, combined breast beam/cloth beam, polyester heddles and super light harnesses, with an adjustable spring-loaded harness return action which raises 12 harnesses with the same treadling effort as it takes to raise two. The Dobby chains are interchangeable — a chain with a particularly good design can be taken off and stored until needed for another series of the same project. Using the Dobby takes a bit of initial effort to learn; the looms are accompanied by a 40-page extremely thorough instruction manual detailing Jim Ahrens' production techniques for warping, threading and setting up. Prime for anyone weaving and designing apparel originals.

—Diana Sloat

Ahrens and Violette Looms
Catalog
free from:
Ahrens and Violette Loom Company
601 Orange Street
Chico, CA 95926
(9 month back-up on orders)

Glimåkra looms

Glimåkra of Sweden, world's largest loom manufacturer, offers the widest selection of excellently crafted, extremely functional floor looms, ranging from enormous rug looms down to small, collapsible 4-harness floor looms that bolt onto a shelf or table. (Looks like half of a loom.)
The 4-harness counterbalance and all countermarch models come with the "button" tie-up system. They have tall rigid side frames, overhead beaters, mortise and tenon joints with lockpins for swift, easy take-down and assembly. Light harnesses with nylon heddles and back-pivoted treadles give smooth, easy maximum harness-lifting action. The only drawbacks are that treadles can be harder to find with the feet because they flap a little in front, and have a ratchet brake system. (Their counterbalance looms use a hard to adjust "horse" system — not recommended). Very versatile and beautiful looms, otherwise.
—Diana Sloat

Glimåkra Swedish Looms
Manufactured by:
Vavstolsfabriken
Glimåkra AB
Box 125
S-28064 Glimåkra
Sweden

Catalog and price list
free from:
Glimåkra Looms and Yarns, Inc.
P.O. Box 16157
Rocky River, OH 44116

Countermarch loom 40" - 64", 4 harness to 10 harness, $995 - $1620.

Lervad looms

Superbly crafted Danish countermarch looms, as much a pleasure to look at as to use. The Lervad family emphasis has been on quality; their followup on requests for information and replacements parts are prompt and caring (and in English).

—Diana Sloat

Lervad Looms
Information — Send 3 International Reply Coupons (about $1.20) from:
Anders Lervad & Son A/S
Askov, 6600 Vejen
Denmark

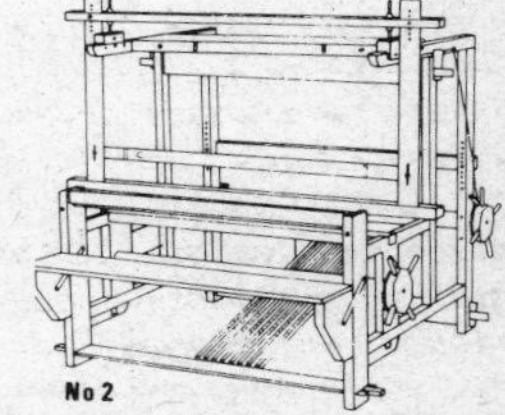

Rasmussen table loom

A compact and inexpensive 25" unfinished 4- or 8-harness table loom with an excellent shed. It's ready to weave on as soon as you bolt the castle upright. The only flaw I've discovered — a cord easily came off one of the rollers under the manipulations of a 2-year-old mechanic, and equally easily slid back in place. It comes with stick shuttle, 12-dent 25" reed and lease sticks. A lot of loom for the price. —Diana Sloat

Rasmussen Table Loom
Information
$ .50 from:
Rasmussen Loom Co.
Box 15451
Seattle, WA 98115

25", 4 - 8 harness, $130 - $185.

Macomber loom

The largest, sturdiest, heaviest, noisiest and most versatile of the jack looms, it has the fastest tie-up system — steel pins snap into place instantly. There's good access to the interior. It's heavy enough for rugs. In fact, moving it is similar to moving a piano — a fact you should consider if your lifestyle is at all mobile. Many professional weavers and artists seem to have them.

—Diana Sloat

Macomber Ad-a-Harness Looms
Catalog
free from:
L.W. Macomber
Beech Ridge Road
York, ME 03909

24" — 72", 4-24 harness, $472 - $3230.

Storz loom

The smaller, graceful but very sturdy weaver-designed jack loom is as handsomely finished as the fireside, available in oak or maple, with 4 or 8 harnesses, 36" or 45" weaving width. The back beam flips up for easy threading; tie-up system is quick and quiet; the harness action is light for metal heddles. There is much thought in design and detailing — excellent for most textiles and very nice to look at. A slanted weaving bench available. There's a 4 month wait on orders.

—Diana Sloat
[Suggested by Sarah Hammond]

Storz Looms
Information
$1 from:
Black Sheep Woodworks
P.O. Box 184
Willits, CA 95490

45", 4 - 8 harness, $820 - $1040

THE RISING SUN
NEIGHBORHOOD NEWSLETTER

In some small Midwestern towns, almost any form of eccentricity is acceptable as long as it is neither political nor sexual.

Texsolv System

A major advance for weavers, and a boon to those of us with older looms with forests of slipping snitch knots. Tie up the trouble spots or the whole loom with a non-stretch, slick, strong, knotless polyester loom cord crocheted in chains of linked loops at standard intervals. The cord can be doubled back on itself through one of the loops and pegged with a small nylon gismo ("peg") or "buttoned" and then pegged into the holes in the treadles with a cotter pin. Such a fast, simple, effective way to standardize spacing on a loom and keep it there! (Has been thoroughly tested in Europe.)

Their new polyester heddles are a major improvement over string as well. They're light, easily threaded, non-stretch, non-slip, slick, with "wide eyes," and no left/right direction to keep track of when installing. Ahrens and Violette looms use the older model; the new ones look even better. —Diana Sloat

Texsolv loom cord and heddles
Kits
$20 - $75 (depending on loom)

Loom cord
$.40/yard
both from:
J-Made Looms and Weaving Accessories
P.O. Box 452
Oregon City, OR 97045

Kits for Glimakra looms
$25 plus shipping from:
Glimakra Looms 'n Yarns, Inc.
(p. 277)

Information
(Include your loom make)
$.50 from:
G. Kinserly,
U.S. Representative
10720 Southwest 30th Ave.
Portland, OR 97219
or C.L. Vlomquist AB
P.O. Box 111
Fritsla, 51020
Sweden

← **Quick-connect nylon peg for adjusting length of linked-loop loomcord.**

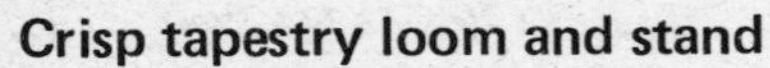

Crisp tapestry loom and stand

Elegant, beautifully made and expensive. They're such magnificent frames people are sometimes reluctant to take off their work when it's finished.

Additionally they are fine tools. They are designed for continuous warping by spinning the frame on the stand with one hand and adjusting warp tension and placement with the other. Height and angle completely adjustable. Joints are mortise and tenon with tapered lockpins for fast dismantling and re-assembly. (Crisp makes a fine "great wheel" as well.) Their deliveries sometimes slow. —Diana Sloat

Crisp looms
$130 - $300 (approx.)

Catalog
$1 from:
Crisp Woodworking Concerns Ltd.
333 Southeast Third Street
Portland, OR 97214

Leclerc vertical table warping mill

Far faster and easier to use than a warping board. Handles up to twenty yards, two yards per rotation. Folds flat for storage. Suction feet anchor it to the table. (If you must have a warping board, Ashford — see p. 282 — makes an inexpensive kit.) —Diana Sloat

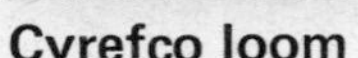

Leclerc vertical table warping mill
$60 (approx.)
Catalog and nearest dealer location
$1 from:
Leclerc Corporation
Highway Nine North
P.O. Box 491
Plattsburgh, NY 12901

Fireside loom

Large weaver-designed, handsomely detailed and finished jack type loom with 4 or 8 harnesses, 40" or 54" weaving width. The back beam pivots up for easy threading; the cloth beam and beater lift out. It's heavy and well-balanced enough for light rugs, and will also go through a 30" door. A friction brake, slots in the treadles for fast tie-up, recessed slots in the cloth beam, large capacity 2/3 yard warp beam and relatively quiet action make this loom an excellent tool as well as a beautiful piece of furniture. Very nice accessories as well. —Diana Sloat

Fireside Looms
Brochure
$ .50 from:
Fireside Looms
Star Route Box 11
Deadwood, OR 97430

40" - 54", 4 harness - 8 harness, $885 - $1485. ↓

Cyrefco loom ↑

So far in my area I've found no counterbalanced loom I'd be thoroughly comfortable owning. The closest is the 45" Cyrefco 4-harness "traditional loom." It's a copy of the Swedish looms with overhead beater, but with friction brake, a choice of rollers or horses, optional adjustable loom bench and horizontal warping mill that fits into the back uprights of the loom for warping. All (loom, bench and mill) are offered in kit form as well as finished, a definite advantage, $-wise; Aliphatic glue, Watco oil, sandpaper and instruction book are included. Major reservation was the rattle of the heavy maple beater; the maker said he would be happy to slot the vertical pieces to put in a wing nut on each side for anchoring the reed and silencing the rattle. —Diana Sloat

Cyrefco 45" Traditional Looms
$510 - $740 (approx.)

Information
$.50 from:
Cyrefco Looms
P.O. Box 1640
Palo Alto, CA 94302

Schacht looms

As a long-time weaver and author of weaving books, I can recommend the four harness loom. It is especially helpful because of the portability, and possibility of a long warp. This equipment is very well made. —Jean Wilson

Schracht Looms
Catalog and price list

$1 postpaid from:
Schacht Spindle Company
2526 49th Street
Boulder, CO 80306

36" - 42", 4 harness - 8 harness, $550 - $850.

Handloom Weaving Technology

Excellent reference work on looms, loom types and weaving equipment in general, if you can get past the royal "we." Good section on dobby looms. Expensive; have your local library order it. —Diana Sloat

Handloom Weaving Technology
Allen Fannin
1978; 336 pp.
$26.50 postpaid from:
Van Nostrand Reinhold Company
Order Department
7625 Empire Drive
Florence, KY 41042

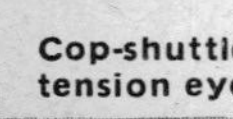

Cop-shuttle tension eye

Tension Eye

Unlike the boat shuttle, the end-delivery shuttle has provision for adjusting and maintaining whatever filling tension is required. This adjustment, once made, will not only remain constant from a full quill to an empty one, but will also remain constant for quill after quill as long as the same yarn is used. Furthermore, no tension changes are encountered regardless of the side of the shed from which the pick originates. The amount of tension required depends on many variables, but as a rule, enough tension should be used to prevent filling loops at the selvages. Several picks should be woven at the beginning of a length of warp to check this. In addition, if more than one shuttle is used, either with the same or with different yarns, the tension on each of them should be adjusted individually so as to produce the same result from shuttle to shuttle.

Warping All By Yourself

Cay Garrett has banished the last warping jitter. Learn to speed warp from the front of the loom, thread from the cross held in one hand, and then go from there using either her system or sharing the warp chain with a friend. Takes you inch by inch, crystal clear diagrams and text giving tips down to sighting, feel and body position at each step. For all levels from the barest novice. —Diana Sloat

Warping All By Yourself
Cay Garrett
1974; 160 pp.
$4.95 postpaid from:
The Handweaver Press
P.O. Box 1271
Sonoma, CA 95476
or Whole Earth Household Store

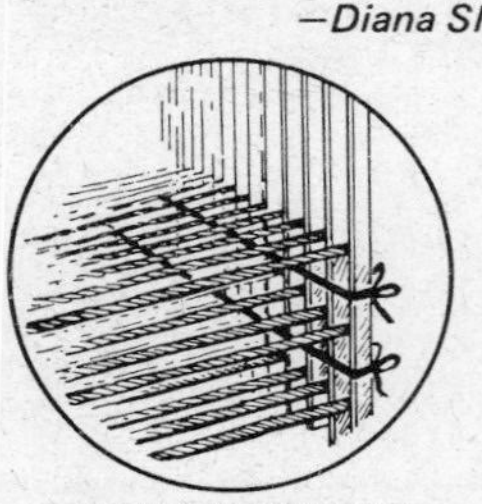

STRINGS SEPARATING THREE WARP ENDS PER DENT

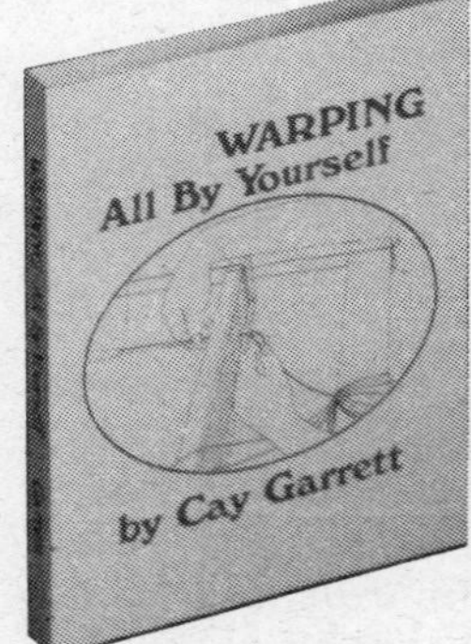

STRING SEPARATING TWO WARP ENDS PER DENT

Pull the knot on the loop that ties the cross and find the one and only warp end (see arrow) that does not have another end in front of it between the "V" of the loop knot, working from the loose play in front of the knot. Then *draw that end out* from the loop tie.

Building the Oregon Loom

David Mathieson has designed his loom and written for the builder with little or no woodworking experience, few tools, and no access to power tools. His loom, of Douglas Fir, is a four harness counterbalance that weaves up to 45" of material. It's good looking and ought to be sturdy. —Norman Potter

Building the Oregon Loom
David Mathieson
1973, 1977; 158 pp.

$4.95 postpaid from:
Serenity Weavers
111 West 7th
Eugene, OR 97401

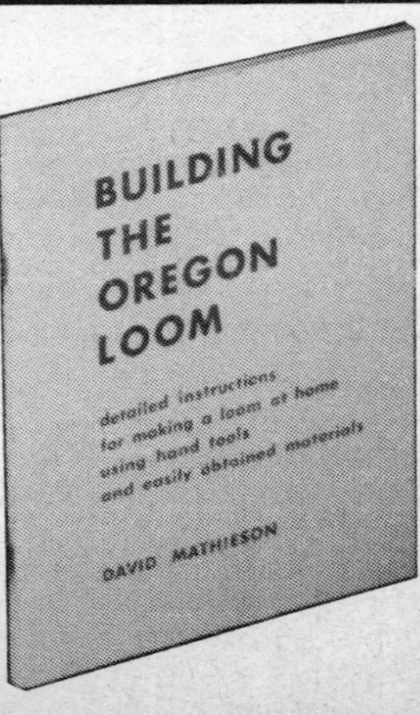

BUILDING THE OREGON LOOM
detailed instructions for making a loom at home using hand tools and easily obtained materials
DAVID MATHIESON

Wholesale-by-Mail Yarn

by Roberta Magid

I have a yarn shop that I am currently closing up. One of the many reasons I am closing my business is that I found out that many of the places I get my yarn from (my wholesalers) can be bypassed and ANYONE (you don't have to be a retailer) can buy yarn cheaper from the mills. Sometimes the retail mill price is below my wholesaler's price! What it amounts to is there is often one price to retailer/wholesaler and the sources are somewhat obscure. The larger yarn distributors are banking on the fact that many people don't investigate sources, and even if they do, it's sometimes difficult to tell what the yarns are really like from the small sample snips. As I found this out I got a sort of sick feeling and didn't feel justified selling the stuff for twice the price anyone could get it for without me. I guess I'm not cut out to be a capitalist.

Here are some sources.

Rammagerdin h.f.
P.O. Box 751
Hafnarstraeti 19
Reykjavik 121 Iceland

This is where Lopi comes from. If you are willing to wait a few weeks it is ½ the price of Reynolds Lopi. Free samples. (Knitting and weaving yarn)

J & H Clasgens Co.
New Richmond,
OH 45157

Good source for worsted wool knitting yarns (and other weights, too) needlepoint yarns. Better prices for bulk orders.

William Condon & Sons, Ltd.
P.O. Box 129
Charlottetown, PEI
Canada C1A, 7K3

This is another source of high quality beautiful wool yarns at cheap, cheap prices. Probably any mill you could find in Canada would be reasonably priced (½ American retail price and the yarns have a lot more character. U.S. yarns are for the most part sort of blah in comparison to the Canadian yarns. Free samples. (Knitting and weaving yarns)

Briggs and Little Woolen Mills
York Mills, Harvey Station
New Brunswick
Canada EOH 1HO

This yarn is marketed under the name Candide by an American distributor for more than double the mill's retail price. Briggs and Little will send free samples and pay postage on retail orders over 5 lbs. Their 2/12 leather knitting wools are my favorite yarn and some of the nicest I've ever seen and worked with at low prices. (They have weaving yarn, too.)

PASA Yarns
P.O. Box 279
Uxbridge, MA 01569

This place is wholesale only, so you could ask a local shop about their stuff. Mostly weaving yarn, some knitting yarn. They had an 8 ply worsted (8/8) cotton that would retail $4 - $5/lb. The same yarn with different dyes is sold by 2 import companies for knitting (Takhi and Pingouin) for about $2.35/50 gram ball — 4 times the price. (That's a $7 sweater vs. a $24 sweater!) It's just a matter of recognizing the stuff! Samples to wholesale accounts only.

Wood Forms
Foster Hill Road
Henniker, NH 03242

A source for beautiful exotic wood buttons — the perfect finishing touch for a hand-made garment. Retail or wholesale for larger quantities.

Ironstone Warehouse
P.O. Box 196
Uxbridge, MA 01569

A $100 minimum 1st order (any quantity afterwards) for cheap prices on rug wools, novelties, cottons mostly for weaving. Their mohair is the same yarn that is balled by yarn companies to knit with at about three times the price. Even if you buy mohair on the cone from a retailer at $25 - $30/lb. it's still about ½ price of the preballed yarn and it's the same thing. Free samples.

Wondercraft
1 Constitution Street
Bristol, RI 02809

Good prices on yarns for weaving — cottons, rug wools, and synthetics. Prices vary with quantity — but even smaller quantities are very reasonable. Quality is varied. Free samples.

Dk. Sheep
Med. Sheep
Lt. Sheep
Natural
ROVINGS (pencil)

Bartlett Yarns
Harmony, ME 04942

This is a wholesale/retail wool mill with good prices. Nice wools for knitting and weaving. Custom spinning for those with sheep who want yarn from their fleece. Free samples.

Daft Dames Handcrafts
13384 Hain Road, Rt. 5
Akron, NY 14001

These women are retail and wholesale. Their retail prices are fantastic. The pearl cotton they supply retails for less than Lily's wholesale price and the quality is the same. Mostly weaving yarns/supplies, an incredible variety and quality varies. Samples $.50. (Tell them what you're interested in.)

PRIMITIVE (Navajo Style)
560 yards per 1 lb. cone

Medium Green R-83
Dark Green R-84
Nile Green R-85
Sheeps Grey R-86
Charcoal R-87
Oxford R-88
R-89
Red Mix R-90
Blue Mix R-91
Green Mix R-92
Multi-Mix R-93

—Bartlett yarns

Oriental Rug Co.
214 S. Central Avenue
P.O. Box 917
Lima, OH 45802

Great source for carpet warp. One price to all and they are quick and pay postage. Other weaving supplies too. Free samples.

There are more sources. A good place to look is the supply section of a weaving book. An excellent "supplier's directory" is put out by the Handweavers Guild of America, 65 La Salle Road, P.O. Box 7 - 374, West Hartford, CT 06107. Free to members who pay dues, $4.50 to non-members. ■

Paula Simmons natural yarns

Yarn like this really makes it worth one's while to weave or knit. Undyed, unbleached yarns that come in many shades and mixtures of cream, red, brown, grey and black — the Simmons sheep grow that way. The yarns are in many thicknesses so you can make a bear sweater or a delicate baby garment. Mrs. Simmons also weaves from her yarn and sells the product as well as giving you advice on knitting or weaving with it yourself.

Will's brown sweater is super warm, soft, nearly waterproof and BEAUTIFUL. —Janet Bloch

Besides selling fine yarn, Paula Simmons is a considerable author — **Spinning and Weaving with Wool** *(our p. 280);* **Handspinner's Guide to Selling** *(our p. 280);* **My Secret Cookbook**; **The Zucchini Cookbook**; *and* **Raising Sheep the Modern Way** *(our p. 113).* —SB

Yarns
(13 colors)
$1.35/oz.

Yarn samples
$1 postpaid

both from:
Ross & Paula Simmons
Box 12
Suquamish, WA 98392

Natural color yarns

Paula Simmons and her favorite sheep, "Mary"

Cheryl Kolander silk

Source of silk of all descriptions. The best new source of anything I've found in recent years. Truly incredible selection. —Sarah Hammond

Speaking of incredible, check out Cheryl Kolander's **A Silkworker's Notebook**. *The full story — from legend to technique to suppliers — printed on hand-laid paper with tipped-in silk fabric samples throughout. Classy.* —SB

Silk yarn samples
$5 postpaid

A Silkworker's Notebook
Cheryl Kolander
1979, 120 pp.
$50 postpaid

both from:
Cheryl Kolander
276 North Myrtle
Myrtle Creek, OR 97457

•

What are the qualities of silk that make it so esteemed? Paramount is its beauty: the natural beauty of the fibre, and the extraordinary colours it takes. Not only is it beautiful, it's also useful: silk makes the most comfortable clothes, and silk, while seemingly delicate, is actually one of the strongest, toughest fibres. And, too, silk is not the most abundant of stuffs. It takes proverbial effort and care to produce, process and weave it.

Silk is the most lustrous of the natural fibres. This lustre is probably its most well known attribute. The lustre comes from the way silk is formed. It is spun by the silk caterpillar as a semi-liquid, continuous filament that hardens on contact with air. The smooth surface of the silk fibre reflects light, and the reflected light is seen as lustre.

Knotted, naturally dyed silk cord: CLOUD PATTERNS by Diane Itter

Lacis

"We are the only shop specializing in lace and lace-making with materials and supplies for bobbin, needle and Battenberg lace, tatting, filet and Irish crochet. Our bobbin lace kit for the beginner is $8.50. Also specialized tools for Kumi Himo (Japanese braiding) and weaving." —Lacis
[Suggested by Jeanie Darlington]

Lacis
Catalog
$.50 from:
Lacis
2990 Adeline Street
Berkeley, CA 94703

Bobbin lace kit

THE RISING SUN
NEIGHBORHOOD NEWSLETTER

Kathy and I were talking to two guys who liked boats a lot and saying we thought they should be more interested in the stuff that was under the water. They didn't so much disagree with us as not understand what we were talking about. Kathy decided they had to repress the fact that there was stuff below the surface because they were afraid of how deep it was.

That reminded me of when we went on the whale watch trip and when Andrea went all white and wide eyed when we left the Bay and after a few minutes I realized it wasn't nausea but fear of heights. Stewart told me that his new boat has a window in the bottom and any boat could but very few do. You can't even see as far as the rudder in the Bay, but out on the ocean you can sometimes see dolphins dancing eighty feet down.

Handspinner's Handbook

Superb wheel-spinning instruction — she gives the kind of information usually left out of "how-to" books. Not only does she tell you the principles involved, but how it looks and feels when it's right or wrong, and how to correct it. It's like having a personal lesson from Bette Hochberg herself.

The "long draw," the fastest, most efficient and consistent method of spinning is covered in depth, as is how to condition and adjust a wheel, and how to prepare and spin some 20 different natural fibers, animal and vegetable.
—Diana Sloat

Handspinner's Handbook
Bette Hochberg
1976; 66 pp.

$6.50 postpaid from:
Straw Into Gold
5533 College Avenue
Oakland, CA 94618

•

THE DRAWING-OUT TRIANGLE. You must learn to observe what happens in the area where the fibres are being drawn out of the mass, and being twisted. This area usually assumes a somewhat triangular shape. The triangle must be long enough to allow the individual fibres to slide freely past each other as they are being drawn into the twist. So the length of the triangle will change from one fibre to another.

The number of fibres that are in the triangle at any moment determines the thickness of that portion of yarn.

Keep your eyes always on the drawing-out triangle as you spin:

If the twist runs up too far and the triangle becomes shorter than the length of the staple of fibre, you won't be able to continue drawing back the mass of unspun fibre.

If you draw the triangle out longer than the length of the staple, the yarn will get thin and drift apart or break.

If suddenly there are too many fibres in the triangle they will form a lump.

If suddenly too few fibres are in the triangle, that portion will become thin.

When you understand this, you will find it really very easy to spin anything. There are no "difficult fibres" — only inadequate understanding of them.

When you spin a short to medium staple fibre carded into a rolag, hold it firmly but don't clutch. Let the wheel draw the fibres from the end of the rolag.

To spin a loose mass of short-staple fibre like cotton or cashmere, hold it loosely cradled in your hand. Let the tug of the wheel pull the fibres from under your thumb. The drawing-out triangle will be very short.

When spinning a short staple roving like cotton or ramie, hold it lightly between your thumb and forefinger. Hold just enough so the wheel doesn't pull it out of your hand. The drawing-out triangle often is not visible.

With long-staple roving fold a length about six to eight inches long over your right forefinger. (Lay starting cord in center of fold and pinch until twist catches.) Keep forefinger in center of fold and the fibres will be drawn off the end of it like a funnel. The drawing-out triangle will be long.

Your Handspinning

Still the classic on flax handspinning.

The book commences with a discussion of wool and sheep, then come chapters devoted to sorting a fleece, learning to make a continuous yarn and the art of carding and spinning wool. There is an excellent section on the construction, use and maintenance of spinning wheels and hints on buying a wheel. There is information on the cultivation and preparation of flax, and the spinning of fibers such as silk, angora rabbit, camel and other animal hairs. There is a chapter on plying and the making of fancy yarns and a section devoted to the preparation of spun yarns for use — washing, bleaching, etc. The book concludes with a chapter on machine spun yarns: counts/ qualities and defects/fiber identification. —SB
[Suggested by Victoria Becker]

Your Handspinning
Elsie Davenport
1953, 1964; 130 pp.

$5 postpaid from:
Select Books
P.O. Box 5145
Ojai, CA 93023
or Whole Earth
Household Store

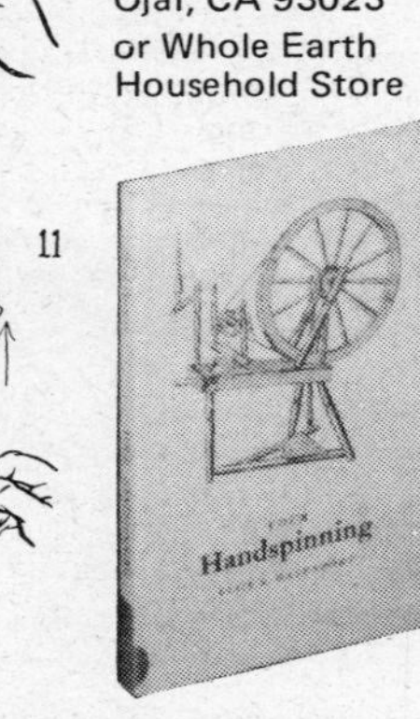

•

Linen yarn is spun from the long inner fibres of the flax plant which remain when the outer straw and the inside pith have been rotted away. It has been used from very early times — evidence of flax has been found in several excavations of pre-historic sites, and fragments of linen cloth from Egyptian tombs testify to the amazing skill with which the cultivation, preparation and spinning was done as early as 2000 B.C. Flax is frequently mentioned in the Old Testament, and conditions in some areas of the Middle East — in the Nile valley in particular — were undoubtedly favourable to the growing and dressing of the very fine flax which must have been used for some of the surviving fragments of linen.

Spinning and Weaving with Wool

Unique book — obviously, how to card and spin, with photographs, specifications and access on a wide variety of available wheels (no pros and cons), but best of all, plans for building your own rough but inexpensive handcarder, drum carder, handcranked table spindle wheel, bicycle wheel mounted on a sawhorse base, counterbalanced loom (well-designed), warping reel, and umbrella swift. And in case that's not enough, an excellent source list.
—Diana Sloat

Spinning and Weaving with Wool
Paula Simmons
1977; 221 pp.

$12.95 postpaid from:
Pacific Search Press
222 Dexter Avenue North
Seattle, WA 98109
or Whole Earth
Household Store

↑
Another possibility for a homemade spinning device is one in which you use a bicycle wheel for the drive wheel. Although it is shown here with a double belt propelling a flyer and bobbin, it is even simpler to make if it turns a spindle because it then needs only a single belt. With flyer and double belt, keep in mind that the spinning fork (with hooks for yarn guides) is fixed to the spindle shaft and that the bobbin must turn freely on that shaft. The bobbin pulley groove must be smaller than the flyer pulley groove. About a 2:1 pulley ratio for finer yarn.

Handspinner's Guide to Selling

Extremely thorough, authoritative book. Information on everything from woolwashing tubs, drying racks, "cradle" or "corsican" wool picker (with plans for same) to the how-to's of pricing, selling, mail order, and advertising. Indispensable. —Diana Sloat

Handspinner's Guide to Selling
Paula Simmons
1979; 110 pp.

$8.95 postpaid from:
Pacific Search Press
222 Dexter Avenue North
Seattle, WA 98109
or Whole Earth
Household Store

•

The "cradle" wool picker does a faster and more uniform teasing of wool than if it were done "by hand." In building the picker from these plans, hardwood is preferable, but high quality softwood could be used for all except the cards, which will hold the picker teeth. There may be considerable stress on these cards during the teeth-bending process, and the grain of a tough hardwood will resist splitting. This picker weighs about thirty pounds and is portable.

The top card frame picks up wool from the front bin and the teeth propel the wool from front to rear, where it drops out. You should have a box or basket there to catch the picked wool as it emerges. ↓

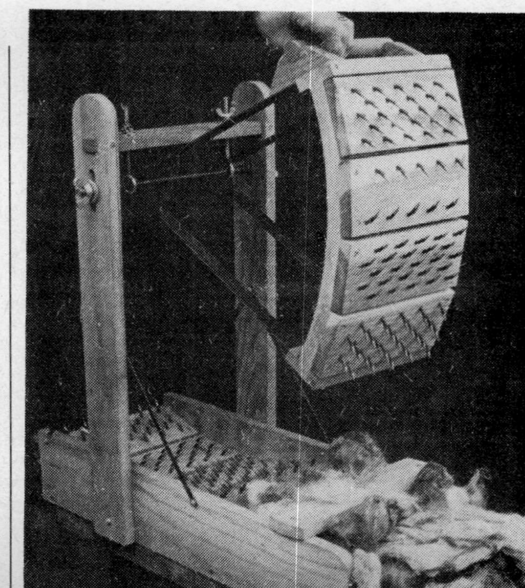

Handspindles

So-called "primitive" people have developed very fast and efficient methods of hand spinning with the simplest equipment. This is the best, most thorough (and only) book on the types, history, and use of handspindles in different cultures. Also for teaching yourself to use drop spindles of different kinds, supported spindles, and a distaff! You'll find the same precision and clarity as her wheel-spinning instructions in **Handspinner's Handbook**. *The section on preparation of natural fibers for spinning overlaps with it, so buying two books isn't necessary if your're starting out.* —Diana Sloat

← **The simplest form of distaff is a forked stick with one or more smaller branches growing from it. A mass of short uncombed fibres can be nestled into the branch, as in a basket, or combed fibres can be wrapped around the branches. This style is excellent for short staple wool, uncombed cotton or linen tow.**

Handspindles
Bette Hochberg
1977; 73 pp.

$7.45 postpaid from:
Straw Into Gold
5533 College Avenue
Oakland, CA 94618

Using a drop spindle
↓

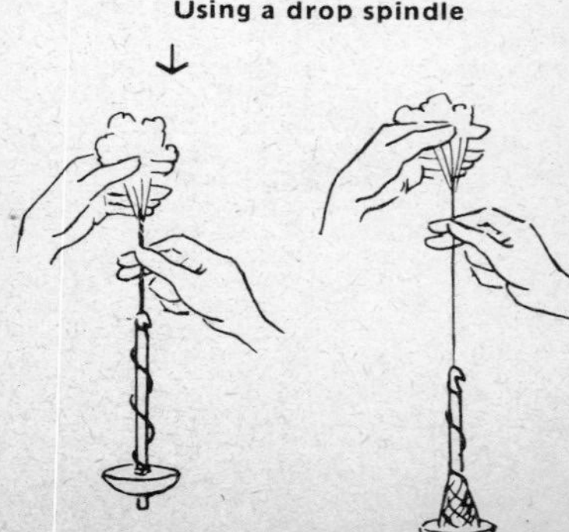

earing
piece

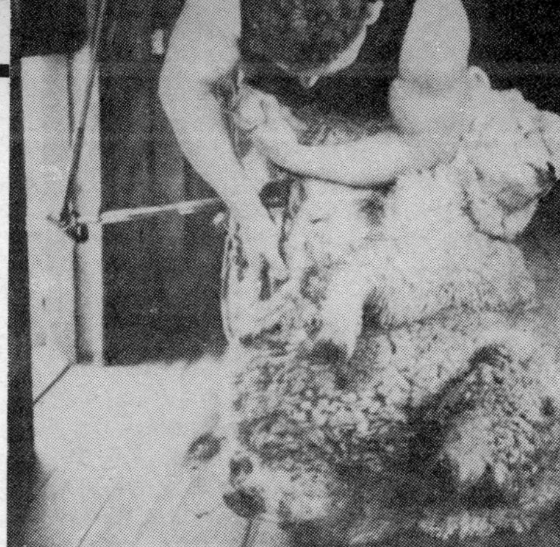

The start of the belly. ↑

Wool Away

The book for the inexperienced (not the unexperienced) as well as the accomplished sheep shearer. Godfrey Bowen, a world renowned shearer, goes into depth in his coverage of the shearing of sheep. He has a "blow-by-blow" account of shearing a sheep complete with photographs of each step, discusses shearing gear in terms of the proper use and care of the equipment, gives a good discussion on the breeds of sheep, and he even talks of the correct diet and dress of the sheep shearer. He then takes the reader into a totally new world of sheep shearing competitions. There is a bit of a problem with many colloquial terms, but Bowen realizes this and has provided the reader with a glossary. All in all, truly the book for those really into sheep. —Carol Mortensen

Wool Away
(The Art and Technique of Shearing)
Godfrey Bowen
1974; 192 pp.

$4.95 postpaid from:
Van Nostrand Reinhold Co.
Order Department
7625 Empire Drive
Florence, KY 41042
or Whole Earth Household Store

•

A good shearer can be likened to a good billiards player — he won't make one shot unless the next one is waiting. Have your sheep moving into position the whole time. This is especially important in machine shearing, as position and the lie of the sheep is everything. In controlling sheep watch balance. Sheep and shearer between them make up approximately three hundred pounds weight. They are either on balance or off. Keep the legs apart, get down over your sheep, becoming almost part of it, and handle it with body co-ordination resembling a graceful slow waltzing movement. It will take young shearers years to get this but it is the goal to aim at.

Fleece in Your Hands

A classic, back in print. For years it was a xeroxed "hand-to-hand" among spinners. Describes general wool characteristics of a sheepbreed and its texture, gives tips for spinning it, and then sets out instructions for a project (knitted, woven, crocheted, etc.) appropriate to that fleece. Timeless and invaluable — even the projects are superb. I wish it had reached my hands, not just my ears, years sooner. —Diana Sloat

Fleece in Your Hands
(Spinning with a purpose: Notes and Projects)
Beverly Horne
1979; 69 pp.

$5.95 postpaid from:
Interweave Press, Inc.
306 North Washington St.
Loveland, CO 80537

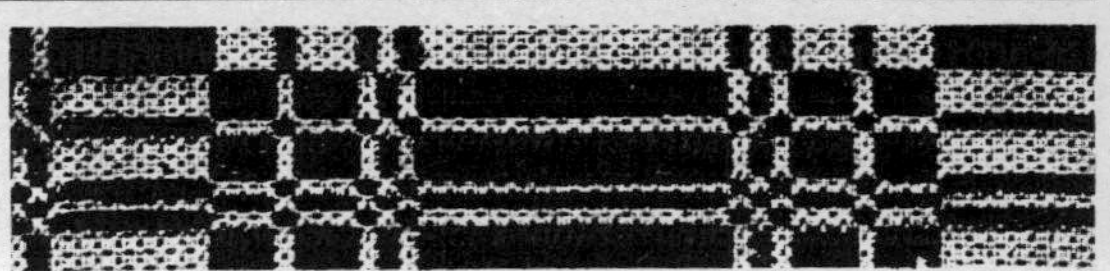

•

Romney. The Romney was brought to New Zealand in 1853 from the south of England and quickly established itself under New Zealand conditions to become the most predominant breed of sheep and probably the most familiar and popular breed for spinners. It produces a heavy quality fleece but many spinners do not realize the many possibilities of this breed and the count range it covers. It is the most versatile available to spinners . . .

Recommended Uses. A good, general purpose wool for children's to high-fashion garments. One of the most versatile New Zealand breeds. Has a nice lustre, washes and wears well. Can be spun into many types of yarns: thick or thin, novelty yarns, warp yarns, worsted yarns or woolen yarns. A weight loss after washing 10% and a take-up of only 3/4 - 1" per yard, makes this a good wool for weaving. It dyes well without uncontrolled matting.

British Sheep Breeds

Fleece from different breeds differs widely in qualities of the fiber, in how it feels, works up, and how it can be used. For me, the breeds would be a jumble of random names without this book and its samples. Now when a catalog arrives I read the description, "fine Romney top," look at the sheep portrait, feel the sample, dream a little, plan the project and then order. It's particularly important now that most of us live a continent or two away from the source of the fibers we spin.

The British Wool Marketing Board will sell you on the utility, diversity, and romance of wool in delightfully glossy language and paper. They've been spinning, weaving, knitting and crocheting with wool for a long time. —Diana Sloat

British Sheep Breeds
The British Wool Marketing Board
1976; 80 pp.

$7.40 postpaid from:
Handcraft Wools, Ltd.
Box 378
Streetsville, Ontario
Canada L5M 2B9

Fleece samples
write to inquire price from:
British Wool Marketing Board
Kew Bridge House
Kew Bridge Road
Brentford, Middlesex
England TW8 OEL

↑
Sheep have been a familiar sight on Romney Marsh since the thirteenth century or earlier. The bleak climate of the area and the perennial rye grass and wild white clover pastures have no doubt combined to develop the tough constitution of the Romney breed as we know it today. They are big, sturdy, fine-looking animals, with unusually hard hooves which enable them to resist foot rot and survive successfully in marshy conditions. A further special characteristic is their habit of spreading out evenly over the available grazing area, and so making the best possible use of the pasture. The breed has also become established in many countries overseas, especially in New Zealand. Romney wool is denser and finer than that of other Birtish Longwool breeds, and it has a decided crimp. Demand for this wool is always high and it is used in the manufacture of a wide range of high quality products, including hosiery and hand-knitting wools, worsted cloth, woollen cloth, blankets, and carpets.

Feltmaking

"Fanciful and functional" — best description of this delightful book to carry one well past the stomping stage into art for the body or house. (You could make your own weatherstripping, but . . .) —Diana Sloat

Feltmaking
Beverly Gordon
1980; 152 pp.

$17.50 postpaid from:
Watson Guptill Publications
2160 Patterson Street
Cincinnati, OH 45214

•

Felt is a pressed, matted fabric formed by the interlocking of certain unspun fibers, most notably wool. No spinning, weaving, or knitting is involved. Rather, through a combination of heat, moisture, and pressure, each individual fiber becomes completely entangled with the other fibers around it. The tangled mass forms a natural, self-tightening, *felted* mat.

↓ **Laying the Batt. Lay the rolags or batts next to one another on a piece of nylon mosquito netting. They should overlap slightly at the edges. Lay the second layer of rolags so it is 90 degrees, or perpendicular, to the first layer. All subsequent layers should be put on in alternate directions: the third layer perpendicular to the second, and so on.**

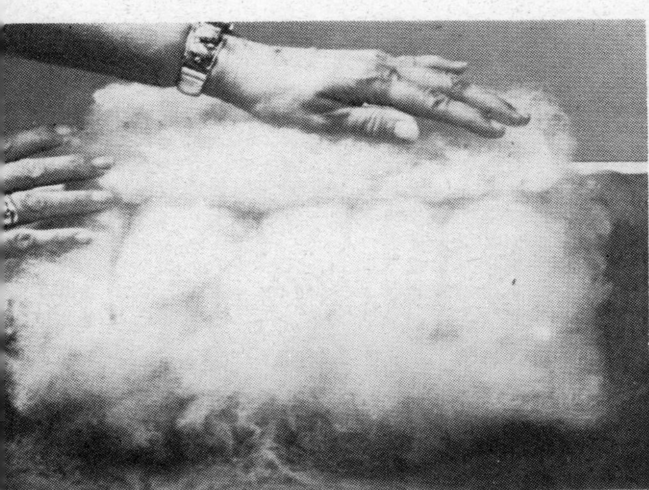

The Incredible Rope Machine

Why braid when you can twist? You can make a living with this little gadget — try rugs. This one works the best of those I've seen. —Diana Sloat

The Incredible Rope Machine

$15 postpaid from:
Schacht Spindle Company
2526 49th Street
P.O. Box 2157
Boulder, CO 80306

→
Cloverleaf Rope Rug by Gale Litvak

Handspinning Cotton

If you already spin, here's a very good "how-to" for preparing and spinning cotton, and (equally important) handling it after the spinning's done — sizing, dying, warping and weaving it. Plans for Harry Linder's simple, excellent Pakistani wheel are included. —Diana Sloat

Handspinning Cotton
Olive and Harry Linder
1977; 50 pp.

$6.25 postpaid from:
The Cotton Squares
1347 East San Miguel Ave.
Phoenix, AZ 85014

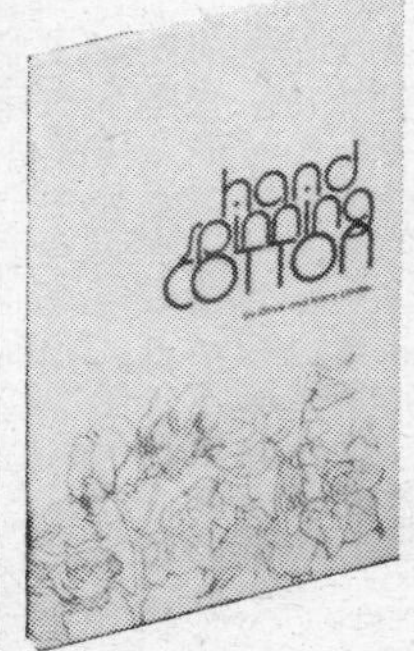

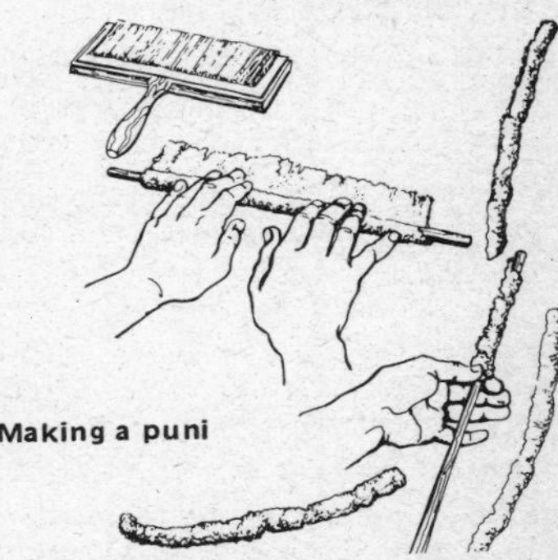

Making a puni

THE RISING SUN
NEIGHBORHOOD NEWSLETTER

The difference between spinning and weaving is you take a big bunch and turn it into a fine line, then you take a fine line and turn it into a big bunch. Spinning is the first and weaving is the second. —Kathleen

SPINNING WHEELS

Pennsylvania Dutch spinning wheel from plans.

Colonial spinning wheel from plans.

The Great Wheel

Back in print, revised, and inexpensive, in case Great Aunt Martha's wool wheel is decorating the family fireplace unused: introduction, technique, strengths and limitations of this beautiful and efficient tool.
—Diana Sloat

The Great Wheel
(Introduction and Technique)
Alden Amos
1977, 1980; 24 pp.

$4 (approx.)
Write for exact price from:
Straw Into Gold
5533 College Avenue
Oakland, CA 94618

Spindle head

Your imagination's the limit on bulk and novelty yarns with this attachment for Saxony wheels. Clamps on the wheel bed with a "C" clamp, allows you to make any size or texture yarn on your own wheel since you're no longer bound by size of orifice or hooks. You have both hands free to draw out and wind on as you treadle. It's also possible to convert it for a Nagy Castle wheel by drilling slots in the spindle head base identical to those on the base of the Nagy mother-of-all. Just bolt it on in place of the mother-of-all. Very simple, versatile gadget. Instructions included for mounting and spinning with it. Available in 4 different sizes. *—Diana Sloat*

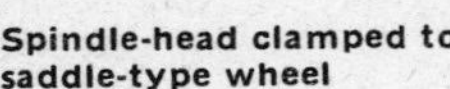

Spindle Head
$15 postpaid from:
Handcraft Wools Ltd.
Box 378
Streetsville, Ontario
Canada L5M 2B9

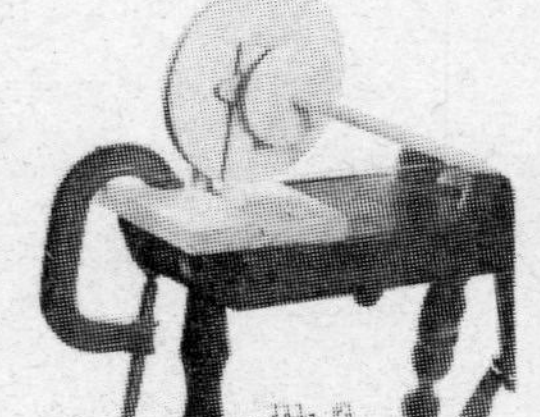

Spindle-head clamped to saddle-type wheel

Spinning wheel plans

All the considerations of buying a wheel, plus a lot of skill and access to a very complete woodshop equal challenge!

Here are two good sets of plans. They've been checked out by a professional wheel maker for workability of design, completeness of detail, etc., and will result in good-sized, functional wheels.

Colonial Spinning Wheel Plan

Pretty saxony, full-scale plans, several photos, fairly detailed instructions and diagrams, materials and parts list. Small orifice, bobbin and hooks.

Pennsylvania Dutch Spinning Wheel

Full scale plans for a walking wheel with spindle head. Photo shows head mounted incorrectly, but fairly detailed instructions and diagrams are correct. Materials and parts list included. Easiest to build. *—Diana Sloat*

Colonial Spinning Wheel Plan No. 379

Pennsylvania Dutch Spinning Wheel Plan No. 404

$2.20 each postpaid from:
Wildflower Fibres
205 Northwest
Second Street
Portland, OR 97209

Here's another source for plans. We have the drawings for the Welsh, Norwegian and English wheels; they look OK to good — very British and stuffy plans. They're listed in the Project Supply Catalog from Woodcraft (p. 143).
—Alden Amos

Quailcraft Spinning Wheel Plans
(English upright, No. 40B01-FJ; Norwegian double-table, No. 40B02-FJ; Welsh sloping, No. 40B03-FJ)

$10 each postpaid from:
Woodcraft Supply Co.
313 Montvale Avenue
Woburn, MA 01888

or

Information
£1 (about $2.30) from:
Quailcraft Products
Five Poplars
Pankridge Street
Crondall, Farnham,
Surrey, England

Amos handspindles

Alden Amos makes very efficient handspindles as well as wheels. The notched, slotted head at the top of the shaft allows the yarn to feed off from dead center giving a prolonged continuous spin. The bottom of the shaft is slim enough to stay put if you spin sitting and unwind the yarn holding the spindle upright on your thigh, and is notched for resting on a jeans watch pocket if you wind off standing up holding the spindle horizontally.

The beanpot spindles are made of exotic hardwoods for density and weight; the extra weight and design give a very fast spin for fine, hard-twisted yarns. The flat whorl spindles come in two weights — light to medium, and medium to heavy for spinning more conventional yarns, and are of various hardwoods with birch shafts. All have shaft and whorl lathe-turned as a unit for perfect balance.

These spindles rotate without a wobble if correctly used: wind yarn 3 - 4 turns up the shaft, under the notch and pull up through the slot. Do not loop yarn under the whorl.
—Diana Sloat

Amos Handspindles
Student spindles
$2 - $3 plus shipping
Flat-whorl spindles
$10 - $12 plus shipping

Beanpot and double-whorl spindles
$15 - $20 plus shipping
all from:
Straw Into Gold
5533 College Avenue
Oakland, CA 94618

Ashford Almanac

How to finish, assemble, troubleshoot and "fine-tune" your Ashford (or any) wheel. Indispensable for good performance and good spinning! *—Diana Sloat*

Ashford Almanac
Alden Amos
1980; 102 pp.

$12 (approx.)
Write for price from:
Straw Into Gold
5533 College Avenue
Oakland, CA 94618

Choosing a spinning wheel

A wheel, as any other fine tool, is a very personal thing. Which one to buy depends on a number of things: the kind of spinning you want to do, the variety of fibers you want to spin, quantity of output, size, portability, esthetics, etc.

Here are a few tips on wheels in general:

- *A double drive band wheel is good for learning because the ratio of flyer to bobbin revolution is fixed. By turning a single screw you adjust tension (speed of takeup) by adjusting the distance of the bobbin and flyer assembly from the wheel — a whole lot easier when hands and feet are trying to co-ordinate their action!*
- *A single drive band wheel with a brake on bobbin or flyer (often called "scotch tension") allows fine adjustment of the ratio of bobbin to flyer revolution. You can "slow" the bobbin or flyer revolution to nearly zero for spinning very short staple fibres like cotton, that require lots of twist. Or you can "speed" it up to nearly equal the other for a very fast takeup with little twist for spinning flax. So, you have to adjust two things, the distance of your whole bobbin-flyer assembly from the wheel and the amount of braking action you want. More versatile system but more complex to learn.*
- *With the double drive band you adjust yourself to the wheel and fiber; with the scotch tension you adjust the wheel. So it's up to you — feelings run high in both camps.*

About size and portability, the castles are smaller, have the bobbin and flyer assembly mounted above the wheel, and ride well seat-belted in the car. The saxonys are larger, less portable, but faster. The tradeoff is in diameter and weight of the wheel — the large wheels produce more bobbin and flyer RPMs per treadling effort, hence more speed. Without some initial skill they can also be more difficult for a beginner to control.

Here are the wheels and their strong points; they're each quite different in feel and function:

The Clemes *(double drive band) is an excellent slow castle wheel for beginners. It's compact, beautifully finished, good for fine to medium weight yarns, small apartments and portability. Its action is excellent; the 16" wheel is heavy enough to balance the large (3/8") orifice, hooks and capacious bobbins. Easy to learn on and an excellent buy!*

The Paragon *is a very pretty oil-finished oak horizontal wheel. The wheel is 20" on a ball-bearing axle with a double drive band. It's not so portable nor polished in finish as the Clemes, but has very smooth treadling and bobbin action. Price is steep but it's the only medium-range wheel (not for beginners but not as advanced as the Amos Saxony) that can handle short staple fibers like cotton. A good wheel.*

The Woolspin *(single drive band) is the most versatile of the castles, taller, smoother action, more beautifully finished than the others. It was originally known as the Nagy wheel. Made of Kauri wood, mahogany-stained or walnut-stained and superbly finished, it spins medium to fine yarns.*

The Amos *is a very large, plain, extremely fast Canadian saxony wheel of oak. Technical details: wheel 27" x 2", orifice ½", bobbins 4" x 6", 2-speed whorl, single drive band. This is no dainty fireside piece; it's a powerful workhorse for production spinning. Unique, versatile, and downright exciting to spin on! He also makes a large 18" castle wheel. Currently there is a 2 - 3 year wait for them.*

Alden Amos has also developed other innovations: 1. A "level-winder" for the Ashford and other wheels, which eliminates the "hook-feed" system on the flyer. Very fast, it allows a continuous winding of yarn onto the bobbin without stopping to change hooks. Yarn placement is adjusted with a tap of the finger. The only complaint has been eventual spinner arm fatigue from the continuous draw! 2. A handsome oak "banjo spinner" for cotton, similar to the charka. 3. Wheel conversions to electric, for those thoroughly into production.

The Indian Valley Spinner *(single drive band) is the most handsome and best of the bulk spinners — great for plying rope and spinning heavy yarns. Walnut frame handrubbed with cast-iron wheel heavy enough to draw on any weight yarn that'll go through orifice and hooks. Single drive band with scotch tension. Bobbin holds 2 lbs. wool yarn in the grease. Its action is a bit rough for long periods of spinning.*

The spinner heads can be bought separately for mounting on a treadle sewing machine base — cheaper, but somewhat awkward since the orifice is mounted at right angles to the treadle.

The Ashford Kit Wheel *(single drive band) is your best buy as a beginning wheel. They improved their basic kit wheel (already good) recently, and implemented the suggestions of a master wheel maker: the flyer is better balanced, it has nylon bushings, a solid crank, improved treadling system and a built-in speed kit. It's a much faster, more versatile wheel and costs barely over $100, with only small increments in price planned. Similar improvements have been made on their Treadle Mark II castle wheel that, with newly increased wheel diameter (18"), make it a good fast inexpensive castle wheel that will spin short-staple fibers, like cotton.* *—Diana Sloat*

Clemes Castle Wheel
$235 plus shipping
Information
$1 from:
Clemes and Clemes
Spinning Wheels
650 San Pablo Avenue
Pinole, CA 94564

Paragon Wheel
$350 plus shipping
Information
$1 from:
Paragon Wheels
2309 Laguna Road
Santa Rosa, CA 95401

Woolspin Wheels
$325 (approx.)
Information — Send 3 International Reply Coupons (about $1.25) — from:
Woolspin Industries Ltd.
107 Daniell Street
P.O. Box 9637
Wellington, New Zealand

Amos Spinning Wheels
Canadian Saxony Wheels
$400 - $600 plus shipping
Castle Wheels
$300 (approx.) plus shipping
Level-Winder (includes tune-up)
$100 (approx.) plus shipping

Banjo-spinner
$200 (approx.) plus shipping
Information (write detailing your specific needs)
$1 from:
Alden Amos
Straw Into Gold
5533 College Ave.
Oakland, CA 94618

Indian Valley Spinner
$195 plus shipping
Spinner head
$78 plus shipping
Information
$1 from:
Thomas and Dorothy Ricci
Route 2, Box 17
Bradfordsville, KY 40009

Ashford Spinning Wheels
$100 - $200 (approx.)
Information
$1 from:
Ashford Handicrafts Ltd.
P.O. Box 180
Ashburton, New Zealand
or
Straw Into Gold (p. 276)
5533 College Avenue
Oakland, CA 94618

WHO WAS THAT MASKED RAM? I WANTED TO THANK HIM.

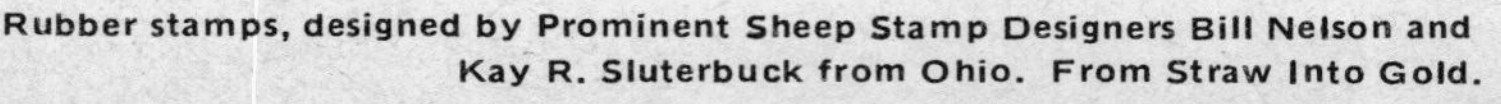

Rubber stamps, designed by Prominent Sheep Stamp Designers Bill Nelson and Kay R. Sluterbuck from Ohio. From Straw Into Gold.

One Pot Dye and Mordant Method

ction	Ingredients	Time
Soak gether	plant, scoured textile, water — all together	Overnight
immer	All Together	15 Minutes
emove	Textile from Pot	Temporarily
dd	Mordant: Alum (A), Cream of Tartar (C of T)	
eturn	Textile to Pot	
immer	A, C of T — all together	30 Minutes
ool	All Together	Overnight
inse	Textile	
ry		

One pot dye and mordant method ↑

Nature's Colors

Most exciting natural dye book for the Westerner. Extensive coverage of all aspects of dyeing. Ms. Grae's free-wheeling experimental approach will lead you to anything as a dye source: trees, weeds, shrubs, and garden plants.

—Diana Sloat

Nature's Colors
(Dyes from Plants)
Ida Grae
1974, 1979; 229 pp.

$6.95 postpaid from:
Macmillan Publishing Co.
Order Department
Front and Brown Streets
Riverside, NJ 08075

Dyes from Natural Sources

An impressive little book by British craftswoman Anne Dyer; well designed and readable, it will not overwhelm the beginner with obscure technicalities in this inevitably unpredictable process. Every statement in the book is founded on the author's own testing, and an outstanding feature is the chapter on methods and techniques of testing. Other possibilities of dyeing from such diverse substances as anthracite soot from cooking range flues, sawdust, and steel filings are detailed.

Among listings of species are some native to New Zealand, Australia and the U.S., besides those of England.

A country woman who runs 200 acres of forest, Dyer advocates a respectfully conservationist attitude about the taking of wild plants. —J. Prestianni

Dyes from Natural Sources
Anne Dyer
1976; 86 pp.

$7.25 postpaid from:
Charles T. Branford
19 Calvin Road
P.O. Box 16
Watertown, MA 02172

•

One of the charms of vegetable dyes is the complete uncertainty of the results, not just year to year and country to country, but day to day and plant to plant. I was experimenting with hawthorn leaves one day and obtained orange from one bush and rust from the next, both apparently growing in identical conditions of light and soil, and both of the same variety. The only way to forecast results exactly would be to analyze the plants chemically, and, even if one had the skill, I think it would be quicker to do a test boiling.

•

Never, anywhere, consider picking anything that is not obviously plentiful; never pick more than a quarter of any group of plants, and try to make the picking as well spread out and inconspicuous as possible. And be sure that you are aware of local and national legislation on picking or digging up wild plants; your Local Government office or Conservation Trust branch can give you this information.

Mushrooms for Color

MUSHROOMS? Rich earthy colors. Why not for inks and textile printing as well as for yarns. (Must admit I haven't tried 'em yet, but I am intrigued!)

The book contains identification, mordanting, dyeing instructions, extensive table of species with colors obtained and tear-out cards for cataloging your own experiments. (Note: Author's instructions on handling poisonous mushrooms — "DON'T.") —Diana Sloat

Mushrooms for Color
Miriam C. Rice
and Dorothy Beebee
1980; 145 pp.

$8.43 postpaid from:
Mad River Press
Route 2, Box 151-B
Eureka, CA 95501

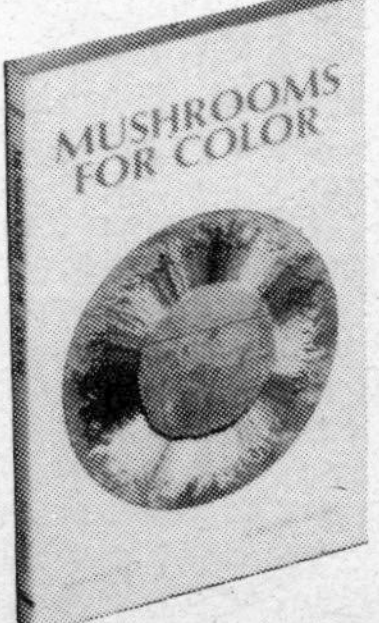

Dye plants and other useful herbs drying in a craftsman's attic.

Dye Plants and Dyeing

This book I consider about the best that is available on its subject and would make an excellent basic handbook for the beginner. It contains historical information as well as the basic steps to dyeing, recipes, and articles about dye plants from various regions and countries. So, no matter what part of the country you live in, you will find a variety of plants and recipes which you would be able to use. There is enough information in this book to enable you to start your own dyeing and end up with satisfactory results, which is not true of all natural dye books. The one difficulty in using it, however, is that there is no index. —Carole Beadle

Dye Plants and Dyeing
(A Handbook)
EthelJane McD. Schetky, Editor
1964; 100 pp.

$2.55 postpaid from:
Brooklyn Botanic Garden
1000 Washington Ave.
Brooklyn, NY 11225

or Whole Earth Household Store

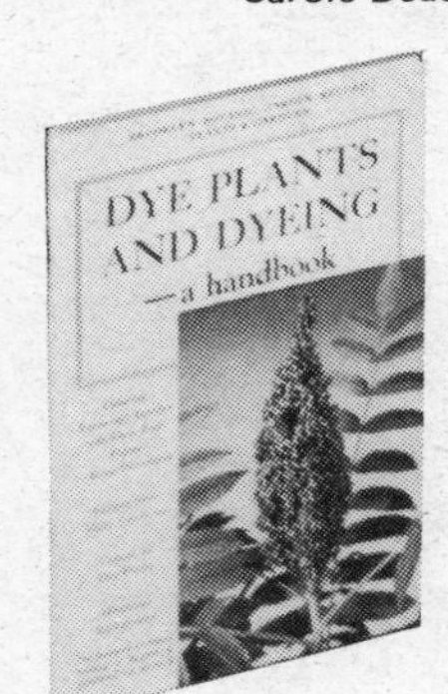

Natural Dyes and Home Dyeing

Wonderful for its wealth of historical information, more than 150 recipes with special attention given to color-fastness, and an excellent chart for top-dyeing. Includes recipe for iron buff dyeing. In one of the five interesting appendices, the dye materials listed by D'Ambourney read like poetry and send one off into the fields and forests with clippers and basket! —Sarah Kahn

Natural Dyes and Home Dyeing
(A Practical Guide with over 250 Recipes)
Rita J. Adrosko
1971; 154 pp.

$2 postpaid from:
Dover Publications, Inc.
180 Varick Street
New York, NY 10014
or Whole Earth Household Store

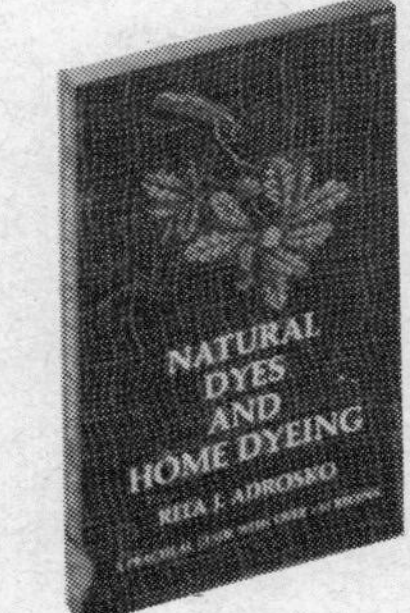

•

Vigogna, (colour of Vigogna wool.)

From the shoots of the Siberian acacia.
From the dry shoots of the elder.
From the leaves of artichoke.
From rest harrow, *Ononis arvensis.*
From wild angelica, *Angelica sylvestris.*
From tuberose crowfoot, *Ranunculus bulbosus.*
From common bladder sena, *Colutea arborescens.*
From flowers of balsamine.
From the water parsnip, *Sium latifolium.*
From *Gallium verum*, lady's bedstraw.
From the round leaved bell flower, *Campanula rotundifolia.*
From the sea holly with pinnated cut leaves, *Eryngium campestre.*
From the blue berried upright honeysuckle, *Lonicera caerulea.*
From the common hedge honeysuckle, *Lonicera periclimenum.*
From the pasque flower, *Anemone pulsatilla.*
From the seven leaved colutea, *Coronilla glauca.*
From the branches of the fig tree, *Ficus carica.*
From the rose flowering raspberry, *Rubus odoratus.*
From the barked wood of the common ash, *Fraximus excelsior.*
From the heart of the common broom, *Spartium scoparium.*
From the yellow everlasting pea, *Lathyrus aphaca.*
From the *Valantia aparine.*
From the thorny hedge gooseberry, *Uva crispa . . .*

Lichens for Vegetable Dyeing

Your own subtle, aromatic "Harris" tweed! E. Bolton's small, excellent handbook on lichen dyeing is in print again, now expanded to aid the U.S. dyer. For identification you'll find the most thorough descriptions of many species, their habitats and growth patterns, and several pages of color drawings. Good collecting, extracting and dyeing instructions, too. Because many species grow very slowly, 50 - 100 years to produce a palm-sized patch, collect with care, and with use in mind.

—Diana Sloat
[Suggested by Suzanne Lainson]

Lichens for Vegetable Dyeing
Eileen Bolton
1972; 63 pp.

$6.95 postpaid from:
Robin & Russ Handweavers
533 North Adams Street
McMinnville, OR 97128

Natural Plant Dyeing

Companion to Brooklyn Botanic Garden's earlier, indispensable handbook **Dye Plants & Dyeing** *this latest offering augments rather than supplants the first book, but makes one hope they'll continue to publish on this subject. (As I write, carrot tops simmer on the stove — somehow this hadn't occurred to me.) Rich in lore, the booklet is an anthology of excellent articles on collecting and storing, classroom dyeing with clear photos of each step (useful to a first-time dyer trying to learn from a book), preparation of fleece, a folk tale on Liberian indigo dyeing, lichens, regional information, the chemistry of dyeing, a list of dye plant suppliers. The recipe for Madder Root unfortunately omits the importance of temperature control for obtaining various reds. The center color spread shows lovely hues obtained from lichens, how different mordants bring diversity from the same dyebath, and an illustration of color-fastness tests. Indexed by dye-sources.* —Diana Sloat

Natural Plant Dyeing
(A Handbook)
Palmy Weigle, Editor
1973; 64 pp.

$2.55 postpaid from:
Brooklyn Botanic Garden
1000 Washington Avenue
Brooklyn, NY11225

or Whole Earth Household Store

THE RISING SUN
NEIGHBORHOOD NEWSLETTER

When I was in elementary school, I knew we were the first generation raised with The Bomb and we were supposed to worry about it a lot, but I hardly thought about it. Even though we were sold identification dog tags when we were in the second grade and even though we went to the school basement twice a year and squatted down with our heads between our knees and our hands over our heads and even though there was at least a movie a month on tv about the last two to five people on earth, being bombed was not something I worried about, and I worried a lot. I worried about wearing the right clothes (the ones that would make me not shy) and whether people liked me and would I get my school work done in time and before I went to sleep I thought about this housefire I'd heard about. The fire had started inside the walls of the house and the family had gone about its business all day and in the night when they were sleeping when the flames leaped out of the walls and burned them alive. It was an old house we lived in and you could hear it creaking all night long.

The Dyer's Art

Rich, eye-dazzling, and sensuous. It's for inspiration not technique. Ninety full-color plates of some of the world's finest examples of resist-dyeing — batik, tie-dye, and ikat — with descriptions of the techniques, some of the history of the work and the workers. —Diana Sloat

The Dyer's Art
(ikat, batik, plangi)
Jack Lenor Larsen, et al.
1976; 272 pp.
$37.50 postpaid from:
Van Nostrand
Reinhold Company
Order Department
7625 Empire Drive
Florence, KY 41042
or Whole Earth
Household Store

← Although limited to stripes of one type or another, bound resists are as effective as they are simple. The loosely constructed cloths are rolled into a rope and so firmly bound with cords as to resist dye during a prolonged dye-bath. The challenge is to obtain a thorough and even penetration deep into the center of the cloth. This Indian example is a turban cloth from Rajasthan. The very special checks are the result of multiple resists and dyeings in two directions. A variety of stripe widths adds to the interest.

↑ The arrowhead, one of the oldest and most universal of warp-ikat patterns, can be manipulated in many ways. In a detail from a Turkistan half-silk hanging, it is shown as a subsidiary form, multiplied to build up a larger floral motif which becomes the all-over pattern repeat. Here, the arrow is determined in the tieing. In most cases, the arrow is "pulled," that is, tied as a simple rectangle then adjusted or pulled at center to form an arrow shape.

↑ The dyers of the Ivory Coast take the free approach of smearing an entire cloth surface with rice paste, then scraping it with a comb in the manner of fingerpainting. Since even the scraped areas are partially covered, the blue color tends to be softly tone-on-tone.

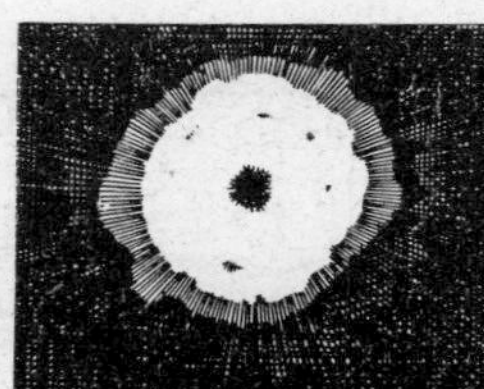

Plangi — Raising portions of an open cloth

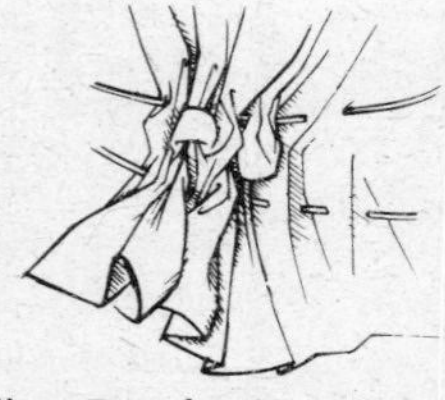

Tritik — Drawing thread through the fabric

Robin Grey's Batiker's Guide

Good practical studio workbook. Primarily a technical guide covering all phases of batik production with procion dyes. Does not attempt instruction in design of motifs, but has a substantial amount of information on color theory, color combinations, integrations, value and hue, etc. —J. Prestianni

Robin Grey's Batiker's Guide
(A Guide to Using Procion Fiber Reactive Dyes for Batik, Fabric Painting and Tie-Dye)
Robin Grey
1976; 76 pp.
$5.65 postpaid from:
Dharma Trading
Company Publications
P.O. Box 916
San Rafael, CA 94902
or Whole Earth
Household Store

Use rapid brush strokes so that wax doesn't penetrate all areas. This creates a feeling of movement.

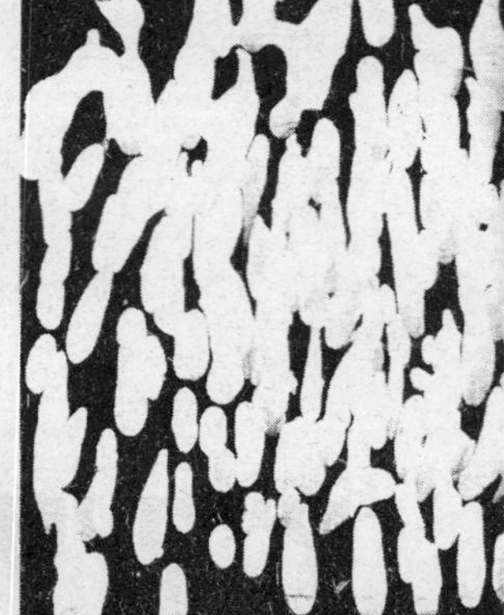

Dribble wax onto the fabric. Allow the wax to run by holding up the cloth while the wax is still liquid.

Contemporary Batik and Tie-Dye

If you like a book that can give you a feel for a whole range of ways to work with dyes on cloth, this is the one you should pick up. The pictures (alas that there aren't more in color) give you diverse and exciting examples of what you can make. The step-by-step illustrations throughout help to clarify procedures that words can't convey. For a newcomer to the art the major problem will be trying to pick out which techniques to try first. Along with an extensive glossary, bibliography, supply source list and index, this book becomes a real tool for the craftsperson. —Susan Mehra

Contemporary Batik and Tie-Dye
(Methods, Inspiration, Dyes)
Dona Z. Meilach
1972; 280 pp.
$6.95 postpaid from:
Crown Publishers
One Park Avenue South
New York, NY 10016
or Whole Earth
Household Store

Rewaxing and overdyeing — Now all unwaxed areas will have your first color. Put the fabric on the frame again. The second waxing will cover all areas that will remain pink. They appear dark here because of the translucence of the wax. Soaking and dyeing procedures are repeated for the second color, which is bright red. ↓

↓ **Sunflower — Sister Mary Remy Revor. A batik with very little crackle is created by applying dyes directly to the fabric rather than dipping waxed fabric into dye. Very controlled lines and shapes can be achieved by applying the wax with a tjanting tool originally used by the Javanese.**

Testfabrics, Inc.

Testfabrics, Inc. offers a very complete selection of hard-to-find white, scoured fabrics for dyeing, printing, painting, etc. The selection includes 100 percent cotton in an astonishing variety of weights and textures, silks, wools and synthetics. Prices vary according to type of fabric and how many yards you buy. A sample book of 4" x 6" swatches is available for $4.50 ($4 with order). —Marilyn Green

Testfabrics, Inc.
Price list
$.50 from:
Testfabrics, Inc.
P.O. Drawer O
200 Blackford Avenue
Middlesex, NJ 08846

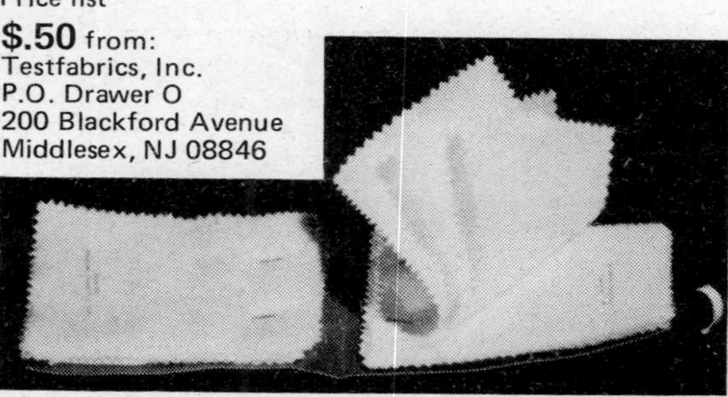

Batik Supplies

by Robin Grey

Sources — *There isn't space to list all the available mail order sources. Batik suppliers are continually changing. Therefore I suggest looking in craft magazines and newsletters for additional sources. I especially find* **The Surface Design Journal** *good for this.*

The Surface Design Journal
Stephen Blumrich, Editor
$20/year (4 issues)
includes membership
from:
Surface Design Assn.
Sonya Whiddon
North Texas
State University
P.O. Box 5098
Denton, TX 76203

Suppliers have price lists or catalogs and fabric samples, which they will send upon request. A source's willingness to give advice, its experience and quality supplies are more important than its prices.

Here are some sources that may sell any or all of the following: dye, fabrics, waxes, tools, chemicals and books.

The Batik Art Place, 530A Miller Avenue, Mill Valley, CA 94941. Price list free

Batik International, P.O. Box 4382, Medford, OR 97501. Information $1

Cerulean Blue, Ltd., P.O. Box 5126, Seattle WA 98105. Brochure $.50

D.Y.E. Textile Resources, 5629 West Adams Boulevard, Los Angeles, CA 90016. Price list $.50

Fabdec, 3553 Old Post Road, San Angelo, TX 76901. Information $1

Pro Chemical and Dye, Inc., Box 14, Somerset, MA 02726. Brochure $.50

Straw Into Gold, 5533 College Avenue, Oakland, CA 94618. $1 (See p. 276)

Keystone Ingham Company, P.O. Box 669, Artesia, CA 90701. Information $1

FABRICS ONLY

Horikoshi New York, Inc., 55 West 39th Street, New York, NY 10018. Information $1. Silk - bulk orders only. Test samples for batikable fabrics

Oriental Silks, 8377 Beverly Boulevard, Los Angeles, CA 90048. Silks only. Test samples for batikable fabrics. Information $1

Testfabrics Inc., P.O. Drawer O, Middlesex, NJ 08846. Information $.50.

Fabric Printing: Screen Method

Dynamite! Years of experience packed into this informative book. It strides through a vast amount of material easily and in the simplest language. Make your own screens and printing table, cut your own stencils, set up a darkroom and do your own photo stencils. It's all there: complete instructions with properties of fabrics, dyes, pigments, and other chemicals thoroughly and efficiently presented along the way. Extensive supplier's list included. Hurrah for authors, artist and publisher — for $3.95 it's a people's book and pretty, too! —Diana Sloat

Fabric Printing: Screen Method
Richard Valentino and Phyllis Mufson
1975; 49 pp.
$3.95 postpaid from:
Bay Books
1643 North Beverly Glen Boulevard
Bel Air, CA 90025
or Whole Earth Household Store

Put your design into a non-rectangular format. You are doing this because a design with a straight edge looks static to the eye when printed and also creates problems in printing, because it makes any flaw in registration more obvious. An irregular edge deceives the eye and creates the illusion of flow. Make sure the unit links from top to bottom and from side to side. One way to check that the linking is correct is to roll your drawing into a cylinder from top to bottom and from side to side.

Net Making

This is the only book I know of on net making. It includes instruction for making string bags (as an alternative to paper bags), fishing nets, hammocks, etc. I recently used the book to make several nets for pea and bean vines to climp up in my garden. Materials are cheap; basically, all you need is some twine and a few netting needles (which you can make yourself) and you can begin. —Marilyn Green

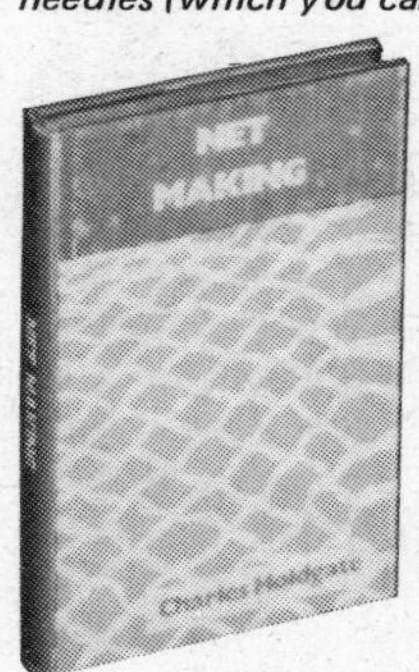

Net Making
Charles Holdgate
1970; 136 pp.
$7.95 postpaid from:
Emerson Books
Reynolds Lane
Buchanan, NY 10511

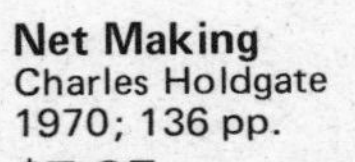

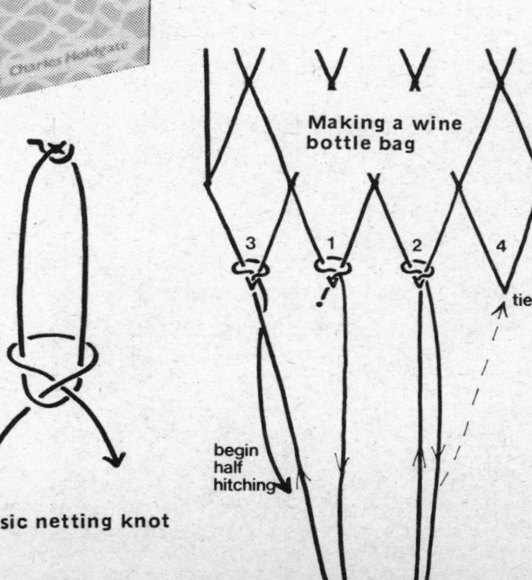

The basic netting knot

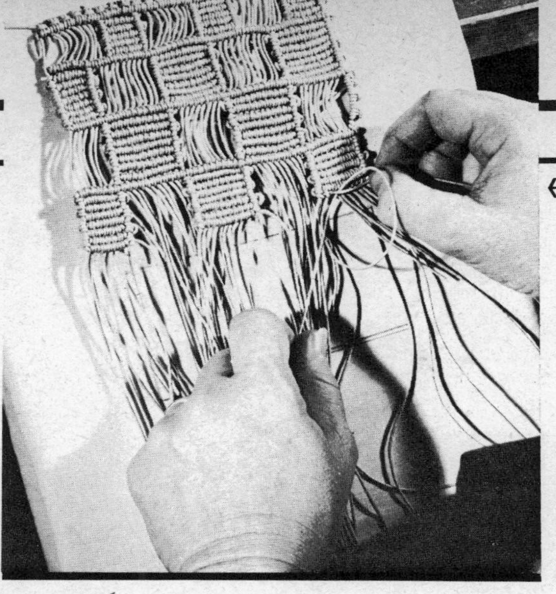

Macramé

Although designs for knotted pieces differ according to locale and use, there are very few individual knots. Virginia I. Harvey has collected photographs of traditional knotted pieces throughout the world and presents them in **Macramé: The Art of Creative Knotting**. *She carefully diagrams the half-knot, square knot, double half-hitch, diagonal double half-hitch, vertical double half-hitch and other knots. The basic knots are described in detailed instructions for making a sampler. Following the pattern for the sampler will give the beginner experience in doing the knots, and show how combining just a few types of knots can offer large pattern variation.*

This book is the best reference manual of knotting technique available. It offers information on all facets of macramé, including discussion on planning, mounting, shaping and finishing a knotting project. Tools and materials are displayed. There are photos exhibiting how different fibers worked in the same pattern can vastly alter visual and textural effects. The pictorial history of macramé and examples of contemporary knotting projects offer plenty of design ideas for the more advanced macramé craftsperson. —Sue Boyle
[Suggested by Alexandra Jacopetti]

← **A piece of stiff cardboard padded with polyurethane foam and covered with cotton sheeting is used as a base. The lines marked on the surface of the covering are a guide to keep the work square and straight.**

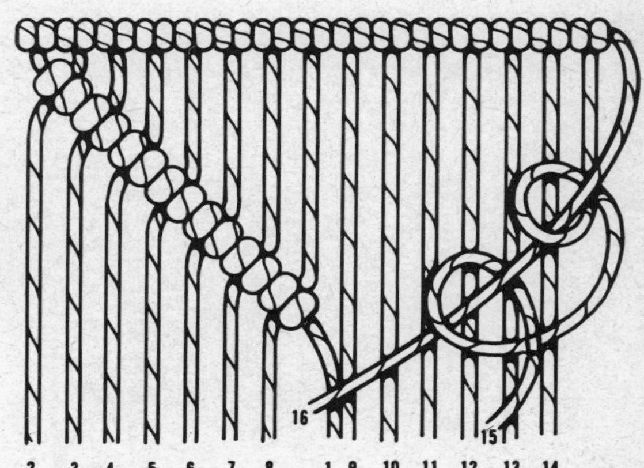

Diagonal double half-hitch

Macramé
(The Art of Creative Knotting)
Virginia I. Harvey
1967; 128 pp.
$6.95 postpaid from:
Van Nostrand Reinhold Company
Order Department
7625 Empire Drive
Florence, KY 41042
or Whole Earth Household Store

Square Knot Handicraft Guide

This book antedates the recent enthusiasm about knotting homemade goodies. Well illustrated, providing enough projects to get you through this winter, at least. —J.D. Smith

Square Knot Handicraft Guide
(Square Knotting or Macramé)
Raul Graumont and Elmer Wenstrom
1949; 212 pp.
$4.95 postpaid from:
Random House
455 Hahn Road
Westminster, MD 21157
or Whole Earth Household Store

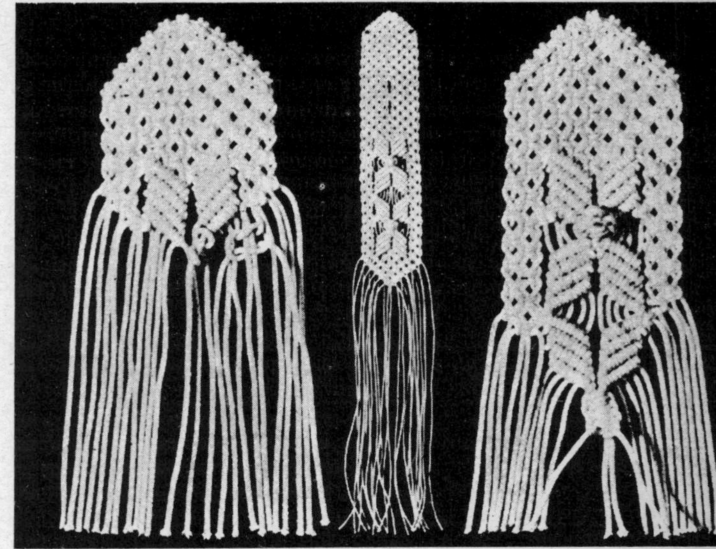

→ **Shell Knot Design**

Illustrated construction of the basic square knot

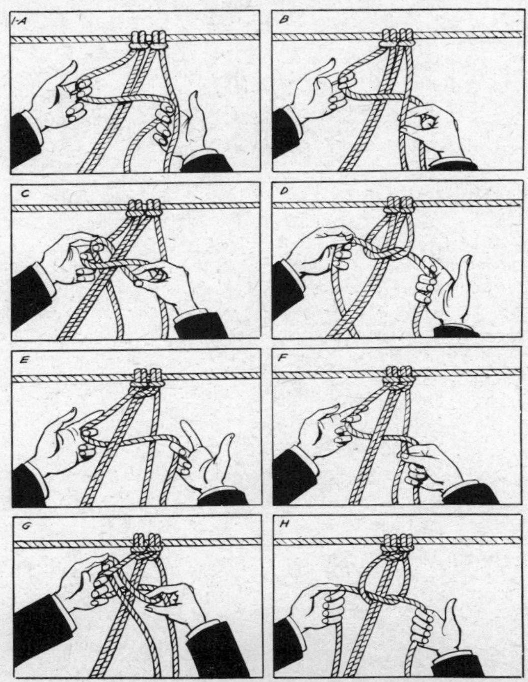

P. C. Herwig Co.

Calls itself Square Knot Headquarters, has cords, belt buckles, rings, beads. —SB

P.C. Herwig
Information
$1.00 from:
P.C. Herwig Company
Route 2
Milaca, MN 56353

DREADNAUGHT CORD No. 120
Highest Tensile Strength

THE RISING SUN
NEIGHBORHOOD NEWSLETTER

The rest of the country looks at California the way the rest of the world looks at America — rich, decadent, silly, great place to live at the expense of everyone else.

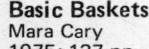

Basic Baskets

The detailed step-by-step illustrated instructions on the making of a round basket in this book are the result of the author's own teaching sessions which she tape recorded and photographed. This format carries a beginner through and outlines successful projects for those teaching. You might say all the bugs have been worked out. Variations of shapes and weaves along with synthetic and natural dye information are included.

—Susan Spalding

Basic Baskets
Mara Cary
1975; 127 pp.
$4.95 postpaid from:
Houghton Mifflin Co.
Wayside Road
Burlington, MA 01803

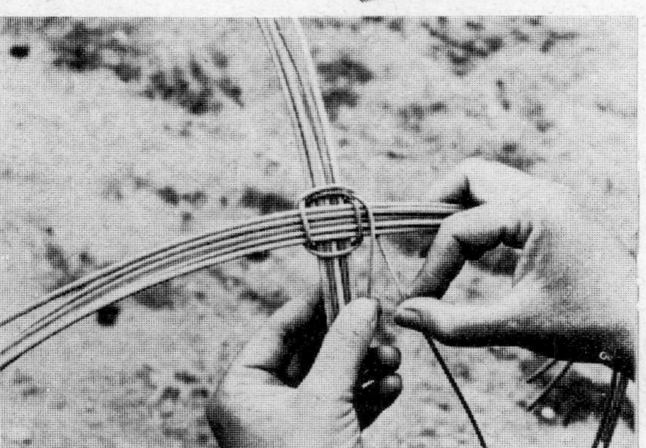

First steps in starting to weave a basket

Earth Basketry

Earth Basketry *I recommend highly if you are into using natural materials you can gather. Ms. Tod covers purchased materials but also gives information on preparing honeysuckle vines, grasses, willow rods, splints, pine needles, etc. A chapter lists 103 plants used by the Indians in basketry, where in the U.S. they grow, where to find and how to prepare them. Instructions for varieties of coiling and twining stitches are complete, with diagrams located close to the text describing the technique. There's even a chapter on basket birdhouses.*

—Susan Druding Jones

Earth Basketry
Osma Gallinger Tod
1972; 169 pp.
$9.95 postpaid from:
Olivia Gallinger Tod
Weaving Studio
219 Mendoza Avenue
Coral Gables, FL 33134

I Two-Rod With Overlay

J Multiple Foundation

•

Grasses and Stems

Beach Grass — (Eastern Coast as far as N. and S. Carolina). Split white stems make coarse patterns in spruce root baskets.
Brome Grass — (Western Canada). Split white stems used for patterns in split root baskets.
Broom Corn — (Cultivated, mainly central West). Seed heads of broom corn and other sorghums are borne on long fine straw-like stems that make bundles for coiled baskets. Several strands laid side by side may take place of a flat weaver to be used for plaiting.
Cane — (Cultivated, southern states). Strips cut from outer stalk make flat plaiting material. Fine split strands used as weavers over spokes. A slight blow crushes the large grass-like stalk, the spongy pith is scraped away and the outer strips or splints are ready for use.

Baskets As Textile Art

This book will cure your narrow mind about baskets. The range of human basketry is awesome, ingenious, gorgeous. You can't beat it, but you can join it.

—SB

Baskets as Textile Art
Ed Rossbach
1973; 144 pp.
$9.95 postpaid from:
Van Nostrand
Reinhold Company
Order Department
7625 Empire Drive
Florence, KY 41042

(Possibly out of print — write for information.)

•

Pleasure can be derived from observing how the vigorous, flowing curves, which some materials take naturally, are used for handles; how the smooth surface of materials is kept where it must be touched in using the basket; how fragile grasses of especially desired colors are placed sparingly as accents among sturdier materials; how elements are forced to radiate from a center without causing bulkiness and yet without leaving holes; how willow is placed so that its natural curve works with the curve of the basket; how elements strong enough to serve as a base are replaced by more fragile and pliable elements when the direction changes in forming the sides; how the weave and materials vary from one part of a basket to another for reasons sometimes structural, sometimes decorative.

↑ **Plaited palm basket, Pnape, Micronesia. The palm leaflets are left free, to be held in plaiting only along the base of the basket. The plaiting is brought up as sides, and then carried through the rim to act as handles.**

Detail of wickerwork basket, Korea. Certain elements of the plaited rim swing out of the construction in great flowing curves to act as handles. ↓

Basketry of the Appalachian Mountains

This book tells how baskets were used in everyday Appalachia and includes instructions for making them today. It's exceptionally well-written, well-researched and intertwined with the author's stories of growing up in the area. The author tells you which baskets are hard to make and why, discusses preparation of materials brought in from field and forest, and tells how to make basketry tools. Sections at the end deal with hearth brooms, dyes, cleaning and conservation of old baskets, advice to collectors and supply sources. I like the book for its solidness.

—Marilyn Green

Basketry of the Appalachian Mountains
Sue H. Stephenson
1977; 112 pp.
$9.95 postpaid from:
Van Nostrand
Reinhold Company
Order Department
7625 Empire Drive
Florence, KY 41042

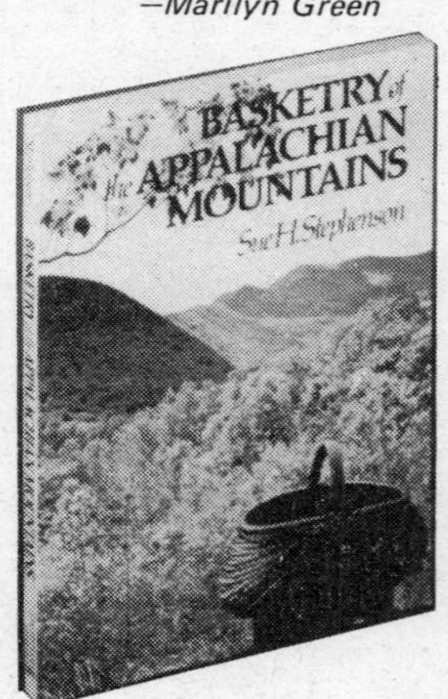

Twin-bottomed egg basket. The most common style of basket of the Appalachian Mountains.

Indian Basket Weaving

The most valuable feature of this book is the descriptions of materials to be gathered in the wild and details of their preparation: sedge root, willow, redbud, yucca, etc. The author has lived and woven baskets with weavers from each of the four tribes covered. She has a gift for transmitting not only the actual technical information, but also the emotional experiences of working with these natural elements. This book will be especially valuable for basket weavers who have the knowledge of the stitches, but have wanted to explore using native plant materials. Ms. Newman also suggests substitutes for materials found only in limited geographical areas for weavers outside of the western states.

—Susan Druding Jones

Indian Basket Weaving
(How to Weave Pomo, Yurok, Pima and Navajo Baskets)
Sandra Corrie Newman
1974; 91 pp.
$5.95 postpaid from:
Northland Press
P.O. Box N
Fort Valley Road
Flagstaff, AZ 86001

Plain basket start in conifer root.

Kern, Inyo, and Tulare Bowls. ←

Aboriginal Indian Basketry

For those interested in American Indian basketry there is one thorough classic originally published as **Aboriginal American Basketry: Studies in a Textile Art Without Machinery** *(1902), with 248 plates, 48 in color. It's hard to say a few words about this book — it's very thorough. A sampling of what is covered: materials by Latin and common names, basket making symbolism, uses and ethnic varieties from all over the Americas. There are photographs of many basket types and of Indian women with their work. Although there are no "instructions," experienced basket makers will find inspiration and ideas from illustrations and line drawings. (I might mention that this and all the Rio Grande books are large with sturdy bindings and washable covers. They will hold up well as reference books.)* —Susan Druding Jones

Aboriginal Indian Basketry
Otis Tufton Mason
1972; 592 pp.

OUT OF PRINT
Rio Grande Press

Get this book back in print

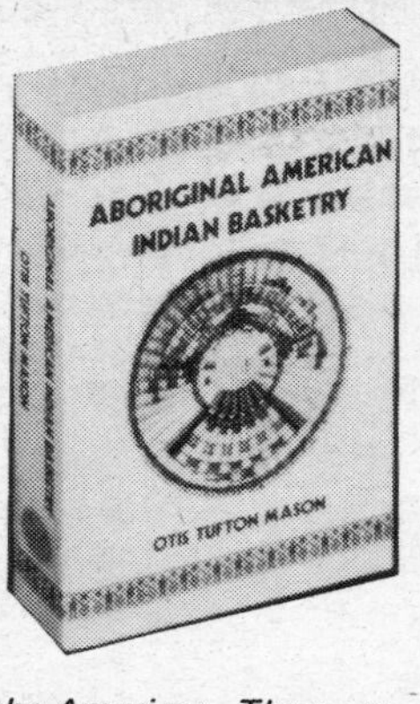

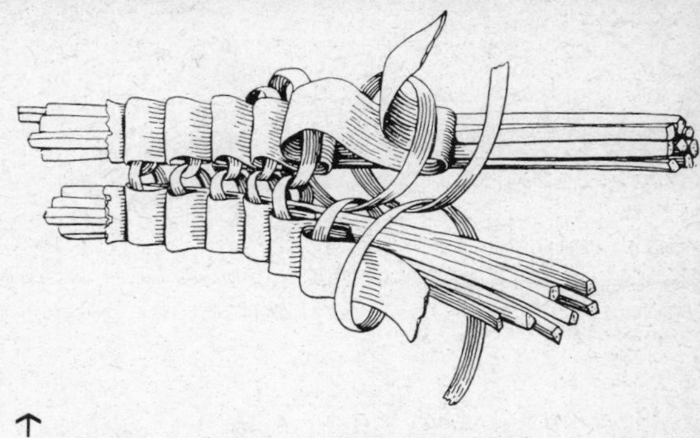

↑

In a small area on Fraser River, in southwestern Canada, on the upper waters of the Columbia, and in many Salishan tribes of northwestern Washington, basketry, called imbricated, is made. The foundation, as said, is in cedar or spruce root, while the sewing is done with the outer and tough portion of the root; the stitches pass over the upper bundle of splints and are locked with those underneath. On the outside of these baskets is a form of technic, which also constitutes the ornamentation. It is not something added, or overlaid, or sewed on, but is a part of the texture effected in the progress of the manufacture.

Perkins Reedcraft

Reedwork takes time. That's probably why there are so many cane bottom chairs sitting around with the bottoms poked out.

My dad learned how to weave reeds a few years ago, had a lot of trouble finding literature on the craft. The Perkins people sell reed and provide the newcomer with good lessons on the basic weaves as well as carrying a complete line of weaving materials. —J.D. Smith
[Suggested by Judy Rock]

Perkins
Catalog
free from:
H.H. Perkins Company
P.O. Box AC
Amity Station
Woodbridge, CT 06525

FINE-FINE — 7/16" MESH

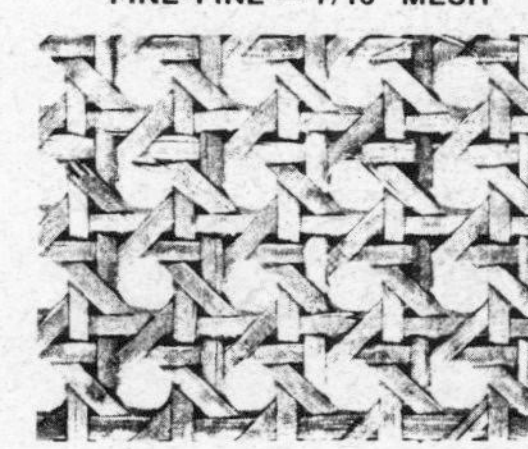

CANE WEBBING

This is used for chairs that do not have holes thru which the cane is drawn. There is a small groove around the edge of the chair into which the ready woven webbing is driven and held in place with a piece of reed called spline. Spline should be ordered with every piece of webbing. For sizes of webbing compare samples with illustrations.

Width	Per Running Foot
12"	**$2.80**
14"	**3.25**
16"	**3.75**
18"	**$4.20**
20"	**4.65**
24"	**5.60**

Collecting and Restoring Wicker Furniture

With a renewed interest in craftsmanship and handmade things, has come a renewed interest in wicker furniture. Its lightness and natural squeaky character has an undeniable charm, especially in modern sterile architecture. This book is both a gallery of traditional 19th century designs, and a fine manual of how to repair any restorable items you might find in Aunt Minnie's attic. I hope this book and the wicker revival are successful; fine wicker-work is beautiful, while at the same time allowing some of the grossest design excess ever seen in furniture. —J. Baldwin

Collecting and Restoring Wicker Furniture
Richard Saunders
1976; 118 pp.

$6.95 postpaid from:
Crown Publishers
One Park Avenue
New York, NY 10016
or Whole Earth
Household Store

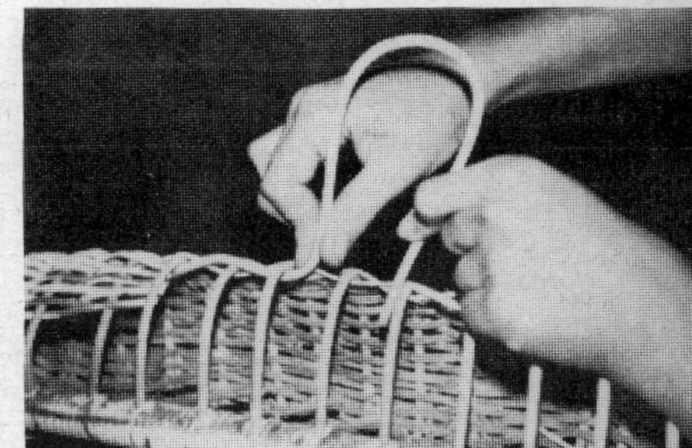

→ **When weaving, be careful not to put too much pressure on any of the spokes or they may be pulled out of the framework. It is helpful to brace the reed next to the spoke with one hand while guiding the end of the reed through the spokes with the other hand.**

Bamboo

The adoration and utilization of a towering weed.

Civilization as seen by a material.

Every single thing that plastic isn't. —SB

Bamboo
Robert Austin, Dana Levy, Koichiro Ueda
1970; 215 pp.

$27.50 postpaid from:
Charles E. Tuttle Company
28 South Main Street
Rutland, VT 05701
or Whole Earth
Household Store

← **Dish scourer of split bamboo**

•

Regarded as a material to work, bamboo shows itself "grateful" — to use the artisan's term. It is flexible yet tough, light but very strong. It can be split with ease, in one direction only, never in the other; it may be pliant or rigid as the occasion demands; it can be compressed enough to keep its place in holes; after heating, it can be bent to take and retain a new shape. It is straight and possessed of great tensile strength.

•

Bamboo is one of the most extraordinary plants that exists. It flowers perhaps once in a hundred years, and then it dies. It grows faster than anything in the world. In fact, it is sometimes possible to *see* it growing, just as one can see the hands of a large clock moving: there are recorded instances of bamboo's growing four feet in a single day. In a grove in spring the vitality of the surrounding green pillars is almost palpable. While the stem is growing above ground, the root stops: when the stem has finished, then comes the turn of the other. Bamboo also possesses the characteristic of making its complete growth in about two months only. Thereafter it remains the same size as long as it lives.

But bamboo is interesting for much more than this: it is the most universally useful plant known to man. For over half the human race, life would be completely different without it. The East and all its peoples can hardly be discussed without bamboo's being taken into account. Accepted as a mere fact of life or prized for aesthetic reasons, it touches daily existence at a thousand points which vary as widely as its employment in literary metaphor and its use in the walls of houses. It serves the most mundane purposes, and the most refined: dwellings are constructed from bamboo; it is widely used for eating and drinking utensils and for countless other household implements. Ubiquitous, it provides food, raw materials, shelter, even medicine for the greater part of the world's population. The interlocked roots of a bamboo grove restrain the river in flood and during earthquakes support the insubstantial dwellings of country villages.

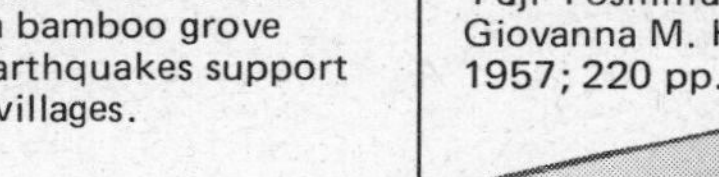

Bamboo is used as scaffolding all over the East, as in this Hong Kong scene. The intersections and joints are lashed with rattan, which is tied on wet and shrinks to take a very tight grip. ↓

The Japanese Art of Miniature Trees and Landscapes

This is the ultimate in model-making. Tiny trees in tiny scenes, and a careful, happy person hovering in the sky nearby. This book is really thorough on the science and the art of bonsai. The standard work. —SB

The Japanese Art of Miniature Trees and Landscapes
Yuji Yoshimura and Giovanna M. Halford
1957; 220 pp.

$13.75 postpaid from:
Charles E. Tuttle Company
28 South Main Street
Rutland, VT 05701
or Whole Earth
Household Store

Bonsai tree

THE RISING SUN
NEIGHBORHOOD NEWSLETTER

"We couldn't get a permit for a block party, so we got a parade permit and kept everybody moving."

COMMUNITY IS ONE OF OUR CATCH-ALL SECTIONS ("learning" is the other), but on scrutiny, two themes emerge. One is that living well and living free bear a lot of relation to living cheap. The second is that living cheap and living happily are all wrapped up with the complex life of neighborhood, family, friends, lovers, co-workers — community.

—SB

The Four Illusions of Money

and the non-money truths they hide

by Michael Phillips, Rasberry and Andora Freeman

*Ex-banker Michael Phillips is the author (with Rasberry) of **The Seven Laws of Money** (p. 308). The clip art is from the peerless Hart Picture Archive **Humor, Wit, & Fantasy** (p. 464).*

—SB

Why do people work at jobs they don't like? Why is it common to hear people say their goal in life is to "make a lot of money?" These are the most frequently given answers:

"A lot of money will let me be free to do what I want."

"People with a lot of money command more respect from others."

"I need more money for my family."

"Money is necessary for security in old age."

THESE STATEMENTS ARE ILLUSIONS. They are inaccurate perceptions of the world we live in.

When we look at the average graduating class of high school students, we are distressed to know that nearly all of them hold these values: they seek "a lot" of money as a lifetime goal. Less than five percent of these students will become wealthy. The remaining 95 percent will shape their lives around these inappropriate values.

How do *you* feel about these four statements? Read them over and see if you find them completely agreeable. For most people they are.

"A lot of money will let me be free to do what I want."

You can really feel this way when you're working at a job that you don't like, when you're unhappy with the way things are going in your life, and when there is some object, experience, or service you desperately want to buy.

The alternative is to deal with these feelings, directly and positively. Write down the specific things you want to do with your life. Describe the things you need to shape the kind of person you want to be (the experiences you need, knowledge, skills, talents, etc.) Make sure what you write down doesn't include money itself. When you look at your list you'll find that there is a way to accomplish all of it in your lifetime without any more money than you now have. Most things require that you actively pursue them and LEARN in the process. If you want to be a world traveller, join the crew of a sailing ship and be useful in a way you know now. Later you'll be useful as a sailor and have the necessary great stories to tell at night about hitting sharks on the nose in the Bahamas.

What you may find from the list that you make is that having a lot of money may allow you to achieve goals a little sooner, but the effort of going out and earning money to make something happen sooner is not worth the time, and more importantly the person you may become may have lost vigor and joy.

Back in the late '50s a young woman who desired a doctorate degree won over $100,000 on a TV quiz show. Years later, in reflecting on the effect of the prize money, she said it made little difference in her life although it may have accelerated her degree by a few years. She was a strong woman and knew what she wanted to do with her life. She's Doctor Joyce Brothers.

Her experience is not uncommon. People who know what they want to DO with their lives go ahead and do it. They don't make the money first doing something else. It often turns out that money and the possessions which go with making lots of money are responsibilities and restrictions that inhibit freedom. The possessions unrelated to your livelihood are often amassed to help you feel better about yourself.

Check your list again and see how many possessions are listed there. Most possessions on your list are abundantly available. Many things can be borrowed from friends who are willing to share. That includes everything from a ski condominium in Snowmass to an Aston-Martin race car. With a good network of friends, nearly anything is possible. The alternative to investing your energy in making money is developing strong friendships. This means being an interesting, trustworthy and helpful person yourself.

When you are unable to locate something you need among your friends, consider renting the piece of equipment. Finding and restoring "discards" can be an alternative to save both money and resources. Perhaps you have possessions you can trade to a friend or neighbor in exchange for something more useful. Service bartering can be an even more rewarding experience. It costs no more than time and energy spent with a friend. If you have a skill, share it with others.

In writing and examining your values it's helpful to talk to someone who is wise. The wisdom of millions of our ancestors has been very consistent on this point, and wise people constantly pass it on to us. The goal of amassing (getting a lot of) money is traditionally called "greed" and regardless of your motives in getting the money (freedom, charity, or anything else) the results will not be what you hope for. Instead the wise teachers of tradition tell us to go ahead and do the things we want and become good at them. In that lies our freedom.

"People with a lot of money command more respect from others."

If you know that the first statement about money and freedom is false, then it will help you to see the fallacy behind money equaling respect. In looking at the big cars and the big houses we often believe that their owners can do much more than we can. If indeed the people with big cars and houses can do more than we can, then it probably isn't their money, it's other qualities that they may have such as knowledge, experience, and friends. It isn't their money. A common experience in business is the person who builds a successful company, goes broke, and then builds up a new company again starting from scratch.

If we believe we personally want respect, it helps to make a list of the qualities we want to have, qualities that lead others to respect us, qualities that we want our children to have or our friends to have. Do words such as loyal, honest, and generous occur on your list? A careful examination of these qualities reveals that each of them has to do with how we conduct our daily lives and not how much money we have.

Now make a list of the people you love. Bob, Annie, Carole, and David. Examine the list to see if it's ranked in the order of how much money they have. There is probably no relationship between love and the amount of money they have. The same criteria we apply to others can be applied to us. Money isn't a reason for friendship or respect.

"I need more money for my family."

Why shouldn't people be generous with their families! This seems like reasonable parental behavior. It's when people use this concept as an excuse for doing something that they would rather not do that it is a fallacy. When someone works at a job that they find unpleasant, monotonous (too demanding), stressful, or frustrating and say they do it for their family, they're talking nonsense.

Many people work long hours, develop ulcers and live with great stress because they believe their family benefits. Stop and ask your family what they want. Would your children rather have a Winnebago camper (which may mean the main wage earner works a lot of overtime) or would they rather have you at home to spend time together or go on a camping trip with ordinary sleeping bags and tents? Give your family the choice between those possessions and the time and peace of mind you are diverting from them to earn it.

Another useful technique is to look at a picture of two houses – one a glamorous mansion, the other a modest home with a bicycle near the front door. Which one of the houses has a happier family? Most people would say "I can't tell" when the question is posed this way because we know in our hearts money and possessions have nothing to do with happiness.

"Money is necessary for security in old age."

Michael is blessed with a father who is a living contradiction of this. When he was 65, his father retired from teaching anthropology and social sciences with a modest pension and Social Security income of $300 a month. He sold his home and all his belongings, including a lifetime collection of tools and books which brought almost no revenue. He bought a van in England and proceeded to drive east with his wife (Michael's parents were divorced 15 years earlier). He got teaching jobs along the way and stopped anywhere he found interesting.

Driving as far east as they could go, they ended up in Malaysia where they bought part of a South China Sea island near Singapore for $2,000. They now live part time on their island with a sandy beach, coconut trees, fresh fish, and lots of Malaysian and Chinese friends. They live on less than $100 a month and save the rest for numerous trips they take to all parts of the world including back to the U.S. One of the most surprising benefits is that they see many of their old friends from all over the world regularly. Everyone wants to visit their tropical paradise for a vacation. With Singapore nearby, they have all the comforts of a major international city with its cuisine, culture, and excitement.

Michael's father could live on any amount of money. In the seven years since he retired he hasn't touched his savings. How about health care and medicine? One of his closest friends is chief of a major research hospital in Malaysia that is better than 98% of the hospitals in the U.S. Friendship is more powerful than money.

From the Grey Panthers to people in retirement villages the ones who are happy in their old age are the ones that have the same qualities that Michael's father has: being friendly and flexible. Money makes no difference at all. With friends, especially ones of all ages, you can solve the problems that arise, whether it's tax increases, inflation or legal hassles – problems that other people can't handle because times have changed and their lifetime experiences and contacts are inappropriate. Friends also provide vitality, emotional support and new friends – which is especially valuable after age 75 when one out of ten old friends die each year.

Flexibility in attitude is also essential as your body becomes less reliable. We all know old people who say, "Close the window, the draft is terrible," "I can't sleep in that bed, it's too soft," and "I don't like to be around those kinds of people." With that attitude, who wants to be around THEM?

Michael's mother, who is also a positive example for him, has been living on her own for the last 20 years. She built a small contemporary house for herself and has always been gregarious and flexible. Even past seventy, she's involved in the politics of her city, art-related projects, and is the local fund raiser for the ACLU. (Any of her friends can call her for help on anything and she'll do it.) When she comes to visit San Francisco, several of Michael's friends always insist on spending time with her and showing her around. She travels regularly, often being invited on global trips just for her company and knowledge. You don't hear her complaining about comfort issues or how terrible the world is today.

The three of us have worked with many older people who had lots of money. In a case where the husband had earned the money we frequently find that the husband is confident and secure but the wife is anxious and often hysterical. He has earned the money in the first place and knows he could do it again even in his old age; the woman has no such experience and dreads the day when her husband will die and she has to face the world alone. No amount of money that we have seen can calm this kind of fear.

How do you prepare for old age? How do you prepare for inflations, wars, and depressions of the future? By being the kind of person other people want to be around. Competent, helpful, flexible, curious, generous, and experienced in dealing with the world.

The Moral

If you have friends and make an effort to be an interesting person, money is irrelevant. You can have a great deal of freedom and respect during your life and security in your old age. However if you are a loner, rather selfish, with narrow interests in life, then making a lot of money may be your only way to make it through life. ■

Bibliography

Seven Laws of Money, Michael Phillips, (p. 308).
Briarpatch Book, (p. 306).
Inland Whale, Theodora Kroeber.
Zen Mind, Beginner's Mind, Suzuki-Roshi
Tassajara Bread Book, Ed Brown, (p. 367).

Possum Living

Dolly Freed has published a "first of its kind." Her book is a top-flight guide to simple living that is wonderfully written, explains the basic concept and speaks from personal experience.

I think she deserves folk hero status; the book is emotionally exciting and is very persuasuve. It is worth noting that Ms. Freed is 19 years old, didn't go to high school and lives with her father (he is an important figure whom detective story readers will try to identify). It all takes place in Pennsylvania. —Michael Phillips

Possum Living
(How to Live Well without a Job and with Almost No Money)
Dolly Freed
1978; 176 pp.

$3.95 postpaid from:
Universe Books
381 Park Avenue South
New York, NY 10016
or Whole Earth Household Store

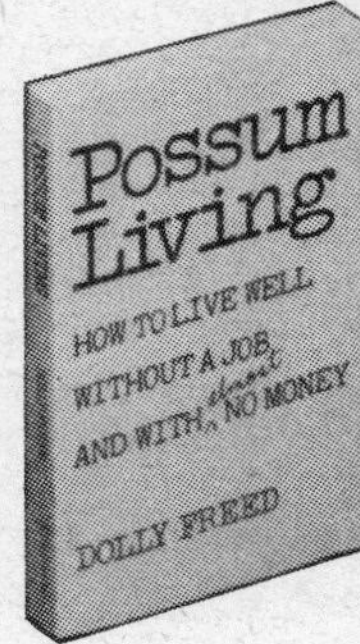

•

Vacations, another common expenditure, are not required – our whole life is just one big vacation. We don't need to "get away from it all" because there's nothing we want to get away from.

Hobbies don't cost us much. Mine, birdwatching, requires a pair of binoculars and book for identifying them, but they both last for many years. We both have $17 running shoes, but they last pretty long. We bought a badminton set for $11 (listed under "Luxuries"), but that, too, should give us years of enjoyment.

Christmas doesn't exist for us. December 25 is just another day here. 'Tis the season to be greedy, ostentatious, treacly sentimental, frenzied, hysterical, morbidly drunk and suicidal, and we see no reason to pretend otherwise.

•

Owning your own home free and clear – that's the key to all the rest. Once you have your snug harbor, your safe base, all else comes easy. You can tell the rest of the world to go to hell if you want, once you own the roof over your head. I believe that some parents who are willing to scrimp and save to give their kid a college education would be doing the kid a better turn by giving him that money to buy a house instead. Once he realizes he doesn't have to worry about his future – once he has security and leisure to think about it, instead of having his future rammed down his throat – he'll make his own future.

•

Ordinary pump-air rifles or CO_2 rifles are efficient tools for getting pigeon meat. You don't have to own one yourself, for invariably some neighborhood kid will. Tell him you like pigeons, and he gets to gratify his killer instinct, guilt-free, and you get that good meat. Everyone's happy but the pigeons.

We haven't tried it ourselves, but I've read of people scattering liquor-soaked bread, and gathering up the pigeons when they get too drunk to fly. Often at night we planned to do this but then next morning we'd find there wasn't any liquor left.

People who raise pigeons as a hobby often simply destroy unsatisfactory birds (such as homing birds that take too long to come home). If you ask these people they might either give them to you or sell them for a nominal price. These birds are referred to as culls.

•

Before you make extensive repairs on the tumble-down hobo shack you bought (get used to using those kinds of terms), go to the tax assessor's office and cry on his shoulder. Chances are the assessment was made before the place became dilapidated, and you might get it lowered. Compare your assessment with those of others in your neighborhood against their last sale prices. (One property here sold for five times what ours went for, and yet had a lower assessment. Daddy made sure the tax people knew ours should be lowered!) A zoning change from commercial to residential, as in the cases of the grain elevator and our country store, also lowers the value of a property, which should be reflected in the assessment.

THE RISING SUN
NEIGHBORHOOD NEWSLETTER

A guy who travels a lot has given many people at the San Francisco airport those little metal clickers. The idea is if you get approached by a moonie or krishna or see some innocent approached, you start clicking your clicker and everyone around who has one (lots of staff do) starts clicking their clickers and keep doing it until the smiling religous person shuts up. It worked so well it got the krishnas out of SFO, at least for a while.

– The Examiner

The Ecotopian Encyclopedia for the '80s

I prefer the title of its 1972 incarnation, **Living Poor With Style**, *but since Callenbach is the author of the surprisingly influential visionary novel* **Ecotopia** *(reviewed on p. 378), it's understandable he would try to theme-coordinate his* *oeuvre*. *(Will his* **Film Quarterly** *soon become* **Ecotopian Film Review?)**

Gossip aside, this completely rewritten and expanded encyclopedia is a wonderful book on how to be alive today. It has all in one place most of the lore that one spends one's entire twenties and thirties picking up — all that fundamental stuff they don't tell you in school and which the advertising media obscure. The nuts and bolts of enlightened self-interest. The cheap transportation, housing, food, clothing, etc. which is better than most of the expensive stuff. How to get jobs, think about family, travel, learn skills. Kind of like the **Whole Earth Catalog**, *maybe better.* —SB

The Ecotopian Encyclopedia for the Eighties
(Based on Living Poor with Style)
Ernest Callenbach
1980; 352 pp.

$9.95 postpaid from:
And/Or Press
Box 2246
Berkeley, CA 94702

or Whole Earth Household Store
(Available Spring 1981)

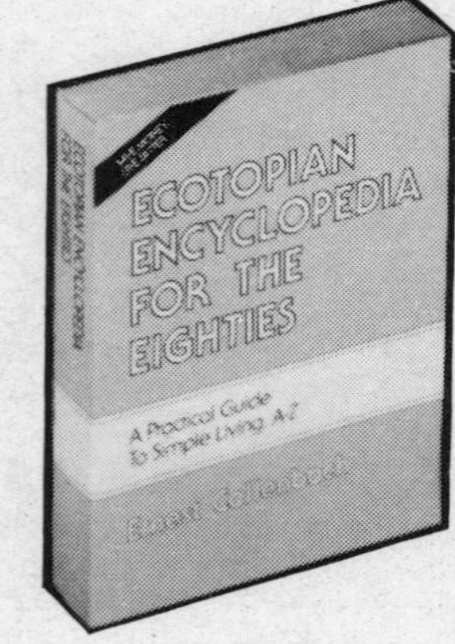

•

People planning to build a house themselves in the country often find it a good idea to live in a mobile home while they're doing it, and in town, if you plan to do a serious remodeling job, you might want to park a trailer in the driveway and live in it for the period when the house is totally torn up. Generally urban trailer "parks" are depressing places, however, though some of the new ones (which generally have only around 150 - 175 sites) have trees, green areas, and a spacious feel. Since many parks provide a central recreation area where laundry, play grounds and other common facilities are located, they often generate quite a feeling of community. Traffic inside generally moves slowly (if road bumps aren't installed, they should be) and children are safer than on ordinary streets. Check out a possible park on a hot day, however; the expanses of asphalt and close proximity to other people's windows (and radios) can be hopeless disadvantages.

Some parks are mainly inhabited by older people, or by very conservative folks. It is time for parks to be established to cater to other tastes as well: students, professional couples. Such parks would generate a market for mobile homes with higher design standards.

•

Bartering is also a way of cementing friendships in a way that buying and selling things for cash somehow just doesn't do. You don't even necessarily have to get a return on an item right away. Some experienced barterers know that if they say, "Well, just take it now — you'll discover something you can give me for it," they will seldom be disappointed. Barterers have to take each other's tastes and personalities into account; they have to deal with each other as human beings.

But the financial side is often gratifying too. If, for example, you go into a store to buy something new, you'll pay, let's say, $50 for it. Plus maybe $3 in sales tax. But to get that $53, you probably had to *earn* about $75 (considering the impact of income tax). On the other hand, if you can find somebody who'll give you the item in barter, you "pay" for it with an item of yours on which you've already gone through the financial preliminaries; you are, so to speak, recycling your previous investment. So your effective outlay for the item you want is probably less than half of what it would be if you bought it new. (And, depending on how you value your time, it might be even less if you trade a service for an object.)

One of the reasons to grow vegetables, or keep bees or chickens, is that they tend to provide you with more than you can use, so you have surpluses to use in bartering. That can be, in fact, half the fun.

Barter: How to Get Anything from Automobiles to Vacations without Money, by Constance Stapleton and Phyllis Richman. Scribner, 1977.

Let's Try Barter, by Charles Morrow Wilson, Davin, 1980.

•

The best deals in housing are always gotten by word of mouth. You hear from relatives or friends that a good place is going to be vacant. Or you're talking to a storekeeper and he or she mentions that a relative has a place for rent. Give yourself as much time to look as possible, so you can take advantage of these informal leads. It takes weeks of steady looking to find anything you'll really like.

Author shopping for dinner.

Tom Duckworth was one of the very first employees of **The Whole Earth Catalog.** *He and his family lived in the back of a truck by the precepts of this piece he wrote in 1969 or so. Tom was a travelling, don't-give-'em-a-standing-target Libertarian. Interestingly, his precepts hold steadily true 11 years later. We've updated the prices. Tom, where are you? You get $50 for having this article reprinted.* —SB

On Getting by Without Money

by Tom Duckworth

Disassociation with the economic bag of any society is difficult unless you are very rich or a Trappist monk. This article is for those who have no savings, no inheritance, no trust funds and no desire to remain in a money-oriented rut (there are so many other ruts to explore).

What I have to offer here is not all-inclusive — just merely information that I have acquired firsthand as my family (wife and 2 kids) and I have tripped along.

When we first started on the trip, our first concern was food — a needless concern in this country — we went to the local grocery store and asked for the vegetable and fruit discards. Every day grocery stores — all of them — throw away about 4 garbage cans full of edible food. Food that is "spotted," "overripe," "bruised," or ugly, or dairy food on its "pull-date." The quality and quantity of the throw-away food depends very much on the type of ownership of store and its clientele. One-man operations or family owned stores keep everything — chain operated stores throw away good food all the time. The easiest way to get vegetables from a store is to ask for them. Sometimes you score, sometimes not. The store I got vegetables from gave me enough to feed 31 people, 10 chickens and start a good compost pile — 2 - 3 boxes every day. Stores catering to the elite of this society have the most throwaways — no blemishes or bruises allowed — but they tend to be selfish with their garbage. Stores like Safeway, etc. are best bets.

Another source of food is government food stamps. In San Francisco County, a person with no income is "entitled" to $63 worth of free food per month (as of October 1980). A four-person household is "entitled" to $209. The place to check in the phone book is the U.S. Department of Agriculture's local Food Stamp office. The food stamp prices and rates change frequently.

Food is a good trade item — we traded for eggs and non-food items. For example, we made arrangements with a group living on a farm. They didn't "qualify" for welfare food but had an abundance of barnyard stock. We traded. We had food, another made sandals. We traded. We had cornmeal, someone raised a lamb — we had meat, they had meal. The best way to trade is to give it all away — when it's time, it will come back.

Next to free food, you need cheap food. Most bakeries sell day-old bread — we get about 5 loaves of french bread for $1. (This helped feed the chickens too.) Egg processing companies and ranches sell flats of eggs below market value — we got cracked eggs for less than 4 cents each (cheap enough to feed the dogs) — though they do spoil quickly and there's some danger of *Salmonella*. Also, farmers markets and flea markets are good places for cheap good produce. Most important of all — bulk purchases of wheat and rice are very wise investments.

Cheap clothes are available at the Goodwill, army surplus stores, rummage sales and flea markets. Rent is the real bummer and we never solved it completely until we moved into our camper. However, rent can be lessened on a trade for rent basis. I got 3 weeks free rent in agreement to clean up the house I was moving into. One friend got a big house for 3 months in exchange for repairs. Another got a year's free rent — the first 6 months in exchange for repairs and the last 6 months in trade for a sculpture he did. With the camper, rent is not the problem it once was.

I built my camper for about $125. I got nearly all of the lumber at the city dump and at construction sites (you could start a lumber company from their scrap pile). The stove in the camper came from a trash pile and I traded a window for the sink. The icebox was given to me. The $25 foam rubber mattress on our bed cost $10 at the flea market. Four of the five tires on my truck were free — I got them from behind the Santa Cruz County auto maintenance building. They use tubeless tires and they don't repair them. They throw them away — it's covered by taxes. Service stations and department stores sometimes throw away usable tires.

Transportation is hard — mostly luck. I've been given 1 car, 1 truck and I bought an excellent running car for $20 trade.

Medicine. In emergency, go to the county hospital, look for trade situations. I know of a dentist who did work at cost or trade for long-haired people. Another friend worked at a veterinary hospital to pay for his dog's operation. Look behind the doctor's office. I found 700 tranquilizers at the dump.

Tools and furniture may be gotten at Goodwill, flea markets and rummage sales.

If you look around, you may be able to find a mechanic who will work for exchange of things other than money — there are lots of things you can do. ■

Living Free

Son of **Preinform**, *son of* **Vonulife**, *this endearing newsletter is a practical guide to living in America in such a way as to be invisible to its government. The idea is dogged Libertarian. The practice looks like fun and is surely cheap and mobile.* —SB

Living Free
Jim Stumm, Editor

$6 /year (6 issues) from:
Living Free
Box 29
Hiler Branch
Kenmore, NY 14223

•

While it is nice to find ways to survive in our mad society by dropping back to a simple lifestyle, I think it is all too easy to get caught in a trap of negative returns for the expended effort. We only have so much allotted time. If we are stuck out in the boonies raising our food and trying to exist w/o some decent technology, it just kills the hell out of our time. If a person can find a mate willing to live the "back to basics" life, then such time can be enjoyable. If not, forget it. Few women in society can "drop out" and most inwardly seek security in other directions.

Friend R.E. is specialized. He travels through the larger city areas attending auctions and looking through newspaper ads. His prey is the gas refrigerator under $35. On his journeys north he loads up half a dozen or so and gets over $200 for every one he has. He diddles and piddles along in gorgeous back country and lives the same life a wealthy traveller would live in many ways.

I have a neighbor down the road with a wife and family who travels around with his truck looking for driveways to pave with asphalt or gunk. He makes a good living and never sees any of his loot split with the tax man.

The point of these and many examples left out is that there are still enough cracks in the System as it stands to enable anyone with a good brain to find their niche and enjoy themselves w/o "dropping out."

—John Freeman

SARAH HARTIGAN

←
Bau Graves at the back door of his home-made home-financed home. Look at the speed of events in this ingenious, heart-warming episode. The appeal went out August 5, 1978. On September 25 construction began. On November 22 Graves moved into his new house. He footnotes, "My friend on whose land I built my house read this piece and commented that he thought I should have said more about the pleasant community feelings that were generated by my project — the fact that many people felt a sense of participation in my house and my life."

Typesetter Evelyn refers to this article as "The Chutzpa House."

How to Finance a Home (or anything) Without Job, Capital, Bank, or Crime

Use your real worth. Your friends and your word.

by Bau Graves

WHEN MY CAT AND I DECIDED, after our twelfth move in nine years, that we'd better get ourselves a more permanent place to live, I visited the bank. I told the man at the bank that since I wanted to own my home but had no money I would like to borrow $5,000 from him. He asked me some questions about myself and my income, which is rather sporadic. I run a small music store part of the time, but the bulk of my income comes from working one day per week at a publishing firm, which nets me very little, and playing for occasional dances or concerts, which nets me even less. Eventually he told me that he was sorry but; a) the bank didn't believe that a habitable home could be built for $5000; b) no bank in its right mind would consider lending ANYTHING to a person like myself with a small and uneven income and no credit; and c) why didn't I just work hard for a few years and try to make lots of money, then come back and see him.

I next visited the Farmer's Home Association, an organization ostensibly established to provide mortgage loans to low income rural people who could not get them through regular banks. The man there told me that their MINIMUM income requirement is more than twice the $2600 which I'd made in 1977. He further stated that there was "no way" I would ever be able to secure a mortgage from ANY established source without doubling or trebling my income.

Realizing that I was a terminal case as far as traditional money sources were concerned, I got to wondering whether I could raise enough money to build a house by borrowing ten bucks from everybody I knew. In China it was once traditional for all of the hundreds of relatives of a new couple to pitch in a little money which amounted to enough to build them a home (probably still works that way in some culture, somewhere). Why wouldn't it be possible for MY extended family of friends and acquaintances to provide my mortgage?

With that in mind, last August I wrote a letter detailing my sources of livelihood and my experience with the banking world. I pointed out that I was living a very low-key, non-consumption oriented lifestyle and was being penalized as a result of what I considered to be responsible and patriotic behavior. I then asked for a loan, saying:

> **If you will loan me $10 now, I promise to pay you back $11 sometime within the next ten years. In addition you will be invited to the very best house-warming party in Maine's history! I promise to pay all my loaners back, a few each month (just like paying rent!) in the order in which I receive the contributions. If, for some reason, I fail to raise sufficient funds, I promise to repay all loaners within one year.**

I sent copies of the letter to everyone I could think of who knew me or anything about me. I distributed them to customers in my store and passed them out at meetings of the Brunswick Folk Club which I organize. I feared that my project would fail and nearly gave it up when my parents refused me permission to send it to ANY of my relatives or their friends, thus cutting me off from hundreds of potential donors. It seems they assumed that their friends and kin would believe they had refused to lend me the money, which would embarrass them. However, by this time money was already pouring in (in the stamped, self-addressed envelopes I had enclosed), so I thought I'd see how much would accumulate.

This was the most interesting part of the project. All of a sudden there was a financial "issue" between me and virtually everyone I knew. People reacted to my proposal in some strange and varied ways.

Many people applauded my audacity and were pleased and proud to contribute. I received many notes like "Far out for you! I hope everything works out!" or, "Your idea is great. We are always willing to help friends who have no use for welfare and/or mortgage people." There was one which read: "Good luck Bau! Here's $10 from me and $10 from my mother who also thought your idea was great!" I received several donations from complete strangers who happened to read my letter: "I don't know you at all, but picked up your letter at the Chocolate Church (Performing Arts Center at Bath). Best of luck in your endeavour. Enclosed find loan of $10." Many of my donors asked that I not bother with repayment: "Enclosed is some money for your 'build your own house fund.' Consider it a gift. Some day you can buy me a beer and we'll be even."

Not all of the response was positive, however. Several friends expressed anger (not to me, usually — but things get around) that I should ask THEM for house money when they had been saving for a home for years. The fact that I had asked for money DID put a certain amount of tension into my relationships with a few people who didn't want to contribute but probably felt like I might hold it against them or something. A couple of reluctant contributors cared enough to comment: "I've been debating about whether to send this or not," wrote one, "not because I don't trust you, but because it raised some issues in my mind about feeling that if I had somehow managed to get money together in my life then I was rather a sucker . . ." Another wrote: "My mental response to your letter was, 1) Huh! Get a job yourself; 2) Look for/create a land trust; and 3) Your marriage dissolved, now you want the world to take care of you. . . ." Two other people wrote refusing to contribute, I received one empty envelope (no return address), and was asked by three people to buy into a chain letter instead.

All in all, I distributed about 500 letters. I raised a little over $3,900 which was contributed by 131 individuals, many of whom voluntarily gave more than the $10 I requested. In the process of collecting money, however, another fringe benefit of my fund raising method became obvious. People have ALL KINDS of things just laying around waiting for someone to use them. By tipping off hundreds of people to the fact that I was building a house I saved enormous amounts of money — people were anxious to just get rid of things which I needed. I was GIVEN a gas stove, a refrigerator, a composting toilet, two-thirds of my windows including a big picture window, my kitchen counter, all of my interior wiring, and virtually all of my furniture. I was let in on terrific bargains on all of the wood used in the house and most of the shingles. Best of all — two close friends offered to let me build on their property, which I eventually did with a lease arrangement by which I pay a portion of their annual taxes.

I started construction of my house on September 25. So many people knew I was building that I had constant free assistance from friends who wanted to lend a hand and advice from experienced carpenters. I moved in the day before Thanksgiving and have been warm and snug in my own home ever since. The total cost of the house came to less than $3,400. It is a small house, just a little over 400 square feet, but it is comfortable and beautiful, sitting on the edge of a ravine about 1/2 mile through the woods from Maquoit Bay. A civil engineer friend calculated all the stress factors and beam sizes, so I know it'll be here for a long time to come.

As I work through my list of contributors, paying a few back each month, it is a pleasure to think of them individually and thank them for making it possible for me to have my own home. I imagine it's nice for them too — receiving a check from out of the blue and thinking of the wonderful service of friendship they've performed. ■

THE RISING SUN
NEIGHBORHOOD NEWSLETTER

"The Indians in Northern California didn't have a concept of fighting. They just died, mostly of disease."

Sermon 1: Local Dependency

"Self-sufficiency" is an idea which has done more harm than good. On close conceptual examination it is flawed at the root. More importantly, it works badly in practice.

Anyone who has actually tried to live in total self-sufficiency — there must be now thousands in the recent wave that we (culpa!) helped inspire — knows the mind-numbing labor and loneliness and frustration and real marginless hazard that goes with the attempt. It is a kind of hysteria.

The trouble is that self-sufficiency looks good and tastes good and gets swallowed whole — clear down into one's premise structure, where it becomes a design guideline. When a problem comes up, we check the various solution alternatives against the criterion of whether this solution will help make us more self-sufficient. And each time we make a mistake.

Because: self-sufficiency is not to be had on any terms, ever. It is a charming woodsy extension of the fatal American mania for privacy. "I don't need you. I don't need anybody. I! am self-sufficient."

It is a damned lie. There is no dissectable self. Ever since there were two organisms life has been a matter of co-evolution, life growing ever more richly on life. Any "self" is strictly a term of convenience for one's mildly discontinuous local set of body and mood considerations. Any "privacy" is a temporary incremental respite from the big dance. I cherish privacy, even live alone, so it's a bit of a jump to realize how unbasic it is.

Now our poor rich nation wants energy self-sufficiency — a stupid chimera. We nations all are in total dependency on systems which have no respect for national boundaries — atmosphere, oceans, ocean life, biotic provinces and our daily Sun, without which nothing. Cultural flow, language, economic flow — this stuff slows up at national boundaries and probably should, but it never stops. To refute George Washington, "Life IS entangling alliances."

So where does this come out for one's premise structure, design guidelines, and such? It would seem that the more fundamental statement is one of dependency. We can ask what kinds of dependency we prefer, but that's our only choice.

For example, is it preferable to be dependent on institutions we don't know, and which don't know us, or on people, other organisms, and natural forces that we do know? . . . local dependency.

I'm betting that abandonment of illusions of self-sufficiency will free us to accept and enjoy local dependency, by preference.

And since our world is increasingly cultural, and proportionally ever less physical, the meaning of "local" is not geographic, at least not only.*

—SB

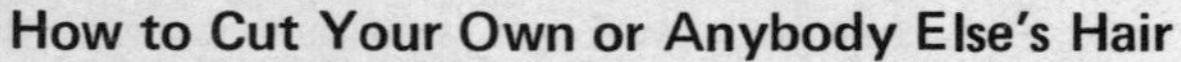

*On re-reading this rant, written in 1976, it occurs to me that the worthy part of the idea of self-sufficiency is better called self-reliance. That term has the responsibility and the pride, but it's not hermetically sealed.

Sermon 2: "Voluntary Simplicity"

. . . has become a buzzword of late, but it goes back a ways. Thoreau called it "voluntary poverty" in **Walden.*** Around 1936 an admirer of Gandhi named Richard Gregg wrote an influential article called "Voluntary Simplicity," about the healthy balancing of inward and outward life.† In 1976 SRI International, the behemoth think tank near Stanford University in California, came out with a Business Intelligence Report which asserted that "Voluntary Simplicity" was the wave of the future in the American marketplace. Authors Arnold Mitchell and Duane Elgin advised the businessmen to get ready for buyers who wanted fewer things and better ones.§

Now, in the summer of 1980, the **Wall St. Journal** has page-one articles reporting that shoppers are responding to recession and inflation by buying only quality goods, much of it of the do-it-yourself sort — hardware, gardening implements, and such.

Meanwhile environmentalists and other do-gooders have been talking up Voluntary Simplicity as the benign way to redress the wealth inequities and exploitive practices of American mega-consumption. (Personally I don't like the term or the argument. I'm more comfortable with the idea of "right livelihood," which is one of the folds of the Buddhist Eight-fold Path to enlightenment. It's less of an exhortation than an observation — greedy behavior makes a sour life. The idealism of "Voluntary Simplicity" is okay I suppose, but it obscures what I find far more interesting — the sheer practicality of the exercise.

Living below your means is a cheap way to be rich. It's the only easy way to be rich.

If you don't want much and don't get much, you can nearly always get whatever you want.

We're talking about quality, the kind of quality that money would like to buy. Few enough things to have fine ones and take good care of them. Time to do your work well enough to be proud of it. Time for an occasional original idea and time to follow it. Time for community.

And here's an odd corollary I discovered when invited by chance to a motley gathering of Adirondack guideboat builders in upper New York state. The guideboat is considered the Stradivarius of boatbuilding. The meeting was at a palatial lakeside estate into which the wood surgeons fit energetically. Motley as they were, they were used to such surroundings, it turned out, because if you do something at all well the rich will court your company far more than they will someone who has merely money.

There's a couple of hazards in Voluntary Simplicity. One is arrogance. Another is success (artistic, commercial, personal) which leads to temptations which lead back again to Involuntary Complexity — too much going on to do anything right. The worst is doing it because someone said to.

—SB

> The gods are those who either have money or do not want it.
> —*Samuel Butler*

*"Most of the luxuries, and many of the so called comforts of life, are not only not indispensable, but positive hinderances to the elevation of mankind. With respect to luxuries and comforts, the wisest have ever lived a more simple and meager life than the poor. The ancient philosophers, Chinese, Hindoo, Persian, and Greek, were a class than which none has been poorer in outward riches, none so rich in inward. We know not much about them. It is remarkable that *we* know so much of them as we do. The same is true of the more modern reformers and benefactors of their race. None can be an impartial or wise observer of human life but from the vantage ground of what *we* shall call voluntary poverty."

—**Walden**

†Reprinted in **Manas** (see our p. 516) 4 September 1974 and in **CoEvolution Quarterly**, Summer 1977.

§"Voluntary Simplicity," Duane Elgin and Arnold Mitchell, **CoEvolution Quarterly**, Summer 1977, pp. 4-19.

Living on the Earth

The original book on how to be a hippie by one of the original hippies. (Both meanings of "original" — "early" and "creative.") A classic of fundamental funk technique, astonishingly undated.

—SB

Living on the Earth
(Celebrations, Storm Warnings, Formulas, Recipes, Rumors and Country Dances)
Alicia Bay Laurel
1970; 214 pp.

$3.95 postpaid from:
Random House
455 Hahn Road
Westminster, MD 21157
or Whole Earth Household Store

shelter . . .

clear and make level a floor space. dig holes 2 feet deep along the sides and insert tall poles. choose a site out of wind and possible falling trees.

bend poles to meet as arches lash them together. lash one long pole along the top of all the arches and additional poles along the sides.

cover with a tarp or some plastic or an old tent or even a blanket.

turn the cover under the Bottom transverse pole (which is lashed to the outside of the frame) and sew it together.

if rain is imminent: cover with plastic with 2 feet extra on the sides. Dig a ditch around shelter and bury extra plastic so rain will run off top and into ditches.

How to Cut Your Own or Anybody Else's Hair

If you want to go the next step beyond the self-administered razor trim to a real hair cut, with scissors, this book is just about all you'll need. I've been cutting my own hair for a few years now (admittedly harder than cutting someone else's) and have turned out a creditable job every time. I learned how from this extremely clear, well illustrated, and cheaper-than-a-single-professional-haircut book.

—*Donald Ryan*

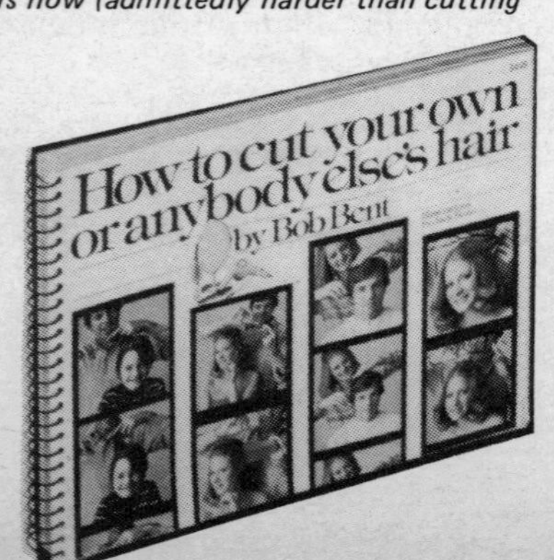

How to Cut Your Own or Anybody Else's Hair
Bob Bent
1975; 126 pp.

$5.95 postpaid from:
Simon and Schuster
Attn: Order Department
1230 Avenue of the Americas
New York, NY 10020
or Whole Earth Household Store

Comb the hair straight out and cut it on an angle conforming to the shape of the head. Do this all the way to the center of the back of the head.

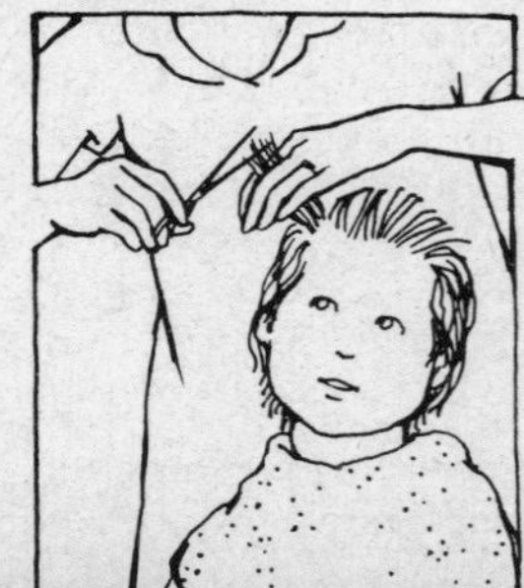

Hairtrimmers

Quickest and cheapest of all haircuts. Compact enough to live in a backpack. So simple you can do it yourself — wet your hair a bit, chop at it with the wide or narrow side, depending. Double-edged razor blades within are replaceable.

—SB

Hairtrimmers
$1 (approx.)
Manufactured by:
Gold Coast Company
Los Angeles, CA
Check your local pharmacy.

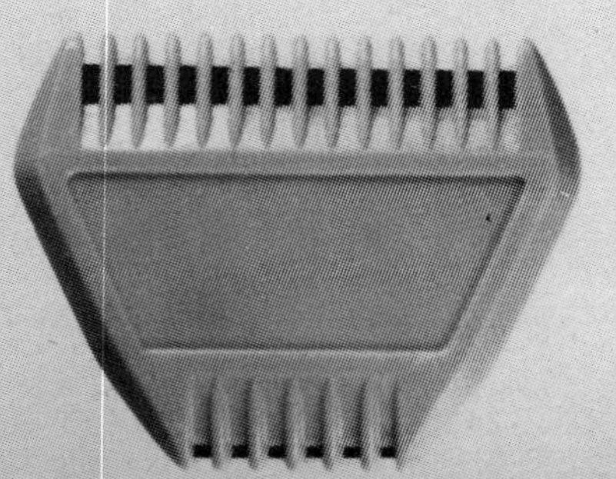

Law Books for Non-lawyers

SOME GENERAL COMMENTS: By design, the entire legal system (civil, criminal and governmental) is an attempt at compensating for people's inability to relate to each other in understanding and trusting ways. It tries to do this by imposing a set of formal and technical rules and procedures as "solutions" to human problems — perhaps, sadly, a necessary evil. But unless you enjoy dealing with personal problems in this way, your trying to negotiate the system is going to be an unpleasant and unnerving experience and you're likely to discover that you're not much good at it. For this reason, if you must resort to the system to work out a personal problem, you probably should let a lawyer help you. If someone else has snared you into the system to work out theirs, definitely don't try to do it yourself.

You can greatly improve on the quality of assistance you'll be able to get from a lawyer, and keep the fees to a minimum, by educating yourself beforehand. People who are not aware of the general legal problems confronting them and who have not personally assessed the relative values of the alternate solutions waste a lot of lawyer's time (equals dollars) and generally end up with less satisfactory results. This is the value of the various "be-your-own-lawyer" books.

Remember, just because you consider the legal trip to be a cynical artificial game and a rip-off is no assurance that your opponent (be it some government bureaucrat, a creditor or an estranged spouse) is not getting off on it.
—Andrew Fluegelman

Everybody's Guide to Small Claims Court

This is a superb book, flawless! No small business should be without it. If you like to sue other people and businesses, then you'll also find it helpful.
—Michael Phillips

Everybody's Guide to Small Claims Court
Ralph Warner
1978, 1980; 264 pp.
$6.95 postpaid from:
Addison-Wesley Publishing Company
Jacob Way
Reading, MA 01867
or Whole Earth Household Store

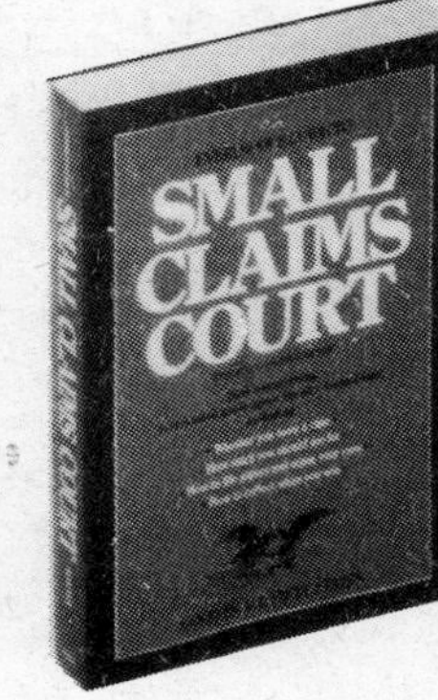

•

The purpose of Small Claims Court is to hear disputes involving modest amounts of money, without long delays and formal rules of evidence. Disputes are normally presented by the people involved. Lawyers are not prohibited in most states, but the limited dollar amounts involved usually make it uneconomical for people to hire them. The maximum amount of money for which you can sue (in legal jargon this is called the "jurisdictional amount") is $750 in California, and $1,000 in a number of states, including New York. These amounts are about average, although there is considerable variation. Some states allow Small Claims Court cases involving thousands of dollars, and others limit Small Claims Court to cases worth no more than two or three hundred dollars.

In recent years the maximum amount for which suits can be brought has been on the rise almost everywhere. Don't rely on your memory, or what a friend tells you, or even what you read here. Call the local Small Claims Court clerk and find out exactly how much you can sue for. You may be pleasantly surprised and find that the maximum is more than you thought.

There are three great advantages of Small Claims Court. First, you get to prepare and present your own case without having to pay a lawyer more than your claim is worth. This right to self-representation should be radically expanded to types of cases not permitted in Small Claims Court. Unfortunately, such expansion runs counter to the self-interest of lawyers, who, like the czars of old Russia or the French nobility at the time of the Revolution, will fight to the death rather than ease the way for sensible reform.

The second great advantage to bringing a dispute to Small Claims Court is simplicity. The gobbledygook of complicated legal forms and language is kept to a minimum. To start your case, you need only fill out a few lines on a simple form (e.g., "Honest Al's Used Chariots owes me $1,000 because the 1977 Chevette they sold me in supposedly 'excellent condition' died less than a mile from the car lot."). When you get to court, you can talk to the judge without a whole lot of "res ipsa loquiturs" and "pendente lites." If you have documents or witnesses, you may present them for what they are worth, with no requirement that you comply with the thousand years' accumulation of fusty, musty procedures, habits and so-called rules of evidence of which the legal profession is so proud.

Third, and perhaps most important, Small Claims Court doesn't take long. Most disputes are heard in court within a month or two from the time the complaint is filed. The judge makes his or her decision on the basis of what is presented in the courtroom, and normally renders a decision within a few days.

ACLU Handbooks

Knowing what your rights are won't keep you from having them violated, but you'll stand a much better chance of protecting yourself when someone tries. The ACLU is publishing, (12 out of 15 so far) an excellent series of handbooks on the basic legal rights of the poor, students, teachers, servicemen, mental patients, women, suspects, etc. Essential information if you (or a dear one) are in any of these categories. And since any one of us may suddenly find ourselves being stopped, questioned and searched by the police, the handbook on suspects' rights is required reading for every citizen.
—Andrew Fluegelman

•

What if you are walking along, stopped and ordered to empty your pockets?

Perhaps you can start by politely saying that you know that that is an illegal search, that you do not consent to such a search, but that you will not struggle if the police persist in ordering you to submit to the search. If the police persist, which they probably will, and if you have contraband on you, you should then start preparing for trial. If there are two police officers, get both badge numbers (but without writing them down, memorize them), since only one policeman will be the arresting officer and the other officer may be inconsistent in his testimony, which sheds doubt on the testimony of both. If the contraband was wrapped in something like a cigarette pack, an eyeglass case, or even paper, that can be helpful at a motion to suppress and you should try to retrieve any wrapping that the police leave behind. Most importantly, look around you for witnesses, even witnesses who just saw you go in and out of a building. If you can, tell your name to people standing nearby so that if anyone wants to, they will be able to find you. If you get out of jail come back to the scene as soon as possible, and if it is a residential neighborhood talk to people who hang around, visit all the apartments with windows that face the street and ask people if they saw you. If the scene of the arrest is a business area, it may be fruitful, if you know that some people saw the arrest, to distribute leaflets to passersby who are on the street at approximately the same time of the day that the arrest took place. Finding one independent witness, who does not know you and has no stake in the outcome, is something even the most biased judges find difficult to ignore.

At the point of asking you to go with them, the police will usually act very friendly and say that they just want to discuss some matters with you; don't be misled into assuming that they want to talk to you as a friend. Even in states which have the Uniform Arrest Act, covering another type of circumstance, it seems probable that, unless there is an actual arrest, the citizen has the right to refuse. You can ask if you are under arrest, and if they say no you can tell them politely that you refuse to accompany them and that, if they order or force you to go with them, this means that they have arrested you and according to the Fourth Amendment to the United States Constitution, they cannot arrest you unless they have probable cause. If they then insist you must, of course, obey unless you want to risk being forced and/or beaten. At the police station, you can again ask if you are under arrest and if you are not, you should say that you are leaving and begin to walk out the door. If the police do not let you leave, you should insist on having a lawyer and if you cannot afford one, you can tell them that they have the responsibility to get you a lawyer free of charge. You should refuse to answer any questions; this may result in your release since, if they did not arrest you in the first place, it means that they might not have sufficient evidence to hold you.

The Supreme Court has held that the police do not have the right to round up people against whom they have no evidence and take the fingerprints of those people. See *Davis vs. Mississippi, supra,* discussed on page 19. Should you be picked up, not formally arrested and directed to submit to fingerprinting, you have the right to refuse; the police will be unable to take your fingerprints against your will since the slightest movement will spoil the print.
—**Rights of Suspects**

The Rights of Prisoners
David Rodovsky, et al.
1973, 1977; 128 pp.
$1.75 postpaid

The Rights of Students
Alan Levine, Eve Carey, Diane Divoky
1973, 1977; 160 pp.
$2 postpaid

The Rights of Women
Susan C. Ross
1973; 384 pp.
$2 postpaid

The Rights of the Poor
Sylvia Law
1974; 176 pp.
$1.50 postpaid

The Rights of Mental Patients
Bruce Ennis and Loren Siegel
1973; 336 pp.
$2 postpaid

The Rights of Teachers
David Rubin
1972; 176 pp.
$1.75 postpaid

The Rights of Military Personnel
(Formerly the Rights of Servicemen)
Robert S. Rivkin and Barton F. Stichman
1972, 1977; 154 pp.
$1.50 postpaid

The Rights of Suspects
Oliver Rosengart
1974; 122 pp.
$1.50 postpaid

The Rights of Reporters
Joel M. Gora
1974; 254 pp.
$1.50 postpaid

The Rights of Aliens
David Carliner
1977; 255 pp.
$2.20 postpaid

The Rights of Gay People
E. Carrington Boggan, et al.
1975; 268 pp.
$2.20 postpaid

The Rights of Hospital Patients
George J. Annas
1975; 246 pp.
$2 postpaid

Book list
$1

all from:
American Civil Liberties Union
Literature Department
132 West 43rd Street
New York, NY 10036
or Whole Earth Household Store

The Living Together Kit

I have been legally married, have done my own legal divorce, have been common law married, and am participating in a common law divorce. My daughter was born out of bureaucratic, regulatory wedlock, which, to all you oldtime assholes, makes her a bastard. I am glad this book has come along, because, like the mouse chasing the elephant, it means that some attention is being paid by someone in the legal profession to the rights of us folks who can't muster up enough confidence in any government to sign papers concerning our own damn business. As well as setting out suggestions for do-it-yourself forms for many kinds of agreements between folks living together, this book breaks the legal terminology down into its human form at the heads of chapters, so there is a step-by-step understanding system at work which leads me, for one, to trust what the lawyer-authors were telling me. Should be real helpful to anyone who wants to live right out in the open with a partner without paper vows or wedding dresses. If your eyes are getting a little pink around the edges because you have been in the closet too long, try this book and get acquainted with your rights as a cohabitor.
—J.D. Smith

The Living Together Kit
(Formerly Sex, Living Together and the Law)
Toni Ihara and Ralph Warner
1974, 1979; 224 pp.
$6.95 postpaid from:
Fawcett Books
600 Third Avenue
New York, NY 10016
or Whole Earth Household Store

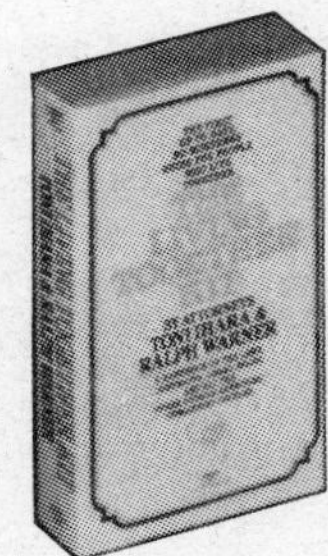

•

We suggest written agreements for major purchases. . . . The purpose of the agreement is not to have something to show an attorney so he can fight for you, but to prevent this kind of action.

THE RISING SUN
NEIGHBORHOOD NEWSLETTER

One time Al Capp was at a prayer breakfast Nixon had at the White House and he asked a butler for coffee with one lump of sugar and milk not cream. Two years later Al Capp was talking to Nixon in the Oval Office and when it was time for refreshments, Nixon said, "I know what you want, coffee with one lump of sugar and milk not cream." Al Capp told his brother this story when his brother asked him if he thought Nixon knew what was going on during Watergate.
—Story told by E.J. Kahn in *About* The New Yorker *and Me*

Shared Houses, Shared Lives

Far cheaper than living alone or as a closed family, somewhat freer (due to related tasks), considerably more adventurous. True book. —SB

Ten years ago, I reluctantly joined a commune. It was my ex-husband's idea; he moved on, I stayed. I left the household just this last Christmas. The other oldest member and I used to joke that we had "lived together" longer than many people stay married. We watched a lot of living groups come and go, some were formed with high ideals and goals, others were haphazard and unplanned, still others had hedonistic purposes. Few have survived. Again I hear people becoming interested in sharing homes and lifestyles, but uncertain about how to begin. Reading this book would be a good way to start. It discusses the often vital problems many communes have run into, ways to deal with or circumvent them, and how to make it all work for you. —Evelyn Eldridge-Diaz

Shared Houses Shared Lives
$6.50 postpaid from:
Houghton-Mifflin Co.
Wayside Road
Burlington, MA 01803
or Whole Earth Household Store

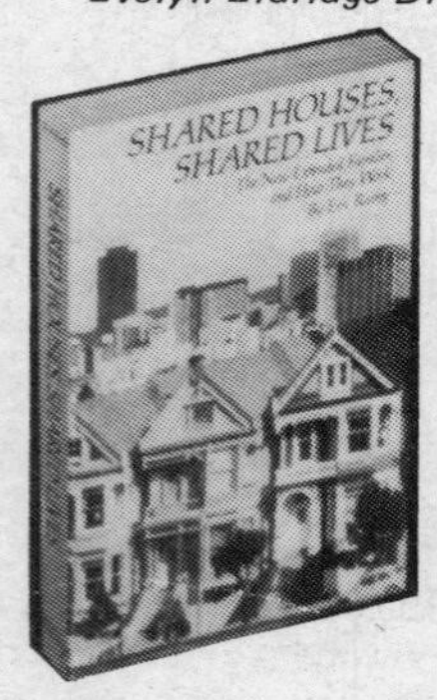

•

One motive is economic. For example: three families or six or seven single people may share a gracious, older house — the kind of house that was built with plenty of space for the much larger families of two or three generations ago. Everyone gets a private bedroom and shares ample living space. But the rent or house payments are split three, six, or seven ways. A single member's share of the housing costs may be as little as a hundred dollars a month or even less in certain cases. Because utility and food costs are shared, they are sharply reduced as well. The two families who rent a house together in Seattle found that communal living cut their utility and food bills by about 40 percent.

The low cost of communal living allows people with modest incomes to live in the kind of home that, alas, has grown far too costly to build today — a solid house with carved woodwork, high ceilings, a fireplace, and a stained-glass window, with trees and a backyard, and in a pleasant neighborhood of similar houses. Many people are able to enjoy life in such a house only because they live communally.

People with moderate or high incomes accumulate an impressive cash surplus while living communally. Often they spend it on travel or on a country home (sometimes the group buys one together). But people who are drawn to communal living for the economic advantages alone tend to be disappointed. Communal living seems to work when people have a genuine desire to become involved with one another as people, not just as partners in a plan to acquire possessions or enjoy a more luxurious lifestyle.

Efficiency is another motivation for living communally. People who don't like having to spend several hours a week keeping house find that shared housekeeping requires only a fraction of that time. Most commune members clean their own room plus one common room. Because they take turns cooking and grocery shopping, members of most groups cook one night a week and shop about once a month. When a group has small children, members can take turns baby-sitting. Parents who once had to stay home with their kids now hold a job or attend classes.

Some Americans feel trapped in a high-consumption lifestyle that supports a high rate of industrial production, which in turn causes continued pollution. These people are motivated to live communally because of their concern for the environment. Three families who decide to share a house no longer need three stoves, three blenders, three washers and dryers, three swing sets, or three newspaper subscriptions; one of each will do. Communal households surveyed in Minneapolis had far fewer appliances per capita than the average family household. Per capita natural-gas consumption was 40 percent less than that of the average household.

Concern for personal growth is another motivation for living communally. At work people learn to function as a polite and efficient team and to avoid more personal contact. Almost inevitably, they gain in self-understanding and in the ability to communicate and to be assertive.

Some people are motivated to live communally because it can open the door to another kind of personal growth. These people find their jobs dissatisfying and yearn to do more fulfilling work. Because of the decrease in their living costs, commune members find it possible to give up their nine-to-five jobs and do something more rewarding. Before I lived communally, I was a newspaper reporter. When I fell asleep in a school board meeting that I was supposed to be covering, I was forced to admit to myself that I had grown bored with my job. I joined a communal household, cutting my living expenses to less than four hundred dollars a month. With the emotional support of my housemates I got up the courage to quit my job and began writing books. Other commune members abandon traditional careers to support themselves by making crafts, leading growth workshops, or pursuing some other form of self-employment. Commune members who want to make a more conventional career change are often able to finance a return to school. Members who have become disillusioned with careers sometimes take part-time jobs, using the rest of their time to launch artistic or political projects, or to follow their creativity in some other direction.

There are many motives for living communally. But there is one underlying motivation that is the most important reason people join or start communal households. When a sociologist asked members of Boston households about the satisfaction of communal living, the great majority checked one box on the questionnaire. It read, "companionship, security, and a supportive atmosphere."

The Integral Urban House

Like the Farallones Institute's Integral Urban House in Berkeley, CA, this fat book offers a basic education in the good stuff: gardening without chemicals, energy saving, solar retrofits, composting, grey water management, etc. If you've elected to be an urban citizen and not flee to the country, you'll need to know much of what is presented here. The house has given many thousands of people their first look at real people doing all the "alternative" things so often seen in the media but so rearely seen in the everyday life of most of us. The book serves in much the same way but in more detail: offering in addition to advice, a number of working plans for such things as windowbox greenhouselets. A good bibliography will serve those who desire more detailed information. The house and the book share a lack of tight economic discussion and largely ignore political aspects of the project; that's what's being worked on now. —J. Baldwin

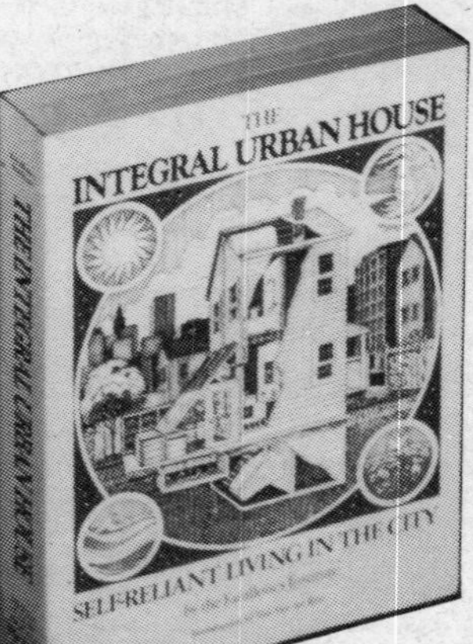

The Integral Urban House
(Self-Reliant Living in the City)
The Farallones Institute Staff
1979; 494 pp.

$12.95 postpaid from:
Sierra Club Books
Box 3886
Rincon Annex
San Francisco, CA 94119
or Whole Earth Household Store

•

Electric blankets use about 175 to 200 watts on an intermittent basis, and using them — as opposed to heating the entire house for the purpose of keeping the bed warm — can save a great deal of energy. A relatively low house temperature setting of, say, 60 degrees can be made tolerable by an electric blanket with a lightweight insulated cover. The idea is to get the heat to where it is needed. If you are going to purchase one of these appliances, get the best model available. (Check the ratings given by consumer testing services such as Consumers Unions.) Safety is an important consideration in selecting any electrical appliance, and careful shopping is therfore vital.

The shock of getting out of bed into the cold to go to the bathroom can be offset by keeping a potty or watering can near the bed or by the use of spot heaters where needed. Again the strategy is to focus on the heat needs rather than to heat the entire house.

Figure 14-2. **Yearly Energy Budget of a Lawn Compared to an Alfalfa Patch**

Lawn 20 square meters — Grass clippings (95.000 Kcal); Trash can; Labor (2.500 Kcal); Fuel (10.000 Kcal); Fertilizer, pesticides (2.500 Kcal)

Alfalfa 20 square meters — Alfalfa hay (110.000 Kcal); Composted manure; Labor (5.000 Kcal); 1 lb fryer; 21 lbs rabbit meat (15.000 Kcal)

	Energy Input, Kcal	*Energy Yield, Plant*	*Kcal: Human food*
Lawn	15.000	95.000	—
Alfalfa	5.000	110.000	15.000

Sharing the Children

The problem: to distribute the duties of child-rearing more equitably, to alleviate the tensions in family life resulting from the needs of children and to do a better job of raising the children. Solution: cooperative child care, re-creation of the village within the city, a group of parents sharing their children by organizing an unorthodox day care center that is non-institutional, uncertified, time-funded, self-equipped, and determined only by the participating persons (miniature and large economy size). This is not an instructional book that outlines how to start a day care center — except as an account of a particular long lasting successful one in the Morningside Heights area of New York City. The story is well-written and uplifting. I was entranced and I don't even have children. —Diana Fairbanks *[Suggested by Lester Natzger]*

Sharing the Children
(Village child rearing within the city)
Nora Harlow
1976; 154 pp.

OUT OF PRINT
Harper and Row
Get this book back in print!

•

It wasn't being mothers that we hated so much. It was that being a mother at this particular time and particular place meant isolation, meant only being able to use your mind in a very limited way, meant spending years of your life in the company of child minds and child emotions. The structure of the relationship with the child was wrong. Banding together as women with young children, we quickly found that our fears of separation were groundless. We hadn't separated at all. We had just included more people in the circle of mother and child.

Urban Homesteading

This is an outstanding guide for urban homesteaders and policy makers involved in housing. Unfortunately it is five years too late for most people. "Gentrification" (return to the inner cities by the rich and powerful) has already eliminated urban homesteading in most U.S. cities.

If you're interested in the years of hard work of repairing an abandoned house and you're willing to live in the few northeastern cities that are still experiencing inner city decay (Rochester, Newark, Harrisburg) this is the definitive book with examples from four cities. —Michael Phillips

Urban Homesteading
James W. Hughes and Kenneth D. Bleakly, Jr.
1975; 276 pp.

$15 postpaid from:
Center for Urban Policy Research
Rutgers University
Building 4051
Kilmer Campus
New Brunswick, NJ 08903

•

The concept is a simple one which borrows from past experience. The homesteader "purchases" his parcel by the agreement to reside in the unit and improve it over a certain period of time. For this he receives title to the property free, or for a nominal charge. The central thesis underlying this program is that homeownership fosters a higher degree of parcel maintenance and specific attachment. The objective is to make previously unattractive units available to qualified owners for little or no initial cost, with the result that parcels which have been economically nonviable can come back on the market simply for the cost of rehabilitation. Implied, but not stated, it is the hope that new residents will be young, upwardly mobile people whose present income does not really reflect their potential. Ideally the program will draw these people back into the central city where, through hard work and a large amount of "sweat equity," the homesteaders will rebuild their homes and, indirectly, the city. Thus, by increasing the number of homeowners, especially in a mix of income brackets, improvements can be made in the quality of life in urban areas.

How to Inspect a House

A valuable little book on what to look for in buying a house. How to evaluate foundations, dry rot, electrical and plumbing systems. If you can make an accurate estimate of repairs needed, you'll know better what you're getting into and how much to offer.
—Lloyd Kahn

Pretty valuable information if you're selling a house or keeping a house, too. *—SB*

How to Inspect a House
(formerly Don't Go Buy Appearances)
George C. Hoffman
1972, 1979; 198 pp.

$4.95 postpaid from:
Delta Books
One Dag Hammarskjold Plaza
245 East 47th Street
New York, NY 10017
or Whole Earth Household Store

↑
In two or three rooms, remove the plate from an electric outlet on the exterior walls only. Wedge the scredriver between the box and the wall covering. Push the screwdriver gently through to the exterior wall. Feel for a slight resistance; you're determining whether or not there is insulation in the wall. Move the instrument about a little. Nothing? Okay. Try in a few more rooms. One test is not conclusive. You'll know if you meet a spongy resistance; if so, you've got insulation in that wall. It's good to know, for it tells you of hidden quality.

•

Thousands of articles have been written on how to change washers to stop drippy faucets, but few mention bonnet packing. Changing washers won't prevent leaking bonnets. If you're going to do the job yourself, here is one simple remedy. Remove the old packing and wrap the stem with ordinary cotton string to fill the void of the bonnet. With this method there's no need to have a certain size of bonnet gasket. String can be wrapped to fit any size. It will last five years or more. I've never known a plumber who didn't carry a ball of cotton string. With that he can meet most emergencies. He uses strings many times in place of gaskets in the large chrome nuts on the drainpipes beneath sinks. You can too.

Essex Forge floor lamp

If you've ever shopped for a floor lamp, you know that it's near impossible to find a versatile durable lamp at a reasonable cost. Most of what can be found in furniture stores looks like something that escaped from a hospital operating room or a minimal sculpture exhibition.

I came across Essex Forge in a New Yorker ad and damned if their catalog didn't have a fine, simple adjustable floor lamp that won't tip over, for less than sixty bucks. A real find, and it comes with a decent shade. Essex also makes a lot of other useful items, adapted from colonial designs. *—Sim Van der Ryn*

Essex Forge, Inc.
Catalog

$1 from:
Essex Forge, Inc.
One Old Dennison Road
Essex, CT 06426

Bridge lamp — $56.50

Home for Sale by Owner

You have a home to sell, and you don't like realtors and their habits, and you don't know zip about selling a home. What do you do? A real good start is to read this book. Might be a good idea to read it if you're thinking of buying too, for it is a very good presentation of both ends of the deal. It's also somewhat of an indictment of the realty trade (which could use a bit of public scrutiny these days in my opinion). The tricks, pitfalls, forms, procedures and trade secrets all are shown and in a relatively readable manner, fortunately. Reading it left me with a sense of outrage though. Too bad a book like this is necessary. *—J. Baldwin*

Home for Sale by Owner
Gerald M. Steiner
1976; 200 pp.

$7.95 postpaid from:
Hawthorn Books
260 Madison Avenue
New York, NY 10016
or Whole Earth Household Store

•

If your home needs $1,000 in repair work, you'll have to drop your selling price by at least $3,000 unless you decide to invest the money to remedy the condition.

The Household Pollutants Guide

We all know that "they" are trying to kill us, right? But how? This nasty little book will show you where the dangers lie in your very own home. It's presented in a non-hysterical way, but the cumulative effect of reading the whole book is to run . . . someplace. Paranoids will find all this delightful. The rest of us will be more careful and I hope be inspired to put some heat on the people who sell us poison by whatever name. The book is from the Center for Science in the Public Interest. We should thank them. *—J. Baldwin*

The Household Pollutants Guide
Albert J. Fritsch, Editor
1978; 309 pp.

$3.50 postpaid from:
Doubleday & Company
501 Franklin Avenue
Garden City, NY 11530
or Whole Earth Household Store

•

Even if fiber glass is ultimately exonerated of carcinogenesis, the inhalation of airborne fibers can still injure sensitive lung tissue. Those working regularly with this material have a tendency to develop such respiratory tract ailments as bronchitis, pharyngitis, rhinitis, asthma, laryngitis, sinusitis, and nosebleed.

There is little disagreement that fiber glass is also a potent skin irritant. This material is by far the most important cause of mechanical contact dermatitis. Although many people suffer only minor discomfort from this disease, others may have severe reactions. Fiber glass dermatitis is no longer just an occupational hazard for insulation workers, but a significant problem for the consumer. This is because of the increasing influx of fiber glass products into our homes over the past fifteen years: curtains, draperies, tablecloths, etc. The problem does not usually arise in their use, but in their cleaning. When these items are laundered, large numbers of glass fibers may be released to contaminate other fabrics in the same (or future) wash load. Physicians have reported entire family outbreaks of dermatitis from contaminated sheets, towels, etc.

The Mother Earth News

A great country wishbook for city dwellers who are thinking of cutting out to the woods — a lot of people; over 500,000 use it, they say. As the beginnings of the magazine are somewhat connected with **Whole Earth***'s early success, I have a mix of feelings about it that might be better expressed by frankness than by faint praise. No one we know that actually lives in the country uses the thing. It's no longer among the 60 or so publications that* **CoEvolution** *subscribes to because the yield turning its innumerable pages looking for a bit of news is too low. Trust wilts amid the overwhelming ad space and uncritically enthusiastic articles ("Recycled Floor Mats!") and cornpone language (energy writer Wilson Clark still winces about an article of his that* **Mother Earth News** *"translated into babytalk").*

On the other hand, founder John Shuttleworth's heart is mostly in the right place environmentally. The "Plowboy" interviews often are quite good and with non-celebrities of real interest. There's a conversational interaction that encourages readers to write and get published, often for the first time in their lives. Some of the ideas work. And there's that itchy audience. Solar designer Steve Baer noted, "When **CoEvolution** *publishes something about Zomeworks, all I get is a good feeling. When* **Mother Earth News** *does, I get a lot of orders."* *—SB*

If you're a struggling artist in need of cash, Gary Nelson suggests you paint "House Portraits." ↓

The Mother Earth News
Bruce Woods, Editor

$15/year (6 issues)
from:
The Mother Earth News
P.O. Box 70
Hendersonville, NC 28739

•

Plowboy: The biointensive farmer will have to face the same kinds of problems that most gardeners tackle, then.

John Jeavons: Exactly, and the *last* thing I'd want anyone to do is read this interview . . . say, "Wow, that sounds fantastic!" . . . and invest his or her life savings in trying to set up a commercial mini-farming operation.

Such a person would be far better off to start with a single bed the first year and — if that project is a success — expand to between five and ten plots the following year . . . continually learning and expanding, as long as the venture proves successful, until he or she is able to work part time as a mini-farmer and part time at a "normal" job.

Naturally, the *ultimate* goal would be to quit all outside work and step into an established, minimal risk, "pocket farming" operation. The approach is cautious, but we're talking about dealing with living biological systems. Growing crops — by *any* method — can't be approached like a paint-by-number picture.

Of course, a lot of folks have no interest in commercial farming at all. But I really encourage everyone who has the *slightest* curiosity about the method to try one small raised bed — it doesn't have to be more than three by three feet — in his or her back yard. Beacuse — after a little practice — he or she should be able to grow enough carrots, for instance, for one person for a full year . . . right in that tiny nine-square-foot plot in the course of a three month growing season. And even such a small step toward self-sufficiency can be an incredibly exciting and inspiring experience.

Judy Sizemore reveals a cash-producing craft for the ecology-minded. Make recycled-glass wind chimes. →

THE RISING SUN
NEIGHBORHOOD NEWSLETTER

Growing up in Cincinnati during the Cold War, I got mixed up about which Reds the headlines were talking about.

Living in One Room

Small is in fact beautiful, or at least it can be if you're clever at using space. This happy collection of ingenuity shows what can be done. Some of the ideas border on being downright fiendish; disappearing kitchens and beds abound. Most rooms show that compact living need not mean lowered living standards. (I can vouch for that, I've been living in a 17-foot Airstream trailer, the Silver Turd, for 7 years now and like it fine.) It would be nice if the work shown here signifies the beginning of a trend away from Buick Architecture. —J. Baldwin

Living in One Room
Jon Naar and Molly Siple
1976; 150 pp.

$5.95 postpaid from:
Vintage Books
455 Hahn Road
Westminster, MD 21157
or Whole Earth
Household Store

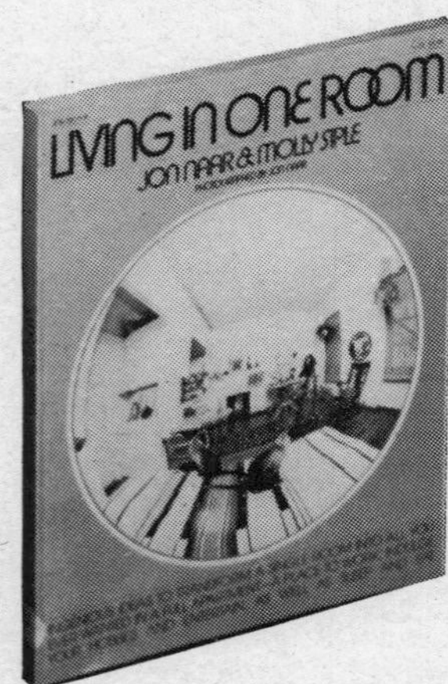

Painter Kas Zapkus created this ingenious dish drainer to drip water directly into the sink, via a shaped rubber mat, saving valuable space and eliminating the bother of sponging the counter. ↓

Instant Furniture

Though not quite as instant as a Middle Sears Roebuck couch from Salvation Army, these designs might help you take on a somewhat different attitude towards furniture and other objects that are expensive to buy, own and move. It might be the start of a New American Colonial style. The instructions are remarkably easy to deal with. —J. Baldwin

Instant Furniture
Peter S. Stamberg
1976; 160 pp.

$8.95 postpaid from:
Van Nostrand
Reinhold Company
Order Department
7625 Empire Drive
Florence, KY 41042
or Whole Earth
Household Store

Hosonaga table. Designer: Kazuhide Takahama

The Spacemaker Book

Another excellent collection of ideas intended to make living in relatively tight places seem less tight. The ideas here are less oriented towards one-room living than towards general canniness in space use and visual spaciousness Most of this will be old hat to mobile home dwellers and to Europeans (especially Scandinavians) who have been doing this sort of thing for years. Replace expensive, resource-eating volume with compact cleverness. Exceptionally good drawings. —J. Baldwin

The Spacemaker Book
Ellen Liman
1977; 120 pp.

OUT OF PRINT
Viking Press
New York, NY

Xerox it at your library.

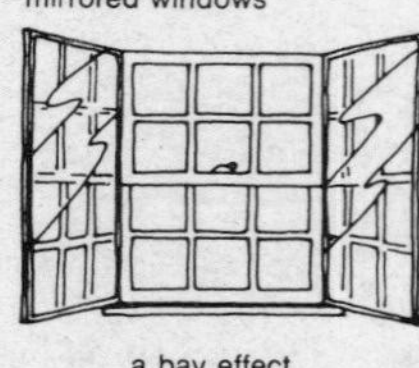

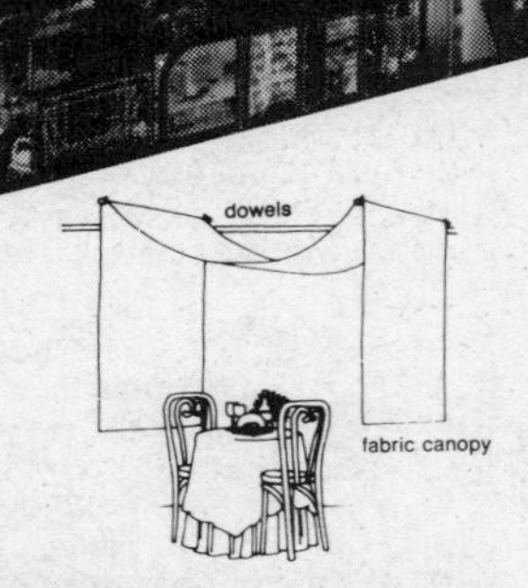

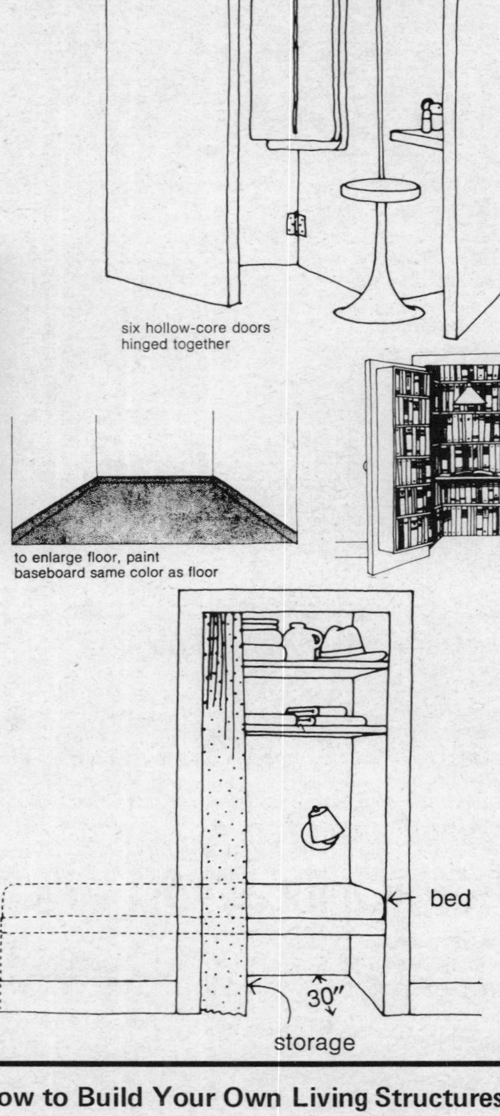

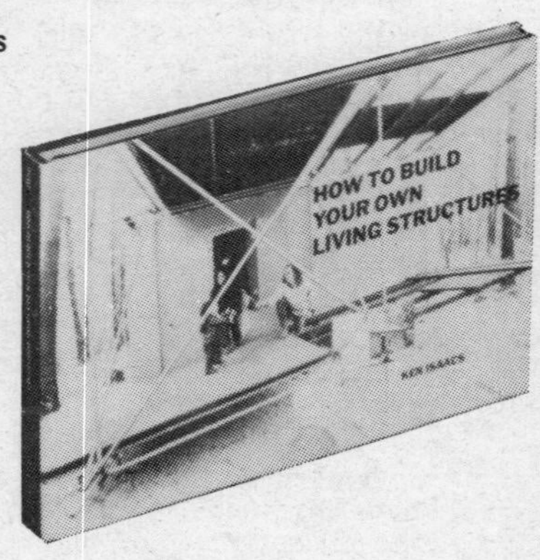

Manhattan Ad Hoc Housewares

Many high tech household items are well suited to small or frequently changed living areas. This is one source. They are middlemen of course. For the raw goods, see our pp. 148 - 154.

(Stephanie Mills, resident aesthete, says, "I hate Hi Tech; nevertheless there are some things in this catalog which interest me.") —SB

Manhattan Ad Hoc Housewares
Catalog

free from:
Manhattan Ad Hoc
Housewares
842 Lexington Avenue
New York, NY 10021

Scotty cart — Made for factories, classrooms, toolrooms, garages. Fire-engine red or black baked-enamel finish. For dining room, kitchen, pantry, office. Light weight for maneuverability. 3" casters with rubber treads. Three shelves for generous storage. Drawer 24" x 14½" x 3" H has a padlock eye. Disassembled. Overall dimensions: 29"W x 18"D x 34" H $155.

Poppy Shiki-buton (Japanese folding bed)

Pattern and instructions for the fabric-covered hinged foam mattress that folds into a sofa, in single, camper and queen sizes. Diana Sloat

Poppy Shiki-buton
Pattern and instructions

$4 postpaid from:
Poppy Fabric
2072 Addison Street
Berkeley, CA 94704

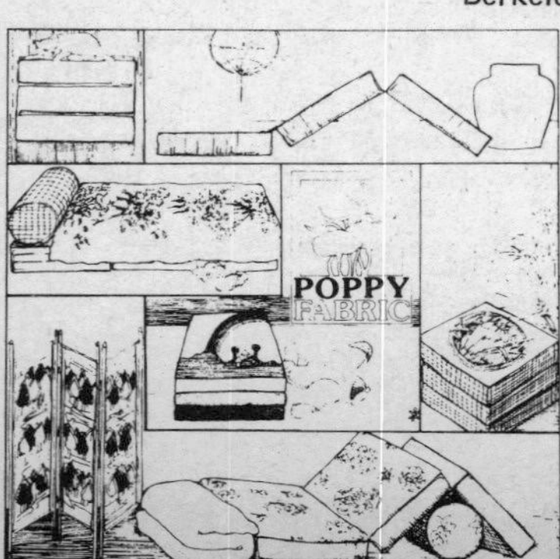

How to Build Your Own Living Structures

You may remember Ken Isaacs from Popular Science Blueprint Projects of the late '60s series. He has compiled his years of micro living structure construction into a work manual at long last. Included are detailed plans for his famous Superchair, the Microdorm and the Space Module, to name a few. Using his book and a handful of 12 year olds equipped with a second-hand drill press, we have built four such structures using discarded motorcycle crates as the raw material. It's the ol' Tinker-Toy-basic-module-building-unit trip. One soon learns elementary mass production techniques in creation of one's own personal Industrial Revolution. The book assumes that the reader knows nothing of woods, tools and connections — this I appreciate. Buying tools at farm sales, understanding wood terminology and identifying a "real" hardware store are all part of his package, along with a rap on the most important tool, "Head-tooling." Here is nomadic, modular, 3D living on a "2X4" budget. —Joe Eddy Brown

How to Build Your Own Living Structures
Ken Isaacs
1974; 136 pp.

$6.45 postpaid from:
Crown Publishers
One Park Avenue South
New York, NY 10016
or Whole Earth
Household Store

3-D LIVING. Living Structures are a way for close people to be close in a single space without getting in each other's hair. The level change really does it.

High-Tech

I have no doubt that if I were acquisitive I would be equipping my life actively with high tech house gear and decor. The stuff is sturdy, highly practical, often cheap, and — except for right now — outside of fashionability. The fashion is understandable — the clarity of the high tech approach is often quite beautiful. But I think sewer manhole covers and military architecture are beautiful and Regency furniture is strictly for unfrequented museums.

This well-made book lavishly covers the range of high tech possibilities, with a generous if unannotated directory of suppliers — over 2,000! —SB

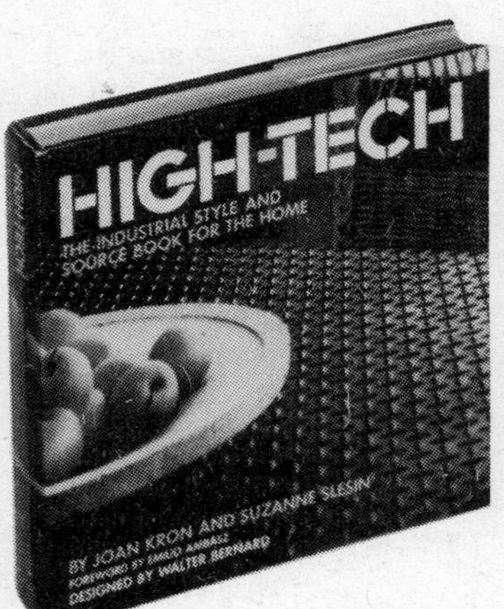

High-Tech
(The Industrial Style and Source Book for the Home)
Joan Kron and Suzanne Slesin
1978; 286 pp.

$30.50 postpaid from:
Clarkson N. Potter, Inc.
Crown Publishers
One Park Avenue South
New York, NY 10016
or Whole Earth Household Store

Containerization — Styrofoam, usually used as packing material, has been carved into kitchen utensil-shaped niches by Rome architect Lino Schenal. ↑

Bookish — Eighty-four-inch-high oak library ladder is $98 from Putnam Rolling Ladder Co. Track is $2 a foot uninstalled. →

Designer Tim Romanello used movers' pads from Rennert ($3.50 to $5.50 per square yard) to cover the bed, floor, and cabinets in his one-room apartment. This fabric must be sanitized before use.

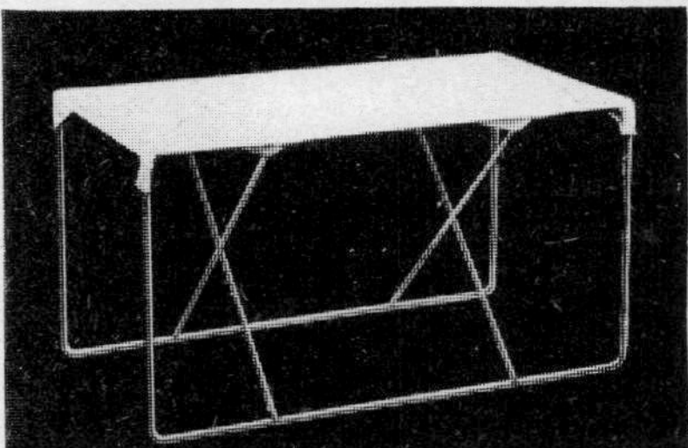

Laundry — Canvas work-top table/bench, 18 inches high, from Steele Canvas Basket Company. Retails for $13 at A. Liss.

Air Ionization and Air Ion Generators

by David Sobel, M.D.

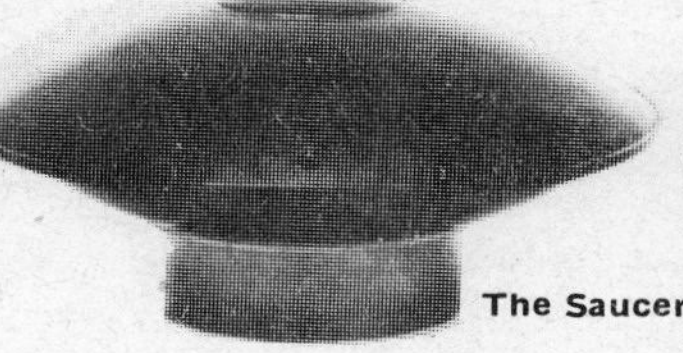

The Saucer

Pro Team ionizer

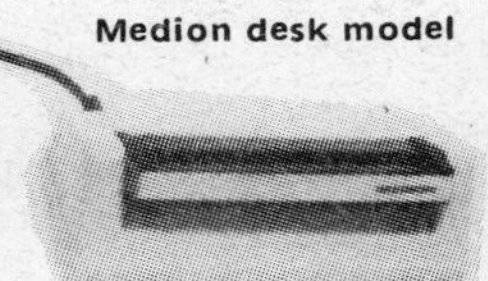

Medion desk model

Modulion

Omega 700

Have you ever wondered about that particular freshness in the air after a thunderstorm or the invigorating atmosphere around waterfalls or in the mountains? This "extra something" in the air may be due to electrically charged gas molecules called small air ions. These minute and short-lived charged molecules are created in nature by radioactive elements in the soil, cosmic and solar ultraviolet radiation, the shearing of water droplets in waterfalls, and the friction of wind over land.

In fresh, unpolluted air there are usually between 1000 to 4000 small ions per cm^3 with a slight predominance of positively charged ions. Certain health spas and vacation areas (e.g. Yosemite Valley) have higher concentrations of ions, particularly negatively charged ions, which may, in part, account for some of the reported health benefits. On the other hand, certain weather complexes — the "winds of ill-repute" like the Santa Ana of California, the *foehn* of southern Europe, or the *Khamsin* of Israel — cause weather-sensitive people to have headaches, respiratory distress, nervousness, and other complaints. These "winds of ill-repute" are marked by a dramatic upset in the air ion balance with an increase in positive ions.

In general, it appears that negatively charged ions have desirable effects, while positive ions, or ion-depleted air, has ill effects. The biological activity of this subtle, often overlooked environmental factor is remarkable, ranging from lethal effects on some bacteria, to stimulation of plant growth. Air ions also affect various neurohormones and may decrease the incidence and severity of migraine headaches, respiratory infections, asthma, hay fever, and various nervous disorders.*

The urban environment wreaks havoc on the delicate natural air ion balance. Air pollutants and cigarette smoke deactivate small air ions. Air conditioning and central heating strip the air of ions. Asphalt and concrete land coverings prevent new ion production by the natural radioactive elements in the soil. The result is that we are likely to spend most of our time in ion-depleted environments particularly deficient in negative air ions.

Air ion levels can be restored and improved with negative air ion generators. These small "black boxes" were introduced in the 1950's in the U.S. and aggressively marketed. Unsubstantiated health claims were made for air ionization from relieving constipation to curing cancer. Also, some of the early machines produced unsafe levels of ozone. The FDA acted swiftly, banning all health claims and setting ozone safety limits.

Recently there has been a resurgence of interest in air ionization and the availability of negative air ion generators. They are now marketed as air purifiers to freshen the air, remove pollutants, pollen, smoke and odors. Many different models are available for cars, single rooms, and larger areas.

For a standard-sized room, most cost between $80 and $250. Some of the generators use higher voltages and produce a larger static electric field around the machines. This may produce a mild static discharge similar to the spark when you shuffle your feet on a carpet and then touch a metal object. All ion generators will precipitate dirt particles from the air, which may create a difficult-to-clean dirt film on walls and other objects near the ionizer. This can be a nuisance, but most people seem to prefer the dirt on the walls rather than in the air.

Unfortunately, there are no accepted industry standards for comparing the various ion generators in terms of ion output or effective room concentrations of ions. Some generators do produce more ions, but more is not necessarily better. The size of the room, amount of smoke and pollutants, number of people, placement of the ionizer, etc., as well as the ionizer's output will determine the effective ion concentration. Ion levels above 10,000 to 50,000 ions per cm^3 have not been shown to be desirable for long term exposure. I have not had the opportunity to do extensive comparative testing of the various ion generators now available. However, I have put together a chart comparing some of the better models designed for single room use. The listing is by no means complete. The prices are approximate, and all these models come with a 1 or 2 year warranty. I should repeat that, at present, these air ionizers are intended for cleaning the air and restoring natural air ion balance, not for therapeutic applications. ■

*See "Air Ions and Health" by A.P. Krueger and D.S. Sobel, in **Ways of Health: Holistic Approaches to Ancient and Contemporary Medicine**, edited by D.S. Sobel, Harcourt Brace Jovanovich, 1979.

NEGATIVE AIR ION GENERATORS

Manufacturer	Model	Price	Noise	Emitter Element	On/Off Switch	Indicator Light	Power Source	Variable Output Control	Static Discharges
Amcor, Ltd.* 350 Fifth Ave. New York, NY 10011	Modulion	$ 80	quiet	recessed needles	yes	yes	wall current	no	no
Clean Air Technology 165 University Palo Alto, CA 94310	Clean Air Machine (900)	$ 85	buzzes	needles	no	yes	wall current	no	no
	Clean Air Machine (1200)	$100	buzzes	needles	no	yes	wall current	no	yes
DEV Industries 5721 Arapahoe Boulder, CO 80303	Air-Care-I	$100	quiet	soft brushes	no	yes	wall current	yes	no
Ion Environments Box 33165 San Diego, CA 92103	The Saucer	$150	buzzes	protected needle	no	yes	wall current	yes	yes
ION Systems* 940 Dwight Way Berkeley, CA 94710	Ionosphere	$ 90	hisses	bristles	no	no	wall current	no	yes
	Omega 700	$255	quiet	needles	yes	yes	wall current	yes	no
Medion International* 261 Hamilton Ave. Palo Alto, CA 94301	Desk	$ 85	quiet	concealed needles	yes	yes	wall current	no	no
	Portable	$175	quiet	needles	yes	no	wall current/ battery	no	no
	Standard	$265	quiet	concealed needles	no	yes	wall current	no	no
PRO-TEAM 4425 Carson St. Oakland, CA 94619	Ionizer	$ 90	buzzes	needles	no	yes	wall current	no	no

*Car ionizer also available.

THE RISING SUN
NEIGHBORHOOD NEWSLETTER

The first time Kathy saw a hummingbird when she was a kid, she told her mother she'd seen a little duck, because mallards were the only birds she'd seen with colors that bright.

Ladies' Home Journal Art of Homemaking

Comprehensive reference for those whose mothers never taught them. Its focus is on staying organized behind a myriad of household chores; its strongest point that it covers care of current fabrics, furniture, and appliances mother never heard of. It gives concise how-to instructions for every imaginable routine, and then encourages you not to be too compulsive — an attractive paradox.
—Diana Barich

Ladies' Home Journal Art of Homemaking
Virginia T. Habeeb
1973, 1978; 588 pp.
$6.95 postpaid from:
Simon & Schuster
Attn: Order Department
1230 Avenue of the Americas
New York, NY 10020

•

Avoid the use of chrome near the seashore, as salty air is apt to corrode it. Stainless steel is a more durable material and will not corrode. To clean it, use a little ammonia and water, a spray glass cleaner, or a special stainless steel cleaner.

Tip: Leftover carbonated water or club soda is excellent for cleaning chrome and stainless steel. We learned this trick from a friendly bartender!

•

WHEN YOU USE A CLOTHESLINE

Despite the increased popularity in the use of automatic dryers, many still prefer to use the clothesline, or if they don't prefer it, they are doing it out of necessity. While it is harder to lug the laundry to the clothesline, drying out of doors does give clothes a lovely fresh smell. An indoor line is also necessary for those bad-weather days. If you don't have an area where you can leave the line up at all times consider one of those indoor retractable types. Hang it in a spare room or bathroom.

To hang sheets, fold them double, hem to hem. Turn about three or four inches over the line and pin, or fold in half if that is easier for you (make sure the pins are snag free and clean). Run your fingers down the selvage edges to make sure they are smooth. If you hang them this way, sheets will dry evenly and will be easier to iron. As a matter of fact, they may well be smooth enough so that ironing is unnecessary if you fold while faintly damp (only enough to feel coolish to the touch). If they are permanent press sheets, then your ironing worries are over!

To hang men's shirts, first fold double by bringing the two shirt fronts together, then hang by the tail, folding three or four inches over the line. Pin at the ends.

We like to hang permanent-press shirts on hangers for drying. Secure the hangers to outdoor lines with clothespins.

To hang towels, fold either one third or double over the line. Shake them vigorously, to restore softness and fluffiness. Never hang by one corner.

Understanding conquers all, even the indomitable cockroach. This article by the Olkowskis (see their ***Integral Urban House*** *on p. 294) is reprinted from the* ***IPM Practitioner*** *(p. 106).* —SB

"A cockroach is always wrong when arguing with a chicken."
—*Old Spanish proverb*

Ecological Cockroach Management

by William Olkowski, Helga Olkowski, Linda Laub

A simple view of the world pits humans and insects in a war for the Earth. The major weapon in the war is intelligence — the cerebral intelligence of humanity against the genetic intelligence of the insects. If intelligence is the ability to modify behavior as a result of experience and the cerebral vs. genetic biological mechanism is the test, we humans are not doing well at all. The cockroach battleground tells the story.

At great cost we have invented numerous insecticides for use against roaches — to no avail. Insecticide treatments are regularly used in kitchens, basements, bathrooms, restaurants, theaters, buses, trains, schools, hospitals, etc., throughout the nation. At best, what is gained is only temporary relief. The eventual result is the presence of roaches and pesticides everywhere, from the grade school down the block to the congressional cafeterias. The introduced toxicants, which persist longer indoors than outdoors because of the lack of the principal degrading agent, ultraviolet light, are respired by humans along with the household dust and other air pollutants. The effects upon the inhabitants are unknown, but could hardly be beneficial.

The latest produced by cerebral intelligence (our side) is a decision-making process called Integrated Pest Management, or IPM. The following is a suggestion on how this process might be adopted to your own private and public battles with this ancient human cohabitant.

The components that comprise an IPM program are basically not new. What is new is their integration and application. A cockroach IPM program begins with correct species identification and biological knowledge of the pest. Other components include: easy-to-use monitoring techniques, habitat modification, and the safest, most effective chemical tool, if necessary. Together, they make up the IPM program. No single element alone is likely to produce useful long-term results.

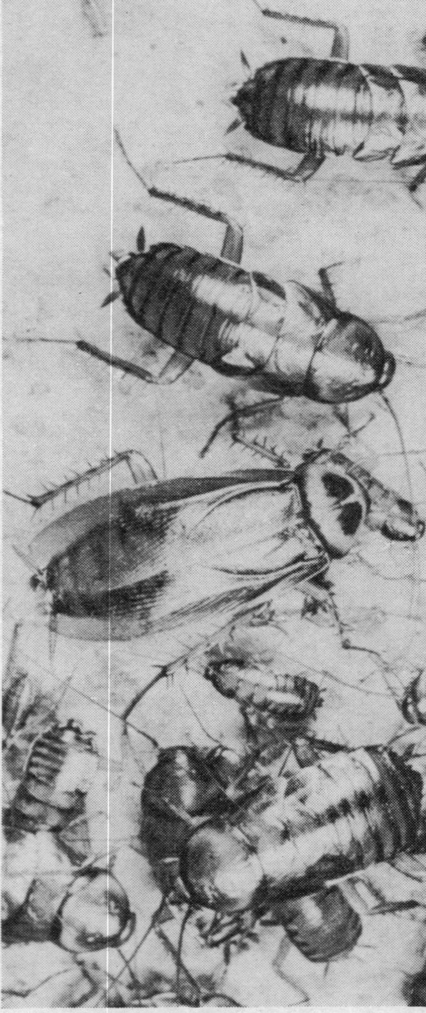

Different stages of growth of the American cockroach. In the middle is a fully developed insect. The females of this species are winged.

COCKROACH BIOLOGY

COCKROACHES HAVE CHANGED little since their beginnings in the Devonian period of the Paleozoic era 400 million years ago. In the world today, there are more than 3,500 species, 57 of them in the United States. As many as 4,000 additional species are still undescribed. Cockroaches, which are closely related to termites, are found in caves, mines, animal burrows, and ant and termite nests, as well as more familiar places.

Of all these species of cockroach, only four are considered significantly pestiferous. These are the German cockroach, *Blattella germanica* (Linnaeus), the brown-banded, *Supella longipalpa* (Fabricius), the oriental, *Blatta orientalis* (Linnaeus), and the American, *Periplaneta americana*

Mend It!

Not many people these days know how to darn a hole in a sock, reverse a collar, let down a hem, or any of the everyday necessary skills my mother and grandmothers had to use to keep their families decently clothed on almost no money. I'm convinced that we are again going to have to make clothes last longer, and more and more folks will be wondering how to go about it. Mending, darning, patching, remaking by hand and machine methods; all those thrifty lessons and more are covered in this guide. For once a book lives up to its claim to be complete. —Evelyn Eldridge-Diaz

Mend It!
(A Complete Guide to Clothes Repair)
Maureen Goldsworthy
1979; 127 pp.
$5.95 postpaid from:
Stein and Day, Publishers
Scarborough House
Briarcliff Manor, NY 10510
or Whole Earth Household Store

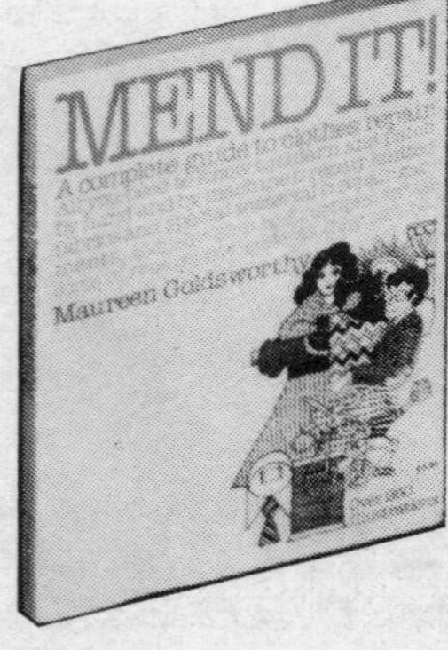

•

The Felled Patch

This is also known as the *Calico Patch.* It is used on plain fabrics where great firmness is needed.

1. Cut the patch large enough to cover not only the hole, but also any thin area around it, and allow 3/8 in. all round for turnings. Fold the turnings to the right side of the patch and press.

2. Place the patch wrong side up on the wrong side of the garment, exactly matching the direction of warp and weft threads. Tack in place. Fell by picking up only a thread or two of the garment, but taking a longer stitch through the fold of the patch. A stitch should fall at each corner.

3. Turn over to the right side. Cut away the fabric inside the patch to a width of 5/8 in. from the stitching.

4. Clip 1/4 in. into each corner, fold under the raw edges, press, and fell.

1 2 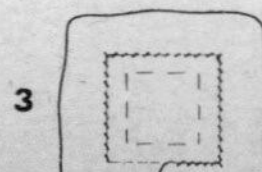 3 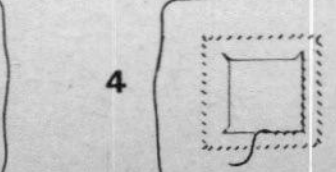 4

Hand washers

A beautiful washing machine is made out of using a "plumber's helper" — pumping it up and down in any sudsy laundry container from bucket to bathtub.
—Norman Soloman
Berkeley, California

We asked Dale Fritz, a Peace Corps agricultural specialist and former Volunteer for Technical Assistance (VITA), who has years of experience overseas.

As it turned out, Fritz himself is the father of a simple hand-operated washing machine that has been featured for years in the **Village Technology Handbook** (our p. 180). "What is the operating principle of the machine?" we asked Fritz.

"Agitation, just agitation," he replied.

"You could take a stick and stand there and stir it," he added, "It's just the motion of the water. The clothes don't even have to move at all . . . It's just the water moving back and forth through the clothing that does the cleaning. The soap breaks down the dirt; and the water carries it away."

"Well," we asked, "if that is the principle, are there any other solutions to the washing problem that are simpler than yours?"

"Sure," he said. "If you have a vehicle, throw your clothes into some kind of a closed container — like a milk can — add soap and hot water and put the container onto the back of your machine. Leave it there all day as you make your rounds — preferably over the roughest available roads — and when you get back in the evening you'll have a load of clean clothes."

That method has been used by bachelor ranchers in the western United States for years.
—**Volunteer Magazine**
published by the Peace Corps (1970)

James clothes washer

I don't know anybody who's used one of these. It looks like it would do the job. May need a little bracing, the legs look flimsy. —SB
[Suggested by Reed Plankenhorn]

James clothes washer
$99.45 plus shipping
James clothes wringer
$48.95 plus shipping
Information on both
$1 postpaid
all from:
S & H Metal Products
RR No. 1
Box 57
Topeka, IN 46571

(Linnaeus). It is their ability to hide by day in small cracks and crevices in or near human dwellings and to feed by night on water and small bits of food and waste which have made these four species of cockroach highly successful residents in human dwellings. The adults are winged, though they seldom fly, range in size from 9/16 to 1-3/4 inches and vary in color from reddish or yellowish-brown to black. While their common names point to various countries, all originated in regions of Africa.

Cockroaches are among the most disagreeable of domiciliary insects. Besides inducing psychological distress and social embarassment in those whose dwellings are infested, cockroaches cause distinct physical problems. They either consume or contaminate human foodstuffs with saliva and excrement and produce secretions which impart a persistent, fetid odor to materials they contact. Cockroaches have been shown to carry many microbial organisms mechanically on their bodies, including human pathogens such as the bacterial species *Salmonella enteritidis*, *S. typhimurium*, *S. montevido*, and *S. oranienburg*, agents of dysentery, enteric fever, food poisoning, and gastroenteritis, and the protozoan species *Toxoplasma* sp., agent of toxoplasmosis, a disease which causes congenital defects in the unborn children of infected mothers. In addition, cockroaches carry hepatitis B antigen – the cause of infectious hepatitis – in their feces. Finally, roaches have been known to induce allergic reactions in humans.

Cockroach infestations can occur in any home and are often accidentally introduced as egg cases in shipped materials, groceries, or secondhand appliances, rugs, furniture, etc.

IDENTIFICATION

Although cockroaches are similar to each other in their requirements and habits, knowledge of the variations among species can lead to more effective pest management.

The German cockroach is probably the most commonly found domiciliary species. Its need for warmth, moisture, and food causes it to be found in kitchens and bathrooms. The female carries her egg case and drops it 1 - 2 days before hatching. Under ideal conditions, the population can have as many as 3 or 4 generations per year. The German cockroach is easily identified by two vertical dark stripes on its pronotum (dorsal side between head and base of wings).

The brown-banded cockroach is less prolific than the German and can be found anywhere in the house, particularly in high, warm, dry areas, in appliances, and behind furniture. Egg cases are glued to vertical surfaces in dark secluded areas.

The oriental cockroach can tolerate lower temperatures than the others can and lives oudoors during the summer months in colder climates and year-round in warm climates. It prefers the basement and first floor of dwellings. The female is practically wingless. This species is a solid dark brown to black in color.

The American cockroach is the largest of the domiciliary species and has a high reproductive potential. Like the oriental cockroach, it can live outdoors, but it cannot survive cool temperatures.

MONITORING TECHNIQUES

Monitoring and record keeping show (1) where cockroach population density is highest and, therefore, where habitat modification efforts should be concentrated, and (2) whether these efforts are actually reducing the cockroach population. A non-toxic cockroach trap developed by the Zoecon Corporation, a division of Occidental Chemical Company, is useful for monitoring purposes. Sold commercially under a variety of trade names, it consists of a small, rectangular (5" x 2" x 1-3/4"), black cardboard box, inside of which are three bands of sticky glue and a dark strip of cockroach attractant. Initial observations have found it to be quite attractive to the German cockroach but less so to the brown-banded.

Trap placement is most important, for cockroaches will not seek them out if they are placed outside their normal travel areas. Cockroaches prefer enclosed spaces and usually travel along the periphery of walls and other objects. Cockroaches rarely venture out into the center of the room for food, even when hungry.

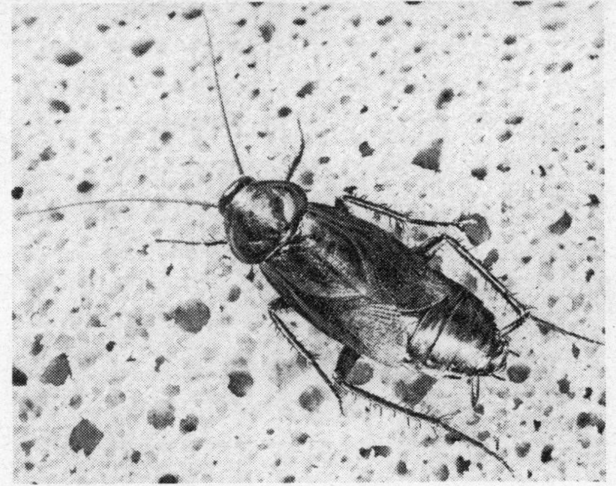

American cockroach

Cockroach feces, called *frass,* look like grains of pepper, and can be an indication of brown-banded cockroach harborage. Another, more toxic, technique is to use a pyrethrin spray to flush out populations behind appliances and in hard-to-reach areas, but this technique should be resorted to only if trapping or visual inspections have been unsuccessful. The best places to monitor are known harborages. Each infested area may have its own particular harborage sites.

By keeping records of numbers and life-stages of cockroaches trapped, numbers killed, and egg cases found, one can tell if the situation has improved. Many adults and egg cases would indicate that the habitat can still support reproduction. Nymphs and egg cases with few adults may indicate a population decline, as egg cases will continue to hatch over time after the adult populations have been killed.

INJURY LEVEL

Although tolerance of pest abundance may vary a great deal according to the type of institution (warehouses can be more tolerant than restaurants), standards of sanitation, and individual predilection (some persons are highly excited by even small numbers of insects), high population levels may represent risks of disease from microbial agents harbored by the roaches.

HABITAT MODIFICATION

Reduction of food, water, and harborage are vitally important in cockroach management. These factors affect the carrying capacity of the environment. If they can be reduced, the ability of the room, house, or structure to support roaches is reduced, hence fewer roaches. Cockroaches evolved as scavengers on dead plant material and as a result prefer carbohydrates to protein and fat. They will discriminate if given a choice but when hungry will eat almost anything. Some products that are not usually considered food – such as starch-based paints, wallpaper paste, envelope glue, and bar soaps – do contain carbohydrates, hence are food for cockroaches. Buildings provide cockroaches with microclimates similar to their native habitats. Most important to their survival is a source of moisture and warmth, although some species, particularly the brown-banded, are adapting to require less heat and water.

INDOORS

Once cockroach harborages are found, accessible areas can be washed down and vacuumed to eliminate egg cases, fecal material, and bits of food waste that may have accumulated. Suspected materials also can be steam-cleaned. Dispose of vacuumings by burning, deeply burying, or place in tightly closed containers for disposal, or compost after safe disinfection (e.g. use of household ammonia).

To remove sources of food, clean up the kitchen, especially after each meal and in areas where grease accumulates, such as drains, vents, ovens, and stoves. Store all food, especially sweet, starchy, or fatty food, in tightly sealed metal, glass, or heavy plastic containers, as cockroaches can infest food in open bags or cardboard or cloth containers. Empty household garbage and pet litter boxes and wash dirty dishes or submerge them in sudsy water before retiring at night. Don't leave pet food out between feedings. To remove sources of water, fix dripping faucets and any other leaks. Provide drainage or ventilation to eliminate moist areas. Do not leave water on kitchen surfaces and remove pet water bowls at night.

Finally, it is essential to reduce harborage. Plug all small cracks around baseboards, wall shelves or cupboards, pipes, sinks, and bathtub fixtures with putty or caulk (paint may also be used alone or in conjunction with either of these). Three general types of caulk are available: (1) cartridge caulk (which requires a caulking gun) is useful for big jobs, such as along floor boards or behind cabinets; (2) squeeze tube caulk is good for sealing around water faucets, vents, etc.; and (3) ropelike caulk is most useful for quick temporary seals and hard-to-reach spaces. Latex caulk is best because it is water soluble before drying and, once dry, stays flexible. Although new urethane foams in aerosol cans are also available, they are difficult to use. Large holes or cracks will require special cements or other substances which match existing materials, depending upon how visible the repairs will be. Since older dwellings often have many cracks, crevices, and hard-to-reach places, start by concentrating on kitchen and bath areas, or wherever populations are heaviest. Work on these areas bit by bit as time and energy allow. Every five inches of hiding place plugged up reduces the number of roaches a house can support. Caulk or weatherstrip cracks and crevices through which pests can enter the home, replace broken windows and screens, and seal door frames. Screen all air vents, particularly those in the kitchen around the stove.

OUTDOORS

Reduce outdoor roach populations by moving debris, firewood, and garbage away from the house. Prevent access to indoor spaces with screens. Commonly available aluminum window screen is adequate to repair existing screens. Silicone seal is an excellent material for filling holes in window screens. Seal cracks around pipes and windows. Compost or bury pet manure, or use a commercial pet waste disposal system. Use garbage cans with tightly fitting lids held on by a spring mechanism to prevent wind and dogs or other animals from scattering the contents.

USE OF INSECTICIDES

These factors are considered when using a poison: safety, effectiveness, and pest resistance. Cockroaches are repelled by pesticides they can smell, but are least repelled by boric acid and have not developed resistance to it in over 10 years of use. The advantages of this inorganic compound are that it does not vaporize and is an effective, slow-acting (7-14 days) stomach poison if placed where cockroaches *normally* travel. Cockroaches treated with boric acid are more visible in the daytime than usual a week to ten days after treatment. It has been surmised that this is due to the disorientation induced in the cockroaches by the poison. Boric acid is best used undiluted. Although, diluted, it can be applied as a wash, cockroaches more easily pick up the boric acid dust. This material can be blown into wall voids or placed beneath appliances where roaches harbor. This may need to be done by a trained applicator. Remember, boric acid is poisonous to people as well as to cockroaches. About 1 ingested tablespoon can kill a child and it can also be absorbed through skin lesions. Wear a dust mask if application methods throw boric acid dust into the air. Keep boric acid away from food, children, and pets. Dependence on boric acid alone is not an IPM approach. ■

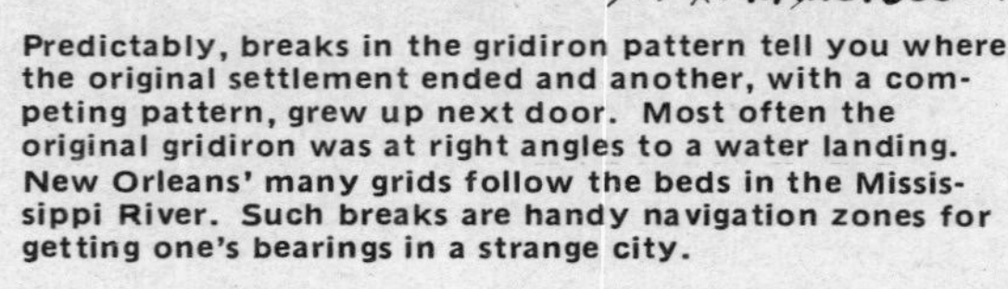

Predictably, breaks in the gridiron pattern tell you where the original settlement ended and another, with a competing pattern, grew up next door. Most often the original gridiron was at right angles to a water landing. New Orleans' many grids follow the beds in the Mississippi River. Such breaks are handy navigation zones for getting one's bearings in a strange city.

Close-Up

Now (after reading this) I know why my neighborhood developed the way it did — and why cities I've lived in previously developed the way they did. And now I know better how to find the parks, streets, culture, turf, beats around any new city which will help me make the neighborhood into my neighborhood — and what to look for in a neighborhood the next time I move. —Art Kleiner

Close-Up
(How to Read the American City)
Grady Clay
1973, 1980; 192 pp.
$6.95 postpaid from:
University of Chicago Press
Department PK
5801 South Ellis Avenue
Chicago, IL 60637
or Whole Earth Household Store

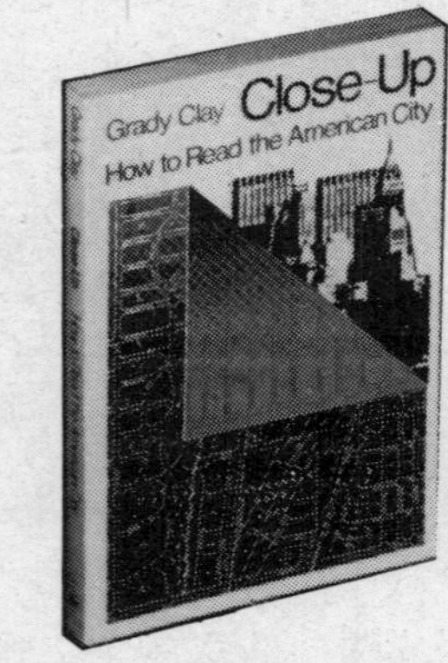

•

Quite by accident, mixed into a long search, I stumbled upon one of the more important epitome districts to be found in any city that is still linked together by an establishment, power elite, or power structure. This is the distinct pathway or network of paths along streets, sidewalks, and corridors followed by central-city movers and shakers, influentials, wheelers and dealers, and hangers-on.

Despite the rise of electronic communications, much important person-to-person business is still transacted out in the open, between office and lunch, courtroom and conference, bench and bar, desk and drinks.

The process of my own discovery is worth looking into, for it tells something about the ways in which downtown epitome districts work, and suggests clues to their futures. In writing about my own city, Louisville, I found it essential to move about on foot, to pay personal calls on as many political, financial, and other key figures as possible, to see them in their own haunts and lairs, to probe their attitudes and experience, and, as a journalist, to move in public places, observing who was with whom for clues to future alliances, deals, and consortia.

After repeated exposure, I discovered that one particular stretch of sidewalks, doors, and corridors in the financial-civic district was extraordinarily productive in contacts, tips, suggestions, reactions, observations, and gossip.

•

No city considers itself sufficiently armed to entice footloose tourists or industrialists without a new sort of epitome district called Six Flags Over Ourtown, or Vacation Village, Frontierland, Pioneerland, Butchertown, German Village, Old(e) Town(e), or local imitations of Vieux Carre, Williamsburg, Sturbridge Village, Bavarian Alpine Village, and Old Salem.

These new epitome districts usually have most if not all the following indicators: a name; well-defined boundaries or a boundary zone; local history made evident in maps, pamphlets, etc.; a mythology; a central zone of action; gatekeepers or at least symbolic entrances; and a variety of signs and symbols. A significant indicator is an increase in neighborhood celebrations. New York City in three years increased the number of street-closing permits from some 700 to over 5,000 in 1972 — mostly for neighborhood festivals. There is no limit to size: Disney World's 56,000 acres combined with its promoters' political power to collect highway interchanges and dominate the source of much of Florida's underground waters forecast a whole new scale of epitome districts which, under single managements, may become world meccas for tourism.

Travelers may discover themselves in a yet-to-be-defined epitome district through the presence of old place names, ethnic foods, religious carnival preparations; and become amateur historians by that simple device of trying to follow the old shore line in a waterfront city. ("There is Dock Street, we must be getting close.")

Surrounded by this mixture of newly emerging identity and old-style puffery, we need constant vigilance so as to match what we see happening against what is being artificially manufactured for us. Windbaggery — an airy form of packaging dear to chambers of commerce and tourism promoters — can easily blind us to the true nature of what is going on around us.

The "success" of any of these environments depends on a very special sort of exchange between it and us. The environment I call an epitome district must be information rich, and packed with visible evidence of complexities beyond itself.

The Death and Life of Great American Cities
The Last Landscape

These are the two best books on land use planning I know about. Both writers became involved with the subject because of concern for particular places. Jane Jacobs was concerned to keep her neighborhood from being bulldozed away by the urban renewers. She learned enough about the subject to write this book, a classic, old but fortunately not out-of-date. Her books challenge the assumptions of most city planners. She understands that a city is a human ecology, and that city planning is a problem in self-government. She has written a later book, **The Economy of Cities***, which is interesting but not as good as* **The Death and Life of Great American Cities.** *William H. Whyte does for suburbia and the countryside what Jane Jacobs does for the city. He was concerned about the desecration by developers of his native place, Chester County, Pennsylvania. Previously he had been a business writer and wrote* **The Organization Man.** *Now he is concerned with people in the landscape even more than people in organizations. Both he and Jane Jacobs provide tools for understanding land use on the level of the local planning commission where, like it or not, most land use decisions are being made.* —Phillip Ebersole

Better still, see **A Pattern Language**, *p. 217.* —SB

The Death and Life of Great American Cities
Jane Jacobs
1961; 448 pp.
$3.95 postpaid from:
Vintage Books
Random House
455 Hahn Road
Westminster, MD 21157
or Whole Earth Household Store

The Last Landscape
William H. Whyte
1968; 402 pp.
$2.95 postpaid from:
Anchor Books
Doubleday & Company
501 Franklin Avenue
Garden City, NY 11530
or Whole Earth Household Store

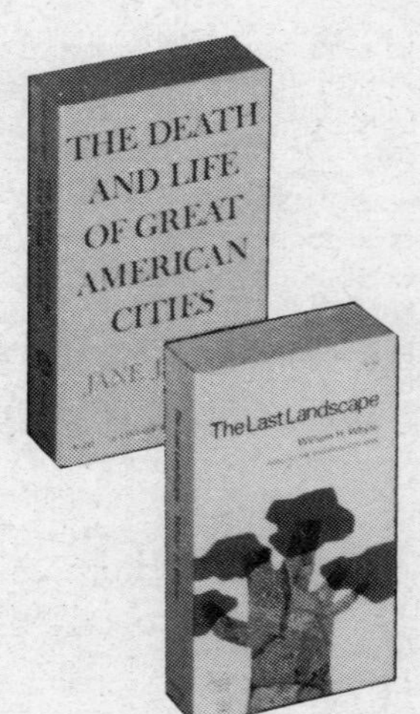

•

To generate exuberant diversity in a city's streets and districts, four conditions are indispensable:

1. The district and indeed as many of its internal parts as possible must serve more than one primary function; preferably more than two. These must insure the presence of people who go outdoors on different schedules and are in the place for different purposes, but who are able to use many facilities in common.
2. Most blocks must be short; that is, streets and opportunities to turn corners must be frequent.
3. The district must mingle buildings that vary in age and condition, including a good proportion of old ones so that they vary in the economic yield they must produce. This mingling must be fairly close-grained.
4. There must be a sufficiently dense concentration of people for whatever purposes may be there. This includes dense concentration in the case of people who are there because of residence.

•

"I know how you feel," he said, "I often go down there myself just to walk around the streets and feel that wonderful, cheerful street life. Say, what you ought to do, you ought to come back and go down in the summer if you think it's fun now. You'd be crazy about it in summer. But of course we have to rebuild it eventually. We've got to get these people off the streets."

•

There is a quality even meaner than outright ugliness or disorder, and this meaner quality is the dishonest mask of pretended order, achieved by ignoring or suppressing the real order that is struggling to exist and to be served.

•

How big, in functional terms, must an effective district be? I have given a functional definition of size: big enough to fight city hall, but not so big that streeet neighborhoods are unable to draw district attention and to count.
—The Death and Life of Great American Cities

•

What makes driving along back roads such a delight? It is more than the scenery; it is the tightness of scale. You go around abrupt curves, up sudden crests, under a canopy of overhanging foliage. Sometimes the view opens up to distant hills; sometimes it narrows down almost to a tunnel as you pass through woods. But always the edge of the landscape is close by — stone fences, a line of maples, a barn — so close by that we tarry where else we would speed.

This thightness of scale is what gets improved away. Curves are straightened, crests flattened, the trees and stone fences moved out of the harm's way. The edge of the landscape gets moved back. **—The Last Landscpe**

Community Technology

Karl Hess and friends worked for five years to transform the Adams-Morgan neighborhood in Washington, D.C. into a self-sufficient model of what could be done. There were fish farms, solar collectors, vegetable gardens and all the "good stuff" you could wish for. Thousands of people were involved in a town-meeting democratic direct-participation self-governing system. It sounds great! It failed. Karl Hess tells what happened with sometimes heart-breaking honesty, and finishes the book by describing what could be done next time to make it keep working. As grand experiments are attempted, it is essential that chronicles such as this one are written both to record events and to give the subsequent efforts the benefit of experience. Thanks Karl. (See **Return to the City,** *p. 313.)*
—J. Baldwin

Community Technology
Karl Hess
1979; 107 pp.
$2.95 postpaid from:
Harper & Row
Keystone Industrial Park
Scranton, PA 18512
or Whole Earth Household Store

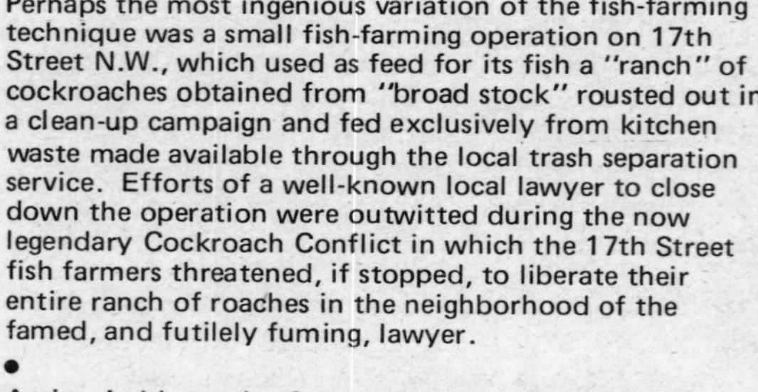

•

Perhaps the most ingenious variation of the fish-farming technique was a small fish-farming operation on 17th Street N.W., which used as feed for its fish a "ranch" of cockroaches obtained from "broad stock" rousted out in a clean-up campaign and fed exclusively from kitchen waste made available through the local trash separation service. Efforts of a well-known local lawyer to close down the operation were outwitted during the now legendary Cockroach Conflict in which the 17th Street fish farmers threatened, if stopped, to liberate their entire ranch of roaches in the neighborhood of the famed, and futilely fuming, lawyer.

•

An inevitable result of an undiscussed rising crime situation was the deterioration of the neighborhood and the easing of entry for the next wave of residents, the ones who could afford better security and who did not mind living in a small fortress so long as the address was fashionable. It happened in Adams-Morgan.

But could neighborhood people have coped with crime? I certainly think so. It would mean first coping with their own children, facing them down, creating families that would absorb their energies and deserve their loyalities. Not easy. Not likely. And particularly not likely when parents are opiated by a welfare existence, and where schools are simply disciplinarian baby sitters, offering young people no creative alternative to violence as the way to get out, to get up, to get even.

•

The culture of poverty will run its course. How long that course is, I have no idea. I am convinced, however, that if the culture of poverty is to be broken in any black neighborhood it will be broken by black people, not by starry-eyed whites talking soul patter.

Tools on loan from public libraries

More libraries are getting into the tool rental business: patrons of the three-branch Grosse Pointe, Michigan, Library System have access to a 200-item, $9000 tool collection that was started 30 years ago by the local Rotary Club. Tools like power sanders are loaned out for three days and no deposit fee is required.

Ohio's Canal Fulton Public Library has a collection that includes an auto tune-up kit, slide rule, microscope, guitar, four cassette players, several movie projectors, and a ventriloquist's dummy.

The Plainedge, New York, Public Library is loaning out pocket electronic calculators, rototillers, dwell meters, strobe lights, tree pruners, aluminum extension ladders, hedge trimmers, saber saws, belt sanders and electric sewing machines.

Reports indicate that most patrons take care of equipment, though some losses and damages have occurred.
(Reprinted from **Library Journal**)

by Ray Jason

Ray Jason

Suggs the Mime

IF YOU ARE A FREE SPIRIT with a penchant for performing, then street entertaining could provide you with an actual *vocation* in an age that usually offers only *jobs*. You'll get to work out of doors in the fresh air and sunlight. You'll be unharried by bosses and unconcerned with timeclocks. As a busker you'll be the essential democrat — of the People, by the People, and for the People. You'll be adding to the festiveness of your community, helping to deflate the rapidly rising cost spiral of the entertainment industry, and liberating your fellow citizens from their T.V. addiction. In the eyes of some folks you will be nothing but a show-off and a free-loader, but in the eyes of others you may very well become a minor celebrity and a folk hero. Here are some tips to get you started.

Is your talent too tiny?

Ideally, the aspiring street performer should have an act that is really special. But if it is not extraordinary it should at least be good. However, due to the deceptive nature of subjectivity, this is sometimes difficult to determine. So just apply Jason's Threefold Test:

1. Do the people stop to watch your act?
2. Do they applaud and laugh?
3. Do they put money in the hat?

If yes, proceed.

Wanted: Street Xylophonist

Perhaps you're wondering whether your particular specialty would be successful in a sidewalk venue? Well, here's a listing of all of the acts that I can recall seeing in my nine years on the streetcorners. It should clearly illustrate how vast the range of possibilities open to aspiring street performers is.

Acrobats, actors, bagpipers, bellydancers, bluegrass musicians, children's theatre groups, classical musicians, clowns, conga drummers, country and western serenaders, dixieland jazz bands, escape artists, fiddlers, fireaters, folksingers, hammered dulcimer players, human anvils, human juke boxes, javelin twirlers, jug bands, jugglers, magicians, marionette manipulators, mimes, mind readers, modern dancers, one man bands, opera singers, organ grinders, pick-up truck pianists, poets, political theatre troupes, punch and judy shows, puppeteers, rock 'n roll bands, rollerskating accordionists, singers, snake charmers, stand-up comics, steel bands, strongmen, tap dancers, tightrope walkers, trained dog acts, unicyclists, and vibraphonists.

The jug band plays the Opera House (steps).

So where should you take your xylophone if you want to start regaling audiences? There are certain standard locations, but like all other aspects of street performing this is an area that is open to personal experimentation. The usual spots include: parks, crafts fairs, shopping malls, flea markets, commercial districts, theatre lines, civic plazas, transportation terminals, college campuses, pedestrian malls, and county fairs.

Commercial districts are noontime venues. Your clientele is mostly businessmen and secretaries on their lunch breaks, so you'll need to do short, walk-by acts. Civic plazas around city halls, museums and opera houses usually abound in row after row of steps which can be easily utilized as natural amphitheatres. Transportation terminals include subway stations and ferry docks. Greyhound bus terminals are only recommended if you want a lot of recycled chewing gum in your hat. College campuses work best at noontime somewhere near the Student Union where everyone goes for their midday refreshment.

*Read about street juggler Ray Jason in the **Rising Sun Neighborhood Newsletter** on p. 61. A nine-year veteran of the asphalt, he is a patriarch of San Francisco and American street performing. This year he juggled his way around the world.* —SB

Short is Beautiful

How long should your act be? Well, the secret to making a moderately comfortable living as a street performer is to fill the hat with dollar bills. It takes an awful lot of quarters to make a living. So you should try to develop an act that is long enough and good enough to merit a greenback but not so long that people leave because they are tired of standing. So if you have an act with a beginning and an end, 20 to 30 minutes is a good time frame. If you have a walk-by act where people listen to a couple of tunes, drop something in the hat and then move along, you'd do best to play fairly continuously and only take breaks when exhaustion warrants it.

Always standing room only

Crowd gathering techniques fall into three main categories: Noise — whistles, drums, trumpets, etc. Verbal — ballyhoo, bluster, or courteous enticements. Visual — outrageous costumes, mechanical mimes standing perfectly still, or grown men juggling rubber chickens.

Silent offerings preferred

The single most important factor in getting people to donate generously is to make 'em laugh. When making your hat pitch do it humorously. For instance while innocently and imploringly holding your hat you might say, "If you can give — give. If you can't give — don't give. But, please, whatever you do — don't TAKE!"

Some performers actually walk amongst the audience passing their hats, others stand in one place cradling it in their hands and others just leave it in a conspicuous spot. The San Francisco Mime Troupe used to surround their crowd, thus lessening the chance for the people in the back to escape without contributing.

You will enhance your chance of getting dollar bills if you wave one around and make a joking reference to it such as, "Don't forget — whenever possible I do prefer SILENT OFFERINGS!"

Sergeant Friday, I presume . . .

At some point the police will probably hassle you. The usual charges are begging, disturbing the peace, and obstructing the sidewalk. (I totally support the vigorous enforcement of this last infraction. Dozens of times I've watched street acts fail to control their crowds, thus forcing people to walk in the street. I've yet to see a performer who was worth getting hit by a truck for.)

You need not fear any rat-infested dungeons. In fact, you'll probably spend only a few hours in jail, so resist the temptation to view yourself as a martyr. Instead, try to look at it as comic theatre. Your ability to remain calm will both benefit you and baffle the police.

District Attorneys rarely prosecute street performers. Usually the charges are dismissed before they ever reach the Court. However, if you verbally abuse the arresting officer, your predicament becomes much more serious and the D.A. might press charges. At the time of the confrontation there will be a strong temptation to wise-off to the gendarmes because your audience will probably be vehemently defending you. Such support is certainly pleasing, but don't forget that these fans are in no real jeopardy, and remember that they will not offer to take the rap and go to jail for you. As much as this outcry bolsters your ego it actually only aggravates the situation. I've never heard of an instance where the taunts and protests of the crowd kept the police from hauling the busker off to the station house.

Here are some practical suggestions you might find helpful. Try to get some names and phone numbers of people in the audience to use as possible witnesses. Keep a couple of dimes stashed in your socks for jailhouse phone calls. Carry the phone numbers of a good bail bondsman and a lawyer. Keep small index cards in your wallet with the names and phone numbers of three friends on them. Give these cards to folks in the audience, instructing them to keep calling these accomplices until they reach one. Prearrange with the people listed on the cards the things they will have to do to hasten your release.

If you want to vigorously protest your arrest and make yourself a test case, you will need the power of the press behind you. This shouldn't be too difficult if you have a fairly good act, because such a story makes good copy. The little guy versus harsh, recalcitrant authority always arouses the interest and ire of readers. You'll also need a good lawyer. If you can't afford such counsel, try the Public Defender's office or the American Civil Liberties Union.

After my first arrest my lawyer dressed me in a convict's costume, complete with ball and chain, and sent me back out to my corner to perform my juggling act. Both the major newspapers and several T.V. stations reported this, and the story generated so much support and sympathy that it became very difficult for them to prosecute me. The charges were dismissed.

For my finale . . .

In conclusion I should say that basically street performing is a fun way to make a living. However, it also has some noble results. It can help undermine almost everything that is evil in America: consumerism, waste, bigness, greed, energy gluttony, distrust, impersonalness, despair, disparity of wealth, etc. It's not going to topple the system, but combined with other private, personal and heartfelt commitments it can have a tremendous impact. ■

THE RISING SUN
NEIGHBORHOOD NEWSLETTER

Paul Newman is color blind and can't tell his eyes are blue.

Sylvia Porter's New Money Book

Sylvia Porter is not kidding. This is about money, not so much how to make it but how to keep, save, and judiciously spend it. There is advice and information on every purchasing decision, and it is usually good advice.

—Paul Hawken

Sylvia Porter's New Money Book for the 80's
Sylvia Porter
1975, 1979; 1,305 pp.
$24.95 postpaid from:
Doubleday and Company
501 Franklin Avenue
Garden City, NY 11530
or Whole Earth Household Store

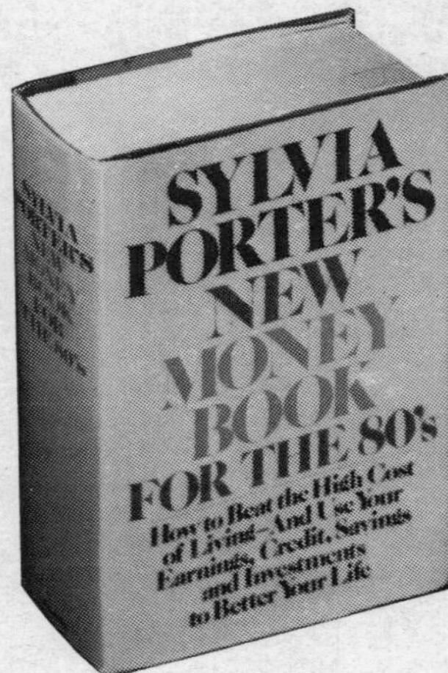

•

How To Find The Right Site

Before you invest a penny in your dream house you must find the right property on which to build. Here's how to go about it:

- Find out from the town clerk's office the zoning regulations in the neighborhood in which the property you like is situated.
- Ask for a survey of the lot. Exactly where are the boundaries? (Walk the lines yourself.)
- Plan to invest in a title search, no matter how little the lot costs.
- Find out from local lenders whether they will make home-building loans in your neighborhood. A good source of information is the Federal Housing Administration's nearest branch office. The FHA considers the neighborhood as well as the individual house when it insures loans.
- Inspect the lot after a heavy rain; if possible, after several days of downpour. That will show how rapidly surface water leaves the site. If a plot is filled, the fill may settle and take the house along with it.
- Be wary of land subdivisions still in the "blueprint stage." These always are a gamble.

•

What Fund For You?

Every investor certainly should investigate funds. Many of you will find the funds are suitable for achieving your investment goals.

To help you determine the kind of mutual fund that is best suited for you, here are broad guidelines.

Specifically, if you are:

- *Single,* earning under $15,000, with a savings-oriented (conservative) temperament: you should own an income fund with a dual goal of providing some longer-term capital growth.
- *Single,* earning under $15,000, with a chance-taker's (aggressive) temperament: yours should be a "total return" fund, concentrating on high-growth common stocks or a long-term growth fund.
- *Married,* with two or three dependents, earning $15,000 to $25,000, with a conservative temperament: the best for you would be a blue-chip, common stock fund, for long-term growth of both capital and income.
- *Married,* with two or three dependents, earning $25,000 and up, with a growth-oriented temperament: yours should be either a pu·e "income" fund, a "money-market" fund, or a bond fund.
- *Working couple,* earning $25,000 and up, with growth-oriented temperament: obviously, a growth fund is for you, so the investments can help you accumulate resources for future tuition needs, travel and other recreation, retirement, etc.
- *Older person,* income coming from Social Security and some savings, with a conservative temperament and a goal of preservation of capital and more current income: ideally, the medium should be an income fund of the more conservative type which pays dividends and has some appreciation possibilities. Or a money-market fund which will preserve capital and offer a satisfactory yield.

Why Should You Buy Mutual Funds?

If I were to tell you that the investment advice given to the small investor in the United States is far inferior to that given to the big guy, and that the men and women who give that advice agree the above is true, wouldn't you be deeply disturbed? Okay, I'm telling you that this is the opinion of an overwhelming percentage of the nation's security analysts. According to a recent survey:

- A shocking seven out of ten security analysts have "reservations about the advice available to the small investor as compared with that given the large one."
- Only one in three believes that "the quality of investment advice now available adequately serves all types of investors."
- Nearly half favor "some form of blanket registration of security analysts" (in short, greater control).

MORE IMPORTANT MISTAKES ARE made about personal finance — about money in general — than maybe any other easily correctable area of human folly. It's one of those things that majoring in English, or being on the Left, or seeing yourself as a noble artist, scientist, or spiritual person can prevent you from ever getting right — to the vast detriment of your writing, politics, art, science, or spiritual practice.

Money ain't bad. Money is good. Restart from there and it's no big problem, just a somewhat interesting chore, like personal health. —SB

Successful Investing

Just as the idioms of energy became the language of the seventies, economic terminology is suffusing us now. For a good read into the basic terms and concepts that inform the business section of the paper, **Successful Investing** *will supply you with a lot of information quickly. If you have some money to squirrel away, it is also laden with advice as to how to do it. It is a basic conservative approach.*

—Paul Hawken

Successful Investing
(A Complete Guide to Your Financial Future)
Ronald K. Mills, Editor
1979; 507 pp.
$8.95 postpaid from:
Simon and Schuster
Attn: Order Department
1230 Avenue of the Americas
New York, NY 10020
or Whole Earth Household Store

•

The thoughts have all been expressed at least once before in this book; some will be expressed again. By bringing them together here, we provide a yardstick against which you can measure future investment decisions. Read them carefully. Commit them to memory. Recite them whenever you have an investment decision to make. If you are a compulsive investor, tempted by every hot tip that comes your way, tattoo them to the back of your hand. Ignore them at your peril.

The five: Set your goals. Buy the best-known companies. Invest for the long term. Avoid fads. Diversify.

•

Index Funds

The Vanguard Group introduced the First Index Investment Trust — the first index fund to be offered to the public — in August 1976. This fund, in common with a number of other index funds that are not available to the general public, seeks to provide investment results that correspond to the price and yield performance of the Standard & Poor's 500 Composite Stock Price Index. The trust holds more than 400 of the issues in the S&P.

Although the investing public has not warmed up to the notion of indexing, a number of major institutional investors have. The main target of the index fund marketers is the giant pension fund market. With tens of billions of dollars of assets, over half of which are invested in equities and with yearly contributions tending to run to more billions, the money flowing into private pension funds each year is roughly equivalent to a third or more of the total assets of the mutual fund industry.

Although a fund may mimic a popular market average in a low-cost manner — index funds are "managed" by computer programs — there are many mutual funds that have outperformed any and all market averages over the long term. If you are content to ride the coattails of the Standard & Poor's 500 and have no hopes of ever doing better than average in your investments, then index funds are for you. Otherwise, stick to managed mutual funds, where good judgment pays off in good performance.

•

A list of good quality growth funds would include these:

David L. Babson Investment Fund	Pioneer Fund
Johnston Mutual Fund	Putnam Investors Fund
National Investors Corp.	T. Rowe Price Growth Stock Fund

Here's a sampling of funds that stress high current income:

David L. Babson Income Trust	American General Bond Fund*
Northeast Investors Trust	Fort Dearborn Income Securities*
Rowe Price New Income Fund	Montgomery Street Income Securities*

Here are some that emphasize both growth and income:

Affiliated Fund	Financial Industrial Income Fund
American Mutual Fund	Guardian Mutual Fund
Decatur Income Fund	Windsor Fund

Here's a potpourri of funds that tend to invest in speculative stocks. These funds are not for the faint at heart:

Acorn Fund	Pioneer II
Mathers Fund	Putnam Voyager Fund
Over-the-Counter Securities	Scudder Special
Value Line Special Situations	

Money, Honey, 1980

by George von Hilsheimer

In the month or so since Art Kleiner phoned me to ask for a 10 year anniversary comment on my "Money, Honey" article in **The Last Whole Earth Catalog,** *I've had fun diddling around modeling all the strategies I might have used following my own advice in 1970.*

$30,000 invested at maximum leverage in bags of U.S. silver dimes could have been cashed in this year for $2,000,000 — that's figuring worst case interest on the leverage and having just left it all alone to fatten the bankers whilst it fattened you.

Our commune invested exactly that amount in 1969, but bailed out in three years to buy farmland. The farmland has not appreciated at all, at all, but we are not complaining. We've essentially had no money hassles. We are grateful that JFK and his co-thieves had such a delirious money policy. The Feds recently sold silver "dollars" for 45 to 65 paper "dollars." My. A rose is a rose but a dollar isn't a dollar.

The second option I suggested 11 years ago made us a mere 1000% profit. Two bars of silver we bought at $1.55 per ounce in 1969 were sold in 1979 for $16 an ounce, less 5% smelter's fee. With a little bit of luck we could have sold them at $50 an ounce in February, but that's crap shooting. In silver, just follow your long term plan, using YEARS or catastrophes as your selling semaphore.

I couldn't advise you to buy gold in 1970; but had you done so when it became legal for "free" Americans to own gold, then your money would have appreciated at an annual rate of 22.65% (this is the real return, adjusted for inflation).

The three best investments in the last decade have been gold, silver, and stamps. The best money investment has been Swiss francs which earned a real adjusted return of 3.7% each year.

Honey Money for 1990

I assume that anyone with good sense has some silver coin buried in the back 40 against the day everything falls apart and people refuse the politicians' printed promises they laughingly call "money." Silver on downswings is still a good buy if you don't plan to read the financial pages and do plan to keep the silver until at least 1990 or the balloon goes up. I prefer silver to gold because of the ease of investing in it, the ready recognizability of a genuine U.S. silver dime, and the availability of small denominations.

A dime minted from 1916 through 1965 contains .07234 of an ounce of pure silver. When silver is $49 an ounce, a real dime is worth $3.54; whereas on the historical silver/gold average ratio of 20:1 a gold Krugerrand will be around $900 — a little big to use to pay for a pound of hamburger.

The silver market has been discovered by the lemmings, and for anything other than survival or planning in decades, silver as an investment is a crap shoot — maybe a bit less honest. However, I don't think anyone who bought silver at $40 in February, and buried it and stopped reading newspapers and digs it up in February 1990, is going to be unhappy.

Reliable Old Gnomes, Making Honey Better'n Bees

Unfortunately, there is in 1980 no analogous madness to the insanity organized by the late sainted JFK when he decided to sell off the largest accumulation of silver in history. I have nothing as safe and wonderful as leveraged U.S. dimes to recommend in 1980.

Therefore, it's the Swiss gnomes as your honey bees for 1990.

It used to be that a prudent fellow could purchase an annuity through an assurance society and reliably plan his fading years in the safety and glory of the U.S. dollar. These days you might as well use toilet paper for an umbrella. In 1970 had you bought a fixed annuity of 1,000 U.S. dollars each month from a U.S. firm dealing in U.S. dollars, by 1979 you would need 700 extra dollars to keep even; but your assurance society would be paying you only the same little grand.

An annuity bought the same year from a Swiss Assurance Society would be paying more than $2,600 in 1979. Your style of living would have jounced merrily upward, gilded by Swiss good sense and a commodity (gold) backed currency. There never has been a failure of a Swiss Assurance Society; the same ethics and legal protection of legal confidentiality hold as obtain for Swiss banks. There are no nasty penalties as in holding Swiss francs outright; and the downside risk is very small. With a Swiss annuity you are betting on 300 years of stability

and a 5,000 year record of gold being better than politicians' promises.

In my dear unhumble opinion (remember, had you bet $1,000 with me in 1970 you'd be laughing all the way to the banco with a mere $66,666.67 in your dear fist), all bets in bonds, stocks, and other traditional passive investment ventures in the U.S. market are betting on Jimmy's two smiles.

Fun Ways of Shooting Craps

Did you ever figure out that if gold reaches $1,000, then the Feds' gold holdings will offset the entire foreign dollar holdings. When gold reaches $3,900 the U.S. government's gold holdings will offset the entire national debt. You think gold won't reach $3,900 before 1990? You believe in the tooth fairy, don't you?

An interesting thing is that as the lemmings have swirled around in the gold market, making it an unesthetic place for us cranky folk who preached gold's virtues a decade ago; the stocks of gold mining companies have not gone up in the same dizzy way (nor have they swooped down as vertiginously). Many companies which have to buy gold and silver may find it cheaper to mine it, and eventually the great horde of "investors" will hear that gold and silver come out of the ground and then, whee. You might want to get into an interesting crap shoot, the "penny" gold and silver stocks. Mind you, this is for fun; don't sell your assurance policy, and by no means dig up the Krugerrands or dimes. A fun way to participate in the dismantling of Western Capitalism by the Trilaterals is to play in these cheap stocks — who knows, you might make some money, and if you just have to read the paper, what a nice way to adrenalize the day.

SILVER AND GOLD

Nice courteous folk who have been in the business for years and don't bite too hard on your dimes.

Bramble Coins
information

free from:
Bramble Coins
1604 Michigan
National Tower
Lansing, MI 48933

SWISS ANNUITIES

***The Autumn Annuities** is Junior High School lucid, utterly persuasive, and gives you all the info you need. At $15 the book is overpriced as a book, but it includes application forms and information otherwise unavailable. A U.S. broker cannot legally sell a 'free' American a Swiss annuity; but you can still buy on your own. PF sells the book with a money-back guarantee. Don't like it, send it back. **Personal Finance** is the ideal letter for folk into making and hiding money. **Tax Angles**, same address, is $44 for 12 issues. At the very least see that your library gets it. Read all about how the wily capitalist hunts the elusive loophole; how smiley Jimmie the Georgia Pecan Deacon hasn't plugged anything. These are probably the most lucid, and least gung ho, of the multitudes of letters advising you how to make and squirrel away money whilst the Fed fiddles and burns.*

The Autumn Annuities
(A Life Income in Swiss Francs)
Jean-Pierre Bernard
1979; 76 pp.
$15 postpaid

Personal Finance
Jim Kelder, Editor
$65/yr. (24 issues)

Tax Angles
Vernon K. Jacobs, Editor
$44/12 issues
all from:
Personal Finance
901 North Washington
Street #605 W
Alexandria, VA 22314

*While I am at it, all you libertarian types might like to make a $15 donation to the National Taxpayers Union for a subscription to **Dollars and Sense**, $15/year (12 issues including membership) from: National Taxpayers Union, 325 Pennsylvania Avenue, Washington DC 20003. It may just drive you insane with its tales of Fed funnies.*

PENNY MINING STOCKS

*For $6.50, **Western Mining News** sells a collection of charts on all the registered and many of the over-the-counter stocks sold in the Spokane Exchange. As of the end of February 1980 there are 22 stocks at less than 11 cents a share. Just think, spend $100 and own 100 shares each of ten mining companies. Silver Beaver. Painted Desert. North Star. King of Pine. Lucky Star. "Well, one of my companies dropped 50% yesterday, but I'm getting well with my Silver Beaver shares, oh sure." Wheeeee.* ■

Western Mining News
R.R. Rutcasky, Editor
$26/yr. (52 issues)
postpaid from:
Western Mining News
227 Peyton Building
Spokane, WA 99201

WESTERN MINING NEWS
GOLDEN TRIANGLE MAY BE AMERICA'S NUMBER 1 GROWTH STOCK

Earning Money Without a Job

Many people want to leave their traditional 40 hr. a week jobs. For most of them, starting a business or buying one are the alternatives they dream of. Unfortunately the skill to run a business is very scarce and most people fail. The real answer to being your own boss is many small jobs. This book is the best guide available.
—Michael Phillips

Earning Money Without a Job
Jay Conrad Levinson
1979; 204 pp.
$4.95 postpaid from:
Holt, Rinehart and Winston
383 Madison Avenue
New York, NY 10017
or Whole Earth Household Store

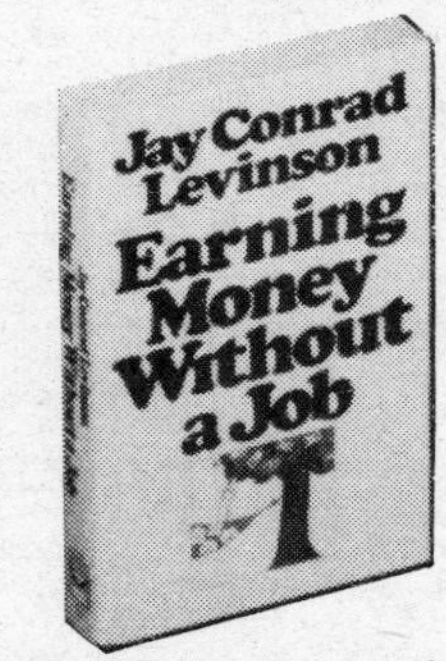

•

I have been without a job for over seven years, yet I never have been without work. I have earned considerably more money without a job than I did with a job, yet I rarely work more than three days a week. I have tasted freedom and quickly grew addicted to its pleasures.

•

Become aware of the immense amount of information provided to you by the Yellow Pages. Through study of them you will learn of voids in your area, shortages, needs, and growth opportunities.

•

The more amazing you are, the more you will succeed. When you do not have the brute force of a gigantic advertising budget, you must turn to the brute force of your own imagination to communicate your abilities or goods.

And the way to exercise that force is to be as amazing as you can.

There are some people who are paid large sums just to be amazing. Jim Moran is one. He sold refrigerators to Eskimos to prove how amazing he is. A young couple who had just opened a boutique lacked the money to advertise it properly. So they got married in their boutique. The ceremony was covered on TV and in the newspaper. All free publicity — and just because they were amazing. It does not require talent or brains to be amazing, merely courage.

Go Hire Yourself An Employer

How to get a job doing what you want to do. Everyone who has ever been unemployed knows that help wanted ads, employment services, and their ilk, don't do you much good. This book shows some better approaches. Advice on interviews, how to write a good resume, what to do when you quit (or get fired). The style is brusque and slang-ridden, and sometimes sounds pretty stupid. But don't be fooled. There is a solid core of real information here.
—William Bonney

Go Hire Yourself An Employer
(Revised Edition)
Richard K. Irish
1972, 1978; 238 pp.
$4.50 postpaid from:
Anchor Books
501 Franklin Avenue
Garden City, NY 11530
or Whole Earth Household Store

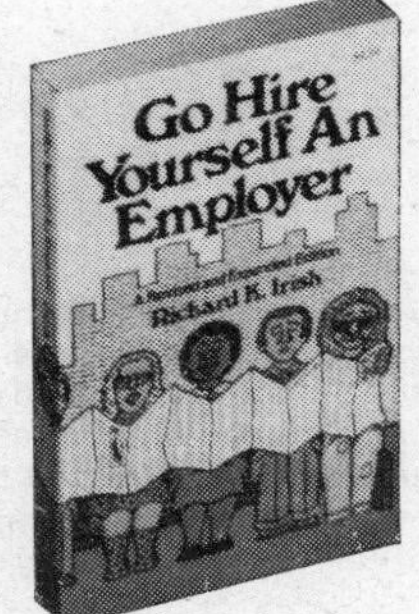

•

What happens if I begin a job, and the job I really want is offered two months later?

Quit and take the second job.

It's crackers to be "obligated" to employers. Betcha he/she will congratulate you on your good luck.

•

Never, never, never look for a job — always interview for information. Let's say, biostatistics is your trade. You work for a small, wealthy, but stagnant firm whose management will never admit you to its ownership. You want to find a firm — the same size — with growth potential where you can own a piece of the company. Because Uncle Sam takes more than he deserves (and you can afford) after the first $25,000 in salary, you know a piece of the stock action is the only way you're going to survive.

So, spend your early mornings, lunch hours, or the late afternoons checking out firms you might want to work with and who might need your skill. (Remember, one of your skills is knowing how to find a job.) You stake out the key people in each company, the men and women you would want to work for and from whom you can learn, and ask their advice on how to move up in your field. Always obtain the names of four more key people and companies from each person you interview and before long you've snowballed your job campaign into fifty interviews and, I bet, four hidden job offers.

How to Get Control of Your Time and Your Life

Almost a parody of the self-help genre, this glib book nevertheless can shake your bad habits and start better ones. I've used it and wasn't sorry. I've fallen away from the proper list keeping, but I work out of better priorities now — more realistic and more what I want — and I'm glad. Last time I saw author Lakein he was headed for an indefinite vacation at Big Sur — proving something, I would say.
—SB

How to Get Control of Your Time and Your Life
Alan Lakein
1973; 204 pp.
$1.95 postpaid from:
New American Library
P.O. Box 120
120 Woodbine
Bergenfield, NJ 07621
or Whole Earth Household Store

•

The 80/20 rule suggests that in a list of ten items, doing two of them will yield most (80 percent) of the value. Find these two, label them A, get them done. Leave most of the other eight undone, because the value you'll get from them will be significantly less than that of the two highest-value items.

These examples, drawn from everyday life, should enable you to feel more comfortable about concentrating on high-value tasks, even at the cost of ignoring many lower-value tasks:

80 percent of sales come from 20 percent of customers
80 percent of production is in 20 percent of the product line
80 percent of sick leave is taken by 20 percent of employees
80 percent of file usage is in 20 percent of files
80 percent of dinners repeat 20 percent of recipes

•

If you have to procrastinate, I'm going to show you how to do it positively.

Sit in a chair and do nothing. That's right — nothing. Don't read a book, don't shuffle papers, don't tackle your knitting, don't watch TV — just sit completely still.

If you sit doing nothing for fifteen or twenty minutes (don't cheat — you must do absolutely nothing), you should become very uneasy. That A-1 is staring you right in the face. And you're doing nothing. Precious minutes that you can use accomplishing a lifetime goal are slipping by. And you're sitting in a chair — doing nothing. Whenever I find myself procrastinating, this is the technique I use. Believe me, after ten minutes I'm off and running on my A-1.

Landlording

This is very valuable. Even though it includes California law, it is applicable in most states. The advice is clear, concise and based on experience in Berkeley, California, a tough area.
—Michael Phillips

Landlording
(A Handymanual for Scrupulous Landlords and Landladies Who Do It Themselves)
Leigh Robinson
1975, 1978; 254 pp.
$12.50 postpaid from:
ExPress
P.O. Box 1373
Richmond, CA 94802
or Whole Earth Household Store

•

In landlording, you use more supplies than the homeowner do-it-yourselfer does, and many retailers know it. Your local hardware store may give you charge privileges and a 10 percent discount to boot. Ask. Sears has a contract sales department which offers rental property owners special discounts on catalog sales and on other merchandise, like coin-operated laundry machines. Ward's offers trade discounts in certain of its retail departments. Other firms are anxious to do business with you, too, if you let them know who you are and what your requirements are. Take advantage of these privileges. It's good do-it-yourself landlording and it's good business.

THE RISING SUN
NEIGHBORHOOD NEWSLETTER

The Crowells were the first people I met who never said something was red. They'd say a thing was puce or mauve or magenta or vermillion and I wouldn't know if that was more like red or green. They called me color deaf.

The Incredible Secret Money Machine

For seven years I have actively advised and observed over 400 small businesses. This is the book that would have been helpful to nearly all of them. There is nothing comparable in wisdom, wit and genuine experience that I've seen in writing. On pages 5 & 6, he tells whether the book is for you: it is if you are in business "on a total lifestyle basis." "You want to stay in control" of your business, you are doing it," so . . . (you) can continue doing what you like in the direction you want to go. . ." and your business is intended to be "gentle on yourself, gentle on people and gentle on the environment." Out of hundreds of books I've read on small business practices, this is the front runner by a large distance. It's fun to read and exciting.

—Michael Phillips

[Suggested by Seren Bach]

The Incredible Secret Money Machine
(A How-to Cookbook for Setting Up Your Own Computer, Craft or Technical Business)
Don Lancaster
1978; 159 pp.

$6.95 postpaid from:
Howard W. Sams and Company, Inc.
4300 W. 62nd Street
Indianapolis, IN 46268
or Whole Earth Household Store

●

Having enough advance financing for your money machine is about the *worst* possible thing you can do and is almost certain to scuttle the whole machine.

A glib but accurate reason is that if you have the money, you are only going to spend it. And spend it on things that are totally unnecessary and in ways that will commit you down the road to even higher future costs. For your money machine to work, you have to start out scared, lean, and hungry. Such frivolities as food, clothing, and shelter should be totally forgotten in getting your money machine started.

There are lots of good reasons for studiously avoiding excess money when you start your money machine. It's real difficult for any beginner to increase the amount of money he is handling by more than 20% or so a year without starting to do stupid things with it or worrying too much about it.

●

If a person seeks you out, he has made an ego decision that he will defend. Should he buy from you, he will defend this decision, even if what he bought doesn't meet his needs. No way will he ever admit he got taken.

Oppositely, if a person feels he was "sold" something, he will easily find minor and even unreasonable faults with it to vent his displeasure.

●

Find out everything you can about possible antagonists, detractors, or competitors of any form. Anticipate what they are going to do and then completely change the rules of the game to something they simply won't understand.

●

Be hardnosed to freeloaders — if someone is using up more of your time, energy, or money than you'd like, tell them to shove off, walk away, ridicule them, or give them a dose of incompetence.

●

Screw off a lot — Go for a bicycle ride. Daydream. Go back to bed. Shoot pool. These are the times when things jell, when problems solve themselves, when new ideas happen.

●

The way around the copyright protection dilemma is to make your product so low in cost that no one can afford to duplicate it on their own in small quantities. A $4 to $9 technical paperback is unlikely to get widely copied. The same stuff in a $40 hardback book is almost certain to, particularly if it's required for a university course. A $5 cassette software program won't get ripped off because it takes more than $5 worth of hassle to duplicate a single copy.

Small-Time Operator

***Small-Time Operator** is most of the financial record-keeping information you need for a small business plus the lined paper for one year with excellent instructions on how to use it; along with good advice on the key issues that are related to them (such as when the IRS is likely to consider someone your employee).*

Bear (Bernard Kamoroff) lives the advice in the book. You can order a copy directly from him in Laytonville. He will package and ship it to you after he feeds the chickens and tends the garden. The first chapter has excellent general business advice that Bear collected in interviews with his clients.

—Michael Phillips

Small-Time Operator
(How to Start Your Own Small Business, Keep Your Books, Pay Your Taxes, & Stay Out of Trouble)
Bernard Kamoroff
1976, 1980; 189 pp.

$7.95 postpaid from:
Bell Springs Publishing Company
P.O. Box 640
Laytonville, CA 95454
or Whole Earth Household Store

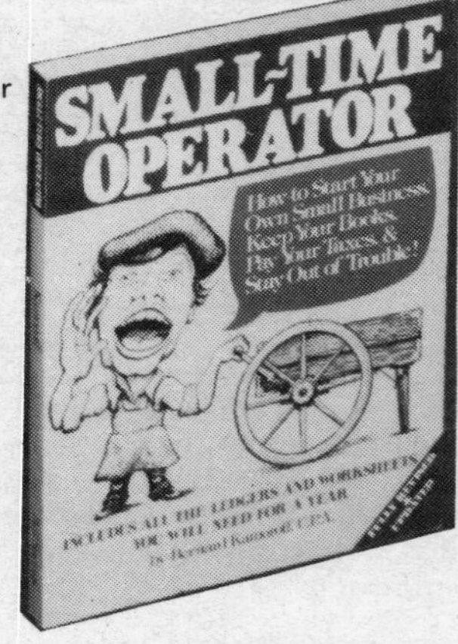

●

You can start out easily and simply. You don't have to make the Big Plunge, selling everything you own and going into debt. Start slowly, try it out, and learn as you go. You'll get there.

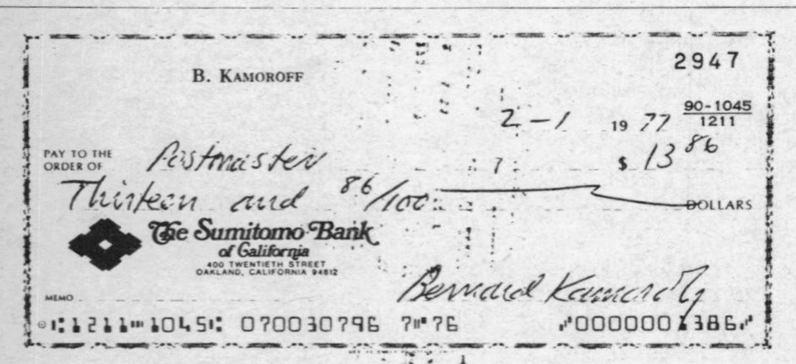

Another possible error if your bank account won't balance: compare the amount of the check to the computer-punched amount in the bottom right-hand corner of the cancelled check. They should be the same.

●

Things worked well for Joe. But if they had not — if he really did not have it in him to be in business for himself, or if he just picked the wrong thing at the wrong time — he could easily have stopped anywhere along the way with little or no loss. And maybe try it again some time.

●

If you're going to start a business, any business — the first and most important characteristic, I feel, is a clear head and the ability to organize your mind and your life. The "absent-minded professor" may be a genius, but he will never keep a business together. In running a small business, you are going to have to deal with many different people, keep schedules, meet deadlines, organize paperwork, pay bills, and the list goes on. It's all part of every business. So if balancing your checkbook is too much for you, or you just burned up your car engine because you forgot the oil, maybe you're not cut out for business. The work in a small business is rarely complicated, but it has to be done and done on time. Remember, this is going to be <u>your</u> business; it's all up to you.

Charlie Lee, Farmer and Farrier

Working for Yourself

Are you ready to quit your job and be self-employed? This book will give plenty of encouragement. It is based on several hundred interviews with people who are sucessfully working for themselves. The author has a very clear writing style and is supportive of the readers' interests. Good advice and wonderful examples ranging from many in farming to several in crafts and a few unusual things like inventing and editing.

—Michael Phillips

Working for Yourself
(How to Be Successfully Self-Employed)
Geof Hewitt
1977; 320 pp.

$7.95 postpaid from:
Rodale Books
33 East Minor
Emmaus, PA 18049
or Whole Earth Household Store

●

Charlie told me that he does his own billing. I asked if he ever has trouble collecting. "Yup. Some folks don't pay. Curiously, it's the wealthy people. I'd rather work for the farmers—they're more easy going, and they pay on time. If I had my way, I'd have a shop right here on my farm, and work only on horses that were brought to me. But I don't figure I can do that quite yet. I feel I need more experience before the business will come to me, but ideally, I'd work only draft horses.

"Part of the job is meeting so many different kinds of people," he said as we were driving to Enosburg, where he would shoe Harvey, a racehorse. Figuring up the day's profits: Charlie gets $18 for a regular shoeing job if he provides the shoes; $12 if the owner's shoes are used. This had been a fairly typical day; three clients in his date book with a total of five horses. Charlie had supplied all the shoes today, and the tally came to $90. "Not bad for a sweaty old blacksmith," he chuckled.

●

Surely one of the reasons for the Colemans' success in their quest for independence has been their thoroughness in doing every job right the first time, and keeping their efforts limited to their real capabilities. In starting with a plot of wooded land, the kind of land which — if ever cleared — is usually farmed for nothing more than blueberries, the Colemans wisely limited the size of their garden to only a quarter-acre. The garden, and the income it fetches, has grown with every season. Their first summer of selling vegetables, the Colemans earned only $350, living on savings from Eliot's years of teaching. Their economic yield, after seven years, was $4200 from three-and-one-half acres, which for them is just fine. Outside expenses are limited to gasoline, grains, sweeteners, and, right now, a new root cellar, contracted to a concrete firm — the only contracted project on their homestead.

The Colemans' Organic Vegetable Farm, near Penobscot, Maine.

Mail Order Moonlighting

This is the authoritative and best up-to-date word for anyone in the mail order business or planning to start one. No baloney, the real thing in a field full of phony books. Every useful detail is covered. Cecil Hoge, Sr. deserves the title "Sr."

—Michael Phillips

Mail Order Moonlighting
Cecil C. Hoge, Sr.
1976; 399 pp.

$7.45 postpaid from:
Ten Speed Press
Box 7123
Berkeley, CA 94707
or Whole Earth Household Store

●

An axiom of mail order is that you should never change any element of any successful mail order advertisement in any future advertising schedule, except for new tests of variations. This means every word, picture, layout element, or slightest variation in offer.

You can become a mail order scientist measuring *exactly* what happens when you change element in an advertisement.

There have been tremendous improvements, in recent years, in mail order testing methods. Yet, many advertisers and some agencies still do not realize exactly what could happen in sales if they slightly changed certain elements of the mail order advertising.

Test after test, for product after product, has shown conclusively that the apparent difference between overpoweringly effective advertising and ineffective advertising is far slighter than most people have any inkling. Again and again, seemingly slight variations have made the difference.

Mr. Roebuck started first, selling *one item only . . . watches,* and only one basic kind of watch with very little choice of styles and sizes. Mr. Sears took over and sold one additional item after another, until he spread or, it is said, rather sprawled his operation all over Chicago . . . in lofts and cellars and small offices . . . and initially *without* a catalogue. Mr. Sears, like some mail order men today, was said to be a bit of a mail order buccaneer. Not all his items would pass the laboratory tests Sears now requires. Not all of his first advertising copy (and it was often longer then) would now clear through the Sears internal censorship for factual truth and accuracy. Mr. Sears ran ad after ad in the same issue of individual magazines; sometimes up to thirty or forty of them. The catalogue seemed to come into being as an overgrown cluster of package enclosures, which in turn started one by one.

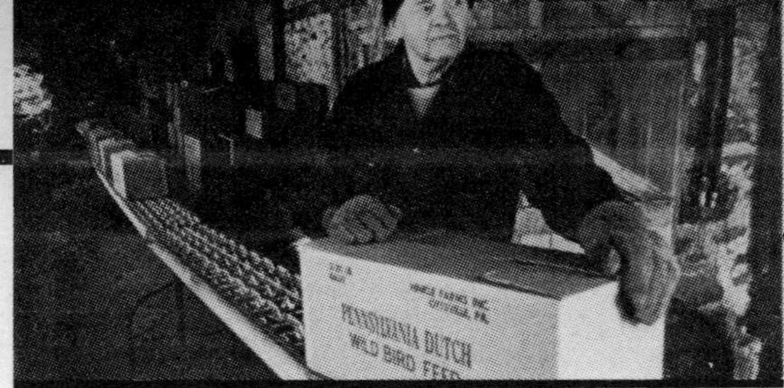

From a total investment of $2,600, Peyton Hinkle now operates a flourishing bird feed business, supplying area grocery and hardware stores.

In Business

A national magazine for small, warm entrepreneurs. Encouragement, advice, and perspective where it's most needed. This here issue includes a piece on bookkeeping by the author of **Small Time Operator** *(opposite page), access to and evaluation of low-cost long distance phone services, microcomputer programming, the business history of Brookstone Tools (p. 143), and new business opportunities in beneficial insects.*
—SB

In Business
Jerome Goldstein, Editor
$14 /yr (6 issues)
postpaid from:
In Business
Box 323
Emmaus, PA 18049

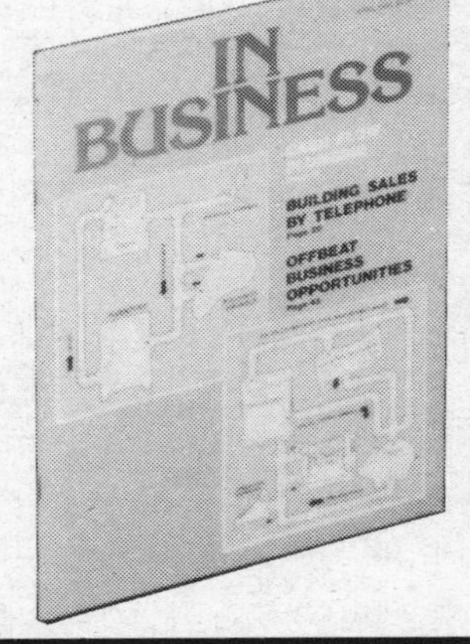

•

If your monthly phone bills are $400 or more, you probably should consider some kind of long distance telecommunication system.

•

A savvy farmer gave me this cash flow advice: "Never spend more in a month than you make in a week and you'll always come out okay."

•

Harold Brossman is a small apple grower. He's so small, in fact, commercial packers or buyers don't want to bother with him. On top of that, he lives in an area where roadside markets for selling fruit outnumber grocery stores. So he solved his apple marketing problem by making dried apples. Commonly called schnitz in the Pennsylvania Dutch country, the dried apples are wholesaled to the surrounding roadside market operators and to area groceries.

Not far away, Robert Kime and his wife also found they weren't faring very well with only 30 acres of apples. They looked around and decided to make them into apple butter. Demand for the product has grown to the extent they now are obliged to buy apples from their neighbors, mostly large growers.

Peyton Hinkle operated a small egg farm until business got so competitive only large operators could show a profit. Hinkle looked around for another way to survive. He came up with the idea of growing and mixing bird feed for sale to area grocery and hardware stores. Today he has a flourishing route business that requires two trucks to handle. He has added gourmet lines of processed fruits and condiments as a way of making each stop more profitable.

Robert Thayer sells dried weeds for floral arrangements. But at one time he and his brother grew vegetables for the wholesale market. Then labor and other problems became too much of a burden. Thayer looked at all the weeds he used to fight every year and decided to put at least some of them to work for him. Today his dried weed business is so extensive he hasn't time to harvest them anymore. He buys from other weed pickers—some of them a couple of thousand miles away.

How to Open Your Own Shop or Gallery

A good detailed book on retail business, with step-by-step examples. The advice is based on experience, the motives are very American. The author writes for **McCall's** *and* **Better Homes and Gardens.**
—Michael Phillips

How to Open Your Own Shop or Gallery
Leta W. Clark
1978; 229 pp.
$2.95 postpaid from:
Penguin Books
299 Murray Hill Parkway
East Rutherford, NJ 07073
or Whole Earth Household Store

•

If your shop's decor permits, try to include a community bulletin board. Become a regular stop for everybody who has a poster to put up or kittens to give away. Work to establish your store as a viable, caring part of your community. Also, if your budget is too limited to permit donations to every worthy cause, offer the use of your bulletin board as your contribution. It helps, and it works.

In retailing jargon, events that bring people into your shop are called "traffic builders." Time-honored ones are the Santa at Christmas time, and the free demonstration or giveaways. The idea behind traffic builders is based on the strength of numbers—the more people that trek through your store, the higher your chances are for sales.

One of the funniest traffic-builder stories is told by Ben Rosenthal, of the Small Business Administration's Service Corps of Retired Executives. He tells of a shop he and some partners opened in a small town in Texas during the Depression, with no pre-opening promotion budget, and a slim purse to carry them through the beginning months. They needed a terrific promotion to kick it all off, and he was very worried.

They finally took stock of the town and discovered that the townspeople were very religious. Every other block seemed to have a church in it, and attendance at services was high. This gave them their big idea. The store owners put all their excess efforts into building a big grandstand directly in front of the shop. Then they went around to every church they could find and announced that they were sponsoring a singing contest between the town's many church choirs.

The churches responded enthusiastically, and the store owners proceeded to the local newspaper office with a written notice of the contest, the names of the participating churches and the hours each choir was set to appear—coinciding, of course, with the opening week of the store. The clincher was that the winning choir would be selected by votes cast by the community. Anybody who wanted to vote was eligible, and the ballot box was placed inside the store.

The newspaper ran several major articles about the big contest. Religious leaders announced it from every pulpit in town. Extra choir practice sessions were prepared, and the entire network of church communication carried news of the big competition—and at the same time, news of the new store.

Obviously, the event was a smash. The store swarmed with voters who soon became customers, the store owners had generated untold waves of good will, "certificates of excellence" were awarded to some of the choirs, and the newspaper circulation increased. Rosenthal finishes his story by pointing out that the cost was virtually nil—they disassembled the grandstand and eventually used the wood for other purposes!

Starting a Small Restaurant

This is an extraordinary book in many ways but it will be most useful to those people who think their cooking is great and that they should do it in their own restaurant; next in line will be those who read it and still want to open a restaurant. No other comparable book exists. This is a unique and tough hands-on guide to doing it. It is fun for all those people who like good restaurants, think they know why some are good and others aren't and for those people who wonder how the complexity swirling around them in a restaurant gets translated into a profitable business.
—Michael Phillips

Starting a Small Restaurant
(A Guide to Excellence in the Purveying of Public Victuals)
Daniel Miller
1978; 180 pp.

$6.95 postpaid from:
The Harvard Common Press
The Common
Harvard, MA 01451
or Whole Earth Household Store

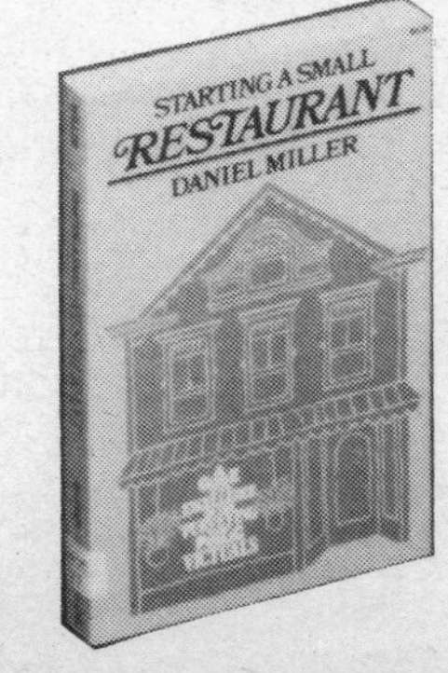

•

All your friends, who have just been treated to another of your wonderfully warm parties with delicious food and drinks, are urging you to open your own little place. Do not listen to them. Not unless you realize many years will pass before you spend another full evening with them, either as host or guest.

•

The layout of the restaurant should allow the server to proceed to the pickup point, take the order ticket, pick up the meal plates, and deliver them, all in less than a minute. In sixty seconds, a hot meal loses little flavor or heat. In 180 seconds it can lose its "piping hot" quality, and the dinner partially loses its initial delicious aroma as well. The main advantage of a small dining establishment is that it can fulfill this implied promise to its customers: hot food will be served hot and cold food will be served cold. Your servers must understand this principle. If you wish to infuriate a chef, design your kitchen so that orders cannot be picked up within forty-five seconds after the call.

•

If your restaurant is dependent on transient customers, one of the tricks of the trade on a slow day is to have all employee vehicles parked in front of the place.

Where the Money Is & How to Get It

Methods of raising capital. Accurate, simple, clear, short and precise as opposed to bright, wise, sensitive, comprehensive. Expensive, but most public libraries should get a copy.
—Michael Phillips

Where the Money Is & How to Get It
2nd Edition
Ted Nicholas
1973, 1976; 186 pp.
$3.95 postpaid from:
Enterprise Publishing Company
Hippocrene Books
171 Madison Avenue
New York, NY 10016
or Whole Earth Household Store

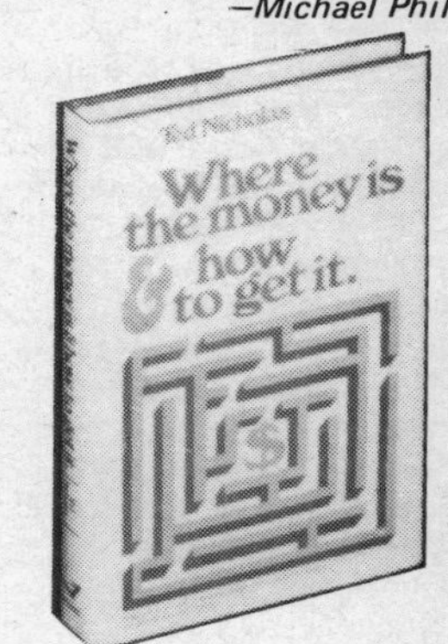

•

A big mistake often made by entrepeneurs whose venture fails is to start off under-capitalized.

To figure your start-up costs, estimate all expenses. Add up all disasters that are likely to happen — *because they will.* Then *double* it. This is how much capital you should have.

In your planning, forget any grandiose ideas about your "image." Expensive facilities or fringe benefits for employees will cause you to go broke before you start.

Keep your operating expenses to a minimum. Use your home for an office. If you must, rent a small, inexpensive office. Furnish it second-hand. Do not put in executive benefits and other frills. You must be willing to postpone rewards until the company is a success.

Cut every corner you can. Order a small quantity of stationery. Type letters yourself at first. Buy supplies in small quantities. Find the least expensive way to test your product or service. Work on methods of selling your product or service.

A quick way to kill a venture capitalist's interest is paying yourself a higher salary than your former job or by establishing company headquarters in, for example, an attractive tropical place without a sound business reason.

THE RISING SUN
NEIGHBORHOOD NEWSLETTER

I'm one of the few people I know who can deal with something at the beginning of a movie like MCMXXXIX without fear because I really enjoyed Roman number day in elementary school. But it is real weird — in MCMXXXIX you have a subtraction problem followed by an addition problem followed by a subtraction problem — and everyone knows that number reading is supposed to be addition and multiplication only — higher and higher. (1000 plus 1000 minus 100 plus 10 plus 10 plus 10 plus 10 minus 1 is a real strange way to get to 1939.) But it's a bad time to be reading Roman numerals in — first the whole century is a little bizarre, starting off with the MCM stuff and now here at the end of the century things are getting longer and messier by the year — this year is MCMLXXX and it's an even year — think of 1988 — MCMLXXXVIII, followed by MCMLXXXIX, followed by — get this — MCMXC — short but odd. It's hard to think their way — I was thinking of 1999 being MCMXCIX and sort of getting off on it — subtraction all the way, but really 1999 is MIM, followed by MM followed by MMI and MMII and all the gang. For a while things will be kind of short — MMX and stuff like that and you'll be able to date movies at a glance by the verbosity of their copyright dates — if it goes on and on it's twentieth century. I have faith that our grandchildren, if any, will be able to read Roman numbers, if they're still being used, better than we because their's will all start with MM which is a way of saying 2000 even we might have thought of.

My favorite Roman date in this millenium is MDCCCLXXXVIII which is the longest one there is if you follow the rules. Of course, not every one follows the rules, though movie people seem to. For example, Sather Gate says Erected by Jane Sather MDCCCCVIIII which is saying 1909 the hard but clear way.

The Effective Executive

Wherever there's a bunch of people doing something, somebody is bearing executive relation to the group, usually badly, therefore unhappily for everyone, and nothing much is going on besides frustration. But some leaders are good, and with them a lot happens and everybody feels good. This book takes a deep look into how "good" executives behave in common. The generalizations that emerge are useful to anybody with responsibility, from the honcho of a commune to the goddam Pope.
—SB

The Effective Executive
Peter F. Drucker
1966; 178 pp.
$10.95 postpaid from:
Harper & Row
Keystone Industrial Park
Scranton, PA 18512
or Whole Earth
Household Store

•

1. Effective executives know where their time goes. They work systematically at managing the little of their time that can be brought under their control.

2. Effective executives focus on outward contribution. They gear their efforts to results rather than to work. They start out with the question, "What results are expected of me?" rather than with the work to be done, let alone with its techniques and tools.

3. Effective executives build on strengths — their own strengths, the strengths of their superiors, colleagues, and subordinates; and on the strengths in the situation, that is, on what they can do. They do not build on weakness. They do not start out with the things they cannot do.

4. Effective executives concentrate on the few major areas where superior performance will produce outstanding results. They force themselves to set priorities and stay with their priority decisions. They know that they have no choice but to do first things first — and second things not at all. The alternative is to get nothing done.

5. Effective executives, finally, make effective decisions. They know that this is, above all, a matter of system — of the right steps in the right sequence. They know that an effective decision is always a judgment based on "dissenting opinions" rather than on "consensus on the facts." And they know that to make many decisions fast means to make the wrong decisions. What is needed are few, but fundamental, decisions. What is needed is the right strategy rather than razzle-dazzle tactics.

These are the elements of executive effectiveness — and these are the subjects of this book.

•

The definition of a "routine" is that it makes unskilled people without judgment capable of doing what it took near-genius to do before; for a routine puts down in systematic, step-by-step form what a very able man learned in surmounting yesterday's crisis.

•

We know very little about self-development. But we do know one thing: People in general, and knowledge workers in particular, grow according to the demands they make on themselves. They grow according to what they consider to be achievement and attainment. If they demand little of themselves, they will remain stunted. If they demand a good deal of themselves, they will grow to giant stature — without any more effort than is expended by the nonachievers.

•

To tolerate diversity, relationships must be task-focused rather than personality-focused. Achievement must be measured against objective criteria of contribution and performance. This is possible, however, only if jobs are defined and structured impersonally. Otherwise the accent will be on "Who is right?" rather than on "What is right?" In no time, personnel decisions will be made on "Do I like this fellow?" or "Will he be acceptable?" rather than by asking "Is he the man most likely to do an outstanding job?"

•

There is serious need for a new principle of effective administration under which every act, every agency, and every program of government is conceived as temporary and as expiring automatically after a fixed number of years — maybe ten — unless specifically prolonged by new legislation following careful outside study of the program, its results and its contributions.

The Briarpatch Book

What really happened to the '60s generation? We nearly all got into small business. Businessmen were the first non-stoned Americans to accept us, and many of us entrepreneured in the dope black market. Small wonder that we evolved our own version of the admirable small-business ethic. Its expression came to greatest clarity in the Briarpatch — a loose association of San Francisco Bay Area new-age businesses.

The name and practice of the Briarpatch has become famous but hard to find and examine. Here it is, declared and exampled. Michael Phillips, whose opinions pepper the adjoining pages, was and is in the thick of it. (See his "Four Illusions of Money," p. 288.)
—SB

The Briarpatch Book
(Experiences in Right Livelihood and Simple Living)
Briarpatch Community
1978; 313 pp.
$8.95 postpaid from:
New Glide Publications
330 Ellis Street
San Francisco, CA 94102
or Whole Earth
Household Store

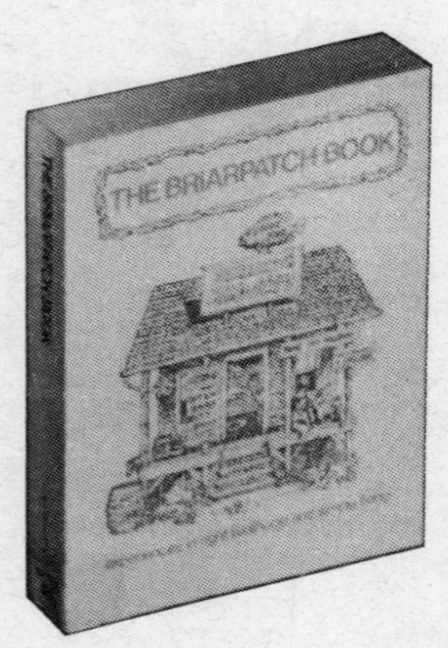

•

The Briarpatch is a network of small-business people who have three values in common: we are in business because we love it; we find our reward in serving people rather than in amassing large sums of money; and we share our resources with each other as much as we can, especially our knowledge of business. We share management and marketing information, legal and technical know-how, names of suppliers, and what general practices work and do not work. We are committed to keeping our books and financial records open. Our customers, employees, friends, and relatives know how much we earn, how much our supplies cost, and anything else they want to know about the financial workings of our businesses.

We share naturally because we love what we are doing, and we are open because our practices are honest. If you share these values, then you, too, are a Briar.

•

There are only two ways to search out a storefront: ask other shopkeepers in the area you like (realty companies also if you come across any); and locate dimly lit, painted over, or unused-looking stores.

The name of the owner or landlord will never be posted on such stores. So how do you find out whom to contact? First, call the Public Library and ask to speak to the office that has the "City Directory." This book is the opposite of the phone book — it has street addresses (from 1 Broadway to 3001 Broadway, for example) listed first, followed by people and phone numbers. So if you know the address, you can call the number at that address. If there is no listing for that address in the City Directory, don't give up — there's another approach: call the Assessor's Office at City Hall and ask for the owner's name and number listed in the "Realty Index." This book is organized the same way as the City Directory except that it has names of owners, not renters.

Why S.O.B.'s Succeed and Nice Guys Fail in a Small Business

So many people of good heart start a small business only to have it fail miserably. Most of the failures I have known and/or been a party to would have had a lot better chance of making it if this unscrupulous book had been handy. Oh, there's nothing here that is against the law, but the fine line is certainly approached. All of the advice comes under the heading of "sound business practice" but it is definitely aggressive stuff, and many will find it offensive in every way. On the other hand most of what is presented is normal business procedure for large corporations, which are the enemy. (The customer is not considered the enemy; it isn't that kind of unscrupulous.) If you are struggling along with a small business or are about to, a look here might prove mighty useful.
—J. Baldwin

Personally I find the tone and much of the advice of this book odious and its premise incorrect. (Of 300 Briarpatch businesses dedicated to "right livelihood" only two have gone out of business, says Mike Phillips.) Nevertheless a lot of the realities of small business depicted here may be found in no other book, but keep a firm grip on your conscience while reading.

Additional comments: Michael Phillips, "Follow the advice and go to jail." Paul Hawken, "People I know starting in business use this book to discover the real as opposed to ostensible practices of business — they're fully capable of sorting out the morality for themselves."
—SB

Why S.O.B.'s Succed and Nice Guys Fail in a Small Business
Financial Management Associates, Inc.
1976; 374 pp.
$22.81 postpaid from:
Financial Management Associates, Inc.
3824 East Indian School Road
Phoenix, AZ 85018
or Whole Earth
Household Store

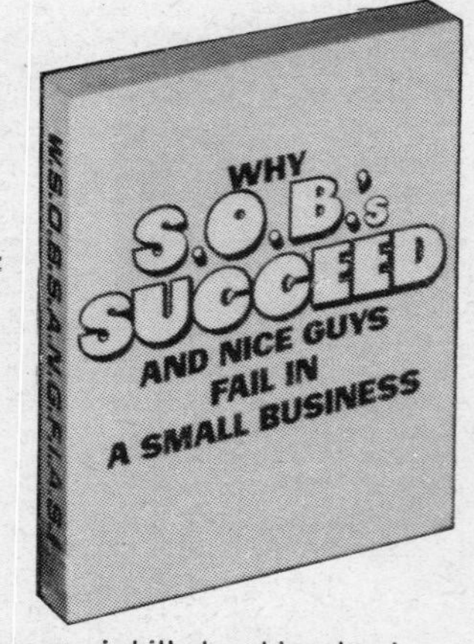

•

For the "grunt" jobs, those semi-skilled and low-level positions in your organization, one of the best sources of potential employees is from your own employees. Almost all of them probably know people who would make better than average employees, and by simply letting them know what you are looking for, you can get a great number of people to interview at no expense to yourself.

You should not, however, use this source too often for judgment jobs. Here you could get into a problem with the perception of your employees as to what a job requires. For judgment or management position jobs, you need to deal at arms' length with everyone. You don't want to risk upsetting or irritating your employee by turning down the individual who they consider perfectly suited for the job, and who have gone out and shot their mouth off by telling this individual that they can get him this particular job because they have great influence with you.

•

The one person who can rate lawyers from the standpoint of ability and responsibility is a judge. When a judge is your confidant and your friend, he will give the names of lawyers for particular situations who can do the job for you. They'll even pick up the phone and call them and make an appointment for you assuring you of red carpet treatment when you arrive at the office.

Many times a judge can give you legal advice that would cost you several hundred dollars to get from a lawyer, just talking to him over cocktails.

Up the Organization

This book has an amazing amount of truth, some of it pretty radical truth, about how to run an enterprise.
—SB

Up the Organization
Robert Townsend
1970; 202 pp.
$2.85 postpaid from:
Fawcett Books
Columbia Book Service
32275 Malley Road
P.O. Box FB
Madison Heights, MI 48071
or Whole Earth
Household Store

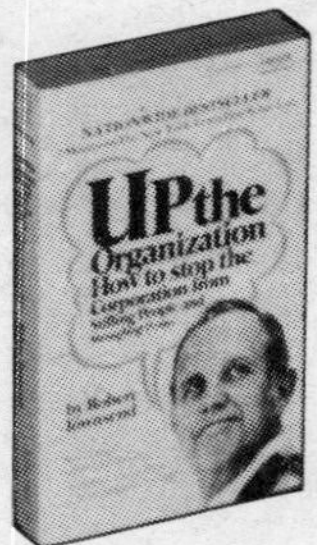

•

A lesson very few have learned: If you want to approach the head of XYZ Corporation, call him cold. Tell him who you are and why you want to talk to him. A direct and uncomplicated relationship will follow.

The common mistake is to look for a mutual friend — or a friend's friend on his board, in his bank or investment bank or law firm — to introduce you. This starts all sorts of side vibrations and usually results in a half-assed prologue by the intermediary, who is apt to grind both edges of his own ax.

•

All decisions should be made as low as possible in the organization. The Charge of the Light Brigade was ordered by an officer who wasn't there looking at the territory.

There are two kinds of decisions: those that are expensive to change and those that are not.

•

If you can't do it excellently, don't do it at all. Because if it's not excellent it won't be profitable or fun, and if you're not in business for fun or profit, what the hell are you doing here?

•

Admit your own mistakes openly, maybe even joyfully.

Encourage your associates to do likewise by commiserating with them. Never castigate. Babies learn to walk by falling down. If you beat a baby every time he falls down, he'll never care much for walking.

•

To keep an organization young and fit, don't hire anyone until everybody's so overworked they'll be glad to see the newcomer no matter where he sits.

Business Week

By far the best journal for staying abreast of international and domestic business news, with analyses superior to any other commentaries in competing publications. Economic analysis is much less dated than other business journals, all of which are still bogged down in "flat Earth economics."
—Hazel Henderson

Business Week
Lewis H. Young, Editor
$30.50 /year (51 issues)
from:
Business Week
P.O. Box 506
Hightstown, NJ 08520

•

In his new book, **Managing in Turbulent Times**, Peter Drucker admonishes that during inflation "the figures lie." Drucker argues that the illusion of record profits "leads to the wrong actions, the wrong decisions, the wrong analysis of the business" — in short, "gross mismanagement."

Now, thanks to the Financial Accounting Standards Board's new pronouncement on inflation accounting, investors and managers can begin to measure how sharply inflation has sliced into the seemingly handsome but deceptive record sales and earnings for some 1,300 of the nation's largest publicly owned corporations. A new study, released on June 5 by Price Waterhouse & Co., one of the nation's largest CPA firms, analyzes that impact on 157 giant industrial companies in 14 key industries plus 58 other companies in finance, retailing, transportation, and utilities.

The broad conclusions:

- Inflation-adjusted earnings of most of these broad business groupings are 40% to 70% lower than the traditional profits reported under historical-cost accounting.
- Effective tax rates typically are 15 to 25 percentage points higher with inflation adjustments — often far exceeding the U.S. statutory maximum rate of 46% on corporate income.
- Return on assets in real terms is only one-third to one-half that under more familiar historical-cost measures.
- Many industries are paying out twice as much in dividends as commonly thought; for retailers and utilities, dividends exceed inflation-adjusted income, which amounts to paying dividends out of capital.
- Sales growth during the past four years, after adjusting for inflation, has been less than half as strong as initially calculated. And dividend growth for most groups after adjustment shows even a more pronounced lag.

The Drawing Board

A good source of cheap, functional business stationery, note-o-grams, address labels, business notebooks, etc.
—SB

The Drawing Board
Catalog

free from:
The Drawing Board, Inc.
256 Regal Row
Dallas, TX 75221

Amazing but true: Note-O-Grams can actually cut your correspondence costs in half. Even more amazing: they save you up to 90% in preparation time! Take your choice of 3 formats: unruled 8-1/2" x 7-3/4" with carbonleaf or NCR Paper; ruled 8-1/2" x 7-3/4" with carbonleaf or NCR Paper; or ruled 8-1/2" x 9-1/4" with carbonleaf only. All formats in 3-part style, imprinted in red or black with your company's name and address, as shown below. The built-in follow-up system allows you to circle the month and day you expect a reply on your yellow file copy.

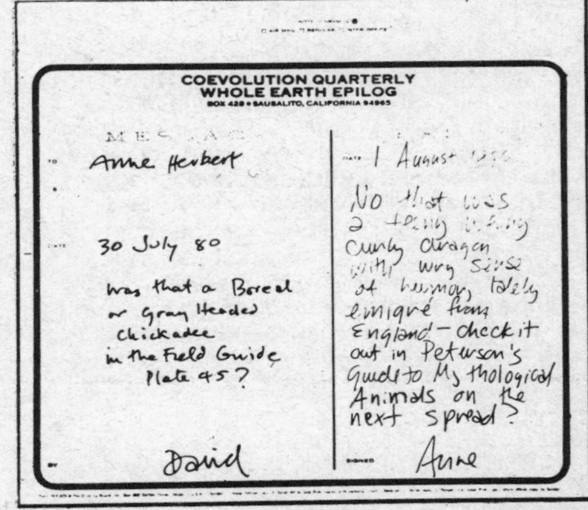
COEVOLUTION QUARTERLY
WHOLE EARTH EPILOG

Anne Herbert

30 July 80

Was that a Boreal or Gray Headed Chickadee in the Field Guide Plate 45?

David

1 August 1980

No that was a flying talking Cunky Oragon with wry sense of humor, lately emigré from England — check it out in Peterson's Guide to Mythological Animals on the next spread?

Anne

Pert/CPM Guide

PERT means Program Evaluation and Review Technique. CPM means Critical Path Method. Two versions of the same idea that emerged in the late '50s to keep complex projects on schedule. The trick is to figure out which parts of the work can go on concurrently and which have to happen in sequence. The longest necessary sequence is the Critical Path — work there sets the real pace. This method allows you to anticipate, map, and adapt your activities around that Critical Path spinal cord. We used a crude form of it to organize work on this ***Whole Earth Catalog.***

Of the numerous books, computer programs, etc. on the subject, I like this quick hard summary best. The author also offers puffed-up kits and handbooks at ridiculously high prices. But if you're doing a lot of PERT work, you might get some use out of his overpriced plastic Critical Path Computer.
—SB

PERT/CPM Guide
James Halcomb
1980; 17 pp.
$5 postpaid

Critical Path Computer
$23.50 postpaid

both from:
Halcomb Associates Inc.
510 E. Maude Avenue
Sunnyvale, CA 94086

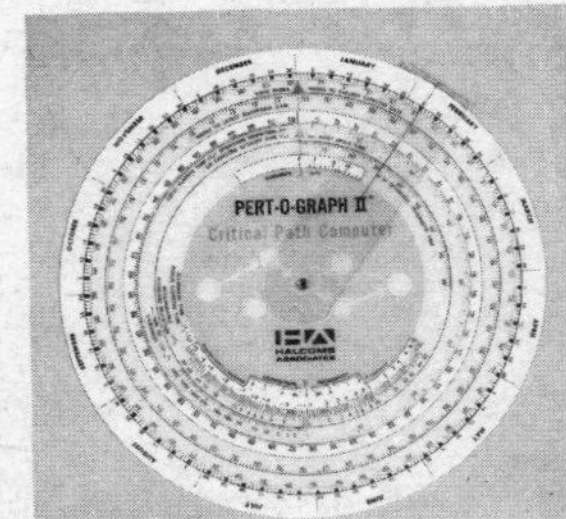

•

A PERT/CPM network analysis for a project is complete when all milestones are laid out in a logical sequence, time estimates are made for each activity, and when Earliest/Latest Dates, Slack, and the Critical Path is computed. The network plan becomes a "road map for managers" to monitor future progress. As the network is tracked, it is marked up in green to show normal progress, in yellow to show observed minor delays, and in red to show serious delays requiring urgent management corrective action. Management's job is to plan the work, then to work the plan.

↓

SII
SURVEY INSTRUMENTS INC
MODEL 32 NEW PRODUCT INTRODUCTION CYCLE

CRITICAL PATH

GREEN Normal progress
YELLOW Observed delay
RED Serious delay

PERT-O-GRAPH SYSTEM

Fidelity Business Supplies

Cheap good office gear — especailly a myriad of cardboard filing drawers, shelves, flat-boxes, bins, etc. ALL of my filing gear comes from Fidelity.
—SB

Fidelity Business Supplies
Catalog

free from:
Fidelity Products Co.
705 Pennsylvania Ave. So.
Minneapolis, MN 55426

Low As
$49.95

Desk-Side Roll File

Fidelity's heavy-duty corrugated fiberboard cabinet has a steel-reinforced frame for added stability. Forty-five 3-inch-square openings. Positive-locking door latch included. Metal index card holder. Master index chart inside door makes locating a particular rolled plan or print easy. Stand file on either end . . . for either right or left-handed convenience. Shipped set-up. Measures 15¾" wide, 31¼" deep and 27½" high. F.O.B. Minneapolis plant, freight collect or billed.
Model S4531 Shpg. wt. 25 lbs. . . . . **$54.95;** 3 or more **$49.95 each**
Optional Metal Base. Holds cabinet 2" above floor, protects against soil and moisture (raises top surface to 29½" off floor—flush with most desk tops).
Model S4532 Shpg. wt. 5 lbs. . . . . **$13.95 each**

Platform Trucks

An easy way to move parts, materials and unfinished products through manufacturing, production and shipping departments. Heavy-duty trucks are right for any moving job. They're lightweight and inexpensive. Tongue-and-groove seasoned hardwood platforms with heavy cross battens. Reinforced 26"-high handle for heavy loads. Two double-ball swivel casters and two matching rigid casters. Semi-steel or vulcanized rubber-tired wheels. Handle adds 4" to overall length and 26" to overall height. Built to last for years of use

- Reinforced Tongue and Groove Hardwood Decks
- Easy To Push and Maneuver
- Steel or Rubber-Tired Wheels
- Double-Angle-Iron Steel Framing

Model	Wheels	Platform L x W x H	Load Capacity	Shpg Wt	Price, Each 1 or 2	3 +
S8500	4x1½	42x24x7¼	800 lbs	61 lbs	$94.95	$89.95
S8501	5x1⅝	48x27x8½	1000 lbs	85 lbs	114.95	109.95
S8502		54x27x8½	1100 lbs	102 lbs	124.95	119.95
S8503		60x30x8½	1200 lbs	114 lbs	134.95	129.95
S8504	4x1½	42x24x7½	800 lbs	61 lbs	104.95	99.95
S8505	5x1⅝	48x27x8½	1000 lbs	85 lbs	124.95	119.95
S8506		54x27x8½	1100 lbs	102 lbs	136.95	129.95
S8507		60x30x8½	1200 lbs	114 lbs	146.95	138.95

Platform trucks shipped F.O.B. Neenah, Wis. plant, freight collect or billed.

Office Organizers

Tray Style

Our Most Popular!

Low As **$21.88**

- 12 slide-out trays (choose Letter or Legal size) store product sheets, pens and pencils, note pads, etc.
- Multi-ply corrugated fiberboard cabinet is steel reinforced
- Metal channels on middle shelves protect edges from wear
- Label Holders and I.D. Cards included
- Rich walnut woodgrain finish

Model	Size	12 Trays W x D x H	Overall W x D x H	Shpg. Wt.	Price, Each 1 or 3	4 +
S7161	Letter	9x11⅞x4	28¼x12¼x20⅞	14 lbs	$26.88	$21.88
S7163	Legal	9x15x4	18¼x15⅞x19⅞	16 lbs	29.88	26.88

THE RISING SUN
NEIGHBORHOOD NEWSLETTER

I've never lived on a maid's line, though I'm getting closer all the time, but sometimes when I go to visit friends I ride to work with the maids. I hear them talking about getting the kids ready for school at 6 so they can leave at 6:30 so they can catch three buses to make it to work by nine and get docked an hour's pay for being 5 minutes late, and about trying to buy enough groceries to feed five kids when every item goes up 5 cents a week and eating the moldy baloney the lady left for lunch and I wonder if someone offered them a better life in another country would they take the chance? Do they have dead friends or grandkids who did? I hope there's an everlasting life of simple unremitting justice pouring down right now on the soul of Reverend Jones. (I don't think my friends and I are ready for it yet, though.)

THERE ARE ONLY THREE THINGS TO DO WITH MONEY: SPEND IT INVEST IT OR GIVE IT AWAY!

The Bread Game

If you're raising money from foundations, this blunt little book is indispensable. I've been on both sides of the breadline enough to cherish its succinct candor in the bullfart atmosphere of granting. There's now a whole literature on fundraising, but this book was first (1973), and its forthcoming third edition (Fall 1980) is likely to still be the best. —SB

The Bread Game
(The Realities of Foundation Fundraising)
Herb Allen, Editor
1973, 1974; 96 pp.

$7.70 postpaid from:
New Glide Publications
330 Ellis Street
San Francisco, CA 94102
or Whole Earth Household Store

•

Wealthy Individuals. Many wealthy individuals do not have foundations of their own, but often make tax-deductible contributions to projects. There are all sorts of weird ways of finding these people: contribution reports of liberal political candidates, society pages of newspapers, friends and relatives, etc. They can be an excellent source of funds: first, because you don't have to go through a bureaucracy to contact them; second, because they need the contact from non-wealthy people. Before you approach them, have everything together to make it easy for them to make a tax-deductible contribution to your group. Read carefully the legal and fiscal sponsor material in this book!

•

Do It Right the First Time

The importance of good accounting procedures for all organizations cannot be overstated. Too many groups tend to feel that anyone can keep a set of books. Don't be sucked into this attitude — it can be your undoing. Keep good records from the beginning. Ask the help of a good accountant to at least get the books set up in good order. Even though you may write your own checks, make all your own deposits and do your own posting. Check back with your accountant every three months so that your books can be reviewed and checked over for accuracy. A good set of books will go a long way toward convincing foundations and other contributors that you are a responsible group.

•

Developing Skills in Proposal Writing is written by Mary Hall, and is available from Continuing Education Publications, Waldo 100, Corvallis, Oregon 97331. This is the best, economically priced, proposal writing manual that we have seen. $10

On Free Money

FROM MY LIMITED EXPERIENCE, the realm of foundations and grants is one of the most cynical in the American economy, though it's improving a little of late. Generally when you approach a foundation they are friendly and half-receptive. They consider your project promising if a little naive, and they'd like you to write up a proposal on it. You spend a month learning how to write proposals and a month writing this one. They keep it six months. Your idea has died of dry rot. Then they request that you re-write the proposal to accommodate (whatever) and it might go through next time the board meets. Do this three times, and you have died of dry rot.

Most actual grants I know of were initiated by the donors, not the donees. The most effective way to get grant money is to be Highly Visible.

I don't know why foundation and government money is so often toxic to projects. Maybe because the process becomes so easily dishonest. Do me no favors, and I'll tell you no lies. Or is it the belief that there's such a thing as a free lunch that is the root lie? —SB

The Foundation Directory

The reference book of foundations. Gives addresses, finances, officers, purposes and activities. Foundations are listed by state, which is intelligent, since grants are usually given locally. (For non-foundation fundraising see **The Grass Roots Fundraising Book**, *p. 394.)* —SB

The Foundation Directory
7th Edition
Marianna Lewis, Editor
1967, 1979; 594 pp.

$15 postpaid from:
Columbia University Press
Stock Department
136 South Broadway
Irvington-on-Hudson, NY 10533

The Seven Laws of Money

Ex-banker Michael Phillips — also ex-director of POINT, the foundation that publishes this **Catalog** *and gave away the million bucks that we got from sales of the* **Last Catalog** *— tells all. It's a bit New Age, but it's wise, smart, and original on a subject that usually fights those qualities. The book has made a lot of people cheeky enough to try stuff, and it's helped them get away with it. (See his "Four Illusions of Money," p. 288.)* —SB

The Seven Laws of Money
Michael Phillips
1974; 194 pp.

$4 postpaid from:
Random House
455 Hahn Road
Westminster, MD 21157
or Whole Earth Household Store

•

THE FIRST LAW
Do it! Money Will Come When You Are Doing the Right Thing

THE SECOND LAW
Money Has its Own Rules: Records, Budgets, Saving, Borrowing

THE THIRD LAW
Money is a Dream: A Fantasy As Alluring As the Pied Piper

THE FOURTH LAW
Money is a Nightmare: In Jail, Robbery, Fears of Poverty

THE FIFTH LAW
You Can Never Really Give Money Away

THE SIXTH LAW
You Can Never Really Receive Money As A Gift

THE SEVENTH LAW
There Are Worlds Without Money

•

Money, which represents the prose of life, and which is hardly spoken of in parlors without an apology, is in its effects and laws, as beautiful as roses.

—Ralph Waldo Emerson

•

When you open a checking account, open it with the largest amount of money you possibly can. I'm not kidding! Even if the average balance in your account is only going to be $50, try to borrow a friend's $10,000 home payment for *one day* so you can use it to open your account. You don't have to go that far, but anything over a couple of thousand dollars looks good. You can withdraw most of the money a few days after the account is opened. Really! The reason for this is that the bank records your opening balance on your signature card (and often in other places, too), believing that it is representative of your financial status. I did a study when I was a banker and found absolutely no correlation between opening balances and the kind of balances that appeared later on in the same account. It's such a strong tradition to do it this way (at least a hundred years old) that bankers still judge people by their opening balance. Try it; the branch manager will smile on you forever more.

•

When you're asleep and dreaming, that's a world without money.

•

An example of foundations gone wild occurred recently. I funded Margo St. James to organize a prostitutes' collective to protect street prostitutes from the inhuman daily abuse they get from the police, the courts, and hypocrites. I advised her to let a few local foundations know what she was up to so they would be aware of her project if in the future she should need to go to them for funds. I read the letter she sent to them; no request, just a friendly letter saying what she was doing. One liberal foundation, Pacific Change, invited her over to lunch and grilled her cruelly and mercilessly the same way they do groups they regularly screen. They berated her for not being serious, not being a member of a minority and not being poor enough. Fortunately, she told them to go to hell and left. Another foundation simply sent her a letter of rejection, although she hadn't applied for money. These institutions are examples of how most foundations are so structured that they become numb in the process of dealing with the pain people feel in the donor/grantee relationship.

Robin Hood Was Right

An inspiration and advice kit for rich kids. How to not feel bad about being born to wealth, and how to treat the burden as a creative resource for others. I'm a great supporter of private wealth — through no other means can you get really original and really radical giving in the society. This good book shows how. —SB

Robin Hood Was Right
(A Guide to Giving Your Money for Social Change)
Vanguard Public Foundation
1977; 148 pp.

$5 postpaid from:
Vanguard Public Foundation
4111 24th St.
San Francisco, CA 94114

•

If you publicly give away money, you have to face the fact that you're going to get hustled. People will invite you to "parties" that are really fundraisers; others will make it their business to get to know you on a friendly basis. You'll receive tons of letters in the mail and occasional knocks on your door asking you to pay the rent of families facing eviction or bail someone out of jail in Peru, sponsor trips to Tahiti or support a struggling young poet. In short, you'll be asked to fill an entire spectrum of heartrending and sometimes whacky needs that have nothing to do with projects you want to fund. You may wonder, "Am I really this popular?" The answer is no.

In response to this pressure, many rich people have simply disconnected the phone, closed the checkbook, and stopped giving money away altogether. There are better ways to deal with the problem.

•

The ways of giving anonymously are fairly simple:

• Register a fictitious name with the IRS, get a Post Office box and a bank account in that name, and start writing checks. For your tax accountant's purposes, the checks are written by you, but the organizations you give to will think they are from Merdley A. Scrump, or whatever name you choose. Or you can arrange for a lawyer to be your agent. He or she will make donations and sign the checks, telling the grantees they are from an anonymous client.

• It is much better, however, to work out a relationship with an existing foundation or consultant. You will be working with people who are accustomed to keeping secrets and who have the mechanisms set up to channel money from an anonymous donor. One advantage of this method is that it provides you with a more effective cover. If your favorite local tenants' union receives a grant from, say, the Liberty Hill Foundation, the group will think of it as a grant from the Foundation itself, even though they may be told it is a "donor-specified" grant. On the other hand, if the same group suddenly gets a check from Merdley A. Scrump — who is not in the phone book and is not known by anyone — or from a lawyer representing an "anonymous donor," that's an open invitation to start trying to find out who the mystery person might be. A visible passion for secrecy mainly attracts publicity, as Howard Hughes and the CIA have discovered.

One important caution: resign yourself to the fact that partial secrecy is impossible. You cannot expect to give money to organization A in your name, tell them "don't say it was from me," and expect your secret to stop there. It never will.

San Francisco Opera House. Annual budget: $6,637,981

The San Francisco Mime Troupe is an alternative political theater collective which has performed original comic satire nationwide since 1959. Here they perform free False Promises-Nos Enganaron. **Low-budget, community-based arts projects often must struggle to secure funding. These projects involve and educate the community and are important to ethnic groups with different cultural heritages which are frequently ignored by traditional arts groups.**

The Small Towns Book

Two city people who have gone back to the town advise others like themselves on how not to destroy what they came to take part in. Case studies of six small towns in danger of being loved to death by bureaucrats, tourists, or urban exiles. There's enough detail that it might help you in your fights and enough good general ideas that it might change your mind about what to fight for.

—Anne Herbert

The Small Towns Book
(Show me the way to go home)
James and Carolyn Robertson
1978; 208 pp.

$5.95 postpaid from:
Doubleday and Company
501 Franklin Avenue
Garden City, NY 11530
or Whole Earth Household Store

•

AN OPEN LETTER TO VISITORS

First be assured that it is not you, personally, we are questioning. Person-to-person, had we a quiet context, we would probably become friends; certainly not enemies.

Our problem is that the flood of tourists recently has passed beyond what a small town can handle and still function as a community. Noise of automobiles drowns out sounds of the ocean, even late at night. We now smell exhaust instead of salt air. Streets are littered. Townspeople cannot find places to park. Many young, creative people have had their rents increased and must now move. Taxes are rising and many oldtimers now must sell. The quiet, creative ambience of the town is dissolving, replaced by a growing number of antique stores and other tourist-oriented businesses.

We realize growth is inevitable; most of us moved here realizing M — had an active tourist industry already. We accept that visitors have a legal right to come here and that property owners have a legal right to develop their land as they see fit.

But we also profoundly cherish the fact that M — is a living community; this is our home; families live here. This is still a creative center where artists, poets, actors and students come to live and work and experiment.

We do not mind a reasonable number of visitors, especially visitors who will pause long enough to get to know the town, the people — will trouble themselves to *feel* the real M — beneath the commercial veneer. We mind the innundation of the town by hordes flashing through for a few minutes or hours. We mind the rapid and sudden investment in M — as commercial-enterprise, especially by those who live elsewhere.

So we urge you to come here infrequently, sensitive to the fact that you are entering a fragile community of real people. If you do come back, we urge you to consider staying for more than a night or two — long enough to realize that basic functions of communities are deep and personal . . . and that window dressing is not the real product. Look for the authentic work of *local* people. Question what you buy, whether it is locally made, or just shipped here for the tourist industry.

Please do not encourage others to come here. Present facilities — and basic services — are overloaded. We do not want more facilities to further destroy the fragile fabric of community that still exists here. Consider — and we say this respectfully — your own backyard. If you spent the time and energy *there* that you are spending here, wouldn't you, your family, your neighborhood, and the planet, be better off? Then, perhaps we could someday visit *you* and have something to gain from it.

Community in America is getting to be a lost art. Commercial, phoney tourist traps are increasingly prevalent. Help us protect, maintain, and develop the former.

—The M—SCAT Committee
(Sensible Citizens Against Tourism)

Small Town

A little magazine bound to be useful to any community large enough to have a town hall. It's about character, controlled growth, and planning. —SB

Small Town
Clayton Denman and Ann Smith Denman, Editors

$25/year (6 issues) from:
Small Towns Institute
P.O. Box 517
Ellenburg, WA 98926

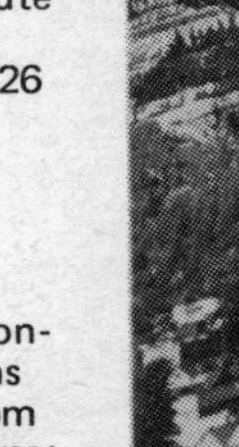

•

The planning environment of small towns as distinguished from cities usually involves:

1. A small circle of decision makers who can be easily reached if not easily persuaded;
2. A slower tempo of development pressure;
3. A greater proportional impact of major development if it occurs;
4. Fewer resources (staff, libraries, research capabilities, and consultants) to cope with major planning problems when they arise;
5. Less reliance on government and more of a *laissez faire* attitude by citizens and their representatives;
6. Less power of organized environmental and consumer groups (which often are closely affiliated with public planners).

Sa-So catalog

Town equipment. Signs, trash cans, paint, flags, office supplies, auditorium stuff, playground stuff, radios, searchlights, badges, handcuffs, guns, prison stuff, uniforms, stretchers, fire equipment. Fascinating catalog. See excerpts and access on p. 149. —SB

[Suggested by Sam Halstead, former Mayor of Portola Valley]

The Country of the Pointed Firs

One of the reasons that I keep reading the humanist journal **Manas** *(p. 516) is that nearly every week it has some good old book to recommend. As a rule, good old books are better than good new ones. Also there's more of them. Why are they so seldom reviewed?*

Anyway here's one. Written by a New England woman mostly about New England women, it contains in its stories more of the craft of lucid writing and of honorable living than any other fiction I've seen. Willa Cather remarks in the preface, "If I were to name the three American books which have the possibility of a long, long life, I would say at once **The Scarlet Letter**, **Huckleberry Finn**, *and* **The Country of the Pointed Firs**. *I can think of no others that confront time and change so serenely."*

The stories are set in Maine seacoast towns early in this century. You can smell them and hear the voices. The lives make large distinct patterns, turning on single events and lifelong strengths. These are old virtues. Their joys are slow and deep and far from simple. Here in California I miss them like thunderstorms. —SB

[Suggested by Sally Brooke]

The Country of the Pointed Firs
(And Other Stories)
Sarah Orne Jewett
1896, 1956; 320 pp.

$2.95 postpaid from:
Doubleday and Company
501 Franklin Avenue
Garden City, NY 11530
or Whole Earth Household Store

•

"I wish I had known her; Mrs. Todd told me about your wife one day," I said.

"You'd have liked to come and see her; all the folks did," said poor Elijah. "She'd been so pleased to hear everything and see somebody new that took such an int'rest. She had a kind o' gift to make it pleasant for folks. I guess likely Almiry Todd told you she was a pretty woman, especially in her young days; late years, too, she kep' her looks and come to be so pleasant lookin'. There, 't ain't so much matter, I shall be done afore a great while. No; I sha'n't trouble the fish a great sight more."

The old widower sat with his head bowed over his knitting, as if he were hastily shortening the very thread of time. The minutes went slowly by. He stopped his work and clasped his hands firmly together. I saw he had forgotten his guest, and I kept the afternoon watch with him. At last he looked up as if but a moment had passed of his continual loneliness.

"Yes, ma'am, I'm one that has seen trouble," he said, and began to knit again.

LUFKIN
CITY LIMIT
POP. 15135

Turkey Drop

by Terrence Williams

Last Saturday the Junior Chamber of Commerce in the small town nearest us held a Farmer's Appreciation Day to let us know how much they love us. Their love is matched only by that of politicians in an election year. They have a free dinner and all the store clerks dress up in funny clothes. The merchants drag out the seconds and imperfect goods, jack up the price thirty-five percent, put up a red bargain sign, and we lap it up.

This year as an added fillip they decreed a turkey drop. This was a gimmick thought up in the late forties where they took a hundred ping pong balls, put special marks on six, and dropped them over a town. The finders of the six specially marked balls got turkeys. The Junior Chamber had heard of the turkey drop, but not about the ping pong balls.

The advertising said Catch Your Easter Turkey. Alas, this was not to be.

Turkeys don't fly very well, and never more than a few feet off the ground. So when the earnest young men pushed six of them out of a light plane 3000 feet above main street, the birds knew they they were doomed. They accepted their fate with great dignity. They folded their wings and dropped straight down on to the crowd below like six huge black rocks. One hit the roof of the bank where it will doubtless remain until the directors can see a way to profit by its removal. The rest hit the pavement with enormous splats at intervals along the full length of the street. Fortunately no one was hit because being hit by a forty pound tom at terminal velocity would be fatal to man and bird. As it was, it was abundantly fatal to bird.

One tight skinned matron was standing a few feet from the second to strike, and her south-west exposure was instantly and generously covered with blood and fowl guts and two fronds of entrails festooned her hat. She was able to contain her glee better than I.

In fact I thought the day a complete success. The town cats and I have suggested that next year the Junior Chamber provide us farmers with an Easter dinner of ham. After all, hogs fly about as well as turkeys. ■

The author may be found at Williams Farms, Gettysburg, South Dakota, founded 1884. His account, unlike some animal stories, is true. —SB

THE RISING SUN
NEIGHBORHOOD NEWSLETTER

At the Food Company I was reading this picture book about logging called *Big Timber/Big Men* and the waitress, Debra, opened it up to a picture of a 1909 logging crew and said, "That looks just like my old boyfriend's crew. He's a smoke-jumper, parachutes into forest fires to put them out. Boy, the people who do that really know how to party, and there's never any bullshit either. They tell you exactly what they think because they just don't care." I asked her some questions and she said, "He was gone about 4 months a year and came back with money in 5 figures, I couldn't say exactly how much. Of course, they couldn't get insurance. A lot of the planes are real old, World War II, and they don't fix them up, so there are always crashes. Of course, the jumpers have their chutes, but they lose a lot of pilots that way. Sometimes when they go down even on regular jumps they have to stay in the wilderness for weeks till they find a place to be picked up so they need really good survival skills. Look at the pants in that picture — those are just like my boyfriend's. Pants like that are like iron — they'll last forever. You don't see anything like that on men around here. Men around here are dressed better than you or me or anyone we know."

Next time I went in the Food Company she didn't work there anymore.

COMMUNITY FIRE AND EMERGENCY MEDICAL SERVICES

by Gerald Myers

Gerald Myers is Chief of the Beginnings Fire Company, Redway, California. If you find this article useful, you will want their new book **Homestead Fire Prevention and Suppression**, *mentioned below.* —SB

The myth of the totally self-sufficient homestead dies hard, but the first time a 10 or 100 (or 10,000) acre fire heads toward your 40 — or the old man or lady falls off the roof and is laying in a broken, unconscious heap on a pile of lumber — you may begin to expand your vision of self-sufficiency to community self-sufficiency. Disaster freaks ("survivalists") continue to try to find a tucked-away hideout in the woods where they can stock up and ride out the coming apocalypse — an ego-tripping fantasy akin to the bomb shelters of the '50s. Rural (or urban) community self-help organization for fire and medical emergencies, under disaster conditions or not, is another story, and an old one. The Reading, Pennsylvania Rainbow Volunteer Fire Department was formed in 1773 and is still going strong.

In Northern California several of the new rural communities have put together the people, communications, skills, and tools to handle community emergencies. Organization varies from a summertime only hand-tool fire crew to year-round fire and medical emergency fire departments. It's down home, country funk, grass-roots, 99% tedium and 1% adrenaline, but when the stuff hits the fan even a modest amount of teamwork, training, and tools can accomplish a great deal. It beats feeling helpless and waiting for the "experts" to arrive, especially when the experts may not show up in your neck of the boonies come apocalypse.

Listed here are my evaluations of some of the publications and suppliers in the fire/emergency medicine field. My biases are rural, forested, western, and poor — equipment is specialized and not cheap.

Two warnings: 1. As with all good exercises with the universe, fire and emergency medical services are open ended. You can never have all the skills, tools, or experience you want. With luck, you will have what you need.

2. No matter how well trained, how good the teamwork and equipment, and how fast the response time, the very nature of emergency services means YOU CAN'T WIN 'EM ALL. It's a hard lesson.

Locating the line for line construction with hand tools.

Wildfires: Prevention and Control

Big (319 pages, 229 illustrations), expensive, and thorough, this book tells you 5 times as much as most of you will ever want to know about wildfires. However, every community should have a copy — must reading for crew leaders. Nitty-gritty, fine-grain detail of how to do it in a variety of situations. The illustrations of working firefighters show them working without gloves — you'll only make that mistake once! I'll be re-reading this one for a long time. (Women's Lib note: The only women illustrated are being led to safety by male firefighters.)

Wildfires
(Prevention and Control)
Harry P. Gaylor
1974; 319 pp.

$15.95 postpaid from:
Robert J. Brady Co.
Routes 197 and 450
Bowie, MD 20715
or Whole Earth Household Store

(Brady puts out many other other books and training materials for fire and medical emergencies. Get their catalogs free.)

FIRE PUBLICATIONS

There are a lot of fire books and magazines, most oriented to urban problems and equipment (and budgets). In order to determine their usefulness to rural communities trying to get a new trip together (or re-establish an old, out-of-steam dead or dying small town department), visit your nearest local fire agency. Talk to the folks (usually full-time paid professionals) who respond to fires in your area now. Find out what they think your community can do to assist itself and them on different types of fires and/or medical emergencies. Expect a condescending attitude, grit your teeth and smile, drop in during the quiet part of the year — persevere. They will probably have many of the publications listed here for you to look over, take subscription cards from, borrow reader service cards from, and generally evaluate before you commit your dollars to my evaluation of their worth.

Homestead Fire Prevention and Suppression

The best book for the busy rural homesteader with many bases to cover. Brief, cheap, covers the basics of fire ecology, fire theory, homestead fire prevention, individual fire suppression, and organizing a neighborhood fire crew. Individual and crew safety, handline construction, and some "typical" fire situations are also covered, as well as communication systems and an itemized list for a do-it-yourself first aid kit. The book's orientation is the forested northern California area, but most of it is applicable to other rural ecosystems. It is one of the few fire books that does NOT assume you are male and have a fire truck to play with — just that you are intelligent people with hand tools. This book was written and copiously illustrated by a friend of mine, who has organized a local fire crew, and I wrote the introduction — you are warned of my bias. However, if you are a rural community dweller interested in fire safety and/or in starting or helping to start a local fire crew, this book is for you. Profits (if any) on the sale of this gem go to the Crooked Prairie Fire Crew equipment fund. Help my next-watershed-over neighbors buy a fire truck.

Homestead Fire Prevention and Suppression
Larry Heald
1980; 100 pp.

$4.50 postpaid from:
Larry Heald
Crooked Prairie Fire Crew
Star Route Ettersburg
Garberville, CA 95440

Hitting the head of a small fire with water will stop its spread

Forest Fire Fighting Fundamentals

Published in the 1950s by the California Department of Forestry and National Forest Service, this jewel is out of print (and some unmentionable S.O.B. has stolen my last copy of it). Your local fire agency or library may have it or something similar free for the asking. ASK. Covers fire behavior, fire line safety, and basic hand tools and hand crew fire suppression.

FIRE PERIODICALS

For starts, many states have a firefighters' lobbying association that publishes a monthly magazine. Orientation is usually to the full-time, paid firefighter, but the association may offer insurance to volunteers and may have useful articles. Check yours out.

State Fire Office publication(s) are also useful. Get on the mailing list of your state (or national forest) fire agency or agencies and get their monthly periodicals. Usually covers fire fatalities and serious injuries with enough detail to maybe prevent a similar accident happening to you. May also have "refresher" articles on specifics of how to handle a certain incident. Best part is it's "free" — get some of your tax bucks back.

Most fire periodicals are oriented to urban structure fires and the BIG fires — the three alarm department store, the overturned toxic chemical rail cars (lots of those lately), the oil refinery fire, etc. All the fire magazines have tear-out, postage paid "Reader Service Cards" which allow you to circle a bunch of numbers and shortly receive a huge stack of manufacturer's literature and catalogs to pile somewhere for your Equipment Reference file. All those periodicals also have monthly columns on politics, new publications, and new products. All of them (like the big city departments they aim towards) are horrendously sexist. Here are the ones I read. Each has a certain usefulness to a rural fire company with fire and medical emergency responsibilities.

Fire Command

Published by the non-profit National Fire Protection Association (NFPA), this monthly has as its stated purpose, "To communicate to fire service leaders those technology concepts and applications that result in effective management of public fire protection." It does just that. Oriented to urban/industrial fires, it offers enough nitty gritty detail here and there to be useful to anyone involved with structure fire protection. The style is "Pay attention class" text-booky formal for the most part, but one of these little details may save my ass some day, so I pay attention. NFPA publishes many other fire texts and training materials. Ask for their free "Fire Service Catalog."

Fire Command
(The Magazine for Fire Service Leaders)
Rex Jordan, Editor

$10 /year (12 issues) from:
National Fire Protection Association
470 Atlantic Avenue
Boston, MA 02210

Western Fire Journal

Affordable, usually good editorials, and almost always at least one article with specific, useful information for the rural firefighter. The covers are usually spectacular as well, with the visceral, anus-clenching quality of reality.

Western Fire Journal
(The Magazine for the Progressive Fire and Rescue Service)
David K. McKnight, Editor

$8 /year (12 issues) from:
Western Fire Journal
Subscription Department
9072 East Artesia Blvd.
Suite 7
Bellflower, CA 90706

Firehouse

Five years old and just through a management change, **Firehouse** *is edited (and now published) by Dennis Smith, author of* **Report from Engine Co. 82** *and* **Glitter and Ash** *AND a New York City fireman — busy.* **Firehouse** *is somewhere between a firefighter's magazine and a fire buff's magazine, with an urban, Eastern, big-city, union-man orientation. Most articles lack the fine-grain detail useful for learning much in the way of specifics — BUT the monthly columns on Tools, Hotline, and Training are good to excellent, the photography (mostly color) is excellent, editorials are usually more than platitudes, and this is the only fire magazine that consistently deals with the people problems of the fire service as well as the technical ones. Unionization, management hassles, the difficulties of integrating minorities and women into big-city departments, and the frustrations and sometimes anger of the guys on the tailboards —* **Firehouse** *talks about the stuff the "nice" fire magazines omit. Every issue has a few articles written by free lancers who sometimes have a painful lack of experience, which shows, but the magazine is definitely improving.* **Firehouse** *is not the most useful of the fire magazines, but it is the most entertaining, and I like it the most because it reflects the strengths (and weaknesses) of an editor who really gives a passionate damn about fire protection and the people who provide it. Find a copy and tear out the new subscriber's introductory subscription rate card and save about a third.*

Firehouse
Dennis Smith, Editor

$15 /year (12 issues) from:
Firehouse Magazine
Subscription Department
P.O. Box 2434
Boulder, CO 80321

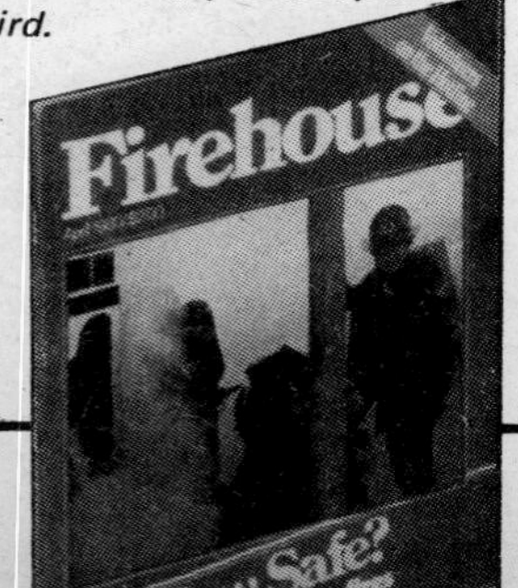

EMERGENCY MEDICINE

Once you have a community communications net, be it horn signals, CBs, telephones, radio-telephones, or some combination of all these, and a team of people trained to respond to fires, it is inevitable in a rural community that you will be called to medical emergencies. Textbooks and periodicals are no substitutes for trained people with a jump kit of basic emergency first aid equipment, which in turn is no substitute for an ambulance and hospital, but you have to start somewhere. Basic first aid is a minimum, EMT (Emergency Medical Technician) training for several community members a worthwhile goal. Check around — you may have a big city burnt-out paramedic, ex-military medic, or nurse willing to serve. The field of pre-hospital care has seen enormous changes in the last 10 years, with EMS (Emergency Medical Service) programs being developed all over the country, and ambulance drivers turning into paramedics who can start IVs and do cardiac defibrillation in the field. Lots of growing pains, lots of learning, and a lot of training and techniques that can be transferred to the back woods. The further out in the boonies your community, the more important emergency medical capability becomes. If you're starting from scratch, contact the ambulance service, hospital and health service that serves your area. Find out when and where first aid and/or EMT classes are conducted. If you're qualified and the ambulance service rules allow it, volunteer for ambulance duty one day a month. You can't learn emergency medical care from books — it takes good training and good practice. Once you have these basics, experience and periodic review will keep your hand in.

Emergency medical care is a continuum from home first aid to hospital recovery room. In between basic first aid and the hospital emergency room is EMT and EMT/Paramedic training. The 80 (or so) hour EMT 1 course is offered variously as a two-week cram course, a one-semester college course, or a one-year college course, usually with hospital emergency room observation time required. Taken mostly by ambulance attendants, fire-fighters, and cops, it ain't for dilettantes, but it's a valuable skill to carry around in your head and hands. There are three textbooks for EMT training which are all good — which one you prefer will probably depend on which one is/was required for your training. Any of these books without the training can still be useful, if you really dig into them ahead of time and work at it. (I'll be drummed out of the corps for saying that!) Buy yourself an inexpensive medical dictionary at the same time. (See also **Advanced First Aid for All Outdoors**, *p. 415.)*

The Family Medical Handbook

There are many home first aid books. What's "best" for you depends on your training and living situation. This inexpensive paperback is excerpted from the larger **How to Be Your Own Doctor — Sometimes.** *(See review on our p. 321.) Simple, readable, up-to-date home treatment guides for the most common illnesses and injuries. Treatment index, Symptom/Concept index, and Testing index are excellent simple treatments of complex stuff. If you have no first aid training, this is probably the best self-help medical book.*

The Family Medical Handbook
Keith W. Sehnert, M.D. and Howard Eisenberg
1975, 1979; 127 pp.

$2.95 postpaid from:
Grosset & Dunlap Inc.
51 Madison Avenue
New York, NY 10010
or Whole Earth Household Store

Emergency Care and Transportation of the Sick and Injured

The basic, standard textbook for the DOT (Department of Transportation) Basic Emergency Training Course, required in many states. For a textbook, it is remarkably well written and illustrated. I've read most of mine twice or more — it covers a lot of ground. We had to buy the companion **Workbook** *as well — most people like it for the review/feedback it provides, but I stopped using mine after the fourth or fifth week — your choice.*

Emergency Care and Transportation of the Sick and Injured
American Academy of Orthopaedic Surgeons
1977; 481 pp.
2nd Edition
$10.50 postpaid

Workbook for Emergency Care and Transportation of the Sick and Injured
American Academy of Orthopaedic Surgeons
1977; 245 pp.
$2.50 postpaid
both from:
American Academy of Orthopaedic Surgeons
P.O. Box 7195
Chicago, IL 60680
or Whole Earth Household Store

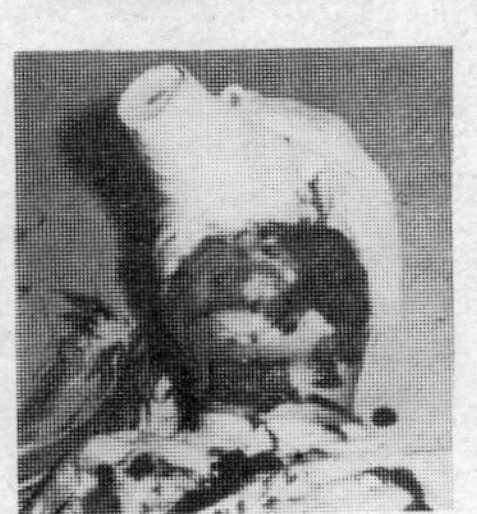

An extruded eye sometimes occurs in an accident. Pressure should never be applied on the eye. It may be covered with a paper cup or cone to protect it while the patient is being transported. Both eyes should be bandaged to help the injured eye remain still.
—Emergency Care and Transportation of the Sick and Injured

Emergency Care

Another textbook with student workbook to cover the DOT 81-hour course. I have only seen the advertising blurb for it, but my paramedic EMT lab instructor recommends this text as being better organized than **Emergency Care and Transportation of the Sick and Injured.** *A catalog with other related texts is free.*

Emergency Care
Harvey Grant and Robert Murray
1978; 542 pp.
2nd Edition
$12.50 postpaid

Self-Instructional Workbook for Emergency Care
J. David Bergeron
1978; 272 pp.
2nd Edition
$6.95 postpaid
both from:
Robert J. Brady Co.
Routes 197 and 450
Bowie, MD 20715
or Whole Earth Household Store

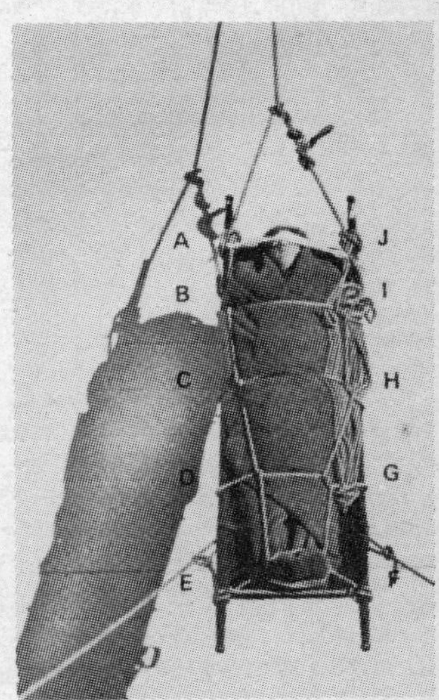

A properly lashed pole stretcher.
— Emergency Care

Emergency Care: Principles and Practices for the EMT-Paramedic

Written by three Orange County, California doctors who helped develop their county's EMS program, this new textbook is more words and much more detail, particularly for advanced tools and techniques such as MAST trousers and cardiac monitors/defibrillators. My copy is on order — I've skimmed it and like it a lot, but it's more expensive and has more information than a rural part-timer may wish to handle. If you ride ambulance part-time or are considering going from EMT I to EMTII/Paramedic, or if you already have EMT training and are way out in the boonies, you will find this the best of the EMT texts. My EMT instructors are trying to get this established as the standard county textbook.

Emergency Care
(Principles and Practices for the EMT-Paramedic)
Alan B. Gazzaniga, et al.
1980; 704 pp.

$19.95 postpaid from:
Reston Publishing Company
Prentice-Hall, Inc.
Box 500
Englewood Cliffs, NJ 07632
or Whole Earth Household Store

EMERGENCY MEDICINE PERIODICALS

Emergency

A volunteer first aider or EMT serving a rural area doesn't get enough day-to-day experience to keep the booklearning fresh. This monthly, published by Dyna Med, offers the best refresher around, and many articles do not assume you have an ambulance to play with. The monthly features "Drug Capsule" and "An Emergency Revisited" are top-notch: clear, well written, technical, but not top-heavy with medical terminology. The monthly "Beyond the Roadhead" is often right on for rural areas. If you have not had EMT training, you may have to run a bit at times to keep up, with medical dictionary in hand, but it's worth it. Excellent graphics and photographs, reader service card. If you are a part-timer and can only afford time or money for one magazine — this is the one.

Emergency
(The Journal of Emergency Services)
Lorraine Musil and Rick Minerd, Editors

$12.98 /year (12 issues) from:
Emergency
P.O. Box 28897
San Diego, CA 92127

Emergency Medical Services

This bi-monthly is bigger, more detailed, and oriented to ambulance attendants. It has some information of use to field first aid and community EMT people, many advertisers and a reader service card. At $25 a year, I read borrowed copies. Look a few copies over to see if the information is worth it to you before you buy.

Emergency Medical Services
(The Journal of Emergency Care and Transportation)
Carol Summer, Editor

$25 /year (6 issues) from:
Emergency Medical Services
12849 Magnolia Blvd.
North Hollywood, CA 91607

jems (A Journal of Emergency Medical Services)

Formerly **Paramedic International, jems** *was purchased early in 1980 by Backdraft Publications and is now published and edited by James O. Page, author of* **Effective Company Command** *(fire service),* **The Paramedics,** *and many articles in the emergency service field. Page is also Executive Director of ACT (Advanced Coronary Treatment) Foundation, which provides education and technical assistance to people concerned with EMS, and has been a strong and vocal critic of sloppy field work and "certain multi-billion dollar federal agencies, committed by law to serve health care providers and organizations — not to mention consumers — (which) had become little more than transfer agents." Page has recruited (stolen?) the former managing editor of* **Emergency** *for the new* **jems,** *and I expect an already good magazine to get a lot better. It is easy to read, has lots of photographs and several good articles each month on field care, with an orientation to the working professional. I like it enough to read borrowed copies. Now that Page is at the helm, I'm subscribing.*

Page is promising to be a "credible advocate for the emergency patient and those systems that can give him the best possible chance to survive" and more stuff on "street-level experience in the real world of providing emergency rescue and medical services . . . ." If past history and the first issue of **jems** *is any indication, he will also be taking a critical look at systems that aren't working so well, with some in-depth analysis of why. Take a good look at this one — you'll probably like it.*

jems
(A Journal of Emergency Medical Services)
James O. Page, Editor
$12.40 /year (12 issues) from:
jems
P.O. Box 152-M
Morristown, NJ 07960

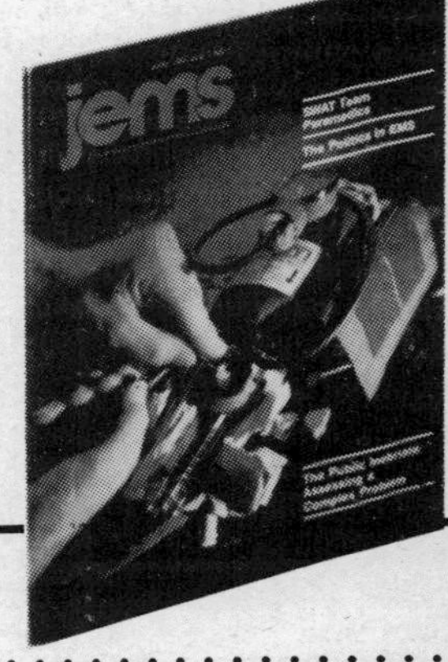

More on emergency services on next spread

THE RISING SUN
NEIGHBORHOOD NEWSLETTER

When Chuck Yaeger became the first person to break the sound barrier, some people thought that breaking the sound barrier would cause the human body to disintegrate. Right before the first ever atomic bomb test, someone asked Fermi what he thought the odds were that the bomb would start a spontaneous nuclear reaction of the atmosphere that would destroy the world in less than a minute. He said, "Fifty-fifty." Both men were strangely brave but Yaeger was brave for himself and Fermi was brave for everyone.

Continued from p. 311

FIRE AND MEDICAL EQUIPMENT SUPPLIERS

Emergency equipment is relatively low volume, specialized, and high quality. That equals E-X-P-E-N-S-I-V-E. Building an all-volunteer (no tax base) fire/rescue capability from scratch requires a lot of scrounging, making do, improvising, and shopping around — as well as a carefully thought out list of priorities. Just like low-budget homesteading, in fact. Here's what I've learned in seven years.

FIRE EQUIPMENT

Every rural building should have a minimum of at least one dry chemical 2A 40BC extinguisher near an exit; and each vehicle should have a minimum of one 1A 10BC extinguisher aboard. Smaller sizes than this, which are the usual case, often ain't enough folks — trust me. Kidde, General, and Sears all make good refillable ones (don't get the one-shots), shop for sales OR check the local outfit(s) that refill extinguishers — they may have used, re-conditioned extinguishers for sale, which are perfectly OK. Garden hose long enough to reach around your buildings and up on the roof, equipped with a pistol-grip type stream/spray garden nozzle, is also a wise idea, especially if you are more than 5 minutes away from your nearest fire truck.

Every homestead should also have a 5 gallon back pump. The first thing that usually goes in a wildfire is the above ground plastic water line to your place. The collapsible rubber backpumps require too much maintenance for most homesteaders and are usually empty when you need them the most. Sioux, General, Chapin, and Parco all make good metal ones. I've used them all, and the best cost-benefit for the occasional user (or more — our fire truck has two of them) is the PARCO Model 400 (galvanized tank) with combination nozzle. This model has a metal "holster" to hold the pump vertically, which simplifies carrying the thing in your vehicle or through the brush. Get together with some neighbors and order six or more (order up some extra gaskets and nozzles at the same time) for BIG savings from PARCO.

PARCO Back Pack Fire Pump
$60 - $80

Information
free from:
PARCO
Blue Mountain Products, Inc.
P.O. Box 250
New Hartford, NY 13413

PARCO Model 400
5 gallon back pump

Western Fire Equipment Company

If you are involved in any aspect of wildfire control, no matter what the ecosystem, you have GOT to have this catalog/wishbook. Specialized, absolutely trust-your-ass top quality gear with hair-raising prices. They don't discount to small customers, only big ones (unless you're a better con artist than I am). Service to us has been only fair, back orders can take forever, billing is confusing — and I love 'em. If you can get it anywhere else, do, because it will be cheaper. BUT, when you need that specialized piece of gear, they've got it (and you). Their slip-in units are the best, and the most expensive. Their Roadrunner unit has been the mainstay of our little fire company for going on four years now — in an ungaraged pickup yet — and it has never failed us. Somehow, the price doesn't seem so steep when you roll up to a vehicle that is really cooking and you need stuff to work, without fail, right NOW. I have a lot of equipment catalogs which I keep (and use) in a reference file. I've carried the Western Fire catalog in my briefcase for the past three years, and I have learned the hard way never to loan it to another firefighter — it disappears.

Western Fire Equipment
Catalog

free from:
Western Fire Equipment Company
440 Valley Drive
Brisbane, CA 94005

When you take the step to a neighborhood fire crew with hand tools, organization and training, a "Uniform" is useful to distinguish crew members. Nomex turnout gear is too expensive unless you get a lot of action, but headgear is not. Start with matched hard hats of the same color, add goggles and nomex earlaps as the need is felt (which will be immediately after your first hot fire). We standardized on yellow Bullard Utilyte 2000 hard hats (about $5) with Beuten goggles (about $4) from Bullard, goggle retainers from MSA ($3), and nomex earlaps from Western Fire ($9). HINT: Some (not all) safety equipment sales reps are often very sympathetic to the struggling new fire organization and will discount to you — experience has taught them that community emergency organizations grow. Another HINT: OSHA requirements on fire gear are requiring that paid departments buy new, improved turnout gear — older, unimproved but very usable gear may be obtained if you scrounge long and hard enough — find a neighbor who knows a fireman in the city. We have tried a bunch of suppliers over the last few years. These are the ones we have found the best for us.

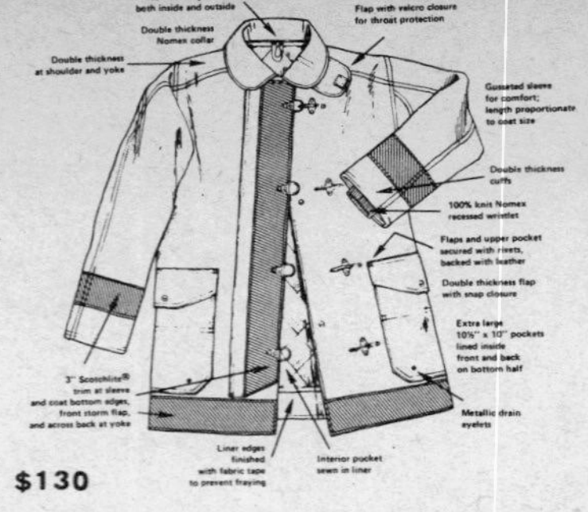

$130

Firecraft protective turnout coats and pants are constructed of new, first quality, 7.5 oz. 100% Nomex.

Bullard Safety

Nice folks, a complete line of personal and industrial safety gear. They gave us credit when we were new and struggling. I trust my head to their hard hat on fires — and that, dear friends, is one hell of a recommendation.

Bullard Safety
Catalog

free from:
E.D. Bullard
2680 Bridgeway
Sausalito, CA 94965

Mine Safety Appliances Company

Write the address below for a catalog (tell them your interests) and the address of your nearest branch office. I trust my head to their metal hard hat when I'm working in the woods — another plug. MSA breathing apparatus will be our choice for the fire company if we can ever afford it.

Mine Safety Appliances Company
Catalog

$1 from:
MSA
600 Penn Center Blvd.
Pittsburgh, PA 15235

Havis-Shields

The only outfit I've found that offers out-front discounts on emergency lights and sirens. They have been good to us — our next fire truck (now a-buildin') will probably be equipped as much as possible with gear from them.

Havis-Shields
Catalog

free from:
Havis-Shields Equipment Corporation
P.O. Box 533
Willow Grove, PA 19090

MEDICAL EQUIPMENT

A good rescue/emergency medical capability is within the financial grasp of any rural community, IF a trained, willing person or persons is into it, because much of the gear can be home-made. You can also spend a LOT of bucks. Some of the medical equipment our community uses lives on our fire/rescue vehicle (backboards, splints, oxygen, burn kit, and climbing gear). But the lifesaving guts of emergency medicine in a rural area is a trained, skilled person with a jump kit. Unless you have lots of bucks to blow, avoid the ready-made first aid and trauma kits as the plague — they are over priced and have stuff you will never need. By putting together your own jump kit, you get an education in what you need, and you will know where it is when you need it in a hurry. Our jump kits are nylon "day packs" that we can carry "over the bank" with us on car wrecks. You may require a "hard" box to take the beating of a kit kicking around in a vehicle. Locally, the PLANO line of tackle boxes is preferred for "hard" trauma kits. Check out their model 747. Try your local fishing outfit stores or Plano Molding Company, Plano, Illinois 60545.

What you put into the kit depends on you, but a basic CHEAP start would include:

Clean towels cut to various sizes and placed in baggies
A bunch of big safety pins
Sterile 4 x 4 and 8 x 10 dressings
Triangular bandages (non-sterile)
Roller bandages (2" and 4" Klings are nice)
Penlight
Space blanket
Small stuff (bandages, etc.)
Miscellaneous, various depending on individual, budget, and training
A quart of clean water nearby

Under $50 and you are in business. Cardboard and wood wooden splints can be made at home "free." Three spineboards (or two spineboards and 2 shortboards) 16" wide can be cut from one 3/4" sheet of plywood. Portable oxygen and O_2 powered suction units are expensive, but used gear can possibly be had for $100 - $250. The next step is an ambulance, advanced life support gear and training, and communication with a hospital. However, minimum equipment and maximum training can be truly life-saving, especially when you are a long way out. There are many medical supply distributors — here are the outfits I'm familiar with.

W.S. Darley & Co.

From firetrucks to flashlights, Darley has a complete line of municipal-type fire gear. Prices are a bit lower than most, service to us has been good. Get their catalog and look it over.

W.S. Darley & Co.
Catalog

free from:
W.S. Darley & Company
2000 Anson Drive
Melrose Park, IL 60160

Dyna-Med

A big, colorful, slick, photo-packed, mouth-watering catalog of goodies at top prices. Get this catalog, figure out what you need from the pictures and price comparisons between brands, and order from Life Assist. Dirty trick, but it IS your money. Dyna Med has some specialized goodies that are going to hook you anyway. Good service to us.

Dyna Med
Catalog

free from:
Dyna-Med, Inc.
11630 Rockfield Court
Cincinnati, OH 45241

Build-A-Board

Features and Benefits: Helps immobilize victims with suspected spinal injury and permits extrication of auto accident victim in a seated position. Can be used as conventional scoop stretcher. The first stretcher designed to be built around the victim. It's a combination spine board and scoop stretcher. Unit aids in minimizing body movement when spinal or neck injuries are possible. Tubular aluminum construction. Stores compactly. Upper section measures 17 x 24-3/4 inches; seat section measures 17 x 18-3/4 inches; lower torso section is 17 x 49 inches. Upper and seat sections coupled is 17 x 42 x 1¼ inches. Upper and lower torso sections coupled measure 17 x 72¼ inches.

Ordering Information: Complete with patient restraint straps. Available with lower torso section or without.

A11501—(1) With Lower Torso Section	**$290.75**
A11500—(2) Without Lower Torso Section	**207.40**
A11515—Leg and Waist Strap	**3.85**

—Dyna-Med

L.N. Curtis & Sons

Safety and fire equipment distributors — every metropolitan area has one or more outfits that specialize in such gear. Go in person. When I told the salesman at Curtis about our piteous finances during the order of one turnout jacket, he not only discounted the price on the coat, but made a couple of long-distance calls to some fire chief friends to try to line up some used, surplus turnout gear for us! Thanks, Al.

L.N. Curtis & Sons
Catalog

free from:
L.N. Curtis & Sons
4133 Broadway
Oakland, CA 94611

Life Assist

Their "catalog" is a non-fancy price list only — you have to know what you need. The service is good and the prices are the lowest I've found on cross-comparisons of identical, brand-name gear. My first choice.

Life Assist
Catalog

free from:
Life Assist, Inc.
11357 Pyrites No. 5
Rancho Cordova, CA 95670

Rockford Safety Equipment Co.

Prices mostly in-between Life Assist and Dyna-Med, catalog has lots of black and white pictures. Service to us on two orders was slow, might be better if you live in eastern part of United States.

Rockford Safety Equipment Company
Catalog

free from:
Rockford Safety Equipment Company
P.O. Box 5166
Rockford, IL 61125

There are many, many more suppliers of fire and medical equipment than are listed here, but these, in conjunction with suppliers listed in the various magazines, will give you a good start on an open-ended process of preparing yourself, and your community, for any emergency. Organize, train, and plan ahead — then hope like hell you never need it. ■

Old Glory

Your town has origins. So does your family. This is a splendid book about how to find and preserve and parade them. There is such a thing as cultural good ecology. Savor your own peculiar community's weirdness. Savor some other people's. —SB

Old Glory
(A Pictorial Report on the Grass Roots History Movement and the First Hometown History Primer)
James Robertson, Editor
1973; 191 pp.

OUT OF PRINT
Warner Paperback Library

Get this book back in print!

•

Every town should have at least one great old building to show off to visitors, and there certainly ought to be at least one amazing story that goes along with it.

•

The Self Help History Test

Rate yourself. Score two points for every correct answer. One point for each answer partially correct. No fair cheating. Answers must come from memory. Above 38 points, excellent. Between 24 and 37 points, passable. Below 23 points, dismal, better get to work.

1. Where was your father born? (Town and state)
2. When was he born? (Date and year)
3. Where was your mother born? (Town and state)
4. When was she born? (Date and year)
5. Where and when was your father's father born? (State and year)
6. Where and when was your father's mother born? (State and year)
7. Where and when was your mother's father born? (State and year)
8. Where and when was your mother's mother born? (State and year)
9. What was the chief occupation of your father's father? Your father's mother?
10. What was the chief occupation of your mother's father? Your mother's mother?
11. What is the origin of your family name? Has it been changed?
12. What is the country of your father's family's origin?
13. What is the country of your mother's family's origin?
14. When did your family first come to this country?
15. Where did they land? (Port of entry)
16. Where did they settle? (Town and state)
17. Are there still relatives in that place?
18. Did your family migrate after arriving in this country?
19. How many states were home before the present one?
20. When was the town or city nearest you founded?
21. Who founded it and for what reason?
22. Were Indians living there? What nation or tribe?

Beloit, Wisconsin — One of the boys on the roof is Ron Dougan, whose memories of the old schoolhouse have helped restoration efforts. Some of his memories have also enriched the folklore that surrounds the old building: "At times the mothers would try to send things for a hot meal. One day there was a pot of soup heating on top of the stove, and it blew the cover off, putting soup all over the ceiling." Besides a soup-stained ceiling, the schoolhouse had a blackboard at one end, and a raised platform for the teacher's desk. There was no provision for lighting (when it got dark, school was over), and heat came from the wood-burning stove. "There was a ventilation pipe which went from the jacket of the stove through the outside wall. When someone had to stay out and there was to be some excitement inside the school, two children could get their heads down by the ventilation pipe and hear what was going on inside."

The destruction of the Portland Union Station was the call to action for city preservationists. It remains a symbol for all of us to remember. →

Return to the City

The middle-class movement in America for historic preservation of old buildings has expanded to the broader concept of urban conservation. This book lovingly charts that progress, by rich and poor, and in cities you might not think of — Pittsburgh, St. Paul, Portland and Galveston.

This recent social and economic phenomenon spawned its own buzzword — gentrification (from gentry: in Britain, the class of landowning people ranking just below the nobility). In terms of race and class it frequently means blacks out and whites in, the same effect that many of the grandiose and misguided urban renewal projects of the last two decades had. But as author Richard Reed demonstrates in text and photos, it doesn't have to be that way. This is a book about community, and neighborhoods, and is full of the details of what groups in other cities did to stop the bulldozer and wrecker's ball.

For more on these matters see our pp. 235-236 and 300.
—Richard Nilsen

Return to the City
(How to Restore Old Buildings and Ourselves in America's Historic Urban Neighborhoods)
Richard Ernie Reed
1979; 191 pp
$8.95 postpaid from:
Doubleday and Company
501 Franklin Avenue
Garden City, NY 11530
or Whole Earth Household Store

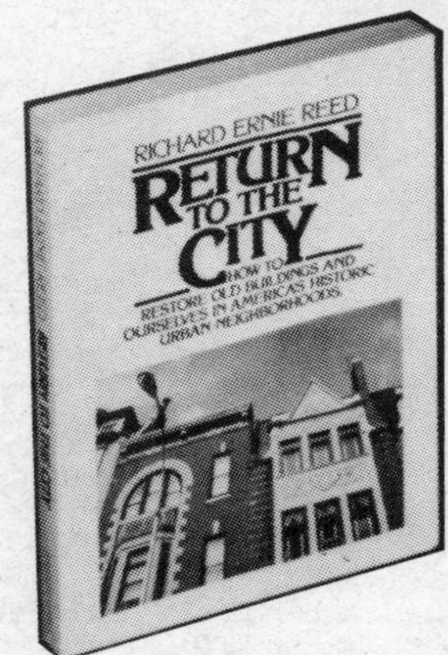

It takes a special kind of person to see beauty in a burned-out, abandoned building. But preservationists in Charleston saw the potential and realized it as these before and after photos prove.

•

The Renegades of Harlem, whose twenty Black and Puerto Rican members range in age from eighteen to thirty-five, converted their first six-story, 23-unit tenement for an average cost of $15,000 per unit in just one year's time. Universally poor and uneducated, almost all with criminal records, the gang members were able to not only personally rehabilitate the building, but they also managed the dispersement of funds from the mortgage loan for materials and supplies. The gang went by the book, learning all the traditional business rules as they went along, even forming a corporation.

Ancestor worship

After reading the review of **Old Glory** in your **Whole Earth Epilog**, I became interested in tracing my family tree. Luckily, the college here — University of Arkansas at Little Rock — offered a non-credit course for $2. Wow! A whole new dimension opened up. Now I spend most of my spare time in the archives, in old courthouse records and in the genealogy room at the library. Not only can you learn about your ancestors but see history in a whole new light.

The Everton Publishing Company, P.O. Box 368, Logan, UT 84321 has any supplies you might need. They have a free catalog. Also the Superintendent of Documents, U.S. Government Printing Office, Washington, D.C. 20402 offers these: **Where to Write for Marriage Records**, Publication No. 630B, $ .15; **Where to Write for Birth and Death Records**, Publication No. 630A, $ .15.

Paige Mayer
Little Rock, Arkansas

The Latter Day Saints, who don't like to be called Mormons, have the most complete genealogical records in the world on microfilm in Salt Lake City. They also have regional archives around the country which are useful in themselves and which can get you microfilm you need from Salt Lake City. You can get a free list of the regional libraries by writing: Genealogical Library, 50 East North Temple Street, Salt Lake City, UT 84150. Anyone, Latter Day Saint or not, can use these archives and I hear the librarians are really helpful.

—Anne Herbert

22 x 26 inches, folds to 8½ x 14, punched to fit the 9 x 15 binders. May also be used for framing. Permalife paper.

10 Generations 1022 Ancestors

The largest pedigree chart we have ever offered. It is a double-fan arrangement with the paternal ancestors on one side and the maternal ancestors on the other. There is room on the first five or six generations for small pictures to be placed by the name and data of each of your ancestors. Enough space is also provided to record 20 or 30 descendants of the first couple on the chart (Nos. 2 & 3) and by using the corners of the sheet you may enter several additional generations — making it possible to get as high as 12 to 15 generations of ancestors on some lines.
—Genealogical Supply Catalogue, Logan, Utah

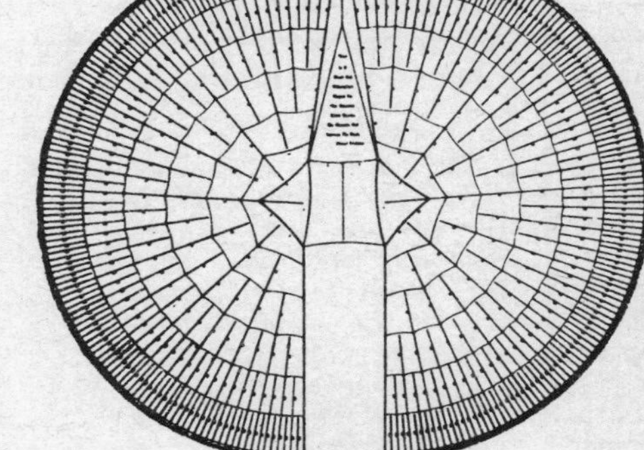

The Tape Recorded Interview

Some of your local history is in records, but a lot more of it is in minds. Here's how to ensure it's in both. When you're an old geezer, wouldn't you like to be asked what really happened back in 1980? —SB

The Tape-Recorded Interview
(A Manual for Field Workers in Folklore and Oral History)
Edward D. Ives
1974, 1980; 130 pp.
$5.50 postpaid from:
University of Tennessee Press
293 Communications Building
Knoxville, TN 37916
or Whole Earth Household Store

•

I remember one young girl, interviewing an old woodsman, who asked what they cut down the trees with. 'Well, girlie,'' he said with a kind of amused contempt, "we used an ax, that's what we used!" Girlie looked him right in the eye: "Poll or double-bit?" she said. You could feel his attitude change. "Well, mostly poll axes, but later on. . . ." It comes down to this: The more you know about your informant's life, work, and times, the better equipped you will be to carry on the interviews — and the more you will enjoy your work!

THE RISING SUN
NEIGHBORHOOD NEWSLETTER

Long ago when a bunch of people were sailing from England to Ireland, they decided that the first person to touch land would get first choice of good land. So as they approached land, O'Neill, ancestor of all the O'Neills, cut off his hand and threw it on shore, so he was first. So that's why the O'Neill coat of arms has a red hand on it and why O'Neills are not to be trifled with.

BEFORE 1970, THE QUESTION OF WHAT TO DO with a city's garbage was never asked. The answer was obvious: to the dump! to the incinerator! Now, dumping sites are scarce or defended by lovers of marshes; existing sites overfloweth; pollution from burning plastic or leached car bodies has met some opposition; and some people even believe "solid wastes" are useful. Food wastes could be compost. Aluminum, steel cans, glass, rubber tires, or newspapers can all be reused.

Each year the average American citizen discards 1,400 pounds of waste (154 million tons for 1978). This is close to 4 pounds per person each day. Only 1 out of every 4 aluminum cans is recycled. Only 25% of soft drink and beer bottles are returnable. (In 1950, 99% of the soft drink bottles and 70% of the beer bottles were returnable. Some made 40 round-trips before they got dumped.) Only 20% of all discarded paper products become born-again paper products; only 3% of all the glass and only 2% of all the iron. Whatever happened to Benjamin Franklin's "Waste not; want not?" We have a long way to go. Here's the bookish beginnings. —Peter Warshall and Sonoma Community Recycling Center

Recycling: The State of the Art

This collection of papers from a recycling conference deals with every aspect of recycling. You'll find papers on municipal composting, mobile recycling centers, debate between low tech and high tech recycling methods, and many proven programs. Nice book. Printed on recycled paper too. —J. Baldwin

Recycling: The State of the Art
Christine Olsen, Editor
1978; 132 pp.

$10 postpaid from:
Community Environmental Council
P.O. Box 448
Santa Barbara, CA 93102

or Whole Earth Household Store

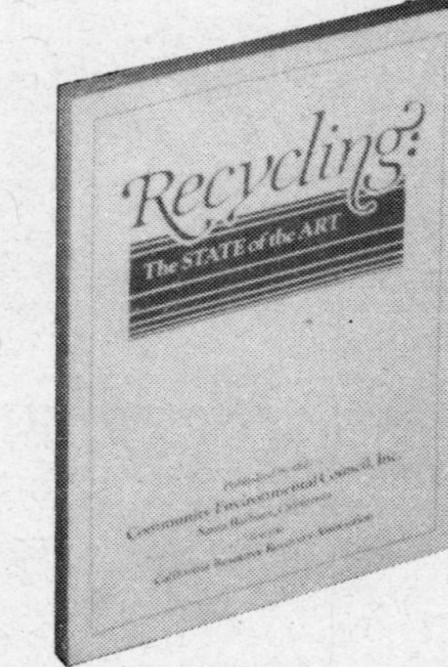

•

I don't like the trend of garbage being considered as a source of energy. It would be a much better policy to recover fibers that can either be reused or that can be converted to insulation, thus saving much more energy than can be created by burning the papers. Other organic material should be reclaimed and returned to the soil. Perhaps for organics a bio-gas system, where gas is created for energy and a concentrated sludge that can be returned to the soil, would be best.

Compost Science/Land Utilization

Keep up-to-date on composting garbage, land application of sewage sludge, appropriate technology for each kind of waste recycling, and government policies. In short, this is it for the nouveau miners of garbage gold. —Peter Warshall

Compost Science/ Land Utilization
(Journal of Waste Recycling)
Jerome Goldstein, Editor

$20 /year (6 issues) from:
The JG Press
Box 351
18 South Seventh Street
Emmaus, PA 18049

•

In California, which is putting more into its recoverable waste effort than the entire federal government is appropriating, the Santa Barbara Recycling Center is a leader. If there is another community of 150,000 that recycles 125 tons a week of reusable resources, the Santa Barbara area hasn't heard of it.

The Center estimates that 70 percent of all the newsprint delivered to the county's South Coast residents finds its way to the recycling bins. Last year that amounted to 4,500 tons of newspapers. In addition, there were 20,000 telephone books, 500 tons of high grade (office) paper, 500 tons of glass, 300 tons of metals and 330,000 pounds of aluminum.

Garbage-to-Energy: The False Panacea

The battle continues: Gold Cadillac vs. Home Energy. In this case, Gold Cadillac is represented by the centralized "refuse recovery" factory that burns the plastics and paper and sometimes recovers the iron and metals. They require huge capital investments and are more often more costly than beneficial because of breakdowns, complicated technological machinery, and resulting environmental damage. Home Energy is represented by the "source separators" that find it economic to have each household or community divide the organics, paper, glass and metals before collection. They are the local recyclers with negligible costs and damages compared to the Gold Cadillac. Their problem is that they educate Americans that the throw-away mentality is bad news. Such education is subversive to the industries (like bottling companies) that profit from your waste. This report is the best technical and political summary of the problem. —Peter Warshall

Garbage-to-Energy: The False Panacea
Tania Lipshutz, et al.
2nd Edition
1979; 90 pp.

$5 postpaid from:
Sonoma County Community Recycling Center
P.O. Box 1375
Santa Rosa, CA 95402

Here's How To Prepare Your Recyclables:

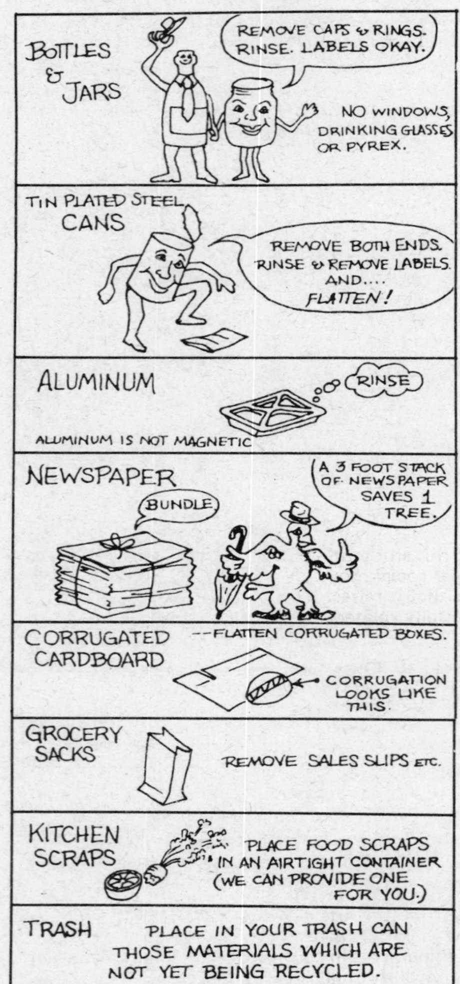

BOTTLES & JARS
REMOVE CAPS & RINGS. RINSE. LABELS OKAY.
NO WINDOWS, DRINKING GLASSES OR PYREX.
TIN PLATED STEEL CANS
REMOVE BOTH ENDS. RINSE & REMOVE LABELS. AND.... FLATTEN!
ALUMINUM
RINSE
ALUMINUM IS NOT MAGNETIC
NEWSPAPER
BUNDLE
A 3 FOOT STACK OF NEWSPAPER SAVES 1 TREE.
CORRUGATED CARDBOARD
--FLATTEN CORRUGATED BOXES.
CORRUGATION LOOKS LIKE THIS.
GROCERY SACKS
REMOVE SALES SLIPS ETC.
KITCHEN SCRAPS
PLACE FOOD SCRAPS IN AN AIRTIGHT CONTAINER (WE CAN PROVIDE ONE FOR YOU.)
TRASH
PLACE IN YOUR TRASH CAN THOSE MATERIALS WHICH ARE NOT YET BEING RECYCLED.

Institute for Local Self-Reliance

Many of us are well aware of the New Alchemy Institute (p. 177) and its attempt to find small-scale, self-reliant ways to conduct our affairs. The Institute of Local Self-Reliance is the urban equivalent of New Alchemy. They are a non-profit, research and consulting organization promoting neighborhood self-reliance. They have done an amazing number of good works: rooftop gardens for elderly citizens in an apartment house; a task-force to provide insulation and energy conservation for low-income neighborhoods in Newark; community-based solid waste collection and recycling; research on community-controlled banking and on and on. The Institute issues a jam-packed newsletter, **Self-Reliance**, *every other month. They have a great, free publications list. Available publications include* **Municipal Composting** *on how cities can recycle the organic waste stream by composting and how to use the compost ($4) and* **Economic Feasibility of Recycling** *which stresses the importance of separating garbage at home ("source separation"). It was prepared for the Economic Development Administration of the U.S. Department of Commerce ($3).*

You can become a member of Self-Reliance for $25 (individuals) or $40 (groups). —Peter Warshall

Self-Reliance
David Macgregor, Editor

$8 /year (6 issues)

Publications list and information
free

both from:
Institute for Local Self-Reliance
Attn: Publications
1717 18th Street NW
Washington, DC 20009

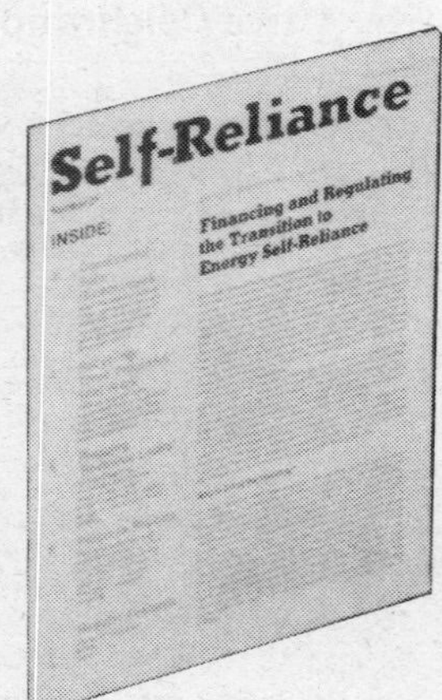

Christiania

Outside of Copenhagen, Denmark, is an old military barracks and arsenal recycled by squatters into probably the roughest and readiest free community in the world. Liberated since 1971, the place has sustained and earned its independence. Vividly photographed and warmly told, this tabloid-size account may help inspire more such healthful blemishes on the monocultural landscape. I believe there will be more. —SB

Christiania
(A Publication About Europe's Free Town)
Mark Edwards
1979; 20 pp.

30 Krones (about $6)
postpaid from:
Johannes Feil
Information Forlag
Store Kongensgade 40
1264 København K
Denmark

•

Outside a Christianit is catching apples aimed at police and handing them over to the men, urging them to throw them back through the second-floor windows in Løvehuset, where they came from. Christiania is rich in moments of pure surrealism. I have never lived anywhere that rivals Christiania in this respect, and it was one of the compelling attractions that drew me into the weird community.

Communitas

This book has been around for a good while, and it's still holding its own as a lucid gathering of the elements to think and design with on the subject of community.
—SB

Communitas
(Means of Livelihood and Ways of Life)
Paul and Percival Goodman
1947, 1960; 248 pp.

OUT OF PRINT
Random House

Get this book back in print!

•

A major problem of every intentional face-to-face community is its 'cash-crop,' its economic role in the great society that has no integral way of life but has a most integrated cash nexus. Usually the problem is not enough money or credit to buy needed mass-produced machinery. But let us mention a touching example of a contrary problem. The Macedonia (pacifist) community made pedagogic toyblocks for cash, and distributed them, at cost of production, to like-minded groups like progressive schools; but the blocks became popular and big commercial outfits wanted a large number. Macedonia was then faced with the following dilemma: these commercial jobbers would resell at a vast profit; yet if Macedonia itself charged them what the market would bear, the community would itself be contaminated by commercialism.

The Joyful Community

The person who ought to review this book is Ramon Sender, who grew up in a Bruderhof community in New England and honors his education there. Ramon is the most thorough commune personality I've known. A consummate tape-music composer and grass-reed musician, for years he's been the gentle fiber of some of the wooliest anybody-come communes ever. Did Bruderhof give him his skill and his joy? I now believe it.

Ramon's out of reach of telephones, so I'll have to make my own assertion: This is the best and most useful book on communes that's been written.
—SB

The Joyful Community
Benjamin Zablocki
1971; 537 pp.

OUT OF PRINT
Penguin Books

Get this book back in print!

•

The Bruderhof is a community unlike any I have ever seen. When I first visited it in the winter of 1965, I felt as if I had wandered in a dream into a medieval village, or into a world outside of history where neither time nor space existed. Never before or since have I felt the presence of brotherly love so permeating a place that I felt I was breathing it. I have visited close to a hundred contemporary communes and studied the history of those of the last century. The Bruderhof can be classified with neither the new nor the old. It is not at all a typical case. I present this study not as a key to the understanding of some larger social movement, but because I feel that the problems that it raises and the solutions that it offers are fundamentally related to our society's quest for *fraternité*.

•

A most striking thing about the Bruderhof is the people. Here are no rugged, bearded Amish peasants transplanted from another age but, for the most part, sophisticated, middle-class, college-educated individuals. The population is highly diversified in background — ex-millionaires and ex-tramps, holders of post-graduate degrees and grade-school dropouts, a dozen nationalities, and as many religions. Unlike the Hutterians and Amish, the Bruderhof has never become a blood-related ethnic group. The community still has some of its original members and is beginning to raise a fourth generation of *'sabra'* children but it has remained constantly open to a stream of new members from the outside world. At the time of this study, the majority of Bruderhof members were converts who had joined within the past ten years. This combination of survival through at least three generations with a continually open membership policy is a major accomplishment, often striven for but rarely achieved among communitarian groups.

Alternative Celebrations Catalogue

Voluntary Simplicity sort of personally institutionalized, the authors of this perennial (now in its 4th edition) noticed that a lot of American consumer madness goes on around public special occasions — Mother's Day, Christmas, Valentine's Day, etc. When the occasions are made more personal and creative, the consumer part not only drops away, a feeling of wanting to give help to others replaces it. Ideas and encouragement and a thorough roster of do-good groups.
—SB

Alternative Celebrations Catalogue
Alternatives Bookstore Staff
4th Edition
1973, 1978; 243 pp.

$5 postpaid from:
Alternatives
P.O. Box 429
Ellenwood, GA 30049

or Whole Earth Household Store

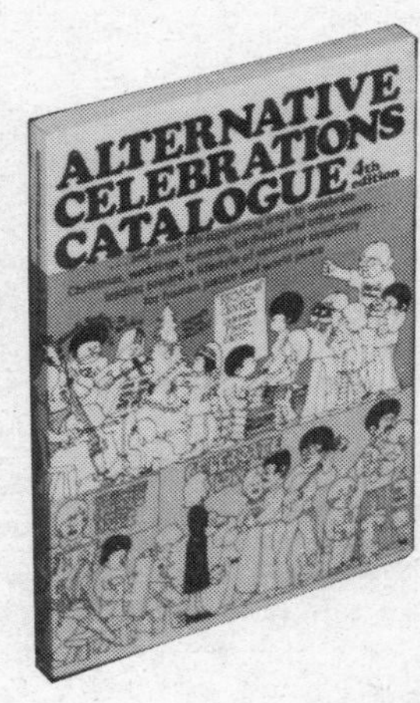

•

How to make the most effective use of this book depends on who you are and what you've been up to. If you're one of the growing number who have been actively working on "kicking the commercial habit," then you may be more interested in the material on how to organize your city or the articles on giving your town the gift of a food cooperative or recycling center. Or the vision of the city of the future, of the urban village, or the article on voluntary simplicity may be the necessary ingredients to stimulate your mind.

The Farm

By any measure this is far the most successful of any communal effort in America ever. It started in San Francisco in the late '60s as "Monday Night Class" — a standing-room-only weekly lecture by one Stephen Gaskin. By 1980 it is 1350 people on a huge farm near Summertown, Tennessee, pursuing a sort of religion of competence. They publish, besides the teachings of Stephen such as in **This Season's People**, *or* **Mind at Play**, *a number of the best how-to books (reviewed elsewhere in this* **Catalog — Spiritual Midwifery**, *p. 347;* **A Cooperative Method of Natural Birth Control**, *p. 343;* **The Big Dummy's Guide to CB Radio**, *p. 523.) and others). They have a considerable international do-good effort called "Plenty."*

I figure you can join 'em, or get the idea and go do it your way, or just be cheered by the Farm's existence.
—SB

Mind at Play
Stephen Gaskin
1980; 192 pp.

$10 postpaid

This Season's People
Stephen Gaskin
1976; 168 pp.

$3 postpaid

Catalog and information
free

all from:
The Book Publishing Co.
156 Drakes Lane
Summertown, TN 38483

•

Darwin said that competition is what causes the species to evolve, and that theory was taken over by businessmen as a justification for power politics and power economics. But at the same time that Darwin published, a fellow named Kropotkin also published, and everything that he published says that *cooperation* is how animals make it. He points out that there aren't any more sabre-toothed tigers, but the cockroach has lived unchanged for a hundred and thirty-six million years.

If the dirt in a can of worms gets dry, the worms all crawl up close together to share what moisture they have. It seems that if a can of worms can cooperate when the earth gets dry, mankind ought to learn to cooperate too.

If you're going to say we're all One, let's give up competition at that level of food and life and death and housing, and things like that.
—This Season's People

← Communities Journal

Put out by the accomplished Twin Oaks Community (80 people on 500 acres and a $500,000/year hammock business), this is the only survivor of the plethora of commune periodicals of a decade ago. It survived on its own perseverance and its value — encouragement and advice to other communers.
—SB

Communities
(Journal of Cooperative Living)
Mikki Wenig, Editor

$7.50 /year (5 issues)
from:
Communities
Box 426
Louisa, VA 23093

•

For many of us, the early '70s allowed us to dream and taught us to struggle and to fight against something: anti-war, anti-draft, anti-institutions and anti-establishment. The struggles were painful but clear; it was one thing to demand 'health care is a right; not a privilege,' but quite another when we were confronted with the reality of actually providing health services. Free clinics, alternative institutions, community controlled health centers sprang up by the hundreds throughout the country. Professionals worked with community people to bring patient care back to the forefront of medicine. Alternative health care became associated with such things as collective decision making, hippies, wholistic health, relaxation techniques, herbal medicines — often serving the very groups of people most alienated from the main stream of America. By the mid '70s many of these institutions, caught in the squeeze between economic survival and the refusal or inability to compromise to the excessive demands of public funding, were forced to close.

The Fair Haven Clinic also began as an alternative — as an alternative to the big city hospitals which included long waits, high expenses and the frustrations of fragmented care. People were asking for a health center to call their own, a place they could afford to go when they were sick, a place that would treat them with dignity. The Clinic began seeing increasing numbers of families in the early years with problems such as sore throats and stomach aches and requests for basics such as family planning, pre-natal care, immunizations and care for their chronic problems such as hypertension and diabetes and arthritis. Much of the work was outreach work, and helping people to get appointments and to get better housing and welfare assistance. It is more important to get heat in an apartment than to continue to treat a variety of respiratory complaints, or to help a family move to a new apartment than attempt to 'cure' lead paint poisoning.

•

The Rainbow Gathering Caravan is planned to begin in the Northwest on the 3rd of June and head for the '80 Gathering in West Virginia. Joining with others there, the caravan will make its return trip through South Dakota to support the Black Hills Alliance. This Alliance is composed of traditional Indian and AIM People, and white ranchers, and anti-nuclear activists planning to stop the scheduled depletions and contamination of the area's water. The Alliance was formed to protect the irreplaceable beauty of the Black Hills area from becoming what has been termed a "national sacrifice area."

THE RISING SUN
NEIGHBORHOOD NEWSLETTER

From the February, 1979 *Atlantic* about Lyda Masterkova, exiled Russian artist. "In Paris she has seen many films without knowing the language on the sound track. When she talked to people who had seen the same films and understood the dialogue, 'I was surprised that they had missed some very important details that I had seen. I think the word is a signal that limits the horizon and breaks continuity of thought.' "

— quote from the article "Alone Abroad" by Anthony Astrachan

shramadana giving energy

A Sri Lanka invention good anywhere

by Joanna Rogers Macy

Earth moving, shramadana-style, ↑ to cut a jungle road.

↓ Though shramadana was begun by Buddhists, these Tamil Hindus in northern Sri Lanka are in shramadana to make irrigation ditches.

It does not require oil, gas, coal or nukes; it empowers people not machines; it is *shramadana*. Literally meaning the giving (*dana*) of human energy (*shrama*), this source of power is widely used in rural Sri Lanka. In more than two thousand villages over the past twenty-two years that is how roads have been built, irrigation canals dug, markets and meeting halls erected. Note the name: neither the purchase of energy through tariffs, taxes, tolls, nor the forced conscription of human labor, *shramadana* is rather its free gift — *dana* denoting both gift and the virtue of generosity itself, the supreme and most meritorious "perfection" in the ancient Buddhist tradition of this land.

Over the centuries the notion of *dana* had become largely identified with alms-giving to the Sangha or order of Buddhist monks. It was almost forgotten that long before the colonial rulers came with their Western ways, the great irrigation systems that had made of this island the "granary of the East" were constructed and maintained through the voluntary sharing of human energy. This was recalled, however, as a glory of the past that could be reappropriated. Then in 1958 a young Buddhist schoolteacher organized the first *shramadana* work camp in one of the island's poorest, most backward communities.

The campaign launched then by A.T. Ariyaratna and his friends has grown into a national movement for rural development. Sarvodaya Shramadana, its name meaning the "awakening of all" through the "giving of energy," is now the largest non-governmental program in the country. While its activities have branched out into many forms, from preschools and craft centers to alternative marketing schemes, shramadana remains a central feature. The financial aid from foreign countries that has poured in in recent years, affording handsome headquarters, training centers, motor vehicles, has been attracted by the movement's energy on the grass-roots level — a vitality which springs from shramadana and which money cannot buy.

Any day, any week, there will be several shramadana work camps underway around the island — one or two may go on for months but most occur on Sundays, when folks are free from jobs and school. You can cut a two-mile road through the jungle on three Sundays, if you rally enough people. And "people" does not mean just able-bodied men, but children too, and mothers and grandparents, everybody can contribute. If you are not big and strong enough to wield the heavy mammoty or to loosen, lasso and pull over a palm tree, you can rake the dirt or carry the kettle of hot sweet tea that goes the rounds. Except for the elephant borrowed on the first Sunday to haul out the heaviest trees, all the power is people power. There is no roar of bulldozer or drill to compete with the music that blares from the loudspeaker set up in the temple compound — or with the laughter. Toward the temple's open preaching

I have a feeling this idea and this melodious Sanskrit word will be turning up all over in the next few years. Shramadana camps in Sri Lanka have increased from 104 in 1974 to over a thousand in 1979. We're grateful to Eric Utne for sending the article and author our way. The piece also appeared in **Resurgence.** *—SB*

Making a rural playground.

hall pots full of rice and curries, with fresh banana leaves tied on for tops, are carried from each household. Come noon, you leave your tool and converge there with the others for a cooperative meal and the traditional Sarvodaya "family gathering." You can sit then on a straw mat as the hottest part of the day slips by, sharing the curry a neighbor cooked and the songs and prayers and talks which follow.

Then it is back to work to see if we all can finish the section of road as far as the paddy field before we quit until next week's or next month's Sunday shramadana. As you collaborate to lever up some roots, you may find yourself in a team with someone you hardly know. He may be from the other side of the village and from a caste different from yours. But you work together now, learning to know and trust each other's strength; and, as you heard done in the "family gathering" and as you were urged there to do, you call him *malli*, brother.

Shramadana campaigns proved so effective in organizing villagers, that in the mid-60s the government started conducting some of its own. It even briefly formed an office of National Shramadana Service. To ensure that people showed up to work and to keep them at it, material rewards were sometimes offered, in cash or kind – perhaps a ration of rice or some powdered milk. According to Sarvodayans they were not very successful. Those camps, they say, lacked both discipline and laughter; people did not sing together or call each other brother and sister; they did not choose the project themselves or take charge of their own work. When the project is one the villagers want – and know they want, having chosen it, additional rewards can be unnecessary and even counterproductive. The two-mile road that will connect the village of Jambureliya to the Colombo road means an hour's less walk to buses and schools, two hours less wait when a doctor must be fetched. That meaning can be present in each shovel-load of dirt – along with pride in the doing of it and gratitude for each other.

Last Sunday's shramadana in the hill town of Avissawella was one of a series to clean and beautify the grounds of the district hospital. A committee of long-term patients had asked local Sarvodayans to help them organize an action, get the trash picked up and construct a lotus pond by the front entrance. Unlike cutting a road or digging a canal, this had no economic merit; no one's livelihood or convenience would be benefited – yet the spirit was the same. The long line I joined to pass down the pans of dirt excavated for the pond was hot, sweaty, and high-spirited. Ten- and twelve-year-olds, including a little girl on my left in a lacy pink party dress, kept up the pace and younger children raced the empty pans back to the diggers. Young bucks in stylish Sunday bell-bottoms or more sensible in sarongs, showed off a bit, tossing and twirling the pans to each other, while saried ladies in their sixties joined the brigade for shorter spells. So did patients from the hospital and nurses in starched white saris, neither group showing concern for the fresh red soil that would spill on them. To my right I slung the dirt to a public official from the Ministry of Health. Discovering my interest in Buddhist philosophy, he engaged me in a disjointed discussion of the no-self doctrine. "Ah, see," he said, half joking, "with every load of dirt, I wear away the illusion of ego." He was also a little annoyed that Sunday visitors to the hospital would watch us without joining in. For me, however, still relatively fresh to shramadana, it was wonder enough that *we* were doing it.

Veteran Sarvodaya organizers say that it is sometimes questionable whether the actual work accomplished in a camp is worth the amount of time, effort and frequent subsidiary costs which are required to set it up. What is considered definitely worth the price, however, are the other results of shramadana. These are manifold and nonmaterial. They are reflected in the Sarvodayan saying, "We build the road and the road builds us." If the villagers now have a road where there was no road before, they have also that which the road built – a new sense of unity across the caste, class and political barriers that so frequently fracture village life. A widow of forty with three children, having moved here to Markandana two years back, had decided to leave and seek elsewhere to settle. Now, after the village's first shramadana, she and her family choose to stay. They have friends now, she tells me, and it is a better place to be. After shramadana in the village of Galapitemadama, the young people now draw lots each week to select the house where they will work together – fixing the well or repairing the roof.

The road, then, also builds a new sense of power and possibility. This is evident in the local Sarvodaya *haulas* or committees that often constellate in the course of the first shramadana or two – youth committees, elders' committees, or committees of mothers to start a preschool or community kitchen. The collective action combined with the fresh respect it breeds for manual labor can generate a personal commitment to the development of the village that no government programs or foreign aid projects appear able to duplicate. Public reforestation schemes, for example, often founder because villagers neglect the seedlings, let goats and cattle eat them. But when undertaken as shramadana, with the sense of ownership and responsibility that brings, the plants are watered and protected.

With the experience that the Sarvodaya movement has accrued with more than three thousand shramadana camps, and well over a half million participants, certain methods have evolved as most effective for long-term results. Here is how – if you are a Sarvodayan in Sri Lanka – you organize a shramadana.

1 Go to a village and start making a survey of its needs. Go from house to house and then get folks together, say in the temple or in the school, to talk about what they want. Talk till agreement is reached on the choice of an initial project.

2 Contact district government officials to see if they can provide needed material – tools, seeds, truck. They are usually not hard to persuade when you have a lot of free labor to offer.

3 If cement, bricks, elephant, or right-of-way over a piece of land are needed, get the wealthier parties in the village to offer them. In the course of the meetings, to their own surprise and out of competition or desire for good will, they often will.

4 Be sure to involve the local priest. Usually to bless so generous an effort, his presence both legitimates and inspires.

5 Meanwhile a local family or two will be taking the lead in organizing the day's collective meal. A mass potluck is always fun and sometimes the start of a community kitchen, which can make a real difference in awareness of nutrition needs.

6 See which city folk and foreign visitors to Sarvodaya headquarters want to join the shramadana. They often enjoy this contact with village life and in the eyes of the locals their presence – and their actual physical labor – adds lustre to the occasion.

7 When the day comes, start early while it is cool; this also saves time for the midday and evening "family gatherings." Begin with a brief meeting for meditation and chant. It helps collect the energy that will be given this day.

8 At the family gatherings, as folks relax, speak about the meaning of *dana*, the power of the free gift, the merit of generosity. Remind people they can remake their world out of their own caring and power. Recall for them the glories of the past when Sri Lanka was *Danyagara* and *Dhammadvipa*, granary of wealth and island of righteousness. These can be restored when they work as brother and sister; as you have from the start, you continue, of course, to address them in these terms and treat them in this fashion.

9 Remember to provide in these gatherings both space and encouragement for the participation of the villagers. They enjoy this opportunity to perform for their neighbors in song or dance, which, of course, is great for community spirit; and the experience of giving an impromptu talk on their perception of village needs raises their awareness of their own leadership capacities.

10 When it is all over, stay in close touch – for shramadana is often just beginning.

It is just the beginning because people have tasted what they can do together – and there is no limit to that. As a visitor from a far-away land I tasted it too. It stirred in me old memories of my grandparents telling about husking bees and barn-raisings, stirred also recent memories of the potlucks and collective gardens we started in upstate New York. In America, too, there was shramadana and there also now the sanity of the past is being reappropriated. Not having seen it, though, on a scale like this, I find myself wondering if we could not move more systematically and full-tilt into the giving of human energy. There is healing, hope and deep community in such sharing, perhaps because, in the last analysis, that is what we are – pure energy. ■

THE RISING SUN
NEIGHBORHOOD NEWSLETTER

"I used to hate to go to parties but if she was there when you got there it was a good party. She does things for reasons so real you can't understand them."

—Stewart about Margo St. James

Running must be the most benign fad in history. Apparently superficial, as any craze, it nevertheless goes deep into the practitioner and possibly into the society as a whole. Harmful effects are hard to find. The gear is too minimal to be a distraction. Competition is optional. Health and good spirits bloom. OK.

Tom Ferguson, editor of **Medical Self Care** *(p. 322) went from reluctance to enthusiasm to obsession about running, as you can tell from his appraisals of the current best of the running literature.*

—SB

The Aerobics Way

Ken Cooper has had more positive impact on the lives of more Americans than any other living physician. Since the publication of his first book, **Aerobics***, in 1968, 60 million Americans have started exercise programs, many of them using his book as a guide. During this time the death rate from heart disease has declined ten percent. Between 1970 and 1974, the average American's life span increased from 70.9 to 72.0 years. Since '68, Cooper has been continuing his exercise research at the Aerobics Center in Dallas. This new book includes his experiences in the intervening nine years. It is a much superior book.* **Aerobics** *was based on Cooper's work with young and middle-aged Air Force men.* **The Aerobics Way** *reflects his work with women, older people, and people with special medical problems, including obesity. There is a much more complete treatment of diet. More sports are included. There is a self-scoring coronary risk profile, and an excellent bibliography.*

The basic program has changed in two ways: endurance points have been added (so that three miles run together are now worth more than three miles run separately), and there is more emphasis on starting out very slowly and gently. Cooper argues persuasively for a treadmill stress test — especially for men over thirty-five — before starting a new program, and at regular intervals afterward. Such testing was not widely available when the first book was published. Now — largely because of Cooper's efforts — they are becoming increasingly so. **The Aerobics Way** *lists 151 centers, nation-wide, which specialize in such testing. The most interesting new resource this book offers is corresponding membership in the new Aerobics International Research Society. People exercising regularly are encouraged to join. Members receive a blank exercise log which is filled out daily and periodically mailed in. Your exercise information is added to the AIRS data bank. You receive a monthly printout of your activity with aerobics points calculated, and copies of the Society's newsletter. You'll also be asked to fill out an occasional health questionnaire, so that the effects of your exercise program can be documented. There is a nominal yearly membership fee. "I hope you will join," Cooper writes, "since it will be motivational for you and will provide our research institute with an invaluable source of data." Membership information is available from AIRS, P.O. Box 22359, Dallas, Texas 75222.*

The best book currently available on getting in shape.

—Tom Ferguson, M.D.

The Aerobics Way
(New Data on the World's Most Popular Exercise Program)
Kenneth H. Cooper, M.D., M.P.H.
1977; 311 pp.

$10 postpaid from:
M. Evans and Company
E.P. Dutton and Co.
Two Park Avenue
New York, NY 10016
or Whole Earth Household Store

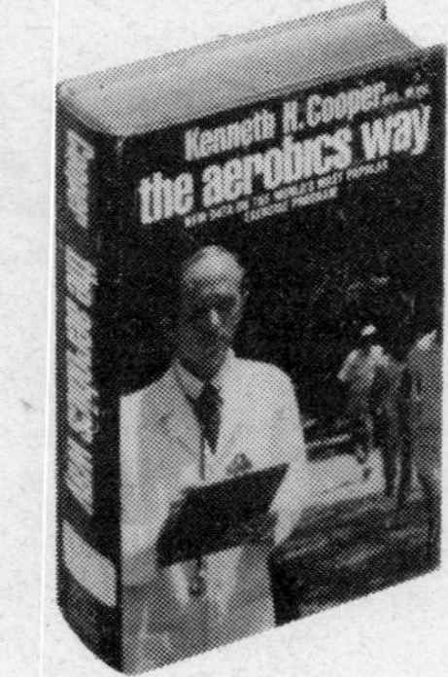

•
Another important phenomenon of exercise is the seemingly contradictory fact that vigorous exercise actually depresses the appetite, thus making dieting easier.

Total Fitness in 30 Minutes a Week

This book's title put me off for a long time, but people kept recommending it and I finally read it and, lo and behold, it's a very useful book, though it could more accurately be entitled "Relative Fitness in 30 Minutes a Week." The point is that if you don't exercise at all, 30 minutes a week devoted to Dr. Morehouse's program will probably bring you to above-normal fitness for your age and sex.

Reading this book made me aware of my own prejudices in the direction of high levels of fitness. It also made me realize that I have never been completely out of condition. Moorehouse has you start small — standing instead of sitting, taking the stairs instead of riding the elevator, running in place for five minutes before your daily bath or shower. An excellent book if you are just starting to exercise, or if you have limited time to devote to an exercise program.

—Tom Ferguson, M.D.

Total Fitness in 30 Minutes a Week
Laurence E. Morehouse, Ph.D. and Leonard Gross
1975, 255 pp.

$2.45 postpaid from:
Pocket Books
Attn: Order Department
1230 Avenue of the Americas
New York, NY 10020
or Whole Earth Household Store

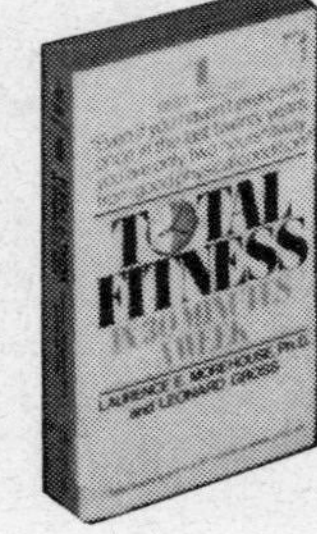

•
To double your physical strength and endurance and bring you to par with a trained athlete requires a minimum of two hours a day of strenuous exertion. That's not a realistic goal; you haven't got the time, patience, inclination, or need. You'll do extremely well with less.

Skipping the Rope

If you're trapped indoors, this is a good quick way to fit up without going anywhere (jogging machines seem madness to me). Though the scenery is limited, rope skipping offers more things you can try than running does — cross overs, spins, twirls, flips, double turns, cross foots, alternating sideward leg flings, and heel clicks. No propaganda here, just technique.

—SB

Skipping the Rope
(For Fun and Fitness)
Frank B. Prentup
1963; 36 pp.

$2.25 postpaid from:
Pruett Publishing Co.
3235 Prairie Avenue
Boulder, CO 80301

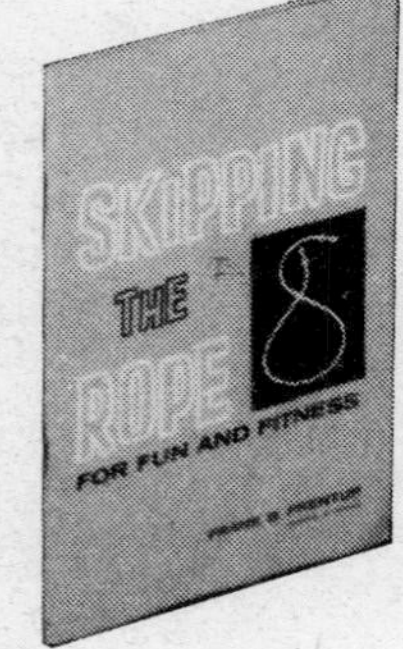

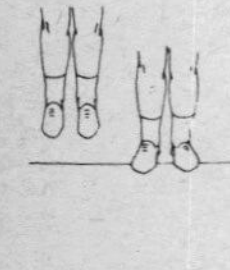
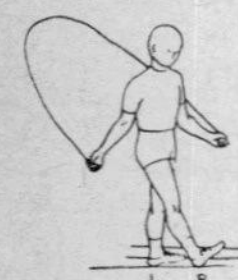
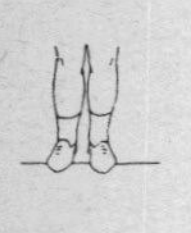
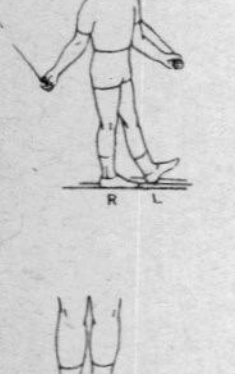
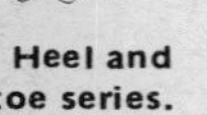

Heel and toe series.

Measuring the Rope — Stand in the loop with the feet together and stretch the ends of the rope to the armpits.

Women's Running

For beginning and advanced women runners. Good sections on sox, bras, cold and wet weather clothing. Evaluates shoes by brand name and gives names of companies which sell extra-narrow running shoes (a problem for many women, since most companies make only small versions of wider men's shoes). The author, a physician who runs, communicates the feeling of camaraderie of running with women and offers practical tips on running with men.

—Gatha Hesselden

Women's Running
Joan Ullyot, M.D.
1976; 155 pp.

$4.95 postpaid from:
World Publications
Box 366
Mountain View, CA 94040
or Whole Earth Household Store

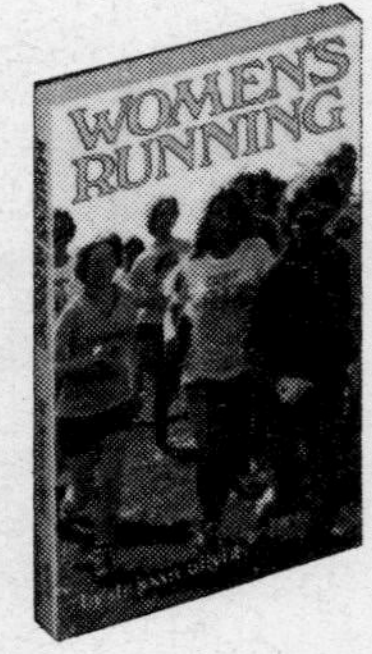

•
One of the sad facts of life is that even a paunchy, beer-drinking, smoking, middle-aged slob, if he's male, can almost always run a mile faster and more easily without practice than a woman. It's discouraging to you and can lead to understandable feelings of resentment if you set out together. It's unjust, but there it is — your horribly unfit husband is a better miler than you at the start. . . . He may wish to run with you and guide your steps. Say no. Pleasant as it may be to have company, it is unwise to run with a man until you are reasonably fit and can run under 10 minutes per mile.

The Complete Book of Running

This chatty, highly readable runner's gazetteer covers an amazing number of the big and little details — practical, physiological, philosophical, from transcendence to jock-straps — that take on increasing importance as running becomes an integral part of your life.

—Tom Ferguson, M.D.

The Complete Book of Running
James F. Fixx
1977; 315 pp.

$10.95 postpaid from:
Random House
455 Hahn Road
Westminster, MD 21157
or Whole Earth Household Store

•
The easiest time of day for running, the time least likely to be disrupted by unexpected intrusions, is early morning. All that's needed is to rise a bit earlier than usual. Even in winter there's a special joy in being outdoors at dawn, a peaceful sense of privacy found at no other time. In summer there's the advantage of getting your run in before the heat of the day.

The Joy of Running

Dr. Kostrubala has you start big — running/walking for three one-hour periods a week. You end up joining a running group — or forming your own — and running 10 miles a day in training for a marathon. The author started out 50 pounds overweight, unable to run 100 yards. The story of his progress — interspersed with physiological and anthropological asides — is delightful and inspiring. His account of his first marathon will make you feel as though you had run one yourself.

I started marathon training after reading this book. (I'd worked my way through Ken Cooper's **The Aerobics Way** *program already.) I'm now up to 15 miles. Training for a marathon takes a long time — often a year or longer. It becomes a sort of benign addiction. There's certainly a point where it becomes something more than just keeping in shape. In my case it was some things I started noticing at and beyond the three-mile mark. A kind of physical and emotional second wind. Near the point of exhaustion, I'd suddenly find myself sprinting, transported. Or, other times, suddenly crying for no apparent reason. Something happens when you start running long distances. I don't understand what it is, but I'm out there every day because of it. This personal, quirky book comes as close to describing it as anything I've seen.*

—Tom Ferguson, M.D.

The Joy of Running
Thaddeus Kostrubala, M.D.
1976, 1977; 176 pp.

$2.20 postpaid from:
Pocket Books
Attn: Order Department
1230 Avenue of the Americas
New York, NY 10020
or Whole Earth Household Store

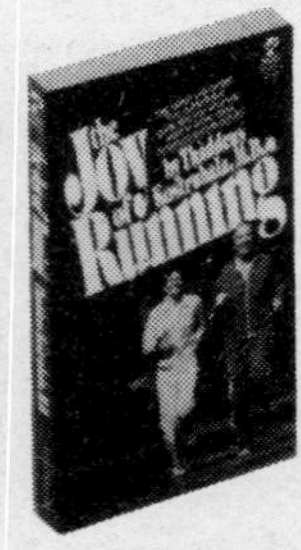

•
The slow, long-distance runner experiences a part of his unconscious. It is an altered state of consciousness. . . . There is often a complete relief of tension and anxiety. The runner is washed out from within.

Beyond Jogging

Advanced running. Breathing techniques, running meditation, and altered states. Mike Spino studied with the great running coaches Percy Wells Cerutty and Mihaly Igloi, and passes on some of their secrets. An additional bonus is the fine afterword, "Sport as Yoga," by Michael Murphy, who has spent the last few years talking to high-performance athletes about the special powers, similar to the yoga siddhi, that arise during the performance of one's sport.

—Tom Ferguson, M.D.

Beyond Jogging
Mike Spino
1976; 111 pp.

$4.95 postpaid from:
Celestial Arts
231 Adrian Road
Millbrae, CA 94030
or Whole Earth Household Store

Altitude training has become a tradition, but almost no one knows for sure if it works.

Runner's World

The present glut of running literature leads one to debate whether further ingestion of the stuff will bring enlightenment or just befuddlement, and as a 20-year runner and former fanatic who once read every word published on the topic I've finally been overwhelmed. Now I just rely on my local running club newsletter. After all, the only thing you really need to know is the race schedule.

But for a person passing from the old-tennies-and-cutoffs stage into Serious Running there's much to be said for learning from the mistakes of others, and that means hanging out with runners who know more than you, and reading the literature.

For years the literature meant **Runner's World**, *top dog in a pack of 1. It was a slightly funky magazine which balanced contradictory training programs and typographical errors with shallow interviews and a West Coast bias, while also producing a new message that many heard. Editor Joe Henderson laid out his personal philosophy of non-competitive running, a ridiculous idea that not only worked, but caught on, for the readership was composed not of champs but the rank and file, the middle of the pack runners. Medical advice came from wise old Dr. Sheehan (author of* **Dr. Sheehan on Running**), *who'd personally experienced every ache, pain and malady known to sports medicine. The overall effect was to offer people a new personal truth — if you ran three miles a day in the park you were just as worthy as the guy who was first at Boston.*

Times have changed, running's gone mainstream, and **RW** *shows the price of success. There's still some genuine Soul there, hidden away among the full-color ads of non-running New York models peddling chic clothes and unneeded gadgets, but it's become a Slick Product. Although the competition* (**The Runner, Running Times**) *is closing in,* **RW** *is still the standard by which it's judged.*
—Dick Fugett

Runner's World
Bob Anderson, Editor
$16 /year (12 issues)
from:
Runner's World Magazine
P.O. Box 366
Mountain View, CA 94042

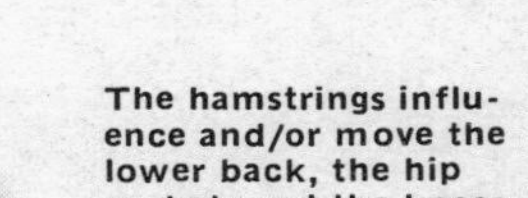

The hamstrings influence and/or move the lower back, the hip sockets and the knees.

●

Police polled in a number of major American cities agree that crime is running out in big-city parks. A spokesman for the Chicago Park District, for example, said that while exact statistics are unavailable, crime in Chicago parks has "probably gone down" over the past several years because of the growing number of runners. "The more runners and joggers out there," he said, "the less chance of people being robbed or murdered." Additionally, citizens can better enjoy park recreational facilities with runners about. "People tell me they feel more secure in Golden Gate Park when they see runners," Sgt. Walter Garry of the San Francisco Police Department said. "I'm a runner and I know sometimes when I've approached people from behind they hear the footsteps and turn anxiously around. When they see a runner, they smile. As a police officer I find it ironic that a fully dressed male would be a threat, but a half-dressed male is not. Runners draw positive responses."

Track and Field News

This is the only periodical I read from cover to cover! It contains all important news about world and national class track and field events, all new national and world records, periodical reviews of the best times in various events through history, personal news of leading athletes (how they are training, what their goals are, etc.), assessments of various events, training routines, sports arenas, etc. Because I am especially interested in the human body's capacity for transformation and supernormal performance, this becomes a periodical I cannot do without. To my knowledge, there is nothing so thorough covering any other sport in which world records are being broken with regularity.
—Michael Murphy

Track and Field News
Bert Nelson, Editor
$13.50 /year (12 issues)
from:
Track and Field News, Inc.
Box 296
Los Altos, CA 94022

Stretching

A lot of athletes — pro and amateur — are getting into mixing "hard" sports (football, swimming, running) with "soft" ones (yoga, stretching, t'ai Chi). P.E. teacher Bob Anderson teaches stretching clinics for professional and college athletic teams. His straightforward home-published book is a fine introduction to combining tension exercises with relaxation exercises. It includes special stretching routines for use before, during, and after running, swimming, cycling, football, tennis, basketball, etc. I've been doing his stretching routines before and after running. It makes quite a difference.
—Tom Ferguson, M.D.

Note. I've got to admit I do this stuff too, and it works. The author offers a set of stretching charts (for 26 specific activities, at $2 each) and Stretching Cards (for Running, Everyday, and Traveler's Stretches, $2.95 each) from: Stretching, Inc., Box 767, Palmer Lake, CO 80133. Stretching is American yoga, is all.
—SB

Stretching
Bob Anderson
1975; 183 pp.
$7.95 postpaid from:
Random House
455 Hahn Road
Westminster, MD 21157
or Whole Earth
Household Store

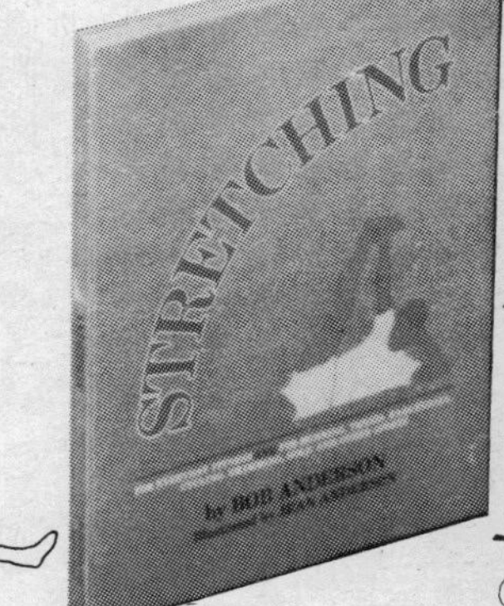

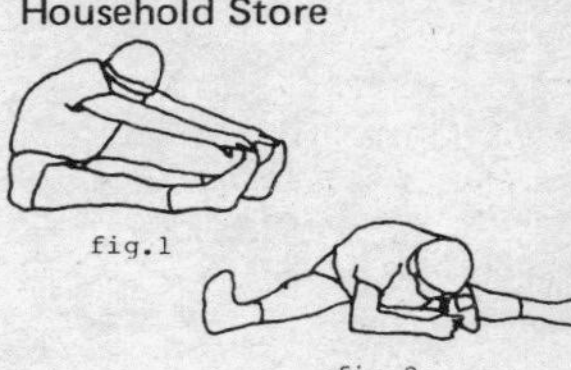

●

A minimum test of flexibility sometimes used is sitting with legs straight, fingers touching toes (fig. 1) and sitting with legs spread, forehead on top of fists on the floor (fig. 2), holding each stretch comfortably for about fifty to sixty seconds.

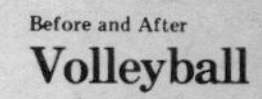

25 seconds each leg *(page 71)*

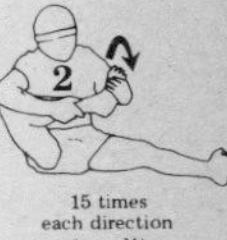

15 times each direction *(page 31)*

30 seconds *(page 56)*

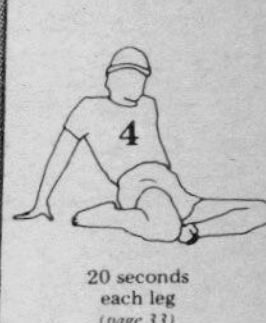

20 seconds each leg *(page 33)*

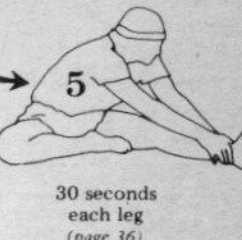

30 seconds each leg *(page 36)*

30 seconds *(page 93)*

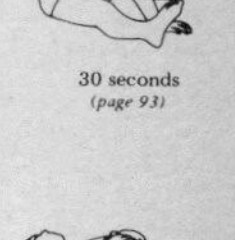

30 seconds *(page 24)*

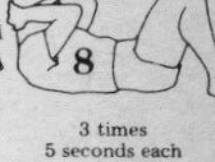

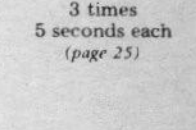

3 times 5 seconds each *(page 25)*

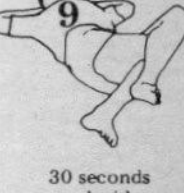

30 seconds each side *(page 24)*

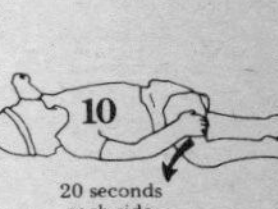

20 seconds each side *(page 29)*

3 times 5 seconds each *(page 28)*

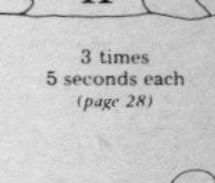

10 seconds each leg *(page 47)*

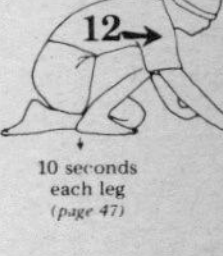

25 seconds each leg *(page 48)*

THE RISING SUN
NEIGHBORHOOD NEWSLETTER

Across from the UC Theatre where they have a new double feature of old movies every day and *The Rocky Horror Picture Show* on Fri. and Sat. at mid. is the Berkeley Violin Store where after any show you can see the backs of basses gleaming in the street light as they hang from the ceiling. I wondered and wondered about that store and the other morning I went in. Inside you can see that not only are there the 8 or 10 basses hanging in the front, but there are 40 or 50 violins hanging in the back over the repair area. An 18 - 20 year old was crouched over a violin in the back, and in the front under the basses another young guy was playing a guitar, the only one in the shop, though there were recorders for sale. I asked him what the cheapest and most expensive violins in the shop were and he told me that the cheapest would be about $85 used and it wouldn't be much and the most expensive they had would be maybe $3000 though violins went way higher than that, they mostly sold to students. He also told me they got customers from all over because not that many shops around sold in that price range — some in San Francisco started about where they stopped and went up from there.

Violins should always be made out of spruce on the top and maple on the sides and back; sometimes manufacturers experiment with other woods but they don't work. The Japanese make small violins for kids mostly, and the wood is often cut too thin so they don't sound good. Basses are often made of plywood; it's not a great idea but even a plywood bass runs $600 and carved basses (carved out of spruce and maple) can cost much more, starting maybe $1500. Not all grownups use full sized violins; small players may use a 7/8 (pronounced seven eight) all their lives — that's the next to the largest size, 4/4 is the largest. I asked him if smaller violins sounded different than full size and boy, was that a stupid question. No violin in the world sounds like any other violin in the world or even close. When people buy a violin they never come in and just pick one. They take a series of violins home for a week or so and try them out, looking for the right sound for them.

Fit or Fat?

Regardless of diet, the main message your metabolism gets from your behavior is: muscle or fat. Aerobic exercise makes muscle, replaces fat, and alters the metabolism to maintain that. Lack of aerobic exercise does the opposite. The book makes the case pretty unavoidably, like a boot in your fat ass.
—SB

Fit or Fat?
(A New Way to Health and Fitness through Nutrition and Aerobic Exercise)
Covert Bailey
1977, 1978; 119 pp.
$3.95 postpaid from:
Houghton Mifflin Co.
Wayside Road
Burlington, MA 01803
or Whole Earth
Household Store

→

Above 25 percent fat, people float easily.

At 22 - 23 percent fat (healthy for a woman), one can usually float while breathing shallowly.

At 15 percent fat (low for a woman, healthy for a man), one will usually sink very slowly even with a full chest of air.

At 13 percent fat, one will sink readily even with a full chest of air, even in salty ocean water.

●

All I am really saying is that aerobic exercise is the *most efficient* way to remove the marbling fat, which in turn is the most efficient way to change your metabolism so you won't get fat anymore.

●

The main criterion of aerobic exercise is that it be continuous and steady. We don't know exactly why it works, but it does. There is something about pushing a muscle to work hard at a steady pace that leads quickly to a firming of the muscle and a loss of its marbling. Stop-and-go exercises just don't do the same thing as quickly. There are very strong weight lifters who cannot run a mile and whose muscles are loaded with fat. These are people who "go to fat" if they become inactive.

●

After the age of forty, you should switch exercises from day to day. (For example, run on Monday, Wednesday, and Friday, and cycle on Tuesday, Thursday, and Saturday.) The reason is that muscles can't repair as quickly when you get older. By switching exercises, you give the set of muscles you stressed on Monday time to build up while you stress another set on Tuesday. By Wednesday, the "Monday muscles" are not only repaired but also stronger than ever.

●

If you're in a hurry to get in shape, *exercise longer, not harder.*

Fat Floats!

Hot Tubs
Hot Tubs, Spas and Home Saunas

These two books demonstrate how far the phenomenon of hot tubs has come — from a bohemian invention of Southern Californians in 1958 to a practically de rigeur luxury item for the financially or hedonistically rich. **Hot Tubs** *is by the bohemians and tells why to, with very sketchy practical advice.* **Hot Tubs, Spas & Home Saunas** *is by* **Sunset** *magazine, that citadel of upwardly mobile niftiness, and has superb how to diagrams and advice and not a single naked human being. (What kind of hysterical prude would wear a bathing suit in a hot tub? Why not wear a raincoat?)*

If you get or make a hot tub, your friends will love you the more. It can be expensive. For a practical very-low-cost alternative, see my own "Better Bathtub" on p. 332.
—SB

Hot Tubs
(How to Build, Maintain and Enjoy Your Own Winter & Summer All Year Round)
Leon Elder
1973, 1978; 111 pp.
$4.95 postpaid from:
Vintage Books
Random House
455 Hahn Road
Westminster, MD 21157
or Whole Earth Household Store

Hot Tubs, Spas and Home Saunas
(Sunset Ideas for Landscaping and Design)
Jack McDowell,
Barbara G. Gibson, et al.
1979; 80 pp.
$3.95 postpaid from:
Lane Publishing Co.
Menlo Park, CA 94025
or Whole Earth Household Store

—Hot Tubs

The Basic Hot Tub

Tubs offer a surprising range of choices in size and shape, as well as equipment.

—Hot Tubs, Spas & Home Saunas

•

The best time is at night, in windy rain, an old oak groaning and creaking overhead. Naked and shivering, you stare at the steaming pool and put one foot in. The stinging tells you it's being cooked, yet other people are in up to their chins, laughing and beckoning. The cold rain encourages you in the cauldron. A searing line slowly rises to your chin and you don't dare move. Then within five minutes you feel melted and happy, even into your bones. Someone passes a glass of wine. Pelted by rain, it bubbles like champagne. Fifteen minutes later you rise into the wind — it feels delicious. Now you understand how the Finns can run naked from a sauna to hurl themselves into the snow. You sink easily back into the water again and gaze at the nude people, some standing in halos of steam, others hunched down to their chins. They all appear curiously pleased with themselves, and you think — what bliss!
—Hot Tubs

The Sauna Book

I'm not a bit sure whether increasing use of saunas is a sign of advanced civilization or advanced decadence. Either way, everything needed is here — how to enjoy, how to build, unusual sauna lore, and detailed review and access on manufacturers. A nice job. One tip: if you're building a house and sauna, build the sauna first and you'll have a nice place to relax from house construction.
—SB

The Sauna Book
Tom Johnson and
Tim Miller
1977; 193 pp.
$7.95 postpaid from:
Harper & Row
Keystone Industrial Park
Scranton, PA 18512
or Whole Earth Household Store

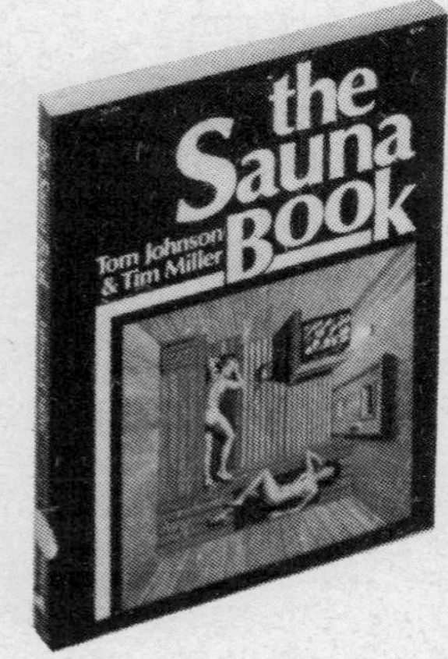

The Best Cheap Stove You Can Get

We spent a long time trying to figure out how you could get an electric or gas sauna stove without spending much money. For a while we played with a homemade stove utilizing the heating element from the oven of an abandoned electric stove but never quite got the kinks worked out of it. Then Gerhard Zuther, who lives right in the neighborhood, showed us his. Friends, he has the answer.

Gerhard's stove is made from an old water heater. Water heaters are normally abandoned because the tank has a small leak, not because the heating unit (be it electric or gas) is faulty. This means that they are just fine for our purposes, since what we're after is something that will (a) heat and (b) hold stones. water heaters hold 20 or 30 gallons; 10 gallons of volume will be plenty for your stones. At this point you will probably have to get some help, unless you have a cutting torch, but at any rate the cost should be low. Gerhard bought his gas water heater in a junkyard for $2.50, and the proprietor made the necessary cut for an additional two bucks.

Incidentally, contemporary water heaters are usually lined with fiberglass, but many old ones are not. You will want one that is not.

Nippa Sauna Heater

The Japanese-type hot bath, with a wood-burning firebox, is excellent, but the fireboxes are hard to make and impossible to buy from Japan. The Japanese bath also uses a lot of water, which can be a problem if you have to pump or carry water any distance.

One answer is the sweat-lodge/sauna. An earth-lodge will do, or better a cedar-lined room with a high bench and a drain in the floor. Carrying hot rocks can be tiresome; the best arrangement we've found is this wood-burning sauna stove made by the Nippa company in Michigan. We use the WC 22 model, holds a lot of wood, heats 15 gallons of water to a rolling boil in 20 minutes, heats the rocks on top at the same time, doesn't use much wood actually, and keeps the sauna room hot for hours. Expensive, but will last several lifetimes and keep maybe 2 dozen people clean and happy. (Another wood-burning sauna heater on p. 207.)
—Gary Snyder

Nippa Sauna Heaters
WC-18, 18" deep
$339.95 plus shipping
WC-22, 22" deep
$359.95 plus shipping
Brochure
free from:
Nippa Sauna Heaters
P.O. Box 213
Bruce Crossing, MI 49912

Native American sweating

The Native American sweat house ritual is varied and complex — some groups separate the sexes, i.e., don't sweat together (Nez Perce for example); others sweat communally. The social, psychological and physiological advantages of sweating are numerous and not to my knowledge adequately researched (Finnish data is *best*). This Nez Perce (contemporary) sweat house will sweat four to six:

You need:
- 5 - 7 green, usually deciduous, poles, approximately 15' in length
- 1 ball sturdy twine or if a purist, rawhide strips
- blankets — Nez Perce use blankets of wool; old coats, clean gunny sacks, any pliable insulating material of cloth will do, get plenty!
- 2 pitch forks
- 1 20-gallon can — not absolutely necessary
- 2 18" - 20" sticks, 1" or so in diameter

1
You will need a location near water (usually a stream) — cleared of all brush and undergrowth. An area 30' in diameter will do depending on local conditions. Stream must be deep enough to allow submergence of one's body.

2
The shape of wickiup-type lodge will be semi-hemispherical about 8' or so in diameter. Construct the frame by holding green poles in proper shape over a fire (small) and slightly dry poles which will hold curved shape better. Tie the poles together with twine thereby maintaining shape.

3
Cover the frame with insulating material — 3 or 4 layers will suffice. Leave no spaces! The lodge must be nearly air-tight. I use an initial layer of plastic tarping to aid in heat retention — although I dislike its negative appeal. Leave a door just big enough to enter — you can hitch a cross-piece to the frame of the lodge and hang several blankets off it making sure an adequate seal is formed.

4
Dig a small depression inside the door and to the right — this becomes the receptacle for the red-hot rocks. Should be 10" deep and 25 - 30" in diameter. Line this hole with good rocks (see definition of a good sweat rock, which follows).

5
Gather 30 or so sweat rocks. A good rock is hard to find. My best luck has been with slightly vesicular basalt, subangular and about twice the size of a brick. Test rocks by heating over fire to a red hot glow — sprinkle over with water. If the rocks spit and hiss but do not explode or crack — you *may* have a good rock. River rocks have been my best source, i.e. subangular basalt cobbles. Granite is too heterogeneous.

6
Gather wood — the best wood is usually the hardest to procure. Most deciduous wood burns hotter but it is harder to find. I use anything I feel right about. *Never* cut a green tree for firewood or for any stupid reason. Use dead wood, stumps. You need a lot. Build your fire place next to, but too close to, your sweat lodge, which is hopefully next to, but not too close to, the water. Stack your fire logs, crisscrossing to achieve a sturdy and fairly flat top, on which you evenly distribute your rocks. Fire is fairly big and hence you will need adequate precautionary measures.

7
Light fire. Usually this takes 45 minutes to an hour or even longer depending on wood. The rocks fall through to the ground and become ash-covered. This is where the pitch forks come in. The rocks should actually be red hot and you will need them to pass the rocks into the house. One individual must receive and arrange the rocks in the receptacle pit so he will need the two sticks. By the way, the house is only about 3½' high in the center so this individual is on his knees. The pitch fork will facilitate cleaning burning ashes and embers from the rocks in the transferring process — these ashes would cause smoke in the lodge. Line floor of lodge with clean gunny sacks — cheap and available at any feed store.

8
After the rocks are all in place, all can climb in (naked of course) and enjoy. The host tends the rocks by sprinkling small amounts of water on top which cause increased humidity. I use pungent water, made by using certain roots; these cause a delightful fragrance. Sweat house lore says you should be serious or at least not *too* playful. When you are well heated and feel ready for the water — do indulge. Most serious sweaters consider the plunge into the water and the accompanying sensations to be the best part of sweating. Three times in the sweat house should be enough — an effective contraceptive too.

—Greg Cleveland
Albuquerque, New Mexico

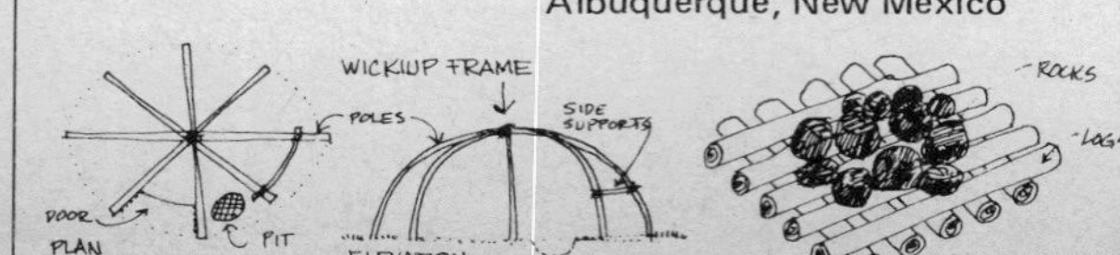

Cold Comfort

This book is so useful and sensible that it makes you wonder why somebody didn't write it a long time ago. It's about colds — and the flu — and it's written to be read while you have a cold or the flu.

Describes exactly what's happening to make you feel that way — including anatomy and physiology and a brief elementary course in viruses. Bennett, co-author of the **Well Body Book** *describes the pros and cons of commercial cold remedies, and the benefits of relaxation, acupressure, vitamin C, hot lemon tea, hot ginger milk, and "Grandmother Pelton's chocolate-molasses cookies." Also offers tips on how to distinguish between colds and flu and the onset of more complicated illnesses.*

Sure to become a classic. I've already loaned it out to several friends with colds. Their verdict — (Sniffle. Cough.) — A+.
—Tom Ferguson, M.D.

Cold Comfort
(Colds and Flu: Everybody's Guide to Self Treatment)
Hal Zina Bennett
1979; 155 pp.
$6.45 postpaid from:
Clarkson N. Potter, Inc.
Crown Publishers
One Park Avenue South
New York, NY 10016
or Whole Earth Household Store

•

Take a very hot bath, as hot as you can stand, and then snuggle up in a nice warm bed. Remain there the whole day and through that night, even if doing so means you're neglecting your family. Read a good book or write letters to special friends who are far away. Drink lots of fluids.

. . . The main ingredient here is warmth, a subject we investigated in our discussion of temperature. We know that heat increases the body's production of natural substances to reduce the viruses' ability to reproduce. Moreover, it speeds up the body's metabolic rate, creating an active rather than a sluggish system, for cleansing away dead cells and creating new cells to replace those damaged by the viruses. And by raising your body temperature you make a less inviting environment for the viruses. In addition, the warmth relaxes you. This absence of stress, we know, is particularly therapeutic — not only because it opens tiny capillaries throughout your body, thus increasing the flow of blood to areas of infection, but also because it keeps down your production of the hormone cortisol, which can reduce antibody production.

•

Q: What does it mean to let a cold or flu "run its course"?

A: The *course* is the period of time it takes your body to identify the virus, build antibodies, and render the virus noninfectious. You get over a cold not because the virus gets tired of your company and decides to move on to the next person but because your body does some very definite things — it identifies the virus, it synthesizes substances that make it impossible for the virus to spread (sort of like feeding the virus a birth control pill), and it repairs tissue damaged by the infection, which it accomplishes by reproducing healthy body cells at a more rapid rate than usual.

Q: What about using antihistamines, decongestants, and the other cold medicines advertised in the media and sold in drugstores and supermarkets?

A: Minimize your use of these drugs. None of them shorten the period you have the infection, and many can cause symptoms of their own. My own experience is that they frequently cause further discomfort and can prolong the period you have a cold or flu.

The Well Body Book

Already widely known and well beloved, this beautifully designed book has become so popular it's easy to overlook how good it really is. It combines a deep emphasis on the feeling side of things — sensitivity, coping, communication — with excellent sections on preventive medicine and diagnosis and treatment. Their section on the physical examination is one of the best I've seen.
—Tom Ferguson, M.D.

The Well Body Book
Mike Samuels, M.D. and Hal Bennett
1973; 350 pp.
$7.95 postpaid from:
Random House
455 Hahn Road
Westminster, MD 21157
or Whole Earth Household Store

•

Herpes Simplex (Also called "Fever Blisters," or "Cold Sores").

Symptoms: Small blisters on the mouth, genital areas or skin. Affected areas may itch or be painful.

Physical Exam: You will see, in the mouth, genital areas or skin, small raised blisters which turn into "punched out" sores. They may look like round sores with little holes punched out, which then become scabbed over. You may find them singly or in clumps. They can crust over and "weep" (become runny) toward the end of the herpes infection. Swollen lymph nodes in the area may be more disturbing to the person with Herpes than the actual disease itself.

What's Going On? Herpes is a viral infection. Some people believe that the virus is on the skin from early childhood; others believe that you catch it from other people who have it.

Herpes infections are known to be aggravated by certain things: another infection somewhere in your body that lowers your resistance (like when you have a cold), windburn, or nervous tension. In my experience, Herpes occur occurs and reoccurs for a certain period of time in a person's life, and then the person simply stops getting it, and is not troubled with it again.

Treatment: I've found that drying agents such as cornstarch or baby powder work to relieve symptoms on external infections. Herpes is self-limited (stops itself) and usually lasts from one to three weeks. If you find Herpes-type sores in the genital area, I'd advise getting a blood test to make sure it's not Syphilis. The symptoms of Herpes and Syphilis often appear the same, and can be difficult to differentiate. Look upon Herpes as your body's message to you asking you to pay attention. Then take care of it the best way you know how.

Your Doctor As a Resource: Your doctor can give you a blood test for Syphilis if Herpes appears in your genital area (or mouth).

Prevention: Herpes takes place most often in times of tension and stress. Relaxation is an essential part of prevention. Avoid touching Herpes sores on other people.

Take Care of Yourself

One of the most useful tools to come out of the new paramedic training programs is the clinical algorithm — big, detailed flow charts, one for each of the common medical complaints (such as sore throat, dizziness, low back pain) that might bring a person into a medical clinic. They tell you the key questions to ask to decide whether the person needs to see the doctor NOW, needs to see the doctor sometime soon, or if home remedies are indicated.

The heart of this book is the 68 most commonly used clinical algorithms, presented in full-page size with nice graphics. There are some additional chapters on "Skills for the Medical Consumer" — Choosing a Doctor, The Home Pharmacy, etc., and a little gem of an essay on Giving a Good Medical History.
—Tom Ferguson, M.D.

Take Care of Yourself
(A Consumer's Guide to Medical Care)
Donald M. Vickery, M.D., and James F. Fries, M.D.
1976; 269 pp.
$6.95 postpaid from:
Addison-Wesley Publishing Company
Jacob Way
Reading, MA 01867
or Whole Earth Household Store

•

Home Treatment

The rational approach to a skin lump is to observe it to see if it changes size or color, bleeds, or gets inflamed. Otherwise, don't worry so much. In the absence of these characteristics, the only reason to have lesions removed with commercially available over-the-counter preparations if used consistently and carefully (Compound W, Vergo). On your next routine visit to a doctor, ask about any skin lumps which bother you.

Skin, Bumps & Lumps — 33

Is the bump tender and inflamed? — yes → Is there only one bump? — yes → Refer to Boils, Problem 30.
Is there only one bump? — no → Make appointment with physician.
Is the bump tender and inflamed? — no → Is the bump enlarging, changing color, or bleeding? — yes → Make appointment with physician.
Is the bump enlarging, changing color, or bleeding? — no → Apply home treatment.

How to Be Your Own Doctor — Sometimes

How to use a stethoscope, measure blood pressure, look at an ear drum, take a pulse. Not just another handy-dandy guide to common medical problems — though it contains an excellent one as an appendix — this book teaches basic medicine in language folks outside the medical profession can understand. Dr. Sehnert is the pioneer in teaching medical self-care. He calls medically-trained laymen Activated Patients. In China they call them barefoot doctors.
—Tom Ferguson, M.D.

How to Be Your Own Doctor — Sometimes
Keith W. Sehnert, M.D.
1975; 353 pp.
$5.95 (paperback price) postpaid from:
Grosset and Dunlap
51 Madison Avenue
New York, NY 10010
or Whole Earth Household Store

•

Take the sphygmomanometer, an instrument that no home should be without. When I gave them to patients in my mostly black class at Northeast-Georgetown Medical Center in Washington, I knew they'd turn up plenty of hypertension, because it runs rampant in the black community. So that was my homework assignment: "Take these blood pressure cuffs home. Try them out on family members, friends, acquaintances — each of you check a minimum of half a dozen people." Nationally, statistics on high blood pressure are 6% for whites and four times that high for blacks, buffeted as they are by inner city stresses and tensions. My students exceeded national figures. A startling 30% of those they examined had this aptly named "silent disease" hypertension — and most didn't even know it.

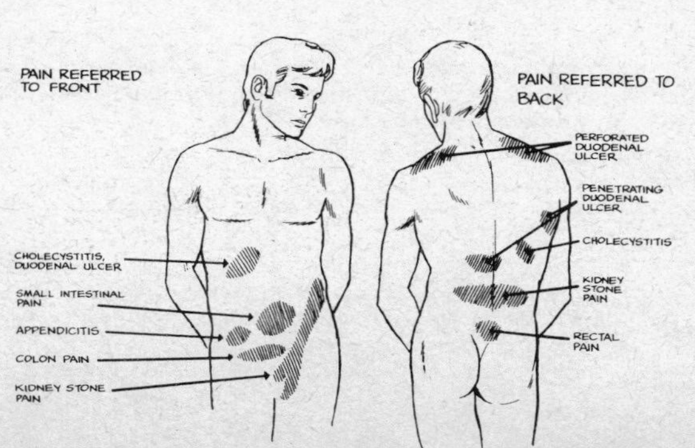

THE RISING SUN
NEIGHBORHOOD NEWSLETTER

I completely see through people I hate; I can predict with amazing accuracy how people who get on my nerves are going to get on my nerves again. People I like I pretty much understand but they surprise me sometimes; people I love are almost wholly mysterious. It's probably a matter of how much data you collect. Physics was pretty sure of itself there in the middle with balls striking each other and planets rotating and causes effecting, but now that they know about all these little particles, they know that all of these little particles are being random all the time, doing what they want who knows why, though balls and planets are still predictable. I know why my truelove quit his last job and why he took his current one, and I was sure he was going to do both before he was, but I can't figure out why he smiled that way, in that place, about that sentence and the more I think about it, the stranger it is.

Medical Self-Care Magazine

Editor Tom Ferguson lives close to us at **Whole Earth** *in more ways than one. His home is just over the hill. His philosophy is identical with ours — empower the individual. And he writes reviews for us (many of them also appear in his magazine and book).*

Hell, 80% of what goes on in medicine can be better handled by the potential patient — not to mention the horrendous matter of cost. (Inappropriate professional expertise costs just as astronomically as the useful stuff.) Most of it's prevention. Most of the rest is awareness and doing something about what you notice. I like the operational word in Tom's title — "care."

The magazine is a friendly, wide-ranging thing. The issue on my desk has information on pollution hazards, auto safety, rape, negative ions, cancer, Mexican barefoot doctors, and TV set hypnosis. Medical self-care is a rapidly growing movement. This is its magazine. Proof: insurance companies are hot for it. —SB

Medical Self-Care Magazine
(Access to Medical Tools)
Tom Ferguson, Editor
$15 /year (4 issues)
from:
Medical Self-Care
P.O. Box 717
Inverness, CA 94937

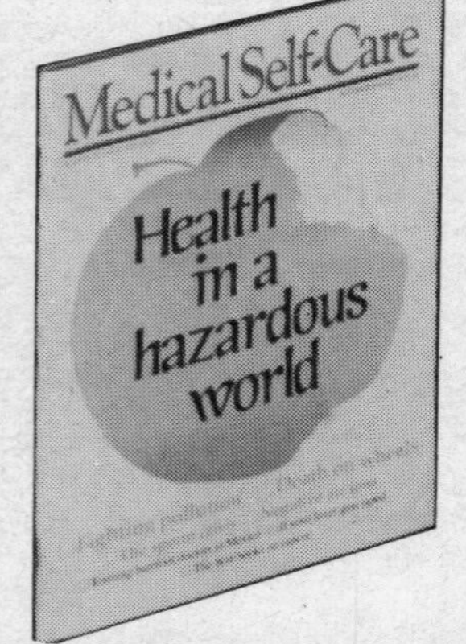

Medical Self-Care

It's an anthology (boo!), but it's a pretty great anthology (yay!). Drawn from many sources as well as his own magazine, Ferguson has a couple of articles and many book reviews each on this gamut of topics: Self-Care Concept, Being Your Own Paramedic, Birthing, Body Work, Clinical Sciences, Couples, Drugs, Dying, Eating, Elders, Exercise, Health Workers, Sex, Children, Medical, Consumerism, Men's Health, Psychological Self-Care, Classes, Stress, and Women's Health. That'll keep you busy for a while, and if you still get sick, instead of feeling sorry for yourself you'll feel stupid. As it should be.

If you find you're really using this medical part of the **Next Whole Earth Catalog**, *you should get Ferguson's full treatment in this book.* —SB

Medical Self-Care
(Access to Health Tools)
Tom Ferguson, Editor
1980; 288 pp.
$8.95 postpaid from:
Summit Books
Simon and Schuster
Order Department
1230 Avenue of
the Americas
New York, NY 10020
or Whole Earth
Household Store

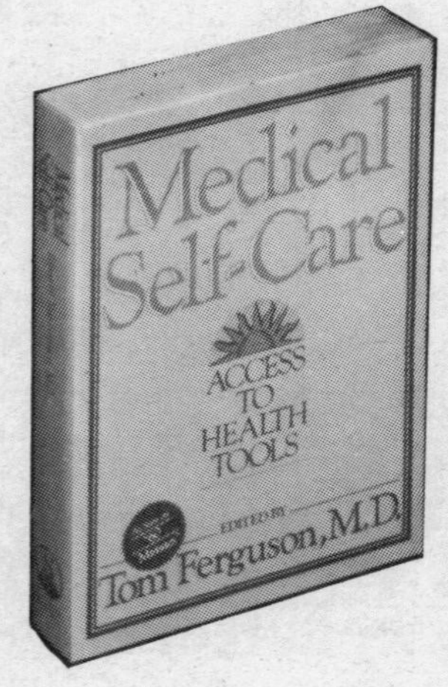

•

I'll have to admit, I've been stunned by the way **Medical Self-Care** magazine has been accepted by health workers and health workers' organizations. I got into this work very disillusioned with conventional medicine, and I expected to be considered a real rebel, attacked by the AMA, the whole bit. It's been absolutely the contrary. In fact, I've just been invited to speak to the AMA's Annual Rural Health Conference.

•

One researcher who set out to study exercise addiction ran into problems which illustrate just what an important part of life exercise can become. He wanted to look at physiological changes in athletes who *stop* exercising. After interviewing a great many people who exercised regularly, he was forced to give up his project. He could not find enough people who exercised regularly who were willing to stop.

"Notwithstanding the fact that they were being offered higher pay than usual," he wrote, "many prospective subjects (especially those who exercised daily) asserted that they would not stop exercising for *any* amount of money."

More cancers may be caused by personal behaviors such as smoking and diet than by external physical and chemical hazards

•

Medical and Dental X-Rays: A Consumer's Guide to Avoiding Unnecessary Radiation Exposure, Priscilla W. Laws, 1974; 74 pp., Health Research Group, 2000 P Street, NW Washington, D.C. 20036.

A consumer's guide to evaluating risks of X-rays, deciding when and when not to have them, and keeping records of radiation exposure. Also lists federal agencies and other organizations concerned with protecting consumers and workers from unnecessary radiation exposure. Highly recommended.

•

Roughly half of all traffic deaths in the United States involve the heavy use of alcohol.

•

A Florida State University professor recently found high levels of four toxic chemicals in semen samples from 132 student volunteers. Three of these chemicals are recognized as carcinogens (substances causing cancer) or teratogens (substances causing birth defects). In addition, the students' sperm counts averaged only 20 million sperms per milliliter, compared to 60 million found in a 1974 study, and 100 million found in a study conducted in 1929. 23 percent of the students had sperm counts so low that they were classified as functionally sterile. The Florida study supported earlier findings showing that the proportion of men with sperm counts of 100 million per milliliter or more has decreased from 80 percent in 1929, to 44 percent in 1950, to 22 percent in 1977. —Michael Castleman

•

Healthwise Handbook: A Guide to Responsible Health Care, Toni Roberts, Kathleen McIntosh Tinker, Donald W. Kemper, 1979; 250 pp., $6.95 postpaid from Doubleday & Co., Garden City, New York, NY 11530.

Everybody seems to agree that self-care classes are a great idea, but hardly anyone's doing them. The bottleneck has been the lack of good course materials. Developing a curriculum from scratch can take months or even years.

Well, friends, no more excuses. Here it is — a bonafide textbook of self-care medicine. With a cooperative nurse, doctor, physician's assistant, or a health educator and a copy of this book for each student, you could have a self-care class in your neighborhood next month.

The book limits itself to conservative traditional medicine — how to do a physical exam, common ailments, injuries, emergencies, eating, dental care, developing a home medicine- and medical-tool chest. The elementary course: Self-Care 101. Makes you wonder what advanced courses will be like — probably more detailed teaching about more chronic diseases, more extensive treatment of stress, exercise, counseling skills, human sexuality, medical consumerism, and healing traditions other than traditional Western medicine.

But that's all a little further down the road. For getting a first class started, this book seems just right. —Tom Ferguson

Talk Back to Your Doctor

The principles of good medical care, spelled out and explained so that you can judge the care you yourself receive. The process of diagnosis, the standard steps in a doctor's visit, lab tests, seeking a second opinion, going in for surgery. Best book on medical consumerism we've seen. —Tom Ferguson, M.D.

Talk Back to Your Doctor
(How to Demand
[& Recognize]
High Quality
Health Care)
Arthur Levin, M.D.
1975; 245 pp.

OUT OF PRINT
Doubleday and Company
Get this book back in print!

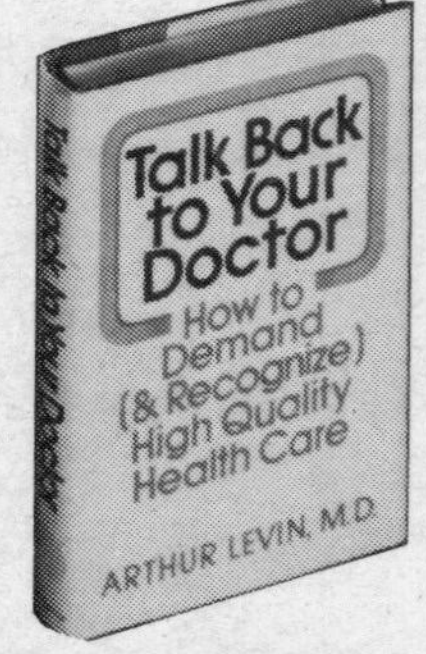

•

Principle: You should choose a hospital which trains interns and residents and, if possible, one which is also affiliated with a medical school.

In the **Ladies' Home Journal** list of "best" hospitals, all were "teaching hospitals" (interns and residents), and all except a couple were medical school-affiliated.

Overwhelmingly, doctors themselves choose such hospitals for their own or their families' care. And with good reason. In the Columbia hospital studies, chances of getting sub-standard care were *more than three times as high* in hospitals without medical school ties.

Family Black Bag

Someone has finally put together a serviceable and sensibly-priced black bag of professional-quality doctor's tools. This kit contains stethoscope, blood pressure cuff, otoscope (for looking into ears), high intensity penlight, oral and rectal thermometers, tongue depressor, dental mirror, a self-help medical guide by self-care pioneer Keith Sehnert, M.D., and a sturdy vinyl bag to carry everything in. Family health record forms and instructions for using tools are included. Women may want to add a plastic speculum. —Tom Ferguson, M.D.

Family Black Bag

$82 postpaid from:
Health Activation
Network
P.O. Box 923
Vienna, VA 22180

Prevention

Long before most of us knew that white sugar wasn't the best kind or that the red dye No. 2 might cause cancer, **Prevention Magazine** *was writing about, researching and sharing ways to stay in good health. They report on new research on vitamins, unusual therapeutic methods, the inside story of some of the horrible things done to food, as well as reports on physicians, spas, or clinics where new methods of healing seem to be working.*

Their bias is to keep you away from M.D.s who do not understand nutrition and to make you more aware of your own responsibilities for staying alive. They also watchdog legislation and regulations which may affect your health. The writing is not technical and the advice is usable. —Jim Fadiman

Prevention
(The Magazine for
Better Health)
Robert Rodale, Editor
$7.97 /year (12 issues)
from:
Prevention
Rodale Press
33 East Minor
Emmaus, PA 18049

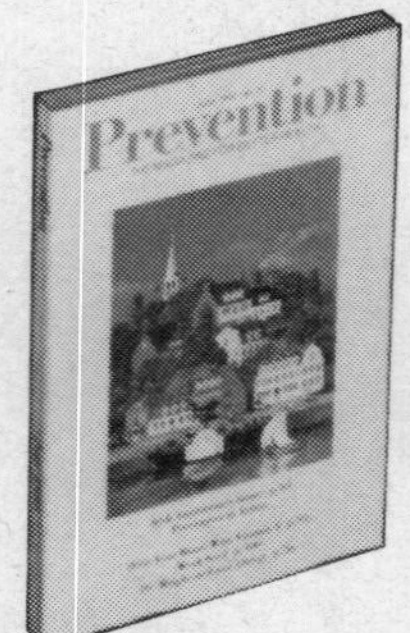

•

Marijuana smokers have abnormal sperm, too — what's left of them. Experiments showed that young men who smoked marijuana at least four times a week for six months had a decrease in sperm numbers in proportion to the amount smoked, falling to almost zero in some very heavy users (**Keep Off the Grass**, Pergamon Press, 1979).

•

After 60 days, all 20 men taking the vitamin C preparation (one gram per day) had impregnated their wives, while none of the men in the control group had. And not only had the vitamin C preparation reversed the sperm-agglutination, but it had also raised sperm *counts* by 54 percent (**Fertility and Sterility**, October, 1979).

•

"PABA protects against the UVB wavelengths of the sun," Dr. Lorincz told **Prevention**. UVB is the form of ultraviolet radiation which causes sunburn and other skin problems to flare. At the same time, PABA permits UVA rays, which are the less dangerous, tanning rays, to travel through to the skin.

The superiority of PABA as a sunscreen has been documented in various laboratory tests. In 1969, Harvard scientists found that, of 24 screening agents tested, a solution of five percent PABA in alcohol provided the best protection against ultraviolet radiation (**New England Journal of Medicine**, June 26, 1969).

•

Principle: You should beware of any doctor who treats by injection.

This is particularly true if the doctor is unwilling to tell you what he is injecting, or if he says you need a "series of shots" to cure your illness.

There are very few adult conditions (with the exception of an acute asthma attack, heart attack, and other real emergencies) which require injections. Diabetics need injected insulin, but they can be taught to give it to themselves at home. Patients with "pernicious anemia" do need monthly B12 injections, but this is the only disease for which B12 is needed — and it is a very rare diagnosis indeed.

Mercurial diuretics are injected drugs which are used in patients with heart failure and fluid retention. These drugs, too, can be self-injected, like insulin, after instruction. *They should not be used as "diet" drugs, however.*

With these and a few other exceptions (cancer chemotherapy, for example, and desensitization shots for various allergies) the use of injected drugs by a doctor in the long-term treatment of adults is cause for suspicion.

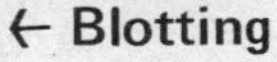

T Fingers on Chin- PLACE Bristles Crevice- BLOT Gums as Shown

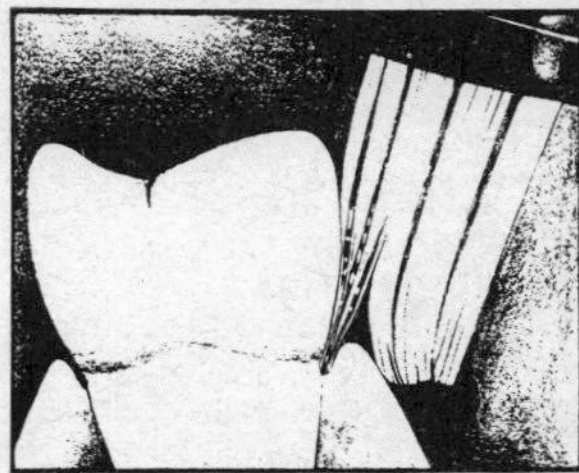

Bristles DON'T MOVE in Crevice

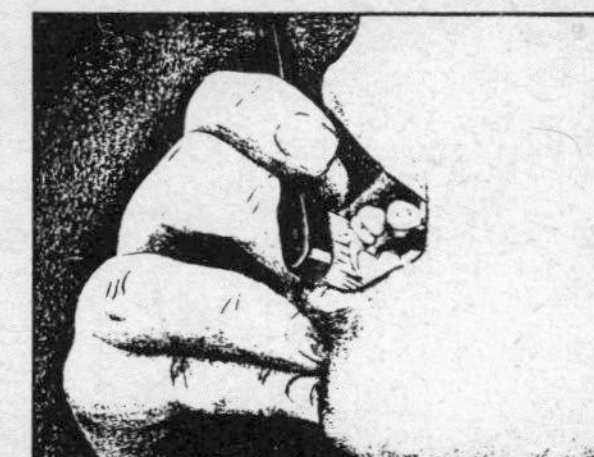

PUT- PLACE- BLOT

SIP- Keep the Brush Damp-dry

← Blotting

Better dental health through a superior new toothbrush (the Periodontal Health Brush) and a superior form of brushing called blotting. Since it requires no toothpaste or rinsing, you can do it anywhere (I blot while commuting). The brush is designed to travel easily in shirt pocket, purse, glove compartment. The secret of the technique is fine bristles on the brush which get the placque-bearing juices out from between the teeth and gums. You sip the brush and move on to the next couple teeth.

There are other items available here — a talking book (cassette plus booklet and two brushes), brushes alone, and a forthcoming little book (called **The Skin of My Teeth** *— not yet available at this writing). The technique is enough different from standard brushing to warrant getting the talk book for now.*

—SB

"If Ya Got 'em . . . Blot 'em!"
(A Guide to the Blotting Method of Mouth Care)
Dr. James H. Shipley
1979; 34 pp. (plus cassette tape and two blotting brushes)
$13.95 postpaid
Blotting Brush
$1.25 each
$6 (set of six)
all from:
Truth Publishing Co.
6641 University Avenue
Middleton, WI 53562

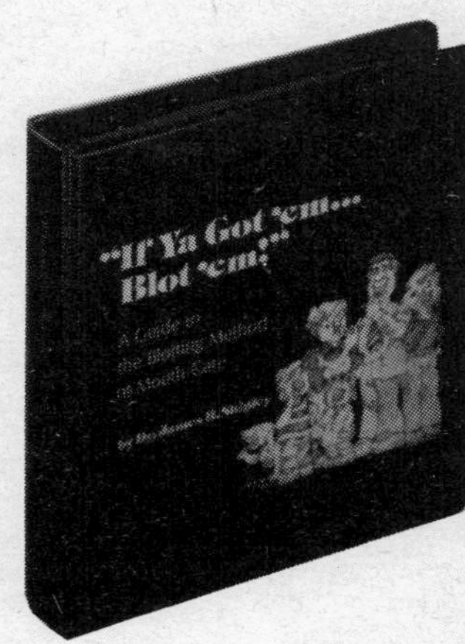

The Tooth Trip

Dr. McGuire's book is an exhilarating and informative book about your teeth, gums and mouth. Exhilarating because of its charming, hip and humorous approach to a traditionally ignored subject. This is the first of the "how to" books about your teeth, and it often seems to turn people on. Several controversial chapters, one on flourides and the other about "the Dentist as a con artist" need to be interpreted cautiously. The cost of the book is reasonable if it has an impact on improving your home care and thereby reducing costly dental bills. The book is indeed, a TRIP.

—Daniel Phillips, D.D.S.
[Suggested by Annie Bradford]

The Tooth Trip
(An Oral Experience)
Thomas McGuire, D.D.S.
1972; 233 pp.
$4.95 postpaid from:
Random House
455 Hahn Road
Westminster, MD 21157
or Whole Earth Household Store

•

Healthy gums do not bleed. If your gums bleed when brushing or eating, they are *not*, I repeat, *not* normal or healthy. No matter what your friends say — your teacher, your family or anyone else. Most people's gums have been bleeding for so long that they think that bleeding is either normal or inevitable. Well, it's damn well not!

•

Used properly, the water pick is the most far-out dental invention since the tooth brush. I have heard dentists say they don't like it, and others who say it harms the gums. Sure, anything can be harmful if abused, and the water pick is no exception.

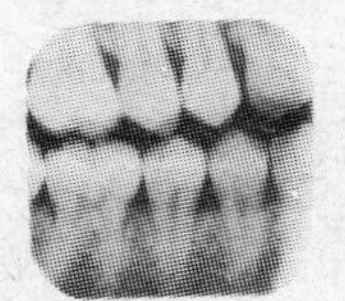

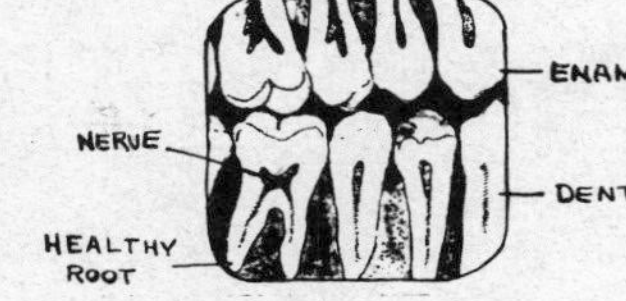

Look on the x-ray for the details noted on the drawing.

2) Bone loss due to gum disease and resulting decay. The white portions of the teeth are fillings.

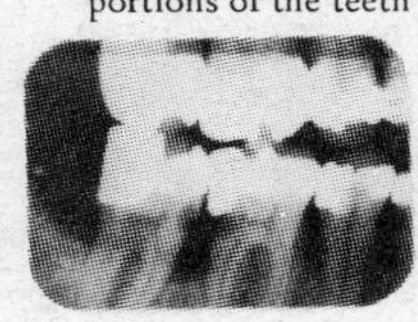

Healing at Home

A course in basic pediatric medicine, by parent, psychologist, pediatrician, and self-care advocate Howell. Includes chapters on "Taking a Health History," "The Physical Examination," "Remedies — Old and New," "Common Illnesses and Injuries," "Nutrition, Relaxation, Exercise," and "Dealing with Medical Professionals."

A warm, readable book. Especially good in guiding parents to help their children develop their own self-care skills.

—Tom Ferguson, M.D.

Healing at Home
(A Guide to Health Care for Children)
Mary Howell
1979; 287 pp.
$5.95 postpaid from:
Beacon Press
Harper and Row
Keystone Industrial Park
Scranton, PA 18512
or Whole Earth Household Store

→

How to "mummy" a child. If you must do something to a child who is frightened or protesting, you will begin by trying to soothe and explain. Young children who don't use language well will not be very comforted by explanations. Generally, the longer the child anticipates in fear, the more panicky s/he will be. In this situation it is kindest to use swift and effective restraint, and get done what you have to get done. (An example: examining a child's eye to be sure that it has not been injured by a scratch or a blow.)

To mummy a child, fold a sheet lengthwise into a strip a little less wide than the child is tall. Lay one end of the strip on a bed or table, lying horizontally. Lay the child on the end of the strip so that her/his shoulders are even with the top edge of the strip and the vertical edge is under the left arm. Pull the long end of the strip up between the right arm and body, then wrap the strip over the right arm and under the back. Bring the strip up between the left arm and body, then over the left arm and under the back. The remaining end of the strip is wrapped around and around the child's body.

With a light child of 35 pounds or less this maneuver can be done quickly by one person. Practice it when you don't need it, when it can be a game for you and the child. With a heavier child who is struggling you may need help with the wrapping. It is very secure and not unpleasant for the child, except for the indignity of being restrained. In general, the indignity of restraints at a hospital or clinic is so much more demeaning to the child that it is a kindness to do whatever needs to be done at home.

"Mummying" a Child ↓

1. Lay the child with right arm at right edge of the sheet.
2. Sheet is drawn over the left arm, under body, and up between body and right arm.
3. Sheet goes around right arm and back under the body.
4. The rest of the sheet is wrapped around the child's body at bottom.

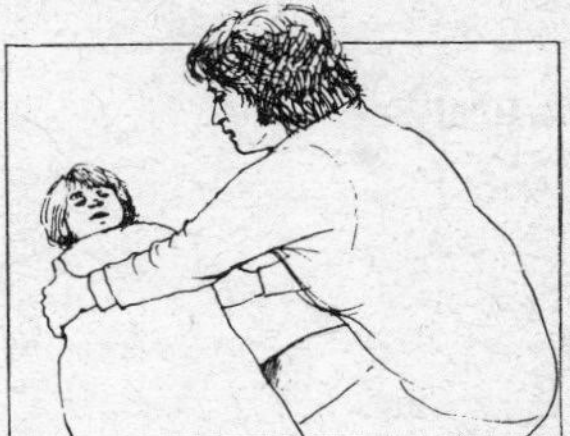

THE RISING SUN
NEIGHBORHOOD NEWSLETTER

Lord Greystoke announced his discovery that black holes are the elephant graveyard — the elephants go off to this whirlpool at the source of the Nile and are whooshed into a black hole in space (different black holes for different elephants) and are recycled and their tusks become stars and their hides become cloudy days and their souls become planets which explains why planets seem to be moving really slow even though they're moving really fast because that's how elephants move. Mostly Greystoke was back to look for Jane, found out that she had been able to get National Geographic to front the money for her to hang out with chimps, something he'd never thought of, but now she couldn't because her station had to be manned by blacks because of political pressures, which he didn't understand because of how he'd always been real nice to the natives. When he found out she was supporting efforts to teach chimps human sign language he was really p.o.'ed — "That's like teaching Shakespear to talk like a sociology professor — you and me knew what they were saying all the time, didn't we, Janie?" But she talks different now too, she knows how to get grants, and he was last seen heading for the source of the Nile, naked as an elephant.

In his prepared statement, he had said, "You guys keep shooting the elephants instead of letting them go off to die, you gonna be further up shit crik than you ever dreamed possible. Elephants do a lot after they leave here, not just being stars, like anything good that happens against the odds, half the time it's an elephant at work.* Like you think there ain't been a nuclear war because Brezhnev and Nixon were nice guys, cause Jerry Ford was smart maybe? There's two elephants out in Andromeda Galaxy (M31/ 21 and 43 on your star map) been working their asses off to keep the missiles in their silos but they've been dead a long time and they're tired. They need help and shooting bunches of elephants to save the corn crop or resell them in pieces in the back of *The New Yorker* sure as hell ain't the way they're gonna get help so watch out is about all I got to say, and I don't expect you to listen."

*The rest of the time it's chipmunks or good intentions. —Ed.

Just in Case

At no time is the difference between being part of the problem and part of the solution more acute than in an emergency. This book aids solution — your own and thereby everybody's. Both for cost and effectiveness it's a big improvement over insurance. (Might take a little more work — reading and heeding — but it's exciting reading.) —SB

Just in Case
(Everyone's Guide to Disaster Self-Help)
John Moir
1980; 200 pp.

$4.95 postpaid from:
Chronicle Books
870 Market Street
San Francisco, CA 94102
or Whole Earth Household Store

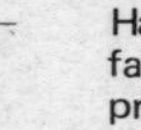

•

Having the proper equipment on hand is often a decisive factor in an emergency. There is no better time than the present to invest in the necessary equipment. While no one needs every item mentioned in this book, there are a few to which special consideration should be given. The eight most important items to have are:

1. Flashlight
2. Battery-operated radio
3. Fire extinguisher
4. Smoke detector
5. Emergency food and water
6. Water purification supplies
7. First aid kit
8. First aid manual

•

General Preparations for a Disaster

Regardless of where you live or what type of disaster you may encounter, there are some standard preparations you can make. The nine most important are:

1. Post a list of emergency numbers near your phone.
2. Fill out an Emergency Information Card and carry it in your wallet.
3. Locate your utility shutoff valves and switches.
4. Plan where to go in case of an evacuation.
5. If you have school-age children, be familiar with your school district's emergency plans.
6. Have a fire escape for your home.
7. Take a first aid class.
8. Keep your typhoid and tetanus immunizations up to date.
9. Keep this book in an accessible location

•

When making an emergency call, force yourself to speak calmly and slowly. Give the following information in this order:

1. State that there is an emergency and briefly describe what it is.
2. Give the telephone number you're calling from, your location, the nearest crossroad if you know it, and your name.
3. Provide any information that dispatcher asks you for.
4. Most importantly — do NOT hang up until the dispatcher tells you to. That way you can be certain he or she has all the needed information.

Emergency Medical Guide

Henderson's **Emergency Medical Guide** *is a useful book. including illustrated sections on bandaging techniques, mouth-to-mouth resuscitation, injuries to extremities, poisoning, snake bites, emergencies of infancy and childhood, and home care of the ill. Emphasis is placed on the prevention of accidents and disease. Some situations are covered which are not generally considered emergencies (except by the patient) such as painful menstruation. A chapter on normal human anatomy and physiology is included in order to make the rest of the book more intelligible to those giving first aid.*
—Eugene Schoenfeld, M.D.

Emergency Medical Guide
John Henderson, M.D.
1963, 1978; 556 pp.

$4.95 postpaid from:
McGraw-Hill Company
Princeton Road
Hightstown, NJ 08520
or Whole Earth Household Store

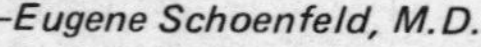

•

EPILEPSY

It is important to keep the victim of the attack from aspirating or choking on vomited matter, but since most attacks will terminate harmlessly by themselves, regardless of what you do or do not do, just protect the victim from injury and bide your time. When he recovers, do not be unduly sympathetic — you may only embarrass him. Give him a drink of water or tea, protect him from curious onlookers, and be sure that he is well enough to go on his way or that he is taken home. If the condition is more serious, see that he gets to a hospital.

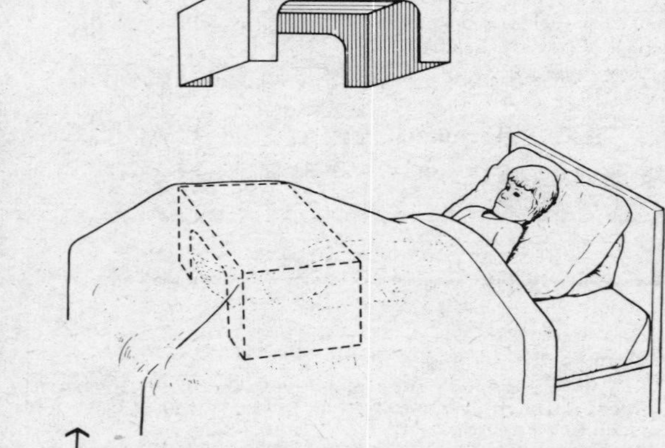

↑ A cradle to keep bedclothes off legs and feet, made from a cardboard carton.

← Procedure for reducing a simple dislocation of a finger, applying pull on each side of the affected joint.

Thumb — Do not attempt to set a dislocation of a thumb. Because of its complicated anatomy, reduction may require a minor operation. Cover the thumb with a protective compress, support the hand in a sling, and seek medical aid.

Heimlich maneuver

To prevent choking to death on something caught in your throat, have a friend embrace you from behind just under your ribs and squeeze really hard and suddenly. That thing flying through the air is what was strangling you.

Ten people a day die in the U.S. choking on food. The procedure invented by Dr. Henry J. Heimlich at The Jewish Hospital, Cincinnati, Ohio, has saved over 100 lives. This booklet explains the details. —SB
[Suggested by Dr. and Mrs. Karl Menninger]

Heimlich maneuver
(Clinical Symposia reprint)
Henry J. Heimlich, et al.
1979; 32 pp.

$1.50 postpaid from:
Ciba Pharmaceutical Co.
P.O. Box 1340
Newark, NJ 07101

↑ Standard Heimlich Self-Save Technique — Victim positions his own hands slightly above the navel and below the rib cage, and presses his fist into his abdomen with a quick upward thrust. Thrust is repeated several times if necessary.

Advanced First Aid

This is the stuff all of us should know, and we should know it before *confronting the friend or stranger who is unconscious or bleeding or broken or gasping. If you know the basics of what to do, you won't be freaked at the time and you won't feel hideous later.*

Get the book. Take some courses. Encourage the people around you to do both. They're the ones who will give you first aid when you need it most. —SB

Advanced First Aid
(& Emergency Care)
The American National Red Cross
1973; 318 pp.

$3 postpaid from:
Doubleday and Company
501 Franklin Avenue
Garden City, NY 11530
or Whole Earth Household Store

•

The use of a tourniquet is dangerous, and the tourniquet should be used only for a severe, life-threatening hemorrhage that cannot be controlled by other means. Tourniquets are used far too often and are rarely required; they should not be used except in critical emergencies when direct pressure on appropriate pressure points fails to stop bleeding. *The decision to apply a tourniquet is in reality a decision to risk sacrifice of a limb in order to save a life. Once a tourniquet is applied, care by a physician is imperative.* (NOTE: A tourniquet should be at least two inches wide.) ↓

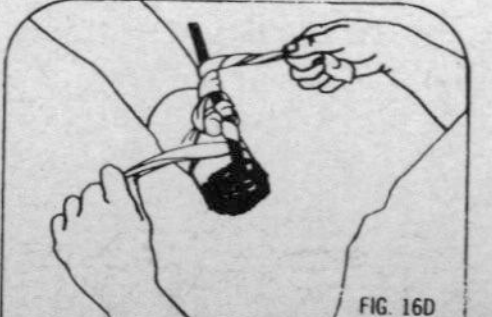

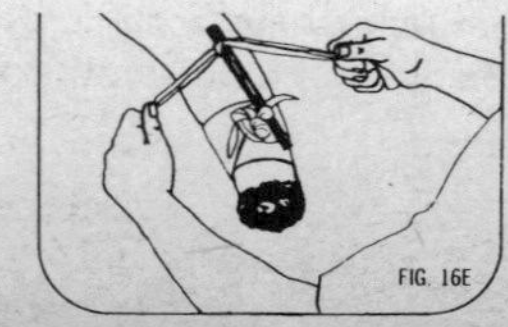

Nursing at Home

What an invaluable book! Here's everything to give you the skill and confidence to replace the expensive hospital room with a healing home, the overworked rotating nurses with a steady personal caring. Equipment, when to call the doctor, what the doctor needs to know, bed handling skills, sanitation, grace with bedpans, nutrition, prevention and treatment for bed sores, taking temperatures, blood pressure, etc. And there's a whole section of instruction for the patient to read.

A real family tool, this. —SB

Nursing at Home
(A Practical Guide to the Care of the Sick and the Invalid in the Home)
Page Parker and Lois N. Dietz, R.N., M.P.H.
1980; 344 pp.

$16.45 postpaid from:
Crown Publishers
One Park Avenue South
New York, NY 10016
or Whole Earth Household Store

•

Never push a patient away from you. Always move or "pull" your patient toward you. ↓

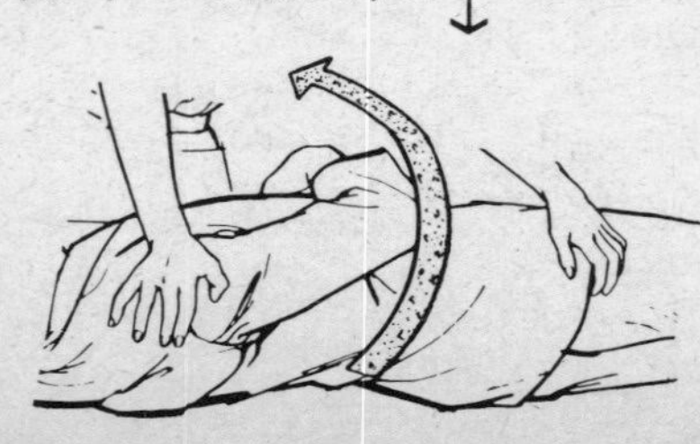

•

If your condition permits it, a very good way to show that you feel better is to return as much as possible to your normal behavior. Go all out, even though some of your relatives and friends, even your nurse, may not approve of the way you dressed and behaved. It may be that their disapproval without being willing to stop you (remember, you still are sick and require some indulging) will add a bit of beneficial spice to your life.

•

Most patients who can be taken home will usually respond better there to nursing care than they will if kept in an acute hospital or a convalescent or long-term hospital. There are several reasons for this. Sick people are more comfortable in their own environment. At home they are not bound by rigid hospital routine. They can relax and be themselves. And, being nursed by a member of the immediate family, or by a close personal friend, usually gives sick people a sense of security.

How much nursing experience you have is of minor importance. If you and your patient are willing, you can learn what is necessary.

→ Trapeze bars give physically disabled patients a practical means for helping themselves in changing position in bed, moving from bed to commode or wheelchair, and so forth. Trapeze bars are also excellent for exercising the hands, wrists, arms, shoulders, and possibly other parts of the body.

Anatomy of an Illness

Peerless reading for the hospital bed. Norman Cousins, long-time editor of **Saturday Review**, *acquired a second fame a couple of years ago with an article in the prestigious* **New England Journal of Medicine** *chronicling his self-inflicted recovery from a crippling and supposedly irreversible ailment (his spine was disintegrating).*

With the aid of his unusual doctor Cousins got the hell out of the hospital, took full responsibility for his own treatment, and began trying stuff — massive vitamin C, massive cheerfulness (the famous home-showing of Marx Brothers and Candid Camera films).

The miracle of cure plus Cousins' intellectual and lively presentation has made this one of the most influential medical documents ever. Patients read it and act differently. So do doctors. So do hospitals. —SB

Anatomy of an Illness
(As Perceived by the Patient: Reflections on Healing and Regeneration)
Norman Cousins
1979; 173 pp.

$9.95 postpaid from:
W.W. Norton & Company
500 Fifth Avenue
New York, NY 10036
or Whole Earth Household Store

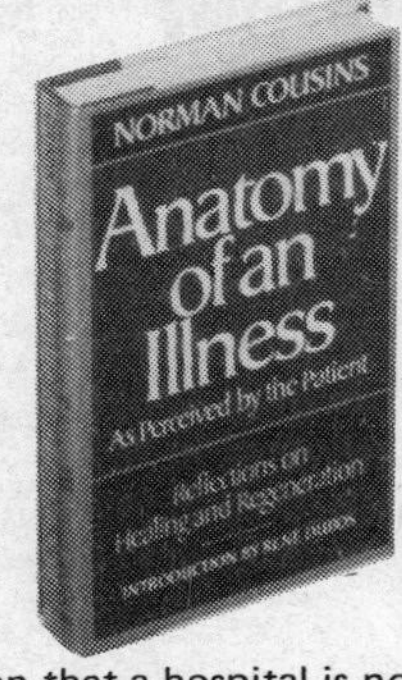

•

I had a fast-growing conviction that a hospital is no place for a person who is seriously ill. The surprising lack of respect for basic sanitation; the rapidity with which staphylococci and other pathogenic organisms can run through an entire hospital; the extensive and sometimes promiscuous use of X-ray equipment; the seemingly indiscriminate administration of tranquilizers and powerful painkillers, sometimes more for the convenience of hospital staff in managing patients than for therapeutic needs; and the regularity with which hospital routine takes precedence over the rest requirements of the patient (slumber, when it comes for an ill person, is an uncommon blessing and is not to be wantonly interrupted) — all these and other practices seemed to me to be critical shortcomings of the modern hospital.

•

I made the joyous discovery that ten minutes of genuine belly laughter had an anesthetic effect and would give me at least two hours of pain-free sleep. When the painkilling effect of the laughter wore off, we would switch on the motion-picture projector again, and, not infrequently, it would lead to another pain-free sleep interval. Sometimes, the nurse read to me out of a trove of humor books. Especially useful were E.B. and Katharine White's **Subtreasury of American Humor** and Max Eastman's **The Enjoyment of Laughter**.

The Merck Manual

In 2188 type-packed pages this book covers most of the possible illness and injuries that can occur to human beings. Each difficulty is described, symptoms are discussed and suggested treatments are indicated.

The writing is extremely technical and is designed as a ready reference for practicing nurses and physicians. Unless you are at ease with the unusually colorful language of modern medicine you will need a medical dictionary to fully understand this book.

While a considerable portion of the advice given is sensible and does not require a doctor's presence, much of the book will not be of use to persons who do not have access to medical supplies. This book is not intended in any sense for primitive or simple living conditions; it does not describe alternatives if medical treatment is not available nor does it suggest folk treatments in lieu of hospitalization. However, if you want to understand what is going on when a member of your family or community is seriously ill, this volume can be helpful. There is an excellent index as well as a special section devoted to specific prescriptions and special therapies. The excerpts given below illustrate both the common-sense and the technical aspects of this volume. —James Fadiman

PETIT MAL SEIZURE
Synchronous 3/sec spikes & waves

The Merck Manual
(Of Diagnosis and Therapy)
1899, 1977; 2188 pp.

$9.75 postpaid from:
Merck and Company
P.O. Box 2000
Rahway, NJ 07065
or Whole Earth Household Store

•

HEAT PROSTRATION
(Heat Collapse, Exhaustion, or Syncope)

A syndrome resulting from exposure to excessive heat, characterized by prostration and circulatory collapse.

Etiology

Heat prostration results from failure to adjust to the dilation of the skin blood vessels, a primary response to heat. Alcohol intake, dehydration, excessive sweating, vomiting, and diarrhea increase the probability of its development. Heat prostration may complicate surgery performed in a hot environment.

Symptoms and Signs

The patient is listless, apprehensive, and often semicomatose or unconscious. The skin is ashen, cold, and damp; sweating may be profuse, blood pressure depressed, and peripheral vascular failure evident. Premonitory symptoms — weakness, dizziness, vertigo, headache, nausea, dim or blurred vision, irritability and mild muscular cramps — may precede the attack. The pulse rate is usually under 100; body temperature is normal.

Diagnosis and Prognosis

Heat prostration is differentiated from food or chemical poisoning by the history and rapid response to treatment. It is usually transient, and the prognosis is excellent although death can occur from uncorrected circulatory failure or subsequent hyperpyrexia.

Prophylaxis

Physical exertion with profuse sweating must be avoided by unacclimatized persons. Fluid intake should be sufficient to maintain a urinary volume of at least 1 L/day. Light, loose, well-ventilated clothing is generally advisable, although insulated clothing may be preferable in hot, dry, desert conditions or in enclosures with high wall temperatures (e.g., boilers or kilns). Unacclimatized persons should increase their sodium chloride intake by taking 1 or 2 Gm orally with water q.i.d., especially in hot dry environments.

Treatment

The patient should be placed in a recumbent position, in a cool environment, with clothing loosened. Cool water may be given orally. Management of acute circulatory failure is the essential problem. Patients in profound collapse should be given isotonic saline solution 1500 ml IV slowly and cautiously to avoid overloading an already embarrassed circulation. Cardiac stimulants (e.g., epinephrine 1:1000, 0.3 to 1 ml s.c.), plasma volume expanders (e.g., albumin, dextran), and O_2 may be given. Sodium bicarbonate is contraindicated.

Notes on Nursing

From home care to special ward, this guide to "think how to nurse" by Florence Nightingale, first published in 1859, is still the finest book on nursing, according to Dr. Richard Lamerton of St. Joseph's Hospice in London. It articulates the basics of bedside care in a way no advance of technical medicine has been able to improve on. —SB
[Suggested by Richard Lamerton]

Notes on Nursing
(What it is, and what it is not)
Florence Nightingale
1859, 1969; 140 pp.

$3 postpaid from:
Doubleday and Company
180 Varick Street
New York, NY 10014
or Whole Earth Household Store

•

I knew a very clever physician, of large dispensary and hospital practice, who invariably began his examination of each patient with "Put your finger where you be bad." That man would never waste his time with collecting inaccurate information from nurse or patient. Leading questions always collect inaccurate information.

In watching diseases, both in private houses and in public hospitals, the thing which strikes the experienced observer most forcibly is this, that the symptoms or the sufferings generally considered to be inevitable and incident to the disease are very often not symptoms of the disease at all, but of something quite different — of the want of fresh air, or of light, or of warmth, or of quiet, or of cleanliness, or of punctuality and care in the administration of diet, of each or of all of these.

•

One hint I would give to all who attend or visit the sick, to all who have to pronounce an opinion upon sickness or its progress. Come back and look at your patient *after* he has had an hour's animated conversation with you. It is the best test of his real state we know.

•

There is no better society than babies and sick people for one another.

Getting Well Again

This is the famous "Simonton imaging technique" that the families and friends of cancer patients are urgently telling each other about. Since many patients are in no shape to read, the Simontons offer an excellent set of cassettes, available from: Cancer Counseling and Research Center, 1300 Summit Avenue — Suite 710, Fort Worth, Texas 76102. Phone: (817) 335-4823. —SB

Getting Well Again
(A Step-by-Step, Self-Help Guide to Overcoming Cancer for Patients and Their Families)
O. Carl Simonton, M.D., Stephanie Matthews-Simonton, James Creighton
1978; 268 pp.

$10.20 postpaid from:
J.P. Tarcher
9110 Sunset Boulevard
Suite 212
Los Angeles, CA 90069
or Whole Earth Household Store

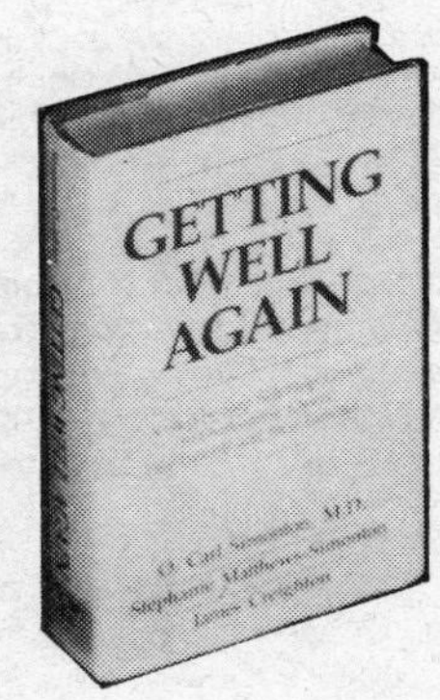

- Picture your body's own white blood cells coming into the area where the cancer is, recognizing the abnormal cells, and destroying them. There is a vast army of white blood cells. They are very strong and aggressive. They are also very smart. There is no contest between them and the cancer cells; they will win the battle.
- Picture the cancer shrinking. See the dead cells being carried away by the white blood cells and being flushed from your body through the liver and kidneys and eliminated in the urine and the stool. This is your expectancy of what you want to happen. Continue to see the cancer shrinking, until it is all gone. See yourself having more energy and a better appetite and being able to feel comfortable and loved in your family as the cancer shrinks and finally disappears.
- If you are experiencing pain anywhere in your body, picture the army of white blood cells flowing into that area and soothing the pain. Whatever the problem, give your body the command to heal itself. Visualize your body becoming well.
- Imagine yourself well, free of disease, full of energy.

Betty's Initial Imagery, Showing Anger and, Hostility.

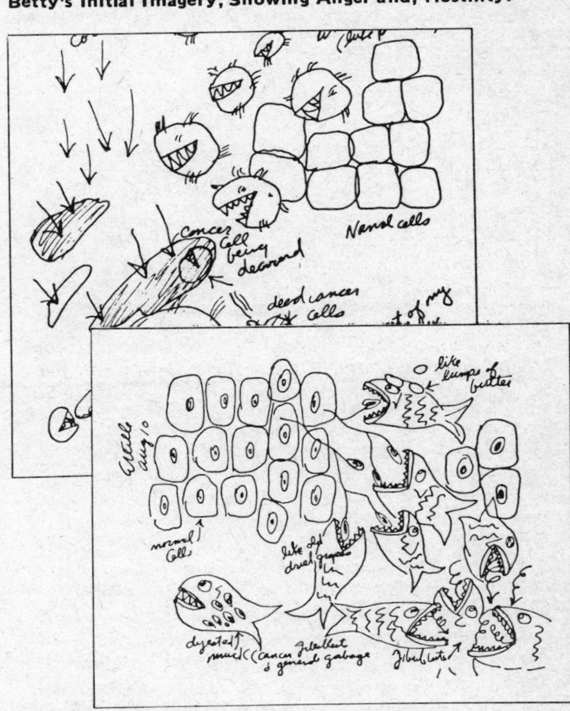

Betty's Imagery Six Months Later

THE RISING SUN
NEIGHBORHOOD NEWSLETTER

Florence Nightingale was named Florence because she was conceived in Florence, Italy, and it wasn't a person's name before that and then she became famous and many people were named that.

Where There Is No Doctor

A pioneering self-care handbook based on practices developed by the author and co-workers over the past sixteen years — while organizing a self-care health network in a remote, doctorless area of rural Mexico. Every page is crammed with useful basic information, some of it specific to the problems of underdeveloped countries, most of use to anyone. Includes a fine chapter on being a lay health worker. Spanish edition also available.
—Tom Ferguson, M.D.

*This is an amazingly fine book. Perfectly organized, highly graphic, concise, honest, shocking at times, really comprehensive. As Henderson (***Emergency Medical Guide,** *p. 324) is the book to have around the house, this is the one to have when you live or are traveling out of immediate reach of ambulances.* —SB

Where There Is No Doctor
(A Village Health Care Handbook)
David Werner
1977; 447 pp.
$7.50 postpaid

Donde No Hay Doctor
(Spanish Edition)
David Werner
1973, 1977; 299 pp.
$7.50 postpaid

both from:
The Hesperian Foundation
P.O. Box 1692
Palo Alto, CA 94302

or Whole Earth Household Store
(English edition only)

SKIN PROBLEMS — A Guide to Identification

IF THE SKIN HAS:	AND LOOKS LIKE:	YOU MAY HAVE:	SEE PAGE:
small or pimple-like sores	Tiny bumps or sores with much itching—first between fingers, on the wrists, or the waist.	scabies	199
	Pimples or sores with pus or inflammation, often from scratching insect bites. May cause swollen lymph nodes.	infection from bacteria	201
	Irregular, spreading sores with shiny, yellow crusts.	impetigo (bacterial infection)	202
	Pimples on young people's faces, sometimes chest and back, often with small heads of pus.	acne, pimples, blackheads	211
	A sore on the genitals, without itching or pain.	syphilis venereal lymphogranuloma	237 238

Deep Wounds in the Abdomen

Any wound that goes into the belly or gut is dangerous. **Seek medical help immediately.** But in the meantime:

Cover the wound with a clean bandage.

If the guts are partly outside the wound, cover them with a clean cloth soaked in lightly salted, boiled water. Do not try to push the guts back in.

If the wounded person is in shock, raise his feet higher than his head.

Give absolutely nothing by mouth: no food, no drink, not even water.

If the wounded person is thirsty, let him suck on a piece of cloth soaked in water.

Treatment for cough:

1. **To loosen mucus** and ease any kind of cough, **drink lots of water.** This works better than any medicine. (However, potassium iodide may help. See page 370.)

Also **breathe hot water vapors.** Sit on a chair with a bucket of very hot water at your feet. Place a sheet over your head and cover the bucket to catch the vapors as they rise. Breathe the vapors deeply for 15 minutes. Repeat several times a day. Some people like to add mint or eucalyptus leaves or *Vaporub*, but hot water works just as well alone.

- Aspirin and hot soaks (p. 195) help calm most kinds of back pain.
- For low back pain that comes from lifting or straining, quick relief can sometimes be brought like this:

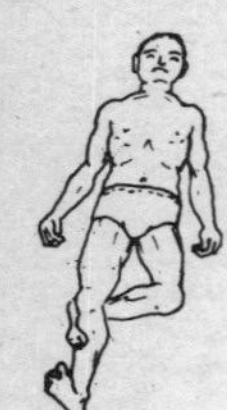

Have the person lie with one foot tucked under his knee.

Then, holding this shoulder down,

forcefully push this knee over so as to twist the back.

Do this first on one side and then the other.

IF YOU DO NOT HAVE A TOOTHBRUSH:

Use the twig of a tree, like this:

Sharpen this end to clean between the teeth.

Chew on this end and use the fibers as a brush.

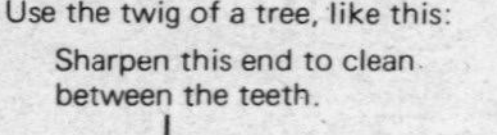

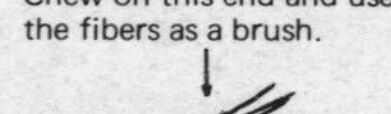

14 True Words on Health and Malpractice Insurance

You will stay healthier without health insurance.

Doctors give better care without malpractice insurance. —SB

The Essential Guide to Prescription Drugs

The most detailed available consumer's encyclopedia on the 200 + most commonly prescribed drugs — mode of action, side-effects, contra-indications, time required for benefit, recommended follow-up examinations, interactions with other drugs, and — especially hard to find — use during pregnancy and breastfeeding. No opinions on controversies here, just the facts.
—Tom Ferguson, M.D.

The Essential Guide to Prescription Drugs
(What You Need to Know for Safe Drug Use)
James W. Long, M.D.
1977; 752 pp.
$8.95 postpaid from:
Harper and Row
Keystone Industrial Park
Scranton, PA 18512
or Whole Earth Household Store

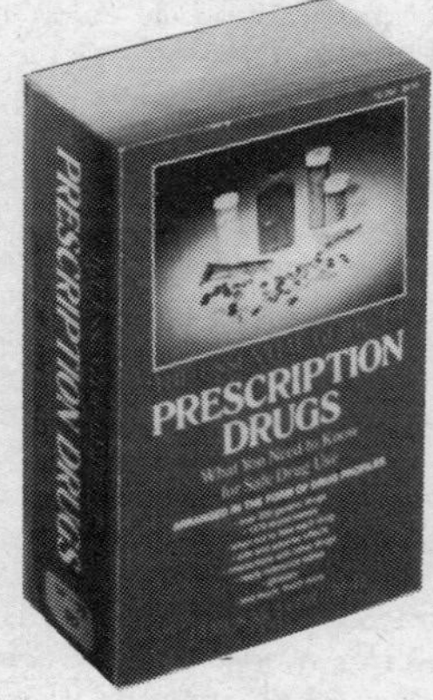

•

Aspirin — Use During Pregnancy — Studies indicate that the regular use of salicylates during pregnancy is often detrimental to the health of the mother and to the welfare of the infant. Excessive use of salicylate drugs (aspirin) can cause anemia, hemorrhage before and after delivery, and an increased incidence of still births. It is advisable to limit the use of aspirin during pregnancy to small doses and to brief periods of time.

Aspirin — Use in Breastfeeding — This drug is present in milk and may cause adverse effects in the nursing infant. It is advisable to avoid use if nursing.

Health for the Whole Person

Whew. A measure of how wide and deep holistic medicine has reached in the last couple years is this great big attempt to surround the field. Family therapy, medical self-care, environmental toxins, biofeedback, hypnosis, meditation, psychic healing, exercise, chiropractic, homeopathy, nutrition, vitamins, music and color, childbirth, dentistry, hospice, and sundry overviews. Each subject has a substantial essay followed by a richly annotated bibliography. I'd say the attempt succeeds.

If you've had it with conventional hospitals and conventional docs, shop here. —SB

Health for the Whole Person
(The Complete Guide to Holistic Medicine)
Arthur C. Hastings, James Fadiman, James S. Gordon, Editors
1980; 529 pp.
$12.95 postpaid from:
Westview Press
5500 Central Avenue
Boulder, CO 80301
or Whole Earth Household Store

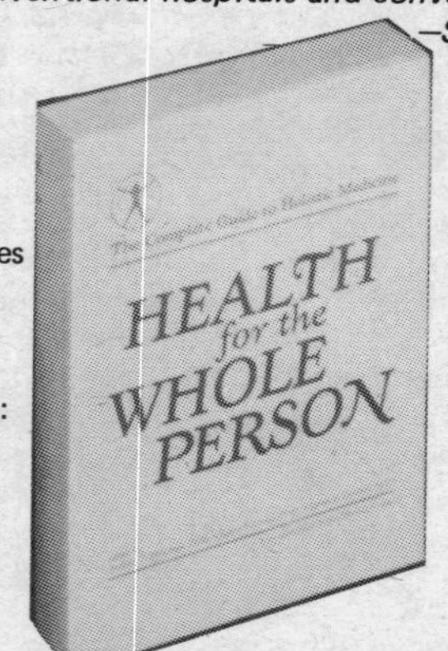

•

A person who has suffered a traumatic injury or who is critically ill can be considered to be in a spontaneous hypnotic state. Frightened people need no formal induction to hypnosis; they are already in the hypnotic state when we see them. This makes them wonderfully responsive to helpful suggestion, even though they may appear apathetic or even unconscious.

These principles may be helpful in using this state for the benefit of the patient (Cheek, 1969):

- Learn to recognize and enhance the signs of hypnotic behavior in the critically ill.
- Use all your power to communicate hope and optimism; do it sincerely because phony reassurance is easily recognized by the critically ill.
- Collect your thoughts and marshal a plan of action; don't be rushed. Give some instructions to bystanders before touching or speaking to the patient. This allows time to regain your poise.
- Tell the patient what has happened and that he will be all right. Outline what you are doing and what your reason for doing it is. Tell what your plan is for him tomorrow and in the future. With unconscious people, even if they show no pupilar reflex to light, give instruction and promises of a future. Congratulate the person for being so relaxed. Tell him specifically how long you expect him to remain relaxed before awakening with feelings of hunger or thoughts of food. Give instructions for the body to relax and for it to deal as necessary with physical needs and recovery.
- Give medication for pain if possible. Tell the patient what you are giving and why. This communicates constructive action.
- Get a conscious patient to talk about work, hobbies, family, and experiences if he is able to talk. This directs the mind to concern itself with times and places where pain and fear did not exist.

•

Kuntzleman, C.T., and *Consumer Guide* Editors. **Rating the Exercises.** New York: Penguin, 1980.

Charles Kuntzleman is a former national director of YMCA athletic programs, including the popular and effective Fitness Finders Program. He is the author of several other fitness books and has experience in designing specific physical regimes for varied groups throughout the United States. I worked with him one summer and enjoyed his approaches and techniques in person as much as I enjoyed his books.

In this book, possibly his best, Dr. Kuntzleman rates every major exercise program from aerobics to yoga. He identifies fuzzy thinking, transparent claims, ripoff approaches, poor research, and old wives' tales. His most important criterion for effectiveness is whether an exercise provides adequate cardiovascular effects. Steamrooms, saunas, hot tubs, and other passive devices are enjoyable but unproductive for strengthening the heart, lungs, and major muscle groups; for decreasing body weight; or for increasing the ratio of lean muscle to fat content. The book, which devotes an entire chapter to discussing the utility of health spas and other health and fitness enterprises, is especially valuable as a reference document.

Activated charcoal

Certain (not all) water supplies contain chlorinated hydrocarbons — a carcinogen. They are formed when your water supply company chlorinates your water and the water contains large amounts of organic compounds like petroleum. In New Orleans, the most downstream city on the Mississippi, chlorination has increased cancer rates because of all the petroleum products dumped into the river upstream. Poughkeepsie, New York suffers the same problem because of upstream dumping. Everyone in these cities (and others) should run their drinking water through activated charcoal. This is the oldest and best filter of chlorinated hydrocarbons. Distillation does not work! Anyone who suspects high amounts of chloroform or other carcinogens in their water supply should force their water supplier to test for all the possibilities. No one knows "safe" amounts. Walnut Acres provides high quality activated charcoal and good instructions. Slightly too expensive. —Peter Warshall

Granulated Activated Carbon
$2/lb. (Instructions included) from:
Walnut Acres
Penns Creek, PA 17862

NRTA—AARP Pharmacy

Biggest and best source for mail order drugs. Offers both prescription and non-prescription items at a great discount. Especially good for vitamins if you buy the NRTA-AARP Formula that's equivalent to nationally advertised brands. Also has a good selection of elastic stockings and hearing aid batteries.

They say their service is only for members of the National Retired Teacher's Association-American Association of Retired People. The scrupulous among us will join (they don't check) for an annual fee of $4. Well worth it for a confirmed pill popper. You don't have to be old, after all, to be retired.

Interestingly enough, I've been led to believe by an official of NRTA-AARP that, despite the really good discount given, the co-op pharmacy is a real money-maker for the organization; so don't feel like you're robbing a bunch of old people by taking advantage of this. Other good things: they will give you credit with no delay for credit clearance and there are no postal charges.
—James Thorsen

NRTA-AARP
Catalog

free from:
NRTA-AARP Pharmacy
1224 24th Street, NW
Washington, DC 20037

The Family Circle Guide to Self-Help

Self-help groups provide a low-cost, low-technology, consumer-intensive alternative to expensive, high-technology, expert-intensive models of providing human therapy and services. The self-help movement is large (500,000 groups, 5 million members in the U.S.) and largely invisible.

This inexpensive paperback is a readable, helpful introduction to the theory and practice of self-help groups. Includes listings of 450 self-help groups in the U.S. and Canada. —*Tom Ferguson, M.D.*

The Family Circle Guide to Self-Help
Glen Evans
1979; 240 pp.
$2.25 postpaid from:
Ballantine Books
455 Hahn Road
Westminster, MD 21157
or Whole Earth Household Store

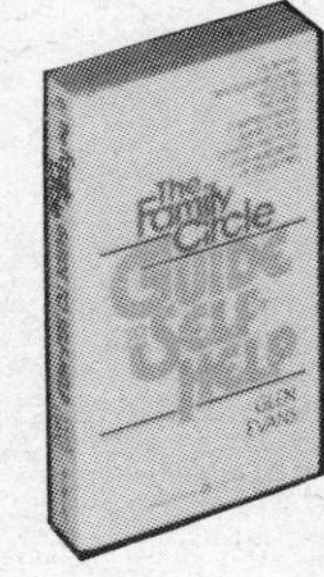

•

I have seen self-help group members reach out to neurotics, gamblers, alcoholics, drug abusers, phobics, ex-convicts, and child abusers, to name a few, and lead them out of their enormous emotional anguish and overwhelming stress and guilt. Many of these people had been unable to deal with the bureaucracies of programs sponsored by professional agencies. Others had been tragically ignored, stigmatized, and ridiculed for years. It was a revelation to me to see how they responded to people in self-help groups who had been "down the line," who shared their anxieties and concerns with them and offered encouragement and support.

•

As one group of self-helpers put it (the Integrity Groups), "You alone can do it, but you can't do it alone."

How to Live with Schizophrenia

Here is the book that spells out the idea and practice of treating schizophrenia with a recently developed medication, nicotinamide — vitamin B-3 — in massive doses. It's not universally successful, but for those it works on it is a miracle cure. As it's a matter of restoring a chemical balance, it may take weeks or months to take effect, and the patient will probably need it for life, as a diabetic does insulin. The drug is cheap. For the sufferer it would be cheap at any price. —*SB*

How to Live with Schizophrenia
Abram Hoffer and Humphry Osmond
1978, 177 pp.
$5.95 postpaid from:
University Books
120 Enterprise Avenue
Secaucus, NJ 07094
or Whole Earth Household Store

•

Treatment of Schizophrenia

Perhaps you have been depressed for the past few months. For no good reason that you can think of you suddenly burst into tears, or you have moments of panic you can't explain. Your work no longer interests you. You are fatigued and miserable.

At the same time you may be having frightening experiences, such as seeing flashing lights, noticing changes in people's faces, or feeling peculiar changes in your body. Something is happening to you and no one has been able or willing to tell you what it is.

Perhaps you are now taking tranquilizers and occupational therapy at a clinic? You are possibly making regular visits to your psychiatrist for deep therapy to "root out the source of your troubles buried in your psyche." Although you are willing to cooperate with your doctor to the best of your ability, you are frightened because you are not feeling any better, and you are convinced that you never will.

What can you do now? Where can you go for help?

Help is available. It is up to you to see that you get that help. We will describe here a treatment program for schizophrenia which we have developed and found effective in our own work, and which we think is the best available. We will furthermore examine what part other members of the treatment team — hospitals, nurses, family, community, and yourself — must play in this effort. For effective treatment of schizophrenia requires all the resources that can be made available to you . . .

Madness Network News
Madness Network News Reader

I've never gone crazy enough at the right time for somebody to grab my ass, lock me up, and pump me full of social drugs and electricity, so that I might be a milder member of modern American culture. Thousands of folks are sleeping behind bars tonight because they got a little weird once too often, or let their mind shine through a little too strongly at the wrong time, or pushed a relative just a little too far.

Madness Network News Reader *is a digest (1974) of the* **Madness Network News,** *and represents the collected efforts of a few folks who are trying "to put an end to the degrading and alienating practices of the psychiatric system and to create instead a process that validates human beings and their right to express themselves."* **MNN** *is a tool in that direction. The publications are full of scary things, funny things, crazy things, revolutionary things, all having something to do with the overthrow of the mind control industry.* —*J.D. Smith*

Madness Network News
$5/6 issues from:
Madness Network News
P.O. Box 684
San Francisco, CA 94101

Madness Network News Reader
Sherry Hirsch, et al., Editors
1974; 192 pp.
$7.29 postpaid from:
Glide Publications
330 Ellis Street
San Francisco, CA 94102
or Whole Earth Household Store

•

Lonely, hell!
I feel crowded.

•

Atwake we keep our dreams of sleep
because we see life's seems are cheap.

•

Sometimes Catatonia
sits with me for hours.

I do not speak to her.
She does not speak to me.

We communicate this way.

•

A jolt of power jars you into the darkness of temporary death. It's a darkness you can't see or perceive. It's the equivalent of death, except you wake up again. You wake up upstairs in your cell and they feed you breakfast. It destroys some of the cells in your brain and erases your treasured memory. The war-criminal doctor gives you not one of these but 15, and one guy got 100!

It completely shuts off the light in your brain to temporary darkness that feels like it lasts one day, but actually lasts about 20 minutes. It's horror!!

After my treatment, given to me because I punched an attendant, I couldn't even remember what my mother looked like and one patient couldn't even remember the names of his kids. One patient asked me if he "died" in the shock treatment room. One patient said he got a "little glimpse of eternity and there's nothing out there." One girl after her treatment said, "Where's my brains at, where's my brains at?" Yes, girls get shock treatments, too. Once, in Montana a patient DIED on the table, and never got up.

I lost my treasured memory, and much of my mental ability. I used to be good at mathematics, now I am just mediocre. I used to be the best Bridge player at the hospital, now a retarded patient plays better. I used to be able to memorize all the cards in a Pinochle game, now I just coast through. I used to be good at Art, now I quit because I lost the knack. Now I am always forgetting things and I used to have a good memory. I'm stopped at getting choice jobs and professions. (The treatments give you Epilepsy, too.)

And every doctor applying electricity to the flesh knows it harms. His sins are seen by the Skies, and *by himself.* He's worse than an Auschwitz fanatic.

•

What are the real issues? "I don't like what you are doing, stop it . . . and this is what I'm going to do if you don't." If more people said that and meant it then there would be less need for psychiatric hospitals to do other people's dirty work. —**Madness Network News Reader**

You Are Not Alone

A tough-minded primer of emotional problems and mental health, and guide to seeking professional psychological help. Part One leads you through methods of treatment and diagnostic categories while at the same time questioning whether some diagnoses (e.g., schizophrenia) serve any useful purpose. Part Two is a consumer's guide to mental health resources likely to be available in your community, and includes a useful chapter on paying for such services. Part Three, entitled "Outrage — And How to Use It," is a guide to making the mental health establishment meet your needs.

Park is the mother of an autistic child. She's been there. Park and Shapiro's book is a model consumer's guide — crammed full of relentlessly practical information and a wealth of well-chosen resources. —*Tom Ferguson, M.D.*

You Are Not Alone
(A comprehensive guide for people who want reliable information about emotional problems, mental illness, and how to get professional help)
Clara Claiborne Park and Leon N. Shapiro, M.D.
1976; 496 pp.
$6.95 postpaid from:
Little, Brown and Co.
200 West Street
Waltham, MA 02154
or Whole Earth Household Store

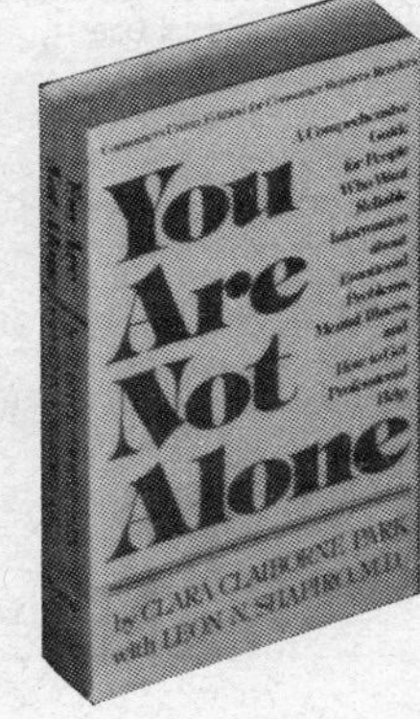

•

The professional's first allegiance is to his patient. The professional's trust is something that relatives have to earn. How can you earn it then? You don't do it as you might elsewhere, by sounding knowledgeable, even if you are. Mental health professionals are more interested in who you are than in what you know. If you establish that you're open, reasonable, and not too full of yourself, they'll be more ready to accept you on their turf. Avoid fancy psychiatric terms, at least at first, even if you've read them in this book. It's surprising how well you can make out in plain English. Though psychiatric professionals use those words continually, they don't seem to like them nearly as well when they hear them from us.

Sane Asylum

The spectacular success of John Maher's Delancey Street, the place of turnaround for social wreckage such as cons, junkies, hookers in San Francisco, is not just reported but made understandable — maybe even replicable — in this riveting book. Read it for dialogue, read it for method. —*SB*

Sane Asylum
(Inside the Delancey Street Foundation)
Charles Hampden-Turner
1976; 291 pp.
$10 postpaid from:
San Francisco Book Company
2311 Fillmore Street
San Francisco, CA 94115

•

On the issue of radicalism versus traditionalism, John has grasped important truths from Martin Luther King and Cesar Chavez. As you try to change a social system, you must calm it *as* you change it, or it will go into shock and you will lose all control. Accordingly, you must especially emphasize tradition and continuity with the past in order to create a sense of movement *from* that past into the future.

•

"Tell me, Your Lordship, you construct theories in which even we may have a place?"

"Yes."

"You make connections between distantly related events?"

"When I can."

"And from this activity you get pleasure — even a few highs?"

"Why, yes I do!" It feels so good to be understood that I'm almost gushing.

"See!" he turns to the others in triumph. "Mad! *Absolutely* mad. Answers tangentially, shuts himself away and theorizes, makes connections, gets high: a theory addict! He's one of us. Welcome to the club!"

THE RISING SUN
NEIGHBORHOOD NEWSLETTER

"I was in the Navy and all you can do on a ship is play poker in different places."

Alcoholism

by a member of Alcoholics Anonymous

TWENTY QUESTIONS

Are You an Alcoholic?

To answer this question, ask yourself the following questions and answer them as honestly as you can.

1. Do you lose time from work due to drinking?
2. Is drinking making your home life unhappy?
3. Do you drink because you are shy with other people?
4. Is drinking affecting your reputation?
5. Have you ever felt remorse after drinking?
6. Have you gotten into financial difficulties as a result of drinking?
7. Do you turn to lower companions and an inferior environment when drinking?
8. Does your drinking make you careless of your family's welfare?
9. Has your ambition decreased since drinking?
10. Do you crave a drink at a definite time daily?
11. Do you want a drink the next morning?
12. Does drinking cause you to have difficulty in sleeping?
13. Has your efficiency decreased since drinking?
14. Is drinking jeopardizing your job or business?
15. Do you drink to escape from worries or troubles?
16. Do you drink alone?
17. Have you ever had a complete loss of memory as a result of drinking?
18. Has your physician ever treated you for drinking?
19. Do you drink to build up your self-confidence?
20. Have you ever been to a hospital or institution on account of drinking?

If you have answered YES to any **one** of the questions, there is a definite warning that **you may be an alcoholic.**

If you have answered YES to any **two**, the chances are that you **are an alcoholic.**

If you have answered YES to **three or more, you are definitely an alcoholic.**

Reprinted with permission of A.A. World Services, Inc.

ABOUT FIVE YEARS BEFORE I made it to AA, I answered fourteen of those questions yes. Because I didn't relate drinking to the damage that was already underway, I decided that the test must be bullshit. Denial, they tell me, is characteristic of alcoholics.

I had a great life. I didn't enjoy it much. I had *reasons* to drink. (Only alcoholics need reasons to drink, they tell me.) I drank because everyone else did. I drank because I was sensitive.

I was depressed, hung over, and incapacitated a lot. (Not surprising, considering that alcohol is a depressant, and toxic.) After another couple of years of prodigious daily drinking, I began to think that I might have a drinking problem after all.

Somebody told me that if I could quit drinking for two weeks without getting DT's, I wasn't an alcoholic. I quit for exactly two weeks, saw no snakes, and started drinking again. (Later, I learned that not drinking doesn't equal sobriety. Some alcoholics can make it for a year without a drink on a white-knuckle basis, but it's not much fun.)

By this time, my 24-year-old heart was beating erratically, my digestion was so screwed up that I took belladonna regularly, and the perpetual hangover required aspirin daily. I usually drank at lunch, frequently had a few on the way home, and always had wine with dinner. Very high class. I concluded many festive evenings by heaving my guts. Very sexy. I thought this was all normal. (I heard one AA say, "I thought everybody over thirty vomited blood in the morning.") I was not a happy lush. I was paranoid and deeply pessimistic. I had no idea that these feelings were connected with my drinking.

LIFE *WITHOUT* ALCOHOL HAD become inconceivable, but I sure wished I could drink less. I rarely intended to get drunk. I generally did, and expended a lot of energy on trying to seem sober.

Another friend, a psychologist working with alcoholics, told me that personality changes and blackouts (memory losses while drinking) are considered definitive symptoms of alcoholism. Although I usually felt that I could be a lot nicer person than I was, I didn't understand what she meant by personality changes . . .

. . . Until I entered a steady relationship with a real prince. It was bliss, marred only by our getting drunk together every night, and my sadistic verbal assaults on his character, his aspirations, and his friends and relations. More than once I made him cry. I was remorseful by midnight and self-justifying by noon. And I really couldn't stop.

He put up with this for a while (alcoholism in a relationship requires teamwork). But the mind-fucking got old fast, and he told me so. By now I figured I was a moral failure, unable to stop hurting him — and myself — so badly; and, by no coincidence, unable to control my drinking. Things had got hopeless enough for me to admit my alcoholism. It was obvious that I couldn't quit drinking by myself, and obvious that if I continued to drink my health, my psyche and my life were guaranteed to deteriorate till I died.

For some reason, Ann Landers' good advice probably, I believed that Alcoholics Anonymous was how to quit drinking. (Most cities of any size list AA in their telephone directories and AA's General Service Office, Box 459 Grand Central Station, New York, NY 10017, will help alcoholics in remoter places by mail.) So. I called Alcoholics Anonymous, and found that there was a meeting in my neighborhood that night. I went.

That was a year and a half ago. With the help of AA, I haven't taken a drink since. Because I consider my sobriety to be a daily reprieve from a deadly progression, I go to at least a couple of AA meetings every week, and I try not to drink between meetings no matter what.

"Forever non-professional", AA is pure mutual aid. AA meetings are endlessly interesting and usually funny while providing ongoing discussion of the homely business of facing life without booze.

THE GENERAL IDEA IS TO CHOOSE life. Unchecked, alcoholism is fatal. Your average drinking alcoholic lives about fifty-five years. That's short because alcoholism has destructive effects on the liver, the pancreas, the gut, the brain, the nerves, and the heart, to say nothing of the soul. The majority of fatal car accidents, fire deaths, drownings, and fatal falls involve alcohol. Over half of the murders and incidents of child abuse, and a third of the rapes and suicides committed in the US are attributable to alcohol misuse. This totals a hell of a lot of destruction and human misery, much of which could be avoided.

In this country, seven out of ten people drink. One out of ten is an alcoholic, just like me. We don't choose to be alcoholic any more than others

I'll Quit Tomorrow

Alcoholics start out from a million different situations and head in the same direction — towards insanity and death. The progression of alcoholism, and the personality changes it brings about are predictable. This straightforward book describes that progression. Johnson presumes that alcoholics are incapable of recognizing what's happening to them and why. Therefore he advises intervention by the alcoholic's family and describes how that, and subsequent hospitalization for group therapy, can be done.

Thomas Szasz, **The Myth-of-Mental-Illness** *man, would shit a brick; Vernon Johnson is no psycholibertarian. But he, like Szasz, has got a big piece of truth here, and has written a book which is helping to save lives.*

—Stephanie Mills

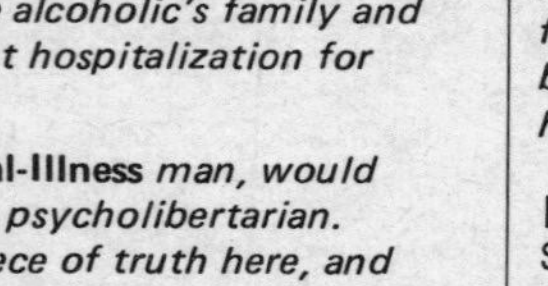

I'll Quit Tomorrow
(A Practical Guide to Alcoholism Treatment)
Vernon Johnson
1980; 182 pp.

$9.95 postpaid from:
Harper and Row
Keystone Industrial Park
Scranton, PA 18512
or Whole Earth
Household Store

•

As the drinking continues, the learning process continues, and a lot of it is unconscious learning. But if it is subtle, it is thorough. The drinker learns that alcohol *works every time*, and continues not only to *use* alcohol, but to develop a *relationship* with it. This whole experience is absorbed, and in due time the drinker knows that one drink can greatly improve a bad mood. Or if it isn't enough, and the mood needs more improving, one or two more will do the trick. This relationship with alcohol is *positive* rather than negative. It is based on implicit trust, built in more and more strongly as experience proves that booze will do its job every time. Experience builds on experience and consolidates it, and the result is a *deeply imbedded relationship which the drinker will carry throughout life.*

•

We believe in intervention because a person's life is in danger. It is as necessary as surgery when peritonitis is inevitable. The chief misconception is that spontaneous insight may occur. When you examine the lives of those who claim to have had it, you discover that a buildup of crises has forced them to look at the reality of their condition. The only way back to reality is through crisis.

Love and Addiction

This is what Art Kleiner calls a "metabook." It's one that provides entry to a whole field. Its starting point is that addiction is a type of relationship, one which can obtain between people, as well as between people and things like booze, heroin, or cigarettes.

Peele describes the social and familial factors which help form addict personalities, then suggests pathways for maturing out of addiction. It's definitely a get better book, written with enough respect for the person that he or she might actually get better as a result.

—Stephanie Mills

Love and Addiction
Stanton Peele and
Archie Brodsky
1975; 309 pp.

$2.50 postpaid from:
The New American
Library
P.O. Box 120
120 Woodline
Bergenfield, NJ 07621
or Whole Earth
Household Store

•

The addict is a person who never learns to come to grips with his world, and who therefore seeks stability and reassurance through some repeated, ritualized activity. This activity is reinforced in two ways — first, by a comforting sensation of well-being induced by the drug or other addictive object; second, by the atrophy of the addict's other interests and abilities and the general deterioration of his life situation while he is preoccupied with the addiction. As alternatives grow smaller, the addiction grows larger, until it is all there is. A true addict progresses into a monomania, whether the object of addition is a drug or a lover.

•

Today, alcoholism is considered our largest-scale drug problem. Explaining the reasons for alcohol misuse, David McClelland and his colleagues discovered in **The Drinking Man** that heavy, uncontrolled drinking occurs in cultures which explicitly value personal assertiveness while at the same time suppressing its expression. This conflict, which alcohol eases by offering its users the illusion of power, is precisely the conflict which gripped America during the period when opiate use grew and was outlawed, and when our society had such a hard time deciding what to do about alcohol.

•

Practically speaking, we can only make the personal decision to treat something as an addiction on the basis of how much we see it hurting us, and how much we want to be rid of it. More philosophically, we can accept a degree of ambiguity in our lives and relinquish the need for certainty and for perfect solutions that is itself a facet of addiction. Accepting ourselves in our imperfection, though with insight and determination to change, we are ready to become free, responsive beings.

choose to be colorblind. Alcoholism's the existential card we're dealt. We have to play it, one way or another. I tried drinking for fifteen years and sobriety for one and some. I like sobriety better. If, like me, you passed that twenty questions test, I hope you'll save yourself a lot of time and trouble and find the help you need to deal with your drinking problem today.

Alcoholics Anonymous is a fellowship of men and women who share their experience, strength, and hope with each other that they may solve their common problem and help others to recover from alcoholism.

The only requirement for membership is a desire to stop drinking.

There are no dues or fees for AA membership; we are self-supporting through our own contributions.

AA is not allied with any sect, denomination, politics, organization or institution; does not wish to engage in any controversy; neither endorses nor opposes any causes. Our primary purpose is to stay sober and help other alcoholics to achieve sobriety.

—Copyright by the AA Grapevine, Inc.; Reprinted by permission of Alcoholics Anonymous World Services, Inc.

Check your telephone book for an AA listing

Or write AA World Services, Inc.
P.O. Box 459
Grand Central Station
New York, NY 10017

AA will send three to four pamphlets free and a Public Information Material Order Form listing titles and prices of various books and pamphlets ■

Alcoholics Anonymous

Known to most AA's as the Big Book, **Alcoholics Anonymous** *is the bible of the program. It explains briefly how AA came into being and how it works. It describes AA's program for living (and thriving) sober. It also contains accounts by 42 AA's of their alcoholism, from progressive drinking to hitting bottom to entering AA and on to recovery.*

Two other AA books — In **Twelve Steps and Twelve Traditions** *"A co-founder of Alcoholics Anonymous tells how members recover and how the society functions."* **Living Sober** *has "some methods AA members have used for not drinking." —A member of Alcoholics Anonymous*

Alcoholics Anonymous
1939, 1976; 575 pp.
$5.65 postpaid

Living Sober
(Some methods AA members have used for not drinking)
1975, 1979; 87 pp.
$1.75 postpaid

Twelve Steps and Twelve Traditions
(A co-founder of Alcoholics Anonymous tells how members recover and how the society functions)
1952, 1953; 192 pp.
$4 postpaid

all from:
Alcoholics Anonymous World Services, Inc.
P.O. Box 459
Grand Central Station
New York, NY 10017

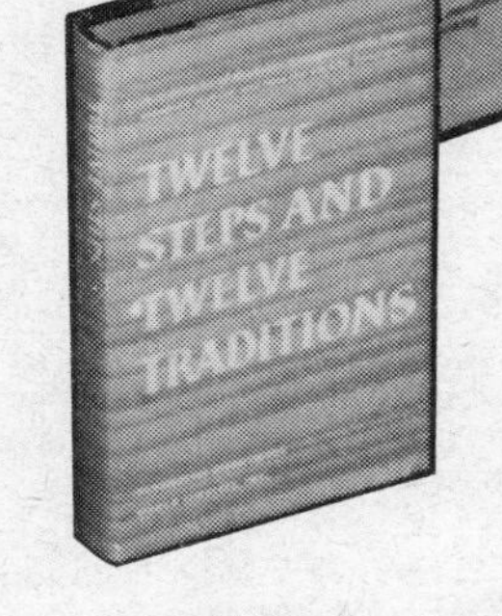

•

We have three little mottoes which are apropos. Here they are:

First Things First
Live and Let Live
Easy Does It.

—Alcoholics Anonymous

•

Much later when I had progressed to full-blown alcoholism, people told me I should quit. Like most other alcoholics I have known, I *did* quit drinking at various times — once for ten months on my own and during other interludes when I was hospitalized. It's no great trick to stop drinking; the trick is to *stay* stopped.

To do that, I had come to AA to learn how to handle sobriety — which is what I could not handle in the first place. That's why I drank.

—Alcoholics Anonymous

•

THE TWELVE STEPS

Step One
"We admitted we were powerless over alcohol — that our lives had become unmanageable."

Step Two
"Came to believe that a Power greater than ourselves could restore us to sanity."

Step Three
"Made a decision to turn our will and our lives over to the care of God *as we understood Him*."

Step Four
"Made a searching and fearless moral inventory or ourselves."

Step Five
"Admitted to God, to ourselves, and to another human being the exact nature or our wrongs."

Step Six
"Were entirely ready to have God remove all these defects of character."

Step Seven
"Humbly asked Him to remove our shortcomings."

Step Eight.
"Made a list of all persons we had harmed, and became willing to make amends to them all."

Step Nine
"Made direct amends to such people wherever possible, except when to do so would injure them or others."

Step Ten
"Continued to take personal inventory and when we were wrong promptly admitted it."

Step Eleven
"Sought through prayer and meditation to improve our conscious contact with God *as we understood Him*, praying only for knowledge of His will for us and the power to carry that out."

Step Twelve
"Having had a spiritual awakening as the result of these steps, we tried to carry this message to alcoholics, and to practice these principles in all our affairs."

—Twelve Steps and Twelve Traditions

From Sad to Glad

You've heard things like this said before: this book may save your life. More important (because dead men do not feel), it may save you months and years of dreadful and irrelevant suffering.

This book is of potential interest to many people — to the colleagues, lovers, friends, and relations of depressives; to psychiatrists, doctors, social workers; to the curious. It's unique and unprecedented, a discussion of what is known of this malady written by a man who is, by experience, scholarship, and gifted observation, reassuringly qualified to write such a book. (There are a bewilderingly few other books on depression. I can't be certain that I've seen them all, but the others I have seen are either idiosyncratic and wrong or stupid and wrong.)

I went through six shrinks and a couple ordinary doctors before I began to get even a whiff of what was wrong with me, and I'm a classic, regulation manic-depressive if ever there was one. Thousands and thousands of hours I suffered, because they didn't know and thought they did.

Kline covers a lot: the history of depression as a medical entity; famous depressives (Darwin, Abe Lincoln, etc., etc.); the best current theories as to the nature of the "biochemical storms," as he calls them, which are depression; manic-depressive illness; forms of treatment (including shock treatment, which a stomachful of ignorant badmouthing to the contrary, may be profoundly beneficial in depression). The book is conversational, almost simple; but it's thorough and informative. (If, after reading it, you want more detail and sophistication, you now have a good basic knowledge with which to approach the **Archives of General Psychiatry**.*)*

But I'm really here to say that this book is, urgently, for depressives themselves. Buy it, beg it borrow it, check it out: get it. Most doctors and most psychiatrists are not qualified to treat depression because they don't know anything true about it. They think it's something else. So you better know. Get this book.

The heart of the experience that is depression, the universal symptom, is the absence of all pleasure. From the fragile prettiness of a spiderweb to the melting savor of a truly great steak to the corruscating delights of lovemaking: all pleasures vanish. If you won the Nobel prize, the wine country of France, the loving esteem of all humankind, a Maserati, and another Nobel prize, all on the same balmy, sundrenched summer morning, you'd feel . . . perhaps fear, perhaps bewilderment, perhaps horror. But no pleasure. Depression is to the sensor of pleasure as blindness is to the eye.

If yours is a mild depression, it may be no more than the simple absence of pleasure. The world goes flat, and nothing calls to you. Whatever you loved, you don't love it anymore. You don't want to go running through the meadows, dancing, bodysurfing, backpacking. You feel awkward around people, inferior because you have no spark to give them, no life. If you used to be witty, you aren't. Nothing is funny. Challenges become burdensome, unpleasant chores loom like dead Sequoias. You feel always either saggingly bored or hardpressed. Sex is without attraction, like the prospect of dining on birdseed. You initiate nothing, not adventures, not conversations.

Unaccountably, it seems desperately important that you appear to other people as if nothing were wrong. Your polite smile is like wet clay stuck to your face, for you are inwardly paralyzed with dread and for you there is no such thing as play or even casual civility. Every gesture and every word must be forged, manufactured with as much difficulty and more concentration than goes into an entire Chevrolet. Any decision, whether to leave your door open or closed, to have salad with dinner, to put a book back on the shelf, to take a coat — is agony, irresolvable. There is no criterion on which to base a decision, for all the feelings and preferences of ordinary life have been usurped by dread, and dread cannot tell you whether you want to wear green socks or blue ones.

This despair may bring along a friend, terror, known in the trade as "anxiety." It is fear like acid, permeating the black ocean as the black ocean permeates your life, fear of nothing and fear of everything. Terror shrieks around you, recoiling off the edges of the universe, off your front door, off your pillow. It screams up out of the gutters and boils out of gasoline pumps. Fear blazes through your head like bullets, but there's nowhere to run, because it's there, too.

Except there is one place to run, and that's death. Some people do.

It's like nothing else, depression. It's horrible. But the right medication may dissolve the horror, and restore you to forests, and giggling, hot pastrami, Bach, moral outrage, sleeping late, and even falling in love.

—Judith Van Slooten

From Sad to Glad
(Kline on Depression)
Nathan S. Kline, M.D.
1974; 250 pp.
$2.50 postpaid from:
Ballantine Books, Inc.
455 Hahn Road
Westminster, MD 21157
or Whole Earth Household Store

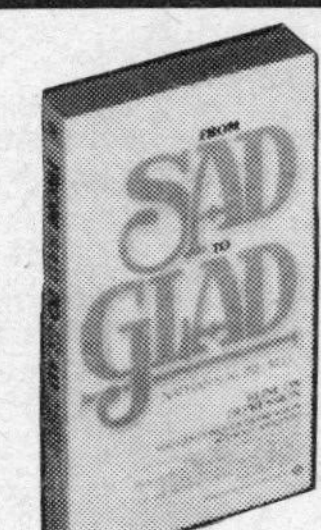

•

True depression. . . requires treatment, and that brings us right back to the question of what kind of illness it is. I am convinced that it's usually a biochemical disorder, and I find that in most cases it responds well to drug therapy. I believe that some cases probably do truly arise from a neurosis, but I consider these to be exceptional instances. I estimate neurotic depression to constitute a very small percentage of the truly severe cases. . . . The really important thing is that in most cases the medication works. . . .

Curiously enough, some patients feel guilty about achieving that kind of recovery. They have been thoroughly indoctrinated in the idea that emotional disturbance must reflect psychic ills, and they expect the treatment to require a prolonged, painful search through deeply buried layers of their unconscious. When they obtain relief without that effort, they feel that they didn't earn recovery because they haven't paid the psychic price. However, that is a disappointment that most can adjust to readily enough.

I recall a particular patient, a prominent radio personality, who was a manic-depressive. For fifteen years he sought a remedy in psychoanalysis, all the while enduring moods that swung erratically and irrationally from elation to despair. "I think the analysis was valuable," he told me later. "I gained a lot of insight into myself. I was probably the most insightful manic-depressive you ever met. But I was still a manic-depressive." I placed him on chemotherapy, and the problem was cleared up in about two months. . . .

THE RISING SUN
NEIGHBORHOOD NEWSLETTER

Art says that he reached a moment when he had to decide how much he wanted to be involved with computers because if he didn't want to be very very involved he had to stop right then.

On Death and Dying

On Death and Dying *establishes a psychological fact that most people close to a dying person already know, even if they can't admit it: one tends to turn away. Even from husbands, even from wives, even from one's own children. Dying people are casualties of life. Their dying, especially if it is a long, drawn-out affair, is a reminder of how vulnerable we all are, and that's something most people want to forget.*

This is a powerful book, because it forces the reader into the point of view of someone dying. Suddenly you're on the other side of that glass between the living and the dying, and it's not comfortable. But, as Elisabeth Kubler-Ross points out, the point is not always to "comfort" the healthy. That tendency is a major cause of the intense psychic suffering dying people must endure, in addition to the physical failures that are killing them. This book speaks for the dying in a way they are unable to speak for themselves. It's disturbing; but then so is all education. I'd say this book is indispensable for all people who are living in the presence of someone else's gradual death. —Gurney Norman

What Rachel Carson's **Silent Spring** *did for pesticides, this book did for the subject of death. Unlike Carson's book, it hasn't dated a line, although the author maybe has.* —SB

On Death and Dying
Elisabeth Kubler-Ross, M.D.
1969; 260 pp.

$2.45 postpaid from:
Macmillan Publishing Co.
Order Department
Front and Brown Streets
Riverside, NJ 08075
or Whole Earth Household Store

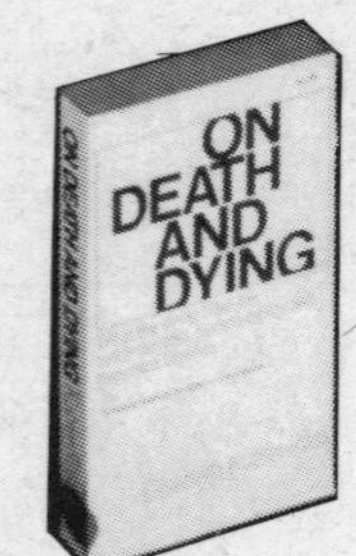

•

I remember as a child the death of a farmer. He fell from a tree and was not expected to live. He asked simply to die at home, a wish that was granted without questioning. He called his daughters into the bedroom and spoke with each one of them alone for a few minutes. He arranged his affairs quietly, though he was in great pain, and distributed his belongings and his land, none of which was to be split until his wife should follow him in death. He also asked each of his children to share in the work, duties, and tasks that he had carried on until the time of the accident. He asked his friends to visit him once more, to bid good-bye to them. Although I was a small child at the time, he did not exclude me or my siblings. We were allowed to share in the preparations of the family just as we were permitted to grieve with them until he died. When he did die, he was left at home, in his own beloved home which he had built, and among his friends and neighbors who went to take a last look at him where he lay in the midst of flowers in the place he had lived in and loved so much.

•

He was quite aware that his days were numbered, and his greatest wish was to be moved into different positions (he was paralyzed to his neck). He begged the nurse never to put the siderails up as it reminded him of being in a casket. The nurse, who was very hostile to this patient, agreed that she would leave them down at all times. This private duty nurse was very angry when she was disturbed in her reading, and she knew that he would keep quiet as long as she fulfilled this wish.

•

Everybody expected her to die soon, but day after day she remained in an unchanged condition. Her daughter was torn between sending her to a nursing home or keeping her in the hospital, where she apparently wanted to stay. Her son-in-law was angry at her for having used up their life savings and had innumerable arguments with his wife, who felt too guilty to take her out of the hospital. When I visited the old woman she looked frightened and weary. I asked her simply what she was so afraid of. She looked at me and finally expressed what she had been unable to communicate before, because she herself realized how unrealistic her fears were. She was afraid of "being eaten up alive by the worms." While I was catching my breath and tried to understand the real meaning of this statement, her daughter blurted out, "If that's what's keeping you from dying, we can burn you," by which she naturally meant that a cremation would prevent her from having any contact with earthworms. All her suppressed anger was in this statement.

•

First Stage: Denial and Isolation
Second Stage: Anger
Third Stage: Bargaining
Fourth Stage: Depression
Fifth Stage: Acceptance

The Wheel of Death

Sentimentalizing death is a disservice. This book by the author of **Three Pillars of Zen** *assembles sundry anecdotes and quotes primarily from the Buddhist tradition, which treats death as a lesson.* —SB

The Wheel of Death
(A Collection of Writings from Zen Buddhist and Other Sources on Death, Rebirth, Dying)
Philip Kapleau, Editor
1971, 110 pp.

$3.50 postpaid from:
Harper and Row
Keystone Industrial Park
Scranton, PA 18512
or Whole Earth Household Store

•

It cannot be stressed too often that the funeral rites are for the benefit of the deceased himself, and that the family must comply with his expressed wishes as to who shall perform them, and how. Similarly, his instructions for the disposition of his own body and the performance of subsequent rites must not be ignored.

•

Socrates:

To fear death, gentlemen, is nothing other than to think oneself wise when one is not; for it is to think one knows what one does not know. No man knows whether death may not even turn out to be the greatest of blessings for a human being; and yet people fear it as if they knew for certain that it is the greatest of evils.

•

Riding this wooden upside-down horse,
I'm about to gallop through the void.
Would you seek to trace me?
Ha! Try catching the tempest in a net.

—Death verse of Master Kukoku

Life After Life

Truth is qualitative but proving something requires numbers. The author has investigated the experience of over 100 people who have clinically died and then recovered. They all had a similar experience, and none had further fears of death. That may be sufficient proof for you to relax now about dying. Or you can wait for the truth. —SB

Life After Life
(The Investigation of a Phenomenon — Survival of Bodily Death)
Raymond A. Moody, Jr.
1975, 187 pp.

$2.50 postpaid from:
Bantam Books
414 East Golf Road
Des Plaines, IL 60016
or Whole Earth Household Store

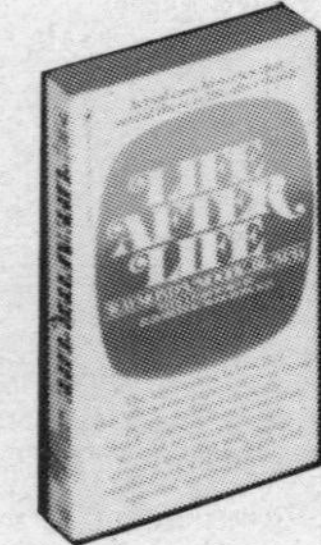

•

What is perhaps the most incredible common element in the accounts I have studied, and is certainly the element which has the most profound effect upon the individual, is the encounter with a very bright light. Typically, at its first appearance this light is dim, but it rapidly gets brighter until it reaches an unearthly brilliance. Yet, even though this light (usually said to be white or "clear") is of an indescribable brilliance, many make the specific point that it does not in any way hurt their eyes, or dazzle them, or keep them from seeing other things around them (perhaps because at this point they don't have physical "eyes" to be dazzled).

Despite the light's unusual manifestation, however, not one person has expressed any doubt whatsoever that it was a being, a being of light. Not only that, it is a personal being. It has a very definite personality. The love and warmth which emanate from this being to the dying person are utterly beyond words, and he feels completely surrounded by it and taken up in it, completely at ease and accepted in the presence of this being. He senses an irresistible magnetic attraction to this light. He is ineluctably drawn to it.

•

The reason why death is no longer frightening, as all of these excerpts express, is that after his experience a person no longer entertains any doubts about his survival of bodily death. It is no longer merely an abstract possibility to him, but a fact of his experience.

•

Many persons report being out of their bodies for extended periods and witnessing many events in the physical world during the interlude. Can any of these reports be checked out with other witnesses who were known to be present, or with later confirming events, and thus be corroborated?

In quite a few instances, the somewhat surprising answer to this question is "yes." Furthermore, the description of events witnessed while out of the body tend to check out fairly well. Several doctors have told me, for example, that they are utterly baffled about how patients with no medical knowledge could describe in such detail and so correctly the procedure used in resuscitation attempts, even though these events took place while the doctors knew the patients involved to be "dead."

•

I know a few cases in which a suicide attempt was the cause of the apparent "death." These experiences were uniformly characterized as being unpleasant.

As one woman said, "If you leave here a tormented soul, you will be a tormented soul over there too." In short, they report that the conflicts they had attempted suicide to escape were still present when they died, but with added complications. In their disembodied state they were unable to do anything about their problems, and they also had to view the unfortunate consequences which resulted from their acts.

Busy dying

So far I've been told that my time on this planet as a conscious being was;

- not important because I'm going to die anyway
- very important because soon enough I'll be dead
- serious business because I'll be born again
- no big deal because there is no death

ho hum

Max Krimmel
Boulder, Colorado

Vital Signs

Taking a journalist's approach, John Langone reports what's going on around deathbeds, very accurately, often shockingly. This book lands us right here, where we are, rather than up there ahead, where we want to go. Thanks. —Diana Barich

Vital Signs
(The Way We Die in America)
John Langone
1974; 363 pp.

$3.95 postpaid from:
Little, Brown and Company, Inc.
200 West Street
Waltham, MA 02154
or Whole Earth Household Store

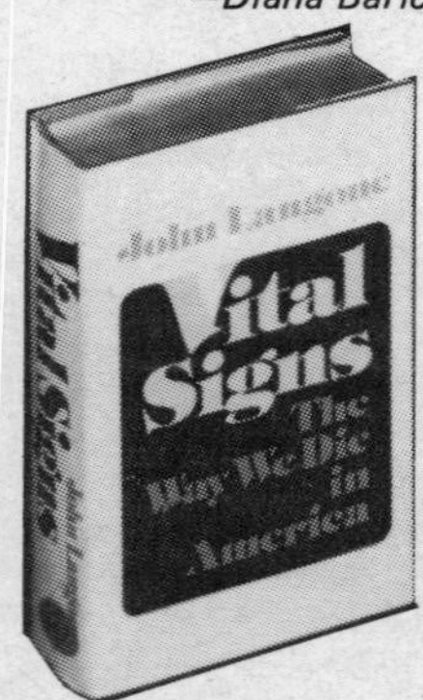

•

"All I want to know is that there is someone to hold my hand when I need it. Death may be routine to you, but it is new to me." —A dying woman to her doctor

•

She was just crying and crying. She said, what am I going to do, I'm dying. I have little children. What am I going to tell them? And she said, I'm really sorry to be crying. And I said, Oh, it's all right, it's all right. You can cry, and I'm sitting there, of course, really trying not to cry myself. And she said, when my husband's here I can't cry, I have to pretend that I'm not worried when he's here, because he doesn't think that I am dying. Well, I knew her husband knew, but he apparently had been denying it all the time, and she had been going along with him, and they had to play this elaborate little game, pretending it wasn't happening. At this point — she had been crying for five or ten minutes — and one of the nurses came in and said, oh what a baby, cut out that crying. What's the matter with you? Cheer up, buck up. What if your husband could see you like this? And there it went, you know, sort of like all the freedom and honesty that she had been allowed for those few minutes completely evaporated and she had to put on her little game again.

A Hospice Handbook

With astonishing speed the hospice movement is investing America. More and more communities have the service, sometimes as part of a local hospital, sometimes not. It means that dying is acknowledged finally, that the dying are acknowledged. If you're dying, find a hospice. If you're living, help make one.

Of a number of books on the subject, this one I think covers the ground most thoroughly and insightfully.

—*SB*

A Hospice Handbook
(A New Way to Care for the Dying)
Michael Hamilton and Helen Reid, Editors
1980; 196 pp.

$4.95 postpaid from:
Eerdmans Publishing Company
255 Jefferson Avenue S.E.
Grand Rapids, MI 49503
or Whole Earth Household Store

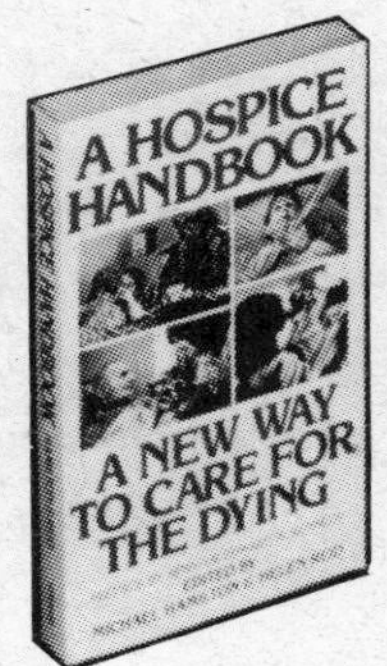

•

The dying are often lonely, frightened, and in pain. They deserve special care and attention, and this book describes a new, humane way to help them. All of us will die one day, and we need to prepare for that time.

The Hospice for the Dying movement began in England in the late fifties and early sixties with the opening of St. Christopher's Hospice in London. It was primarily the creation of Dr. Cicely Saunders, who recognized that many patients were receiving inadequate care in hospitals and that relatives were having problems in caring for the dying at home. Dr. Saunders saw the need for supporting and counselling the patients and their families before death as well as after death. She inaugurated programs by which patients, knowing their death was inevitable and imminent, could enter the hospice program and receive only symptomatic control. Instead of using heroic technological methods which prolonged the dying process, Dr. Saunders gave only sophisticated and effective pain relief. She provided medical, nursing, and spiritual care for hospice resident patients and also for those who, having someone to look after them, could die comfortable and happily in their homes.

•

The aim of treatment should be to control pain so that it will not return. This can be compared to the control of blood sugar in diabetics where the physician does not wait for symptoms of distress or coma before giving insulin. Breakthrough, or recurring pain is unnecessary pain. Additionally, recurrence of pain erodes the patient's confidence in his physician while generating anxiety and fear. Constant pain control is achieved through appropriate dosage given at regular, well-timed intervals.

Ease of administration is a significant consideration because it has substantial impact on the patient's way of life. The patient taking oral medication is free to move around, travel in a car and, most importantly, be at home.

The Business of Dying

A guide to dealing with the legal and financial aspects of dying — wills, estate planning, probate, funeral services. Divided into two parts — Preparing for Your Own Death, and Coping with a Death in the Family. Unsentimental, last-minute, nuts-and-bolts advice on putting your affairs — or a loved one's — in order. For a more long-term preparation and planning, see **A Manual of Death Education and Simple Burial.**

—*Tom Ferguson, M.D.*

The Business of Dying
(A Practical Guide)
Yaffa Draznin
1976; 228 pp.

$3.95 postpaid from:
Hawthorn Books
E.P. Dutton and Co.
Two Park Avenue
New York, NY 10016
or Whole Earth Household Store

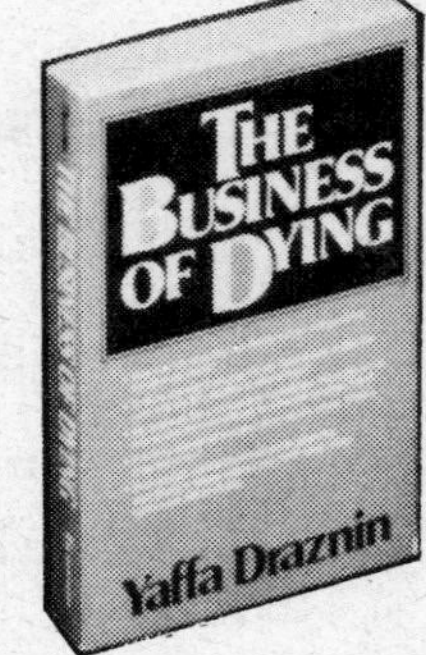

•

When you die intestate (without a will) the probate court (or "surrogate court" or "orphans court" or whatever the name in your state) appoints an administrator to supervise the distribution of the property. The administrator appointed often is the closest inheriting next of kin (which may or may not be good for your estate, depending on how complicated its business affairs are and your relationship to that person).

. . . Then there's the way the state statute determines who inherits what. The rules are determined by marriage or blood relationship; and how the formula is applied is based on the number of relatives alive when you die, how close their relationship was to you, and whether or not you live in a community property state.

The formula is predetermined and rigid — and while the distribution may be just the way you would have apportioned your estate, the chances are that it won't be. The number of "typical" family situations upon which the intestate laws are based are very few in real life. And once you die, the impersonal process set into motion is unalterable.

Bequests to charity are given no recognition. Persons with whom you're very close, either taking care of you or living with you, get no part of your inheritance if they are not related by blood or law. Neither does your divorced spouse nor her or his children, nor any number of persons with whom you may have a special relationship.

Your business may have to be liquidated, your estate may be subject to federal and state taxes at the highest rate, and your heirs may have to wait an inordinate length of time until your assets are freed to pass to them.

You can see why now is the time to make out your will.

Care of the Dying

In bad times, a friendly culture has customs and traditions and etiquette and folklore and rituals that tell you what to do with pain and love. Our culture isn't friendly with dying and the only advice it gives is to lie a lot. If you decide to be honest and loving with a dying person, it's hard to know what to do specifically. Dr. Richard Lamerton works at St. Christopher's Hospice in England, and he has advice for medical people and family and friends about exactly how to help when they feel very helpless.

—*Anne Herbert*

Care of the Dying
Richard Lamerton
1973; 160 pp.

$8.95 postpaid from:
Technomic Publishing Company
265 Post Road West
Westport, CT 06880
or Whole Earth Household Store

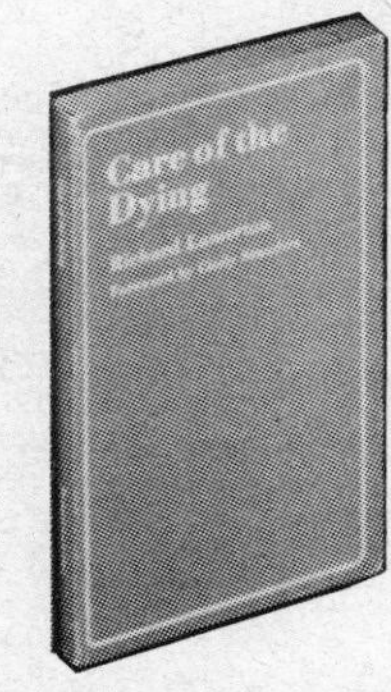

•

On their death beds many men mature wonderfully. Priorities fall into place, tolerance and courage may grow in the most unlikely soil and more amazing still is the serenity which so often comes to one from the dying. Much of the work of those caring for the dying is to prevent anything arising which may hinder this growth in the patient's being. He must be free from pain, but still alert; he must be told as much of the truth about his condition as he can cope with, but no more; he must be encouraged to turn his attention away from himself, and must be given a clean example of real service.

When a man's responsibilities drop away, either by reason of physical weakness or of senile dementia, there remains a great beauty which has been covered by the busy-ness — or laziness — for many a year. Death removes the covers: this unmasking can be a thrilling revelation.

•

People feel helpless beside the dying because they do not realize that what counts is their presence, not their activity. They may feel guilty because the mind plays with irrelevant thoughts, taking attention off the dying person. They should be encouraged to touch the patient — hold his hand for instance — for this will be one of his last channels of reassurance. To the last he can be assumed to hear all that is said. Often a flicker of a smile or a faint squeeze of a finger will confirm that the message has been received.

Distress in the last hour is rare and the fear of it is a morbid twist in our culture. The idea of suffering may well be projected on to a person by distressed spectators who are in fact dreading their own imminent bereavement. There is, on the contrary, almost always a rather beautiful giving-in. The person withdraws serenely and willingly, as gently as an ocean liner slips away from the quayside. Sometimes there may be a brief period of complete lucidity, as in the case of Mr. B. who, when I went to say good-bye, suddenly opened his eyes and said to me, "I'm joining your flock now, Doctor. I hope the coffin is ready. Cheerio!"

A Manual of Death Education and Simple Burial

Not everybody has an opportunity to depart this world gracefully, and those that do usually blow it. The people left behind fumble just as badly, for largely the same reasons: ignorance, fear, a lack of foresight and preparation. None but the dead can know for sure the full consequences of the failure. But even if there are no consequences for the dead, there are enough of them for the survivors in the forms of trauma and ruptured bank accounts, to make this **Manual of Simple Burial** *seem something like a life-saver.*

For this little manual of death is firmly on the side of life. As part of the literature of funerals, it's like a living rosebud in a bouquet of plastic flowers. In 64 pages it quietly tells you how to avoid the ghastly system of converting human left-overs into products packaged as "funerals." In simple language backed by intelligent sympathy, it suggests ways to surround the act of passage with appropriate rites of passage that offer real meaning to people in need of meaning.

According to the manual, the main alternative to expensive, hastily-improvised funerals is membership in a memorial society. A memorial society is "a voluntary group of people who have joined together to obtain dignity, simplicity and economy in funeral arrangements through advance planning." The manual provides a list of several societies by name and address. It also has information on cremation, autopsies, eye banks, bequethal of bodies, and the business and legal matters that usually attend a death, as well as chapters with titles like "Interpreting Death to a Child," and "What to do When Death Occurs."

People choose their horrors. We choose war. We choose pollution. And, by default, we choose to make the rituals surrounding death grotesque. But what is chosen can be unchosen, once an alternative is clear. **The Manual of Simple Burial** *describes a clear alternative to one of our chosen horrors.*

—*Gurney Norman*

A Manual of Death Education and Simple Burial
Ernest Mortan
9th Edition
1968, 1980; 64 pp.

$3 postpaid from:
The Celo Press
Burnsville, NC 28714
or Whole Earth Household Store

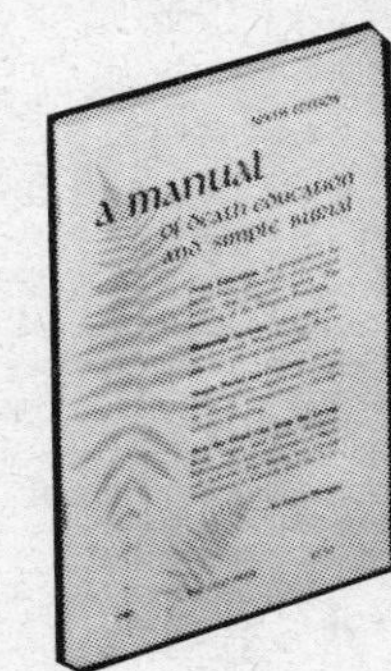

•

At time of death the immediate family is under great strain. Ordinary things like shopping, cooking, child care and minor chores suddenly become "just too much." This is a time when thoughtful friends should rally in a coordinated way, with food, errands, child care, hospitality for relatives, chores, etc. Done skillfully, in the right context, this is a comforting and heart-warming experience. Ineptly done, it can be an extra burden. Don't say, "If there's anything I can do, just let me know."

These functions usually fall within the scope of the church, neighborhood or other social group, but someone is needed to "spark" the action.

•

Modern cremation is a clean, orderly process for returning human remains to the elements. Unless encumbered by unnecessary trimmings it is economical. With the rising cost of land burial and (in some areas) shortage of land, it is finding increasing use. Many prefer it for aesthetic reasons. Between 8% and 10% of those who die in America are now cremated and in Sweden, Denmark, England and West Germany the figure is now above 50%. Crematoria are increasing in number.

The ashes (actually pulverized bone fragments) are clean and white and may be stored indefinitely or mailed parcel post for distant interment. Some families prefer to scatter them in a favorite garden or woods, or from a mountain top. (First make sure they are pulverized, to avoid visible bone fragments. This is not difficult.) Some crematories now have equipment which leaves no ashes at all. A few states have laws prohibiting the scattering of ashes. Such laws are commercially motivated and serve no hygienic or esthetic purpose.

Bodies may be delivered to the crematory, in most cases, in a plain container; in some, on a pallet. Inexpensive fibreboard containers are manufactured for this purpose. Some crematories require a regular casket and this requirement is sometimes mistakenly quoted as law. The container is placed in the retort with the body. Crematory charges range from $75 to $150. In some places religious groups or private citizens may obtain the necessary death certificate and permits for transportation and cremation, usually provided no one is being paid. In other places a funeral director is required.

THE RISING SUN
NEIGHBORHOOD NEWSLETTER

Libraries will get you through times of no money better than money will get you through times of no libraries.

Common-Sense Suicide

This book says old people should be able to stop being alive when they want. Says it very well, too.
—Anne Herbert

Common-Sense Suicide
Doris Portwood
1978; 142 pp.
$6.95 postpaid from:
Dodd, Mead and Company
79 Madison Avenue
New York, NY 10016

•

There is a continuing increase in suicide by the under-24 age group and few would argue against the need for suicide prevention centers, counselor hot-lines and research projects. When you are under 24, there is so much time to change your mind. People with many productive years to live should be helped to have that chance.

Equally, older persons should be accorded the courtesy of an assumption that we know what we want. By the time we reach 65 most of us have made many decisions. On a private decision we deserve the dignity of a respectful concurrence. When an older woman leaves a social gathering — perhaps an hour after dinner and when younger guests are settling down to a game or a fresh drink — no one urges her to linger on. Someone may call a cab or offer a lift. She will receive thoughtful words during the process of departure, but no insistence on her staying. There is the assumption that she has, in fact, some good reason for going.

When we have a good reason for voluntary departure from life, similar courtesy would be appreciated, but we cannot count on it.

•

"Maybe he's death, the great lover," she says. "Anyway, he carries two guns and we have our rendezvous in a saloon-like bar. But luxurious — you know? Ripe leather and polished wood. He buys me a neat whisky and we talk about his beautiful guns. They *are* beautiful. Lots of intricate design in the metal. And heavy. I lift one. He speaks of Russian Roulette. I believe that there are no empty chambers in this heavy gun. And then there is a sound of firing. I notice the men at the bar turn their heads toward our table. Slowly, like a replayed sport detail. And — well, that's all."

"The man — gun-toting Death or whoever. Is he young or old?"

"Funny," she says. "I never noticed."

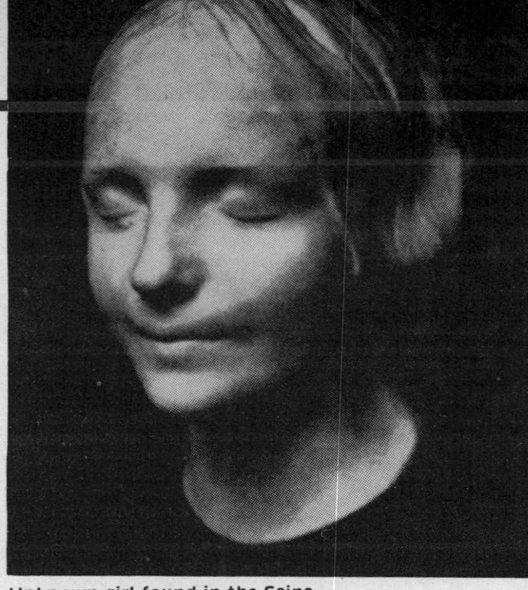

Unknown girl found in the Seine

Last Rights

A classic apologia both for euthanasia and for a less isolated way of treating the elderly and the ill. All the reasons why we ("society") should reform our attitudes and laws; very little about the personal and social weaknesses that have created them. *—Diana Barich*

Last Rights
(A Case for Good Death)
Marya Mannes
1973; 150 pp.
$1.50 postpaid from:
New American Library
P.O. Box 120
120 Woodbine
Bergenfield, NJ 07621
or Whole Earth Household Store

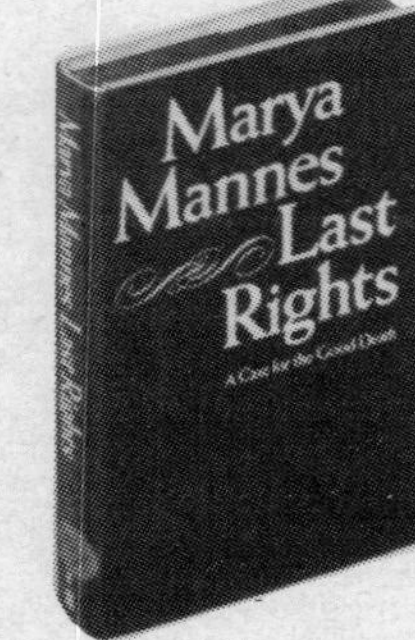

•

If you want to die "well" and be sure of freedom from heroics and antipain-killer doctors, the best thing to do is pick your doctor with care. Agree on your right to know the truth and share in decisions about care. Remember that most doctors are compassionate men. They are not sadists or ogres.

•

For his last three years, Swift sat and drooled, and at least five years before he died in fits of convulsion lasting thirty-six hours, he had written to his niece: "I am so stupid and confounded that I cannot express the mortification I am under both of body and soul."

Garnett concludes: "The story of this man's death points us directly to the broad problem of suicide, as well as to the more particular problem of euthanasia. We get a glimpse of this paradox in our present customary morality, that it sometimes condemns us to live, or, to put it another way, destroys our moral being for the sake of just *being*."

There is also a common ambivalence in the attitude that suicide is a form of cowardice. To evade self requires no courage: to face self and perform the act of consciously destroying it demands great courage. No reversal is possible.

And if aiding and abetting suicide is a crime, then mercy and compassion are both crimes. And the men who withheld the knife and the drug from the raging Jonathan Swift are heroes and saints.

Counsel for a suicide's friend

Dear Prof. Bateson: 23 May

I talked with you yesterday morning and near the end you asked me if I had any specific questions I did but couldnt bring myself to ask them, but find that I really do want to ask them so this letter.

First unasked question has to do with something said to the effect that "if your heart's in the frying pan, then you cant go wrong." Well, obviously, nothing much can be done if your heart's not in the frying pan, but what if you guts are in it and things go wrong.

What I'm talking about is I was introduced to a young woman about two years ago but my ex-shrink because he was feeling a bit stuck with her ef on the othe - her craziness reminded him of mine.

Anyway she suicided eight months ago. At 21.

I am not willing to accept the premise that we were not really friends as I know I was there and was paying attention. So I'm stuck, amongst other things, with trying to sort out how I can legitimately (to myself mainly) aspire to trying to help others with their crazinesses? Have I the courage — yes and no. That is, I still think I understand some of it, but doubt whether that understanding is sufficient. And if it isnt, what is?

Which brings me to unasked question #2. One thing that looks to me as if it had the possibility of being sufficient is small communities like Kingsley Hall, the Granville Road house, etc. What mostly worries me about them is how do you get a community stable enough to sustain itself and support people working on their maps but not get tangled up in questions of stability and/or minimizing chaos as to interfere with people's working?

Respectfully

Dear ____________ 27 May 1973

I am sorry I did not manage to answer your letter while I was in Seattle.

I suggest that you consider and complete in your imagination the following scenario (after all, it is in your imagination that change is requested or needed):

Your friend has achieved her suicide and arrived at the Pearly Gates, where she is challenged by St. Peter, who notes that she has come too soon. She says that it was all ____________'s fault.

There are many ways of completing the scenario, but one way or another, your friend has to demonstrate that she had no free will but you had. I suggest either that you both had free will or that neither of you had.

Of course it is gratifying to you and to all therapists to believe that they have more free will than their patients. But it won't do.

Your problem is to stop the boat rocking between the arrogance of "I had the power and the knowledge to help" and the self repudiation of "I failed."

Your second question is much more difficult, but the answer is I suppose really a corollary following from what I have just said. You will always be terrified of the things which will inevitably happen in any therapeutic community if you start out with a false estimate of the power and the wisdom of whoever it is that runs the community (especially if it's you). What one human being can do for another is not quite nothing, but it probably sometimes helps the helpee when the helper is clear about how little help can be given. Some temporary protection from the cold winds of an insane civilization, some shared tears and laughter, and that's about it.

Yours sincerely, Gregory Bateson, Santa Cruz, California

A Better BathTub

by Stewart Brand

You don't need to know why this item is here instead of somewhere more logical, but you might be interested. It got squeezed off the cockroach and cheap living spread by lack of space, and nothing else really wanted to be on the suicide page, so I volunteered. Besides, if I was going to die on purpose, I'd like to do it in my tub. (Afterward my friends could drain out the water, replace the plug, and float it and my carcass aflame into the Bay, chanting Viking sea burial hymns the while.) This piece is adapted from a column in the New Scientist, June, 1980. For more on hot tubs and saunas, see p. 320. *—SB*

It's not hard to improve on the traditional tub, that miracle of rotten design. Uncomfortably hard. Dangerously slippery. Boringly ugly. Unmanageably heavy. Forbiddingly expensive. They're usually so short and shallow that some part of you is out in the cold. There's no room for company. What warmth there is in the water rapidly conducts out through the enamel and metal, leaving one in that homely dilemma of a cooling tub and no more hot water coming yet.

My idea of the good life has as its central tenet the availability of baths, long, hot, and frequent. In 1974 I realized that I had been spoiled by too many ecstatic dips in the wild hot springs of the West to any longer suffer the medical esthetic of standard bathtubs. Down with phoney hygiene, up with genuine healing. Being in California, I figured: Right, get a hot tub.

The hot tub is this state's most currently famous and infamous invention, and with reason on both counts. Its worthy ancestor is the Japanese *ofuro* — a simple, beautiful box of fragrant wood into which scalding water is cycled through an elegant heater. To keep the bathing water pure, the Japanese bather showers before and after. This exquisite device was noticed, sped up, and vulgarized by West Coast Americans into the hot tub. Such tubs first appeared during the '50s on Mountain Drive, a bohemian community near Santa Barbara, California. Most of the early efforts were splendidly crude. I had two that consisted solely of leaky wooden sides, a metal bottom, and an open fire underneath simultaneously cooking, steaming, and smoking the happy missionaries in the pot.

The bathers are always plural. That's the whole hidden agenda of hot tubs — ogling, bumping, diddling, possibly writhing about with other naked bods. Many a newcomer to California remembers forever the trauma of first being invited — at a perfectly ordinary party — to strip and enter a steaming tub full of strangers. As for two people alone, there's no surer prelude to getting laid, and if on rare occasion it doesn't work the bath is a soothing compensation and substitute. (There's carefully no sexism in that remark. It was a lady, delighted with her new tub, who pointed the fact out to me.)

By 1974 hot tub design had become elaborate and expensive. (Now, 1980, I can call any of the 37 hot tub manufacturers in the San Francisco Bay Area and get estimates ranging from $1500 to $10,000. For installation add another $3000.) Figuring I'd better build my own, I sought the

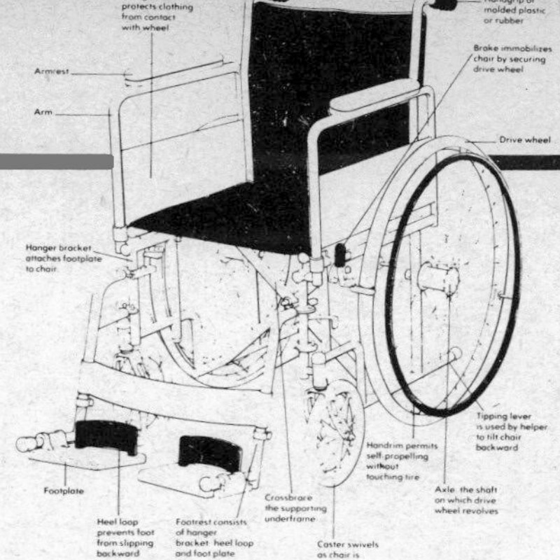

The Source Book for the Disabled ↑

This is an artful, comprehensive starting point for people who are disabled and need to help themselves; or for people who have just become disabled and are learning to live independently; or for parents of disabled children; or for those who simply want to learn what's going on. There are a lot of day-to-day details you might never suspect — how to redesign a kitchen for wheelchair access, or how to toilet-train children with cerebral palsy. It's all here.

It should be said that disabilities-from-birth are (apparently) becoming increasingly common, and this book (plus a lot of love) will be needed. The book's exceptional in every way; it can't be recommended highly enough. The service-to-the-disabled agencies which we called agreed.
—Art Kleiner

The Source Book for the Disabled
(An Illustrated Guide to easier more independent living for physically disabled people, their families and friends)
Glorya Hale, Editor
1979; 288 pp.

$14.95 postpaid from:
W.B. Saunders
West Washington Square
Philadelphia, PA 19105

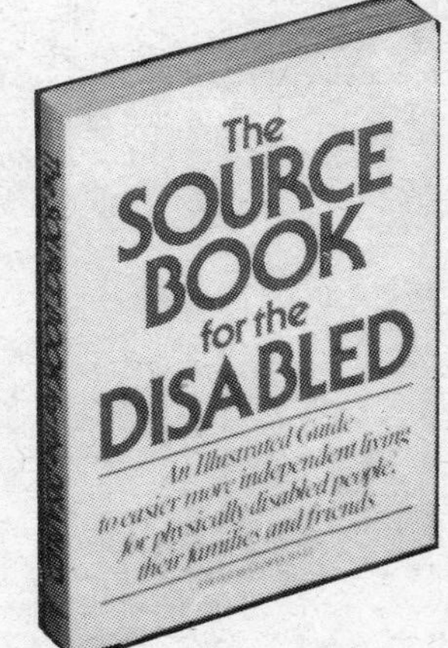

•

The Wheelchair Pilots Association (International) formed in 1970 and headquartered in Largo, Florida has more than two hundred members in the United States, Canada, Great Britain, Germany, Australia and Japan. In the United States there are now four manufacturers of hand controls. The apparatus fits several Cherokee models as well as Cessna and Grumman aircraft.

All aspiring pilots, handicapped or able-bodied, must have a third-class medical certificate before they are permitted to fly solo. Although disabled pilots-to-be almost certainly encounter more difficulty than average able-bodied applicants, they can rely on an objective appraisal of their physical ability to safely handle a plane.

How to Build Special Furniture and Equipment for Handicapped Children

With prices for special equipment (when available) approaching the obscene, and quick obsolescence brought on by the children growing, this book should be most welcome to those with handicapped children. Plans are simple and assume only rudimentary skills, tools and materials. The book also makes it clear that there's a wide open opportunity for anyone interested in designing for the handicapped.
—J. Baldwin
[Suggested by Jane Ritter]

How to Build Special Furniture and Equipment for Handicapped Children
Ruth B. Hofmann
1970; 87 pp.

$7.50 postpaid from:
Charles C. Thomas
301-327 East
Lawrence Avenue
Springfield, IL 62717

Access

A good where-is-it guide, which could save years of hunting for the right newsletter, agency, or document. Services for the disabled are notoriously hard to find; they usually don't have much money for advertising. Though the writing in this book is sometimes too preachy, there are lots of specifics on every service they recommend — a good model for any directory — plus encouraging suggestions on how to ask for what you need, and print in large type. (See also **Communications Outlook**, *p. 536).*
—Art Kleiner
[Suggested by Ken Cowan]

Access
(The Guide to a Better Life for Disabled Americans)
Lilly Bruck
1978; 251 pp.

$6.95 postpaid from:
Random House
455 Hahn Road
Westminster, MD 21157
or Whole Earth Household Store

ACCESS THE GUIDE TO A BETTER LIFE FOR DISABLED AMERICANS
BY LILLY BRUCK
Preface by Betty Furness
Introduction by Frank G. Bowe

•

The disabled audience in this country is a large and potentially powerful one. "Eighteen percent of the population," estimated President Jimmy Carter in his address to the White House Conference on Handicapped Individuals, in May 1977. That is one American in six. There are 332,000 veterans of World War II, Korea and Vietnam; 2 million children with orthopedic handicaps; 250,000 Americans of all ages use wheelchairs; 13.4 million are hearing impaired, 750,000 of them deaf; 6.5 million are vision impaired, 1 million of them blind; 6.5 million mentally retarded; 100,000 babies each year are born with congenital impairments; 22 million people a year are injured in home accidents: disabling injuries occur at the rate of 1.2 million a year. Every day, 1,000 Americans pass their 65th birthday, entering the sphere of geriatric diseases, arthritis, heart disease, problems with vision and hearing.

↓
Using the Creeper

Place child on back board. Fasten the harness — sides, tail, and top. Tighten the straps. Turn the frame over so that the child is suspended from the frame. If the child's knees do not touch the floor, loosen the straps. If the child is too heavy to turn over while strapped in the frame have the child kneel and position the frame over his body. Buckle the harness in place.

As the child grows, the creeper can be made higher by bolting on longer legs.

I Can Do It Myself!

What a nice idea — specially designed clothes for disabled children and adults. Mindful, caring, kindly facing tough reality.
—Stephanie Mills

Prices are reasonable, too, which is rare in this type of business.
—Art Kleiner

I Can Do It Myself!
(Clothing for Special People with Special Needs)
Brochure
free

Fabric samples
$1 postpaid

both from:
I Can Do It Myself
3773 Peppertree Drive
Eugene, OR 97402

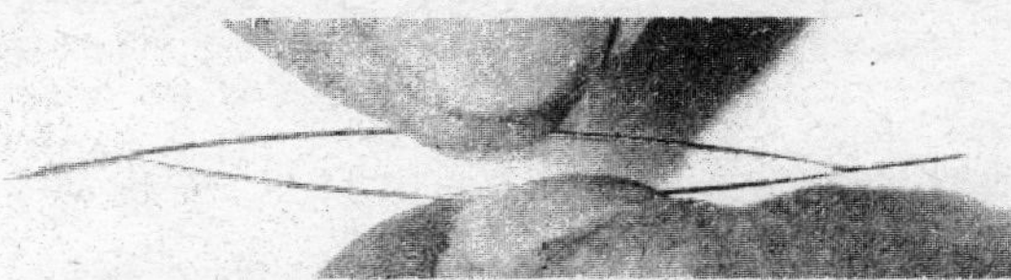

Spread eye needle — easy to thread needle with a long split down its center.

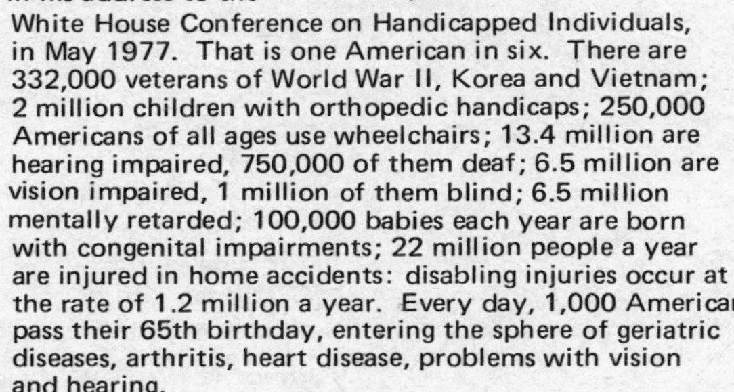

Hi Marks makes 3 dimensional markings on cloth woods or metal.

← Products for People with Vision Problems

From a design standpoint, as well as a humanitarian one, this is one of the most fascinating catalogs I've seen. Pretty reasonable prices. It's printed in large type. Braille edition of the catalog is available.
—SB

Products for People with Vision Problems
Catalog

free from:
American Foundation for the Blind
Consumer Products Department
15 West 16th Street
New York, NY 10011

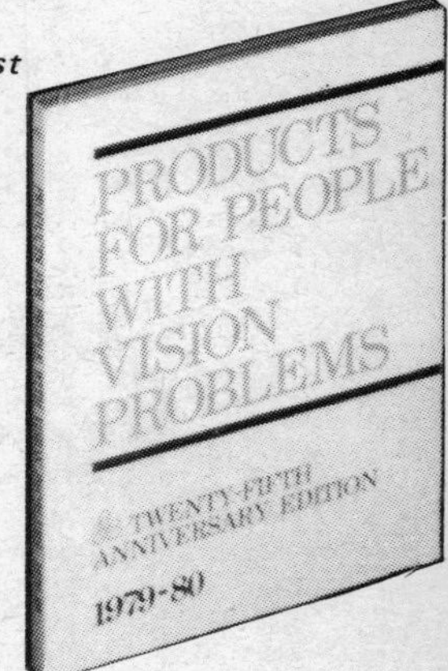

advice of one Ed Stiles, considered at the time to be the best designer and builder of hot tubs in Marin County, the hot tub capital of the galaxy. He advised me not to build a hot tub.

Look, he said, a hot tub wastes too much energy and money, and it's a lot of trouble to make, install, and maintain. Besides the tub itself — a big deal — you have the behemoth heater, a deck, a cover, extra plumbing, a thermostat, a filter system without which everything turns to slime, and suddenly more friends more often than you may want. The whole mess is like having a very hot very small swimming pool.

There's easier ways to sit in hot water with weather and a friend, he said. Go to Sears Roebuck and get a regular largish water heater. Hook it up in series with your existing hot water heater. Run the water in when you want a bath. Feed it to the garden when you're done. So I did. I lazily didn't even put in a cold water line — I just fill up with all the hot and enough cold to make the temperature perfect. (Mind you, there's nothing to prevent such a tub from being indoors, hooked up to regular plumbing. All it is is a better bathtub.)

It stays perfect because the tub is wood, but nothing fancy. Five pieces of 5/8" plywood, sized and angled to fit my body and one other facing me. A rectangular bottom piece about the length of my legs. Two rectangular ends, torso length, leaning back comfortably with plenty of support for langorous heads. And vertical sides; 26 inches apart allows room but maintains human contact. The ensemble is screwed and glued (marine glue), with 2" x 2" lumber stiffening outside each joint. Also 2" x 2" along the outside of the rim to provide a horizontal surface for soap, shampoo, bath toys, and perching one's butt. Any leaks: wedge in a bit of oakum from a fisherman's supply house. Plywood is truly the major achievement of the 20th century. The stuff I got wasn't even marine grade (which has no rottable voids supposedly), and of course it's raw — not coated with anything. Six years of constant use later it's doing fine.

With a deep enough outdoor tub, weather is irrelevant. Does it sometimes rain where you are? Or cool off in the evenings? Subside in your glorious tub till just a periscope of nose and eyes remains above water, sensitive to the delicate kiss of the snowflakes. And should your landlord tell you to go away and stop being so happy, take your better bathtub with you. It's portable. ■

THE RISING SUN
NEIGHBORHOOD NEWSLETTER

The Golden Gate Bridge cop said one thing they do is watch cars parked at Vista Point and under the bridge and if they see one parked for more than 2 or 3 hours they start looking on the bridge to see if anyone seems upset. People often think a long time before jumping. He said usually anyone who's thinking of suicide, if you speak to them at all, they break down. Of course, he is a very fatherly and kindly man and I'm sure people who wouldn't break down for just anyone cry on his shoulder.

Not a Marginal Act

Talking with Mimi Farina, Lucie Alexander and Dan O'Neill

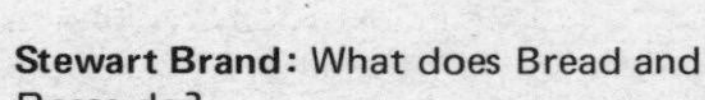

DARYL L. SCHIFF

Mimi Farina at Hillhaven Convalescent Home in Mill Valley, California: "What she was saying to me — she said it about ten times — was, 'You know what I'm gonna do when I get my social security check? I'm gonna go out and get a nice tall cold glass of BEER!' "

Every community has massive institutional walls around its prisons, convalescent homes, hospitals, mental institutions, etc. While many on the inside, patients, inmates, staff, are trying to reach out, very few on the outside try to reach in. (It's too real in there for most people.) Working as a volunteer in the places is the most direct way in. Here's another one.

Since 1974 Bread and Roses has brought free entertainment to the institutions of Marin County (across the Golden Gate Bridge from San Francisco). Founder Mimi Farina is a singer (a little less well known than her sister Joan Baez, which is probably a nuisance for both of them) and top flight cultural inventor, as this interview should demonstrate. The interview was done in 1978 with Mimi, her co-founder Lucie Alexander, and an occasional grump from cartoonist Dan O'Neil.

One element of the conversation that print leaves out and that you may want to resupply is Mimi's skill as a comedienne. She worked a year with the San Francisco improvisational comedy group, The Committee, and she talks like it. Her discourse is mostly imagined or remembered dialogue, all of it spoken in the various characters, including parody of herself, the sensitive, vulnerable, innocent idealistic singer.

Bread and Roses largely funds itself from autumn to autumn with a sensational acoustic music festival in Berkeley, California, where some of the greatest names in the business donate their talent. If all this puffery sounds like I'm on the Bread and Roses Board or something, I am. I was honored to be invited shortly after this interview.

We've done a detailed how-to booklet for this sort of service, available for the cost of handling. It covers funding and working with institutions, finding and working with ideal entertainers, and running an enjoyable office. Some of the why-to is in this interview. The rest is in your community. —SB

Bread and Roses Handbook
1979, 28 pp.

$.50 postpaid from:
Bread and Roses
78 Throckmorton Ave.
Mill Valley, CA 94941

•

BREAD & ROSES PERFORMER GUIDELINES

1. *Promptness is very important* for people confined in institutions. They are on regular schedules. In most circumstances, the patients or inmates become anxious and unhappy if the expected and anticipated entertainment is late.

2. Communicating with the audience is as important as entertaining them. We encourage you to visit with the residents before or after a performance. However, please be aware that expressing personal beliefs and philosophies (religious, social, political, etc.) is inappropriate and perhaps alienating. The quality of your performance itself will express inherent beliefs and messages.

3. Please don't make promises or commitments to the inmates or patients that you don't intend to keep; i.e., future visits or continued correspondence.

4. Cleanliness and good health are *most important,* particularly when you are visiting a health care facility. Many residents have a very low resistance to disease. If you are not feeling well the day before a scheduled performance, call the office to rearrange your visit.

CINDY CHARLES

The Jamie Miller Troupe bellydances at another Hillhaven Convalescent Home in San Rafael.

Stewart Brand: What does Bread and Roses do?

Mimi Farina: It takes 30 live shows per month into institutions in Marin County. What shows go where are determined by auditions. We see if the performer will be appropriate for the institutions and will feel comfortable in the setting that we take them to. Some people are afraid of hospitals and not afraid of juvenile hall, and you don't know that until you ask. You might take a piano bar singer into an old folks' home because she or he will know all the melodies that the older people know.

Brand: Is sticking strictly in Marin County out of some principle?

Farina: It's out of the principle to stay small. One of the things that people in institutions lack most is a sense of trusting anybody — the guards, each other, the nurses, the administrators. So if there can be a sense of rapport and trust with one source on the outside, it's better than having no trust at all. We want to establish a friendship amongst patients and the staff and ourselves, and going back repeatedly is what establishes that friendship. First visit around maybe it went well and maybe they'll remember you, but if you never go back, so what?

Brand: How much are you going back now?

Farina: Monthly. Generally. It's something like 20 shows that we do definitely once a month and then the other 10 are off and on different places — experimenting with new ones, or some of the places close out, like when some of the Drug Rehabilitation Centers stopped being funded.

Brand: What's the range of institutions?

Farina: There are supposedly 300 institutions in Marin. Mostly convalescent homes, drug rehabilitation centers, psychiatric day care centers, mental wards (some of them lock-up, some of them not), and then we also go to Napa Mental Hospital once a month. And there's a new thing called Nutrition Sites. It's where they feed old people lunch and/or dinner, with a bus that'll take them to the site. We've been entertaining there — those are more like parties than situations where the old folks are stuck in their chairs. What else?

Lucie Alexander: Well, there's juvenile hall, a couple of big prisons — San Quentin Vacaville. Is Vacaville in the county? Close enough. The Honor Farm. There are some children's centers for retarded children or children with learning disabilities. Also the kids who've just been in or who are about to go into juvenile hall, kids who won't or can't do well in school because they just have too much energy and anger.

Brand: Who are the artists you use?

Farina: Right now we've worked with 400. Most of them are local people who don't have credibility in the industry — meaning that they don't have albums out or are not professional in the sense of being on the market. Some of them have been professional entertainers in the past, like Ah Wing who is a Chinese comedian, used to entertain the troops, and now doesn't have a whole lot to do with his life — he's 60-some years old. Other people who are aspiring to be professional performers. Others who are teachers who give lessons, piano lessons, voice lessons. And a lot of just San Francisco street musicians, performers, jugglers, tightrope walkers, and fire eaters and so on.

Brand: For these artists there's no remuneration or expenses?

Farina: No. My theory was . . . Bread and Roses was really formed as a result of my anger towards the industry and finding out that it was the third largest money-making business in the country.

Brand: Which industry?

Farina: Music.

Brand: I didn't know that.

Farina: Yeah. I've got a lot of wealthy friends. I'm not so wealthy. Now when I look back I think it was an active non-violent approach to my resentment, to my anger, which I think was healthy and good, because I might never have played the guitar again or performed again. I really wanted to get famous people in the institutions to expose them to institutional life, because I felt that they had a platform which most musicians don't use at all. And so it's still an ambition of mine to use more famous artists, more people who have the ability to be heard by the public and might have more to say if they had experience with these institutions. Plenty of famous artists performed at our Bread and Roses Festival last fall, but it was a big party for a lot of people to get together and have a good time. It was a public event so they're sure of being in the news. If you go to an institution, nobody's ever liable to hear about it except those poor people who are falling out of their wheelchairs.

Alexander: Unless it's a famous prison like San Quentin or Soledad or Folsom, what's the point of going to a little old convalescent home?

Brand: What is the point?

Farina: For us? Or for them? For me the

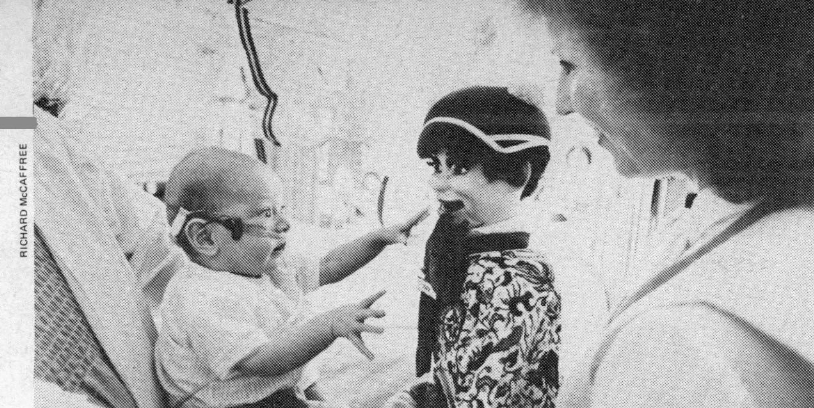

RICHARD McCAFFREE

On the children's ward of Moffitt Hospital, University of California Medical Center, San Francisco — Phyllis Barnard and "Joey."

point is to bring some sense of joy, freedom, beauty — whatever art has to offer. And I think also for an artist, there is a sense of participating in a community that's not there for them usually.

Brand: Have you been able to drag any famous folks besides yourself to the institutions yet?

Alexander: Steve Goodman, who is not as famous here but is more famous on the East Coast, came out and did a benefit for us. He performed in the county jail in San Francisco and was so enthusiastic about it that the next time he came out said, "I'll play anywhere, convalescent home, children's home, I'll make the music that's appropriate to the situation."

Brand: Why? What was in it for him?

Farina: He got turned on. He sang at the county jail in San Francisco and an old Bojangles type character . . . it's a good story. Steve was playing in front of different cells, and sometimes walking while playing. It's a little complicated to perform in that jail, because people could only look through the bars of the cell and hang their arms out. They couldn't really see him once he got past. One old man was doing a shuffle inside the cell, and things got quiet. There's always that din, people talking and even when everyone else is quiet some cocky guy is always speaking up. I used to like to walk along and sing, and especially on gospel tunes or hymns, all of a sudden the guys'd be singing along. And if you sort of pretend you don't notice, they really chime in with do-wahs and everything and sometimes it's very beautiful. In this case this old guy was doing a shuffle, and I said to the guard, "Can we let him out to dance in the hall?" He said, "Mmgghhmm." I said "No, really, it won't cause any disturbance and look how quiet they're being. They want to hear him." The guard said no no no no, but finally we convinced him and so he let the old man out and a friend of his handed him a little paper cup of salt which he poured on the floor, like this, because you can hear it better when you're dancing. So Steve would play one chord and the guy would dance out the four bars to the measure, and then he'd play another chord and the guy would dance out the next four bars. Each one was different, he never did one the same. He was really a soft shoe-er. He was incredible.

Alexander: Another one was Jesse Colin Young. He played at Napa Mental Hospital for us one afternoon. Jesse is very particular about his performances. He tuned his guitar for an hour before the performance at Napa, which I thought was conscientious. There must have been 400 people in the audience, most of them young adults. And they really got into it. They shouted and screamed and yelled and sang along on every song, and finally he let some of them come up and sing with him, which must have been heaven for them. He went on an hour longer than he was supposed to, letting people come up and sing with him and encouraging them to do it. It was really a very warm, generous afternoon. He was quite surprised himself. He was very nervous about being there.

Brand: Because . . .

Alexander: Mostly because the people look different. It's quite shocking sometimes.

Farina: And in every institution there are bright fluorescent lights on.

Brand: How are your relations with the institutional staffs?

Farina: In general, lately I think they're very good. I hit some bad ones. Marin County is very proud of the fact that they have a lot of small homes to keep the mentally ill rather than one large institution, and that's a good idea, but what goes along with it is that they encourage the patients to take on responsibility for everything. Which means that when Bread and Roses calls we have to speak to a patient to set up our gig. Which means often that we arrive and somebody forgot. Or only two people are there because the rest went to a movie, or they are all out playing a basketball game. So that's a nuisance. In some cases it's not just rude but dangerous. There was one young magician who was 17, very good, very clever, and he was going through his magic tricks. He held out a handful of cards and said, "Okay, who wants to come up and do a card game with me?" And two guys walked up. One was very withdrawn, very shy, hunched over, and the other looked like a big thug from Oakland. He looked like he could kill you by looking at you. So the kid said to the thug, "Okay, you go first, pick a card, any card. Not that card." And the guy's face dropped when he heard, "Not that card." He didn't know it was a joke. And I suddenly thought oh my god there should be someone in the room here, there should be some staff. Fortunately the kid was quick. "I was just kidding. *Any* card!"

Alexander: Mostly the staffs are very cooperative and very happy to have the entertainment. It's the real break in their month.

Farina: The good ones get everyone in one room, and in chairs, and ready for a show. The crummy ones, you get there and they say, "Oh yeah, well, we'll turn the Muzak off, and would you like to help us bring the patients out?" But the good ones are enthusiastic. It's volunteers and the occasional hard workers on the staff who care that make these places livable.

Brand: Are there other groups like yours working? Or others that you've inspired?

Farina: When we started there was one group called Hospital Audiences from New York. They've grown and are trying to start on the West Coast as well. There's four or five throughout the country. I know of one that was a direct result of Bread and Roses, called Sunflowers, in Stockton — it's been going for a year and they do about 20 shows a month. In Santa Cruz there were some CETA workers working under the name of Living Arts Express — one branch of it was doing institutional shows, and when they heard about us through our festival they came and we had an interview and they modeled themselves after our program. And in San Francisco two people came out to the festival — a lady who had been an actress and a guy who had been an accountant and also a music critic for a San Francisco music magazine. We put the two of them together and before any paper work got done they had people in institutions performing. They got so excited about the idea, once they met each other and realized that they could work together, it was like a sudden overnight marriage, it got going so fast. They're calling their group COMITY. And in New Jersey an ex-Bread and Roses performer, Will Charette, has started a group called Good Works Music, modeled after our program, as well.

We've always claimed that each community is different and therefore each project should be different. And I've never wanted the responsibility of having Bread and Roses expand and be associated with people that I don't know. The San Francisco group has been taking ethnic music into ethnic situations — in a Chinese old folks' home they will take Chinese music. That doesn't exist in Marin.

Brand: Don't you have an unusual pool of talent in Marin?

Farina: It's unusually rich with famous people who hide out, who want to be here on vacation and don't want to be found, which is a drag for us, but every once in a while Dan Hicks says he wants to do something, or Maria Muldaur will come by. We took Paul Krassner into the Centerpoint Drug Rehabilitation Center. Paul went in, I think, with nothing in mind, just to go in and talk. And talk and talk and talk and talk. They loved him. The drug rehab center has a lot of the people, very bright, very well read, and when they heard Paul Krassner was coming in, they must have got **Realists** from 15 years ago. It was a very interesting political discussion. One staff member called me after that and said that a lot of people asked questions, spoke up, who never talk at all. That happens with music too. So and so will get up in a convalescent home at the end of a show and play the piano, and everyone will say, "We didn't know she played the piano." The piano sits there month after month. No one is inspired. They're drugged, they're bored, they're angry, they're fighting — it's something when you see two old women fighting in wheelchairs. It's like chickens going at each other — they're scrawny and they're twisted and they can't move very well, and they're so furious, when they're not drugged too much, and they will whack at each other, and the wheelchairs spin. They can really get mad.

Brand: Say more about what happens for the audiences.

Alexander: I took one show into a retarded home — belly dancers, and we brought champagne. Champagne and belly dancers. What happens in a lot of these homes is there are different sections of people — some of them are physically handicapped, some of them are mentally handicapped, and some of them are neither, they're just in a retirement home, and none of the groups will mix with any other groups. It's just like in a prison, there's a real segregation of who will talk to whom and who will sit by whom, and they have special places, special people that'll talk to me and won't talk to the other people. Well this time with our champagne and belly dancers they all got up and danced together. Which was very unique. They all got drunk together, and they all slept the next morning right through breakfast. The director told me they had such a good time, they had more physical activity than they'd had in months.

Farina: It was a retirement home rather than a convalescent home, so it was easier to get alcohol in.

Brand: What is a convalescent home exactly?

Alexander: It's people who are either there to die or they're there convalescing from being in a hospital and they have no one to take care of them.

Farina: They're really the hardest to sing or perform for.

Alexander: Because they're very depressed.

Farina: But, oh, they love children. And children are not afraid of them. I mean, I object to their urine on the floor and the smelliness, but kids have less apprehension I think. Marilyn — the secretary of Bread and Roses — her kids and some neighbor friends formed a singing group called "Biscuits and Buds" over the summer. They did 12 convalescent homes, and at the end of the summer they were all charged up and they said, "Oh, we'll do it on our Christmas vacation," and Marilyn asked which ones they wanted to go back to, and it's true that the ones that they didn't like were the smellier and the less well kept ones.

Alexander: In some of the convalescent hospitals they're very uncared for. They don't dress them. The people are wearing nightgowns and one sock.

Dan O'Neill: I saw an old woman being beaten. There's a convalescent home across the street from my house. This lady got out and she could hardly move, mhm mhm mhm mhm mhm. The matron came running out and grabbed her and put her back in. Three times she did that. And the fourth time the matron started cuffing her — bang bang. The woman was somewhere in her 80s.

Farina: I'm aware of one man who died from pills, the wrong medication. The male nurse was pretending not to be aware of it, and when the activities director

←
"Biscuits and Buds" — seven girls age 8 to 15 — sang at twelve convalescent homes during their summer vacation. Here, at Bayside Convalescent Home.

THE RISING SUN
NEIGHBORHOOD NEWSLETTER

Jonathan says it's bad luck to look behind the refrigerator because it means you'll clean there.

questioned it, he said, "We'll check the book later." She said, "I think those are the wrong pills." It happened that we hired this activities director to come and work at Bread and Roses, and after a couple of months she started telling us stories. We were dumbfounded at the things that she knew that weren't getting out and I was saying, "Why didn't you do something?" All she could say was, "It was my job and I'm divorced and I have two kids to raise, and what was I supposed to do?"

Brand: That's interesting, because one of Governor Brown's arguments about getting volunteers into these institutions is that they'll find out things and say so on the outside.

Farina: That's perfect. Unfortunately, with Bread and Roses we cannot, because of our tax-exempt status, do anything openly political. That's why I want to take entertainers into those situations. Entertainers are creative, they're not stupid, and when they are confronted with that kind of thing, I think that they're sensitive enough to have a feeling of response.

Alexander: We did go to some hearings on convalescent hospitals and testified on the problems. A lot of things are not necessarily illegal, they're just inhumane. They move people from room to room without telling them. They'll come back after lunch and they'll be in another room. It's confusing having to be without your things when you're older.

O'Neill: And we're all gonna be there in 30 years.

Farina: I know some of the reasons why the convalescent homes are so bad. They are like restaurants; there are chains of convalescent homes. The owners exchange jobs, and the dirty dealings that they do can be hidden because they all cover for each other. Little things like when somebody dies, you can go on collecting their social security after they've died until it's reported by the mortuary to the state. So they make deals with the mortuary, "We'll bury this guy but don't tell 'em for two months and I can collect so-and-so many dollars, and you can have a percentage of that." A girl who worked in our office was fired from her old job because she refused to sign a number of social security checks. Someone on the staff has to sign the checks before they're cashed. An operator of a home can get somebody to sign illegally, go cash their checks, keep them for himself, and never tell anybody. She said no, and he said, "Do you want to continue working here?" She went home, called several activities directors and friends of hers and said, "What should I do?" They all said, "Look, you're good enough that you'll be hired somewhere else if you get fired, you have a good reputation in the county, don't sign the checks." So she went back and said, "I'm not gonna sign the checks," and he said, "Okay, you're fired." So she called a friend who was working in the state Health Department, and within 24 hours they came and investigated. It was in Mill Valley, a place that we had complained about because they had been so rude at one of my performances. They closed the place down and had everyone shifted to other hospitals. Which is healthy in the sense that it hits the news and the public hears about it, but unhealthy in the sense that all those people are totally lost. In the middle of the day or night they're shifted, like from one concentration camp to the next. They miss all their friends, all the things that have surrounded them and they're accustomed to.

Alexander: And chances are they're in another hospital which again is overcrowded.

Farina: Gary Goodrow and I went to a home — he went to read poetry and I went to sing — and throughout the entire hour there was a voice and we never could figure out where it came from, of an old woman saying *[sepulchral gasp]* "Nuurse! . . . Nuurse! . . ." — which was very creepy, in and out of his poems and my song. At the end of the hour we were leaving, sort of gliding out through the urine — it was not the cleanest place — and an aide was wheeling a lady to in front of the TV. She was a tiny little woman, so frail, skin that was almost transparent. She was just at the edge, she was like a little leaf, in fall, when the leaves are so crackly. And she, raising one arm — it was about all the strength she had — and she was saying, "I don't wanna watch television. I don't wanna watch television." And the aide was saying, "It's only 8:15, bedtime's 8:30. You're gonna watch TV till 8:30." And he crammed her in front of the TV set. Gary just stood there and went UAUGGHH. At the end of our wonderful performance to hear that, that was the end of my day. All the way home in the car Gary kept saying, "Nuurse! . . . Nuurse! . . ."

Brand: Do you get some one-time performers that can't hack it again?

Alexander: I don't know if it's that they can't hack it or that their performance wasn't quite appropriate or captivating enough or something like that. Usually if their performance is good they'll come back to do it again.

Brand: What things go over best?

Alexander: I would say comedy, and songs. Children's songs for children, older people's songs for them. Popular songs and also the artist's own material. It's special to hear somebody's creation, but it's also special to hear something that you can sing along with, that's familiar to you. Comedy goes over very well with groups that are alert.

Farina: The mental patients relate so well to it because they see somebody in front of them acting out of his mind and they register, "If he can act that crazy on the outside and earn a living doing it, what am I doing in here? If I can laugh and relate to that, I must have something going for me." At juvenile hall someone like Paul Krassner or people from the Committee go over beautifully.

Alexander: Workshops work better than performances sometimes. The first one I remember, was for a music instructor at San Quentin.

Farina: The first jam session was in the dining hall with Hoyt Axton, Verlin Sandals, Merle Saunders, and people from "Evolution of the Blues." It was especially funny because Hoyt has rifles in his bus, and at the last minute my pacifist girlfriend Martine was seen carrying six rifles to hide in the trunk of her car at the Howard Johnson's so that we could get in. Nevertheless the show went on very well. But it was rough because of the din and activity.

Alexander: Also, we brought a lot of acts. They want you to please every group, so you have to bring something for the Samoans, and the Filipinos . . .

Farina: Black, White, Chicano, Mafia. And some added. There's at least four separate groups.

Brand: No Chinese?

Farina: I guess there's no Chinese comedians and no Chinese prisoners. The jam session was so incredible. We got Jules Broussard, and who else?

Alexander: Nick Gravenites, Mark Naftalin, that bass player from Booker T.

Farina: Just a handful of people who were in town.

Alexander: And a drummer from Jesse Colin Young's group. Going in, the bass player was so nervous. He hadn't had any dope for at least an hour. He was shaking, saying, "How long is this gonna be? Where are we going?" Poor guy.

Farina: This is a character who normally gets up on a stage 45 minutes late and he's hot shit all the way. "Could I have some more lights please?" All of them, "When will we get out?" was the main question. That's what is fascinating to me about taking rock 'n' rollers into San Quentin. At first it's just, "Oh boy my name in San Quentin," but all of a sudden it's keys and gates and locks and guards and guns and big rolls of barbed wire, and then they're inside and really they're panicked. And performers normally, particularly rock 'n' roll, are so used to performing with either alcohol or dope, either on stage or right available whenever necessary during the show. I'm not talking about the old jazzers who are professional musicians and who really have a completely different attitude, but the rock 'n' rollers who I personally resent because of their non-professional attitude.

The Flying Karamazov Brothers

Alexander: They're used to playing to adoring teenagers.

Farina: Yeah, and suddenly they've put themselves — which I think is courageous — in the position of being in front of another audience, who may or may not like them, they don't know.

So here was a handful of people who didn't know each other that well, had heard each other's names, maybe some of them had jammed together, they walk in, we set up the sound, everything's getting plugged in, they're tuning up, and they're sort of saying, "Well, what's gonna happen next?" And we're saying, "Why don't you just rehearse, go ahead and play a little bit." They start to play and because of nervousness, they're suddenly playing harmoniously together as if they've known each other all of their lives. They get going for about 10 minutes and then in walk about 60 inmates.

Brand: So these guys were already cooking when . . .

Farina and Alexander: They were COOKING!

Farina: Oh boy, it was neat. They played for about an hour — incredible music. Then there was a break and we announced that inmates with instruments could get up and jam. There was one of the prettiest moments, and I regret not having it on tape. Jules Broussard sat in the middle with a horn player on each side of him, one was white and the other was black?

Alexander: That's right.

Farina: And they traded horn parts. Jules would be playing along, and he would turn to the guy on the right and they would play something together. They'd end that and then Jules would play a little more and turn to the guy on the left. And then in the end they all played together and Jules played two horns at the same time, which he can do. It was spectacular, and the inmates, who were really caught off guard, were listening without any self-consciousness by that time. It was beautiful to see their faces. I'll never forget one young white guy who'd been kinda bored with the whole affair but came nonetheless, and he didn't know who Nick Gravenites was on sight, he only knew the name from records. He got up and he was playing along on a guitar, and somebody must have told him that he was playing Nick Gravenites's guitar. He looked down and he looked around and he said in this loud voice, "This is Nick Gravenites's guitar?!"

But now that music instructor is gone, and the new one won't permit a large workshop. And there's a new warden who's much more stern.

Brand: Staff turnover is greater than the prison population turnover?

Alexander: Definitely.

Farina: With convalescent homes as well as everywhere else. They can't stand it, so they keep switching around. It's an ugly existence for them.

Brand: How long have you guys been doing this now?

Farina: Since '74. It's frustrating. I was just thinking, in all these stories of good moments there are intertwined all these general complaints. And what's frustrating for me is to know that Bread and Roses can only exist if we don't open our mouths and complain. At the same time I am so uncomfortable. The more I find out, the more I realize that change has to take place, and somebody has to speak up. Somebody once said, "Well, if that's your goal why don't you take a bunch of businessmen in? They're the people who have all the money and who run society." And I said, "You're absolutely right, but they are also the ones who lack imagination. It's the entertainers and sensitive artistic types who can come up with alternatives faster than businessmen who are out to gain a buck, not for anyone else's benefit but to raise funds for their own life. I still have as a goal to get more "famous" people, but I do think that they are kept away from society, kept away from community life, family life, a kind of normal home life that most people have to deal with. Being on the road, in planes, in elevators, in hotel rooms, in back stages, you really are hidden, just the way an institutionalized person is hidden from society. Having watched one entertainer after another come out of an institution saying, "Boy, there but for fortune . . . ," I can't help but think some of those creative minds will have to respond, maybe not now, maybe twenty years from now.

Brand: Maybe we're down to the why this thing began and how it looks four years later in terms of the aspirations.

Farina: Well, I'm thinking it's time we did some sort of seminar or conference — I don't know yet what to call it — that deals with the public, and people who work in institutions, and people who have been institutionalized. Have them all in a setting where they can talk to one another. Every single time I go to an institution I come away having found out

Nick Gravinites jams with inmates

RICHARD McCAFFREE

Performing at St. Vincent's School for Boys, San Rafael

something that I want to change, something that makes me just irate.

Brand: Was it anger that started you on Bread and Roses in the first palce?

Farina: Yes, a different anger. In 1973 there was an oil shortage. Oil is part vinyl which is what record albums are made of. I was in the process of separating from a singing partner, and the record company said, "Don't worry about signing a new contract, just make demonstration tapes, and if we approve, then you can make a solo album." So we put together a demonstration tape which cost $10,000 — that was the company's assumption that if it was good enough we would use parts of it to become an album.

It took a long time to do that because I was doing it bit by bit, one song at a time, and I would go to L.A. when everyone was available and when I had the time. The engineer was really the person who was pulling together the musicians, but that also meant that while I was in the studio he was on the phone with Paul Horn and talking to other people making other arrangements. He was getting things done, but I needed lots of attention — being very very insecure — so I would sing for a half an hour, go to the bathroom and cry for half an hour and come back and sing. It wasn't what you'd call a comfortable situation. I did not feel invited. I didn't think I was good enough, didn't think I belonged, was getting no encouragement, and finally I was told that I was a marginal act, and the marginal acts that year had to be put aside because of the fact that there simply was not enough vinyl to go around. The President said to me, "Now, all you artists are the same. Nobody believes me, but these are the facts." I said, "That's a great thing to say to me. It relieves a lot of my worries, and I am more than willing to accept it. I thought you didn't like me. So tell me, what's going on? Am I so much of a marginal act that I'm not gonna be allowed to make any albums here or do I have to wait for 5 years, what's gonna happen?"

"Well, maybe you can find a producer. Maybe the right producer could give you the right sound." So there was about a year of those meetings. I was then setting up tours with my manager's assistant who was something of a sloth and so I was putting a lot of energy into it and becoming an organizer, although I didn't know it, which was great for me. And during the concerts I would say to the audiences, "We're in the midst of an energy crisis, that means we're out of oil, that means there are fewer records gonna be sold, that means you have more choice. You've gotta speak up. Currently I'm not being invited to make any albums. If you'd like to hear my first solo album, would you like to write to my company, here's the address. . . .

So at Madison, Wisconsin, they started a petition, and at the end of the week they showed it to me. There were a thousand signatures, and it read very politely, "We the undersigned would like to see a solo album by Mimi Farina," and some other nice things. A girl came up very shyly and said, "Is this okay? I just wanted to know if it was polite enough, because you kept stressing being polite." I said, "It really is polite enough and I can't tell you how delighted I am." Then it happened again in Boston, only this time I provoked it. I said, "This is what they did in Madison." So, another petition went out — 1,000 signatures. And then in New York I opened a Phil Ochs concert, and from that I know that a lot of letters went in, and one phone call. And for the first time on this month-long tour my manager called me. I don't know how he found me because he never knew where I was. He said, "I've gotta talk to you." I said, "Oh, what is it?" He said, "There's some business about you talking on the stage." I said, "What, who said what?" And he said, "I'll just give it to you the way they told it to me. What they said at the company was that some bull dyke from the Bronx called up and said, 'On behalf of Mimi Farina, fuck you!' Did you tell her to say that?"

I said, "Is that all they said? Did they tell you anything about the letters and the petitions and so on?" "No, not a word." "You mean they didn't mention anything except this phone call?" "No, they said nothing else." I said, "That is so typical!"

Brand: That's interesting. That says a lot about what works, between thousands of signatures and one fuck-you.

Farina: I have a cousin Skipper Henderson who has a restaurant in Larkspur now, and he has lots of ideas. He was working in a halfway house at that time, and we were out to dinner, and I was saying, "Oh the industry," and "Going out on the road is so hard," and "I hate clubs because you have to stay up so late and wait in between shows and you go home smelling like a cigarette butt, and nobody cares anyway, and the company's awful." And he said, "Why don't you sing where you know it would be useful, where you know people would appreciate it. You might come away with a different feeling, and a different sense of your own music, and self, and so on. Why don't you come to my halfway house?"

So I did. It was certainly not inspiring, but it sparked something. I saw a real need for music in those places, and it got me thinking about all the people — 40 to 50 acts — being dropped from labels because of the oil crisis. I thought, I can't be the only one, there must be people who are feeling just as rejected and are not sure what to do. And at the same time there must be stars who somewhere in their heart of hearts are feeling a little guilt for some of it, and I'd like to use that and put them in a setting where none of the industry exists, where just human beings exist, and they sing for the sake of singing and give for the sake of giving.

I am always going back to the fact that I feel that contributions should be just that — a charitable act. I really like the idea because it is so out of this media society to do something for the sake of doing it, not for what the reaction will be in the future, not for what you'll take home with you, but for the moment that it happens.

It really pains me to see people who were inspired when they were young, who got chills all over at the sound of music or a piece of art, something that inspired them to want to do it themselves. Or maybe they never saw anything. Maybe it came completely from inside, but it made them excited and made them gleeful and happy and energized and vital, and to watch that go down the drain for the sake of the industry, for the sake of money, for the sake of receiving future funds that'll enable them to live until eternity in a happy house with a pool and a sauna, that is uninspiring to me and takes away from the value of the art. Maybe one can create wonderful songs on cocaine but it is short lived, and maybe someone can become a star overnight but that's probably gonna be short lived. And we're so prone to getting the most the quickest, that most of what we do is short lived. Most of the good things we do don't have lasting quality, and that's what I'm after, not just for me but for anybody.

Brand: Do you get it from this?

Farina: Oh yeah. A sense of security, identity, schedule — there were so many things that I did not have before Bread and Roses that I have now. Somebody asked me, "What does it feel like to be a do-gooder?" I said I had never thought about it but to me do-gooders were people who did good for others and not for themselves, but there was no way to describe the Bread and Roses that way. Bread and Roses did me good, because I needed it in my life to know that I was doing something other than getting profit, and needed a schedule. I wasn't good at getting up in the morning and facing an empty day and having to decide moment by moment what to do. I'm a very organized person, I came to discover, and so that this has saved me from endless days of hopeless hours of not knowing what to do and sticking my thumb in my mouth and having that terrible feeling of limbo added to the feeling of insecurity of being a little sister to somebody who's famous. This gave me purpose in life and a framework within which to use it.

Brand: So how does Bread and Roses look four years later?

Farina: I didn't have any expectations, I had an idea. People are always saying, "Has Bread and Roses lived up to your expectations?" I didn't have a vision in mind, I didn't have a picture, but I just had a feeling and an idea and it was so exciting that nothing could stop me from getting it going.

Brand: Was the idea whole or fragmentary? Did it come all in one piece?

Farina: Well, Lucie was the first person I called. She said, "Oh, yeah, what a neat idea, I've got free time, I'd like to help." I never went to college, I barely finished high school. I had a bad time in school, so I was very nervous about the fact that I couldn't make whole sentences or type and lots of things. So I kind of said, "Fuck all that, I've got this idea. I know a guy who knows a guy . . ." I at least have enough friends who can assist me and enough friends have graduated from college. So Lucie and I got together and I found a tiny room in Larkspur that was available. Lucie came over with a typewriter and we sat down and started inventing a brochure. And it was like dynamite, it had to come out of me.

Then we began fund raising and I went on KTIM and said, "I've started this group and this is what we're going to do and this is why and we have a room and a desk and a typewriter and a telephone and we need a secretary. So then there was a phone call and this girl came and she was wonderful and she became the secretary. It just kept moving faster than my thinking, so every time a new problem would come up, I was there with my notebook and I'd go home and think it through and come back the next day with a solution. I never had a moment to rest for the first year. And the first year it was all females, so it looked as though we were a feminist organization, which really irritated me. And they were all as beautiful as Lucie, so sometimes going into prisons it looked like we were a fashion show.

Brand: How did all this relate to your career?

Farina: Sometimes I worried about it. I thought, "Ooawhh if I do that, then I'll not only become a social worker but I'll lose any kind of respect as a performing artist."

Brand: It's the opposite, isn't it?

Farina: It turned out to be the opposite.

Brand: How does someone who's inspired by your example do it, start a Bread and Roses?

Farina: I think 50 percent of it is inspiration. That comes from some unknown force, so that part I can't talk about. Or be responsible for. But as far as logistics and how to set up a nonprofit organization, we are producing a pamphlet that describes how anybody in any part of the country could set up a program like this. I think that the approach is to start by working, not by getting the paperwork done. The success of a group is determined by the inspiration of the people. If the people see only the how-to's in order to get a project underway, it seems as though that slows them down. The red tape and the paperwork gets in the way of inspiration. But if you're inspired, in spite of everything you get the work done and then the paperwork follows. ■

Grand finale of the Bread and Roses Festival, October, 1977. On "Just a Closer Walk With Thee" — left to right — Gary Goodrow, Josh White, Jr., Jayotis Washington, Richie Havens, Terry Garthwaite, Freebo, Jackson Browne, Tubo Rhoad, Jerry Lawson, Joan Baez, Theodore Bikel, Pete Seeger, David Lindley, Terry Reid, John Herald, Gay Mentin, Mimi Farina, Jimmy Hayes, Arlo Guthrie. "Through days of toil and snares/If I fall, dear Lord, who cares?/Who with me my burden shares?/None but Thee, dear Lord, none but Thee."

A nice double album of the occasion, "Bread and Roses," is available from Fantasy Records.

THE RISING SUN
NEIGHBORHOOD NEWSLETTER

"Don't tell me to change the world. Change your clothes!"

— Heard by Izzy at a punk fashion show

A Good Age

The best, most accessible work on the facts and fictions of oldness. Novelist, poet, gerontologist, and author of **The Joy of Sex**, *Alex Comfort makes it clear that a good deal of what we think of as aging is not biological but social and psychological. Certain roles and patterns are imposed on people who have been around longer than some of the rest of us. They are arbitrarily defined as unintelligent, unemployable, crazy, and asexual, despite all evidence to the contrary. Dr. Comfort calmly suggests revolt.*

Beautifully designed and illustrated with portraits of robust oldsters. Fine marshalling of facts to show that a good deal of what I believed about aging was nonsense. In the long view, there are no young. Only the present old and (myself included) the new old.

—Tom Ferguson, M.D.

A Good Age
Alex Comfort
1976; 224 pp.
$5.95 postpaid from:
Simon & Schuster
Attn: Order Department
1230 Avenue of
the Americas
New York, NY 10020
or Whole Earth
Household Store

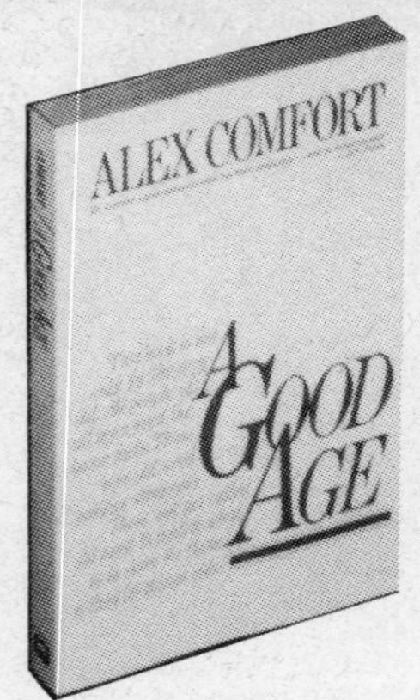

Karen, Baroness Blixen, the supremely gifted short-story writer, was Danish, but wrote most of her books in English under the pseudonym Isak Dinesen. Her first book, Seven Gothic Tales, **was published in 1934, when she was forty-nine.** Shadows in the Grass, **her last, appeared when she was seventy-six, one year before her death.**

•

Dignity. Stand on this. If other people don't recognize it, put them down — other older people depend upon the degree to which you ensure that anyone who thoughtlessly displays agism doesn't get away with it. React to people who talk slightingly about seniors ("old buffer," "old biddy," "dirty old man," "old lady in tennis shoes") in the way that black people have learned to react to people who talk slightingly about "niggers." Tell them you don't appreciate that sort of language. Your reaction will give them a salutary shock. Usually they mean no harm, but need their heads changed, to see older people as people, and only incidentally or secondarily as old. Don't put up with being addressed by nurses, aides and others as "Granny," "Pop" or the like. Point out acidly that you have a name and if they don't know it they can damn well ask, and that you were earning a living when they were still eating baby food.

•

When I was young I was amazed at Plutarch's statement that the elder Cato began at the age of eighty to learn Greek. I am amazed no longer. Old age is ready to undertake tasks that youth shirked because they would take too long. —W. Somerset Maugham

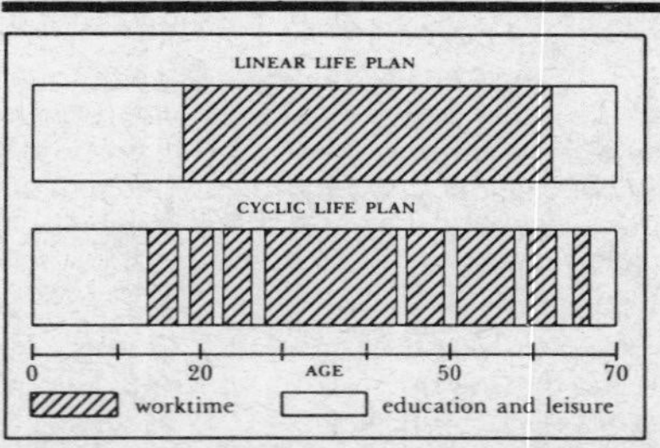

What Do You Want to be When You Grow Old?

It's always nice when someone marshals the facts to debunk some weepy liberal bummer. Dienstfrey and Lederer do that and more. Their cleanly-written book presents a compassionate and positive picture of old age, a condition very different from the alienated gray nightmare we may assume. **What Do You Want to be . . . ?** *contains revisionist information on retirement communities and trailer camps, remarriages, relationships between the old and their children, and the prospects for rehabilitation after stroke; it describes the value of senior centers and hospices; it explains the social security system and a proposal for its radical revision.*

The book's design (by Yolla Bolly press) is very high-class for a paperback. It gracefully integrates photographs, cartoons, and several types of marginalia.

Anyone who is planning to live past retirement or caring about older parents or grandparents might find this book useful. It challenges the reader to consider what she wants her old age to be, and offers an array of true options, success stories, and possibilities.

—Stephanie Mills

What Do You Want to be When You Grow Old?
Harris Dienstfrey and
Joseph Lederer
1979; 301 pp.
$2.75 postpaid from:
Bantam Books
414 East Golf Road
Des Plaines, IL 60016
or Whole Earth
Household Store

•

More than 80 percent of the people sixty-five and over see their children at least once every two weeks. Note that the statistic speaks of parents *seeing* their children. They live close to one another; the children aren't scattered helter-skelter over the country. (For the record, the physical contact extends to the third generation: Three-fourths of the people over sixty-five see their grandchildren at least once every two weeks.)

•

Even with general agreement between husband and wife about where to live in retirement, they may not be ready for a future of unrelieved togetherness. It is not unusual for newly retired couples to be found constantly bickering.

The Massage Book

People rubbing people is always nice. People rubbing people with skill is an order of magnitude nicer. This was the first book on massage-for-pleasure, and it is still far and away the best. Everyone should have this skill. It's easily gotten from the book — plus a friend, telling you how you're doing. "Mmmmhh." —SB

The Massage Book
George Downing
1971; 200 pp.
$4.95 postpaid from:
Bookworks
Random House
455 Hahn Road
Westminster, MD 21157
or Whole Earth
Household Store

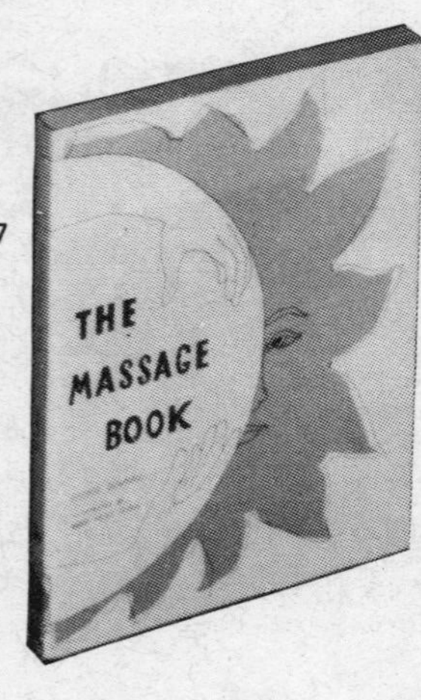

Over 50

An excellent book that warrants its subtitle, "The Definitive Guide." It's for anyone who is thinking about their own problems of growing old. —Michael Phillips

Over 50
(The Definitive Guide
to Retirement)
Auren Uris
1979; 613 pp.
$17.95 postpaid from:
Chilton Book Company
Sales Service Department
Chilton Way
Radnor, PA 19089
or Whole Earth
Household Store

•

There are all those things you've planned to give away or bequeath eventually anyway. Why not start to do it now? Not only will the donees get more pleasure out of them (hopefully), but you'll be able to observe their pleasure, while being relieved of the necessity to maintain, make room for, insure or otherwise spend money on them. And to the extent that your gifts are to approved charities, the tax benefits can be much more important now than they will be later.

For other things, the years between now and retirement may be the best time for a gigantic "garage sale," so to speak. It goes without saying that you won't get as much for anything as you really know it is worth. But selling something when you have time to say yes or no to an offer can bring in a lot more than selling it in those last few hurried months or weeks before you take off for the South Seas. A detailed household inventory can prove invaluable at this point. By marking each item "sell," "keep," "give away," or just "?" you can begin on paper the process of trimming your excess baggage, and getting into shape for traveling light.

•

Protection from stretching

When washing the face, use as little manipulation as possible. You face doesn't need scrubbing. Washing using only the fingertips is a good method. And, when cleansing the face, avoid any pulling of the skin in the eye area. Any eye rubbing habit should also be broken.

Another culprit is smoking. Aside from being generally bad for the health, it causes many small wrinkles because of associated facial movements. (Just another good reason to quit.)

•

1 Before anything else I like to hold my palms lightly against my friend's forehead for a few moments. Cover the forehead with the heels of your hands, letting the fingers extend down the temples. Apply no pressure. Pause as long as seems right and comfortable to you; a few seconds, half a minute, whatever. Center yourself. Let your friend grow accustomed to your touch.

2 Now begin massaging your friend's forehead with the balls of your thumbs. First mentally divide the forehead into horizontal strips about a half an inch wide. Then, starting with your thumbs at the center of the forehead just below the hairline, glide both thumbs at once in either direction outwards along the topmost strip. Press moderately; use about the pressure it takes to stick a stamp on an envelope. Continue all the way to the temples, a surprisingly sensitive place, and end there by moving your thumbs in a single circle about half an inch wide. Immediately pick up your thumbs, return them to the center of the forehead, and begin the next strip down, again moving your thumbs from the center outwards. Then, working progressively downwards, do each of the others in turn, ending with a strip running just above your friend's eyebrows. Remember to conclude each strip with another small circle on the temples — a flourish not strictly necessary, but your friend will feel it's very 'right.'

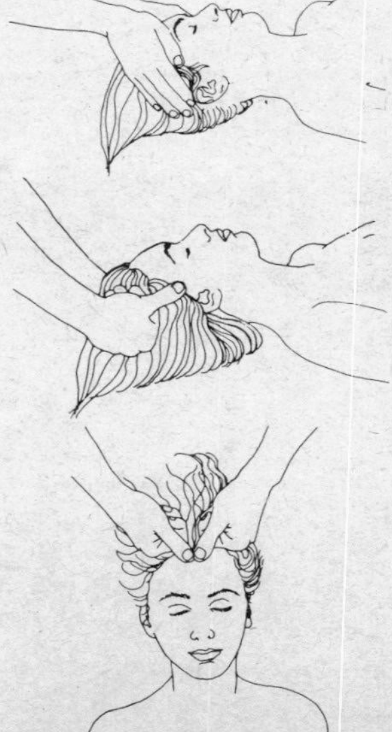

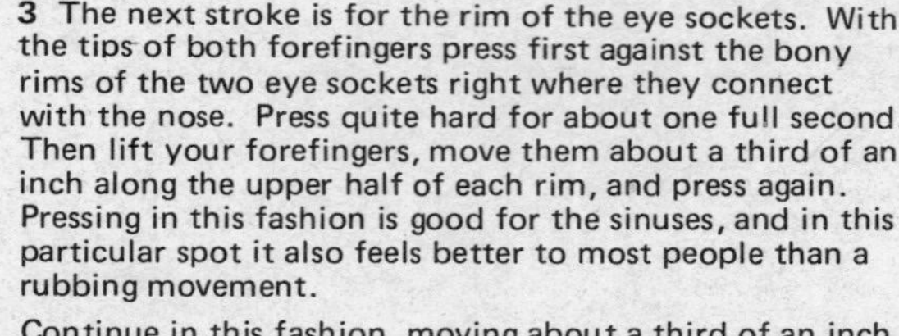

3 The next stroke is for the rim of the eye sockets. With the tips of both forefingers press first against the bony rims of the two eye sockets right where they connect with the nose. Press quite hard for about one full second. Then lift your forefingers, move them about a third of an inch along the upper half of each rim, and press again. Pressing in this fashion is good for the sinuses, and in this particular spot it also feels better to most people than a rubbing movement.

Continue in this fashion, moving about a third of an inch each time you press, until you have reached the outermost point of each eye socket (i.e., the point farthest from the nose). Then return to the point nearest the nose and begin again, this time working the length of the lower half of the rim.

•

Finally, for the *coup de grace*, tell your friend to listen to the sound inside his head. And then, moving with extreme slowness and gentleness, close both his ear channels with the tips of your forefingers. (Be sure to close both sides at once; nothing will happen if one ear is closed alone.) Keep them closed for about fifteen to thirty seconds. Although some people don't care for this, many enjoy a brief but pleasant journey.

TWO OF THE TOP LINES ON my public agenda have to do with averting nuclear war and averting overpopulation. Whether sex has anything to do with war I'll leave to the Freudians. But sex has plenty to do with population. I figure, the more attention and sophistication that goes into sex as recreation, the less we will all be saddled with the effects of accidental procreation. Now there's a workable program. —SB

The Joy of Sex

If a book is judged on how profoundly it affects people's lives, and how many lives it reaches, this book is one of the all time greats. You can't read it without trying some of the ideas in it, and those lead to others, and human relations grow steadily warmer. In the writing, the content, and the illustrations, warmth is what the book is about. And imagination, and variety. Contact. Health. —SB

The Joy of Sex
(A Gourmet Guide to Love Making)
Alex Comfort, Editor
1974; 254 pp.

$8.95 postpaid from:
Simon and Schuster
Attn: Order Department
1230 Avenue of the Americas
New York, NY 10020
or Whole Earth Household Store

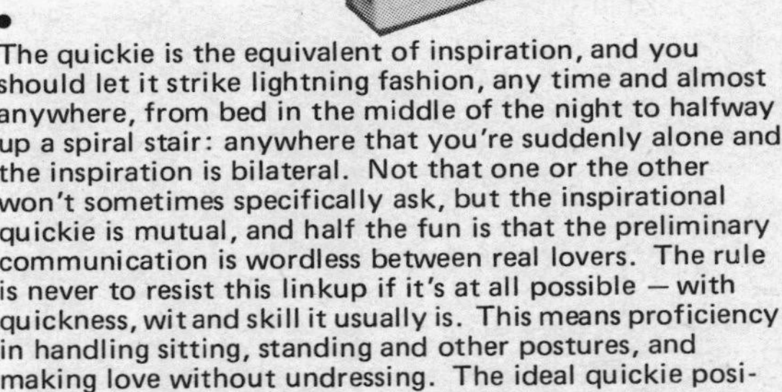

•

The quickie is the equivalent of inspiration, and you should let it strike lightning fashion, any time and almost anywhere, from bed in the middle of the night to halfway up a spiral stair: anywhere that you're suddenly alone and the inspiration is bilateral. Not that one or the other won't sometimes specifically ask, but the inspirational quickie is mutual, and half the fun is that the preliminary communication is wordless between real lovers. The rule is never to resist this linkup if it's at all possible — with quickness, wit and skill it usually is. This means proficiency in handling sitting, standing and other postures, and making love without undressing. The ideal quickie position, the nude matrimonial, will often be out. This may mean on a chair, against a tree, in a washroom. If you have to wait and can go straight home, it will keep up to half an hour. Longer than that and it's a new occasion. Around the house, try not to block, even if you *are* busy.

•

Bondage

Bondage, or as the French call it, ligottage, is the gentle art of tying up your sex partner — not to overcome reluctance but to boost orgasm. It's one unscheduled sex technique which a lot of people find extremely exciting but are scared to try, and a venerable human resource for increasing sexual feeling, partly because it's a harmless expression of sexual aggression — something we badly need, our culture being very up-tight about it — and still more because of its physical effects: a slow orgasm when unable to move is a mind-blowing experience for anyone not too frightened of their own aggressive self to try it.

Sexual Honesty

I believe this book has found its way to the very center of interest in sex books: What do other people do? — details please. Textbooks, including **The Joy of Sex**, *try to generalize satisfaction for everybody. Kinsey found, and Shere Hite proves, that wild variety throbs in American bedrooms. Furthermore immeasurable human unhappiness goes with painting oneself into a sexual corner. The out is sexual honesty. Start with this exciting book. (Her later book,* **The Hite Report**, *is more interpretive and less interesting.)* —SB

Sexual Honesty
(By Women for Women)
Compiled and edited by Shere Hite
1974; 294 pp.

$1.95 postpaid from:
Warner Paperback Library
Book Order Department
Independent News Co.
75 Rockefeller Plaza
New York, NY 10019
or Whole Earth Household Store

•

40. I would like to try having sex outside in a setting like the warm, luxuriant garden I mentioned before, and I would like to spend a whole day with my husband having prolonged and repeated sex. I would like to have sex more than we do now, and I would like the part before intercourse to last longer. I would like to change our bedroom scene so that my husband would treat sex in a less routine way.

•

If it's one of those nights when I just want EVERYTHING in me, we get into a missionary position where he has his penis in my vagina, and I have room to play with the clitoris, and then we put the vibrator in my anus. Wow! Blows my mind!

•

41. My first lesbian experience was incredibly electrifying — and a brief affair I had later with a woman who was an unbelievably tender and romantic lover. Also Susan!

My Secret Garden
Forbidden Flowers

By female and male acclaim these are the horniest books in print. They are made of letters to Nancy Friday by innumerable women telling their sexual fantasies in vivid detail. They're liberating and a turn-on for women — completely defusing any lingering guilt about having such fantasies — and enlightening and a turn-on for men, dissolving what was long thought to be a major difference and barrier between the sexes (also tangentially educating males on how to be a sensitive and imaginative lover rather than a narrow-minded clod).

The second book, **Forbidden Flowers**, *is even more explicit since the women are responding to the excitement of* **My Secret Garden**. *A number of the correspondents announce gleefully that they are masturbating as they write. Nice books to read alone, or aloud with a good friend.* —SB

My Secret Garden
(Women's Sexual Fantasies)
Nancy Friday
1973; 336 pp.
$2.95 postpaid

Forbidden Flowers
(More Women's Sexual Fantasies)
Nancy Friday
1975; 324 pp.
$2.95 postpaid

both from:
Pocket Books
Attn: Order Department
1230 Avenue of the Americas
New York, NY 10020
or Whole Earth Household Store

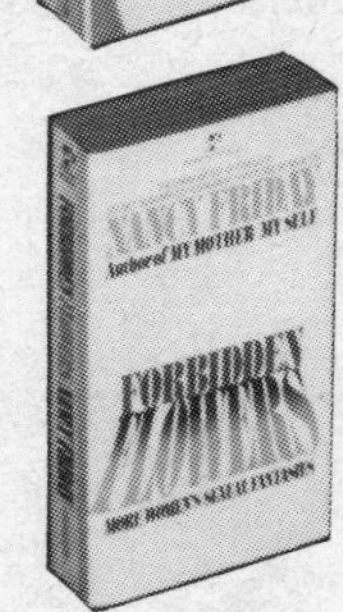

•

I've agreed to help a bachelor friend paint his new apartment, and since it's a hot day we've both shed our clothes to do the job. He's up on a high ladder slapping paint on the ceiling with a broad brush, while I'm standing below painting the walls with a roller. It's a water paint, pale grey; and at one point as we are laughing at some joke — we've been smoking a joint, and the record player is on loud — I glance up at him as he grins down at me, and from below his balls look so funny (and nice) even though he and I have never been to bed together and I don't really know him well enough to know how he'll take it — even so I reach up with my roller dripping grey paint and slather his bouncing balls, and on up to his collarbone. He lets out a yell, and risking his life he's down the ladder like a flash and lets go — slap! slap! — with his brush, on my tits, left then right, and I go spinning around and he whops me on the can, left then right, with his big fat brush. So I run my roller up one of his sides from ankle to armpit, so he dabs me in the navel, and I double over laughing and he's on top of me, and we go down in a puddle of grey paint, writhing and wrestling and struggling and both of us suddenly aroused, hot as hell and panting and I'm saying "Put it in" and he's trying to get me in position so he can, and I get my legs up around his neck in a frenzy so he can find my cunt and it's all impossible with all the goddam paint, and suddenly I see his eyes widen with panic and I feel it the same second: the paint is burning us up, but it's only the first second we mind it, then it becomes the greatest sensation in the world and we both start sliding together and the slimy stuff on all our surfaces glues us together and we get it in, and we slide around fucking and fucking and FUCKING and FFFUUUCCCKKKIIINNNGGG . . . [aaaarrrrggggghhhh] [Taped interview]

—**My Secret Garden**

•

. . . I'm spread-eagled on a huge roulette wheel that hangs on a wall. As my partner penetrates me, the wheel spins faster and faster and faster . . .

. . . I am attacked by a pack of German Shepherds (sexually, that is) . . .

. . . I have been smuggled into a male prison and am being passed from cell to cell. It is the "long-termer" section (they are ravenous!) . . .

. . . I am completely passive having things done to me against my will. It is not actually rape, I don't struggle, I enjoy it but against my will. Sometimes I hear a voice, like on a PA system, describing what is being done to me and my reaction . . .

. . . I am out on the street with no underwear. I approach two men walking together, lift my skirts, and offer to do anything . . . —**My Secret Garden**

•

I am rising up toward the starry sky. It seems as close as a ceiling. The moon is glowing light bulb. I can see for miles, lights and buildings, roads and mountains, rivers and seas. Down below me, hundreds of miniature people stare upward in wonder and awe. A big safety net is being quickly constructed on my acre of space (which seems only a few feet to me now). My squadron of deep-sea divers stand ready and waiting at its edge. They are naked except for suitably shaped helmets on their heads (like the reddish tips of penises — outsized to them, but now quite suitable to me — a six- or seven-inch cock . . .). Dance music has been turned on over loudspeakers, but it is faint and far away to me. "Turn up the music, please," I say, and my voice, louder than any loudspeaker, reverberates over the landscape. The Lilliputians below clasp their hands over their ears. The music is turned up, and I can hear the drumbeat. I sway to the rhythm. I am a beautiful giantess-sex-goddess. No one has ever seen anything like me before. I pull down one side of my bra, exposing a soft white mountain of breast. I draw down the other side, and two heavy, mountain-breasts swing over the crowd, joggling as I dance. Some of the little men (overcome with the sight, it would seem) faint or collapse. I feel very heavy, but it is a pleasant, slow heaviness like slow-motion films. I have a beautiful, monstrous, symmetrical body. I put my fingers on the top of my panties and begin to push them down. I push them down to my thighs, exposing a naked, slowly gyrating pelvis of unbelievable size. Little heads crane upward. I can see their wide open eyes and mouths. I have to be careful when I draw up one leg (I'd hate to lose my balance and step on anybody). I pull my panties off, one leg and then the other, stand with my legs spread apart. "So, Little People . . ." I whisper very softly, although my voice still echoes from mountaintop to shining sea. "You've never seen anything like this before?" I rock my pelvis and spread my legs wider apart as I bend my knees. For a moment, my bedsized clitoris is exposed above them. They jump up and down with excitement. "Let's see it again . . . again . . ." I can hear them crying in little voices like mewing kittens. "Please, Great Sex Goddess . . . show us again!" I fingertip my labia apart for a few seconds, smiling down on them. The moisture of my excitement creates drops of falling rain. Giant Goddesses do everything on a grand scale.

"Well, my cocky astronauts . . ." I whisper to my crew. "Are you ready for your journey?"

—**Forbidden Flowers**

THE RISING SUN
NEIGHBORHOOD NEWSLETTER

Andrea's grandmother worked in an American flag factory and if she was one minute late, they locked her out for the whole day.

Liberating Masturbation

Betty Dodson, sex educator, erotic artist-feminist, having explored virgin territory with a smile, has translated her findings into a new form of power based on self-pleasure and self-knowledge.

Through her teachings, her Bodysex Groups and her nude drawings Betty has brought us a treasure — the gift of our own exquisite orgasms — any way we want 'em. —Salli Rasberry

Liberating Masturbation
Betty Dodson
1974; 80 pp.

$5 postpaid from:
Betty Dodson
P.O. Box 1933
New York, NY 10001
or Whole Earth Household Store

•

Most of us are conditioned to negative body images, shame about body functions, and guilt about sex and pleasure. To reverse this conditioning I recommend that we have intense love affairs with ourselves. With frequent practice of selflove rituals we can discover and create new sexual response patterns, healing ourselves with massive doses of love and orgasms. Each of us can set up a personal program for "do-it-yourself-at-home" sexual liberation.

•

MASTURBATING TECHNIQUES

PRESSURE: Some women achieve orgasm by pressing the thighs together and squeezing and tensing the muscles. This is done in different positions, squeezing and pressing rhythmically. It is impossible for me to experience orgasm this way, but some women do. I require more direct stimulation. The pressure technique is great for buses and planes and sitting in waiting rooms.

WATER: Some women have orgasms by letting water run on their genitals. The amount of pressure can be controlled and the water is symbolically pleasing. This is especially good for women who find it difficult to touch their genitals, and the bathroom offers privacy and security. Never use your vibrator in the tub or shower. Water and electricity, as you know, do not mix.

HAND: This is perhaps the most common form of self-love. I always use an oil or cream. Saliva works but it dries too quickly. Also, reaching inside and using your own lubrication is fine. For me the slippery, moist feeling of oil on my genitals is a turn on. You can use one finger or your whole hand. Try circular motions, above the clitoral body, below, on top, or to the side. Every woman is different, so different strokes for different folks. Experiment with several techniques, observing the arousal potential of each — going slow, fast, soft, firm. You can lie on your stomach, your side, your back. Try putting your legs up and also stretching them out. Try sitting up, standing up, watching in a mirror.

VIBRATORS

by Joani Blank

Owner/Operator of Good Vibrations, The Vibrator Store, and Down There Press

Until quite recently, access to vibrators was pretty much limited to so-called "adult" bookstores and mail-order business, largely advertising in "men's" magazines. Electric vibrators have also been sold for years in department stores and some beauty supply shops, but many people wanting to use them for masturbation or sex with a partner have been very reluctant to shop for them there.

Over the last few years, several retail outlets have been established which sell vibrators and other sensual supplies in a non-exploitive, non-sexist, sex-positive and open environment. Although none of these stores is exclusively for women, all are places where women will be comfortable shopping. Some of these stores have mail order catalogs, and all will send items by mail on request.

There are four basic kinds of vibrators. Battery-operated penis-shape vibrators are lightweight, portable, relatively inexpensive, and they vibrate quite gently. Many now have variable speed controls. Most are made in Hong Kong and they are not the most reliable. Those manufactured in Europe are of higher quality, more expensive and much less widely available in the U.S. Back-of-the-hand or Swedish type massager/vibrators are heavy and strong. They shake up the hand a lot, making them considerably less desirable than other electrics for sexual use. Compact, silent electric (line voltage) vibrators with multiple attachments are manufactured by several different U.S. and Japanese companies (Oster, Wahl, General Electric, Norelco, Conair, Clairol) and in Hong Kong as well. There is nothing magic about special attachments designed for clitoral stimulation. One of the standard attachments usually works just fine. Wand-type electric vibrators (especially the Hitachi Magic Wand) are strong motor-driven vibrators that are good for whole body massage as well as both solo and partner sex.

In my store (Good Vibrations) we are often asked the question, which is the best vibrator? Since individual preferences vary so much, it is impossible to recommend one that is best for everyone. Recent "surveys" published in popular magazines tell more about the effectiveness of certain companies' advertising than about the effectiveness of the vibrators. We only can tell you that most women who switch from battery-operated to electric vibrators do not go back, and that hardly anyone who switches to the wand-type electric ever goes back.

For the person or couple who has never tried a vibrator before, almost any one will do for starters. For the person who knows what she/he wants, there's no substitute for holding the vibrator in your hand to check out its weight, shape, sound and intensity. So, if you live anywhere near one of the stores listed below, try to get there. If not, try your local Sears or other store that carries small appliances. (Don't worry, nobody will ask you what you are going to use it for.) If you prefer, request catalogs from the places listed here. All have reasonable exchange and/or return policies. If you want to read more about vibrators before trying one, order my book **Good Vibrations**. Order it directly from Down There Press or with your vibrator from one of the places listed here. ■

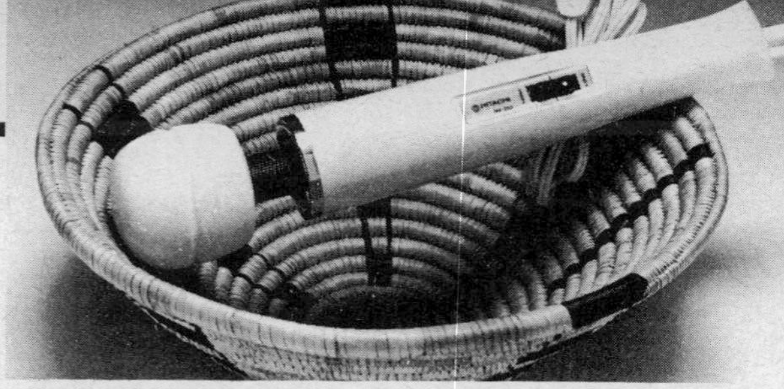

Hitachi Magic Wand (the Cadillac of vibrators) $24.95 from Xandria

Good Vibrations
(The Complete Woman's Guide to Vibrators)
Joani Blank
1976; 43 pp.

$2.50 postpaid from:
Down There Press
P.O. Box 2086
Burlingame, CA 94010

Good Vibrations
Catalog

$.25 from:
Good Vibrations
3416 22nd Street
San Francisco, CA 94110

Eve's Garden
Catalog

free from:
Eve's Garden
104 Greene Street
New York, NY 10012

Come to Your Senses
Catalog

free from:
Come to Your Senses
321 South Cedar
Minneapolis, MN 55454

The Xandria Collection
Catalog

$3 postpaid from:
The Xandria Collection
P.O. Box 7685
San Francisco, CA 94120

The Love Shops
Gourmet Lover's Guide and Catalog

$2.95 from:
The Love Shops
Box 200
Station A
Vancouver, B.C.
Canada V6C 2V2

Lovecraft, Ltd.
Catalog

$1 from:
Lovecraft, Ltd.
63 Yorkville
Toronto, ON
Canada M5R 1B7

Whirling Derby & Friend $14.95 from Eve's Garden

Adam & Eve

How about eight inches of hot, slick — catalog? Adam & Eve's mail order service offers athletic supplies for varsity fucking. Skimpy outfits for ladies and men, porn to help the fellas get it up, rubbers to cover it when it's up, industrial strength sex lubricants and more dildoes than you can shake a stick at. If all the electric pleasuring devices available herein were plugged in simultaneously, both coasts would be browned out. So much the better. —Stephanie Mills

Adam & Eve
(Division of Population Planning Associates)
Catalog

free from:
Adam & Eve
P.O. Box 800
Carrboro, NC 27510

The best sexual lubricant

Coconut oil.

Saliva dries up. K-Y jelly is a mineral oil. Kama Sutra oil and its imitators are expensive, cloying, and untasty.

Sex without lubrication easily tends toward discomfort, brevity, and unimaginativeness.

Coconut oil is cheap, organic, odorless, flavorless, and easily available (at any organic food store, where it's sold as cooking oil). Coconut oil in the jar is semi-solid, like butter, but it melts to a clear oil at the touch of human skin, warm and slippery. Afterwards it absorbs into the skin. Some users melt the oil in the jar for personal repackaging in cold cream jars, camper's squeeze tubes, etc.

An oil footnote: The Woman's Movement has done well in educating men in such matters as due (but not exclusive) attention to the lady's clitoris, avoidance of chafing away at a dry vagina, etc. Therefore it is surprising how few women are sensitive about the male equivalent — dry friction on the penis, ambivalently welcome at best compared to friendly oil. —SB

[Suggested by Toni Ayers]

Screw
Sex Sense

What vibrators are to female masturbation, pornography is to the males. The problem is that pornography is quasi-illegal, with all the cop/underworld convolutions that implies, including routine rip-offs (who do you complain to?). The answer is **Screw**, *a raunchy cheery tabloid out of deepest New York City which subjectively but honestly rates the scene. Along with sundry outrageousness (remember the nude pix of Jackie O.?),* **Screw** *grades the quality of romp you'll get at New York sex parlors, the quality of action in porno films in circulation, and so on. For more limited specific consumer product evaluation* **Screw** *publishes* **Sex Sense**, *a bi-monthly whose main attraction is an updated list of which mail order suppliers are Dirty Dealers and which are Safe Sellers.* —SB

Screw
(The Sex Review)
Al Goldstein, Editor

$39.95 /year (52 issues)

Sex Sense
John Milton and Jay Blickstein, Editors

$10 /2 years (11 issues)
both from:
Milky Way Productions
Subscription Department
P.O. Box 432
Old Chelsea Station
New York, NY 10011

Frederick's of Hollywood
Ah Men

I used to wonder what my friends and acquaintances looked like naked. Now I imagine what they'd look like in the clothes from these catalogs. —Art Kleiner

Ah Men
(Shop for Men)
Catalog

free from:
Ah Men
8900 Santa Monica Blvd.
Hollywood, CA 90069

Frederick's of Hollywood
Catalog

$1 postpaid from:
Frederick's of Hollywood
6608 Hollywood Blvd.
Hollywood, CA 90028

The Casablanca $25.95 from Ah Men

D
Natural Look under Knits and Slinkies

Natural Nipples Bra $10.50, Seductress Provocative Garter Belt $9, or both for $17.44 from Frederick's

The Atlas of Sexual Pleasures

Far the best photographic sex book. Entirely in color — good quality at that — full range of bodily details and human practices, and charming models (German). People seize this book and don't put it down till they've checked clear through it. Good for all ages; I imagine the curious young would gain the most from having one around.
—SB

The Atlas of Sexual Pleasures
(Acts, Practices & Deviations)
Gunther Hunold
1972; 173 pp.

$9.95 postpaid from:
Crescent Books
1646 South La Cienega Boulevard
Los Angeles, CA 90035
or Whole Earth Household Store

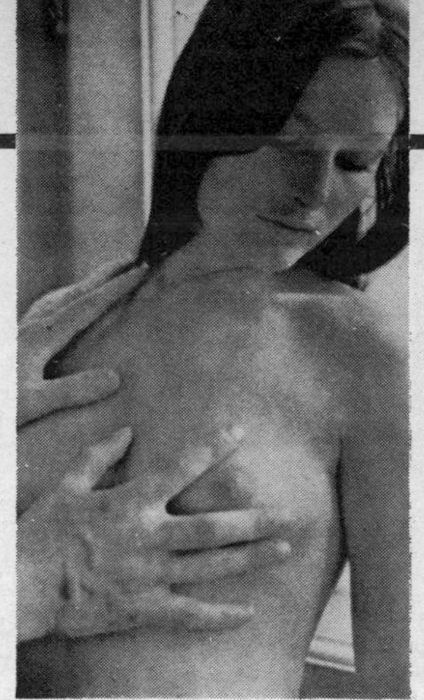

Multi-Media Resource Center

Warm, friendly, informative, wholesome porn — that is, genuinely educational sex films and books of straights, gays, olds, groups, paraplegics, various races, expectant couples, masturbators, etc., all doing it and loving it. Expecially important for such sex advisors as ministers, doctors and high school teachers, to whom all of this healthy variety is usually news.
—SB

Multi-Media Resource Center
Catalog and book list
free from:
Multi-Media Resource Center
1525 Franklin Street
San Francisco, CA 94109

•

Reflections

Filmmaker: Laird Sutton, 1976. Co-facilitators: Margo Rila, Berry Kugler,. Soundwoman: Salli Rasberry. Production Assistants: Bob Durham and Greg Gollihur. Production Consultant: Ted McIlvenna. Producer: National Sex Forum. Color/Sound. 25 minutes.

Eight friends, some of them in couple relationships, some single, share through discussion and lovemaking their experiences and understandings of swinging and group sexuality. The film provides a positive, endorsing insight into what it is like to be involved in this aspect of the human sexual spectrum. Their lovemaking includes delight in the reflections of each other's bodies in a mirrored room.

This documentary film about group sex provides a realistic look at group sex in both the discussion and actual sexual activities. The film is useful for de-mystifying an aspect of human sexual behavior that many people have fantasized about. Suggested use is for sexual enrichment discussion groups, couples' groups, and college level human sexuality courses. This film is an excellent discussion starter on what group sex is really like, what happens and how people feel about it.
16MM Rental $55/Sale $330. E53

GAY ACCESS

by Dan Allen and Richard Hall

The world of publishing has exploded with gay materials in the last five years. Not only have gay periodicals, newsletters and quarterlies appeared by the dozens, but book publishers, large and small, have brought out a torrent of gay-related works — compensating for the silence of centuries. The love that dare not speak its name, in Lord Alfred Douglas' famous phrase, is now the behavior with a thousand annotations in both fiction and non-fiction. Every major bookstore now has a "Gay" section (usually near the Women's bookshelf), and there a are four major purveyors of gay reading matter to mail buyers. They are:

Lambda Book Club
P.O. Box 248
Belvidere, NJ 07823

Books Bohemian
P.O. Box 6246
Glendale, CA 91205

Paths Untrodden Book Service
P.O. Box 459
New York, NY 10014

Elysian Fields Booksellers
81-13 Broadway
Elmhurst, NY 11373

What follows is a brief sampling of some of the varied wares on homosexuality, male and female, of the past few years. We think these titles and services are important — but remember, they're just the tip of the iceberg. If they don't interest you, write to one of the mail order houses for a wider selection, both new and used, current and out-of-print.

Positively Gay: New Approaches in in Gay Life

About two dozen essays on all aspects of gay life — identity, parenting, coupling, religion, coming out, aging, jobs, voting and finance. The idea is to consult gay experience and culture for models in life — and this book is an almanac of options that gay readers will find valuable.

Positively Gay
(New Approaches in Gay Life)
Betty Berzon and Robert Leighton, Editors
1979; 192 pp.

$5.95 postpaid from:
Celestial Arts
231 Adrian Road
Millbrae, CA 94030
or Whole Earth Household Store

The Gay Report

This is the Kinsey Report of gay life, answering the perennial question, "What Do You People Do, Anyway?" Over 5000 lesbians and gay men answered a detailed questionnaire on every aspect of love, sex and relationships. Books like this and **The Spada Report** *mean an end to supposition and innuendo, and a brass-tacks, statistical approach to gay lovemaking.*

The Gay Report
(Lesbians and Gay Men Speak Out About Sexual Experiences and Lifestyles)
Karla Jay and Allen Young
1979; 816 pp.

$14.95 postpaid from:
Summit Books
Simon and Schuster
Attn: Order Department
1230 Avenue of the Americas
New York, NY 10020

Men Loving Men

This is a sex manual for gay eroticism, full of warmth, gentleness and humor. Because gayness is viewed not only as a way to go but a way to grow, the book also talks about consciousness, spirituality and becoming more yourself.

Men Loving Men
(A Gay Sex Guide and Consciousness Book)
Mitch Walker
1977; 160 pp.

$8.95 postpaid from:
Gay Sunshine Press
Bookpeople
2940 Seventh Street
Berkeley, CA 94710

Hidden Heritage

An anthology of 2000 years of gay writing, from Plato to Andre Gide, much of it forgotten, suppressed or neglected. The best overview of our gay past now available.

Hidden Heritage
(History and the Gay Imagination)
Byrne R.S. Fone, Editor
1980; 323 pp.

$19.95 postpaid from:
Avocation Publishers
50 King Street
New York, NY 10014

The Advocate

The only "national" gay newspaper distributed in stores and on newsstands across the country, bi-weekly, 25 times a year. The most general of all the gay publications, it covers news, politics, personalities, books, theater on a continuing basis. If you are located out of the main current of American gay life, this may be your lifeline.

The Advocate
Robert J. McQueen, Editor
$18 /year (25 issues) from:
The Advocate
1730 South Amphlett
Suite 225
San Mateo, CA 94402

Our Right to Love

A work of love, this anthology is the biggest and most thorough study of the lives of lesbians. The list of writers is an all-star cast: Kate Millett, Alma Routsong, Karla Jay, Phyllis Lyon, Del Martin, Audre Lord, among others, with support statements from Florynce Kennedy, Lily Tomlin, Shere Hite and Bella Abzug. Rita Mae Brown writes in the foreword:

Lesbians as a group can be very confusing. There are lesbians whose politics are to the right of Genghis Khan. There are lesbians who make Maoists look moderate. There are lesbians who can only be described as dowdy dykes. There are lesbians who can't be described, they simply knock you out with their beauty. . . . There are poor lesbians and rich lesbians. There are dumb lesbians (yes, I hate to admit it but there are) and there are smart lesbians. We come in all colors, too. Lesbians are everywhere, even in the morgue. We die like anyone else.

Our Right to Love
(A Lesbian Resource Book)
1978; 319 pp.

$6.95 postpaid from:
Prentice-Hall, Inc.
Box 500
Englewood Cliffs, NJ 07632

The Joy of Lesbian Sex

Companion to **The Joy of Gay Sex** *(the handbook extolling the sheer delight of gay male sex by Silverstein and White). The writers present a dictionary of lesbian sex from "Alcohol and Sex" through "Massage" to "Water, Water, Everywhere" (on how to bathe together, a lesson for lesbians who like it clean and are into whirlpool baths and fancy showerheads). On the clitoris they state, "It is the only part of the human anatomy, male or female, that serves no other function than to produce sexual pleasure." While this is not quite accurate — male nipples also have only a pleasure function — it's intriguing that those pleasure points are often considered attributes of the opposite sex, with some people considering male tits as feminine and the clitoris as a vestigial penis. All of Sisley and Harris' dictionary entries are exciting and can teach a few tricks to more staid lesbians than the authors apparently are.*

The Joy of Lesbian Sex
(A Tender and Liberated Guide to the Pleasures and Problems of a Lesbian Lifestyle)
Dr. Emily L. Sisley and Bertha Harris
1977; 191 pp.

$7.95 postpaid from:
Simon and Schuster
Attn: Order Department
1230 Avenue of the Americas
New York, NY 10020
or Whole Earth Household Store

THE RISING SUN
NEIGHBORHOOD NEWSLETTER

—"How's it going between you two?"
—"I guess it would be a good book but a lousy porno flick."

—bus voices

CONDOMS, These Days

by Salli Rasberry and Laird Sutton

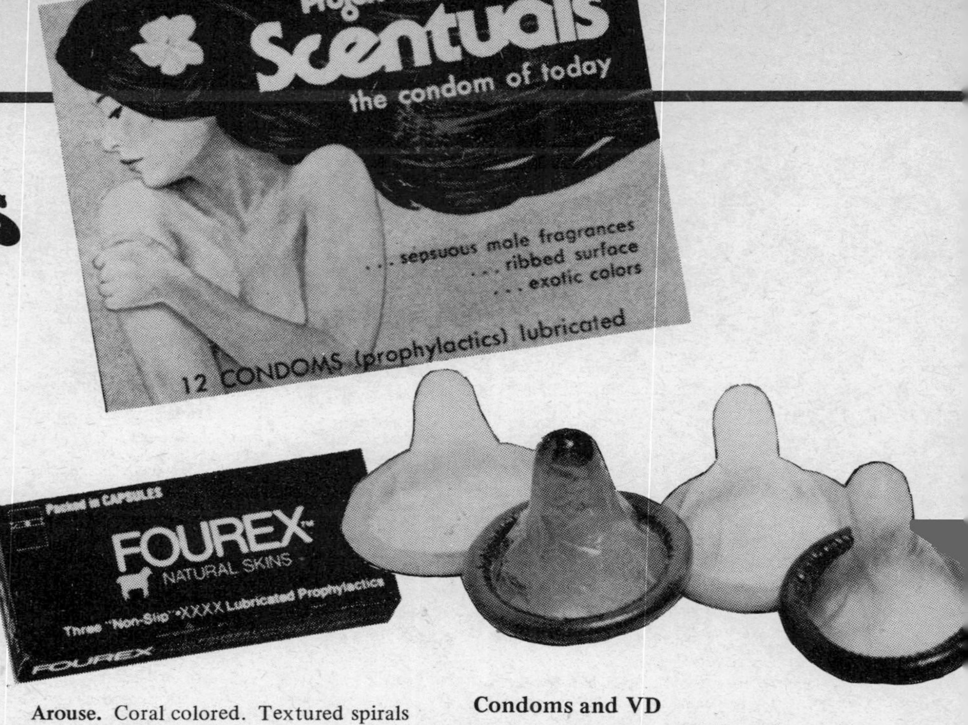

AFTER UNHAPPY EXPERIENCES with the birth control methods I was using, my partner and I decided to reassess what was available. The pill caused me to have 24-day periods. When I switched to the IUD, my body protested strongly from the moment it was put in. Two tries it took to make it stick and then there was an almost constant nagging pain. After encountering horror stories and alarming statistics I had my IUD removed. My options were now narrowed to foam, surgery, diaphragm, lunaception or condoms. Sex is so wonderful, but when you don't want anymore children and birth control becomes a hassle, the future of your sex life begins to look a little grim.

We decided to give shared birth control a try and see what condoms were all about. We reasoned they were convenient, offered peace of mind, there were no harmful side effects, and we could have a lot of fun experimenting. Our local country drug store offered slim pickins. There we found the opaque, dry condoms of our youth unappealingly labeled "For the prevention of disease only." Luckily we found an ad for mail order contraceptives in **Penthouse** magazine, and one week later we were eagerly opening our package of one hundred assorted condoms.

What fun! Coral ones, black ones, dry ones and wet ones. Pre-shaped, ribbed, textured, contoured, and scented – we tried them all. We blew them up, tried them on, measured how long they were, how thick, filled them with water and made a barometer out of one. Our friends got into the spirit when they saw that condoms had a brand new look and we had a contest to determine the favored brands.

Here is some of what we found out during our adventure with condoms.

Do they work?

Planned Parenthood says that when the condom is used by itself it is theoretically 97% effective, but in actuality it's 80 - 85% effective. The difference seems to be in terms of lack of knowledge of how to use condoms to the best advantage. The 3% method-failure rate can be reduced even further by using vaginal foam along with the condom. During my most fertile days (the middle portion of my menstrual cycle) we use a birth control cream.

Where do you get them?

Drugstores, discount stores, some family planning centers, and mail order houses are the main sources at present. A bill has been passed in California to allow their sale in a variety of public places, but as yet condoms may not be dispensed from a vending machine. Availability is considerably greater in other countries. In Japan (where the Pill and IUD are not legally sanctioned) 70% of the couples who use contraception use the condom, which Japanese women sell door to door.

Drug stores are handy, but for the largest selection and economy mail-aways are the best source. The two mail-order catalogs we use are:

Adam & Eve
P.O. Box 800
Carrboro, NC 27510

Federal Pharmacel
Laboratories
6652 N. Western Avenue
Chicago, IL 61645

Both companies are dependable and fast and offer a good selection of fresh, tested condoms. It's a good idea to order both catalogs and check the prices, which vary a good deal. We have come across nine different firms making condoms. They cost about a cent to make, but packaging and middle people raise their price to about $ .20 to $ .90 each, depending on quantity and type.

Varieties

Choosing a condom is a matter of personal preference. They all work. There are two main types of condoms – skin (made of sheep intestines) and latex (rubber). Many users of the "skins" feel they are more natural and provide greater sensation. Skins cost two or three times more than latex and smell a bit too much like sheep for our taste.

There are a lot of different colors available in latex. Color adds a visual dimension which we use occasionally for an added turn on. At the other extreme are the opaque white ones which look like an old rain coat. No wonder they were often called "rubbers."

Some condoms are dry and are harder to put on and in. There's nothing like a dry piece of rubber in your vagina or feeling the skin of your cock pulled and pinched to diminish your sexual ardor. Some condoms are initially very wet yet dry quickly. The best feeling ones are lubricated with a dry silicone, sometimes called S-K 70. These condoms are silky and sexy. In addition we sometimes use saliva or K-Y jelly, this lubrication providing a thermal zone to effectively transmit feeling.

The old fashioned condom did not have a reservoir end to catch the semen, which contributed to leakage and breakage. Most of the modern latex condoms have a reservoir end, and we highly recommend these. Many of our favorite brands are contoured to cling to the head of the penis. Latex condoms can be extremely sensitive or amazingly dull. When we miked them (measured them with a micrometer) we found the thickness ranged from .0015 in. to .0035 in. Two Asian brands, Geisha thins and Skinless Skin are .0003 in. thick. Thinness does make a difference in sensitivity. We hear it bandied about that the best thing about condoms is that they dull sensation, helping the man to last longer. We found one condom that even had a delay cream inside to "extend" lovemaking. Sensation is the name of the game. Why have a numb one when sex feels so good. Men are not studs for female enjoyment. If you are coming faster than you want, try learning to relax, especially your legs, thighs and small of your back or come again later. (If you do come several times use a new condom each time.) There is no need to put yourself down for coming or to buy thick condoms.

We have found several condoms of the sixty or so we encountered that incorporated all the best features.

Texture Plus. Textured rings on the head and hundreds of raised pleasure dots on the shaft. This textured surface massages the sensitive vaginal tissues in the first third of the vaginal barrel where most of the feeling is. Complete with instructions.

Geisha Thins. So thin we used foam at first until we were convinced they wouldn't break. Mesh pattern on the shaft for added stimulation. They are expensive so we use them for special occasions.

Jade. Comes in green, blue, gold and red. Reasonably priced, preshaped, sheer – good all around condom.

Scentuals. Ribbed, colorful and they smell good.

Arouse. Coral colored. Textured spirals at reasonable price.

Fourex. Everybody's favorite skin condom.

We recommend trying one of the samplers until you find a condom that suits you, then order in quantity. Condoms are significantly cheaper by the gross.

How big?

Condoms normally come in one size and are advertised to fit any size penis. There are several brands that are smaller in both length and diameter, and some men prefer the way they hug the contour of their penis. The average length of an erect cock is a little over six and one-half inches. The condoms with reservoirs are almost all seven inches long. Condoms appear to be made only for the circumcised male. The uncircumcised man has up to two extra inches of skin to account for. Uncircumcision discrimination?

Storage

Proper storage of condoms is important for their effectiveness, as they are made primarily of latex rubber which if kept too long or too hot can ROT. Many are dated, and these dates indicate a shelf life of four years. Planned Parenthood suggests a shelf life of two years, which seems right to us. Keeping them in your billfold or glove compartment for very long is NOT a good idea. Often condoms kept this way will either rot or the foil package breaks and perforates the rubber. Keep one for show in your billfold if it makes you feel good, but have a fresh one handy for use.

Putting it on

Put your condom on before there is any penetration, even "just for a moment." There is a pre-ejaculate fluid secreted by the Cowper's gland which prepares the tubes for ejaculation. This pre-ejaculate often contains sperm, hundreds of them, and it only takes one sperm to become pregnant. If you use a separate lubrication, other than what is on the condom, stay away from petroleum-based jelly or oil. Vaseline or baby oil can weaken the latex and can irritate the vagina. Use saliva or K-Y jelly.

Make it a fun thing to do. Either partner can put it on. Squeeze the end of the condom slightly to release the air (this increases sensitivity and helps to eliminate breakage). Roll the condom over the head of the penis and unroll slowly until the entire penis is covered. If you are uncircumcised, retract your foreskin, which makes rolling the condom over your penis more comfortable. Condoms are made for the erect penis. It is best to remove the penis from the vagina while the penis is at least semi-hard, otherwise the condom may slip off. Grasp the ring of the condom against your body during withdrawal to avoid spillage. As the rubber tends to cling to your skin, pulling your condom off by the tip may spray your partner. If you are concerned about the possibility of VD, wash your cock or vagina and surrounding area, and urinate after sex.

Condoms and VD

At this time condoms are the only form of birth control that also provides protection against venereal disease and trichomonas (vaginal infection that gets passed back and forth between partners and can be hell to get rid of). There is some indication that some foams may also help, but this is not well researched yet.

An estimated one in ten teens will have VD before graduating from high school, and it is now epidemic among people between the ages of 15 and 24. Doctors may legally treat persons of *any* age for VD without informing the parents or guardian.

VD clinics *could* give out condoms to those who come for VD treatment, as it can still be passed even though treatment has been started. Studies indicate that once teenage boys are introduced to the condom, they are likely to continue using them.

Pregnant Drop Outs

Being pregnant is the single biggest reason for girls dropping out of high school. There are 786,000 unintended teenage pregnancies annually. One in sixteen women who have pre-marital sex become pregnant. Teens account for one third of all legal abortions in the U.S. and one half of out-of-wedlock births. One half of Aid to Dependent Children (welfare payments – some forty-seven billion dollars annually) goes to households in which the mother had given birth as a teenager.

Many young women feel it can't happen to them, are careless, forgetful. Often young men leave contraception up to the woman. There is a feeling that if you do get caught there is always an abortion possible. When a young person takes precaution the first time they have intercourse, 78% continue to do so. If they do not use protection the first time, only 49% get it together for the future. Only about one-third of sexually active females under 20 uses a reliable method of birth control. Under the California Schmitz Act a teaching credential can be revoked if a teacher does not willingly inform the parents in writing or by phone of *any* classroom discussion of sex. Children want sex information from their parents. They want fact without arguments or need to reveal their sex lives. They often feel that they cannot afford or find birth control devices.

The facts are alarming, the chasm between adult information and experience and the needs of youth is widening. Children have their own values yet lack the ability to see into the future. A groovie fuck tonight without precaution may be an unwanted child forever. As long as parents and other adults are uptight and judgmental of the young, communication will strangle and die. Our children are developing mature bodies at an early age. They are ripe, and their biological urges to reproduce seem strong. Yet the brain is an important sex organ. Who is going to take the responsibility for actions that affect the whole of mankind? ■

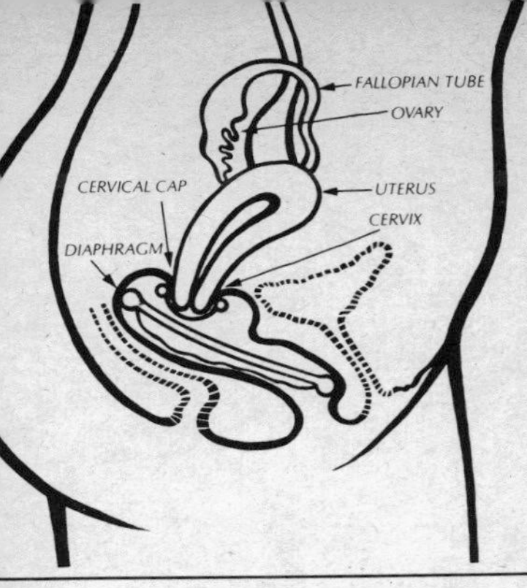

John Ellis

Birth Control

by Stephanie Mills

THESE DAYS, WHAT'S NEW in birth control is you and me as active participants. Not so long ago, it looked like automatic birth control had arrived. Just re-wire the woman's cycle with synthetic estrogen and/or progesterone, install an IUD, or have a vasectomy, and get ready for years of hassle-free, non-procreational sex.

. . . Wrong. With birth control, as with anything else that matters, we offload responsibility at our own peril. As more is learned about the side effects of those no-think birth control methods and the true costs of the trade-offs are understood, more women and men are beginning to substitute motivation for high technology. Regardless of the method you choose, it's the decisive factor.

This may mean some sacrifice in convenience but a lot more closeness and creativity. For instance, Natural Family Planning, a method I once considered suitable only for infertile fundamentalists, is becoming increasingly popular, and rightly so. It's a careful sympto-thermal method which does require some abstinence from penis-in-vagina intercourse. It works best with a lot of cooperation and, its proponents say, helps you to really know one another.

The more you know about yourselves, your fertility, and your contraceptive options, the freer you'll be of modern medicine and its perils. Louise Lacey, who pioneered Lunaception, says, "Any woman can get to know her body so well that she'll know ahead of time when she's fertile." The effort involved is worth it, whether or not you opt for natural family planning. Knowing you're ovulating, you might want to intensify your contraception — say, add foam to condoms — or you might decide to make a baby. It's your choice.

Realistically, probably the most reliable way to know what your contraceptive options are and to grasp their advantages and disadvantages is to volunteer at a family planning clinic and pay attention to the gossip. The state of the art changes rapidly, and doctors aren't always the first to know — or tell. What's more, family planning practitioners have vastly more experience with a wider range of methods than your average private Ob/Gyn, and often their sexual politics are better.

No single book or periodical can tell you everything you need to know. A serious student of the politics of health might want to subscribe to the **National Women's Health Network News** *($25 for 6 issues a year and network membership from the National Women's Health Network, 2025 I Street NW, Suite 105, Washington, D.C., 20006). A professional publication which reflects establishment thinking is* **Family Planning Perspectives** *($25 for 6 issues a year from the Alan Guttmacher Institute, 515 Madison Avenue, New York, NY 10022). You might simply want access to them and other specialist publications; many family planning clinics and medical centers have libraries which carry them.*

In spite of all the richly deserved bad press, pills are still the most popular contraceptive method in the U.S., followed by IUDs. Nevertheless, most of the fam plan types I talked to feel that barrier methods (condoms, diaphragms, cervical caps, and foam) are the best options, and the ones they use.

One compelling reason to use condoms, if you're the multiple partner type, is Pelvic Inflammatory Disease (PID). Slowly simmering PID is a common consequence of gonorrhea (which goes undetected by most women) or other infections. It causes 35 to 80 thousand involuntary sterilizations a year. Between 15 and 40 percent of women are sterilized by one bout, often unwittingly. An IUD can double or quadruple the risk. PID sterilizes by scarring the Fallopian tubes, which is why all the interest in test tube babies: in vitro fertilization offers a way to get egg and sperm together in spite of a blocked tube.

Non-gonoccocal urethritis, which can cause prostatitis in men, cervicitis and salpingitis in women, and conjunctivitis in babies born to infected women, is even commoner than gonorrhea, and another great argument for condoms. The VD capitals of the U.S. are Atlanta, Baltimore, and San Francisco. Approach lovers from these towns with extreme caution and much latex.

For a more monogamous woman who seeks an alternative to the diaphragm, there's the cervical cap, a golden oldie which is currently enjoying renewed interest. Caps fit over the cervix, rather than barricading the whole back portion of the vagina. Consequently they are for some women much more comfortable than diaphragms. For others though they are impossible to insert. Like diaphragms, they require thorough instruction and practice. Held in place by suction from the uterus, caps require little or no spermicide (depending on who's advising).

Caps have been used in various forms for thousands of years. They have been made of opium, beeswax, lemon rinds, gold, silver, aluminum, and lately, of latex. Being made of latex obviates what was, in the golden age, their greatest advantage namely that you could leave them in all month. Latex caps, says Felicia Guest, "set up a right powerful stink after 24 to 48 hours." Work is in progress on caps made out of less porous materials, but it's likely to be a while before they're generally available. The FDA in its (dubious) wisdom, has banned the use of caps as contraceptives.

Nevertheless, there are a number of nurse-practitioners, doctors, and clinics fitting caps. The National Women's Health Network will mail a list of these providers. Please send them a nice contribution for their trouble. Calculate your savings on jelly and give them a healthy cut.

*Another classical revival is mutual masturbation. Doctors Sadja Goldsmith and Alan Margolis, two respected innovators in family planning, have lately been urging their cohorts to teach Outercourse as a birth control method. (They and we are indebted to Lonnie Barbach for that coinage.) Goldsmith and Margolis say that Outercourse is "99% effective, free from side effects, simple to use and teach, and lowers the risk of sexually transmitted diseases." What's more, they say, "It's always at hand." In addition to these virtues, Outercourse is one way to expand one's concept of sexual expression beyond penis-in-vagina sex.**

I think it's also worth liberating oneself from the notion that sex necessarily has to be genital. Sex can enhance intimacy or substitute for it. There was a time when it seemed that the groovy new birth control methods would enable us to have all the sex we wanted, with no thought before or after. That whole approach was fun, but expensive. No trust necessary.

It may still be fun, but it doesn't seem nearly as interesting as trying to establish honest relationships which allow bodily self-determination. And sometimes that means saying — or hearing — no.

**Creative couples have always found abundant alternatives to the penis-comes-in-vagina rut, which explains why the world is not overrun with Frenchmen and Greeks. Consider. For the clitoris and/or vagina there is tongue, lips, thumb, forefinger, middle finger, of the right hand, left hand, both hands, own hand, thigh, forehead, vibrator. . . . For the penis there is mouth, right hand, left hand, both hands, own hand, ass (slowly, with plenty of oil), pubis, hair, sundry cleavages, vibrator. . . . A wonder that anyone ever conceives.* —SB

A Cooperative Method of Natural Birth Control

The method is a combination of three different rhythm systems. They are: the calendar method, which strives, however unreliably, to predict ovulation based on a menstrual history; the basal body temperature method, which tells when ovulation has occured by measuring a slight temperature increase; and the mucus method, which identifies the fertile period by observing changes in the cervical mucus.

As Margaret Nofziger points out, this method requires cooperation between partners. Some instruction would also be helpful, and many family planning clinics are beginning to offer it. Some of them even recommend this book. No wonder. It's accurate, responsible, and friendly. Just the thing for people who want birth control without technology. —Stephanie Mills

A Cooperative Method of Natural Birth Control
Margaret Nofziger
1976; 127 pp.

$5 postpaid from:
The Book Publishing Company
156 Drakes Lane
Summertown, TN 38483

She ovulated on day 14. Her first higher temperature wasn't high enough to call "number 1." The next day it rose more and this temperature was high enough to be called "1" (at least .3° higher than 6 temperatures before the rise.) On the 3rd morning of higher temperatures, she was infertile for the remainder of the cycle.

Basal Temperature and Mucus Chart

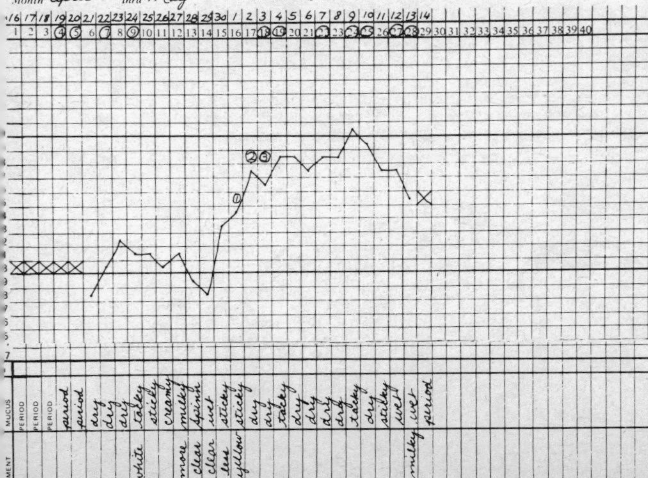

Women and the Crisis in Sex Hormones

Synthetic estrogens were first administered to women at Auschwitz by Nazi experimenters in fertility control. That was just a part of genocide. Since then, they have been hailed as panaceas for contraception, threatened miscarriage, and menopause. And, as SB has observed, panaceas are poison.

Reading this book made me feel that my six years on the Planned Parenthood Federation Board were an unwitting collusion in gynocide. Using anecdotal and other evidence, the Seamans tell the story of the pill's development (which PP's founder, Margaret Sanger spurred and the organization abetted), and of its disastrous consequences for the health of many women.

The pill's pervasive side effects were anticipated, but the risks to individual users were deemed negligible in light of the general urgency of population control, which seemed to call for a technofix. It was also assumed that a full warning of the pill's possible consequences might scare off prospective users. Yes, indeed.

The Seamans also provide the shameful story of DES in full, and argue strongly against the use of estrogen replacement therapy by menopausal women. Not surprisingly, they recommend the use of barrier methods of contraception, including the cervical cap. However, according to one family planner the book overstates the testedness of the cervical cap. It isn't quite the "complete guide to birth control" that the cover claims: more like a complete guide to the sexual politics of drug development. Rub it up against **Contraceptive Technology** *for a spark or two of controversy.* —Stephanie Mills

Women and the Crisis in Sex Hormones
Barbara Seaman and Gideon Seaman, M.D.
1977; 621 pp.

$3.50 postpaid from:
Bantam Books
414 East Golf Road
Des Plaines, IL 60016
or Whole Earth Household Store

Contraceptive Technology

I'd recommend **Contraceptive Technology** *in addition to* **My Body, My Health** *(p. 344) because in order to avoid mayhem and bitter feelings, patients have to become their own physicians. What better way to do that than to read a practitioner's handbook?*

CT *sets the standard for careful medical procedure — an activist patient should expect no less than what's described here.* **CT**'s *biannual update makes it especially valuable. Medical practice in this field must change according to new information, and you can't always depend on your doctor to keep up.* —Stephanie Mills

Contraceptive Technology 1978-1979
Robert A. Hatcher, M.D., et al.
1978; 192 pp.

$3.95 postpaid from:
Halsted Press
John Wiley and Sons
One Wiley Drive
Somerset, NJ 08873

THE RISING SUN
NEIGHBORHOOD NEWSLETTER

A church bell is kind of like an electric can opener or a dishwasher. When you don't have one you think you don't need one, but once you have it, you find yourself using it all the time. Take the jamboree, for instance. A church bell mounted on its own handy portable (by three strong people) stand could have been standing on a hill above the event and some power-hungry kid or grownup would've been ringing it all the time because it really is a kick to make a large noise like that and even a small church bell makes a really large noise. I happen to know because I used to have one outside my bedroom door and ringing it was how my family got my attention. It worked, and the noise is loud enough that the jamboree bell would've had to have been fairly far away from everything else or it would've driven those close to it nuts, but as a distant ding dong it would've been nice.

continued on next spread

My Body, My Health

This will be welcomed by both health professionals and women interested in self-care and quality gynecological care. Written by several people long-respected in gynecology and family planning circles, its concise yet surprisingly thorough chapters cover the gamut of women's most frequently encountered health concerns: pregnancy, birth control, abortion, surviving a pelvic exam, common infections, menstrual problems, abnormal pap smears, breast self-exam, breast lumps, cancer, sexual problems, menopause, surgery, etc.

I appreciated the up-to-date coverage of DES exposure and rape, and the special section (available in the clinician's edition only) on developing patient education programs and obtaining legal consent. The sections on teenage sexuality, vaginal hygiene, recognition of early signs of pregnancy, facing surgery, and special help in choosing a method of birth control are sensitively written and cover topics not easily found elsewhere.

Lists of good references for some topics — particularly DES — are included, as is a list of recommendations for further reading. The only improvements I could suggest would be more explanations of alternative or holistic approaches to women's health concerns, and more consideration of women's lifestyles, stress, exercise, and nutrition.

All in all, this is a fine piece of work — our first lay gynecology textbook. I'd like to see a copy in every library, every women's clinic, and every gynecologist's waiting room. —Carol Berry, R.N., N.P.

[Suggested by Tom Ferguson, M.D.]

My Body, My Health
(The Concerned Woman's Guide to Gynecology)
Felicia Stewart, M.D., Felicia Guest, Gary Stewart, M.D., and Robert Hatcher, M.D.
1979; 566 pp.

$7.95 postpaid
(Regular Edition)

$14.50 postpaid
(Clinician's Edition)

both from:
John Wiley and Sons
One Wiley Drive
Somerset, NJ 08873
or Whole Earth Household Store
(Regular Edition only)

•

Taking Minipills is a method of birth control that many women would seriously consider if they only knew about them. Estrogen-free Minipills offer many of the benefits of regular Pills, with fewer side effects and a lower overall dose of hormone. Although Minipills are relatively new and detailed studies of Minipill safety are not yet completed, this method seems to deserve a more prominent place among contraceptive options than it now has. If manufacturers' marketing policies were altered to give Minipills the exposure that regular Pills now receive, it is likely that many women who now choose Pills might decide to try Minipills instead.

•

I've examined my breasts each and every month for at least ten years, and I still have to *make* myself do it every time! I always do it *in the morning of a weekday*; so I can call my doctor *immediately* if I find anything. I don't think I could do it at night. —Woman, 33

It would be less frightening to find a lump that wasn't there a month ago than to find a lump that wasn't there a year ago. Two recent breast cancer studies estimate that there may be a 15% to 24% increase in survival after breast cancer for women who do monthly breast self-exams compared to women who do not. Investigators believe that regular breast self-exams clearly helped women find breast cancer at an earlier, more treatable stage.

•

Breast lumps are fairly common, and about nine out of ten lumps are *not cancer*. See your clinician at once if you find a lump. You may avoid anxious, worrying nights. There is absolutely nothing to be gained by waiting to see if your lump goes away.

↓

Lie down and put one arm behind your head. You will first examine the breast on the same side as your raised arm. (Putting your arm behind your head stretches chest muscles so that you will have a firmer surface to press downward on.) *Feel every part of your breast by pressing the flat part of your fingertips on a spot and then moving your whole hand in a small circle so that the breast tissue slides back and forth under the skin.*

Our Bodies, Ourselves

If anyone has any doubts left that women can really get it together, they should have a look at this book. It's written by and for women and is a masterpiece. The subject is our bodies — our relationship to them, to ourselves, to men, to each other, and to our society. It makes me feel very special but in no way unique — a warm and wonderful feeling.

It's a political book in the best sense of bringing it all back home and making it clear how we got here and where we need to go. It's full of good solid information which is presented in a tone totally different from either the usual medical presentations, or the "just relax sweetie, and I'll tell you where it's at" tone of some women authors. If you don't think you have any questions about your body, you'll probably be surprised. And if you're looking for a stronger, clearer sense of yourself as a woman, you'll be satisfied. What it reminds me of most is a woman's body — intelligent, warm, soft, inviting. —Diana Barich

[Suggested by Jane Pincus]

With over a million copies sold since 1970, this much-copied book has been a banner success for the Women's Movement and for self-publishing. The second edition (1976, 1979), with 50% new material, continues the excellence. —SB

Our Bodies, Ourselves
(A Book by and for Women)
Boston Women's Health Collective
1971, 1979; 383 pp.

$6.95 postpaid from:
Simon and Schuster
Attn: Order Department
1230 Avenue of the Americas
New York, NY 10020
or Whole Earth Household Store

At Highest Risk

It's a wipeout to read, but a necessary one. What Ms. Norwood is on the track of, with a fine comprehensivity, is no less than some of the subtlest evil around. The widely reported increasing evidence of human-caused cancer is only an indication of the much deeper damage turning up in our children. Chromosomes, fetuses, and children are far more susceptible than adults to the genotoxic effects of new chemicals, heavy metals, X-rays and other radiation, parental smoking and alcoholism, and even asbestos. —SB

At Highest Risk
(Environmental Hazards for Young and Unborn Children)
Christopher Norwood
1980; 280 pp.

$10.95 postpaid from:
McGraw-Hill Book Co.
Princeton Road
Hightstown, NJ 08520
or Whole Earth Household Store

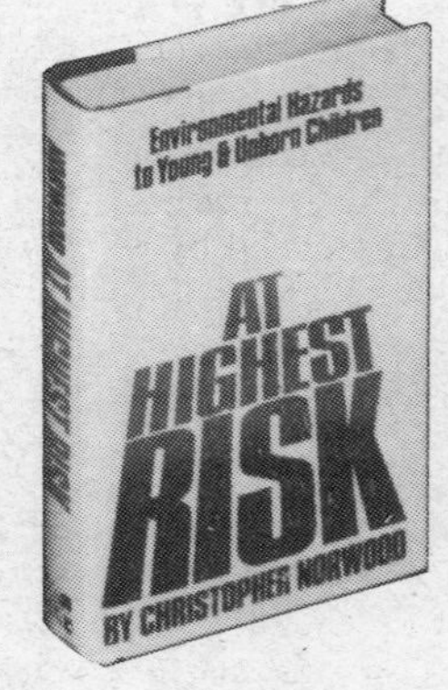

•

Why are hormones evidently teratogenic after brief use, while the teratogenicity of alcohol seems to depend on chronic use? On the other hand, why are perhaps 30 percent of the children of alcoholic, or "heavy drinking," mothers born with congenital malformations, while even the daily use of hormone supports seems to elicit relatively few serious malformations? After all the investigations of operating rooms, alcohol, and hormones, the hows and whys of birth defects remained as elusive as ever. Scientists still could go no further than the exasperated statement of a government scientist that most defects were probably "the result of teratogenic agents acting on susceptible individuals by mechanisms known only to God."

•

The federal Environmental Protection Agency now estimates that there are about 2,500 similar toxic landfills and open dumps scattered across the United States, and that perhaps eight hundred of these pose as serious a health threat as the Love Canal — either potentially or, perhaps, at the present moment. As other states begin to contend with their industrial waste sites, will their health departments find as many deaf and retarded and malformed children as were found near the ditch William Love left behind?

•

In a brief outline, the Meyer team first concluded that "the risk of perinatal death increased directly with the smoking level" — by 22 percent when a mother smoked less than a pack a day, and by 44 percent when a mother smoked more than a pack a day. The Meyer team next learned that mothers who had smoked had more low-birthweight children (infants who weigh less than 2500 grams, or 5 pounds 8 ounces) and more preterm children (those born before thirty-eight weeks' gestation) than women who didn't smoke.

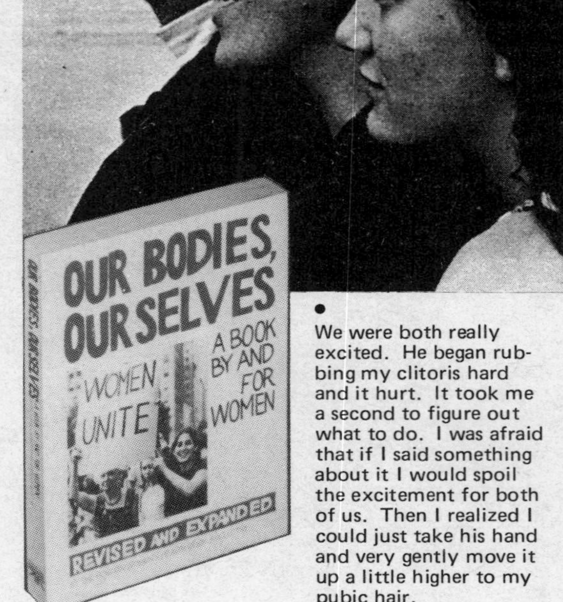

•

We were both really excited. He began rubbing my clitoris hard and it hurt. It took me a second to figure out what to do. I was afraid that if I said something about it I would spoil the excitement for both of us. Then I realized I could just take his hand and very gently move it up a little higher to my pubic hair.

•

When estimates of the number of rapes that go unreported are combined with the rising rape rate, we find that as many as *1 out of every 3 women in the U.S. will be raped during her lifetime.*

•

Here are some precuations against rape by a stranger, used by many women:

- We can get together with other women in the same neighborhood or apartment building. We can establish a signal (e.g., a special whistle) as a call for help, exchange phone numbers, find out those times we can accompany each other while walking on the streets at night, and of any ways we can help one another to avoid situations where rapes might occur.
- If we live alone we can list only our first initials in the phone directory and on our mailboxes. Also, we might add the names of fake roommates or housemates to our mailboxes.
- On all outside doors, we can use dead-bolt locks that are harder to jimmy. We should be sure we know who we are letting in *before* we let them in.
- We can keep our windows locked, especially at night, and obtain special iron grids for windows on the first floor (this is particularly important for windows that we want to keep open).
- We should keep all hallways and entrances brightly lit. (Sometimes we need to pressure our landlords in order to get adequate lighting.) Also, we should try to have our keys ready before we reach the door.

•

I left the clinic with my friend, feeling two ways about the whole experience: one, that I'd had as good and supportive an abortion experience as a woman could have; and two, I would never put myself in the position of having to go through it again.

Is My Baby All Right?

A surprisingly candid and sensible guide to birth defects. All prospective parents should read it, because it informs without scaring. Birth defects are much more common than we'd like to think, and genetic counseling far less available than we'd want. This book explains a lot the ways that things can go wrong, treats the major defects extensively, and tells you what can or can't be done about them. —Diana Barich

Is My Baby All Right?
Virginia Apgar, M.D., M.P.H. and Joan Beck
1973; 542 pp.

$14.95 postpaid from:
Simon and Schuster
Attn: Order Department
1230 Avenue of the Americas
New York, NY 10020

Corrective shoes held in position by a metal bar may be worn by a baby to treat mild degrees of clubfoot, or following removal of corrective plaster casts.

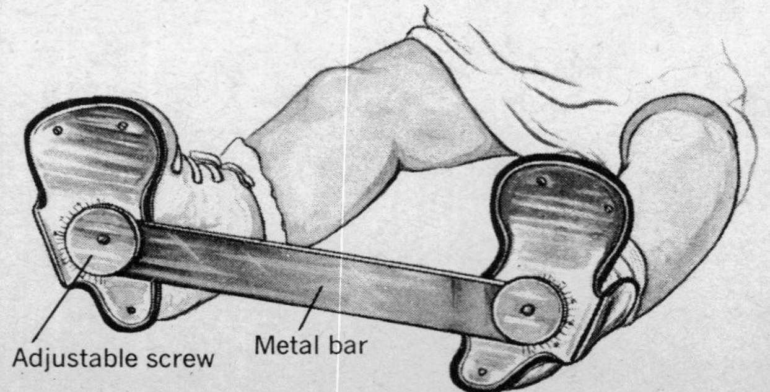

ANDREW FLEUGELMAN

Lynn Mathison has a nice family underway with her one-year-old daughter Brook Lyn Mathison. The only thing unusual about Brook is the manner of her conception. Three of Lynn's gay male friends made a joint sperm donation and then waited attentively to see who the child would resemble. The other women in the house Brook shares cavorted around behind the camera to help with the first published portrait of a family made by amateur artificial insemination. The root of the word "amateur" is "love."

You have to get all kinds of permission to kill somebody, but anyone can start a person that wants to. I think that's great. Now, thanks to the growing expertise in amateur insemination by the San Francisco Bay Area gay community, the possibilities for person-making are even wider. We're having a boom of turkey-baster babies among the lesbians, is what's happening.

Susan Stern reported at some length on the phenomen in the Summer 1980 ***CoEvolution****, "Lesbian Insemination." In the piece here she focuses mainly on technique. Where all this will lead remains to be seen. The gossip is that a high (2/3?) proportion of the babies are boys. Last year one Armand Karow told a Houston meeting of the American Association for the Advancement of Science that artificial insemination significantly reduces miscarriage and dramatically reduces birth defects. He added that sperm that have been frozen up to fifteen years have successfully conceived. Any year now, I expect, we'll have a black market in frozen sperm from (or allegedly from) famous donors. Hm! Would I rather father my own kid, or, say, Gregory Bateson's, or Miles Davis', or, um, Charles Darwin's? Something to think about.* —SB

AMATEUR INSEMINATION

by Susan Stern

With a little help from your friends you can get pregnant in your own home without having sex. You can use artificial insemination. Doctors have been doing it for decades to impregnate the wives of sterile men. But now lesbian and heterosexual single women are bearing children outside the closet of heterosexual wedlock. In doing so they have brought artificial insemination out of the Ob-Gyn suite and into the bedroom.

Artificial insemination is a three-act procedure. A man ejaculates into a clean glass jar. The semen is delivered to the woman. Lying with her legs slightly raised, the woman squirts the semen into her vagina with an eyedropper, turkey baster, or needleless syringe.

Artificial insemination is not complicated, but there are techniques that definitely improve its success. A glass jar for the semen is preferable to a plastic container because the petroleum in plastics has been known to kill some sperm. Using a wide mouthed shallow jar will make it easier to remove semen with the eyedropper, turkey baster, or syringe.

The semen should be used as soon as possible, within 1-2 hours. If it is going to be carried from one house to another it should be protected from light and cold, which may kill some sperm. In other words, put the jar in a paper bag and carry it close to your body's warmth. Don't worry if the amount of semen looks small. About 2 cc (a half teaspoon) of semen is a normal ejaculation, quite capable of impregnating.

In order to get the semen to flow toward your egg rather than down your leg, lie down with your legs slightly raised (on a pillow, chair, wall, friend's or lover's lap). By tilting your pelvic area up, gravity will help pull the sperm into your uterus.

Whatever you use to put the semen into your vagina, make sure it doesn't take the semen back out with it. It may seem obvious, but don't release the bulb of the eyedropper or baster or pull back the plunger of the syringe until you have removed it from yourself. If you use a turkey baster, don't insert it more that 1½ inches. A turkey baster expells a lot of air. If it is inserted too far, the opening of the cervix could be hurt. Lying down for about thirty minutes after the insemination will keep the sperm inside you. If you have to get up immediately, put a diaphragm in first and squirt semen *behind* it, between it and your cervix.

That's it for the mechanics. But artificial insemination, like "natural" insemination, is more than mechanics. You will also have to chart your ovulation-menstruation cycle to find your fertile period. Then you will have to find a donor(s) and decide what role, if any, he will play in your and your child's future.

Sperm can stay alive in the fertile cervical mucus for about four days. The egg, however, begins to disintegrate 24 hours after ovulation. You should try to inseminate as many times as possible during the fertile period from four days before to one day after ovulation.

Determining the day you ovulate is one of those things that is easier on paper than in practice. Ovulation occurs at different times for different women and may vary for each woman from month to month, but you can start with the premise that ovulation usually occurs from 12 - 16 days prior to the beginning of your period. The best way to pin down your own pattern of ovulation is to chart the daily changes in your basal body temperature and cervical mucus for a couple of months before you start inseminating. After a couple of months of watching these ovulation indicators, the pattern of your particular ovulation will become fairly clear.

Your basal body temperature is your body temperature taken at its lowest ebb (immediately upon waking) with a specially gradated thermometer. Most drug stores sell basal thermometers, complete with directions for estimating ovulation, for about $6. Your basal body temperature will zig-zag up and down from day to day throughout your cycle, but the approximate day of ovulation will be distinguished by a sharp drop in temperature immediately followed by a sharp, steady rise. The exact moment when ovulation occurs is debatable, but most sources agree that when your temperature has risen, ovulation is over.

The color, texture and quantity of the cervical mucus in your vagina will change along with your body temperature during your fertile period. At the beginning and end of your menstrual cycle, when your estrogen level is low, the mucus will be scant, tacky, opaque and infertile. As your estrogen level increases the mucus also increases and becomes at first thinner and milkier and then clearer, more watery and more fertile. Just prior to ovulation, when the estrogen level peaks, the mucus will become profuse, slippery and very fertile. It will look something like egg white and stretch between your thumb and forefinger in an unbroken strand.

While you're getting your ovulation time pinpointed, you can be lining up your donor(s). This may prove to be the hardest part of artificial insemination. Since VD can be transmitted through the sperm, it is a good idea to ask your donors to get themselves tested. You may also want to ask him/them to complete a medical history questionnaire. You would want to ask what diseases, allergies or impairments members of the donor's family (siblings, parents, aunts and uncles, grandparents) have suffered from, in order to eliminate donors with clearly undesirable heriditary conditions. You might also want to know what chemicals the donor is exposed to on his job and what drugs he takes. Various chemicals and drugs have been proven to cause sterility, decrease the sperm count or cause inheritable damage in the chromosomes of the sperm.

To make sure your donor's sperm count is as high as possible, you may also want to ask him to forgo hot baths or saunas for 24 hours before donating. and refrain from ejaculating for 24 - 48 hours before donating.

Being a sperm donor is clearly no casual affair. Once you have found a donor or donors that pass your inspection, you will want to warn them that, even via "natural" insemination, conception often takes six to eight months of trying. Some women prefer to use men they know and like. If you and your donor know each other, it is crucial that you agree upon exactly what his rights and responsibilities to your child will be. Some women draw up contracts spelling out these areas of potential conflict, but lesbian rights lawyers warn that even these contracts may not stand up in court if either the mother or donor changes her/his mind when the baby becomes flesh.

If you know that you don't want the donor in your future, the safest route is to use anonymous donors. This, however, makes the process a little more complicated. If you live in a community with a large "out" gay population, there may be women who are running artificial insemination services who can set you up. Call your local women's center or women's clinic. If there are no such services in your community, your friends can be enlisted to find and screen donors and transport the semen without revealing their or your identity. Even if your donor is a friend, you may want another friend to transport the semen.

If you don't get pregnant after several months of concerted effort, you might want to take your donor's semen to a local laboratory for a sperm count. You can find a lab in the phone book. If you don't get pregnant after a year of effort, it may be time to get professional medical advice and perhaps have your own fertility tested. But the important thing is, as they say, to "stay relaxed." Stress and ill health can be a barrier to conception. ■

The pamphlets listed below can give you more information on artificial insemination. They also detail some techniques that women have been trying out to select the sex of their child. None of these techniques, however, have been proven successful, and some may even decrease your chances of conception.

Lesbian Health Matters
Mary O'Donnell and Kater Pollock, et al.
1979; 101 pp.
$3.75 postpaid from:
Santa Cruz Women's Health Center
250 Locust Street
Santa Cruz, CA 95060

Woman Controlled Conception
Mary Anonymous and Sarah Anonymous
1979; 25 pp.
$2 postpaid from:
Womanshare Books
P.O. Box 1735
Grants Pass, OR 97526

THE RISING SUN
NEIGHBORHOOD NEWSLETTER

continued from last spread

But who has a church bell? Privately owned church bells are rare and how my family got ours was from a defrocked church. Churches like the Methodist used to be based on tiny country churches established with great trouble by pioneers and then everyone moved to the city, and later when they moved back from the city they didn't go to church at all or if they did, went to suburban churches where people with similar kids and ambitions were and the little country church since 1823 would have an average attendance of 8, five from the same family, and they'd finally give up or the larger church organization would make them give up, and there'd be a closing ceremony with hundreds of people who used to be connected with that church, and it was all one of those things that was fairly sad but so inevitable you didn't really want to think about it much and one of these churches closed and was sold for something fairly commercial (I'd love to say Col. Sanders but since I can't remember, that would be cheating) but before it was sold one of its former ministers took the bell (no small task, it was a heavy son of a bitch) kept it in his garage for 2 years and then gave it to another minister, my father, because my father is good at using things.

continued on next spread

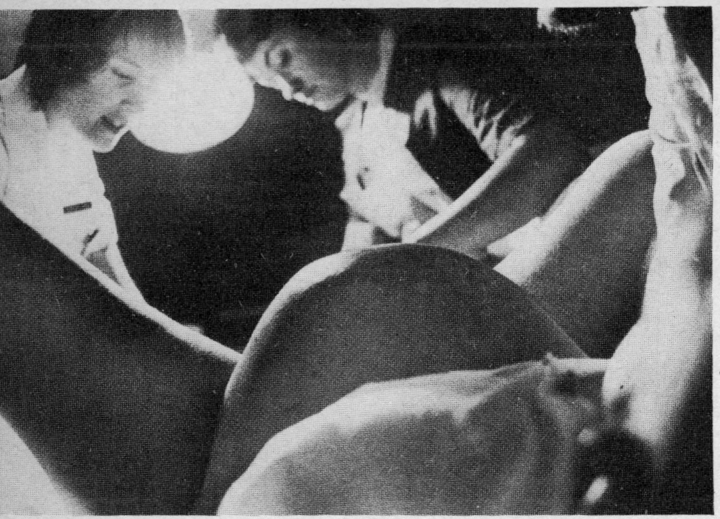

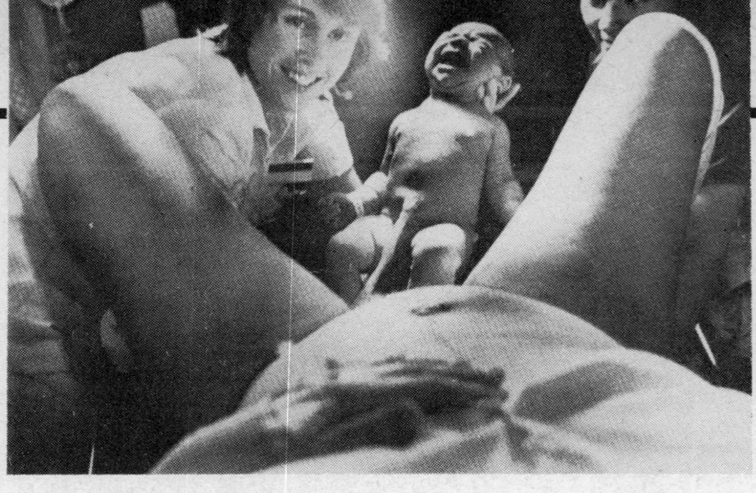

← The final stage of the delivery as seen by the mother, just before and just after. ↑

A Child Is Born

*"Visualization" is a buzzword in holistic medicine, deservedly, and you'll never visualize health more precisely than in these gorgeous color photos by Lennart Nilsson (***Behold Man**, *p. 26) of the baby as it develops in the womb. This 1977 revised edition has complete information for prospective parents, including fine photo-journalism of the whole pregnancy/birth/parent process. A nice present for a mate or a friend.*

—SB
[Suggested by Salli Rasberry]

A Child Is Born
Lennart Nilsson, Mirjam Furuhjelm, Axel Ingelman-Sundberg, Claes Wirsen
1965, 1976; 160 pp.

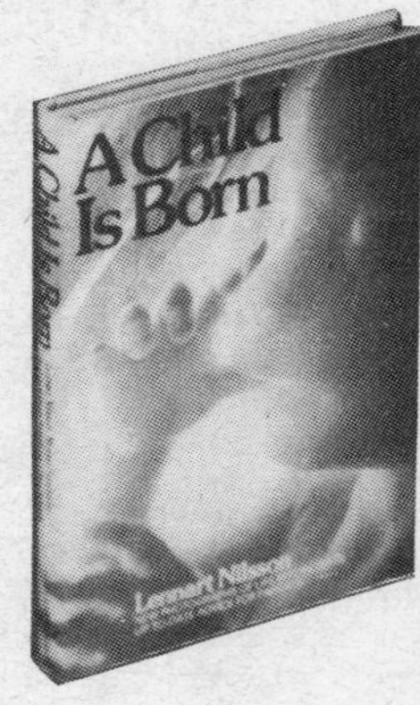

$6.95 postpaid from:
Dell Publishing Co.
1 Dag Hammarskjold Plaza
245 East 47th Street
New York, NY 10017
or Whole Earth Household Store

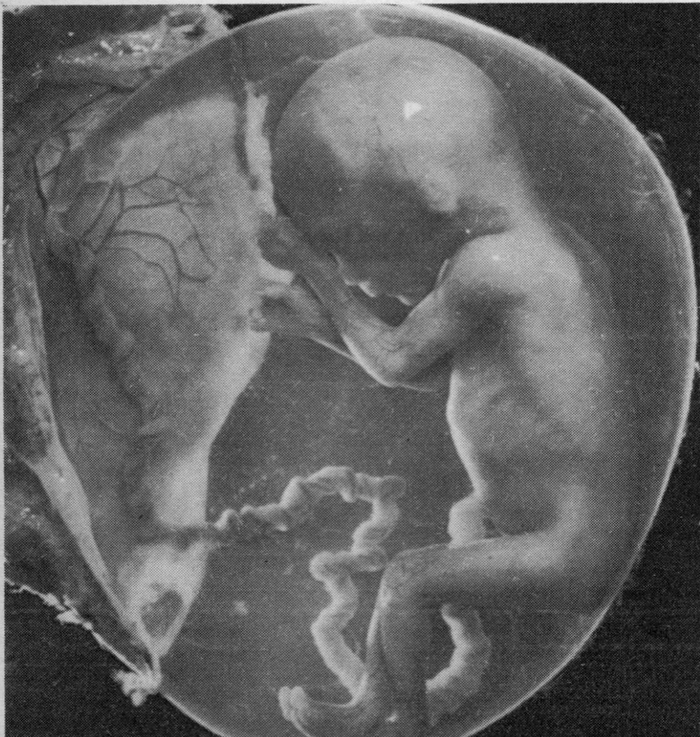

← At 16 weeks, 16 cm (6.4 inches). Through the two umbilical arteries, fetal blood is pumped out to the placental root threads, to get rid of carbon dioxide and waste products. At the very tips of the root threads, the blood receives oxygen and nourishment from the fresh arterial blood of the woman, and then starts its journey back. In the umbilical vein the blood is given an additional push, the pulse of the coiled arteries acting like an auxiliary pump.

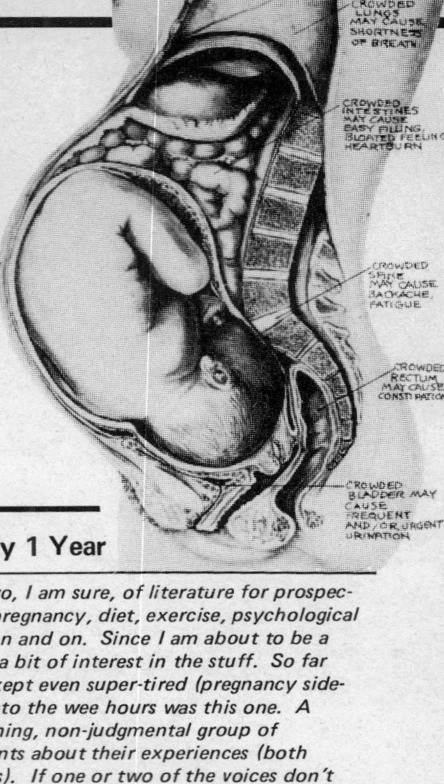

9 Months 1 Day 1 Year

There is a ton or two, I am sure, of literature for prospective parents about pregnancy, diet, exercise, psychological development, and on and on. Since I am about to be a parent I have quite a bit of interest in the stuff. So far the one book that kept even super-tired (pregnancy side-effect) me awake into the wee hours was this one. A totally non-threatening, non-judgmental group of thoughts from parents about their experiences (both fathers and mothers). If one or two of the voices don't appeal, certainly some will. It covers pregnancy (the 9 months), birth (1 day), and after (1 year). The book is organized into little anecdotal sections like "images of baby," "maternity clothes," "thinking ahead: diapers," "circumcision," "when to start solids," etc. Each section has several people's voices and the range is from the cosmic (how it felt the first time it kicked) to the mundane (how to avoid stinky diaper smell). I kept reading parts aloud to my husband until he said he'd read it. Definitely captures the high humor and pathos of it all. There are also appendices containing other reading suggestions, each with a mini-review, and an annotated baby paraphernalia section. —Andrea Sharp

9 Months 1 Day 1 Year
(A Guide to Pregnancy, Birth and Babycare)
Jean Marzollo, Editor
1975; 191 pp.

$4.95 postpaid from:
Harper and Row
Keystone Industrial Park
Scranton, PA 18512
or Whole Earth Household Store

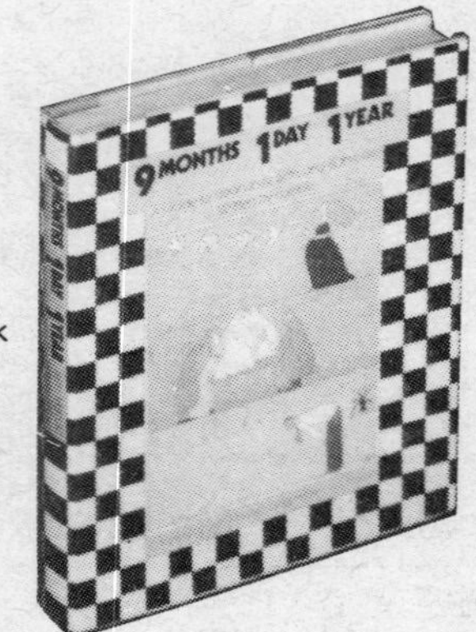

•

Take a big suitcase and don't fill it up. You can use the room later for gifts and free hospital supplies. D.M.

Pack the minimum: one washable dressing gown, two washable nightgowns, slippers and a pot of honey for tea. Visitors can bring anything else you need. I.K.

Take beautiful nighties and robes for frequent changes. Splurge on as many as you can afford. It's a time to feel indulged. B.T.H.

Pack your bag in advance. Some babies come in a hurry! K.T.

Basic birthing kit

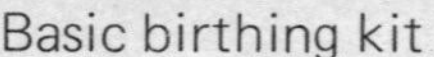

Dear Art and others,

The home birth movement in the U.S. — of which we are a part — has suffered from the poor availability of professional birthing supplies at reasonable prices to mothers and birth attendants. Patricia Pedigo, home birth educator certified by the Association for Childbirth at Home International, and Christopher Junkin have established Moonflower Birthing Supply to bridge this gap. We provide professional birthing supplies through the mail at prices well below retail stores. Many other people in the birthing field feel there is a real need for this service, so we hope you'll include an item about it in **The Next Whole Earth Catalog.**

I'll list below our basic birthing kit that will be the primary unit of our business:

2 plastic sheets (40" x 72")
16 absorbent underpads
6 pairs of sterile gloves
6 packets of lubricating jelly (2.7 grams)
30 sterile gauze pads (4" x 4")
1 sterile bulb syringe (3 oz.)
2 strands of sterile umbilical cord tape (18" long)
15 alcohol preparation pads
1 sanitary belt
12 maternity-size sanitary napkins
1 Peri bottle (8 oz. squeeze bottle)
4 oz. Betadine solution
1 oral thermometer

Our current price for this kit is $14, postage not included. With our inflation rate, we expect our costs to rise by **Catalog** publication time, forcing us to raise prices as well.

We offer all of the birthing kit items individually along with surgical scissors, instruments, fetal stethoscopes and books — all at prices well below retail. We'll send a brochure and price list free upon request.

Sincerely,
Patricia Pedigo
Christopher Junkin

Moonflower Birthing Supply
1636 South Downing
Denver, CO 80220

Re babies

The items reviewed here focus on pregnancy and childbirth. For a shower of stuff relating to the baby and beyond, *turn to p. 540.* —SB

Birth Without Violence

The idea is to have the delivery room dimly lit, warm, and inviting, and the infant is placed on Mom's belly with umbilical still intact between them. Then baby is gently massaged and washed in warm water. Such kids are said to be born smiling instead of howling. Whether such "trauma-less" birthing really makes a difference has yet to be determined, but a lot of parents want it, so some hospitals are offering "Leboyer" delivery scenes, sometimes cosmetically at best, sometimes sincerely and well. Surest way to get it is do it at home with a doctor or midwife you like and trust. —SB

Birth Without Violence
Frederick Leboyer
1975; 115 pp.

$9.95 postpaid from:
Alfred A. Knopf, Inc.
455 Hahn Road
Westminster, MD 21157
or Whole Earth Household Store

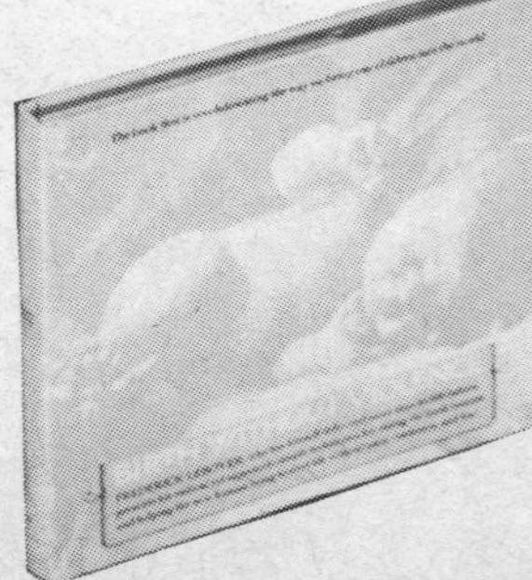

Childbirth Preparedness Kit

Seems a sensible item. The supplier has a small catalog which also offers nursing bras, washable, re-usable bra pads, hard-to-find pure hydrous lanolin, a breast milking and feeding unit, and other infant goodies. —SB

Childbirth Preparedness Kit

$22 postpaid from:
Happy Family Products
1252 S. La Cienega Blvd.
Los Angeles, CA 90035

•

KIT CONTAINS:

1 **Emergency Childbirth Manual,** 62 pages, very helpful.
1 pair disposable sterile gloves
1 disposable sheet — 40" x 72"
2 Prep pad alcohol — to wipe and clean the birth opening before delivery
2 towelettes
2 cord clamps — to clamp umbilical cord before cutting
1 disposable scalpel — to cut the umbilical cord
6 oversponges 4" x 4" — to wipe the mucus from the baby's mouth
1 bulb aspirator — to remove fluid from the baby's mouth and throat
1 receiving blanket
1 obstetrical pad — to be used after delivery
1 plastic bag — to carry the placenta to the hospital for inspection
6 disposable towels — 13" x 18"
2 Nylon tie offs — for use in cases of enlarged umbilical cord

Spiritual Midwifery

The most accessible and thorough of the home birthing books, based on experience with hundreds of births by now. There's quite a lot of the spiritual trip of Stephen Gaskin's Farm (see p. 315), which may delight you or may not. It doesn't affect the practicality of the book and does make it more entertaining.
—SB

Spiritual Midwifery
Ina May Gaskin
1978; 480 pp.

$10 postpaid from:
The Book Publishing Company
156 Drakes Lane
Summertown, TN 38483
or Whole Earth Household Store

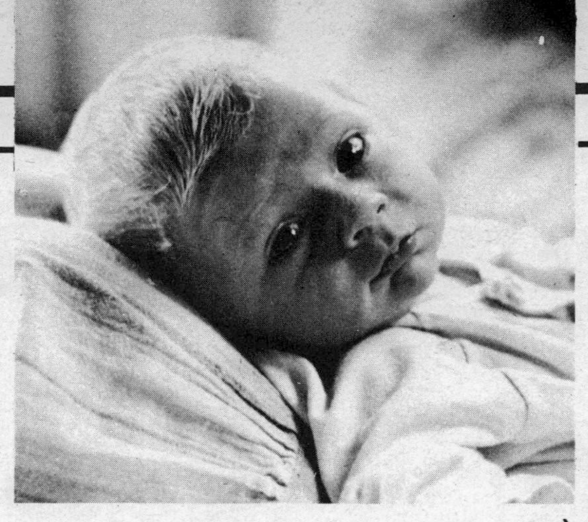

While the mother is pushing, have her keep her knees open wide, so that the baby will have plenty of room to move down. Have the mother keep her bottom firmly placed on the bed, especially during crowning rushes, as this will keep her muscles more relaxed than if she's lifting her bottom up. →

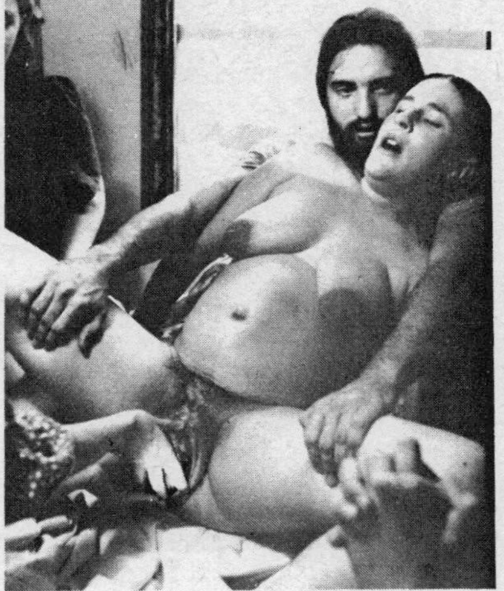

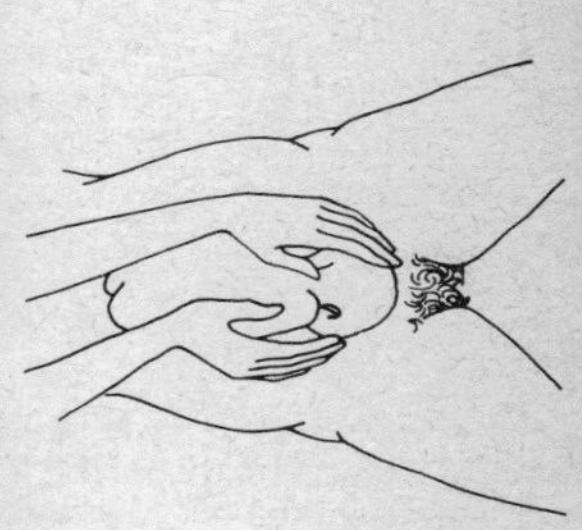

Feeling the Forehead ↑

Emergency Childbirth

Say you and your partner are going to have a baby. You've done lots of reading, gone to the classes, feel reasonably sure of yourselves. What if for some reason you can't get to the hospital or the doctor can't get to you when the baby decides to come? Suddenly you realize that all that reading has just flown out of your memory. **Emergency Childbirth** *is exactly the book to have on hand.*

It's clear, concise, and covers nearly every situation — normal delivery, abnormal presentations, injury or illness of the mother, premature delivery, etc. Cautions are given where called for, and the few illustrations are simple and easy to read. One of the best features of the book is the index of emergency instructions at the back — each condition and what to do for it is outlined in a sentence or two, with page references for the complete instructions.
—Evelyn Eldridge-Diaz

Emergency Childbirth
Gregory J. White, M.D.
1958, 1973; 62 pp.

$4.75 postpaid from:
Police Training Foundation
3412 Ruby Street
Franklin Park, IL 60131

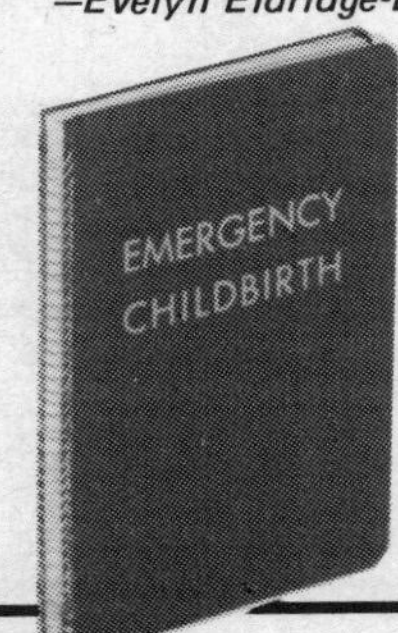

•

Perhaps the most important thing for the lay assistant to know is that labor and the delivery of a child are normal functions which nature always tends to complete successfully. Statistics show a loss of less than one mother in a thousand, less than four babies in a hundred — and these statistics are for all deliveries in large hospitals and therefore include mothers who have been ill for years and premature babies too tiny to live. An attendant without medical training called upon suddenly to assist at a birth should have results at least as good as those of the hospitals because he is usually dealing with the least complicated cases. Mothers who have been ill for some time are ordinarily hospitalized. Women with prolonged or obstructed labors do get to the hospital in time. The women who deliver in taxicabs, ambulances, and police squad cars are usually those with short labors, and these are nearly always easy, normal deliveries. Since the babies in these circumstances are not suffering from the effects of anesthetics or pain-relieving drugs given to the mother, they rarely require resuscitation.

•

When delivery becomes imminent in automobile, ambulance, or police car, the person most important to the safety of the mother and child is the driver. Nature unaided will usually conduct a successful delivery; but all her efforts may be canceled and the mother and baby lost if the driver goes too fast or too recklessly and smashes up the car. Childbirth is not nearly so dangerous as a wild ride in an automobile.

•

Snotty babies and colds: A baby can seem snorty and snotty, but sometimes it sounds worse than it is. A baby's nasal passages are narrow, so just a little snot can make a racket. A baby can catch a cold, though, and have a runny nose that makes it hard to breathe while he nurses or sleeps. You can suction out a baby's nose several times a day with a rubber syringe to clear it, but don't overdo it, because that in itself can be irritating. If a baby is otherwise healthy, being snotty isn't serious. You could mix 1 tsp. of salt in half a glass of water. Put 2 - 3 drops in each side of his nose, then suction out his nose. If he's still noisy, suction it out again in five minutes. The salt water helps thin the snot. Do this 2 - 3 times a day for 3 to 4 days. You wouldn't want to use it longer than this, as syringing can be irritating and cause more snot to be made. You could also try sleeping him in one of those little baby seats.

Textbook for Midwives

From England, where midwifery is widely practiced and legal, this is an encyclopedia on birth. Long sections on anatomy and physiology, pregnancy, abnormalities of pregnancy, normal labor, abnormal labor, the puerperium (post-partum), the newborn baby. Full of pictures and diagrams and highly technical (medical) terminology. It's meant as a textbook to teach midwives their jobs; it can teach anyone who's interested in the process, and is a must for those involved in home deliveries. It's especially strong on the knowledge necessary to deliver in remote areas, and unequivocal about when to seek medical/hospital help.
—Diana Barich
[Suggested by Annie Hines]

Textbook for Midwives
1953, 1974; 827 pp.

$18.75 postpaid from:
Longman, Inc.
19 West 44th Street
New York, NY 10036

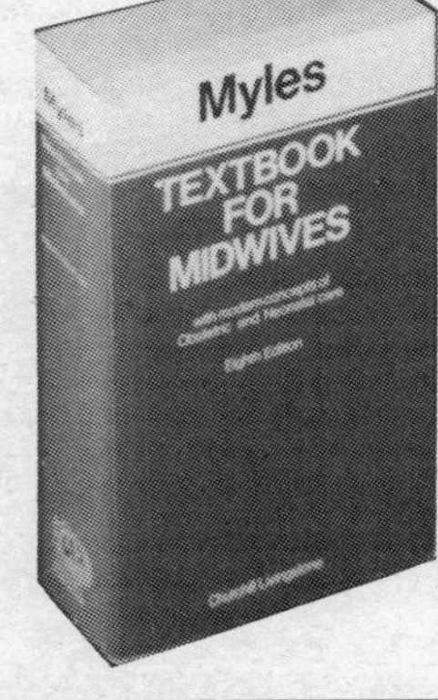

•

The Uterine Contractions

True Labour	False Labour
1. Are always present.	1. Are not always present.
2. Are accompanied by abdominal tightening, discomfort or pain.	2. Are not always painful.
3. Rarely exceed 60 seconds.	3. May last three to four minutes.
4. Recur with rhythmic regularity.	4. Are erratic and irregular.
5. Are often accompanied by backache.	5. Are not accompanied by backache.

The Cervix

True Labour	False Labour
1. The cervix is shortened.	1. The cervix is not shortened.
2. The os is dilating.	2. The os is not dilating.
3. The membranes feel tense during a contraction.	3. The membranes do not become tense.
4. Show is usually present.	4. There is no show.

—Textbook for Midwives

The Adoption Adviser

Adoption is simply a way to have a child yet add zero to the population. It's more and more popular these days — so much so that white infants are sometimes scarce and older, non-white and disabled children are increasingly in demand. (Adopting a special kid can be a great happiness-expanding deed.) **The Adoption Adviser** *is considered the best introduction to adoption in general. It walks prospective parents through the entire process, from legal maneuvers to emotional changes. It doesn't exactly try to talk you out of adopting, but it does ask you to articulate your reasons. It's also full of names and addresses of groups who can help you make the next step.*
—Art Kleiner

[Suggested by Mary Bohan, Director of the Association for the Adoption of Special Kids]

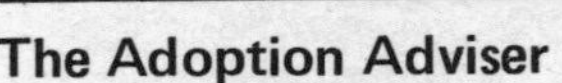

The Adoption Adviser
Joan McNamara
1975; 231 pp.

$4.95 postpaid from:
Hawthorne Books, Inc.
260 Madison Avenue
New York, NY 10016
or Whole Earth Household Store

•

The Holt Book, Holt Children's Service, Eugene, Oregon

Holt, one of the leading international adoption agencies, puts out the Holt Book, sometimes called the Blue Book, which contains pictures and descriptions of children in the agency's custody. The children listed — from Korea, South Vietnam, or other foreign countries — generally are considered difficult to place because of age, racial background, or medical problems, or because there are brothers or sisters who must be adopted together. People who inquire about these children usually must meet the Holt agency's own standards for adoptive applicants in order to have their inquiries seriously considered. Unlike most other groups that maintain adoption exchanges, Holt directly places the children it lists.

•

In looking at these books together, you can talk of how excited and anxious you were for your child's arrival, how you sat in the agency office or at the airport waiting. You can tell your child about how you laughed and cried at the same time because you were so happy. All of the funny-sad stories about how you adjusted to each other, and the colorful details that make the past vivid and important, will tell how you worked to make a family and learned to love each other in a special way that still grows every day. Children cherish stories of themselves and how they are loved. A memory book is one personal, creative, yet simple way to share and explain the adoption story.

THE RISING SUN
NEIGHBORHOOD NEWSLETTER

continued from last spread

Cleaning the bell — It was dull black and I remember that Comet didn't work and auto polish didn't work and paint remover didn't work and Zud Brass Cleaner didn't work, but I do not remember what did work because whatever it was, what mainly worked was me, rubbing for hours. We were using the church bell in our Fourth of July church float and it needed to look shiny. It did look shiny sitting on a wagon with a long rope and Hank trying to get people along the parade route to ring it as it passed. They didn't much want to, not as much as you'd think but then much of my father's life has been devoted to trying to get people to be more participatory than they are and it's basically a good fight. We used it in other Fourth of July parades, inside a Conestoga wagon loaned by Harvey who owned the all-you-can-eat-for-a-dollar place in Miamisburg with eight people including ineffectual me pulling it and my sister inside with ear guards ringing the bell, and another year it was inside a chicken wire and tissue paper replica of our red brick imitation castle church tower with me inside with ear guards ringing it.

continued on next spread

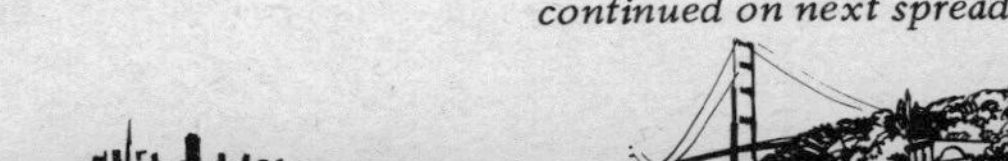

Sears Roebuck and Company

We used to run Sears and Wards together. Since Wards seems to be steadily declining, we're not any more. By mail order or in person, Sears has more variety and more high quality than any other retailer in the world. It's worth having the most recent big catalog (1570 pages these days) just as a price guide when you're shopping for (or selling) anything. Often you'll be surprised by a better price in the Sears catalog, as we were when looking for a good cheap overhead Casablanca fan. (See our p. 235.) They have excellent service followthrough, especially on tools, as we noted on p. 147 — if your Craftsman tool breaks, they replace it with no further questions. You get the big catalog, along with sales announcements, etc., regularly so long as you're ordering at least $25 worth of goods every three months or so. Sears also has specialty catalogs for: Window Fashions, Men's Apparel, Uniforms, Western stuff, Home Health Care, Farm & Ranch, Home Improvement, Business Equipment, Floorcoverings, Tools, Boating & Fishing, Truck & Recreational Vehicle gear, Photographic Supplies, Toys, Winter Sports, and Hunting.

The catalog works in over 100 countries. If overseas, write to Sears in Chicago. —SB

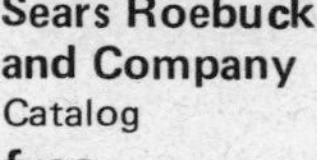

Sears Roebuck and Company
Catalog
free

Check your phone book under Sears or write for location of nearest mail order plant from:
Sears Roebuck & Co.
925 South Homan Avenue
Chicago, IL 60607

MURAPHONE® Remote Telephone Unit has cordless receiver so you can answer your phone from up to 400 feet away

Muraphone, 3K 3486C $89.99

Solar-powered Electric Fences. No electrical costs. . . Uses "free" energy from the sun $160.99 25-mile Fencer. →

Gable roof steel storage building $254.99 to $654.99

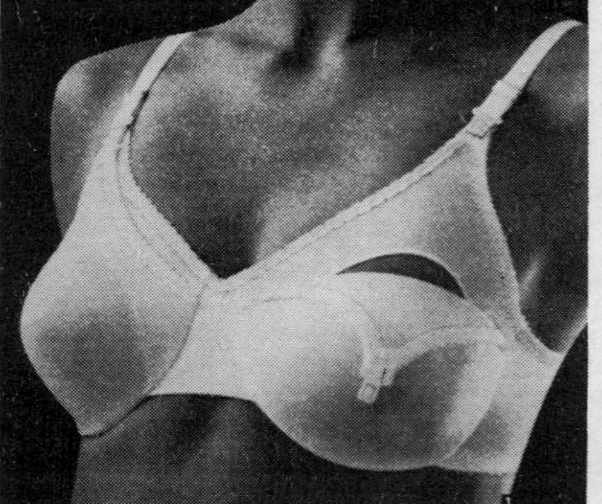

Maternity-Nursing Underwire Bra B Cup, $9.00

Our finest Power-Mate Vac has 4 pile heights, the versatility of 2 speeds plus 3.6 HP (peak) motor . . . the most powerful vac suction motor we sell. $294.95.

Three-blade Fan with sleek contemporary design.

Construction: White molded polystyrene blades and housing. Smooth 38-inch blades. Extends 12 inches from ceiling. Does not take swag kit or light kit: must be wired to ceiling outlet box. Hardware and assembly instructions included. 66-watt motor. $64.99

The Wholesale by Mail Catalog

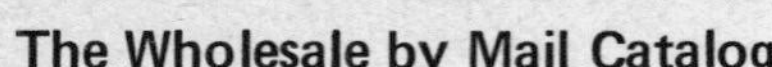

Describes 350 sources of mail order goods 30% to 90% off list price. Nicely done (though graphically dull). We immediately sent for 50 catalogs in our own interest and in the interest of **The Next Whole Earth Catalog.** *The catalogs poured in, proving out the evaluations and reminding us once again of the genuine excitement of life by mail order.* —SB

The Wholesale by Mail Catalog
Prudence McCullough, Editor
1979; 203 pp.
$5.95 postpaid from:
St. Martin's Press, Inc.
175 Fifth Avenue
New York, NY 10010
or Whole Earth Household Store

•

Wolff Office Equipment

Wolff backs up the goods they sell with a 15-man service department that does complete repairs. They sell typewriters, calculators, dictating machines, telephone answering machines, and office furniture. Some of the brands they carry include SCM, Olivetti, Olympia, Royal-Adler, Remington, IBM (rebuilt), Sharp, Hewlitt-Packard, Texas Instruments, Victor, Phillips-Norelco, Sanyo, and Phone Mate. They have a large selection of office furniture by Steelmaster, Cole, and other leading manufacturers. They do price quotes, and also have a free price list — just write or call.

Wolff Office Equipment
1841 Broadway
New York, NY 10023
(212) 581-9080
Price List: free
Discount: 20 to 50%
Goods: name brand
Minimum Order: none
Shipping, Handling, Insurance: extra, UPS or FOB New York City
Guarantee: by manufacturer
Payment: MO, MC, Visa, AC, DC
$$$$

•

Freeport Music

Freeport has been in business since 1921 and will probably be here in 2021 because you can't beat great prices and a good selection. There are Ludwig drums at 40%-off list, drums by Pearl, Slinger Land, Earth amps and mixers, electronic equipment made by Fender, Marshall, Kingston, Marlboro, Morley, and Shadow, Shure mikes, Seth Thomas and Franz metronomes, etc. There are also guitars and accessories by Martin, Fender, Gibson, Guild, Ovation, and Yamaha. Freeport carries Olds brass instruments, Leigh woodwind accessories. Benge brass, Armstrong flutes, Arp electronics, Hohner harmonicas, and disco lighting and stage effects for rock groups. They also have good buys on used instruments and coupon "specials" — don't buy an instrument or another set of strings before you get this catalog.

Freeport Music
114K Mahan St.
W. Babylon, NY 11704
(516) 643-8081
Catalog: $1
Discount: 30 to 60%
Goods: name brand
Minimum Order: $25 on charges
Shipping: extra
Sales Tax: NY residents
Guarantee: defective goods replaced or refunded
Payment: check, MO, MC, Visa, AE, CB, DC
$$$$

•

Contrary to popular belief, prices on cameras and photographic equipment are, for the most part, better here in the United States than they are in Hong Kong. Even a firm that has only a small camera department in addition to an extensive appliance or audio inventory can probably offer discounts of up to 40% off list prices. The large camera and photographic supply houses carry much more than cameras, bulbs, and film. Some of the specialized goods available from these firms are lighting equipment, screens, film editors, splicers, projection lamps, batteries, projection tables, lenses, filters, adapters, meters, albums, camera bags and cases, enlargers, color analysers, darkroom equipment and supplies, and film processing services.

Even if you don't need custom work done, you can have your film processed by a mail order discount lab at about half the price a drugstore or retail outlet would charge, and you usually get credit for unprintable negatives.

•

Executive Photo, 884 Sixth Ave., New York, NY 10001, (212) 532-1277. Catalog: $3. Discounts: up to 50%. Goods: name brand. Minimum Orders: $25. Shipping: extra. Sales Tax: NY residents. Guarantee: by manufacturer. Returns: within 2 weeks. Payment: check, MO, MC, Visa, AE. $$$$

Executive sells all the name brands in cameras and accessories — Nikon, Pentax, Sigma, Hassleblad, Minolta, etc. Unlike most U.S. camera discounters, they have a catalog, which saves you the trouble of writing or calling for a price quote. Their discounts are true wholesale — 50% and more off list price.

Hong Kong

Hong Kong used to be the place to look for amazingly great deals in cameras, tape recorders, motorcycles, binoculars, calculators, suits and other items commonly imported from Japan. From what we can tell now, some deals are still worth the five-week wait: a Seiko watch which costs $175 in the U.S. is $100 including postage and customs duties from T.M. Chan. But other goods, like cameras, are only a few dollars cheaper than you can get them here. The store prices may vary in different parts of North America, too; probably best to write for these catalogs and check the prices against stores near you.

We've had exactly no complaints about any of these firms.
—Art Kleiner
[Suggested by Terry Link, Thomas Dixon, Jas Hayden, Anne, Jim Kessler]

T.M. Chan & Co.
Catalog
free from:
T.M. Chan and Company
P. O. Box 33881
Sheungwan Post Office
Hong Kong

Far East Company
Catalog
free from:
Far East Company
P.O. Box 97335, TST
Kowloon, Hong Kong

Universal Suppliers
Catalog
free from:
Universal Suppliers
P.O. Box 14803
General Post Office
Hong Kong

Albert White & Co.
Catalog
free from:
Albert White and Co.
K.P.O. Box K-202
Kowloon, Hong Kong

Woods Photo Suppliers
Catalog
free from:
Woods Photo Suppliers
60 Nathan Road
Kowloon, Hong Kong

SEIKO 7820-8050
"QUARTZ" Long life battery, thin dress watch, with yellow gold-plated case and leather strap. US$100
—T.M. Chan & Co.

The Cumberland General Store

Tools that last because they HAVE lasted, available new from where they're still manufactured. A better investment than gold. It's all here — shop tools, garden and farm tools, kitchen tools; much that is merely nostalgic, much that is strong, simple, and cheap. An exciting catalog. —SB

The Cumberland General Store Wish & Want Book
Catalog
$3.75 postpaid from:
The Cumberland General Store
Route 3
Crossville, TN 38555

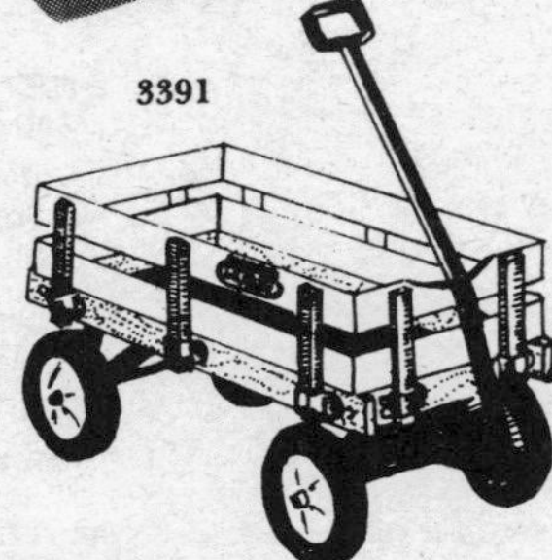

3391

RADIO FLYER RODEO
A sure winner with 4 to 8 year-olds. Improved "Easy-Turn" steering assembly assures carefree playtime. Semi-pneumatic rubber tires. Finest natural hardwood body; red side-boards. All-weather protected. Easy to assemble.
Body: 28" x 14½" x 7". Steel Wheels 7" x 1¼". Shipping wt. 25 lbs.
3391 .... $41.60

Surrey with Fringe Top
Model H-10
7052 steel tires $4,050
7053 rubber tires $4,225

OLD STANDBY
An ideal instrument, popular everywhere. 10 single holes, 20 reeds finely nickel plated covers. Packed in neat hinged box. Length 4". Ship. wt. 1 lb.
7364 Key of C $11.10
7365 Key of G $11.10

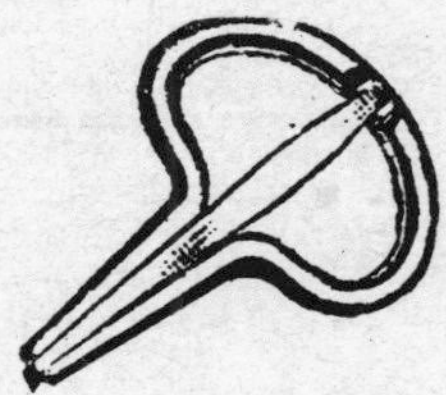

JUMBO JAW HARP
The finest harp that has been produced in this country for several hundred years. Made of steel. 3¾" tongue. Shipping wt. 1 lb.
3312 .... $3.25

GLASS ROLLING PIN

Hollow glass rolling pin has smooth surface. Fill with crushed ice or cold water to keep pie crust cold and to prevent dough from adhering to the roller. Ideal for making the finest and thinest pie crust possible. Rolling pin measures 15 inches long and 2¾ inches in diameter. Cap is made of cork. Shipping wt. 3 lbs.
3641 .... $10.14

Pennsylvania craftsmen make our cookie cutters in Early American designs. Our basic assortment of 13 small cutters includes a boy, girl, rabbit, tree, star, dog, bell, turkey, owl, Santa, angel, heart, and deer. Shipping wt. 1 lb. →

HAY BUCKERS' APRON ALL LEATHER—SPLIT LEG
Heavy pearl splits. Top grain cowhide adj. belt and crotch reinforcing. Popular design for hay and heavy cargo handlers. 4 leather leg straps with harness snaps. 36" long Shipping wt. 3 lbs
6352 .... $52.48

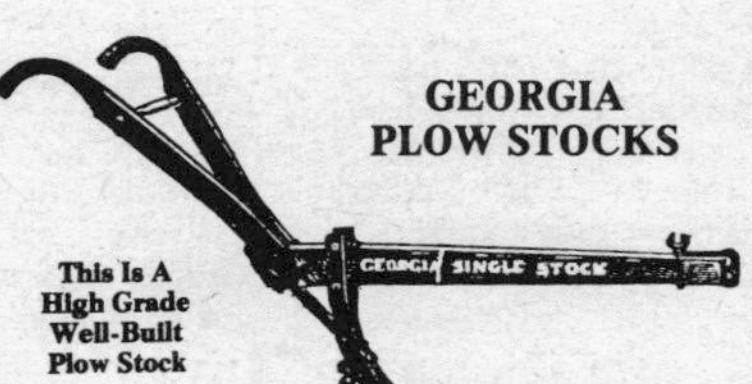

GEORGIA PLOW STOCKS

This Is A High Grade Well-Built Plow Stock

Varnished beam and handles, wrought iron standard, replaceable handles. The standard moves on a pivot which passes through it and the brace, and can be set at any angle by loosening the bolts by which standard is fastened to beam and moving standard forward and backward as desired. Any kind or style of blade that takes a heel bolt can be used on these stocks. Georgia Plow Stocks measures 1¾"x3¼"x42". Shipping wt. 20 lbs
7190 .... Ea. $75.99

Goat Harness
With some modification this could be used for a large dog also.
6196 $69.95.

The Vermont Country Store

Called "The Voice of the Mountains," it is an old-fashioned mail-order catalog which has "revived" many quality cotton yard goods for sewers, including 100% cotton American Calico and matching solid colors, huck toweling, and damask by the yard. This may well be the only mail-order source for such fabrics. Also from Vermont Country Store are various homey kitchen and personal items — first piece of pie lifter-outer; cotton lisle stockings; foundry worker gloves; New England food specialties, etc. Fun to browse through. —Evelyn Eldridge-Diaz

Voice of the Mountains
(The Vermont Country Store)
Catalog
free from:
The Vermont Country Store
Weston, VT 05161

Old-fashioned Calico Apron — With full calico ties in back, this apron, ruffled at bottom, will fit most normal women. They're made for us in Vermont homes by Vermont seamstresses: not a factory product. Comes in Yellow, Blue, Green, Red, Pink and Lavender. (Please state second choice when you order.) No. 704. Calico Apron, $12.95.
↓

Pot Cleaning Chain
The kind grandma used, heavy steel, never wears out. For scouring and cleaning iron pans and dishes, 5½ by 9 inches. No. 11508. Pot-chain, $1.50*. Ship. wt. ½ lb.

↑
Hand Churn Popcorn Popper for Top of Your Stove — This old-fashioned do-it-yourself Popper produces perfectly popped corn on your own stove top. The 9" diameter black steel heats quickly (use medium heat). Concave bottom sits up off the stove burner, thus trapping the heat to pop corn without burning. Put in 1 teaspoon oil and ¼ cup of our Bear's Paw White Popcorn. Snap on lid and turn crank.

Our Own Authentic Early American Calico — These charming, colorful, small patterns are in excellent taste for children's garments and for women's dresses, aprons, blouses and skirts. Ideal, of course, for historic celebrations, as well as for window drapes, curtains and quilts. Light Blue, Dark Blue, Light Green, Dark Green, Light Red, Dark Red, Yellow, Pink. Set of swatches No. 600 50¢ postpaid. No. 700. Calico, $1.99 yard. 36" wide.
↓

Heavy Leather Heat-proof Gloves Used by Welders & Foundry Men Now Handy for Wood Fire Use — The chrome tanned, heavy duty leather is lined at the hand area with flannel to stand off high temperatures. Long 5" wide gauntlets protect forearms from sides of hot stoves when you put in wood. No. 1406. Wood Stove Gloves $14.95 pair. Ship. wt. 1 lb.

↑
First-Piece-of-Pie Lifter Outer. Remember this handy gadget from years ago? Now it's being made again. Place the wedge-shaped spatula in empty pie plate before baking. Then lay the bottom crust over it and proceed as usual. When pie is baked and ready to serve, cut along outline of spatula and lift out a perfect first piece, easy as pie! Use as spatula for rest of pie. Made of tin.
No. 14028 Two Pie-Piece Lifters $3.25
Shipping weight ¼ lb.

THE RISING SUN
NEIGHBORHOOD NEWSLETTER

continued from last spread

Living with the bell — Between parades it mostly sat outside my room being rung occasionally to bug me and amuse visitors. I will now explain what its stand was like because someone might wonder, and because explaining odd physical objects is supposed to be good for a writer's soul but if you're in it for the amusing anecdotes, you can skip down to the asterisk on p. 353.

continued on next spread

Good Garb

A well-researched, consumer-oriented book dealing with selecting and caring for practical clothing. The authors focus on all aspects of durable clothing from underwear to shoes. The book includes a chapter on what to wear when it's really hot and how to keep warm in cold weather — and why. Also includes information on how to buy good down-filled and other insulated garments and how to care for them once you do. Complete information on mail-order sources and even some addresses of firms that will accept your dirty sleeping bag or down jacket for cleaning by mail if your local cleaner won't do it. (At **Next Catalog** *press time we did not have a printed copy of the book, so we can't show its copious illustrations.)* —*Marilyn Green*

Good Garb
(A practical guide to practical clothing)
William Dasheff and Laura Dearborn
1980; 279 pp.

$8.95 postpaid from:
Dell Publishing Company
One Dag Hammarskjold Plaza
245 East 47th Street
New York, NY 10017
or Whole Earth Household Store

•

To a large extent, the really high quality functional clothing exists in a realm off the beaten trail. For the most part, you just can't walk into a department store or shopping mall and start buying the kinds of clothes presented in this book. Small specialty shops here and there may carry some items but the main source is mail-order catalogs.

•

The C.C. Filson Company has been delivering top quality clothing since 1897. Garments manufactured thirty or forty years ago are practically identical to those being made today. Filson has had many imitators but no one, as far as we know, has ever matched the quality and outstanding value that Filson steadfastly delivers.

•

For mass-manufactured utility footwear, Chippewa is just about the best you'll find. Workmanship and materials are first-rate. Selected models are available from Todd's or contact: Chippewa Shoe Company, Chippewa Falls, Wisconsin 54729, (715) 723-1012 for the name of a dealer near you.

•

In terms of practicality, members of the American Armed Forces have been among the best-dressed people in our society.

•

One of the most telling signs about a garment is the finish work. After all, all garments, from the worst to the best, basically consist of just a few simple seams. The cost of the material itself, with a few exceptions, is relatively small. The main cost and the part that is most time-consuming is the finish work. How well are the buttonholes made and the buttons sewn on; is the stitching small, neat and even, with no skipped stitches and no puckering of the fabric; are the seam edges cleanly finished; have stress points been reinforced with bar tacks of good quality?

•

Oiled wool is more water-repellent than regular wool which has had most of its natural lanolin removed. Oiled wool garments should never be dry cleaned as this will remove all the oil. Gently hand wash as you would any fine wool sweater.

•

Howard Geiger was the man who made, among other superb leather flight clothing, the famous G-1 goatskin flight jacket for the Navy's pilots during World War II. While he has long since ceased making them for the Navy, he continues to produce the finest version of the G-1 available in the United States and most probably in the world. It is without doubt the best of its kind.

Available from Dennis Connor, Dunhams of Maine and OMS or contact: Willis and Geiger, 45 W. 36th Street, New York, NY 10018.

L.L. Bean

The Bean catalog was the model for the **Whole Earth Catalog.** *Mr. Bean had a directness and integrity that still shows in the catalog, the products, and the service. Though the catalog carries a range of outdoor equipment, it's real forte is durable, practical clothing. I'm a hat shopper; I notice that 3 of my 4 main hats — the knit watch cap, the adjustable baseball cap, and the flaps-that-tie-down-over-the-otherwise-frozen-ears brim cap — are all from L.L. Bean.* —*SB*

L.L. Bean
Catalog
free from:
L.L. Bean, Inc.
Freeport, ME 04032

•

Watch Cap

Traditionally worn by merchant seamen, the Watch Cap is a handy item for outdoorsmen in cold weather. Tightly knit of 100% virgin wool yarns for extra stretch and warmth. Cuff is doubled and pulls down over forehead, ears and neck.

Weight 4 oz.

One size fits all. Color, Navy.

1241C Watch Cap, $4.50 postpaid.

•

Bean's Blue Rock Sweater

Body and sleeves are herringbone knit in a vertically striped pattern of blue and light gray. Collar, cuffs, and waistband are rib-knit in solid light gray. Blended 3-ply yarns of 85% wool and 15% nylon make hard wearing, medium weight outdoors sweater.

Weight about 16 oz. Hand wash or dry clean.

One pattern, Light Gray with Blue stripes.

Men's sizes: Sm. (36 - 38), Med. (39 - 41), Lg. (42 - 44), XLg. (45 - 47).

1766C Blue Rock Sweater, $21.50 postpaid.

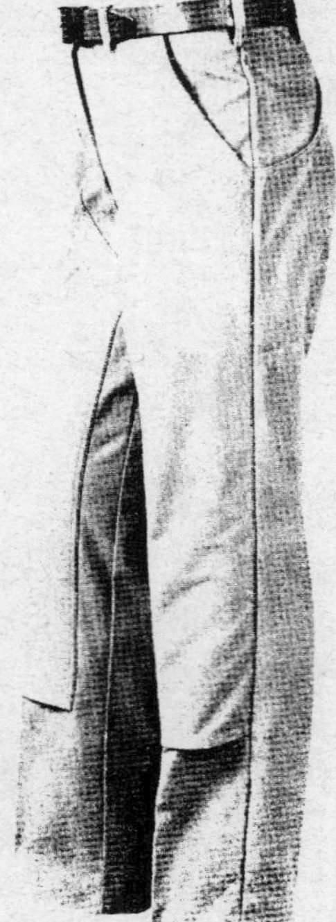

•

Chouinard Double Seated Trail Pants

Originally used by iron workers and adopted by Yvon Chouinard as highly functional rock climbing pants. For outdoors use where a tough, comfortable, non-binding pant is required. Made of 12 oz. polyester-cotton duck, double stitched and bartacked at all points of stress with polyester wrapped cotton thread for extra strength. Deep front pockets. Roomy double seat forms two large rear pockets secured at top by velcro. Double layered front provides for long wear and will not bind. Machine washable and dryable.

Color, Straw. Weight 21 oz. Men's even waist sizes 28 to 38 (state finished inseam length desired).

1821E Chouinard Double Seated Trail Pants, $25.50 postpaid.

Filson outdoor clothes

Cars are tinny, silverware is stainless steel, and fiberboard boxes are palmed off as houses. Contemporary economics seem designed to diminish standards of excellence. Even the durability and construction of clothing has deteriorated: Levi's will not stand four months of normal work; "Can't-bust-ems" have disappeared, and except for Ben Davis' polyester gorillas, there's hardly a tough, trim line of clothing available at all, especially in natural fibers.

Hardly, but the C.C. Filson Co. of Seattle is an exceptional line of clothing and outerwear for loggers, game wardens and outdoor workers. Filson is to work clothes what White is to workboots. Their all-wool shipcords at $59 a pair will survive four or five Levi's at $25 a pair. Filson canvas or "tin" pants and coats are waterproof and extremely resistant to wear.

The top of the line is the Filson "Cruiser," an all-wool, water-repellant coat with nine pockets, in a rich forest green. It is tough enough for the woods but elegant enough for town — warm as a toaster and handsome as a Douglas Fir.

The company responds promptly to requests for their free catalog. —*Peter Coyote*

Filson outdoor clothes
Catalog
free from:
C.C. Filson Company
205 Maritime Building
Seattle, WA 98104

←
Women's Mackinaw Cruiser

"Equal Protection for Outdoor Women"
A companion jacket to the men's model Lot No. 110 including the double back feature. Superbly tailored in classic lines that combine roomy comfort with flattering style and drape. Cut from women's patterns. Double lower pockets combine a utility pocket and hand warmer pocket with side opening. Double upper left front pocket. Button front closure with snap fasteners on all pocket flaps.

Colors: *Plaids;* Red/Black
Solids; Forest Green, Navy Blue, Scarlet $90

→
Filson Whipcord Trail Pants

"A Backpacker's Delight"
Specially designed "all purpose" outdoor pants full cut for freedom. Pockets a-plenty; two bellows pockets with flaps over two deep cargo pockets in front, plus two large back pockets with snap flaps. All pockets are double stitched. Men's model has eight sturdy belt loops, women's model has seven — both easily accommodate a 1½" belt. Heavy-duty zipper fly. Women's model has concealed elastic waistband in the back assuring a comfortable fit. Patterned for real move-around comfort plus flattering good looks. The very best in utility and durability. A casual item for the smart set.

Color: Forest Green, Sage Gray $58.50

↑
Filson Olympic Cruiser

"Medium weight for Town & Country wear"
Styling is smartly casual in a beautiful brown heather shade. An especially woven 21 ounce virgin wool gives this cruiser coat a classic beauty all its own. Features a cape front and a double back for extra protection. Special double lower pockets combine a utility pocket and concealed hand warmer pocket with side opening. Top front pockets and a full carrying pocket in the back provide exceptional utility. Added inside pocket. Button closures throughout. A rare combination of rugged good looks offers an excellent choice for all around use.

Color: Brown Heather $95

← Blanket lined overshirts — $18.59

Gohn Brothers

Gohn Brothers supplies chiefly the stricter Mennonite orders and the various orders of the Amish Mennonite people all over the country. Since the Amish have managed communal living successfully for about 350 years, I figure at least some of their practices must be valid. Their clothing in particular is comfortable, durable and of low price. I can recommend from experience their broadfall work pants (no fly: broad button flap like lederhosen in front), overshirts (plain jacket with two roomy pockets on the inside) and overcoats (heavy dark wool, with cape). Many hard-to-find practical items listed, as well as a broad selection of rather plain yard goods. Service is fast and courteous. Once on their mailing list you get about four to six catalogs a year.

—Peter R. Hoover

Gohn Brothers
Catalog
free from:
Gohn Brothers
Box 111
Middlebury, IN 46540

BLANKET-LINED OVERSHIRTS .... **$18.59 ea.**
10-oz. Sanf. Blue Denim. Sizes 32 to **44** chest measure. Hooks and eyes. No outside pockets. Sewn with black thread. Cut with roomy armholes and wide sleeves. Two inside pockets. Sizes 46 to 50. $2.00 extra.

SHEEPSKIN VESTS
Zipper front. Patch pocket. Sizes S, M, L, XL.
Natural color. Not dyed .... **$46.98 ea.**
Dk. brown. Dyed .... **$48.98 ea.**

CLOTH OF GOLD PERCALE, Solid Colors, 45" **$2.09 yd.**
— 100% COTTON - SANFORIZED - MERCERIZED —
Guaranteed color fast. Lt. blue, yellow, lt. green, pink, navy white, med. green, kelly green, scarlet, dk. yellow, gold, beige, rose, orange, orchid, cream, brown, tan, moss green, black, wine, royal, red.

MEN'S BROADFALL WORK PANTS
No. 1190 10 oz. Sanf. Blue, 35% Dacron .... **$11.49 pr.**
No. 55 10 oz. Sanf. Blue Saddle Denim, 100% cotton . **$10.98 pr.**
No. 66 10 oz. Sanf. Grey Saddle Denim, 100% cotton . **$10.98 pr.**
No. 66 and No. 55 are solid colors. No white in it. Dressier than regular denim, but make excellent work pants.

AMISH OVERCOATS **$126.00**
With Cape .... **$15.00 extra**
100% navy blue melton. Made in single or double breasted style. Send for samples. Complete instructions on how to measure are furnished on request.

Functional Clothing Limited

We haven't seen any of their stuff, but it looks promising. Considering British weather, I tend to trust British weather clothing.

—SB

Functional Clothing Limited
Catalog
$2 (cash only) from:
Functional Clothing Ltd.
Causeway Avenue
Wilderspool Causeway
Warrington WA4 6QQ
England

→
Coat
Six pockets
Weight — About 30 oz.
Length — About 37"
Fitted for optional Contour Hood and Belt and Winter Warm Liner

Barbour raingear

Here in California, Barbour all-weather gear looks hopelessly exotic. Appropriate dress for leaning against the helm or sneaking into East Germany in November and other romances. Outstanding for motorcycles. Waterproof without condensation because the garments have a real oil dressing on them — raindrops actually bounce off. When the dressing eventually wears off, send the item back to Barbour for redressing or do it yourself. Lifetime rain gear.

—SB

[Suggested by Jerome Skuba]

Barbour
Catalog
free from:
J. Barbour and Sons, Ltd.
Simonside, South Shields
Tyne & Wear
NE34 9PD England

↑
Barbour British International motorcycle suit

J. Jill Ltd.

My favorite mail order catalog for women's clothing. Clothes are well designed, simple and very reasonable in price. Most are made from good quality natural fabrics (100% cotton, fine wool, silk, etc.) and are extremely well made. Most styles are loose fitting and comfortable and can be ordered in sizes small, medium or large only which makes the chances good that what you order will fit. A good alternative to Macy's.

—Marilyn Green

J. Jill Ltd.
Catalog
free from:
J. Jill Ltd.
Stockbridge Road
Great Barrington,
MA 01230

Traditional "Sankta Lucia" Gown. →
Pure white 100% cotton broadcloth and dainty lace. Extra long sleeves and fullness for toss-and-turn comfort. Machine wash.
No. 2100-768
Sizes S-M-L
$24.95 ppd.
Size XL
$26.95 ppd.

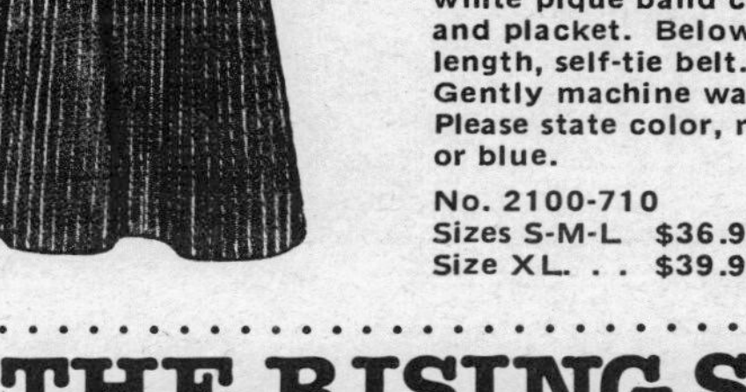

← **Pinstripe Slipover Dress.**
Woven chalk-white pinstripes accent the clear blue or red ground of a full-bodied, hand-loomed Indian fabric of 100% cotton. Long floaty sleeves from narrow shoulder and deep arm hole. Chalky buttons, white pique band collar and placket. Below knee length, self-tie belt. Gently machine wash. Please state color, red or blue.
No. 2100-710
Sizes S-M-L $36.95 ppd.
Size XL . . . $39.95 ppd.

U.S. Cavalry Store

One of the more fascinating catalogs you can get. It's designed for people in, around, and after the tanks part of the U.S. Army — a bizarre mix of wonderful military boots and clothing, grotesque military memorabilia and decorations, kid's stuff, and oddments findable nowhere else.

—SB

U.S. Cavalry Store
Catalog
$2 postpaid from:
U.S. Cavalry Store, Inc.
1375 North Wilson Road
Radcliff, KY 40160

↑
British Regimental Sweater. Best woolen pullover on the market. Olive drab, rib knit. Certified approved for optional purchase. Approval No. 27-77. 100% new wool. Matching shoulder and elbow patches. Sizes 32 through 46.
G01-1051 USMC Sweater .... $28.75 ppd

↑
USCG Deck Jacket. Genuine issue (jacket, cold weather, permeable). 50% nylon, 50% cotton. Water repellent, machine washable. Deep front pockets, snap chest pocket. Zipper front with button down front flap. Knit cuffs, sleeves and body olive drab blanket lined. Sizes S, M, L, XL, XXL.
G05-1067 .... $49.50 ppd

USN Leather Flight Jacket. USN contract. Rugged leather, Dynel collar, knit wristbands. Brown only. Sizes 36-38-40-42-44-46-48.
G04-1001 .... $174.50 ppd

←
Zipper Paratrooper Boot. We make it for you. High quality and wearability. Side zipper, steel shank. Use size chart "A."
G03-1005 .... $47.00 ppd

Miller Stockman

Dude western wear. Surprisingly well made.

—SB

Miller Stockman
Catalog
free from:
Miller Stockman
P.O. Box 5407
Denver, CO 80217

←
Shooting Stars accent these great new separates from two of your favorite manufacturers.
SHIRT is permanent press cotton/polyester chambray. Stars are appliqued on front and back yokes. Dyed-to-match pearlized snaps. Miller's famous tapered fit.
MEN'S SHIRT has extra long tails. Sizes 14½ (sleeves 33), 15 (33, 34, 35), 15½ (33, 34, 35), 16 (34, 35), 16½ (34, 35), 17 (34, 35). $30.00
6-2080-41 Blue 6-2080-25 Brown
JEAN from Farah is prewashed 100% cotton denim. Four-pocket western style with embroidered star on back pocket. Riveted at stress points. Boot cut legs with 38" inseams. Unfinished hems are easy to alter. Waist sizes 29 - 38. $20.00
BUY THE SET and save $5 $45.00

THE RISING SUN
NEIGHBORHOOD NEWSLETTER

continued from last spread

First off, you may not know what a bell is like and how it gets rung, so I'll tell you. A bell is like a bell and how it gets rung is it's hanging from the axle of a cart wheel. The cart wheel has a rope around it in a shallow yo-yo-groove and one end of the rope is attached to the wheel, and you pull on the other end of the rope, wheel moves, axle moves, bell moves, clapper inside bell stays still (gravity, ya know), bell hits clapper, ding. But all of the above could not happen unless cart wheel, axle and bell were all off the ground and able to move freely.

How, you may, if you're insatiably curious, ask, did they get off the ground? Well, my father and two other men lifted them onto this here triangular stand, this stand made up of two triangles and cross beams. Let me put it to you like this. Take a swing set, shrink it down, ditch the swings, put the ends of the bell axle on those two cross pieces at the end of the swing set, bell hanging down between the triangles, cartwheel on the outside of one of the triangles, and you've basically got it.

In this case, the swing set is made of wood and about four feet tall, the bell is about a foot and a half tall and the wheel is about 2 feet tall. (Am I asking you if you care? I am not. I'm in this for my soul, you remember. I missed fully half of Ivanhoe because I skipped the descriptions and here I am with bells, exactly as fascinating as how many drawstrings in your typical rough Saxon ensemble, I'm sure.)

continued on next spread

Consumer Reports

***Consumer Reports** is a comfort. When the time is come to buy some goodie — color television, or a hi-fi, or a sewing machine — CU (Consumers Union) is there with the information on what's the best, or the best buy, or the healthiest of the brands available. **Consumer Reports** is a monthly magazine with articles on various classes of products and various cases of marketing misbehavior; the December issue is the **Buyer's Guide** — a dense compendium of all the quality/price information.* —SB

Consumer Reports
Consumers Union
Staff, Editors
$12/year (11 issues and one Buyer's Guide)

Consumer Reports Buyer's Guide
Consumers Union
Staff, Editors
$3.50/year (annual)

both from:
Consumer Reports
Consumers Union
256 Washington Street
Orangeburg, NY 10962

•

The new *Honda Civic* was a pleasant surprise. It's a much more civilized car than its predecessor. It's larger and quieter, and it rides and handles better, too. What's more, its fuel mileage is the highest available outside of a diesel engine.

The *Civic 1500* turned in 48.8 mpg on the expressway and 28.2 mpg in the city. Over a year's time (or 15,000 miles of mixed highway and around-town driving), the little car would use about 390 gallons of fuel.

Consumer Union News Digest

*From the makers of **Consumer Reports** a nice bi-weekly collection of synopses of consumer articles gleaned from 150 periodicals. An unusually pleasant digest to scan.* —SB

Consumers Union News Digest
(An information service prepared by the library staff of Consumer Reports Magazine)
$36/year (24 issues)
from:
Consumers Union
News Digest
Blaisdell Road
Orangeburg, NY 10962

•

Now It's "No Frills" Supermarkets

If you like the idea of "no frills" groceries, you may be even more excited by the prospect of a "no frills" supermarket. "No frills" outlets keep down prices by cutting services to a minimum. You choose your groceries from cartons stacked on the floor, bring your own paper bags, and pay cash — no check-cashing service provided. Since these outlets buy in volume to keep overhead low, customers generally have to buy in bulk too. The market may not always have everything on your shopping list; but if you have the space to stock up and a large family to feed, you may find the savings worthwhile. For small families with limited space, having to take a giant size box of detergent or a two-pound jar of honey may simply not be worth the trouble. "Saving Dollars At 'No Frills' Supermarkets," by Loraine Serravillo, Christian Science Monitor 3/21/79 p. 18.

•

Fireplaces May Be Friendly Fuel Savers After All

Ever since the energy crisis, the fireplace, traditional symbol of warmth and security, has suffered disparagement. Armchair experts delight in revealing that a fireplace actually wastes heat because the warm air it draws from the interior of the house has to be replaced by cold outside air that must be heated by the furnace. Now there are signs that the fireplace's sullied reputation may be redeemed. A study at Auburn University in Alabama shows that if the outside temperature is above 15 degrees F. or the furnace is turned off, the typical fireplace will contribute more heat than it consumes. Not to be minimized, either, is the fireplace's ability to lure the whole family into one room. It is then easy to save on fuel by turning down the heat in the rest of the house. "Fireplace's Reputation Defended," by David F. Salisbury. Christian Science Monitor 3/21/79 p. 3.

•

Consider "natural" potato chips. They are often cut thick from unpeeled potatoes, packaged without preservatives in heavy foil bags with fancy lettering, and sold at premium price. Sometimes, such chips include "sea salt," a product whose advantage over conventional "land" salt has not been demonstrated. The packaging is intended to give the impression that "natural" potato chips are less of a junk food than regular chips. But nutritionally there is no difference. Both are made from the same food, the potato, and both have been processed so that they are high in salt and in calories.

Sometimes the "natural" products may have ingredients you'd prefer to avoid. *Quaker 100% Natural* cereal, for example, contains 24 percent sugars, a high percentage, considering it's not promoted as a sugared cereal. (*Kellogg's Corn Flakes* has 7.8 percent sugar.) Many similar "natural" granola-type cereals have oil added, giving them a much higher fat content than conventional cereals.

Brand and model	Price	Weight	Size	Cutting	Sawing	Prying	Smashing	Manipulation [1]
Oversized shackle locks								
CITADEL [3]	$28	2 lb.	4¼ in.x½ in.	Excellent	Good	Excellent	Excellent	Very good
KRYPTONITE 4 [3]	25	2	4x½	Excellent	Good	Excellent	Very good	Very good
MAGNUM II 1001 [3]	16	2¾	3⅛x½	Excellent	Fair	Excellent	Excellent	Very good
ABUS 42HB/110-300	22	3¼	2¾x½	Good	Excellent	Excellent	Excellent	Very good
TECH LOCK	14	2¼	4¼x½	Excellent	Excellent	Excellent	Very good	Poor
SUPER-LOCK	16	2¼	4¼x½	Excellent	Excellent	Excellent	Very good	Poor
KRYPTONITE 3	19	1¾	4x⅜ [4]	Excellent	Poor	Excellent	Very good	Very good

Excellent / Very good / Good / Fair / Poor

↑
If, as the FBI reports, bicycle theft has decreased somewhat in recent years, the decline can hardly be attributed to the overall quality of bicycle locks on the market. More than half of the 171 models tested for this report were rated Not Acceptable because they could be yanked, stomped, or sprung apart without the use of tools.

In bolt-cutter country, the first choice would be one of the oversized shackle locks. In our tests, the three top-rated models of that type — the *Citadel*, the *Kryptonite 4*, and the *Magnum* — could easily resist the attacks commonly launched by bike thieves.

Gadget

*This "newsletter for grown-up kids" features highly subjective user reports of the latest technological temptations available to the American consumer. The tests are in marked contrast to the pickynit documented programs of **Consumer Reports**. **Gadget**'s total criticism might consist of a laconic "nobody on our staff liked it." This is thin soup, considering that **Consumer Reports** costs $3 less per year. But **Gadget** reports on products as soon as they appear. Sometimes they show something that has only been on the market a matter of weeks. This can be an advantage if you value being the first on your block to have the latest equipment, or if you are into electronic devices which obsolete themselves quickly. **Gadget** has no ads.* —J. Baldwin

Gadget
$15/year (12 issues)
from:
G.A. Publications, Inc.
116 West 14th Street
New York, NY 10011

•

More of us are attempting to stay fit through strenuous bouts of exercise, be it jogging, tennis, racquetball or sessions at the local health club. This inevitably means more of us are experiencing aches and pains of bruised and and battered muscles. And, when there's an ache, you can bet someone will be there with a product designed to make that ache go away. In this case, that someone is *The Gillette Company (Prudential Tower, Boston, MA 02199)* and they call their contemporary ache-remover the *Heat Wrap*, a thin lightweight heating pad which Gillette likes to think of as the first major innovation in heating pad design in years. The Heat Wrap features a long narrow shape, measuring 20" x 6" with Velcro fasteners, and belt and shoulder loops to facilitate wrapping and keeping heat around large and small muscle areas. Although a bit narrow for use on general backaches, the Gillette Heat Wrap works well with knees, elbows, ankles and wrists, as well as other areas. The Gillette Heat Wrap features a sponge insert for optional moist heat and three heat settings. Price: $17.99. →

Hamilton Beach 794

↑
Hamilton Beach 794 Drip Coffee Maker. This 2-10 cup ADC unit (with lighted switch) is a good, reasonably priced, no-frills machine with ample capacity for home use and an unusually attractive design. A new model (795) is just like this one, but has a timer that allows you to set it to start brewing a specified number of hours later (about $45). (Hamilton Beach Division, Scovill, Inc., Scovill Square, Waterbury, CT 06720)

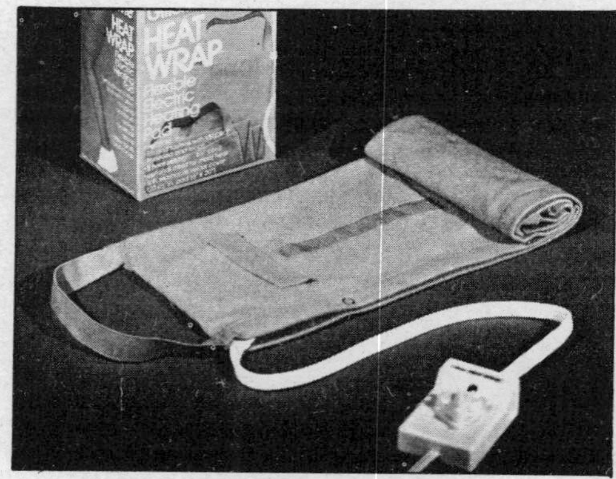

Heat Wrap

The best shave is the cheapest

Unless you're a real little leaguer we must share the memory of barbers and civilians caressing each others' faces or the left and right sides of one face or some other comparison, ad nauseum. The point is that the barber shave has been conceded to be the best by anyone that has had one. It isn't the basis of comparison anymore because nobody remembers. Well, let me tell you, it's still great.

I bought a straight razor for $2 and a strop for $5, both used from (of all people) a barber. I went to the old style barber shop (with the moose head somebody shot before it was disgraceful) where I went when I was little (and where I quit going when I wanted longer hair and found I couldn't trust them). These guys all seem to have a drawer full of old razors that lost their shine. They try out new ones like you'd try out flavors of ice cream. When I bought my razor I had 10 - 15 different razors to choose among from the guys in the shop. They were all happy to unload them and even discounting the ones that were worn out, there was quite a choice (if you go to buy one new it will cost 5 - 10 times as much and don't expect a selection). All the guys in the shop gave me tips for sharpening and using the thing too — I was an instant expert.

You do need to be initiated by someone who knows but it is worth the trouble. It takes less than $15 capital (razor, strop, stone, brush, soap) and you're set for 10 years' shaving.

It might cost another dollar or two per year for soap but that's all. You get the best shave, complete self-sufficiency, and a tremendous bargain at a stroke. If you drop $50 on an electric, $10 per year on tune-ups (plus pre-shave, electricity, etc.) — no bargain for a 2nd class shave (and a new razor in 5 years). The safety razor is no prize either. An endless supply of blades, aerosol foam, etc. — the expense is staggering. You become a stainless steel junkie. And that is clearly a second-class shave too. It might get as close (the double blades *still* don't win, guys) but it takes narrow, short strokes. A straight razor can take you your whole face in big, wide (and wear-saving) strokes. And did you ever try to cut off sideburns, go around a beard — square it off underneath. A couple of strokes through real hair and a safety razor looks like a paint brush (and cuts as well). A straight razor can't clog. You get the same shave in the same time whether your last shave was yesterday or 20 years ago.

Talk about common sense, perishable resources, crass commercial exploitation . . ., if there was ever a case of people's habits being reoriented to generate consumption for its own sake. . . .

Roger Hyde
Los Angeles, California

Editor's question: any reports from women on straight razor advantages? —SB

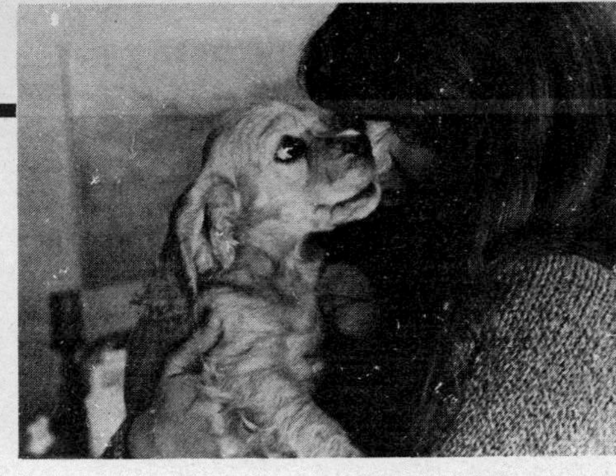

Goethe in the Pea Patch

And Other Animal Stories by J.D. Smith

Hannelore and I had a dog we named Goethe. Goethe wasn't any bristling, nasty, fanged, Kraut, killer. He was, rather, an anemic, wheezy, drippy-eyed poor-man's puppy imitation of the Tramp that Lady loved. We had, on one late winter's Saturday morning, ridden the bus into some Boston suburb and rescued him from the SPCA. (You'd better be kind to animals, so we don't have to gas them in our pounds.) He got his name partly because Hannelore was European, trilingual, hopelessly classic, and partly because the first thing the pup did after we had smuggled him into our Cambridge apartment was to Goethe the terlet all over a Navaho rug.

Hannelore worked as a librarian and translator at Harvard's Museum of Comparative Zoology, where she learned that clean skeletons were produced by throwing cadavers into a room full of omnivorous beetles. I worked the graveyard shift in a twenty-four-hour bookstore, where I learned that I could keep Rodger the Smackhead in spending money by sleeping a few minutes each week while he filled his briefcase with fancy European art books, that there is nothing wrong with working with a gay man if you are a eyefucking womanwatcher (we would split the couples fifty-fifty), and that the doughnuts delivered to the cafeteria next door came two hours before they opened. (Note to prospective all-night book-store owners: No literature gets sold from two a.m. to eight a.m. If you want the shelves restocked during those hours, hire a neutered speedfreak who desperately wants to learn the alphabet.)

Goethe and I were afternoon regulars in Harvard Square. I'd roll out about two, and we would wander out among the tourists and the scholars, grab a snack and a newspaper, then find a nice chunk of sod over by the Radcliffe tennis courts, where I'd watch leg muscles while Goethe pestered picnickers, tried crab-grass herbal remedies on his worm problems, and shat on the footpaths. Ah, Freedom. When the university bells rang the quitting-time carols, the pup and I would putter back through the eye contact and pant legs to our house for trick time. Over the course of a couple of months of Goethe's puppyhood, we learned how to sit up, shake hands, and an amazing diving act, during which I would make tight kissing sounds and Goethe would fling his furry self off the mantle above the fireplace and into my trustworthy arms. Eventually, Hannelore would be home from work to cook supper for us.

Living the decadent-yet-misunderstood, proletarian, artist's life can, even in a college community, become a wretched energy sink. Hannelore gradually seemed to be picking only the "loves-me-not" petals from my activities. I began to wonder why I hadn't stayed back home and become a railroader. Hannelore pricked herself with pins and bled on the bathtub to scare me. I kicked the guts out of our television set. Our eyes found the alarm clock each night after supper. We both became flagrant masturbators. I blamed our mess on city living. She blamed Amerika. Finally we decided to move a little farther out of the bustle, to a place with a yard, for Goethe's sake.

In a couple of weeks we had rented a bright, windowed, third-floor flat, overlooking a good, green, fenced yard, with little garden plots all around the edge of the house. It was a full moist spring. Goethe loved his yard. I stole a bicycle for Hannelore to ride to work. She brought bright curtains home from the museum. Our neighbors were friendly, intelligent, older, almost sane. Things were looking up for us. I began to learn music. She began to translate Creeley and Olson into German and French. I tried to remember how my folks' gardens looked, read books on vegiculture, bought a shovel and some seeds. Goethe began to learn deportment from a spayed golden retriever.

Well, like my Grandad used to say, "You can't stick your foot into the same shoe twice." I began to spade up the plot, hauling gook from the edge of the Charles river and working it into the sandy fill along the house. The mailman took to getting barked at by Goethe and the retriever, but not with total joy, so on this sunny, soily day, I had left my pup up-stairs in the apartment, with the windows open so he could watch my farming. I had just powdered up what was to be the pea patch, when, with what must have been Henny Penny's basic awareness, I looked up to see Goethe halfway between the third floor window and me, front legs extended, expecting me to catch him. He broke his neck right beside me. I hadn't had time to let go of the shovel, so it didn't take long to bury him. Never had the heart to plant anything else there. Not long afterward, Hannelore and I went our separate ways. ■

CHARLIE THE GOOSE

(heard in Burgdorf, Idaho, July 1976)

"A year ago last Spring, my oldest daughter's boyfriend gave her a little bitty wild Canadian honker, and she raised it up on mush and milk out on the back porch with our three dogs. That goose got housebroke pretty soon, and would come up to the back door just like the dogs, and he'd peck on it, and we'd let him in, and he'd beg food from the table, and it even got to the point where when my daughter was loading the dogs in the back of the pickup she'd just call "Charlie, Charlie," and that blamed goose would fly right up in the back of the truck and ride there, like a dog.

"Well, we worried ol' Charlie through hunting season that Fall, and kept him warm by the fire all Winter, then this Spring he started being gone overnight and the first time we figured out what he was up to was when one of our neighbors called up and said that our goose was down there bothering his dogs, and keeping folks awake all night. We figured he was trying to mate with a dog since he probably had never seen another goose.

"Finally he was gone for a couple of weeks and we started believing he'd flown up to Canada or somewhere, when my daughter was driving about fifteen miles from our place, and saw a wild goose out in back of this old fellow's place, and stopped and it turned out to be Charlie with his wings clipped. She and the old man had quite an argument about whose goose it was, but she eventually proved to him that the goose would follow her any-where she would go, so she helped him up in the back of the truck and brought him home and put him out on the porch with the dogs, and, you know, believe it or not, we got up the next morning and our own dogs had eaten that goose. Musta had something to do with his wings being clipped."

HOW TO FIX A DOG RACE

My Grandpa Frary took a dogfever pilgrimage from Colorado to Florida to learn how greyhounds are trained to run. He found out that many trainers work the dogs in low pens with live rabbits. Real rabbits rarely run in perfect halfmile ovals like their mechanical cousins at the track do. Real rabbits dart and weave and slow down just a little before they change directions. The dogs sense the move coming and break their own strides to make the turn with the real rabbits. At the track the mechanical rabbit runs on a rheostat setup, so that the person who is controlling the speed of the track bunny can slow it down at just the right time, the lead dogs think the rabbit is going to take a ninety degree turn, break their stride a little, and the hind dogs catch up. This knowledge didn't keep my Grandpa from betting on the dogs.

COONDOG MEMORY

(heard in Rutledge, Missouri, about ten years ago)

"Now, this dog is for sale, and she can not only follow a trail twice as old as the average dog can, but she's got a pretty good memory to boot. For instance, last week this old boy who lives down the road from me, and is forever stinkmouthing my hounds, brought some city fellow around to try out ol' Sis here. So I turned her out south of the house and she made two or three big swings back and forth across the edge of the woods, set back her head, bayed a couple of times, cut straight through the woods, come to a little clearing, jumped about three foot straight up in the air, run to the other side, and commenced to letting out a racket like she had something treed. We went over there with our flash-lights and shone them up in the tree but couldn't catch no shine off a coon's eyes, and my neighbor sorta indicated that ol' Sis might be a little crazy, cause she stood right to the tree and kept singing up into it. So I pulled off my coat and climbed up into the branches, and, sure enough, there was a coon skeleton wedged in between a couple of branches about twenty foot up. Now as I was saying, she can follow a pretty old trail, but this fellow was still calling her crazy or touched 'cause she had hopped up in the air while she was crossing the clearing, until I reminded him that the Hawkins' had a fence across there about five years back. Now, this dog is for sale."

MOUSE DISCOUNT

(heard in Burgdorf, Idaho, 1974)

"I was the manager of the Penney's store in Nampa for a few years. One year business got a little slow, so I took a piece of plywood, drilled about fifty inch-and-a-half holes in it, randomly numbered them either ten, twenty, thirty, or forty percent, nailed mason jar rings to the bottoms, and screwed pint jars into them. The idea was that when a person had something figured out that he wanted to buy, he'd bring it to the mouse board, and I'd let out this little mouse and whatever hole the mouse would run down, that is how much discount the person would get. Now the trick is this: a mouse won't go into a hole where no mouse has ever been, so by taking a few mouse turds and dropping them down the ten percent holes, and say one turd down one of the forty percent holes, I could provide a little excitement for the customers, and a little for myself, as long as I only marked up the goods fifteen or twenty percent."

THE RISING SUN

NEIGHBORHOOD NEWSLETTER

continued from last spread

*Anyway, for a while there was a bell outside my room and a long bell rope hanging over the stair-well into the downstairs, which my family would pull if they wanted me. It was useful, because though my parents' current house shocked me by being one of those one-floor plans where hiding from company means you can't pee or talk, this was a 150-year-old, two-story, internal brick wall yell producer, and I was always reading or trying to figure out the truth about the truth and God (really, and to think I could've been masturbating, although, on the other hand, there were two doors into my bedroom from two different locales and although my family was pretty good about knock-ing, two doors, though certainly not causative of a jumpy personality, cannot be said to be a cure). Also, the bell was good to impress, entertain, or weird out visitors. "Wanna see the church bell?" and they'd say yeah, but they never expected it to really be a church bell, or so loud, or for my father to ring it so long. And when my parents were counselors at a tent camp with fairly scat-tered tents it was a good way to call the campers for things, and another privilege to dole out (no bell ringing without permission was a necessary rule).

continued on next spread

OF ALL THE SUBJECTS in the **Catalog,** *I have the least confidence in our coverage of the pet scene (except for Lorenz and* **The Complete Dog Book**). *Nothing on cats here at all. How about some advice from pet-knowledgeable readers, so our next edition won't be so lame in this area? We pay $10 for suggestions and for reviews that are used.* —SB

Giving a "line" signal to a dog on the Directional Retrieve.
—The Pearsall Guide to Successful Dog Training

King Solomon's Ring
Man Meets Dog

The classic animal books by the originator of ethology, the study of animal behavior. Lorenz loves his pets and understands them, and they seem to respond in kind. —SB

King Solomon's Ring
Konrad Z. Lorenz
1952; 202 pp.

$1.95 postpaid from:
New American Library
P.O. Box 120
120 Woodbine
Bergenfield, NJ 07621
or Whole Earth Household Store

Man Meets Dog
Konrad Z. Lorenz
1954; 198 pp.

$3.70 postpaid from:
Penguin Books
299 Murray Hill Parkway
East Rutherford, NJ 07073
or Whole Earth Household Store

•

Why has the dog the inhibition against biting his fellow's neck? Why has the raven an inhibition against pecking the eye of his friend? Why has the ring-dove no such "insurance" against murder? A really comprehensive answer to these questions is almost impossible. It would certainly involve a *historical* explanation of the process by which these inhibitions have been developed in the course of evolution. There is no doubt that they have arisen side by side with the development of the dangerous weapons of the beast of prey. However, it is perfectly obvious why these inhibitions are necessary to all weapon-bearing animals. Should the raven peck, without compunction, at the eye of his nest-mate, his wife or his young, in the same way as he pecks at any other moving and glittering object, there would, by now, be no more ravens in the world. Should a dog or wolf unrestrainedly and unaccountably bite the neck of his pack-mates and actually execute the movement of shaking them to death, then his species also would certainly be exterminated within a short space of time.

The ring-dove does not require such an inhibition since it can only inflict injury to a much lesser degree, while its ability to flee is so well developed that it suffices to protect the bird even against enemies equipped with vastly better weapons. Only under the unnatural conditions of close confinement which deprive the losing dove of the possibility of flight does it become apparent that the ring-dove has no inhibitions which prevent it from injuring or even torturing its own kind.

— King Solomon's Ring

An everyday occurrence: you are walking along the front of a garden fence and a big dog is growling and barking behind it. Judging by the behavior of the animal, which is snarling and biting the fence with brutally bared fangs, it is only the railings that keep him from your throat. On such occasions I am not intimidated by these threats of violence and I always open the garden gate without hesitation. The dog demurs; unsure what to do next, he continues to bark but in much less menacing tones, and his demeanour plainly betrays that he would never have exhibited so much fury had he foreseen that I should not respect the inviolability of the fence. It may even happen that when the gate is opened, he flees several yards and then keeps up his barking in a different tone and from a safe distance. And conversely a very shy dog, or wolf, which shows no sign of enmity or mistrust from behind the bars, may attack in deadly earnest anyone appearing in the doorway.

These apparently opposite types of behaviour can all be explained in terms of the same psychological mechanism. Every animal, particularly every large mammal, will flee before a superior rival as soon as it comes within a certain fixed distance. The 'flight distance,' as Prof. Hediger, its discoverer, calls it, increases proportionately with the degree of fear which the animal possesses for its opponent. There is an exactly predictable point at which an animal will turn tail when an enemy starts to encroach on the flight distance, and there is a similar point at which it will fight if the enemy gets very close. Under natural conditions, such an overstepping of the 'critical distance' (Hediger) only occurs in two instances, either when the animal is taken by surprise or when it is cornered and so unable to flee.

— Man Meets Dog

The Pearsall Guide to Successful Dog Training

Neither rough nor punishment-based, this guide for "obedience from the dog's point of view" goes from house-breaking the puppy to advanced training, with basic, novice, open, and utility training along the way. A highly regarded method and book. It looks like fun; the old harsh methods weren't. —SB

The Pearsall Guide to Successful Dog Training
(Obedience from the dog's point of view)
Margaret E. Pearsall
1973, 1976; 351 pp.

$11.95 postpaid from:
Howell Book House
230 Park Avenue
New York, NY 10017
or Whole Earth Household Store

•

We can generally classify the voice in four categories:

a. **Coaxing:** Used to excite the pup into doing something.

b. **Happy:** For a job well done, especially after a correction has been applied.

c. **Harsh:** *Never* to be used, even if the pup is slow to learn. *You* just might be the one to blame.

d. **Demanding:** To be used only when you are positive your pup knows what you want but refuses.

•

Let him know you mean business when you demand something from him, but don't let any harsh correction or punishing tone creep into your voice. A coaxing or pleading voice will not get the desired response, will not encourage respect and obedience; nor will you get anywhere with a sharp, cross voice, as this can convey just as much unpleasantness as physical punishment. You want your Buddy as a companion and, still more important, *he* wants *you* as one. Don't let your emotions show in your voice (other than what is required when you're working with him) and don't try to fake anything with him. He will be able to see through you every time, so why bother trying to fool him? It proves to be wasted time and energy. Also, an unusually loud command is unnecessary, as a dog's normal hearing is so acute that it is one of his outstanding attributes.

If a more severe tone of voice should be needed as a correction, clip your words off as you say them, to get more immediate attention. In doing this be careful you do not accompany this with glaring or staring at your dog. Remember this all through training: *Whenever you are facing your dog, always look above his head or a bit to his side, never at his eyes.*

Right now we want to have you become familiar with commands you will be using, teaching your dog different exercises as you go along through the basic part of his education and on into the more advanced phases. Always use your dog's name for attention, then follow with a command that you want him to carry out. Some of these are *"Heel," "Sit," "Stand," "Down," "Stay," "Wait,"* and *"Come."* Another word we would like to have you get in the habit of using is not a command but is extremely important in your training. This is the word *"Good!"* for it is so easy to inject your feelings and pleasure into it and let Buddy know you are happy with his performance.

At heart of the Pearsall training methods is a constant awareness of what we are asking of the dog. Here a class literally sees signals from the dog's point of view.

The Complete Dog Book

I hate dogs and like this book. Scanning through the breeds recognized by the American Kennel Club (whose official publication this is) I find myself commencing to shop. Hm, would I like a Siberian Husky (fastidiously clean, amiable), a French Bulldog (intelligent, not noisy), a Mastiff (one brought down an elephant), an Otter Hound (sagacious, devoted, web-footed)? The brief authoritative introductions to care, training, health, breeding, etc. seem manageable. I even like this kind of book — co-evolved with its users and its dogs through sixteen editions, cheap, restrained and proud. —SB

The Complete Dog Book
(The photographs, history and official standard of every breed admitted to AKC registration, and the selection, training, breeding, care and feeding of pure-bred dogs)
American Kennel Club
1941, 1979; 768 pp.

$11.95 postpaid from:
Howell Book House
230 Park Avenue
New York, NY 10017
or Whole Earth Household Store

Schipperke. The name is Flemish for "little captain" and is properly pronounced "skeep-er-ker" (the last r almost silent). Though called a canalboat dog, the Schipperke was as popular with shoemakers and other workmen as it was on the canals . . . While usually an excellent ratter, the Schip is not a powerful fighter, though he can hold his own with most dogs of his weight and will tackle anything in defense of his household or of his master. He is not aware of the limitations of his size. . . This breed is usually long-lived for a small one, many instances of dogs living to be fifteen and sixteen years old being recorded; one dog, bred in Rothesay, Scotland, was reputed to have lived twenty-one years. Schips are very fond of children and in some cases have served as guards; and they have taken the place, to some extent, of human nurses, so devoted are they to their small charges.

The Schipperke is often called "the best house dog" (le meilleur chien de maison).

A TRAINED DOG IS A JOY and a pride. An untrained dog is an infernal nuisance to everybody. Most dogs are untrained.
—SB

Koehler Method of Dog Training

This is more a dog correcting book than training. Here are techniques, many of them harsh, for correcting a problem dog — barking, biting, bolting, chasing cars and joggers, howling, digging up the garden, etc. The author trains most of the movie dogs, so you've already seen his results. I'd start with the Pearsall book and fall back on Koehler.
—SB

Koehler Method of Dog Training
W.R. Koehler
1962, 1977; 208 pp.
$8.95 postpaid from:
Howell Book House
230 Park Avenue
New York, NY 10017
or Whole Earth
Household Store

One good correction will do the job where many tentative ones fail.

•

This book differs from others in two ways: it openly acknowledges that not all dogs "want to please," and that some are even viciously resentful of efforts to train them; and it takes the stand that these viciously resentful problem dogs, since they are bred and influenced by man, have a moral right to the training that may be necessary to rehabilitate them.

The book's methods are applicable to those dogs that resist training, as well as to the tractable dogs, which are in the great majority.

Thought by thought and act by act, the objective of this book is to enable the reader to train the dog he now has, regardless of its conduct and character, to a point where he and his dog will enjoy the fullest companionship.

•

The Chase-Happy Biter

This type of dog, with the tremendous drive he expresses in chasing and biting at people who are running, skating, or riding such things as bikes, scooters, motorcycles, and horses, needs basic obedience — but plenty. After you've added to his restraint and conscience by having him hold lots of stays while exposed to the temptations, you can stimulate him with the same distractions without his being told to stay. What you do with the stays is to make him think well before charging anything.

Be certain of two things: first, that he is equipped with a good strong line; second, that if he moves one inch aggressively, he'll wish he hadn't. Remember, you are liable if his charge, with or without a bite, should cause someone to fall and be injured. So grab the line and give him about five minutes of the hardest tanning you can administer. Use a belt heavy enough to make him really feel your efforts. Sometimes the long duration of a spanking is a big factor in making an indelible impression. *Since you are dealing with a dog that could cause the death or serious injury of a person, let there be no compassionate trembling before the necessity of stern measures.*

Stromberg's pets

Exotic animals, armadillos to peacocks. Reviewed on p. 110.
—SB

FLYING SQUIRRELS $35.00 PAIR
2 Pair $60.00—3 Pair $75.00

Bill Boatman and Company

Hunting dog stuff. Collars, pens, training devices, medicines, and coonhunting paraphernalia, such as super flashlights.
—SB
[Suggested by Charley Kroner]

Bill Boatman and Company
Catalog

free from:
Bill Boatman and Company
Bainbridge, OH 45612

→

Shoulder Length Rubber Gloves. Muskrat trappers can avoid cold hands and arms. Even "icy water" can be worked in comfortably with these shoulder length, gauntlet gloves.

Avoid exposure that leads to "time losing" bad colds or even pneumonia. Work your line regardless of the weather. Take advantage of new areas after others quit. Eyelets to tie or snap up. 31" long. No. 1121 $19.95

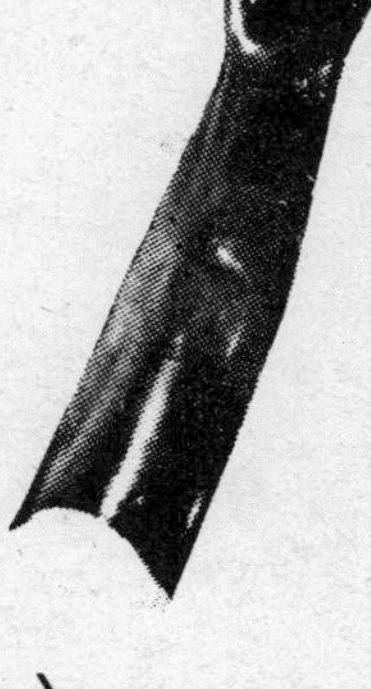

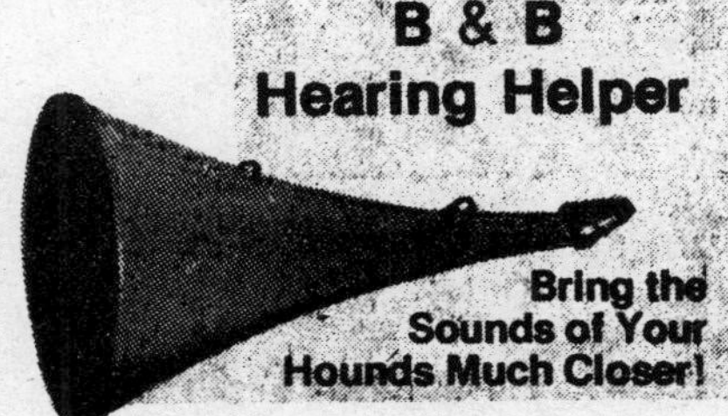

B & B
Hearing Helper
Bring the
Sounds of Your
Hounds Much Closer!

→

Pick out the front running hound in a race. Don't be fooled by a noisy hound running second. Helps you "really place" a new hound in your pack. You can quickly and easily tell whether he is running ahead or behind the hounds you normally hunt.

"Direct" your hearing toward the hounds. By slowly turning the hearing helper in different directions you can actually determine which way they are going. Lets you zero in on the hounds and away from unwanted highway noise, low flying airplanes, or the sounds of a babbling brook or a rampaging river.

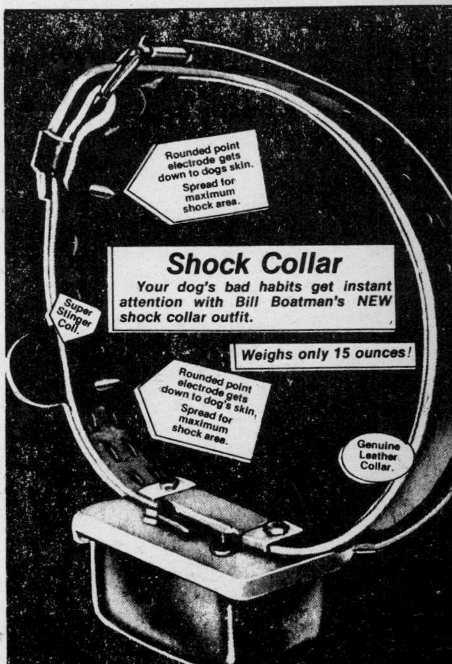

Rounded point electrode gets down to dogs skin. Spread for maximum shock area.
Shock Collar
Your dog's bad habits get instant attention with Bill Boatman's NEW shock collar outfit.
Super Stinger Coil
Weighs only 15 ounces!
Rounded point electrode gets down to dog's skin. Spread for maximum shock area.
Genuine Leather Collar.

→

Fault buster, Jr. Medium range, with dry cell (non re-chargeable) receiver batteries. Complete outfit includes powerful transmitter, shock collar, dummy collar and "how-to-use" booklet with training tips by Bill Boatman and other experienced hunters. No. 2094 $199.95.

Feather Finder Bird Dog Training Kit. Start your pups right in your own backyard. Teach them to retrieve the durable training dummy. Then add bird scent to the dummy. Hide it. They'll learn to locate and point. Train for one game bird at a time. Feather Finder Kits are sold exclusively by Boatman's. Order now for step-by-step systematic training. Specify: Quail, Pheasant, Grouse or Duck.

Training Kit includes Scent, Canvas Dummy, Training Whistle and instructions. No. 620 $8.95

↓

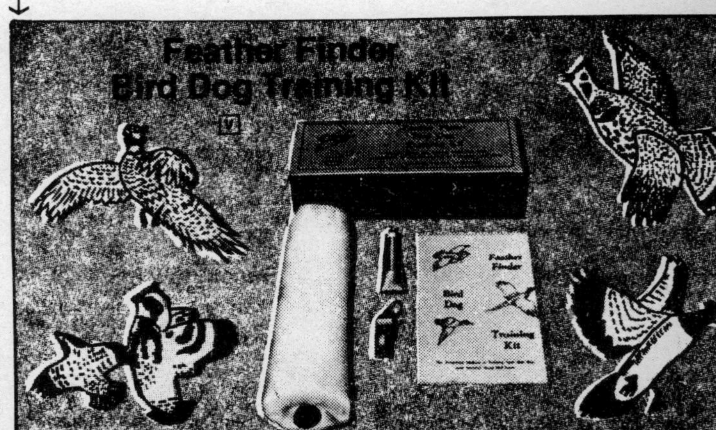

How to Raise & Train Pigeons

Pigeon fanciers say this is the best book on the subject. One advantage of pigeons over dogs is they make a more pleasant sound. Another is you can eat them. Racing the homers looks like fun. Nice city rooftop pet.
—SB
[Suggested by William L. Cassidy]

How to Raise & Train Pigeons
William H. Allen, Jr.
1959, 1974; 159 pp.
$8.95 postpaid from:
Sterling Publishing Co.
Two Park Avenue
New York, NY 10016

If you hand-feed your pigeons, you will get to know each other and the birds will become very tame.

THE RISING SUN
NEIGHBORHOOD NEWSLETTER

continued from last spread

Getting the church bell down around the hairpin steps from outside my room to the project of the hour was a nice short difficult challenge for strong people. I notice strong people like to use their strength really a lot now and then — when Luke's antsy from ordering too many books I figure it would be nice if he and David could move the church bell from the front office to the back office or something. They might have to get Stewart to help, church bells are really heavy, but then we don't have a church bell. Even my father doesn't have a church bell now. When he moved out of that eight room house to the present one-floorer he gave the bell to Arnold Watkins, co-owner of the hardware store, who put it in his garage and rang it for a while that very night, and someone called the cops, and the cops came and they heard it, but they couldn't figure out where the noise was coming from. Not everyone should have a church bell, but people who could use it properly should certainly consider it.

continued on next spread

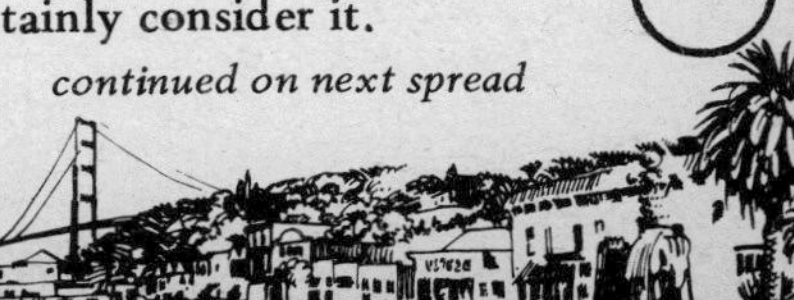

The Complete Indoor Gardener & Grow It Indoors

Although unaffiliated, these two books together are the best source of houseplant information so far. ***Complete*** *could be the workbook and Langer's book the text.* ***Complete*** *has several useful color pictures per page and excellent instructions. If I could buy only one, I'd buy that. Langer goes deep into indoor gardening technique, and horticulturally, it's even better than his classic homesteading book* **Grow It!** *(p. 120).*

—Rosemary Menninger

The Complete Indoor Gardener
Michael Wright, Editor
1974, 1979; 256 pp.
$8.95 postpaid from:
Random House, Inc.
455 Hahn Road
Westminster, MD 21157
or Whole Earth Household Store

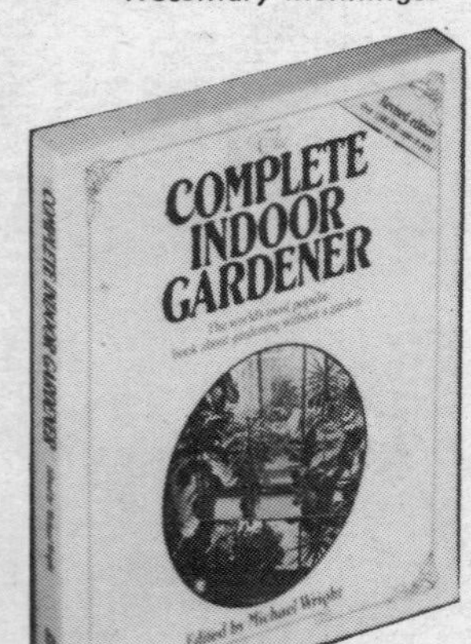

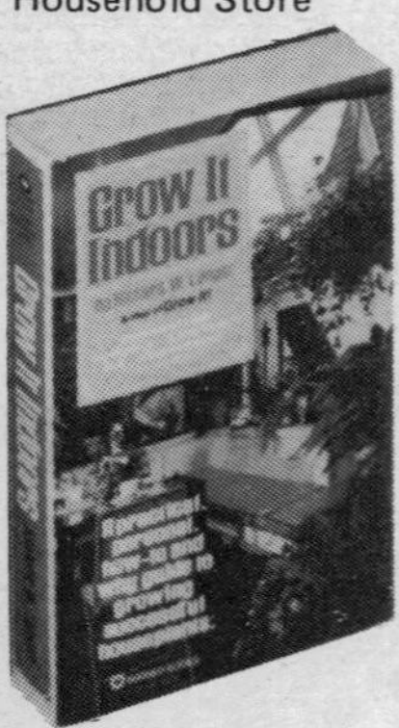

Grow It Indoors
Richard W. Langer
1975; 243 pp.
$4.95 postpaid from:
Warner Books
75 Rockefeller Plaza
New York, NY 10019
or Whole Earth Household Store

Ginger; coffee
If you can find a fresh ginger root in a food shop, you can grow it into an extremely handsome indoor foliage plant, with glossy dark green leaves. **below** Simply suspend the root in water until it sprouts, and then plant in a pot of good potting mixture. Keep it warm and light.

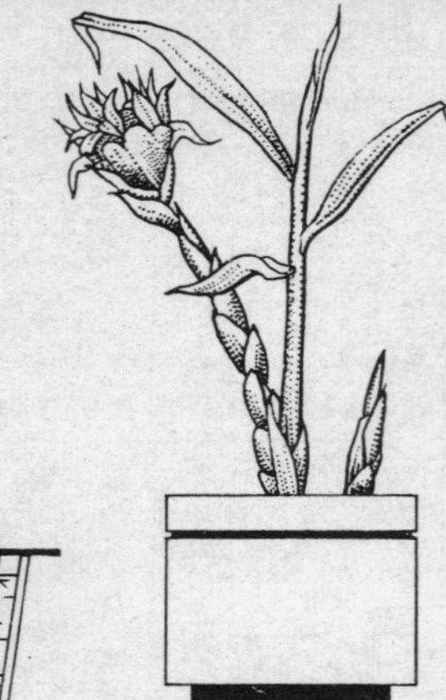

Ginger

You can also grow a plant from a fresh unroasted coffee bean. It needs warm, damp potting mixture to germinate, but once you have a coffee plant it likes only moderately warm conditions – a minimum of 10°C (50°F) – and prefers shade and plenty of air. The leaves are a coppery colour when they first emerge, and turn a dark, glossy green. The small white flowers smell sweet, and are followed by red berries that contain coffee beans. Once mature, prune the bush to keep it neat for the house.

← **Watering cans; sprayers**
A watering can is a vital piece of equipment. For watering pot-plants and window boxes, choose one with a fine nozzle and long spout **right below**.
It is wise to have two sprayers **right** – one for water and the other for pesticides. There are neat hand models suitable for treating plants indoors in confined spaces. The sprayer used for clean water should be clearly marked and used for nothing else. Many plants benefit from an occasional fine overhead spray, especially in the dry atmosphere of the home.

Coffee

—**The Complete Indoor Gardener**

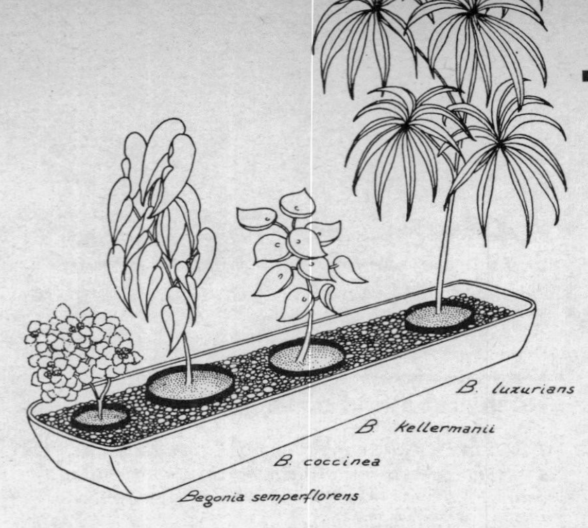

Leaf variation in begonias

—**Grow It Indoors**

Recently while perusing the English version of the May 1973 **Doklady Akademii Nauk SSSR**, an obscure Russian scientific journal, I came across a fascinating little article still somewhat out of science fiction. Somewhere in their vast bureaucracy the Russians must have plans to colonize the moon, for here were described the beginnings of research on how to feed the emigrants.

The article, "Growth and Development of Plants with a Lunar Period," discussed the fact that most annual plants, if they even survived being subjected to a period of darkness lasting three or more days, lost not only their photosynthetic pigments, but their reproductive ability as well. Cereals were particularly sensitive to the light deprivation, a two- to three-day period of darkness being sufficient to eliminate development of the grain for which the plants were grown.

The phenomenon would present quite an agricultural problem on the moon, where the days and nights are each fifteen earth days long. Artificial lighting could be used to grow the plants, of course, but the energy demands and cost would be tremendous.

Scientists reasoned, however, that sharply reduced night temperatures might slow down the plant's metabolic rate enough to avoid the disastrous damage to the reproductive system. It worked. So far as lunar wheat harvests went, the particular problems of extra long nights, at least, had been solved.

What I found just as interesting, from a houseplant point of view, was that plants used in the experiment made up for lost time during the fifteen-day days. Overall the wheat plants grown on a lunar time-table matured as quickly as their more normal earth-environed cousins.

—**Grow It Indoors**

Mother Earth's Hassle-Free Indoor Plant Book

Basic and easy, and surprising that this book that's half (good) cartoons should give so much important information that many "serious" houseplant books overlook.

—Rosemary Menninger

I recommend leaving most ivy outdoors. Spathiphyllum is particularly good for those who love to water.

Mother Earth's Hassle-Free Indoor Plant Book
Lynn & Joel Rapp
1973; 114 pp.
$3.95 postpaid from:
J.P. Tarcher, Inc.
9110 Sunset Blvd.
Los Angeles, CA 90069
or Whole Earth Household Store

Mushroom trees

Here's an easy and virtually guaranteed way to grow delicious mushrooms at home without having to sift buckets of manure or devise other growing mediums. The Kinoko Company has developed kits for four types of mushrooms — common button (the kind you get in the grocery store), velvet stem, tree oyster, and the much-prized oriental Shiitake (commonly used in Chinese and Japanese cooking). See also **Mushroom Growing for Everyone** *(p. 98) and* **Growing Mushrooms,** *(p. 418).*

—Evelyn Edridge-Diaz

Kinoko Mushroom-Mate Kits
$9.95 - $14.95
postpaid
Information and price list
free from:
The Kinoko Company
P.O. Box 6425
Oakland, CA 94621

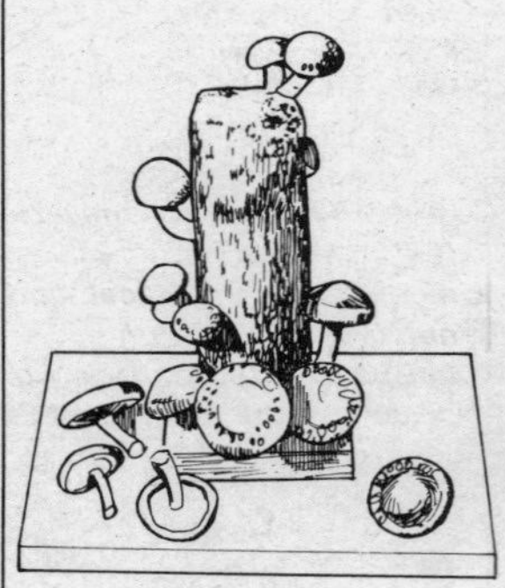

VELVET STEM

TREE OYSTER

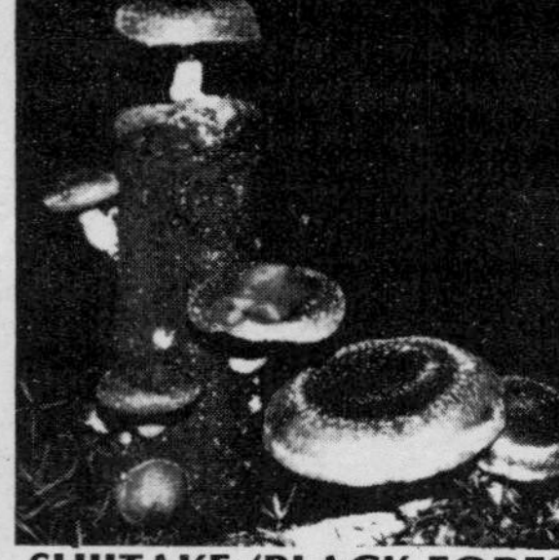

COMMON BUTTON

SHIITAKE (BLACK FOREST

Mushroom-Mate Kit in a Complete Package:

Common Button	$ 9.95
Velvet Stem	$ 9.95
Tree Oyster	$ 9.95
Shiitake	$14.95

Outside continental U.S./Alaska and Hawaii — $2 extra.

Garbage diverter

One of the handiest gadgets in electric kitchens, as any upper middle class housewife can tell you, is the garbage disposer. Chuck onion peels, egg shells, moldy yogurt, et cetera into it, flip the switch, and presto! All the stinky wet garbage disappears down the drain, borne by clean water.

As the ecologically enlightened know, that stinky garbage is also potentially rich garden soil. There is something in my Scot's cells that rebels against this kind of waste. So the other day I asked a mechanic friend to create for me a device I had designed to capture the ground-up organic material before it goes down the drain. He did it. Now I am using the disposer's ground-up output plus the water in my garden instead of running it out into Bolinas lagoon.

I call the gadget Margot Doss's Little Jim Dandy Garbage Diverter and have applied for a patent.

The gung-ho back-to-nature buffs may shriek:

1. That it uses electricity
2. That you can do the same thing in a blender
3. That composting does the work in time

The answer to all these is yes, of course. Apart from that, a blender must be cleaned after every use, and the gunk that comes out of the Diverter is ground so fine it speeds up the composting considerably. I hope the Little Jim Dandy Garbage Diverter will introduce a lot of people to the mystique of organic gardening.

If your readers seem interested, I will also sell the plans for one sawbuck. Anyone who wants a reservation on this trip should send a self-addressed legal sized envelope and $1 to Little Jim Dandy Garbage Diverters, Box 447, Bolinas, CA 94924.

Cordially

Margot Patterson Doss
Bolinas, California

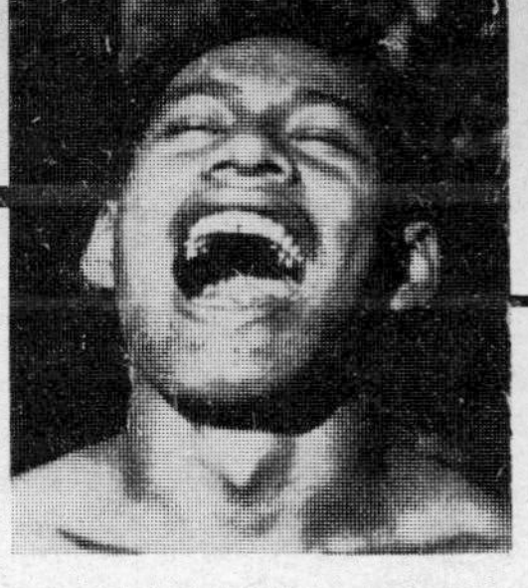

Polynesians are a beautiful race and physically sturdy. They have straight hair and their color is often that of a sun tanned European. They have perfect dental arches.

Wherever the native foods have been displaced by the imported foods, dental caries becomes rampant. A typical modernized Tahitian.

Nutrition and Physical Degeneration

Of all the books written on nutrition, I still find this the most interesting. Dr. Price was a practicing dentist who noticed the marked decline in his young patient's health and dental condition. In 1930, he began a 150,000 mile trek around the globe seeking out healthy primitive peoples whose teeth (and health) were excellent. In his book 14 tribal diets are completely examined, diets which give their people almost perfect dental and physical health. Wonderfully, each diet is radically different from the other. What is consistent is not the foods, their proportion or kind, but the fact that each of the diets is completely indigenous and totally derived from a direct relationship to the person's environment. The Gaels of the Outer Hebrides ate little but fish, oats, barley, and some seaweed. The Kikuyus of Africa ate primarily sweet potatoes, corn, beans, and bananas. While the Indians of the Pelly mountain country in northwest Canada ate almost solely wild animals.

In contrast to the racial stock that was eating indigenous foods, Price sought out a neighboring tribe or group that had been exposed to foods of western civilization, particularly refined foods such as flour, sugar, as well as canned foods and meats. The comparisons between the "control" and the newly civilized group invariably showed a rapid deterioration of teeth, malocclusion, a rise in infectious diseases, and even more startling, a rapid change in the skeletal and racial characteristics that are supposedly genetic. Flat nosed Indians had aquiline noses within two generations, and sinus troubles as well. New Zealand Maori would not only find that their dental arches would narrow, but that their pelvic arches would contract causing pain, injury and even death at childbirth. Again, Price found these changes within one generation of change in diet.

All of the foods grown and gathered by primitives were taken and analyzed. While diets differed widely, all were high in protein, vitamins, and minerals. Corresponding foods grown by primitives were in many cases 10 - 50 times as high in minerals as the similar foods in our own culture. Just as important was the observation that when primitive peoples reverted back to their original diets, their health improved, dental caries halted, and the physiology of their offspring resembled again their racial origins. He never found a healthy child that wasn't breast fed. No book written since has as effectively demonstrated the relationship between good health, nutrition and the environment. —Paul Hawken

Nutrition and Physical Degeneration
(A Comparison of Primitive and Modern Diets and Their Effects)
Weston A. Price, D.D.S.
1945, 1970; 526 pp.

$20.50 postpaid from:
Price-Pottenger Nutrition Foundation
P.O. Box 2614
La Mesa, CA 92041

Item No.	Food and description	Water	Food energy	Protein	Fat	Carbohydrate Total	Carbohydrate Fiber	Ash	Calcium	Phosphorus	Iron	Sodium	Potassium	Vitamin A value	Thiamine	Riboflavin	Niacin	Ascorbic acid
(A)	(B)	(C)	(D)	(E)	(F)	(G)	(H)	(I)	(J)	(K)	(L)	(M)	(N)	(O)	(P)	(Q)	(R)	(S)
		Percent	*Calories*	*Grams*	*Grams*	*Grams*	*Grams*	*Grams*	*Milligrams*	*Milligrams*	*Milligrams*	*Milligrams*	*Milligrams*	*International units*	*Milligrams*	*Milligrams*	*Milligrams*	*Milligrams*
	Squash:																	
	Summer:																	
	All varieties:																	
2191	Raw	94.0	19	1.1	0.1	4.2	0.6	0.6	28	29	0.4	1	202	410	0.05	0.09	1.0	22
2192	Cooked, boiled, drained	95.5	14	.9	.1	3.1	.6	.4	25	25	.4	1	141	390	.05	.08	.8	10
	Crookneck and Straightneck, Yellow:																	
2193	Raw	93.7	20	1.2	.2	4.3	.6	.6	28	29	.4	1	202	460	.05	.09	1.0	25
2194	Cooked, boiled, drained	95.3	15	1.0	.2	3.1	.6	.4	25	25	.4	1	141	440	.05	.08	.8	11
	Scallop varieties, white and pale green:																	
2195	Raw	93.3	21	.9	.1	5.1	.6	.6	28	29	.4	1	202	190	.05	.09	1.0	18
2196	Cooked, boiled, drained	95.0	16	.7	.1	3.8	.6	.4	25	25	.4	1	141	180	.05	.08	.8	8
	Zucchini and Cocozelle (Italian marrow type),																	

Composition of Foods

Since natural food does not come with a list of ingredients on the label, the Department of Agriculture has kindly prepared this authoritative analysis of everything edible. If you're serious about nutrition, it's a buy. —SB

[Suggested by Tassajara Zen Center]

Composition of Foods
(Raw, processed, prepared)
Bernice K. Watt and Annabel L. Merrill
1963, 1975; 190 pp.
No. 001-000-00768-8

$4 postpaid from:
Superintendent of Documents
U.S. Govt. Printing Office
Washington, D.C. 20402
or Whole Earth Household Store

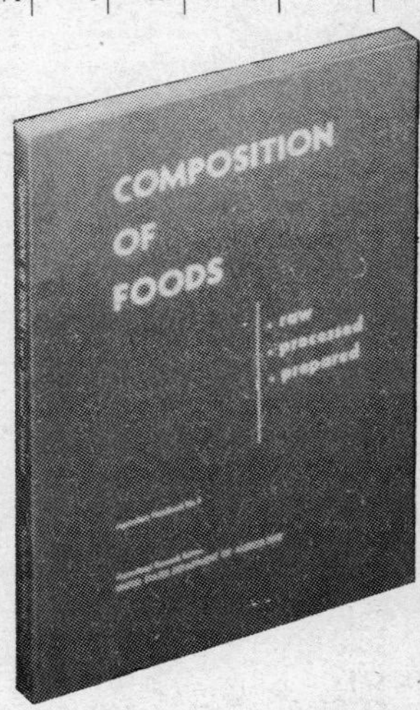

Aurora Book Companions

Largest mail-order supplier of health and nutrition books. Some of the dumbest (macrobiotics) and smartest (beware sugar) things you can do are abundantly covered. —SB

Aurora Book Companions
Catalog

$ .15 from:
Aurora Book Companions
Box 5852
Denver, CO 80217

Whole Foods Magazine

Each dinner I look at my plate and say: Where does this food come from? What soils? Water? Nutrients? I have yearned for someone to be able to tell me what happened to this food from seed to shop to stomach. **Whole Foods** *does it. A buyer's guide and detective work on all kinds of food — from olive oils to cereals. Its attitude is like the* **Wall St. Journal**. *If people know what's good, they'll buy it and, if they buy only good food, then the natural foods industry will prosper. Fine summaries of contemporary USDA, FDA and other food-related politics. Brief summary of crop and marketing conditions throughout the country. Special articles like problems of ginseng quality and regulation.* —Peter Warshall

[Suggested by Gay Leslie]

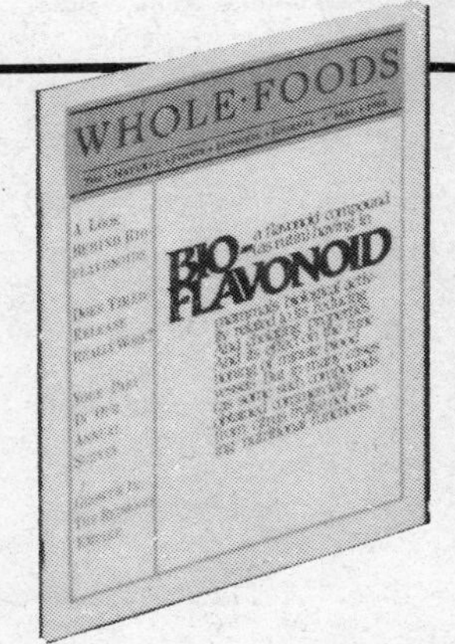

Whole Foods
(The Natural Foods Business Journal)
Jim Schreiber, Editor

$24 /year (12 issues)
from:
Whole Foods
2600 Eighth Street
Berkeley, CA 94710

L & H Natural Vitamins

They sell all kinds of vitamins, minerals, enzymes, and other nutritional aids at a 20% discount. (When you get into multiple dollar a day nutritional programs, it adds up quickly.) You can order by WATS line, (800-223-1892) and use charge cards for fast delivery. Local stores never have a fraction of L & H Vitamins' selection, either. —J. Garwood

L & H Natural Vitamins
Catalog

free from:
L & H Vitamins
1064 Lexington Avenue
New York, NY 10021

•

Item	Size	Retail	Your Price
Timed Release Niacin, 500 mgs.	50	$ 3.25	$ 2.60
	100	5.75	4.60
Niacinamide, 100 mgs.	100	1.60	1.28
	250	3.25	2.60
Niacinamide, 250 mgs.	100	2.25	1.80
	250	4.75	3.80
Niacinamide, 500 mgs.	100	3.25	2.60
	250	6.95	5.56
Chewable Vitamin C With Acerola, 150 mg.	100	2.95	2.36
	250	6.50	5.20
Chewable C With Acerola, 500 mg.	100	4.95	3.46
	250	9.95	7.96
500 C Plus	100	4.95	3.96
	250	11.50	9.20

Journal of the Nutritional Academy

Pretty sane looking magazine. It surveys the gamut of medical, quasi-medical, and nutritional goings on — holistic health, in other words. —SB

[Suggested by J. Garwood]

Journal of the Nutritional Academy
Cameron Stauth, Editor

$10 /year (12 issues)
from:
Journal of the Nutritional Academy
1238 Hayes
Eugene, OR 97402

•

Chronic diseases, the most alarming of which is cancer, are indeed on the rise amongst young people. One study recently said cancer is now the *leading* cause of death in children under the age of 15. For many years, traumatic accident was the major cause of death in this age group. In fact, 50 years ago a case of malignant disease in childhood was such a rarity that it was generally written about in medical journals. Now we see large numbers of our young succumbing to leukemia, Hodgkin's disease, other lymphomas, and osteogenic sarcomas, to name a few of the most common childhood cancers. Nearly everyone has experienced a case of childhood cancer within his or her family or group of friends and acquaintances. Something is obviously very wrong.

THE RISING SUN
NEIGHBORHOOD NEWSLETTER

continued from last spread

It may not be necessary to acquire your own church bell if you are associated with a church that has a church bell. You will find that if it is being rung on a regular basis, the person who is doing it thinks the task is boring. So you can offer to help or to do it, and suggest other occasions that would be appropriate, that you will do yourself, of course. If it is not being rung regularly, you can offer to call the faithful to worship Sunday morning and move out from there. It wouldn't be fair to be as bizarre as you would be in the privacy of your own home or office, but a bell is a good minor sense-of-community creator, so you figure out when the folks near the church are or might want to be feeling like a community and help them. Remember that the people near the church are more important than the church members, as they are the ones stuck hearing it when you do it times other than Sunday morning. We (my sister and I and sometimes my father and sometimes other kids) rang it on New Year's Eve at exactly midnight (a semi appropriate number of times, like how many years since 1900), and Christmas Eve, and the Fourth of July (how many years has the Republic stood), Election Day sometimes, for some funerals, and very occasionally to show off to friends — that had to be in broad, wide-awake daylight. We tolled the number of years for some church members and Bobby Kennedy and Martin Luther King — something I'm sure wouldn't have happened in that town without us — our church was a mere six blocks from an old '20s KKK rallying site, and many of the ralliers still lived and had raised kids who weren't that different. On the day King died, Billy and I collected money at school for a memorial gift to Save the Children (we figured it had to be that innocuous or we didn't have a chance) and only three people said they were glad he was dead, and we figured we were doing good. Anyway, it seemed nice to toll for King so the people who gave a shit could have something besides TV for a minute.

continued on next spread

Putting Food By

Even a tiny garden can grow more than one family can immediately use. **Putting Food By** *is 500 pages of readable instructions on drying, freezing, canning, smoking and root cellar storage. The book is laid out with frequent topic headings and charts, making it handy for quick reference. Freezing is by far the easiest method, and feasible for nearly every type of food, even eggs. Sun-drying is ideal for fruit, except where it's humid; so there are instructions for making an indoor box dryer. With nearly two-thirds of every food dollar going to processing and marketing, it is easy to see that home processing saves money. This book, with suggestions on freezing TV dinners from leftovers and storing pre-cooked meals, even shows how it can save time.* —*Rosemary Menninger*

Putting Food By
Ruth Hertzberg,
Beatrice Vaughan, and
Janet Greene
1973, 1975; 500 pp.
$8.95 postpaid from:
The Stephen Greene Press
P.O. Box 1000
Fessenden Road
Brattleboro, VT 05301
or Whole Earth
Household Store

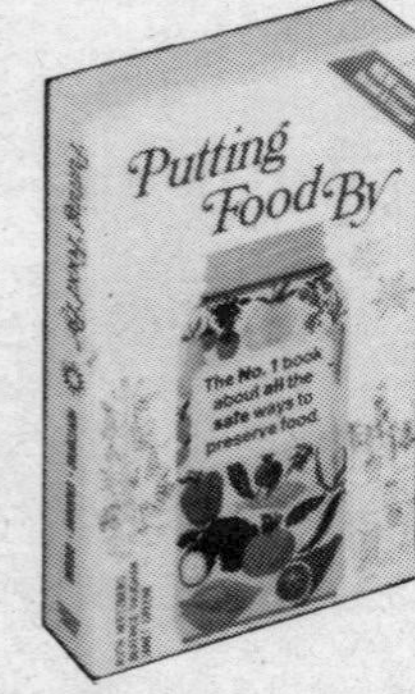

→

The beauty of root-cellaring is that it deals only with whole vegetables and fruits and there are no hidden dangers; if it doesn't work, we know by looking and touching and smelling that the stuff has spoiled, and we don't eat it.

On the other hand, it's something that sounds a lot more feasible than it may really turn out to be.

First, the householder must learn something about the idiosyncrasies of the fruits and vegetables he plans to store on a fairly large scale: for example, apples and potatoes — the most popular things to carry over through winter — can't be stored near each other, and the odor of turnips and cabbages in the basement can penetrate up into the living quarters, and squashes want to be warmer than carrots do.

Some modern glass canning jars may also be used for freezing most fruits and vegetables. The wide-top jars with tapered sides are advised for liquid packs: the contents will slide out easily without having to be fully defrosted.

•

The WHY of Pressure Canning

Every vegetable except tomatoes (q.v.), every meat, every seafood that is canned at home MUST BE CANNED IN A *PRESSURE* CANNER.

Or put it this way:

Pressure canning is the ONLY process that is able to destroy the tough spores of bacteria like *Clostridium botulinum* which can grow and produce deadly poison in jars or cans of *any* low-acid food.

—Or this way:

Dangerous spoilers can live through even a long Boiling-Water Bath at 212 F./100 C. in containers of food with a natural acidity of 4.5 on the *pH* scale, but *they are killed by higher temperatures that can be reached only in a Pressure Canner.*

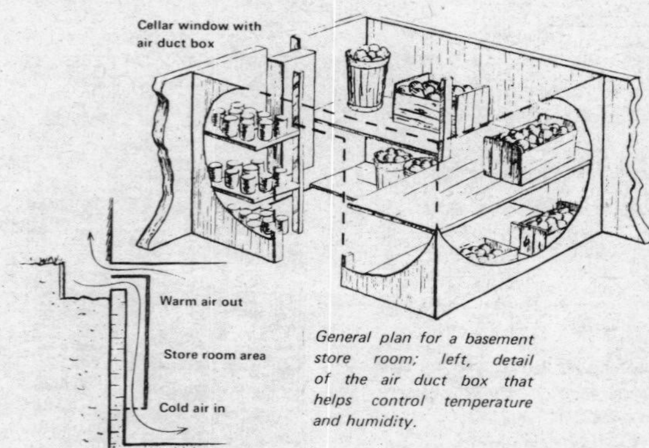

General plan for a basement store room; left, detail of the air duct box that helps control temperature and humidity.

Ball Blue Book

Though this guide to home canning (by the biggest maker of canning jars) has been in print since 1905, it easily avoids the Grandma image and gets you into your own canning. It has illustrated, step-by-step directions and recipes and handy guides for jar estimating. When something goes wrong, there's trouble-shooting guides. If you have a good growing summer, this book can help you have a well-fed winter. —*SB*

Ball Blue Book
(The Guide to Home Canning and Freezing)
1905, 1979; 96 pp.
29th Edition
$2.50 postpaid

Ball Libro Azul
1979; 142 pp.
Spanish Edition
$2.95 postpaid

both from:
Ball Corporation
Consumer Affairs Dept.
P.O. Box 2005
Muncie, IN 47302

INSTRUCTIONS FOR USING IDEAL JARS WITH WIRE BAILS AND GLASS LIDS

1. Visually examine sealing surfaces of jar and glass lid for nicks, cracks and sharp edges. Examine wire bail to make sure it works properly. Discard any defective jars or lids.

2. Wash jars, lids and rubbers in warm, soapy water and rinse in hot water. Let stand in hot water until needed.

3. Pack food into jar, leaving head space recommended in recipe. Eliminate air bubbles with non-metallic kitchen utensil. Wipe away any food residue from sealing surface of jar with clean damp cloth.

4. Fit wet rubber on shoulder of jar, stretching only enough to fit over mouth of jar.

5. Place glass lid over mouth of jar so that it rests on rubber.

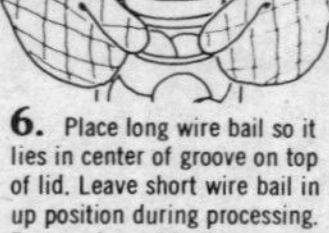

6. Place long wire bail so it lies in center of groove on top of lid. Leave short wire bail in up position during processing. Process jars of food as recommended in recipe. When jar is removed from canner, push lower wire bail down against side of jar to complete seal.

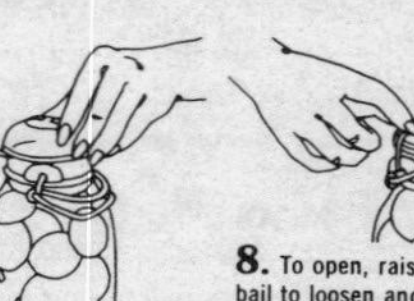

7. When jars are fully cooled, tip jars to check for leaks. Store properly sealed jars in cool, dark, dry place.

8. To open, raise lower wire bail to loosen and then place both bails on side of jar. Run dull table knife between rubber and shoulder of jar to let in air and break seal. Discard rubber; it is not reusable.

Making Your Own Cheese and Yogurt

Max Alth wrote this book for people who don't know anything about making cheese or yogurt. It covers lots of different kinds of cheese ranging from harder, more aged cheeses to the softer types. Lots of different recipes and information about cost of things use, and suggestions about where to get them. —*Shannon Slate*

Making Your Own Cheese and Yogurt
(Complete instructions for making numerous varieties of cheese and yogurt in your home)
Max Alth
1973, 1977; 226 pp.

$4.50 postpaid from:
T.Y. Crowell
Harper and Row
Keystone Industrial Park
Scranton, PA 18512
or Whole Earth
Household Store

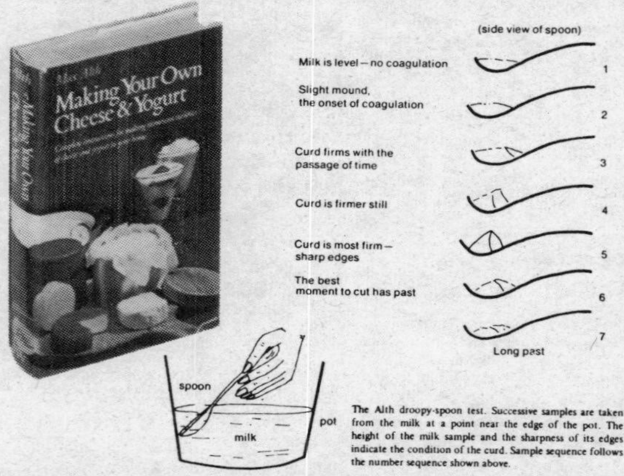

The Alth droopy-spoon test. Successive samples are taken from the milk at a point near the edge of the pot. The height of the milk sample and the sharpness of its edges indicate the condition of the curd. Sample sequence follows the number sequence shown above.

Make Your Own Soap!

Making your own soap is a highly satisfying worthwhile endeavor. With a minimum of ingredients and gadgetry, a novice can produce relatively pure laundry soap that is non-pollutant and very effective. A further motive for soapmaking is the opportunity to recycle such household throwaways as bacon fat and milk cartons . . . plus the personal reward of creating an attractive, useful product for your daily life.

This book is the best buy: she gives positive advice including why something is done the way it is. Historical background, recipes, and information on scent, color and shape of soaps is given. She favors using materials at hand whenever possible, and includes sections on soap sculpture and imaginative ideas for gift containers. —*Lorna Jones*

Make Your Own Soap!
Dorothy Richter
1974; 137 pp.
$1.95 postpaid from:
Dolphin Books
Doubleday and Company
501 Franklin Avenue
Garden City, NY 11530
or Whole Earth
Household Store

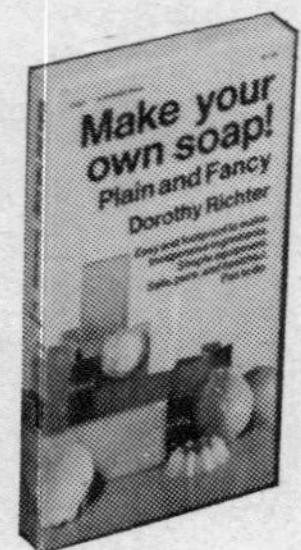

•

Causes of Imperfections and Variations in Soap

1. A greasy layer on top of soap indicated that too little lye was used for the amount of fat.
2. Streaked soap shows that the fat and lye solution were not thoroughly mixed.
3. Cracks in the soap may be due to too much stirring or too much free lye; or drying too quickly.
4. A white deposit on the soap may be due to the use of hard water in making the lye solution; a little free lye; or the addition of too much borax.
5. If too cold or too hot temperature is used, or if soap is too vigorously or not thoroughly mixed, a separation may occur. A separation may also result from using exceedingly rancid fat or fat containing salt. Greasy soap forms on top while liquid settles to the bottom.

Garden Way's Guide to Food Drying

Drying is a good way to preserve food if canning and freezing are not viable options. **Garden Way's Guide to Food Drying** *gives the best overview of preserving food in this fashion. They review commercial dehydrators and alternative methods such as sun drying or oven drying. A plan is included for building your own electric dehydrator. Detailed instructions are given for drying many fruits, vegetables, meats, dairy products, grains, herbs, and blossoms (for potpourris and herbal teas). Included are storage techniques, recipes, and other uses for the drying equipment such as bread raising and yogurt making.* —*Evelyn Eldridge-Diaz*

Garden Way's Guide to Food Drying
(How to Dehydrate, Store and Use Vegetables, Fruits and Herbs)
Phyllis Hobson
1980; 216 pp.
$5.95 postpaid from:
Garden Way Publishing
Charlotte, VT 05445
or Whole Earth
Household Store

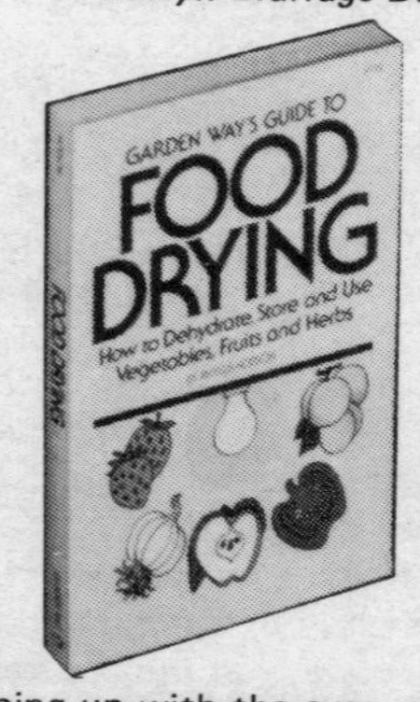

•

If you're having trouble keeping up with the ever-increasing cost of food, a selection of dried foods on your pantry shelf can save your food budget as much as $1,000 a year.

You can save the most money, of course, by drying fruits and vegetables from your own garden or foods that otherwise would go to waste. Drying is not only a safe, easy way of preserving your excess garden harvest; it also is an inexpensive method. Drying costs less than canning and freezing in equipment, energy and storage space.

Even if you don't plant a garden, you can still save money by drying foods at home. During the harvest season fruits and vegetables can be purchased cheaply by the bushel at the country markets and roadside stands.

Equiflow Food Dehydrators are manufactured by B & J Industries, 514 State St., Marysville, WA 98270. They also make the lower cost Garden Way 10 Tray Food Dehydrator available from Garden Way Catalog, Charlotte, VT 05445.

Three models are produced — a compact, five-tray dehydrator with five square feet of drying area for $109.95, a ten-tray model with fourteen square feet of drying area for $169.95 and a twenty-tray floor model with forty-one square feet of drying area for $329.95. ↓

Champion juicer

Advertised as world's finest. We've used ours for four years and have found the claim to be true.

Most juicers only juice, the Champion does all the following:

- *Juices: vegetables (carrots, leafy greens); fruits — all kinds (with seeds and skins if desired)*
- *Purees and homogenizes: raw apple sauce, healthful baby foods, creamy nut butters (date butter, etc.)*
- *Grates: coconut, nuts, carrots*
- *Homogenizes: frozen ripe bananas (making delicious "banana delight" with the consistency of soft ice cream), frozen orange sections (making pure "orange sherbet").*

Most other juicers, being centrifugal, will only juice a limited amount of food at a time, then the pulp has to be cleaned out from the body. In the Champion, one can juice indefinitely because of its unique structure. It has a horizontal shaft which is fed from above. The pulp is ejected out one end and the juice comes out down below through a fine screen. It's easy to clean and an excellent kitchen tool.

We use ours at least once a day. Comes with a recipe book. G.E. 1/3 HP capacitor type motor. 100% Dupont nylon and stainless steel. Colors. 5 year guarantee.

—Bruce and Hasmig Meyer

Champion juicer
$208.95 plus shipping
Brochure

free from:
W.R. Laboratories
639 E. Lockeford Street
Lodi, CA 95240

Mil-Rite flour mill

The best bread is made from wheat ground just before baking.

This is a small electric grain grinder manufactured by an old dependable company. A unique feature of this machine is that it grinds the entire grain kernel, including the germ and bran, into fine flour. You fill the hopper and an automatic feed admits the proper amount of grain into the stone grinding chamber. The carborundum grinding stone never needs redressing, the mill does not get warm enough to impair the nutritional value of the flour, and fresh stone ground flour . . . pass the bread!

—Lloyd Kahn

Mil-Rite Flour Mill
$230 (approx.)
Information

free from:
Retsel Corporation
Box 47
McCannon, ID 83250

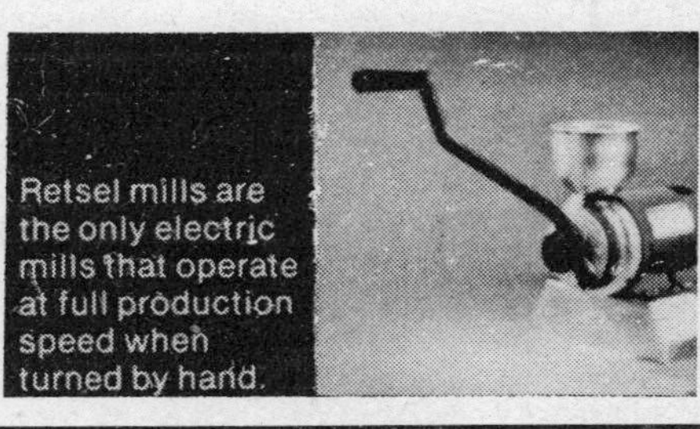
Retsel mills are
the only electric
mills that operate
at full production
speed when
turned by hand.

Mehu-Liisa steam juicer

One advantage of the steam juicing fruit is that the residue is palatable — make fruit leather, ice cream, ketchup. And you can run the juice hot into bottles, put on a rubber cap that the firm sells, and it'll seal on for storage or giving.

—SB

Mehu-Liisa steam juicer
$79.50 postpaid

Rubber caps
$7-13 (per 100) postpaid

Fruit Season
(Suddenly it's fun; an idea-book to use with your steam juicer)
Greta Ashdown
1975; 42 pp.
$2 postpaid

Information
$.50 postpaid

all from:
Ashdown House
612 East Pheasant Way
Bountiful, VT 84010

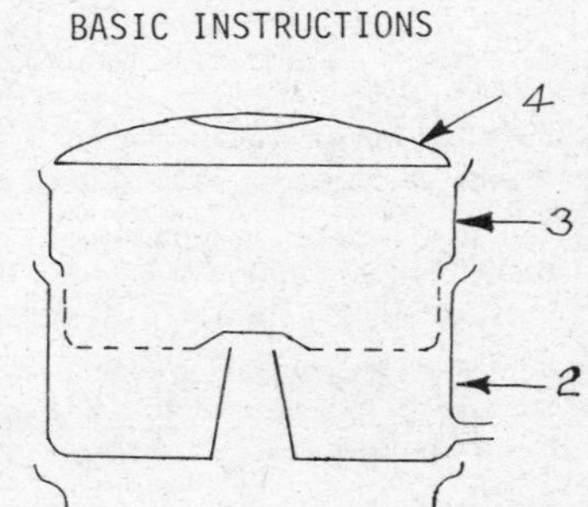

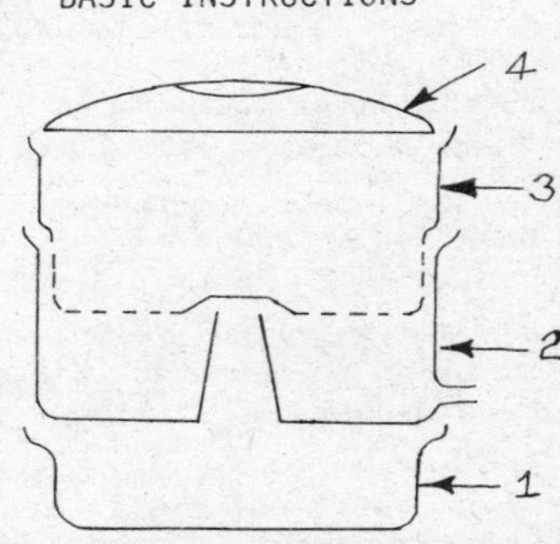
BASIC INSTRUCTIONS
4
3
2
1

Juicing Process

Step 1 — Fill the water container (1) about ¾-full of water. Place it on the stove to start heating while you prepare the fruit. If you have an aluminum juicer, do use untreated tap water, as water that has gone through a water softener is corrosive to aluminum.

Step 2 — Place the juice container (2) in position above the heating water. Be sure the tube is in good condition and the clamp securely in place.

Step 3 — Fill the fruit basket (3) with washed and drained fruit. Place the basket in position above the juice container.

Step 4 — Put the lid (4) on and bring the water to a boil, then reduce the heat to a medium setting. The water must continue to boil to produce steam, but it does not need to boil violently.

Phantasmagoria

Good discount prices on Mil-Rite Mills (20% off), the Champion Juicer (25% off), ice cream freezers (30% off), Aladdin Lamps (20% off), etc. The "R/" is retail price, the "O/" is their discount price.

—SB

Phantasmagoria
Catalog
$.50 postpaid from:
Phantasmagoria
311 South 11th Street
Tacoma, WA 98402

<u>White Mountain Ice Cream Freezers</u>

Triple action, metal gears, New England pine tubs w/ maple finish, self-adjusting Beechwood scrapers; all metal parts coated w/ pure tin. Good looking, excellent quality.

Hand Crank	-2 qt.	-R/$59.95	-O/$51.
	-4 qt.	-R/$64.95	-O/$52.
	-6 qt.	-R/$79.95	-O/$64.
	-8 qt.	-R/$134.95	-O/$95.
Electric	- 4 qt.	-R/$105.95	-O/$83.
	- 6 qt.	-R/$120.95	-O/$90.

F.O.B.- Calif. 10-20#

Discount-14--30%

<u>Champion Juicer Grain Grinding Attachment</u>

Fits on Champion motor in place of juicer. Has adjustable steel grinding plates that will grind anything. A snap-on bag catches the flour. Grinds wheat at 60#/hr. It runs at higher speed & with higher heat than the Mil-Rite, and to our minds seems overpriced, but, of course, if you already have the juicer, its less of an investment.

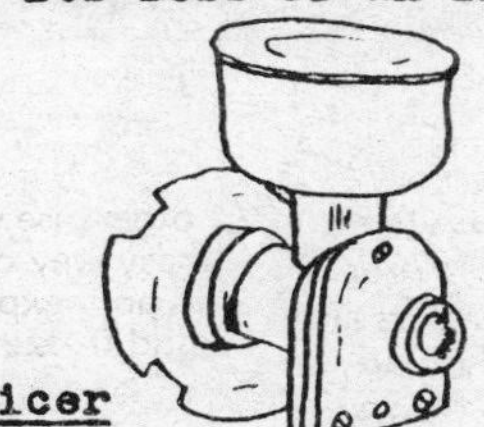

<u>Champion Juicer</u>

-R/$89.95 -O/$77.-

F.O.B. - Portland - 10#

colors- white only

Discount-15%

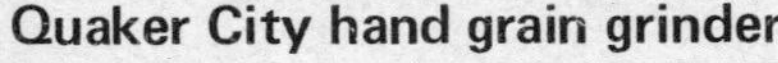

Quaker City hand grain grinder

Tight competition, but this is considered the best of the hand grain grinders these days. Important if you want to still eat your wheat (etc.) when central power floweth not. (Though the Mil-Rite mill does have a hand crank attachment.)

—SB

Quaker City
hand grain grinder
$19.95 postpaid
Information

free from:
Nelson and Sons, Inc.
P.O. Box 1296
Salt Lake City, UT 84110

THE RISING SUN
NEIGHBORHOOD NEWSLETTER

continued from last spread

Tolling, FYI, is different than ringing. It's done with a different rope, attached to a toller, a hammer that hits the inside lip of the bell. (Picture — hammer with a pivot in middle like seesaw, rope pulls down on one end of seesaw, other end with hammer head goes up inside bell and hits it.) That way you can hit it as slow as you want and count how many times you've hit it. Once you're ringing a bell with the old cartwheel technique, you've got lots of inertia and gravity stuff going on and you can't really make it go slow. Also, when you're ringing, not tolling, you can only sound it an odd number of times, not an even number.

continued on next spread

Tuesday Dinner

↑

Hors d'oeuvres No. 27
Green cream soup No. 70 and No. 73
Thin sticks No. 9
Wheatburgers No. 35
Oven-cracked wheat No. 46d
Soft ice cream No. 83 with caramel syrup No. 84
Barber pole sticks No. 90
Cold milk

•

No. 19, Creme Gluten A La Emergency

Gluten No. 12b — Wheat grass No. 6
Cream Sauce No. 70

Form the gluten in marble-size balls. Bake and simmer in stew broth No. 77. Mince wheat grass grown in soil and cut when 1½ inches high. Add gluten balls and grass to cream sauce and serve immediately.

•

Packaging the four survival foods — wheat, milk powder, honey and salt — in five-gallon cans has been a project of different groups who have been awakened to the need for emergency storage. Each can contains one month's food supply for one adult person: 27 lb. of wheat, 5 lb. of powdered skim milk, 3 lb. of honey, up to 1 lb. of salt.

•

Fat-free powdered milk, when kept dry and reasonably cool, stores with little change for over 15 years.

Fat Years, Lean Years

One of the big issues that arises for virtually everyone when they think of food storage and reserves is the question of hoarding. In a world of growing scarcity is it ethical to have plenty? **Fat Years, Lean Years** *tackles that question first, since the authors had the same initial doubts about selfishness and greed. Their conclusion is that it is better to acknowledge survival instincts and deal with them creatively than to suppress them and deal with them negatively in a crisis.*

The Mormons of course have been storing food for decades. On the other hand, there is a Buddhist saying that one should not store food, simply grow it. My opinion is that storing food is a big hassle and that it would be unnecessary in a society that took better care of itself. That society doesn't exist right now and food storage, rather than being a hoard, represents the building of resiliency into the overall system. Carrying extra provisions is like having a little fat on the bones. Good idea for winters. **Fat Years, Lean Years** *suggests a simple, no-nonsense approach, emphasizing just four foods: Wheat, legumes, salt, and honey. It is written by people who have been through the entire process of trying to locate, obtain, and store simple foods on a simple budget. Full of practical advice, good tips, and a generous attitude towards life.*
—*Paul Hawken*

Fat Years, Lean Years
(A food storage compendium for the 1980s)
Ann Elliott, et al.
1980; 17 pp.

$2 postpaid from:
Creative Living Center
P.O. Box 478
San Andreas, CA 95249

•

Altogether, the specific per day per person rations are:
¾ pound grain (wheat, corn, rice*, barley, rye, and millet).
¼ pound legumes (beans — kidney, white, pinto, lima, garbanzos — soybeans, split and black-eyed peas, and lentils).
1½ ounces honey.
¼ ounce salt.
(optionally) 1 pint (reconstituted) or 1/10th pound dry-weight skim milk.

*In storing rice it needs to be noted that brown rice easily becomes rancid unless purchased in vacuum-packed cans. Therefore, if putting up your own, buy white rice.

A TWO-WEEK SUPPLY FOR ONE PERSON — If you are just one individual and not buying as part of a cooperative group, you could begin with the following that would see you through a short-term food crises:

12 pounds of grain
4 pounds of legumes
1 and 1/3 pounds honey
3 and ½ ounces salt
1 and ½ pounds instant powdered skim milk (optional)

A TWO-WEEK SUPPLY FOR A FAMILY OF FOUR can be similarly determined and the amounts rounded off:

50 pounds grain
16 pounds legumes
5 pounds honey
1 pound salt
6 pounds powdered skim milk (optional)

From these minimal reserves you can multiply for larger families or for reserves for longer periods of time. For instance, A ONE-YEAR SUPPLY FOR ONE PERSON:

300 pounds grain
100 pounds legumes
35 pounds honey
6 pounds salt
36 pounds powdered skim milk (optional)

Passport to Survival

The four foods for survival are wheat, powdered milk, honey and salt — they will keep indefinitely when properly stored. Mrs. Dickey bases her survival diet on these ingredients and enhances them with 40 more supplementary foods varying in degrees of storability and nutritional value. Then she gives more than a hundred recipes that almost all use only these four basic survival foods and water.

There's no question that you'd eat well on this diet. From wheat flour, honey and warm water you can grow yeast and thus make bread. Derive wheat gluten from wheat kernels and eat a very high-protein, incredibly versatile meat substitute. Every thing from spaghetti and tacos to puddings and taffy is produced rather miraculously. Supplementing with yogurt (from powdered milk) and bean and seed sprouts gives a fairly rounded regimen.

Emergency procedures and the forethoughts stored here will serve you come holocaust, catastrophe, or unemployment.
—*Hal Hershey*

Passport to Survival
Esther Dickey
1969; 180 pp.

$5.95 postpaid from:
Bookcraft Publishers
1848 West 2300 Street So.
Salt Lake City, UT 84119

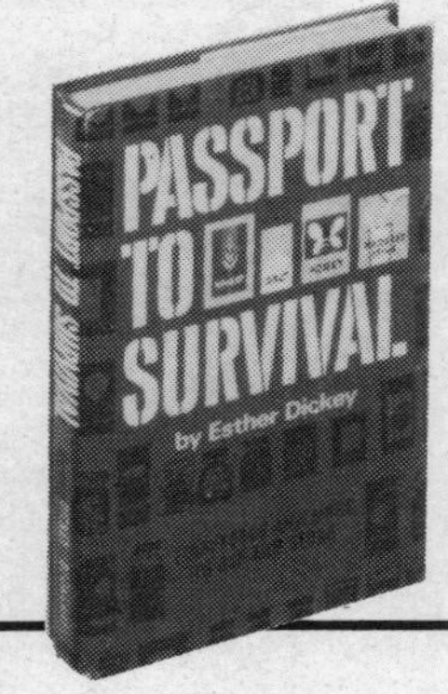

Mormon Advice

A bow is in order to the Mormons, who have developed not only the practical state-of-the-art of food storage but also an admirably realistic and humane approach to any major emergency. A glimpse of that is visible in these guidelines to members of the Marin Stake by their then (1973) president, Weston L. Roe.
—*SB*

Listed below are some specific suggestions that will be helpful in making preparation for the future, if and when a problem may arise:

1. Get one year's supply of food, including some permanent type storage as well as rotatable stock. If this cannot be done get as much as you can, a little at a time.

2. Get yourself and family out of debt. Avoid unwise debt. (Do not charge anything you cannot pay for in full when the bill is presented.) Be sure each member of the family understands the family finances and knows where important papers are kept.

3. Plant a garden and fruit trees. Use part of your lot to develop a home garden. Plant fruit trees in place of general type shade trees so that we can produce fruit to eat and for canning purposes.

4. Get a supply of wood that can be used for heating and cooking if gas and electricity should be lost.

5. Have some candles and a supply of dry matches on hand. A kerosene lamp, kerosene (this must be stored safely) in a tight metal container.

6. Arrange a source of water in case of an emergency. Store many gallons in Clorox bottles or similar containers to be used in emergency for drinking and preparing food. If possible a well on your lot may be beneficial.

7. Learn how, and prepare food for storage and use over the winter by canning or drying. Have on hand some bottles and caps for home canning.

8. Talk with your neighbors about cooperation. Find out their resources and how you can help them and they in turn help you.

9. Be ready and willing to cooperate with your police, firemen and civil defense in their efforts to meet emergency situations.

10. Be prepared to show true brotherly love and service to others by sharing with those truly in need. True brotherly love in harmony with the gospel would be to share rather than fight and drive people away.

11. Have all necessary shovels, spading forks, hoes, rakes, hammers, nails and other tools that may be needed.

12. Have on hand a roll of plastic material that could be used to cover windows, if broken.

13. Have on hand a year's supply of clothing, extra blankets, shoes, etc., to share with those who may have lost everything.

14. Be ready to take someone into your home, and care for those injured or in need.

15. Be ready to care for the sick, have some medical supplies and provisions on hand (including special medicines, vitamins, insulin, etc.) if needed.

16. Know and understand sanitary procedures and how to implement them in case of need.

17. Know who your home teachers are and how to get in touch with them.

18. Be ready to work for what you get. Do not expect a handout so long as you are able to work. Seek to repay in labor or services for all help received. Be ready to help others without repayment.

19. Have a year's supply of money on hand where it could be available in case an emergency should arise.

20. Have an emergency kit prepared (food, clothing, bedding, medicines, first aid) on hand, so you could move to temporary quarters if circumstances warranted doing so.

Survival food catalogs

All the catalogs listed below carry "reserve" and "storage" foods intended for use during food shortages, emergencies, or even more unthinkably, famines. They are an interesting statement of what happens when the idea of "self-sufficiency" filters through the mesh of fear and uncertainty that may hold for the future. The old Whole Earth Truck Store used to sell its Aladdin lamps next to their Snow and Nealy axes. In the Alia catalog, the Aladdin lamps are sold next to the Smith & Wesson 357 Magnum Speed Loader. Nevertheless, most carry pre-packed selections of freeze-dried goods, grains, seeds, and mixes. They make a lot of sense for remote cabins, long ocean voyages, and any place else that has tenuous supply lines (like the cities?).
—*Paul Hawken*

Alia, Inc.
P.O. Box 8411
Asheville, NC 28804
Coins, grain mills, guns, Gerber Knives, seeds, and food. New company.

SamAndy
525 South Rancho
Colton, CA 92324
Has the biggest variety of foods, mostly in smaller containers, many of which are dehydrated complete meals. Expensive.

Perma-Pak
40 East 2430 South
Salt Lake,City, UT 84115

The Simpler Life
Arrowhead Mills
P.O. Box 671
Hereford, TX 79045
Good grains and seeds from these people since they are growers too.

James Ito
Intermountain Freeze Dried Foods
3025 Washington Blvd.
Ogden, UT 84401

Reliance
1900 Olympic Blvd.
Walnut Creek, CA 94596
The best catalog of the lot. Good selection of tools, foods, stoves, water purifiers, cookware, books and seeds.

3. ESSENTIAL UNIT • *One Year Supply For One Person* **OR** *Six Month Supply for Two People*

Contains 11 cases of No. 10 cans, totaling 66 cans.

#10 Cans:

2	Peanut Butter Powder	1	Raisins, Low Moisture	1	Onions, Chopped
2	Beef TVP	1	Date Bits	1	Soup Base, Beef
2	Chicken TVP	3	Apple Slices	3	Carrot Dices
1	Eggs, Scrambling	1	Mixed Fruit	2	Split Peas
1	Cheese, Cheddar	4	Potato Slices	2	Corn Meal
2	Pinto Beans	2	Tomato Crystals	2	Rolled Oats
2	Baby Lima Beans	1	Green Garden Peas	2	Macaroni
6	Milk, Regular Nonfat	1	Soup Mixture	2	Brown Rice
6	Milk, Instant Nonfat	1	Cabbage Dices	1	Cereal, Fruit & Nut
2	Banana Slices	2	Potato Granules	3	Cracked Wheat Cereal
		2	Cut Green Beans	2	Potato Dices

$ 707.00

—**Alia, Inc.**

VEGETABLES

	401	Cabbage Dices	1½	12.
	402	Carrot Dices	1¾	9.
	403	Corn, Sweet	3	19.
	404	Peas, Garden	2¾	21.
	405M	Potato Granules with Milk	5½	6.
	406	Potato Dices	2	6.
	408	Beans, Green Cut	1	11.
	S409	Celery, Cross Cut	1	12.
	410	Potato Slices	1¼	5.
	S411	Spinach Flakes	½	6.
	412	Onions, Small Sliced	1¼	6.
	S413	Beet Dices	2¾	12.
	S415	Carrot Slices	1¼	7.
	S416	Sweet Potato Granules	4	9.
	S417	Tomato Powder	4¼	25.
	S421	Vegetable Soup Blend	1¾	12.
	S422	Vegetable Stew Blend	1¾	12.

—**SamAndy**

FOODS BY MAIL AND BY TRUCK— WHOLESALE

by Paul Hawken

Very few companies in the United States still mail order food, particularly the natural kinds. There are so many retail outlets that there just isn't much need. Even in the country, small towns have natural food stores, co-ops, and other types of food outlets that stock commodities and foodstuffs not found in the supers. Most of the companies on this list started small not so many years ago and still welcome a new customer and a friendly face at their door. Some have grown large, perhaps too quickly, and you may have to work your way past the teamsters, diesel rigs, and cases of organic deodorants before you find the oatmeal. There is a Δ by the ones that are small, but all of them will sell wholesale to groups if they present themselves in an organized way. Wholesalers sometimes refuse to sell directly to consumers for two reasons: one, they get so big that they don't want the hassle; two, they are afraid of getting their retailers mad. To avoid those considerations, present yourself with an already made out list of exactly what you want. If the distributor doesn't split cases, don't ask him to. If you are a food buying club or conspiracy, try to select the same person to deal with the same company each time. Distributors crave consistency. Don't try to pay in food stamps, coins, third party checks, or postal money orders. Collect your funds into one source and make out a check there. Have a name. Any name: The Food Wave. Fruits and Nuts. Smith Co-op. The minimums at most of the distributors are small enough so that even a family of two who plans ahead could well buy at wholesale.

Walnut Acres Mill & Store
Penns Creek, PA 17862

The one major company that still does and always has mail-ordered is also the only company that actually produces most of the foods on its list. The smaller sizes are a bit pricey, but if you can order in bulk, their prices are competitive, and their quality is unsurpassed. Still family-owned and run, the Keenes have set a standard for honesty in a business where "organic" still means different things to different people. Catalog free.

New Items

WALNUT ACRES AMISH CHEDDAR CHEESE —
Approx. Wts. — 1 lb. - 2.87; 2½ lbs. - 6.61; 5 lbs. - 12.48

A great new find! Right into our own back yard there moved recently a cheesemaker from a Swiss family of long-time cheesemakers. And he's making cheese for us from milk produced mostly by local Amish farmers. This is raw milk cheese, processed at low temperatures, using vegetable enzymes only! It has been aged at least 60 days, as required by law, and ranges from mild to medium in sharpness.

***WALNUT ACRES SAUERKRAUT — in #303 (16 oz. tins) - 1 tin - .80; 3 tins - 2.38; 12 tins - 9.41; 24 tins - 18.24**
(Sh. wts. 1 lb. 3 oz.; 3 lbs. 9 oz.; 15 lbs.; 30 lbs.)

From our very own organic cabbage, of course. Cabbage and salt only, plus time to "ripen". Delicious as always.

***WALNUT ACRES FARMERS BEANS — #303 (16 oz.) tins - 1 tin - .57; 3 tins - 1.69; 12 tins - 6.70; 24 tins - 13.00**
(Sh. wts. 1 lb. 3 oz.; 3 lb. 9 oz.; 15 lbs.; 30 lbs.)

We invented these lovely beans. Well, we recall our mother making them for us well over half-a-century ago! We left regular tender green beans on the plants until the beans in the pods were swollen and ripening. Then we harvested them in this stage, and canned them, adding our deep well water and salt only. What an unusual texture and flavor. Salted or unsalted, state choice.

Δ **Deer Valley Farm**
R.D. 1
Guilford, NY 13780

Another mail order company which also grows some of its products. The Carsten family has been growers for over fifty years using Bio-dynamic methods. Good source for grains, cereals, flours, meals and seeds. Their bakery products use their own fresh milk, eggs, honey and flour. Catalog free.

Lifestream
12411 Vulcan Way
Richmond, B.C.
Canada V6V 1J7

The largest distributor in Canada. Carries most basics and its own brands as well. Foods from U.S. are exceedingly expensive there because of taxes and duties. Customers will do better to find Canadian sources for their grains. Lifestream has some but not many. Catalog $.50.

Erewhon
3 East Street
Cambridge, MA 02141

The largest natural foods company since in many ways it was one of the first. Unfortunately, its very size makes it a more formidable place to do business and less likely to produce a sense of place or person. Best known for their rice, pastas, granola, and oils. Catalog free.

Δ **Shiloh Farms**
P.O. Box 97
Sulphur Springs,
AR 72768
and
White Oak Road
Martindale, PA 17549

Shiloh is a Christian community that has been growing and manufacturing foods for nearly 40 years. They are best known for their organic meats (frozen) and their nitrate free hotdogs, sausages, and luncheon meats. They deliver just about anywhere in the Eastern U.S. in their own tractor-trailor. Catalog $.50.

Arrowhead Mills
P.O. Box 866
Hereford, TX 79045

Frank Ford, who started Arrowhead in a railroad boxcar next to the sewage treatment plant in Hereford twenty years ago, has made his company the largest producer of whole grains in the natural foods business. Arrowhead's wheat comes from Deaf Smith County, famous for its mineral rich soils and fluorine laden waters. Being producers and close to the source, their prices are good. On large orders, they have been known to give discounts, although it is not advertised. The four best items they sell are their wheat, the corn, the oils, and the peanut butter from neighboring Las Cruces. Catalog free.

Δ **CC Grains**
6749 East Marginal
Way South
Seattle, WA 98108

I have a stong prejudice for these distributors who have not computerized their price lists nor made large warehouses full of playfoods. CC Grains sells the basics only at good prices and is dead honest about what they are. Catalog free.

Δ **Starflower**
885 McKinley Street
Eugene, OR 97402

Like CC Grains in Seattle, Starflower is a worker-owned and managed, feminist collective that has managed to secure a firm foothold in the new old-boy network of the natural foods business. Actively serves buying clubs and food networks with a complete list of basic foods. Catalog $.75.

Δ indicates small company

Δ **Sunburst Farms**
Goleta, CA 93017

These are the only distributors who virtually do everything. Sunburst farms organically with horses, grows and bakes wheat into bread, and even goes out to sea in its squarerigger to nab fish once in awhile. And they do it well. For people in southern California, they have six outlets in Santa Barbara County as well as a warehouse in Los Angeles. They also wholesale to other stores, buying clubs and co-ops. Catalog free.

Laurelbrook Foods
P.O. Box 47
Bel Air, MD 21014

Family-owned and operated in a small town. Good eye for quality and righteous prices. They will deliver on orders over $500 for free, and for a small charge under. Lots of basic foods. Price list free.

Δ **Country Life Natural Foods**
Route 1, Box 86D
Chisholm, MN 55719

A tiny company that has most of what you need. Good prices and good food for Wisconsin and the Dakotas. Catalog. $.50.

Westbrae Natural Foods
4240 Hollis Street
Emeryville, CA 94608

Although Westbrae does not "make" any of their foods, they are fastidious purchasers and uphold a standard of quality that is becoming scarce. The only supplier listed to print a glossary of foodstuffs offered telling about sources, quality, and ingredients. Catalog free.

Δ **Stow Mills**
Box 1030
Greenfield, MA 01302

Stow Mills is the result of three small distributors, (Stow Mills, Llama Trading Company, and Harvest Trading Company) merging into one big one. Straightforward wholesaler with a vast assortment of vitamins, cosmetics, and edibles. Catalog free.

Δ **Eden Foods**
4597 Platt Road
Ann Arbor, MI 48104

Midwest company with good sources, prices and quality. Also direct importers from Japan and China. Catalog free.

Δ **Covalda Date Company**
Coachella, CA 92236

Run by the Anderson family since the Depression, Covalda is the best supplier of dates in the country. Lee and Ruth Anderson are old pros when it comes to growing without chemicals. Price list $.50.

Δ **Jaffe Bros.**
28560 Lilac Road
Valley Center, CA 92082

Good prices on dried fruits, nuts, and sesame and olive oils. Jaffe's does mail order and all prices quoted are for mail order. Catalog free.

Δ **Manna Foods**
112 Crockford Road
Scarborough, Ontario
Canada M1R 3C3

Manna started out as Erewhon in Canada and later changed its mind and became a small, quality wholesaler serving the Toronto area. Gene Newman is both meticulous and conscientious to his customer's needs and gladly serves all. Catalog free. ■

Inside word here. 'Twas Paul Hawken who founded Erewhon, the pre-eminent mail order food supplier of the late 60's, early 70's. Now he purveys good tools (Smith & Hawken, p. 129). —SB

Lundberg rice

The best rice this side of Japan is grown by the Lundberg Brothers: Harlan, Eldon, Wendell, and Homer (all named after Supreme Court justices). They work and live in Richvale, California and pioneered organic rice-growing in this country. Even if you aren't satisfied that organically grown rice is "better," the few extra dollars you pay for Lundberg rice is worth it in taste and keeping qualities alone. They're friendly people with unswerving integrity. They also produce the most delicious catfish I've ever tasted, but only the rice can be sent to you through the mail or by truck. —Paul Hawken

Lundberg Rice
Price list and nearest dealer location

free from:
Wehah Farms, Inc.
P.O. Box 13
Richvale, CA 95974

Whitmer wheat

For twenty years the best red, hard, spring wheat in North America has been produced by Ted Whitmer and his sons. Decades ago, wheat was normally 14% or better in protein content. Nowadays, you're lucky to see 10 - 11% sometimes. Whitmer's is consistently 16% and better. He has rotated with clover since he started. Last time I was there, he picked up an old bone on the side of the road. When we got to his place, he threw it on a large stack of bones which he grinds and dusts the soil with. All his tricks and great effort produce a wheat noticeably different in taste, color, and mineral content. Like fine wines, you won't see it in the stores. —Paul Hawken

Whitmer Wheat
Nearest distributor location

free from:
Whitmer and Sons, Inc.
P.O. Box 48
Bloomfield, MT 59315

THE RISING SUN
NEIGHBORHOOD NEWSLETTER

continued from last spread

(Another step to heaven, she tries to explain.) When you are ringing a bell, you are only in control of it half the time. You pull on the rope, ding, you're in control. Then you let go the rope, the bell swings back the other way, dong, and you really didn't have anything to do with it. After it's been going a while, it's doing its little pendulumish thing and you're encouraging it every other noise (ding) to keep going. So, if you want to stop it, and you're on the ding and you're pulling on the rope, it's easy. You pull really hard on the rope, hold it, keep the bell at that angle, let it down gently so the clapper doesn't hit anything, and it's all over. But what if it's donging, doing the other half of the swing where you aren't pulling. Well, after it hits on that side, dong, there's no way you can stop the swing of the pendulum at that point, having donged it will inevitably inertially swing back and ding and then you can stop it by holding down the rope, etc. Which is why our Fourth of July and New Year's belling were accurate only in odd number years. (The down pulling stroke is the first stroke, one, and every other stroke thereafter.)

continued on next spread

HOW TO USE ROAD KILLS

by Douglas Elliott

THERE ARE FEW OF US who don't feel a twinge of pain or sorrow when we pass a dead animal on the road. Some express their pain by sporting, "I brake for animals" bumper stickers. Braking for animals is of course a fine idea, but in most cases an animal traffic fatality is so sudden that neither the animal nor the driver knows what hit them. The blame must be shared by all of us who participate in this high speed mechanized society. Finding ways to respectfully atone for these casualties is important.

I have taken to picking up many of these animals, using their fur and feathers and dining on the meat if it is fresh. Using road kills in this manner nourishes my being in many ways. I can eat good organic meat, and my surroundings are enriched by furs and feathers. More importantly, this is a relatively non-violent way to tap into and savor another aspect of the spirit and wildness of the natural world.

When skinning, gutting, and preparing an animal for food, one is engaged in a very ancient and honorable endeavor — that of providing meat. There is a certain completeness and dignity that can be attained by taking an animal through this universal age old process — a completeness and dignity to the person who does the butchering as well as to the physical remains of the animal-being which would otherwise have been rather disharmoniously ground into the pavement.

Recently I've found that others are out there doing the same thing and thanks to Gary Snyder, roadside scavenging has been transformed into poetry.

How did a great Red-tailed Hawk
come to lie — all stiff and dry —
on the shoulder of
Interstate 5?

Her wings for dance fans

Zac skinned a skunk with a crushed head
washed the pelt in gas; it hangs,
tanned, in his tent

Fawn stew on Hallowe'en
hit by a truck on highway forty-nine
offer cornmeal by the mouth;
skin it out.

Log trucks run on fossil fuel

I never saw a Ringtail til I found one in the road:
case-skinned it with the toenails
footpads, nose, and whiskers on;
it soaks in salt and water
sulfuric acid pickle;

she will be a pouch for magic tools.

The Doe was apparently shot
lengthwise and through the side —
shoulder and out the flank
belly full of blood

Can save the other shoulder maybe,
if she didn't lie too long —
Pray to their spirits. Ask them to bless us:
our ancient sisters' trails
the roads were laid across and kill them:
night-shining eyes

*The dead by the side of the road.**

→
Douglas Elliot with baby opossum. He lives in Burnsville, North Carolina. For more road kill techniques, see **Getting the Most from Your Game and Fish**, *on p. 450.*
—SB

*"The Dead by the Side of the Road" from **Turtle Island** by Gary Snyder, 1974 New Directions Books, 333 6th Ave., New York, NY 10014.

THERE ARE SEVERAL THINGS that I consider when I'm deciding whether to take some tender young beastie home to dinner. The first thing I look for is a warm body. In the case of warm-blooded animals (especially in cool weather) this indicates that the animal was killed very recently. Another good indicator is the blood. If the blood is still somewhat liquid, the animal is fresh. I examine the eye to see if it is still clear and holding its form. As the time after death increases, the eye gets cloudy and soft, and after a day or so it starts to cave in. **

If you pick up an animal and it later gets stiff with rigor mortis, you can take comfort in this. Rigor mortis sets in a few hours after death as the muscles cool, and it indicates that the animal is fairly fresh. Of course smell is one of the best indicators. If an animal smells "ripe," I won't eat it. There is often a strong visceral smell that is associated with the cleaning out of the entrails from the body cavity. This is different from the smell of decomposition and with a little experience and discriminating nose work, the difference will come clear. ***

Perhaps you are new to the delights of carrion eating and you are a little unsure of your judgment in these matters. Just what are the consequences of eating spoiled meat? Apparently there are none if it is sterilized by cooking. According to my research, "spoilage" is a relative, cultural term. It is caused primarily by bacteria and other organisms but these are all killed by the heat of thorough cooking.

There are some basic techniques of wild meat cookery that you can use to turn this raw material into gourmet fare. It is regularly accepted that the quality and taste of an animal's flesh is often characterized by its diet. Generally it is considered that vegetarian, herbivorous creatures have milder tasting flesh than carnivorous animals. Duck hunters will tell you that plankton and algae-feeding ducks are better eating in the dead of winter than in the summer when there is a higher percentage of animal life in the water. Mergansers and other fish eating birds are known for their strong tasting flesh. A traditional way of preparing an opossum is to keep it in a cage for a few weeks and "clean it out" with a diet of corn meal, milk, molasses and other delights. (It sort of reminds me of the Inca sacrifices of the child-kings.) To me, a mild gamy flavor provides a taste thrill. However, like most good herbs, spices, and other flavorings, there is such a thing as too much. Moderating this gaminess is one of the tasks facing the aspiring wild meat chef.

I USE SEVERAL TECHNIQUES. First I soak the meat in salt water for a few hours to draw out the blood. Apparently this is a custom of American origin, because many European game recipes call for saving the blood and stirring it in later to make gravy. Then there's marinating. This means soaking the meat for eight to twenty-four hours in a solution of vinegar (or wine), oil, herbs, and spices. Marinating tenderizes as well as flavors the meat. There are as many kinds of marinades as there are cookbooks. My recipe goes something like this: a cup or two of good vinegar, a dribble of flavorful oil (olive is great), two or three crushed cloves of garlic, a small sweet onion, a couple of crumpled bay leaves, a pinch of celery seed, a sprig of thyme, basil and rosemary, a few crushed juniper berries, and a crushed spicebush berry. Parboiling is a way of dissipating some of the flavor of the meat as well as tenderizing it. All you have to do is boil the meat thirty minutes at the most before using it in whatever recipe you decide to follow.

As for preparing the skins, there are particular problems related to the various types of animals you might find. With mammals there are basically two methods of skinning — the case and the opened-skin method. (See *Figs. 1 & 2.*) The best blade for skinning is either a razor or a very sharp knife. Cut along the lines indicated, trying to cut just through the skin and not into the body cavity. This keeps the job cleaner. The basic method after the incisions are made, is to pull firmly on the hide and to use the blade to cut the translucent tissues that connect the skin to the body (*Fig. 3*). If the animal is bleeding and you are concerned about protecting the skin, sprinkle the bloody areas with cornmeal as an absorbent. As you get to the head go carefully around the ears, eyes and mouth.

Your first skinning job will probably be sloppy and time consuming. But experience is the best teacher and after you've done a few, the rest will come much easier and faster. On the Eastern Shore of Maryland during the height of muskrat season, there is the Annual World Championship Muskrat Skinning Contest. In recent years, it has been won by a trapper from the Louisiana bayou country. The record time is five muskrats in less than one minute, and the skins are all in good condition. I feel like I'm doing well if I get one done in less than half an hour.

One handy tool for skinning out the tails of animals like fox and raccoon is an old umbrella rib, which is a narrow strip of steel shaped like a "U" in cross-section. This is slipped under the skin and slid down

** Fred Funk, taxidermist at California Academy of Sciences, also cautions that all birds, except the English sparrow and rock dove (common pigeon), are under Federal protection. This means that if you pick up that dead bird beside the road, and a game warden sees you do it, you may be subject to fine. If he sees you. However, you could say that you are going to give it to a local wildlife museum, etc. He also warns that anything which has been washed up on a beach is very dubious. Chances are they have died from disease, and may have been dead for a long time. Seals can give humans a severe skin irritation called seal finger.

There are several things to check for in dead animals. The first place to begin deteriorating is the abdomen. If the animal has been killed by impact, the viscera is usually ruptured, which releases the digestive juices, setting in motion deterioration. You can tell if that has begun by grabbing and tugging the skin. If there's any slippage, check further up, to determine how far the spoilage has gone. There is usually something that can be salvaged, even if only skeletal and skull. Even if the skull is crushed the skin is often intact, and a whole skin can be obtained.

Things to check for in dead animals:
1. Are there any abscesses in the muscle tissue (sores)? Discard this meat.
2. Are there signs of parasites in lungs, heart, stomach, liver, muscle tissue? Cook this animal's meat well.
3. Be careful handling rodents, especially rabbits. They can carry such things as bubonic plague and Tularemia, which can be transferred to humans.
4. Keep an eye out for the game warden.

—Evelyn Eldridge Diaz

*** Peter Warshall requests that even if you decide not to harvest the corpse you're inspecting, you'll do a service if you toss it out of the way of traffic. Numerous predators beside yourself are interested in the meat, and it would be well if they were not smooshed while dining. Failure to perform this courtesy can lead to a two-dimensional pavement display of the local food chain. — SB

DOUGLAS ELLIOT

the length of the tail. Once in place, it will serve as a mini-trough or guide for the blade to follow. This will assure a straight cut the whole length of the tail (*Fig. 4*).

Once removed, the open skin is stretched by tacking fur side down onto a board (*Fig. 5*). The remaining bits of flesh are scraped off with a knife, a sharpened spoon, or whatever tool you can improvise. This is called "fleshing." After the hide is fleshed, a little borax may be rubbed in as a preservative and the skin put in a warm place to dry. This usually takes a few days to a few weeks depending on the humidity and temperature and the thickness of the skin.

The case-skinned hide is treated basically the same except you have to improvise a flat, bullet-shaped stretcher sized in proportion to the animal hide in question. This can be cut from a board or made from a bent piece of springy steel wire (*Fig. 6*). I once cut one out of a piece of stiff cardboard for a weasel skin. The hide is slipped like a glove over the stretcher. For the fur market, cased hides are usually stretched with the flesh side out, but for my personal use, I usually leave the fur out.

AFTER THE ANIMAL IS SKINNED and if you plan to eat it, then the entrails must be taken out. This involves cutting into the abdominal cavity, reaching in and pulling out the guts. It may seem a little yucky at first but there are ways to get into it. Look at those colorful organs! You've got a basic anatomy course right before you. Can you identify them? Sometimes I open the stomach to see what the animal has been eating. The stomach contents of plant-eating animals usually have a pleasant herbal smell that's a refreshing contrast to the strong visceral smells wafting from the body cavity. You may want to save the liver to cook or add to the gravy. If you do, carefully remove the gall bladder which is on the underside of the liver. Don't allow any of its contents to drip onto the meat. (You've heard the expression, "bitter as gall.") Above the diaphragm in the chest cavity are the heart and lungs. These parts can also be used in gravies and stuffings.

Some mammals have scent glands on various parts of their body that can adversely affect the taste of the meat. Deer have glands in the hock or "elbow" of the hind legs. Be careful not to touch or cut into these while preparing the meat. Certain other small animals have four waxy corn kernel-shaped glands. If you take note of these and remove them, most of your battle against excessive gaminess is won. In the muskrat, there is one gland under each fore and hind leg. In the opossum, raccoon, woodchuck, and porcupine there are two glands in the small of the back and one in each front "armpit." (You thought *you* had gamy pits.)

DEER

YOU ARE REALLY INTO A BONANZA if you find a fresh killed deer. In most states however you can be busted for possession of a deer out of season if you don't have a hunting license. This is true of any game, but the penalties for deer tend to be the heaviest. Deer are also harder to conceal. If you want to pick up the road killed deer and appear legal during the hunting season, you can buy a license and the proper stamps and tags and say that you shot it. Out of season, there is usually no legal channel. If you report it to a game warden, their common policy is to confiscate the meat and donate it to a government financed institution such as an old folks home or a school.

With fresh venison, the longer it is cooked, the tougher it gets. The recipe I use goes something like this. Heat a skillet till red hot. Put a dab of grease on it and then rub half an onion over the surface. Throw a thin slab of venison in such a manner that it skids lightly over the surface of the pan and is caught on a waiting dinner plate where it is to be served immediately. (This is hardly an exaggeration.) I also recommend venison jerky. Lean meat is cut into shoelace-like strips and hung over sticks in the smoke of a fire till it is dry. The venison shouldn't be so close to the fire that it cooks. It takes on a delicious smoked flavor and makes a tangy, high-protein trail munchie.

THE BUCK-TOOTHED VEGETARIANS

RABBITS AND SQUIRRELS are mild flavored and hardly need any preliminaries. They can be fried, stewed or even stuffed and roasted. Rabbits have a particularly thin, delicate hide that tears easily when skinning, so don't be discouraged if you have trouble getting it off whole.

In some parts of the country (the west and southwest in particular), rabbits sometimes carry tularemia (spotted fever) and bubonic plague, so it is important to know the area where you pick up rabbits. (Check with local wildlife people, game wardens, or veterinarians.) Wearing rubber gloves is often recommended when dressing rabbits. It's all right to eat a rabbit with tularemia as long as it is well cooked; it's only in the raw state that it can cause problems.

Other rodents like muskrats, porcupines and woodchucks are also good eating, however, a little parboiling and marinating is in order with these.

THE CARNIVORES AND OMNIVORES

RACCOONS AND OPOSSUMS are common highway fatalities. Since they have a varied diet, the flavor of their meat is often a function of what they've been eating. The salt soak and vinegar marinades as well as parboiling is usually called for.

I have eaten fox meat on one occasion and it was quite good. After soaking and parboiling, I browned the pieces in a skillet with onions and simmered them in their own gravy. We cooked up some potatoes and steamed some wild amaranth and lambs-quarter to round out the meal.

WILDFOWL

CLEANING AND DRESSING BIRDS: the main question is — to pluck or not to pluck. To remove the feathers you can either pluck the bird or skin it. There are advantages to each. When the bird is plucked with its skin left on, it has a tendency to cook better because the skin usually holds in the moisture as well as the fat. Plucking the bird dry is somewhat messy because the feathers fly about and also stick to your hands. (This is less of a problem with small birds.) The best way to remedy this situation is to scald the bird in a pot of boiling water with a little detergent added if the bird is oily (especially in the case of waterfowl). The detergent cuts the oil so the water can soak through to the skin.

I usually prefer to skin the bird for a couple of reasons. First of all, it is less time consuming. Secondly, I like to keep the feathers for decoration, etc. This way they are anchored, won't blow around, and are in the same arrangement as they were on the bird. Soaking the feathers makes them difficult to reclaim. Also, with some fish-eating birds, the strong flavor is in the skin and fat and they should be removed even if the bird is plucked.

If you want to save the skin, rub it with borax and dry it. I don't usually stretch bird skins but I often pin the wings out-spread till they dry. These are great for fanning fires and for ornamental or ceremonial purposes.

Pheasants, grouse and quail are the real prizes of the prolific pavement. They are mild tasting, have large breasts of white meat, and, like turkey, are well suited to stuffing and roasting. These as well as other birds can be cooked the same way that you cook any poultry. I have eaten doves, ducks and railbirds, as well as various songbirds. I even ate crow once and found it delicious enough to be worth losing election bets on a regular basis.

ILLUSTRATIONS BY KATHLEEN O'NEILL

REPTILES

SNAKES are often highway casualties, especially in the spring and fall when they crawl onto the roads to absorb a bit of extra warmth. All kinds of snakes are edible. I have tried rattlesnakes, copperheads, and rat snakes and have found them all quite good. Filet mignon, which is considered to be the best cut of beef, comes from the muscle right along the backbone. When you look at a snake, you will realize that it is practically all filet mignon. Snakes should be at least a couple of feet long to have enough meat on them to be worth eating.

I usually skin a snake by cutting around the neck and then down the belly. The skin pulls off rather easily and the entrails literally drop out, making it one of the easiest animals to clean. The skin should be tacked out and fleshed before it has a chance to dry. The meat is white and mild flavored but tough. It should be cut in pieces and parboiled for about twenty minutes. After which I usually like to roll the pieces in flour and fry them like chicken. ■

THE RISING SUN
NEIGHBORHOOD NEWSLETTER

continued from last spread

There's a whole bunch of other stuff about church bells in churches that has to do with the fact that they're high up and you have to climb narrow steps to ring them and tall ladders to see them (the ringing rope is long) and a certain natural exclusivity is built into these activities. My dad had a confirmation class that met for a year in a bell tower by the bell and really fixed it up and invited their parents at the end but some parents never saw the club room because they were scared shitless, but that actually belongs with climbing stories not ringing stories, and I can't think of any other ringing stories right now, except *The Nine Tailors*, a good and oppressive mystery story by Dorothy Sayers, all about change ringing which, dare I tell you involves 9 bells and lots of non-random number sequences and lots of difficult description, and I read and liked the whole thing even the description and even the numbers, two of my unfavorite things.

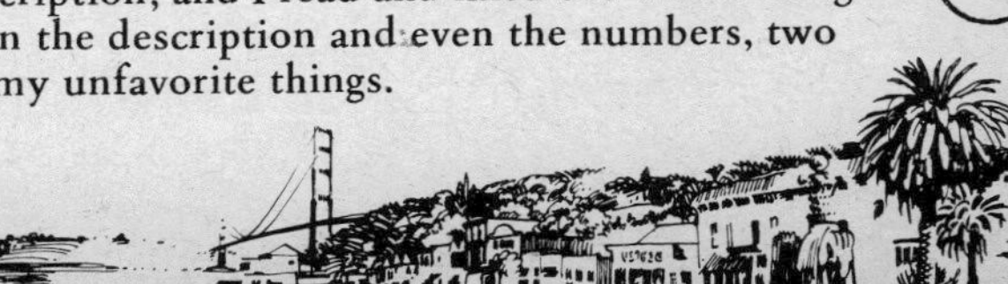

The Books of Tofu, Miso, Tempeh, Kudzu

An ever-expanding opus on how to make soybeans not only palatable but gourmet fare. The books translate centuries of Asian sophistication into accessible how to — how to make at home, how to cook with, even how to produce in commercial quantities. Also why to — getting meat-equal nutrition and gustatory delight lower on the food chain means more food for everybody.

Tofu is a Japanese protein-rich light cheese-like soybean derivative that handily takes on the flavors of whatever you cook it with. Miso, also Japanese, is the paste derived from fermented soybeans and is used in all manner of cooking and seasoning. Tempeh is an Indonesian tofu, distinctly meat-like — it has as much protein as steak (20%). Kudzu is the Japanese vine that is burying the American south, fought tooth and nail by the inhabitants. Since the Japanese make food, medicine, and cloth out of it, why don't we?

Good food. Good books. A major dietary improvement under way here. —SB

The Book of Tofu
(Food for Mankind)
William Shurtleff and Akiko Aoyagi
1975; 336 pp.
$7.95 postpaid

The Book of Miso
(Savory High-Protein Seasoning)
William Shurtleff and Akiko Aoyagi
1976; 255 pp.
$8.95 postpaid

The Book of Kudzu
(A Culinary and Healing Guide)
William Shurtleff and Akiko Aoyagi
1977; 104 pp.
$4.95 postpaid
all from:
Autumn Press
1318 Beacon Street
Brookline, MA 02146

The Book of Tofu
(New Americanized Edition)
William Shurtleff and Akiko Aoyagi
1975, 1979; 434 pp.
$2.95 postpaid from:
Ballantine Books
455 Hahn Road
Westminster, MD 21157

The Book of Tempeh
(A Super Soyfood from Indonesia)
William Shurtleff and Akiko Aoyagi
1979; 158 pp.
$6.95 postpaid from:
Harper and Row
Keystone Industrial Park
Scranton, PA 18512

Tofu and Soymilk Production
(The Book of Tofu, Volume Two)
William Shurtleff and Akiko Aoyagi
1979; 336 pp.
$17.95 postpaid

Tempeh Production
(The Book of Tempeh, Volume Two)
William Shurtleff and Akiko Aoyagi
1980; 154 pp.
$13.95 postpaid

Miso Production
(The Book of Miso, Volume Two)
William Shurtleff and Akiko Aoyagi
1977; 62 pp.
$8.95 postpaid

Tofu Kit
$14.95 postpaid

Catalog
free

all Shurtleff books and soy items from:
New Age Foods Study Center
P.O. Box 234
Lafayette, CA 94549

all books also from
Whole Earth Household Store

•

Today, throughout much of Asia, tofu is by far the most important way of using soybeans as a daily food. Indeed tofu is as much a part of Oriental culture, language, and cookery as is bread in the West. In America, a country with twice the population of Japan, there are 19,000 bakeries and the average annual consumption of bread is 73 loaves per person. The tofu made in Japan's 38,000 tofu shops provides the average Japanese with about seventy 12-ounce cakes each year. And there are an estimated 150,000 tofu shops in China, 2,500 in Taiwan, 11,000 in Indonesia, 1,400 in North and South Korea, and still more in the Philippines, Thailand, and Vietnam. Now imagine how strange it would seem if, in the world's largest wheat producing country, most of the people had never tasted bread. Yet no less unusual is the present situation in America, the world's largest producer of soybeans, where the majority of people have not yet tasted, seen, or even heard of tofu.

America now produces about two-thirds of the world's soybeans. They are one of our largest and most important farm crops, second only to corn (and ahead of wheat!) in dollar value, and third in total acreage.
—**The Book of Tofu**

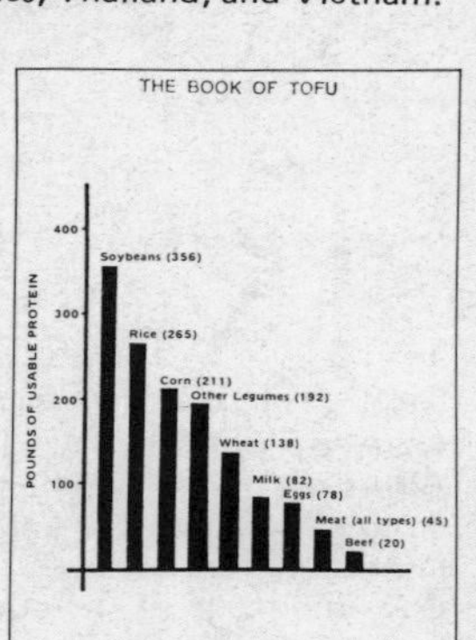

Per-acre Yields of Usable Protein from Different Food Sources

•

Tifton B. Merritt, a southern journalist, gives the following advice for cultivating kudzu:

Choosing a plot: Although kudzu will grow quite well on cement, you should select an area having at least a little dirt.

When to plant: Kudzu should be planted at night to avoid neighbors seeing you and throwing rocks.

Fertilization: Forty weight, nondetergent motor oil applied to the underside of tender leaves prevents their scraping when kudzu begins its rapid growth.

Mulching: For best results, as soon as the young shoots begin to appear, mulch heavily with concrete blocks.

—**The Book of Kudzu**

Kudzu's future in America lies in the use of its root.

Soycraft

A new magazine confidently serving the growing population of soyfood makers. I can see it gets to be a way of life all right. —SB

Soycraft
(The Journal of the Soycrafters Association of North America)
Richard Leviton, Editor
$15 /year (4 issues)
from:
Soycraft
Sunrise Farm
Heath Road
Colrain, MA 01340

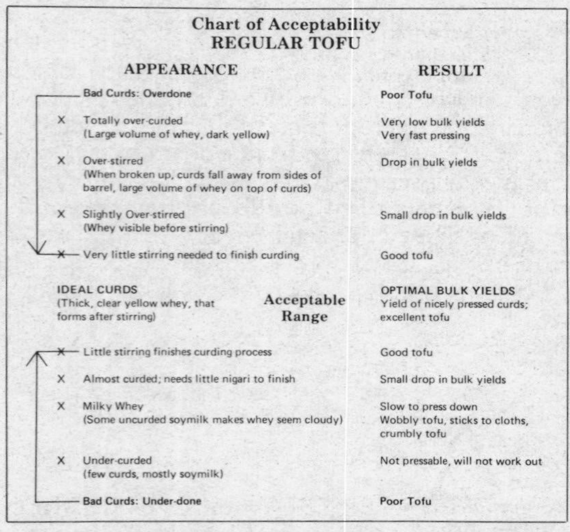

Chart of Acceptability
REGULAR TOFU

APPEARANCE	RESULT
Bad Curds: Overdone	Poor Tofu
X Totally over-curded (Large volume of whey, dark yellow)	Very low bulk yields Very fast pressing
X Over-stirred (When broken up, curds fall away from sides of barrel, large volume of whey on top of curds)	Drop in bulk yields
X Slightly Over-stirred (Whey visible before stirring)	Small drop in bulk yields
X Very little stirring needed to finish curding	Good tofu
IDEAL CURDS (Thick, clear yellow whey, that forms after stirring) — Acceptable Range	OPTIMAL BULK YIELDS Yield of nicely pressed curds; excellent tofu
X Little stirring finishes curding process	Good tofu
X Almost curded; needs little nigari to finish	Small drop in bulk yields
X Milky Whey (Some uncurded soymilk makes whey seem cloudy)	Slow to press down Wobbly tofu, sticks to cloths, crumbly tofu
X Under-curded (few curds, mostly soymilk)	Not pressable, will not work out
Bad Curds: Under-done	Poor Tofu

•

The key to miso's extraordinary nutritional value is the process of fermentation, a process which, throughout its long and varied history around the world, has served three fundamental purposes: the improvement of a food's digestibility; the transformation of its flavor and aroma, color and texture; and its preservation without refrigeration. Watching the drama enlarged a thousandfold and presented in time-lapse color photography, one witnesses a near-miraculous world in which tiny spores burst into blossom like elegant and complex flowers, enzymes reach out inquisitively like long fingers melting solid particles at their touch, and populations of mold explode until they have totally enveloped the foods — or "substrates" — which support their life. Just as Western craftsmen have fermented milk to form cheese and yogurt, or grapes to form wine, Eastern craftsmen have fermented soybeans and grains to form miso and shoyu.
—**The Book of Miso**

Tempeh-Filled Pot Stickers or Gyoza

MAKES 33

Now quite popular at Chinese restaurants in the West, these half-moon-shaped delicacies are called Steamed Dumplings (chiao-tzu) in their simplest steamed or boiled form, and Pot Stickers (kuo-t'ieh or kuo-teh) in their more popular crispy fried form. Both represent nice ways to use leftover tempeh; we feel they would also make excellent commercial products, especially for the vegetarian market.

Making tempeh-filled pot stickers or gyoza

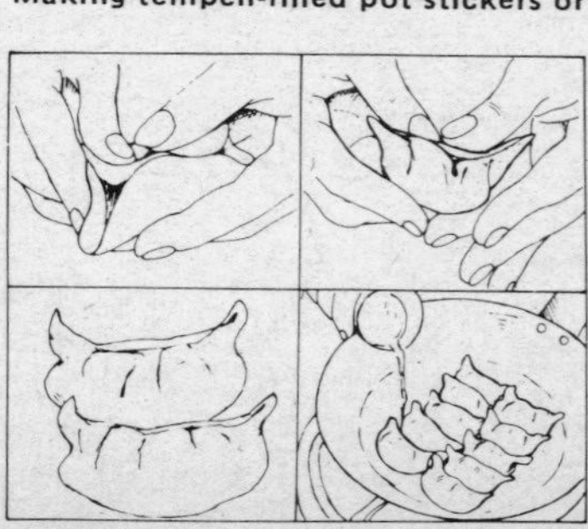

6 ounces (170 grams) tempeh, cut into ½-inch cubes, and deep- or shallow-fried (page 52–54)
3½ ounces (100 grams) cabbage or Chinese cabbage (2½ to 3 leaves), parboiled and minced
2 tablespoons chopped chives
¼ cup minced leek (or scallion) whites
1 clove garlic, crushed or grated
½ teaspoon grated gingerroot
¼ to ½ teaspoon salt
Dash of pepper (optional)
1 tablespoon cornstarch, arrowroot, or kudzu powder
33 wonton or gyoza skins or wrappers, each 3¼ inches in diameter (storebought or homemade)
4 to 6 tablespoons oil
6 to 8 tablespoons water
Dipping Sauce. For each person:
1½ tablespoons shoyu (natural soy sauce)
1 teaspoon (rice) vinegar
½ teaspoon sesame oil or rayu (red-chili oil)
¼ teaspoon hot mustand (optional)

Mash tempeh, then combine with the next eight ingredients, mixing well. Place 1½ teaspoons of the mixture at the center of each of 11 wonton skins. (Wrap the remaining skins temporarily with plastic wrap to prevent their drying.) Moisten the perimeter of each skin with water, fold over like a turnover, and seal the edges as shown above, then arrange on a plate and cover with plastic wrap. Proceed to fill the remaining 22 skins in the same way.
—**The Book of Tempeh**

Prime grade Commercial grade

Because Commercial grade beef comes from older animals, it is not naturally tender — even though it is well-marbled and could be mistaken by the uninformed for Prime grade (compare the pictures). Commercial grade beef requires long, slow cooking with moist heat to make it tender. But when prepared in this manner it can provide delicious and economical meat dishes. — and it will have the rich, full flavor characteristic of mature beef.

Food Co-ops for Small Groups

How to bypass the supermarket and buy food direct from farmers and wholesalers. Joining or organizing a food co-op has other benefits too — a chance to meet your neighbors and to work together toward a common goal.

This book does a good job of telling how a small group, regardless of location, food preferences, or prior experience, can start and operate. —*Tom Ferguson, M.D.*

Food Co-ops for Small Groups
(How to Buy Better Food for Less)
Tony Vellela
1975; 173 pp.

$2.95 postpaid from:
Workman Publishing Company, Inc.
1 West 39th Street
New York, NY 10018

or Whole Earth Household Store

•

Locating the people you need is easier than it seems. They need not all be from the same group. Food co-ops have formed from friendships made in dozens of groups, in dozens of situations. Consider neighborhood groups, tenant associations, day care centers, church or other spiritual groups, office and factory workers, PTA groups, block associations, community centers, service clubs, the gang at the laundromat, the regulars at the health food restaurant, the area chapter of NOW, members of the union local — any of these groups can be sources for your food co-op's membership.

•

The Yellow Pages list wholesale food distributors in all areas under such headings as:

Bakers Suppliers
Bakers — Wholesale
Dairy Products Brokers
Eggs, Cheese, Butter
Food Brokers
Food Products — Mfrs. & Distrs.
Fruits and Vegetables — Wholesale
Grocers — Wholesale
Health Food Products — Wholesalers/Manufacturers
Meat, Wholesale
Milk and Milk Products
Natural Foods
Nuts, Edible — Wholesale
Oils, Vegetable
Poultry — Wholesale
Restaurant Purveyors
Sugar Brokers & Wholesalers

•

Finally, a very, very important and wise consideration: make every effort to contact area farmers directly. Your local or regional branch office of the Department of Agriculture might help. Or else post a sign at stores where farmers would shop for supplies; ask regional 4-H Club leaders for help; Future Farmers of America might supply some names. Dealing with farmers would give them a friendly, direct market and give you a friendly, minimal markup. You'd be supporting a small operation which may be facing the threat of losing its holdings if forced to accept corporate prices for crops; by selling to people close by, the farmer could get a price higher than the corporate price, and the co-op could get a price lower than the wholesale price. And you'd know exactly where some of your food is coming from.

How to Buy Food for Economy and Quality

A collection of U.S. Dept. of Agriculture publications including information on fresh meat, fish, dairy products, fruits and vegetables and frozen and canned goods. Also has sections on what government gradings mean; pointers on when higher quality is worth the price, on storing food — where and for how long, and seasonal bargains. All in all informative and full of reassuring rules of thumb.
—*Laura Besserman*

How to Buy Food for Economy and Quality
(Recommendations of the United States Department of Agriculture)
Valerie Moolman, Editor
1970, 1975; 160 pp.

$1.50 postpaid from:
Dover Publications
180 Varick Street
New York, NY 10014

or Whole Earth Household Store

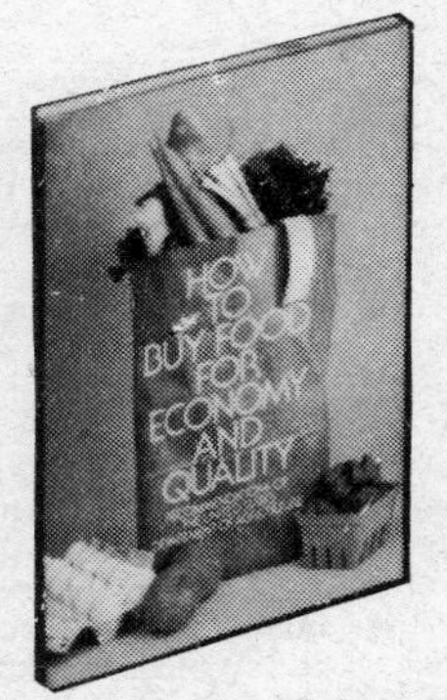

How to Save Money Through Group Buying

Co-ops are good because they spread the responsibility and the information more evenly among consumers, handlers, and producers, so that they do not all treat each other solely as economic things. Better service cheaper is the result. This is the best book on the remarkable range of co-oping going on and how to do some. —*SB*

How to Save Money Through Group Buying
Albert Lee
1977; 302 pp.

$4.95 postpaid from:
Stein and Day, Publishers
Scarborough House
Briarcliff Manor, NY 10510

or Whole Earth Household Store

•

We could save hundreds, even thousands, of dollars each year. Save as much as 40 percent on many food products. Save a third on rent. Save by avoiding usurious revolving charges and long-term high-interest financing. Save money, anxiety, and even pain by being able to take advantage of preventive medicine, preventive legal advice, and counseling to avoid consumer frauds. We would save by knowing what we were getting and by getting only high-quality goods free of gimmicks. You and I could have a higher standard of living not by working more hours but by getting more out of the income we now have.

Butterflies in My Stomach

This book about edible insects (and not anxiety, which one might think from the title) gives evidence of a priceless offering of protein to the human diet from bugs. It points out that for centuries both primitive and highly cultured societies have straightforwardly served meals of insects and that today a good part of the planet's people still do. But not in America. Interestingly enough the occidental who once went forth to hunt meat and fowl and now searches and researches with camera, may lay aside his notebook and take to the field as hunter again . . . with a net. It appears the insect world is a land-o-plenty, plenty of protein. Even the vegetarian is informed of the great quantity of insect flesh s/he has inadvertently partaken of. Bulletins are cited disclosing the percentages of permissible insect parts in many marketed foodstuffs and also the efficiency of food conversion rate is shown with insects compared to meat, fowl, fish and shellfish.

Canned insects are judged (low), information is offered on searching out insects and specifics are given on cultivating one's own "herd" and where to send for "stock."

There is an appendix of over 250 known edible insects and spiders. This book appears designed for the average American, but it is written informatively by an entomologist. Who could ask for more? **Butterflies** *is the definitive work on such of recent date.*
—*Eava Mayanna*

Butterflies in My Stomach
(Insects in Human Nutrition)
Ronald L. Taylor
1975; 224 pp.

$8.95 postpaid from:
Woodbridge Press
P.O. Box 6189
Santa Barbara, CA 93111

or Whole Earth Household Store

•

Jonathan Swift once said, "He was a bold man that first ate an oyster," and I fully agree. A more loathsome-looking creature would be hard to find. And yet people eat them *alive* — their muscles contracting, their heart beating, fecal material passing through them. Or, consider the lobster. There perhaps isn't a more foul-feeding animal on the surface of the earth. Lobsters eat every kind of putrid flesh and fish they can find. In fact, some lobster fishermen bait their traps with putrid flesh. Nevertheless, lobsters are highly prized as human food. (Putrid flesh is the best bait for crayfish and for prawns, too.)

•

Virtually all insects found in nonpolluted fresh water are edible and delicious. The larvae and aquatic adults of beetles, bugs, mayflies, stoneflies, caddisflies, damselflies, dragonflies, and others are edible.

↓

Fried Grasshoppers. Most people liked this product comparing its flavor to sardines or at least to fish. One person thought these insects would be good on pizza. Some tasters found the grasshoppers to be sweet.

Butchering, Processing and Preservation of Meat

If you are going to go native or at least semi-fringy, you had better figure out a way of beating Safeway to the price of a pork chop. In other words, if you are going to beat the system, Ashbrook's book will show you how. (At least in the meat department.)

Want to butcher a steer? Ashbrook tells you how to do it in the minute detail you need if you have never done something like this before. Same goes for hogs, sheep and lambs, game animals and poultry and wild fowl. After you have the animal cut up he tells you how to freeze it, can it, salt it and even smoke it. Want to make your own sausage? He tells you how. This is the most complete book I've ever seen on the subject. From how to select the right knife to what to do with all the leftover fat (make soap with it — he shows you how).

Ashbrook knows what he is talking about after 40 years as animal husbandman and biologist with the U.S. Dept. of Agriculture and Interior. You can forget about all those 15 cent pamphlets from the USDA, this one book is all you need. —*Arthur Keim*

Butchering, Processing and Preservation of Meat
(A Manual for the Farm and Home)
Frank G. Ashbrook
1955; 318 pp.

$4.95 postpaid from:
Van Nostrand-Reinhold
Reinhold Company
Order Department
7625 Empire Drive
Florence, KY 41042

or Whole Earth Household Store

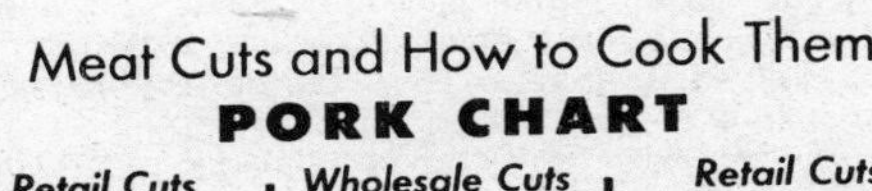

Meat Cuts and How to Cook Them
PORK CHART

THE RISING SUN
NEIGHBORHOOD NEWSLETTER

"She was definitely the leave-four-eggs-in-a-pot-of-boiling-water-and-go-upstairs-and-go-to-sleep kind of roommate." —Art

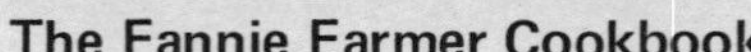

Joy of Cooking

You really only need one book in the kitchen. This book. Along with everything (!!) else, it is the only cookbook with two handy red ribbons to mark your place.

—SB

Joy of Cooking
Irma S. Rombauer and
Marion Rombauer Becker
1931, 1979; 915 pp.

$12.95 postpaid from:
Bobbs-Merrill Company
4300 West 62nd Street
Indianapolis, IN 46268
or Whole Earth
Household Store

[Note. There are two paperback versions of the **Joy.** *Don't bother with them. They are earlier editions, and as paperbacks they will not survive kitchen duress.]*

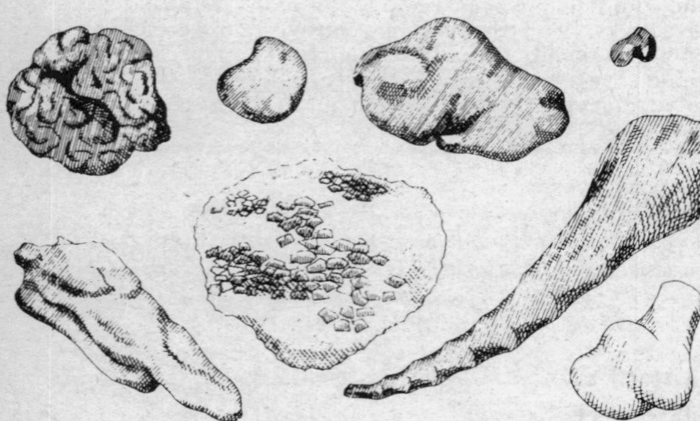

About Variety Meats

Variety, we know, is the spice of life. And variety meats provide welcome relief from the weekly round of beef, pork, veal, chicken and fish. They include organ meats like sweetbreads, brains, lamb kidney, calf and chicken liver, shown from left to right in the upper row. Muscle meats like heart, tongue and tripe; and very bony-structured meats like oxtails and knucklebones and their delicious marrow centers, seen in the lower row. Time was when most of these tidbits were ours almost for the asking simply because most Americans had built-in prejudices against them. But in recent years, the American passion for travel has developed more cosmopolitan tastes in food, and more of us have learned to appreciate the odds and ends from which European cooks prepare some of their most celebrated dishes. There are practical reasons, too, to serve these delectable oddments: with the exception of calf liver and sweetbreads, now in the higher-priced bracket, they are still gentle to a fragile budget; and last but not least, they contribute significantly to our well-being; although some of those formerly used, like lungs, are now outlawed. But even the muzzle of beef can be prepared as for tongue. It is essential that variety meats be fresh. They are highly perishable; use them at once.

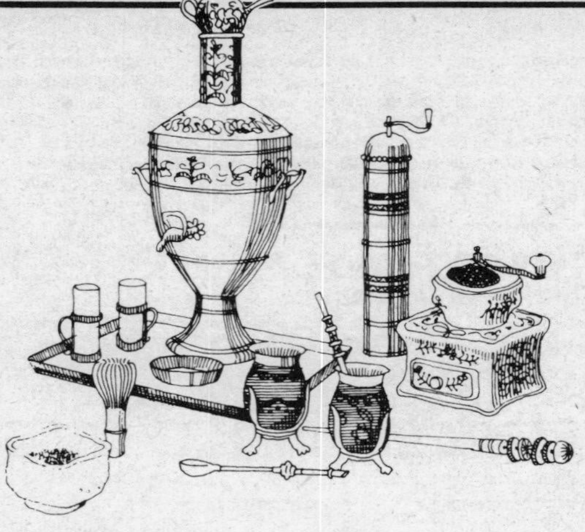

↑

As our friend the late Edgar Anderson pointed out in his stimulating book, **Plants, Man and Life,** primitive man located the only sources of caffeine known to this day: tea, coffee, cola, cocoa and yerba maté and its relatives. Subsequent generations have adopted social rituals and created special equipment to enhance the cheer and communicativeness that these plants release. Shown here is a massive Russian samovar with its charcoal pipe, the tea essence above, the hot water container below, and a few typical metal-encircled serving glasses: a strong cultural contrast to the Japanese teabowl and whisk nearby. Illustrated, too, is a charming porcelain coffee mill from Central Europe which makes a much coarser grind than does its tall Turkish counterpart. Rounding out the assembly are two examples from south of the border. From Mexico comes a wooden chocolate-stirrer, or molinillo; from South America, carved gourds for yerba maté. The gourd is supported on a silver stand, but after it has been filled with maté leaves and boiling water it becomes a communal cup and is passed from hand to hand, each guest taking a sip through the bombilla, a metal "straw," finely perforated at its bulbous base to strain out the herbs.

•

About Corn Breads

Anyone who grew up on southern corn breads hankers for a rich brown crust and a light but slightly gritty bite. We can assure you that without stone-ground cornmeal and a heavy, hot pan, the end product will be pale and lifeless. For a very crisp crust, grease the pan well and heat it in a 425° oven before filling. Whether you bake as muffins, sticks or bread, you may vary the corn and wheat proportion within a 2-cup limit, to your own taste. We like 1¼ cups cornmeal to ¾ cup all-purpose flour. Try, if you like, adding a little minced onion, shredded cheddar cheese, cream-style corn or bits of cooked ham or bacon. Many southern cooks use no sugar, but for a distinctive flavor, try dark brown sugar instead of granulated.

When baking corn breads at high altitudes, reduce the baking powder or soda by one-fourth. But do not reduce soda to less than ½ teaspoon for each cup of buttermilk or sour cream used.

•

In baking, round pans will give you more even browning; square pans tend to cause heavier browning at the corners. Note, too, that shiny metal baking pans deflect heat and that dark enamel or glass ones both catch and hold the heat more. Therefore, food cooked in glass or enameled pans needs at least a 25° reduction in the oven temperatures given in our recipes. While vitreous or dark metal materials may brown cookies too rapidly, they will ensure better browning for pies and puff pastes. If cooking fuel is scarce, a great saving can be effected by the use of these heat-retaining pans.

The Fannie Farmer Cookbook

Recently **The Fannie Farmer Cookbook** *(The Boston Cooking School Cookbook) underwent a complete renovation by Marion Cunningham and Jeri Laber. The renovation reflects the changes in attitude towards cooking we have seen in the past two decades.* **Fannie** *is probably the best starting place for a beginning cook. From it you can learn the skills and procedures needed for nearly any cuisine. James Beard hails it as a "rebirth of the principles of good cooking that Miss Farmer established at the turn of the century."*

—Norman Shea and Evelyn Eldridge-Diaz

The Fannie Farmer Cookbook
Revised by
Marion Cunningham
with Jeri Laber
1979; 811 pp.
12th Edition

$14.95 postpaid from:
Alfred A. Knopf, Inc.
455 Hahn Road
Westminster, MD 21157
or Whole Earth
Household Store

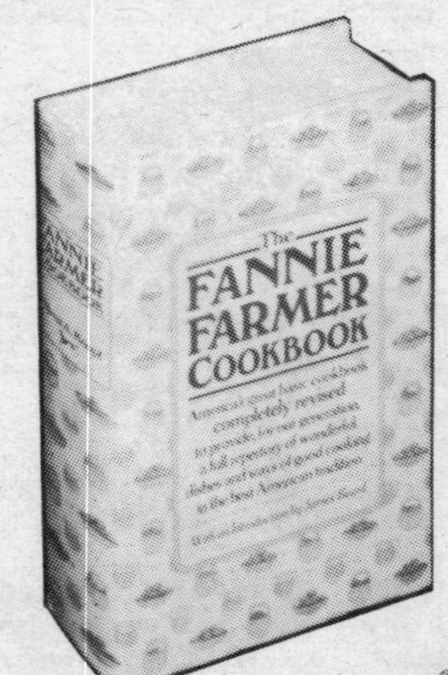

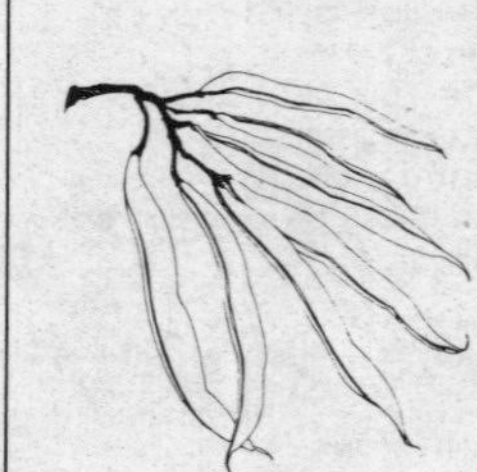

Vegetables from Fannie Farmer Cookbook, **from top: garlic, mushrooms, scallions, asparagus, shell beans, broccoli, artichoke, and kohlrabi.**

↑

About Green Beans

Availability: Year round, especially in spring and summer.
What to Look For: Crisp, firm beans, with good, fresh color; should snap when broken.
Uses: Hot or cold, boiled or steamed, as an appetizer, salad, or vegetable; add leftovers to soups or salads, or puree. *As a vegetable accompaniment,* good with just about everything.
Amount: One pound serves three or four.
Alternatives to Fresh: Frozen preferable to canned, but will be limp.

Green beans were once called string beans. Today they are stringless; just break off the ends as you wash them. Green beans, wax beans, and pole beans may all be cooked the same way, until just tender but crunchy. Try them fried whole in a beer batter for a change sometimes.

•

The way tea is served in most public places — a cup of hot water with a tea bag alongside it — is an insult to anyone who cares about tea and should be protested because it is impossible to produce a decent cup that way.

The important points to remember in making tea are:

- The water you use should always be cold and freshly drawn — not water that has been boiled before or has sat around in a kettle. Bring it to a rolling boil and use immediately.
- Earthenware or china pots are best. Metal is apt to alter the flavor ever so slightly.
- Warm the teapot (mug, or cup) by pouring boiling water in and swirling it around, then discard.
- Put 1 teaspoon of tea into the steaming pot (or a tea bag into the warm cup or mug) for every cup of water, then gently pour over the leaves water that has just come to a rolling boil. Give a good stir, cover, and let steep 5 minutes. (For the single cup or mug, use a saucer to cover; 3 - 4 minutes of quiet steeping should be enough; don't dunk the bag.)
- Give a final stir to the pot, let the tea settle, and pour — through a tea strainer or not, depending on whether you mind a few leaves in your cup.
- If the tea is too strong when you pour it out, add boiling water. You may find that for your own taste the proportion of 1 teaspoon per cup for certain strong blends like Irish Breakfast is too strong and that you want to use slightly less tea. But remember that it is easier to weaken tea with boiling water after it is made than to try to add more leaves after it has been brewed.
- Serve with cream or milk, slices of lemon, and sugar on the side for those who want them. Always have available a pot of hot water.

The Art of Eating

If you have a curiosity about how food and cooking fit in with love and war, death, joy and sorrow, M.F.K. Fisher is the source to consult. More of a philosopher and memoirist than recipe mongerer, Fisher is the dean of California food writers and strikes me as a cross between Julia Child and Lillian Hellman.

How to Cook a Wolf *was published nearly 40 years ago to enable people to cope with wartime food shortages. Much of its advice has stood the test of time and can be welcomed if we want to enter a new era of limitations with a sense of grace. Vintage Books has done a great service by compiling five of Fisher's books (including* **How to Cook a Wolf***) of the 30's and 40's into one thick $6.95 paperback entitled* **The Art of Eating.**

—Norman Shea
[Suggested by Elizabeth Logan]

The Art of Eating
M.F.K. Fisher
1937, 1976; 749 pp.

$6.95 postpaid from:
Random House
455 Hahn Road
Westminster, MD 21157
or Whole Earth
Household Store

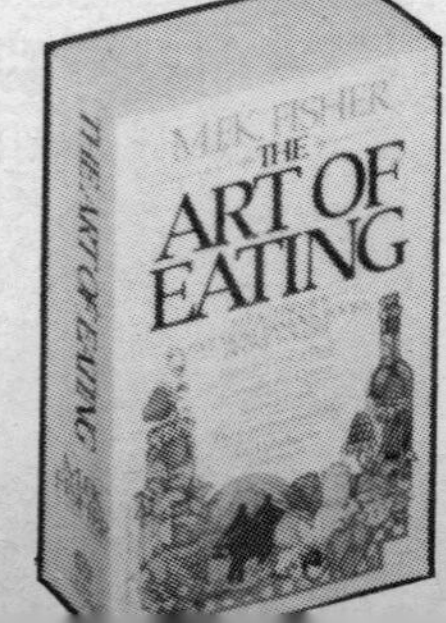

•

I have eaten a great many pigeons here and there, and I know that the best was one I cooked in a cheap Dutch oven on a one-burner gas-plate in a miserable lodging. The wolf was at the door, and no mistake; until I filled the room with the smell of hot butter and red wine, his pungent breath seeped through the keyhole in an almost visible cloud.

Supper took about half an hour to prepare (I could have done it more quickly, but there was no reason for it), and long before I was ready to put the little brown fuming bird on my one Quimper plate, and pour out my second glass of wine, I heard a sad sigh and then the diminishing click of his claws as he retreated down the hall and out into the foggy night. I had routed him, because of the impertinent recklessness of roasting a little pigeon and savoring it intelligently and voluptuously too.

This is the way I cooked that innocent brown bird, and the way, with small variations, I have often treated other ones since then:

Roast Pigeon

1 pigeon
1 lemon
2 slices fat bacon (or 2 tablespoons butter or oil)
parsley
red wine (or cider, beer, orange juice, tomato juice, stock . . .), about a cupful
water
salt, pepper

Melt the fat. [If bacon is used, cook it until crisp, and then remove it until time to serve it alongside, over, or even under the little bird.] See that the bird is well plucked, and rub her thoroughly with a cut lemon and the seasoning. Push the parsley into the belly. Braise well in the hot fat.

Add the liquid, put on the lid quickly, and cook slowly for about 20 minutes, basting two or three times. If you are going to eat the bird cold, put into a covered dish so that it will not dry out. [And if hot, make a pretty slice of toast for each bird, butter it well (or spread it with a bit of good *pate de foies* for Party!), and place the bird upon it. Swirl about one cup of dry good wine and 2 tablespoonfuls butter in the pan, for 4 birds, and spoon this over each one immediately, and serve.

The Tassajara Bread Book

Here's a breadmaking guide that stands on profound respect for simple, wholesome ingredients and a "rip-ening, maturing, baking, blossoming" process, that turns a glob of dough into a fragrant food fit for anyone's meal. Good bread is always magically more than the sum of its ingredients.

There are recipes for breads yeasted and unyeasted, fruit-filled loaves, sourdough, pancakes, pastries, muffins, and various favorite snacks from the Tassajara kitchen. This zen cook knows the true nature of bread.

—Hal Hershey

The Tassajara Bread Book
Edward Espe Brown
1970; 146 pp.

$6.50 postpaid from:
Shambhala Publications
P.O. Box 271
Boulder, CO 80306
or Whole Earth Household Store

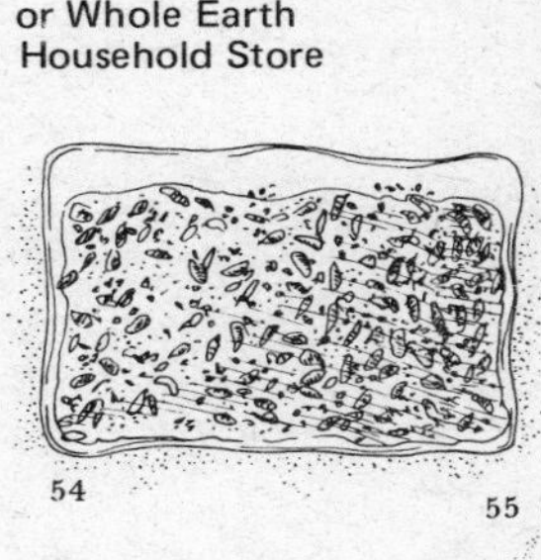

54

55

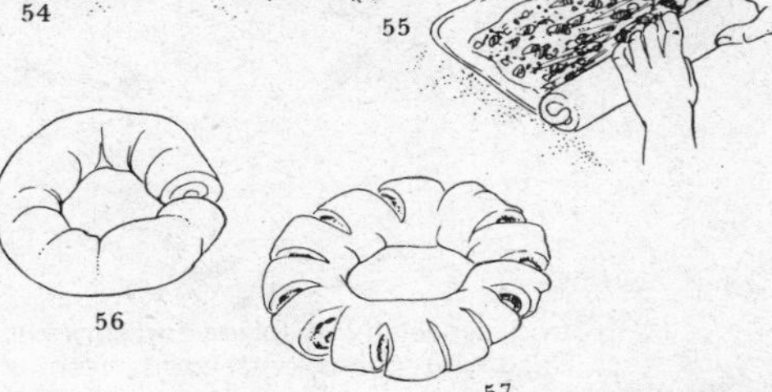

56

57

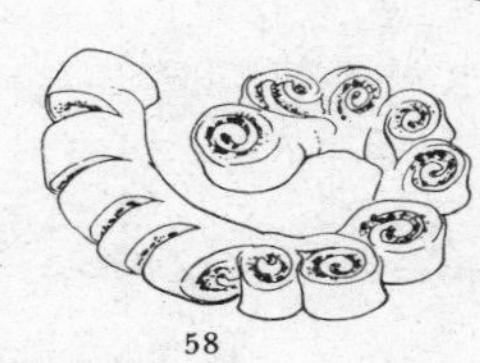

58

59

↑

Swedish Tea Ring (see illustrations)

Looks so good, a blossoming flower of fruit-filled bread. (Serves 4 - 6)

Use Yeasted Breakfast Bread Dough recipe No. 19. As dough is rising, simmer until thickened:

1 c chopped pitted prunes or dates or raisins
½ t cinnamon (nutmeg or allspice are good too)
1 T lemon juice (or orange)
¼ c brown sugar (or 1 t vanilla extract)
1/8 t salt

After dough has risen, roll out to 12" x 14". Spread with fruit mixture (Figure 54). Roll as for jelly roll (Figure 55). Place on greased sheet and join ends (Figure 56). Cut 1" slits with scissors (Figure 57). Twist if you wish (Figures 58 and 59). Allow to rise double in bulk. Brush with egg wash. Bake at 350° for 30 - 40 minutes until golden brown. Frost with liquidy mixture of beaten egg white sweetened to taste with powdered sugar.

Tassajara Cooking

***The Tassajara Bread Book** showed what else goes into outstanding bread besides flour. Now Ed Brown and the Tassajara Zen Center are back to show us the rest of the kitchen. These ascetic Bay Area zennies continually smite my secularity with the best cooking I've ever eaten. Some asceticism. They cook a good cookbook too. Universally acclaimed.*

—SB

Tassajara Cooking
Edward Espe Brown
1973; 242 pp.

$7.50 postpaid from:
Shambhala Publications
P.O. Box 271
Boulder, CO 80306
or Whole Earth Household Store

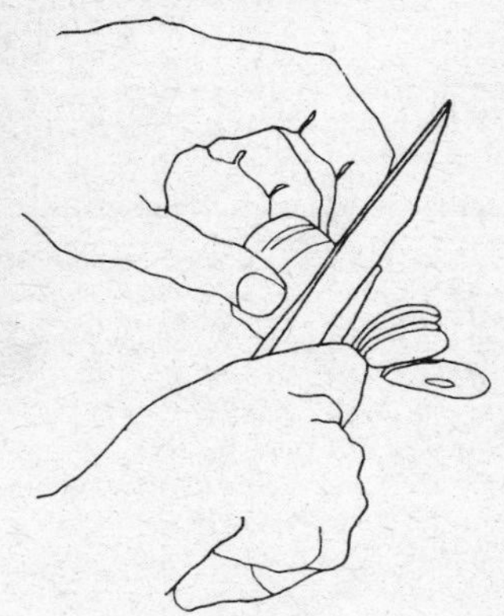

About Guiding the Knife ↑

Keep your right hand dumb. It's just going to cut cut cut, always guided by the last knuckle of the middle finger of the left hand. Either the left hand walks back along the vegetable, the knife following, moving over just as far as the retreating knuckle, or the left hand inches the vegetable forward, maintaining its own position.

•

Being good friends with the knives, clean and replace them in the knife rack after use.

Being good friends with the sponge, rinse and wring it out; with the towels fold and hang them up, and wash when dirty, or before.

Being good friends with the counter, wipe it after use, and scrub sometimes; with the floor, sweep and mop. Get into the corners, and when you're done, stand the broom on end or hang it on a hook. After cleaning a greasy floor sprinkle some salt where it's still slippery.

Being good friends with the dish sponge, don't use it on the floor. Use the dish towel for dishes, and have another for face and hands.

Being good friends with the scraps and trimmings, make some stock.

Clean the sinks! Clear the drains!

•

Outline for Making Salads

Background Ingredients:
lettuce, cabbage, carrots, spinach, cucumber, cauliflower, broccoli, potatoes, sprouts, beets, tomatoes, green beans, asparagus, other?
beans: kidney, lentil, garbanzo, other?
grains: rice, bulgur wheat, other?

The ingredient upon which a particular salad is based is the "Background," which is how the salad gets its name, for instance, "Potato Salad."

Foreground Ingredients:
green, yellow or purple onions, celery, green peppers, red radishes, capers, dill or sweet pickles, olives, cheese, nuts, seeds, fruit and dried fruit

These are employed to compliment each other and the basic ingredient, adding color, shape, taste, zest. The ingredients listed under "Background" could also be used in lesser amounts as "Foreground" ingredients.

If a salad is kept fairly simple, say three or five ingredi-ents, each ingredient can have some prominence, but it is also intriguing to "hide" ingredients in a salad. Consider how to cut each thing. How does it look? How well does it taste when bitten into? Can it be easily chewed? Does it need cooking?

Consider how to arrange the ingredients: Mixed together? Separate rows? Circles? Layers? Dressing in the middle surrounded by the salad ingredients? If each ingredient to be used is kept in a separate bowl, some of them may be arranged decoratively on top of the salad rather than being mixed in.

Laurel's Kitchen

*There are lots of vegetarian cookbooks around. The big difference here, the one which makes this book superior, is that **Laurel's Kitchen** has a giant 180-page section on nutrition. There are complete descriptions of the different food components, analyses of foods, calorie-computation tables, and a good bibliography. You can cook a recipe from the front of the book, then refer to the back to see how much of which minerals, carbo-hydrates, etc., you gave your family that day. Tasty recipes, too. Tom Ferguson, our medical editor, gives it an A+.*

—Evelyn Eldridge-Diaz

Laurel's Kitchen
(A Handbook for Vegetarian Cookery and Nutrition)
Laurel Robertson, et al.
1976; 508 pp.

$3.95 postpaid from:
Bantam Books
414 East Golf Road
Des Plaines, IL 60016
or Whole Earth Household Store

•

Don't let the time factor keep you from fixing hot whole-grain cereals for your family's breakfast. Many of us are in the habit of setting up the coffee pot as soon as we can grope our way to the kitchen — it takes no more effort to get the cereal started, and within a half hour (while you're dressing or meditating) it's cooked. Measure out the water and cereal the night before, so it's all ready to go. Even faster is the thermos method: Put ¾ cup or so of cereal into a preheated pint-sized thermos, fill it up with boiling water, cap it, and let it stand overnight. By breakfast time, the cereal is cooked and piping hot. If it's thick, thin it to taste with more hot water.

The Vegetarian Epicure

*The pages of our copies of **The Vegetarian Epicure, Parts I & II**, are spattered with sauces and memories, to my mind one of the best recommendations for a cookbook. They are used more than any other cook books in our house of gourmet cooks and critical eaters. Anna Thomas has a delightful, innovative way with spices and herbs, and we have yet to cook an unsatisfactory dish from her recipes (with the possible exception of parsleyed eggs — they're green and weird looking). Her text is informative, informal, and easy to follow, with suggested menu plans, a discussion of handy and necessary tools, and basic instructions at the beginning of each chapter. The line drawings are delightful, and convey the spirit of the books; a sense of joy in both the preparation and eating of epicurean vegetarian meals.*

—Evelyn Eldridge-Diaz

The Vegetarian Epicure
Anna Thomas
1972; 305 pp.

$5.95 postpaid

The Vegetarian Epicure
(Book Two)
Anna Thomas
1978; 401 pp.

$6.95 postpaid
both from:
Alfred A. Knopf, Inc.
455 Hahn Road
Westminster, MD 21157
or Whole Earth Household Store

•

People have approached me, puzzled, and asked how vegetarians eat. Their puzzlement is genuine. They try to imagine their own meals without meat and shudder. But when I imagine their meals I shudder too, because the standard American diet is so appalling in its lack of imagination. Even in finer cooking, the variety is largely limited to the preparation of the main course, almost without exception meat or fish. The menu is thus rigidly standardized. There is one important item: the entree. In a very secondary place, really playing the role of uninspired accompaniment to the meat, are such things as salad, vegetables, and bread. The standard menu is served with but little change from day to day or week to week, the "square" meal certainly is.

Vegetarian cookery is not a substitute for anything. It is a rich and various cuisine, full of many marvelous dishes with definite characteristics not in imitation of anything else — certainly not in imitation of meat.

—The Vegetarian Epicure

•

To make an individual omelet, two eggs are generally sufficient, but three can be used if the appetite warrants it. Beat the eggs briefly in a bowl with a pinch of salt and a smaller pinch of pepper, as well as a dash of milk or cream if you like. Heat an 8- or 9-inch omelet pan and melt about 1 tablespoon butter in it, swirling the butter all over the bottom of the pan. When the butter has melted and foamed and the foam has begun to subside, set a medium flame, pour in the beaten eggs, and tilt the pan around gently so that the eggs spread evenly over the bottom. In a moment, the eggs will begin to set. When they do, run the spatula once around the edge of the omelet to loosen it, and shake the pan a bit. Then start carefully lifting the edges with your spatula and tilting the pan to let the uncooked eggs on top run to the bottom.

In less than a minute, the omelet will be nearly done. Give the pan another quick shake to keep the eggs from sticking. The top of the omelet, at this point, should be moist but not runny. If you are filling your omelet, spoon in some of the prepared filling now. Then slip a spatula under one side and fold it over the other. Leave the omelet in the pan just a few seconds more before sliding it out onto a warm plate. The omelet should be golden in color and tender and creamy inside. And it must be served immediately!

—The Vegetarian Epicure, Part Two

THE RISING SUN
NEIGHBORHOOD NEWSLETTER

"I'd like something Brian Eno would wear please."
—David in the clothes store

One Bowl

Get in touch with what and how you eat and the way it feels to your body; you'll eat what's good for you and in a quantity appropriate for your own metabolism. In fifty-four pages of simple, clear prose, Don Gerrard offers concepts and practices to eliminate distractions from our eating and make it meaningful. There's not a word devoted to magic lists of foods to avoid or panacea substitutes. And the daily moment-of-truth on the bathroom scales is abandoned since it focuses on external rather than internal feedback. —Andrew Fluegelman

One Bowl
Don Gerrard
1974; 54 pp.
$1.45 postpaid from:
Random House
455 Hahn Road
Westminster, MD 21157
or Whole Earth
Household Store

•

Try to make yourself comfortable eating this way — from your bowl, in courses — before you move on to develop this diet concept further. For example, it takes time to figure out how to eat a breakfast of cereal, eggs, sausage and toast all from a bowl. It takes time for it to feel okay to eat foods one at a time. It also takes more time to do the eating. You will be surprised, however, just how satisfying this can be. After a meal, each food will linger more distinctly in your memory, and eating will have been a series of gifts, linked together by your bowl.

•

The next development in this concept is to begin eating alone. Maintain your same diet of foods as before, eating from your bowl, in courses. But now begin eating alone. Pick a favorite room or area of your living space and go there alone with your bowl. Make yourself comfortable in all the ways you know you like, and eat. Once you think about it, you might choose to eat in bed, or on your back porch, or in a corner of the living room. Help yourself. You need not always eat in the same place, but do always eat in a place you like.

The Ten Talents

For at least a hundred years the Seventh Day Adventists have practiced vegetarianism as part of their religion. For years before any other westerners they were turning soybeans into edible food. ***The Ten Talents*** *reflects their concern that their food be good to eat as well as vegetarian. An excellent cookbook.* —Evelyn Eldridge-Diaz

A Good Cook . . .
Ten Talents
Frank J. Hurd, D.C. and
Rosalie Hurd, B.S.
1968; 369 pp.
$9.95 postpaid from:
Ten Talents Press
P.O. Box 86A
Route 1
Chisholm, MN 55719
or Whole Earth
Household Store

Simple Bread Roast
(Really good!)

Bread—hard, day old, leftover, any kind
McKays or Washington Broth
Onion, chopped fine sauteéd in oil (3 lg. onions for every loaf bread)

1. Sauté onions in oil using large skillet. When tender and not brown add broken bread (small cubes) a little at a time till soaked and steamed through.
2. Add poultry seasoning and salt to taste. Mix.
3. Make a broth of McKays or Washington seasoning. Pour this slowly over bread and onions in skillet turning over with fork till bread is moistened and mixed evenly. Add enough broth so it will not be too dry after baking.
4. Brush top with oil. Bake in shallow covered pan at 300° for 30 minutes. Uncover, and bake for 10 minutes.

VARIATIONS: This roast may be packed in a loaf pan with sautéed celery, and finely chopped nuts. Bake in oiled pan. Slice.

•

Beverages may be made with sprouts. Liquify them with tomato juice, fruits, or milk. No one will ever suspect that he is eating sprouts. Drinks made with sprouts are highly nourishing. If he appreciates good nourishment, tell him. If not just serve him quietly. He will appreciate it some day when he feels like a million! Try these luscious drinks.

Pineapple Juice
Sprouted
Sunflower Seeds

Tomato Juice
Alfalfa Sprouts

Carrot or Celery
Juice
Alfalfa Sprouts

Strawberries
or Pears
Sprouted
Sunflower Seeds

Prune Juice
Wheat Sprouts

Hot Carob
(soy or cashew)
Sprouted
Sunflower Seeds

How to Cook and Eat in Chinese

Chinese cookbooks always make me feel like I have two left hands, and cooking from them like I have four feet. Not this one. Ms. Chao makes it all simple, amusing, and delicious. Hundreds of recipes, every Chinese dish I've ever heard of, plus. Rant, rave. Health, variety, probably long life. —Diana Barich

•

Sizzling — Sizzling is the act of throwing fried rice toast into hot clear soup. There are various forms of this. Usually, you make a clear soup with Szechwan *cho-ts'ai*, a tasty, slightly hot salted vegetable. Rice toast is the burned-bottom layer of rice which is formed by continued heating after the rice is done. (The burning of neglected rice at the *beginning* of boiling is a different affair and does not give such a good smell.) After the rice toast is dry after some hours, it is deep-fried and then sizzled into the soup at the table. In Chungking this dish has recently been named "Bomb Tokyo."

How to Cook and Eat in Chinese
Buwei Yang Chao
1945, 1972; 249 pp.
$2.45 postpaid from:
Vintage Books
Random House
455 Hahn Road
Westminster, MD 21157
or Whole Earth
Household Store

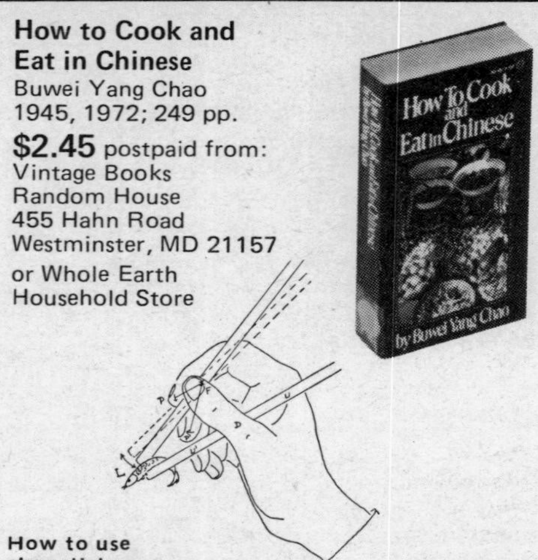

How to use chopsticks

Quantity Recipes • Simplified Quantity Regional Recipes

In a commune I lived in in New Mexico we had two major problems: food and sex. These books will go a long way to helping you solve the first. What a drag to take down the ***Joy of Cooking****, find something really great to fix for yourself and friends and have to spend a half an hour multiplying all the ingredients by seven or eight knowing that you couldn't possibly need a cup of oregano in the chili, but that's what your figures say. We ate some pretty bad experiments and several of the women and men shied away forever from anything but the lettuce salads. Enormous pots of food take a certain skill or they become enormous pots of glop.*

In my opinion the recipes in these books are basic — that is, I would add here and there seasonings, etc. to make the food special, new, hopefully an experience and not just another meal. Like all cook books they finally become a guide rather than a road. After a few weeks, or months, cooking creatively can get a bit strained. Then other cook books will pull you through with the advantage of already being adjusted for a large group. —Steve Katona

Quantity Recipes
Marion A. Wood and
Katherine A. Harris
1945, 1973; 233 pp.
$2.50 postpaid from:
Distribution Center
Seven Research Park
Cornell University
Ithaca, NY 14850

Simplified Quantity Regional Recipes
Mabel Cavaiani, Muriel
Urbashich and
Frances Nielson
1979; 214 pp.
$13.95 postpaid from:
Hayden Book Company
50 Essex Street
Rochelle Park, NJ 07662

BOSTON BAKED BEANS
(New England)

YIELD: 50 portions (about 3 gallons) **PORTION SIZE:** 1 cup
PAN SIZE: Roaster **TEMPERATURE:** 350°F Oven

INGREDIENTS	WEIGHTS/MEASURES	FOR_____	METHOD
Dry great northern or pea beans Cold water	8 pounds (4 2/3 quarts 2 1/2 gallons		1. Pick over beans. Remove any dark or discolored beans. Wash thoroughly with cold water. Drain well. Cover with cold water and bring to a boil. Boil 2 minutes. Remove from heat. 2. Cover beans and let stand 1 to 2 hours.
Hot water	As necessary		3. Bring beans and water in which they were soaked to a boil. Add hot water, if necessary, to cover beans. Cover and simmer 1 1/2 hours or until beans are tender but not mushy.
Chopped onions Salt Brown sugar Molasses Vinegar Ground mustard Ground cloves Salt pork with rind removed and cut into 1/2-inch pieces Hot water	1 quart 1/4 cup 2 1/2 cups 2 cups 1/4 cup 1/4 cup 1 teaspoon 2 pounds As necessary		4. Add onions, salt, brown sugar, molasses, vinegar, mustard, cloves, and salt pork to beans. Mix thoroughly and place in roaster. 5. Cover roaster and bake 3 to 4 hours. Add extra hot water, if necessary, to keep beans just covered with juice the first 3 hours. Remove the cover the last hour to allow beans to brown. Stir beans once during the last hour to mix the brown top into the beans.

DIETARY INFORMATION:
May be used as written for general, high-fiber, and bland diets.
Low-cholesterol: Delete salt pork and add 1 pound margarine in step 4.

—**Simplified Quantity Regional Recipes**

The Thickening of Sauces and Gravies Made Easy
The melted fat and flour are first cooked together, then poured into the hot liquid and cooked until thickened. Stirring with a wire whip throughout prevents lumping; cooking over hot water prevents scorching.
—**Quantity Recipes**

The Art of Making Sausages, Patés, and Other Charcuterie

Charcuterie is the French name for the art of pork alchemy. It's ancient (Grigson includes a Roman recipe for ham, recorded by Cato in 200 B.C., that is still usable). Most people who eat meat love ham and sausage. It can be a miraculously low capital industry. My investment was a 25 dollar first-class hand meatgrinder with a sausage-horn and a 35 dollar electric smoker from Sears' catalog. —Birrell Walsh

The Art of Making Sausages, Patés and Other Charcuterie
Jane Grigson
1967, 1976; 376 pp.
$6.95 postpaid from:
Alfred A. Knopf, Inc.
455 Hahn Road
Westminster, MD
21157
or Whole Earth
Household Store

•

Probably the English pig — which is called a "bacon-type" pig in the United States — is now being taken too far toward leanness, at any rate for the finer points of *charcuterie*. He has become too much a factory animal: we neglect his ears, his tail, his trotters, his insides, his beautiful fat, and his flavor (pig's ears by the hundred thousand are fed to mink, from one of the Wiltshire bacon factories, which is a bit like feeding caviar to canaries). But with a little care and persistence the English housewife can bully out of her butcher what is known as "overweight pig," and for very little money she can obtain the fat parts, as well as the extremities and the offal — the basis of many of the most delicate and delightful dishes it is possible to make. The American housewife, on the other hand, I am told, has it easier, because the pork sold in the United States comes from "butcher-type" pigs, which have much more fat than our English ones. The skillful and economical housewife can buy a pig's head for $2 to $2.50; this is what she can make from it — pig's ears with a piquant sauce, brains in puff pastry, Bath chap, 1½ lbs. of sausage meat for making pate or *crepinettes*, and some excellent *rillons* which are more usually made from belly of pork. There is an average 4½ lbs. of boneless meat on a pig's head. And an excellent clear soup or aspic jelly is to be made from the bones.

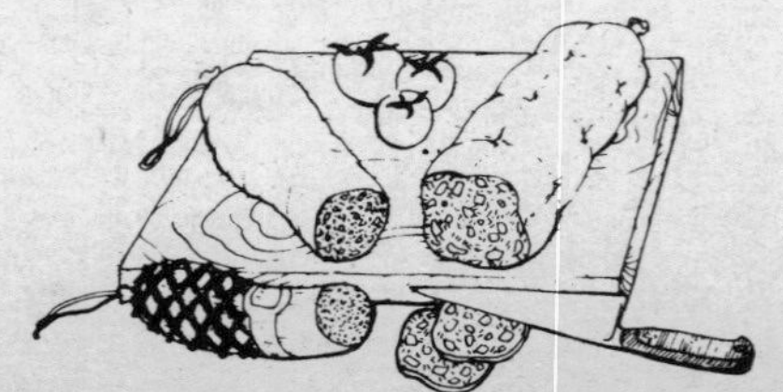

Unmentionable Cuisine

This engrossing book of lore and recipes makes a great contribution to eco-cuisine which ain't of the vegetarian persuasion.

Unmentionable Cuisine *gives the how and why of eating all the icky parts of conventional livestock, then goes on to suggest that eating surplus dogs, cats, starlings, and giant African snails could be a way for Americans to have protein while muddling towards frugality. I say Americans, because other cultures have been eating weird things for millenia, and with gusto. In fact, most of the recipes Calvin Schwabe presents are traditional, some of them dating way back into Europe's pagan past, when communicants drank real blood.*

Eaters of road kills, pet haters, eco-hunters, and truly serious cooks should find this book indispensable. It suggests savory ways to get your goat (or eel or porcupine), and how to do it sanitarily and in good taste.

—Stephanie Mills

Unmentionable Cuisine
Calvin W. Schwabe
1980; 423 pp.
$20 postpaid from:
University Press of Virginia
Box 3608
University Station
Charlottesville, VA 22903

•

Broiled Puppy/Hawaii

The delicate puppy meat usually is prepared by flattening out the entire eviscerated animal and broiling it over hot coals. It also may be spitted on sticks. The traditional Hawaiian accompaniment for dog cooked in any way is sweet potatoes.

•

Lampreys

The lampreys, or cyclostomes, are primitive, smooth-skinned, eel-shaped cartilaginous fish with suckerlike mouths by which they attach to and feed on other fish. The completion in 1921 of the Welland Canal bypassing Niagara Falls permitted lampreys to enter the Great Lakes of North America, where they have played havoc with valuable commercial and sports fisheries. Lampreys, which also are distributed widely in rivers on both coasts of the United States, are themselves excellent eating, a fact that is little appreciated by Americans. The flesh of lampreys is particularly delicate, and they are prized highly in France. This is another instance where consumption at our dinner tables could help to keep a very destructive pest species under control.

Basic Preparation

Before cooking, lampreys often are bled first, then scalded briefly in boiling water, and skinned by scraping with a knife. The spinal cord is removed by cutting off the end of the tail, then hooking the cord through an incision behind the gills and drawing it out. Lastly, the animal is eviscerated.

•

Shark with Raisins and Pine Nuts *(Tiburon con pasas y pinones)*/**Spain**

From the nutritional standpoint the 23 percent protein and 0.2 percent fat of shark meat compares with 14.7 and 32.1 percent, respectively, for T-bone steak. Shark fillets are also one of the cheapest fish meats available today, and they may be prepared to advantage by virtually any recipes suitable for firm-fleshed fish. The only shark recipes I have included, therefore, are just a few more unusual recipes, including two shark classics from the cuisines of Iceland and China.

Shake small pieces of shark in a paper bag containing flour and fry them in very hot olive oil. Add chopped onion and brown it well. Throw in a chopped tomato, some raisins, pine nuts, crushed garlic, chopped parsley, paprika, and black pepper. Simmer a few minutes and serve.

Better Than Store Bought

Emphasizing recipes for foods that are usually thought of as "store bought," the authors demonstrate the wide variety of foods that can be made better and cheaper at home. They include everything from condiments, sausages, and cream cheese to marshmallows, hot dog buns, and hot fudge sauce. The authors know their stuff and have put together a cookbook that is fascinating to read and fun to use. *—Norm Shea*

Better Than Store Bought
(A Cookbook)
Helen Witty and
Elizabeth Schneider Colchie
1979; 325 pp.
$12.95 postpaid from:
Harper and Row
Keystone Industrial Park
Scranton, PA 18512
or Whole Earth
Household Store

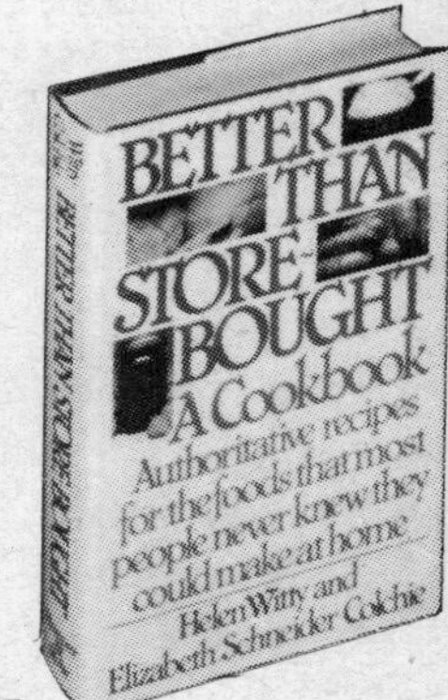

HOT FUDGE SAUCE

This is the way we think hot fudge should be. It is thick and bittersweet and hardens *just* enough when you spoon it over ice cream.

Makes about 2½ cups

¾ stick (6 tablespoons) unsalted butter
6 ounces (6 squares) unsweetened baking chocolate
1 cup boiling water
2 cups sugar
½ cup light corn syrup
¼ teaspoon salt
1½ teaspoons vanilla extract

1. Combine the butter and chocolate in a heavy saucepan and stir over low heat until melted. Stir in the water, sugar, corn syrup, and salt.

2. Turn the heat to medium and bring the mixture to a boil, stirring. Boil the sauce gently, without stirring, for about 8 to 9 minutes, or until it is thickened and smooth. Stir in the vanilla extract and serve hot. (Or you may store it in the refrigerator for months.)

Mastering the Art of French Cooking — I & II

The authors — Julia Child, Simone Beck, Louisette Bertholle — wrote these cookbooks because they felt and wanted to prove, that anyone, anywhere, could learn classical French cuisine techniques if they were provided with the correct instruction. By following their basic recipes carefully step by step you will find when you've finished that you have not only created a delightful dish, but also mastered a skill which can then be used in combination with many other techniques to continue creating masterpieces. One of the nice features is that wherever possible they tell you when something can be made in advance, or when the process can be interrupted, say overnight or for a few hours. All the ingredients are readily available in American supermarkets, so there's no tearing your hair out about unavailable esoteric condiments. These are definitely the books to start with if your tastes lean to classical French cooking.

—Evelyn Eldridge-Diaz

Mastering the Art of French Cooking
(Volume One)
Julia Child, Louisette Bertholle, Simone Beck
1961, 1979; 716 pp.
$15 postpaid

Mastering the Art of French Cooking
(Volume Two)
Julia Child and Simone Beck
1970, 1979; 618 pp.
$15 postpaid
both from:
Alfred A. Knopf, Inc.
455 Hahn Road
Westminster, MD 21157
or Whole Earth Household Store

How to Truss a Chicken

A whole chicken should be trussed so the legs, wings, and neck skin are held in place during its cooking, and the bird will make a neat and attractive appearance on the table. The following French method calls for a trussing or mattress needle and white string. There are two ties, one at the tail end to secure the drumsticks, and one at the breast end to fasten the wings and neck skin.

Tie Number 1 — Thrust the needle through the lower part of the carcass.

Come back over one drumstick, through the tip of the breastbone, and over the second drumstick. Tie.

Tie Number 2 — Push the needle through the carcass where the second joint and drumstick join, coming out at the corresponding point on the other side.

Turn the chicken on its breast. Fold the wings akimbo. Go through one wing, catch the neck skin against either side of the backbone, and come out the other wing. Draw the string tightly and tie.

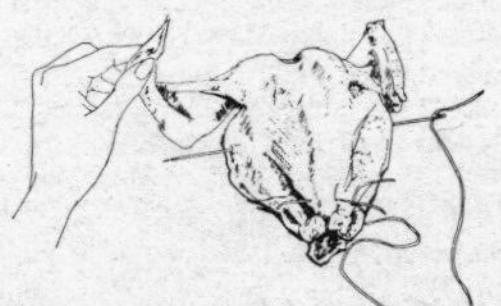

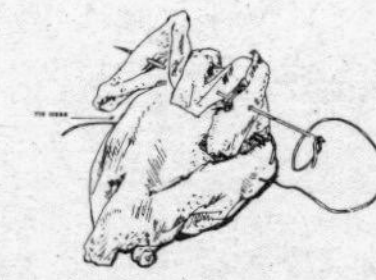

The chicken is now ready for oven roasting, spit roasting, or poaching.
—Mastering the Art of French Cooking (Volume One)

Simple French Food
French Provincial Cooking

These two volumes should be companions on the book shelf. Both deal with the types of foods you will find at French cafe routier, country inns and farmer's tables rather than the haute cuisine of the city restaurants. David's book contains deliciously simple recipes requiring a minimum of ingredients and explanations. Olney's has both simple and complex recipes, but his erudition in the subject of French cooking is superb. If you have to choose between the two, I recommend David's. *—Paul Hawken*

•

A whole unboned stuffed roast rabbit may be a thing of beauty, but it is impossible to carve; the stuffing is crushed and scattered and the flesh shredded as one attempts to sever sections of the backbone and the large quantity of stuffing engulfed by the rib cage can only be reached with a spoon once the initial carnage is finished. A boned stuffed saddle is cut into neat slices without further ado.

—Simple French Food

•

Potage Bonne Femme

This old-fashioned French soup is the cheapest and one of the nicest of all vegetable soups.

1 lb. potatoes, 3 carrots, 2 large leeks, 1½ oz. butter, 2 pints water, seasoning. To finish the soup, a little cream, parsley, or chervil when available.

Melt the butter in your soup pan, put in the cleaned and finely sliced leeks and the diced carrots. Let them get thoroughly hot and saturated with the butter; add the peeled and diced potatoes, the water, a little salt, a lump or two of sugar. Cook steadily but not at a gallop for 25 to 30 minutes. Sieve through the finest mesh of the *mouli*, twice if necessary. Taste for seasoning, and when ready to serve add the cream, and parsley or chervil chopped very, very finely. Enough for four.

The carrots are not essential to the soup, but they add a little extra flavour and colour.

—French Provincial Cooking

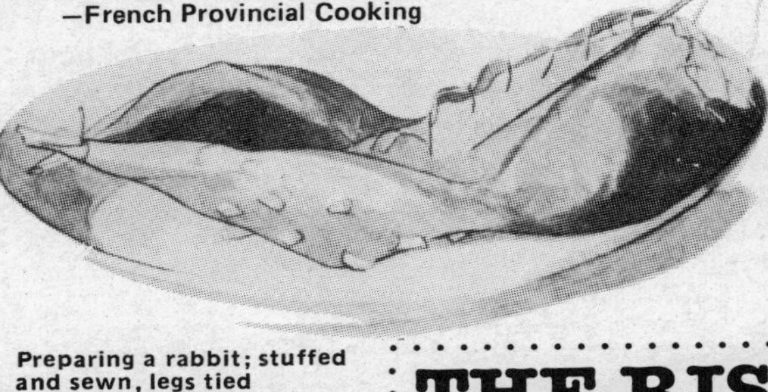

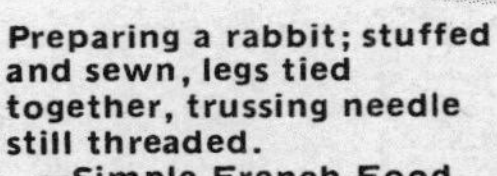

Preparing a rabbit; stuffed and sewn, legs tied together, trussing needle still threaded.
—Simple French Food

Simple French Food
Richard Olney
1977; 433 pp.
$5.95 postpaid from:
Atheneum Publishers
Book Warehouse, Inc.
Vreeland Avenue
Totowa, NJ 07812
or Whole Earth
Household Store

French Provincial Cooking
Elizabeth David
1960, 1970; 584 pp.
$3.50 postpaid from:
Penguin Books
299 Murray Hill Parkway
East Rutherford, NJ 07073
or Whole Earth-Household Store

THE RISING SUN
NEIGHBORHOOD NEWSLETTER

The first concert in a new concert hall is called the hard hat concert and is for people who built it. —Nancy

Woodstove Cookery

I learned to cook on a woodstove and have been adjusting my methods to gas and electric ranges ever since. There are definitely things to know and do and things not to do with a woodstove. (I burned off my eyelashes and eyebrows once when I poured kerosene on what I thought was a dead fire.) **Woodstove Cookery** *is a good way to find out what those rules are. Jane Cooper tells: how to choose a stove; how to use it properly; safety precautions and checks; and how to build fires for different kinds of cooking. What I like the best is that she has put down a lot of old-timers' hints and comments — some of them I recognize from my childhood. Many of her recipes have been culled from turn-of-the century cookbooks, when woodstove cookery was the only option. (More on woodstoves, see pp. 203 - 210.)* —Evelyn Eldridge-Diaz

Woodstove Cookery
(At Home on the Range)
Jane Cooper
1977; 196 pp.
$5.95 postpaid from:
Garden Way
Publishing Company
Charlotte, VT 05545
or Whole Earth
Household Store

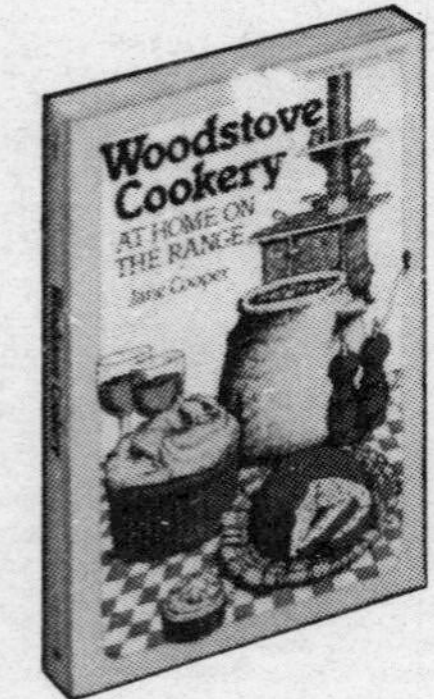

•

If you don't already own a wood range, some consideration should be given to what you might expect. Foremost, expect versatility. The stove's surface will provide any kind of heat, from blazing-hot to soothing-to-the-touch, accommodating any kind of frying, simmering or warming, be it food or wet socks. Warming ovens and water reservoirs perform numerous jobs, and some wood stoves are even capable of heating the domestic water supply.

Also, expect flavor. Foods can cook for hours, allowing time for the different ingredients to mingle and harmonize, a service the more frugal-minded might be reluctant to utilize on a stove powered by electricity or gas.

As well as fulfilling a functional role, a wood cookstove also appeals to the senses. Well-polished and clean, it is a pleasure to behold. The feel of its heat is soothing and steady, and the expanding metal ticks with contentment. The aromas from the burning wood and cooking food enrich the air, and citrus peels or cloves, scattered in the back, release a rewarding fragrance.

•

"Cooking on a wood stove changes your timing. It's a different rhythm. You start the fire, put on a pan, and cut your onions. By the time they're cut, the stove is hot enough to start sautéing. Between every cooking juncture, check to see if you need more wood. You have to adjust to the rhythm of the stove rather than the stove conforming to you." —Victoria Weber, Bethel, VT

•

"Many test their ovens this way: If the hand can be held in 20 - 25 seconds, it is a 'quick oven,' 35 - 45 seconds is 'moderate,' and 45 - 60 seconds is 'slow.' All systematic housekeepers will hail the day when some enterprising Yankee or Buckeye girl shall invent a stove or range with a thermometer attached to the oven, so that the heat may be regulated accurately and intelligently."
Practical Housekeeper, 1884

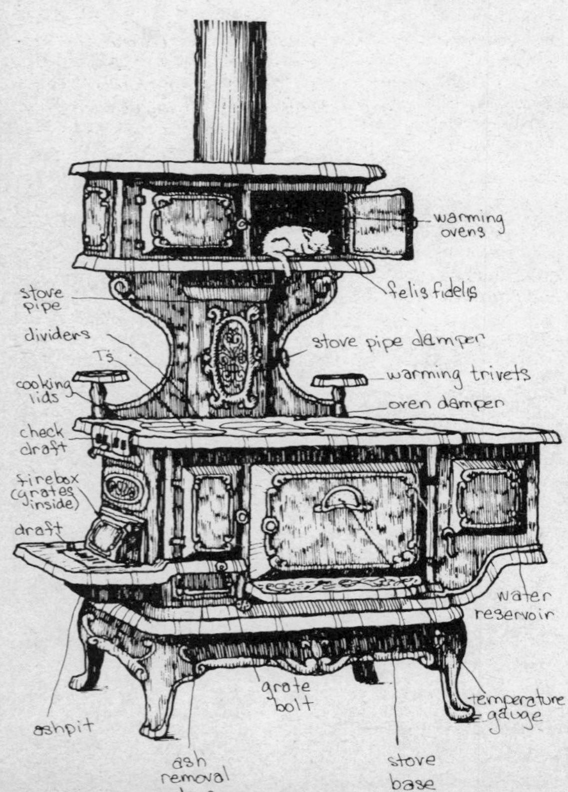

Garden Way Country Kitchen Catalog

Kitchen things I haven't seen since helping my grandmother and aunts put up fruit and vegetables, at prices they would still like. Old-fashioned tools and newfangled time-savers. —Evelyn Eldridge-Diaz

Garden Way Country Kitchen Catalog

free from:
Garden Way Catalog
Charlotte, VT 05445

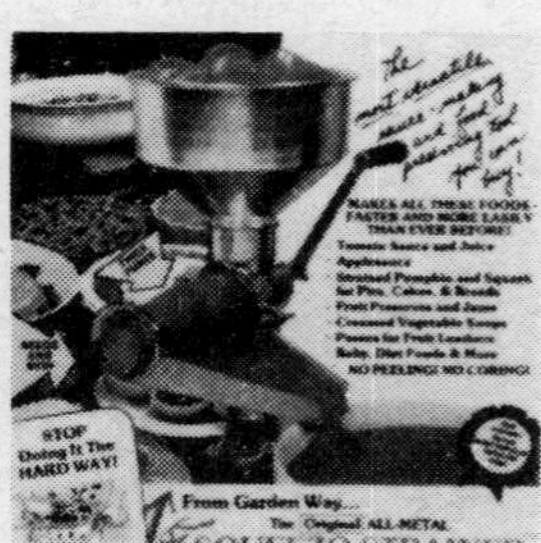

← **The Squeezo Strainer has become the tool used most to make the thickest smoothest tomato or apple sauce you've ever tasted! All without a trace of seed or skin — and without ever having to peel or core a single tomato or apple!**

No. 101 Squeezo Strainer with 1/16" Standard Screen $35.90

Though not designed for big jobs, this all-metal sheller is an efficient time-saver. As you feed pods through rollers, shelled peas fall into bowl. Hand crank or power with your mixer or drill.

Clamp-On Sheller ↓ $14.95

↑ **Blackbird-in-a-pie**

What a dainty dish to set before a king! And this ceramic blackbird in your pie serves a very practical purpose. As your pie bakes, its juices enter the bird's hollow interior instead of flowing over the edge of the pan. No need to puncture your crust — steam escapes from the bird's mouth. This delightfully old-fashioned baking helper is from New England. 4½" tall.

Ceramic Pie Bird $4.98

A. Stainless Vollrath Bucket

Experienced cheesemakers insist on mixing and setting cheese curds in heavy-gauge, stainless steel containers like this long-lasting, all-purpose 12½ qt. Vollrath bucket. It's seamless for greater sanitation, and its strong handle won't bend or come loose under the heaviest loads. 12" rim dia. x 10" h.

No. 3509 Stainless Vollrath Bucket $27

B. Stainless Curd Knife

The stainless blade of our curd knife is over a foot long to reach right to the bottom of deep cheese pails. Hardwood handle stays free of "set" milk, so important for cutting the curd evenly.

No. 3501 Stainless Curd Knife ↓ $14.50

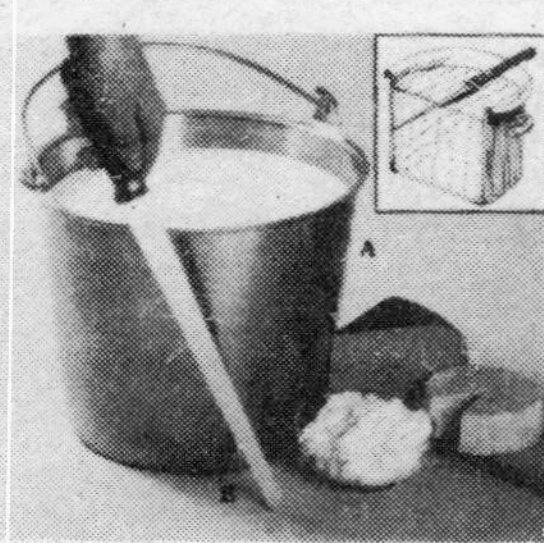

↑ **Cast-iron Kettle**

Keep this large, fine-looking 6 qt. kettle simmering on your woodstove. It serves as an efficient humidifier. And because it's cast-iron, it radiates all the warm good feelings we have when we think of the old kettle steaming on grandmother's kitchen hearth. Made to last for generations.

No. 624 Cast-Iron Kettle $47.95

Basic Living Products

Wowee. A whole gamut of food preparation and other gear (building, stoves, energy stuff) at very low prices. —SB

Basic Living Products
(Formerly Whole Earth Access Company)
Catalog
free from:
Basic Living Products
2990 Seventh Street
Berkeley, CA 94710

6-pc. 12" Wok Set (wok, aluminum cover, reversible ring, wood steam rack, chopsticks, booklet)

Manufacturer's Suggested Price	Basic Living Products Price
$30.24	$24.19

The Cooks' Catalogue

This is a wish book, listing over 4000 items, loaded with folklore, recipes, and some useful information about evaluating kitchen tools. From it, you will get an idea of the fantastic elaborations of cuisine. The editors list multitudes of esoteric devices which could well become mandatory if one developed certain culinary fetishes.

If you are a cook of the funkadelic variety however, you'd welcome this book as a gift, wish it were in your public library, and buy it if you came into money. This latter condition is not just because **The Cook's Catalogue** *is itself a bit of a high-ticket item, but because the dreamy stuff it lists is mostly expensive.* —Stephanie Mills

The Cooks' Catalogue
James Beard, Milton Glaser, Burton Wolf, et al., Editors
1975, 1979; 565 pp.
$9.20 postpaid from:
Avon Books
Mail Order Department
250 West 55th Street
New York, NY 10019
or Whole Earth
Household Store

Soft-boiled Egg Cutter — aluminum; 4" long. $2.90.

Compulsive consumers of soft-boiled eggs like to make neat work of slicing through the shell — not for them the jagged edge left by an ordinary spoon. Having tested various eggshell cutters that work on the scissors principle, our experts have vetoed them all in favor of this doohickey. The small metal cup is topped by a knob — the maker calls it a "spring hammer" — which is attached by a strong, flat spring. Place the cup over the small end of the egg, pull up on the knob twice, and whang! the top of the shell is neatly excised by vibration. No shell fragments to mar the golden liquid of the yolk or to lie disguised in the white, and no burnt fingers. You might even be able to lure your little ones away from their customary bowl of sugar-frosted crunchy munchies to a healthful soft-boiled egg for breakfast with the promise of using this gadget.

Baking Soda

For $ .49/lb. you can buy a humble tool that replaces a lot of fancy-priced ones: Arm and Hammer baking soda.

Potential uses —

1. *Toothpaste.* Mix soda with salt, for the kind of toothpaste oldtime Texas dentists used to say was better than storebought.
2. *Acid indigestion tablet substitute.* Just take a little soda with a glass of water.
3. *Scouring powder.* Especially good in refrigerators, because it deodorizes.
4. *Sunburn ointment substitute.* Spread on paste of soda and water.
5. *Putting out kitchen fires.*
6. *Deodorizing rugs and upholstery.* Sprinkle on, vacuum off. As good as that fancy spray-on stuff.
7. *Maybe even baking?*

—Anonymous

Bibble Ledbetter adds:

For those who still smoke you can put some on your car ash trays to absorb the odor and safely snuff your cigarette out.

It's a great refresher when added to your bath.

Use it when I clean my iron skillets, cutting boards, knives, etc. It not only helps to remove baked on foods but it does not leave a detergent taste to the equipment like the above that tend to absorb odors.

Bibble Ledbetter
Washington, D.C.

Home Beermaking

by Donald Ryan

Barley was humankind's first cultivated grain and was probably fermented into beer somewhat before the first baker made the first loaf of bread. There's a lot of literature available to help you become part of that history.

The World Guide to Beer serves as an excellent introduction to the product, if you need one, and any of the home brewing guides can lead you through the process and the alternatives. The ingredients will be found at any of the stores that carry home wine and beer making supplies, and most of the utensils are probably already in your kitchen. Malt solution must be boiled only in a stainless steel or enameled steel pot. A plastic wastebasket makes a dandy primary fermenter and the traditional secondary fermenter is a 5 gallon glass water bottle with a fermentation lock on the top. A hydrometer must be used to test the progress of fermentation.

A Treatise on Lager Beers

This is one of the books most frequently recommended by other home-brewing authors. Eckhardt has obviously spent a great deal of time and thought on beermaking and especially on the relatively long, refrigerated, secondary fermentation called lagering, and as such this book is a good complement to the British books with their emphasis on the relatively quicker and warmer fermenting ales. There are recipes for ales and steam beer and the "your first simple beer" recipe calls for corn sugar as a major ingredient, but Eckhardt pushes the advantages of using all malt and makes it clear what he considers to be the True Path. Included is an interesting matrix-type recipe for thirty German-style beers — all one page spread! Very competent book. Eckhardt is also the editor of **The Amateur Brewer**.

A Treatise on Lager Beers
(How to Make Good Beer at Home)
Fred Eckhardt
1970, 1979; 53 pp.
5th Edition

$2 postpaid from:
Fred Eckhardt Associates
P.O. Box 546
Portland, OR 97207

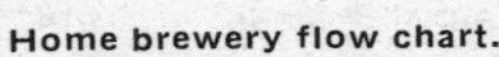

Home brewery flow chart.

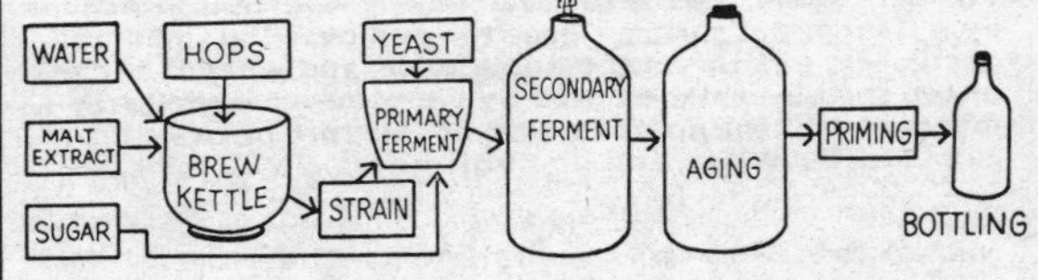

The World Guide to Beer

Whether you favor a Henry's after a dusty volleyball game on Gate Five Road or take an icy Coors in one hand as you finesse your way through afternoon traffic on Pacific Coast Highway in your Speedster or remember a shared Bière d'Alsace in the gently quaking shade of an ancient chestnut, you'll LOVE this book. It has all the malty warmth of Optimator and the rosy fragrance of dry-hopped Anchor Steam. It has lore galore. **The World Guide** *is at once literate, humorous, thorough, and graphically arresting as Jackson traces the History and the histories, and identifies the personalities behind the world's breweries and their beers. There's enough technical detail to interest the home brewer though the book in no way attempts to even introduce that craft; this is a book for the consumer. There is tremendous variety in the hundreds of breweries and beers produced on every continent from the straits of Good Hope and Magellan and from New Zealand through the torrid and intemperate zones of Great Consumption to the Arctic Circle. They're all here and the flavor comes right through. Makes me thirsty.*

The World Guide to Beer
Michael Jackson, Editor
1977; 255 pp.

$7.95 postpaid from:
Ballantine Books
455 Hahn Road
Westminster, MD 21157
or Whole Earth Household Store

The *Kalevala*, the national epic of Finland, manages to describe the creation of the world in 200 verses, but requires 400 in which to explain the origins of beer. No wonder Julius Caesar described it as "a high and mighty liquor."

Quality Brewing

One of the competent straightforward beermaking books with little of the chumminess of the English books and none of the giggly humor of a whole raft of American homebrew books (none reviewed here) whose sometimes-good recipes and competent advice are buried by cutesy titles (usually involving plays on words), long anecdotes, and lots of back- and thigh-slapping jokes. Burch has a very thorough section on procedures and quite a detailed description of the properties of various hop varieties. And he has some terrific recipes. I brewed a batch of his "Full Bodied Brown Bitter Ale" that brought tears to the eyes of Anglomaltophiles (good tears, not bad tears), and my "Irish Type Stout" from his recipe was proclaimed by one who had been there to be as good as any that'd flowed from behind St. James Gate, Dublin (that's Guinness, mates). The latest edition of **Quality Brewing** *includes the recipe for the stout that won Burch the gold medal in international competition in Spring 1980.*

Quality Brewing
(A Guidebook for the Home Production of Fine Beers)
Byron Burch
1974, 1979; 50 pp.

$3.25 postpaid from:
Great Fermentations
87 Larkspur Street
San Rafael, CA 94901

A quiet revolution has been taking place these last few years in the world of home brewing. So sweeping have been the changes that a practitioner of ten years ago would hardly recognize his craft (had he not kept up in the meantime). Fortunately the new developments have resulted in vastly better beers. Significant advances have been made in the twin realms of technology and ingredients. The home brewer can now appropriate virtually all beneficial practices of the commercial brewery. By applying these techniques to top quality malts, hops, and yeasts, he can create superb beers.

Mail order brewing supplies

Read one of the brewing books before you send for catalogs. Look for local suppliers in your Yellow Pages under "Brewer's Equipment and Supplies" or "Winemaking Supplies." The following list is only a sample.

Wine and the People, 907 University Avenue, Berkeley, CA 94710. *Great newsletter.*

E.C. Kraus, P.O. Box 7850, Independence, MO 64053.

Semplex of U.S.A., 4805 Lyndale Ave. N., Minneapolis, MN 55430. *Old company with European origins.*

Duane Imports, Ltd., 508 Canal St., New York, NY 10013.

Brick Store Brewer's Supplies, The Common, Stratford, VT 05072. *Simple, clear catalog.*

Home Beermaking

Can't get much simpler than this. Another of the inside-every-homebrew-supply-store-there's-a-writer-tired-of-answering-questions-for-free books. Covers ingredients, process, refinements, alternatives, equipment and starts you with six classically simple recipes for ales, lagers, or steam beer. Crystal-clear and dry as the best pilsner, and spare of words — Moore says in mere paragraphs what Dave Line takes chapters to cover. And — blessed relief — the recipes are all malt — NO white or corn sugar except for priming. Looks great.

Home Beermaking
(The Complete Beginner's Guidebook)
William Moore
1980; 43 pp.

$2 postpaid from:
William's Brewing
P.O. Box 461
Oakland, CA 94604

San Francisco Steam Beer

A full-flavor lager beer with a strong hop aroma. For authenticity of flavor, ferment at 60 to 70 degrees F.

5 pounds light dry malt or 6 pounds light malt extract syrup
3/4 pound crushed crystal grain
4 ounces American Cascade hops
2 packets lager yeast
1 teaspoon gypsum
¼ teaspoon citric acid
4 ounces corn sugar (for carbonation)

Starting gravity 43, finishes at 14 or less. Alcohol 3.8%.

The Big Book of Brewing

None of the amateur brewers books are very big — many are almost brochures — but this one is bigger than most. For the home brewer this must be ranked as the most complete-in-one-place manual and includes malting (which is the sprouting of the grain barley — the very first stage of the starch-to-fermentable sugar conversion process — probably attempted by only the most adventuresome brewer), and esoterica such as reconditioning of old wooden casks. Line has devoted whole chapters to subjects discussed in mere paragraphs in most books. There is some technical discussion and a little math but nothing that should tax the intelligence of even most beer drinkers. With one caution the book is logically laid out and literate in the English fashion. The caution relates to that English fashion. Anyone who got a kick out of word-playing with the mis-translations that used to appear in the instructions for Japanese toys, for instance, will love English brewing books. It's a different language, my fellow Americans. But, like learning Japanese while reading **Shōgun**, *you'll pick it up as you go along. Lots of recipes and discussion of beer types, and also in the English fashion, too much white sugar.*

The Big Book of Brewing
Dave Line
1974; 256 pp.

$5 postpaid from:
Great Fermentations
87 Larkspur Street
San Rafael, CA 94901
or Whole Earth Household Store

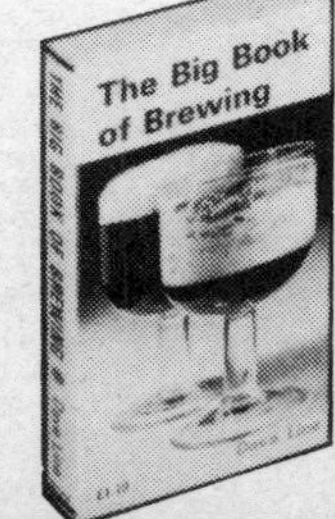

The Amateur Brewer

This is allegedly a quarterly "for the serious home brewer." You'd have to be a patient home brewer too. Editor Eckhardt's years get a little stretchy. As of summer 1980, his summer 1979 is still the current issue. But if you subscribe you get four issues anyhow — however long it takes. And it's worth waiting for. Very rich in technical tidbits and news from the commercial front, giving us access to the biggest research labs. Long articles discuss single beer types or arcana such as growing hops. Number Six, for instance, is devoted to articles about yeasts. Each issue has brewery news, club news, and book and product reviews. Not stylish and not humorous, but you'll appreciate what Eckhardt is doing.

The Amateur Brewer
Fred Eckhardt

$5.95 /four issues from:
Amateur Brewer
P.O. Box 546
Portland, OR 97207

THE RISING SUN
NEIGHBORHOOD NEWSLETTER

If you can tread on six daisies with one step, you know that summer is here.
—David's mother

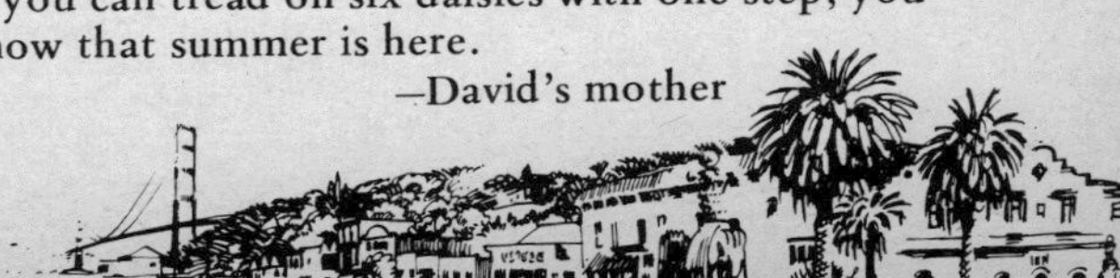

Home Fermenter's Digest

Published by a supplier of home fermenting goods, it talks to the winemakers and distillers (allegedly for fuel only — an in-joke of constant amusement to the home distillery crowd) as well as brewers. Friendly, supportive and readable. —Donald Ryan

Home Fermenter's Digest
Georgia M. Weathers, Editor
$6/year (6 issues) from:
Home Fermenter Publications
2761 Teagarden Street
San Leandro, CA 94577

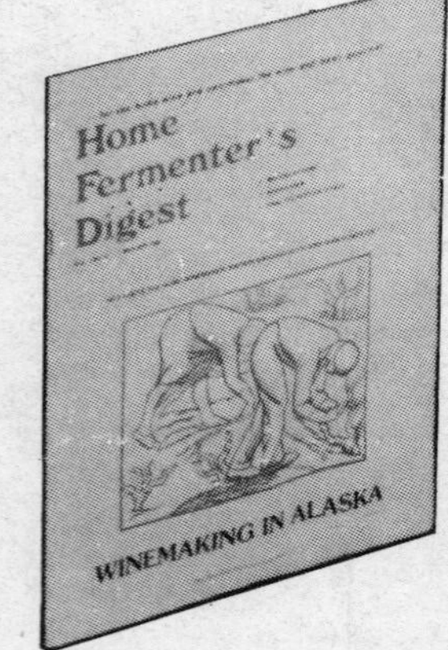

•

Gasohol

If you have an available copy, read Gil Russell's article on Gasohol in the first issue of **Home Fermenter's Digest**.

Then read **The Lore of Still Building** subtitled **Getting to Know Your Local Sheriff** by Gibat and Gibat, a husband and wife team living in Ohio. Before the current gas shortage, **Lore** was selling at the rate of about 8,000 copies, which is not bad. Since the shortage, sales have jumped to over 20,000 per year, even though the basic, original purpose of the book was to simply inform the reader about the history and state of the art or producing distilled alcohol for consumption. Since the end product is the same, whether you plan to drink it or burn it in your gas tank, people have been buying the book up in droves to make the popular substitute fuel, gasohol.

Home winemaking suppliers

The gear available to the home winemaker has become almost as sophisticated as that used in commercial operations, from high speed hand corkers to crushers that also take the stems off the grapes. Most large cities now have at least one store with a good line of winemaking equipment and chemicals. Check the yellow pages. Or write one of the following mail order suppliers and ask for a catalog. —Mike Palmer

The Compleat Winemaker
1201 Main Street
St. Helena, CA 94574

Danenberger Food Market
P.O. Box 276P
New Berlin, IL 62670

Great Fermentations
87 Larkspur Street
San Rafael, CA 94901

Lundberg's Wine Supplies
9562 Tamarind Avenue
Fontana, CA 92335

Oak Barrel Winecraft
1201 University Avenue
Berkeley, CA 94702

Semplex of U.S.A.
4805 Lyndale Avenue No.
Minneapolis, MN 55430

Wine and the People
907 University Avenue
Berkeley, CA 94710

Oak Barrel Winecraft

•

European Oval Oak Barrels, Best:

1 gal. 6 Black Hoops w/Bung, Spigot & Stand	$40
2 gal. 6 Black Hoops w/Bung, Spigot & Stand	$59
3 gal. 6 Black Hoops w/Bung, Spigot & Stand	$69
5 gal. 6 Black Hoops w/Bung, Spigot & Stand	$79
10 gal. 6 Black Hoops w/Bung, Spigot & Stand	$140

Weiner's Herbal

About 170 plant medicines with scientific updates on chemistry and modern medicinal experience. No info on collecting. Good info on preparations and dosages. —Peter Warshall

Weiner's Herbal
(The Guide to Herb Medicine)
Dr. Michael A. Weiner, et al.
1980; 224 pp.
$9.95 postpaid from:
Stein and Day, Publishers
Scarborough House
Briarcliff Manor, NY 10510
or Whole Earth Household Store

ALOE: Used for treating burns since the time of Cleopatra, this remarkable plant was found to be effective in treating radiation burns in the early 1950's.

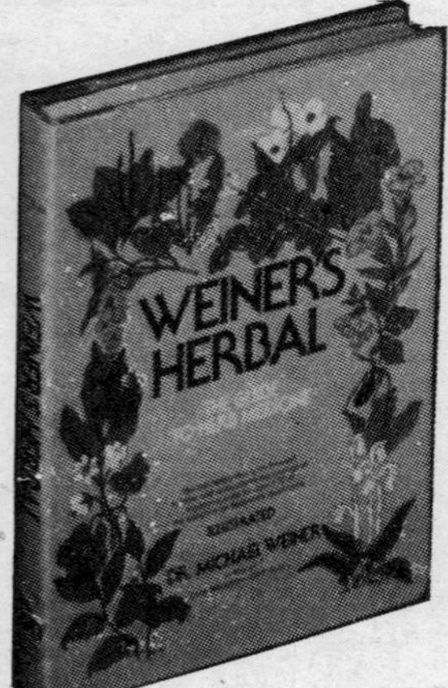

←
OAK, WHITE: Acorns are employed for their tonic and astringent properties. When applied locally, they tend to shrink hemorrhoids and often accelerate the healing of flabby ulcers.

RHUBARB: Here is an unusual medicine that combines cathartic with astringent properties. It first relieves constipation and then checks bowel evacuation through its astringent property. See cautions in text.

SQUILL: This Mediterranean bulb is a dangerous plant, making an excellent rat poison. When disguised in a mixture with other herbs as an encapsulated medicinal, it may be unintentionally fatal.

Medicines from the Earth

This extravagantly priced book is extravagantly the best. 250 of the Earth's most used plants for complaints and ailments. You can look them up by plant; by illness; by preparation into salves, teas or compresses; by constituents that have been identified thus far by science and by the best part for collection and the best season for collection. A lovely respect for the past combined by a delight in what we still have to learn from plant powers. —Peter Warshall

Medicines from the Earth
William Thomson, Editor
1978; 208 pp.

$29.95 postpaid from:
McGraw-Hill Book Co.
Princeton Road
Hightstown, NJ 08520
or Whole Earth Household Store

It has been estimated that only 10 percent of the organic constituents in the Plant Kingdom have been discovered. Modern phytochemistry, with extraordinarily new sophisticated techniques, must assure astonishing new finds in the next few years, when larger segments of the Plant Kingdom are thoroughly examined. For, to date, chemical studies have been desultory, erratic, and incomplete.

Ginseng and Other Medicinal Plants

Perhaps the most mystical symbiosis of human and plant physiology. The best book to home grow ginseng, Goldenseal and some others. Lovely prose. —Peter Warshall

Ginseng and Other Medicinal Plants
A.R. Harding
1972; 385 pp.
$4 postpaid from:
A.R. Harding Publishing Company
2878 East Main Street
Columbus, OH 43209

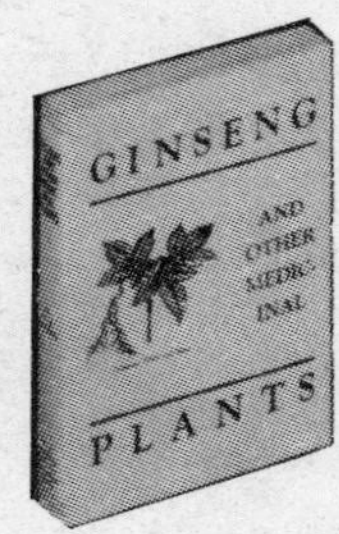

•

Ginseng is truly and wholly a savage. We can no more tame it than we can the partridge.

Ginseng — a very good shaped root but it is immature and will not bring more than half what the same root of the same size would bring had it been matured so as to show the rings around the root.

The Ginseng Report

You will be hearing a new word more and more — "adaptogen." It's simply a plant product or substance that helps buffer the body against the stress of daily ups and downs. They work in preventative more than curative ways. The king of the adaptogens is ginseng. Its popularity in the U.S. (it's always been popular in China, Japan and Korea) has of course, led to weak, adulterated or even non-products. The worst are "instant teas" or a species of Rumex called "wild American ginseng" which has nothing to do with Panax (the medicinal plant). The real, American wild ginseng has been so over-harvested that it is extinct in many states. Where are the growers? This is the best book — especially on analyzing the ginseng products and varieties and their uses. —Peter Warshall

The Ginseng Report
Walter Ziglar
1979; 127 pp.
$4.95 postpaid from:
International Institute of Natural Health Sciences
P.O. Box 5550
Huntington Beach, CA 92646
or Whole Earth Household Store

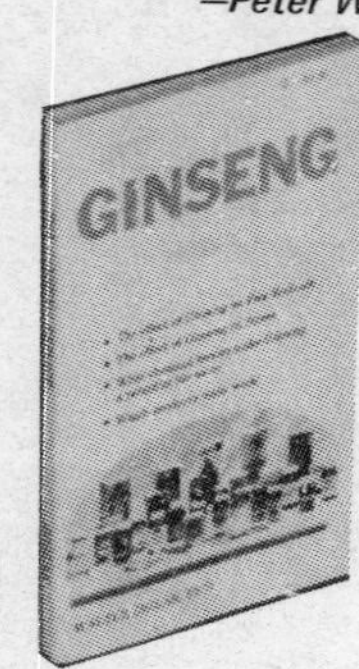

•

Listed are some of the claims of the therapeutic activity of ginseng cited and verified by this study.

- A first class adaptogen.
- Has a marked stimulant and tonic action, e.g. builds zest, energy, stamina and endurance; increases mental and physical work activity; helps combat everyday weariness; improves appetite and sleep; relieves signs of brain fatigue; improves mental and physical reflex action.
- Delivers a therapeutic effect in functional nervous disturbances, e.g. chronic irritability, depression, nervous exhaustion, hypochondria and menopausal neurosis.
- Has a remarkable protective effect against most types of stress.

← Leaves of sweet cicely resemble ferns. The green seeds have a spicy taste and are mixed with other herbs. They are used in certain liqueurs.

Handbook on Herbs

In the Brooklyn Botanical Gardens I learned my first botany and first love for plant life and powers. It's no wonder. The Gardens produce clear and thorough pamphlets. This one on herbs is essential for the herb gardener and initiate. —Peter Warshall

Handbook on Herbs
Brooklyn Botanic Garden
1958, 1971; 93 pp.

$2.55 postpaid from:
Brooklyn Botanic Garden
Brooklyn, NY 11225
or Whole Earth Household Store

Potted fresh herbs. From left to right: marjoram; rosemary topiary; thyme (front); opal basil (rear); chives (front); lemon balm (rear); orange mint; and sage (far right).

The Forgotten Art of Growing, Gardening and Cooking with Herbs

This book is for herb lovers, and if you never thought about loving herbs, consider a garden devoted to scent and supplying fresh seasonings for every meal. Seems like a luxury, except herb gardens are low-maintenance and can be stuck in minimal places, outdoors or in. Poor soil is fine, as long as it has good drainage, and intense heat brings more oil into the leaves. The practicality of herbs is described; not in medicines, but in dyes, potpourris and organic pesticides. The chapters on herb cooking are straightforward with easy recipes. —Carolyn MacDougall

The Forgotten Art of Growing, Gardening and Cooking with Herbs
Richard M. Bacon
1972; 121 pp.

$5.95 postpaid from:
Yankee, Inc.
Main Street
Dublin, NH 03444
or Whole Earth Household Store

Herbs and spices, teas and coffee

Green Mountain Herbs
P.O. Box 2369
Boulder, CO 80306

Fmali Company
Wildcraft Herbs
831 Almar Avenue
Santa Cruz, CA 95060

Best suppliers of ginseng in U.S.

McNulty's Tea & Coffee
109 Christopher Street
New York, NY 10014

If you live in the sticks and are tired of Maxwell House, these people have the answer. They have extended selections of rare, unusual, exotic and good tasting coffees. Also large selection of black teas.

The Black Swan Trading Company
245 South Boulevard
Oak Park, IL 60302

Herbs.

The Whole Herb Co.
250 East Blithedale
Mill Valley, CA 94941

Herbs.

Penn Herb Co, Ltd.
603 North 2nd Street
Philadelphia, PA 19123

Charles Loeb Distributors
615 Palmer Road
Yonkers, NY 10701

Spices.

Murchie's
1008 Robson Street
Vancouver, B.C. V6E 1A7

Teas, coffees, and spices. —Paul Hawken

—Fmali

hinese
ed Ginseng
the Original

Shiu Chu
Kirin

—Fmali

BLENDED COFFEES

FOLLOWING ARE SOME OF THE MORE POPULAR BLENDS. THEY ARE LISTED IN ORDER OF STRENGTH, BEGINNING WITH THE MILDEST. EACH IS GIVEN WITH ITS FORMULA WRITTEN IN OUNCES (16 OZS. PER POUND).

	PER POUND
DELMONICO (6 MA - 6 JA - 4 MO)	4.75
MOCHA - JAVA (5⅓ MO - 10⅔ JA)	4.75
OLD TIMES (5⅓ CO - 5⅓ MA - 5⅓ SAN)	4.75
MOCHA - COLOMBIAN SUPREMO (10⅔ SUP - 5⅓ MO)	4.85
MOCHA - COLOMBIAN (10⅔ CO - 5⅓ MO)	4.75
MARIANNE'S BLEND (7 MO - 6 SUP - 3 (FR) AL)	4.85
RESTAURANT BLEND (11 CO - 3 MO - 2 (FR) CO)	4.80
WILLIAM & MARY (12 AL - 4 (FR) AL)	4.75
TOLTEC (4 MO - 4 SA - 4 AL - 4 (FR) AL)	4.75
SCANDINAVIAN	4.75
TURKISH BLEND (6 JA - 6 MO - 4 (FR) CO)	4.80
VIENNESE (4 MO - 4 JA - 4 CO - 4 (FR) CO)	4.80
FRENCH - MOCHA (8 MO - 8 (FR) CO)	4.80
FRENCH ROAST DELUXE	4.85
NEW ORLEANS (12 (FR) CO - 4 (UT) CO)	4.87

* PLEASE SPECIFY GRIND OR TYPE OF COFFEEMAKER IF YOU PREFER GROUND COFFEE. OTHERWISE WE WILL MAIL BEANS *

GROUND, DARK-ROASTED CHICORY 1.95

—McNulty's

The Herb Quarterly

The first magazine devoted entirely to the propagation and cultivation of herbs. It has a simple format and sensitive graphic touch. Becoming better with each issue as it starts to link up the herbalist lore scattered across the land. —Paul Hawken

The Herb Quarterly
Sallie Ballantine, Editor

$10/year (4 issues) from:
The Uphill Press
Green Road
Wilmington, VT 05363

Caswell-Massey

Caswell-Massey is an old-fashioned apothecary in New York that does a whopping mail-order business. They have an international assortment of exotic (herbal and otherwise) soaps, ointments, toothpowders, plasters, sponges, handmade combs. If you are a member of the celebrated cucumber cult, they have the largest selection of cucumber products (emulsion; soap, shampoo, cold cream, cologne, etc.) I have found anywhere. They have a battery of esoteric items, like the goose quill toothpicks I bought 4 years ago that are still in the prime of their picking. —Jeanne Campbell

Caswell-Massey
Catalog

free from:
Caswell-Massey
320 West 13th Street
New York, NY 10014

← A truly superior dentifrice base expressly prepared for its stain-effacement capabilities. Clinomyn's flavor, likewise, is calculated to swiftly renew the cleanliness and freshness of your mouth in an instant.

Clinomyn Smoker's Toothpaste.
(56005) $2.50

Herb suppliers

Wild World Herbs, Ltd., 11 St. Catherine Street East, Montreal, Quebec, Canada H2X 1K5

Free catalog for over 2000 herbs, roots, barks, dyes, etc. Minimum $5 order. Also essential oils, known for its dyes. Retail only.

ATTAR, Playground Road, New Ipswich, NH 03071

Wholesales and retails high quality culinary herbs, herbal teas, roots and barks (like ginger, kava kava and burdock), gums and resins (primarily for incense), scented herbs (primarily for sachets and potpourris), essential oils (the botanical essences or "attar" that are used as the base for perfumes) and others. Catalog $.25

Indiana Botanic Gardens, P.O. Box 5, Hammond, IN 46325

A very far-out free catalog and herbalist's almanac which will tell you the best days to plant, what the weather will be like and other useful tidbits. Sell teas, medicines, herbs and spices, seeds, beans, nut oils, vitamins, cosmetics, perfumes, formulas for liquor or tobacco addiction.

Meadowbrook Herb Garden, Wyoming, RI 02898

Catalog is a beautiful piece of printing and calligraphy. Sell herbs and teas, spices, seeds, toiletries, books, and misc. Into anthroposophy and Bio-Dynamics. Catalog $.50

The Flower Essence Society, P.O. Box 586, Nevada City, CA 95959

Followers of a school of herbalists that believe the essences derived from flowers are gentle, yet powerful health catalysts. They have a free catalog of bottled flower essences and a quarterly magazine on flower therapies — **The Flower Essence Quarterly**, *edited by Richard Katz, $10/year.*

For more on herbs, see p. 100.

—Peter Warshall

•

Whenever I see an expanse of golden dandelion heads buzzing with bees in the sun, I wonder how frequently the plant would be grown in flower beds if it were scarce and considered exotic. Children whose souls have not yet been benighted by such pejorative terms as "weed" immediately appreciate the beauty of dandelions; they gather bouquets and blow fluffy seed heads with charmed absorption. You can expand their taste buds by sharing a dish of dandelion greens with them.

THE RISING SUN
NEIGHBORHOOD NEWSLETTER

When Art and a friend of his used to spend hours discussing their friends and how they acted and why they acted the way they did, they called it "talking about people's shadows," to remind themselves they really didn't know.

THE THIRD WAVE

by Ron Jones

What follows is a true story.
It took place at Cubberly High School, Palo Alto, California, on five days in April, 1969 – the height of "do your own thing." —*SB*

For years I kept a strange secret. I shared this silence with two hundred students. Yesterday I ran into one of those students. For a brief moment it all rushed back.

Steve Coniglo had been a sophomore student in my World History class. We ran into each other quite by accident. It's one of those occasions experienced by teachers when they least expect. You're walking down the street, eating at a secluded restaurant, or buying some underwear when all of a sudden an ex-student pops up to say hello. In this case it was Steve running down the street shouting, "Mr. Jones, Mr. Jones." In an embarrassed hug we greet. I had to stop for a minute to remember. Who is this young man hugging me? He calls me Mr. Jones. Must be a former student. What's his name? In the split second of my race back in time Steve sensed my questioning and backed up. Then smiled, and slowly raised a hand in a cupped position. My God. He's a member of the Third Wave. It's Steve, Steve Coniglo. He sat in the second row. He was a sensitive and bright student. Played guitar and enjoyed drama.

We just stood there exchanging smiles when without a conscious command I raised my hand in curved position. The salute was given. Two comrades had met long after the war. The Third Wave was still alive. "Mr. Jones do you remember the Third Wave?" I sure do, it was one of the most frightening events I ever experienced in the classroom. It was also the genesis of a secret that I and two hundred students would sadly share for the rest of our lives.

We talked and laughed about the Third Wave for the next few hours. Then it was time to part. It's strange, you meet a past student in these chance ways. You catch a few moments of your life. Hold them tight.

Then say goodbye. Not knowing when and if you'd ever see each other again. Oh, you make promises to call each other but it won't happen. Steve will continue to grow and change. I will remain an ageless benchmark in his life. A presence that will not change. I am Mr. Jones. Steve turns and gives a quiet salute. Hand raised upward in a shape of a curling wave. Hand curved in a similar fashion I return the gesture.

The Third Wave. Well at last it can be talked about. Here I've met a student and we've talked for hours about this nightmare. The secret must finally be waning. It's taken three years. I can tell you and anyone else about the Third Wave. It's now just a dream, something to remember, no it's something we tried to forget. That's how it all started. By strange coincidence I think it was Steve who started the Third Wave with a question.

We were studying Nazi Germany and in the middle of a lecture I was interrupted by the question. How could the German populace claim ignorance of the slaughter of the Jewish people. How could the townspeople, railroad conductors, teachers, doctors, claim they knew nothing about concentration camps and human carnage. How can people who were neighbors and maybe even friends of the Jewish citizen say they weren't there when it happened. It was a good question. I didn't know the answer.

In as much as there were several months still to go in the school year and I was already at World War II, I decided to take a week and explore the question.

STRENGTH THROUGH DISCIPLINE

ON MONDAY, I introduced my sophomore history students to one of the experiences that characterized Nazi Germany. Discipline. I lectured about the beauty of discipline. How an athlete feels having worked hard and regularly to be successful at a sport. How a ballet dancer or painter works hard to perfect a movement. The dedicated patience of a scientist in pursuit of an idea. It's discipline. That self training. Control. The power of the will. The exchange of physical hardships for superior mental and physical faculties. The ultimate triumph.

To experience the power of discipline, I invited, no I commanded the class to exercise and use a new seating posture. I described how proper sitting posture assists concentration and strengthens the will. In fact I instructed the class in a mandatory sitting posture. This posture started with feet flat on the floor, hands placed flat across the small of the back to force a straight alignment of the spine. "There, can't you breathe more easily? You're more alert. Don't you feel better?"

We practiced this new attention position over and over. I walked up and down the aisles of seated students pointing out small flaws, making improvements. Proper seating became the most important aspect of learning. I would dismiss the class, allowing them to leave their desks, and then call them abruptly back to an attention sitting position. In speed drills the class learned to move from standing position to attention sitting in fifteen seconds. In focus drills I concentrated attention on the feet being parallel and flat, ankles locked, knees bent at ninety degree angles, hands flat and crossed against the back, spine straight, chin down, head forward. We did noise drills in which talking was allowed only to be shown as a distraction. Following minutes of progressive drill assignments the class could move from standing positions outside the room to attention sitting positions at their desks without making a sound. The manuever took five seconds.

It was strange how quickly the students took to this uniform code of behavior. I began to wonder just how far they could be pushed. Was this display of obedience a momentary game we were all playing, or was it something else? Was the desire for discipline and uniformity a natural need? A societal instinct we hide within our franchise restaurants and T.V. programming?

I decided to push the tolerance of the class for regimented action. In the final twenty-five minutes of the class I introduced some new rules. Students must be sitting in class at the attention position before the late bell; all students must carry pencils and paper for note taking; when asking or answering questions a student must stand at the side of their desk; the first word given in answering or asking a question is "Mr. Jones." We practiced a short "silent reading" session. Students who responded in a sluggish manner were reprimanded and in every case made to repeat their behavior until it was a model of punctuality and respect. The intensity of the response became more important than the content. To accentuate this, I requested answers to be given in three words or less. Students were rewarded for making an effort at answering or asking questions. They were also acknowledged for doing this in a crisp and attentive manner.

Soon everyone in the class began popping up with answers and questions. The involvement level in the class moved from the few who always dominated discussions to the entire class. Even stranger was the gradual improvement in the quality of answers. Everyone seemed to be listening more intently. New people were speaking. Answers started to stretch out as students usually hesitant to speak found support for their effort.

As for my part in this exercise, I had nothing but questions. Why hadn't I thought of this technique before? Students seemed intent on the assignment and displayed accurate recitation of facts and concepts. They even seemed to be asking better questions and treating each other with more compassion. How could this be? Here I was enacting an authoritarian learning environment and it seemed very productive. I now began to ponder not just how far this class could be pushed but how much I would change my basic beliefs toward an open classroom and self directed learning. Was all my belief in Carl Rogers to shrivel and die? Where was this experiment leading?

STRENGTH THROUGH COMMUNITY

ON TUESDAY, the second day of the exercise, I entered the classroom to find everyone sitting in silence at the attention position. Some of their faces were relaxed with smiles that come from pleasing the teacher. But most of the students looked straight ahead in earnest concentration. Neck muscles rigid. No sign of a smile or a thought or even a question. Every fibre strained to perform the deed. To release the tension I went to the chalk board and wrote in big letters "STRENGTH THROUGH DISCIPLINE." Below this I wrote a second law "STRENGTH THROUGH COMMUNITY."

While the class sat in stern silence I began to talk, lecture, sermonize about the value of community. At this stage of the game I was debating in my own mind whether to stop the experiment or continue. I hadn't planned such intensity or compliance. In fact I was surprised to find the ideas on discipline enacted at all. While debating whether to stop or go on with the experiment I talked on and on about community. I made up stories from my experiences as an athlete, coach and historian. It was easy. Community is that bond between individuals who work and struggle together. It's raising a barn with your neighbors, it's feeling that you are a part of something beyond yourself, a movement, a team, La Raza, a cause.

It was too late to step back. I now can appreciate why the astronomer turns relentlessly to the telescope. I was probing deeper and deeper into my own perceptions and the motivations for group and individual action. There was much more to see and try to understand. Many questions haunted me. Why did the students accept the authority I was imposing? Where is their curiosity or resistance to this martial behavior? When and how will this end?

Following my description of community I once again told the class that community, like discipline, must be experienced if it is to be understood. To provide an encounter with community I had the class recite in unison, "Strength Through Discipline." "Strength Through Community." First I would have two students stand and call back our motto. Then add two more until finally the whole class was standing and reciting. It was fun. The students began to look at each other and sense the power of belonging. Everyone was capable and equal. They were doing something together. We worked on this simple act for the entire class period. We would repeat the mottos in a rotating chorus, or say them with various degrees of loudness. Always we said them together, emphasizing the proper way to sit, stand, and talk.

I began to think of myself as a part of the experiment. I enjoyed the unified action demonstrated by the students. It was rewarding to see their satisfaction and excitement to do more. I found it harder and harder to extract myself from the momentum and identity that the class was developing. I was following the group dictate as much as I was directing it.

As the class period was ending and without forethought I created a class salute. It was for class members only. To make the salute you brought your right hand up toward the right shoulder in a curled position. I called it the Third Wave salute because the hand resembled a wave about to top over. The idea for the three came from beach lore that waves travel in chains, the third wave being the last and largest of each series. Since we had a salute I made it a rule to salute all class members outside the classroom. When the bell sounded ending the period, I asked the class for complete silence. With everyone sitting at attention I slowly raised my arm and with a cupped hand I saluted. It was a silent signal of recognition. They were something special. Without command the entire group of students returned the salute.

Throughout the next few days students in the class would exchange this greeting. You would be walking down the hall when all of a sudden three classmates would turn your way each flashing a quick salute. In the library or in gym students would be seen giving this strange hand jive. You would hear a crash of cafeteria food only to have it followed by two classmates saluting each other. The mystique of thirty individuals doing this strange gyration soon brought more attention to the class and its experiment into the German personality. Many students outside the class asked if they could join.

STRENGTH THROUGH ACTION

N WEDNESDAY, I decided to issue membership cards to every student that wanted to continue what I now called The Experiment. Not a single student elected to leave the room. In this the third day of activity there were forty-three students in the class. Thirteen students had cut other classes to be a part of The Experiment. While the class sat at attention I gave each person a card. I marked three of the cards with a red X and informed the recipients that they had a special assignment: to report any students not complying with class rules. I then proceeded to talk about the meaning of action. I explained how discipline and community were meaningless without action. I discussed the beauty of taking full responsibility for one's action. Of believing so thoroughly in yourself and your community or family that you will do anything to preserve, protect and extend that being. I stressed how hard work and allegiance to each other would allow accelerated learning and accomplishment. I reminded students of what it felt like being in classes where competition caused pain and degradation. Situations in which students were pitted against each other in everything from gym to reading. The feeling of never acting, never being a part of something, never supporting each other.

At this point students stood without prompting and began to give what amounted to testimonials. "Mr. Jones, for the first time I'm learning lots of things." "Mr. Jones, why don't you teach like this all the time." I was shocked! Yes, I had been pushing information at them in an extremely controlled setting but the fact that they found it comfortable and acceptable was startling. It was equally disconcerting to realize that complex and time-consuming written homework assignments on German life were being completed and even enlarged on by students. Performance in academic skill areas was significantly improving. They were learning more. And they seemed to want more. I began to think that the students might do anything I assigned. I decided to find out.

To allow students the experience of direct action I gave each individual a specific verbal assignment. "It's your task to design a Third Wave Banner. You are responsible for stopping any student that is not a Third Wave member from entering this room. I want you to remember and be able to recite by tomorrow the name and address of every Third Wave Member. You are assigned the problem of training and convincing at least twenty children in the adjacent elementary school that our sitting posture is necessary for better learning. It's your job to read this pamphlet and report its entire content to the class before the period ends. I want each of you to give me the name and address of one reliable friend that you think might want to join the Third Wave."

To conclude the session on direct action, I instructed students in a simple procedure for initiating new members. It went like this. A new member had only to be recommended by an existing member and issued a card by me. Upon receiving this card the new member had to demonstrate knowledge of our rules and pledge obedience to them. My announcement unleashed a fervor.

The school was alive with conjecture and curiosity. It affected everyone. The school cook asked what a Third Wave cookie looked like. I said chocolate chip of course. Our principal came into an afternoon faculty meeting and gave me the Third Wave salute. I saluted back. The librarian thanked me for our 30′ banner on learning which she placed above the library entrance. By the end of the day over two hundred students were admitted into the order. I felt very alone and a little scared.

Most of my fear emanated from the incidence of tattletaling. Although I formally appointed only three students to report deviate behavior, approximately twenty students came to me with reports about how Allan didn't salute, or Georgene was talking critically about our experiment. This incidence of monitoring meant that half the class now considered it their duty to observe and report on members of their class. Within this avalanche of reporting one legitimate conspiracy did seem under way.

Three women in the class had told their parents all about our classroom activities. These three young women were by far the most intelligent students in the class. As friends they chummed together. They possessed a silent confidence and took pleasure in a school setting that gave them academic and leadership opportunity. During the days of the experiment I was curious how they would respond to the egalitarian and physical reshaping of the class. The rewards they were accustomed to winning just didn't exist in the experiment. The intellectual skills of questioning and reasoning were nonexistent. In the martial atmosphere of the class they seemed stunned and pensive. Now that I look back, they appeared much like the child with so-called learning disability. They watched the activities and participated in a mechanical fashion. Where others jumped in, they held back, watching.

In telling their parents of the experiment, they set up a brief chain of events. The rabbi for one of the parents called me at home. He was polite and condescending. I told him we were merely studying the German personality. He seemed delighted and told me not to worry. He would talk to the parents and calm their concern. In concluding this conversation I envisioned similar conversations throughout history in which the clergy accepted and apologized for untenable conditions. If only he would have raged in anger or simply investigated the situation I could point the students to an example of righteous rebellion. But no. The rabbi became a part of the experiment. In remaining ignorant of the oppression in the experiment he became an accomplice and advocate.

By the end of the third day I was exhausted. I was tearing apart. The balance between role playing and directed behavior became indistinguishable. Many of the students were completely into being Third Wave members. They demanded strict obedience of the rules from other students and bullied those that took the experiment lightly. Others simply sank into the activity and took self-assigned roles. I particularly remember Robert. Robert was big for his age and displayed very few academic skills. Oh he tried harder than anyone I know to be successful. He handed in elaborate weekly reports copied word for word from the reference books in the library. Robert is like so many kids in school that don't excel or cause trouble. They aren't bright, they can't make the athletic teams, and don't strike out for attention. They are lost, invisible. The only reason I came to know Robert at all is that I

THE RISING SUN
NEIGHBORHOOD NEWSLETTER

David talking on the phone said, "It's not such a good time to visit, you know, because we're making this 600 page book and there are all these people going around with words in their heads and if they see a new face, they forget the word and have to find it again on a little piece of paper."

found him eating lunch in my classroom. He always ate lunch alone.

Well the Third Wave gave Robert a place in school. At least he was equal to everyone. He could do something. Take part. Be meaningful. That's just what Robert did. Late Wednesday afternoon I found Robert following me and asked what in the world was he doing. He smiled (I don't think I had ever seen him smile) and announced, "Mr. Jones, I'm your bodyguard. I'm afraid something will happen to you. Can I do it Mr. Jones, please?" Given that assurance and smile I couldn't say no. I had a bodyguard. All day long he opened and closed doors for me. He walked always on my right. Just smiling and saluting other class members. He followed me everywhere. In the faculty room (closed to students) he stood at silent attention while I gulped some coffee. When accosted by an English teacher for being a student in the "teacher's room" he just smiled and informed the faculty member that he wasn't a student, he was a bodyguard.

STRENGTH THROUGH PRIDE

N THURSDAY I began to draw the experiment to a conclusion. I was exhausted and worried. Many students were over the line. The Third Wave had become the center of their existence. I was in pretty bad shape myself. I was now acting instinctively as a dictator. Oh I was benevolent. And I daily argued to myself on the benefits of the learning experience. By this the fourth day of the experiment I was beginning to lose my own arguments. As I spent more time playing the role I had less time to remember its rational origins and purpose. I found myself sliding into the role even when it wasn't necessary. I wondered if this doesn't happen to lots of people. We get or take an ascribed role and then bend our life to fit the image. Soon the image is the only identity people will accept. So we became the image. The trouble with the situation and role I had created was that I didn't have time to think where it was leading. Events were crushing in around me. I worried for students doing things they would regret. I worried for myself.

Once again I faced the thoughts of closing the experiment or letting it go its own course. Both options were unworkable. If I stopped the experiment a great number of students would be left hanging. They had committed themselves in front of their peers to radical behavior. Emotionally and psychologically they had exposed themselves. If I suddenly jolted them back to classroom reality I would face a confused student body for the remainder of the year. It would be too painful and demeaning for Robert and the students like him to be twisted back into their seat and told it's just a game. They would take ridicule from the brighter students that participated in a measured and cautious way. I couldn't let the Roberts lose again.

The other option of just letting the experiment run its course was also out of the question. Things were already out of control. Wednesday evening someone had broken into the room and ransacked the place. I later found out it was the father of one of the students. He was a retired Air Force colonel who had spent time in a German prisoner of war camp. Upon hearing of our activity he simply lost control. Late in the evening he broke into the room and tore it apart. I found him that morning propped up against the classroom door. He told me about his friends that had been killed in Germany. He was holding on to me and shaking. In staccato words he pleaded that I understand and help him get home. I called his wife and with the help of a neighbor walked him home. We spent hours later talking about what he felt and did, but from that moment on Thursday morning I was more concerned with what might be happening at school.

I was increasingly worried about how our activity was affecting the faculty and other students in the school. The Third Wave was disrupting normal learning. Students were cutting class to participate, and the school counselors were beginning to question every student in the class. The real gestapo in the school was at work. Faced with The Experiment exploding in one hundred directions, I decided to try an old basketball strategy. When you're playing against all the odds the best action to take is to try the unexpected. That's what I did.

By Thursday the class had swollen in size to over eighty students. The only thing that allowed them all to fit was the enforced discipline of sitting in silence at attention. A strange calm is in effect when a room full of people sit in quiet observation and anticipation. It helped me approach them in a deliberate way. I talked about pride. "Pride is more than banners or salutes. Pride is something no one can take from you. Pride is knowing you are the best . . . It can't be destroyed. . ."

In the midst of this crescendo I abruptly changed and lowered my voice to announce the real reason for the Third Wave. In slow methodic tone I explained what was behind the Third Wave. "The Third Wave isn't just an experiment or classroom activity. It's far more important than that. The Third Wave is a nationwide program to find students who are willing to fight for political change in this country. That's right. This activity we have been doing has been practice for the real thing. Across the country teachers like myself have been recruiting and training a youth brigade capable of showing the nation a better society through discipline, community, pride, and action. If we can change the way that school is run, we can change the way that factories, stores, universities and all the other institutions are run. You are a selected group of young people chosen to help in this cause. If you will stand up and display what you have learned in the past four days . . . we can change the destiny of this nation. We can bring it a new sense of order, community, pride and action. A new purpose. Everything rests with you and your willingness to take a stand."

To give validity to the seriousness of my words I turned to the three women in the class whom I knew had questioned the Third Wave. I demanded that they leave the room. I explained why I acted and then assigned four guards to escort the women to the library and to prevent them from entering the class on Friday. Then in dramatic style I informed the class of a special noon rally to take place on Friday. This would be a rally for Third Wave members only.

It was a wild gamble. I just kept talking, afraid that if I stopped someone would laugh or ask a question, and the grand scheme would dissolve in chaos. I explained how at noon on Friday a national candidate for President would announce the formation of a Third Wave Youth Program. Simultaneous to this announcement over 1000 youth groups from every part of the country would stand up and display their support for such a movement. I confided that they were the students selected to represent their area. I also questioned if they could make a good showing, because the press had been invited to record the event. No one laughed. There was not a murmur of resistance. Quite the contrary. A fever pitch of excitement swelled across the room. "We can do it!" "Should we wear white shirts?" "Can we bring friends?" "Mr. Jones, have you seen this advertisement in Time magazine?"

The clincher came quite by accident. It was a full page color advertisement in the current issue of Time for some lumber products. The advertiser identified his product as the Third Wave. The advertisement proclaimed in big red, white and blue letters, "The Third Wave is coming." "Is this part of the campaign, Mr. Jones? Is it a code or something?" "Yes. Now listen carefully. It's all set for tomorrow. Be in the small auditorium ten minutes before 12:00. Be seated. Be ready to display the discipline, community, and pride you have learned. Don't talk to anyone about this. This rally is for members only."

STRENGTH THROUGH UNDERSTANDING

N FRIDAY, the final day of the exercise, I spent the early morning preparing the auditorium for the rally. At 11:30 students began to ant their way into the room, first a few scouting the way and then more. Row after row began to fill. A hushed silence shrouded the room. Third Wave banners hung like clouds over the assembly. At twelve o'clock sharp I closed the room and placed guards at each door. Several friends of mine posing as reporters and photographers began to interact with the crowd taking pictures and jotting frantic descriptive notes. A group photograph was taken.

Over two hundred students were crammed into the room. Not a vacant seat could be found. The group seemed to be composed of students from many persuasions. There were the athletes, the social prominents, the student leaders, the loners, the group of kids that always left school early, the bikers, the pseudo hip, a few representatives of the school's dadaist clique, and some of the students that hung out at the laundromat. The entire collection however looked like one force as they sat in perfect attention. Every person focusing on the TV set I had in the front of the room. No one moved. The room was empty of sound. It was like we were all witness to a birth. The tension and anticipation was beyond belief.

"Before turning on the national press conference, which begins in five minutes, I want to demonstrate to the press the extent of our training." With that I gave the salute, followed automatically by two hundred arms stabbing a reply. I then said the words "Strength Through Discipline," followed by a repetitive chorus. We did this again, and again. Each time the response was louder. The photographers were circling the ritual snapping pictures, but by now they were ignored. I reiterated the importance of this event and asked once more for a show of allegiance. It was the last time I would ask anyone to recite. The room rocked with a guttural cry, "STRENGTH THROUGH DISCIPLINE!"

It was 12:05. I turned off the lights in the room and walked quickly to the television set. The air in the room seemed to be drying up. It felt hard to breathe and even harder to talk. It was as if the climax of shouting souls had pushed everything out of the room. I switched the television set on. I was now standing next to the television directly facing the room full of people. The machine came to life producing a luminous field of pale blue light. Robert was at my side. I whispered to him to watch closely and pay attention to the next few minutes. The only light in the room was coming from the television and it played against the faces in the room. Eyes strained and pulled at the light but the pattern didn't change. The room stayed deadly still. Waiting. There was a mental tug of war between the people in the room and the television. The television won. The glow of the test pattern didn't snap into the vision of a political candidate. It just whined on. Still the viewers persisted. There must be a program. It must be coming on. Where is it? The trance with the television continued for what seemed like hours. It was 12:07. Nothing. A blank screen. It's not going to happen. Anticipation turned to anxiety and then to frustration. Someone stood up and shouted.

"There isn't any leader is there?" Everyone turned in shock, first to the despondent student and then back to the television. Their faces held looks of disbelief. In the confusion of the moment I moved slowly toward the television. I turned it off. I felt air rush back into the room. The room remained in fixed silence, but for the first time I could sense people breathing. Students were withdrawing their arms from behind their chairs. I expected a flood of questions, but instead got intense quietness. I began to talk. Every word seemed to be taken and absorbed.

"Listen closely, I have something important to tell you. There is no leader! There is no such thing as a national youth movement called the Third Wave. You have been used. Manipulated. Shoved by your own desires into the place you now find yourself. You are no better or worse than the German Nazi we have been studying.

"You thought that you were the elect. That you were better than those outside this room. You bargained your freedom for the comfort of discipline and superiority. You chose to accept the group's will and the big lie over your own conviction. Oh, you think to yourself that you were just going along for the fun. That you could extricate yourself at any moment. But where were you heading? How far would you have gone? Let me show you your future."

With that I switched on a rear screen movie projector. It quickly illuminated a white drop cloth hanging behind the television. Large numbers appeared in a countdown. The roar of the Nuremburg Rally blasted into vision. My heart was pounding. In ghostly images the history of the Third Reich paraded into the room. The discipline. The march of super race. The big lie. Arrogance, violence, terror. People being pushed into vans. The visual stench of death camps. Faces without eyes. The trials. The plea of ignorance. I was only doing my job. My job. As abruptly as it started the film froze to a halt on a single written frame. "Everyone must accept the blame – No one can claim that they didn't in some way take part."

The room stayed dark as the final footage of film flapped against the projector. I felt sick to my stomach. The room smelt like a locker room. No one moved. It was as if everyone wanted to dissect the moment, figure out what had happened. Like awakening from a dream and deep sleep, the entire room of people took one last look back into their consciousness. I waited for several minutes to let everyone catch up. Finally questions began to emerge. All of the questions probed at imaginary situations and sought to discover the meaning of this event.

In the still darkened room I began the explanation. I confessed my feeling of sickness and remorse. I told the assembly that a full explanation would take quite a while. But to start, I sensed myself moving from an introspective participant in the event toward the role of teacher. It's easier being a teacher. In objective terms I began to describe the past events.

"Through the experience of the past week we have all tasted what it was like to live and act in Nazi Germany. We learned what it felt like to create a disciplined social environment. To build a special society. Pledge allegiance to that society. Replace reason with rules. Yes, we would all have made good Germans. We would have put on the uniform. Turned our head as friends and neighbors were cursed and then persecuted. Pulled the locks shut. Worked in the "defense" plants. Burned ideas. Yes, we know in a small way what it feels like to find a hero. To grab quick solutions. Feel strong and in control of destiny. We know the fear of being left out. The pleasure of doing something right and being rewarded. To be number one. To be right. We have seen and perhaps felt what these actions taken to an extreme will lead to. We each have witnessed something over the past week. We have seen that fascism is not just something those other people did. No, it's right here. In this room. In our own personal habits and way of life. Scratch the surface and it appears. Something in all of us. We carry it like a disease. The belief that human beings are basically evil and therefore unable to act well toward each other. A belief that demands a strong leader and discipline to preserve social order. And there is something else. The act of apology.

"This is the final lesson to be experienced. This last lesson is perhaps the one of greatest importance. This lesson was the question that started our plunge in studying Nazi life. Do you remember the question? It concerned a bewilderment at the German populace claiming ignorance and non-involvement in the Nazi movement. If I remember the question, it went something like this. How could the German soldier, teacher, railroad conductor, nurse, tax collector, the average citizen, claim at the end of the Third Reich that they knew nothing of what was going on? How can a people be a part of something and then claim at the demise that they were not really involved? What causes people to blank out their own history? In the next few minutes and perhaps years, you will have an opportunity to answer this question.

"If our enactment of the Fascist mentality is complete, not one of you will ever admit to being at this final Third Wave rally. Like the Germans, you will have trouble admitting to yourself that you came this far. You will not allow your friends and parents to know that you were willing to give up individual freedom and power for the dictates of order and unseen leaders. You can't admit to being manipulated. Being a follower. To accepting the Third Wave as a way of life. You won't admit to participating in this madness. You will keep this day and this rally a secret. It's a secret I shall share with you."

I took the film from the three cameras in the room and pulled the celluloid into the exposing light. The deed was concluded. The trial was over. The Third Wave had ended.

I glanced over my shoulder. Robert was crying. Students slowly rose from their chairs and without words filed into the outdoor light. I walked over to Robert and threw my arms around him. Robert was sobbing, taking in large uncontrollable gulps of air. "It's over." "It's all right." In our consoling each other we became a rock in the stream of exiting students. Some swirled back to momentarily hold Robert and I. Others cried openly and then brushed away tears to carry on. Human beings circling and holding each other. Moving toward the door and the world outside.

For a week in the middle of a school year we had shared fully in life. And as predicted we also shared a deep secret. In the four years I taught at Cubberley High School no one ever admitted to attending the Third Wave Rally. Oh, we talked and studied our actions intently. But the Rally itself. No. It was something we all wanted to forget. ■

Ron Jones now lives in San Francisco, is a member of The Briarpatch Network, and publishes and edits the excellent **Deschool Primer** *series of workbooks available from Zephyros, 1201 Stanyan St., San Francisco, CA 97117.* *(Reviewed on p. 571.)*

Another true story by Jones, **The Acorn People**, *is published at $4.95 by Abingdon Press, 201 Eighth Avenue South, Nashville, TN 37202.*

THE RISING SUN

NEIGHBORHOOD NEWSLETTER

One time a friend of Kathleen's got tired of taking all that acid without learning the truth, so he decided it was time to take the trip. He went into the back bedroom, closed the door, turned off the lights – no visual or audio stimulus. He saw himself sitting in front of a door. He got up and opened that door and there was a hall with a door at the end and he opened that door and kept on like that opening doors and getting, he could tell, closer and closer till he finally reached the door that he could just tell was the door with the answer and as he reached to open it the door knob in the real bedroom he was in started to turn and his roomate walked in and said, "What's happening?"

He decided he wasn't supposed to know the truth.

Many Dimensional Man

Every so often a book of social analysis comes along that reorients many people's sense of what is intelligent and right to do with their lives. McLuhan's **Understanding Media** *did that. So did Schumacher's* **Small Is Beautiful** *and Marcuse's* **One Dimensional Man**, *off which this book bounces its title.*

Ogilvy's finely-wrought argument is that the old battle of Man against Nature has been essentially won by Man thanks to the tools of Politics and Technology. Now Man's battle is with the uncontrolled wilderness of Politics and Technology, to be fought with tools yet to be invented. Ogilvy suggests paratechnology and parapolitics as the tools and portrays a many-dimensional man who could sharpen and wield them.

I'm thrilled by it. (According to him, I would be.) The book has special political relevance because it declares the Presidency is dead — in the same sense and for the same reason Nietzsche declared God dead. The over-centralized state, overcentralized religion, and overcentralized personality all have become grotesque, infinitely less than the sum of the whole life of their whole parts.
—SB

Many Dimensional Man
(Decentralizing Self, Society and the Sacred)
James Ogilvy
1977, 1979; 386 pp.

$5.95 postpaid from:
Harper and Row
Keystone Industrial Park
Scranton, PA 18512
or Whole Earth Household Store

•

The paraprofessional mediates between those who need care and an increasingly esoteric system of medicine that seems increasingly unable to help. The paraprofessional does not create new tools; he provides access to already available tools. **The Whole Earth Catalog** is subtitled "Access to Tools." **The Whole Earth Catalog** is an example of what we might call, to coin a new and necessary word, paratechnology.

What about parapolitics? The ratio, patient-paraprofessional-professional to man-?-politics suggests at least the linguistic appropriateness of 'parapolitics' as the name for the social practice mediating between man and the new alien environment. The prefix "para-" connotes both "beside" and "against." What theory defines the practice so named? Surely not the theory of anarchism, more an antipolitics than a parapolitics. The stance of the anarchist is too close to that of the political ascetic, too reminiscent of the will to turn one's back on the alien environment rather than work both beside and against it. Yet the anarchist remains more likely than others to see the sense in which the tools of politics will turn on their modern manipulators and tie them more tightly into the knots they wished to escape.

To complete the preliminaries, the naming of the problems prior to their attempted solutions, what of the new man? What sort of person will flourish in these parapolitical enclaves carved out of the political-technologal wilderness? Both the professional's practice and the theory to be developed show him to be a many dimensional man, pluralized and multi-selved. A decentralized parapolitics calls for decentralized people.

•

What is the difference between the power of the entrepreneur and the "power" of the technocrats? Most briefly it is the difference between the power of the yes and the "power" of the no.

•

The proliferation of human tribes and languages marks freedom's triumph over the uniformity of nature, not reason's fall from uniform grace.

•

Were Socrates alive today would he declare the over-examined life not worth living? Our passions to plumb the depths of our private psyches and our rage to affix our personal identities run the risk of generating false identities in the process of asking and too eagerly answering the question, "Who am I?"

Could it be that we are not the autonomous individuals we take ourselves to be? Could it be that we are, in our dispersion into privatism, symptoms of a sickness in the history of man, victims of an illusion? Could our passion to find "personal identity" be like the paranoiac's need to identify "the enemy"? If so the question, "Who am I," can only deepen the sickness, at least until it leads to the further question, "Who are we?"

•

Cultures of interdependence like the Olympian pantheon contain *greater variety* of polytheistic ideals to which one might conform. In place of this variety the unity of value implicit in the *Normalgott* of monotheism makes the freedom of the monotheistic ego turn over into its opposite: "Our society gives far more leeway to the individual to pursue his own ends, but, since *it* defines what is worthy and desirable, everyone tends, independently but monotonously, to pursue the same things in the same way." Monotheism takes its toll in monotony.

Shining Examples

Examples is the word! A very inspiring collection of renewable energy projects is presented in a dowdy, less-than inspiring manner. The details include things that many observers have forgotten or glossed over: financing, community involvement, impact, economics, complexity, local climate, and how long it took to do the job. This sort of thing is very useful for convincing local bankers and boards of supervisors that they are not stepping into the vote-losing, money-risking unknown. A large variety of projects is shown in categories such as agricultural, community, industrial, education, financing, government, and housing. If you can get by the format there's some hot stuff here. A big cheer for the reasonable price too.
—J. Baldwin

(For more local energy models, see our p. 175.)

Shining Examples
Kathleen Courrier, et al., Editors
1980; 210 pp.

$6.95 postpaid from:
Center for Renewable Resources
1001 Connecticut Avenue N.W.
Washington, DC 20036
or Whole Earth Household Store

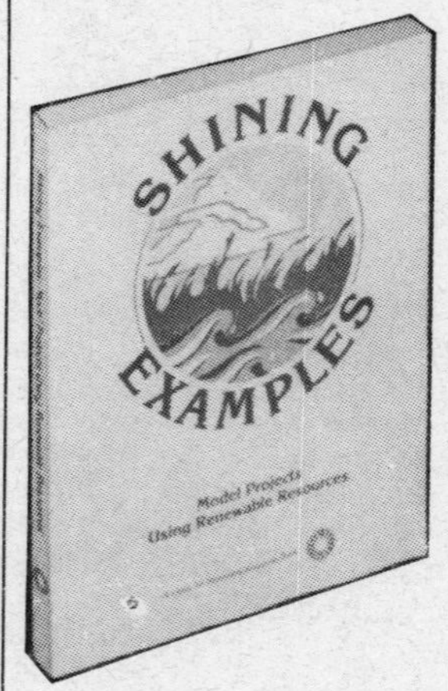

Renewable Resources—
A National Catalog
of
Model Projects

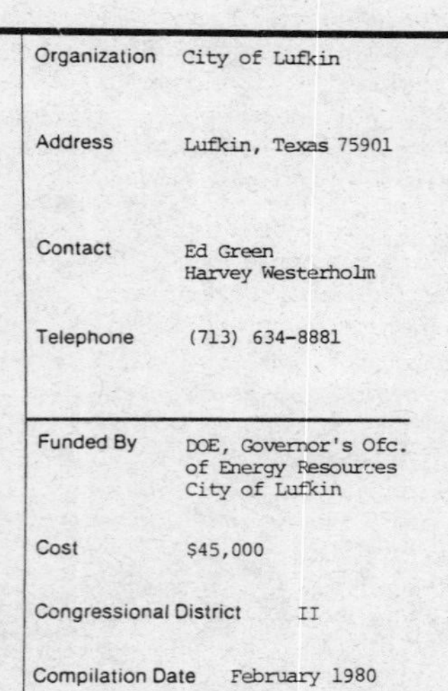

Category Cities
State TX
Project Name Lufkin Worm Ranch

Organization City of Lufkin
Address Lufkin, Texas 75901
Contact Ed Green
Harvey Westerholm
Telephone (713) 634-8881

Funded By DOE, Governor's Ofc. of Energy Resources City of Lufkin
Cost $45,000
Congressional District II
Compilation Date February 1980

The Lufkin Worm Ranch uses worms to process city sewage sludge, in the process producing more worms, larger worms, worm castings for fertilizer and a near-mineral soil for use in potting plants.

The project was inspired by the work of Ed Green, a farmer with a large earthworm farm in Shelbyville. Green discovered that his worms thrived on sewage sludge and, in August of 1977, he and his 30,000 square feet of worm beds began treating the overburdened waste-treatment system of nearby Center, a town of 5,000 people.

Now the City of Lufkin has started the first phase of its own municipal worm waste-treatment farm. They were prompted by the desire for less expensive waste treatment, more energy conservation, and the desire to transform waste into potting soil. The mayor, city council, and city management enlisted the help and advice of the Texas Department of Health, the Department of Water Resources, and the Environmental Protection Agency to ensure that the system was safe and effective. Then, armed with a $15,000 grant from the Governor's Office of Energy Resources and a $30,000 U.S. Department of Energy grant, the City bought its first 5,000-6,000 pounds of worms at $1.50/lb. to seed the worm cells, which will eventually hold 10,000 pounds of worms and process 10 percent of the city's sewage. The program is already handling 5 percent of the sludge, and operating at 50 percent of capacity. When fully operating it expects to save the city of 30,000 up to $65,000 per year in energy costs alone. The initial phase should require one full-time operator, with only two skilled or semi-skilled people required to eventually run the full-size farm.

The worm cells now used are covered with 12 greenhouses (totalling 22,800 square feet of earthworm culture) to protect the beds from rain

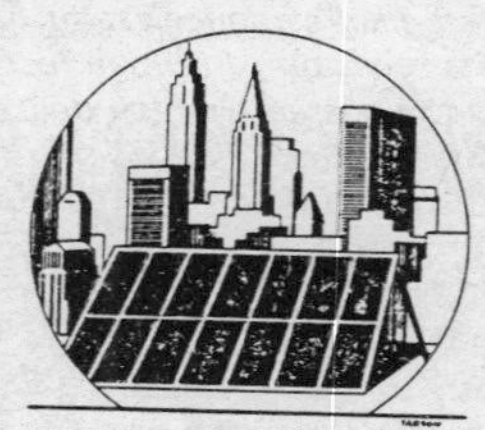

Center for Renewable Resources

Ecotopia

This enjoyable work of fiction is listed here in Politics because it is the best integrated <u>positive</u> *vision in print of how our civilization might fall into balance. It makes people mad enough to change their behavior. They see no reason why we can't live like Ecotopians NOW. —SB*

It doesn't really matter when things don't happen on time in Ecotopia. People grease and paint their bodies and cheer over spilled blood in the ritual war games. "The family" means some dozen or twenty folks coming and going and sharing the chores but no woman has a child unless she chooses the man. And it's not that things are sexually promiscuous at all . . . they're easy. (Organized promiscuity is limited to a few days on either side of the soltices and equinoxes, meaningful times of the year.) William Weston doesn't think of himself as the square reporter from New York, United States, the first foreigner to enter Ecotopia since the great war of succession in 1980, but as we develop a feel for Ecotopia, we the reader readers and Weston our narrator all begin to pick up vibes of our own squareness. What was once northern California, Oregon and Washington has become (by the year 2000) bucolic, calming, rhythmical and sensible. Climaxes (both sexual and violent) are there but they occur at reasonable, natural intervals. It is a question of values.
—Lynn Margulis

(See Callenbach's **Ecotopian Encyclopedia**, *our p. 290.)*

Ecotopia
(The Notebooks and Reports of William Weston)
Ernest Callenbach
1975; 212 pp.

$2.75 postpaid from:
Bantam Books
414 East Golf Road
Des Plaines, IL 60016
or Whole Earth Household Store

•

(May 18) Marissa says I am squeamish about violence. Makes fun of American war technology, claims we had to develop it because we can no longer bear just to bayonet a man — have to spend $50,000 to avoid guilt, by zapping him from the stratosphere. This because last night I expressed dismay at the ritual war games. "Listen, you'll *love* it," she said gaily, "You're just ripe for it!"

•

"Probably our greatest economies were obtained simply by stopping production of many processed and packaged foods. These had either been outlawed on health grounds or put on Bad Practice lists."

This sounded like a loophole that might house a large and rather totalitarian rat. "What are these lists and how are they enforced?" I asked.

"Actually, they aren't enforced at all. They're a mechanism of moral persuasion, you might say. But they're purely informal. They're issued by study groups from consumer co-ops. Usually, when a product goes onto such a list, demand for it drops sharply. The company making it then ordinarily has to stop production, or finds it possible to sell only in specialized stores."

"But surely these committees are not allowed to act simply on their own say-so, without scientific backing or government authorization?"

The Assistant Minister smiled rather wanly. "In Ecotopia," he said, "you will find many many things happening without government authorization."

•

After some drinks the conversation got livelier and more personal. Thought I'd do some probing. "Doesn't this stable-state business get awfully static? I'd think it would drive you crazy after a certain point!"

Bert looked at me with amusement, and batted the ball back. "Well, don't forget that we don't have to be stable. The system provides the stability, and we can be erratic within it."

•

Ecotopians treat as severe breaches of the peace many actions we consider white-collar crimes seldom deserving of police or court action. Deliberate pollution of water or air is punished by severe jail sentences. "Victimless" crimes such as prostitution, gambling, and drug use are no longer on the books, but embezzlement, fraud, collusion, and similar "gentleman's crimes" are dealt with just as severely as crimes like assault and robbery — which are, by the way, rare in Ecotopia, perhaps because of the personal nature of their neighborhoods and the virtual impossibility of anonymity in them. (Strangers get a lot of attention in Ecotopia, but the motives for this may not be entirely friendliness.) Ecotopian courts mete out fines very seldom, it appears, preferring to rely on imprisonment, which is felt to affect convicted persons more equally. I hope to visit an Ecotopian prison soon; I am told that all prisons require the inmates to work, and rumors have circulated that some verge on slave-labor camps.

ANARRES URRAS

Mutual Aid

First published in 1902, this is considered to be Kropotkin's classic. Kropotkin himself was a classic; a Russian prince abashed by the arbitrariness of his own privilege. After he'd done his stint as a page at the Tsar's court, when the time came for him to choose a regiment, he unfashionably headed for Siberia and became an explorer. His researches led him to a new concept of Asia's geography. Publication of his theory would earn him international scientific prominence. Another thing Kropotkin discovered in Siberia: anarchism — it was there he met Madame Bakunin, who introduced him to her husband's ideas.

After resigning his commission and retiring into scholarly penury in St. Petersburg, Kropotkin got into trouble with the Tsar for lecturing to gatherings of workers. For this he was jailed. Two years later a number of friends contrived an elaborate plan for a daring daylight escape and freed him. His flight took him through Switzerland and France (where he was jailed again), and finally to London, where he went to work for the magazine **Nature.**

In the late eighties the vulgarization of Darwin's thought into social Darwinism began to dismay Kropotkin. After having meditated on the evidence at length, he took to print to refute Huxley's image of nature as a "continuous free fight"; a Hobbesian "war of all against all." In **Mutual Aid** *Kropotkin assembled evidence of cooperation in all animal societies, including man's. There are descriptions of animal behavior substantiating the notion that the survival of a species is often furthered not by internecine warfare, but by the banding together of its members for hunting, migration (which he perceived as a means of avoiding competition), and sociability. Kropotkin and the observers he quotes were anthropomorphising ethologists; their science was so new that it was unaffected by the quantification fetish; they were willing to interpret animal behavior in terms of feeling, even tender feeling.*

If **Mutual Aid***'s ethological evidence seems quaint by today's standards, its re-vision of human history is illuminating, particularly the passages which deal with the history of medieval free cities. They* <u>were</u> *utopias, their infrastructures were shaped by craftsmen's ethics — guild charters; their citizens worked together in myriad ways to support the communes — not merely out of altruism or necessity. Decency just happened to be an elegant way of achieving homeostasis. It took considerable ruthlessness on the part of nationstates to subjugate these cities and destroy their wholesome autonomy.*

—Stephanie Mills

Mutual Aid
(A Factor of Evolution)
Peter Kropotkin
1902, 1976; 362 pp.
$4.50 postpaid from:
Porter Sargent Publishers
11 Beacon Street
Boston, MA 02108
or Whole Earth
Household Store

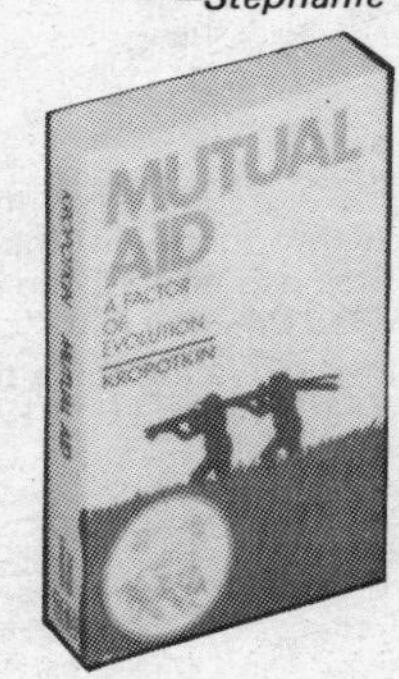

•

The absorption of all social functions by the State necessarily favoured the development of an unbridled, narrow-minded individualism. In proportion as the obligations towards the State grew in numbers the citizens were evidently relieved from their obligations towards each other.

•

When the parrots start hunting, they display the most wonderful intelligence, prudence, and capacity of coping with circumstances. Take, for instance, a band of white cacadoos in Australia. Before starting to plunder a corn-field, they first send out a reconnoitring party which occupies the highest trees in the vicinity of the field, while other scouts perch upon the intermediate trees between the field and the forest and transmit the signals. If the report runs "All right," a score of cacadoos will separate from the bulk of the band, take a flight in the air, and then fly towards the trees nearest to the field. They also will scrutinize the neighbourhood for a long while, and only then will they give the signal for general advance, after which the whole band starts at once and plunders the field in no time. The Australian settlers have the greatest difficulties in beguiling the prudence of the parrots; but if man, with all his art and weapons, has succeeded in killing some of them, the cacadoos become so prudent and watchful that they henceforward baffle all strategems.

There can be no doubt that it is the practice of life in society which enables the parrots to attain that very high level of almost human intelligence and almost human feelings which we know in them. Their high intelligence has induced the best naturalists to describe some species, namely the grey parrot, as the "bird-man."

As to their mutual attachment it is known that when a parrot has been killed by a hunter, the others fly over the corpse of their comrade with shrieks of complaints and "themselves fall the victims of their friendship," as Audubon said; and when two captive parrots, though belonging to different species, have contracted mutual friendship, the accidental death of one of the two friends has sometimes been followed by the death from grief and sorrow of the other friend. It is no less evident that in their societies they find infinitely more protection of beak and claw. Very few birds of prey or mammals dare attack any but the smaller species of parrots, and Brehm is absolutely right in saying of the parrots, as he also says of the cranes and the sociable monkeys, that they hardly have any enemies besides men; and he adds: "It is most probable that the larger parrots succumb chiefly to old age rather than die from the claws of any enemies."

•

Under the present social system, all bonds of union among the inhabitants of the same street or neighbourhood have been dissolved. In the richer parts of the large towns, people live without knowing who are their next-door neighbours. But in the crowded lanes people know each other perfectly, and are continually brought into mutual contact. Of course, petty quarrels go their course, in the lanes as elsewhere; but groupings in accordance with personal affinities grow up, and within their circle mutual aid is practised to an extent of which the richer classes have no idea.

The Dispossessed

Not so many books have changed my mind politically. **Brave New World** *did (away with Utopia).* **Dune** *did (toward a politics of stressed systems). And* **The Dispossessed** *has (toward Kropotkin and Mao).*

Ursula K. LeGuin is the daughter of the eminent Berkeley anthropologist Alfred Kroeber. It shows. Her work has a textured believability, depth of insight, and complexity of character seldom found in science fiction, and which can carry her idea far into your life. The idea in this book is of a two-planet system. One is rich and "free" — a kind of Ur-America. The second is almost a desert, granted to the rebels from the first planet to play out their biological metaphor ("The Analogy") of social mutual-aid against a harsh environment. The two societies have not communicated in centuries. Now, in the person of a remarkable physicist, they reconverge. LeGuin's skill as a storyteller is to progressively buffet the reader's opinion as to where the goods and evils are in these diametric systems. Simplistic she is never.

As in **Dune, Lord of the Rings,** *or* **The Once and Future King,** *one wants to live in her world.* *—SB*

The Dispossessed
Ursula K. LeGuin
1974; 311 pp.
$2.50 postpaid from:
Avon Books
Mail Order Department
250 West 55th Street
New York, NY 10019
or Whole Earth
Household Store

•

"Excess is excrement," Odo wrote in the *Analogy*. "Excrement retained in the body is a poison."

•

Some way before him, down the darkening path, a person sat reading on a stone bench.

Shevek went forward slowly. He came to the bench and stood looking at the figure who sat with head bowed over the book in the green-gold dusk under the trees. It was a woman of fifty or sixty, strangely dressed, her hair pulled back in a knot. Her left hand on her chin nearly hid the stern mouth, her right held the papers on her knee. They were heavy, those papers; the cold hand on them was heavy The light was dying fast but she never looked up. She went on reading the proof sheets of *The Social Organism.*

Shevek looked at Odo for a while, and then he sat down on the bench beside her.

He had no concept of status at all, and there was plenty of room on the bench. He was moved by a pure impulse of companionship.

He looked at the strong, sad profile, and at the hands, an old woman's hands. He looked up into the shadowy branches. For the first time in his life he comprehended that Odo, whose face he had known since his infancy, whose ideas were central and abiding in his mind and the mind of everyone he knew, that Odo had never set foot on Anarres: that she had lived, and died, and was buried, in the shadow of green-leaved trees, in unimaginable cities, among people speaking unknown languages, on another world. Odo was an alien: an exile.

The young man sat beside the statue in the twilight, one almost as quiet as the other.

•

We have nothing but our freedom. We have nothing to give you but your own freedom. We have no law but the single principle of mutual aid between individuals. We have no government but the single principle of free association. We have no states, no nations, no presidents, no premiers, no chiefs, no generals, no bosses, no bankers, no landlords, no wages, no charity, no police, no soldiers, no wars. Nor do we have much else. We are sharers, not owners. We are not prosperous. None of us is rich. None of us is powerful. If it is Anarres you want, if it is the future you seek, then I tell you that you must come to it with empty hands. You must come to it alone, and naked, as the child comes into the world, into his future, without any past, without any property, wholly dependent on other people for his life.

•

There were no rules of parliamentary procedure at meetings in PDC. Interruptions were sometimes more frequent than statements. The process, compared to a well-managed executive conference, was a slab of raw beef compared to a wiring diagram. Raw beef, however, functions better than a wiring diagram would, in its place — inside a living animal.

•

The sunlights differ, but there is only one darkness.

THE RISING SUN
NEIGHBORHOOD NEWSLETTER

Her problem was she was translucent (more sometimes than others, more noticeable to herself than others) and when, for example, she held her hand up to shield her eyes from the sun and the sun shone through a little, she found it to be an inconvenience as well as a star in the middle of her hand. Some things passing through left traces, such as the nearly new moon on the sticking out bone of her left wrist months after she'd pointed at it and the cow's nose she'd petted one summer's afternoon and glimpsed faintly on the back of her hand on yearly anniversaries of whatever day it was. There was also an owl she'd stared at for hours one moonlit night staring out of the back of her head but it was only seen by the guy who cut her hair who took it as a sign to take less drugs and move to Oregon (but he was probably going to move to Oregon anyway) and a couple of lovers (who were probably going to stop being lovers anyway). Everyone's skin looked so cold and clammy through hers, except on some sunny beaches, that she tended to send all lovers away until sooner or later she met someone opalescent which was better — faint rainbows showing through her knuckles made touching more fun — but also disconcerting because when their whole bodies touched at the same time it turned out they matched, every other molecule, and they fell right through each other. "Maybe if I wore pantyhose and sold real estate these things wouldn't happen to me," she thought, but it was too late for that, and she and her lover learned to do controlled falls and stop in the middle of each other to let some molecules change bodies if they were bored, and pretty soon both of them were both translucent and opalescent and found each other's bodies about the best thing to look at the world through — hidden spectrums found, beauty of shapes revealed through simplification, the funny fuzzy texture of human skin over it all. They still used their naked eyes some for old times sake and contrast but one time when they were watching the sunset through each other they disappeared.

Amnesty International

It's always a shock to learn that God is not interested in your pain. The best you can hope for is the help of other people.

The use of torture is steadily increasing world-wide. It is difficult to find out about and nearly impossible to check. So far the only deterrent is public opinion. That requires a respected international investigative organization. Amnesty International delivers.

Torture is a runaway phenomenon — far from preventing fanaticism, it increases fanaticism, which leads to more torture, and so forth. It will not cease until indeed it becomes as universally unthinkable as slavery. If we're going to have an intelligence and espionage establishment, let it work on this one.

You can participate in Amnesty International with donations, letterwriting campaigns, and attention to their various publications: ***Matchbox****, sundry special reports, the* ***Annual Report****, and their book* ***Report on Torture****.*

—SB

Amnesty International Report on Torture
1973, 1975; 285 pp.
$4.95 postpaid

Amnesty International Annual Report
$4.50 postpaid from:
AIUSA Publications
Mid-Atlantic Book Service
5 Lawrence Street
Bloomfield, NJ 07003

Matchbox
Amnesty Action
(Amnesty Action Newsletters)
$20 /year (11 issues includes membership)

Publications List
$1
all from:
Amnesty International U.S.A.
Amnesty Action
304 West 58th Street
New York, NY 10019
or
Publications List
£1 from:
Amnesty International
International Secretariat
10 Southampton Street
London WCZE 7HF
England

•

AMNESTY INTERNATIONAL OBJECTIVES

I detest your ideas but I am ready to die for your right to express them. —Voltaire

Amnesty International was founded in 1961 in the belief that every person has the right to hold and to express his convictions and has an obligation to extend the same freedom to others. It is now a worldwide human rights movement which is independent of any government, political, ideological or religious grouping.

Amnesty International works for the release of men and women imprisoned anywhere for their beliefs, colour, sex, language, ethnic origin or religion, provided they have not used or advocated violence. These are termed "prisoners of conscience."

Amnesty International opposes the use of torture and the death penalty in all cases and without reservation. Since 1973 Amnesty International has been conducting an international Campaign for the Abolition of Torture.

Amnesty International advocates fair and early trials for all political prisoners and works on behalf of persons detained without charge or without trial and those detained after expiry of their sentences.

Amnesty International seeks observance through the world of the United Nations Universal Declaration of Human Rights and of the UN Standard Minimum Rules for the Treatment of Prisoners.

•

Every day the dead are less docile

What's going on?
These dead are different than in the old days.
Today they are ironic
They ask questions.
It seems to me that they have begun to realize
That they are the majority.

—Roque Dalton Garcia
"El Descanso de Guerrero"
La taberna y otros lugares, 1976

Roque Dalton Garcia was a member of El Salvador's People's Revolutionary Army who was executed in 1975 — by whom remains a mystery.

Index on Censorship

Even if you're sure the news is being censored, you're a prisoner of your own particular brand of paranoid speculation unless you know exactly what is being left out. This magazine reports on stories not covered and why they weren't from all parts of the world and political spectrum. The style is calm, careful, well-researched, and horrifying.

—Anne Herbert

Index on Censorship
Hugh Lunghi, Editor
$18/year (6 issues)
from:
The Fund for Free Expression
205 East 42nd Street
New York, NY 10017
or
£9 /year (6 issues)
from:
Index on Censorship
21 Russell Street
Covent Garden
London WC2B 5HP
England

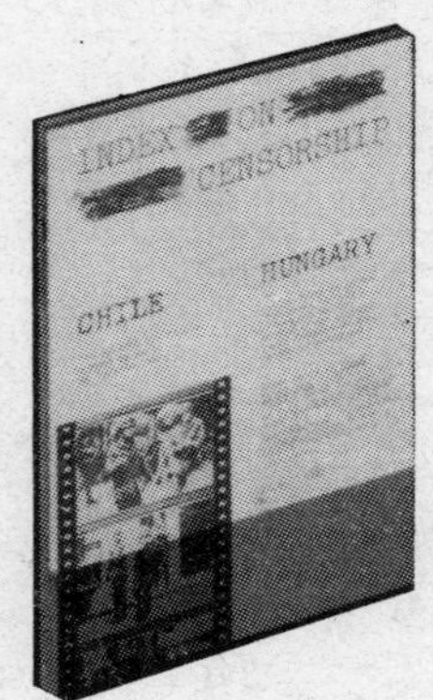

Argentinian cameraman, Leonardo Hendriksson, films the shots which killed him during the attempted "Tancazo" coup of 29 June 1973. The sequence appears in Part 1 of Patricio Guzman's La Batalla de Chile.

•

The most influential theoretical writing on the Cambodian society and its problems was the Ph.D. thesis submitted by Khieu Samphan (now Cambodian Head of State) to the Faculty of Law and Economics of the University of Paris in 1959. In his thesis, **The Economy of Cambodia and its Problems of Industrialisation**, Khieu Samphan argues that the only way the Cambodian economy could be independent and self-sufficient would be to cut itself off from the international economy for a period of time. Because Phnom Penh and other provincial cities owed their expansion to French colonialism, Chinese commerce and the bureaucracy, they were a drain on national wealth. Khieu Samphan estimated that over 80 per cent of city dwellers were unproductive and only served the elite. He proposed to transfer them to productive sectors of the economy, basically to agriculture, and form them into cooperatives. His main argument is that only by expanding agricultural production can the base be provided for industrialisation.

—Lek Hor Tan
Cambodia's Total Revolution

Resurgence

British-based journal of the Fourth World. International perspectives on decentralism, alternative technology, small communities, ethnic cultures. Editor Satish Kumar was a very early publisher of the ideas of E.F. Schumacher and now administers the Schumacher Society. ***Resurgence*** *provides a forum for spiritual, philosophical, and ecological debate as well as the practical and political dimensions of social change.*

—Hazel Henderson

Resurgence
Satish Kumar, Editor
$20 /year (6 issues)
from:
Resurgence
Ford House
Hartland, Bideford
Devon, England

•

Revolutions begin when people who are defined as problems achieve the power to redefine the problem.

A critical point in the development of the civil rights struggle was the Black movement's capacity to declare the central issue the "White problem." A people, declared deficient and in need, unshackled their labels and attempted to lock them on their oppressors.

There was a revolutionary insight in that strategy. It recognized that the power to label people as deficient and declare them in need is the basic tool for control and oppression in modern industrialized societies. The agents with comprehensive labelling power in these societies are the helping professionals.

New Internationalist

If economic development for the Third World means increased industrialization, why is it those very developing nations with "successful" industries also have a corresponding decline in real wages and employment opportunities? The ***New Internationalist*** *addresses the mechanisms that permit this trend to occur, but most importantly it emphasizes the effects on the lifestyle of the poor who comprise the increasing percentage of the world's population. What sorts of adjustments must a rural peasant make when he finds himself with his family on the streets of New Delhi without a job or home? How do the urban poor in Nairobi create their own jobs? It is rare that such questions are dealt with in detail as they are in this magazine. Each issue also provides access to international activist groups in a campaign directory and contains ads for needed professionals in various developing countries. A useful and credible publication for those who not only wish to learn about the nature of world poverty but want to do something about it.* *—Angela Gennino*

New Internationalist
$15 /year (12 issues)
from:
New Internationalist
113 Atlantic Avenue
Brooklyn, NY 11201
or
£9 /year (12 issues)
from:
New Internationalist
Montagu House
High Street
Huntington
Cambridgeshire
England PE18 6EP

•

You wouldn't know it from the literature on population growth, but babies are made by women and men having sex together. Debbie Taylor reports that the denial of women's economic and political rights is reflected in the denial of their right to enjoy sex and control their own fertility.

Foreign Affairs

An establishment publication but eclectic in its choice of authors (Kissinger but also Nyerere). Very long and useful list of new books in each issue with brief reviews.

—Witold Rybczynski

Foreign Affairs
William P. Bundy, Editor
$18 /year (5 issues)
from:
Foreign Affairs
P.O. Box 2615
Boulder, CO 80322

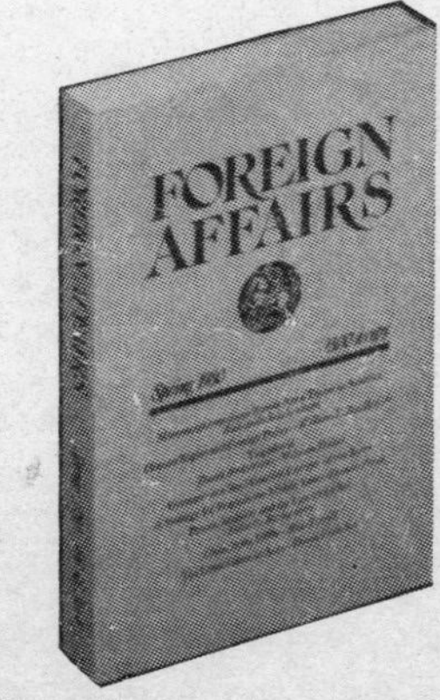

•

To begin with, there is the careless and inaccurate use of the words "Russia" and "Russian" in place of "U.S.S.R."

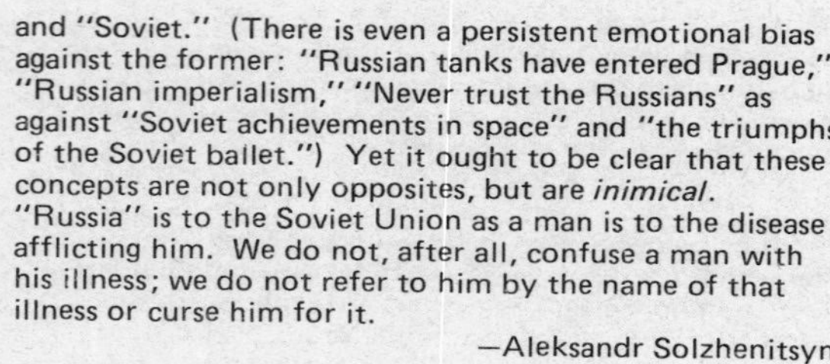

and "Soviet." (There is even a persistent emotional bias against the former: "Russian tanks have entered Prague," "Russian imperialism," "Never trust the Russians" as against "Soviet achievements in space" and "the triumphs of the Soviet ballet.") Yet it ought to be clear that these concepts are not only opposites, but are *inimical*. "Russia" is to the Soviet Union as a man is to the disease afflicting him. We do not, after all, confuse a man with his illness; we do not refer to him by the name of that illness or curse him for it.

—Aleksandr Solzhenitsyn

•

Tourism: Passport to Development? By Emanuel de Kadt. New York: Oxford University Press (for UNESCO/World Bank), 1979, 360 pp., $14.95 (Paper, $5.95).

Second only to oil as a currency earner for poor countries, tourism has a thin literature, so this volume is welcome. Professor de Kadt, a sociologist from Sussex, provides a good survey; the dozen or so papers prepared for a seminar range from how to plan, through some interesting case studies of a number of countries, to prescriptions for defense mechanisms. The tone is positive, with more emphasis on jobs than culture conflict.

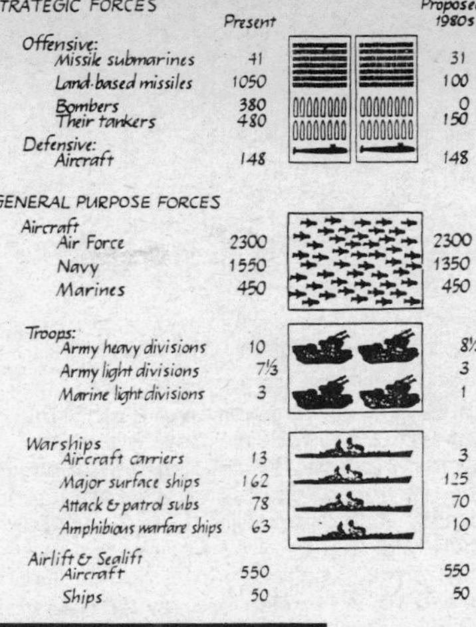

A PROPOSAL FOR THE MILITARY FORCES

	Present	Proposed 1980s
STRATEGIC FORCES		
Offensive:		
Missile submarines	41	31
Land-based missiles	1050	100
Bombers	380	0
Their tankers	480	150
Defensive:		
Aircraft	148	148
GENERAL PURPOSE FORCES		
Aircraft		
Air Force	2300	2300
Navy	1550	1350
Marines	450	450
Troops:		
Army heavy divisions	10	8⅓
Army light divisions	7⅓	3
Marine light divisions	3	1
Warships		
Aircraft carriers	13	3
Major surface ships	162	125
Attack & patrol subs	78	70
Amphibious warfare ships	63	10
Airlift & Sealift		
Aircraft	550	550
Ships	50	50

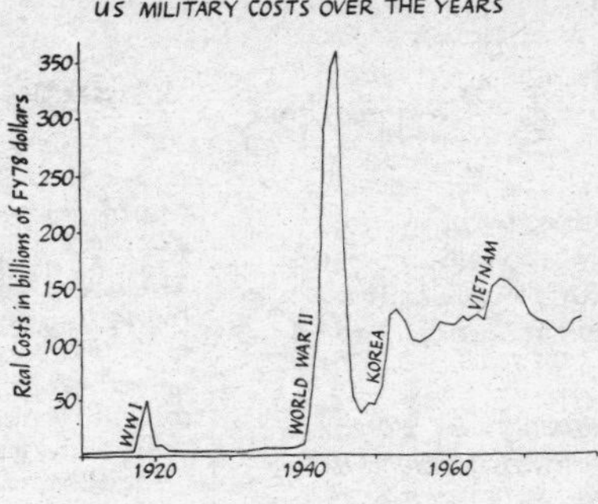

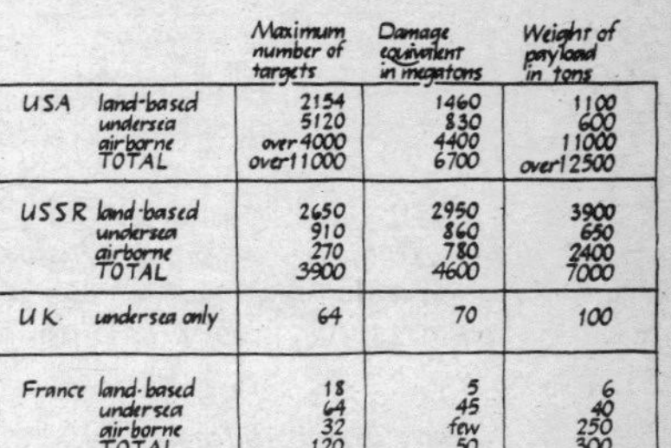

WORLD STRATEGIC NUCLEAR FORCES COMPARED

		Maximum number of targets	Damage equivalent in megatons	Weight of payload in tons
USA	land-based	2154	1460	1100
	undersea	5120	830	600
	airborne	over 4000	4400	11000
	TOTAL	over 11000	6700	over 12500
USSR	land-based	2650	2950	3900
	undersea	910	860	650
	airborne	270	780	2400
	TOTAL	3900	4600	7000
UK	undersea only	64	70	100
France	land-based	18	5	6
	undersea	64	45	40
	airborne	32	few	250
	TOTAL	120	50	300
China	land-based	50-80	20-60	30
	airborne	80	200	250
	TOTAL	150	250	300

The Causes of War

Nuclear proliferation is at hand — many small nations with short-term governments with little to lose . . . and the Bomb. All the more reason to take a searching non-rhetorical look at War, wars, and try to discern what sense they operate by. Geoffrey Blainey has investigated every international war since 1700. His conclusions are fine hard aphorisms that can be navigated by. —SB

The Causes of War
Geoffrey Blainey
1973; 278 pp.
$5.95 postpaid from:
Macmillan
Publishing Company
Order Department
Front and Brown Streets
Riverside, NJ 08075
or Whole Earth
Household Store

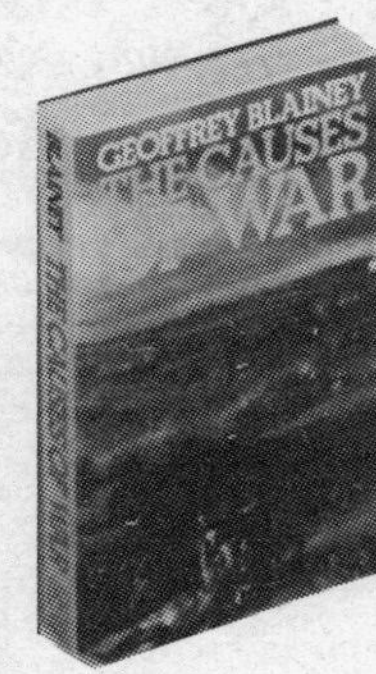

•

11. Wars usually begin when two nations disagree on their relative strength, and wars usually cease when the fighting nations agree on their relative strength. Agreement or disagreement emerges from the shuffling of the same set of factors. Thus each factor is capable of promoting war or peace.
12. A change in one factor — the defection of an ally or the eruption of strife in the land of the enemy — may dramatically alter a nation's assessment of its bargaining position. In the short term that factor could wield an influence which seems irrationally large.
13. When nations prepare to fight one another, they have contradictory expectations of the likely duration and outcome of the war. When those predictions, however, cease to be contradictory, the war is almost certain to end.
14. Any factor which increases the likelihood that nations will agree on their relative power is a potential cause of peace. One powerful cause of peace is a decisive war, for war provides the most widely-accepted measure of power.
15. Even a decisive war cannot have permanent influence, for victory is invariably a wasting asset.
16. A formula for measuring international power is essential: ironically the most useful formula is warfare. Until the function of warfare is appreciated, the search for a more humane and more efficient way of measuring power is likely to be haphazard.

•

The hope, so widely held between 1860 and 1914, that mechanised methods of warfare were making long wars an impossibility, has not been fulfilled. That hope was revived in 1945 when the first nuclear bomb was dropped on a Japanese city, but so far it has not been fulfilled. Even if two main nuclear powers went to war, the web of their alliances would probably turn it into a general war; and present knowledge offers no strong probability that a general war would be short. Even if it began with nuclear attacks there is no strong probability that it would end quickly. Although there seems a chance that a general war could end in a month, a disastrous month, there seems a greater chance that it would continue for years.

Defense limitation publications

Even if you subscribe to the **New York Times,** keeping up on the arms race and the defense establishment in general can be difficult. Two other sources are particularly helpful.

The Defense Monitor, $15 (contribution)/year, 10 issues, from Center for Defense Information, 122 Maryland Ave., NE, Washington, D.C. 20002; "The Center for Defense Information supports a strong defense but opposes excessive expenditures or forces. It believes that strong social, economic, and political structures contribute equally to national security and are essential to the strength and viability of our country." Each issue features a particular aspect of defense policy.

Arms Control Today, $20/year, 11 issues, from The Arms Control Association, 11 Dupont Circle NW, Washington, D.C. 20036, focuses more generally on strategic weapons and weapons systems, and related areas (e.g., nuclear proliferation). Each issue contains a few pages of essays on relevant topics by different authors. Roughly half of each issue is given over to "Arms Control in Print" — bibliographies of recently published articles in a variety of arms control subject areas.

If you're a serious student of arms and defense issues, or simply want to keep reasonably informed in these areas as part of your regular general input (as do I), these two publications are invaluable. Those of us interested in more social, political, spiritual, and/or appropriately technological issues would do well to remember that the world remains on the edge of blowing itself up. Until we solve *that* one, all the rest may be academic.

Antidefenseestablishmentarianly,
Phillip Greenberg
Mill Valley, California

The Price of Defense

I know of no more important subject and no more graspable handle on it than this book. There is considerable news here, news to me at least — U.S. defense expenditures are not for defense; the expenditures can be reduced by half without reducing military effectiveness for major U.S. goals; the U.S. practice of "extended deterrence" (threatening first use of nuclear weapons in behalf of allies) is inflammatory at best. Our present military stance is that of an empire, not a nation, and costs accordingly.

Prepared in part by my heroes Philip and Phylis Morrison (of **Scientific American***), the book is a superb introduction to modern warfare in terms of its weapons and national stances, though it does not particularly address the secret war of intelligence and counter-intelligence. A book of equal quality about that battlefield would be especially welcome now that we have* **The Price of Defense.** —SB

The Price of Defense
(A New Strategy for Military Spending)
The Boston Study Group
1978; 228 pp.
$15 postpaid from:
Times Books
Harper and Row
Keystone Industrial Park
Scranton, PA 18512
or Whole Earth
Household Store

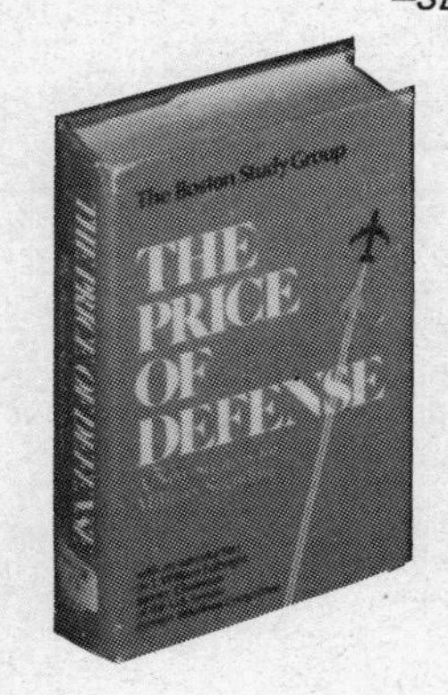

•

Briefly put, we recommend that half of the present military establishment aimed mainly at responding to aggression by the Soviet Union should be left unchanged or improved, while most of the other half, not useful for countering Soviet military threats or accomplishing other acceptable goals, should be eliminated.

The three major items which we cut back are:

- *the vast excess in the quantity of nuclear weapons,* over and above the number needed to deter a nuclear attack;
- most of the *aircraft carriers, amphibious landing ships* and *lightly equipped land-combat forces,* which are primarily useful not against the U.S.S.R. but against the lesser military powers in the poorer half of the world, like Vietnam; and
- the *unnecessary investment in development of new weaponry,* which has long made the United States the driving force behind the rapid, destabilizing and costly advances in world military technology.

The forces we propose to retain are:

- a relatively *small but invulnerable nuclear-weapon force,* to deter Soviet nuclear attacks by threatening retaliation;
- the *heavily equipped land-combat forces* presently assigned to help defend Western Europe against possible Soviet aggression together with
- *most of the current tactical combat aircraft,* which are intended to provide air cover in the event of a war in Europe and to protect the ocean approaches to Japan; and
- an *unchanged force of surface ships and attack submarines,* to protect the freedom of the seas.

The changes we propose are meant to be introduced over a period of five to ten years. This gradual transition is intended to preserve international stability and to permit a smooth conversion to civilian employment. We also assume that a major revamping of U.S. military policy would be preceded by several years of national publicity, reflection and debate.

Giving Up the Gun

Our culture feels oddly helpless about its bad habits. Remember the population harangues of the '60s? — no one, pro or con, imagined that birth rates might actually decrease anything like the way they in fact have. Similarly the Arms Race is treated as a given, like Original Sin.

From 1543 to 1879 the highly sophisticated culture of Japan gave up the gun, and they didn't even have to (as we do). Read this short wholly fascinating book and take heart. —SB

Giving Up the Gun
(Japan's Reversion to the Sword, 1543-1879)
Noel Perrin
1979; 122 pp.
$5.50 postpaid from:
Shambhala Publishers
P.O. Box 271
Boulder, CO 80306
or Whole Earth
Household Store

•

What the Japanese experience *does* prove is two things. First, that a no-growth economy is perfectly compatible with prosperous and civilized life. And second, that human beings are less the passive victims of their own knowledge and skills than most men in the West suppose.

World Military and Social Expenditures 1979

The most godawful facts in the world, assembled with care, presented strikingly but without rhetoric. None is needed. Half an hour with these charts and you're ready to take your own soapbox downtown and rail at strangers. —SB

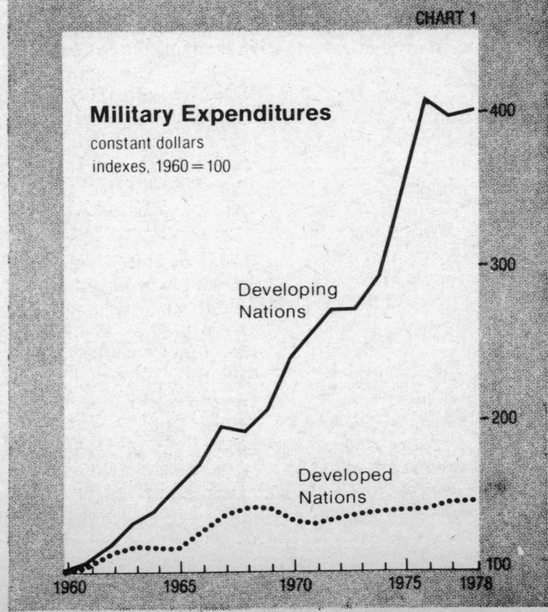

World Military and Social Expenditures 1979
Ruth Leger Sivard
1979; 36 pp.
$3.50 postpaid from:
World Priorities, Inc.
Box 1003
Leesburg, VA 22075
or Whole Earth
Household Store

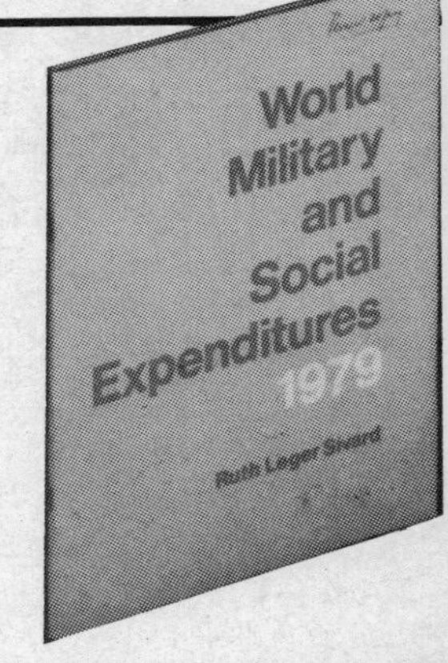

THE RISING SUN
NEIGHBORHOOD NEWSLETTER

Muni buses run at B flat. Most mechanical things run at B or B flat. —Nancy

The Effects of Nuclear War

The latest word, and a fine job of it. This 1979 report was prepared by the Office of Technology Assessment for the Senate Committee on Foreign Relations. Unlike many such government documents, it is imaginatively presented. It seems we know quite a lot by now about the effects of nuclear explosions on human affairs. And while much is guessed at about the broad effects of a general nuclear war, the authors admit that mostly they don't know.

I figure that real prevention of real nuclear war will require a lot of personal thinking about the unthinkable and knowing as much as possible about the unknowable. It is an abstract evil — nuclear war — dissolvable not by counter abstraction but by sane attention to gritty detail.
—SB
[Suggested by Shannon Bush]

The Effects of Nuclear War
Office of Technology Assessment
1979; 151 pp.
No. 052-003-00668-5

$4.75 postpaid from:
Superintendent of Documents
U.S. Government Printing Office
Washington, DC 20402
or Whole Earth Household Store

•

The entire United States has facilities to treat 1000 or 2000 severe burn cases; a single nuclear weapon could produce more than 10,000.

Approximate footprint coverage of Soviet attack.

•

The combined populations of Charlottesville and Albemarle County rose to 150,000 in the 7 days after the nuclear attack. Slowly, hostility and resentment wedged a gap between residents and refugees who attempted to join the group shelters. The refugees, still in a daze from their experience, believed that they had priority rights after all they had suffered. The local residents viewed the outsiders as a threat to their own survival, particularly as the extent of the war damage was becoming evident.

(For anti-nuclear reactor information, see **No Nuclear News** *p. 500.)*
—SB

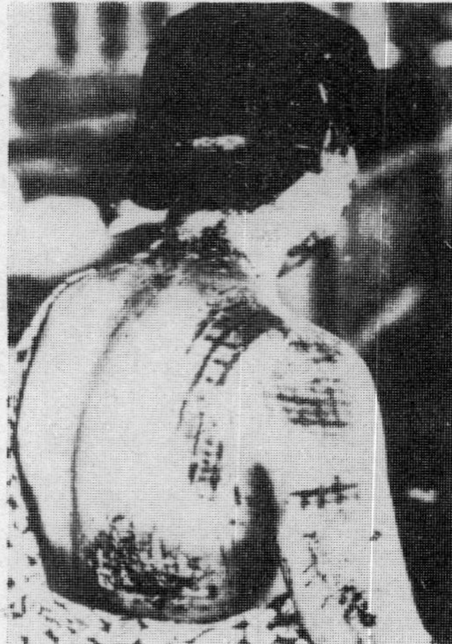

The patient's skin is burned in a pattern corresponding to the dark portions of a kimono worn at the time of the explosion.

Nukebuster

I was M.C. in D.C. for the March on Washington/No Nukes rally April 26th, 1980. About 40,000 demonstrators braved a torrential downpour to witness 26 speakers and 13 musical acts. It was an incredible achievement to run a full sound stage under water. Your cover must be absolute or musicians will fry like eggs. A lot of the credit goes to the Farm folks in Tennessee. Stephen Gaskin was one of the speakers and played drums for The Nuclear Regulatory Commission, the new farm band. Those farmers also worked security and helped coordinate. Meanwhile their kids were running from trailer to trailer dosing rock and rollers with tofu, except for the few who toured the Smithsonian (right across the street) with a Nukebuster! The Nukebuster is a sophisticated geiger counter that continually detects the ambient level of radiation. These farm kids aimed that sucker at the uranium sample in the geology wing and the pointers damn near jumped off the dial. Perhaps a citizen's arrest?
—Wavy Gravy

Nukebuster
$280 plus shipping
Information **free** from:
Solar Electronics
156 Drakes Lane
Summertown, TN 38483

→

Nukebuster Gamma, Beta, Alpha with Meter @ $280.00

BU1 - Battery pack attachment for intermittent portable use @ $24.95

CA2 - Cigarette Lighter adapter for plugging in two units @ $9.95

WP-110V - Adapter for home use; wood pedestal AC adapter @ $24.95

METER · ALPHA WINDOW · MODE SW · AUDIO · NORMAL · x10 · NUKE BUSTER · COUNT LIGHT · ALARM LIG

	MODE SWITCH	
	NORMAL & AUDIO	x1
METER LIGHTS UP	.04 mR/hr (3-4 times background*)	.4 mR (30-40 times b
ALARM GOES OFF	.1 mR/h (10 times background*)	1 mR (100 times ba

*Normal averaged background at sea level is approximately .01 mR/ Some counts will always occur due to background radiati

The Dangers of Nuclear War

American activists are in orderly transition from work on curbing just nuclear energy to the harder and far more momentous task of curbing nuclear weapons. Some of the resistance techniques will transfer and some won't. With nuclear reactors, what to stop and how to stop it was a relative known. With nuclear weapons what to stop is less well known, and how to stop it is an utter unknown.

Therefore instead of jumping to ideological conclusions a more effective path for the movement for now may be to raise questions and court ideas — encourage brainstorming on a world-wide scale. If all parties are welcomed to that discussion, a fair step toward resolution may already have been taken.

The critical ingredient is information. Political groups out of power fall into sectarian squabbling because their political life is restricted to theory and conflicting assertions. Parties in power are somewhat more convergent because the realities of daily responsibility force them to be; theory is secondary. The reason Dan Ellsberg is such a potent anti-nuclear spokesman is because he marshals his facts as if he were still Establishment.

I don't know the best texts for a budding activist against nuclear weapons. I grabbed this one out of the river of books flowing by my desk. It's the papers from a Pugwash Symposium held in 1976 and 1977 (the 30th of that noble lineage). Damn near every page changes my mind somewhat, and I thought I had my mind made up on this subject.
—SB

The Dangers of Nuclear War
Franklyn Griffiths and John C. Polanyi, Editors
1979; 197 pp.

$5.95 postpaid from:
University of Toronto Press
33 East Tupper Street
Buffalo, NY 14203
or Whole Earth Household Store

•

In effect, acute super-power crisis is now and will doubtless remain a precondition for the occurrence of general war. To inquire into the likelihood of general war is therefore to consider the likelihood and character of super-power crises — the potential they present for miscalculation, for inadequate control of national strategic forces, and for mutual loss of control over escalation of the crisis itself. John Steinbruner's account of the vagrant strategic anti-submarine warfare operations of the U.S. Navy during the Cuban missile crisis of 1962 shows just how things might begin to go wrong. And this was at a time when political leaders sought to exercise intense political control over military forces far less complex and elaborate than exist today.
—Franklyn Griffiths

•

Many millions who die in the aftermath of a massive nuclear exchange will die most horribly in a society that can no longer offer the comforts of warmth, shelter, food, uncontaminated water, and medication. The millions of injured who survive in a condition of reduced health (blinded, burnt, maimed, or weakened by the effects of radiation) will provide a fertile ground for plagues of contagious disease. Those fortunate enough to escape the war and its aftermath without visible scars will live in fear that their long-term health may have been impaired, their environment poisoned, and their future progeny imperilled for generations to come. The sense of demoralization, and its consequences for the orderly process of reconstruction, defy imagination. No parallels can be drawn (though sometimes they are) with the deaths and carnage of previous wars. The compression into a matter of hours of events more terrible than those that took place in other times over a period of years will shred the fabric of society rather than — as previously — severely strain it.
—John C. Polanyi

The Battle

by Peter Blue Cloud

They were so angry that they decided to have a battle. So terrible was their anger that they would not wait, but declared that the fight must be fought now, immediately, on this very spot. Fox blamed what he considered to be the crime on Badger. Badger in turn was all for placing the blame on Cougar.

Jackrabbit hopped in agitation, calling for Mole and for Mouse, and for Deer and Bear to fetch their sharpest arrows and their heaviest warclubs.

By the time Coyote arrived the sides had already been chosen, the battle lines formed, and the smell of hate and future bloodshed permeated the very air.

He, Coyote, listened to all the threats and promises of broken bodies to be. He walked out and stood between the enemies, declaring very solemnly, and in a very soft voice:

"No, I cannot allow this great fight to happen just yet. There has been no battle-preparation dance. There has been no pipe of cleansing. No, the Creation does not wish this battle to take place just yet."

And some say it was Bear, but strangely, no one actually remembers just who it was. Bear denied the accusation, but someone ran from one of the lines and struck Coyote dead!

And Coyote fell and indeed lay there, very dead. And the cry for immediate battle resumed, and the menacing cries for blood again filled the air,

when, from the opposite end of the battle lines, Coyote again stepped out, dancing and brandishing a huge club.

He ran to his dead self and struck a tremendous blow upon the body, then turned to face the creatures, shouting: "Who killed this person? Who struck him down before I did? Was that person purified? Did he sweat himself and think of the children? Did he dance to assure that the life cycle continue?"

"Enough talking!" someone shouted and ran to Coyote and struck him dead.

And again, much later, no one remembered who or what struck the blow which killed Coyote for the second time.

Then from the left hand side of center, Coyote ran out swinging a great club and struck at his fallen selves until all that remained were two masses of fur and blood and broken bones and twisted sinew.

Then Coyote danced the dance of victory over his own fallen selves, pledging their death to his own great anger, Oh, he danced, he really danced.

"Now then," said Porcupine, "how is it that this one who dances the victory in battle dance, when it was not himself who killed himselves? Is it within reason for him to claim this doubtful victory?"

"If I did not kill these two, then who did kill them?" demanded Coyote. "Let him step forward to claim these deaths, that I may kill him too in revenge."

When no one stepped forward, Coyote declared, motioning to his dead selves, "Then obviously, these kills are mine!"

"It seems to me," began Elk, who was interrupted by Skunk, who also began, "It's quite obvious to me that . . ." "Now hold on a moment," said Badger. And Coyote wheeled on Badger, shouting, "Hah! Don't you know that you can't hold onto a moment, let alone a minute?"

And so they argued, all the animal creatures, about the finer points of who might or might not claim a kill.

And the women of these great warriors, at the urging of Coyote, prepared a great feast, so that these mighty warrior-debators might continue on full stomachs.

And soon, the recent anger was set aside for the more important battle of words leading to reason.

And by this time, everyone having forgotten all about Coyote,

he, Coyote, took his fallen selves by their tails and dragged them away uphill.

Then he took a good hot sweat bath and then sang a song of renewal known only to himself, and soon his other selves revived. "Now," said one of them, 'that's what I'd call making your point the hard way. You know, it really hurt when you killed me."

"Yes," said the other self, standing up and stretching, "the next time this happens, don't forget it'll be your turn to be killed."

"Hey, maybe this won't ever happen again, huh?"

"Oh, it will happen again." Coyote said, "Yes, it always seems to happen again."

Then he merged into himselves and walked away, far away. ■

← Photo from Critical Mass Journal, the energy publication of Ralph Nader's Public Citizen, Inc.

Groups Active in Environmental Politics

by Peter Warshall

League of Women Voters

If the word "responsible" means anything in the United States, it means the League of Women Voters. Understanding with great wisdom that education and politics are identical, the League has taken action on water and air quality, solid waste management, land use, and energy. The California League's mimeo pamphlet on water politics for $1.50 contained more direct and clear information than the state's $35 atlas. That's how good they are. They publish **The National Voter** *which tells you what the Big Boys are up to.*

The National Voter, Susan Hayes Coughlin, Editor, **$8**/year (4 issues), from League of Women Voters of the United States, 1730 M Street N.W., Washington, DC 20036

Planned Parenthood

Right out there among the people, Planned Parenthood operates medically supervised clinics to help women and their husbands create the family they desire. In an atmosphere of abortion hysteria and world over-population, they remain the calm and practical voice.

Planned Parenthood, Information **free** from Planned Parenthood, Education Department, 810 Seventh Avenue, New York, NY 10019

Friends of the Earth

Under the chairmanship of David Brower, FOE has again and again put itself in difficult and controversial environmental politics and come out as admirable warriors for preservation, restoration and rational use of our planet. Many overseas affiliates — especially a fine branch in France. 23,000 members. Publishes **Not Man Apart** *(p. 51). It needs to have better local (vs. national) organization.*

Friends of the Earth, Information **free** from Friends of the Earth, 124 Spear Street, San Francisco, CA 94105

Environmental Defense Fund

More than Sierra Club or even Friends of the Earth, EDF has been the legal lion of the environmental movement. Tough and innovative legal suits have forced government agencies to pay closer attention to U.S. citizen's health, welfare, and future. I know of their excellent work in toxic substance regulation, but EDF also works hard on projects in pest control, water resources, land use, transportation and wildlife. Their bimonthly newsletter is short, sensible, and always informative.

Environmental Defense Fund Letter, Norma H. Watson, Editor, **$15**/year (6 issues — includes membership), from Environmental Defense Fund, 475 Park Avenue South, New York, NY 10016

Public Interest Research Group

Inspired by Ralph Nader, so you know what it's about. Consumer-citizens trying to get their two cents in while the heavies (corporations-bureaucrats-politicians-organized labor) shuffle the big bucks among themselves. Their recent work on toxic substances has been truly revelatory.

New York Public Interest Research Group, 5 Beekman Street, New York, NY 10038. Information $1.

Nader's own umbrella group, Public Citizen, Inc., includes a host of similarly-minded gadfly groups and some thoroughly-researched publications. —Art Kleiner

Multinational Monitor, Jonathan Ratner, Editor, **$15**/year (12 issues), from Multinational Monitor, P.O. Box 19312, Washington, DC 20036

Public Citizen Health Publications, Catalog **$.50**, from Health Research Group, Department 222, 2000 P Street NW, Washington, DC 20036

Critical Mass Journal (The Energy Publication of Ralph Nader's Public Citizen, Inc.), Whayne Dillehay, Editor, **$7.50**/year (12 issues), from Public Citizen, Inc., P.O. Box 19404, Washington, DC 20036

The Congress Watcher (Newsletter of the Congress Watch Locals), Gene Karpinski, Editor, **$5**/year (6 issues), from Public Citizen, Inc., P.O. Box 19404, Washington, DC 20036

Public Citizen, Information **$.50**, from Public Citizen, Inc., P.O. Box 19404, Washington, DC 20036

National Audubon Society

The strength of Audubon since 1905 has been its naturalist backbone. More than any other environmental organization, its members actually know the animals and plants they try to conserve. Not only that, they seem to love their knowledge with early naturalist enthusiasm. The educational aspects of Audubon are truly admirable. Their politics vary locally and, if you contribute, it's good to earmark your contribution for a particular purpose, especially for specific sanctuaries. **The Audubon Leader** *is the burgeoning political newsletter and, so far, very solid.* **Audubon** *magazine is reviewed on page 51.* **American Birds** *is wonderful for me — a true avian addict.*

Audubon Leader, Robert C. Boardman, Editor, **$10**/year (26 issues), from National Audubon Society, 950 Third Avenue, New York, NY 10022

American Birds, Robert S. Arbib, Editor, **$10**/year (6 issues), from National Audubon Society, 950 Third Avenue, New York, NY 10022

Natural Resources Defense Council

47,000 members support this heavy duty group of scientists and eco-lawyers as it monitors government bureaucrats to see that they're doing what the laws require, file suits when they aren't and educate its members on the new rules concerning the environment as the courts and Congress churn them out. The chatty N.R.D.C. magazine **Amicus** *(p. 51) focuses on major concerns from water projects to wildlife protection. A typical publication is* **Land Use Controls in the United States**.

Land Use Controls in the United States (A Handbook on the Legal Rights of Citizens), Elaine Moss, Editor, 1977; 362 pp., **$8.45** postpaid from Natural Resources Defense Council, 122 East 42nd Street, New York, NY 10017

N.R.D.C. Publications List, **free**, from Natural Resources Defense Council, 122 East 42nd Street, New York, NY 10017

Ducks Unlimited

This 350,000-member organization has been responsible for the preservation of more waterbird breeding grounds (especially marshlands) than any government or other group. Working internationally (ducks haven't learned about Canada, U.S. and Mexican boundaries), Ducks Unlimited restores, manages, and purchases wetlands throughout North American waterfowl flyways. They say they're not political. That's what a bad name the word "politics" has these days. Non-profit, tax-exempt.

Ducks Unlimited, Lee Salber, Editor, **$10**/year (6 issues), from Ducks Unlimited, Inc., Box 66300, Chicago, IL 606 IL 60666

Soil Conservation Society of America

Over one million acres of prime farmland disappear in urban development each year. In the Great Plains and the Pacific Northwest, 85 percent of the farms lose 5 tons of their topsoil yearly. The SCS provides a meeting ground for all the specialized interests who are interested in preserving the ultimate strength of this nation: its soil. They publish a technical but, for my interests, totally absorbing magazine — **The Journal of Soil and Water Conservation**. *It's a mature group, organized in 1945.*

The Journal of Soil and Water Conservation, Max Schnepf, Editor, **$20**/year (6 issues), from Soil Conservation Society of America, 7515 Northeast Ankeny Road, Ankeny, IA 50021

Izaak Walton League of America

An old conservation group with a distinct midwestern twang. Rooted morality. Never upstarts. They are hard, persevering workers who conserve, maintain, protect, and restore soil, forests, water and air. A wholesome 52,000 membership. Publishes **Outdoor America** *(formerly* **Walton News**). *Has an endowment fund to purchase unique natural areas.*

Outdoor America, Frederick A. Vallejo, Editor, **$5**/year (6 issues), from Izaak Walton League of America, 1800 North Kent Street, Suite 806, Arlington, VA 22209

American Rivers Council

The major national organization dedicated to the preservation of America's free flowing rivers. There are fewer intact free flowing rivers of large size than there are California condors, and there are only about 30 condors. The Council works on legislation to protect wild and scenic rivers at federal and state level and helps local groups interested in river conservation.

American Rivers Council, Information **$1**, from American Rivers Council, 317 Pennsylvania Avenue SE, Washington, DC 20003

International Union for the Conservation of Nature and Natural Resources (IUCN)

The original authors of the **Red Book** *— giving IUCN's list of all the rare, endangered, and threatened animals of the whole Earth. Has 105 member countries working in all aspects of regional conservation and ecology. Essentially,* **CoEvolution's** *biogeographical map of the Earth (p. 21) was born within the IUCN. An admirable group of scientists and professionals. Many publications.*

International Union for the Conservation of Nature and Natural Resources, Robert I. Standish, Editor, **$20**/year (12 issues), from I.U.C.N., Avenue du Mont Blanc, CH - 1196, Gland Switzerland

Conservation Directory

From the publishers of **Ranger Rick** *(p. 547) comes the most useful catalog of private and public organizations, governmental agencies and officials (like Senators or department heads) concerned with natural resources, wildlife, and their management. Anyone trying to coordinate their activities (such as stream restoration for fish) with other groups or wanting to know all the conservation groups within their state or trying to contact the relevant Washington authority can use this catalog. Good price too.* —Peter Warshall

Conservation Directory
(A List of Organizations, Agencies, and Officials concerned with Natural Resource Use and Management)
Jeannette Bryant, Editor
1980; 290 pp.
$4 postpaid from:
The National Wildlife Federation
1412 Sixteenth Street NW
Washington, DC 20036

Sierra Club National News Report

Sierra Club's NNR is basic reading for conservationists interested in following national policy developments. (At **Not Man Apart**, *we often developed our news section out of it and the New York and L.A.* **Times**.)

It is an excellent example of the newsletter genre. Newsletters are less daunting than magazines and quicker to reach the point. The time-space coordinates they operate on demand brevity and currency. Newsletters afford entry to their editors' networks. They are almost as specific as computer networks but are artifacts and so can be re-perused in leisurely thumb-through fashion. Newsletters are to magazines as stand-up comedy is to plays. —Stephanie Mills
[Suggested by Harry Dennis]

Sierra Club National News Report
Gene Coan, Editor
$12 (35 issues, approx.)
from:
The Sierra Club
530 Bush Street
San Francisco, CA 94108

The Sierra Club

The Sierra Club has many parts which provide different services. They have integrated their politics with the Big Boys so well that sometimes I think the leadership loses touch. This occurred, for instance, when the Sierra Club supported a huge water project in California (the Peripheral Canal) which its membership overwhelmingly hated and its defense fund was essentially trying to halt. The Sierra Club is also the "hated" symbol for those who feel environmentalists are commie extremists. Caught in all these cross-currents, they can use more input and support from their membership. The voice of John Muir needs a 1980 broadcast system.

The Sierra Club Foundation, Information **free**, from Sierra Club, Information Services, 530 Bush Street, San Francisco, CA 94108

THE RISING SUN
NEIGHBORHOOD NEWSLETTER

Then there was the guy who made his fortune, a large one, by thinking of avocado as a color for appliances.

Groups Concerned About Biohazards

by Peter Warshall

—From Common Knowledge **by Commonweal**

Environmental Action, Suite 371, 1346 Connecticut Ave. N.W., Washington, D.C. 20036. *There are 430,000 generators of hazardous wastes in the U.S. Ninety per-cent of the waste discharged does not meet EPA standards. EA has an inventory of these polluters. Write them and ask for your state list. EA also publishes a biweekly of political updates, especially in their major field of interest, conservation political lobbying.*

Federation of Homemakers, Inc., P.O. Box 5571, Arlington, VA 22205. *Lobbies against biohazardous food additives. Great people. About to tackle Coca Cola and Pepsi. Newsletter, $10/year (4 issues).*

Environmental Defense Fund, 1525 - 18th St. N.W., Washington, D.C. 20036. *Leading group in bringing lawsuits to stop use of biohazardous pesticides and other consumer products. Major work on water supplies contaminated with substances harmful to human health. In short, litigation, research, and newsletter ($20/year for six issues and membership).*

Society for Occupational and Environmental Health, 1341 G St. N.W., Suite 308, Washington, DC 20005. *Professional society of doctors and scientists that holds conferences and supplies information on improving the quality of working and living places.*

Western Institute for Environmental/Occupational Sciences, Inc., 2520 Milvia St., Berkeley, CA 94704. *An activist group of concerned medical people. Screened thousands for asbestos-related health problems using mobile medical units. Now working on the effects of microwaves on workers.*

Commonweal, Box 316, Bolinas, CA 94924. *A non-profit group concerned with all kinds of human stress. Hopes to have clinic for chronic diseases and seeks methods of treating them. Produces excellent quarterly newspaper* **Common Knowledge**, *the only publication dealing completely with biohazards and you — $10/year.*

Citizens Against Toxic Sprays, Inc. (CATS), 1385 Bailey Ave., Eugene, OR 97402. *The best effective grassroots group against chemical spraying of forests and people.*

Northwest Coalition for Alternatives to Pesticides, Box 375, Eugene, OR 97440. *A Pacific Northwest group fights the use of chemical spraying of forests and people. Expanding its interest to other biohazards. Grassroots networking so everyone knows what everyone else is doing. Meetings and newsletter ($7/year for 4 issues).*

Coalition on Environmental and Occupational Health Hazards, 106 K Street, Suite 200, Sacramento, CA 95814. *Fledgling group to educate and influence the public on policy issues relating to biohazards.*

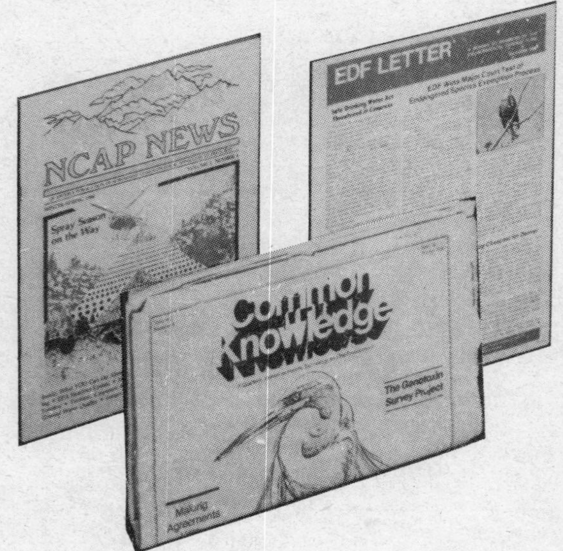

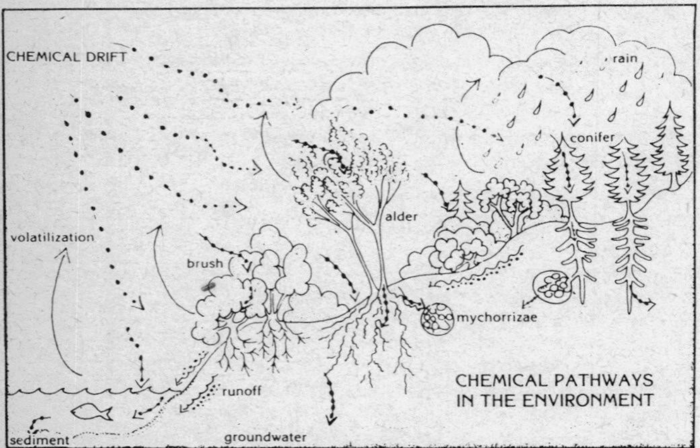

—**NCAP News**

Environmental Impact Assessment

Today, both State and Federal Environmental Impact Statements are the heaviest political, educational and, in many ways, religious tools of the American citizen. Politically, the Environmental Impact Statement forces humans to consider the consequences of their acts. You can't shoot buffalo or sell redwoods to Japan without stating the social and economic impact of human life on the natural world. The EIS has stopped the Kaiparowits Power Complex by simply making the industrial consortium aware of all the side effects of coal mining in southern Utah. The EIS slowed Warm Springs Dam in California by taking the Army Corps of Engineers to court. And even when projects were not stopped, the EIS put rational ecological guidelines on what could have been a "waste the Earth" devastation (e.g., the Alaska pipeline).

Educationally, the EIS has melded science and the citizen. Scientists are tested for honesty and thoroughness by non-academic naturalists and planners. Citizens have plunged into the subtle realities of scientific thought ("carrying capacity," "indirect and direct impacts on food chains," etc.). The result: by far the most refreshing rhetoric and dialogue in contemporary America. A dialogue where words have meaning, are connected to land and sea, and, when effective, give that special good feeling that comes in aiding a forest or river or mammal or bird.

In this book "The Practical Appendix" and Johnston's essay "Assessing Social and Economic Impacts" are the most useful tools to present-day EIS writing I know.
—*Peter Warshall*

Environmental Impact Assessment
Patrick H. Heffernan, Ruthann Corwin, Editors
1975; 267 pp.

$12.95 postpaid from:
Freeman, Cooper & Co.
1736 Stockton Street
San Francisco, CA 94133

Chain of impacts associated with dam construction.

Neighborhood preservation is an ecology issue

What bulldozers do to an existing human community is no different from what they do to any other climax biological community — wetland, woodlot, or streambed. A complex mature meta-life is crippled or killed and replaced by a simplistic early successional non-community, and then at great expense kept that way.

The process is always called improvement.

To measure whether it is improvement, count the variety of life before and after. Count the number of species. Count the number of kinds of people, kinds of jobs, services, interactions, ages, incomes. Decrease in variety is ecological damage. It's called improvement because it isn't.

Neighborhood preservation is an ecology issue. Count the variety. If it's going to be diminished, start phoning.
—SB

Land, Private Property Public Control

A Canadian textbook. Its examples of how land ownership forms evolved, did or didn't work, whether for primitive tribes, Rome, or contemporary U.S.A., along with philosophical discourses, make it the best I have found to provoke a better understanding of the relationships between people and the land. It is small of print and is tedious at times, but worth reading, especially for those who are into the destiny of the community/world landscape.

The working ideas and vocabulary in it unravel a lot of mysteries so that a reader can cope with concepts like leases, land banks, less-than-fee ownership, various taxation approaches, etc., in the reader's private or community land problems.
—*Huey Johnson*

Land, Private Property Public Control
R.W.G. Bryant
1972; 377 pp.

$12.50 postpaid from:
Harvest House Ltd.
4795 St. Catherine St. W.
Montreal, Quebec
Canada H3Z 1S8

•

Every society must establish its own equilibrium between private rights and social responsibilities. Perhaps equilibrium is not quite the correct term. There is a broad zone of interaction between private and public interests. Even within the general framework of Western democracy, the line of demarcation within this broad zone varies enormously as between Sweden and Texas. In the Netherlands, for example, it is normal and acceptable for the public authorities to intervene in the use and disposition of land, to an extent that would be considered unthinkable in the United States -- yet both are democratic countries in the generally accepted sense of that term. . . . In the United States habits of thought dating from the days of the expanding frontier, and the concomitant notion that space is limitless are still extant. To a degree, the persistence of this outmoded mental climate is very largely responsible for the difficulties experienced by the U.S.A. in adapting its forms of government to modern requirements, and in developing effective means of controlling development, other than the basically crude and clumsy device of the zoning by-law.

The Health Effects of Environmental Pollutants

Written for the practicing clinician, this volume is filled with useful data that can help doctors do the difficult detective work involved in tracking down the often delayed and disguised health effects of environmental pollutants, particularly airborne pollutants, in the population at large.

Waldbott covers a wide spectrum of pollutants — pulmonary irritants (ozone and chlorine), fibrosis producing agents (silica, iron, cobalt, barium), asphyxiating pollutants (carbon monoxide and hydrogen sulphide), systemic poisons (lead, mercury, fluoride, and cadmium), allergic agents, radioactive contaminants, carcinogens, and mutagens, as well as smoke.

The Health Effects of Environmental Pollutants *is vastly informative. It stands out as eminently readable in a field known for its jargon-ridden and impenetrable prose.*
—*Steve Lerner*
[Editor, **Common Knowledge***]*

The Health Effects of Environmental Pollutants
George W. Waldbott
1973, 1978; 360 pp.

$16.95 postpaid from:
The C.V. Mosby Company
Times Mirror Company
11830 Westline
Industrial Drive
St. Louis, MO 63141

The Nature Conservancy

Many people (especially on nature tours) ask me what group does the most to help preserve the natural beauty and diversity of the Earth. Without hesitation I say: "If you give money to one conservation group, give it to Nature Conservancy." They have been responsible for preserving over one and a half million acres of forests, marshes, prairies, mountains, islands, as well as innumerable rare and endangered plants, butterflies, and other wildlife. They carefully research their financial priorities, move with coyote-like wiliness and roadrunner speed in real estate transactions, and, for my money, manage their purchases with the best network of volunteer and professional land stewards in the U.S.A. So far they have completed 2,200 conservancy projects. Your grandchild's view of a prairie falcon in Idaho, Audubon's Caracara in Florida, native prairie in Ohio, or even the rare Massasauga rattlesnake in New York make Nature Conservancy my idea of a solid investment. One of the fringe benefits is the four-color newsletter. —Peter Warshall

The Nature Conservancy News
Sue E. Dodge, Editor

$10 /year (6 issues — includes membership) from:
The Nature Conservancy
1800 North Kent Street
Arlington, VA 22209

→

Wildhorse Island

Few people associate islands with the State of Montana. But the "Big Sky Country" contains the largest freshwater island in the western U.S. — 2,156-acre Wildhorse Island, lying in the west's biggest freshwater lake, Flathead Lake.

Wildhorse Island contains the only remaining stretch of undisturbed shoreline — eight and a half miles long —

Wildhorse Island

on the lake. Its rugged hills, which rise steeply to 1,000 feet above "lake level," support a herd of 210 Rocky Mountain bighorn sheep, one of the largest contained populations in the nation. In addition, there are active bald eagle and osprey nests. Coyotes, black-tailed deer, and occasional black bear roam the island. Wildhorse's vegetation is predominantly grassland and forest of towering ponderosa pine and Douglas fir.

A project endorsed by the American Land Trust, Wildhorse Island was acquired in late 1977 and will be transferred in a series of transactions to the State of Montana for management in cooperation with the University of Montana. **—The Nature Conservancy News**

The Trust for Public Land
Institute for Community Economics, Inc.

More and more, people are being excluded from land because of its cost and concentration among relatively few owners. Short of a revolution, one solution to this problem that works is the land trust. There are two types of land trusts, and while structurally they look much the same — non-profit corporations with by-laws and boards of directors — they serve different purposes. The first is the conservation land trust, designed primarily to protect a land resource. The best known example is the Nature Conservancy, reviewed above. Another is the Trust for Public Land. It was founded in 1973 and works in urban neighborhoods to convert vacant land into community-built parks and gardens. For residents in rural and suburban communities, it has developed special training materials directed at building local land trusts which can acquire and manage lands with open space or resource value to the surrounding community. Recently, The Trust for Public Land has begun working with Western farming communities who have elected to form land trusts as a way to ease the speculative pressure on productive lands and restrict the land's use to agriculture.

The second type of organization is the community land trust. Access to land by people is the major goal, either to live on or work on. There are fewer of this kind of land trust, and the Institute for Community Economics serves as a clearinghouse. They know where groups already exist, and can help you start your own. Many land trusts are small and not well publicized — there may already be one formed near you. —Richard Nilsen

The Trust for Public Land
Information
$1 from:
The Trust for Public Land
82 Second Street
San Francisco, CA 94105

Community Land Trusts
Information
free from:
Institute for Community Economics, Inc.
120 Boylston Street
Boston, MA 02116

Getting People Together in Rural America

If city and country are two very different places, then the way to go about organizing in rural areas will differ from the methods that work in cities. The distilled experience here is centered around consumer issues like utility rate increases, but the concise techniques are equally applicable to environmental issues. —Richard Nilsen

Getting People Together in Rural America
(A Beginner's Guide to Consumer Organizing)
Barbara Swaczy
1979; 40 pp.

$3 postpaid from:
Northern Rockies Action Group
9 Placer Street
Helena, MT 59601

•

It would be ideal if issues in agricultural areas could wait until winter, when farmers and ranchers aren't in the fields from sunrise until sunset. But year-round there is always something a person could be doing besides joining a group. If you have a choice, January is a good time to start an organization in cattle or grain country. Otherwise, wet weather will tend to keep farmers in their homes. And there can be one or two breaks in the haying each summer.

Farmers *can* come to evening meetings in mid-summer if it's important enough. But schedule meetings for 8:30 p.m. and get your business done in one-half hour, because the people are tired.

One of the classic techniques of farm organizing was that employed by the Non-Partisan League in North Dakota in the 1910s. The Organizers hired able farm hands who went with them into the fields. The hand would replace the farmer on his tractor while the organizer talked to the farmer about the League.

—Akwesasne Notes

Indian Nationhood *by Jerry Mander*

Three publications by Native Americans — one short philosophical/historical tract, and two newspapers — brilliantly express a newly revived "traditional" radicalism among Indian people. After a very long period during which the U.S. government succeeded in installing colonial-type puppet governments on Indian reservations — committed to economic development policies along American corporate lines — the voices of traditional Indian leadership have begun to emerge. A coalition, of sorts, has been formed between tribal elders — people who have retained the old ways, language and values — and young activists who have tried out the joys of Western techno-life and found it wanting and suicidal. This coalition is in opposition to the tribal leaders, installed by the Bureau of Indian Affairs, who tend to form the "progressive" block of Indians seeking to sell land for money, make leases for coal and uranium mines, follow American models of health, education and organization, and go for the American dream.

The new opposition has re-introduced the term "sovereignty," by which some of them mean economic self-sufficiency along traditional subsistence lines but many of them literally mean separate nationhood. They voice the position that this nationhood was never lost. Treaties confirm it, and a new young breed of Indian lawyers are achieving some success in arguing the cases. More than 22 Indian nations are taking the legal argument that the land was never lost in any legal sense, and they are refusing all monetary settlements. The hoped-for result of this activity will be the re-recognition of Indian treaties, the re-establishment of their land base, with all rights attached thereto, the re-installation of traditional Indian governments, and the rejection of American development corporations — oil companies, uranium companies, agribusinesses which have insinuated themselves into effective control of Indian land and resources. The new mottos are "Land, not money, sovereignty not integration, Indian nations, not Americans."

A Basic Call to Consciousness *is a bound reprint of the position paper of the Six Nations (Iroquois Confederacy) presented at the UN Conference on Indigenous People, Geneva, 1977. Largely the work of John Mohawk (who also edits* **Akwesasne Notes***) in collaboration with the elders of the Six Nations, this book is a clearly stated analysis of the inherent values of Western culture which have led to the destruction of Indian people in the past, and continue to do so in the present. Many such analyses have been written by whites, but this one by a brilliant young Indian contains perspectives and a passion that have been absent before. An interesting distinction, for example, is that this book celebrates Indian* **political** *forms as being the most "advanced" in the world and the most relevant to today's problems. Reference is also made to the fact that the Iroquois Constitution was bastardized to become the basis for the American constitution and also Marxism, a fact that too few scholars have noted.*

Akwesasne Notes *is the largest and most thorough Indian newspaper, carrying current events and perspectives concerning Indian people. These days, the paper is especially emphasizing the crunch between technological society's need for scarce resources and the fact that many of them are on Indian land. 65% of the so-called uranium reserves, and a comparable percentage of coal, natural gas, oil, and precious minerals are on Indian land, which is why so much attention is being paid by the U.S. government to who runs the reservations. The newspaper goes into great depth on these matters and is supportive of the resistance to U.S. corporate efforts to get the Indians to cooperate.*

Native Self-Sufficiency *is published six times per year by the Tribal Sovereignty Project, an organization which gives material and educational support to a variety of Indian groups and projects which have in common a desire for separation from America politically, culturally, and spiritually. It is devoted to the "quiet building of the political and economic infrastructures of our communities that would make sovereignty a practicality." The paper concentrates on (1) land and natural resource issues, (2) self-sufficiency and alternative technology and economics, (3) the re-establishment of traditional Indian governments.*

(See more on Native American culture, pp. 44 - 45 and 452.)

A Basic Call to Consciousness
(The Hau de no sau nee Address to the Western World)
1978; 55 pp.
$1.25 postpaid

Akwesasne Notes
$5 - $10 /year (optional contribution — 5 issues)
both from:
Akwasasne Notes
Mohawk Nation
Via Rooseveltown
New York, 13683

Native Self-Sufficiency
Paula Hammett, Editor
$6 /year (6 issues) from:
Tribal Sovereignty Program
P.O. Box 10
Forestville, CA 95436

THE RISING SUN
NEIGHBORHOOD NEWSLETTER

Rob said that in New York now dealers are taking the seeds out of marijuana so people won't grow their own. Izzy said that was like a lot of artists in New York now won't invite anybody to their studios for fear they'll steal their ideas.

Freedom Inside the Organization

Most people who work for large institutions are aware of the fact that for 40 hours a week they are deprived of many Constitutional Amendment rights. This book examines the issues and begins the long 20 - 40 year battle ahead of us to bring civil liberties to the institutionalized employee. —Michael Phillips

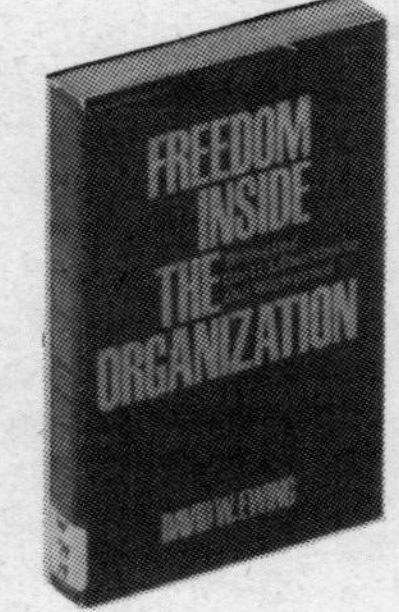

Freedom Inside the Organization
(Bringing Civil Liberties to the Workplace)
David W. Ewing
1977; 246 pp.

$3.95 postpaid from:
McGraw-Hill Book Co.
Princeton Road
Hightstown, NJ 08520
or Whole Earth Household Store

•

At Connecticut Mutual Life Insurance Company, a worker can get a free lunch by sitting at an executive's table in the cafeteria and taking part in a rap session where no questions are out of bounds.

•

In England, reports business writer Nancy Foy, the president of a large process company made significant changes in operations after he began sitting down with employees, leveling with them, and listening at length to their most devastating criticisms of management. Despite lack of cooperation from middle managers, the interchange led to significant changes in production and personnel policies, with the company going from a static, break-even level to a very profitable one.

•

In 1974 the **Wall Street Journal** reported that Combustion Engineering, its management incensed by a **Journal** article describing certain terms of nuclear power contracts negotiated by the company, was requiring officers and employees to submit to lie detector tests. "Do you know anybody at the **Wall Street Journal?**" was one question asked by the polygraph operator. "Did you give any information to anybody at the **Wall Street Journal?**" was another.

•

According to Ralph Nader, a U.S. Senate study in 1974 estimated that between 200,000 and 300,000 lie detector tests are administered each year in companies. Nader also reported that two surveys showed that the loyalty of about one worker in every five is checked by eavesdropping or other means.

Of Acceptable Risk

How safe is that bag of Barbeque Potato Chips? Who says so? Has anyone checked? Have the studies been scientifically valid? Have the results been suppressed? Has anyone tested for interactions with other foods? Does anyone care? This disquieting book tells what's being done and what should be done. What will be done is up to us as citizens. I found the lack of emotional cause-hustling refreshing. There should be more research done. This tells why. —J. Baldwin

Of Acceptable Risk
(Science and the Determination of Safety)
William W. Lowrance
1976; 180 pp.

$5.95 postpaid from:
William Kaufmann, Inc.
One First Street
Los Altos, CA 94022
or Whole Earth Household Store

An array of considerations influencing safety judgments

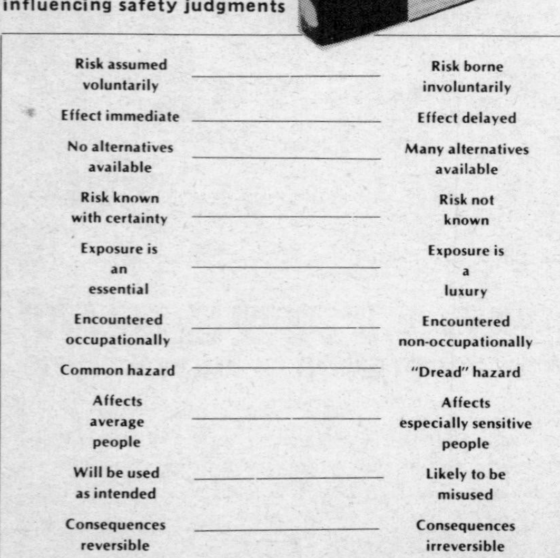

Risk assumed voluntarily
Risk borne involuntarily
Effect immediate
Effect delayed
No alternatives available
Many alternatives available
Risk known with certainty
Risk not known
Exposure is an essential
Exposure is a luxury
Encountered occupationally
Encountered non-occupationally
Common hazard
"Dread" hazard
Affects average people
Affects especially sensitive people
Will be used as intended
Likely to be misused
Consequences reversible
Consequences irreversible

The Strip Mine Handbook

In 1977, after a ten year battle, the federal Surface Mining Control and Reclamation Act became law. As a result, the notorious abuses involved with strip mining coal are now controlled by the new Office of Surface Mining (OSM), a branch of the Interior Department.

This **Handbook** *is done so well it could serve as a model of its kind. It takes a technical subject, and an even more complex set of federal regulations, and makes them comprehensible to the average concerned citizen. How to spot, document, and report violations, and the entire grievance procedure, from an OSM inspection to a federal court suit, are superbly summarized. Since all the tough language in the world means nothing if there is no enforcement, citizen participation is going to be crucial to the success of the new law.* —Richard Nilsen

The Strip Mine Handbook
(A Citizen's Guide to the New Federal Surface Mining Law. How to Use It to Protect Your Community and Yourself)
Center for Law and Social Policy and Environmental Policy Institute
1978; 107 pp.

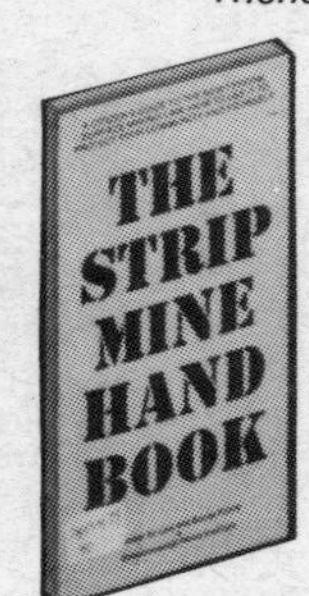

$2.25 postpaid from:
Environmental Policy Institute
317 Pennsylvania Ave.
Washington, D.C. 20003

Medical Nemesis

High tech medicine is making us sick, not well, and the essence of that sickness is passivity. Overblown industrialism shames traditional methods of healing, education, locomotion and social organization. Exporting the monster model plunges traditional cultures into a hopeless abyss of underdevelopment and condemns them to ecological insanity. Human abilities to self heal, indeed to self sustain, have been traded off for or expropriated by Big Brother's quasi-benevolence. Illich, fatalistic, says that to regain control of our health, we will have to re-learn how to suffer pain; to regain our autonomy we'll have to forfeit our "envious, greedy, and lazy" dreams. (See more on Illich, p. 40.) —Stephanie Mills

Medical Nemesis
(The Expropriation of Health)
Ivan Illich
1975; 183 pp.

$2.75 postpaid from:
Bantam Books
414 East Golf Road
Des Plaines, IL 60016
or Whole Earth Household Store

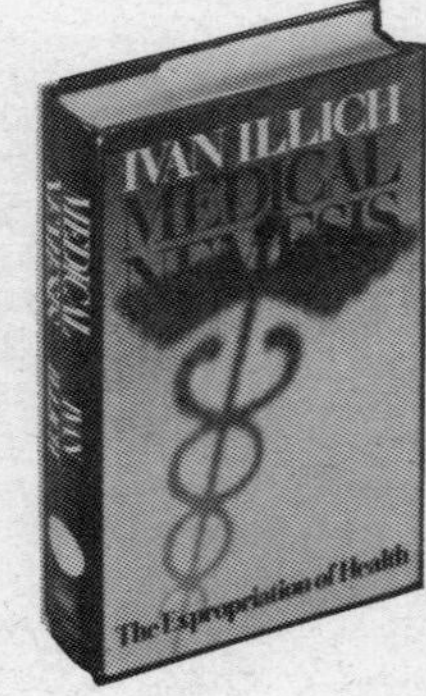

•

Increasing and irreparable damage accompanies present industrial expansion in all sectors. In medicine these damages appear as iatrogenesis *[disease caused by treatment]*. Iatrogenesis is clinical when pain, sickness and death result from medical care; it is social when health policies reinforce an industrial organization which generates ill health; it is structural when medically sponsored behaviour and delusions restrict the vital autonomy of people by undermining their competence in growing up, caring for each other and aging, or when medical intervention disables personal responses to pain, disability, impairment, anguish and death.

•

In many a village in Mexico I have seen what happens when social security arrives. For a generation people continue in their traditional beliefs; they know how to deal with death, dying, and grief. The new nurse and the doctor, thinking they know better, teach them about an evil pantheon of clinical deaths, each one of which can be banned, at a price. Instead of modernizing people's skills for self-care, they preach the ideal of hospital death. By their ministration they urge the peasants to an unending search for the good death of international description, a search that will keep them consumers forever.

← Look to determine if the pond is unduly full of sediment. Do you see "islands" of sediment building up under the surface of the pond? If so, there is probably a violation.

If the pond is full of sediment, then water flowing into it will simply flow through without losing its pollutants. They will go into the receiving stream. This is also a violation.

•

Acid water (low pH) is caused by the exposure of pyrite to air during the mining process. Pyrite is often contained in the rock which makes up the overburden.

Acid is one of the most damaging pollutants. It kills fish and other aquatic life, eats away metal structures and destroys concrete, and increases the cost of water treatment for power plants and municipal water supply and renders the water unfit for recreational use. Low pH also causes other pollutants (such as iron) to become soluble and these in turn cause more damage. Thousands upon thousands of miles of streams have been degraded by acid mine drainage and runoff.

Council on Economic Priorities

One of the most effective checks on American corporate mischief is this non-governmental research organization. Their reports have earned such confidence that they are routinely transmitted through the economic pages of the **New York Times, Wall St. Journal,** *etc. What the reports detail is the actual anatomy of corporate activity in terms of pollution, worker's rights, defense contracts, relations with South Africa, energy, pricing, political activity, etc., etc. Credit is given where it is due and blame likewise. A quiet, pointedly effective service.* —SB

Council on Economic Priorities Reports and Newsletters
$15 /year
(10 newsletters)

$25 /year (2 reports and 10 newsletters)
from:
Council on Economic Priorities
84 Fifth Avenue
New York, NY 10011

•

The single most dramatic development in this year's annual meeting season is the submission of a large number of anti-nuclear resolutions by individuals and groups around the country. No other single topic has provoked such a large number of resolutions from such a wide variety of individual filers. Thirty-three nuclear-related resolutions have been filed so far, up from six last year. Undoubtedly the Three Mile Island accident, which came in the heart of last year's annual meeting season, played a major role in triggering this tremendous upsurge in shareholder actions. The high votes received by last year's nuclear resolutions (all over 5%, five of the six qualifying for resubmission) almost certainly encouraged more submissions. Moreover, the National Council of Churches, after a three year energy policy study, has for the first time taken a formal stand opposing the use of nuclear power, resulting in the filing of 15 anti-nuclear resolutions by church groups for the first time this year.

• Top 25 Foreign Military Sales Contractors, FY 1978
(Thousands of Dollars)

	1978	1977 (rank)
1. General Dynamics Corp.	$1,475,524	$ 303,302 (4)
2. Litton Industries, Inc.	523,212	120,941 (10)
3. Textron, Inc.	441,456	73,540 (15)
4. Lockheed Corp.	297,292	305,226 (3)
5. McDonnell Douglas Corp.	273,857	446,134 (2)
6. Raytheon Co.	188,950	149,028 (8)
7. Northrop Corp.	266,978	846,002 (1)
8. General Electric Co.	175,657	220,958 (6)
9. Ret Ser Engineering A.G.	167,791	*
10. Hughes Aircraft Co.	156,188	156,092 (7)
11. United Technologies	115,302	87,102 (12)
12. Vinnell Corp.	103,726	*
13. FMC Corp.	70,683	*
14. Grumman Corp.	69,992	252,814 (5)
15. Ford Motor Co.	65,642	42,260 (17)
16. Harsco Corp.	63,684	39,698 (18)
17. Westinghouse Electric Corp.	56,403	70,986 (16)
18. Mi Ryung Construction Co.	43,323	137,710 (9)
19. Hyundai Construction Co., Ltd.	41,193	*
20. Chamberlain Mfg. Co.	37,761	26,099 (21)
21. Honeywell, Inc.	32,879	*
22. General Motors Co.	31,969	*
23. Hercules, Inc.	30,519	19,879 (25)
24. American Telephone & Telegraph Co.	28,176	26,773 (20)
25. Teledyne, Inc.	26,871	21,241 (24)
Total, Top 25 Companies	$4,867,532	$3,695,277
Total FMS Awards	$5,805,480	$4,449,536

*Not among top 25 FMS contractors in FY 1977.

Human Fahrenheit, Inhuman Celsius

It'll be a hot one in the Valley today — 90 to 95 degrees. That's, uh, 32 to 35 Celsius...

by Brian Toss

April first, 1794: the French National Assembly adopts the Celsius temperature scale, giving it an official relationship with the Metric system, though of course providing it with no rational one. The scale as adopted is an *upside-down* version of Andres Celsius's 0° boiling point of water and 100° melting point of ice calibration. Is the legislation's timing an obscure example of Gallic humor?

Copenhagen, 1708: A young instrument maker, Daniel Gabriel Fahrenheit, meets with astronomer Ole Rømer to discuss thermometers. The century prior to their meeting has seen countless experiments with a bewildering and sometimes ludicrous variety of tubes, pots, gauges, ethers, and wines that have failed to produce a single thermometer that is both accurate and consistently reproducible. Rømer's experiments have shown the necessity of exact calibration and the use of unvarying points to measure from, and Fahrenheit subsequently devises a method for producing a mercury-filled thermometer tube of constant diameter and *two* fixed points (originally body temperature and the melting point of ice, the former soon replaced by the boiling point of water[1]), a method which is the basis of all thermometer fabrication today.

His instruments win him wide acclaim and a steady income, allowing further and more extensive research. He is an artisan, not a scientist,[2] his shrewd good sense unconstrained by the dogma of his day. He discovers properties of super-cooled water, the effect of barometric pressure on the boiling point of water, and refinements in hygrometer construction. These are significant achievements, but perhaps no more important than the fundamental assumption that the Fahrenheit scale should have an immediately perceivable relation to the human physicality. To do this he had recorded extremes of temperature for Europe and bracketed the 0° to 100° section of his scale with them. This range is appropriate for habitable climates, and stands as an elegant reference point for temperatures outside ordinary human experience, as found in inhospitable times and places (the poles, deserts, sun, space, etc.).

This significant 0 to 100 range, unfortunately misused in the Metric system, is best suited to high-definition measurements which can be conveniently divided by ten and which "peak" at one hundred. Thus we have a hundred dollars, miles, years, or degrees of temperature indicating significant amounts. Measurements requiring numerous divisors and/or which bear no innate relation to one hundred have other ranges, thus twelve inches, feet, months, eggs, hours, or sixteen ounces or four quarts. In general, arbitrary, person-made sums can be referred to conveniently, some of the time, by tens and hundreds, while *interface* with the world favors more fractionable systems, the more simply to describe portions or multiples of a given value.

The Fahrenheit scale belongs, of course, in the former category. It is a high-definition system of great *humanness*, immediately understandable and easily used, since its "metric section" relates specifically to humans, and not just the characteristics of water. Unlike the Celsius scale it is a reflection and extension of ourselves; it does not have the effect of squeezing us into a sterile, high-tech worldview, residents of a minus 15 to 40 degree niche, a fraction of scale having little to do with our daily lives. ■

REFERENCES

1. *Dictionary of Scientific Biography, Vol. IV*, p. 517.
2. *History of the Thermometer and Its Uses in Meteorology*, W. E. Knowles, p. 66. A fine book.

Stop Metric Madness T-shirt

In bright rainbow colors on 100% cotton, this is the most remark-provoking T-shirt you can wear. Little old ladies come up and warmly agree with you. Strangers open conversation. Even the rare metric proponent is delighted to see this hidden issue addressed in public.

Against 75% citizen opposition or disinterest, some American multi-national corporations, some government bureaucrats, and some educators are trying to sneak metric into general usage. ("Sneak" is the word used by an avid metricizer on the California Metric Conversion Council with me. She isn't kidding. She and one cohort alone managed to get the California Education Department to require exclusive use of metric by California schools from kindergarten to fourth grade. Hearings did not support the move. The press did not report it. It's a repeat of the New Math disaster.)

Quietly in schools and quietly in government. Many federal bureaucracies now require metric specifications in contracts with private industry. The Department of Defense is moving toward 100% metric (when a cost-cutter took metric out of the MX missile specs, it saved $25 million). Nothing in the press on this either.

Metric conversion has never been voted on in any nation, province, or community in the world. Proponents know it would lose. Except for specialized uses in scientific abstraction and technological micro-measure, metric is an inferior system to customary measure. This T-shirt is a vote.

In a market democracy such as the U.S., metric has no chance to become the standard measuring system. What is possible however is being manipulated part way so that we are left hanging with an eternally confusing and alienating "dual system." This is what happened in England, which balked half-way in, with dual direction hostility to match. The same is now happening in Canada.

The former scientific proponents of metric have withdrawn their support. Good liberals are now embarrassed by the issue. You can head off the whole thing by complaining at school (British school kids, trained exclusively in metric, have to be re-trained to customary measure when they look for jobs); at any propaganda from the government directed at you through newspapers, radio, bank clocks, etc; and at gas stations, some of whom are trying to sell gas by the liter (worth boycotting on this one is Shell Oil, who is putting the pressure on the other companies).

Why do schools and governments fall for ideas like metric and nuclear energy that make sense so long as you don't think about them for more than 30 seconds?

—SB

Stop Metric Madness T-shirt

$8 postpaid from:
Americans for Customary Weight and Measure
47 West Street
Penthouse
New York, NY 10006

Games Mother Never Taught You

Learning and applying Harragan's information is tantamount to "cracking the code" of business success. Most women need to approach big business as though it were foreign territory because until recently it was — only men were allowed into the policy-making ranks. Harragan makes a superb spy, and her book explains the jargon and system of the corporate world. Reading it, you can anticipate moves and plot at the same informed level as your male colleagues who usually have absorbed the basic strategic information as part of their upbringing.

Harragan emphasizes the fact that corporations are modeled after the military and women must understand this model to function in any business. She also dissects the myth of "sleeping your way to success" and the myth that "good performance equals success." Why didn't we have this book ten years ago? It would have saved me and my women business colleagues from re-inventing the wheel! Read it now, and you'll have the opportunity to invent a new game or at least succeed at the old one.

—Anne Kent Rush

Games Mother Never Taught You
(Corporate Gamesmanship for Women)
Betty Lehan Harragan
1977; 399 pp.

$2.95 postpaid from:
Warner Books
Book Order Department
75 Rockefeller Plaza
New York, NY 10019
or Whole Earth Household Store

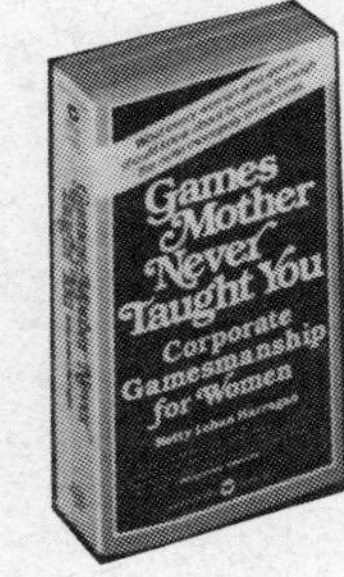

•

While you're at your salary research, if you discover that a man who held your job previously got paid more than you or that a man doing substantially the same work as you (never mind his title, the job functions are the key) is getting paid more, don't go home in fury and frustration. Pick up the phone book, look under U.S. Government, Department of Labor, Wage and Hour Division. Call up and ask about the simple process to file an Equal Pay Complaint. No one will ever find out because this agency, which enforces the Equal Pay Act, operates in secrecy and confidentiality.

•

Once you've slept with your boss, you've ended your upward mobility in that company — and the reason has nothing to do with sex. *That* particular career path is closed because you violated the chain-of-command relationship. I've even seen this happen to men who were close friends when the subordinate man failed to observe the mandated deference and distance required once his friend became his boss.

•

Everybody knows that long-time affairs between secretaries and their bosses can go on without repercussions, always providing the woman remains in her subservient, noncomplaining role of the dutiful doormat. Those sexual relationships are possible because secretarial jobs have no place in the hierarchy; as presently constituted, they are extraneous servant positions. A secretary has no upward mobility and the job is not a team position.

Privacy — How to Protect What's Left of It

A traveller's guide to the Mystery Land out among the credit bureaus, government computer systems, and new lie detector technologies. This is the definitive reference book on potential privacy invaders and what effects they could have on your life. It will either calm or confirm your fears; more likely both. The tone is a bit Naderishly self-righteous, but that's preferable to the paranoid cynicism of most of its competitors. Each chapter ends with a list of what you can do to protect yourself — mostly raise hell, gently but relentlessly.

—Art Kleiner
[Suggested by Sandy Emerson]

Privacy
(How to Protect What's Left of It)
Robert Ellis Smith
1979; 319 pp.

$4.95 postpaid from:
Anchor Books
501 Franklin Avenue
Garden City, NY 11530
or Whole Earth Household Store

•

If you suspect that your telephone is being monitored, make sure that you can find a motivation for someone to do this to you. Is there family disharmony? Are you involved in political action? Would you be perceived as a threat — using the broadest possible stretch of the imagination — by a government agency or a political opponent? Do you belong to an organization that interests the FBI, the Department of Defense, or local police? Would your employer suspect you of leaking information or cheating?

Next, try to prove that information learned by someone else could have come *only* from telephone conversation on your telephone. One way to do this is to talk deliberately about false (but believable) information on the telephone you suspect is being monitored. Then watch where the information surfaces. If you continue to do this, you may have much more fun than discovering the physical evidence of the surveillance.

THE RISING SUN
NEIGHBORHOOD NEWSLETTER

Multiple choices:

1. Individual human beings think of, create, originate ideas.

2. Ideas occur. Sometimes they occur where one person's mind is, sometimes they happen in several minds at once. *continued on next spread*

Womansplace Booklist

This looks to be your feminist bookstore by mail. The list is comprehensive and intriguing, offering basics and surprises both. Equality-wise, they even have a section of books on men's liberation. What's more there's fiction, science fiction, children's literature, music, poetry, and access to periodicals and other feminist bookstores (how's that for solidarity?)

Best of all, as with any good bookstore, there's a distinct taste and intelligence evidenced in their selection and annotation. A quick glance at their book list excited my book lust. —Stephanie Mills

[Suggested by Joani Blank]

Womansplace Booklist
$1/year (6 issues)
from:
Womansplace Bookstore
2401 North 32nd Street
Phoenix, AZ 85008

●

SEXISM

Sexual Shakedown — Lin Farley — $2.50 — examination of sexual harassment on the job, plus what you can do about it.

For Her Own Good: 150 Years of the Experts' Advice to Women — Barbara Ehrenreich and Dierde English — $3.95 — shows how the experts usurped women's age old skills and set themselves up as authorities on everything from work to love.

Language and Woman's Place — Robin Lakoff — $2.50 — uncovers roots of language that classify and delineate the sexes.

Words and Women — Casey Miller and Kate Swift — $2.50 — new language in new times; comprehensive survey of various ways in which sex bias is built into English language.

Sexual Politics — Kate Millett — $2.95 — devastating analysis of literary sexism.

Sex, Gender and Society — Ann Oakley — $2.95 — shows the insidious ways gender roles of Western society hinder our free choices.

Myth America — Carol Wald, et al. — $8.95 — picturing women 1865 - 1945; graphic collage documenting myths of popular culture and images of how it shaped women's experiences.

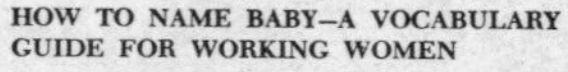

HOW TO NAME BABY—A VOCABULARY GUIDE FOR WORKING WOMEN

Media Women—New York

If A Person Is:	Call Her	Call Him:
Ingratiating	Sweet	Ass-Licker
Supportive	Bright	Yes-Man
Intelligent	Helpful	Smart
Helpful	Good Girl	Helpful
Innovative	Pushy	Original
Insistent	Hysterical	Persistent
Tough	Impossible	Go-Getter
Cute & Timid	A Sweetheart	A Fairy
Sexy	A Piece	Handsome
Dumb	Not Too Bright	An Idiot
Plain Looking	Homely, Ugly	no comment
Successful	Ball-Breaker Up-Tight Hard Dame Bitch The Only Successful Woman I've Ever Met Who Isn't A——(Ball-Breaker, Up-Tight, Hard Bitch, etc.)	Successful
Politically Involved	Over-Emotional	Committed
Supportive Helpful Ingratiating Passive Gentle	A Real Woman	A Minister's Son
Invisible	Nice Chick	Never Heard of Him

Sisterhood is Powerful

This benchmark anthology, assembled ten years ago, set an agenda for women's liberation. Many of the articles in it deal with structural manifestations of patriarchy: discrimination in employment, academia, and the military; the biases of psychiatry and medicine; the never-ending struggle to equalize the responsibility for housework; and the bitter prejudice against lesbians.

It no longer seems so radical to address these problems (which is not to say that they've been solved). Indeed, that struggles for change on all these fronts are underway is inspiriting. But the horizon keeps receding. The frontier of liberation tends from the secular to the spiritual and on to a reconciliation of the two. Once equal opportunity to work is obtained, it then becomes necessary to fight sexual harassment on the job. When that is done, freeing oneself from internalized patriarchy must begin.

Some of the freshest material in **Sisterhood is Powerful** *is in the "Historical Documents" section: statements from various covens of WITCHES and the uproarious SCUM manifesto. Other articles, by Florynce Kennedy, Eleanor Holmes Norton, and Robin Morgan; poetry by Rita Mae Brown and Marge Piercy; plus contributions from a host of other women make* **Sisterhood is Powerful** *a rich sourcebook for contemporary feminism.* —Stephanie Mills

Sisterhood is Powerful
(An Anthology of Writings from the Women's Liberation Movement)
Robin Morgan, Editor
1970; 648 pp.
$4.95 postpaid from:
Random House
455 Hahn Road
Westminster, MD 21157
or Whole Earth Household Store

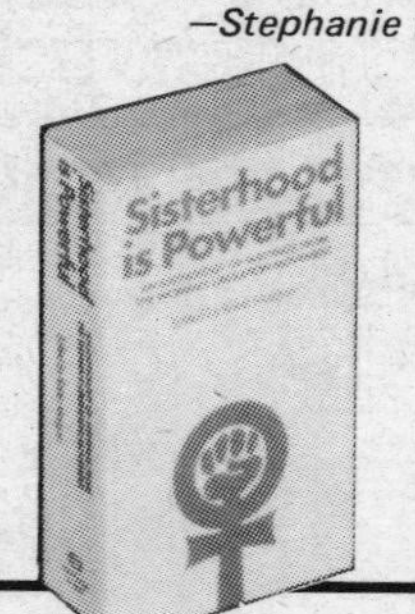

●

"I don't mind sharing the work, but you'll have to show me how to do it."

Meaning: I ask a lot of questions and you'll have to show me everything everytime I do it because I don't remember so good. Also don't try to sit down and read while I'm doing my jobs because I'm going to annoy hell out of you until it's easier to do them yourself.

"I *hate* it more than you. You don't mind it so much."

Meaning: Housework is garbage work. It's the worst crap I've ever done. It's degrading and humiliating for someone of *my* intelligence to do it. But for someone of *your* intelligence . . .

●

You are a Witch by saying aloud, "I am a Witch" three times, and *thinking about that.* You are a Witch by being female, untamed, angry, joyous, and immortal.

Intimatalk

Whenever I hear the word "share" I would reach for a gun if I had one. "Share" is frequently followed by the word "feelings," and I have enough of my own thank you; please do us both a favor and repress yours.

Given that prejudice, and other maleness, how pleasant to be won over by this female confidence of a magazine. It's tiny, devoid of advertising, regular as menses, and fascinating as reading other people's mail. Here the ladies convene in print at Louise Lacey's invitation (she researched and wrote **Lunaception***) to discuss one subject or another in highly personal terms. Depression; success; friends; humor; fear (and courage); power; dreams; love letters; good marriages. A mail order woman friend. Readers can also contribute.* —SB

Intimatalk
(formerly Woman's Choice)
Louise Lacey, Editor
$24/year (12 issues)
from:
Intimatalk
P.O. Box 489
Berkeley, CA 94701

●

Sexual Responsibility

In my experience, it's been more difficult for women to get what they want than it has been for me. For one thing, I didn't care what they wanted. All I was concerned with was proving myself. Also, most of the time, most of the women were passive, allowing me to do whatever occurred to me. And even if I asked, a lot of them really didn't know what they wanted . . .

It must be the way we're brought up. The women, as little girls, had the prize. I, as a little boy, was the potential prize winner. You don't learn to get what you want out of your prize when her whole game is based on withholding it from all but the highest bidder. And little boys get all the practice at bidding. I can recall times when my intuition said 'No,' but my mind said, 'Go,' because it was obeying some internalized cultural imperative to prove myself. All these opportunities didn't do much toward sensitizing me to women's needs. But women just didn't know, or wouldn't say, what they really wanted. And I was too busy proving to listen. —Al Einhorn

●

Creativity

My times of greatest creativity have been when I gave birth to my daughter, and one time when I was singing, and another time when I was screaming my head off. During those times I was frightened that if I let these things pass through me, like letting the baby out, I would disappear and be gone and just cease to exist. The more I opened up and let the child out, or the music or the scream out, it was as though my body was opening and I was losing the concept of myself as I usually think of it, with the head telling the hands what to do. The head was not making any judgements or controlling what I was doing. I was just letting it out. That required suspension of the mind, which required a lot of will power and a lot of respect for raw emotions and raw force. I had to tell the head, this is not the place or the time for you now. It's a really intense struggle. The fear comes in from the conscious mind and says, 'You're losing control, get back.' So the direction creativity takes is coming not from the head, where things usually come from, but from the heart or the soul. It's all so new and so powerful for me that it's just awesome. —Cathy Powell

Gyn/Ecology

Ordinarily, I don't read feminist statements: Ordinarily, I don't stare into the Sun. That doesn't mean I don't love the light. I didn't set out to read **Gyn/Ecology***; I feared it would change my accomodations. By chance I picked it up. It has yet to put me down.*

It is an anti-male book. In an anti-female world, this is a refreshing perspective. After feeling paranoid for thirty years, finding out that I had, rather, been a realist feels not good, but true. Mary Daly talks about Be-ing a Self-Identified woman. Reading this, I realized that in thirty years, every major decision I'd ever made was made in relation to a patriarch: Father, Lover, or God. Daughter was turned against Mother early on. If definitions of sanity are male-ordained, then it is insane to take the word of a woman. Later you learn to disbelieve women (who, Steinem observes, tell the truth by speaking personally) at the risk of colluding in your own mutilation.

That Mary Daly's threats to the established order haven't met with censorship may have to do with Tolstoy's dictum that there is only one thing men (sic) love more than freedom, and that is slavery. Speaking for myself only, I don't love slavery. I dislike the contortions I have assumed to please the fathers who spring up in my life like dragon's teeth. Nevertheless, this has become a Practice. Damned Daly, thorn in my mind's side, reminding me that charm is futile and integrity the hardest work of all. Her book has made me furious. It hasn't made me free, but it has made me think. She wrote it as a challenge. Read it if you dare. —Stephanie Mills

Gyn/Ecology
(The Metaethics of Radical Feminism)
Mary Daly
1978; 485 pp.
$7.95 postpaid from:
Beacon Press
Harper and Row
Keystone Industrial Park
Scranton, PA 18512
or Whole Earth Household Store

●

Why has it seemed "appropriate" in this culture that the plot of a popular book and film (*The Exorcist*) centers around a Jesuit who "exorcises" a girl who is "possessed"? Why is there no book or film about a woman who exorcises a Jesuit? From a radical feminist perspective it is clear that "Father" is precisely the one who cannot exorcise, for he is allied with and identified with The Possessor. The fact that he is himself possessed should not be women's essential concern. It is a mistake to see men as pitiable victims or vessels to be "saved" through female self-sacrifice. However possessed males may be within patriarchy, it is *their* order.

●

There is every reason to see the mutilation and destruction of women by doctors specializing in unnecessary radical mastectomies and hysterectomies, carcinogenic hormone therapy, psychosurgery, spirit-killing psychiatry and other forms of psychotherapy as directly related to the rise of radical feminism in the twentieth century.

One Answer to Rape: Humiliate the Raper

Robert Gnaizda, a lawyer with the San Francisco public interest firm Public Advocates, pointed out a couple years ago that there might be an easier way to convict rapists than by the chancy ordeal of a standard rape trial. Accuse the man of *indecent exposure.* If you've been raped and can identify the guy, say he grabbed you and took out his penis and showed it to you. Results: 1) The cops will not treat you weird but will treat him weird; 2) You're not embarrassed before the world, 3) The man will be humiliated by his friends and the other prisoners; 4) He'll probably plead guilty, because juries don't need much evidence for such crimes; 5) Even if there's a trial, your personal life will be no part of it; 6) The man will ever after have to register as a sex offender wherever he goes.

It might be worth it just to watch the guy squirm at not being able to say what he really did. Or it may be an effective way to get him to confess.

I realize this proposal appears to trivialize what is one of our most vicious crimes. But what if it works? So far as I know no one has tried this approach. If you try it, *let us know what happens.* —SB

OPPRESSIVE DICHOTOMIES BY JAY KINNEY

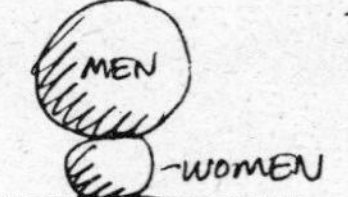

THE FEMINIST VIEW OF THE WORLD:

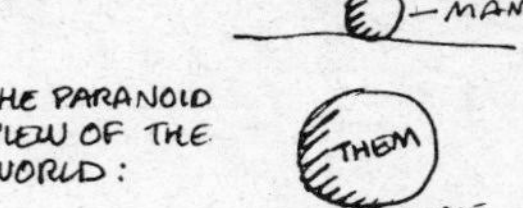

THE BLACK NATIONALIST VIEW OF THE WORLD:

THE NAZI VIEW OF THE WORLD:
NON ARYANS

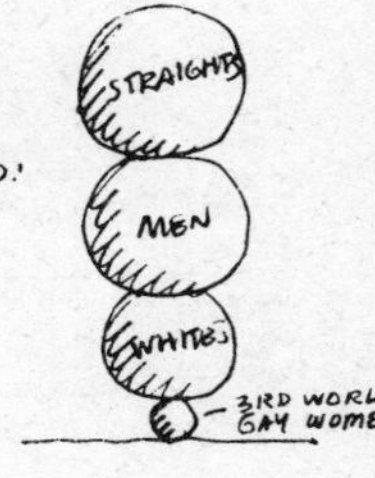

THE PACIFIST VIEW OF THE WORLD:

THE BLACK RADICAL LESBIAN VIEW OF THE WORLD:

3RD WORLD GAY WOMEN
THE PET'S VIEW OF THE WORLD:

MAKE UP YOUR OWN COMBINATIONS!

ENJOY THE RIGHTEOUS INDIGNATION OF DUALISTIC THINKING.

THE GAY VIEW OF THE WORLD

THE ANARCHIST VIEW OF THE WORLD:

LIBERAL'S VIEW OF THE WORLD:

In These Times

And they said it couldn't be done! **In These Times** *is an intelligent socialist weekly newspaper which presents world, national and local news in a non-sectarian, non-rhetorical manner. Attractively laid-out and professionally written,* **ITT** *is a pleasure to read, not a punishment. Sports, ecology, movies and books are regularly discussed in its pages, in contrast to most other Left newspapers where internecine wrangles and "Politics" seem to define the boundaries of the universe. Dedicated to helping forge a democratic Left majority in the U.S.,* **ITT** *clearly has its work cut out for itself . . . a fact it acknowledges by an optimism tempered with realism. Apolitical cynics be forewarned:* **ITT** *can be habit forming.* —Jay Kinney

In These Times
(The Independent Socialist Newspaper)
James Weinstein, Editor
$19.50/year (42 issues)
from:
In These Times
1509 North Milwaukee Ave.
Chicago, IL 60622

•

How do you see the relationship between your writing and your political opinions?

People on the left always ask that question. The right does not bother to ask or to answer that question.

On the left I think there is a great deal of confusion, wishful thinking and sentimentalism about this. First I think one has to realize very, very clearly that in almost all circumstances, if you are urgently, politically committed, and you give absolute priority to the political transformation of society or the political progress of a class, then you shouldn't be in one of the arts.

•

So what is the political duty of the writer?

It seems to me that it is to describe the world we live in as not being inevitable. Life with its enormous and crushing necessities often does not allow for something that is happening to be other than what it is.

—John Berger

•

And I've never tired of re-reading Garcia Marquez's moving anecdote, when on a visit to a Cuban village, he met a group of peasants who asked him what he did for a living. "I write," he answered. "What've you written?" a *campesino* asked. "I wrote a book called **One Hundred Years of Solitude**," Garcia Marquez replied — at which point the awestruck villagers shouted in chorus, "Macondo!"

—Gene Bell-Villada

BIOREGIONAL NEWSPAPERS AND MAGAZINES

by Peter Warshall

Cultural Survival

Cultural Survival *is an organization of concerned anthropologists and other citizens trying to preserve threatened cultures and explore ways in which native peoples can accommodate to the twentieth century without too great a loss of their own uniqueness. They rent an introductory slide lecture kit ("Indigenous People in Search of a Future"); coordinate, report, and gather funds for a host of projects for Amazonian native peoples, the Kalahari bushmen, Mayan peoples of the Chiapes/Guatemalan region, etc. They have a fine newsletter with access to much of their recent work concerning cultural survival.*

Cultural Survival
Jason Clay, Editor

$15/year (4 issues, includes membership)
from:
Cultural Survival, Inc.
11 Divinity Avenue
Cambridge, MA 02138

High Country News

Everything up to date west of the 100th meridian. A deep heart connection to the Western landscape and its peoples. Bioregional journalism at its best. *(See p. 51)*

Econews

Voice of the Oregonian temperate woodlands — especially in northern California. Network for groups concerned with logging, herbicides, policy decisions, and watershed settlement.

Econews
(Newsletter of the Northcoast Environmental Center)
Michael Matthews, Editor
$6/year (12 issues)
from:
The Northcoast Environmental Center
640 Tenth Street
Arcata, CA 95521

The Texas Observer

Bi-weekly newspaper covering the Texas grasslands, the Chihuahuan desert and the broadleaf woodlands of Texas and the Gulf Coast. Fiercely independent with articles on Tejano corridos, clearcutting the Texas forests, or the hot chili in Texas corruption.

The Texas Observer
Jim Hightower, Editor

$14/year (26 issues)
from:
The Texas Observer
600 West Seventh
Austin, TX 78701

Dry Country News

A magazine covering the desert bioregions (Sonoran, Chihuahuan, Mojave and Great Basin) but, at present, concentrating in the Arizona/New Mexico (Mexico) areas. This is the up-and-coming, located journal on dry land agriculture or raising goats in the desert or the creosote brush rebellion. It includes access to books, organizations, and a few poems and philosophy.

Dry Country News
Gordon Solberg, Editor
$7.50/year (4 issues)
from:
Dry Country News
P.O. Box 23
Radium Springs, NM 88054

Blackberry

Blackberry *is about the Gulf of Maine which runs from Cape Cod to the Gulf of Sable and includes the only Canadian Taiga in the lower 48 as well as some of the richest off-shore fishing grounds.* **Gulf of Maine** *is a collection of* **Blackberry's** *history, poems, old-timer reflections, fishing politics, whales and tidal pool photos. An elegant beginning in bioregional love.* ■

Gulf of Maine
(A Blackberry Reader)
Gary Lawless, Editor
1977; 134 pp.
$4.95 postpaid

Blackberry
Gary Lawless, Editor
$15/year (7 issues)

both from:
Blackberry
P.O. Box 186
Brunswick, ME 04011

All Alone Stone

An exquisite magazine of the Sitka rainforest peoples (ancient and modern) trying to preserve the integrity of the lush forested islands from Vancouver Island up to the Alaska peninsula. Presently focused on the Queen Charlotte Island area. Filled with intelligent writing, muckraking truths, respect for indigenous peoples, passion, and beautiful photographs.

All Alone Stone
Dan Bowditch, et al., Editors
Irregular
$6.50/issue from:
All Alone Stone Islands Protection Society
P.O. Box 302
Masset, BC
Canada V0T 1M0

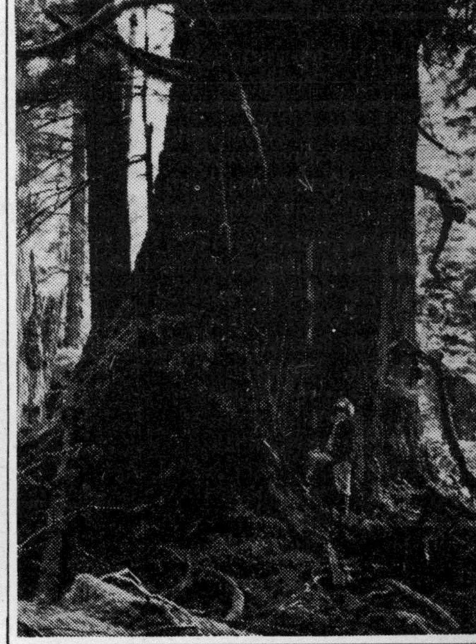

Virgin forest with giant cedars slated to be logged soon.
—All Alone Stone

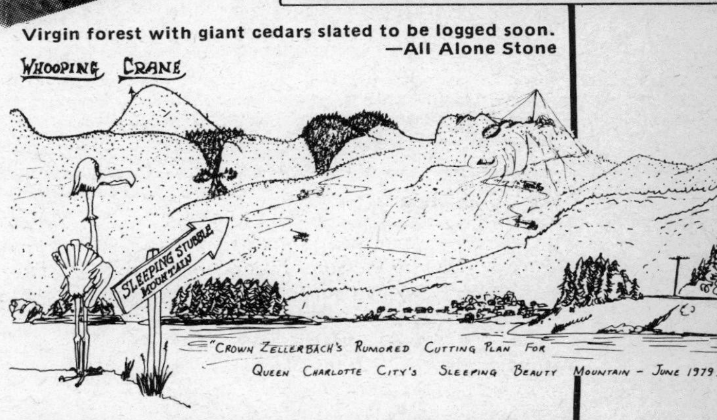

WHOOPING CRANE
SLEEPING STUMBLE MOUNTAIN
"CROWN ZELLERBACH'S RUMORED CUTTING PLAN FOR QUEEN CHARLOTTE CITY'S SLEEPING BEAUTY MOUNTAIN – JUNE 1979."

THE RISING SUN
NEIGHBORHOOD NEWSLETTER

Multiple choice continued from last spread

3. Ideas emerge from conversation. It can be a conversation between different parts of one person, one person and the world, several people in the same room, several people on the same planet sensing each other, between different parts of the world and maybe an individual transcribes the conversation — what does the civil rights movement say to bored housewives, what do roses say to glass, what did Genghis Khan say to the Transamerica Pyramid? Were you there when the Chiffons stole My Sweet Lord?

continued on next spread

Let me try to be as ambiguous as possible. I am an Anarchist and I am not. I am a Socialist and I am not. I am a Communist and I am not. I am a Libertarian and I am not. I am not what I say I am, I am what I say. I vacillate and I do not. I am all these things and I am not. I can be pinned down and I can't. I like to label others. I do not like to be labelled by others. I believe in the masses and trust no one. I believe that I am God and I am an atheist. I believe that you are God and let you get away with murder. Clarity only arrives when one realizes that it is impossible. All emphatic statements I make are false. All qualifiers are cowardly. All negotiations are bad vibes, man. Got that? Good. Let's start over. —Jay Kinney

Intro

COMMON SENSE TELLS US that politics is a complex area not easily understood, and cynicism further suggests that we leave politics to the politicians while we get on with *real* life. There's some truth to both notions. However, politics left to the "experts" has a way of abruptly re-entering our lives, whether invited or not – witness the draft – and elementary self-defense would suggest at least a passing acquaintance not only with the present system but with the most commonly proposed alternatives, as well.

The following survey of the Left is a tentative attempt to shed some light on one set of alternatives and its advocates. The Left today is not the left of the '60s, and even a veteran of the anti-war movement is bound to be puzzled by the plethora of new groups that have appeared in the '70s. While my survey is far from complete (and unavoidably subjective), I have tried to set out the main categories and summarize the most notable groups therein.

Some of the political formations commonly associated with the Left (such as the Women's, Third World, and Gay movements) have not been covered in this survey, in part because they cut across the political and economic categories used here and partly due to my own limited familiarity with their complexities. That they fall outside the confines of this survey in no way diminishes the importance they hold for the Left as a whole.

And now, without further delay, let's dive in and see what we find.

Liberals

Most numerous of all inhabitants of the Left are the **Liberals**. Traditionally associated with the Democratic party, and more recently with lobbying groups like Common Cause or Ralph Nader's armies, the liberals need little introduction. Broadly speaking, they share the assumption that a just and generous life is possible for all under the present economic/political system, if only the right reforms and laws are enacted. Welfare and busing are two familiar liberal programs to combat poverty and segregation – programs which have had decidedly mixed results.

Cartoonist Jay Kinney, routinely our best-informed and most objective source of news on the Left, has a comic book history ranging from **Young Lust** *to* **Corporate Crime** *and* **Anarchy Comics.** *Researching this 1980 field guide nearly finished him off. The Left is an elusive and slippery subject (and, like the South, will rise again).* —SB

Throughout the '70s, the liberals have been gradually splitting into two tendencies. One tendency has drifted rightward, acquiring more and more conservative characteristics. This approach has been particularly popular with politicians campaigning to be all things to all people. The second tendency, observable with some labor leaders such as the United Auto Workers'(UAW) Doug Fraser, has been to shift further left, advocating more drastic reforms – even toying with (gasp!) the nationalization of some industries.

Since liberal groups get the best media coverage and have the most pervasive publicity on the Left, I'll not bother to cover them in detail here. As the coalition to end all coalitions, the recently formed **Progressive Alliance** is worth mentioning, however. Originally called together by UAW prexy Doug Fraser in the fall of 1978, and consisting of leaders from over 30 labor groups, numerous Dem. political organizations, every liberal issue group imaginable (National Organization for Women, National Association for the Advancement of Colored People, Friends of the Earth, Americans for Democratic Action, etc.) as well as two socialist groups (the Democratic Socialist Organizing Committee and the New American Movement), the Alliance began in a flurry of rhetoric about the need for "a vigorous counterattack against the right-wing corporate forces and the political system they dominate." The Alliance has yet to solidly implement such intentions, however, and in the absence of any mechanism for support from grass-roots activists seems unlikely to.

The Progressive Alliance best indicates the pressure felt by established liberal groups that their past reforms are not enough – especially in the face of growing economic crisis. Largely committed to Democratic Party channels, their search for more radical solutions is nevertheless leading them to lend an ear to groups like DSOC and NAM.

Democratic Socialists

This leads us to the **Democratic Socialists,** who have probably gained more visibility and influence on the national scene than any other left grouping in the late '70s. Whether advocating "economic democracy," greater corporate "accountability," or a growing role for "public ownership of vital resources," the democratic socialists are united in their commitment to structural change in government and economy through the ballot box and legal channels.

This "evolutionary" strategy is most commonly associated with the old pre-WWI Second International, and indeed many democratic socialists look back fondly to the days when the Socialist Party could pull nearly a million votes in presidential elections, as well as elect mayors in 56 cities and towns, including Milwaukee, Schenectady, and Flint.

The democratic socialist vision usually sees the future election of socialists on both a local and national scale leading to the public control of major corporations and a greater institution of democracy both in government and the workplace.

Because this vision is predominantly a moral one based on the ideal of the expansion of democracy within existing institutions, it is quite possible to be a democratic socialist and have no need of Marx at all.

The **Democratic Socialist Organizing Committee** (DSOC) under the leadership of Michael Harrington has the goal of working through the "leftwing" of the Democratic Party to try and push it towards a socialist position. DSOC has a number of politicians and labor leaders as members (Rep. Ron Dellums, Gloria Steinem, Machinist Union President William Winpisinger) and prides itself on dealing with "real possibilities in the real world" – an approach which usually boils down to trying to influence the writing of the Dems' platform, and stumping for liberal Dem. re-election campaigns. Exactly who is using whom here is unclear, and a more cynical outlook might call this all "politics as usual."

Democratic Left, Michael Harrington, Editor, **$5**/year (10 issues), from Democratic Socialist Organizing Committee, 853 Broadway, Suite 801, New York, NY 10003

In These Times, "the independent socialist newspaper" has of late increasingly lined up with the DSOC strategy. Begun in Fall, 1977, with James Weinstein as editor and a staff heavily drawn from NAM, **ITT** has attempted to be a rhetoric-free source of national and world news, as well as a forum for discussions among democratic socialists. 1979 saw **ITT** affiliate with the Washington, D.C.-based, left-liberal think-tank Institute for Policy Studies, as well as the appearance of an editorial line explicitly dissociating the paper from most other left groups and "sects." Design-wise, one of the best weekiles around. (Reviewed on p. 389.)

Hovering in this same area is the **Campaign for Economic Democracy** (CED), the organization founded by Tom Hayden and Jane Fonda in the wake of Hayden's unsuccessful run for U.S. Senate. Avoiding explicit reference to "socialism" altogether, the CED prefers the euphemistic term "economic democracy," which Hayden juggles with attacks on bigness and a hazy defense of small-time capitalism. CED has concentrated its efforts in California on local campaigns for things like rent control and city council seats, while making inroads into Jerry Brown's bureaucracy. Tom & Jane's national CED roadshow in late 1979 barnstormed against nuclear power while attempting to spread CED nationwide, but the organization's strength remains close to home in California for now.

CED News (Campaign for Economic Democracy Newsletter), Sam Hurst, Editor, **$15**/year (12 issues, includes membership), from CED, 409 Santa Monica, CA 90401

Meanwhile, the granddaddy of democratic socialism, the **Socialist Party**, is still surviving, though barely. Long identified with the late Norman Thomas, and then with Michael Harrington, the SP has suffered a spate of internal disputes and defections in recent times. (DSOC is the direct descendant of a former SP caucus.) Seventy years ago the SP was the major voice for socialism in the U.S. – but these days it serves mainly as a loose umbrella for several local and state organizations.

The People (Newspaper of the Socialist Labor Party), **$4**/year (26 issues, from Socialist Labor Party, 914 Industrial Ave., Palo Alto, CA 94303

The **New American Movement** is posed somewhat uneasily with fingers in several pies. Proponents of DSOC-style politics mix in NAM's ranks with Euro-communist enthusiasts, community organizers and academic Marxists. Perhaps better than any other group on the Left, NAM has maintained an open-ended, multi-caucus approach which harks back to the days of the '60s' New Left. NAM calls itself a socialist-feminist organization and has been active in trying to stress the importance of fighting both sexual and class oppression simultaneously.

As its optimistic name suggests, NAM believes that only a mass-movement in favor of socialism can successfully revolutionize the U.S. However for the last decade NAM's membership has stabilized at about 600 people, indicating that NAM's unique complexity may also be keeping it from achieving mass appeal. Whatever its long-range dreams, for now NAM remains an organization of activists engaged in a variety of local battles.

Moving On (Monthly Magazine of the New American Movement), **$5**/year (10 issues), from New American Research Institute, 9244 North Clark Street, Chicago IL 60657

Ranking groups across a right-to-left spectrum is tricky at best but as we proceed leftward it is pretty safe to say that each new group criticizes the ones to its right as not going far enough in advocating social change. (Thus the oft-used derogatory term "Reformist.")

Communists

For the **Communists**, a socialist society is only a transitional stage on the way to a classless, stateless, "free" society, not an end in itself. Yet to reach even that transitional stage a revolution must occur, to throw out the (please excuse the rhetoric) ruling class. And revolutions are not voted in – Allende's Chile being the exception that proves the rule.

Lenin, building on Marx's theories, developed an organizational plan for revolutionaries which posited a strong centralized party to "lead" the revolution. (He also developed the analysis of Imperialism which sees advanced Capitalist nations depending on their exploitation of less-developed countries in order to further their own growth.) Followers of Lenin's strategy and accompanying theories are usually called Marxist-Leninists, though as a catch-phrase that label is most often claimed by Maoists and Stalinists. (See below.) Not all communists are Leninists, it should be noted, and the more libertarian non-Leninists are discussed towards the end of this survey.

The most famous U.S. Leninist party, and the one the late J. Edgar Hoover loved to hate, is the **Communist Party U.S.A.** (CPUSA). It was originally founded in

1919 in response to the inspiration of the Russian Revolution. CPUSA members were active in unemployment organizing and union work during the Depression – particularly within the CIO. This was the Party's heyday, when its prestige and influence both with workers and intellectuals were strongest.

Yet tied as it was to the defense of the Russian Revolution, and consequently to Stalin's foreign policy, the CPUSA had to perform a series of sudden about-faces (most notably following the Hitler-Stalin pact of 1939), which cost it its credibility. Moreover as the post-WWII Cold War grew, with help from the likes of Nixon and McCarthy, the Party came under heavy government attack as a "nest of spies." It is still almost impossible to tell to what degree such allegations had a basis in fact; recent evidence, for example, indicates that the Rosenbergs may well have been framed, while Alger Hiss' guilt is still up for grabs. Whatever the case, the CPUSA was once again devastated. One imagines that when Krushchev denounced Stalin in 1956 and ushered in the era of "peaceful coexistence," CPUSA leaders were only too happy to temper their menacing image accordingly. The Party's current strategy, so un-menacing as to be positively toothless, is the "Anti-Monopoly People's Coalition" which aims to bring together trade unionists, the poor and small business people in opposition to "Big Business."

The '60s' New Left denigration of the CPUSA as a bunch of old has-beens had its core of truth. However, the Party is still the largest on the Left, publishes a daily newspaper (the **Daily World**), has thousands of members spread across the country and remains active (if low profile) in labor and community struggles. And, for better or worse, the CPUSA is still the organization against which most others (especially Maoists and Trotskyites) feel obliged to favorably compare themselves.

Daily World (Continuing the Daily Worker) Carl Winter, Editor, **$12**/year (365 issues), From Long View Publishing, P.O. Box 544, Old Chelsea Station, New York, NY 10011

People's World (A Weekly Associated with the CPUSA), Carl Bloice, Editor, **$10**/year (52 issues), from Pacific Publishing Foundation, 1819 Tenth Street, Berkeley, CA 94710

Trotskyites

The longest-running Leninist critics of Soviet-aligned communism are the Trotskyites. As Commander of the Red Army during the Russian Revolution, Trotsky was one of the top leaders in the U.S.S.R., until he came into strong conflict with Stalin, in part over Stalin's policy of "Socialism in One Country," the slogan under which Russia stabilized itself in the '20s and moved towards heavy industrialization. Trotsky felt that it was Russia's foremost duty to push for revolution worldwide – "Permanent Revolution" – and he differed with other leaders in the Russian CP over how far and how fast such revolutions could be pushed – believing that they should be "one-stave" revolutions which would not cease until true Communism was instituted and thus "permanent." Expelled from the CP in 1927 and from Russia in 1929, Trotsky became a prime critic of Stalin and his methods. (Whether Trotsky in power instead of Stalin would have made much real difference remains a matter of historical second-guessing.) In the '30s Trotsky formed the Fourth International, a network of communist groups around the world in agreement with his views, as a rival to the Stalinist Third International. On August 20, 1940, Trotsky was assassinated by an ice-axe-wielding Soviet agent in Mexico City.

The **Socialist Workers Party** is the largest and oldest Trotskyite group in the U.S. (In the '50s and '60s it was second only to the CPUSA in drawing fire from the FBI.) Like the CPUSA it has downplayed the role of revolution – preferring to field candidates regularly for local and national office. During the Vietnam war, the SWP, along with its youth affiliate, the Young Socialist Alliance, thrust itself into the thick of the anti-war movement, where it won much resentment from others in broad coalitions through the SWP's penchant for take-over ploys.

The Militant (Newsweekly of the Socialist Workers Party), **$24**/year (52 issues), from The Militant, 14 Charles Lane, New York, NY 10014

The SWP spent much of the '70s working with women's, gay and anti-racist struggles, but 1979 saw a major shift in SWP strategy with members being encouraged to get industrial jobs as lead-ins to rank & file organizing among workers. Two other Trotskyite groups have already made some inroads in this area, the Sparticist League and the International Socialists.

The **Spartacist League** (SL) began as a splinter from the SWP in the early 60s, and has since stacked up a reputation as the most sectarian group on the Left (no mean feat in itself!). An enormous amount of energy is spent by SL members dogging the heels of the SWP and other communist groups – often with picket signs or leading questions intent on demonstrating the bankruptcy of its rivals' positions. The SL's approach to its potential supporters is equally unsubtle, with the SL paper **Workers Vanguard** commonly running headline commands such as "Hate Carter!"

Yet despite such shenanigans the SL is not as isolated as one might imagine. It has militant caucuses organized in a number of union locals, most notably in The Communication Workers of America (the Phone Co. union). Using the union meetings, elections, and conventions as forums, the caucuses attempt to expose the "sell-out" nature of the unions, posing their own militant leadership as an alternative.

Workers Vanguard (Marxist Working-Class Biweekly of the Spartacist League of the U.S.), Jan Norden, Editor, **$3**/year (24 issues), from Workers Vanguard, Box 1377, GPO, New York, NY 10116

The **International Socialists** (IS) took a somewhat similar approach a few years ago when it helped organize the Teamsters for a Democratic Union (TDU) as a reform movement in that corrupt labor empire. At that time IS was the least rigid of the Trotskyite groups, eschewing the usual tight party discipline. However this was IS's peak and following an attempt to more thoroughly Leninize, it suffered some crippling splits. The remaining group, considerably reduced in size, has had to retrench considerably. In contrast to SL's combative purism, IS has, of late, been showing interest in uniting with any other Left groups with which it can reach certain minimum agreements. IS, one suspects, is not long for this world.

Changes (Magazine of the International Socialists) Marilyn Danton, Editor, **$10**/year (12 issues), from Changes Socialist Monthly, 17300 Woodward Avenue, Detroit, MI 48203

There are several other "Trot" groups, such as the Revolutionary Socialist League (an IS splinter) and the Workers League, with sizes ranging from tiny to small, whose unique qualities elude me. While Trotskyism is the predominant Left tendency outside of the Labour Party in England, over here it remains just one among many.

Maoists and Post-Maoists

Maoism is a relative newcomer to the U.S. Left, dating back to 1961 - 62 and the Sino-Soviet split. This geopolitical schism reverberated in the ranks of the CPUSA, precipitating the departure of a group of 50 or so members who were sympathetic to China. This group, under the leadership of Milt Rosen, was to become the Progressive Labor Movement, later the **Progressive Labor Party**. Just as Lenin had added his own theories to Marx's, Mao added his to theirs; the result, most familiarly distilled into his "Little Red Book," was "Mao Tsetung Thought."

At a time when most of the Old Left, New Left, and student movement were downplaying or oblivious to a "class analysis," the PLP, in the mid '60s, was making it their central concern. Only the Working Class (Proletariat) could make "the Revolution," PL maintained in orthodox fashion. From 1966 to 1969 PL made a concerted effort to push this analysis in the Students for a Democratic Society (SDS), the biggest and most influential New Left group. Through manipulation and grandstanding PL played a key role in SDS's 1969 splintering, going so far as to maintain its own "SDS" for a few years following the blow-up. PL subsequently parted ways with China in 1971, and today is a shadow of its former self, visible mainly through its strident front, the Committees Against Racism.

Challenge (Newspaper of the Progressive Labor Party), **$7.50**/year (26 issues), from PLP, Box 808, GPO, Brooklyn, NY 11202

SDS's demise was the crowning blow to the amorphous New Left which had prided itself on its skepticism towards dogmatic Marxism. As the '70s got underway there was a general knuckling down by the ex-student Left and a demand for more structure and theoretical coherence which made many reconsider Marxism (and Leninism in particular). It is more than a little ironic that some of the SDS leaders who had fought most vehemently against PL's encroachments in '69 are now proselytizing Maoists themselves. In fact, with PL no longer promulgating Maoism, the field has been dominated by two groups both led by former SDSers – the **Revolutionary Communist Party** (RCP) under Bob Avakian, and the **Communist Party (Marxist-Leninist)** (CPML) headed by Michael Klonsky.

The RCP began in 1969 as the Bay Area Revolutionary Union, a local SDS Leninist study group. By linking up with similar study groups and collectives around the country it went national in 1970 as the Revolutionary Union (RU). RU played an important role in early efforts by the "New Communist Movement" (as the various independent Maoist groups and pre-parties called themselves) to build a new vanguard party to succeed the hopelessly "revisionist" CPUSA. However RU's sectarianism, combined with some unpopular political lines – RU opposed busing to integrate schools, for instance – led to the group's virtual exile from the rest of the Left by October, 1975. At that time it decided that party-building was over and unveiled itself as the fruition of its own dreams – the RCP!

The Revolutionary Worker (Voice of the Revolutionary Communist Party), **$12**/year (52 issues), from Revolutionary Worker, Box 3486, Merchandise Mart, Chicago, IL 60654

The CPML which began as a L.A. study group called the October League (OL) in 1970, went national in 1972 and thereafter followed a course similar to RU's. Members of both groups have gotten jobs in basic industries, attempting rank and file organizing with only sporadic success. In the wake of Mao's death in 1976 and the purge of the "Gang of Four" in 1977, OL loyally followed the new Chinese regime's policies. The RCP, on the other hand, after a prolonged silence on the matter announced its defense of the Gang of Four, and declared that China was now on the road back to Capitalism.

Thus when OL became the CPML in 1977 (as the *real* vanguard party, of course) it received blessings from Beijing, with Klonsky personally sharing toasts with Hua Guofeng at official banquets. The RCP, for its part, sustained a giant split on the issue, with nearly half its membership resigning in early 1978 to form yet another Maoist group, the Revolutionary Workers Headquarters (RWHq). Since then, the RCP has mobilized its remaining membership around a succession of special big events (Mao Memorial Services, May Day Celebrations) which serve to keep the cadres busy and built the personality cults of Avakian and Mao.

The Call (Organ of the Communist Party Marxist-Leninist), **$12**/year (52 issues), from The Call, P.O. Box 5597, Chicago, IL 60680

The RCP and CPML, of course, are not the only Maoist groups, merely the largest. The **Communist Workers Party** (CWP) – formerly the largely East Coast based Workers Viewpoint Organization – has been active in anti-Klan organizing and made national news when 5 of its members were tragically killed in ambush by Klan/Nazi forces in Greensboro, N.C. in November, 1979.

The Workers Viewpoint (Political Organ of the Communist Workers Party), **$13**/year (50 issues), from Communist Workers Party, GPO Box 2256, New York, NY 10116.

The **League of Revolutionary Struggle** formed in 1978 from the merger of the mainly-Chicano August 29th Movement, the Chinese-American I Wor Kuen, and several local collectives. It has recently entered into discussions of uniting with the CPML and the RWHq. *If* this occurs (and one must remember that the path of true love never runs smooth) the resulting party would probably dwarf all previous Maoist groups.

Unity (Newspaper of the League of Revolutionary Struggle), **$7.50**/year, (26 issues), from Getting Together Publications, P.O. Box 127, Oakland, CA 94604

Stalinists and Miscellaneous Leninists

Beyond the Maoists there are still other M-L groupings that should be noted. Many of these are groups formerly faithful to China who broke with Maoism at varying points in the recent past.

For instance, there are now at least two separate vanguard parties who cling to tiny Albania as the last "Bastion of World Revolution." These are the **Marxist-Leninist Party of the USA** (MLP) and the **Communist Party USA (Marxist-Leninist)** (CPUSA-ML). The MLP is notable for publishing what is surely the dreariest newspaper on the Left, **The Workers' Advocate**. (Sample headline: "Lies and slanders of the bourgeoisie will never stop the growing influence of Marxism-Leninism and the Communist Party of Trinidad and Tobago among the working class and people.") The CPUSA-ML, for its part, has given special attention to defending Stalin, proudly peppering their paper, **Unite!**, with quotes from the old butcher.

The Worker's Advocate (Voice of the MLP), **$11**/year (6 issues), from Marxist-Leninist Publications, P.O. Box 11972, Fort Dearborn Station, Chicago, IL 6061[illegible]

Unite! $8/year (24 issues), from Unite! P.O. Box 6206, Chicago, IL 60680

Finally there is another handful of Leninist groups not aligned with any one country who are still engaged in mutual discussions towards (surprise!) building a new party. Many of these discussions began in the pages of the **Guardian** ("the independent radical newsweekly") througout the last decade. The leading New Left tabloid of the '60s, the **Guardian** went Leninist at that decade's end, maintaining a loyal readership through

THE RISING SUN
NEIGHBORHOOD NEWSLETTER

Multiple choice continued from last spread

4. Ideas emerge from silence. The reason you think of things right before you go to sleep is that you've finally shutup so the idea that's been knocking at your head all day can come in.

continued on next spread

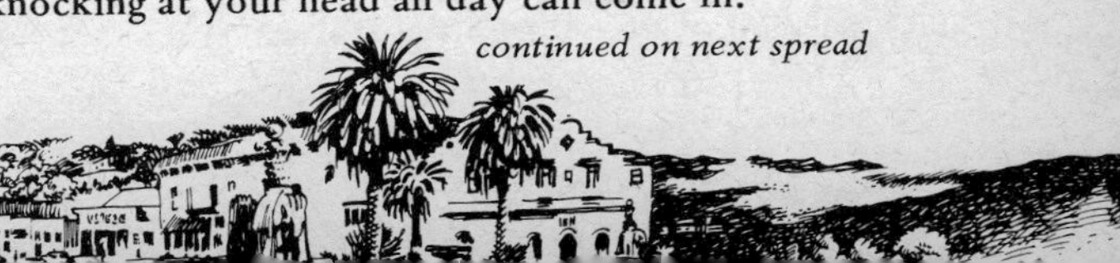

extensive coverage of both U.S. and Third World politics. When Irwin Silber, the **Guardian's** executive editor and film critic split with the paper in 1979, many of the Guardian Clubs (a network of support groups for the paper) left with him.

These clubs, now known as the **National Network of Marxist-Leninist Clubs** (NNMLC) believe that the remaining New Communist Movement must get its theoretical chops together before a Party can be built. This is called the "Rectification" Line and is in apparent conflict with the **Organizing Committee for an Ideological Center** (LC/IC) whose "Fusion" Line calls for the remaining M-Lers to "fuse" with the working class while building the Party. The founding force behind the OC/IC is the **Philadelphia Workers Organizing Committee**, led by Clay Newlin.

The Guardian (Independent radical newsweekly), Jack A. Smith, Editor, **$17**/year (50 issues), from Guardian, 33 West 17th Street, New York, NY 10011

The Line of March (Journal of Rectification of the National Network of Marxist-Leninist Clubs), **$12.50**/year (24 issues), from Institute for Scientific Socialism, 964 Valencia Street, San Francisco, CA 94110

The Organizer (Newspaper of the Philadelphia Workers Organizing Committee), **$10**/year (12 issues), from PWOC, Box 1168, Philadelphia, PA 19101

Like a small island of relative sanity in the middle of this arcane madness, the **Tucson Marxist-Leninist Collective** publishes the **Theoretical Review**, a modest bimonthly which prints firsthand accounts of Leninist groups' histories, along with debates between M-L groups involved in these party-building talks.

Theoretical Review (A Journal of Marxist-Leninist Theory and Discussion), **$8**/year (6 issues), from The Theoretical Review, P.O. Box 3692, Tucson, AZ 87522

Libertarian Left

The problems of the Leninists are a source of some relief to another strain of aspiring revolutionaries who have opposed Leninism and its hierarchical, centralized party all along. Leninism's decline has been matched by the slow but steady growth of an outlook often called **Libertarian Socialism** (or Libertarian Communism or sometimes Ultra-Leftism). Some ultra-leftists trace their roots to the "Council" Communists of the post-1918 period who proposed rule by mass assemblies (e.g., Workers' Councils) as an alternative to either State or Party rule following the Revolution. Others emphasize the importance of balancing personal autonomy with social cooperation. Most see the task of revolutionaries as agitation and clarification of ideas rather than "leadership." But all agree that without the abolition of wage labor and the State a revolution is just a changing of the guard. To the libertarian left, the countries usually labeled socialist or communist are no such thing, but exploitative class societies where bureaucrats call the shots instead of corporate execs.

While in the U.S. such views are held by a minority on the Left, they have become quite popular in parts of Western Europe recently. The most notable case is the Italian "Autonomy" movement of the mid-'70s, which brought together tens of thousands of young workers and unemployed in a revolt against both the Christian Democrat government and the Communist Party.

There is no uniform attitude toward Marx among the libertarian left. Some groups call themselves Marxist, and stick closely to their own interpretation of Marx's social-economic analysis. Others draw eclectically on Marx to varying degrees.

Internationalism is the North American section of the International Communist Current (ICC) – the largest organization on the ultra-left, linking groups in 9 different countries. The ICC holds that labor unions, "National Liberation" struggles, and the "socialist" countries as well as the democratic-socialist and Leninist Left are all thoroughly integrated into the world capitalist system. Thus workers can look only to themselves to organize a revolution. While there is a certain elegance to the ICC's across-the-board critique, this is undercut by a turgid writing style and sectarian demeanor virtually guaranteed to alienate everyone not already convinced.

Internationalism, $4.50/year (4 issues), from Internationalism, P.O. Box 961, Manhattanville Station, 365 West 125th Street, New York, NY 10027

Root and Branch, "A Libertarian Marxist journal" from the Boston area, holds views similar to the ICC's although they diverge on one or two significant points. For instance, the two groups hold differing versions of Marxian "crisis theory" – pointing at different causes for the present crisis of the System. In general R&B's approach is more flexible and open-minded than the ICC. The journal publishes excellent in-depth analyses of current world events as well as expositions of economic theory.

Root and Branch, $8/year (4 issues), from Root and Branch, Box 236, Somerville, MA 02143

Red Menace is a tabloid published irregularly by the Libertarian Socialist Collective in Toronto, Canada. It features extensive debates between various groups and individuals within the libertarian left, both socialist and anarchist, particularly over the validity of Marxian ideas. It has a stronger emphasis on "personal politics" than **R&B**, and its most interesting features are firsthand accounts of work-place and community organizing.

The Red Menace (A Libertarian Socialist Newsletter), **$3**/year (12 issues), from The Red Menace, P.O. Box 171, Postal Station D, Toronto, Ontario, Canada

Most growth on the libertarian left has been in local groups such as **Philadelphia Solidarity.** Originally part of a split-off from the Socialist Labor Party (see below), this group has an anti-authoritarian brand of politics heavily influenced by Cornelius Castoriadus, the French radical critic of Marxism. The group's main activity is a local libertarian socialist bookstore, Wooden Shoe, and mail-order book service. In addition it co-edits a newsletter **Synthesis** with the **League for Economic Democracy,** another SLP breakaway.

Synthesis (An anti-authoritarian newsletter of citizen-worker self-management ideas and activities), Published irregularly, **$.40**/1 issue, from League for Economic Democracy, P.O. Box 1858, San Pedro, CA 90733

Most of these groups are heavily involved with the printed word as their main propaganda medium. An exception, and perhaps a sign of things to come, is the Bay Area based **Union of Concerned Commies.** The UCC began as a one-shot collaboration between libertarian communists around the 1979 Three Mile Island protests. Since then it has continued to be active in the anti-nuke/anti-draft movement in various ways. The UCC is most notable for its ventures into street theatre which feature sardonically funny attacks on the straight left, the military, wage labor, and organized religion. Most recently, the group has extended its satirical style into cable TV, an upcoming series on the listener-owned radio station, and a rock band, the Funktionaries.

Union of Concerned Commies, Information **free** from UCC, Box 1200, 2000 Center Street, Berkeley, CA 94704

By far the oldest group on the U.S. libertarian left is the **Socialist Labor Party.** Founded by Daniel DeLeon in 1897 as a radical breakaway from the Socialist Party, the SLP advocates a "Socialist Industrial Unionism," their plan for society to be administered by the workers through a system of democratic, industry-based organizations. The similarity of these ideas with those of the newer groups is obvious, especially since several of them came out of the SLP itself. However, while the SLP continues to publish a fairly intelligent and readable paper, the **People**, its schema for the new society looks a little cobwebby since the majority of U.S. workers are now employed in "industries" like insurance, chain stores and fast food.

The People (Newspaper of the Socialist Labor Party), **$4**/year (26 issues), from The People, 914 Industrial Avenue, Palo Alto, CA 94303

The SLP attempted early on to become the political arm of the **Industrial Workers of the World** (IWW), a revolutionary labor union founded at the turn of the century which once claimed tens of thousands of members among loggers, miners, textile workers and migrants. The old-time "wobblies" have been in the spotlight recently as the subject of a new documentary film. Less well known is the small but continuing presence of the IWW as organizers of low-paid workers in the U.S. and Canada. The union, which rejects "politics" but stands for the abolition of the wage system and against "business unionism," publishes a newspaper, the **Industrial Worker**, out of its Chicago headquarters.

The Industrial Worker, $4/year (12 issues), from 3435 North Sheffield, Suite 202, Chicago, IL 60657

Anarchists

Libertarian socialism used to be a term used interchangeably with **Anarchism,** and even now it is difficult to make a solid distinction between the two. There are probably as many varieties of anarchism as there are anarchists, from the hard-core individualist types who follow the lead of Max Stirner (author of **The Ego and His Own**), to anarchist-communists who owe some debts to Marx and work side by side with groups like the UCC. For all of them, though, maximum individual freedom is the ultimate goal against which all political schemes should be measured. Government and laws are coercion, so is wage-labor, and the sooner we realize this and abolish them, the better. In the absence of a State, anarchists believe that a "natural" order will emerge among humans – an extension of the cooperative tendency which makes it possible for people to live and work together in the first place.

The anarchist position is an uncompromising one and there is little love lost between anarchists and the rest of the left, whom they are fond of criticizing for authoritarian tendencies.

After a stretch of scattered demoralization in the early '70s, anarchists are presently on an organizational upswing. Like libertarian socialists they are active in anti-nuke affairs, and a strong "anarcha-feminist" current is becoming influential in the more aggressive wing of the Women's Movement.

The **Social Revolutionary Anarchist Federation** (SRAF) was the first major attempt by local U.S. anarchist groups to federate about seven years ago. The groups and individuals have kept in touch through the "anything goes" **SRAF Bulletin** which often features intense arguments between every kind of anarchist under the sun. These days SRAF is on the wane and the letters in the Bulletin tend to express individual obsessions, worn-out debates and obscure points of dogma, with little connection to social and political reality.

The SRA Federation Bulletin for Anarchist Agitators, $6/year (6 issues), from SRAFPrint, Box 52, Cottage Grove, OR 97424

In 1978, six or seven of the more militant SRAF affiliates became fed up with SRAF's lack of cohesive activities and split off to form the **Anarchist Communist Federation** (ACF). The ACF publishes the **North American Anarchist**, the only bi-monthly anarchist newspaper on the continent, and is involved in anti-nuke, labor and prison organizing here and in Canada. As its name suggests, the federation, now numbering a dozen member groups, has a much stronger "class" orientation than SRAF, and identifies itself with the Spanish anarcho-syndicalist labor confederation, the CNT.

North American Anarchist (The Newspaper Devoted to Direct Action), **$5**/year (6 issues), from The North American Anarchist, P.O. Box 2, Station O, Toronto, Ontario, Canada M4B 2B0

While the ACF's newspaper and propagandizing style (such as reprinting 60-year old essays as pamphlets) are all too reminiscent of other leftist circles, there is another North American anarchist paper whose visual dazzle, varied articles and non-sectarian posture make it stand alone on the Left in conveying a mood of self-assured professionalism. This is **Open Road** from Vancouver. **OR** was started in the summer of 1976 and has come out with 12 issues so far – averaging about 3 per year. In its efforts to be non-sectarian, **OR** has shown a tendency to cheerlead every challenge to authority from most any quarter, as if all were equally commendable, though this has been changing for the better with recent issues.

Open Road, 2 hrs. wages/year (3-4 issues), from The Open Road, Box 6135, Station G, Vancouver, BC, Canada V6R 4G5

If the ACF paper and **OR** are the mass-oriented periodicals of the movement, **Black Rose**, out of Boston, is its best theoretical journal. Elegantly produced on a small budget, **BR** features intelligent open-minded articles on world politics, psychiatry, art and literature, as well as the theory and philosophy of anarchism.

Black Rose, $6/year (4 issues), from Black Rose, P.O. Box 1075, Boston, MA 02103

Last but not least, is the **Fifth Estate**, an occasional tabloid-format journal. **FE** used to be Detroit's main underground rag in the '60s but in 1973 was taken over by a group of anarchists, libertarian communists, and assorted hard-core radical crazies. Its evolution from that time on has moved through flirtations with ICC-type Ultra-leftism, and exotic French post-marxist theorists, to its present total critique which might be best summed up as "anti-civilization." Throughout its evolution away from all "isms," FE has maintained a wicked sense of humor, often running pointed ad satires and mock posters which are then reprinted and posted by their readers. Strictly speaking, **FE** isn't purely anarchist in the traditional sense, but like the UCC, an expression of a local left-libertarian milieu which has also spawned rock bands, theater, and various illegal and semi-legal direct action tactics.

Fifth Estate, $4/year (6 issues), from The Fifth Estate, 4403 Second Avenue, Detroit, MI 48201

Outro

Any long-term, *meaningful* social change, be it reform or revolution, is never imposed from above but comes from our own determination and desires. To the degree that it is open to mass participation the Left has a role to play. Whether that role will shrink or grow in the days ahead is up to us. ■

LIBERTARIAN PERIODICALS

by Jay Kinney

Inquiry
Williamson Evers, Editor
$15 /year (20 issues)
from:
Inquiry
P.O. Box 2500
Menlo Park, CA 94025

HATS OFF!

Libertarian Vanguard
Justin Raimondo, Editor
$10 /year (12 issues)
from:
LPRC
199 Dolores Street No. 7
San Francisco, CA 94114

Frontlines
Robert Poole, Jr. and
Marty Zupan, Editors
$15 /year (11 issues)
from:
Box 40105
Santa Barbara, CA 93103

RIVETING

Reason
Robert Poole, Jr., Editor
$15 /year (12 issues)
from:
Box 40105
Santa Barbara, CA 93103

EH!

Liberty
Milton Mueller, Editor
$8 /year from:
Students for a
Libertarian Society
1620 Montgomery Street
San Francisco, CA 94111

THUMBS UP

Libertarian Review
Roy A. Childs, Jr., Editor
$15 /year (12 issues)
from:
P.O. Box 28877
San Diego, CA 92818

SOLID

We hold that all individuals have the right to exercise sole dominion over their own lives, and have the right to live in whatever manner they choose, so long as they do not forcibly interfere with the equal right of others to live in whatever manner they choose.

— from the Statement of Principles, 1980 Platform of the Libertarian Party

To try and sum up any political movement or philosophy in the course of a handful of magazine reviews is to do a disservice not only to the movement but to the reader as well. That would certainly be the case with libertarianism, a movement whose increased intellectual and electoral activity is coupled with as bewildering an array of publications, feuds, caucuses, shifting alliances, and offshoots as one usually associates with the more traditional Left or Right. Yet with the recent Libertarian candidate for Governor in California drawing nearly 400,000 votes at the polls, and the Libertarian Party (LP) second only to the GOP-Dems nationally, one can hardly ignore the movement much longer.

Right off the bat it should be noted that the libertarian of today is not the same as those answering to that moniker in times past. Traditionally, "libertarian" has been a synonym for "anarchist," implying an opposition not only to the State but to Capitalism as well. Most current users of the term however (particularly those associated with the LP or the journals mentioned below), usually champion the notion of minimal government (often called "minarchist") while singing the praises of laissez faire capitalism (a la Ayn Rand or the Austrian economist Ludwig von Mises). It's an ideology with particular appeal for small businessmen and the broad middle class whose pursuit of the American Dream has met increasing obstacles in the last decade.

With some hard-line anarchists determined to maintain their own use of the term "libertarian," things can get pretty confusing. Increasingly, though, common usage is favoring the newcomers and the new definition.

For the reader curious to figure out this recent political hybrid, several periodicals can be recommended. **Inquiry, Libertarian Review, Liberty,** *and* **Libertarian Vanguard,** *all published in San Francisco, represent the more radical wing of the movement, while* **Reason** *and* **Frontlines** *from Santa Barbara, California, represent the more conservative wing. Attention should be paid to both poles to get a full picture of the libertarians.*

INQUIRY *has my vote as the most consistently interesting political magazine around. Published by the Cato Institute, the "non-political" foundation set up by libertarian oil millionaire Charles Koch,* **Inquiry** *prints muckraking and opinions by liberals and conservatives as well as libertarians. The common thread throughout is a jaundiced distrust of government and vested interests, and a keen devotion to civil liberties. The result is an unpredictable (and graphically handsome) "united front" package which puts libertarianism's best foot forward in a refreshingly undogmatic manner.*

While **Inquiry** *has the brash flash of a two-year old,* **REASON,** *a libertarian old-timer at age eleven, follows a more stolid path.* **Reason's** *columns, ads, and readers' letters display an ongoing concern with individual economics — protecting investments, fighting inflation, and saving that "hard money." Yet within this conservative context which constantly threatens to revert back to the traditional far right, some worthwhile truths are revealed: intriguing interviews with anarchist Murray Bookchin and Mormon doomsayer Howard Ruff; a bold investigative report on curious United Farm Workers funding; and monthly news briefs on government shenanigans around the world. Yet if* **Inquiry** *seems intent on seducing disaffected rad-libs,* **Reason** *has about it the air of a slightly stiff suburban Rotarian loosening his tie while he excitedly discusses abolishing the Income Tax.*

Interestingly enough in view of this, **FRONTLINES,** *the monthly "newsletter for libertarians" published by* **Reason,** *is another story altogether. Lively, gossipy, and informal,* **Frontlines** *covers all camps in the movement, giving blow-by-blow accounts of internecine tiffs, threatened firings, libertarian victories and defeats. At $1.25 for 8 pages, the price may be a bit high except for avid political sports fans. On the other hand, there's probably no better way to gain a compact overview of the libertarians. Highly recommended.*

In a movement as relatively recent and tightly knit as the libertarian, one might wonder at the existence of yet a third slick-covered magazine, this called the **LIBERTARIAN REVIEW.** *Like* **Inquiry** *and Cato Institute,* **LR** *exists in large part due to Charles Koch's financial generosity. Originally an east coast tabloid,* **LR** *was purchased by Koch a couple of years ago and moved to San Francisco, with offices a block from Cato and Co.*

In **LR***'s 48 monthly pages, major issues confronting libertarians are examined at length (Abortion, Nuclear Energy, the Draft) while lengthy letters from readers and Milton Mueller's regular column on "The Movement" hash out different positions and strategies.* **LR** *can perhaps be best characterized as the movement's general theoretical journal.*

Sharing **LR***'s offices is the national headquarters of the Students for a Libertarian Society, a fledgling SDS-styled organization with over 80 campus chapters. Active in anti-draft demonstrations, SLS has gained much publicity recently. Their monthly tabloid* **LIBERTY** *primarily serves as a rostrum for SLS leaders to present their positions on hot topics such as nuclear energy and Iran. Whether libertarianism will catch on with students remains to be seen (though the impending Draft can't hurt). Following a recent facelift,* **Liberty** *is one of the most attractive libertarian publications around and if it can be faulted on any count it would be that it seems very much the production of a central committee in San Francisco and is slim on SLS or campus news.*

Another increasingly significant tabloid is the **LIBERTARIAN VANGUARD,** *published by the Radical Caucus of the Libertarian Party (LPRC). The LPRC (which includes* **Inquiry** *editor Williamson Evers and indefatigable libertarian theoretician Murray Rothbard among others and represents approximately 7 - 10 percent of LP membership) acts as an inner-party lobby for strictly cleaving to ideological principles in the face of myriad opportunities to dilute them for electoral gain or expediency. The caucus portrays itself as revolutionary and, with Rothbard's guidance in particular, has evolved a Lenin-like notion of the need for "cadres" to work full-time for libertarianism. The* **Libertarian Vanguard** *under Justin Raimondo's editorship sports a rather intense vehemence in its editorial stance: traitors are denounced and the unrighteous condemned. In the* **Libertarian Vanguard** *the enthusiasm and fury of the libertarian movement's early days (when YAF drop-outs, Objectivists, and anarcho-SDSers predominated) lives on.*

Postscript: The libertarians are intriguing. I find their idealism (and disdain for the traditional Left and Right) attractive, and their economics simplistic. But one thing is certain — we haven't heard the last of them. ■

READINGS ON THE FAR RIGHT

by Jay Kinney

Reading the other camp's publications may be considered beyond the call of duty for most of us, but I've renewed my subscription to all three of these publications at least once, so I must find something worthwhile in them.

THE SPOTLIGHT is the weekly tabloid of the Liberty Lobby, the superconservative Washington, D.C. pressure group. I first read of Carter's Trilateral Commission connections here, before they were mentioned anywhere else. I also found out who in Congress was for and against the "Canal Giveaway," and I keep up on the latest doings of Anita Bryant, the Tax Revolt, and the Gun Grabbers. Isolationist and anti-Zionist, they maintain that the Holocaust didn't happen. Not recommended for those with sensitive political stomachs. However keep in mind that **The Spotlight** *claims 200,000 in paid circulation, a number that beats any comparable Left paper 10 to 1.*

THE AMERICAN SPECTATOR, on the other hand, is less immediately threatening — at least at first glance. It's a witty monthly much like a **NY Review of Books** *for Conservatives. Regular fare tends to include choice roasts of vulnerable liberals and shrill reformers, paeans to Mencken, and raised eyebrows for everyone else. One of my favorite magazines, politics be damned.*

THE COUNCILOR, so I'm told, began as an official publication of the Louisiana Citizens' Councils, though it has long since gone independent. Yes, it's racist, and wary of Jewish ("Khazar") control of International Finance, but for advanced students of conspiracy theories it's a treasure-trove of trivia. Tidbits about the Illuminati are stuck between "I told you so" articles on the Kennedy Assassination and genealogical rundowns on the Rothschilds. Editor Ned Touchstone maintains a detached yet folksy tone throughout, reminiscent at times of the Old South's allegedly genteel xenophobia.

The Spotlight
Bernard R. DeRemer, Editor
$16 /year (51 issues)
from:
The Spotlight
300 Independence Ave. S.E.
Washington, D.C. 20003

The American Spectator
R. Emmett Tyrrell, Jr., Editor
$12 /year (12 issues)
from:
The American Spectator
P.O. Box 1969
Bloomington, IN 47402

The Councilor
Ned Touchstone, Editor
$5 /year from:
The Councilor
P.O. Box 3567
Shreveport, LA 71103

THE RISING SUN
NEIGHBORHOOD NEWSLETTER

Multiple choice continued from last spread

5. "Sometimes I see the image whole in my head before I start and sometimes it's time to start something new and I start drawing on some paper and something happens." (Ideas are answers to questions you ask and leave silence after.) ○

continued on next spread

The Grassroots Fundraising Book

Joan Flanagan tells how to put some power in your organization's purse, without worrying about strings that may be attached to government or foundation grants. (See p. 308.) The book methodically outlines the planning process for fundraising events of all sizes, from a neighborhood book sale to a $50-a-plate dinner, and it offers suggestions for year-round fundraising like membership dues and setting your group up in business.

In a comforting, conversational style the book helps you confront the stark realities of your group's bottom line without hysteria, whether you're plotting a political campaign, saving seals, or keeping your volunteer fire company afloat. As treasurer of an organization struggling to meet a $55,000 budget, I refer to Flanagan's book for both inspiration and nuts-and-bolts advice.

—Nancy E. Dunn

The Grassroots Fundraising Book
(How to Raise Money in Your Community)
1977; 219 pp.

$5.75 postpaid from:
The Youth Project
1555 Connecticut Avenue
NW Washington,
DC 20036

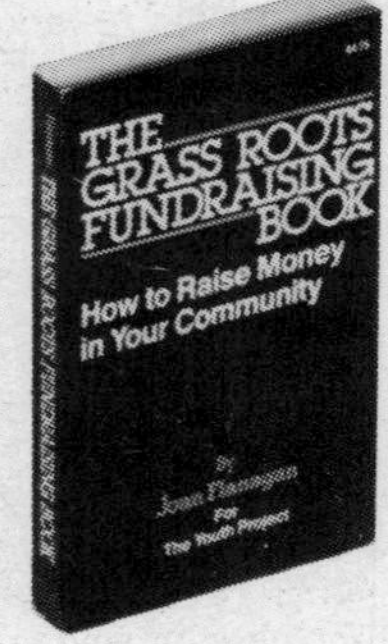

•

There are a lot of benefits from doing your own fundraising besides the cold, hard cash. When you map out your fundraising strategy, consider all that you can gain from raising your own budget by your own work.

You gain self-sufficiency. A well-planned, long-range fundraising campaign will guarantee that you can pay your staff, buy your supplies, and run your program. It's a good feeling to know you can take care of yourself, whether you are a not-for-profit corporation or an individual.

You gain independence. When you have an income from a wide variety of fundraising events, you know you have the talent and the techniques to raise money. No one can threaten to cut off your funds. You are free to plan and run whatever programs the members choose.
You gain peace of mind. Knowing you can plan and control your income will take away the anxiety of the leaky roof, or the horror of a missed payroll. You can use your energies to make things happen, rather than worry about which creditor to put off. As any coach will tell you, "Winners decide what they want to do. Losers worry about what they don't want to have happen to them"

You gain pride. Remember how proud you felt when you got your own first paycheck? The pride of raising your own money, and sharing the success, will boost the morale of your group in the same way. Grass roots money is honest money. Everyone in the group can be proud of his or her part in raising the money. You can answer any questions from a new member, a donor, or the press honestly and easily from your own open, up-to-date reports. Raising your money from a variety of sources will also reduce the temptation to accept money from any single donor who could compromise the organization.

•

Last, but certainly not least, decide to have fun while you raise the money. Plan the fun just like you plan the work. Make up your mind to have a good time, and your volunteers will be chomping at the bit to start the next project.

Human Development Training Manual

Some of the densest wisdom I've seen on conducting meetings — direct, concise, and honorable. I wish I'd had it two years ago when we began work on our conference on technology. Rave review.

—Stephanie Mills

Human Development Training Manual
William Meacham
1980; 21 pp.

$4 postpaid from:
Human Development Training
Training
1004 Elm Street
Austin, TX 78703

•

Our culture doesn't stress the importance of telling people when you appreciate them, assuming such things don't need to be said. Well, they do. *Appreciation is as important as criticism*, and it is wise to be open and direct with both.

•

Giving criticism can be hard, but it's important. Usually it's something about what a person does or the way they do it that we don't like, rather than the person him/herself, so it is important to *give specific examples.*

Vague	Specific
"The kitchen was a mess this morning!"	"There was a dirty frying pan and three dishes in the sink, and I didn't like it."

How to Make Meetings Work

It always amazes me how a group of otherwise pleasant people can go collectively insane as soon as they get in a meeting together. Anyone who suffers through the wrangling and frustration of poorly run meetings will find this book very useful. It analyzes common problems and suggests a straightforward, practical approach to improving the situation. I particularly like its emphasis on achieving consensus, a worthy goal that lots of people talk about without knowing much of how it can be achieved. It's good to finally find some concrete techniques for this process.

I worked for the authors of this book for a while and had a chance to try their method with several groups. It works! In fact, in one case a group of high school English teachers who hated department meetings became so turned on by achieving consensus that their principal interpreted their new found energy and enthusiasm as subversive and threatened to transfer three of them if they didn't elect a chairman and give up consensus immediately.

—Linda Williams

How to Make Meetings Work
(The New Interaction Method)
Michael Doyle & David Straus
1976, 1977; 300 pp.

$2.50 postpaid from:
Playboy Press
Simon & Schuster
Attn: Order Department
1230 Avenue of the Americas
New York, NY 10020
or Whole Earth Household Store

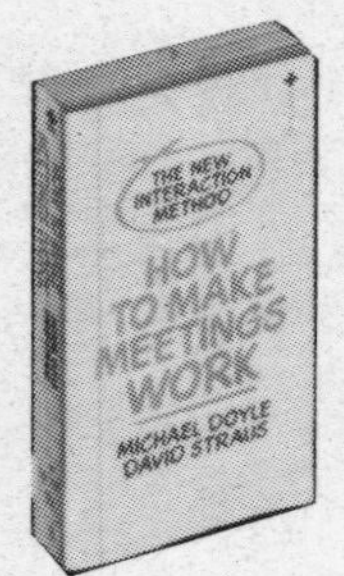

A clearly legible record of the key ideas of the meeting taped to the walls is called a group memory.

↑

The very presence of the group memory has many beneficial effects. It provides a physical focus for the group. Rather than sitting in a closed circle around a conference table, channeling their energies toward each other, the members sit in a semicircle and automatically focus their energies on the problem as represented by the group memory. This simple change can make a tremendous difference.

The group memory can also be a great benefit to you personally. You no longer have to hold on to an idea in your short-term memory. Once you have had a chance to express it to the group and have seen it recorded in the group memory, you know that your idea is captured and "remembered." You will feel a great psychic release—you can let go because you know that the group has heard you and that you can recall your ideas simply by looking up at the record in front of you. There they are up on the wall in full view of everyone—they won't be forgotten.

•

Here are some ways to avoid or *cut down on meeting time:*

Spread information by sending around a memo to all who need to know, or posting it on a central bulletin board.

Make a decision by sending a written proposal around with space for agreement, comment or proposed changes. Have a meeting only if disagreements are serious enough to need discussion to resolve them.

Use individual, pair, or committee work instead of meetings with the whole group.

Keep the number of people working on a project to the minimum needed to get it done; don't tie up the whole group needlessly.

Don't have a meeting without preparation (see specific guidelines).

If what you really need is a social event to build group morale, have a party or picnic, etc., instead of a meeting.

How to Use the Freedom of Information Act

In the historic American tradition of governmental checks and balances, the Freedom of Information Act lets the citizen participate in maintaining governmental candor. Ask, and if they know and it won't sink the republic to tell, they have to tell you. This is a modest run-down on the federal procedure.

—SB

How to Use the Freedom of Information Act (FOIA)
L.G. Sherick
1978; 138 pp.

$3.50 postpaid from:
Arco Publishing Company
219 Park Avenue South
New York, NY 10003
or Whole Earth Household Store

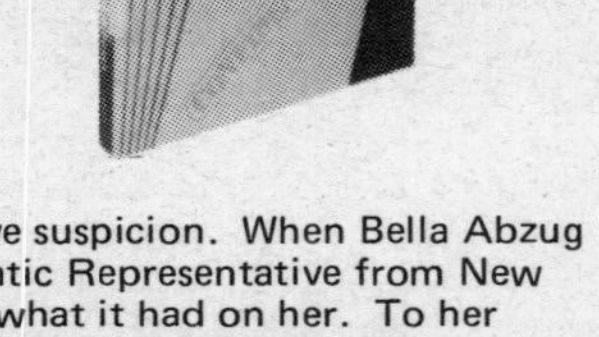

•

No one seems to be above suspicion. When Bella Abzug was serving as a Democratic Representative from New York she asked the CIA what it had on her. To her surprise she found out that for 22 years the CIA — an organization charged with overseas intelligence gathering as it concerns national security — had been monitoring her activities as a lawyer and politician.

•

Sample Request

(Name and Address of Government Agency)
Washington, D.C. Zip Code

Re: Privacy Act Request

Dear (agency head or Privacy Act Officer):

Under the provisions of the Privacy Act of 1974, 5 U.S.C. 522a, I hereby request a copy of (or: access to) (describe the record or records you want and provide all the relevant information you have concerning them).

If there are any fees for copying the records I am requesting, please inform me before you fill the request. (or: . . . please supply the records without informing me if the fees do not exceed $ ____.)

If all or any part of this request is denied, please cite the specific exemption(s) which you think justifies your refusal to release the information. Also, please inform me of your agency's appeal procedure.

In order to expedite consideration of my request, I am enclosing a copy of ____ (some document of identification). If you wish to discuss the matter, my telephone number is (Area Code +_____).

Thanking you in advance for your time and consideration, I am,

Sincerely,

Loompanics

Yes, there are books about the skills of apocalypse — spying, surveillance, fraud, wire-tapping, smuggling, self-defense, lockpicking, gunmanship, eavesdropping, car chasing, civil warfare, surviving jail, and dropping out of sight. Apparently writing books is the way mercenaries bring in spare cash between wars. The books are useful, and it's good the information is freely available (and they definitely inspire interesting dreams), but their advice should be taken with a salt-shaker or two and all your wits. A few of these volumes are truly scary. Loompanics is the best of the Libertarian suppliers who carry them. Though full of "you'll-wish-you'd-read-these-when-it's-too-late" rhetoric, their catalog is genuinely informative.

—Art Kleiner

Loompanics
Catalog

$2 from:
Loompanics Unlimited
P.O. Box 264
Mason, MI 48854

•

Fundamentals of Physical Surveillance

Here is an excellent addition to our best-selling line of police manuals — a how-to-do-it book on shadowing and spying!

Law enforcement personnel are only one of many groups who will find this book to be an invaluable guide to physical surveillance. It will also be useful to government agency investigators who operate without police power, to private investigators, and to personnel employed in investigative capacities for industrial concerns, insurance companies, and law firms.

Is Big Brother watching *you*??? Or do you want to spy on someone? This comprehensive and important book has many uses. *Highly recommended.*

Rules for Radicals

Toward a science of revolution. Much radical literature is aimed at fighting. This book is aimed, by an expert, at winning. —SB

Rules for Radicals
Saul D. Alinsky
1971; 196 pp.
$2.45 postpaid from:
Vintage Books
Random House
455 Hahn Road
Westminster, MD 21157
or Whole Earth
Household Store

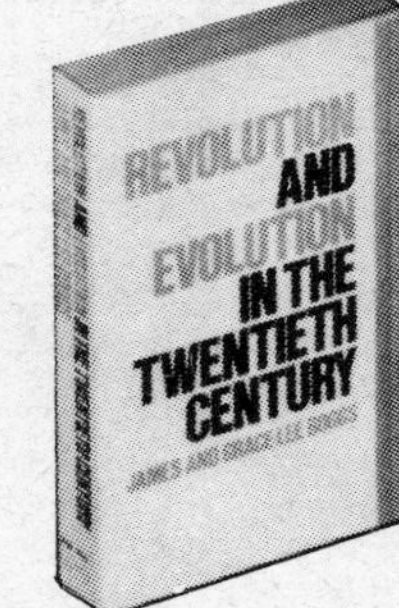

•

For an elementary illustration of tactics, take parts of your face as the point of reference; your eyes, your ears, and your nose. First the eyes; if you have organized a vast, mass-based people's organization, you can parade it visibly before the enemy and openly show your power. Second the ears; if your organization is small in numbers, then do what Gideon did: conceal the members in the dark but raise a din and clamor that will make the listener believe that your organization numbers many more than it does. Third, the nose; if your organization is too tiny even for noise, stink up the place.

Always remember the first rule of power tactics: *Power is not only what you have but what the enemy thinks you have.*

The second rule is: *Never go outside the experience of your people.* When an action or tactic is outside the experience of the people, the result is confusion, fear, and retreat. It also means a collapse of communication, as we have noted.

The third rule is: *Wherever possible go outside of the experience of the enemy.* Here you want to cause confusion, fear, and retreat . . .

The fourth rule is: *Make the enemy live up to their own book of rules.* You can kill them with this, for they can no more obey their own rules than the Christian church can live up to Christianity.

The fourth rule carries within it the fifth rule: *Ridicule is man's most potent weapon.* It is almost impossible to counterattack ridicule. Also it infuriates the opposition, who then react to your advantage.

The sixth rule is: *A good tactic is one that your people enjoy.* If your people are not having a ball doing it, there is something very wrong with the tactic.

The seventh rule: *A tactic that drags on too long becomes a drag . . .*

The eighth rule: *Keep the pressure on,* with different tactics and actions, and utilize all events of the period for your purpose.

The ninth rule: *The threat is usually more terrifying than the thing itself.*

The tenth rule: *The major premise for tactics is the development of operations that will maintain a constant pressure upon the opposition.*

The eleventh rule is: *If you push a negative hard and deep enough it will break through into its counterside;* this is based on the principle that every positive has its negative. We have already seen the conversion of the negative into the positive, in Mahatma Gandhi's development of the tactic of passive resistance . . .

The twelfth rule: *The price of a successful attack is a constructive alternative.* You cannot risk being trapped by the enemy in his sudden agreement with your demand and saying, "You're right—we don't know what to do about this issue. Now you tell us."

The thirteenth rule: *Pick the target, freeze it, personalize it, and polarize it.*

Revolution and Evolution in the Twentieth Century

The left-wing youth movement is showing vitality these days, especially on anti-nuke and anti-draft themes. The new leaders have a useful tool in the non-violent organizing techniques of the mid-1970s. They are called various names but are actually highly structured guerrilla management. The new theories are grounded in the Boggs' writings. This one is their best. The name of their own organization is The New Organization for the American Revolution. James is black, Grace is Asian. Their final views are very close to most environmentalists and the "simple livers" like me. The book is 1) well written, 2) full of good ideas, 3) very important. —Michael Phillips

Revolution and Evolution in the Twentieth Century
James Boggs and
Grace Lee Boggs
1974; 266 pp.
$5.95 postpaid from:
Monthly Review Press
62 West 14th Street
New York, NY 10041
or Whole Earth
Household Store

•

There has to be some sense of *process* — that doing things takes time and that there is a logical and temporal relationship between various steps of the activity. And there has to be a sense of *workmanship,* i.e., that the quality of the results depends upon the quality of the effort. It is inconceivable that humankind could exist without work. The new ethic of work starts out in the first place with the idea that work is a necessity for the human personality.

Raising Hell

It's all too easy while muckraking to overlook important statistics or ramifications because the data is hidden in the collective memory of some obscure agency. This booklet, published by **Mother Jones**, *makes finding that data an accessible process. It's not the comprehensive tactical manual that the subtitle would imply, but it does provide an inexpensive introduction to reference books, places to call, and what to ask for when you get 'em on the phone. As reporter Nancy Dunn suggested, your next step should probably be a glance at* **Finding Facts Fast** *(p. 496).* —Art Kleiner

Raising Hell
(A Citizens Guide to the Fine Art of Investigation)
Dan Noyes
1978; 32 pp.
$1.35 postpaid from:
Mother Jones Magazine
625 Third Street
San Francisco, CA 94107

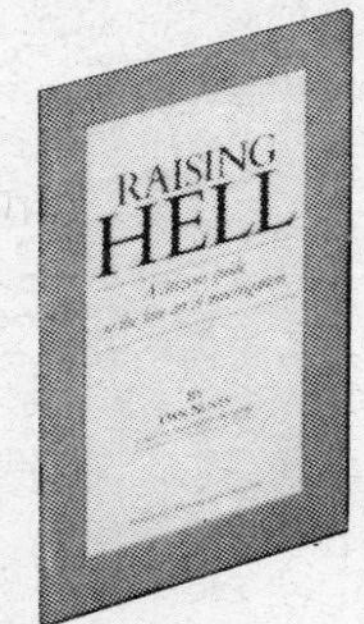

•

Remember the phone book! It's surprising how many times this essential directory is overlooked in trying to research someone. Use it to check the spelling of a name, address and phone number. Many larger cities have reverse phone books that list telephone numbers by address. Use it to obtain a phone number if you only have an individual's address, verify an address or find other phone numbers for the same address.

For the People

An excellent how-to-do it book for consumer action ranging from surveys of drugstore pricing to evaluating nursing homes. Complete details and examples including how to run a news conference when you finally blow the whistle. —Michael Phillips

For the People
(A Consumer Action Handbook)
Joanne Manning Anderson
1977; 379 pp.
$5.95 postpaid from:
Addison-Wesley Publishing Company, Inc.
Jacob Way
Reading, MA 01867
or Whole Earth
Household Store

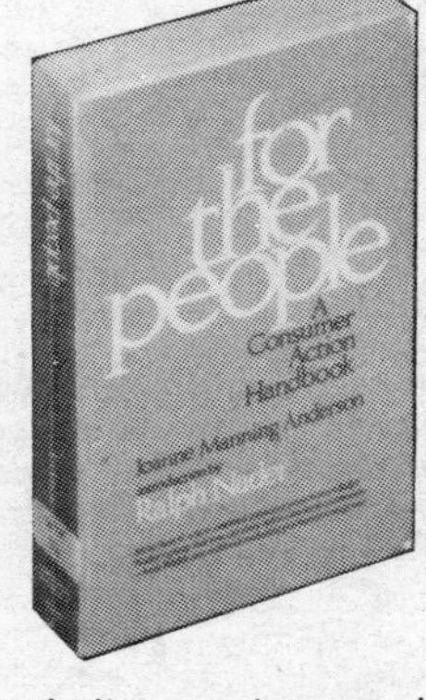

•

One of the purposes of a doctor's directory is to provide consumers with basic information — information about education, availability, fees, and services — that will enable them to make a more informed choice when selecting a doctor. In addition, a doctors' directory can help demystify the medical profession in the minds of consumers by arousing consumer consciousness about questions to ask doctors. A directory provides a first step towards a more open relationship between doctor and patient, and the willingness or reluctance of doctors to cooperate may indicate their attitude towards such a relationship. The directory outlined in this project should not be viewed as an attempt to evaluate the medical competence of doctors.

•

Legislators may be influenced by any of the following: a genuine interest in your issue, favorable publicity, the stand taken by committee chairpeople and other legislative or political party leaders, views of staff people, and loyalty to friends, lobbyists, and campaign contributors. But for most legislators, the desire for the support of the voting public proves the most important motivating factor. Reelection or election to a higher office is never far from their minds, and only public support can elect. Votes talk and legislators listen.

Eight Sneaky Ways to Get Information About Groups You're Investigating

1. Make up wildly exaggerated lies. Call the people in charge (or in charge of talking to outsiders) and ask them if this rumor you've heard is true. When they correct it, they may inadvertently tell you something less extreme which you nonetheless needed to know.

2. Ask their competitors, their critics, their enemies, and anyone else who has investigated them for leads and ideas. A good source on businesses are stock analysts who pick up Wall Street gossip. Ask the people in charge about what their critics said, without mentioning the critics by name.

3. Find as many people as you can who work in the organization, and talk to them all, even those who annoy or intimidate you. Ask all your friends if they know anyone. Ask each person if they know others. Be honest but mild about who you are and why you're there. If they won't talk to you, be gentle but persistent until they agree to say something, if only to get rid of you. Ask each person about what the others said.

4. Be considerate of the feelings of the people whom you interview. If you have time, tell them you will call to check the facts before your final report (and do). If your consideration shows, they will tell you more. Agree to keep sensitive stuff off the record if they specifically ask you to, but ask someone else to confirm it, without saying who told you originally.

5. Read everything you can about the organization before talking to people in person. Particularly good are in-house newsletters or magazines, if you can get them, and trade journals. Being prepared shows in the directness of the questions you ask, and shows that you care enough to take the trouble. (On the other hand, don't be afraid to ask dumb questions. Trying to prove you're an expert during an interview gets in the way of learning what you need to know.)

6. Don't ask yes-or-no questions. Ask questions that require lengthy answers no matter what the answer is. "Why" and "how" questions are best.

7. Try to hang around a place during its daily business and observe. Be genuinely interested in the day-to-day affairs, or pretend to be, while you're there. Never interview people over the telephone if you can see them in person.

8. Assume that all your starting assumptions will be wrong.

— **Art Kleiner**

A Ninth Way: Make arrangements for followup, either by phone or in person, to clarify confusion in your notes or your head, to verify titles and figures, to get the essential data you forgot to ask for despite all your preparation. *(See The Craft of Interviewing, p. 499.)* — **Nancy E. Dunn**

THE RISING SUN
NEIGHBORHOOD NEWSLETTER

Multiple choice continued from last spread

6. Elias Howe who invented the sewing machine and to whom Help is dedicated got really stuck part way through inventing the sewing machine, because the needle had a hole in the top at the dull end because needles always had the hole in the top at the dull end but the machine wouldn't sew with it that way and one night he dreamt about a bunch of Africans running around with spears and all the spears had a hole right in the tip and Howe woke up and knew that putting the hole in the pointed part of the needle would make the sewing machine work and it did.

continued on next spread

THERE ARE STARTING to be a few books on how to politic at the state and national level — that's great — but there is zilch about the really important stuff, local politics. How do you get on the school board? How do you do good things there? How do you lose a mayoral election in a way that's good for the community? County/town relations — what are they, how can they be better? How can I get the goddamn real estate types that are selling Sausalito off of our City Council?

Write such books. Send them to us. We'll review them big. —SB

In Our Own Interest

Here is the finest operative introduction to the process of legislative politics that I have seen. Our political system, like our marketplace, is based on an odd mix of cut-throat competition and genuine honor. A good political idea will not defend itself. Financial clout counts for something in lobbying but not as much as savvy and integrity. Much of the savvy is here. —SB

In Our Own Interest
(A Handbook for the Citizen Lobbyist in State Legislatures)
Dorothy Smith
1979; 137 pp.
$4.95 postpaid from:
Madrona Publishing
2116 Western Avenue
Seattle, WA 98121
or Whole Earth Household Store

•

Integrity and professionalism are the cornerstones of all fruitful legislative activity. There is no place where a person's word is more important, and no place where personal integrity is more relied upon and more appreciated than in the legislature.

Partisanship is expected at every turn; when the opportunity arises, try to take every advantage according to the rules. But there is an "honor of the House" that is the very real foundation of processes that must rely, at root, on trust and accurate communication.

The more the citizen seeking change recognizes the reality and the strength of the rules by which the game is played (and by which he will be judged), the greater the respect he will have for the worth of our legislative processes — and the greater success he will have in dealing with those who are involved in public business.

•

Reserve judgment about the people with whom you must deal until you have had sufficient personal experience to know them. If you are wise, you won't censure those who oppose you on specific matters — today's foe may become tomorrow's colleague. *The ability to see your opposition in realistic terms is essential to the achievement of workable legislative solutions.* It is almost impossible to come to agreement with an enemy. Compromise with an opponent is possible and often desirable. Reaching agreement with a truly hostile antagonist is next to impossible. Fight your opponent intelligently. But do not hate him. To permit yourself to hate a person is, after all, to become to some degree his prisoner.

How You Can Influence Congress

A good intro to the subject; gives the basics and some extras. The material is clearly presented, and examples are given throughout, making it easy reading. If you're not interested in lobbying for specific legislation, there are chapters on organization building, preparing your arguments, your publications, tactics, and hearings, which make up about half the book and would be useful to anyone doing any kind of grassroots organizing. Not just for beginners. —William Bitsas

How You Can Influence Congress
(The Complete Book for the Citizen Lobbyist)
George Alderson and Everett Sentman
1979; 360 pp.
$9.95 postpaid from:
E.P. Dutton and Company
Two Park Avenue
New York, NY 10016
or Whole Earth Household Store

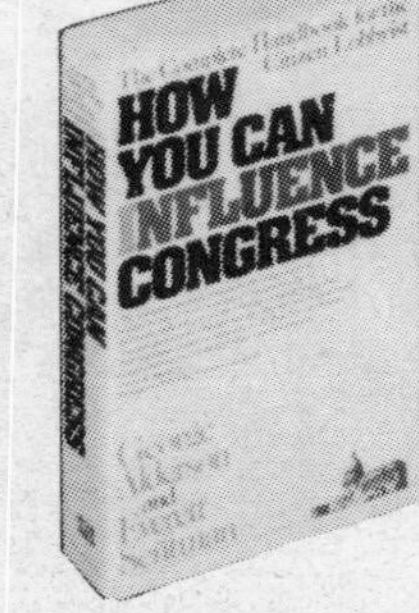

•

1. Make your cause respectable. Get scientists, economists, prominent local citizens, labor and ethnic leaders to speak up for your side.

2. Make your opponents' position unrespectable. Reveal who really benefits from their cause. Try to provoke them into "blowing their cool."

3. Make sure everybody knows your side is the underdog. You get more sympathy and help if you're seen as fighting a good fight against great odds.

4. Get help from friends in high places. Ask local and state politicians to talk to your congressman and to raise your issue in friendly local forums, such as the city council or county board.

5. Stay ahead of the opposition. Keep taking the initiative with interesting tactics that show you've got the facts on your side. Don't be sucked into a role of constantly responding to your opponents' charges.

6. Show public support through letter-writing campaigns, petitions, rallies, etc. Your objective is to make your issue so ubiquitous that the congressman hears about it everywhere he goes in his district, and gets letters and calls about it every day he's in Washington.

7. Get help from local VIPs who have special access to or credibility with your congressman. These include people who have power or money, people who are friends of the congressman, people who helped in his campaign, and people he respects. Get them to speak to the congresman.

8. Use all events for your purpose. Look ahead to holidays and ceremonial occasions, and plan ways to use them in your campaign.

9. Raise your issue in the election campaigns. Get the congressman's opponents to challenge his position, or his lack of one.

10. Build long-term influence by giving the congressman opportunities to learn more about your issue and to do something about it often, so he will come to identify himself with the issue. *Praise him when he does the right thing.*

•

"If there's any rule for effective actions, it's 'Be Creative!'," says Troutman. "Almost any group has a person who thinks creatively." Just as an indication of the range of possible actions, consider this example:

Protesting the lack of rat-control measures in poor neighborhoods in Washington, D.C., activist Julius Hobson threatened to trap large numbers of rats and release them in the posh Georgetown residential area. He then drove through Georgetown with cages of rats atop his car, to make the threat more dramatic.

The Almanac of American Politics

Who did what, where, when. For each state and district a recent political history; for every Senator and Representative, a profile, ratings by political interest groups (who his friends and enemies are), his/her voting record on key issues, and federal funds outlaid in his district. True inside dope, know your Congressman. —Diana Barich

The Almanac of American Politics
Michael Barone, Grant Ujifusa, and Douglas Matthews
1972, 1979; 1055 pp.
$10.95 postpaid from:
E.P. Dutton and Company
Two Park Avenue
New York, NY 10016
or Whole Earth Household Store

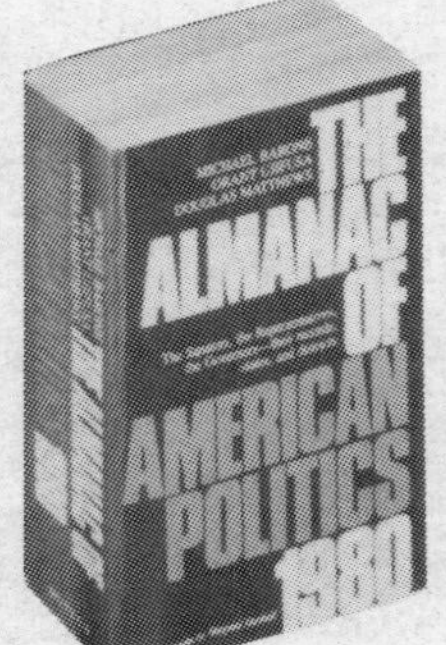

•

California, Twelfth District

It was only after his first election that McCloskey became known as an ultra-liberal Republican. And that was really only because of his views on the war; on economic issues he has tended to reflect the caution of his upper income constituents and their aversion to organized labor. Even his opposition to the Vietnam war came from an unlikely source: his feelings, as a decorated Marine veteran, that the war was perverting the Corps and the military generally. With a fervor that may only come from experience in battle, McCloskey argued against unnecessary war and bloodshed, and made as strong a case as was made against the Vietnam adventure.

McCloskey has reason to feel much more comfortable in the Republican Party today. He believes strongly in the free market economic system, and has no problem supporting Republican positions like deregulation of natural gas or the Kemp-Roth bill. Much of his legislative effort has been concentrated on the Merchant Marine and Fisheries Committee, on which he became ranking Republican in 1979. McCloskey opposes efforts to subsidize the U.S. shipping industry — the primary business of the Committee — and he successfully led efforts in 1977 to kill the bill requiring that 9.5% of oil imported into the U.S. be shipped in U.S. carriers. McCloskey was able to get most Republicans and many younger Democrats on his side; against him was organized labor and the maritime unions and companies. McCloskey gets about 50% voting records from labor and liberal groups — far higher than the average Republican, but low enough to suggest that he is by no means a Democrat-in-disguise.

After all the turbulence and expense of his earlier campaigns, this must seem an easier time for McCloskey. He had no primary opposition in 1976 and beat another Republican easily in 1978. A Democrat spent substantial time and money against him in 1976 and won only 32% of the vote; McCloskey won even more easily in 1978. The 12th is just about evenly split in presidential contests — it gave Richard Nixon in 1972 and Gerald Ford in 1976 the same 53% — but it seems to be utterly safe for McCloskey for the foreseeable future.

Rep. Paul N. McCloskey, Jr. (R) Elected Dec. 12, 1967; b. Sept. 29, 1927, San Bernardino; home Portola Valley; Occidental Col., Cal. Inst. of Tech., 1945-46, Stanford U., B.A. 1950, LL.B. 1953; Presbyterian.

Career Navy, 1945-47; USMC, Korea; Deputy Dist. Atty., Alameda Co., 1953-54; Practicing atty., 1955-67.

Offices 205 CHOB, 202-225-5411. Also 305 Grant Ave., Palo Alto 94306. 415-326-7383.

Committees *Government Operations* (5th). Subcommittees: Environment, Energy, and Natural Resources.

Merchant Marine and Fisheries (Ranking Member).

Key Votes

1)	Increase Def Spnd	AGN
2)	B-1 Bomber	AGN
3)	Cargo Preference	AGN
4)	Dereg Nat Gas	FOR
5)	Kemp-Roth	FOR
6)	Alaska Lands Protect	DNV
7)	Water Projects Veto	FOR
8)	Consum Protect Agcy	FOR
9)	Common Situs Picket	FOR
10)	Labor Law Revision	FOR
11)	Delay Auto Pol Cntrl	AGN
12)	Sugar Price Escalator	FOR
13)	Pub Fin Cong Cmpgns	FOR
14)	ERA Ratif Recissn	AGN
15)	Prohibt Govt Abrtns	AGN

Who Runs Congress?

Not surprisingly, the answer to the title's question comes in the first few pages: Big Business and Habit. The medium of Big Business is lobbyists (and that obscene new phenomenon, Political Action Committees); and the medium of Habit is, well, habit. Since we're all disillusioned about Congress by now anyway, we have two choices. We can give up and ignore national politics (in which case this book is still a good read, as fascinating as watching an anthill, and it makes you understand why all those young lawyers in Washington dress and talk and act alike). Or we can grit our teeth and dig into lobbying ourselves to make something good happen on a big scale. In that case, Ralph Nader's staff people, masters at the game, offer the necessary how-to news here. This is such an un-dreary book it even makes Congress seem interesting, not merely important. —Art Kleiner

Who Runs Congress?
Mark Green and Michael Calabrese
1972, 1979; 343 pp.
$2.95 postpaid from:
Bantam Books
414 East Golf Road
Des Plaines, IL 60016
or Whole Earth Household Store

•

Whatever their diversity, the members of Congress are not very representative of the American people. Almost one third of the Senate are millionaires. Almost half the Congress is composed of lawyers, who make up less than one-third of 1 percent of the population. Blue-collar workers may get to Congress, but usually as tourists passing through the guided tours. Women and minority groups are, for the most part, severely underrepresented. This institution will order over $400 billion of your money to be spent this year and use or refuse to use vast amounts of your power to affect your way of living and our relations with other nations. That is enough reason for this book.

•

Congress devotes itself to what it was not essentially designed to do — running small favors for complaining constituents. What Congress *is* supposed to do — legislate — it does not do well. It is the executive that now initiates most legislation, and it is the Supreme Court that has made many of the important human-rights breakthroughs in the past twenty-five years — equal education for blacks, reapportionment, rights for criminal defendants, near abolition of the death penalty, the right to an abortion. To get major legislation passed often require requires a major national trauma: the 1937 and 1962 drug amendments followed the Elixir and thalidomide scandals; President Kennedy's death gave impetus to his successor's civil rights and Medicare achievements.

The Craft of Power

An astounding treatise on the naked wielding of naked power — how to get it, hold it, use it. Appearing more brutal than it is (Siu's bottom lines reflect on compassion and nobility), the argument proceeds from a torrent of Machiavellian aphorisms to instruction and anecdote. If you have a talent for power, this book may set it resonating. If you have no taste for power, you'll find that out more quickly here than in the polite corridors of the real thing.

Siu is the author of the **Tao of Science** *(p. 29), a translation of the* **I Ching**, *and other works. He has been head of numerous research departments for the U.S. military. This book is the first of a trilogy on leadership.*

—SB

The Craft of Power
R.G.H. Siu
1979; 255 pp.
$14.95 postpaid from:
John Wiley and Sons
One Wiley Drive
Somerset, NJ 08873
or Whole Earth
Household Store

•

The seasoned bureaucrat is adept at servo-bureaucrato viscosity: to every challenge there is an equal and frustrating viscosity. He dwells in the nirvana of historical momentum: reversing a bureaucrat is tantamount to reversing history.

Accommodate to the bureaucrat; he will then ease your life and extend your power. But do you otherwise; he will then drive you out of office and out of mind.

•

People are to be used like fuel in the furnace of power, or cleared away like worn-out gears for more efficient replacements.

So that they burn with the requisite intensity, cleanse them of incombustible allegiances.

•

Let the cadre prove its selfless commitment and offer up their persons as signed undated blank checks in your strongbox.

•

Do not place undue weight on that course of action promising maximum gain, if successful. Limit the choices to those preventing a fatal blow to yourself, no matter what the opposition may feasibly do.

•

Credibility is the greatest obstacle to many an overture to power.

Repeat your thesis often, for people tend to shun the unfamiliar and embrace the familiar. Use phrases mellifluous to the ear, for people like to identify with the pleasant. Make it sound vital, for people incline to align with the important. Announce your intentions to accomplish something, which is actually well on the way. Promise something that seems difficult but is within ready reach of your unseen reserves.

Then let the people conclude for themselves that you are truly a man of your word.

•

Propitiousness There is nothing more important in imparting elegance and style than the art of being propitious. The essence of propitiousness is good timing. More failures in the exercise of power have been due to poor timing than any other single factor.

When Catherine the Great ascended the throne she tried to introduce the liberal ideas of Charles de Montesquieu. But the Russian state of mind was not receptive. Her ministers balked, and the peasant uprising of Emilien Pugachev of 1773 forced her to drop the idea. It took another 120 years before the time was ripe for even a semblance of parliament.

In our own day, there are relatively few executives who possess a really keen sense of timing. Most of them do not know how to use the instrument of time. They are unable to allow precisely for lead time, lag time, incubation time, time to build up a head of steam, time to forget, time to get bored, time to stop talking, and so on. They do not have the feeling for matching the duration of different acts to come into fruition against their respective times of need. They fail to lay the basis for the resolution of conflicts before their actual onset. As a result, they only struggle with the fortitude of facing crisis after crisis. They never glide with the art of de-existing them.

Transcending the Power Game: The Way to Executive Serenity

This sequel to **The Craft of Power** *is as benign as the other book is fierce. It consoles, congratulates, advises balance and pace, even gives practical guidance about eventual retirement. Where before Siu was talking about his bosses, here, one senses, the old Chinese gentleman is talking about himself. He speaks thus comfortably and with authority from the longest, soundest bureaucratic tradition on Earth. Badly needed ginseng in headlong America.*

(The last book in his trilogy will be called **The Master Manager.***)*

—SB

Transcending the Power Game: The Way to Executive Serenity
R.G.H. Siu
1980; 249 pp.
$14.95 postpaid from:
John Wiley and Sons
One Wiley Drive
Somerset, NJ 08873
or Whole Earth
Household Store

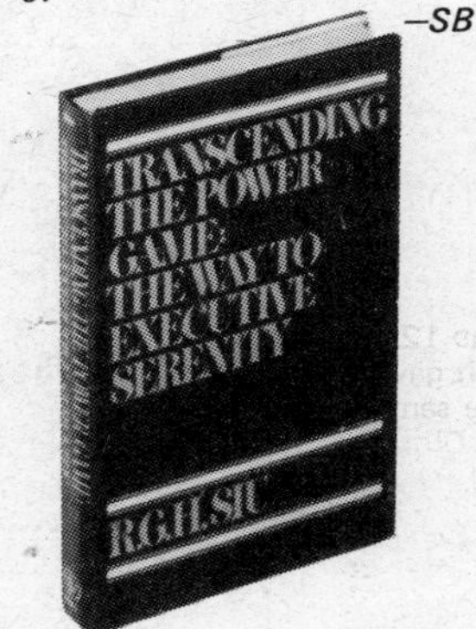

•

A person travels farther, lasts longer, and acts more equably if he taxes himself at a fraction of his capabilities. Because of the resulting large reserve, he is not apprehensive over possible emergencies. His body is not fatigued and his mind not numbed. He dwells in the midst of difficulties, feeling no despair; brings his goals within ready reach, regretting no rewards passed over. There is no need for sycophancy before superiors, nor abuse before subordinates. His is an easy-going discipline, a genial demeanor, absorbing attention. He induces an airiness of festive calm. His presence is a pleasance.

Cruising is prerequisite to the life of graciousness.

•

A creature in pain is more pain than creature. To remove the pain is to restore the self.

There can be no greater good than that a man or beast be given back his self.

Let the reduction of suffering be the foundational expression of your relating to others on earth.

•

If you plant for a season, plant budgets. If you plant for a decade, plant reorganizations. If you plant for a century, plant people.

•

The annealing of an act into a gracious one requires a certain all-absorbing attention on the recipient, a certain sincerity of forgetfulness of oneself, a certain fitness to the fineness of the moment, and a certain genuineness about it all.

Action from gov't

I've found that one of the best ways to get anything out of the national government is by writing directly to your congressperson; the best way to gain results with a state agency (unless you have an unusually good state representative) is through a letter to the governor's office, although this approach may vary from state to state.

Bob Murphy
Sierra Club volunteer
Boston, Massachusetts

Congressional hit record

Note to pragmatic existentialists: no matter how whole your particular earth, there's always somebody in Washington that wants to deal it away. Protect yourself with the **Congressional Record.** A bit windy but you'll learn how to read it with a little practice. And burns slowly with good heat for after use in the fireplace. Write your Congressman and Senators first, to see if they can add you to their comp list. If not: $75 per year, 50 cents per copy, payable in advance. Check or money order payable to Superintendent of Documents, Government Printing Office, Washington, D.C. 20402. Well worth the investment.

MY
Union, Maine

Thoughts

It used to be said that the only safe political behavior (nevermind one's pronouncements) was to be economically liberal and socially conservative. Jerry Brown reversed that formula, made it work, and it's becoming the new conventional wisdom.

This collection of remarks, chosen from the press by poet Lawrence Ferlinghetti during the first year or so of Brown's governorship of California, conveys the freshness of thought he brought to a stale game. The special appeal of the man, besides his intelligence, is his willingness to learn before your very eyes and include you in the process.

—SB

Thoughts
Edmund G. Brown, Jr.
1976; 79 pp.
$2 postpaid from:
City Lights Books
1562 Grant Avenue
San Francisco, CA 94133
or Whole Earth
Household Store

•

I'm going to be very reluctant to approve of spending which does not require basic fundamental structural reforms wherever possible, because just pumping more money into the machine is not going to turn around the very difficult situation that we face in the schools. If you look at the reading scores, look at the achievement scores, talk to kids, talk to teachers, there is something wrong in the classroom. Now much of it reflects a certain malaise in the society, and I don't really hold the teachers accountable because of the failures of the system. It's a problem for those in government and those in a position of responsibility to make the changes.

I'd like to see some changes. And when people come for the money, that's the opportunity to make the change. If you just give it away without requiring this kind of change then you lose an opportunity. I don't want to see that opportunity lost in the event we can make some constructive changes.

•

There is an elephantiasis that takes over that you get so big you can't function. I think if you look at the classical world, as the political entity expanded its role and responsibility, it ran into problems both in Greece and Rome that it could not handle. And it was accompanied by these generalized and mystical feelings that as the borders expanded, as the discipline weakened, as the decadence increased, as the classes that were in the leadership position lost their nerve, then those on the perimeter ultimately came through. In 410, when Mr. Alaric walked through, where we had this wonderful civilization, there was grass and wild dogs wandering around. That is not, you know, a lesson that is ignored with impunity.

•

If they [politicians] would just kind of jump out for a while, and then maybe come back. But they stay long beyond their time. The Greeks had that — ostracism. Ostragon is the potsherd that's dropped in the pot. If the majority drop it in then you're out. There was a fellow named Aristides the Just. Aristides the Just was going through his ostracization process, and he stood there and as some Athenian came by to drop in the potsherd which was an indication for him to exile, Aristides said, "Why are you doing that? Haven't I been a good man?" And the Athenian said, "Look, we're tired of hearing the name of Aristides the Just."

I think there's a certain amount of truth to that . . . once in power, no one ever likes to give it up. Because it becomes addictive. It becomes co-terminous with your own identity with yourself, and so it becomes very hard to shake loose from. So all this detached philosophizing, but when the moment of separation comes, I suppose . . . they say they throw you out or carry you out. But I think it's probably good to make it a relatively brief period.

•

You don't have to *do* things. Maybe by avoiding doing things you accomplish quite a lot. Maybe if Kennedy had avoided the Bay of Pigs or Vietnam, that would have been quite an accomplishment.

THE RISING SUN
NEIGHBORHOOD NEWSLETTER

Multiple choice continued from last spread

7. "Regard everything as an experiment." Corita Kent's 6th law of teaching and learning; (Ideas emerge from relaxation but on the other hand some of us can't relax until we've put it off three months past the last minute and decided it will prove our basic worth or lack of and then by putting it off we've proved lack of and then given up and relaxed and let the idea happen, but I suppose one could relax at the beginning.)

continued on next spread

TO TRAVEL, YOU MIGHT want a Swiss Army Knife (p. 132), but all you really need is a self-editorial that begins, "Fuck it . . ."

—SB

The Art and Adventure of Traveling Cheaply

We've seen plenty of travel books. All have been competent and a few downright enticing, but none have really tangled with the unmentionables — border trouble, bribes, black markets, and other sub-official situations. This handbook tells you not only what you should do and what you should not, it tells you what you can get away with. As a bonus, there is a chapter (by a woman guest editor) on women's special concerns such as how to deal with hassling by foreign men. The money-saving tips promised in the title are served up as advertised. Most of the information shown in other general travel books is there too. Nice job. —J. Baldwin

The Art and Adventure of Traveling Cheaply
Rick Berg
1979; 226 pp.
$4.95 postpaid from:
And/Or Press
1409 5th Ave.
Berkeley, CA 94710
or Whole Earth Household Store

•

"For men of honor there are no borders." Told to me by a Colombian border guard who had just accepted my bribe.

•

Even when prices appear to be fixed, haggling is the rule in almost every country. Vendors in markets will usually come down about 25 per cent on food and other staples (other than canned and bottled stuff), and 50 per cent or more on clothes and tourist items. You'll do worse if you look rich and have a lot of newly purchased goods with you that show you're an eager buyer. Never act eager. And never pull out a wad of cash.

•

To really make big money, you can perform in simulated sex shows in Tokyo for several hundred dollars a night. Attractive women are almost begged to work as waitresses or escorts in Singapore and Hong Kong. These jobs involve no further obligations and pay up to $100 a night.

No one who had ever worked at one of these jobs has left without at least one outrageously funny experience. A woman from Iowa who was making big money at a club in Hong Kong was offered $1,000 by a Chinese gentleman as an inducement to find a more respectable job, even though her work never went farther than waiting on tables. She gratefully accepted the money, quit her job, and resolved never again to live in sin.

•

Once the hustle is over, the boys can be mighty interesting. In Morocco, for example, most of the young hustlers speak five languages and have more street savvy than any of us ever will. They know all the tricks and can tell you where the bargains are. All over the world they'll climb palm trees for you and catch you a fish dinner. A small tip will suffice; be sure you don't give a boy more than his father earned last week.

The Bed & Breakfast League

The cheapest way to travel is have travellers come and stay with you. Rather than move out of your house when the kids grow up, use their rooms for interesting income. Help kick the Motel Moloch's shins. Become a Bed & Breakfast host (or guest). Contact the Bed & Breakfast League, 20 Nassau St., Princeton, NJ 08540. —SB

[Suggested by Eric Utne]

International Home Exchange Service

Published three times a year, this is a shopping list of places and people to temporarily swap your home with. What a good idea. 400 listings so far. —SB

International Home Exchange Journal
$25/year (four issues plus one home's registration)
from:
International Home Exchange Service
P.O. Box 3975
San Francisco, CA 94119

•

No hotel tab at the end of your vacation is just one of the benefits of exchanging. You can cut down on restaurant costs by cooking your own meals, and you can frequently include a car in your exchange. "Exchangers" give each other helpful hints that only a native can give about where to go or not go; where to shop and where to play. Friends and neighbors can sometimes be called upon as hosts. The worries about your vacant home being robbed, your plants or even your pets being properly cared for are greatly reduced.

How to Be an Importer and Pay for Your World Travel

An excellent, readable, complete and wise book. —Michael Phillips

How to Be an Importer and Pay for Your World Travel
Mary Green and Stanley Gillmar
1979; 181 pp.
$5.95 postpaid from:
Celestial Arts
231 Adrian Road
Millbrae, CA 94030
or Whole Earth Household Store

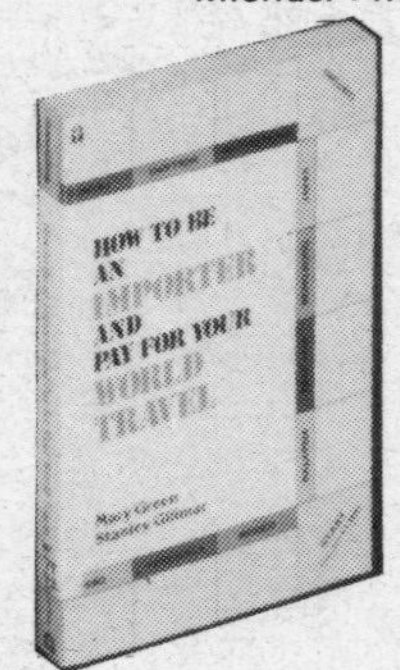

•

You are on a plane, daydreaming on your return flight from Nepal. Your suitcase is filled with potentially salable treasures. If you sell them your trip will be paid for. Then you remember that you've never sold anything in your life since the fourth grade school magazine drive. Don't panic. Your first sale may be the the friend picking you up at the airport, who, seeing the lovely antique coat you are wearing, wants one immediately. How convenient that you just happen to have one in your luggage and offer it to her, for a price above your cost and considerably below the cost in a retail store. That was easy. She was a friend. Now she is also a customer.

•

Many small museums have shops attached to them with items for sale from all over the world. You may be able to interest them in some of your purchases. The people working there most frequently are easy to approach as they are often there in a volunteer capacity. We find such people often have a real interest in the store and its merchandise.

The cure for jet lag

According to my sources NASA did a major study a few years ago on the causes, disturbing effects, and possible cures of jet lag — the psycho-physical dislocation that goes with travelling rapidly across time-zones. Apparently the study turned up an at least partial cure for jet lag, but NASA refused to publish it.

The cure for jet lag is orgasm.

Whole Earth *readers who travel are invited to do individual research on this subject — how soon after arrival, how often, during arrival, instead of travelling, alone versus with somebody (preferably a local?), what else works, etc. Also does anyone know more about the NASA research, or is that apocryphal?* —SB

How to Fly for Less

The annual update of this most useful manual on how to fly cheap. If you're thinking of flying, this book is a must. All current update too. —J. Baldwin

How to Fly for Less
(Consumer's Guide to Low Cost Air Charters and and Other Travel Bargains)
Jens Jurgen, Editor
$5/year (1 issue)
from:
Travel Information Bureau
44 County Line Road
Farmingdale, NY 11735

•

"What is the lowest fare to Europe?" or "Just tell me the cheapest way to fly to XYZ?" I must have had questions like these in my mail a hundred thousand times over the years, with most travelers asking about fares to Europe.

In the 1960s and '70s, the answers usually were: A charter flight, Icelandic Airlines to Europe or a regular excursion or group tour fare, sometimes utilizing a so-called "throw-away tour," paying for a voucher to a remote guest house or pension you did not plan to use, merely to qualify for a lower "tour basing" air fare.

In the 1980s, we have many more low fare alternatives both for domestic and international travel. The lowest fares now for about a hundred popular routes between the U.S.A. and Europe, to certain South American and Pacific destinations and even for an "Around The World" flight, are so-called BUDGET or STANDBY Fares. These rates usually save you at least 50% over normal Economy fares and often much more! Repeating my warning that the lowest fare is not always your best fare (no stopovers, etc.), let's delve deeper into the standby/budget fare concept. You must have this extra over-all knowledge in order to take full advantage of these incredible air travel bargains and avoid disappointments and inconvenience. Commissions on "inexpensive" fare tickets are often so low that most travel agents simply cannot afford the time to research all you fare options and their specific conditions and do the planning for you. You must do much of it yourself!

The Travel Catalog

Would you like to spend your vacation at Bluegrass festivals? Or perhaps visiting the greatest roller coasters? Or at a ranch run by bird watchers? How about a nude beach, film festivals, whitewater running or the finest in scenic drives? You name it, you'll probably find it in this fascinating collection of things to do and see. In fact, you'll likely find things here you've never even heard of let alone wished for. Addresses are given as well as pertinent travel information. This book is now standard equipment in my car's map department. Now if you'll excuse me, I have a few things to pack. —J. Baldwin

The Travel Catalog
Karen Cure
1978; 191 pp.
$6.95 postpaid from:
Holt, Rinehart and Winston
383 Madison Avenue
New York, NY 10017
or Whole Earth Household Store

•

The Magic Table

There exists, in New York City, a sort of Round Table at the Algonquin for magicians. Lovers of magic, whether prestidigitators in their own right or merely fans, are welcome. But if you go, be prepared to get a live dove when you ask for salt to put on the melon (inside which you just found a playing card). Magicians back from Europe are often on hand to relate their experiences with ghosts. You may play magician's assistant to some of the world's greatest — it depends on who's around when you go. The Magic Table is at the Scandia Restaurant in the Piccadilly Hotel at 227 West 45th Street in New York — from about noon until two.

•

Toy Collections

They're there in numbing profusion — at the Museum of Yesterday's Toys, 52 George Street in St. Augustine 32084; at the Museum of the City of New York in New York City; at the Shelburne Museum in Shelburne, VT 05482; at the Perelman Antique Toy Museum, 270 South Second Street, in Philadelphia. It's a subject that holds such fascination for so many people that you'll find some sort of display in almost every area that gets any visitors.

The Freighthopper's Manual for North America

Making a big comeback with college age. "Yeah Ma, I'll be home for Thanksgiving. Uh, no I don't know when I'll be getting in." Cheap travel, real adventures, often good company. Some lines and yards are still too hot, but many a railroad is operated largely by aging hippies these days, who will help you. A fine little book, all you need. —SB

The Freighthopper's Manual for North America
(Hoboing in the 1980s)
Daniel Leen
1978, 1979; 96 pp.
$5.45 postpaid from:
Capra Press
P.O. Box 2068
Santa Barbara, CA 93120
or Whole Earth Household Store

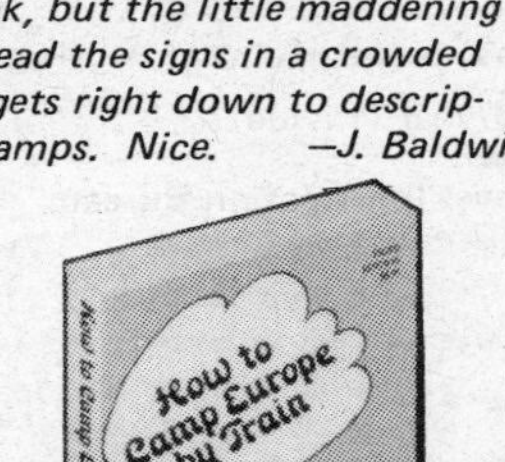

•

"When you're running on the ground you're in one frame of reference, and when you're in the boxcar you're in another. But when you're leaving one and not yet in the other — that's reality!"

•

All trains originate, run to their destination, and terminate. In the yards however, the switchmen say a train is "made up." This involves an hour or more of switching cars onto a particular set of tracks in a particular order, putting a caboose on the back end, one or more engine units on the head end, and connecting and pressurizing the air line. A train may stop and switch along its route but it is still the same train until it terminates or "breaks up." Theoretically the switching out in the yards and the preparation of the engines in the roundhouse are timed so that the engines will roll out of the roundhouse just as the last boxcar slams into place. Thus, when you find out when the engine is called for, you have a general idea of when your train will pull out.

Youth Hosteler's Guide to Europe

An excellent guide to 22 European countries for the shoe string traveler and outdoor enthusiast. Includes 60 detailed tours, maps, and charts, walking and cycling tours through cities and countryside; lists and locations of youth hostels, and mountain trails for backpackers and campers. The section on each country starts off with background data on the geography, climate, people, language, religion, history, government, and so forth. Next is touring info covering transportation, maps, money, restaurants, clothing, and various outdoor activities. The major data on each country though, consist of the Touring Route schedule, main excursion routes through the country with mile-by-mile descriptions, side trips, excursion activities and hostels to stay at. Quite a guide for $4.95. —Al Perrin

Youth Hosteler's Guide to Europe
Youth Hostels Association
1973, 1977; 491 pp.
2nd Edition
$4.95 postpaid from:
Collier Books
Order Department
Front and Brown Streets
Riverside, NJ 08075
or Whole Earth Household Store

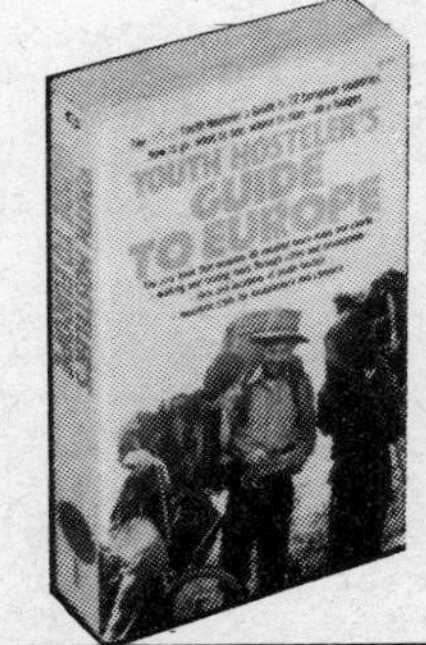

How to Camp Europe by Train

Train information

Using a Eurailpass to jump from campground to campground is one of the cheapest and most satisfying ways to see Europe. Not only are the expected things covered in this comprehensive handbook, but the little maddening things are too; like how to read the signs in a crowded train station. The detailing gets right down to descriptions of specific trains and camps. Nice. —J. Baldwin

Tickets

How to Camp Europe by Train
Lenore Baken
1975, 1979; 384 pp.
3rd Edition
$6.95 postpaid from:
Ariel Publications
P.O. Box 255
Mercer Island, WA 98040
or Whole Earth Household Store

Entrance

Exit

Snack bar

Don't drink water

•

Eurail Youthpass can be bought by anyone under 26 and its first day of use must occur before the 26th birthday. It is issued for a two month period only for a cost of $260. It gives unlimited travel in the same countries as does the Eurailpass but in the second class cars. The pass can only be bought outside of Europe. Almost all the bonuses of the Eurailpass are included in the Eurail Youthpass with the most notable exception being that the express service on the Rhine River can't be taken without paying a supplement but there are other boats to take anyway.

Drinking water

Waiting room

•

In northern Europe, a cafeteria represents considerable saving over a restaurant and is a fine buy. Switzerland and Germany have the cafeteria counter which culminates in stand-up tables, but the more common cafeteria is similar to the U.S. Both department stores and super markets often have a cafeteria. A cafeteria meal cost about $3 - $4 in northern Europe, less so in southern Europe.

Seat reservations

Currency exchange

For meals in southern Europe, we recommend eating in a restaurant for the noon meal rather than in the evening. It is the "table d'hote" lunch which vies for the patronage of the businessman, bureaucrat, shopgirl and office-worker on his lunch hour. This is the daily special which changes each day, incorporates seasonal foods and is served more quickly than anything on the regular menu. It goes by a different name in each country such as "menu a '25' franc" in France or "el pranzo" in Italy. Usually it will be listed on a half-page dittoed sheet sometimes attached to the regular menu and sometimes not. Though often the regular menu is multi-lingual or else there is a separate English one, the table d'hote menu isn't translated from its native language in most cases.

Post office

Public phone

Women's restroom

Restroom

Men's restroom

Car rentals

Luggage storage

Luggage lockers

Baggage registration

Pick up baggage

Restaurant

Smoking permitted

No smoking

Lost and found

The Magic Bus (Europe and east)

Dear Whole Earth,

There's a travel service in Europe called the Magic Bus that provides transportation between Paris and many European points (including London) at a price substantially less than the regular bus/train fares. The Bus also makes trips to Morocco, Yugoslavia, Greece, Turkey and India. In the fall of 1979 the one-way fare from Paris to Delhi, India was $250 (not including food or lodging), and that fare allowed stops in Athens, Istanbul, and Teheran (before the most recent troubles in that country).

I've heard some wild stories about the longer trips — Afghani outlaws and border hassles — but my buses between London and Paris and Lyon, France were on time, modern, and peopled with a very agreeable mix of ages and nationalities (except for the lady from L.A. who giggled long and loudly over the fact that the Frenchman taking our tickets in Paris had a French accent).

The parent company organizing the Magic Bus is called 'Les Voyageurs Associés' and they also organize a number of other package tours and charters all over the world.

Bon Voyage,

Steve Dunnington
Seattle, Washington

Magic Bus
Ticket information
free from:
Magic Bus
15600 Roscoe Boulevard
Van Nuys, CA 91406

Magic Bus
66 Shaftesbury Avenue
London W1
England

The Magic Bus
Damrak 87
Amsterdam, Holland

Les Voyageurs Associes
28, rue du Pont-Louis-Phillipe
75004 Paris France

The Magic Bus
24 Kidathineon
Plaka Athens
Greece

Michelin maps and guides

If you're gadding about Europe or Africa these are the standard maps and guides. —SB
[Suggested by Joe Godwin]

Michelin maps and guides
Catalogs

free from:
Michelin
P.O. Box 5022
New Hyde Park, NY 11040

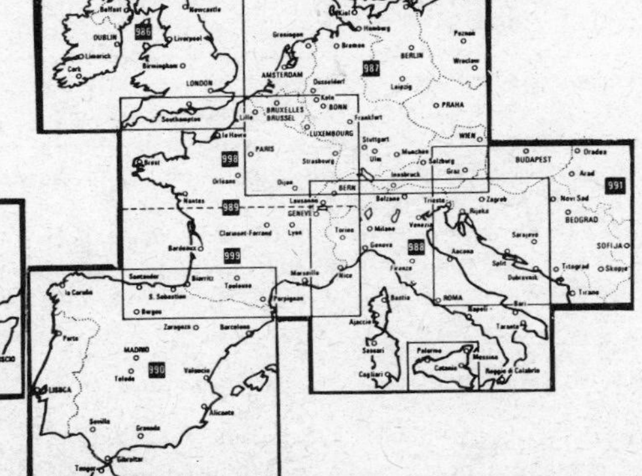

American Youth Hostels Handbook

Now you can read up on hosteling without becoming a member of AYH (American Youth Hostels), though you might want to join after you see what they offer. A membership lets you stay at more than 200 inexpensive hostels in the U.S. and something like 5000 more around the world. You'll meet all sorts of other travellers, exchange lies, make alliances, and perhaps modify your plans after hearing of some more interesting option from someone who's just been there. This book has some mediocre general tips on trip planning and travel, but its main use will be the comprehensive listing and descriptions of all the hostels in this country and their associated customs. I can tell you from considerable experience that hosteling can be a good way to go, especially if it's your first time out. All ages are welcome. —J. Baldwin

American Youth Hostels Handbook
American Youth Hostels
1980; 192 pp.
$2.25 postpaid from:
American Youth Hostels, Inc.
Delaplane, VA 22025

•

1. Graded hostels may charge the following maximum rates or they may charge less:

	Summer	Winter
Shelter	$2.00	$2.50
Simple	$3.00	$3.75
Standard	$4.00	$5.00
Superior	$5.00	$6.25

Summer is defined as April 16 to October 14. Winter is October 15 to April 15.

2. Home Hostels may accept a donation of up to $2.50 for each overnight, $1.00 for each supper provided (if any), and $.50 for each breakfast provided (if any).

Little America Youth Hostel. Truro, MA.

THE RISING SUN
NEIGHBORHOOD NEWSLETTER

Multiple choice continued from last spread

8. "I waited on the Lord; he took his own sweet time."

continued on next spread

Vat Sra Sri, a monastery in Sukhothai, former capital of Thailand, the buildings include the chedi with viharn, a mandop, a prang and a bot.

TRAVELLING IN ASIA

by Kevin Kelly

First, get the book: **The Budget Traveler's Asia** *by David Jenkins. Read the introduction thoroughly, then purchase some* **Bartholomew's Maps** *of Asia, for where you're headed. You'll need at least $10 per day of travelling — I don't see how you can do it for less. Even if you just hang around you'll wind up spending it on something, or you can easily spend more. Convert all but $100 of it into travellers' checks, either American Express or First National City (both are universally accepted, but equally spotty in service). If it doesn't sting your patriotism, buy them in German marks so that you won't hurt each time you go to the bank and exchange your checks at a lower, sinking dollar rate. American Express checks are also available in Japanese, French and Swiss currency. Ask for the checks in a mix of small and large denominations. You don't want to be stuck with only large ones when all you need is $3 to pay an airport tax or the bus fare to the border. It is a big headache to break a large one into smaller units, and you lose money doing it. Carry the remaining $100 in cash — in $10 and $20 bills, and a few $1 bills to use in emergencies such as the many desperate days official banks are closed, or in places where they don't exist, as at borders. Five or ten dollar bills will prove invaluable at some time on your trip.*

If you are getting a new passport, ask for one with 48 pages in it (no extra cost) to avoid running out of space. (Some artistic custom officers enjoy imprinting just one entry or exit stamp per page.) You can have extra, awkward, fold-out pages added to your existing passport at any American embassy, also at no cost.

Where to carry all this paperwork of checks, passport, vaccination card, cash, tickets, youth hostel card and other valuables is a problem that receives a different solution by different travellers. I hid my passport, one $50 check, one $20 bill and vaccination card in my secret place. The rest — all those travellers' checks, cards, the rest of the cash — I put in an old bag with my cameras and kept it near me as best I could. Money belts are hot and a nuisance to use. My secret place was an inside pocket sewn in my pants, which was very safe and not noticeable to me or a potential pickpocket. There are other possibilities, with pluses and minuses. Anything that could fall off, be torn off, or forgotten behind should be avoided. I would avoid example No. 2 in the illustration. I kept one copy of my travellers' checks' numbers in my secret place. It is very important to have more than one copy of those numbers in various places, even one at home, because you can't replace them on your trip unless you have those numbers! For many years there were all kinds of rackets being played with travellers' checks and banks in Asia make it as difficult as possible to replace them there.

Forget about having money sent over: it's unsure and time-consuming and in some countries near hopeless. The best solution to the problem of running out of money is not to let it happen — bring enough.

Rates for converting your dollars or marks into local currency are given up-to-date in current issues of **Newsweek**, *which can be found in any larger Asian city. Avoid the black market; it is dangerous, not for your life so much (that is possible) as for the safety of your money. The people who deal in that business know every trick that works, and it's a good way to lose your whole bankroll. I could write a book on some of the maddening and foolish stories I have heard first-hand about the skill of these con men. Besides, I can think of only two Asian countries where the black market rate is substantially better than the official one. Stick to banks, but do shop around because bank rates vary; very often banks at borders and airports have less lucrative rates. In many Eastern countries, there is a curious custom of refusing to deal with broken, ripped or taped bills, and you will find it hard to have someone accept them from you. There is little choice but to join in the game. So don't accept them from anyone else, especially from a bank!*

Some things to bring besides money: lots of passport size photos. You almost can't have too many — the few you don't use you can give away to people you stay with. Some countries require 4 or 5 photos for one visa, so you can really go through a bunch of them. A good idea is to bring the **negative** *of your photo and have an Asian studio print them up for you very inexpensively if you need any more on the way.*

As a rule, it is easier and cheaper to get visas along the way. It is usually quicker than getting them in the U.S., and there is little chance of the visa expiring as you dawdle on a beach somewhere.

Bring at least two rolls of toilet paper. Bring very few clothes; it is simple and cheap to buy or have clothes made in Asia (cheap labour). Do bring a coat and very sturdy shoes, which you cannot find there. Don't bring a raincoat — bring a folding umbrella. Bring a small padlock to lock rooms in guesthouses or inns. (One with a "combination-lock" is very effective because it is unfamiliar to local lockpickers, and useful with a partner — no key to share or lose.) Don't bring any medicines. Most prescription drugs are available there, by brand name, over the counter, and inexpensively. **Lomotil** *is the standard "plug" for diarrhea symptoms. You would need an antibiotic or antiamoebic for more serious diarrhea or dysentery. Check one of the guide books or* **Staying Healthy in Asia** *(see below) for more information on maintaining your travelling body.*

All these things are very important, but after 4 years of wandering around the back roads of Asia, what became most important to me was mail. Three ways to receive mail are: c/o American Express, c/o your embassy, or c/o Poste Restante. American Express requires that you be using their checks and holds mail 1-2 months. Your embassy is safe but out of the way and sometimes troublesome to get into. Mail goes there via the local postal system, the same as Poste Restante, which is a general listing. Poste Restante mail is shelved alphabetically, so check all possible letters of your names. Poste Restante can be used at any post office, not just ones in large cities. They hold for 1-3 months. People writing you just address your name, last name very clearly, c/o Poste Restante, and name of a town or city in the country.

Sending packages is another art. Every country has its own traditions and methods, some ridiculous, but it's always in your self interest to follow them exactly. Don't trust anyone to do it for you. I have sent scores of packages of all sizes, from all countries, most full of exposed film (up to 50 rolls in one). They have all arrived safely and most were unopened by either our or their customs. The key is doing the boxing, wrapping, affixing stamps, and paperwork yourself, and to do it in the main post office of a large city. Most handmade merchandise made in Asia is exempt from duty. Write that on the box: **Handmade, Exempt from Duty.** *Sea mail takes 2-3 months. Air mail costs about 1 million dollars per package.*

How to Get There

To the Mideast, fly Laker to London. Check the city guides and "underground" newspapers for cheap flights to the Mideast, usually such carriers as Aeroflot, Jordan Airlines or Syrian Airlines, all non-members of international price agreements.

To the Far East, join OC-Tours, a "charter" group that was originally for overseas Chinese visiting relatives, and now flies several thousand flights a year to Japan, Hong Kong, Taiwan and other Asian cities. Current fares (1980) include: San Francisco to Hong Kong—$309, one way, $579 roundtrip. OC-Tours, 828 Airport Road, Burlingame, CA 94010. Telephone (800)-632-4734 or (800)-227-5988.

When To Go?

Summer is obviously hot, but with plenty of visitors about, wild. Almost any city, except a few notorious spots, is far safer than any large town in America. Things are changing quickly in Asia: go now. By far your best source of guidance is the network of new gypsies wandering in all parts of Asia. They have just come the way you are headed, and will gladly share their hard won knowledge.

Passp… photo… negati…

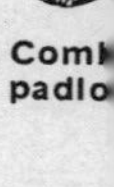

Comb… padlo…

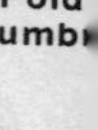

Fold… umb…

Sources:

The Budget Traveler's Asia

Definitely the most useful guide to Asia in print. Well worn copies have passed from veterans leaving to newcomers arriving. All my copies were eagerly bought by new initiates hard up for usable information. It happily covers every country from Turkey to Japan, except mainland China, supplying basic advice and solid tips to travelling in the East in general and minute particulars such as the $2 hotels available in Kabul, Afghanistan, or the sequence of trains and buses connecting India and Nepal. The book lacks maps and much on languages, but does have a short bibliography of general reading for each country. As a whole the guide is honest and dependable and very popular among travelers.

The Budget Traveler's Asia
(Formerly Student Guide to Asia)
David Jenkins
1975, 1979; 415 pp.

$4.95 postpaid from:
E.P. Dutton and Company
Two Park Avenue
New York, NY 10016
or Whole Earth Household Store

The On-Your-Own Guide to Asia

This book is superior to the **Budget Traveler's Guide**; *however, it only covers a portion of the same area, that is Thailand east to Japan, also excepting the communist countries, but it presents this area thoroughly and substantially. It has good language rudiments, good bibliographies, decent maps, and an amazing amount of information that is simply not available anywhere else. It is written by young people who have lived there, and is the best travel guide to anywhere I have ever encountered.*

The On-Your-Own Guide to Asia
(The Budget Handbook to East and Southeast Asia)
Alison Davis, Editor
1979; 347 pp.

$3.95 postpaid from:
Charles E. Tuttle Company
Rutland, VT 05701
or Whole Earth Household Store

Bartholomew's Physical Maps

The five relevant maps are the Mideast (Greece to Iran), Indian Subcontinent (Afghanistan to Bangladesh), Southeast Asia (Burma to Indonesia), China (including Mongolia and Korea, Taiwan) and Japan. Smaller towns and secondary roads are charted and physical features are indicated by color and contours, making it indispensible for someone unfamiliar with the geography. Includes index of major place names. Available in some Asian cities.

Bartholomew's Maps
(30" x 40", scale 1:4 million)
$5.95 each

Catalog #604 **free** from:
American Map Company
1926 Broadway
New York, NY 10023

Staying Healthy in Asia

Combining common sense and the experience of students living in Asia for extended periods, this book teaches preventative health care, dealing with special illnesses of Asia, and using medicines yourself to help. The success of your Asian journey hinges on your health. Don't be ignorant. Your family doctor will not be able to supply you with this valuable information because he doesn't know anything about it.

Staying Healthy in Asia
(formerly VIA Health Handbook)
Ann Huckins, Editor
1979; 96 pp.

$2.50 postpaid from:
Volunteers in Asia
P.O. Box 4543
Stanford, CA 94305
or Whole Earth Household Store

The Complete Guide to China

Just the very idea is tempting, isn't it? Since going over there on your own and traipsing around isn't permitted, a guidebook such as this one can be very useful. Dr. Saunders starts with the essential visa and the mechanics of getting together the required group. He tells you what to expect at the border, how to be polite Chinese style, and how to get along with your interpreters and guides. There will probably be some culture shock, so there's a bit about that. (How would it feel to be walking down the street in a big city and have a mob following you?) In short, a typical, competent guidebook but with a very personal touch stemming from his recent firsthand experience. I've left the best to last: the color photographs are enough to inspire you to rash action!

—J. Baldwin

The Complete Travel Guide to China
Hilliard Saunders
1979; 179 pp.
$8.95 postpaid from:
China Publishing Company
P.O. Box 342
Seal Beach, CA 90740
or Whole Earth Household Store

•

The Chinese are honest people. As a result, travelers need not worry about articles being pilfered from their hotel rooms or pockets. On the contrary, you will find it difficult to throw away worn articles; the Chinese will return them to you.

↓ Scenery along the Li River

A Traveler's Guide to El Dorado and the Inca Empire

Colombia, Ecuador, Peru, Bolivia — the four countries on the northwest shoulder of South America — are made warmly accessible and inviting by this unusually sound travel book. Neither stiff nor cute, it reads like a letter from a good friend with all the advice you need to kick your excuses and trepidations in the head and get south for some Andean Adventures. —SB

A Traveler's Guide to El Dorado and the Inca Empire
Lynn Meisch
1977, 1980; 446 pp.
$8.95 postpaid from:
Penguin Books
299 Murray Hill Parkway
East Rutherford,
NJ 07073
or Whole Earth
Household Store

•

Although it's hard to generalize, my experience has been that you settle on sixty to eighty percent of the initial price. This surprises people who are used to bargaining in Mexico and Guatemala, where you often arrive at a price equal to half the asking price. In South America people seem to name a price much closer to what they actually want, unless they think you're an idiot and will pay anything.

•

Pre-Columbian Textile Heritage. Peru is a textile-lover's paradise for several reasons. First, the Peruvian Indians have retained their traditional dress and textile techniques far more than the Indians of highland Colombia and Ecuador. Second, Peruvians are fortunate to have had the use of a wide variety of fibers — especially the cameloid fibers, alpaca, llama and vicuna — in addition to sheep's wool and cotton. The ancient Peruvians also made use of viscacha (an *altiplano* rodent), rat and mouse fur, human hair, sisal, kapok, spider webs and various grasses. Third, many of the incredibly fine textiles produced by the ancient Peruvians now reside in museum collections, so it's possible to study the general continuities in Peruvian textile production over a span of about 4200 years. Fortunately for us textile fanatics, the dryness of the coastal desert has helped preserve some of the finest textiles the world has ever known. Due to the lack of moisture, artifacts buried in graves don't decay.

Nagel's Encyclopedia-Guide to China

Essential for anyone going to the People's Republic of China and extremely valuable to those who want accurate and entertaining summaries of Chinese geography, demography, history, religion, literature, games and art, along with detailed physical descriptions of every major city and province. The whole thing was written by a group of young French scholars passionately devoted to Chinese civilization, and they show the French genius for lucid compression.

Price is a drawback: $65. But, for the price, you get 1500 pages, 92 plans, 15 large colored maps and 25 pages of Atlas in color. You also get a deep sense of China. —Ed LeFevour

Nagel's Encyclopedia-Guide to China
Anne L. Destenay, translator
1973, 1979; 1504 pp.
$65 postpaid from:
China Books & Periodicals
2929 24th Street
San Francisco, CA 94110
or Whole Earth
Household Store

Building a palapa

A palapa (hut, also ramada, choza or jacal) is basically a shelter made of sticks and palm fronds (also called palapas). They are very common on all the coasts of Mexico.

The People's Guide to Mexico

The best 360° coverage of traveling and short term living in Mexico that's going. Reading the book is almost like being there and going through the problems and frustrations, pleasures and wonders of dealing with a new environment, new people and new ways of doing things, but by golly every page, every step of the way you're learning something. Carl is candid, to the point, and leaves few, if any, questions unanswered in telling you how to handle just about everything: border crossing, driving in Mexico, public transportation, hitching, camping, indigenous living (living on the beach, building a hut, stove, digging a well, etc.) and scrounging for food, renting a house, restaurants, markets, stores, health, legal hassles, communication services, car repairs, the language and customs, cantinas and whorehouses, buying things, and so forth. A fantastic book, well written and really interesting. —Al Perrin

The People's Guide to Mexico
(Wherever You Go . . . There You Are!)
Carl Franz
1972, 1979; 625 pp.
$10 postpaid from:
John Muir Publications
P.O. Box 613
Santa Fe, NM 87501
or Whole Earth
Household Store

•

A friend flew from New York to Yucatan with his bicycle, pedalled to a small village, and then sat there quite happily for two months. The cost of living in the village was about equal to the tax on his airplane ticket. He not only had a wonderful time but was able to keep his *overall* expenses within his limits and still enjoy the luxury of flying to and from Mexico.

The Maya World

If you're planning on travelling through Southern Mexico and Central America, pack this little book along. Natasha and Gregorio share the insights, out-of-the-way finds and practical tips of seasoned, leisurely, thorough nomads. After being completely frustrated at getting their information published, they've turned self-publishers with fine results. —Andrew Fluegelman

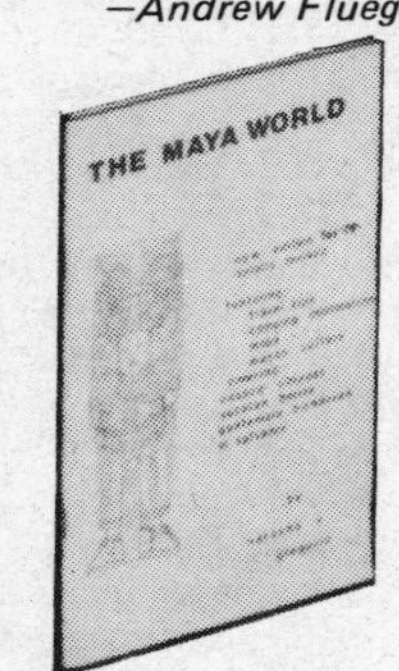

The Maya World
Natasha y Gregorio
1976, 1979; 68 pp.
$2.95 postpaid from:
Intermundial Research, Inc.
Box 518
Inverness, CA 94937

•

Belize City has a party atmosphere and to get in the spirit of things we recommend 3 Barrel Rum. Also eat conch fritters at the swinging bridge market and watch the produce being brought in by boat from the many small communities only accessible by water. Belize City is built at 3 feet above sea level so many of the streets are actually canals which lends an old world look to this black city. The English spoken here is musical and rhythmical and will take some getting used to, but it is a pleasant break after many months of Mexican Spanish.

The South American Handbook

This small, hardbound, fine print book is absolutely packed with information on South and Central America, the Caribbean and Mexico. For each country there are maps, information on climate, geography, history, food, holidays, and best of all, city by city and town by town — how to get around, what to see, and where to stay and eat. Furthermore, the **Handbook** *isn't just for ricos. It includes listings for good 50¢ meals and two dollar a night hotels with hot water. For most of us, the "how to get around" information is most valuable: what bus lines to take (and which to avoid), which border crossings are easiest, what to expect on long train rides (pack food), and which little airlines go where.* —Lynn Meisch

The 1980 South American Handbook
(A traveller's guide to Latin America and the Caribbean)
John Brooks and Joyce Candy, Editors
1924, 1980; 1273 pp.
$24.95 postpaid from:
Rand McNally Retail Store
23 East Madison Street
Chicago, IL 60603
or
£6.95 postpaid from:
Trade and Travel Publications
The Mendip Press
Parsonage Lane
Bath BA1 1EN England

Madrigal's Magic Key to Spanish

How to guess your way through Spanish. This very thorough textbook tells you how to change most of the words you already know into Spanish — the rules are simple and consistent. Correct Spanish word order is regularly reinforced by translation into incorrect English ("to me he delivered the book"). Exceptions to rules are dealt with unhysterically. At the end is a compilation of common Spanish expressions and a good vocabulario. An address is given where one can send for records to complete the immersion.

Madrigal's style of instruction is breezy and beguiling, belying the great volume of vocabulary you gain right away (over 450 words in the first chapter). With the panic of speechlessness out of the way, the rest is almost easy. —Sally Brooke

Madrigal's Magic Key to Spanish
(An exciting, new approach to the study of a foreign language)
Margarita Madrigal
1951, 1953; 496 pp.
$9.95 postpaid from:
Doubleday & Company
501 Franklin Avenue
Garden City, NY 11530
or Whole Earth
Household Store

•

Note: if pronouns seem at all complicated to you, don't worry about them. In fact, forget you ever heard of them. They will come up so often in future lessons that before you know it you will be using them automatically.

•

Remember that if a word ends in "tion" in English, change the "t" to "c" and, presto, you have a Spanish word.

TION = CION
the nation = la nacion

"La" means "the"; "una" means "a, an."

la informacion
la constitucion
la operacion
la preparacion
una invitacion
una institucion
una indicacion
una composicion

THE RISING SUN
NEIGHBORHOOD NEWSLETTER

Multiple choice continued from last spread

9. Ideas rise from messy desks and messy minds where objects and concepts and memories that would not meet in an ordered universe bump into each other and start new and different disordered universes and boy is that self righteous coming from me.

continued on next spread

Home Is Where You Park It

What's it like to live only in an "RV" (recreational vehicle)? Thousands of people do these days. Some are retired, some are "boomers" who work here and there as they go. None have a home base. Their travel trailer or motor home (not mobile home) is IT. So what about mail, medical help, taxes, parking, schools for the kids, attack, banking, credit, appliance warranties, driver's license and insurance? What kind of RV is best for you? How much does living this way cost? Kay Peterson answers all the above questions and about 200 more as she describes life on the road. Having done this bit myself, I can vouch that her advice is pretty good. If you're thinking of living this way, giving her a listen will save you many hassles. —J. Baldwin

Home Is Where You Park It
(A Guide to RV Living as a Life-Style)
Kay Peterson
1977; 192 pp.

$5.95 postpaid from:
Follett Publishing Company
1010 W. Washington Blvd.
Chicago, IL 60607
or Whole Earth Household Store

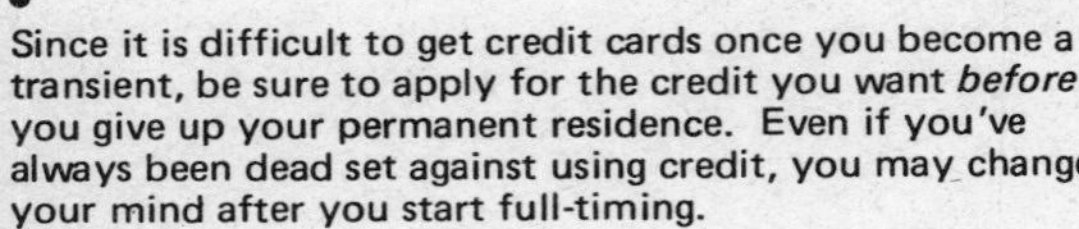

•

Since it is difficult to get credit cards once you become a transient, be sure to apply for the credit you want *before* you give up your permanent residence. Even if you've always been dead set against using credit, you may change your mind after you start full-timing.

•

The total expenditure at the end of our first year of living in an RV was slightly more than half as much as it had been in 1969, when we lived in a house. Why does it cost so much less to live in an RV than it did to live in a conventional house? . . .

The most noticeable differences in my own records occur in clothes, home repairs, and major purchases. We bought so many more things when we lived in a house! . . .

Another savings is in clothes. Because of the limited closet space in an RV, we buy fewer clothes now. . . .

Day-to-day living costs are much less when you live in an RV. Because a trailer occupies about one-tenth the interior space of a house, heating and electricity cost less. We use a small portable electric heater to supplement our propane furnace because we've found it is cheaper to heat with electricity than with propane gas. The cost of propane has soared since the energy crisis started in 1973. It is expected to continue to rise along with the cost of gasoline, electricity, and fuel oil. But one of the advantages of living in an RV is that you have wheels under your home. You don't have to stay in cold climates!

•

Some people make their goal the attainment of an executive position. This attitude is not compatible with booming because supervisory positions are a reward given to permanent employees. Some people need the security that comes with a steady job and a predetermined paycheck. Boomers cannot have those guarantees, nor can they count on a pension.

So boomers have to be the type of people who find security in their abilities and talents. And they must be able to sell those abilities to new employers. In order to do that, they must truly believe in themselves. They must be people who enjoy challenges and who aren't afraid to take chances. It takes more than just a love of travel to make a boomer; it takes a willingness to experience whatever adventures life has to offer.

Roll Your Own

A joyous book on life on the road in buses and vans: How to build one, what it's like living in one, equipment, repairs, special places to go, war stories, lots of photos of machines and nice people. The data and style are a bit dated by now. —J. Baldwin

Roll Your Own
Jodi Pallidini and Berverly Dubin
1974; 192 pp.

$3.95 postpaid from:
Collier Books
Macmillan Publishing Co.
Order Department
Front and Brown Streets
Riverside, NJ 08075
or Whole Earth Household Store

•

In the five years we've lived in this van we've had different concepts of what it is we're doing with ourselves and the van. We prefer to have our furniture easily rearrangeable rather than built in. If you have a built-in interior you are stuck with that arrangement, while your living concepts keep on changing.

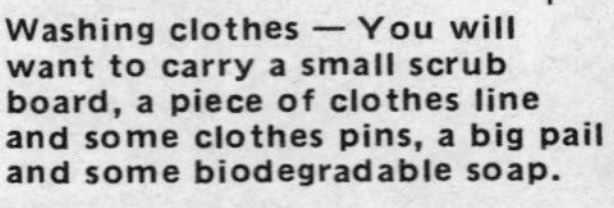

Washing clothes — You will want to carry a small scrub board, a piece of clothes line and some clothes pins, a big pail and some biodegradable soap.

This was a moving van originally, '53 Chevy, 6500 feet, 18 inch rails.

Hitchhiking, the homilies

Use a sign. Have a map.

Look like who you want to pick you up.

Wait where it's easy for drivers to see you and stop.

Be of use to the driver, or at least no bother.

Don't take it personally when they don't pick you up. See it as their problem.

Stay on the curb, and off freeways. Don't rob or murder or rape anybody; it makes it hard for the rest of us. —SB

Truck stop men's room

Here I sit with a
broken heart,
Took my last little pill,
now my truck won't start.

Start truck first, Then take
Pill, Dummy!

If your pills
were worth a fuck,
You'd go out
and pull your truck.

—Sequence of graffiti seen at the 4-WAY TRUCK STOP, Wells, Nevada by Richard Nilsen

Viking Camper Supply
Fredson RV Supply

Working with owner-responsible power sources or attempting to "live small" can be frustrating when it comes to hardware: you either can't find any, or you are stuck with the outrageously expensive yacht equipment that is much overdesigned for land use. A useful compromise can be found in recreational vehicle hardware, but it is often hard to find too, especially in an array that makes a choice possible. These catalogs present an array that makes a choice possible, to say the least. If you've "always wondered where to get one of those . . ." try here. —J. Baldwin

Viking
Parts and Accessories Catalog

free from:
Viking Camper Supply
99 Glenwood Avenue
Minneapolis, MN 55403

Fredson RV Supply
Catalog

$1 from:
Fredson RV Supply
815 North Harbor Road
Santa Ana, CA 92703

MINI HAMMOCK
Lightweight 100% nylon storage hammock.
For out of the way storage in recreational vehicles, tent, boat or at home.
Strong and compact — stretches to 40" long x 16" deep with tie strings to hold in place.
No. 36401
$4.49

Waterproof
Bathroom Tissue Holder
A really unique and necessary convenience for recreational vehicles with compact shower-toilets!
The counter-balanced tissue roll holder automatically covers itself when not in use, shielding the paper from both mist and spray, even when the shower is turned on full force. The Waterproof Bathroom Tissue Holder comes in 3 compatible decorator's colors and can be securely mounted on any smooth surface in minutes without tools!
10-2905-05 Waterproof Tissue Holder - Avocado $7.49
10-2905-23 Waterproof Tissue Holder - Harvest Gold $7.49
10-2905-40 Waterproof Tissue Holder - White $7.49

Bullet
Lights
This light is highly efficient, and it is low in cost. Uses attractive high impact white plastic shade with drawn base. Excellent for almost any suitable application - map reading, dinette, etc. Overall width and height, when mounted 4½" x 5".
02-5668-33 Single Bullet Light - Satin Gold $10.29

—Viking Camper Supply

Airstream Travel Trailer

Well, Stewart lived in one for three years and we've lived in ours for six years (never paying rent), so I guess we can fairly be rated as experienced in matters Airstream. Ours is 21 feet (that's 17 inside), has a separate bedroom, a shower, sink and potty, 6 feet of kitchen counter, stove, oven, sink, fridge (gas or electric), hot water heater, wood stove (FreeFlow, p. 207), photovoltaic array for electricity (and wired for a portable wind generator), ten feet of desk, 20 feet of bookshelf, stereo, a one-person couch, and lots of nook-and-cranny storage. It's like a boat in many ways. Yes there are no-goods too: mostly having to do with condensation in very cold weather and pipe freezing likewise. That's below 20°F. Above that, it's fine. Even without air conditioning, it never gets hotter in there than it is outdoors. All in all it's been a very good house, though this size is a bit cramped for two. Yet the smaller sizes are more easily parked and consequently find a welcome where a bigger one would be too gross. The best part of Airstream ownership is the remarkably sturdy and maintenance-free running gear and aerodynamic body. They tow with very good behavior. A cheaper version, "Argosy," is similar in most ways except they don't have the natural aluminum finish. Used Airstreams can be a bargain. —J. Baldwin

Airstream Travel Trailers
$10,000 - $31,000
(approx.)

Information
free from:
Airstream
419 Pike Street
Jackson Center, OH 45334

AAA (American Automobile Association)

If you own a car or if you're likely to be driving one much, an AAA card is worth its weight in battery charges. For $29 a year you get: 1) free towing, battery jumps, emergency gas delivery; 2) the best up to date maps available for the U.S., plus booklets of camping sites, plus help in choosing travel routes; 3) insurance discounts; 4) bail for misdemeanor traffic charges. Our AAA has paid for itself in the first 3 months of every year we've had it.

AAA offices in every major city. —Michael Wells

In this larger pool the water cools down to about 95 degrees, ideal for a long soak.
—Hot Springs and Pools of the Northwest

The Good Book
Hot Springs Gazette
Hot Springs and Pools of the Northwest

There are hundreds of bathable hot springs in the American West, many, maybe most, of them utterly untamed. I'm not about to tell you where my favorites are, though I could thrill you for three evenings straight with hot springs adventures. These books tell. **The Good Book** *is a facsimile copy of the U.S. part of the famed (and out of print)* **Thermal Springs of the United States and other Countries of the World** *by the U.S. government. Good data on each spring — name, location, temperature, flow — and very general maps. Still the definitive text. It is published by* **The Hot Springs Gazette,** *an overly chatty but informative source, sort of periodical, somewhat on different regions each issue (3 so far).*

Hot Springs and Pools of the Northwest *tells all — detailed access maps, photos, comments — for Washington, Oregon, Idaho, Montana, Wyoming, Utah, Colorado. (Stay out of Nevada, you bastards). Nicely done book. After an hour in some of these springs, you'll be nicely done too.*
—SB

The Good Book
(Thermal Springs in the United States)
Norah D. Stearns, Eric Irving, et al.
1939, 1979; 46 pp.
$3 postpaid

The Hot Springs Gazette
Eric Irving, Editor
Published irregularly
$2/issue
both from:
The Doodley-Squat Press
P.O. Box 40124
Albuquerque, NM 87106

Hot Springs and Pools of the Northwest
Jayson Loam
1980; 159 pp.
$7.95 postpaid from:
Capra Press
P.O. Box 2068
Santa Barbara, CA 93120
or Whole Earth Household Store
(**Hot Springs and Pools of the Northwest** only)

↑
#109 Olympic Hot Springs
Near the town of Port Angelus

Several primitive springs in Olympic National Park, on the side of a steep ravine, surrounded by lush rain forest greenery. Elevation 1600 ft. Open all year except when road closed by snow.

Natural Mineral Water flows out of the ground at 100 to 110 degrees. Volunteers have built primitive rock soaking pools below the spring flows, holding the water in the 95 to 105 degree range. There is no posted clothing policy, which leaves it up to the mutual consent of those present.

No services on the premises. A tents-only campground is 200 yards away. 8 miles to cafe and grocery store. 20 miles to motel, service station, RV facilities and public bus.

Source maps: Olympic National Park; U.S.G.S. — Mt. Carrie, Washington.
—Hot Springs and Pools of the Northwest

	Clallam County				
2	14 miles by road southwest of Crescent Lake, NW¼ sec. 32, T. 29 N., R. 9 W., Olympic National Forest.	Sol Duc Hot Springs......	132......	50......	3 main springs in group covering 1 acre, 8 others in river bed; resort.
3	11½ miles by trail southwest of Elwha post office, SW¼ sec. 27, T. 29 N., R. 8 W., Olympic National Forest.	Olympic Hot Springs......	120-125..	135......	17 springs covering 5 acres; resort.

—The Good Book

Temporary car

A good way to move from city to city on little money is by driving a car for an auto transport agency, which you can find in your yellow pages or newspaper classifieds. Call and ask if they need any cars driven near to where you want to go. If they say yes, go to their office to apply. They usually require that you be 21 years old or more, carry a valid driver's license, and provide local references. They take a deposit of about $100, but refund that plus your gas expenses when you reach the other end. (They'll also refund repair expenses if they weren't caused by your negligence. Sometimes there are a few cars available and you can shop around for one that doesn't look like it's falling apart. Waiting a couple of days and checking regularly with the agencies will often turn up a good car.) On the road, keep your agency sticker with you, and if you choose not to pay the border taxes which some Western states levy on commercial vehicles, drive slowly so you don't get stopped. The only other problem is wanderlust — there's usually a time limit which doesn't let you make any sidetrips or visit too long anywhere. If you check your local university's ride board, you may even find someone to share expenses and experiences on the trip.
—Art Kleiner
[Suggested by Arn]

National Directory of Budget Motels

A directory of chain motels in the U.S. that cost $12 - $17 a night for a single.
—SB

1980-81 National Directory of Budget Motels
(A Nation-Wide Guide to Low-Cost Chain Motel Accommodations)
Raymond Carlson, Editor
1980; 72 pp.
$3.50 postpaid from:
Pilot Books
347 Fifth Avenue
New York, NY 10016

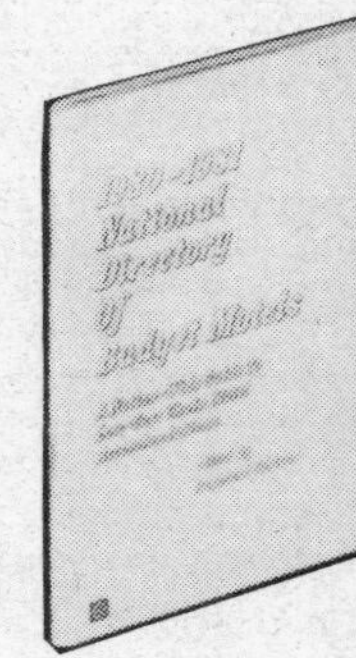

INDIANA

ANDERSON
Kings Inn, 583 B'way, (46012), 317-643-6685
Motel 6, I-69 & Rt. 109 N., 5810 Scatterfield Rd., (46013), 317-642-3333
ANGOLA (46703)
Best Western Redwood Center Motor Inn, I-69 to US 20 E., 219-665-9451
AUBURN (46706)
Starlite Motel, I-69 & Hwy. 8, 219-925-0500
BEDFORD (47421)
Rosemount Motel, Hwy. 50 & Rt. 37, 812-275-5953

To Hell on Wheels

You'd expect from the name and cover that this is a four-wheeler's tear-up-the-desert book. It isn't. The author wants you to be able to get out into the desert, stay there, and return safely. Driving technique, survival, tools, first aid, navigation, and vehicle extraction are all covered neatly by a man who's done it.
—J. Baldwin

To Hell on Wheels
(The Illustrated Manual of Desert Survival)
Alan H. Siebert
1974, 1976; 64 pp.
$3.50 postpaid from:
Brown Burro Press
P.O. Box 2863-D
Pasadena, CA 91105

Wheels spinning

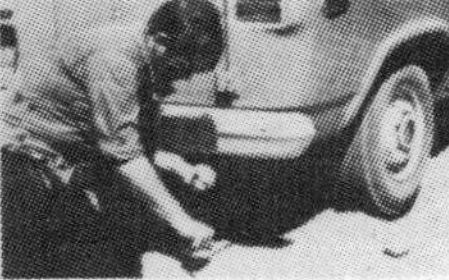

Jack and jack pads

Clearing the way

Sand mat in place

Reduce tire pressure

Ease it out

•

All by yourself and stuck?

1. Jack up vehicle, have someone watch the vehicle to warn you if the jack is slipping off the jack pad. You did put the jack pad under the jack? Be sure to block the unjacked wheels with handy stones.

2. Start digging a gentle ramp the car can back out of, or go forward, whichever way there is hard earth.

3. Place the sand mats, planks or carpet on the ramps in the direction of the run-out.

4. **Clear sand from front or rear of tires** in the direction you are heading.

5. Let the car down.

6. Let a little air out of **both front and rear tires.** Bring them down so they slightly bulge out on the sides; not flat, or even half flat, but almost flat (about 9 - 12 pounds).

7. Make sure the undercarriage is clear, If not, dig it out. You may have to jack it up again to do this but don't get too far under the vehicle with your body.

8. Get back in and **move out gently,** braking slightly to avoid a sudden burst of spinning that will end you where you started.

•

To Tell Direction from Barrel Cactus: The plane of the top of the plant leans to the Southwest. The blossoms are on the south side of cacti.

•

Equipment:

1. A good jack or two (be sure your jack fits your bumper). An axle jack may also come in handy here.

2. A strong tow chain 3/8" link or 12-foot polyester rope. (A nylon or polyester rope can spring free, etc.)

3. Jack pads (one per jack), 3/4" ply — 12" square.

4. Sand mats (can be old carpet with strong backing) or planks. These should be at least 4' long by 11" wide.

5. Good, short-handled shovel, a GI intrenching tool or a straight neck with the handle shortened (for digging under the tire).

6. Tire pump (spark plug type) for reinflating tires.

Use multiple signal systems when you think a search party may be near.

THE RISING SUN
NEIGHBORHOOD NEWSLETTER

Multiple choice continued from last spread

10. "I did stuff over and over again for a while but then I found out I could get a lot of the same effect by letting time pass — on Monday whether or not I wrote 12 drafts in between." So much of the process is subterranial, subcranial anyway that how much you suffer as the idea happens and grows may be related to how much you like to suffer rather than to helping the idea. Some of the 99% perspiration that genius is supposed to be made of may be attributed to a muscular inability to be patient. Gertrude Stein said, "It's hard to be a genius, you have to sit and not think so much."

continued on next spread

CARS - NOW

by J. Baldwin

IT'S TOO LATE. The U.S.A. has been settled and built up in a way that requires most people to have access to a car. Those who don't own a car use someone else's car anyway — a taxi, a piously hitchhiked trip, a borrowed machine, a rental. As you may have noticed, buying and running a car is a major item in the family budget. It has always been. In the 1950s, owning a car took proportionately more of the total family income than it does now, though that is hard to believe. Most people have not looked very carefully at what their car really costs them anyway. It works out to about 10 cents a mile for an old VW to maybe 35 cents a mile for a new $7000 model. More than you'd probably think.

There are ways of reducing the costs of automobiling. Start by driving less. I've managed to whip my mileage down to about 5000 a year from 30,000 or more. I've done this mostly by combining trips (planning a bit) and by using my bike a lot for minor errands. I don't live where there is mass transit from where I am to where I wish to go; a common failing of that transportation method. Reducing driving may raise your cost per mile because such things as insurance remain about the same, but *overall outlay* can be reduced dramatically and your energy conscience will feel better.

Another way to reduce costs is to car pool. If you are reasonably sure you will be keeping the same schedule for awhile, then a car pool can be good sense. A van is ideal for this despite the poor mileage because the passenger mileage per dollar and per gallon is still very good. Van pooling can have tax advantages. Some states have special express lanes for vans. Parking fees are cut too. A few areas have van jitneys you can call or subscribe to. In many cases, such a service will save you money as well as reducing national Arab troubles.

Obviously, a way to reduce car expenses is to drive a small economy model, but you should examine this option carefully. For instance, a friend of mine recently considered giving up her old Dodge because it got terrible gas mileage. A little calculator pounding showed that a new Honda Civic would pay itself off in gasoline saved compared to the Dodge in 200,000 miles over an 18 year period. The *interest* on the new Honda would more than pay for a complete overhaul of the Dodge. The payments, license, and insurance on the new "economy car" would add up to *doubling* the cost per mile she now thinks is excessive! As long as there is no rationing, the old reliable gas pig may be the best way to go if you already have one. And one must keep in mind that the smaller cars are not as safe as the bigger ones, though this will not always be so.

A compromise might be to buy a used pre-smog control compact car. (Smog controls tend to age awkwardly.) A '66 Dodge Dart would be a good choice. It is easy to justify a $1000 overhaul of such a car. In effect you recycle it, thus saving the energy that was required to manufacture it. Your miles per dollar would likely be as low as you can get. But what if an old hungry car isn't for you? What is a good car these days?

In my not particularly humble opinion, one of the front wheel drive cars would be a good choice. I'd go Honda as first pick. Their reputation is deservedly good. Rabbit, Fiesta, Subaru (now much improved and with 4 wheel drive in sedans too), Toyota Tercel, Le Car, Champ — all offer interior space rivaling that of much larger cars, trunk included. Front drive gives a number of important advantages: wind stability, good traction in snow and mud, larger interior in a given size car, and inherently safe handling. If you haven't taken a test drive in such a car, you may be surprised. General Motors' so-called "X" cars are of similar layout and offer similar advantages in a larger car, as does Saab. There will be more and more such cars until most are of this configuration. That's good. I would advise waiting a few years before buying an all-new model though. Many manufacturers (I was about to say reputable manufacturers but in the car business there aren't any) use the first batch they make as a field test. You don't want one of those, new or used. A good place to check the reputation of a make and model is in **Consumer Reports** magazine (p. 352). Their annual auto issue and their Annual Buying Guide (at your local library) show reliability for recent models. You can check the Buying Guide for past years to see about older ones. You local independent mechanic also knows.

Honda Civic Wagon. The 1980 Wagon has much more total cargo room than its predecessor. Stowage space behind the rear seat has been increased by almost five cubic feet. There's more passenger room. The rear doors are wider. And the tailgate is bigger for easier loading.

Citroen Visa is roomy, very economical (40-50 mpg), and lively, all with the typical Citroen big-car smooth ride. Not imported, alas.

A hatchback or wagon is the best way to go for most people, as these bodies have more room and versatility — critical in a smaller car. You'll want radial tires. They last longer, are safer, and give about three more miles per gallon because they roll easier. Rustproofing treatment that is sprayed into the doors and frame (*not* mere "undercoating") will make the machine last a lot longer if you live in salt country. "Polly glop coat" and other special wax jobs do not help; don't waste your money. Five speed transmissions will pay their way if you do a lot of highway work. City mice need not bother; in fact a five speed may actually worsen city mileage. Buy a light, bright, non-metallic color. White, for instance, reflects the sun and may make an air conditioner unnecessary even in hot climates. (Air conditioners commonly eat 3 to 5 miles per gallon.) My measurements show a white car to be about 35 degrees cooler than a black one under the same conditions. Lighter colors are generally easier to see and are thus safer. Stay away from silver and other metallic colors. Not only are they less visible, the metallic content of the paint tends to deteriorate faster thus encouraging cancer of the panel. If you need a roof rack, use a "Quik-N-Easy" (p. 447) or some other removable type — racks steal about one mile per gallon just sitting there with nothing on them. If a smaller car won't carry your stuff, perhaps it's time to think about what it is you are carrying. If you need a van once a year, rent it; you'll still come out ahead.

Keeping tires at the right pressure uses less fuel, is safer, and saves on tire wear. Gas station gauges are often very inaccurate. Having one of your own is best. Here's a good one: Accu-Gage, $12.49, manufactured by G.H. Meiser and Company. Check your local auto supply store.

What about a diesel? They don't cost any less to run than a gasoline car after you figure in the expensive fuel filter replacements, more frequent oil changes, larger battery and heavy-duty starter maintenance. Moreover, diesels DO need what amounts to a "tune-up" despite what the ads say. That's a tune-up that you cannot do yourself either. A careful reading of the ads will also reveal that no claim of longer lifespan for the diesel is made. Oh yes, they *imply* it, but don't claim it. Truck diesels do last longer but car diesels may or may not, depending on conditions. Olds, for instance, comes right out and says that their diesel lasts about the same as a gasoline engine. Diesels do get better fuel mileage, but the diesel price advantage is rapidly on the way out as demand increases. Most diesel cars must be driven 40,000 miles or so before the fuel saved pays for the premium price paid for the motor. If you keep your diesel till overhaul time, the added costs of working over the injector pump and other special parts will soon reduce any overall economies to approximately the gasoline level.

Then there is the matter of fuel availability, especially on Sunday night on the way back from Lake Tehatchapoocoo. And the fuel congeals in cold weather, making all sorts of witchcraft necessary to keep things humming, assuming you can get things started at all. What it adds up to is that a diesel only makes sense for someone who commutes in mild weather. That's not very many of us. Even the supposed smog reduction has turned out to be mostly myth. I'll stick to gasoline or some version of it.

What other ways are there for cutting auto expense? Maintain it! With the cost of repairs and new cars getting out of hand, good maintenance will pay more than ever. Change the oil when you should and oftener in winter or under other bad conditions. If your car has grease fittings, hit them often, even every day if you are driving on gravel or salty roads. Use good oil. Castrol, Quaker State, Pennzoil are good brands. Buy it by the case at K-Mart and change it yourself. It costs half as much as having the gas station do it, it gets done right, and doing it yourself takes less time too. Another advantage is that you can inspect your machine for incipient troubles like loose muffler clamps.

Try to avoid short trips, especially in cold weather. Running a car less than six to ten miles doesn't let it work up enough to evaporate the acid by-products of cold starts, contributing greatly to engine wear. Keep an eye on your tires. Check the pressure often and watch for uneven wear. When the battery wears out, replace it with one with caps. The "maintenance-free" models are a lot more trouble than the "old fashioned" types. I've had good luck with the Sears Die Hard (see **Sears Catalog**, p. 348) under very poor operating conditions. Generally speaking it pays to keep a car in good shape overall. Otherwise, it gets too discouraging and you become vulnerable to new car fever, an expensive malady. The whole idea is to avoid becoming the slave of the car.

Of course we are all slaves of the cars anyway with our society set up as it is. Unless there are some unexpected changes, we will soon be *forced* to do something about our car habit. Driving less, keeping an economical car longer, and flapping your legs a bit will reduce the need for your car, and consequently make the transition away from a car-wastrel existence easier. There will soon be no choice. ■

Cherries & Lemons

Good advice: get a used car. Good advice: which ones to consider, how to buy, and how to maintain. Take the low road, save and be smug. Enjoyable reading. —SB

Cherries & Lemons
(The Used Car Buyer's Handbook)
Joe Troise
1979; 175 pp.
$1.95 postpaid from:
Warner Books
75 Rockefeller Plaza
New York, NY 10019
or Whole Earth Household Store

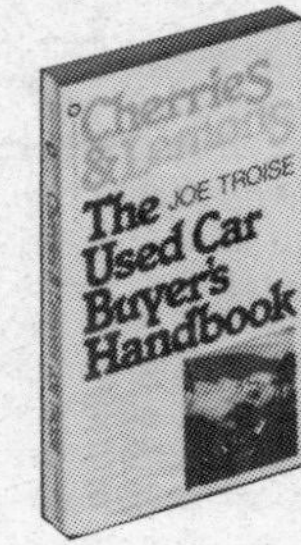

•

English cars can be very beautiful. English cars can be fun to drive. English cars can also be an incredible nuisance.

Regrettably, I cannot recommend *any* English auto for you. This includes the *Plymouth Cricket.*

•

Since the "Blue Book" is a bit hard to obtain, sold only by subscription to people who read them like a poker hand, you might consider buying a copy of **Edmund's Used Car Prices,** available at most local newstands or by writing to Edmund's Subscription Dept., USC-478, 515 Hempstead Tpk. West Hempstead, NY 11552. Ask for the current issue and send them $1.95 plus 50 cents ransom money for the U.S.P.S. This book is not used as often as the blue book in professional circles, but it can be useful protection against over-payment for your prospective car.

Ratings For General Motors Cars

EXCELLENT

Oldsmobile F-85/Cutlass	1964–1972
Buick Special/Skylark	1964–1969
Chevrolet, Full Size	1955–1956
Chevy II	1964–1968
Chevrolet Nova	1968–1971
Chevrolet Camero	1967–1971
Chevelle	All Years to 1971
Malibu	All Years to 1971
Corvette	All Years to 1967

GOOD

Chevrolet, Full Size	All Years (*)
Chevelle	1972 on up
Chevy Malibu	1972 on up
Corvette	1968 on up

American Built Cherries Hall Of Fame

Dodge Dart	1963-1969
Plymouth Valiant	1963-1969
Chevrolet Chevy II	1964-1967
Chevrolet, Full Size	1955-1956
Ford Falcon	1964-1967
Ford Mustang	1964-1966
Ford Fairlane	1965-1967
Checker	1959-1964

Explosafe gas can

A gasoline can that can't explode no matter what, even in in a crash or fire. If you are antzy about carring a full gas can in your car or boat or even having such a potential bomb in your garage, this thing should make you feel better. —J. Baldwin

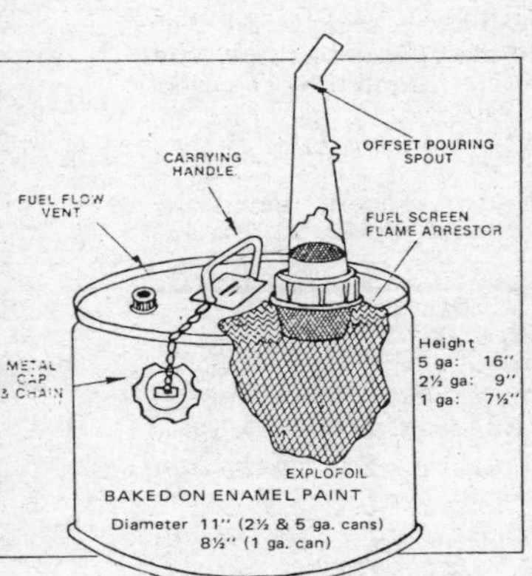

Explosafe gas can
5 gallon can
$42 postpaid
2½ gallon can
$34 postpaid
1 gallon can
$27 postpaid
all from:
Jens Jurgen Wegscheider
Travel Information Bureau
14 Mulberry Drive
Huntington, NY 11743

Superwinch

A winch that can pull a 3500 lb. Jeep up a 30% hill and yet weighs less than 20 lbs and is breadloaf size. Egad! But here they are. One model uses electric drill for power. Most use 12 volts. —J. Baldwin

Superwinch
$129 and up

Information
free from:
Superwinch, Inc.
Connecticut Route 52
at Exit 95
Putnam, CT 06260
or check your local auto supply dealer.

Once A Week

CHECK THE FOLLOWING, ADD AS NECESSARY:

Engine Oil
Automatic Transmission Fluid
Radiator Coolant Level
Battery Water
Brake Fluid
Power Steering Fluid
Tire Pressure
Look for water and oil leaks on or under engine and transmission.

It only takes 10 to 15 minutes to do the above checks, and doing them regularly could save you an inconvenient, expensive breakdown.

Drive It Till It Drops

By the same author as **Cherries and Lemons,** *here's the on-going saving advice. Once you really give up on showing off, you save* thousands *of dollars. And frapped cars got soul. Even more enjoyable reading.* —SB

Drive It Till It Drops
(How to Keep Your Car Running Forever)
Joe Troise
1980; 117 pp.
$3.95 postpaid from:
And Books
The Distributors
702 South Michigan
South Bend, IN 46618
or Whole Earth Household Store

•

The Stillman Zero-Maintenance Theory

The idea is this: first, you shop around for ugly, neglected, socially abhorrent used cars in the $200 - $500 range. When you find one, you don't waste any money paying a mechanic to check it out (remember, this is the "Zero" theory). Instead, you start it up, maybe five or six times. This proves that it starts cold. Then you drive it a bit, to see if it accelerates and stops without too much hassle. If it spits and sputters, or smokes and clatters, or if the brake pedal plunges to the floor, that's it. REJECT. If the car passes the start and stop test, take it out on the highway speed. Drive along for 5 miles or so, then go back to your starting point, lift the hood and look around for oil leaks, water gushing out of something, or horrible noises. If everything seems ok, then start it up again while it's still hot. If it starts, then buy the thing. The Stillman theory supposes that any car capable of doing these simple tasks without blowing up will probably run for quite a while.

Now for the important part. As long as you own this car, you don't do *anything* to it. ZERO. Just check the water and oil and other fluids, and add a little here and there. When the door handle comes off, it stays off. No heater? Leave it. If a safety item is involved, and it doesn't cost much, well, ok, then do it. But only out of dire necessity. No tune-ups, no oil changes, no nothin! You keep this up until something awful happens. Then you sell the car to someone who might want to repair it (somebody always does). Next step? Buy another clunker.

The Stillman theory actually works quite well, because there are lots of good running cars out there that just happen to look like disasters. If a car like this will run for just one year, with zero maintenance, you will have paid very little on a per-mile basis for your transportation. Remember, one does not even consider looks, gas mileage or size when using the Stillman theory. The whole idea is to achieve a low cost-per-mile figure by keeping your initial investment and maintenance costs way down.

•

The Rabbit Versus The Hog, After 3 Years

	1980 Rabbit	1968 Pontiac
Original Down Payment	$ 1,400.00	$ 1,350.00
Total Bank Payments	6,876.00	—
Total Insurance	1,500.00	675.00
Total Fuel	1,228.00	3,340.00
Maintenance and Repair	450.00	675.00
Total Expenses	11,454.00	6,040.00
Less Resale of Car	-5,000.00	-500.00
Total Out-of-Pocket Expense:	**$ 6,454.00**	**$ 5,540.00**

Why Trade It In?

As car prices become increasingly insane, a book encouraging you to keep the old one going is more than welcome. The authors are correct in assuming that the need for a new car is most often psychological, and a lot of this modest book is devoted to opening your eyes to the subtle forces making you unhappy with your present wheels. Under most conditions, it is always cheaper by far to fix the old unreliable than to get a new one (which may also be equally unreliable). It's overall the most sensible book I've seen on buying and keeping a car, though experienced mechanics will already be well aware of most of the necessarily pretty general information given. For nonmechanics and the easily manipulated, this book could be a boon. I can vouch for their economic analysis. My car is 12 years old with 270,000 miles on her and is still not too bad. I have no intention of ever selling it; even with a major overhaul coming up it will still be the cheapest transportation I can get. My maintenance has closely followed what they suggest. Nuff said. —J. Baldwin

Why Trade It In?
George and Suzanne Fremon
1976; 247 pp.
$5.95 postpaid from:
Liberty Publishing Co.
50 Scott Adam Road
Cockeysville, MD 21030
or Whole Earth Household Store

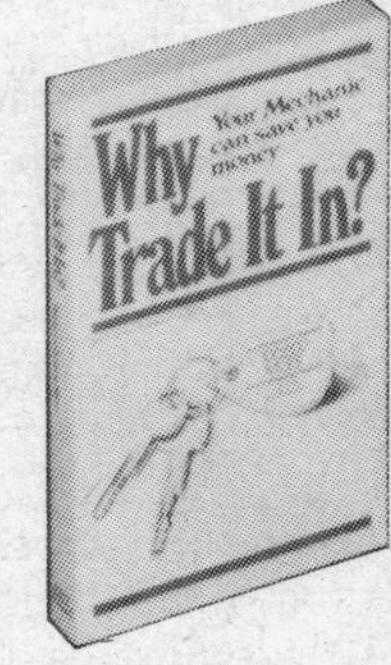

•

Another myth the notebook may dispel is the myth that repairs are eating you up, and so perhaps you should get a new car. The notebook may show that you have actually spent only $200 over the past year for repairs, and that the remainder of the $500 in garage bills actually went for tires, tune-ups, oil changes, and other things that a newer car would require just as frequently.

The Book of Expert Driving

Techniques for safe and skillful driving by a real pro, written in a style that happily is not reminiscent of most driving instructors. Wish I'd had this to read when I was sixteen. —J. Baldwin

The Book of Expert Driving
E.D. Fales, Jr.
1970, 1979; 192 pp.
$4.95 postpaid from:
Hawthorn Press
E.P. Dutton and Co.
Two Park Avenue
New York, NY 10016
or Whole Earth Household Store

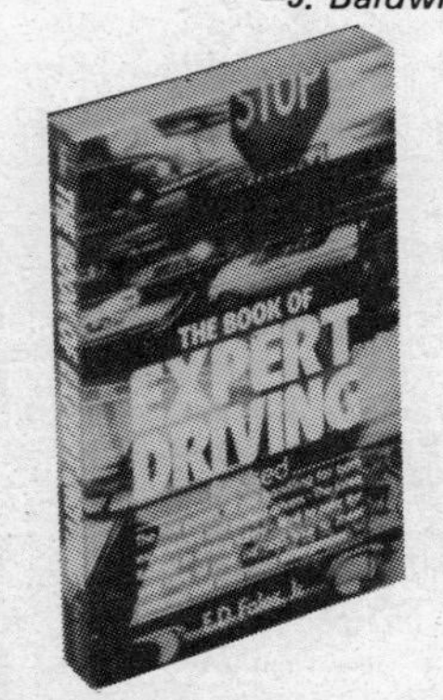

Better Visibility for the Driver behind You

WRONG: When you drive close to the center line, the driver behind you cannot see if someone stops ahead.

RIGHT: When someone ahead of you slows to turn or prepares to stop, pull slightly to the right so the driver behind you can see his brake light.

Gas Mileage Guide

From the Environmental Protection Agency comes a FREE mileage rating of all new cars. —SB

Gas Mileage Guide
(For New Car Buyers)
U.S. Environmental Protection Agency
1980; 35 pp.
free from:
Fuel Economy
Consumer Information Center
Pueblo, CO 81009

SMALL STATION WAGONS (Continued)

Manufacturer	Fuel Economy		Vehicle Description			
Manufacturer Car Line	Estimated MPG	Average Annual Fuel Costs	Engine Description CID/Cyl Type	Transmission	Fuel System	Body Type Interior Space Passenger Trunk or Cargo (Cu Ft)
FORD						
PINTO WAGON	21	$643	140(2.3L)/4 (FFS)	M4	2	2DR-78/31
	21	$643	140(2.3L)/4 (FFS)	A3	2	
HONDA						
CIVIC WAGON	25	$540	91(1500CC)/4	S2	3	4DR-84/27
	29	$466	91(1500CC)/4	M5	3	
LINCOLN-MERCURY						
BOBCAT	21	$643	140(2.3L)/4 (FFS)	M4	2	2DR-78/31
WAGON	21	$643	140(2.3L)/4 (FFS)	A3	2	

THE RISING SUN
NEIGHBORHOOD NEWSLETTER

Multiple choice continued from last spread

11. Art and I had this conversation in which the idea was thought of or occured that ideas need to live in neighborhoods close together so they can bump into other ideas and make new ideas and not in the suburbs with lawns in between them.

continued on next spread

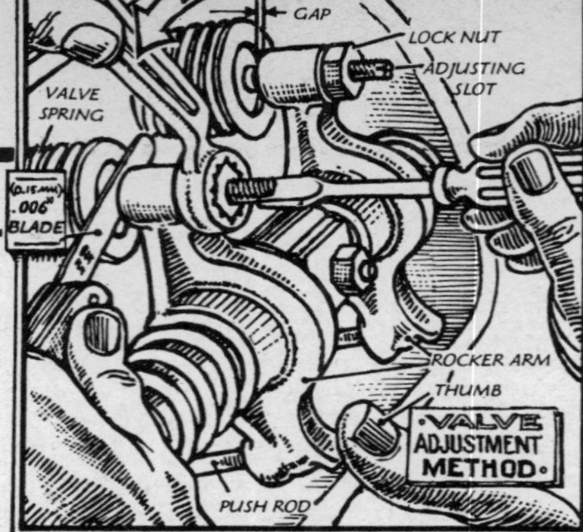

Basic Auto Repair Manual

This manual is intended to be an introduction to automobile mechanics and the more fearsome professional shop manuals. It contains about all the amateur mechanic needs to know in order to diagnose, repair, and maintain domestic cars. It is assumed that the mechanic has no experience at all. All major assemblies are well illustrated and explained both in principle and specifically, with note made of quirks found in certain models. There are chapters or remarks on tools needed and how to use them them, working safely, junk yard technique, on-the-road repairs, and general money saving. There is a very good chapter on logical trouble shooting. "If this is wrong, try this first, this second, etc." Included is most likely diagnosis and prescription. Common repairs like "putting in new points" are covered neatly. Major jobs are presented so that the amateur mechanic can get most of the work done before calling in expensive expert help. It is clearly stated when to give up, and what not to attempt without expertise. They even tell you how much you will save, and how long it will take. This is a great book for that person trying to keep the oldie going and/or who wants to understand cars in general. Well worth the money.

—J. Baldwin

Basic Auto Repair Manual
Spence Murray, Editor
1977; 384 pp.
8th Edition
$12.95 postpaid from:
Peterson Publishing Company
Attn: Book Fulfillment
6725 Sunset Boulevard
Los Angeles, CA 90028

To disassemble this Ford starter, loosen and remove the brush cover band, starter drive plunger lever cover and the cork gasket under it.
↓

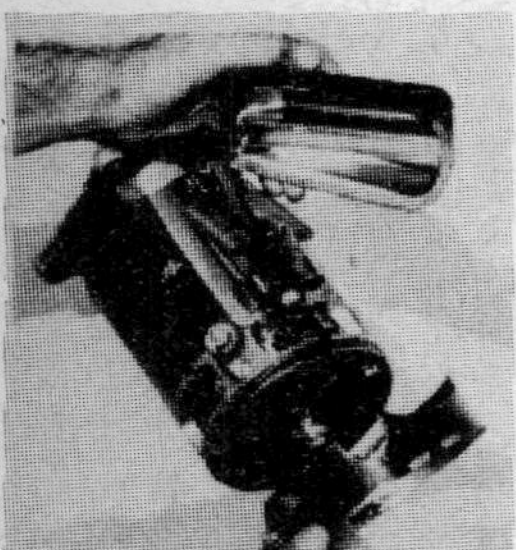

BASIC BEGINNER'S TOOLS

1. Combination box- and open-end wrenches, from ⅜-in. through 1 in. in increments of 1/16-in.
2. ⅜-in.-drive socket set, with ratchet and breaker bar
3. ⅜-in-drive spark plug socket and three extensions—a short one, a long one and a flex-drive
4. Four screwdrivers—one short and one long of both the Phillips type and the regular, flat-tip type
5. Pair of slip-joint pliers
6. Pair of needle-nose pliers
7. Adjustable wrench (Crescent type)
8. Roll of mechanic's wire (cheap and very handy at times)
9. Diagonal cutting pliers
10. Small stock of sundries, such as electrical tape, WD-40 oil, engine degreaser, white-grease lube and spray-can paints
11. Ball-peen hammer
12. Two jack stands
13. Scissors jack (better than bumper jack, but not as expensive as a hydraulic jack)

How to Keep Your Volkswagen Alive

In 1968 John Muir, a 50-year-old dropout NASA engineer who'd settled into a mixed career of science fiction writing and car repair in the wide open spaces between Mexico and Taos, was forced by the pressures of the moment — his own wedding — into writing instructions on how to do a valve job for a friend instead of helping out in person as he usually did. Although the novice mechanic caught her hair in the fan belt as the completed engine was being tested (the book now advises a stocking cap) the operation as a whole was a success. The idea that some kind of book might help out a lot of people who had the desire to do it themselves, but lacked the experience, soon followed.

Publishers disagreed, saying there was no market for such a book, so Muir sold his house to finance the publishing of 2500 copies, and a new outfit in Berkeley called Book-people did the distribution. His book was reviewed in another just-born publication, **The Whole Earth Catalog.** *That was December '69. Since then sales of the Idiot Book, as it instantly became known, have reached 1.3 million, including the German and Spanish translations. A 360-page 21st printing now covers all air-cooled VWs through '79.*

How does a simple, wire-bound book about fixing old cars manage to generate a steady stream of letters over the years that read ". . . your book changed my life."? The Idiot Book did two things well. First it taught a specific skill, one that had been reserved for "experts" who believed in the mystification of their knowledge. But more importantly it opened a door in the mind as those who took the risk were introduced to the rewards of manual skills. When they found they could fix their own car they began to go beyond other previous limitations and take charge of their own lives. After the car was fixed they took on the plumbing, the washing machine, and finally built their own houses. Which is not to say that the Idiot Book is God's Word delivered, but reader feedback from 20 printings has reduced the blemishes to almost nil, and only a small-minded nit-picker could still debate such arcanums as whether clogged heat risers really do produce burned rods.

Howard Palmer, who runs Rveeco (VW engine rebuilders in Berkeley) and knows so much about VWs that Muir went there to learn the fine points, brings up other matters that are familiar to students of the marque, but not emphasized in the book. The Achilles' heel of any aircooled engine is overheating, and as VW began to boost hp their cooling systems failed to keep pace. For those who seldom leave the city there's no problem, but long cruises in the summer can produce bad news in the engine compartment, either the immediate grief of a thrown rod or the slow debilitation that's produced by a toasted valve.

Engine sealing is a good place to start in avoiding those catastrophes, for that little bugger is sucking in 1300 cubic feet of air per minute, and if the rubber engine compartment seal is shot, like most of them are, it'll pull up air from down below that's just passed over the muffler and heater boxes and comes blazing in at 450°. Recycled heat. Assuming you have an oil temp gauge and are aware of the problem, a basic response is to drive slower, but who's got the self control when there's still 200 miles between you and El Paso and the heat is frying your brain?

More effective than self control is an outside oil cooler, but emphasize outside, for if it's inside the engine compartment it's just more recycled heat, you want those BTUs outside. Same with leaks in the fan shrouding and the tin, the tighter the seal the more heat stays off the engine.

So if you can keep it cool, and follow the book's advice on regular oil changes and tune-ups, your VW engine can last indefinitely. Remember Muir's slogan: "Come to kindly terms with your Ass for it bears you."

—Dick Fugett

How to Keep Your Volkswagen Alive
(A Manual of Step by Step Procedures for the Compleat Idiot)
John Muir
1969, 1979; 364 pp.
$10 postpaid from:
John Muir Publications
P.O. Box 613
Santa Fe, NM 87501
or Whole Earth Household Store

•

In the VW engine, the connecting rods splash about in the oil sump and this oils the cylinder walls. While a car sits all night the oil film between the pistons and cylinder walls comes loose due to the action of gravity. In addition to this you always start the engine with a shot of raw gas, either by pumping the accelerator pedal or by choke action and raw gas has a tendency to wash the oil off the cylinder walls. OK? All the super warm-up equipment that VW hangs on their engines doesn't change this one whit. I warm my engine up for the two or three minutes it takes me to roll a cigarette, light it and get it drawing well. I have disconnected my automatic choke so I don't have that worry, but I do pump the accelerator a little to get some gas down there to start the cold engine. In those one-half to three minutes, depending on the weather (the colder, the longer), the rods are doing their thing in getting the oil on the cylinder walls, all the way around; the raw gas that I pumped in has been used, and there is enough of a film of oil protecting my cylinder walls from being excessively worn by the passage of the rings. Now when I put a load on the engine, it is the oil that carries that load, not the metal. The morning warm-up is the nicest thing you can possibly do for your engine.

Poor Richard's Rabbit Book

Well, bugs and buses come, and someday they may go, but there's still 11 million of them on the road, which is 10 million more than there are Rabbits. But the Rabbits are multiplying like mad whereas the "real" VWs are no longer sold in the U.S. There are bugs being built in Mexico and Brazil (has anyone tried bringing one in?) but for most folks who want economical German machinery the Rabbit is the obvious answer.

Muir was 60 now, and a folk hero to boot, but there was this damned new VW coming out, an all new water-cooled engine stuck up in front, black boxes and devious smog devices everywhere, even a diesel option. A new book was called for, a great challenge, but what a drag to start from scratch again. However, the flow evidently aimed at making the Rabbit book. Richard Sealey, a British racing mechanic whom Muir had met on a trip to Europe, wound up in Santa Fe, but as the Rabbit project got under way in 1977 Muir died (attentively, at home, with friends).

John Muir Publications bought the funkiest, rankest Rabbit in town and Sealey crawled underneath to get acquainted. Three years and many Rabbits later he emerged, a Perfected Master, and work on the book began. So now there's another big floppy volume out, 400 pages worth of **Poor Richard's Rabbit Book**, *alias the new Idiot Book.*

Precise, step by step instructions guide us in our struggle with Technological Challenge, along with the wit, philosophical commentary and great illustrations we've come to expect from Muir publications. It's a brand new book and with shop rates in the $25 - $30 an hour range it can't help but sell. For starters the JMP people have a note from a Wisconsin VW dealer they'd shipped copies to for resale. He wanted a second shipment fast since the first batch had been bought out by his own mechanics.

So if you're moving forward (?) into the high tech era of autos, you won't find a better friend. A good number of folks who first met the underside of a VW with Muir's guidance went on, like myself, to careers as mechanics. It will probably happen again. Happy wrenching to one and all.

—Dick Fugett

Poor Richard's Rabbit Book
(How to Keep Your Volkswagen Alive; Being a Manual of Step-by-Step Procedures for the Compleat Idiot)
Richard Sealey
1980; 412 pp.
$13.50 postpaid from:
John Muir Publications
P.O. Box 613
Santa Fe, NM 87501
or Whole Earth Household Store

Volkswagen Official Service Manuals

Resign yourself to the fact that no single manual ever written will cover everything you want to know; it's the same as with cookbooks. But if you've finished the Idiot Book and you still have fire in your eye then check out the **VW Service Manual**, *printed by Bentley. Unlike Muir the book assumes you know a little about what you're doing, and there are plenty of good photos and diagrams to help out. Their dry, technical style makes us long for Muir's wit, but the great color wiring diagrams almost let us forgive them. Good sections on body and frame, front end work and transaxles. They print numerous manuals to cover models from 1966 through the Rabbits, including Super Beetle, Beetle and Karmann Ghia 1970-79; Beetle and Karmann Ghia 1966-1969; Super Beetle, Beetle and Karmann Ghia 1970-1974; Fastback and Squareback 1968-1973; Rabbit/Scirocco Gasoline Models 1975-1979; Station Wagon/Bus 1968-1979; Rabbit Diesel 1977-1980; and Dasher 1974-1979.*

—Dick Fugett

Volkswagen Official Service Manual
$16.50 each from:
Robert Bentley, Inc.
872 Massachusetts Ave.
Cambridge, MA 02139
or your VW dealer

Fixing Cars

Chapter One is entitled: "Women and Cars," and in a book with this one's title, don't expect to find many jokes about sisters running the Buick through the back end of Hubby's garage. This is serious revolutionary mechanics, though still a primer. There is a good rap on how Detroit has messed over the world, and why to go on ahead and try to keep the old lunkers running; there are nice simple illustrations, good tool advice, and nice political auto cartoons by quite a few folks, including Dan O'Neill. Taken as a primer, it is new and good. Taken as an automotive repair book, it still suffers from the attitude that there are jobs (wheel alignment, for instance) which are better left to the experts, whereas I believe that the people might benefit from the realization that the baling wire repairs of depression fame were not so much expressions of Okie idiosyncracy as they were the peoples' way of dealing with an industry based on the myth of technician and tool worship. The basics are here. Decide for yourself how far you can run with them.

—J.D. Smith

Fixing Cars
(A Peoples Primer)
Rick Greenspan, et al.
San Francisco Institute of Automotive Ecology
1974; 191 pp.

$5.50 postpaid from:
Bookpeople
2940 Seventh Street
Berkeley, CA 94710
or Whole Earth Household Store

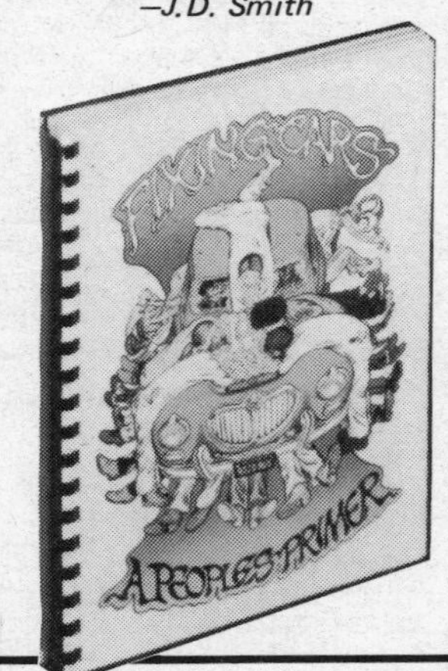

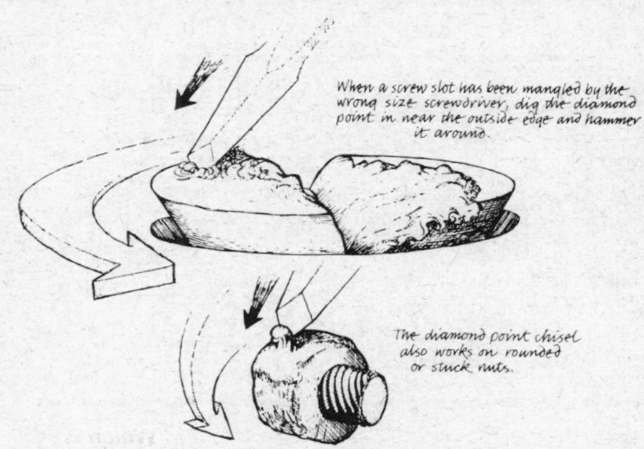

When a screw slot has been mangled by the wrong size screwdriver, dig the diamond point in near the outside edge and hammer it around.

The diamond point chisel also works on rounded or stuck nuts.

Basic Bodywork and Painting

Just about everything you can expect to get from a book on this subject is presented here clearly. But it should be obvious that bodywork is largely a learned skill, and you'll learn it from messing up some metal. If you know nothing about the tools and how to use them, this book will get you started and is well worth the money. Might be useful for those into metal sculpture too.

—J. Baldwin

Basic Bodywork and Painting
Jay Storer, Editor
1973, 1980; 192 pp.
4th Edition

$4.95 postpaid from:
Petersen Publishing Co.
Attn: Book Fulfillment
6725 Sunset Boulevard
Los Angeles, CA 90028
or Whole Earth Household Store

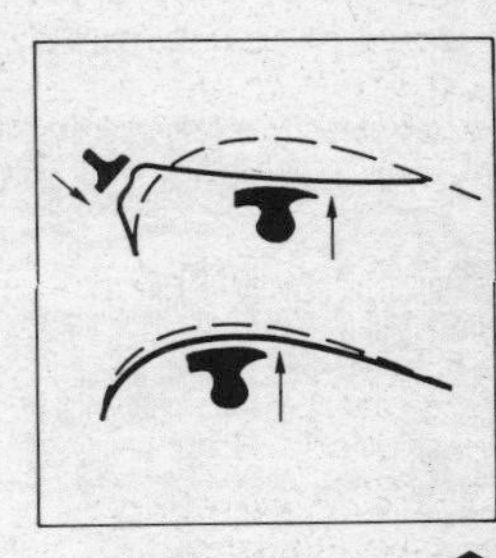

When using the hammer-off technique, the hammer blow should always be on the high metal adjacent to the low spot, never anywhere else! Learning to "see" with the hand palm is part of metal work experience, and feeling to locate the low and high parts of the damage becomes a natural reaction.

Hemmings Motor News

A 450-page magazine full of ads for Ford and non-Ford cars and parts and literature and misc. Lots of pictures make the whole thing worth while for the person with a casual interest in old cars. (Almost all the cars advertised are vintage or antique, but not all of them.) It's monthly and cheap.

—David O. Weaver

Hemmings Motor News
(World's Largest Antique, Vintage and Special-Interest Auto Marketplace)

$9.75 /year (12 issues) from:
Hemmings Motor News
P.O. Box 100
Bennington, VT 05201

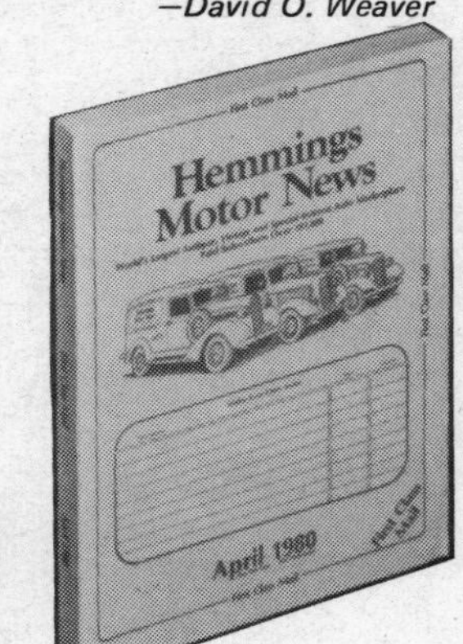

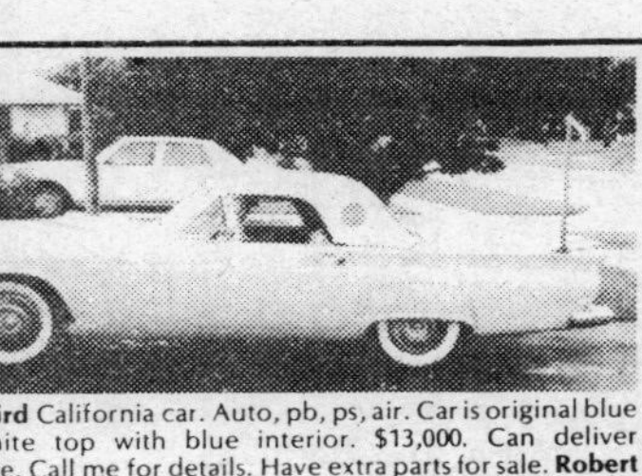

Bird California car. Auto, pb, ps, air. Car is original blue hite top with blue interior. $13,000. Can deliver re. Call me for details. Have extra parts for sale. **Robert** , 301 SE 13 Ct, Pompano Beach, Fla 33060, PH: 305-942-

1930 Model A phaeton. This unique four door phaeton has been in dry storage for the past thirty years and has been in the family for the past twenty-five years. The odometer shows the original 32,000 miles. The body has no rust or dents; this is a rare opportunity to acquire a very nice, clean original phaeton. Price $13,500. **John O'Donnell,** 615 Raymond St, Westfield, NJ 07090, PH: 201-233-5082.

The Vintage Auto Almanac

Vendors and fixers of specific brands of cars are here listed together with the necessary specialized parts manufacturers, car clubs, including international ones, salvage yards with vintage parts, museums, books — every source of information on keeping that oldie on the road or sitting proud for show (shame!) If you're into old cars, you need this.

—J. Baldwin

The Vintage Auto Almanac
David Brownell, Editor
1979; 198 pp.
3rd Edition

$4.95 postpaid from:
The Vintage Auto Almanac
P.O. Box 945
Bennington, VT 05201

PORSCHE

Best Deal 8171 Monroe St. Stanton, Cal. 90680 714/995-0081	**parts** **accessories**

Porsche - 356, 911, 912, 914, 924.

see also: Section 5, salvage yards

Jerry L. Brewster Rt. 2 Bastrop, La. 71220 318/281-2371 Monday-Saturday	**parts** **literature** **car dealer**

see also: Corvette

Steve Harris 2708 S. Arcadian Shores Rd. Ontario, Cal. 91761 714/984-1000	**locator service** **restoration** **coordinator**

see also: Volkswagen

International Mercantile PO Box 3178 Long Beach, Cal. 90803 213/434-9728	**rubber parts** **trim parts**

The Super Catalog of Car Parts and Accessories

Where do you find a water pump for a 1935 Mack truck? An owner's manual for an Allard? Titanium front end parts for a jeep? This catalog of catalogs has the answers. More than 1000 firms, clubs and factories listed with complete description of services and products. Mostly information that is not well known, gathered from a very wide range of sources. Uncommon quality and rarity are stressed, making this a real service for people still enchanted by cars.

—J. Baldwin

The Super Catalog of Car Parts and Accessories
John Hirsch
1974, 1978; 310 pp.

$4.95 postpaid from:
Workman Publishing Company, Inc.
231 East 51st Street
New York, NY 10022

Exhaust gas analyzer from Auto Marine Instruments Corporation.

Auto Marine Instruments Corporation, 6101 Grosse Point Road, Niles, Illinois 60648. Tune-up instruments for the professional or backyard mechanic include power timing lights, tach/dwell meters, alternator/generator/regulator testers, compression and vacuum testers, exhaust gas analyzers, and complete tune-up kits. Free literature.

Edgewood National Off-road Vehicle Parts

Those of you who actually need a 4-wheel drive know that the stock off-road vehicle leaves a lot to be desired. Here's where you find the hardware to beef it up (and adorn it, too).

—J. Baldwin

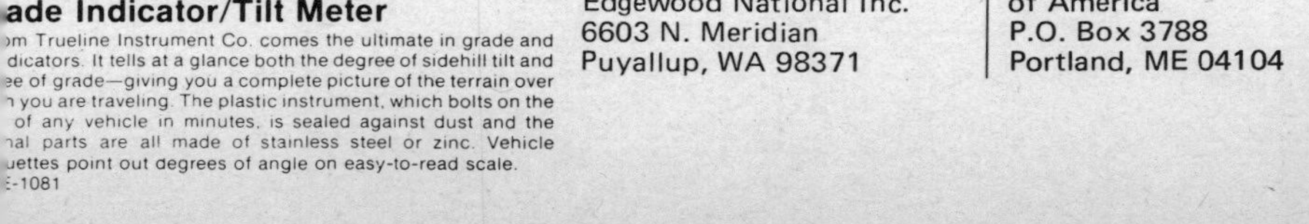

ade Indicator/Tilt Meter

om Trueline Instrument Co. comes the ultimate in grade and dicators. It tells at a glance both the degree of sidehill tilt and ee of grade—giving you a complete picture of the terrain over n you are traveling. The plastic instrument, which bolts on the of any vehicle in minutes, is sealed against dust and the nal parts are all made of stainless steel or zinc. Vehicle uettes point out degrees of angle on easy-to-read scale. E-1081

Edgewood National, Inc.
Catalog and price list

$2 from:
Edgewood National Inc.
6603 N. Meridian
Puyallup, WA 98371

The Carriage Journal

The quarterly magazine of the Carriage Association of America, Inc. Each issue fifty pages containing illustrated articles on horse-drawn carriages, their construction and makers, collections, restoration, harness, etc.

—Dave Patty

The Carriage Journal
Thomas Ryder, Editor

$25/year (4 issues, includes membership) from:
H.K. Sowles, Jr.
Carriage Association of America
P.O. Box 3788
Portland, ME 04104

THE RISING SUN
NEIGHBORHOOD NEWSLETTER

Multiple choice continued from last spread

12. The army guys and the political guys in Germany successfully kept the physicists who were trying to build an A bomb from talking to each other. The army guys in the United States tried to keep the nuclear physicists from talking to each other but they didn't succeed.

continued on next spread

AMERICA is emerging from a period when it couldn't see its bicycles for all the cars. The perception of the bicycle primarily as a child's toy still prevails. Automobiles are certainly more convenient than bicycles, but they need oil, while the bicycle remains the most efficient human-powered form of transportation there is. Bicycles belong to the future.

In the last 15 years, multi-geared balloon-tired bicycles — called clunkers — were hybridized and perfected for off-road use. Our reviewers Gary Fisher and Charles Kelly were part of that process, and as such have designed, raced, written about, crashed, built and repaired clunkers and lightweight bicycles. Their latest endeavor is Mountain Bikes (p. 411). —Richard Nilsen

Takara's Pro-Tour 990 was equipped with the HKK Ultra-6 chain and Sun Tour Ultra-6 freewheel.

Bicycling

Bicycling *evolved from a regional newsletter begun in 1962 to an early 1970s bike boom spinoff whose editorial content closely reflected advertising revenues, to a mature magazine which can be taken seriously by adults. Recently purchased by Robert Rodale, whose Rodale Press also publishes* **Organic Gardening** *(p. 94) and* **Prevention** *(p. 322),* **Bicycling** *covers most aspects of cycling, with the exception of BMX. Articles range from stream-of-consciousness touring accounts to incredibly detailed technical dissertations. Currently the largest circulation of any cycling monthly.*
—Gary Fisher and Charles Kelly

Meet the cyclists who traveled up to a thousand miles to get where the four-wheelers and mountain goats wouldn't go.

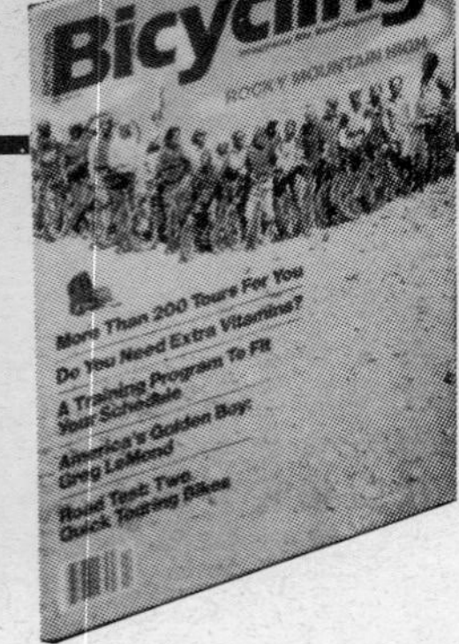

Bicycling
(Incorporating Bike World Magazine)
James C. McCullagh, Editor
$10 /year (9 issues)
from:
Rodale Press
33 East Minor
Emmaus, PA 18049

•

I have been well satisfied with 27 x 1¼-inch Michelin Sports, not only on dirt and gravel roads but in such places as Mexico where even the paved roads are rougher than what we are used to in the United States. The Sports are very sturdy with a wide footprint on the road and sidewalls which withstand much more punishment than the normal skinwall tire. Because they are larger, a greater percentage of the tube is outside the rim, making them surprisingly resilient even at their recommended pressure of 70 pounds. These are also good tires for tourists carrying heavy loads on paved roads when you want maximum stability, reliability and comfort.

League of American Wheelmen

In 1898, this cyclist's organization had over 100,000 members and lobbied for the nation's first paved roads, off of which they were promptly driven by the automobile. Today they have local clubs across the country, and are active advocates for the protection and support of the bicycle as supplemental safe transportation. They're also the best people to contact about joining or organizing a tour. Don't be put off by the name — lots of female peddlers in their ranks. —Andrew Fluegelman

American Wheelmen
(Monthly Publication of the League of American Wheelmen)
Walter K. Ezell, Editor
$15 /year (12 issues; includes membership)
from:
League of American Wheelmen
P.O. Box 988
Baltimore, MD 21203

Cycletouring

Cycletouring *is the official newsletter of the Cyclists' Touring Club, a British organization. Nowhere in the magazine is it suggested that anyone actually races a bicycle. The English cycle tourist is different from his American counterpart; the main reason may be that the English did not recently discover touring. With a century-old tradition in the sport their viewpoint is more conservative and this magazine reflects that. Although the style is stuffy,* **Cycletouring** *represents an evolved type of cyclist, and contains delightful nuggets. Member feedback equipment reviews are informative, and tour accounts cover all parts of the world.*
—Gary Fisher and Charles Kelly

Cycletouring
H. John Way, Editor
$7.20 (or £3)/year (6 issues) from:
Cyclists' Touring Club
Cotterell House
69 Meadrow
Godalming, Surrey
England GU6 3HS

City Cyclist

I've been an urban bicycle commuter on and off for the past eight years, but never realized til now that what I'd always thought were solitary hassles — just part of the rules of the game — were actually shared by my fellow commuters. Some examples: bike lanes that dissolve into traffic, wintry weather, lack of good places to chain bicycles to. Newsletters like **City Cyclist** *really help, particularly when they're backed by a local make-bicycling-better-here group. The group behind this one is Transportation Alternatives in New York, a city that bursts into life on a bicycle (all cities do, actually). If there's no newsletter like this one in your city, maybe you should send for a few copies as a model to use in starting your own.* —Art Kleiner

City Cyclist
$10/year (occasional, subscription includes free classified ads)
from:
Transportation Alternatives
133 West 72nd Street
No. 301
New York, NY 10023

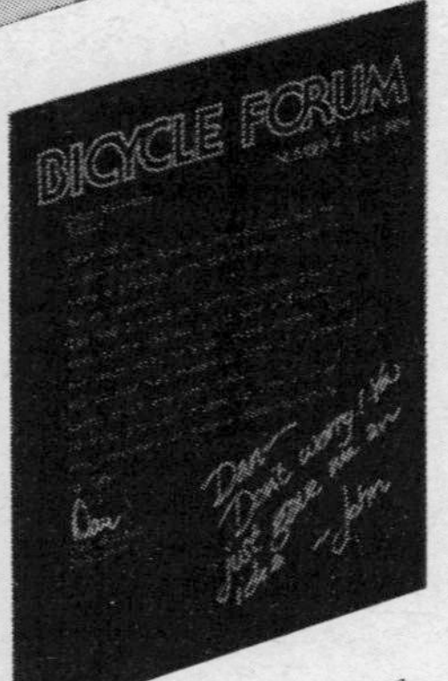

Bicycle Forum

Now under new editorship, this quarterly is intended to help bridge the gap between cyclists and government officials. The first issue is an improvement on the previous mode, and promises to deliver the goods. It has the least hype and the most realistic look at the existing scene; that in itself is uncommon. And it is most refreshing to see harassed officials treated not as enemies or cretins, but rather as citizens with a responsibility for seeing to it that the best thing gets done. It's a true forum too. Those of you trying to increase bike use should get involved here where things ae being debated without rancor.
—J. Baldwin

Bicycle Forum
John Williams, Editor
$10 /year (4 issues)
from:
Bicycle Forum
317 Beverly
Missoula, MT 59801

•

There are four things bearing on facilities which bicyclists need; access to roads, road engineering as if bicycles mattered, parking and storage, and interface with public transport.

Cycling U.S.A.

All American bicycle racers will find **Cycling U.S.A.** *essential for keeping up with results and upcoming events; they can hardly avoid it, however, since a subscription is included in the cost of a racing license.*

The magazine provides considerable treatment of the politics of bike racing, which tend to be convoluted, in addition to thorough coverage of events; there is also some technical and physiological information.
—Gary Fisher and Charles Kelly

Cycling U.S.A.
Robert Carpenter, Editor
$10 /year (12 issues)
from:
United States Cycling Federation
1750 East Boulder
Colorado Springs, CO 80909

Bicycle Motocross Action and BMX Plus!

Bicycle Motocross, or BMX, began with a lot of little kids terrorizing vacant lots on their Stingrays and is now a major force in the bicycle industry, the success story of the decade. Racing bikes have evolved from $5 beaters to $500 custom machines, and the carryover to the other bikes made for children has vastly improved the quality of small bikes.

The racing circuit attracts millions of riders and spectators to what amounts to the Little League of Motocross, with top pros in their teens making as much as $20,000 a year riding events that usually last less than a minute. In identifying with their idols of this sport, and riding better machines, children are more aware of the necessity for riding skills and better equipped to survive in a world of traffic.

These magazines are similar; in fact one is a spinoff of the other, and for that reason they are included in the same review. While readers tend to be restricted to teenage males, these publications cover BMX in all its dimensions and include plenty of technical information as well as race reports. Many photos.

BMX is making a lot of money these days, and manufacturers' interests can sometimes be seen lurking between the lines, but for anyone who follows Bicycle Motocross, **Action** *and* **Plus!** *are required reading.*
—Gary Fisher and Charles Kelly

Bicycle Motocross Action
Bob Osborn, Editor
$14.50 /year (12 issues)
from:
Wizard Publications
P.O. Box 5277
Torrance, CA 90510

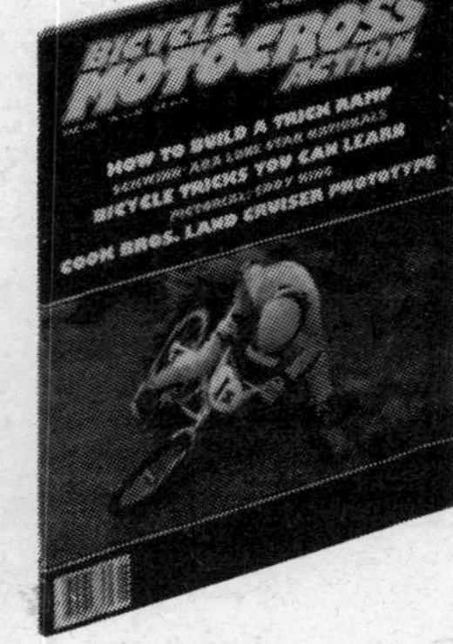

BMX Plus!
$12 /year (12 issues)
from:
BMX Plus!
2458 West Lomita Blvd.
Lomita, CA 90717

Bookin' and cookin' down a trail in the woods. The Quad-Angle can handle ANYTHING you've got the hair to try.
—BMX Action

The Bicycle
(A Commuting Alternative)
Frederick L. Wolfe
1979; 154 pp.

$7.95 postpaid from:
Signpost Books
8912 192nd Street SW
Edmonds, WA 98020
or Whole Earth Household Store

The Bicycle: A Commuting Alternative

This book is actually a short general cycling manual with special emphasis on subjects applicable to commuters, such as big city bike parking, mass transit, and riding at night. One aspect we liked was the assumption that the cyclist is riding for reasons other than sport and will therefore wish to ride under adverse conditions.

—*Gary Fisher and Charles Kelly*

Panic Stops: Bicycling in heavy traffic or in developed areas may require that you stop quickly to avoid another vehicle, a dog, child, toy, or pedestrian. If this maneuver is not handled correctly, it can cause the bicyclist to become airborne resulting in possible injury. To stop quickly, apply both brakes evenly and firmly and sit as far back and as low on the bicycle saddle as possible. Never apply the front brake before applying the rear brake. Practice this panic stop technique in preparation for the actual situation.

•

The economic benefits of bicycle commuting will vary for each individual rider. You save automobile costs including fuel, oil, maintenance, tires, parking, tolls, insurance, and licensing fees. It has been calculated that the cost of operating a bicycle is approximately 1.5 to 2 cents per mile compared to the 20 or more cents per mile for operating an automobile. Using these figures, I currently operate my bicycle at a cost of $52 per year (10 mile roundtrip per day) instead of the $520 it would cost me to drive my car every day to work. This cost does not include annual parking expenses. How much would you save by bicycling to work or school each year?

Bicycle commuting equipment.

1 Bell
2 Saddle Cover
3 License
4 Rear Reflector
5 Pump
6 Pack
7 Toe Clips and Straps
8 Helmet
9 Parka
10 Chapstick
11 Note Pad and Pen
12 Down Vest
13 First-Aid Kit
14 City Street Map
15 Identification
16 Tool Kit
18 Sweat Band
19 Goggles
20 Leg Light
21 Extra Light Batteries
22 Shoe Overboots
23 Safety Vest
24 Rain Suit
25 Lock
26 Gloves

Bickerton Bicycle

This most portable of the portable bikes looked good enough to buy, so we did, and we're glad. Actual city use shows that it really can solve the problems of theft (wad it up and take it in with you) and portability. On public transportation you stuff it into the canvas bag supplied and the conductor will never know it's there. It's light enough at 18 lbs. to stow in the overhead luggage racks in buses! In your car, just flip it into the trunk. Yes, even in a Honda.

The folding-unfolding ritual, which takes about 1 minute with practice, is a rather fiddly and undignified procedure. The riding, however, is beautiful. The little guy is unusually resilient as it eels its way over bumps, and the super-high (3-speed) gearing lets you fly down the road with the effortless ease of a good 10-speed. Mr. Bickerton's background as an aircraft designer shows in the all-aluminum construction which seems sturdy and clever though "not for apes" as he says. Nice job. Mine has been in almost daily use for 4 years now with no real problems.

—*J. Baldwin*

Bickerton Portable Bicycle
$425 (approx.)

Information **free** from:
American Outdoors Co.
282 Old Pickard Road
Concord, MA 01742

Handleman's
Route 22 at
Reservoir Road
White Plains, NY 10603

Bickerton Cycles Ltd.
1314 NW Glisan
Portland, OR 97209

Bickerton Bicycles
Vulcan Ltd.
Moorsom Street
Birmingham, England
B6 4NX

The Schwinn Klunker - 5

It appears that the 26-inch balloon-tired, multi-geared bicycle — commonly known as a clunker or cruiser — is well on its way to repeating the pattern established ten years ago by the 20-inch motocross bikes for kids: a product that begins selling first in California and within two years has caught on nation-wide. (I hope all of you out there realize this is due more to corporate marketing strategies than to any inherent grooviness of Californians.) Schwinn took a back seat on the motocross fad, but definitely has the jump in the clunkers.

In September, 1978, Schwinn took their good old heavy-frame messenger boy bike (which you can see being ridden maniacally in the heart of any large American city) and added a Shimano Positron II 5-speed derailleur, a drum brake in the rear, and side-pull brakes in the front. They christened it the Klunker-5 and expected to sell 3,000 of them in the remaining months of 1978. Those bikes were gone in a week and a half, and Schwinn has been behind ever since.

So the answer to the question "Where can I buy a clunker bike?" turns out to be easy: at your local Schwinn bike shop. The K-5 is selling now for $205, which is a good price.

The weakest part of the design is the front forks, which are not tubular, and can break from heavy riding. This is something Schwinn can easily remedy, and hopefully they will. I have also made a few modifications to the K-5 I have recently purchased, to wit: a 20-inch twelve-gauge seat post (needed by anyone over 6' 0"), a quick-release seat post clamp, Sure Stop pads for the front brakes, and Oakley hand grips (not pictured).

In the meantime, custom-made cruiser bikes costing as much as $1,000 continue to be made here in northern California. The extra money definitely puts you in another league — lightweight, incredibly strong, and parts that will last a lifetime. For most people interested in off-road bike travel, the K-5 is a good place to start.

—*Richard Nilsen*

I got me a clunker and am restored to the True Path. This is a genuine American work bike, suitable for real town (down the library steps) and real country (mountain fire-trails, primrose paths). Using a lightweight 10-speed for such duties is like chopping wood with a violin. —*SB*

The Schwinn Klunker-5
$205 (approx.)

Manufactured by:
Schwinn Bicycles
Chicago, IL

Check your local bike shop.

Golden Bear MK2 bike locking cable

Every little bit helps. This cable is certainly cuttable, but it takes longer because the tiny wires in it are more likely to squash than fracture in the jaws of the enemy bolt-cutter. Moreover, it has to be cut twice, and it's no more vulnerable than the monster chains seen these days.

—*J. Baldwin*
[Suggested by Tom Smerling]

Golden Bear MK2
$8.95 postpaid from:
T.E.R. Corporation
2950 De La Vina,
Suite 2
Santa Barbara, CA 93105

Or check your local bike shop.

•

When we first started using this cable we were concerned that the medium-sized diameter (3/8") would reduce its effectiveness as a deterrent. It doesn't look very intimidating. But of the 1200 cables we've sold over the last two years, matched with a Master 17 lock, we have had reports of no more than half-a-dozen successful thefts. . . . That's about all you can ask from a cable.

—Tom Smerling
Freewheel Bike Coop
Minneapolis, Minnesota

Richard Nilsen in clunker country

Bicycle Security

- *There is no way to make an exposed bicycle positively theft-proof.*
- *Always lock your bike in a place where attempts at lock-busting will be obvious to passers-by.*
- *A lightweight cable or chain will foil only a jump-on-and-pedal thief.*
- *An un-locked, un-attended bicycle will disappear.*

—*Andrew Fluegelman*

THE RISING SUN
NEIGHBORHOOD NEWSLETTER

Multiple choice continued from last spread

13. Sometimes you have to build the altar in order that the fire from heaven may come down someplace near us. The way to catch a unicorn is to sit very still and to have not worn yourself out doing other things. Catching unicorns has to be it for you, whether you catch one or not. You'll have to like sitting as much as you like catching since you'll be spending so much more time at it.

—Many of the choices were thought of or occurred in conversations Kathleen and I have had about thinking of things and having things think of you.

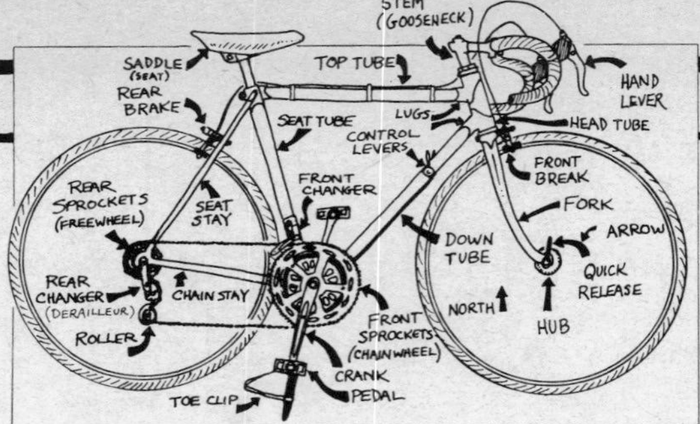

Anybody's Bike Book

Ah. We have here the John Muir of bicycles. Complete introduction, cheerful information on bike use and maintenance. Good advice, reasonable price; that's nice. Cuthbertson on four wheels: see **Anybody's Skateboard Book**, *p. 456.*

—SB

[Suggested by Karen Herold]

Anybody's Bike Book
Tom Cuthbertson
1971, 1979; 200 pp.
$4.95 postpaid from:
Ten Speed Press
Box 7123
Berkeley, CA 94707
or Whole Earth Household Store

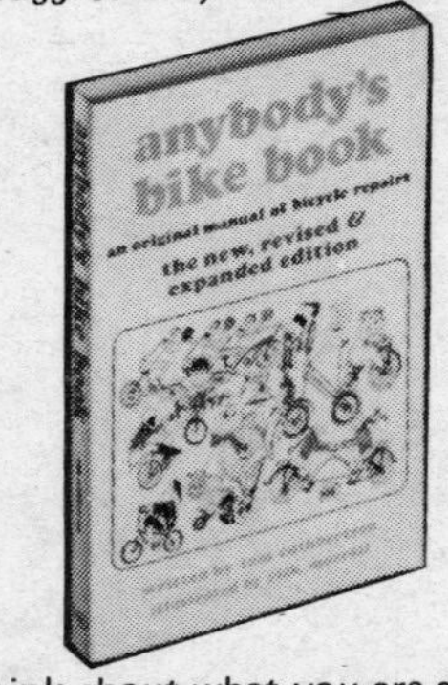

•

Before you buy a bicycle, think about what you are going to use it for. Then look at used bikes as well as new ones that will fit your need. A well-cared-for bike is one of this limited planet's greatest re-cycles!

If you are going to ride over plowed fields, or on sand flats at low tide, or if you plan to take only short rides to the corner store, get a sturdy coaster-brake model, a balloon-tire bomber. Price: two to ten hours work at laborer's wages.

If you plan leisurely shopping jaunts, weekend excursions up to 30 miles, or commuting for short distances, all on reasonably even terrain, get a 3 speed. A good light (25 to 35 lbs.) 3 speed will do just what most of us want and need it to. Price: eight to twenty-five hours work at laborer's wages.

If you plan to cover long distances over varied terrain, and if you are willing to accommodate yourself to a specialized riding position for the sake of vast improvement in cycling speed and responsiveness, get a 10 speed. Price: fifteen to two hundred hours work at laborer's wages, and more if you want to blow it!

•

Find a bike shop that *cares*. They will get you hard-to-find parts, give you advice, and help you when this book can't. There *are* bike shops that care. They aren't necessarily the big and flashy ones — remember, it's the people that count. When you find a good shop, do all your business there. Tell people who want new bikes to shop there. It's the least you can do in exchange for the small-parts hunting that a good shop will do for you.

Cultivate a fine ear so you can hear any little complaint your bike makes, like grindy bearings, or kerchunking chain, or a slight clunking of a loose crank. You don't have to talk to your bike when you ride it — just learn to listen to it affectionately.

Keep all bearings adjusted properly. Your bicycle has between 150 and 200 ball bearings. To keep them all rolling smoothly, you have to learn to adjust the *cups* and *cones* in which they run. Adjustment involves screwing the cone and cup together until they are snug on the ball bearings, then unscrewing the cup and cone slightly. The bearing should revolve smoothly, without any "play" or looseness between the cup and cone.

The Custom Bicycle

When a store-bought bicycle isn't as good as you are, then it's time to start saving your money for a custom job. Matching a bicycle exactly to your particular requirements has become a fine art, and riding a machine made especially for you can be one of life's rare moments of rightness. But what are "your requirements"? Can they be met? This book is a good place to find out. As you might expect, the authors review materials, design details, components, and gearing. Less expected, and most welcome, they personally interview a number of the world's better builders. There's also a highly detailed chapter on fitting the beast to your physique. Illustrations abound. I'm sure that some of their information is controversial, but so what? This book combined with your experience should enable you to order what you need. (Note that this is not an instruction book on how to build frames.)

—J. Baldwin

The Custom Bicycle
(Buying, Setting Up, and Riding the Quality Bicycle)
Michael J. Kolin and Denise M. de la Rosa
1979; 274 pp.
$8.95 postpaid from:
Rodale Books
33 East Minor Street
Emmaus, PA 18049
or Whole Earth Household Store

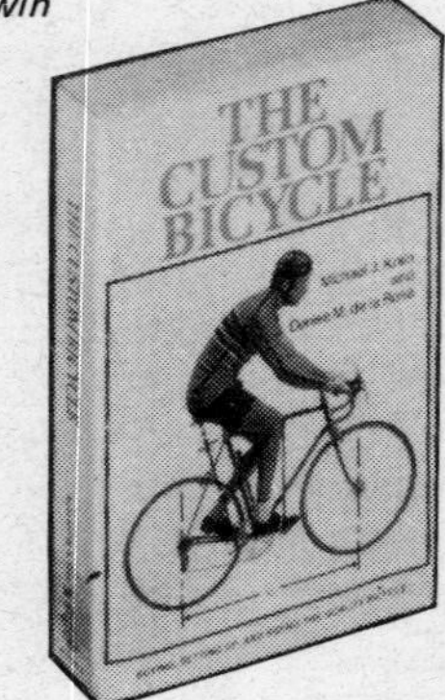

•

Rule of thumb: if the gear you have selected is too high, your legs will fatigue before your lungs. If the selected gear is too low, your lungs will fatigue first.

DeLong's Guide to Bicycles and Bicycling

Fred DeLong is a veteran of American biking. A professional engineer, he has been technical editor of **Bicycling** *magazine and* **The American Bicyclist and Motorcyclist**, *a trade magazine. For years he has been sent products to test, and his book is marked by his progressive views. Many offbeat and unusual parts are discussed along with traditional ones. The approach is general, aimed at the beginning and recreational cyclist, with a generous treatment of the actual art and skill of cycling as well as a good section on repairs. Racing is mentioned only in passing. Profusely illustrated.*

—Gary Fisher and Charles Kelly

DeLong's Guide to Bicycles and Bicycling
(The Art and Science)
Fred DeLong
1974, 1978; 278 pp.
$9.95 postpaid from:
Chilton Book Company
Sales Service Department
Chilton Way
Radnor, PA 19089
or Whole Earth Household Store

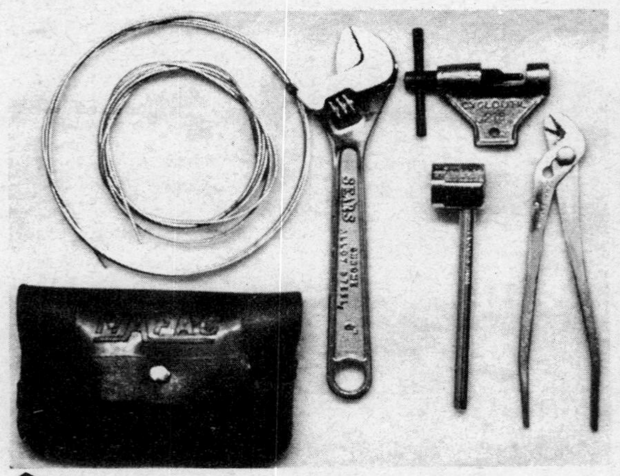

↑ **A portable tool set that has proved ample in tens of thousands of miles bicycle touring is shown. It consists of a 6-inch, thin Crescent wrench, a Mafac 49 tool kit, a chain tool, a small pliers, a 1/8-inch screwdriver, a cotterless crank socket wrench, plus a spare chain link and a spare rear brake and a spare derailleur cable. Every one of these tools has been used, including the freewheel remover, often in remote locations far from shops. There have been almost no occasions where this tool set has been inadequate.**

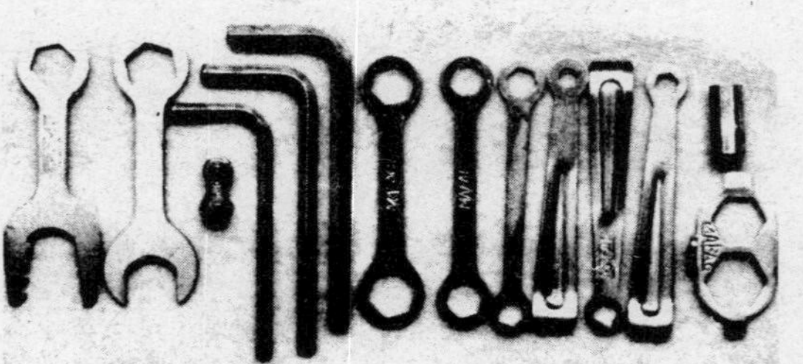

→ **Contents of Mafac kit (less tire patches): wheel-bearing cone wrench, pedal wrench, spare chain link, metric allen wrenches (for stem, derailleur, and seat bolt), three metric box wrenches, three tire irons (with smaller metric box wrench openings), socket wrench (for brake lever nut), spoke wrench, a screwdriver, and a seat bolt tool.**

Effective Cycling

John Forester is one of the most politically involved cyclists in the country, currently president of the League of American Wheelmen and former president of the California Association of Bicycle Organizations, also the author of numerous engineering tracts on the dynamics of bicycle and auto traffic. His book, **Effective Cycling** *belongs on every fanatic's bookshelf, but be warned, it isn't light reading.*

The book is arranged as a teaching text for a 30-hour course; the advantages of it are the thorough treatment of the subject, from traffic tips to first aid to major repairs. The disadvantage is the extremely dry presentation, reminiscent of government, and the cheap printing with an absence of good illustrations.

—Gary Fisher and Charles Kelly

Effective Cycling
John Forester
1975, 1979; 215 pp.
3rd Edition
$10 postpaid from:
Custom Cycle Fitments
726 Madrone Avenue
Sunnyvale, CA 94086

2-2-7

NORMAL TURN
WHEEL TRACK
BODY TRACK
SHARPEST TURN
EASY ENTRY
INSTANT TURN
WHEEL TRACK
BODY TRACK
SHARP TURN ALL WAY ROUND
STEERING LEFT FORCES MAXIMUM RIGHT LEAN IMMEDIATELY

↑ **INSTANT TURNS. The spiral turn has one disadvantage — it takes too long to prepare. Suppose a car coming towards you at an intersection turns left on a collision course with you. You want to whip into that cross street to get away. Here's how. You turn your front wheel left — the wrong way, towards the car. By doing this you've got a good lean started, a tenth of a second or so, turn your front wheel right and you'll find yourself in a tight right turn. To make a right turn you must lean right, so to hurry up the leaning process you made your bike track to the left a few inches. Then you are leaning over properly and can steer a right turn.**

Sutherland's Handbook for Bicycle Mechanics

The first and only book that comes to grips with the fact that international bicycle parts are woefully unintercbangeable. A complete lexicon of very technical specifications (what parts can be made to fit and what looks like it might work but won't) — all presented in an elegantly clear format. This handbook is obviously of no use to you unless you own a half-dozen different bicycles, but you should bring it to the attention of your local bike shop, because with it they'll be able to give you vastly better service. Also a valuable reference book to carry in a "sag wagon" supporting a group of cross-country tourists.

—Andrew Fluegelman

Sutherland's Handbook for Bicycle Mechanics
Howard Sutherland
1974, 1980; 205 pp.
3rd Edition
$27.50 postpaid from:
Sutherland Bicycle Shop Aids
P.O. Box 9061
Berkeley, CA 94709
or Whole Earth Household Store

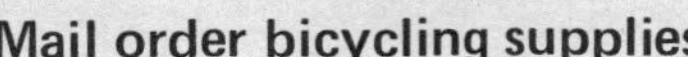

Mail order bicycling supplies

William Allen, Bookseller, P.O. Box 315, Englewood, CO 80151. *A complete assortment of bicycle books, including all current and many old and out of print titles; also books for collectors. Catalog free.*

Bikecology, P.O. Box 66-909, Dept. B-6, Los Angeles, CA 90066. *A big, slick catalog full of high quality racing and touring supplies, also a separate BMX catalog. Catalog and technical information, $1.*

Bicycle Bell — from Germany. Hard-to-find small bell. Only 2 inches in diameter with a sharp, clear ring. More civilized than yelling at pedestrians and other bike riders. In many European countries a bicycle bell is required by law. Weight 1½ oz. $3.50 postpaid

—Touring Cyclist

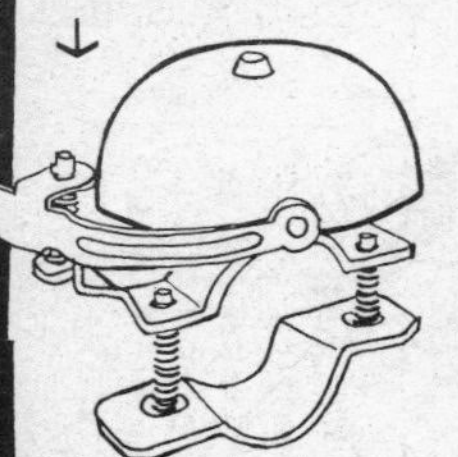

HALT!

Just the thing to curb dogs. Works up to 10 feet away Clips on belt or HB bag. Large Size, AR-H $2.40

CANNOT BE SHIPPED OUT OF THE COUNTRY

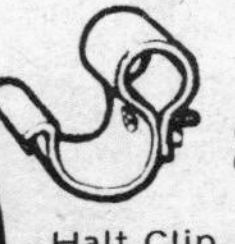

Halt Clip, of lightweight plastic attaches to handlebars. Holds Halt secure within quick and easy reach. AR-C $1.40

BMX Tires & Tubes, 1837 Sting Ray 20 x 2.125" tire.

1837

Bike Warehouse, 215 Main Street, New Middletown, OH 44442. *Racing, touring, camping supplies, books, ski-touring equipment. Catalog $ .50.*

Byron's Bicycle Shop, Inc., 299 Glenwood-Lansing Road, Glenwood, IL 60425. *Strictly BMX supplies, parts and clothing. Catalog $1.*

Cove Bike Shop, No. 1 Blackfield Drive, Tiburon, CA 94920. *Off-road bicycle supplies, including framesets and complete bikes. Catalog $2.*

Cyclo-pedia, 121 South Main Street, Mount Pleasant, MI 48858. *European racing and touring supplies. Send $3 for catalog, which includes many useful tips and product information.*

Flying Dutchman Ltd., P.O. Box 20352, Denver, CO 80220. *Racing and touring bicycles and parts, clothing, accessories and tools. Catalog $2.*

Handbook of Cycl-ology, 2735 Hennepin Avenue South, Minneapolis, MN 55408. *Racing, touring and utility bicycle parts and accessories. Very complete. Catalog $4.*

Hutch BMX Racing, 731 Swan Cove Lane, Pasadena, MD 21122. *Strictly BMX supplies, framesets and bikes. Catalog $ .25.*

International Pro Bikeshop, Inc., 3733 Wilmington Pike, Kettering, OH 45429. *Intermediate to high quality racing and touring supplies; framesets and used parts. Catalog $2.*

Jones Cycle Wear, 24 Brown Avenue, Lunenburg, MA 01462. *Racing and touring clothing. Catalog $.25*

Kirtland Tour Pak, P.O. Box 4059, Boulder, CO 80306. *Touring racks and bags. Catalog free.*

No. 90-3 Competition Saddle. A new Ideale saddle. Hand treated according to the recommendations of Daniel Rebour. Needs no "breaking-in." The suppling is done for you in the factory before the leather top is fitted to the frame and is the equivalent of many miles of riding without the chance of the top becoming misshapen. Size: 10½ x 5-3/4". Wt. 26 oz. $30.50

—Cyclo-pedia

Lickton's Cycle City, 310 Lake Street, Oak Park, IL 60302. *Intermediate to high quality racing, touring and BMX parts and clothing. Catalog $1.*

Mountain Bikes, P.O. Box 405, Fairfax, CA 94930. *Intermediate to high quality off-road bicycles and parts. Catalog $ .25.*

Palo Alto Bicycles, Inc., P.O. Box 1276, Palo Alto, CA 94301. *High quality bicycles, parts and clothing. Catalog free.*

Quicksilver Racing Supply, P.O. Box 28348, Washington, D.C. 20005. *Specialists in high quality Italian racing products. Price list free.*

Redwood Cycling apparel, 1593 G Street, Arcata, CA 95521. *High quality cycling clothing. Custom fits available. Catalog $.25.*

The Third Hand, 1259 Siskiyou Boulevard, Ashland, OR 97520. *Bicycle tools and books. Catalog free.*

Touring Cyclist's Shop, P.O. Box 4009, 2639 Spruce Street, Boulder, CO 80306. *Bicycle touring and camping supplies, tools, clothing and books. Catalog $ .35.* —Gary Fisher and Charles Kelly

1714

Sew Up Tires

1714 Clement Griffo Cycle Cross butyl tube 340 g

1764 Schwinn Super Record 27 x 1-1/8" 300 g. 90 lb. $9.50.

1687 Continental Cotton Latex Rib Tread 415 g
1705 Hutchinson Cross TR cotton, butyl tube heavy Diamond tread 380g
1752 Clement No. 3 Track silk, latex tube, smooth 175 g

—Lickton's Cycle City

Park Third Hand. An inexpensive contraption made of spring steel that effectively holds caliper brake pads against the rim which takes the tension off the brake cable which frees both your hands to play with that same cable. It is one of the primary repair tools of all bicycle mechanics. We feel that Park makes the best of the available inexpensive third hands on the market. Item No: 2-BT1, $2.25.

—The Third Hand

The overall size of this envelope-type briefcase is 15½" x 11½". The main compartment (15½ x 11½) and the outside pocket (15½ x 7) are both closed with hooded zippers — hooded to keep out rain. An aluminum stiffener is firmly riveted in its own pocket. This pocket is left open to give you an extra filing compartment.

The Touring Cyclist Brand Briefcase is made of rugged 11.5 oz. Cordura with Super K-Kote water-repellent coating. Weight: 18 oz. Color: Navy blue with handle of Red webbing. $25 postpaid —Touring Cyclist

1764

The Nomad Handlebar Pack

Here's a quality front bag designed for the tourist/commuter who requires a stable, functional, and versatile handlebar pack. It employs the famous Eclipse suspension system and offers these features:

Constructed of durable 5 oz. nylon pack cloth with waterproof coating.

Has two compartments: a large roomy main compartment, with the same volume as our Pro bag, and a large nylon net front compartment, handy for stowing those little items you need to get at quickly.

1687

Nomad Handlebar Pack 3683. Weight: 15.20 oz (430.92 gr.) Volume: 450 cu. in. (7375.5 cu. cm.) $24

—Lickton's Cycle City

King of the Road

As you might expect, bike people will find this lavishly illustrated history most interesting. But for me the interest comes from the presentation of the bike as a social phenomenon as well as a piece of hardware. Bikes started out being very controversial, and there has been a noticeable class-struggle aspect to them since their invention. This is one of those histories that you can really learn something from as you compare past to present. The book is also an unusually clear look at a developing technology and its impact on the society that must deal with it. There's a good chapter on tricycles too. Trikes are sort of looked down upon these days, but at one time, it was the other way around when they were transport for nobility and bikes were for the proletariat. With trikes beginning a comeback as urban transportation, a look at the past is more than mere idle curiosity. Books like this and **Bicycling Science** *are already getting a lot of people into making their own. Good.* —J. Baldwin

King of the Road
Andrew Ritchie
1975; 192 pp.

$7.95 postpaid from:
Ten Speed Press
900 Modoc Street
Berkeley, CA 94707

A West London club member on the road in the early eighteen eighties.

A copy of Kirkpatrick Macmillan's velocipede made in about 1860 by Thomas McCall, a joiner and wheelwright of Kilmarnock, who was born and brought up near where Macmillan lived. He sold the velocipedes he made for £7 each. (Note horse head! — JB)

Bicycling Science

The human being used as an engine may not be the way you look at a bicycle, but that's how nature looks at it. This exceptional book analyzes, compares and judges the measurable aspects of people-power and the bicycle being ridden. Did you know that a loosely flapping shirt can add 30% to your air drag?; that the radical designs featuring a rider low down with a backrest aren't as efficient as traditional frames?; that until a grade is 15% you use less energy riding up than pushing the bike? The authors are engineers and have performed exhaustive tests to back their graphs and conclusions. Happily, they haven't hidden the findings in a mass of jargon. The chapter on bicycle physics will get most readers to a useful level of understanding. The chapter on people-powered devices other than bicycles is fascinating; there's even a lawnmower!

1705

Sharp editing and careful research have made this book important to those bicyclists who wish to know what they are talking about. It's sure to stir controversy, and equally sure to result in better bicycles. —J. Baldwin

1752

Bicycling Science
(Ergonomics and Mechanics)
Frank Rowland Whitt & David Gordon Wilson
1974; 247 pp.

$5.95 postpaid from:
MIT Press
28 Carleton Street
Cambridge, MA 02142
or Whole Earth Household Store

Racing-bicycle ergometer

THE RISING SUN
NEIGHBORHOOD NEWSLETTER

"Well, thank God for small favors. There isn't a quote from *The Procedure Handbook for Arc Welding.*"

—Evelyn

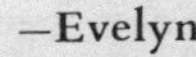

Bike Tripping

Tom Cuthbertson's companion volume to his maintenance/repair book (p. 410) is a joyful, unpretentious, and highly informative introduction to the proper and efficient use of a bike for transportation/recreation. Good pointers on cycling technique and a crucial life-and-limb-saving chapter de-mystifies the dynamics of the frame, written by master frame-builder Al Eisentraut.

—Andrew Fluegelman

Bike Tripping
Tom Cuthbertson
1972; 172 pp.

$3.95 postpaid from:
Ten Speed Press
Box 4310
Berkeley, CA 94704
or Whole Earth
Household Store

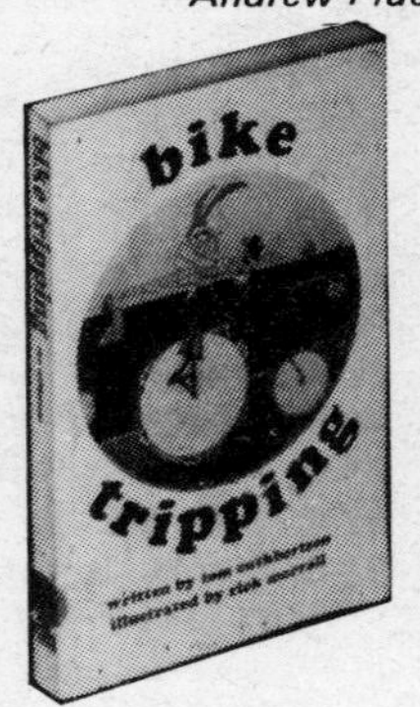

•

A great alternative to a 20 pound bike with a 20 pound lock and chain is a 40 pound "trashmo" special. Rick the artist bought a used one speed for me at a flea market for five bucks. Works like a charm. And nobody ever tries to steal it. For short around-town trips, commuting and shopping, or for school, the trashmo is the only way to go.

If you use a fancy bike for those trips, you have to get a huge lock and chain, or get ulcers, or both. Why not have two bikes — a trashmo for local errands, and a super-bike for joy rides and longer trips. Just make sure you tend to the maintenance needs of your lovable old trashmo.

When passing a whole row of parked cars, look into the cars for drivers who might open their doors or pull out suddenly in front of you.

Winning Bicycle Racing

The major author is a man who, if not the ultimate authority, is close enough for you and me. Jack Simes is a third generation bicycle racer, silver medalist in World Championships, multiple National Champion, professional, and successful coach of the U.S. National team.

Training advice is comparatively brief; emphasis is on tactics, technique, psychology, and the use and maintenance of the machine. Although the style is folksy and casual, every paragraph contains real information based on experience rather than theory.

—Gary Fisher and Charles Kelly

Winning Bicycle Racing
Jack Simes and
Barbara George
1976; 195 pp.

$5.95 postpaid from:
Contemporary Books
180 North Michigan Ave.
Chicago, IL 60601
or Whole Earth
Household Store

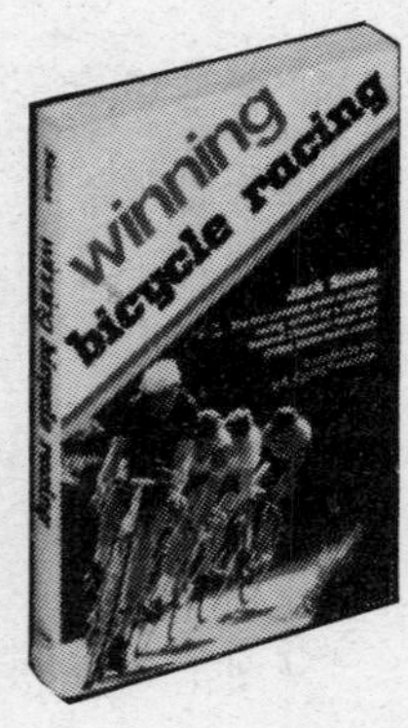

•

The way to prevent the other riders from knowing when you are suffering is to keep your mouth closed and look alert. Inside, your guts may be falling out, but you look fresh as a daisy.

Sometimes, on the other hand, it's beneficial to appear tired. You can pull a lot on your bars and wrestle with your bike. Breathe hard and try to look red in the face. People will notice this. They are watching and their eyes are flicking around all the time.

→

The sport of cyclocross provides valuable training in bike handling because of the difficult courses and tricky surface conditions.

Bike Touring

***Bike Touring** offers solid, detailed technical advice on touring, from the most elementary aspects (riding a bike) to the more complex (building wheels). Bridge gives a thorough treatment to purchase and mechanical details, including maintenance both at home and on the road. Other subjects treated include training, clothing, camping gear, accessories, and safety.*

—Gary Fisher and Charles Kelly

Bike Touring
(The Sierra Club Guide to Outings on Wheels)
Raymond Bridge
1979; 456 pp.

$6.95 postpaid from:
Sierra Club Books
Box 3886
Rincon Annex
San Francisco, CA 94119
or Whole Earth
Household Store

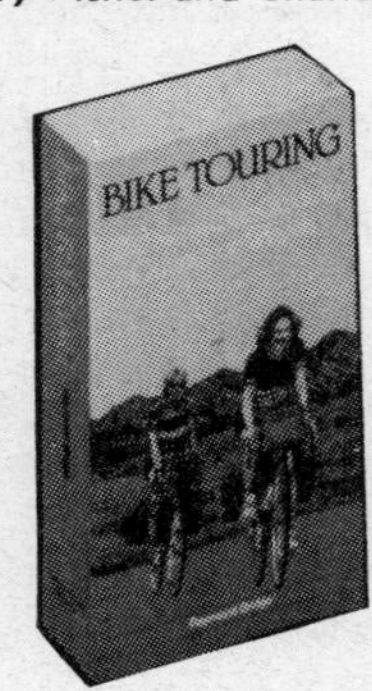

•

I prefer a headlamp that straps around your forehead or helmet, pointing where you are looking. A headlamp has several advantages over a light that clamps to the bike. It is very convenient for camping and for unloading your bike in the dark because the light moves with you but leaves your hands free. This feature is especially welcome when you are digging in your panniers for small items, pitching a tent in the rain, or lifting the lid off a pot to stir the stew. It also is useful when you are reading road signs (usually at the wrong angle for conventional bicycle lamps), looking for chuckholes, or trying to attract the attention of a car approaching from the side. With a headlamp, you can wiggle your head in the direction of the driver and create a flashing effect. The battery case for a headlamp usually is carried in your pocket, where it stays warm, so the batteries operate at maximum efficiency. Finally, the headlamp receives a gentler ride than a light attached to the handlebars would.

Drafting, a technique that enables two or more riders to ride considerably faster, yet with less effort, than the solo tourist. One rider breaks the wind, and each succeeding cyclist follows closely behind.

A Great Safety Device: The French Arm-band Light.

Bikecentennial

Bikecentennial is a non-profit, membership-supported organization for cycle tourists. Anyone interested in extended touring in the U.S. or Canada should look into their services, which include books, trip planning, maps, and group tours.

*The Bikecentennial people have researched and compiled an impressive library of maps designed especially for cyclists, with routes chosen to utilize secondary and scenic roads. Their **Cyclist's Yellow Pages** lists planning resources, clubs, shops, publications, accomodations, map sources, and so on. Members receive a newsletter, personal trip planning service, discounts on maps, t-shirts and books, and a number of free pamphlets including the **Yellow Pages**.*

—Gary Fisher and Charles Kelly

Bikecentennial
Membership
$15/year

The Cyclist's Yellow Pages
(A complete resource guide to maps, books, routes, organizations and group tours)
Bikecentennial
1979; 48 pp.

Bikecentennial Publications List
both
free (with membership)

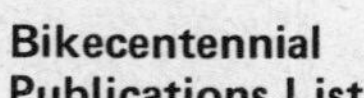

all from:
Bikecentennial
P.O. Box 8308
Missoula, MT 59807

The Bicycle Touring Book

Several years the authors rode across the country with their children, then aged 9 and 2. While the Sierra Club book is written by and for a rugged individualist, this book is aimed at more typically American types. Equipment is presented in a general fashion for the less technically oriented reader, and the dynamics of group tours are discussed in detail. Other good chapters cover physiological aspects of touring, determining and improving physical condition, diet, hazards of altitude, and exposure.

The last chapter is a priceless tale of a man who broke every rule in the book (old geezer, old bike, heavy luggage) and off-handedly biked across America.

—Gary Fisher and Charles Kelly

The Bicycle Touring Book
(The Complete Guide to Bicycle Recreation)
Tim Wilhelm and
Glenda Wilhelm
1980; 303 pp.

$9.95 postpaid from:
Rodale Books
33 East Minor
Emmaus, PA 18049
or Whole Earth
Household Store

•

Preferred All-Around Pannier Set
Eclipse Transcontinental ($85)

Preferred All-Around Handlebar Bag
Eclipse Professional ($46)

Preferred All-Around Front Pannier
Eclipse Superlite ($40)

Best Overall Value (Panniers)
R.E.I. Pannier II ($42)
A.Y.H. ($32)
Karrimor ($45)

Best Overall Value (Handlebar Bag)
Cannondale Casey ($15)

Best Overall Value (Front Pannier)
Karrimor ($20)

To determine correct frame size, straddle bike with no more than 1½ inches clearance. ↓

U.S. Geological Survey maps

Nigh indispensible hiking tools 1) for not getting lost, 2) for finding the most interesting places to not get lost in, 3) to pace your travel. Our p. 24 tells all.

—SB

Baron Von Mabel's Backpacking

Just had to throw this in. It's a rare pleasure to have a bit of humor shown for a subject all too often taken with a seriousness bordering on the tedious. The advice is sound, the information delivered painlessly, and the drawings look an awful lot like they were done by Gilbert Shelton.

—J. Baldwin

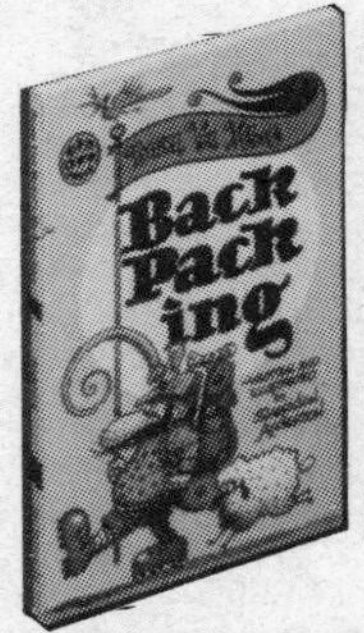

Baron Von Mabel's Backpacking
Sheridan Anderson
1980; 96 pp.
$4.95 postpaid from:
Rip Off Press
1250 17th Street
San Francisco, CA 94107
or Whole Earth
Household Store

The New Complete Walker

Though its 1974-most-recent-revision-date makes the equipment advice a bit off the mode, this is still the most civilized hiking book in print. Taken to heart, where it's written from, it obsolesces the house, the automobile, the Recreational Vehicle, the snowmobile, and most of the 20th Century.

—SB

The New Complete Walker
Colin Fletcher
1974; 485 pp.
$11.95 postpaid from:
Alfred A. Knopf, Inc.
455 Hahn Road
Westminster, MD 21157
or Whole Earth
Household Store

→

Office-on-the-yoke

Because I often walk without a shirt and therefore without a front pocket, I have had a 5-by-6-inch pocket sewn onto the front of my yoke strap, roughly where the shirt pocket comes. Into it go notebook and map, and sunglasses when not in use. Pen, pencil and thermometer clip onto the rear, between pocket and strap, where they are very securely held — not, as they used to, in front, where removing map or notebook can flip them out unnoticed. I cannot imagine how I ever got along without such a pocket. Mine is made of ordinary blue-jean material, but anything stout will do.

On desert afternoons a strong wind often blows for hour after hour. When it does, the continuous flapping of the poncho makes a hideous din, always threatens to tear grommets loose, and sometimes does. One way of reducing both noise and strain is to secure only three corners of the poncho to fixed points and to tie a large rock on the downwind corner with a cord of such length that the stone will just rest on the ground under normal conditions but will lift, and so ease the strain, when the poncho billows under an especially strong gust.

Backpacking One Step at a Time

This book has been needed for a long time. It isn't a manual intended for paramilitary survival combat with the elements, nor is it a "my experiences and methods of wilderness camping." It's a book intended to provide the basic information needed to get ready for the trail and have a fine time while on it. The author speaks to people who haven't done it before, particularly families. Discussions are geared to contemporary conditions and currently available equipment, so the information can be easily put to use. Where there is controversy about equipment (you can get into a considerable argument in any mountaineering store) the most commonly accepted solution is offered. Choices and reasons for them are given where performance requirements might differ enough to make trouble. All in all a very fine way to get into trail hiking if you're not already into it or if your technique has a tendency to leave you cold, wet, tired, bitten and hungry.

—J. Baldwin

Backpacking One Step at a Time
Harvey Manning
1973, 1980; 368 pp.
$4.95 postpaid from:
Vintage Books
Random House
455 Hahn Road
Westminster, MD 21157
or Whole Earth
Household Store

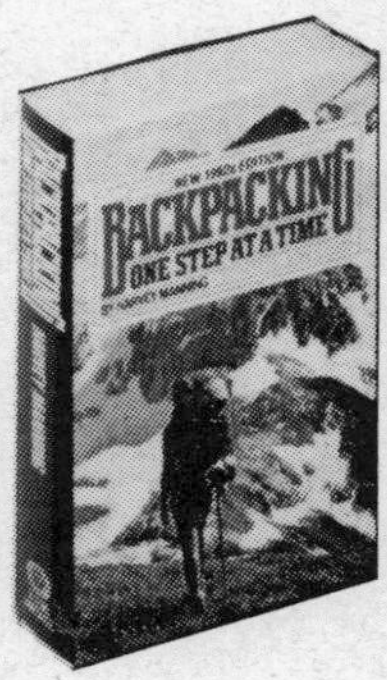

•

Through use of dried foods and those naturally low in water content, shucking cardboard packaging, and moderately careful menu planning, it is possible to feed the average hiker to repletion on 2 pounds of food per day. By more precise planning the job can be done with 1½ pounds. And if the party members are willing to leave a bit of lard along the way and endure pangs while stomachs shrink, with 1 pound. At this point, though, about the fifth evening the hiker will look into the setting sun and see not the majestic drama of day's end but only a great fried egg dripping hot butter.

Backpacking on a Budget

Two experienced campers — co-directors of the Climbing School of North Country Mountaineering in Hanover, New Hampshire — describe the state of the art (including Gore-Tex) in packs, boots, tents, sleeping bags, parkas and stoves, all in **WEC/Consumer Reports** *style. Money-saving ideas for acquisition (used equipment; cooperative buying; inflation trends; and state-by-state guide to leading shops with annual sale dates, manufacturers' seconds outlets, and rental services) and maintenance of the gear.*

—William Gifford

Low-cost yes. I question their state-of-the-art judgement.

—SB

Backpacking on a Budget
Anna Sequoia and
Steven Schneider
1979; 304 pp.
$4.95 postpaid from:
Penguin Books
299 Murray Hill Parkway
East Rutherford, NJ 07073
or Whole Earth
Household Store

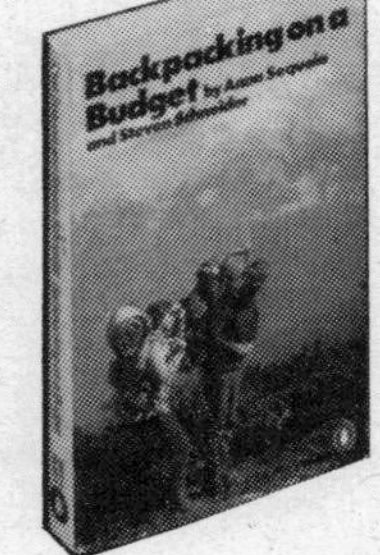

AMC Field Guide to Trail Building and Maintenance

Proudman draws heavily on the experience accumulated by members of the Appalachian Mountain Club trail crew, a group that's been dealing effectively with trail problems in New Hampshire's rugged but heavily travelled White Mountains for over fifty years. He covers the nuts-and-bolts of trail design and construction, from initial planning to the legal brushcutting involved in getting permission to route a trail across private land. Best of all, he stresses the use of natural materials for any necessary reconstruction and the use of non-motorized tools, neatly avoiding the tendency of some agencies to turn popular footways into little Interstates.

The text is nicely illustrated with black and white photographs, and some fine pen-and-ink drawings. While the book was written with Eastern backcountry in mind, most of the techniques described apply equally well to other parts of the country. Required reading for anyone involved in the care and feeding of a foot trail, and recommended for anyone else who wants to understand what they're hiking on.

—Jon Vara

AMC Field Guide to Trail Building and Maintenance
Robert D. Proudman
1977; 193 pp.
$5.95 postpaid from:
Appalachian Mountain
Club Books
5 Joy Street
Boston, MA 02108

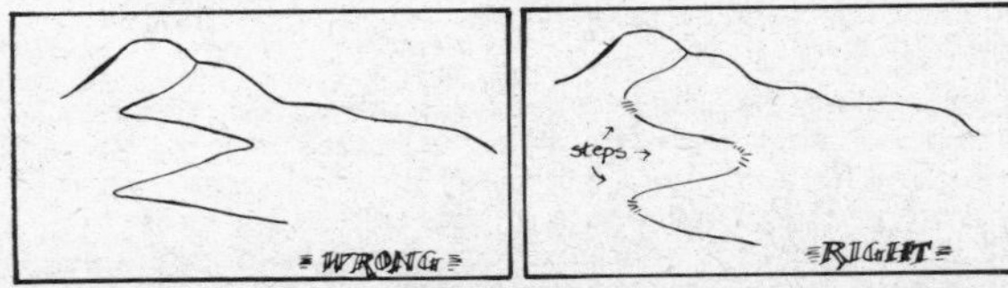

Left: narrow switchbacks are prone to shortcutting. Right: wide turns fortified with steps prevent shortcutting.

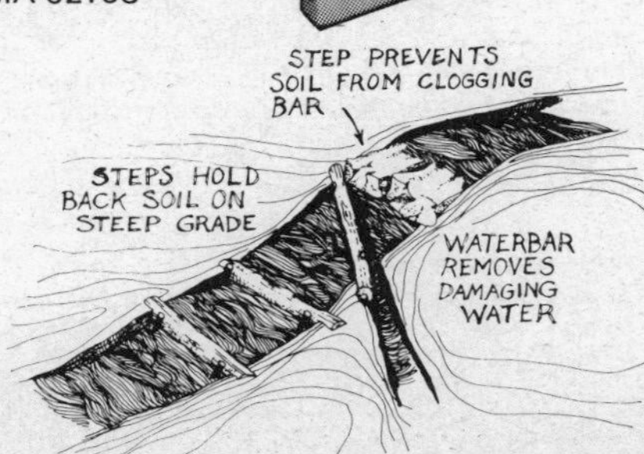

THE RISING SUN
NEIGHBORHOOD NEWSLETTER

I always figured that the thing that made a neighborhood other than a proximity was a certain lack of choice. In a neighborhood, you deal with people you wouldn't otherwise deal with or deal with some people more than you would deal with them. A neighborhood takes the dilettantism out of human relationships, so you find out you actually like people you wouldn't otherwise have chosen to spend 3 minutes with or you hate some initially innocuous soul more than you ever would have suspected possible. Mind broadening and all. Which is why work is the last neighborhood — it is the last place where you don't choose every little person you deal with. Which is why it doesn't necessarily seem so great for computer terminals to end the need for going to work — think of all those people you wouldn't have met, but then I guess you'd meet other people on the computer network, right, Art?

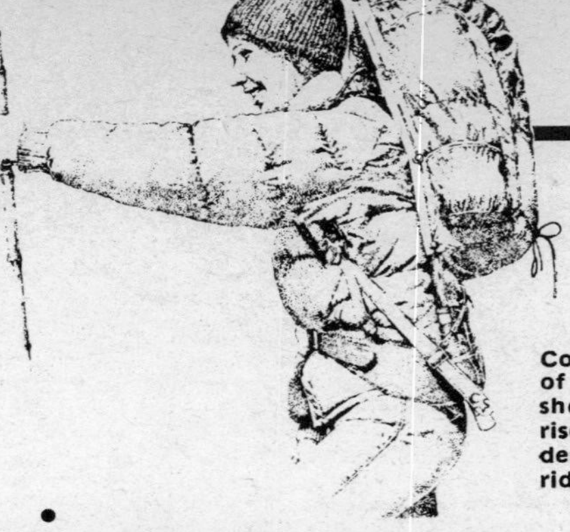

Correct fitting of frame pack: shoulder straps rise over shoulders, hip belt rides on hip bone.

Number of minutes to cover 1 MILE	HIGHWAY	OPEN FIELD	OPEN WOODS	MOUNTAIN & FOREST
WALK	15	25	30	40
RUN	10	13	16	22

Walking Softly in the Wilderness

Thorough, competent, and very up-to-date with respect to equipment and newly emerging standards of wilderness etiquette. —J. Baldwin

Walking Softly in the Wilderness
(The Sierra Club Guide to Backpacking)
John Hart
1977; 436 pp.

$7.80 postpaid from:
Sierra Club Books
Box 3886
Rincon Annex
San Francisco, CA 94119
or Whole Earth Household Store

•

Many hikers adjust the lacing of their boots depending on the slope of the hill. At the start of a climb, they loosen the toe and tighten the heel. which tends to shift and chafe in uphill travel. On the downslope they loosen the heel and tighten the toe. Again, only your experience will tell you whether you need to bother. This kind of adjustment is most easily done on boots that lace around hooks, rather than through D-rings or eyelets. The trick: run the laces around each hook in a loop. Laces set up this way won't slip around the hooks; they stay tight where you want them tight and loose where you want to ease the pressure on your foot.

← Loop pattern vs. normal lacing.

•

Pay attention to the heel, the outside of the big toe, and the sides of the foot at the base of the toes. If you feel a spot of irritation forming as you walk — a "hot spot" — don't wait. Sit down, pull off the boot, and find out what's going on. Put on moleskin or tape; if you have some on already, make sure that it hasn't developed wrinkles (they can cause extra irritation) and add another layer. Make sure that your boots are very snugly laced, particularly in the upper part of the lacing pattern, and that your heel is not rising too far inside the rear of the boot as you stride. If the fit seems loose, try adding another pair of inner socks.

•

Campfires these days are not popular with wilderness conservationists, nor with wilderness managers. The impact of fires on the land — so many people have come to feel — is simply too great. Fires can sterilize fertile ground for decades, leave ugly scars, and consume down wood that should be left to rot and replenish the soil. But in this, as in so many of these questions, common sense must be the guide. A fire in an old ring of stones in a middle-elevation forest littered with down logs can't possibly be called an attack on the land. A similar fire built (illegally) of green wood on a peak in the crowded Catskills, or built (illegally) against a granite boulder in an uscarred alpine meadow, is an atrocity.

Be Expert with Map and Compass

Don't fuck around. Be expert with map and compass. This experienced book is the introductory classic. —SB

Be Expert with Map and Compass
(The Orienteering Handbook)
Bjorn Kjellstrom
1955, 1976; 214 pp.

$7.95 postpaid from:
Charles Scribner's Sons
Vreeland Avenue
Totowa, NJ 07512
or Whole Earth Household Store

One way of orienting map with compass is to place the edge of the base plate parallel with the magnetic-north line, then turn the map until the compass on it is oriented.

Nature Is Your Guide

Once in awhile I get a book that just blows my socks off. Little mysteries solved; distant departments suddenly connected; totally unfamiliar matters discussed openly — something to stop you on every page. This book is one of those. A professional pathfinder tells the secrets of past pathfinders and navigators, teaching in a logical and gentle manner. Why do lost people walk in circles? How can you prevent doing so? How can you navigate using waves and swells as your guide? I read the whole thing in one sitting. A real eye-sharpener. —J. Baldwin
[Suggested by Scott Thyborg]

Nature Is Your Guide
(How to find your way on land and sea)
Harold Gatty
1958, 1979; 271 pp.

$3.95 postpaid from:
Penguin Books
299 Murray Hill Parkway
East Rutherford, NJ 07073
or Whole Earth Household Store

•

Objects look much nearer than they actually are when:
Looking up or down hill.
There is a bright light on the object.
Looking across water, snow or flat sand.
The air is clear.
Objects look much farther away than they actually are when:
The light is poor.
The colour of the object blends with the background.
The object is at the end of a long avenue.
You are looking over undulating ground.

•

A simple means of judging distances which can be used either on land or at sea is the finger method. It is based on the principle that the distance between the eyes is about one-tenth of the distance from the eye to the end of the extended finger. When the width of a distant object is known and you wish to determine how far away it is, proceed as follows:

With the right arm extended in front of you, hold the forefinger upright and align it with one eye on the end of the distant object. Without moving the finger, observe with the other eye and note how many feet along the length of the object it appears to have moved. The range of the object will be ten times this distance. When the height of a distant object such as a mountain, a building or a vessel is known, hold the head sideways and follow the same procedure.

Starting Small In the Wilderness

The grim possibility of having to drag a squalling brat down the trail to a rejected dinner and a soggy bed has kept many families from enjoying the beauties of wilderness adventure. Many unexpected problems can arise with the kiddies along, but with this long-needed book you'll likely be able to handle things OK. Common problems such as where to get child-size equipment and what to do about picky eaters are discussed with a convincing knowledge that can only have been gained from the field experience of what must have been hundreds of families. The book deals with bike, canoe, and ski trips too. The tone is encouraging. The quality is high in the expected Sierra Club manner. —J. Baldwin

Starting Small In the Wilderness
(The Sierra Club Outdoors Guide for Families)
Marlyn Doan
1979; 273 pp.

$7.80 postpaid from:
Sierra Club Books
P.O. Box 3886
Rincon Annex
San Francisco, CA 94119
or Whole Earth Household Store

•

Getting children to enjoy carrying a loaded frame pack requires some parental ingenuity. Toting gear is work. Parents must somehow disguise or soften that fact for youngsters.

A good principle is to begin small, both with pack size and weight, and to start young children with some kind of soft, frameless pack (see Chapter 4, "Frameless Packs"). If youngsters carry something every time the family hikes, they will grow up thinking that pack toting is perfectly natural.

Backpacker magazine

Fairly good place to keep up with the coevolution of hiking gear and hikers. The magazine has some on where to hike, some on how to hike, and much on what to hike with. There's a lot of (useful) advertising, so the evaluations are generic and not as fierce as they should be. ["This piece a shit pompous Brandname stove can't hold a flame if a mouse sighs within five feet of it!" (Clank clank clank down the talus slope)]. —SB

Backpacker
(Including Wilderness Camping)
William Kemsley, Jr., Editor

$15/year (6 issues) from:
Backpacker
P.O. Box 2784
Boulder, CO 80302

•

Workmanship is every bit as important as material. So before buying, examine the tent fully erected, if this is possible. Check the seams first. The flat-felled seam is the strongest. It should be used wherever any strain is anticipated. The highest quality tents use nothing else, except at reinforcements and zippers.

Lock stitching is preferred. It is more resistant to abrasion and less likely to unravel when a thread is cut than is the case with the cheaper chain stitching. Chain stitching is adequate for lighter use, especially when well coated with seam sealer.

Stitching and seams should be straight, with no gathers or puckers. Be sure that all seam edges are firmly caught. Stitches should be about seven to twelve to the inch. Fewer may result in a weak seam. More may tend to weaken the fabric. Check *both sides* of each seam. A seam with improper tension may look fine on one side, but be loose and messy on the other.

Watch especially for detail at strain points: guy attachments, peg loops, corners, reinforcements, zipper seams. These may be difficult to sew and hard to see. Poor workmanship may slip by there, until it comes under strain.

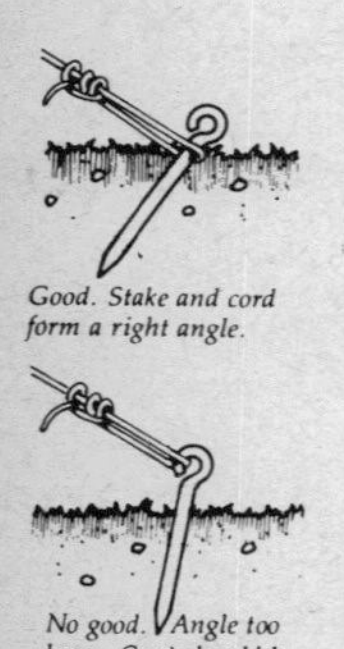

Good. Stake and cord form a right angle.

No good. Angle too large. Cord should be below eye.

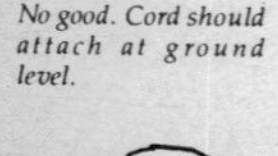

No good. Cord should attach at ground level.

A rock will help hold stake in place.

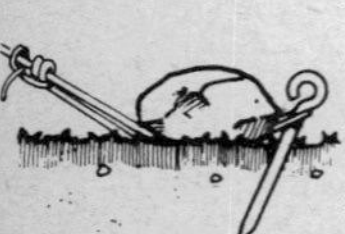

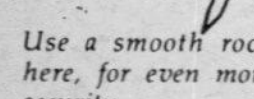

Use a smooth rock here, for even more security.

NOLS Conservation Practices

This 11-page pamphlet published by the National Outdoor Leadership School outlines guidelines for low-impact camping. Information is listed for backcountry travel, camping, fires and stoves, sanitation and waste disposal and includes seasonal and regional modifications necessary for winter conditions, high altitude, desert and coastline environments. Good guidelines by people who know what they are doing. —China Galland

NOLS Conservation Practices
1978; 11 pp.

free from:
National Outdoor Leadership School
Box AA
Lander, WY 82520

•

Toilet paper, if used, should be *completely* burned. In low moisture or high fire hazard areas, toilet paper should be bagged and packed out. When available, snow, leaves and other natural substitutes are preferable to toilet paper.

Tampons must be burned in an extremely hot fire to completely decompose, therefore in most cases they should be bagged and packed out. *Never* bury tampons in a latrine.

Soap must not be used in lakes and streams. Complete soap bathing involves jumping in the water, lathering on the shore, far away from the water, and rinsing the soap off with water carried in jugs or pots. This allows the biodegradable soaps to break down and filter through the soil before reaching any body of water. Clothes can be adequately cleaned by thorough rinsing. Residual soap can cause skin irritation, so we recommend *not* using soap to wash clothes in the backcountry.

The Well-fed Backpacker

You can hike a weekend using only Twinkies for fuel and still get home ok. But if you're going out longer or in harsh weather and high altitudes, you're going to have to do better than junkfood. Turns out that most folks take one of the two obvious choices: they go heavy duty with store-bought food that weighs too much and has heavy packaging, or they go freeze-dried and put up with extreme expense and the, uh, esthetic deficiencies. Most folks also don't know how to properly balance their meals either. Most books intended to help don't. This one does, at least it helps me. Clever, well-balanced recipes from lightweight inexpensive ingredients are dished up by a lady of goode mind with lots of trail experience. This is my choice of all the books on the subject.

—J. Baldwin

The Well-fed Backpacker
June Fleming
1976, 1979; 112 pp.
$4.95 postpaid from:
Victoria House
2218 NE 8th Avenue
Portland, OR 97212

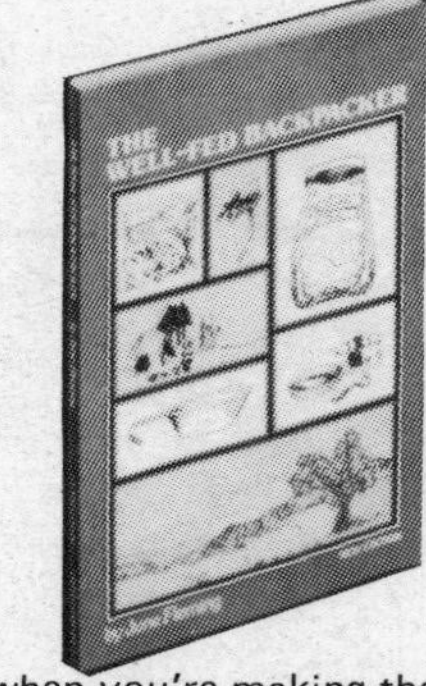

•

Don't scorch melting snow when you're making the water supply; the water will taste burned. Make sure there is always a half-inch or so of water in the bottom of the pan.

RUSSIAN TEA

2 cups sugar
1 cup Tang (powdered orange drink)
½ cup instant tea
½ to 1 teaspoon each cinnamon and cloves
1 quart package lemonade mix

The New Healthy Trail Food Book

If you're not into eating shitfood and you can't afford freeze-dry (which to many also qualifies as shitfood) then you have a problem. What do you eat that fulfills your nutritional requirements and is also light, cheap, easy and fast to prepare, and economical of fuel and water? This comprehensive booklet gets you started towards feeding your face in a righteous manner by explaining the theory of adequate diet before presenting the menus and recipes (which I'll admit I haven't tried). The section of developing menus for extended trips is especially good, which is fortunate. Without experience such planning is most difficult. Miller's estimate of 2 lbs. and about $2.00 a day per person seems realistic to me, as do the recipes. There are other books on this subject, but this one seems unusually easy to actually use.

—J. Baldwin

The New Healthy Trail Food Book
(With All-Natural recipes for good eating outdoors)
Dorcas S. Miller
1976, 1980; 80 pp.
$4.50 postpaid from:
Dorcas S. Miller
Georgetown, ME 04548

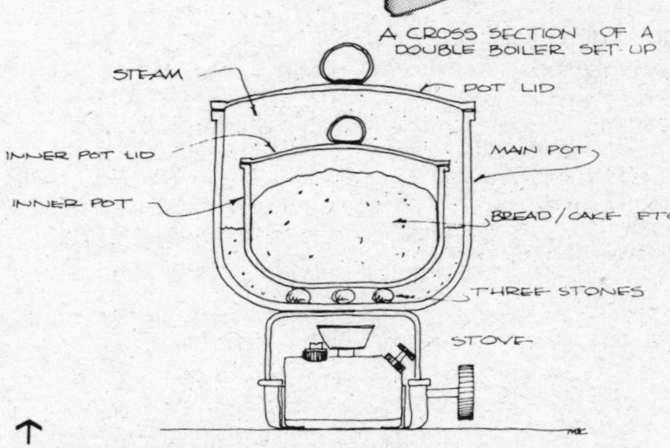

↑

Double Boiler: Baking With a Stove

For a very special occasion, cakes can be baked on a gas stove by using the double boiler principle:

a. Put about 2/3 c water in the larger of two nesting pots.
b. Put the cake batter in the smaller pot, and slip inside the larger one.
c. Put lids on both pots, place whole on stove.
d. Boiler water will steam heat and cook the cake. Make sure the pot does not boil dry.

Because this improvised oven does not reach much over 212 degrees, it takes a long time to bake a cake. So be prepared to wait! Also, try for a thin cake rather than a thick one or else it won't bake well.

NOLS Cookery

The National Outdoor Leadership School is a private, non-profit educational organization dedicated to teaching people how to enjoy and conserve the wilderness. NOLS also happens to publish a small cookbook that's grown out of their years of experience and hundreds of backpacking expeditions over areas as far-flung as Utah, Alaska, Montana, Baja, Wyoming, Mexico and Kenya, East Africa. For $1.95, the revised 1978 version is a bargain hard to beat.

The NOLS cookbook focuses on basic principles and guidelines in nutrition, rationing, equipment, stoves, fire-building and safety. It also includes many helpful tables of basic ration lists as well as a useful food chart based on food needed for 2 people for 10 days. The appendix contains an equivalency table of common backpacking foods. For example, 5 cups of dried apples equal 1 lb., so does 4 cups of raisins, 3 cups of lentils, 5 cups of oatmeal and so forth.

—China Galland

NOLS Cookery
(Planning and Preparation of Food for Backpacking Expeditions)
Nancy Pallister, Editor
1974, 1978; 61 pp.
$1.95 postpaid from:
Emporia State Press
ESU Box 43
1200 Commercial
Emporia, KS 66801

Camping and Woodcraft

How could anything written in 1917 still be so useful? One, it is a masterwork. Two, in Kephart's day when you went camping you really disappeared, so there's a valid nostalgia factor. But the main thing is, the book survives on its wealth of specific practical lore. Game: find the information that is outdated, sort it from the information that is correct and available nowhere else.

—SB

Camping and Woodcraft
Horace Kephart
1917, 1967; 479 pp.
$8.95 postpaid from:
The Macmillan Company
Front and Brown Streets
Riverside, NJ 08075
or Whole Earth Household Store

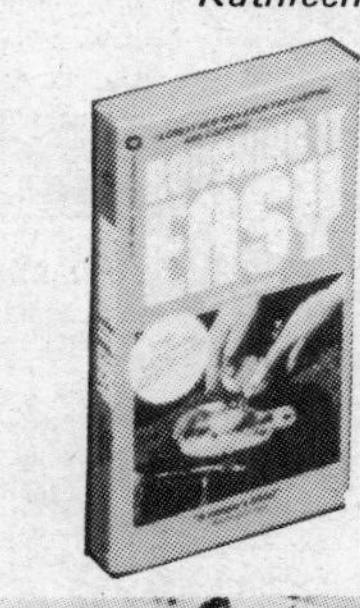

•

Men working hard in the open, and exposed to the vicissitudes of wilderness life, need a diet rich in protein, fats (especially in cold weather), and sweets. This may not agree with theories of dieticians, but it is the experience of millions of campaigners who know what their work demands. A low-protein diet may be good for men leading soft lives, and for an occasional freak outdoorsman, but try it on an army in the field, or on a crew of lumberjacks, and you will face stark mutiny.

•

One glance at a camper's fire tells what kind of a woodsman he is. It is quite impossible to prepare a good meal over a heap of smoking chunks, a fierce blaze, or a great bed of coals that will warp iron and melt everything else.

Roughing It Easy

Mostly for those who like to do ingenious no-pot cooking while outdoors. Really good for car camping, horse packing or scout camping. There's a **Roughing It Easy 2** *which is not so interesting.*

—Kathleen Whitacre

Roughing It Easy
(A Unique Ideabook for Camping and Cooking)
Dian Thomas
1974; 246 pp.
$4.95 postpaid from:
Brigham Young University Press
205 UPB
Provo, UT 84602
or Whole Earth Household Store

Bread baking in see-through cardboard box oven →

Advanced First Aid for All Outdoors

Realistic treatment for quite serious situations — including injections, suturing, stomach-pumping, etc. Dramatic use of anecdotes drives the lessons home. Excellent book. For even more extensive coverage of this sort, get **Where There is No Doctor** *(p. 326), rural emergency information (pp. 310 - 312), and* **Ship's Medicine Chest** *(p. 439).*

—SB

Advanced First Aid for All Outdoors
Peter F. Eastman, MD
1976; 161 pp.
$6 postpaid from:
Cornell Maritime Press
P.O. Box 456
Centerville, MD 21617
or Whole Earth Household Store

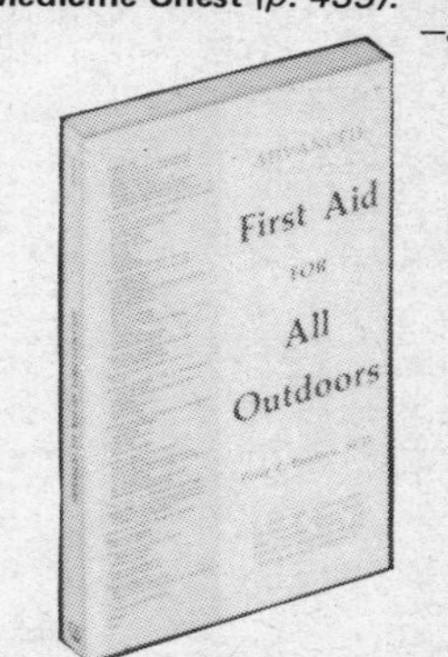

↓

6. Injected the lidocaine into Don's foot an inch behind the dead toe, top and bottom, medial and lateral, four sites in all, a total of 10 cc.
7. Made a circular cut around the base of the toe down to the bone.
8. Suddenly Brian felt dizzy, sat down, began to sweat and nearly fainted. He put his head between his knees and took two or three deep breaths.
9. Presently he felt better, picked up the tin snips and cut off the toe well behind the last joint on the foot. Dierdre tossed the dead toe to the mackeral congregation off the stern.
10. Brian pressed the gauze firmly against the amputation site until the small digital artery stopped spurting, about 10 minutes. (If it had failed to stop in a reasonable time, 10-20 minutes, he might have applied a tight dressing to the foot.)
11. Left the amputation wound wide open. Had an artery continued to bleed, he might have seized it with the forceps and closed it with a stich.

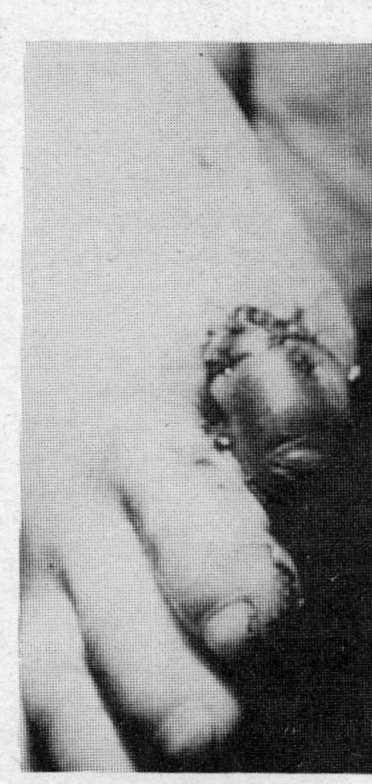

Gangrenous toe 7 days post suture

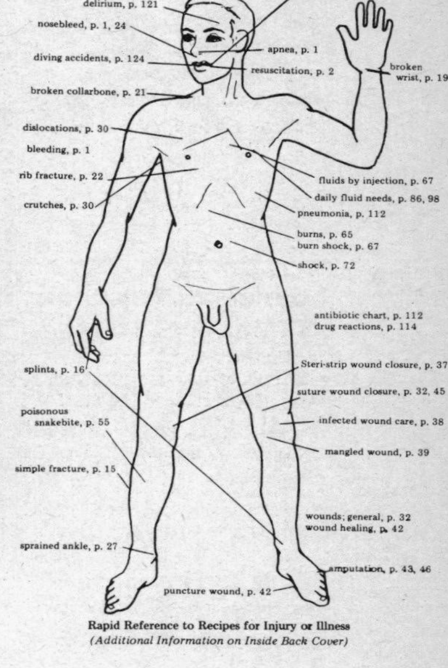

Rapid Reference to Recipes for Injury or Illness
(Additional Information on Inside Back Cover)

THE RISING SUN
NEIGHBORHOOD NEWSLETTER

Jay told a story about when Jim Bowie challenged a guy to a duel and had two pairs of leather breeches with feet in them nailed to a log about three feet apart and they fought it out with knives. Which is sort of like being in this job where you are professionally, morally, personally obligated to be there 60 hours a week with all these other folks whom you might possibly be a little tired of. It feels amazingly like that sometimes only since we all like each other (thank you jesus) you just keep pulling at the breeches and dropping the knife or throwing it out of your own reach or tickling the other person to silliness, but those nails in the feet of the leather pants you put on yourself sure are an interesting feeling sometimes. Just the tiniest sample of the realio trulio neighborhoods of ancient days where you knew your whole life you had to spend your whole life with these 60 people in the manor and that was it. (No wonder they died young.)

ELL, IT'S THE new eco-fad. Everyone wants to eat off the Earth and moon over the wonders of the Earth's gifts. It's true, but this is the twentieth century and 200,000 people cannot all eat nature's bounty. So it becomes crucial that you do not pull up wild edibles if there are only a few in one area. Give the plant a chance to reproduce and to be abundant. Don't pull a plant when its fruit isn't ripe or its root is too small. Most of all, don't yank out any of the endangered plants (such as American ginseng in certain states).

Learning about edible wild plants from books can be difficult. Here's how to separate the wheat from the chaff:

- Does the guide have good pictures of the plant?
- Does it picture the plant at the season you want to harvest it?
- Does it picture the part (root, berry, seed) you want to harvest?
- Does it describe the plant's favorite growing places (near ponds, under pines, in sunlight)?
- Does it describe the distribution of the plant — which states? which elevations?
- Does it give you good collecting advice (especially which season to collect) with suggestive recipes?
- Does it describe poisonous species with which you might confuse the edible plant?
- Does the guide have enough species for your locale to make it worth lugging around or keeping as a reference?

Here are the best foraging guides to pass through our hands in the recent years.

—Peter Warshall

Edible Wild Plants of Eastern North America

East of the Great Plains. North of Florida. The best overall guide to edibles. Too big for backpacking but accurate and gentle and thorough. —Peter Warshall

Edible Wild Plants of Eastern North America
Merritt Lyndon Fernald, Alfred Charles Kinsey, Reed C. Collins
1943, 1958; 452 pp.

OUT OF PRINT
Harper and Row

Get this book back in print!

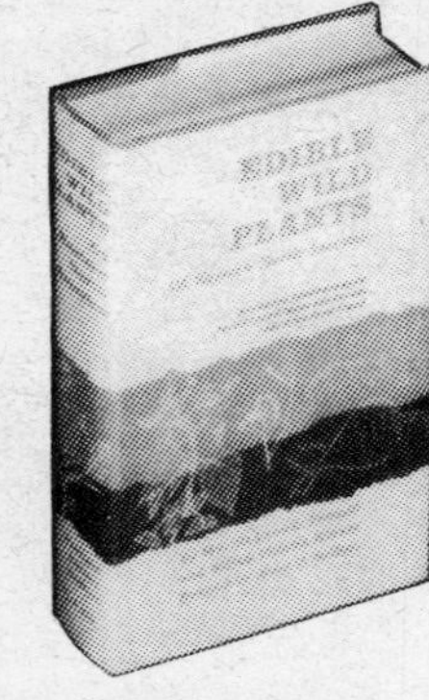

•

BARBERRY FAMILY *(Berberidaceae)*

May-Apple, Hog-Apple, Wild Lemon, "Mandrake," *Podophyllum peltatum.*

Habitat and Range: rich woods of the Central States, eastward to western Quebec and western New England and southward.

Season of Availability: late summer.

Uses: fruit, marmalade, summer drink.

The fully ripe fruit of the May-Apple (because flowering in May) is familiar to every country boy of the regions where the plant abounds and, although Asa Gray described it as "mawkish, eaten by pigs and boys," in its fresh state it has a peculiar flavor very agreeable to most human grown-ups. It makes a luscious marmalade and a beautiful jelly, and, being abundant where it grows, should be experimented with cooked in other ways. In the South a drink is prepared from the juice of the fruit with Madeira and sugar, and a less ardent beverage may be prepared by squeezing the juice into lemonade or other fruit-drinks.

The foliage and root of the plant are poisonous to eat.

Fig. 60, May-Apple

Edible and Poisonous Plants of the Eastern United States
Edible and Poisonous Plants of the Western United States

These color cards can be stuck in your backpack and you can take only those needed for locale and season. Information is the bare minimum. —Peter Warshall

Edible and Poisonous Plants of the Eastern United States
1973; 52 cards

Edible and Poisonous Plants of the Western United States
1970, 1974; 52 cards
$5.95 (each set)
both postpaid from:
Plant Deck, Inc.
2134 S.W. Wembley Park Road
Lake Oswego, OR 97034

WILD ROSE (Rosa species)
Description: Bushes 3-10 ft. tall, usually with prickly, branched stems. The showy, pink flowers usually grow in clusters on young side branches. The compound leaves are toothed. The fruits (hips), which ripen in the fall, are red or orange-red and very conspicuous.
Habitat: Widely distributed throughout the continent, growing in many different situations from sea level to about 6000 ft.
Uses: Few foods are comparable to the tasty rose hips in vitamin C content. Cut them open, remove the seeds and use the fleshy rinds. They make excellent jams and jellies, or they can be dried and used for tea. Because they remain on the plant throughout the winter and can be picked when other fruit is unavailable, they are a good source of emergency food.

Stalking the Wild Asparagus
Stalking the Healthful Herbs

Easy intros. Chatty. Accurate as far as it goes but weak on locations and identifying pictures. —Peter Warshall

Stalking the Wild Asparagus
(Field Guide Edition)
Euell Gibbons
1962, 1970; 303 pp.
$3.95 postpaid

Stalking the Healthful Herbs
(Field Guide Edition)
Euell Gibbons
1966, 1970; 303 pp.
$3.95 postpaid

both from:
David McKay Company
Two Park Avenue
New York, NY 10016
or Whole Earth Household Store

•

I have a friend, a little girl, who is intensely interested in wild foods and herbal remedies. Once we stood before a witch-hazel bush while I explained its reputed therapeutic uses, the controversy over them, and my own ideas on the subject. At the end of a half-hour lecture, she brilliantly summarized all I had said by remarking, "As I understand it, witch-hazel will help nearly everything, but not very much." There you have it! Witch-hazel is useful in a large number of minor complaints, but its action is likely to be gently corrective and unspectacular.

—Stalking the Healthful Herb

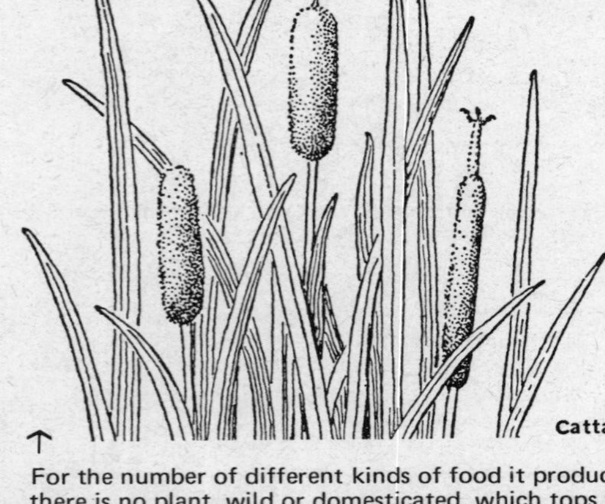

Cattail

For the number of different kinds of food it produces there is no plant, wild or domesticated, which tops the common Cattail. In May and June the green bloom spikes make a superior cooked vegetable. Immediately following this comes the bright yellow pollen, fine as sifted flour, which is produced in great abundance. This makes an unusual and nourishing ingredient for some flavorful and beautifully colored pancakes and muffins. From fall until spring a fine, nutritious white flour can be prepared from the central core of the rootstocks for use as breadstuff or as a food starch. On the leading ends of the rootstocks are found the dormant sprouts which will be next year's cattails. These can be eaten either as a salad or as a cooked vegetable. At the junction of these sprouts and the rootstock there is an enlarged starchy core the size of a finger joint. These can be roasted, boiled or cooked with meat. In the spring, the young shoots can be yanked from the ground and peeled, leaving a tender white part from six to twelve inches long which can be eaten raw or cooked.

—Stalking the Wild Asparagus

Edible wild plants of Canada

Though many of these plants are common in the U.S. there is, of course, only the vaguest description of U.S. locales. Nevertheless, these Canadian publications are the most elegant and informative series of books on wild edibles to be published. They do everything a guide is supposed to do — including wandering into other uses and how the natives employed each plant. —Peter Warshall

Edible Garden Weeds of Canada
(Edible Wild Plants of Canada, No. 1)
Adam F. Szczawinski and Nancy J. Turner
1978; 184 pp.
$9.95 postpaid

Wild Coffee and Tea Substitutes of Canada
(Edible Wild Plants of Canada, No. 2)
Nancy J. Turner and Adam F. Szczawinski
1978; 111 pp.
$6.95 postpaid

Edible Wild Fruits and Nuts of Canada
(Edible Wild Plants of Canada, No. 3)
Nancy J. Turner and Adam F. Szczawinski
1979; 212 pp.
$9.95 postpaid

all from:
University of Chicago Press
Department PK
5801 South Ellis Avenue
Chicago, IL 60637
or:
Publishing Division
Order Services
National Museums of Canada
Ottowa, Ontario
K1A 0M8 Canada
or Whole Earth Household Store

•

Basswood Tea

To make this healthful drink you should start on a sunny, hot day when the basswood trees are in full bloom. Gather the blossoms and spread them thinly on papers in a warm room, or outside in the sun. When dry place them in containers with secure lids. They dry quickly and will store very well.

In brewing the tea, proceed as with any Oriental tea. You should do some experimenting with the amount of dry flowers until a strength suitable to your taste is reached: 15 ml (1 tbsp) per 250 ml (1 cup) of tea is a good average. Sweeten with honey if you wish.

—Wild Coffee and Tea Substitutes of Canada

Edible Native Plants of the Rocky Mountains

Western Edible Plants

The hardback **Edible Native Plants** *is essential to all eaters-from-the-wild. The paperback* **Western Edible Plants** *is a limited number of species from the hard-back. Good drawings. Good advice on collecting. Good recipes. Five stars for accuracy and interest.*
—Peter Warshall

Edible Native Plants of the Rocky Mountains
H.D. Harrington
1967, 1974; 388 pp.
$8 postpaid

Western Edible Plants
H.D. Harrington
1972; 156 pp.
$4.95 postpaid

both from:
University of New Mexico Press
Albuquerque, NM 87106
or Whole Earth Household Store

Roots

A delightfully written guide to a number of roots used in medicine and as food (no dyes). Although it says "North America," **Roots** *focuses on the Atlantic seaboard. Standard West Coast roots like Chenopodium (soap root) and many many other medicinal roots are not even mentioned. But, what's here is grounded: good drawings, botany, Indian uses, pharmacopoeia entries, harvesting, drying and preparing. I keep returning to* **Roots** *to learn something new and turn away hoping the next edition will dig a little deeper into each plant's chemical constituents, medical effectiveness and preparation.*
—Peter Warshall

Roots
(An Underground Botany and Forager's Guide)
Douglas B. Elliott
1976; 123 pp.
$5.95 postpaid from:
The Chatham Press
143 Sound Beach Avenue
Old Greenwich, CT 06870
or Whole Earth Household Store

↓
Apios americana
Leguminosae, Pea Family
Other Common Names:
Indian-potato, Ground-potato, Potato-pea, Pig-potato, White Apple, Traveler's Delight, Wild Bean, Bog Potato.

Groundnut is a vine which can be found spreading over the ground or climbing over bushes to a height of several feet. The compound leaves have five to nine leaflets. In late summer the blossoms spring forth in clusters on spike-like racemes from the junction of the leaf stalks and the stem. The flowers are brownish purple, very fragrant, and shaped like a bean blossom. In autumn the blossoms for form slender, bean-like pods.

Groundnuts were a staple food of the American Indians. Both pilgrims and early colonists often subsisted on them.

The great botanist, Asa Gray, once said that if advanced civilization had started in North America instead of the Old World, the Groundnut would have been the first tuber to be developed and cultivated. Actually, they were taken to France to be cultivated as early as 1635 but were soon forgotten, probably because the roots take two or three years to reach eating size. In Captain John Smith's **Narratives of Early Virginia**, he tells of "Groundnuts as big as Egges and as good as Potatoes, and 40 on a string not two inches underground."

I have never found them quite like Smith described, but then again, he got there first . . .

Groundnuts can be eaten raw or boiled, but I like them best sliced thin with the skin on and gently fried in a little oil with a bit of wild onion or garlic added for additional flavor. They are a relative of the soybean and are reported to contain 25 percent protein.

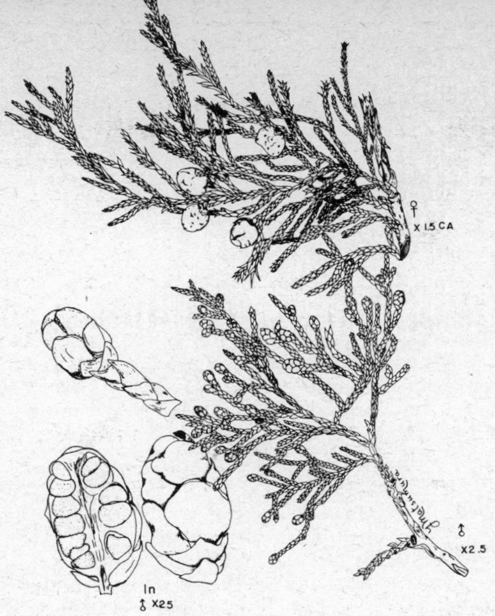

↑
Juniperus scopulorum (Sabina scopulorum)
Rocky Mountain Juniper, Red Cedar

Description: This is a bushy shrub or a medium-sized tree, often with several trunks; leaves scale-like, 1/24 to 1/8 inch long; some plants producing only pollen, others only fruit; fruit blue with a whitish coating, about 1/8 to 1/4 inch wide.

Dry rocky ridges, foothills and bluffs. Grows from Alberta to British Columbia in Canada and south to New Mexico and Arizona.

Use: The junipers have a characteristic, rather displeasing, resinous odor and taste, but fortunately the fruit has less of this than do other parts of the plant. These berry-like fruits vary among the different kinds in size and thickness of pulp. The Indians used these fruits in the late summer or fall, and ate them raw or cooked. They have a high percentage of sugar and are sweet to the taste. The cooking process can be either boiling or roasting. We have tried them raw and found they were strong flavored, but not actually inedible. Since we did not care for the taste we did not try to cook them. However, a few were used to flavor meat and imparted a taste somewhat like sage. As is well known, the berries of some junipers are used to flavor gin. The fruit and the young shoots have been used to make a kind of tea. It may be healthful, but we found it rather potent for our taste, although it is for sale in one grocery store in this area.

The Indians used to dry the fruits, and stored them for the winter. These berries could then be ground into a meal and used to make mush or cakes. They could also be roasted and ground to make a substitute for coffee.
—Edible Native Plants of the Rocky Mountains

American Indian Medicine

The definitive book — all the tribes, all the medicines. The author is looking through the window of Western medicine and Western anthropology, but he is looking with detailed appreciation. Weedmunchers could find no better guide. The people who could use it best probably can't afford a doctor and drugstore and probably can't afford this book — another good reason for libraries.
—SB

American Indian Medicine
Virgil J. Vogel
1970, 1977; 585 pp.
$19.95 postpaid from:
University of Oklahoma Press
Sales Office
1005 Asp Avenue
Norman, OK 73019
or Whole Earth Household Store

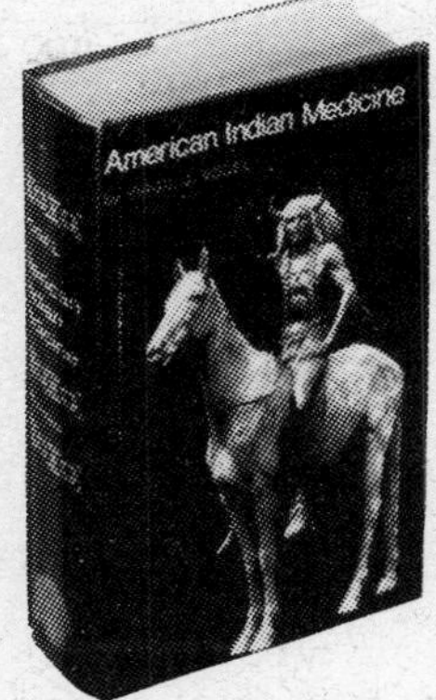

Jimson weed. (Datura meteloides D.C). **The seeds were used to induce visions, for poultices applied to burns and inflammations, and for other purposes. Seeds have been found in pre-Columbian caves. Considered poisonous.**

Wild Edible Plants of the Western United States

The listing of 302 species from Oregon to Mexico is the most attractive feature of this book. Identification and seasonal availability will require another book. Its small size makes it easy to carry.
—Peter Warshall

Wild Edible Plants of the Western United States
Donald Kirk and Janice Kirk
1970, 1975; 328 pp.
$5.95 postpaid from:
Naturegraph Publishers
P.O. Box 1075
Happy Camp, CA 96039
or Whole Earth Household Store

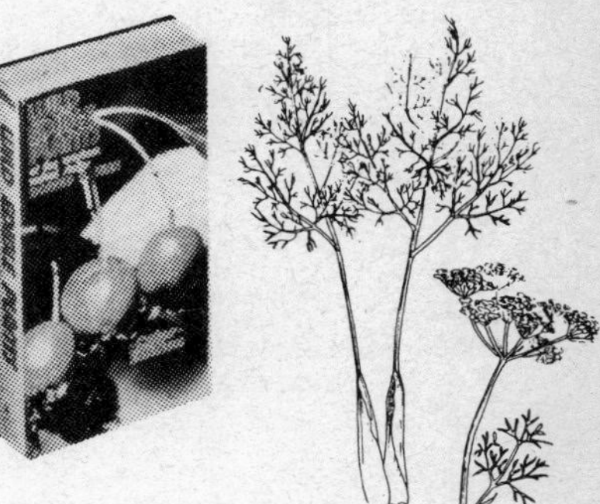

•
Foeniculum vulgare (1) (Carrot Family)
Fennel, Sweet Fennel

Preparation and Uses: The leaf stalks may be eaten raw or cooked.

Habitat and Distribution: The plant is found in waste ground throughout the West.

Description: Fennel is an erect perennial herb with a leafy stem, and an anise odor. The leaves are more than once divided into linear divisions. The yellow flowers are in large compound umbels. The sepals are obsolete.

Northwest Foraging

The seasonal list is the delight on this book. OK (but not outstanding) on other aspects like collecting, cooking, and poisonous species. Just the Northwest.
—Peter Warshall

Northwest Foraging
(A Guide to Edible Plants of the Pacific Northwest)
Doug Benoliel
1974; 171 pp.
$5.95 postpaid from:
Signpost Publications
8912 192nd Street SW
Edmonds, WA 98020

•
Bracken Fern (Brake Fern)
Pteridium aquilinum (L.) Kuhn.
Fern Family — Polypodiaceae

There can be much reward in learning this plant, for it can be harvested from April to July, early in the low elevations and later in the mountains. At sea-level the less than 8 inch tall unfolded leaf can be gathered to be used immediately or stored. The season lasts only a few short weeks. However, the plants emerge from the ground later in the season with an increase in altitude. In June and July a person can gather Bracken Fern at 3000 to 4500 feet in the Cascades and Olympics. This is a plant that the hiker-camper who wants to supplement his diet should know. →

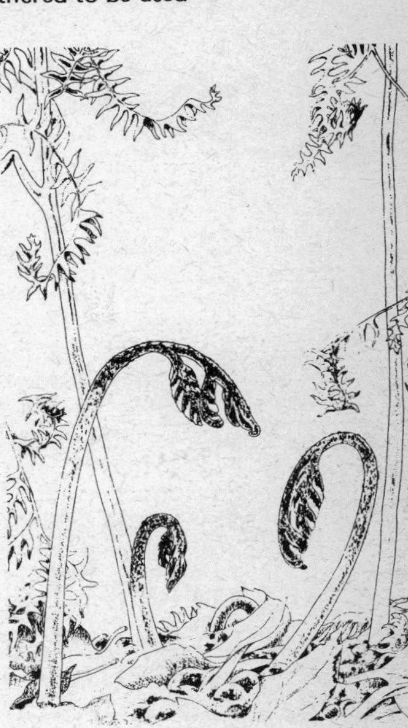

EDIBILITY, excellent *when young.* Cook the young unfolded leaves (fronds) like asparagus. Cook 15 minutes or until tender. The younger they are the more tender and tasteful they will be. Excellent when dipped in a sauce of butter, lemon juice, salt, pepper, chili powder, and onion salt. The fronds can also be boiled, dried, and stored for use later in the year, when they are reconstituted with water.

THE RISING SUN
NEIGHBORHOOD NEWSLETTER

"Time is what keeps everything from happening at once."
—Stephanie

MUSHROOMS
by Peter Warshall

THE INITIATION

Here are the musts:

- *There is no one guide so you must buy a few.*
- *The vocabulary and textures of mushrooms are unique and awe-inspiring. You must begin to learn the weird Latin names.*
- *Mushrooms produce spores that have unique qualities. To begin to learn the different kinds, you must make spore prints.*
- *No mushroom can be identified easily. You must gain patience. Perseverance greatly furthers.*

Mushroom Collecting for Beginners

Simply, a free course by a Mushroom Guru (J. Walton Groves). Beautiful photos show all stages of mushroom growth. Text describes confusions that usually occur among the initiates. I wish, I wish, when I started . . .

Mushroom Collecting for Beginners
J. Walton Groves
1951, 1980; 36 pp.
No. A43-861-1980
free from:
Supply and Services
Canadian Government
Printing Centre
Hall, Quebec
Canada, K1A 0S9

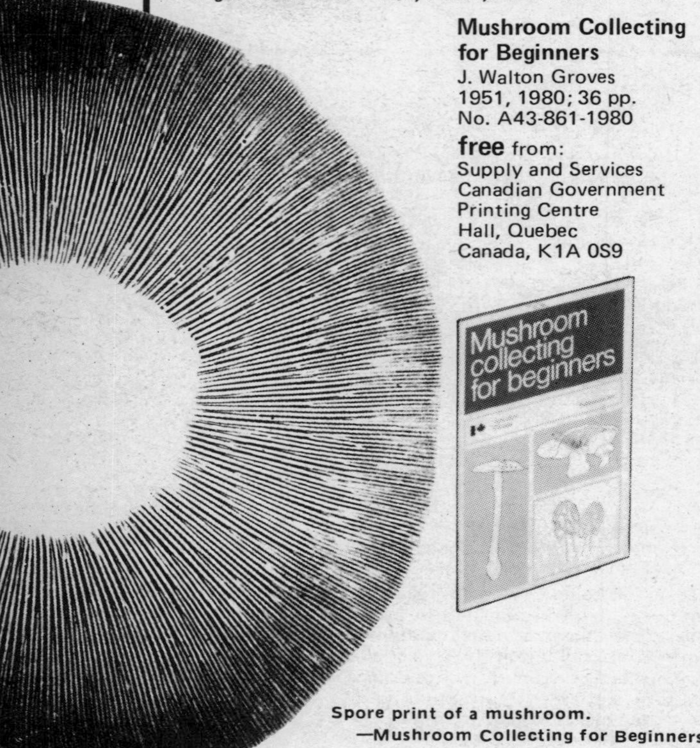

Spore print of a mushroom.
—Mushroom Collecting for Beginners

THE PERIOD OF DANGEROUS FOOD

Armed with a small vocabulary and spore prints, you can probably stay alive and eat pretty well. But, to immerse yourself in the mind-boggling diversity of mushrooms, to discover the deeper loves and secrets of fungi, and to expand your gourmet risks, a second commitment is needed. You must get heavily into Latin names to describe the beast (many mycologists think mushrooms are animals).

How to Identify Mushrooms

The must booklet of the mushroom kingdom. Exquisite line drawings. Uses only spore color and visible features. Other more advanced volumes are **Volume II, Field Identification of Genera,** *$3.50;* **Volume III, Microscopic Features,** *$8.25; and* **Volume IV, Keys to Families and Genera,** *$5.50.*

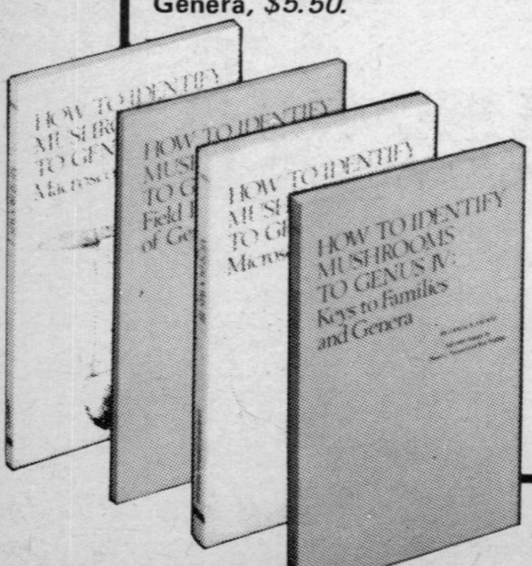

How to Identify Mushrooms to Genus I
(Macroscopic Features)
David L. Largent
1973, 1977; 86 pp.
$4.85 postpaid
all from:
Mad River Press
Route 2, Box 151-B
Eureka, CA 95501

INTERMEDIATE GUIDES

These guides all have advantages and disadvantages. You might want all of them even before you continue into the bliss of impossible mushroom identification.

Alexander Smith's mushroom guides

The Mushroom Hunter's Field Guide *is good for all North America but especially East of the Rockies. It's hard to use. The key is not cross-referenced to page number. 188 varieties.*

Smith's **A Field Guide to Western Mushrooms** *is too complicated to help anybody, but it does include 250 species — more than other guides.*

The Mushroom Hunter's Field Guide
Alexander H. Smith
and Nancy Smith Weber
1958, 1980; 336 pp.
$14.95 postpaid
or Whole Earth
Household Store

A Field Guide to Western Mushrooms
Alexander H. Smith
1975; 309 pp.
$16.50 postpaid
both from:
University of
Michigan Press
839 Greene Street
P.O. Box 1104
Ann Arbor, MI 48106

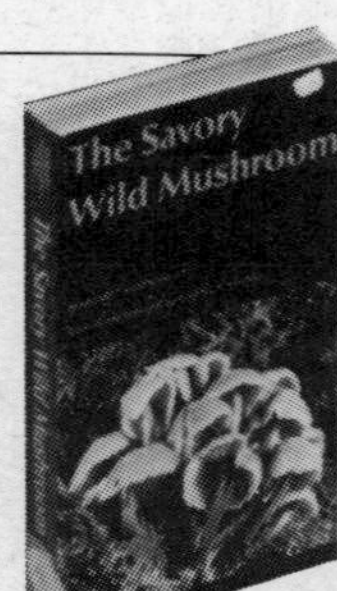

→
Morchella esculenta (Morel or Sponge-Mushroom)
Edible and choice. One of our most popular wild mushrooms and one of the easiest to recognize at sight.
When and where to find it. The habitats are diverse. It frequently grows in old orchards, beech-maple and oak forests, lightly burned areas such as old grassland, lawns (rarely), and swampy ground under elm with a cover of jewelweed, and under ash trees. May is the month for it in the central and eastern states. It is earlier in the southern and later in the northern states. Most farmers look for it when the oak leaves are at the "mouse ear" stage of expansion.
—The Mushroom Hunter's Field Guide

The Savory Wild Mushroom

Great for the West. Key to mushrooms badly set up. Good recipes. 83 varieties. Fine essay on poisons.

The Savory Wild Mushroom
Margaret McKenny
and Daniel E. Stuntz
1962, 1971; 272 pp.

$7.95 postpaid from:
University of
Washington Press
Seattle, WA 98105
or Whole Earth
Household Store

•
A Hunter's Toast
On a tramp through the fields and forests, carry with you a small jar of butter, creamed with salt and pepper. On finding any edible mushroom (except morels or elfin saddles), collect a few dry sticks and fire them. Split a green stick (alder or willow) at one end. Put the mushroom in the cleft, hold it over the fire until tender, season with the butter. Eat from the stick.
—The Savory Wild Mushroom

Growing Wild Mushrooms

Just as pot cultivation drew many Americans into the joys of gardening, psilocybin draws us now into the joys of mushroom growing. Here is the best of the no-fooling-around text on grain-media and compost-media (in-jar and outdoors) of some edible and psilocybe mushrooms. Read it slowly. Read it carefully. Bob Harris knows his mycelia, sterile techniques, and, especially, his compost.

Growing Wild Mushrooms
(Complete Guide to Cultivating Edible and Hallucinogenic Mushrooms)
Bob Harris
1976, 1978; 88 pp.
$5 postpaid from:
Bob Harris
Box 607
Inverness, CA 94937
or Whole Earth
Household Store

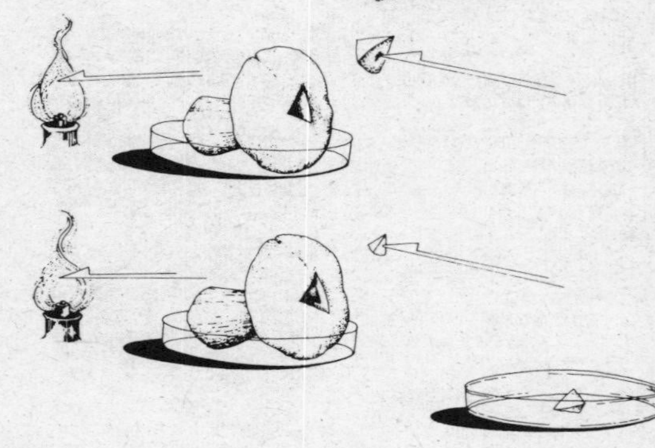

↑
The carpophore is disinfected with an alcohol solution of iodine on the surface. The mushroom is placed on a clean surface in the transfer box. A small blade is flamed in the alcohol lamp. Then a section of the carpophore is sliced and removed (a 1/3 inch by 1/2 inch piece). Flame the knife again and now remove a small piece of tissue from inside the hole just made. This tissue should be sterile, and should be transferred to an agar plate sterilely. The Petri plate can be used to cool the blade between flamings as discussed with the loop. The plate can be set aside and the fungus will grow out of this piece of tissue.

Mushroom growing supplies

Mushroompeople, P.O. Box 158W, Inverness, CA 94937. *Access to agar agar, growing media, spores, mushroom kits, books, tools and supplies. Catalog free. (Also see the mushroom growing kits on p. 356.)*

HEAVY DUTY MUSHROOM LOVE

Edible and Poisonous Mushrooms of Canada

Best advanced book. Great keys using a technical vocabulary. By the man who wrote **Mushroom Collecting for Beginners.** *400 species.*

Edible and Poisonous Mushrooms of Canada
J. Walton Groves
1962, 1979; 326 pp.
No. A43-1112-1979
$11.95 postpaid from:
Supply and Services
Canadian Government
Publishing Centre
Hull, Quebec
Canada K1A 0S9

Mushrooms of North America

422 species. Beautiful photos. Best book on use of staining and microscopic features. As usual, keys and page references are badly cross-referenced. It's a hard book to use. I find a mushroom from other guides, then see what Miller has to say.

Mushrooms of North America
Orson K. Miller, Jr.
1972; 360 pp.
$9.95 postpaid from:
E.P. Dutton
Two Park Avenue
New York, NY 10016
or Whole Earth
Household Store

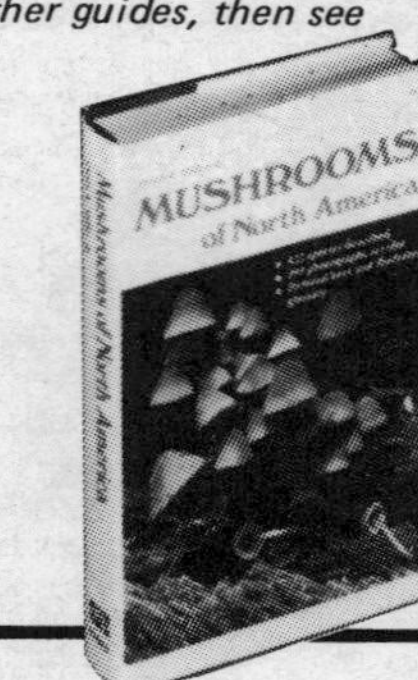

MUSHROOM MISCELLANY

Write the North American Mycological Association, 4245 Redinger Road, Portsmouth, OH 45662 to find out the location of the nearest mushroom society.

For lichen (fungi plus algae) identification, buy **How to Know the Lichens** *(see review on p. 58).*

Kitchen Magic With Mushrooms

Long out of print, this book is magic. Puffball French fries, blewit duxelles, mushroom pirog and piroshki, ceviche marin and on and on.

Kitchen Magic with Mushrooms

OUT OF PRINT
Mycological Society
of San Francisco
Get this book back in print!

THE FUNNY THING about survival books is, the people who have them don't need them, and vice versa.

—SB

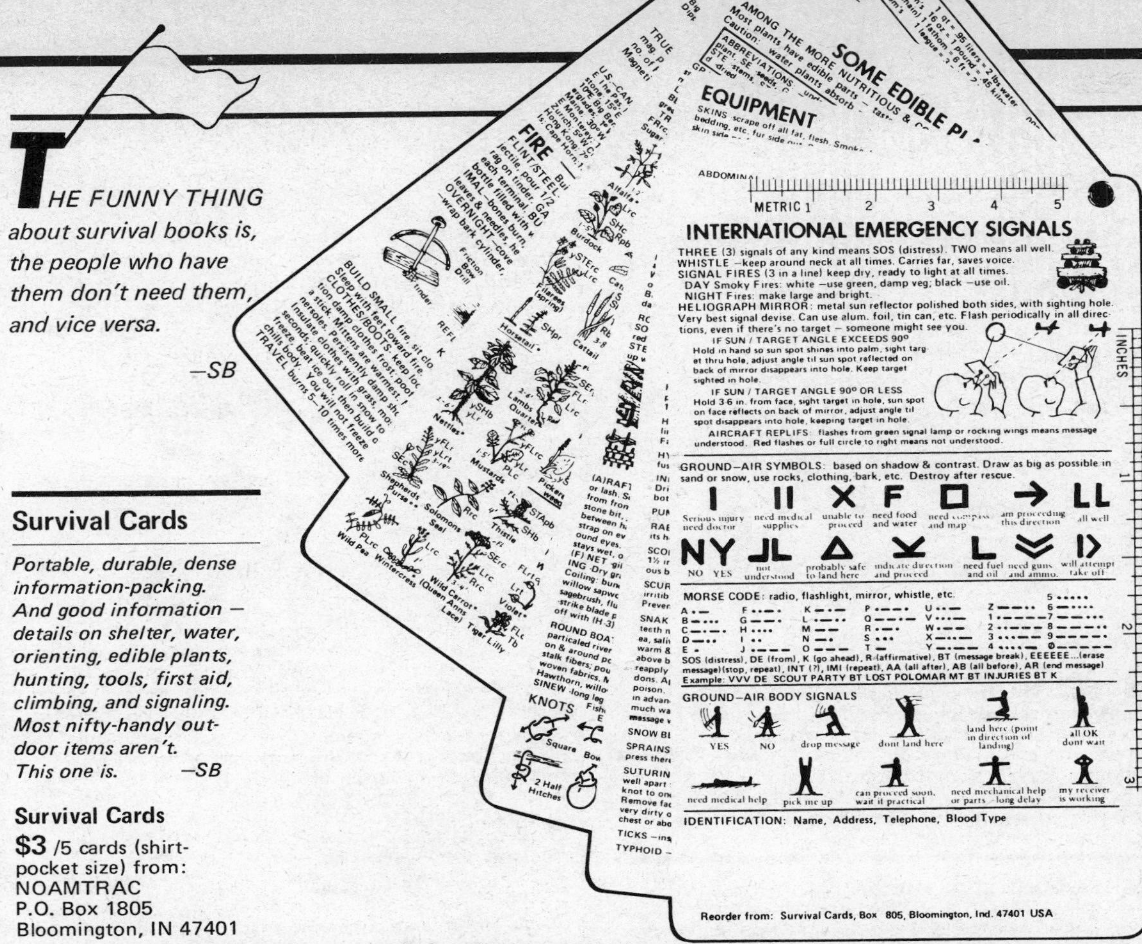

Survival Cards

Portable, durable, dense information-packing. And good information — details on shelter, water, orienting, edible plants, hunting, tools, first aid, climbing, and signaling. Most nifty-handy outdoor items aren't. This one is. —SB

Survival Cards
$3 /5 cards (shirt-pocket size) from:
NOAMTRAC
P.O. Box 1805
Bloomington, IN 47401

The Book of Survival
Survival in the City

The advice is mostly practical, sometimes grotesque, and always fascinating. The style is brilliant — brutal, over-simplified statements and images that you will remember under duress. Are you ready for burning buildings, freaked humans, speeding cars, dogs, floods, electricity jolting your body, poison, burglars, muggers, poverty, terrorism, con men . . . life, sometimes city life. The wilderness is safer, and more boring. —SB

The Book of Survival
(Everyman's guide to staying alive and handling emergencies in the city, the suburbs and the wild lands beyond)
Anthony Greenbank
1967; 223 pp.
$1.95 postpaid

Survival in the City
Anthony Greenbank
1974; 474 pp.
$6.95 postpaid

both from:
Harper and Row
Keystone Industrial Park
Scranton, PA 18512
or Whole Earth Household Store

Fire drill
—The Book of Survival

Buoy position in crowd
—The Book of Survival

At first signs of crowd-surge squirm away from anything solid like wall, barrier or pillar. Undo shirt collar and loosen tie.

In hysterical/swaying/terrified crowd this is all you can do. Note: Most vulnerable position of all is to be caught with hands in pockets. Neither should you clasp hands with interlocked fingers in front of body.

Where crowd is limited — too many trying to get out of emergency exit, say — try to calm panic by shouting humorous understatements.

•

A closed door offers at least twenty to thirty minutes resistance to flames. Remember — the fire may bypass it and not attack it immediately.

Someone should stay by window so that people outside realize the urgency of calling the Fire Department immediately.

Anyone weakening from the heat, fumes and fear should be restrained from jumping. He should be told to lie on the floor while you wait by the window.

Consider alternative action if help cannot reach you in time, and prepare for it by knotting sheets together or throwing down mattresses in preparation for jumping on them.

•

FIGHTING DRUNK

Humor.

If involved in brawl, drunks can offer astoundingly strong grip. Hit hard in stomach and this may make him sick.

—The Book of Survival

Survival Evasion and Escape

Here's one for our customers who plan to jump bail or escape from jail. Thoughtfully prepared by the U.S. Army. Three-fourths of the book is about living off the land, with edible plants illustrated in color. Pretty damn good book. —SB

Survival, Evasion and Escape
1957, 1969; 430 pp.
008-020-00157-1
$6.05 postpaid from:
Superintendent of Documents
U.S. Govt. Printing Office
Washington, D.C. 20402
or Whole Earth Household Store

Hanging snare

•

Casting

Frequently the duplication of buttons, insignia, seals, medals, etc., is necessary to complete an evasion disguise. Casting these items in soft metal generally is the best method, and the procedures involved require very simple materials.

a. Lead, solder, and zinc are the easiest and most common materials to work with. Lead can be obtained from pipe or plumbing fittings, from around underground electrical wire, and from leaded window frames. Solder may be melted from the seams of tin cans. Zinc frequently is used on washbowls, metal fittings, metal containers and some window and roof construction.

b. Make a mold by using clay, soap or a large potato. The material used is cut in half, and half of the design is cut into each piece so that when fitted together the hollowed-out parts will have the form desired. In all molds, a hole must be made in one side through which to pour the metal; a small hole is made in the other side to allow air to escape. Molds made of clay should be baked to harden. After being poured and allowed to cool, finish the casting by trimming with a knife or file and painting or polishing as appropriate.

Outdoor Survival Skills

Olsen assumes that you get stuck out there with nothing but some knowledge — no matches, food, compass, toothpaste, or magazines. Scrounge the tools, food and shelter. Good bunch of pictures and diagrams. Sort of a purists' book. For someone who is thinking about stopping along the road on the way to work some day and just walking out into the wilderness.
—J.D. Smith
[Suggested by W.H. Bayman]

Outdoor Survival Skills
Larry Dean Olsen
1973; 188 pp.
$4.95 postpaid from:
Brigham Young University Press
206 UPB
Provo, UT 84602
or Whole Earth Household Store

Pressure flaking with horn and a pad.

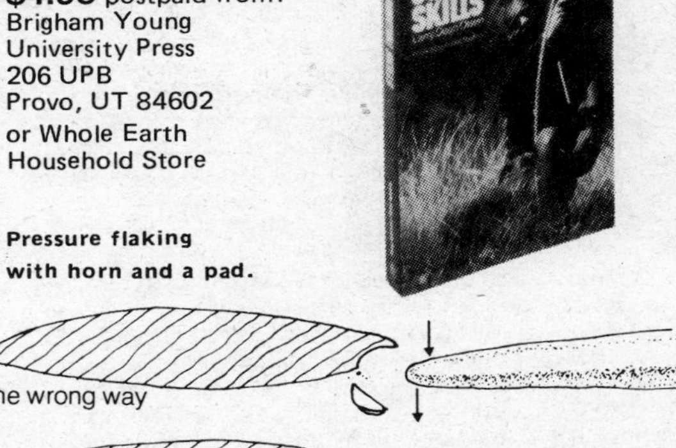

the wrong way

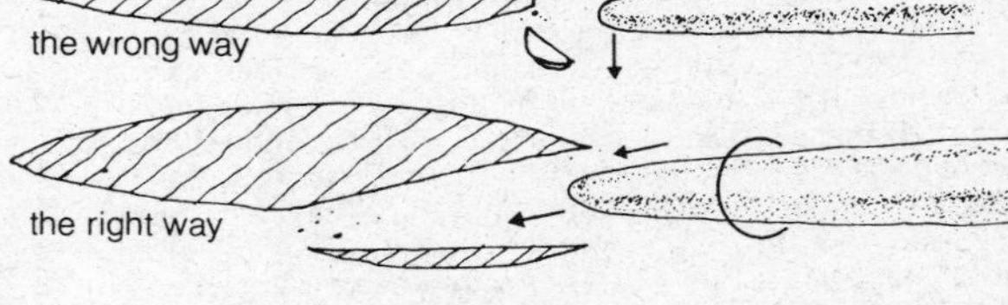

the right way

notching with fine-tipped flaker

Outdoor Living

A practical manual designed to enable you to survive an emergency outdoor situation. The authors assume a short-term problem, and that your immediate action will help assure rescue. Good mental attitude is the name of the game. Basic survival principles are discussed so you can think out clearly what to do. Good book for the money. —J. Baldwin

Outdoor Living
Fear, Simac, Lasher
1973; 109 pp.

$4 postpaid from:
Tacoma Mountain Rescue Unit
P.O. Box 696
Tacoma, WA 98401

•

A review of actual outdoor survival emergencies requiring outside assistance indicates that the majority last only one day, with the weather contributing the greatest danger to life and sustaining energy. It was also noted that the critical period is the first six hours after the situation develops. Decisions made and actions taken during this period will determine the outcome of the experience.

•

RADIATION is a leading cause of heat loss in almost any situation, and the head is the most efficient portion of the body's radiator system. So rapid is the radiation from the head in a cold situation that heat loss from an unprotected, uncovered head can be enormous. An unprotected head may lose up to one-half of the body's total heat production at 40°F; up to three-quarters of total body heat production at 5°. This proves the wisdom of the old mountaineers' maxim: "When your feet are cold, put on your hat." Parkas with attached hoods or balaclavas are essential for protection against this dramatic heat loss in cold, windy and wet situations.

THE RISING SUN
NEIGHBORHOOD NEWSLETTER

Beth was going to serve a woman who hadn't paid her for some artwork with notice to appear in small claims court and I told her I was really impressed that she got it together to do that and she said, "You know, it's just like Bob says, everybody's gotta serve someone."

Ski Camping

Cross-country skiing takes many forms, with most of the publicity going to what I call "slot-car skiing" on prepared trails. This enticing book is for you who crave to ski where you make the first tracks, and to stay out overnight as well. There are other books on this subject, but none so well done, so free of paramilitary macho, and so easily understood. A spare, positive text is backed by exceptionally good photographs. I find the recommendations to be right on the mark. Nordic skiing has been one of my favorite enterprises for 25 years, and this is the nicest introduction to that delight I've seen. —J. Baldwin

Ski Camping
Ron Watters
1979; 154 pp.
$7.95 postpaid from:
Chronicle Books
870 Market Street
Suite 915
San Francisco, CA 94102
or Whole Earth
Household Store

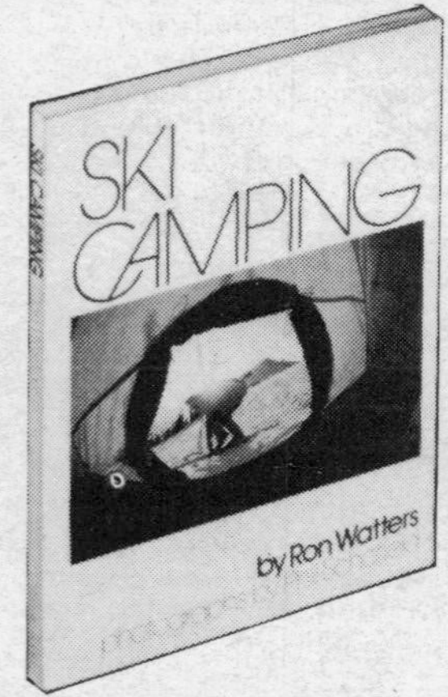

←
Waxless ski bottoms: from top — fishscale, step, mica and radial step.

•
Whether to use wax or waxless skis can produce a difference of opinion among cross-country skiers. Most cross-country ski authorities now agree that a wax ski can outperform a waxless ski on a track. Little, however, has been said of the use of waxless skis in the back-country where minimizing the hassles that come with waxing skis can be a big advantage.

I've always been a wax ski advocate myself. Recently, though, I was on a long ski trek, and encountered a variety of conditions from soft, deep powder, to transitional snow, to coarse, spring snow, to icy, avalanche rubble. One member of our party used a pair of fishscale skis. Many times I watched in amazement from the side of the trail with my waxes spread out while Sandy skied by. Her skis were more than adequate for the great variety of snow conditions we encountered.

Waxless skis are criticized on the basis of glide which, while important for track skiing, is not as important for backcountry skiing.

Carve a domed ceiling in the snow cave.

Sherpa snowshoes

Know what porcupines eat in the summer? Stored snowshoes, that's what. Unless they happen to be one of the newer designs such as these. In addition to being unpalatable to rodents, these snowshoes are unaffected by water and ice, they require no annual varnishing or other maintenance, and they don't loosen as you plod down the trail. Their exceptionally light weight makes them easy to carry and also tends to prevent the dreaded "Mal d' Raquette." These people are not the only ones making modern snowshoes, but they have a very good reputation. Their products are a good example of modern materials and design making the old way seem a bit silly except as a nostalgic handcraft.

I'll concede that these are more energy-intensive to make, but on the other foot, they are less labor intensive to use. Where you draw that line may not be so obvious until you've spent some miles on the trail. After 20 miles, esthetics and philosophy seem to defer to functional elegance. As usual. They are not cheap. —J. Baldwin

Sherpa Snowshoe Products
Manufactured by:
Sherpa Design
Platteville, WI 53818
$71-$78 plus shipping from:
R.E.I. Co-op (p. 426)
or check your local ski supply store.

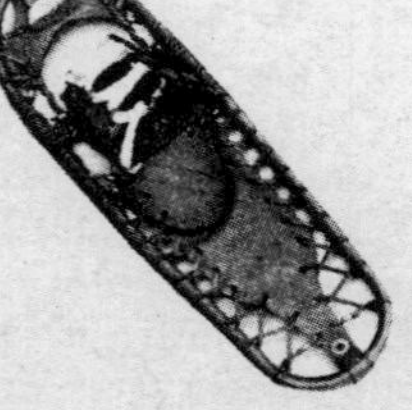

Complete Cross-Country Skiing and Ski Touring

Complete, no. An inviting introduction to cross-country equipment and technique, decidedly. If I were trying to get a friend interested in x-c, I'd give this. "Take a look. If you're interested, we'll rent some skis next weekend and go where the snow is quiet." —SB

Complete Cross-Country Skiing and Ski Touring
William J. Lederer
and Joe Pete Wilson
1970, 1975; 189 pp.
$4.95 postpaid from:
W.W. Norton and Co.
500 Fifth Avenue
New York, NY 10036
or Whole Earth
Household Store

↑
Walking or shuffling the length of the track, the skier should swing his arms, holding the poles loosely by the straps in order to become conscious of how the left arm and right leg move together, and of how right arm and left leg move together. The skier should then go the length of the track, hopping forward instead of shuffling. When he hops off his left leg, he then also pushes back with his right pole. That's all there is to the basic diagonal stride.

Cross-Country Downhill

If you think that cross-country skiing is restricted by the inability to go down steep hills on those skinny planks, then this will be news to you. With the techniques neatly explained in this book, you'll be able to ski in country you wouldn't have approached before, and do it safely too. I can vouch for the moves shown here; they work well. The book is aimed at those who already know how to ski with reasonable skill, and that may be just as well because it isn't a beginner sport. Still, just about anyone who can ski Nordic should be able to pick up the ability to do it. The photographs of each move are very clear rather than being showy. —J. Baldwin

Cross-Country Downhill
(And Other Nordic Mountain Skiing Techniques)
Steve Barnett
1978, 1979; 107 pp.
2nd Edition
$7.95 postpaid from:
Pacific Search Press
222 Dexter Avenue
Seattle, WA 98109
or Whole Earth
Household Store

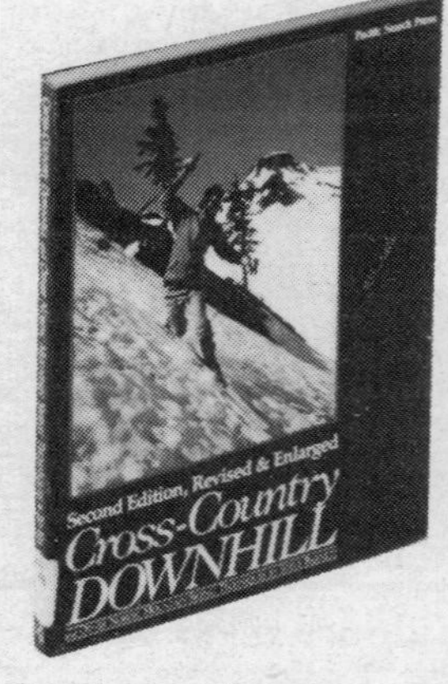

The Snowshoe Book

Excellent guide to snowshoeing! Well illustrated with drawings by Grace A. Brigham. Pertinent info on snowshoe types and uses, bindings, extra equipment and technique, also sections on racing and games plus survival including first aid, avalanches and rescue. Something in here for everyone whether novice or expert. —Al Perrin

The Snowshoe Book
(A complete guide to how, why, when and where)
William Osgood
and Leslie Hurley
1971, 1975; 162 pp.
2nd Edition
$5.95 postpaid from:
The Stephen Greene Press
P.O. Box 1000
Brattleboro, VT 05301
or Whole Earth
Household Store

These snowshoers take a difficult obstacle course with what looks like no effort at all.

Cross Country Ski Gear

A very complete analysis of boots, bindings, poles, clothes, wax, and other stuff you need to ski away from the madding crowd. I don't know whether you need to know all this, but I found the book highly informative even though I've been watching this stuff since my Army ski troop years in the '50s. It's especially good in helping you choose equipment. —J. Baldwin

Cross Country Ski Gear
Michael Brady
1979; 211 pp.
$6.95 postpaid from:
The Mountaineers
719-B Pike Street
Seattle, WA 98101
or Whole Earth
Household Store

•
Twist or warp will cause a ski to *yaw*, that is, always turn or climb out of a track instead of running straight.

Check for twist by holding a pair of skis together and sighting from tail to tip when the tails are held together. Bases should touch over their entire width at the shovel. If there is a v-shaped gap, one or both skis is twisted. Even if the skis meet as they should, both may be twisted. Check for this defect by reversing one ski, holding the pair with one tail against one tip, and resighting.

Check for warp by squeezing the midpoints of the skis together. The waists should meet exactly. If there is an offset, one or both skis are warped. Even if the waists meet exactly, both skis may be warped, in opposite directions. Again, check for this defect by reversing one ski, holding the pair tail against tip (centering at both contact points, as tips and tails are seldom of equal width), and resqueezing the midpoints.

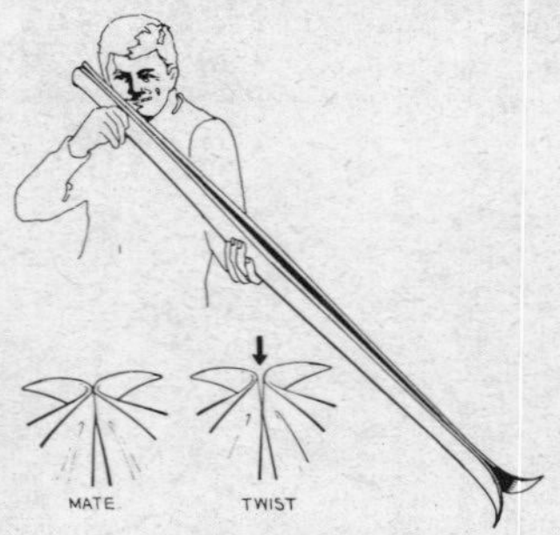

Sight along skis to check for twist.

Mid-ski mismate indicates warp.

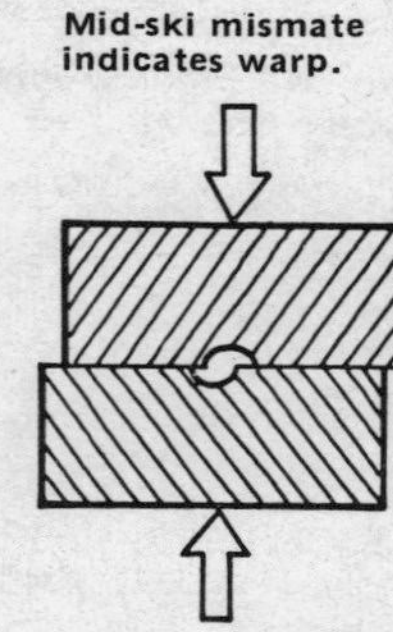

Movin' On

When somebody asks me what's a good book for learning about winter hiking and camping, this is the one I tell 'em about. —J. Baldwin

Movin' On
(Equipment & Techniques for Winter Hikers)
Harry Roberts
1977; 135 pp.
$4.95 postpaid from:
Stone Wall Press
5 Byron Street
Boston, MA 12108

•
If there's a "secret" to pitching a tent on snow, it's this — start with a firm platform. Truck around on your skis or your snowshoes, pack out the kitchen and the tent area and pack out a trail to the area you'll use as a latrine. Be meticulous; be thorough — which means, get to camp on time! Pack the kitchen first, so the cook can start to work, and then do the rest. The tent should be up and the bags out and fluffed at about just enough time before chow call to change into a dry undershirt and a heavy parka.

•
The cardinal rule of snowshoeing technique is to remember to pick up the foot to be moved ahead *over* the edge of the stationary foot and to move this foot far enough *ahead* so it won't encumber the stationary foot . . . Likely somewhere along the way the beginner will take his first spill into the soft, deep snow and wonder how on earth he will ever get back on his feet again. Here the pole can be used as a vertical prop . . . If the snowshoes seem hopelessly snarled and the snow bottomless, the bindings can be unhitched, the snowshoes taken off and set in a good position to use as a platform to get back on your feet again. Don't thrash around needlessly. We should all take a tip from oxen who lie quietly while their drivers arrange for them to get back on their feet, unlike horses who often get panic-stricken after a fall in the deep snow.

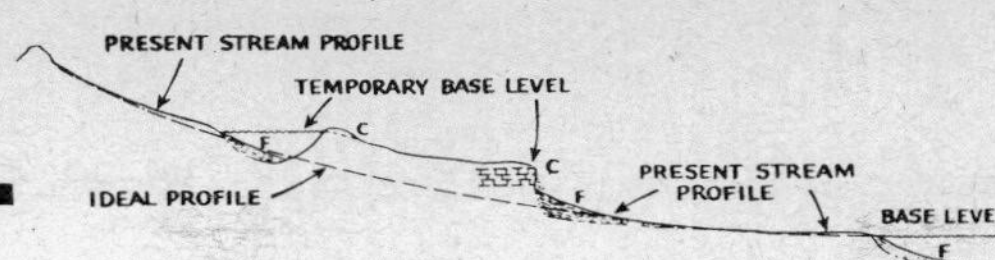

← Graded stream profile and base levels. Stream is cutting at C, filling at F. Dashed line is ideal profile.

•

The supreme aim of a stream is to make its bed form a smooth curve from its headwaters to its mouth, or *base-level*, a curve steep at the upper end, flat at the lower. When the ideal curve is achieved, the stream uses all its energy to carry all the debris dumped into it by side streams and gravity, and the stream is said to be at *grade*. Since perfect grade is elusive, a stream is always in flux, rarely satisfied for long. Lakes and waterfalls are particularly abhorrent. To fill the former the stream slows down (it must) and drops its load; to eliminate the latter it speeds up (it must) and picks up more tools to gouge away at the steep face, causing the falls to migrate upvalley, and leaving behind a deep gorge.

The mountaineer soon learns to avoid the temptation of trail-less riverside routes when marching into the hills, realizing that he may arrive at an impasse of cascading water and damp, sheer cliffs. A lake or waterfall acts as a *temporary baselevel*, and the stream above grades itself in relation to it, meanwhile trying to remove the lake or fall from the true grade curve.

Chimney climbing sequence →

Mountaineering

By far the most complete and sensitive treatment of mountaineering available. Oriented around Pacific Northwest mountaineering, where trails often end miles before the peaks begin, it is particularly relevant to wilderness camping and travel. It is much more than a book on how to climb, it reflects several generations of a respectful relationship with mountains. If you move (or sit) where there are trees, rocks, snow and brush, it speaks to your terrain. One limitation: little about dry, arid areas — glaciers are the local functional equivalent of deserts.
—Michael Templeton

Mountaineering
(The Freedom of the Hills)
Peggy Ferber, Editor
1960, 1974; 496 pp.
3rd Edition

$11.15 postpaid from:
The Mountaineers
719-B Pike Street
Seattle, WA 98101
or Whole Earth Household Store

← Climbing on Cathedral Peak; Cascade Range

Summit
Off Belay

Two classy magazines with gorgeous photos, the latest niceties of mountain technique and gear, and ads. I still mourn the demise of the riskier **Mountain Gazette.**
—SB

[Suggested by Drew Langsner and Al Perrin]

Summit
Jene M. Crenshaw and H.V.J. Kilness, Editors
$9/year (6 issues)
from:
Summit Magazine
P.O. Box 1889
Big Bear Lake, CA 92315

Off Belay
(The Mountain Magazine)
Ray Smutek, Editor
$12/year (6 issues)
from:
Off Belay
15630 S.E. 124th Street
Renton, WA 98055

↑ An exciting fingertip hang is involved at midpoint on the "Juggernaut," a Pueblo classic. Climber: Jeff Achey. —Summit

•

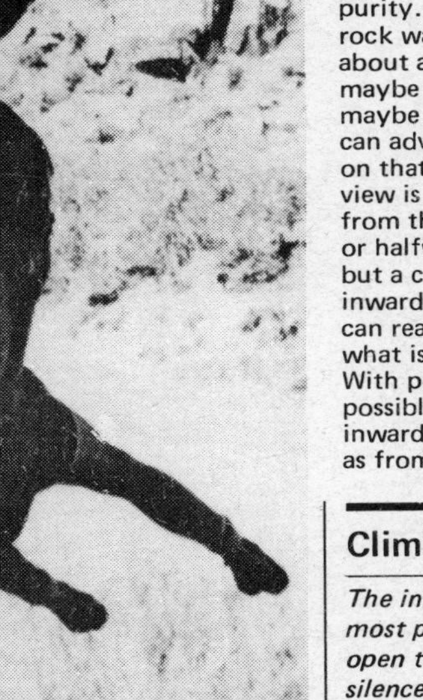

. . . bouldering has a delightful inherent purity. Find a suitable rock wall and you have about all that's required; maybe climbing shoes, maybe some chalk. You can adventure a long way on that little gear. The view is indeed different from the top of Everest or halfway up El Cap, but a chance to peer inward is what a climber can really value, and what is really sought. With perseverence it's as possible to glimpse inward from ten feet up as from ten thousand.

Climbing Ice

The initial reaction of most people when they open this book is total silence! The photographs are so awesome and the risks being taken are so apparently ultimate, that there is just nothing to say. Those few of you interested in trying ice climbing will find a very technical presentation of both strategy and tactics, technique of all sorts explained in detail, and an erudite discussion of equipment. Those of you who have no intention of ever doing this sort of thing may find much of the writing inspiring and exciting anyway, and of course the photographs! Ah yes, the photographs — and a reasonable price too. I've added this to my permanent library.
—J. Baldwin

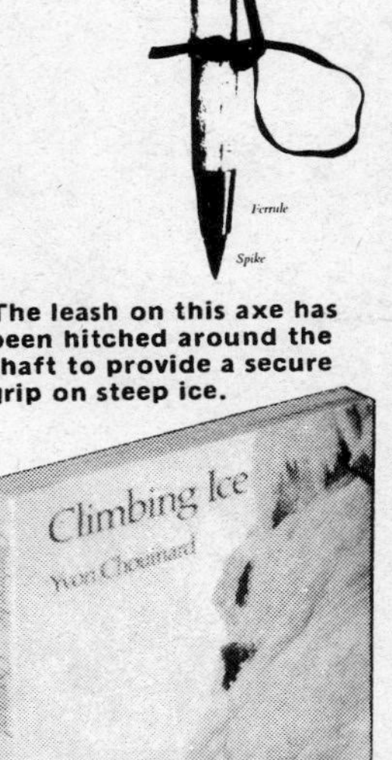

The leash on this axe has been hitched around the shaft to provide a secure grip on steep ice.

Climbing Ice
Yvon Chouinard
1978; 192 pp.
$9.95 postpaid from:
Sierra Club Books
P.O. Box 3886
Rincon Annex
San Francisco, CA 94119
or Whole Earth Household Store

→ Dale Bard and Rob Taylor on a free ascent of the Middle Ice Fall of Mount Fay in the Canadian Rockies. The last six meters actually overhang about fifteen degrees

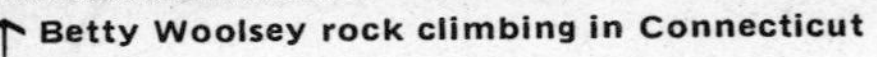

↑ Betty Woolsey rock climbing in Connecticut

Climbing in North America

Non-climbers (me) sometimes have difficulty understanding why climbers climb when it isn't any fun and the risks get ridiculous. Most climbing books don't say much about that, or if they do, it's concealed in a mass of equipment descriptions and jargon as mysterious as the motivations in question. Chris Jones has deftly managed to combine exciting accounts, diaries, and history with a handsome writing style. The result is that you can begin to feel what is behind the willingness to face hardship and death. I was fascinated by the controversies regarding the use or non-use of certain pieces of hardware, and the tough competitiveness underlying most of the expeditions. It's easy to starve while trying to read all about it in one sitting. By the fire.
—J. Baldwin

Climbing in North America
Chris Jones
1976; 392 pp.
$9.95 postpaid from:
University of California Press
2223 Fulton Street
Berkeley, CA 94720
or Whole Earth Household Store

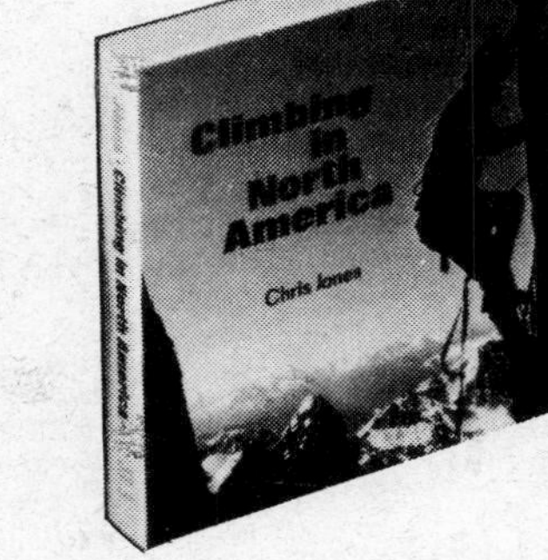

•

Even a single piton placement and removal may alter and scar the rock, and some classic routes are experiencing hundreds of ascents. Europeans never faced this problem because they have a tradition of leaving pitons in place. In the sixties British climbers started to wedge machine nuts into cracks. Later they developed special-purpose, wedge-shaped aluminum "nuts." Robbins advocated their use in 1967, though at that time more as a complement to pitons than a replacement. As climbers gained experience with nuts, they saw in them a way to preserve the rock. Moreover, dispensing with pitons was a new "game." The idea caught on fast. Today's beginning climber is unlikely even to own a piton hammer.

← Climbing Naiset Peak in 1920. Leader Albert MacCarthy belays William Stone, President of Purdue University, who died the next year on the first ascent of nearby Mount Eon. Note the primitive belaying methods.

Jim Bridwell on Butterfingers, Yosemite Valley. His hands are taped against abrasion and chalked to give extra grip. Note the nuts and chalk bag at his waist. ↓

↓ Snowpatch Spire

THE RISING SUN
NEIGHBORHOOD NEWSLETTER

We are as people and might as well get modest at it.

American Caves and Caving

Creeping around underground isn't everyone's idea of fun, but it ranks with technical rock climbing and mountaineering, and often utilizes similar techniques and attitudes. Aboveground, there really isn't much left to explore for the first time, especially in the U.S.A. Underground, the opportunities for true exploration are there, with all the risks and possibilities of reward. This book is a very thorough presentation of methods and equipment as well as the expected yarns and war stories. Vertical caving is especially well shown. Beginners might be a bit put off by the author's emphasis on emergencies (he's an M.D.) but considering where cavers cave, a bit of caution is obviously in order.

This book is already considered a classic and will likely remain so until the sport/art develops considerably more advanced techniques. —J. Baldwin

American Caves and Caving
William Halliday, M.D.
1974; 360 pp.

$12.95 postpaid from:
Harper & Row
Keystone Industrial Park
Scranton, PA 18512
or Whole Earth Household Store

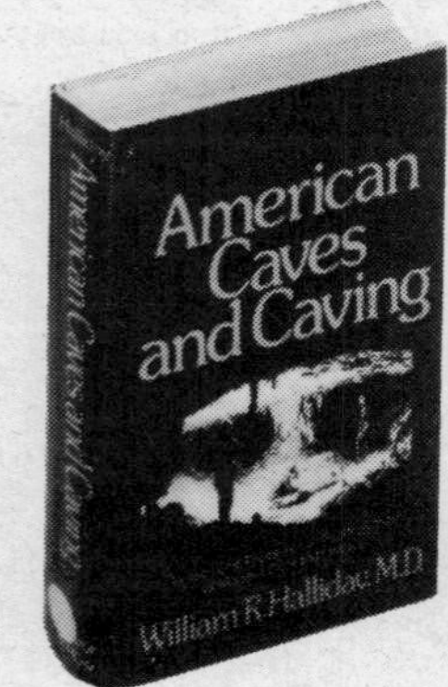

192-foot entrance drop in Stamps Pit Cave, Tennessee, showing vertical ribbing and other features of domepits. Harry White is shown as ascending by a standing rope technique.

•

If a rappel rope doesn't reach the bottom, a knot at the end reduces the incidence of air or ropeless rappelling, a distinctly undesirable technique.

The World of Caves

Ever hear of Ogof Ffynnon Ddu? It's a cave in Wales. I'd like to go there and check it out. I'd like to go to all the caves shown in this collection of the world's most fascinating spelunking. The descriptions are direct from the author's experience, and are accompanied by big, inciting color photographs. The hardships involved are probably more than you or I will likely undertake. Some caves are accessible to the tourist, but most require training and years of underground scrambling before a visit could be attempted. So much the better, then, that this fine volume is available at such a reasonable price. I stayed up all night wandering through its pages.
—J. Baldwin

The World of Caves
A.C. Waltham
1976; 128 pp.

OUT OF PRINT
G.P. Putnam and Sons

Get this book back in print!

A caver descends a thin wire ladder that disappears into the depths of Eldon Hole in the English Peak District.

Mountaineering Medicine
Medicine for Mountaineering

One small, one large, both for serious no-doctor situations. The small one carries easily and works in the field easily. The large one gives you an education and backs it up if you have it with you. Comparing **Medicine for Mountaineering** *to* **Advanced First Aid for All Outdoors** *(p. 415), the mountaineering book is bigger, more authoritative, stodgier, less well illustrated, and harder to use in the field. One thing I learned from the mountaineering book is that if someone can't breathe because of mangled face or a throat obstruction that the Heimlich maneuver (p. 324) won't remove, you can still save their life by poking a hole in their trachea.* —SB

Mountaineering Medicine
Fred Darvill, Jr., M.D.
1966, 1980; 60 pp.

$2.15 postpaid from:
Skagit Mountain Rescue Unit
P.O. Box 2
Mt. Vernon, WA 98273

Medicine for Mountaineering
James A. Wilkerson, M.D., Editor
1906, 1975; 367 pp.

$7.95 postpaid from:
The Mountaineers
719-B Pike Street
Seattle, WA 98101

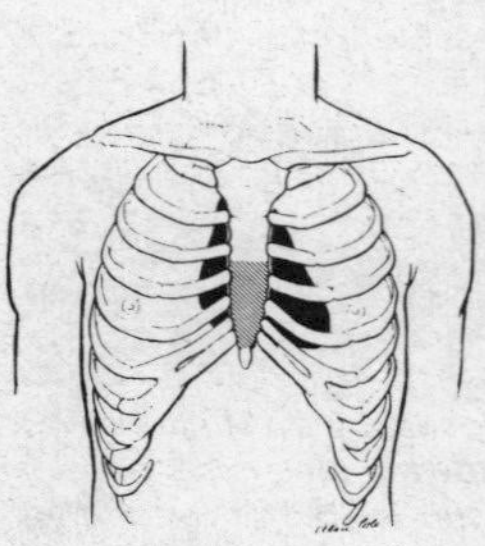

Area of the chest to which pressure is applied during external cardiac massage.

•

Incipient and/or first degree frostbite should be treated by warming the extremity against the warm skin of a companion (abdomen; armpit). More severe frostbite should not be treated until facilities for rapid rewarming are available. A climber may walk many miles on frozen feet, but once rewarming has been performed, he becomes a litter case. Rapid rewarming is achieved by immersing the cold damaged body parts in water at 104 - 108 degrees F. (40 - 42 degrees C.); most authorities recommend the use of a thermometer, feeling the temperature must be exact. However, in a crisis, one can test the water temperature by immersion of a normal hand. The water should be comfortably warm but should not burn the test hand. Severe pain occurs shortly after rewarming and therefore medication for pain relief should be available when rewarming is performed. Continue the soaking until flushing occurs in the tips of the fingers or toes, or for one hour, whichever is shorter. After the rewarming, the extremities should be handled gently to avoid further injury. Careful cleansing with a germicidal soap, padded sterile dressings, splinting, and observation for concomitant dehydration are indicated. Ideally, rewarming should be performed in a hospital where this equipment is available. If rewarming is done in the field, hospitalization must be effected as soon as possible.
—**Mountaineering Medicine**

•

If only one rescuer is present he must give both cardiac massage and artificial respiration. The technique generally recommended is to give fifteen compressions of the heart at a rate of approximately eighty per minute and then two quick breaths of artificial respiration. Repetition of the cycle at this rate provides approximately sixty cardiac compressions a minute.
—**Medicine for Mountaineering**

Great Pacific Iron Works

Almost everyone who goes into the mountains eventually develops an urge to try rock scrambling or climbing of some kind. It is therefore important to be aware of the best safety procedures and climbing aids available. Alpinists Yvon Chouinard and Tom Frost design and fabricate a high quality selection of modern climbing equipment.
—Drew Langsner

Great Pacific Iron Works
Catalog

free from:
The Great Pacific Iron Works
P.O. Box 150
Ventura, CA 93001

Asolo-Chouinard Friction Shoe — We have been working with Asolo in Italy for three years on developing a climbing shoe that will friction and smear on granite and still be able to edge sharp limestone holds. The Chouinard Friction Shoe is the result. For smearing and friction climbing we made tne sole flexible fore and aft but not quite so much as a pure friction shoe so that some degree of comfort and stability is gained in heel and toe chimneys and twisting toe jams. The sole is made of the same proven rubber used in EB's. The rubber rand comes up high on the heel for protection and maximum friction on heel and toe jamming.

The edging qualities come mainly from superb fit and from a thin plastic insole under the ball of the foot which creates a solid base for the rubber. A special last holds the foot tightly in place and does not allow it to roll inside the shoe when edging. Even though the sole profile is extremely narrow under the ball this superb last will accommodate very wide feet comfortably. In fact you can wear the same shoe for climbing 5.12 or walking back to camp. The fit will last through the life of the shoe because non-stretch breathable canvas is used to back up the split leather uppers. The leather covers the entire shoe for maximum durability, and the shoe is resolable. Sizes 3 - 13 incl. ½ sizes. Weight: 28 oz. $80.

REFLECTIONS FROM WITHIN THE OUTDOORS EQUIPMENT INDUSTRY

by Bruce LeBel

"Functional Quality." Never lose this perspective when considering backpacking/mountaineering equipment. I could end now with that general principle for consideration, but the information and detailing which have led to it (and sprung from it) are the tools really needed to make an efficient, effective, and safe trip into the wilderness of equipment purchases.

I have attempted as fair and informed a researching and description of the present state of value in these products as I could make. The result is a brief critical examination of most of the industry and its products. Included as considerations are: Materials; Construction; Features; Buying a Product; Company Reviews; Product Reviews.

And it's all about to be preceded by some non-specific thoughts about manufacturing these goods.

A wide range of approaches and capabilities can be found within the outdoor equipment industry. It is as important to choose the quality of the company whose goods you purchase as it is to choose the product itself. One company may be comprised of a wife and husband while another is a "wholly-owned subsidiary." Some are special specialists in alpine equipment, and others manufacture across such a wide spectrum of products that the specialized requirements of the down bag and parka are neglected. The middle ground between non-industrial craft and craftless industry is where 99% of the finest value will be found, for the following reasons:

1
Economies of scale. *It is simply less expensive to make 100 of something than it is to make one of the exact same thing. On the other hand it will never be possible to make more than a few items using limited resources such as down with a fill power of greater than "550."*

2
A complex of functions: *forecasting, purchasing, scheduling, engineering, quality control, data processing, personnel. There is much more to these products than a designer and a sewing machine operator. When peak efficiency coincides with optimum quality, value in real terms results.*

3
Collective experience: *knowledge and training in marketing, manufacturing, and backpacking/mountaineering throughout the organization is essential for an integral product.*

4
Consistency: *Will this item being considered for purchase have the same construction as the one preceding or the one following it out of production?*

5
Reliability: *Will the company stand behind its product? Will it even be around to do so?*

The purchase of a bag, parka, pack, or tent is an investment requiring no small sum of money, yet it will provide exceptional benefits through use and should be built to last your lifetime. Value is not cheap.

MATERIALS

INSULATORS

Goose Down *The lightest and most efficient insulator known, by reason of its complex structure of plumules and correspondingly large amount of surface area with which to trap air. Goose down's compressability, resilience, organic softness, and excellent breathability have not been duplicated.*

"Fill power" is the often cited descriptor for quality of material used, and is certainly important, but is not the only variable characteristic. Another characteristic to compare is "recovery," or the length of time the material requires to regain its total loft. This is an important aspect to consider as it relates directly to the longevity of the material and also because some "high fill power" downs have awful recovery. Also of importance is the feather content, as all downs have some percentage of feathers — usually between 5% and 20%. Perhaps the key indicator is the size or maturity of the down pods themselves, the larger older geese (European) producing the finest down.

I met Bruce LeBel a few years ago whilst discussing the fine points of a North Face geodesic tent design. Bruce is a manufacturing engineer — he designs the systems whereby the goods get made right. He showed me some of the small details that must be properly attended if quality is to result at a decent price. I learned a lot talking with him and thought his information might be useful to **Catalog** *readers.*

He is open to accusations of bias of course, but if you inspect (as I have) the products he mentions, you will probably agree with his conclusions. He says, "I wouldn't work for an outfit that didn't make good stuff." It's nice to know someone still feels that way. —J. Baldwin

Testing of goose down can be as simple a process as measuring loft in a calibrated cylinder (hopefully in a temperature and humidity controlled environment) or as complex a process as applying a Lorch separator to determine exact percentages of down, feather and "other" content. It is difficult to be sure that you are getting what is claimed unless the manufacturer has a complete materials testing program in-house. Numerous tests throughout a large sample of one company's "700 fill power" down actually filled only 479 cubic inches/ounce. Beware of hype.

As a consumer your best test may simply be to measure (using tape or ruler) and compare the actual loft of the product you may purchase against the maker's claims. Also subjectively test for recovery by stuffing the bag and refluffing it, comparing several bags.

Is there any value to using down with a fill power claim of greater than 550 (550 is the highest fill consistently available as an industry standard, achieved by blending Chinese and European downs)? Or is it simply a high cost for the actual performance? As mentioned previously, the consistency of these materials is also questionable. How critical to you is four to eight ounces? Goose down bags in general are so efficient that it would seem to be in only the most extreme situations that the payback on greater than 550 fill would materialize.

PolarGuard *A polyester pile with its continuous fibers crimped and stacked in layers. It is the only polyester pile which is not chopped and carried by a resin or backing material. Thus, PG better maintains its tensile strength and structural stability through use.*

The thermal efficiency of PolarGuard is "quite high," and its lower cost results in a lower cost for the product. Significantly, PG absorbs less than 1% water by weight and, like wool but unlike down, retains its loft when wet to provide (some) insulation. It is thus a superior insulator in areas of high humidity or much rain. Life expectancy and cleaning are the main problems with PolarGuard, as with all synthetic fills.

Thinsulate *Providing both lightness (compared to other synthetics) and loft efficiency in insulation, thinsulate uses millions of extremely fine polyolefin fibers (finer than human hair) plus supportive polyester fibers affixed to a backing material. The insulative value is approximately twice that of PolarGuard by thickness and 1½ times that of PG by weight, primarily as a result of the increased surface area of the fibers which trap and deaden air, retaining body heat. The result is that insulating garments can be realized with less bulk and better fit for increased mobility and style. Thinsulate absorbs less than 1% water by weight, dries quickly, and retains its loft when wet. As yet there is no thinsulate material appropriate for use in sleeping bags. 3M is working on such a material. Thinsulate is proving to be effective in doing just what it claims, and several manufacturers are making a wide selection of styled and classic outwear which is indeed "full function."*

HoloFill *and* **KodoFill** *are both chopped polyester fibers which have similar insulative properties to PolarGuard but require being sewn to a backing for stability (heavier weight) and have less structural stability (more limited lifetime).*

FABRICS

When searching for value in a product it is important to compare the fabrics used and their relative functional qualities.

On packs, for instance, compare the look and feel of two oxfords. Is one appropriately heavier? Is the other better coated for waterproofness over time? Is a heavier weight cordura more or less appropriate for your needs? Do the manufacturers have thorough material inspection programs?

Compare the performance requirement of the material. The fabric presently requiring closest examination is Gore-Tex, a laminate of an ultra-thin layer of teflon (and either one or two fabrics) which is porous to vapor and (usually) impermeable to liquid. Is Gore-Tex really advantageous for your sleeping bag shell as you will use it?

If you have a tent to sleep in, you certainly don't need to spend any more money on water- and wind-repellancy for your sleeping bag. The value of Gore-Tex is quite high in some applications and nonexistent in others (who needs Gore-Tex gaiters?). Consider carefully the added cost vs. return. Gore-Tex used to lose much of its quality when soiled by dirt or perspiration, but this serious flaw has been mostly overcome by a revised laminate. (Gore-Tex may still leak when the fabric is stressed, such as at the knee in rain pants.) Also, water will always move through sewn seams, unless sealed, and who wants to put liquid plastic all over a $125 good-looking jacket? Personally I consistently use a Gore-Tex Windjammer (by North Face, a pullover with no seams over the shoulder) and have been disappointed (wet) only once. I do not consider GT to be value-adding for sleeping bag shells in the vast majority of situations.

Many manufacturer's products differ from each other mainly in the type of fabric used. A brief comparison of similarly applied fabrics:

- **Ripstop** *vs.* **Taffeta** *Taffeta has the smoother "hand" and a higher thread count. Ripstop has the highest strength-to-weight ratio of any nylon fabric, achieved via extra-strength yarns woven in at regular intervals. Downproofness is achieved in ripstop by "calendering," a process of rolling the piece goods between smooth heated cylinders while applying a small amount of a special treatment. This also increases water repellancy. Beware down-leaking fabric. Flame retardance is achieved (in most cases) by the application of a thiourea-based compound which has proven to be non-carcinogenic.*
- **60/40** *vs.* **65/35** *The former is a 60% cotton (fill) with 40% nylon (warp), has a soft feel, good water and wind repellancy and high abrasion strength. The weave has shown a tendency to fray and separate over time. The latter is 65% polyester and 35% cotton "intimate" blend (blended in the yarn itself). It has highest tear strength, best water-repellancy of blended fabrics, best resistance to ultraviolet rays.*
- **Oxford** *vs.* **Cordura** *Oxford has the greater weave strength and thus a lighter fabric (compared to cordura) and usually meets the need. Cordura has excellent abrasion resistance, is about 25% heavier for similar strength, and has an intriguing brushed look (a bona-fide marketing tailfin). Whichever is on your pack, it should be heavily coated for waterproofness. Cordura is harder to waterproof. For a porosity check, hold one layer of the fabric up to a light and compare fabrics.*

Some other important materials considerations are:

- **Snaps** *A "prong" snap is far superior to a "punch" type snap as the prongs only separate the weave when passing through rather than cutting through it and locally weakening the fabric. The cross-bent prongs also give a more positive attachment, assuring a snap which will stay on for the life of the product.*
- **Webbing** *Is the material the appropriate size, weight, and stiffness for its function? Is it adequately tacked in place and the fabric well reinforced? This "flat rope," a spin-off of WWII research and development, is normally of excellent strength, but some soft and loose material is around which wears and frays quite rapidly.*
- **Zippers** *Of all the components which come together into backpacking products, the highest failure point is in the zipper. A cheap zipper is doom. Tooth zippers provide a sure positive lock. The larger molded plastic tooth zippers are easy starting and sliding, but use them with caution, because a broken tooth is the end for that unit, and any caught fabric is likely to be torn. "Coil" zippers are smooth sliding, self-repairing, long-lived, and won't destroy any fabric they may catch. An example of a proven value-adding expense is North Face's use of the German-made Optilon coil zippers in their down bags. For a product with a lifetime warranty the best zipper available is the only zipper to use.*
- **Buckles, sliders, cordlocks** *Examine the very different hardwares on the products you compare, looking for simplicity of design and operation, durability, and performance. Can you adjust your pack with your mittens on?*
- **Leather** *Should be top grain and chromium-tanned. Check accessory patches for their strength, as a ripped patch is potentially hazardous at the worst, added weight at the best. The cost of leather is soaring, so a leather bottom on a day pack is an example of a feature which is losing its payback.*

CONSTRUCTION

In the actual production of these goods they are all essentially hand made and thus subject to variance. Several companies, large and small, have reduced this variance to a minimum, while too many others allow poor work to slip by.

On many (20%) of the goods I examined from one company, between 6 and 40 stitches per inch were found (6 is a weak seam while 40 has destroyed the fabric.) Eight to 10 s.p.i. is what should be found on nearly every backpacking product — 10 to 12 for tents. Check. Measure. Some parkas from another well known company were found with four s.p.i., showing some serious flaws in their quality control. Consistent with this, this company's packs are known to come apart regularly, although fortunately for the consumer they offer a lifetime warranty.

Look for reinforcing layers of fabric in all stress points and for reinforced stitching on any stressed seam. Top-stitching, double-needle seams, back tacking and bar-, arrow- and X-tacking all have their place and should be there in order to achieve extended performance. A pack of good design but 100% single-needle construction will simply not hold together as well as one which has been reinforced using a heavy-duty (and expensive) cam-automated tacker. These small differences can have the most profound results, as any victim of an untimely failed seam can testify.

In "hot cutting" of fabric a rotary shear with heated blade is used to individually cut every piece of fabric. This is done to prevent "ravelling" or fraying of the fabric. It does. However it is a classic example of high-cost low-return production technique. Constructing a stack cut fabric using proper structural seams such as overlock with safety stitch, double-needle lap feld, bias tape with stopstitch, or even a simple set stitch with proper topstitching accomplishes the same result at a much lower cost. (The last requires care in gentle laundering, which is also a requirement for any down product.) The savings of stack cutting (150 - 400 ply at a time) are a standard in the garment industry and are in no way a hindrance to the longevity of any properly constructed product. In addition, if your seams should fray, most quality manufacturers' warranties will cover repair or replacement. There are wiser investments than hot-cut products.

FEATURES

Design characteristics vary with performance requirements, manufacturers' capabilities, and marketing strategies.

Your own requirements should be well considered before shopping. Within the product lines available there are both functional overlapping and quantum differences in performance capabilities. (E.g., many 3-season modified-mummy down-filled sleeping bags are on the market. When comparing features, do you really need a down "collar" or a double draft flap for such 3-season use? Both are costly additions.) My own strategy is to look for the simplest design with the highest quality material and construction which meets projectable needs. It is as bad to "over buy" as it is to "under buy." Remember, functional quality.

YOU AND THE PRODUCT

- **Performance requirements.** *Know your needs. How cold the nights? How heavy the load? Over what terrain? How diverse the situations to be met? How rugged the use? How much style in your garments?*
- **Budget.** *Know your pocketbook. Spending limits will help guide you to find the most for your money. 20% (list) price differences for similar products from different manufacturers are not uncommon. (If more of us shop wisely for maximum value it just could help hold prices in line.)*
- **Fit.** *Your pack should feel as though it grew out of your hips and shoulders and met mid-back. Before buying, fiddle with the adjustments until you are sure that that model will fit you perfectly. Can the loading be adjusted from shoulders to hips as terrain varies? Your sleeping bag should be neither snug nor airy. Get in it before buying. Compare the fit of different cuts and different lengths. Your parka should be both close-fitting and allow completely unrestricted mobility. The shoulder seam should fall at or just over the point of the shoulder (depending on how much bulk you'll be wearing underneath). The sleeves, when unfastened at the cuff and pulled out straight, should not rise above the wrist more than 1". With your arms stretched out in front the parka should be tight but not strained across your back. Check out the pockets for ease of access.*

Continued on next page

THE RISING SUN
NEIGHBORHOOD NEWSLETTER

Art finally after 6 months on the job and the rest of us failing for years thought of a way to describe the *Whole Earth Catalog* to straight people such as ladies with yarn shops in Iowa: "It's a less formal *Consumer Reports.*" Don said he should say, "Remember all those things you were paranoid about? That's it."

LeBel's outdoor industry survey continued from last page

COMPANY REVIEWS

The North Face, 1234 Fifth Street, Berkeley, CA 94710. *Begun 12 years ago in the back room of a Berkeley store. Now holds 50% market share in the specialty backpacking market in bags and parkas and is rapidly growing in packs and tents. Still independently owned and operated by K. Hap Klopp. (Through an ESOP program all employees share in some portion of company ownership.) The North Face is this industry's primary steady keel and innovative source. Introduced the original internal frame panel-loading rucksack as well as the original geodesic tents. The down-filled gear is incomparable in consistently excellent materials and construction via the extensive quality control program from which the entire product line benefits. Excellent warranty and repairs program. (This is where I work.) Catalog free.*

Sierra Designs, 247 Fourth Street, Oakland, CA 94607. *Founded by two campers looking for a source of quality equipment. George Marks, one of the founders, is still the designer. Sierra Designs is now owned by C.M.L. of Concord, MA. Their stitching is excellent but materials quality is inconsistent. Nice parkas, decent bags (highlighted by several unique construction techniques), funky tents; good people. Catalog free.*

JanSport, Paine Field Industrial Park, Everett, WA 98204. *Owned by K2 (of downhill ski fame). Their frame packs shine, and other product designs are also differable from the crowd. The sewing is inconsistent however, and some of the specialized components (as the pack frame connections) are not known for their longevity. Examine carefully the particular unit you may buy for its workmanship. Catalog free.*

Trailwise, 2407 Fourth Street, Berkeley, CA 94710. *Owned by Boss Industries, Kewanee, IL, a manufacturer of work gloves. One of the original manufacturers of alpine equipment, but too extended in product offering for their scale. Limited recent innovation. Generally acceptable designs and quality, but production inefficiency results in their higher prices. Catalog free.*

Holubar, P.O. Box 7, Boulder, CO 80306. *Owned by Johnson Wax. Still maintains much of the materials and construction consistency well-founded by Alice and Roy Holubar over 32 years of manufacturing. They are, however, relying more and more on outside suppliers as Johnson Wax also owns Eureka tents and Camp Trails. Holubar offers most of its products in kit form as well as ready sewn. Catalog free.*

Marmot Mountain Works, 331 South 13th, Grand Junction, CO 81501. *Independent and claiming to be at the utmost peak of quality, MMW products were found by this reviewer to be functionally inconsistent, mostly from sewing problems, more often than any other manufacturer I have examined. Very disappointing. They seem to emphasize design frills, costly materials, and in my view unnecessarily costly production methods (such as "hot cutting" individual fabric pieces). Cost vs. performance seems to offer a low relative value, except in a few cases such as their vest.*

Class 5, 1480 66th Street, Emeryville, CA 94608. *Owned and operated by the original designer for The North Face, Justus Bauschinger. Another "pinnacle" company that's not quite what it's claimed: again, production inefficiencies primarily as a result of small scale. Good products, but also more costly for little if any gain in actual performance. Catalog free.*

Wilderness Experience, 20675 Nordhoff Street, Chatsworth, CA 91311. *The Thompson brothers run a small scale, reasonable quality operation. Their packs are adequately constructed (could be better reinforced) but seem to be priced more towards what the market can bear rather than from a percentage over costs. Very few in-house designs apparent. They seem to sell through a number of outlets which lack adequate product knowledge. Catalog free.*

Lowe Alpine Systems, P.O. Box 189, Lafayette, CO 80026. *The Lowe family are renowned rock and ice climbers, specialists in climbing gear, and have had some of their innovative designs become industry standards. Their execution of the product shows a lack of manufacturing experience, however. The entirely single-needle construction of their packs predicts limited longevity. Catalog free.*

Stephenson's Warmlite, RFD 4, Box 145, Gilford, NH 03246. *Here is the real pinnacle, at least in their down bag design. You've got to pay for the crafted product, but to some it is certainly a worthwhile expense. This is a family-owned and operated company that has consistently held to its principles and has contributed much to the information needed for highest-performance products. Catalog $3.*

Down Home, West Fork Road, Deadwood, OR 97430. *A young couple manufacturing (crafting) custom down bags of extremely high quality. Several esoteric features. Costly. Catalog $3.*

Recreational Equipment, Inc. (REI, the Co-op), P.O. Box C-88125, Seattle, WA 98188. *One-stop shopping for its 1,000,000 co-op members, but shop carefully! Recent financial problems and changes in management portend a somewhat uncertain future. Emphasis on quality seems to have diminished. The Taiwan-sewn down parkas are a tragedy. The sleeping bags have been dangerously over-rated. REI private label equipment is generally of median price and quality. Product selection and promotion is of variable value. Catalog free.*

Frostline, Dept. C., Frostline Circle, Denver, CO 80241. *Now owned by Gillette Company. If you sew, you could save many dollars by constructing from a Frostline kit, plus have the pride of producing your own gear. The down bag and frame pack designs are weak points; you can get superior value in the marketplace. Many high quality kits, well tested for sewing ease with only a few hang-ups (e.g., hand setting of snaps scars and dents the snap). Complete warranty. Catalog free.*

Kelty Pack, P.O. Box 639, Sun Valley, CA 91352. *Originally the standard against which others were measured, and still of consistent quality. Recent innovations has been limited as it has been sold twice, first to C.M.L. (parent company of Sierra Designs) then recently to Kellwood, the $500 million sales company supplying 90% of its goods to Sears and discount retail stores. Catalog free.*

BACKPACKS

DAYPACKS

Comparing materials and design, construction, and price, there are a large number of excellent daypacks available. Differences are scarcely discernible. JanSport, Kelty, The North Face, and Wilderness Experience are consistently recommendable. Be sure to carefully choose the design which best suits your needs, and do look for reinforced construction and warranty.

INTERNAL FRAME PACKS

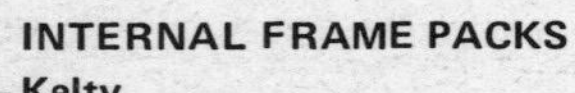

← Kelty

Cinch Packs. *Simultaneously adjust their capacity to your load and compress themselves to your body for comfort and balance, eliminating side-to-side sway and movement of gear.*

Pinnacle. *Expedition-quality pack using 18 oz. Ballistic cloth (to withstand the most extreme use) and a suspension system adapted from their Massif frame. Excellent design, construction and materials; high price.*

The North Face

Ruthsac. *The original panel-loading interior frame pack is still the excellent general purpose unit. Very comfortable fully adjustable suspension system (bend the contoured aluminum stays to fit the shape of your back precisely; no structural weakening). "Conical cut" padded hip belt provides proper weight distribution through hips. Panel-loading allows access to every part of the compartment at any time, but requires careful packing.*

Crevasse. *Designed primarily for skiing and climbing and thus refined in shape, fit, and attachment capabilities, this pack is adapted from the proven performance of the Ruthsac. When compared with similar packs available from other manufacturers, the Crevasse showed better reinforcement, better construction consistency, and a 20% lower price for no sacrifice of features or performance capabilities.*

FRAME PACKS WITH "FIXED" SUSPENSION (hips and packframe are in a fixed position)

Kelty packs have proven to be incontestably superior in design, construction, comfort and durability, and overall performance, primarily as a result of Dick Kelty's extensive experience and ingenuity. Such features as the TIG welded frames with their spoked structure, the frame extension option, and the unique camlock buckle on the waist belt make these packs perform. A variety of sack configurations are available for all three frame systems: Massif, for greatest durability; Mountaineer, for a lighter framepack; StretchFrame, for the growing backpacker.

← Kelty Massif Tioga

FRAME PACKS WITH "INDEPENDENT" SUSPENSION (allows hip motion independent of pack frame)

JanSport. *The waist suspension system on the Dhaulagiri and Alpine Phantom packs is in effect a load distributing (limited) universal joint which allows for motion of the hips independent of the motion of the pack frame and increases the ability for the packer to shift the load from shoulders and back to waist as changes in terrain require. The adjustability of the frame and the suspension system is 100% via machined aluminum cam fittings attaching the pack and waistbelt as well as for positioning frame crossbars. Several packsacks available; examine the stitching carefully as inconsistencies are prevalent.*

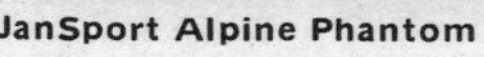

JanSport Alpine Phantom

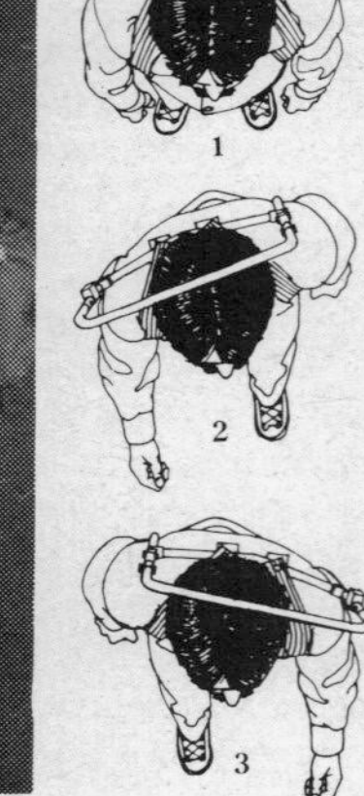

How the frame works

The North Face. *Back Magic independent suspension is realized through a patented joint made of nylon Zytel and a urethane elastomer which interfaces the frame with the waist suspension. The result is an incredibly comfortable load bearing system. Mobility, flexibility, and light weight surpass the JanSport system; however adjustability and load variability are not as great. Some view the joint as a structural weakness and fear its failure on a trek, but extensive research and design and testing of every joint prior to installation insures a reliable and durable frame pack offering the maximum comfort available for carrying a load on your back.*

SLEEPING BAGS

GOOSE DOWN FILL

These bags offer maximum efficiency and comfort for the backpacker who desires the most warmth for the least weight and will be able to protect the bag from becoming wet. There are many differences in materials used, design, construction, and performance capabilities. There is also a lot of hype. Beware marketing "tailfins" such as excessive fill-power claims or superfluous features, for they are often disfunctional and are always costly. Following are descriptions of similar bags (mummy shape, 8" loft total) from five sources with distinctly different approaches to design and production of this artifact.

boxed Down Dipper

Down Home "Dipper." *A custom-designed handcrafted beauty for those with a need for the best and money to burn. The young couple who produce these bags use more complex construction techniques and offer a wider variety of options than any other manufacturer. A floating hood (with 10 separate down compartments!) fully surrounds the head and is available either fixed to the bag or floating for those who sleep on their side. An affixed "boxed" hood is also available. The shoulders of the bag fully surround the upper torso, a truly sculptural form which requires some extremely difficult sewing. A double zipper system (originated by Stephenson's Warmlite) totally eliminates the normal cold line by maintaining similar differential along the zipper as throughout the rest of the bag. Custom options include total loft, bottom loft, hood style, bag girth, bag length, outer shell fabric, inner shell fabric, and removable liner. The Gore-Tex model with vapor barrier liner goes for about $395.*

floating

Holubar "Timberline." *Twenty years of performance have proven the value of this no-frills fully-functional bag. 1.9 oz, ripstop outer and inner shells, blocked channel construction, generous draft flap; the basic bag efficiently produced. The same model is available in a sew-it-yourself kit (as with many Holubar products) which seems to be superior to Frostline's. The ready-made goes for approximately $215; the kit for $50 less. More kits:* **Country Ways,** *p. 427.* ↓

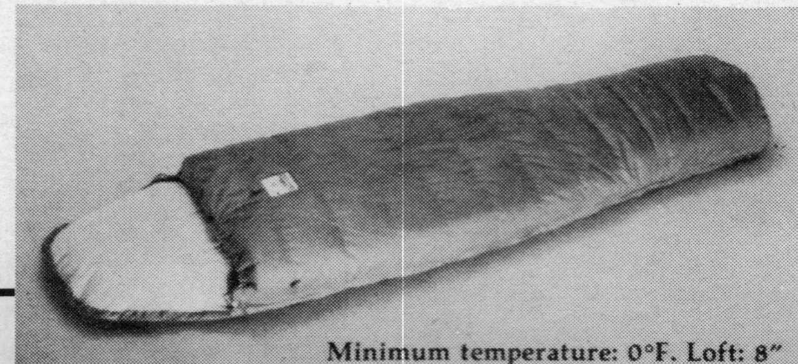

Minimum temperature: 0°F. Loft: 8"

GARMENTS

DOWN-FILLED, FOR EXTREME COLD

"Brooks Range" — North Face. *Simply the warmest, most comfortable and most durable parka available for sub-zero use. 3" wide inner and outer draft flaps, disc velcro cuff and zipper flap closures (no snaps to freeze shut), huge hood and handwarmer cargo pockets and 4" of loft all around. Approximately $195.*

"Expedition II" — Holubar. *Two separate goose down layers in an offset position, five pockets, two down insulated, stretch nylon cuff, waist and hip drawcords, and a generous down fill. Approximately $185, including hood. Expedition II pants are also available for the complete Michelin Man.*

DOWN-FILLED, FOR WINTER USE

The North Face "Serow." *Over the compartmentalized down-filled inner shell is sewn an outer shell of 65/35 cloth, a construction leaving no sewn through seams as cold spots. The finest construction and most consistent materials of any similar product. About $120, plus $17.50 for the hood.*

Sierra Designs "Inyo." *A heavy-duty windbreaking insulator, of similar construction as the Serow with a different fit and fewer pockets. Large No. 10 zipper, 60/40 cloth outer shell, reliable stitching. $125, plus $16 for the hood.*

North Face "Sierra"

Sierra Designs "Thinsulate" 60/40 Parka

DOWN-FILLED 4-SEASON BACKPACKER PARKAS

The North Face "Sierra." *The first of the best, and the last to hold prices under the $100 mark. Excellent fit for freedom of movement, elastic cuffs, double slider zipper, highest quality consistent materials and construction; lifetime warranty. Available in ripstop or 65/35 outer fabrics, with optional hood.*

Sierra Designs "Whitney" and "Toyabe." *Taffeta or 60/40 outer shells, and very little else different between this and The North Face product except a slightly higher price. SD also offers a bargain parka "Sierra" for about $20 less but of nowhere near the same performance or quality.*

Holubar "Ascent." *Generously filled and available in taffeta or 65/35, this parka offers the same durability, protection, and features as the above, with just a bit more down. Also available as a kit at about 35% savings.*

POLARGUARD PARKAS

PolarGuard is a real dog when it comes to garments, both because it is difficult to style and because it doesn't launder well. Holubar and JanSport offer the most stylish models. The North Face offers the best backpacking model.

THINSULATE PARKAS AND VESTS

Once again, look to Sierra Designs and The North Face for the best value in the field. Sierra Designs was the first company to offer a thinsulate parka and they now use it to the exclusion of PolarGuard. Sierra offers a wide range of styles, including an insulated version of their 60/40 Mountain parka, designed for all around use from the woods to the slopes to around town. The versatility of thinsulate is rapidly becoming apparent, and the material itself seems to have a superior durability to any previously available synthetic insulation. (I've worn a North Face all winter, including night rides on my BMW, and have yet to feel anything but warm under a layer of thinsulate.)

Marmot Mountain Works "Gopher." *Marmot uses high loft (high cost) down, individually hot cuts (high cost) the Gore-Tex (high cost) fabric which is sewn entirely by one (high cost) seamstress. Seven baffles in the foot, double draft tubes, and a "shoulder muff" are also included and of questionable worth. At approximately $300 the performance vs. cost equation leads this reviewer to question the value of this bag.*

Sierra Designs "Swallowtail." *The SD bags include several unique functional construction differences which add little to the cost of the product. Innovations include "tuck-stitch" baffling which leaves no thread on the surface to abrade or catch, and longitudinal torso baffles which assure full loft over the upper body (no down migration to the sides of the bag is possible). SD quality of materials varies considerably, however, so be sure to check the fabric and down loft carefully. At about $220, this bag rates high.*

The North Face "Chamois." *Another "basic" bag with several effective details such as the top performing "Optilon" zipper, oversized draft tube, and thoroughly tested materials, plus complete inspection by quality control and a full lifetime warranty. At approximately $200 this bag will perform as well for a lower cost as any of the other bags studied by this reviewer.*

DOWN-FILLED WITH "OTHER THAN DOWN" BOTTOM

"Cascadia" — REI. *With goose down fill on the top and PolarGuard fill on the bottom, this three season bag is theoretically advantageous by joining the loft and stuffability of down with the lesser compressability of PolarGuard. My opinion is that this melding of materials presents the worst of both. Polarguard will age and lose its loft long before the down tires, and the temptation to use the bag in a damp environment will lead to the failure of the down as an insulator. About $150.*

Stephenson's Warmlite "Triple Bag." *"Five bags for the price of one. . ." or only slightly more; anyway it's worth it. Stephenson's engineering background (aerospace) has been well applied to backpacking products, and the "triple" proves out. The foam or "Down Air Mat" bottom beats the down compressability problem, the bottoms, sides and the top of the bag are filled with the highest quality goose down (750 fill is claimed) and the design is pure function. The double zipper system eliminates the normal cold line which draft flaps attempt to inhibit, and lead to the bag's key: two upper layers which can be used either separately or in combination to give comfortable sleep in any condition. Wow! Stephenson also pioneered, and for years was alone in offering, a fitted, attachable vapor-barrier liner (they work). From $275 to $460 depending on size and foam or down air mat bottom, with $100 worth of options available for tropical to snow cave use.*

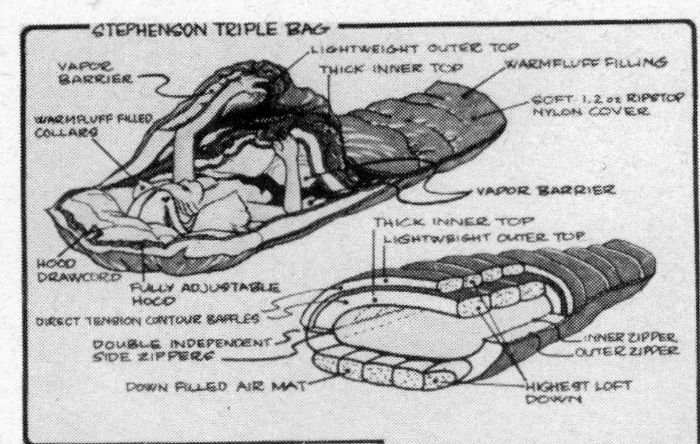

POLARGUARD FILL BAGS

There is little of the differentiation of down bags to be found among the PG filled product, and so the best strategy seems to be to look to the most consistent and reputable manufacturers who offer a complete line to choose from. For this reason, I suggest looking to The North Face or Sierra Designs for your PolarGuard bag, for one of the two will offer the appropriate product at the best price for whatever requirement you may have. ■

Stephenson Warmlite

Jack Stephenson, an aeronautical engineer, began making superior and occasionally radical camping gear more than ten years ago. I went for it then with one of his incredibly light tents (less than half the weight of most competition and better in storms) and I have not been sorry. His sleeping bags are a wonder too. Made with cloth that reflects your radiated heat back to you, they feature a bottom that includes a built-in mattress, and two tops. The light top is good for summer, the heavy one for fall and both for winter. Adjustable. Expensive. Effective. And controversial too in some quarters. I have found Warmlite equipment to be very fine, and the catalog is too: Jack and his family are featured, nude, modeling the goods, while Jack fills your head with the logic behind his designs. Super! (His stuff is available only by mail order. No middle men.) —J. Baldwin

Stephenson Warmlite
Catalog
$3 postpaid from:
Stephenson
RFD 4
Box 145
Gilford, NH 03246

Warmlite 2 RS Billee $265

27 Warmlites, zipped together

Triple bags, all full loft with highest quality 750 down

Girth	52	56	60	64	70	over 70
Foam bottom	$276	$322	$345	$368	$396	$5.75/in
DAM bottom	$333	$385	$408	$431	$460	$6.85/in

Includes foam or Down AirMat, pump and sack
SSSS, Stephenson Super Silver Sleeper, $750
Extra large bag sack with bag order, $5

OPTIONS:
1. Net top for tropical use $35
2. Cotton bottom liner for tropic use $20
3. Waterproof single sheet top cover $20
4. Waterproof bottom cover, zip on $23
5. DAM purchased SEPARATELY without a bag, $75
6. Extra thick top, cost is 50% of foam bottom bag price.

THE RISING SUN
NEIGHBORHOOD NEWSLETTER

"I think people with certain kinds of parents can recognize each other by the fake limp. 'Sorry I exist, Dad, but I'll seem incompetent to make up for it.' "

E.M.S.

Eastern Mountain Sports is the big Back East store. They feature items from many sources, not just in-house brands, and their catalog is among the fattest. They have a particularly good selection of cross country skis and other winter equipment.
—J. Baldwin

Eastern Mountain Sports
Catalog
free from:
Eastern Mountain Sports, Inc.
Vose Farm Road
Peterborough, NH 03458

Double Gradient Density Lens — For unusually intense glare from extra-bright sky or reflection from snow, water. Coating of Inconel, a form of stainless steel, is deposited on lens. It gradually becomes thinner, less dense, from edge to center. Transmission of visible light ranges from 4% at the edge to 31% at center. Coated on both top and bottom areas.
69-0321, Outdoorsman Frame $37.00
69-0149, Large Metal Frame $34.00

Optimus 8R Stove — Scaled-down version of the 111B. Weight saved by dropping pump, cutting fuel tank size. Still a good choice when cooking for 1 - 3 people. Cleaning needle included. Wt. 1 lb. 7 oz.
63-0285, $41.50

MSR Gasoline and Multi-Fuel Stoves — Lightest for their heating power. Work well at all altitudes, temperatures; easy to run. Priming pump, unique flint lighter. Little risk of over-generating. Simple if crude wind screen. Gas model burns Coleman or Blazo; multi-fuel burns Stoddard Solvent, No. 1 stove oil, No. 1 diesel, JP-4, Blazo. In a pinch, both will burn leaded auto gasoline for some 2 hours before gumming up. Can be ungummed in the field. Fuel bottle not included. Wt. less bottle, 1 lb. 5 oz.; wind screen 3 oz.
63-1226, Gasoline Stove, $60.95
63-1242, Multi-Fuel Stove, $65.95
64-1126, Sigg Qt. Fuel Bottle, 6 oz., $6.00

Optimus 111B & 111Stoves — A Veritable blowtorch, right choice when cooking for several people. Stable, rugged. Pressure pump, built-in cleaner, big fuel tank. Model 111B burns Coleman fuel or equivalent; Model 111 burns kerosene. Wt. 3 lbs. 8 oz.
63-0400 111B, $78.60 63-0462 111, $78.60

L.L. Bean
Filsen Outdoor Clothes

Because of the quality of their lines of clothing, these two outdoor suppliers are reviewed on p. 350. Bean has a goodly range of outdoor stuff at medium price and excellent service. Filsen has the best standard outdoor clothing in the business — their wool cruiser jackets and whipcord trousers are unsurpassed.
—SB

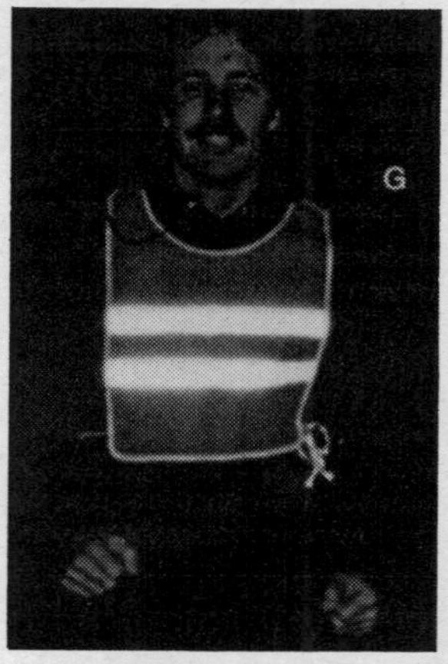

←
Jog-a-Lite Safety Vest — Don't run at dawn or dark without it. Light and bright, with Reflexite stripe on coated iridescent orange nylon webbing, trimmed with iridescent yellow. String ties at the side. One size fits all. Wt. 3 oz.
28-6013 $9.95

R.E.I.

The "co-op" features an astounding variety, ranging from Hong Kong specials of good price but dubious quality, to the finest available from several manufacturers. If you join the co-op, you get a rebate at the end of the year — sort of a delayed discount. R.E.I. is a good place to see what's offered, and their prices are hard to beat.
—J. Baldwin

R.E.I.
Catalog
free from:
Recreational Equipment, Inc.
P.O. Box C-88125
Seattle, WA 98188

←
Backpacker's Flippy Flyer. Foldable, 8½" nylon disc with weights in outside edge so it propels like a flying disc. Fits into back pocket. Color: Yellow /Black. Wt. 2 oz.
F53-600 $2.95

G
Snugli Baby Carrier— Unique frameless carrier can be used as a backpack, front pouch, or nursing sling. Made of heavyweight corduroy. Tucks and darts release to allow expansion as child grows. Padded shoulder straps, adjustable inner pouch. Machine washable. Weight, 1 lb. 7 oz.
B04-6552 — Blue B04-6553 — Rust $41.95

H
Gerry Kiddie Pack— A lightweight baby carrier made of 2-ply cotton duck with an aluminum frame, padded shoulder straps and a portable stand. Baby faces forward in an adjustable seat with space underneath for storage. Wt. 1 lb. 4 oz.
B04-6682 — Blue B04-6685 — Green $23.50

←
Woolrich Chamois Shirt. Warm, durable outdoor shirt made of heavyweight 100% cotton that gets even softer with every wash. Versatile enough to be worn as a single shirt or as an outer shirt over other clothing. Two button-down pockets, nylon-lined button front, extra long tails to tuck in or leave out. Men's Sizes M, L and XL can be ordered in the Tall size in Tan and Light Blue only. Tall size is 3" longer in the body and 2" longer in the sleeves than the Regular size. If the longer body and sleeve lengths are desired, specify Tall size when ordering.

Men's Sizes: S, M, L, XL. Average Wt. 1 lb. 2 oz.
C30-1002 — Light Blue C30-1003 — Rust
C30-1004 — Navy C30-1005 — Green
C30-1008 — Tan $19

Women's Even Sizes: 8-18. Average Weight, 1 lb.
C30-1102 — Light Blue C30-1103 — Rust
C30-1104 — Navy C30-1105 — Green
C30-1108 — Tan $19

Portable water purification

This is the kind of equipment Everest climbers use to keep from getting dysentery trampling through Nepal on the way to the high country above where people live. You can pour red wine in the top and have clear water drip out the bottom.

What makes them work is a silver-infused activated charcoal filter that is good for things down to 20 microns in size. It will get most cysts and bacteria, but the company does not guarantee against viruses, so they suggest and supply chlorine drops (the "Mini-Booster") for pre-treatment — the filter will then remove the chlorine taste from the water.

The Portable Water Washer is compact, weighs a pound, has a 1,000 gallon capacity and a replaceable filter unit. It is also great for anyone trying to wear contact lenses in a place where the water is muddy.

The Super Straw will fit in a large pocket, and has a 40-quart capacity — when you can no longer suck water through it the filter is filled up and you throw it away. This company also makes a line of household filtration systems, including an under-the-sink reverse osmosis unit for about $550.
—Richard Nilsen

Portable Water Washer
M-1000P
$24.70 postpaid

Super Straw with Mini-Booster
M-10S
$5.70 postpaid

both from:
American Water Purification
115 Mason Circle
Concord, CA 94520

Pouring Cup (A)
Funnel Cup (B)
Filter Section (C)
Receiving Cup (D)

Sun Shower

At 12 ounces it's probably a bit much for backpacking, but in car camping, on a boat, on a river, at a cold water cabin, the glory of a hot shower is decidedly worth it. Also handy for sprinkling grumps who disbelieve in solar energy. J. notes that his Sun Shower lasted four years, using it nearly every day.
—SB

Sun Shower
$13.95 postpaid from:
Basic Designs
P.O. Box 479
Muir Beach
Sausalito, CA 94965

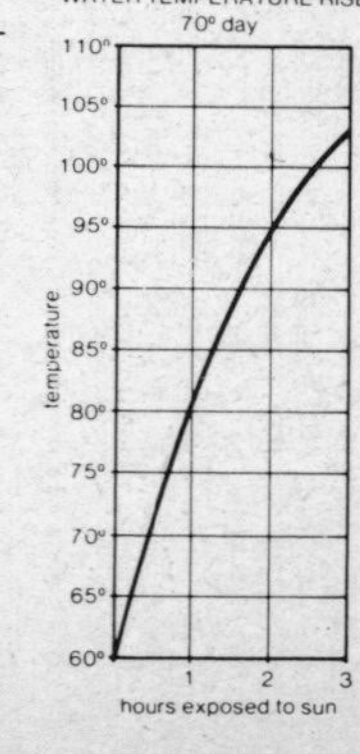

Solus $136

Moss Tent Works

→

Bill Moss has been experimenting with tension structures on this side of the Atlantic for more than 22 years. What interests me most are his recent efforts towards developing fabric structures that feel more like buildings than tents. The expertly patterned contours spill wind and give remarkable rigidity to the assembly as well as considerable beauty. I see a great potential in these: not only are they materials-efficient, they can be easily adapted to a wide variety of climates. They can be shaped to trap or repel solar energy, and can be made to serve as water-catchers. The portability is obvious. Hold-downs can be waterbags for thermal mass. Additions are easily made or subtracted.

Moss is showing the way with a series of commercially available designs ranging from backpackers' equipment to veritable cottages. I view these as the first of a new shelter form. —J. Baldwin

J. has a Moss Star Gazer, I have a Solus, and we're both happy. The Star Gazer uses two poles, has great sky view (without fly). The Solus uses only one pole and has 360° visibility (without fly). Fine, fast, intelligent tents. And the Optimum 200 looks to me to be the solution to most second home problems — cost, maintenance, and vandalism. Build a platform. Put up the Optimum 200 (200 sq. ft.) in 20 minutes when you arrive. Stash it with a neighbor when you leave. —SB

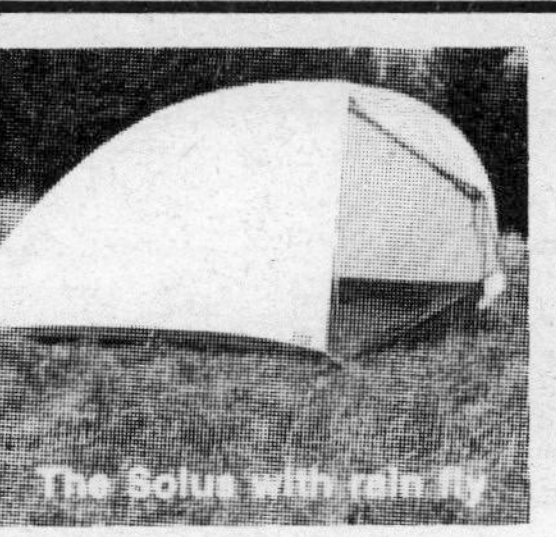

The Solus with rain fly

Moss Family and Backpacking Tents
$54 - $989
Catalog
free from:
Moss Tent Works
Camden, ME 04843

The Optimum 200, $989

Todd's

First-rate boots — Chippewa and Frye, surprising variety in both renowned brands. For ladies too. I wear my Chippewas for country work, Fryes with my three-piece suit. —SB

Frye Jet Wellington $59.95

Todd's
Catalog and price list
free from:
Todd's
5 South Wabash
Chicago, IL 60603

$59.95

↑
Famous Chippewa "warriors" — Fine quality multi-purpose lightweight boots, built for superior comfort and rugged durability. —$64.95

West Coast Shoe Company

Loggers, construction workers, and foresters in the Pacific Northwest need rugged boots with good grip to endure a lot of rough going. One of the boots often used by these men is the 210V built by the West Coast Shoe Company. This company's boots are carried by stores in the Pacific Northwest and can be ordered by mail from elsewhere. The company will send measuring instructions on request. The 210V boot fits the foot with firm support. The boots are carefully constructed of high quality leather which is tough but soft. The leather keeps its shape and dries soft after being wet. The quality of the leather is one reason these boots keep their fit and stay comfortable while giving long service. —R.C. Engle

West Coast Shoe Company
210V Boots
$102.75 postpaid
Information
$1 from:
West Coast
Shoe Company
P.O. Box 607
Scappoose, OR 97056

210 V Boot

White's Boots

White's Shoe Shop has been making hand made shoes for as long as I can remember and I say this because my father wore them for 40 years, in every condition the Pacific Northwest has to offer, he always had three pairs at once rotating them to dry when wet. Also one of the pairs were elk tanned for summer. We Condras have always taken care of our feet and White's shoes are the best bar none. I've had at least one pair on hand since my feet stopped growing. The pair I have now, No. 375 ' "Smoke Jumpers Shoe" are going on three years old, and will go more as long as you sole them, etc. They aren't cheap, but if you ever spent $40 for a pair of shoes and only had them last a year, you'll find them a bargain in the long run. I've fought a lot of forest fires, and good shoes on your feet are as much a necessity as a shovel or pulaski in your hands. If you have hard or very hard to fit feet, they make shoes for you too. A nice little catalog and all the help you need with OLD fashioned quality and service. —Joseph Condra

Whole Earth's cowboy J.D. Smith, long time a White's enthusiast (he got mine when I decided the high "woodsman's heel" hurt my legs and put a trampling strut in my pace), says on a note in our marked up old **Whole Earth Catalog** *that "Danners are better and cheaper." What and where are Danners?* —SB

White's Boots
Catalog
free from:
White's Shoe Shop
West 430 Main
at Stevens
Spokane, WA 99201

$167 $145

Calked Logger $167

Smoke Jumpers $145

Country Ways

You can get good sew-it-yourself outdoor wear from Frostline and Holubar (p. 423). This outfit has a few jackets, pants, shells, etc., but also kits for boats, knives, paddles, packs, musical instruments. . . . —SB

Country Ways
Catalog
$1 from:
Country Ways
U.S. Highway
101 South
Minnetonka, MN 55343

Snowshoe Kits
Small: 10" x 42", for about age 6 to about 130 lbs, $39
Medium: 11" x 54", 120 to about 190 lbs., $42
Large: 12" x 60", 180 to about 240 lbs., $45
↓

Scandian Single Kayak Kit. Measuring 15' 9" by 2' 1" and weighing 35 lbs., the Scandian Single is The boat for extended touring expeditions, etc. The long waterline makes for extra speed and the larger size means more load capacity for bigger people and/or more gear. $240
↓

Craft Manual of North American Indian Footwear

Moccasinmaking. The fellow who put this book together has saved a truckload of good information from being buried in family shoestores around the world. Thirty or forty designs and patterns set out, using length and circumference of whatever pretty foot to be shoed. Step by step instructions for stitching and assembly can be followed by anyone who can read and use a knife and needle. Not recommended for people wanting heavy-soled fringy street shoes or patent-leather leggings. Meant for people who want to build North American Indian footwear like the North American Indians feet wore. —J.D. Smith
[Suggested by David Morris]

Craft Manual of North American Indian Footwear
George M. White
1969; 71 pp.
$3.25 postpaid from:
G.M. White
Box 365
Ronan, MT 59864

THE RISING SUN
NEIGHBORHOOD NEWSLETTER

David and Kathleen said I was wrong to say there were no rectangles in nature because crystals form rectangles, so does fractured gneiss, also super magnified eye lenses look like graham crackers (you saw it second in *The Next Whole Earth Catalog*, p. 27) and leaf veins sometimes form rectangles and the spaces between trees and how about teeth.

GOLD PROSPECTING

by Mack Taylor
Exploration Labs, Sausalito, California

There are still prospectors out exploring and living in the mountains and wild places all over North America. And, surprisingly, there are plenty of ore deposits left to be discovered — as attested to by the monthly announcements of discoveries in mining and geology journals. The rate of ore discovery in the western U.S. — the most thoroughly prospected region on Earth — is as high as it's ever been. As well as can be figured, there seem to be more "finds" made per year now than there were a hundred years ago, when post-Civil War prospecting was at its peak.

The nature of the work has evolved considerably since the then. A certain amount of gadgetry and bookwork have displaced some of the more basic crafts associated with burros and camp life. The surface has been picked over pretty carefully, so most ore is now found by inferring its presence below the surface — sometimes 'way below — and going to a lot of trouble and expense to put a hole down to it. For most metals, successful prospecting has become pretty demanding, principally in terms of experience , money, and luck.

Fortunately, the most obvious and exciting development in the field is the great rise in the price of gold in recent years ($630/oz. today, July 18, 1980). By Mother Nature's Cosmic Coincidence this most sought-after metal is the one ore which can be found by a hard-working individual with a gold pan with as great a likelihood as the most well-financed corporate exploration department. The mineable gold finds in the last few years have been a Pro-Am standoff, with maybe a little edge to the beginner. Despite a great deal of research done in the techniques of mineral exploration, the common gold pan is still the most sensitive and accurate detector of gold. Nothing else even comes close. If there is any significant amount of gold in an area, carefully panning the streams or dry washes will pick it up.

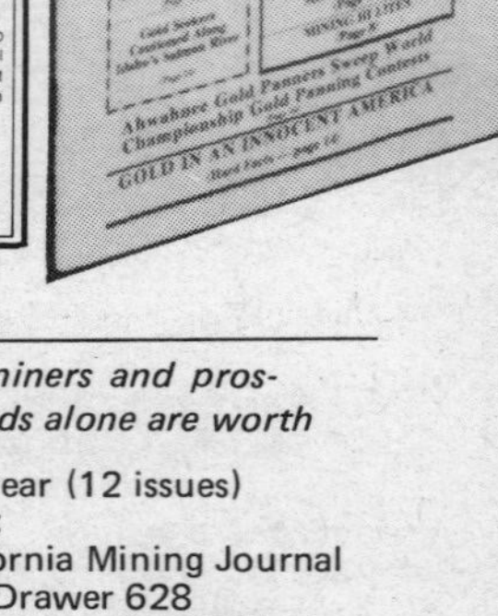

California Mining Journal

The standard magazine for small miners and prospectors for nearly fifty years. The ads alone are worth the subscription.

California Mining Journal
Kenneth L. Harn, Editor

$8/year (12 issues)
from:
California Mining Journal
P.O. Drawer 628
Santa Cruz, CA 95061

The Prospector's Manual

Facsimile reproduction of a charming account by a for-real prospector of the last century. The accumulated experience of a lifetime spent prospecting set down in a practical and heartfelt fashion.

The Prospector's Manual
Arthur J. Burdick
1905, 1970; 156 pp.

$8.50 postpaid from:
The Shorey Book Store
110 Union Street
Seattle, WA 98101
or Whole Earth Household Store

•

The horse is not a good climber, being insecure of foot and too clumsy and timid for the business. Again he must feed heartily and drink frequently or he becomes discouraged, fatigued and incapacitated for travel. The burro, on the contrary, will fast long and will go without water thirty-six to forty-eight hours without serious inconvenience. He is sure-footed, fearless on dangerous and difficult mountain trails, and will dine heartily and satisfactorily on sage-brush or greasewood, or upon bacon rinds and leavings of the camp. He will consider himself well pastured in localities which would afford no forage whatever to a horse.

Handbook for Prospectors

This is a comprehensive manual covering every aspect of the subject concisely and clearly. It is written in plain English and seems intended for the practical amateur.

For more than a generation a manual entitled "Handbook for Prospectors and Operators of Small Mines," by Max W. von Bernewitz served as the bible of the field. It went into the 4th edition after von Bernewitz' death in 1940, but was out of date then. Dr. Pearl has completely rewritten the original — and retitled it — cleaning up the sourdough mentality and adding the new technology such as geophysics and geochemistry. Out of respect for the original, Dr. Pearl calls this the 5th edition. In reality it is the one and only edition he intends to write. But it's a good job, and should serve as a fundamental text and reference manual for at least another ten years.

Handbook for Prospectors
Richard M. Pearl
1954, 1973; 472 pp.

$21.95 postpaid from:
McGraw-Hill Book Company
Princeton Road
Hightstown, NJ 08520
or Whole Earth Household Store

Gold Locations of the United States

A very useful reference for the dedicated gold prospector. The book seems to be an organized collection of thousands of notes on gold locations in the U.S. In conjunction with the federal and state publications, this data should provide a wealth of leads.

Gold Locations of the United States
Jack Black
1975, 1980; 174 pp.

$6.95 postpaid from:
Del Oeste Press
P.O. Box 397
Tarzana, CA 91356

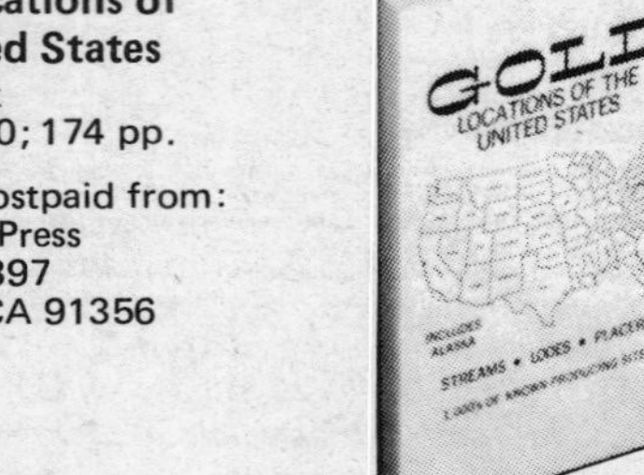

•

Vasquez Canyon

Vasquez Canyon is about nine miles north of Saugus and directly south of Texas Canyon. A gold vein was discovered here many years ago and explored for some distance. There was some gold produced but no record of how much. The mine was about one mile directly south of Texas Canyon diggings.

Dredging for Gold

A magnificent general work hiding behind a specialized title. If you want to go beyond panning a creek, to recover enough gold to sell, then stream placers (sounds like 'plasters' without the 't') are the practical place to find it and Matt Thornton's book is an incomparable guide and inspiration.

The small suction dredge has been developed mainly in California since the 1950s. The early models were heavy, cantankerous dinosaurs — disheartening to all but the most dedicated. Thanks to the perseverance of a small group of enthusiasts, the equipment has evolved into a stable of light, reliable workhorses, so efficient that they have revolutionized the mining of gold placers. Next to the rise in price, this is the major new development in the field. The small suction dredge allows an individual to work with a great increase in efficiency over the old mechanical dredges. Streams can now be worked that used to be too small or rocky. It seems likely that large versions of these dredges will be developed to handle the major placer fields currently lying fallow.

Now that the tools have been developed, and rich 'holes' are getting scarce in California, the wide world calls. Alaska, Western Canada, Mexico, Central and South America are barely touched.

Dredging for Gold
(The Gold Divers' Handbook)
Matt Thornton
1975, 1979; 243 pp.

$7.95 postpaid from:
Keene Industries
9330 Corbin Avenue
Northridge, CA 91324

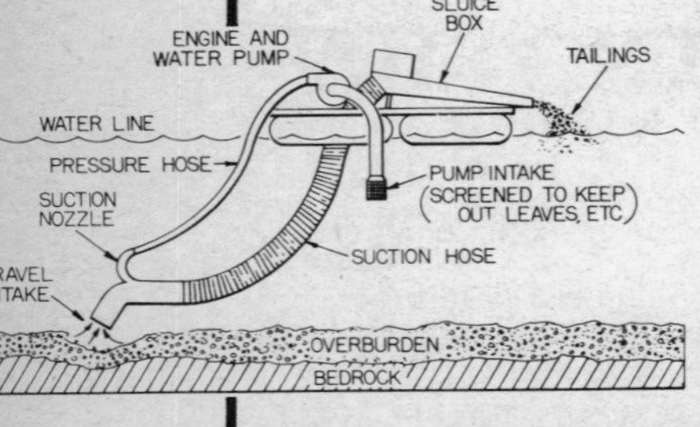

Suction nozzle type of surface dredge —Dredging for Gold

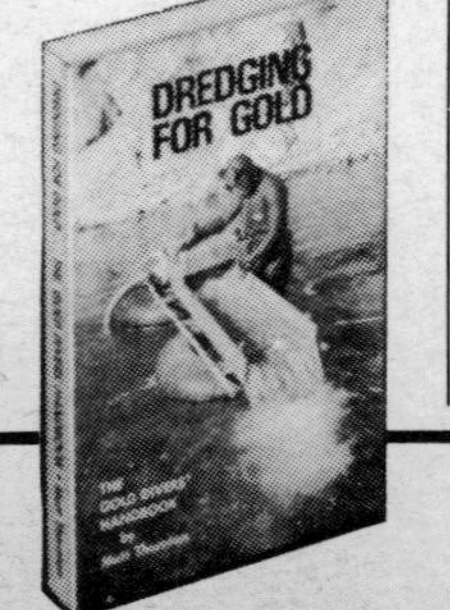

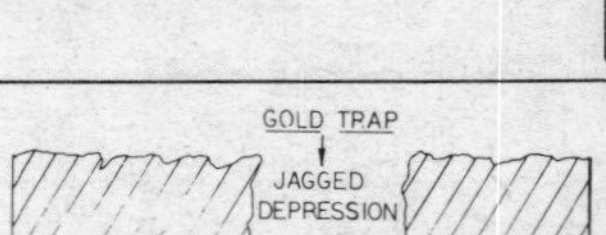

Bedrock "quartz vein" crevice ←

Crevice slanting out toward midstream ↓

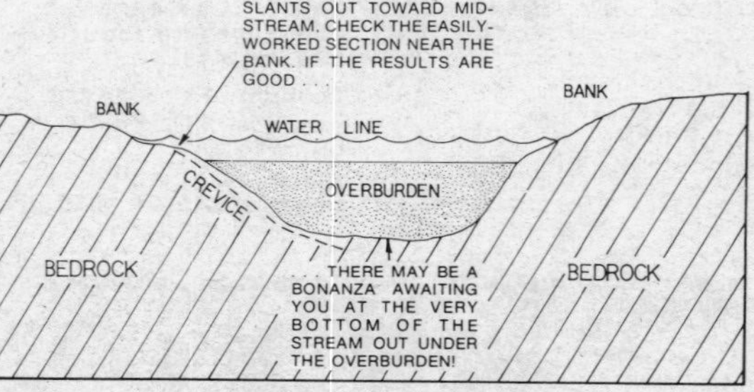

↑

You will find that each time you remove any particular rock it will facilitate the removal of rocks along side of it. It will take time, but eventually you will get to the bottom of the crevice where it starts to narrow down. It is here where you will find the heavier materials that have been settling in the crevice over the years — black sands, old nails, bullets, buckshot, Chinese coins (no, I'm not kidding!), and last but certainly not least, GOLD. The gold will always be at the very bottom of the crevice, and now you will need your *long tweezers* to extract it. Believe me when I say you've never experienced a greater thrill in your life than that of picking nuggets out of a crevice and plopping them into your *sample bottle*, hearing that delightful PLUNK! every time a piece of gold hits the glass.

Diving and Digging for Gold

A short, well-written introduction to the field. All a beginner needs to have fun panning streams on the weekend. The author is thoroughly conversant with the subject. She was the editor of **California Geology** *for twenty years, during which time that publication became one of the most popular and authoritative geology magazines in the country.*

Diving and Digging for Gold
Mary Hill
1960, 1974; 47 pp.

$2.50 postpaid from:
Naturegraph Publishers
P.O. Box 1075
Happy Camp, CA 96039
or Whole Earth Household Store

•

The bed of the stream itself is a very good place to look; for the heavy gold, as it is jigged along, falls to the bottom. There it is pushed along fairly rapidly over smooth rock (such as clean, unweathered granite or slippery serpentine), more slowly where the bottom is rough and uneven. It is wise to look where the bottom is ragged, for here the natural jiggling action of the stream may concentrate gold in the lee of obstructions, which serve as natural riffles. If the bottom is soft and weathered, as in old schist or slate, the particles of gold may burrow deeply; where the bottom is markedly uneven, as in areas of deeply pitted limestone, particles of gold have been known to drop into crevices as much as 50 feet below the general stream bottom.

Gold in hell

. . . about the miner who died and went to heaven where he was met at the gate by Peter who inquired of him what he had done in life. The miner replied that he had been a gold miner. Peter told him that there was a surplus of gold miners and he couldn't come in. The miner asked whether or not he might be allowed to stay if he could get rid of all the other miners to which Peter agreed to let him in for a trial run. Once in, the miner wandered around until he came across a couple of familiar faces. He walked over to them and whispered that there was a gold strike in hell. They shrugged their shoulders and continued on with what they were doing. Instantly the rumor was all over the place and people were leaving in droves. Within seconds it had emptied. A while later the miner, feeling lonely and isolated, went over to Peter to ask for permission to leave because, he explained, "even though I was the one that started the rumor, there just might be something to it . . ."

Dick Donovan
Stamford, Connecticut

GAD POINT

• Double Polished Hammer Faces Lets You Drive Bar Either Way

PRY

ESTWING GAD–PRY BAR

Open seams and crevises easily with this handy, featherweight tool. Forged hard tough tool steel. Unsurpassed temper, balance and finish. I–beam construction. Weighs 16 ounces. Length 18". Shipping weight 2 pounds.

AO 669. $8.96

Miners' Catalog

A good general catalog and supply house oriented toward prospectors.

Miners' Catalog
free from:
Miners, Inc.
P.O. Box 1301
Riggins, ID 83549

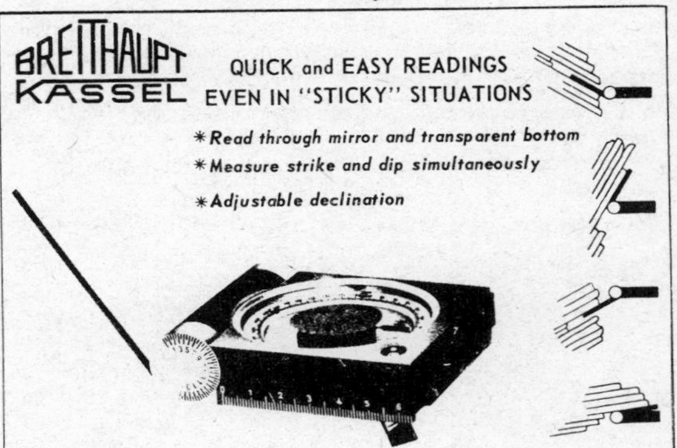

BREITHAUPT KASSEL
QUICK and EASY READINGS EVEN IN "STICKY" SITUATIONS
*Read through mirror and transparent bottom
*Measure strike and dip simultaneously
*Adjustable declination

GEOLOGICAL STRATUM COMPASS

This quality, German-made compass is a versatile instrument for underground mines measurements of azimuth, dip, and strike. In addition to the compass for bearing determination, there is a circular spirit level, a transparent bottom and hinged mirror for making measurements below the compass, a cover and hinge designed to measure dip and strike, and a sighting prism for rapid, coarse sightings. The compass circle is graduated into 360°, graduation interval of 1° and numbered in 10° intervals. A magnet provides eddy-current damping of the magnetic needle, while permanent locking of the needle is provided using a lever on the compass corner. The cover hinge is graduated into 235° quadrantal, with intervals of 5° and numbered intervals of 20°. Actual weight 9 ounces. Closed compass dimensions 2-15/16" x 3-13/16" x 1". Shipping weight 1½ lbs.

A 1724 $544.00

Geological surveys

There are two major sources of help that should not be overlooked — state and federal geological surveys.

Nearly every state maintains an office concerned with its natural resources. These people usually know a great deal about the location of natural resources in their state, likely areas for prospecting, state publications and maps of use to you, and the status of land and mineral rights in these areas. In general, they are very cooperative and will prove to be your best source of information and assistance.

The U.S. Geological Survey does a large amount of research in geology and mineral resources. Probably the most useful of its publications for prospectors are these.

Professional Paper 610: Principal Gold-producing Districts of the United States, A.H. Koschmann and M.H. Bergendahl, 1968; 283 pp. $7 postpaid.

Bulletin 1355: Placer Gold Deposits of Arizona, Maureen G. Johnson, 1972; 103 pp. + map. $2.55 postpaid.

Bulletin 1356: Placer Gold Deposits of Nevada, Maureen G. Johnson, 1973; 118 pp. + map. $2 postpaid.

Bulletin 1357: Placer Gold Deposits of Utah, Maureen G. Johnson, 1973; 26 pp. + map. $1.25 postpaid.

all from: U.S. Geological Survey Center, Eastern Distribution, 604 South Pickett Street, Alexandria, VA 22304.

or over the counter at the U.S.G.S. Public Inquiries Offices listed under topographic maps, our p. 24.

Bulletin 193: Gold Districts of California, William B. Clark, 1970; 186 pp. + map. $6.50 postpaid from: California Division of Mines and Geology, P.O. Box 2980, Sacramento, CA 95812.

Labs

Getting good assays is sometimes a problem. Here are three labs that have done a consistently good job. For comparison, their prices for a standard gold and silver fire assay are listed. They each have sample preparation charges and minimums. They welcome new business from individuals, but get backlogged a month or more during the summer season. Current price lists are sent free on request.

Skyline Labs, Inc., 12090 West 50th Place, Wheat Ridge, CO 80033, and 1700 West Grant Road, P.O. Box 50106, Tucson, AZ 85703. Gold and silver fire assay, $6.50.

Southwest Assayers & Chemists, Inc., 710 East Evans, P.O. Box 7517, Tucson, AZ 85725. Gold and silver fire assay, $6.00.

Union Assay Office, 269 Brooklyn Avenue, Salt Lake City, UT 84101. Gold and silver fire assay, $7.50. ■

Handbook for the Alaskan Prospector

Longstanding fantasy: learn a little about rocks, walk, fly out there somewhere. Set up a placer claim, live happily ever after. Then this book let me know that I had to know more than a little about rocks. But I got five claims. This book is still the best. —J.D. Smith

Handbook for the Alaskan Prospector
Ernest Wolff
1969, 1980; 460 pp.

$8 postpaid from:
The Mineral Industry Research Laboratory
University of Alaska
College, AK 99701

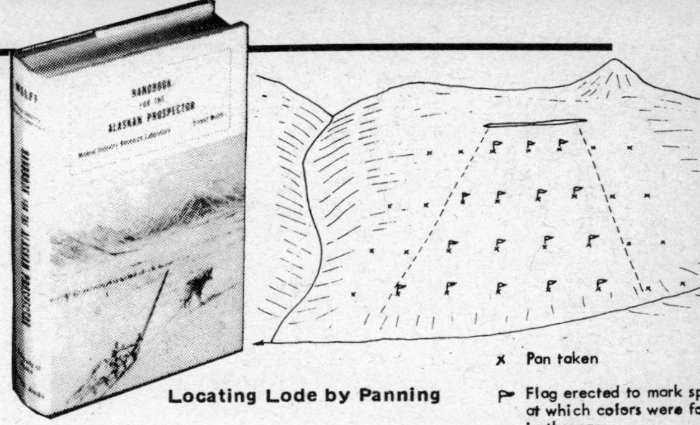

Locating Lode by Panning

The Alaska Catalog

Alaska books tend to accent deprivation and gold. Alaska guidebooks tend to stress the joys of murdering rare animals. The tourist brochures assume you have unlimited money and that you'll go home when it gets cold. Exported stories are vulnerable to Texas-style inflation (except for mosquito stories, which simply can't be exaggerated). So what does one do if one wishes to find out what to expect in Alaska? One buys **The Alaska Catalog**, *that's what. You'll find everything from job hunting tips to patterns for making mukluks, with sources pinned right down to the person's name you should talk to. Unlike many* **Whole Earth Catalog** *look-alikes this is excellent in every respect, including attitude. I can personally vouch (from having lived there) that much of their information is just what you'll need.* —J. Baldwin

The Alaska Catalog
(Living, Working & Traveling in the Northland)
Elizabeth Johannsen, Editor
1977; 140 pp.

$8.50 postpaid from:
Polar Palm Productions, Inc.
P.O. Box 4-907
Anchorage, AK 99509
or Whole Earth Household Store

FOOD STORAGE PIT FOR USE IN PERMANENTLY FROZEN GROUND

•

I would like to add a word of my own, which may prove helpful to the beginning gold panner. After you have filled your pan with likely-looking gravel, drop in a few birdshot from a shotgun shell. When you've finished washing out the tailings, the pellets should still be there. If not, it means that your panning procedure was incorrect.

•

Parka construction is important. Although you should avoid dressing too warmly, you need wind protection for every square inch of your body. The parka should be roomy enough, especially at the armholes, so that you can pull your arms out of the sleeves and into the body of the parka. While no commercial gear is perfectly designed, Eddie Bauer down clothing remains about the best available. Partly because they are designed by people in warmer southern climates, mountaineering-style parkas often don't work very well for severe arctic conditions. Many are glorified ski shells, with poorly-designed, form-fitting hoods. Since your head is the key to thermal regulation (if you cool your head, you cool your trunk and feet), hood construction is important. The hood should be tunnel-shaped and fringed with a ruff to provide wind protection for your face and so that air can become slightly pre-warmed before you breathe it. You should be able to slide the hood back and forth without fancy finger-work, to permit easy cooling and warming of your ears and nose. Sometimes these appendages freeze with little pain; once frozen, they will remain a nuisance for the rest of your life.

Alaska Geographic Magazine
Alaska's Great Interior

The glittery beauty of Alaska beckons many of us, and nowhere is that beauty better shown than in the series of books put out by the Alaska Geographic Society. This one on the interior is especially enticing to me because I lived there for a few years and want to go back. I can hardly sit still with this volume on my desk. The color shots are all one could wish, and the articles are general enough to give a broad idea of what to expect. If you hunger for Alaska, this is your meat. —J. Baldwin

Alaska Geographic
Robert A. Henning, et al., Editors
$20/year (4 issues; includes membership)

Alaska's Great Interior
(Volume 7, No. 1 of **Alaska Geographic**)
Tom Walker, et al., Editors
1980; 128 pp.
$9.95 postpaid

both from:
Alaska Geographic Society
P.O. Box 4-EEE
Anchorage, AK 99509

The Alaska Almanac

If Alaska interests you and you want to do something about it (after reading **Alaska Geographic**, *for instance), just about everything you need to know is included in this little book. Its style is a bit junior high school but the information is there: cost of living, weather, history, laws, land policy, clothes you need, animal life, you name it. A fine bibliography too.* —J. Baldwin

The Alaska Almanac
(Facts about Alaska)
Staff of **Alaska** magazine
1976, 1979; 125 pp.

$3.95 postpaid from:
Alaska Northwest Publishing Company
P.O. Box 4-EEE
Anchorage, AK 99509
or Whole Earth Household Store

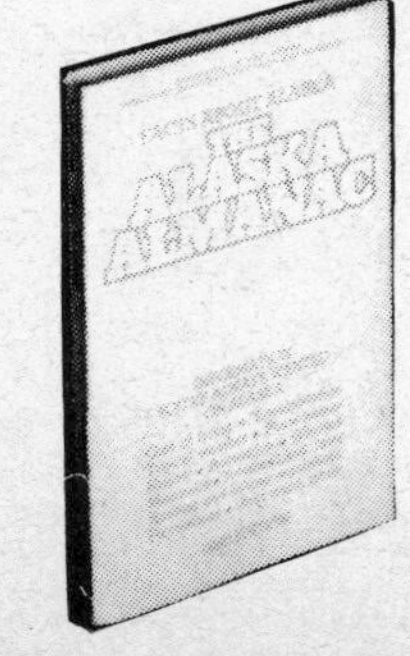

Cache Lake Country

An illustrated seasonal diary of lake country tricks and tips, written by a mellow, contented man, who loves the woods, knows his subject, and writes pretty well too. Kane's illustrations are the nicest I've seen. The book makes me want to learn how to swim. —J.D. Smith

Cache Lake Country
(Life in the North Woods)
John J. Rowlands and Henry B. Kane
1947, 1978; 270 pp.

$5.95 postpaid from:
W.W. Norton and Company
500 Fifth Avenue
New York, NY 10036
or Whole Earth Household Store

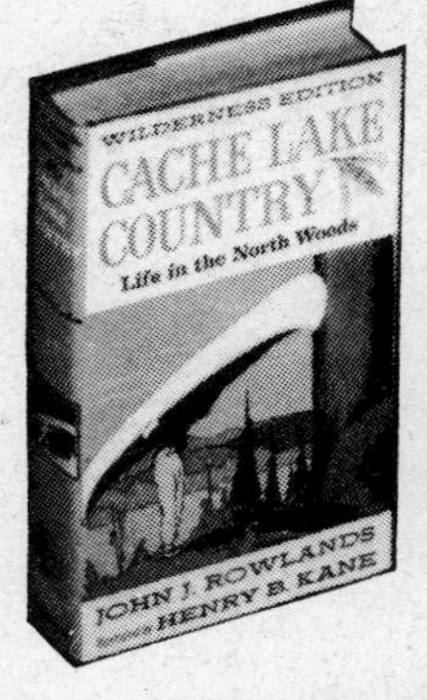

To keep antenna from snapping if attached to swaying trees, carry supporting wire at one end over pulley and weight with stone or sand bag.

THE RISING SUN
NEIGHBORHOOD NEWSLETTER

All the information operators in New York State are now required to say "Have a nice day," Mimi and David have inferred, because they now all do. We were trying to think of alternatives such as "Have a Day" and "24 hours." Having someone with prototypically New York accent and delivery say "Have a nice day" makes the day substantially less nice all by itself.

Earthwatch Research Expeditions

Want to participate in a real scientific expedition? You can by joining one sponsored by this group. Yeah, you have to pay instead of them paying you, but many agree that the money is well spent — you'll learn a lot (including how to do an expedition). Looks interesting! You have to be between 16 and 75 years old. —J. Baldwin

Earthwatch Research Expeditions
Information
free from:
Earthwatch
10 Juniper Road, Box 127
Belmont, MA 02178

←
Astronomers of Machu Picchu
Starting Area: Cuzco, Peru
Disciplines: Astronomy, preColumbian history, engineering
Team I: Jun 16 - 27
Team II: Jun 29 - Jul 10
Share of costs: $1,140

↑
Underground Cities of Tunisia
Tunisia
Passive energy, architecture
Team I: (Bulla Reggia) Mar 24 - Apr 4
Team II: (Matmata) Apr 7 - 18
Share of costs: $860

Expedition Research

As their brochure says: "If you are a scientist, journalist, physician, professional photographer, accomplished mountaineer, registered guide, archaeologist, certified instructor, crew sailor, expert diver, or graduate student in science, Expedition needs your expertise." These guys get you together with someone who needs you or someone you need. —J. Baldwin

Expedition Research
Registration
$20/year
Includes newsletter **Exploration** (monthly)
from:
Expedition Research, Inc.
P.O. Box 467R
Cathedral and Franklin Streets
Annapolis, MD 21404

HOW CLOSE IS ADVENTURE to your tedium? Well, it's 40 yards from ours. While editing this page, word filtered through the office that the beached-whale-looking thing by the road just outside has been rowed across the Atlantic and the Pacific by a crew of two. The reason it's out there is it's being refitted for a single-handed row from California to Australia — a nine-month journey. Looking at it with some **Whole Earth** *staff, I realize that if I wait until I'm old to have adventures again, some kinds of adventure will be ruled out.* —SB

STEWART B

Mountain Travel

An unusually wide range of trips and unusually inviting catalog distinguish this one-among-many of the new adventure-brokers. It's a booming field, with the result there are getting to be a lot of skilled trekkers and travellers loose in the world. You go on a couple of these organized trips and pretty soon you're organizing your your own.

For a sea-going equivalent, check out Ocean Voyages on *p. 576.* —SB

Mountain Travel
Catalog
$1 from:
Mountain Travel
1398 Solano Avenue
Albany, CA 94706

↑
Ecuador Spinning and Weaving Tour
Learning the folk art of the Andes
July 1 - July 23 (23 days)
Leader: Lynn Meisch
Grade: A-1

We will learn to spin with the distaff and hand spindle (Ecuadorian-style) and observe backstrap loom weaving, indigo dyeing, warping, tapestry weaving and Panama hat weaving.

With two weeks in Cuenca, we'll also become familiar with other Cuenca-area crafts, such as embroidery, knitting, macrame and pottery. The last 8 days of the trip are devoted to various individual textile projects in the weavers' homes.

Our intimate contact with the families of Cuenca and our special look at Ecuadorian culture and family life will be an additional plus on this trip. Limit 10.

Land Cost: $1425

•

Noatak River Exploration
400 miles on a wild arctic river
Aug 1 - Aug 21 (21 days)
Leader: Dave Schmitz
Grade: B-2

Using 2-man Klepper kayaks, we will navigate the entire river from its headwaters to the Eskimo village of Noatak near the Kotzebue Sound. En route, we will have plenty of time to fish for delicious arctic char, grayling and salmon, and hike along interesting side streams.

No previous kayak experience is necessary, and this trip is a good chance to become proficient in this skill. All participants must be in excellent physical condition. Limit 10.

Land Cost including charter: $1750

The upper Noatak River

•

The reefs along the north shore of Little Cayman Island descend from the surface to hundreds of feet below. This remarkable coral wall is one of the best diving areas in the Caribbean and is, therefore, well-suited for marine studies.

The purpose of this expedition is to acquaint students with major groups of algae, the foundation of all marine ecosystems and food chains. Field research will be conducted to document the abundance and species composition of algae on coral reefs, on exposed shores, in lagoons, and near mangrove stands.

•

Typical Information Needs Handled by Expedition Research, Inc.

What research vessels are currently available for work off the west coast of Greenland?

Where can I obtain route information for Popocatepetl, Ixtaccihuatl, and El Pico de Orizaba?

What earthquakes occurred this past month, when, and at what magnitude?

Provide a list of trip operators who offer overland expeditions from London to Kathmandu.

What visa requirements apply to Madagascar?

Treasure Hunter's Manual #7

Generally accepted among initiates in the treasure hunting fraternity as the definitive work on the subject. Half of the book is jaw, half good hard core info. —Al Perrin

Treasure Hunter's Manual #7
Karl von Mueller
1972, 1979; 293 pp.
$7.95 postpaid from:
Ram Publishing Company
P.O. Box 38649
Dallas, TX 75238

•

Most instrument work is a slow, tiresome process. You can't take a metal detector into an area and swish it around a couple times and really expect to find anything. Yet, this is what a lot of fellows do. Nine out of ten men are too impatient or allow too little time for the job to be done right. You should allow an hour to scan an area three feet wide and 100 feet long. On the basis of this requirement, if you are to work a farm yard, for example, that is 300 feet wide and 300 feet long, it will take you 200 hours. This is three weeks of everyday work starting at 8:00 in the morning and quitting at 5:00 at night, Saturdays and Sundays included. The average city block covers this area, so you can see that it takes some 'doings' to cover a large area properly.

Part of a bootlegger's cache found in a cellar where it had been hidden over 30 years ago. Some of the gold coins were as clean and perfect as the day they were minted. All of this must have come from selling a bottle or two at a time. Some of the silver coins were bright but most of them were tarnished due to the sulphur in the rubber container.

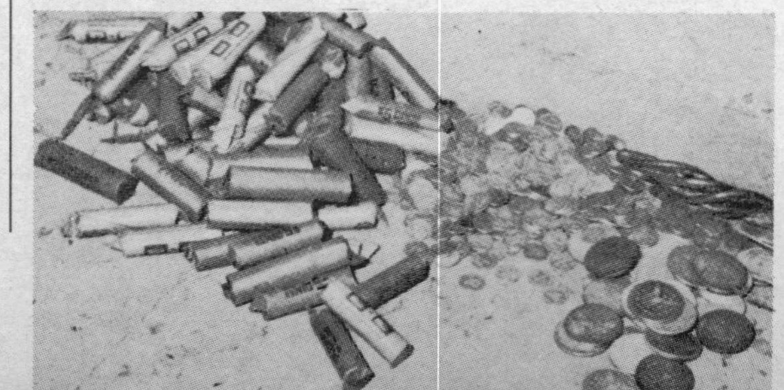

Cellar of a farmhouse, about 1660, at the Allerton Site, Kingston, Massachusetts. (Allerton was the treasurer of Plymouth Colony.) In the upper left corner the cellar intersects an earlier hearth that belongs to a house built about 1635. —The Amateur Archaeologist's Handbook

AMATEUR ARCHAEOLOGY

by Faith Harrington

More often than ever before, archaeologists can be spotted dirtying their hands in cities, along seemingly deserted backroads, and in the remote enclaves which are their traditional turf. Like many other aspects of our natural environment, archaeological sites are precious, non-renewable resources, and their preservation depends on the public's awareness of protective legislation. Archaeological activity increases as these laws are enacted, and more people are getting a firsthand look at what an excavation is really like. Sites excavated in cities receive a lot of public exposure via local newspapers, magazines, radio, and even television stations. The stereotypic image of the archaeologist as a bearded and pith-helmeted sage sifting endlessly through the sands of the ancient world is being updated. Not that archaeology isn't exciting, but a visit to your local excavation where periods of drudgery are interrupted by only sporadic moments of excitement, will remove some of the mystery and romance.

The diggers' continuum stretches from pot hunter to professional archaeologist. The amateur, avocational, or public archaeologist is usually an excavator who is knowledgeable of his or her locale and its history, and perhaps a member of the state or regional archaeological society, but, unlike the professional, is without advanced educational training (today that means without a Master's or a Ph.D.), or a lot of field experience, or a practiced hand at producing publishable reports.

Obviously, the amateur does have a place in this field and anyone curious about archaeology will probably enjoy reading James Deetz's **Invitation to Archaeology**. *Unlike the usual technical, heavily referenced books on the subject, this is a refreshingly brief, perceptive, and inclusive look at what archaeology is and what it is that archaeologists do. Deetz clarifies some of the jargon encountered in the classroom and in the field, and covers bilaterally the prehistoric and historic time periods ("historic" being the archaeology of the time for which we have written records) and their research problems, field techniques, and dating methods. Finally, in a mere thirteen pages, he competently describes the developmental stages from the Paleolithic to the Iron Age in the Old World and the corresponding time periods in the New World.*

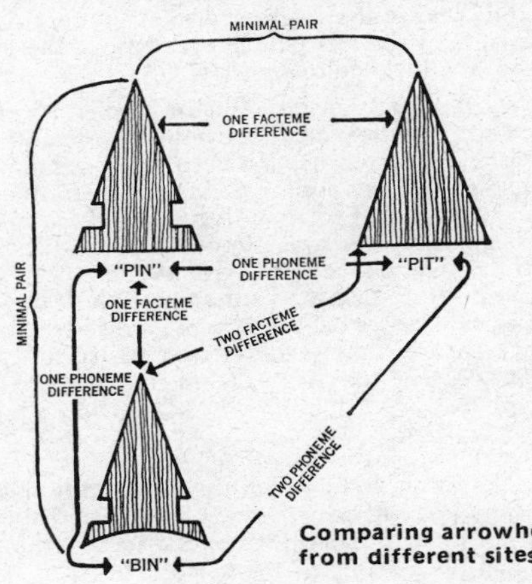

Comparing arrowheads from different sites

Invitation to Archaeology
James Deetz
1967; 150 pp.

$1.95 postpaid from:
Natural History Press
Doubleday and Company
501 Franklin Avenue
Garden City, NY 11530

or Whole Earth Household Store

•

Language, human social organization, fire, shelter, clothing, weapons, and religion, all had their beginnings during the Paleolithic. We do not even know just where or when each of these important innovations took place, but they are all clearly present at the end of the Paleolithic, and were not at the beginning. Man was a hunter during the entire Paleolithic. —**Invitation to Archaeology**

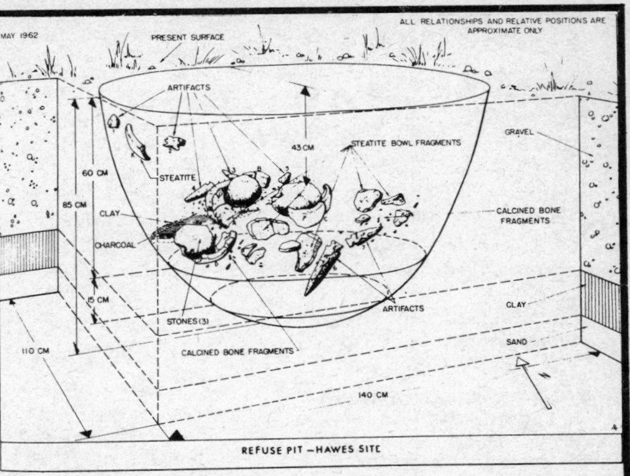

The sketch showing the layering and total content of a feature is an important part of the record. —The Amateur Archaeologist's Handbook

Once you understand *why* *archaeologists do what they do, you'll probably want to know* *how* *they do it. A lucid and serious guide to fieldwork, first published in 1966 and revised in 1973, is Maurice Robbins'* **The Amateur Archaeologist's Handbook**. *It includes a brief survey of the North American culture groups, when and where each one lived, and what each of their distinct artifact assemblages looks like. The gamut of procedures, from planning an excavation to dating the artifacts, is unravelled. Several appendices are included which offer valuable info for anyone who would like to visit sites, museums, join a society, review current legislation, or study this pursuit.*

The Amateur Archaeologist's Handbook
(A Complete Guide for Digging into America's Past)
Maurice Robbins
1966, 1973; 288 pp.

$10.95 postpaid from:
T.Y. Crowell and Company
Harper and Row
Keystone Industrial Park
Scranton, PA 18512

or Whole Earth Household Store

Fossils for Amateurs
Hunting for Fossils

Few readily available experiences offer such a deep sense of continuity as finding a clearly once-alive and exotic pattern staring out at you from a rock. And they're all over the place, once you start noticing. **Fossils for Amateurs** *will educate your eyes and understanding.* **Hunting for Fossils** *tells you where the richest hunting is in the U.S. once you've got the bug. It was such rocks who taught us about evolution.* —SB

•

Ohio is another of those satisfying states where fossils may be found almost anywhere , sometimes just waiting to be picked up, and often in astonishing abundance.

The best places are quarries (to be investigated, of course, only with permission), railroad and highway cuts, old strip mine workings, and areas where the soil has weathered for a long time. Fossils include plants, invertebrates, and vertebrates. The hunter may find whole specimens, casts, molds, tracks, trails, burrows, and coprolites (fossil dung); and the original material may have been replaced by minerals, or the remains — especially those of fishes — may be encased in rocks from which all liquids have been squeezed out. Like numerous other states, Ohio has a gap between Permian and Pleistocene, so that Mesozoic and early Cenozoic fossils are missing. —**Hunting for Fossils**

Fossils for Amateurs
(A Handbook for Collectors)
Russel P. MacFall and Jay C. Wollin
1972; 341 pp.

$7.95 postpaid from:
Van Nostrand Reinhold Company
Order Department
7625 Empire Drive
Florence, KY 41042

or Whole Earth Household Store

Hunting for Fossils
(A guide to finding and collecting fossils in all fifty states)
Marian Murray
1967, 1974; 348 pp.

$2.95 postpaid from:
Macmillan Publishing Co.
Order Department
Front and Brown Streets
Riverside, NJ 08075

or Whole Earth Household Store

Illinois and Indiana are famous for the superb plant fossils found in concretions such as this. When struck on edge, they break along the fossil surface, exposing two halves. Neuropteris gigantea; **Pennsylvanian; Braidwood, Illinois. —Fossils for Amateurs**

Experimentation on a corner showed that the trilobite was harder than a brass bristle brush and the matrix was softer. After most of the matrix was removed with the scraper, a small brass wire brush on the flexible shaft completed preparation of the specimen. —Fossils for Amateurs

Fibre cases

A veritable plethora of special cases for your special whatever (tools, cameras, fossils, instruments, name it). Wide stock, customizing available. —SB
[Suggested by Ron Williams]

Ikelheimer-Ernst Fibre Cases
Catalog

free from:
Ikelheimer-Ernst
Fibre Products Division
601 West 26th Street
New York, NY 10001

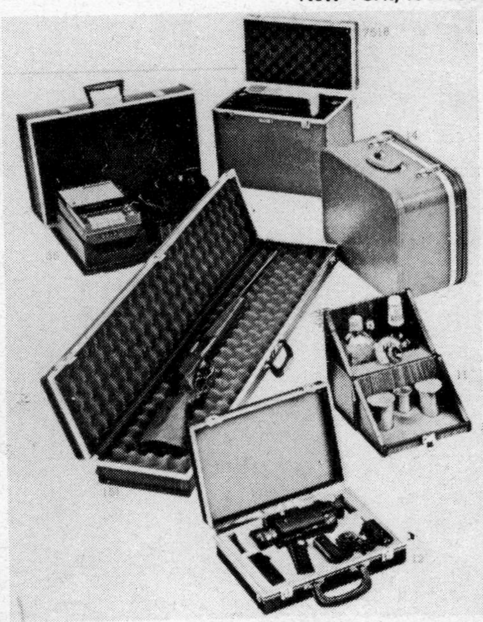

THE RISING SUN
NEIGHBORHOOD NEWSLETTER

"The problem with taking a nap is that after it's over you no longer have the option of taking a nap." —Tom

YOU may be a land animal, but it's an ocean planet. —SB

The Edge of the Sea
The Sea Around Us

Most of us remember DDT, Rachel Carson, and poisoned robins in one short flashback. But Rachel Carson left more: these two exquisitely delicate books about the huge, rough-and-tumble oceans. —Peter Warshall

The Edge of the Sea
Rachel Carson
1955; 276 pp.

$4.95 postpaid from:
Houghton-Mifflin Co.
Wayside Raod
Burlington, MA 01803
or Whole Earth
Household Store

The Sea Around Us
Rachel Carson
1950, 1961; 221 pp.

$2.25 postpaid from:
New American Library
P.O. Box 120
120 Woodbine
Bergenfield, NJ 07621
or Whole Earth
Household Store

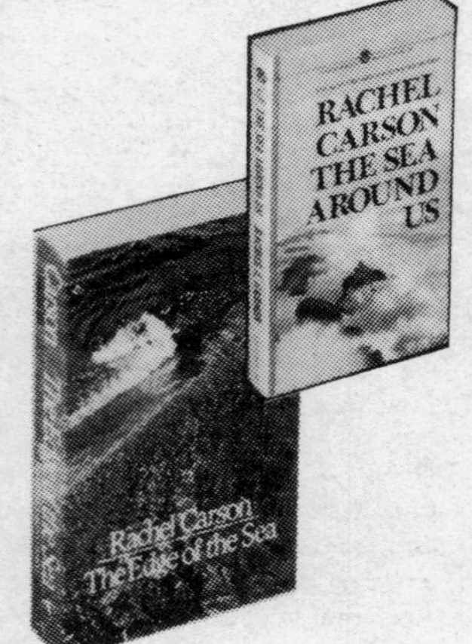

← Janthina is a pelagic snail that drifts on the surface of the open ocean, hanging suspended from a raft of frothy bubbles. The raft is formed from mucus that the animal secretes; the mucus entraps bubbles of air, then hardens into a firm, clear substance like stiff cellophane. In the breeding season the snail fastens its egg capsules to the under side of the raft, which throughout the year serves to keep the little animal afloat.

Like most snails, Janthina is carnivorous; its prey is found among other plankton animals, including small jellyfishes, crustaceans, and even small goose barnacles. Now and then a swooping gull drops from the sky and takes a snail — but for the most part the bubble raft must be excellent camouflage, almost indistinguishable from a bit of drifting sea froth. There must be other enemies that come from below, for the blue-to-violet tints of the shell (which hangs below the raft) are the colors worn by many creatures that live at or near the surface film and need to conceal themselves from enemies looking up from below. —The Edge of the Sea

•

The greatest depth at which the giant squid lives is not definitely known, but there is one instructive piece of evidence about the depth to which sperm whales descend, presumably in search of the squids. In April 1932, the cable repair ship *All America* was investigating an apparent break in the submarine cable between Balboa in the Canal Zone and Esmeraldas, Ecuador. The cable was brought to the surface off the coast of Colombia. Entangled in it was a dead 45-foot male sperm whale. The submarine cable was twisted around the lower jaw and was wrapped around one flipper, the body, and the caudal flukes. The cable was raised from a depth of 540 fathoms, or 3240 ft. —The Sea Around Us

A 100:1 scale model of Oceanside, California, being subjected to large waves at an angle with the shoreline to determine the effectiveness of groins and offshore breakwaters for controlling the movement of sand. —Waves and Beaches

Seashores
Waves and Beaches

Instead of a camera, take your eyes to the beach, watch its form and the forms of the creatures living there. The little Golden book will riffle you through the shore's table of contents. Other Golden nature guides are listed on pp. 59, 60 and 62. The classic Bascom book will introduce you to some of the most dynamic geology on Earth. Watching waves is a lovely blend of meditation and science. —SB

Seashores
(A Golden Guide)
Herbert S. Zim
and Lester Ingle
1955; 160 pp.

$1.95 postpaid from:
Golden Press Division
Western Publishing Co.
1220 Mound Avenue
Racine, WI 53404
or Whole Earth
Household Store

Waves and Beaches
(The Dynamics of
the Ocean Surface)
Willard Bascom
1964, 1980; 366 pp.
2nd Edition

$5.95 postpaid from:
Anchor Books
501 Franklin Avenue
Garden City, NY 11530
or Whole Earth
Household Store

Warty Sea Star 4″-5″

Mud Star 3″-4″

Blood Sea Star 2.5″-4″

Sun Star 16″-20″

Purple Star to 15″

Atlantic starfish

—Seashores

Seashells of North America
Field Guide to Seashells of the World

The primary function of a field guide is quick and easy identification. R. Tucker Abbott and the people at Golden Press don't want you to be flipping through the pages of a book while the incoming tide laps around your ankles. Logical arrangement by family groups, common names in bold type, clear color illustrations, and succinct descriptive information makes **Seashells of North America** *one of the most useful seashore guides around. It covers a representative sample of common marine mollusks found in the intertidal and shallow waters of the U.S. and Canada. Even the shell-less nudibranchs, the sea hares, and the cephalopods are included.*

Although not as neatly organized as the Golden Field Guide, the fine detail and definition of Gert Linder's exquisite color photographs in **Seashells of the World** *measures up to the best of the "showcase" shell books, at half the price. With well over 100,000 species of marine mollusks found world-wide, no single guide could begin to describe them all. Linder has selected nearly 1000, from the California Green Abalone to the Pearly Nautilus of the Indo-Pacific.*

I'd take Abbott to the beach with me, leaving Linder at home for more leisurely reference. —David Burnor

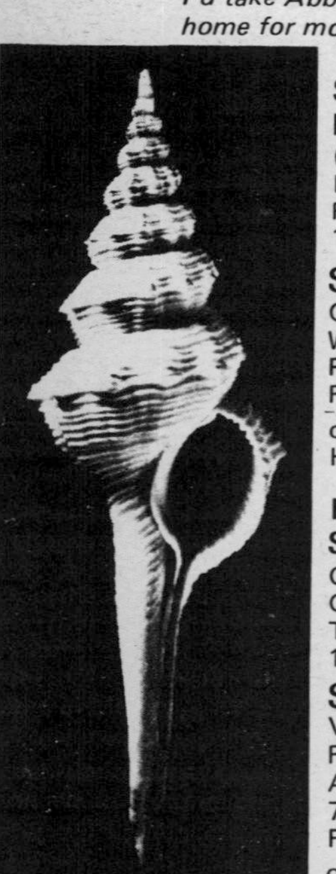

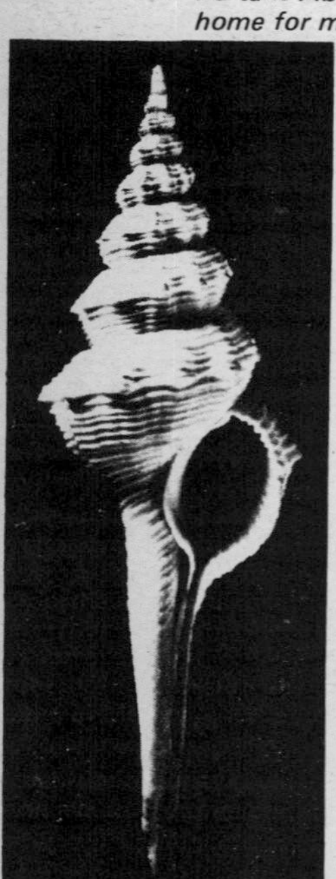

Seashells of North America
(A Guide to Field Identification)
R. Tucker Abbott
1968; 272 pp.

$4.95 postpaid from:
Golden Press
Western Publishing Co.
P.O. Box 700
Racine, WI 53404
or Whole Earth
Household Store

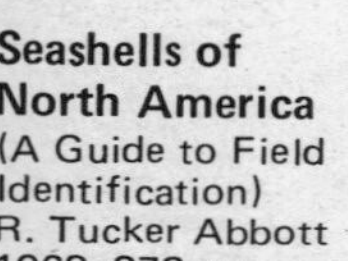

Field Guide to Seashells of the World
Gert Linder
Gwynne Vevers, Translator
1975, 1978; 271 pp.

$9.95 postpaid from:
Van Nostrand
Reinhold Company
Attn: Order Department
7625 Empire Drive
Florence, KY 41042
or Whole Earth
Household Store

↑
Spindle-shaped Fusinus salisburyi Fulton, 1930
—Seashells of the World

→
Channeled Top Shell.
Calliostoma canaliculatum (**Lightfoot**).
Alaska - S. Calif. Shell light; sides and base quite flat. Whorls yellowish tan, with about 9 sharp, weakly beaded spiral cords between sutures. Common; on offshore kelps.
—Seashells of North America

Stalking the Blue-Eyed Scallop

When you go to the shore, just take seasoning, something nice to drink and Euell Gibbons' guidance, and you can dine far better and infinitely cheaper than in those deadly restaurants that grow on coasts. (More Euell Gibbons books on p. 416) —SB

Stalking the Blue-Eyed Scallop
(Field Guide Edition)
Euell Gibbons
1964, 1970; 332 pp.

OUT OF PRINT
David McKay Company

Get this book back in print!

↑
Owl Limpets are seldom eaten in California, but they are highly esteemed by the Mexicans of Lower California, who know a good thing when they taste it. Each Owl Limpet will yield just one small steak about 2 inches across, but when this is properly prepared it is delicious, being of finer grain and more delicate flavor than even the highly prized Abalone. Each little Limpet Steak should be placed inside a fold of muslin and pounded on a wooden surface with a mallet or rolling pin to make it tender, then dipped in egg that has been beaten with a dash of water, dredged in fine bread crumbs, and fried to a golden brown. When cooked perfectly, these limpet steaks can be cut with a fork and have a rich but delicate flavor that is just right.

The next time you are in Southern California and a native son starts bragging about the wonders of Abalone steak, practice a bit of one-upmanship by finding some Owl Limpets and treating him to a taste thrill that makes Abalone seem ordinary. Unless he is a student of marine life, he probably doesn't even know this fine food is available.

Seaweed in Agriculture and Horticulture

Seaweed is a plant that is a fertilizer and a plant food. It's not mined from the earth like many fertilizers, it is harvested from the ocean — a renewable source. Think of plants like comfrey, alfalfa, and the seaweeds as solar-powered fertilizer factories. But seaweed is special because of the rich salty soup it grows in. The list of plant nutrients it contains is very complete, and as a slow-acting meal worked into the soil, seaweed can often be a single solution to many different soil deficiencies — including trace elements. As a fast-acting liquid, it can be sprayed onto the leaves of plants. This book also has a bit of the history of the production process, an excellent short section on "How Plants Grow," and recommended rations for feeding seaweed meal to livestock. —Richard Nilsen

Seaweed in Agriculture and Horticulture
W.A. Stephenson
1974; 241 pp.

$9.50 postpaid from:
Bargyla Rateaver
Pauma Valley, CA 92061

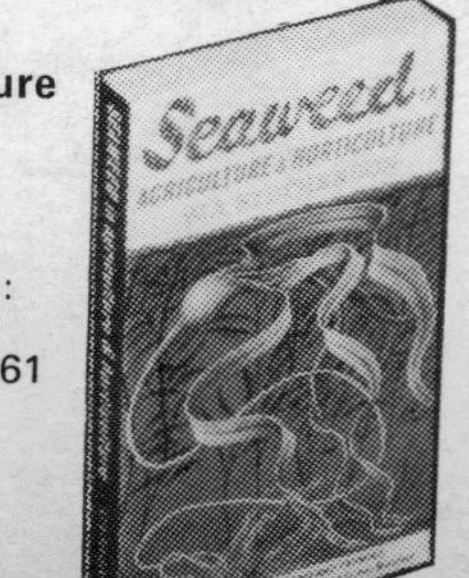

The Seavegetable Book

Attention all coastal peoples. The tidal zone is filled with food. But for some reason us people have not learned to eat and to care for the ocean's edge. This is the book I have always wanted: foraging; cooking; recipes; folk names from England, Scotland, Japan, China, Russia, the United States; uses; nutrients; commercial sources; fine line drawings; habitat; gel and special things to know about varied North American coasts. Seaweed like it was warm homemade bread. —Peter Warshall

The Seavegetable Book
(Foraging and Cooking Seaweed)
Judith Cooper Madlener
1977; 288 pp.

$8.45 postpaid from:
Clarkson N. Potter, Inc.
Crown Publishers
One Park Avenue
New York, NY 10016
or Whole Earth
Household Store

Though the sea palm looks like a tiny palm tree, all parts of it are tender and delicious, when prepared. The Chinese community in San Francisco considers this sea vegetable a special treat!

Collect only fresh sea palms. (Stipes should snap crisply when bent.) Dry the blades for tasty snacks. Rinse the stipes in cold water. Cut into 2-inch lengths. Steam them, then cut again down the center.

BOATS, I'M ABUNDANTLY convinced, are better for building competence and mental health than any other toy — skis, airplanes, performance cars, or interactive graphic computers. It has something to do with operating on the wildly various interface between the two fluids, water and air. It takes balance — whether you're in a kayak or a 75 ft. sailboat — and real or threatened dunkings drive the lessons of balance into your fibre.

And beyond that, if they're lived with, boats teach aesthetics. They can't help it. —SB

The Small Boat Journal

The way to start with boats is small — you learn more and spend way less. And a good way to start small is with this new magazine put out by the venerable **National Fisherman** *(below). It's handsome, traditional, sometimes innovative, and so are the boats it reports on. It promotes fine workmanship, but it's not afraid to deliver an essay of praise for the cheapo aluminum utility outboard.*

My boat madness ballooned from my experience six years ago with a 16-foot traditional Whitehall rowboat. Now, by grotesque happenchance, I own three yachts 26 - 30 ft. (voluntary simplicity). If I had to cut back to the one boat that does the most for me, it would be the 16-foot Whitehall. —SB

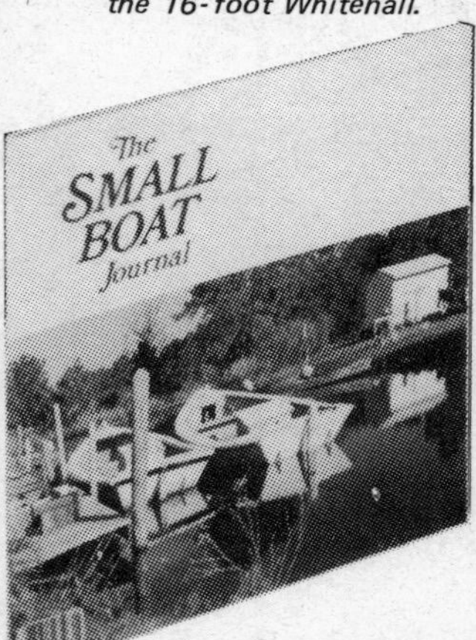

The Small Boat Journal
David R. Getchall, Editor
$12/year (12 issues)
from:
The Small Boat Journal
21 Elm Street
Camden, ME 04843

Boats, Oars, and Rowing

Boat-designer R.D. Culler of Cape Cod here holds forth on the nice details of design and technique that go with enjoying a good pulling boat. Rowing is coming back these days. It beats jogging for exercise, pleasure, and getting into interesting trouble. —SB

Boats, Oars, and Rowing
R.D. Culler
1978; 149 pp.
$10.95 postpaid from:
International Marine Publishing Company
21 Elm Street
Camden, ME 04843
or Whole Earth Household Store

W. COAST RIG

Nearly every boat I have built, with the exception of double-enders, has had a sculling slot; the double-enders can well have an oarlock socket blocked out to be used in place of a slot. Personally, I like the looks of a slot, besides admiring its practicality and simplicity. For those who don't like them, an oarlock socket can usually be placed in any stern. In this country, the slot is usually in the center of the stern; in many other countries, notably the Bahamas, it is offset to port for a couple of good reasons — to account for the method of sculling, which is different from ours, and to allow the oar to be used with a rudder in place, so a sailing craft can be helped out in a calm. Regardless of locality and tradition, I think any small sailing boat should be rigged this way. I don't know which came first, the off-set slot or the stroke of the oar that seems best suited to it. However, I can say that the Bahama method, once you adapt to it, is far superior in most boats to the accepted Yankee method.

One of the great things about small boats is that you don't need a dinghy. Unless you have a keel sailboat, your craft can be its own dinghy. All you have to do is run her up to shore, leap out, tie off to the nearest tree or post and presto! You're docked.

If you use this method where there are winds, waves and tides, however, you've got problems. The wind may bang your boat into the rocks or turn it broadside to the breaking waves and fill it with water. If you're in tidal water and the tide is falling, your boat could end up high and dry. Or if the tide is rising, you'd better be sure your boat is well tied. —John K. Burleson

Loop-line anchoring for camp-cruisers

WoodenBoat Magazine

The success of this magazine (circulation about 40,000 after only five years) says a lot about the increasing sophistication of boat use these days. The magazine is uncompromising in its focus on superb workmanship in what was thought to be a fading medium — wood for boats. It's a question of love I think. If you're mainly racing or mainly partying on occasion, a fiberglass boat makes sense. But if you're romantically involved in your boat, **WoodenBoat** *will feed your infatuation and keep it healthy. A fine magazine on every count.* —SB

WoodenBoat
(The magazine for wooden boat owners, builders and designers)
Jonathan Wilson, Editor
$15/year (6 issues)
from:
WoodenBoat Publications
P.O. Box 78
Brooklin, ME 04616

Intermezzo is a beautiful example of Eddie Crosby's design talents. She was fashioned with care in every step, and contains some exquisite detailing. Her planking is white cedar, except for the mahogany garboards and sheer strakes. Mahogany seats, teak floorboards, and continuous inwales of ash set her off in a unique and distinctive fashion.

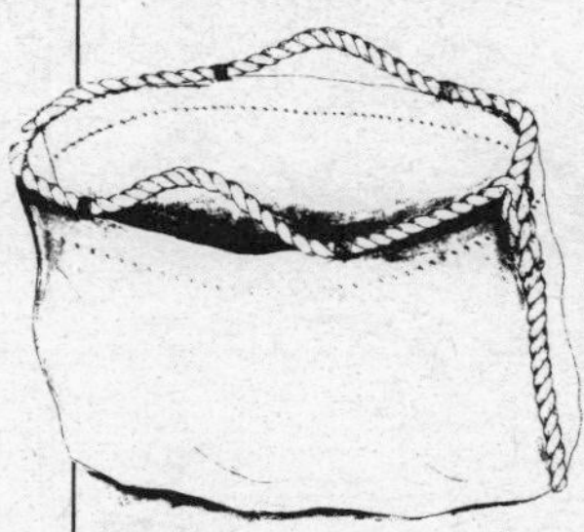

Ballast bag with rope cringles

Sand or ballast bags used to be common around small boats — so common that they were sold commercially by marine hardware companies early in this century. Today's small boat racing rules prohibit shifting ballast, perhaps a legacy of the shift away from sandbaggers in the 1880s and '90s. But the nonracing wooden boat owner isn't bound by any rules, and 25 lbs of sand can do wonders for the small boat. It can hold the bow of a flat-bottomed skiff down and keep it from pounding when only one person is sailing. It can be shifted to weather to relieve some of the effort of keeping a boat on her feet in a breeze. Or the sand in it can be poured over the side when it isn't needed and an empty bag brought home. —Ben Fuller

National Fisherman

The saltiest publication I know. Fishing, boatbuilding, ocean conservation, oceanography, sea news. A trade publication with a dignified nod to the sea buffs. Damn good newspaper. —SB

The National Fisherman
David R. Getchell, Editor
$15/year (13 issues)
from:
The National Fisherman
21 Elm Street
Camden, ME 04848

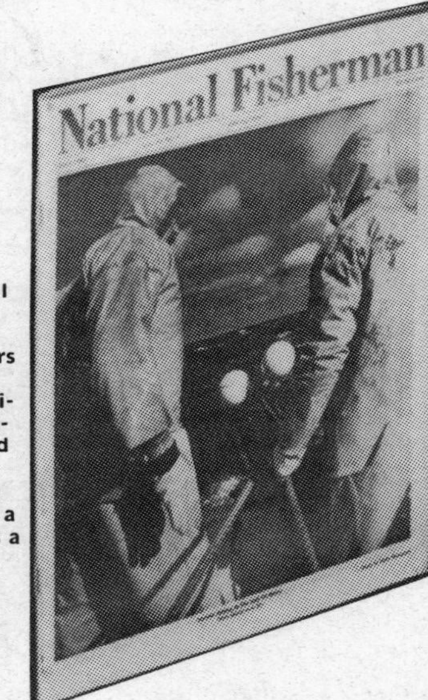

The wearer of this survival suit is also carrying a full complement of auxiliary equipment to help rescuers locate him quickly. He is holding an Electronic Position Indicating Radio Beacon, which is encapsulated in foam for flotation; clipped to his left arm are a chemical light stick and a box of pen flares; there is a strobe light on his right wrist; and he is wearing a whistle at his throat.

Survival Suits

The best protection from cold water is to stay out of it. Survival time is at its maximum when a person is dry. The dry foam survival suits now on the market appear to be the most reasonable equipment for most fishermen. These suits are not expensive; they store easily, are quick to don and are highly buoyant. . . . Three brands of survival suits are currently available in Maine: the Bayley, Fitz-Wright and Imperial. . . .

The Bayley suit is much stiffer than the other two when stored in the cold. When selecting a suit, try on a cold one to determine its speed of entry under the most adverse conditions. A fisherman tested a cold Bayley suit for the authors and was only able to put it on after 3 minutes, 19 seconds. This is well above the maximum 60 seconds allowed by the Coast Guard.

Maintenance and life expectancy of the suits are areas of concern to the purchaser. According to manufacturers, shelf life should be about 20 years. However, there are a few factors that will enhance shelf life.

First, keep the suit in the dark, away from gas or diesel fumes and out of direct salt spray. When the vessel is not to be used for a long period of time, remove the suit from its bag and hang it on a wooden coat hanger in a dark, cool closet. Maintenance of the suit is minimal: it should be washed in fresh water after each exposure to salt water.

—Dr. Andrew M. Longley, Jr. and Gary Anderson

THE RISING SUN
NEIGHBORHOOD NEWSLETTER

— "I really feel like I'm losing my mind."
— "You should be grateful that you've still got a mind to lose — that you're one of the lucky ones who can still feel it going."

—Nancy and Jonathan

Nautical Quarterly

I haven't seen its like since **Eros**. *Elegant design, comes in a box, no advertising. Sumptuous color photos of gorgeous creatures in loving detail, intelligent analysis of their working.*

The sexy creatures are, of course, boats — sensational boats, sensational boating. The magazine doesn't do much in the way of how-to but concentrates on sheer appreciation of good work. Being free of advertising it can even look at the working of the boat biz, how for example the Grand Banks line of power yachts went bust, how Westsail sailing yachts made good. The editorial view is biased neither toward nor away from traditional boats and materials, so old and new styles are placed in interesting mutual context.

The publishers make a reasonable assumption that people who own boats are used to throwing away money and will not cavil at $42.50 for four issues. In fact, that's a pretty good deal. If you're thinking of getting a fancy boat, why don't you just get this magazine instead, and save a lot of expense and aggravation? —SB

Nautical Quarterly
Joseph Gribbins, Editor
$42.50 /year (4 issues)
from:
Nautical Quarterly
141 Lexington Avenue
New York, NY 10016

↓ Harold Payson sells the finished boat for $650 with Wilcox-Crittenden bronze oarlocks and spruce oars leathered and varnished. He also sells Bolger's plans for building a Gloucester Gull at home. These are $10. Asked to estimate cost of materials for a one-off building project, Payson thought $250 was about right for a marine-plywood boat. Building time was a bit less definite because of the time an amateur inevitably wastes, even though he may enjoy every minute. Harold Payson guesses at "three weeks, working every day," and including time for the drying of glue and paint.

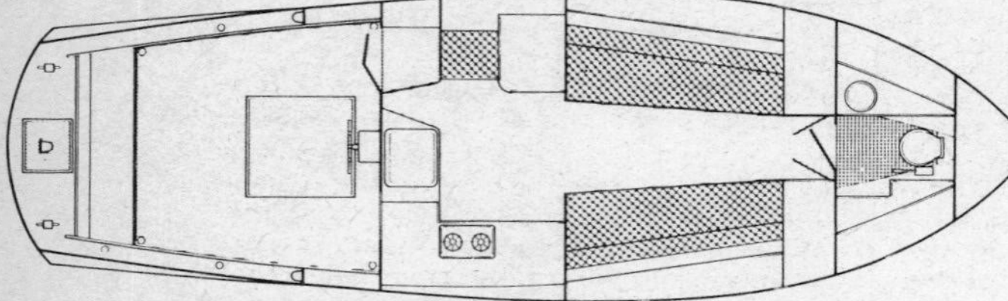

Ken Wenman's Scout 30, an elegant, commodious coastal cruiser ↓

Gloucester Gull by Phil Bolger ↓

Boston Whaler

These are the best and safest utility outboards in the business — well-made, unsinkable, sure-riding, work platforms. When one ship I read of recently sank, the Whaler in davits deck was so bouyant it tore itself loose, floated to the surface and saved an otherwise drowning crew. Whaler publicity people like to cut the boats in pieces and float the pieces. Whole boats go from 9' to 22' and $1315 to $19,800. —SB

•

At the mooring, every Whaler is self-bailing. Pull the plugs and let it rain.

Boston Whalers
Brochure and price list

free from:
Boston Whaler, Inc.
1149 Hingham Street
Rockland, MA 02370

•

Two men standing on the gunwale won't dip the hull six inches.

A 13' Whaler sawed into thirds will support the weight of two thousand pounds and still keep the power head of the engine above water and dry.

Re-started, it can get underway and bail itself in a matter of minutes.

The Case for the Cruising Trimaran

Trimarans have always fascinated us, as have some sailors' fixations on those craft, and like many other monohull fanciers, we've always wondered why anyone would want to build three hulls when one would do, or why the multihull sailor who wrote the definitive multihull seamanship manual went missing in a tri, or why anyone would seriously consider capsize as an option in an offshore passage. Be that as it may, there are plenty of people who must have a trimaran, and for them, Jim Brown, among others, is a guiding light. We don't know for a fact, but there could very well be more Brown-designed cruising tris afloat than any others.

Jim Brown makes **The Case for the Cruising Trimaran**. *His prose reads well, his arguments are more objective than you would expect, and he faces squarely and without obfuscation the bane of the multihull — capsize: why it happens, how to prevent it, what to do when it rears its ugly head, how to survive.* —Peter Spectre

The Case for the Cruising Trimaran
Jim Brown
1979; 214 pp.
$17.50 postpaid from:
International Marine Publishing Company
21 Elm Street
Camden, ME 04843

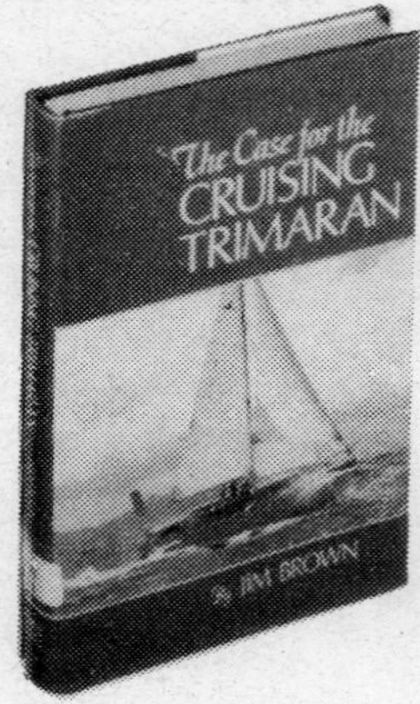

•

I'd like to lay the cornerstone of my case for the cruising multihull. If it is safety that you want, a feeling of security, a justifiable concept, then try cruising in a boat capable of over 20 knots, and when the wind is up, just keep her down to something less than 10. When things get tough, just throttle back for comfort, and gain safety. What, honestly, is the threat of capsize when compared with the threat of going down?

Boats and Harbors

If you want a really funky boating newspaper, then you want **Boats and Harbors**. *It's almost all working boats stuff, thousands of them, and the deals can make you cry. A friend of ours recently found in it (and purchased) a 61-foot oyster smack built in 1907 with a diesel the size of your kitchen for $4,500. And steamed home in her!* —George Putz

Boats and Harbors

$4 /year (36 issues)
from:
Boats and Harbors
P.O. Drawer 647
Crossville, TN 38555

Sea Canoeing

The English call kayaks canoes, thus this title. This being the only book to cover the subject of handling kayaks in the open ocean, it is also the best. The nice thing about it is that if there were a hundred books on the subject, it would probably still be the best. The author is an intrepid sports kayaker whose techniques are grounded in native practice at sea, making it not only the practical manual, but solid ethnography as well. —George Putz

Sea Canoeing
Derek Hutchinson
1976, 1979; 204 pp.
$24 postpaid from:
Transatlantic Arts
88 Bridge Road
Central Islip, NY 11722

Reflected waves and clapotis. If the angle is acute where the reflected wave meets the original wave pattern, and if a big swell is running, the resulting clapotis can be tremendously powerful. The two toppling walls of water will collide almost head on, sending tons of water vertically skywards in a thundering plume that rushes along like an express train. This is not a safe area in which to canoe, and the capsized paddler in the illustration is in a bad position. With his canoe and paddle, he must swim seawards clear of the "break" area. His companions can then give him a rescue outside the danger area, where he should never have been in the first place.

—Sea Canoeing

↓

Surveying Small Craft

Those of us hankering for a boat are most likely to make one or buy a used one. Buying a used one is very tricky. "Surveying" is what hiring a specialist to look it over is called. You can do some of it yourself (though it isn't a job for amateurs) and save money. This book tells how. It's written by an Englishman, and there's a note of translation by an American surveyor to explain things that might not be clear otherwise. If you're thinking of adding a boat to your life, this is required reading. This is "medical self-care" for boats — how to detect the hidden rot, electrolysis, rust, and dumb design that can lead to disaster or huge expense. It won't make you a professional boat doctor — surveyor — but it sure helps good preventive health care. —SB and J. Baldwin

Surveying Small Craft
Ian Nicholson
1974; 224 pp.

$14.95 postpaid from:
Granada Publishing, Inc.
866 UN Plaza, Suite 405
New York, NY 10017

or

£5.95 postpaid from:
Granada Publishing, Ltd.
P.O. Box 9
St. Albans, Hertfordshire
AL2 2NF England

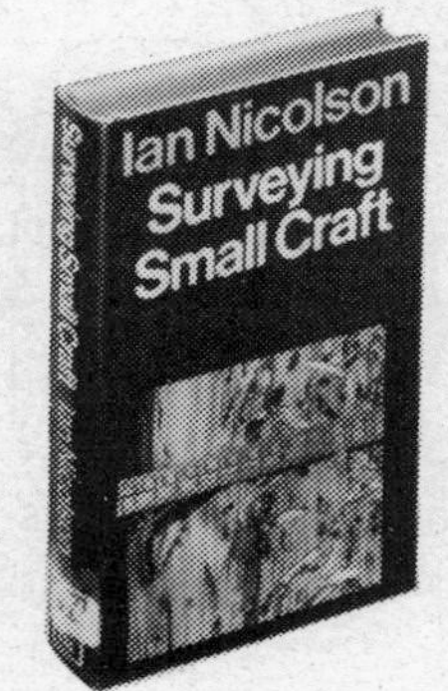

AT WINDOW EDGES
AT BEAM ENDS & CARLINES
BY EDGES OF DRAINING BOARD
BY CHAIN PLATES
BELOW STANCH'NS
AT JOINS IN DOOR FRAMES
IN FURNITURE BELOW HATCHES
IN ENCLOSED SPACES
AT CRACKED FRAME
AT BOLT ENDS
AT KEEL EDGE
PUDDLE BY BUTT BLOCK
AT WOOD FLOORS BY PUDDLES

A search should be made for rot wherever water can become trapped, and particularly where rainwater can seep in. This sketch shows typical vulnerable areas and suggests other comparable danger spots. For instance, stanchions work loose so that rain and spray gets down through their boltholes. The same trouble occurs at other deck fittings, especially those which take a lot of punishment.

•

The second phase of laying up is to protect the boat's permanent fixtures. Wash with fresh water and lubricate all fittings that have moving parts. Oil all hinges, and apply a film of petroleum jelly to any exposed hardware likely to corrode. Find out the yard's policy on fuel tanks: some yards require that tanks be topped off to prevent condensation; others, wary of the fire hazard, want the tanks totally drained. Drain or pump out old, acidic engine oil and replace it with fresh oil. In cold climates, pump antifreeze into the engine's cooling system to avert burst piping. Remove batteries, store them in a warm, dry place and keep them from going dead with "trickle charges" of steady low-voltage current. Most yards will do the latter; but it can be handled at home by purchasing a small charger that can be attached to the battery and plugged into a wall socket.

→

Fishhooks — the nautical term for strands of wire rigging that have broken and curled outward — are a sign of wear, and a menace. They can rip sails and leave painful cuts in bare hands. A fishhook in galvanized wire can be snipped off with cutters and taped over. If a rash of them appears, it means the wire itself is deteriorating. Replace it.

Maintenance

Far more than for a car, a house, or a body, maintenance is required for a boat. Use eats boats, disuse eats boats, and water, both fresh and salt, eats boats with relish. They don't tell you that, and books on boat maintenance tend to be feeble, leaving three choices: turn it all over expensively to the yard, learn personally from an expert, or let the boat dissolve. This surprising book presents an alternative learning source (surprising because it's the only excellent volume in an otherwise wretchedly overwrought, over-priced series from Time-Life). It's pretty comprehensive, splendidly clear, and most important, gives the beginner confidence to begin. —SB

Maintenance
Time-Life Books, Editors
1975; 176 pp.

$12.95 postpaid from:
Time-Life Books
541 North Fairbanks
Chicago, IL 60611

or Whole Earth Household Store

Your Boat's Electrical System

Most boat owners are utterly mystified by the vagaries of their boat's electrical misbehavior — myself included. It is the single source of most of a boat's problems, including serious dangers such as fire and debilitating electrolysis. You'd think there would be a host of books competing for excellence on the subject. Sorry, there's only one, not very good at teaching, but it covers the subject comprehensively if tortuously. I built a troubleshooting tester from it that has shot a lot of trouble on my 30-foot cutter. But some still eludes me. Better books, please. —SB

Your Boat's Electrical System
(The Boatkeeper's Guide to Installation, Care and Troubleshooting of All Electric Gear)
Conrad Miller
1973; 350 pp.

$7.95 postpaid from:
Hearst Books
P.O. Box 1406
Radio City Station
New York, NY 10019

or Whole Earth Household Store

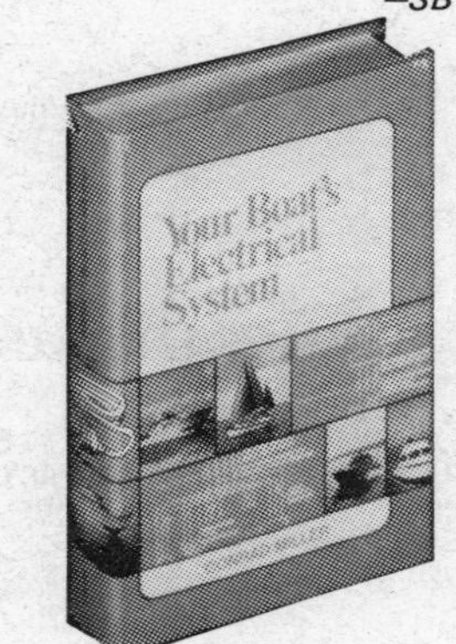

←

Good terminals and connectors are particularly important on a boat's d.c. wiring system because, despite vibration and corrosive environment, they must offer continuity and low resistance to current flow. Terminal lugs recommended most highly are the swaged, or crimped, solderless, tinned copper or brass variety with ring ends. These are better than those with spade or forked ends because they will stay in place even if the stud or nut loosens.

The Galley Book

It's meant for boats, but anybody with any kind of tiny or mobile kitchen will find this an invaluable book. It's far more important than a cookbook. The stove advice alone saved me many dollars and hours (she recommends pressure kerosene over alcohol and LP gas stoves — and I never knew pressure kerosene stoves can manage with plain old diesel oil). —SB

The Galley Book
Janet Groene
1977; 209 pp.

OUT OF PRINT
David McKay Company

Get this book back in print!

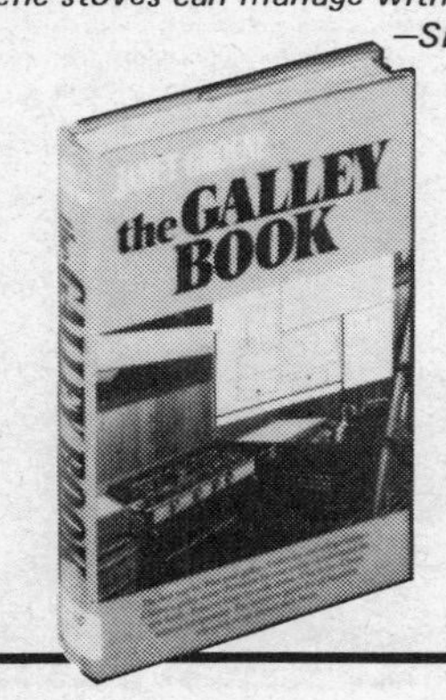

•

Stove-Top Baking

Back in the 1930s a manufacturer of heavy aluminum cooking ware came out with a line of pots and pans, and a sales pitch aimed at American country cooks who were using kerosene wick burners and two-burner gas plates. In a recipe book it was explained how to bake atop the stove — an innovation that at last allowed summertime baking without heating up the big, hot coal cookstove.

The technique is still valid today. Its secret is the use of heavy pans with heavy, tight-fitting lids. The unit, heated evenly throughout, surrounds food with heat, just as an oven does. We haven't found anything superior to heavy aluminum for the job.

•

In our galley we have a 4-quart heavy aluminum pressure cooker and an 11-inch Club Aluminum covered skillet (chicken fryer), both of which are used for baking, and a heavy 2-quart Lifetime stainless-steel saucepan, which is used for stove top casseroles.

The Groenes' stove-top oven consists of this Club Aluminum skillet and lid, pressure cooker rack to keep baking pan from resting on skillet bottom, and appropriate cake and pie pans.

Living Aboard

If you want to keep your simplicity voluntary, there's nothing like a small mobile home on a large mobile environment to enforce it. This is a dense practical guide to boat living, the best of its kind. —SB

Living Aboard
(The Cruising Sailboat as a Home)
Jan and Bill Moeller
1976; 299 pp.

$15 postpaid from:
International Marine Publishing Company
21 Elm Street
Camden, ME 04843

or Whole Earth Household Store

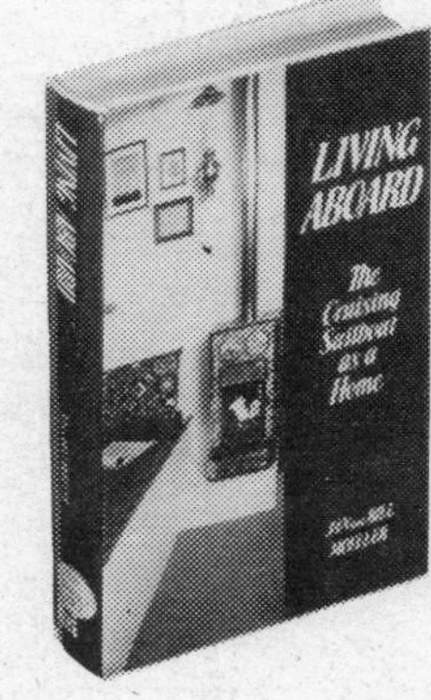

•

One of the best ways to save money is to try to avoid buying supplies and equipment in marine stores. There is much you can't get anywhere else, but there is more that you can. Stove alcohol is a good example. When we were new live-aboards, we asked the price of a gallon in general hardware store that also handled a few marine supplies. The clerk consulted a list and said, "Marine alcohol is $4 a gallon." We asked him if he had any alcohol that was not designated "marine." He said he had several brands. We chose the least expensive of all, which was then $2 a gallon. The label listed its many uses, one of which was stove fuel. In all the years we had an alcohol stove, we never used "marine" alcohol and we never had any problems. Neither will you, if the label on the alcohol you buy lists stove fuel as one of its uses.

•

All our bulkheads are painted with interior latex, which not only is much cheaper than marine paint but also will not harbor mildew, since latex paint "breathes." It also dries in an hour, which is one of our main reasons for using it. Living aboard in a small area is no place to apply paint that takes many hours to dry, unless you can go off and live somewhere else while it is drying.

•

Trailer supply stores are an excellent source for many items that can be used in boats, especially those items, such as light fixtures, that use 12-volt power. We had a good little wall-mounted, stainless-steel reading lamp in one of our boats. It cost $15. We found the very same light for $3 in a trailer supply store. The light was aluminum, with a cheap-looking brass finish. For our live-aboard boat, we bought three of these lamps, and we spray-painted them white to match the bulkheads on which they are mounted. After three years, there is not a sign of rust on them anywhere.

THE RISING SUN
NEIGHBORHOOD NEWSLETTER

—"You're wonderful, Evelyn."
—"No, I'm not, but I would be if I had some chocolate."

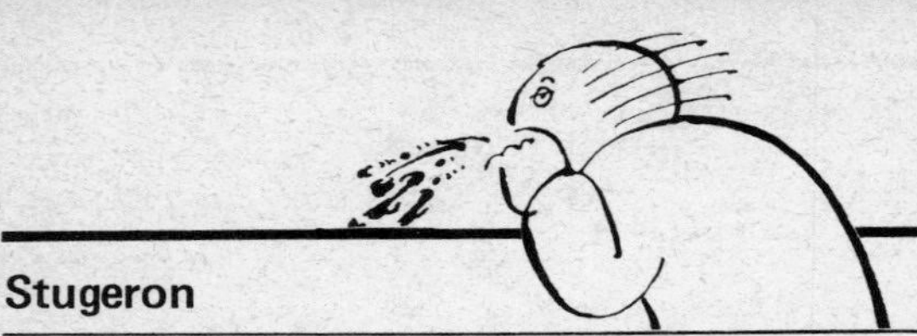

Stugeron

The main thing that you should know about sea-going is that at last an effective remedy exists for seasickness. The British have it and we don't. It's a drug called Stugeron. Have traveling friends pick it up at pharmacies such as Boots the Chemist in England. It doesn't make you sleepy but may make you silly, which I'll take over sick any day. We've used it effectively. The survivors of the Fastnet Race used it effectively (through 360° knockdowns and such). If you've routinely looked at gorgeous ocean sunsets through a brown veil of nausea, as I have, you'll be amazed. —SB

Sailing Illustrated

Probably Royce has taught more people to sail than any other book, and its jam-packed paperback fit-the-hand format, just begging to be taken and kept aboard, shows why. It has a quick-reference thumb index that works, and the emphasis is on showing the procedures rather than talking about them. Good keepaboard fare. —George Putz

Sailing Illustrated
(The Best of All Sailing Worlds)
Patrick M. Royce
1956, 1979; 345 pp.
7th Edition
$9.20 postpaid from:
Western Marine Enterprises
P.O. Box Q
Ventura, CA 93001
or Whole Earth Household Store

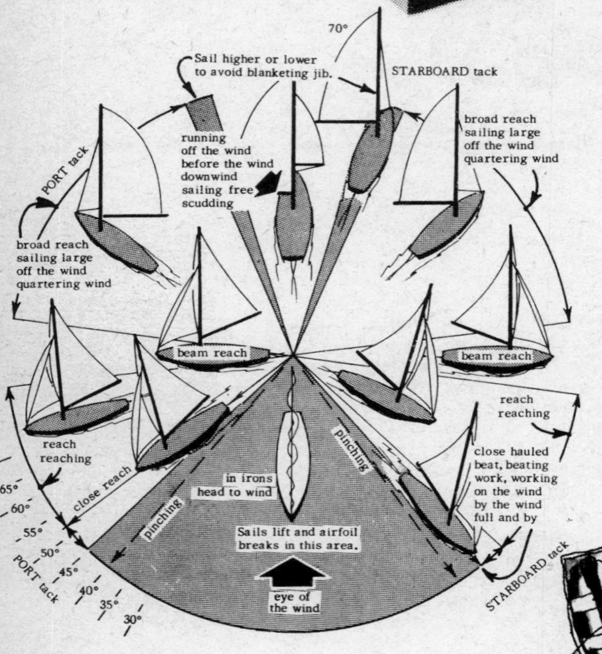

Piloting, Seamanship and Small Boat Handling

For reference on board stick by "Chapman's," (the familiar term for this book, which indicates its vast popularity). In print since 1922, now in its 54th edition, this is the only available one-volume complete introduction to running a boat — from its excellent intro to nautical terminology through navigation, rules of the road, flag bloody etiquette, weather, electronics, boat trailering, the whole wet gamut. That it is not at all restricted to sailboats helps broaden and inform the otherwise narrow windblown mind. —SB

Piloting, Seamanship and Small Boat Handling
Charles F. Chapman
1922, 1979; 640 pp.
54th Edition
$13.95 postpaid from:
Motorboating and Sailing Books
224 West 57th Street
New York, NY 10019
or Whole Earth Household Store

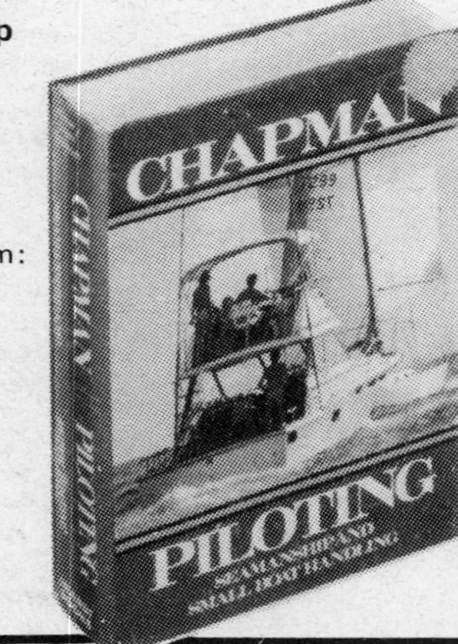

Boats that must cross a bar with breaking waves must avoid "pitchpoling" — being thrown end over end if caught driving hard down the face of a steep sea, burying the bow. This double-ended fisherman just misses being caught on the forward face of a breaker. This is no place for pleasure boats.

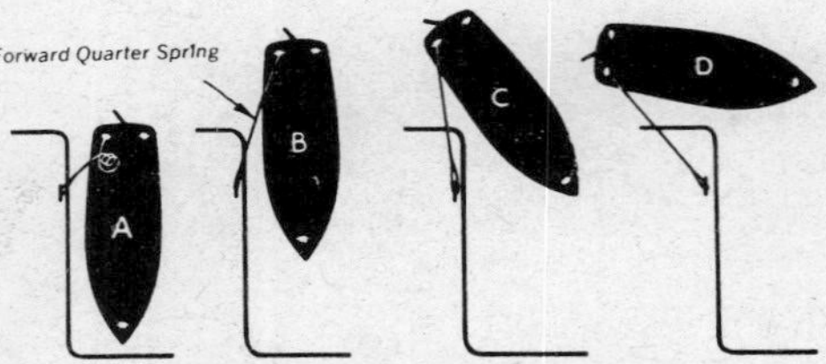

Use of a forward quarter spring when backing a boat out around the end of a dock. When spring is taut, boat reverses with full right rudder.

The Craft of Sail

If you sail and take people along who don't sail, your entire sense of self-worth may disappear when a passenger asks what makes the boat go and you can't explain properly and get huffy and they have to pretend they understand and then sit quietly feeling stupid and unhappy. This book solves all that — it's the only one I've seen that does. Furthermore it has a singular fineness of illustration, writing, and experience that makes old salts study it with the same pleasure as children do. A great first sailing book. More by Adkins, p. 564. —SB

The Craft of Sail
(A Primer of Sailing)
Jan Adkins
1973; 64 pp.
$6.95 postpaid from:
Walker and Company
720 Fifth Avenue
New York, NY 10019
or Whole Earth Household Store

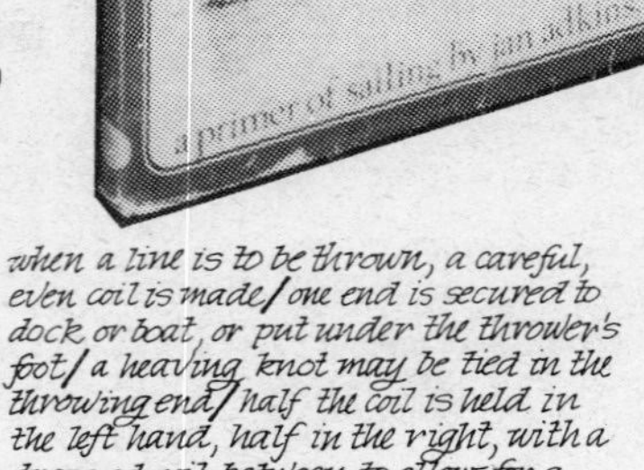

when a line is to be thrown, a careful, even coil is made/ one end is secured to dock or boat, or put under the thrower's foot/ a heaving knot may be tied in the throwing end/ half the coil is held in the left hand, half in the right, with a dropped coil between to allow for a hefty swing/ when one coil is thrown, it strips the remaining coil as it goes

"Back the jib" — another crew member holds the jib out to starboard so the backwinded jib will push the bow around to port. The skipper reverses his tiller so the stern will swing to starboard as the boat backs up.

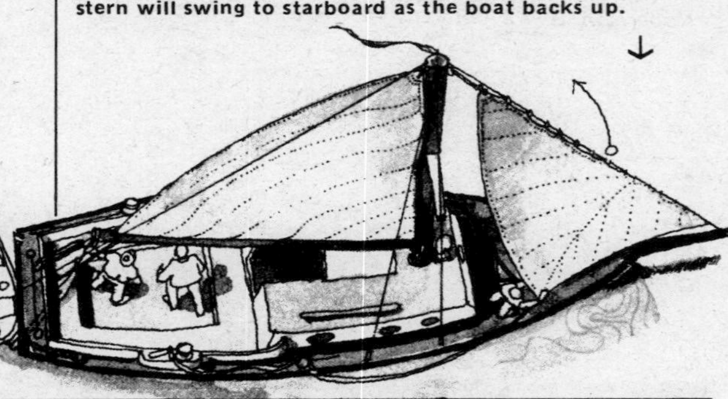

The New Glénans Sailing Manual

From France and years of training experience at the Glenans Sailing Center comes a text so comprehensive and graphic it serves as an example of what "comprehensive" really means. You start with a tiny dinghy ("If there is an instructor around, he should look the other way. At all costs he should not shout advice . . .") and advance by skills to serious passage making. Typical skill: spinnaker handling: twenty pages. —SB

The New Glénans Sailing Manual
James MacGibbon and Stanley Caldwell, Editors
1972, 1978; 782 pp.
$35 postpaid from:
W.W. Norton and Co.
500 Fifth Avenue
New York, NY 10036

→
There are several ways of making a boat luff up or bear away without a rudder, which can either be adopted at one and the same time or separately. They have already been explained, but they are worth repeating here. *A boat luffs up when she heels, when the mainsail is sheeted in, when the centreboard is fully lowered or when she is down by the head.*

A boat bears away when she heels to windward, when the mainsail is eased, when the centreboard is raised, even partially, or when she is down by the stern.

Speed is an influential factor. The faster a boat goes the more weather helm she carries. If she is going slowly, she may develop some lee helm (more likely still if she goes astern).

→
The end of the anchor chain (the *bitter end*) should be made fast to the ring in the chain locker with a number of turns of rope with a total breaking strain equal to that of the chain [four parts of 3/4-in. circ (¼ in dia) nylon = a 3/8 in chain]. The whole lashing should be at least four inches long so that it can be easily cut. Wire and shackles must be avoided, because it takes too long to release them if you need to slip your cable or load in an emergency.

One way of damping down the snatch on a tow rope

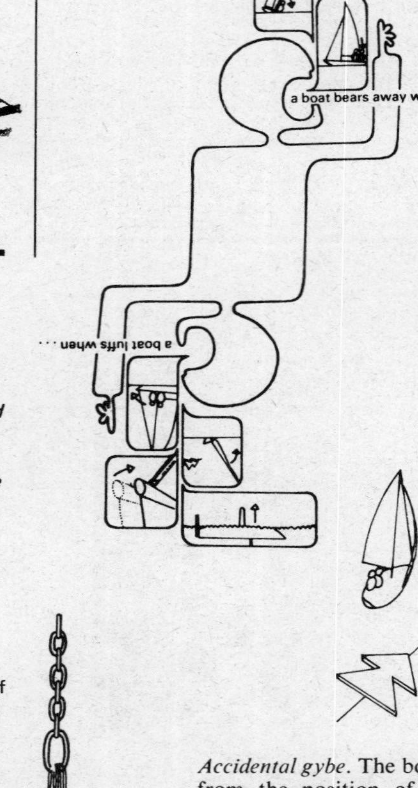

Accidental gybe. The boat has passed from the position of wind astern, unnoticed, and it is sailing by the lee. The sail slams over unexpectedly. This kind of gybe can be violent, breaking something or, quite simply, making the boat capsize

Three other important sea books

Advanced First Aid for All Outdoors, *reviewed on p. 415, is expanded from an earlier book,* **Advanced First Aid Afloat**, *so its emphasis is still salty. It'll equip you to handle nearly any medical emergency at sea, where doctors are seldom on call.*

The overall best weather book, I believe, is **Weather for the Mariner**, *reviewed on p. 20.*

The most wonderful reference book you can have wherever you do your dreaming and reading about the sea is the **Oxford Companion to Ships and the Sea**, *reviewed along with the Horatio Hornblower series on p. 508.*

The absolutely best way to learn to sail is with skilled sailors. You can find them and their boats for hire in exotic locales in Mary Crowley's Sail Training survey on p. 576. Personally I favor Mary's own outfit, Ocean Voyages. —SB

Blue Water

The product of — whew — 200,000 miles under sail, the Griffiths' great book is packed with the lore of serious passage making. They have a lot of highly personal ideas — twin headsails for quartering winds, a deadlight in the bottom for undersea viewing, dynamite on board for blasting out of coral reefs or sticky situations with pirates — and I'm convinced by nearly every one of them. But I want to check them out . . . CHAIN ME TO THE DESK QUICK! (That kind of book.) —SB

Blue Water
(A Guide to Self-Reliant Sailboat Cruising)
Bob Griffith and Nancy Griffith
1979; 267 pp.
$17.95 postpaid from:
W.W. Norton and Company
500 Fifth Avenue
New York, NY 10036
or Whole Earth Household Store

•

On your head, a sou'wester hat is far better than a hood. When you face to windward the brim keeps you from being blinded and stung by driving rain, you can turn your head freely without impeding your vision, and you can hear much better than with a hood on.

•

One of the simplest means of checking for drag is using a leadline, which is lowered to the bottom and made fast with enough slack in the line so it does not drag as the boat swings. If, after a while, the line leads forward when you take it up firm, the boat has dragged. Our leadline has served as an automatic anchor watch on many occasions. We put a tin can or two in a bucket on the cockpit seat and make a bight of the slack leadline fast to it. The clatter of the bucket falling to the deck when the line comes taut announces that the boat has shifted.

For long passages with trade winds over the quarter, jibs flown on twin headstays are the handiest, strongest, and safest rig.

Landfall on San Miguel, Azores. . . . as we approached it took shape; the volcanic peaks, the dark green areas of trees, a patchwork of tiny fields . . . gathered colour and substance.'
—Voyaging Under Sail

Voyaging Under Sail
Cruising Under Sail

The hardcore **Whole Earth** *readership must chaff whenever they see a book called essential or "must reading," but dammit you can't know too much about a boat at sea if you're going to be on one. Hiscock has spent his entire adult life on them (three boats of his own named Wanderer), sailed all seas, and kept his eyes, mind, and friendship open the whole while. His books are technically complete, redolent with examples, and filled with the blood of shared experiences — at least half his wisdom comes from the next boat over. Which is another thing: there is a kind of fifth world out there sailing, a populous, mobile society making the world its neighborhood and with the selfconsciousness and gossip (from the German for God's family) to cover it all.* —George Putz

Voyaging Under Sail
Eric C. Hiscock
1970; 315 pp.
$19.95 postpaid
Cruising Under Sail
Eric C. Hiscock
1950, 1965; 468 pp.
$25 postpaid
both from:
Oxford University Press
16-00 Pollitt Drive
Fair Lawn, NJ 07410
or Whole Earth Household Store

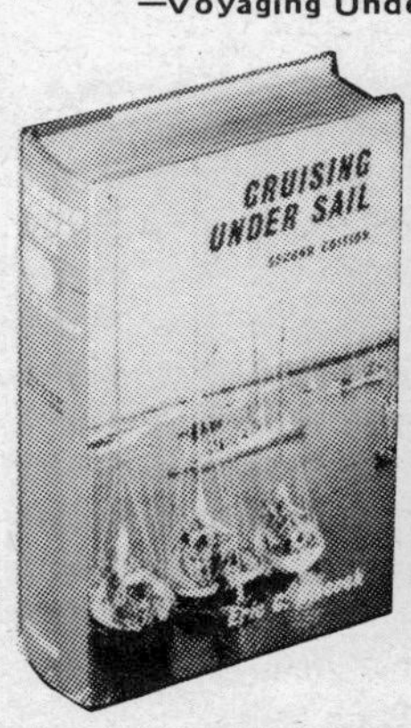

Ocean Passages for the World

The all-time official blood-boiler, this text and set of charts is what you consult when you're deciding where in the world to go — prevailing winds, trade winds, currents, old commercial sail routes, new power shipping routes. If you never sail an inch, these charts will outclass most anything else for your walls. And once your planned passage approaches a thousand miles, you've got to have them. —SB
[Suggested by Mary Crowley]

Ocean Passages for the World
British Royal Navy Commander
H.L. Jenkins et al.
1895, 1973; 258 pp.
plus charts and 1977 supplement

$39.60 postpaid from:
Navigation Equipment Company
228 West Chicago Ave.
Chicago, IL 60610

•

9.07.04. From the equator southward. Having crossed the equator as recommended, stand across the Southeast Trade Wind on the port tack, even should the vessel fall off to about 260°, for the wind will draw more to the E as the vessel advances, and finally to due E at the S limit of the Trade. When in the vicinity of Penedos de Sao Pedro e Sao Paolo, frequent astronomical observations should be made, the current should be watched and allowed for, and a good lookout should be kept, as these rocks are steep-to, and can only be seen on a clear day from a distance of about 8 miles. The same precautions are necessary, if passing westward of Ilha de Fernando de Noronha, when approaching the dangerous Atol das Rocas.

CHART OF THE WORLD
SHOWING
TRACKS FOLLOWED BY SAILING AND AUXILIARY POWERED VESSELS

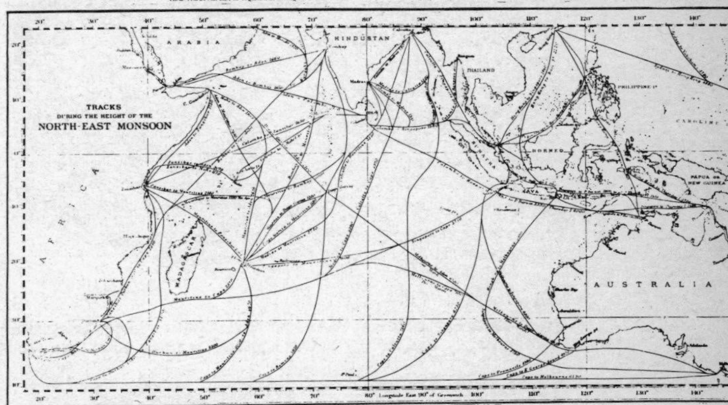

Sea Survival

There are many books and manuals on safety at sea and sea survival in the event of an accident. Almost all books on general sailing or boat handling have a chapter on the subject. Certainly these books and chapters have their value, but compared to Robertson they all pale, because Robertson has been there. He spent days on end in a liferaft after a catastrophe at sea. When he sat down to write this book, he didn't mess around! Every aspect of physical, mental, and emotional survival is here in detail and supported by example and often anecdote. If you take any boat onto any ocean, take this book with you. Inside the back cover are drift and weather charts, shipping lane charts, maps of occupied shorelines, and other arduously friendly dope. —George Putz

Sea Survival
(A Manual)
Dougal Robertson
1975; 148 pp.
$9.95 postpaid from:
Paul Elek, Inc.
Merrimack Book Service
99 Main Street
Salem, NH 03079
or Whole Earth Household Store

•

Foul water which is not poisonous but may cause vomiting can be absorbed rectally by means of a water retention enema. In rain storms, when all containers have been filled, additional water may also be taken in this way not only in order speedily to relieve dehydration but also as an additional method of conserving surplus water, for when the stomach shrinks in survival conditions, it is unable to hold much water. Up to a pint of water may be taken and absorbed through the rectal membrane, but it must be remembered that salt water taken in this way is equally as dangerous as if taken by mouth.

scale:– 0 30ft

Waves
AB: Swell (caused by distant winds)
One every 9 seconds
Height 20 feet
Length 300 feet

CD: Seas (caused by local winds)
One every 3-4 seconds
Height 5-10 feet
Length 50 feet

Swell in this case travels about three times faster than Seas

THE RISING SUN
NEIGHBORHOOD NEWSLETTER

The Stonehenge rocks have worn in them by rain over the years drainage channels in the shape of giant hands and David, who grew up near Stonehenge, thinks that the people who built Stonehenge planned the hands from the beginning.

Alaska Blues

Carlyle said: "The tragedy of life is not what men suffer, it's what they miss." Occasionally a journal of a stranger's intensely lived work season is so immediate that the reader is left with an aching, a longing to pack up everything and be off after the writer. **Alaska Blues** *is this immense a treat. But more. Packed with excellent photograph after excellent photograph, it chronicles an April to November on the inland waterway from Seattle to Skagway. Throughout 228 carefully laid out pages, Joe Upton's journal is beautifully written, an extraordinary work of love; a marvelous mating of time, place, mood and lore.*

Specifically his subject is salmon trolling, with lesser attention paid to gill netting, long lining and market doings. As the central issue is conservation, his conclusions are somewhat grim. But Upton most entertainingly weaves a history of the industry and some of its more colorful practitioners into an account of a working tour along a thousand miles of our last wilderness.

—*David Shetzline*

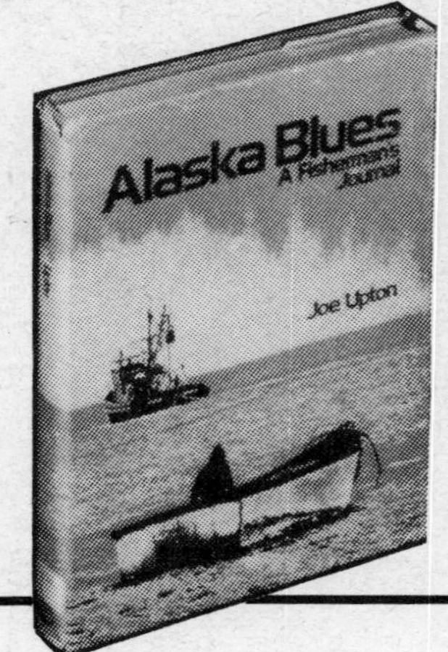

Alaska Blues
Joe Upton
1977; 236 pp.
$15.45 postpaid from:
Alaska Northwest Publishing Company
P.O. Box 4EEE
Anchorage, AK 99509
or Whole Earth Household Store

•

The glass was falling rapidly despite a fair weather report, and there were low fast-moving clouds to the southeast at dawn. Sure enough, squalls started up from the south at 10, raising a nasty short chop. Gave it up without even thinking twice, and ran to the very head of Safety Cove and dropped the anchor. Safety Cove — I guess that's a good name for the first harbor on the north side of Queen Charlotte Sound. And many's the boat that's been glad to make it, with a big souther behind and decks washed clear after a nasty crossing. The first harbor on the south side is nicknamed God's Pocket, so you can guess what the little body of water that lies between is like. A friend told me that one fall he was stuck here for a week, trying to get across; he was beaten back five times. Said he would have starved if a Canadian tug hadn't given him some grub.

The Boat Who Wouldn't Float

Farley Mowat, of **Never Cry Wolf** *(p. 63), etc., once bought a sieve-bottom pocket schooner in Newfoundland and proceeded to get in more hair-raising scrapes — with randomly reversing engines, grim fogs, lethal coasts, nefarious humans, fishplant sewage outfalls, and worse — than any 50 other earnest-but-careless cruising men. The written account stands head and shoulders below any other cruising yarn. I think it's the funniest book I ever read. If one cruises to find interesting trouble, this saga is an inspiration.*

—*SB*

The Boat Who Wouldn't Float
Farley Mowat
1970; 264 pp.
$8.95 postpaid from:
Little, Brown and Company, Inc.
200 West Street
Waltham, MA 01254
or Whole Earth Household Store

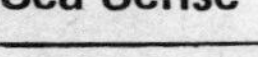

•

And then the main pump jammed.

That pump was a fool of a thing that had no right to be aboard a boat. Its innards were a complicated mass of springs and valves that could not possibly digest the bits of flotsam, jetsam, and codfish floating in the vessel's bilge. But, fool of a thing or not, it was our only hope.

It was dark by this time so Jack held a flashlight while I unbolted the pump's face plate. The thing contained ten small coil springs and all of them leapt for freedom the instant the plate came off. They ricocheted off the cabin sides like a swarm of manic bees and fell, to sink below the surface of the water in the bilges.

•

The boat was lying in a tiny slip dominated by the fish plant. All the effluence, both human and animal, from this plant, which employed one hundred and forty-seven men, women and children, and which processed about 500,000 pounds of fish a day, was voided into our slip through a ten-inch sewage pipe that vomited at us at irregular intervals. At low tide, the pallid guts of defunct codfish formed a slippery pattern all about the boat and festooned all her lines. The air, already pretty noxious, was further poisoned with gases from the meal plant. Such fish offal as was not poured into the water was reduced to stinking yellow powder that sifted down from heaven upon our bared heads like the debris from a crematorium. So awful was the stink that four wooden barrels standing at the end of the stage, wherein Obie was wont to throw the livers of newly caught codfish, so they could rot and reduce to oil under the heat of the sun, gave off a rather pleasant fragrance by comparison. Our clothing, bodies, hair, became slimy with the effluvium of long-dead cod and, of course, every inch of the vessel was thickly coated with . . .

The Compleat Cruiser

This charming classic (1956) is the only book around on enjoying the minutiae of cruising of the sort that most people really do — gadding about one's local bays and islands, ideally with a couple of boats separating for adventures and rejoining at anchorages, indulging in anything-goes races, just messing around. It can be a high art, proves this aristocratic tale.

—*SB*

The Compleat Cruiser
(The Art, Practice and Enjoyment of Boating)
L. Francis Herreshoff
1956, 1980; 372 pp.
$9.95 postpaid from:
International Marine Publishing Company
21 Elm Street
Camden, ME 04843
or Whole Earth Household Store

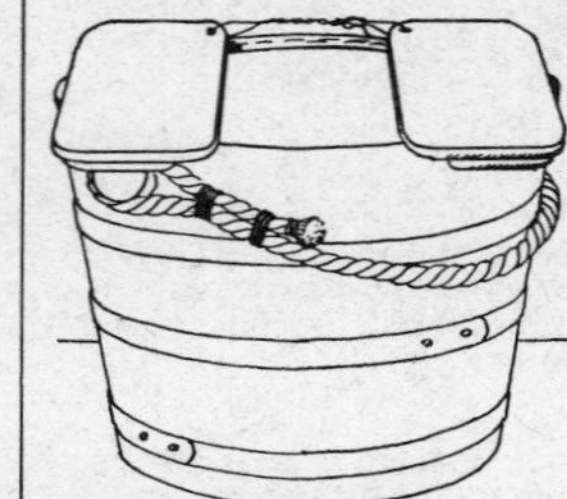

The cedar bucket toilet with seat in place.

•

If Horace Kephart, in his fine book **Camping and Woodcraft**, stresses simplicity on every page, I would just as strongly suggest simplicity in cruising, for I feel that the average small cruiser of 50 or 60 years ago is capable of giving more pleasure for the cost than the usual boat of today. In my youth, the small sailboat or cruiser had no engine, toilet, or electrical devices so that (short of a collision or severe stranding) repairs through the summer season were almost unheard of, while we could cruise in most any direction without thought of expense or fuel consumption.

•

After they had moved out into the cockpit again the sun was drying up the dew so that Weldon hurried as much as he could, wiping off the brightwork, while Jim, who was now fully awake, asked him why he liked to chamois the morning dew so much. He explained: "The dew has been settling on the brightwork all night and has softened up the films of dirt, salt and gum that are on the surface of the varnish." Weldon then chamoised a place in the shade where the dew still remained and it came out as smooth as a piece of amber.

Sea Sense

A very good collection of tidbit type information on boats, designs, surveying, construction, safety equipment, emergency maneuvers (capsizing, running aground, fire, etc.), weather, storm seamanship and heavy weather rigs that it would take the average sailor years of sailing on many different boats in a variety of situations to accumulate. The emphasis is on knowing what to look for or prethinking a potential situation to avoid trouble.

—*Al Perrin*

Sea Sense
(Safety Afloat in Terms of Sail, Power, and Multihull Boat Design, Construction Rig, Equipment, Coping with Emergencies, and Boat Management in Heavy Weather)
Richard Henderson
1972, 1979; 352 pp.
2nd Edition
$17.50 postpaid from:
International Marine Publishing Company
21 Elm Street
Camden, ME 04843
or Whole Earth Household Store

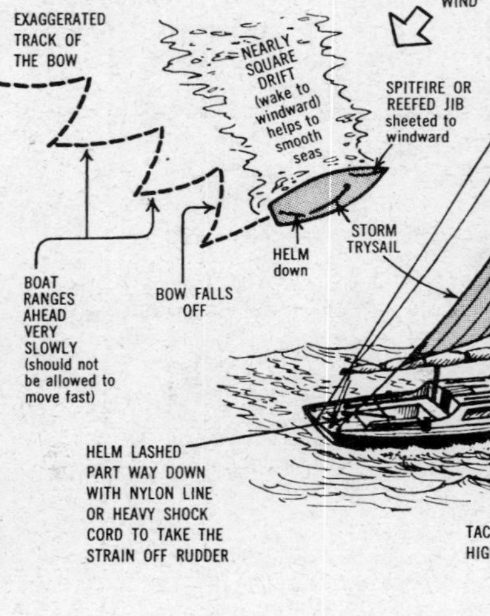
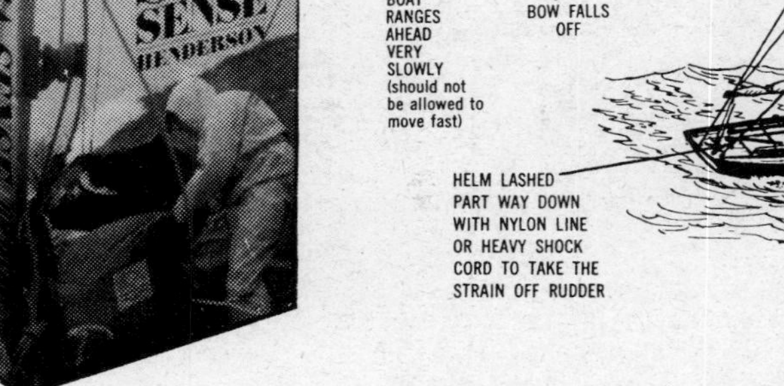

The importance of a self-draining cockpit is dramatized by this heavy-weather photograph. In addition, the lack of a lifeline in such a situation could easily result in the loss of the helmsman.

This sequence of pictures dramatically illustrates why the words "lee shore" fill the hearts of many coastal sailors with dread. The boat shown was reduced to kindling wood within an hour after grounding on the coast of Normandy.

Navigation, Step by Step

There are scores of navigation books in print today. As far as I can see, they can be divided into two neat categories — those that teach both theory and practice, and those that try to simplify things by teaching practice alone. Being a person who believes that understanding the why is as important as understanding the how, I don't think much of the simplified books. What I do like are books that teach me to think my way through a problem. Two that do that are **Coastal Navigation Step by Step** *and* **Celestial Navigation Step by Step** *(the former covers inshore navigation; the latter covers the offshore variety). Both are filled with examples and problems, with solutions, and are written with style, which is unusual for this type of book.* —Peter Spectre

•

The most fundamental idea a navigator must understand is the relationship of time to longitude. Longitude and time have been the Waterloo of many would-be navigators. This need not be if you will just consider hours, minutes, and seconds of time as another system of measuring circles and sectors of circles that can be substituted for degrees, minutes and seconds of arc.
—**Celestial Navigation**

Using the chip log ordinarily requires at least two people. On the old square riggers, casting the log was a ceremony almost as sacred as the noon sight. The master and the mate went to the stern of the ship along with another hand to hold the spool. The first officer held the sand glass. When all was in readiness, the master gave the order to "cast," and the chip was cast over the stern. The log line ran out, pulled by the braking action of the bridled chip, and as the first mark, the piece of red rag, was coming off the spool, the warning "stand by" was given. At the instant the piece of red rag passed over the taffrail, the order "turn" was called and the sand glass was turned. At the exact instant all the sand ran out of the top of the glass the mate sang out "mark." The spool was stopped, and the number of knots at the last piece of fish-line marker was counted. This was the speed of the ship in "knots" or nautical miles per hour. The log line was further marked by pieces of white rag spaced to divide the distance between each piece of fish line marker into five even segments. Thus speed could be measured to the nearest two-tenths of a knot. If the ship happened to be going faster than the log could measure, and the "knots" all ran off before the 28 seconds were up, the log was cast again, and a 14-second glass was used. Twice the number of knots run off in 14 seconds gave the speed of the ship. Today we use a stopwatch instead of a sand glass, and the spool can be mounted on the rail so only one man is necessary to cast the log. After the knots are counted, the chip is reeled in. To break the drag of the bridled chip, before reeling in, give the log line a hard yank. This will pull the peg from the socket and upset the bridle so the chip will come in edgeways.
—**Coastal Navigation**

Figure 9-4. The complete chip log.

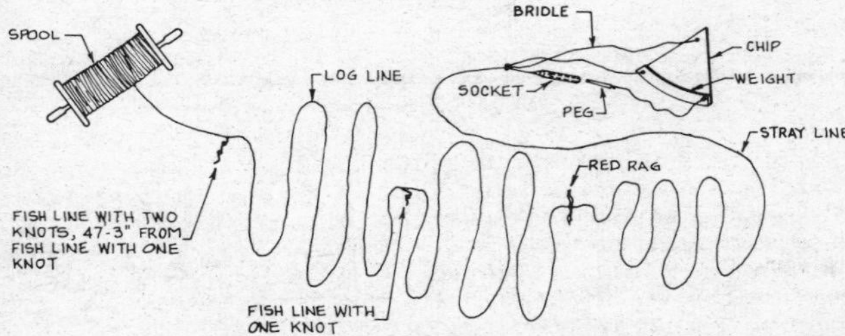

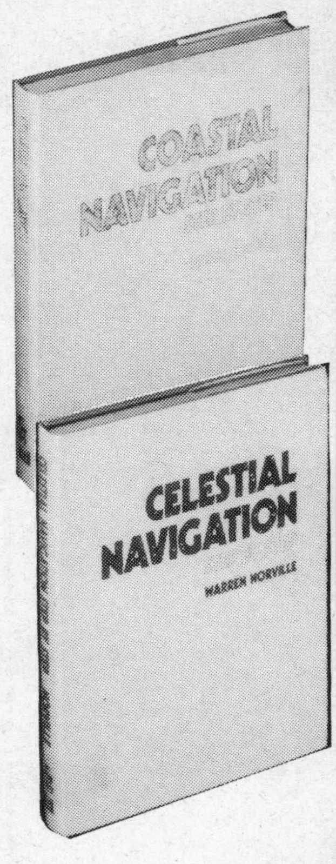

Coastal Navigation Step by Step
Warren Norville
1975; 203 pp.
$20 postpaid

Celestial Navigation Step by Step
Warren Norville
1973; 157 pp.
$17.50 postpaid
both from:
International Marine Publishing Company
21 Elm Street
Camden, ME 04843
or Whole Earth Household Store

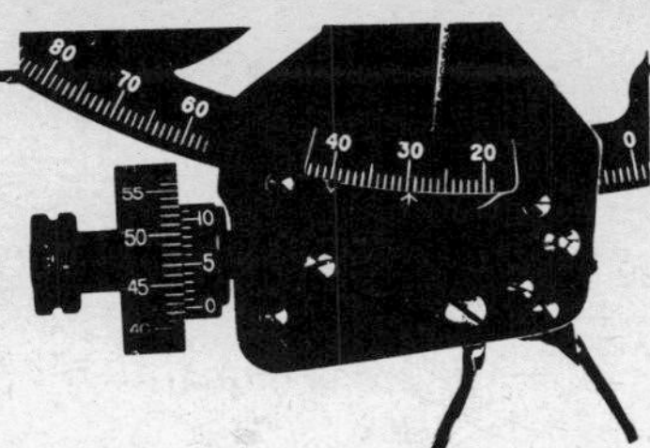

Micrometer drum sextant set at 29°42'5".

American Practical Navigator

There's something eminently satisfying about learning and doing navigation with these volumes which live in unbroken lineage from their 1799 origins. They are THE word, appealingly accessible, and they are shockingly inexpensive (especially considering that various choice portions of the public-domain tomes are reprinted by private publishers at standard high prices). Includes very recent navigational stuff such as satellites and pocket calculators. —SB

American Practical Navigator, Vol. I
(An Epitome of Navigation)
Nathaniel Bowditch and U.S. Defense Mapping Agency Hydrographic Center
1799, 1977; 1386 pp.
$10 postpaid

Volume II
1799, 1975; 716 pp.
$5.80 postpaid
both from:
George Butler Company
633 Battery Street
San Francisco, CA 94111

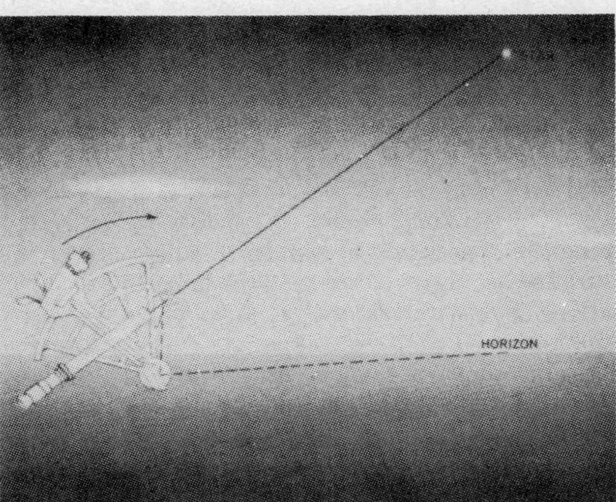

Method of bringing horizon "up" to body.

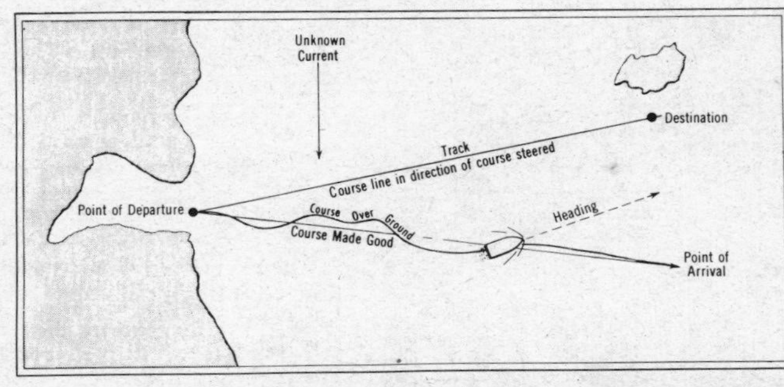

Course line, track, course over ground, course made good, and heading.

The Ship's Medicine Chest and Medical Aid at Sea

The official tome for vessels that have no doctor on board, so you get everything from how to baptize a stillborn baby, to treating rum fits, to diagnosing syphilis (color pix), to minor surgery. An amazing book. A shorter form of this same kind of information is in **Advanced First Aid for All Outdoors**, *p. 415.* —SB

The Ship's Medicine Chest and Medical Aid at Sea
George T. Furlong, Editor
1881, 1978; 474 pp.
No. 017-029-00026-6
$10.25 postpaid from:
Superintendent of Documents
U.S. Govt. Printing Office
Washington, D.C. 20402
or Whole Earth Household Store

•

For hangover symptoms of jitters, tremulousness, coated tongue, thirst, nausea, and severe headache, the patient should be allowed to remain as quiet as circumstances on the ship will allow. A single dose of an antacid may help the nausea. One or two cups of salted tomato juice and a glass of fruit juice, sipped slowly, also may help. Acetaminophen 600 mg may be given every four hours by mouth for headache, if it can be retained without vomiting.

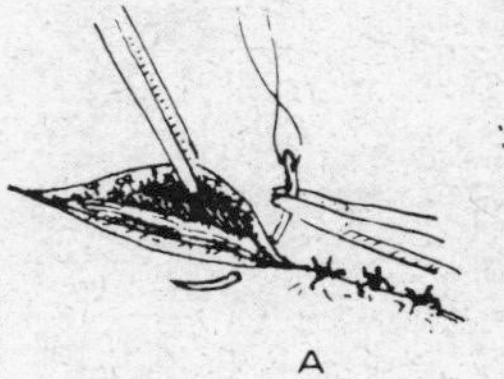

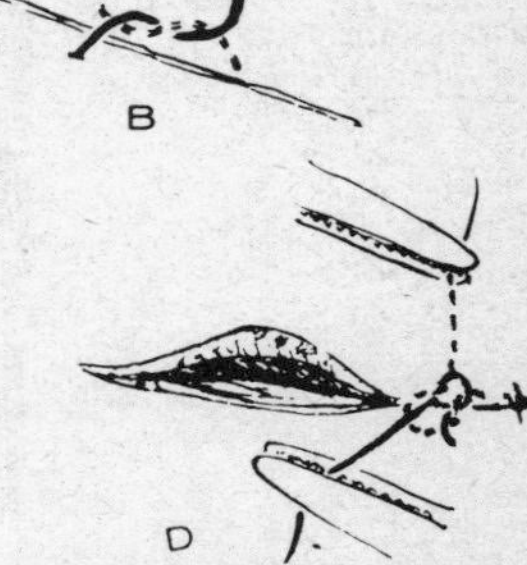

Technique of suturing a wound. A, Method of passing interrupted sutures; B, Tying a nonslip, square knot; C, Tying a granny knot which will slip; D, Suturing a wound with interrupted, square-knot-sutures.

Boatman's Guide to Light Salvage

An overdue book. It used to be if you sank it or lost it, an expensive specialist had to float or find it and tow it home. Now you can. An admirably straightforward little book. —SB

Boatmen's Guide to Light Salvage
George H. Reid
1979; 71 pp.
$5 postpaid from:
Cornell Maritime Press
P.O. Box 456
Centerville, MD 21617
or Whole Earth Household Store

A sailboat "heaved down" and towed to deeper water.

Sager Weathercaster

This clever, proven kit enables you to forecast local weather up to 24 hours in advance. All you need is a barometer and the kit; no radio, TV, or newspaper. The kit consists of an explaining booklet (which includes photographs of cloud types) and a sort of circular slide-rule that you set according to observed conditions and read out the prediction. Looks to me like a great way to learn about weather patterns too. It'll only work for latitudes north of 25° N. (Also see **Weather for Mariners** *on p. 20.)* —J. Baldwin

The Sager Weathercaster
Raymond M. Sager
1942; 26 pp. plus device
$10.45 postpaid from:
Weather Enterprises
P.O. Box 473
Pleasantville, NY 10570

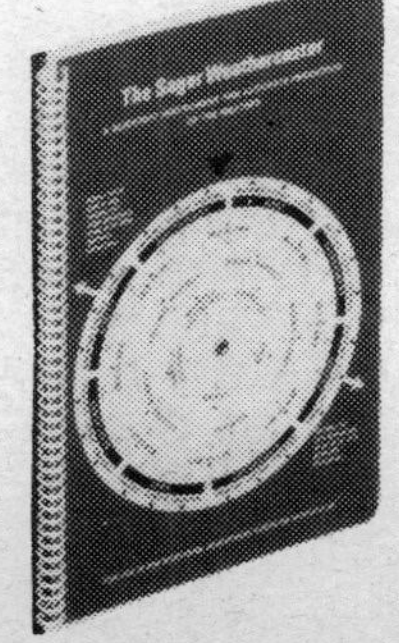

THE RISING SUN
NEIGHBORHOOD NEWSLETTER

People who live near Stonehenge are proud of the fact that they've never been there for the solstice sunrise.

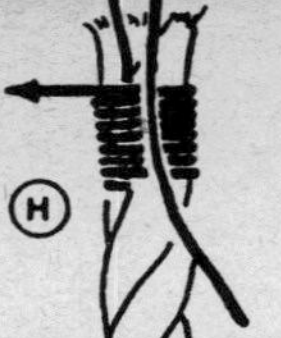

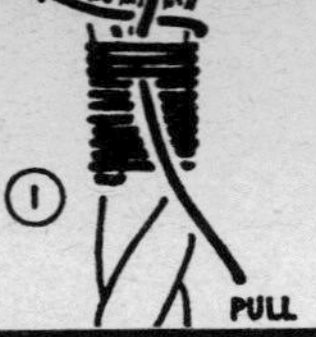

Knots and Lines

The reason this is far the best introductory nautical knot book is that it teaches your hands (rather than just your eyes) how to make knots, and everything in the book is in reference to use on a boat. Photographs of the tier's hands from the tier's point of view do the trick. Who would have thought the invaluable if complex "constrictor knot" could be made by dropping two twisted loops over the item to be constricted instead of by elaborate weaving? —SB

Knots and Lines
(Illustrated)
Paul Snyder and
Arthur Snyder
1967, 1970; 104 pp.

$7.95 postpaid from:
International Marine
Publishing Company
21 Elm Street
Camden, ME 04843
or Whole Earth
Household Store

1

2
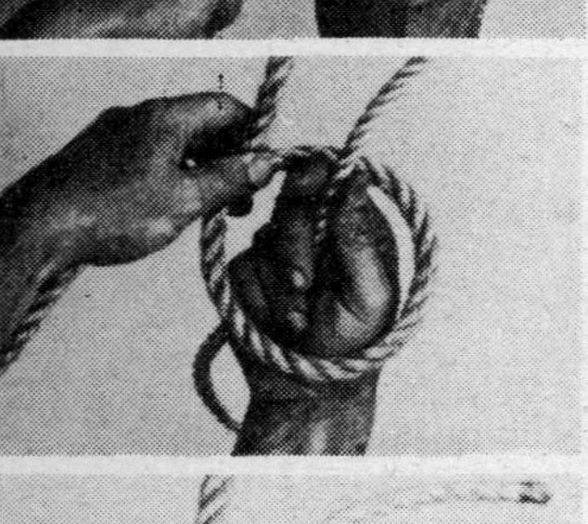
3

4
5
6
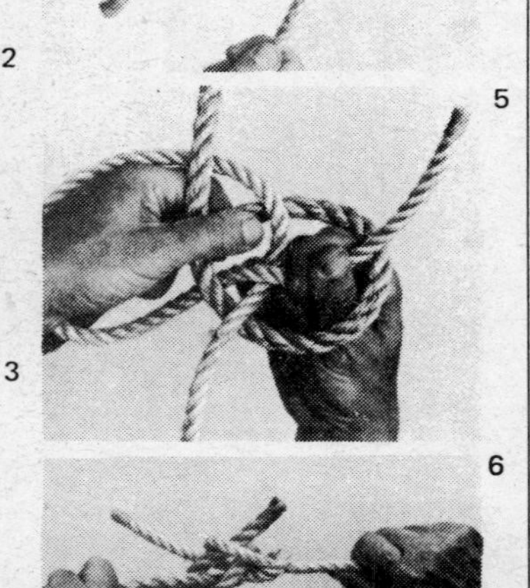

How hands make a "carrick bend." The best knot for connecting two lines. (Forget the square knot — it's worthless.)

Knots and Splices

All the basic knots for all manner of purposes presented simple as pie. Everyone should know these knots. What a clear little book! —SB

Knots and Splices
Percy W. Blandford
1962, 1967; 79 pp.

$1.25 postpaid from:
Arco Publishing Company
219 Park Avenue South
New York, NY 10003
or Whole Earth
Household Store

↓

A very useful variation of the figure eight knot is the *packer's knot*, which the man behind the counter uses to tie up your parcel. It is a slip knot which can be pulled tight and locked. A figure eight knot is made with the end around the standing part. Take care that this finishes with the end standing up, and not the other way. The line is tightened by pulling on the standing part, then a little loop, called a *half hitch*, is made with the standing part over the end projecting from the figure eight knot.

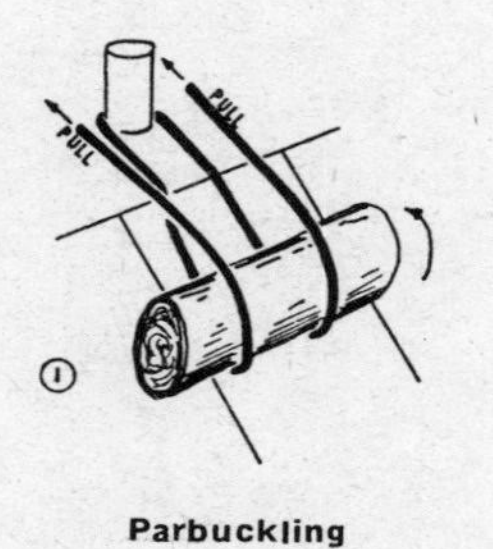

Parbuckling

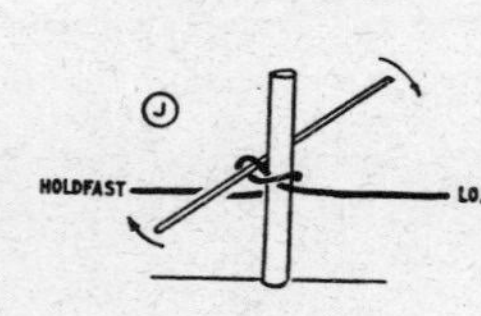

Spanish windlass

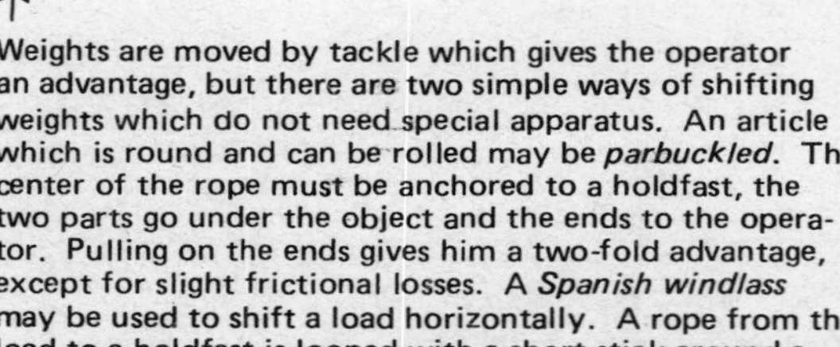

Packer's knot

↑

Weights are moved by tackle which gives the operator an advantage, but there are two simple ways of shifting weights which do not need special apparatus. An article which is round and can be rolled may be *parbuckled*. The center of the rope must be anchored to a holdfast, the two parts go under the object and the ends to the operator. Pulling on the ends gives him a two-fold advantage, except for slight frictional losses. A *Spanish windlass* may be used to shift a load horizontally. A rope from the load to a holdfast is looped with a short stick around a pole being held upright. If the stick is turned around the pole, considerable leverage can be applied.

The Arts of the Sailor

A classy little book of traditional marlinspike seamanship — all the tyings, lashings, sewings, etc. that keep your boat universe shipshape. Nice telling, beautiful illustrating. —SB

The Arts of the Sailor
(A handbook of related skills indispensable to the modern sailor)
Hervey Garrett Smith
1953; 233 pp.

$3.95 postpaid from:
Barnes and Noble Books
Keystone Industrial Park
Scranton, PA 18512
or Whole Earth
Household Store

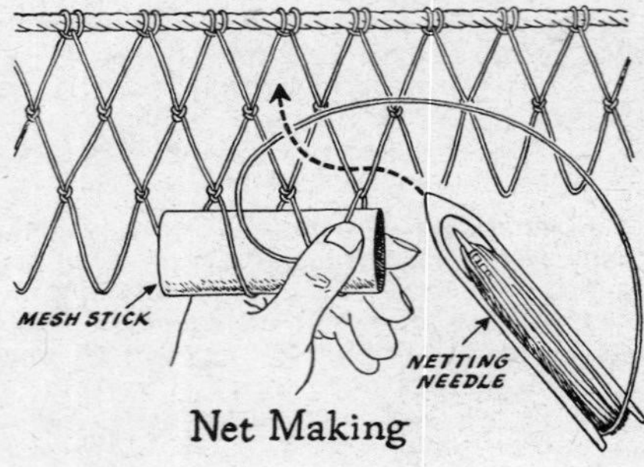

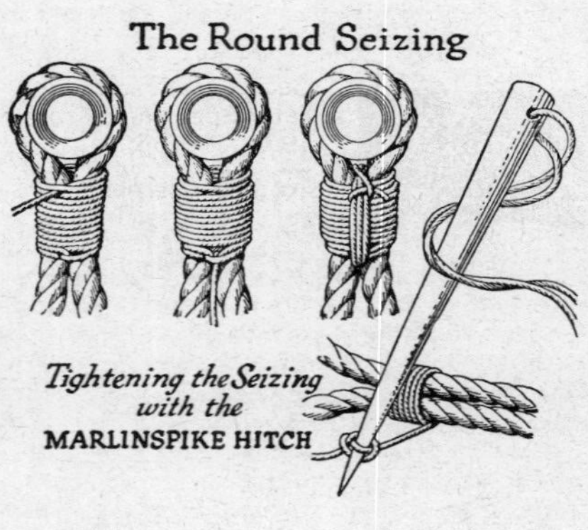

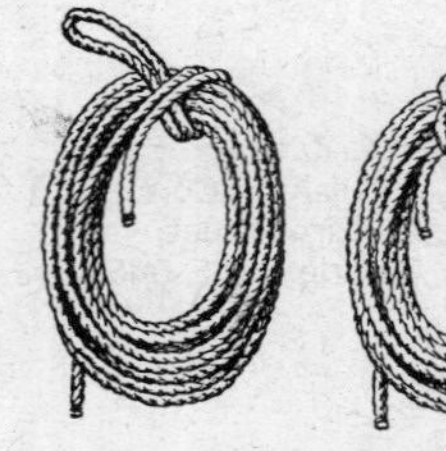

The Ashley Book of Knots

3900 knots and the stories to go with them. Fascinating, deeply useful stuff. Buy a pipe, git out of the sun, and go to it. —SB

The Ashley Book of Knots
Clifford W. Ashley
1944; 260 pp.

$18.95 postpaid from:
Doubleday and Company
501 Franklin Avenue
Garden City, NY 11530
or Whole Earth
Household Store

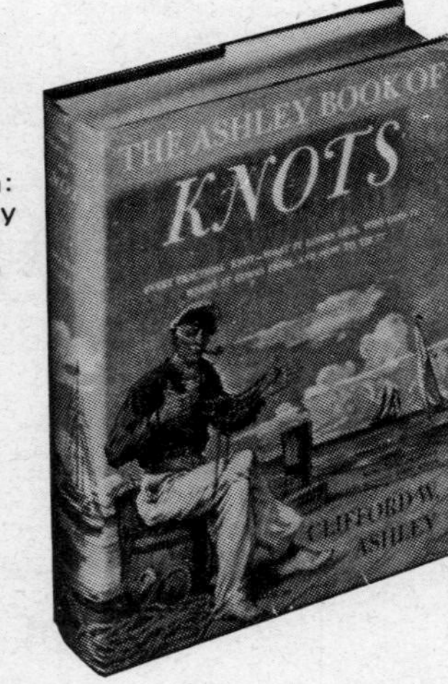

Camel Hitch. The camel is the most ruminative of animals, and he slobbers constantly while he ruminates, particularly on his Picket-Line Hitch, which he believes is provided for the purpose. His knot is always sopping, but it has been very nicely planned; and so, wet or dry, it is never difficult to untie and it does not slip in either direction.

↓

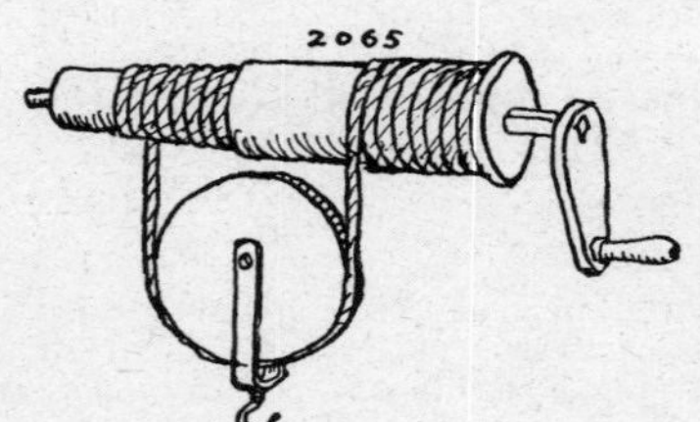

↑

The **Chinese windlass** is the grandfather of the present-day differential chain hoist. One end winds, while the other unwinds, and the right end of the barrel, being larger than the left, winds or unwinds a greater length of rope than the left end, with each revolution of the crank.

→

Latching is an old method of attaching a drabbler to a jib, or a bonnet to a fore and aft sail. Nowadays it is the method employed by circuses in assembling the canvas sections of the tents. A series of eyelets in the upper section of the sail are opposite a series of loops, termed "keys," in the headrope of the bonnet. Starting at one side, a key is rove through the opposite eyelet and hauled to the next eye. The next key is rove through its opposite eye and through the key that was first led. This process is continued until the center is reached. The process is then repeated, beginning at the other edge of the sail. The two center loops, being twice as long as the rest, are reef knotted together. Captain John Smith described them in 1627, calling them "latchets."

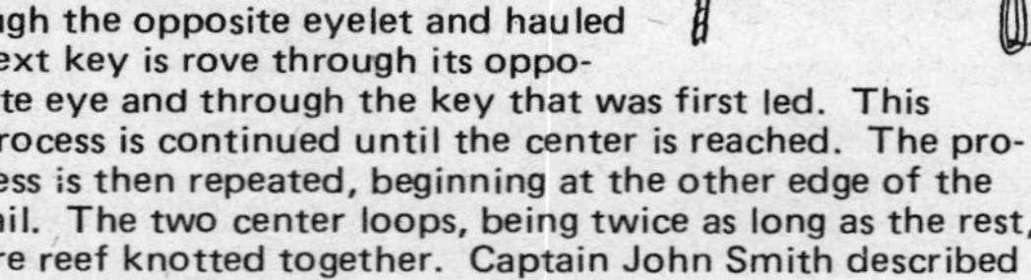

Encyclopedia of Knots and Fancy Rope Work

About the same number of knots as Ashley (3668), less on how to tie them, more on how they're used, more ornamental stuff, more quasi-official. I expect anybody this interested in knots will have both. —SB

Encyclopedia of Knots and Fancy Rope Work
Raoul M. Graumont
and John J. Hensel
1939, 1952; 690 pp.

$17.50 postpaid from:
Cornell Maritime Press
P.O. Box 456
Centreville, MD 21617
or Whole Earth
Household Store

Fig. 131: *The Ladder Rung Knot* is tied with two parts of rope. One part is laid out with a bight at each end. The other part is passed through the top bight on the right as shown. Any number of round turns can be taken, suitable to the length of the rung. The rope is then passed through the lower bight on the left, and the knot is pulled taut.

↓

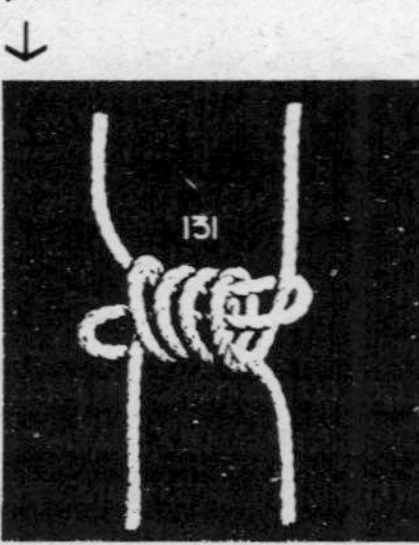

→

Fig. 130: *The Rope Ladder* shown here has its rope rungs made as in Fig. 131. For every other rung, the knot is reversed.

130

The Mariner's Catalog Volumes 2 - 7

Mariner's Catalogs *are most commonly referred to in an indignant howl, e.g., "Where the HELL is my* **Mariner's Catalog?!"** *(Matter of fact I can hear Stewart right now.) About the only way you can keep one is to nail it to the table. Each volume accompanies the items or phenomena with a fine, Maine-flavored personal commentary that's hard to resist. Though it tends to be expensive, yacht equipment is often more efficient and compact than landlubber hardware. Some items can be happily adapted to "living small" uses. We're close to these people. The editors guest-edited an issue of* **CoEvolution Quarterly** *(Fall, 1979); some of their reviews from then appear in this* **Whole Earth.**
—*J. Baldwin*

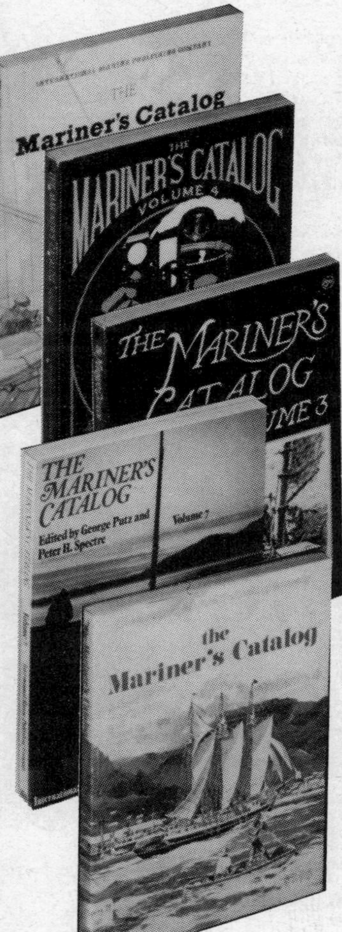

The Mariner's Catalog Volume 2
David R. Getchell, et al., Editors
1974; 191 pp.
$4.95 postpaid

Volume 3
George Putz and Peter Spectre, Editors
1975, 190 pp.
$5.95 postpaid

Volume 4
George Putz and Peter Spectre, Editors
1976; 192 pp.
$6.95 postpaid

Volume 5
George Putz and Peter Spectre, Editors
1977, 192 pp.
$7.95 postpaid

Volume 6
George Putz and Peter Spectre, Editors
1978; 192 pp.
$7.95 postpaid

Volume 7
George Putz and Peter Spectre, Editors
1979; 191 pp.
$8.95 postpaid

all from:
International Marine Publishing Company
21 Elm Street
Camden, ME 04843

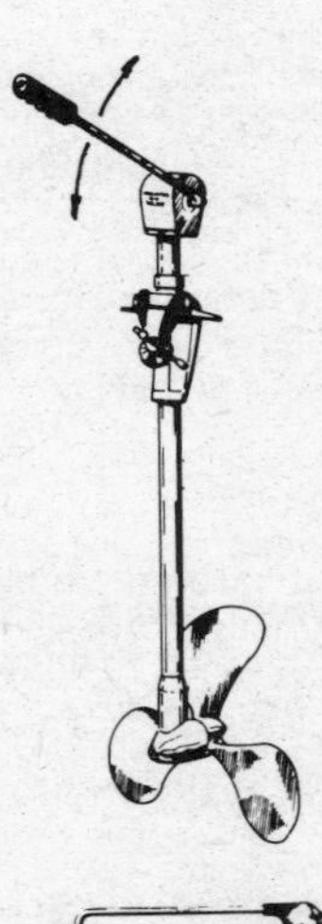

Crank It — Ladies and gentlemen, the hand powered outboard from:

**Finn Machine Products Company
P.O. Box 396
Lithia Springs, GA 30057**

Wholesale from the factory, $59.95; retail is in the $75 range.

Finn Machine's hand-powered outboard. This thing really works.
—Volume 5

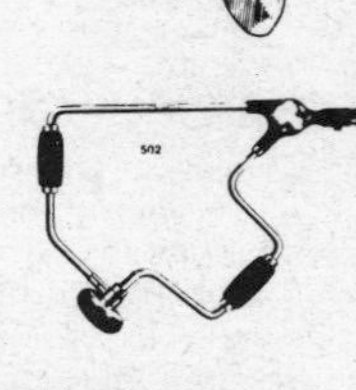

And if ratcheting two feet of bit through oak from a location six inches off the floor or out from the wall is not your cup of kumquat extract, here's a handy item from Miller's Falls:

**Millers Falls Company
57 Wells Street
Greenfield, MA 01301**
—Volume 4

Warmth Plus Beauty — A perfectly beautiful ship's heating stove, burning wood, coal or peat, and made by Lange in Denmark, is distributed in this country by:

**Southampton Stove Company
75 Herrick Road
Southampton, NY 11968**
—Volume 5

You've dreamed of a one-man submarine? Someone the military trusts will make one for you. The K-250 sub is 11' 8" overall, $12,000. Optional are trailer, u/w telephone, bottom floodlight, and mechanical claw. From:

**Kittredge Industries, Inc.
Warren, ME 04864**
—Volume 6

•

Anyway, we were jovially "filling" our canvas, as per instructions, with five coats of marine paint — two primers and three finish coats — when some clerical type in the company mentioned that by so doing we were actually doubling the *weight* of the boat and the *cost* of the boat. "Cripes almighty," somebody said reverently, "we're 'sposed to finish the boat, not the customer!"

And then some bright friend says something like, "Well yer such a dimwit, ya deserve it." He, not knowing that we are only in a dimwit disguise, was promptly cajoled into revealing this awful secret: AIRPLANE BUTYRATE DOPE!

Of course! What idiots we had been! Henceforth, we shall go to our local small-craft airport, locate the supplier of aircraft dope, and (Kapowee) a light, smooth, easy-to-apply, quick-drying, noncracking, tough, controlled-shrinkage surface for kayaks and canoes will be gained.

Colored dopes run about $20 per gallon. Clear dope is less than half that. You can also get thinners, retarders, fungicidals (fungus is always a problem on the canvas undersides in marine craft), and related materials. We received our information from:

Van Dusen Aircraft Supplies
P.O. Box 232
East Boston, MA 02128

Check your local airport. Can you imagine a two-seat biplane trying to get off the ground filled and sheathed with *marine* paint?!
—Volume 4

•

We had been using regular kerosene in our stoves because I object to paying $5.00 a gallon for stove fuel. For the stoves it was fine, for the bulkhead lamp it stinks. It would drive us out of the tiny cabin. This summer we were anchored at Round Island in company with Gordon and Doris Swift aboard their lovely *Madrigal of Exeter*. From Gordon I learned that Thinex, the paint thinner, is a highly refined petroleum product which burns clean and odor-free in kerosene stoves and lamps. Maybe some chemist will tell me some day that the stuff's explosive in a lamp, but Gordon had been using it for a long time and we used it too with great success for the few week-ends that were left of the summer. Thinex doesn't have a picture of a boat on the can, but maybe that's why it doesn't cost $5.00 a gallon.
—Jay Hanna, Rockport, Maine **—Volume 6**

The Ocean Sailing Yacht Volume 1 Volume 2

Don Street has done a **Whole Earth Catalog** *for sea-going sailboats. He focuses mainly on gear and other material matters — rigs, engines, fittings, stoves, refrigeration, electronics, dinghys, anchors — but certain philosophical views come clear. He likes wood. He likes sailboats without engines. Nevertheless he is highly informative on glass, steel, aluminum, and (what's left of) ferro-cement hulls. And his section on engines is the best I've seen. Street has delivered enough yachts, brokered enough marine insurance, written enough letters to manufacturers and sailed his own yawl enough thousands of miles to speak with unusual authority. His access-and-evaluation appendices are invaluable. Street is on my shelf next to all the* **Mariner's Catalogs.**
—*SB*

The Ocean Sailing Yacht Volume 1
Donald M. Street, Jr.
1973; 703 pp.
$25 postpaid

Volume 2
1978; 595 pp.
$27.95 postpaid

both from:
W.W. Norton and Co.
500 Fifth Avenue
New York, NY 10036

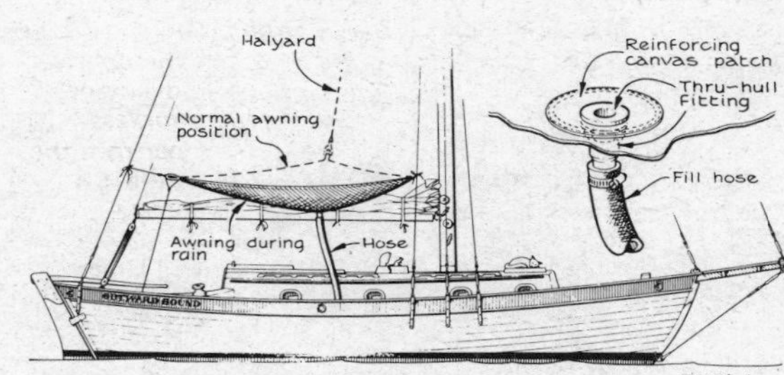

Awning used as rain catcher
—Volume 2

Aquair with air fan in place of log line
—Volume 2

Aquair towed generator
—Volume 2

•

When Oars are too short, the oarsman finds it difficult to get them down into the water, and his strokes develop little power. Throughout the world boatbuilders, old fishermen, old yacht skippers, all mention the same approximate figure for the length of an oar: it should be twice the beam of the boat plus 6 inches.
—Volume 2

The towed generator combined with a wind generator certainly seems to be the answer for the cruising yachtsman who has no engine or who wishes to minimize his engine time. Going to windward the wind generator will work; off the wind on long passages, he can throw the towed generator overboard; and in sum, enough power for normal needs is likely to be available. From the evidence already at hand, it appears that the average boat cruising in the trades will obtain up to 72 ampere-hours per day — more electricity than one can really use unless one is trying to run a very small 12-volt refrigeration system from the unit.

From:

Ampair Products (Hugh Merewether)
Aston House
Blackheath, Guildford
Surrey GU4 8RD, England
—Volume 2

THE RISING SUN
NEIGHBORHOOD NEWSLETTER

It's all very well, sci fi fans, to realize the evil you must fight, are trying to fight, is embodied in your image in the mirror, someone with your very name, your doppelganger walking down the street toward you, your long lost brother sister father mother, but the real life stinger is finding out that the good you must embrace is walking around living in someone who has the other kind of earlobes, feels the other way about anchovies, wakes up with the other amount of energy in the morning, and will probably never read your favorite book.

Defender Industries, Inc.

In a decade's time of collecting marine equipment catalogs, to the point where joists and sills creak, we have found few outfits as good and none better for general marine supplies, at bottom dollar and consistent service, than Defender. —*George Putz*

Defender Industries, Inc.
Catalog

$1 from:
Defender Industries, Inc.
P.O. Box 820
255 Main Street
New Rochelle, NY 10801

•

No. 1030 New Quartzmatic Seasprite II Tide and Time Clock — $57.95

Black wrinkle finish metal case gives it a sharp nautical instrument appearance. Quartz crystal accuracy and weatherproof feature make it a good functional unit on board boats. Red indicators at low and high tides. Jet black 24-hour dial, white markings. Operates on "C" size battery. Diameter 6¼", Depth 3", Dial 4".

FRANCIS BARKER SEXTANT

COMPACT 3"X4" ACCURATE UNIT SET IN ATTRACTIVE LEATHER CASE, AMAZING DESIGN. (C109-6)

NEW DESIGN ROUND POCKET SEXTANT, ONLY 3" IN DIAMETER,, HAS INGENIOUS PLANETARY DRIVE FOR SINGLE KNOB OPERATION. VERY SPECIAL OFFER AT NET OF **$189.95**

(C113-11)

MINI HAND BEARING COMPASS

dampened compass rose allows nearly instant bearings. Tritium gas light provides excellent night readability and an infinity prism eliminates parallax error. A rubber perimeter guard protects the unit from damage during rough usage. A neck lanyard and stowage in a breast pocket makes this new and rugged instrument an essential to the racing and cruising skipper by eliminating the need to carry still another navigation aid into the cockpit. The Mini Compass measures 2 3/4 inches by 1 1/4 inches

LIST PRICE ~~$84.50~~ $56.95

WHITE PLASTIC BRACKET MOUNT $2.95

OPTI/COMPASS AS ABOVE ONLY $58.95 NET.

FOLDING STEPS
FOR TRANSOM OR CRUISERS
CHROMED BRASS
2"X 4" $8.95

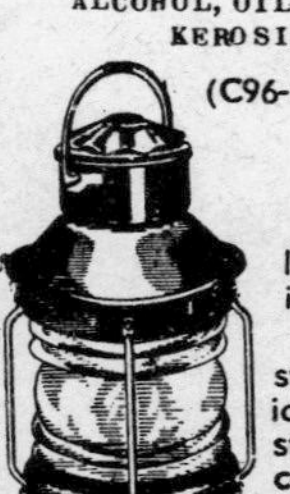

ALCOHOL, OIL KEROSINE

(C96-2)

ANCHOR OR RIDING LIGHT

FOR CLASS 1, 2, 3 BOATS
STORM PROOF

Polished copper finish, clear lens 360°. Height 9½" excluding ring, width base 4⅝".

This light is of all copper construction, has hinged top, it is an ideal light for sailboats and will stand up in any type of weather conditions. Oil burning.

Price .... ~~$76.50~~ $49.95
Spare Globe 12.95

Weatheralert

WX-16

$22.95

Receives National Weather Service broadcasts from as far out as 40 miles.

- Powered by 9V battery (not included) (C126-4)
- Switch-selectable for all 3 weather channels
- LED power indicator, slide volume control

TA-20
3 channel

$38.50

- Continuous beeper alarm and visual warning system

Both continue until reset

- AC-powered *(adapter incl.)*
- Automatic battery back-up feature
- Switch-selectable for all 3 weather channels (C126-5)
- "On" indicator light

Windicator (C153-8)

Find wind direction instantly from almost any position on the boat for sailing efficiency and performance!

Exclusive features of Windicator include:
* Hull Shape Replica at the Vane Location
* Extreme Sensitivity in Light Air of 0.2 Knots
* Calibrated Lockable Tacking Arms
* Lightweight, rugged construction
* Reflective Surface for Night Sailing
* Custom storage case
* Easy assembly and mounting.

LIST ~~$41.50~~ NET $29.95

WINDICATOR 11
FOR RACING OR MEDIUM SIZE BOATS, $24.95
$16.95

(C153-9)

WINDICATOR 111
FOR SMALL BOATS $17.95
$12.95

Boat Technology International

British scientific and use testing of nautical gear — could be the ultimate word on which is the best equipment. We'll see. The magazine incorporates the formerly excellent **Geartest***, which carried no advertising (and died financially). Whether real product truth-telling and product advertising can live together remains to be proven. A worthy and fascinating attempt.* —*SB*

Boat Technology International
(Incorporating **Geartest**)
Brian Grant, Editor

$45/year (6 issues)
from:
Hudson Publications, Ltd.
300 Ashley Road
Parkstone, Poole, Dorset
England BH14 9EF

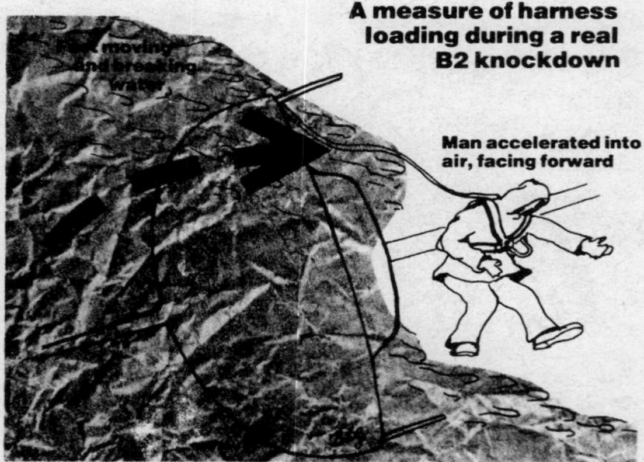

Keel holds in deeper, slower moving water

The Telltale Compass

Jorgensen's four-page newsletter tells all with no holds barred — the inside poop on the boating industry. Who's screwing up, who's doing a good job. Definitely worthwhile information if you can afford the $25 tab. —*Al Perrin*

The Telltale Compass
Victor Jorgensen, Editor

$25/year (12 issues)
from:
The Telltale Compass
18418 South Old River Dr.
Lake Oswego, OR 97034

•

Aluminum repairs have always been best left to experts and exotic equipment. When I heard about a welding technique which can be used on aluminum propellers, engine and refrigeration parts, spars, and boats, and was told it was done with a propane torch, I was interested but skeptical.

After buying a bundle of Hille's welding rod for $12 (72 inches) I tried it on everything from heavy 5052 stock to papery 2024, which can't be joined with arc welding. Because these welds were being done for test purposes, I quenched them before going at them for bending and yanking. Yet in each case, the bond was stronger than the parent metal, even though Hille's instructions say the weld will be even stronger if allowed to cool at room temperature.

For most sailors, the biggest advantage of Lumiweld is its portability. It is carried by float plane pilots in the North country for in-the-field repairs to aluminum floats and I can think of a dozen times I could have used it on remote islands when cruising the Bahamas. In addition to the welding rod, which is available in batches of 72, 360 and 720 inches, all you need is the propane torch and a stainless steel brush.

According to Hille (Alumismiths, Inc., P.O. Box 517, DeLand, FL 32720; Main Office, 215 Commonwealth Avenue, Massapequa, NY 11758), the tensile strength of Lumiweld is as high as 40,000 PSI, shear strength 18-33,000 PSI depending on joint design, and hardness is 55-60 Rockwell B. The repair can be filed, ground, machined, painted, tapped, plated, or painted.

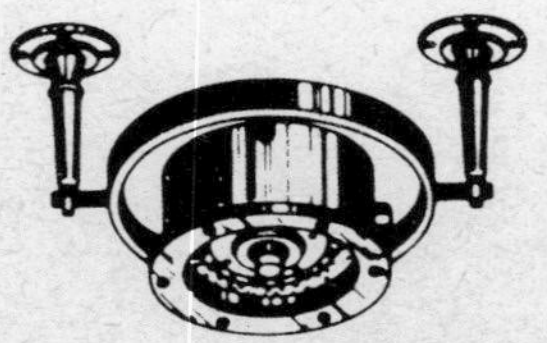

Stephen Lirakis of the USA being towed at 8 knots in his own harness

•

Harness Security

The severe testing to which harnesses were subjected during the 1979 Fastnet Race demonstrated a number of weaknesses. This has naturally caused concern amongst the sailing fraternity as to whether the problems are general or particular; whether forces encountered exceeded those which even the formal testing procedures would have anticipated, or whether they could be attributed to poor design, use and maintenance which fell well below formal standards.

Davis Instruments

Begin small, stay simple, offer lots for little. Years ago Davis listened to **The Graduate***'s homely advice and went into plastics, developing and manufacturing nautical gear and accouterments of plain, solid design and low cost, six dozen or so; range and direction finders, speedometers, sextants, and other navigational aids, wind indicators, spar and rig fittings — all kinds of stuff. Something for the boat on its birthday.* —*George Putz*

Davis Instruments
Information

free from:
Davis Instruments Corp.
642 - 143rd Avenue
San Leandro, CA 94578

•

Standard Mark 3 Marine Sextant. Find your position accurately anywhere on the earth with the Davis Marine Sextant! Full 7" (178mm) arc — instantly adjustable — 4 sun shades — corrosion proof. #011 $22.95.

•

Mark 25 Deluxe Master Sextant *with Full-Field Beam with Full-Field Beam Converger!*

Davis Instruments proudly presents MARK 25 Deluxe Master Sextant incorporating the most significant improvement in sextants in a century — a Full-Field Dielectric Beam Converger replacing the conventional half-silvered horizon mirror.

- A full sighting field makes it easy to find and hold the sun and stars and to observe the horizon.
- Beam Converger is unaffected by salt spray; front surface has protective quartz hardcoat.
- Beam Converger color selection permits better sightings under certain haze conditions.
- MARK 25 Deluxe Master Sextant is molded in a new increased-strength reinforced plastic. Incorporates all features of the Standard Mark 20; LED illumination, telescope, case, etc.

•

Navigation Kit — $56.95

The Navigation Kit provides in one economical package each of the instruments most often used by the navigator. Also included is the booklet "How to Find Your Position With a Sextant" edited by Robert E. Kleid, P.E., showing the beginner simplified techniques which enable him to navigate anywhere in the world. The ideal gift, the Kit is attractively packaged and contains: Sextant, Artificial Horizon, Parallel Rules, Time-Speed-Distance Computer, Three-Arm Protractor, Dividers and Booklet.

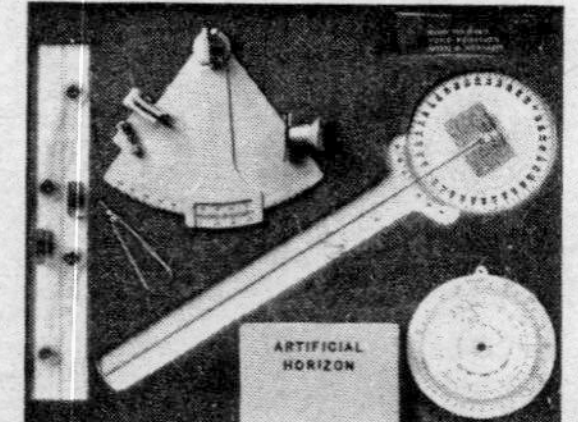

Aladdin kerosene lamps

Coleman lamps are terrible — they hiss and clank and blind you, just like civilization.

Aladdin is the answer if you need good light and 117ac isn't around. It is bright, silent, and requires no pumping. (It does require some babying to keep the mantle from smoking up; it's like not burning toast.) They do use a lot of kerosene, but they'll light a whole cabin, not just the couple feet around them of ordinary kerosene lamps.

You can get them from many hardware stores, or from headquarters in Nashville, or — at the lowest prices we've seen — from Phantasmagoria, reviewed on p. 359. —SB

Aladdin kerosene lamps
Catalog and price list
free from:
ALH, Inc.
Aladdin Industries
P.O. Box 100255
Nashville, TN 37210
or check your local hardware store.

← **Aluminum cabin hanging lamp — $66.95**

Aluminum recreational table lamp — $59.95

NAEBM Westlawn School of Yacht Design

Believe it or not, this school is strictly by correspondence! It's sponsored by The National Association of Engine and Boat Manufacturers, and it has a very good reputation. I count an education in this field as likely to be one of the better ones available; it's a kind of knowledge that gets you into interesting places. A number of famous designers are graduates. It is accredited, and GI Bill is acceptable. They've been at it for 44 years. The course is $595.
—J. Baldwin

NAEBM Westlawn School of Yacht Design
Information
free from:
NAEBM Westlawn School of Yacht Design
733 Summer Street
Stamford, CT 06904

Fiberglass Repairs

A comprehensive look at the tricks of the trade. Recycle that battered boat! The author assumes you know nothing about it. You will soon though. Competent, simple, good photos. —J. Baldwin

Fiberglass Repairs
Paul J. Petrick
1976; 74 pp.
$6 postpaid from:
Cornell Maritime Press
P.O. Box 456
Centreville, MD 21617
or Whole Earth Household Store

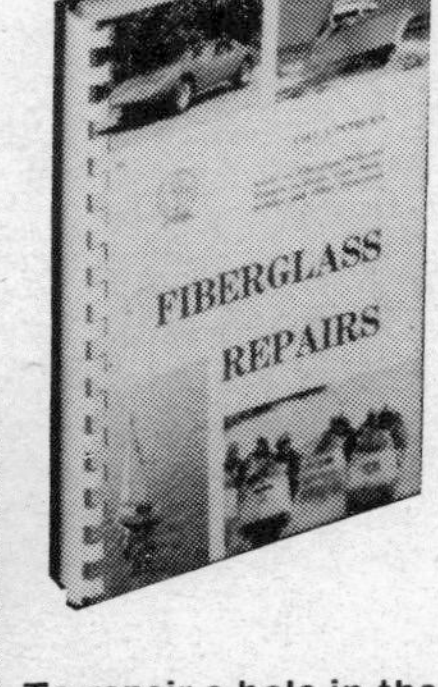

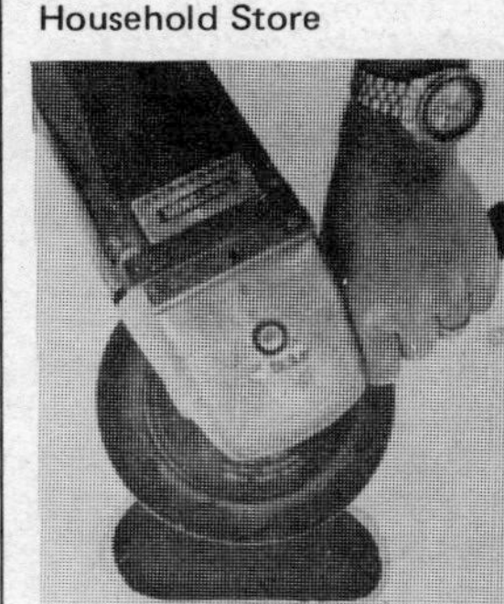

To repair a hole in the hull where the inside of the hull is inaccessible, cut out the damaged area with a saber saw as described in the previous sequence. Featheredge the hole to a "knife edge" from the outside, using a disc sander.

How to Fiberglass Boats

Sheathing plywood with fiberglass is a favorite amateur-builder pastime, as is sheathing worn out broken wooden boats of all types. You will get arguments pro and con about fiberglass used in these ways, but there is no arguing with some of the successful applications (nor is there any arguing over some of the gruesome failures). **How to Fiberglass Boats** *goes into matters like these, as well as how to build laid-up fiberglass craft and how to use Arabol for boat decks.* —Peter Spectre

How to Fiberglass Boats
Ken Hankinson
1974; 120 pp.
$6.95 postpaid from:
Glen-L Marine Designs
9152 Rosecrans
Bellflower, CA 90706

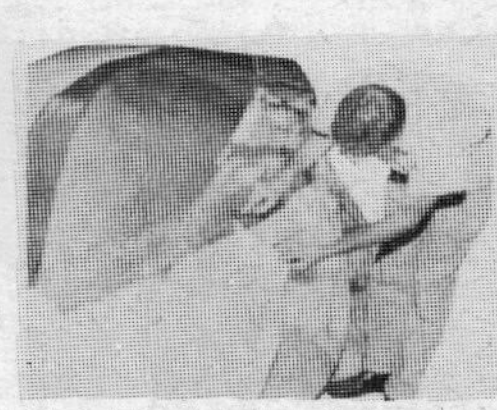

Because the boat is planked with plywood, only one layer of cloth is required. The "dry" method is being used together with polyester resin, although the process would be much the same if epoxy resin was used. The fiberglass cloth is laid onto the bare wood surface which must be clean and dry. Tape, tacks, or staples can be used to hold the cloth in position on vertical surfaces or where it can move. The resin is applied in a series of three coats for most applications, although four coats could be necessary depending on many variables. The fiberglass cloth is saturated with the initial coat of resin to wet out the material and make it smooth. The second coat of resin fills and conceals the weave of the fiberglass cloth. The third coat provides the final finish surface which should be smooth and hard.

Semple steam engines

Develop five to twenty horsepower with wood or coal. Ride up the river. Finished engines or kits. —SB

Semple steam engines
Information and price list
$1 from:
Semple Engine Co., Inc.
Box 6805
St. Louis, MO 63144

Semple Steam Engines

Five Horsepower (single)	
No. 34 DW 3" x 4" - wheel reverse	$ 1,425
No. 34 DL 3" x 4" - lever reverse	1,593
Ten Horsepower	
(compound - 2 cylinders) lever reverse	3,012
Semple Marine Power Units (Engine, Boiler, Accessories)	
Five Horsepower (standard)	4,410
Five Horsepower (special)	4,912
Ten Horsepower	6,703
Twenty Horsepower (twin)	13,407
Condenser (optional on 5 hp)	160

WEST System

Well, it LOOKS like wood. The controversial WEST system of epoxy/wood laminate has many of the advantages of both materials but offends the purists who decry the plastic component of the superstrong, highly durable, esthetically pleasing composite. I find the WEST idea well developed and eminently acceptable. Boats made with it have an aircraft spidery lightness and birdlike beauty to the fine details. The designs realized in WEST technology have, to me, a unique and compelling character to them, and if I were building something that could be built that way, I'd go for it. Boats, car bodies, furniture, and windmill blades are some of the possible uses for this system. The chemicals, their uses (and precautions), the techniques right down to washing the brushes are all now well proven, and well presented in the WEST book. The rumor reputation is pretty good too.
—J. Baldwin

WEST System
Descriptive manual
$2 postpaid
Instruction book
$20 postpaid
Catalog of available plans and materials
free
all from:
Gougeon Brothers
706 Martin Street
P.O. Box 908
Bay City, MI 48707

Cold-molded cedar dinghy built by Steven Loutrel ↓

From a Bare Hull

Those who know better would be the first to point out that building the hull is only a small part of building the total boat. And those who have spent time with their calculators have quickly come to the realization that to buy a mass-produced bare fiberglass hull is almost as cheap as to build th same hull yourself. Enter the bare hull suppliers, and enter **From a Bare Hull** *by Ferenc Matē — a manual on turning an empty shell into a real boat. Some readers have taken issue with some of the author's assertions and with the fact that the book is a shill for Westsail, a manufacturer of bare hulls, but of the two books I know of that cover this aspect of boatbuilding, Matē's is the best.* —Peter Spectre

From a Bare Hull
Ferenc Matē
1975; 534 pp.
$19.95 postpaid from:
Albatross Publishing House
Box 33766
Vancouver, BC
Canada V6J 4L6

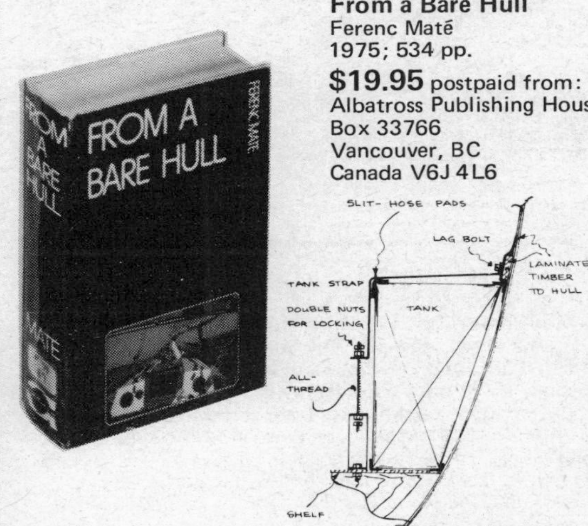

Stainless steel hold-down strap.

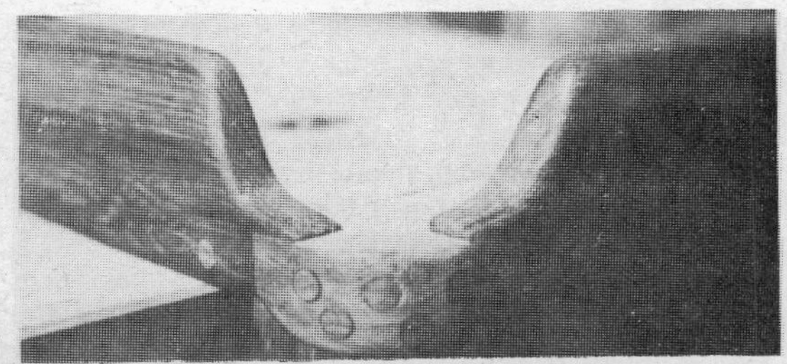

Open searail corner for sweeping out dirt.

THE RISING SUN
NEIGHBORHOOD NEWSLETTER

Geologists have a category of rock called FRGOK, pronounced fergock, meaning, Funny Rock, God Only Knows, which is used enough to occasionally make it into their scholarly journals. (Would that all scientists were so humble.)

—info from Don

Boat Building with Plywood

The welcome and increasing interest in hand-making things from wood will sooner or later turn many to boat-building. It's a skill that soon develops an attitude in the craftsman that can be transferred to other disciplines, housebuilding for instance, with great advantage. This book is sort of a beginner's introduction; real diehard wood boat builders frown on plywood. On the other hand, it's the fastest and easiest way to make a serviceable small boat. Very clear instructions with lots of drawings and photos. The publisher also has a host of other how-to books of similar merit on subjects ranging from boat trailer building to fiberglassing.
—J. Baldwin

Boat Building with Plywood
Glenn L. Witt
1962, 1979; 278 pp.
2nd Edition
$12.95 postpaid from:
Marine Designs
9152 Rosecrans
Bellflower, CA 90706

PLATE 6-C—The "right" way (at left) to drive a screw in plywood, and the "wrong" way (to right). The screw should compress all the veneers in a plywood panel.

Instant Boats

Intermediate technology using modern materials (if you are willing to accept such a contradiction in terms) is best exemplified by the work of Harold Payson in his interpretation of the designs of Phil Bolger. Payson's instant boats are plywood craft that are simple, easy to build, and marvelous to behold and use. His book of the same name is informative, thought provoking, and truly delightful to read. If you can imagine and appreciate a down-east boatbuilder describing how to fuse traditionalism with avant-gardism, you will thoroughly enjoy **Instant Boats**.
—Peter Spectre

Instant Boats
Harold H. Payson
1979; 152 pp.
$12.50 postpaid from:
International Marine Publishing Company
21 Elm Street
Camden, ME 04843
or Whole Earth Household Store

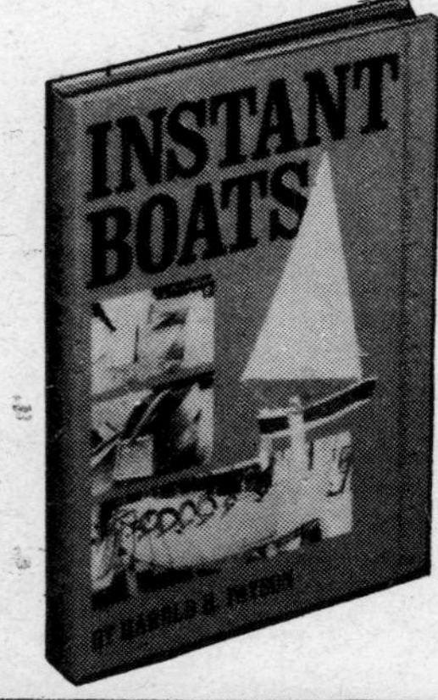

Karin applies resin over the fiberglass tape on the stem. The chines have already been coated with resin. Tacks are placed 4 or 5 inches apart to help secure the cloth. ↓

Glen-L boat plans
Luger boat kits

Looking through Glen-L's 144-page catalog is like wandering around a boat show. They have a huge selection of work boats, sail and power cruisers, ski-boats and house-boats. Most are designed for fiberglass or plywood construction. They also carry frame and accessory kits and camper plans and kits. The boat plans run $10 - $299 and come with full size patterns, eliminating lofting which is usually the most frustrating step for beginners.

For someone who is interested in saving time, and about half the dealer's price of a cruising sloop or daysailer, Luger's bare boat kits may be the way to go. The hulls are pre-formed, molded fiberglass, and are easy to put together. Basic kits run about $2000 - $5000; fittings and hardware are extra and can be purchased from Luger or a nearby chandlery.
—David Burnor

Glen-L Boat Plans
Catalog
$2 from:
Glen-L
9152 Rosecrans
Bellflower, CA 90706

Luger Boat Kits
Catalog
free from:
Luger Industries
3800 W. Highway 13
Burnsville, MN 55337

Voyager 30 "Basic" Sloop, $10, 312.25
Voyager 30 "Interior-Included" Sloop, $13,213.00
—Luger Industries, Inc.

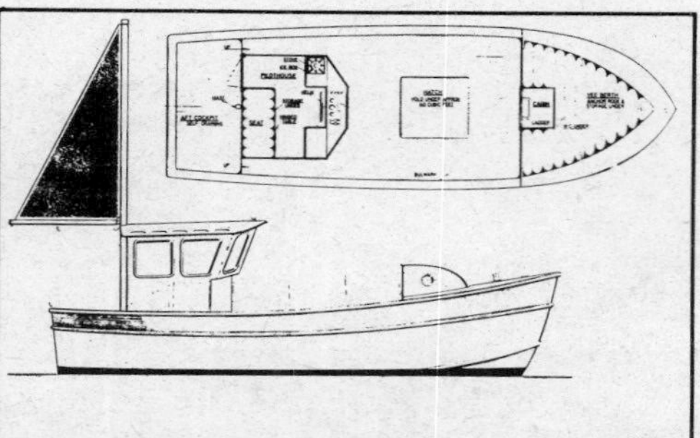

Noyo Trawler, a 24' trailerable workboat. ↑

Our "Noyo Trawler" is a sensible and appealing craft, especially for those who might be interested in turning hobby fishing into a profit making activity, at least part of the time. While compact in size and trailerable, the hold has a surprising 140 cubic feet of volume that will take on a couple of tons of fish or other cargo with ease. Just think! You can trailer your own "Noyo Trawler" anywhere, following the fishing grounds as they change and eliminating the cost of a full-time slip. And you can operate on a shoestring since this economical vessel requires only nominal power using just a little more than one gallon of diesel fuel per hour for a range of about 500 miles!

Complete plans with Bill of Materials, Fastening Schedule, Table of Offsets, and instructions. $40.00

Complete plans as noted plus full size patterns for the breasthook, stem, transom, and frame contours. $60.00
—Glen-L

Instant Boat plans

Winter. Good time to build a first boat in the garage or basement. A first boat had better be simple, if you hope ever to build another. Designer Harold Payson specializes in smart plywood smallcraft designed by Philip Bolger which require no lofting or building jigs. He has nice plans (about $12 each) and patterns for a 15'6" Crab skiff, a 12' Kayak, 8' punt, 31' foot schooner, etc. Sails available.
—SB

Instant Boat Series
Catalog
$3 from:
Harold H. Payson
Pleasant Beach Road
South Thomaston, ME 04858

•
Crab Skiff 15'6" (Surf), $12
Elegant Punt 8', $10
Gloucester Schooner 31', $20
Kaya 12', $10
Teal, 12', $12
Zephyr 20', $12
Pointy Skiff 10'6", $12
Tortoise 6'5", $10
Query 16' - 4'6", $12

31' Gloucester Schooner

•
Instant Boats do pare down the problems to a minimum. If you have average skills with tools and can saw along a penciled line, your Instant Boat will take shape in a surprisingly short time. Builders with no more than a modest amount of skill have built some Instant Boats in one 40-hour workweek. One woman, whose picture appear here, started from ground zero, and even though she had to learn to use tools before she could learn to build boats, she completed her 12-foot sailboat in just 90 working hours.

•
When developing the Instant Boat concept, Phil Bolger showed his usual good judgment and realized that it made sense to design a fleet of small boats using materials that could be had at one stop at the nearest lumber company. That meant specifying 8-foot plywood sheets and 2 x 4s for framing. Because of heavy demand, these are always in stock and always competitive in price, which guarantees a long-time supply. An Instant Boat can always be in the reach of almost any would-be boatbuilder.

Building the Skiff Cabin Boy

Boatbuilding-as-a-worthy-skill-that's-also-good-for-your-head. This book takes you inside the head of a master craftsman as he meticulously constructs a specific skiff. It's the most intimate, highly detailed instruction I've ever seen. If I were a bookstore owner, I'd have this with **Zen and The Art of Motorcycle Maintenance** *(p. 582) in the philosophy department. Nice skiff too.*
—J. Baldwin

Building the Skiff Cabin Boy
Clemens C. Kuhlig with Ruth E. Kuhlig
1977; 140 pp.
$12.50 postpaid from:
International Marine Publishing Company
21 Elm Street
Camden, ME 04843
or Whole Earth Household Store

← **A close-up of the boathook, showing the small leather strips attached to both points to keep the hook from damaging any surface it may hit. The leather also protects the hook itself.**

The finished skiff, with the oars stowed out of the way, yet ready for use.

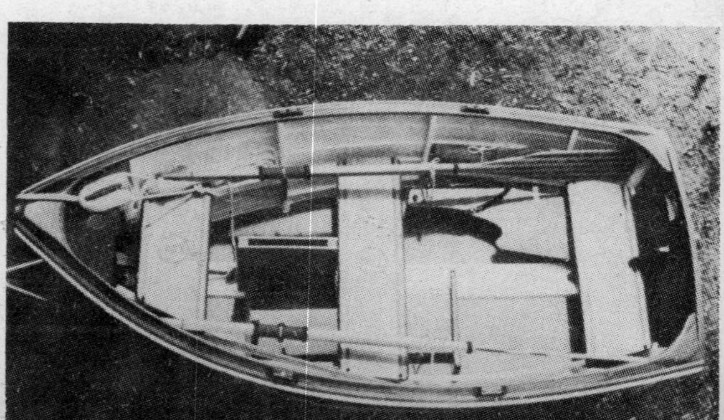

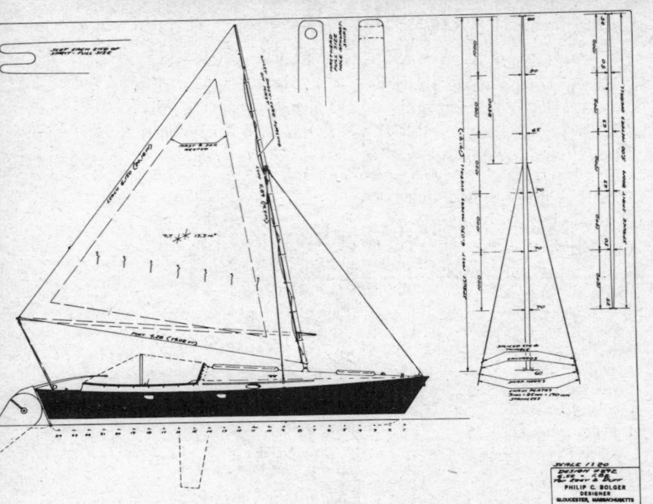

↑
Dovekie is a strenuous attempt to produce a popular family recreational boat that will function without an engine. For this she plainly needed a high enough performance under sail, and tight enough control, to go under sail wherever there is wind and minimum space.

Secondly, she must row well enough, in a calm, to make rowing her a mild satisfaction not leading quickly to frustration or exhaustion; this meant among other things that there could be no underwater surfaces or excrescences not absolutely necessary to float her, and that she must be as low to the water and streamlined as possible, certainly having no spars or wires sticking high in the air.

She was built as a joint experiment with Edey & Duff of Mattapoisett, of Airex foam-sandwich construction. The hull and deck assembly, stripped, weighs four hundred pounds. With normal equipment her displacement without crew is on the order of six hundred pounds. Another five or six hundred pounds of people doesn't seem to affect her performance much, other than making her much stiffer under sail and harder to start and stop under oars. So loaded she draws about four and a half inches of water, whereas empty she floats in about three inches. This sort of draft and upright stance aground were bonuses of the dead-flat bottom, which was mainly meant to give maximum stability for her weight and enough flat surface inside for four people to lie down.
—**The Folding Schooner**

Small Boats
The Folding Schooner

Phil Bolger's books, like his boats, are bold, witty, innovative, exciting, and a cut above everything else. They are an education. —Peter Spectre

Small Boats
Philip C. Bolger
1973; 196 pp.
$15 postpaid

The Folding Schooner
(And Other Adventures in Boat Design)
Philip C. Bolger
1976; 198 pp.
$15 postpaid

both from:
International Marine Publishing Company
21 Elm Street
Camden, ME 04843
or Whole Earth Household Store

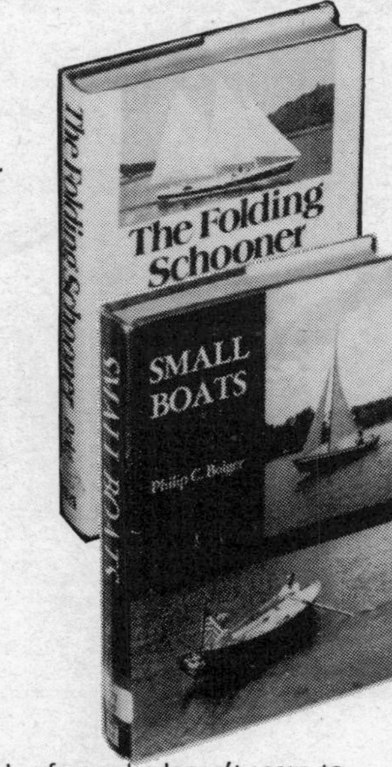

Building Classic Small Craft

For those who wish to build in the smaller sizes — rowing boats, small daysailers, utilities — **Building Classic Small Craft** *by John Gardner is the book. The author is an experienced builder with a solid reputation for skill and the ability to make all processes easy to understand. Though he favors boats of traditional design, he has the good sense to adapt today's materials and techniques where applicable. One is able to have, with a clear conscience, one's cake and eat it too.* —Peter Spectre

Building Classic Small Craft
John Gardner
1977; 314 pp.
$22.50 postpaid from:
International Marine Publishing Company
21 Elm Street
Camden, ME 04843

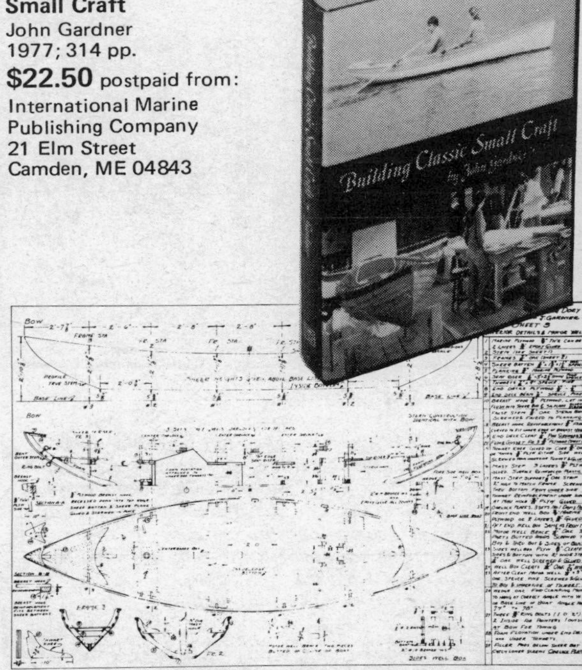

Marblehead gunning dory

↑
Using a gunning dory for lobstering is like hitching a spirited horse to a dump cart. But this superbly beautiful double-ender of ultra-light construction stood the gaff for several years in spite of advanced age and the roughest sort of treatment. Even under huge loads of lobster pots it rode the waves lightly, with infinite grace and with only slight urging on the oars. The gunning dory as perfected in Marblehead by William Chamberlain is the queen of all dories, and one of the handsomest double-enders ever built anywhere, not to mention its easy speed under oars and its unexcelled rough-water ability with capable hands at the oars.

Boatbuilding

The grandpa of boatbuilding books is **Boatbuilding** *by Howard Chapelle. In print continuously since 1941, for many years it was the only game in town, and glassy-eyed dreamers would clutch their copies with a death grip. It features carvel construction, wood naturally, with only a nod to the other methods. Its strengths are plenty of detail and a foundation of traditionalism; its weaknesses are a Byzantine organization, dull style (yes, there are stylishly written boatbuilding books), and nothing on the miracle materials and methods that have been developed since WWII. Nevertheless, if you are at all serious, you must have this book.* —Peter Spectre

Boatbuilding
Howard I. Chapelle
1941; 624 pp.
$20 postpaid from:
W.W. Norton and Co.
500 Fifth Avenue
New York, NY 10036

•
Boiling is more practical than steaming, as few amateur builders care to go to the trouble of building a wooden steam box and then attaching a boiler to it. Steaming is a slower operation than boiling. It is doubtful if boiling harms timber any more than steaming; at any rate, either will kill the dry-rot spores. The boiling tank may be set on loose brick or concrete blocks, and the fire fed with scrap lumber, or a couple of single-burner oil stoves may be used instead. Boiling water is required, not just hot. Incidentally, the plank will be so hot that gloves will be required when handling it.
↓

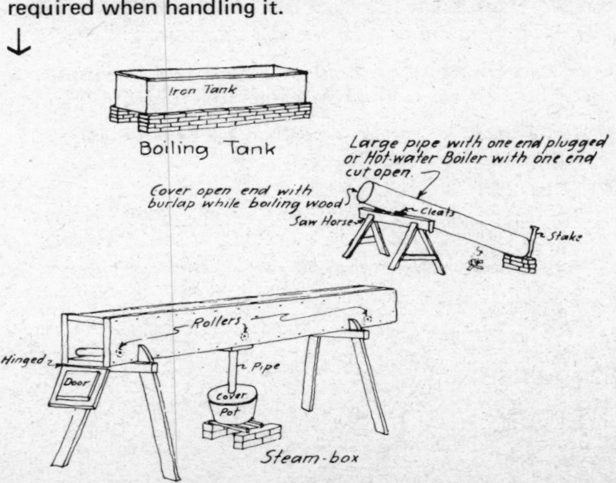

Ferro-Cement Design, Technique and Applications

And then there is ferrocement boatbuilding. For a number of years a cottage industry operated, wherein certain cultists — not unlike dome advocates — hyped ferrocement as the route to inexpensive, easily-built boats. Instead, we got cheap, shoddily-built boats. Part of the blame should be placed on the shoulders of the writers and publishers of f-c building books, who were too quick to tout a good thing before the kinks were ironed out. So ferrocement got a bad name before this veritable encyclopedia on the subject was published. I daresay that if you were to follow Bruce Bingham's advice in **Ferro-Cement Design, Techniques and Application,** *you would have a boat to be proud of. It's too bad it was not the* <u>first</u> *book on ferrocement to be published.* —Peter Spectre

Ferro-Cement Design, Technique and Applications
Bruce Bingham
1974; 444 pp.
$17.50 postpaid from:
Cornell Maritime Press
P.O. Box 456
Centerville, MD 21617

After stretching or rolling the mesh panel onto the hull, smooth the mesh wrinkles toward each other, stapling as you go.

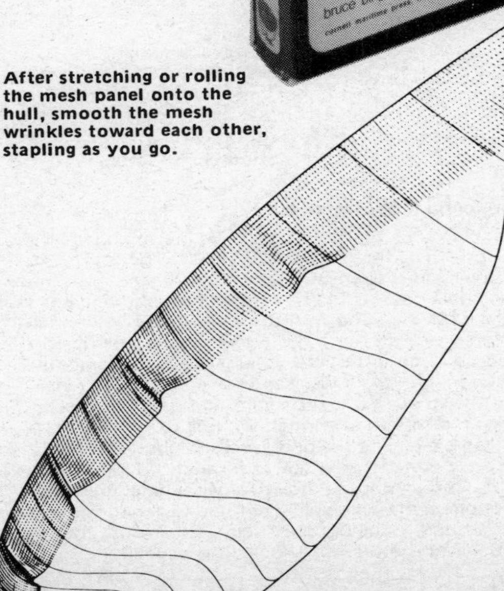

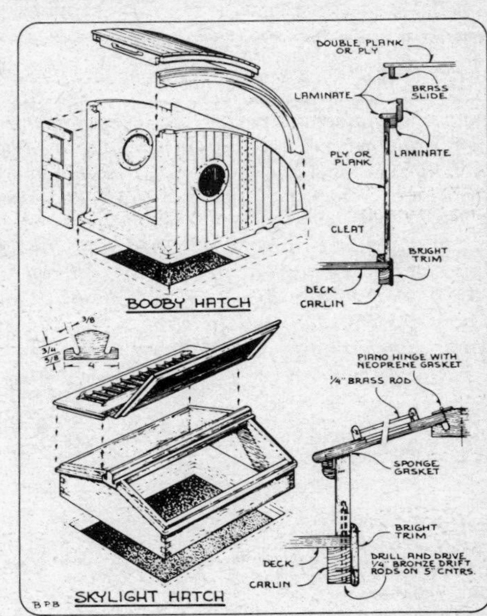

THE RISING SUN
NEIGHBORHOOD NEWSLETTER

One problem Jay used to give people in his design class was to package themselves to be dropped 2 stories and then actually be dropped in the package. Andrea said she'd build a package 2 stories high and climb down it.

The Complete Wilderness Paddler

When books begin to appear on a subject that has had limited media coverage, the first one is usually pretty good. It has no competition, and the lack of public awareness of the subject means that the first book can be relatively rich. That book is followed by many imitators hoping to cash in on its success. The best of those advance the state of the art in tiny increments as various viewpoints and techniques are presented. Then somebody gets it all together and says, "This is it, for now." This is that for now. And a special mention must go to the illustrations, which are quite exceptional. —J. Baldwin

The Complete Wilderness Paddler
James West Davidson and John Rugge
1976; 266 pp.

$10.95 postpaid from:
Alfred A. Knopf, Inc.
455 Hahn Road
Westminster, MD 21157
or Whole Earth Household Store

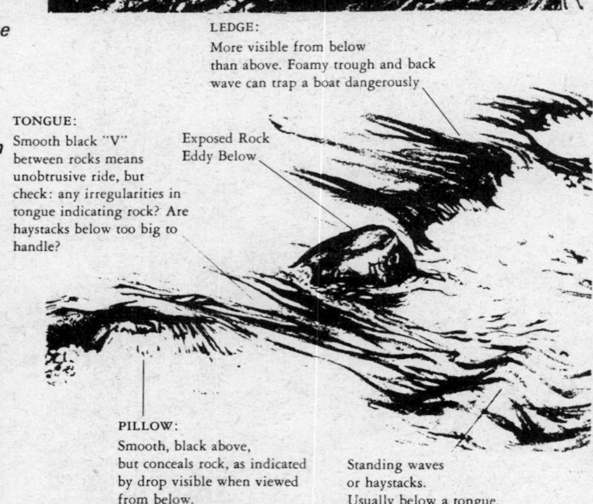
LEDGE:
More visible from below than above. Foamy trough and back wave can trap a boat dangerously.
TONGUE:
Smooth black "V" between rocks means unobtrusive ride, but check: any irregularities in tongue indicating rock? Are haystacks below too big to handle?
Exposed Rock Eddy Below
PILLOW:
Smooth, black above, but conceals rock, as indicated by drop visible when viewed from below.
Standing waves or haystacks. Usually below a tongue.

The Canoeist's Catalog

Canoe know-it-alls will soon find out that they don't quite when they thumb through this marvelous collection of gear, boats, maps and other necessities of the trade. It's the only place that you can find all this information in the same box, so comparisons can easily be made. A very much needed service, very well presented by people who know what they are talking about. —J. Baldwin

The Canoeist's Catalog
William F. Stearns and Fern Crossland Stearns, Editors
1978; 191 pp.

$7.95 postpaid from:
International Marine Publishing Company
21 Elm Street
Camden, ME 04843
or Whole Earth Household Store

•

Twenty maps of rivers in the Colorado River Basin, the Idaho-Wyoming Snake River Basin, the Rogue and McKenzie in Oregon, the Fraser, Canoe, and Columbia in British Columbia are currently available in a series. The maps look like a draftsman's labor of love. A scale of more than an inch to a mile, together with many comments based on experience on the river, campsite locations, rapids and their ratings, make these maps extremely useful for some big water travel. They have an excellent reputation for accuracy.

How to roll Leslie Jones' maps.

It is the physical form of the maps that makes them intriguing: a scroll format, printed on waterproof Mylar, with a river profile paralleling the contour map of the river. The whole thing is packaged in a sealable plastic bag that allows the map to be rolled (or unrolled) to expose several miles of river. It is an idea that more mapmakers should use. For maps contact: Leslie A. Jones, Star Route Box 13A, Heber City, Utah 84032

A.M.C. White Water Handbook

The classic little book on how to handle your kayak or canoe if you were paddling on a flood of water down, say, your basement stairs. If you handle it right, you'll wind up in the attic. A.M.C. (Appalachian Mountain Club) also has nice river guides for all of New England. —SB

A.M.C. White Water Handbook
(For canoe and kayak)
John T. Urban
1969; 76 pp.

$3.70 postpaid from:
Appalachian Mountain Club
5 Joy Street
Boston, MA 02108

•

Eskimo roll

Apart from the direct satisfaction that it brings, mastering the roll has some specific and important benefits. Since you can cheerfully court an upset when practicing bracing strokes and crossing currents, your practice and subsequent style will not be cramped through fear of capsizing; your ability to use the paddle for balance in rough water will be much enhanced; and finally, you will be able to recover from at least some upsets on the river.

Rolling is not the rare feat it was once thought to be. In a well-designed kayak little strength is required for a properly executed roll, and some experts can roll without a paddle using two hands alone, and in some cases, only one hand.

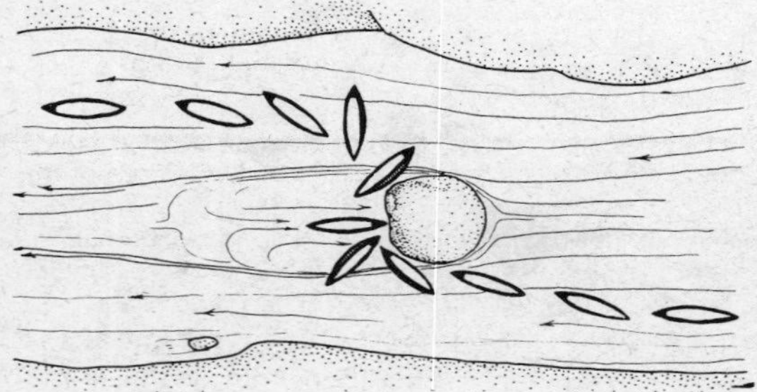

An eddy turn below a midstream boulder, followed by a turn downstream into the current on the opposite side

Water charts

If you're travelling on the water, you're going to need something more than an Exxon roadmap to tell you where you are. For United States waters the best charts (the only ones, really. All the others say something like "refer to the appropriate NOAA chart for navigation data") are the ones issued by various government agencies.

Where to get the charts depends on where you want to go. Charts of the Atlantic, Pacific and Gulf Coasts, the Great Lakes, and the Intra-coastal Waterway come from the National Oceanic and Atmospheric Administration (NOAA). Internal rivers and tributaries are on charts from the Army Corps of Engineers. Cost of individual charts varies; most run about $4. River charts usually come in books.

Index map catalogs for the lakes and coasts are free from the NOAA. Catalog No. 1 covers the Atlantic and Gulf Coasts, Catalog 2 the Pacific, Catalog 3 Alaska and Catalog 4 the Great Lakes and some internal waterways. Write: National Oceanic and Atmospheric Administration (NOAA), Distribution Division C44, National Ocean Survey, Riverdale, MD 20840. They also have sales agents around the country and will tell you where the nearest one is to you.

For river charts, you write the appropriate Corps agency for the river you want, and they send you the book of charts. There's no central source, but the different Corps offices are listed in any of the NOAA catalogs.

Charts are frequently revised, and you should be using a current one, because the changes can sometimes be big ones.

Nautical charts of foreign countries are issued by the U.S. Naval Hydrographic Office, Washington, DC 20390. Write to them about a catalog.

—John M. Ross
St. Louis, Missouri

Canoe Poling

In an unguarded moment a river person will admit that there is one anti-environmental aspect to the bit: going upstream requires a car. But you can do it with a pole too, it turns out. Rivers and swamps that are inaccessible to any other boating technique are made into practical routes either direction by polework. This book reveals the secrets heretofore only known to a few. All you need besides the book is a canoe or similar craft, a pole (they tell you how to make one), and dry clothes . . . Looks good to me! I'm getting a pole right away. —J. Baldwin

Canoe Poling
Al, Syl and Frank Beletz
1974; 148 pp.

$4.95 postpaid from:
A.C. MacKenzie Press
Box 9301
Richmond Heights Station
Richmond Heights, MO 63117

Poling is the fastest way to ascend a stream by human power. ↓

Canoeing

The venerable, dull, unfriendly and outdated Red Cross canoe manual has been totally redone. It's now one of the very best available. The illustrations by Richard Guy are the clearest I've seen anywhere, and show nonwhites in action too for a change. The whitewater section is particularly good. Also included are sections on canoe poling and sailing, and, of course, first aid in the usual Red Cross manner. It's friendly now, too. —J. Baldwin

Canoeing
American Red Cross
1977; 452 pp.

$3.95 postpaid from:
Doubleday and Company
501 Franklin Avenue
Garden City, NY 11530
or Whole Earth Household Store

•

Spin-Around (180-Degree Turn)

The spin-around, or 180-degree turn, is also known as the crash turn. The first part of this stroke is performed in the same manner as the dragging stop. That is, you must jam the pole down a few feet back of your poling position (on the left side if you wish to turn left and on the right side if you wish to turn right). With your upper hand you apply force against the pole, while at the same time you pull in with the lower hand toward your leg that is nearer the stern. You hold your upper body and legs stiffly, therefore transferring the force to your feet. Your foot that is closer to the bow forces the bow to swing toward the poling side while your other foot applies pressure in the opposite direction. If enough pressure has been applied, the canoe will continue to turn until you have turned it in the desired direction. That is, you can stop the canoe at 60, 90, 180, or 240 degrees, or you can make a complete 360-degree turn if you so desire. ⟶

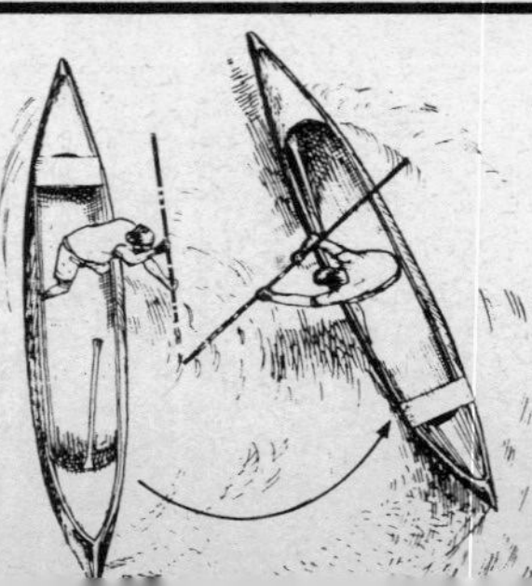

The Survival of the Bark Canoe

The Bark Canoes and Skin Boats of North America

Henri Vaillancourt and the canoes he builds (see below) provide the framework for John McPhee's penetrating tale of an expedition in the Maine woods. **The Survival of the Bark Canoe** *follows Thoreau's route on a trip down the Penobscot River, presenting a history of the construction and use of the native American birch-bark canoe as well as an alluring portrait of the river and the people whose lives it touches. McPhee's characterizations and his unique capacity for fascinating digression makes this rambling* **New Yorker** *profile a joy to read.*

Vaillancourt learned his craft from Edwin Tappan Adney's **Bark Canoes and Skin Boats** *and uses the book as an illustrated catalog. From 1887 until his death in 1950, Adney sought out everything he could learn about the bark canoe of the North Woods and the Eskimo kayak. Compiled by Howard Chapelle for the Smithsonian, this is the ultimate word on the evolution of the first American boatbuilding tradition.* —David Burnor

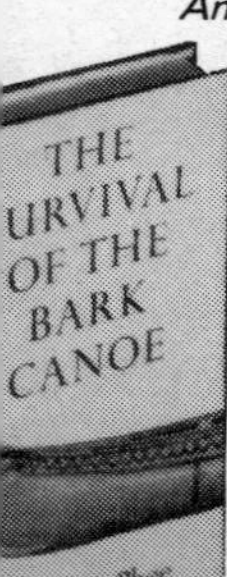

The Survival of the Bark Canoe
John McPhee
1975; 145 pp.
$5.95 postpaid from:
Warner Books
Independent News Co.
75 Rockefeller Plaza
New York, NY 10019
or Whole Earth Household Store

The Bark Canoes and Skin Boats of North America
Edwin Tappan Adney and Howard I. Chapelle
1964, 1979; 242 pp.
No. 047-001-00021-8
$8 postpaid from:
Superintendent of Documents
U.S. Government Printing Office
Washington, DC 20402
or Whole Earth Household Store

•

The river has many riffles, too minor to be labelled rapids. Nonetheless, they are stuffed with rock. The angle of the light is not always favorable. The rocks are hidden, and — smash — full tilt we hit them. The rocks make indentations that move along the bottom of the canoe, pressing in several inches and tracing a path toward the stern. It is as if the canoe were a pliant film sliding over the boulders. Still, I feel sorry and guilty when we hit one. I have been in white water and Rick has not, so he has asked me to paddle in the stern — to steer, to pick the route, to read the river — and I reward his confidence by smashing into another rock. Nothing cracks. If this were an aluminum canoe, it would be dented now, and, I must confess, I would not really care. Of all the differences between this canoe and others I have travelled in, the first difference is a matter of care about them. The canoes can take a lot more abuse than we give them, but we all care. Landing, we are out of the canoes and in the water ourselves long before the bark can touch bottom. We load and launch in a foot of water. The Indians did just that, and the inclination to copy them is automatic — is not consciously remembered — with these Indian canoes.
—**The Survival of the Bark Canoe**

p. 71. Malecite 2½-Fathom River canoe, 19th Century. Old form with raking ends and much sheer.

Fur-trade canoe on the Missinaibi River, 1901

Henri Vaillancourt birch-bark canoes

The birch-bark canoes I make are of the Malecite Indian type described in the chapter on Malecite canoes in the book **Bark Canoes and Skin Boats of North America**, by E.T. Adney and H.I. Chappelle. This book is also the best source of information for anyone interested in the art.

I make both the flare-sided St. Lawrence River type and the tumblehome types with either a high or low end. The beam for a flare-sided canoe is 34 inches, depth 11 inches to 12 inches. For $200 extra, two inches can be added to the depth and width of a flare-sided canoe. The tumblehome types are available in 16-foot and 18-foot lengths only.

In addition, fur trade canoes may be ordered in any length from 20- to 37-feet in any styles shown in the book.

I make these canoes entirely by hand with the axe, crooked knife, awl, and froe, no power tools are used. The woodwork is split from white cedar for ribs, planking, stems, and gunwales, and from ash or birch for thwarts.

The skin is white birch-bark sewn with split pine root in the traditional manner. Pegs and root lashings are used in the fastening of the inwales and outwales. Because of the time involved and scarcity of bark, I make only six or seven canoes a year.

The prices quoted below are only approximations and are subject to change. In placing an order please send your name and address, the length and style of the canoe desired, and a $200 deposit by certified check.

Length	Approximate Weight	Price
10'	40 lbs.	$1100
12'	50 lbs.	$1200
14'	60 lbs.	$1300
16'	70 lbs.	$1400
18'	80 lbs.	$1500
24' fur-trade type		$3600
37' fur-trade type		$5500

—Henri Vaillancourt
Mill Street, Greenville, New Hampshire

A sequence of the 16' Blue Hole OCA pinned, trashed, and untrashed

Blue Hole canoes

There's a problem with white water open canoeing: if you blow it, your boat can be wrecked — $600 worth. Having wiped out a Grumman in about two seconds a long time ago, I was naturally reluctant to invest again in expensive equipment that could be all too easily trashed by a moment of ineptitude. Blue Hole canoes have changed all that. They are made from Royalex, a plastic sandwich that springs back after a hit, rather like a squeeze bottle. In fact, a Blue Hole can be completely wrapped around a rock and still restored to useful life by a heat lamp (or judiciously applied campfire); Royalex "remembers" its shape. Soft aluminum gunwales protect the edge of the plastic and deform with it rather than breaking and initiating a crack. (Other Royalex boats do not share this essential feature.) O.K., so how does it work? After five years of severe abuse, I can report that it all works pretty damned well. Our boat is scarred but unpierced, and it still has all the Blue Hole advantages of maneuverability and good overall performance. They now have a new expedition model that brings this sort of bulletproof reliability to otherwise risky back country trips. And I should add that the folks who make 'em are real nice to deal with too. —J. Baldwin

Blue Hole Canoes
Catalog
free from:
The Blue Hole Canoe Co.
Sunbright, TN 37872

•

OCA 16' Whitewater	$630
17A 17' Whitewater	$655
MGA 17'6" Cruising	$770

Klepper kayaks

Easily the best of the folding kayaks for 1 person ($1360), 2 people ($1390) and even sailing (add $500). Adventure packed in your trunk or closet (take your boat on the bus to the water). —SB

Klepper Folding Boats and Kayaks
Information
free from:
Hans Klepper Corporation
35 Union Square West
New York, NY 10003

Grumman Canoes
Old Town Canoes

Grumman has the best of the aluminum canoes, clanky but durable — 13' to 20', $454 to $722.

Good old Old Town has classic and classy wood canoes ($1300 - $1600), plastic ones (around $800) and some nice kayaks ($500 - $700). —SB

Grumann Canoes
Catalog and price list
free from:
Grumman Boats
General Sales Office
Marathon, NY 13803

Old Town Canoes
Catalog and price list
$1 from:
Old Town Canoe Co.
Old Town, ME 04468

Grumann SD - 20

Old Town Molitor

Quik-N-Easy roof racks

These are the best we've seen. —J. Baldwin

Quik-N-Easy Universal Car Top Carriers
Information
free from:
Quik-N-Easy Products
P.O. Box 278
Monrovia, CA 91016

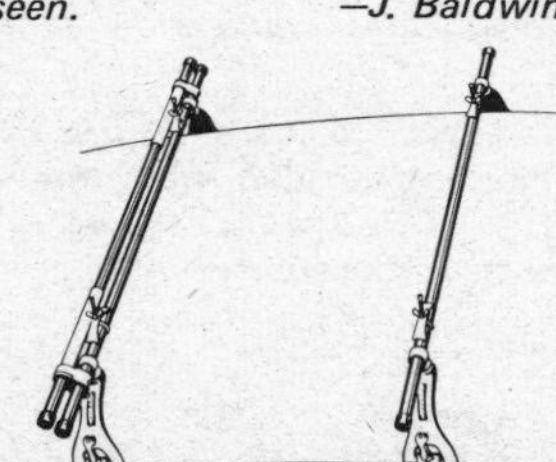

UCS-6 — Universal Standard Side or Rear Loader includes 4 tumbled yokes with levers, clips, tube holders and three 1" steel tubes 60" long (one tube equipped with 2 neoprene sleeves and adapters for use as roller bar to assist in boat landing). Plastic end caps for all tube ends, and one set of 4 Boat Holdown Clamps. $53.14.

Avon inflatable boats

Rafting is sometimes the only way to get down a river. They flow resiliently along as part of the water, and can be packed into remote areas. For mild rapids, a "Hong Kong Special" discount store raft will do if loaded to ½ rated capacity. For serious work you'll need a serious raft from Avon. These aren't cheap: $1850 - $3370. Also fine liferafts ($1430 - $3140), dinghies ($800 - $1260) and sportboats ($2000 - $8800). —J. Baldwin

Avon Inflatable Boats
Catalog
free from:
Avon Inland Marine Co.
79 East Jackson Street
Wilkes-Barre, PA 18701

THE RISING SUN
NEIGHBORHOOD NEWSLETTER

"When he was good he was very, very good, but when he was bad, he was wonderful."
—Evelyn

The Stream Conservation Handbook

"The first practical primer for fishermen — how to protect, preserve, and restore our rivers." Buy it, read it, use what you learn. Don't just sit there shaking your head, mumbling, "Now ain't it just a damn shame."
—Al Perrin

The Stream Conservation Handbook
Michael Migel, Editor
1974; 292 pp.

OUT OF PRINT
Crown Publishers

Get this book back in print!

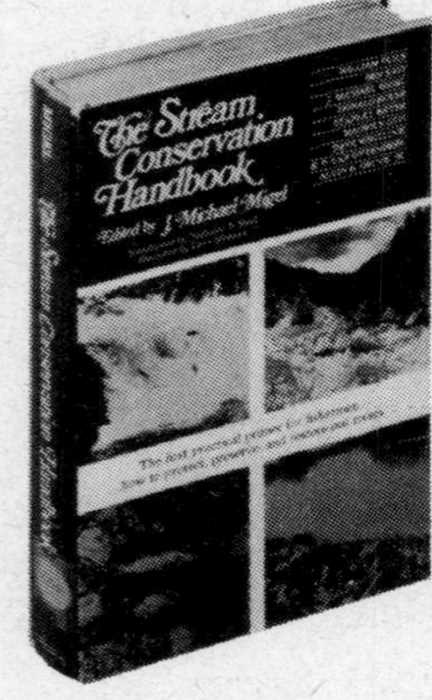

•
In addition to the formidable barriers posed by the dams and their turbines and impoundments, an even graver threat hangs over the river's fish populations: the little understood poisoning of water known as nitrogen supersaturation. Few fishermen have heard of it, but it is a deadly killer.

The Complete Fisherman's Catalog

This is an easily understood guide to quality sport fishing equipment and is the best book on the subject we have read. It covers the history of the equipment being discussed including how and why it evolved. In doing this, it covers the rich history of fishing as an art.

It does have a touch of the snobbishness similar to that experienced in some gourmet cookbooks. And though we rarely can afford the quality of equipment described, it is enjoyable to understand the hows and whys of such gear, while being rewarded by the excellent philosophical discourse woven between descriptions. For the non-fisherpeople, reading this will bring a clearer understanding of why people have and will always enjoy fishing as a hobby. —*Tyler H. Johnson and Huey D. Johnson*

The Complete Fisherman's Catalog
(A Source Book of Information about Tackle and Accessories for Fly Fishing, Spinning, Bait Casting, Surf Casting, Ice Fishing, Offshore Fishing and more)
Harmon Henkin
1977; 463 pp.

$8.95 postpaid from:
J.B. Lippincott Company
East Washington Square
Philadelphia, PA 19105
or Whole Earth
Household Store

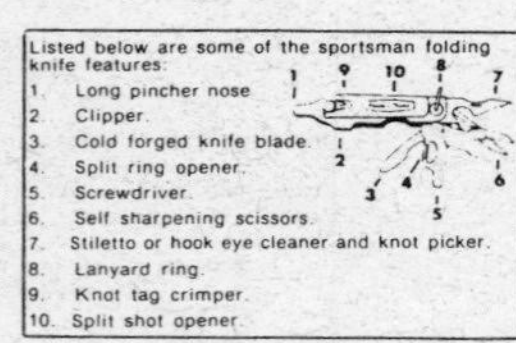
Listed below are some of the sportsman folding knife features:

1. Long pincher nose
2. Clipper.
3. Cold forged knife blade.
4. Split ring opener.
5. Screwdriver.
6. Self sharpening scissors.
7. Stiletto or hook eye cleaner and knot picker.
8. Lanyard ring.
9. Knot tag crimper.
10. Split shot opener.

↑
Walton's Thumb, produced by Colorado's Hank Roberts, is enough to send the confirmed gadgeteer over the edge. Expensive and well-made, the Thumb is to the old angler's clipper what the atomic bomb is to the firecracker. Made from stainless steel and surprisingly light, it has blades that include a tiny pincer pliers, side-positioned clipper, small knife blade, split ring opener, split shot remover, scissors, reel-sized screwdriver, hook eye cleaner, knot tag crimper and bottle opener. The parts are replaceable and it is guaranteed. Really swell. Get one for Christmas.

←
Despite an uncertain marketing future and the great technical advances of Japanese reels like Daiwa and Olympic, the Italian-made Alcedo Micron remains the best of the ultralight reels, according to many hardcore experts. It's an unassuming reel but very solidly made and features a smooth running drag that seldom fails. The extra spools slip on very easily and line hangup behind the bail was pretty much eliminated years before it was an area of concern for other makers. The anti-reverse button is oversized and conveniently located. Alcedo will be the one ultra-light that can last you the rest of your life. Even if they are no longer imported, there are still plenty of them around in supply houses and better stores. Get one before the collectors discover the joy of owning this fine piece of machinery.

Big Roche-a-Cir Creek, Waushara County, Wisconsin. Meadow section before current deflectors and bank "hides" were installed. The deepest place in the stream within view of the photo is a small twelve-inch pocket. Most of the stream, at mid-channel, is only about six to ten inches deep.

The meadow section of Big Roche-a-Cir Creek about two years after current deflectors and bank "hides" were installed. Many places in the picture are now eighteen to twenty-four inches deep; with overhanging cover. Some sections are a full three feet deep.

The Curtis Creek Manifesto

At one time I owned more than 25 books on fly-fishing for trout. Generally, all were confined to a rigid, traditional form and were highly technical or philosophical. Hardly appropriate tools for one of life's more important matters — passing an understanding and appreciation of trout fishing on to others, namely my children. This book's contemporary, simple style, cartoon drawings and and broad overview make it useful for fostering this initial awareness.

The Curtis Creek Manifesto *projects the need of major personal commitment to master the complex concept of new awareness that trout fishing offers. On the one hand the sadness of knowing how fragile and in need of defense trout waters are and on the other — personal level — it offers a chance to immerse one's self and become for at least a little while, closer to nature. To know that the human being, like the trout, is affected by weather, food supply and habitat.*

Fly-fishing, by the way, need not be a matter of killing fish. It's one of the few pursuits where the skilled fly fisherman can catch and release alive the now wiser quarry. This book is an excellent source for general inquiry on the subject. —*Huey D. Johnson*

The Curtis Creek Manifesto
(A Fully Illustrated Guide to the Strategy, Finesse, Tactics and Paraphernalia of Fly Fishing)
Sheridan Anderson
1976; 47 pp.

$3.95 postpaid from:
Salmon Trout Steelheader
P.O. Box 02112
Portland, OR 97202
or Whole Earth
Household Store

FLY CASTING
"FLIP" OR SNAP CAST
IF IT'S EASY, YOU'RE PROBABLY DOING IT WRONG
THE SUCCESSFUL FISHER MUST LEARN TO CAST WELL UNDER DIFFICULT CONDITIONS AND FROM A VARIETY OF AWKWARD AND OFTEN UNCOMFORTABLE POSITIONS — DON'T BE MISLED INTO THINKING THAT BEING ANNIE OAKLEY OR WILD BILL HICKOK ON THE LOCAL CASTING PUDDLE QUALIFIES YOU AS AN ISAAK WALTON...

McClane's New Standard Fishing Encyclopedia & International Angling Guide

This is an epic work, and to my knowledge it is the most comprehensive, all-encompassing fishing book available on this planet. A.J. McClane is the executive editor of **Field and Stream** *magazine, a writer with exceptional wit and style and, without doubt, one of the top authorities on angling in the world today . . . but no one person alone could have written this book. Its scope is too vast and its level of expertise too profound. A.J. has sounded the ramshorn and amassed a formidable array of heavies representing the entire angling spectrum and the result is an extremely impressive and solid work, for the first time, a true angler's bible.*

This isn't the kind of book you read while hanging onto a subway strap. It's as thick as a butcher's block and the weight is commensurate. There are hundreds and hundreds of color photos and illustrations. The total number must run into several thousand. There are more than 6000 entries covering nearly 1500 species of fresh and saltwater fish. There are drawings, charts, diagrams, step by step lessons on how to procure the finny beauties — also how to cook, clean, smoke and mount them . . . There are major articles on such things as algae, insects, diseases and parasites, rod building, flies and fly tying and currents.

If that isn't enough, the international angling guide puts you onto the hot spots in all fifty states, Canada, Central and South America, Europe, Asia, Africa, Australia, Iceland, the Pacific, the Atlantic, etc., etc., etc.

Obviously it would make a superb gift for any fisherperson, but beyond that it would serve as a unique and invaluable reference in any library. Don't let the fifty dollar price tag throw you, this is something you can give your grandkids.

Fishing has been one of mankind's most elemental and necessary pursuits for well over a half million years, and McClane's book is the best single-volume elucidation yet.
—Sheridan Anderson

McClane's New Standard Fishing Encyclopedia and International Angling Guide
A.J. McClane, Editor
1965; 1974; 1156 pp.

$50 postpaid from:
Holt Rinehart and Winston
383 Madison Avenue
New York, NY 10017

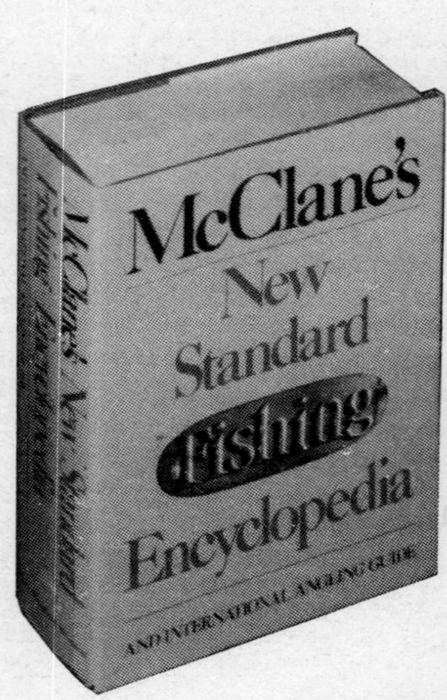

→
The Improved Clinch Knot has many applications in tying flies, lures, bait hooks, and swivels to leader or line, or to tie a line to a reel spool.

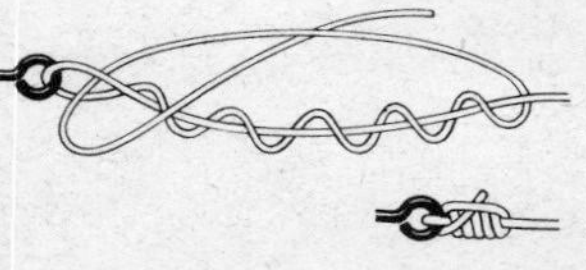

←
Occasionally, prior to death, an octopus will eat its own arms.

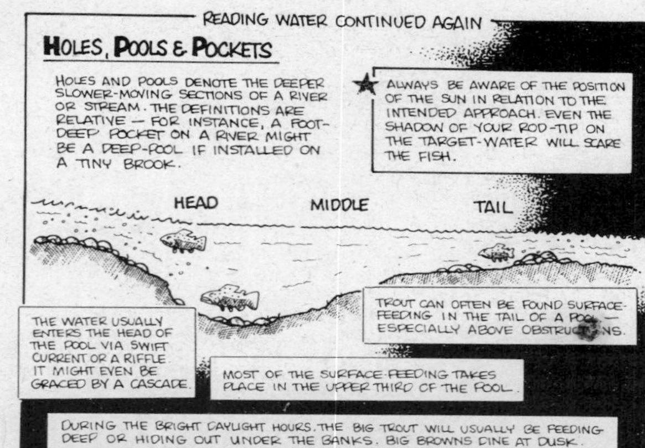

READING WATER CONTINUED AGAIN
HOLES, POOLS & POCKETS
HOLES AND POOLS DENOTE THE DEEPER SLOWER-MOVING SECTIONS OF A RIVER OR STREAM. THE DEFINITIONS ARE RELATIVE — FOR INSTANCE, A FOOT-DEEP POCKET ON A RIVER MIGHT BE A DEEP-POOL IF INSTALLED ON A TINY BROOK.
ALWAYS BE AWARE OF THE POSITION OF THE SUN IN RELATION TO THE INTENDED APPROACH. EVEN THE SHADOW OF YOUR ROD-TIP ON THE TARGET-WATER WILL SCARE THE FISH.
HEAD
MIDDLE
TAIL
THE WATER USUALLY ENTERS THE HEAD OF THE POOL VIA SWIFT CURRENT OR A RIFFLE. IT MIGHT EVEN BE GRACED BY A CASCADE.
TROUT CAN OFTEN BE FOUND SURFACE-FEEDING IN THE TAIL OF A POOL — ESPECIALLY ABOVE OBSTRUCTIONS.
MOST OF THE SURFACE-FEEDING TAKES PLACE IN THE UPPER THIRD OF THE POOL.
DURING THE BRIGHT DAYLIGHT HOURS, THE BIG TROUT WILL USUALLY BE FEEDING DEEP OR HIDING OUT UNDER THE BANKS. BIG BROWNS DINE AT DUSK.

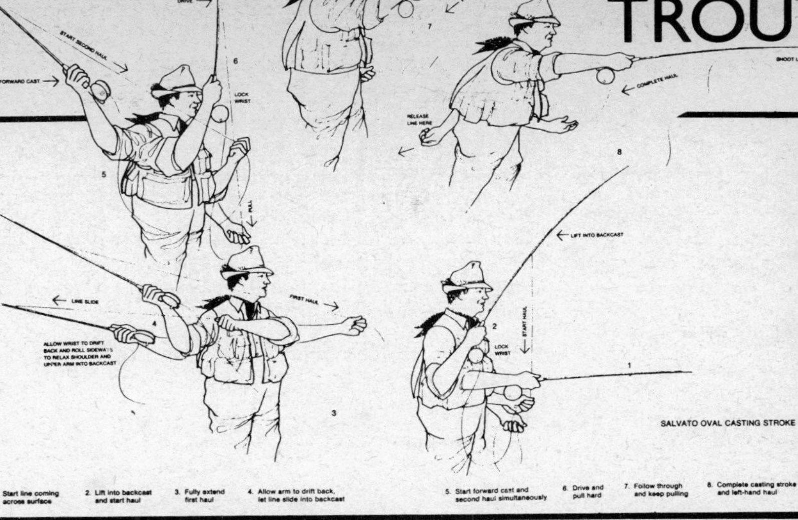

FLY FISHING

by Tom Macy

If you want to catch trout, go to the water, leave your gear behind, and watch them. Unentangled by tackle you will learn their secrets. But watch closely, because "trout do not lie or cheat and cannot be bought or bribed or impressed by power, but respond only to quietude and humility and endless patience." (Robert Traver, **Anatomy of a Fisherman.***)*

Watching them will lead you to loving them (rather than your tackle). Trout are such irresistible beauties; only a heavy dose of love and respect will save them from the expertise gleaned from authors recommended here. Other creatures should be so lucky to have inspired such books; all written by men who have watched as much as fished.

Tom Macy, apart from his weakness for trout, saves huge bodies of land for the Nature Conservancy (p. 383). —SB

The Run

This one is not about trout or even fishing. It is about the author's close, thoughtful observation of alewives (members of the herring family) on their spawning run up freshwater streams to Cape Cod ponds and back to the ocean. **The Run** *is what watching fish is about.*

The Run
John Hay
1959, 1979; 184 pp.
3rd Edition

$3.95 postpaid from:
W.W. Norton and Co.
500 Fifth Avenue
New York, NY 10036
or Whole Earth
Household Store

•

A fish is supported by water — an advantage over cumbersome human beings in their own surrounding medium, the air — its specific gravity being close to that of its own body. The fish is so made as to swim through the water with as little resistance as possible. It also gets energy from the water, orienting itself by the current, with the various changes of pressure in the flow, the way a bird uses currents in the air. Insofar as a bird is streamlined too, and finds in air pressure and weight the means to fly up and forward, their actions have something in common. A bird, like an alewife, may lose its momentum if the angle of climb gets too steep. Swimming and flying take place in fluid surroundings.

Selective Trout

This is the most important recent contribution to the study of aquatic insects for fly fishermen. The drawings and photographs are excellent.

Selective Trout
(A Dramatically New and Scientific Approach to Trout Fishing on Eastern and Western Rivers)
Doug Swisher and
Carl Richards
1971; 184 pp.

$9.45 postpaid from:
Crown Publishers
One Park Avenue South
New York, NY 10016
or Whole Earth
Household Store

•

The cardinal rule of streamside procedure is "get a sample." No matter how well we are acquainted with a stream and its hatches, it is imperative that specimens be caught and examined closely on every trip. General observation of a natural as it floats by or flies overhead is not sufficient. Specimens must be captured and held at close range so that color and size can be determined.

•

As the hatch progresses, a moment is usually reached when most of the trout become partial to duns only. They know exactly what they want and become very selective. This is the beginning of a great frustration for many fishermen, when actually it should be the period when the greatest harvest is reached. This is the time when the trout is most vulnerable if the angler has the right fly and knows how to use it.

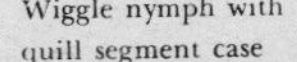
Wiggle nymph with quill segment case

Trout

Above all, this is the one book to buy. It is a window on the entire subject for $75 — just shy of what a top river guide charges for the day. However, no guide will get you through the hard times — the long winter months of the off-season — the way this book will. If there is a college course on fly fishing somewhere, this is the text, for beginners and experts. Unlike a text, each chapter sparkles with fishing tales.

The two volumes of **Trout***, in an attractive slip case, are divided into six separate books or subjects (1693 pages): The Evolution of Fly Fishing; American Species of Trout and Grayling; Physiology, Habitat, and Behavior; The Tools of the Trade; Casting, Wading and Other Skills; Trout Strategies, Techniques, and Tactics. Color plates, drawings, and diagrams are all done by the author*

Eighty-seven pages are devoted to a primer of modern fly-casting. Few books convey flycasting well, because understanding it relies so much upon feel. This section comes as close to imparting feel as a book can.

Trout
Ernest Schwiebert
1978; 1745 pp.
(2 volumes)

$75 postpaid from:
E.P. Dutton and Co.
Two Park Avenue
New York, NY 10016

•

Stealth and cunning are the primary rules. Your approach must be muffled, and you cannot plunge through the stream-side willows and alders without alarming the fish. Your final presentation must be gentle, placing your fly softly in the current so the trout will not be frightened. Careful fishermen will most often approach from downstream on a small river, behind skittish trout, and usually conceal themselves behind willows and tree trunks and grass. It is valuable to watch the reaction of the fish, either taking the fly readily or refusing it. Such lessons are not easily learned on larger streams, where you seldom see the trout at close range.

•

There are moods when the cacophony and leg-wearing power of a big river become oppressive. Difficult wading and countless double hauls can erode both body and soul. Big water holds big trout, and there is a period in the maturing in the career of every fisherman when he is addicted to the pursuit of a trophy-size fish. Once you have that fever in your blood, it is a passion that drives you beyond good judgment. Your behavior is so irrational that only a turned ankle, casting arm stiff and aching from big-river casting, or swollen knees hurt in a fall among slippery rocks will help you regain your senses. After such aberrations, it is time for the tranquility of some unpretentious brook and its peaceful music will restore your perspective.

A River Never Sleeps

Haig-Brown, a famous Canadian sportsman and naturalist, lived on the banks of the Campbell River on Vancouver Island, British Columbia. He describes the wonderful experience it is to know one river well. He knew the Campbell River intimately and he takes you there and to other favorite Pacific Northwest waters, month by month, in pursuit of winter steelhead, spring sea run cutthroat, summer trout, and the fall salmon run. Beautifully written, it is already a classic of modern angling literature.

A River Never Sleeps
Roderick L. Haig-Brown
1974; 191 pp.

$9 postpaid from:
Crown Publishers
One Park Avenue South
New York, NY 10016
or Whole Earth
Household Store

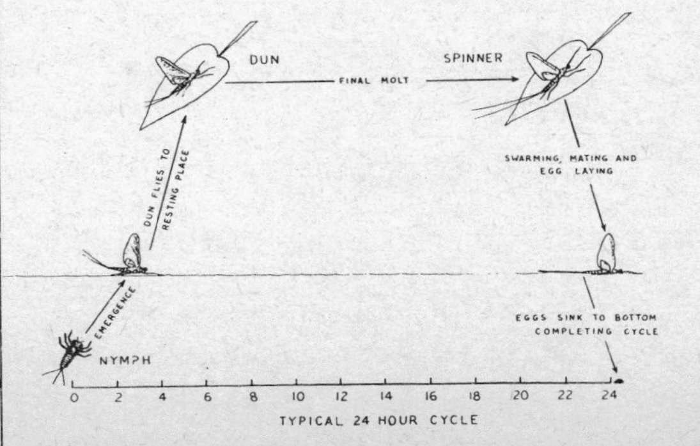

Trout Fishing

Those overwhelmed by **Trout** *and its price tag, particularly beginners, should try this one. It covers all someone new to the sport needs to know, with colorful tales of fishing the world's great rivers. Brooks writes clearly on casting techniques and explains the playing and landing of fish and the art of wading — a good primer. I encourage you to read at least this one book before you wade into the delicate environs of trout.*

Trout Fishing
Joe Brooks
1972; 217 pp.

$15 postpaid from:
Harper and Row
Keystone Industrial Park
Scranton, PA 18512
or Whole Earth
Household Store

Fly Fisherman

Here's the magazine for fly fishermen. Six issues for $11.97, or $1.95 per issue. The 1980 late-season issue contains articles on Floating Nymphs on Spring Creeks, Low Water Trouting, The Tweed Clinch, Matching the Hopperhatch (All Hoppers Are Not Equal), Small Streams of the Northwoods (Fishing the Impossible Places), The Salmon-Fly Hatches (Big Insects That Bring Fish to the Surface), Reaching the Fish on the Salmon-Fly Hatch (Techniques and Tactics), Float Tubes (An Evaluation). The ads will point you to the reputable guides and retailers. The articles will keep you abreast of developments in fly fishing and good fishing spots in your region.

Fly Fisherman
Don Zahner, Editor

$11.97 /year (6 issues)
from:
Fly Fisherman Magazine
Circulation Department
P.O. Box 2705
Boulder, CO 80322

•

Eastern fly fishermen, looking for diversity in their sport, travel to western states, passing in transit western fly fishermen making the pilgrimage to storied eastern waters to sharpen their light tackle skills. I often visualize planeloads of these traveling fishermen at the head of vapor trails that criss-cross the sky as I enjoy another day of fly-fishing on the streams of southwestern Wisconsin. ■

THE RISING SUN
NEIGHBORHOOD NEWSLETTER

I'd like to tell you about Jonah, the guy who lives in the Bible about halfway between Elijah and Luke. A lot of you probably think Jonah is the story of a man and his whale. That's not actually true. Jonah is the story about the joy of hatred. Jonah is the story about that exhilarating feeling you get when you discover someone who is really morally more reprehensible than you are. Jonah discovered that joy, and Jonah's basic thing was hating Ninevites. Ninevites lived far away from him, and he'd never met any of them, but he had a lot of data about them.

continued on next spread

Professional Guide's Manual

If you're eating meat, deerhunting is about the most honest and economical way to go about it. This bargain book from Herter's has all the information you need to find, shoot, and butcher your deer. It's also chocked with tips on fishing, camping, storing stuff, and other sundry.
—SB
[Suggested by Peter Rabbit]

Professional Guide's Manual
George Leonard Herter and Jacques P. Herter
1966; 98 pp.

$1.80 postpaid from:
Herter's, Inc.
R.R.2, Interstate 90
Waseca, MN 56093

To use the "Back Carry" method, slit the skin through each hind leg as the illustration shows. Through these slits put the corresponding front legs. Put sharp sticks through the front legs to lock them in place. To get the deer on your back, set the deer up on his rump in a sitting position. Spread the hind legs apart and sit between them. Grasp a front leg in each hand, lean backward and swing the deer up on your back. Put both arms through the loops formed by the legs. Now go on your hands and knees and lean forward. Bring up first one foot then the other until you are erect. Whistle and sing as you carry out the deer when using this method so no one can possibly mistake the deer on your back for a live one.

Getting the Most from Your Game & Fish

An amazingly thorough and well-illustrated opus on preparing wild meat. It includes taxidermy (especially the brand-new technology of "injectadermy"), preparation of pelts and hides, trapping . . . This is warm-hearted, up-to-date quality from good old Garden Way. (See road kills article, p. 362.)
—SB

Getting the Most from Your Game and Fish
(A Complete How-to from Field to Kitchen . . . and a Lot More)
Robert Candy
1978; 278 pp.

$8.95 postpaid from:
Garden Way Publishing Company
Charlotte, VT 05445
or Whole Earth Household Store

ON RELEASING FISH

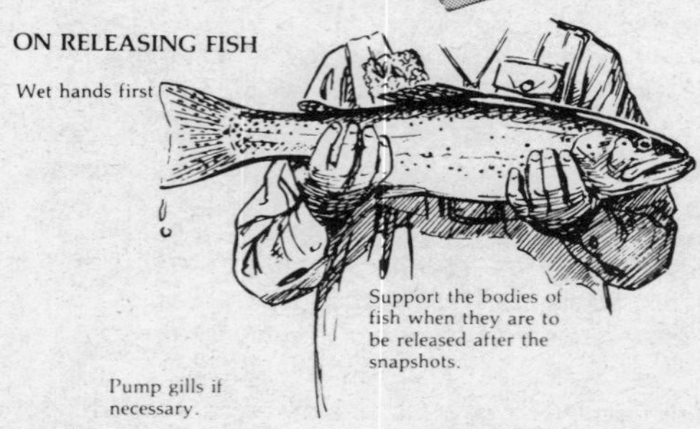

Wet hands first
Support the bodies of fish when they are to be released after the snapshots.

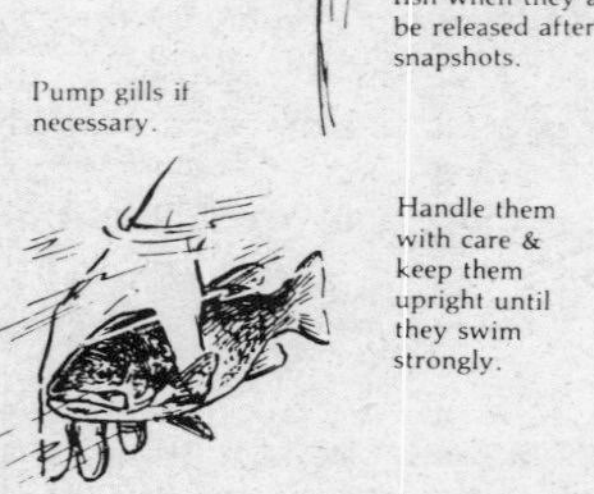

Pump gills if necessary.
Handle them with care & keep them upright until they swim strongly.

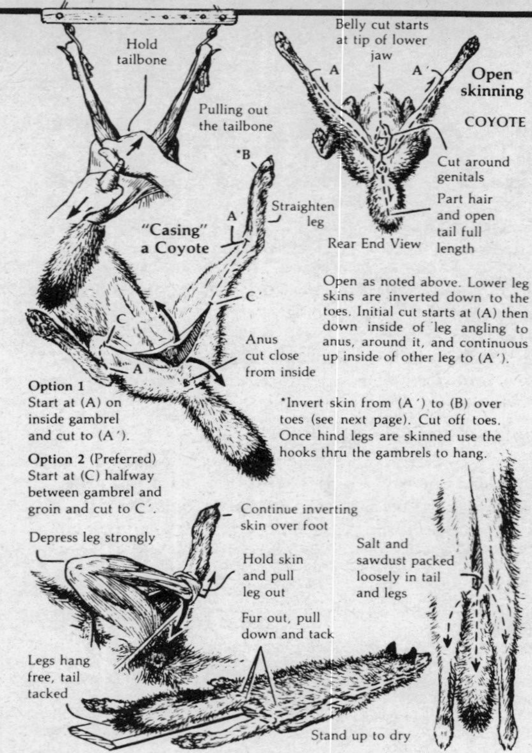

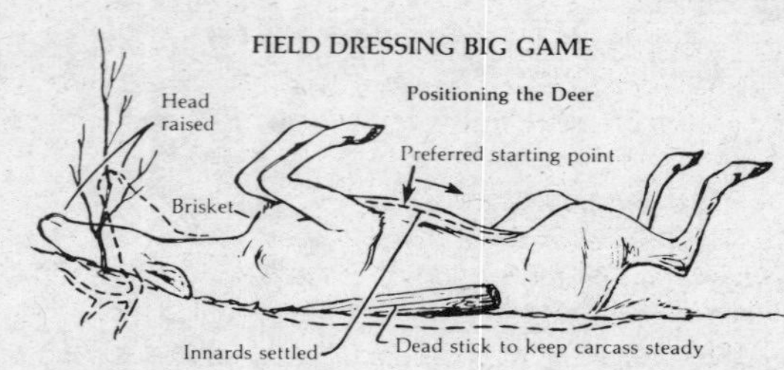

Hold tailbone
Pulling out the tailbone
Belly cut starts at tip of lower jaw
Open skinning
COYOTE
Cut around genitals
Part hair and open tail full length
Rear End View
Straighten leg
"Casing" a Coyote
Anus cut close from inside
Open as noted above. Lower leg skins are inverted down to the toes. Initial cut starts at (A) then down inside of leg angling to anus, around it, and continuous up inside of other leg to (A').
Option 1
Start at (A) on inside gambrel and cut to (A').
Option 2 (Preferred)
Start at (C) halfway between gambrel and groin and cut to C'.
*Invert skin from (A') to (B) over toes (see next page). Cut off toes. Once hind legs are skinned use the hooks thru the gambrels to hang.
Depress leg strongly
Continue inverting skin over foot
Hold skin and pull leg out
Fur out, pull down and tack
Salt and sawdust packed loosely in tail and legs
Legs hang free, tail tacked
Stand up to dry

FIELD DRESSING BIG GAME
Positioning the Deer
Head raised
Preferred starting point
Brisket
Innards settled
Dead stick to keep carcass steady

Venison getting

I don't know anything about sporty hunting. I'm a good poacher. I've thought a lot about it and decided that if there's going to be meat on our table I'm going to put it there. I hunt with a .22 Winchester magnum with a 4x scope. I have a blind overlooking a big block of salt in a creek bottom. The deer come there every morning and evening. I watch them. I call them with a Herter's Deer Call. I ask them if any among them is ready to die. I tell them that we will use the energy we get from eating their flesh in a way that would please them. I don't forget those words. Almost always it is a doe without a fawn or a lone buck that tells me he will join us. I shoot them in the chest from no further than 50 yards. They die almost instantly. I feel their spirit enters me everytime. It feels good. That's all I know about killing deer.

Joy — Love — All Blessings
Peter Rabbit
Libre, Colorado

Orvis

The most prestigious fishing and hunting gear. Very good stuff at occasionally take-your-breath-away prices. Probably worth it sometimes if you use and appreciate like mad.
—SB

Orvis
Spring and Fall Catalogs

free from:
The Orvis Company
Manchester, VT 05254

Camo Gun and Bow Tape

Eliminates the glare that spooks game. Will not harm gun blueing or stock finishes, protects against scratches. May be peeled off and used again. Roll measures 20" x 2" (400 sq. inches), will cover one gun or two bows. Use on vacuum bottles, outboard motors, too.
SH2961-00 — 1 Roll $5.80

Camo Compac

New. Pocket size make up kit contains four colors to mask hands, neck, and face. Unbreakable case has small mirror, fits any shirt pocket. Colors are easily removed with soap and water.
SH2960-00 — 1 Kit $7.95

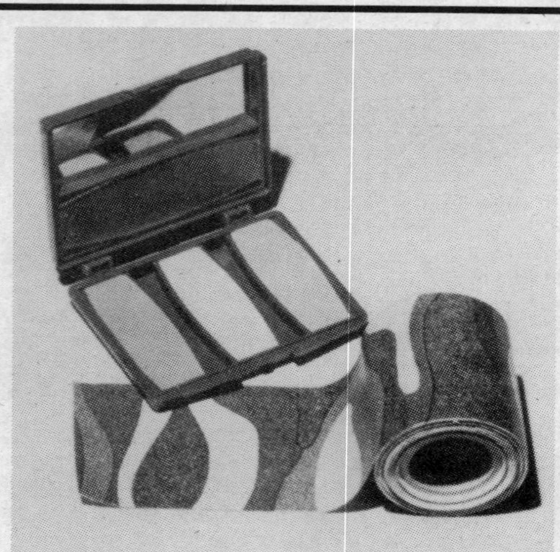

Thos. D. Robinson & Son, Ltd.

Big fat catalog of hunting, fishing, and camping stuff at very good prices. One way to shop is get the critique on quality items from highly selective catalogs like Orvis and then check for the same item in Robinson. Learn where it's expensive, buy where it's cheap.
—SB

Thos. D. Robinson & Son, Ltd.
Catalog

free from:
Thos. D. Robinson
& Son, Ltd.
321 Central Avenue
White Plains, NY 10606

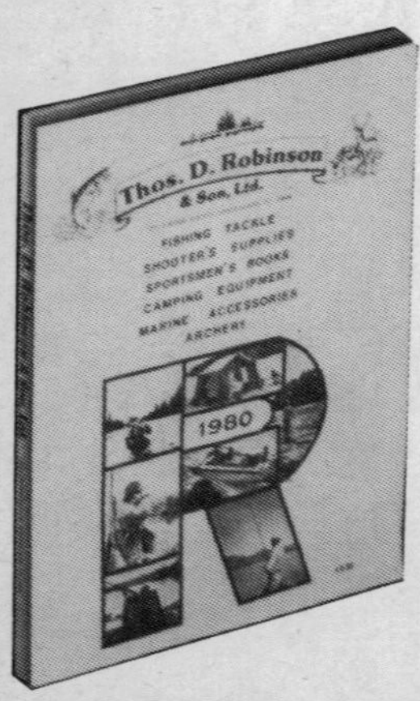

1980

New Penn 450SS Skirted Spool
Light skirted spool reel with exceptionally fast retrieve and internal automatic bail system for both salt and fresh water. All the features of the 550SS, including strong stainless steel bail and Teflon multi-disc drag. Gear ratio 5.1-1 Capacity approximately 250 yds./10 lb. mono. Weight 14 oz. $40.65

Gerber Sportsmen's Knives — **GERBER** — **The Most Useable Knives in Existence**

The Legend as it's Told —The Blade as it's Used

Gerber® Presentation Series	Order No.	Blade Steel	Blade Design	Blade Length	Blade Thickness	Overall Length	Sheath	Price
Skinning	400S	440-C Surg'l. Stnls.	Drop Point	4"	.156"	9"	Yes	$61.99
Hunting & Camping	425S	440-C Surg'l. Stnls.	Trail-ing Point	4¼"	.156"	9½"	Yes	$61.99
Fish & Game	450S	440-C Surg'l. Stnls.	trail-ing Point	4½"	.156"	9½"	Yes	$59.99
Big Game	475S	440-C Surg'l. Stnls.	Trail-ing Point	4¾"	.187"	9¾"	Yes	$63.59
Heavy Duty Hunting	525S	440-C Surg'l. Stnls.	Trail-ing Point	5¼"	.187"	10¼"	Yes	$63.59
Survival Knives Gerber®								
Mark I Survival Knife	MkI	Special Alloy Tool Steel	Compound Curve	5"	.250"	9"	Yes	$33.99
Mark II Survival Knife	MkII	Special Alloy Tool Steel	Compound Curve with Wasp Waist	6¾"	.250"	12"	Yes	$39.59

BROWNING
BL-22 LEVER ACTION RIFLE
Rugged dependability and accuracy . . . classic lines of the legendary Old West.
• Short Lever Throw.
• Will Handle Mixed Loads.
• Available in Two Grades.
• Exceptional Accuracy.
• Three Position Hammer.

Grade I — SUG. LIST $179.95 — SPECIAL $145.85
Grade II — SUG. LIST $204.95 — SPECIAL $165.39

Armorhide® Hunting Knives	Order No.	Blade Steel	Blade Design	Blade Length	Blade Thickness	Overall Length	Sheath	Price
Drop Point Hunter	A-475	High Speed Tool Steel	Drop Point	4¾"	.100"	9⅜"	Yes	$23.59
All Purpose	A-450	High Speed Tool Steel	Straight Back	4½"	.085"	9"	Yes	$19.99
Utility Skinner	A-425	High Speed Tool Steel	Semi-Drop Point	4½"	.100"	8⅞"	Yes	$21.99
Drop Point Hunter	A-400	High Speed Tool Steel	Drop Point	4"	.088"	8½"	Yes	$17.99
Game & Fish	A-325	High Speed Tool Steel	Straight Back	3¼"	.062"	7½"	Yes	$15.99
Pixie	P	Stain-less	Straight Back	3"	.050"	7"	Yes	$9.99
Fishing Knives Gerber®								
Trout & Bird	Tb	Surg'l. Stnls.	Straight Back	3¼"	.050"	8"	Yes	$11.99
Coho	Co	Surg'l. Stnls.	Straight back	6"	.062"	11¾"	Yes	$17.99
Muskie	Mu	Surg'l. Stnls.	Straight back	6"	.062"	11¼"	Yes	$17.99
Fisher-5	F-5	Surg'l. Stnls.	Drop Point	5"	.072"	11"	Opt.	$9.19
Fisher-8	F-8	Surg'l. Stnls.	Drop Point	8"	.072"	14"	Opt.	$10.79

Precision Airgun Guide

Grownup's air guns. A far cry from the two-dollar Daisy, these guns serve the same purpose as a .22, only they do it cheaper and quieter. The European spring-action requires no repetitious pumping, fires the same each shot, and is a lot quieter than a pump-it-up or CO_2-type. Most guns shown in this catalog are of remarkably high quality. Prices range from about $40 for an all-purpose pistol to more than $800 for a match rifle.

—J. Baldwin

[Suggested by Alberto Robles]

Precision Airgun Guide
Catalog
$1 postpaid from:
Beeman's
Precision Airguns
47 Paul Drive
San Rafael, CA 94903

Beeman/Weihrauch model 35

Spec summary

Series:	HW35L
Weight:	8.0 lbs.
Length:	44.7"
Velocity:	755 fps
Accuracy:	.19"
Cocking effort:	35 lbs.
Cat. No.:	1325
	$254.50

Beeman/Webley Tempest

Spec summary

	.177"	.22"
Weight:	2.0 lbs.	2.0 lbs.
Length:	8.9"	8.9"
Velocity:	470 fps	400 fps
Accuracy:	0.8-1.2"	0.9-1.4"
Cocking effort:	25 lbs.	25 lbs.
Cat. No.:	2281	2285
	$89.95	$89.95

•

Pest Chasing: Pest elimination can be considered with small game hunting, but pest chasing is a different matter. Here you may be trying to rout orchard-wrecking deer or annoying dogs without really injuring them. Study the extended range ballistic tables carefully. A low velocity air rifle or, much better, an air pistol is called for. Use light, flat headed pellets to prevent penetration. Experiment by shooting at a grapefruit, potato, or the like at various distances to be sure you are not going to cause cruel wounds. Beeman's hard felt cleaning pellets are great for harmlessly adding exit velocity to pesky dogs, cats, etc.

•

A little imagination and you can supply a whole range of easily obtained, inexpensive plinking targets: Neccos, Life Savers, tiny candy hearts, dry clay balls, hard white mints, soup crackers, etc. all give a satisfying disintegration when hit.

•

Airguns are not subject to the Gun Control Act of 1968 or most other repressive gun laws. There are usually no purchase or ownership problems. Normally you can ship them, mail them, and take them across state and even international lines when traveling and vacationing. . . . Even top grade pellets only cost about $4.00 per 500; the savings over even .22 caliber cartridges would pay for a fine, precision airgun with only 10 to 20 tins of pellets. . . . Human Scale: Finally, the more you use a precision, adult airgun, whether it be to fill the pot or punch targets, or both, the more you may gradually come to realize that here is an arm that is scaled to human sensitivities and perception. This is not easy to define, but it seems that here is a tool that rewards your skill, intelligence, and precision with its own precision and a lack of unnecessary power and disturbance. The intelligent reader will find it intriguing to expand this concept.

Survival Guns

I have about a yard of various gun books on my book shelves and this one unquestionably gives the reader more reliable information for less money than any others that I have seen.

The emphasis of the book is on the practical selection and use of all types of firearms for both defense and securing food. The information is intended for the person who has either a "retreat" or a homestead.

Of equal value are the sections which cover the related fields of accessories, ammunition, maintenance, and non-firearm weapons. Whether for mundane items such as lubricants or exotic accoutrements such as cartridge converters and sub-caliber devices (for, say, firing a .22 rimfire from a 12-gauge shotgun), Tappan has produced a book that is as close to being a good one-volume reference as I have seen. —*John C. McPherson*

Survival Guns
Mel Tappan
1976; 458 pp.
$8.95 postpaid from:
The Janus Press
P.O. Box 75455
Los Angeles, CA 90075

The Savage over/under combination guns are among the most versatile survival tools. Above: Model 24C Camper's Model with takedown case and author's lace-on ammo carrier. Additional rounds are stored in a trap in the butt.

The Charter Arms AR-7 is one of the most useful of all .22 survival guns. It weighs only 2¾ lbs. and stows away in its own waterproof stock. Shown here assembled, taken down and packed for transport or storage.

Gun Owner's Book of Care, Repair and Improvement

A famous gunsmith tells you how to work on your own weapons. The entire book is presented in that detailed, exact way that only a man who <u>really</u> knows can accomplish. The photos and drawings are unusually clear, as is the text. There is particular emphasis on "accurizing" and upgrading your weapon to a level far above the factory standards. I found this book to be detailed to the point where I'd feel at ease actually attempting the work. (Most books are an exposition of the skill of the author and you don't dare really do it yourself.) Just reading through the book will enormously expand your knowledge of guns even if you aren't going to do any work. He covers gunsmith's tools exceptionally well, and there's a passel of useful tables, lists of sources, and a glossary at the back. Exceptionally good job. —*J. Baldwin*

Gun Owner's Book of Care, Repair and Improvement
Roy Dunlap
1974; 336 pp.
$12.95 postpaid from:
Harper and Row
Keystone Industrial Park
Scranton, PA 18512
or Whole Earth
Household Store

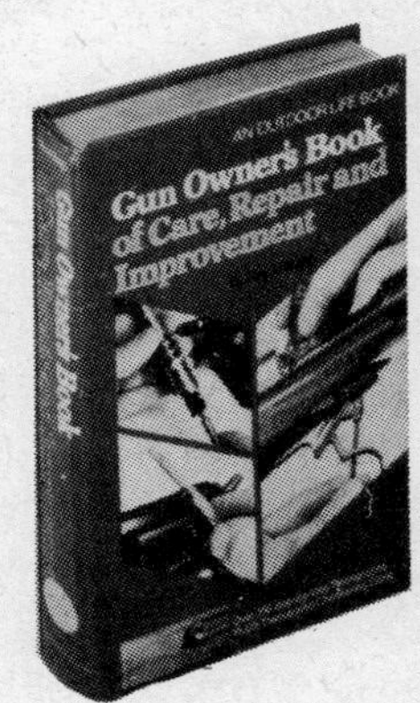

•

Should you wish to teach a small son to shoot, you have problems. Not since the days of custom muzzle-loaders have boys' rifles really been made for boys. Any single-shot bolt-action rifle you can get will have too much stock and too much trigger pull, although the barrel length and weight may be OK. It's best to take the stock off and make a stock yourself, kid-size. It doesn't have to be hard walnut: it can be soft pine, easy to shape with a knife, chisel and file. If you can't find 1¼-inch or 1½-inch soft clear wood at a pattern shop, go to a lumberyard for ¾-inch shelving and glue two pieces together. Make the pistol grip close to the trigger and small in diameter so the child's hand can really fit it.

Air Gun Digest

Just about everything that's known about buying, shooting, and caring for adult air guns is in this handsome, fat book. The author is one of the persons responsible for bringing modern air guns to this country from Europe. Everything is illustrated. (Did you know that Lewis and Clark carried a powerful air gun on their expedition?)

—J. Baldwin

Air Gun Digest
Robert Beeman
1977; 256 pp.
$6.95 postpaid from:
DBI Books, Inc.
One Northfield Plaza
Northfield, IL 60093

•

Spring-air guns make little sound when fired, allowing hunter to take that second shot. Popularity of air guns for hunting small game is on the increase.

Shotgun News

Best paper out for gun bargains.

—Rainbow People

Shotgun News
$7.50 /year (24 issues)
from:
Shotgun News
Box 669
Hastings, NE 68901

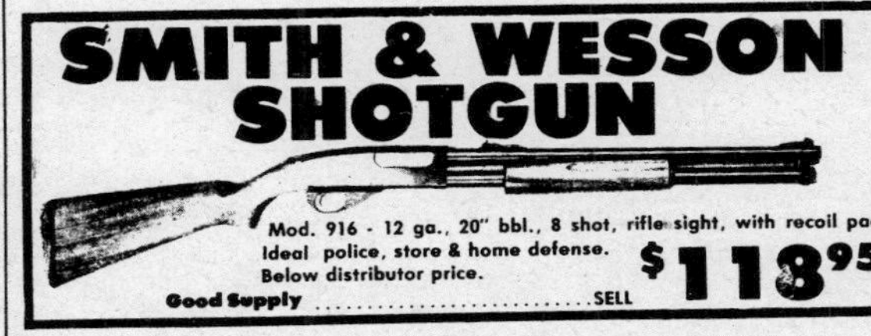

THE RISING SUN
NEIGHBORHOOD NEWSLETTER

continued from last spread

Now, hating Ninevites was not like hating Jews, Catholics, Black people, etc. Hating Ninevites was like hating American Nazis, builders of nuclear reactors, and tuna fishermen. It was a rational, well-researched hatred based on the actual behavior of the hatees. Jonah had a lot of data on Ninevites, and he was building a career on them. He had just had a story about the relationship of Ninevites, the Mobil Oil Corporation, and saccharine on the cover of *Mother Jones*. He was hitting the junior college circuit with a speech about Ninevites, and he was hoping to make the Ivy League soon.

continued on next spread

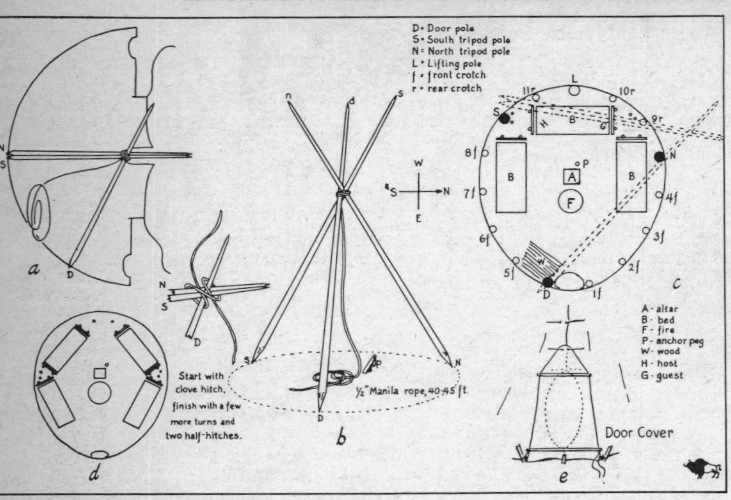

← Erecting the Sioux Tipi

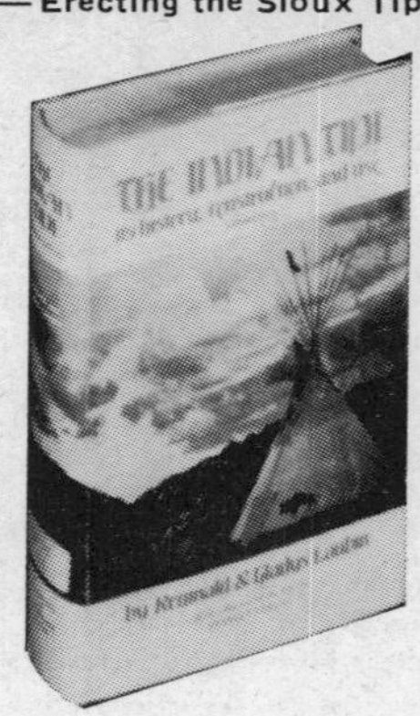

The Indian Tipi

Tipis are cheap and portable. To live in one involves intimate familiarity with fire, earth, sky and roundness. The canvas is a shadow-play of branches by day, people by night. Depending on your body's attitude about weather, a tipi as dwelling is either a delight or a nuisance. Whichever, you can appreciate the elegant design of a tipi and the completeness of the culture that produced it.

The Laubins' book is the only one on tipis, but it is very good. All the information you need, technical or traditional, is here, and the Laubins are interesting people. This second edition greatly expands on the subject. The book has no competition at all (except the paperback, which is the first edition and isn't worth it in light of the new edition). —SB

The Indian Tipi
(Its History, Construction and Use)
Reginald and Gladys Laubin
1977; 350 pp.
2nd Edition

$14.95 postpaid from:
University of Oklahoma Press
1005 Asp Avenue
Norman, OK 73019
or Whole Earth Household Store

• We discovered that the idea of a ventilating pipe underground to the fireplace is the very best way of insuring a clear lodge and the most heat.

40 below

40 above sweltering

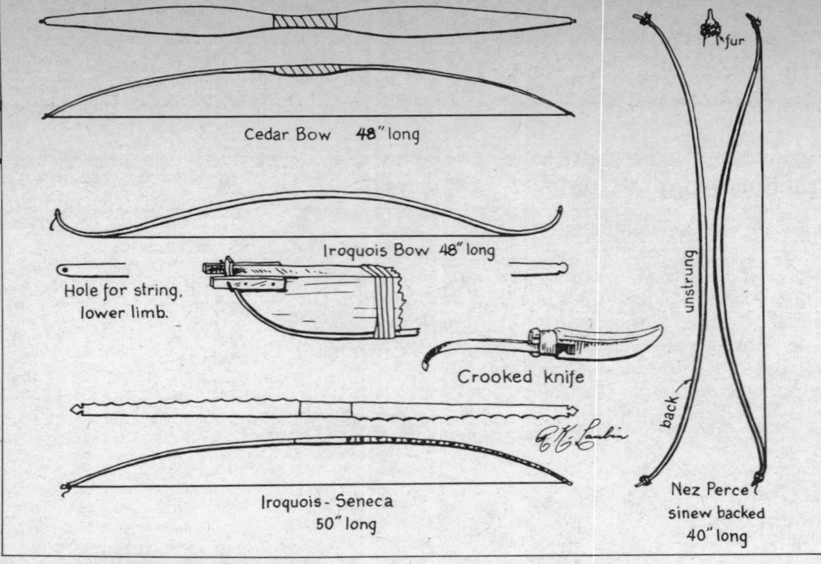

American Indian Archery

Not since Saxton Pope shot arrows with Ishi in 1923 has such a complete book on Native American archery been available. Of more interest to archers than "Indian enthusiasts," the book details kinds of bows, arrows, quivers, strings, and shooting techniques. Sometimes an excessively chatty prose style but lots of good photographs. By the authors of **The Indian Tipi**. *More Native American culture on pp. 44 - 45 and 385.* —Peter Warshall

American Indian Archery
Reginald and Gladys Laubin
1980; 179 pp.

$12.50 postpaid from:
University of Oklahoma Press
1005 Asp Avenue
Norman, OK 73019
or Whole Earth Household Store

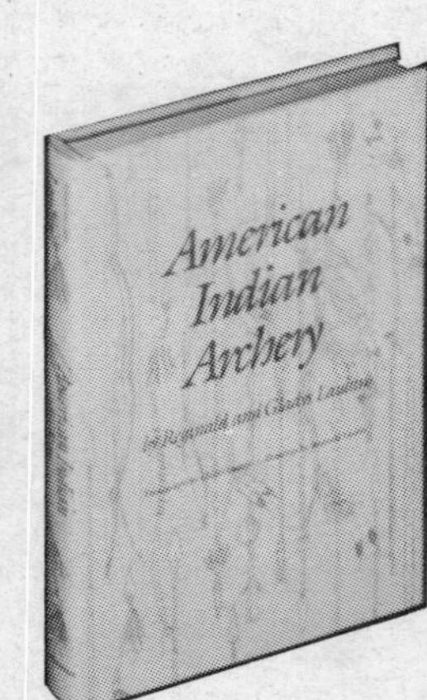

The Complete Book of the Bow and Arrow

The best archery book for competition and hunters. For the archer moderne. Tubular aluminum shafts, fiberglass compound bows, metal stabilizers to reduce vibration, plastic vanes to replace turkey feathers. —Peter Warshall

The Complete Book of the Bow and Arrow
G. Howard Gillelan
1977; 328 pp.
2nd Edition

$9.95 postpaid from:
Stackpole Books
Cameron and Kelker Sts.
P.O. Box 1831
Harrisburg, PA 17105

(Available February 1981)

Tipi suppliers

The joys of living in a tipi are many if the tipi is a good one and you use it intelligently. Here are two good tipi makers. Goodwin-Cole has had a fine reputation for many years (we've known of them for 10 years), and their products reflect not only good design but the proper spirit so important to this sort of enterprise. Nomadics Tipi Makers have also been around that long and are of similar quality and demeanor. They make a kit too, and claim to have sold more than 5000 tipis in the last 10 years! Both outfits sell canvas and other tipi necessities. Jeb Barton at Nomadics suggests avoiding flame retardant tipi covers (expensive and ineffective), but flame retardant tipi liners might be a good idea (though the chemicals may be toxic — they are to his workers). —J. Baldwin

Nomadics Tipis 14' to 26', $221 to $511.

Nomadics Tipi Makers
Catalog
$1

Tipi Kit Instructions
(You can sew your own from these plans.)
$4 postpaid
both from:
Nomadics Tipi Makers
17671 Snow Creek Road
Bend, OR 97701

Goodwin-Cole
Catalog
free from:
Goodwin-Cole Tentmakers
1315 Alhambra Blvd.
Sacramento, CA 95816

↓ **Goodwin-Cole Tipis 14' to 24', $171 to $349.**

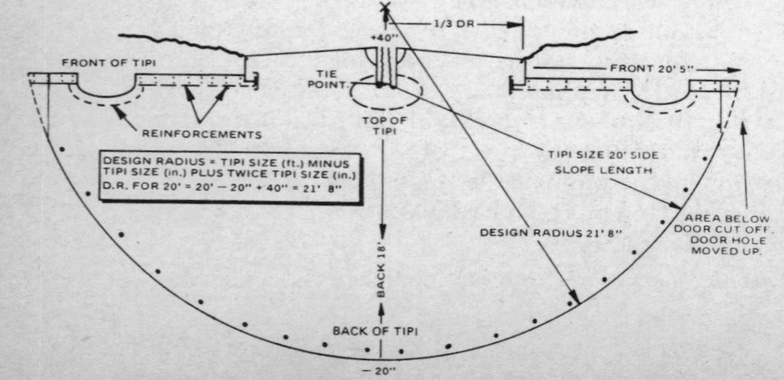

Bow Hunting for Big Game

If you grow up in working-class America, Herman Kahn likes to point out, you are given three guns — a .22 rifle when you are 12, a .410 shotgun when you are 15, and a .30-.30 when you are 18 and considered trustworthy with a deadly weapon. This admirable book offers a worthy alternative. You get all the skills and more that go with rifle hunting, and the meat, plus more pride, and less (but enough) of the killin'. —SB

Bow Hunting for Big Game
Keith C. Schuyler
1974; 224 pp.

$5.95 postpaid from:
Stackpole Books
Cameron and Kelker Sts.
P.O. Box 1831
Harrisburg, PA 17105

• Who said it first is immaterial, but countless hunters today agree that it is a bigger thrill to miss a deer with a bow than it is to kill one with a gun. . . .

It is an awesome thing to release an arrow at a living creature when it is within the usual shooting range. Like hand to hand combat, it becomes a much more personal thing. You are much more emotionally a part of the shot than at the usual gun range. It is a part of you.

Bow & Arrow

Well, maybe the best book for getting into bow and arrow isn't a book, it's a pretty good magazine. The ads will give you all the suppliers (there's scores), and the articles are better than most hobby magazines. —SB

Bow & Arrow
Jack Lewis, Editor

$6 /year (6 issues)
from:
Box & Arrow
Box HH
Capistrano Beach, CA 92624

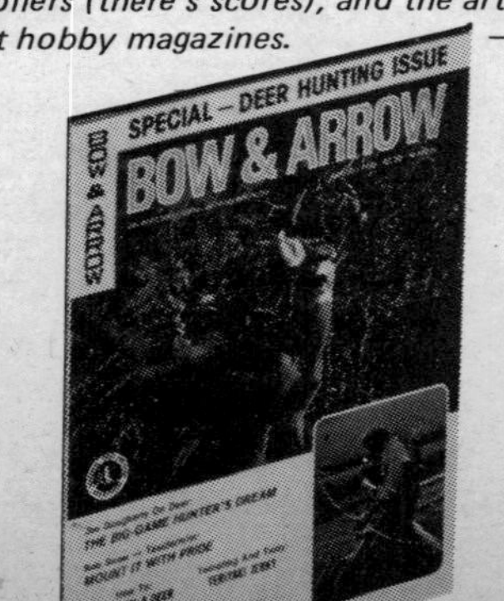

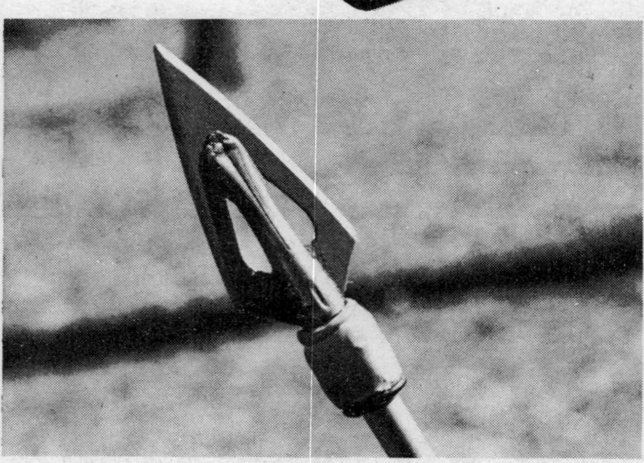

A broadhead and a drug-filled pod. On contact, the rubber covering of the pod peels back and the powdered drug is released.

Archer's Bible

This is the catalog of Kittredge Bow Hut supplies. It has — amid the usual gear (in profusion) — some books and kits for making your own bow hunting tackle. —SB

Archer's Bible
$1 from:
Kittredge Bow Hut
Box 598
Mammoth Lakes, CA 93546

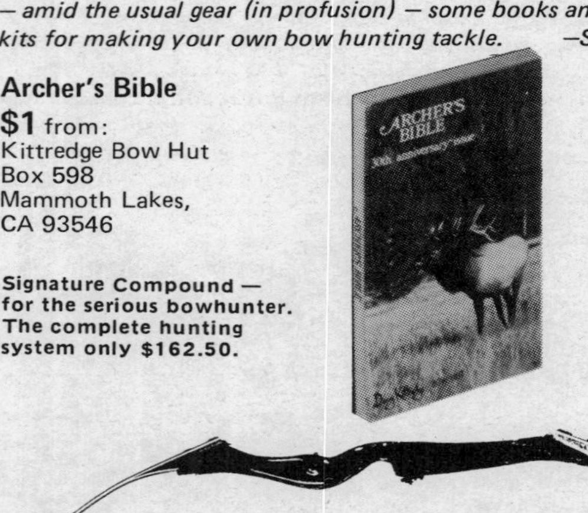

Signature Compound — for the serious bowhunter. The complete hunting system only $162.50.

Randall made knives

It's understandable that males occasionally get their knives confused with their cocks, given the similar shape, activity, and (wish) size. That's the only way I can explain the mania that goes on around "custom" knives. Anyway, at about the pinnacle of the mania is Randall knives, famously famous, and also quite fine knives at reasonable prices. In a field that tends toward the grotesque, Randall stays with a conservative simplicity of design, even in his renowned fighting knives, beloved by military men. For a fascinating treatment of the world of custom knives, see **Knives and Knifemakers** *by Sid Latham (1973; $6.95 postpaid from MacMillan Publishing Company, Order Dept., Front and Brown Streets, Riverside, NJ 08075).*

Personally I prefer Gerber (the whole line is shown on p. 450 in the Thos. D. Robinson review). The All-Purpose Gerber (4½" blade, $20) is the only knife I use for kitchen and camping — thin blade, tough edge, fine design, light weight, easy sheath. I suspect that Gerber's Mark II Survival knife ($40) is a more effective weapon than Randall's (though not much use for anything else, and Randall's are). The over-rated Buck knives you can forget — they shatter. Gerber for use; Randall for pride — and use. I admit to being sorely tempted. —SB

Model 18. "Attack-Survival" — 5½" and 7½" blades of ¼" stock. Sawtooth edge on top. 4¾" - 5" stainless steel tubular handle. 1" diameter, silver-soldered to ¼" oblong brass hilt, fitted with removable, threaded brass butt cap and waterproof "O" ring. (See detail.) Flared holes in top and bottom of hilt accommodate wrist thong and facilitate attachment of rod for conversion to spear. (Name etching and stainless steel blade only extra features available. Manual for combat use available. (Wt. 5½" 10-12 oz., 7½" 12-14 oz.) $128 (One of these knives is displayed in the Museum of Modern Art in New York.)

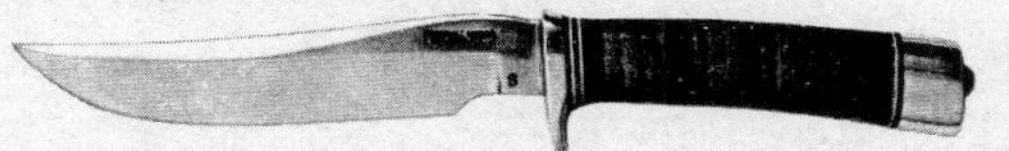

Model 3. "Hunter" — 5", 6" and 7" blades of ¼" stock. 4½" - 3/4" leather handle. Brass hilt. Duralumin butt cap. An ideal all-around heavy duty sportsman's knife. Scientifically designed for every outdoor use. (Wt. 6-8 oz.) $85

Randall Made Knives
Catalog

$ .50 from:
Randall Made Knives
P.O. Box 1988
Orlando, FL 32802

Indian Ridge Traders knife blades

IRT's specialty is a line of unfinished knife blades made by Hopkinson in Sheffield, England. IRT is a small neo-co-op organization which I have dealt with over the last couple of years. Their prices are low, the service fast and friendly, and best of all unlike other knife firms, no far right political bullshit.

Their blades are almost strictly high-carbon steel which although not as classy as 440C stainless is easy to work with and can be sharpened by hand in a finite amount of time, a characteristic not included in 440C's properties. A knife which I made for my own use from one of their blades, a rigger's knife, has seen use in and around fresh and salt water for over a year now with negligible rusting and pitting with only a minimum of care.

Their catalog lists a large variety of blades, mostly tools with only a few weapons. Their line of kitchen blades is especially good. They also list some knife finishing materials and suggest sources for others. One source which they suggest for a variety of weird hardwoods is the back of your friendly neighborhood Oriental motorcycle dealers. Nearly all his thrown-out crates are made of a variety of Eastern hardwoods. —Larry Murray

Indian Ridge Traders
Catalog

free from:
Indian Ridge Traders
P.O. Box 869
Royal Oak, MI 48068

•

The Lightweights

Many hunters and backpackers prefer a very light, small knife of high quality. This group of blades was designed with such people in mind. Each blade has a "cast-on" tang (not in a straight line with the blade) which gives some mechanical advantage when the knife is drawn toward the user in a cutting operation. The tangs are large enough to provide great strength but small enough to be completely inletted in a slab handle allowing the knife crafter to make a handle of any shape or size that suits his needs. Each blade is made of 1/16" steel and is hollow ground, so you know they aren't made for whittling. They are of American Carbon Steel and you can readily hone these like a Surgeon's Scalpel which is the design concept. A very sharp, small, thin blade will work faster and easier than a heavier blade in the usual knife tasks encountered by the small game or bird hunter.

LW-1, Packer, 4" x 3/4" x 1/16", 1 oz, Grind D, American Carbon Steel, KSS-B, $3.70.

LW-2, Bird Blade, 4" x 3/4" x 1/16", 1 oz, Grind D, American Carbon Steel, KSS-B, $3.70.

LW-3, Slicer, 4" x 3/4" x 1/16", 1 oz, Grind D, American Carbon Steel, KSS-B, $3.70.

LW-4, Mini Skinner, 2-3/4" x 3/4" x 1/16", 3/4 oz, Grind D, American Carbon Steel, KSS-B, $3.70.

LW-5, Fish Blade, 4" x 3/4" x 1/16", 1 oz., Grind D, American Carbon Steel, KSS-B, $3.70.

LW-7, Unground Blank, 4" x 3/4" x 1/16", 1½ oz, Not ground, American Carbon Steel, KSS-B. You can put your own shape and basic grind on this fully heat treated blank to create your own custom knife, just grind slowly and cool frequently to protect hardness. $2.00.

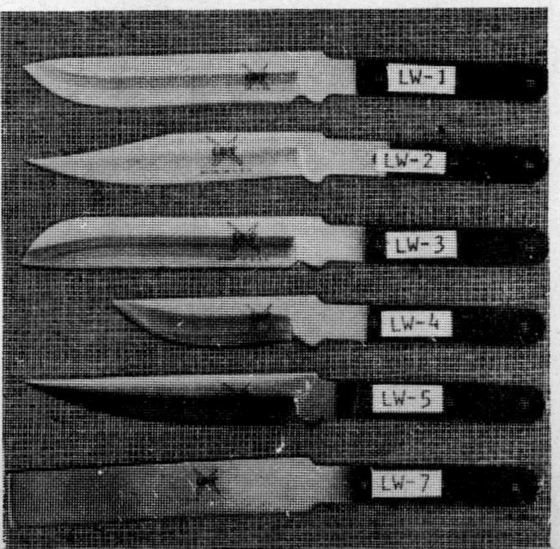

How to Make Knives

Most how-to books concentrate on mystery or history. This one does neither, despite the possibilities present in an old tradition-rich craft. Every step is photographically served, and, surprise, there's even a discussion of metallurgy and tempering! Multiple visiting pros add the interest of several opinions. There's a fine list of tools and resources too. —J. Baldwin
[Suggested by John Ellis, Jr.]

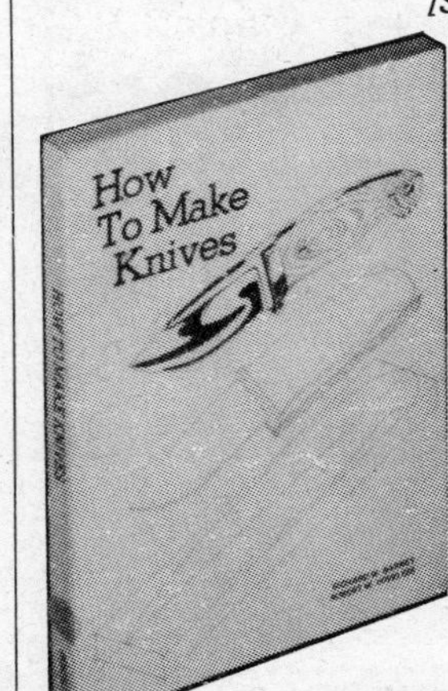

How to Make Knives
Richard W. Barney and Robert W. Loveless
1977; 182 pp.

$13.95 postpaid from:
Beinfeld Publishing, Inc.
12767 Saticoy Street
North Hollywood, CA 91605

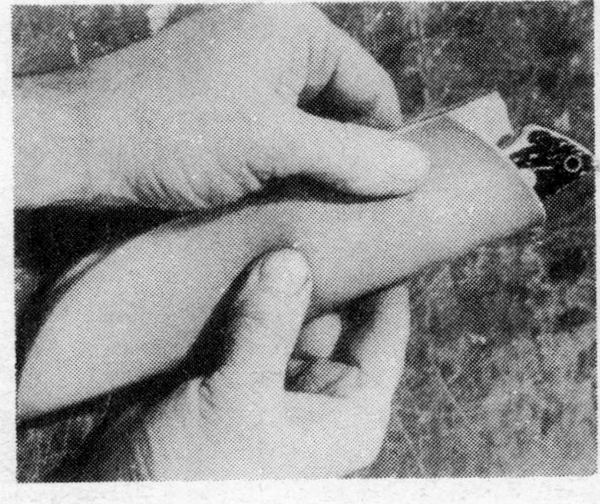

•

Yeah, I know — there are lots of knives around with stamped trademarks. But do this sometime: ask a metallurgist about notch-sensitive tool steels, and stress risers, and stuff like that and you'll learn why I don't stamp my blades, ever.

Trumark Slingshot

"My God! Is that far-out!," was the reaction given to a demonstration of the power and accuracy inherent to my Trumark, an example of what an old innovation, the sling shot, the creative application of a scientific principal, leverage, and a little practice can produce.

The Trumark is an expertly crafted piece of hand weaponry far superior to all others I have ever encountered, short of the firearm. It is completely rust-proof and, if in time the rubber sling should break after hard, long usage, it is easily replaceable with two matching lengths of surgical rubber tubing obtainable from your local dealer. —Joe Eddy Brown

Trumark Slingshot
$6 postpaid

Matched replacement rubbers and leather pouch assembly
$2 postpaid

Information
free
all from:
Trumark Wrist-rocket
P.O. Box 1517W
Boulder, CO 80306

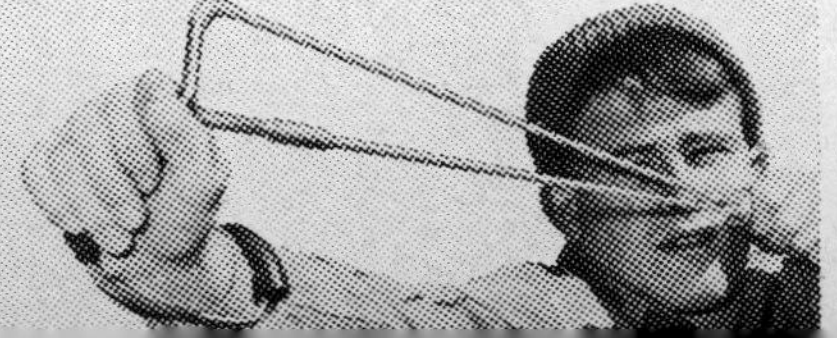

Step-by-Step Knifemaking

A straightforward step-by-step how-to book on knifemaking, and the perfect companion to **How to Make Knives** *by Barney and Loveless. This one manages to be a hair different in that it gets into making and adapting equipment as well as using less of it. The big bonus comes in the chapter on Etching on Steel — everything you need to know for embellishing the blade by etching. What this must do to the school of knifemakers who refuse to so much as stamp a trademark on a blade because of stress risers, etc.! Two opposing camps.*

Boye talks about cutting up vegetables, while Barney and Loveless have a curious line about cutting up people. I guess that does get into the history of knives. These two books should keep the budding knifemaker happy for awhile. —Charlene Modena

Step-by-Step Knifemaking
David Boye
1977; 288 pp.

$7.95 postpaid from:
Rodale Books
33 East Minor
Emmaus, PA 18049
or Whole Earth Household Store

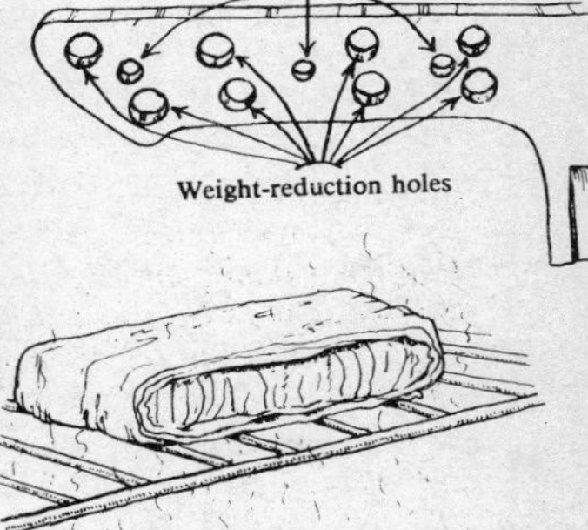

Baking a whetstone

•

Cleaning the Whetstone

It is important to keep the stone clean. Periodically wash the stone with soap and water, or use a solvent and a rag. Occasionally, it may be necessary to clean the pores of the stone if they are clogged up. To do this, soak the stone in kerosene, wrap tightly in a towel, and bake in a slow oven (250°F.).

Now we come to a vital step in the making of a pouch sheath: the first wet forming. Good cowhide possesses a unique property. It stretches when slightly wet, and holds whatever shape you mold it to. So now you turn on the hot water tap (hot water works best, although I don't know why), and put the sheath under it, getting it just wet enough to turn dark in color, but not soaking wet. Fold the sheath side together to form the pocket, and get the knife into it, about in the position you want it to be. Mold the damp leather in against the knife, especially around the guard and around the handle. Press the leather against the blade, on each side, enough to get an imprint of the edge on the surface of the cowhide. Be sure to have your hands clean while you're molding the leather, because any dirt or stains you get on the leather during this operation won't come out, period.

When you are satisfied that you've molded the leather down on the knife to suit you, take the knife out of the wet-formed pouch, and wipe it off dry. Even if your knife is made out of 440C or 154CM, nothing will stain it like hot, wet leather.

THE RISING SUN
NEIGHBORHOOD NEWSLETTER

continued from last spread

So he was not surprised when one day God came to him to talk to him about the Ninevites. He had never spoken to God before, and he wasn't really a God groupie, but he figured God knew who the expert was, right? So God came to Jonah, and said, "Jonah, I'm going to destroy all the Ninevites." And Jonah said, "Wow, you must have read my article." And God said, "Before I destroy them I want to warn them. It seems only fair. Since you know so much about them, I want you to go to Nineveh and tell them I'm going to destroy them, so they'll have a chance to change their ways and save themselves." And Jonah said, "No way in hell. I don't want to go there, they're creepy people, and besides that, what if they change?" So Jonah took off. He took the greyhound bus to the most distant point available, only it wasn't a Greyhound bus at that point in time, it was a boat. He got on the boat, and he thought he would skip town, and all would be cool. He did not know he was dealing with a Whole Earth God.

continued on next spread

SKIN AND SCUBA DIVING

Well, I got Scuba certified four years ago and haven't dived or kept up much since then, so I called around some dive shops for the current gossip. Here it is.

The learning manual of choice, among several, is Jeppesen's **Sport Diver Manual** *— it is really clear and inviting. I'm glad to hear that, since it's the one I learned on, and I loved it. There's also an advanced manual.*

Of the two magazines, **Skin Diver Magazine** *and* **Sport Diver**, *the bi-monthly* **Sport Diver** *is much meatier and more interesting.*

Of all the certifying agencies, one to be a bit wary of is N.A.S.D.S. (National Association of Scuba Diving Schools), because they tend to hard-sell expensive equipment, though the courses are otherwise competent. So stick with N.A.U.I., P.A.D.I., or the YMCA programs. As everyone agrees, the main criterion is the quality of the instructor, and for that you'll have to rely on hearsay and personal impressions.

Equipment by mail order is not so good a deal as it used to be. **New England Divers** *is worth a look to see the range of things available, but you'll probably get better prices at a local shop.* **Marvel** *is used mainly on the East Coast, especially for commercial gear, but their service is poor.*

Since all new regulator equipment is completely safe regardless of cost, and all tanks are really identical (apart from valves, etc.), you can buy whatever low cost line of hardware is available in complete confidence. This is not as true of bouyancy compensators and wet suits, where money may be well spent on durability. At the top of the line, considerable comfort is available — dry suits, jacket-style bouyancy compensators, and the like. And people have been diving long enough now that there's an active market in underwater photography stuff, night diving stuff, and other delights.

Of the four kinds of personal bodily flight — sky diving, hang gliding, skin diving, and dreams — sky diving is worth it a couple of times, hang gliding stays interesting somewhat longer, skin diving is as endlessly interesting as the waters available to you, and I'll take all the dreams I can get. —SB

Lying less than 200 yards off the coast of Curacao in 100 feet of water, this almost intact 150-foot freighter is a popular site for visiting divers. —**Sport Diver**

Sport Diver
Steve Blount, Editor
$15 /year (6 issues) from:
Sport Diver
P.O. Box 2781
Boulder, CO 80323

•

Because they are so large and slow moving, the first impression one gets of a whale underwater is not unlike a London bus emerging from a dense fog.

New England Divers
Catalog
free from:
New England Divers, Inc.
Mail Order Warehouse
Tozer Road
Beverly, MA 01915

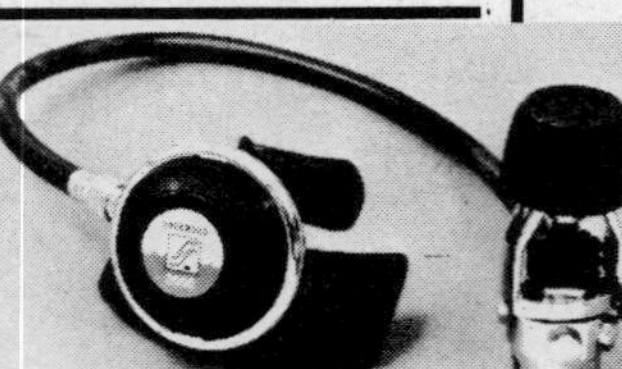

Sherwood SRB-2000. The first stage regulator is of simple, straightforward design. It has heavy duty swivel yoke, a large piston that offers quick breathing response, three low pressure ports for auxiliary attachments, and one high pressure port with a safety orifice to prevent high pressure hose whip. $126.00

Instamatic Housings. This ready to use housing provides complete reliability to 150 feet for the following Kodak Instamatic cameras. This does not include flash or camera as pictured. Flash used is No. 4029.
5315 Kodak X15-X30 $79.95

Sport Diver Manual
Jeppesen Sanderson
1975; 280 pp.
$8.25 postpaid from:
Jeppesen Sanderson
8025 East 40th Street
Denver, CO 80207

Bend at the waist, first.
Then lift your legs up completely out of the water.
Let the weight of your legs force you down.

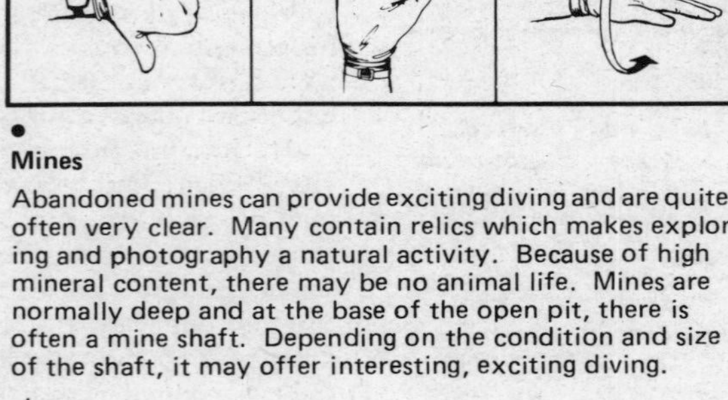

•

Mines

Abandoned mines can provide exciting diving and are quite often very clear. Many contain relics which makes exploring and photography a natural activity. Because of high mineral content, there may be no animal life. Mines are normally deep and at the base of the open pit, there is often a mine shaft. Depending on the condition and size of the shaft, it may offer interesting, exciting diving.

↓

Marvel Diving Specialties
Catalog
free from:
M & E Marine Supply Co.
P.O. Box 601
Camden, NJ 08101

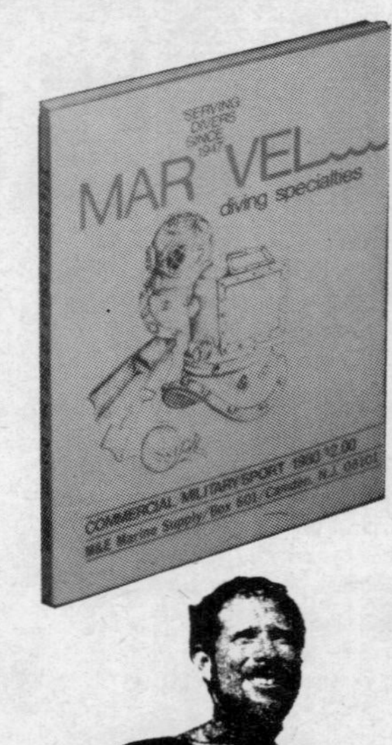

HEAVY DUTY WEIGHT MOLD

Heavy duty means 5 to 12 lb. hip weights made easy. This new mold comes with extra large cylindrical handle, hollow to reduce heat and raised center blocks for easy knock-out.
C-90 .... $29.95

All new Henderson dry suit. This handsome dry suit constructed from only the finest Rubatex foam neoprene has become the most popular choice of cold water divers. Careful tailoring has eliminated the baggy look and created a dry suit with form fit style. Model 2021 — Stock sizes S, M, L, XL in black. Customs in blue, black or orange. $340

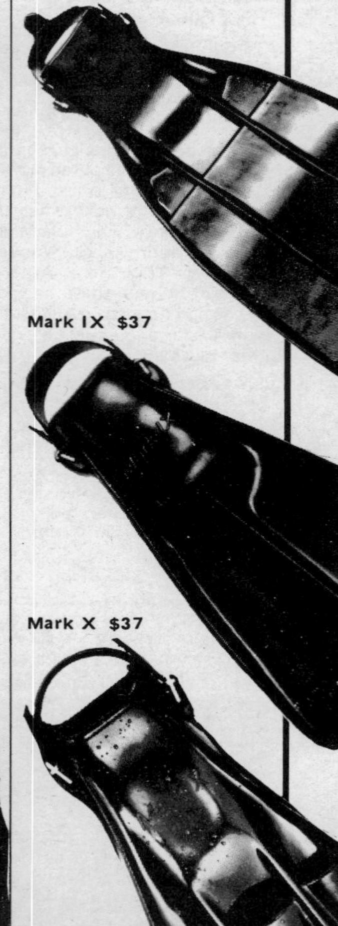

Rocket Fin $32.95

Mark IX $37

Mark X $37

Windsurfing

It's a sensational sport, maybe the best available — you can do it wherever there's wind and a bit of water. I gave up hang-gliding for windsurfing — easier, closer, cheaper, wilder, safer, more interesting places to go, and more interesting weather can be flown in.

There's no rudder. You steer by how you hold the sail. The mast meets the board in a universal joint, so the sail can rotate, lean forward or aft, or side to side. Once you get the hang of it you seldom get wet in light wind unless you want to. You just let the sail fall in the water, stand there on the surprisingly stable board figuring out what you did wrong, then haul up the sail and take off again. Get tired? Lie down on the board for a nap. Wind too strong? Paddle to shore on the board alone. Wind strong enough? Merge with it or get wet again.

Windsurfing in the U.S. is strictly one design. In Europe, where the Windsurfer patent hasn't held up, there are dozens of manufacturers and designs, more competitive prices, and a lot more "sail boarding" as they call it. As I write, a few European boards are starting to show up in the U.S. Good.

Variations in the American product — it was invented here, by the way — include smaller high wind sail and the new Rocket board with footholds, suitable for leaping off waves into the sky. The basic board costs about $895.

The book **Windsurfing** *is a capable job, not brilliant, but you could probably learn with it and a board alone, and the range of activities, ever growing, is apparent. The magazine* **Windsurfer** *would go nicely with one's first year of enthusiasm or with one's competitive or commercial activity.*

You can spend $120,000 on a yacht that won't give a fraction of the enjoyment of a windsurfer. Among other things, the windsurfer is faster than almost anything else that sails. —SB

Windsurfer
Diane Schweitzer, Editor
$10 /year (4 issues, includes membership)

Windsurfer basic board
$895 (approx.)
both from:
Windsurfer Association
1040 Princeton Drive
Marina del Rey, CA 90291

The Complete Guide to the Sport of Windsurfing
(Wherever There's Water and Wind)
Glenn Taylor
1979; 272 pp.
$7.95 postpaid from:
Bay Windsurfing
P.O. Box 776
Menlo Park, CA 94025

This may be the safest of all the modern sports yet invented, far safer than surfing, water skiing, snow skiing, conventional small boat sailing, or even bicycling.

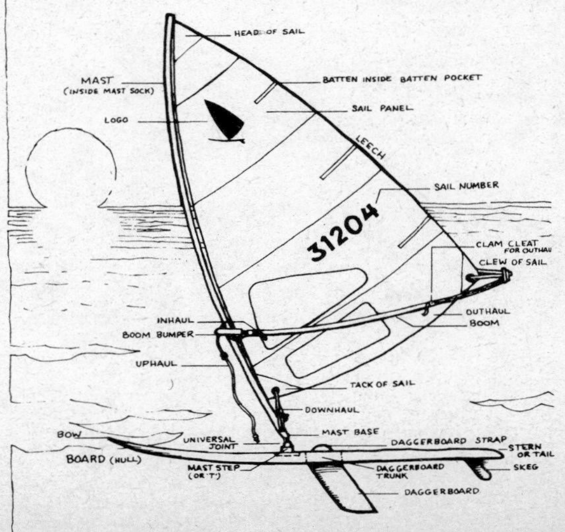

The Art of Bodysurfing

I like this book, written by Presiding Justice Robert Gardner of the court of appeals at San Bernardino. It's terse, knowledgeable, thorough, informative, and agreeably written. I learned a lot, reading it (though I can't refrain from correcting: Makapuu is deprived throughout the book of its final "u"; and "Kaha Halu" is not the Hawaiian for bodysurfing, "kaha nalu" is. Kaha nalu means, literally, roughly, "draw a line in the surf.") At any rate, he tells of many wonders:

History: Gardner surfed Balboa Pier in the late twenties, and he's evidently soaked up his money's worth since, of observation and experience. Learn how bodysurfing gave John Wayne to the movies.

Waves and surf: How waves come to stand up. The greatest wave ever measured by man. And Gardner insists on pre-immersion squat-and-study, so (among other things), you don't go out for the three-foot sweeties playing the intermission between the nine-foot killers. (I did this once. Once.)

Equipment: knowing how to swim. What to wear. For men, why not to bodysurf naked, ha ha. Wetsuits. Fins: make, fit, and how to avoid having to search for yours on the beach the morning after a big day.

Bodysurfing for beginners: Considering that what Gardner does cannot be done, he does it very well. His instructions are clear, explicit, and thorough. The man knows what he's doing.

Modern bodysurfing: surfing different breaks. Cutting. Big Surf. How to stay out of trouble, or handle it if you can't. The trough, oh God. How to pull out of a wave, avoiding a long thumpy shoreward tumble until the white water subsides.

Where to: an impressive list of places he's been himself, Atlantic & Pacific coasts, Baja, Mexico, and (natch) Hawaii. China!

If only we could breathe water.

Dear Stewart, just one more word, please? A moral lesson. "Bodysurfing will always be the supreme test of man's age-old struggle to conquer his most ruthless, dangerous, and implacable enemy — the sea." Happily, this wrongheadedness doesn't permeate the book. But dammit, why do so many surfers of all varieties hold to the notion that when they have successfully and lyrically hitched a ride from the great ocean by virtue of alert sensitivity to what the wave was going to do, with him on its shoulder or without him — why do these surfers fancy that they have conquered the wave? I loved bodysurfing at Makapuu because I mumbly inarticulate loved it. But I also was pleased to think that by bending myself to the waves I was tuning up not just my body but my world view. Americans believe in conquest, and I am an American, so I rejoiced to think as I flapped my Churchills against my thighs, heading into the water, that my friend Makapuu was gonna wash that taint right outa my hair, at least some. A day spent sliding in and paddling back out, over and over, was a varied, unremitting manifestation of the lesson that if I did not fit my way to the way of the tao, I would suffer — if only from a shore-break skinned knee. But if I yielded in a lively way, I had rushing green translucent heaven. —Judith Van Slooten

The Art of Bodysurfing
Robert Gardner
1972; 83 pp.
OUT OF PRINT
Chilton Book Company

Get this book back in print!

Sometimes the waves wall up so critically that they hollow out, and the surfer who is screaming along the face of the wave in a tight cut finds himself in a free fall. This time you simply roll yourself into a tight tuck position, take a long breath, and prepare to battle for your life. This is where you'd better be in good condition. Be sure to hold your breath tight because otherwise, even in a tight tuck, the wind will be knocked out of you. When you hit, you head for the bottom — if you are not already there — then shove off out to sea and try to get beyond the turbulence and into the green water.

This is Steve Barna using the outrigger technique at The Wedge. He has dropped his shoulder for his cut, thrust his left arm out into and, when the shot was taken, out of the wave. —**Photo by Kevin Egan**

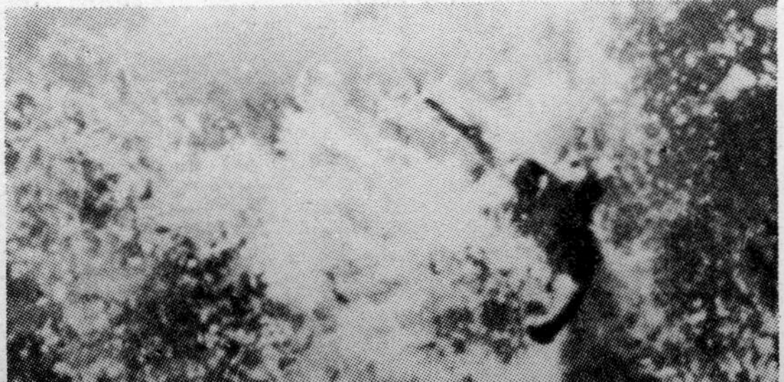

The Science of Swimming

The basic swimming strokes have been totally re-vamped in the past 15 years. Propulsion in the crawl now relies on a bent elbow "pull" under water instead of the old windmill arm action. The flutter kick has been found to contribute nothing to propulsion; it only keeps the body aligned and afloat while the arms are pulling. The new strokes are dissected here in simple diagrams, and the explanation of how they were developed shows that swimming is indeed a science. Author Counsilman is an Olympic coach who is a pioneer in human hydro-dynamics.

I was able to learn the strokes by memorizing the diagrams and watching my arms and legs through goggles as I swam. The biggest change seems to be in the front crawl, which keeps the body higher in the water with less resistance. At times it feels like being a flying fish. —Rosemary Menninger

The Science of Swimming
James E. Counsilman
1968; 446 pp.
$17.50 postpaid from:
Prentice-Hall, Inc.
P.O. Box 500
Englewood Cliffs, NJ 07632
or Whole Earth Household Store

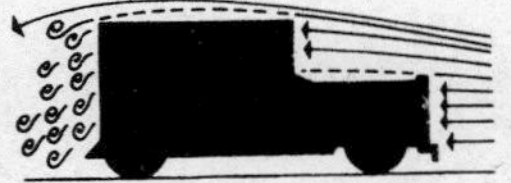

poor streamlining

good streamlining

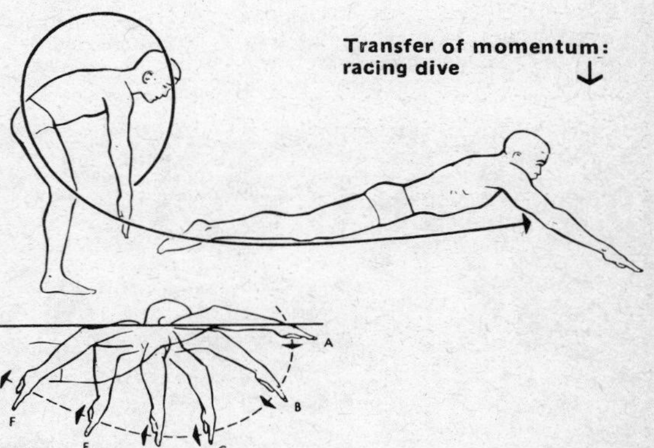

Transfer of momentum: racing dive

The correct pull

THE RISING SUN
NEIGHBORHOOD NEWSLETTER

continued from last spread

God followed him in the boat and started a very large sea storm. The captain of the boat was extremely upset about the sea storm. He was an experienced captain who knew a theological sea storm when he saw it. So he said, "Someone on this boat is not on speaking terms with God. Let's draw lots and see who." Jonah said, "Ah, we don't need to do that, I'm the one, I'll jump overboard because it seems like the only way that I'm going to win." Now it turned out that God knew, as well as any civil rights legislator knows, that the only way to overcome hatred is with brute force. And God doesn't give up easy. So when Jonah jumped over the side of the boat, God had a whale there to catch him. Jonah landed in the whale, stayed in the whale with the rotting fish and the whale digestive juices for three days. Jonah was a stubborn man of principle — it took 72 hours of an unusual smell for him to change his mind, but finally he said, "Oh heck, God, I'll go to Nineveh." So the whale barfed him up on shore near Nineveh and he headed for the world capital of badness.

continued on next spread

Anybody's Roller Skating Book

It's lunch time. A well-dressed man emerges from an attorney's office, locks the door behind him, and stoops for a moment. Bright red wheels pop out of his shoes, and he skates away, presumably to a local restaurant. What the hell? He's just part of the rollerskate madness that is in the process of sweeping this country (and several others). If they aren't skating near you now, they will be soon. In some locales, it has clearly gotten out of hand. I recently attempted to walk through Golden Gate Park. I had to walk on the grass, and even then I wasn't safe from hurtling bodies on their way to a turf landing, often face down. Police say that there were more than 35,000 skaters in the park that day. If you'd like to know more than merely where to rent skates, this timely book will probably answer your questions. (It's by the well-regarded author of **Anybody's Bike Book** *and* **Anybody's Skateboard Book.**) *For the very latest word, you'll have to frequent your neighborhood skate store; like their skateboard cousins, the new street skate technology is advancing faster than the media coverage. And then, of course, there's rollerskate disco, rollerskate Frisbee, skater's armor, and (inevitably) a host of recently-enacted antiskater laws. Join the fun!*

—J. Baldwin

Anybody's Roller Skating Book
Tom Cuthbertson
1979; 188 pp.

$1.95 postpaid from:
Bantam Books
414 East Golf Road
Des Plaines, IL 60016
or Whole Earth
Household Store

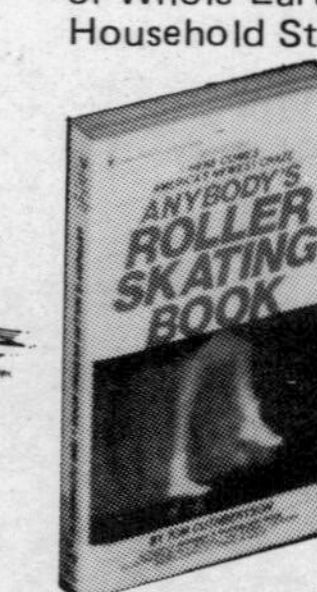

To use this heel stop, you just put that foot forward, tip the toe up slowly, and lean your weight back as you slow down, so you don't pitch forward. It's easy to do, and you'll find that you can stop in a much more controlled manner than you could with a toe stop or with the T-stop, especially on rough pavement. The one trouble with the heel stop is that it adds weight to the skate. If you don't mind a little weight, use it. If you do, learn some of the other braking and stopping maneuvers, or be prepared to change your toe stops often.

Misha Washington low riding

Skate sailing

You rest this thing on your windward shoulder, stand on ice skates on an icy lake, and there you are, sailing 40 mph across the winter afternoon.

—SB

Icicle Skate Sail
$115 - $125
Information
free from:
Waterfun, Inc.
Box 3442 Ridgeway
Stamford, CT 06905

← **Radical turn.**

Anybody's Skateboard Book

Culbertson is particularly good explaining the various hardware, how to choose, use and take care of it. It's by the same author as the excellent **Anybody's Bike Book** *(p. 410) which remains one of the very best.*

—J. Baldwin

Anybody's Skateboard Book
Tom Cuthbertson
1976; 144 pp.

$3.50 postpaid from:
Ten Speed Press
Box 7123
Berkeley, CA 94707
or Whole Earth
Household Store

•

Once you've mastered the slowing-down technique of wedeling, you can mix it in with traverses, some power-slide turns, riding in a crouch, and whatever other moves you want to decorate your downhill dance with. Or you can concentrate on slalom techniques, picking out marks or pieces of dirt or patches on the pavement to use as imaginary gate markers as you go along. The mixture of wide turns and carefully controlled slides is essential in this game; if, for instance, you have to make a wide turn on a steep hill to get speed in the controllable range as you do the wide turn, you'll have to pull two really fast wedel turns in the middle of the wide turn. Many riders call this a "check turn," because of its similarity to a surfing turn.

On the more level portions of a hill, like those that are about one-in-twenty, you can coast in gentle curves, but you can also do a sort of reverse wedeling, known as pumping. Pumping requires a board with some twang and a rider who can use his body english in perfect rhythm with the board as it turns and flexes. If you weight and unweight the board at just the right moments, and twist in such a way that you "pull" the board through each turn, it will actually accelerate as it goes weaving along. Don't let the wheels slide at all while pumping, or you'll lose speed.

Sail trikes

Unlike other landsailers, these rigs have pedals and so are legal on the road. Sail to Utah. People have. Costs range from $565 to $1535.

—SB

Sail Trike Landsailers
Information

free from:
Rans
408 Milner
Hays, KS 67601

PARACHUTING

by Dan Poynter

SPORT PARACHUTING has become a well-organized, well-recognized aviation activity since catching on some twenty years ago. Each weekend, more than 30,000 skydivers take to the air making over 2 million jumps every year over North America. **Next Whole Earth Catalog** editor, Stewart Brand, has made 27 so far.

After leaving a perfectly good airplane, you accelerate for eleven seconds until you reach some 120 mph and "terminal velocity": that speed at which your weight equals your wind resistance. By standing on your head and reducing your frontal area to the air, you can accelerate to 190 mph. It is in this way of altering the body's flying attitude that a long line of fast exiting skydivers are able to end up on the same level to join hands in a circle or other formation. The freefall challenge is to build circles (stars), lines (caterpillars), snowflakes, diamonds and other geometric patterns, one after the other. It is all too easy to transform the delicately balanced formation into a comical human waterfall.

The most common jump is from 7,200 feet for a thirty second "delay" or freefall until it's time to pull the ripcord. Falling flat and stable (face-to-earth like Superman) burns up about 1,000 feet every five seconds and one always pulls the ripcord at 2500 feet. If the main parachute should fail, one now has ten seconds to pull the reserve.

The ride down under the large colorful nylon canopy takes about two minutes, and it may be steered to land almost anywhere you like. The view is incredible and there is no noise as you descend slowly over the countryside. Later you will graduate to the more exciting "ram-air" gliding canopies which are closer to a glider than they are to a parachute.

Landings are like hopping off a cable car, or if you're not from San Francisco, like jumping off the hood of a

Dan Poynter, with over 1200 jumps (at right) behind him, authored **Parachuting — The Skydivers' Handbook, Hang Gliding, Manned Kiting** *and* **The Self-Publishing Manual** *(reviewed p. 504). He's been various sorts of national-level official in the worlds of parachuting and hang gliding. As a self-publisher he's also a self-promoter ("an egotist, but honest," say the organizations we checked with). Letting go of airplanes in flight will give you new relationships to: release, body, air, companions, hazard, death and pride.* →

—SB

—Manned Kiting

← Sensor 210 by Seedwings, 1919-P Castillo, Santa Barbara, CA 93101
—Hang Gliding

Hang Gliding
Hang Flight
Manned Kiting

I never really believed that what airplanes do isn't utterly miraculous until I started hang gliding. There at last my show-me body got the message, from running to build wind speed over the wing and hence lift, from banking the wing with my arms and feeling how the turn progressed, from diving, stalling, crashing gently in the sand, and landing gently like a seagull on a piling, into the wind. Air is not nothing. It is merely transparent, like very dilute water. We don't float but we can surely glide in it, and when the updraft exceeds our rate of descent, we rise. I have seen a person next to me run, take off, rise and keep rising to two thousand feet above me, there to linger for three hours watching the late afternoon light change on California.

The wings have come a long way since my day (1974). Besides the elegant triangular rogallos there are all manner of crescent affairs, stiff wings, even bi-planes, each one more efficient in the air. There's even motor-powered hang gliders now for take off any old where. Dan Poynter's **Hang Gliding** *has the most comprehensive coverage of the field — how-to, history, maintenance, products and suppliers, official matters, and latest trends. For understanding exactly what is going on with the wing in flight I prefer the wonderfully graphic clarity of* **Hang Flight.** *If you are where hills and wind aren't, you still can get up behind a boat or car and can use Poynter's* **Manned Kiting.**

The official organizations are: United States Hang Gliding Association, Box 66306, Los Angeles, CA 90066; Hang Gliding Association of Canada, Box 4063, Calgary, Alberta, Canada, T2T 5M9. —SB

Hang Flight
(A Flight Instruction Manual for Beginner and Intermediate Pilots)
Joe Adleson and Bill Williams
1974; 96 pp.
$3.25 postpaid from:
Aviation Book Company
1640 Victory Boulevard
Glendale, CA 91201

Hang Gliding
(The Basic Handbook of Skysurfing)
Dan Poynter
1973, 1979; 181 pp.
$6.95 postpaid

Manned Kiting
(The Basic Handbook of Tow Launched Hang Gliding)
Dan Poynter
1974; 97 pp.
$3.95 postpaid
both from:
Parachuting Publications
P.O. Box 4232-42
Santa Barbara, CA 93103

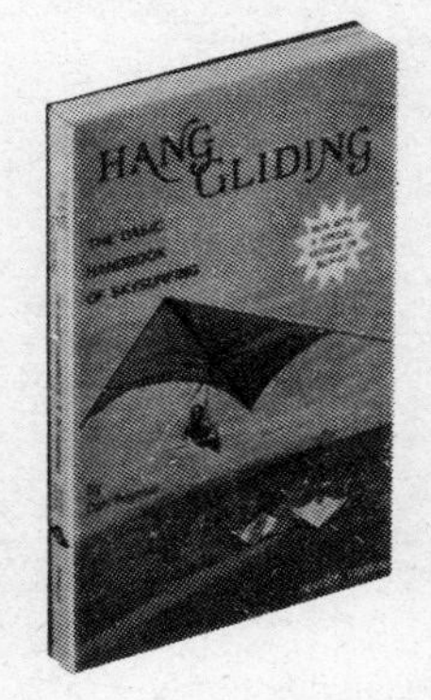

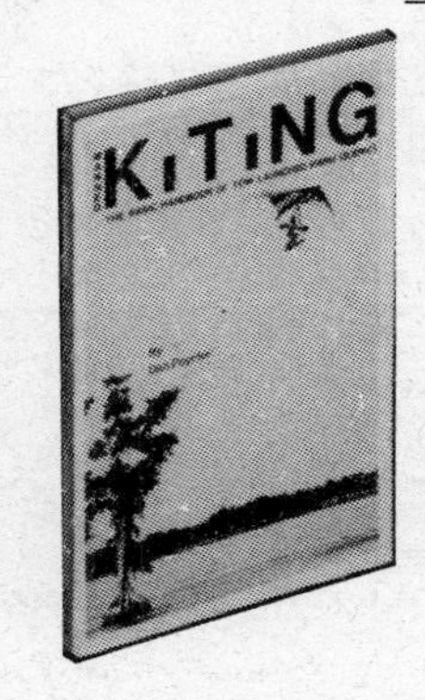

Kent Trimble in a tight turn. Centrifugal force swings the body off plumb and further increases the bank. Pushing the bar forward will further increase the bank and tighten the turn. This type of overcontrol is reserved for the experts. —Hang Gliding

LANDING

—Hang Flight

car moving slowly at three to five miles per hour. Not hard but tricky because of the horizontal movement produced by the wind and forward motion of the canopy. Parachuting isn't as rough and tumble as its Army Airborne heritage would lead you to believe. In the U.S., 15% of the skydivers are women and their percentage is on the increase. Yes, anyone can fall.

Students undergo a thorough half day training session to acquaint them with the equipment, the exit procedure, canopy steering, landings and emergency procedures. The first jump course runs about $75 at most clubs and centers. After the initial jump, aircraft rides cost $5 to $7 plus equipment rental; like skiing, it's cheaper when you own your own gear. The first five jumps are with a "static line" which activates the parachute automatically. From there you will progress from short delays to longer ones from ever higher altitudes.

There is only one up-to-date basic sport parachuting handbook and it is highly recommended. It is not only a great overview of the sport, it provides detailed instruction in all phases of novice to intermediate jumping.

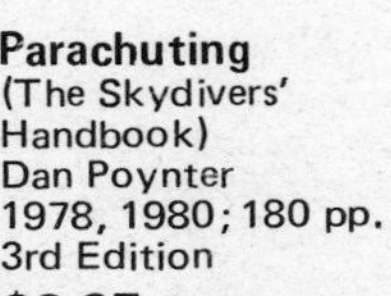

Parachuting
(The Skydivers' Handbook)
Dan Poynter
1978, 1980; 180 pp.
3rd Edition
$6.95 postpaid from:
Parachuting Publications
P.O. Box 4232-42
Santa Barbara, CA 93103

There are some 500 parachute centers across North America and the jumping everywhere is under the control of about 300 Area Safety Officers appointed by the national organizations. Jumpmasters and instructors are licensed by the United States Parachute Association and Canadian Sport Parachuting Association after undergoing rigorous training and testing sessions. Parachutists may pack their own main parachutes but mains to be used by others and all reserve parachutes must be packed only by federally licensed parachute riggers. Both associations offer liability insurance as well as excellent magazines.

For membership information and the name of the jump activity nearest you, write for an information kit ($2):

United States Parachute Association
806 15th Street NW
Suite 444-P
Washington, DC 20005

Canadian Sport Parachuting Association
333-P River Road
Ottawa, Ontario
Canada K1L 889

Freefall parachuting is the closest we have come to pure flight. ■

Even minor tilting of the palms will cause a turn. To turn, twist your body like a propeller.

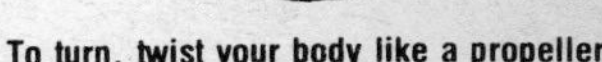

—Parachuting

THE RISING SUN
NEIGHBORHOOD NEWSLETTER

continued from last spread

Now, when he got to Nineveh, he was pleased to see that everything that he'd ever thought about Nineveh was true. I mean they were right there on the streets using sweat shop labor to run a nuclear reactor that powered an ITT plant that made neutron bombs, whale trawlers, and saccharin. He was naturally appalled. So he got into his street-beggar mode, which he had once used to support his Ninevite research, and he started things in a way that not very many people would hear them. He shuffled down the street, leaned against the walls and muttered, "Repent. Repent. In 40 days you will be destroyed if you don't repent." You had to be walking right by him to hear him but the very first person who happened to walk by him happened to be bored with his job as a nuclear reactor janitor and he said, "Wow, you're right, this is really awful, let's all repent."

continued on next spread

The Joy of Soaring

One of the hardest things in making a how-to book is focussing on essentials. However essential they may be to the reader-beginner, they're old hat to the writer, who is naturally far more interested in fascinating details, recent discoveries, personal ideas, etc. This official instruction manual book is a masterpiece of essence portrayal — the fundamental joys and fundamental techniques of soaring. One by-product is that it ages comfortably into classic-hood with no need for fussy new editions all the time. Essences are stable, conservative things.

A book that makes you want to fly, moving to the moving air, quiet and alert as a hawk. —SB

The Joy of Soaring
(A Training Manual)
Carle Conway
1969; 134 pp.
$11.95 postpaid from:
Aviation Book Company
P.O. Box 4187
Glendale, CA 91202

Soaring
Ballooning

Obsessions require magazines. Everyone knows that. How else can you keep up when leisure and technology link up and set off at a brisk gallop?

Soaring, *a trifle staid and official, is the Journal of the Soaring Society of America. They claim more private pilots are interested in soaring since the price of fuel went up.*

Ballooning *is quite a handsome magazine (suggesting there is a population of armchair balloonists). This sport has been coming on strong of late. You can get a used balloon for about $4,000, a spiffy new one for $8,000.* —SB

Soaring Magazine
Doug Lamont, Editor
$23/year (12 issues; includes membership)

Soaring Information Kit
$3 postpaid

both from:
Soaring Society of America
P.O. Box 66071
Los Angeles, CA 90066

Ballooning Magazine
Deke Sonnichsen, Editor
$15/year (6 issues)
from:
Ballooning Federation of America
P.O. Box 66071
Los Angeles, CA 90066

Kit built sailplanes

AmEagle Corporation, 841 Winslow Court, Muskegon, MI 49441. *American Eaglet: foam fiberglass wings, aluminum substructure, self launching on-board 12 hp engine. Also Minibat flying wing: foam and fiberglass construction. Information $5.*

Bryan Aircraft, Inc., Williams County Airport, Bryan, OH 43506. *HP-16, RS-15, HP-18: varying metal and foam fiberglass construction. Sailplane trailer kits also available. Information free.*

DSK Aircraft Corporation, 13161 Sherman Way, Department S, North Hollywood, CA 91605. *2 kits: BJ-1b Duster or Woodstock: wood construction; self-launch engine package planned for Woodstock. Information $5 each.*

Marske Aircraft Corporation, 130 Crestwood Drive, Michigan City, IN 46360. *Pioneer IIB, Monarch Ultralight: wood and fiberglass, flying wing configuration. Information $5.*

Monnett Experimental Aircraft, Inc., 955 Grace Street, Elgin, IL 60120. *Monerai: metal, bonded wings, can be self-launch rigged. Kit $3200. Information $2.*

Sailplane Corporation of America, Box 101, Adelanto, CA 92301. *BG-6, BG-7, BG-12BD, BG-12/16: all wood, plans and bulkhead layouts. Information $5.*

Rand/Robinson Engineering, Inc., 5842 K McFadden Avenue, Huntington Beach, CA 92649. *KR-1B Motorglider: wood and foam construction. Plans $85. Information $1.*

All these designers or manufacturers sell plans, which generally run about $100 per set, give or take a few dollars.
—*John Lee*

•
The Basic Idea

The glider's angle of bank and pitch attitude should be fairly well under the pilot's control, and the glider should be equipped with a variometer, airspeed indicator and altimeter. Thus prepared, the pilot can try his hand at thermaling. When the variometer reads up, the pilot commences circling, keeping a sharp eye on the instruments, the attitude of the glider and the position of other traffic. After a full turn he will know at what point of his circle the lift was best and where it was weakest. Mentally, he draws a line through these points, and then moves his circle toward the stronger lift to improve his rate of climb. When the variometer shows a constant rate of climb for a full circle, the glider is perfectly centered in the lift, so the rate of climb is the best. Oh happy day! (It seldom happens.)

AMATEUR FLYING

by Dick Fugett

1966 was a good year for cheap thrills, and the one I remember best was picking up a shiny new Citabria at the factory. I filled up my $6000 airplane with 42 cents per gallon gas, then me and 371RF headed west for home, where we'd learn aerobatics and other fancy stuff. The same plane today goes for 25 grand, and the gas is $1.50, when you can find 80 octane. Eras come and go, and that one sure has gone.

My monthly bible back in those days was **Flying** *magazine, and the* **Flying** *writer who did it for me best was some guy named Bach. His stuff always had more juice. There were other stories to feed my fantasies, like the Yale professor who stormed thru the skies in his 2400 hp F8F Bearcat going from one airshow to another, knocking out the fans. It was all really very attractive to me.*

But tempus fidgeted, the prof clobbered into a hill, Richard Bach hatched Jonathan Livingston Seagull, and **Flying** *reflected the changes in the aviation scene. It's still the slickest mag of all, but it's going where the action is, and that's the big bucks commercial sector. If you're looking for a good pilot report on the latest model Learjet, or trying to decide how to best spend the $10,000 you've budgeted for updating your old navcom equipment, then* **Flying** *has no peer. America's preoccupation with high tech, high cost, no effort gizmos is as obvious in aviation as anywhere else. But there are other avenues for folks who'd rather fly for fun than tax writeoffs.*

Flying
Richard L. Collins, Editor

$15/year (12 issues)
from:
Flying
P.O. Box 2772
Boulder, CO 80321

The orthodox method of learning to fly is to head for the airport, find a dealer offering flight instruction, and take off. With reasonable skill and $1500 - $2000 for finances you'll end up with a private license after about 50 hours of flight time. A little initiative can open more interesting paths though. Flying clubs are worth looking into. You buy in, pay monthly dues, and have a relatively cheap plane available, maybe an instructor too. Check the bulletin boards at the nearby airports, talk to the local pilots, and watch the Aircraft section of the classified ads. Put up your own notice if necessary, and they'll find you.

Another route is to buy an old plane, find a low-cost instructor, and eliminate the middleman. Because the FAA requires an annual inspection of everything that flies, old planes can be just as safe as new ones. A '47 Cessna is still held together by the correct number of nuts and bolts, unlike many Chevies and Fords made that year.

Low-cost instructors are not found at the local Beechcraft dealer, but circumstances make them numerous none the less. An embarassingly large number of certified flight instructors, more than can find jobs, are hovering at that stage of existence for no other reason than to log enough hours to qualify for an airlines job. Head for the airport bulletin boards again, write 'Have Plane, Need Instructor' on a lot of 3 x 5 cards, and see if you don't get some calls. Larger airports will be more productive on this one. But keep one thing in mind — you're starting off on a major learning experience, and neither the cheapest instructor nor the hottest pilot is the guy you want. Sift through the possibilities and get the best teacher.

As for the plane, flyable old Cessna 150's start around $5000. Figure 100 mph at 5 gph and you've got reasonable economy. Besides, they've virtually quit depreciating. Go halves with a friend, get your private license cheap, then sell the 150 for $4995 and make a down payment on a radio for that $1.8 million, bottom-of-the-line Learjet of your dreams.

Buying and selling used airplanes means **Trade-a-Plane.** *It's been coming out of Crossville, Tennessee with classified ads for planes and equipment for more years than I can remember. It's an invaluable reference and after you've read a few issues nobody's going to fake you out on what a plane is worth.*

Trade-a-Plane
$9.50/year (36 issues)
from:
Trade-a-Plane
Crossville, TN 38555

But before you get to wheeling and dealing and laying out cash, there's another step to consider. Remember the first time you ever bought a used car? Ha! Well, if your recollections cause you to cringe the way mine do, then employ some wisdom and avoid another expensive learning experience by taking a look at **The Aircraft Owner's Handbook.** *Although it's aimed at the same well-heeled crowd that*

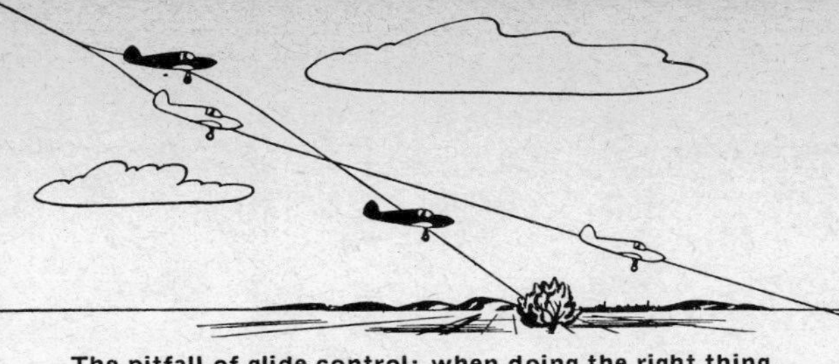

The pitfall of glide control: when doing the right thing, you get the wrong result first, the right result only later. Nosing the airplane up steepens the descent, but first **causes a temporary ballooning. Nosing the airplane down shallows the descent, but first causes an extra sink.**

Stick and Rudder

Writing, illustration, comprehensiveness, insight — it's a full-throated classic. Written in 1944, **Stick and Rudder** *is still the standard text for understanding how to fly. When someone finally musters a Library of Fame of great how-to books, Langewiesche will deserve a special exhibit. I can't help thinking this book is about a lot more than flying. Check the excerpts.* —*SB*

Stick and Rudder
(An Explanation of the Art of Flying)
Wolfgang Langewiesche
1944; 389 pp.
$12.95 postpaid from:
McGraw-Hill Book Co.
Princeton Road
Hightstown, NJ 08520
or Whole Earth Household Store

•

Stick and Throttle. The so-called 'elevator' is really its up up-and-down control. This is hard to believe but is one of the keys to the art of piloting.

•

Flying is done largely with one's imagination! If one's images of the airplane are correct, one's behavior in the airplane will quite naturally and effortlessly also be correct.

Flying *is, it's brimful of practical advice on having a plane, from financing and fixing to owning and operating. Pricing a paperback at $16.95 is the publisher's way of introducing you to one of aviation's basic principles — if it's for an airplane, it costs more. (Boat owners claim there is a maritime corollary.)*

The Aircraft Owner's Handbook
(Everything you need to know about buying, operating and selling an aircraft)
Timothy R.V. Foster
1978; 249 pp.
$16.95 postpaid from:
Van Nostrand Reinhold Company
Order Department
7625 Empire Drive
Florence, KY 41042
or Whole Earth Household Store

Money has always been a factor for plane owners, but lately there's a new uncertainty — fuel. Manufacturers, like their energy wasting cousins in Detroit, have finally understood that the times are changing, but lag time in aviation design is even longer than automotive. So we see sales beginning to slump for the single engine models that individuals buy, but continue climbing for the twins and jets that the corporations, still somewhat insulated from reality, purchase. Time is Money proclaims the executive set as they attempt to Be There Now while their Lear hurtles through the sky guzzling 170 gallons of fuel per hour.

But the air, like the sea and the mountains, will always call, so some of the little guys are trying a different route — do it yourself. Homebuilt aircraft have much to offer. On the material plane they cost less, and better yet, they offer the reward that comes from having created a useful item with your own hands. If you have basic experience in crafts, and manual creation is a challenge you can meet, go build yourself an airplane.

There's a bundle of designs to choose from. For $25 a year you can investigate it all, including the ultralights,

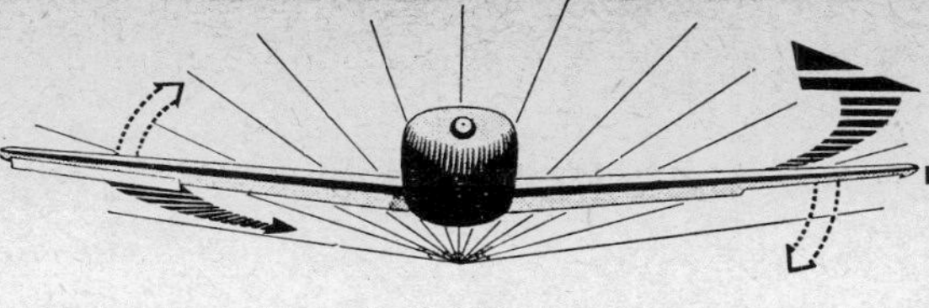

The adverse yaw effect: Ailerons have two **effects.** White arrows: **yawing effect is an undesired by-product of rolling effect. Here, the pilot banks to (his) left, presumably in order to turn to the left, but the airplane at the same time yaws to (pilot's)** right. **That's why this yaw effect is called "adverse." Pilot must kill this effect by using rudder.**

•

As you approach the ground you must keep your vision relaxed and look all around; you must take in the whole scenery, the perspective of the hangars on the side of the field and the other airplanes on the field, the parked automobiles, the trees, the telegraph poles all around, the grass, the horizon; for it is from the perspective and apparent motion of such things that you will get a vivid perception of your height; and a staring eye will not see what matters. When you get tense, you will almost certainly stare; approaching the ground, most students do get tense; that is largely why the landing is so difficult for most beginners.

•

On wings it is safe to be high, dangerous to be low; safe to go fast, dangerous to go slow. Generally speaking, if you want the airplane to go up, you point its nose up a little too much, and you go down in a stall or a spin. In landing an airplane, to make it sink down on the runway and stay down, you move the controls much as for an extreme upward zoom. In the glide, if you want to descend more steeply, you point the airplane's nose down more steeply! And — most spectacular contrariness of all — in emergencies, when the airplane is sinking toward the ground in a 'mush' or falling in a stall or a spin, and you a are afraid of crashing into the ground, the only way to keep it from crashing is to point its nose down and dive at the ground, as if you wanted to crash!

those powered hangliders that require no license to fly, by joining the Experimental Aircraft Association and getting a year's worth of their magazine, **Sport Aviation**. *It's loaded with real life experience, as well as optimism, for many of the articles are written by the people who are pushing the products. If $25 is a little steep for openers, try* **Homebuilt Aircraft**. *Not quite as authentic, but 12 issues come for $17 and it's also on the newsstands for browsing.*

Sport Aviation
Jack Cox, Editor
$25/year (12 issues — includes membership)
from:
Experimental Aircraft Association
P.O. Box 229
Hales Corners, WI 53130

Homebuilt Aircraft
Don Werner, Editor
$17/year (12 issues)
from:
Werner and Werner Corporation
606 Wilshire Boulevard
Suite 100
Santa Monica, CA 90401

The two homebuilt designs that interest me most are both by Burt Rutan, who sits out in the Southern California desert and keeps dreaming up big steps forward. The Quickie, for example. Imagine an 18 hp powerplant pulling a tiny singleseater along at 125 mph, or throttled back to cruise rpm and getting 100 mpg. Then there's also the VariEze, a canard — the wing's in back and the tail is up front — that nears 200 mph with a 100 hp engine. Average building costs have been $10,000 and up for the VariEze, maybe half that for the Quickie. The first time you see either one of these machines you'll rub your eyes and think it's something that escaped from **Star Wars**, *but hundreds of them are flying already and a lot more are being built, so they must be real.*

Quickie kit $4,850 (includes engine) plus shipping. Information kit $8 postpaid. Brochure free. All from Quickie Aircraft Company, Hangar 68, Mojave Airport, Mojave, CA 93501.

VariEze plans $139 postpaid. Kit $5000 (approx. — no engine). Brochure free. All from Rutan Aircraft Factory, Building 13, Airport, Mojave, CA 93501.

Regardless of whether you build it or buy it there may come a time when one of those machines is finally yours, and when you finally own the sky you'll meet many of the realities of flight. You won't need help with the ones that are fun, but there is another reality that's based on the universal principle about free lunches. You'll run into it when that scratchy old radio packs up and dies, and the guy in the shop starts quoting replacement prices, or when your mechanic strokes his chin and calmly announces that it's time to major your engine, and you faint.

Limited assistance is available. First of all there's our old friend **Trade-a-Plane**: *in addition to all the used aircraft*

← Rutan's 'Quickie' **—Homebuilt Aircraft**

Aeronautical Charts

Mack Taylor is a friend who has a fondness for the blank places on other people's continents. He walks into them in his tennis shoes and makes friends with the chief and walks out and tells stories about how the main hazard in the jungle is dead-eye monkeys who shit on you from the trees. Mack says that often the only maps with information in the blanks are the ONC's — Operational Navigation Charts, available for $1.95 apiece. Get them, and other flight charts, by catalog from NOAA. —*SB*

National Oceanic and Atmospheric Administration Aeronautical Charts
Catalog and related publications
free from:
Chart Information and Sales
National Ocean Survey
6501 Lafayette Avenue
Riverdale, MD 20840

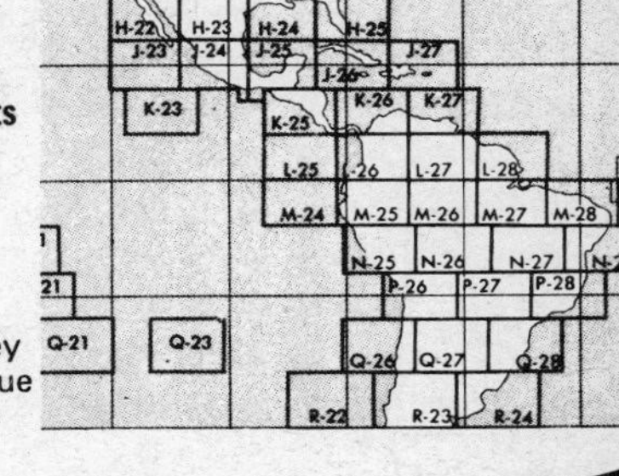

Directional gyro

The trusty altimeter

True airspeed indicator

—The Aircraft Owner's Handbook

they have good listings on services, as well as equipment, both discounted and used. There's also a relatively unknown magazine called **The Aviation Consumer**. *It is to pilots what* **Consumer Reports** *is to the rest of the world. They evaluate products, conduct reader surveys to find out the owner's opinions, and have used airplane guides that range from Cubs to Cessna 310's. Since they carry no advertising they are able to step on a lot of toes that other publications avoid. If you have any major expenses coming up, starting with buying the plane, this little journal could save you a bundle.*

The Aviation Consumer
(The consumer report to pilots and aviation owners)
Richard B. Weeghman, Editor
$39/year (24 issues)
from:
The Aviation Consumer
Subscription Department
P.O. Box 972
Farmingdale, NY 11737

On the other hand, maybe you can't swing financing for either the VariEze or the Learjet until you figure how to pay last month's rent, and you'll settle for a good book to read beside the fireplace. Flying and good writing often go together, and the classic example must be St. Exupéry, whose book **Wind, Sand and Stars** *has never been surpassed.* ■

Wind, Sand and Stars
Antoine de Saint Exupéry
1939; 243 pp.
$2.75 postpaid from:
Harcourt Brace and Jovanich
757 Third Avenue
New York, NY 10017
or Whole Earth Household Store

THE RISING SUN
NEIGHBORHOOD NEWSLETTER

continued from last spread

And that guy started yelling Jonah's message and it turned out that a lot of people were bored with their jobs as neutron bombadiers and saccharin cane cutters and they went to the president of the country and said, "We've been gross and awful, and we're going to repent and you have to, too." They put on sackcloth and ashes, they turned their nuclear reactor into a solar generator and they all planted organic gardens and Jonah was *pissed*. He was just furious and he said, "OK, God, are you gonna be conned by these hypocrites, do you think that just because they're behaving different they're better?" And God said, " 'Fraid so. Behavior counts. You lose."

continued on next spread

INFORMATION: any difference which makes a difference. —Gregory Bateson

A tickle of magnetism on a tape topples an empire of things. The thing is not dead, but long live the tickle. —SB

Ladle Rat Rotten Hut

by H.L. Chace

WANTS PAWN TERM, dare worsted ladle gull hoe lift wetter murder inner ladle cordage, honor itch offer lodge, dock, florist. Disk ladle gull orphan worry putty ladle rat cluck wetter ladle rat hut, an fur disk raisin pimple colder Ladle Rat Rotten Hut.

Wan moaning, Ladle Rat Rotten Hut's murder colder inset.

"Ladle Rat Rotten Hut, heresy ladle basking winsome burden barter an shirker cockles. Tick disk ladle basking tutor cordage offer groin-murder hoe lifts honor udder site offer florist. Shaker lake! Dun stopper laundry wrote! Dun stopper peck floors! Dun daily-doily inner florist, an yonder nor sorghum-stenches, dun stopper torque wet strainers!"

"Hoe-cake, murder," resplendent Ladle Rat Rotten Hut, an tickle ladle basking an stuttered oft.

Honor wrote tutor cordage offer groin-murder, Ladle Rat Rotten Hut mitten anomalous woof.

"Wail, wail, wail!" set disk wicket woof, "Evanescent Ladle Rat Rotten Hut! Wares are putty ladle gull goring wizard ladle basking?"

"Armor goring tumor groin-murder's," reprisal ladle gull. "Grammar's seeking bet. Armor ticking arson burden barter an shirker cockles."

"O hoe! Heifer gnats woke," setter wicket woof, butter taught tomb shelf, "Oil tickle shirt court tutor cordage offer groin-murder. Oil ketchup wetter letter, an den — O bore!"

Soda wicket woof tucker shirt court, an whinny retched a cordage offer groin-murder, picked inner windrow, an sore debtor pore oil worming worse lion inner bet. Inner flesh, disk abdominal woof lipped honor bet, paunched honor pore oil worming, an garbled erupt. Den disk ratchet ammonol pot honor groin-murder's nut cup an gnat-gun, any curdled ope inner bet.

Inner ladle wile, Ladle Rat Rotten Hut a raft attar cordage, an ranker dough ball. "Comb ink, sweat hard," setter wicket woof, disgracing is verse.

Ladle Rat Rotten Hut entity bet rum, an stud buyer groin-murder's bet.

"O Grammar!" crater ladle gull historically, "Water bag icer gut! A nervous sausage bag ice!"

"Battered lucky chew whiff, sweat hard," setter bloat-Thursday woof, wetter wicket small honors phase.

"O Grammar, water bag noise! A nervous sore suture anomalous prognosis!"

"Battered small your whiff, doling," whiskered dole woof, ants mouse worse waddling.

"O Grammar, water bag mouser gut! A nervous sore suture bag mouse!"

Daze worry on-forger-nut ladle gull's lest warts. Oil offer sodden, caking offer carvers an sprinkling otter bet, disk hoard-hoarded woof lipped own pore Ladle Rat Rotten Hut an garbled erupt.

MURAL: Yonder nor sorghum stenches shut ladle gulls stopper torque wet strainers. ■

The true story of "Ladle Rat Rotten Hut"

"Ladle Rat Rotten Hut" is often attributed to Anonymous, but it was actually written by H.L. Chace. He was a professor of French at Miami University in Oxford, Ohio, retired in 1965 and now is living in Cincinnati. He's in his eighties. I talked to him by phone about the story of the story.

"I wrote it about 1940. It was going to be part of a little article I was writing. It was in the days of rationing during the war and I thought about what would happen if we had to ration language. If our vocabulary were cut in half, we'd have to get along with other words. Consequently, I thought I'd see how you'd get along with the other half. I've never written that article, but I've always thought of doing it.

"I taught French, and I used the story in my class to show the importance of intonation in learning a foreign language. You see, if you take these English words and put them in columns like a spelling book and just read them, they have no meaning. However, if you read them with the proper intonation, the meaning appears for certain people. For other people the meaning never does appear.

"I never submitted it to anybody, but it got spread some way or other. It's one of those things that got completely out of control. I showed it to a few friends and to a book salesman who came to see me. He liked the thing because it had to do with words. I think I may have given him a copy, and he must have given it to someone else. It first appeared in print in the Merriam Company's magazine **Word Study**. I think it got in **Stars and Stripes** [U.S. Army newspaper] because I heard from people in Baghdad, Sweden, all over the world. **Sports Illustrated** found it in another publication and gave me $1000 for it. Arthur Godfrey found it in **Sports Illustrated**, and he broadcast it and very generously told any readers that wanted a copy they could have one by sending me postage. To my surprise, I mailed about five thousand of them. After that episode, Prentice Hall asked me to write a series of stories for a book, which I did. [**Anguish Languish** was published by Prentice Hall in 1955.]

"The book sold fairly well for that sort of thing. It went through four printings I think, maybe 14,000 copies total.

"It's used now a good deal in textbooks to demonstrate the phonetic structures of English. The book has been used by some psychologist to determine the ability of people to understand sound, to study the limit of distortion that can be comprehended. That varies from person to person.

"People who like it best are language people, teachers, lawyers, and doctors. That's almost all the people who are interested in it. And children, strange to say. I've had a lot of letters from them."

I asked him if it bothered him that it is often printed without his name. He said, "Well, it doesn't bother me, but it's just that if I had a cent for every Xerox copy, I'd be much better off because I know it's been copied by the thousands."

The book, ***Anguish Languish****, is out of print and very hard to find. Chace himself only has one copy. Dover or somebody should reprint it.* —Anne Herbert

The Graphic Work of M.C. Escher

Geometry set at its own throat via the images of dreams. The subjective frontier. For deepest application see **Gödel, Escher, Bach** *on p. 539.* —SB

The Graphic Work of M.C. Escher
M.C. Escher
1960, 1968; 98 pp.
$7.50 postpaid from:
Ballantine Books
455 Hahn Road
Westminster, MD 21157
or Whole Earth Household Store

Mots d'Heures: Gousses, Rames

Far beyond fractured French is the multi-dimensional bilingual punword of this party favor. Frenchmen HATE it. All others revel. Try "Hickory dickory dock," below. —SB
[Suggested by Gregory Bateson]

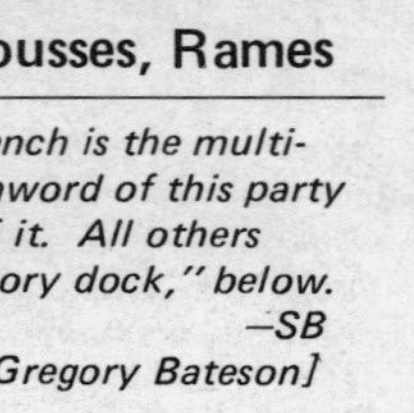

Mots d'Heures: Gousses, Rames
(The d'Antin Manuscript)
Luis d'Antin Van Rooten
1967; 48 pp.
$3.95 postpaid from:
The Viking Press
299 Murray Hill Parkway
East Rutherford, NJ
07073
or Whole Earth Household Store

•
Et qui rit des curés d'Oc?[1]
De Meuse raines,[2] houp! de cloques.[3]
De quelles loques ce turque coin.[4]
Et ne d'ânes ni rennes,
Ecuries des curés d'Oc.[5]

1. Oc (or Languedoc), ancient region of France, with its capital at Toulouse. Its monks and curates were, it seems, a singularly humble and holy group. This little poem is a graceful tribute to their virtues.

2. Meuse, or Maas, River, 560 miles long, traversing France, Belgium, and the Netherlands; raines, **old French word for frogs (from the L.,** ranae**). Here is a beautiful example of Gothic imagery: He who laughs at the cures of Oc will have frogs leap at him from the Meuse river and**

3. infect him with a scrofulous disease! This is particularly interesting when we consider the widespread superstition in America that frogs and toads cause warts.

4. "Turkish corners" were introduced into Western Europe by returning Crusaders, among other luxuries and refinements of Oriental living. Our good monks made a concession to the fashion, but N.B. their Turkish corner was made of rags! This affectation of interior decorating had a widespread revival in the U.S.A. at the turn of the century. Ah, the Tsar's bazaars' bizarre beaux-arts.

5. So strict were the monks that they didn't even indulge themselves in their arduous travels. No fancy mules nor reindeer in their stables. They just rode around on their plain French asses.

The Image

This book is by an economist enchanted with cybernetics. He's after the organizing principle in life, the image that everything comes together through. He scarcely mentions the brain, and he's right. It ain't the brain.

—SB

The Image
(Knowledge in Life and Society)
Kenneth E. Boulding
1956; 175 pp.

$3.50 postpaid from:
The University of Michigan Press
P.O. Box 1104
Ann Arbor, MI 48106
or Whole Earth Household Store

•

The meaning of a message is the change which it produces in the image.

•

Between the incoming and outgoing messages lies the great intervening variable of the image. The outgoing messages are the result of the image, not the result of the incoming messages. The incoming messages only modify the outgoing messages as they succeed in modifying the image.

•

I have never been to Australia. In my image of the world, however, it exists with 100 per cent certainty. If I sailed to the place where the map makers tell me it is and found nothing there but ocean, I would be the most surprised man in the world. I hold to this part of my image with certainty, however, purely on authority. I have been to many other places which I have found on the map and I have almost always found them there. It is interesting to inquire what gives the map this extraordinary authority, an authority greater than that of the sacred books of all religions. It is not an authority which is derived from any political power or from any charismatic experience. As far as I know it is not a crime against the state nor against religion to show a map that has mistakes in it. There is, however, a process of feedback from the users of maps to the map makers.

•

In tracing the effect of images on the course of history, peculiar attention must be paid to the images of time and especially the images of the future. Curiously enough, it may not be so much the actual content of the image of the future which is important in its effect, but its general quality of optimism or pessimism, certainty or uncertainty, breadth or narrowness. The person or the nation that has a date with destiny goes somewhere, though not usually to the address on the label. The individual or the nation which has no sense of direction in time, no sense of a clear future ahead is likely to be vacillating, uncertain in behavior, and to have a poor chance of surviving. Those images of the future which are most persistent and which have had the greatest impact on human history seem to be those which are impenetrable to feedback and which maintain themselves by their own internal beauty and consistency.

Etc.

General Semantics is the art and science of thinking about symbols instead of swallowing them whole and unexamined. **Etc.** *is the quarterly magazine put out by the International Society for General Semantics, and it prints smart, scholarly articles about the dangers of loose thinking and fuzzy talk. It's a good antidote for face value. Your subscription also gets you a monthly collection of additions called* **Glimpse**.

—Anne Herbert

Etc.
(A Journal Devoted to the Role of Symbols in Human Behavior)

$20/year (4 issues, includes membership)
from:
International Society for General Semantics
P.O. Box 2469
San Francisco, CA 94126

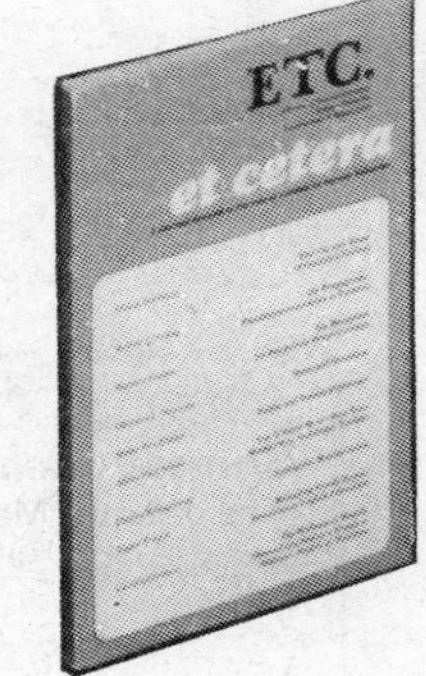

•

In societies with only an oral tradition, it is possible to have almost continuous change — like the perpetual re-editing of a sacred text. For example, if two instances of some hitherto unrecognized form of polygamy — such as a man marrying a mother and her daughter — occurred in the same hamlet among the Arapesh of New Guinea, the rest of the language group might shrug their shoulders and say, "That is becoming the custom in Ahalesmihi."

—Margaret Mead

•

An article in the May/June issue of the "Vegetarian Times" also registered concern for the fate of the world's fauna. Pointing out the need for new expressions to replace the carnivorism in our language, the article suggested some alternatives for expressions of violence towards non-human animals: instead of "There's more than one way to skin a cat," "There's more than one way to slice a cucumber;" instead of "On a wild goose chase," "On a wild mushroom hunt;" instead of "Kill two birds with one stone," "Cut two apples with one slice;" instead of "A dog-eat-dog world," "A hostile world."

—Glimpse

•

To a man asking for money, a tie can be a cash nexus. So indicates an article from "TWA Ambassador" magazine. It tells of syndicated fashion columnist John Malloy's experimental begging in New York's Grand Central Terminal.

Dressed in a three-piece suit, white shirt and polished shoes but without a tie, Malloy approached people and asked for 75 cents train fare. The first hour he collected $7.23. The second hour he told the same hard luck story, but this time he wore a tie. His take the second hour was $26, plus two offers of extra money.

—Glimpse

An Introduction to Cybernetics
Design for a Brain

We are migrating from a world governed primarily by the laws of thermodynamics to a world governed primarily by cybernetics — a weightless world (Fuller says "metaphysical") whose events are the impinging of information on information. Wiener (p. 30) is a good philosophical introduction to this world; Bateson (p. 28) is a peerless cybernetics-inspired philosopher; but Ashby is the profoundest practical introducer, profound enough to be scarcely dated decades later in one of the fastest growing fields we have.

—SB

An Introduction to Cybernetics
W. Ross Ashby
1956; 295 pp.

$9.50 postpaid

Design for a Brain
(The origin of adaptive behavior)
W. Ross Ashby
1952; 286 pp.

$11.95 postpaid

both from:
Methuen, Inc.
757 Third Avenue
New York, NY 10017
or Whole Earth Household Store

•

Thus there exist factors, such as "height of threshold" or "proportion of variables constant", which can vary a large system continuously along the whole range that has at one end the totally-joined form, in which every variable has an immediate effect on every other variable, and at the other end the totally-unjoined form, in which every variable is independent of every other. Systems can thus show more or less of "wholeness".

—An Introduction to Cybernetics

•

What is an amplifier? An amplifier, in general, is a device that, if given a little of something, will emit a lot of it. A sound amplifier if given a little sound (into a microphone) will emit a lot of sound. And a money-amplifier would be a device that, if given a little money, would emit a lot.

Such devices work by having available a generous reservoir of what is to be emitted, and then using the input to act as controller to the flow from the reservoir.

—An Introduction to Cybernetics

•

The development of life on earth must thus *not* be seen as something remarkable. On the contrary, it was inevitable. It was inevitable in the sense that if a system as large as the surface of the earth, basically polystable, is kept gently simmering dynamically for five thousand million years, then nothing short of a miracle could keep the system away from those states in which the variables are aggregated into intensely self-preserving forms.

—Design for a Brain

Number Words and Number Symbols

Suppose you want to help human communication to re-understand itself. So much of that understanding is wrapped up in numbers that if you penetrate the one you may have a foothold to tweak the other onto a new course. Invent language and you invent humans.

This book penetrates numbers.

—SB

Number Words and Number Symbols
(A Cultural History of Numbers)
Karl Menninger
1958, 1969; 480 pp.

$10.95 postpaid from:
The MIT Press
28 Carleton Street
Cambridge, MA 02142
or Whole Earth Household Store

•

In the seaports and market places of the Red Sea, Arabia, and East Africa, merchants have evolved a finger language that is understood in every market of every country in the region. Buyers and sellers come to terms underneath a cloth, a fold of garment or a strip of muslin from a turban, by touching the fingers of each other's hand and thus bargaining in complete privacy.

•

1 2 3 4 5 6 7 8 9 and 0 — these ten symbols which today all peoples use to record numbers, symbolize the world-wide victory of an idea. There are few things on earth that are universal, and the universal customs which man has successfully established are fewer stilll. But this is one boast he can make: The new Indian numerals are indeed universal.

Albrecht Durer's year dates. In writing the dates of the years around 1495, Durer illustrated the development of the 4 into its present form. From three of his drawings dated in successive years.

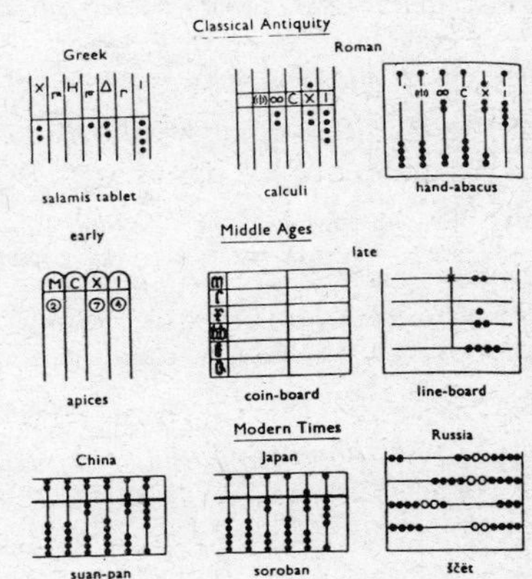

Various forms taken by the counting board throughout history; the number 2074 is represented on all of them.

THE RISING SUN
NEIGHBORHOOD NEWSLETTER

continued from last spread

So Jonah stomped to a hill outside of town and sat under a tree praying for the Ninevites to show their true nature and for God to fry them alive. And all that happened was that God destroyed the tree Jonah was sitting under so he got a sunburn. Jonah said, "God, how come you destroyed this tree? This tree never did nothing." He did a ten minute rap about the tree and how trees are important and you can't just destroy them for no reason. And God said, "How come, Jonah, how come, wherefore why is it, that you care so much about that tree, when you have no pity at all for Nineveh, a city that has a whole lot of folks in it, and some children and animals and you wanted me to kill them all? How come you didn't care about them?" And that's the end of the book in the Bible. You're left there with the question. You never know what Jonah said. And you find out the question is for you. What are you going to do? Can you live without hatred?

Mapping

A map is the meeting ground of drawing, writing, and geometry. No other medium carries such a wealth of critical information at glance readiness. Students of brain and thought design are lately placing more and more emphasis on the matter of Where-Is-It — apparently much of the mind's store, retrieve, and relate systems are based on position relationships in mental space.

This book is a well-made introduction to map use, map construction, and something of the meaning of maps.
—SB

Mapping
David Greenhood
1944, 1964; 288 pp.
$5.50 postpaid from:
University of Chicago Press
11030 S. Langley Avenue
Chicago, IL 60628
or Whole Earth Household Store

•

Maps and charts — you may have noticed in this chapter the repetition of these two words. What's the difference in their meaning? Charts are maps with a special, practical purpose such as navigating, weather forecasting, and population studies. A chart is a map on which to work with protractor, compass, dividers, and gauges — even a densitometer.

← **Land-form map. Accurate information shown with vividness and grace. Drawn by Erwin Raisz for a geography textbook.**

•

Considering how much the mere idea of a map encompasses, maps are probably more *un*confusing than anything else put down on paper. A map should be regarded as an antidote to panic.

•

We can scan the history of civilization as well as of mapping itself simply by observing which direction has topped the map. Erwin Raisz, the Harvard authority on cartography, says, "It seems to be a tendency among map makers of every country to put at the top of the map the direction toward which national attention is turned."

The Romans headed their maps as they so often did their empire-stretching ships, eastward. So did the Crusaders trying to recover the Holy Land. Many medieval wind roses have a cross as an east-mark.

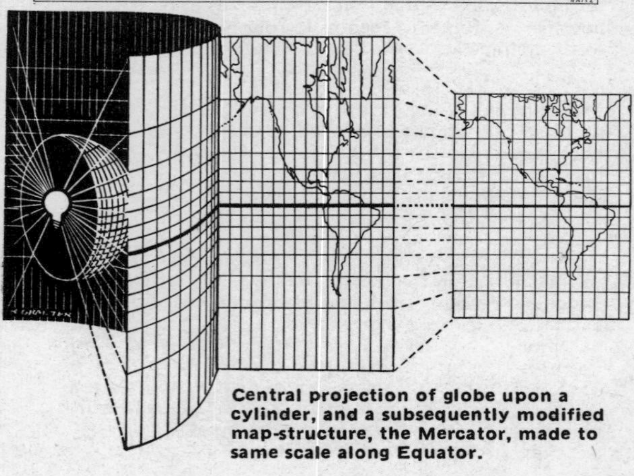

Central projection of globe upon a cylinder, and a subsequently modified map-structure, the Mercator, made to same scale along Equator.

Pen pressed against T square too hard

Pen sloped away from T square

Pen too close to edge. Ink ran under

Ink on outside of blade, ran under

Pen blades not kept parallel to T square

Avoidable troubles of the ruling pen

Graphis Diagrams

Dammit! As usual, the great book is out of print, the lousy book is in print (oops, no longer), and the really needed book doesn't exist at all.

The great book was **Diagrams** *(Watson-Guptill, 1969), of which I wrote, "A diagram is a conceptual map. Elegantly done it can ease comprehension. Thoroughly done it can aid analysis. Done with originality it can remake your internal world."* **Diagrams** *itself had all those qualities.*

Graphis Diagrams, *unfortunately does not. It is far less conceptual in its interest and more "graphic," with emphasis on trendy decadent European overwrought image perversion that actively obscures understanding. But it's the only diagram book available. (Note:* **Graphis Diagrams** *went out of print just as we were going to press.)*

The non-existing needed book is on illustrating how-to books. Nothing serves the kind of books and magazines we review — a mainstay of the publishing market these days — better than excellent explanatory diagrams and drawings, and there's no book on how to do it well. If I were going to be a commercial artist, that is the skill I would master. It's a seller's market. *—SB*

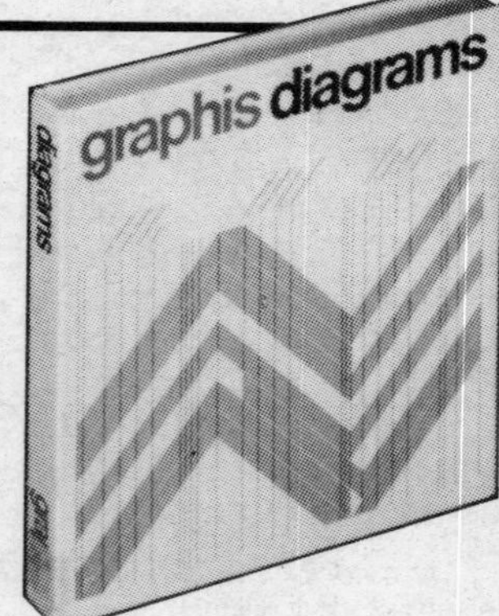

Graphis Diagrams
(The Graphic Visualization of Abstract Data)
Walter Herdeg, Editor
1974; 183 pp.

OUT OF PRINT
Hastings House

Good!

Spiral of the world's energy production. From History of the 20th Century.

Thinking with a Pencil

Good title, wonderful book — an inviting pragmatic introduction to the full range of image-representation. Nelms makes it look easy and great fun. *—SB*

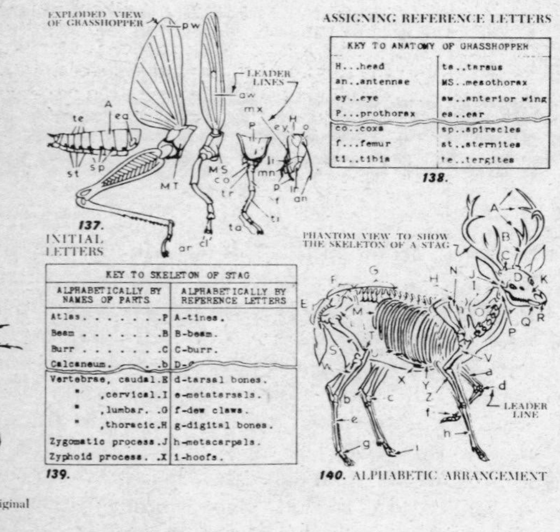

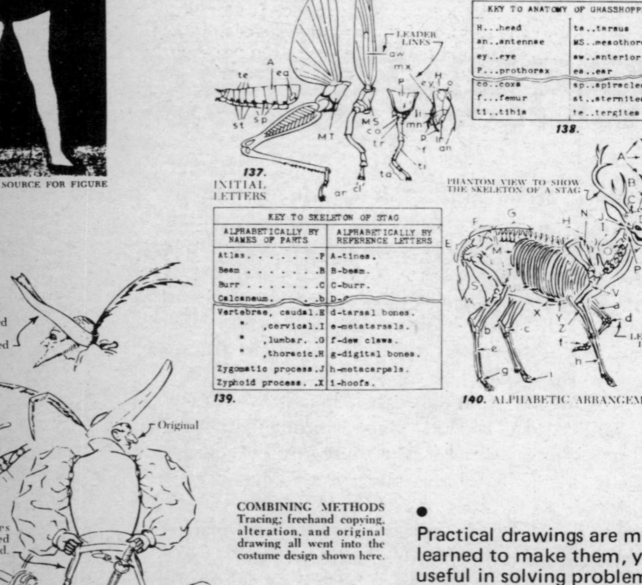

Thinking with a Pencil
(With 692 Illustrations of Easy Ways to Make and Use Drawings in Your Work and in Your Hobbies)
Henning Nelms
1957, 1964; 348 pp.

OUT OF PRINT
Barnes and Noble

Get this book back in print!

•

Practical drawings are mental tools. Once you have learned to make them, you will find that they are as useful in solving problems as saws and hammers are useful in carpentry.

•

Omitting the useless is as important as including the essential. Aristotle stated a fundamental truth when he said that everything which does not add will detract.

Art and Illusion

So much art criticism is so much a vapid waste of time that a book like this one is thoroughly a shock. Every page yields fresh information (did you know that the comic strip was singlehandedly invented by a Swiss gent named Töpfler in the 1820's?) and worthwhile hypotheses about how art and artists gradually teach themselves energies of effect. Furthermore the book is a bargain — it has 319 fine illustrations, 18 in color. *—SB*

•

Max Friedlander tells the revealing story of the bank official who insisted that German bank notes should retain a portrait head in their design. Nothing, he said, was harder for the forger to imitate than precisely the right expression of these artistically quite insignificant heads, nor was there a quicker way of discovering a suspect note than simply observing the way these faces look at you.

•

Only in the realm of dreams has the artist found full freedom to create. I think the difference is well summed up in the anecdote about Matisse. When a lady visiting his studio said, "But surely, the arm of this woman is much too long," the artist replied politely, "Madame, you are mistaken. This is not a woman, this is a picture."

→

True, we can switch from one reading to another with increasing rapidity; we will also "remember" the rabbit while we see the duck, but the more closely we watch ourselves, the more certainly we will discover that we cannot experience alternative readings at the same time. Illusion, we will find, is hard to describe or analyze, for though we may be intellectually aware of the fact that any given experience *must* be an illusion, we cannot, strictly speaking, watch ourselves having an illusion.

→

But no tradition of art had a deeper understanding of what I have called the "screen" than the art of the Far East. Chinese art theory discusses the power of expressing through *absence* of brush and ink. "Figures, even though painted without eyes, must seem to look; without ears, must seem to listen. . . . There are things which ten hundred brush-strokes cannot depict but which can be captured by a few simple strokes if they are right. That is truly giving expression to the invisible." The maxim into which these observations were condensed might serve as a motto of this chapter: *"i tao pi pu tao —* idea present, brush may be spared performance."

Art and Illusion
(A Study in the Psychology of Pictorial Representation)
E.H. Gombrich
1960, 1969; 466 pp.
$9.95 postpaid from:
Princeton University Press
Princeton, NJ 08540
or Whole Earth Household Store

Rabbit or duck?

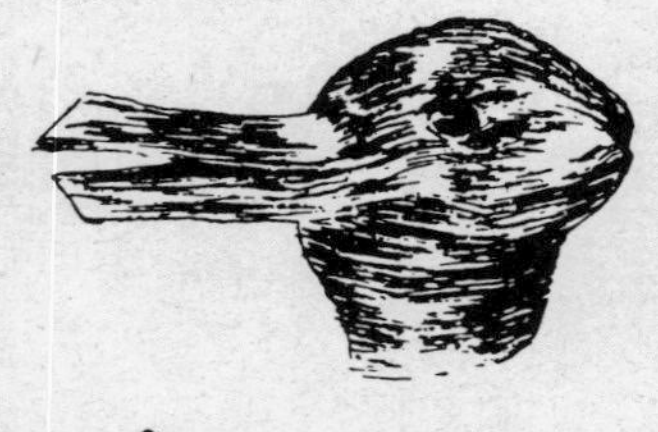

ADDING EYELIDS
CHANGES
THE EMOTION!
HAPPY BECOMES SATISFACTION

MEAN
BECOMES

EVIL

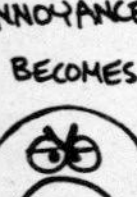

ANNOYANCE
BECOMES

RESENTFUL

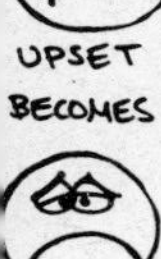

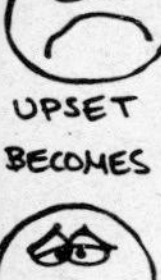

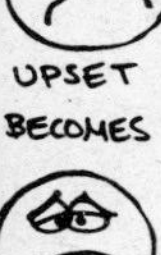

UPSET
BECOMES

TIRED

The Big Yellow Drawing Book

How to cartoon. Dan O'Neill's fiendish plot to free the world — create millions of skilled cartoonists. (And put himself out of business. O'Neill is responsible for the daily strip "Odd Bodkins," "Air Pirates Funnies" — sued by Walt Disney Productions — and two books, **Hear the Sound of My Feet Walking Drown the Sound of My Voice Talking** *and* **The Collective Unconscious of Dan O'Neill.**) *This workbook was co-authored with Dan's father Hugh, an education professor. There's no better introduction to the deadly science.* —SB

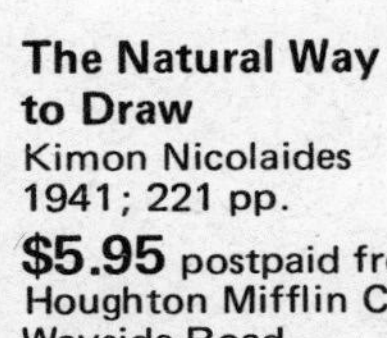
DETAIL- THE 6TH PRINCIPLE OF PERSPECTIVE...
WE SEE SMALL DETAILS ON LARGE OBJECTS CLOSE TO US.. BUT THESE DETAILS DISAPPEAR AS THESE THINGS SHRINK IN THE DISTANCE. THE VEINS ON LEAVES AND BARK OF THE TREES.. THESE ARE DETAILS.
DRAW ONE OF THESE FORESTS

The Big Yellow Drawing Book
Dan O'Neill,
Marion O'Neill and
Hugh D. O'Neill, Jr.
1974; 64 pp.

$3.50 postpaid from:
Hugh O'Neill
and Associates
P.O. Box 1297
Nevada City, CA 95959
or Whole Earth
Household Store

The Natural Way to Draw

This classic work by an outstanding art teacher is not only the best how-to book on drawing, it is one of the best how-to books we've seen on any subject. —SB
[*Suggested by Roy Sebern*]

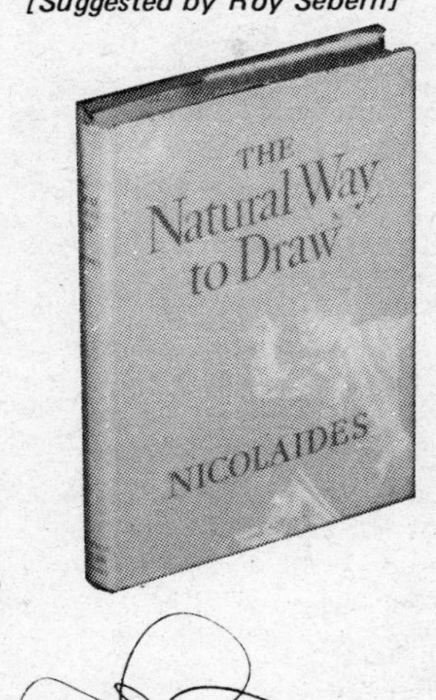

The Natural Way to Draw
Kimon Nicolaides
1941; 221 pp.

$5.95 postpaid from:
Houghton Mifflin Co.
Wayside Road
Burlington MA 01803
or Whole Earth
Household Store

In contour drawing you touch the edge of the form.

In gesture drawing you feel the movement of the whole.

•

The job of the teacher, as I see it, is to teach students, not how to draw, but how to learn to draw.

•

THE SOONER YOU MAKE YOUR FIRST FIVE THOUSAND MISTAKES, THE SOONER YOU WILL BE ABLE TO CORRECT THEM.

A gesture drawing is like scribbling rather than like printing carefully — think more of the meaning than of the way the thing looks.

•

Sit close to the model or object which you intend to draw and lean forward in your chair. Focus your eyes on some point — any point will do — along the contour of the model. (The contour approximates what is usually spoken of as the outline or edge.) Place the point of your pencil on the paper. Imagine that your pencil point is touching the model instead of the paper. Without taking your eyes off the model, *wait* until you are *convinced* that the pencil is touching that point on the model upon which your eyes are fastened.

Then move your eye *slowly* along the contour of the model and move the pencil *slowly* along the paper. As you do this, keep the conviction that the pencil point is actually touching the contour. Be guided more by the sense of touch than by sight. THIS MEANS THAT YOU MUST DRAW WITHOUT LOOKING AT THE PAPER, continuously looking at the model.

•

Changing the Point of View

It is well known that the printed or spoken word has a tendency to take on authority once it is printed or spoken. To get away from it almost takes a revolution. The same thing is true with your own drawing. The very mistakes you make, as they linger on the paper, have this tendency to become authoritative. To combat it, move about the room during the long pose, making occasional scribbled drawings. A thing is factually the same from whatever point of view you see it, but seeing it from different points of view will illuminate the meaning of the forms and lines you have been looking at.

Drawing on the Right Side of the Brain

It is surprising how many adults are terrified when asked to draw. Especially since translating three dimensional objects into drawings and its mirror skill of turning plans into objects are basic tools for everything from carpentry to sewing.

Drawing on the Right Side of the Brain *challenges the concept that drawing is an innate ability and proves it by showing Before and After student drawings. The easily-followed exercises will help you translate what you see rather than what the left side of the brain thinks is there.* —Kathleen O'Neill

Drawing on the Right Side of the Brain
(A Course in Enhancing Creativity and Artistic Confidence)
Betty Edwards
1979; 207 pp.

$8.95 postpaid from:
St. Martin's Press
175 Fifth Avenue
New York, NY 10010
or Whole Earth
Household Store

Tom Nelson
August 8, 1978

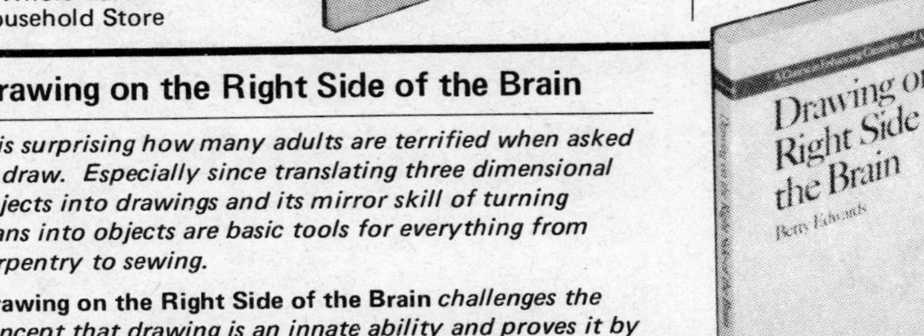

Tom Nelson
September 3, 1978

•

Adult students beginning in art generally do not really see *what is in front of their eyes* — that is, they do not perceive in the special way required for drawing. They take note of what's there, and quickly translate the perception into works and symbols mainly based on the symbol system developed throughout childhood and on what they *know* about the perceived object.

→
In the first drawing, the student had great difficulty reconciling his stored knowledge of what the objects were "supposed to look like" with what he *saw.* Notice in the drawing that the legs of the cart are all the same length, and a symbol is used for the wheels. When he switched to R-mode drawing, using a viewfinder and drawing only the shapes of the negative spaces, he was far more successful. The visual information apparently came through clearly; the drawing looks confident and as though it were done with ease. And, in fact, it was done with ease, because the left hemisphere had been tricked into keeping quiet.

Drawing the Human Form

I usually find how-to-draw books boring because they try to teach you to draw like the author. **Drawing the Human Form** *covers all the basics from theory to anatomy but illustrates them with a variety of master artists' and students' works. Each one is a vivid example of a successful figure drawing and the captions and text help to understand how it was done.*

The step-by-step exercises make it a good book both for beginners and for those who want to hone their ability. —Kathleen O'Neill

Modeling the figure from life with crayon. Forms that recede or turn in space can be pushed back in the drawing by pressing on the crayon, which results in a correspondingly darker tone.

Drawing the Human Form
(A Guide to Drawing from Life: Methods, Sources, Concepts)
William A. Berry
1977; 256 pp.

$12.95 postpaid from:
Van Nostrand
Reinhold Company
Order Department
7625 Empire Drive
Florence, KY 41042
or Whole Earth
Household Store

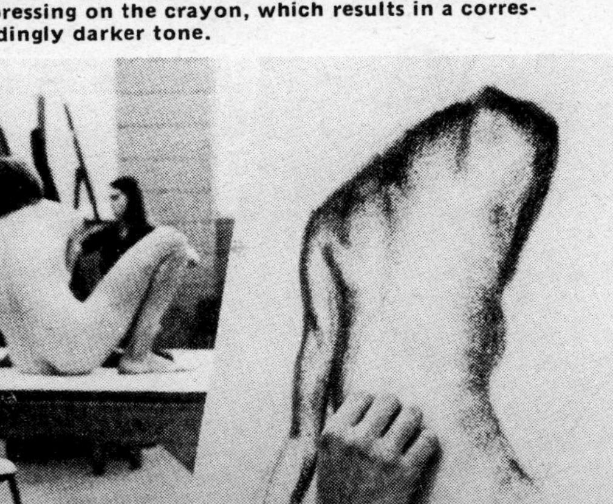

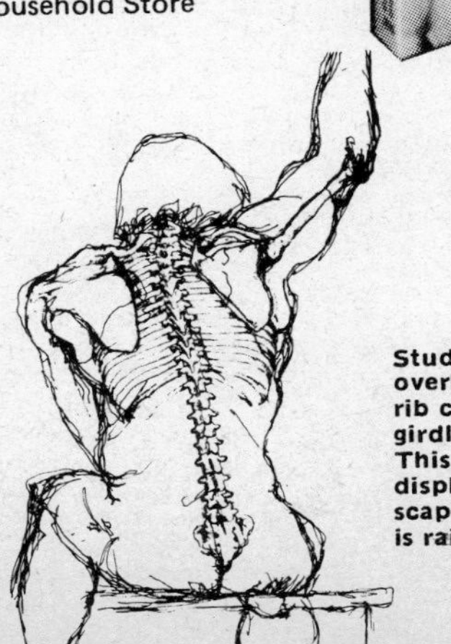

Student drawing with overlay study of the rib cage and the shoulder girdle. Graphite pencil. This study illustrates the displacement of the scapula when the arm is raised.

THE RISING SUN NEIGHBORHOOD NEWSLETTER

Astronomers who look at both stars and planets often train one eye to look at stars and the other eye to look at planets because they are different kinds of seeing. (That training is needed to see anything is obvious to anyone who has looked through a telescope the first time and seen boring little splotches.) Professional astronomers don't look at stars and planets much anymore with their eyes — they mostly read computer printouts and examine spectrograms and things like that, though when they want a break they sometimes go out and look up at the night sky.

ARTISTS' REFERENCE

by David Wills

Learning to see. *A working artist needs visual reference as a tool for inspiration; for seeing visual connections not made before; or as models to draw from or photograph. Inventing images, drawing constructions out of the blue, is helped if you've got a few aids.*

I Spy. *When I was a kid, one way I learned to see was playing "I spy with my little eye, something beginning with C" — "clouds." Then, when we got smarter, it would be I spy O for "owls in the cloud" and they'd have to guess what "O" stood for before the cloud blew away. Now I play I spy in my small library of big picture books and look out for images and inspiration to appear.*

Access. *Big picture books, encyclopedias, and reference tomes are expensive and often out of print. Since art reference is often used as found-art, this is reflected in their purchase — a bit of an old encyclopedia is quite useful in a found-art context. So I buy my books at street sales, the flea market and jumble sales. This means that my entire collection, except for the Dover books, is quite fortuitous — a random lot. Here are a few I've used or have around waiting for the day. Those with ordering information added are worth buying new; the others are examples of what you may find cheap if you look around.*

Cumulus of strong vertical extent

↑

International Cloud Atlas, by the World Meteorological Organization. *This is what the U.S. Coast Guard trained on. My copy is from their library, bought at a street sale on Haight and Ashbury for $ .50.*

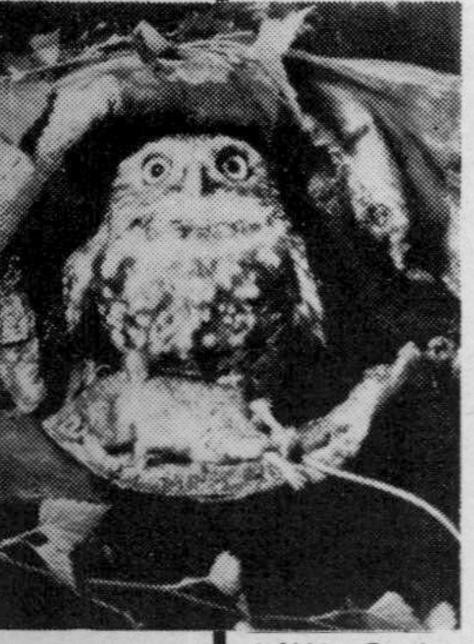

Little Owl

←

A Natural History of Owls, by Michael Everett. *Brother Robin had a pet Little Owl, which used to drip blood while eating moles. This book has good reference to draw the scene.*

Larousse Encyclopedia of the Animal World, 1975; $50 postpaid from Larousse and Company, 572 Fifth Avenue, New York, NY 10036. *Margo Saint James' prostitute rights group "Coyote" button was drawn using art-ref of a red fox I found in Larousse. (At that time it was all I could find, and it looked close enough.)*

←

Red Fox, Canis vulpus

Old Magazines. *A pile of old magazines always comes through when image hunting.* **National Geographic** *and* **Life** *are both good access to the old.* **National Geographic,** *August, 1974, was the issue where I first found detailed pictures of a coyote.*

↓

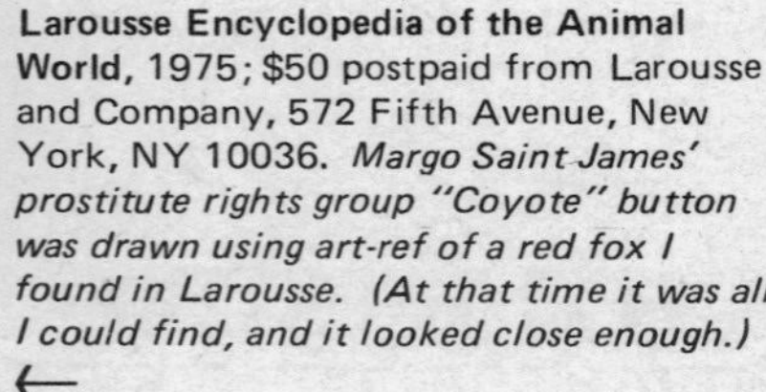

Coyote

Jean-Paul Sartre

↑

The Twentieth Century, edited by Alan Bullock. *An intelligent picture history book. I constantly refer to it, refresh my mind. I used it as art-ref for a picture of Sartre masquerading as a Belgian, in drawings for "I Sing of Thee" in* **CoEvolution Quarterly.**

An ABC of the Work of Hipgnosis ("Walk Away Rene") by Hipgnosis, 1978; $10.95 postpaid from A & W Visual Library, 95 Madison Avenue, New York, NY 10016. *A real pop art; good album covers and their stories. Learn graphic design techniques.*

↓

Album cover Montrose "Jump on It"

→

The Nude, by Kenneth Clark, 1972; $7.95 postpaid from Princeton University Press, 41 William Street, Princeton, NJ 08540. *Nudes on the brain down the ages. A classic look at the form.*

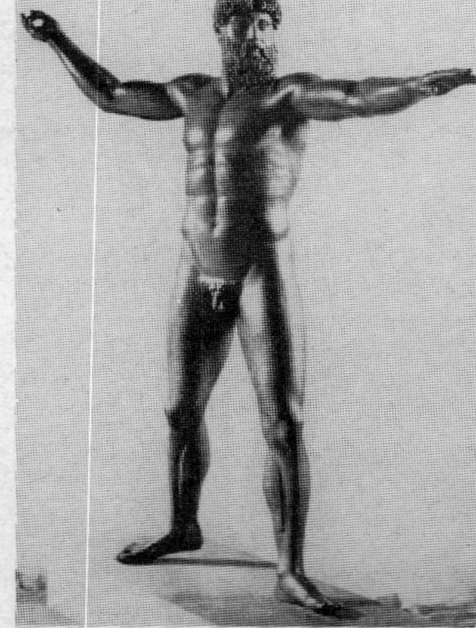

Bearded god of Histiaia, Attic, c. 470 B.C.

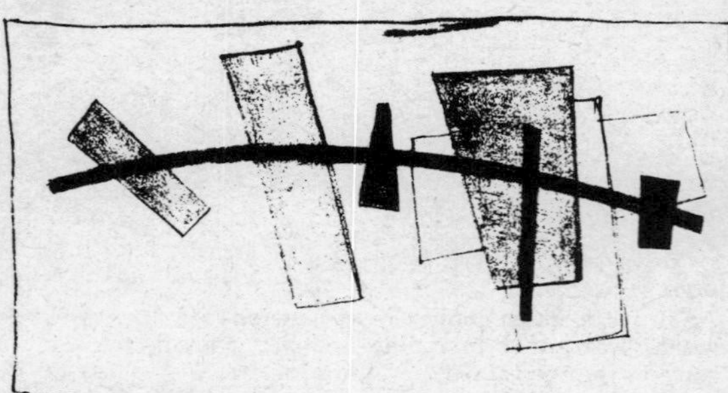

Malevich, Suprematist drawing

↑

Art Exhibition Catalogs and Postcards. *If you go and get off at art, get a good catalog or postcard when you leave. Learn more about what you like. The one in front of me is called* **Constructivism and the Geometric Tradition.** *I'm learning about the Russian suprematist, Malevitch. Usually the words aren't worth a tinker's, but who cares as long as the pictures are well reproduced?*

Punu, mask on stilts

African Art, edited by Albert Beuret, Andre Malraux, et al. *African culture masterpieces.* ←

Paul Klee's Notebooks, published by Lund Humphries, London. *An insight of delightful obscurity into the mind of a teaching genius. These are the class notes.*

Paul Klee, Water Wheel and Hammer

↓

Flood victims, Louisville, Kentucky, February 1937 by Margaret Bourke-White

↑

The Best of Life, edited by David E. Scherman, 1973; $10.20 postpaid from Avon Books, Mail Order Dept., 250 West 55th Street, New York, NY 10019. *The world's best photographers, out on the beat, bringing it all back home. The images many of us (I) culled our (my) view of real from.*

Out of copyright material. *Copyright images may not legally be reproduced photographically but they can often be used as reference for drawing from. The time period for copyright is now the artist's life plus 50 years, and for this reason many graphic aids are culled from old sources — stuff that's available to clip or photograph/photostat for the taking without a by-your-leave, either because it's real old or published specifically for reproduction.*

Four Horsemen of the Apocalypse from The Complete Woodcuts of Albrecht Durer, Dover

↑

The Dover Archives (Dover Pictorial Archive Book catalog free from Dover Publications, 180 Varick Street, New York, NY 10014). *Books come, books go, but few studios get by without something from this vast lucky dip. I count a score of Dover titles I've used and as many more I'd like to. Often well done and to the point — where would deadlines be without them? My dad, a civil servant, used to worry about me working as an artist. "What happens when you run out of ideas?" Picture archives, that's what. Dover is also reviewed on* *p. 511.*

Authentic Indian Designs, edited by Maria Naylor, 1975; $6 postpaid from Dover Publications, 180 Varick Street, New York, NY 10014. *Eugene Curley, the Navajo muralist, borrowed this book for many moons. He said it was good; now he's painting at the gathering of the tribes in New Mexico. (The Coyote button was influenced by the Pueblo pottery.)*

Ancient Pueblo pottery from Chevlon ↑

← **Humor, Wit and Fantasy.** *(See* *pp. 288 - 289* *for example.) The Hart inventory of artist reference books (***Designs of the Ancient World, Oriental Designs, American Designs, Humor, Wit and Fantasy, The Animal Kingdom, European Designs,** *and* **Trades and Professions***) is now remaindered and available at sales and close-outs everywhere.*

Illustrating Priestley's discovery of oxygen

↑

Science for All (An Illustrated Encyclopedia). *Typical of the random reference access methods is the flip-through-and-see-what-gives technique. Take Volume II (which has no date except a stamp from the Gualala, CA Post Office Library of 1923), for instance. Break it open halfway and quickly flip to the front, then back to the middle and flip to the end. Very surprising what you find.*

Library of Natural History, edited by Richard Lydekker (1904). *The be all, end all of crib books — steel engravings up the wazoo, techniques by the dozen and all the animals of creation. I paid $10 for the set at the flea market. Many of these images are reproduced in* **The Animal Kingdom,** *published by Hart.*

↓

Turkey vultures

Around the World Stampbook *(or any postage stamp book). This collection cost me 25 cents. (From it came the logo for the "Street Lightnin' Gang" graffiti artists' union.) Stamps in general give good art-ref; very graphic and basic, these odd cameos, vignettes and symbols of the world in the mail box.* ↓

Professional Picture Research. *For further information about picture research you might try the American Society of Picture Professionals, Box 5283, Grand Central Station, New York, NY 10017. The group includes picture researchers, librarians, photographers and their agents. They co-publish* **Picture Sources Three** *(1975; $17 postpaid from: Special Libraries Association, 235 Park Avenue South, New York, NY 10003).*

Other art reference aids. *Apart from all the other paraphernalia of the artists' studio, here are some that are useful for reference:*

Sketch books *are easily available and necessary. I use one of those anonymous black-bound $4.50 8 x 10s, available at any art store. Draw on one side of a page only — the pen shows through. I use a selection of fibre tip pens: Sandford's Expresso fine, medium and bold are good ($1 each) — the points can take the jolts at the back of the bus without disintegrating. For other graphic supplies, see p. 466.*

A hand-held instant camera *is often useful. Second-hand ones are cheaply available, or you could borrow one from a rich friend who is overloaded with trinkets. A new Polaroid SX70 costs $198 from Solar Cine Products (p. 486), and film $8 for ten shots. It's cheaper by pencil, but you save time.*

A Camera Lucida — *for enlarging the itty-bitty instant images up to wow-sized graphic wonders onto frosted glass where they can be traced. $275 from Flax's (p. 466).*

A pair of binoculars — *I use a Sensi 7x50, 372 ft at 1000 yards which I got in a pawnbroker's for $30. Use them discreetly.* ■

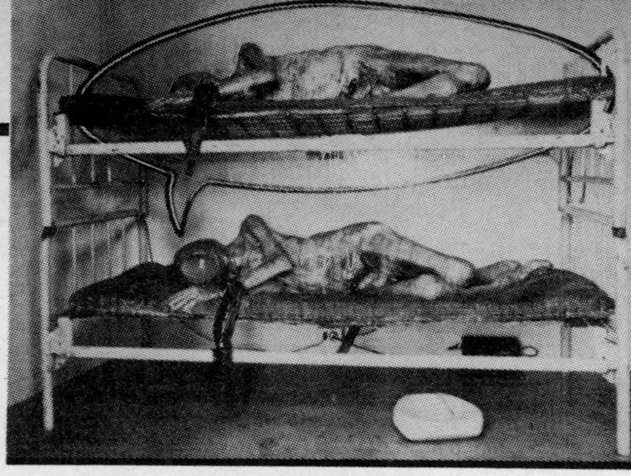

Beyond Modern Sculpture

Jack Burnham is one of the most provocative and perceptive writers on art that I know of. He made his critical debut with **Beyond Modern Sculpture** *and in my opinion it's still his best book.* **BMS** *is nothing less than a total reconstruction of the development of twentieth-century sculpture in light of the transition from a split mechanist-vitalist worldview to an integrated techno-cybernetic systems worldview. From this perspective, scattered trends and stylistic innovations that, in standard art histories, seem merely interesting or idiosyncratic, suddenly gel into a meaningful pattern: What Burnham is describing is a paradigm-shift as profound as the one marked by the emergence of abstract art some 60 - 70 years ago.*

With the rapid expansion of technology in this century, the hand-crafted-object tradition of sculpture finds itself overwhelmed and undermined by the complex artificial systems that characterize industrial society. Looking at the situation with perverse optimism, Burnham sees this as redefining the meaning and future direction of sculpture, not as rendering it obsolete. In order to establish precedents for a certain range of new options, he reviews the development of some long-ignored "subsculptural" genres: mechanical dolls, programmed light displays along the Las Vegas Strip, clocks, calculators, music boxes, Grey Walter's "tortoises," and other modern automata. This material is fascinating, but is included mainly to set the stage for some heavy prognostications:

Unless the world is substantially altered for the worst, the logical outcome of technology's influence on art before the end of this century should be a series of art forms that manifest true intelligence, but perhaps more meaningful, with a capacity for reciprocal relationships with human beings . . . .

Pressing the argument further:

It is a thesis of this book that formalist and vitalist sculpture represent two preparatory steps which symbolically anticipate the re-creation of life through non-biological means, that is, through technology.

And, to polish it off, he cites a book by MacGowan and Ordway called **Intelligence in the Universe** *for some lengthy quotes about the inevitability of the transition from "born-in-the-wild" organic lifeforms to synthetic inorganic lifeforms, once it becomes technically possible.*

*It's a full-blown Faustian vision, intoxicating but chilling. Caught up in the resolving power of his own version of recent art history, and thoroughly awed by the technological juggernaut (***BMS** *was written in 1967), Burnham goes somewhat overboard on the historical determinism angle. Most of his more recent writings have been devoted to counteracting this excess and emphasize the semiotic, ritual and mythic content of art. But whether or not one agrees with him on the future direction of sculpture or its inevitability, his outline of the principles of "systems esthetics" crystalized the paradigm he foresaw as immanent, and that is a real accomplishment.*
—Robert Horvitz

Beyond Modern Sculpture
(The Effects of Science and Technology on the Sculpture of This Century)
Jack Burnham
1968, 1975; 402 pp.
$8.95 postpaid from:
George Braziller, Inc.
One Park Avenue
New York, NY 10016
or Whole Earth Household Store

•

The cultural obsession with the art object is slowly disappearing and being replaced by what might be called "systems consciousness." Actually, this shifts from the direct shaping of matter to a concern for organizing quantities of energy and information. Seen another way, it is a refocusing of aesthetic awareness — based on future scientific-technological evolution — on matter-energy-information exchanges and away from the invention of solid artifacts. These new systems prompt us not to look at the "skin" of objects, but at those meaningful relationships within and beyond their visible boundaries.

←

Rivaling the frightening pathos of the great Counter-Reformation Spanish woodcarvers, the Californian Edward Kienholz has produced some of the strongest and most memorable tableaus of this generation. The moral vantage of Kienholz is keenly evident in *The State Hospital.* Here the artist has reincarnated memories that reflect his experiences as an attendant in an asylum. These are no longer human beings, but fetid bodies and faces represented by cloudy, translucent containers. Even more eerily pathetic is *Birthday* (1964), in which a young woman lies on a portable operating table in an abortionist's office. Everything vibrates muted whites and grays; all surfaces of the tableau are bathed in a sickly sheen of clear polyester resin plastic. The mouth of the young woman on the table emits a plastic bubble containing a floating toy — signifying perhaps the scream of lost motherhood; from her stomach seven giant plastic arrows protrude; the center arrow carries the soul of the dead fetus back to its place of origin.

Leonardo

Most art books and magazines are about the product of art, with lots of four-color pictures to wow you. **Leonardo** *is the opposite. It's pure process, pure tool — TECHNIQUE — of the most advanced, most refined, most in fact modern of arts. (The news stays the same in this world; only science and technology change, and art chases them.) I view this publication with the same contemporary fascination as* **Science** *or* **New Scientist**. *They announce the present (i.e., future).*

Not cheap, not for browsing. Lay out the bucks and make the magazine earn it back in your work or settle it all at your library. —SB

Leonardo
Frank J. Malina, Editor
$20 /year (4 issues)
from:
Pergamon Press
Journals Department
Maxwell House
Fairview Park
Elmsford, NY 10523

•

Abstract — Roy Adzak describes his work after 1968 dealing with the making of negative forms of inorganic and organic objects. He has produced three different series. In the first, the "Dehydration" Series, he obtained imprints of fruits and vegetables in cement and he left them in the hardened cement molds to display them during and following their dehydration. Similarly, fresh fish suspended by nylon threads were dehydrated, their shrinkage following dehydration being revealed by tabs on the threads. The "Textures" series is comprised primarily of shallow imprints of natural objects and artifacts in plaster to display their structural surface characteristics. The series was extended to include photographs of surfaces, such as those on water which cannot be recorded by the imprint technique. The "Anthropometric" series includes imprints in plaster of parts of his body. His major effort, however, was to obtain "interior imprints" — that is, physiological records of organs, bones, etc. inside his body. Illustrations are given from these three series and he describes thoughts he has had that induced him to pursue work in these directions.

↓

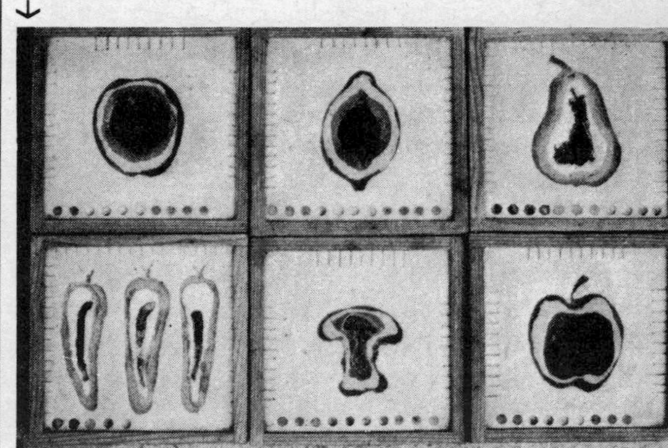

THE RISING SUN
NEIGHBORHOOD NEWSLETTER

Lorrie was handing me back my matches but it looked like she was handing me the cigarette like a joint and I said how if tobacco was illegal and scarce it would be shared too. Yeah, a community thing, she said and said even though she really liked cocaine she didn't like how she felt about it, because it's so expensive and so good you just want to have it all yourself and you have to be really good friends with someone before you feel like sharing it.

GRAPHIC SUPPLIES

by David Wills

Kern ruling pen, Michael's $34.80

Your corner art store is convenient, but if you're looking for 'Skum-X' (a powder you put on drawings so they won't smudge easily), they might not have it on demand. If you have a heavy art supply habit, the way to go is to shop at a larger mail-order house where it often pays to buy in bulk.

Four companies listed here, Michael's, Flax, Friedman and Dick Blick, cover most artists' needs. The other companies cater to the more specialist graphic arts supplies of screen process, letterpress, lithography, etc.

THE STUDIO

Michael's Artist Supplies, 314 Sutter Street, San Francisco, CA 94108. Catalog $3.50. *Good prices, wide variety, informative catalog, quick service. The art store the* **Catalog** *uses.*

Flax's Artists Materials, 1699 Market Street, San Francisco, CA 94103. Catalog $3. *Expensive, specializes in adagency convenience, they often have that wonderful something not available elsewhere. Very complete lines of paper supplies and graphic aids.*

A.I. Friedman Art Supplies, 25 West 45th Street, New York, NY 10036. Catalog free. *They're in New York, they're good. We never got their catalog.*

Dick Blick, P.O. Box 1267, Galesburg, IL 61401. Catalogs (Creative Materials or Graphic Arts) free. *Extensive range of graphic art and other craft materials for schools, including etching, letterpress and lithography.*

CHEAP OIL PAINT

Utrecht Linens Company, 111 4th Avenue, New York, NY 10003. Catalog free. *For student painters and others, a real inexpensive line of oil colors and canvas. Minimum order $40.*

GOOD ACRYLIC

Politec, Inc., 1157 Masonic Avenue, San Francisco, CA 94117. *The best acrylic paint for murals, formulated according to specifications of the Mexican mural masters. A joy to use.*

Politec	Retail Prices				
	2 oz.	8 oz.	pint	quart	gallon
Titanium White	1.60	4.80	8.60	15.50	56.00
Supreme Black	1.60	4.80	8.60	15.50	56.00
Brown	1.60	4.80	8.60	15.50	56.00
Yellow Ochre	1.60	4.80	8.60	15.50	56.00
Red Oxide	1.60	4.80	6.60	15.50	56.00

LIQUID TEMPERA
Pump Kit

Contains six assorted color gallons with pump lids, and 100 disposable Stancups. Shpg 60 lbs.
4509900 .... Each Kit $64.90
4508600 PUMP LIDS ONLY ... Each $ .90
STANCUPS ONLY • Pkg of 100
855500 .... Each Pkg $2.10
5 Pkgs .... Each Pkg 1.95
10 Pkgs .... Each Pkg 1.78

—Dick Blick

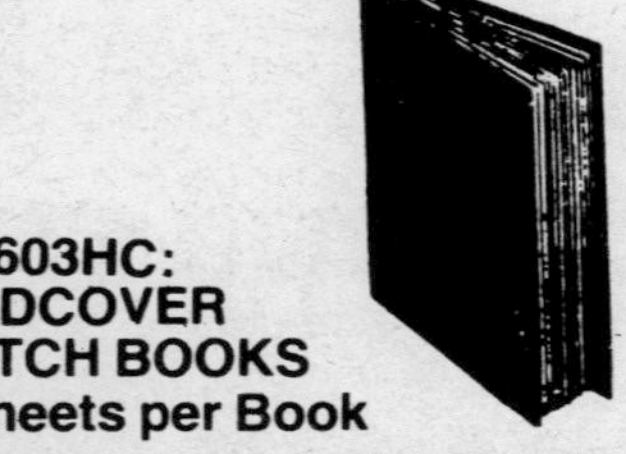

No. 603HC: HARDCOVER SKETCH BOOKS
76 Sheets per Book

Special coated paper made especially for pen and ink and felt tip markers. The surface produces clean, crisp, lines and no bleed through the paper.

Item Number	Sheet Size	Utrecht Price per Carton	Price per Ctn. 4 Cartons & More
• Packed: 12 Books per Carton			
230 992	5½"×8½"	$41.58	$35.64
230 993	8½"×11"	58.38	50.04

—Utrecht

Neoltino drafting table, 37½" x 55". $287.47

← Winsor Newton sable brush — Series 7 #6 $24

Skum-X: A soft granular material that provides a temporary protective coating over drawings during drafting. 66 8160 (Shaker top canister) $1.10

Lino Assortment — No. 1 assortment $3.50

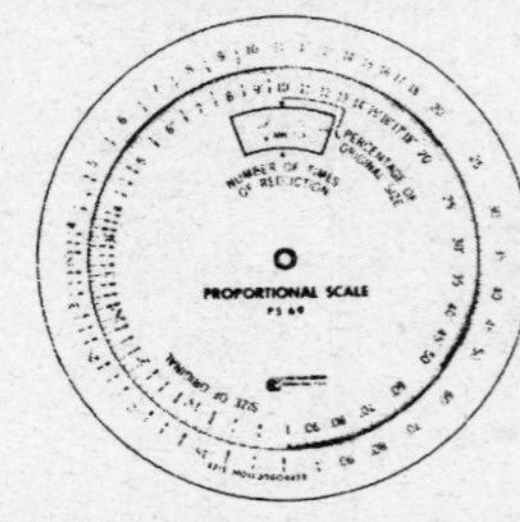

Circular proportional slide rules permit quick calculation of enlargements or reductions of photographs, art work, layouts and blue prints. $3.75

—Michael's Art Supplies

Art Waxer
Unique open-end waxing system applies a coat of pressure sensitive wax to the back of paper to be pasted up. Takes less than one square foot of space. Coats an area 5½" wide by any length; wider sheets, maps, signs, etc. can be coated in stages. Art-waxed copy blocks are easily repositioned. Foot switch, brayer, wax, parts packet included.
13125-06 Art waxer **$288**
Art wax **$24.15**

Camera Lucida
A precision made instrument for enlargement, reduction, or copying photographs, drawings, or objects. A prism projects an image to the paper surface while permitting your eye to see the image, the paper surface, and the pencil at the same time. Lens of different focuses plus the ratio of distance of prism to paper surface and prism to object determine the character and size of the image. An extremely useful, and widely used, instrument for the artist.
1338-07 Complete with case and 12 lenses **275.00**

3M "Post-It"
A revolutionary adhesive note paper that adheres securely to paper and most surfaces, yet removes easily without damage. Eliminates the need for pins or tacks or of damaging the surface with ordinary tape.
13123-11 "Post-It"
#653 100 sheet pad 1½" x 2"
12 pads **$4.40**

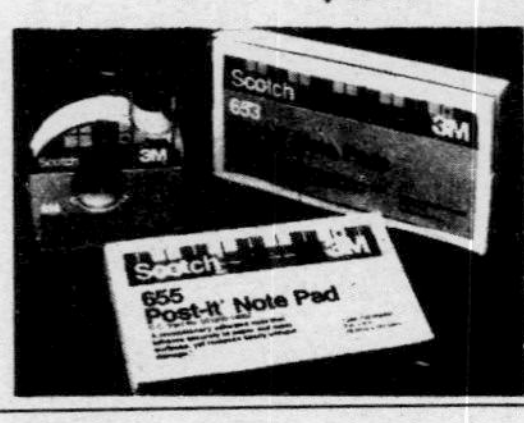

Bracket Dispenser

#104: For rolls up to 4" wide or holds 4 rolls of narrower tape.
13124-08 **$8.25**

—Flax

WOOD ENGRAVING
—T.N. Lawrence and Son

END-GRAIN BLOCKS

Boxwood or Substitute, type high ... Made to any size	26p to 30p per sq. in. According to quality
Pear Tree, type high or similar wood (whichever is available)	20p per sq. in.
Double Sided Blocks	15p extra per sq. in.
Re-Surfacing Blocks	10p per sq. in.

These Blocks must not be stored in rooms with central heating. We do not deal in Centimetre sizes except for Continental orders.

TOOLS for ENGRAVING

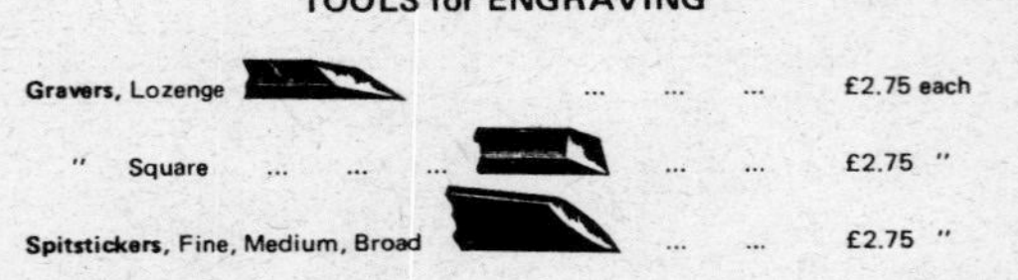

Gravers, Lozenge	£2.75 each
" Square	£2.75 "
Spitstickers, Fine, Medium, Broad	£2.75 "

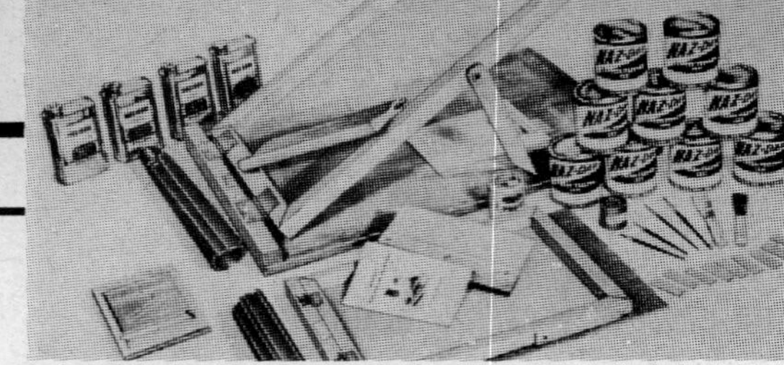

Naz-Dar No. 5358, Commercial silk screen printing kit. $117.15 —Naz-dar

SCREEN PROCESS

The Naz-Dar Company, 1087 North Branch Street, Chicago, IL 60622. Catalog free. *Comprehensive, professional, everything the competent squeegee basher could ever need. Fellow graphic artist Donald Ryan said they supplied him with all he needed when he needed it.*

Inko Silk Screen Printing, 1199 East 12th Street, Oakland, CA 94606. Silk screen printing book $6 postpaid (smaller booklet, $.50). *I have found them to be most helpful. Their wonderful catalog is worth the price, with complete instructions for screen workshop practice.*

LETTERPRESS, LITHOGRAPHY

American Printing Equipment, 42-25 9th Street, Long Island City, NY 11101. Catalog free. *Everything you might need to set up shop as a letterpress or litho printer.* *Also see p. 504.*

Quaker City Typefoundry, R.D. 3, Box 134, Honey Brook, PA 19344. Catalog $.50. *Good prices on metal type fonts.*

ETCHING

Printmakers' Supplies, Graphic Chemical and Ink Company, P.O. Box 27, 728 North Yale Avenue, Villa Park, IL 60181. Catalog $1. *Etching supplies mostly. Rembrandt would gloat over this catalog. They also have the cheapest linoleum blocks.*

WOOD ENGRAVING, WOODCUTS, LINOLEUM

T.N. Lawrence & Son, Ltd., 2-4 Bleeding Heart Yard, Greville Street, Hatton Garden, London, EC1N 8SL, England. Catalog free. *Specialists in engravers' boxwood blocks, tools for wood engraving, wood and linoleum cutting, handmade papers and some etching supplies. Established in 1859 and situated in Bleeding Heart Yard, London, England. Their time-honoured craft is legendary — but beware, their student supplies take three months to deliver.*

PRECISION AMERICAN PROOF PRESS
The ideal press for showcard signs

—American Printing Equipment and Supply

ALL PRESSES HAVE A RETRACTABLE STAINLESS STEEL INKING PLATE.

PROOF PRESS WITH PRESSURE CONTROL UNIT

No. 1-B Proof Press 15" x 19¼"	$ 895.00
No. 2-B Proof Press 15" x 32¼"	1,050.00
Steel Cabinet for No. 2-A and 2-B Presses	135.00

NU-ARC SST1418
The small camera with quality, stability, and results. This fast, compact, easy-to-use camera shoots a full size 14" x 18" image with utmost sharpness.

→ Brass type gauge 12 ins., inch and agate $4.40

Boxed set of burins, $86
—Graphic Chemical & Ink Company

CHELTENHAM BOLD
36 pt. 3 A 4 a
36 Chelt Bd

—Quaker City Type Foundry

The Artist's Handbook of Materials and Techniques

Part of becoming a Rembrandt or DaVinci is creating art work that lasts for several hundred years. Cracking, peeling, fading or darkening colors are usually the result of poor technique.

This book thoroughly covers traditional media from pigment to finishing (the section on fresco sounds enticingly difficult). The new sections on polymers and synthetic organic pigments round it out.

No illustrations — make your own.

—Kathleen O'Neill

The Artist's Handbook of Materials and Techniques
Ralph Mayer
1940, 1970; 749 pp.
$16.95 postpaid from:
The Viking Press
299 Murray Hill Parkway
East Rutherford,
NJ 07073
or Whole Earth
Household Store

•

Encaustic or hot wax painting comes down to us from ancient Greece, where it was a major creative art process for both easel and mural painting. It is perhaps man's earliest formal easel-painting method, and it shares with the ancient process of fresco a certain fundamental purity or simplicity combined with a rather inconvenient and demanding *modus operandi*. Its use was displaced by other mediums (tempera, oil painting, etc.) with the developing and changing requirements of European art and also because of the cumbersome nature of its equipment, so that during the medieval and Renaissance periods it was a genuine "lost art." . . .

The Process

The "classic" or "basic" encaustic method is extremely simple; it consists of painting on any ground or surface with paints made by mixing dry pigments with molten white refined beeswax plus a variable percentage of resin (usually damar), working from a warm palette. The brush or palette knife manipulations can also be assisted by warming and chilling the surface. A final heat treatment, or "burning in" (which is the meaning of the name encaustic) by passing a heat source over the surface, fuses and bonds the painting into a permanent form without altering it, and a light polishing with soft cotton brings out a dull, satiny sheen. When cool, the picture is finished; no further change ever takes place. The work, however, may be set aside at any moment to be taken up again later.

Color Primer I & II

An unusually simple, unusually graphic guide to understanding and manipulating colored light and colored pigment.

—SB

[Suggested by Sarah Fisk]

Color Primer I & II
Richard D. Zakia and
Hollis N. Todd
1974; 142 pp.
$7.50 postpaid from:
Morgan & Morgan, Inc.
Publishers
145 Palisade Street
Dobbs Ferry, NY 10522
or Whole Earth
Household Store

•

We have learned that:

1. The addition of two of the red, green and blue primaries of white light will produce colors having cyan, magenta and yellow hues.

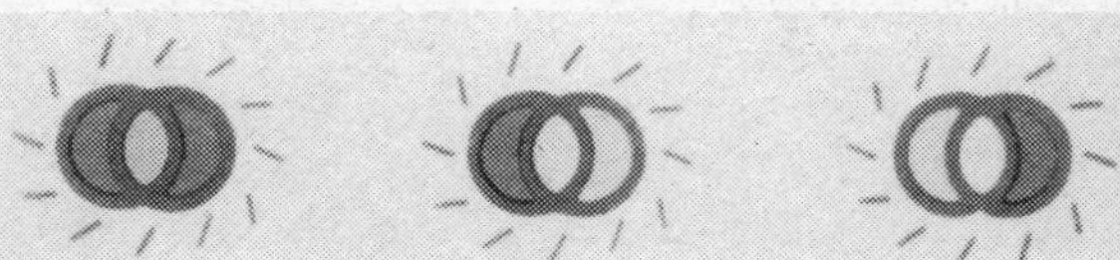

2. The addition of equal amounts of all three primaries of white light will produce neutrals.

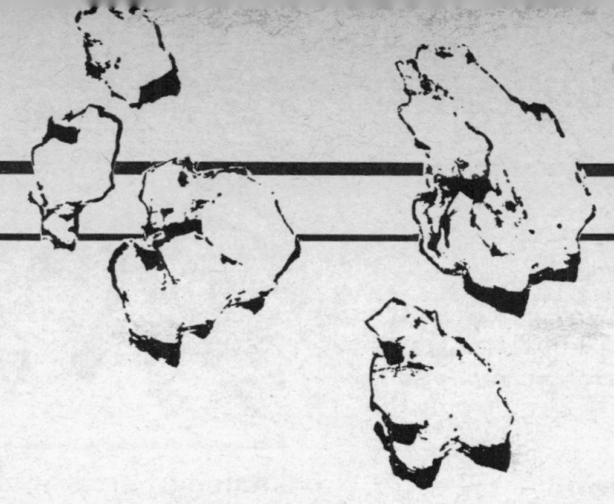

There are not many secret methods in the painting of rocks. If I may sum it up in a phrase: rocks must be alive.

The Way of Chinese Painting ↑

Chinese painters do more with brush, ink, inkstone and paper than western gadgeteers accomplish with their complicated mixing formulas, apprenticeship programs, and didactic traditions. Has a lot to do with thinking simply.

This book can provide you with good access to the tools and ideas of eastern brush painting — things you can carry around in your hip pocket as you move; you provide the practice.

—J.D. Smith

The Way of Chinese Painting
Mai-mai Sze
1956, 1959; 456 pp.
$3.95 postpaid from:
Random House
455 Hahn Road
Westminster, MD 21157
or Whole Earth
Household Store

•

Purifying White

In paintings, the areas where white is used often darken. Chew the heart of a bitter apricot seed, and with the juice wash these spots once or twice. The dark spots will then disappear.

•

The aim of ink painting and its brevity and directness of expression, which has "color" and does not need colors, is well summed up by a statement in the **Li Chi**: "Acts of the greatest reverence admit of no ornament."

—Bk. VIII, Sec. I, 14 (tr. Legge)

•

A lute player plucking his instrument should appear also to be listening to the moon, while the moon, calm and still, appears to be listening to the notes of the lute. Figures should in fact be depicted in such a way that people looking at a painting wish they could change places with them. Otherwise the mountain is just a mountain, the figures mere figures, placed by chance near each other and with no apparent connection; and the whole painting lacks vitality.

Art Objects

An excellent technical book on how to keep Time away from your collection of whatevers.

—SB

Art Objects
(Their Care and Preservation, A Handbook for Museums and Collectors)
Frieda Kay Fall
1971; 332 pp.
$17.50 postpaid from:
Laurence McGilvery
P.O. Box 852
La Jolla, CA 92037
or Whole Earth
Household Store

This case was designed especially for the shipment of the bronze sculpture. Note the constructed wood support for the base of the sculpture and the padded wood bracing. Before shipment the space within the crate was filled with a shock-mitigant material. Instructions for unpacking were lettered on one end of the crate.

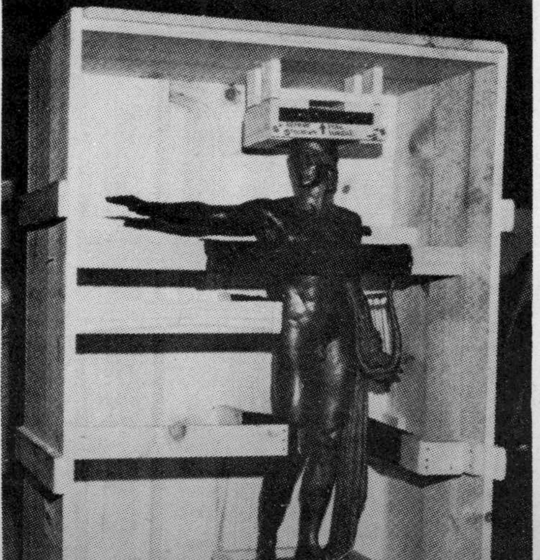

How to Care for Works of Art on Paper

An excellent, low-cost pamphlet for ordinary art- and book-loving people who want to preserve and protect their treasures. Reveals the "enemies" that attack and destroy paper (light, moisture, heat, pollution, insects) and how to guard against them with proper care, handling, and museum-standard matting and framing (not difficult and well worth it to anyone who has lost or damaged a favorite print or drawing through sloppy framing). Also describes the inherent qualities in poor and high quality paper which contribute greatly to its longevity. A chapter describing the processes and techniques of the professional art restorer has been included, as well as a comprehensive listing of art and book conservation materials and suppliers, and a selected bibliography of books and technical articles.

A must for anyone who owns or makes works of art on paper (don't forget that photographic prints come into this category.)

—John Prestianni

How to Care for Works of Art on Paper
Francis W. Dolloff and
Roy L. Perkinson
1971, 1979; 48 pp.
3rd Edition
$3.95 postpaid from:
Museum Shop
Boston Museum
of Fine Arts
479 Huntington Avenue
Boston, MA 02115

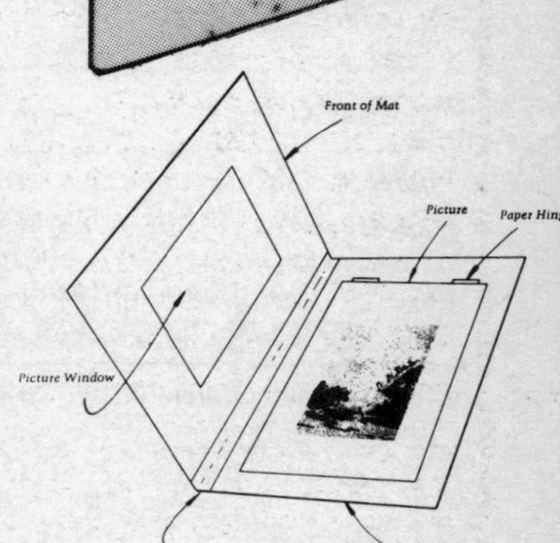

•

A mat serves to protect a picture, whether framed or stored, and to enhance its aesthetic qualities. Since the mat is in close contact with the picture, the collector and framer should be particularly careful about the quality of the materials used in its manufacture. False economy leads many inexperienced framers to use wood-pulp matting board, which is acidic and contains a high percentage of unrefined groundwood pulp that inevitably disintegrates. The picture absorbs some of the destructive chemicals and becomes stained. Mat board of this type is usually faced on both sides with a paper of better quality (even pure rag stock may be used) to make the discoloration less apparent. When an opening for the picture is cut, however, the inner core of inferior material is exposed, and the corrosive chemicals soon migrate into the picture. Pictures that have been kept in such a mat for just a few years begin to show a characteristic brown stain that corresponds with the inner edge of the mat opening.

Talas

A mail order source for all types of art conservation materials and bookbinding supplies. They sell everything from Limousine car polish to a whole range of acid-free boxes for storing paper documents and textiles. Prices are very reasonable. Minimum order is $3.

—Marilyn Green

(See "Bookbinding," p. 505.)

Talas
Catalog
free from:
Talas
130 Fifth Avenue
New York, NY 10011

Leather Protector

2.50	½ pint
4.00	pint
7.40	quart
25.30	gallon

•

Leather protector developed by the British Museum gives triple protection; its potassium lactate counteracts acids absorbed by the leather from its surrounding atmosphere, and neutralizes acids introduced during most tanning processes (both conditions cause leather to become brittle and dry). Its p-nitrophenol protects against molds and mildew, prevalent in moist, hot environments. It also cleans leather.

THE RISING SUN
NEIGHBORHOOD NEWSLETTER

We were talking about cigarette ashes and Lorrie said, "I remember our high school prom, it was the whole thing with your first sexual experiences. Someone's parents were away for the weekend and everyone went there to fuck and have a good time except this one guy who was there but wasn't into it. In the middle of the night he burst into the room and turned on the lights and shouted he had a perfect ash. He did, an ash almost as long as a cigarette with just a little end left to hold it by, but nobody appreciated it."

Exhibits for the Small Museum

I used to work in exhibit design and can affirm that this is a right handy little book for the friendly task of making stuff visible, interesting, understandable, and protected. Great primer for a first-time museum. (Don't tear down that old building. Do this book to it.) —SB

Spring clip for suspended ceiling track

Brass snap swivel (used for fishing)

PULL TIGHT

Nylon fishing line

To suspended object

MONOFILAMENT (NYLON) KNOTS

Mirror B

Rear-projection screen

Mirror A

Furnace filter

→ A closet with a slide projector, mirrors and translucent rear-projection screen can be a useful set-up. By "bending" the projector's beam with mirrors, it is possible to get the equivalent of a 6'9" projection distance in a closet that is only 30" deep.

Exhibits for the Small Museum
(A Handbook)
Arminita Neal
1976; 169 pp.
$8 postpaid from:
American Association for State and Local History
1400 Eighth Avenue South
Nashville, TN 37203
or Whole Earth Household Store

Catalog of art prints

Since 1949 UNESCO has been trying to update and internationalize the world of art prints. They have a central archives of prints, and a committee of experts who decide which prints to include in their catalogs. The criteria are: quality of print, significance of the painter, and importance of the painting.

There are two UNESCO print catalogs: **Catalogue of Colour Reproductions of Paintings Prior to 1860** *and the same of paintings from 1860 to 1973. Both are understandably limited in scope by what quality prints are available, and the choice of painters and paintings is often poor. Too much trivial or repetitive work by minor painters takes the place of better paintings by major artists. The catalog does function as a useful access device, and includes reproductions of many inspired paintings, not all of which are expensive. Each entry includes the artist's name, dates, a black and white photo of the painting, its title, date, medium, size and collection in which it rests. In addition, there are lists of publishers and printers, and information on purchasing prints.*

Catalogs are trilingual in French/English/Spanish and print dimensions are given in both inches and centimeters. But price conversions are not given so you must deal with each foreign price.

—Joe Bonner and Annie Helmuth

Catalogue of Colour Reproductions of Paintings Prior to 1860
1979; 346 pp.
$18.75 postpaid

Catalogue of Colour Reproductions of Paintings 1860 - 1973
1974; 525 pp.
$15 postpaid
both from:
Unipub
345 Park Avenue South
New York, NY 10010

1.

2.

3.

1. Kandinsky — Perpetual Line, **1923. Oil on canvas, 54¾ x 78-9/16 inc. Private collection. Reproduction: Collotype, 24½ x 35¼ in., UNESCO Archives: K. 16-14, Verlag Franz Hanfstaengl, München, Bundesrepublik Deutschland, DM 50.**

2. Cassatt — La Partie de Canotage, **1894. Huile sur toile, 90,2 x 117,5 cm. Chester Dale Collection, National Gallery of Art, Washington. Reproduction: Letterpress, 8½ x 11 in., UNESCO Archives: C. 343-4, Beck Engraving Co., National Gallery of Art, Washington, 25 cts.**

3. Daumier — La Insurrección. **Huile sur toile, 87 x 112,2 cm. The Phillips Memorial Gallery, Washington. Reproduction: Collotype, 22¼ x 28¾ in., UNESCO Archives: D. 241-3, Arthur Jaffé Heliochrome Co., The Twin Editions, Greenwich, Connecticut, USA, $15**

Publications from the AASLH

A catalog of books about how to find and appreciate and show other people the artifacts and history around you. Seeing the historic stuff of your community can change your life. In the George-Washington-slept-here town where I grew up, we kids hung out in the historic museums, where we felt like we were breathing mystery and learning about our special-ness, alone and together. We knew the adults had to be prodded every now and then so they'd see it. The people who set up those shrines probably used these books. (More on local history, see p. 313.)
—Art Kleiner
[Suggested by Ric Haynes]

Publications from the AASLH
Catalog

free from:
American Association for State and Local History
1400 Eighth Avenue So.
Nashville, TN 37203

•

Recreating the Historic House Interior
From Concept to Completion
William Seale

Anyone interested in recreating the interior of an old house will appreciate this book's no-nonsense discussions of floors and wall coverings, transient objects, furniture, lighting, window treatments, and arrangements of a room's elements.

William Seale skillfully leads the reader to historical authenticity with clear-cut descriptions of the research to be done preparatory to the necessary report listing hoped-for acquisitions, items on hand, and themes to be carried out.

With its 108 historical photographs, this book is an invaluable aid for the transformation of the past into the present.

Fall 1978
$22
96 photographs, 12 color plates

artscanada

During the past ten years of her editorship, Anne Brodzky has made **artscanada** *the most informative, most unpredictable, and best designed art mag published in the English language. Every issue is built around a theme: shamanism, West Coast art, maps, contemporary drawing, etc. Writers are brought in as needed to contribute their special expertise; regular contributors are few in number and more or less relegated to the gallery review section in the back pages. This policy of high diversity from issue to issue has prevented* **artscanada** *from institutionalizing itself as an arbiter of taste and value within the art marketing system, has kept it free and credible as an information source.*
In general, the emphasis is on research rather than gossip, ethnography rather than trendwatching. Some issues are so extraordinary (like the shamanism issue, Dec. '73/Jan. '74) that they reappear as hardcover texts at ten times the original newsstand price. Their coverage of Eskimo and Northwest Indian culture is particularly good — to the point where white "mainstream" artists in Vancouver and Toronto complain about being slighted. Since **artscanada** *receives a partial subsidy from the national government (as do most Canadian art organizations), such complaints can translate into political pressure. A growing subscribership is their best defense.* —Robert Horvitz

artscanada
Anne Trueblood Brodzky, Editor
$25/year (6 issues)
from:
Artscanada
Society for Art Publications
3 Church Street
Toronto, Canada
M5E 1M2

A Huichol shaman demonstrates the concept of metaphysical equilibrium by "flying" from rock to rock at the edge of a spectacular waterfall.

Art in America

The only periodical I know that consistently makes art seem like something worth bothering with. —SB

←
Robert Graham: Untitled, 1979, bronze and white paint, 93 inches high. Robert Miller Gallery.

Art in America
Elizabeth C. Baker, Editor
$29.95/year (10 issues)
from:
Art in America
542 Pacific Avenue
Marion, OH 43302

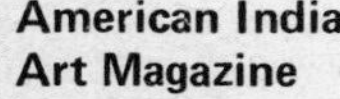

•

More and more sculptors have turned to casting in metal — particularly in bronze — motivated by a desire for permanence, a renewed interest in "touch," even by by economics.

American Indian Art Magazine

From the luxury of Scottsdale, Arizona, comes a quarterly magazine bridging the old crafts of Native Americans with the new, amazing commercial growth of contemporary Indian Art. Luscious photographs and thoughtful articles are sandwiched between ads for the most popular and, sometimes, the best galleries showing today's jewelry, blankets, baskets, silkscreens, paintings and sculpture — all in the native American tradition. (Request the Autumn 1978 issue for Bill Benton's article on the late T.C. Cannon — one of the finest painter-lithographers this continent has ever nurtured.) —Peter Warshall

American Indian Art Magazine
$14/year (4 issues)
from:
American Indian Art Magazine
Circulation Department
7333 E. Monterey Way No. 5
Scottsdale, AZ 85251

← **T.C. Cannon self-portrait**

Foundation creme stick make-up complete/student (jr) size $15. Bob Kelly Cosmetics, Inc. 151 West 46th Street, New York, NY 10036.

No other special effect has the dramatic impact of a bottle broken over an actor's head or smashed against the wall. Rosco breakaways are specially formulated to shatter realistically without any danger to actors, technicians or equipment. They are available in wine, scotch, whiskey, beer or cola bottles, water, beer glasses and champagne stem glasses.

Simon's Directory

Where to find play leases, actors' agents, costumes, make-up, scenery, curtains, projection systems, lighting, props, sound equipment, signs, photographers, books, foundations, and so forth. Covers U.S. and Canada. —SB

Simon's Directory
(Of Theatrical Materials, Services and Information)
1980; 320 pp.
6th Edition

$16.95 postpaid from:
Package Publicity Service
1501 Broadway, Rm. 1314
Room 1314
New York, NY 10036

Theatre House

Lovely junky stage stuff. Fine for amateur theater or for inexpensively tricking yourself out for all-the-world's-a-stage performing. —SB

Theatre House
Catalog

$2 from:
Theatre House
P.O. Box 2090
Covington, KY 41012

FAKE BRICK
Size of a real brick, made of foam rubber.
#1764 - 2.75

FAKE ROCK
Approximately size of a grapefruit, made of foam rubber.
#1765 - 2.75

King
#960
17.25

Queen
#961
14.65

Matching full crowns, 7" diameter, 4 1/2" high, jewel trimmed.

PADRE OR QUAKER

Black - Full size
Paper felt - #1165 - 2.50
Wool felt - #2788 - 13.25

←
Mini Follow Spot

The Mini Spot has an axial mounted 500 watt bulb which gives a very high efficient white light. This is excellent for Night Clubs and small Showcase Theatres. The unit includes a spotlight with Iris, stand and dimmer with extra receptacle. Uses EHD lamp.

Height: 30"; Length: 14"; Dimmer: 500 w
#2769 — $260

Theatrical equipment and supplies

Oh my goodness! A mouth-watering catalog of stage stuff, much of it easily adapted for other uses. (As you might guess, because stage equipment is by its nature always being adapted for this or that). Hide my checkbook!
—J. Baldwin
[Suggested by Dick Dillman]

Theatrical Equipment and Supplies
Catalog

$2 postpaid from:
Mutual Hardware Corp.
5 - 45 49th Avenue
Long Island City, NY 11101

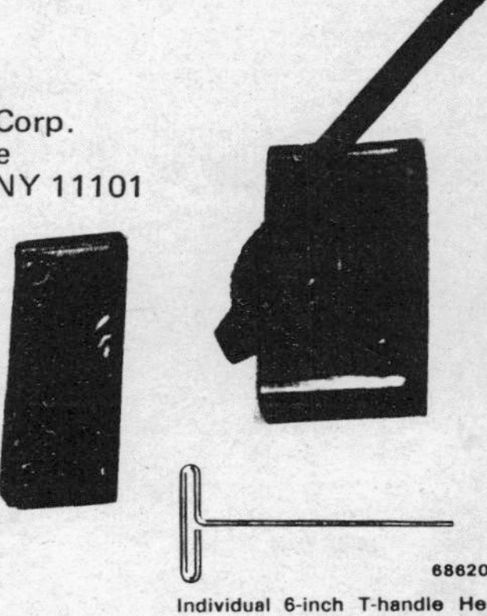

68620
Individual 6-inch T-handle Hex Keys

↑
Coffin/Roto Lock — $2.75

The Coffin/Roto Lock is an excellent device for locking platforms and panels together. Can be recessed or surface mounted. Can be used for right angle connections. It's turned with hex wrench or screw driver. No springs. It operates simply.

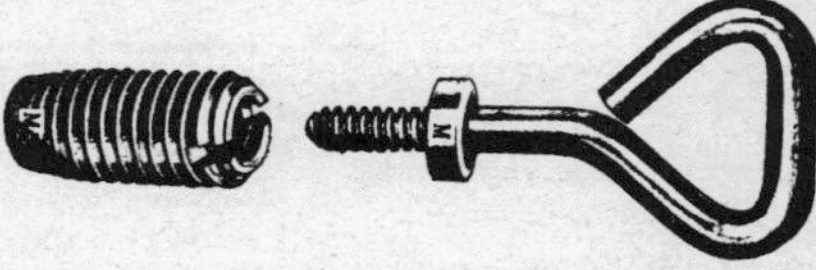

↑
Improved Stage Screw and Plug — $4.25

The new Improved Stage Screw and Plug were developed to eliminate the destruction of stage floors. A ½ inch hole is drilled into stage floor to accomodate a threaded Stage Plug. A vise type thread on Stage Screw allows quick and easy insertion. An unused plug can easily be removed and the hole filled with a 9/16 inch dowel. Holding power is approximately 5 times that of any old style stage screw.

Fig 9000 Plastic Snow is designed to create authentic snowfall effects and set dressings for all stage, television and display work. So real, Eskimos can't tell the difference. 5 pounds equal 1 cubic ft. $2.30/lb.

P-CUSTOM DESIGNED PATTERN TEMPLATES → Can be used with any Ellipsoidal Spotlight

City Alley
P210

City Skyline
P211

Old City Skyline
P212

Industrial Skyline
P213

Bare Trees
P215

Picket Fence
P214

Bare Branches
P216

Jungle Leaf
P217

Realistic Leaves
P218

A. Brill's Bible of Building Plans

Amuse your cows with a 43-whistle circus calliope? Join a carnival as a knife thrower or 'shake-em-up' ride owner? What A.K. Brill sells is methods of making fantasy less improbable. His **Bible** *is part book, part catalog. The 30-page book portion ranges from the economics of carnivals to the recipes for raunchy carnival food (like a "mashed potato center covered with chocolate"), to a method of arthritis relief. The catalog portion offers for sale all the plans and info required to entirely recreate the midway of a sleazy county fair: scary rides, fair games of skill, and curious concessions.*

The building plans he sells are uncommon. They convey the old builder's art of scrounging up the parts needed from what's lying around. It's kind of like hunkering down with the old builder and hearing: "Now you can build this out of a surplus gear box or this way out of an old truck differential and this part can be made of a fly-wheel and front wheel spindle and here is how to figure the gear ratios to get the speed you want . . ." A typical twenty-buck building plan might be twenty dittoed legal size pages. Ten pages of single-spaced monologue, the rest sketches plans and drawings. You learn the cheapest ways of building it in Muncie or Micronesia, how to build the equipment, to decorate it, and how to operate it as well.

On top of some 200 building plans there are offered for sale tricks of the trade — the Magic Horseshoe (No. 719, $5) actually enables anyone to letter large signs easily. In his spare time, A. Brill also sells the 4-foot-tall "giant running chicken" and the "smartly dressed rooster," as well as other oddments. —Alan Kalker

28 NOTE "MINI" CALLIOPE
IS POWERED BY ANY CANISTER TYPE VACUUM CLEANER
Complete Drawings and Instructions
$10
627
ONLY 20½" LONG, 9½" WIDE AND 16" HIGH
CAN BE HEARD FOR A QUARTER MILE
Imagine, an instrument that can be carried in a suitcase size box, giving true tone to 28 individually tuned whistles, in so great a volume. It has safety valves that permits the sweeper to run continuously.
Can be tuned to play with a band, or slightly out of tune, for a clown act. Piano type keyboard.
You can use it for bally or build an entire act acount it. Note: it does not reproduce calliope tones, but that of tuned whistles. All whistles are 3/4" diameter tubing of varying length. Requires considerable lathe work, but not expert machining. Uses auto fittings and street "L", and very little welding.
A.B. Enterprizes BOX 875, PEORIA, ILLINOIS, 61601 U.S.A.
74

A. Brill's Bible of Building Plans
(And Collection of Much Information Useful to Showman, Carnie, Fairman and Amusement Park Operator)
Catalog

$1.50 postpaid from:
A.B. Enterprizes
P.O. Box 875-W
Peoria, IL 61652

Clouds and fog to order

We thought you might be interested in knowing about our company, which makes clouds.

Clouds, fog and mists have many applications in display, decoration, advertising and special effects. Mee Industries can produce these phenomena in size, quantity and even color to meet your requirements.

This firm of cloud physicists has made some major breakthroughs in cloud generation so that these special effects can now be tailored to meet your requirements. One exclusive Mee Industry capability is the generation of real cloud or fog banks from pure water. This can be used to advantage where chemical additives are undesirable.

Mee Industries will work with your designers, engineers and contractors to put clouds to work for you. Call for a quotation on any job with a cloud in its future.

Mailing Address: Post Office Box 365, Altadena, California 91001. Phone: (213) 794-2577

Thomas R. Mee

THE RISING SUN
NEIGHBORHOOD NEWSLETTER

Something that's happening in the Haight is that the cops are coming down pretty hard on public selling and consumption of drugs. The reason for this is some of the 30-year-old young professionals got grossed out by some of the drug-related activities of some of the 19-year-olds, which, almost needless to say, are not without resemblance to the drug-related activities of the 30-year-olds themselves when they were 19. Though the indignation may have been originally aimed at things like visible cocaine deals in local restaurants and visible junkies nodding off on the sidewalk and rumored violence, the effect has been that people have been arrested for smoking marijuana at the corner of Haight and Ashbury and it is much harder to buy marijuana on the streets. Which ain't a big hardship for people our age because we know someone, or know someone who knows someone, or know someone who knows someone who knows someone who's a marijuana farmer (we are in the ownership class), but it's tough for those dumb kids just off the bus from Illinois who came for a bit of the dream that made the 30-year-olds move there in the first place. But it's the American way — once you achieve the dream, you want to clean it up and sand off the rough edges and make it convenient and nice for you.

—Information from Kathleen

Mime

A superior introduction to the art because it's absolutely graphically clear and teaches you tricks quickly enough that you begin with competence and confidence the craft of embodiment. —SB

Balloon Flight

Stand with your knees slightly bent. The balloon you're holding on a string starts pulling your arm up, stretching it higher and higher. Your body follows up . . . up . . . up . . . to your tip toes. You're floating in space.

Look down to see how far you've come (about three inches!).

Mime
(A Playbook of Silent Fantasy)
Kay Hamblin
1978; 192 pp.

$6.95 postpaid from:
Doubleday and Company
501 Franklin Avenue
Garden City, NY 11530
or Whole Earth Household Store

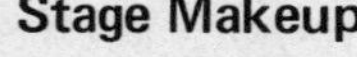

↑
Easy Walk

Stand in neutral with your feet about nine inches apart, your weight on the balls of your feet. Only your heels will move in this walk.

Raise your right heel, bending your right knee. Feel the shift in your pelvis as your right hip moves forward too. The ball of your foot remains stationary, as if glued to the floor.

As you lower your right heel, raise your left heel. Do this simultaneously. Don't wait for your right heel to settle before moving your left.

Repeat, lowering your left heel, raising your right. Again, feel the movement in your hips. All the action is taking place from your waist down. Your head remains level, not bobbing up and down. Direct the movement in your knees forward rather than upward. Both knees remain flexed, not locked tight, and your toes are firmly in place.

Let your arms swing naturally with the movement. Usually the left arm moves forward with the right knee and vice versa.

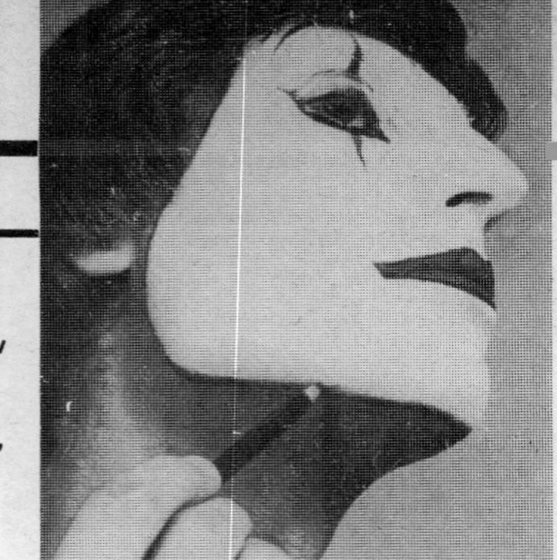

Outline your whiteface with a black line. This line should follow and enhance the natural shape of your face. Your "mask of silence" is now complete.

Dancing

Dance may not be something to learn from a book, but this book serves as a great introduction to those of us who are beguiled and yet intimidated by the idea of dancing. Addressed both to the hesitant adult beginner who prances around the house when nobody's looking and to the young adult considering a career in dance, **Dancing** *cuts through a lot of the mystique and mistaken glamour with practical, specific advice: choosing a style of dance, finding a good teacher and getting the most out of a class, preventing injury, and even viewing dance.*

A real aid for parents who want to get their youngsters started off on the right foot — both daughters and sons (plenty of photos of men dancing, though most of the pronouns are "she"). Competent directory of dance resources around the country, with special emphasis on New York. (Jacob is responsible for the annual guide **Dance in New York.***)*

Dancing *does what no elegant dance picture book can do: makes it plain that you can dance even if you don't look like a Capezio ad.* —Nancy E. Dunn

Dancing
(The Complete Guide)
Ellen Jacob
1980; 320 pp.

$9.95 postpaid from:
Danceways Books
393 West End Avenue
New York, NY 10024
or Whole Earth Household Store

•

A good class has a thorough warm-up with adequate time to establish alignment and placement. The teacher should be constructive and inspiring, and should push you beyond your limits physically by increasing your range of movement and strength; and mentally, by breaking through barriers of fear. Avoid an inhibiting atmosphere in which too much discipline prevents you from making mistakes and learning from them; a frustrated, negative teacher; overcrowded classes, and rushed classes, especially the warm-up. Also stay away from classes that are so slow and intellectual that the body has no chance to incorporate what is learned into its muscle memory. Dancing is nonverbal. Words can help, but eventually you have to understand in your body.

—Sara Maule
American Ballet Theatre

•

In most dance classes the more advanced students stand in the front line during center work and go first across the floor. They serve as models for students who are less sure of the combinations. Use them as examples, but with a grain of salt: They are students too, and they can make mistakes. If you get overdependent on following others, you'll never know how to do anything yourself. And you'll be in trouble when you are moved to the front line.

Once you feel comfortable in a dance class, it's a good idea to periodically change your spot at the barre or in the center. Some teachers assign places for students to stand; but if placement is left up to you, don't get stuck in the back left corner of the room every day. During one class each week try standing on the right side, or in the center. You don't want to learn the routines from one perspective only, or to be hidden most of the time from the teacher's correcting eye. If you always rush to the front, other dancers won't get their turn for the teacher's attention.

•

You cannot dance well unless you have clear intentions — a sharp attack that comes from a precise idea of the steps. Learning to see and pick up movement is thus a critical part of dancing.

•

Modern dance attire is the simplest and least expensive because you work barefoot. Leotards and tights or leg warmers are all you need. Heavy socks with the heels and toes cut out can also be added to keep the ankles warm. Special footless tights are sold for modern dance, but many dancers prefer to cut the heels and toes off their ballet tights, or to slit the foot seams, so they can be used both ways (thin white ankle socks can be worn with footless tights to make the reverse change for classes that require shoes). If you bruise easily you may want to buy a pair of knee pads to protect your knees during floor work. These should not be too tight, and can be purchased at any sporting goods store.

Stage Makeup

This is one art that would require a hell of a book to put across with the printed page alone. **Stage Makeup** *does it. Step-by-step close-up photos, in color where needed, make it look easy enough to try, and when you find it isn't easy, the photos help you learn where you went wrong. Not all the tricks of the trade are here, but enough to get you work.* —SB

Stage Makeup
Herman Buchman
1971; 208 pp.

$21.50 postpaid from:
Watson-Guptill Publications
2160 Patterson Street
Cincinnati, OH 45214
or Whole Earth Household Store

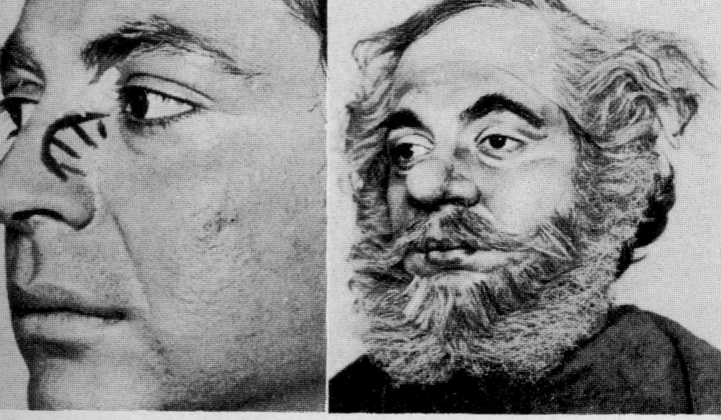

←

There are two major illusions which need to be created in the extreme stout technique: (1) All wrinkles and folds of flesh will be shaped as horizontally as possible to make the face seem wider. This will apply also to the use of wig, mustache, and beard. (2) We will create the illusion that the face is larger than it actually is by making many features appear smaller than they actually are. Therefore, carrying the facial lines horizontally, making the features smaller, plus creating specific optical illusions of roundness, will contribute to the extreme stout effect we seek.

To make the bridge of the nose shorter and wider, carry the shadow from the corner of the eye onto the bridge in an arc, moving down to the nostril. Apply a strong highlight in the corner of the eye.

The Use and Training of the Human Voice

Everything you need to understand, train, improve and enjoy your voice is here in this wonderful book. Lessac's method is uncomplicated and precise . . . a basic system for actors, speakers, singers, everyone who uses the voice as an instrument beyond simple communication.

One of the best features of Lessac's approach is the way he relates the voice to general health and the total person. Many people who never get near a stage or a microphone can use the book to make real gains in self-awareness and well-being.

Best of all, perhaps, the book is designed for self-teaching. It takes nothing for granted, but exposes every vital aspect of the use and training of the voice.

—Scott Beach

The Use and Training of the Human Voice
(A Practical Approach to Speech and Voice Dynamics)
Arthur Lessac
1960, 1967; 297 pp.

$12.50 postpaid from:
DBS Publications
150 West 52nd Street
New York, NY 10019

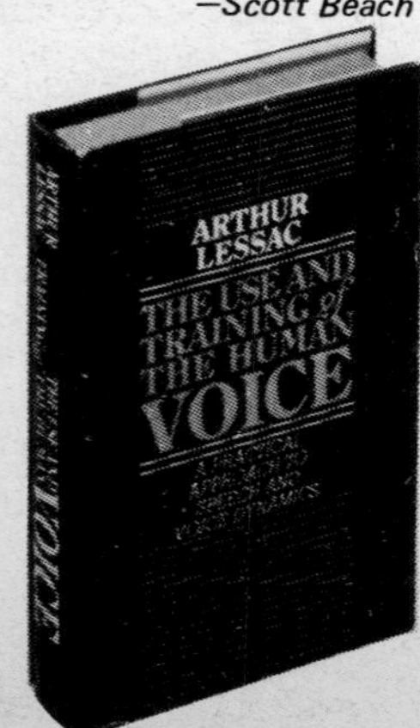

•

When the word *characteristic* is spoken with the C's felt as light, tapping drumbeats and the S as a sustained sound effect, it takes on new rhythm and a new quality of expression. The same principle applies to words like *environment, demand, questioned, contract,* and *scientists.*

•

Character Calls

Play each of these roles with a clear, comfortable, sustained resonant call. Find your own pitch and your own motivation.

1. *Train conductor:* All Aboard — Tacoma . . . Emporia . . . Tuscahoma . . . Roanoke . . . Daytonsburgh . . . Baltimore . . . Philadelphia . . . Williamsburg . . . Buffalo . . . Dover . . . New Brunswick . . . and all points north — A-a-a-all abo-o-o-o-o-o-a-rd
2. *Street vendor:* Apple . . . Potato . . . Watermelon . . . (Pronounced: Epaw . . . Pohtehtoh . . . Wawtahmelohn . . .)
3. *Captain of a sailing schooner:* Ahoy there *Marco Polo* — Can we help you?
4. *Construction worker:* Okay, Joe . . . Let 'er go-o-o-o-o-o-o-o! Okay, Bill . . . take 'em away-ay-ay-ay-ay-ay!

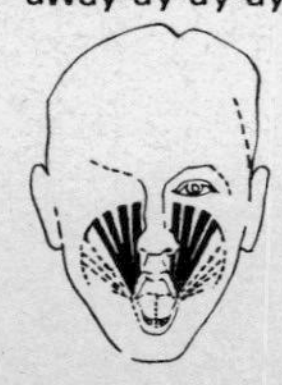

Triangular patches of muscle that help form the inverted megaphone shape.

IDENTITY IS A FRAME; death is a curtain; we are all actors. Those who "act" the identity of others are directly connected to the lineage of Paleolithic shamans; first transformers; first knowers that identity is mutable.

That their magic is fundamental is proven time and time again by the power available to even the puffiest bourgeois theatrical when it brushes this charged ground.

A study of the following books will put stretch in your sense of self, aid the development of penetrating observation, and do for your human interactions what jogging does for the cardiovascular system. Become your own transformer. Practice throwing your own switches. You'll be surprised what your little electric train can do. —Peter Coyote

Audition

Michael Shurtleff, casting director for such hits as **The Graduate, Beckett, The Sound of Music,** *and* **Pippin,** *offers a montage of useful observations from a life spent discriminating winners and losers. Not as technique-oriented as Stanislavski, but a well-built compass indicating specific directions, and his tone and bits of show-biz lore are honest as a good comedian and quite in tune with the times.* —Peter Coyote

Audition
(Everything an Actor Needs to Know to Get the Part)
Michael Shurtleff
1978; 187 pp.
$3.95 postpaid from:
Bantam Books
414 East Golf Road
Des Plaines, IL 60016
or Whole Earth Household Store

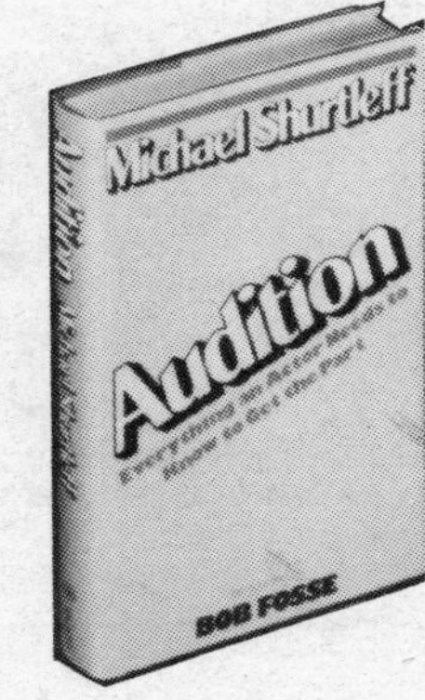

•

An actor cannot play boredom or he will be boring. He must find what it is that the character wants instead of the boring condition he's in, and he must fight for that. I use the word *fight* because the actor must find the strongest, most positive goal possible. Nothing less will do.

•

Humor is not being funny. It is the coin of exchange between human beings that makes it possible for us to get through the day. . . . One would sometimes think actors are trying to reverse the life process by what they do onstage. They take humor out instead of put it in. That's what makes acting unlifelike.

An Actor Prepares

The Source Text. Stanislavski's studies of the techniques of the best actors of his day are the basis of all subsequent teachings. His dedication and worship of nature are an inspiration. —Peter Coyote

An Actor Prepares
Constantin Stanislavski;
Elizabeth Reynolds Hapgood, Translator
1936, 1948; 295 pp.
$9.95 postpaid from:
Theatre Arts Books
153 Waverly Place
New York, NY 10014
or Whole Earth Household Store

•

When you speak to the person who is playing opposite you, learn to follow through until you are certain your thoughts have penetrated his consciousness. Only after you are convinced of this and have added with your eyes what could not be put into words, should you continue to say the rest of your lines.

Impro

Most theater texts are like books on learning to ride a bike. Only after you have the hang of it are they valuable. This book is a rare peek into genius. Keith Johnstone, associated with George Devine and Tony Richardson of the Royal Court Theatre in London, creator of the Theatre Machine, comes across as a true magician, an inspired innovator of techniques for plugging people into the wellsprings of their own imaginations. One of the most useful and provocative books I have ever read on theater. —Peter Coyote
[Suggested by Pat Ryan]

Impro
(Improvisation and the Theatre)
Keith Johnstone
1979; 208 pp.
$11.95 postpaid from:
Theatre Arts Books
153 Waverly Place
New York, NY 10014
or Whole Earth Household Store

•

There are people who prefer to say "Yes" and there are people who prefer to say "No." Those who say "Yes" are rewarded by the adventures they have, and those who say "No" are rewarded by the safety they attain. There are far more "No" sayers around than "Yes" sayers, but you can train one type to behave like the others. . . . Fred Karno understood this. When he interviewed aspiring actors he'd poke his pen into an empty inkwell and pretend to flick ink at them. If they mimed being hit in the eye, or whatever, he'd engage them. If they looked baffled and "blocked" him, then he wouldn't.

•

"Try to get your status just a little above or below your partner's," I said, and I insisted that the gap should be minimal. The actors seemed to know exactly what I meant and the work was transformed. The scenes became "authentic", and actors seemed marvellously observant. Suddenly we understood that every inflection and movement implies a status, and that no action is due to chance, or really "motiveless". It was hysterically funny, but at the same time very alarming. All our secret manoeuvrings were exposed. If someone asked a question we didn't bother to answer it, we concentrated on why it had been asked. No one could make an "innocuous" remark without everyone instantly grasping what lay behind it. Normally we are "forbidden" to see status transactions except when there's a conflict. In reality status transactions continue all the time. In the park we'll notice the ducks squabbling, but not how carefully they keep their distances when they are not.

Respect for Acting

Uta Hagen's book is an indispensable companion to Shurtleff's, Stanislavski's and Boleslavsky's. A consummate actress and teacher, she offers precise methodologies for developing one's intuitions, perceptions and responses, and coaxing open the doors of the subconscious as reservoir for solutions to acting problems. (Which are real-life problems, no?)

Her style is passionate, and her standards are demandingly high, offered to what is best in world theater. She has also written an inspiring cookbook called **Respect for Cooking.** —Peter Coyote

Respect for Acting
Uta Hagen
with Haskel Frankel
1973; 227 pp.
$7.95 postpaid from:
Macmillan Publishing Co.
Order Department
Front and Brown Streets
Riverside, NJ 08075
or Whole Earth Household Store

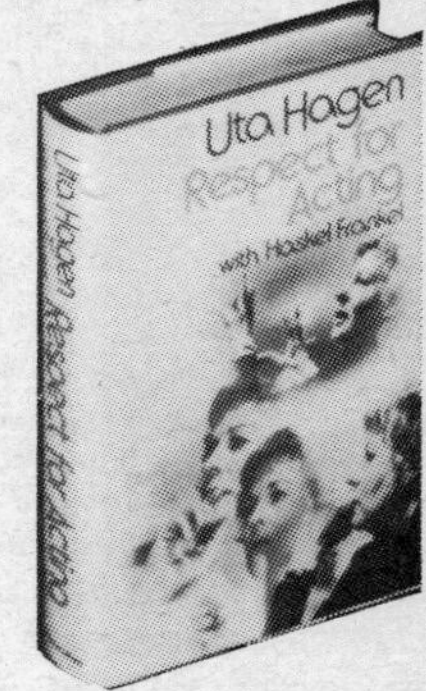

•

You must *justify* your character not judge him, or you will fall into one of two traps. Either you will soften and sentimentalize the character to prove that "I'm not really like this," or you will bring about illustrative actions to tell an audience "look how evil *he* is."

Improvisation for the Theater

Widely considered the best source for getting non-rote life seething on the stage. Take the chances, interact, make it through the lameness into originality that is. —SB
[Suggested by Scott Beach]

Improvisation for the Theater
Viola Spolin
1963, 1973; 397 pp.
$12.50 postpaid from:
Northwestern University Press
1735 Benson
Department S80
Evanston, IL 60201
or Whole Earth Household Store

•

Hidden Conflict

Two or more players.

Where, Who, and What agreed upon. Each player takes a conflict and states it to himself in the first person without letting the other know what it is.

POINT OF CONCENTRATION: never to verbalize the problem (conflict).

EXAMPLE: Where — kitchen. Who — husband and wife. What — breakfast.

Hidden conflict: Husband — I am not going to work. Wife — I want him to leave. I'm expecting a visitor.

POINTS OF OBSERVATION

1. Let audience know each player's hidden conflict.
2. When the hidden conflict is stated, the scene is over.
3. Variation of this is to write a series of hidden conflicts on slips of paper and let actors pick after they have decided on Where, Who, and What.
4. HIDDEN CONFLICT forces use of objects and was one of the early exercises that started the semantic shift from "conflict" to "problem," thus opening up new doors of inquiry.

Acting: The First Six Lessons

This book, about teaching a young lady, "The Creature," what acting is about, is recommended for all anthropologists, psychologists, and others who are impressed with the ridiculousness and grandeur of people. It's done in the form of a dialogue between Boleslavsky and the creature and is almost impossible to quote because what the book has to say is mostly in the way the dialogue is put together. —Gregory Bateson

Acting: The First Six Lessons
Richard Boleslavsky
1970; 122 pp.
$5.95 postpaid from:
Theatre Arts Books
153 Waverly Place
New York, NY 10014
or Whole Earth Household Store

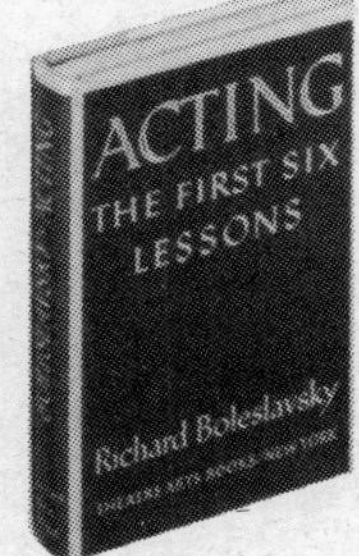

•

The Creature: Do you mean to say that Ophelia should not think?

I: I wouldn't be so rude as that, but I would say that Shakespeare did all the thinking for her. It is his mind at work which you should characterize while acting Ophelia, or for that matter, any Shakespearean character. The same goes for any author who has a mind of his own.

The Creature: I never thought of that. I always tried to think the way I imagined the character would think.

I: That is a mistake which almost every actor commits. Except geniuses — who know better. The most powerful weapon of an author is his mind. The quality of it, the speed, alertness, depth, brilliancy. All of that counts, without regard to whether he is writing words of Caliban or those of Jeanne d'Arc, or those of Osvald. A good writer's fool is no more foolish than his creator's mind, and a prophet no more wise than the man who conceived him. Do you remember Romeo and Juliet? Lady Capulet says about Juliet, "She's not fourteen." And then a few pages later Juliet speaks.

"My bounty is as boundless as the sea,
My love as deep; the more I give to thee,
The more I have, for both are infinite."

Confucius could have said that, or Buddha, or St. Francis. If you will try acting Juliet's part in a way which characterizes her mind as a fourteen-year-old mind, you'll be lost. If you try to make her older you'll ruin Shakespeare's theatrical conception which is that of a genius. If you try to explain it by the early maturity of Italian women, by the wisdom of the Italian Renaissance, and so forth, you will be all tangled up in archaeology and history, and your inspiration will be gone. All you have to do is to grasp the characterization of Shakespeare's mind and follow it.

The Creature: How would you describe the quality of it?

I: A mind of lightning-like speed. Highly concentrated, authoritative, even in moments of doubt. Spontaneous, the first thought is always the last one. Direct and outspoken. Don't misunderstand me, I'm not trying to describe or explain Shakespeare's mind. No words can describe it. All I am trying to do is to tell you that whatever character of Shakespeare you perform, its mind (not yours but the character's) must have those qualities in its manifestation. You don't have to think like Shakespeare, but the outward quality of thinking must be his. It is like portraying an acrobat. You don't have to know how to stand on your head, but all the movements of your body must convey the idea that you are able to turn somersaults whenever you wish to do it.

THE RISING SUN
NEIGHBORHOOD NEWSLETTER

Don told me that Captain James Cook presented some island king with a turtle and the turtle is still alive and in the same family.

Oak Publications

THE publisher when it comes to down home funky music.
—Andi Lewis

Oak Publications
Quick Fox Books Catalog

free from:
Oak Publications
33 West 60th Street
New York, NY 10023

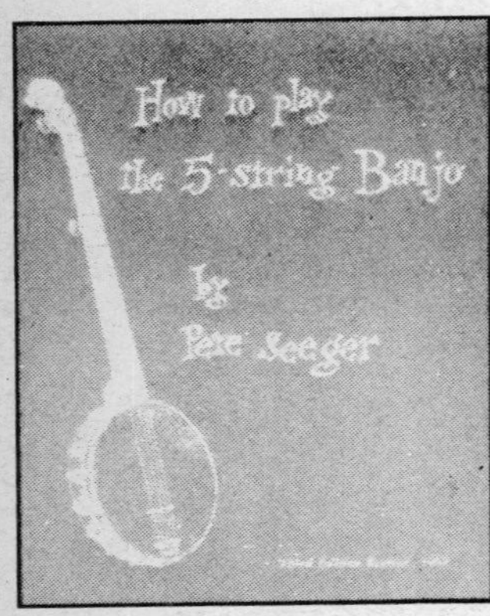

—From Folk Style Autoharp, **Oak Publications.**

How to Play the Five-String Banjo
by Pete Seeger

The unique qualities of the five-string banjo are captured to perfection in this instructional manual by one of the greats of American folk music. This is the basic manual for banjo players at any level. Beginners can work at their own pace, learning all the fundamentals of strumming, hammering-on, and pulling-off. More advanced players can brush up on their technique or explore new areas (blues, jazz, Spanish and South American music). In addition to practice exercises, there are many favorite folk and traditional songs all with melody line, lyrics, and banjo accompaniment, and solos in standard notation and tablature. Discography and bibliography included.

ISBN: 0-8256-0024-3 *72 pages/$2.95* *000024*

•

How to Play Nearly Everything
by Dallas Cline

Dallas Cline, author of **Homemade Instruments**, has compiled a new book that teachers, parents, kids, and anyone who loves making music will want to have. Chapters are written by specialists in their fields, and cover how to make and play such folk instruments as the wash-tub bass, kazoo, washboard, spoons, bodhran (Irish drum), jaw harp, musical saw and more. Each instrument constitutes a complete project, with instructions on how to construct and play it, plus a song in tab to learn. Here's a book that's filled with history, illustrations and fun, particularly good for classroom use, but appealing to just about anyone interested in music as well.

ISBN: 0-8256-0199-1 *80 pages/$3.95* *000199*

Blowin' In The Wind

Words and Music by
BOB DYLAN

In singing a slurred note, keep in mind that the human voice is like a trombone. I don't know about you, but I like to hear a voice that moves around easily and smoothly, without yoo-hooing. You know what I mean by a "yoo-hooer"? It's the kind of singer who sings,

"He's got the whole wur-hurld
In his hands"

Maybe some like it. You make up your own mind about it.

Henscratches and Flyspecks ↑

What a wonderful book! Pete Seeger has brought joy and pleasure to millions of folks with his singing. And now, he's whomped-up this easy guide to understanding the sign-language of music. Everybody who's itched to be able to look at those confusing spots, squiggles, swoops and lines and sing the song they stand for will have a ball.
—Scott Beach

Henscratches and Flyspecks
(How to read melodies from songbooks in twelve confusing lessons)

Peter Seeger
1973; 256 pp.

OUT OF PRINT
G.P. Putnam and Company

Get this book back in print!

Musical Saw

I play saw. It's the easiest instrument to learn except maybe for kazoo — you can get into it in a week or two well enough to show off. People generally eat it up: "Hey look . . . he's playing a SAW!" What I like best is being able to sit in on some good bluegrass (the slow numbers). Hank Williams tunes are just right. You can get together with other saw-ers and do barbershop harmony too. Yes, you can probably play the saw you have hanging in the garage, but even the best of them (Sandvik or Disston) will only give you an octave or so. This professional saw gets a good two octaves, and sounds fine wailing along as harmony with a fiddle. No particular skill needed except you have to be able to carry a tune. These are very nice saws. *—J. Baldwin*

Musical Saw
$20 postpaid

Kit with bow, case, etc. in addition to the saw
$42.50 postpaid

Information
free

all from:
Mussehl and Westphal
130 South 4th Street
Delevan, WI 53115

J. Baldwin howling and shimmering away on his Messehl and Westphal.

Autoharps

I think autoharps are easier to play than guitars, mainly because the chording is done mechanically. Thirty-six strings and twelve or fifteen bars of felt pads. Push down a bar, and all the strings you don't want in your chord, are felt padded out, so you are left to figure out how to keep thirty-six strings in tune, and what to do with the hand that isn't pushing down bars.

Autoharps are cheap: $70 to $125 from Sears (p. 348). The Oscar Schmidt Company, which makes Sears' also has their own line available at music stores for $155 to $280. *—J.D. Smith*

Oscar Schmidt Autoharps
Catalog

free from:
Fretted Industries
1415 Waukegan Road
Northbrook, IL 60062

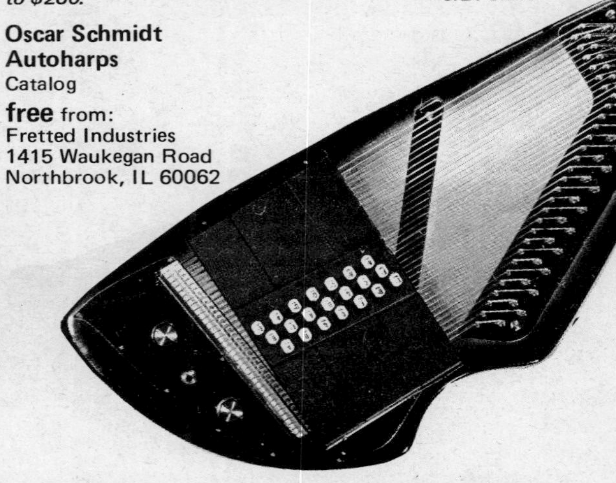

The Mountain Dulcimer
The Hammered Dulcimer

These book-record combinations correct the craziness of most music books — trying to convey expertise in an ear medium through exclusive use of the eyes. Mostly you learn music from other people and from instruments. With these items you can start with neither, make the instrument and become the people. And Folk Legacy Records are nice, uh, folks. See p. 480. *—SB*

The Mountain Dulcimer
(How to make and play it — after a fashion)
Howard Mitchell
1965, 1966; 50 pp.
plus 12" record
$8.98 postpaid

The Hammered Dulcimer
(How to make it and play it)
Howard Mitchell
1971; 50 pp.
plus 12" record
$8.98 postpaid

both from:
Folk Legacy Records
Sharon, CT 06069

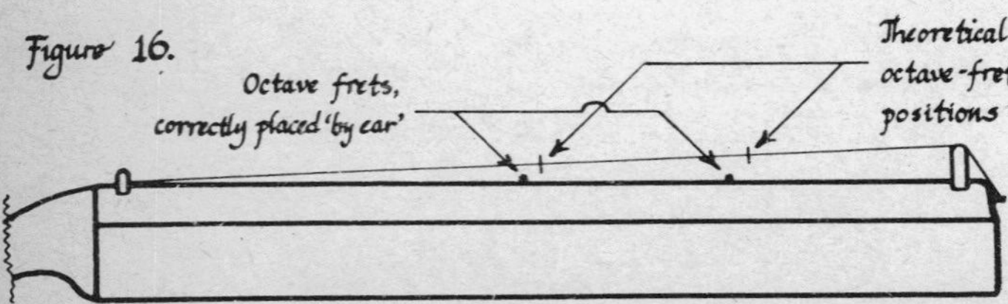

Stewart-MacDonald Banjo

Their particular claim to fame is their line of banjo and mandolin kits which provide musicians with great sounding instruments in easy-to-build money-saving form. Mandolin kit $150. Banjo kits $142 - $289.
—David Burnor

Stewart-MacDonald Banjos and Mandolin Kits

Catalog
$ .50 from:
Stewart-MacDonald Manufacturing Co.
P.O. Box 900
Athens, OH 45701

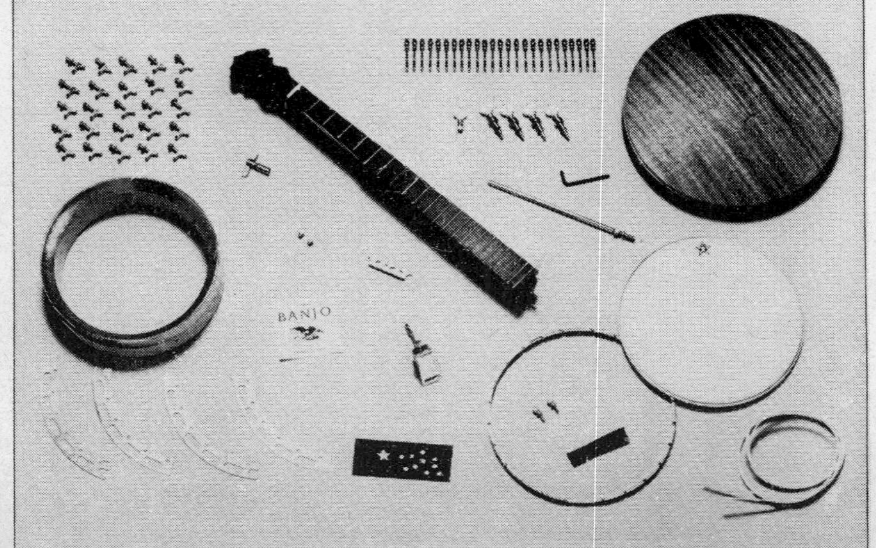

1 Triple pipe, earthenware, Mexico, c. 500 AD (Veracruz Museum, Mexico)
2 Triple reed whistle, South America
3 Gling-bu, wood, Tibet

Triple flutes. The Mexican triple flute (1) has one longer pipe that was probably unfingered and used as a drone. The South American triple whistle (2) has sound holes near the center of the pipes. The Tibetan gling-bu (3) has identically placed finger holes on each pipe.

Musical Instruments of the World

With sufficient cleverness I daresay you could cobble together some damned interesting instruments just by close attention to the illustrations, profuse (4000) and detailed as they are, in this absorbing survey of the world's noise-makers.
—SB
[Suggested by Otis Reed]

Musical Instruments of the World
(An Illustrated Encyclopedia)
The Diagram Group
1976; 320 pp.
$24.95 postpaid from:
Facts on File
119 West 57th Street
New York, NY 10019
or Whole Earth Household Store

Hughes instrument kits

Nice cheap shoddy instrument kits. I believe I'd try a few of these before I took on a Burton Harpsichord.
—SB
[Suggested by Charles Benecke]

Hughes Dulcimer Co.
Catalog
free from:
Hughes Dulcimer Co.
4419 West Colfax Avenue
Denver, CO 80204

Double or courting dulcimer played by the courting couple — no chaperon was needed as long as the sound of the dulcimer was heard. D37W8 $76; spruce top $16.

The Amateur Wind Instrument Maker

Robinson has put together an excellent guide, both for craftsmen and for musicians. The book includes lucid descriptions of the materials and methods for making a number of wind instruments, and includes detailed plans for making flutes, recorders, oboes, shawms, trumpets, and many others. This is not a handbook for whittling hobbyists, but a how-to-do-it manual for serious craftsmen.
—Scott Beach

The Amateur Wind Instrument Maker
Trevor Robinson
1973; 132 pp.
$8.95 postpaid from:
The University of Massachusetts Press
P.O. Box 429
Amherst, MA 01002

Vibrations

How to make your own musical instruments, and a good book, too. Ceramic flutes, bamboo flutes, tin can fiddles — some traditional and some downright weirdo noise-makers are presented with clear instructions, sharp drawings, and lots of encouragement. Exceptionally nifty: a nice gift for someone you like.
—J. Baldwin

Vibrations
(Making Unorthodox Musical Instruments)
David Sawyer
1977; 102 pp.
$9.95 postpaid from:
Cambridge University Press
510 North Avenue
New Rochelle, NY 10801
or Whole Earth Household Store

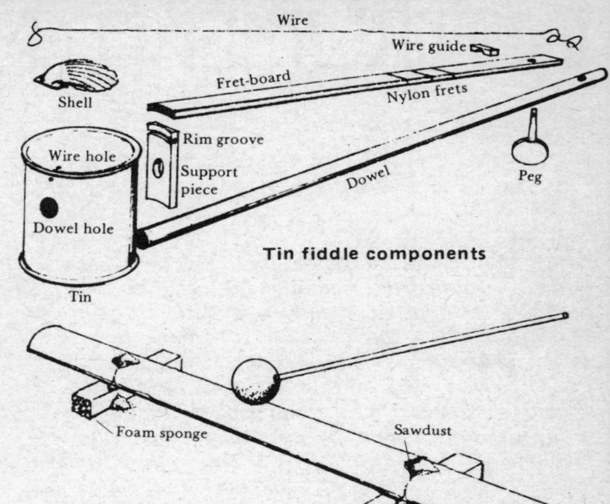

Tin fiddle components

Foam sponge
Sawdust

Sawdust method to find the nodal points where the bar will be supported

Horns, Strings, and Harmony

This is a very clear and fairly comprehensive introduction to musical physics, with suggestions for experiments to be performed by the reader at home. The author is a physicist and musician; the book is written for musicians and amateur physics teachers.
—Peter Lynn Sessions

Horns, Strings, and Harmony
Arthur H. Benade
1960; 269 pp.
$2.50 postpaid from:
Doubleday and Company
501 Franklin Avenue
Garden City, NY 11530
or Whole Earth Household Store

•

Once again the flute is different from other woodwinds; it needs no bell for two reasons: first because the vibration recipe of any flute, old or new in style, is so lacking in the higher components that very little sound energy is present above the change-over frequency, and, second, the very large holes of the modern Boehm flute serve to cut off the tube so effectively that *all* the notes think of themselves as coming out of the end of an ordinary pipe!

The size of a side hole affects a pipe's vibrational frequencies. The extent of the effect is illustrated here by comparing different hole sizes with pipe lengths that give matching frequencies. Each pipe in the lower row has a frequency matching that of the holed pipe immediately above it.

Making a Simple Violin and Viola

Another first-rate book by the author of **Musical Instruments Made to Be Played**. *Ronald Roberts takes a thorough and practical approach to instrument making. The designs, explanations and illustrations are clearly presented so that anyone with minimal workshop skills can produce a respectable instrument.*

There's no pleasure quite like that of finishing an instrument and playing it for the first time. My first such experience was with a dulcimer I made under the guidance of Lyn Elder, another excellent teacher and craftsman. I've made two other instruments using Roberts' plans and methods, and the results have been delightful.

The uncomplicated violin and viola designs in this book will probably horrify purists of the Amati-Guarneri-Stradivari school. But Roberts isn't talking to them. His designs and steps are directed toward the average person who may never dream of making one of those super-difficult traditional instruments, but who'd be very happy to make and play a thoroughly serviceable violin or viola.
—Scott Beach

(See **Make Your Own Musical Instruments**, *p. 544.)*

Making a Simple Violin and Viola
Ronald Roberts
1976; 112 pp.
$13.95 postpaid
Violin and Viola plans
$5 postpaid
both from:
David and Charles, Inc.
P.O. Box 57
North Pomfret, VT 05053

←
A spade head and tuning gear fitted to a violin made of maple and spruce

H.L. Wild

Good wood is getting scarce. It takes a good while to grow a mahogany tree. Wild has a fine selection of instrument maker's woods, and the plans, tools, and books to go along with them.
—J.D. Smith

(Wild's was all set to send us their catalog so we could show you some of their marvelous materials, but at the last minute their catalogs were stolen from the printshop. Alas!
—Art Kleiner)

H.L. Wild
Catalog
free from:
H.L. Wild
510 East 11th Street
New York, NY 10009

THE RISING SUN
NEIGHBORHOOD NEWSLETTER

Mammals and such are hot blooded, meaning they make their heat inside their bodies. Reptiles are cold blooded, meaning they get their heat from the outside environment. When I was in elementary school, they taught us that this means that reptiles are the same temperature as the air around them, but this is not true in real life. It is only true in laboratories, where there is no sun. When reptiles are in the sun, they can keep their internal temperature within a 2 degree area (like 110-112 F. for lizards) by changing their relationship to the sun. In the morning they put their bodies lengthwise to the sun to catch all the rays they can and in the hot afternoon they face it head on or go under rocks so they don't burn up. Every movement has something to do with maintaining body heat and body heat is maintained. But if you put them in a lab lit by fluorescent lights and heated by the radiator, they just lie there and become room temperature, and lead you to lie to young children.

—Information from *Hot Blooded Dinosaurs* by Adrian J. Desmond

INSTRUMENT MAKING

by Doug Roomian

*I asked luthier Doug Roomian for this survey after we saw an article in the San Francisco **Examiner** about him which said he started instrument making because he read about it in **The Last Whole Earth Catalog** in 1971. He trained himself, co-managed a music store in San Francisco, and now he makes, plays, and repairs fine guitars and dulcimers full-time.*
—Art Kleiner

NO BOOK will enable you to become a master luthier. Guts, patience, commitment for a lifetime of hard and rewarding work, and a great desire to see more fine instruments in the world are really more important factors. There is no one consensus among builders or musicians about what constitutes a great instrument. Each book reviewed here is good enough that if you follow the outline diligently you will make a quality instrument. The key is that you will make the instrument, not the author. So read the books well, keep your mind open and seek help (if possible) when in trouble. Handmaking your own instrument is a task greater than many people aspire to. Playing an instrument paid for not by dollars but by your own commitment to beauty and music is something worthy of your aspiration.

Classic Guitar Construction

A book that I'm sure you would find in every guitar maker's library. Why? Because Sloane's book is an accurately detailed outline of the Spanish method of constructing a classical guitar. The Spanish developed the guitar as we know it, and the Spanish guitar is, to this day, considered the standard among classical musicians. There are other ways to build a guitar, but the chances are good that a classical performer will want it built this way.

Classic Guitar Construction
(Designs, photographs, and step-by-step instructions)
Irving Sloane
1966; 95 pp.
$10.95 postpaid from:
E.P. Dutton and Co.
Two Park Avenue
New York, NY 10016
or Whole Earth Household Store

Rosette — The mosaic inlay around the sound hole identifies the Byzantine heritage of the Spanish guitar.

Classic Guitar Making

I like the Overholtzer book. Imagine Yankee ingenuity set loose on the classical guitar. Inside you'll find a plethora of information and many neat jigs that the woodworker schooled in America will appreciate. It may not be the design most guitar makers would choose, but if you plan on making any guitar you will find this technique very useful. Available from Williams Tool Company who also offer for sale many luthier tools designed by Mr. Overholtzer. (Williams Tool Company, 5531 San Juan Avenue, Citrus Heights, CA 95610.)

Classic Guitar Making
Arthur E. Overholtzer
1974; 325 pp.
$14.95 postpaid from:
Brock Publishing Company
P.O. Box 1685
Chico, CA 95927
or Whole Earth Household Store

Yacobi
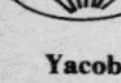

Esteso

Torres

Amadeo

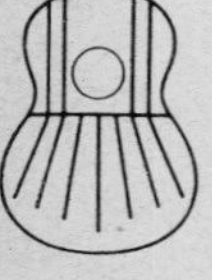
Bouchet

Tatay

← Different styles of top bracing

↓ Carpenter square as straightedge

Complete Guitar Repair

The set-up, maintenance, restoration and construction of the acoustic and electric guitar by a master craftsman. Soft-spoken Hideo Kamimoto is a well-respected repairman in the Bay Area. This book shows why. Lots of well-thought-out approaches to the types of repairs you as a repairperson will have to deal with. I recommend practicing the more difficult repairs. If you can turn that flea market special into something that plays and looks like a concert model, you're ready to tackle that 1910 Martin. Side note: it's been my experience that instruments are rarely broken in the hands of the people who own them. Few people will respect your guitar as you do. Please be careful whom you loan it to.

Complete Guitar Repair
Hideo Kamimoto
1975; 192 pp.
$7.95 postpaid from:
Oak Publications
33 West 60th Street
New York, NY 10023
or Whole Earth Household Store

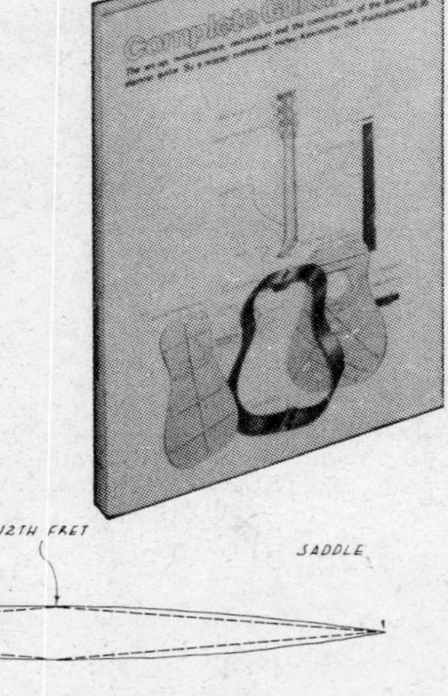

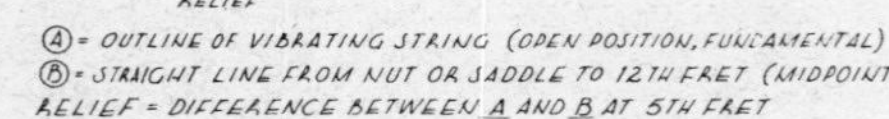

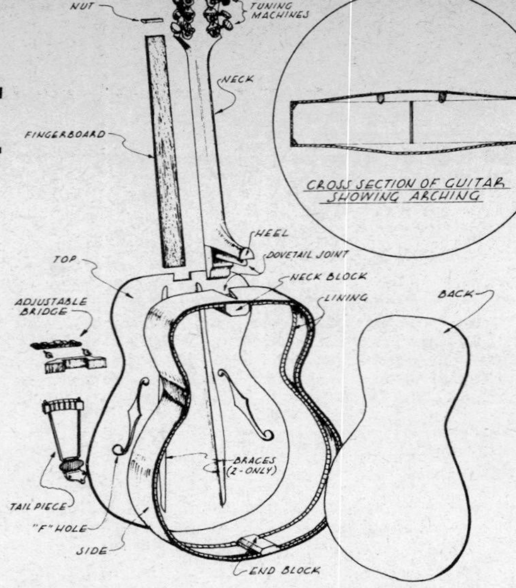

PLECTRUM GUITAR – EXPLODED VIEW

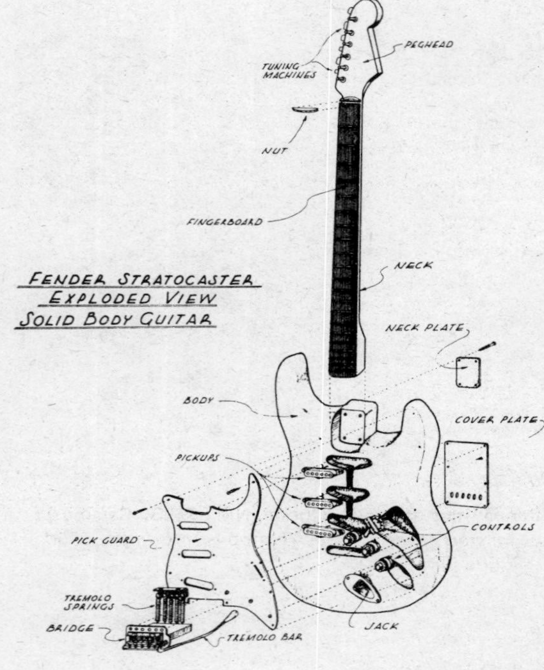

SUPPLIERS

Gurian, P.O. Box 595, West Swanzey, NH 03469. Catalog $1. *One of the larger suppliers of musical instrument materials, Gurian sells to everybody, from basement luthiers to large factories. Prices are among the best and although the quality does vary, it is never unacceptable. For one dollar you receive a catalog of parts and materials for guitars, mandolins, lutes, viola da gambas, banjos, and both plucked and hammered dulcimers.*

The Luthier's Mercantile, P.O. Box 774, Healdsburg, CA 95448. Catalog $4.60. *Formerly the Bill Lewis Supply Company of Washington, Luthier's is now run by Tom Peterson, who is working very hard to make his business the most complete supplier of wood, parts and tools for the stringed instrument maker. Slightly more than a catalog, this publication has articles on wood, workshop tips and other goodies.*

KMP Larry Kass Music Products, P.O. Box 4111, San Rafael, CA 94903. Price sheet free. *Larry Kass Music Products is a smaller wood supplier than Gurian and as such, his prices tend to be higher. This outfit is of interest for that hard-to-find piece of wood, such as ebony bass fingerboard and ebony in log form. Orders are shipped prepaid within 48 hours.*

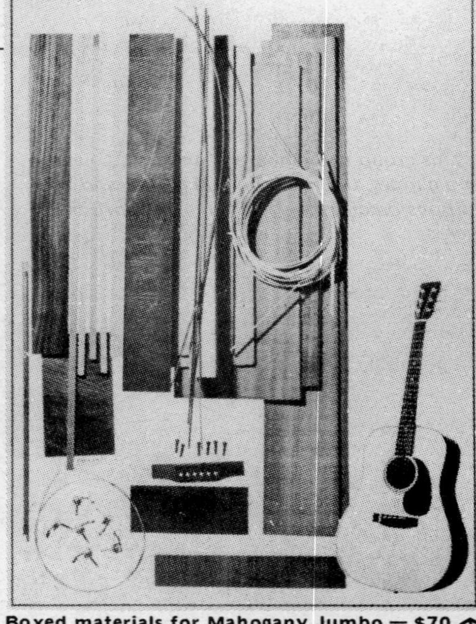
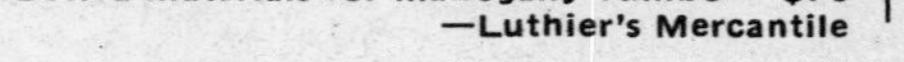

Boxed materials for Mahogany Jumbo — $70 —Luthier's Mercantile ↑

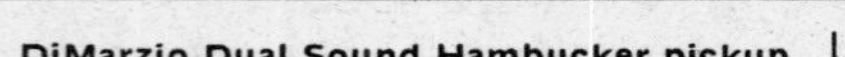

Inlaid guitar made with materials from Luthier's Mercantile ↑

ELECTRIC GUITAR KITS

DiMarzio Instrument Pickups Company, 1388 Richmond Terrace, Staten Island, NY 10310. Catalog $1. *In the early '60s, many musicians I knew bought Fender guitars unassembled from the factory, screwed them together the way they wanted them, and saved a few bucks in the process. For whatever reason Fender discontinued this option. Recently, however, a rash of independent companies have begun making and selling exact replacement bodies and parts for the most popular guitar designs. Hotter pickups, more wiring options, fancier woods, and in some cases higher quality hardware are the benefits to be gained from kit guitars, not to mention uniqueness. Prices vary depending on whether the kits are made here or in the Orient. Assembly is not difficult, and it's not prohibitively expensive if you elect to let your local repairperson do it. Larry DiMarzio pretty much started the whole ball rolling, and he carries the most complete line of American-made parts. Also they're damn nice people. You cannot buy direct from DiMarzio, but I'm told that if you send them $1 you'll receive their color catalog and a list of their distributors near you.*

DiMarzio Dual Sound Hambucker pickup ↓

INSTRUMENT MAKERS

Factory instruments are getting very expensive of late. Higher overheads and extensive distribution networks force the price of the instrument way up by the time you see it. Contrast this with the fact that if there is a dollar to be saved in construction at the factory it has already been saved. However, smaller companies (let's hear it for small companies), though by no means less expensive than factories, tend to have their prices more closely reflect actual labor and materials. Also custom instruments are the only way to go if you want something other than an off-the-rack model. This list, though far from complete, is comprised of instrument builders who have been in the business long enough to establish themselves and their market. They can be counted on to deliver the instruments as ordered and to respect any guarantee they may offer.

Hammond Ashley Associates, 19825 Des Moines Way South, Seattle, WA 98148. No catalog but inquiries are welcome. *These people make, repair, and restore all bowed stringed instruments. In addition they produce many sizes (treble, soprano, mezzo, alto, tenor, baritone and bass) of what they call the "new violin family." I heard the tenor violin and loved it. Sort of a cross between the violin and the cello.*

Black Mountain Instruments, P.O. Box 779, Lower Lake CA 95457. Catalog free. *Reasonably priced dulcimers and dulcimer kits of a very nice design. Instruction book for the kit is very complete.*

R.E. Brunê, Luthier, 800 Greenwood Street, Evanston, IL 60201. Catalog $1. *Harpsichords $3500 to $10,000, lutes $1100 to $1500, baroque guitars $2875 and classical guitars $1400.*

Capritaurus, P.O. Box 153, Felton, CA 95018. $3/year for catalog, almanac and supplements. *Originally Capritaurus started with fine affordable dulcimers. Now they offer a total line of folk instruments including zithers and Irish harps.*

Dillon Guitars, Box 441, Questa, NM 87556. Catalog $1. *Custom steel string acoustic flat-top guitars in the $900 to $2000 range.*

Lynn Ellsworth (Captain Boogie), 10719 128th Street, East Puyallup, WA 98371. Inquiries welcome. *As the name implies, it's all electric guitars here, purchased complete or in kit form. Lynn is noteworthy as the maker of the world's largest guitar.*

Gurian Guitars Ltd., P.O. Box 595, West Swanzey, NY 03469. Catalog $1. *Acoustic guitars $600 to $1600. The largest company listed here, Gurian now offers a very fine acoustic cutaway guitar.*

Guitars Friend, Route 1, Box 200, Sandpoint, ID 83864. Catalog $1. *This group is the home of the R.L. Givens mandolins and guitars, the Franklin OM guitar, and the Musical Traditions dulcimers. Nice folks, nice prices, nice instruments.*

Higgins & Sons, 2530A California Street, San Francisco, CA 94115. Inquiries welcome. *1) Baroque guitars — Voboam style, 2) Cittern — 6 course, 3) Rebecs — 13" scale length, 4) Viols — bass, tenor and treble, and 5) Arch-top guitars. All on special order.*

Matthew Klein Classical Guitars, c/o Gruhn Guitars, Inc., 410 Broadway, Nashville, TN 37203. Inquiries welcome. *Very fine classical guitars, one model with a unique cutaway.*

Steve Klein, Designer and Builder in Wood, 22522 Burndale Road, Sonoma CA 95476. Catalog $1. *$1800 to $3000. A well-known maker of acoustic and electric guitars, Steve's instruments are of an unusual design incorporating many of Professor Kasha's scientific theories on changes for the acoustic guitar. I've seen a $10,000 Eagle guitar made by Steve that had to be seen to be believed.*

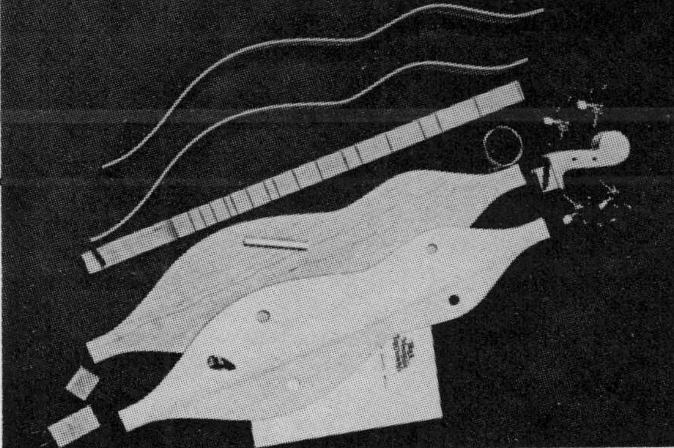

Black Mountain dulcimer kit $95

Mittenwald hammer dulcimers (hackbretts) are made in Germany, are fully chromatic dulcimers with more than two octaves ranging from G to B. They have four strings per course and a total of 112 strings. They are available in veneered dark maple, veneered mahogany or maple and rosewood. Available only by special order from Germany — at the time of printing this catalog prices ranged between $600 and $800. —Capritaurus

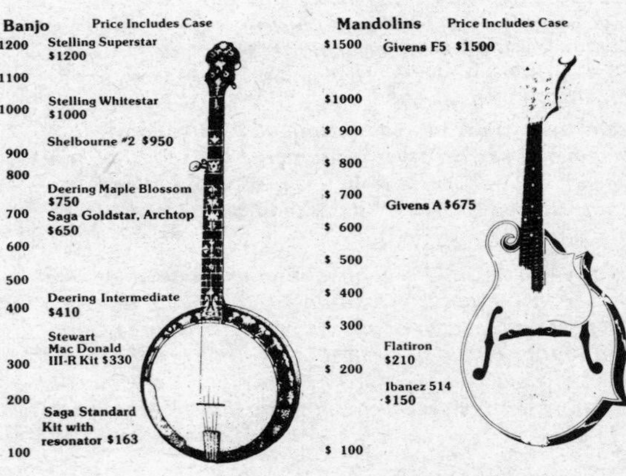

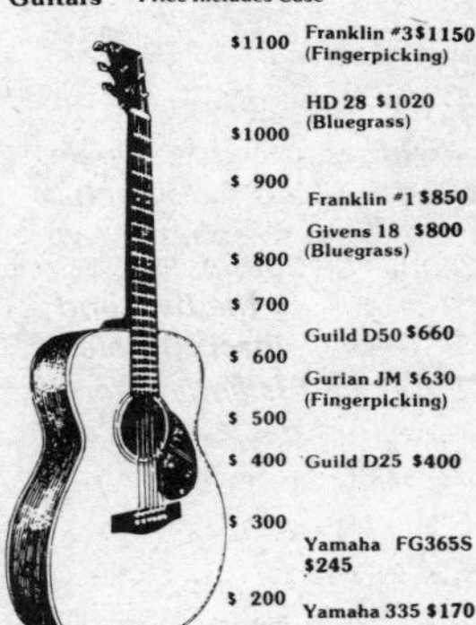

Over the years a lot of folks have asked us what we thought were the "hot deals" in different instruments and prices, etc.

With that in mind we have put together the following charts which should make our recommendations a bit more graphic. —Guitar's Friend

Francis M. Kosheleff, P.O. Box 634, Los Gatos, CA 95030. Inquiries welcome. *Francis makes many strange zither-type instruments, but I believe his folding guitar called the pack axe will be of the most interest to* **Whole Earth** *readers.*

Max Krimmel, Krimmel Guitars, Salina Star Route, Boulder, CO 80302. Send stamp for catalog. *Very fine acoustic steel-string guitars (six-string). Max has a model with a cutaway and midnight blue sunburst finish that is a real show-stopper. Guitars are $1200 - $3000.*

Lane Moller Custom Guitars, 1275½ Chestnut Street, Chico, CA 95926. Catalog $1. *Custom 6- and 12-stringed acoustic guitars, electric guitars, basses and double necks, $2000 - $4000. Lane offers the Nasty cordless electric transmitter on all models.*

John Monteleone, Custom Mandolin and Guitar Maker, 41 Degnon Blvd., Bayshore, NY 11706. Inquiries welcome. *Some of the nicest mandolins I've seen: $2000 - $3000.*

David John Morse, 1833 Soquel Avenue, Santa Cruz, CA 95062. Send stamp for catalog. *Custom built handcarved arch top guitars, built one at a time for the jazz guitarist.*

Olsen Lutherie, 8222 Park Street, Tacoma, WA 98408. Inquiries welcome. *Classics, flat-tops, solid body guitars, acoustic flat-top basses. Tim Olsen's flat-top guitar bass is quite an instrument — with 5 strings, a 34" scale length and a very large body, this bass really puts out.*

Musical Instruments of the Andes, 426 22nd Avenue No. 1, San Francisco, CA 94121. Send stamp with inquiries. *Sikus (pan pipes), charangos (small ten-string guitars) and quenas (flutes) made by Gabor Schoffer. His charango, though without the traditional armadillo shell back, is the finest made in America.*

George Peacock, Peacock Music, 2200 15th Street, San Francisco, CA 94114. Inquiries welcome. *$800 - $1200 classical, flamenco and steel-stringed guitars.*

Richard Raimi, Luthier, 4028 Woodland Park North, Seattle, WA 98103. Inquiries welcome. *Frailing banjos, $265 to $295. Acoustic guitars, $800 and up.*

Robinson's Harp Shop, P.O. Box 161, Mount Laguna, CA 92048. Inquiries welcome. *Irish and Paraguayan harps. R.L. Robinson is also the editor of the* **Folkharp Journal** *($8/year for four issues, from his shop) and as such is one of the leading experts on the rich culture surrounding the harp.*

→

Paraguayan

The Paraguayan harp is unique among folk harps. The neck is made in two halves and the strings are suspended between the halves, thus no lateral tension is exerted on the neck. The box is lightly constructed, resulting in a superb tone and a volume not possible on other folk harps. The neck design provides for an even tension throughout the range, and a proper length for the heavy bass strings. String spacing is a bit narrower than on conventional Irish harps. No semi-tone levers are used. Deluxe model includes inlays and purfling on neck and soundboard. $650

—Robinson's Harp Shop

Roomian Instruments, 3121 20th Street, San Francisco, CA 94110. Catalog $1. *Finest quality rosewood, maple, and spruce acoustic guitars in two sizes, $800 to $1200. Fretless electric basses, $375 to $475. Fretted electric basses, $1500 to $1650. Various electric guitars $450 to $850. Concert-sized and -toned dulcimers, $225 to $325. Medium-sized sound wood dulcimer, $150. All custom work available. This is my shop.*

Ervin Somogyi, 3052 Telegraph Avenue, Berkeley, CA 94705. Inquiries welcome. *Six- to twelve-string guitars with or without cutaways, classical guitars and baroque lutes.*

Maish Weisman, P.O. Box 1241, Laguna Beach, CA 92652. Inquiries welcome. *Maker of lutes, ulhuelas, baroque and renaissance guitars, orpharians, bandoras, citterns, harps and rebecs.*

Witcher Harps, 7406 Gravenstein Highway, Cotati, CA 94928. Inquiries welcome. *Three models of celtic harp, from 38" to 44" in height. Made with walnut and spruce woods.*

There you have it. Enough instrument makers for you? No? Looking for someone closer to you? Contact an organization called the Guild of American Luthiers, 8222 South Park Street, Tacoma, WA 98408. This guild with over 1300 members may know of someone in your neck of the woods. Better yet, why not join the guild? You don't have to be a luthier to join. You just have to be interested. The membership fee is $15 annually. For this sum, you'll receive the quarterly booklet full of information concerning handmade instruments. Also, you'll receive the package of data sheets sent in by luthiers around the globe. These sheets dispel the old notion that instrument builders are excessively secretive about their work. Here they detail new ideas, jigs and techniques, making this guild very useful if instrument-making is of more than passing interest to you. ■

Stars Guitars, 818 Folsom Street, San Francisco, CA 94107. Catalog $.50. *Stars has been providing expert service and advice to builders, musicians, and major manufacturers for over 5 years now. They have had a hand in many of the design developments of recent years. They offer pre-amped electronics and state-of-the-art hardware. More importantly, they have the ability and the inclination to build custom guitar systems to your specs.*

Stars has developed a one-of-a-kind string return pickup for acoustic or electric instruments. Utilizing the string itself for the signal, the string return system provides increased harmonic range and touch sensitivity. Inquiries are welcome though the device is not on the market at this time.

← **The FRAP triaxial transducer**

FRAP-Flat Response Audio Pickup, P.O. Box 40097, San Francisco, CA 94140. Information sheets $1. *The finest of the Piezo (vibrational and pressural) electric pickups for stringed, brass and woodwind instruments. The FRAP is a professional quality alternative to the microphone for use in live gigs or in the recording studio. Arnie Lazarus, inventor of the FRAP, has pioneered the development and the usage of vibrational pickups beyond all others — his data sheets have real information in them, saving us all a lot of time. The guy has recorded the moans and groans of the Golden Gate Bridge with them. Prices are high, making these units feasible only for those who respect and need that extra amount in an acoustic pickup.*

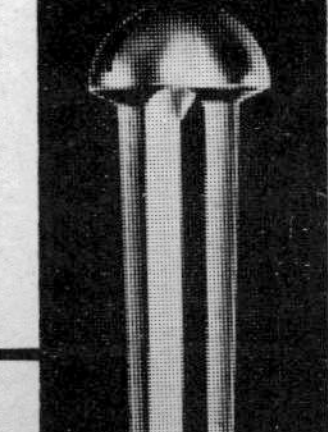

← **Caviar Brass Bridge Pins**, 225 Piper Street, Healdsburg, CA 95448. *I thought I'd include this tiny company for yuks value. Their only product is a patented brass acoustic guitar bridge pin, guaranteed to dress up your axe. The company claims an improvement in brightness and protection. I only know that most people who use them like them. Catalog is free, pins are $9 including shipping for a set of six.*

THE RISING SUN
NEIGHBORHOOD NEWSLETTER

The accepted way to get the attention of a deaf person who isn't looking at you is to stamp on the floor really hard. They feel the vibrations.

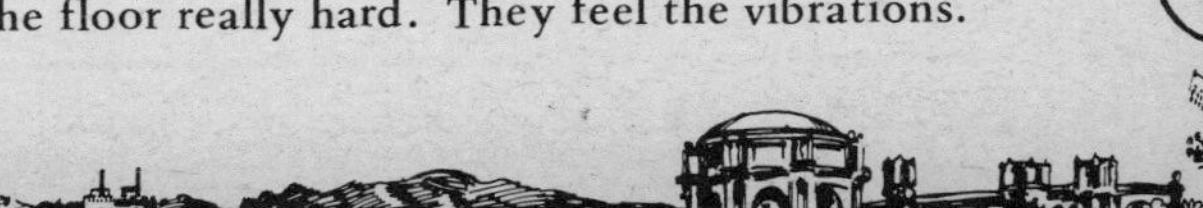

Early Keyboard Instrument Kits

by Harold R. Langland

Hubbard harpsichord kit "cut to fit"

Finished Hubbard Harpsichord

E LIVE IN AN AGE OF NOISE and speed. Wherever we go, loudspeakers blast the three chord thumps of pop music at us, but the owner of a harpsichord can turn off the radios, close the windows, and ease into a gentler time. A harpsichord in the home is the center of musical evenings, alone, with a few recorders or violin, or just voices. It speaks of a time when there was more time, more quiet, more sensitivity to the small beauties.

It is no wonder that harpsichord making has become big business in this country and abroad. A firm in Australia that makes harpsichords costing over $900 each is seven years behind schedule, such is the demand. In the U.S. there are over 100 full time harpsichord makers trying to keep amateurs and professionals supplied.

But there are also several manufacturers of kits. An instrument in kit form suddenly becomes affordable by cutting the cost 2/3 or more. It also eliminates the usual long waiting time for a finished instrument, and it gives the builder an intimate knowledge of the workings of it, so it can be easily and well maintained. But perhaps the biggest plus is the pride in having built a genuine musical instrument yourself.

It is not my aim here to attempt any kind of list of makers of finished instruments — that job has been tackled by Igor Kipnis, and will appear in his new book on harpsichord technique. Rather I will deal only with makers of kits.

But first some explanation is necessary. There are many different kinds of keyboard instruments offered by kit makers. The main one is the harpsichord itself, which comes in several types. Italian harpsichords are the smallest, with a bright, crisp tone, and always just one keyboard. Flemish instruments are more like the usual picture of a harpsichord and come with either one keyboard (singles) or two (doubles). French style harpsichords, usually thought of as the epitome of the art, again come as either singles or doubles, with the "French Double" more or less the standard for serious concert and recording work. In addition one will find English and German harpsichords, which do not differ significantly enough to worry about here.

Mention will also be made of spinets and virginals. These were smaller harpsichords of various shapes, but with the strings running either across or at an angle to save space. They are cheaper and simpler to build than a harpsichord, and, though less versatile, make a full bold sound.

And then there are clavichords. I, actually, am a clavichord addict. These marvels "touch" the string instead of plucking it, giving a very soft sound but the most sensitive control of any keyboard instrument. In 1768 Jacob Adlung said, "A good clavichord, well played, is sweeter and more heart-stirring than any other instrument." But that "well played" is the catch, as their extreme sensitivity shows up bad technique, and builds good technique like no other instrument. On top of all that, they are the cheapest to buy, easiest to build and maintain. Some weigh only 20 lbs. and can be tucked under the arm for toting around.

When Mozart and his contemporaries sat down at what was then a rather new instrument, the piano, it was not at all like the great curving black creatures of today, able to balance a symphony orchestra at full throttle. Mozart's piano, which we now call a "Fortepiano" to distinguish it from modern ones, was of all wood construction with two light strings (not 3 heavy ones) per note, and a very simple, but lightning-fast action. The tone was softer, and different, more like woodwinds. Wonderful kits for fortepianos are now being made. Imagine having a grand piano in your living room, and saying, "I made that." Better yet, imagine dashing off some quicksilver Haydn runs on it.

Kits come in a variety of states of completion. The cheapest form, requiring the most work, is the "basic kit." This is just the guts of the instrument — the keyboards, jacks, jack guide, strings, curved parts, etc. You buy the lumber for the case and plane and cut and join it yourself. If you're good at woodworking and have a shop full of tools, you might try it; otherwise you'd do well to buy a more complete kit. For example, some makers make a "dimensioned" kit, where the lumber is included, cut roughly to size, and you cut the joints. Better still, and the most common form, is the "cut to fit" kit, where you get everything you need and just start right in gluing it all together. If even that scares you, you can usually buy a "case assembled" kit, where it arrives all glued together looking like an instrument, and you do all the fiddly bits of the action, string it, apply the finish, and brag.

To make some sense of all the variations in price, I will quote only "cut to fit" kits, and will generally just quote for a French Double, but will also indicate other instruments available from each maker. If you are sincerely interested in an instrument, write to the different makers and get their brochures, compare, and see all the options they offer, because there are plenty. But do me and them a favor — don't write off to all these makers and get them to mail you their expensive brochures just for your own amusement. I'm sure you'll understand.

THE KIT MAKERS — U.S.A.

Frank Hubbard Harpsichords, Inc., 185 A Lyman Street, Waltham, Massachusetts 02154

Frank Hubbard is the grand old firm of harpsichord making. It was he who wrote the definitive book on the subject, **Three Centuries of Harpsichord Making,** *and apprentices from his shops are many of the major makers today. His were the first kits to make a really professional instrument. You might find kits as good as these days, but none better.*

Yet, surprisingly, they are not the most expensive. His big French Double, in the "cut to fit" form, is $2200. There are, of course, lots of options, but this kit, made carefully, will yield an instrument ready for a concert artist. Also in his line are French singles, a Flemish single for $1575, a lovely English Bentside Spinet, and a fine Fortepiano. Very highly recommended.

Zuckermann Harpsichords Inc., 15 Williams Street, Box 121, Stonington, Connecticut 06378

If Frank Hubbard wrote the definitive book on old harpsichords, Wolfgang Zuckermann wrote the definitive book on new ones, **The Modern Harpsichord.** *And, as far as I know, the first harpsichord kit ever produced was produced by him. It was a small, rather unhistorical job that went for just $150, which lots of people bought and which really spread the harpsichord bug.*

Today Zuckermann produces a line of nine different instruments, each very accurate historically and each stunningly beautiful. Naturally this firm knows how to make kits that fit and write instructions that instruct, so you won't go wrong with these.

His big French Double is $2600, a bit more than Hubbard, but in this league one worries about more important things than money.

The Zuckermann range also includes three kinds of Flemish harpsichords, a lovely Italian one, an Italian Virginal for $935 (that's the one I covet), two types of clavichord, and a fortepiano. Also very highly recommended.

B & G Instrument Workshop, 318 North 36th Street, Seattle, Washington 98103

This West Coast outfit is making a serious run at the two big boys just mentioned. They produce historically accurate instruments in an even wider range than Zuckermann. And their prices are very good. Their big French Double goes for $2300, just above Hubbard and below Zuckermann, but there is a big difference. B & G supply all their kits "in an advanced state of completion where all the woodworking has been done." So these are really "case assembled" kits, and compare with a price of $2490 for the same thing from Hubbard.

Their range of instruments also includes a Flemish single, English double, a pedal harpsichord (to be placed under a regular one), an Italian, two sorts of English spinets, two sizes of clavichord, and a fortepiano.

In addition they produce a line of parts, such as keyboards, jacks, jack guides etc., if you want to build an instrument without a kit.

Burton Harpsichords, 4921 North 57th Street, Box 80222, Lincoln, Nebraska 68501

This is an old reliable firm who make kits of less historically imitative instruments, designed to be lower in cost, and more suitable for the home. Their big double, for example, is only $1575. In addition they make a single in three different stringings, a small spinet (basic kit only $315), and a clavichord. They have a lot of experience and produce a well thought out and buildable kit. They also claim to ship the same day the order is received.

Carl Fudge, Harpsichord Maker, 208 Ridge Street, Winchester, Massachusetts 01890

He makes only two kits at present, both for clavichords — a small one at $495 and a large one at $850. But he is the clavichord king, having spent more time specializing in this instrument than most other makers. He does, though, make a wide variety of custom built harpsichords, and he is planning to bring out yet another clavichord kit and a Flemish virginal kit. Very fine workmanship.

The Williams Workshop, 1229 Olancha Drive, Los Angeles, California 90065

S.R. Williams has been in the kit business a long time and specializes in not overly historic, but certainly affordable, kits for the person who will use the instrument primarily in the home. He does not have a kit for a double, but has a small Flemish single in basic form for only $345! Case Complete is $895. He also offers a triangular spinet, Italian Virginal, and small clavichord ($290). I would not recommend these for professional musicians, but they could be excellent as a first instrument.

ENGLAND

John Storrs, Hunston, Chichester, Sussex P0206NR, England.

He is the major kit maker in England. Though I haven't seen his instruments personally, they appear to be well researched and carefully done. His big double (Flemish, in this case) is about $2450, depending on the current rate of exchange. This instrument comes in a variety of finishes, and the price is for the fancy one. He also makes a Flemish single, an English Bentside spinet, a Triangular Spinet which will fit virtually any dwelling, and a clavichord.

But he has a delightful bonus. He offers courses in building his kits. Taking only 10 people at a time, he works

The Italian Virginal

The Italian Virginal Kit	$ 935
The Assembled Italian Virginal Kit, ready for painting and installation of action	1,535
The Italian Virginal, with action installed, regulated and voiced, ready for painting	1,920
The Finished Italian Virginal	2,520

Zuckermann Italian Virginal

The Italian Virginal. Length 64 in. (162.5 cm); width 17¼ in. (44 cm); depth of case 7½ in. (19 cm). Disposition 1 x 8', no buff. 54 notes, GG/BB-e'''. Boxwood naturals, stained wood sharps. Sixty to one hundred twenty hours.

Carl Fudge Small Clavichord Kit

Small Clavichord Kit

Complete kit, ready for assembly	$ 495
Partially assembled kit	575
Arcades for key fronts (rosewood)	30
Listing board	20
Printed paper for inside of rim	5
Canvas carrying cover	75
Canvas carrying cover with extra padding	90
Instrument custom-built, natural finish	1,900
Instrument custom-built, painted finish	2,100

United Parcel Service shipping charges: Northeast $12, South and Midwest $15, West $20.

How to Love Your Flute

inspire *1a. archaic:* to breathe or blow into or upon *b. archaic:* to infuse (as life) by breathing . . . *2b.* to exert an animating, enlivening, or exalting influence upon.
—Webster's

Mark Shepard's soul-felt passion for the flute resonates through his book like music. It's a comprehensive guide, with something for everyone from novice to professional, and so well written that it's a pleasure just to browse through it. I'm not sure how he managed to present so much information so simply and clearly, but it's clean as a whistle. This book inspires. —Diana Barich

How to Love Your Flute
(A Guide to Flutes and Flute Playing)
Mark Shepard
1980; 97 pp.

$6.95 postpaid from:
Panjandrum Books
11321 Iowa Avenue
Suite 8
Los Angeles, CA 90025
or Whole Earth Household Store

•

Among North American companies, the reputable companies include Armstrong, Artley, and Gemeinhardt; in the handmade flute category, Haynes and Powell are well known names. In Europe the list includes Couesnon, Hammig, Marigaux, Monnig, Selmer, U.S.A., and Rudall, Carte. In Japan, Yamaha and Muramatsu are considered good.

•

There is not a great deal I can tell you about learning free improvisation, because it's a fairly personal matter, but I will tell you two of my own favorite ways to do it. One is playing free improvisational duets with another flutist. The other is playing in a place with a lot of echo — an enclosed stairwell, a parking garage, a tunnel, a cathedral. Paul Horn, a well-known flutist, will actually travel to the other side of the world to try out an echo!

with them on their kits in his shops, assuring a correctly finished product. You stay in Chichester, with its charming cathedral (one of my favorites) and the 10 day course (for spinets and clavichord), costs only $400 plus kit. That includes full room and board. The 17 day course, for the harpsichords, is only $605. So, for $3055 plus air fare you get 17 days living and working in southern England, plus a finished Flemish double. Tempting, eh?

Sandy Rogers, Warren House, Stone Street, Faversham, Kent, ME13 8PS, England

Sandy Rogers makes kits for three instruments — two kinds of Italian harpsichord and a clavichord. The large Italian is $1375, the clavichord is half that. Sorry, but no courses there.

Steer Instruments, 23 Denmark Road, Carshalton, Surrey, England

I ran into this firm at a fair of early instruments in London. They make just parts — keyboards, jacks, even a "Gothic Stool" — for those building without a kit.

Gough & Davy Ltd., 13 - 15 Savile Street, Hull, North Humberside, England

These people are representatives for a Dutch firm which makes a pipe organ kit. These are genuine chamber organs, with various numbers of ranks of pipes, and based on Baroque models. The usual one is modelled on an 18th Century "Kabinet" organ, with three sets of pipes. As their brochure charmingly states, "Build it yourself for harpsichords is usual already for a long time, which for house organs is taking a high flight more and more."

Alan Gotto and John Perkins, Briar Hall, Bramerton, Norwich, England

These two makers produce a line of five instruments, four of which can be purchased in semi-completed form. These are an Early English single, and Italian, a Flemish Virginal and an Italian Virginal. Their biggest is around $2075, in England. By semi-completed, they mean all carpentry done, you just assemble jacks, string, and play. The instruments are very good, very historical, and very beautiful.

One final word: I've encountered many people who never built anything before. For some reason they summoned the courage to buy an instrument kit, and such is the state of the art today, that they succeeded in finishing lovely instruments which proudly dominate their homes. The outlay in money and time is considerable, but the rewards of owning the very embodiment of civilization and grace are more than worth it. ■

Japanese Shakuhachi Flute

A wonderfully breathy flute, the shakuhachi expresses the player more directly and delicately than any instrument I know. Monty Levenson has American-made shakuhachis ($20 - $80), Japanese-made ($195 - $1275), books, accessories, guidance, and the right attitude. Nice work. —SB

Japanese Shakuhachi Flute
Catalog
$.15 from:
Monty H. Levenson
P.O. Box 294
Willits, CA 95490

•

The Shakuhachi is an end-blown flute tuned to a pentatonic (5 note) scale. By various fingerings, half- and quarter-holings, and by controlling the angle of the mouthpiece against the lip all of the twelve tones of the western chromatic scale can be produced. The mouthpiece consists of an oblique blowing edge cut diagonally toward the outside of the flute. It is unique in that it enables the player to control the pitch by changing the angle at which the flute is being blown. This, in turn, produces a delicate change of intonation — a swelling or bending of notes characteristic of the traditional music. The timbre of the instrument is almost always described as "mellow" in its low tones, although it is equally capable of producing shrill, penetrating, and breathy tones in its upper and middle registers. Little can be said of the tone of the shakuhachi without first hearing its beautiful ring.

The Piano Owner's Guide

If you're going to buy a piano, new or used, get this book first. It tells you everything to look for and to look out for. It's so easy to get burnt (as in buying a car) that I'd say this book is a necessity. If you already own a piano, the book will show you all its parts, tell you how it's made, how it works, and what it needs to keep working well.

Schmeckel, a piano tuner-technician and rebuilder for over forty-five years, writes clearly and has divided the book into numbered sections for easy cross-reference. This is the first and only book of its kind — finally. —Dave Potvin

The Piano Owner's Guide
(How to Buy and Care for a Piano)
Carl D. Schmeckel
1971, 1974; 127 pp.

$3.95 postpaid from:
Charles Scribner's Sons
Vreeland Avenue
Totowa, NJ 07512

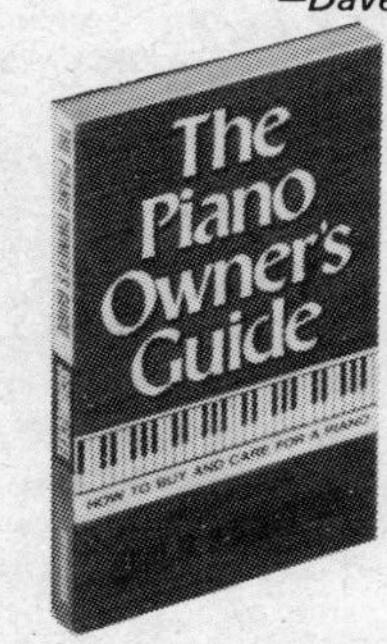

•

If you must purchase a small piano, it is strongly recommended that you settle for nothing smaller than *console* size with a direct-blow action.

•

Any make or style of piano, regardless of its use or location, should be tuned a *minimum* of twice a year.

•

The string tension in a typical piano at American Standard A-440 cycles-per-second (cps) pitch can easily approximate 20 tons (40,000 lbs.) of pull. This is enough to lift a double garage off its foundations!

How to Buy a Violin

It has a lot to do with who to trust, including your own objective ear. The violin is a barbarous instrument, and so is the shopping. Good to have a native guide like Reuter. —SB

How to Buy a Violin
(Reuter's Consumer Report on Violins, Violas, Celli, Basses and Bows)
Fritz Reuter, Jr.
1971; 30 pp.

$3 postpaid from:
Fritz Reuter and Sons
1565 Howard Street
Chicago, IL 60626

•

More than ninety per cent of all violin teachers, orchestra and band directors, and a large number of music administrators in public and private schools, music schools and universities are employed on a commission basis by one or more musical instrument dealers.

•

A $500 violin if tonally compared with a $15,000 violin can be more beautiful in sound than the more expensive one. This principle has been demonstrated numerous times with modern violins when compared with most fine old master violins.

The *maximum amount* of money one would have to pay if *only* interested in finding a violin fulfilling all individual requirements of tonal beauty is $1000 to $2000, depending on the sales method of the seller. Only a *very few* violins of the finest old masters are tonally superior, but in *no way* as much as the difference in price may indicate.

Elderly Instruments

I had seen the Elderly catalog around for a few years, so liked its looks and had heard so many good things about the company, I just normally supposed we here (who are supposedly in the know) had already run a review of Elderly somewhere in the past ten years. Well, we hadn't. Till now.

If you are at all interested in a mail order source of quality musical instruments, accessories, parts, books, records, cases, and lore — at discount prices, then send for this catalog. Their motto is: "Music self-played is happiness self-made." —J.D. Smith

[Suggested by Marc Bristol]

Elderly Instruments
Catalog
free from:
Elderly Instruments
541 East Grand River
East Lansing, MI 48823

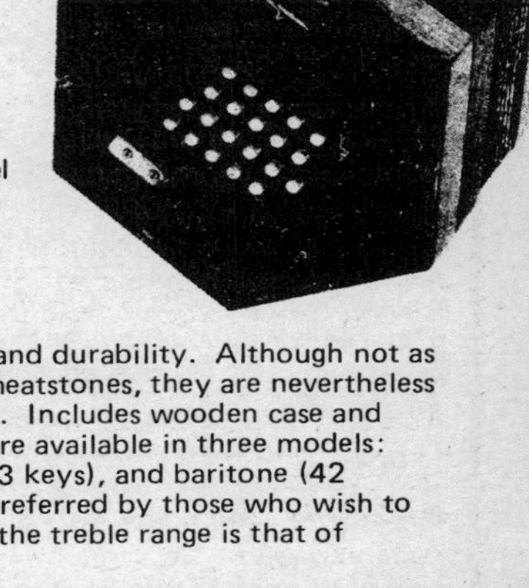

•

Concertinas

The New English Concertina features Swedish steel reeds, 8 fold bellows with leather corners and edges covered with leather inside and out. Made in Italy, these concertinas are of good quality and durability. Although not as finely made as the old Wheatstones, they are nevertheless a good value for the price. Includes wooden case and instruction book. They are available in three models: treble (48 keys), tenor (43 keys), and baritone (42 keys). Treble is usually preferred by those who wish to play with a fiddler, since the treble range is that of the violin.

Bagpipes

For those who may be interested in bagpipes — acquiring them or playing them, there is an excellent company in Scotland: Hugh MacPherson Ltd., 17 West Maitland Street, Edinburgh, Scotland, EH12 5EA

Importing them yourself is about 4 times cheaper than buying one over here. Furthermore, the quality is better and the service is extremely courteous although slow. (It takes 3 months to get your bagpipe after ordering it.) It is worth it however. A full sized bagpipe, full mounted in imitation ivory, costs about $400 in American money (at the current rate of exchange). That's another thing they'll do for you. They'll translate their prices into recognizable money symbols for Americans. Since MacPherson's things are made of selected African blackwood and constructed with an old fashioned pride-of-craftsmanship, there can be no comparison. They sell also practice chanters, instruction books, collections of the Ceol Mor, maintenance accessories and even superfluous goodies like highland costumes for performers. They will send you a catalog (of sorts) if you write them. I highly recommend the practice chanter for starting. An excellent beginners instruction book is the **College of Piping Tutor Book I**, by Seumas Macneill and Thomas Pearston. Also order extra reeds with your chanter. The plastic types last a long time.

Tiny Alice
Los Angeles, California

THE RISING SUN
NEIGHBORHOOD NEWSLETTER

Beth went to a masquerade party as a Hadassah lady — with correct hairdo, dress, ear rings and comments — and a friend of hers liked it so much he invited her to a dinner party as the Hadassah lady and not herself. Beth wants to write a short story called "Becoming the Hadassah Lady," about that happening more and more until the Hadassah lady gets all the invitations and has all the friends.

Electronic Music Synthesizers

Electronic Music Synthesizers Electronic Music Synthesizers

by Bernard L. Krause

PARASOUND, INC.
SAN FRANCISCO, CALIFORNIA

KATE KLINE MAY

Nyle Steiner on EVI

If you go to movies or hear pop music, you've been listening to Bernie Krause for a long time. He's scored or participated in the sound tracks of dozens of major films and TV shows and side-manned with all the top pop groups. Lately he also hangs out musically and academically (Ph.D. in progress) with whales and dolphins. As knowledgeable a word on electronic music as we're likely to find. **–SB**

WITH THE ADVENT OF CONTEMPORARY synthesizers fifteen years ago, composers or sonic artists found that the old definitions of music had evolved to mean control of sound. All the parameters of sound became controllable: (1) pitch or frequency, (2) loudness or amplitude, (3) color or timbre, and (4) time/amplitude or envelope or gate. An entire expanded range of sound and aural subtlety was opened up to the sonic artist.

The concepts of modular instruments and voltage-control, developed at about the same time in the 1960s on the East Coast by Robert Moog and in the West by Donald Buchla, represented two major developments which helped lead to the wide acceptability of the analog systems in both academic and commercial music environments. However, analog systems, while still popular, contain within them many limitations. In context of the more recent digital technology, the sonic artist has available even greater latitudes of expression — cleaner and more accurate reproduction of aural visions and information storage capabilities heretofore unavailable in the analog precedents. It is quickly coming to pass that many of the constrictions extant in the former systems have now been mitigated and much, much more is promised for the 1980s.

In this survey I wish only to touch on some of the available analog and digital instruments in several price ranges with a brief discussion of some of the outstanding features of each. Because of time and space there will be no attempt to be comprehensive. Most of my comments will be based on field reports of users and dealers of currently available instruments and apply to those which best represent quality technology, human engineering, field service, overall value, and imaginative function concepts. Since prices are so volatile these days, only general ranges will be mentioned, leaving the kind and ever-curious reader the option of pursuing the matter directly with the various companies where further in-depth information is sought.

A few caveats however, if you plan on buying a synthesizer. Play the instruments yourself or have them demonstrated by one who really knows what variables to look for. Each instrument brand has its own unique sound and playing characteristics. Be certain that you can live with your purchase, particularly if you are spending upwards of $1500 on your system. Also, you might want to make sure that the system you're investing in is serviceable.

UNDER $200

Casiotone 10, Casio, Inc., 15 Gardner Road, Fairfield, NJ 07006. *Casio, the pocket calculator company, makes this item. This 32-key, 2½ octave, 8-note polyphonic instrument has four voices consisting of piano, organ, flute, and violin. It has a built-in speaker, is battery operated, weighs 4 pounds, and also comes with a 2-way AC/DC power source (household current or DC batteries).*

Casiotone 10

$450 - $800

Korg MS 10 & 20 Series, Unicord, 89 Frost Street, Westbury, NY 11590. *Both are monophonic. The Model 10 has one fully variable voltage Control Oscillator (VCO) and the 20 has two. The 10 and 20 are completely open systems, meaning that they are expandable. The 20 has an External Signal Processor module which will allow any external instrument (or signal) to play it. This module will follow both envelope (amplitude/time functions), trigger and pitch of incoming signals. Both these instruments are flexible and just fine for education and limited studio work. Sequencers are optional.*

EVI (Electronic Valve Instrument), Steiner Instruments, 2736 South 2700 West, Salt Lake City, UT 84119. *Nyle Steiner of Steiner Instruments in Salt Lake City put this one together. It was used extensively on Francis Ford Coppola's recent film, "Apocalypse Now," and was designed for those who favor breath controlled instruments rather than keyboards. This means, of course, that any horn player can now play a synthesizer. The fingering is the same as for trumpet, tuba, or french horn. It is compatible with most synthesizers, has a seven-octave range without re-tuning and an over-all possible range of seventeen octaves! The EVI is designed so that the sonic energy spectrum changes in a manner similar to that of many acoustic instruments when played over a wide range. This instrument, because of its design, is probably the most expressive of the monophonic analog synthesizers, yet, in its basic form, comes in a compact case not much larger than that which holds a standard flute.*

Moog Prodigy, R.A. Moog, 2500 Walden Avenue, Buffalo, NY 14225. *A closed system instrument, the Moog Prodigy is a quality performance system with the 4-pole (24 dB/octave) filter that has made Moog instruments unique and outstanding in the field of analog audio subtleties. It is reliable and serviceable, but like all closed systems, limited.*

Casiotone 201

Casiotone 201, Casio, Inc., 15 Gardner Road, Fairfield, NJ 07006. *For a presettable, closed system instrument, this is one that a little extra attention should be paid to. It contains 49 keys, four octaves, 8-note polyphony, and 29 different voices (including different timbres of strings, winds, brass, organs and effects) that sound pretty real. It also has a pre-settable four-tone memory. Weighs 15 pounds, is AC powered, and has an internal 2W speaker.*

Yamaha CS 20, Yamaha International, P.O. Box 6600, Buena Park, CA 90622. *Often referred to as a Mini-Moog with programming capabilities, this instrument is a single-voice, two-oscillator unit which is an eight-voice memory cassette interfaceable synthesizer. It has a 37-note keyboard and is backed by Yamaha's excellent field service reputation. It is well-built, reliable, and can stand some rough handling. A good performance instrument.*

$1000 - $2000

Roland 100M Series, Roland Corporation, U.S., 2401 Saybrook Avenue, Los Angeles, CA 90040. *In the modular analog systems group of instruments currently on the market in this price range, few have the value and flexibility of this well-thought-out series. The system is totally expandable and one can add a whole plethora of options such as keyboards, sequencers, a micro-processor (16 kilobyte capacity where 8 independent voices or up to 5200 single-voice notes can be programmed). Relative to the operator's abilities, studio requirements, and budget, Roland offers as part of its package a complete semi-professional studio (sans tape recorders and boards) including equalizers, a phaser, vocoder, reverberation, echo, mixers and jack panels.*

$2000 - $5000

OBX - Oberheim, Oberheim Electronics, Inc., 1549 9th Street, Santa Monica, CA 90401. *The "Oberheim sound" is a standard in the world of disco and pop music these days. It seems to "cut" as they say, mostly because of the Oberheim 2-pole (12 dB/octave) filter. (A 4-pole 24 dB/octave switch is available as an option.) The OBX is polyphonic and comes with a cassette interface for programming. It has a spring-loaded pitch band, a unique unison "fire-in-parallel" feature. It is an expandable, open system, and has the option of from 4-8 voices by simply adding circuit boards. It tunes itself very quickly.*

Polyfusion 2000

$7000 +

Polyfusion 2000 Series, Polyfusion, 160 Sugg Road, Buffalo, NY 14225. *As modular analog instruments have been refined, several have evolved that are worth taking note of. One, the Polyfusion 2000 is extremely well-built and flexible. Every signal and control output and input is made available from control panel jacks and internal printed circuit edge connectors such that any imaginable patch can be made temporarily, semi-permanently, or permanently. Although basically monophonic, the player can get a two-voice or polyphonic 8-voice keyboard (with interface) as an option. The instrument sounds good, meaning that the filter system can handle subtleties of expression, and it is low noise. It comes with all kinds of options and is recommended for the advanced studio composer desiring to remain with analog systems.*

Other synthesizer systems which should be mentioned are Moog, Buchla, ARP and E-mu. All are standards in their own rights and have within their catalogs fine instruments in all kinds of configurations. Unlike the other companies I've reviewed, their designs have remained on much the same track during the last five years or so. They're covered in **Synthesis**, *reviewed below.*

R.A. Moog, 2500 Walden Avenue, Buffalo, NY 14225.
Buchla Associates, Berkeley, CA. *(Don Buchla requested we not list his address.)*
ARP, 320 Needham Street, Newton, MA 02164
E-mu Systems, 417 Broadway, Santa Cruz, CA 95060.

Fairlight CMI

DIGITAL SYNTHESIZERS

↑ **Fairlight CMI,** 15 Boundary Street, Rushcutters Bay, Sydney, Australia 2011. *Australians make this item. Find a sound you like. Put it up on an oscilloscope. Trace the waveform with a light-pen on the graphics display screen of the Fairlight or play back a sound off a tape recorder or mike. Enter the program on floppy disc and you've got that retrievable sound forever. You can create any waveform with this unit. The use of floppy disc assures the sonic artist that all is absolutely repeatable. Program complex musical compositions and hear them retrieved and played back without the keyboard. "Look, ma . . ." Having eight-note polyphony means that eight different voices can be played at the same time. You won't need any previous knowledge of computers or programming. There's lots more but you'll have to write them.*

TO-BE-INTRODUCED-IN-1980-BUT-NOT-YET-ON-THE-MARKET (April, 1980)

Yamaha TRX (Touch Response X), Yamaha International, P.O. Box 6600, Buena Park, CA 90622. *The TRX is a performance-oriented, 88-key system that looks like a small baby grand in a walnut case. It is 16-note polyphonic. In order to produce a sound, you have four tone modules (equivalent to four synthesizers/note in analog terms). This means, for instance, that for the same note you can have possible a plucked sound, a percussive sound, a string or organ sound. The keyboard scaling allows all characteristics of sound to be changeable across the entire range of the keyboard. Depending on how you change your touch you will get a plucked string, an organ, or percussive feels. The key result here is that this instrument truly sounds acoustic and therefore is a remarkable adjunct to performance and recording synthesizers.*

Audity, E-mu Systems, 417 Broadway, Santa Cruz, CA 95060. *The Audity is a totally computer-controlled polyphonic synthesizer system planned for release in the summer of 1980 by E-mu Systems, Inc. It is designed to allow the sonic artist to rapidly realize complex multi-line orchestrated music without the aid of tape recorders or orchestras. The user can create a library of sounds on magnetic disk and assign any combination of these sounds to any combination of musical lines played either live or by the polyphonic sequencer. The system stores not only single sounds but entire orchestrations and groups of orchestrations. For the first time the sonic artist can experiment with voice assignment in real time, while his composition is actually being played. With the touch of a button the artist can change a single voice or the entire orchestration and hear the results immediately. The system consists of three elements: an electronics rack containing the disk drives, the main system CPU (Central Processing Unit), and up to 64 voice cards; a console containing the synthesizer control panel, controls for sound storage and retrieval, and an alphanumeric display; and a polyphonic keyboard/sequencer with the capacity to store up to 6000 notes.*

Synclavier II, New England Digital Corporation, Main Street, Norwich, VT 05055. *About the size of a Mini-Moog, this exceptional digital instrument manufactured by New England Digital Corporation in Vermont is available in 8, 16, 24 and 32 voices. Up to 96 different harmonics can be programmed for one polyphonic voice; also, multiple vibratos and portamentos. Sixty-four sounds are pre-programmed any of which can be modified or create your own aural visions. And here's the kicker! This instrument is equipped with a 16-track digital memory recorder giving the sonic artist virtually the same controls as with a 16-track tape recorder in sync. Storage is unlimited and accomplished with floppy disc. It goes without saying that the sounds of violins, celli, xylophones, bells and brass "sound" almost indistinguishable from the real thing. It should be said that this instrument will be on the market by the time the* **Catalog** *is in print.*

Prophet 5, Sequential Circuits, 3051 North First Street, San Jose, CA 95134. *Sequential Circuits makes this analog/digital hybrid. It is a 5-voice (they also have a 10-voice instrument called the Prophet 10), closed system. The unit features a digital storage memory with all functions programmable. It also includes an "edit" mode. Portable, cosmetically and functionally well-designed, the Sequential Circuits people really understood the meaning of human engineering and elegant simplicity. The updated version contains a built-in cassette interface for unlimited storage of settings and a variable scaling program which allows each note or key to be scaled independently.* ↓

Prophet 5

Oberheim OB-X programmable polyphonic synthesizer

BOOKS

Although nothing replaces "hands on" experience when working with synthesizers, I can recommend three books out of many excellent ones that might help clarify some of the myths, mysteries, expressions and techniques with regard to the control of sound and synthesis.

For beginners: **The Nonesuch Guide to Electronic Music,** by Paul Beaver and Bernard L. Krause, 1968. New edition to be released by Nonesuch records in 1981; $14.88 postpaid from King Karol or Moby Music (p. 482). *Includes three 12" records of sounds and a book of what sound is all about in lay terminology. Also, an extensive bibliography and glossary of terms. Available through Nonesuch Records.*

Beginner - Intermediate: **Synthesis, An Introduction to the History, Theory, and Practice of Electronic Music** by Herbert A. Deutsch, 1976; $6.95 postpaid from Alfred Publishing Company, 15335 Morrison Street, Sherman Oaks, CA 91403. *Includes a 7" record. It is comprehensive in its explanation of musical synthesis.*

Intermediate - Advanced: **Electronic Music, Systems, Techniques, and Controls** by Allen Strange, 1972; $7.95 postpaid from: William C. Brown Company, 2460 Kerper Blvd., Dubuque, IA 52001. *Clear and comprehensive explanations of the understanding and control of sound. Includes an excellent bibliography.*

Digital information — it is usually the case that each manufacturer of digital equipment has an application manual or application notes. I can't imagine any worth their salt that wouldn't. There might be a slight charge, but write to them. If you are interested it will be worth every penny. ■

Computer Music Journal

The acknowledged place to look for ongoing news about computer-generated music and its makers. Innovations in computer music come so quickly that a journal is needed. **CMJ** *was long published by the People's Computer Company, but recently moved to the MIT Press. The first issue from MIT has been delayed, so we haven't seen it yet, but all the issues we've seen up till now have been first-class.* —Art Kleiner

Computer Music Journal
Curtis Roads, Editor
$20 /year (4 issues)
Journals Department
The MIT Press
28 Carleton Street
Cambridge, MA 02142

•

Up until recently, all music was real time, in that musicians played their instruments and the music was heard immediately. Now with the computer, it is not only possible, but it is usually essential to compute the numbers representing the sound first, store them on some medium, such as rotating disk storage, then play them back later. This separation of the computing phase and the listening phase is a bit annoying in that it means you cannot listen to your piece as it is produced, but it gives us the aforementioned advantage that pieces of arbitrary complexity can be realized. They just take more and more computer time. With analog synthesizers, one eventually runs out of modules (oscillators and filters and such). With the computer, one simply runs out of patience or computation time.

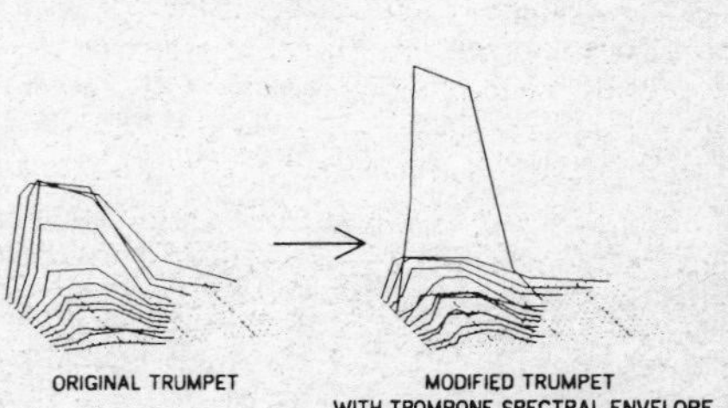

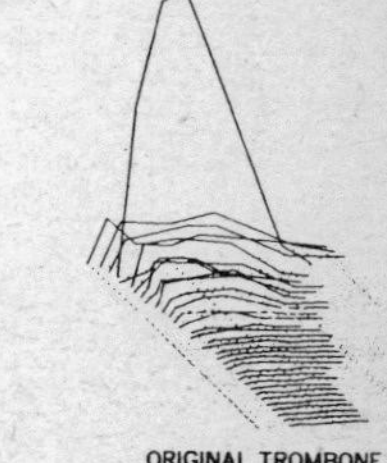

Exchange of spectral envelopes between the trumpet and the trombone to form the modified trumpet and modified trombone (not shown).

THE RISING SUN
NEIGHBORHOOD NEWSLETTER

If Woody Allen never dies, he's going to feel really silly.

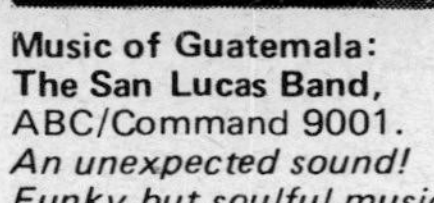

An Introduction to World Music: 100 Records to Start With

by Susan Ohori

Going across the radio dial almost anywhere in the U.S.A., you get a pretty homogeneous and unexciting idea of music that is current, available, listened to, and accepted by Americans. Uniform whether it is classical, rock, jazz, folk, or country. But today more than ever, ironically, a great wealth of the world's varied music is available through records. We have only to open our ears and minds to enjoy these cultural treasures. I believe that they have much with which to enrich us and inspire us. And these different cultures deserve our support and recognition — partly to encourage their very survival and preservation, especially in this century where there is a definite trend toward a homogeneity of culture and life.

Because western European-American culture today has enjoyed the greatest material wealth and world political superiority, people almost everywhere in the world have been made aware of that culture and have often abandoned or modified ("westernized") their traditional forms of music, as well as other arts and even their traditional way of life, their traditional values, for the western forms and values. But "it is a curious irony that two powerful factors in the destruction of the indigenous cultures and their musics — the European colonial empires and the modern age of advanced communication and technology — have also given us hope for their preservation." In how many places from Alaska to the Tierra del Fuego are there only a few survivors who remember the traditional music? Beautiful traditions are vanishing in our lifetime.*

So it's high time to start listening and delve into the world of music. There's a large number of records available and it may be difficult to know where to begin — so I offer a mere 100 Top Records of World Music to get started. It's a huge field and so I've sharply limited its scope. It includes the broad categories of folk, tribal, classical, and some popular musics. It does not include most popular musics, folklorico renditions, folk interpreters, or political songs. It does not include European-American music of the classical tradition, or any music of the United States except Native American music and a few examples of ethnic groups in the U.S. (an area of music that has been growing in strength and deserves a list of its own). The large field of current European folk music is excluded except for a small number of records representative of an authentic, historic tradition. The "Top 100" aims at being representative, with the criteria of authenticity and enjoyability, the best widely available records — reflecting also my personal tastes.

Start wherever your fancy chooses — and enjoy!

***David Reck,** Music of the Whole Earth, **1977, Charles Scribner, NY.**

Eskimos of Hudson Bay & Alaska, Folkways FE4444. *Especially nice children's game songs, hunting calls and songs.*

Songs of Earth, Water, Fire & Sky: San Juan Pueblo, Seneca, N. Arapaho, N. Plains, Cree, Yurok, Navajo, Cherokee, S. Plains. New World NW 246. *An excellent sampling of a number of varied styles.*

Chippewa Grass Dance Songs, Canyon 6106. *Exciting & dramatic vocal & drumming style.*

Songs of the Warm Springs Indian Reservation (Oregon), Canyon 6123. *One of few recordings of Indian women — a fine recording.*

Washo Peyote Songs, Folkways 4384. *One of the best of peyote song albums — extended performances.*

Night & Daylight Yeibi chei, Indian House 1502. *Interesting vocal style with glissandi. Long, fascinating songs.*

Indian Music of the Southwest, Folkways FE8850. *Includes a good variety of styles — Hopi, Papago, Zuni, Pueblo, Apache, Navajo & more.*

Una Historia de la Musica de la Frontera — Texas-Mexican Border Music — Vol. I. Folklyric 9003. *An excellent introduction to this lively, popular music — including some of the finest performers. Excellent notes included.*

Indian Music of Northwest Mexico: Tarahumara, Warihio, Mayo, Canyon 8001. *Lovely, gentle music — matachin dance with 5 violins; pascola with harp, violin & rattles.*

Yaqui Dances, Folkways 6957. *Haunting, enchanting, beautiful music — with violin & guitar.*

Music of the Tarascan Indians of Mexico, Folkways 4217. *Some very fine guitar & violin music, chirimias & flutes from one of the most musically interesting areas of Mexico.*

Modern Maya: The Indian Music of Chiapas, Mexico, Folkways 4379. *Soulful & plaintive music, recorded at various fiestas — violins, harps, guitars.*

Fiestas of Chiapas & Oaxaca, Nonesuch 72070. *An excellent selection ranging from church music to brass band, small string ensemble, solo singer and guitar.*

Music of Guatemala: The San Lucas Band, ABC/Command 9001. *An unexpected sound! Funky but soulful music.*

Caribbean Island Music — Songs & Dances of Haiti, the Dominican Republic, & Jamaica, Nonesuch 72047. *Excellent field recordings of black folk music. Best album of Caribbean music available.*

Bongo, Bakra, & Coolie — Jamaican Roots, Vol. I, Folkways 4231. *Magico-religious songs, Jamaican east Indian music.*

Return on Wings of Pleasure — Pedro Padilla y su Conjunto, Roundup 5003. *A mellow group from Puerto Rico recently recorded.*

Sacred and Profane Music of the Ika — Colombia, Folkways 4055. *Music of the mountain Indians of N. Colombia. Dance music played on accordion with rasp.*

Music of the Jivaro — Ecuador, Folkways 4386. *Music of a very interesting jungle tribal people showing aspects of their lives.*

Los Chiriguanos of Paraguay, Nonesuch 72021. *Bright, lively music played on guarani harps sometimes with singing.*

Instruments and Music of Bolivia, Folkways 4012. *Raucous, strong, sometimes discordant music, but with great dignity and charm.*

Traditional Music of Chile, ABC/Command 9003. *Music for guitarron, accordion, guitars, singers — mestizo music.*

Amerindian Ceremonial Music of Chile, Philips 6586 026. *Music for panpipes, curing ceremony of a shamaness. Lengthy selections.*

Mountain Music of Peru, Folkways 4539. *Most interesting & comprehensive collection of Peruvian music — Quechua and mestizo.*

Fiestas of Peru: Music of the High Andes, Nonesuch 72045. *Flutes, harps, guitars — festive music.*

Music from Mato Grosso, Brazil, Folkways 4446. *Especially interesting for animal calls, 8'-long flutes. From Xingu area.*

Bresil — Musiques du Haut Xingu, Ocora 558 517. *Interesting long horns, animal songs, flutes. Fascinating people fast disappearing.*

In Praise of Oxala & Other Gods — Black Music of South America, Nonesuch 72036. *Festive music from Colombia, Ecuador, and Brazil.*

Anthology of Central & South American Indians, Folkways 4542. *A good sampling from Yaquis in the north all the way to the Tierra del Fuego.*

Songs of Aboriginal Australia & Torres Strait, Folkways 4102. *Vocal songs & didgeridoo music.*

Fataleka & Baegu Music, Malaita, Solomon Islands, Philips 6586 018. *Very interesting & beautiful vocal polyphonics and panpipes.*

Gamelan Semar Pegulingan: Gamelan of the Love God — Bali, Nonesuch 72046. *An excellent recording of a full, rich, classical gamelan.*

Golden Rain — Balinese Gamelan Music, Ketjak: the Ramayana Monkey Chant, Nonesuch 72028. *Most famed for introducing the wonderful monkey chant which knocked people off their feet.*

Gamelan Music from Seloatu — Bali, Archive 2533 130. *A dramatic, shimmering, precise & exciting gamelan.*

Java: Historic Gamelans, Philips 6586 004. *Some old, rare, varied & interesting types of gamelans.*

Javanese Court Gamelan from the Pura Paku Aleman, Jogjakarta. Nonesuch 72044. *Some extended stately & beautiful pieces by a classic court gamelan.*

Sunda (West Java), Philips 6586 031. *Gamelan music & music for small kecapi suling ensemble.*

Musiques de l'asie traditionelle, Vol. 6, Borneo, Playa Sound 33506. *Hindu-influenced music as well as gong-ensemble music.*

The Music of the Magindanao — Philippines, Folkways 4536. *Examples of gongs used in a gamelan-like ensemble, jew's harps, flutes, vocal chants, boat lute, percussion beams.*

A Bell Ringing in the Empty Sky — Japanese Shakuhachi Music — Goro Yamaguchi, Nonesuch 72025. *Haunting, quieting, evocative solo shakuhachi (bamboo flute). Two lengthy selections.*

Japan — Semiclassical & Folk Music, EMI C064-17967. *Good recordings of nagauta, koto, & shakuhachi. Especially good selections of folk music.*

The Koto Music of Japan, Nonesuch 72005. *Nice solos for koto. Especially nice music for sankokyu ensemble — shakuhachi, koto, and shamisen.*

Japan II: Gagaku, Baren Reiter BM 30L 2013. *Dramatic & beautiful ensemble music for the court.*

P'Ansori — Korea's Epic Vocal Art & Instrumental Music — Kim So-hee, Nonesuch 72049. *Music for oboe-like piri, chang go, kae yugeum. Especially fine, strong singing by Kim So-hee.*

Korean Music, Philips 6586 011. *Prominent are the oboe-like hyang-piri played in small court ensemble & taegum flute, both expressive and virtuosic.*

Hong Kong: Instrumental Music, EMI C064 17965. *Mostly solo performances — excellent: p'i p'a, yeng-chin, hsiao, ti, ch'in, sheng, erh-hu, cheng.*

China: Shantung Folk Music & Traditional Instrumental Pieces — Lu Sheng Ensemble, Nonesuch 72051. *Excellent examples of folk & classical music played on sona (oboe), drum/cymbals, sheng, cheng, k'un-ti, nan-hu, ti-tzu.*

Southern Laos: Traditional Music, Philips 6586 012. *Music for khenes (mouth organ), singer; pi-phat orchestra; wedding orchestra; buffalo sacrifice, gong with singer. Exciting and interesting.*

Laos, Baren Reiter BM 30 L 2001. *Khenes, pi-phat orchestra, nice love songs.*

Royal Music of Cambodia, Philips 6586 002. *Long piece by pinpeat orchestra — wooden-keyed xylophones predominating with gongs. Various smaller ensembles & mohori orchestra.*

Thailand: The Music of Chieng Mai, EMI C064 18080. *Three lengthy complete pieces by pi-phat orchestra; ceremonial orchestra of monastery, old Thai ensemble with fiddles, zither, flute, and percussion.*

Ramnad Krishnan: Vidwan — Songs of the Carnatic Tradition, Nonesuch 72033. *Vocal with violin & mrdangam. Extended performances, lengthy alap.*

Sarangi, The Voice of a Hundred Colors — Instrumental Music of North India — Rain Narayan, Nonesuch 72030. *Excellent performances on the sweet sarangi, bowed-string instrument.*

India III: Dhrupad — Moinuddin & Aminuddin Dagar, Baren Reiter BM 30L 2018. *Strong performance of Dagar brothers singing in Dhrupad style.*

Ravi Shankar, Capitol ST 10504. *One of the best recordings of this excellent sitar player.*

T. Viswanathan — South Indian Flute, World Pacific WPS 21451. *Viswanathan in top form.*

Tibetan Buddhism: Tantras of Guyto: Sangwa Dupa, Nonesuch 72064. *Chord-like vocal effect is evidenced in chanting. Extended selections.*

Music of Tibet: Tantric Ritual, Anthology 4005. *Excellent example of chord-like vocal phenomenon in this type of chanting. Extensive notes.*

Ladakh/Songs and Dances from the Highlands of Central Tibet, Nonesuch 72075. *Lovely folk songs and instrumentals.*

Music of Afghanistan, Argo ZFB 57. *Fine selection of vocal and instrumental music.*

Afghanistan Folk Music, Vol 2, Lyrichord 7231. *Very interesting selection of vocal and instrumental folk music.*

Georgia I, Baren Reiter BM 30L 2025. *Polyphonic religious music with surprising and strange harmonies, "yodeling." Beautiful music.*

Azerbaijani Mugam: Bahram Mansurov, tar, Philips 6586 027. *Virtuosic performances of several "mugams" on the stringed tar.*

Arabian Music: Maquam, Philips 6586 006. *Very fine performances on 'ud.*

Kurdish Music, Philips 6586 019. *Dramatic, exciting music. Excellent recording.*

A Persian Heritage/ Classical Music of Iran — Faramarz Payvar and Ensemble, Nonesuch 72060. *Excellent performances on santour, tar, kamancheh, zarb.*

The Pan-Islamic Tradition — Vol. 3, Music of Morocco, Lyrichord 7240. *Drums & chanting, powerful music — flutes & double-reed oboe.*

Algeria (Sahara), EMI C064 18079. *Strong tribal music.*

Jewish Music, Philips 6586 001. *Religious chants from the Mediterranean-Middle Eastern area — from Gibraltar and Morocco to Turkey and Yemen.*

Escalay: The Water Wheel — Oud Music of Nubia — Hamza El Din, Nonesuch 72041. *Extensive selections of a unique style of music personally developed by the soloist — vocal, oud, and tar.*

Ethiopia II: Music of the Cushitic Peoples of Southwest Ethiopia, Baren Reiter BM 30L 2305. *Interesting selections of a tribal people — especially Gidole flute ensemble, interesting vocal techniques.*

Ethiopia II: Music of the Desert Nomads, Tangent TGM 102. *Very interesting vocal selections, love song, work song for hauling water, trance music.*

Musique d'Afrique Occidentale, Vogue LDM 30.116. *An excellent sampling from West Africa with xylophones, women's chorus, flutes, drums, musical bow.*

Alhaji Bai Konte, Roundup 5001. *Virtuosic, exciting performances on the kora, 21-string harp from Gambia.*

African Journey: Roots of the Blues in Africa, Vanguard SRV 73014-5. *Very interesting brass band music, Christian choral singing, kora, mandingo drumming.*

Banda Polyphony, Philips (French) 6586 032. *Fascinating polyphonic horn and flute ensembles, vocal ensembles.*

Ba Benzele Pygmies, Baren Reiter BM 30L 2303. *Excellent, vigorous storytelling. Beautiful polyphonic singing, women singing into one-note flute.*

Aka Pygmy Music, Philips 6586 016. *Beautiful vocal music — solos, duets, larger ensembles of beautiful polyphonies; head and chest voice singing.*

Music from the Heart of Africa — Burundi, Nonesuch 72051. *Music for enanga (zither) and other tribal music.*

Africa — Drum, Chant & Instrumental Music — Niger, Mali, & Upper Volta, Nonesuch 72073. *Strong and interesting drumming, chants, lutes, and flute.*

Valiha — Madagascar, Ocora 18. *Lovely music for valiha (bamboo tube zither) with guitar, violin, singer, flute.*

Mail order records

THE MOST INCREDIBLE news for your ear is seldom available at record stores. To Susan Ohori's splendid list of sources I would add only: **Folk-Legacy Records** *(mentioned on* *p. 472**) and* **Musical Heritage Society**, *14 Park Road, Tinton Falls, NJ 07724 (catalog of 1200 recordings, $1.25).*
—SB

Basque Songs & Dances, Lyrichord 778. *Choral songs. Music for flute and drums. An unexpected sound from Spain.*

Early Cante Flamenco (1934-1939), Folklyric 9001. *Includes the classic Nina de las Peines. Historic recordings.*

Anthology of Portuguese Music, Folkways 4538. *Nice, simple and heart-felt songs sung by various women, as well as instrumental music.*

Italian Folk Music — Vol. I, Piedmont, Emelia, Lombardy, Folkways 4261. *Nice songs and small instrumental ensembles with clarinets, accordion.*

Sicily, Argo ZFB 71. *Short selections but great variety of folk music, some surprising and raucous, some plaintive and charming.*

Folk Music of Albania, Topic 12T154. *Interesting selection of songs and instrumental music.*

Music from the Island of Krk, Folkways 4060. *Vigorous vocal music for a wedding with strange harmonies. Interesting music for oboe-like pipe.*

Islamic Ritual Music from Yugoslavia — Zikr of the Rufai Brotherhood, Philips 6586 015. *Strange, ecstatic, trance-like music.*

A Harvest, a Shepherd, a Bride — Village Music of Bulgaria, Nonesuch 72034. *Very strong women's music. Music for kaval, gaida, gadulka.*

In the Shadow of the Mountain: Bulgarian Folk Music — Pirin — Macedonia, Nonesuch 72038. *Excellent folk ensembles playing dance music, strong women singers.*

Songs & Dances from Czechoslovakia, Argo ZFB 89. *Panpipes, fiddles, string orchestras, and vocals — interesting selection.*

Musique Populaire Hongroise, Ocora 54. *Rich and varied old music — songs, music for stringed instruments, flutes.*

Rumania: Traditional Folk, EMI C064 18120. *A good selection — with panpipes, a very moving lamentation.*

Ukrainian-American Fiddle & Dance Music — 1926-1934, Vol I, Folklyric 9014. *Re-issues of historic recordings — lively music.*

With Shawm & Bagpipe — The Traditional Music of Brittany, Musical Heritage Society MHS 3342. *A living tradition that carries the thread from medieval Europe — very interesting.*

The Irish Pipes of Finbar Furey, Nonesuch 72048. *A modern piper, sometimes with guitar, flute.*

Irish Dance Music, Folkways 8821. *A historic collection.*

Irish-American Dance Music & Songs (late 1920s), Folklyric 4010. *Historic recordings.*

Scottish Tradition 2 — Music from the Western Isles, Tangent TNGM 110. *Some "waulking" songs by women, bagpipes and flutes. Good notes.*

INTERESTING COLLECTIONS AND ANTHOLOGIES OF WORLD MUSIC

THE MUSIC OF AFRICA SERIES, by Hugh Tracey, Kaleidophone

Musical Instruments 1: Strings, KMA-1
Musical Instruments 2: Reeds (Mbira), KMA-2
Musical Instruments 3: Drums, KMA-3
Musical Instruments 4: Flutes & Horns, KMA-4
Musical Instruments 5: Xylophones, KMA-5
Musical Instruments 6: Guitars 1, KMA-6
Musical Instruments 7: Guitars 2, KMA-7
Rhodesia 1, KMA-8
Tanzania 1, KMA-9
Uganda 1, KMA-10

Music from Uganda, Tanzania, Rhodesia, Malawi, Mozambique, Congo, Rwanda. (Order by mail from Kleidophone. See addresses.)

MUSIC IN THE WORLD OF ISLAM, by Jean Jenkins & Paul Rovsing Olsen; Tangent.

1: The Human Voice, TGS 131.
2: Lutes, TGS 132
3: Strings, TGS 133
4: Flutes & Trumpets, TGS 134
5: Reeds & Bagpipes, TGS 135
6: Drums & Rhythms, TGS 136.

North Africa, Middle East, India, to Indonesia. (Available from Roundup Records and Down Home Music.)

MUSIC FROM MEXICO FROM THE INSTITUTO NACIONAL DE ANTROPOLOGIA Y HISTORIA

1. Testimonio Musical de Mexico
2. Danzas de la Conquista
3. Musica Huasteca
4. Musica Indigena de los Altos de Chiapas
5. Musica Indigena del Noroeste

— and more through Vol. 19.

(Available from Down Home Music — cheaper than from Mexico.)

UNA HISTORIA DE LA MUSICA DE LA FRONTERA — TEXAS-MEXICAN BORDER MUSIC, Folklyric

Vol. 1: An Introduction, 1930-1960, 9003
Vol. 2: Early Corridos — Part 1, 9004
Vol. 3: Norteno Accordion — Part 1 — 1930s, 9006
Vol. 5: The String Bands, 9007
Vol. 6: Cancioneros de Ayer — Part 1, 9011

— and more through Vol. 16.

(Available from Down Home Music.)

FOLK MUSIC IN AMERICA, Library of Congress

Vol. 1: Religious Music — Congregational & Ceremonial
Vol. 2: Songs of Love, Courtship & Marriage
Vol. 3: Dance Music: Breakdowns & Waltzes
Vol. 4: Dance Music: Reels, Polkas & More

— and more through Vol. 15.

Reflecting popular and ethnic influences. (Order by mail from the Library of Congress. See addresses.)

ADDRESSES OF RECORD COMPANIES AND DISTRIBUTORS

Canyon Records
4143 N. Sixteenth St.
Phoenix, AZ 85016

Indian House
P.O. Box 472
Taos, NM 87571

Folkways Records
43 W. 61st Street
New York, NY 10023

Lyrichord Records
141 Perry Street
New York, NY 10014

Nonesuch Records
665 Fifth Avenue
New York, NY 10022

Monitor Recordings, Inc.
156 Fifth Avenue
New York, NY 10010

Balkan Arts
514 W. 110 St. No. 3
New York, NY 10025

Kaleidophone Records
Traditional Music Documentation Project
3740 Kanawha St., N.W.
Washington, DC 20015

The Library of Congress
Music Division
Recorded Sound Section
Washington, DC 20540

Roundup Records
Box 474
Somerville, MA 02144
(Roundup also distributes Topic, Tangent, Folk-lyric and more.)

Festival Records
161 Turk Street
San Francisco, CA 94102
(Carries wide selection of European folk and dance music.)

Peters International
619 W. 54th Street
New York, NY 10019
(A major distributor for imports.)

Graeme Vanderstoel
P.O. Box 599
El Cerrito, CA 94530
(Books and records — carries Ocora, Tangent, UNESCO, more.)

Down Home Music, Inc.
10341 San Pablo Avenue
El Cerrito, CA 94530

Muskadine Music
212 Pier Avenue
Santa Monica, CA 90405
(Down Home and Muskadine specialize in traditional American music but have excellent sections of world music — Ocora, UNESCO, Vogue, more.)

A NOTE ON IMPORTS: I have refrained from including many records on imported labels in the list of the "Top 100" because of the difficulty in obtaining them nationwide. Otherwise, many would have been on the list — in particular, those on the Ocora or Vogue labels. If you see them in your record shops, you can be sure they're excellent. There is a great need for better distribution of world music. ■

A Basic 10 Records of American Composers

by Peter Garland

American writing and painting are generally known and acknowledged to be among the most significant of the 20th century. So was its music, though many composers (Ives, Ruggles, Varèse, Rudhyar, Partch, Nancarrow) suffered incredible neglect in their lifetimes. People often ask me where to get started with this music: here. These records are all easily available (if not at your record store, try the mail order houses we list on *p. 482**). And granted, re "American" music, this is one side of the picture, only.*

Complete Music of Carl Ruggles, Buffalo Philharmonic, Michael Tilson Thomas, conductor, $11.98, Columbia M2 34591. *Carl Ruggles (1876-1971), one of our greatest composers, illustrates the neglect contemporary American music still suffers: his life-work, which comprises about 1½ hours only was only recorded in 1979! Incredible, "damn fine music," as Ruggles himself said — 12 pieces in a lifetime of 95 years.*

Piano Music: Henry Cowell (played by Cowell) Folkways FM 3349. *Cowell (1897-1966) "invented" many new piano techniques: the tone cluster (played by the forearm or palm), playing inside the piano, etc., back in the 1910s-1920s! Sixty years later, these pieces have lost none of their freshness.*

Americas, Arcana, Ionisation: Edgard Varèse, NY Philharmonic, Boulez, conductor, $6.98, Columbia M 34552. *Varèse! (1883-1965)* **The Rite of Spring** *has always seemed slightly tame to me compared to* **Americas**. *No one has ever written better for an orchestra — or more powerful, convulsively beautiful music.*

Paeans, Stars, Granites: Dane Rudhyar. **Piano Works**: Ruth Crawford Seeger, Masselos (Rudhyar), Block (Seeger), piano, $7.95, Composers Recordings, Inc., S247. *Rudhyar (1895 -) is perhaps better known as an astrologer. Yet he was also one of this century's important composers (especially for the piano) — still is. These three pieces are some of his greatest. Ruth Crawford Seeger (1901-1953) was the most significant woman composer to date of the century: likewise, these are some of her finest pieces.*

Three Places in New England: Charles Ives. **Appalachian Spring**: Aaron Copland. St. Paul Chamber Orchestra, D.R. Davies, conductor, $16.50; Sound 80 Records DLR-101. *Charles Ives (1874-1954) needs little introduction. This piece is one of his best, combining both his experimental and Americana sides. Copland's (1901 -) music does not excite me personally as much as others' — but his contribution to American music cannot be overlooked. He is our most famous composer. Try these pieces. Nice ones.*

Sensemaya, Redes, Caminos, Itinerarios, Janitzio: Silvestre Revueltas, New Philharmonia Orchestra, Mata, conductor, RCA (not currently available). *Revueltas (1899-1940) was the most important composer Latin America has produced yet. These pieces are similar to the murals of Orozco or Rivera: in a populist vein, colorful, vigorous, passionate.*

Complete Studies for Player Piano: Conlon Nancarrow. $9.98; 2-1750 Arch Records S-1768. *In the 1940s Nancarrow (1912 -) renounced performers, and simultaneously went into political exile in Mexico. He then created his own self-sustaining musical world, working exclusively with the player piano. He has suffered as much neglect as any American composer, yet his music has the power and impact of Varèse's. The keyboard has never sounded like this!*

Pacifika Rondo, Four Pieces for Harp, other works: Lou Harrison, Oakland Youth Orchestra, Hughes, conductor. $7.98; Desto Records DC-6478. *Non-western musics and cultures have had a tremendous influence on American music, and nowhere is that more wondrously evident than in the work of Lou Harrison — combined with his wonderful lyrical gift!*

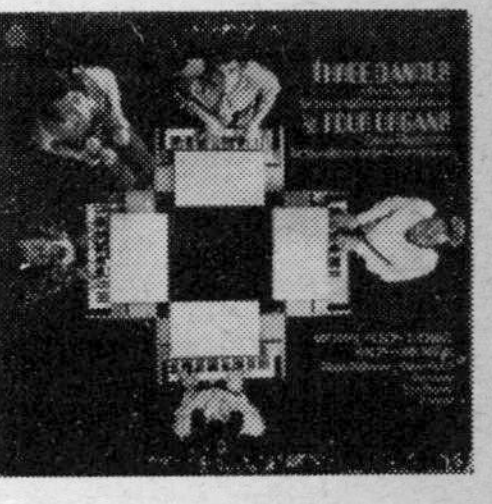

Delusion of the Fury: Harry Partch, Unique Instrument Ensemble, Mitchell, conductor. $11.98; Columbia M2-30576. *Partch (1901 - 1974) was the most revolutionary composer of the past 500 years of Western music! This work, a large-scale dance/mime theater piece, is based on a Japanese Noh drama, and an African folk tale. Written for the incredible orchestra of instruments (and in the special tuning) that Partch created to perform his unique music. And what music!*

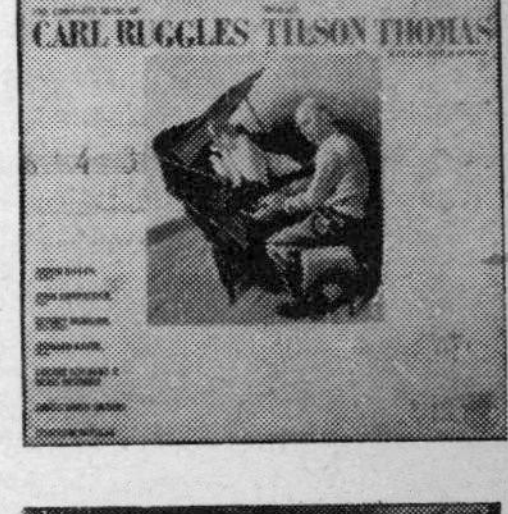

Three Dances for Two Prepared Pianos: John Cage. **Four Organs**: Steve Reich. Thomas, Grierson, pianos; Thomas, Grierson, Kellaway, Reich, organs. $8.98; Angel S-36059. *Cage (1912 -) is again, unique. Perhaps best known for his aesthetic of chance, these pieces predate that, and are from the 1940s; some of his finest music, for the prepared piano (where nuts, bolts, etc., are put in/on the piano strings, to alter the sound), an exotic, beautiful sound-world in itself. To get a taste of what's happening today, try Steve Reich (1936 -). This music is both intellectually satisfying, and quite accessible, "likeable." And he especially is starting to attract a wider public to this kind of music — at last!* ■

Music of the Whole Earth

This is the most beautiful and essential book on music I have ever seen! Perfectly accessible to the music-lover as well as the music-maker, this is a book that everyone seriously interested in music should read. David and Carol Reck have done a stunning job of tackling an ambitious subject: the charting of "an exquisitely beautiful and relatively unexplored country: the musical landscape of the whole earth." And this book comes at a most urgent time: traditional musics of the world rank high on the list of endangered species. They too, once gone, will never reappear.
—Peter Garland

Music of the Whole Earth
David Reck
1977; 545 pp.
$9.95 postpaid from:
Charles Scribner's Sons
Vreeland Avenue
Totowa, NJ 07512
or Whole Earth Household Store

THE RISING SUN
NEIGHBORHOOD NEWSLETTER

People who didn't die include Elijah, who went to heaven in a chariot of fire and in the Middle Ages often returned to ask rich people and poor people for a potato and the rich people wouldn't give it to him and soon got poor as punishment and poor people would give it to him and soon found a pot of gold as a reward when they were digging up their back yard to plant more potatoes. There is a chair for him at all Seders and some wine but he never shows up, probably off asking for spare change.

The New Listener's Companion and Record Guide

Make no mistake, this is not the book for the casual listener — someone who thinks that a counter-tenor is a singing soda jerk and that largo is an island off the coast of Florida. B.H. Haggin assumes that his readers share his love of classical music and are interested in developing critical insight. He begins with musical procedures and forms, explaining the development of form in sound — the ways in which sound conveys thought. He analyzes selected pieces, using prose and musical notation. Next is a survey of the literature of music and chapters on performance and criticism. The second part of the book is a guide to recorded performances of the music discussed in the survey. Recordings are evaluated on the basis of quality of performance and sound reproduction. The list has been updated to include recordings issued through 1978. Haggin's critical judgments are well-reasoned, well-written and all-pervasive — an open invitation to listen and form your own opinions. If that doesn't tempt you, at least you'll know that contrapuntal procedure isn't football jargon for a 4th down defensive maneuver.

—Diana Fairbanks

The New Listener's Companion and Record Guide
B.H. Haggin
1956, 1978; 456 pp.
5th Edition

$6.95 postpaid from:
Horizon Press
156 Fifth Avenue
New York, NY 10010
or Whole Earth
Household Store

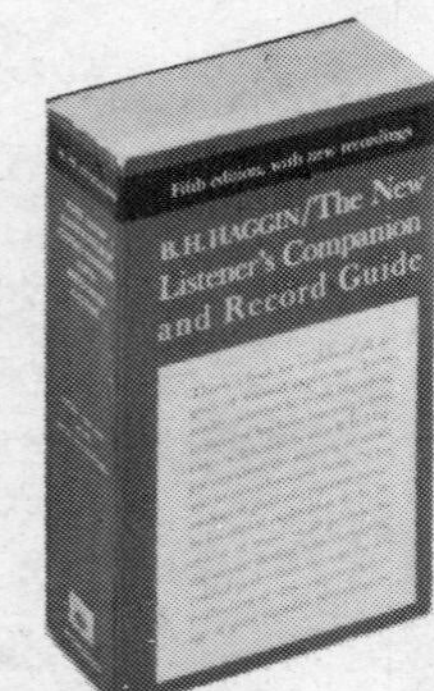

•

Thomson

The Mother of Us All, one of the very few American operas worth listening to (the others being Thomson's *Four Saints in Three Acts* and Copland's *The Tender Land*), is available on records at last on New World NW-288/9, performed by the Santa Fe Opera. Mignon Dunn is not the right singer for the central role of Susan B. Anthony, whose high notes are beyond Dunn's range of agreeable sound; but the other singers are good, and Leppard conducts effectively.

World Around Songs

World Around Songs, of Celo, North Carolina, offers a service that might be very useful to any group that was getting together, being neighborly and in the process, singing a few songs. They publish more than 100 stock songbooks such as the ones shown here (all in pocket-sized format), as well as specializing in the production of custom songbooks for various groups. World Around Songs is the new name for the old Cooperative Recreation Service, Inc., of Delaware, Ohio. They have a library of some 2000 songs, including many timeless favorites as well as an excellent body of songs from many foreign countries (usually collected and transcribed from native singers).

—Chris Joyner

World Around Songs
Catalog

$.50 from:
World Around Songs
Route 5
Burnsville, NC 28714

•

Songs of All Time, $1.15;
Tent and Trail Songs, $1.15;
101 Rounds for Singing, $.80;
Little Book of Carols, $.80;
Sing Together Children, $1.20;
Sacred Canons, $.55;
Having Fun the Polish Way, $.90;
Handy Play Party Book, $4.00 (plastic binding)
plus shipping . . . .
Discount rates begin with order of 10 books.

This Old Man

This old man, he played one, He played knick-knack on my thumb. Knick-knack pad - dy - wack, Give your dog a bone. This old man came roll - ing home.

2. On my shoe
3. On my knee
4. On my door
5. On my hive
6. On my sticks
7. Up in heaven
8. On my pate
9. On my spine
10. Once again

—Sing Together Children

More records by mail

Mail order record houses from large cities often give better prices than what you can find locally, and they usually send hard-to-find records and tapes faster than a local store can deliver them. King Karol in New York and Moby Music in Los Angeles are reputable, reliable, comprehensive and cheap (for a $7.98 list price LP, King Karol charges $6.49 and Moby charges $5.59). Both have good special sales. Both will supply any record or tape in Schwann's, the catalog of all American albums-in-print. (For Classical or current releases, ask for Schwann-1; for other music, ask for Schwann-2.)

Two highly recommended specialty record-by-mail stores are Down Home (folk music, blues, jazz, old-time country, vintage rock'n'roll) and Rather Ripped (new wave and rock esoterical). Both are in the San Francisco Bay Area, the center for the independent recording industry.

—Art Kleiner

(See p. 571 for children's records.)

King Karol
Schwann's catalog

$1 from:
King Karol Records
P.O. Box 629
Times Square Station
New York, NY 10036

[Suggested by Tom Ferguson]

Moby Music
Brochure

free

Schwann's catalog

$1.25
both from:

Moby Music
14410 Ventura Blvd.
Sherman Oaks, CA 91423

[Suggested by Annette LeBette]

Down Home
Catalog

free from:
Down Home
10341 San Pablo Avenue
El Cerrito, CA 94530

[Suggested by Arhoolie Records]

Rather Ripped Records
Catalog

free from:
Rather Ripped Records
1878 Euclid Avenue
Berkeley, CA 94709

[Suggested by Jonathan Evelegh]

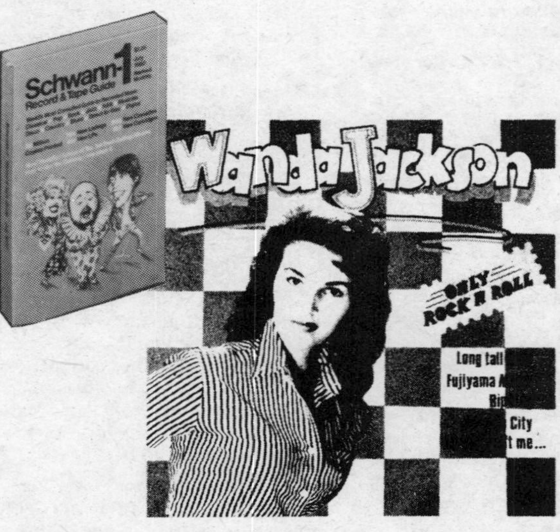

Wanda Jackson. Probably the best of all the female rock 'n' roll singers with a really tough raspy voice. She had several rockin' hits in the early '60s and later went on to singing straight country.

Starline 5120 PIONEERS OF ROCK (Let's Have A Party /Money Honey/Mean Mean Man/Tongue Tied/Honey Don't/Long Tall Sally/Honey Bop/Rip It Up, etc. $6.98

Capitol (U.K.) 1007 ROCKIN' WITH WANDA (15 of her best — Hot Dog! That Made Him Mad/Baby Loves Him/Mean Mean Man/You've Turned To A Stranger /Don'a Wan'a/I Gotta Know, etc.) $8.98

—King Karol Catalog

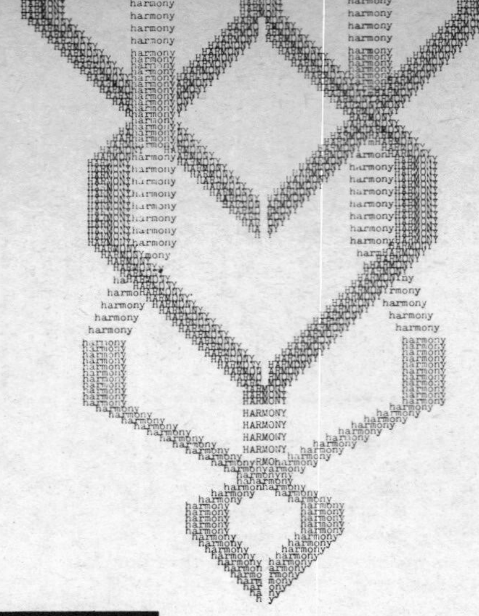

Ear Magazine

Although I am a musician, many of the articles in **Ear** *go over my head, or perhaps "in one ear and out the other." However, the editors are abreast of what is happening in modern classical music, and are aware of what frontiers are being explored. Although based in New York, there is some nationwide coverage and the magazine appears to be growing rapidly.* **Whole Earth** *readers will applaud the philosophy of encouraging reader input, and as a result,* **Ear** *provides a forum for young composers. Some of the events covered in recent issues include the 12th International Sound Poetry Festival, New Music America at the Twin Cities, and organizations that have been covered include the Public Access Synthesizer Studio, the Experimental Intermedia Foundation, Ringling Bros. Barnum & Bailey Circus. The interviews are good, and the reviews of performances and recordings are usually short and informative without excluding the layman. The magazine is a must for experimental composers.*

—Otis Read

Ear Magazine
Michael Cooper, et al., Editors

$10 /year (5 issues)
from:
New Wilderness Foundation
210 Sullivan Street
Apartment 2C
New York, NY 10012

•

The genre of music introduced by Reich, Glass, Reilly, etc., has opened the listener to the power of repetition. It is often credited with having reformed the listener's expectation for rapidly evolving thematic data. This music still relies on listening "in time" wherein the repetition gathers meaning and sonic ideas unfold at a much slower pace. It seems that the composers that I am writing about have abandoned the idea of theme and development altogether. This music is designed to be heard in the present without regard for its past or future. This environmental sound quality has been dismissed by many as a non-viable tool for composition and yet there are many people coming from different traditions (jazz, experimental, and electronic music) who are working with this sound.
One of the most interesting examples of this type of music is Brian Eno's album, "Music for Airports." Eno calls this music "ambient music" and he writes on the album sleeve about its ability to function as a sort of enlightened musak. "Ambient music must be able to accommodate many levels of listening attention without enforcing one in particular; it must be as ignorable as it is interesting." This album is more interesting than ignorable though I like his point. The subtle timbres and almost mysterious textures show Eno's marvelous dexterity and facility with the electronic idiom.

Goldmine

Well, some of those old records do appreciate, you know. You just got to figure out the price you have to have to pry the vinyl from your paws, and then find a buyer. **Goldmine** *is a place to start. About 80% ads for yesterday's sounds from both pro and amateur dealers; you could find your desert island discs on almost any page. Informatively rounded out with collectors' stories, interviews with classic vinyl creators and reviews of today's $6 item (maybe tomorrow's collector's delight).*

—Jonathan Evelegh

Goldmine
(The Record Collector's Marketplace)
Rick Whitesell, Editor

$15 /year (12 issues)
from:
Goldmine
P.O. Box 187
Fraser, MI 48026

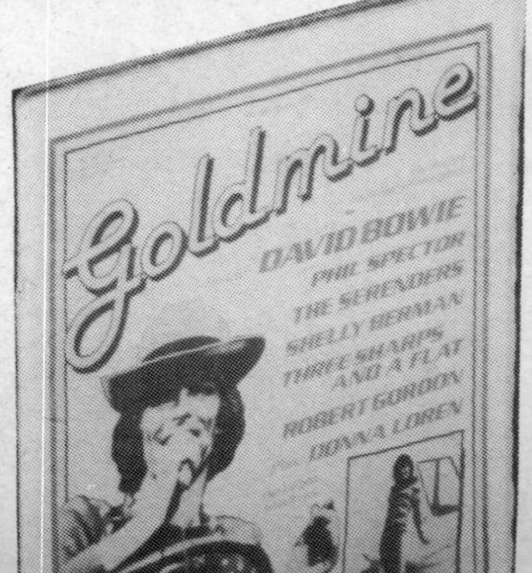

FOLLOWING 45 s ALL WITH PIC. SLEEVES,SLEEVES GRADED FIRST MB 2$ UNLESS NOTED

56. ATCO 6140-BOBBY DARIN--DREAM LOVER VG+/M
57. CAPITOL 4637-JACK SCOTT--ONE OF THESE DAYS VG++/M MB5
58. CARLTON 493-JACK SCOTT--GOODBYE BABY M-/M- MB5
59. DECCA 31703-RICK NELSON--A HAPPY GUY VG/M(DJ)
60. DECCA 31093-BRENDA LEE--IM SORRY M-/M
61. DECCA 30314-B. HALEY&COMETS--BILLY GOAT VG++/M(DJ)
62. DECCA 31231-BRENDA LEE--YOU CAN DEPEND ON ME VG+/M
63. EPIC 9615-ROLF HARRIS--NICK TEEN&AL K. HALL M-/VG+(DJ WOL)
64. LIBERTY 55581-BOBBY VEE--A LETTER FROM BETTY VG+/M(DJ)
65. LIBERTY 55246-THE CHIPMUNKS--COMING ROUND THE MTN. M-/M
66. RCA 7035 ELVIS--JAILHOUSE ROCK VG++/M MB4
67. RCA 7155-TONY PERKINS--JUST BEING OF AGE VG++/M
68. ROULETTE 4090-JIMMIE RODGERS--ARE YOU REALLY MINE VG++/M(DJ)
69. 20th FOX 311-MARILYN MONROE--RIVER OF NO RETURN VG+/M(DJ)

FOLLOWING 45s POP,ROCK,MISC. 50 sAND EARLY 60 s MB 2$

TOWER
Reg. U.S. Pat. Off.
RB 404
BIG NOISE FROM WINNETKA
THREE SHARPS AND A FLAT
1266
MANUFACTURED FOR RICHARD BRADLEY AND ASSOCIATES, CHICAGO

MUSIC BUSINESS
(For Musicians)

by Diane Sward Rapaport and Jonathan Evelegh

The authors prepared this material independently, but their work blends nicely, which I did. Diane Sward Rapaport is the author of the exemplary **How to Make and Sell Your Own Record.** ***Jonathan Evelegh, British, tall and redheaded, has been working around grass roots music business since pop became punk became new wave. Prior to that he was a music agent and promoter in his native England. He also handles much of the office business for Whole Earth.***

Dear Diane and Jonathan: is there any guidance in any of this material that can help keep the successful rock-type musician from acquiring one of the most repulsive personalities alive? Rewarding youthful impulsiveness with infinite attention, money, drugs, and sex seems an abundantly fatal prescription. When I got to sit next to Linda Ronstadt at a poetry reading once, I remarked that the aging beatnik poets such as Gary Snyder, Allen Ginsberg, Philip Whalen, etc. seemed unusually sane, balanced, competent people. "They're either sane or dead," mused Ronstadt. "The same is true in my business."
—SB

THE RECENT INCREASE in the number of musicians working for themselves — booking their own gigs, promoting their own concerts, producing and selling their own records, copyrighting and publishing their own songs — is good news. It means that the musicians are not only communicating directly with the people who buy and promote their art, but that they control their own budgets.

The business role is not easy for many musicians to assume. They've had to overcome any resistance they have to selling their own art and any conditioning that leads them to believe that artists are incapable of being competent business people.

Fortunately, the musician who tries has many allies. Classes, seminars, and lectures in music business and recording are increasingly available in major cities through numerous sources — adult education and community college programs; music stores and recording studios; local songwriter or musicians' collective organizations. Both cheap and good, these programs are taught by working music business or recording professionals within the community.

When such programs are not accessible, several good books deliver specific, useful information. Here are the best ones. —*Rapaport*

This Business of Music
More About this Business of Music

The legal nuts and bolts of the music industry. It's all the same whatever style of music you're into. Nitty-gritty discussions of what seem like minutiae until you multiply out thousands of units tinkling their way into the world's eardrums. If you're serious about communicating on a wide scale with your, or anyone else's, music, there's no way around the first of these books. (You may be able to avoid the second, depending on the areas you're working in.) Not light reading but there are indexes. —*Evelegh*

(See Modern Recording and Music, p. 521.)

This Business of Music
(A practical guide to the music industry for publishers, writers, record companies, producers, artists, agents)
Sidney Shemel and M. William Krasilovsky
1977; 575 pp.
4th Edition
$18.50 postpaid

More About this Business of Music
Sidney Shemel and M. William Krasilovsky
1974; 341 pp.
$12.95 postpaid

both from:
Watson-Guptill Publications
2160 Patterson Street
Cincinnati, OH 45214
or Whole Earth Household Store

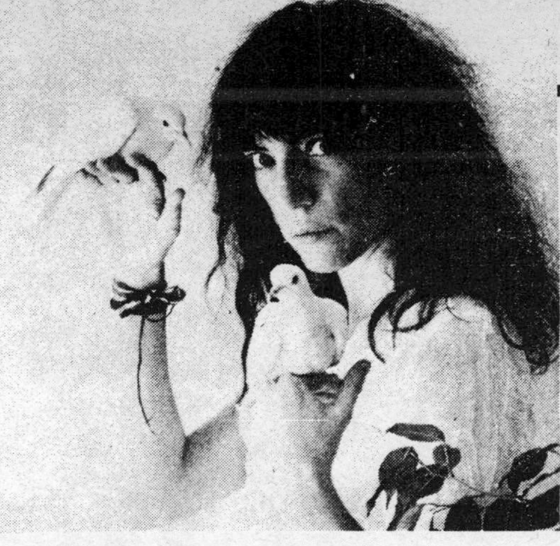
Patti Smith — Contemporary Music Almanac

The Broadcasting/Cable Yearbook
Contemporary Music Almanac 1980/81
New Youth Productions International Directory

The names and addresses of some of the forces behind modern popular music. **The Broadcasting/Cable Yearbook** *is an expensive way of getting names, addresses, and other pertinent data for radio and TV stations right across the United States and Canada. But if you're in the business of getting your record played or selling expensive electronic equipment to those stations, it's convenient to at least have access to a copy.*

The Contemporary Music Almanac *is a monster hodgepodge of names and addresses of prominent members of the Found Music Industry, as well as being crammed with statistics, trivia, bios, charts and other fascinations including standard contracts and advice to the star struck. Its major failing is the old missing index.* **The New Youth Productions International Directory** *is another hodgepodge of information, covering radio stations, stores, clubs, fanzines, etc. in the punk/reggae scenes around the world — updated punkerly. The best value out of the three if it's your scene and it's hard, usable information you need. Should be cross-referenced with* **OP Magazine.**
—*Evelegh*

—Sound Mixers, New York

Contemporary Music Almanac 1980/81
(Awards, Events, Trends, Trivia, Hit Singles and Albums, Who's Who, Calendar, Films, Directories)
Ronald Zalkind
1980; 948 pp.

$9.95 postpaid from:
Schirmer Books
MacMillan Publishing Co.
Order Department
Front and Brown Streets
Riverside, NJ 08075
or Whole Earth Household Store

•
1979
February: Sid Vicious dies in New York. The new wave reaches its Altamont.
—**The Contemporary Music Almanac 1980/81**

•
Brand-name institutions, such as Bob Dylan, ABC, or the Ford Foundation, are hung up on the glamour of their names. They are unlikely sources of money for beginning music business entrepreneurs. Practically all brand-name institutional money goes to similarly respectable brand-name institutions or brand-name causes, such as the world peace movement, CARE, and Lincoln Center for the Performing Arts.
—**The Contemporary Music Almanac 1980/81**

The Broadcasting/Cable Yearbook
Saul Taishoff, Editor
1980; 1184 pp.

$55 postpaid from:
Broadcasting Publications, Inc.
1735 DeSales Street NW
Washington, DC 20036

New Youth Productions International Directory
(of independent, non-aligned creators and promoters of music and the visual arts)
$6/year (4 issues)
from:
New Youth Productions
P.O. Box 6029
San Francisco, CA 94101

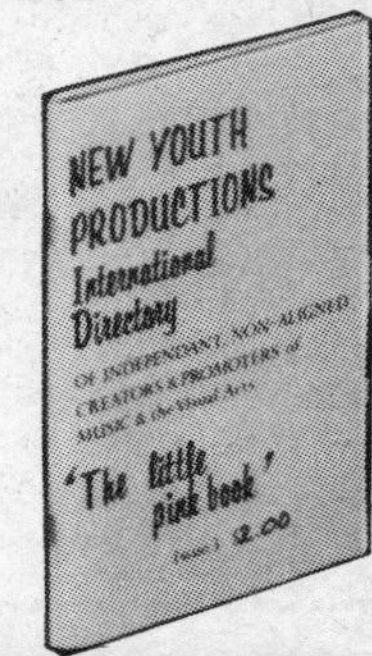

—New Youth Productions International Directory

CONTINUED ON NEXT PAGE

The Art of Deduction

A handy outline of federal income tax laws as they apply to individual artists (rather than partnerships or corporations) and good examples of their applications in specific instances. —*Rapaport*

The Art of Deduction
(Income Taxation for Performing, Visual and Literary Artists)
Kim Marois, Editor
1979; 27 pp.

$4.50 postpaid from:
Bay Area Lawyers for the Arts
Fort Mason Center
Building B
San Francisco, CA 94123
or Whole Earth Household Store

The CAMEO Dictionary of Creative Audio Terms

This book offers precise definitions of commonly used audio terms for people who are not technically inclined. Nice graphs and charts for the more difficult terms.
—*Rapaport*

The CAMEO Dictionary of Creative Audio Terms
Gary Davis and Associates
1979; 99 pp.
$5.95 postpaid from:
CAMEO
10 Delmar Avenue
Framingham, MA 01701

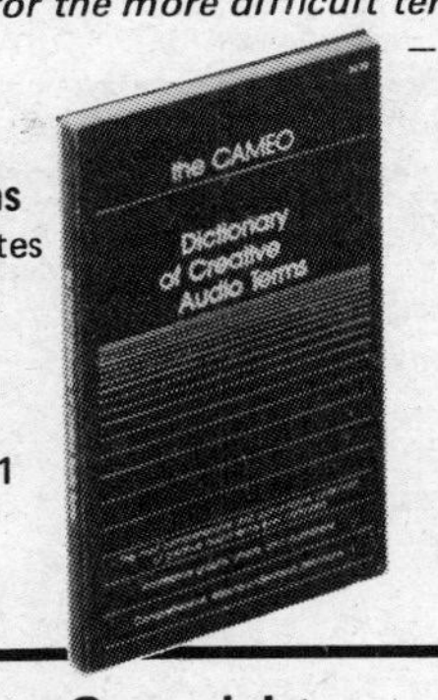

Musician's Guide to Copyright

Written by three lawyers, this book answers the majority of questions songwriters have about copyrighting and publishing in no-nonsense, plain talk. It's primary purpose is to de-mystify copyright laws so that musicians can understand them. —*Rapaport*

Musician's Guide to Copyright
J. Gunnar Erickson, Edward R. Hearn and Mark E. Halloran
1979; 85 pp.

$6.95 postpaid from:
Bay Area Lawyers for the Arts
Fort Mason Center
Building B
San Francisco, CA 94123
or Whole Earth Household Store

THE RISING SUN
NEIGHBORHOOD NEWSLETTER

King Arthur didn't die but floated down the river as ladies sang sad songs, to an undetermined location, or Avalon, from which he will return when he is really, really, I mean seriously, needed. When Merlin told young Arthur that they were both going to come back much later, Arthur was silent for a long time and said, "Will we know anyone then, Merlin?"
(The Once and Future King)

CONTINUED FROM LAST PAGE

How to Make and Sell Your Own Record

An indispensable guide for those who wish to go vinyl on their own behalf. Gets in the groove of the independent recording business and stays there from early planning of promotion right through to tax returns. Read it before you book your studio time. —Evelegh

How to Make and Sell Your Own Record
(The Complete Guide to Independent Recording)
Diane Sward Rapaport
1979; 167 pp.
$11.50 postpaid from:
Headlands Press
Box 862C
Tiburon, CA 94920
or Whole Earth Household Store

↑
We chose to do an EP in accordance with our budget ($2000, which ended up $2500 plus) — not wishing to have such an important step to us result in only a two-song single, but not being able to afford an LP. Also, the record was an experiment to see whether our established audience would come through for record sales, as well as the already proven aspect of ticket sales. Fortunately, we found success.

The New Miss Alice Stone Ladies Society Orchestra
Harmony Club Records

Speck 800-C mixing console

- A Sub output meters (1 - 8)
- B Main output meters (1, 2)
- C Input sections (1-16)
- D Monitor control board
- E Main output section
- F Pushbutton buss assigns (1 - 8)
- G Pseudo-parametric equalizers
- H Solo switch
- I Pad
- J Cue sends (2)
- K Echo send
- L Mic/line switch
- M Tape monitor/ program switch
- N Monitor gain
- O Pan pot
- P Fader
- Q Talkback mic
- R LEDs (2 - power, solo)
- S 2-track play (1, 2)
- T Cue echo return (1, 2)
- U Cue prompt (1, 2)
- V Talkback gain and EQ
- W Slate (talk to tape)
- X Talk (studio monitors)
- Y Studio monitor volume
- Z Control room monitor volume
- A' Dim pad (—30dB)
- B' Sub out master pots (1 - 8)
- C' Echo returns (1, 2)
- D' Cue master pots (1, 2)
- E' Cue solo switches (1, 2)
- F' Master fader

•

A great deal of work needs to be done in advance of making your record. You need to identify your potential audience, to acquire a working knowledge of the media, to assemble mailing lists, and to design and print promotional materials, such as album covers, posters, or photographs. In addition, money should be set aside to meet expenses for promotional materials and such ongoing costs as telephone and postage. So many independents have spent their last dimes making their records sound beautiful and then have no money left to pay for an effective cover, much less for postage to send records to people on their mailing lists.

You will need to acquire a rudimentary knowledge of the promotional methods open to you and use them to gain performances, reviews, and airplay. By adding persistence, imagination, and old-fashioned *chutzpah*, you'll be surprised at the attention you can attract.

Rock 'n' Roll is Here to Pay

And this is how it pays — BIG. And when something pays big the big boys are playing. And when the big boys play they want things their way. This book is a fascinating chronicle of how the big boys have got their way over the years. Essential reading for an understanding of modern popular music and the forces behind it. Needs updating to cover the last four years when many interesting things such as punk and the small label eruption occurred, but I hope that this book can never be considered totally up to date. —Evelegh

Rock 'n' Roll is Here to Pay
(The History and Politics of the Music Industry)
Steve Chapple and Reebee Garofalo
1977; 345 pp.
$10.95 postpaid from:
Nelson-Hall
111 North Canal Street
Chicago, IL 60606
or Whole Earth Household Store

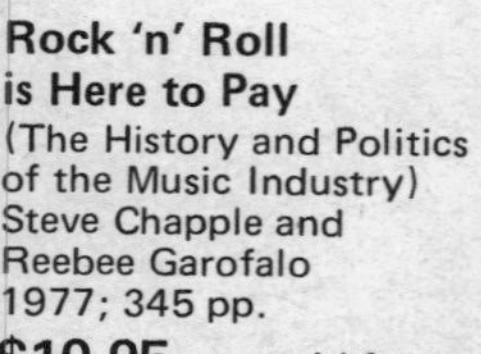

OP magazine

If you have an interest in the music the mega corporations of the pop culture are ignoring, this is the magazine for you. Published by the non-profit Lost Music Network, **OP** *presents a vibrant mix of letters from local scenes all over the country, information lists of sympathetic stores and radio stations, reviews of a multitude of small label pressings with no genre boundaries, and tales of others' experiences with the vinyl mistress/master. Good balance of arty entertainment, culture, and utility.* —Evelegh

OP magazine
John Foster, Editor
$6/year (12 issues) from:
Lost Music Network
P.O. Box 2391
Olympia, WA 98507

Star-Making Machinery

Chronicles the ups and downs of Commander Cody and his lost Planet Airmen through a few years of their major label rollercoaster glide. Trucking along like a good novel — exciting story line, flavorsome dialogue, tension and drama, love and hate — the book succeeds in capturing the emotional tenor of recording and promoting hit records with all the attendant shocks, knocks and humors. "The rock chain may begin with a musician strumming his guitar in a tenement walk-up," writes Stokes, "but it includes a bewildering array of technology, armies of lawyers and accountants, and considerable wheeling and dealing in money and drugs." —Rapaport

Star-Making Machinery
(Inside the Business of Rock and Roll)
Geoffrey Stokes
1976; 234 pp.
$4.95 postpaid from:
Vintage Books
Random House
455 Hahn Road
Westminster, MD 21157
or Whole Earth Household Store

Home Recording for Musicians

Aimed at musicians who have purchased recording equipment for home use, this book introduces technical terms and operating procedures in plain, conversational language, and provides easy to follow illustrations. Chapters include: Studio Basics; Creating the Home Studio Environment; The Console; Microphones; Recording Techniques; Mixing and Assembling the Master Tape; Projects for Home Recording. —Rapaport

Home Recording for Musicians
Craig Anderton
1977; 182 pp.
$9.95 postpaid from:
Guitar Player Books
20605 Lazaneo
Cupertino, CA 95014
or Whole Earth Household Store

The Mix

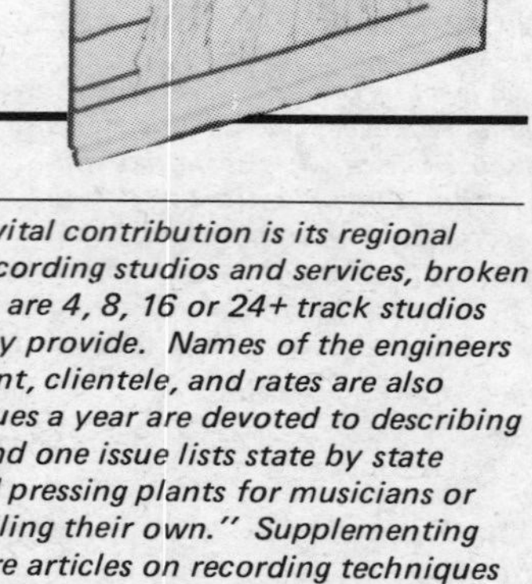

This magazine's most vital contribution is its regional directory listings of recording studios and services, broken down by whether they are 4, 8, 16 or 24+ track studios and the equipment they provide. Names of the engineers operating the equipment, clientele, and rates are also given. At least two issues a year are devoted to describing new audio products, and one issue lists state by state mastering facilities and pressing plants for musicians or small label owners "rolling their own." Supplementing the directory listings are articles on recording techniques or new technology or interviews with producers, engineers, or musicians. —Rapaport ■

The Mix
William I. Laski, Editor
$20/year (12 issues) from:
The Mix
Box 6395
Albany, CA 94706

The Photographer's Handbook

I was a photogger before I was a catalogger, and long I've deplored the dearth of practical/comprehensive books on photography. You either had excellent but highly specialized items like Minor White's **Zone System Manual** *or the absurdly overpriced and overproduced Time-Life series of photography books.*

The one book I long relied on, Feininger's **Total Picure Control**, *has now been surpassed by this beautiful new book. It's quite wonderful to use, rewarding the browser as well as the photographer who has a special problem. I went to sleep on the subject of photography years ago. This book makes me think about waking up and trying some of its myriad ideas and techniques.*

The book replaces about eight others I might have reviewed.
—SB

The Photographer's Handbook
John Hedgecoe
1977; 352 pp.
$17.95 postpaid from:
Alfred A. Knopf, Inc.
455 Hahn Road
Westminster, MD 21157
or Whole Earth
Household Store

•

Uprating film

One way to help solve the exposure problems when shooting under very dim conditions is to "uprate" the film, so that effectively you are under-exposing. The film is then given increased development. Some films, especially fast film like Tri-X and HP5, respond better to this treatment than slower films, although uprating tends to give all films an exaggerated grain pattern and increased image contrast. Subjects which are flatly lit with soft, diffused illumination therefore lend themselves to this technique more than contrasty, harshly lit subjects. The latter often produce excessively hard negatives which are impossible to print. . . . Most fast and ultra-fast films can be "pushed" to between three and four times their normal ratings.

Nikon F, 180 mm, Tri-X uprated, 1/250 sec f2.8

↑

Freezing action

In some areas of athletics, notably gymnastics, it is important not to blur the picture. You need to show the precise attitude of the contestant at a crucial moment in the performance. For indoor events this means using widest aperture and pushing the film speed to allow the shortest possible exposures.

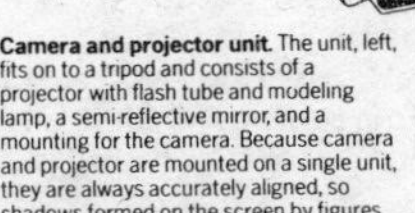

Camera and projector unit. The unit, left, fits on to a tripod and consists of a projector with flash tube and modeling lamp, a semi-reflective mirror, and a mounting for the camera. Because camera and projector are mounted on a single unit, they are always accurately aligned, so shadows formed on the screen by figures in the studio cannot be seen by the lens.

Front projection units

With a front projection unit, right, you can combine a figure in the studio with a background which has been photographed on a previous occasion. For this, you need a special screen, designed to reflect back light narrowly along its original path. A semi-reflective mirror is mounted in front of the camera lens at an angle of 45°, with a small projector below it for the background transparency. The projected image is reflected from the mirror down the studio to the screen. From the camera viewpoint the shadow cast by the figure is always hidden. The background image will not record on the figure as long as the model wears non-reflective clothing. The model should be lit separately by carefully regulated studio lighting.

Front projection set-up. The picture, right, was taken with a front projection unit with the screen and lighting arranged as shown above. Notice the masking screen carefully positioned to prevent the light spilling onto the projection screen.

Combining images. The background for the image, right, was made by projecting a transparency on to a sheet of torn white paper and re-photographing it. The resulting transparency was projected, and the subject positioned in front of the screen.

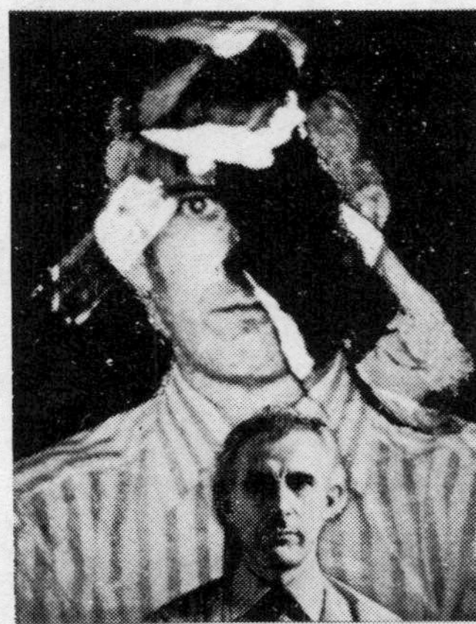

Field Photography

I contend that any photographer — creative, journalistic, amateur — can triple their range and pleasure by acquiring the technical skills of nature photography. This here is the definitive book.
—SB

Field Photography
(Beginning and
Advanced Techniques)
Alfred A. Blaker
1976; 451 pp.
$25.95 postpaid from:
W.H. Freeman
and Company
660 Market Street
San Francisco, CA 94104
or Whole Earth
Household Store

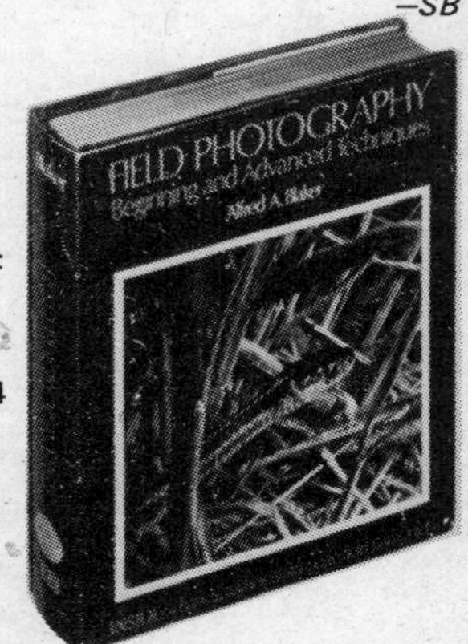

Flash exposure technique — A Western Garter Snake at Mendocino, California, in motion among grass blades, shown here five times actual size. (The original image magnification was x½; the original Kodachrome slide was enlarged when it was copied into black-and-white.) This photograph, with good depth of field and with action stopped, was made by using an M3B flash bulb, synchronized at 1/1000th of a second, with a lens aperture of f/32.

Index to Kodak Information

Lessons in eye-hand coordination. Keys to holding your camera steady. Learning photographic terms. How to record eclipses and starlight. Choosing the right film. In the darkroom: theory and technique. Photomacrography. Graphic arts techniques. Infrared. Pictures in extremes of weather (and of extremes of weather). Projection, filters, extra-long exposures. Scientific photography. Low prices and good mail service make it profitable to pick the brains of Kodak's researchers and staff photographers. Information useful to novice and pro alike.
—Gary Braasch

Index to Kodak Information
(Publication No. L-5)

free from:
Eastman Kodak Company
Department 454
Rochester, NY 14650

•

Using Photography to Preserve Evidence; 1-76; $2.50. Presents techniques for using photography to collect, abstract, or preserve evidence for criminal cases or other legal processes.

Kodak Infrared Films; 7-77; $1.75. Discusses the photographic properties and discriminating effects of infrared radiation in terms easily understood by practicing photographers. Includes a complete description of films and processing for infrared photography.

Documentary Photography

*Every now and then we see something which sets a new level of excellence in how-to writing. That's what this book does. The author is one of the best photographers around (***Suburbia; Our Kind of People; Working***), known for the kind, brutal frankness of his eye. The same goes for his writing. It's all on the table, every inner trick and turn of how to be a photographer with your life. All the unspeakable stuff like getting published, getting grants, getting the confidence of subjects and the attention of audience, and not paying out too much immortal soul in the process.*
—SB
[Suggested by Michael Phillips]

Documentary Photography
Bill Owens
1978; 64 pp.
$5.95 postpaid from:
Addison House
Morgan's Run
Danbury, NH 03230
or Whole Earth
Household Store

•

The best place to get a start is the small town or suburban newspaper. These papers are often "throw aways." Basically they carry supermarket advertisements, but they also have an editorial department and use photographs. As a small town photographer I photographed everything; editorials, women's pages, sports, features, and advertising. It was an experience more enriching than a big newspaper because I did seven to ten assignments a day, on a large city paper you seldom do more than two assignments a day.

Some excellent photojournalism is being done on the small town paper. There you have the freedom to use good photography and develop your talents. If you can take a good picture of Little League Baseball teams, you can take a good picture of the Oakland A's. Perhaps the best jobs in photography today are on the small town newspaper because here you have personal freedom and, more important, *space* to publish your photographs. . . .

Finally, make friends with other photographers and writers. Share your information with them. Other photographers can help you get started by helping you understand editors and magazines. It's tough work to compete and sharing information is an important part of photography. . . .

←

These photographs illustrate the difference between the use of natural light and strobe light. The photograph on the left was taken with natural light. The print is 40% black; half the man's face is in deep shadow. As you can see, the print is dark and contrasty. And the high contrast presents the couple in an unattractive way. Both their faces are lit dramatically, and the woman's hand looks more like a claw than a hand.

The strobe lit photograph on the right reverses the situation. Both faces are well lit, and one can see textures in their hair and clothing. The shadows now serve to define rather than distort, and a more even three dimensional quality is created in the image. If **Suburbia** had been photographed with natural light exclusively, the deep shadow effect would have dominated the book, and it would have been difficult to read many of the photographs. (As it was, too many people thought **Suburbia** was a put-down of suburban life styles.)

THE RISING SUN
NEIGHBORHOOD NEWSLETTER

continued from last spread

Merlin didn't die but was enchanted by this seductive person named Nimuë who wasn't a better magician than him but befuddled his mind with love and lust and things so she could zap him asleep for centuries with a cheap spell, but he'll come back with Arthur. When Merlin came back in *That Hideous Strength* by C.S. Lewis, he was amazed that you couldn't hit serfs when they were cheeky and that all men of all social ranks wore drab clothes — in his day, only serfs wore brown and black — and he was amazed that the woods wouldn't listen to him like they used to. He could still do major magic but he couldn't mess around with plants and little animals like he used to, because they had become more themselves and people had become more people and spirits had become more spirits and the middle ground where all these things met and overlapped was almost gone — Merlin had no place to stand.

continued on next spread

The Photography Catalog

A knowledgeable, critical survey of the world of photo equipment. Considering that it was done in 1976, it is not particularly dated, and the intelligence of Snyder's evaluation approach would be useful to learn even if the data were obsolete. Camera stores are buzzing, greedy places. Shop here first.

According to the publisher, there are no plans to update this worthy volume, but a somewhat more technical book is coming in winter 1980: **In Focus: A Rated Guide to the Best in Photographic Equipment,** *by Simon Nathan, 1980, 224 pp., $9.95 postpaid.* —SB

The Photography Catalog
Norman Snyder, Editor
1976; 256 pp.
$7.95 postpaid from:
Harper and Row
Keystone Industrial Park
Scranton, PA 18512
or Whole Earth
Household Store

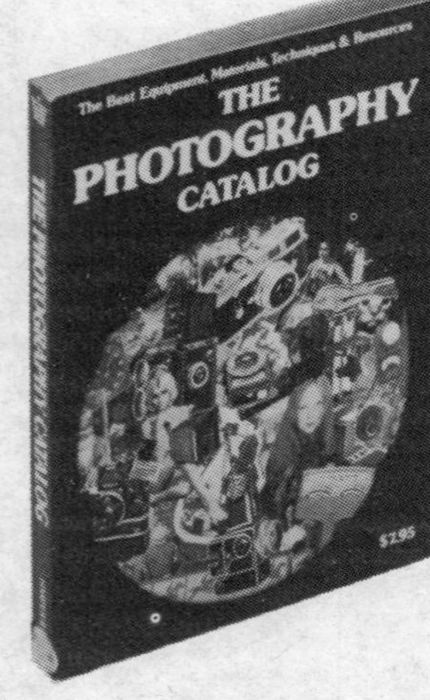

•

Use Your Head

With a pair of adjustable vise-grip pliers and a Leitz head, you can make an immensely versatile clamp that is ideal for cramped or unusual quarters. Use a carbide bit to drill into one arm of the pliers. Insert a ¼ inch X 20 bolt and screw the head onto the pliers. Now, you can clamp a camera or light source in awkward situations, since the vise-grip will tighten around practically anything. One photographer used this device to secure a motorized Nikon onto motorcycle handlebars. Though the bike scrambled over some rough terrain, the pliers held, and he got some dramatic shots.

•

There is something mysterious — some magic, some marvel — about the class of cameras named Leica (from E. Leitz's Camera) that has set men and women to doing things and feeling emotions that no other camera quite has. One thinks of the enthusiasm with which Model A and Model T Fords are driven and of how old, green-glass, six-ounce Coca-Cola bottles are cherished.

•

From Dust We Come, With Dust We Live

Unless you photograph, develop and print in a room designed for the assembly of missile computers, you can count on winding up witn white specks on your prints from dust that has settled on or embedded itself into the negative. Fight the dust . . . then learn to spot. Use a magnifying glass; any clean paper used to lean on to protect the print from skin oil and dirt and a good No. 00 or No. 000 red sable artist's brush, twirled on the tongue to keep it pointed. Special dyes, shown below, are mixed in to match the image tone of each particular brand of paper. Hint — after mixing the dye, combine it with a water puddle on a 4 x 5-inch (11 x 13 cm) glass plate. When it's dry, you will have various densities of dye available to lift off the plate with a tongue-moistened brush. Build up the image SLOWLY by stippling, not by painting. Beginners always go too far.

Photographic spotting dyes penetrate completely into the print emulsion, leaving no surface residue. Always use a dye dilution that is *lighter* than the area to be matched; it can always be made darker by successive applications. Retouch Methods, Inc., makes a kit of five different "Spotone" black dyes: Marshalls' Spot-All set is identical. Kit directions indicate mixing proportions for various papers, toned and untoned.

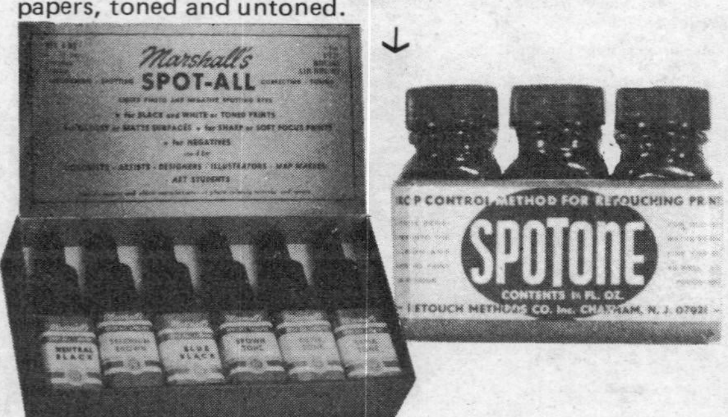

Shutterbug Ads

This is the nationwide marketplace for anything photographic: professional, amateur, antique. There is hardly anything you would ever need that couldn't be bought used or traded for in the pages of **SA.** *Every month the pages are jammed full of photographic items at fair prices. They use a grading guide, published in each issue, so everyone knows what everyone else is talking about when something is described as "very good" or "mint," etc. For me it's been a good way to trade for or buy what I need and sell what I don't need. A certain amount of trust is involved but people you can't see should be just as honest as people you can see.* —John Nichols

Shutterbug Ads
(The Nationwide
Marketplace for
Anything Photographic)
$8 /year (12 issues)
from:
Shutterbug Ads
P.O. Box F
Titusville, FL 32780

BLACK NIKKORMAT ELW body. SA excellent. Boxed in original packing with manual. A super camera! $250. 10 MBG. SASE. I pay postage and insurance. **Dan Harper,** 160 Robideaux Rd., Aptos, CA 95003; 408-688-4637.

PENTAX K1000 with 50mm f2 and case like new. $150. Will trade for top of line SX-70 Sonar or Alpha I or Minox 110S or Canon 110 ED-20(?). **Gerald Borel,** 2207 Hazel, Westlake, LA 70669.

NIKON F2A Black, warranty papers, box, SA-mint. MD-2, MB-3, boxes, SA-EXC, $925. **Fred Hull,** 100 Cheek Rd., Nashville, TN 37205; 1-615-356-5431.

Solar Cine Products

Used to be we sent photo gear buyers to Hong Kong (p. 348) for the best prices. Now the U.S. discount houses are better. This is one. We know the prices are good; we don't know if the service is. We don't know who Solar's best competition is. With your experienced advice, all this could be improved in the next edition of **The Next Whole Earth Catalog.** —SB

Solar Cine Products
Catalog
free from:
Solar Cine Products
4247 South Kedzie Ave.
Chicago, IL 60632

← **POLAROID's SX-70 SONAR OneStep**

- **Automatic and precise Sonar focusing in any light conditions.**
- **Manual focusing too.**
- **Single-lens reflex pre-viewing feature.**
- **4 element, 116mm precision glass lens.**
- **Sharp, clear pictures from 10.4" to infinity (flash to 20').**
- **Variable aperture from f:8 to f:74.**
- **Built-in low-light indicator.**
- **Automatic time exposures up to 14 seconds.**
- **Never needs batteries.**
- **Compact, lightweight, folds.**
- **Elegant chrome and black leather finish.**

H-6776 ....Retail $269.95..wt. 4 lb..**Solar Price $198.00**
B-129 FlashBar (10 flashes per bar)....wt. ¼ lb..Solar Price 2.52

Camera available All-Black body only. Comes with battery, strap and eyecup. Optional Flash and Motor Drive illustrated but not included.

E-6619	A-1 w/1.8 lens	wt. 5 lb	Solar Price $416.90
E-6620	A-1 w/1.4 lens	wt. 5 lb	Solar Price 462.00
E-6621	A-1 w/1.2 lens	wt. 5 lb	Solar Price 563.20
H-6622	A-1 Body Only	wt. 4 lb	Solar Price 342.10
E-6623	A-1 eveready case	wt. 2 lb	Solar Price 29.34
E-6628	A-1 case (for body with 1.2 lens)	wt. 2 lb	Solar Price 29.44
C-6624	Canon 199A Speedlite	wt. 2 lb	Solar Price 104.53
H-672	Set of 4 AA Alk. batts. for above	wt. ½ lb	Solar Price 2.84
C-6625	Canon Motor Drive MA (requires either battery pack below)	wt. 2 lb	Solar Price 164.09
C-6627	Battery Pack MA w/o batts	wt. 1 lb	Solar Price 76.82
H-672	Set of 12 AA Alk. batt. for above	wt. 2 lb	Solar Price 8.52
C-6626	Ni-Cad Pack w/charger & batts	wt. 3 lb	Solar Price 159.53
C-5993	Power Winder A	wt. 1 lb	Solar Price 93.47
H-672	Set of 4 AA Alk. batts for above	wt. ½ lb	Solar Price 2.84

OLYMPUS XA CAMERA OUTFIT - A 4" x 2½" x 1½" rangefinder, full-frame 35mm with an Olympus f:2.8 Zuiko 6-element, 5 group lens with an internal focusing system permitting the front element to remain stationary and hermetically sealed. The camera has a dome-shaped dust cover that slides open to reveal lens, rangefinder, eyepiece and viewfinder. When closed, all is protected. It has an aperture priority automatic exposure system with a speed range of 10 to 1/500th second and backlighting compensation of 1½ stops. ASA range of 25 to 400. Aperture range of f:2.8 to f:22.

Comes with exclusive A-11 Electronic flash which operates when camera's aperture selector is set to flash symbol. Then all you do is focus and shoot for perfectly exposed flash pictures.

OTHER FEATURES: Auto-reset frame counter, 12 second self-timer. **Outfit comes with camera, flash and 2 S-76 batteries (for camera).**

G-6955 ....Retail $233.00..wt. 2 lb..**Solar Price $153.89**

★ VARIOUS PINHOLE CAMERAS ★

FLAT BOX,
"WIDE ANGLE"

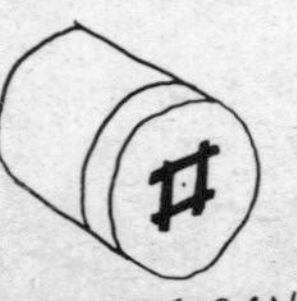

LONG BOX
"TELEPHOTO"

The Hole Thing

Photography minus equipment. Looks like fun. —SB

The Hole Thing
(A Manual of
Pinhole Fotografy)
Jim Shull
1974; 64 pp.
$2.95 postpaid from:
Morgan & Morgan, Inc.
145 Palisade Street
Dobbs Ferry, NY 10522

•

One readily apparent possibility is the wide-angle effect. For a "normal" photo you should have about a 6" focal length which amounts to about a 40° - 50° angle view. If you have a 4" focal length you will get a wide-angle effect of about a 60° angle of view. And if you have a 3" focal length you get an 80° angle. This means that a type of photo that is considered to be real keen these days is a very simple thing. Even greater wide-angle effects can be obtained by curving the flim so that more angle of vision is brought into the act. This also more or less equalizes the exposure over the film area. Such a camera can be made from a Quaker Oats box. For 8" x 10" format, use an ice cream box.

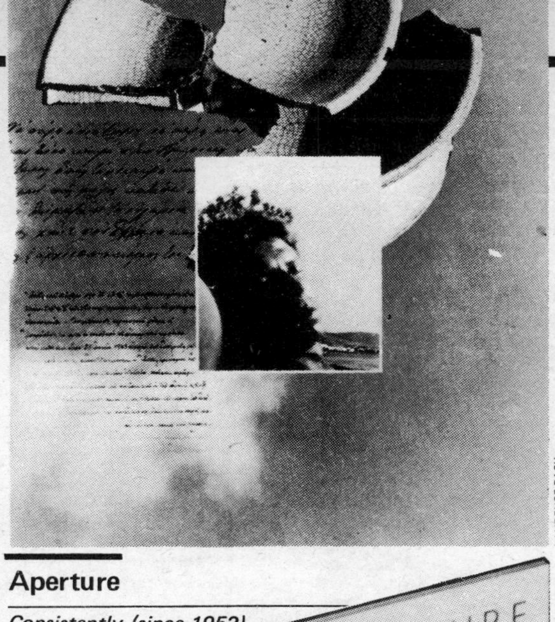

MICK LASKA

LAURENCE BACH

American Photographer

I like making photographs. I despise photography magazines. If they are not pornographic forums for the display of useless expensive shit, they are pre-Raphaelite salons for the idly rich. The introductory propaganda for **American Photographer** *promised something different and, egad, they've done it! Now two years old, the magazine has come in with revealed growth and maturity in every issue, specifically, a magazine that reflects and actually tries to build a community for serious photographers. There are three regular features using solicited thematic photographs from readers. The careers of at least two photographers, one "classic" the other "new" are covered in detail in each issue. There's nicely covered photographer's gossip (photographers get into really wierd situations). And the technical articles deal with real photographs of distinction and how they were made. It has reawakened my interest in the business and given it some much-missed respect.*

—George Putz

American Photographer
Sean Callahan, Editor
$18 /year (12 issues)
from:
CBS Publications
1515 Broadway
New York, NY 10036

The New Zone System Manual

The manual for highest quality black and white photos, with details in the black and in the white. The key is ***previsualization****, which is looking at reality through an accurately imagined photographic print, then knowing how to make the calculations and mechanical and chemical adjustments so the print has what you saw, plus any divine grace that happened by.* *—SB*

The New Zone System Manual
Minor White, Richard Zakia and Peter Lorenz
1961, 1980; 140 pp.
$8.95 postpaid from:
Morgan and Morgan, Inc.
145 Palisade Street
Dobbs Ferry, NY 10522
or Whole Earth Household Store

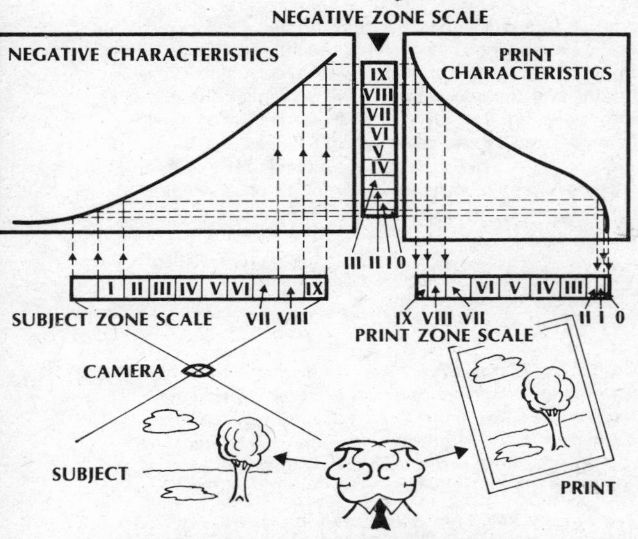

Aperture

Consistently (since 1952) the profoundest of the photography-as-art publications, **Aperture** *has very high quality reproductions of significant seeing.* *—SB*

Aperture
Michael E. Hoffman, Editor
$28 /year (4 issues)
from:
Aperture, Inc.
Millerton, NY 12546

Homegrown Holography

The ideas of holography — of interference patterns, coherent light, and the amazing properties of a hologram — are so mentally liberating that even a little of the excellent technique in this manual can inspire a lot of philosophy. *—SB*

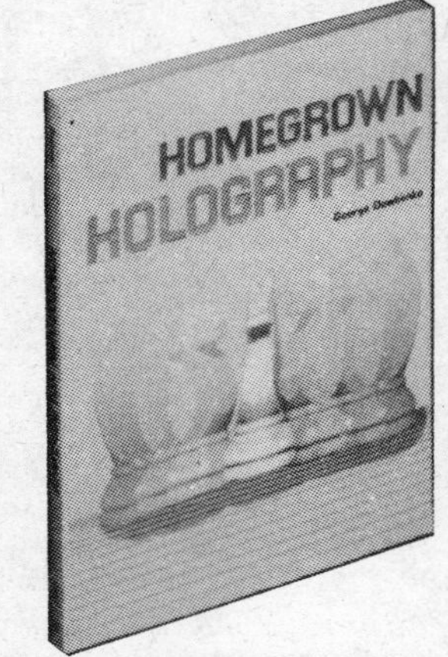

Homegrown Holography
George Dowbenko
1978; 160 pp.
$8.95 postpaid from:
American Photographic Books
Watson-Guptill Publications
2160 Patterson Street
Cincinnati, OH 45214
or Whole Earth Household Store

Museum of Holography Bookstore Catalog

Seems esoteric, a museum devoted only to holography; but so they might have said about a museum of television in the 1930s. The catalog is itself a survey of this three-dimensional photographic art form; it explains a little of how it works, lists a progression of how-to books, and offers books and holographic objects for sale (most from $7 - $50). This is a fascinating laser-based technology which has yet to establish itself to outsiders as more than a novelty, but its creators have already brought it far beyond that holographic woman who winks at passersby. There's still a distance to go, though: imagine a holographic model of an entire town! (Or transmitting holograms through fiber-optic cables . . .) *—Art Kleiner*

Museum of Holography Bookstore
Catalog
$ .50 from:
Museum of Holography Bookstore
11 Mercer Street
New York, NY 10013

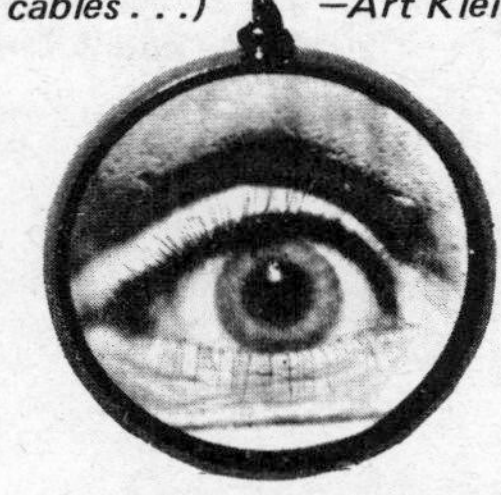

Eye, M, L (No. 4408) $18.00.

Afterimage

Very nice gossip-and-peek tabloid for the photo art world. One way to get ahead is keep up with the trends double fast. The other is ignore and learn steadily. Not mutually exclusive approaches. *—SB*

Afterimage
(A Publication of the Visual Studies Workshop)
Charles Hagen, Editor
$15 /year (9 issues, includes membership)
from:
Visual Studies Workshop
31 Prince Street
Rochester, NY 14607

Family Portrait on My 32nd Birthday.

The photos I am holding were given to me by my parents several years ago. My father was very proud of his, a publicity photo for his job. My mother had her picture taken by a photographer in a shopping center who specialized in daguerreotype-style polaroids. I no longer speak to my parents. This is probably the only picture of the three of us taken in the last 10 years. —Linda Lindroth

Collection, Use, and Care of Historical Photographs

A good solid technical treatment of the labor and joy of working with old photographs. Some illustrative why and a lot of detailed how. *—SB*

Collection, Use, and Care of Historical Photographs
Robert A. Weinstein and Larry Booth
1977; 222 pp.
$16 postpaid from:
American Association for State and Local History
1400 Eighth Avenue
S. Nashville, TN 37203

An ambrotype showing its simultaneous negative and positive characteristics. Half the normal black paper backing has been removed for this photograph to reveal the negative portion of the ambrotype. →

Rockland liquid light

Print photographs directly on brick, wood, aluminum, tile, eggs, leather, concrete, cloth . . . Liquid Light costs $25/pint. → *—SB*

Rockland Liquid Light
Brochure and price list

free from:
Rockland Colloid Corporation
302 Piermont Avenue
Piermont, NY 10968

THE RISING SUN
NEIGHBORHOOD NEWSLETTER

continued from last spread

That's one of Lewis' ideas in that book — that if you look at any person, group of people, institution, over time, you can see that earlier on, it was any number of things all mixed up but as time goes on it becomes more and more itself and less and less anything else. We keep living our lives and making our choices and becoming more intensely what we are until we're these intensely focused pinpoints of whatever — and we can touch other things but we can't really become other things in the way we could when we were a bit fuzzier and less dense. *continued on next spread*

On Photography

If you have any interest in photography you must read Susan Sontag's book. The six essays were originally published from 1973 to 1977 in **The New York Review of Books**, *but they are more interesting when read as consecutive chapters. It is fascinating to watch Sontag's well-honed intelligence trying to make sense out of the seemingly "simple and mechanical" medium of photography. There are lots of false starts and contradictions between essays, but that is the fun of it. Sontag must have written a hundred sentences beginning "Photography is . . ." before she got it right: ". . . photography is not, to begin with, an art form at all. Like language, it is a medium in which works of art (among other things) are made."*

Books on photography aren't supposed to win the National Book Award, but this one did.

—Andrew Williams

On Photography
Susan Sontag
1978; 207 pp.

$3.95 postpaid from:
Dell Publishing Company
One Dag Hammarskjold Plaza
245 East 47th Street
New York, NY 10017
or Whole Earth Household Store

•

In these last decades, "concerned" photography has done at least as much to deaden conscience as to arouse it.

•

The lure of photographs, their hold on us, is that they offer at one and the same time a connoisseur's relation *to* the world and a promiscuous acceptance *of* the world.

•

While paintings or poems do not get better, more attractive simply because they are older, all photographs are interesting as well as touching if they are old enough.

•

To photograph is to appropriate the thing photographed. It means putting oneself into a certain relation to the world that feels like knowledge — and, therefore, like power. A now notorious first fall into alienation, habituating people to abstract the world into printed words, is supposed to have engendered that surplus of Faustian energy and psychic damage needed to build modern, inorganic societies. But print seems a less treacherous form of leaching out the world, of turning it into a mental object, than photographic images, which now provide most of the knowledge people have about the look of the past and the reach of the present. What is written about a person or an event is frankly an interpretation, as are handmade visual statements, like paintings and drawings. Photographed images do not seem to be statements about the world so much as pieces of it, miniatures of reality that anyone can make or acquire.

Light Impressions

Looks to me like the best mailbox place to shop for photography books — big wide stock, accurate descriptions, nice sample images. *—SB*

[Suggested by Andrew Williams]

Light Impressions
(Books, Slide Sets and Archival Framing Supplies)
Catalogs

free from:
Light Impressions Corporation
P.O. Box 3012
Rochester, NY 14614

•

Minor White: Rites & Passages. "His photographs accompanied by excerpts from his diaries and letters." Autobiographical essay by James Baker Hall.

"Amid the static its name lies in the images that have an affinity for one another./Many readings flicker until suddenly one reading is unequivocal." — Minor White. Issue no. 80 of **Aperture**, the magazine founded by the late Minor White in 1952, has been issued as the final collection of his work which he planned before his death. "To see the sacred in the profane is to see the eternal in time: that was the controlling quest of Minor White's life, the search for an imagery that was in perfect register with the stillness of the still photograph, for a communication between people that was most articulate in silence." — the conclusion of Hall's essay. An elegant and carefully executed tribute to one of the world's great photographers, with beautiful reproductions, a chronology, bibliography and list of plates.

Untitled/Minor White

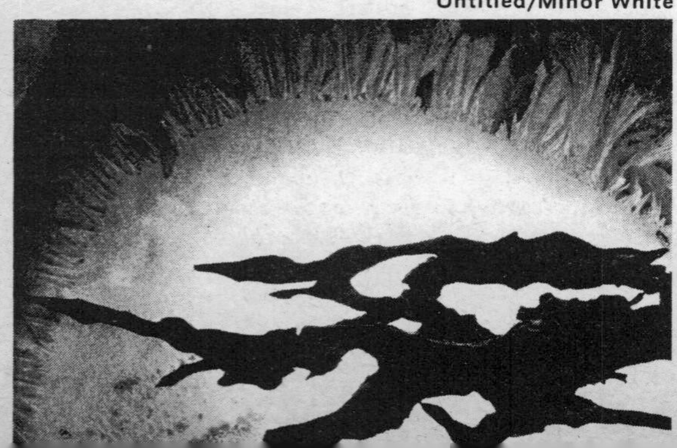

Magnifications

Photographs as beautiful as any by Ansel Adams or Eliot Porter. The eye is that of a gentle man with a good sense of humor who has mastered a new tool: the electron scanning microscope. Not satellite perspective (too far away). Not x-ray crystallography (which abandons my sense of life for the mineral lattice). Just right . . . the eye travels from familiar, everyday life into the expansive detail of marijuana resin droplets, feathery thrips, gold-coated aspirin, pollen grains and gladiola petals.

—Peter Warshall

Magnifications
(Photography With the Scanning Electron Microscope)
David Scharf
1977; 119 pp.

$10.95 postpaid from:
Schocken Books
200 Madison Avenue
New York, NY 10016
or Whole Earth Household Store

The Friends of Photography

In the world of photography, bargains and excellence are usually mutually exclusive concepts. However there does remain one great bargain of the highest quality, a membership in The Friends of Photography.

For a twenty dollar fee, less than most photographic books today or a little more than one-third the price for one hundred sheets of printing paper, one gets twelve monthly issues of The Friends **Newsletter**, *four issues of the journal* **Untitled**, *discounts on photographic books, a chance to participate in the annual members-only juried exhibition, and for a very reasonable fee a weekend workshop for Friends of Photography members.*

The journal, **Untitled**, *is one of the liveliest and best presented publications in photography today. The format varies from collections of essays to the presentation of work by a single photographer. The quality of the reproduction of photographs is excellent, and the writing is always penetrating and provocative.* **Untitled** *itself more than justifies the membership fee.*

All of this emphasis on quality comes as no surprise since the Friends was founded in 1967 by people like Ansel Adams, Wynn Bullock, Beaumont and Nancy Newhall, and Brett and Cole Weston. The marvel is that access to all this quality work in photography comes at such a reasonable price. Don't be fooled into thinking that only classic west coast photography is allowed. The Friends have encouraged contemporary innovations with exhibitions of the work of Robert Rauschenberg and Robert Heinecken as well as by sponsoring traveling exhibitions on 3M Color-in-Color process and on photographs made with a plastic "toy" camera called the Diane.

For those with a bit more money and a desire to collect original photographic prints at very reasonable prices the Friends has a $150 membership which includes all of the above plus one of five original prints. This year the selection includes prints by Marsha Burns, Francis Frith and Lou Stoumen. In the past prints by Ansel Adams, Duane Michaels, Jerry Uelsmann, Minor White, and many others have been offered. This is the ultimate bargain.

—Andrew Williams

The Friends of Photography
Membership
$20

Membership information
free from:
The Friends of Photography
P.O. Box 239
Carmel, CA 93921

Honeybee's Eye – Compound eye. Note ocellus (simple eye) in background.

Worlds Within Worlds

A catalog of all the new "photographic" techniques and projects happening on and off Earth. Holograms, neutrography, Kirlian photography, x-ray, field emission microscope, sonography, false color, infra-red and ultra-violet, the linescan, weather radar . . . to name just a few. Each technique is explained and a "classic" example of the technique portrayed. Some photos are amazing; some ho-hum. A basic text to the state-of-the-art.

—Peter Warshall

Worlds Within Worlds
Michael Marten, John Chesterman, et al.
1977; 208 pp.

$7.95 postpaid from:
Holt, Rinehart & Winston
383 Madison Avenue
New York, NY 10017
or Whole Earth Household Store

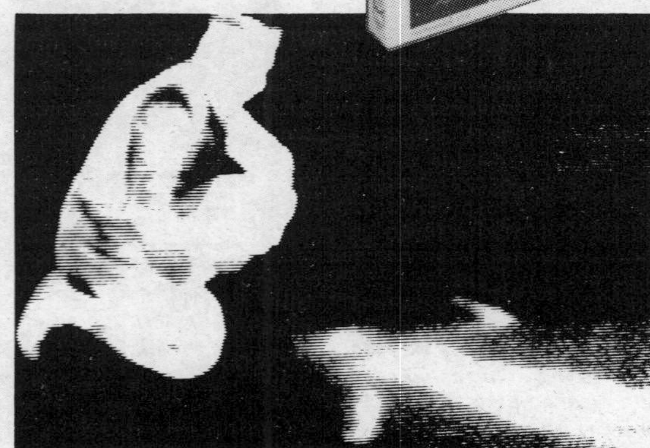

This picture illustrates the uses of infrared photography in police work. Though the murder victim's body is gone, thermography reconstructs its position from the heat it left on the floor. The policeman sees only a rug; the thermogram sees the heat image of a corpse.

Cheap, great photos and films at the Library of Congress

For a minimum fee and for private use, the Library of Congress will make copies of any of the individual prints which are catalogued there. The Library is a tremendous resource. People who pay $1,000 and up for "original" photographs can sometimes find the same images available at the Library for $10 per gallery-quality print, often made in fact from the original negative. Accordingly, anyone buying photographs would be wise to check the Library's resources first, and then check to see if the "original" being offered by any gallery didn't indeed originate at the Library. Historical societies, museums, universities and state libraries also usually offer quality photographic prints for sale, on request, at a minimum price.

Write:

—Elihu Blotnick
Berkeley, California

Library of Congress
Photo Duplications Service
Washington, D.C. 20540

Note: The Library does not publish a catalog of their prints; you have to know what photograph you are looking for before you write. Also, a small number of their eight million photographs cannot be copied, for copyright reasons or because the original donors restricted their circulation.

The Library of Congress also keeps prints of every motion picture ever copyrighted, including those which can't be publicly released for one legal reason or another. (One example is "Rope," a 1948 Hitchcock movie filmed entirely in one shot.) If you want to see a specific film and are willing to travel to Washington, D.C. to do it, you can write the Library of Congress Motion Picture, Broadcasting and Recorded Sound Division, Washington, D.C. 20540, for an appointment. Admission is free. Scholarly inquiries are particularly encouraged. They won't project the film; you run it through a motorized desk-top film editing machine in their back rooms. Similar services exist for broadcast and sound recordings. *—Art Kleiner*

Seeing the Light

I wish everyone would do a book like this, made of the things they say to themselves to keep themselves doing what they do well. Embarrassing stuff — bombastic, personal, and wholly invaluable to anyone else trying to do something well. The revelant here is avant-garde filmmaker James Broughton. —SB

•

Excellent strategy: do what you are most afraid of doing. Look what Brakhage did. He has always feared death intensely, it has been a constant threatening imminence for him. So, with the courage that has always made him a trailblazer, he took his camera tightly in hand and went into the city morgue of Pittsburgh and looked closely and filmed unforgettably the forms of death as they had never been seen before: **The Act of Seeing With One's Own Eyes.**

•

The avant-garde task is to deal with what nobody else is attending to. This keeps widening human consciousness and keeps balance in the universe.

•

Oz is a place all poets should visit once a year. . . .

Oz is of a different order of nonsense from Zen.

Zen is where you see what is. Oz is where you see what isn't.

Zen is here, Oz is there. Far out there.

Oz is where there are no parents, no teachers, no preachers, no police, no experts, no press, and no need of them.

•

Making a film is a more hazardous act than looking at one. For you will create a dream. Whereas dreams themselves are natural events which happen to us. You will create a dream for others to dream and to be dreamed by.

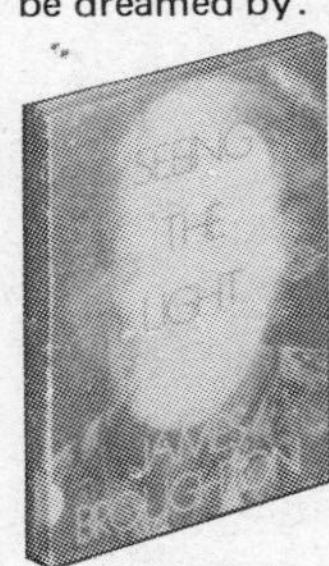

Seeing the Light
James Broughton
1977; 80 pp.

$3 postpaid from:
City Lights Books
1562 Grant Avenue
San Francisco, CA 94133
or Whole Earth
Household Store

Superior Bulk Film

A reliable mail order service (and store) for 8 mm and 16 mm film, processing, equipment for home processing labs, and most equipment and supplies for amateur filmmakers who desire control and versatility at low cost. Their film and processing package deals are as cheap or cheaper than any I've seen, probably more reliable than most. They also have excellent specials frequently. Discounted film stocks, spliced reels, etc. — check it out! Good catalog available, newssheets run down specials, new stuff, changes, etc. This place isn't one of these Jumbo-Junk Filmailer houses.

—Bruce Schmiechen

Superior Cine Manual
Catalog

free from:
Superior Bulk Film Co.
442-450 N. Wells Street
Chicago, IL 60610

Ultra Fast B&W Film
Superior 1000
(ASA 1000 Tungsten)
Superior 1000
8/8mm 25' Spool, $6.49
8/8mm 100' Bolex, $19.95
16mm is available "B" wind for sound.

The Filmgoer's Companion

Any movie-user will find this guide indispensable. Splendid succinct reviews — summaries of every noticeable movie, film-title biographies of sundry stars, directors, etc. — each with thumbnail sketch. Fine piece of work at bargain price. Might get used more than any other reference book in your house. Also see **Movies on TV**, *on p. 490.* —SB

The Filmgoer's Companion
Leslie Halliwell
1965; 1978; 828 pp.
6th Edition

$9.95 postpaid from:
Avon Books
Mail Order Department
250 West 55th Street
New York, NY 10019
or Whole Earth
Household Store

Burt Lancaster. He grew gracefully into an excellent character actor, but this is the image one remembers with most affection: the ex-circus acrobat with more vitality than a dozen normal men. →

SMALL INDEPENDENT FILM DISTRIBUTORS

by John Hoskyns-Abrahall, Bullfrog Films, Inc.

There's a host of informative, artistic, enjoyable, educational, and stimulating films being made by independent filmmakers. They need you and, I think you'll find, you need them. If you're seriously interested in renting or buying films, write to the distributors below and ask for a copy of their latest catalog. Most of these small distributors have special interests as noted.

Appalshop Films, P.O. Box 743, Whitesburg, KY 41858. *Excellent documentaries by and about Appalachians — their music, culture, coal, crafts and unions. (Also fine June Appal recordings.)*

Bullfrog Films, Oley, PA 19547. *Good selection of films on solar and other renewable energy sources, and the food/farming/land use/nutrition connection.*

California Newsreel, 630 Natoma, San Francisco, CA 94103. *Outstanding collection of films on Southern Africa, labor and the economy.*

Canyon Cinema Cooperative, 2325 3rd Street, Suite 338, San Francisco, CA 94107. *Some important works by film artists included in this long-standing cooperative's collection.*

Creative Film Society, 7237 Canby Avenue, Reseda, CA 91335. *Fine selection of art shorts ranging from old-time comedy to contemporary film art.*

Direct Cinema Ltd., P.O. Box 69589, Los Angeles, CA 90069. *A showcase of good films by American independents, including some features.*

Filmmakers' Cooperative, 175 Lexington Avenue, New York, NY 10016. *The first film distribution cooperative organized so that independent filmmakers could retain control over their films. Some well-loved films.*

←
Save the Planet: The story of the atomic age. 18 minutes, color, 16mm & 35mm, produced by Green Mountain Post Films for MUSE, Inc. 1979. 16mm rental $25, B: $40, C: $55. Sale: $350, 35mm.

Flower Films, 10341 San Pablo Avenue, El Cerrito, CA 94530. *Les Blank's evocative films on ethnic American people, food and music.*

Green Mountain Post Films, P.O. Box 229, Turners Falls, MA 01376. *An important collection of films from the worldwide anti-nuclear movement.*

Hartley Productions, Cat Rock Road, Cos Cob, CT 06807. *A unique collection of films on spirituality, eastern religions, new age communities, and holistic health.*

Kartemquin Films, 1901 West Wellington, Chicago, IL 60657. *Films tackling major social issues in the Chicago area.*

Maysles Films, 250 West 54th Street, New York, NY 10019. *Outstanding cinema verité documentaries including "Salesman," "Grey Gardens" and two films on Christo.*

New Day Films, P.O. Box 315, Franklin Lakes, NJ 07417. *Ground-breaking feminist film collective, with rousing films on feminism, social change and unions.*

New Front Films, c/o Elaine Archer, 1409 Willow Street, Suite 505, Minneapolis, MN 55403. *New independent features and documentaries including "Northern Lights" and "The War at Home."*

New Time Films, 1501 Broadway, Suite 1904, New York, NY 10036. *Political films including "Paul Jacobs and the Nuclear Gang."*

Serious Business Company, 1145 Mandana Blvd., Oakland, CA 94610. *Fine selection of independent films — avant-garde, feminist, health and sexuality, animation, children and anthropology.*

Third World Newsreel, 160 Fifth Avenue, New York, NY 10010. *Social issues films on minority and women's rights, labor relations, housing, international affairs and community organizing.*

Unifilm, 419 Park Avenue South, New York, NY 10014. *The former Tricontinental Film Center and Latin American Film Project. Comprehensive collection of important films on, and often by, Third World people.*

Zipporah Films, 54 Lewis Wharf, Boston, MA 02110. *Fred Wiseman's unique series of PBS documentaries on American institutions.*

Of the larger companies, the following deserve special attention:

National Film Board of Canada, 1251 Avenue of the Americas, New York, NY 10020. *Home of brilliant documentaries and animation.*

New Yorker Films, 16 West 61st Street, New York, NY 10023. *Important international and U.S. feature films, shorts and documentaries, many on social issues. Excellent selection of African, Brazilian and Japanese films.*

Pyramid Films, P.O. Box 1048, Santa Monica, CA 90406. *Excellent collection of cinematic shorts and documentaries.*

Time-Life Films, 100 Eisenhower Drive, Paramus, NJ 07652. *The BBC/Time-Life connection. "Civilization," "The Ascent of Man," "Connections" etc.*

Finally, if you know the name of a film but not the distributor, these people are the best source of information, and can probably help you out:

Educational Film Library Association, 43 West 61st Street, New York, NY 10023.

And for information about films and other media on food and land, contact:

Earthwork, 3410 19th Street, San Francisco, CA 94110.

THE RISING SUN
NEIGHBORHOOD NEWSLETTER

continued from last spread

Which goes along with Lewis' idea that all you have to do to imagine heaven and hell is to assume eternal life. If you look at some people and imagine them being more and more themselves forever, it's clear that for them to live with themselves bring more and more themselves forever would be hell — no flames necessary — whereas for other people to get more so forever would probably be pretty neat for themselves and others, maybe even heavenly.

continued on next spread

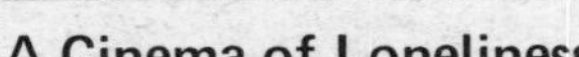

FILM

by Tom Schneider

A two-word description of American filmaking: No center.

Hollywood, the old center, is still there. But now it's just the place to go to get the money, and later, to pick up your awards. Films are made where the story is: Texas, North Dakota, or a glacier in Finse, Norway. Filmmakers live where they want to live; mostly Northern California — it looks like from here in Northern California.

Is the craft any better for the change? Yes, if vigor, diversity, new talent, are what is wanted. If the films themselves are sometimes disappointing, we can still look forward to reading about why they didn't quite meet their mark. See Eleanor Coppola's **Notes** *(about the making of* **Apocalypse Now***), a particularly scorching example.*

The success of **Notes** *points up another remarkable aspect of the current filmmaking scene: the manufacturing has become as interesting as the product. Just as novels reach an audience filled with aspiring novelists, movie theaters seem to be jammed with future filmmakers, all wanting to know: "How was it done?" Once they find out, will there be room at the top for more George Lucases and Francis Coppolas? Those are exceptional successes. And the outer reaches, the riskier reaches of filmmaking — documentary, shorts, animation — are getting riskier every day. Jean Renoir dreamed of film becoming as plentiful as sketchbooks. Not likely, when every aspect of film-making is energy-intensive and the funding comes from the driest of venture capital pools. And yet daring films continue to be made. Witness* **Northern Lights, Goodnight Miss Anne,** *and* **Word is Out.** *These are powerful films made by strong individuals or groups of individuals. They are not adaptations; they were conceived as films.*

It's not an unhealthy time for film making. The center may be gone, but there's much life around the edges. We may see fewer films but better.

(See "Filmmaking for kids," p. 570.)

The Films in My Life

Remember the scene in **Day for Night** *when Truffaut, playing himself, unwraps a shipment of film books from America? There he is, in the middle of an exhausting production, still clearly delighted to spend his only free time reading about the process that is making him miserable.*

That same kind of tireless passion infuses his own book. Here are the films and filmmakers who moved him, first as a critic and then as a director. To read Truffaut, the accomplished master, enthusing over the works of others is warmly satisfying. I feel surrounded by geniuses.

The Films in My Life
François Truffaut
1975, 1978; 358 pp.

$5.95 postpaid from:
Simon and Schuster
Attn: Order Department
1230 Avenue of
the Americas
New York, NY 10020
or Whole Earth
Household Store

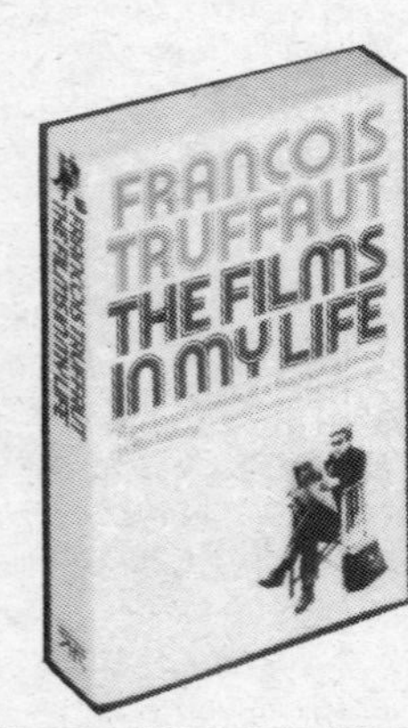

Film Makers on Film Making

The pioneers of cinema already seem so ancient that it surprises me to find that Louis Lumière was interviewed for French television in 1948, and that David Wark Griffith wrote an article for **Collier's** *on "Film 100 Years from Now." ("Now" was 1924.)*

These pieces are here, along with selected articles or interviews with a total of 30 filmmakers whose own words are not often seen in print. It's as close as we can get to having a conversation with Edwin S. Porter, Mack Sennett, or Jean Cocteau. And setting these illuminations next to each other makes for added sparks. A refreshing way to absorb film history.

Film Makers on Film Making
(Statements on Their Art by Thirty Directors)
Harry M. Geduld, Editor
1967; 302 pp.

OUT OF PRINT
Indiana University Press
Get this book back in print!

A Cinema of Loneliness

Bonnie and Clyde, A Clockwork Orange, The Conversation, Three Women, Taxi Driver*: films about isolation, made by filmmakers who work in isolation. Is there a connection?*

That is one of the intriguing questions raised by this book.

These films could not have been made in the Old Hollywood. The themes are too daring, the aesthetics too adventurous, the morality too unclear. These are films of great quality. That is our gain. Is there also something lost?

The Old Hollywood provided a community of administrators, superb technicians, and experienced artisans who could be called on in support of each new production. Now, each production is an island. Its sole support is itself. The studio bosses are gone, and in their place is the agent, the talent broker. "The 'deal' and the contract," writes Kolker, "loom over the production, affecting it perhaps more than any boorish old studio head ever did."

A Cinema of Loneliness
(Penn, Kubrick, Coppola, Scorsese, Altman)
Robert Phillip Kolker
1980; 395 pp.

$15.95 postpaid from:
Oxford University Press
16-00 Pollitt Drive
Fair Lawn, NJ 07410
or Whole Earth
Household Store

Screens and buttons ("2001").

Men, therefore, have a reason to be passive: they are the servants of a higher order, slaves of a predetermined plan so precisely calculated that only a precise calculator, the HAL 9000 computer, realizes its full meaning and gets, quite literally, emotional about it and goes crazy (I don't mean to underplay this: I find the confrontation of HAL and Bowman, the latter undoing the computer's thought patterns while it cries "I can feel it," to be one of the most powerful and ironic sequences in the film — an agon between a man and a construction with a human voice in which the latter wins our sympathies).

—A Cinema of Loneliness

The Silent Clowns

A work of genius about the work of geniuses. Walter Kerr has gifted us with a remarkably deep study of silent film comedians Buster Keaton, Charlie Chaplin, Harold Lloyd, and others.

"This is a book as much about comedy as about movies, about eyes and ears and how and why we laugh."
—Thomas Willis
Chicago Tribune

The Silent Clowns
Walter Kerr
1975; 369 pp.

$9.95 postpaid from:
Alfred A. Knopf, Inc.
455 Hahn Road
Westminster, MD 21157
or Whole Earth
Household Store

It scarcely matters what the inanimate object is. Buster fits it.

TECHNIQUE

Caligari's Cabinet and Other Grand Illusions

This book has done something irreversible to the way I look at films. I'm reminded of that Charles Addams cartoon of two grey-flannel commuters, jaws dropped, staring out the train window at a giant Lionel transformer, a huge knee, and monstrous sneakers.

Barsacq's book suggests that film designers are like Addams' child-god: always at the controls; seldom, if ever, noticed. They toy with our vision, and if they are very good, their work disappears. But here, with great confidence, Barsacq pulls back the cameras to show the guy wires, the scaffolding, the false perspective. The master magician reveals his secrets. Are we disillusioned? No, oddly, the amazement increases. Suddenly we're aware of the incredible patience and cleverness and talent that has gone into the deceit.

René Clair describes a street scene that Barsacq designed for his film "The Gates of Paris." The set was so perfect, that the director planned to intercut shots of the actual street with shots of the replica. It didn't work. Everyone agreed that the real thing was nowhere near as authentic and convincing as the set.

A large miniature designed by Leon Barsacq for Carmine Gallone's Michael Strogoff (1956). —Caligari's Cabinet

Caligari's Cabinet and Other Grand Illusions
(A History of Film Design)
Leon Barsacq
1970, 1976; 264 pp.

$5.95 postpaid from:
New American Library
P.O. Box 120
120 Woodbine
Bergenfield, NJ 07621
or Whole Earth
Household Store

Nonfiction Film

Feature filmmaking is so pervasive, and our entertainment appetite so large, it's easy to forget there's a whole other segment of filmmaking, loosely called "documentary." That's everything from travelogues to television news specials.

Film critic Andrew Sarris suggests that all films are documentaries: in the sense that they document someone, something, some time, some place. There's an equal but opposite ambiguity in the common assumption that a documentary film is one that tells the truth. In reality, selectivity and bias begin the moment you pick up and point the camera. Richard Meran Barsam appears to have put aside the semantic puzzle by calling his book **Nonfiction Film.** *Not so. It seems that much of the history and vitality of this kind of filmmaking turns around the problem of definitions: Establishing what is truth of a scene: Is it real? Is it too poetic to be believed? Will it look like propaganda? The questions arise for Flaherty on "Nanook of the North" (1922), and they also bother the Maysle brothers ("Gimme Shelter," 1970). I come away from this survey believing that non-fiction filmmakers have far more formal, structural, might as well say artistic, problems than directors of fictional works. From all that is there that could be shown, their problem is how to decide what relatively little will be shown.*

Nonfiction Film
(A Critical History)
Richard Meran Barsam, Editor
1973; 382 pp.

$4.95 postpaid from:
E.P. Dutton and Company
Two Park Avenue
New York, NY 10016
or Whole Earth
Household Store

Screenplay

Arrgh! I want so much to recommend an exceptional book on the basics of screenwriting. **Screenplay** *is a good book. My problem is I can't imagine Colin Higgins (who praises this book) could have given us "Harold and Maude" by subscribing to this "one, two, three," pedantic approach. (Maybe Higgins wrote "Harold and Maude," then read this book and wrote "Foul Play.") There's the difference. One film is inspired, the other pleasant but mechanical.*

The danger is, you can put reading about script writing ahead of writing one. And when you read that every script must follow a model (paradigm is the new word): "setup, confrontation, resolution;" and that the "plot point" usually happens between page 27 and 29 (figuring one page per minute of screen time) you may just want to turn your typewriter over to automatic pilot.

This book is a useful reference. The missing ingredient is inspiration. If you want something to get a fire going, read "The Wild Child" by Truffaut, or the screenplay of some movie that you love. Go to the masterpieces for models. Then refine your work by consulting an expert engineer, like Syd Field.

Screenplay
(The Foundations of of Scriptwriting)
Syd Field
1979; 212 pp.

$4.95 postpaid from:
Delta Books
c/o Montville
Warehousing Company
Change Bridge Road
Pine Brook, NJ 07058
or Whole Earth
Household Store

LEARNING

Biases and Idiosyncrasies of the Reviewer

There are too many film schools. I read manuals on filmmaking and get irritable. I read biographies of film pioneers and feel lifted, wide-open. (Very few pioneers attended a film school.) Reading screenplays, and novels, is better preparation for writing than reading books about screenwriting.

Learn to make films by making films. And by looking at films. And by teaching others, especially children. Continually renew your resources: that is . . . don't read **American Cinematographer** *as much as you read novels, biographies, short stories.*

The professional filmmakers I know have had varying amounts of formal training, apprenticeship,— the traditional learning and preparation routes. What is more compelling about their activity is the drive they bring to it, the compulsion to work into the night, ignore mates and children, and generally act like people in love, not in business.

Without this kind of passion, and a sizeable ego, I don't think you can make it against all the competition, rejection, and indifference you will meet.

FILM ACCESS

Movies on TV

*This is the guide I most frequently grab to connect a director's name to a film, find out what year it was made, or get a capsule review to jog my memory. The listing is surprisingly complete on feature films and goes beyond those that have already been released to television to anticipate those that someday may be. The star ratings match my taste pretty well, though some of my friends think that Leonard Maltin (**TV Movies**, 1979; $2.95 postpaid from: New American Library, P.O. Box 120, 120 Woodbine, Bergenfield, NJ 07621) is on point more often. Of course the book was originally designed as a companion to TV movie viewing. All I can say is good luck. Less and less do the films you see on TV bear any resemblance to the version released to theaters. It is not uncommon in current production to shoot two versions of some scenes. One to cut into the theatrical release, another for home consumption. Even the ending may be different!*

Movies on TV
Steven H. Scheuer, Editor
1958, 1977; 816 pp.
8th Edition
$3.95 postpaid from:
Bantam Books
414 East Golf Road
Des Plaines, IL 60016
or Whole Earth
Household Store

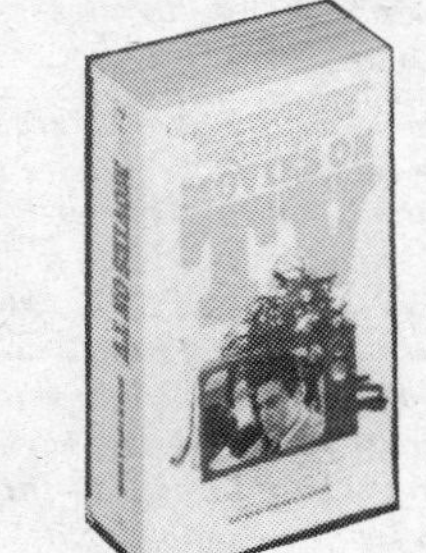

Film Programmer's Guide to 16 mm Rentals

The Magnolia Moving Picture Club meets in my basement every three months or so. Our specialty is Buster Keaton features and shorts. Most of Keaton's early films are an exclusive of Raymond Rohauer/Audio Brandon, distributors. Without this book, I might have assumed "The General" was in the same category, and paid $75 to rent it.

The listing in **Film Programmer's Guide** *tells a different story. The lesson is: shop around. Your savings could quickly pay for the book.*

"She's Oil Mine" is another exception; a 1941 Keaton that I've never seen. Found it in the back of this book, where there are complete filmographies by director and star.

Film Programmer's Guide to 16 mm Rentals
Kathleen Weaver, Editor
1972, 1980; 318 pp.
$20 postpaid from:
Reel Research
P.O. Box 6037
Albany, CA 94706

The Movie Collector's Catalog

A few years ago FILMEX, the Los Angeles film expo, wanted to show the classic "Oliver Twist" (1922). No prints were located, and the film's producer claimed the original had been burned many years ago to salvage $80 worth of silver content. A frantic call went out to collectors, and what may be the only existing print was found in Yugoslavia!

It's a common story. Collectors, even film pirates, have done more to save examples of film history than either libraries or studios. Interested? **The Movie Collector's Catalog** *has individual listings of collector's items and their trade value, an exhaustive listing of film rental catalogs, (so you can rent before you buy) and a thorough discussion of projectors and film maintenance equipment. All good to look at before you leap.*

The Movie Collector's Catalog
(How to Collect 8 and 16 mm Movies)
Ken Weiss
1977; 160 pp.
$5.95 postpaid from:
Cummington
Publishing, Inc.
17 Old Orchard Road
New Rochelle, NY 10804

Independent Filmmaking
The Super 8 Book

No book will give you the wisdom and confidence you'll get from completing some films. You just have to wade in. But reading Lenny Lipton can help. It's like having a good friend who's an auto mechanic. Lipton takes the arcane practice of filmmaking and makes it much less mysterious. He's got a warm style and solid information.

Independent Filmmaking *has been revised once and is needing it again, but it's still the most-used, friendliest guide.*

The Super 8 Book *has not been revised since 1975, and that's a real handicap in the rapidly changing super 8 world. Since* **Independent Filmmaking** *covers super 8 as well as 16 mm, if you can only get one, it's the best choice.*

Independent Filmmaking
Lenny Lipton
1972; 431 pp.
$8.95 postpaid

The Super 8 Book
Lenny Lipton
1975; 308 pp.
$7.95 postpaid

both from:
Simon and Schuster
Attn: Order Department
1230 Avenue of
the Americas
New York, NY 10020
or Whole Earth
Household Store

Cinematography

Studio oriented but useful in other ways. Especially clear on lighting, lens selection, and A-B rolling. The authors know their stuff.

Cinematography
J. Kris Malkiewicz and
Robert E. Rogers
1973; 216 pp.
$9.95 postpaid from:
Van Nostrand
Reinhold Company
7625 Empire Drive
Florence, KY 41042
or Whole Earth
Household Store

Making Films Your Business

Reality therapy. Don't read it until you've nailed down your dream. The very hopefulness of this book — that videotapes and especially videodiscs open up new markets for small scale distribution of films ($3 per disc, instead of $300 per 16 mm print) — is also grounds for increased paranoia. It opens many new and original paths for plagiarism and exploitation. But how are you going to protect yourself from the monsters out there if you don't know what they look like? Lots of positive information too, on proposals, grants, financing.

Making Films Your Business
(Covering: Proposals, Grants, Distribution, Financing, Budgets, Copyrights, Video, Contracts, and the Future)
Mollie Gregory
1979; 256 pp.
$6.95 postpaid from:
Schocken Books
200 Madison Avenue
New York, NY 10016
or Whole Earth
Household Store

MAGAZINES

American Film

The **New Yorker** *of film magazines. From the simple, elegant covers to back page news of prestigious workshops, and forthcoming grants. Read it and savor the impression that all is lively and well with American film thanks to the panache of the American Film Institute and the largesse of the National Endowment for the Arts. Raise your sights.*

American Film
Hollis Alpert, Editor
$15/year (10 issues)
from:
Subscription Service
American Film
P.O. Box 966
Farmingdale, NY 11737

Super 8 Filmaker

Lenny Lipton writes for **Super 8 Filmaker**. *John Korty subscribes to it. Sure it's eclectic and often amateurish, but that's where we all start, and very often it's where really fresh ideas come from.* **American Cinematographer** *shows technical problems solved with big crews and big bucks.* **Super 8 Filmaker** *is more likely to get you the same effect with tissue and a comb.*

Super 8 Filmaker
Richard J. Jantz, Editor
$15/year (8 issues)
from:
Super 8 Filmaker
609 Mission Street
San Francisco, CA 94105

American Cinematographer

This is the magazine that will acquaint you with the professional filmmaking community. Reading **Cinematographer** *you'd think that Hollywood is still the center of the film universe. Yes, they are chauvinistic, but they're also really good at their work. Besides finding out how Robert Altman records overlapping dialog using up to fourteen wireless microphones, a typical issue might include an interview with the cinematographer of a current (usually big box-office) feature, plus technical tips, readers' questions answered, workshop announcements and maybe a deal on some used equipment from the classifieds.*

The ads will keep you posted on the latest equipment, so at least you won't sound like a complete novice in the camera store. ■

American Cinematographer
Herb A. Lightman, Editor
$9/year (12 issues)
from:
American Cinematographer
P.O. Box 2230
Hollywood, CA 90028

THE RISING SUN
NEIGHBORHOOD NEWSLETTER

continued from last spread

What this has to do with Merlin is he had been functioning pretty early in the identification/separation process so, for example, trees and people were both living things on the Earth so they could do things to each others' spirits but by the time Merlin came back, trees were into being wood and people were into going to shrinks and they didn't have a hell of a lot to say to each other. So Merlin couldn't do all his sleight of hand type tricks, just only got to do one trick the whole time he was here, but that was a good 'un — pulled a Tower of Babel number on the bad guys at the critical moment — made it so nothing they said made sense and they couldn't talk to each other. Since the bad guys were sociologists and government planners, bringing them to this state was only a minor exaggeration of their existing state and it didn't hardly take nothing for old Merlin to pull it off — just made them become what they were — total mushmouths — a little faster than would otherwise have been the case.

continued on next spread

Videowest is a group of media people producing, from a San Francisco-based UHF-TV station, the type of programming they couldn't find elsewhere: fast-paced magazines weaving news features, on-the-street interviews, personality profiles, off-the-wall comedy, and the latest rock'n'roll music.

For more information about Videowest programs (soon available on videocassette), write: **Videocassette Productions**, 735 Harrison Street, San Francisco, CA 94107.

The reviews were written by Fabrice Florin with help from Ron Compesi, Tim Curry, Betsy Miller, Scoop Nisker and Phyllis Uppman.

—The Video Guide

VIDEO

by Fabrice Florin and Videowest, San Francisco, California

TELEVISION, THE MOST POWERFUL MEDIUM of our times, has only been used so far to convey simple messages to the largest possible audience, shaping the minds of millions to serve the purpose of a happy few. Broadcast TV, as we know it, programs for the lowest common denominator, filling our screens with what has been described by network executives as the "least objectionable programming."

The long-awaited emergence of video may change this whole picture. As a highly technological future creeps upon us, new gadgets appear on the market which seem to offer more viewing options than the three networks did: VHS or Beta home video recorders, color cameras, giant screens, cable and pay TV, video games, videodisks, etc. Whether this avalanche of hardware will affect immediately the quality of the software remains to be seen. The trend, however, certainly seems to lead towards a decentralization of the medium: "narrowcasting," as it is called, or special-interest programming aimed at smaller audiences. With hands-on access to the new technologies, viewers may soon produce, select and distribute programs of their choice, changing our passive television set into a more convivial tool just like the telephone. For good or bad, video is here to stay and will affect deeply, along with home computers, the next cultural revolution.

We decided not to evaluate any specific video products for two reasons: (1) There is such an abundance of similar but distinct pieces of hardware and software in the market today that a proper review would take more space than we have; and (2) by the time you get this book, our selections may well be outdated, considering the present pace of technological development. Furthermore, the publications listed below will do a much better job than we could in guiding you through the ever-expanding video jungle. Happy trails!

The Video Guide

An excellent overview of small format video production with extremely detailed operating procedures on many of the most popular ENG (Electronic News Gathering) and home video systems (for 1/2" and 3/4" tape). Well illustrated and very up-to-date, with state of the art field production equipment. Charles Bensinger applies "new age" consciousness to video technology with interesting results. A "must" for aspiring videographers.

The Video Guide
Charles Bensinger
1977, 1980; 254 pp.
$16.95 postpaid from:
Video Info Publications
P.O. Box 1507
Santa Barbara, CA 93102
or Whole Earth Household Store

•

Video then is *decentralization of media.* It can become a very personal statement, reflecting ideas and events and communicating information for perhaps only a single city block of people. What we have here is a true medium for the people and for individual applications. It can serve the small folks and the nation as well. And that's why it excites a lot of people and motivates them sufficiently to somehow get their hands on a portapak, or whatever, and *make tapes!*

Four Arguments for the Elimination of Television

Former adman Jerry Mander proposes a radical solution to the negative aspects of television: get rid of the damned thing altogether. Despite solid research to back the arguments, Mander's crusade against the all-American drug reminds one of Don Quixote and the windmills. While recognizing that he wouldn't know how to eliminate television in the first place, Mander proceeds to demonstrate how it distorts our perception of reality, pointing out the inherent dangers in a system where information is controlled by commercial interests. Great topic for thought and discussion. Keep it by your bedside if you're a heavy TV viewer.

Four Arguments For the Elimination of Television
Jerry Mander
1977; 371 pp.
$4.95 postpaid from:
William Morrow and Co.
Wilmor Warehouse
6 Henderson Drive
West Caldwell, NJ 07006
or Whole Earth Household Store

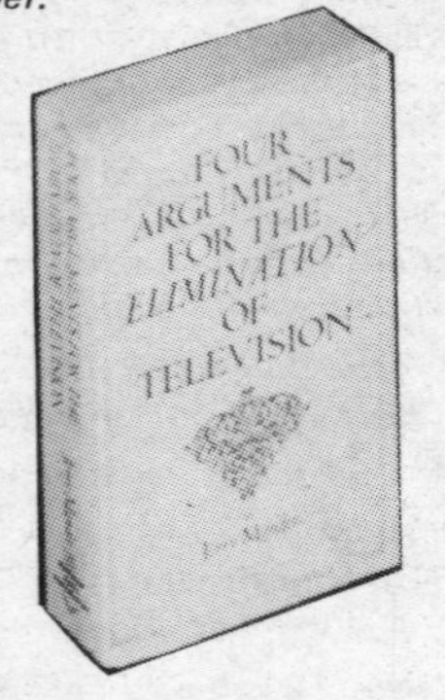

TV Guide Almanac

A good research tool for the trivia buff, compiled by the editors of **TV Guide**. *With all the depth and insight of a phone book, the* **Almanac** *lists everything from commercial TV stations to Emmy Award winners to college programs in broadcasting across the United States. Mainly facts and figures, but good reference material for those who care.*

TV Guide Almanac
Craig T. Norback and Peter G. Norback
1980; 680 pp.
$10.95 postpaid from:
Ballantine Books
455 Hahn Road
Westminster, MD 21157
or Whole Earth Household Store

•

The big year for CBS turned out to be 1951, with the debut of *I Love Lucy*. Although the show from its inception looked to be a success, there was some question whether it would ever get on the air. Lucille Ball had to insist that CBS sign Desi Arnaz before the network would do so. Moreover, the couple wanted to do the show before a live audience, an idea that the network rejected. Ball and Arnaz produced the first show themselves to demonstrate their conception of *I Love Lucy* to the network. The upshot was that they invented the situation-comedy format. —TV Guide Almanac

The Cool Fire: How to Make It in Television

An insider's look at the television industry. Bob Shanks, the producer of The Great American Dream Machine and The Jack Paar Show (among others) and a vice president of ABC, takes the reader on a grand tour of a business he loves. He describes, with colorful anecdotes, the history of the networks, how programs are developed and sold, how ratings work, and how talent agencies, advertisers, producers, directors, and technicians collectively shape contemporary television. A great working tool with first-hand tips for the aspiring television producer.

The Cool Fire
(How to Make It In Television)
Bob Shanks
1976; 318 pp.
$3.95 postpaid from:
Vintage Books
Random House
455 Hahn Road
Westminster, MD 21157
or Whole Earth Household Store

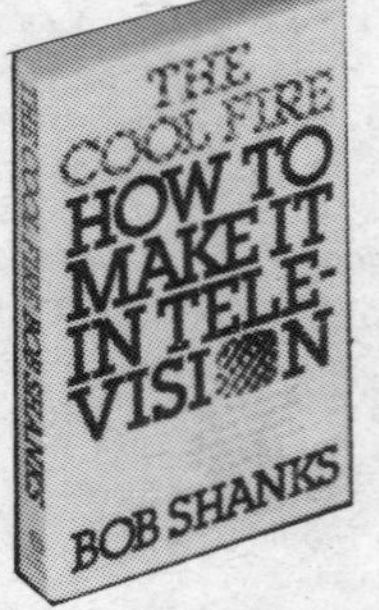

The Technique of Television Production

A classic textbook on broadcast television production, covering in detail both technology and aesthetics, with over 1,000 quick-guide diagrams. Emphasizes heavy television studio operations, leaving aside small format field production techniques. Recommended for would-be television engineers.

The Technique of Television Production
Gerald Millerson
1961, 1980; 440 pp.
10th Edition
$17.95 postpaid from:
Focal Press
10 East 40th Street
New York, NY 10016
or Whole Earth Household Store

The Home Video Handbook

Charles Bensinger has adapted his **Video Guide** *into a consumer-oriented manual for those only interested in ½" home video systems (Beta or VHS). Includes several chapters on production techniques and aesthetics for beginners.*

The Home Video Handbook
Charles Bensinger
1979; 304 pp.
$8.95 postpaid from:
Video-Info Publications
P.O. Box 1507
Santa Barbara, CA 93102
or Whole Earth Household Store

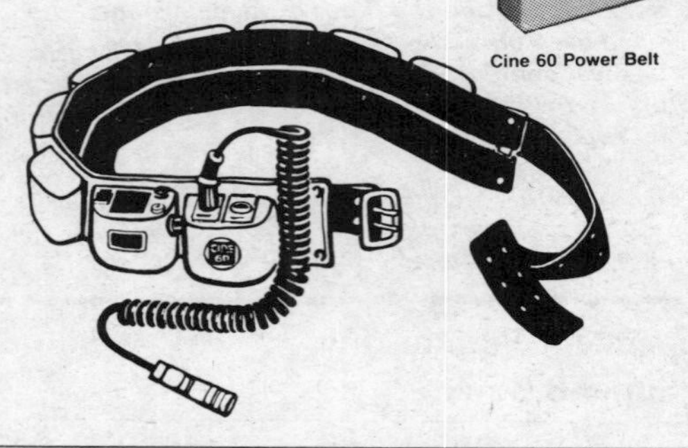

Cine 60 Power Belt

CHEATED SUBSTITUTES. This sequence of illustrations shows a fugitive climbing a cliff-face, seeking escape from his pursuers. The fugitive looks up at the cliff-face. Hearing his pursuers, he decides to climb. We have a shot of the possible route, followed by one of running feet.

Fig. 18.5. Pt 2.

The fugitive seeks a handhold then, turning to see if his pursuers have seen him, he climbs. They stop at the cliff-base, his foot dislodges a stone, and they look up ...

Fig. 18.5. Pt.3.

And the studio set-up for this sequence. *Left:* A gravel-strewn floor. *Centre:* A photo-caption of a cliff-face. *Right:* And a surface-contoured flat, over which the fugitive crawls. The shot is canted to suggest vertical climbing.

The Video Source Book

By far the most comprehensive catalog of prerecorded programs available on videotape: over 15,000 titles, from horror movies to rock concerts or instructional tapes. Doesn't review the programs or list prices, but provides basic information on format, availability, and distributors.

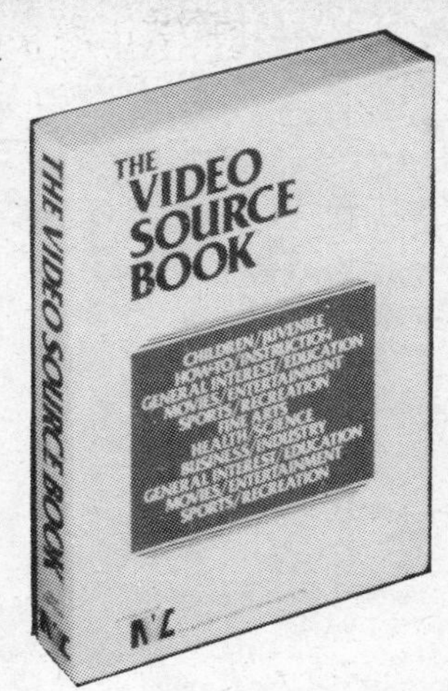

The Video Source Book
Maxine K. Reed, Editor
1979; 685 pp.

$25.95 postpaid from:
National Video Clearinghouse
P.O. Box 3
Syosset, NY 11791

Home-Satellite TV Reception

Every day half a dozen satellites beam down to earth a smorgasbord of first run movies, exclusive sports events, religious, educational, and children's programs, business conferences and 24-hour superstations from Atlanta and elsewhere. For $15,000 you could have an Earth-receiving station installed in your own backyard and tune in on any of those channels for free. Bob Cooper's **Home-Satellite TV Handbook** *tells you how to build your own for under $4000. (See also* **Coop's Satellite Digest** *on p. 523.)*

Coleman's Under $500 Terminal — Robert Coleman of South Carolina has created, using surplus electronics equipment, his own version of a home terminal. Antenna is ten foot diameter; all electronics is outside, largely spread on ground, which he covers up with plastic sheet to keep water out!

Home-Satellite TV Reception Handbook
Bob Cooper, Jr.
1979; 72 pp.

$7.50 postpaid from:
Satellite TV Technology
P.O. Box G
Arcadia, OK 73007

MAGAZINES

The state of the art of video hardware and software is changing so fast that most books on the subject may become dated after a few years. To keep up with the latest news, your best bet is to check out some of the following publications.

Panorama

An expanded **TV Guide** *for sophisticated viewers and video consumers. Slick but substantial,* **Panorama** *will provide you with easy reading on new programs, along with the usual mix of celebrity interviews and behind-the-scene reports. If you can afford a home video recorder or a cable subscription, you may be interested in their reviews of latest videocassette releases and upcoming programs on pay TV, subscription TV or even PBS.*

Panorama
Roger Youman, Editor
$12/year (12 issues) from:
Triangle Communications, Inc.
850 Third Avenue
New York, NY 10022

Videography

A solid publication for the professional videographer, with an emphasis on industrial and broadcast video production technology. Also informative interviews with people in the industry and some good tips for the independent producer.

Videography
Peter Caranicas, Editor
$12 /year (12 issues)
from:
Videography
475 Park Avenue South
New York, NY 10016

Home Video

A home consumer version of **Videography**, *including reviews of new equipment and programming, as well as home video production techniques.*

Home Video
$7.50 /year (6 issues)
from:
Home Video
Circulation Department
P.O. Box 2651
Boulder, CO 80322

Variety

Still the official publication of show business, covering the entertainment industry in its own original teletype language. A working tool for people in the business of film, television, or music, it is starting to feature well-informed articles on the burgeoning video revolution. ■

Variety
Syd Silverman, Editor
$25 /year (52 issues)
from:
Variety
154 West 46th Street
New York, NY 10036

Amateur Television in a Nutshell
Amateur Television Magazine

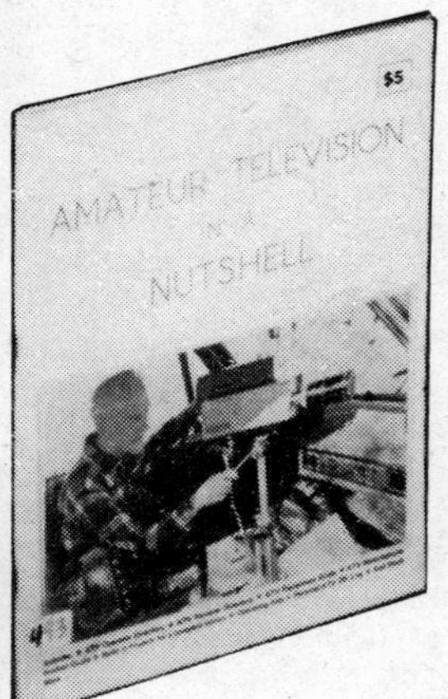

Ham TV?!? It's actually a next logical step, combining home video, home ham radio and home computers (for captions, special effects and switching controls.) It's very conversational; you set a date with someone far away and at the appropriate moment exchange pictures — either moving pictures of whatever you've pointed your camera at (called fast-scan) or still pictures in 8-second successive intervals (slow-scan, which is somewhat less expensive). The experience is surprisingly intimate and the exchange is exciting to watch. Plus it leads to all sorts of technical and artistic experiments in creating and manipulating images, building equipment, and linking with voice and satellites. Henry Ruh's **Amateur Television Magazine** *has been around a long time — 14 years — and has a nice, direct, amateur-oriented tone to it, plus all the technical authenticity you could ask for. His book is the hardware authority. Ham TV is one avocation that started in the center of the continent and is just now spreading out towards the coasts. It's how television should be; a creating medium, not a watching medium.* —Art Kleiner
[Suggested by Jane Veeder]

Amateur Television in a Nutshell
(Everything you need to know to build or operate your own ham TV station)
Henry B. Ruh
1978; 72 pp.
$5 postpaid

Amateur Television Magazine
Henry B. Ruh, Editor
$7/year (6 issues)

both from:
Amateur Television Magazine
P.O. Box 1347
Bloomington, IN 47401

Ham TV operators introduce their broadcasts to each other with their call numbers and an identifying graphic.
—Amateur Television Magazine

The New Communicators
Community Television Review

An admittedly presumptuous opinion: the purpose of cable TV is neither improved reception nor Home Box Office. The purpose of cable TV is locally originated good TV, focused on local matters, with lots of participation and feedback from people in the community. In Canada, local TV programmers have been doing this for some time; **The New Communicators** *is a manual developed out of a cable network in Ottawa.* **Community Television Review** *is published by the (deep breath) National Federation of Local Cable Programmers, the United States group which by all accounts is best helping would-be local programmers get good stuff on cable. Their newsletter covers the process thoroughly and un-boringly.* —Art Kleiner
[Suggested by Carolyn Perkins]

The New Communicators
(A Guide to Community Programming)
Dorothy Forbes and Sanderson Laying
1977, 1978; 117 pp.
$7 postpaid

Community Television Review
Tom Borrup, Editor
$12 /year (4 issues)

both from:
National Federation of Local Cable Programmers
P.O. Box 832
Dubuque, IA 52001

THE RISING SUN
NEIGHBORHOOD NEWSLETTER

Lilith, Adam's first wife, never died. Well, actually not wife probably, but a woman before Eve, the original bad woman. What was bad about her? She wasn't made out of part of Adam but out of the Earth itself, so she was sort of wild and uncontrollable like the Earth itself, and she distracted Adam from whatever he was supposed to be doing by her pervy practices — she liked sex in other words — and she didn't want to live in the same place as Adam but just visit him sometimes. For one or all of these things she was banished from where nice people hang out, both Eden and the next place, and was mainly known after that for trying to kill little kids and babies and make pregnant women miscarry because she couldn't have kids (since everyone knows fun, sex and kids don't go together and was jealous). So she's lived forever mostly as a reason to be worried about your kids, and a carrier of the evil eye, but anyway she didn't die and now some folks are trying to say she wasn't so bad, old Lilith, a strong and jolly person and maybe she wasn't trying to kill the kids but tell them about sex which their Eve-ish mothers would try to keep from them for years. Anyway, the reason God and Adam started with Adam's rib for the next lady was they hoped to get something a little more manageable, but I don't see how they figured they could if they couldn't even kill Lilith but had to settle for libel.

(Lilith didn't make it into the Bible, she's a Jewish folktale.)

Since Sputnik there is no Nature. Nature is an item contained in a man-made environment of satellites and information. Goals have now to be replaced by the sensory reprogramming of total environments and DNA particles, alike. The earth is an old nose cone.

If nature didn't, Warner's will.

Understanding Media

Everybody talks about McLuhan, and everybody does something about him, and that makes it subjectively harder to get at him. He's got other insights than what you hear about, so it's worth the trouble to track him down, both his current sayings and his prime collections. The primest is **Understanding Media**. —SB

Understanding Media
((The Extensions of Man)
Marshall McLuhan
1964; 318 pp.

$1.75 postpaid from:
New American Library
P.O. Box 120
120 Woodbine
Bergenfield, NJ 07621
or Whole Earth Household Store

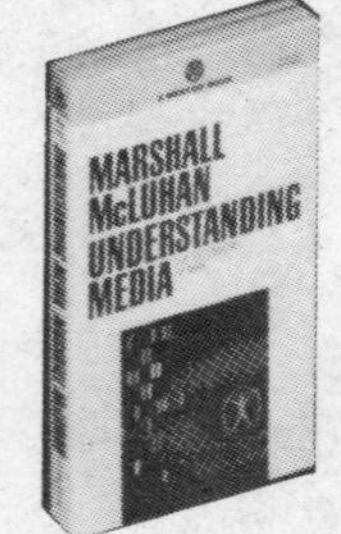

•

As W.B. Yeats wrote of this reversal, "The visible world is no longer a reality and the unseen world is no longer a dream."

•

Meantime, the countryside, as oriented and fashioned by plane, by highway, and by electric information-gathering, tends to become once more the nomadic trackless area that preceded the wheel.

•

"Work," however, does not exist in a nonliterate world. The primitive hunter or fisherman did no work, any more than does the poet, painter, or thinker of today. Where the whole man is involved there is no work.

•

Everybody experiences far more than he understands. Yet it is experience, rather than understanding, that influences behavior, especially in collective matters of media and technology, where the individual is almost inevitably unaware of their effect upon him.

Culture Is Our Business

McLuhan's best format. Each pair of pages has a reprint of an ad on the right, and fresh McLuhan aphorisms, quotes, and misquotes on the left. The resulting energy across the spread is economic and multi-directional — i.e., you make it.

This book should be restored to print, ideally with some new McLuhan additions. His news stays news. —SB

Culture Is Our Business
Marshall McLuhan
1970; 336 pp.

OUT OF PRINT
McGraw-Hill Book Co.

Get this book back in print!

•

Ads are the cave art of the twentieth century. While the Twenties talked about the caveman, and people thrilled to the art of the Altamira caves, they ignored (as we do now) the hidden environment of magical forms which we call "ads." Like cave paintings, ads are not intended to be looked at or seen, but rather to exert influence at a distance, as though by ESP. Like cave paintings, they are not means of private but of corporate expression. They are vortices of collective power, masks of energy invented by new tribal man.

•

Poets and artists live on frontiers. They have no feedback, only feedforward. They have no identities. They are probes.

•

Today, through ads, a child takes in all the times and places of the world "with his mother's TV." He is gray at three. By twelve he is a confirmed Peter Pan, fully aware of the follies of adults and adult life in general. These could be called Spock's Spooks, who now peer at us from every quarter of our world.

•

Psychically, art is valuable only when new.

Commercially, new art is kooky and worthless.

The gap between the kooky and the commercially valuable is closing fast.

•

Invention is the mother of necessity.

•

If the phonetic alphabet was a technical means of severing the spoken word from its aspects of sound and gesture, the photograph and its development in the movie restored gesture to the human technology of recording experience.

•

Man the food-gatherer reappears incongruously as information-gatherer. In this role, electronic man is no less a nomad than his paleolithic ancestors.

•

It is a principal aspect of the electric age that it establishes a global network that has much of the character of our central nervous system. Our central nervous system is not merely an electric network, but it constitutes a single unified field of experience. As biologists point out, the brain is the interacting place where all kinds of impressions and experiences can be exchanged and translated, enabling us to react to the world as a whole.

The Best Thing on TV: Commercials

If you watch television you'll love this book. It's about something you know all too well — the ads — and that no other book or critic (besides McLuhan) has given proper attention to. Considering the amount of sheer cultural effort and cost that focuses into those few-second spots, with the encouragement of this book you can look through them like portholes upon a universe of media empire and nuance. Behind the great ads are great stories. —SB

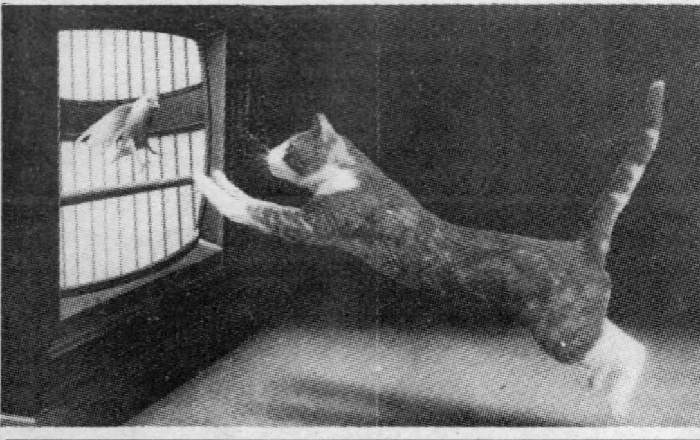

The Best Thing On TV: Commercials
Jonathan Price
1978; 184 pp.

$8.95 postpaid from:
Penguin Books
299 Murray Hill Parkway
East Rutherford, NJ 07073
or Whole Earth Household Store

•

The door opens, and out gets the man. "Yea, you're here!" we yell. "Oh God, God, oh God," he says and falls down. And we rush out to meet him to find out what's wrong. We got within twenty feet, and then we all started saying, "Oh God." The bear had been carsick for one hundred and forty miles. He had vomited and defecated all over the inside of the van, all over both the driver and the assistant, and they just had to hang in there and drive. We got the doors open, and the bear is lying there with his feet up in the air. Ohhhhh. It knocked a day out of our shooting, the bear lying there moaning.

The 100 Greatest Advertisements

All the tricks, guilt trips and assumptions-between-the-lines in advertising today have their roots somewhere in this book. It's the kind of book you can pore over, like a family album. Its most recent ad ran in 1959, and its earliest ones go back to the dawn of Advertising itself, in the 1850s. Yet the book's still in print and I refer to my copy often. The editor's unabashed commentary and the ads themselves are full of unintentionally revealing glimpses into a profession with one of the weirdest built-in attitudes around — a mix of creativity, craftsmanship and unashamed prostitution. The attitude is quite charming at times, especially in some of its little-old-New-York manifestations.

Oh yeah, the book was intended to teach how to write ad copy, and you can use it that way. But its value, its heartbreaking importance, lies in the way it bares the roots of those media tendrils which poke their way so deeply into most of us. —Art Kleiner

The 100 Greatest Advertisements
(Who Wrote Them and What They Did)
Julian Lewis Watkins
1949, 1959; 233 pages

$5.50 postpaid from:
Dover Books
180 Varick Street
New York, NY 10014
or Whole Earth Household Store

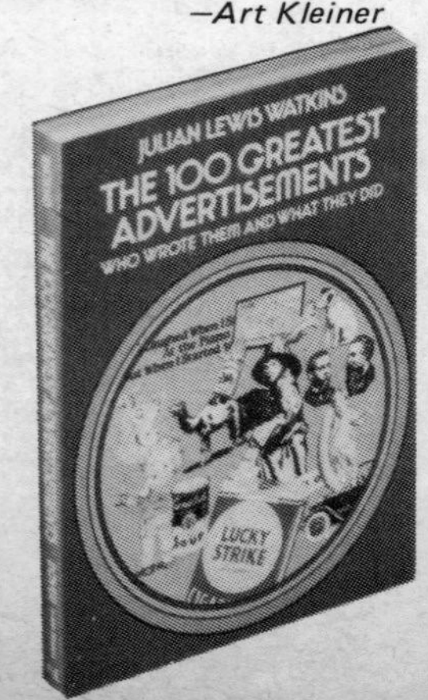

↓

You didn't have to wait to learn the results to know this ad was great. Its greatness hit you right between the eyes, and you tore it out of the newspaper and pinned it to your wall, and stole a look at it every once in a while, and hoped like hell you could do something near as well.

So I wrote David Ogilvy for the story and this is what he sent me:

"When I presented this headline to the senior Rolls-Royce executive in New York, that austere British engineer said: 'We really must do something to improve our clock.'

"At 60 miles an hour the loudest noise in this new Rolls-Royce comes from the electric clock"

LITTLE KNOWN TELEPHONE BARGAINS & REFINEMENTS

by Art Kleiner

Telephone services change so quickly and quietly in the United States that specifics go out-of-date within weeks and changes aren't reported in the newspapers. To confuse matters more, service from each local phone company is apt to be different, whether or not it is a division of American Telephone and Telegraph (The Bell System). To choose your type of service, check out some of the options mentioned here, decide what you want, and then ask in person at either the new phone center stores or at your phone company office. Some of the new options are money-savers; others make sophisticated new communications media out of the telephone systems we take for granted.

Optional Residence Telephone Service (ORTS) eliminates toll charges (message units) for calls to specific areas within a specific distance (usually less than 40 miles, but sometimes as large as an entire state). Instead, you pay a $5 - $10 monthly rate. It's only available in metropolitan areas, but it's great for those who speak regularly to someone in the next suburb. Also a boon for people who share a telephone and are fed up with figuring out who made those picayune message unit calls. Regrettably, ORTS isn't offered over long distances.

Optional Calling Measured Service (OCMS) is the rural version of ORTS. You pay a monthly fee which covers tolls for medium-distance calls to specific areas.

Foreign Exchange Service (FEX) lets you set up your telephone number in a different community than where your telephone is located. You can make local calls to the area where your number is listed and others can dial you there as a non-toll call. More expensive than ORTS.

Limited Service. Most phone companies have two or three limited (or reduced) service plans. You pay less and are allowed fewer free calls per month. Good for

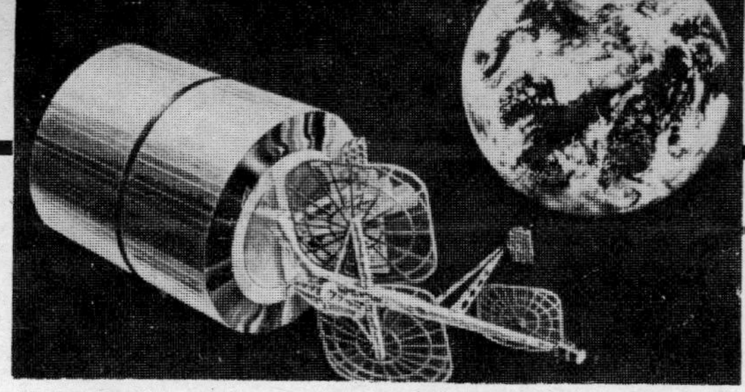

INTELSAT IV-A, also twelve transponders of 36 MHz, designed for intercontinental transmission.

Future Developments in Telecommunications

With his high-powered seminars and prolific writings, James Martin has become a lord high guru of telecommunicationsdom. In keeping with this reputation, his **Future Developments in Telecommunications** *has the twin virtues of being both meaty and accessible. The writing style is clean and you can't help but get a sense of the breadth and scope of the field while scanning through the pages.*

The book is divided into three parts: the first provides an overview of the telecommunications scene today; the second offers a "synthesis" that blends emerging technologies into a scenario of the future; and the third gets down to a hard look at the technology of the technology.

Future Developments *can be used as both an introductory telecommunications text and as a reference work. It's well worth the hefty price tag.* —*Michael Schrage*

Future Developments in Telecommunications
James Martin
1971, 1977; 668 pp.
2nd Edition
$34.95 postpaid from:
Prentice-Hall
Box 500
Englewood Cliffs, NJ 07632
or Whole Earth Household Store

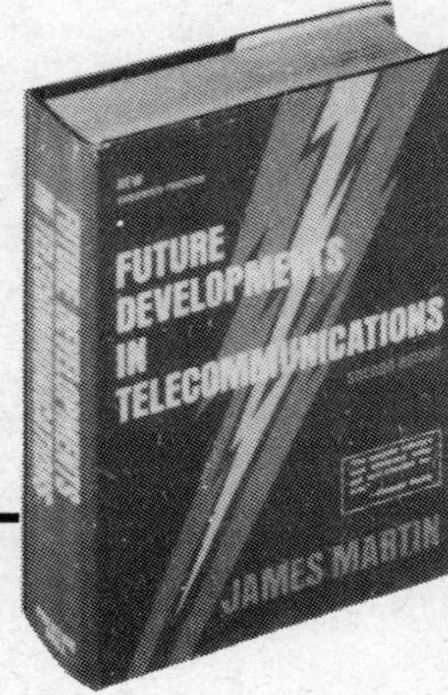

The communication satellite. Satellites have provided telephone and television links to the underdeveloped world. The satellite antennae in some underdeveloped countries stand next to fields ploughed by oxen. Now satellites have the potential of revolutionizing corporate communications both nationally and internationally.

Low-cost satellite earth stations. Planar microwave circuits make it possible to mass-produce satellite receiving equipment at very low cost. Satellite receivers cheap enough for home purchase have been used in Canada, Japan, and India.

Demand-assigned multiple-access equipment. Satellite or high-capacity channels can be shared by multiple goegraphically dispersed users in a highly flexible manner, portions of channel capacity being allocated to users according to their instantaneous needs.

The helical waveguide. A pipe, now operating, that can carry 250,000 or more simultaneous telephone calls or equivalent information, in digital form, over long distances.

The laser. This means of transmission has the theoretical potential of carrying many millions of simultaneous telephone calls or their equivalent. It is being used with optical fibers to carry several thousand.

Optical fibers. A thin flexible fiber made of extremely pure glass which can carry a thousand times as much information as a copper wire pair. Optical communication fibers are now on the market; some are in use carrying public telephone calls. Many thousands of such fibers can be packed into one flexible cable.

Large-scale integration (LSI). A form of ultraminiaturized computer circuitry that probably marks the beginning of mass production of computerlike logic circuitry. It offers the potential of extremely reliable, extremely small, and, in some of its forms, extremely fast logic circuitry and memory. If large-enough quantities can be built, this circuitry can become very low in cost.

On-line real-time computers. Computers capable of responding to many distant terminals on telecommunication lines at a speed geared to human thinking. They have the potential of bringing the power and information of innumerable computers into every office and eventually every home.

Microcomputers. Mass-producible miniature computers of low cost.

Video telephones. Telephones with which subscribers see as well as hear each other or can see still images.

Large TV screens. TV screens that can occupy a wall if necessary.

Cable TV. A cable into homes with a potential signal-carrying capacity more than one thousand times that of the telephone cable. It can be used for signals other than television.

Voice answerback. Computers can now assemble human-voice words and speak them over the telephone. Voice answerback and the pushbutton telephone set, makes every such telephone a potential computer terminal.

Millimeter-wave radio. Radio at frequencies in the band above the microwave band can relay a quantity of information greater than all the other radio bands combined. Chains of closely spaced antennas will distribute these millimeter-wave signals.

Cellular mobile radio. A system organization that will permit many radio telephones or other mobile radio devices in a city.

Packet radio. Radio systems for computer terminals that will make pocket terminals, or other small mobile terminals practicable.

Data broadcasting. Information can be broadcast in digital form at VHF or UHF frequencies for reception on home TV sets, special terminals, or portable devices.

Pulse code modulation. All signals, including telephone, Picturephone, music, facsimile, and television, can be converted into digital bit streams and transmitted, along with computer data, over the same digital links. Major advantages accrue from this.

Codecs. Circuits which convert signals such as speech, music, and television into a bit stream, and convert such bit streams back into the original signal. Codecs will become increasingly inexpensive and efficient.

Computerized switching. Computerized telephone exchanges are coming into operation offering many new services, and computerlike logic can be employed for switching and "concentrating" all types of signals.

Data banks. Electronic storage for huge quantities of information that can be manipulated and indexed by computers and that can be accessed in a fraction of a second.

Packet switching networks. One way of building generalized switched data networks interconnecting computers and terminals. A widely accepted standard CCITT x .25 exists so that packet switching networks of different countries will be interconnectable.

Major inventions and developments which, in combination, have the potential of changing the fabric of society

•

An extensive use of EFT (Electronic Fund Transfer) will reduce the "float" money within a country, like taking up the slack in an anchor rope. It will make the float available for people or corporations to spend. Economists use the phrase "velocity of money" to refer to the rate at which money turns over. Today one dollar issued by the government might be spent 17 times in the course of the year. With EFT, the velocity would be higher, perhaps much higher; the same dollar issued would be spent many more times. Unless compensating controls were devised this increase in the velocity of money would probably have an inflationary effect. As with a vehicle, the faster the velocity the tighter the controls must be. Today's mechanisms would provide inadequate control.

Express Mail

If you are as bad about meeting deadlines as I am, or if you live in a perpetual state of last minute, or if your lover lives in San Francisco and you are in Manhattan — the U.S. Postal Service Express Mail Service may be just what you need.

It works like this: bring your letter or package to a designated Express Mail Post Office by 5 p.m. and it will be delivered to the Express Mail Window of the designated Post Office near the area of your choice by 10 a.m. the next day. To find the nearest Express Mail Post Office, call your local Post Office or check your phone book.

It's up to you to notify someone to pick up the mail.

A regular letter (up to one pound) is roughly $6 (ask for A-Label Service). For an additional $2 the Postal Service will deliver it to the addressee by 3 p.m. the next day (ask for B-Label Service). Rates vary a little depending on distance.

There is Express Mail service in many metropolitan areas now. —*Rick Fields*

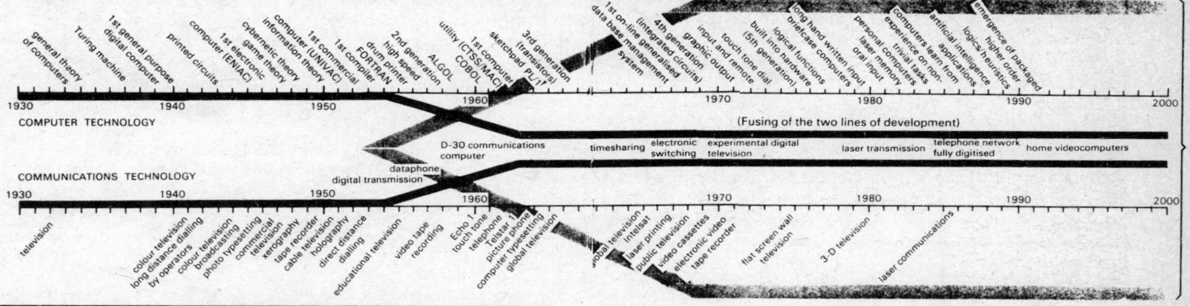

people who make few outgoing calls. Party lines, a long-time staple of cheap telephone service, are being phased out.

Custom Calling Services I. AT&T is quite proud of these new features; they're interesting but I wonder about their usefulness. "Call Forwarding" means the Bell System, on your instruction, automatically transfers incoming calls from your phone to another phone. "Three-Way Calling" lets you set up a simultaneous chat between yourself and people at two other phone numbers. "Call Waiting" is a residential version of putting someone on hold while you take another call. "Speed Calling" sets up short-cut two-digit codes for your most frequently called numbers. Rates for these sub-options vary from $5 to $20 per month. One friend who has all four services plays them against each other, speed-dialing three-way conversations which he then puts on hold to take another call – all from someone else's phone to which he's had his calls forwarded.

Custom Calling Services II. Not yet available but planned for late 1980/early 1981. They seem more useful and also a bit scarier. "Call Answering" will record messages when you're not there, like an answering machine built into the central AT&T switching system. "Voice Storage" will record your message and, at a specified time, dial someone else's number and replay the message for them. (Wait till teenagers and telephone solicitors get to experiment with it . . .) "Personal Identification Number" (PIN) cards will replace AT&T credit cards next year. The PIN number will be a general identification number, issued by the phone company, for telephone-call billing, shopping by phone, and banking by phone. "You can travel all over the country, and if you leave word the central switching computer will find you when it needs to," the representatives from Pacific Telephone (an AT&T subsidiary) told me.

If this prospect seems more threatening than promising, you may want to look into the services of AT&T's competitors, the independent long-distance phone companies. They can provide substantial savings over the Bell System if you make $100 or more worth of long-distance calls per month. (Incidentally, some people feel outraged at the thought of spending so much money on long-distance telephoning. However, I and many of the people I know are cross-continentally mobile, and we depend on the telephone to keep in touch. Uses much less energy than a 3000-mile trip, too.)

To use an independent phone company, you dial their number, then your account number, and then the number you want to reach. The advantage is the huge savings (30 - 60% of regular rates) and the mobility of making calls on your account from anywhere. Also the small companies break the bill down by destination – a much simpler to read format. The disadvantages are those extra digits to punch, plus poorer overall service than the Bell System – bad connections, sudden disconnections, and echoed voices. (When it comes to transmission quality, U.S. citizens are spoiled, as anyone who has tried phoning home from Tierra del Fuego will attest.) In addition, the independents operate only in large city areas. They don't have the millions of dollars to invest in circuitry that AT&T has. Reportedly the smaller companies are improving their service each year, especially over medium distances. Information on each of them is free.

Sprint, Southern Pacific Communications, P.O. Box 974, Burlingame, CA 94010. The easiest to use and the service most directly aimed at home users. It's managed by the Southern Pacific Company, which transmits on microwave links strung along their old railroad tracks. Many have suggested the service to us; some are annoyed with the poor quality and others don't notice it. It apparently depends on luck.

Microwave Communications, Inc. (MCI), 1621 Euclid Avenue, Suite 1414, Cleveland, OH 44115. MCI uses more satellites, probably has slightly better service, is a little more difficult to use than Sprint.

ITT City Call, International Telephone and Telegraph, Two Broadway, 21st Floor, New York, NY 10004. Attn: Len Seasonwein. ITT discourages non-business use, but if you can get an account with them, it's worth it, because their technical connections are almost as good as Ma Bell's, and they're cheaper. Especially good for those who make $300 or more long-distance calls a month, or for a commune or shared household. ■

The Changing Information Environment ↑

Planet implodes! Everything is changed! Few notice! This book notices. —*SB*

The Changing Information Environment
John McHale
1976; 117 pp.
$18 postpaid from:
Westview Press
5500 Central Avenue
Boulder, CO 80301
or Whole Earth Household Store

•

Information and knowledge, as resources in themselves, are not reduced or lessened by increased use or wider sharing — rather they may gain in the process.

THE RISING SUN
NEIGHBORHOOD NEWSLETTER

"We're keeping our place clean by keeping some-place else dirty — with electricity."

—Daniel

Yellow Pages

No reference book matches the practical currency of the Yellow Pages in your telephone directory. On any subject you can browse, call, inquire, ask who else would have information, and proceed to the heart of any matter. Many of the evaluations expressed in this **Catalog** *are based on exactly such research, and those are the evaluations I trust most. As J. Baldwin notes on p. 516, the best yellow pages of all are in the Manhattan phone directory, available at the library or Mother Bell.*
—SB

Information Please Almanac
The World Almanac and Book of Facts

Every home or office needs an up-to-date, general-reference almanac. Despite a few recent entries in this field, these two still lead the pack in accuracy, completeness, and ease of locating information. Each contains some information that the other doesn't, and annual revisions are usually slight. So, over the last 20 years, I've found that buying one almanac every other year and switching back and forth between the two yields the best data-to-dollar ratio.

From space to sports, politics to postage, discoveries to disasters (you get the idea), either book will answer thousands of questions, settle hundreds of arguments, give you background details on scores of newspaper articles, and provide dozens of hours of browsing pleasure. Keep it next to the john for entertainment. —Randy Alfred

Information Please Almanac
(The Answer Book)
Theodore B. Dolmatch, Editor
Annual; 1000 pp.
$3.95 postpaid from:
Simon and Schuster
Attn: Order Department
1230 Avenue of the Americas
New York, NY 10020
or Whole Earth Household Store

The World Almanac and Book of Facts
George DeLury, Editor
Annual; 1000 pp.
$4.50 postpaid from:
Newspaper Enterprise Association
200 Park Avenue
New York, NY 10017
or Whole Earth Household Store

•

Teen-Age Spending

Teen-age spending in 1978 reached $32.2 billion, almost 10% higher than in 1977, reported the Rand Youth Poll.
—Information Please

NTIS

The National Technical Information Service (NTIS) of the U.S. Department of Commerce is the information storage and dissemination machine of the U.S. Government's massive scientific community. Subjects regularly covered in NTIS publications include energy and environment, NASA and aerospace, government-developed computer software, and technical political news from other countries. Many of the technical books reviewed in our Soft Tech and Land Use sections come from NTIS. Their inventory is so huge that their general catalog describes product lines, not individual items. From that you might choose to order their Energy catalog, which lists energy-related publications; or one of their monthly Tech Notes, a series of scan sheets on new developments in applied technology; or one of the NTIS abstract newsletters, which reviews new publications on technical subjects.

Finally, NTIS keeps dial-in bibliographic computer-search files. A custom-made computer search costs $100 or more; not cheap but much less arduous than poring through the reference lists yourself. For $30 each you can send for one of NTIS's "Greatest Hits" searches on often-requested topics. Their book, **Currently Published Searches** *has the details on all computer-based reference.*

All of the above are just NTIS' methods for pinpointing the exact book or manual or pamphlet you need; then you have to order that. But in many cases, the information is available nowhere else; and knowing the range of what's been written about a technical subject is often as important as reading any one book. Most NTIS publications are available on microfiche. —Art Kleiner
[Suggested by Chuck Missar]

Finding Facts Fast

A basic handbook for laymen it has beautiful 2 and 3 page descriptions of how to treat hundreds of problems in research from very elemental to very advanced levels. From "Finding the Right Library" to "Government as an Information Source" to "Oral History Collections" and "Obtaining Out-of-Print Books." Every time I get lost in the world of information I use Todd to ground me. (See **Raising Hell**, *p. 395.)* —Richard Green

Finding Facts Fast
(How to Find Out What You Want to Know Immediately)
Allen Todd
1972, 1979; 121 pp.
$3.95 postpaid from:
Ten Speed Press
900 Modoc Street
Berkeley, CA 94707
or Whole Earth Household Store

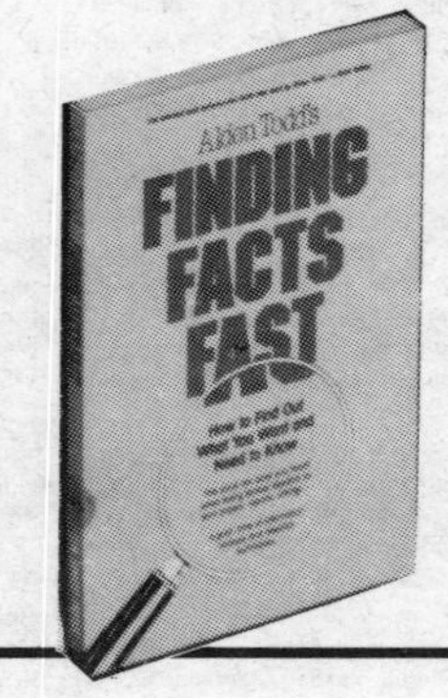

Help

This is a new breed of almanac, to be distinguished from the general-reference, astrological, planting, or fun-to-read types. **Help** *is a consumer almanac, and it's well named indeed. Every bit of information in it will help you deal with big government or big business — abuses to be wary of, how to report them, how to get more help, how to find and choose lesser evils, or how to opt out altogether.*

If the sections on spending wisely don't help, there's info on better jobs, better banking, lower taxes, and government financial assistance. And if the data on the hazards of food, clothing, cosmetics, wiring, travel, etc., don't keep you alive, **Help** *will at least steer your survivors clear of funeral frauds.*

Taken as a whole, this is a necessarily depressing catalog of all the ways we're all being ripped off, but the details and advice in each individual section will save you from the worst. —Randy Alfred

Help
(The Indispensable Almanac of Consumer Information)
Arthur E. Rowse, Editor
Annual; 600 pp.
$9.95 postpaid from:
Consumer News
813 National Press Bldg.
Washington, DC 20045
or Whole Earth Household Store

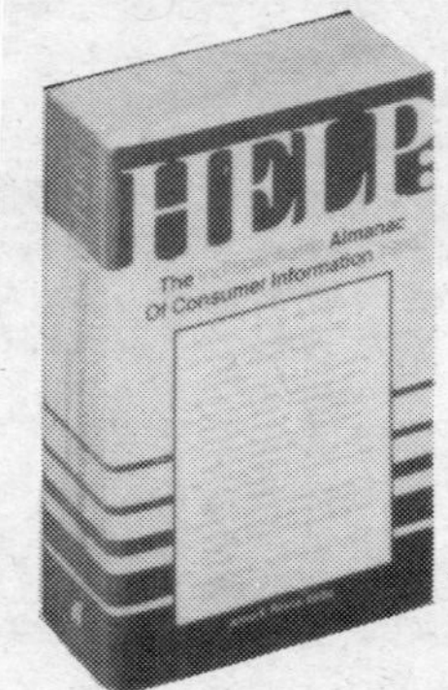

RATING THE STATES ON TAXES
Where the Bite's the Biggest

State	Income Tax as Pct. of Personal Income	Sales Tax (cents)	Beer Tax (dollars)[1]	Cigarette Tax (cents)[2]	Gasoline Tax (cents)[3]	Motor Vehicle Registration Fee[4]	Real Estate Deed Tax[5]	Per-Capita Tax Burden	Overall Grade[6]
Alabama	1.20%	4¢	$16.53	12¢	7¢	$13.75	.50	$ 455	B+
Alaska	3.68	none	7.75	8	8	30.00	none	1,896	C−
Arizona	1.24	4	2.48	13	8	8.00	2.00	731	B
Arkansas	1.42	3	7.51	17.8	8.5	26.00	.55	454	D+
California	1.92	4.75	1.24	10	7	11.00	none	964	B+
Colorado	1.93	3	2.48	15	7	15.20	.05	728	B−
Connecticut	.22	7	2.50	21	11	21.00	.55	778	D−
Delaware	3.46	none	2.00	14	10	20.00	10.00	768	D−
Dist. of Colum.	3.25	5	2.25	13	11	79.00	5.00	924	F
Florida	0	4	12.40	21	8	36.50	2.05	566	D
Georgia	1.50	3	10.00	12	7.5	15.00	.50	549	B
Hawaii	2.98	4	(*)	(*)	8.5	21.06	.25	935	F
Idaho	2.11	3	4.65	9.1	9.5	30.15	none	590	C+
Illinois	1.47	4	2.17	12	7.5	30.00	.50	769	C
Indiana	1.23	4	2.95	10.5	8	12.25	none	588	A
Iowa	2.17	3	4.34	13	7	69.05	.55	701	D+
Kansas	1.30	3	6.51	11	.8	26.50	none	651	B−
Kentucky	1.59	5	2.50	3	9	15.50	.50	549	A−
Louisiana	.57	3	10.00	11	8	3.00	none	610	A−
Maine	.91	5	7.75	16	9	15.00	.55	671	D
Maryland	2.77	5	2.79	10	9	30.10	3.05	814	F
Massachusetts	3.18	5	3.30	21	8.5	7.00	1.14	903	F
Michigan	1.84	4	6.30	11	9	26.85	.55	749	D
Minnesota	3.47	4	4.00	18	9	67.75	1.10	823	F
Mississippi	.99	5	13.23	11	9	20.75	none	486	C
Missouri	1.19	3.125	1.86	9	7	25.50	none	570	A

NTIS Information Services General Catalog, 1979; 97 pp. NTIS-PR-154. Free.

The NTIS Energy Catalog (Energy Research and Energy Information Services Available from the National Technical Information Service), 1979; 14 pp. NTIS-PR-378. Free.

NTIS Tech Notes (In Computers, Electrotechnology, Energy, Engineering, Life Sciences, Sciences, Machinery, Manufacturing, Materials, Ordnance, Physical Sciences, Testing and Instrumentation). $35 each/year (12 issues), $200/year for all 12 categories.

Tech Notes Information, Brochure. NTIS-PR-365. Free.

NTIS Abstract Newsletters, Brochure. NTIS-PR-205. Free. *(There are 26 newsletters on different topics ranging from $65 to $265 yearly.)*

Current Published Searches (From the NTIS Bibliographic Data File), 1980; 144 pp. NTIS-PR-186. Free.

All from NTIS, U.S. Department of Commerce, 5285 Port Royal Road, Springfield, VA 22161.

•

In research in history, biography and events of the recent past, particularly when you are looking for printed material, you can frequently get results if you play detective and ask yourself:

Who would know?
Who would care?
Who would care enough to have put it in print?

By following this procedure, the researcher might quickly come up with conclusions like these in specific cases:

What was the dollar value of the property loss in a recent big fire, or hurricane? Because insurance companies paid the property loss claims, they cared enough to compile their loss records. And because several companies must have been involved, the total loss figure is likely to have been compiled by the trade association of insurance companies — the American Insurance Association.

•

Of all the lists of reference books available, I find the most useful and best edited is **Reference Books: A Brief Guide** (pub. by Enoch Pratt Free Library, 400 Cathedral Street, Baltimore, MD 21201). This 180-page paperback costs $2.50. If you cannot find it locally in bookstores that service a school of library science, you can order it by mail from the Enoch Pratt Free Library. New editions appear at intervals of four or five years.

Encyclopaedia Britannica

The **Britannica***'s vital statistics are impressive: 15 years in preparation, 160 lbs., 43 million words, 33,141 pages, $32 million to develop (excluding printing). Fortunately, the contents are impressive as well. Don't be put off by the high-sounding titles of the three sections into which the 30 volumes are divided — this new format works well. The Micropaedia (Ready Reference and Index) carries a comprehensive set of 102,000 shorter articles; 40,000 of these entries are cross-referenced to longer articles in the Macropaedia (Knowledge in Depth). The Propaedia (Outline of Knowledge) is a one-volume study guide which classifies human knowledge within ten categories, then subdivides the topics within those basic areas. It is a highly organized index to the information in the Micropaedia and Macropaedia — a great aid in exploring a subject in depth and on through its related fields. In fact,* **"Britannica 3"** *has been conceived as a tool for teaching oneself, in a systematic way, the range of man's accumulated knowledge. It is still the definitive reference work — a worthy successor in a proud line.*

The **Britannica** *regularly retails in a standard binding at $899 plus tax and shipping. It's better to buy them from local representatives, whom you can find in the phone book or by writing Britannica in Chicago. Besides saving shipping charges, local reps often offer promotional deals which include bookcases or other reference works.*
Yearly updates to **Britannica** *are also available at approximately $14 each.* —Doris Herrick

Encyclopaedia Britannica
1974; 33,141 pp.
(30 volumes)
$899 plus tax and and shipping
Information
free from:
Encyclopaedia Britannica
425 N. Michigan Avenue
Chicago, IL 60611

Figure 1: Roman aqueduct at Segovia, Spain, probably built under Trajan (c. AD 100-110). Still in use, the 2,700-ft. structure carries water from the Rio Frio to the city of Segovia.
↓

Earthbooks Lending Library

How to borrow books that aren't in your public library — join this private mail order library and rent the books for a dollar each. They stock good books (many of our titles) and let you buy the book if you really like it (the rent is deducted from the price). They're nice to deal with, and they've created a world-wide community out of their membership. —Art Kleiner

Earthbooks Lending Library
Catalog
$1
Mini catalog
free
Lifetime membership
$5

all from:
Earthbooks
Lending Library
Allegheny Branch
Box 556
Harmony, PA 16037
or
Northern Rockies Branch
Sweet, ID 83670

Inter-library loan

You don't have to buy any of the books listed in our **Catalog.** Your local library can borrow any book they do not carry through the *inter-library loan system.* Many people are not aware of this service. Thelma Percy, our local librarian says often a person will come in, ask for a book, and she'll reply, "We don't have it, but we can get it for you."

"You can?"

You may have to wait a few weeks and pay postage, but it's a way to see books you're not sure of or can't afford. An outstanding service of the American library system, which, as Mrs. Percy says, is the best in the world.

—Lloyd Kahn

The Federal Information Center

For once (I'm glad to say) there is a governmental agency that knows what it is doing. These people are so fast at finding information that I have been unable to receive their answer . . . I was so flabbergasted. They are fast, extremely courteous, and accurate. This is like a phone-in **Whole Earth Catalog.** One time I called the Los Angeles City Hall to find out where the county was going to present their sewer proposal to the South Coast Regional Planning Commission (whew!). After being transferred around about twenty times I gave up and called the FIC . . . BINGO, they had it. They will frequently take your number and, after researching a question, call you right back. Saves on the phone bill. I think they deserve peonies of praise. Write to General Services Administration, Washington, DC 20405 for brochure giving FIC office nearest you.

Scott Bryson
Malibu, CA

They've often answered my vague questions with specific answers that targeted right in on the information that I couldn't articulate I needed. —Art Kleiner

Library Journal

Simply the best periodical on books in America. Best reviews, widest coverage, least nonsense. To stay current in any field I'd call it essential. —SB

Library Journal
John N. Berry III, Editor
$27 /year (22 issues)
from:
Library Journal
R.R. Bowker Company
Subscription Department
P.O. Box 67
Whitinsville, MA 01588

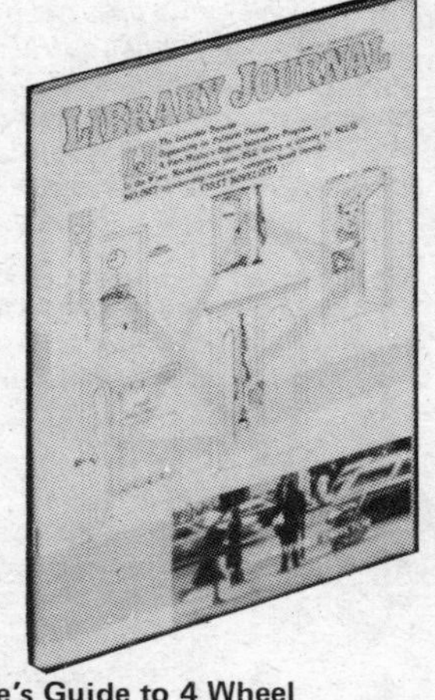

•

Hampton, William. **Everyone's Guide to 4 Wheel Drive.** Contemporary Bks. Jun. 1980. illus. index. LC 79-8755. $9.95; pap. $4.95.

This book is aimed at the person buying his or her first vehicle and considering the merits of four-wheel drive. However, parts of it would be very useful even to the experienced driver. The book is flawed by many trite or obvious statements and the text doesn't set any new literary standards. As an example: "But the first time you slide behind the wheel of that four wheelin' rig and head out with those four wheels pawing the ground. . . ." In spite of these problems, the book is recommended for public libraries, as there is little other material on the subject. — *Charles M. Falco,* **Midwest Antique & Classic Motorcycle News,** *Hinckley, IL.*

•

Denk, Roland & Anne Kimball, eds. **The Complete Sailing Handbook.** Mayflower Bks. Jun. 1980. 344p. fwd. by Richard Henderson, illus., some color, bibliog. index. ISBN 0-8317-1600-2. $29.95.

This very attractive book, first published in Germany in 1976, is a fine all-purpose encyclopedia of sailing for the novice as well as the avid sailor. It compares quite favorably with **The New Glenans Sailing Manual** (**LJ** 2/1/79), and it has many more color photographs and diagrams than that book. In format and appearance it is not unlike Richard Creagh-Osborne's **This Is Racing** (**LJ** 6/15/77). Included is a good chapter on the relatively new sport of windsurfing, which began in the United States and has reached its greatest popularity in Europe. A little expensive for smaller libraries, but nevertheless a worthwhile purchase for those libraries serving sailing enthusiasts. — *John Kenny, San Francisco P.L.*

Science Books & Films

Published by American Association for the Advancement of Science (the people who publish **Science**, *p. 33), most of the reviews are specific and quite nitty-gritty; if they don't like a book they often cite better books on the same subject. It reviews books right on down to kindergarten level; very helpful in locating non-anthropomorphic, factual, logical, and withal delightful books for young ones.* —John Lord

Science Books & Films
$17.50 /year (5 issues)
from:
Science Books & Films
1515 Massachusetts Ave
Avenue N.W.
Washington, DC 20005

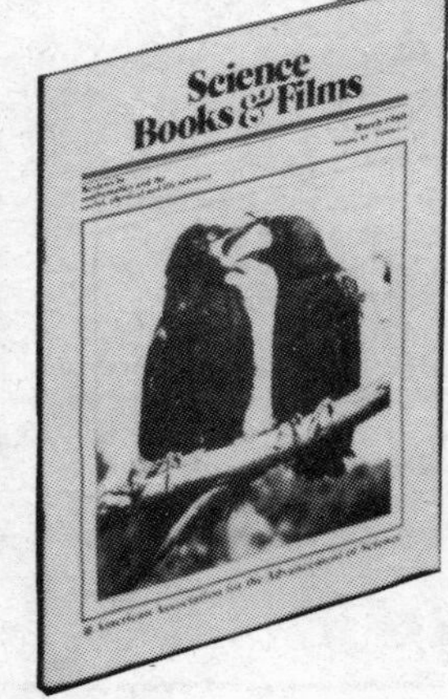

•

Philosophy and Related Disciplines

120 Knowledge, Cause, and Purpose

Bateson, Gregory. **Mind and Nature: A Necessary Unity.** (Illus.) NY: Dutton, 1979, xii+238pp. $11.95. 78-14796. ISBN 0-525-15590-2. Glossary; Index; C.I.P.

C-P★★ **Mind and Nature** should be read by every student of philosophy and life sciences. The concepts, however, cannot be assimilated by casual reading. Bateson's avowed task is to picture the world (Nature) as it is unified in its "mental aspects" (Mind), but his definition of "mind" radically expands the conventional one. When he asks, epistemologically, "How can we know anything?," "we" includes starfish and forests, and "know" incorporates how to grow into five-way symmetry and how to survive a forest fire. The chapter "Every Schoolboy Knows" elucidates 16 concepts that many schoolboys' professors know only slightly. Other chapters explore multiple versions of the world and relationships, stochastic processes, and the differentiation between classification (idea coding) and processes. Concepts are developed to project Bateson's grand premise, although it is a challenge to keep abreast of the development and to grasp the premise. The last chapter, "So What?" is a repeated critique of fragments of a conversation with his daughter. Among them: "Daughter: 'So what? Why write the book?' Father: '. . . a feeling that if we are all going down to the sea like lemmings, there should be at least one lemming taking notes and saying, "I told you so." . . .' Daughter: 'I think you are talking nonsense, Daddy. . . Nobody is going to buy a book by a sardonic lemming.' " This sardonic lemming may not stem the tide, but his notes will stimulate numbers of seldom-used nerve synapses to function. —William B. Peck

•

Blassingame, Wyatt. **Wonders of Crows.** (Illus.) NY: Dodd, Mead, 1979. 96pp. $5.95. 78-21633. ISBN 0-396-07649-1. Index; C.I.P.

EI-EA-JH★★ This attractive little book, with excellent black-and-white photographs, could serve as an introduction to the bird world for children. Their attention will be captured by many anecdotes about pet crows. Most of these emphasize the crow's intelligence, occasionally its seeming stupidity. Imprinting, courtship, flocking, reaction to hunters, migrant and nonmigrant populations are all described well. Experiments by Lorenz and others and a drawing and brief account of *Archaeopteryx* give an idea of the scientific method. Such words as "rookery" and "ravenous" are a heritage of our long acquaintance with corvids. The many variations of the basic "caw" of the crow are explained as signals. The author introduces the concept of ecology through the crow as a scavenger, white grub eater and corn puller. A brief description of all species and subspecies of North American corvids is interesting, but the Latin trinomials seem out of place here.

—Sidney Hyde

Government Printing Office

The best buys in books in the United States are from the U.S. Government, which prints all manner of fascinating non-fiction. A good starting point is the brochure **A Consumer's Guide to Federal Periodicals,** *which is free and comes with an order form (and a list of Government Bookstores around the country). It also lists free bibliographies available on a huge range of topic areas, from Accident Prevention to Food Storage to Tax Appeals to Foreign Languages to Graphic Arts to Telecommunications. There's also a free catalog of government periodicals (Price List No. 36), and another for posters, charts and pictures (No. SB-057). For keeping up with totality, there's the massive* **Monthly Catalog of Government Publications** *($65/year). For highest interest, there's the free monthly catalog* **Selected U.S. Government Publications,** *which contains only the new and consistently popular items. All from: Superintendent of Documents, U.S. Government Printing Office, Washington, DC 20402.* —Art Kleiner

Demco Library Supplies

After 12 years of handling books I've come to understand and appreciate library hardware — card catalog drawers, bookends, magazine protective covers, book trucks, book repair fabric, record-keeping cards. Noble stuff, right up there with firemen's hats as far as I'm concerned. Some of this stuff might be handy for a home library. —SB

Demco
Catalog
free from:
Demco
Box 7488
Madison, WI 53707

Wood Book Display Table

Promote new titles and best-sellers with both display table and framed bulletin board mounted in the center. Use space wisely. Table has room for books on both sides.

Finish	Price
Light Maple	$349
Walnut	349
Light Oak	349
Medium Oak	349

← **Record/Picture-Book Shelving**

Four shelves with 20 compartments create storage for records and large picture-books awaiting processing. More than 400 records can be placed in this shelving unit. 63" high, 36" wide, 11-3/4" deep (160cm x 91.4cm x 28.5cm). 115 lbs., $86.50

New key lock assembly makes units easy to assemble or take apart for storage. Denser particle board provides greater strength and durability.

THE RISING SUN
NEIGHBORHOOD NEWSLETTER

Stephanie was saying one reason condoms don't work is one size doesn't fit all — sometimes they're too large and they fall off and stuff like that, so they should actually be available in sizes like large, extra large and enormous — even as with olives, there should be no small sizes — then we started thinking of various names for the sizes such as delicious, delightful and incredible; gosh, o my god and I don't believe it; huge, gigantic and beyond human imagining — and then a male human being walked into the room and Stephanie blushed and quickly went back to her office to write about birth control for *The Next Whole Earth Catalog*. (Steph got the size idea from Barbara Seaman, no shit.)

SURFACE BARRIER

conduction band
conduction e
ionized donors
energy gap (E
valence band

Energy diagram of a surface barrier as employed in an n-t semiconductor. W = Fermi le ϵ = highest energy level of surf state filled by electrons wher surface is electrically neutral; energy of bottom of conduct band; E_v = energy of top of valence band.

heather
Calluna vulgaris

opossum
Didelphis marsupialis

The American Heritage Dictionary of the English Language

The most interesting and usable English dictionary in print. Bowker's outstanding **Dictionary Buying Guide** *(1977; $16.50 postpaid from R.R. Bowker Company, Fulfillment Department, P.O. Box 1807, Ann Arbor, MI 48106) says:*

The American Heritage Dictionary of the English Language, first published in 1969, is the newest general dictionary of substance on the American scene. In many ways it is an innovative dictionary which has caused the same sort of lexicographical waves that the now tired **American College Dictionary** did 30 years ago. Among **American Heritage**'s outstanding qualities are "readability" (not usually associated with dictionaries) and the absence of excessive dictionary symbols and abbreviations (or "dictionary shorthand"), excellent typography and inviting format, clear and up-to-date treatment of the 155,000 total vocabulary which derived from a computer sample of one million words, and provision of some 4,000 interesting and informative graphics, including many photographs and locator maps of countries.

In the back of the dictionary is a highly valuable etymological appendix of Indo-European word roots, where you learn the rich history of any word you are taking seriously. At the root of "whole," for example, is "kailo," which leads forward and back to words meaning "healthy" and "holy."

An advantage of the dictionary is currency and boldness in the accurate coverage of slang, including dirty words. I well recall being upset as a child when I tried to look up such words as "fuck" in the dictionary, found that they didn't exist, and began to wonder if I didn't exist. Oddly enough, only the unabridged editions of **The American Heritage Dictionary** *have the naughty words. Happily the abridged editions have the word root appendix; unhappily, it is also abridged.*

Of the seven or so editions available, I recommend only three. The "New College Edition" is the best of the unabridged; it is smaller (handier) and cheaper than the deluxe and large format editions, but has all the same contents and illustrations, even a thumb index. There are two paperback editions, both abridged (55,000 entries instead of 155,000), identical in content but different in size, binding and price. For rare use I'd take the cheap one, for constant desk reference the sturdier one.
—SB

[Suggested by Clifford Barney, Marilyn Green and Stephanie Mills]

health·ful (hĕlth'fəl) *adj.* **1.** Conducive to good health. **2.** Healthy. —**health'ful·ly** *adv.*
health·y (hĕl'thē) *adj.* **-ier, -iest. 1.** Possessing good health. **2.** Conducive to good health; healthful. **3.** Indicative of a constructive frame of mind: *a healthy attitude.* **4.** Sizable; considerable: *a healthy portion.* —**health'i·ly** *adv.* —**health'i·ness** *n.*
heap (hēp) *n.* **1.** A group of things haphazardly gathered; a pile. **2.** Often **heaps.** A great deal; lots. —*v.* **1.** To put or throw in a heap. **2.** To fill to overflowing. [< OE *hēap.*]
heart-rend·ing (härt'rĕn'dĭng) *adj.* Causing anguish or deep sympathy.
heart·sick (härt'sĭk') *adj.* Profoundly disappointed; despondent; unhappy.
heart·strings (härt'strĭngz') *pl.n.* The deepest feelings or affections.
heart-to-heart (härt'tə-härt') *adj.* Personal and candid.
heart·y (här'tē) *adj.* **-ier, -iest. 1.** Expressed with warmth of feeling; exuberant. **2.** Complete or thorough. **3.** Vigorous; robust. **4.** Nourishing. —**heart'i·ly** *adv.*

—$2.25 edition life size

health·ful (hĕlth'fəl) *adj.* **1.** Conducive to good health. **2.** Healthy. —**health'ful·ly** *adv.*
health·y (hĕl'thē) *adj.* **-ier, -iest. 1.** Possessing good health. **2.** Conducive to good health; healthful. **3.** Indicative of a constructive frame of mind: *a healthy attitude.* **4.** Sizable; considerable: *a healthy portion.* —**health'i·ly** *adv.* —**health'i·ness** *n.*
heap (hēp) *n.* **1.** A group of things haphazardly gathered; a pile. **2.** Often **heaps.** A great deal; lots. —*v.* **1.** To put or throw in a heap. **2.** To fill to overflowing. [< OE *hēap.*]
heart-rend·ing (härt'rĕn'dĭng) *adj.* Causing anguish or deep sympathy.
heart·sick (härt'sĭk') *adj.* Profoundly disappointed; despondent; unhappy.
heart·strings (härt'strĭngz') *pl.n.* The deepest feelings or affections.
heart-to-heart (härt'tə-härt') *adj.* Personal and candid.
heart·y (här'tē) *adj.* **-ier, -iest. 1.** Expressed with warmth of feeling; exuberant. **2.** Complete or thorough. **3.** Vigorous; robust. **4.** Nourishing. —**heart'i·ly** *adv.*

—$3.95 edition life size

heart·sick (härt'sĭk') *adj.* Sick at heart; profoundly disappointed; despondent. —**heart'sick'ness** *n.*
heart-strick·en (härt'strĭk'ən) *adj.* Also **heart-struck** (-strŭk'). Overwhelmed with grief, dismay, or remorse.
heart·strings (härt'strĭngz') *pl.n.* **1.** The deepest feelings or affections. Often used facetiously: *a performance geared to tug at the heartstrings.* **2.** In notions of anatomy held before the 17th century, sinews and tendons bracing and sustaining the heart.
heart-to-heart (härt'tə-härt') *adj.* Personal and candid; frank.

—New College Edition

American Heritage Dictionary of the English Language

New College Edition
William Morris, Editor
1969, 1978; 1555 pp.

$11.95 postpaid from:
Houghton Mifflin Company
Wayside Road
Burlington, MA 01803
or Whole Earth Household Store

Paperback Edition
Peter Davies, Editor
1969, 1976; 820 pp.
$3.95 postpaid

Small Paperback Edition
Peter Davies, Editor
1969, 1979; 820 pp.
$2.25 postpaid

both from:
Dell Publishing Company
1 Dag Hammerskjold Plaza
245 East 47th Street
New York, NY 10017
or Whole Earth Household Store

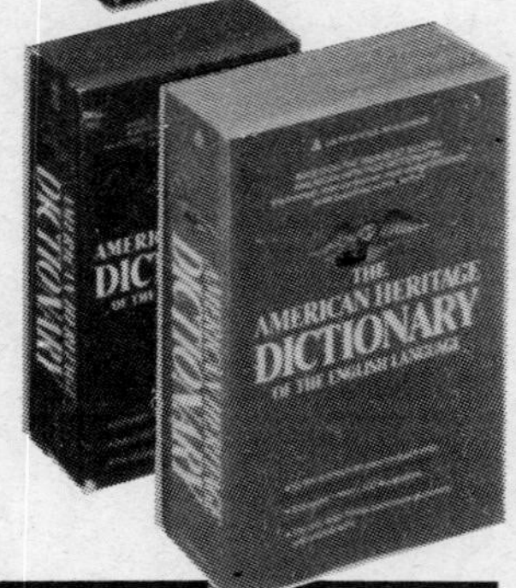

Dictionary of Scientific and Technical Terms

*As technology becomes more complex, the language involved is increasingly laced with specialized words. Web_ r's isn't much help with these. McGraw-Hill's is. As might be expected, you sometimes have to look up the words in the given definition too before you get the meaning, e.g., "***restiform body:** *See interior cerebellar peduncle." Generally, though, the book is concise, clear, well illustrated, and easy to read. The discipline generating the word is indicated which makes it easy to tell where you can find out more about the subject in the definition. And the range of subject matter just has to be seen to be believed! Even as a technocrat, I've never before felt so strongly the immensity of technology. Insist your library get one.*
—J. Baldwin

McGraw-Hill Dictionary of Scientific and Technical Terms

Daniel N. Lapedes, Editor
1960, 1978; 1840 pp.
2nd Edition

$42.50 postpaid from:
McGraw-Hill Book Company
Princeton Road
Hightstown, NJ 08520
or Whole Earth Household Store

Origins

AT LAST BACK IN PRINT, this classic dictionary of word origins is so standard a text among professional and amateur wordcrafters that it is usually referred to personally — "Partridge."
—SB

Origins

(A Short Etymological Dictionary of Modern English)
Eric Partridge
1958, 1977; 970 pp.

$39.95 postpaid from:
MacMillan Publishing Company
Order Department
Front and Brown Streets
Riverside, NJ 08075
or Whole Earth Household Store

•

whole, whence **wholly**—cf **whole cloth (out of), wholemeal, wholesale, wholesome; hail,** v, and **hale,** adj; **heal** (whence **healer** and pa, vn **healing**)—**health,** whence **healthful, healthless** (obsol), **healthy** (whence **healthiness**).

1. The n *whole* derives from the adj *whole,* ME *hole* (*hoole*), earlier *hale,* OE *hāl,* sound (complete), healthy: cf OFris *hēl,* OS *hēl,* OHG-MHG-G *heil,* Go *hails,* MD *hiel,* MD-D *heel,* ON *heill,* syn OSl *cělŭ,* OP *kail*ustikan, health, Gr *koilu,* the beautiful (prop, neu adj). The OGmc etym is **khailaz*; the IE, **koilos*; the IE r, **kail-,* **koil-.*

2. From *whole cloth,* a (large) uncut piece of cloth, derives (of a story, a lie) 'made *out of whole cloth*'—a sheer fabrication; *whole meal=meal* (grain coarsely ground) of *entire*-wheat; *wholesale,* goods sold in large quantities, hence the corresp adj, whence the sense 'both extensive and undiscriminating or indiscriminate'. *Wholesome* is much older; it derives from ME *holsum,* itself perh from ON *heilsamr*—cf MD *heilsam,* D *heilzaam,* G *heilsam.*

3. From ON *heill,* sound, healthy, comes ME *heil, hail,* used in greeting (cf *wassail*), whence ME *heilen, hailen,* to greet, whence 'to *hail*' or greet. With *Hail!,* cf G *Heil!* and Go *Hails!*: for 'Be *hail*' or well, 'Long Life!' But from E *hāl,* sound, healthy, comes ME *hal,* later *hale,* retained by E.

4. Akin to OE *hāl,* healthy, is OE *hǣlan,* ME *haelen, helen,* E 'to *heal*': cf the syn OFris *hēla* and OS *hēlian,* and OHG *heilēn,* to become, also to make, well, MHG-G *heilen,* to cure, Go *hailjan,* MD *heilen, hielen, helen,* MD-D *heelen.*

5. OE *hāl,* well, has derivative *hǣlth* (abstract suffix *-th*)—ME *helthe*—E *health.*

The Compact Edition of the Oxford English Dictionary

Not a bad deal for a home reference — in magnifying glass size type the entire 12-volume 1933 **OED**. *Words in literary usage, contexts shimmering down the generations.*
—SB

The Book-of-the-Month Club regularly offers the **OED** *compact edition at an incredibly reduced rate as an introductory membership premium. The last ad we saw offered it for $19.95 plus your agreement to buy four more books in the next two years. Makes joining worth it, even if you don't like book clubs. For information write to: Book-of-the-Month Club, Inc., Camp Hill, PA 17012.*
—Mimi Abrams

The Compact Edition of the Oxford English Dictionary

1971; 4116 pp.
(plus magnifying glass)

$125 postpaid from:
Oxford University Press
16-00 Pollitt Drive
Fair Lawn, NJ 07410

Evolution (evōliū·ʃən, īvōliū·ʃən). [ad. L. *ēvolūtiōn-em* (recorded in the sense 'unrolling of a book'), n. of action f. *ēvolvĕre*: see EVOLVE. Cf. Fr. *évolution.* The pronunciation (īvŏ-) is not sanctioned by any Dict., but is now somewhat common.]

I. The process of unrolling, opening out, or disengaging from an envelope.

1. The opening out or unfolding of what is wrapped up (*e.g.* a roll, a bud, etc.); *fig.* the spreading out before the mental vision (of a series of objects); the appearance in orderly succession of a long train of events. Also *concr.* 'the series of things unfolded or unrolled' (J.).

1647 H. MORE *Poems* 150 Evolution Of outward forms spread in the worlds vast spright. **1667** — *Div. Dial.* i. § 15 The whole evolution of..ages, from everlasting to everlasting, is..represented to God at once. **1678** CUDWORTH *Intell. Syst.* 878 The Periods of Divine Providence, here in this World, are commonly Longer, and the Evolutions thereof Slower. **1742** YOUNG *Nt. Th.* iv. 510 Beyond long ages, yet roll'd up in shades..What evolutions of surprising fate! **1762** — *Resignation* ii. xxxvi, Flowers..When ev'ning damps and shades descend, Their evolutions close. **1759** JOHNSON *Idler* No 70 ¶ 11 He whose task is to reap and thresh will not be contented without examining the evolution of the seed. **1843** G. S. FABER *Sacred Cal. Proph.* (1844) I. p. xv, The evolution of time has served only to confirm me in.. the honest persuasion, that, etc.

2. Emergence or protrusion from the folds of an envelope. Frequent in *Biol.*

1762 HUDSON in *Phil. Trans.* LII. 500 Our author asserts, That every Fungus is contained in an entire and perfect state..in the egg, or as it is called, the seed, and wants nothing but evolution, in order to imbibe the necessary juices. **1800** *Med. Jrnl.* III. 5, I determined to leave Nature undisturbed, to effect the evolution of the child. **1817** T. SAY *Hessian Fly*, Entom. Wks. 1859 II. 7 The specious circumstance of its evolution from the pupa itself of the destroying larva. **1887** *Gray's Anat.* (ed. Pike) 85 The first appearance of the eye consists in the protrusion or evolution from the medullary wall of the..interbrain of a vesicle.

Scott, Foresman Beginning Dictionary

Better even than the **MacMillan Dictionary for Children**, *this dictionary stands out for its conceptual grace, graphic liveliness, and wit.* **Dictionary Buying Guide** *remarks, "The* **Scott, Foresman Beginning Dictionary** *has the most impressive illustrations and design of any dictionary currently on the American market."*
—SB

Scott, Foresman Beginning Dictionary

E.L. Thorndike and Clarence Barnhart
1945, 1976; 718 pp.

$12.95 postpaid from:
Doubleday and Company
501 Franklin Avenue
Garden City, NY 11530
or Whole Earth Household Store

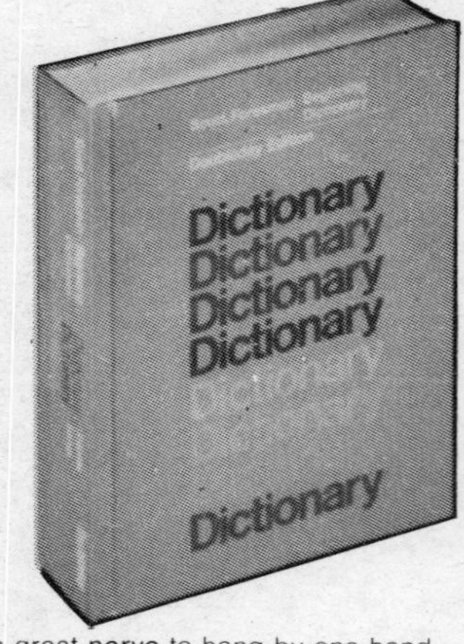

•

nerve (definition 2)—It takes great nerve to hang by one hand from an airplane.

Effective Promotion

How to Publish Community Information on an Impossibly Tight Budget

What people haven't heard about they can't decide about or take action about. Uncommunicated issues don't exist. For local broadcast on the quick and dirty and cheap, here's two quick, dirty, cheap, and excellent pamphlets of how-to.
—SB

Effective Promotion
(A Guide to Low Cost Use of Media for Community Organizations)
Michelle Cauble
1977; 22 pp.
$.50 postpaid

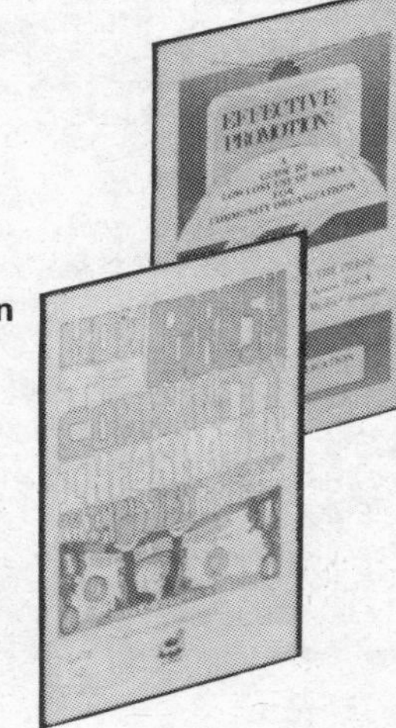

How to Publish Community Information on an Impossibly Tight Budget
Vic Pawlak
1976; 23 pp.
$.50 postpaid

both from:
Do It Now Foundation
Institute for
Chemical Survival
P.O. Box 5115
Phoenix, AZ 85010

•

In general, gaining access to media depends on your own personal development of important skills: cultivating personal contacts at newspapers and stations; working on a friendly basis with the local media professionals; learning your local media by format and audience; presenting yourself and your issue or interest in such a way as to attract, rather than distract, the media; being fully informed on the issues yourself; understanding the proper TIMING for releases, conferences, PSA's and so forth; learning what is newsworthy and interesting to the public; and — of great importance to the success of any media effort — coming on coolly, competently, and professionally, knowing what you're doing. Don't be afraid of the media . . . they rely on you for information.
—Effective Promotion

•

The biggest single mistake most people make in designing a brochure or publication is not using a standard size. Unless it is somehow a multiple or division of 8½ x 11 or 14, you will probably get ripped off. For example, a brochure that is 9½ x 12 will cost a lot more than 8½ x 14 even though it is relatively the same number of square inches of paper. This is because the company must cut up larger sheets that are also multiples of 8½ x 11 or 8½ x 14, and you pay for the wasted odd pieces. A standard size for offset paper, for example, is 23 x 35, which would cut down to 8 sheets of 8½ x 11 paper. Other types of paper have various basic sizes. Always check with your supplier before ordering odd sizes.
—How to Publish Community Information on an Impossibly Tight Budget

A Conference and Workshop Planner's Manual

The best conferences are on new subjects by new people. The worst conferences are by new people who don't know what they're doing. This straightforward text — it's basically a well-experienced checklist — can make the difference.
—SB

A Conference and Workshop Planner's Manual
Lois B. Hart and
J. Gordon Schleicher
1979; 143 pp.
$15.95 postpaid from:
AMACOM
P.O. Box 319
Saranac Lake, NY 12983
or Whole Earth
Household Store

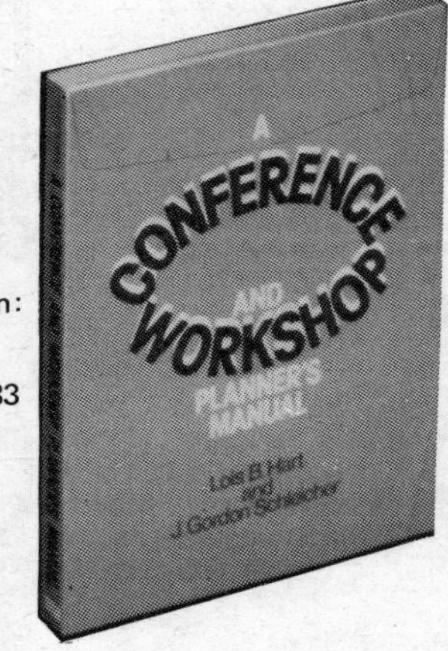

•

Follow-Up Letter to Resource Person

After the resource person has confirmed his or her willingness to participate according to the terms of the contract, you should send a follow-up letter. In this letter, you will provide the resource person with the following:

- A current agenda, including names of other speakers and their topics
- Information on housing, meals, airport pickup arrangements, directions, and maps
- Information on the design of the assigned meeting room
- Feedback from the planning committee on information the resource person sent regarding the design, required materials, or other requests
- Information on any pre-event or post-event activities
- Any required registration procedures
- Information on whether a member of program committee or a facilitator has been assigned to him or her and how contact will be made

Ask the resource person to provide:

- The signed contract, completed forms, and biographical information requested in the first letter
- Exact arrival time and requests for pickup at airport, train station, or bus depot
- Housing needs

Blackboard
Speakers Table
Mike Mike
Movie Screen
Tables Tables Tables
Mike Mike

Room setup for 30 - 50 reporters.

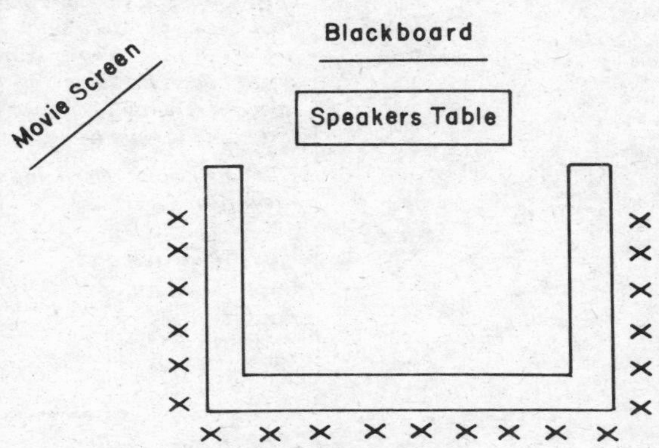

Room setup for 15 - 20 reporters

The Executive's Guide to Radio and TV Appearances

If the electronic press doesn't like you in front, and you're not skilled at meeting press, you will be disemboweled in public.

This book confers the skills to not only survive a media flash but flourish in it, educate with it. And once you do that, you'll be asked back, no matter what your message.
—SB

The Executive's Guide to Radio and TV Appearances
Michael Bland
1979, 1980; 144 pp.
$14.95 postpaid from:
Knowledge Industry Publications
Two Corporate Park Drive
White Plains, NY 10604
or Whole Earth
Household Store

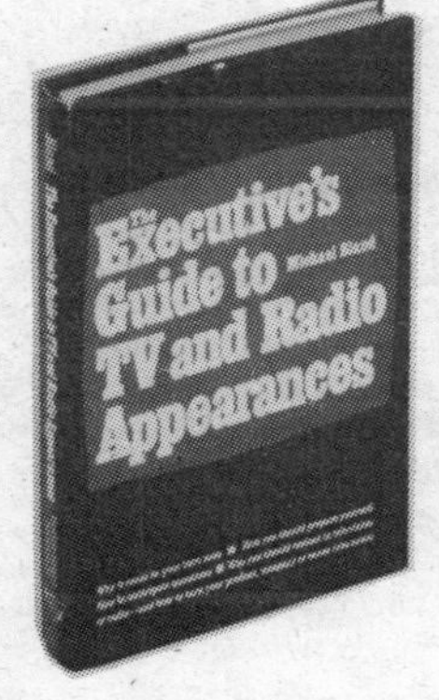

•

1. Think of something you'd like to say if you were given 15 seconds of free television time.
2. Think up the nastiest, most loaded, antipathetic question about the subject.
3. Put the two together!

Watch the pros doing it. Next time you see a politician getting away with murder, look for the techniques:

'Racial discrimination *is* a problem, I agree, and it has a bearing on what I was about to say . . .'

'I can't really answer that question without explaining some of the background . . .'

'Sure, some people say we made a mistake, but we mustn't let it cloud the real issue, which is . . .'

•

HANDLING THE INTERVIEW
Golden Rules

1. Don't let the interviewer butt in without a fight.
2. Refute any incorrect statements.
3. Don't use jargon.
4. Stay off the defensive.
5. Remember there is only *one* viewer.
6. Don't get sidetracked.

How to Be Heard

A must for anyone who ever needs to use or deal with publicity. Provides an x-ray view of the making of the news, preaches a sound ethic (be well prepared) for dealing with its purveyors; lists resources for cranking up an effective movement. Pithy, handily indexed, and full of tidbits about situations where Davids trounced Goliaths by doing their homework.
—Stephanie Mills

How to Be Heard
(Making the Media Work for You)
Ted Klein and
Fred Danzig
1974; 346 pp.
$9.95 postpaid from:
MacMillan Publishing Co.
Order Department
Front and Brown Streets
Riverside, NJ 08075
or Whole Earth
Household Store

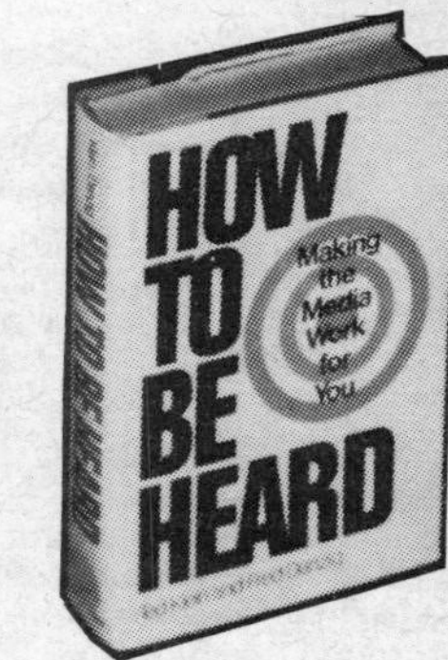

•

The papers that you deal with will be more receptive to your stories if you supply useful information in complete form. Your press release should include a name, address, and telephone number for the reporter's follow-up questions. If possible, provide alternate names and numbers. If the contact named on your release is not able to be at that number for periods of time, arrange to have another person receive the call and supply information, or find out the needed information and relay it to the reporter. Promptly. Reporters who are racing deadlines — and you must assume that they *always* are racing deadlines — do not like to be told that the person listed as the contact isn't around and won't be back for a few hours or will call back tomorrow.

The Craft of Interviewing

Not a brilliant book but plenty competent enough to vastly improve the level of most dumb-question-dumb-answer published conversation. It also helps if interviewers have studied and done a bit of field anthropology.

If you find yourself being an interviewee, these skills are even more important, since it's your ass on the line.
—SB

The Craft of Interviewing
John Brady
1976, 1977; 244 pp.
$3.95 postpaid from:
Random House,
455 Hahn Road
Westminster, MD 21157
or Whole Earth
Household Store

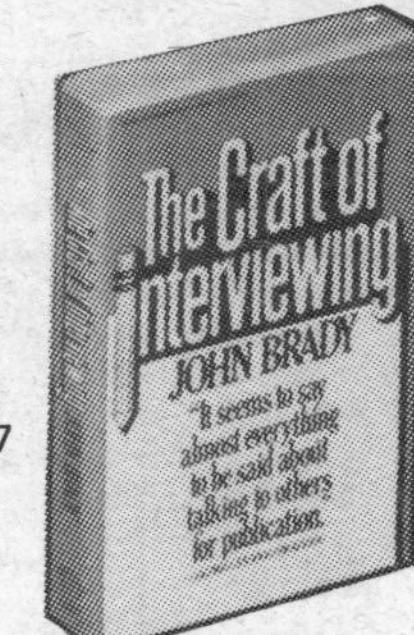

•

"I think it is very important for a person to do his homework," explains Manchester. "There's nothing more insulting than to ask a man, like a President of the United States, a question that he's answered many times before. Then he's quite likely to dismiss you. So what you want to ask are the questions he's never been asked before, questions that show that you have a great familiarity with his life. And then he's likely to respect you and be interested in the exchange, the colloquy." In preparing for his initial interview, Manchester went through a list of the appointments that President Kennedy had made with special assistants and cabinet advisers. He found that over 80 percent of them were within a few years of the President's age. So he asked Kennedy if he were a "generation chauvinist." "Now, he'd never thought of this," says Manchester, "but he liked the idea and he played with it, and it was entertaining for him. A really first-rate interview with an articulate man can be fascinating for him. And if he is fascinated, then it will go on and you will learn more from him. It all depends on how much time you spend in advance."

THE RISING SUN
NEIGHBORHOOD NEWSLETTER

There was a guy I grew up knowing and I thought his main handicap was having a club foot and then years later I found out his main handicap was that he was a homosexual in an isolated small town where everyone thought homosexuality didn't exist and was horrible if it did and he agreed. Although I still don't know if that was his main handicap — maybe he saw everything in four dimensions all the time without drugs or anyone to talk about it, or maybe he saw seven other colors than anyone else and his favorite made his eyes hurt almost, but not quite, unbearably or maybe he couldn't see cars but could only hear them so spent a lot of time being scared but he wasn't sure what of.

How to Do Leaflets, Newsletters and Newspapers

There's no leverage like local publishing — it's cheap, fast, relatively easy, and outrageously effective if done well. In this booklet is all you need to do it well. (Technically, at least; the rest is character.) The booklet is its own best demonstration. I wish I'd had it when we started.

—SB

•

Editing is mostly a matter of reading and watching your own reactions. Here are some questions to ask yourself about an article which you are editing:

Did you understand it all the way through? If you're confused for a while and only start to get the idea at the end, some facts or ideas are probably in the wrong order. A less sympathetic reader won't take the trouble to figure out what the story means. Did you get confused because the writer made you think s/he was going to talk about one thing, and ended up talking about another?

Are there extra words that don't sound like normal speech? If someone said to you, "The MBTA announced it will begin a new evening security program," that would sound pretty strange. "More police will patrol subway stations after 5:00 PM." is simpler and gives real information.

How to Do Leaflets, Newsletters and Newspapers
Nancy Brigham
1975; 44 pp.

$2.45 postpaid from:
Boston Community School
10 West Street
Boston, MA 02111
or Whole Earth Household Store

Too much body type
½ body type

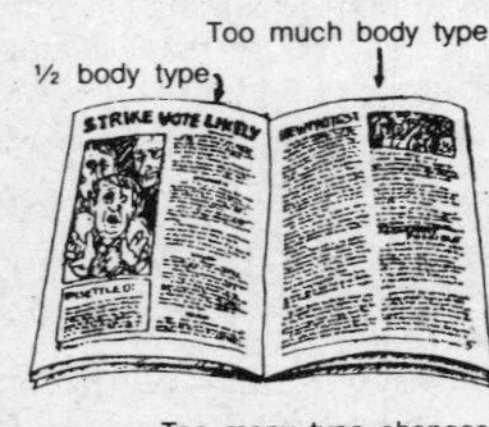

Too many type changes
Column too wide

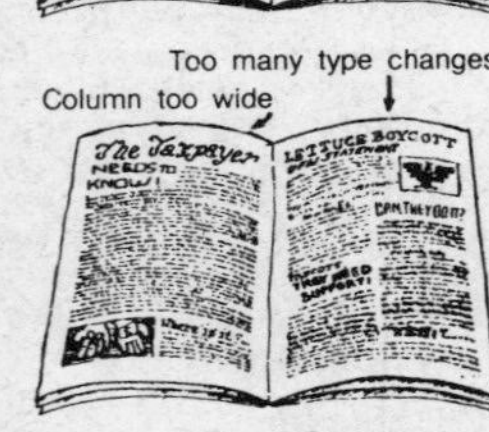

Bad use of space — Better

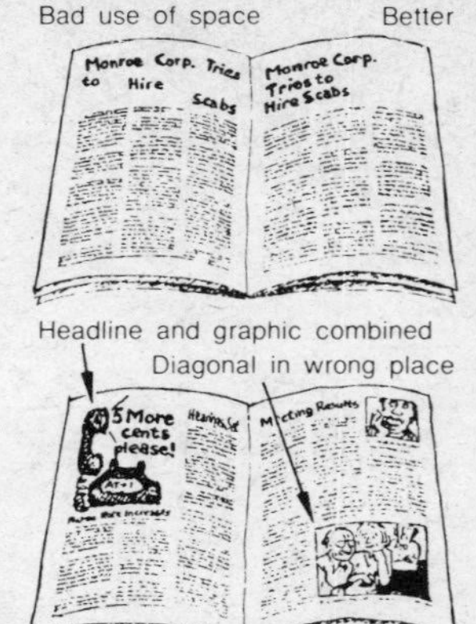

Headline and graphic combined
Diagonal in wrong place

Diagonal in right place
Competing headlines

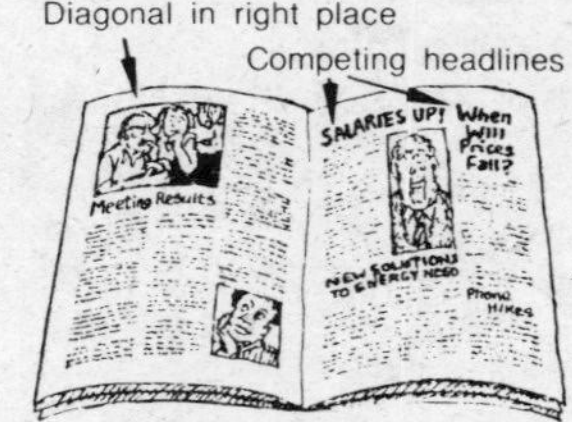

Graphic in the middle of type columns creates confusion

Confusion: would you start computer article here or here?

Interruption: big jump from bottom to top of page to finish article
Messiness

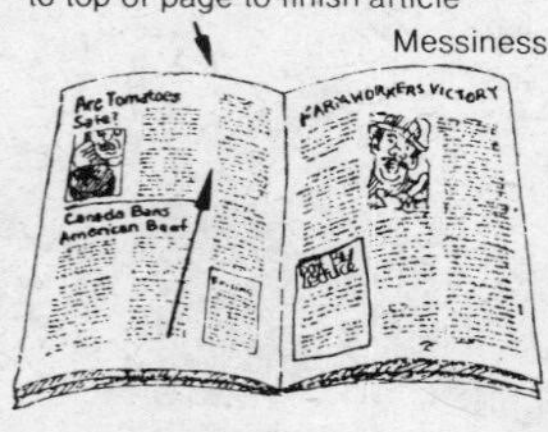

Spanish mayors protest against nuclear plant

In brief:

Nucleares No Gracias

6000 protest nuclear plant

No Nuclear News

A shard of the Boston Clamshell Coalition, **No Nuclear News** *describes itself as "a participatory newsclipping service in the form of a monthly paper." The idea is that people around the world send in local news clips on nuclear issues,* **NNN** *pastes them up, and the movement gets a clear look at how it's doing. People who are regular in sending clips get a free subscription. Pretty neat.*

—SB

No Nuclear News
$6/year (10-12 issues) from:
Boston Clamshell Coalition
595 Massachusetts Avenue
Cambridge, MA 02139

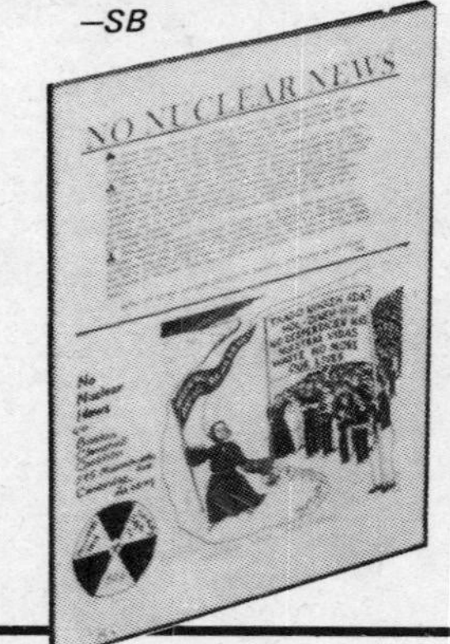

Designing with Type

Whether it's a poster or a book, designers have to work with words. Letters come in all shapes and sizes, each with its own personality and charm. But they all have the same purpose — transferring ideas and information.

Legibility and impact are not accidental. Starting with alphabetical history, families of type and units of measurement, and finishing up with leading and copy fitting, the clear examples in this book will add new meaning to the words you see. —Kathleen O'Neill

Designing with Type
(A Basic Course in Typography)
James Craig
1971, 1980; 175 pp.
2nd Edition

$15.95 postpaid from:
Watson-Guptill Publications
2160 Patterson Street
Cincinnati, OH 45214
or Whole Earth Household Store

Designing with type

Words set in lowercase have a more distinct outline and are therefore more quickly recognizable. →

HOW DO WE READ?

how do we read?

For Two Celebrity Reps, It's a War of Nerves

PROVINCETOWN ADVOCATE
Benson Bares Fire Fault Report
SCRAM Suit In Hearing Monday
Nude Ban Demonstration Saturday

The newspaper at left chooses a large, bold headline style, and breaks up the type page by the use of subheads and excerpts from the article set in a smaller display type. This is a useful alternative when pictures are lacking. At right, a good example of how to use one traditional type style imaginatively in headlines to keep a varied but unified appearance.

How to Produce a Small Newspaper

I can't imagine why anyone would dream of starting a small restaurant or a small bookstore when it's possible to start or take over or work for a small newspaper. As art and news media go, nothing else can give you as much freedom, creativity, responsibility, effectiveness, contact, and home-town adventure.

This fine book tells all and not a bit more. Picked up a few tips myself.

—SB

How to Produce a Small Newspaper
Editors of the Harvard Post
1977; 158 pp.

$5.95 postpaid from:
Harvard Common Press
The Common
Harvard, MA 01451
or Whole Earth Household Store

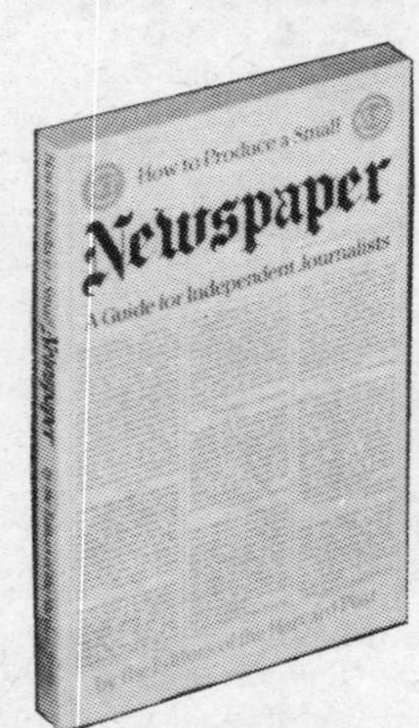

The Magazine

Many people dream of starting their own magazine. If your dreams get past this book, they're probably worth pursuing. The book's oriented to Madison Avenue magazines which hope to make lots of money some day; so small press publishers may justifiably get impatient with all the discussion of selling ad space and surveying readers. And it's almost useless on graphics (try **Editing by Design** *instead). But it has an uncommonly accurate picture of the financial priorities and ambiance of big-time print media, much of which is useful for small-time as well.* —Art Kleiner

It occurs to me this book might be of great interest to magazine readers. —SB

•

A magazine has a lifetime — ten, twenty, or fifty years. (Witness the death of the original **Life, Look,** and **Saturday Evening Post.**) The editor must constantly infuse the magazine with the dynamism that will keep readers stimulated. There must always be an atmosphere of excitement in the magazine — in its graphics and in its writing. Many readers subscribe to magazines out of force of habit, year after year. Compare them to the readers who anxiously await each issue. The successful editor is the one who innovates, who takes chances all the time.

•

The would-be editor or magazine writer can begin by becoming familiar with the local city magazine. What may begin as a small free-lance assignment can often lead to a full-time editorial job. These staffs function very much like any other magazine but often rely on local "stringers" (part-time reporters) for leads and ideas for new articles. As a training ground for editors, the city magazine is excellent, and it does not require the writer to leave his or her home and relocate to New York to find quality-magazine employment.

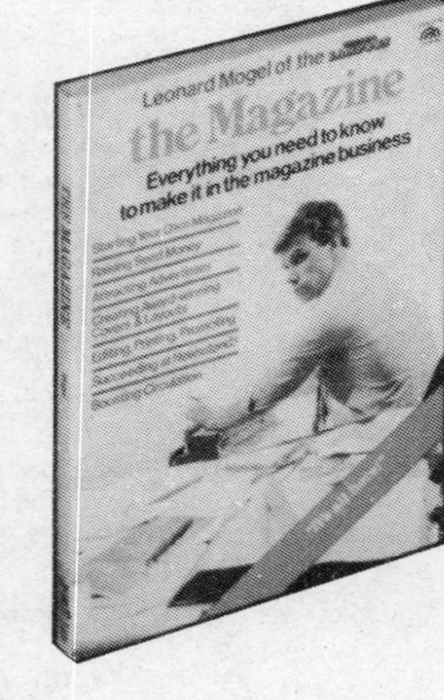

The Magazine
(Everything you need to know to make it in the magazine business)
Leonard Mogel
1979; 192 pp.

$7.95 postpaid from:
Prentice-Hall, Inc.
Box 500
Englewood Cliffs, NJ 07632
or Whole Earth Household Store

Production for the Graphic Designer

Getting your finally-published work back from the printer can often be disappointing. Explaining what you want is as frustrating as figuring out what went wrong.

Find out what the printer means by "gripper edge," "work and tumble," and "ghosting," and which tools will save you time, and what process will reproduce your work best. —Kathleen O'Neill

Production for the Graphic Designer
James Craig
1974; 207 pp.

$21.95 postpaid from:
Watson-Guptill Publications
2160 Patterson Street
Cincinnati, OH 45214
or Whole Earth Household Store

Ink hickies

Moiré caused by rescreening a halftone

Scaling art using a diagonal line →

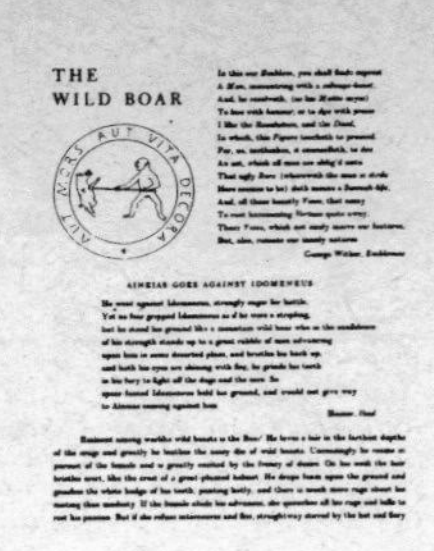

A title page in complete harmony with the text. Design by Joseph Blumenthal.

Bookmaking

This peerless book heads off all the common mistakes of fragmented publishing crafts by teaching the whole of bookmaking — editing, design and production — as a single discipline. It's the book I learned from, which may account for the chutzpah with which the original **Whole Earth Catalog** *sprang whole and self-published into the world.*

Not least, **Bookmaking** *is exemplary, is very well made itself. I'm glad author Lee and publisher Bowker came out with a brand new second edition. A one-step shop for making effective sense in print.* —SB

Bookmaking
(The illustrated guide to design/production/editing)
Marshall Lee
1965, 1979; 485 pp.
2nd Edition

$25 postpaid from:
R.R. Bowker Company
Fulfillment Department
P.O. Box 1807
Ann Arbor, MI 48106

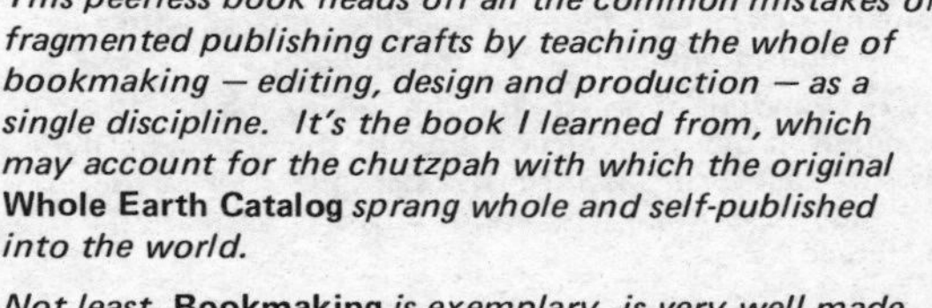

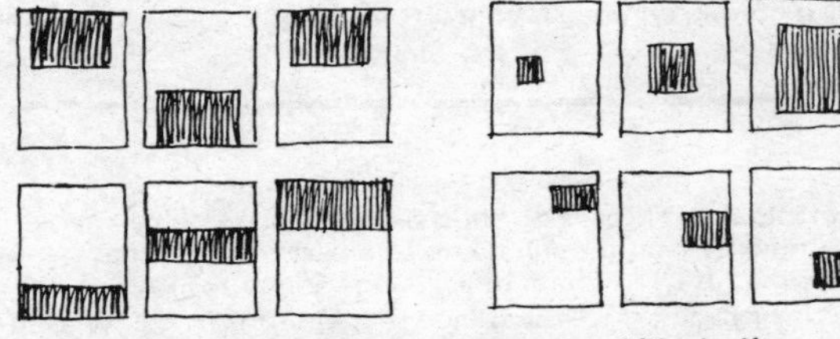

Thought must be given to the sequence of illustration position and size, as well as to the layout of each spread. Variety, rhythm, and order should be planned in terms of the whole book — which has a consecutive order more like a motion picture than a series of separate frames. For example, illustrations might be placed alternately at top and bottom, or they might repeat a sequence of bottom, middle, top, etc.

↓

Long lines of type, especially when well leaded, look graceful — just as tall, slender models do. But the models are too skinny for anything but modeling, and long lines of type are not efficient for reading.

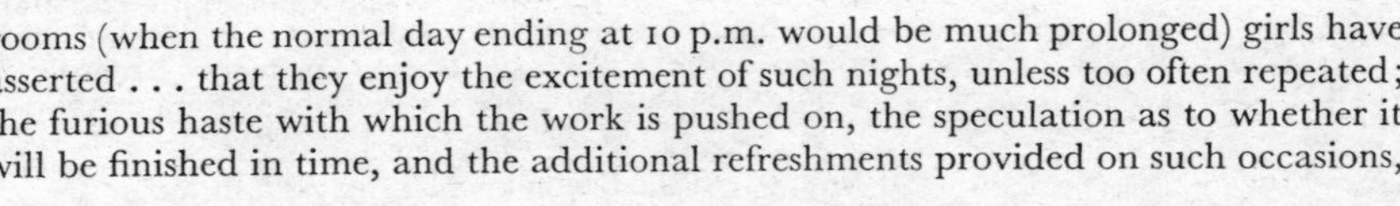
rooms (when the normal day ending at 10 p.m. would be much prolonged) girls have asserted . . . that they enjoy the excitement of such nights, unless too often repeated; the furious haste with which the work is pushed on, the speculation as to whether it will be finished in time, and the additional refreshments provided on such occasions,

Editing by Design

Outstanding book on design — using the image and images of the page to carry a message with pure clarity. This one book, heeded, could cure the rotten design of most home publishing — build the communicative base to evolve upon. —SB

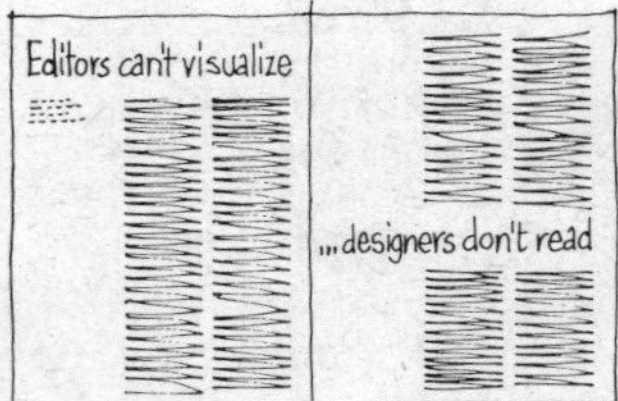

Editing by Design
(Word and picture communication for editors and designers)
Jan White
1974; 230 pp.

$18.50 postpaid from:
R.R. Bowker Company
Fulfillment Department
P.O. Box 1807
Ann Arbor, MI 48106

Example of a picture story about pictures: the gist: a wide-angle lens camera attached to driver automatically photographs the action during the race. The dramatic pictures were enlarged to full-spread size, shown against a black background, their corners were rounded — and they were placed on the pages at random angles to increase their surprise value.

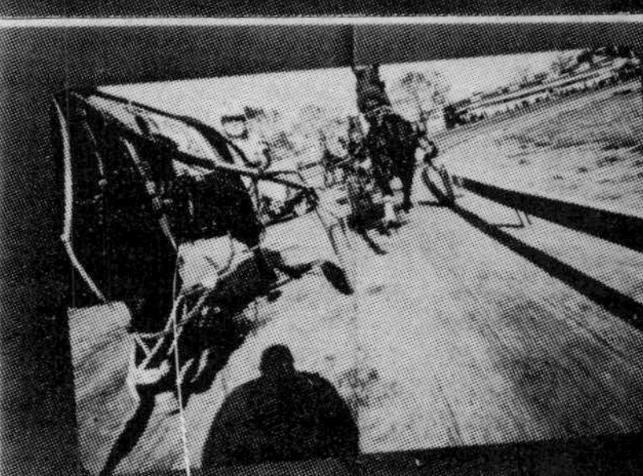

Editors can't visualize ...designers don't read

Split Headlines — If the headlines allow themselves to be split by phrases, it is possible to place the phrases in separate positions on the spread, and thereby achieve unexpected results. An even better (because more functional) application of this principle is to allow the headline to flow from one spread onto the succeeding one, thus forcing the reader to realize that the story continues.

By Design

So useful a book that I had to wrest it from the cumulative grasp of our art department, which was using it. They were ordering drawers for our page flats and considering other cutting and inking implements than the ones we use, comparing their judgments with Jon Goodchild's, doing what you do in a real good catalog or sourcebook: SHOP. If you're making anything graphic, you'll revel. —SB

By Design:
(A Graphics Sourcebook of Materials, Equipment and Services)
Jon Goodchild and Bill Henkin
1980; 255 pp.

$12.95 postpaid from:
Quick Fox
33 West 60th Street
New York, NY 10023
or Whole Earth Household Store

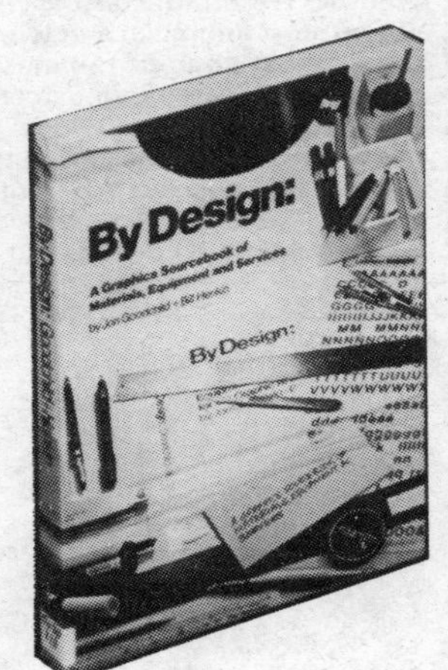

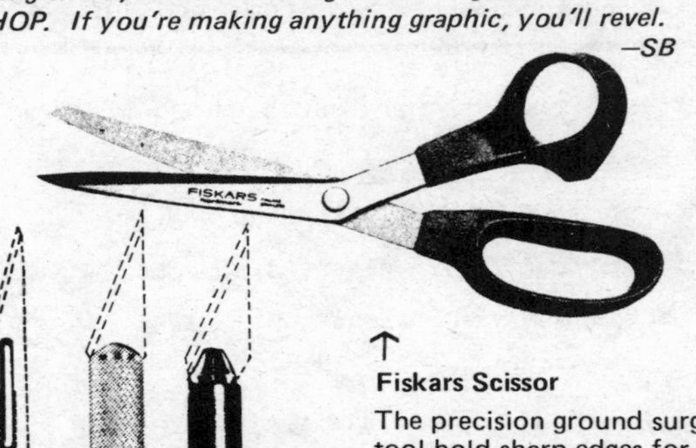

↑
Fiskars Scissor

The precision ground surgical steel blades of this Finnish tool hold sharp edges for years. This is a lightweight version of tailor's shears, with molded plastic handles, available in 8" right or left hand models.

Cost: $8.95

Most art, craft, and hardware stores

←
Knives

It's not the body, but the blades that cost you money over the years, and if you've used the standard No. 11, you know they don't last long at all. Our advice is to invest in surgical steel blades and a fine oilstone, and you can stop running out to the store for those endless packs of 100 ordinary blades.

→
Britta System

A basic solid pine drawer and divided cube, also solid pine, comb-jointed and glued and finished in clear lacquer. The adjustable internal divisions make four open shelves. Combinations of these two units make a flexible system that looks good anywhere.

Cost: drawer unit, $69; cube units, $59

Conran's

THE RISING SUN
NEIGHBORHOOD NEWSLETTER

Me and Art and Kathleen were talking about how a lot of people don't understand what design is which has a lot to do with a lot of people don't get that everything made by people is the way it is because of a series of decisions made by somebody — by some particular person or people — none of it is given from on high not the bold lines across the top of the reviews or the fine lines between reviews or illustrations bleeding off the bottom or the 457 other things that make a spread seem like it's one thing when it's really just a bunch of ink that never met before.

I first noticed that not everyone knows about the decisions that make things happen when I was about 7 and my friends in church were really shocked that I helped choose the hymns we sang on Sunday and that if I really really wanted a certain hymn on a certain Sunday I could lobby for it and get it. They thought God chose the three hymns out of the book of five hundred or so, but what happened was they had to be chosen by Wednesday night for the choir to run through for Sunday so Wednesday at supper we'd sit around and everyone in the family would flip through a hymn book and come up with a four/four hymn to march the choir in to, a quiet one to lead into the main prayer and a fairly strong one to end things up on. The other important thing that I learned from that other than it ain't such a big deal to decide on things is that if you do decide on things sometimes the constraints of reality, such as 3 hymns a Sunday, 52 Sundays in a year and not wanting to sing my three favorite hymns 52 times, lead to accepting and sometimes even pushing for things you don't like such as "Crown Him With Many Crowns" which though ugly and boring is at least some kind of change.

NOTHING SO FITS A PERSON for a life of dedicated useless unhappiness as four years of majoring in English.
—SB

The Elements of Style

With a few well cared-for tools and direct unshowy motions the craftsperson keeps the work moving steadily toward completion. The result looks as if it must have been easy to do, 'surprisingly inevitable.' You can write like that. Here are the tools.
—SB

The Elements of Style
William Strunk, Jr.
and E.B. White
1935, 1979; 85 pp.

$1.95 postpaid from:
MacMillan Publishing Co.
Order Department
Front and Brown Streets
Riverside, NJ 08075

or Whole Earth
Household Store

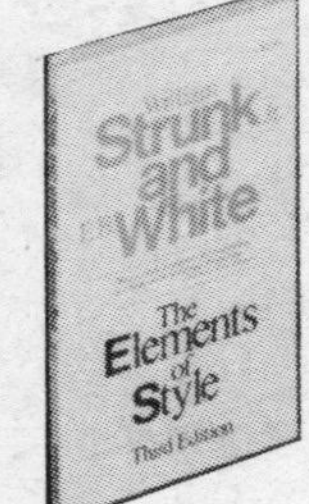

•

14. Use the active voice.

The active voice is usually more direct and vigorous than the passive:

I shall always remember my first visit to Boston.

This is much better than

My first visit to Boston will always be remembered by me.

The latter sentence is less direct, less bold, and less concise.

•

15. Put statements in positive form.

Make definite assertions. Avoid tame, colorless, hesitating, noncommittal language. Use the word *not* as a means of denial or in antitheses, never as a means of evasion.

He was not very often on time.	**He usually came late.**
He did not think that studying Latin was much use.	**He thought the study of Latin useless.**

•

16. Use definite, specific, concrete language.

Prefer the specific to the general, the definite to the vague, the concrete to the abstract.

A period of unfavorable weather set in.	**It rained every day for a week.**
He showed satisfaction as he took possession of his well-earned reward.	**He grinned as he pocketed the coin.**

•

22. Place the emphatic words of a sentence at the end.

The proper place in the sentence for the word or group of words that the writer desires to make most prominent is usually the end.

Humanity has hardly advanced in fortitude since that time, though it has advanced in many other ways.	**Humanity, since that time, has advanced in many other ways, but it has hardly advanced in fortitude.**
This steel is principally used for making razors, because of its hardness.	**Because of its hardness, this steel is principally used in making razors.**

•

The breezy style is often the work of an egocentric, the person who imagines that everything that pops into his head is of general interest and that uninhibited prose creates high spirits and carries the day. Open any alumni magazine, turn to the class notes, and you are quite likely to encounter old Spontaneous Me at work — an introductory paragraph that goes something like this:

Well, chums, here I am again with my bagful of dirt about your disorderly classmates, after spending a helluva weekend in N'Yawk trying to view the Columbia game from behind two bumbershoots and a glazed cornea. And speaking of news, howzabout tossing a few chirce nuggets my way?

This is an extreme example, but the same wind blows, at lesser velocities, across vast expanses of journalistic prose. The author in this case has managed in two sentences to commit most of the unpardonable sins: he obviously has nothing to say, he is showing off and directing the attention of the reader to himself, he is using slang with neither provocation nor ingenuity, he adopts a patronizing air by throwing in the word "chirce," he is tasteless, humorless (though full of fun), dull, and empty. He has not done his work. Compare his opening remarks with the following — a plunge directly into the news:

Clyde Crawford, who stroked the varsity shell in 1928, is swinging an oar again after a lapse of thirty years. Clyde resigned last spring as executive sales manager of the Indiana Flotex Company and is now a gondolier in Venice.

This, although conventional, is compact, informative, unpretentious. The writer has dug up an item of news and presented it in a straightforward manner. What the first writer tried to accomplish by cutting rhetorical capers and by breeziness, the second writer managed to achieve by good reporting, by keeping a tight rein on his material, and by staying out of the act.

Writing Without Teachers

According to Elbow, writing is sculpted from a rocky mass that you've generated freely, rather than wrought from an agony of cerebral ozone. His advice on how ranges from the specific to the sublime. Read the book literally — you'll write. Then read **Writing** *as a metaphor and just enjoy his widsom.*
—Stephanie Mills
[Suggested by Jim Moore]

Writing Without Teachers
Peter Elbow
1973; 196 pp.

$2.95 postpaid from:
Oxford University Press
16-00 Pollitt Drive
Fair Lawn, NJ 07410

or Whole Earth
Household Store

•

Another reason for starting writing and keeping writing: If you stop too much and worry and correct and edit, you'll invest yourself too much in these words on the page. You'll care too much about them; you'll make some phrases you really love; you won't be able to throw them away. But you *should* throw lots away because by the end you'll have a different focus or angle on what you are writing, if not a whole new subject. To keep these earlier words would ruin your final product. It's like scaffolding. There is no shortcut by which you can avoid building it, even though it can't be part of your final building. It's like the famous recipe for sturgeon: soak it in vinegar, nail it to a two-inch plank, put it in a slow oven for three days, take it out, throw away the fish, and eat the plank.

•

The essence of editing is *easy come easy go.* Unless you can really say to yourself, "What the hell. There's plenty more where that came from, let's throw it away," you can't really edit. You have to be a big spender. Not tightass.

•

Iago's work is almost done once he gets Othello to the point of needing certainty: only one answer is acceptable — infidelity. Fidelity is incapable of being determined with certainty. The need for certainty, then, tends to carry in itself a drift toward certain kinds of investigations and certain kinds of results. There are some kinds of data and propositions and insights a person cannot benefit from if he has no tolerance for working with uncertainty.

•

Trying to get the beginning just right is a formula for failure — and probably a secret tactic to make yourself give up writing.

•

It is a class of seven to twelve people. It meets at least once a week. Everyone reads everyone else's writing. Everyone tries to give each writer a sense of how his words were experienced. The goal is for the writer to come as close as possible to being able to see and experience his own words *through* seven or more people. That's all.

On Writing Well

The fact that William Zinsser has revised his excellent **On Writing Well** *a mere four years after its first publication says more about writing well than anything I can think of. Writing, to be good, cannot be writ as if in stone, not even by a professor of it. It's got to be honest, responsive, and current, mindful, above all, of the reader's impatient intelligence.*

This second edition includes a chapter on writing on the job, advice crucially needed. He counsels the business writer to be self-revealing, which is not the same thing as self-indulgent. Elsewhere in the book, he does his best to smite the morbid passive tense, favored voice of the faceless corporation. Still elsewhere he makes a manful attempt to advise on the pronomial and titular changes demanded by feminism, predictably scoffs at some of them, and fails to grasp that it's not about equality. This is one of the few bits of his advice I wouldn't regard as gospel.

As for the rest, any writer, at any point in his or her career, can benefit from Zinsser's instruction. If you are serious about communicating with your readers, this book belongs on your shelf right next to Strunk and White's **Elements of Style** *and the dictionary of your choice. It's that good.*
—Stephanie Mills

On Writing Well
(An informal guide to writing nonfiction)
William Zinsser
1976, 1980; 187 pp.
2nd Edition

$6 postpaid from:
Harper and Row
Keystone Industrial Park
Scranton, PA 18512

or Whole Earth
Household Store

The writer must therefore constantly ask himself: What am I trying to say? ~~in this sentence?~~ Surprisingly often, he doesn't know. ~~And~~ Then he must look at what he has ~~just~~ written and ask: Have I said it? Is it clear to someone encountering ~~who is coming upon~~ the subject for the first time? If it's not, ~~clear,~~ it is because some fuzz has worked its way into the machinery. The clear writer is a person ~~who is~~ clear-headed enough to see this stuff for what it is: fuzz.

I don't mean ~~to suggest~~ that some people are born clear-headed and are therefore natural writers, whereas others ~~other people~~ are naturally fuzzy and will ~~therefore~~ never write well. Thinking clearly is a ~~an entirely~~ conscious act that the writer must force ~~keep forcing~~ upon himself, just as if he were embarking ~~starting out~~ on any other ~~kind of~~ project that requires ~~calls for~~ logic: adding up a laundry list or doing an algebra problem. ~~or playing chess.~~ Good writing doesn't ~~just~~ come naturally, though most people obviously think it does. ~~it's as easy as walking.~~ The professional

•

Two paragraphs of the final manuscript of this chapter. Although they look like a first draft, they have already been rewritten and retyped — like almost every other page — four or five times. With each rewrite I try to make what I have written tighter, stronger and more precise, eliminating every element that is not doing useful work, until at last I have a clean copy for he printer. Then I go over it once more, reading it aloud, and am always amazed at how much clutter can still be profitably cut.

•

OVERSTATEMENT. "The living room looked as if an atomic bomb had gone off there," writes the inexperienced writer, describing what he saw on Sunday morning after a Saturday night party that got out of hand. Well, we all know that he's exaggerating to make a droll point, but we also know that an atomic bomb *didn't* go off there, or any other bomb except maybe a water bomb. "I felt as if ten 747 jets were flying through my brain," he says, "and I seriously considered jumping out the window and killing myself." These verbal high jinks can get just so high — and I'm already well over the limit — before the reader feels an overpowering drowsiness. It is like being trapped with a man who can't stop reciting limericks. Don't overstate. You didn't really consider jumping out the window. Life has more than enough truly horrible funny situations. Let the humor sneak up so that we hardly hear it coming.

The Writer's Craft

A writer (John Hersey) collecting the writings of other writers (Faulkner, Cummings, Conrad, Kipling, Solzhenitsyn, Mailer, Gorky, Ellison, etc.) on writing. A craft examining itself. Admirable selections. —SB

The Writer's Craft
John Hersey, Editor
1974; 422 pp.

$9.95 postpaid from:
Random House, Inc.
455 Hahn Road
Westminster, MD 21157
or Whole Earth Household Store

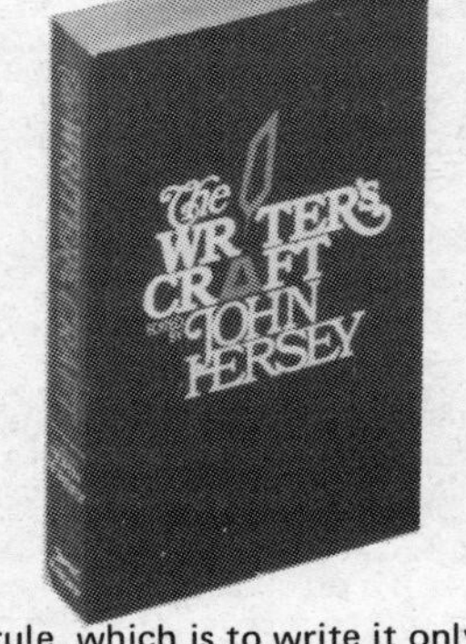

•

I have, myself, one simple rule, which is to write it only when it is hot, and always stop before it cools off so I will have something to go back to; never to write myself out. But there is somewhere, whether you realize it or not, there is the policeman that insists on some order, some unity in the work. But I would say to never force yourself to write anything. Once you do that you begin to think, "Well, I might as well force myself to write something and make a little money out of it." And then you are sunk — you are gone, you have stopped being a writer. You must be an amateur writer always.

—Faulkner

•

In Russian, proverbs about *Truth* are favorites. They persistently express the considerable, bitter, grim experience of the people, often astonishingly:

One Word of Truth Outweighs the World.

On such a seemingly fantastic violation of the law of the conservation of mass and energy are based both my own activities and my appeal to the writers of the whole world.

—Solzhenitsyn

•

I think that words are an around-the-world, ox-cart way of doing things, awkward instruments, and they will be laid aside eventually, probably sooner than we think. This is something that will happen in the space age. Most serious writers refuse to make themselves available to the things that technology is doing. I've never been able to understand this sort of fear.

—Burroughs

Verbatim

An intriguing little quarterly of correspondence, mini-articles, book reviews, etc. on the world of verbal expression. Hobbyist manic glee is rife throughout. —SB

Verbatim
Laurence Urdans, Editor

$7.50/year (4 issues) from:
Verbatim
P.O. Box 668
Essex, CT 06426

•

Mr. Eisiminger states that a green room is "the actors' waiting room, painted green to soothe eyes strained by harsh stage lights."

While this may be so in some cases today, the origin of the term is unrelated to the color any such room may have been painted. As I learned it (though I don't recall the source of the information), the room where actors met to discuss details of a production was originally called the "agreeing room." This became the " 'greeing room" which became the " 'greein' room" which then became the "green room."

Of the many green rooms I've been in over the years, none was painted green. Any green to be seen was in the actors' faces, not on the walls.

Sylvia Bursztyn
Los Angeles, California

SIC! SIC! SIC!

Sign at a neighborhood recreation center in Hawaii: "Do Not Sit On Balls. Use For Intended Purposes Only." [Submitted by Alfred G. Hoel, University of Hawaii, Pearl City]

Fiction Writer's Handbook

People with writing pretensions, aspirations, ambitions, and especially talents, should read. Read the writers you hope to rival; read good books most of all; but read good books about the art you hope to master, too. **Fiction Writer's Handbook** *is just such a one. The author and her late husband, with whom she shares credit for authorship, were longtime co-editors of* **STORY** *magazine and teachers of fiction writing. They speak eloquently and advisedly of the work and commitment demanded of the writer of fiction. They offer (as claimed) practical advice for an impractical calling, and more: insight into the workings of good fiction, illustrated with excerpts from a wide array of mostly modern classics. Indeed,* **Fiction Writer's Handbook** *is a classic in its own write.*

—Stephanie Mills

Fiction Writer's Handbook
(Practical advice on every aspect of writing novels and short stories with illustrations from modern and past fiction writers)
Hallie and Whit Burnett
1975; 200 pp.

$3.95 postpaid from:
Barnes and Noble Books
Keystone Industrial Park
Scranton, PA 18512
or Whole Earth Household Store

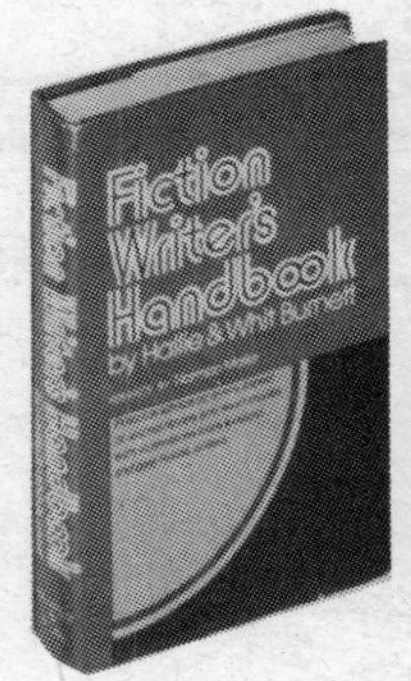

•

Jean Cocteau has said, "The spirit of creation is the spirit of contradiction. It is the breakthrough of appearances toward an unknown reality."

•

Too often young writers believe that a sensitized state of mind is enough for a story. That is enough for a state of mind, but that's about all. Since all fiction must have some narrative interest, underuse of plot can be a defect. All editors have felt hope, in beginning a story written well and even arrestingly, only to find it comes to nothing in the end. We then send the story back, and sometimes on rejection slips we write, "Too slight." And the author never seems to know what we mean!

A Manual of Style

It's reassuring to know that such time-worn standardization exists, even if your first (and best) instinct is to mischievously deviate from it. Advises on setting the more esoteric and scholarly type (poetry, letters and diaries, "Citing Public Documents"), and helps you completely understand the mysteries of Rights and Permissions (requesting, granting, "Fair Use" common law, etc.) Slick glossary; good reference tool for the whole production crew. If you need to know the correct type style to set your favorite TV serial in, and much, much more, this is your book.

If you wait till 1981, you can get the new 13th Edition.

—Pam Cokeley

A Manual of Style
(For authors, editors and copywriters)
The Editorial Staff of the University of Chicago Press
1906, 1969; 546 pp.
12th Edition

$15 postpaid from:
The University of Chicago Press
Department PK
5801 South Ellis Avenue
Chicago, IL 60637
or Whole Earth Household Store

•

The chief reason for any style book, of course, is to ease the work of the writer, the editor, and the typesetter in achieving clarity and consistency within a publication. To say, for instance, that *Congress* is always spelled with an initial capital letter and that the titles of plays are given in italics is to remove two cases from the list of those that must be decided on their own merits — such decisions to be remembered from the beginning to the end of the work. When style rules go beyond their role of achieving clarity and consistency, when they become precious or merely doctrinaire, they must be changed or eliminated.

How to Write and Publish a Scientific Paper

A surprisingly enjoyable treatise on how to meet the demands of one of the most demanding forms of communication by print, harder than a sonnet and more routinely failed at. The author is a managing editor of 25 years experience; he knows whereof he rejects and accepts. —SB

How to Write and Publish a Scientific Paper
Robert A. Day
1979; 160 pp.

$8.95 postpaid from:
Institute for Scientific Information (ISI) Press
325 Chestnut Street
Philadelphia, PA 19106

•

DeBakey said it, "the contents of an article shall be *new, true, important,* and *comprehensible.*"

•

While on the subject of misspellings, I recall the Professor of English who had the chance to make a seminal comment on this subject. A student had misspelled the word "burro" in a theme. In a marginal comment, the Professor wrote: "A 'burro' is an ass; a 'burrow' is a hole in the ground. One really should know the difference."

Examples of full and shortened references

5. John P. Roche, *The Quest for the Dream: The Development of Civil Rights and Human Relations in Modern America* (New York: Macmillan Co., 1963), pp. 204–6.
6. J. H. Hexter, "The Loom of Language and the Fabric of Imperatives: The Case of *Il Principe* and *Utopia*," *American Historical Review* 69 (1964): 945–68.
7. Stevens to Sumner, 26 August 1865, Charles Sumner Papers, Harvard College Library, Cambridge, Mass.
8. James Losh, *The Diaries and Correspondence of James Losh*, ed. Edward Hughes, 2 vols., Publication of the Surtees Society, vols. 171, 172 (Durham, England: Andrews & Co. for the Society, 1962–63), 2:200–212.
9. Roche, *Quest for the Dream*, p. 175.
10. Hexter, "Loom of Language," p. 949.
11. Stearns to Sumner, 28 August 1865, Sumner Papers.
12. Losh, *Diaries and Correspondence*, 1:150.
13. Ibid., 2:175.
14. Ibid., p. 176. [The same volume number as the preceding note.]
15. Ibid. [The same page as the preceding note.]

THE RISING SUN
NEIGHBORHOOD NEWSLETTER

The Quakers weren't always anti-slavery. Used to be everybody, including the Quakers thought slavery was kind of naughty but would quietly fade away as all poor taste things should — without much effort on anyone's part. Part of the compromise about slavery in the Constitution was the part that said that no slaves would be imported after 1808 which anti-slavery folks comforted themselves with — thinking it would all quietly fade away but just as importation stopped the cotton gin was invented and made slavery really profitable and owners thought of the interesting new concept of breeding.

Anyway, the Quakers were like everyone else, waiting for the withering away of the icky when along came John Woolman, who thought slavery was very bad and not to be compromised with and that God's people, notably Quakers, shouldn't own slaves and he went around saying so all over, taking advantage of those Quaker meetings where you can say anything and also did jolly things like standing outside the meeting houses and as people entered busting a previously concealed bladder of blood in his hands saying all Quaker slaveowners and people who permitted slaveowners in the meeting were covered with blood.

After he did stuff like this fifteen or twenty years and got covered with spit and hatred, Quakers decided that no Quakers could own slaves and all Quakers were abolitionists (as opposed to gradualists, which is what they'd been before). Anyone who got lonely being an abolitionist could become a Quaker or hang out with Quakers. Almost anything you read about John Woolman would convince you he wasn't a fun person to be around — no small talk, all "The Lord's wrath will visit the land which permits man to own man," and such like, never a relaxed moment, but he did do the job as the vanguard of the vanguard, which can't be relaxing. Did you know we were the second to the last country, next to Turkey, to have legal slavery, and you gotta admit that that ain't entirely uncharacteristic of this land of the ironic.

The Self-Publishing Manual

Self-publishing is still sometimes seen as a sour grapes response to rejection from big publishing houses. That's not true at all any more. One of the best reasons to publish yourself is because you know it'll be done right. Dan Poynter, whose books on hang gliding and parachuting are reviewed on p. 457, has clearly done it right; he has a percentage record of good sellers that Random House might envy. (Then again, he only publishes books he personally cares about.) Poynter's chapters on writing and designing are recipes for making books just like his own, which seems limiting. But the bulk of **The Self-Publishing Manual** *is terse nuts and bolts for promotion and distribution — crucial stuff, covered nowhere else with such thoroughness and good sense. (P.S. — When you get your book published, don't forget to send us a review copy.)* —Art Kleiner

The Self-Publishing Manual
(How to write, print and sell your own book)
Dan Poynter
1979, 1980; 174 pp.
$9.95 postpaid from:
Parachuting Publications
P.O. Box 4232
Santa Barbara, CA 93103
or Whole Earth Household Store

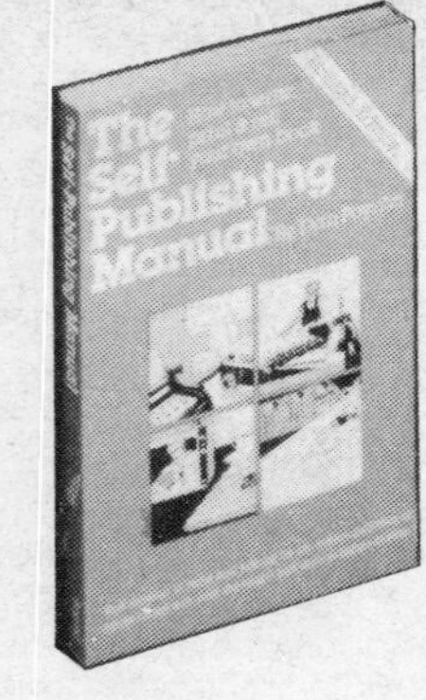

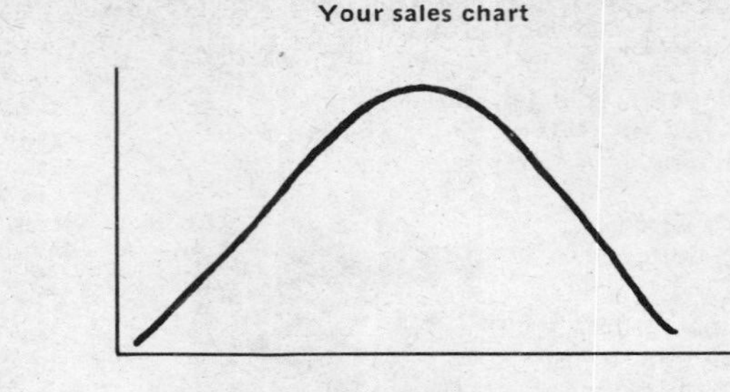

Your sales chart

Typical big firm individual book sales chart

•

You can expect your sales to take on an airfoil shape if your prior promotion is good. Sales will climb rapidly, level out, taper off and become steady. Thereafter you will notice bumps in response to seasonal changes or when your advertising or promotional work is successful.

The big initial jump is due to your pre-publication publicity and resulting orders; they all hit at once. By contrast, the big New York publishers market books in the same way Hollywood sells a motion picture. They throw it out on the market to see if anyone likes it. If it gets a response, they dump in a lot of promotional money. Then they push it for a couple of months. When the interest cools, they bring out another film and start all over.

As a small publisher, it makes more sense to market your book like breakfast food or soap. Develop your product, pour on the promotion, carve a nitch in the market and then continue to sell at the same level for years. This can be done with a non-fiction book which is revised at each printing.

•

"Good judgement comes from experience, and experience — well, that comes from poor judgement."

The Publish-It-Yourself Handbook

New York is not Publishing. Your home and some work can be. Here are some recent experiences, home-published of course. Damned inspiring. Damned useful. —SB

Interestingly, Harper and Row now co-publishes the new edition. Publish it yourself, but get help with distribution wherever you can. (The **Next Whole Earth Catalog** *is self-published, Random House distributed — best of both worlds.)* —Art Kleiner

The Publish-It-Yourself Handbook
(Literary tradition and how-to)
Bill Henderson, Editor
1973, 1980; 365 pp.
$6.95 postpaid from:
Harper and Row
Keystone Industrial Park
Scranton, PA 18512
or Whole Earth Household Store

•

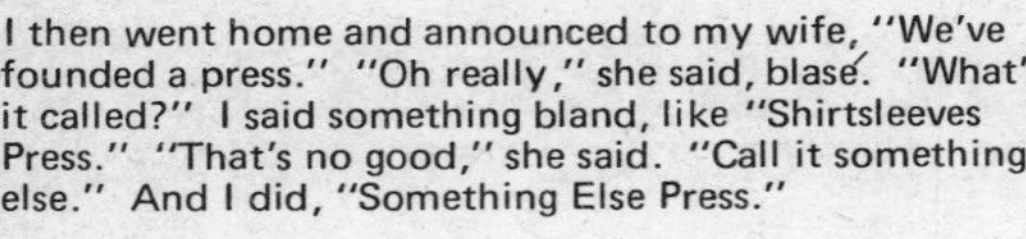

I then went home and announced to my wife, "We've founded a press." "Oh really," she said, blasé. "What's it called?" I said something bland, like "Shirtsleeves Press." "That's no good," she said. "Call it something else." And I did, "Something Else Press."

•

Barbara, since I spoke to you last, you've had a book published the conventional way.

Yes [sigh], the most conventional way possible. Hard cover (Doubleday) followed by soft cover (Penguin).

How did your experience with **All the Livelong Day** *compare to your experience with* **MacBird**?

One big difference is right there in the title. I had originally called my new book, about tedious routinized jobs, **Whistle While You Work**. This wasn't just satiric. The book is about human ingenuity, the games people play to keep from going crazy on these jobs. But **Whistle While You Work** is a Walt Disney song and that worried Doubleday. It's true titles aren't copyrightable. And anyway, during the Second World War half the country walked around singing "Whistle while you work/Hitler is a jerk." Nevertheless, Doubleday pointed out, quite correctly, that those Disney Land characters have lots of lawyers and can be plenty mean. But as a self-publisher I would have taken the chance.

Lithographer 1 & C
Lithographer 3 & 2

If you want someone to teach you to be a first-class pressman or lithographer, join the Navy. If the military life isn't your cup of tea, you can teach yourself by using the same books the Navy does. It may seem odd to learn about half-tones by looking at pictures of destroyers and Donald O'Connor look-alikes, but for a general understanding of offset lithography or for specific instructions on camera or press operations, these are the most complete, the most clearly illustrated and well-written manuals available. They cover everything from job planning and layout through printing and binding.

Take the case of Don Donahue, my partner in the comix biz. With nothing but the Navy books and a large supply of Korbel brandy to guide him he mastered the techniques of camera work and stripping, and achieved masterpieces of full-color art on his antique multi-1250. Don has since graduated to larger, more sophisticated presses, but he still keeps the Navy books handy. Their trouble-shooting charts on press and darkroom problems alone are worth the price. —Susan Goodrick

Lithographer 1 & C
No. 008-047-00077-4
Bureau of Naval Personnel
1970; 337 pp.
$4 postpaid

Lithographer 3 & 2
No. 008-047-00190-8
Naval Education and Training Command
1975; 557 pp.
$10.50 postpaid

both from:
Superintendent of Documents,
U.S. Government Printing Office,
Washington, D.C. 20402

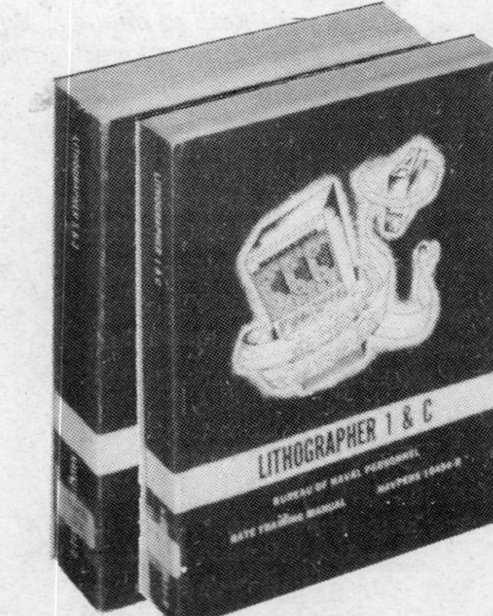

density density density
CORRECT — INCORRECT —

The image areas of a negative appear sharp and clear when it has been properly exposed and processed.

Pocket Pal

History, the printing processes, art and copy preparation, graphic arts photography, platemaking, printing, binding, paper, printing inks, graphic arts terms. This tasty book has been around since 1934 and has been continually revised as the printing biz evolved. **Pocket Pal** *will teach you the language you need to know to keep your local printer from bullshitting you overmuch. You will also learn a healthy respect for his art and the myriad events which transpire in a complicated printing job. Life is a two-way street. Printing paper merchandisers who handle the International Paper line will often have copies in stock. Talk to a salesman.* —E. Todd Ellison

Pocket Pal
(A Graphic Arts Production Handbook)
1934, 1979; 204 pp.
$3 postpaid from:
International Paper Company
220 East 42nd Street
New York, NY 10017
or Whole Earth Household Store

Halftone dots enlarged

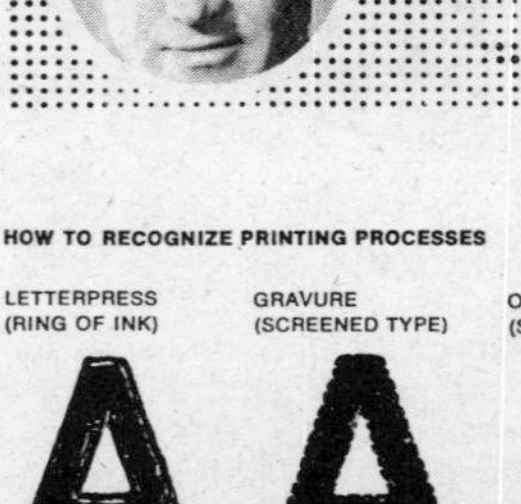

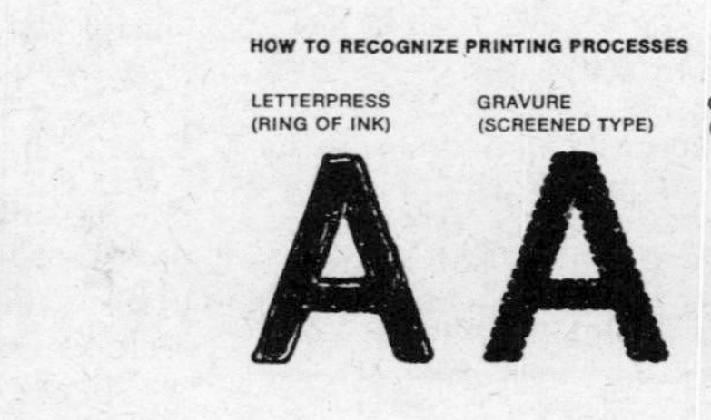

HOW TO RECOGNIZE PRINTING PROCESSES

LETTERPRESS (RING OF INK) — GRAVURE (SCREENED TYPE) — OFFSET (SMOOTH PRINT)

A A A

Cheapest printing equipment

Good prices on direct mail order mimeographs ($200 - $300) from **Vari-Color Duplicator Company**, 435 South Lincoln, Shawnee, OK 74801.

Used printers supplies (and smaller new machines) available from: **Turnbaugh Printers Supply Company**, 104 Sporting Hill Road, Mechanicsburg, PA 17055.

—Vari-Color

Printing It

Not much money on hand, and you're gonna make a book? Clifford Burke, an impecunious bookmaking craftsman himself, has the basics bite-size. —SB

Printing It
Clifford Burke
1972; 127 pp.
$3.50 postpaid from:
Wingbow Press
2940 7th Street
Berkeley, CA 94710
or Whole Earth Household Store

•

The one sound bit of training that will do most to help you prepare good camera-ready paste-ups is the knowledge of what the offset camera can "see." . . . For our purpose in this book the rule is *the camera sees anything black on a white ground*. While this rule is variable, it is also absolute. For example, because of their reflective qualities the camera sees pale blue as white, and it sees red as black. It also sees green thumbprints, red wine stains, and flecks of gray cigarette ash. It sees little white specks in the blackest letter, and rough edges on the most carefully made drawing. In offset printing the camera is the taskmaster, and only after this is learned can laying out "black" copy on "white" paper be really money saving and creative.

Printer's Supply Book

A look at the **Whole Earth Catalog** *or any other piece of printing confirms that the items sold by the Kelsey Company are obsolete. Today good, cheap quick printing is done offset. And Kelsey sells only letterpress equipment. But they have a full line — everything. Good and reasonably prices.*

—Will Powers

(See "Graphic Supplies," p. 466.)

Printer's Supply Book
$1 from:
The Kelsey Company
P.O. Box 941
Meriden, CT 06450

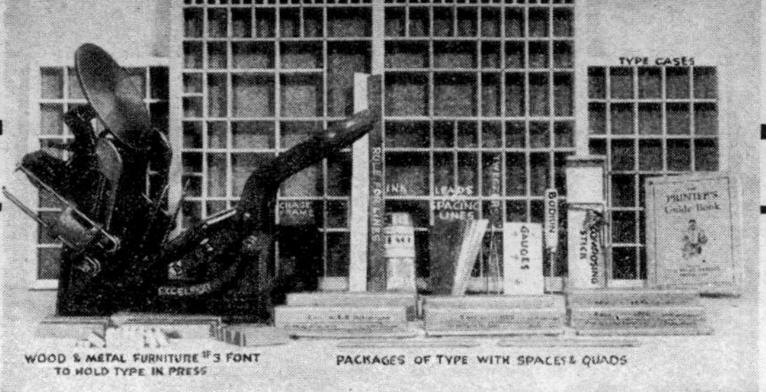

•
Outfit No. 2C, with 5 x 8 Press

5 x 8 Press
Type (your selection or ours) with spaces and quads
3 California Type Cases
Composing Stick
Furniture Font No. 5
Tube of Black Ink
Leads, Guage Pins
Bodkin, Tweezers
Shipping Weight: 108 lbs.

Fine Print

It's probably a sign of advancing age, but I am coming to honor the wellmade book. If you're a similar anachronism, this precise little publication of "the Arts of the Book" will hone your intolerance fine.

—SB

Fine Print
(A Review for the Arts of the Book)
Sandra Kirshenbaum, Editor

$20/year
(4 issues)
from:
Fine Print
P.O. Box 7741
San Francisco, CA 94120

→
THE ARION PRESS
566 Commercial Street, San Francisco, California 94111

Melville, Herman. *Moby-Dick; or, The Whale.* 1979. 38 x 25.5 cm. (15 x 10), 576 pp. Full blue goatskin. Sewn on tapes inserted into split boards with title stamped in silver color on spine. Blue cloth slipcase. $1000
Out of print.

Colophon: . . . printed and published by Andrew Hoyem at The Arion Press, San Francisco, California.

The edition is limited to 265 copies of which 250 are for sale. The type is handset Goudy Modern. The Leviathan capitals used for the title and initial letters were designed by Charles Bigelow and Kris Holmes. The illustrations were drawn and engraved by Barry Moser. The paper was handmade by Barcham Green at Hayle Mill in England.

CHAPTER 63 THE CROTCH

OUT of the trunk, the branches grow; out of them, the twigs. So, in productive subjects, grow the chapters.

The crotch alluded to on a previous page deserves independent mention. It is a notched stick of a peculiar form, some two feet in length, which is perpendicularly inserted into the starboard gunwale near the bow, for the purpose of furnishing a rest for the wooden extremity of the harpoon, whose other naked, barbed end slopingly projects from the prow. Thereby the weapon is instantly at hand to its hurler, who snatches it up as readily from its rest as a backwoodsman swings his rifle from the wall. It is customary to have two harpoons reposing in the crotch, respectively called the first and second irons.

But these two harpoons, each by its own cord, are both connected with the line; the object being this: to dart them both, if possible, one instantly after the other into the same whale; so that if, in the coming drag, one should draw out, the other may still retain a hold. It is a

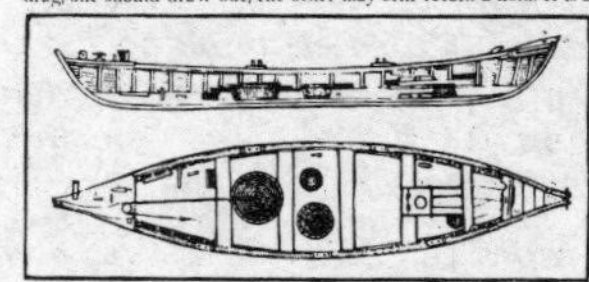

Typical New Bedford Whale Boat: A. Steering oar brace, B. Cuddy board, C. Knife, D. Lion's tongue, E. Loggerhead, F. Whale line going to the loggerhead, thence to the harpoon, G. Large line tub, H. Small line tub, I. Water keg, J. Mast hinge, K. Bucket, L. Clumsy cleat, M. Knife, N. One inch cut used for straightening harpoons, O. Chocks.

doubling of the chances. But it very often happens that owing to the instantaneous, violent, convulsive running of the whale upon receiving the first iron, it becomes impossible for the harpooneer, however lightning-like in his movements, to pitch the second iron into him.

296

HERMAN MELVILLE

MOBY-DICK;
OR, THE WHALE.

THE ARION PRESS. San Francisco 1979

↑
This book has no preface, foreword, or introduction. Except for a detailed colophon, the book is pure Melville. Perhaps only one other edition in a century-and-a-quarter can be cited as a great typographic, illustrated edition, and that is the Lakeside Press edition illustrated by Rockwell Kent.

If one were directly influenced by the tradition of the finest California printers, it would be difficult to be anything but another great printer. This is precisely where Andrew Hoyem stands. His folio edition of *Moby-Dick* upholds the high standards of book design of the best American fine printers.

BOOKBINDING BIBLIOGRAPHY AND SUPPLY

by Robin Rycraft (April 1980)

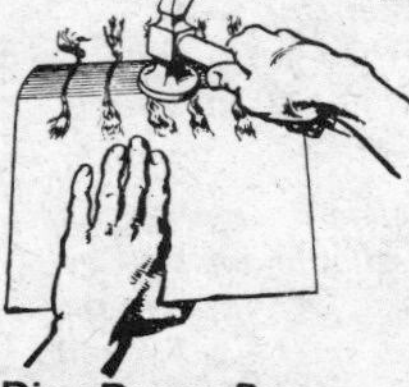

—Bookbinding and the Care of Books

This list updates one compiled in April, 1974. The most notable changes in the past six years are the increased availability of American handmade paper and decorated paper on one hand, and the decrease in quality and selection of European and Japanese handmade papers on the other. Although American handmade and decorated papers remain expensive, the quality is equal to or better than the European counterpart.

The availability and cost of bookbinding materials fluctuate. There are many instances where new technology is replacing old methods and traditional materials. Some of these changes work to our advantage and some do not.

This is not likely to change. When desirable materials become available, take advantage of the opportunity to obtain them.

BOOKBINDING ORGANIZATIONS

Center for Book Arts,
15 Bleecker Street,
New York, NY 10012

Designer Bookbinders,
12 Cornwall Mansions,
33 Kensington Court,
London, W8 5BG, England

Guild of Bookworkers,
663 Fifth Avenue
New York, NY 10022

The Pacific Center for the Book Arts,
157 Bluxome Street
San Francisco, CA 94107

BOOKS

Bookbinding and the Care of Books
Douglas Cockerell
1978; $9.95
postpaid from:
Taplinger Publishing Co.
200 Park Avenue South
New York, NY 10003

Good reference book for anyone interested in bookbinding and decoration.

Marbling
Robert Akers
1976; 45 pence
(about $1.25 U.S.)
postpaid from:
Dryad Press
Northgates, Leicester
LE1 4QR, England

The basics of English marbling techniques, ostensibly for children.

Bookbinding, Its Background and Technique
Edith Diehl
1946, 1979; $60
postpaid from:
Hacker Art Books
54 West 57th Street
New York, NY 10019

Good reference material on history and technique. Two volumes.

Paper
Quentin Fiore
1958; $1
postpaid from:
Tamarind Institute
108 Cornell Avenue SE
Albuquerque, NM 87106

Excellent pamphlet on Eastern and Western methods of papermaking.

Cleaning and Preserving Bindings and Related Materials
Carolyn Horton
1969; $5
postpaid from:
American Library Association
50 East Huron Street
Chicago, IL 60611

Very nice book for librarians. Helps organize the approach to preventive maintenance within the library.

Writing, Illuminating, and Lettering
Edward Johnston
1906, 1977; $9.95
postpaid from:
Taplinger Publishing Co.
200 Park Avenue South
New York, NY 10003

A classic work about the writing and decorating of manuscripts. Although more detailed technical information is now available, the spirit in which this book is written is a guiding light for many people today. (Also reviewed on p. 506.)

Creative Bookbinding
Pauline Johnson
1965; $10.95
postpaid from:
University of Washington Press
Seattle, WA 98105

An excellent reference book on traditional bookbinding and teaching projects that relate to bookbinding, portfolios, decorative papers, etc.

Papermaking
1968, 1977; $6.95
postpaid from:
Library of Congress
Information Office
Washington, DC 20540

Nice historical bit about papermaking, mainly American.

The Restoration of Leather Bookbindings
Bernard Middleton
1972; $10
postpaid from:
American Library Association
50 East Huron Street
Chicago, IL 60611

Technical details for advanced binders.

Bookmaking: A Practical Guide for Beginners
Robin Rycraft
To be published in 1981; $5 postpaid from:
Robin Rycraft
4205 SW 53rd Street
Corvallis, OR 97330

Help for the beginner.

MATERIALS AND EQUIPMENT

Gane Brothers and Lane
218 Littlefield
South San Francisco, CA 94080

Tools for handbookbinding, bindersboard and miscellaneous supplies.

Process Materials Corporation
301 Veterans Boulevard
Rutherford, NJ 07070

Specialty products for the preservation and conservation of archival materials.

Russell Bookcrafts
Hitchin,
Hertsfordshire
England

English source for supplies and equipment.

Talas
130 Fifth Avenue
New York, NY 10011

A very good all-around source for anything needed in the fields of handbookbinding, conservation work. Bindersboard, paper, tools, etc. Many of the books mentioned above are available here. (Also reviewed on p. 467.)

PAPER

Andrews, Nelson and Whitehead
(Imported Papers)
38-10 48th Avenue
Long Island City, NY 11101

Reliable source for imported handmade, mouldmade, and machine-made paper. Quantity orders only.

Daniel Smith
1111 West Nickerson
Seattle, WA 98119

European handmade papers. Quality printing inks. Small quantity orders accepted. Reasonable prices.

Dieu Donne Press and Paper, Inc.
3 Crosby Street
New York, NY 10013

Linen and cotton rag papers. Unusual high quality and character.

Faulkiner Fine Paper Ltd.
4 Mart Street
London WCZE 8DE
England

Handmade, mouldmade, and machinemade paper. Small and large quantities. Excellent European source.

New York Central Supply
62 Third Avenue
New York, NY 10003

Fine selection of handmade papers, and hard-to-find handmade papers.

Talas
(See above)

Send for catalog of various handmade paper available.

Twin Rocker Handmade Paper Inc.
R.F.D. 2
Brookston, IN 47923

Beautiful American handmade paper.

Yasutomo
24 California Street
San Francisco, CA 94111

Japanese papers. Great variety available.

DECORATIVE PAPERS

Aiko Art Materials Import
714 North Wabash Ave.
Chicago, IL 60611

Japanese handmade and decorative papers. Ask for catalog.

Don Guyot
1902 North 44th
Seattle, WA 98103

Experienced marbler and bookbinder, offering complete marbling supplies and equipment. Some bookbinding supplies. Workshops also available.

Talas
(See above)

Write for catalog on available papers. Great variety of American and European printed, paste, marbled papers.

LEATHER AND VELLUM

H. Band and Co., Ltd.
Brentway, High Street
Brentford, Middlesex,
England

Vellum for writing, illuminating, or binding.

J. Hewitt and Sons, Ltd.
97 St. John Street
London, EC1 England

Fine leather for bookbinding. Also brass tools and general supplies.

Talas
(See above)

Many kinds of leather and vellum available. Ask for catalog. ■

THE RISING SUN
NEIGHBORHOOD NEWSLETTER

"Almost only counts in horseshoes and hand grenades."

—Stephanie

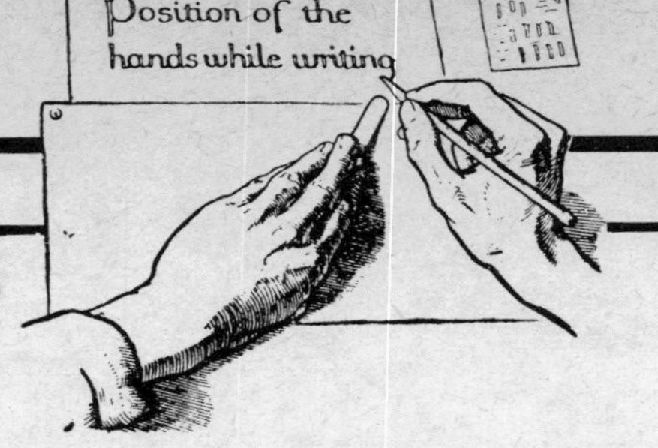

d. "Slanted pen" free flourishes

Writing & Illuminating & Lettering

When this book was first published in 1906, the printers who did the job were so impressed by it that they told the author that a copy of it should be kept in every printing office. Sydney Cockerell declared it to be the best handbook ever written on any subject. And it has certainly held an undisputed position as the best book on the craft of lettering for over seventy years. Continuously in print since its initial publication, it is a text that anyone involved in the lettering arts ought to have.

The importance of this work can be better appreciated when one learns that the craft of broad-edged pen calligraphy was retrieved from oblivion by Edward Johnston, who, through study of medieval manuscripts in the British Museum rediscovered the dynamic properties of the square cut pen as the essential letter making tool. Singlehandedly he revived an art that had been killed by the invention of printing in the 15th century. What is perhaps even more remarkable is that he wrote this rather encyclopedic book only ten years after beginning his his research.

Culturally Johnston belongs to the 19th century Arts and Crafts movement begun by Socialist William Morris — but his influence was deeply felt on the continent, where his type design for the London Underground stimulated the development of sans-serif typography. This was taken up by the Bauhaus group and others (Eric Gill among them) and has revolutionised the practice and philosophy of contemporary bookarts.

Though somewhat dated in appearance, the thinking in this book remains sound; its spirit is pervasive: "For all things — materials, tools, methods — are waiting to serve us and we have only to find the 'spell' that will set the whole universe a-making for us." —John Prestianni

Writing & Illuminating & Lettering
Edward Johnston
1906, 1977; 439 pp.
$9.95 postpaid from:
Taplinger Publishing Co.
200 Park Avenue South
New York, NY 10003
or Whole Earth Household Store

The Irene Wellington Copy Book

How is the essential skill of handwriting to be preserved in an age which sees the keyboards of the typewriter and computer terminal assume ever-growing importance in our daily lives? Yet there are many humanizing factors in the cultivation of fine handwriting, not the least of which is a simple and legitimate pride in something of one's own which is in a very real sense handmade.

This I feel is the best and most practical of the italic handwriting copybooks currently available, written by one of England's greatest calligraphers. Anyone who studies and practices from the models in this book can attain at least a very legible if not beautiful cursive hand. While most italic models are derived from 16th century Chancery hands, which tend to narrow angularity and spikiness, these letters are based on rounder, more open forms. They lend themselves to a more rhythmically graceful movement that will not break down under the pressure of speed.

Direct, clear, and logical, the copybook can be used to teach even young children how to write; many of the exercises consist of old rhymes, poems and country calls, notable for their charm as well as their instructive value, and suitable for recitation. —John Prestianni

The Irene Wellington Copy Book
(An Omnibus Edition)
Irene Wellington
1957, 1977; 80 pp.
$3.95 postpaid from:
Pentalic Corporation
132 West 22nd Street
New York, NY 10011
or Whole Earth Household Store

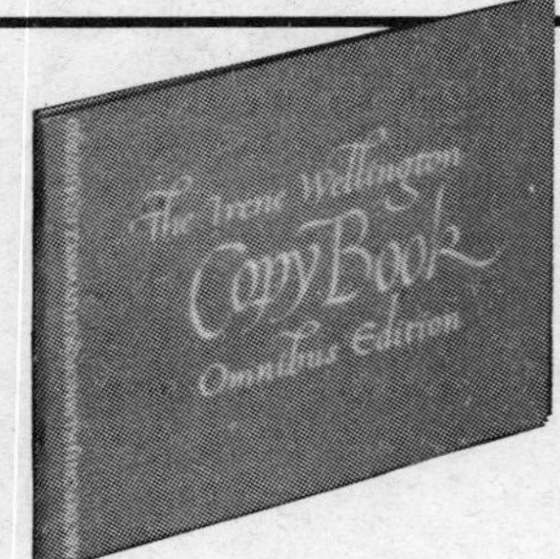

Some calls used by country people in England to coax or drive their animals home.

for cows	Coop! Cush, cush! Hoaf! Hobe! Mull! Proo! Proochy! Prut!
for calves	Moddie! Mog, mog, mog! Pui-ho! Sook, sook! Pui-ho!
for sheep	Co-hobe! Ovey! Co-hobe! Ovey! Co-hobe! Ovey!
for pigs	Check-check! Cheat! Dack-dack! Giss or Gissy!
pigs	Tantassa, tantassa pig, tow a row, a row! Tig, tig, tig!
and still for pigs	Lix! Ric-sic! Ric-sic! Shug, shug, shug!

Pen Lettering

Regarded by many as the best small book on lettering and calligraphy, this classic gains more admirers with each passing year.

It is one of the most penetratingly clear analyses of the Roman capital and minuscule hand that I've ever seen and used, presented with logic and authority — and free of the intrusion of any personal idiosyncrasies on the part of the author; other factors which recommend it are its restricted format, which makes it enormously accessible for the student and practical for the teacher; and that it's cheap.

While it does not enter into the historical roots of calligraphy, nor into the complexities of the production of fine work, much is compressed into the seemingly simple information contained here. —John Prestianni

Pen Lettering
Ann Camp
1957, 1978; 83 pp.
$3.95 postpaid from:
Pentalic Corporation
132 West 22nd Street
New York, NY 10011
or
£1.35 postpaid from:
Dryad Press
P.O. Box 38
Northgates, Leicester
LE1 9BU England

A PIECE OF WRITING MIGHT BEGIN WITH SEVERAL LINES OF CAPITALS

These capitals could be in black the same as the text, or they could be in colour, Red, Blue or Green. The text must be carefully studied first and emphasis only be made where it assists the meaning. It is wrong to emphasise any part of the text for decorative reasons alone.

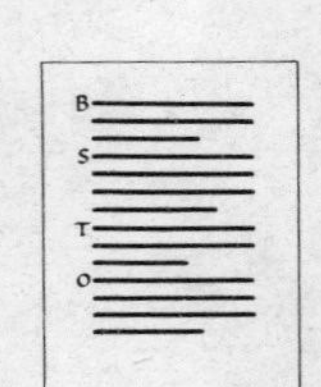
Capitals in margi

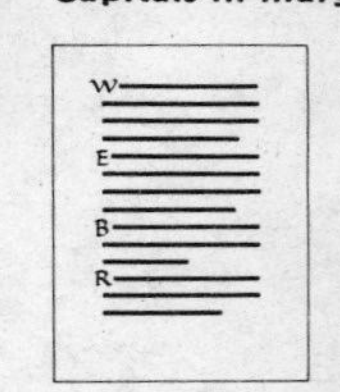
Capitals partly in

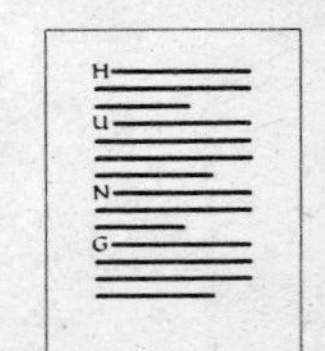
Capitals square w left-hand margin

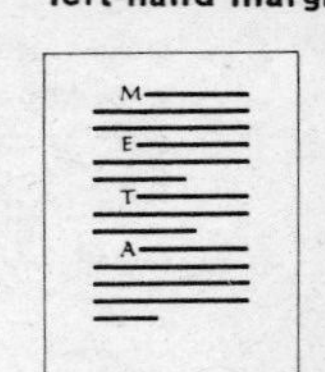
Capitals complet indented

WRITTEN LETTERS

Here is a calligraphy book that communicates a real warmth and joy about making letters. Jackie Svaren has created 22 handsome alphabet worksheets, each surrounded with exquisitely tiny italic notes and comments and stories. The book is large (feels like a portfolio) and laid out beautifully in black and red with lots of marvelous empty space. The writing has had no reductions and no white paint touch-ups. How wonderful to discover ~~an author~~ a calligrapher who admits (and loves) her mistakes.

"Notice that a letter was left out of one word. The correction was put in above. REJOICE IN HUMANESS! Machines can't make mistakes. If you compete with a machine on its terms, YOU LOSE! so don't reduce your writing to being like type. YOU ARE NOT A TYPEWRITER. (Admit mistakes, correct them & go right on."

This book transmits a feeling of ease and calm around a core of calligraphic discipline. It's a fine space to write from. BARBARA BASH

Written Letters
Jacqueline Svaren
1975; 56 pp.

$14.20 postpaid from:
The Bond
Wheelwright Company
136 Main Street
Box 296
Freeport, ME 04032
or Whole Earth Household Store

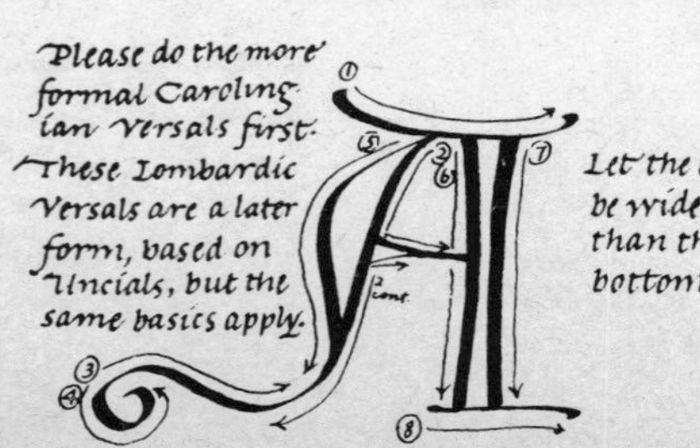

Please do the more formal Carolingian Versals first. These Lombardic Versals are a later form, based on Uncials, but the same basics apply.
Let the top be wider than the bottom.

Calligraphy

JOHN PRESTIANNI

by Antonia T. Smith

PEN NIBS

Although Speedball is well known, there are other, better brands. Brause nibs are excellent. They are well designed and easy to use. Just make sure the well (a small metal piece that attaches to the nib to hold ink) doesn't extend past the end of the nib. These German-made nibs are now available from Pentalic Corp. Be sure to keep the nibs clean. After each use, rinse them with water or a solution of water and ammonia, brushing them with a toothbrush as well. They will last a long time if well cared for. If, after much use, your letters have lost their nice sharp edges, you can sharpen the nib on Crocus cloth (the finest sandpaper). Hold the pen at a specific angle and make figure eights on the cloth.

For larger letters, Coit or Automatic pens are available in sizes up to one inch across. Automatic pens are available through Pentalic. Coit pens can be purchased from Bridgeport Pen Company.

FOUNTAIN PENS

There are several: Pelikan, Platignum, and Osmiroid. Pelikan fountain pen nibs come in fine, medium and broad widths only. The other pens have nibs that range in size from extra fine to B-4 (the fourth size in broad) which is about 2½ mm wide.

Nothing is better for handwriting than a fountain pen. The ink flows constantly without the need for frequent refills and if the pen nib is of good quality, it glides easily over the paper. Unfortunately, my experience with fountain pens during the past few years of teaching calligraphy has not always been good. Quality varies from nib to nib. This is especially true of the now popular Platignum pens. Sometimes nibs can be rough or have prongs out of alignment. Besides problems with the nib itself, some nibs don't work well until they are broken in and others work better with certain inks or specific paper-ink combinations. The most successful combination for me has been Pelikan 4001 ink with Strathmore #5 series Layout Bond. Special pads labeled "Calligraphy Paper" are usually a poor buy, especially "parchment" paper which does not take ink well. One notable exception is the Italic Calligraphy Practice Pad put out by Pentalic.

SOCIETIES

There are at least 34 calligraphy societies in the U.S. and Europe. If you would like a complete list, you can write the Society of Scribes and Illuminators c/o FBCS, 43 Earlham Street, London WC2H 9LD. Send 3 international money order coupons (about $1.25 U.S.) to cover postage and time.

The P
Callig

BATHROOM LITERATURE

by Jan Adkins

ACCEPTING THE CLICK of the bathroom door's latch as a respite from the confusion beyond it, the material for the Contemplative Library near the toilet should be light, non-sequential, random, varicolored and of many moods. I suggest a few titles.

Bartlett's Familiar Quotations

Endlessly and instantly entertaining, its chronological format gives it an order of contemporaries, and its brief entries remind a writer of the power in the short, terse statement. It has a truly useful index and the best cast of characters in publishing.

Bartlett's Familiar Quotations
John Bartlett
1968; 1750 pp.
14th Edition
$24.95 postpaid from:
Little, Brown and Company
200 West Street
Waltham, MA 02154
or Whole Earth Household Store

•

A good marriage is that in which each appoints the other guardian of his solitude. —Rainier Maria Rilke

•

If parents would only realize how they bore their children! —George Bernard Shaw

The Oxford Book of Literary Anecdotes

A literate, 1300 year issue of **People** *magazine, catching famous and obscure ink-fish at their wittiest and at their most foolish, with their wigs off, their pants down, and at their hour of death. A book that greatly expands your list of ideal dinner guests.*

The Oxford Book of Literary Anecdotes
James Sutherland, Editor
1976; 500 pp.
$2.95 postpaid from:
Pocket Books, Inc.
1230 Avenue of the Americas
New York, NY 10020
or Whole Earth Household Store

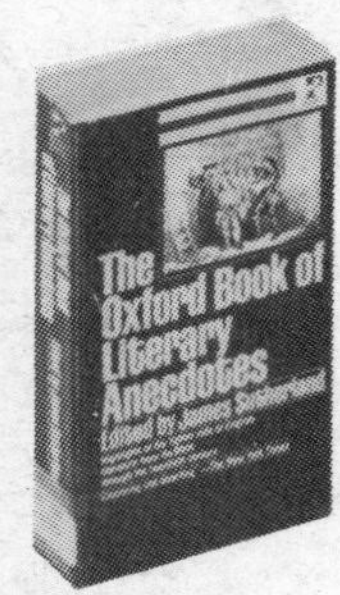

•

Colley Cibber, they say, was extremely haughty as a theatrical manager, and very insolent to dramatists. When he had rejected a play, if the author desired him to point out the particular parts of it which displeased him, he took a pinch of snuff, and answered in general terms — "Sir, there is nothing in it *to coerce my passions*."

•

When Tennyson entered the Oxford Theatre to receive his honorary degree of D.C.L., his locks hanging in admired disorder on his shoulders, dishevelled and unkempt, a voice from the gallery was heard crying out to him, "Did your mother call you early, dear?"

Brewer's Dictionary of Phrase and Fable

Dipping into **Brewer's** *to net examples for this review I was caught by the undertow and surfaced again (by an act of stern will) an hour later; it is a dangerously seductive book. It is an encyclopedic reference to the maddeningly obscure phrase, the curiously opaque line, and the abstruse story.* **Brewer's** *is a necessity for reading books your grandfather read, explaining the vernacular that was part of his language but is, alas, lost to us poor solemn birds; Grandpa's Billingsgate (see* **Brewer's***) and high-blown metaphor is reduced in his grandchildren's time to a very few Anglo-Saxon verbs and some earnest Freudian similes. This book, taken with an infusion of Bret Harte's and Damon Runyon's filigreed stories, is guaranteed to bring color to your language and whimsy to your correspondence. It lacks only a hole bored through the pages, upper left, to be the ideal privy counselor, the best bathroom book published.*

Brewer's Dictionary of Phrase and Fable
(Centenary Edition)
E. Cobham Brewer and Ivor H. Evans
1971; 1175 pp.
$22.95 postpaid from:
Harper and Row
Keystone Industrial Park
Scranton, PA 18512
or Whole Earth Household Store

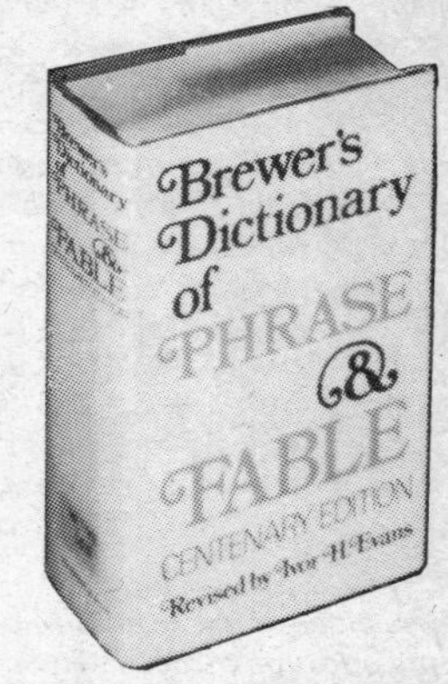

•

Googly. In CRICKET, a deceptive delivery depending on hand action by the bowler in which an off-break is bowled to a right-handed batsman with what appears to be a leg-break action. *Cp.* CHINAMAN.

It was invented and developed by B.J.T. Bosanquet from 1890 and he used it against the Australians in 1903. In Australia it is called a "BOSEY."

(These capitalized words in the quotes are the undertow: they are references found elsewhere, and they have references found elsewhere, and pretty soon it's two a.m.)

•

Billingsgate. The site of an old passage through that part of the city wall that protected London on the river side, named from an early property-owner in the area. The site of a fish-market for many centuries, where porters were famous for their foul and abusive language at least four centuries ago.

Add to these a good anthology of poetry (a paperback textbook, **Sound and Sense***, Harcourt, Brace & World, is the smallest and cheapest and best I know of), a* **Complete Poems of Carl Sandburg** *(or T.S. Eliot or Wallace Stevens, if they suit your ear, though I opt for the less strenuous bards in the bathroom), a well-finished rosewood toilet seat and you cannot avoid being rested — even ennobled — by your small sabbatical amidst the plumbing.* ■

Imperial Messages

Writers are writing more very short stories — one-paragraph to three-page complete tales. Many are as strong as they are short. I've had one collection of them, **Imperial Messages***, for a year and I love it and I still haven't finished it. It sometimes takes weeks to absorb a story that took a few minutes to read.*

Imperial Messages *has one hundred stories in about three hundred pages. It includes familiar and unfamiliar authors like Kafka, Dostoevsky, Bob Dylan, Jakov Lind, Isak Dinesen, Mark Halperin, and Italo Calvino. And titles like "The Tramp's Sin and Charlie Chaplin," "The Glass Blower," "A Tale from the Old Buzzard's Youth," "King Solomon and the Sea," "A Very Old Man With Enormous Wings," and "The Motorcycle Social Club." There are some profound ideas in the words and between the lines of these stories. The ideas sneak up on you because the stories themselves seem so straightforward. Most of them have very traditional forms, with beginnings, middles, and ends, and complete sentences throughout. But when they're over you're left with something strange and unexpected that you can't quite define or forget.*
—*Anne Herbert*

Imperial Messages
(One Hundred Modern Parables)
Howard Schwartz, Editor
1976; 348 pp.
$2.50 postpaid from:
Avon Books
Mail Order Department
250 West 55th Street
New York, NY 10019
or Whole Earth Household Store

SUPPLIERS

All these companies do mail order business and have catalogs:

Fahrney's, Suite 503, 123 North Pitt Street, Alexandria, VA 22314. *Complete collection of writing instruments, also calligraphy books, inks and some papers. Catalog $1.*

Bridgeport Pen Company, Box 1206, Fairfield, CT 06430. *Coit pens. Catalog free.*

Calpen, 176 West Jaxine Drive, Altadena, CA 91001. *Offset pen holders for copperplate felt pens ½" to 3" wide, especially designed for calligraphy, cut bamboo and reed pens, cut turkey quills.*

Murray's Frame Shop, P.O. Box 1787, Monterey, CA 93940. *Paper, pens, quills, vellum, inks, gilding supplies. Catalog free.*

New York Central Supply Company, 62 3rd Avenue, New York, NY 10003. *Catalog free.*

Art Media, 820 SW 10th Avenue, Portland, OR 97205. *Catalog free.*

Pentalic Corporation, 132 West 22nd Street, New York, NY 10011. *Excellent source of calligraphy materials as well as an extensive selection of books. Catalog free.*

M. Schwartz & Son, Inc., 45 Hoffman Avenue, Hauttauge, NY 11787. *Complete supply of feathers in all sizes and varieties. Catalog free.*

Italimuse, 3128 Burr Street, Fairfield, CT 06430. *Calligraphic supplies, newsletter, complete set of books on how to teach italic handwriting to elementary school children. Catalog $1.* ■

←
Goose Quills

For calligraphers who are interested in adding a certain old-style character to their work, N.Y. Central now carries genuine goose quills. These quills are available
Uncut Quills — $.30 ea. / $2.50 dozen
Hand Cut Quills — $1.50 ea. —**New York Central Supply**

A Certain World

The best prose writers and selectors are invariably poets. This collection of W.H. Auden's favorite quotes (prose and verse) belongs on the shelf by the toilet for rewarding serendipity. —*SB*

A Certain World
(A Commonplace Book)
W.H. Auden
1970; 438 pp.
$10 postpaid from:
The Viking Press
625 Madison Avenue
New York, NY 10022
or Whole Earth Household Store

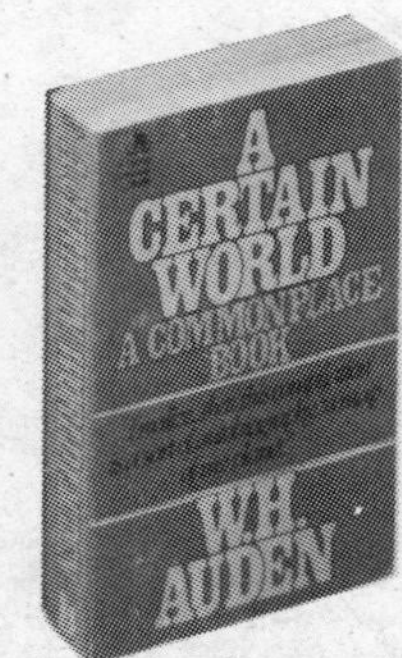

•

Letting rip a fart —
It doesn't make you laugh
When you live alone.
—Anonymous Japanese (trans. Geoffrey Bownas)

•

Tradition means giving votes to the most obscure of all classes — our ancestors. It is the democracy of the dead. Tradition refuses to submit to the small and arrogant oligarchy of those who merely happen to be walking around. —G.K. Chesterton

The Harvest of a Quiet Eye

The highest yield-per-page of any of the quotation books I've seen (dozens). If you like the samples here you'll want the book for further sampling. A bathroom, rather than a bedside book this is. —*SB*

The Harvest of a Quiet Eye
(Scientific Quotations)
Alan L. Mackay
1977; 192 pp.
$19.50 postpaid from:
Crane, Russak and Company, Inc.
Three East 44th Street
New York, NY 10017
or Whole Earth Household Store

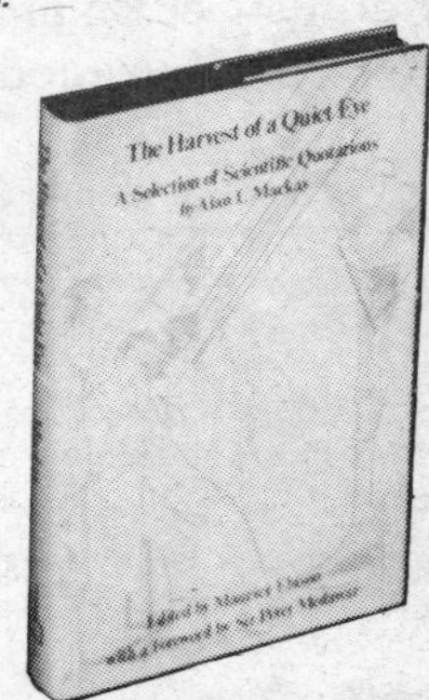

•

'Life is very strange,' said Jeremy. 'Compared with what?' replied the spider. —Anonymous

•

All the streams in the world could not, like the Virgin, build Chartres. —Henry Brooks Adams 1838-1918

•

An intellectual is someone whose mind watches itself. —Albert Camus 1913-1960

•

Genius . . . means transcendent capacity of taking trouble. —Thomas Carlyle 1795-1881

•

The manuscript in the drawer either rots or ripens. —Maria von Ebner-Eschenbach 1830-1916

•

[Occam's Razor] *Entia non sunt multiplicanda praeter necessitatem.*

It is vain to do with more what can be done with less. —William of Occam 1300-1349

THE RISING SUN NEIGHBORHOOD NEWSLETTER

We were looking at a book of old magazine ads and noticing how silly they were and how much they were like the same stuff today and I realized that about 80% of all ads say "Lonely? Why not buy something in a cardboard box?"

WHAT DO THE WORKS *below have in common with James Jones'* **From Here to Eternity**, *James Clavell's* **Shogun** *and* **Taipan**, *Ayn Rand's* **Atlas Shrugged**, *T.H. White's* **Once and Future King** *(p. 593), Frank Herbert's* **Dune** *trilogy, Isaac Asimov's* **Foundation** *trilogy, and some of the deeper detective series? Each presents a world so complete and engrossing that the reader becomes immersed and suffers the fictional events personally. Each goes on long enough that normal personal growth takes on the flavor of the reading. As with favorite childhood books, we are changed. We must be glad of it, because these are the books which are re-read.*

—SB

Lord of the Rings, etc.

*I think no other fictional world matches the depth of Tolkien's. This children's tale (***The Hobbit***) seized the Oxford mythologist and ancient languages scholar Tolkien and hurled him and us into a saga so vast that he never did encompass it all. The three-volumed* **Lord of the Rings** *is the central masterpiece — the journey of the hobbits, men, and elves, and wizard Gandalf to destroy the Ring of Power of the dark Lord Sauron. It is a tale of surprising invention, subtlety, and insight. Among the glorious details of the work are no less than fourteen whole languages. (See* **The Languages of Middle Earth** *by Ruth S. Noel, 1980; $4.95 postpaid from: Houghton-Mifflin, Wayside Road, Burlington, MA 01803.) The enormous success of Tolkien's work has happily inspired a fervent interest by the current young in living mythology, the phenomenon of "Dungeons and Dragons" — see our p. 552.*

For proper immersion in Middle Earth, you may want some additional tools. The most important I feel is **The Pictures of J.R.R. Tolkien**, *the author's own paintings and drawings of significant places and moments in the story. Expensive but worth it. Then there's* **The New Tolkien Companion**, *by J.G.A. Tyler, a sort of glossary-in-depth of the creatures, characters, terms and place names of Middle Earth — handy (does not cover* **The Silmarillion**). **The Silmarillion**, *endlessly fiddled with but not completed at Tolkien's death in 1973, was assembled adroitly by his son Christopher. It chronicles the huge doings of the First Age. A more biblical feeling book, it ends with a few pages covering the whole of the* **Lord of the Rings** *story.*

To connect you back to this world it may be necessary to read the biography, **Tolkien**, *about a nice man, serious scholar, interested in dragons.*

—SB

←

Orthanc. 'A peak and isle of rock it was, black and gleaming hard: four mighty piers of many-sided stone were welded into one, but near the summit they opened into gaping horns, their pinnacles sharp as the points of spears, keen-edged as knives.'

•

'Hold it up!' said Gandalf. 'And look closely!'

As Frodo did so, he now saw fine lines, finer than the finest penstrokes, running along the ring, outside and inside: lines of fire that seemed to form the letters of a flowing script. They shone piercingly bright, and yet remote, as if out of a great depth.

'I cannot read the fiery letters,' said Frodo in a quavering voice.

'No,' said Gandalf, 'but I can. The letters are Elvish, of an ancient mode, but the language is that of Mordor, which I will not utter here. But this in the Common Tongue is what is said, close enough:

One Ring to rule them all, One Ring to find them,
One Ring to bring them all and in the darkness bind them.

It is only two lines of a verse long known in Elven-lore:

Three Rings for the Elven-kings under the sky,
Seven for the Dwarf-lords in their halls of stone,
None for Mortal Men doomed to die,
One for the Dark Lord on his dark throne
In the Land of Mordor where the Shadows lie.
One Ring to rule them all, One Ring to find them,
One Ring to bring them all and in the darkness bind them.
In the Land of Mordor where the Shadows lie.'

He paused, and then said slowly in a deep voice: 'This is the Master-ring, the One Ring to rule them all. This is the One Ring that he lost many ages ago, to the great weakening of his power. He greatly desires it — but he must *not* get it.'

Frodo sat silent and motionless. Fear seemed to stretch out a vast hand, like a dark cloud rising in the East and looming up to engulf him. 'This ring!' he stammered. 'How, on earth did it come to me?'

—The Fellowship of the Ring

The Hobbit
(or There and Back Again)
J.R.R. Tolkien
1938; 317 pp.
$6.95 postpaid
Hardcover edition
$18.95 postpaid

The Lord of the Rings
J.R.R. Tolkien
1955; 1180 pp.
(3 volumes)
$13.95 postpaid
Hardcover editions
$39.95 postpaid

The Hobbit and The Lord of the Rings
(Paperback boxed set)
$18.95 postpaid

The Pictures of J.R.R. Tolkien
J.R.R. Tolkien
1979; 100 pp.
$30 postpaid

all from:
Houghton-Mifflin Company
Wayside Road
Burlington, MA 01803
or Whole Earth Household Store
(Paperbacks only)

The Silmarillion
J.R.R. Tolkien and Christopher Tolkien
1977; 458 pp.
$2.95 postpaid from:
Ballantine Books
455 Hahn Road
Westminster, MD 21157
or Whole Earth Household Store

The New Tolkien Companion
J.E.A. Tyler
1976, 1979; 531 pp.
$14.95 postpaid from:
St. Martin's Press
175 Fifth Avenue
New York, NY 10010
or Whole Earth Household Store

Tolkien: A Biography
Humphrey Carpenter
1977; 287 pp.
$2.50 postpaid from:
Ballantine Books
455 Hahn Road
Westminster, MD 21157
or Whole Earth Household Store

"The Tree of Amalion" from The Pictures of J.R.R. Tolkien.

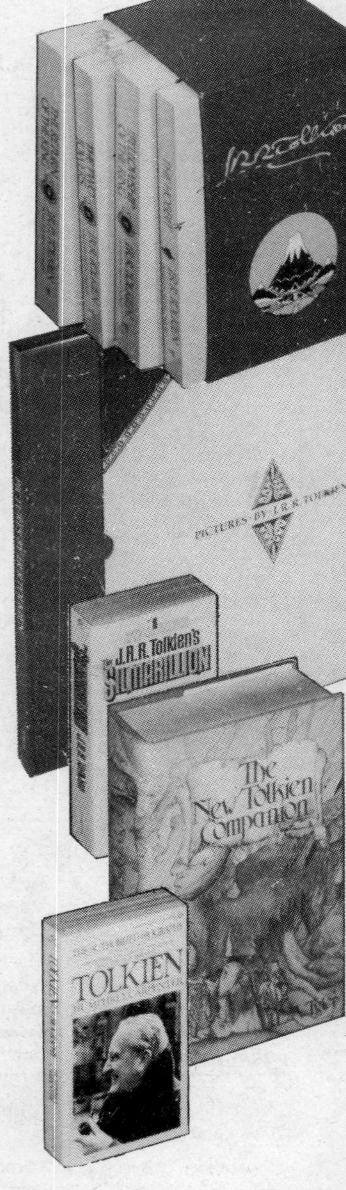

The Hornblower Saga
The Hornblower Companion
The Oxford Companion to Ships and the Sea

These eleven novels cover the professional life of British naval officer Horatio Hornblower from June, 1794 to October, 1823 — from midshipman to admiral; from battling the French revolutionary navy, through the entire epic decades of war with Napoleon, to a campaign against the pirates of the Caribbean. This was the British Navy of Nelson, the pinnacle of wooden fighting ship seamanship in the world's history. Great yarns, grippingly told.

The reason I'm presuming to review the series in this catalog of tools is because of two additional books. One is somewhat expectable — **The Hornblower Companion** *— a book of charts showing the routes and actions in each of the Hornblower books, along with explanatory text by author C.S. Forester. It is Forester's obsessive attention to nautical and historical detail that makes the second additional book so useful and absorbing. The* **Oxford Companion to Ships and the Sea** *is one of the most interesting reference books around anyway, but in company with Hornblower it is completely fascinating. Every piece of a ship, every maneuver, every salty term, every named admiral even, has a whole real story behind it. Soon, when Hornblower bellows, "Main tops'l aback!" you'll know exactly what's going on and why it stops the ship and advances the story.*

—SB

•

A bullet struck the barricade beside him as Hornblower trained the gun down, but he gave it no thought. Surely the top was swaying more even than the heavy sea justified? No matter. He had a clear shot at the enemy 's quarterdeck. He tugged at the lanyard. He saw men fall. He actually saw the spokes of the wheel spin round as it was left untended. Then the two ships came together with a shattering crash and his world dissolved into a chaos compared with which what had gone before was orderly.

The mast was falling. The top swung round in a dizzy arc so that only his fortunate grip on the swivel saved him from being flung out like a stone from a sling. It wheeled round. With the shrouds on one side shot away and two cannon balls in its heart the mast tottered and rolled. Then the tug of the mizzen stays inclined it forward, the tug of the other shrouds inclined it to starboard, and the wind in the mizzen topsail took charge when the back stays parted. The mast crashed forward; the topmast caught against the mainyard and the whole structure hung there before it could dissolve into its constituent parts. The severed butt-end of the mast must be resting on the deck for the moment; mast and topmast were still united at the cap and the trestle-trees into one continuous length, although why the topmast had not snapped at the cap was hard to say. With the lower end of the mast resting precariously on the deck, and the topmast resting against the mainyard Hornblower and Finch still had a chance of life, but the ship's motion, another shot from the Frenchman, or the parting of the overstrained material could all end that chance.

—Mr. Midshipman Hornblower

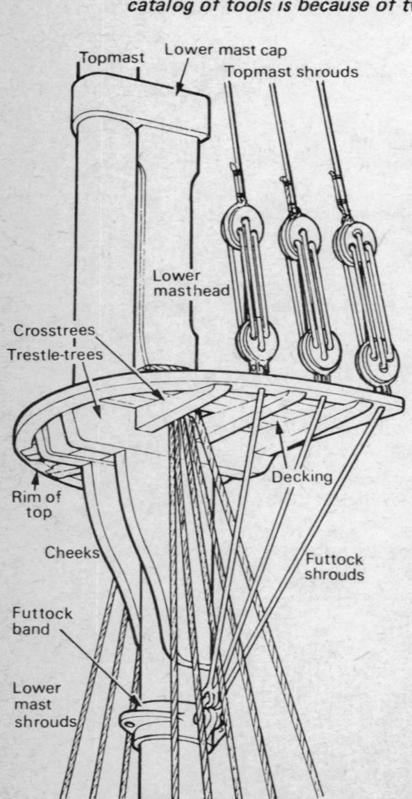

—The Oxford Companion to Ships and the Sea

The Hornblower Saga
C.S. Forester

Volume 1: Mr. Midshipman Hornblower, 1948; 266 pp., $1.50
Volume 2: Lieutenant Hornblower, 1951; 306 pp., $1.50
Volume 3: Hornblower and the Hotspur, 1962; 342 pp., $1.50
Volume 4: Hornblower and the Atropos, 1953; 310 pp., $1.50
Volume 5: Beat to Quarters, 1937; 215 pp., $1.50
Volume 6: A Ship of the Line, 1938; 233 pp., $1.25
Volume 7: Flying Colors, 1938; 210 pp., $1.50
Volume 8: Commodore Hornblower, 1945; 315 pp., $1.50
Volume 9: Lord Hornblower, 1946; 243 pp., $1.50
Volume 10: Admiral Hornblower in the West Indies, 1957; 312 pp., $1.50
Volume 11: Hornblower During the Crisis, 1950; 168 pp., $1.50

The Hornblower Companion
C.S. Forester and Samuel H. Bryant
1964; 178 pp.
$1.95

all postpaid from:
Pinnacle Books
One Century Plaza
2029 Century Park East
Los Angeles, CA 90067

The Oxford Companion to Ships and the Sea
Peter Kemp, Editor
1976; 972 pp.
$39.95 postpaid from:
Oxford University Press
16-00 Pollitt Drive
Fair Lawn, NJ 07410

(See our seagoing section, pp. 433 - 445.)

Zen in English Literature and Oriental Classics

One of the strangest books alive, a genuine hybrid of East and West and robust as hell for it. Blyth's Zen has been deemed limited, but his selector's and translator's eye is unsurpassed, and a form of literary analysis emerges that has spark. Nowhere else have I seen Robert Louis Stevenson's mystical story "The Poor Thing." I think this is an ideal book for someone who is just starting to read seriously. Bring back the paperback! —SB

Zen in English Literature and Oriental Classics
R.H. Blyth
1960; 446 pp.

$21 postpaid from:
Hokuseido Press
Heian International Publishing Company
P.O. Box 2402
South San Francisco, CA 94080

or Whole Earth Household Store

180 ZEN IN ENGLISH LITERATURE

One definition of Zen, given me by a man who had done zazen for eight years, is worth recording. "Zen is a trick of words." How true it is! And poetry too is nothing more and nothing less. Here are some examples from the New Testament:

> He that findeth his life shall lose it: and he that loseth his life for my sake shall find it. (Matthew, x 39)
>
> And whosoever will be chief among you, let him be your servant. (Matthew, xx 27)
>
> For whosoever hath, to him shall be given, and he shall have more abundance: but whosoever hath not, from him shall be taken away even that which he hath. (Matthew, xiii 12)

Compare this last to the 44th Case of the *Mumonkan*:

> Bashô said to the assembled monks, "If you have a stick, I will give you one. If you have not a stick, I will take it away from you."
>
> 芭蕉和尚示衆云儞有柱杖子我與儞柱杖子儞無柱杖子我奪儞柱杖子。 (無門關、第四十四)

For Zen the most important thing in these lofty ethical pronouncements is the paradox itself. A paradox is not a kind of pun, to be resolved by explaining the double meaning of the word. It does not spring from a desire to mystify the hearers or oneself. It arises from the inability of language to say two things at once. A doctor cuts off a leg causing pain and loss, which is evil, but saves a life, which is good. If we speak of the good-bad action, the mind unavoidably interprets this as partly good and partly bad. In this way music is greater than language. We can say two things at once, and the two separate melodies become one single indivisible harmony. Pater says, "All art aspires towards the condition of music." Action does the same, and when it reaches it, it is the activity of Zen.

PARADOX 181

Take for example Bach's Organ Passacaglia (Joh. Seb. Bachs Werke für Orgel, Band VI, Breitkopf and Härtel). On the pedal is given out the ever-recurring

This is the Absolute, the Voice of God, the Wheel of the Law, Nature. Then, hesitantly, in syncopation, begins the Relative; in grief and pain, from the end of bar 16, dying away to bar 24 where the soul reaches its lowest point, the same C as in the basso ostinato. From there, the resurrection, new life and hope; but the bass continues the same as ever. "There is no resurrection," it says, "there was no death;" only, "I am that I am." "Before Abraham was, I am":

> "Nature, with equal mind,
> Sees all her sons at play."

Yet the Absolute plus the Relative equals something else, which breaks through all language. Because

> Eternity is in love with the productions of time,

the unchanging bass of the pedal and the ever-changing melodies of the two manuals *together* express Something which is hinted at in the 2nd Case of the *Hekiganroku*:

> Once you speak and use words, there is relativity
> or absoluteness.
> *But I Jôshu am not to be found in this region of Absoluteness.*[1]
>
> 纔有語言是揀擇是明白。老僧不在明白裏。 (碧巖錄、第二則)

[1] Robert Bridges, in *Nightingales*, expresses his desire for the absolute:
"O might I wander there,
Among the flowers, which in that heavenly air
Bloom the year long!"

Haiku

Japanese traditional form seeking maximum impact from minimum words in highly formal structure. Renowned translation and comment by R.H. Blyth in four lovely volumes. Indeed like cherry blossoms on a very old very tough branch. J.D. Salinger raved about these books in one of his stories. —SB

白魚やさながら動く水の色 來山
Shirauo ya sanagara ugoku mizu no iro

The whitebait,—
As though the colour of the water
Were moving. Raizan

古池に草履沈みてみぞれかな 蕪村
Furuike ni zôri shizumite mizore kana

The old pond;
A straw sandal sunk to the bottom,
Sleet falling. Buson

秋の暮烏もなかで通りけり 几湫
Aki no kure karasu mo nakade tôri keri

An autumn evening;
Without a cry,
A crow passes. Kishû

Haiku
R.H. Blyth

Volume 1: Eastern Culture
1949; 422 pp.

Volume 2: Spring
1950; 382 pp.

$8.95 each postpaid

Volume 3: Summer-Autumn
1952; 443 pp.

Volume 4: Autumn-Winter
1953; 396 pp.

$8.95 each postpaid
(Volumes 3 - 4 available Spring 1981)

all from:
Hokuseido Press
Heian International Publishing Company
P.O. Box 2402
South San Francisco, CA 94080

or Whole Earth Household Store

America: A Prophecy

In this fascinating new anthology Brother Rothenberg and Brother Quasha have recast modern American poetry, and its rich antecedents, along broad new lines. A new "ethnopoetic" tradition that includes the early work of the dadaists and surrealists, the early "field hollers" and gospel songs and the modern blues lyrics and great street talkin' con man voice of Black America, the extraordinary Origin myths and brilliant "imagism" of Native American healing songs, and the scattered writings of early isolate white hobos and visionaries and assorted crackpots, as well as generous sampling of modern American poetry — a poetry now well schooled in the revolutionary implications found in the early work of William Carlos Williams, HD and the venerable Ezra Pound. And through it all — through the terrific urgency and excitement of the text, through the radical sometimes chaotic experimentation, through the waterfall of pure speech both "shocking" and "shocked" — the presiding fact of Prophecy — a foretelling of the return of the Old Gods. Released through the translations of these ancient and magical texts, The Old Gods, we are told, are again walking among us in the West.
—*Robert Callahan*

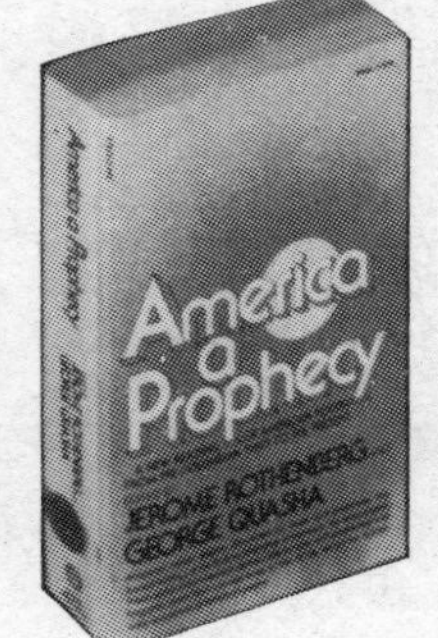

America: A Prophecy
(A New Reading of American Poetry from Pre-Columbian Times to the Present)
George Quasha and Jerome Rothenberg, Editors
1973; 603 pp.

$4.95 postpaid from:
Vintage Books
Random House
455 Hahn Road
Westminster, MD 21157

•

From the half
of the sky
That which lives there
Is coming, and makes a noise.

—Anonymous Chippewa Song
Francis Densmore Translation

Technicians of the Sacred

These are songs from the center, from the middle. (The cortex of humanity is convoluted, each fold patriotic, distinct on the outside, connected in the middle.) Superb editing by Rothenberg. A book to take with you. —SB

Technicians of the Sacred
(A Range of Poetries from Africa, America, Asia and Oceania)
Jerome Rothenberg, Editor
1968; 521 pp.

OUT OF PRINT
Doubleday and Company

Get this book back in print!

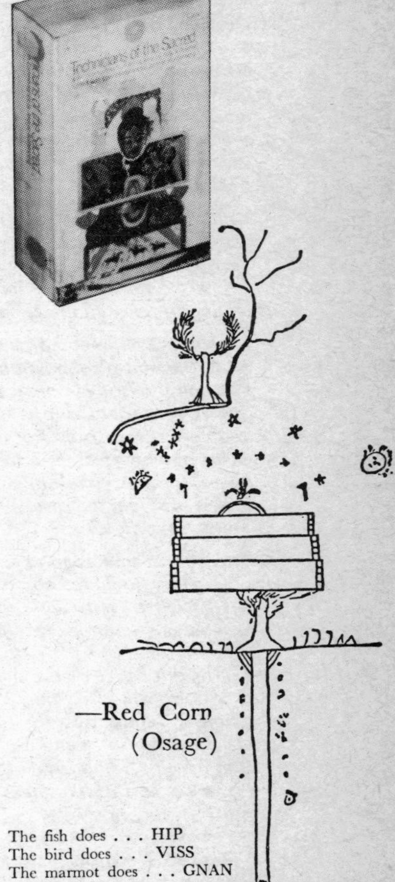

•

There is no one; there are no people. It is desolate, it lies desolate. There is nothing edible. Misery abounds, misery emerges, misery spreads. There is no joy, no pleasure. It lies sprouting; herbs lie sprouting; nothing lies emerging; the earth is pressed down. All die of thirst. The grasses lie sprouting. Nothing lies cast about. There is hunger; all hunger. It is the home of hunger; there is death from hunger. All die of cold; there is freezing; there is trembling; there is the clattering, the chattering of teeth. There are cramps, the stiffening of the body, the constant stiffening, the stretching out prone. —Aztec

An Eskimo Poem against Death

I watched the white dogs of the dawn.

What are you saying to me & am I
in-my-senses?

(Ojibwa)

I throw myself to the left,
I turn myself to the right,
I act the fish,

—Red Corn
(Osage)

The fish does . . . HIP
The bird does . . . VISS
The marmot does . . . GNAN

I throw myself to the left,
I turn myself to the right,
I act the fish,
Which darts in the water, which darts
Which twists about, which leaps—
All lives, all dances, & all is loud.

The fish does . . . HIP
The bird does . . . VISS
The marmot does . . . GNAN

(Gabon Pygmy)

Sens-Plastique

What is this astounding collection of one-liners? Chazal is French, lives on the island of Mauritius, has been publishing these things since 1947. Translator Weiss calls the prose poems "science fictions, extensions of present knowledge, visionary statements. Chazal keeps crossing the border between literature and prophecy, language and the ineffable, for the whole enterprise of **Sens-Plastique** *is dedicated to descrying in nature's oneness exactly how everything may be understood as everything else."* —SB

Sens-Plastique
Malcolm de Chazal
Irving Weiss, Translator
1948, 1979; 163 pp.

$5 postpaid from:
SUN
456 Riverside Drive
New York, NY 10027

or Whole Earth Household Store

•

The model of marching in step is the rhythmical bounce of the female breasts.

•

People will believe anything that mystifies them. To gain conviction, speak softly.

•

Every artist makes the mistake of eventually wanting to turn his art into a science. Of doing what Adam did when, dissatisfied with his enjoyment of Paradise, he wanted to know "what made it tick" and how the formula was arrived at.

•

Light is never dirty except in the human glance.

•

The emptied container of a sick man's voice.

THE RISING SUN
NEIGHBORHOOD NEWSLETTER

"A journey of a single step begins with a thousand miles."

ABC of Reading

In grade and high school I was taught how to hate Shakespeare, most novelists, and all poetry. College merely burnished my ignorance, adding the ability to hate in French. Ezra Pound, where were you when I needed you? Through Pound, literature becomes a place to revel, confirm, maybe even grow. —SB

[Suggested by Frank Deis]

ABC of Reading
Ezra Pound
1934; 206 pp.
$3.25 postpaid from:
New Directions
Publishing Corporation
William Morrow and Company
Wilmor Warehouse
6 Henderson Drive
West Caldwell, NJ
07006
or Whole Earth
Household Store

•

It doesn't, in our contemporary world, so much matter where you begin the examination of a subject, so long as you keep on until you get round again to your starting-point.

•

"Literature is news that STAYS news."

•

Men who do not understand BOOKS until they have had a certain amount of life. Or at any rate no man understands a deep book, until he has seen and lived at least part of its contents. The prejudice against books has grown from observing the stupidity of men who have *merely* read books.

•

Chaucer and Shakespeare have both an insuperable courage in tackling any, but absolutely any, thing that arouses their interest.

Selected Writings of Gertrude Stein

Gertrude Stein is not as weird as you think she is. She and her writing have a reputation for bizarre inaccessibility that started in the twenties when an expatriate lesbian who didn't use commas seemed strange beyond words to most Americans. If you actually read what she wrote, you'll find that a lot of it is straightforward, easy to understand and funny. The lack of commas is its only strangeness besides high quality.

And the stuff that is strange isn't that scary. Her word games are fun to read, especially out loud. You don't need a James Joyce-style line-by-line commentary to get it. You just need to be a speaker of English who's willing to relax and have some fun with the native tongue.

Gertrude Stein met words on an equal basis. She didn't bully them into submission nor did she let herself be bullied by past lives and meanings they may have had. She greeted them as interesting playmates and gave them and herself freedom. For a writer, reading Gertrude Stein is the perfect cure for school. In school, you feel like you can only say things that are safe and stale. Stein makes you feel that every time you use a word it's new if you'll let it be.

This collection has good examples of all of Stein's ways of writing. Included complete is the best introduction to her straightforward style — **The Autobiography of Alice B. Toklas.** *(I admit that the fact that it is written by Stein in the first person as if she were Toklas is a little tricky, but other than that it's perfectly clear and full of scrumptious Paris-in-the-'20s gossip.) Also included whole is* **Tender Buttons**, *which is the best place to start in Stein's fun and games, preferably aloud, with a liter of wine. And if you like either of those, there's lots more sort of like them in this very book, and even more in the library.* —Anne Herbert

Selected Writings of Gertrude Stein
Carl Van Vechten, Editor
1933, 1972; 706 pp.
$5.95 postpaid from:
Random House, Inc.
455 Hahn Road
New York, NY 10022
or Whole Earth
Household Store

•

I always say that you cannot tell what a picture really is or what an object really is until you dust it every day and you cannot tell what a book is until you type it or proof-read it. It then does something to you that only reading never can do. A good many years later Jane Heap said that she had never appreciated the quality of Gertrude Stein's work until she proof-read it.

—**The Autobiography of Alice B. Toklas**

The Reader's Adviser

If you throw darts at a world map and go where they point, you'll have a much more interesting vacation than anything the travel bureau can offer. Likewise if you throw one of these hefty volumes at a bed, examine the open pages and read in the direction indicated, your mind will meet minds a bookstore dare not carry. Every goddamn page (2616 all told) has fascinating people and works that I've never heard of in my high rent liberal education, warmly and searchingly remarked upon, with all the access information you need to waltz cheerfully through library procedures to the goods. —SB

The Reader's Adviser
(A Layman's Guide to Literature)
Sarah L. Prakken, Editor

Volume I
(The Best in American and British Fiction, Poetry, Essays, Literary Biography, Bibliography and Reference)
1921, 1974; 808 pp.
12th Edition
$29.95 postpaid

Volume II
(The Best in American and British Drama and World Literature in English Translation)
1921, 1977; 774 pp.
12th Edition
$29.95 postpaid

Volume III
(The Best in the Reference Literature of the World)
1921, 1977; 1034 pp.
12th Edition
$29.95 postpaid

Three-volume set
$69.95 postpaid

all from:
R.R. Bowker Company
Fulfillment Department
P.O. Box 1807
Ann Arbor, MI 4806

•

Walton, Izaak. 1593-1683. **The Compleat Angler**, one of the most famous books in English, was written by a self-educated ironmonger. Walton wrote it for his own pleasure as well as that of others; it not only describes the technique of angling, but is a contemplative essay on the peace and quietude attained by the fisherman. After its first appearance in 1653 there were frequent revisions adding new material during the author's lifetime. George Saintsbury called Walton's style one of a "singular and golden simplicity." In spite of Walton's background he became recognized as a "gentleman" of cultured tastes and learning. An Anglican and Royalist, he was overjoyed with the Restoration. In his own time, Walton was known as a biographer, author of the **Lives of John Donne, Sir Henry Wotton, Richard Hooker, George Herbert and Robert Sanderson** (Oxford $4.25).

Kenneth Rexroth wrote a charming essay on **The Compleat Angler** in the **Saturday Review** of Sept. 16, 1967, which catches the secret of its enduring appeal — and that of its author shining through it: "Izaak Walton, above all other writers in English, owes his enormous popularity to his virtues as a man, and these virtues are what condition his style and give his work its fundamental meaning. Millions have read him with joy who have never caught a fish since childhood, if at all. Indeed, . . . in America at least, most of the kinds of fish he talks about are left to small boys. The second half of the **Compleat Angler** was added in late editions and written by Charles Cotton as a guide to trout fishing in rough water. Those who want to know how to catch fish can learn most from Cotton's additions. We read Izaak Walton for a special quality of soul . . . for his tone, for his perfect attunement to the quiet streams and flowered meadows and bosky hills of the Thames valley long ago. . . . It may sound outrageous to say that Izaak Walton wrote one of the Great Books — and that about catching fish — because he was a saint, but so it is. . . . He is, in fact, an unusual embodiment of a quietly powerful tradition, that of the contemplative laymen, St. Thomas More, Nicholas Ferrer, William Law, Gilbert White. After the eighteenth century this type is more commonly found in the sciences than in religion. And like Gilbert White's **Natural History and Antiquities of Selborne**, Walton's **The Compleat Angler** is in a sense, a scientific work, an outstanding example of the piety of science."

The Compleat Angler, or The Contemplative Man's Recreation. 1653-1676. *Dutton* Everyman's 1906 $3.95 pap. $1.50; ed. by John Buchan *Oxford* 1914 World's Classics 1935 $4.25; *Rowman* 1962, 1974 $7.50.

—**The Reader's Adviser, Volume III**

Gravity's Rainbow

It took America's best book reviewer, Philip Morrison at **Scientific American** *to bring my reluctant attention to this most ambitious novel of Thomas Pynchon's. It became a book I lived in for months. Occasionally I put the book down to applaud, or stare amazed at a wall or ceiling while some perverse scientific insight sank in — or some shock of identification of Pynchon's late-World War II stateless European "zone" with the lineaments of chaos, amid which heavings of control systems all is Plot, vast conspiracy, the kind of paranoid heaven that a Nixon must live in. It is an adventure book, a victim's book, a revolutionary technological treatise (Gravity's Rainbow is the parabolic path of a V-2 rocket from Peenemunde to London; the chief villain is an experimental Pavlovian behaviorist; the major quarry is a vicious fleshlike plastic, Imipolex G).*

Tour de force. —SB

Gravity's Rainbow
Thomas Pynchon
1973; 887 pp.
$3.95 postpaid from:
Bantam Books
414 East Golf Road
Des Plaines, IL 60016
or Whole Earth
Household Store

•

The straight-ruled boulevards built to be marched along are now winding pathways through the waste-piles, their shapes organic now, responding, like goat trails, to laws of least discomfort.

•

If there is something comforting — religious, if you want — about paranoia, there is still also anti-paranoia, where nothing is connected to anything, a condition not many of us can bear for long.

•

"Temporal bandwidth" is the width of your present, your *now.* It is the familiar "Δt" considered as a dependent variable. The more you dwell in the past and in the future, the thicker your bandwidth, the more solid your persona. But the narrower your sense of Now, the more tenuous you are. It may get to where you're having trouble remembering what you were doing five minutes ago, or even — as Solthrop now — what you're doing *here*, at the base of this colossal curved embankment. . . .

•

Where you cannot feed, you take away weapons. Weapons and food have been firmly linked in the governmental mind for as long as either has been around.

The Pushcart Prize

Printing good (and bad) writing is easy and cheap these days, but getting it to where people can buy it is still complicated and expensive. That hurts small, worthy presses, and it also hurts you since you're missing a lot, no matter how many bookstores you go to.

Here is a way to miss less of what's being published by groups smaller than Time, Inc. and **Mother Jones.** **The Pushcart Prize** *is a collection of good writing nominated annually from hundreds of small press publications. Strange good things by people you wouldn't otherwise see. And it lists where the pieces were originally published so you can use it as a guide to small magazines you might be interested in.* —Anne Herbert

The Pushcart Prize
(Best of the Small Presses)
Bill Henderson, Editor

Volume I
1976; 437 pp.
$6.95 postpaid

Volume II
1977; 527 pp.
$5.95 postpaid

Volume III
1979; 543 pp.
$6.95 postpaid

Volume IV
1979; 589 pp.
$7.95 postpaid

all from:
Avon Books
Mail Order Department
250 West 55th Street
New York, NY 10019
or Whole Earth
Household Store

Blackwell's Books New and Forthcoming

An account with Blackwell's of Oxford is worth it just for the catalogs of new books in whatever field you choose. Since most American bookstores now refuse to single-order paperbacks, Blackwell's provides a service unlike any other — a mailorder service for monks in the new Dark Ages. Write:

Blackwell's of Oxford
Broadstreet
Oxford, England

—*William Irwin Thompson*

SPECIAL OFFER SAVE 50%

The Annotated™ Shakespeare

Edited by A.L. Rowse. These popular definitive editions of Shakespeare's works are the most up-to-date, containing much newly discovered material, and are the most convenient as well as authoritative editions ever published for the modern reader. 8½" x 11". Each illustrated with over 1,400 prints, drawings, and engravings and contain over 750 pages.

Pub. at $20.00

Only $9.98 each

Limited Quantity of these Slightly Damaged Odd Volumes

320495. Vol. I The Comedies

The Comedy of Errors
Two Gentlemen of Verona
The Taming of the Shrew
Love's Labours Lost
A Midsummer's Night Dream
Merchant of Venice
As You Like It
Much Ado About Nothing
The Merry Wives of Windsor
Twelfth Night
Troilus and Cressida
All's Well That Ends Well
Measure for Measure

320509. Vol. II The Histories, Sonnets and Other Poems

The First Part of King Henry VI
The Second Part of King Henry VI
The Third Part of King Henry VI
King Richard III
King Richard II
King John
The First Part of King Henry IV
The Second Part of King Henry IV
King Henry V
King Henry VIII
A Lover's Complaint
Venus and Adonis
The Rape of Lucrece
The Sonnets
The Phoenix and the Turtle

—Marboro

Remaindered and used books

As we've discovered again and again to our chagrin while compiling the **Next Whole Earth Catalog**, *not every good book remains in print (particularly in these days of conglomerate publishing and revolving-door bookstore shelves). When a book I want is no longer available, (especially if it's relatively recent), the first place I turn to is the remaindered-book firms. When publishers clean out their warehouses, that's where they send the castaways.* **Publisher's Central Bureau** *and* **Marboro Books** *are the least expensive (usually about half what you'd pay for the books new) and have the most interesting catalogs. I've been poring over them eagerly since I was 15. The attraction is the sheer quantity of trashy books — murder mysteries which never unravel, biographies of the uninteresting, ptomaine-inspiring cookbooks — with a true gem at very cheap price every other page or so. The real values are in art and picture books — the kind David Wills visually refers to on page 464 — as well as reference books and last year's bestsellers.*

The two companies are virtually identical; I slightly prefer Publisher's Central Bureau, but that's only because Marboro sold psychedelic posters back in the sixties, and always seemed a bit seedier for it. Their free catalogs (so free that once on their mailing list you'll feel inundated) are available from: **Publisher's Central Bureau,** One Champion Avenue, Avenel, NJ 07131; *or* **Marboro Books, Inc.**, 205 Moonachie Road, Moonachie, NJ 07074.

The **Strand** *is classier; they operate out of a huge, dusty warehouse/store just east of Greenwich Village in New York. Every impoverished student in Manhattan knows about them. Their prices aren't as good as the remainder houses, but they have better books, and list them by author's name. Most useful if there's a book you already know you want. Here again, the best deals are in picture books. Between catalogs they release bulletins with "Strand Specials" which are truly incredibly priced. Regrettably, the catalog doesn't have the same browse-appeal of the store itself; but this way, you get to keep the money you save instead of walking out with four other books. Their booklists are free from:* **Strand Book Store,** 828 Broadway, New York, NY 10003.

We're not listing used book dealers because we don't know any who are reputable by mail; but for out-of-print books you really want, a good alternative is book search services. Generally, you send them the title, author and edition of a book, plus a fee (about $2). During the next 2 - 3 months, they put ads in book-search publications (which only accept ads from registered book dealers) and when they find the volume, they send you a price quote. You're under no obligation to buy it. One good firm (suggested by Mimi Abrams) is **Academy Library,** 2245 Larkin Street, No. 2, San Francisco, CA 94109. *They say there's a 90% chance of finding any book. Other such firms can be found in the classifieds of* **Library Journal** *(p. 497), the* **New York Times Book Review, Atlantic Monthly,** *and other high-rent literary magazines.*
—*Art Kleiner*

Also — check your library. I've known people who would call 17 book stores to find a book and never go down the street to the library. At the library, it doesn't matter if books are out of print. They're there, and the price is right.
—*Anne Herbert*

•

Cumming, W.P. et al. — **The Exploration of North America 1630-1776.** With superb maps and illust. Putnam. 1974. 272 p. (pub$30.00) $9.95

Dalton, S. — **Borne On the Wind.** An extraordinary collection of photographs of insects in flight. Reader's Digest. 1975. 160p. (pub$18.95) $5.95
—**Strand**

Dover Publications

This press resurrects saviors — books which, though supposedly dead and out of print, have acquired lives of their own, tattered library lives, faded xerox lives. Dover gives them high quality new paperback bodies to live in, and they go on forever. They're about everything. The original half-mad books that opened whole new subject areas. Old time how-to books. Copyright-free great-illustration books of clip art. Kids' classics. Get their catalog. (See an artist's notes about Dover on p. 464.)
—*SB*

Dover Publications
Catalog
free from:
Dover Publications
180 Varick Street
New York, NY 10014

↑
Adams, Percy G. — **Travelers and Travel Liars**

This book is a fascinating, scholarly account of the deceptions and exaggerations found in many authentic (and some not-so-authentic) travel accounts of the 18th century; of the motivations behind these deceptions; and of the far-reaching effects these "travelers and travel liars" had on Europeans and Americans of the times. Professor Adams, Director of Graduate Studies in English at the University of Tennessee, introduces a colorful cast of rogues and scholars, ranging from Voltaire, who gave little credence to the 9-foot Patagonians, to Defoe, who made up travel accounts under various names. Adams' lively exploration of human credulity in the Age of Reason will delight lovers of travel lore and anyone interested in the history of the period. "A work of industrious and amusing scholarship." — **Times Literary Supplement,** (reviewing the first edition). Unabridged republication of the University of California Press edition, 1962. New Preface by the author. 9 illustrations. 320pp. 5-3/8 x 8-1/2. April 1980. 23942-X Paperbd. $4.50 (tent.).

•

Muybridge, Eadweard — **The Human Figure in Motion**

"Unparalleled dictionary of action for artists" (**American Artist**) contains more than 4500 stopped-action photographs, in series, showing undraped men, women, children jumping, lying down, running, sitting down, throwing, wrestling, carrying objects, and similar actions. Taken by the great 19th-century photographer, Muybridge, these are among the finest action shots ever taken. 4789 photographs. xvii + 390pp. 7-7/8 x 10-5/8. 20204-6 Clothbd. $13.50.

•

Tashlin, Frank — **The Bear That Wasn't**

Delightfully humorous, yet with serious implications; a fable for our time and an utterly charming children's story. In sum, a book that defies classification. Profusely illustrated. v + 51pp. 20939-3 Paperbd. $1.50.

•

Bentley, W.A. and W.J. Humphreys — **Snow Crystals**

Over 2,000 beautiful, clear snowflakes (and occasional ice formations) enlarged from photomicrographs. Brief text on methodology of research. Can be used for decorate in many contexts. 202 plates. 226pp. 8 x 10¼. 20287-9 Paperbd. $7.50

Books on Tape

I am an American, therefore I commute. My company on the road used to be 18-wheelers and stale news radio. Then I discovered Books on Tape, offering over 300 complete books read by actors and actresses on cassette tapes — Americana, classics, fiction and science fiction, history and war, non-fiction, travel and adventure. They have recently added children's books to their list. The readers are instructed not to over-dramatize the books — "if Dickens and Maugham could leave something to the reader's imagination, we can too." The books average 7 - 14 one-hour tapes, and cost between $6 - $15 to rent for one month. When you have finished listening to them, just put them back in their self-mailing box, drop it in the mail box and wait for the next one. We share the cost and listening with a couple of friends.
—*Evelyn Eldridge-Diaz*

Books on Tape
Catalog
free from:
Books on Tape
P.O. Box 7900
Newport Beach, CA
92660

•

The Adventures of Sherlock Holmes (1109) by Arthur Conan Doyle.

Adventures of world's first consulting detective. Twelve famous short stories. 7 - 1½ hr. cassettes. Read by Richard Green. $9.50

•

Papillon (1116) by Henri Charriere

Daring escape from island prison. 12 - 1½ hr. cassettes. Read by Michael Prichard. $10.50

Spoken Arts

A fine big collection of records and cassettes of poets, stories, exotic song, drama, and so forth. Records are $8.98 each, cassettes $9.95 each. Play Rikki-Tikki-Tavi again. Play Wallace Stevens again.
—*SB*

Spoken Arts
Catalog
free from:
Spoken Arts
Department E
310 North Avenue
New Rochelle, NY 10801

•

An Informal Hour With Dorothy Parker, read by Dorothy Parker, Record 726; Cassette 44-3.

The celebrated poet-critic-writer reads her story "Horsie," and recites twenty-six of her bittersweet poems. "All this — and the Parker voice too — make for a very special evening." —**Hi-Fidelity.**

•

Anne Frank: The Diary of a Young Girl, read by Julie Harris, 2 Records, 1116 A/B; 2 Cassettes 7201/02; Book $1.95.

The stirring true drama of a family in Amsterdam who had to hide from the Nazis for two years. Julie Harris recreates those touching words. Accompanying paper-back book. 2-record set.

Large print books

Large print books exist and are wonderful. Libraries often have lots of them — classics and popular novels and kids' books and fact books. They're relaxing to read if your vision is perfect and a re-entry to a lost world if your vision is poor. A good thing to pick up at the library for someone who doesn't get around much, and also nice for you. **Large Type Books In Print,** *also at the library, lists 3300 titles, and is a good place to find out what there is if you're gift giving.*
—*Anne Herbert*

Large Type Books Books In Print
(Subject Index, Author Index, Title Index)
Annual; 674 pp.
$19.95 postpaid
from:
R.R. Bowker Company
1180 Avenue of the Americas
New York, NY 10036

Library of Congress Talking Book Service Choice Magazine Listening

These two services are only available to the blind (or those certified with a physical disability that makes reading hard). They're free spoken-word records and cassettes. (Record players and/or cassette players are available free to those who can't afford their own.) The Library of Congress service is an index to recorded books, and a list of the libraries nationwide where they're available. **Choice** *is a magazine, excerpted from the likes of* **Smithsonian,** *the* **New Yorker,** *and our own* **CoEvolution Quarterly.** *We've heard good reports about both; they're real world-openers. I bet it's flattering for the authors whose works are chosen, too. (See more resources for the disabled, p. 333.)*
—*Art Kleiner*

Talking Book Service
Information
free from:
National Library Service for the Blind and Physically Handicapped
Library of Congress
Washington, D.C. 20402

Choice Magazine Listening
Information
free from:
Choice Magazine Listening
P.O. Box 10
Port Washington, NY
11050

Instant Hardcover

For $2.75 to $3.75 (higher price only for largest size books) Hartzberg will convert any paperbound book up to the size of the **Next Whole Earth Catalog** into a sturdy, long-lasting hardbound. Buy cheap. Convert to hardbound.

I find that my books are easier to handle with the new binding — open easier; don't fight me. They feel good.

Nirvana — knowing that my autographed copy of **Utopia or Oblivion** will last forever, and for only $2.75 over the purchase price of $1.25. Cheap preservation.

You do have to send a minimum of 15 books or there is a $15 service charge.

Hartzberg — New Method
Vandalia Road
Jacksonville, IL 62652

Rick
Freeport, Texas

"Some one with a good deal of intelligence," remarked Poirot drily.

THE RISING SUN
NEIGHBORHOOD NEWSLETTER

Stephanie said the biggest thing she learned from fasting for four days in the Liferaft Earth event was that food structures time and without food time just goes on and on.

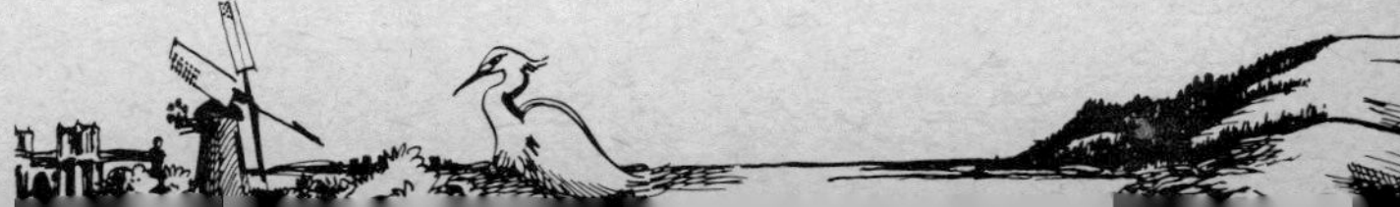

NEW WAVE IN PRINT

by Jay Kinney

PRINT IS AT BEST A CLUE. If a punk group's record is a far cry from the immediacy of its live performance, then reading a printed article about that record is twice as abstract.

Nevertheless, few of us have the opportunity (or stamina) to be front and center at every punk/new wave show in every urban scene. Similarly, the proliferation of groups with self-produced 45s, EPs (extended-play records), and small (as well as major) label albums makes it difficult to keep track of the best recorded sounds. In some circles, word-of-mouth does the job, and the enthusiasm of a trusted friend is still the best testimonial.

However, failing that, there are several new wave publications which share news, reviews, and interviews — often in a visually-tactile style which is a graphic analog to the music. There are also a number of allied publications falling within the vague new wave genre that traffic in areas besides music: ads as art, art as style, and life-style as put-on. To the degree that there is an all-encompassing new wave sensibility developing (an arguable notion), it is at least partially reflected here too.

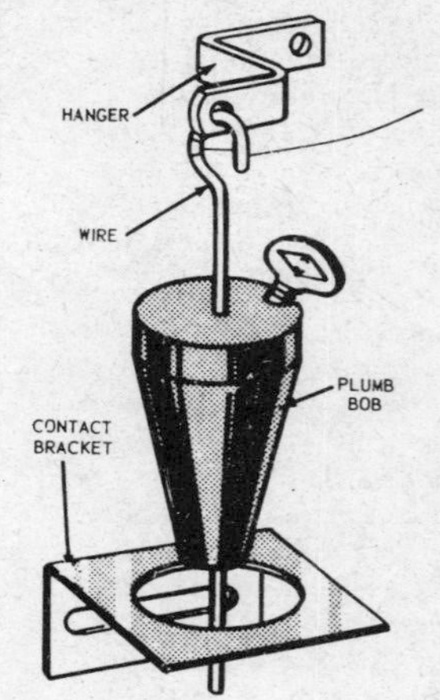
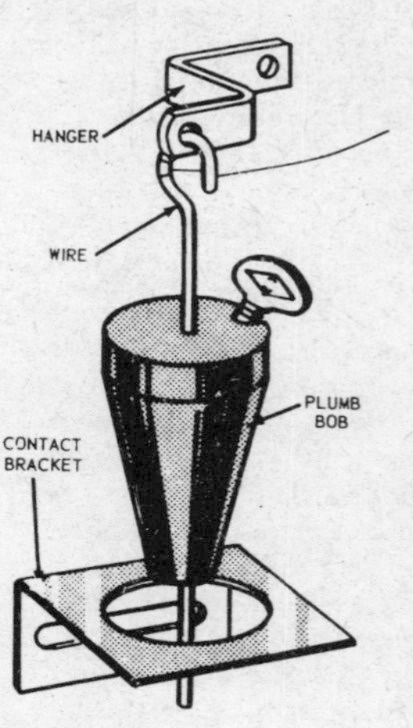

The tilt mechanism

Katherine Latanville by George Whiteside, Impulse

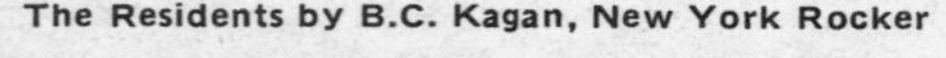

The Residents by B.C. Kagan, New York Rocker

The Slits by Fran Pelzman, NY Rocker

Slash

Slash is an irreverent and snotty monthly tabloid from L.A. which somehow manages to convey an honesty and intelligence that is certainly absent in 99% of the slick media. Kickboy Face, Chatty Chatty Mouth, Ranking Jeffrey Lea and other staff writers review local concerts, mounds of 45s and LPs, and interview a wide range of musicians and performers. Correspondents in London and San Francisco keep tabs on those scenes, while **Slash**'s own "Local Shit" column does the same for southern California. Cartoonist Gary Panter is on hand each issue with a bizarre comics page featuring neanderthal punker Jimbo. Highly recommended.

Slash, P.O. Box 48888, Los Angeles, CA 90048. $12/year (12 issues), Claude Bessy and Philomena, Editors.

New York Rocker

New York Rocker is fatter than **Slash** and increasingly pop-oriented, probably a reflection of its location in N.Y. where the scene is older and, by now, more jaded. Its editorial stance is slightly removed from it all and of late there has been an upsurge of perfunctory pop-journalism in its pages. A central new wave organ nevertheless.

New York Rocker, 166 Fifth Avenue, New York, NY 10010. $11/year (11 issues). Andy Schwartz, Editor.

Trouser Press

Trouser Press began over 6 years ago as an Anglophilic rock fanzine and has since grown into a color-covered slick with a strong new wave and progressive rock coverage. The **TP** tends to take a historical approach to the groups covered with often exhaustive attention to chronology and background of the musicians. **TP** is still heavily weighted in favor of British groups with record contracts, but columns also cover domestic "underground" 45s, other rock media, and plenty of new LPs. Narrow but deep.

Trouser Press, P.O. Box B, Old Chelsea Station, New York, NY 10011. $12/year (12 issues). Scott Isler, Editor.

New Musical Express

New Musical Express, the long-running English rock weekly, is the best means of keeping up on the ever-changing contours of the British punk and new wave scene. The leftist-tinged staff manages to keep readers aware of the machinations of the music industry as it interacts with bands. New groups are touted early by **NME**, though they subsequently come in for heavy criticism for "selling out" by the time said groups release their second albums. If this route seems a bit pat, still it is in unique contrast to say, **Rolling Stone**, where the difference between ads and editorial content is often hard to discern.

New Musical Express, Room 2613, Kings Reach Tower, Stamford Street, London SE1 9LS, England. $52/year (52 issues). Jim Watts, Editor. Make checks payable to IPC Magazines.

ALL OF THE ABOVE periodicals are professional to one degree or another and make stabs at keeping their readers informed of new wave developments in at least the major cities. Legions of small-circulation punk fanzines and papers serving local scenes in smaller cities may have a more limited scope but often beat the larger rags for vitality. Since fanzines are produced by fans, not journalists, they tend to rise and fall following the trajectory of enthusiasm. Xeroxed or quick-printed, their circulations rarely exceed a couple of hundred (if that), and to list them here would be akin to promoting your grandma's kitchen in the Michelin Restaurant Guide. The point is to keep your eyes open for your hometown fanzine(s) or start your own. Neverthless, a few scene-binding publications look like they'll be around for awhile (maybe) and are worth noting. This selection merely scratches the surface.

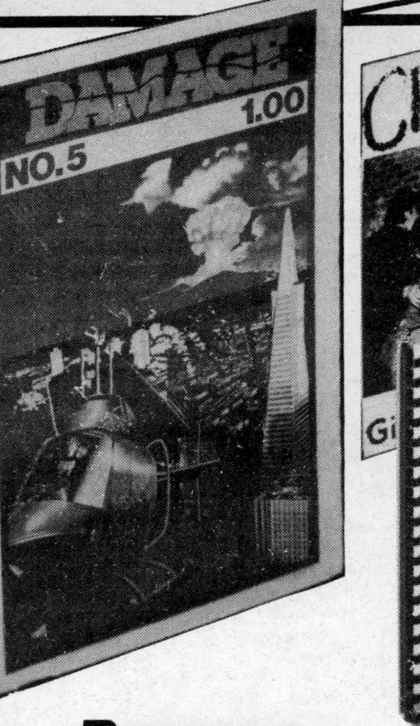

Damage

When **Search and Destroy**, the groundbreaking S.F. punk tabloid ceased publication early in '79 ("mission accomplished"), **Damage** stepped in to fill the gap. A heavy emphasis on group interviews is being increasingly supplemented with opinion pieces, fiction, articles, trend news, and criticism. Compared to the semi-monolithic **Slash**, **Damage**'s identity is loose and diffuse – perhaps mirroring San Francisco itself.

Damage, P.O. Box 26178, San Francisco, CA 94126. $10/year (12 issues). Brad L., Editor.

Creep

Creep, another S.F. punk rag is smaller, more personal, less regular than **Damage**. A fanzine, not a tabloid, **Creep** presents interviews, exhortations, lists, and gossip with unrelenting first-person honesty.

Creep, P.O. Box 5528, San Francisco, CA 94101. $ .75/ issue (no subscriptions).

Sluggo

Sluggo!, which just moved from Austin, Texas, to San Francisco, is an amazing offset fanzine in various colors of inks and paper. Energy fairly drips off the pages, where cultural, political, *and* musical opinions and news vie for space. Plenty of strange art, comic strips, and interviews. And they print it in their own basement!

Sluggo!, 530 Stanyan Street, San Francisco, CA 94118. $7.50/year (4 issues). Nick Modern, Editor.

Quasi-Substitute

Quasi-Substitute is a somewhat scruffy San Diego fanzine. Your standard reviews of live shows, new plastic, and band interviews, emphasizing San Diego's scene. Around 16 pages of teeny typewriting plus photos and art.

Quasi-Substitute, 4307 Date, La Mesa, CA 92041. $3/ 6 issues. Checks payable to M. Toombs.

AN UNEXPECTED side effect of the languishing death of "fine art" has been the shifting of art activity out of galleries and museums and into the media. Enter ads as art wherein surrealism hovers over grids of boomerangs selling you the addresses of boutiques. Ads as interior brain decoration. Perhaps this interchangeability of ads, art, and editorial matter is nothing new – yet the recent appearance of publications willing to admit it (and frankly exploit it) is.

With immediacy, fashionability, and crisp aesthetics as the common denominators, the following publications approach the antithesis of the original punk impulse, yet for better or worse they are part of the new wave mix. Fashion obsolescence being what it is, by the time this sees print they may have moved on; but for now . . .

Another Room

Cancel the above. Most urban ad tabloids start out free, with populist notions of "cheap media access for the (un)common man," and a certain raw excitement. Of all such attempts in the Bay Area, **Another Room** alone has kept the faith (so far) – it's still free and still worth a regular glance-through. Ads for bands and artists predominate, with a constantly improving smattering of puzzling graphics, art/music interviews and reviews spread throughout.

Another Room, 1640 18th Street, Oakland, CA 94607. $6/year (12 issues). Lucy Childs and John Gulak, Editors.

Boulevards

Boulevards, on the other hand, has gone from similar humble origins (monthly ad tab for gay and punk boutiques) to the lofty realms of a 52-page, saddle-stitched magazine with columnists, feature articles, color covers – the works. For a buck. The scattershot unpredictability of the very first issues has long since gone, replaced with a certain chic reliability.

Boulevards, 1008 Sutter Street, San Francisco, CA 94109. $8/year (12 issues). Kevin Jenkins, Editor.

Wet

One more rung up the ladder of commercial success resides **Wet**, formerly the magazine of Gourmet Bathing. **Wet** has long since left hot tubs behind for the greener pastures of life styles. The '50s meet Japan meet post-disco spif meet New Wave and all go out for an expensive drink. Simultaneously striking and vapid, **Wet** is dandy intellectual cotton candy.

Wet, P.O. Box 1017, Venice, CA 90291. $10/year (6 issues). Leonard Koren, Editor.

Impulse

Far better is **Impulse**, from Toronto, which is graphically experimental, relatively ad-free (7 pages out of 68, compared to **Wet**'s 42 out of 84), and editorially wide-ranging. An art magazine above all else (video, microfiche, performance), **Impulse** also covers new technology, architecture, music, and organized crime, sometimes in surprising depth.

Impulse, P.O. Box 901, Station Q, Boston, MA 02115. $10/year (4 issues). Eldon Garnet and Shelagh Alexander, Editors.

Subway News

Finally, this tabloid combines elements of all of the above into a package whose contradictions fascinate while they confuse. Leave it to Boston to spawn this mish-mash of new wave music, fashion pix, first-person reviews and gossip, and comic strips (by Mark Beyer, America's best primitive cartoonist). Page layouts look, in turn, like the **New Yorker**, the **National Enquirer**, and the weekend entertainment section of any big city daily paper. Yet, on the whole, the **Subway News** works in its quirky way, and by its very eclecticism may escape the usual degeneration into a pat formula. Good luck!

Subway News, P.O. Box 149, Boston, MA 02115. $1/ issue. Doug Simmons, Editor.

Photo by Brian Hagiwara, Wet

A word of caution on ordering these periodicals – as with the underground press of the '60s many new wave publications have appeared to fill a need or express a mood – which they do far better than turn a profit. Except for **New Musical Express, Wet, Trouser Press**, and **Boulevards** I'm unsure I could predict the continued existence of the reviewed publications by the time this sees print, much less months later. Moreover, subscriptions, while great in theory, are often screwed up in practice. (The **New York Rocker** never did get mine straight. I'm now back to buying them at my local record shop.) If ordering sample copies, add $ .50 to single copy price for postage. ■

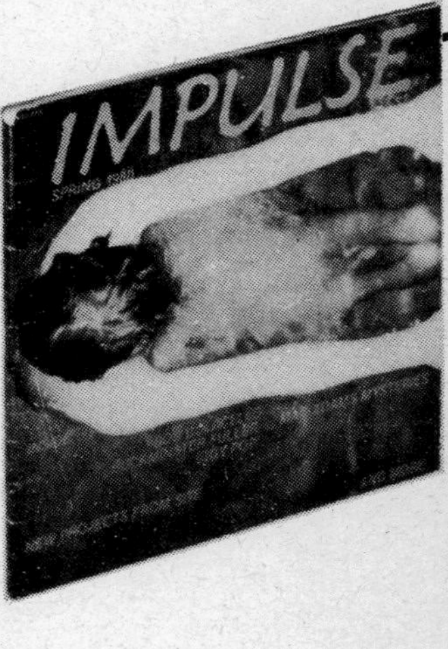

THE RISING SUN
NEIGHBORHOOD NEWSLETTER

Susan asked me if I was a backpacker and Ben said, "Do bears read poetry in the woods?"

UNDERGROUND COMIX

CARTOONISTS AND POETS TEND TO BE EXCELLENT WRITERS — MAYBE BECAUSE THEY HAVE TO MANAGE WITH MINIMUM WORDS. CARTOONIST KINNEY IS MOST SEEN THESE DAYS IN ANARCHY AND YOUNG LUST COMICS.
—SB

by Jay Kinney

Most of the "underground" media serving the counterculture in the '60s have either long since disappeared or metamorphosed into slick-format ad-vehicles retailing narrow slices of life-style. Not so underground comix.

Originally started by a loose network of self-publishing cartoonists in 1968, these comix soon developed into an energetic if tiny industry. As most of the UG cartoonists lived in or migrated to San Francisco and Berkeley, 3 of the 4 main comix publishers sprang up there as well. (The fourth was located in Milwaukee!)

The earliest UGs emphasized personalized humor about those great participant sports of the youth culture — sex and drugs. A third obsession, violence, was added soon, reflecting the atmosphere created by Manson, Altamont, and the war. This triumvirate of taboos in varying combinations monopolized most of the comix throughout the early '70s.

There were, of course, exceptions. Comix edited and drawn by many women UG cartoonists took as their focus the real-life experiences and fantasies of women living in a male dominated culture. A number of "theme" comics spotlighted ecology, drug addiction and similar topics, as well.

Sales faltered in '73-'74, due in part to the 1973 Supreme Court ruling on obscenity which left decisions as to what was obscene up to local "community standards." UGs were suddenly too risky, for many distributors and outlets were not willing to stick their necks out for the meagre profits the UGs earned. Moreover, the market was increasingly flooded with low-quality comix (many of which were published by those same fickle distributors), and many formerly enthusiastic readers were driven away.

The next few years were characterized by several attempts by the publishers and the best UG artists to develop mass-circulation comic magazines. **The Funny Papers, Arcade,** *and* **Comix Book** *all failed in their tries at a winning format. Expensive to produce and advertising-poor, these magazines were ill-suited for a national newsstand distribution system which shreds up unsold copies and forces publishers to rely on ad income for survival.*

Amazingly enough, in the wake of these blows, UGs have rebounded and survived. With some of the cartoonists only now hitting their stride, and the publishers maintaining stricter standards of quality, the comix of the last 3 - 4 years have been among the best ever.

Whether due to widespread cultural satiation, inevitable artistic "maturity," or simply boredom with old kicks, the venerable themes of sex, drugs, and violence are far less in evidence now. Humor, social satire, history, and educational strips rule the roost these days.

Distribution, through alternative channels, is as spotty as ever, and the comix can be better found in some midwestern college towns than in Manhattan, for instance. Accordingly, mail order has grown in importance, with most publishers carrying each other's titles in addition to their own. Since availability (and prices) can change as time goes by, your best bet is to order the current catalogs from the publishers and mail order firms below before sending for specific comix.

For news of UG comix as they come out, plus reviews and artist interviews, the following two publications are worth checking out:

Cascade Comix Monthly, Everyman Studios, 432 South Cascade, Colorado Springs, CO 80903. $5/year (6 issues). *A handsome, offset fanzine with color covers.*

Comix World, Clay Geerdes, Box 7081, Berkeley, CA 94707. $6/year (24 issues). *A single-sheet newsletter full of news, tips, gossip, "opinions."*

Below is a listing (with telegraphed descriptions) of some of the best UG comix of the last few years.

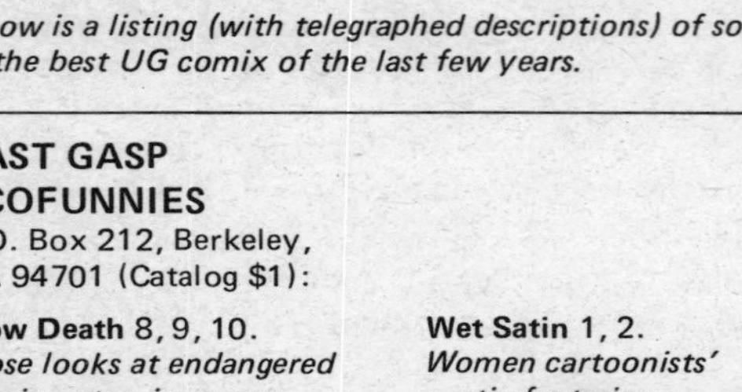
YOU'RE RIGHT! THIS IS A CRUCIAL TIME. WE CAN'T AFFORD TO BE PASSIVE SPECTATORS — IF WE SIT BACK AND LET THEM GET AWAY WITH THIS... ONE DAY WE WILL WAKE UP TO FIND OUR FREEDOM
HAS PASSED AWAY LIKE A DREAM!

—from Class War Comix, Kitchen Sink Enterprises

RIP OFF PRESS
P.O. Box 14158, San Francisco, CA 94114 (Catalog $.50):

Rip Off Comics 1 - 6. *Anthology comic with the latest Freak Brothers and Wonder Warthog stories.*

40 Year-Old Hippie 1 - 2 by Ted Richards. *Tales of the best burn-out still navigating the streets.*

Cartoon History of the Universe 1 - 4 by Larry Gonick. *Impressive scope, wry humor, a top-notch series for both adults and kids.* *(See p. 566.)*

Comanche Moon by Jack Jackson. *Fine paperback collection of true tales of Indian life. Co-published with Last Gasp.*

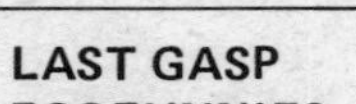

LAST GASP ECOFUNNIES
P.O. Box 212, Berkeley, CA 94701 (Catalog $1):

Slow Death 8, 9, 10. *Close looks at endangered species, atomic power, and cancer, respectively.*

Anarchy 1, 2. *New wave political humor and history.*

No Ducks 1, 2. *Funny animals for adults . . . but no ducks.*

Young Lust 5, 6. *Romance parody as springboard for social satire.*

Wet Satin 1, 2. *Women cartoonists' erotic fantasies.*

Dr. Atomic 4, 5 by Larry Todd. *The UG's favorite mad scientist and dope fiend.*

Yow 1, 2 by Bill Griffith. *Zippy the Pinhead adventures in depth.*

Wimmens' Comix 6, 7. *Honest stories by women for everyone.*

KITCHEN SINK
P.O. Box 7, Princeton, WI 54968 (Catalog $.50):

Corporate Crime 1, 2. *Entertaining (?) dramatizations of corporate rip-offs.*

Snarf 6 - 8. *One of the best anything-goes anthology comics around.*

Bizarre Sex 6 - 8. *Sometimes bizarre, sometimes sexy, usually amusing.*

Dope Comix 1 - 3. *Dope humor refined to its pure essence.*

Snoid Comics by R. Crumb. *Mr. Snoid throws tantrums for women with big legs.*

EDUCOMICS
P.O. Box 9090, Boulder, CO 80301 (Catalog $1):

Energy Comics 1. *Energy alternatives to nukes and fossils.*

All-Atomic Comics by Leonard Rifas. *Chock full of anti-nuclear arguments and facts.*

Gen of Hiroshima by Keiji Nakazawa. *The first of a 20-volume series on Japan before and after the Bomb.*

Mama Dramas. *True tales of motherhood from cartooning mothers.*

THE PRINT MINT
830 Folger Avenue, Berkeley, CA 94710 (Catalog $.50):

Zap 9. *With Crumb, Wilson, Moscoso . . . the oldest anthology comic in the UG.*

Moondog 4 by George Metzger. *Post-hippie fantasy of post-industrial life.*

OTHER PUBLISHERS

APEX NOVELTIES
353 Frederick Street, San Francisco, CA 94117.

Best Buy Comics by R. Crumb. *Crumb's recent best work . . . from the pages of* **CoEvolution Quarterly.**

KRUPP MAIL ORDER
P.O. Box 9090, Boulder, CO 80301 (Catalog $1).

THE AMAZING REALM OF SELF-PUBLISHING

Honkytonk Sue 1, 2 by Bob "Boze" Bell, 707 West MacKenzie, Phoenix, AZ 85013. *Splendid satire of cowboy culture, UFOs, Hollywood, featuring "The Queen of Country Swing."*

BOB SIDEBOTTOM
481 Alvarado, Monterey, CA 93940 (Catalog $.25).

BUD PLANT, INC.
P.O. Box 1886, Grass Valley CA 94945 (Catalog $1). ■

—Fat Freddy's Cat by Gilbert Shelton ↓

ME OUT! PROWL NOW!

WOW! ME OUT? ME OUT?

HUNH? WHAT? DO YOU WANT ME TO OPEN THE DOOR?

I SWEAR, THEY'RE SO STUPID THEY DON'T EVEN SEEM TO UNDERSTAND WHEN YOU SPEAK TO THEM IN THEIR OWN LANGUAGE!

National Geographic

Nine *million* *circulation. Ninety-two years old. A magazine success story that re-earns its success with each fascinating issue. And each year it takes a few more chances with environmental and political issues. The readership could care less; like with* **Playboy**, *they're in it for the pictures, the sheer planetary range of human activity. Also good maps* *(see p. 22)* *and not-bad science sometimes, with a nice element of common people feeling involved.* —SB

NATIONAL GEOGRAPHIC

National Geographic
Gilbert M. Grosvenor, Editor
$9.50/year (12 issues, includes membership) from:
The Secretary
National Geographic Society
P.O. Box 2895
Washington, DC 20013

Transplanted in the desert from China's crowded east, Han Chinese families work at state farms on former wastelands and help swell the population along the sensitive border with the Soviet Union.

Lofty solitude was the reward of 14th-century monks who thwarted plunderers by dwelling atop rocky outcrops in Thessaly's Meteora region. A walkway now leads to Rousanou Monastery, right center, once reached by ladders and nets.

Situated at the edge of the Atlas Mountains, Marrakech is a sprawling, labyrinthine city of courtyards and casbahs.

GEO

Decidedly the hottest of the new slickies. Like **National Geographic** *on LSD,* **GEO** *covers the planet with a definite flair for detail, sometimes enlightening, sometimes grotesque, commonly both. If I were once again a young photographer,* **GEO** *(and* **Zoom**) *is where I would be looking for work. It's a mid-Atlantic publication, most of its roots in Germany, many of its leaves in the U.S. Despite its success the magazine is maintaining an atavistic rawness in the photographs and even in the text — jolting ideas as well as images.* —SB

GEO
H.J. Kaplan, Editor
$36/year (10 issues)
from:
Neodata
P.O. Box 2552
Boulder, CO 80322

The centerpiece at Harvard's annual Kirkland House Christmas banquet.

Zoom

There was an English-language edition of this high-style photo magazine around for a while, but I don't think anybody noticed because they were too fascinated by the pictures. So now it's only available in French. But it's one of the most (if not the most) visually spellbinding magazines in the world. —Art Kleiner

Zoom
(Le magazine de l'image)
Joël Laroche, Editor
$55/year (12 issues)
from:
Zoom
2, rue du Faubourg
Poissonnière
75010 Paris, France

Le travail de Knut Bry semble reposer sur ces ambiguités consenties.
↓

→
Le voyeur des cimetières ne rapporte que des photos dont on sourit ou dont on s'écarte, par peur. Bernard Pierre Wolff, lui, se pose en voyageur et en compagnon.

Communication Arts

The image magazine for American professional image makers — designers, illustrators, advertising agencies, etc. Much of it is outstanding anyway, much is indicative of what the culture is seeing or wants to see — always a visual treat. —SB

Now restricted to two small areas in and around San Francisco, this lovely little butterfly has been deprived of its only food supply, the lupine leaf, which has been bulldozed almost out of existence by developers. It is now on the verge of extinction.

Communication Arts
Richard Coyne, Editor
$30/year (6 issues)
from:
Communication Arts
P.O. Box 10300
410 Sherman
Palo Alto, CA 94303

Galapagos Giant Tortoises (Geochelone elephantopus), mating.
↓

THE RISING SUN
NEIGHBORHOOD NEWSLETTER

The dryers at the laundromat next to the 7-11 near Fred's are called Ted, Hal, Tom, Bob, Jim, Ric, Flo, Kim, Sue, Ann and Pam in silver on black background letters such as one may buy at a dime-store. I thought it was charming surrealism till someone told me it was to help you remember which dryer your clothes were in. I was surprised that I thought that some of them sounded like dryer names and some didn't.

The Wall Street Journal

The only daily NEWSpaper. Perhaps because it's harnessed to real events (namely price changes, the relatively uncontrollable democracy of the market), **The Wall Street Journal** *has an honesty. Having an honesty it has an originality (maybe those qualities are not separable). I know that if I were restricted to two periodicals for all my news, I would take* **Science** *(p. 33) and* **The Wall Street Journal**. *—SB*

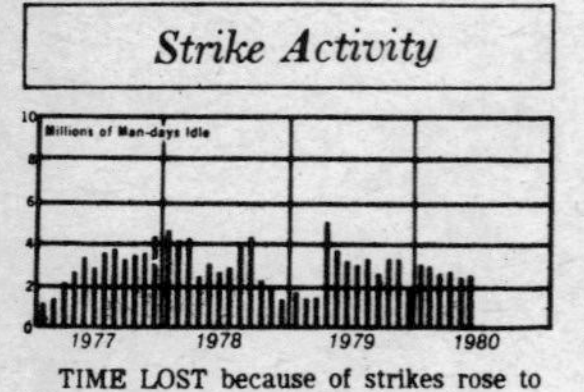

TIME LOST because of strikes rose to 2.6 million man-days idle in June from 2.5 million man-days idle a month earlier, the Labor Department reports.

The Wall Street Journal
$63/year (260 issues)
from:
The Wall Street Journal
200 Burnett Road
Chicopee, MA 01021

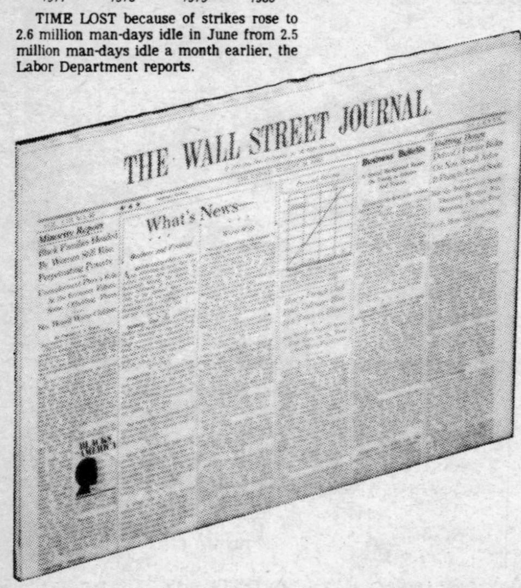

•

Portland, Ind. — Preacher Townsend looks positively bewitching on the pulpit this evening. He's wearing a red evening jacket with velvet lapels, ruffled shirt, red bow tie and two-toned shoes. A small embroidered rabbit is popping out of a small embroidered hat on his right lapel.

His sermon is enchanting, too. "Thy word is a lamp unto my feet," he says, and his Bible bursts into flame.

Wait a minute. Is this the Portland Friends Church or a magic show?

It's both.

This, folks, is show biz, Bible-belt style. Some churches are using unorthodox methods to increase attendance in the face of televised church services, changing ways of life and a general religious lethargy among many young people. Magic — either hiring such touring performers as the Rev. Charles Townsend or taking up sorcery themselves — is the ministers' favorite, but they are also trying ventriloquism, clowning and puppetry.

Quest
Robert Shnayerson, Editor
$12/year (10 issues)
from:
Quest
1133 Avenue of the Americas
New York, NY 10036

Quest

Like **GEO**, *a brand new slick success. The idea of* **Quest** *(shocking that it should be shocking) is to present good news, "the pursuit of excellence." And that it does, without being very predictable or at all sentimental. Since our magazine* **CoEvolution** *is also in the good news business, there's a certain competitive zest in watching* **Quest** *comparatively. It's a good magazine to be published in; they pay handsomely. We got $3500 for seven pages worth of* **Next Whole Earth Catalog** *excerpts.* *—SB*

•

Lifesigns/80 — A digest of relatively good news, offering modest evidence that the world may yet survive.

The bus went out of control and skidded almost — but not quite — over the edge of the rain-soaked Calumet Expressway near Chicago. It carried no passengers. The driver escaped through an emergency exit. He was a little banged up. He's not complaining. What didn't happen to you today? →

↑ **"You had to watch the traffic," Keech says of these two photographs, which were taken in Pennsylvania. "When it's opening time, you'd better be out of the area. But dives like these are so well organized that it usually works out." Forty to fifty men dove from two planes for what Keech thinks may be his best shots to date. "But wait," he says. "You never know what I'll try tomorrow."**

Manas

Henry Geiger's philosophical humanist journal. A weekly thoughtful delight, these are the good thoughts that lead to and emerge from good actions. It's also one of the few places you hear about old books used in renewed ways — Gandhi, Ortega y Gasset, Tolstoy — and new and promising activities and publications. *—SB*

•

All the gears of the march of progress in the Western world have signs which say *Keep on going or the machine will break down,* but as we keep it going the little troubles grow into big ones, and the choices open to the individual are fewer and fewer because technological efficiency means that you get what you need in just one way or not at all. So there is increasing dislike, if not distrust, of the "system" on which we so completely depend.

•

The **Nation** had no large funds to pay for "investigative journalism," but its editor kept gathering material on major questions that deserved attention — the policies of the FBI under J. Edgar Hoover, the munitions business, the political corruption of New York City, the prosecution and perhaps the martyrdom of Alger Hiss, what the CIA was doing, the persecution of J. Robert Oppenheimer, and the lying by government informers in the trials of supposed communist sympathizers — and found capable writers to put it together. The readers of the **Nation** have probably known more about what was actually going on in the area of national and international affairs than most other citizens.

Manas
Henry Geiger, Editor
$10/year (44 issues)
from:
Manas Publishing Company
P.O. Box 32112
Los Angeles, CA 90032

The Economist

Requisite reading for serious predictors. For over a hundred years this lively magazine with a stodgy name has published in London. Coverage is truly international, though strongly focused on the USA and UK. The staff is anonymous but has included Barbara Ward and those of her ilk. They are brutally truthful and accurate, but often tell their tale with understated British humor. Events of which I have had knowledge were more perceptively reported in **The Economist** *than in the American press. 52 times a year you get about 125 pages of future and current news, politics and finance reported in depth. About 10 times a year a 25-page survey of a specific area, such as Hong Kong, oil or computers, is included. Even deeper surveys are available at extra cost from The Economist Intelligence Unit. If a forecaster could receive but one publication,* **The Economist** *would be a good choice.*
—Alan Kalker
[Suggested by Richard Baker]

•

Neutron bombs — Now a French bid

With scarcely a whisper of domestic opposition and little more than a stern glance from Mr. Brezhnev, France has built and tested the weapon that kicked off a major Russian propaganda campaign three years ago and caused a serious rift within Nato when the United States first insisted on and then abandoned it: the neutron bomb. The underground test on Muroroa atoll on June 16th means that the French have made a workable model; they should be able to package it inside a missile warhead in about a year.

The Economist
$48/year (52 issues)
from:
The Economist
54 St. James's Street
London, SW1A 1JT
England

Periodical Scanning

by J. Baldwin

ABOUT ONCE A YEAR, I check out a **Manhattan Yellow Pages** from the local university library (you can order one for yourself from your Bell Customer Service Office too). Just about everything in the world is there, including useful listings not found in other Yellow Pages; for instance Finders. Finders, together with Factors, will get you together with people of mutual business interest. For example, let's say I need 10,000 used gallon jugs for a solar storage unit. Someplace there is somebody with 10,000 used bottles to sell. The Finder gets us together and takes a small cut as his fee. If you're the man with the bottles to sell, you call a Factor, who then lists his goods with the Finder. Like that.

I give the **Sears Catalog** (p. 348) the once-over quarterly too. That's where you first see verified "consumer acceptance" of fads, trends, and conventional wisdom. Sears watchers who have been at it for many years have an advantage; the glacier moves ever so slowly. The catalog is also an interesting social document as you note subtle changes in the type of models used, and their poses. It's a good place to establish a base line for product prices and availability, too. I read lots of catalogs besides Sears, including university course catalogs.

But what I've found most useful about periodicals is their variety. Several times a year, I reserve an entire day to peruse the stock of a large magazine store. I snoop into everything from **Modern Hair Styles** to **Supermarket Manager's Monthly**. **Beautiful Ten-Year-Old Boys, Battles of World War II, CB, Kung-fu, Jack & Jill,** Hollywood magazines of all stripes, **Motor Trend, Four Wheel Drive, Orchid Raising, Consumer Reports, Playboy** and **Playgirl, Woman's Day, Art News, Modern Camera, Ski, Bicycling, Vogue Patterns, Field & Stream, Dogs, Cats, Horses** . . . egad! Snoop-reading gives me a cross-section of what is going on in this vast country. Perhaps it's a bizarre idea, but I have found over the years that the habit really does seem to reveal trends. I usually make peace with the magazine store by buying one now and then as the day progresses. I am limited, finally, by curvature of the spine, clatter from the mental storage-retrieval system, and squint.

This game can also be played in the periodical room of a big library. If it is a university library, you will soon be into things you have never even *heard* of, let alone suspected that there were enough people interested in to make

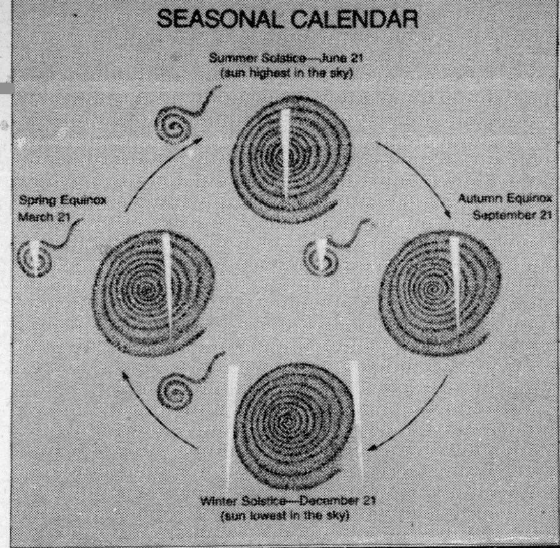

Science 80

For the lay reader it may become the best science magazine in print. So far we only have one year by which to judge this carefully considered infant brother of **Science**, *both published by the Olympian "triple-A-S" — the American Association for the Advancement of Science. For handy comparison last Fall, both* **Science** *and* **Science 80** *had cover stories on Fajada Butte, the exquisitely subtle sun calendar made by rather early Americans on a Southwest cliffside. For me the* **Science** *treatment, thick with technical detail, was a mildly interesting skim. But reading the article that* **Science 80** *titled "The Anasazi Sun Dagger" and described so — "A chance discovery of a stunningly sophisticated solar marker in New Mexico rivals the unveiling of Stonehenge" — I found myself buying it. I was wowed, inspired, proud for my continent.*

So it went throughout the issue. There're recognizable heavyweights here — Lewis Thomas, Carl Sagan, Lynn White, Jr. — along with people I've never heard of writing very well indeed. Of real news, science provides about 70% these days. —SB

Science 80
Allen L. Hammond, Editor
$15/year (10 issues)
from:
Science 80
Subscription Department
P.O. Box 10790
Des Moines, IA 50340

•

The Chacoans built irrigation systems with canals and small dams to collect and channel the ephemeral runoff. And they constructed a remarkable system of hundreds of miles of roadways, the full extent of which is only now being documented through the use of such space-age techniques as remote sensing and analysis . . .

Scientific American

Articles cover a whole variety of subjects in astronomy, physics, medical biology, geology, archeology, resources. Written for the well-trained layman, the articles are never easy but aim at making complicated matters understandable. The most condensed explanations of current technology and ideas in science that are to be found anywhere. —Luna Leopold

Scientific American
Dennis Flanagan, Editor
$21/year (12 issues)
from:
Scientific American
415 Madison Avenue
New York, NY 10017

•

Unless the current negotiations in Geneva succeed in prohibiting the development, production and stockpiling of chemical weapons, a new and more dangerous phase of the arms race may be in store.

↑

Nerve gas is stored as a liquid in metal containers at the Tooele Army Depot in Utah. The containers hold a total of about a million gallons of Agent GB, or sarin, a highly toxic organophosphorus compound chemically related to certain pesticides. The lethal dose of sarin for an adult human being is about a milligram. The buildings in the distance contain additional nerve-gas supplies in the form of filled munitions. The objects stacked between the warehouses are 160-gallon aircraft spray tanks, filled with another nerve gas, agent VX. Approximately 40 percent of the total U.S. stockpile of poison gas, which includes both nerve gas, is stored at this site and others at the Tooele depot.

The New Yorker

The best popular magazine in the world. For Borges or Lem, Steinberg drawings, or "Reporter at Large" essays on cybernetics and family therapy, there is nothing remotely in its class. In our new world of high-tech electronic kitsch and behavioral/science banality, it remains as literate as we used to be.
—William Irwin Thompson

The New Yorker
William Shawn, Editor
$28/year (52 issues)
from:
The New Yorker
25 West 43rd Street
New York, NY 10036

"The meeting will come to order."

•

The " Portrait of Gertrude Stein" obsessed him for months. Stein submitted to eighty or ninety sittings in the winter and spring of 1905-06, but before Picasso went away on vacation to Gosol, in the Pyrenees, he became dissatisfied with the head and painted it out. When he came back to Paris in the fall, he finished the painting without asking Stein to sit again. The masklike, "Iberian" face is truer than any likeness. ("We all know that art is not truth," Picasso said in 1923. "Art is a lie that makes us realize truth.") As Stein once wrote, the portrait "is the only reproduction of me which is always I, for me."

The New York Review of Books

From the late Hannah Arendt to Emma Rothschild, with some of my hairy-chested intellectual heroes like Christopher Lasch, **NYRB** *first brought me the word on the new narcissism and goodies like the world armament markets. Often, The First Ever to notice undercurrents and windshifts. Harumpf.* —David Shetzline

•

Meanwhile Picasso had the good fortune to spend his formative years in a city that was one of the most progressive in Europe. Thanks largely to Gaudi, Barcelona had become a hotbed of art nouveau, and the young artists and poets who befriended Picasso kept in touch with the latest developments in Paris, London, and Vienna. Passionate admirers of Nietzsche, they subscribed — some of them at least — to a semi-serious belief that the century about to dawn would see the emergence of a glorious new art and the coming of a Messianic artist: a Nietzschean superman with a Dionysiac style. A self-portrait of this period (not in the show), which the artist inscribed three times over with the words *"Yo el Rey,"* suggests that Picasso so implicitly believed in his divine right as an artist and also saw himself fulfilling this regal role — *stupor mundi*! And two other prophetic drawings which *are* in the show, both entitled *Pierrot Celebrating the New Year*, and which, it is significant, are dated January 1, 1900, hint that the "King" might on occasion double as a clown.

The New York Review of Books
Robert B. Silvers and Barbara Epstein, Editors
$16.50/year (22 issues)
from:
New York Review
Subscription Service Dept.
P.O. Box 940
Farmingdale, NY 11737

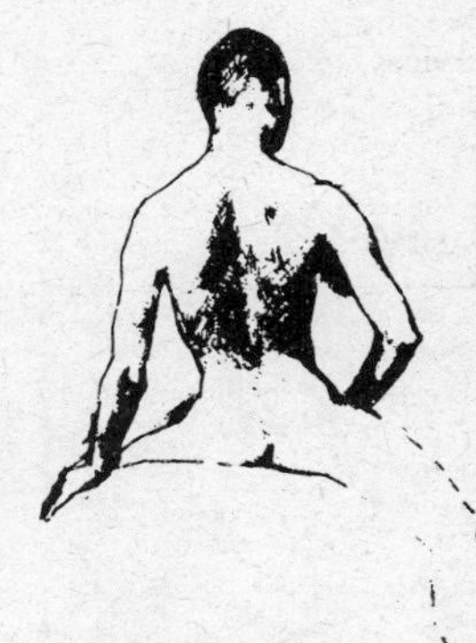

Picasso, a study for "The Watering Place"

possible a specialized magazine. There must be a "Journal of" for every possible subject of human endeavor in nearly every language. Must universities admit anyone at all to the periodical room without an ID, and furnish you with good light and a nice chair too. Whenever I get to feeling provincial, I hie me to the nearest one and settle in for a spell. Makes me feel good all over. I've found that a significant number of the successful ideas and good times of my life have come rather directly from being able to say, "I remember reading about some people that were . . ." Specialist periodicals are also the best place to establish access to further knowledge in that field; not so much from facts given in the feature articles, but in the *ads*. Advertising has reduced the theory to practical usefulness, if that's what you need. As I get more and more into interdisciplinary design work, such information is not only useful, but essential. That's where I find new catalogs too.

Tip: In the above wideband snooping tactics, it is useful to develop a speedreading style appropriate to the task. Most articles size up the subject matter at hand in the first few paragraphs, and sum it up in the last few. If there are illustrations, the captions will help you decide if you want to read every word. Many specialist publications also include a summary or abstract, sometimes in the table of contents. This is just as well, as the sort of journal that has abstracts is likely to be one of the sort that requires a concept to be imbedded in "academese" which you don't have the time (or inclination) to read. You can test your "screen" by trying it out on a few articles and then reading them more carefully to see if you missed something important. After you get your screen adjusted to a useful mesh, you can really roar along. You won't miss much, because mostly all you want is to be informed of the existence of a phenomenon, not to become an expert in the field. Hope this helps. ■

THE RISING SUN
NEIGHBORHOOD NEWSLETTER

— "Being a cashier at Safeway, if you're more than 10 cents off two days in a row, you're fired. And they do all that punching keys by Braille — if you watch them, you'll see they never look at the keys. They really earn their money."

— "I dunno — $15 an hour — that's what they're making since the strike. I think nurses should get more than people who charge for groceries."

— "Yeah, but cashiers are working for a profit making things and nurses aren't."

— "Don't you believe it. That's just the way hospitals keep their books. You look in the parking lot at UC Med at the doctors' cars and the nurses' cars and tell me somebody isn't making a profit — but it's not the people who hold your hand at 2 a.m., I'll tell you that."

—Conversation overheard at California Surplus

The Futurist

In a field excessively professional, **The Futurist** *is blithely amateurish, enthusiastic, open to contradiction, interested. It used to be strictly optimistic and technoid, but in recent years, editor Cornish has increasingly welcomed gloomy views and soft path scenarios. The World Future Society has cells everywhere, no doubt one near you. I'm glad the magazine has survived so well, but I'll admit my favorite periodical on the subject is* **Future Life** *(p. 548).*
—SB

The Futurist
Edward S. Cornish, Editor
$18 /year (6 issues)
from:
World Future Society
P.O. Box 30369
Bethesda Branch
Washington, DC 20014

•

The Co-op movement around the U.S. may get a helping hand from the recently opened National Consumer Cooperative Bank in Washington, D.C. The bank will offer low-interest loans to co-ops of all kinds, and may give an especially valuable boost to the growing number of energy co-ops, which help their members save money by providing such services as bulk purchasing of heating fuel and firewood, non-profit maintenance of boilers and furnaces, and installation of storm windows and insulation. If the bank succeeds in encouraging co-ops around the U.S., the federal involvement will eventually be phased out and the bank will be wholly owned and operated by the co-ops it helped establish. For further information, write: National Consumer Cooperative Bank, Washington, D.C. 20220.

•

Many banks — including some of the biggest — will fail. Thousands of depositors may suffer financial losses and major inconveniences, despite the Federal Deposit Insurance Corporation (FDIC) and other agencies and safeguards maintained by the government.

A number of big U.S. banks are widely reported to be already in a highly weakened condition due to bad loans carried on their books. A severe downturn would inevitably add to this load of bad debt and push some banks into bankruptcy. The FDIC and other U.S. government agencies will find it extremely difficult to cope with the massive bank failures likely to occur during a major depression. The FDIC has only about $10 billion in reserves to protect deposits totaling more than one *trillion* dollars.

Early American Life

Technically accurate American nostalgia for your home, crafts, and life. I like the gentle use of color photos on non-slick off-white pages.
—SB

Early American Life
Robert G. Miner, Editor
$12 /year (6 issues)
from:
The Early American Society
P.O. Box 1607
Marion, OH 43302

Tom found the central staircase, which was from an old New Hampshire house, stored in a hen house. The Daniel Munroe tall case clock is especially fine, mahogany veneer on cherry, with a painted face and brass finials. The fire-buckets belonged to a ship captain who took some of the first missionaries to the Sandwich Islands.

The Village Voice

For vicious irresponsibility, I read **The Village Voice.** *In the absence of H.L. Mencken and the rarity of Hunter Thompson, it has Alexander Cockburn, master of the multidirectional insult. "The case of New Zealand remains deplorable. Cannot this country ever do anything interesting? If only its army were to install a right-wing dictatorship, then at least William Buckley could recommend some PR man to explain its case to the world."* **The Voice** *also offers the continuing story of NYC politics, in gruesome detail, which is far enough away from affecting me and being affected by me that it's slightly entertaining as well as being totally depressing.*
—Anne Herbert

→

A sensory assault. Sounds: lockers being slammed and kicked, voices calling back and forth, showers spattering followed closely by a shriek about icy water, a whoosh as the steam room door is opened, hair dryers roaring into action, pleasure groans from the directions of the massage cabinets. Smells: chlorine, urine, Visine. Wafts of any perfume ever hawked, which never quite conceal the permanent funky odors of the locker room — fresh sweat, old sweat, stinky feet, stale armpits, menstruation, farts. And sights: dozens of milling, naked women. Teenagers, mothers, grandmothers. Black, white, Latin, Oriental; Jamaican, Italian, Cuban, Jewish, Arabic, Irish. But — the first rule of a women's locker room is Don't Stare. (Peek discreetly.)

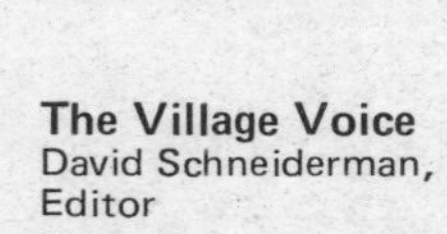
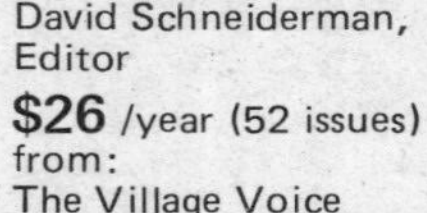

The Village Voice
David Schneiderman, Editor
$26 /year (52 issues)
from:
The Village Voice
Subscription Department
643 Ryan Way
Marion, OH 43302

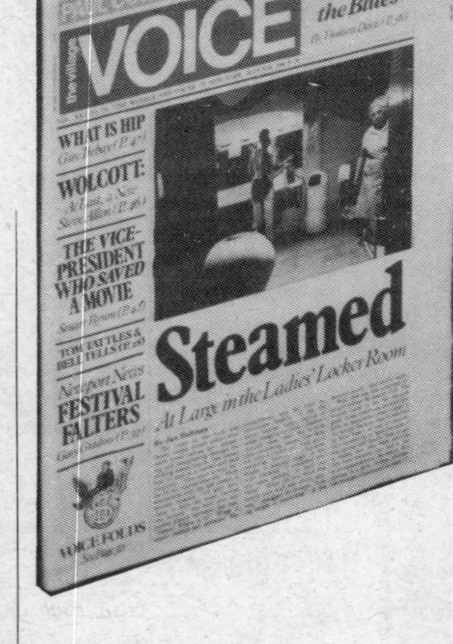

New Age Journal

Best magazine linking human potential movement ideas, news with political activism, and good, solid grounding that evaluates the helter-skelter, sometimes faddish "consciousness movements" with keen balance and common sense.
—Hazel Henderson

New Age Journal
Peggy Taylor, Editor
$12 /year (12 issues)
from:
New Age
Subscription Department
32 Station Street
Brookline Village, MA 02146

•

Richard Grossinger's **Planet Medicine: From Stone Age Shamanism to Post-Industrial Healing** (Doubleday, $5.95) illuminates numerous contemporary alternative healing systems by showing their historical ties to ancient medical approaches. Grossinger provides brief yet comprehensive historical contexts for each alternative healing system, examines its modern relevance (often through personal encounters with healers), and lets readers draw their own conclusions. Balanced and fair-minded in tone, his writing is rich with literary and anthropological associations and psychological data from various world cultures. Every chapter challenges counter-cultural cliches and assumptions while revealing a deep sympathy for — and the necessity for — alternative modes of healing. This book provides a comprehensive philosophical and historical overview of healing throughout the planet.

Serials Review

When I asserted, once, that **CoEvolution** *and* **Library Journal** *are the only magazines that review magazines, I asserted in ignorance.* **Serials Review** *has been doing it in spades for five years (there is also* **The Serials Librarian** *— "of interest primarily to libraries," says our suggester). What a pleasure to see really detailed examination of periodicals, how they differ and what they are good for. A regular feature, "Serials Digest" by David Walker Lupton, is pure informative gossip of what's changing on the magazine scene. This is a quarterly that could direct you knowledgeably down some unexpected paths.*
—SB
[Suggested by Stephen Rilke]

Serials Review
C. Edward Wall, Editor
$25 /year (4 issues)
from:
Pierian Press
P.O. Box 1808
Ann Arbor, MI 48106

Magazines for Libraries

You don't believe us? You shouldn't — we're upstarts. Check with the old hands at your library — Bill Katz and Berry Richards' working tome of magazine evaluation. They cover 6500 periodicals "which the editors and contributors believe to be the best of the more than 65,000 titles now available."
—SB
[Suggested by Michael O. Engel]

Magazines for Libraries
Bill Katz and Berry G. Richards
$39.95 postpaid from:
R.R. Bowker
Fulfillment Department
P.O. Box 1807
Ann Arbor, MI 48106

•

Freedom Today. 1975. m. $15. Diane Nobel. Freedom Fellowship Church, 30 W. Pasadena, Phoenix, AZ 85013. Illus., adv. *Bk. rev:* Notes. *Aud:* Ga.

A libertarian-alternative culture magazine of some 30 pages, this is directed to young people and adults who "want to learn how to achieve the freedom you need to do what you want. And how to combat the fears, pressures and obligations that keep you from changing the course of your life." Unlike many of the genre, its short articles are grounded in practical affairs, e.g., articles on how to live to 100, civil liberties, reviews of investment letters, 14 methods to achieve self-freedom, "Making an Abilities Inventory," etc. Other numbers trace the history of the tax revolt and suggest ways of living on a boat. Sometimes dangerously close to a Dale Carnegie revisionist program, but most of the material should be of value to those thrashing around seeking identity and how to fit into, or escape, the system. Recommended.

Audio Equipment

by Jim Stockford

Model 144 Portastudio

Dear Art:

I am forced to cut way back on the audio material for the reason that so much of the equipment out is undistinguished in any sense from the rest of the pack. Major differences really boil down to front panel design and choice of knob colors. Progress in the design of analog gear has been pushed far beyond the limits of the transducers (microphones and speakers), and further development will be boring. To hell with it. I cannot get behind a medium-priced cassette player that is no different from twenty others.

I am drenched in statistics that compare highly technical data which merely reflect design around solid state devices that are available to all manufacturers. Only the very high end professional gear has any meaningful differences, depending upon its application. This means comparison of machines that cost thousands and tens of thousands of dollars, with appeal only for someone working full-time and competing heavily with someone across town for scarce dollars sticky from wet dreams. The appeal is ultimately to a goon mentality.

With the record industry sick and dying, stinking of cocaine, a victim of its own machismo, audio stores are switching to video fast. Novelty for its own sake will be the only impetus for sales until digital techniques take over completely.

Yet, when the dust settles there are a few items that will stand the test of time. Some of the following equipment may necessarily vanish shortly, but I've made an effort to describe mostly basic, high quality goods with an eye to dollar value. Hopefully most of these pieces will stay with us until the technology fades. Readers should write the manufacturers for the location of the distributor nearest them or check their local audio equipment store.

AUDIO EQUIPMENT

RC-550 Radio Cassette Recorder. $280 (approx.), Japan Victor Corporation (JVC), Home Entertainment, 1011 West Artesia Blvd., Compton, CA 90220. *Tuned to music or tuned to the police, on the beach or on the bus, low-priced and loud, here is an FM/shortwave/medium wave portable radio with a cassette player-recorder complete with a microphone (which means that this set can be used as a PA system to boot). Powered by a mighty seven watt amplifier that covers the entire audio range from 100 Hz to 10 kHz at no more than 10% THD, the self-contained Three Way Speaker System (10" woofer, 4" midrange, 2" tweeter) sounds astonishingly good for the price.*

RC-550 ↑

Advent Model 300 FM Stereo Reciever ↑

Advent Model 300 Stereo FM Receiver. $370 (approx.), Advent Corporation, 195 Albany Street, Cambridge, MA 02139. *Do you want a very, very fine system for a moderate price? Would you like a system that sounds great in your living room, that won't rattle the windows or give you a headache? Go out and buy the Advent Model 300 FM Stereo Receiver. This receiver only puts out about 15 watts per channel. This is a plus in this world of 100, 200, up to 1000 watt amplifiers. The reason? Because you can develop a full, beautiful sound at home without having to turn your system up so loud that you can't talk or think or hear the phone. Systems with a lot of wattage generally don't even tinkle until they are turned up to a devastating point. The amplifier has excellent frequency response and distortion figures, and the FM radio section is superlative.*

Crown FM1 Tuner. $1000 (approx.), Crown, 1718 West Mishawaka Road, Elkhart, IN 46514. *Crown is one of the very few manufacturers that has over decades consistently produced equipment that can be rated as the finest in the world. Their FM 1 stereo tuner really and truly belongs in that class. An FM tuner for well over one thousand dollars, it features a station memory that remembers your favorite stations even with the plug pulled from the wall; its tuning is ultra sensitive, with variable muting to select out stations that have a low signal to noise ratio. There is a search and scan for all stations or for stereo only stations, and a level adjust to allow you to set the level of your preamp to match the levels put out by your other equipment. Much more is included in this package, but suffice it to say that this is the finest FM tuner in the world and deserves the name FM 1.*

Pixoff record cleaner. $20 (approx.), Sonic Research, Inc., Danbury, CT 16810. *A wonderful tool which helps you take care of your records better than anything else. The Pixoff record cleaner is a small roller that is covered with a specially designed adhesive covering that reaches to the very bottom of your record grooves. Roll this across your records and it picks up all of the dirt, completely, and it doesn't leave a sticky residue of cleaning fluid. When the adhesive covering gets too dirty, simply remove it to expose the next one underneath. Don't settle for anything less.*

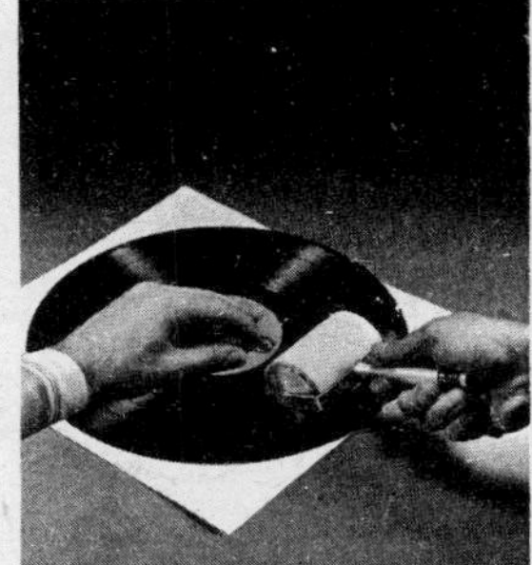
Pixoff Record Cleaner

PZM microphone. $360 (approx.), Crown, 1718 West Mishawaka Road, Elkhart, IN 46514. *Until now, all of the technology for changing sound energy into electrical energy and back was based on theoretical work done in the twenties and thirties. The PZM (Pressure Zone Microphone) is a new and exciting breakthrough in microphone technology which offers the possibility of much truer response characteristics than traditional microphony.*

Here is the short story. A microphone element is placed in a capsule and suspended within a few millimeters of a large homogeneous surface. The theory is that the surface, or plate, will transmit to the microphone front and rear sound waves that are in phase, eliminating much of the cause of uneven response. The instrument has had much success in acoustical piano work and seems to be able to provide a very true signal from a live orchestra. Much lies between. This instrument has been getting rave reviews across the country, and anyone seriously interested in recording must take a long look at it.

Teac Model 144 Portastudio, a four track cassette recorder. $1600 (approx.), Teac Corporation of America, 7733 Telegraph Road, Montebello, CA 90640. *I walked into the establishment of one of the local purveyors of audio equipment and asked to be shown around. They told me that they were busy making deals. I said, "C'mon, guys, show me one good thing. What's your hottest piece of equipment?" "The Teac Model 144 Portastudio," they said, "now get out of here."*

The Teac Model 144 Portastudio was designed for the immense number of people who wish to record at home and who are knowledgeable enough about recording techniques to be critical of their equipment. This machine includes as much of everything-you-could-ever-want-in-a-recording-studio as is wise to put on an easy-to-use cassette deck. The main features are that it records four channels of program onto a cassette with Simul-Sinc (sound on sound, so you can add new material to your already recorded program), and that it allows punch-ins (so you can re-do small parts of any track without having to re-do the entire track).

A word of warning: this is not a wet dream studio with glowing lights and lots of signal processing. It is a basic, easy-to-use machine for doing the kinds of sketches most working musicians are interested in getting down, including professional demos. I have heard music done solely on this machine that was as good as any commercial product I have ever heard. Of course, the guys who did it knew what they were doing.

TOOLS

Paladin Stripex Wire Strippers (No. PA 1100). $29.95 (approx.), Paladin Corporation, 31332 Via Colinas, Westlake, CA 91361. *For anyone at an active electronics bench the Stripex PA 1100 is a new tool that must be tried. This is a nose-feeding wire stripper that will automatically sense and strip any solid, stranded, or multiple cable wire from size 12 to size 30 AWG, and includes a built-in wire cutter. The stainless steel stripping blades are self-adjusting and will last for over one hundred thousand strips. Front-loading, small, and tough, this fiberglass reinforced nylon bodied tool is designed to operate in tight places, with insulation against shock hazards. It is a top contender in the arena of overall lowest cost per thousand stripping operations.*

Stripex PA 1100

Paladin Corex coaxial cable stripper (No. PA 1204). $30 (approx.), Paladin Corporation, 31332 Via Colinas, Westlake, CA 91361. *This tool strips coaxial cable with an outside diameter of from 0.14" to 0.30" in such a way that in one operation the outer jacket is stripped, the shield and dielectric sheath are stripped and exposed to a length beyond the jacket set by the operator, and the inner conductor is stripped beyond the dielectric to any length set by the operator. Interchangeable blade cassettes allow for different stripping length configurations, and the replaceable blades are rated for up to 5000 cuts.*

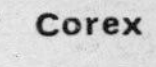
Corex

Paladin Desoldering Tool (No. PA 1700). $15 (approx.), Paladin Corporation, 31332 Via Colinas, Westlake, CA 91361. *One way to tell an electronics bench technician is to look for the dents in his forehead. Small dents about the size of a nickel are the result of his using long spring-loaded solder sucking tools from which, upon being triggered, the inner piston handle pops back and strikes him in the forehead.*

As these vacuum operated tools have advantages over bulbs and wicks, it is nice that there is a well made alternative to the head denters. The Paladin Desoldering Tool features a sturdy metal body, teflon tips, and a heavy duty spring and plunger. Best of all is its compact size, which makes it convenient as a bench tool and handy in small or large equipment. ■

Desoldering Tool

Jim Stockford is a semi-amateur, semi-professional audio/electronic aficionado, who co-manages a performance space/recording studio called Valencia Tool and Die in San Francisco. He dashed around the local electronics shops to compile these reviews for us, then typed them up in his office, a tiny room piled high with cables, amplifiers, parts, tools, recorders, microphones . . .

—Art Kleiner

THE RISING SUN
NEIGHBORHOOD NEWSLETTER

"Nurses give good heart." —David Wills

Heathkit

The Heathkit company is the only source of high grade electronic equipment in kit form. The kits meet or exceed their catalog specifications and are famous for very clear instruction manuals. Heavy-duty printed circuit boards, made by Heathkit, are stamped with a picture and the value of the components to be mounted, and the printed circuit board foil is extra heavy-duty to prevent the repeated reinstallation of components from lifting the foil. Semiconductor devices are individually tested and provided with socket mounting for installation onto the boards. Components are mostly U.S. made, and all parts carry a ninety day warranty. With rosin core solder provided in all kits, kit building is virtually fool-proof. The result is rugged, high quality equipment that is easy to repair.

Heathkit retail centers throughout the U.S. stock most kits and display a large number of demonstration models. Retail store features include a "jiffy bench" set up with Heathkit test instruments for the customer's use, a phone consultation service, a repair service, and a replacement parts stock. Mail orders can be placed at the local stores either pre-paid or C.O.D. —Jim Stockford

What can you build? Excellent hi-fi equipment, ham radio gear, shortwave radios, television sets, marine depth sounders and radio detection finders, electronic instruments, programmable door chimes, metal detectors, telephone accessories, intercoms, and pretty good computers. —SB

Heathkit
Catalog

free from:
Heathkit
Heath Company
Benton Harbor, MI 49022

Heathkit hand-held digital multimeter $94.95

Heathkit Screen Star Projection TV
- Three-tube projection for a brighter, more vivid picture
- 6-foot diagonal high-reflectivity, washable viewing screen for a big, bright, lifelike image
- A full 5 watts of clear, low-distortion sound
- Built-in adjustments for easy self-service $2195

4-Band Shortwave Receiver — just right for the beginning kit builder — your introduction to the fascinating world of shortwave listening $99.95

Herbach & Rademan

Herbach & Rademan offers good prices on a wide range of industrial reject components, overruns, and discontinued models. Recent offerings include computer keyboards, Norden bombsights, solar cells, video recorders, prisms, and varied electro-mechanical thinga-magigs. To deal with their ever-changing inventory, they put out their catalog in periodical sections, issued every month or so. If you save the last few issues you have an idea of what they have on hand. The items are clearly photographed and described, though some may require minor tinkering to get working. If an item cannot be immediately used by a novice, they often offer an accessory kit of instructions and parts. —Alan Kalker

Herbach & Rademan
Periodical catalog

free from:
Herbach & Rademan
401 East Erie Avenue
Philadelphia, PA 19134

SOLAR BATTERY ***HANDY SIZE***
Delivers 3, 6, or 9 VDC @ 50 mA
Solar generating panel designed to charge 9 Volt, 6 Volt, or 3 Volt rechargeable batteries or operate 9 Volt transistor radios. Output 50 mA maximum under full sunlight. Utilizes concentrating lens system and double light reflecting mirrors to provide maximum output. Output voltages selected by means of jack and plug selector arrangement. Plug has 24" cord for connection. Panel, 5-3/4" H x 4-1/8" W x 17/32" thick. Reflecting mirrors, 5" H x 4" W x 3/32" thick. Shipping Wt, 1 lb.
CAT. NO. **S11-104** ______ **$19.95**

Allied Electronics

After considerable mail and discussion by **Whole Earth** *users, it is clear that Allied is the best mail order source for electronic gear. They also print an industrial electronic catalog that is particularly rich in components. Plug in, link up, discorporate.* —SB

Allied Electronics
Catalog

$1 from:
Allied Electronics
401 East 8th Street
Fort Worth, TX 76102

Soldering Irons for Microelectronic Circuits

Mfr's Type	L. In.	Wt. Oz.	Power Watts	F Temp. Range	Price
C-3	6½	3	15	650-750	11.70
G-3	6½	3	18	650-700	12.26
X25-3	8¾	4	25	650-700	14.35

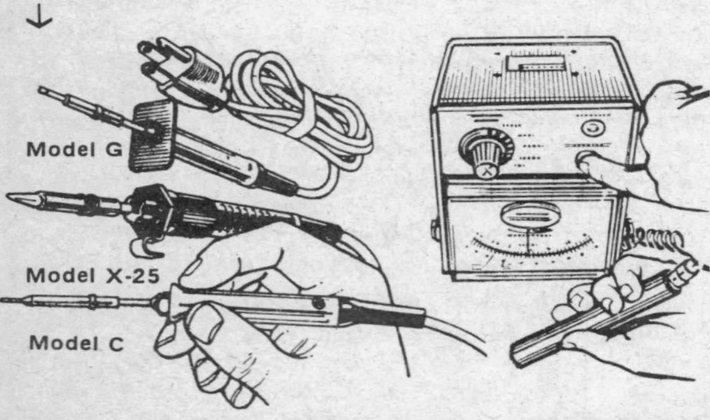

Portable Photo Tachometer — Model 891. Reads speed of motors, engines, grinders, SCR controls, etc. without contacting shaft. Provides instant rpm measurement, ¼" to 25" away from rotating object, with beam of light. Mark object's shaft with reflective tape (materials included), then direct light from probe on the mark. $160.

Amplified Communication System — Series 3400 Communication System. Ideally suited in situations where voice communications are necessary, but background noises and/or distance makes it virtually impossible to communicate. Because it is a self-contained, portable and easy-to-operate system it can be used to communicate on construction sites, crane operations, oil rigs, large manufacturing facilities, steel mills, mines, sporting events, rock concerts, racing, large open work area, around noisy equipment or anywhere you need to be heard above the noise. Master stations $352.50. Remote junctions $112.50. Headsets $94.75 and up.

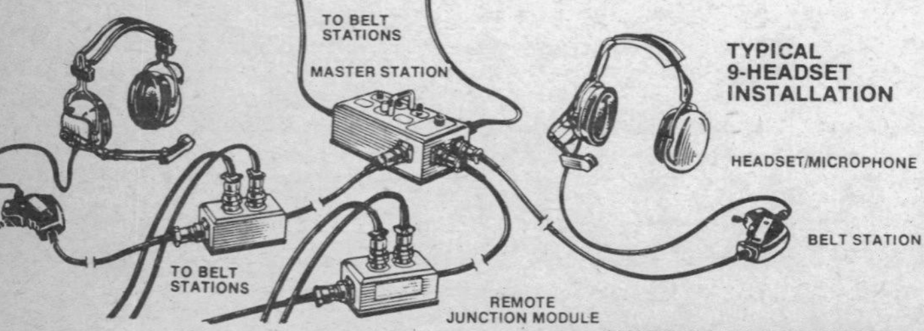

ELECTRONICS MAIL ORDER HOUSES

by Jim Stockford

Electronics parts mail order houses are a species unto themselves: They're informal, with breezy catalogs. They pick up surplus, outmoded and otherwise used and unused stock, and often go out of business. Here is a list of a few of the operations that have been around for several years and which are expected to be around for a while to come.

John J. Meshna, Jr., Inc., P.O. Box 62, East Lynn, MA 01904. *My hands-down favorite catalog. My copy sits in the bathroom with my old* **Whole Earth Catalog**, *and they get my vote for inclusion in the Sunday paper. Their prime customers would seem to be inventors and experimenters who can put together odd modules with half of a police infra-red viewer and incorporate an intervalometer and a surplus Wang Lab core memory to make an instrument of delight. Where do they get this stuff? Industry and the military. You can't imagine the strange uses people build machines for until you open these pages. Excellent prices on hardware, and a scanty selection of components such as resistors, capacitors, and semiconductors, as they pick them up from production lines. Catalog free.*

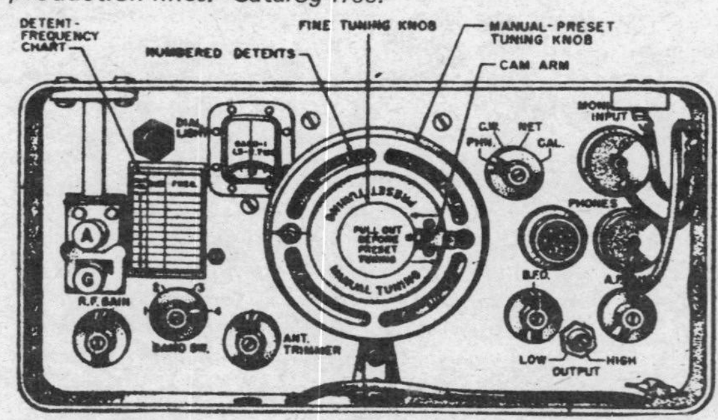

Short wave receiver SPL 18-L $55. —Meshna

Edlie Electronics, 2700 Hampstead Turnpike, Levittown, NY 11756. *Where Meshna offers industrial surplus, the Edlie catalog features test instruments, tools, speakers, a variety of transistors, and, hold your breath, a vast selection of tubes! Yes, tubes — those glass things that used to make table top radios work. A small selection of semiconductors at moderate prices. Catalog $1.*

HERE'S XCELLITES MOST COMPETE TOOL KIT AND EDLIE SLASHES THE PRICE.
Reg. $471.40 EDLIE PRICE $269.95
THE MODEL TC-100ST
DG814

PRC-6 walky talky — US Military hand held walky talky AN/PRC-6 $25 or two for $45. Antenna $5 each. —Meshna

Marlin P. Jones and Associates, P.O. Box 12685, Lake Park, FL 33403. *Their catalog lists mostly hardware in the form of switches, connectors, heatsinks, and fans — the kinds of things that most people in electronics need drawers full of. Nothing glamorous like I.C.s or counters; still, it's necessary hardware at excellent prices. Catalog free.*

Digital Research: Parts, P.O. Box 401247, Garland, TX 75040. *One can only assume that with a name like "Digital Research" these people have another catalog with digital listings. This catalog presents the classic electronics mail order inventory and reads like a newspaper insert from the local Valu-Land discount store. Caps, transistors, transformers, diodes, I.C. power amps, crystals, with a few gismos (e.g., clock modules, power supplies, motors, etc.). Prices are very good. Catalog free.*

Quest Electronics, P.O. Box 4430, Santa Clara, CA 95054. *Now here is a digital mail order house about which I am going to give away a secret. But first: their catalog lists a real variety of hardware and devices, from breadboards to wire wrapping tools, from oscilloscopes to motherboards and mainframes. They have an extensive list of transistors, microprocessers, and I.C.s, almost all for digital applications, and theirs are among the very lowest of semiconductor prices I've been able to find.*

Here is the secret: of all the home computer systems available, Apple is one of the most sought after, and Quest is the place to make your deal for good service and good price, but don't mention my name. Catalog $.50. *(For more on home computers, see our p. 529.)*

Babylon Electronics, P.O. Box 41778, Sacramento, CA 95841. *Babylon sends out a few pages filled mostly with digital semiconductor listings but also including caps, resistors, transistors, a few switches, and a few knick-knacks. Moderate prices. Catalog free.*

All Electronics Corp., 905 South Vermont Avenue, Los Angeles, CA 90006. *Back to basics: switches, caps resistors, lamps, very few semiconductor devices, and those mostly house marked. Still, these are at very low prices for the things we all need, and with a few specialty items listed their catalog is a steal for the price (free).*

Solid State Sales, P.O. Box 74, Somerville, MA 02143. *Another free catalog, more basics, more semiconductors (but with a fairly broad line including RCA, National, Motorola), more specialty items.*

Digi-key Corp., P.O. Box 677, Highway 32 South, Thief River Falls, MN 56701. *With a telephone WATS line and a 48-page catalog with an index, this large mail order house seems to exist mainly for hobbyists. They feature the basic selection of semiconductors for both linear and digital applications, with most of their catalog space devoted to breadboards, tools, batteries, books, and a variety of digi-clocks. I'm sorry to say that their prices are not so good, but their selection is broad, and their catalog will be useful for someone who doesn't have access to a large urban area. Catalog free.*

Crutchfield

Car stereo equipment by mail. Their catalog is very informative and straightforward with useful comments on each item. The selection is good, and the prices beat most downtown stores even including the postage. I have personally found their service to be fast and crap-free.
—J. Baldwin

Crutchfield
Car Stereo Buyer's Guide

free from:
Crutchfield
1 Crutchfield Park
P.O. Caller 1
Charlottesville, VA 22906

Pioneer KP-575 (Cassette Only) — If you park your car in a high crime district, a KP-575 mounted in the glove box is a sure way to enjoy quality car stereo while you thwart would-be thieves.

- **mini size**
- **auto reverse**

Major specifications — power output: 4.4 watts per channel; best tape frequency response: 40-14,000 Hz; best tape signal to noise ratio: 52 dB; wow and flutter: .15%. List price: $159. Our price: $125.

Modern Recording and Music

This one hits the nail on the head in opening up what goes on in making records from the engineering side and it does it in plain language. Interviews with recording stars, producers, engineers. Equipment reports, record reviews. Beginners, don't miss this. See *"Music Business for Musicians" p. 483.*
—Dan Dugan

Modern Recording and Music
H.G. La Torre, Editor
$14/year (12 issues)
from:
Cowan Publishing Corporation
14 Vanderventer Avenue
Port Washington, NY 11050

Popular Electronics

PE *offered the Altair microcomputer as a construction project in January, 1975, and ignited the microcomputer boom. Really neat construction projects like laser and microwave communication links, computer interfaces. Major construction articles usually include source of parts kits. Good tutorial articles on basic electronics and design. Audio equipment reviews, some TV, radio technology, and hobbies.*
—Dan Dugan

Popular Electronics
Arthur Salsberg, Editor
$14/year (12 issues)
from:
Popular Electronics
P.O. Box 2774
Boulder, CO 80302

A low-cost analog audio delay line. Full-size etching and drilling guide for the main printed-circuit board.

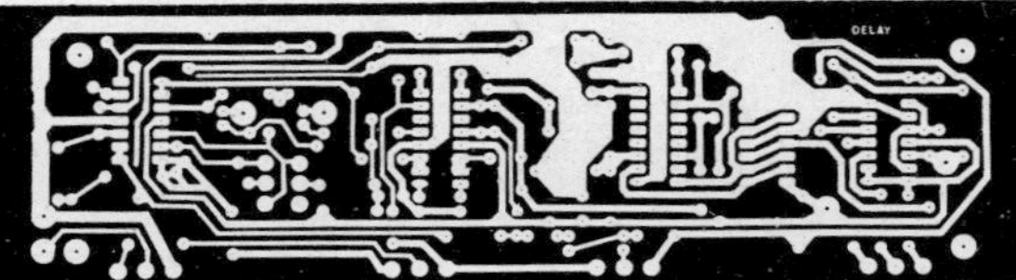

•

With so many readily available, low-cost surplus transmitters around for sale, it doesn't take much money at all to set up for this illegal venture, which is usually low powered. The undergrounders don't follow the program pattern set by legal stations. For example, they often play forefront music on obscure records. It's claimed that new-wave rock and even disco were introduced on illegal radio before the FCC-licensed stations picked them up. Weekends and holidays are reported to be prime underground broadcast times because FCC agents are inactive then. Telephone "loops" are employed, too, for interactive programs. This makes it difficult for the FCC to trace calls.

There are also some TV undergrounders around. The article noted that some engineering students at Syracuse U. followed a "Saturday Night Live" program when the local station switched off for the night, with a three-hour porno movie under the banner of "Lucky 7."

According to an article in **Electronic Mail & Message Systems** (EMMS), a newsletter, electronically transmitted pornographic material is appearing over Viewdata and similar home information services. The British Post Office, too, has been embarrassed by an offer over the British Prestel viewdata service of a "Dirty Books Guide." EMMS points out that MicroNet, a computer timesharing service, has a Pornotrap that detects obscenities used by computerist game players. Players are immediately cautioned on this when detected, and a reprimand is addressed to them on the service's electronic bulletin board. (If you'd like a free copy of its analysis of "Teleporn on Home Information Systems," write EMMS at 30 High Street, Norwalk, CT 06851.)

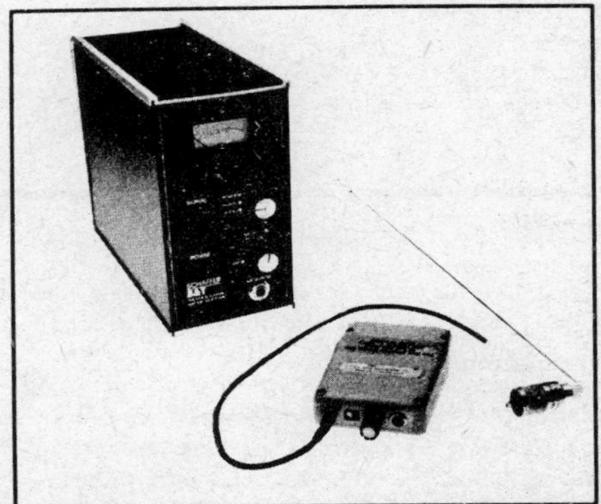

Schaffer B&T

Many professional users of wireless systems for "live" performance applications consider the Schaffer-Vega Diversity system to be the Cadillac of wireless systems, but unfortunately the system also carries a Cadillac-like price tag somewhere on the far side of $3400. The Ken Schaffer Group recently announced the availability of a new, lower-cost wireless system known as the Schaffer B&T.

Electronics

The cream of the world of electronic manufacturing. The latest techniques in analog, digital, and integrated circuit components, systems design and manufacturing methods. By and for professionals. World news and trade gossip. New components and products. Advanced manufacturing machinery. Advanced networks. Test and measurement equipment and methods. Inventions. Very expensive color advertising. Economics of industry and international trade. Respectful of women. Six handy circuit design quickies in each issue. Controlled circulation (send your order on a letterhead or check your library).
—Dan Dugan

Electronics
Samuel Weber, Editor
$18/year (26 issues)
from:
Electronics
P.O. Box 514
Hightstown, NJ 08520

•

The bar codes that leer incomprehensibly at customers from many packages in today's supermarkets and department stores might start to disappear if a fast new optical-character-recognition scanner from West Germany's Scantron GmbH catches on. Early next year the small Frankfurt company will field-test a number of scanners capable of reading an alphanumeric price and identification label whatever its position in relation to the machine — upside down, skewed, or right way up.

TV-camera-like scanner uses 8-bit microcomputer to read 22-character label in less than a second.

Fluke digital multimeter

The Fluke 8020A Digital Multimeter now seems to be the industry standard for hand-held DMMs. The forecast is that the overload protection circuitry protects the device from the inevitable connection of the resistance function to the power line, which would reduce any other meter to a spaceman's breakfast. The instrument can withstand up to 500 volts on the resistance, 1000 volts dc and 750 volts ac on the voltage ranges, 2 amps on the current ranges, and transients of up to 6 kHz. A second important feature is that the instrument measures two ranges of conductance at 200 nS and 2mS, which allows testing of leaky diodes, capacitors, insulators, and dialectrics as well as measurement of transistor gain. Other features include resistance measurement up to 10,000 Megohms, 0.1% accuracy on basic dc, a diode test function, as well as standard voltage and amperage ranges. The package is easy to use and virtually indestructible, with a 3½ digit easy to read display.
—Jim Stockford

Fluke Digital Multimeter
No. 8020A
$179 (approx.)
Information and nearest dealer location

free from:
John Fluke Manufacturing Company
P.O. Box 43210
Mountlake Terrace, WA 98043

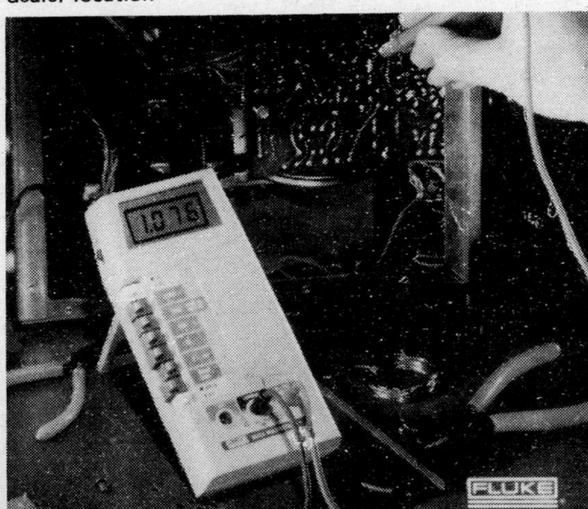

Audio Amateur

The hi-fi pioneers of the '50s (guys who built their houses with the living room wall a giant exponential horn, the speaker buried in a 55-gallon steel drum — 1953-4 **Audio** *magazines are a real treat) became the stereo component manufacturers of the '60s, responsible for the full-color-ad brochures that masqueraded as audio-hobby magazines of the '70s. In diametric opposition to this herd is* **Audio Amateur**, *dedicated to enticing us to build rather than consume, to experiment enjoy learn grow, to write articles for the magazine (I'm in the middle of writing a series on electronic music systems for live performance). Maximum pleasure for minimum $, to help us through the 25-year depression.*
—Larry Greisel

Audio Amateur
Edward T. Dell, Jr., Editor
$14/year (4 issues)
from:
Audio Amateur
P.O. Box 576,
Department WE
Peterborough, NH 03458

THE RISING SUN
NEIGHBORHOOD NEWSLETTER

Kathleen said she learned about making decisions and changing things in her obligatory series of shitty jobs like working for the State of Wisconsin and in restaurants where the way things were being done was so inefficient and backwards and not right that she couldn't stand it and she'd go to the person in charge and make suggestions and the next thing she knew she'd be sort of in charge or very in charge of several people — deciding how things should be done. Seems like some people don't want to decide because it's all very complicated but others have not realized that they can decide, that everything is decided by someone and why not them?

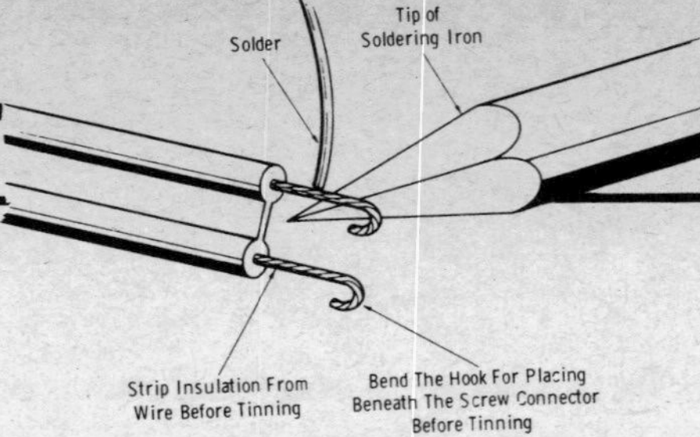

Preparation of ribbon lead-in for screw terminals

Learn Electronics Through Troubleshooting

This book is a one-of-a-kind for people who wish to get started in electronics. The book is written simply and clearly and assumes no knowledge on the part of the reader. Beginning with simple troubleshooting techniques, it takes you through basic arithmetic, simple electrical laws, an explanation of tools to be used, pictures and explanations of the various devices used to make electronic equipment, and finally some simple examples of circuits found in everyday household appliances such as radios and phonographs. Each chapter ends with questions and answers which really help.

—Jim Stockford

Learn Electronics Through Troubleshooting
Wayne Lemons
1969, 1977; 608 pp.

$10.95 postpaid from:
Howard W. Sams and Company
4300 West 62nd Street
P.O. Box 7092
Indianapolis, IN 46206
or Whole Earth Household Store

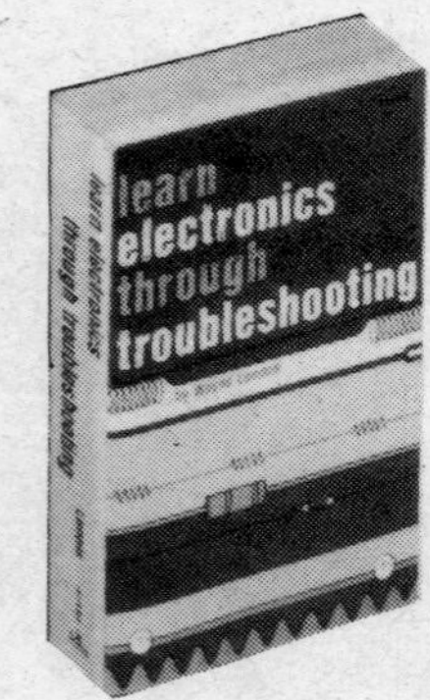

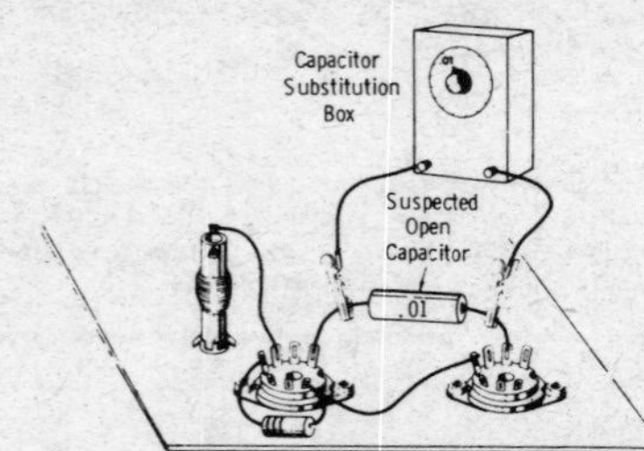

Method for testing a suspected open capacitor

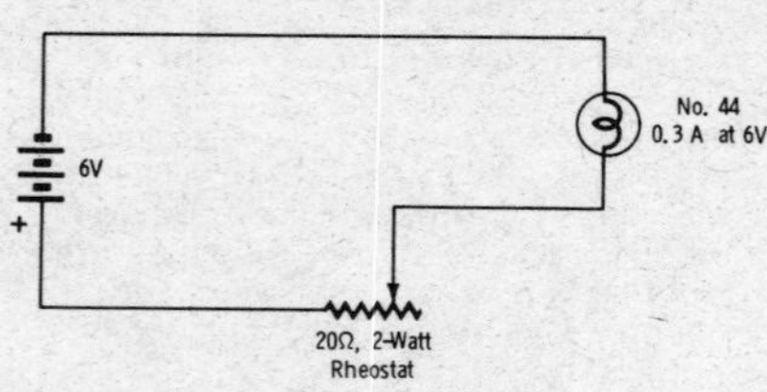

Rheostat used to control lamp brightness

Audio Cyclopedia

Written for professionals in the audio field, this is a Herculean effort by one man and deserving of a tribute. This book provides comprehensive coverage of all modern technologies that affect sound transmission. With a very light use of math there is a heavy reliance on tables, charts, schematics, waveform comparisons, and exploded drawings, with the bonus of an excellent index. This is the most important and most used book in my library.

—Jim Stockford

Audio Cyclopedia
Howard W. Tremaine
1959, 1979; 1757 pp.
2nd Edition

$39.95 postpaid from:
Howard W. Sams and Company
4300 West 62nd Street
P.O. Box 7092
Indianapolis, IN 46206
or Whole Earth Household Store

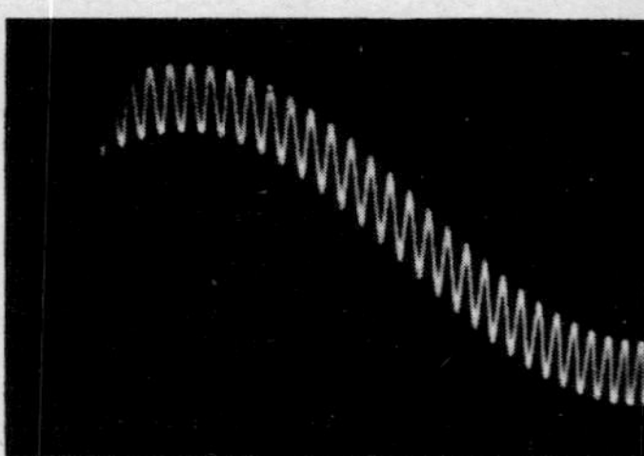

Fraction of a cycle of the intermodulation signal at "send" terminals of the send section. The waveform has been expanded to show the high-frequency signal on the low-frequency carrier (f_1 equals 40 Hz, and f_2 equals 2000 Hz).

Don Lancaster's Cookbook Library

These books provide the home brew tinkerer with a, um, grounding in the basics of micro circuits — with which you can build your own calculators, amplifiers, meters and terminals, and get a start on building your own computer. Each book deals with a different type of component. CMOS circuits are building-block electronic switch circuits out of which computer choice pathways are woven. TTL circuits are simpler, more often used to build clocks, meters and peripherals. Getting through TTL is a good step towards learning CMOS. Active filters are useful in amplifying or controlling sound frequencies. TV typewriters are, in Marc LeBrun's words, "the medium of choice for communicating with your personal computer." (They're basically home brewed terminals.) Cheap video (in this case) means graphically refined TV typewriters. Lancaster takes pride in teaching you to make things that are more useful and versatile — more artistic, really — than what you can buy commercially. You'll need some electronics experience, or lots of time, or both.

—Art Kleiner

CMOS Cookbook
Don Lancaster
1977; 416 pp.

$10.50 postpaid

TTL Cookbook
[A Complete Guide to The Understanding and Using of Transistor-Transistor Logic (TTL) Integrated Circuits]
Don Lancaster
1974; 335 pp.

$9.50 postpaid

Active Filter Cookbook
Don Lancaster
1975; 240 pp.

$14.95 postpaid

TV Typewriter Cookbook
Don Lancaster
1976; 256 pp.

$9.95 postpaid

Cheap Video Cookbook
Don Lancaster
1978; 288 pp.

$5.95 postpaid
all from:
Howard W. Sams & Co.
4300 West 62nd Street
P.O. Box 7092
Indianapolis, IN 46206
or Whole Earth Household Store

•

A newer logic family is called CMOS, short for Complementary-Metal-Oxide-Silicon. CMOS has some very important advantages over earlier logic families. As we'll see in detail later on, these benefits include very low cost (from 3 cents per gate and up), ultralow and non-critical power needs, wide logic swings, "down-the-middle" transfer characteristics, open-circuit inputs, lots of "fan-out" drive, good noise performance, and lots of different devices available from many highly competetive sources.

—**CMOS Cookbook**

•

1. Leave the existing microcomputer system nearly as you find it, making only a bare minimum of minor changes.

2. Use a plain old TV set, also leaving it nearly as you found it, again making only a bare minimum of minor changes.

3. Put some hardware between the microcomputer and the TV set that lets them talk to each other. Keep the hardware as simple and flexible as possible. Use PROMs as needed to give flexibility from μP system to system. . . .

What we really want to do is to eliminate anything at all between the microprocessor and the TV set. Since this is not quite possible, we reduce the size, cost, and the "dedicatedness" of our interface as much as we possibly can. Typically, an alphanumeric interface can end up with three hex inverters, two baby PROMs, a shift register, and a character generator.

—**The Cheap Video Cookbook**

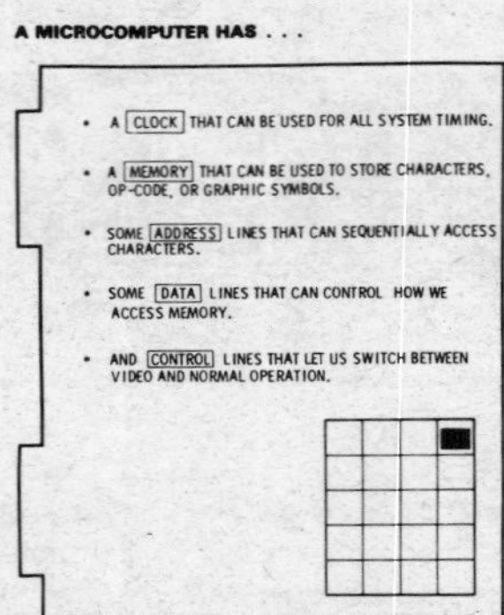

(A) Microprocessor-based video displays get us from here . . .

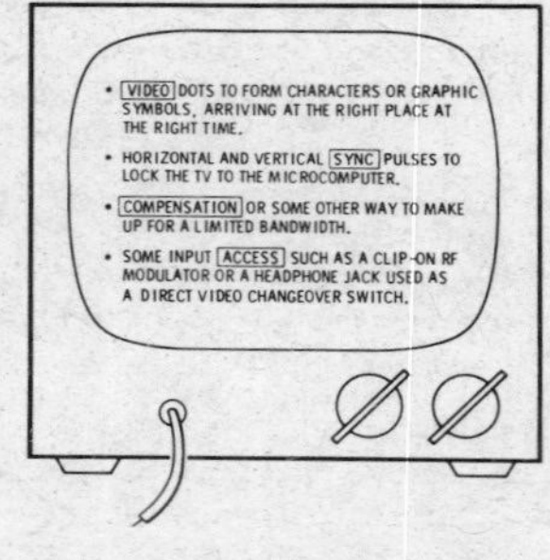

(B) . . . to here, with . . .

—**The Cheap Video Cookbook**

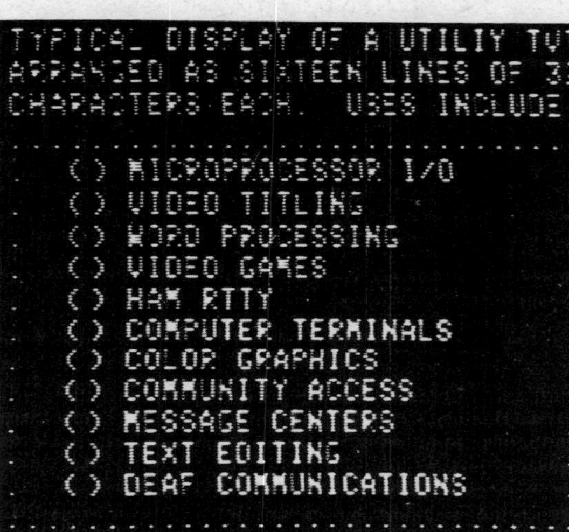

Typical page display of utility tvt.

—**TV Typewriter Cookbook**

Don Britton electronic plans

A catalog of electronic construction plans of all sorts of devices which can be built by amateurs. The plans are workable, detailed and although some of the claims seem outrageous, they do work provided you take care and approach the construction in a conscientious manner. They're not easy, but nothing worthwhile is. Some of these devices are quite useful, such as the portable radio phone. Others appeal to the sneaky low-down bastard in all of us.

—Wolfgang Drohsler

Don Britton Electronic Publications
Catalog

free from:
Don Britton Enterprises
P.O. Drawer G
Waikiki, Hawaii 96815

•

Automatic Police Dialer

When triggered this device connects to your telephone line and dials the police advising them of the emergency. Unit can be built for under $30, and is totally solid state. Order plan set #SC3S6S5 at $6.50.

•

Infra-Red Surveillance TV Camera

A miniature device

This camera measures just 4" x 3" and transmits complete picture by VHF radio. Unit is ULTRA Sensitive and features a "Fish Eye" wide angle lens. Uses non-standard scanning rates and a specially modified TV Receiver to provide security in surveillance. Can be used in apparent, total darkness with appropriate Infra-Red light source. Total cost of construction is under $100. Plans include Camera, Lens, and Receiver Modification. Order plan set SO10SO $10.

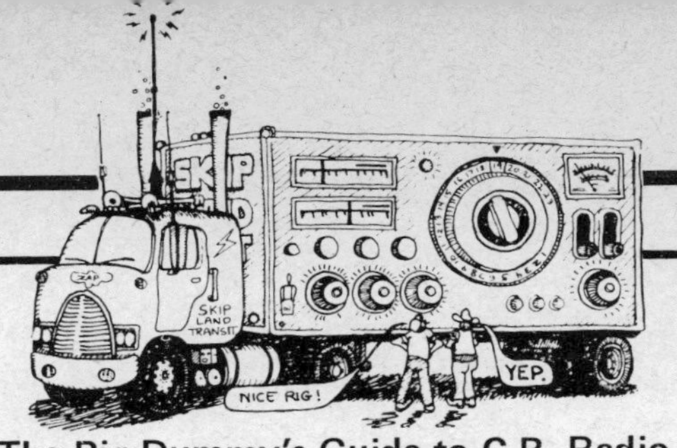

The Big Dummy's Guide to C.B. Radio

The Citizen's Band radio craze (that's the word) continues to expand at a pace that has even the manufacturers of the equipment surprised. No wonder; CB is real revolution — true people's communication. Surprisingly, the government has not seen fit to overregulate the phenomenon. Instead, more channels are being opened in an effort to accommodate the millions of users and reduce the increasing confusion. Perhaps this effort will be like building more freeways to reduce traffic congestion, which doesn't because it encourages more users. We'll see. Then there are the side effects which are not yet sorted out and may never be. CB assisted crime and CB interference with other communications and electronic devices such as garage door openers and auto fuel injection systems are a few of the problems. But for sure CB is here to stay. And a good way to find out about it is by means of this book. There are others like it but this one seems to be more oriented to non-technical users than most. It covers what you need to know: equipment, regulations, lingo (which is working its way into everyday speech) and how it all works out. —"Bluejay" Baldwin

The book doesn't say so, but it comes from Steve Gaskin's Farm commune in Tennessee (p. 315) — they needed CB for their bus convoys. Andrew Main, familiar with Farm gossip, says they've sold 250,000 copies (75,000 to the Army). It's a major cash crop of the Farm. —SB

The Big Dummy's Guide to C.B. Radio
The Book Publishing Company
1976; 128 pp.

$2.95 postpaid from:
The Book Publishing Company
156 Drakes Lane
Summertown, TN 38483
or Whole Earth Household Store

Radio frequency spectrum

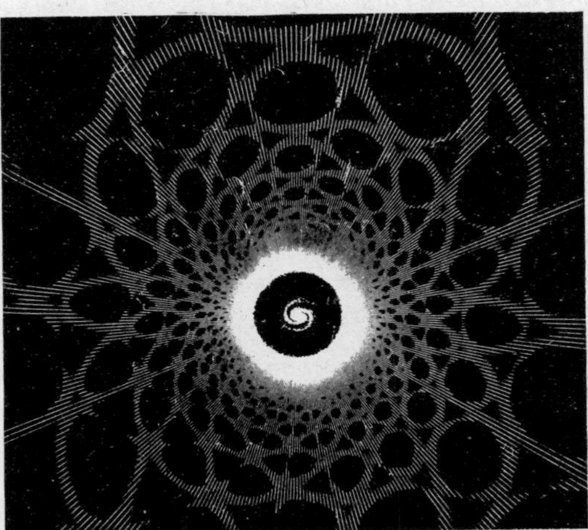

Now everybody get ready. We're getting out on the antenna now and we're about to leap on out there into the sky. We'll radiate on out there, travel at 186,000 miles per second for thousands of miles out into the Universe, ending up heaven knows where.

Ham publications from ARRL

I'm not a ham (in the radio sense), but if I had the money and the time, I probably would be. The American Radio Relay League is the organization that coordinates amateur radio activities and their publications are the best way to get into the field. Here are some titles that looked interesting to me:

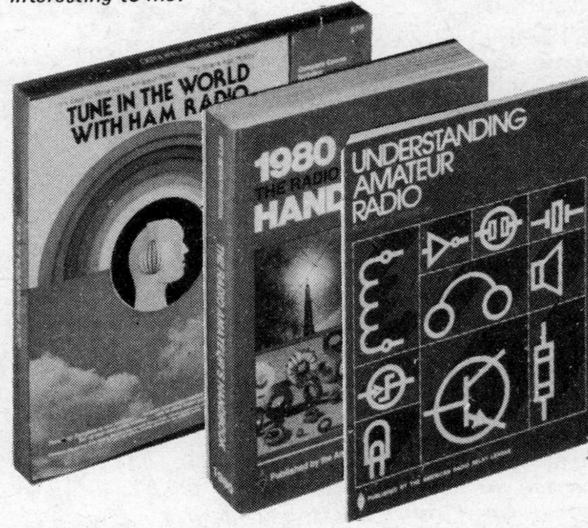

The Radio Amateur's Handbook. *"Internationally recognized, universally consulted. The all-purpose volume of radio. Packed with information useful to the amateur and professional alike. Contains hundreds of photos, diagrams, charts and tables. 56th Edition." $10 U.S., $11 Canada. $12.50 elsewhere.*

A Course in Radio Fundamentals. *"Twenty-six chapters present the electrical and electronic principles that are basic to understanding radio circuit operation. 5th Edition." $4 U.S. $4.50 elsewhere.*

Understanding Amateur Radio. *"Explains in simple language the elementary principles of electronic and radio circuits. Includes how-to-build-it information on low-cost receivers, transmitters and antennas. A 'must' guide for the newcomer. 3rd Edition." $5 U.S. $5.50 elsewhere.*

Tune in the World with Ham Radio. *"The complete beginner's package. Everything needed to obtain a Novice license: theory, rules, how to assemble a station, and operating practices. With one-hour code cassette. 2nd Edition." $7.*

In addition, they publish a slick monthly magazine, **QST**, *that will keep you up-to-date on amateur activities, equipment, meetings, gossip, etc.* **QST**, *$18/year, 12 issues. All publications from:*

American Radio Relay League
225 Main Street
Newington, CT 06111

—Robert Horvitz

Hank Greenberg W2LTP, of Cranford, NJ, saving lives and fighting to keep his antennas. Photo courtesy of The Daily Journal, Elizabeth, NJ. From 73, May '77. →

Coop's Satellite Digest

No doubt about it: the era of home satellite TV reception has begun. In August, 1979 the first Satellite Private Terminal Seminar (SPTS '79) drew an enthusiastic crowd of over five hundred backyard tinkerers, equipment suppliers, Gyro Gearlooses, and prospective dish owners from as far away as Alaska and Mexico to Oklahoma City for a state-of-the-art trade fair and information swap. In September, 1979, I got a press release from the Canadian Department of Communications proudly announcing, "Canada First Nation to Start Direct-to-Home TV Broadcasting Service by Satellite" (service began on September 25, 1979). And in October, 1979, the FCC decided to stop requiring that U.S. satellite receiving stations be licensed at all. According to the **Wall Street Journal** *(10/19/79), this will eliminate the three-month wait and the $1500 - $3000 it used to cost to undergo the licensing process. It will also make it next to impossible for program suppliers to identify who is receiving their programs. Hardware costs for receive-only stations are plummeting.*

The man at the center of all this activity is Bob Cooper, who organized SPTS '79, and who has just started a newsletter for people who want to follow this rapidly evolving field, **Coop's Satellite Digest**. *The first issue, October, 1979, began with a reprint of Arthur C. Clarke's classic "Extra-Terrestrial Relays" essay from 1945, and the rest of the issue was devoted to technical correspondence, circuit diagrams, and explanations of two low-cost terminal designs. There has been a very dense discussion of the legal and economic issues involved in the deregulation of satellite reception, loaded with facts about what's currently available and what commercial distributors' attitudes are about the sudden opening of the reception field. This is the most exciting magazine I've seen all year.*

Coop also has available many videotapes of seminars and his own satellite-distributed weekly TV show, plus how-to to-built-it manuals. Write to Arcadia for a current list of what's in stock. —Robert Horvitz

Portable solar radio communications

Another item from The Farm, who did **The Big Dummy's Guide to CB Radio** *and the Nukebuster on p. 382.* —SB

Solar Electronics of Tennessee, USA, is manufacturing a line of solar-powered radio equipment, tailor-made to provide rural and emergency communications in developing countries at a fraction the cost of telephone or other conventional communications systems. This line includes a solar-powered base station, portable backpack radio with self-contained solar panel, and mobile unit. The equipment features simple snap-lock connectors for rapid assembly in the field by local non-technical labor. A range of radio equipment is available, including VHF, AM, single sideband, and UHF, depending on the individual situation in your particular country.

VHF FM Solar Backpack (complete)
For export use $1770
For FCC type accepted for U.S. use $1970

25-35 MHz AM SSB Solar Backpack (complete) $1670

Solar Backpack Kit Includes:

Radio: Low Band AM or Single Sideband; 26-27 MHz in the United States; 25-35 MHz in Developing Countries; VHF FM for Developing Countries; VHF FM for U.S. use.

Solar Panel: 18 volt, 600 milliamp.

Battery: 14 volt rechargeable sealed battery.

Carrying Case: All-weather-proof, impact resistant, with lock.

Antenna: Collapsible antenna; Cigarette lighter charge plug; Charge circuit; Circuit breaker; External antenna connection; External antenna mount; AC 120 charge circuit; Hardware, wiring, and clamps.

Comes with complete instructions. All prices include total labor charges.

VHF FM Solar Base Station Kit (complete)
For export use $1860
FCC type accepted for U.S. use $2060

25-35 MHz AM SSB Solar Base Station Kit (complete) $1560

VHF FM Mobile Radio System (complete)
For export use $895
FCC type accepted for U.S. use $1045

25-35 MHz AM SSB Mobile Radio System (complete) $745

All from:
Solar Electronics
156 Drakes Lane
Summertown, TN 38483

Coop's Satellite Digest
Bob Cooper, Editor

$50 /year (12 issues)
from:
Satellite Television Technology
P.O. Box G
Arcadia, OK 73007

(See **Home-Satellite TV Reception**, *p. 493.)*

•
Being free of FCC licensing is important. It will add a tremendous amount to the foundation we are all trying to build upon. Watching TV is unnerving enough without having to post guards out front to warn off the approach of 'revenue agents.' Having a clear-cut, legal right to own satellite TV receiving equipment without a license will bring dozens of new hardware amnufacturers into the field. Rapidly. It provides the foundation of legitimate operation which, missing to date, has scared many reputable but capable firms away.

THE RISING SUN
NEIGHBORHOOD NEWSLETTER

She is now painting the river that runs through all three worlds.

—World Radio TV Handbook

SHORT WAVE LISTENING

by Robert Horvitz

THERE ARE MANY REASONS for listening to short wave radio broadcasts. If you're interested in international politics and culture, you can get up-to-the-minute reports and commentaries from dozens of countries, in English, pretty much any time you turn on the radio. (The best time to listen is the "prime time" hours of 2200-0600 Greenwich mean time, and there are more stations reachable from the East Coast.)

If you're interested in a particular country or region (say your ancestors are from there, or you're planning a trip), you can tune in to the local situation, to events and details too "small" to be reported by the international news agencies. If you know a language that no one around you speaks, and you don't want to lose your fluency, you can listen to daily broadcasts in that language. (Or you can learn a new language: many countries offer lessons in their native tongue via short wave.) Like exotic music? Much of the air time of Third World stations is filled with folk, indigenous pop, and traditional music – and the eerie electronic murmurs and cackles between the broadcasting bands put all so-called avant-garde composers to shame (these noises remind me of how a mother's body must sound to an infant in the womb).

Short wave is truly a magic carpet, and it's surprising that so few Americans take advantage of it (we have the lowest proportion of SW listeners to overall population among the industrial nations) particularly now that faraway events intrude so forcefully and so regularly into our lives. Last year, if you had a SW receiver, you might have heard the Voice of the Islamic Republic of Iran's own broadcasts about the revolution and its aftermath, including the seizure of the American Embassy and the holding of the hostages. You might have followed the Russian invasion of Afghanistan, as I did, by tuning from Radio Moscow to Radio Pakistan, to the BBC, to Peking, to All India Radio, to the Voice of America, to several European stations, to hear what each was saying – and not saying. Short wave is unbeatable for following crises as they happen, and for gaining multiple perspectives on complex events. Trying to understand the patterns of change and conflict in today's world solely on the basis of the coverage provided by the American mass media, is a lot like trying to understand life in a very large, old city without leaving the Hilton Hotel. It doesn't have to be that way! Almost all nations have external broadcasting services (they *want* to be heard) and the ongoing revolution in solid-state electronics has made the current crop of SW receivers more rugged, more portable, more sophisticated, and cheaper than earlier models.

The air is so full of signals nowadays that you need a receiver with very accurate tuning, so you know exactly what frequency you're getting. (In some bands, being off only .005 MHz will yield a different station.) For that reason (as well as the time-saving glance-check convenience) I'm sold on digital frequency displays. Sensitivity and selectivity are also important: a good receiver should be able to pick weak signals out of background noise, but at the same time should be able to reject signals overlapping the one you want to hear. Portability (size) is a factor for many people, and of course you want to get the best deal for your money. For my money, the best deal currently is the **Panasonic RF-2900**. *Its frequency display consists of five easy-to-read LEDs, which can be turned off to save power, once you've found your station, if you're running the set on batteries. SW band coverage is continuous from 3.2 to 30 MHz, plus local AM and FM. There's a large, two-rate tuning knob: push it in for racing across the spectrum, pull it out for fine tuning. Sound quality, especially on FM, is excellent (but be aware that SW channels are generally noisier and more distortion-prone than local AM). Other features include single-sideband capability, for listening to ham, CB, and other transmissions in that mode, as well as earphone, external speaker, and recording jacks (good SW receivers don't have built-in tape players/recorders). The only criticisms I can make of the RF-2900 are minor: the tuner tends to drift off-frequency when the set is first turned on (takes about half an hour to stabilize completely), it's a bit bulky to travel with, and the knobs stick out of the cabinet just far enough to make me nervous about bashing them whenever I carry it by the shoulder strap. If you plan to do most of your listening at home, the latter two points are irrelevant, and even the first is forgivable, since this is otherwise the best-designed, best priced, easiest-and-most-pleasant-to-use portable currently on the market.*

The RF-2900 is supposed to retail in the $250 to $300 range, but **47th Street Photo** *has been offering it for $190 to $195 for over a year, and that's the lowest price I've seen anywhere. Check their ads in the "Arts & Leisure" section of every Sunday's* **New York Times**, *or write to their mail order department at 36 East 19th Street, New York, NY 10003. Even with shipping charges, they may be your best bet.*

People who travel a lot and who live on tight budgets might also want to consider the **Sony ICF-5900W**. *This is the radio that the U.S. International Communication Agency (which runs the Voice of America) unofficially recommends for its field personnel. It's less than half the size of the RF-2900, much cheaper (only $119.50 at 47th Street Photo last spring), and in my experience, it's more sensitive as well. The first time I saw one in use was in a steel and concrete highrise; the building silenced my RF-2900, but a friend's ICF-5900W pulled in stations like it was outside. The main reason I can't recommend this model for everyone is that tuning it is so extraordinarily difficult. It's a two-step process that takes practice to master, and then it's still a nuisance. Another problem is that the set is designed to run only on batteries: there's no provision for an outside power source. Finally, production of the model is either at a low ebb right now or has ceased altogether, so it's getting hard to find in stores. I only mention it because of its good points (size, sensitivity, and price), which are indeed exceptional.*

MAIL ORDER EQUIPMENT

Not many audio or electronics stores carry a broad selection of SW equipment, so you should know about these two specialized mail order companies. Both have reputations for fast, competent service (I can vouch for Gilfer's, but have never tried Radio West's), both are technically knowledgeable about the equipment they sell, both sell only quality brands and models (sometimes with modifications to improve performance), both sell at prices that are reasonable but not cheap (47th Street Photo is cheap because of their volume and limited service: all the they do is ship the goods), both will be happy to tell you what they offer:

Gilfer Shortwave
Catalog
free from:
Gilfer Shortwave
P.O. Box 239
Park Ridge, NJ 07656

Radio West
Catalog
free from:
Radio West
3417 Purer Road
Escondido, CA 92025

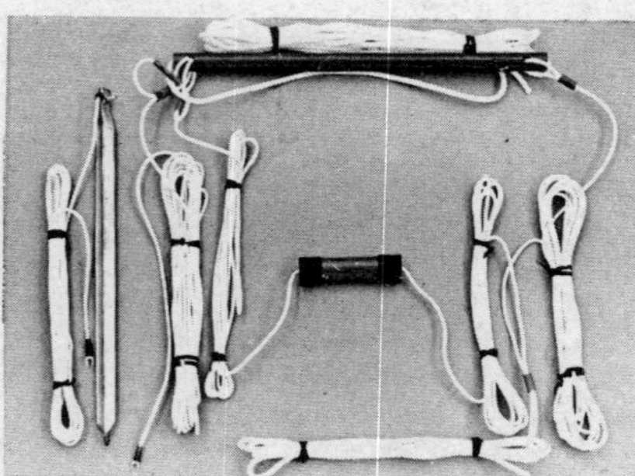

An outdoor antenna in only 20 to 22 feet of space: RAK Listener-1 $24.75 —Gilfer

FINDING THE BROADCASTS

Once you have a receiver, the next step is getting the most out of it. There are so many international broadcasts on so many frequencies, with such frequent schedule changes, that keeping track of who's audible when and where is a problem . . . with many solutions.

Most serious SW listeners keep a logbook by their radio in which to record the time, frequency, station, and audibility of the programs they hear. This takes some discipline, but pays off in a very useful guide tailored to your specific listening habits and reception conditions. At the very least, it will help you find stations that you want to hear again, and remind you when a program you like is on the air. You can "refresh" your log by spending a few hours a month making "spectrum sweeps," in which you catch up on previously unnoted schedule changes by systematically tuning from one end of the SW spectrum to the other.

Another good, free source of timely information can be found on the radio itself: the "DX" programs carried by many SW stations at least once a week. These shows are aimed at hard-core SW enthusiasts for the most part, especially those who enjoy hunting for rarely-heard, exotic stations. Formats vary, but the typical DX program includes brief schedule notes for perhaps a dozen stations (think of the altruism: they help you tune in to other, competing stations!), reception reports from various parts of the world, predictions about reception quality for the coming weeks, and answers to technical questions mailed in by listeners. Many shows go beyond that to give short tutorials on radio science, antenna design, or equipment repair, news about SW publications, listeners' clubs and gatherings, etc. Because this information is often rather rapidly presented, many listeners tape record DX programs for later reference and/or transcription.

You can often get the schedule of a particular station simply by writing to them and asking for it – though I've heard many complaints about slow response (most stations are understaffed). The **World Radio TV Handbook**, *which is published annually, contains all the addresses, as well as a lot of other information. The 34th edition (1980) can be found at many radio stores or mail-ordered from specialists like Gilfer. (Gilfer touts the* **Handbook** *as "The 'Must' Book for Every Listener," but I've done quite well without it, thanks.)*

World Radio TV Handbook
(A Complete Directory of International Radio and Television)
J.M. Frost, Editor
1980; 550 pp.
$15.95 postpaid from:
Watson-Guptill Publications
2160 Patterson Street
Cincinnati, OH 45214
or Whole Earth Household Store

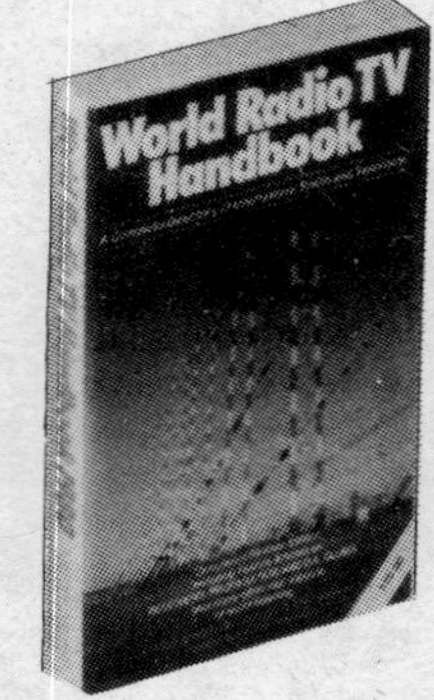

In my experience, the richest source of SW information is other SW listeners – friends who call you at 2 a.m. to say, "Quick! Turn on your radio and tune to ####!" as well as the many club newsletters and noncommercial publications. Best among the latter – in a league by itself, actually – is the **Review of International Broadcasting.** *Most SW magazines are like DX programs: they emphasize schedules and technics, and ignore broadcasting content altogether. Questions of style, subject treatment, editorial stance, credibility and import are never raised.* **RIB**, *edited and published by Glenn Hauser, stepped into this vacuum just over three years ago. Basically it's a monthly montage of "Listener Insights on Programming," press clippings, short essays (mostly written by subscribers. In the April, 1980 issue: a reply by the Voice of America's Acting Director to a critical article in the previous issue, a transcript of a talk aired on Radio Moscow comparing the VOA and RM, "Short Wave Listening in the Arctic – Northern Canada's Cultural Clash," a ballot for the 1980 RIB Awards for Excellence in International Broadcasting, etc.), and a variety of centerfold features. The centerfold in April, June, October, and December is a comprehensive schedule of English-language broadcasts arranged by country; in February and August, a similar schedule of DX programs in English, arranged by time; and in the remaining months, "Stuff We Like," lists of the RIB readership's favorite programs. Except for these (and other) regular features by the editor,* **RIB** *is an open forum, so the quality of the essays and comments varies from the flaky to the fascinating. The long-term trend is definitely upward as more people find out about the magazine and contribute. I've had recurring fantasies of starting a SW magazine myself, but have set them aside as I doubt if I could improve upon* **RIB**. *Though it's designed to be of maximum use to the serious SW listener, it's also a good way to tell if SW is something that will maintain your interest before you shell out money for a set, and to follow what's being broadcast even if you never do buy a set.*

Review of International Broadcasting
Glenn Hauser, Editor
$12/year (12 issues)
from:
Glenn Hauser
University Radio WUOT
Knoxville, TN 37916

Panasonic RF-2900

ANTENNA BOOKS

The final suggestion I can make for getting the most out of your SW receiver is to put the most into it: all portables come with built-in "whip" antennas, but if you do most of your dial-turning in one spot, you can easily boost your set's signal capture ability by putting up a larger antenna. SW antennas are easy enough to make that there's little reason to buy a prefab (unless you're so short on space that you need something called an "active" antenna, in which case you should consult someone more knowledgeable about such things than I). There are many books that explain how to build the basic designs. A good one for beginners (because it emphasizes practical, physical details and requires no math or radio theory) is Rufus Turner's **The Antenna Construction Handbook for Ham, CB & SWL.** *The book has a variety of proven designs and clever suggestions (like using a windowscreen as an antenna), and gives due attention to safety (lightning protection, grounding). Another book for the more technically-minded is Orr and Cowan's* **The Radio Amateur Antenna Handbook.** *Gilfer considers it "the best book we've seen on this subject." For a broad take on the literature, you might write to the Ham Radio Book Store, Greenville, NH 03048, and ask for their catalog.*

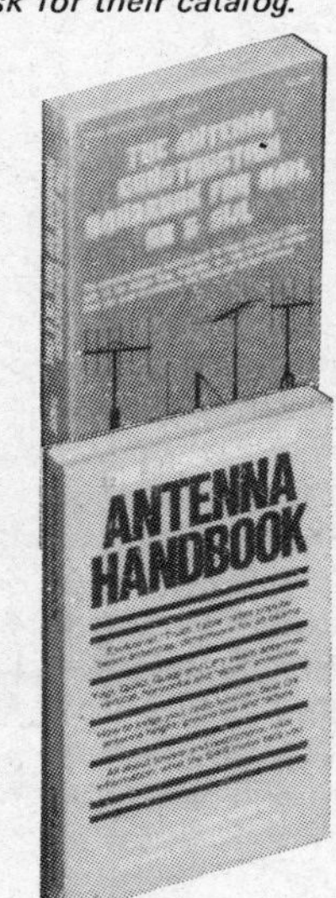

The Antenna Construction Handbook for Ham, CB and SWL
Rufus P. Turner
1978; 230 pp.

$5.95 postpaid from:
TAB Books
Blue Ridge
Summit, PA 17214

The Radio Amateur Antenna Handbook
William I. Orr and
Stuart D. Cowan
1978; 190 pp.

$6.95 postpaid from:
Gilfer Shortwave
P.O. Box 239
Park Ridge, NJ 07656

There's no substitute for a monoband beam placed high and in the clear! This 21 MHz three element Yagi at 56 feet has worked plenty of DX at W6SAI.
—The Radio Amateur Antenna Handbook

VHF/UHF LISTENING

Not all of the voice transmissions that you hear in the SW bands are broadcasts aimed at foreign publics. Some are semi-private conversations between radio amateurs (hams), land mobile units, CBers, etc. These can occasionally be interesting, but not often. A much richer selection of specialized communications is to be found above SW, in the VHF band ("very high frequency," from 30 to 300 MHz) and the UHF band ("ultra high frequency," 300 to 3000 MHz; the SW band, also known as "HF" or "high frequency," runs from 3 to 30 MHz). We're all familiar with VHF and UHF as the home of television channels 2 to 69 and FM radio (88 to 108 MHz), but large chunks of these bands are also reserved for the use of private industry, utilities, and government agencies. Although these channels are not "open to the public" in the broadcasting sense, it is perfectly legal to own receivers capable of tuning them in as long as you do not divulge anything you hear. In fact, the police-and-fire-band scanners made by companies like Electra (Bearcat), Radio Shack, and Regency can easily be adapted to let you listen to a wide variety of unusual, confidential transmissions by boats and airplanes, the Coast Guard, NASA, the military, the FBI, the Nuclear Regulatory Commission, NOAA, the Army Corps of Engineers, private construction and repair crews, etc. **Z-Tech Enterprises** *(P.O. Box 70, Hauppauge, NY 13901) specializes in crystals for tuning in government frequencies; they pop right in to the ordinary scanner's crystal-bays. The newer "programmable" scanners require no crystals to receive any frequency within their intended band coverage. These are more expensive than crystal scanners as an initial investment, but if you end up buying more than a dozen crystals for the cheaper kind, the overall price difference may be insignificant. For the more ambitious,* **VHF Engineering** *(320 Water Street, Binghamton, NY 13901) sells receivers, already assembled or in kit form, that enable you to explore regions of the VHF spectrum not accessible to ordinary scanners, and for the really ambitious,* **The Radio Amateur's VHF Manual** *($4 from the American Radio Relay League, 225 Main Street, Newington, CT 06111) contains plans and how-to tips for probing these bands as a sender as well as a receiver. (Sorry I'm not familiar enough with this technology to make specific hardware recommendations.)*

What you can find in these bands depends mainly on where you live. VHF and UHF signals are limited in range, and mobile transmitters are not very powerful, so if you live way out in the country, you're not apt to hear much at all. But if you live in or near a city, an airport, a harbor, or a military installation, you're apt to hear quite a bit — particularly during a local emergency (flood, black-out, earthquake, riot). While some channels carry messages in an unlistenable form (radioteletype, computer code), a surprising number are in plain old voice. Even FBI channels, which you'd think would be coded or scrambled, often are not. It's even possible (not likely, but possible) to pick up conversations transmitted from a surveillance "bug," if it isn't too far away — and you know what frequency it's using.

Knowing the frequency — that's the big trick, since government frequency assignments aren't made known by the government. Most agencies like the FBI rely on the lack of public information about their radio systems, the slight inconvenience involved in getting access to their part of the spectrum, the brevity of their normal transmissions, and the shifting of message traffic among their available channels — and not much else — to keep their radio communications secure. (Beyond that, many regular radio users speak in a slang familiar only to their cohorts, like CBers, so you may not understand a message even if you hear it clearly.) These are genuine obstacles to the would-be listener, but they're hardly insurmountable, especially to an avid VHF buff like Tom Kneitel. He's been monitoring government use of the band for more than thirty years, and has compiled **The 'Top Secret' Registry of U.S. Government Radio Frequencies,** *which lists over 3800 frequencies from 25 to 470 MHz, and the 50+ agencies that use them. Aside from those I've already mentioned, there are listings for the Postal Service, the Red Cross, the Federal Bureau of Prisons, the CIA, and several agencies concerned with the environment (Bureau of Land Management, EPA, Fish & Wildlife Service, Forest Service, etc.), though the vast majority are military. As a bonus, Kneitel includes the frequencies of 37 U.S. government satellites, and 23 more put up by foreign governments. There's even a listing for a frequency used in military "death ray" experiments (388 MHz)! An unknown number of these frequencies are not in use at any particular moment, an unknown number are used only sporadically, and some of the agency attributions are just hunches. Nonetheless, this is the best key I've seen for unlocking the treasure-house of government radio communications. In the same way that SW is unbeatable for following distant crises, Kneitel's Registry and a VHF scanner are unbeatable for following crises nearby (not too nearby, hopefully).*

The 'Top Secret' Registry of U.S. Government Radio Frequencies
Tom Kneitel
1979; 34 pp.

$4.95 postpaid from:
CRB Research
P.O. Box 56
Commack, NY 11725

For a current and quite extensive listing of frequencies used by local "public safety" and state government agencies (including police, fire, highway patrol and repair, hospitals, etc), get hold of Radio Shack's **Police Call Radio Directory.** *It comes in nine different volumes, each for a specific region of the country. In most places, it is these local agencies rather than the federal government which dominate the airwaves.*

Police Call Radio Directory (Including Fire and Emergency Services), Gene Hughes, Editor, Annual; 150 pp.

Volume 1 (Connecticut, Maine, Massachusetts, New Hampshire, New York, Rhode Island, Vermont)

Volume 2 (Delaware, Maryland, New Jersey, Pennsylvania)

Volume 3 (Michigan, Ohio)

Volume 4 (Illinois, Indiana, Kentucky, Wisconsin)

Volume 5 (Iowa, Kansas, Minnesota, Missouri, Nebraska, North Dakota, South Dakota)

Volume 6 (District of Columbia, Florida, Georgia, North Carolina, South Carolina, Virginia, West Virginia)

Volume 7 (Alabama, Arkansas, Louisiana, Mississippi, Oklahoma, Tennessee, Texas)

Volume 8 (Arizona, Colorado, Idaho, Montana, New Mexico, Nevada, Utah, Wyoming)

Volume 9 (California, Oregon, Washington)

$5.95 each postpaid, all from Hollins Radio, P.O. Box 35002, Los Angeles, CA 90035, or check your local Radio Shack. ■

Weather radio

During the last five years or so the government has built a network of radio broadcast stations to give 24-hour, updated weather reports, specialized for each region of the country and the people living there (more marine-oriented along the coastlines, for instance). To tune in the broadcasts you need radios which can pick up the 162.40 - 162.55 megaHertz "Weather Band." Most radio-stereo stores carry the equipment for around $20 - $40. For more information and a list of operating stations write: National Oceanic and Atmospheric Administration, Weather Network, National Weather Service, Attn: W112, 8060 13th Street, Silver Spring, MD 20910. —Art Kleiner

Some plain old portable AM-FM radios have a weather band feature. It's worth having! That's how I start my day. "Small craft advisory for westerly winds 25 - 30 mph in the afternoon. High tide at the Golden Gate will be at . . ." —SB

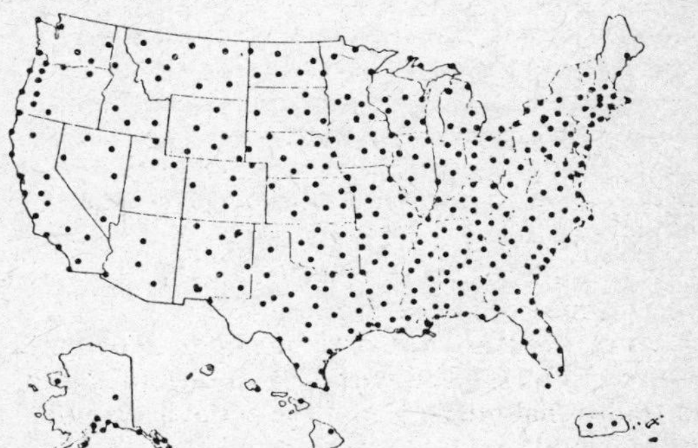

NOAA weather radio transmitters as of 1980

Radios that Work for Free

How many of you have had a crystal set radio? Not many I'll bet. Mine (about 1940) drove me bananas because when I was listening to "Gangbusters," a forbidden fruit in our family, the gunshots at the finale would cause the catwhisker to jump off the crystal, and I'd never find out whodunnit. Anyway, this book elegantly tells how to construct one. Though the author tells how to make the battery by sticking electrodes into a lemon (!), he isn't fuddyduddy. There's a lot about utilizing modern diodes instead of the crystal and catwhisker. I found the whole business possessing a strange esthetic. It's presented nicely too. —J. Baldwin

Radios that Work for Free
K.E. Edwards
1977; 147 pp.

$6 postpaid from:
Hope and Allen
Publishing Company
P.O. Box 535
Belmont, CA 94002
or Whole Earth
Household Store

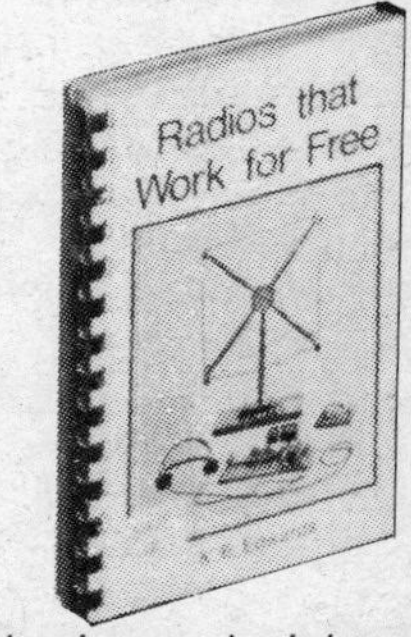

●
These radios work for free, that is, you don't have to plug them in, nor do you put batteries into them. So, where does the power come from? The power comes from the broadcast station who is transmitting.

U.S. Frequency Allocations Chart

It's not as pretty as a land map, but it's even more essential to find your way around electromagnetic territory. The whole allocations table, from 10 kHz to 300 GHz — minus all the footnotes, technical specifications, exceptions, etc. — is presented graphically, using patterns and colors to identify the various services. I must say the colors are harsh — pungent pinks, greens, blues, reds — but that gives the chart an appropriately non-decorative impact. I can't say what exactly I've learned from having it on my wall, but it does keep me aware of how much of the world is beyond direct perception.
—Robert Horvitz

U.S. Frequency Allocations Chart
Department of Commerce
Office of
Telecommunications
1975; 32" x 55"
No. 003-000-00469-4

$1.35 postpaid from:
Superintendent
of Documents
U.S. Government
Printing Office
Washington, DC 20402

THE RISING SUN
NEIGHBORHOOD NEWSLETTER

"I'm so hungry I could eat the last member of an endangered species." —Stephanie

How to Lie with Statistics

In these days of polls and "proof" furnished by testing by "independent laboratories," it might be well to bear in mind the lessons given by this simple book. It's been around a long time, but it's still deadly.

—J. Baldwin

[Suggested by Jonathan Katz]

How to Lie with Statistics
Darrel Huff and Irving Geis
1954, 1973; 142 pp.

$1.95 postpaid from:
W.W. Norton and Co.
500 Fifth Avenue
New York, NY 10036
or Whole Earth Household Store

Simply change the proportion between the ordinate and the abscissa. There's no rule against it, and it does give your graph a prettier shape. All you have to do is let each mark up the side stand for only one-tenth as many dollars as before.

That *is* impressive, isn't it? Anyone looking at it can just feel prosperity throbbing in the arteries of the country. It is a subtler equivalent of editing "National income rose ten per cent" into ". . . climbed a whopping ten per cent." It is vastly more effective, however, because it contains no adjectives or adverbs to spoil the illusion of objectivity. There's nothing anyone can pin on you.

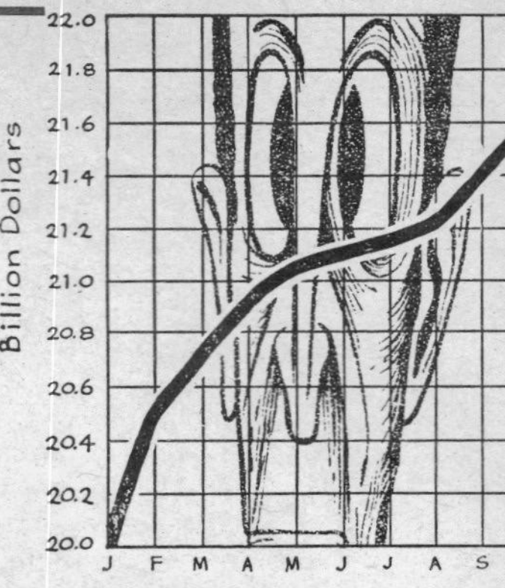

Prof. E. McSquared's Calculus Primer

It sometimes seems a bit ironic that it is necessary to have mathematical skills in order to understand certain natural phenomena, but that's how it goes. The necessity of learning calculus keeps rearing its ugly head. For me that meant 4 to 6 hours a night of laborious homework and a rather highly refined hatred. I don't know if this book would have helped me, but I'll bet it will help lots of other folks. Martin Gardner, resident mathematician at **Scientific American** *likes it too, which is good enough for me. If calculus is hanging you up, it might be worth the reasonable price of this book to see if it can unhang you.*

—J. Baldwin

Prof. E. McSquared's Original, Fantastic & Highly Edifying Calculus Primer
Howard Swann and John Johnson
1971, 1977; 215 pp.

$7.95 postpaid from:
William Kaufmann, Inc.
One First Street
Los Altos, CA 94022
or Whole Earth Household Store

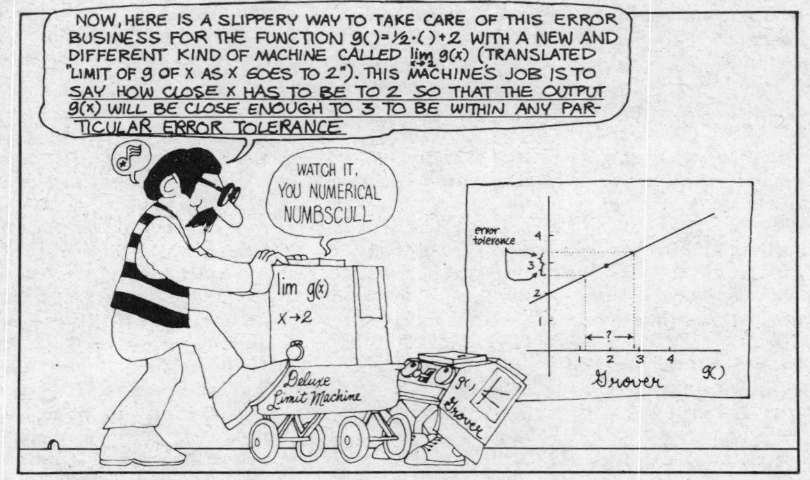

How to Solve It

This is the best book I know of for lining up a problem for a logical solution. The emphasis is on math, but it is simple logic and can easily be applied to all forms of problem identification and analysis. Better yet is that the methods shown really work even on personal decision-making binds. Essentially it's a head-straightener.

—J. Baldwin

How to Solve It
(A New Aspect of Mathematical Method)
G. Polya
1945, 1971, 253 pp.

$3.95 postpaid from:
Princeton University Press
Princeton, NJ 08540
or Whole Earth Household Store

•

Inventor's paradox. The more ambitious plan may have more chances of success.

This sounds paradoxical. Yet, when passing from one problem to another, we may often observe that the new, more ambitious problem is easier to handle than the original problem. More questions may be easier to answer than just one question. The more comprehensive theorem may be easier to prove, the more general problem may be easier to solve.

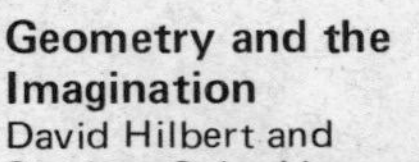
(See **Mathematics as a Human Endeavor**, *p. 566, and* **Fingermath**, *p. 570.)*

Geometry and the Imagination

While reading over a list of books considered by Gregory Bateson to be special, I came across this old friend, a book that had been recommended to me by Bucky Fuller 20 years ago. As I perused it again, I was struck by how much it had affected the way I use my mind. It's still an adventure: geometry understood intuitively rather than through abstract logical constructs. Here is where I learned to exercise and trust my intuition. Even if geometry isn't your thing, you may find the approach enlightening in the best sense.

—J. Baldwin

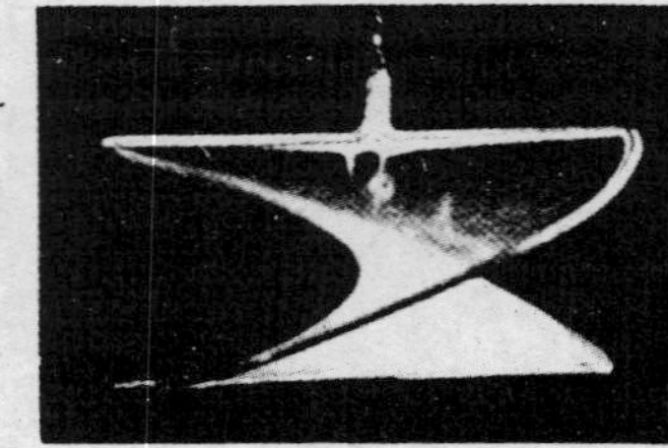

Geometry and the Imagination
David Hilbert and Stephan Cohn-Vossen
1932; 357 pp.

$12.95 postpaid from:
Chelsea Publishing Co.
432 Park Avenue South
Room 503
New York, NY 10018
or Whole Earth Household Store

→

The most general helicoid is the surface swept out by an arbitrary space curve performing a uniform screw motion about a fixed axis. Thus our particular ruled helicoid is obtained when the generating curve is a straight line intersecting the axis at right angles. This surface is called a right helicoid. An examination by analytic methods reveals that the right helicoid is a minimal surface.

Fractals

Many natural phenomena worth study are highly irregular. The central notion presented in this engagingly written volume, the concept of fractional dimensions, is both profound and useful in areas involving such disparate subjects as Brownian motion, coastline lengths, the density of matter in the universe, curdling, moon craters, the distribution of salaries and the meanders of rivers. The book is beautifully produced, and is filled with computer graphics illustrating the various ideas. It is also here and there decorated with appealing graphics accidentally produced by programs containing bugs. As with René Thom's Catastrophe Theory, Benoit Mandelbrot's **Fractals** *is a heartening and illuminating application of advanced mathematics to the beautiful, irregular, enigmas of the world.*

—Marc Le Brun

[Suggested by R.W. Gosper]

Fractals
(Form, Chance, and Dimension)
Benoit B. Mandelbrot
1977; 365 pp.

$21 postpaid from:
W.H. Freeman and Company
660 Market Street
San Francisco, CA 94104
or Whole Earth Household Store

•

Curdling will designate any cascade of instabilities resulting in contraction.

Curd will be used to designate a volume within which a physical characteristic becomes increasingly concentrated as a result of curdling.

Whey will therefore be a natural choice (incidentally, a choice Miss Muffet should not mind) to designate the space not occupied by curds.

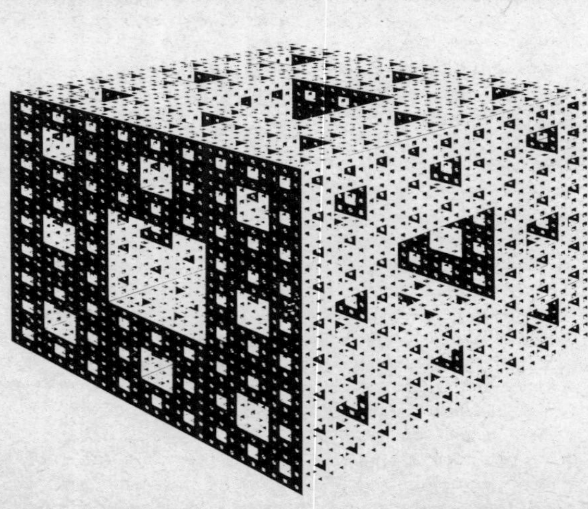

The Sierpinski Sponge — Each of its external faces is known as a Sierpiński carpet (Sierpiński 1916). Its area vanishes, while the total perimeter of its holes is infinite.

Mathematical Snapshots

The most graphically insightful math book in print. Most math feeds proof; this lovely stuff feeds understanding, and is no less rigorous. If someone were going to see only one mathematics book in their life, this would be the best.
—SB

Mathematical Snapshots
H. Steinhaus
1950, 1969; 328 pp.

$15.95 postpaid from:
Oxford University Press
16-00 Pollitt Drive
Fair Lawn, NJ 07410
or Whole Earth
Household Store

↑
To determine the centroid of a stick, we place it horizontally on the edges of our palms and then we bring our hands closer together; finally they meet in the center of gravity. The stick never loses its equilibrium because when the centroid, which is initially between the palms, approaches one of them, the pressure on the nearer palm becomes many times greater than the pressure on the other palm; its product by the coefficient of friction must finally surpass the analogous product for the other palm; when this happens, the relative movement of the first palm ceases and the relative movement of the other one starts. This play continues alternately until both palms meet; the centroid is always between them and it is there at the final stage. The trick is done automatically without any conscious effort.

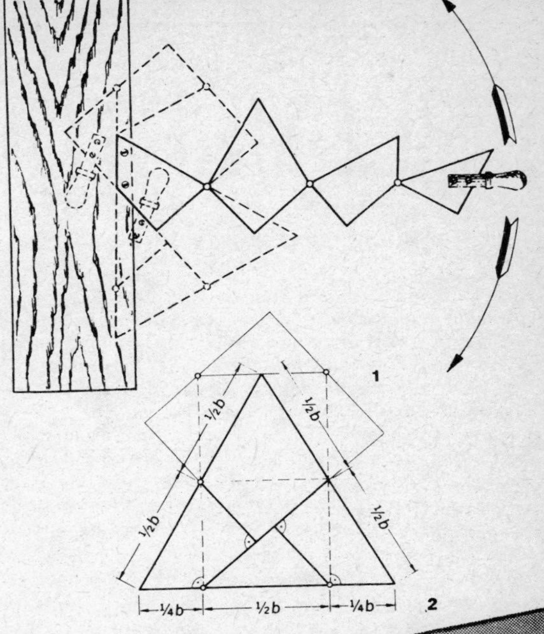

From these four small boards (1) we can compose a square or an equilateral triangle, according as we turn the handle up or down. The proof is given by sketch (2). →

Structural Stability and Morphogenesis

It will be some time before the catastrophe theory work of René Thom, like the work of Einstein or Newton, will come to be fully apprehended and integrated into the structure of scientific thought. Aware of this, the reviewers make no claims regarding the completeness of their comments. —Marc Le Brun

This is an incredible, poetic book. It has already started a cascade of new work in biology, physics and neurophysiology, and it is going to transform all of the sciences now grappling with phenomena too complex to be described in the old Newtonian language. It is a very difficult, knotty, book, a weaving together of aesthetic vision, personal insight, and very tough math.

Thom has made a fundamental connection between the mathematics of form (differential topology) and forms as they appear in science and human experience. His conjectures are proving out experimentally — the language of forms he provides can guide the researcher and the designer.

Further, his language describes the dynamic of form: birth, differentiation, predation, fertilization, parturition, death. Prigogine and others are linking Thom's catastrophe theory up to the thermodynamics of open systems and the theory of self-organizing systems. The door is opened; at last we have a language which respects the diversity, subtlety and complexity of organic form, while providing a bridge to the tools and knowledge of classical quantitative science.
—Jed Harris and John Nash
[Suggested by Paul Ryan]

Structural Stability and Morphogenesis
(An Outline of a General Theory of Models)
René Thom
1975; 348 pp.

$19.50 postpaid from:
Addison-Wesley Publishing Company
Jacob Way
Reading, MA 01867
or Whole Earth
Household Store

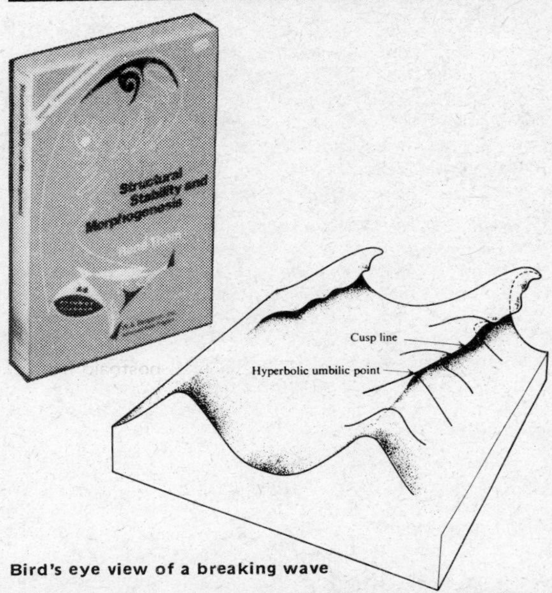

Bird's eye view of a breaking wave

The World of Mathematics

An infectious multi-faceted telling of math stories — pure, applied, ancient, recent: a fine and complete collection.
—SB

•

1. This Book has 597 Pages.
2. The Author of this Book is Confucius.
3. The Statements Numbered 1,2, and 3 are all False.

•

Problem 36 of the papyrus begins: "Go down 1 times 3, 1/3 of me, 1/5 of me is added to me; return 1, filled am I." What is the quantity saying it?

The World of Mathematics
James R. Newman
1956, 2469 pp.
(4 volumes)

$39.95 postpaid from:
Simon and Schuster
Attn: Order Department
1230 Avenue of the Americas
New York, NY 10020

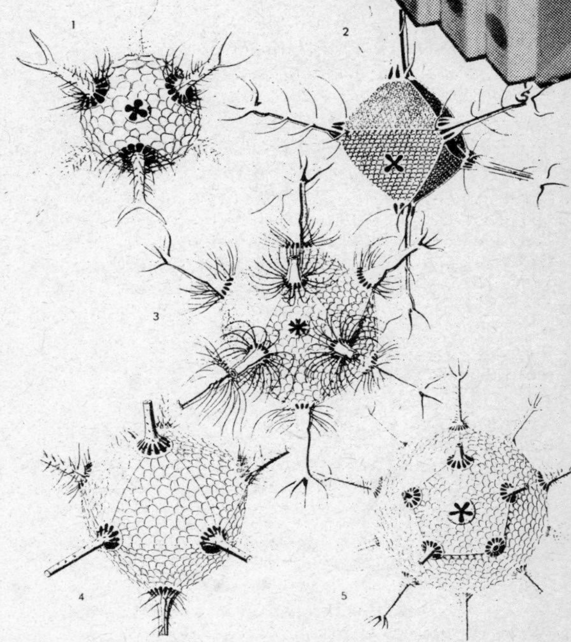

Here is a page from Heckel's Challenger Monograph **showing the skeletons of several Radiolarians. Numbers 2, 3, and 5 are octahedron, icosahedron, and dodecahedron in astonishingly regular form; 4 seems to have a lower symmetry.**

The Geometrical Foundation of Natural Structure

After reading Ken Kern's **Owner Built Home** *(p. 223) I began to wonder why no one had written a good book on geometry and form which would liberate our imaginations when we build shelter. Last year a friend turned me on to this book. It is the finest, most complete book on the subject I have found.*

Once the central concept of the book is stated, it seems simple and beautiful. It should have been self-evident. Geometric forms make up a "language" which is spoken, in a sense, by those of us who make buildings. We have to know the "form language" before we can understand what we are doing when we build. The book has a first chapter containing a discussion of the idea of the "form language." The chapters that follow contain all of the information necessary to understand the ways to organize two and three dimensional spaces from circle packings and tessellations of polygons, to polyhedra and how they pack. All of these geometries are derived from natural structures like crystals and soap bubbles. There is enough information to go into the minutest detail. If this isn't enough, the last chapter shows the methods for creating countless more forms. There are even examples of a few buildings and how these methods were used to make them. The author is interested in design, but the book doesn't push any particular forms down our throats. It just presents possibilities for expanded thinking and leaves all of the decisions about building to us. It is a book to live with and grow with. —Donna Cheney

The Geometrical Foundation of Natural Structure
(A Source Book of Design)
Robert Williams
1972; 263 pp.

$6.70 postpaid from:
Dover Publications
180 Varick Street
New York, NY 10014
or Whole Earth
Household Store

Examples of simple distortions of 4.6^2

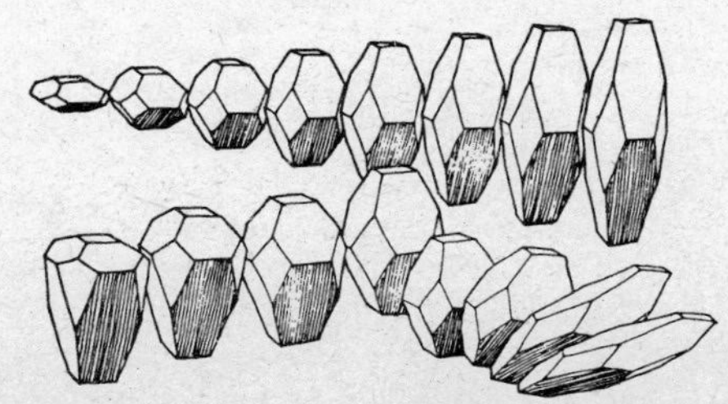

THE RISING SUN
NEIGHBORHOOD NEWSLETTER

Peter Bird, the man who's rowing alone to Australia (p. 430), was selling velvet paintings in England when he met a man who had just rowed around Ireland and he thought that sounded like an interesting thing to do. A year later he and the other man rowed across the Atlantic. Selling velvet paintings was pretty boring. He went door to door with a partner trying to convince people that paintings that were made with a template and cost 75 cents to make were artists' originals worth $20 and also convince them that the paint on the back of some of them where they'd been all piled up in bundles was actually paint that had soaked through when the artist was working on it. He didn't realize when he started selling them that they were made by template and finding out was one of the things that soured him on the job and made him ready to quit and start rowing across the Atlantic.

continued on next spread

CALCULATORS

by Mike Malone and Art Kleiner

Since the great calculator price wars of 1975, when dozens of small calculator manufacturers were underpriced out of business by Texas Instruments (T.I.) the business has been dominated by two American companies (T.I. and Hewlett-Packard) and some new Japanese contenders (most notably Casio). In the meantime, semiconductor technology has steadily improved. Thanks to better integration, batteries, and displays, calculators are now available the size and thickness of a credit card, or built into a watch or pen, or capable of complex programming available just twenty years ago only on computers the size of a small building.

Nevertheless, the characteristics of good craftsmanship hold true even for pocket brains. A well-built calculator keyboard will have keys that are firmly set in place and preferably will feature a click-action to safeguard against multiple entry. The key symbols should be legible and set deep into the keys so they don't wear off. It doesn't matter how small the keys are as long as they are spaced properly. The display, whether liquid crystal (silver, with black numbers) or light-emitting diode (illuminated, usually red numbers), should be readable. Particularly with LED, twist the calculator around to make sure you can read the display at a comfortable viewing angle for you. The packaging should be well-sealed and sturdy.

Finally, turn on the calculator and fill up the display with numbers; then multiply that number by 10. Does the display switch to an overflow mode with two places for exponents on the right? If not, you may never know you've gone off the display. Now divide by 0. The machine should tell you you've made an illegal operation.

SPECIFIC MODELS

If you're just going to calculate mileage and stuff, why spend a lot of money to get a calculator that will compute hyperbolic sine? If it's going to be sitting around the house, you might want one with a little heft to it; if you plan to keep it in your pocket, get an ultrathin one. The best-liked credit card models are the **Casio MQ 12** *(about $50), and the so-called "melody card," the* **Casio ML71** *(about $45). Even though it's the same model with music, the 71 is cheaper because more of them are produced.*

For regular sized pocket four-function calculators, get any that's cheap and disposable. Everybody's got more or less equivalent models: the **Texas Instruments TI1750** *(about $18), the* **Sharp SP8159** *(about $16) and the* **Commodore CIL-30** *(about $13) are all fine. For about $40,* **Casio** *offers the pocket-sized NQ11 with good human interface: two timers, two alarms, a watch, and a calendar.*

In higher-priced scientific and financial calculators, you should probably get a programmable model. Programming can make a simple but repetitious operation a helluva lot easier. If the programs are keyboard-entry only, keep in mind that the program you're using will be lost when you turn off the machine. For that reason you might want to spend a little more and get a CMOS-chip based programmable — it will store a program for a year or so after the machine is turned off. A good programmable calculator will offer the full spectrum of programmer's aids, including subroutining, lopping, flagging, and pausing. The top notch ones even let you redefine the keyboard to make individual keys represent entire programs. The very best programmable calculators also have such external (peripheral) goodies as magnetic card readers, devices that optically read printed code, printers, added memory, and even video displays. These can be built into the calculator or attached via wires.

In programmables, Hewlett-Packard (HP) and Texas Instruments are the names. HPs are more expensive but better built. The models to look at are the **HP-38C** *(about $145) and* **41C** *(about $290), both with CMOS-based continuous memory. The* **HP-41C** *is the most powerful pocket calculator that exists. The* **Texas Instruments TI58C** *(about $105) is roughly comparable to the Hewlett-Packards, but less expensive.*

Programming may scare you or seem unnecessary: in that case, choose a non-programmable based on what functions you need. If you're working with computers, the **TI Programmer** *(about $55) is best. If you're a physicist or mathematician, you can probably use the* **Commodore SR-1800** *(about $18). For general scientific applications it's hard to beat the* **Hewlett-Packard 32** *(about $65). The best financial non-programmable calculator is the* **HP 37-E** *(about $80). A good printing calculator is the* **Sharp 1166** *(about $85).*

Commodore's calculators are usually available through **Mr. Calculator** *— there are stores all over, with a mail order outlet at 160 East El Camino Real, Mountain View, CA 94041. Two good mail-order sources for the rest (if you can't find them locally) are* **Markline***, P.O. Box 1750F, Waltham, MA 02154; and* **Olympic Sales Company***, P.O. Box 74545, Los Angeles, CA 90004 also carries a full line of other consumer-oriented electronic gear — electronic games, watches, toys, clocks, radios, phone accessories, etc.* ■

The TI 58C programmable calculator
$99.95
—Markline

HP 41C — Hewlett Packard's most powerful personal calculator
$289.95
—Markline

This small calculator is packed with performance — it does it all! Complete calculator functions PLUS ultra-portable digital alarm clock with timer and calendar, precision stopwatch, and special melody feature. In MUSIC mode, you can play a complete scale and have your calculation results played back to you in music tones as well as displayed. Wake or sleep to your choice of two pre-programmed melodies. Set for musical tone on the hour to remind you of scheduled events and appointments. Verify entries with audible tones or just have fun "playing" favorite tunes.
$49.95
—Markline

Video World

There's definitely a glut of video magazines, but this "Magazine of Electronic Living" serves as the best running scorecard on electronic gadgetry. That's probably because it's British; British consumers tend to get new products like Videotext (a television-based information system) a few years before we do. That's OK; we get to learn from their mistakes. **Video World** *covered the January, 1980 Las Vegas Consumer Electronics Show (by all accounts a milestone of silicon decadence) with more verve and insight than any American publication. Also keeps up with the news in other foreign countries.*

—Art Kleiner

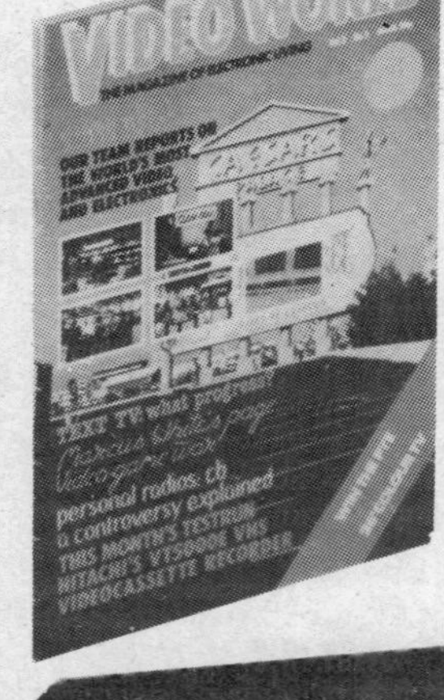

Video World
John Sanders, Editor
£9.50 (about $22)/year (12 issues) from:
Galaxy Publications Ltd.
Hermit Place
252 Belsize Road
London NW6 4BT
England

Typewriter for drunks? Rubber safety keyboard for astronauts? No, it's a specially designed "ergonomic" typewriter keyboard. Ergonomics is the science of fitting machines to people rather than the other way round which seems to be the aim of the rest of science. Called the 'Maltron', presumably after Lillian Malt, the keyboard trainer and designer, the machine is made by PCD Ltd of Farnborough.

Key heights have been made to fit the unequal lengths of people's fingers so that unnatural stretches are no longer necessary. Keys for the middle fingers are set deeper into the keyboard than the keys for the shorter ones. The thumbs, which have been under-used all this time are given up to eight keys each all within easy reach. Not only does the keyboard also compensate for unequal strengths of the fingers but due to the shape of the keys it becomes almost impossible to strike the wrong keys.

The limitations of the 'Qwerty' layout are avoided in the Maltron, which uses 90 percent of the letters of the 100 most used words in English in the home row (Qwerty uses 44 percent). Similar ratios have been worked out for six other European languages.

The high keying speed (up to 40 percent faster) makes it possible to take dictation directly in plain language.

Scientific Analysis on the Pocket Calculator

When I'm working on an application involving really serious "number crunching" (any highly mathematical use of a computer), I almost invariably consult Richard Hamming's 1962 classic **Numerical Methods for Scientists and Engineers** (1973; $22.50 postpaid from McGraw-Hill Book Company, Princeton Road, Hightstown, NJ 08520), *sometimes just for inspiration. Jon Smith has recast Hamming's computer-oriented methods into forms more suitable for implementation on a pocket calculator and has included substantial material covering additional topics.*

Careful attention was paid to making the book as useful as possible to a wide spectrum of users — algorithms are designed to minimize keystrokes to reduce error and fatigue and are given in both algebraic and reverse polish notations. Most of the methods work on even the simplest of calculators but variations and ramifications for more sophisticated models are also treated. For those about to take on some of the heavy stuff armed only with their trusty calculator this well-written, well-designed book is a definitive ally.

—Marc Le Brun
[Suggested by W. James]

Scientific Analysis on the Pocket Calculator
Jon M. Smith
1975, 1977; 445 pp.
2nd Edition
$16.95 postpaid form:
John Wiley and Sons
One Wiley Drive
Somerset, NJ 08873
or Whole Earth Household Store

The Home Computer Revolution

No other introduction book to personal computing comes close. It's not really about specific machines, but about the heart and soul of this devilishly involving avocation/vocation. Except for the author's previous book, **Computer Lib/Dream Machines** *(p. 536), it's the most entertaining computer book around. And it's gleefully low-priced. Ted Nelson is an artist.*

—Art Kleiner

•

Your computer store — you *do* have one, almost anywhere in the USA — if you don't mind driving, that is — your computer store, anyway, gives advice, sells equipment, and helps you with repair. They also may sell prebuilts, possibly even prebuilt S-100 machines, assembled in the back room and guaranteed by themselves. There you can see the machines in operation, daydream with other customers, or get advice from the staff.

An important function of the computer store is to provide free information; and an attitude of general helpfulness without regard to sales, with frank answers, appears to be a widespread norm. Naturally they will try to sell you the computers they prefer to sell, but in general the computer stores seem to be fairly straightforward and honest about facts and advice.

They have to, to establish a reputation for integrity; because the hobby grapevine is ferociously efficient.

The Home Computer Revolution
Ted Nelson
1977; 224 pp.
$2.50 postpaid from:
The Distributors
702 South Michigan
South Bend, IN 46618
or Whole Earth Household Store

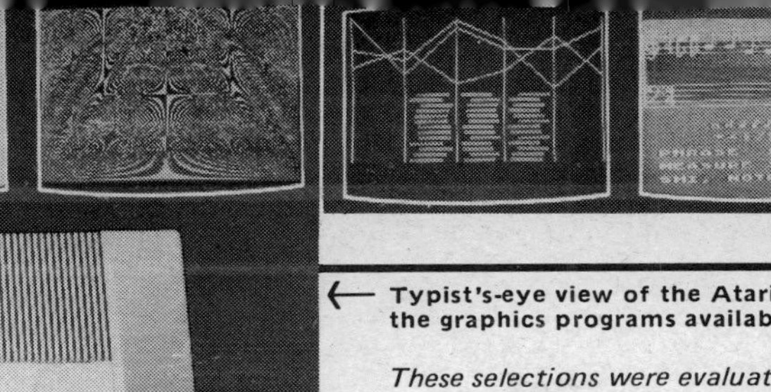

← Typist's-eye view of the Atari 800 computer, plus some of the graphics programs available. $1080 and up

BUYING A PERSONAL COMPUTER

by Art Kleiner

"Which small computer should I buy?" is the question everybody asks and nobody's willing to answer. The computers described here are all good models, but your choice should depend first on what you want to do with it. It's worth checking any potential use out specifically with your dealer, no matter how far down the road it seems now. The padded cells are piled high with people who figured it wouldn't be hard to make some routine adjustment later on to add a certain piece of equipment or use their machine as a networking terminal or run a particular program. Finding a dealer you can trust in your area is often more important than finding any one specific brand.

Despite all the talk of ten-dollar chips, you'll need to spend at least $10,000 (and probably more) if you have regular small business use in mind. Any less, and you'll feel frustrated constantly by what your machine can't do. However, home use, experimenting, learning, game-inventing, networking, music and graphic making, word processing, light programming and personal business handling can all be done on home computers, which sell for $400 and up (most in the $800 - $2000 range). Printers and disk drives usually cost extra and often seem essential before long. If you can't afford $10,000 but need business computing done, get a terminal and printer and use someone else's bigger time-sharing computer through your telephone. Since they are so expensive, we're only showing a couple of the really special business systems here. There are other good ones with full write-ups in MicroWorld's **Micro Shopper** *(below) and in the computer magazines.*

These selections were evaluated with the help of Larry Press (Small Systems Group); Louis Ewens (Marin Computer Center); Bob Albrecht, Dave Caulkins, and Dennis Allison (all loosely connected with the People's Computer Company); J.D. Sharp (Bananas at Large); Alan Hald (MicroWorld); and Jim Whitescarver, Mike Heines, Tom Hargadon, and Steve Heitmann from the EIES computer network (p. 535). Information on all these machines is free from the manufacturers.

Rockwell Aim-65. $415 and up, manufactured by Rockwell International, P.O. Box 3669, Anaheim, CA 92803. *Single-board computers are made for experimenters; they're the least expensive, but they require electronic expertise and machine language programming. The machine to get depends on which type of chip you want to learn the language for. Unlike the other single-boards, the Rockwell AIM 65 has a full keyboard (the others have calculator keypads) and can be adapted for use as a terminal. There's no screen; just an LED display like that of a calculator. A version of BASIC is easily added as an attachable component. The biggest plus is a built-in thermal printer. Another highly respected single-board is the Kim-1, made by Commodore, which also manufactures the PET.*

Atari 800. $1080 and up. Manufactured by Atari Consumer Division, P.O. Box 427, Sunnyvale, CA 94086. *A surprisingly well-designed personal computer with canned programs on plug-in cartridges. The cartridges make it easier for people to use the machines without programming at all (although you can program on the Atari). The problem with cartridge programs is they can't be modified within the cartridge; you can copy them onto a tape or disk and change them there, but then they run more slowly. It's surprising to the uninitiated how much difference a second of sitting at an immobile screen can make. Atari's machines were only released in 1979, but already there's a lot of good software and accessories available, including top-notch small computer graphics and music making. Documentation could be better.*

Commodore PET. $1090 and up. Manufactured by Commodore, 3330 Scott Blvd., Santa Clara, CA 95050. *The PET's unique feature is still its keyboard — most keys can produce a specific graphic symbol, which makes low-level graphics easy to work with. Kids like it. There's also good screen-editing and a nice keyboard to type on (make sure you get the full typewriter keyboard, and not the old calculator-keys model, which is awful). The cassette tape drive, standard on most machines, is optional on the PET; without it your programs will fade into air, so the price above includes it. Because it's got a widely-used industrial interface (the IEEE-488), lots of PETs are being adapted into test instruments or other industrial machines.*

TRS-80 Model I Level II. $619 and up. Manufactured by Radio Shack, Tandy Corporation, Fort Worth, TX 76102. *Were it not for Bob Albrecht's enthusiastic recommendation, the TRS-80 would probably be omitted from this page, even though it's the most popular personal computer. That's its advantage — lots of Radio Shacks which sell and service it and lots of TRS-80 users writing programs for it. It thus has more cottage-industry software than any other home computer. Though it's not good for graphics or sophisticated programming, it's a good machine to learn the basics on. The most useful TRS-80 model for the price is probably the TRS-80 Model I Level II.*

Apple II. $1200 and up. Manufactured by Apple Computer Company, 10260 Bandley Drive, Cupertino, CA 95014. *A very highly praised personal computer. Its main flaw is that it's more difficult for beginners to work with than the TRS-80, PET, or Atari; but it's got a wide selection of good programs and accessories (including VisiCalc, the universally acknowledged Rolls Royce of personal computer programs). Graphics and music are particularly good, and it's expandable into a more powerful business system (approaching but not quite equalling systems like North Star). Apple has the fastest disk drive and most agreeable keyboard of the personal computers. Good manuals, too. While putting this survey together, I decided to buy an Apple II. Bell and Howell plans to market an adapted Apple II for $200 more which is easier for beginners and teachers to work with; there will be jacks on the outside for plugging in joy sticks or video output. For information write Computer Division, Bell and Howell, 7100 McCormick Road, Chicago, IL 60645.*

North Star Horizon. $7000 and up. Manufactured by North Star Computers, 1440 Fourth Street, Berkeley, CA 94710. *A dependable business system with a wide range of available software, and a lot of people writing more. Very reasonably priced. It's particularly good for word processing. The main drawback is the disk drive, which uses mini-floppies — "not for the impatient," Steve Heitmann notes. But it expands into more effective systems easily, and Northstar is noted for good repair service.*

Other high quality business computer makers include Dynabyte, Altos, Cromemco and Vector Graphic.

Onyx. $20,000 and up. Manufactured by Onyx Systems, 73 East Trimble Road, San Jose, CA 95131. *The most powerful small business computer system available — so good that orders backed up as soon as the word spread. (They're designed and made by a small firm in San Jose.) For $20,000 you get a computer which can run Unix, a complex operating system developed by Bell Labs which usually runs on hundred-thousand-dollar mainframes. Four people can use the Onyx at once, and it can be expanded to eight. This is what people recommended when I asked them to name the ultimate in small computers.* *(See also mail order electronic supplies, p. 520.)* ■

The Apple II computer, with video monitor, cassette data recorder, and two joystick controls. → $1200 and up

Computers by Mail

As with other tools, computer stuff is often cheaper by mail (though sometimes cheaper at your local computer shop or Radio Shack). In many cases, you're better off shopping locally because you can get the machine serviced and because computer shops are often jumping-off points for finding people (and computer clubs) with the same machine, who can swap programs, lend peripherals, and consult on programming.

But sometimes you may need mail service. Bob Albrecht uses **CompuMart** *and says they have an uncommonly good reputation in the busines for reliability. Their catalog is also very complete.* **Jade**'*s catalog has more boards and parts and is considerate to new computer users. Jade specializes in putting systems together out of components, the way hi-fi places match stereo gear.* **Micro World** *has the most completely annotated catalog I've seen on any product — a* **Whole Earth Catalog** *of computer equipment in its own right.* —Art Kleiner

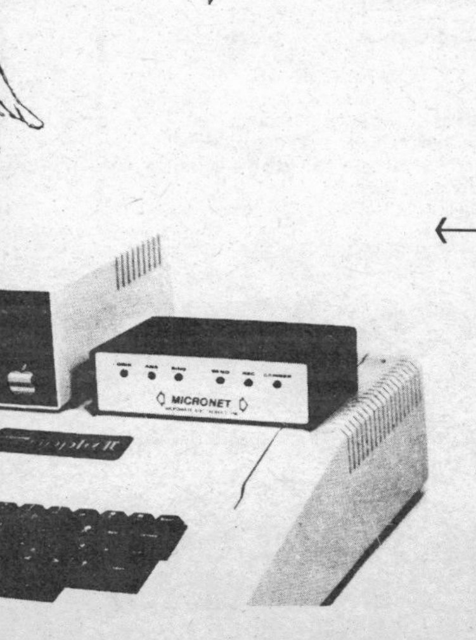

← This modem has more features for the money than any Apple II modem on the market today! It is a Bell Systems compatible 110/300 baud, FCC-certified, crystal controlled, stand alone unit.

And best of all, it plugs directly into your Apple's game I/O connector, and any standard modular phone jack. The Micronet modem operates in originate or answer/auto-answer mode, all under software control. The practical front panel display lets you know at a glance the operating conditions of the modem and the network.

The software (included, on disk) is simple to operate, well-documented and allows immediate and deferred modes of operation.

Join the information revolution today and hookup to the world with the Micronet modem. Shipping weight 3 lbs. Available June/July, 1980.
IOM-2020A A&T $284.95
—Jade

CompuMart
(Formerly NCE Compumart)
Catalog
free from:
CompuMart
270 Third Street
Cambridge, MA 02142

Jade Computer Products
Catalog
free from:
Jade Computer Products
4901 West Rosecrans Ave.
Hawthorne, CA 90250

Micro Shopper
(The Guide to the New Computers)
$9.95 postpaid from:
Micro World
1425 West 12th Place
Tempe, AZ 85281

THE RISING SUN
NEIGHBORHOOD NEWSLETTER

continued from last spread

Peter had never done any rowing before he started thinking about going across the Atlantic and he says that he didn't even train much for that trip — a few miles up and down the Thames is all. That may be the famous British understatement, but he says that doing long distance ocean rowing is its own training and there's no point in starting sooner. The first four hours of the trip are the roughest because that's when you have to beat the tide or be ignominiously washed back ashore. After that you just row and row — about half the time. It's not the type of thing an athlete who's a rower would do, Peter says, because it's too sloppy — no style. It was hard to even do it with another person in a big long boat because such different things are happening to the two rowers it's very hard to pull together. *continued on next spread*

Personal Computing Magazines

by Dan Dugan

The microcomputer or personal computer boom is moving so fast that magazines are the only way to keep track of it. The slick ones have a three-month lead time and better writers, the funky ones are more current and audacious. All of them suffer from the problem that microcomputers come in several popular but incompatible forms that each has its own programming techniques and technical problems. If you have BASIC, articles on PASCAL are of academic interest only; if you have a TRS-80, PET programs have to be modified extensively for your machine; if you have CP/M, all the articles on fun graphics you can do with the more consumer-oriented machines are useless to you. Special-interest mags are springing up (see **S-100 Microsystems**, *below), but the field isn't quite big enough for them to be professional yet. I think this will continue for several more years until the micro industry (like radio and Hi-Fi) gets de facto standards established and the turkeys drop out or find niches.*

Byte

I've been reading **Byte** *since late '75. It's a consistent source of quality information. Out of a dozen feature articles there are usually a couple of real winners that open new areas or tell me how to do something I've been dying to know about. Last year they published a fantastic series of articles on the brain. All suppliers of consequence advertise here. Articles frequently include program listings, often in BASIC, though PASCAL and other languages appear also.*

Byte
(The small systems journal)
Carl Helmers, Editor
$18/year (12 issues)
from:
Byte
P.O. Box 590
Martinsville, NJ 08836

•

The Apple III's graphics capabilities go considerably beyond the Apple II's, offering 80 columns by 24 lines of text on the monitor screen — a must for serious word processing. The character dot-matrix is 8 dots high by 7 wide. Graphics modes include 560 by 192 lines (black and white only) and 280 by 192 lines featuring sixteen high-resolution colors or sixteen shades of gray. (Compare this with the 280-by-160 line resolution in the limited-color, high resolution mode of the Apple II.) Another mode offers forty characters with color-on-color; moreover, the Apple III offers the three Apple II graphics modes (yes, Apple II programs will run on the Apple III — more about this later).

The Apple III, a new 6502A-based personal computer with built-in 5-inch floppy disk drive, up to 128 K bytes of memory, and high-resolution color graphics. Pascal and Apple Business BASIC are built-in, and the machine features a new Sophisticated Operating System called SOS. The Apple III will sell in the premium price range of $4500 to $8000, which includes a complete software and hardware system with peripherals. Reportedly FORTRAN will be available for the unit later in the year. Although the Apple III can be used for a wide range of general applications, the keyboard has been designed with financial, small-business, and word-processing applications in mind. An Apple II-emulation mode is included to enable Apple II software to run on the Apple III.

Dr. Dobb's Journal

DDJ *is the best of the "community-oriented" computer magazines. Its subject matter is wide-ranging, often including assembly language listings and listings of language interpreters like "Tiny-C." Tutorial stuff for beginners too, good dialogue, and general great vibes. Reluctantly accepting advertising with many protestations that they will not be corrupted. They talked about getting serious and changing the title but the subscribers like it the way it is.*

Dr. Dobb's Journal of Computer Calisthenics and Orthodontia
(Running Light Without Overbyte)
Janet Payne, Editor
$19/year (10 issues)
from:
People's Computer Company
P.O. Box E
1263 El Camino Real
Menlo Park, CA 94025

Kilobaud Microcomputing

First the bad news: editor Green has fascist tendencies. In his editorial column he actually encouraged customers of his Instant Software business to try to induce people to buy illegal copies of his programs, then bust them and collect the reward he offers. And then he had the gall to blame "computer error" (Ha! Cybercrud!) for subscription screw-ups.

So why do I support this guy? The magazine has a lot of useful articles, particularly heavy on small- and medium-sized application programs in BASIC with complete code. Useful "fixes" for particular systems that are invaluable when you need them. Published a complete BASIC data-base management system in three parts Jan-Feb-Mar '80. March '80 page 68 has a BASIC program that computes solar heat potential hour by hour including the effect of scattered sky radiation and reflectance from the glass collector angle.

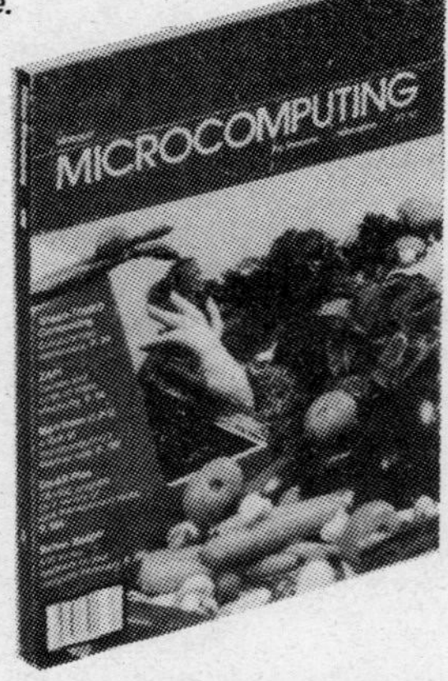

Kilobaud Microcomputing
(For business. . . education . . . FUN!)
Wayne Green, Editor
$18/year (12 issues)
from:
Microcomputing
Subscription Department
P.O. Box 997
Farmingdale, NY 11737

Periodical Guide for Computerists

This booklet provides a detailed index by category for most of the hobbyist publications listed in this section. Besides articles, editorials, book reviews and even letters are cataloged. Also included are some of the "mainstream" computer publications such as **Digital Design** *and a number of the ham radio mags such as* **'73** *as well. A nice feature is that letters of correction aapear in the listing immediately after the entry for the corrected (or commented upon) article. For those who do not feel quite ready to subscribe to the twenty odd available publications this guide could provide another level of detailed information. It is of course also extremely useful as a global index to the literature.* —Marc Le Brun

Periodical Guide for Computerists
E. Berg, Editor
Annual; 80 pp.
$2.50 postpaid from:
E. Berg Publications
622 East 3rd Street
Kimball, NE 69145

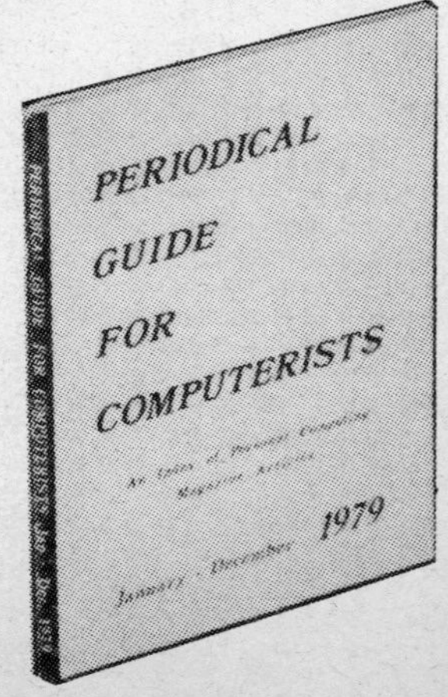

mathematics
mathematics
mathematics
mathematics
mathematics

Adjusting the letters to coarser rasters

S-100 Microsystems

This is a brand new one finding its way. As the populations of particular machines increase, more machine-specific mags will appear. They save skipping all the articles that don't apply to your system. First issue contained engineering definition of industry-standard IEEE S-100 bus (one of several styles of connectors between a microcomputer and its attachments; S-100-based machines are compatible only with each other). The second issue had an interesting program in PASCAL for linear programming (technique applicable to many real-world situations where you want to optimize a mix of many variables with arbitrary limits). Promising.

S-100 Microsystems
Sol Libes and Russell Gorr, Editors
$10/year (6 issues)
from:
S-100 Microsystems
P.O. Box 1192
Mountainside, NJ 07092

Recreational Computing

Funky potpourri. The free-wheeling student side of micros. Allows space for first-time and semi-coherent authors with something to say. Doesn't always give enough specifics on a topic. Games for BASIC students. A good magazine for the novice or casually interested. Was formerly called **People's Computers**, *and may go back to that title.*

Recreational Computing
(For the imaginative small computer user!)
Joan Hiraki, Editor
$10/year (6 issues)
from:
People's Computer Company
P.O. Box E
1263 El Camino Real
Menlo Park, CA 94025

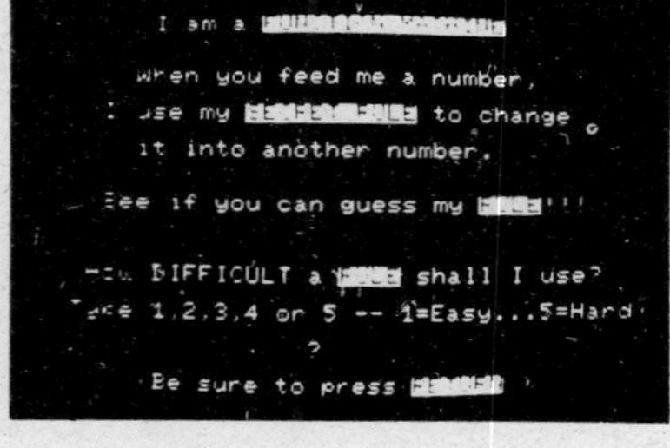

For less than $5, the author built an A/D converter for his COSMAC system.

There's me with the whole setup. The perfboard just to the left of the enclosed keyboard is the A/D circuitry. On the screen is an example of what can be done with the etch-a-sketch program and a little practice. ■

↓

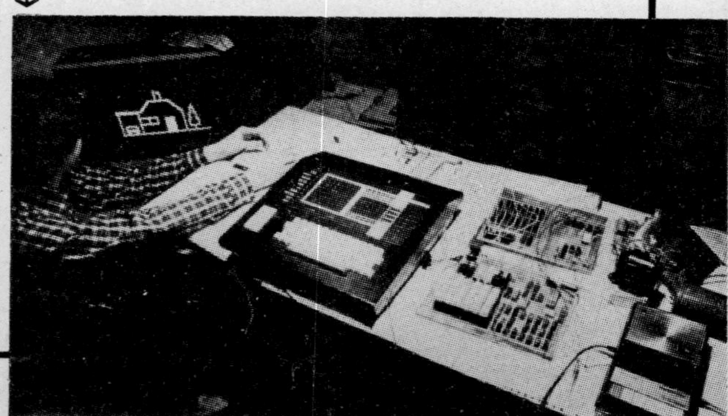

More Personal Computing Magazines

by Art Kleiner

Info World

A tabloid newspaper about the world of personal computing that gets better with each issue. It has almost no how-to material and concentrates on what the industry is doing and what innovations are likely to emerge next. It also has the best coverage of computer networks seen anywhere, and a nice muckrakingly philosophical sensibility left over from the days when it was the **Intelligent Machines Journal**. *Indispensable.*

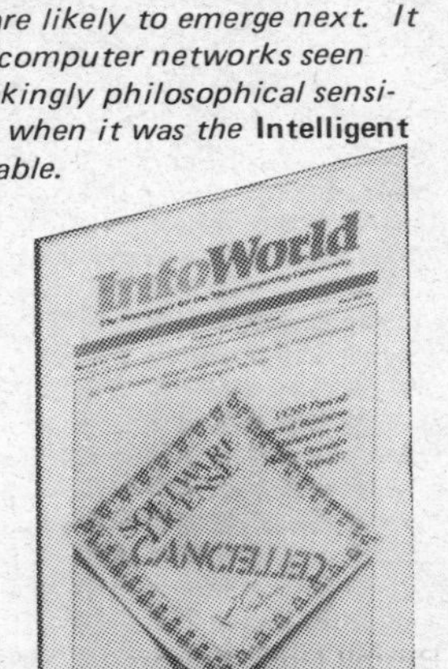

InfoWorld
(The Newspaper for the Microcomputing Community)
Tom Williams, Editor
$18 /year (26 issues)
from:
Popular Computing, Inc.
530 Lytton Avenue
Palo Alto, CA 94301

•

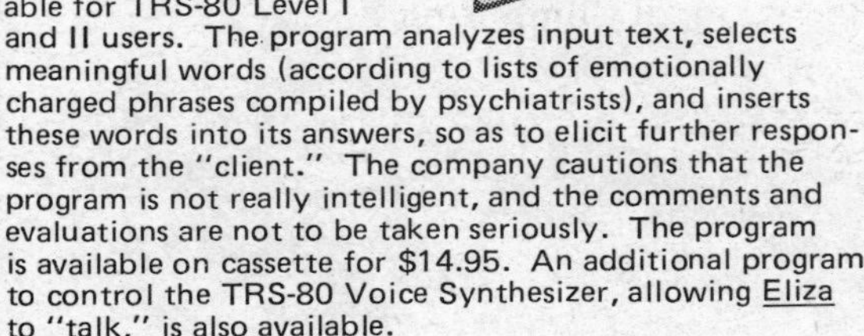

Eliza, the simulated psychiatrist program developed by Dr. Joseph Weizenbaum at the MIT Artificial Intelligence Lab, is now available for TRS-80 Level I and II users. The program analyzes input text, selects meaningful words (according to lists of emotionally charged phrases compiled by psychiatrists), and inserts these words into its answers, so as to elicit further responses from the "client." The company cautions that the program is not really intelligent, and the comments and evaluations are not to be taken seriously. The program is available on cassette for $14.95. An additional program to control the TRS-80 Voice Synthesizer, allowing Eliza to "talk," is also available.

Creative Computing

Published by prolific computer-writer David Ahl (and now co-edited by Ted Nelson, whose **Home Computer Revolution** *and* **Computer Lib** *are reviewed on these pages),* **Creative Computing** *has a wider range of small-computer articles than any other publication, and a lot of devotees. However, we've heard that they're not careful about verifying everything they print, and they've been accused of using material from other publications without credit.*

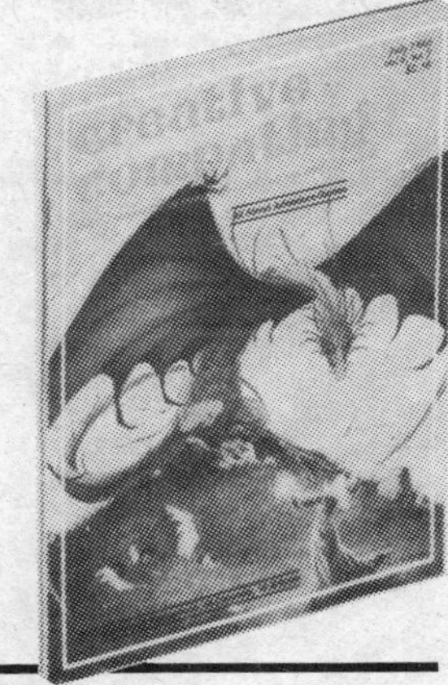

Creative Computing
David Ahl and
Ted Nelson, Editors
$15 /year (12 issues)
from:
Creative Computing
P.O. Box 789
Morristown, NJ 07960

Computer Shopper

Where to buy used computer gear, pure and simple. In a field which changes so rapidly, there are great bargains in old-but-still-usable equipment, and "old" is often measured in weeks, not years. Also includes listings for computer fairs, incipient newsletters, and software.
[Suggested by Larry Press]

Computer Shopper
(The Nationwide Marketplace for Computer Equipment)
$10 /year (12 issues)
from:
Computer Shopper
P.O. Box F
Titusville, FL 32780

•

TRS-80 Phone Dialer — Any number, any sequence — automatically! Will redial, time calls. Level II Basic, 4K up. Complete doc. $4.95. Cassette $9.95. Computerrent, 6074A Egg Lake Road, Hugo, MN 55038. VISA, MC. 800-228-2024 Ext. 410.5.

The Best of the Computer Faires

The fifth volume in what I hope will be an infinite series of annual anthologies from this Bay Area personal computer expo. These collections of micro-computerists' papers are one of the best sources around of information on computer networks, computer education, new microcomputer languages, and all sorts of strange experiments (like simulating the environment of spaceship flight or creating your own videodisks) that don't even make it into the magazines until later. Back volumes are still useful but increasingly dated as they get older; start with the most recent first.

The Best of the Computer Faires, Volume V
(Conference Proceedings of the Fifth West Coast Computer Faire)
Jim C. Warren, Jr., Editor
1980; 238 pp.
$14.75 postpaid

Volume I (1976)
Volume II (1977)
Volume III (1978)
Volume IV (1979)
$14.75 each postpaid

all from:
Computer Faire
345 Swett Road
Woodside, CA 94062

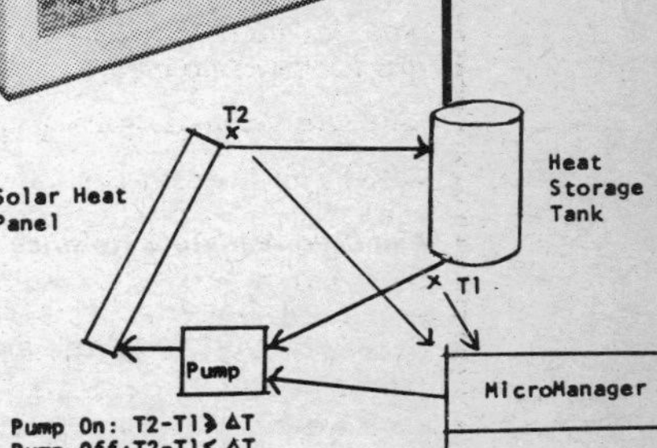

→ Diagram of the Solar Heat Control portion of Helion's Prototype MicroManager.

Datamation

This is where the professionals get their gossip about the industry, and it's useful for anyone who needs to investigate the world of the computer giants. "Twits IBM," wrote Ted Nelson in 1973, and the magazine is also hearteningly cynical about AT&T, GTE and the other large firms it writes about. If you're a professional or can convince them you are, you can get a free subscription.

Datamation
John L. Kirkley, Editor
$36 /year (13 issues)
from:
Technical Publishing Circulation
666 Fifth Avenue
New York, NY 10019

•

Our second computer, BINAC, was two computers working in tandem, each one checking the other. Forty years ago that system was more fail-safe than the analog system they were using at Three Mile Island. ■

Purser's Magazine

This magazine fills a real need excellently. It reviews and gives access to good software (computer programs) for the most popular personal computers: the PET, Apple, TRS-80 and Atari. The reviews are fun to read even if they're not for your machine. Especially recommended for the new computer owner who doesn't know what to do *with the computer once it's uncrated. Weighted heavily toward games and learning, but also includes text editing and other more "practical" programs. For a while each issue had a different name — "Computer Cassettes Review" and the like — but now editor Bob Purser seems to have settled on* **Purser's Magazine** *so people can track it down.*
[Suggested by Bob Albrecht]

Purser's Magazine
(Software Directory for the Level II TRS-80, Apple, PET and Atari)
Robert Elliot Purser, Editor
$12 /year (4 issues)
from:
Purser's Magazine
P.O. Box 466
El Dorado, CA 95623

↓

Three Mile Island, Apple II 48K Disk. The Muse Software Company, 330 North Charles Street, Baltimore, MD 21234.

I thought this was a game. It is not.

Muse's Three Mile Island is an educational program. It is a simulation of a nuclear power plant. And it is very well done.

In my opinion, there are just two ways to learn about a nuclear power plant. One way is to run a nuclear power plant. The other way is to operate a simulation of a nuclear power plant. No amount of reading can give you the understanding that this program will give you in just a few hours.

The next time some "expert" tells you about the safety of nuclear power plants, ask them if they have ever run one. You can in your own home. Why be in the dark about this very important issue when all you need is this program? . . .

This program will be a classic. Every school will need a copy. The only thing you must realize is that it is not a game. Rather it is an educational tool for school or personal development.

I recommend this program.

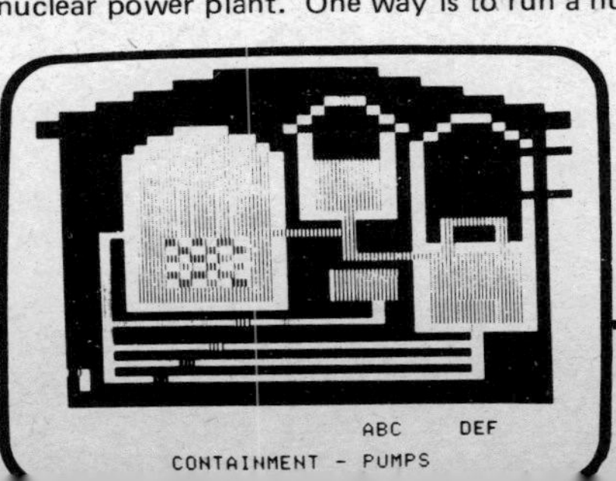

Computers and People

An eccentric magazine of thought and news about the relation of computers to the human beings who use them. It deals mostly with "established" IBM-type computer systems, the kind that only professional programmers or academics normally work with — but the issues it raises filter down to all levels of computing and other technologies as well. Editor Edmund C. Berkeley was one of the first people to see that there even were *issues here. Often the best new books about the implications of computing are excerpted in this magazine.*

Computers and People
(Formerly Computers and Automation)
Edmund C. Berkeley, Editor
$14.50 /year (10 issues)
from:
Berkeley Enterprises
815 Washington Street
Newtonville, MA 02160

•

The prevention of all errors in computer applications (and elsewhere) is of overriding importance and extreme difficulty. Why? Because there is no good, regular, usual method for making sure that all errors have been removed. The real world sits on our doorstep unorganized for the prevention of errors.

THE RISING SUN NEIGHBORHOOD NEWSLETTER

Peter said the most important kind of reading to take along are memory joggers. Not novels that you just read and you're done with but things like maps of places he's been so he can look at them and remember more and more of what's there and what happened when he was there. He likes books with lots of different facts in them (like almanacs and the *Catalog*) because it helps jog his memory for more facts that he knows. "Sometimes you think you'll run out of yourself out there, but with all that time, you remember amazing amounts and it's fairly interesting, some of it."

Crash Course in Microcomputers

Here at the **Whole Earth** *we've been dodging a deluge of smarmy new books about buying and operating small computers. Many seem like they've been written right from last year's manufacturer's handouts. Even the good ones are often out of date before the ink dries.*

Here's the considered consensus of those I've consulted: if you're thinking of buying a computer, and you expect to follow the advice of a book and get a readymade system, you're asking for trouble. You'll be taking your own individual needs and fitting them to someone else's standardized set-up.

The best course involves a little work: read enough so you know what you're talking about, figure out what your needs are, and find a computer store near you (or the few reputable mail order stores listed on p. 529) who can help you choose what you need. If you want to know what machines are available, follow **Byte** *or* **Recreational Computing** *for a few issues (pay particular attention to the ads and letters). If possible, arrange to practice and play on someone else's machine, even if it's only to run some programs.*

To get that quick know-what-you're-talking-about intro, the best book we've seen is **The Howard Sams Crash Course in Microcomputers.** *It's a step-by-step garden path introduction to all the mystifying jargon (and it even makes it seem like not-jargon). It doesn't talk about specific machines, but in an evening or two's reading it will give you the understanding to talk back to folks at the computer shop. And when making a $1000 - $20,000 purchase, it's better to talk back smartly than dumbly, yes?*

—Art Kleiner

•

The major investment in any programming project is the *programmer's time.* A significant amount of time is usually required to develop a useful piece of software. That is why software is so expensive. In fact, the hardware turns out to be the least expensive part of the system in most computer installations. *Software* is always the major expense.

Software is supplied in a variety of media such as paper tape, magnetic tape, hard disk, or floppy disk.

The Howard W. Sams Crash Course in Microcomputers
Louis E. Frenzel, Jr.
1980; 264 pp.

$17.50 postpaid from:
Howard W. Sams and Company
4300 West 62nd Street
Indianapolis, IN 46268
or Whole Earth Household Store

An Introduction to Microcomputers

Designing and programming microcomputers at the assembly language level is the core of much of the hobbyist and small-computer inventing work of the past five years. It's an ever-expanding territory, and the standard atlas (as Marc Le Brun calls it) is this three-volume set. Volume One has the universal principles; Volume Two describes specific circuit designs made by different designers and how to program with them; and Volume Three deals with support devices like terminals and memory storage systems. All three volumes used to be paperbacks; then Volumes Two and Three became looseleaf-bound, updated into 1980 with bimonthly supplements. Henceforth, supplemental "handbooks" will be published to keep them from obsolescing. Adam Osborne is one of the most charming computer writers around, with a regular column in **InfoWorld** *(p. 351). His program listings and other publications are also reputable.*

—Art Kleiner

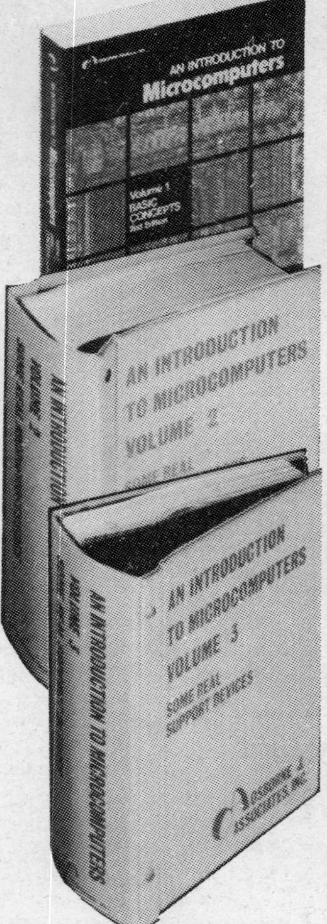

An Introduction to Microcomputers
Volume One: Basic Concepts
Adam Osborne
1975, 1980; 480 pp.
2nd Edition
$13.75 postpaid

Volume Two: Some Real Microprocessors
Adam Osborne and Jerry Kane
1975, 1979; 1400 pp.
$56.25 postpaid
(Includes binder and updates)

Volume Three: Some Real Support Devices
Jerry Kane and Adam Osborne
1975, 1979; 700 pp.
$46.25 postpaid
(Includes binder and updates)

Publications catalog
free

all from:
Osborne/McGraw-Hill
630 Bancroft Way
Department UB
Berkeley, CA 94710

Computer Graphics Primer

A good book on the possibilities in small computers for interactive and animated graphics. Many of the possibilities are just beginning to be explored. There is probably no more exciting a reason for getting a computer of your own (or playing on someone else's). This book is the manual you'll need; it shows some of what high-powered graphics labs are doing, then provides lots of beginners' techniques which aim towards emulating them. The book depends on BASIC and to a lesser extent Apple computer graphics — having access to both would help.

—Art Kleiner

•

The best way to approach learning graphics is by tying it into an existing project you are already turned on about. For example, if you're into electronics you may wish to develop a 24-trace digital storage scope for designing and trouble-shooting computers. You could use a graphics computer to draw the traces on the television that were picked up by your custom interface. If you're into astronomy you might wish to computerize a starmap and have a microplanetarium in your bedroom. If you like playing with the stock market you could get a high-resolution computer to spit out accurate Dow Jones reports just like the graphs in the newspaper.

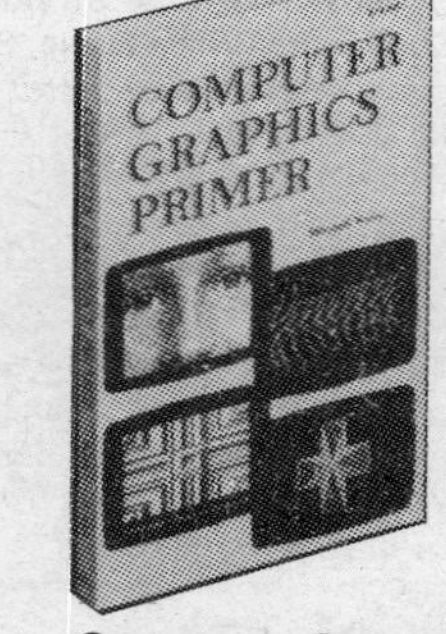

Computer Graphics Primer
Mitchell Waite
1979; 184 pp.

$12.95 postpaid from:
Howard W. Sams and Co.
4300 West 62nd Street
Indianapolis, IN 46268
or Whole Earth Household Store

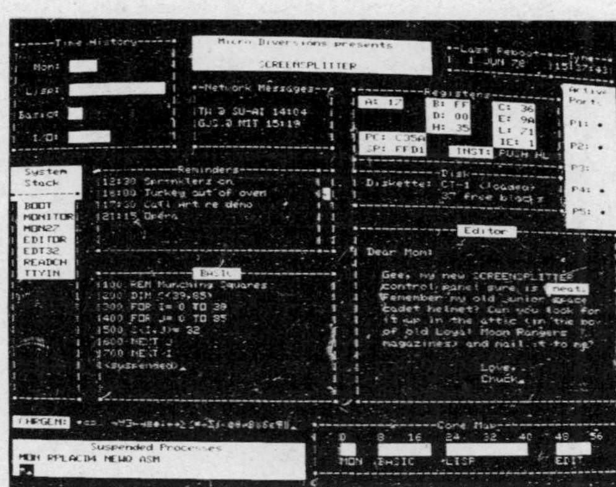
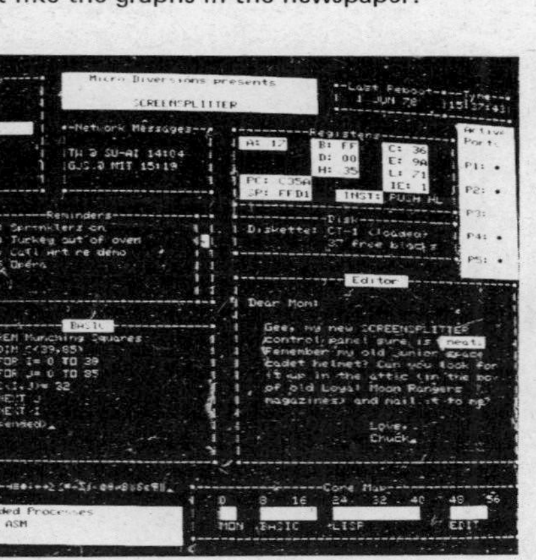

This example of a memory-mapped video display has 40 lines and 86 characters per line.

Tektronix, inc., 4051 Graphic Computing System, $6000 with 8K RAM, 3M tape drive. Storage tube-type crt means selective erase of screen graphics is not possible; however, this computer offers more dot resolution for the money than anything else on the market. Has powerful graphics software for bargraphs and piecharts, as well as HP-like graphic commands.

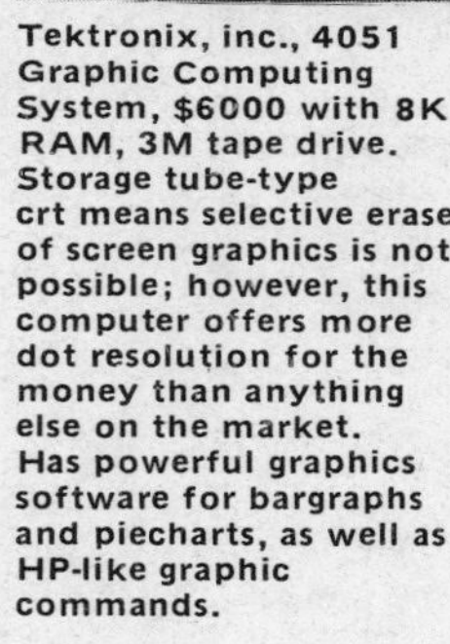

← **Example of output of digital plotter**

Good Small Computer Resources, Games, and Software

by Bob Albrecht & the ComputerTown, USA Staff

Cursor Magazine
P.O. Box 550
Goleta, CA 93017
Monthly cassette magazine for Commodore PET computer. $36/year (12 issues).

Cload Magazine
P.O. Box 1267
Goleta, CA 93017
Monthly cassette magazine for Radio Shack TRS-80. $36/year (12 issues).

Adventure, International
P.O. Box 3435
Longwood, FL 32750
Best source of adventure games for TRS-80. Soon will add adventure games for other computers. Catalog free.

Cybernautics
P.O. Box 40132
San Francisco, CA 94140
Their games — Taipan, Galactic Empire, Galactic Trader and Galactic Invasion — are far superior to older games such as Hammurabi, Kingdom, Star Trek, etc. (for TRS-80). Catalog free.

Don't Bother Me, I'm Learning
Available for purchase or rent. Contact:
David Shepardson,
One Pass
900 Third Street
San Francisco, CA 94107
A one hour TV documentary aired on PBS January 6 & 7, 1980.

Computer Information Exchange
Box 158
San Luis Rey, CA 92068
CIE publishes a newspaper called **S-80 Bulletin, S-80 Computing Magazine** *and* **People's Software** *— inexpensive cassettes with lots of programs. Information free.*

TRS-80 Software Source
Computermat, Box 1664
Lake Havasu, AZ 86403
Latest edition lists more than 4000 software items for TRS-80. Catalog free.

Swordquest from
Fantasy Game Software
P.O. Box 1683
Madison, WI 53701
One of the favorite games of kids in ComputerTown, USA! Someone should write a book about what kids can learn from this game! Hmmm . . . maybe we will. Catalog free.

The PET Program Exchange
Box 516,
Montgomeryville,
PA 18936
$1 per program plus $1 per cassette. Up to 12 programs on a C-30 cassette.

Compute Magazine
900-902 Spring
Garden Street
Greensboro, NC 27403
Specializes in PET, Atari, and Apple Computers. If you are a teacher and have a PET, do get the Jan-Feb 1980 issue. It has a page which shows all educational stuff published in a full year of **CURSOR** *broken down by grade level and skills.*

The Computing Teacher
Computing Center
Eastern Oregon
State College
LaGrande, OR 97850
$10/year (7 issues).

Interface Age Magazine
16704 Marquardt Avenue
Cerritos, CA 90701
I believe this will be the best general magazine for beginners to intermediates in the 1980s. $18/year (12 issues).

The Software Exchange
P.O. Box 68
Milford, NH 03055
Probably the most complete source of software, books, magazines for the TRS-80. Catalog free.

80 Software Directory
Howie D. Blasi
ComputerMat
Box 1664
Lake Havasu, AZ 86403
Latest edition has over 5000 TRS-80 Software listings from over 450 vendors.

Iridis
Box 550
Goleta, CA 93017
Cassette magazine for the Atari. New, I haven't seen a copy yet. ■

SMALL COMPUTER PROGRAMMING LANGUAGES

by Art Kleiner

By now there are probably more computer languages than human ones — each with its devotees and detractors, and some with a horde of dialects evolved for different types of machines. Unless you're interested in programming in the computer's circuit-based assembly language (in which case see Adam Osborne's **Introduction to Microcomputers***), you'll need to learn some of these. University and other large, time-shared computers frequently have several languages available. On personal computers, you usually have to buy the program which makes that language work (except for BASIC, which is ubiquitously supplied by the manufacturers). In both cases, the manuals provided are often not complete or comprehensible. These books and resources should help.*

BASIC (A Self-teaching Guide), by Robert Albrecht, et al., 1973, 1978. $6.95 postpaid from John Wiley and Sons, One Wiley Drive, Somerset, NJ 08873. *There are more efficient and artful beginners' languages (like LOGO and PASCAL), but BASIC is the standard for home computers, with more programs already written in it (and hence adaptable to your needs) than any other. Bob Albrecht was one of the first to recognize and popularize the need for human-forgiving computer languages (around 1972, when he founded the People's Computer Company). His introductory books have yet to be topped. They come in separate editions for dialects like TRS-80 BASIC or Atari BASIC.*

Basic BASIC (An Introduction to Computer Programming in BASIC Language) by James S. Coan, 1970, 1978. $10.95 postpaid from Hayden Book Company, 50 Essex Street, Rochelle Park, NJ 07662. *More utilitarian and comprehensive than Albrecht's books. Elegantly written. Highly praised by everyone I've asked.*

Programming Proverbs (BASIC with Style, PASCAL with Style, FORTRAN with Style, or COBOL with Style), each by Henry F. Ledgard, et al., 1978 - 1980. $6.95 each postpaid from Hayden Book Company, 50 Essex Street, Rochelle Park, NJ 07662. *Henry Ledgard's books lay the groundwork for good style in writing programs, with the same tart directness that Strunk and White's* **Elements of Style** *(p. 502) employs to teach writing English. Programs thought through this way have fewer bugs, are comprehensible to other people, and don't look like a labyrinth of foreign codes six months after they're written. Each edition is the same book adapted to a different language; the FORTRAN and COBOL languages are best avoided unless you need them in your work.* [Suggested by Larry Press]

•

The Programming Proverbs

A Good Start Is Half the Race

1. Don't Panic!
2. Define the Problem Completely.
3. Start the Documentation Early.
4. Think First. Code Later.
5. Proceed Top-Down.
6. Beware of Other Approaches.

Keeping Logical Structure

7. Code in Logical Units.
8. Use Functions and Subroutines.
9. Don't GOTO
10. Prettyprint.

Coding the Program

11. Use Mnemonic Names
12. Comment Effectively.
13. Make Constants Constant.
14. Get the Syntax Correct Now.
15. Don't Leave the Reader in the Dust.
16. Produce Good Output.
17. Hand-Check the Program.
18. Prepare to Prove the Pudding.

And of Course . . .

19. Have Someone Else Read the Work.
20. Read the Manuals Again.
21. Don't Be Afraid to Start Over!

—Pascal With Style

Heathkit digital techniques program

To really get into digital electronics to the point where you can wire up a functioning digital circuit you also need to know a lot more about how the logic chips actually operate inside their black boxes. And you will need to know a good bit about the rules by which they are interconnected. There is quite a lot of information to cover at this point, and any number of ways you could go about doing it — from taking university or community college courses to buying books on specific aspects of digital design and plowing through them on your own, hoping that it'll all come together eventually.

The best single source for all this that I've found is Heathkit's "Digital Techniques" course. Their course covers a lot of territory in its 800 or so pages but it's all broken down into small sections with frequent quizzes and includes lots of experiments using logic chips you wire up on the accompanying electronic trainer. It is a very well written course laid out with the customary Heathkit thoroughness and helpfulness. At the completion of the course you will be able to design logic circuits from scratch and have a good understanding of how they work. The last section of the course introduces microprocessor chips and includes a few lessons in machine language programming. To do the experiments you will need to assemble the trainer, which requires a soldering iron and a few hand tools, and you will need an inexpensive multimeter. You will not need an oscilloscope even though it is recommended in their catalog. The course only has a few experiments which need a scope and you can easily skip them. You will need a scope or access to one if you're going to do a lot of circuit building, but that can come later.

—Bud Spurgeon

Advanced Digital Techniques Training Kit
Electronic trainer in kit form, two manuals and cassette tape
No. EES-3201

$149.90 postpaid from:
Heath Company
Benton Harbor, MI 49022

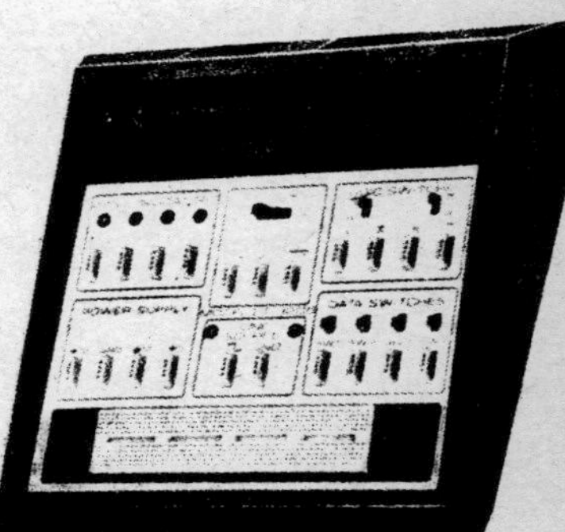

Heathkit electronic trainer

ComputerTown, USA!

Basically what's going on beneath this zealous name is that computers are now in the public library in Menlo Park, California. People can use them free of charge, and there is lots of effort made to training available at a low cost (or free). Frequently kids teach other kids and learn in the teaching. Adults can use the machines too, try things out before investing in their own computers. You can do the same in your town. This fledgling newsletter will encourage and help. It's associated with the People's Computer Company (of Dr. Dobb's Journal and Recreational Computing) and put together by Bob Albrecht and Ramon Zamora, the Pied Pipers of computer accessibility.

—Art Kleiner

ComputerTown, USA!
(A News Bulletin Bringing Computer Literacy to the Entire Community)
Published occasionally

free from:
Computertown, USA!
P.O. Box 310
Menlo Park, CA 94025

•

Begin by doing it! Just start. Don't wait for the right time, or the right place, or enough people, or the grant that you could get. Just start by starting.

If you have a small computer, and if you have a few friends that have small computers, go to the public library (or local bookstore, or pizza place, or . . . anyplace will do) and tell them you want to hold about a three hour meeting once a month. Give them a copy of this bulletin to read. If all else fails, set it up in your home for the first few months.

When you have a goodly number of people attending, ask your local computer store people to drop by and bring computers and software for demonstrations. If they have any old or used equipment, ask them to donate it to the project. The same goes for the user groups. They often have old machines that they can donate to such a project.

Comparison of CP/M Word Processing Programs

Buying computer hardware is relatively easy; it's judging good software that's a problem. (Bad software is worse than useless.) There are good evaluations around of games and such, like **Purser's Magazine***, but not much for business software, like word processors (which cost $200 and up these days). Larry Press' comparison of word processors is readable and gives you enough information to make a choice with. It's the first of a series.*

—Art Kleiner

A Comparison of CP/M Word Processing Programs
Lawrence Press
1980; 49 pp.

$15 postpaid from:
Small Systems Group
P.O. Box 5429
Santa Monica, CA 90405

Beginner's Guide for the UCSD PASCAL System, by Kenneth L. Bowles, 1980. $11.95 postpaid from McGraw-Hill Book Company, Princeton Road, Hightstown, NJ 08520. *PASCAL is a language reminiscent of outline form — boring to some but easily organized and adaptable from machine to machine. The University of California at San Diego (UCSD) PASCAL is a version developed to make PASCAL work on small computers. As a result, there's been much talk of PASCAL becoming favored over BASIC as the most-used language of personal computers, with strong sentiment on either side (and other voices claiming both are outdated). This is the best small-computer PASCAL book.*

APL in Exposition, by Kenneth E. Iverson, 1980. $2 postpaid from APL Press, 220 California Avenue, Suite 201, Palo Alto, CA 94306. *APL (A Programming Language) is an elegant, dense language made up mostly of symbols. Here's a line written in APL:*

```
Z←2=+/[1]0=(⍳⌈/S)∘.|S∇
```

Poor Logical Structure **Better Logical Structure**

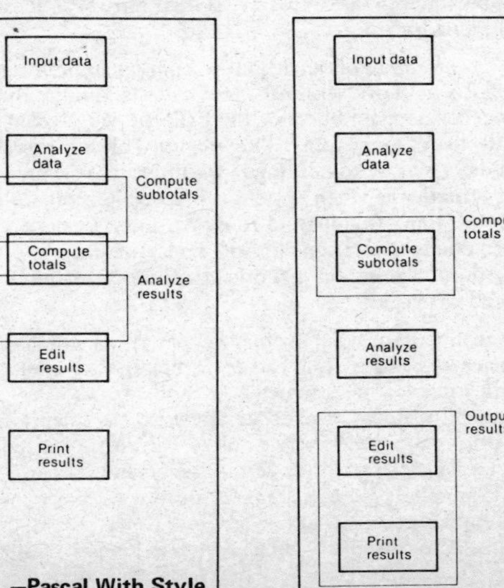

—Pascal With Style

Those who work with it refuse to return to any other language, because it describes complex operations in brief formulas. This booklet introduces APL and refers you to other books which go into more detail. [Suggested by Marc Le Brun]

FORTH Dimensions, newsletter of the FORTH Interest Group. $12/year (6 issues) from FORTH Interest Group, P.O. Box 1105, San Carlos, CA 94070. *FORTH is said to be ten times faster than BASIC and more compact than assembly language. FORTH programmers are fond of comparing how many microseconds they've shaved off their programs' running times. This newsletter is how to find out what's going on. There are no books yet.* [Suggested by Matthew McIntosh]

Other computer language information: Patrick Winston's **Artificial Intelligence** *(p. 539) provides a starting point in LISP, the most-used language of Artificial Intelligence. Seymour Papert's* **Children, Computers and Powerful Ideas** *(p. 536) introduces LOGO, an interesting language used mostly for learning.* **Dr. Dobb's Journal, Byte, InfoWorld** *and the* **Computer Faire** *proceedings (p. 531) cover these and other languages regularly.* ■

THE RISING SUN
NEIGHBORHOOD NEWSLETTER

continued from last spread

Peter intends to go all the way to Australia without landing anywhere because it's always most dangerous near land. Also once you're on land it's easy to make excuses to not leave and just sit there day after day. Kathleen and I asked him if he was afraid of storms and things like that and he said, "Well if you got caught in a hurricane in an island chain, that would be a bit shitty." Later, a reporter asked him what he was most afraid of and he said, "Loneliness." Another reporter asked him why he was doing it and he said so he could be with what he liked the best in all the world. "The sea?" asked the reporter. "No. Myself," said Peter.

LIFE ON THE COMPUTER NETWORK FRONTIER

Likely to change our lives more than any technology since the automobile

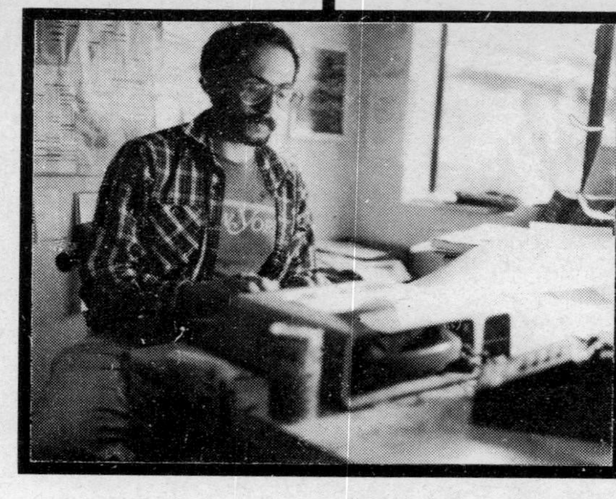

Whole Earth research editor Art Kleiner blitzing his friends on the EIES Network for the latest word on home computer preferences. The terminal is a Computer Devices Miniterm (telephone receiver plugs into the back). For the network's advice, see p. 529.

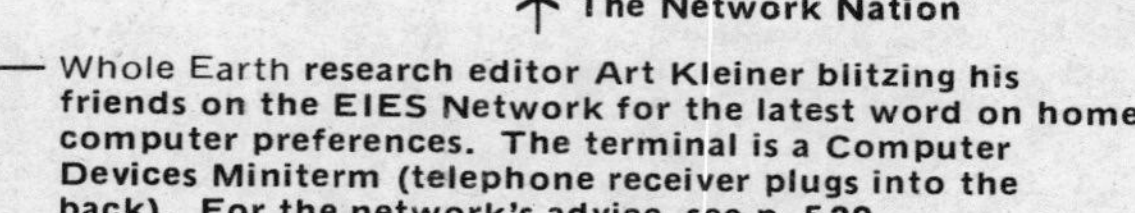

The Network Nation

JOE DIETER/ASIS

by Art Kleiner

"When I log in I 'go' into the network. I'm not here in my room any more. Ask my family. I'm in another place. In formal geographic terms, I'm inside a single point. Yet inside that point is all the space I need to meet with other people – plus my files, my records, and my entire office. And the behavior in there is what you might expect from people who have been wrenched into a fourth dimension."

–Einar Stefferud, consultant for the U.S. Army, the Federal Communications Commission and other groups in Washington, D.C, who does much of his work via a computer terminal in his Huntington Beach, California, home.

COMPUTER NETWORKS are new telecommunications media for transmitting words and pictures. They're used to send messages, pass on news and gossip, search vast indexed data files, manage multinational businesses, bring together faraway compatriots, and take part in interactive fantasy games. They're being promoted hard by an army of international dreamers and at least 20 major corporations. They seem likely to change our lives more than any technology since the automobile.

"If your prime minister were here," writer James Martin (p. 495) told an Australian television audience, **"I'd say, Mr. Fraser, you're building freeways all over the place. An absolutely superlative communications system would cost as much as 100 miles of freeway in all. People could move out of cities and back to villages, because they would get their work, their quality education, and their culture through the terminals. The cities would remain, but only the people who really wanted to be there would have to stay."**

The technology which makes this possible is a hybrid of computers, inexpensive digital transmission links, and telephones. The preferred vehicle is the computer terminal – a typewriter keyboard with a video display screen attached and some provision for plugging in a telephone. Sometimes computer terminals print on paper instead of displaying characters on a screen. Networks vary in how they look and what you can do with them, but the procedure for logging into all of them is roughly the same. You dial a telephone number, plug the telephone receiver into your terminal, wait for your terminal to recognize the high-pitched tones coming out of the phone, and then type in the correct codes:

1. A code for the address of the particular network you wish to enter (if you're entering a network across the country, you use high-speed data transmission lines, whose rates are much cheaper than dialing direct – $3 to $10 for each hour connected. If you're dialing a local network, you don't need an address code).

2. Your name or identification number, by which the network will recognize you from any terminal-and-telephone in the world.

3. Your secret password, so no one else can enter under your I.D.

Then the network welcomes you, asks if you wish to see the messages waiting for you, and delivers any other relevant news. From there, you type in the commands which tell the network what you want to do: send a message, play a game, scan an electronic news wire for stories about a particular subject, leave an item on a computerized bulletin board or conference, edit a paper, find out who else is on-line at that moment, zip off a few quick one-line comments to them, do all of the above at once, or simply sign off.

Computer networks are best used for keeping in touch with people. Far away colleagues coordinate long-range projects, people with similar interests substitute computer networks for newsletters or telephone trees (and end up keeping in touch more personally as a result), and soul-searching friendships develop between those who have never met in person. Some members log on to get a sympathetic response in an emotional crisis. Others make long distance trips to meet in person those they've only seen on the network. There have been typed flirtations which developed into full-fledged romances and idle dreams which suddenly became high-commitment businesses.

There are, of course, other potentials which network designers have only begun to explore. There's shopping via the terminal, voting through it, personalized news on tap, new town-meeting-type promise for public participation in local politics – and also real possibilities for invasion of privacy and monitoring-from-on-high. The companies with big financial stakes in networks are among the biggest in the world – Exxon, Xerox, American Telephone and Telegraph, International Business Machines, General Telephone and Electronics, Warner Communications, American Express. And there's an equally determined grassroots movement, with many small bulletin board networks already established on personal computers, whose members believe this will give individuals more power over their lives than any other technology. A movement is growing for community information centers, which would link neighborhoods for better barter and politics.

Ultimately, it's likely that many of the details of civilization – directory assistance, letters and mail order, travel information – will be handled by networks, and people will belong to five or six networks each – local and nationwide – depending on their needs. The possibility that people who can't or won't participate in networks may be shut out of work or other opportunities is a very real one. Hopefully, libraries and public access centers will acquire terminals so people who want to can use networks even if they can't afford a terminal.

There are probably about 50,000 computer network members now. They range in age from 14 to 90. Many are professional computer programmers, but a fair number never saw a terminal until they joined the network. Many join to keep in touch with far-flung colleagues in scientific or professional fields. Nearly everyone finds it making great changes in their personal lives. Joining a network can be like moving into a new community. Addiction is common. Turning off the terminal can be like waking up from a dream. Network members wonder about their compulsion, as in this late night message from programmer Jim Clark:

"I feel a sense of purpose and connectedness when on the system and even if I haven't been on in a while (2 days) I miss using it. I have encountered an entire new world of good people. I find it more important than the telephone (which I never use), the TV (even less use), the radio (lots of use) and even (self-horror) the on-campus computers (constant use). Is the network addictive? Perhaps regulatory measures are necessary to keep people from becoming addicts and ruining (enhancing?) their lives. Or perhaps there are pre-addiction symptoms that the computer can look for. I don't know. I only know that I have been awake on-line for twenty-five hours now and my last experiment died horribly. It is going to be a long night."

People can use networks without becoming addicted, but there isn't a network without some addicts. Elaine Kerr, who coaches new members of the EIES network, compiled this list of symptoms: **"Signing on at least several times a day (maybe something is waiting). Physically evident impatience when system is inaccessible. Inability to write off-line. Inability to think off-line. Lack of desire to conduct relationships off-line. Inability to sleep without signing on just one last time. Dreaming about the network."**

Users get impatient with ordinary typewriters which don't backspace to correct errors or pick up the mail and with ordinary mail, which takes four days to ship a letter cross continent, and especially with the telephone, which often requires five tries before the person at the other end is reached. Since communication is easier, network members keep in touch with four or five times as many people as they would otherwise. Since the computer stores transcripts of what passes through it, network users don't keep many paper files. Since people aren't there physically, things like shyness, physical disabilities, race, religion, sex, and body language are invisible.

"I worked with someone here on line for some time and then had occasion to talk with him on the phone," one user said. **"The accent suggested he was black. I'd never had reason to think of it before that, and still could be wrong, but the possibility is now in my consciousness where it had not been before."**

Networks open up possibilities for new kinds of games. At the Xerox Palo Alto Research Center there's a form of computerized Star Trek which never starts or ends. People join in from their desk terminals, searching around the videoscreen-simulated universe for someone else who's already playing and drawing them into cospaceship battle. On the Electronic Information Exchange System (EIES), there's a collaborative soap opera – a short story in progress, written under pen names, each member writing a segment in turn.

There's a different quality to news and information when it's pulled out of the system with commands that seek out specific interests. **"Listening to the radio,"** Hudson Institute staff member Douglas Cayne wrote last November, **"I heard a one-line news bulletin saying that South Korean President Park Chung-Hee had been assassinated and his government overthrown. The evening paper had already been delivered, I don't have a TV, so I turned to the UPI news wire on the Source network . . . I was able to monitor reports from Korea all last night and today, and feel much more secure about what actually happened. There's nothing like being able to see that the story you are reading was written only minutes earlier . . ."**

People's reactions to networks depend most on the way they're designed. Airline reservation and bank teller systems use the same technology as more sophisticated networks, but the clerks and bank tellers get frustrated because they can't send messages or do anything but type in the same numbers by rote. A lot depends on how quickly the system responds. The best networks reply as fast as a person would in conversation. A slow system is as frustrating as driving a string of red lights. And a too-fast system takes getting used to:

"One company set up some clerks on a data base," said psychologist Marilyn Albin, who advises business managers about designing networks for people. **"After a while they refused to use it. They claimed it was reading their mind. The response was instantaneous with the last keystroke – before people realized they'd finished asking a question, the machine already had the answer."**

Large corporations are starting to find their empires unmanageable without networks. **"I can get on the system and maintain contact with people in Paris, London, and Singapore,"** said Sal Suniga, Vice President of PLANET, a commercial network based in Palo Alto, California. **"When we set up our system in France, we drafted a contract there, transmitted it here to have it looked at by our lawyer, and transmitted it back there to be signed two days later."**

The technology does have its paranoia-inspiring qualities. The utility-sponsored Electrical Power Research Institute uses a computer network to organize its nuclear power media campaigns – so that next time there's a Three Mile Island, they'll have their news story coordinated. The President's Office of Preparedness uses a computer network to coordinate crisis-handing; the technology makes it easier to build up files of searchable gossip on strike leaders and dissidents. And the National Security Agency (NSA), which handles electronic surveillance for the FBI and CIA, reportedly uses a series of high-powered computers to scan data transmission lines, sifting out messages with particular keywords in them. Corporate systems are often designed to control or monitor the people who use them. **"One grocery system set up for checkout terminals keeps track of how many mistakes each checker makes,"** Marilyn Albin said. **"It's called performance monitoring, and it makes the checkout clerks afraid of the cash registers."**

But the technology also innately encourages freedom. Encryption methods known as public-key codes promise a cheap method of coding computer signals that even the

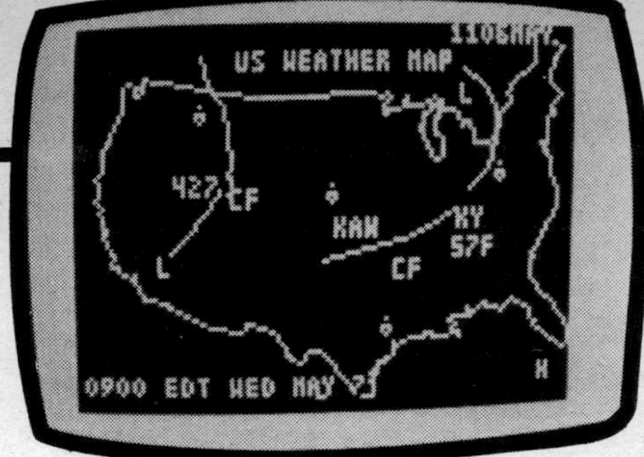

Weather information on PLATO

NSA won't be able to break. People on message systems tend to flow through the holes in a rigid hierarchy, forming new loyalties to other departments and companies. Managers who depend on rank for their authority tend to lose it on computer networks to those who really do the work. Even carefully controlled networks can't entirely avoid this tendency.

"PLANET has a control feature where the managers can inhibit private communication," Suniga said. **"They can prevent staff members from sending private messages and force them to put everything in the group conference. When they do that, though, the length of the conference entries increases dramatically. People sneak their private messages in between the lines."**

Networks take employees out of the physical office and will probably make commuting unnecessary more than once or twice a week. Many people work for groups around the country without leaving home – like Elaine Kerr, who counsels people worldwide from her kitchen table in Worthington, Ohio.

"Sometimes I do miss the 'coffee breaks' that would be a part of a normal office working environment," she said. **"Because, yes, sometimes working this way IS lonely. The tradeoff, however, is well worth it. My work literally spills over into the rest of my life. Here I am now, for instance, very much at home and very much working; with my newspaper on my lap for when the network is slow, the dog sleeping on the couch just a few feet away, and my son about to come home from school in an hour to me rather than a babysitter. Most people, including some of my friends, don't understand. To me, this is a far saner way of living than I've ever had before."** ■

ACCESS TO COMPUTER NETWORKS

The most technically advanced computer networks are closed to the public. For instance the Arpanet (named after the Advanced Research Projects Agency) is limited to people who work on projects sponsored by the Departments of Defense and Energy. It's a free-form linked universe of varied computer subnetworks and the arena where most of the technology for computer networks was first developed. (The method for splitting computer messages into packets, sending across different routes simultaneously and recombining them at the other end was originally developed for the Arpanet – to keep computer signals safe from nuclear attack. Now it's the most efficient way of keeping any single link in a transmission system from getting overloaded.) Many of the most exciting technical and social breakthroughs happen on closed corporate systems, such as those of Citibank in New York or Xerox in Palo Alto.

However, there are a number of networks which you can join if you have a terminal or an adapted computer. The most interesting are these:

The Source, Telecomputing Corporation of America, 1616 Anderson Road, McLean, VA 22101. $2.75/hour (evenings and weekends) plus $100 entry fee. Information free. *The first home terminal consumer information and mail network in America, and certainly the most ambitiously promoted. People with terminals or personal computers can call up versions of the UPI news wire or the bibliographic New York Times information bank. The Source also offers electronic mail and bulletin boards, programs which analyze statistics off the Wall Street stock index, and a clientele (mostly computer hobbyists and small businessmen) which is hungry to communicate with each other.*

According to many users, some of the Source's most promised features – such as airline reservation guides or on-line discussions of different topics – have been slow to materialize or haven't lived up to expectations. The network is also plagued by slow response time and frequent breakdowns. However, the Source deserves credit for bringing the idea of a home-based computer network with open-ended options out into the open. Its managers recently signed a contract with a national library network (OCLC of Columbus, Ohio) to link terminals in public libraries around the country.

Micronet, Personal Computing Division, CompuServe, 5000 Arlington Center Blvd., Columbus, OH 43220. $5/hour ($7/hour in some smaller cities) plus $9 entry fee. Information free. *This home terminal network piggybacks on the CompuServe Timesharing system; during evening hours when their industrial computers are empty, consumers can use them. Micronet is younger than the Source and concentrates on business programs, file editing and electronic mail. Its fledging newswire is pulled from a Columbus newspaper and Associated Press. Micronet's commands are more technically complex than those on the Source, but the system operates more quickly and is more satisfying once you learn how to use it. Their clientele is slightly more technically oriented, but that will probably change on both networks.*

Electronic Information Exchange System (EIES), New Jersey Institute of Technology Computer Conferencing and Communications Center, 323 High Street, Newark, NJ 07102. $3.75/hour plus $66/month. Information free. *EIES is a community of about 900 cross-continental members and is hoping to expand now into a series of such communities, each on a separate computer linked to the others. Most EIES members enter as part of groups working toward specific purposes, such as sharing news about technology for the handicapped or setting up national projects. But members are encouraged by the system to communicate with as many others as they have time and interest for, and to participate in on-line conferences. EIES' mix of participants – from corporations, government, nonprofit groups, the arts, and computerdom is unique among computer networks. It's also the site of specially designed experimental programs for weaving interactive stories, for filtering through masses of technical information quickly, and for corresponding anonymously or under pen names. EIES' founders, Murray Turoff and Roxanne Hiltz, wrote* **The Network Nation** (1978; $17.50 postpaid from Addison-Wesley Publishing Company, Jacob Way, Reading, MA 01867), *which is still the only book to give a true feeling of what it's like to be on a computer network.*

CBBS – *The simplest networks for personal computers to use through the telephone are Community Bulletin Board Systems. Most of the Bulletin Boards carry want ads, greetings, and general graffiti, although some have branched out to concentrate on specific subjects, such as genealogy. Anyone with a terminal can dial in and read anything there. They're financed by contributions and out of the owners' pockets.*

The operators of CBB Systems have an informal network to keep track of the new systems and ideas. The list of phone numbers to reach CBBS's constantly changes. CBBS lists are available for $1 each from Peripherals Unlimited (3450 East Spring Street, Suite 206, Long Beach, CA 90806), People's Computer Company (P.O. Box E, Menlo Park, CA 94025) or AMRAD (524 Springvale Avenue, McLean, VA 22101). *The three lists are updated independently and probably overlap but aren't exactly the same.*

PCNet, PCNet Committee, People's Computer Company, P.O. Box E, Menlo Park, CA 94025. Information free.

A committee of volunteers, founded by David Caulkins of Los Altos, California, has developed an electronic mail system for Commodore PET personal computers which operates over telephone lines. Users start with "PCNet PAN" programs which dial the other person's phone number to send and receive messages. A more sophisticated program called "PCNet" is needed to transfer files and programs without losing characters. Users can arrange for their computer to send the mail late at night when they're asleep and the phone rates are lower. "Easy-Mover" is a similar program for Apple Computers, developed by a private software company (Information Unlimited, 730 Vicente Avenue, Berkeley, CA 94707. Information free). *Others are also being developed – all presumably with different protocols, thus unable to send messages to any but the same type of computer with the same program running. Too bad – like having a hundred different types of incompatible telephones. The PCNet Committee is making some effort to set standards so that doesn't happen.*

PLATO, Control Data Corporation, HQA01A, P.O. Box 0, Minneapolis, MN 55440. Information free. *Originally developed for computer-assisted instruction systems at the University of Illinois, PLATO produces its "lessons" one page at a time in brightly colored letters and line drawings that compose themselves as if someone were twiddling a full color etch-a-sketch behind the screen. PLATO pages are interactive – the page asks a question, the user replies, and the answer determines what page is shown next. A specially designed (and expensive) terminal is required, and these days PLATO is only available at "learning centers" in cities around the country. While taking a lesson users can send messages to other people who are also on-line. Up to five conversations can scoot across the bottom of the screen at any one time. Control Data, the parent company, is noted for its benevolence (PLATO terminals in prisons) and its despotism (PLATO centers in rural areas near Control Data owned land, where CDC is accused of trying to control the farm commodity price markets through the network and to sell the information that the farmers share to third-world countries).*

A music synthesizer linked to a PLATO terminal provides drill and practice so class time can be spent on concept development.

Some interesting proposals for computer networks which don't exist yet:

Datacast, Wireless Digital, 345 Swett Road, Woodside, CA 94062. Newsletter $5/year (12 issues). *Starting in San Francisco sometime in 1980, Datacast will transmit words and pictures over Subcarrier Authorization channels, which are unused FM frequencies linked to existing radio stations. Datacast will be a steady stream of wire service news, financial data, real estate listings, classified ads, weather and library resources. To receive it, users will need a modified personal computer with a radio receiver ($400 or less above the cost of the computer). The computer will pull out only those items which it has been programmed to catch. Until it gets going, Datacast will be covered in its own newsletter, edited by Jim Warren, who organizes the West Coast Computer Faire (p. 531).*

Project Xanadu, P.O. Box 128, Swarthmore, PA 19081. Information $1. *Ted Nelson, who published the milestone book* **Computer Lib/Dream Machines** *(p. 536) in 1972, described there his plan for a computer network system in which people would edit alternate versions of text, jump back and forth between the versions, and make royalties based on how many people would call for their writing. His current plans call for such a system to begin running by the end of this year, possibly through locally franchised "Information Centers." Xanadu will be used for conferencing, writing, editing, and reading. Rather than a single index to everything on the system, users will be encouraged to create their own indexes to what interests them and publish them for others.*

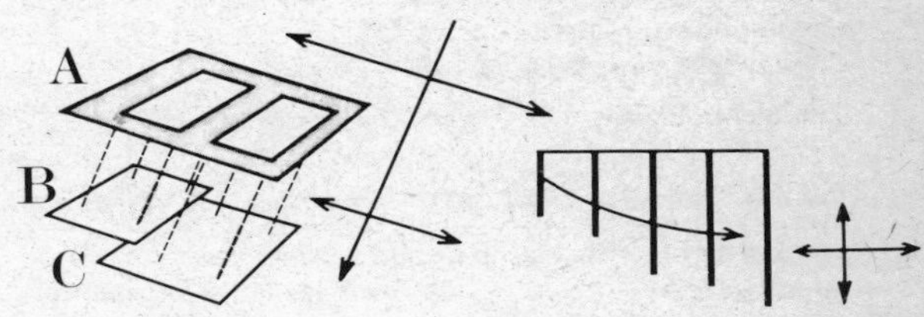

While the user of a customary editing or word processing system may scroll through an individual document, the Xanadu-System user may scroll in time as well as space, watching the changes in a given passage as the system enacts its successive modifications. —Xanadu Prospectus

Nelson said they are looking at hourly costs of $2 and $5 depending on the rate of transmission. Xanadu may use a transmission system like Telenet or Tymenet; or the Xanadu systems may only operate locally.

The Community Memory Project, 916 Parker Street, Berkeley, CA 94710. Information $1. *Convinced that computer networks should be decentralized, open to everyone and service oriented, Community Memory put interconnected terminals in Berkeley public places between 1973 and 1975. People used the system as an electronic bulletin board for news, messages, classified ads, and poetry. Others used the terminals to pull out information with the appropriate key-words, or to add*

CONTINUED ON NEXT PAGE

THE RISING SUN
NEIGHBORHOOD NEWSLETTER

Stewart's brother-in-law flew in airplanes regularly for several years before he ever landed. He was a parachutist in the Army and he was poor, so the Army would take him up and he would jump out but he never traveled by air off duty. When he finally did take a civilian airplane he was really worried about landing – ground coming up fast in a different way and him in a huge metal container that was clearly too heavy and didn't have a parachute.

COMPUTER NETWORKS CONTINUED

comments to existing messages. A new similar system will be established in a Bay Area neighborhood sometime in 1981. Up to 20 terminals will be placed in community centers and neighborhood gathering places. All information in the system will be entered by the people who use it, and no one will connect to Community Memory through private terminals. In the meantime, some of the text editing and file-arranging programs which will compose the Community Memory system are being offered for sale separately. Some of the people involved are associated with the **Journal of Community Communications** *(below).*

ACCESS TO TERMINALS

For networking, you need a terminal which can send and receive through the telephone. If you already have a personal computer you can adapt it into a telephone terminal with a device called a modem (modulator-demodulator). Check with your computer shop, your computer's manufacturer, or scan the magazines for a modem which fits with your machine. Sometimes a special program or board is also needed.

For the rest of us, a printing terminal is usually a better buy than a video-screen model. It's easier to cope with the mass of paper generated than to watch everything flash by too fast to read. (The ideal, of course, is both; a videoscreen terminal with a printer attached that can make paper copies at will. Such a device does not exist cheaply yet.)

Computer Devices Miniterm 1203, $2000 (approx.)

Computer Devices *portable printing terminals are good for networking. They're fun to type on, easy to carry around, and not susceptible to frequent breakdown. I use their Miniterm with satisfaction. The printhead should be kept fresh by running a sheet of paper dampened with rubbing alcohol through the paper feed every now and then.* Information free from Computer Devices, 25 North Avenue, Burlington, MA 01803.

TI Silent 743. $1695 or $100/month

Texas Instruments *makes a good second choice — not as versatile but cheaper to buy and available for reasonable rental. The disadvantages are that it only inputs in upper case, and the paper is poorer quality. But it is a reliable machine. TI also has a bubble-memory version which permits composing off-line, then transmitting to the computer network in one flash, saving minutes of connect time. Some people like this a lot; others find the commands confusing.* Information free from Texas Instruments, P.O. Box 1444, M/S 7736, Houston, TX 77001.

Radio Shack *recently announced a video-screen terminal for computer networks for $395 — cheaper than any other teleterm to date. Rumors are the price will drop to $250 by next year. The terminal is marketed in conjunction with both Micronet and Viewdata but it should work with any network. It's too new for us to have heard any first-hand reports yet, but Radio Shack computer equipment is made with consistently high quality. Now if they can only come up with a $100 printer for it.* Information free from Tandy Corporation, Fort Worth, TX 76102. ■

Radio Shack's TRS-80 Videotex

Computer Lib/Dream Machines

The subtitle of this 128-page paper-bound underground publication is, "You can and must understand computers NOW." It is a spirited, complex and very personal statement, an information packed message from someone who cares about people, machines, life, and dreams. Though it was written back in 1974, what it has to say is still fresh. The two halves of the book are printed in opposite orientations so that **Dream Machines** *is literally the "flip-side" of* **Computer Lib**, *with a duality of content that is suggestive of those qualities associated with the two halves of the brain. Something for everybody, both of you.* —Marc Le Brun

(See **The Home Computer Revolution**, *p. 528.)*

Computer Lib/ Dream Machines
Theodor H. Nelson
1974; 127 pp.

$7 postpaid from:
The Distributors
702 South Michigan
Suite 836
South Bend, IN 46618
or Whole Earth
Household Store

•
That reminds me. Nowhere in the book have I defined the phrase "computer lib." By Computer Lib I mean simply: making people freer through computers. That's all.

Mindstorms

In many ways Seymour Papert pioneered the use of artificial intelligence as a learning tool. His book is a statement about how computer work makes kids more creative, if they're allowed to experiment, dream, and solve problems without someone's preconceived solutions imposed on them. Such creativity is bound up with a new kind of literacy made possible by the responsive math of computing. Kids who have grown up computing are different. Few are the social klutzes people expect computer kids to be; instead, they're aware, self-reliant, and as adult (in a good way) as any adult I've ever met. —Art Kleiner

Mindstorms
(Children, Computers, and Powerful Ideas)
Seymour Papert
1980; 178 pp.

$12.95 postpaid from:
Basic Books
10 East 53rd Street
New York, NY 10022
or Whole Earth
Household Store

•
In a traditional school setting, the beginning student encounters the notion of variable in little problems such as

$$5 + X = 8. \text{ What is X?}$$

Few children see this as a personally relevant problem, and even fewer experience the method of solution as a source of power. They are right. In the context of their lives, they can't do much with it. In the LOGO encounter, the situation is very much different. Here the child has a personal need: To make a spiral. In this context the idea of a variable is a source of personal power, power to do something desired but inaccessible without this idea. Of course, many children who encounter the notion of *variable* in a traditional setting do learn to use it effectively. But it seldom conveys a sense of "mathpower," not even to the mathematically best and brightest. And this is the point of greatest contrast between an encounter with the idea of variables in the traditional school and in the LOGO environment. In LOGO, the concept empowers the child, and the child experiences what it is like for mathematics to enable mankind to do what no one could do before.

The first thing to understand about APL is the fiendishly clever system of notation that Iverson has worked out. This system (sometimes called Iverson notation) allows extremely complex relations and computer-type events to be expressed simply, densely and consistently.

The notation is based on operators modifying things. Let's use alphabetic symbols for things and play with pictures for a minute.

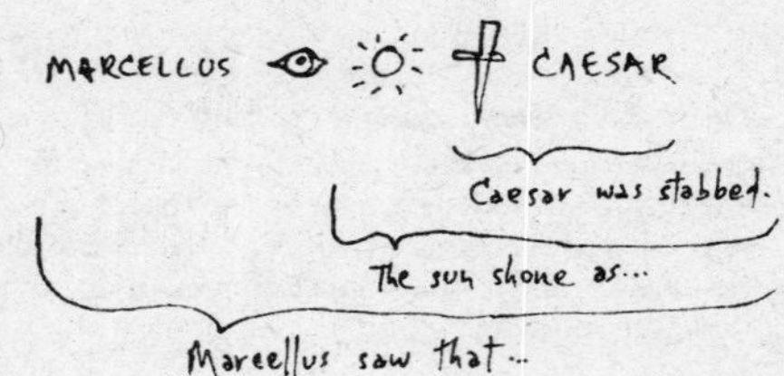

In considering the successive meanings of this rebus we are proceeding from right to left, as you note, and each new symbol adds meaning. This is the general idea.

Communication Outlook

A surprising amount of mainstream telecommunications was originally designed for the physically disabled or for people with cerebral palsy. For instance, computer terminals were developed from tele-typewriters used by the deaf. "Speak-and-Spell" owes its inspiration to voice-output machines which read to the blind. Even the telephone was originally intended to help the hard-of-hearing communicate. Therefore, if you want to know what's coming next in computerized communications, this newsletter will be one of your most valuable sources of leads and ideas. And if you or someone you know is disabled, it will help keep track of new machines you can use, and provide encouragement and perspective besides. It has the most human tone I've seen in any technical journal. —Art Kleiner
[Suggested by Don Selwyn]

Communication Outlook
(Focusing on Communication Aids and Techniques)
Yvonne Danjuma, Editor

$10 /year (4 issues)
from:
Communication Outlook
Artificial Language Lab.
Computer Science Dept.
Michigan State University
East Lansing, MI 48824

Visual Line of Gaze Device — Tufts New England Medical Center is developing a communication device that uses eye movements for control. This device is intended to be used by severely physically involved individuals who are nonvocal. The device monitors eye movements and calculates where in the visual field the user is looking. (This is referred to as the visual line of gaze of the user.) The user is allowed head movement within a one cubic foot range. Visual line of gaze is continually calculated independent of head movements.

Journal of Community Communications

Despite all the glossy promises of "Computopia," it's rare to find anyone writing about communications systems who remembers that there are supposed to be people on the other end(s). But that's the premise of this entire magazine. It covers everything from technology like CB and computer systems to community networks like alternative barter exchanges and anti-nuclear alliances — always with an eye towards what effects they're having on the local politics and their users. Editor Sandy Emerson maintains a consistently healthy skepticism. —Art Kleiner

Journal of Community Communications
Sandy Emerson, Editor

$9 /year (4 issues)
from:
Village Design
P.O. Box 996
Berkeley, CA 94701

Robotics Age

Robots are creeping into the world so stealthily that most people still aren't aware how many exist (thousands) or how intriguing they can be, particularly for the home-brew tinkerer with access to both a machine shop and a microcomputer. There's a lot to tinker with — artificial intelligence, simulated senses, and the mechanical challenge of building an arm that will move only as far as you want it to and no further. By our stereotyped sci-fi standards robots are simple-minded but still potentially useful — both to large corporations and small workshops with repetitive or dangerous jobs. (Auto companies are beginning to use $20,000 industrial robots to weld cars — they look like giant hairdryers, move with the jerky grace of the old "Lost in Space" robot, and work in a cloud of shooting sparks. Models made by independents are less threatening and more interesting.)

The books we've seen on robots and robotics are out-of-date or fluff; but **Robotics Age** *is current and solid. It's for people who make their own. Even in its reports on heavy industry it pays attention to the low-budget applications of high-budget ideas. To a casual observer, the possibilities and implications of this technology are, well, riveting.*

—*Art Kleiner*

Robotics Age
Hugh Bartel, Editor

$8.50 /year (4 issues)
from:
Robotics Age
P.O. Box 801
La Cañada, CA 91011

The MiniMover 5 tabletop arm is a unique instrument that attaches as a manipulative device to an inexpensive personal computer. It enables individuals or groups — such as schools and technical-interest clubs — to acquire "hands-on" experience with computer controlled automation, artificial intelligence, and robotics. The MiniMover 5 may be used for such applications as: 1) computer games, in which the arm moves game pieces on command; 2) computerized construction, in which building components may be arranged into a wide variety of configurations or mathematically programmed designs; 3) computer assembly, simulating automated factories of the future; 4) computer art, using graphic instruments such as paint brushes, felt tip pens, etc. directly.

Further information on the MiniMover 5 can be obtained from Microbot, 1259 El Camino Real, Ste 200, Menlo Park, CA 94025.

•

Mr. Taft told Robotics Age that Milton Bradley is currently spending over $600,000 per year for research on robot- and computer-related products. *(This is roughly comparable to the entire NASA robotics research budget — ed.)*

All this should be important news to Robotics Age readers. As the toy industry, already past masters at producing inexpensive mechanisms, discovers the vast potentials of robotics, we can expect to see an increasing array of cheap, practical devices suitable for computer interfacing, providing an attractive alternative to time-consuming hand-built items and expensive commercial equipment.

One final note — Mr. Taft tells us that Milton Bradley licenses the designs of about half of the devices it uses in its toys from outside sources, so you may want to send them that unique new sensor you've built!

Cybernetics for the Modern Mind

Computers grew out of information theory and cybernetics, grew so fast the origins (and fundamentals) somehow got left behind. "History" around computers means last year. I will bet that's a shallowness error, that deeper experimentation and sounder future sense would come from a thorough grounding in the pre-micro basics and exciting origin story of this particular Captain Marvel.

A British color-graphic candy box, this book does nicely as a compleat guide for the compleat idiot. (Genius is made of routinely asking idiot questions; genius has no shame whatever.)

—*SB*

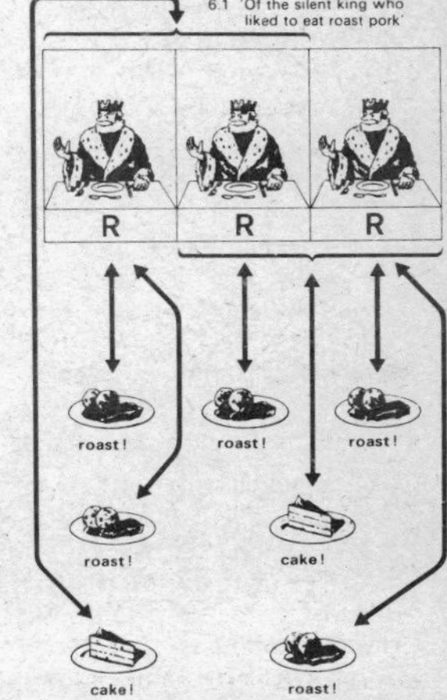

Cybernetics for the Modern Mind
Walter R. Fuchs
1968, 1971; 357 pp.

OUT OF PRINT
Macmillan
Publishing Company

Get this book back in print!

6.1 'Of the silent king who liked to eat roast pork'

R R R

roast! roast! roast! roast! cake! cake! roast!

The first codification attempt of the little fairy-tale king turned out to be ambiguous. Raising his right hand three times in succession could be interpreted as "three times roast," or "roast" followed by "cake," or "cake" followed by "roast."

II Cybernetic Frontiers

Computer people usually hate anything journalistic that's written about them. One measure of this book's value is that they still remember it with affection. The book opens two worlds to the casually interested — the world of hard-core computer hackers (explored in 1972 but still true to life) and the world of Gregory Bateson's cybernetic thought (explored in 1973 but agelessly informative). The book was written by Stewart Brand, who's my boss, but I liked it before I started working here. Bargain priced.

—*Art Kleiner*

II Cybernetic Frontiers
Stewart Brand
1974; 95 pp.

$2 postpaid from:
The CoEvolution Quarterly
P.O. Box 428
Sausalito, CA 94966

•

Legends abound from early ARPA days, full of freedom and weirdness. Here's one of many from Project MAC (Multiple Access Computer) days. Alan Kay: "They had a thing on the PDP-1 called 'The Unknown Glitch.' ["Glitch" — a kink, a less-than-fatal but irritating fuck-up]. They used to program the thing either in direct machine code, direct octal, or in DDT. In the early days it was a paper-tape machine. It was painful to assemble stuff, so they never listed out the programs. The programs and stuff just lived in there, just raw seething octal code. And one of the guys wrote a program called 'The Unknown Glitch,' which at random intervals would wake up, print out I AM THE UNKNOWN GLITCH. CATCH ME IF YOU CAN, and then it would relocate itself somewhere else in core memory, set a clock interrupt, and go back to sleep. There was no way to find it."

System Incoherence

by Marc Le Brun

Computer systems are *environments*, or, if you prefer, *ecologies*. They have a past and a future, functional niches, finite resources and many other properties associated with complicated systems which occur in nature. Yet, few installations take this fact into account as a general policy. As a result the systems are subject to the same sorts of degeneration caused by neglect (or out-and-out rapacity) as their more organic counterparts.

A typical (and costly) result of this is that it takes at least as much effort to instantiate a process on the system as it did to produce the original solution design in the first place. I am not referring to the usual tooling costs incurred in any engineering venture, but the unnecessary aggravation caused by attempting to use a polluted resource.

Ultimately, I suppose, the blame for this lies with conventional attitudes towards the world around us, but in the short range I believe it is because system "health" is never budgeted for, which in turn is because it is not perceived as a "real" property of the system, even though it can account for tremendous losses in time and efficiency.

Installations are in general enslaved to the past and irresponsible of the future. An all too common scenario goes like this: (1) Project A writes some software, completely with self-use in mind. The software is not "clean," but was only intended to "do the job," and has various strange and peculiar side-effects, which however, are of no concern to Project A. (2) After a while Project B develops a need for some similar software and to "cut costs" uses Project A's. The side-effects, while inconvenient, are easily managed. (3) Projects C, D, E . . . follow suit and soon the software has become The Software. (4) Finally, Project Z comes along. Project Z is fantastic, worthwhile, very useful and promises great things for the future except for one thing: the side-effects from The Software are pure poison to it — and the system has developed its first allergy. On older and larger systems *every* new project is like "Project Z," there's *always* some major or minor implementation conflict.

I once did some low-key work on a system that had to meet some "crash priorities" and was under tremendous pressure to justify its continued existence. The main systems group began to modify key portions of the software to expedite their job and help meet deadlines. Less than vital projects had to fend for themselves as various parts of the system ceased to function reliably. Eventually of course, they painted themselves into a corner, since their *own* software began to fail, and the system *had poisoned itself with the metabolic by-products of its own too-rapid growth.*

I believe that this kind of nonsense may be greatly reduced by a little planning at the start, and in particular, *budgeting for the maintenance of system health.* Systems do get old and cranky and die of course, but a lifetime of "sickness" is another thing entirely. ■

University publications lists

Much of the most far-ahead computer science work is done at a few universities. To find out what's going on without becoming a student (which may be inconvenient, difficult, boring, or unnecessary), you can read the reports published by their computer centers. Separating the wheat from chaff when you order may be a problem, but the paper titles are explicit and the listings are sometimes annotated. The two best schools to write to are MIT and Stanford.

—*Art Kleiner*
[Suggested by Marc Le Brun]

MIT Laboratory for Computer Science
Technical Report List and Technical Memoranda List

free from:
Massachusetts Institute of Technology
Laboratory for Computer Science
545 Technology Square
Cambridge, MA 02139

Stanford Department of Computer Science
Bibliography

free from:
Department of Computer Science
Publications Office
Stanford University
Stanford, CA 94305

TAP

This ten-year-old newsletter for telecommunications junkies is still the best source of information on the hidden byways of the telephone and other communications networks. It's expanded its focus since the old make-phone-calls-for-free days; now it covers computers, telex, cable TV, and the postal system. Use it at your own risk; most of it is written under pen names. But that doesn't make it any less fascinating to read.

—*Art Kleiner*

TAP

$5 /10 issues from:
TAP
Room 603
147 West 42nd Street
New York, NY 10036

THE RISING SUN
NEIGHBORHOOD NEWSLETTER

Probably it turns out that having a miracle happen to you is just like having anything else happen — might be great, might be awful, might be OK but ill timed, but there it is — it happened and you have to cope with it.

Computer Power and Human Reason

This book is a center of controversy amongst computerists, especially those working in the field of artificial intelligence. It has received extensive praise and criticism, stimulated a heated and often bitter debate in the technical journals and generally raised a ruckus. It accomplished all this by raising serious moral and ethical questions regarding the use and social impact of computers.

My own attitude about this work is mixed — I feel the topic is important but the treatment is lacking. However it is unquestionably significant, if only because of its effects on the information processing community.

—Marc Le Brun

This was one of the first books I ever read on the subject of computing. Though I agree that its argument isn't completely convincing, I can't think of a better introduction to the psycho-social issues in computer programming and artificial intelligence. *—Art Kleiner*

Computer Power and Human Reason
(From Judgement to Calculation)
Joseph Weizenbaum
1976; 300 pp.
$7.95 postpaid from:
W.H. Freeman and Co.
660 Market Street
San Francisco, CA 94104
or Whole Earth Household Store

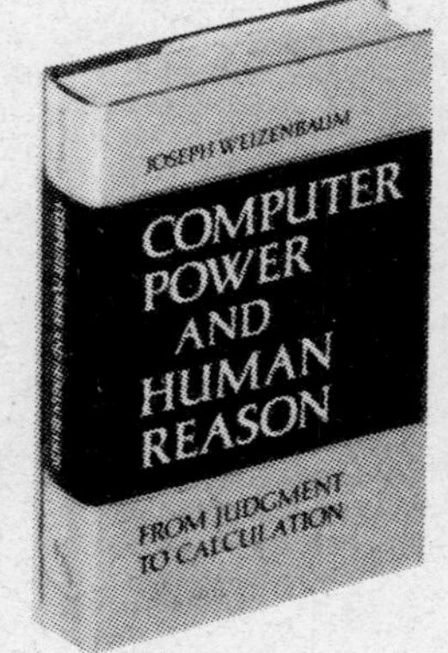

•

For my first experiment, I gave ELIZA a script designed to permit it to play (I should really say parody) the role of a Rogerian psychotherapist engaged in an initial interview with a patient. The Rogerian psychotherapist is relatively easy to imitate because much of his technique consists of drawing his patient out by reflecting the patient's statements back to him. The following conversation between a young lady and ELIZA playing doctor illustrates both the Rogerian technique of encouraging a patient to keep talking and the operation of the computer program ELIZA. The first to "speak" is the young lady. The computer's responses are printed entirely in capitals.

Men are all alike.

IN WHAT WAY

They're always bugging us about something or the other.

CAN YOU THINK OF A SPECIFIC EXAMPLE

Well, my boyfriend made me come here.

YOUR BOYFRIEND MADE YOU COME HERE

He says I'm depressed much of the time.

I AM SORRY TO HEAR YOU ARE DEPRESSED

It's true. I am unhappy.

DO YOU THINK COMING HERE WILL HELP YOU NOT TO BE UNHAPPY

I need some help, that much seems certain.

WHAT WOULD IT MEAN TO YOU IF YOU GOT SOME HELP

Perhaps I could learn to get along with my mother.

TELL ME MORE ABOUT YOUR FAMILY

My mother takes care of me.

WHO ELSE IN YOUR FAMILY TAKES CARE OF YOU

My father.

YOUR FATHER

You are like my father in some ways.

WHAT RESEMBLANCE DO YOU SEE

You are not very aggressive but I think you don't want me to notice that.

WHAT MAKES YOU THINK I AM NOT VERY AGGRESSIVE

You don't argue with me.

WHY DO YOU THINK I DON'T ARGUE WITH YOU

You are afraid of me.

DOES IT PLEASE YOU TO BELIEVE I AM AFRAID OF YOU

My father is afraid of everybody.

WHAT ELSE COMES TO MIND WHEN YOU THINK OF YOUR FATHER

Bullies.

DOES THAT HAVE ANYTHING TO DO WITH THE FACT THAT YOUR BOYFRIEND MADE YOU COME HERE . . .

The shocks I experienced as DOCTOR became widely known and "played" were due principally to three distinct events.

1. A number of practicing psychiatrists seriously believed the DOCTOR computer program could grow into a nearly completely automatic form of psychotherapy.

2. I was startled to see how quickly and how very deeply people conversing with DOCTOR became emotionally involved with the computer and how unequivocally they anthropomorphized it. Once my secretary, who had watched me work on the program for many months and therefore surely knew it to be merely a computer program, started conversing with it. . . .

3. Another widespread, and to me surprising, reaction to the ELIZA program was the spread of a belief that it demonstrated a general solution to the problem of computer understanding or natural language. In my paper, I had tried to say that no general solution to that problem was possible, i.e., that language is understood only in contextual frameworks, that even these can be shared by people to only a limited extent, and that consequently even people are not embodiments of any such general solution.

[Note: the ELIZA program is available. *See p. 532.]*

Design and Memory

A wise book about how civilization will adapt to computing and vice versa. The authors are among the first to notice in print that the styles and practices of programming are already influencing the rest of the culture. The book looks forward to a shared intelligence between humans and computers, on the order of (but more interwovenly complex than) this dialog: Computer: "A and B have 4 similarities and 1,317 dissimilarities." Person: "Yes, but the differences aren't important."

Peter Huyck and Nellie Kremenak are programmers who write English wittily and literately even by **New Yorker** *standards. There's a gem of insight into the human-machine relationship on practically every page of their book.* *—Art Kleiner*

Design and Memory
(Computer Programming in the 20th Century)
Peter H. Huyck and Nellie W. Kremenak
1980; 152 pp.
$11.95 postpaid from:
McGraw-Hill Book Company
Princeton Road
Hightstown, NJ 08520
or Whole Earth Household Store

•

Exercise for students

We have some code which allows the banks to know more about us, but where is the code which allows us to know more about the banks? Write this code.

•

Lewis Mumford described the clock as the "key-machine" of the modern industrial age and considered its invention more significant than that of the steam engine.

"The clock, moreover, is a piece of power-machinery whose 'product' is seconds and minutes: by its essential nature it dissociated time from human events and helped create the belief in an independent world of mathematically measurable sequences: the special world of science."

•

In the case of human/television interaction, the human is the more adaptive partner, and so there is a tendency for the human to adapt to the TV (watch whatever is on) rather than for the TV to adapt to the human (programming changes), which involves a long and complex feedback loop. The same problem arises in a human/program-in-computing-machine partnership. The human can adapt quickly, but the feedback for the machine to adapt (particularly if the human is not a programmer) is long and complex.

What is on television is due largely to accidents of history and the subsequent skewing of evolution by considerations of the marketplace. Current human/machine systems are also early accidents, and the systems of the future will evolve from them. We should tamper with existing systems in the direction of incorporating more sophisticated assumptions than are found in the average bit of FORTRAN so that the systems of the future will have evolved from happier accidents. As a minimum step toward this goal, the feedback loop for machine adaptation must be shortened so that machines will be at least as adaptable as humans — a tall order. Otherwise, the machines will win out as we adapt to them. It will not be an exotic win of the sci-fi type, but a win of drudgery, inconsequence, boredom, and stacks of output.

Principles of Interactive Computer Graphics

The Bible of Computer Grafix. This is the second edition, and it's really up-to-date with state of the art stuff.

—Christopher Kent

Principles of Interactive Computer Graphics
William M. Newman and Robert F. Sproull
1973, 1979; 541 pp.
$26.95 postpaid from:
McGraw-Hill Book Co.
Princeton Road
Hightstown, NJ 08520
or Whole Earth Household Store

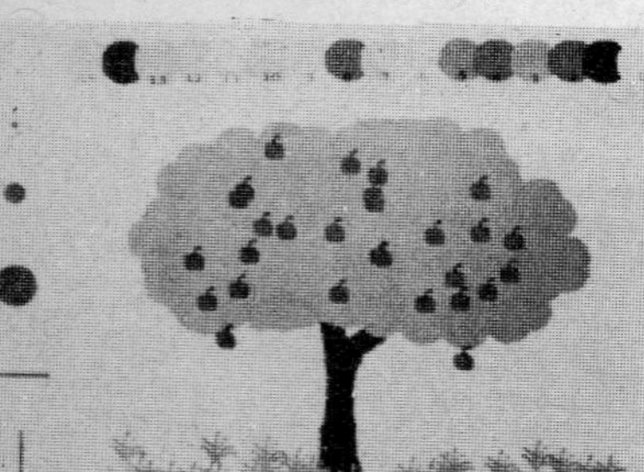

← Use of a menu of colors for painting

A computer-generated image of a teapot with simulated specular reflections of light entering through a window ↓

COMPUTER PARANOIA CUTS BOTH WAYS

by Dirk Hanson

A report compiled for the business community by Stanford Research Institute's Business Intelligence Program has this to say: "The reason (distributed processing) computer networks will not be available to the general public at an earlier date is primarily one of security. *At present, fraudulent input or access to a data base management system cannot be prevented.*" (Italics mine.)

This is a vital piece of information that the industry does *not* want you to know. There's this security problem. Large, flexible time-shared computer systems are swiss cheese. Ask a programmer. Computer crime is a growth industry. Computer security is a myth. For every new data encryption system, there's a programmer out there somewhere who can crack it. A program that sneaks you into an operating system is called a Trojan Horse. At most computer centers, the Trojan Horse is already inside the gates.

Some grim worst-case scenarios might just be floating through corporate corridors these days. Striking British civil servants recently turned off key government computer systems, and the result was chaos. Some of the information and assets probably will not be recoverable. The strikers simply pulled the plugs. Crude, but effective.

But what about the likelihood of more sophisticated guerilla tactics, as computer know-how spreads throughout the populace?

Quite a quandary for industry people: They want you as a customer, but can they trust you? They need to sell you computers and teach you the mechanics of programming, but they don't want to let you *too* far into the distributed processing loop. They need your business, but they're scared of you. No kidding. As time goes by, you could become too smart for their own good.

Computer paranoia cuts both ways. The industry may be nervous about widespread consumer participation in future networks, but it seems much less concerned about consumer privacy abuses in current systems. It's common knowledge — at least it *should* be — that information which goes into such systems, information about you, your habits and activities, information from which your preferences can be deduced, is accessible to almost anyone. Credit records, criminal records, medical records, driving records, financial data — the whole gamut. Right now, most of it is fair game.

It's a muddy affair. Who decides who gets access to what? There's reason to be wary of controls and limitations on access to digitized information, and equal reason to worry about what will happen if there are no such controls. The deciding *in theory* will be a sociopolitical matter; the accessing *in truth* will be by those who know how. And the *what* being accessed will be almost everything. ■

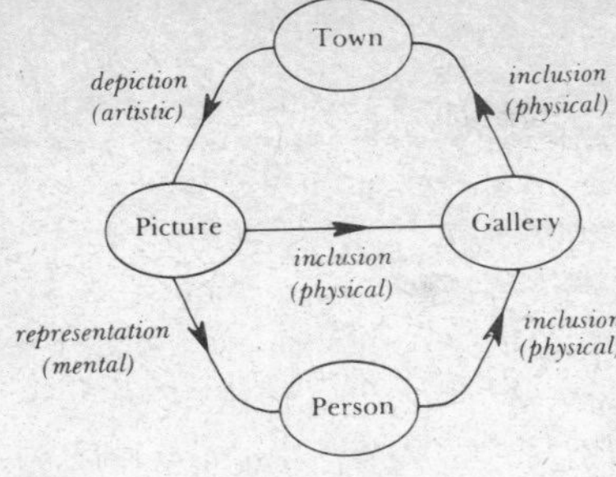

← A strikingly beautiful, and yet at the same time disturbingly grotesque, illustration of the cyclonic "eye" of a Tangled Hierarchy is given to us by Escher in his **Print Gallery**. What we see is a picture of a ship in the harbor of a small town, perhaps a Maltese town, to guess from the architecture, with its little turrets, occasional cupolas, and flat stone roofs, upon one of which sits a boy, relaxing in the heat, while two floors below him a woman — perhaps his mother — gazes out of the window from her apartment which sits directly above a picture gallery where a young man is standing, looking at a picture of a ship in the harbor of a small town, perhaps a Maltese town — What!? We are back on the same level as we began, though all logic dictates that we cannot be. Let us draw a diagram of what we see.

What this diagram shows is three kinds of "in-ness." The gallery is *physically in* the town ("inclusion"); the town is *artistically in* the picture ("depiction"); the picture is *mentally in* the person ("representation"). . . .

Now are we, the observers of **Print Gallery**, also sucked into ourselves by virtue of looking at it? Not really. We manage to escape that particular vortex by being outside of the system. And when we look at the picture, we see things which the young man can certainly not see, such as Escher's signature, "MCE", in the central "blemish". Though the blemish seems like a defect, perhaps the defect lies in our expectations, for in fact Escher could not have completed that portion of the picture without being inconsistent with the rules by which he was drawing the picture. That center of the whorl is — and must be — incomplete. Escher could have made it arbitrarily small, but he could not have gotten rid of it. Thus we, on the outside, can know that **Print Gallery** is essentially incomplete — a fact which the young man, on the inside, can never know. Escher has thus given a pictorial parable for Gödel's Incompleteness Theorem. And that is why the strands of Gödel and Escher are so deeply interwoven in my book.

Gödel, Escher, Bach: an Eternal Golden Braid

"Every few decades an unknown author brings out a book of such depth, clarity, range, wit, beauty and originality that it is recognized at once as a major literary event." So wrote Martin Gardner in the July, 1979 **Scientific American** *in an entire article devoted to this book.*

The subject of the book — and the frequent preoccupation of its deities, mathematician Kurt Gödel, artist M.C. Escher, composer J.S. Bach, and writer Lewis Carroll — is self-reference, what the author calls "strange loops" or "tangled hierarchies." It is the domain of extreme paradox, where math, art, religion (lots of zen in the book, honestly employed), and epistemology collide. It is the fearless exploration of black holes of the mind.

Hofstadter set out to make Gödel's Incompleteness Theorem accessible to the lay thinker, and happily he succeeds in that. Along the way he illuminates a world of music, mathematics, computer intelligence (and gossip), and philosophy. The book confirms the suspicion I've had for years that perhaps the most adventurous and fruitful human frontier we have these days is the hall of mirrors, Lewis Carroll's looking glass.

The unusual form of this book, thick with graphic devices, deserves comment. We may be seeing a development as profound as the invention of the cartoon strip. Hofstadter's images do not illustrate his words, and the words are not caption to the pictures — they are both the text. It's interesting that we have here the first popular work by a computer bum, and it is a masterpiece. Could his imaginative form of discourse be a by-product of the new tool he lives with? —SB

[Suggested by R.W. Bigham]

(See **The Graphic Work of M.C. Escher**, *p. 460.)*

Gödel, Escher, Bach: an Eternal Golden Braid
(A metaphorical fugue on minds and machines in the spirit of Lewis Carroll)
Douglas R. Hofstadter
1979, 1980; 777 pp.
$8.95 postpaid from:
Vintage Books
Random House
455 Hahn Road
Westminster, MD 21157
or Whole Earth Household Store

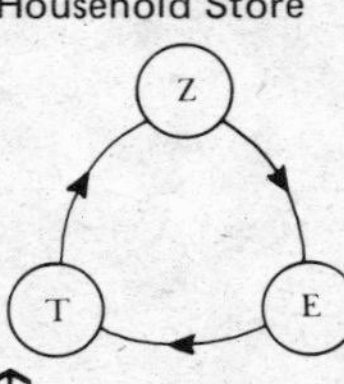

↑ There are three authors — Z, T, and E. Now it happens that Z exists only in a novel by T. Likewise, T exists only in a novel by E. And strangely, E, too, exists only in a novel — by Z, of course. Now, is such an "authorship triangle" really possible?

Of course, it's possible. But there's a trick . . . All three authors Z, T, E, are themselves characters in another novel — by H! You can think of the Z-T-E triangle as a Strange Loop, Or Tangled Hierarchy; but author H is outside of the space in which that tangle takes place — author H is in an inviolate space. Although Z, T, and E all have access — direct or indirect — to each other, and can do dastardly things to each other in their various novels, none of them can touch H's life! They can't even imagine him — no more than you can imagine the author of the book *you're* a character in. If I were to draw author H, I would represent him somewhere off the page. Of course that would present a problem, since drawing a thing necessarily puts it *onto* the page . . . Anyway, H is really outside of the world of Z, T, and E, and should be represented as being so.

At first it looks like a collection of somewhat random blobs, but if you step back a ways and stare at it for a while, all of a sudden, you will see seven letters appear in this . . . ↓

Artificial Intelligence

Patrick Winston's **Artificial Intelligence** *has become something of a classic in the computer field and deservedly so. It makes a wonderful complement to Hofstadter's* **Gödel, Escher, Bach.**

The first half of the book provides a conceptual overview of several of the major research efforts in artificial intelligence, including scene analysis, pattern recognition and pattern-directed inference systems. The second half is a LISP language tutorial (LISP is probably the most important computer language used in artificial intelligence research today) which develops some rather sophisticated AI programs.

Surprisingly, perhaps what's most intriguing are some of the exercises that Winston assigns at the end of the chapters. His questions are structured to elicit and provoke both insight and understanding into the nature of the subject material and its relation with other segments of the book.

Overall, a very, very useful guide to AI.

—*Michael Schrage*

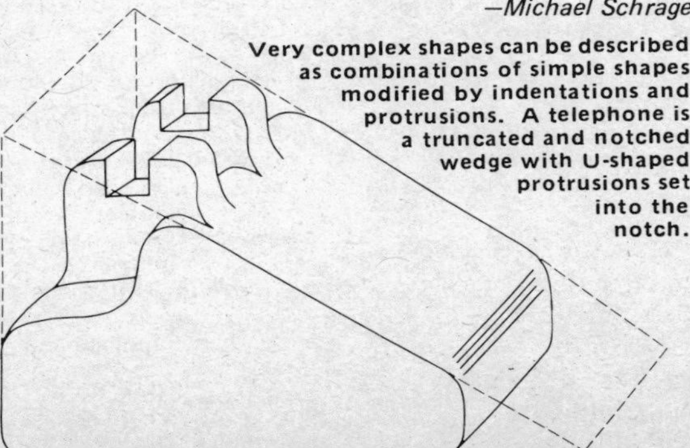

Very complex shapes can be described as combinations of simple shapes modified by indentations and protrusions. A telephone is a truncated and notched wedge with U-shaped protrusions set into the notch.

Machines Who Think

Reading the sloppy writing on artificial intelligence in most magazines and newspapers (even computer magazines!) makes you realize how valuable this book is, and how much more good reporting is needed. Though far from flawless, the book's a gripping piece of gossip about a debate that cyberneticians and computer scientists have argued for twenty years — whether active intelligence in machines is possible, if so whether it's desirable, and how to go about pursuing it. Expect the debate to ripple out into everyday life as smart machines appear around us. This is a good starting point for those outside the field. —*Art Kleiner*

Machines Who Think
Pamela McCorduck
1979; 375 pp.
$14.95 postpaid from:
W.H. Freeman and Co.
660 Market Street
San Francisco, CA 94104
or Whole Earth Household Store

•

As a freshman at Haverford College in 1918, McCulloch remembers being questioned by the Quaker Rufus Jones:

"Warren," said he, "what is thee going to be?" And I said, "I don't know." "And what is thee going to do?" And again I said, "I have no idea, but there is one question I would like to answer: What is a number, that a man may know it, and a man that he may know a number?" He smiled and said, "Friend, thee will be busy as long as thee lives."

—McCulloch, 1965

•

Artificial intelligence as science has been less *apparently* successful than its founding fathers hoped, but its progress in the twenty or so years of its existence has been enough to confound its critics — it performs better and better, slowly breaking down each barrier the critics declared could never be surmounted. Whether it will surmount them all remains to be seen. Each step toward a fully realized intelligent artifact suggests that it can be done, but it hasn't been yet. Each of these steps, however, forces us to refocus our view of ourselves, and at such points people who ponder the human condition have the right, the responsibility, to consider our proper place in the universe, our possibilities and limitations, our individual and collective purposes.

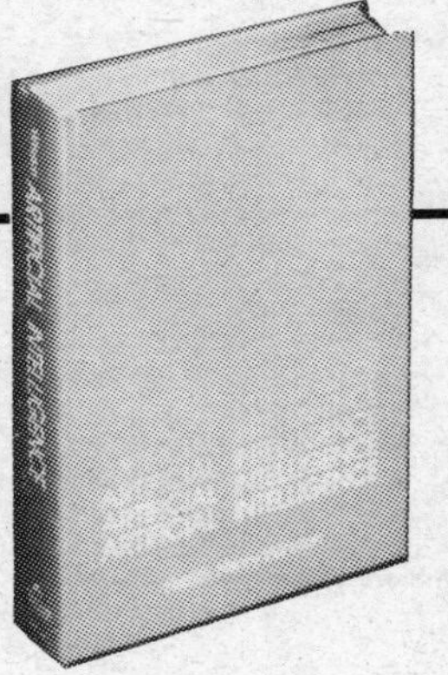

Artificial Intelligence
Patrick Henry Winston
1977; 444 pp.
$18.95 postpaid from:
Addison-Wesley Publishing Company
Jacob Way
Reading, MA 01867
or Whole Earth Household Store

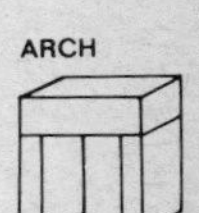

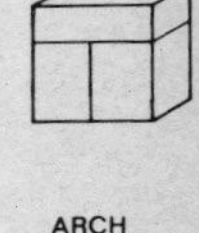

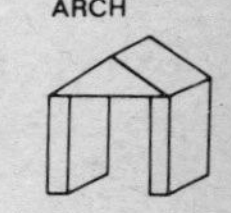

A learning sequence for the arch concept. The first sample conveys the general idea. The others reinforce it by emphasizing that there must be support, that the sides must not touch, and that the top need not be brick. →

•

Myth: Computers Can Do Only What They Are Programmed to Do

Intelligent computers do not organize themselves out of nothing, so in some uninteresting sense their abilities descend from human programmers. But it is equally true that humans are indebted to the genetic code. Somehow there must be enough information processing power to get beyond the threshhold above which learning from the environment takes place. Once humans bring computer intelligence up to this level, computers will no doubt augment their directly programmed gifts by the same means humans do: by being told, by reading, by asking questions, by doing experiments, and by being curious.

THE RISING SUN
NEIGHBORHOOD NEWSLETTER

—"If everyone in the world would wash two dishes, there would be no war."
—"But they won't."

—Stewart and me talking.

Some rules and hints for teachers and students

RULE ONE: Find a place you trust and then, try trusting it for awhile.

RULE TWO: General duties of a student — pull everything out of your teacher; pull everything out of your fellow students.

RULE THREE: General duties of a teacher — pull everything out of your students.

RULE FOUR: Consider everything an experiment.

RULE FIVE: Be self-disciplined — this means finding someone wise or smart and choosing to follow them. To be disciplined is to follow in a good way. To be self-disciplined is to follow in a better way.

RULE SIX: Nothing is a mistake. There's no win and no fail, there's only make.

RULE SEVEN: The only rule is work. If you work it will lead to something. It's the people who do all of the work all of the time who eventually catch on to things.

RULE EIGHT: Don't try to create and analyze at the same time. They're different processes.

RULE NINE: Be happy whenever you can manage it. Enjoy yourself. It's lighter than you think.

RULE TEN: "We're breaking all the rules. Even our own rules. And how do we do that? By leaving plenty of room for X quantities." (John Cage)

HINTS: Always be around. Come or go to everything. Always go to classes. Read anything you can get your hands on. Look at movies carefully, often. Save everything — it might come in handy later.

—Corita Kent

Baby and Child Care

Baby and Child Care *by Dr. Benjamin Spock is an excellent book to have handy, especially with a first child. The advice and explanations Dr. Spock gives regarding fever, rashes, coughs, innoculations, and clothing for the infant is presented in simple language, somewhat wordy and repetitious, but in such a manner that you cannot misunderstand or confuse his instructions. The chapters on illness, first aid, and special problems are excellent and probably the most read and re-read chapters in the book. Not only do you get lots of psychological guidance in the areas of toilet training, weaning, thumbsucking, and bed wetting but, as may be expected, there are sermons on aggressive children, no-war toys and growing up in a bomb-oriented world. You couldn't possibly agree with everything Dr. Spock says but after reading this book you are left with the feeling that you should relax, enjoy your baby, do what seems right and natural, and that Spock is speaking from experience and common sense.*

—Connie Duckworth

Baby and Child Care
Dr. Benjamin Spock
1946, 1976; 666 pp.
$5.95 postpaid from:
Pocket Books
Attn: Order Department
1230 Avenue of the Americas
New York, NY 10020
or Whole Earth Household Store

Better to remove and distract him than just to say, "No, no!"

•
More babies are overdressed than underdressed. This isn't good for them. If a person is always too warmly dressed, his body loses its ability to adjust to changes. He is more likely to become chilled. So in general, put on too little rather than too much and then watch the baby. Best guide is the color of his face. If he is getting cold, he loses the color from his cheeks.

•
To some degree, the first pregnancy spells the end of carefree youth — very important to Americans. The maidenly figure goes gradually into eclipse, and with it goes sprightly grace. Both eclipses are temporary but very real. The woman realizes that after the baby comes there will be distinct limitations of social life and other outside pleasures. No more hopping into the car on the spur of the moment, going anywhere the heart desires and coming home at any old hour. The same budget has to be spread thinner, and her husband's attention, all of which has gone to her at home, will soon be going to two.

•
It's a good idea to begin offering a sip of milk from the cup from the age of 5 months, so that the baby gets used to it before he is too opinionated.

The Well Baby Book

This book will be especially appreciated by parents of babies who want to apply the principles of self-care to parenting. Covers normal child development, dealing with common illnesses and emergencies, dietary do's and don'ts. Also includes some sections you won't find in Dr. Spock — there is a strong emphasis on more natural approaches to childbirth; breast feeding is encouraged; and parents are advised to respect and nurture their child's own natural healing process, and to avoid major medical intervention (e.g., tonsillectomies and adenoidectomies) whenever possible. The authors feel that medications and some surgical and diagnostic interventions are overused in pediatric practice. But they are also very clear that there are times when a doctor's help is necessary. They supply some useful guidelines to help the reader decide when, and when not, to consult a doctor. The book is particularly strong in its use of relaxation and visualization exercises to support both the well-being of child and parent alike.

My only caution about this book is that readers who didn't experience labor as exhilarating, who had a C-section, or who aren't breastfeeding could get the feeling that they had done their child some terrible harm — although I'm sure that wasn't the author's intention. But that's a minor reservation, and on the whole this is a valuable and unique baby book.

—Lewis Engel, PH.D.
[Suggested by Tom Ferguson, M.D.]

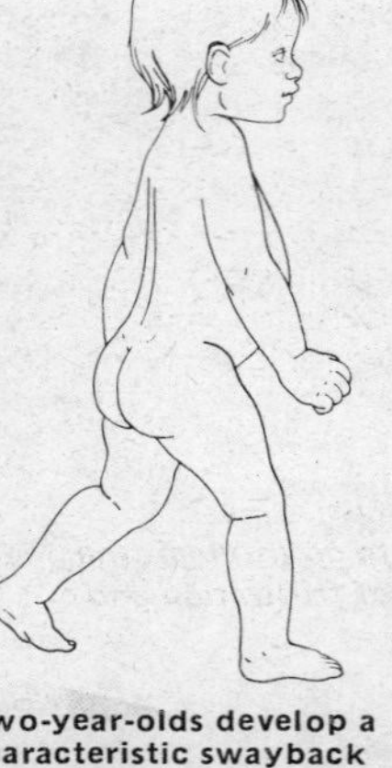

Two-year-olds develop a characteristic swayback and potbelly, which they will lose toward the fourth year.

The Well Baby Book
Mike Samuels, M.D. and Nancy Samuels
1979; 400 pp.
$9.95 postpaid from:
Summit Books
Simon and Schuster
Attn: Order Department
1230 Avenue of the Americas
New York, NY 10020
or Whole Earth Household Store

•
Diaper rash is one of a number of *primary irritant contact dermatitises.* That is, it is an inflammation of the skin due to direct exposure to an irritating agent. The redness and swelling are the result of increased blood flow and greater amounts of moisture in the skin cells. The fatty junctions between cells are replaced by water, the cells are stretched apart, and the normal protective barrier of the skin is broken. The body deals with this situation by bringing in increased amounts of white blood cells to prevent or fight infection.

Suggestions for Treating Diaper Rash

Change diapers more frequently than normal or put baby in double diapers.

Gently rinse or wash the diaper area with lukewarm water and mild soap, especially after a bowel movement.

Dry the diaper area thoroughly after washing, using a blotting action, never rubbing.

Expose the diaper area to air, heat lamps (at a safe distance), or sunlight. The sun's ultraviolet rays actually kill bacteria, as well as dry the skin.

Apply a nonprescription cream or ointment such as *A and D, Diaparene,* or *Vaseline.* These basically form a barrier to protect the skin from irritating agents and may also be healing or antibacterial. (Note: The baby's skin must be completely clean and dry or the cream simply traps moisture and bacteria against the skin and aggravates the problem.)

Let baby go without diapers whenever possible.

The Complete Baby Book

A consumer guide for parents-to-be and parents of children up to about three years, this book provides a thorough introduction to nearly every subject which concerns parenting. There are articles on pregnancy, nutrition, birthing, selecting a pediatrician, and a guide to determining when to call the doctor for your child. In the back are lists of additional readings, a directory of special help agencies, and a directory of sources and manufacturers mentioned in the text. Large sections are devoted to evaluations of maternity products and infant and children's supplies such as nursing aids, toys, clothing, cribs, car seats, etc. Each item is judged for safety and practicality. Since new products come on the market daily, and safety standards are being constantly revised, these kinds of evaluations become a must for responsible parents.

This book way outclasses its competition, **Good Things For Babies.**

—Evelyn Eldridge-Diaz

The Complete Baby Book
(A Total Guide to Buying Products, Toys and Medical Services)
Editors of Consumer Guide
1979; 320 pp.

$7.95 postpaid from:
Simon and Schuster
Attn: Order Department
1230 Avenue of the Americas
New York, NY 10020
or Whole Earth Household Store

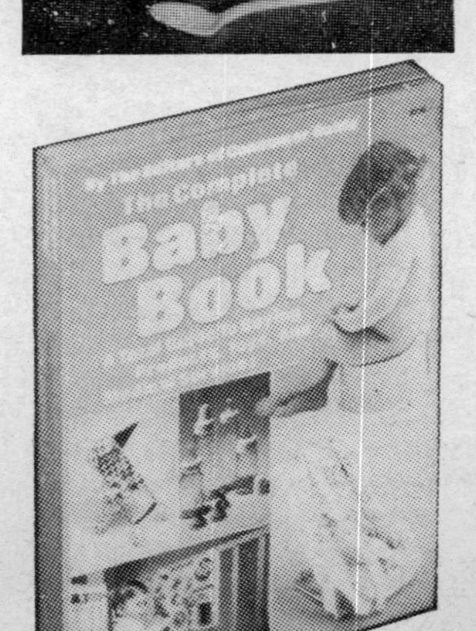

←
Happy Baby Food Grinder

This is the original baby-food grinder invented by a physician 23 years ago. The bowl is wide, the blades are constructed of stainless steel, and the fit of the neck cylinder and the blades against the strainer disc is smooth. Unbreakable and able to withstand cleaning in a sterilizer or dishwasher, the Happy Baby Food Grinder outperforms its many competitors. Price range: $6 - $7.50. From: **Bowland-Jacobs International, Inc.,** Fox Industrial Park, Yorkville, IL 60560.

→
Safe-T-Seat

This (Model 78) is a very new, dynamically tested car seat which shouldn't be confused with other Peterson seats (such as the Safety Shell or the Safe-T-Seat Model 60) which are not considered safe. The Peterson Safe-T-Seat 78 features thick foam padding on the seat body with a soft upholstery that has seams that are sewn rather than heat sealed. The seat offers seven positions from upright to reclining. It is adjusted by means of a metal tab on a tight spring which is lifted up and placed into notches on a semi-circular metal piece on the side of the seat. The seat has a high back and is positioned high enough to permit toddlers to see out of the car. The seat faces rearward for infants up to 17 pounds and forward for children weighing between 17 and 43 pounds. It requires tethering in the forward position. . . . Overall, this is a superior design to all other seats on the market. Price $50. From: **Peterson Baby Products,** 2525 State Street, Columbus, IN 47201

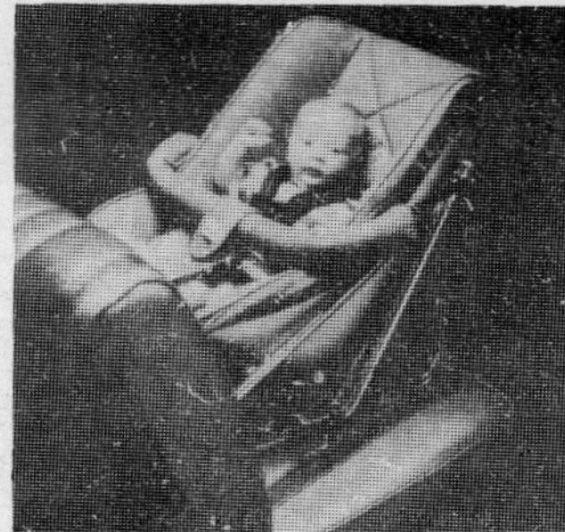

Peterson Safe-T-Seat (infant position)

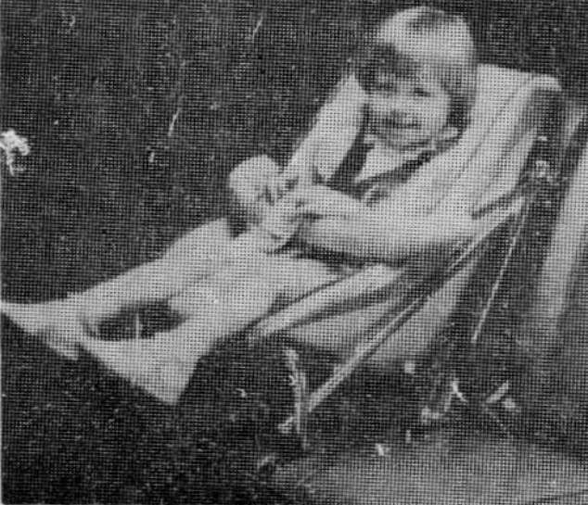

Peterson Safe-T-Seat (child position)

Nursing Your Baby

By common acclaim the best book on the subject, better even than La Leche League's worthy **The Womanly Art of Breastfeeding**. *And updated/revised in 1973.*

Interesting gossip: the author is a noted dolphin researcher (see her **Lads Before the Wind**) *and daughter of the late novelist Philip Wylie.* —SB

Nursing Your Baby
Karen Pryor
1963, 1973; 289 pp.
$2.50 postpaid from:
Pocket Books
Attn: Order Department
1230 Avenue of
the Americas
New York, NY 10020
or Whole Earth
Household Store

•

Birth control pills prevent ovulation by tinkering with the body's hormonal system. Some women who have taken birth control pills during lactation find that their milk supply is definitely reduced. Others notice no effects; lactation is maintained normally by suckling, even in the presence of hormones sometimes used to "dry up" the milk.

We do not yet fully understand the effects and possible hazards of routine use of birth control pills and other hormones. It would seem wise to be conservative, if possible, during lactation, and to use contraceptive methods which do not have an effect on the mother's whole system. Therefore, because of the unknown factor of future effect on the baby, mothers ought to seriously consider another form of contraception while they are lactating.

•

Lactation is the final chapter of a woman's biological functioning. It is an oversight to consider (as Kinsey did) that sexual intercourse and its variations are the only significant form of female sexual behavior. Men, indeed, have only one biological function related to their sex: intercourse. Women have five: the ovarian cycle, intercourse, pregnancy, childbirth, and lactation. Each of these events has a powerful effect on the woman's life.

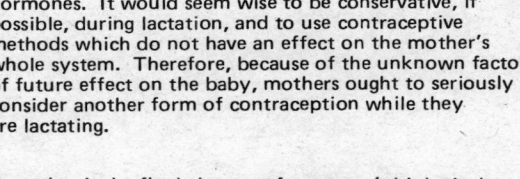

The classic nursing pose, with the infant supported on the mother's raised knee. Egypt, about fifteenth century B.C.

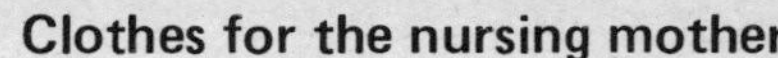

Clothes for the nursing mother

Breastfeeding one's baby is an option being chosen by more women today, but until recently there was no real choice of suitable clothing; it was either a shirt to unbutton to pull up, or an elasticized neckline to pull down. Designers are finally beginning to pay some attention to this need. Here are three sources.
—Evelyn Eldridge-Diaz

Baby Love, P.O. Box 127, Laguna Beach, CA 92652. *Several styles of tops and dresses with a unique velcro fastening on side flaps which lift for convenient, discreet nursing. Washable fabrics, sizes 32 - 40. Free brochure.*

Mothercare-by-Mail, P.O. Box 228, Parsippany, NJ 07054. *Mothercare is a British-based firm. Seven nursing nightgowns in washable fabrics are offered, as well as maternity and infant supplies. Free catalog.*

Sears (p. 348). *Sears now offers nursing nightgowns in several styles. They are still selling their superior nursing bras.*

$28.45 $16.20 $16.20

Happy Nursing from Baby Love

Toilet Training in Less Than a Day

I can't comment on **Toilet Training in Less Than a Day** *but can say a bit about the method. Our daughter, Jessica, served as one of the subjects in the research that led to the book. Dick Foxx did the training.*

It works — beautifully! We had all kinds of problems with Jessica's toilet training. A friend of ours (another prominent B-mod practitioner at Anna State Hospital, a colleague of Foxx) recommended we call Foxx. We did. Foxx showed up about nine or ten one morning, trotted off to the john with 20 month old Jessica and a bag of M&Ms and spent the next four or five hours conditioning her. By the end of that time, she was performing the ritual consistently and "appropriately." Dick came back the next day and spent another couple of hours making sure she was properly programmed. She was. And has been for the last three yeras.

We had all sorts of fears about the effects B-mod might have on our kid — would she turn into a reward freak, expecting goodies every time we asked that she perform to our expectations? Would the reward system impair her ethical development? Would we wake up some morning to find our lovely spontaneous child had been turned into a restrictively programmed robot?

None of that happened. She just learned the ritual and that's all. Through this experience and through the information we've gotten from our friends that work in the field, we've come to accept limited operant conditioning intervention as a powerful tool for individual growth. We still fear the possibility of a world in which operant conditioning would be the dominant educational method. What we fear, we think, is the loss of magic and fantasy. The operant definition of the person would lead to a moral, ethical and cultural reductionism that would ignore the element of Chaos present in the imbedding Suprasystem.

Anyway: Yes, the book is probably very good, judging from the way it was researched. The method saved us a lot of hassle and saved Jessica the trauma of having to go through what probably would have been a period of frustration and confusion.

—Dave and Maria Dix

Giving the doll a treat for urinating in the potty

You did it right! You did it!

Toilet Training in Less Than a Day
N.H. Azrin and
Richard M. Foxx
1974, 1977; 160 pp.
$2.25 postpaid from:
Pocket Books
Attn: Order Department
1230 Avenue of
the Americas
New York, NY 10020
or Whole Earth
Household Store

Soakers

Soakers are knitted or crocheted garments to put over a baby's diapers. They act as a kind of wick, drawing moisture away from the baby, and keeping it nominally dry on the outside. They are not plastic pants, don't misunderstand. They will not keep the baby as dry as modern miracle products but they are a pleasant alternative, especially if your child has adverse reactions to plastic or rubber pants. Handspun Fibers and Fables has patterns for making knitted or crocheted soakers, and also sells natural wool — wool untreated with chemicals, so it retains its natural oiliness, and its natural water-repellent qualities. *—Evelyn Eldridge-Diaz*

Handspun Fibers and Fables
Soaker patterns
$ .75 postpaid from:
Handspun Fibers
and Fables
512 South Mechanic
Pendleton, SC 29670

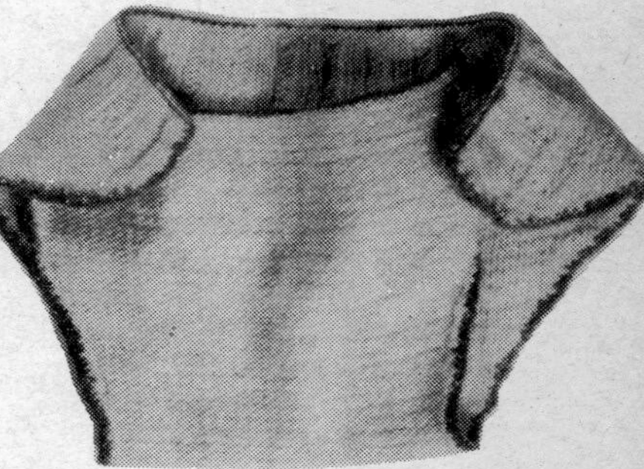

↑

Nuk Orthondontic Exerciser

Similar to the Nuk nipple, the Nuk pacifier has been approved by some dentists because it is designed to fit flat against the tongue so that no pressure is applied against the baby's front teeth. We highly recommend this pacifier.
Price Range: $1 - $1.20
From **Reliance Products Corp.**, 108 Mason Street, Woonsocket, RI 02895.

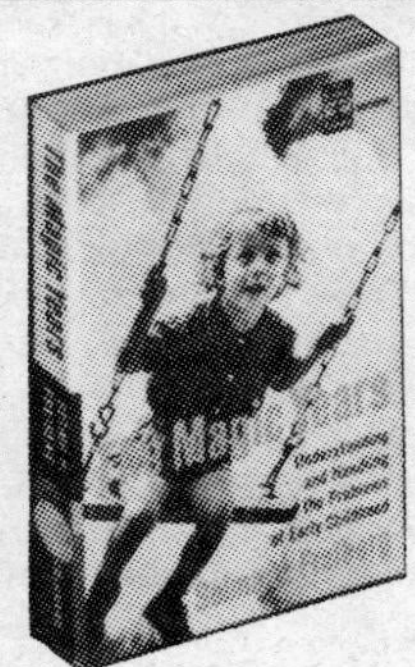

The Magic Years
Selma H. Fraiberg
1968; 302 pp.
$4.95 postpaid from:
Charles Scribner's Sons
Vreeland Avenue
Totowa, NJ 07512
or Whole Earth
Household Store

The Magic Years

I love this book because it has a rare sort of wisdom. Listening to children as Fraiberg listens is an art; like a good detective she probes for clues till seemingly meaningless behavior makes sense. The result is that she's able to appreciate a child's point of view and to offer considerable insight into his/her behavior. She offers not only valuable information on emotional development but, more importantly, she models an approach to understanding children which takes them seriously and respects their diversity. Each time I read a part of her book, I find myself listening more closely to my daughter, trying to hear what she's really telling me.

—Linda Williams

•

Well-equipped modern households in Brobdingnag keep a monster in their closets. When hooked up to an electrical wall outlet it inflates with a deafening roar and sucks everything in its path into its chromium-plated jaw. "It's nothing, dear. Only a vacuum cleaner!" *Only* a vacuum cleaner. Dear Lady, I can only hope that one morning you will rise from your bed and encounter a roaring iron monster twice your size, steadily eating a path toward you, its monster guts shrieking with the labor of unspeakable digestion. I can only hope, Madam, that you will ignore the sales talk and take to your heels.

•

The panda's eye has fallen out. An empty socket and the first glimpse of the cotton entrails that pull out easily now in an urgent, sickening search. And suddenly the panda is a flaccid sack and horror spreads over you. The panda is no more. He is a nothing, and for the first time the thought comes over you that *you* could lose your stuffing and become a nothing. "Never mind, dear. Don't cry so. We can get another panda." "NO! NO! NO!" And no words can be found in this new tongue, the English language, to tell of the dreadful secret tugged from the bowels of the panda.

•

Thirty-month-old Julia finds herself alone in the kitchen while her mother is on the telephone. A bowl of eggs is on the table. An urge is experienced by Julia to make scrambled eggs. She reaches for the eggs, but now the claims of reality are experienced with equal strength. Her mother would not approve. The resulting conflict within the ego is experienced as "I want" and "No, you mustn't." and the case for both sides is presented and a decision arrived at within the moment. When Julia's mother returns to the kitchen, she finds her daughter cheerfully plopping eggs on the linoleum and scolding herself sharply for each plop, "NoNoNo. Mustn't dood it. NoNoNo. *Mustn't* dood it!"

THE RISING SUN
NEIGHBORHOOD NEWSLETTER

David often sketches people on buses and other kinds of public places and gives them the sketches. Poor people, he's noticed, expect to pay for the sketch and rich people expect to get it free.

WHY ARE THESE four the most popular books on child rearing? What they have in common is that each reports warmly a wide range of actual family experience — different kinds of kids, parents, situations, what seems to work and what doesn't. This is practical advice from peers, minus experts or ideology (or all that but not the paid kind). Parents encouraging and helping each other — in the books it's right useful, around you in life it's even better. —SB

Ourselves and Our Children

America today is so wrangled and tangled that most parents must struggle with feeling bewildered and lost. This book addresses itself to them, to the incredible isolation that new parents feel. It is about the new forms of parenthood and families, shared parenting, communes, gay parents, lovers, single parents, and stepparents.

Society does not automatically take care of us or our children. Families feel ignored as second class citizens among the growing population of childless adults. Children in American today are treated with suspicion, fear, over-control, and mindless criticism on a mass level.

Raising kids is a potent force in our personal development, part teaching, part Zen kamikaze future dabbling, part pure survival. Parents often need help getting through the crises and despair, the isolation and entanglements. They need to hear the groans and cries of joy from other parents who are, after all, just kids too, all learning the Great Game together, growing up together. Parents have parents too. In the endless cycle, the beat goes on.

The authors have written collectively, collaborating on the whole, yet individualizing their experiences. (They also did **Our Bodies, Ourselves**, *p. 344.) The impact of simple truths, realized collectively, illuminates the message in this work. It is feminist, it is full of love, it is carefully considered, and right on the money.*
—Mountain Girl

Ourselves and Our Children
(A Book By and For Parents)
Boston Women's Health Book Collective
1978; 288 pp.
$6.95 postpaid from:
Random House
455 Hahn Road
Westminster, MD 21157
or Whole Earth Household Store

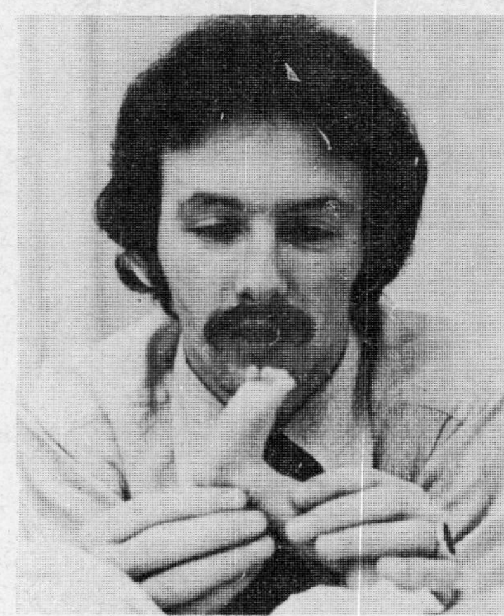

•

The early years are perhaps the most intense period of parenting. They are both crazy and wonderful. In the middle of them you constantly think, I'll never, ever live through this. They are driving me nuts, draining me dry. Occasionally, something happens to let us know that we're different for having survived them — maybe better because of them. Having cared for our own kids through strained peaches and fevers and tantrums and nightmares, we may have grown a capacity to notice and respond:

I was shopping in the food co-op late one afternoon. There was a woman there with a child who was screaming with exhaustion. She was trying to weigh vegetables and tend the child all at once. The bag over the handles of the stroller was overloaded and threatened to tip the baby out onto the floor. All around her other adults went about their shopping as if nothing was happening. I don't know how they could ignore her. I'd been there before and could remember what I'd wanted. I went over, and began to get the groceries she still needed, while she picked up the baby and walked him round and round. In two minutes he was asleep and she could be at peace.

Kids: Day In and Day Out

A wonderful big fat book containing a tremendous amount of good ideas and advice for parents. Much of the information is quite good and some pieces of advice are completely contradictory to others — a piece advising never to strike your child next to one which describes exactly how to hit your kid. It gives one the liberating feeling that there is no "one right way," no formula for successful child rearing. Whatever choices are made must simply be appropriate to the particular parents and children involved. A fascinating, helpful book.
—Lewis Engel

Kids: Day In and Day Out
(A parents' manual)
Elisabeth Scharlatt, Editor
1979; 531 pp.
$7.95 postpaid from:
Simon and Schuster
Attn: Order Department
1230 Avenue of the Americas
New York, NY 10020
or Whole Earth Household Store

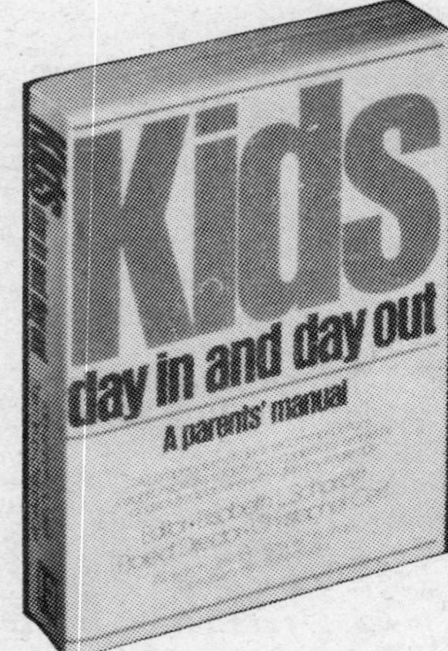

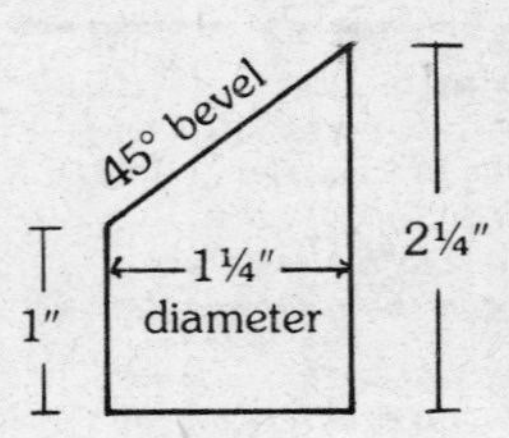

How can you tell if a toy is too small to be trusted in the hands of a child under three years of age? According to the Toy Manufacturers of America, a plaything presents an unacceptable risk of being swallowed if it fits, "in an uncompressed state," inside a "truncated right cylinder" with these dimensions.

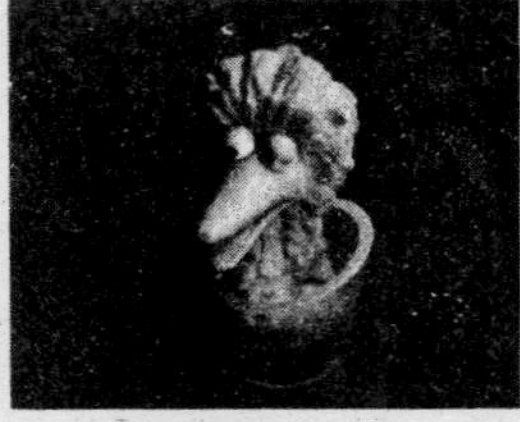

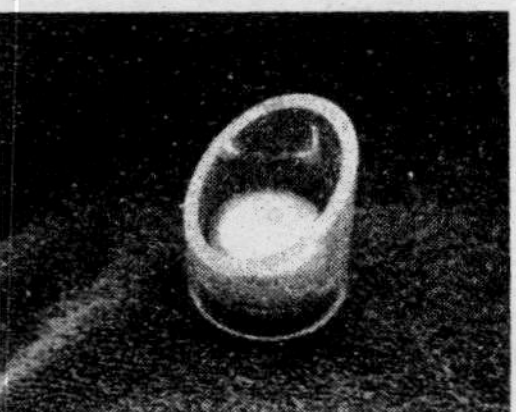

The truncated right cylinder. A Big Bird finger puppet passes with flying colors, but a sterling silver Tiffany yo-yo fails to make the grade. (No need to fret: if you've passed your third birthday, you're entitled to use the yo-yo.)

•

Try a Little Craziness

I've found that when a kid is acting in a really irrational way, it's pointless to be rational. You have to do something just as crazy. Once my friend's child was having a terrible temper tantrum and was kicking and screaming and totally uncontrollable. Finally I took her in my arms, wrapped her in a towel like a straightjacket, carried her into the bathroom, and sprinkled water on her. She was so startled she just looked at me and said, "Why did you do that?" And I said, "Because I didn't know what else to do." Then I asked her what she would have done if I had been kicking and screaming like that. She thought for a minute — and had no answer. We laughed about it and a few minutes later she asked, "Would you do that again?"

She still says to me (two years later) "Remember that time you wrapped me in a towel?" And we laugh.

•

The Mother Strike

One of my most strategic mother-moves is to go on strike. A strike is better than "I'm going to have a nervous breakdown," 'cause they know you ain't about to have a breakdown without a sitter. . . .

About my strikes. First I make sure there's enough food in the refrigerator and all the clothes are clean. And you can't strike when one of the children has a cold. . . . While on strike, it's a good idea to wear something flashy . . . I have a red mini dress I wear each time 'cause it dazzles them. Stay on strike 'til you get a definite commitment on things like sweeping the floor, making beds without being told, watering the plants, etc.

The Parenting Advisor

Advice and viewpoints on child rearing compiled from over 800 sources. A good resource if you feel you'd like to have more than one opinion. Topics covered range from medical advice to physiological and psychological development, to modern aspects of parenting such as the changing role of the working mother. At the bookstore where my husband works, this is the number 1 most-asked-for guide, even over Dr. Spock!
—Evelyn Eldridge-Diaz

The Parenting Advisor
Frank Caplan, Editor
1976; 569 pp.
$6.95 postpaid from:
Doubleday and Company
501 Franklin Avenue
Garden City, NY 11530
or Whole Earth Household Store

•

Choosing a Pet

If you want a pedigreed dog, locate a reputable breeding kennel. If you want a mongrel, try the pound. Since there are so many homeless cats, why not adopt one from your local animal shelter?

Before you acquire a dog or cat, make sure your child is not allergic to animal fur. Let her handle the pet; if her face turns red or if she has a sudden coughing spell, you may have an allergic child. In that case, wait an hour or so to see if the symptoms persist. If you are in any doubt, consult with your doctor before buying a pet.

Rodents are easily cared for and are clean and docile enough to be handled. They require less care than cats or dogs, are soft and warm, and make good companions for children. Their food requirements are simple: rabbits, guinea pigs, hamsters, mice and gerbils eat prepared food pellets, seeds, fruits, and vegetables.

Rabbits are very gentle and love to be held and stroked. Indoors, their cage should be all-wire with a removable metal tray-type bottom for easy cleaning. If your rabbit is kept outdoors, it should live in a hutch constructed of wood, with a wire mesh floor and door, and an enclosed section that offers protection from severe weather conditions.

Guinea pigs and mice are social animals; several of these can be caged together without fear of their fighting except during and right after pregnancy and birth.

Infants and Mothers

If you buy only one book when your baby is born, it should be this one. Brazelton treats infants and their parents as individuals. Other books seem to assume that all newborns are pretty much alike; Brazelton shows that from birth each baby has its own style, its own patterns of activity and response. "The baby" in other books always made me uneasy because it never did the crazy things my baby did; but in Brazelton's portraits of three types of babies and their parents I found glimpses of my daughter and myself that enlightened and comforted me and helped me recognize and respect my child's individual style. When her behavior bumped into my preconceptions, Brazelton reminded me that it was my expectations that were wrong, not the baby.

Brazelton squashes the ideal mother myth. He recognizes that there are as many ways of parenting as there are parents. While he offers plenty of suggestions for dealing with specific problems, he also offers support for parents in finding their own best way. **Infants and Mothers** *is probably the most complete book on the first year of life. It covers the kind of information you find in Dr. Spock and is far more enjoyable to read. Brazelton has a second book,* **Toddlers and Parents**, *that deals with the second and third years. It's also terrific; but I'm not reviewing it because once you've read his first book, you won't need any encouragement to pick up the second.*
—Linda Williams

Infants and Mothers
(Differences in Development)
T. Berry Brazelton, M.D.
1969; 296 pp.
$7.95 postpaid from:
Dell Publishing Company
1 Dag Hammarskjold Plaza
245 East 47th Street
New York, NY 10017
or Whole Earth Household Store

←
All of these bits of play at feeding time may be exasperating for a mother who is in a hurry. They are solid gold for the infant. It is his most receptive time. His physiological needs are being met. He is in a satisfied, receptive state, and each experience that occurs at this time must take on a heightened value. A baby savoring these moments is like a chubby old man savoring his cigar at the end of a delicious, filling meal.

How to Parent

So many child psychology books leave an unsure new parent more anxious or even guilty feeling. This one builds confidence.

How to Parent *is both a practicable review of child psychology and an excellent catalog of toys, books, records, equipment, parental survival, and inexpensive do-it-yourself materials and projects useful in a child's physical, emotional and intellectual development.*

The text concentrates on the different stages of development from birth to six years, offering the most basic findings of behavioral science in relation to each stage, and usable advice on how to help a child structure his self-concept to become a self-regulating person. Most important, the author insists the application of these findings and advice be guided by the feel of childhood — a contact with the child within you that you once were, and that parents must have the wisdom to follow their own hearts, no matter what the "experts" say.

—*Faye Kesey*

More Dodson: **How to Father** (1974; $2.50 postpaid from New American Library, P.O. Box 120, 120 Woodbine, Bergenfield, NJ 07621) *and* **How to Grandparent** (1980; $8.95 postpaid from J.B. Lippincott Company, East Washington Square, Philadelphia, PA 19105).

—*SB*

How to Parent
Fitzhugh Dodson
1973; 444 pp.

$2.50 postpaid from:
New American Library
P.O. Box 120
120 Woodbine
Bergenfield, NJ 07621
or Whole Earth
Household Store

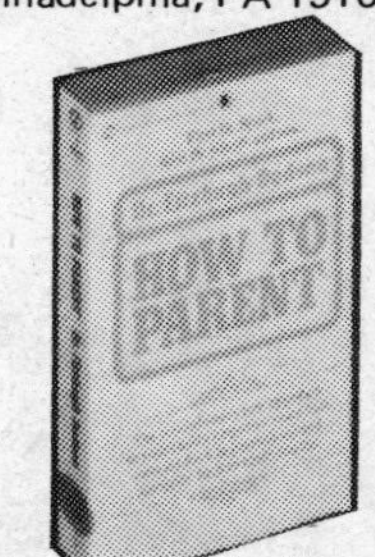

•

Let's be very clear: *you cannot spoil an infant.* Cuddle your infant as much as you want; you won't spoil him. Sing and coo to him as much as you want; you won't spoil him. Pay attention to him as often as he cries; you won't spoil him. The best thing that can happen to your baby psychologically speaking is to have as many of his needs gratified and to have as few frustrations as possible. His ego or sense of selfhood is too tender and immature to be able to cope with much frustration now. There will be plenty of time for life to teach him about frustrations when he is older.

•

Threats deal with the future, but children live in the present. Therefore, threats are useless in improving the future behavior of a child.

The Open Family Books

Six so far in this noteworthy series of books for parents and children together addressing some of the toughest episodes of real-life family soap opera — death, divorce, handicaps, adoption, phobias, and serious illness.

Each is an interesting story with good photographs, a big text for kids, a small text for parents (kids welcome), and remarkable insight. On subjects where the child is afraid to ask and you're unsure how to begin to explain, these books can break the ice.

—*SB*
[Suggested by Alice Gerrard]

The Open Family Books
(For Parents and Children Together)
Sara Bonnett Stein

About Dying
1974; 47 pp.
$7.95 postpaid

About Handicaps
1974; 47 pp.
$7.95 postpaid

About Phobias
1979; 47 pp.
$6.95 postpaid

The Adopted One
1979; 47 pp.
$6.95 postpaid

A Hospital Story
1974; 47 pp.
$7.95 postpaid

On Divorce
1979; 47 pp.
$6.95 postpaid

all from:
Walker and Company
720 Fifth Avenue
New York, NY 10019
or Whole Earth
Household Store

Like the dead bird,
he was put in a box.
It was called
a coffin.
Eric wondered what
he looked like now.
He wanted to keep
the coffin,
with Grandpa in it.

—**About Dying**

Taking Care of Your Child

A companion volume to Vickery and Fries' **Take Care of Yourself: A Consumer's Guide to Medical Care** *(p. 321),* **Taking Care of Your Child** *includes decision charts — clinical algorithms — for the 91 most common childhood medical problems. Additional brief, solid chapters on pregnancy, birth, physical and psychological development, school problems, and immunizations. Includes a log for recording your child's immunization records.*

The best available home medical guide for parents.

—*Tom Ferguson, M.D.*

Taking Care of Your Child
(A Parents' Guide to Medical Care)
Robert H. Pantell, M.D.,
James F. Fries, M.D., and
Donald M. Vickery, M.D.
1977; 409 pp.

$7.95 postpaid from:
Addison-Wesley
Publishing Company
Jacob Way
Reading, MA 01867
or Whole Earth
Household Store

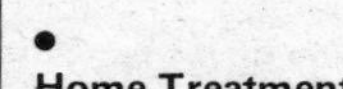

•

Home Treatment

The home treatment for recurrent abdominal pain requires a common-sense approach. Care may include clear liquid feedings, some time in a hot tub, and some gentle rubbing of the belly. A child will often tell you what makes him or her feel better. In addition, an effort should be made to link the cause of the abdominal pain with the symptom. Talking with your child about what is going on in school and what may be upsetting him or her can often be profitable. Children sometimes exploit abdominal pain in order to get attention or get their own way. Your own judgment will guide you in these cases.

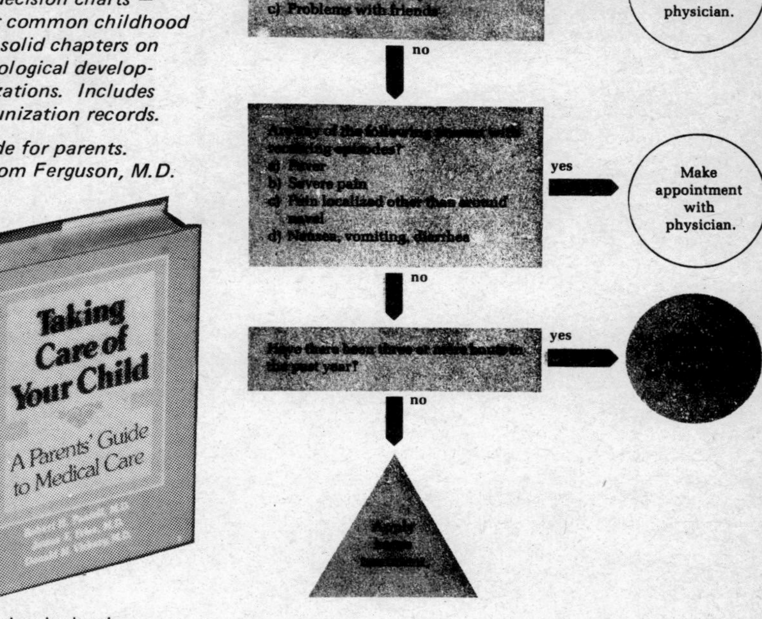

P.E.T.

For parents looking for an alternative to being strictly authoritarian, overly permissive, or oscillating between the two extremes, this book presents a systematic way to change your parental style. Called a "no-lose" method for resolving family and generational conflict, Parent Effectiveness Training teaches "active listening" — the language of acceptance, rather than that of moralizing, dictating, blaming, ridiculing, and all the other vocabularies of control. Dr. Gordon relates numerous stories in which parent-child tensions were resolved in creative and healthy ways, using techniques which are spelled out in detail in this book. Gordon's suggestions are eminently reasonable — they require only that parents put some energy and perseverance into changing the way they deal with their children.

—*Doris Herrick*

P.E.T.
(Parent Effectiveness Training: The Tested New Way to Raise Responsible Children)
Dr. Thomas Gordon
1970; 338 pp.

$2.95 postpaid from:
New American Library
P.O. Box 120
120 Woodbine
Bergenfield, NJ 07621
or Whole Earth
Household Store

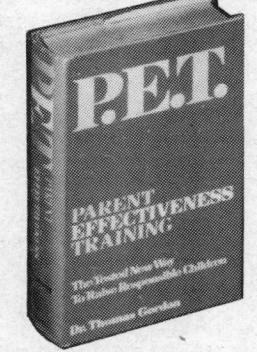

•

If parents could learn only one thing from this book, I wish it were this: Each and every time they force a child to do something by using their power or authority, they deny that child a chance to learn self-discipline and self-responsibility.

Charles, a seventeen-year-old son of two very strict parents who used their power constantly to get Charles to do his homework, made this admission; "Whenever my parents are not around, I find it impossible to pull myself out of the chair in front of the TV set. I am so used to their making me go do my homework, I cannot find *within myself* any power to make me go do it when they are not at home."

How to Start Your Own Preschool Playgroup

Parents of young children will find here delightful, commonsensical advice on solving one of their biggest problems: how to manage time for a job/studies/preservation of sanity, by providing child care that is affordable/reliable/beneficial to the child. Harriet Watts' answer is the organization of preschool playgroups of five or six children, with each parent supervising the group for one morning a week and having the other four weekday mornings free. She gives complete, nitty-gritty advice on legal, psychological and logistical concerns, with suggestions on how to get started, what equipment to have, what activities to plan, and how to make the experience a rewarding one for both children and parents. A warm, practical book obviously written out of a desire to share personal experience, meeting a real need at a very moderate price.

—*Doris Herrick*

How to Start Your Own Preschool Playgroup
Harriet M. Watts
1973; 153 pp.

$2.95 postpaid from:
Universe Books
381 Park Avenue South
New York, NY 10016

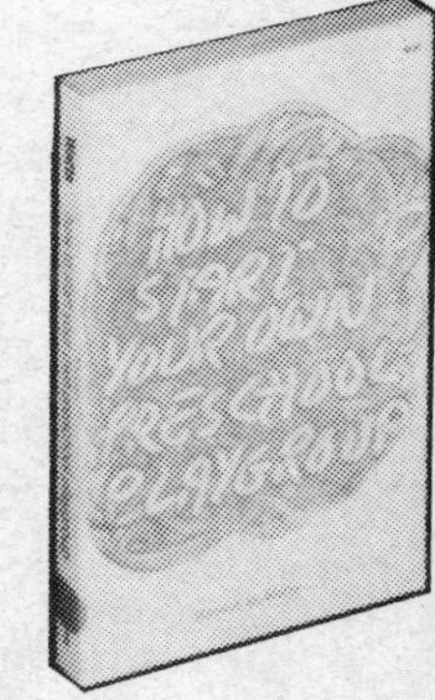

•

When casting about for members, you will have fewer problems if you are careful to limit the age span. The difference between a two-year-old and one age three is great, as any mother knows. A child of two will try to destroy what his three-year-old friend creates. He tires more easily and has a span of concentration of what seems like 30 seconds. In other words, put the two in the same pot and you can expect all sorts of toil and trouble to bubble up. The injection of a four-year-old might seem more successful, but I feel the older child tends to get cheated. His coordination and understanding are just that much more highly developed, and even if he does not show his boredom, his time would be more fruitfully spent with his peers. It is also extremely difficult for a mother to compensate for this difference with individual attention or separate projects. A group of three-year-olds can become one terrible tornado if neglected for any length of time.

THE RISING SUN
NEIGHBORHOOD NEWSLETTER

Stewart and Patty hiking around San Quentin found an old prisoners' graveyard with gravestones that had no names, no dates — only numbers.

Community Playthings

Solid, long-lasting, great looking toys — quality goods. The catalog includes a variety of furniture and toys for disabled kids. Everything has a one year warranty. These toys are the products and income of the Rifton New York Bruderhof Community. It shows. —SB

Community Playthings
Catalog
free from:
Community Playthings
Rifton, NY 12471

Workhorse Tricycle — $74.50

Unit Block Family Sets
F135 Three-Year-Old Set Unit Blocks, 32 blocks in 7 shapes. 18 lbs. $21.50

Rifton Wheelmobile — $74.50

Affectionately named by the children who first tested this movement facilitator for us, it enables otherwise non-ambulatory children to play actively at floor level. The vehicle tips forward to allow self mounting by the child and then tips back onto a rear swivel caster for further maneuvering. Child propels vehicle by turning 8" wheels in a forward or backward direction. Ideal for the spina bifida child, it helps in the development of the upper torso as well as being an aid to the child's mobility. High back and handle allow the child to be pushed "wheelchair" fashion when necessary. The Wheelmobile comes with a seat belt, and can be folded up for convenient storage.

Child Life Play Specialties

Playground-type stuff from doorway gym to elaborate swing sets. Kits available that save 20%. —SB

Child Life Play Specialties
Catalog
free from:
Child Life Play Specialties, Inc.
55 Whitney Street
Holliston, MA 01746

Complete Fire Chief Swing Set, 4 place, as pictured but without 8 ft. slide. This includes Double Bronko, Toddlers Swing (not the Leapin Lena as pictured). Trapeze Bar & Rings, Light-n-Flexi, 2 Cleated Boards, Net, Pole and Knotted Rope. Age 2 to 12. (truck 315 lb.) $495

Kids and Cash

Money is still the last taboo subject. Not gold prices, stocks, and house costs but what you earn and how you place it. Kids have to deal with money usually without much help and without any clear guidelines of what to do with it or how to think about it.

Here's a book, written by two financial consultants, which gives you straight advice, procedures, and suggestions for dealing with all the issues as kids grow up. From buying kid's love to the actual purposes of allowances to over a hundred ways for kids to earn their own, it's filled with up-front advice.

If you're afraid of money, in awe of money, think of it as the root of all evil, or love it, this book might blow some of the soot out of your mind and prevent your passing on your madness to the next generation. The book could help parents to teach children how to handle money and understand its value. The section on kid businesses is thrown in for the capitalists of tomorrow. —Jim Fadiman

Kids and Cash
(Solving a Parent's Dilemma)
Ken Davis and Tom Taylor
1979; 280 pp.
$8.95 postpaid from:
Oak Tree Publications
1175 Flintkote Avenue
Suite C
San Diego, CA 92121
or Whole Earth Household Store

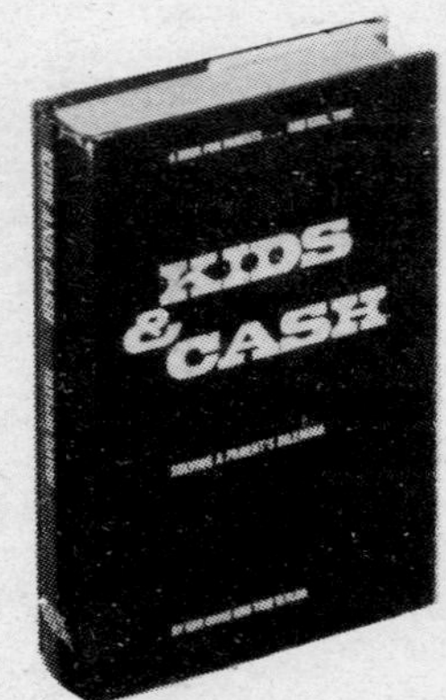

•

You'll probably never become an expert at any job unless you learn how to ask for help. What better person to ask than someone who has already become an expert at what you're interested in doing. Experts can tell you things you will never find in a book, and probably things your parents don't know either. Does your mother clean her kitchen walls with a cleanser she bought at the supermarket? If so, she's using the wrong thing. She could use tri-sodium phosphate (TSP), which can be purchased at a hardware store and probably do a much better job in half the time or less. What's the best wax for floors? How do you clean oil off concrete?

A store that sells janitorial supplies can give you the answers to these and many other questions. Why should they bother? Because you're probably going to be one of their customers and buy your supplies from them.

In addition, you will find that most adults are both flattered and pleased when a youngster shows some interest in how they make their living. Most people are very happy to help a kid get a start doing something on his own. Don't forget that, once upon a time, all adults were kids themselves, so don't be afraid to ask them for help. Ask your nurseryman for advice on plants and gardening, the hardware store for tips on how to sharpen knives and tools. A little advice can start you off earning a lot more money with a lot less frustration.

Constructive Playthings

Fat catalog. Lotsa toys, playground gear, and especially classroom and learning stuff — from great (Montessori) to stupid (metric). Especially handy for home teaching (p. 568). —SB

Constructive Playthings
Catalog
$1 from:
Constructive Playthings
2008 West 103rd Terrace
Leawood, KS 66206

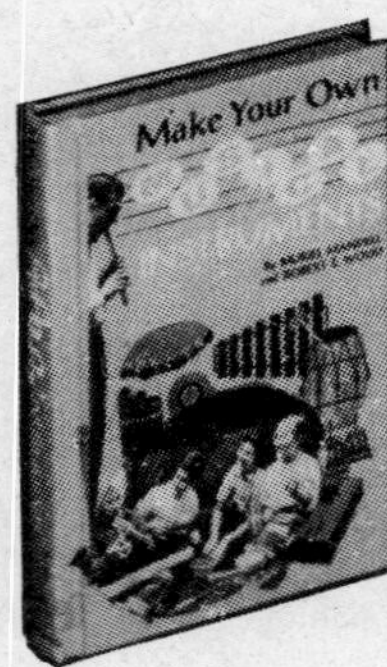

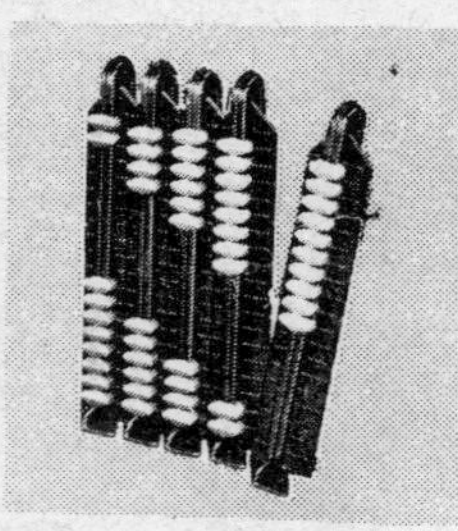

ARITHME-STICKS
Used individually, sticks are used for counting and number fact building. Joined together, the sticks are an abacus or number panel. 5 sticks 8½" tall, 100 plastic counting beads which fit on sticks, complete manual.
No. MB-7601 ..... **$10.00**

TUNABLE TOM TOMS
These double head tom toms represent quality in sound and appearance. Tough styrene plastic shells have replaceable heads that are not affected by humidity. Tuning is by an adjustment device that increases cord tension. Mallet included.
No. RB-1113 Small 5" x 4½" **$6.00**
No. RB-1114 Medium 5" x 6½" **$7.30**
No. RB-1114X Large 5" x 8½" **$9.60**

Make Your Own Musical Instruments

This book is full of ideas for making musical instruments out of flower pots, coconuts, cheese boxes, bottles, cans, shells, hoses . . . junk. Best of all, perhaps, the authors encourage young people to have fun with music, avoid the intimidation that often turns kids off to learning an instrument. (See instrument making, pp. 473 - 475.) —Scott Beach

Make Your Own Musical Instruments
Muriel Mandell and Robert E. Wood
1957; 128 pp.
$6.95 postpaid from:
Sterling Publication Co.
Two Park Avenue
New York, NY 10016
or Whole Earth Household Store

↓
Box Banjo

Raid the kitchen for the main ingredient for a box banjo. It can be cooked up in a matter of minutes but it sounds surprisingly like the real instrument.

Search for a sturdy small carton — from cereal or dry milk or whipped butter, for instance. It may be square or round but should not be more than 2 inches deep. Use scotch tape or gummed paper to anchor the cover on or to seal the spout.

Lay the box flat on its widest surface and carve away. One inch from the left edge, cut out a semi-circular sound hole. Another inch down to the right, cut a 1-inch slit. To make a bridge, cut a 2-inch square of heavy cardboard. From two corners remove half an inch squares. Your bridge will have a one-inch tab.

Fit the bridge into the slit, and string your banjo with 4 rubber bands of different sizes. The smaller ones will stretch more and play higher notes. Pluck them gently with your fingers or with a used kitchen match.

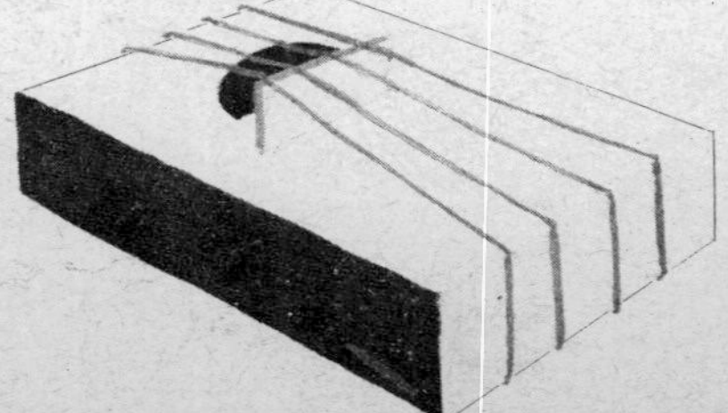

CoEvolution Quarterly
SUBSCRIPTIONS AND PRODUCTS

(For Whole Earth Household Store Book Orders see blue order form)

the ongoing Whole Earth Catalog

We enthusiastically review **Serials Review** on p. 518 of this **Catalog.** They reviewed us in their April/June 1979 issue:

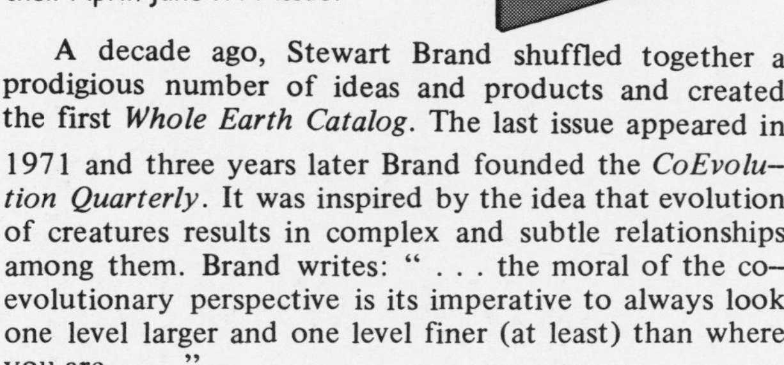

A decade ago, Stewart Brand shuffled together a prodigious number of ideas and products and created the first *Whole Earth Catalog*. The last issue appeared in 1971 and three years later Brand founded the *CoEvolution Quarterly*. It was inspired by the idea that evolution of creatures results in complex and subtle relationships among them. Brand writes: " . . . the moral of the co-evolutionary perspective is its imperative to always look one level larger and one level finer (at least) than where you are . . . . "

Reflecting this unifying formula, *CQ* is a sophisticated descendent of the *Catalog*. Every fan will recognize the similar organization and the same personalized approach of the reviews. Even the openness of the staff has carried over with gossip and complete financial reports. *CQ*'s sophistication is apparent in its disciplined and coherent presentation of widely eclectic ideas, problems, and techniques.

Each issue is organized into ten or so sections and most issues emphasize a particular subject. For example, a recent issue began with a 90-page analysis of broadcasting, while another examined solar heaters used at the turn of the century. Typically, think pieces are followed by several capsule reviews of related books, periodicals, tools, and other items. Articles range from an indictment of the metric system to using road kills in research, and from science fiction by J.G. Ballard to remarks on death by Dr. Elisabeth Kubler-Ross. Authors are a satisfying mix of the famous and the unknown. A comic strip by R. Crumb and other cartoon contributions round out the offerings.

There are no advertisements. Despite the low budget this prohibition must cause, the editing, layout and printing are uniformly meticulous and readable. *CQ* features sturdy covers and strong binding, but the paper is only newsprint quality.

As a book review medium of the kind libraries favor, *CQ* is an excellent companion for a quiet evening by the fire. In a year, about 180 titles were described in the familiar *Catalog* fashion: full bibliographical information, an illustration, an excerpt, and a very brief signed review. Many reviews are written by staffers. The reviews are organized into the same subject sections as the articles. Occasionally, a long review is printed or a book review essay will be featured. For example, a special story-telling essay reviewed 15 titles. Timeliness is respected and most books are only a year or two old. The table of contents serves as a rough title index, but otherwise access is best achieved by browsing. *CQ* is a good, but limited, source for reviews of periodicals and pamphlets.

The clientele of most public libraries is as eclectic as the makeup of *CQ*. It is highly likely that a small but dedicated readership will materialize for this unusual periodical, especially in rural libraries. And it's a good value for the $14.00. Brand reports that *CQ* prints about a half million words a year. Some back issues are still available. Indexing is currently provided by *New Periodicals Index*, itself a very recent effort. On occasion, *CQ* publishes collections of its articles as separate books.

Barbara Conaty

SERIALS REVIEW April/June 1979

CoEvolution Quarterly Subscriptions Back Issues and Products
FOR YOURSELF
(For gifts, see over)

Total For Yourself
$
Total Enclosed For Yourself and Gifts
$

CoEvolution Quarterly Subscriptions and Back Issues

All subscriptions start with current issue unless you indicate otherwise, and are sent via surface mail.

☐ **1 Year** CoEvolution $14 (foreign $16)

☐ **2 Years** CoEvolution $25 (foreign $29)

☐ **Renewal** *Please check if this is a renewal*

☐ **First Class** U.S. & Canada, *add $5 for each year*
Air Mail, *for each year add:* Mexico & Central America $6; South America $9; Europe $9; all others $12.

☐ **Back Issues, $3**
See over. List by number:

Name ______

Address ______

zip ______

Please make sure your address is correct and complete, including zip or postal code number. Allow 5-6 weeks for delivery. Sorry, we don't bill.

CoEvolution Products

☐ **Next Whole Earth Catalog** $12.50

☐ **Post cards** $3 for ten cards

T-shirt $6, please indicate size and quantity:

☐ X-Small
☐ Small
☐ Med
☐ Large
☐ X-Large

☐ **One Million Galaxies Poster** $5 (sent UPS in continental U.S. All others $7.50) *See inside back cover of* **Catalog**

☐ **Biogeographical Map** $3.50 *See inside front cover of* **Catalog.**

☐ **Space Colonies Book** $4.50

☐ **Two Cybernetic Frontiers** $2

See over for product descriptions

6271

TEAR ALONG PERFORATIONS TO SEPARATE ORDER FORM AND ENVELOPE

Is your check enclosed?

NO POSTAGE NECESSARY IF MAILED IN THE UNITED STATES

BUSINESS REPLY MAIL
FIRST CLASS PERMIT NO. 103
SAUSALITO, CA

POSTAGE WILL BE PAID BY ADDRESSEE

COEVOLUTION
P.O. Box 428
Sausalito,
California 94966

From:

Zip

CoEvolution Quarterly

GIFTS

ORDERS FOR YOURSELF SEE OVER
(For Whole Earth Household Store Book Orders see blue order form)

Total this gift
(Add to total for yourself)
$

TO Name ______________________

Address ______________________

______________________ zip ______________________

Please make sure your address is correct and complete, including zip or postal code number. Allow 5-6 weeks for delivery. Sorry, we don't bill.

CoEvolution Quarterly Subscriptions and Back Issues

All subscriptions start with current issue unless you indicate otherwise, and are sent via surface mail.

- ☐ **1 Year** CoEvolution $14 (foreign $16)
- ☐ **2 Years** CoEvolution $25 (foreign $29)
- ☐ **Renewal** *Please check if this is a renewal*
- ☐ **First Class** U.S. & Canada, *add* $5 *for each year*
  Air Mail, *for each year add:* Mexico & Central America $6; South America $9; Europe $9; all others $12.
- ☐ **Back Issues,** $3
  See opposite. List by number:

____

CoEvolution Products

- ☐ **Next Whole Earth Catalog** $12.50
- ☐ **Post cards** $3 for ten cards

T-shirt $6, please indicate size and quantity:

- ☐ X-Small
- ☐ Small
- ☐ Med
- ☐ Large
- ☐ X-Large

- ☐ **One Million Galaxies Poster** $5 (Sent UPS in continental U.S. All others $7.50) *See inside back cover of* **Catalog.**
- ☐ **Biogeographical Map** $3.50 *See inside front cover of* **Catalog.**
- ☐ **Space Colonies Book** $4.50
- ☐ **Two Cybernetic Frontiers** $2.

6272

Send gift card from:

Name: ______________________

the artist cat goes crazy while the hand of fortune gives him the "craziness is money" award

CoEvolution Quarterly

BACK ISSUES AND PRODUCTS

See over for order forms

No. 26, Summer 1980
Native American running, an extensive article on amateur insemination by lesbians, Ivan Illich on vernacular values, Lynn Margulis on a new theory of how evolution happens, and "Some Peculiarities of the Cat, Harley."

No. 25, Spring 1980
Turning back the desert by planting trees, using light rail to revive public transportation, James Lovelock on being a self employed scientist, "Our Enemies, Ourselves" (on Russia), and an article on Shramadana —sharing energy.

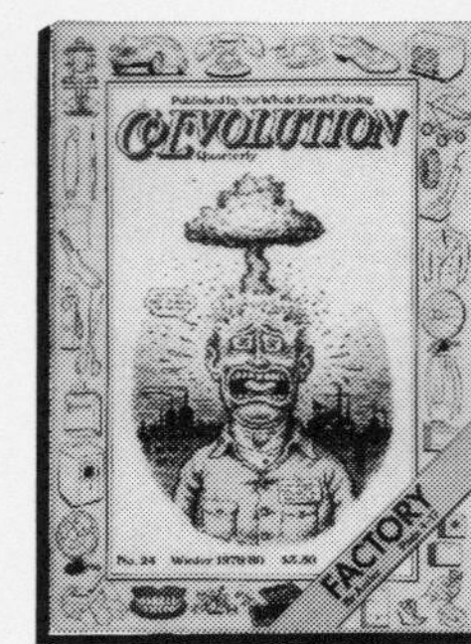

No. 24, Winter 1979/80
How corporate patenting o seeds will cause hundreds o plant species to be los forever, good solar buildin designs used throughout his tory, Gregory Bateson o ending the arms race, and a major poem on the de humanizing horror of factor work.

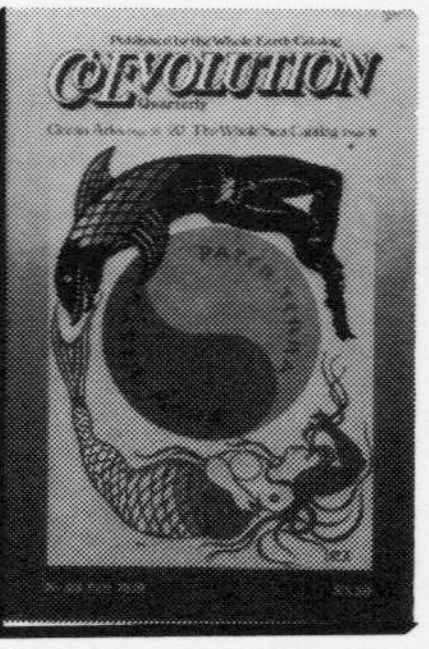

No. 23, Fall 1979
Special oceans issue—John Todd on ocean arks, articles on wooden boat restoration, the future of the fishing business, and antisubmarine warfare, and 30 pages of access to boat tools in the Whole Sea Catalog.

No. 22, Summer 1979
The Oregon women who forced the EPA to ban herbicides that cause birth defects, E.F. Schumacher's belief that tree crops could save British agriculture, what's happening in international radio, and details on Dungeons and Dragons and other fantasy games.

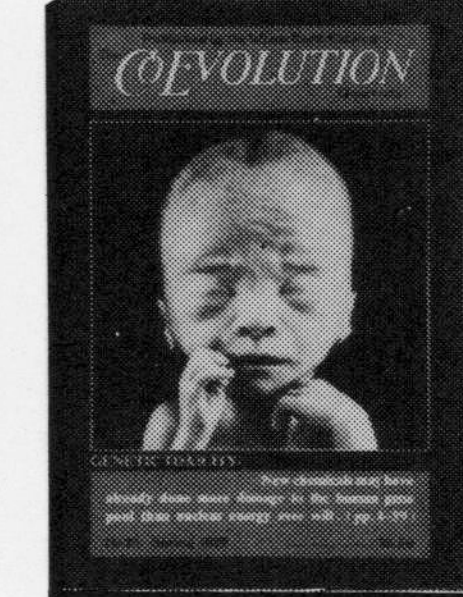

No. 21, Spring 1979
How chemicals are harming our genes, Dan O'Neill defying the Supreme Court by drawing Mickey Mouse, Judy Chicago on "Revelations o the Goddess," and 50 pages of reviews of important and unusual magazines.

Back issues are $3.
Issues 14, 15, 16, 17, 18, 19, and 20 are also available.
The current issue of The CoEvolution Quarterly is $4.

↑ **Whole Earth Postcards**
Ten Cards — **$3**

Space Colonies $4.50
The space colony dream, reviewed on p. 16

Two Cybernetic Frontiers $2
"Gregory Bateson" and "Computer Bums" reviewed on p. 537

World Biogeographical Provinces Map
22½″×39″ $3.50
See inside front cover of Catalog.

One Million Galaxies
39″×47″
$5 continental US. All othe $7.50
See Catalog inside back cover.

CoEvolution T-shirt $6
Dark blue, 100% cotton (will shrink slightly) with light blue and white winged Earth. Five sizes to fit every body.

Vhole Earth
Iousehold Store

3OOK ORDERS

*r CoEvolution Quarterly subscriptions and
oducts see ivory colored form*

RDERING INSTRUCTIONS

e these forms to order *books*
ed in the **Catalog** which
e "or Whole Earth
usehold Store" underneath
m.

ok Orders, by mail
ole Earth Household Store
ilding D, Fort Mason Center,
Francisco, California 94123

lephone orders
15) 441-7250
ISA/Master Charge
yment only)
00 am–4:30 pm Pacific Time

e Whole Earth Household Store
s formerly the Whole Earth
ck Store)

1 Print name and address to which you want the order shipped.
2 Print in the titles and quantities of the books you want, their **Catalog** page numbers and prices.
3 Total the prices of the books you are ordering.
4 For delivery in California add 6% tax (6½% for BART counties).
5 Add $2 to each order for packaging and delivery.
6 For rush orders UPS in the United States, add 40¢ for each book.
7 For foreign orders add 50¢ postage per book for each book over five. We also recommend International Registry Insurance, which costs an additional $3 per order.
8 Enclose payment in full with check or money order. VISA/Mastercharge customers print name from card, account no., Interbank no., Expiration Date, and sign your name.

ar along here to open order form

**Whole Earth
Household Store**

BOOK ORDERS FOR YOURSELF

(For gifts see below left)

Telephone orders
(415) 441-7250
(VISA/Master Charge payment only)
10:00 am–4:30 pm Pacific Time

FOR YOURSELF

Name
Address
Zip
Country
Telephone ( )

Quantity	Catalog page no.	Title	Price each	Total

hole Earth Household Store

GIFT BOOK ORDERS

rders for yourself see above right)

Name
dress
Zip
untry
ephone ( )

talog ge no.	Title	Total

ase make check or money order payable to:
ole Earth Household Store
Payment enclosed, check or money order
VISA ☐ Mastercharge
ount number
iration date Interbank no.
t name from card
ature

Total of Books	$
For delivery in California 6% tax	
6½% BART counties	
Packaging & delivery	$ 2.00
Rush orders (UPS) 40¢ per book	
International Registry see '7' above	
Total amount	$

*ry, no C.O.D.'s
reverse side for shipping details*

d Gift Order from: Name

Is your payment enclosed?

STAMP

From: Name
Address
Zip

**Whole Earth
Household Store**
Building D
Fort Mason Center
San Francisco,
CA 94123

Whole Earth Household Store

OUR STATEMENT

WE WILL DO OUR BEST to try to get your books to you as soon as we can. If for any reason you are dissatisfied with our products or service, please return the books to us and we will promptly refund your money.

Prices
Please bear in mind that prices are likely to change. If they do we will either ask you to make up the difference or return your check informing you of the new prices and ask you to reorder.

Our Location
If you would like to visit us please follow the map to our store in Fort Mason Center, San Francisco.

From the North—Take the Golden Gate Bridge and follow the signs to Marina Boulevard. Enter Fort Mason Center at Marina and Buchanan Streets.

From the South—Take Route 101 and get off at Franklin. Follow Franklin to Bay and turn left on Bay. Follow Bay to Laguna and turn right. Follow Laguna to the Fort Mason Center Entrance at Buchanan.

From the East Bay—Take the Bay Bridge and get off downtown at Broadway. Follow Broadway to Franklin and follow the directions from Franklin as given above.

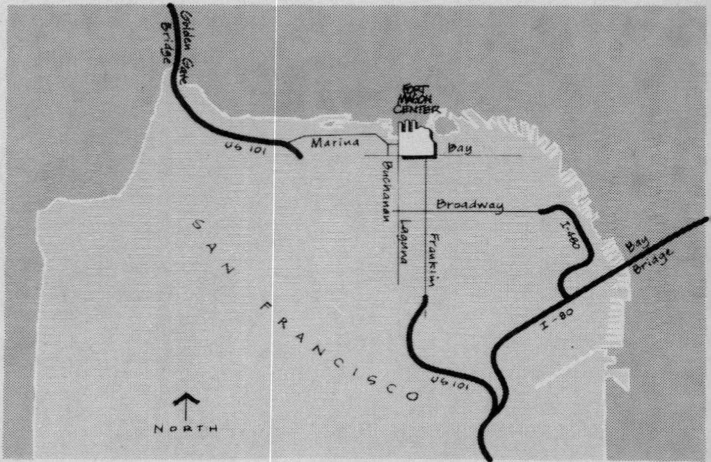

SHIPPING INFORMATION

Packaging and delivery
We ship U.S. Mail fourth class, Book Rate.
We will try to mail your package within 48 hours of receiving your order. Allow up to 4 weeks for delivery.

Rush Orders
For faster delivery we ship UPS. Please add 40¢ per book. Your package will usually reach you within 5-7 working days after we receive your order. All UPS shipments are automatically insured up to $100. Remember, UPS cannot deliver to post office boxes and rural route boxes. *We do not ship Express Mail.*

International Shipping
We ship foreign orders International Book Rate. For six (6) books or more please add 50¢ per additional book for shipping. If you would like to register your books (recommended), please add $3.00 for registry. *Please remember checks must be payable in U.S. dollars on a U.S. bank.*

Sorry, no C.O.D.'s.

Total of books	$
For delivery in California 6% tax	
6½% BART counties	
Packaging & delivery	$ 2.00
Rush orders (UPS) 40¢ per book	
Foreign orders—Add postage and insurance. See #7 in ordering instructions.	
Total amount	$

Please make check or money order payable to:
Whole Earth Household Store
☐ Payment enclosed, check or money order
☐ VISA ☐ Mastercharge

Account number ____________

Expiration Date ____________ Interbank no. ____________

Print name from card ____________

Signature ____________

Sorry, no C.O.D.'s
See reverse side for shipping details

Making Things

Hundreds of art/craft improvisations for hands of any age. Simple drawings and words show how to turn odds and ends into masks, puppets, toys, weaving looms, paper hangings. Most materials are either household salvage or minimal cost. Activities include paper making/9 kinds of printing/skate scooters/ spinners/cardboard racing turtles/pasta and paper clip beads/candle casting/ bread dough sculpture. Instructive and FUN.
—Betty Moss

Making Things
(The Hand Book of Creative Discovery)
Ann Wiseman
1973; 159 pp.

$4.95 postpaid from:
Little, Brown and Co.
200 West Street
Waltham, MA 02154

←
Cardboard Racing Turtles

My mother introduced this game to us as children and I've never seen it played anywhere. Yet it is so simple and such fun especially when grown-ups join in.

Use: A shirt cardboard. Trace a dish circle, draw head, tail, arms and legs.

Decorate with crayons or paint — make both sides like the front.

Cut out the turtle. Make string hole. Measure 10′ of string. Tie one end of string to table leg. Thread string through turtle. Pull string taut, and turtle will stand. Release and he'll flop forward. Pull-flop to the top of the string, flip him over and pull-flop home. Make 3. Find 2 friends and have a race.

←
Tin Can Lanterns

1. Fill can with water.
2. Put cans to freeze (approx. 2 days).
3. Draw design on can with crayon or marker.
4. Put frozen can on pillow or towel so it won't roll.
5. Use big and small nail holes for variation.
6. Use thin coat hanger wire for handles & hanging loops.

Learning for Little Kids

Ambitious book. How to make toys, toys to buy, books to consider, and advice — all organized by subject: self-care and safety, language, cooking and nutrition, sex and birth, death, illness, art, nature, music, fantasy, etc. Pretty neat.
—SB

Learning for Little Kids
Sandy Jones
1976; 232 pp.

$7.95 postpaid from:
Houghton-Mifflin Co.
Wayside Road
Burlington, MA 01803
or Whole Earth Household Store

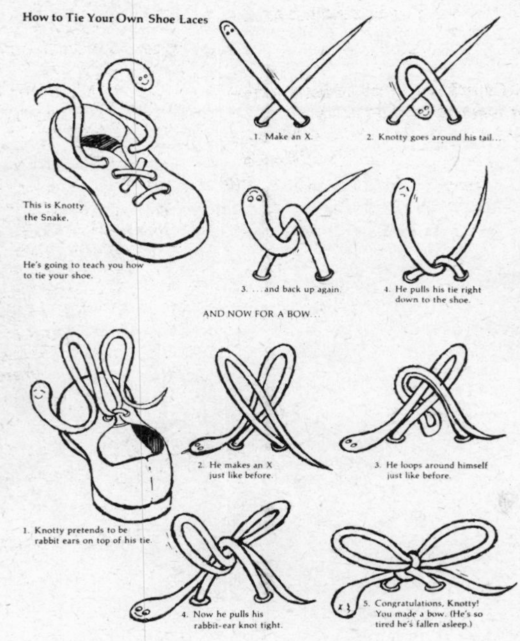

Tools for Water Play: Egg Beater, Eye Dropper, Plunger, Pump and Pitcher, Ping-Pong Balls, Corks, Funnel from the Top of a Plastic Jug, Shower Hose, Ladle

↑
Monkey Birthing Doll

A handmade sock doll that gives birth to a tiny baby. The umbilical cord snaps off and the baby may be snapped to the mother's breast to nurse. The company also offers a tiny backpack for the mother to carry the baby and a backpack for a child to carry both the baby and mother. Directions for making your own dolls, $1.25. Dolls demonstrating a caesarean delivery and specific operations such as a tonsillectomy or appendectomy can be ordered. Please send a stamped, self-addressed envelope for more information.

Monkey Business, Rt. 3 Box 153A, Celina, TN 38551. (Finished doll, $15; Backpack set, $2.)

←
Tweety Bird

A bubble bird that blows bubbles and tweets at the same time. Did you have one when you were a child? This bird is made of plastic. From the Childcraft "Toys that Teach" catalog. Price subject to change.

Childcraft Education Corp., 20 Kilmer Road, Edison, NJ 08817 ($2.50 ea., 6 for $11.95 + $1.95 shipping and handling).

•
Quiet Bedtime Stories and Beautifully Illustrated Picture Books

Goodnight Moon, Margaret Wise Brown, Harper & Row Pubs., Inc., Keystone Industrial Park, Scranton, PA 18512 ($3.95). A quiet sharing book about a bunny settling down for a night's sleep. Watch the little mouse creep across the pages!

Mr. Rabbit and the Lovely Present, Charlotte Zolotow, Harper & Row Pubs., Inc., Keystone Industrial Park, Scranton, PA 18512 ($3.95). Mr. Rabbit helps the little girl pick a present for her mother. Beautiful soft, dreamy pictures by Maurice Sendak.

Crayons

"Stockmar Wachsfarben" (wax-crayons). I have used them both in school and privately for many years. They are very clean to use, especially important for children, and have the most pure colors I have ever seen. If you want to have a real color-experience and do not only want to color objects pedantically, then these lend themselves to it. You can use them in many imaginative ways, many techniques. They come in a basic block-form or in sticks. They last a very long time. Nice modeling wax too.
—Hanna Wilson

Beeswax Crayons and Supplies
$3.50/8 colors (crayons)
Price list
free from:
St. George Book Service
The Melnickers
P.O. Box 225
Spring Valley, NY 10977

The Anti-Coloring Book

The authors believe that conventional coloring books lead to stereotyped art work and destroy creativity. They have produced an antidote — 45 pages of clever ideas and frames for pictures that the young artists can create themselves. There's enough variety to make this book fun for anyone. If anything could wean children from conventional coloring books, this series (there are two others) might.
—Alice Gerrard

The Anti-Coloring Book
Susan Striker and Edward Kimmel
1978; 48 pp.

$3.95 postpaid from:
Holt, Rinehart and Winston
383 Madison Avenue
New York, NY 10017
or Whole Earth Household Store

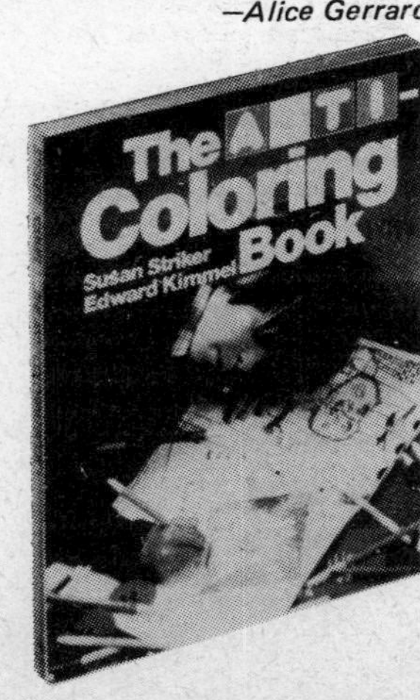

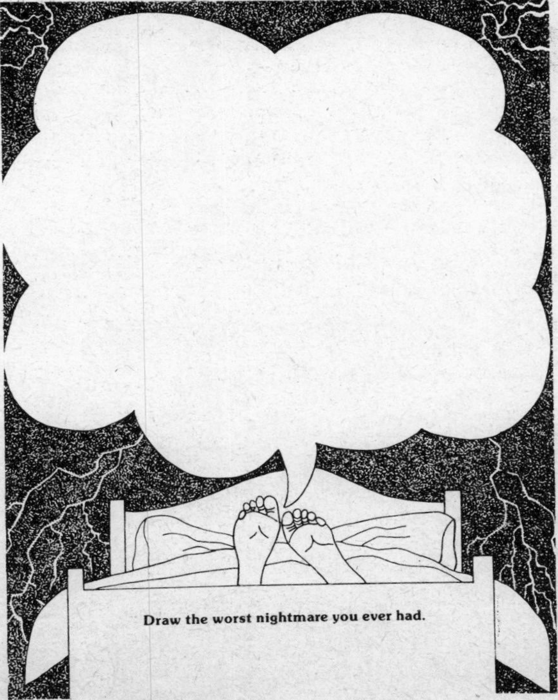

Draw the worst nightmare you ever had.

THE RISING SUN
NEIGHBORHOOD NEWSLETTER

I've noticed that when I meet people my own age who seem to have had a truly incredible number of adventures, they turn out to have not gone to college, so instead of doing one thing for four years they started doing two or three things a year as soon as they left high school.

Toy Book

*Want to make a waterscope and magnifier, or a hexaflexagon, or a rope machine (that makes real rope)? Simple instructions for these and 48 other toys and games, with plenty of photos and diagrams, make the **Toy Book** a must for kids and anybody else interested in conjuring up delightful playthings out of odds and ends and scraps of stuff around the house. Make your own discovery toys, pretending toys, games, building toys, action toys and design toys without spending much (if any) money. All the toys were designed and tested on a whole herd of children by a professional designer and toy consultant who helped design the Boston Children's Museum. For kids age 1 through 11 and parents of all descriptions.*

—Sylvia Jacobs

Toy Book
(Turtle Racers, Moustaches, and More Than 50 Other Good Toys to Make with Children)
Steven Caney
1972; 176 pp.

$5.95 postpaid from:
Workman Publishing
One West 39th Street
New York, NY 10018
or Whole Earth Household Store

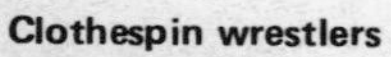

←
Clothespin wrestlers

Place your bets. Wind up the wrestlers — not too tight — and carefully put them down. Now quickly let go. For a few seconds the wrestlers will knock each other all over the place, but in the end, one wrestler will land on top of the other and be the winner. Sometimes neither wrestler will win. Is it a game of chance or a game of skill? Can you predict which wrestler will win? Does it make any difference how much you wind up the wrestlers or the way you put them down? Play is the process of finding out. You might try having clothespin wrestling contests, with winners playing winner. Maybe you know how to make a champion wrestler.

Materials: 2 clothespins, fat rubber band

Construction

Decorate each of the clothespins a different color, with the meanest looking faces you can draw. Round wood clothespins work best. Look carefully at the illustration, and hook the rubber band around both clothespins as shown. Now you're ready to wrestle.

Naturally Powered Old Time Toys

Believe it or not, there was once a time when moving toys were not battery users! I remember using some of the toys shown in this happy collection. Some were endlessly fascinating and some were frankly more interesting to the adults who brought them. All were great rainy afternoon whiler-awayers. This book categorizes the various devices by power source; rubber bands, gravity, steam, etc. and . . . (heh heh) Mystery. (The only one missing is the fly-powered airplanes we used to make. I guess the S.P.C.A. would frown on such things these days.) Anyway, it's well-illustrated with very clear directions and even some full-size patterns. I've added it to my own bookshelf.

—J. Baldwin

Naturally Powered Old Time Toys
(How to Make Sun Yachts, Sail Cars, a Monkey on a String, & Other Moving Toys)
Marjorie Henderson and Elizabeth Wilkinson
1978; 128 pp.

$6.95 postpaid from:
J.B. Lippincott Company
East Washington Square
Philadelphia, PA 19105

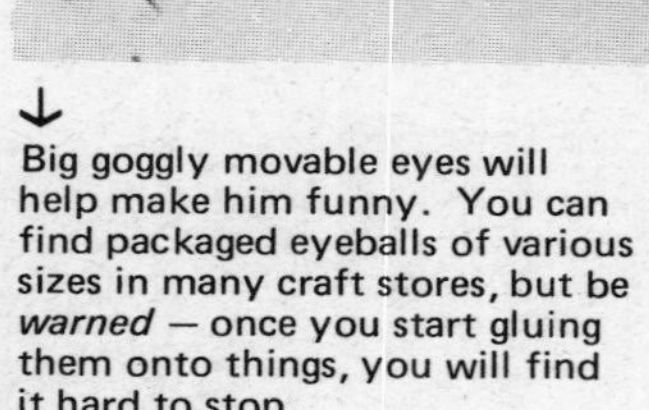

↓
Big goggly movable eyes will help make him funny. You can find packaged eyeballs of various sizes in many craft stores, but be *warned* — once you start gluing them onto things, you will find it hard to stop.

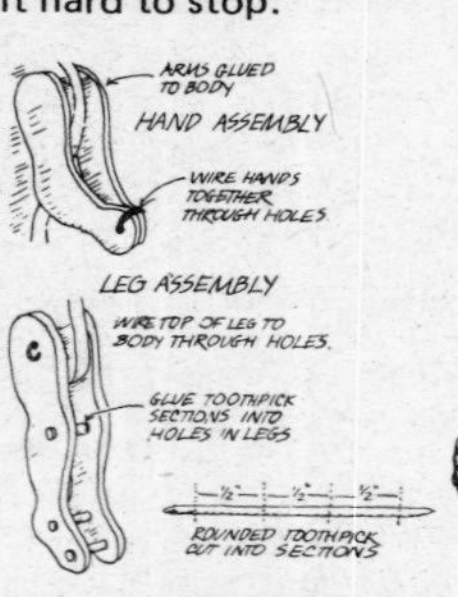

Uniquity

Adult therapy toy catalog that found out kids love the stuff too. Punchers, bashers, thrashers, exercisers, noise makers, and rambunctious games. Great. —SB

[Suggested by Dave Potvin]

Uniquity
Catalog

$ .25 from:
Uniquity
P.O. Box 6
Galt, CA 95632

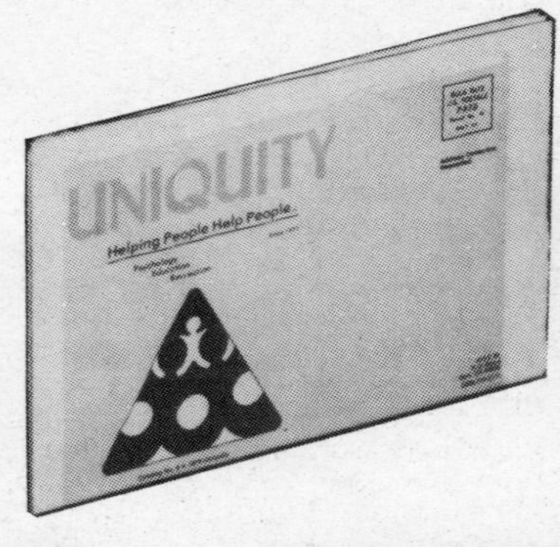

EncounterBat

Wanna Fight? Fighting is OK with EncounterBats. They provide a satisfying release from Anger, Hostility, Frustration, Stress and Excess Energy. For fun or serious fights. Perfect for Assertiveness Training, and for some, a real turn-on. The bats make a loud WHOMP when they hit, and the sound adds satisfaction to a good fight. Most people can be hit without feeling any pain. Kids love to use the bats between themselves and adults. School systems, institutions from preschools to penitentiaries, hospitals, mental health clinics, and people at home have used EncounterBats as an effective aid to anger release.

$35/pair

Sandtiquity

There's no better way to learn about space, form, and time than building sand castles. This book takes one method of sand castle construction and explains eloquently and with style how to build like the grand masters of gravity. (Somewhere there should be a book on the drip method — which gives rise to the Gaudi *[p. 215]* *Barcelona cathedral style of dribbled gothic. For this you dribble wet sand through your fist to make sand stalagmites of surprising ingenuity.)*

—David Wills

Sandtiquity
(Architectural Marvels You Can Build at the Beach)
Connie Simó, Kappy Wells and Malcolm Wells
1980; 111 pp.

$4.95 postpaid from:
Taplinger Publishing Co.
200 Park Avenue South
New York, NY 10003
or Whole Earth Household Store

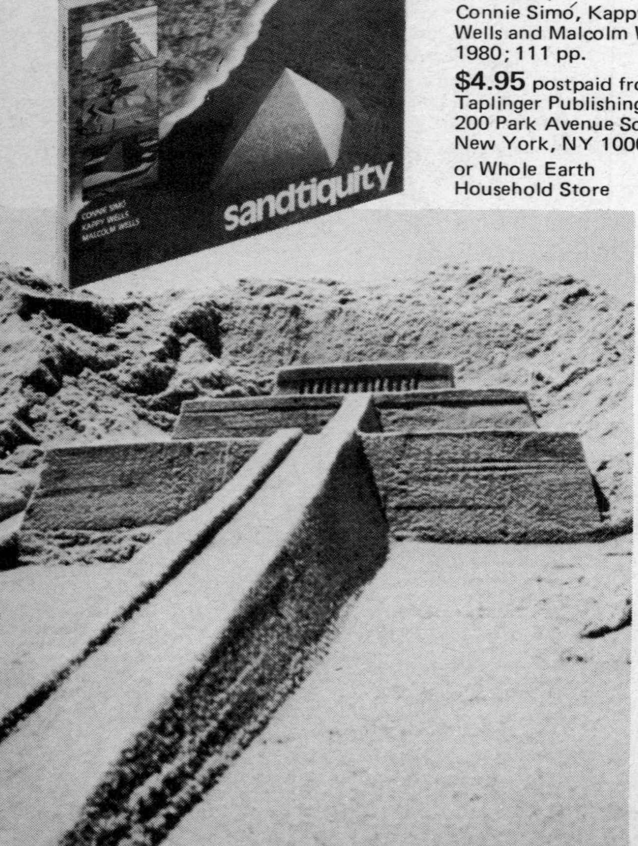

←
First we brush away the dry surface sand and heap up the damp sand into a mound half again as high as the finished size.

Then we pat it into a rough shape, compacting the sand as we work.

We begin to carve the sides with our straightedge. A bold, confident stroke works best.

We go over each face several times, packing the sand tighter with the flat side of our stick to give it that look of solid magnificence.

American Folk Toys

Dick Schnacke has gathered together instructions, diagrams, and materials lists for a number of early American folk toys that are fun and easy to make: apple dolls and cornstalk fiddles, whimmydiddles, Flap Jacks and Skyhooks.

—Dorothy Atkins

American Folk Toys
Dick Schnacke
1973; 160 pp.

$4.95 postpaid from:
Penguin Books
299 Murray Hill Parkway
East Rutherford, NJ 07073
or Whole Earth Household Store

•
Flipperdinger

Materials:

1 Blowpipe, elder branch 5/8" diam. x 12" long
1 Jet Tube, elder branch 1/4" diam. x 1-3/4" long
1 Plug, piece of small cork that fits the end of the blowpipe
1 Pith Ball, cornstalk center pith
1 Wire, hard-drawn copper 26 ga. (.016" diam.) x 2-3/4" long
1 Wire, copper 16 ga. (.051" diam.) x 18" long
Glue, white

The Top

Definitive top book. Spin out. —SB

The Top
(Universal Toy, Enduring Pastime)
D.W. Gould
1973; 271 pp.

$9 postpaid from:
Clarkson N. Potter, Inc.
One Park Avenue South
New York, NY 10016

a. The Twirler **started by twisting action of fingers or hands upon the axis.**

b. The Supported-top **started by cord while top is held upright.**

c. The Peg-top **cast, and the twisting action of a cord on the body of the top imparts spin.**

d. The Whip-top — **the body of the top is lashed to give continued motion.**

e. The Buzzer — **bidirectional motion through twisting of the cord.**

f. The Yo-yo — **bidirectional motion due to inertia and successive energy input.**

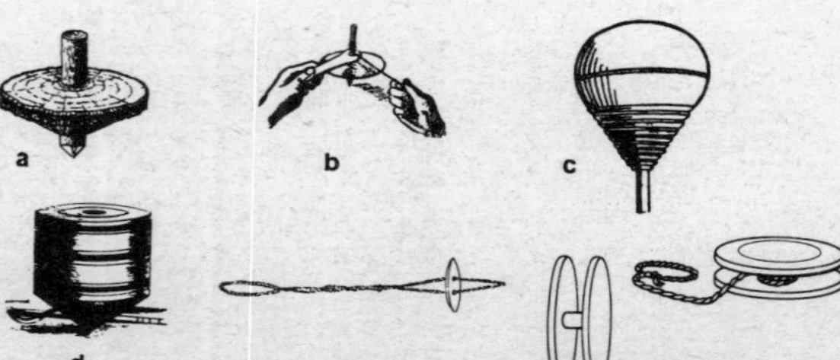
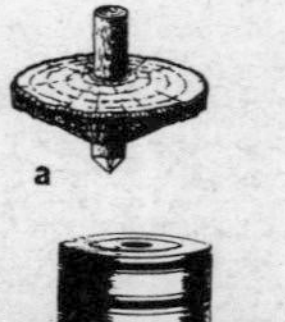
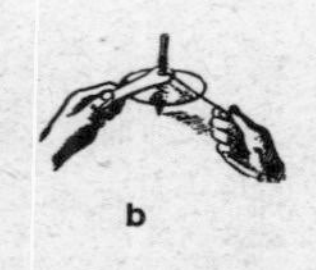

Knock knock
Who's there?
Pencil
Pencil who?
Pencil fall down if you don't wear a belt.

Cricket

The quality and diversity of **Cricket***'s articles and the excellence of its artwork will please children from pre-school to junior high and all discriminating adults. The editorial staff and board includes Clifton Fadiman, I.B. Singer, Kaye Webb and other lights of children's writing. The editors recognize that young people care about everything and so there are folk tales, animal stories, stories in translation, poetry, riddles (what children's magazine or what child can do without them?), puzzles, things to make, explanations of scientific facts, book reviews, reminiscences and articles about sports and sport figures. My children do not read yet, but they faithfully execute craft projects and the illustrations are springboards for stories they make up until mother or father has time to read to them. Older children have been known to read them from cover to cover, over and over (the library types); and others read only the articles that interest them but I have never heard of an issue of* **Cricket** *being thrown away.*

There is a healthy mix of the old favorites such as Ogden Nash, and Laura Ingalls Wilder with contemporaries like John Ciardi and Jane Yolen. In a regular feature called "Meet Your Author," a writer gets to talk to his/her audience about the craft of writing ("How Mary Poppins Found me," by Kaye Webb). Children can learn that stories don't just appear but that they are written, crafted by real people with families, allergies, animal pets, and favorite things.

Cricket *does not talk down to young people. It is sensible, talks sense and knows what good nonsense is. The adults in* **Cricket** *stories are realistic. Parents yell and forget*

Knock knock
Who's there?
Nobel
Nobel who?
Nobel, so I knock knock.

things important to children not from malice but because their lives are busy and full of responsibility. These children and adults tease, love, scold, laugh and learn from one another.

If you have only fifteen dollars to spend on your children or someone else's children this year, invest your money in **Cricket***. Neither you nor the child will be disappointed.*

—Rose A. Doherty

Cricket
Clifton Fadiman, Editor
$15 /year (12 issues)
from:
Cricket
P.O. Box 100
La Salle, IL 61301

Sesame Street Magazine

My two and a half year old is a Sesame Street Freak. The discovery that the mailman brings a magazine about Bert and Ernie and Company is absolute magic for her. Since it's designed to cover a range of ages, some activities are too advanced and others too simple; but that doesn't bother her since she makes up her own games anyway.

—Linda Williams

Sesame Street Magazine
$7.95 /year (10 issues)
from:
Sesame Street Magazine
P.O. Box 2896
Boulder, CO 80322

Draw a circle around all the Y's.
Make the Y's look like this: Ⓨ
Now count the Y's.
Draw a square around all the Z's.
Make the Z's look like this: [Z]
Now count the Z's. ↓

Ranger Rick's Nature Magazine

Gorgeous color pictures of animals, good articles on wild-life and ecology, good magazine for parents and teachers and kids to have around. Aimed at people 8 to 12 years old — direct without being condescending. See also pp. 560 - 561.

—Anne Herbert
[Suggested by E. Gerald Bishop]

Ranger Rick's Nature Magazine
Robert Dunne, Editor
$9 /year (12 issues)
from:
National Wildlife Federation
1412 16th Street N.W.
Washington, DC 20036

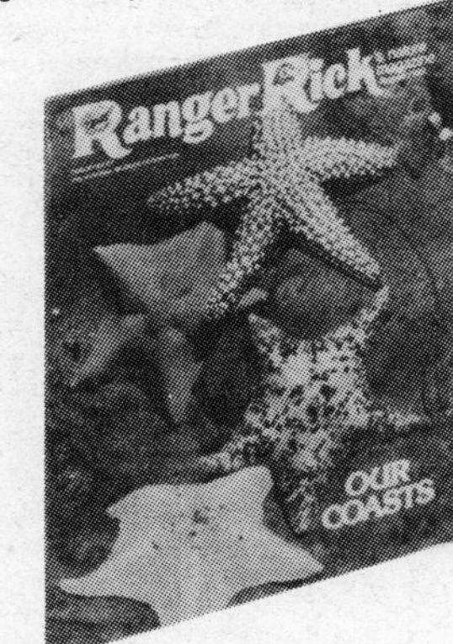

•

Dear Wise Old Owl: Can you really hear ocean waves when you hold a seashell up to your ear?

Joni Naputan
Baton Rouge, LA

The noise in a seashell sure sounds like ocean waves crashing on the shore, Joni, but it's not. The loud roar you hear is just normal sounds echoing back and forth inside the shell. The spiral shape of a seashell makes the sounds seem louder because the sounds bounce off the many curved sides. The shell even picks up sounds that you normally couldn't hear at all.

If you hold a can or bottle up to your ear, you can also hear a dull roar. But these sounds are not as loud as those inside a seashell, because a can is not spiral-shaped.

Starfish

Many Happy Returns

Undocumented observation confirms that there is a little latent boomeranger in all of us. It won't be latent long if this book crosses your path; being a closet boomeranger just isn't practical. The author is the same man that got the Smithsonian into the sport.

—J. Baldwin

You can get a free newsletter on boomerangs (on Oct. 20, 1979, a Pennsylvanian threw a new world's record returning boomerang flight — 123 yards) from the author, Benjamin Ruhe, 1882 Columbia Road, N.W., Washington, DC 20009.

—SB

Many Happy Returns
(The Art and Sport of Boomeranging)
Benjamin Ruhe
1977; 105 pp.
$4.95 postpaid from:
The Viking Press
299 Murray Hill Parkway
East Rutherford, NJ 07073

A Miniature Cardboard Boomerang

This boomerang is simplicity itself. With scissors, cut the boomerang out of a stiff card, such as a used playing card, a file card, or a cardboard folder. Three to six inches in length is about right, and any reasonable banana shape will do. Now bend up a wing tip as shown. Place it on a book for launching, and flick it sharply with a pencil or a finger.

Kite Lines

The tug of the string that catenaries up to the swooping kite is a kid experience that lasts a lifetime. In recent years kite interest has proliferated, and the materials span continents and centuries. Keep up with this nice magazine.

—SB

Kite Lines
Valerie Govig, Editor
$9 /year (4 issues)
from:
Kite Lines
7106 Campfield Road
Baltimore, MD 21207

↓
One of the thrills of a large kite like my 100-foot centipede is the overwhelming spectator interest and desire to participate. Ask for eight volunteers to help you and you end up with 25.

THE RISING SUN
NEIGHBORHOOD NEWSLETTER

The first official surveyors of the Himalayas in 1852 found after taking six cold high uncomfortable measurements that Everest was 29,000 feet high, but they thought that would sound too much like they had guessed to the folks back home, so they said it was 29,002 feet high. (Probably decided 29,001 wasn't enough of a difference and 29,003 was too much of a lie.) The people who lived in the Himalayas never had a name for Everest because they didn't think it was special. It doesn't look as high as it is until you get really close and they could never think of a reason to get really close. (In 1954, an Indian Survey found that it was really, as of 1954 methods, 29,028 feet.)

Future Life

What **Omni** *grandiosely fails at is accomplished with considerable zest by* **Future Life** *— hallucinating the future. Disguised as a science-fiction film fanzine and thereby saved from pretentiousness, this magazine ambles with intelligent curiosity among the fantasies, new technologies, and scientific notions of the day. It's aimed directly at the young, whose youthful enthusiasms will most underlie the human programs of the actual future. This is one of my favorite magazines.* —SB

Future Life
Ed Naha and
Robin Snelson, Editors

$13.98/year (8 issues)
from:
Future Life
475 Park Avenue South
New York, NY 10016

Where no man has gone before intelligent machines like NASA's Mars rover will forge the way for human exploration of the solar system. Will they delay human entry into the cosmos?

•

One Small Step for Humanation

The human in future space ventures may be replaced by a population of self-breeding robots, weaned upon extraterrestrial resources, spreading across the solar system and throughout the universe.

This picture of replicating machines marching about the cosmos isn't drawn from the mind of a science fiction aficionado; it comes straight from NASA administrator Dr. Robert Frosch.

In a speech before the Commonwealth Club in San Francisco, the top NASA official outlined a plan to establish a "productive machine economy" by using our mechanized brethren to build Earth orbiting industries, Moon and planetary bases, including space colonies.

"The key to this idea," stated the administrator, "is the construction of a machine which either totally automatically, or with minimal human intervention and guidance, can use solar energy and local materials on the Earth, or on the Moon, or on an asteroid or elsewhere in the solar system to build a replica of itself."

Generation after generation of machines would then follow, added Frosch, with the total quantity of machines growing exponentially, just as biological generations grow.

Emphasis on nuts and bolts over flesh and bone is partly based on findings of a NASA/Jet Propulsion Laboratory (JPL) study team. In its investigations, the group came to the conclusion that future space operations should rely heavily on machine intelligence and robotics. Not only are long voyages to the planets likely missions for robots, but near Earth operations should be considered as well.

According to Dr. Ewald Heer, organizer of the study, "Without additional automation and increased productivity in the space program, we will not be able to do many of the things we are contemplating."

Will robotics "de-humanize" space, lessening the need for us mortals? "We will not be able to replace the human," claims Heer. "However, we can enhance many human functions, placing individual workers in more supervisory roles." —Leonard David

← This past New Year's Eve, Harrah's Hotel in Reno used lasers to create an animated billboard.

•

Malcolm Brenner: Has the work of science fiction writers influenced you in any way?

John Lilly: When I was doing the early tank work, I began to look for people who had the freedom and imagination I was finding. And people like Olaf Stapledon and Frank Herbert were obviously getting into the same realms of thinking and experience that I was already in. So I used them as examples. Herbert's now on the Board of Advisors of the Human-Dolphin Foundation. I also asked the staff of Project Janus to go see the movie **Alien**, because it presented such an *alien* alien. Something utterly unhuman. Nothing like a dophin, of course.

Listen to Us

This Kids Klassic is the distillation of 2000 children between the ages of 6 and 13 in round table discussion without adult supervision. It is a moppet molotov cocktail that blasts away an adult preconception about where kids are coming from. Volatile topics include runaways, incest, justice, school, divorce, sex, money, friendship etc. The underlying philosophy of **Children's Express** *(now defunct), can be summed up in four words: Kids can do it. To paraphrase Art Linkletter, "Kids say the damndest things," and salvation as a species may well depend on our ability to listen.* —Wavy Gravy

•

Sex: Real Life Versus Fantasy
Linda and Gina, both 13.

CE: Let's say you're horny and boys provoke you, do you get mad because you know you can't have sexual intercourse?

Gina: I get mad because I know that I can't just have sex. The boy's over there with his legs open and provoking you — I mean, it really pisses me off! It's like having food in front of you when you haven't eaten for days.

CE: Do you think that applies to boys? Some people think that boys are always horny when there are pretty girls around. Do you think it's like that?

Gina: They *always* are horny. But they don't have to break their backs.

Linda: They don't have to worry about breaking their hymens or getting pregnant or having babies or having your period.

Listen to Us
(The Children's
Express Report)
Dorriet Kavanaugh, Editor
1978, 255 pp.
$5.95 postpaid from:
Workman
Publishing Company
1 West 39th Street
New York, NY 10018
or Whole Earth
Household Store

HOW DO YOUR PARENTS EMBARRASS YOU?

Steffi, 8:
1. When my father runs around in his underwear.
2. When he tells sick jokes in front of my friends.

Kelley, 10:
1. We were in a restaurant and my mom went to the juke box and put on a bunch of old songs and then some people were staring at us.
2. Sometimes she gets upset at me in public.

Kathy, 10:
1. When my dad answers the phone and he goes on and on talking to my friends.

Jeff, 11:
1. When my dad starts yelling or talking loudly and everyone is looking at us.

Karen, 9:
1. Sometimes my mom tells private things about me to her friends and I get embarrassed.
2. My mom doesn't like rock 'n' roll.
3. My dad smokes too much.
4. Sometimes they're too overprotective.

Stone Soup

Stone Soup *says it is a "magazine by children," and so it seems to be, with some adult help with things like printing, subscriptions, mailing, etc., but with no sign that the children's writing has been edited. The writing is frequently imaginative, sometimes derivative (it's good fun to try to guess what the authors have been reading). Some of the best of the funny stuff is hilarious. It reminds me that while part of the special character of kids' writing may come from writing skills only partly developed, the other part comes from a view of the world fresh, sharp and amused. For parents or teachers who wish, there is available a companion publication, "The Editor's Notebook — a guide for teachers who subscribe to* **Stone Soup**.*"* —George Cope

Stone Soup
(The magazine
by children)
William Rubel and
Gerry Mandel, Editors
$12/year (5 issues)
from:
Children's Art Foundation
P.O. Box 83
Santa Cruz, CA 95063

•

My cat is dead.
He's not sick or old or dying
He's dead.
And there's no time for a last silent moment,
For a last all-encompassing purr,
For a last stroke on soft cat fur,
There's only frozen reality
And tears burning slushily down my face
And my stomach like a clenched fist
And a voice, myself, saying
Shh, now, this is it,
This is real, so don't fight it
So I don't fight — I cry
Broken into softly falling lumps
That will reassemble tomorrow
A little different.

Alison Van Egeren, 13
Glenview, Illinois

Action Now

Spun off of **SkateBoarder** *magazine is this new "sports/lifestyle magazine" of balls-out kid macho — skateboarding, surfing, bicycle moto-cross, high volume music, go-for-it-all-now adolescent hormone and adrenalin gusher.*

Might not last a season. —SB

Harley Flanagan

Where does Harley Flanagan, a 13-year-old from NY's East Village district, go after he's been in one of the Big Apple's most popular live bands, rubbed shoulders with some of rock's current greats and been profiled in Andy Warhol's **Interview** magazine? Well, according to our NY source Glen E. Friedman, to school (though he probably won't admit it) and to a lot of rock clubs (though he's not quite of age).

A drummer since age five and, for the past year, a member of the punkish dance band, the Stimulators, Harley is often playing those notorious venues when he's not just hanging out at them. Together with Denise Mercedes (guitar), Anne Gustavson (bass) and Patrick Mack (vocals), the boy helps lay out some incendiary rock typified by the group's single, "Loud Fast Rules" (flip side, "Run, Run, Run"). Harley also likes to draw, cut hair and listen to records, his favorite bands including 999, the Sex Pistols, the Buzzcocks, the Damned and the Undertones.

From here, it's more summer city gigs and then off to Ireland in August for a punk music conference. No doubt, this rowdy kid will be covering even more ground in the next few years.

SkateBoarder's Action Now
(The Sports/Lifestyle
Magazine)
Brian Gillogly, Editor
$12/year (12 issues)
from:
Surfer Publishing Group
P.O. Box 1028
Dana Point, CA 92629

•

"As far as the military goes, we dig their styling but not their intent."

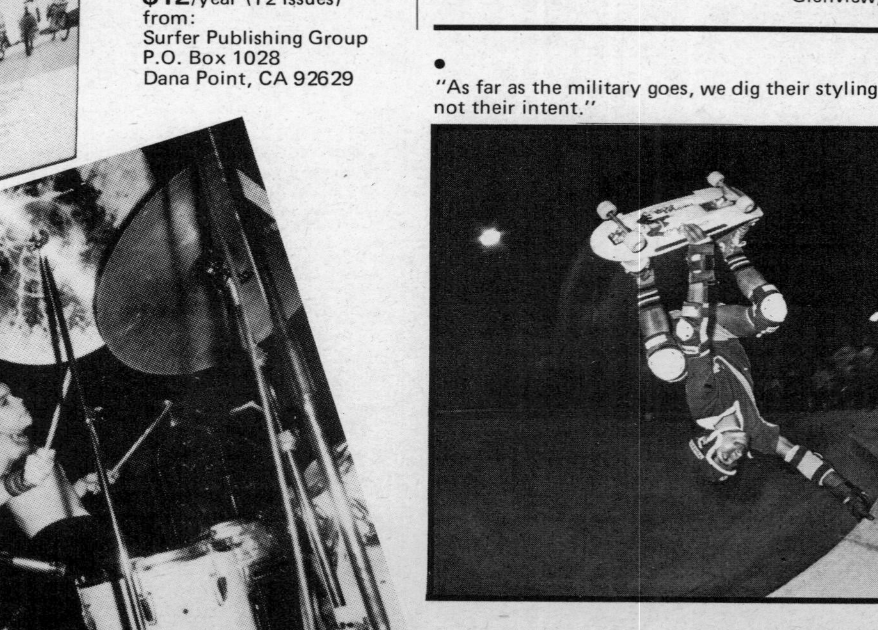

Eggs as usual breakfast etc.

Read this hilarious book (aloud, with audience) and you'll never tell a tightass story to a child again. Go ahead, ride your impatience, start telling a homemade story anyway, and watch it take you into real myth with blood monsters and a personal happy ending. In story-making, looseness is all. This shocking book has it. —SB
[Suggested by Joanna McClure]

Eggs as usual breakfast etc.
Nidra Poller and Gentiane Gaussot
1979; 28 pp.
(also available in the original French)
$10 postpaid from:
Lawrence Hill and Company
520 Riverside Avenue
Westport, CT 06880
or Whole Earth Household Store

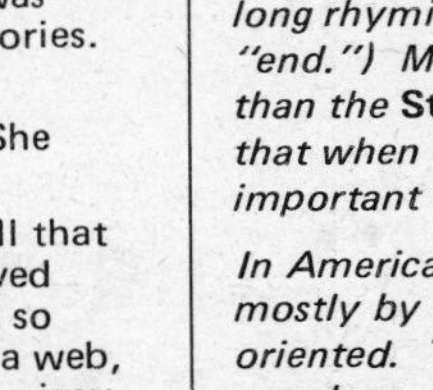

•

Once upon a time there was a mother whose children liked homemade stories better than anything. Better than homemade ravioli, homemade cake, banana splits or home brew beer or homemade scuppernong wine or rough hewn shirts or rough hewn homemade haircuts.

She offered homemade anything else many nights when she was tired or her brain I mean her imagination was empty. No. No to all substitutes. They wanted stories.

•

She went to bed. At eight o'clock. They didn't. She tried so hard to dream.

They plotted. All she could dream was a white wall that went from below ground to above the sky and curved around in a complete and utter circle, allowing not so much as a single corner where a spider could build a web, attract an ant, and start the beginnings of a creepy wispy webby buggy story. Not so much as a corner. Not even a tiny almost invisible crack in the white wall surface where a drop of water could drip down into a small clear globule of a drip of a story. Not so much as a crack. Not even a little rough spot where bits of dust could accumulate and make the foundation for a scattered puffy grey fuzz of a dirty story. Not even a rough spot.

Storytelling
The World of Storytelling

Telling stories eye to eye without reading from a book creates a special excitement for both speaker and listener. Here are two books that can help you to begin and get better.

Storytelling: Art and Technique *is simple, straight-forward advice on how to make it through the story hour. Practical, specific, helpful and not scary. It lists lots of sources for good stories to tell.*

The World of Storytelling *looks at storytelling in different cultures and times. It has interesting comparisons like how Angolans and Turks and Norwegians and Japanese solve the problem of ending the story. (Some do it with long rhyming formulas and some do it with one word — "end.") Much of this book is less immediately practical than the* **Storytelling** *book, but it gives you the feeling that when you tell a few stories, you're part of a long and important tradition.*

In America, storytelling has been practiced and preserved mostly by librarians. So both of these books are library oriented. That's not bad — librarians happen to be the members of our tribe who tell the stories, and it's nice of them to let us in on their secrets. An easy way to see what good story telling is like is to drop by the story hour at your local library.

But you don't need to do that or to buy any book to get started. Tell your kids something that happened to you when you were a kid, and you're on your way. —Anne Herbert

Storytelling: Art and Technique
Augusta Baker and Ellin Greene
1977; 142 pp.
$8.25 postpaid

The World of Storytelling
Anne Pellowski
1977; 296 pp.
$17.25 postpaid

both from:
R.R. Bowker
Bowker Fulfillment Department
P.O. Box 1807
Ann Arbor, MI 48106

Fifth World Tales

I love the murals in Mexico and in San Francisco and have had for a time the fantasy of transforming them into books for children. Murals tell tales. Because they are so large it is possible to range over space and time on a single wall. They are full of detail and reference and visual tricks — all the things that make for books that interest children. My fantasy has been realized. The **Fifth World Tales** *is a series of books for children that seem to flow out of the murals. The books consist of legends from Guatemala, the Philippines, Costa Rica, Mexico, Peru, Bolivia, Nicaragua, Puerto Rico, Chile and Colombia, adapted into modern English and Spanish by Harriet Rohmer, Mary Anchondo, and Jesus Guerrero. Each book was illustrated by a different painter or group of painters. Most of them are muralists; nearly all of them are Latinos (one Filipino). The work is bold and exciting, full of movement and detail. The books are printed in four colors and seem so delicious that a number of children I read them to tried to lick their pages. Each artist does something different with the stories and the collective work is as modern as the work of Sequiros and as old as Maya and Aztec and Inca. The books are magical for children and for us too. I've been crazy enough to buy two sets, one to read and one to cut up and hang on the walls to decorate my study.* —Herb Kohl

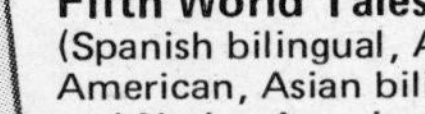

Fifth World Tales
(Spanish bilingual, Afro-American, Asian bilingual and Native American stories for all children from the many peoples of the Americas)

How We Came to the Fifth World
(Mexico; 1976)
The Magic Boys
(Guatemala; 1975)
Cuna Song
(Panama; 1976)
The Headless Pirate
(Costa Rica; 1976)
Land of the Icy Death
(Chile; 1976)
The Little Horse of Icy Colors
(Nicaragua: 1976)
The Mighty God Viracocha
(Peru and Bolivia; 1976)
Atariba and Niguayona
(Puerto Rico; 1976)
Skyworld Woman
(Philippines; 1975)
The Treasure of Guatavita
(Colombia; 1976)
My Aunt Otilia's Spirits
(Spanish; 1978)
The Adventures of Connie and Diego
(Spanish; 1978)
The Iron Moonhunter
(Chinese; 1977)
Don't Put the Vinegar in the Copper
(Chinese; 1978)
The Little Weaver of Thai-Yen Village
(Vietnamese; 1977)
Looking for Ifugao Mountain
(Filipino; 1977)
Aekyung's Dream
(Korean; 1978)
Daxius
(Afro-American; 1977)
The River that Gave Gifts
(Afro-American; 1978)
The People Shall Continue
(Native American; 1977)

$3.95 each postpaid

Catalog
free

all from:
Children's Book Press
1461 Ninth Avenue
San Francisco, CA 94122
or Whole Earth Household Store

Rootabaga Stories

Epistemologist Gregory Bateson said they're the best thing Carl Sandburg ever did. They are definitely the strangest — haunting encounters of characters such as The Potato Face Blind Man, Blixie Bimber, Johnny the Wham, Slip Me Liz, and the Gold Buckskin Whincher. Something powerful is going on amid the whimsy making it peerless aloud-reading, even to yourself. —SB
[Suggested by Gregory Bateson]

Rootabaga Stories
Carl Sandburg

Part 1
1922; 230 pp.
$2.25 postpaid

Part 2
1922; 218 pp.
$2.50 postpaid

both from:
Harcourt Brace Jovanovich
757 Third Avenue
New York, NY 10017
or Whole Earth Household Store

•

One Story — "Only the Fire-Born Understand Blue"

. . . "For some people shadows are comic and only to laugh at. For some other people shadows are like a mouth and its breath. The breath comes out and it is nothing. It is like air and nobody can make it into a package and carry it away. It will not melt like gold nor can you shovel it like cinders. So to these people it means nothing.

"And then there are other people," Fire the Goat went on. "There are other people who understand shadows. The fire-born understand. The fire-born know where shadows come from and why they are.

"Long ago, when the Makers of the World were done making the round earth, the time came when they were ready to make the animals to put on the earth. They were not sure how to make the animals. They did not know what shape animals they wanted.

"And so they practised. They did not make real animals at first. They made only shapes of animals. And these shapes were shadows, shadows like these you and I, Fire the Goat and Flim the Goose, are looking at this morning across the booming rollers on the east sky where the sun is coming up.

"The shadow horse over there on the east sky with his mouth open, his ears laid back, and his front legs thrown in a curve like harvest sickles, that shadow horse was one they made long ago when they were practising to make a real horse. That shadow horse was a mistake and they threw him away. Never will you see two shadow horses alike. All shadow horses on the sky are different. Each one is a mistake, a shadow horse thrown away because he was not good enough to be a real horse . . .

Away off where the sun was coming up, there were people and animals.

See Saw Book Club

How about a copy of **Where the Wild Things Are** *or* **The Snowy Day** *for 75¢! If you're a lover of children's books or the parent of a lover of children's books, you know what an amazing bargain that is. Well, you can thank Scholastic Book Services; that's right, the folks your teacher ordered books from when you were a kid in school. They have a book club for preschool and younger elementary age kids, and they offer some of the best children's books in paperback for less than a dollar apiece. That's the good news; the bad news is that they're not set up for individual orders; however, if you're part of a nursery school or you can get a group of other parents together, you can set up your own club. Each month you get a set of folders describing the ten or so books being offered that month; each member orders what (s)he wants, and someone collects the money and orders and sends them in together. It's like Christmas once a month.* —Linda Williams

See Saw News
Information
free from:
See Saw Book Club
Scholastic Book Services
50 West 44th Street
New York, NY 10036

THE RISING SUN
NEIGHBORHOOD NEWSLETTER

"England is full of peculiar things — a shell fish stall saved by popular request (a petition) on Cambridge Circus at Shaftesbury Avenue. Statues of industry and commerce outside Buckingham Palace with hammer and sickle. Beautiful pink women and skinny bright-eyed men talking so elegantly on the top of a double-decker bus. I'm in love with the shiny wet streets."
—David writing on his first trip back in 5 years

The Most Unusual Letter We've Ever Received

A real person, Carol Van Strum lives over a ridge from Tidewater, Oregon amid a swarm of animals and kids. She wrote the treatise on home teaching on p. 568. This letter to **CoEvolution** *in 1977 opened the way to her becoming a Learning evaluator for* **Whole Earth.**
—SB

by Carol Van Strum

Sirs:

Your article on the Hoedads (p. 85) reminds me of my own extraordinary experience with these remarkable workers – and with the fuzzy boundary between "reality" and illusion.

For twenty-five years I worked as a librarian at the university. After my husband left to live with one of his students twelve years ago I began exploring all the areas I had never ventured into for fear of intruding in his domain or inspiring his ridicule. I took up music again where I had dropped it at our marriage and joined a small chamber group. I adopted a cat. I bought buckets of white latex and painted the dark paneling of our house. I filled the trash bins with phony pre-columbian dolls and useless colonial hinges and latches. I sold all the Herman Hesse and Carl Jung. Not a particularly adventurous life, but comfortable and ordered.

One remnant I kept of our life together was the collection of children's books we had begun when we were expecting our first and only child. After the baby died we had kept it up in a mechanical sort of way, pretending there would be other children some day. To my husband it was another collection, to be made as impressive as possible; it embarrassed him that I actually enjoyed reading the books. After he left I continued to add to the collection and began writing about the books. I was asked occasionally to lecture on the subject. Once or twice a year I still enjoy traveling and speaking to college students. They are a responsive audience; it affords them some comic relief, no coubt, to hear the Babar books presented as Utopian novels.

One lecture last winter was in Oregon. There had been a pleasant, if somewhat ordinary, dinner at the home of a professor of communications theory. The lecture – "Children's Literature, A Place on the Shelf" – had gone well. The weather was dreadful, as usual. Afterward I rented a car to drive out to a motel on the coast at Florence, where a year ago I had spent a pleasant weekend with a violinist friend. My throat had been sore after the lecture, but I attributed that to the speaking and the communications professor's dry wine. After an hour or so of driving, however, my back became unbearably painful; my neck was stiff, my head throbbing, my eyes burning and streaming as if from hay fever. My clothes were damp with sweat, and I began to shake uncontrollably. What a time to come down with flu. The rain beat on the car. I had driven so long without seeing lights I worried I had taken a wrong turn. I became truly frightened when I realized that the road was now unpaved; a pitted gravel track, it bumped and wound through an endless forest of dripping trees, up and down steep grades and switchbacks. In panic, I drove on, fevered, afraid to stop. It must go somewhere, it must go somewhere, I told myself. The first light I see I'll stop. Strange figures waved and stumbled in my headlights, dwindling into stumps and shrubs as I passed.

Finally, miraculously, there was a light. A yard light, a driveway, a pen of ducks with a small pond and a shelter. A neatly trimmed hedge, a lawn, a well-pruned rose garden, bare now in the winter storm. And a house – a cottage it would be called in England – a mossy stone house with broad chimneys and a slate roof. I sat and stared through the windshield. A slate roof? In Oregon? My head buzzed. A dog barked. The ducks in their shelter lifted their heads from their wings and stared into the headlights with small eyes. A light flashed on in one window. I felt a great wave of relief and opened the car door. My legs were so weak I could barely command the strength to get out of the car. I staggered to the house. The door opened as I fumbled for the bell, and someone caught me as I fell.

"Who is it, dear?"

"I don't know. But help me bring her in. She's sick."

"My god, she's soaked."

"And burning with fever. Here, in the spare room . . ."

Warm, gentle hands undressed me. The cool sheets were a shock.

"Here, a warm towel for her back. There. And a wet cloth for her head. How awful, she must have got lost, so sick and in this storm . . ."

"You stay with her, dear, while I fix some broth and tea. We'll get something warm into her . . ."

I tried without success to open my eyes, to see this benevolent couple who ministered to me, bringing quilts and holding my head to trickle warm liquids down my aching throat. I sank into the comfortable mattress. The fever heat spread to the bedding, and I slept.

I woke later in a spasm of chills and trembling. A shawled figure rocked softly in a rocking chair by the bed, her face in shadow. A candle flickered on a small stool next to a still-steaming cup. The light flashed and blotted on the backs of books that lined the room; shelf upon shelf of books, broken only by the windows and the door. Most astonishing, at least half of them were children's books, mixed at random among an untidy collection of great literature. On top of one shelf a stuffed figure – Piglet perhaps – lay on a dusty violin case. I lay and stared in surprise and delight at meeting old friends in the wilderness. The shawled figure rose and placed a cool hand on my forehead.

"Are you amazed at the books?" Her voice was soft, as if afraid of waking someone. "They were our son's. He was killed in Vietnam six years ago. He kept all his favorites for his own children. Now of course there will be no children, but we keep the books . . ."

I stared at the books, ponderously sorting this information. Many of them had been published in the last six years; so they continued to collect them, too. A son. I tried to speak, to tell her of my own son, whom I had held but once in his brief lifetime. So alive and perfect a thing to lose. But to have raised him through the colic, the teething, the Christmases, the fears of the dark, to have built the person who shared this house, these books – I sobbed and the woman comforted me, wiping my forehead with a cloth. I slept again.

Later, the smell of tobacco smoke wakened me. The husband sat in the rocking chair now, reading by the candlelight. He brought me more tea and moistened the cloth on my forehead again.

"Does the smoke bother you?"

I shook my head. I actually liked the smoke; there was something reassuring about it. I tried to tell him how grateful I was to them, how lucky I had been to find their house.

"You like it? We built it ourselves. Long ago we saw a house like this in Dearborn. And old Cotswold cottage and smithy that Henry Ford imported stone by stone from England. He even imported the workers to assemble it. When we finally came to build our own house we modeled it on our memory of that place. We did all the work ourselves, and we ordered seeds from England to plant here. We had hoped to clear more land and farm it, but now we're getting old . . ."

He sat, rocking and smoking, staring at the careful woodwork of the beams and window frames. All night I woke and slept, and always he or his wife was there, ready with a drink, a towel, a word of comfort. It was a long night. I woke at last to shafts of sunlight pouring through trees whose tops soared and vanished in mist outside the window. The room brightened as the mist lifted, and suddenly the room – the house, too, and forest – boomed with the opening of Bach's Magnificat.

I was too feverish now to be surprised. I lay awash in sweat and music.

"Do you mind the music?" the woman bent over my head. "Our son was a musician. This was a favorite piece of his. If it bothers you, though, we needn't play it this morning . . ."

I tried to smile, to tell her how perfect it was. She moved into the next room and stood by the window with her husband, silhouetted against the mist and sunlight. This must be the way they begin their day, I realised.

The voices began, each clearer than the last. The walls receded and the ceiling soared in a succession of vaults. In tier upon tier of galleries the singers stood, and I recognized them all. Wordsworth with an armful of flowers. Coleridge looking guilty about something. Shakespeare, Huxley, Beatrix Potter with a hedgehog in a wicker cage. Joyce, the Brothers Grimm, Ola and Blacken. Harold drawing windows on the wall with a purple crayon. The Frog Prince, Hans Andersen, Homer, Euripides, Marx, Frog and Toad hunting for buttons. Brecht and Little Bear arm in arm, wearing fur hats. Faulkner, Sam Pig, Walter Mitty, Peter Rabbit, Virgil, Lassie. B.F. Skinner launched Gayneck from outstretched hands; the bird soared in circles, higher and higher, past more and more singers. The Swallows and Amazons with a jug slung over an oar. Lucretius, Richard Scarry, Hugo and Josephine. In a row on a railing stood the little folk, Arrietty and Spiller holding hands, Stuart Little, Josephine the Singer, the schoolmaster with his people from Mistress Masham's Repose, Nils astride Morten Goosie-Gander, Thumbelina, Tom Thumb, Mopsa the Fairy, Peter Peabody Pepperell III and Gus the gull.

The faces and the music were all so clear. Ishi stood alone. Melville, Tin-tin and Snowy, Farley Mowat, Pogo, Dido and Simon, Huck Finn, Marcuse, Voltaire, Eloise, Mike Mulligan. The Bastables shifted uneasily on their feet – peas in their shoes again, perhaps. Rabelais, the Tin Woodman, Bertrand Russell. Laura and Pa with his fiddle. Thoreau, Henry Miller, Charlie Bucket, Ezra Pound, Dickens, Beckett, Whitman. Among them stood the animals singing too: Amos and Boris, Tracy's Tiger, Freddy the Pig and Mrs. Wiggins, the lively little rabbit, the poky little puppy, Mrs. Oldknowe and the green deer, Babar and Zephir, Curious George, Pooh, Eeyore, Mr. and Mrs. Mallard, Ping, the Snow Goose, Nicholas Nye. In a corner next to Mrs. Malone a kid in a diamond-patterned sweater bent to tie a broken sneaker, The Tomten, Mr. Biswas, Johnny Tremain, Mowgli, Branwell and the Twelves, the White Knight, the Jumblies, Bambi, Max in his wolf suit, John Clare. Tasha Tudor with a baton led a band of singing Corgis.

"Deposuit potentes de sede et exultavit humiles."

Rank upon rank they stood and sang. It was not an irreverent vision. I wept again, suddenly and feverishly homesick for someplace too far away to recall. The music ended and the sun burst unbearably on my eyes.

"Here, it's too bright. It hurts her eyes . . ."

". . . fever . . . all night . . . doctor . . ."

The curtains closed mercifully. I slept again.

I woke in the familiar whiteness of a hospital room. There were no books. The nurses were professionally cool. I had only to lie passively and recover. The nurse looked at me oddly when I asked about the people who brought me in.

"Oh, they're OK. Paid your room, so's you wouldn't be treated like welfare."

I took the hint and reached for my purse to dig out insurance cards. Everything was tiring. I slept and woke.

"Are we up to having visitors this afternoon? It's the fellow that brought you in."

Finally I was to meet my unknown benefactors. But no. She ushered in a kid wearing baggy overalls. He had a scraggly beard and long hair, which curled from under a dirty, loose-knit tam-o-shanter. He wore a row of ball-point pens clipped to the pocket of his denim shirt. He introduced himself, holding out a crusted hand. There were furrows between the long muscles of his arm. "They said you were awake so we thought we'd see how you're doing. You sure look better than when we found you . . ."

"Found me?"

"Yeah. You were really out, you know. You must of got lost up on the old logging roads. You were lying in your car there at the end of the road by a unit in Alsea we're planting. That's where we found you."

"We – ?"

"Hoedads. Tree planters." He grinned and perched comfortably on the foot of the bed, knocking dry mud off his cleated boots before resting them on the frame. "You don't come from around here. Say, I parked your car in the lot. Rented, isn't it? You're low on gas. Had her running all night, I guess – lights were on, too, and your door was open. The nurse says she got your clothes dry OK, though."

He explained about the Hoedads, as you have told in your articles. We talked of labor-intensive agriculture and forestry, economics, the second law of thermodynamics, decentralization, child-rearing, sun-worship and vegetarian diets. It was exhilarating. Like playing tennis with someone better than yourself, I found I remembered and understood much that I hadn't given thought to in years. He pointed out the window at a truck in the parking lot. A small boy sat in the driver's seat, pretending to drive it. A woman dressed in the same overalls and denim shirt stood next to it with another man wearing an old fatigue jacket and a cowboy hat. A child sat on his shoulders, waving a pinwheel. The side of the truck was emblazoned with gaudy letters, like a carnival van:

CHEAP THRILLS
Fast, deep, and often
Reforestation

I glanced back at him, and his eyes twinkled. Nice blue eyes behind all that grubby beard.

"We all got our own names," he said. "Each crew, I mean"

I laughed and choked, and he slapped my back. I tried to explain what had happened to me in the night: the stone house, the ducks in the yard, the solicitous couple, the vision of the singers, how real it had all seemed. He listened, his eyes wide with interest.

"Yeah, I can believe it. You know once when I was at Yale – "

"Yale!"

"You mean you can't tell?" He looked pleased. "Usually people spot it – the way you talk or hitch up your socks or something – it takes years to get rid of it, like a disease. Well, once when I was there I got so drunk at the Harvard-Yale game I passed out in the men's room at the stadium and got locked in there. I woke up in the pitch dark – I mean I didn't know there could be darkness so dark, it was like absolute nothingness. I couldn't tell if my eyes were open or shut. I was lying there on a damp concrete floor and there was this terrible smell. I thought I'd been buried alive. All of a sudden it seemed as if I could remember the whole thing – the doctors, the stethoscopes, my parents weeping, the hearse ride, the coffin lowered into this grave. I really remembered it, every bit. I tried to yell but my throat was too dry. I put my hand out and it landed on the slimy wall of the urinal – ugh! Stygian, I can tell you. I couldn't think what it was. Then I thought I was blind . . ."

"But what did you do?"

"Figured it out finally, and got to thinking about the Harvard man and the Yale man taking a leak – you don't know that one? – the Yale man says, 'At Yale they teach us to wash our hands after we urinate.' And the Harvard man says 'At Harvard they teach us not to piss on our hands.' I laughed so hard thinking about it I got sick. I sobered up finally and felt around for a window and climbed out. I didn't do a whole lot of drinking after that . . ."

He stood up. "Well, I'm glad you're OK. We're movin' on to a new unit tonight. I can fill your tank for you, though, before we go. It's a gypsy kind of life . . ." He paused in the doorway. "You know, it all seems so real because it is real, the music and everything, it's all part of what you know already. You really thought you were in a cathedral somewheres when we found you. And on the way in you said something really far out."

"I did?"

"Yeah. I remember it, it was so far out. You sat up all of a sudden like and said, 'Oh god, I have lived too long in cities of the West.' Loud and clear you said that, and then you went to sleep again." He smiled and held up his hand. "Well, take care, Mother."

I spent the rest of that hospital stay with a collection of real estate catalogues. In what strange ways we make our new beginnings! ■

THE RISING SUN
NEIGHBORHOOD NEWSLETTER

"Everywhere I go, I find a poet has been there before me."

–Freud

World Tales

Once upon a time, there was a peasant woman with such kindly neighbors that she lacked for no comfort save one, and that was her regret that she had nothing to offer in return for their many favors.

One night a voice came to the peasant woman in her dream, saying, "Unto you will be given a treasure of inestimable worth that will increase its value insofar as you share it with your neighbors." The woman wondered exceedingly at this. And the next day a brown messenger delivered a book to the peasant woman. Being of humble origin, the woman did not perceive that the volume was bewitched, and could not know the nature of its enchantment. Seeing only that it was lovely to behold, she called her neighbors and opened the volume to display to them the good fortune which had so unexpectedly befallen her. But the nature of the book's enchantment was this; that when she had begun to read the very first page, her heart was filled with such delight and wonder that she could not stop reading, and the hearts of her neighbors were likewise so filled with delight and wonder that they gathered like crows in the corn and caused her to read until her voice crept into a corner of her throat to hide, and then they took it in turns to read among themselves to each other. And always when the last page was turned, there were newcomers in the multitude desiring to hear the pages they had missed, and thus the book fulfilled its enchantment in that from the day of its opening it was never closed again, and the tales from its pages were ever told and told anew by the neighbors and the neighbors' neighbors, and the neighbors' neighbors' neighbors of that realm. And the peasant woman lived her days in joy for the gift of a treasure whose worth increased by sharing it.

Interpretation: the brown messenger was the UPS man, and the book, **World Tales**. *The peasant woman is me. All the rest is true. This is a rare and magical book, beautiful to look at and impossible to put down. Each story is more wondrous than the last, embellished — adorned, really — with extravagant pictures by a variety of artists in the tradition of the illustrated book or illuminated manuscript. Idries Shah's tales about each tale, showing where and when each story has unaccountably occurred in widely diverse cultures over vast reaches of time, are as mysterious and wonderful as the tales themselves.*

—*Carol Van Strum*

World Tales
(The Extraordinary Coincidence of Stories Told In All Times, In All Places)
Collected by Idries Shah
1979; 259 pp.
$19.95 postpaid from:
Harcourt Brace Jovanovich
757 Third Avenue
New York, NY 10017
or Whole Earth Household Store

Jonathan Livingston Seagull

A Blood woman told me, "Behind the Sun is the real Sun." This book is about flight that way. Beyond perfection of technique is another perfection, a further freedom, another discipline. Jonathan eventually has to insist he is not the Son of the Great Gull. —*SB*

Jonathan Livingston Seagull
Richard Bach
1970; 93 pp.
$2.50 postpaid from:
Avon Books
Mail Order Department
250 West 55th Street
New York, NY 10019
or Whole Earth Household Store

•

And so they flew in from the west that morning, eight of them in a double-diamond formation, wingtips almost overlapping. They came across the Flock's Council Beach at a hundred thirty-five miles per hour, Jonathan in the lead, Fletcher smoothly at his right wing, Henry Calvin struggling gamely at his left. Then the whole formation rolled slowly to the right, as one bird . . . level . . . to . . . inverted . . . to . . . level, the wind whipping over them all.

The squawks and grockles of everyday life in the Flock were cut off as though the formation were a giant knife, and eight thousand gull-eyes watched, without a single blink. One by one, each of the eight birds pulled sharply upward into a full loop and flew all the way around to a dead-slow stand-up landing on the sand.

↑

The Silent Couple

Once upon a time there was a newly-married couple; still dressed in their wedding finery, they relaxed in their new home when the last of the guests at their feast had left.

"Dear husband," said the young lady, "do go and close the door to the street, which has been left open."

"Me shut it?" said the groom, "a bridegroom in this splendid costume, with a priceless robe and a dagger studded with jewels? How could I be expected to do such a thing? You must be out of your mind. Go and shut it yourself."

"So!" shouted the bride, " you expect me to be your slave: a gentle, beautiful creature like me, wearing a dress of finest silk — that I should get up on my wedding day and close a door which looks onto the public street? Impossible."

They were both silent for a moment or two, and the lady suggested that they should make the problem the subject of a forfeit. Whoever spoke first, they agreed, should be the one to shut the door.

There were two sofas in the room, and the pair settled themselves, face to face, one on each, sitting mutely looking at one another.

They had been in this posture for two or three hours when a party of thieves came by and noticed that the door was open. The robbers crept into the silent house, which seemed so deserted, and began to load themselves with every portable object of any value which they could find.

The bridal couple heard them come in, but each thought that the other should attend to the matter. Neither of them spoke or moved as the burglars went from room to room, until at length they entered the sitting room and at first failed to notice the utterly motionless couple.

Still the pair sat there, while the thieves collected all the valuables, and even rolled up the carpets under them. Mistaking the idiot and his stubborn wife for wax dummies, they stripped them of their personal jewels — and still the couple said nothing at all.

The thieves made off, and the bride and her groom sat on their sofas throughout the night. Neither would give up.

When daylight came, a policeman on his beat saw the open street door and walked into the house. Going from room to room he finally came upon the pair and asked them what was happening. Neither man nor wife deigned to reply.

The policeman called massive reinforcements and the swarming custodians of the law became more and more enraged at the total silence, which to them seemed obviously a calculated affront.

The officer in charge at last lost his temper and called out to one of his men: "Give that man a blow or two, and get some sense out of him!"

At this the wife could not restrain herself: "Please, kind officers" she cried, "do not strike him — he is my husband!"

"I won!" shouted the fool immediately, "so you have to shut the door!"

The Man Who Kept Cigars in His Cap

Life is made of peculiar events — not hilarious as TV would like us to believe — but peculiar. The stuff of stories worth listening to, if they are well told. Jim Heynen, most recently of Idaho and now living in Port Townsend, Washington, can tell a good story. His new book contains forty-odd stories of the old tradition: short, touching renditions of youths finding out how the world works and adults struggling to stay in it. Such tales can arise from urban settings and do so, but these happen to be of a rural nature. Mr. Heynen had the good fortune to be raised in a farming community, where life is richer and includes the amazing feats of animals and the odd behavior of tolerated neighbors (even if The Man Who Sharpened Saws had the unfounded reputation for being a communist, he nevertheless was too good a craftsman for anyone to ignore).

"The Boys" in **The Man Who Kept Cigars in His Cap** *move through their families and community, bearing witness and generating changes. They watched the men try to save a bloated cow and then came up with their own method. It worked. They spied on the woman who made such perfect little waves on the edges of her pie crusts and found out how she did it. They attempted to deliver justice and found the world to be more complicated than it appeared. Their best efforts could not save a wounded animal.*

The portrayal of the man who walked his stallion around on the breeding circuit evokes equal amounts of dignity and tragedy. Are these stories nostalgic? I suggest no. Based as they are on experiences and responses occuring anywhere at anytime, they resemble legends more than anything. Any good story is but a skillfully reworked legend, adapted to local conditions. And legends don't age. —*Terry Lawhead*

The Man Who Kept Cigars in His Cap
Jim Heynen
1979; 61 pp.
$4.50 postpaid from:
Graywolf Press
P.O. Box 142
Port Townsend, WA 98368
or Whole Earth Household Store

DUNGEONS & DRAGONS®

When my son Aaron, 15, began to neglect most of his homework and talk gravely of his activities in "D & D" as if they were important, I decided to take a look. He and his friends were certainly not louting around doing nothing, they were completely serious and spending as much time as they could at the game. It turns out that they are not alone. A vigorous subculture phenomenon based on D & D and other fantasy war games is spreading across the USA and the world. The thousands of players are served by a host of books, a growing number of specialty magazines, and retail outlets purveying the necessary trappings for interesting play. Though it is possible to play a shallow game by hard and fast rules as in chess, the fascination is in top-level games that exercise the imagination and require accumulated expertise. Aaron, who is considered to be a top-level player, asserts that most grownups would quickly meet their match. It is far beyond being kid stuff. If you think it is, I invite you to give it a try.

What makes D & D a challenge is that the rules are incredibly complicated, and they are constantly evolving. Then too, there is "game time" and "real time"; for instance, if two characters marry, they have to wait a realtime month before the baby can be played. There are escalations in weapon and counterweapon, changes in the powers of characters and a constant development of traps and tricks. If a player doesn't participate for a month, he may be severely obsolete! Characters accumulate "experience" from game to game as they gather or lose points. The shifts in power are recorded in a book that players keep and carry to the game no matter where the location. The magazines keep everyone informed as to latest developments.

The complexity and time demands of D & D effectively make the players into an elite that is open to the uninvolved only to the extent they are willing to participate in depth. Many are not willing, though there is a growing adult contingent. (Not many women though . . . the game tends to the macho.) Staid adults are excluded even more thoroughly from the D & D culture than they were from hard rock in a previous generation; you can't just listen in or play a tape while the kid is away. An extensive jargon also adds to the exclusive aspect of D & D.

I'm not a psychologist, but I think it may be significant that the players are so deeply into the realization of a fantasy world consisting mainly of contest, violence and aggression, and that they do this with a spirit noticeably missing from most of their other duties in the real world. I'm not sure if it's good or bad or if it matters. (Aaron says it's no worse than chess or Go.) Certainly putting a lot of effort into something that encourages imaginative thought can't be all bad, and frankly I think the players may be learning more from D & D than from much of what passes as education these days. I can tell you that if I were 15, I'd be into it up to my ears! —*J. Baldwin*

Dropping in to an RPG (role-playing game) store is the easiest way to glimpse the kaleidoscopic surface of the D & D phenomenon. (Check your phone directory under "games.") The store is usually busy with obsessed kids

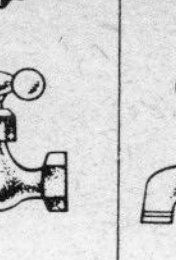

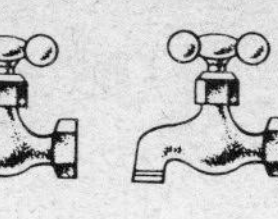
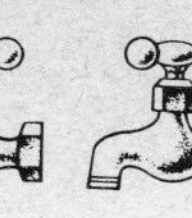

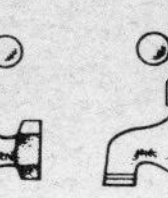

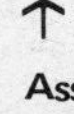

Games

By games they mean brain games — puzzles and pencil games and board games that require cogitation. Some of the magazine is about games — a report on the Fourth National Wargaming Convention and a play-by-play analysis of a championship Scrabble game. But mostly it is games — good games that you can play alone or with others. A crossword puzzle with two sets of clues — very hard and very easy, non-math logic puzzles by **Scientific American's** *Martin Gardner, miscellaneous shapes from maps for you to identify, historic misprinted stamps reprinted for you to find the flaw, a 554-dot connect the dot puzzle, endless mindboggling word games and on and on. Also reader participation contests that make the ones in other magazines seem tame, and detailed reviews of new board games. The super slick, super graphic presentation seems appropriate in this case — hooks you right into playing as you leaf through.*

The games are consistently original and fun and funny. It seems as though game nuts and smart kids and teachers should consider subscribing. People embarking on long trips or mild illnesses should buy or be given at least one issue with warning that addiction may result. **Games** *in the house might make games a time-passing alternative to TV. You don't have to have a history of game fever to like it — I'm having trouble finishing this review because everyone in the office keeps stealing the magazine.* —Anne Herbert

Games
Michael Donner, Editor
$5.97 /year (7 issues)
from:
Games
515 Madison Avenue
New York, NY 10022

Assembly Line Blues

"So Big John the foreman is breathing down my neck about quotas, and Quality Control is squawking over customer complaints about defects. Meanwhile, it's like the conveyor belt is going faster each week. I tell you I've had it. I quit."

Now it's your turn to punch in. Using the model on the left as a guide, demonstrate your level of productivity by spotting and marking all defective items on each belt. There may be one or more in each line, or there may be none. You never know.

Games Afghans Play

For sheer spunk, consider "Castigation," in which the Afghan child who is "it" is bound hand and foot, and thrown to the ground. The other players kick at him while he tries to spit on them. If he succeeds in spitting on another player, that unfortunate becomes "it," is bound hand and foot and thrown to the ground so the other players can try to kick him.

If that's the *children's* idea of fun, we'd hate to be Russians playing for keeps with their big boys.

This drawing is a fanciful cartoon "signature" or rebus puzzle of a well-known person. Can you name the name?

Harry Reasoner

Strategy & Tactics

Board war gaming. The whole Dungeons and Dragons phenomenon (below) began with the inventiveness set loose by this publisher's magazine and historically detailed war games. Each issue of the magazine has a game of interest. It's quality goods — even SPI's fantasy games derived from Tolkien's **Lord of the Rings** *("Sauron," "Gondor," and "The War of the Ring") are considered the best of the Tolkien genre.* —SB

Maximum size of Guerrilla Units

Guerrilla units come in three sizes: *groups, brigades,* and *divisions* (Partisan only). Brigades and divisions are created from smaller guerrilla units. When creating brigades and divisions, any unused brigade or division counter may be employed.

At the beginning of the game and in all succeeding Game-Turns until *brigade-strength* is achieved, the maximum size of any guerrilla unit on the map is the group.

At the end of each Guerrilla Status Phase, the Yugoslav Player should total the number of Partisan and the number of Chetnik groups currently on the map.

Strategy and Tactics
(The Magazine of Conflict Simulation)
James F. Dunnigan, Editor
$15 /year (6 issues)
from:
Simulations Publications, Incorporated
257 Park Avenue South
New York, NY 10010

speaking of utterly arcane matters. The clerk may explain that some of the customers get their first jobs to support their Dungeons and Dragons habit. They buy dozens of pamphlets offering new levels of complexity in spells, weaponry, character, plot turns, etc. They buy hundreds of the lead miniature characters and lovingly paint them. They buy and borrow obscure adult texts on medieval warfare, sorcery, etc., and neglect school to study them.

Dungeons and Dragons was born in approximately 1973 in Wisconsin, begun as a commercial product by TSR Games, Box 756, Lake Geneva, WI 53147. TSR's introductory D & D basic set costs $9.95, the **Advanced Dungeons and Dragons Players Handbook** costs $9.95, and their complete catalog of fantasy, science fiction, and historical games and rules costs $2 — add $1 for handling.

Though many feel that D & D has been surpassed for playability and ingenuity, as the original RPG it still has the most players. Something to graduate from, into grander games, soon of one's own making. —SB

(See Tolkien's **The Lord of the Rings**, etc., p. 508.)

GAMES

This list of Role Playing Game (RPG) games, magazines, and figurine sources was compiled by **Different Worlds** *($10.50/year, 6 issues) and updated for us by them in July, 1980. I'm sure there've already been changes.* —SB

Archive Miniatures, 1111 South Railroad Avenue, San Mateo, CA 94402. *Star Rovers.*

Balboa Game Company, 630 West Willow, Long Beach, CA 90806. *Warlock.*

Chaosium, Inc., P.O. Box 6302, Albany, CA 94706. *RuneQuest (RQ), Dark Worlds, Elric RuneQuest.*

Excalibre Games, Inc., P.O. Box 29171, Brooklyn Center, MN 55429. *Adventures in Fantasy (AIF).*

Fantasy Games Unlimited, Inc. (FGU), P.O. Box 182, Roslyn, NY 11576. *Chivalry & Sorcery (C&S), Bunnies & Burrows (B&B), Flash Gordon & the Warriors of Mongo, Starships & Spacemen (S&S), Villains & Vigilantes (V&V), Gangster!, Skull & Crossbones, Odyssey, Land of the Rising Sun.*

Fantasy Productions, Inc., P.O. Box 27259, Indianapolis, IN 46227. *High Fantasy.*

Flying Buffalo, Inc. (FBI), P.O. Box 1467, Scottsdale, AZ 85252. *Tunnels & Trolls (T&T), Monsters! Monsters! (M!M!), Starfaring.*

Game Designers Workshop (GDW), 203 North Street, Normal, IL 61761. *En Garde!, Traveller.*

Gamescience, 01956 Pass Road, Gulfport, MS 39501. *Knights of the Round Table, Space Patrol, Superhero 2044, Empire of the Petal Throne (EPT), Old West Gunfight.*

Grimoire Games, P.O. Box 4363, Berkeley, CA 94704. *Arduin Grimoire.*

Heritage USA, Inc., 9840 Monroe Drive (Bldg. 116), Dallas, TX 75220. *Star Trek, Heroes of Middle Earth.*

Legacy Press, 217 Harmon Road, Camden, MI 49232. *Legacy.*

Metagaming, P.O. Box 15346, Austin, TX 78761. *The Fantasy Trip (TFT).*

Simultations Publications, Inc. (SPI), 257 Park Avenue South, New York, NY 10010. *Commando, DragonQuest.*

TSR Hobbies, Inc. (TSR), P.O. Box 756, Lake Geneva, WI 53147. *Dungeons & Dragons (D&D), Advanced D&D (AD&D), Gamma World (GW), Metamorphosis Alpha (MA), Star Probe, Star Empires, Boot Hill.*

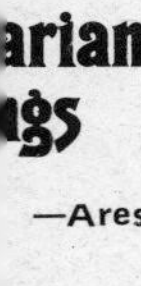

Citadel Miniatures, Ltd., is a British company that is not well known in the U.S. as yet, but won the award for best fantasy figures at the Games Day convention this year. Their address is 48 Millgate, Newark, Nottinghamshire, United Kingdom. Write for an illustrated catalog and tell them you read about it in Different Worlds.

MAGAZINES

Alarums & Excursions (A&E), Lee Gold, 3965 Alla Road, Los Angeles, CA 90066.

APA-DUD, Robert Sacks, 4861 Broadway (5-V), New York, NY 10034.

The Apprentice, David Berman, 24 Sequin Street, Ottawa, Ontario, Canada K1J 6P3

Ares, Simulations Publications, Inc., 257 Park Avenue South, New York, NY 10010.

The Dragon (TD), Dragon Publishing, P.O. Box 110, Lake Geneva, WI 53147.

Gryphon, Baron Publishing Co., P.O. Box 820, La Puente, CA 91747.

The Journal of the Travellers' Aid Society, P.O. Box 432, Normal, IL 61761.

The Judges Guild Journal (tJGJ) and **The Dungeoneer**, Judges Guild, 1165 North University Avenue, Decatur, IL 62526.

The Lords of Chaos (TLOC), Nicolai C. Shapero, 728 South Atlantic Blvd., Alhambra, CA 91803.

Sorcerer's Apprentice (SA), Flying Buffalo, Inc., P.O. Box 1467, Scottsdale, AZ 85252.

The Space Gamer (TSG), P.O. Box 18805, Austin, TX 78760.

White Dwarf (WD), 1 Dalling Road, Hammersmith, London W6 0JD, England.

The Wild Hunt (TWH), Mark Swanson, 71 Beacon Street, Arlington, MA 02174.

Different Worlds (DW), and **Wyrm's Footnotes (WF)**, Chaosium, Inc., P.O. Box 6302, Albany, CA 94706.

MINIATURES

Archive Miniatures, 1111 South Railroad Avenue, San Mateo, CA 94402.

Broadsword Miniatures, 1691 South Hidden Hills Parkway, Stone Mountain, GA 30088.

Citadel Miniatures, Ltd., 48 Millgate, Newark, Nottinghamshire, England.

Gamescience, 01956 Pass Road, Gulfport, MS 39501.

Greenwood and Ball, Ltd., Unit 27, Bon Lee Trading Estate, Thornaby-on-Tees, Cleveland, England.

Grenadier Models, Inc., P.O. Box 305, Springfield, PA 19064.

Heritage USA, Inc., 9840 Monroe Drive (Bldg. 116), Dallas, TX 75220.

Hinchcliffe Models, Inc., 4824 Memphis, Dallas, TX 75207.

Stan Johansen Miniatures, 4249 East 177th Street, Bronx, NY 10465.

Tom Loback General Artwork, 150 West 26th Street (502) New York, NY 10001.

MacCrea Miniatures, 80 Park Street, Medford, MA 02155.

McEwan Miniatures, 840 West 17th Street, Salt Lake City, UT 84104.

Martian Metals, P.O. Box 388, Cedar Park, TX 78613.

Miniature Figurines, Ltd., P.O. Box P, Pine Plains, NY 12567.

Ral Partha Enterprises, 3726 Lonsdale, Cincinnati, OH 45227.

THE RISING SUN
NEIGHBORHOOD NEWSLETTER

"I admire explorers, but I like mapmakers better because they help the timid." —Birrell

This cast bronze statuette of a game of wari is the work of the Ashanti tribe of Ghana. The woman, who is winning, is shown to be a person of high rank by the ceremonial stool on which she is seated.

Shogi pieces

A snakes and ladders board based on a classic Indian design, can be made in a few hours. Serpents of painted clay coils may be added around the board, to make this game of good versus evil appear even more dramatic. Symbolically, a game of snakes and ladders is a moral journey through life to heaven. The path is shortened by virtue and good deeds, lengthened by evil and vice.

Games of the World

This is, I daresay, the most wonderful games book ever made. Handsomely researched, written, illustrated and designed, there is here a game from every age and place for every age and weather. —*SB*

Games of the World
(How to Make Them, How to Play Them, How They Came to Be)
Frederic V. Grunfeld, Editor
1975, 1977; 280 pp.

OUT OF PRINT
Ballantine Books

Get this book back in print!

The Way to Play

I was snowbound for a few winters at an abandoned hot springs resort in the mountains of Idaho, along with five to ten other isolationists. We played cards and ping-pong, did handcrafting, and floated in the hot pools. This book would have been useful, because along about half way through each winter, the games we knew were getting a little old, and gossiping and petty quarrelling became the big sports. Games provide convenient structures through which some folks can get the losing out of their systems.

There are two thousand games quite fully explained, everything from musical chairs to chemin de fer, well illustrated with strategies discussed, which makes it much more useful than just a book of rules would be. It is especially recommended to groups of people who need new ways to scramble up their intramural success standings. Learn a new game together. —*J.D. Smith*

The Way to Play
(The Illustrated Encyclopedia of the Games of the World)
The Diagram Group
1975; 320 pp.

$7.95 postpaid from:
Bantam Books
414 East Golf Road
Des Plaines, IL 60016
or Whole Earth Household Store

Shove ha'penny

Shove ha'penny is an old English game sometimes played in public houses. Two players or pairs attempt to position ha'pennies or metal disks on a marked board. A game is won by the first side to "shove" three ha'pennies into each of the board's nine "beds."

Poker

Probably the best strategy book around. This is a precision textbook on how to be ruthless. Just reading it is a little frightening.
—*Rosemary Menninger*

Poker
(A Guaranteed Income for Life, by Using the Advanced Concepts of Poker)
1968, 1980; 400 pp.

$7.95 postpaid from:
Warner Books
75 Rockefeller Plaza
New York, NY 10019
or Whole Earth Household Store

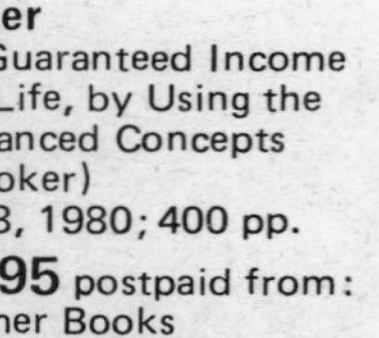

•

The good player is seldom characterized as a tight player. His betting pattern is generally (but not always) aggressive, and often lopsidedly aggressive. Pushing hard whenever he has an advantage (favorable investment odds) and quickly dropping against genuine strength lets him maximize his wins and minimize his losses. A lopsided aggressiveness quickens the betting pace and offers the good player psychological advantages (builds fear in opponents).

World Wide Games

WWG is a small woodworking company that makes and sells games: mostly wooden; some expensive ones (up to $80); mostly inexpensive ($1 to $10). About half of their games are American (old and new); the others originated overseas. For the games they make, they sell replacement parts. The woodworking is clean, smooth, and solid.

Our family has been buying WWG's inexpensive games for several years. Their mail-order service is fast. Their catalog is free. —*R.W. Radl*

World Wide Games
Catalog

free from:
World Wide Games
P.O. Box 450
Delaware, OH 43015

Box Hockey is an exciting and noisy game for 2 or 4 players. Each holds a stick in one hand and attempts to knock the puck through the goal to his left. Game is played on the floor — no table needed. Box Hockey is sturdily built with sides and ends of white oak lumber, bottom of hardwood plywood. It contains 6 sticks and 2 pucks. Box measures 18 x 60 inches open and folds to 18 x 30 x 6. Brass hinges and leather handles make Box Hockey an excellent carrying case for other games.

Go

According to Paul Goodman at the San Francisco Go Club these are the best books on playing the game. They are available in America from the Go Club, or directly from their publisher, the Ishi Press in Japan.

In the Beginning *covers the methods and principles of opening play starting with the very first moves of the game.*

The Direction of Play *explains how the direction of each stone or group of stones exerts its main influence in the game.*

Tesuji *are the tactics of in-fighting. Gives over 300 examples and problems aimed at training the reader to spot the right play in any tactical situation.*

Lessons in the Fundamentals of Go — *connectivity, good and bad shape, the way stones should "move," the difference between territory and influence, how to train yourself to read, where to start looking in a life and death problem, how to study joseki — these are the fundamentals which Kageyama writes about and which every Go player, from beginning to professional, should master.*

The American Go Journal *provides news, game commentary, instruction, general interest articles, and local club news for Go players of all strengths.*
—*David Theis*

In the Beginning
(The Opening in the Game of Go)
Ikuro Ishigure
1973; 152 pp.

$6.50 postpaid

The Direction of Play
Takeo Kajiwara
1979; 248 pp.

$6.50 postpaid

Tesuji
James Davies
1975; 200 pp.

$5.50 postpaid

Lessons in the Fundamentals of Go
Toshiro Kageyama
1978; 268 pp.

$6 postpaid
all from:
San Francisco Go Club
1881 Bush Street
San Francisco, CA 94109

American Go Journal

$12/year (6 issues)
includes membership
from:
American Go Association
P.O. Box 397
Old Chelsea Station
New York, NY 10113

Ishi Press
Catalog

Send 2 International Reply Coupons (about $.80) to:
Ishi Press
CPO Box 2126
Tokyo, Japan

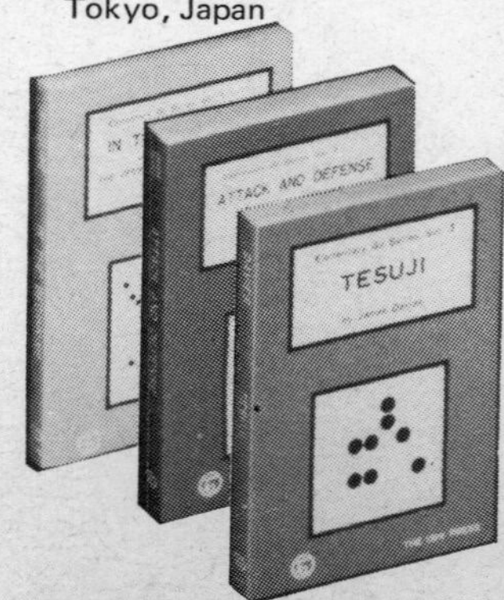

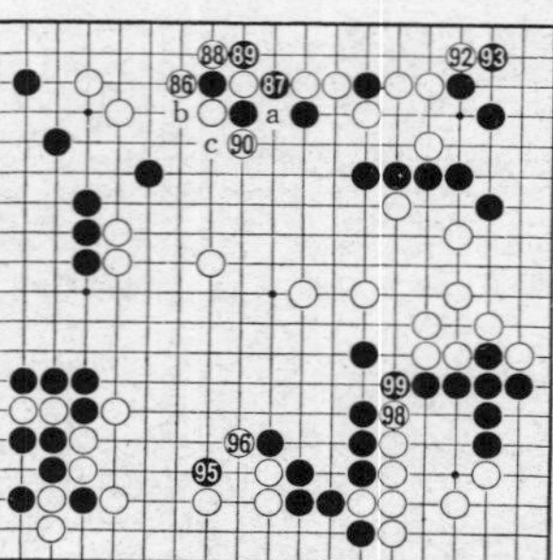

91, 94, 97 and 100: take ko

If White had played 86 at 'a,' then Black 'b,' White 90, Black 'c' would have started a ko. We investigated this, too, after the game but could find no good way for White to play.

I was all ready with what I thought was a good ko threat at Black 95, but White 96 stung sharply. Even now it makes me shudder. There I was, creating difficulties on my own. I was trying too hard. If I had lost, Black 95 would have been the game-losing move.

—Lessons In the Fundamentals of Go

The New Games Book

A compendium of demonstrably playable "new games" — easy-to-join imaginative roughhouse mixing games which have evolved from the New Games Tournaments. (The first one, in 1973, was put on by us.) There are sixty-six games described and abundantly illustrated and named — Hunker Hawser, Slaughter, Earthball, The Mating Game, Prui, Snake-in-the-Grass, etc. The reader-player is given encouragement and guidance to invent further.

It's a **CoEvolution** *and family production. Our Whole Earth business advisor Andrew Fluegelman conceived and edited the book. That's former staffer Beth Fairbanks on the cover. We've run various fractions of the book in our magazine. I wrote a chapter on "Theory of Game Change." If you want objective judgment look elsewhere. We like it.* —SB

The New Games Book
New Games Foundation
Andrew Fluegelman,
Editor
1976; 191 pp.

$4.95 postpaid from:
Doubleday and Company
501 Franklin Avenue
Garden City, NY 11530
or Whole Earth
Household Store

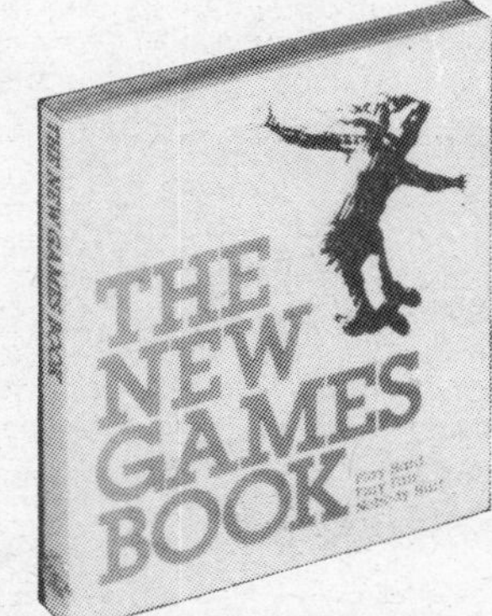

•

You can start with an idea from an old game and follow it wherever it takes you. That's how most of the games in this book evolved. If you're going to invent a new game, try changing or devising one rule at a time. Play the game that way for a bit, then look for the least exciting part of that game and make a rule to correct that. Keep going, and soon you'll have a completely new game.

Earthball

↑
Tweezli-Whop

You'll need two burlap sacks filled with straw and a wooden rail perched high enough to keep your feet from touching the ground. The area beneath the rail should be generously cushioned — a minor haystack will do. You and your partner straddle the rail, face-to-face, and have a go at "whopping" each other with the sacks until one (and frequently both) fall off.

•

Keep an eye out for spectators. Most people who stand around watching a game really want to be playing with you. Invite them.

Kick the Can

Violence! Competition! Vigorous games with plenty of both that have lived far longer than any human being. The vividest sound from my youth is the call echoing through every summer evening in the Michigan pines — "RUN SHEEP RUNNN!"

Nice old book ('50s). No trendy interpretation. —SB

Kick the Can
(And Over 800 Other
Active Games and
Sports for All Ages)
Darwin A. Hindman
1951, 1956; 430 pp.

$3.95 postpaid from:
Prentice-Hall, Inc.
P.O. Box 500
Englewood Cliffs, NJ
07632
or Whole Earth
Household Store

•

Kick-the-Can (Kick-and-Hide. Kick Hide-and-Seek)

All gather around an old tin can placed on the ground inside a two-foot circle. An odd man is selected and one of the other players kicks the can as far as he can. The odd man retrieves the can and places it in the circle while the others run and hide, and then he goes in search of them. When he spies one he calls, "I spy ———," and the two race for the can. The first to reach the can kicks it as far as possible, the other racer immediately becoming odd man. As he retrieves the can, any who have come out of hiding run and hide again. Thus the game continues indefinitely. Of course an old ball or some other object can be substituted for the can.

New Games Resource Catalog

From the New Games Foundation, the tree that grew out of our acorn New Games Tournament in 1973, comes a fine catalog. The best books of how-to and why-to, and plenteous gear: boffers — foam sabres ($16), 6-foot Earthball ($315), loco balls ($5.95), all balls ($5). Invigorate a summer, enthuse a school. —SB

New Games Resource Catalog
(A Playful Guide to
Literature, Games
Equipment and
Materials)

$1 from:
New Games Foundation
P.O. Box 7901
San Francisco, CA 94120

Boffers

You can hit each other endlessly with Boffers and it never hurts, but it does make a very loud, cracking sound (known as a boff). It's a safe way to vent your hostility, with shades of Errol Flynn.

Sword-play games, from Three Musketeers to Star Wars, are what Boffers are all about. They are not for clubbing, but for dueling and also swatting (as in Swat Tag).

Warning: **If Boffers are used like clubs, the tips are likely to break off. Kids really love Boffers, but frankly, if unsupervised, kids quickly demolish them. With care, Boffers will last for many a duel.**

Boffers are white styrofoam swords. They come in a set containing two swords and two eye-and-ear guards. Boffer Sets, 2 lbs. $16

Animal Town Game Company

Friendly organic educational enjoyable board games about small farms, whales, bees, beavers, and the Peter Principle. Cooperation wins. —SB

Mail Order Catalog of Boardgames

free from:
Animal Town Game Co.
P.O. Box 2002
Santa Barbara, CA 93120

→
Part of Nectar Collector ($12). Other Animal Town games include Back to the Farm ($13), Save the Whales ($18), Dam Builders ($13), and Peter Principle ($12).

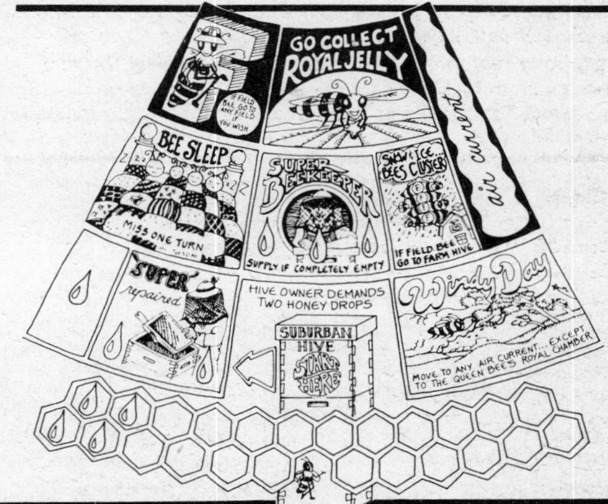

Earthball Canvas Pushballs

OK, it's expensive, we admit it, and there's a lot of games you can't play with it. Baseball, for example, would be difficult to adapt.

But, there's a "Pied Piper" effect to an Earthball. Taking an Earthball to a playing field is like tuning up a band. People can see or hear whatever it is from far away and have an irresistible desire to come closer.

Now, of course, once you've gathered people together, you can do a lot of things with an Earthball that you just can't do with any kind of band. You can push it, roll it, and jump on it; and a group of people can lift it up and pass it, or volley it across a net, or kick it into the air while lying on their backs.

Furthermore, it looks like the whole earth. You can locate yourself on its surface, and sense all the different lands and oceans around you. Anyone for "Planet Pass" while singing, "He's got the whole world in his hands . . .?"

Earthballs are durable pushballs, six feet in diameter, and are guaranteed for one year. They consist of a vinyl lining inside a canvas cover silkscreened with an outline of the world's continents. Each Earthball comes with a set of fabric paints you can use to permanently paint the colors of the earth on the ball. It also comes with a vinyl repair kit. Earthball Canvas Pushballs, 48 lbs. $315

Homo Ludens

Huizinga contends that civilization owes its existence to the play element — to special rituals apart from the daily grind which are joyful, contained in time, space, and rule structure, uncertain in outcome, requiring of fair play, participated in by all. To the roster of convivial tools that Ivan Illich fosters I would add widespread renewal of convivial gaming — play rituals at every level from family to planet. The more frivolous, the more essential to homo ludens. —SB

Homo Ludens
(A Study of the Play
Element in Culture)
Johan Huizinga
1950; 220 pp.

$4.95 postpaid from:
Beacon Press
Harper and Row
Keystone Industrial Park
Scranton, PA 18512
or Whole Earth
Household Store

•

Inside the play-ground an absolute and peculiar order reigns. Here we come across another, very positive feature of play: it creates order, *is* order. Into an imperfect world and into the confusion of life it brings a temporary, a limited perfection. Play demands order absolute and supreme. The least deviation from it "spoils the game," robs it of its character and makes it worthless. The profound affinity between play and order is perhaps the reason why play, as we noted in passing, seems to lie to such a large extent in the field of aesthetics. Play has a tendency to be beautiful.

THE RISING SUN
NEIGHBORHOOD NEWSLETTER

Speaking of office relationships, she said,
"Familiarity breeds attempt."
—Art's friend Sheila who also thought
of the name Next Whole Earth Catalog

Children's Games in Street and Playground

Suppose you were trying to replace war. Would you be interested in "games in which children may deliberately scare each other, ritually hurt each other, take foolish risks, promote fights, play ten against one, and yet in which they consistently observe their own sense of fair play" (dust jacket blurb)? The games are not learned from adults but passed on through the generations of children. This study comes from England, which looks to have a much richer game cycle than American kids usually experience. A product of ten years' research, the book thoroughly describes the rules of play and the popularity of more than a thousand fascinating games.
—SB

Children's Games in Street and Playground
Iona and Peter Opie
1969; 370 pp.
$38 postpaid from:
Oxford University Press
16-00 Pollitt Drive
Fair Lawn, NJ 07140

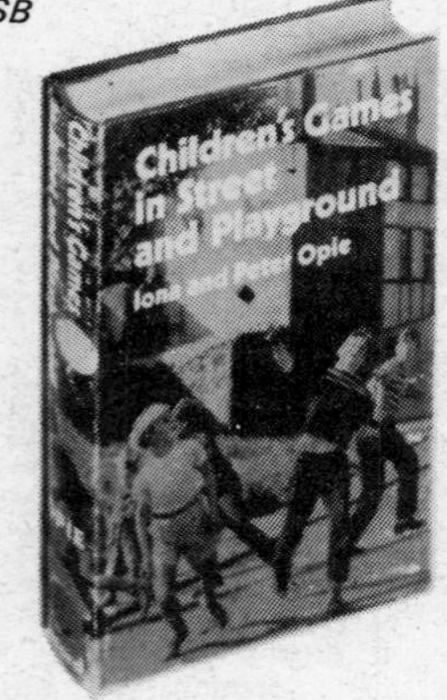

Kingy

This fast-moving game has all the qualifications for being considered the national game of British schoolboys: it is indigenous, it is sporting, it has fully evolved rules, it is immensely popular (almost every boy in England, Scotland, and Wales plays it), and no native of Britain appears to have troubled to record it.

"Kingy" is a ball game in which those who are not He have the ball hurled at them, without means of retaliation, and against ever-increasing odds, an element that obviously appeals to the national character. Anyone who is hit by the ball straightway joins the He in trying to hit the rest of the players. Those who are throwing may not run with the ball in their hands, but pursue their quarry by passing the ball to each other. Those being thrown at may run and dodge as they like, and may also punch the ball away from them with their fists. For this purpose players sometimes wrap a handkerchief round their hand, as "fisting" the ball can be painful. The game continues until all but one have been hit and are "out," and this player is declared "King." When the contestants are skilled (and boys of fifteen and sixteen readily play the game), the ball gets thrown with considerable force; it shoots back and forth across the street or playground, and the game can be as exciting to watch as a tennis match.

As befits a sport in which so much energy is expended, the preliminaries are sometimes wonderfully ritualistic. At Bishop Auckland, for instance, one person shouts "King" to start the proceedings, and two others follow up by crying "Sidey." The players then form a circle round the King, with the two who shouted "Sidey" standing on either side of him like heirs-apparent. The players making the circle stand with legs apart, each foot touching the foot of their neighbour on either side. The King picks up the ball and bounces it — or, as they say in Bishop Auckland, "stounces" it — three times in the ring, and then lets it roll. Everyone watches to see whose legs it will go through. If it does not roll through anybody's legs the King picks it up and bounces it again, and if his second turn fails he has a third try. If the ball still has not passed between anyone's legs, he hands it to the first sidey (the "foggy-sidey") who, as necessary, repeats the performance — for the moment the ball does pass between someone's legs that person is "on," and everyone runs. At the end of the game whoever becomes King takes the place in the centre of the ring to start the next game, and the first two people to shout "Sidey" stand beside him. . . .

The Rules. Although the ways of choosing the chaser are numerous, the game itself is played with little variation. Reports from more than fifty places have been so similar, it is as if a mimeographed sheet of rules was carried in every grubby trouser pocket. Such a set of rules would read as follows:

1. The number of players shall be not less than six or more than twenty: the best number is about twelve.

2. The boundaries of the game shall be agreed on before the game begins. A flat area of 20 x 20 yards, or a length of street of about 20 - 30 yards, depending on the number of players, is ample.

3. One person shall be chosen chaser, and the game shall start immediately he is chosen. The chaser shall, however, bounce the ball ten times before he throws it at anyone, to give the players time to scatter.

4. The chaser may not run with the ball; but while he is the sole chaser he may bounce the ball on the ground as he runs.

5. A player shall be "out" when the ball hits him on the body between his neck and knees (or, as may be agreed, between his waist and ankles). It shall be determined beforehand whether a hit shall count if the ball has first bounced on the ground or ricocheted off a wall; or whether only a direct hit shall count.

6. As soon as a player is "out" he shall assist the chaser in getting the other players out.

7. When there are two or more chasers they may not run with the ball, but may manoeuvre as they wish by passing it to each other.

8. Players being chased may take what action they like to avoid being hit by the ball, including "fisting" it, i.e., punching it away with their fist. They may also pick up the ball between their fists and chuck it away.

9. Should a chaser catch the ball when it has been "fisted," or touch a player while he is holding the ball in his fists, the player shall be "out."

10. Should a player kick the ball, or handle it other than with his fists, he shall be "out."

11. Should a player run out of bounds when trying to avoid being hit by the ball he shall be "out."

12. The last player left in shall be "King," and shall officiate at the selection of the next chaser.

Orienteering

The word means finding your way with map and compass; a good thing to know how to do. Sharpening your skill permits confident "bushwhacking" away from the increasingly crowded trails. Some people make a contest of it, which is a good way to gain skill while giving you a good excuse for wandering around outdoors. Some make a race of it as a true test. This book is mainly aimed at the racers and is intended to promote orienteering as a sport. My problem is that I can never remember where I left my compass. The authors don't mention what to do about that, but they cover about everything else. (Bengtsson's excellent **Be Expert with Map and Compass** *is reviewed on p. 414.)*
—J. Baldwin

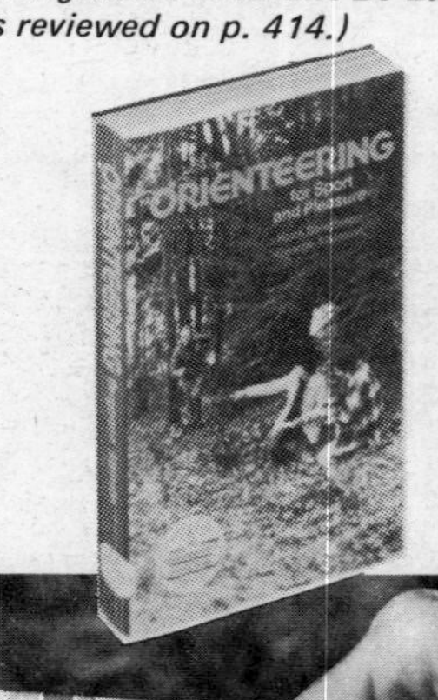

Orienteering
(For Sport and Pleasure)
Hans Bengtsson and
George Atkinson
1977; 224 pp.
$6.95 postpaid from:
The Stephen Greene Press
P.O. Box 1000
Fessenden Road
Brattleboro, VT 05301
or Whole Earth
Household Store

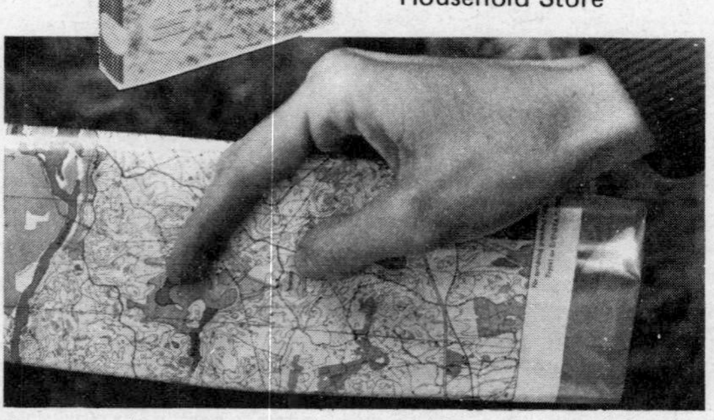

↑
The best way to carry the map is to fold it inside a clear plastic pocket of medium-thick poly. The thick plastic prevents permanent creases from forming regardless of how the map/map case is folded.

This flexible map case also enables you to use the popular and time-saving technique called "thumbing." This is the technique of folding and holding the map so you can use your thumb as a continual pointer to your then current location. *As you move over the land, your thumb moves (with you) over the map.* In this way, every time you look at the map you can fast-focus on your current position instead of having to search over the entire map area. Thumbing not only saves time during a race but also eliminates most chances of parallel errors, i.e., mixing up two adjacent (or nearly so) areas with basically the same main features.

With this technique and some practice you should be able to become quite proficient at running and map reading simultaneously.

Cowstails & Cobras

I love this stuff. A summer camp I went to had an obstacle course against which I would pit myself with unending serious glee. Then in training as an infantry officer I encountered the famous and wonderful group problems — get everyone across the water hazard dry in ten minutes with only a rope, two poles, and a spare tire; staaart now. Etc.

This splendid book has scores of such things — how to make and use. Surely no one has to explain why. Ingenuity learned by the body sticks. Courage too.
—SB

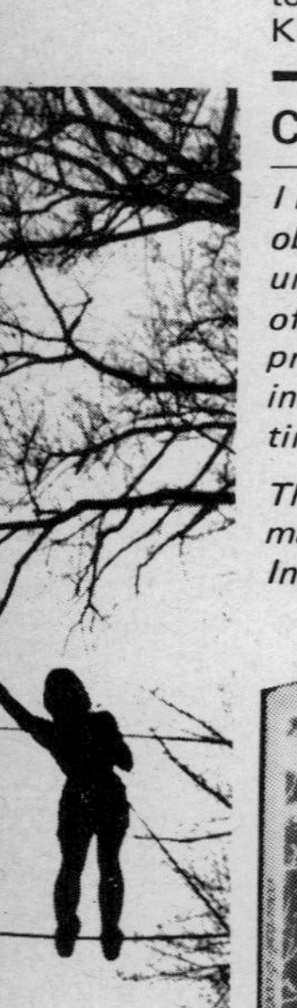

Cowstails & Cobras
(A Guide to Ropes Courses, Initiative Games, and other Adventure Activities)
Karl Rohnke
1977, 157 pp.
$7.25 postpaid from:
Project Adventure
P.O. Box 157
Hamilton, MA 01936

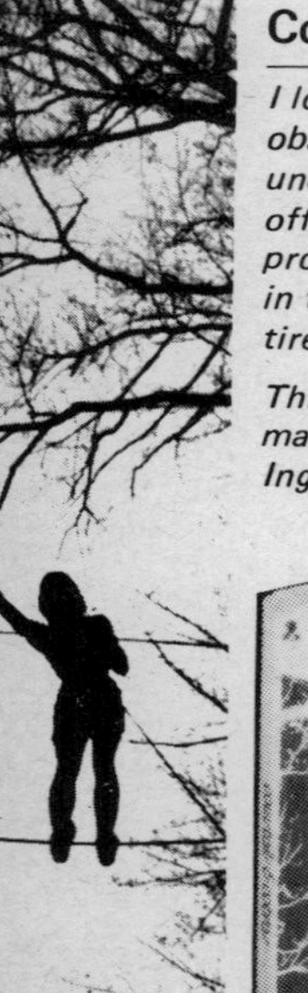

← Two line bridge

Tire traverse ⟶

↓
Tire Traverse

Object: To get the entire group and a "bomb" over a series of suspended tires without touching the ground. (Devise your own bomb, but it should weigh about 30 pounds. A metal ammunition box full of rocks makes a good bomb.)

Rules:

1. The students must proceed from a starting line in front of the first swing rope and end at the finishing line past the last tire.

2. No member of the group may step over the start or finishing line at any time to help. Verbal help may be given at any time.

3. If an individual touches the ground he must return to the starting line and begin again. If the bomb touches the ground, the entire group must begin again.

4. The bomb may not be thrown over the finish line.

5. No knots may be tied. However, a bight in the swing rope may be taken.

6. The available beam may be used in any manner, but if it touches the ground anywhere between the start and finish lines, the group loses further use of it.

7. The horizontal support wire may not be used in any way.

8. No other aids may be used.

9. There is no limit to the number of participants on the tires.

10. Some of the tires may be suspended horizontally to add variety to the passage.

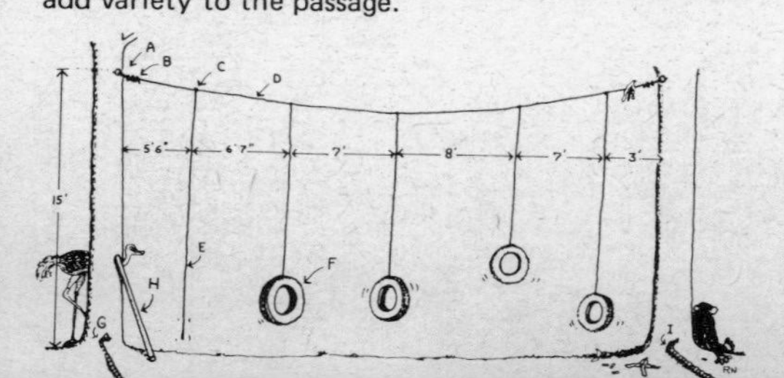

Indian Crafts and Lore

If Boy Scouts and Germans make better Indian gear than most Indians (it's true: ask at any pow-wow), this book may be why. Thorough research and splendid illustration trip you right on in. Good book.
—SB

Indian Crafts and Lore
W. Ben Hunt
1954, 1976; 104 pp.
$2.95 postpaid from:
Golden Press
Western Publishing Co.
1220 Mound Avenue
Racine, WI 53404
or Whole Earth
Household Store

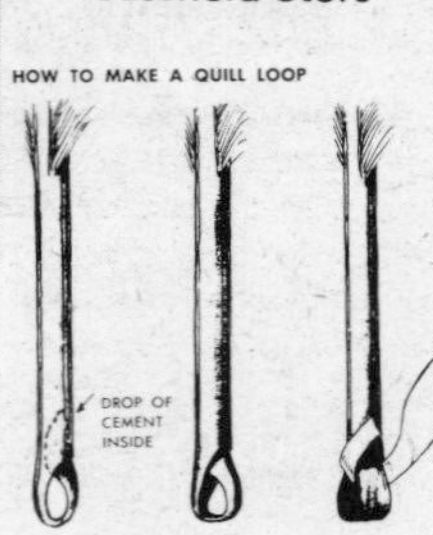

HOW TO MAKE A QUILL LOOP
DROP OF CEMENT INSIDE
1. SOFTEN END OF QUILL IN HOT WATER AND CUT AS SHOWN WITH SHARP KNIFE.
2. PUT A DROP OF CEMENT ON END AND TUCK IT UP INTO THE QUILL.
3. LET IT DRY. ANCHOR TAPE AND WRAP AS SHOWN ABOVE

Grey Owl Indian Craft Supplies

Indian outfit gear, materials, and kits. Suit up, sneak off the reservation, help America start over.
—SB

Grey Owl Indian Craft Supplies
Catalog

$1 from:
Indian Craft Company
113-15 Springfield Blvd.
Queens Village, NY 11429

Grow Flesh Eating Plants

Venus Fly Trap. The most popular of carnivorous plants. Eats flys, other insects. Exotic, beautiful plant snaps shut on anything: finger, pencil, bugs. Watch amazing natural phenomenon as your full grown plant traps & eats its live prey. Single bulb ready to grow. Plants grow several inches high with 10-15 traps, lovely flowers.

☐ **5011. Venus Fly Trap Bulb $1.19**

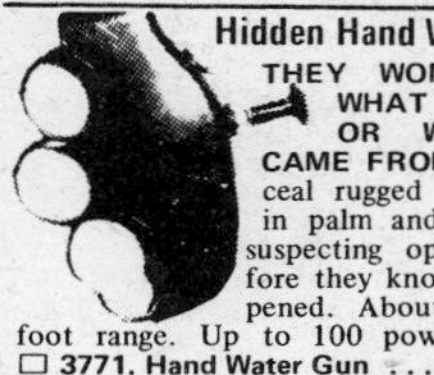

Hidden Hand Water Gun

THEY WON'T KNOW WHAT HIT THEM. OR WHERE IT CAME FROM. You conceal rugged water pistol in palm and drench unsuspecting opponents before they know what happened. About 20 to 30 foot range. Up to 100 powerful blasts.

☐ **3771. Hand Water Gun .... 79¢**

REPLICA DIAMOND RING

LOOKS REAL! MEASURES OVER 1-INCH ACROSS. Stunning ring to give or wear. **Realistic copy of HOPE DIAMOND RING.** Has the sparkle & fire of real thing. Causes sensation. Attractive mounting. Adjustable size. Gift box.

$3.95

☐ **8210. Simulated Hope Diamond... $3.95**

Deluxe Bottle Cutter $3.95

Make beautiful glassware from old bottles. Make your own glasses, vases, lamps, ash trays, candy dishes, etc. Easy-to-do. Ready-to-use. Preassembled cutter. **Newest advanced technique. Clean cuts.** Cuts most bottles up to gallon jugs.

☐ **4016. Bottle Cutter $3.95**

The Johnson Smith Catalog

If you were ever a kid, you remember Johnson Smith. But you may have forgotten just how relevant Johnson Smith could be to your present happiness, not to mention your spiritual development.

They've been around for 65 years. Remember the lists you used to make of all the things you wanted? Well, surprise! You'll still want the same things: secret agent pen radio, juggling kits, X-ray Spex, Magic Money Maker, joy buzzers and, of course, VENTRILO ("BOYS! BOYS! BOYS! Learn Ventriloquism and Apparently THROW YOUR VOICE! Into a trunk, under the bed, under a table, back of the door, into a desk at school, or anywhere. You'll get lots of fun fooling the teacher, policemen, peddlers and surprise and fool your friends besides.")

Yes, Johnson Smith is alive and well in Mt. Clemens, MI. Johnson Smith hasn't changed. But what about you? Get with it, kids!

—Robert Goldman

TELEPHONE SET

Talk from room to room, home to garage, office to shop, house to house, indoors and outdoors. Convenient, practical French-type phones. Electric, dry cell battery operated. **Just lift receiver, ring and talk. Carries voice clearly.** Set of 2 phones, each with electric speaker and earphone, bell to signal call, 25 feet of wire. Easy to connect. Ready to operate immediatel,.

☐ **6809. Home Desk Phone Set. Pair $17.95**

Sucker Coin Trick

FAST MONEY MAKER FOR YOU! Friend drops coin into slot in small plastic box. First it rattles, then disappears. You can make it re-appear in your pocket (or their pocket) if you wish, or keep it and say: "Thanks, Sucker!" Fun & profitable pocket trick.

☐ **3151. Sucker Coin Trick .... 49¢**

The Johnson Smith Catalog
Catalog
free from:
Johnson Smith
35075 Automation Drive
Mt. Clemens, MI 48043

America's Hobby Center

AHC is legendary. They have to publish a separate catalog for each type of ware they stock (model trains, planes, boats, and cars), because their inventory is overwhelmingly huge. Making models can involve the same kind of destiny-controlling creativity as writing a good story. My own obsession was once model trains; now I cry out with nostalgia and sheer covetousness when I look through their train catalog. Prices are low, sale prices are amazingly low, and service is always good.

—Art Kleiner

Airplanes
Catalog
$1.50

HO and N Gauge Model Railroads
Catalog
$1.50

Wood and Plastic Ships
Catalog
$1.50

Set of Catalogs and Bulletins
$3.99

all from:
America's Hobby Center
146 West 22nd Street
New York, NY 10021

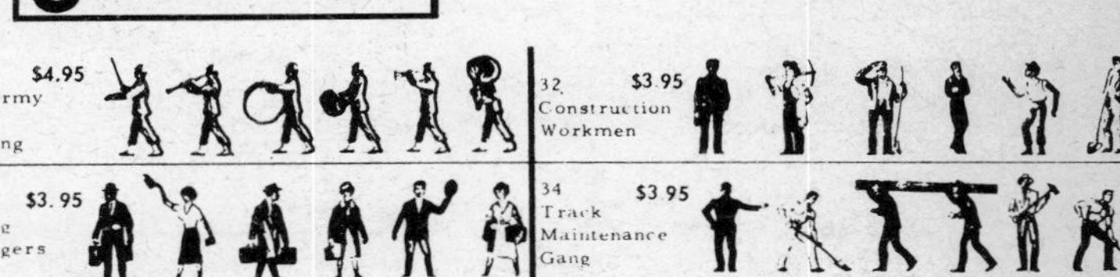

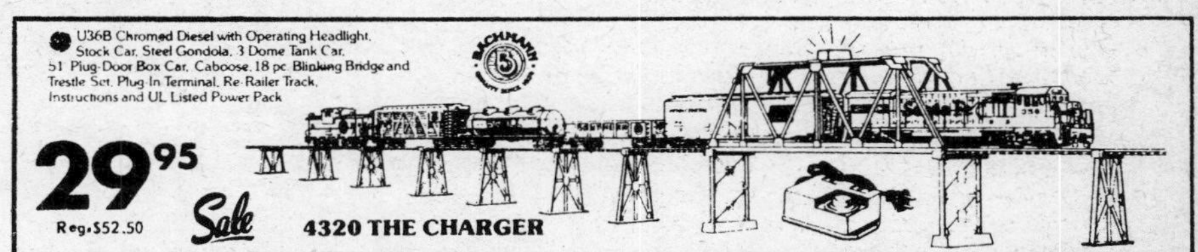

Campaigns

The fascinating world of military miniatures. There's a level of skill, art, and fanaticism here I never dreamed of.

—SB

[Suggested by Jodie Evans]

Campaigns
(An International Magazine of Military Miniatures)
Donald Burgess, Editor
$15/year (6 issues)
from:
Campaigns
P.O. Box 76087
Los Angeles, CA 90076

←
The Soldier Centre's Carthaginian war elephant, by Howard Wolf, bronze medal winner

The Puppet Theatre Handbook

The great-grandmother of all puppet-making manuals is **The Puppet Theatre Handbook** *by Marjorie Batchelder. If you can invest in only one book to get you started with puppets, this is it. It covers the four major kinds of puppets — hand, rod, shadow, marionette; how to work puppets, how to make puppet theaters, write scripts and put a show together. It's the Bible.*

—Joanne Forman

The Puppet Theatre Handbook
(A complete guide for the puppeteer)
Marjorie Batchelder
1947; 289 pp.
$9.95 postpaid from:
Harper and Row
Keystone Industrial Park
Scranton, PA 18512
or Whole Earth Household Store

•

Humanettes

A standard side show novelty, the humanette, has invaded everything from vaudeville to night club floor shows. Simplicity of construction and operation make it a good act where space is limited; besides, it is fun to make, to work, and to watch.

Actually, it is no more than a cloth-and-cotton-filled body that fits around the operator's neck so that when he stands behind a table, bed, or specially built box or stage, the illusion is that of a midget body with normal sized head and hands.

A cloak or jacket is constructed as shown in *Figure A.* The drawstring is tied around the operator's neck while his hands fit through the short sleeves. The cloth body of the puppet *B* is about 28" high, with joints at the waist and knees. It is sewn to the cloak. This creates the impression of a puppet *not* worked from behind, and helps hide the operator's body which will be almost invisible if a stage is used and the jacket is of the same color as the backdrop. Care should be taken to keep as little light as possible from falling on the backdrop *(figure C).*

A favorite trick is to fasten a ring to the center of a length of string or fishline and attach the opposite ends to the knees and shoulders respectively. These rings are slipped over a finger on each hand, thus enabling the operator to move the humanette's legs and feet *(figures C* and *D).*

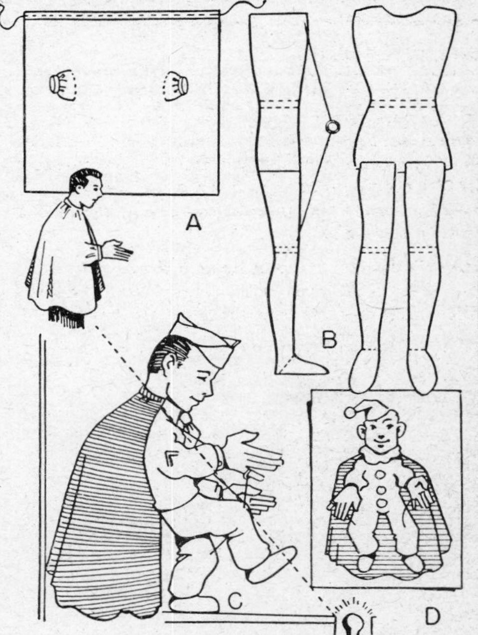

Construction diagram of a humanette by Douglas Anderson

Making Puppets Come Alive

How do you bring puppets to life? With detailed instructions, easy-to-do exercises, and beautiful demonstration photographs (that indicate motion), Larry Engler and Carol Fijan show beginners how to develop the skills to make puppets jump, cry, sneeze and snore. They also show you everything necessary for putting on a full-scale puppet production. A first-rate introduction to puppetry.

—Dorothy Atkins

Making Puppets Come Alive
Larry Engler and Carol Fijan
1973; 192 pp.
$9.95 postpaid from:
Taplinger Publishing Company
200 Park Avenue South
New York, NY 10003
or Whole Earth Household Store

↓
Running. To give the illusion of running, your arm must move up and down rapidly and in a choppy manner, while moving the puppet quickly across the stage. The puppet that merely zooms across the stage is not seen. The choppy movement of the arm gives the necessary feeling of rapidity.

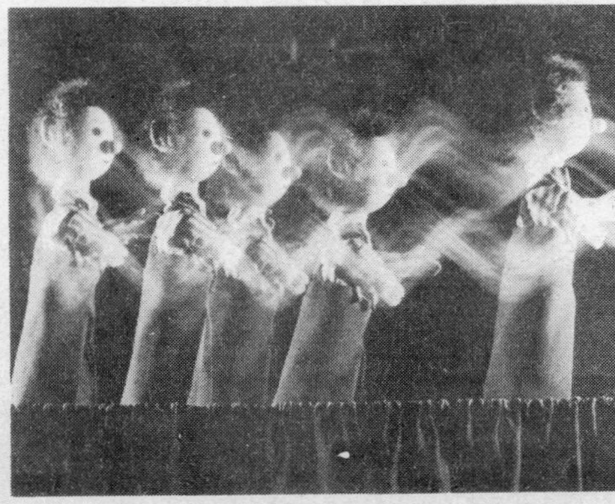

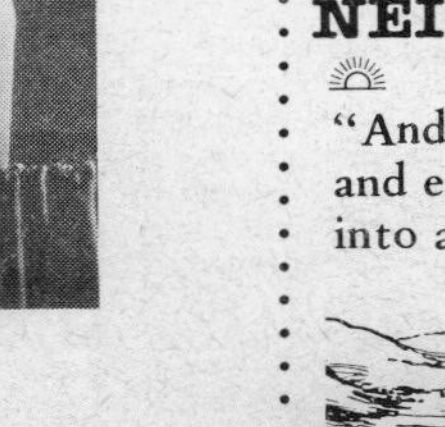

THE RISING SUN NEIGHBORHOOD NEWSLETTER

"And then you leave home and you come back and everything in your refrigerator has turned into a science project."

—Tom Waits

The Juggling Book

I've found juggling to be a sport/meditation-in-action/ training superbly suited for the balancing act and juggling of energies required for staying aloft. When I juggle I am either focused and centered or I drop me balls. Simple as that. Instant bio-feedback. If I'm ON I can step back and watch my hands put out continuing displays of patterns and form change.

All of which is good practice for what for me is the real high of juggling — doing passes with a friend or friends. Now there are 6 balls in front of you instead of 3. One must lock into the other person's timing and flow. At which point you sort of disappear and as long as you don't stop to think how it happens the patterns just continue to unfold effortlessly. It's a great way to warm up and get your timing together if you are a musician, which is my trade.

The best book out is **The Juggling Book** *by Carlo. It should only take you 30 minutes to an hour at the beach or on a large grassy area (saves on furniture) to get started. If you don't know anyone who juggles, Carlo's book seems lucid and thorough enough to do the trick. There's a wealth of material here, some nice advanced stunts — the progression from 3 to 4 ball juggling is clear and logical — and the emphasis on inner states and mind-set is right on. My only complaint is not enough pictures. (For more on juggling as a vocation see p. 301.)*

—Jon Scoville

The Juggling Book
(Everything You Need to Know to Master This Exciting Circus Art and Learn a Lot About Yourself in the Process)
Carlo (Charles Lewis)
1974; 102 pp.

$4.95 postpaid from:
Vintage Books
Random House
455 Hahn Road
Westminster, MD 21157
or Whole Earth Household Store

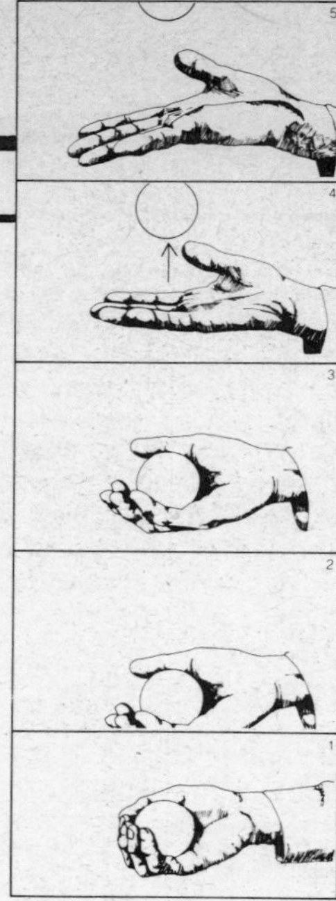

Popping the ball

Louis Tannen's Catalog of Magic
Hank Lee's Magic Factory

Hank Lee has nice stuff for young magicians and parties. Louis Tannen has the biggest magic catalog around, with all manner of tricks, equipment, and work plans for larger gear.

—SB

↑

Wunderbar — a four-star effect, bar none!

Look, Ma, no hands. This reputation-maker by Steve Dusheck is not to be confused with the Silver Stick. Wunderbar is a close-up floating bar effect. Throughout the floating routine the hands need NEVER move, but nevertheless the bar bobs and rises and falls. Wunderbar is the closest thing to real magic we've ever seen. A test tube is introduced, with a 2½" shiny rod inside, supposedly made from moon minerals. It bounces up and down inside the test tube and eventually knocks the cork out. Then Wunderbar proceeds to float up and out of the tube, do an aerial ballet in the air (with NO hand movement whatsoever), and finally floats into your hand. Your close-up audience will believe they've experienced true levitation, and this effect is surprisingly easy to do. Get Wunderbar today. The greatest bargain in magic today! $9.00.

—Louis Tannen's Catalog of Magic

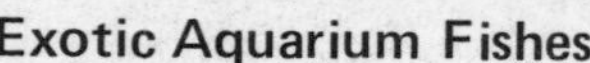

Hank Lee's Magic Factory
Catalog

$1 from:
Hank Lee's
Magic Factory
24 Lincoln Street
Boston, MA 02111

Louis Tannen's Catalog of Magic

$5.95 postpaid from:
Louis Tannen, Inc.
1540 Broadway
New York, NY 10036

↑

A spectator is asked to help with a magical experiment. He places his arm into the chopper. A large solid blade is forced down through his wrist and his hand (his ACTUAL hand!) is seen to drop off into the bag below! One of the most startling effects imaginable. Very well made and only $47.50 (10-702).

—Hank Lee's Magic Factory

Magic Digest

Great magic tricks anyone can perform without special equipment. Everyone should have at least four of these for tedious or tense moments. Every kid should be able to dextrously prestidigitate (baffle grown-ups) by the age of 12.

—SB
[Suggested by Robert Bowie]

Magic Digest
(Fun Magic for Everyone)
George B. Anderson
1972; 288 pp.

$6.95 postpaid from:
DBI, Inc.
1 Northfield Plaza
Northfield, IL 60093
or Whole Earth Household Store

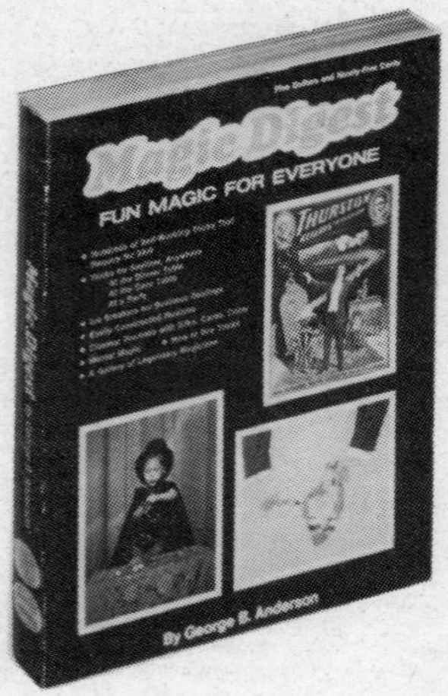

→

Sheer Nerve

Annemann did one card location that was so nervy, magicians couldn't believe it — but he always got away with it. He had a spectator remove a card and remember it. Then, his head turned away, he took the face down card in his right hand, deck in left hand, and put both hands behind his back, saying, "I'm going to put your card into the deck while the cards are behind my back, so that you know I can't look at any of the other cards or put it in any particular spot."

With the deck behind his back, he very deliberately put the chosen card on top of the deck and pulled an indifferent card out about an inch from the middle of the pack. Then he brought his hands to the front, observing, "It's not quite at the middle of the deck." He quickly shoved the protruding card square with the rest of the pack. The selected card was, of course, on top.

He did numerous tricks with this daring substitute for the pass. One simple one was to have the spectator deal four piles of cards from the top of the deck, as many cards in each pile as he chose. Then, picking up each pile and apparently weighing it in his hand, he would declare that the chosen card was in one of the four piles. He carelessly fanned that pile, cutting it and handing to the spectator to acknowledge whether or not he had been correct. The card is, of course, always at the bottom of the first pile. In fanning and cutting the pile, Annemann glimpsed the chosen card.

When the spectator acknowledged the correctness of his selection, Annemann told him to form a mental picture of his card, and then, in dramatic fashion, told him what it was.

Another variation, used at a card table, was to ask a spectator to hold his right hand under the card table, about six inches beneath the table top. "Now," he said, "move to the center. I'll show you." Deck in his right hand, he deliberately put both hands under the table, grasped the spectator's wrist with his left hand, and moved the hands to about the center of the table. He deliberately thumbed off the top card of the deck, holding it against the underside of the table top with his left protruding forefinger, the spectator's wrist being held with the other fingers.

He held the deck in his right hand and slammed it down firmly on top of the table, and let it drop into the spectator's hand.

It doesn't sound sensational, but if you're the spectator, you're absolutely dumbfounded when that chosen card lights on your face-up palm.

•

The Ground Rules of Magic

1. Decide on a style of performance and stick with it.
2. Make your personal appearance indicate the quality of your performance.
3. Never do a trick in public unless you can do it well.
4. Routine your tricks.
5. Never, never NEVER expose a trick under any circumstances.
6. Amateur or professional, you extend professional courtesy to other performers.
7. Accept prevailing performance conditions.
8. Don't embarrass anyone in your audience.
9. Keep it clean.
10. Never do tricks with dangerous items in front of children.
11. Have a definite terminal point.

Exotic Aquarium Fishes

More than 70% of the Whole Earth's surface is under water, with proportional animate population, our ancestral home. Some people immerse themselves in this ecological dimension swimmingly. Others box a bit of it and keep it in their homes for observation, education, fascination, fun. Aquarists have been long aware of environmental balances and such, playing god. How you keep your tanks will show you to be curious, careless, callous, compassionate, concerned, or what.

The dean of American aquarists is Dr. William T. Innes, whose classic manual with its exquisite color photographs, updated by assistants and now published cheaply, unfolds scientific insight, practical lore, wry humor, and humane wisdom.

—Tom Wertenbaker

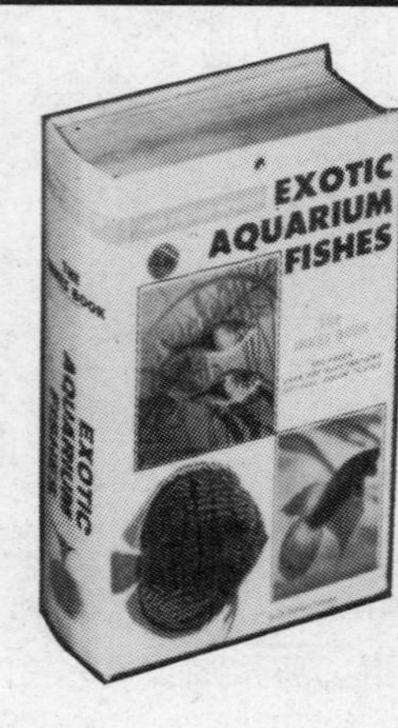

Exotic Aquarium Fishes
Dr. William T. Innes
1938, 1966; 590 pp.

$9.95 postpaid from:
T.F.H. Publications
211 West Sylvania Avenue
Neptune City, NJ 07753
or Whole Earth Household Store

Aqua Engineers

Looks like an unusually low-priced mail order supplier of aquarium stuff.

—SB

Aqua Engineers
Catalog

free from:
Aqua Engineers
335 Mill Street
Ortonville, MI 48462

About the Power Master 300. This rugged filter is designed to pump 300 gallons per hour continuously for many years without a decrease in output or any increase in noise level. You would use it on 20-gal. to 75-gal. tanks. For larger tanks, you could use two. Self priming, never needs oiling. $42.04 →

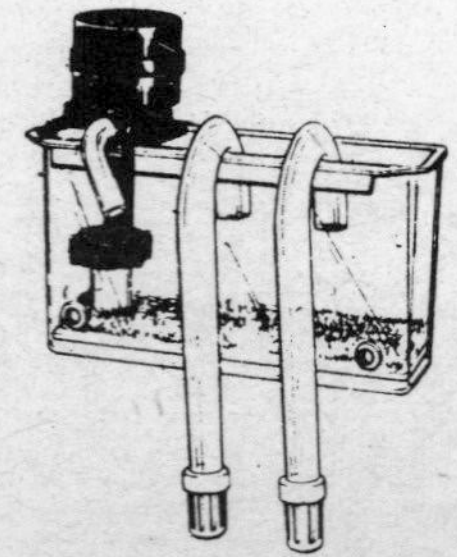

Boy Scout Fieldbook

The Scouts continue their tradition of excellent feedback from an increasingly enormous membership. Their **Fieldbook** *may well be the best value around. Of course, the context is short term camping out in the continental U.S., but much more is afoot. In taking us sure-handedly from the root-hog-or-die survival situations through toward gourmet ecology, the* **Fieldbook** *shows how far we've come and certainly what to do next. The spirit of the Boer War appears to be giving way to that of enlightened naturalism (don't go blazing trees — the landowner will never have us back). Full of recipes, checklists, buying guides, patterns and plans, close-up photographs in how-to-do-it sequence. If you'll need to know something, it's there.*

Having put us at home outdoors, the book opens up into biology, geology and astronomy, and what to do about them. I especially like two sections: one has pictures of which plants to eat where you're starving to death, and the page that tells you not to apply the tourniquet except as a last resort. —Dave Guard

•

Nosebleed is usually from a small vein in the middle partition of the nose. Fold a clean piece of paper into a pressure pad and tuck it under your upper lip. If the blood continues to flow, add to the thickness of the pad and press your index finger across your upper lip.

Rock Tripe (Gyrophora dillenie) can be scrambled like egg in a little water or fat. ←

↓ Have you some steel wool — a scouring pad, maybe? And a two-cell flashlight with live cells? Hold the two cells in one fist, top touching bottom in a firm contact. Shred out pad and tuck one end under the bottom cell. Touch the upper end of pad to the bright contact pole of the upper cell. It will glow and burn hotly. Catch in tinder.

Naturally you want to be physically fit, but are you willing to make the effort?

Boy Scout Field Book
(A Practical Guide For Everyone to Life in The Outdoors)
Boy Scouts of America
1967, 1978; 566 pp.

$4.95 postpaid from:
Workman Publishing Co.
One West 39th Street
New York, NY 10018
or Whole Earth Household Store

Drownproofing

The product of most warnings about water is: "Well, I've fallen in the water, now I'm supposed to start drowning."

New program: "No need to drown." Sinkers, non-swimmers, cripples, children; cramped, exhausted, injured, no rescue in sight. "No need to drown."

The book is sufficient for you to learn or teach the techniques appropriate for floaters, sinkers, and sundry special circumstances. Good medicine for anxious parents. Teach your kids and yourself and stop worrying. —SB

(See **The Science of Swimming**, *p. 455.)*

Drownproofing
Fred Lanoue
1963, 1978; 112 pp.
$3.95 postpaid from:
Prentice Hall, Inc.
P.O. Box 5001
Englewood Cliffs, NJ 076 07632
or Whole Earth Household Store

•

Panic makes you throw your head back, reach up, make gurgling noises, horrible faces and kick and wave your arms frantically. None of these moves will do you the slightest good. Now is the time to learn the following, because *this is what really makes drownproofing work:*

Whether your nose and throat are full of water from lips to stomach, the stroke or the kick will *always* get you to the surface . . .

If you do it in the same manner as you had been doing it, *if* you blow out through your nose, with your lips clamped tightly together as you break the surface with another kick or stroke, whether air or water comes out, you will be somewhat relieved and you will be ready for the inhale.

If your eyes are open and *if* you inhale through your mouth, whether you end up with all air, half air and half foam, you will be better off, and *if* you continue the cycle, *no matter how much water you shipped*, things will get better much sooner than you think.

If this procedure is stuck to and mastered, 90 percent of those involuntary swallows of water will be forgotten three cycles (15 seconds) later. The other 10 percent may take 10 cycles to completely recover from, but if you force yourself to repeat the cycle properly, you are sure to be all right. What counts is that you get yourself out of trouble.

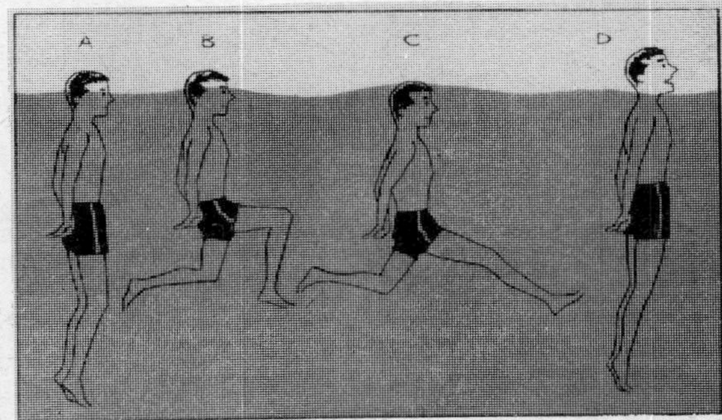

Scissors kick

American Boys Handy Book

Dan Beard's **American Boys Handy Book** *was first published in 1882. After it was out of print for a long time, Tuttle finally reprinted it. This is barefoot-boy-with-cheek-of-tan stuff, detailed lore on how children may make their own worlds. Extraordinary book.* —SB

[Suggested by Arthur Brand]

The American Boys Handy Book
D.C. Beard
1882, 1970; 391 pp.
$10 postpaid from:
Charles E. Tuttle Co.
Rutland, VT 05701
or Whole Earth Household Store

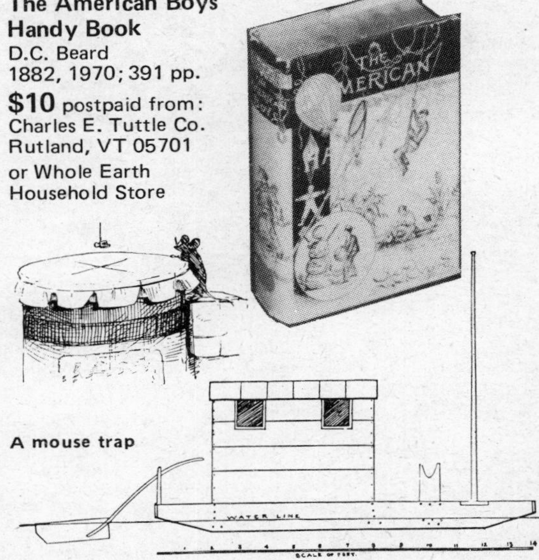

A mouse trap

Side view of flat-boat

Set a seat in front of the rowlock with a hole in it for the "jack-staff" to pass through. The jack-staff should be made so that it can be taken out and put in at pleasure.

Shelters, Shacks and Shanties

A unique little book on primitive structures, sheds, treehouses, Indian buildings, cabin hardware and wilderness shelter. The building diagrams are complete and detailed. Written for Boy Scouts by an American sportsman-outdoorsman in 1914. How simple things were then. —Lloyd Kahn

Shelters, Shacks and Shanties
D.C. Beard
1914, 1972; 243 pp.
$5.95 postpaid from:
Charles Scribner's Sons
Vreeland Avenue
Totowa, NJ 07512
or Whole Earth Household Store

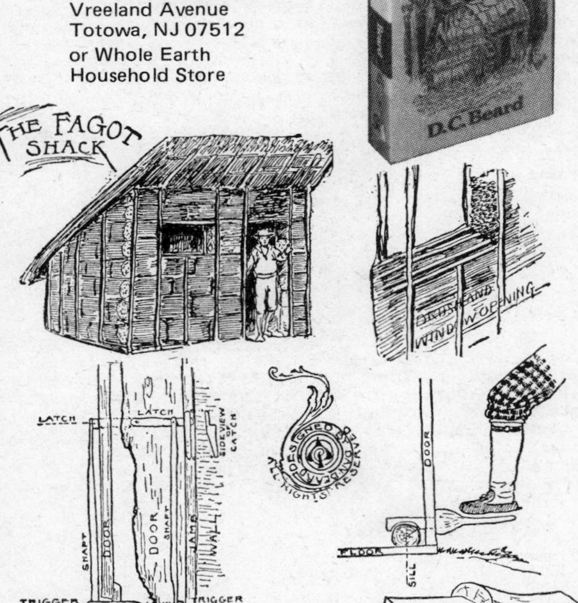

Audubon bird call

Dear Whole Earth:

This one you cannot pass up. This is the best damn $3.50 I ever spent. The Audubon Bird Call works. It won't do ducks or crows or turkeys — but it will do every song bird I've come across. I am not a bird fan (i.e., watcher, listener) in the classic sense. I'm a composer and sound freak. That's why I bought this thing in the first place. For $3.50 it was cheaper and more efficient than a Buchla synthesizer — my 2nd favorite source of bird simulations. I bought it sound unheard but it was a gem. In the middle of one night there was a wiseacre bird outside my house singing like crazy. I got out my trusty Audubon Bird Call and matched this bird, note for note, phrase for phrase for over an hour and neither of us ever repeated a phrase. I would answer him unless he stopped. Then I would lead off with something I thought idiomatic and he always jumped back in. I still don't know what kind of bird it was and really don't care. But I really talked to that bird and learned his sense for variation and development in his singing. It was tremendous.

Now the thing takes a little practice and a musical ear is clearly an asset; but it is the simplest musical instrument I ever played and probably the most versatile and pregnant. I used the thing for a movie soundtrack (for background) in a film I was scoring and it was perfect. Talk about absolute control!

If you have a passing interest in birds (as I do) or more, you'll love this thing — take it on hikes, picnics, whatever. If you hate birds — this may be the key to telling them to buzz off in language they'll understand — no shit. It costs $3.50 from Roger Eddy, Newington, Connecticut 06111 — a real deal.

Roger Hyde
Los Angeles, California

Marine Aquarium Keeping

For the more ambitious aquarium keeper and student of marine life, this book comprehensively covers scientific, technical aspects of aquaria and their ecology. The price is a bit steep, but the information on equipping and maintaining aquaria, choosing and caring for the fish, and creating an attractive marine environment, is detailed and complete. Format and illustrations are excellent — if you are a serious aquarium hobbyist, or plan to be, this could be a worthwhile investment. —Doris Herrick

Marine Aquarium Keeping
(The Science, Animals, and Art)
Stephen Spotte
1973; 171 pp.
$14.50 postpaid from:
John Wiley and Sons
One Wiley Drive
Somerset, NJ 08873
or Whole Earth Household Store

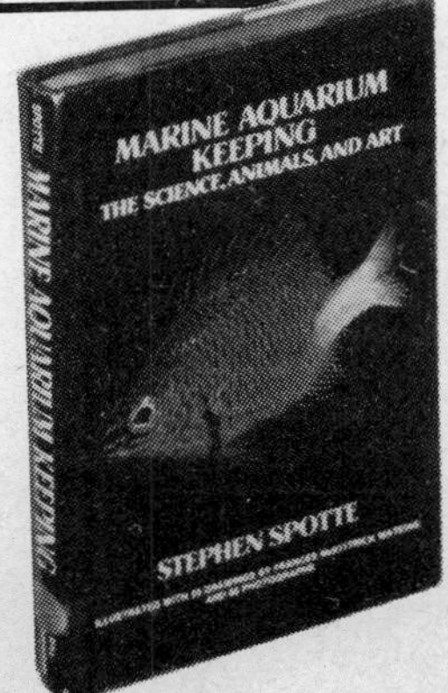

THE RISING SUN
NEIGHBORHOOD NEWSLETTER

One time Ralph Waldo Emerson was carving a roast and talking about the evil of cannibalism, Bronson Alcott said, "But Mr. Emerson, if we are to eat meat, why not eat the best?"

—Information from *Louisa May: A Modern Biography* by Martha Saxton

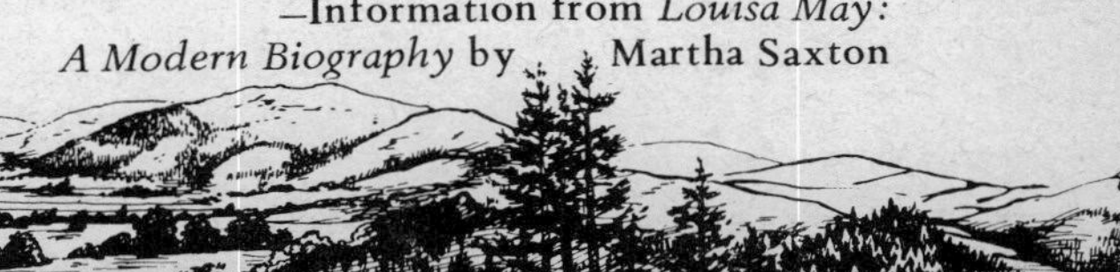

Care of the Wild, Feathered and Furred

The time-tested techniques and practical suggestions. My survival rate soared after discovering this handbook. The writing is easy and grass-roots. —Peter Warshall

Care of the Wild, Feathered and Furred
(A Guide to Wildlife Handling and Care)
Mae Hickman and Maxine Guy
1973; 143 pp.

$5.95 postpaid from:
Unity Press
P.O. Box 1037
Santa Cruz, CA 95061
or Whole Earth Household Store

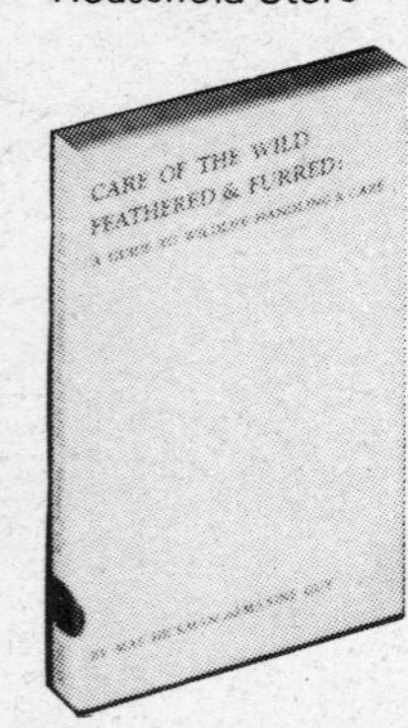

↑ **Red squirrel**

A baby squirrel raised in captivity can be very susceptible to colds. Never bathe the animal. Do not use cedar shavings sold in local pet shops for hamster and mouse cages as they may cause a coating of cedar dust to settle on the animal, clogging the nostrils and causing discomfort. If it is necessary to clean him, use tissues with a bit of baby oil or white petroleum jelly. Never use cotton. Cotton may leave moisture, adding to the danger of pneumonia.

Mockingbird fledglings

↑

The first and most important step when you have a fledgling brought to you is to warm the bird as soon as possible. Nestlings, out of their nests and exposed to the elements, are highly vulnerable to death by pneumonia and need special care until they recuperate. Use a hot water bottle or heating pad (turned on low) or, if you do not have either of these, jars of hot water will do. Plastic bottles that hold liquid detergents and shampoos make excellent hot water bottles. Otherwise use glass jars. Fasten the lids tightly, wrap them in paper and snuggle the tiny birds in a nest of facial tissue directly against the jars. I suggest using two jars, one on either side of the bird, to supply more even heat to the body. The bird will benefit more from the heat if the nest is put directly on top of a padded hot water bottle or heating pad. The heating pad is really preferable to either the hot water bottle or glass jars since the latter will become cool and have to be refilled, while the heating pad will supply an even heat for as long as it is needed.

Snakes: The Keeper and the Kept

I'm not big on pets, but if you're going snake hunting and want to make the captive a domestic friend, this book provides all the lowdown necessary to bring 'em back and keep 'em alive. Lots of hunting stories. —Peter Warshall

Snakes: The Keeper and the Kept
Carl Kauffeld
1969; 248 pp.

$8.95 postpaid from:
Doubleday and Company
501 Franklin Avenue
Garden City, NY 11530
or Whole Earth Household Store

Trans-Pecos Rat Snake, Elaphe subocularis. **Note the ladder pattern, or H-markings; also note the large eyes that bespeak its nocturnal habits.**

A weathered cedar log, a hiding box covered with cedar bark, peat moss, and pine needles covering the floor produce a rustic effect pleasing to both the snakes and the keeper. Note the sliding framed-glass panel door.

102 Bird Houses, Feeders You Can Make

A collection of neat plans for bird houses, bird baths, nesting boxes, and feeders — each designed to attract specific species of birds. If you want to increase the bird population in your area, here are lots of clever, easy-to-execute ideas. —Doris Herrick

102 Bird Houses, Feeders You Can Make
Hi Sibley
1967, 1976; 96 pp.

$4 postpaid from:
Goodheart-Willcox
123 West Taft Drive
South Holland, IL 60473
or Whole Earth Household Store

Feeder on post

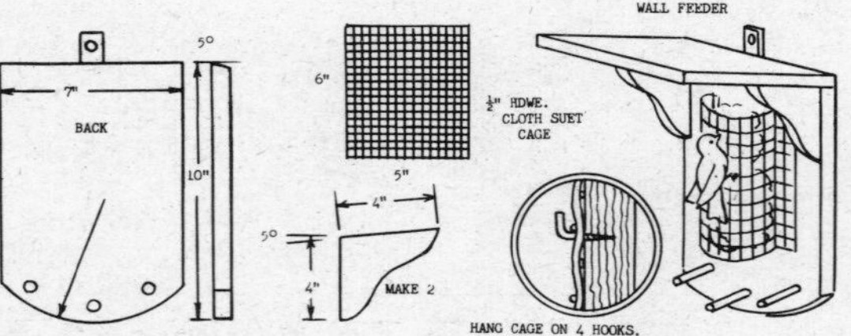

The Hotel Martin which accommodates 58 families juts into Cincinnati, Ohio, skyline. Photo was taken with Leica and 135 mm lens.

The Nature Company

A very fine assortment of gentle tools for natural history — binoculars, magnifiers, bird feeders, weather instruments, sundials, good books, kits, etc. —SB

The Nature Company
Catalog

free from:
The Nature Company
Department E
P.O. Box 7137
Berkeley, CA 94707

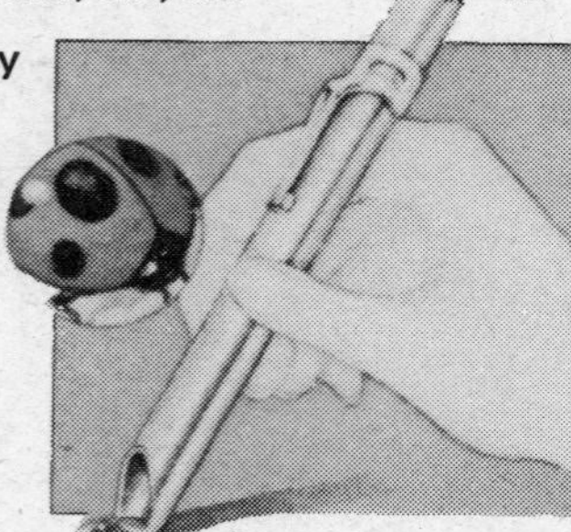

Pocket Microscopes — Great nature tools for all ages and remarkably fine optical instruments. With cases of lightweight aluminum, they clip in your shirt pocket for ready use in home, office or field. Examine practically anything at close range. 20x is the most popular model for general use. 40x lens for use where great magnification is required. 20x (1 oz.) $6.95; 40x (1 oz.) $8.95.

Spectrarc (TM) Window Prism

Nothing short of color photography can describe accurately the beauty and effect of this combination sculpture/mobile and prism. It is a unique, hand-cast optical instrument, incorporating the properties of a prism in its long 12" curved triangular bar to transform light into rainbow colors; and the principles of lenses to shape and focus the resulting spectrum. An adjustable method of suspension lets you change the direction and configuration of the spectrum projected on nearby surfaces. Each Spectrarc is tinted in either blue or red for aesthetic purposes. Each will produce a full color spectrum, with a very slight emphasis toward the tinted color.

0212 Spectrarc (TM). Specify Red or Blue. $24.95

↓

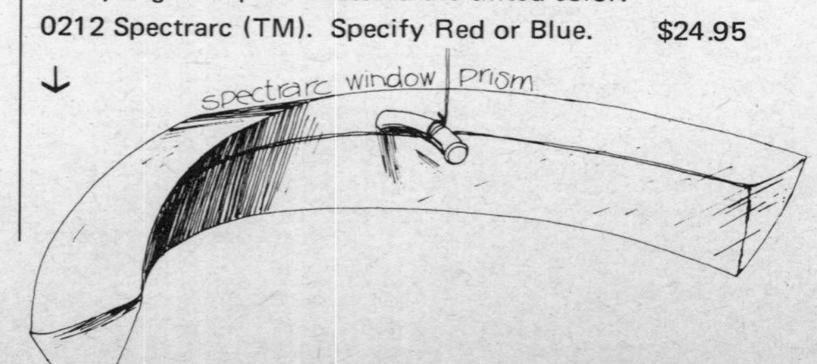

The Naturalists

Serious natural history tools from England, where being a naturalist is a way of life. (A pound equals about $2.40 these days.) —SB

The Naturalists
Catalog

Send 3 International Money Order Coupons (about $1.25) to:
Watkins and Doncaster
Four Throws
Hawkhurst, Kent
England

Beginner's Butterfly Net — 12-inch handle, wire frame complete with bag. 12" diam. £1.95 →

Lenses — Folding pocket type — X10. Foreign, chrome plated, £1.53; General purpose, £1.70; Compound lens, £3.30; Achromatic, £10.80; X15. Compound lens, £8.60; X20. Compound lens, £9.15; Triple folding. Large field approx. X5. £4.50. ↓

Audubon Workshop

Full line of sophisticated bird feeders, bird houses, and bird seed. Low-maintenance high-delight way to have animals around. Remember, once you start feeding birds through a winter, you have to stay with it or they die of starvation. —SB

Audubon Workshop
(The Wild Bird Specialists)
Catalog

free from:
Audubon Workshop
1501 Paddock Drive
Northbrook, IL 60062

Windowpane Intimacy — The "Big Daddy" of suction cup feeders has 3 advantages: (1) 1½ qt. seed hopper lets you leave for a weekend without worry. (2) You get a clear view of the birds on either side — no looking through the feeder. (3) Two models — Thistle Feeder with 6 slotted ports, and Standard Model with 1" diam. ports & flow control baffle. Roof flips up for filling. Clear acrylic, 6-¾" square x 7" high. Two suction cups.

8801 Standard Chalet (1" ports)	$19.95
9981 Std. Chalet + 3 Lb. Shelled Sunflower	$22.50
8805 Thistle Chalet (Slotted Ports)	$19.95
9985 Thistle Chalet & 3 Lb. Thistle Seed	$25.50

"No-Waste" Mixed Seed — Proven winners: Sunflower Meats, Peanut Hearts, Cracked Yellow Corn, Grey Millet and White Colorado Proso — the five most accepted seeds by actual field testing. Economical because there are no fillers; only seeds they like and that are best for them!

2150 Ten Lbs. of "No-Waste"	$6.75
2151 Twenty Lbs. of "No-Waste"	$11.50
2152 Forty Lbs. of "No-Waste"	$21.95

The Wild Inside

Like the book says, "You're never home alone." Natural history abounds indoors whether you want it or not — bugs, mice, pets, molds, indoor weather, and all manner of science alive in the plumbing, static electricity, etc., etc. First rate idea book. —SB

The Wild Inside
(Sierra Club's Guide to the Great Indoors)
Linda Allison
1979; 144 pp
$5.95 postpaid from:
Sierra Club Books
P.O. Box 3886
Rincon Annex
San Francisco, CA 94119
or Whole Earth Household Store

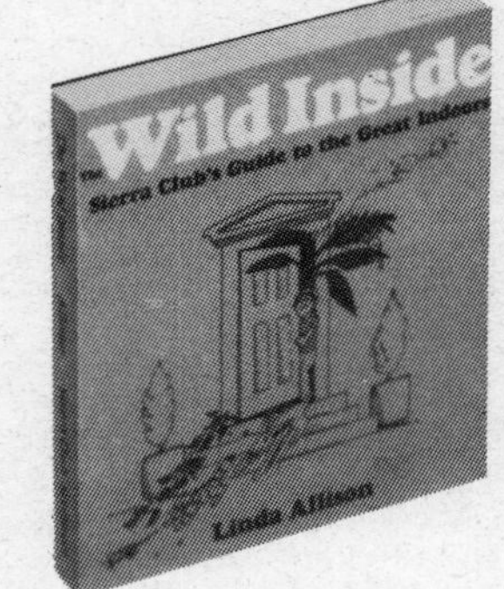

SPIDER WATCH

KEEP WATCH ON A SINGLE SPIDER IN YOUR HOUSE. HOUSE SPIDERS HAVE SMALL TERRITORIES SO YOU CAN VISIT THE SAME SPOT AND EXPECT TO FIND IT HOME. NOTICE WHAT IT EATS. WATCH FOR MOLTING. SEE IF YOU CAN TELL IF IT'S A MALE OR A FEMALE. IF YOUR HOUSE HAS MORE THAN AN OCCASIONAL SPIDER, WATCH FOR MATING. YOU MIGHT NOTICE A FEMALE CARRYING AN EGG. WATCH FOR SPIDER BABIES.

THE AMAZING HOUSE MOUSE

IS A GREAT LEAPER AND CAN JUMP 1 FOOT STRAIGHT UP INTO THE AIR.

CAN JUMP DOWN FROM HIGH PLACES (AS HIGH AS 8 FEET) WITHOUT HURTING ITSELF. AND YOU WONDERED HOW MOUSE TRACKS GOT ON TOP OF THE FRIDGE!

CAN WALK ALONG A WIRE LIKE A TIGHTROPE WALKER AND CAN RUN UPSIDE DOWN ON MESH.

• CAN SQUEEZE THROUGH OPENINGS BARELY 1/4-INCH WIDE.

• HAS FEET THAT WALK UP WALLS (UNLESS THE WALLS ARE VERY SLICK).

• HAS WHISKERS THAT HELP IT GET AROUND IN THE DARK.

Man In Nature

This book is exactly as subtitled: "America Before the Days of the White Man," and "A First Book on Geography." No other book (for kids or adults) spells out North American bio-regional life like **Man In Nature**. *It creates "locale" like Thoreau or John Muir. Read it to a child for your own pleasure.* —Peter Warshall

(More on Native Americans, pp. 44 - 45, 385, 452.)

Man in Nature
(America Before the Days of the White Man)
Carl O. Sauer
1975; 269 pp.
$9.95 postpaid from:
Turtle Island Foundation
2845 Buena Vista Way
Berkeley, CA 94708
or Whole Earth Household Store

Girdling trees

↑

Making a new field was a good deal of work. These people had no plows, no animals for pulling, and no good tools for cutting wood. But they had a very good way of making a new field.

The men took their stone axes and cut or broke the bark around green trees. Captain Smith calls it bruising the bark. Actually, nothing more was necessary than to beat the bark to pieces, so that the sap could no longer flow to the branches and leaves.

If this was done in summer the trees usually died over winter. The next spring they stood bare and leafless.

That was all that was necessary for the first planting. The sun then could shine through the dead tree trunks on the ground. The ground was rich with dead and rotten leaves. Such ground was fine for corn and beans and pumpkins.

More on animals

More on birds, reptiles, natural history in general, pp. 56 - 63.

For pets, see pp. 354 - 355.

Nature at Work

The British have always had a lovely way with Nature: gentler, more at ease and a more persistent curiosity than the American approach. Here is a beautifully illustrated paperback that doesn't flash "we know it all." It slowly draws the reader (high school and up) into the flow of energy created by the sun through the intricate webbing of community ecosystems. A fine reference for all teachers — elementary school on up. —Peter Warshall

(More on ecology and conservation, p. 48 - 53.)

Nature at Work
(Introducing Ecology)
British Museum (Natural History)
1978; 84 pp.
$5.95 postpaid from:
Cambridge University Press
510 North Avenue
New Rochelle, NY 10801
or Whole Earth Household Store

If we choose an area and study . . .

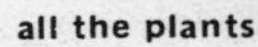

all the plants

all the animals

and the non-living surroundings . . .

. . . we can find out how the plants and animals interact with each other and with their non-living surroundings to form a natural system — an ecosystem.

Dandelion, Pokeweed, and Goosefoot

Kids can learn how early settlers used dandelion, and 62 other plants: horsetail to scrub pots and pans, oxalis for stomach ache, teasel to brush up soft nap on wool, yarrow to stop bleeding (a remedy as old as the Trojan War). Identification is made much easier by detailed drawings and by grouping those in pastures, those in swampland. Plants in these general habitats are then sub-grouped into uses — medicinal, food, or household. 1, 2, 3 directions are given for kids who want to plant an herb garden, collect and dry plants, make teas and salads from herbs, or dye cloth. CAUTION: If you are taking kids to eat off the land, check with a source on poisonous plants. Some plants have their problems — although young pokeweed greens are edible, older leaves are not, and as few as two or three uncooked pokeweed berries can fatally poison a small child. Suggestion: **Know Your Poisonous Plants**, *by Wilma Roberts James.* —Betty Moss

Dandelion, Pokeweed, and Goosefoot
Elizabeth Schaeffer
1972, 1979; 96 pp.
$5.95 postpaid from:
Young Scott Books
Addison-Wesley Publishing Company
Jacob Way
Reading, MA 01867
or Whole Earth Household Store

Dandelion Taraxacum officinale

It is hard to believe, but no dandelion had bloomed in North America until the colonists brought dandelions with them for food and medicine. Remember the meaning of officinalis? The dandelion was once the official remedy for illness that came on in the winter. The same qualities in the plant that make it such a persistent pest now, made it a rich and much-needed source of vitamins for the early settlers. The dandelion stays green long into the winter and grows green again with the first warm sun of early spring. It can do this because of the food it stores in its deep taproot. The settlers used the greens as spring tonic and as a vegetable. They used the youngest leaves in salads and boiled the less tender ones. They roasted the roots to make a coffee-like drink. They even made wine from the blossoms! Now we see dandelions all over North America, even in the cities. The familiar yellow flowers come mostly in the spring, but you can usually see a few blooms all summer and into the fall.

My Garden Companion

Maybe because it's written for children this is better than most books for adults. I learned the answers to some things I've wondered about for years. For instance, what do ants do — good and bad — in a garden? (They're scavengers, keeping things clean but also eating occasional roots and seeds.) This is a gardener's almanac; it even tells how to gear your crops for a harvest party. —Rosemary Menninger

(See Gardening, pp. 92 - 98.)

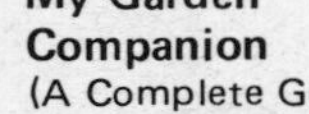

My Garden Companion
(A Complete Guide for the Beginner)
Jamie Jobb
1977; 336 pp.
$5.80 postpaid from:
Sierra Club Books
P.O. Box 3886
Rincon Annex
San Francisco, CA 94119
or Whole Earth Household Store

→

Often, plants don't come up in a beginner's garden because the seeds are planted either too deep or too shallow. Seed packs usually tell how deep the seed needs to be. But if you don't have that information, you can still tell how deep to plant most seeds. Here's the rule to remember:

Plant each seed so that three more seeds exactly the same size could be placed on top of it. You'll need to guess more for odd-shaped seeds (watermelon, squash, bean, pumpkin).

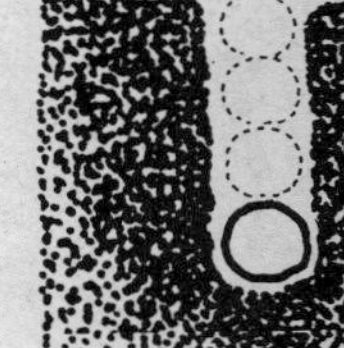

THE RISING SUN
NEIGHBORHOOD NEWSLETTER

"An elderly man that I talked to said that he was happiest in his garden these days. He said, when you're 84 and your only vocation is just being alive, you get a real affinity for flowers and vegetables."

—Patricia

The Brown Paper School Books

Appealing exploration of omnipresent subjects — body, weather, thinking, games, stars, local history. There is approximately no way to read these books and just sit there. Try this, notice that, well what about the other.
—SB

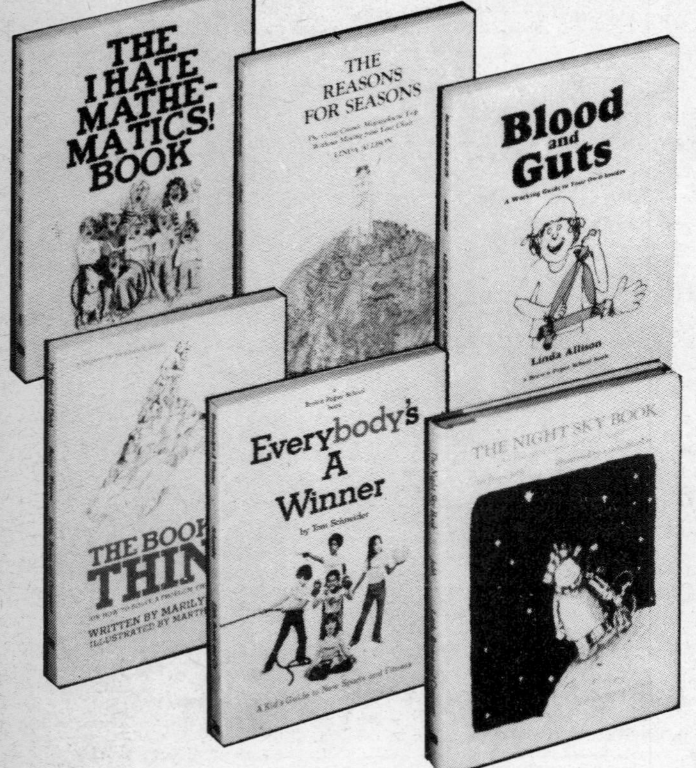

The Brown Paper School Books

My Backyard History Book, by David Weitzman, 1975

The I Hate Mathematics Book, by Marilyn Burns, 1975

The Reason for Seasons (The Great Cosmic Megagalactic Trip, Without Moving from Your Chair), by Linda Allison, 1975

Blood and Guts (A Working Guide to Your Own Insides), by Linda Allison, 1976

The Book of Think (Or How to Solve a Problem Twice Your Size), by Marilyn Burns, 1976

Everybody's A Winner (A Kid's Guide to New Sports and Fitness), by Tom Schneider, 1976

The Night Sky Book (An Everyday Guide to Every Night), by Jamie Jobb, 1977

I Am Not a Short Adult (Getting Good at Being a Kid), by Marilyn Burns, 1977

This Book is About Time, by Marilyn Burns, 1978

Good for Me! (All About Food in 32 Bites), by Marilyn Burns, 1978

$5.95 each postpaid

all from:
Little, Brown and Company
200 West Street
Waltham, MA 02154
or Whole Earth Household Store

Spore prints — To make a spore print, remove the stem from a ripe mushroom and place the mushroom head face down on a sheet of paper. →

•

Tube Race

Get old inner tubes from a company that sells truck tires. (Car tires are mostly tubeless these days.) Stage a tube race by having contestants sit on the tubes and try to make them move. Touching the ground directly with feet or hands is not allowed. **—Everybody's A Winner**

↑

Super Slide

Get a 10-by-20-foot sheet of plastic from a hardware or builder's supply store (about $4.50). Unroll it on the ground, flood it with water from a garden hose, and you've got a dandy Super Slide.

—Everybody's a Winner

•

The Dictionary Game

The rules: One person looks in the dictionary for a word that no one knows. There are plenty to choose from.

Then each person invents a possible definition of that word and writes it down. The person with the dictionary writes the real definition. Even if there are several definitions in the dictionary, one is enough. Or it may be shortened if it's really long.

All the definitions go to the dictionary person. That person now reads all the definitions. Including the real one. Each player then has to try to guess the right definition.

—The Book of Think

PEOPLE FROM HOT, DRY CLIMATES HAVE LONG NOSES INCREASING THE LENGTH OF MOISTURIZING.

PEOPLE FROM COLD CLIMATES HAVE LONG NOSES TO WARM AIR.

PEOPLE FROM WARM, STEAMY CLIMATES HAVE SHORTER NOSES.

—Blood and Guts

Edmund Scientific

The handiest source for low cost popular scientific gadgetry (especially optics gear). 4000 items, they say. They've declined a bit in excitement and variety in recent years. (See Nasco, p. 571.) —SB

Edmund Scientific Catalog
$1 from:
Edmund Scientific Company
101 East Gloucester Pike
Barrington, NJ 08007

↑

Headband Loupe Magnifier — Hinged lens bar and lens pivot that are totally adjustable so that you can shorten or increase working distance. It has a non-reflective vinyl headband, ophthalmic quality lens, and can be worn with bifocals or trifocals. Select the power and working distance that best suits your needs.

Power	Work. Dist.	Number	Price
1.75X	14 in.	42,797	$17.50
2.25X	8 in.	42,798	17.50
2.75X	6 in.	42,799	17.50
3.5X	4 in.	42,800	21.50

← **High performance Electronic Parabolic Microphones magnify signals 100 times more than regular omnidirectional mikes so you can hear a songbird or similar sounds up to ½ mile away! $299**

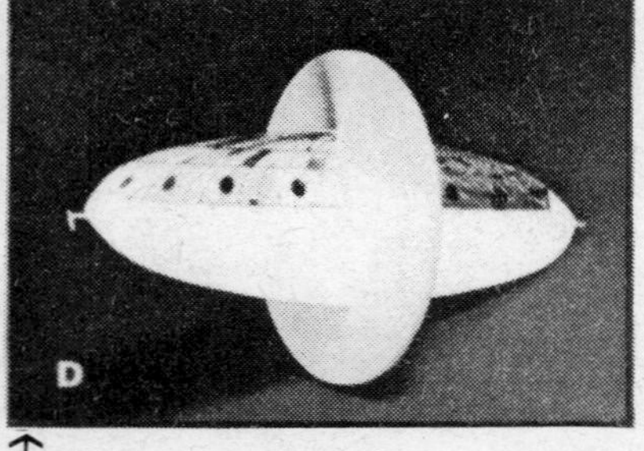

↑

UFO Invader Turbo Kite — Experience galactic space action with a kite that rotates and makes a whirring sound. Printed with flying saucer detail on bright mylar, it emits strobe-like reflections in bright sunlight. 24" wingspan, 14" stabilizing saucer. Easy to assemble. Fly it with a hand line or fishing rod and reel.
No. 72,418 $3.98

← **Make Your Own 9 Foot Hot Air Balloons! — What fun these colorful paper balloons make. When fully inflated, they rise to about 200 feet on just hot air! 9 feet tall and 5 feet wide, they can lift model airplanes or almost anything up to ½ lb. Use them over and over: they're easily repaired if needed. Kit comes complete with 10 pre-cut red & white gores made of No. 1 model paper, 6 feet of 14 gauge wire for bottom ring, cord and instructions.**

9 Foot Kit No. 60,691 $4.95
Two 6 Foot Kits (they're easier to inflate) No. P-71,866 6.95

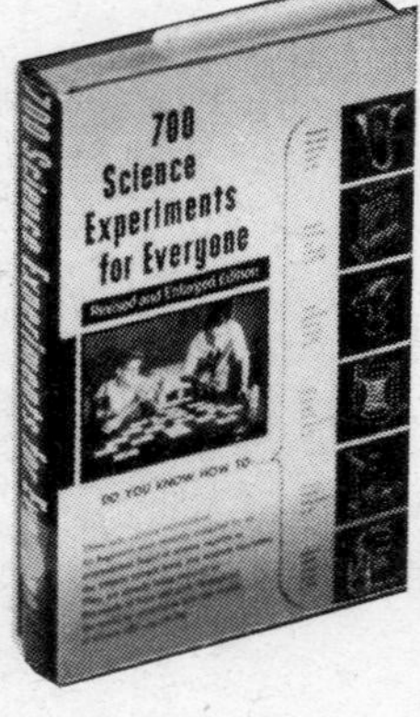

700 Science Experiments for Everyone
1958, 250 pp.
$7.95 postpaid from:
Doubleday and Company
501 Franklin Avenue
Garden City, NY 11530
or Whole Earth Household Store

700 Science Experiments for Everyone

This book grew out of a smaller volume called ***Suggestions for Science Teachers in Devastated Areas*** *whose production was sponsored by UNESCO right after World War II. It was meant for use in schools whose buildings and labs had been destroyed and soon found its way into the hands of people who had never had these things to begin with. Thus it solves the problem of schools, communities — people — who want to do "live" science without money or equipment. There isn't any experiment in it which would be too costly for any of us to do. The book tells you how to put together the equipment you need: real clever ways of making glass cutters, balances, burners, telescopes, microscopes, etc. A lot of what you need to do the experiments is just stuff you'd have around the house. The rest can be gotten (very low cost stuff) at the drugstore, hardware, junk yard, etc.*

Also the book is unusually well written. There's no bullshit in it and it doesn't talk down to the reader. Just very straightforward instructions with illustrations that are highly readable. In most cases you aren't told the outcome of the experiment, an aspect which makes you much more interested in doing it. —Jane Burton

How the lungs work

Cut the bottom off a large bottle. Fit a cork to the neck with a Y tube in it. On each of the lower limbs of the Y tie a rubber balloon or some small bladder.

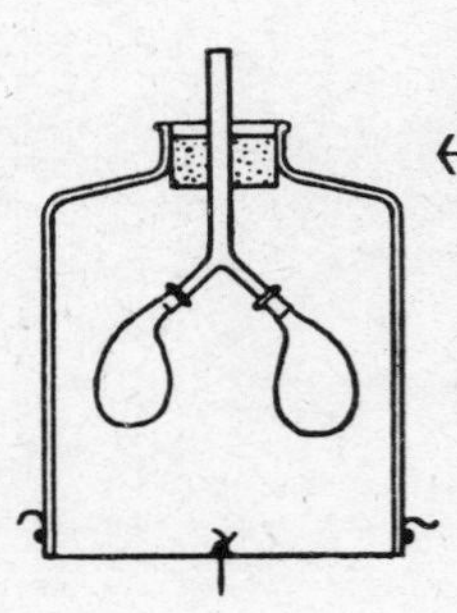

← Tie a sheet of brown paper or sheet rubber round the bottom of the jar, with a piece of string knotted through a hole and sealed with wax. Pulling this string lowers the diaphragm and air enters the neck of the Y piece causing the balloons to dilate.

Pressing the diaphragm upwards has the opposite effect.

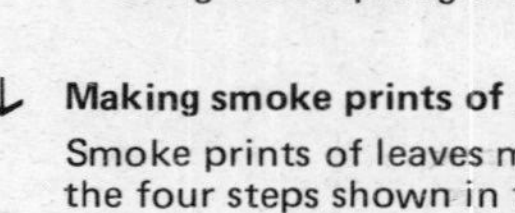

↓ **Making smoke prints of leaves**

Smoke prints of leaves may be easily made by following the four steps shown in the diagrams.

Cover the side of a smooth, round bottle with a thin layer of grease or vaseline. Fill the bottle with cold water and cork it tightly. Hold the bottle over a candle flame until it is covered evenly with soot. Place a leaf, vein side up, on a layer of newspaper and roll the sooty bottle over the leaf. Remove the leaf and lay it vein side up on clean newspaper. Cover the leaf with a sheet of white paper. Next, roll over the white paper and leaf with a clean round bottle or other roller.

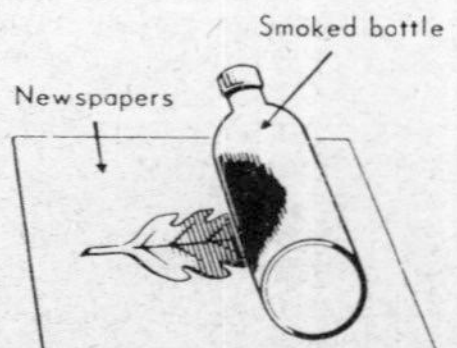

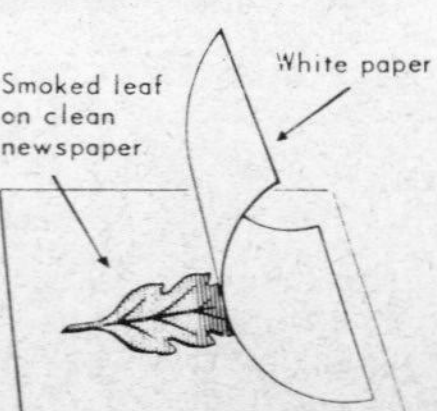

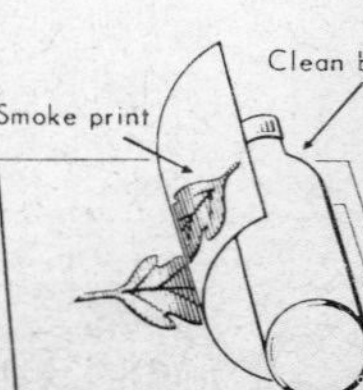

How to learn things: A handy tip

If you're starting to learn about a field that you know nothing about, go to the children's library and get some fifth, sixth, seventh grade books about it before you go into grownup books. Basic books for grownups tend to be aimed at college freshmen taking required courses — and everybody knows that they're supposed to suffer, including the people who write the books. Basic books for kids are aimed at kids browsing in libraries who don't have to be there and could leave anytime. The books have colors and pictures and a will to sell the subject; the good ones assume you know nothing without being condescending. You can get some vocabulary and feel for the shape of the subject before you get into the stuck-up real books. Kids' books can also help you if you are one of those freshmen in one of those required courses.
—Anne Herbert

The two outstanding series of children's how-it-works books are from Golden Press and from Ladybird (British). I think the **Golden Guides** *are the more brilliant. They're economical in size and cost, intelligently researched and edited, well illustrated in color, thoroughly indexed, with good bibliographies. In any of their subject areas I would (and often do) start with a* **Golden Guide.**

Big Dipper as seen from different latitudes: In central Canada (top) it is higher than as seen at the same time from Long Island (bottom). Here it is near the low point of its revolution.
—The Sky Observer's Guide (Golden)

Where the Goldens can incite an interest, Ladybird "How It Works" I would use to feed an already existing interest. More literal and lineal, less (but still nicely) graphic, they sound like a Mary Poppins type of extremely knowledgeable nanny explaining how things are done. There are more Ladybirds — 500 or so — including fiction and history. Sometimes their Britishness is an attraction. "I don't know what a 'verge' is, honey. Maybe we can figure it out from the illustration." —SB

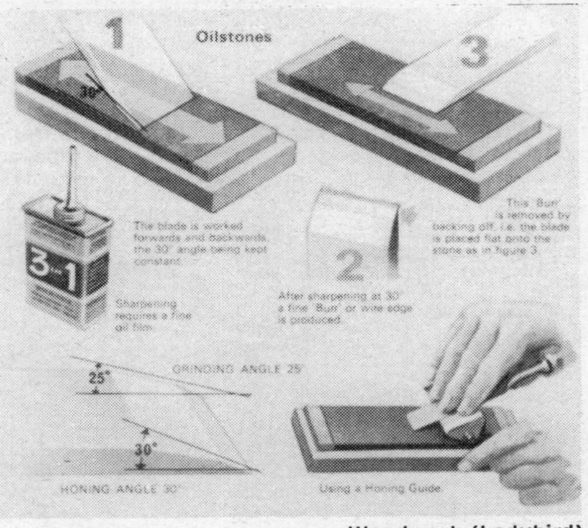

—Woodwork (Ladybird)

Golden Guides

The Rocky Mountains, Fishing, Sky Observer's Guide, Non-Flowering Plants, Families of Birds, Insect Pests, Pond Life, Spiders, Indian Arts, Kites, Geology, Landforms, Oceanography, Weeds, Cats, Cacti, Casino Games, Tropical Fish, Hallucinogenic Plants, American Antique Glass, Herbs and Spices, Weather, Zoology, Gamebirds, Seashells of the World, Fossils, Butterflies and Moths, Exotic Plants for House and Garden, Birds, Flowers, Insects, Stars, Trees, Reptiles and Amphibians, Seashores, Mammals, Fishes, Rocks and Minerals

$1.95 each postpaid

Golden Field Guides

Amphibians of North America, Trees of North America, Seashells of North America, Rocks and Minerals

$4.95 each postpaid

all from:
Golden Press
Western Publishing Company
1220 Mound Avenue
Racine WI 53404
or Whole Earth
Household Store

Ladybird "How It Works" Series

The Motor Car, The Rocket, The Aeroplane, Television, The Locomotive, The Hovercraft, The Camera, Farm Machinery, The Computer, The Telescope and Microscope, Printing Processes, The Telephone

$2.50 each postpaid

Other Ladybird series include **Crafts and Hobbies** (Woodwork, Cooking, Taking Photographs, etc.); **Conservation** (Wildlife in Britain, Disappearing Mammals, Understanding the Sea, Nature in the Town, etc.); **Natural History** (The Honey-Bee, Prehistoric Animals, Story of the Spider, etc.); **Nature** (The Weather, Garden Birds, The Night Sky, etc.); plus series on **Animals, Fiction, Beginning Reading, History, Myths and Legends,** and **The Arts.**

Catalog
free
all of the above from:
Leicestershire Learning Systems
Chestnut Street Hill Mill
Lewiston, ME 04240
or catalog and information
free from:
Ladybird Books Ltd.
P.O. Box 12
Loughborough, Leicestershire
England

Archosauria

My love of evolution started with dinosaurs. Just about every boy I know loves dinosaurs. This is the new testament of dinosaur life. Beautifully illustrated. Clearly and light-heartedly truthful. As with all books like this, it's just as interesting to adults as youngsters.*
—Peter Warshall

**(All the girls I knew liked dinosaurs, too.*
—Evelyn)

Archosauria
(A New Look at the Old Dinosaur)
John C. McLoughlin
1979; 117 pp.
$10.95 postpaid from:
The Viking Press
299 Murray Hill Parkway
East Rutherford, NJ 07073
or Whole Earth
Household Store

Iguanodon possessed defensive spines on its thumbs, with which it must have struck at the eyes of carnivores — there was no other spot at which predatory dinosaurs would be vulnerable to these little weapons.

Show Me!

A very well-made book on sex for kids. The text is as intelligent as it is brief, and concepts are presented quite whole — including graphic acknowledgement that kids too young and grown-ups too old may be disgusted by "all those naked people."

The point, of course, is the photographs — big beautiful pictures of nearly everything — children and adults petting, nursing, peeing, kissing, fucking, giving birth, studying each other's each-perfect bodies. —SB

Show Me!
(A Picture Book of Sex for Children and Parents)
Will McBride and
Dr. Helga Fleischauer-Hardt
1975; 176 pp.
$7.95 postpaid from:
St. Martin's Press
175 Fifth Avenue
New York, NY 10010
or Whole Earth
Household Store

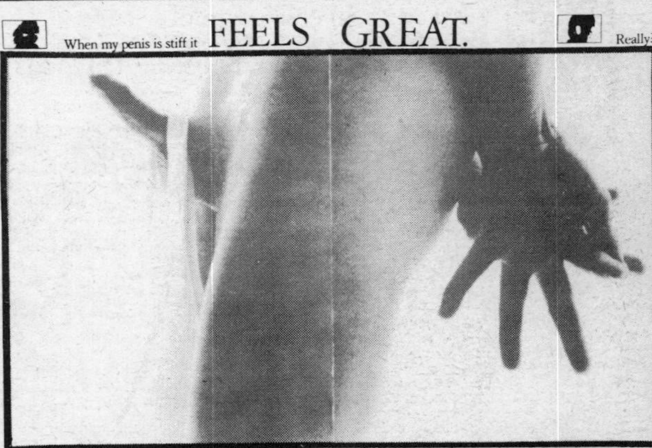

When my penis is stiff it FEELS GREAT.
Really?

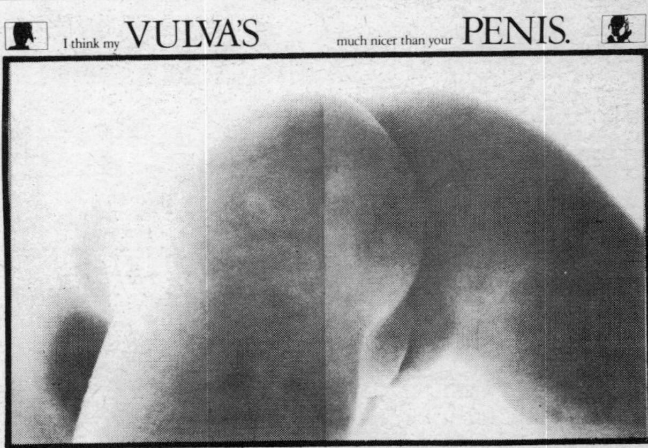

I think my VULVA'S much nicer than your PENIS.

Guinness Book of World Records

An astonishing amount of conversation in the Western World is spent agreeing or disagreeing on the extremes of experience. Maybe it's some primordial urge to know where we are in the universe. Whatever, it's deep. This book is automatic conversation, whoever's reading it has to start reading aloud. And whoever's around has to listen and respond. Weird. Painless education though. —SB

Guinness Book of World Records
1956, 1980; 608 pp.
$2.95 postpaid from:
Bantam Books
414 East Golf Road
Des Plaines, IL 60016
or Whole Earth
Household Store

Heaviest Twins — Benny and Billy McCrary together weighed almost 1,500 lbs. Billy died in July, 1979, while making a personal appearance at Niagara Falls, Ontario, Canada.

Smallest Bicycle — Charlie Charles rides this bicycle in his act in Las Vegas.

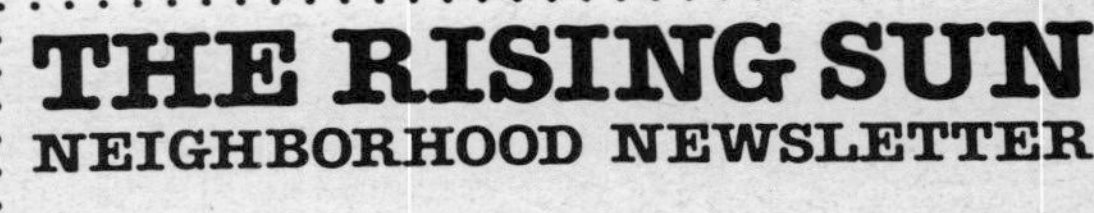

Where do people look when they talk on the phone and what do they see?

THESE ARE THE THREE GREATEST author/illustrators for explaining how things work to kids. MACAULAY does epic projects — cathedrals, castles, pyramids (except for **Great Moments in Architecture**, *which is a hoot). ADKINS does homey stuff — sandcastles, baking, wood tools (also see his* **Art and Ingenuity of the Woodstove** *on p. 203,* **Moving Heavy Things** *on p. 157, and* **The Craft of Sail** *on p. 436). HOLLING tells great stories with full page color illustrations and fascinating diagrams and maps;* **Paddle-to-the-Sea** *is practically an American myth now.* —SB

Books by David Macaulay

Castle, 1977, $9.95 postpaid; **Cathedral: The Story of Its Construction**, 1973, $9.95 postpaid; **City**, 1974, $9.95 postpaid; **Great Moments in Architecture**, 1978, $5.95 postpaid; **Pyramid**, 1975, $9.95 postpaid; and **Underground**, 1976, $9.95 postpaid. All from Houghton-Mifflin Company, Wayside Road, Burlington, MA 01803 or Whole Earth Household Store.

Books by Jan Adkins

The Art and Industry of Sandcastles, 1971, $7.95 postpaid; **Toolchest: A Primer of Woodcraft**, 1973, $6.95 postpaid; and **Symbols: A Silent Language**, 1978, $7.95 postpaid. All from Walker and Company, 720 Fifth Avenue, New York, NY 10019 or Whole Earth Household Store.

The Bakers, 1975, $5.95 postpaid; **Luther Tarbox**, 1977, $5.95 postpaid; and **Moving On: Stories of Four Travellers**, 1978, $6.95 postpaid. All from Charles Scribner's Sons, Vreeland Avenue, Totowa, NJ 07512 or Whole Earth Household Store.

Wooden Ship, 1978, $6.95 postpaid from Houghton-Mifflin Company, Wayside Road, Burlington, MA 01803 or Whole Earth Household Store.

Books by Holling Clancy Holling

Minn of the Mississippi, 1951, $3.95 postpaid; **Paddle-to-the-Sea**, 1941, $10.95 postpaid; **Pagoo**, 1957, $10.95 postpaid; **Seabird**, 1948, $4.95 postpaid; and **Tree in the Trail**, 1942, $4.95 postpaid. All from Houghton-Mifflin Company, Wayside Road, Burlington, MA 01803 or Whole Earth Household Store.

PLEASE PUT ME BACK IN WATER
I AM PADDLE TO THE SEA

"I made you, Paddle Person, because I had a dream. A little wooden man smiled at me. He sat in a canoe on a snowbank on this hill. Now the dream has begun to come true. The Sun Spirit will look down at the snow. The snow will melt and the water will run down-hill to the river, on down to the Great Lakes, down again and on at last to the sea. You will go with the water and you will have adventures that I would like to have. But I cannot go with you because I have to help my father with the traps."
—Paddle-to-the-Sea

→
In a time not so long ago when one craftsman was largely responsible for building an entire home, several master carpenters presented their toolchests to a prospective client. He inspected their tools: the newness of the edges and the wear of the handles, the art of wood-joining in the chests, the strength of the joints, the cleverness of construction. The client chose a carpenter by the condition of his tools; it told him something about the way tools and craftsman worked together.
—Toolchest

Two men powered the great wheel which lifted the wooden centerings. The centerings supported the cut stone ribs of the vaulted ceiling until the mortar was dry. ↑

→
Stone cutters and sculptors finished the moldings and capitals while masons laid the stone slabs that made up the floor. They created a maze pattern in the floor. Finding one's way to the center of the maze was considered as worthy of God's blessing as making the long pilgrimage through the countryside that so many had to make in order to worship in a cathedral such as Chutreaux's.

While the windows were being installed, plasterers covered the underside of the vault and painted red lines on it to give the impression that all the stones of the web were exactly the same size. They were eager for the web to appear perfect even if no one could see the lines from the ground.
—Cathedral

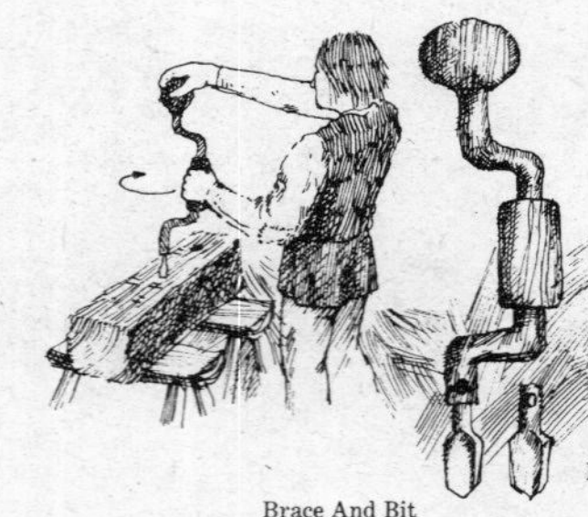

—Cathedral

SHOOTING an edge is another, more positive, method of trying. The piece is clamped flat on a workbench, raised by a thin piece beneath it. The plane is laid on its wing and stroked along the board's edge, depending on the right angle between sole and wing to form a right angle between edge and face. ↓ —Toolchest

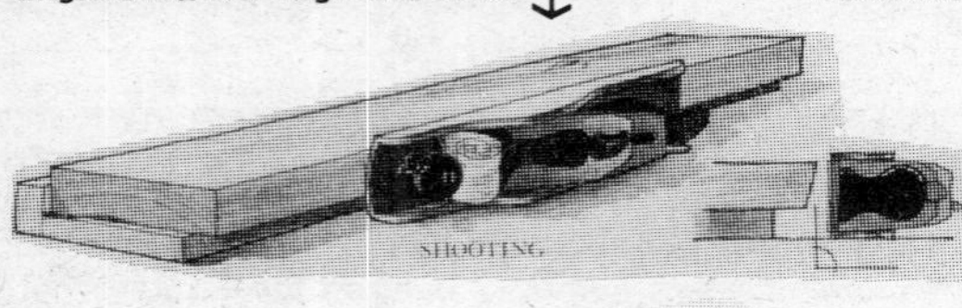

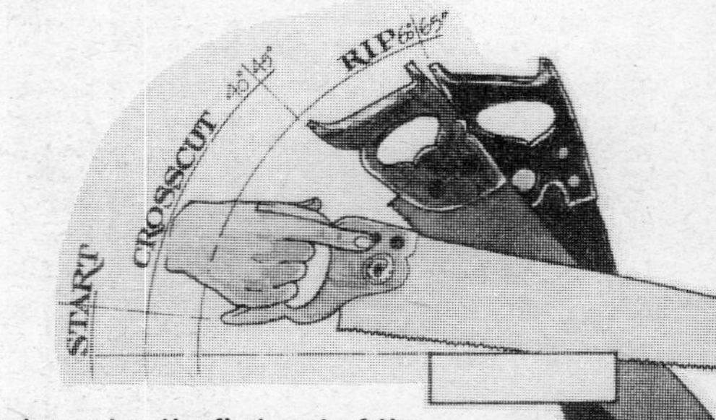

→
The carpenter makes the first part of the cut at a shallow angle. After a few strokes the saw is brought up to its normal angle.
—Toolchest

The World's Last Mysteries

A peerless browse, this collection of fascinating color photos and sufficiently brief explanations of the still half-understood goings-on around Atlantis, the discovery of the New World, El Dorado, sundry megaliths, lost empires of South America, Africa, and the Mideast, Easter Island, Zimbabwe, Angkor Wat, etc. give any reader itchy feet and itchy mind. —SB

The World's Last Mysteries
Reader's Digest
1976, 1978; 320 pp.
$16.95 postpaid from:
W.W. Norton and Company
500 Fifth Avenue
New York, NY 10036
or Whole Earth Household Store

Extraordinary patterns of scrolls, spirals and zigzags cover the surface of these dressed stones forming the passageway to the funeral chamber of a burial mound on the island of Gavrinis off the coast of Brittany. Generations of archaeologists have been unable to decipher these designs.

Things Maps Don't Tell Us

This seductive book — each page has a big simple illustration and accompanying text — teaches you to see what's happening in a piece of landscape. The mountain range is rising or diminishing. The lakes are lined up because the strata are. The atoll is there because a volcano was, and then sank. Geology cycles slow, but big. —SB

Things Maps Don't Tell Us
Armin K. Lobeck
1956; 160 pp.
$6.95 postpaid from:
Macmillan Company
Front and Brown Streets
Riverside, NJ 08075
or Whole Earth Household Store

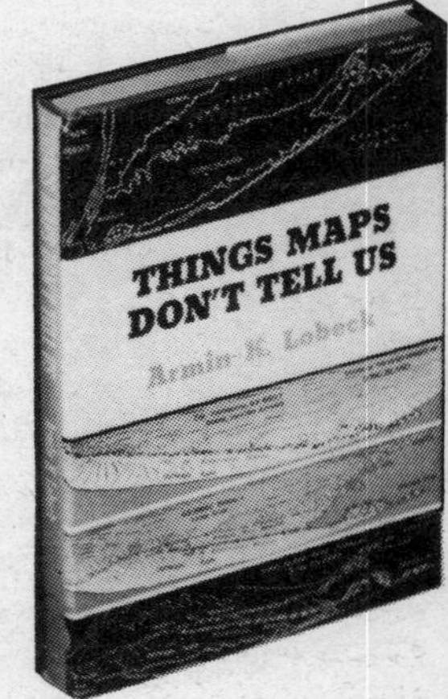

The clue to the origin of Croton Point is the Croton River. During the waning stages of Glacial Time, when this part of the continent stood somewhat lower than it does now, because of the great weight of ice upon it, the Hudson River was about 80 feet deeper in Haverstraw Bay than it is at present. The Croton River, pouring out from the melting ice front, carried great quantities of sand and gravel into Haverstraw Bay and built there a large delta which reached halfway across the river. Like most deltas built into quiet estuaries, the Croton Delta was more or less round in shape, with distributary streams flowing outward in all directions toward its margins.

Following the final disappearance of the ice and the removal of this great weight, the crust of the earth in this part of the United States gradually rose above sea level. In the Croton Delta region the elevation was about 80 feet, with the result that the flat top of Croton Point stands now 80 feet above sea level. An important result of this rising was the invigorating effect it had upon the Croton River. This stream, therefore, flowed more swiftly, and eroded its valley extensively. Much of the delta was removed by the river, so that now only the northern half remains. This is clearly revealed by its present shape.

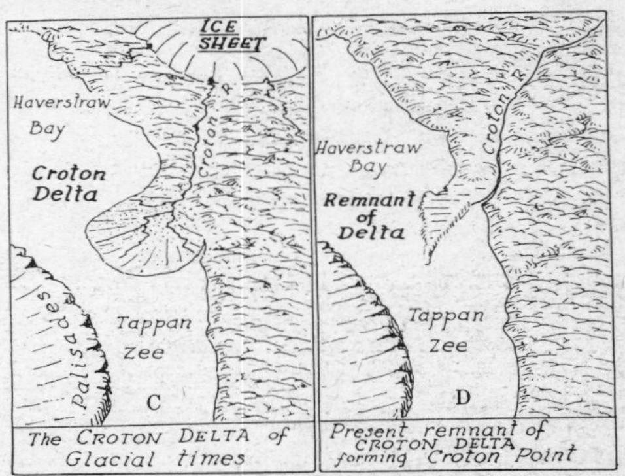

The Stars

Universally considered (in this part of the universe anyway, where the stars make these configurations) the best star and constellation teacher, Rey's book will invest a lifetime of night skies with recognition and reassuring familiarity. Knowing how to find the Pole star may be our most basic planetary understanding. From this book you can move right on to **Astronomical Calendar** *(p. 10).* —SB

The Stars
(A New Way to See Them)
H.A. Rey
1952, 1976; 160 pp.
$5.95 postpaid from:
Houghton-Mifflin Company
Wayside Road
Burlington, MA 01803

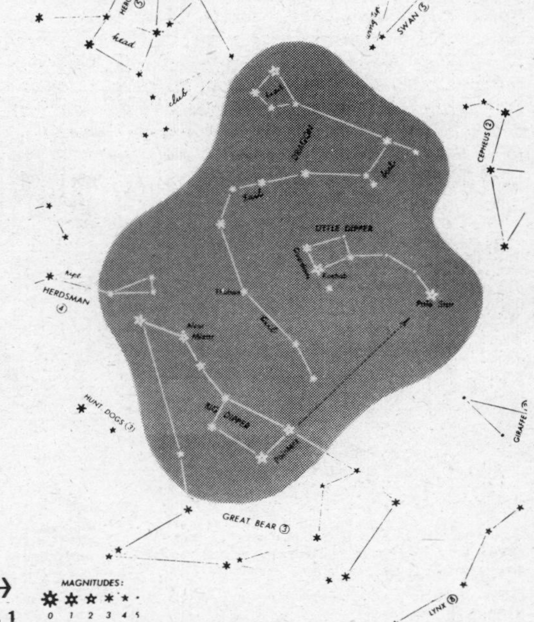

Constellation Chart No. 1

The UFO Handbook

Mind you, I have no use for UFO's (yeah, I've seen 'em too — so what?), but it's great to have a genuine workable UFO birdwatcher's handbook — how to recognize all the Flying Objects that weren't Unidentified after all, how to document a genuinely strange case, how to doubt and how to prove. I figure anything that encourages people to keep an eye on the lovely sky is healthy. Ditto for anything that encourages homegrown scientific rigor. —SB

The UFO Handbook
(A Guide to Investigating, Evaluating and Reporting UFO Sightings)
Allan Hendry
1979; 297 pp.
$8.95 postpaid from:
Doubleday and Company
501 Franklin Avenue
Garden City, NY 11530
or Whole Earth Household Store

"I had the strange feeling that it was trying to say something" — case 227 — an advertising plane — 22% of all NL-IFO's — Nocturnal Light Identified Flying Objects.

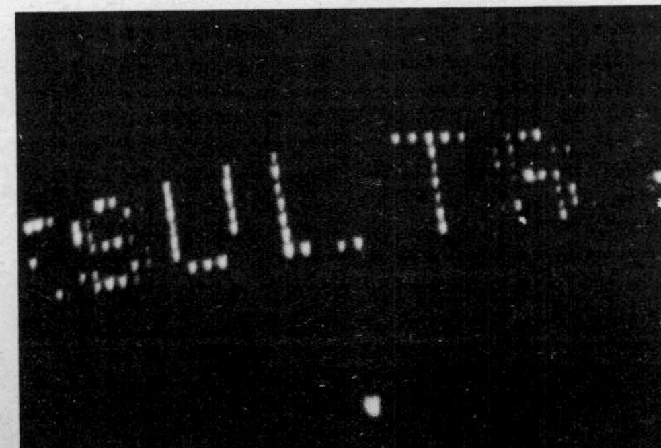

Frontier Living
Colonial Craftsmen
Colonial Living

Are these fine Edwin Tunis books really practical? No, not on the face of it. They tantalize you with detailed sketches but sketchy details of old crafts and tools, those very crafts which have long been obsolesced by machinery.

So what's the value? The value to the **Catalog** *is nostalgia. These books service the desire of much of our market to back the hell out of 20th century confusion. And nostalgia may not only be powerful, but in the big picture very practical, if carried out. One educational route out of a dead end is indeed back. Go back, start over where it feels good, get it right this time. Not for everybody; just enough to unstack the deck a little, enhance the variety of mistakes and opportunities available.*

The dolphins went back, and they're doing all right. (See **Antique Woodworking Tools**, *p. 161.)* —SB

Frontier Living
Edwin Tunis
1961; 166 pp.
$10.95 postpaid

Colonial Craftsmen
(And the Beginnings of American Industry)
Edwin Tunis
1965; 159 pp.
$12.95 postpaid

Colonial Living
Edwin Tunis
1957; 156 pp.
$10.95 postpaid

all from:
T.Y. Crowell Company
Harper and Row
Keystone Industrial Park
Scranton, PA 18512

—Frontier Living

THE RISING SUN
NEIGHBORHOOD NEWSLETTER

The subtitle of *Children's Games in Street and Playground* is "Chasing, Catching, Seeking, Hunting, Racing, Duelling, Exerting, Daring, Guessing, Acting, Pretending," which seems to cover all the games there are, even for grownups.

The Cartoon History of the Universe

Larry Gonick is a tireless researcher who also happens to be a fine cartoonist and considerable wit. His magnum opus, now approaching Volume 5 — "Brains and Bronze: The Rise of Ancient Greece," is a cartoon history of the universe. It's a genre-shattering event equivalent to the Who's rock-opera "Tommy." Neither cartoons, history, nor us avid readers are likely to be quite the same afterwards. —SB

—Vol. 1

—Vol. 2

The Cartoon History of the Universe
Larry Gonick

Volume 1
(The Evolution of Everything Including Sex!)
1978; 50 pp.
$1.25 postpaid

Volume 2
(Sticks and Stones: The Descent of People)
1979; 50 pp.
$1.25 postpaid

Volume 3
(River Realms: Sumer and Egypt 5000 - 12,000 B.C.)
1979; 50 pp.
$1.25 postpaid

Volume 4
(Part of the Old Testament)
1979; 50 pp.
$1.25 postpaid

Book One
(Volumes 1 - 3 in paperback form)
1978, 1980; 109 pp.
$6.95 postpaid
all from:
Rip Off Press
P.O. Box 14158
San Francisco, CA 94114
or Whole Earth Household Store

—Vol. 2

Experiences in Visual Thinking

If you're a poor visualizer, you're working without one of the most important mental tools. Fortunately, visual thinking is an ability one can develop and improve, and Bob McKim has provided a manual for doing just that. The book is both informative — good background information on creativity and problem-solving — and experiential, full of excellent exercises structured to develop specific aspects of visual thinking. A fine balance of about and how to. It's one of the very few books with exercises to do that I've actually managed to work my way through.
—Linda Williams

Experiences in Visual Thinking
Robert H. McKim
1972, 1980; 250 pp.
$12.95 postpaid from:
Brooks-Cole Publishing Company
10 Davis Drive
Belmont, CA 94002
or Whole Earth Household Store

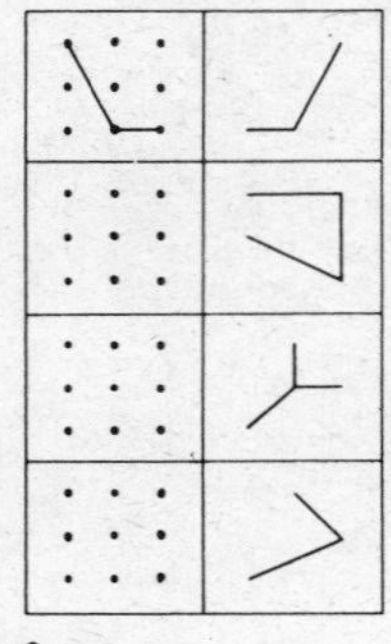

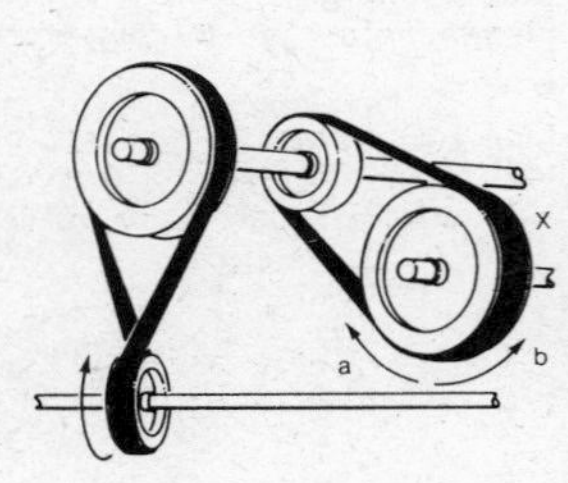

↑
The top drawing on the left is the top right drawing seen reversed. In the remaining squares, draw the inverse of the drawings on the right.

Now mentally rotate the image of a three-dimensional object in space.

←
Which way (a or b) will pulley "x" turn?

Did you trace the motions of the pulleys with your finger, or feel some sort of inner muscular involvement, as you came to the correct conclusion that pulley "x" goes in direction b? If so, you were experiencing the importance of kinesthetic imagery to active thinking operations.

•

Tower of pulp

With two sheets of newsprint and 24 inches of Scotch Tape, construct the tallest tower that you can in 30 minutes. You may cut, fold, or form these materials any way you like. Other challenges, using the same materials: the longest bridge, the largest enclosed volume (open or closed), or the strongest 12-inch-high support structure (add increments of weight to test).

Mathematics — A Human Endeavor

If I were going to teach mathematics, or learn it, I'd want this book. It's unusually enjoyable as well as big, and thorough. Also see the goods on pp. 526 - 527.
—SB

Mathematics
(A Human Endeavor)
Harold R. Jacobs
1970; 529 pp.
$11 postpaid from:
W.H. Freeman and Company
660 Market Street
San Francisco, CA 94104
or Whole Earth Household Store

↑
Three golfers named Tom, Dick, and Harry are walking to the clubhouse. Tom, the best golfer of the three, always tells the truth. Dick sometimes tells the truth, while Harry, the worst golfer, never does.

Use deductive reasoning to figure out who is who and explain how you know. (Hint: First, figure out which one is Tom.)

•

Inflation of the value of money is a serious economic problem. In 1946, inflation of the currency was so bad in Hungary that the gold Pengo was worth 130 quintillion paper pengos. Write this number in scientific notation. (The pengo was replaced that year by another unit of money.)

The Flying Circus of Physics

I'm always looking for good physics books because I personally feel that in this day and age a person ignorant of physics simply can't understand much of what is going on. But physics isn't usually considered an easy subject, and many people seem to need an approach that is different than the usual clothed-in-mystery book that ends a particularly difficult discussion with "we leave it to the student to work this out." (No answers in the back of the book either.) Here's yet another way to get into it: twang the curiosity with a maddening question and then give the bibliography that holds the answer. This will mean more library work than many will be able to hack, but for some this book will be just the goad necessary to bridge the gap between pure what-good-is-it abstraction and reality. I found it fascinating.
—J. Baldwin

The Flying Circus of Physics
Jearl Walker
1975; 224 pp.
$10.95 postpaid from:
John Wiley and Sons
One Wiley Drive
Somerset, NJ 08873
or Whole Earth Household Store

→
What causes the rainbows seen on dew-covered grass fields (dewbows) and on ponds with oily surfaces? In particular, can you explain their shape? Why do dewbows formed by streetlights have yet another shape?

•

The next time you're mulling over a glass of milk, examine the milk film at the edge of the milk as you tip the glass. Between the film on the bottom of the glass and the milk there is a clear area a few millimeters wide. Why is the clear band present?

Satterly, J., "Casual Observations on Milk, Pickled Beet-Root, and Dried-Up Puddles," **Am. J. Phys.**, 24, 529 (1956).

↑
While watching TV in an otherwise dark room, quickly run your eyes from about a foot to the left of the screen to about a foot to the right. You will see a bright, detailed, ghostlike image of the TV picture floating in space to the right of the screen. You may even see three or four images, all right-tilted parallelograms. Why are these ghost images formed, and what's responsible for the tilt? Do you see the same sense of tilt if you move your eyes in the opposite direction? Are there ghost images for a rapid vertical scan of your eyes?

Crookes, T.G., "Television Images," **Nature**, 179, 1024 (1957).

Teaching as a Conserving Activity

The **Wall Street Journal** *gloated over this book, hailing a reversal of Mr. Postman's previous work (***Teaching as a Subversive Activity** *— 1969) as gleefully as the Church over Galileo's recantation. I'm not sure* **WSJ** *appreciated the fact that Postman's "conserving activity" is ultimately as subversive as the readings of Dickens and Proust in Bradbury's* **Fahrenheit 451**, *and for the same reason: both literature and formal education are important mechanisms for "subverting the prevailing biases of the culture."*

There is little doubt that the prevailing bias of our culture is the media, in particular, television, and that its influence over the minds and behavior of our children far exceeds that of school, church, family or any other learning experience. The significant distinction between television and school learning lies in their different — and perhaps antagonistic — modes of codifying information. Postman defines television as an analogic form of information, and language (be it words or numbers) as a digital form, each requiring and generating substantially different intellectual and perceptual activities. He does not propose to eliminate television. He emphasizes the need for an education to provide ballast against it and explores the profound consequences for civilization of a culture dominated by analogic perception and expression.

The organizing and controlling element of civilization, as well as of individual experience, is language, "The instrument of civilized discourse." To be able to read fluently is to have access to the experience, ideas, perceptions and emotions of many generations of diverse cultures and times; to put words together coherently is to bring some semblance of order to one's own experience, ideas, perceptions and emotions and thereby exert control over them. There is ample evidence that fewer and fewer of our children are finishing school with even minimal skill — to say nothing of interest — in speech, reading, or writing, on any subject whatever. Postman describes the results in alarming detail and concludes that "articulate language is our chief weapon against mental disturbance."

In 1963 Jules Henry pointed out that more than 50% of the educated "class" in this country were engaged in one way or another with what he called "the culture of death" — the defense industry and its many direct or indirect contributors. "The forces of death," he wrote, "are confident and organized while the forces of life — the people who long for peace — are, for the most part, scattered, inarticulate, and wooly-minded, overwhelmed by their own importance."

It is time — if there is time — for the forces of life to become confident and organized. That is, articulate. Neil Postman offers hope that our schools, if they turn off the video long enough to read his book, can accomplish this. Pray God they will. —Carol Van Strum

Teaching as a Conserving Activity
Neil Postman
1979; 244 pp.

$9.95 postpaid from:
Delacorte Press
1 Dag Hammarskjold Plaza
245 East 47th Street
New York, NY 10017
or Whole Earth Household Store

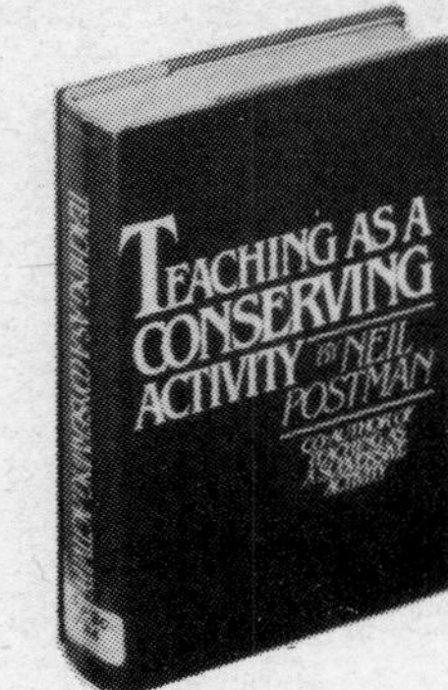

●

The effects to which I am alluding can be observed not simply in the fragmented, impatient speech of the young or their illogical, unsyntactical writing but in the rapid emergence of an all-instant society: instant therapy, instant religion, instant food, instant friends, even instant reading. Instancy is one of the main teachings of our present information environment. Constancy is one of the main teachings of civilization. But constancy presupposes the relevance of historical precedence, of continuity, and above all, of complexity and the richness of ambiguity. A person trained to read a page in three seconds is being taught contempt for complexity and ambiguity. A person trained to restructure his or her life in a weekend of therapy is being taught not only contempt for complexity and ambiguity but for the meaning of one's own past. And a person who abandons a five-thousand- or two-thousand-year-old religious tradition to follow a fourteen-year-old messenger from God has somehow learned to value novelty more than continuity.

Where does the seeming plausibility of instancy as a way of life come from? It is at least a reasonable hypothesis that it emerges from the "world view" advanced by our present information environment.

●

Our youth have no head for historical facts, and probably very little interest in history; which makes history, as I have stressed, particularly relevant to their education.

●

The classroom *is* a nineteenth-century invention, and we ought to prize what it has to offer. It is, in fact, one of the few social organizations left to us in which sequence, community experience, social order, hierarchy, continuity, and deferred pleasure are important.

School at Home

Encouragement and experienced advice on home teaching, including coverage of home study courses by mail and sundry state laws about compulsory school attendance. (For more on home teaching, see next page.) —SB

School at Home
(An Alternative to the Public School System)
Darcy Williamson
1979; 91 pp.

$9.95 postpaid from:
Maverick Publications
P.O. Drawer 5007
Bend, OR 97701
or Whole Earth Household Store

<u>Introduction</u>

I dont go to public school or boarding school, I have school at home. Everywhere I go, my school goes. Mom has a home Instruction book she teaches me from.

My favorite subjects are reading and Greek mythology I also have math, science, and spelling. I know how to do addition, subtraction, division, and multiplication. I have learned how to do lots of other things, too.

Mom and I work a lot. We travel and travel. We have a truck that Mom drives. The truck pulls our trailer. We look for book stores where we can sell Moms books.

Wayde
3 rd. grade

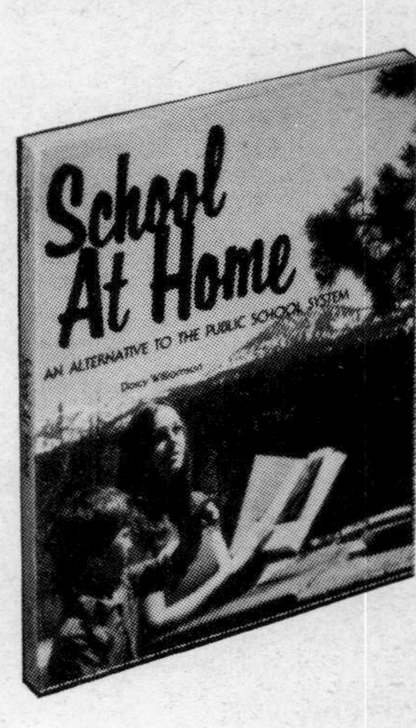

Growing Without Schooling

John Holt's newsletter about not sending children to school. Letters from people who are doing it, advice about what to do and not do with kids at home, the latest legal news, and a directory of unschoolers so they can get in touch with each other. Looks essential if you're not public schooling your kids. —Anne Herbert

Growing Without Schooling
John Holt, Editor

$10 /year (6 issues) from:
Growing Without Schooling
Holt Associates
308 Boylston Street
Boston, MA 02116

●

If I had children, and wanted to teach them at home, I think I would ask someone from out of town, perhaps even out of state, to write the local School Board saying, in effect, "I am now teaching my children at home, am thinking of moving to your area, and am looking for a school district in which I can go on doing this. What requirements and conditions would I have to meet in order to be able to do this in your community?"

To put the question this way puts the School Board in a bit of a spot. If they say, "It doesn't make any difference what you do, you can't teach your children at home under any conditions," they may be violating state law. In any case, such a statement will not look very good if the matter ever goes to court. If they say, "You must meet such and such conditions," and you later meet them, it will be harder for them to say no. If they begin asking prying or hostile questions, or do not answer at all — well, there is your answer. Whatever you decide to do next, you will not have revealed yourself to them.

●

In **Blackberry Winter**, Margaret Mead (who did not attend school regularly until she was eleven) said that children used to be brought up by means of stories. I thought I'd like to try that with my children but didn't know how to start until Sean began to ask me questions last summer about the origins of man and the universe. He would ask me, "How did God make Adam and Eve?" or "How did God make the earth?" Knowing nothing, I knew everything, and I began to enjoy answering his questions, which I did with stories.

Deschooling Society

Very few parents look at teachers and schools with Illich's true understanding of their powerful influence within our society today. He gives a devastating analysis of the ways in which educational institutions act to minimize learning and maximize conformity and social stratification. When we look for positive moves, are Illich's solutions practical, or in fact real, given the current state of education? **Deschooling Society** *clarifies many of the problems, but if readers are anxiously looking for ready answers, they might be in trouble. Or is this what Illich meant to achieve? If so, he has done a good job.* —Diane and Eddie Grayson

(For more on Illich, see p. 40.)

Deschooling Society
Ivan Illich
1970; 186 pp.

$2.50 postpaid from:
Harper and Row
Keystone Industrial Park
Scranton, PA 18512
or Whole Earth Household Store

●

We have come to realize that for most men the right to learn is curtailed by the obligation to attend school.

●

School initiates, too, the Myth of Unending Consumption. This modern myth is grounded in the belief that process inevitably produces something of value and, therefore, production necessarily produces demand. School teaches us that instruction produces learning. The existence of schools produces the demand for schooling. Once we have learned to need school, all our activities tend to take the shape of client relationships to other specialized institutions. Once the self-taught man or woman has been discredited, all nonprofessional activity is rendered suspect. In school we are taught that valuable learning is the result of attendance; that the value of learning increases with the amount of input; and, finally, that this value can be measured and documented by grades and certificates. In fact, learning is the human activity which least needs manipulation by others. Most learning is not the result of instruction. It is rather the result of unhampered participation in a meaningful setting. Most people learn best by being "with it," yet school makes them identify their personal, cognitive growth with elaborate planning and manipulation.

An Education Handbook for Parents of Handicapped Children

Hard as it is to have a handicapped child, most parents will tell you the hardest part is dealing with all the bureaucratic red tape of getting the child educated. Just learning what programs and opportunities are around could occupy a full-time detective — and since they vary by locality, no one sourcebook (p. 333) could guide you. Though it's dry reading, this book has the information you need: how to find a school, how to find the right treatment, how to get funds. Too bad it has to be such a struggle — an inevitable byproduct, perhaps, of education for the disabled moving out of the Stone Age. —Art Kleiner

An Education Handbook for Parents of Handicapped Children
Stanley I. Mopsik and Judith A. Agard, Editors
1980; 287 pp.

$18 postpaid from:
Abt Books
55 Wheeler Street
Cambridge, MA 02138

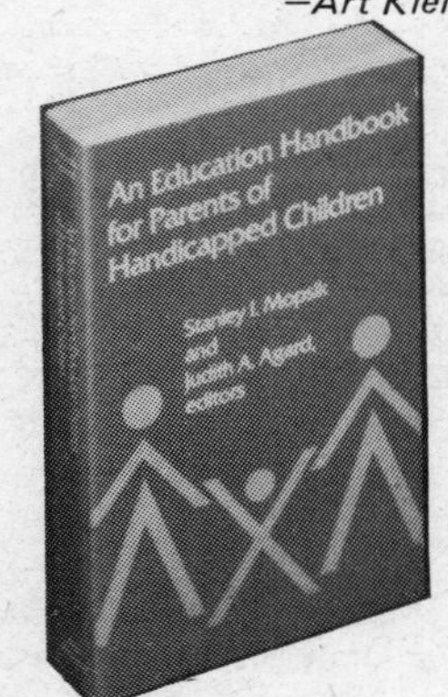

●

Where can I send for information about handicaps?

There's probably no greater asset to parents than good information about their child's handicap and about the people and places designed to help the handicapped. A good source of general information is a national information center for the handicapped called *Closer Look*. It provides information to parents on the various handicapping conditions, lists of parent organizations for each disability in each state, information about coalitions for the handicapped, the names of state-level special education personnel through whom a parent can get information on local special education offerings, helpful guidelines on getting needed services, valuable information on the rights of parents and their children, and a superb newsletter. To receive information and/or the newsletter, write to:

Closer Look
Box 1492
Washington, D.C. 20013

THE RISING SUN NEIGHBORHOOD NEWSLETTER

"Probably the main thing I learned by being a stripper was that, yes, acting out one's fantasies was enlightening and healthy but (Catch-22) once you are *living* a fantasy it is no longer a pretend thing but an actuality. It's a good way to dispel many of your imaginary devils and meet a hell of a lot of real ones. Also you have to be careful of getting stuck — that would be like stepping through the looking glass and not being able to get back or being in a dream where you can't wake up."

—Patricia

Teaching Your Child at Home

by Carol Van Strum

CECELIA CRANE

Carol Van Strum (in the CAT hat) wrote "The Strangest Letter We Ever Received" (p. 550). She taught four children at home and then most of the neighbor kids in a one-shack schoolhouse in the Oregon hills. —SB

Many people have asked about teaching children at home as an alternative to sending them to school. It's a big order, and shouldn't be undertaken lightly, any more than having children in the first place should be. Not that it is so very difficult; anyone who knows something can teach it, and teaching reading, math, etc., is really no different from teaching a child to tie a shoelace. It does, however, require time, energy and consistency, which are available to few parents any more, and sending a child off to school needn't be so awful a fate. You can't expect miracles of schools, though; they cannot undo apathy toward learning that a child brings with him from home. This is a list of publications that I put together for people who ask about teaching at home. It should also be helpful to those with children in, or about to be in, public school, for it's never too late to add to your own life in ways that will help your children.

As far as how one sets about formally teaching children at home, I can't offer any definitive system. For each child it has been different. Of course they were learning all the time, but for two hours of the day that was the focus of our life. During those two hours the phone went unanswered, visitors were discouraged, and all other activities suspended. When the kids were small, those two hours were a time to enjoy each other's undivided attention, reading aloud, drawing pictures and writing captions for them, writing letters, playing word and number games, learning words, simple arithmetic, spelling, exploring the outdoors with field guides. Before long I was working as hard as they just to keep up with them, having to review algebra and geometry, chemistry, etc. I learned physics, mechanics, and music right along with them. In fact, I learned more by "teaching" than I ever learned in school myself. Their exuberance was infectious, and it was very exciting for me.

The thing is, excitement about learning is infectious, and no matter where a child goes to school, if he lives in a home where people are always learning, are excited about discovering new things and communicating them, he will be, too. The biggest favor you can do your child is to keep reading, and share what you read, reading aloud from newspapers, books, magazines, letters, odd trivia from a dictionary or encyclopedia, the awful jokes they put in with the phone bill — anything that amuses, angers or astonishes you. And when a question comes up that you can't answer, look it up together — do you know where Iran is, what its boundaries are? Or what causes the northern lights? Or how fast light travels? Or what an X-ray is? Or what's funny about all multiples of nine? If you are learning all the time, your kids will be, too, and any school will have a hard time undoing it.

The following list is by no means exhaustive. Most of the texts I have come by fortuitously, so there are probably others equally good or better, but this should give an idea of the possibilities. We always made constant use of local libraries as well as state and university libraries for particular subjects of great interest that we couldn't find at home (the state library, on separate occasions, filled our mailbox with books on electronics, the Loch Ness Monster, Irish folklore, and timber practices).

Useful books to have around the house:

Mathematics for Self Study, James E. Thompson, 1967. 5 volumes, 1 each on Arithmetic, Geometry, Trigonometry, Algebra and Calculus. $5 each postpaid from Benjamin-Cummings Publishing Company, Addison-Wesley, Jacob Way, Reading, MA 01867. *These are very useful references for teaching, or at any time, when you find you can't remember how to multiply fractions or figure the volume of a container. There are interesting historical notes as well. Mathematical operations are clearly and concisely described, with examples, and problems for the reader to tackle on his own (the chapter on binary arithmetic in Volume I is a good sample for anyone interested in how computers operate). This is mathematics for anyone who knows how to read.*

Geometry, Harold R. Jacobs, 1974. $12 postpaid from W.H. Freeman and Company, 660 Market Street, San Francisco, CA 94104. *There's no way to describe this except to say it's great fun. The first part of the book is a short course in logic, which kids, relentless logicians that they are, appreciate and immediately put to use in arguing with their peers and parents. Principles of geometry are then explored, their logical bases clearly explained. Illustrated throughout with cartoons, drawings, literary excerpts, and wonderfully loony anecdotes.*

The above math books are for parents as well as children (who are already reading). For teaching simple computations — addition, subtraction, etc., most elementary school texts are boring and repetitive. You can teach these far more effectively yourself, and for practice, I've found dime-store Whitman workbooks to be perfectly adequate, so long as you stay at hand to praise correct work and help correct mistakes. One important thing: encourage the child to feel that not knowing an answer is not bad but on the contrary, exciting; it is the prerequisite to discovering something new.

Basic Concepts in Music, Gary M. Martin, 1966. $12.95 postpaid from Wadsworth Publishing Company, 10 Davis Drive, Belmont, CA 94001. *An interesting and useful programmed text designed to accommodate both the absolute ignoramus and the person with any degree of musical experience. Covers basic components of music notation; notational components of rhythm and melody; harmonic structure of basic intervals and chords; major and minor scales, chords and keys; and the basic structure of music. The child who can read can progress through the book at his own rate; the parent with a piano or penny-whistle and some sheet music at his disposal can learn much to pass on to his children.*

Biology: An Inquiry into the Nature of Life, edited by Stanley Weinberg, 1974. $16.95 postpaid from Allyn and Bacon, Inc., 470 Atlantic Avenue, Boston, MA 02210. *A good, basic biology text, with especially interesting chapters on behavior, genetics, ecology, and "human ecology." Very readable, well illustrated, with good glossary and index. A good reference, and useful to have around when you can't remember what hemoglobin does, or what exactly Mendel did. Lab manual available.*

Elements of Biology, Charles K. Levy, 1978. $17.95 postpaid from Addison-Wesley Publishing Company, Jacob Way, Reading, MA 01867. *Another good biology text, organized around functions common to all living systems. It has an excellent short review of organic chemistry designed for the non-science college student. This is a well written, readable reference. There are also an instructor's guide and a study/guide workbook available.*

Chemistry, George W. Watt, Lewis F. Hatch and J.J. Lagowski, 1964. $12.95 postpaid from W.W. Norton and Company, 500 Fifth Avenue, New York, NY 10036. *A good all-round chemistry text intended "for those students who may take only one course in college chemistry." A useful reference for most of the questions about chemicals that everyday life inspires.*

Alistair Cooke's America, Alistair Cooke, 1974. $20 postpaid from Alfred A. Knopf, Inc., 455 Hahn Road, Westminster, MD 21157. *One man's view of American history, irritating sometimes but always interesting. Lots of good and unusual pictures.*

One good and not often exploited source for particulars of history: the government — congressmen, senators, the Treasury Department (identification of the gentleman on the $2 bill, for instance), etc., for copies of the Constitution, Declaration of Independence, etc., as well as local and state governments and historical societies.

Life World Library, Nature Library, and Science Library. Information free from Time-Life Books, 777 Duke Street, Alexandria, VA 22314. *I wouldn't have expected it, and never would have purchased these, but since someone donated them to us, they have competed well with comics and picture books. Even the smallest kids will plunk down with one and pore over it endlessly, demanding explanations of every picture.*

Encyclopedia Brittanica *(p. 496). Almost any fairly recent edition can be purchased used at a good price. Indispensible for looking up anything that comes along. (Do you know who King Wenceslaus was, for example?)*

Oxford Junior Encyclopedia, 1976. $200 postpaid from Oxford University Press, 16-00 Pollitt Drive, Fair Lawn, NJ 07410. *"Junior" in England, maybe! This is what I would choose if I could have only one encyclopedia in the house. Arranged by subjects in 12 volumes (Mankind, The Universe, The Arts, etc.). Well illustrated and excellently written. I use the Farming and Fisheries volume continually; it is a complete reference for self-sufficient agriculture and animal husbandry. (Volumes are available separately or as a set, with an excellent index volume.)*

You Learn to Type, Alan C. Lloyd and Nathan Krevolin, 1966. $9.80 postpaid from McGraw-Hill Book Company, Princeton Road, Hightstown, NJ 08520. *A spiral-bound programmed course in typing, complete. If you know how to read and are willing to commit yourself to a half hour a day, you can learn to type by proceeding through this book. Kids love it, and learning to type gives them a great thrill. (Interesting: kids learn to spell better by learning to type.)*
(See also Constructive Playthings, p. 544.)

Books by Geraldine Lux Flanagan: **The First Nine Months of Life**, 1962. $7.95 postpaid from Simon and Schuster, Attn: Order Department, 1230 Avenue of the Americas, New York, NY 10020. **Window into an Egg**, 1969. $6.95 postpaid from Addison-Wesley, Jacob Way, Reading, MA 01867. **Window into a Nest**, 1976. $7.95 postpaid from Houghton-Mifflin Company, Wayside Road, Burlington, MA 01803. *Three jewels, beautifully written, illustrated with photographs. The first covers human embryological development from conception to birth, including photos of fetal behavior in utero. The second is a chronology of the growth of a chick, photographed through a "window" in the egg shell. The third shows the life of a nest of tits, from courtship to mating, nest-building, egg laying, etc. These are informative, accurate books, but also far more: they are celebrations of life, of the essential, wonderful mystery of its origins.*

Useful publications to subscribe to for kids: **Natural History** *(p. 56),* **National Geographic World** *(See* **National Geographic**, *p. 516),* **Science 80** *(p. 517),* **Cricket** *and* **Ranger Rick** *(both p. 547), and one of their favorites — and free, the* **Edmund Scientific Catalogue** *(p. 562).*

TEACHING READING

For the very young child, I don't have any particular method. One of the most important things I think is always — from toddlerhood on — to have paper and drawing materials on hand, lots of them. Encourage kids to draw, do sketches yourself (they'll love them, no matter how awful!), and write (print) captions for even the wildest scribbles. It doesn't take long for even a very young child to make a connection between a picture of something and a written symbol (word) for it. Those little magnetized plastic letters are great, too, for kids to play with on the refrigerator, and they like to trace the outlines of them with colored pencils.

The book that I've used most for little kids is a simple Doubleday workbook, **Teach Me to Read**, *that I got at the dime store.* (Also available for $2.20 postpaid from Doubleday and Company, 501 Franklin Avenue, Garden City, NY 11530.) *It uses rhymes to start a child right off with phonetic relationships, as well as introducing important sight words, tense and plurals. It is easy and fun, and I've never had a child get more than halfway through it before tackling "real" books. (Not one of the kids here ever learned to read from any of the Dr. Seuss-type easy readers, although they enjoyed them immensely long after learning to read. Their "first books" have been unexpected choices:* **The Call of the Wild, The Handbook of Organic Gardening, The Tomten . . .***)*
If your child needs something more structured, two of the best things I've found are the **Sullivan Readers** (Cynthia D. Buchanan, 12 volumes, $3.50 each postpaid from Sullivan Associates, Behavioral Research Laboratories, P.O. Box 577, Palo Alto, CA 94302) *and* **Programmed Reading Books** (Cynthia D. Buchanan, 7 books, $3.50 each postpaid from McGraw-Hill Book Company, Princeton Road, Hightstown, NJ 08520). *These are excellent, so long as you don't fall into the trap of expecting them to do your job for you, which is to ensure that reading (i.e., learning) is rich and exciting enough that a child will tackle it as eagerly as he does a new toy.*

For the child who is truly having difficulties learning, whether at home or at school, I can't recommend highly enough the Distar Reading, Language (speech) and Math programs, developed by Siegfried Englemann, University of Oregon, Eugene. (Information free from Science-Research Associates, 155 North Wacker Drive, Chicago, IL 60606.) *These programs have been successful with many severely "educationally handicapped" children as well as kids with only moderate problems. If your child is in public school, you have a right to request their use.*

READING ALOUD

You can see from the above list that I haven't made much use of standard elementary school texts. These are designed for mass teaching of 30 or 50 kids at a crack, and may be excellent for that purpose, but do not at all suit the single child or several children learning from (or with) an attentive parent.

My own "philosophy" of teaching, if I have one at all, is that if a child can read, and read well and enjoy it, there is nothing in the universe of human experience that he cannot have access to. By "read well" I mean the ability to comprehend and appreciate the language, in all its richness and variety of form and vocabulary. It is exceedingly difficult to read a language without hearing it, and the child's best access to the vast diversity of rhythm, syntax, grammar, etc. in our language is through literature, read aloud and enjoyed as a daily family event. There is nothing to equal it, and its worth goes far beyond the realm of teaching. How many difficult days we have weathered by knowing that at the end there will be at least this one happy constant: the next chapter of Dickens, or E.B. White, or Arthur Ransome.

Following is a very partial list of books we have read aloud and loved, and often reread again. Most of them are available at libraries or in paperback editions, and I've given the paperback publishers when possible.

GOOD READING

For younger kids:

The Tomten, The Tomten and the Fox, Christmas in the Stable, Astrid Lindgren and Harold Wiberg; Coward, McCann & Geoghegan.

Mike Mulligan and His Steam Shovel, Virginia Lee Burton; Houghton Mifflin.

The Bee-man of Orn, Frank R. Stockton; Holt Owlet.

Father Fox's Pennyrhymes, Clyde and Wendy Watson; Scholastic Book Services.

The Sam Pig Storybook, Alison Uttley; Merrimack Book Service (Faber).

Make Way for Ducklings, Robert McCloskey; Penguin.

The Little Red Lighthouse and the Great Gray Bridge, Hildegarde H. Swift and Lynd Ward; Harcourt Brace Jovanovich (Voyager).

Once Under the Cherry Blossom Tree, Allen Say; Harper and Row.

The Golden Egg Book, Margaret Wise Brown and Leonard Weisgard; Golden Press (Western Publishing Company).

Goodnight Moon and **The Runaway Bunny**, Margaret Wise Brown; Harper and Row.

The Poky Little Puppy and **The Lively Little Rabbit**, Little Golden Books.

Corgiville Fair, Tasha Tudor; Crowell.

Rabbit Hill, Robert Lawson; Dell Yearling.

The Rise and Fall of Ben Gizzard, Richard Kennedy; Atlantic (Little, Brown and Company).

The Story About Ping, Marjorie Flack and Kurt Wiese; Puffin (Penguin).

And Beatrix Potter, always (most published by Creative Education Books).

For older or even elderly kids:

The Mouse and His Child, Russell Hoban; Avon Camelot.

The Borrowers, The Borrowers Afield, etc., Mary Norton; Harcourt Brace.

The Story of the Treasure Seekers, The Wouldbegoods, The Railway Children, etc., E. Nesbit; Puffin (Penguin).

The Children of Green Knowe, A Stranger at Green Knowe, etc., Lucy Boston; Harcourt Brace Jovanovich.

The Witch of Blackbird Pond, The Bronze Bow, Elizabeth George Speare; Dell or Houghton-Mifflin.

The Wolves of Willoughby Chase, Black Hearts in Battersea, etc., Joan Aiken; Dell Yearling.

Swallows and Amazons, Swallowdale, We Didn't Mean to Go to Sea, etc., Arthur Ransome; Puffin Books or Jonathan Cape.

The Story of Doctor Doolittle, et al., Hugh Lofting; Dell Yearling.

The Book of Three, The High King, etc., Lloyd Alexander; Dell Yearling.

Charlotte's Web, Stuart Little, The Trumpet of the Swan, E.B. White; Dell Yearling.

The Animal Family, Randall Jarrell; Dell Yearling.

No Way of Telling, Emma Smith; Atheneum.

The Secret Garden, Frances Hodgson Burnett; Dell.

Naftali the Storyteller and His Horse, Sus, Isaac Bashevis Singer; Dell Yearling.

The Moon in the Cloud, The Shadow on the Sun, The Bright and Morning Star, The Seal Singing, Rosemary Harris; Macmillan.

The Little House in the Big Woods, Farmer Boy, etc., Laura Ingalls Wilder; Harper and Row.

Tuck Everlasting, Natalie Babbitt; Bantam.

Kim, Rudyard Kipling; Dell.

Inside My Feet, Richard Kennedy; Harper and Row.

The Fledgling, Jane Langton; Harper and Row.

David Copperfield, Great Expectations, Charles Dickens; Penguin.

Freddy the Pig Books, Walter R. Brooks; Knopf (out of print, some reissued in paper).

Mistress Masham's Repose, T.H. White; G.P. Putnam's Sons (Berkeley).

The Fabulous Flight, Robert Lawson (not in print currently).

Meet the Austins, The Young Unicorns, The Arm of the Starfish, A Ring of Endless Light, Madeline L'Engle; Dell or Vanguard.

The Adventures of Tintin, Herge; French and European Publications, Inc. *(Watch out for these, they are addictive to adults, and some children may also be affected.)*

Special Books to Keep:

The Oxford Book of Children's Verse, Iona and Peter Opie; Oxford University Press.

An Inheritance of Poetry, edited by Gladys L. Adshead and Annis Duff; Houghton-Mifflin.

Fun With String Figures, W.W. Rouse Ball; Dover.

String Figures and How to Make Them, Caroline F. Jayne; Dover.

Take Joy, Tasha Tudor; Collins/World. ■

Teacher

Teacher is as unphony, warm, and appealing as the grubby, tear-streaked face of a child; it is also an important technical notebook for educators. Miss Ashton-Warner's organic approach to reading and writing is a detailed enough account to be explored further by teachers anywhere. It is of especial value to teachers working with primary children, students with a cultural or language barrier, and adult illiterates.

—Carol Guyton Goodell

Teacher
Sylvia Ashton-Warner
1963; 224 pp.
$2.25 postpaid from:
Bantam Books
414 East Golf Road
Des Plaines, IL 60016
or Whole Earth Household Store

●

Noise, noise, noise, yes. But if you don't like noise, don't be a teacher.

●

But there are two kinds of order, and which is the one we wish for? Is it the conscious order that ends up as respectability? Or is it the unconscious order that looks like chaos on the top? There is a separate world on each side of this question mark.

Human Characteristics and School Learning

It's Bloom's contention that differences in school learning are largely man-made and not due to a natural stratification of talent; the differences persist because the organization of education is designed to make them persist.

Bloom offers an alternative whereby nearly everyone gets "top grades" without lowering standards: students are given periodic feedback on their progress and opportunities to correct mistakes or inadequacies. Most of the studies Bloom draws on for evidence deal with elementary and high school level coursework, but he believes the theory is applicable to all areas of learning (with some reservation about the fine arts).

This is one of the most exciting books I've run across in my studies (for an M.A.). The man has impeccable credentials — any education major will have run across his name dozens of times. His emphasis on the importance of feedback is what originally made me think of submitting the book to you. *—Steven A. Kvaal*

Human Characteristics and School Learning
Benjamin S. Bloom
1976; 284 pp.
$17.95 postpaid from:
McGraw-Hill
Book Company
Princeton Road
Hightstown, NJ 08520
or Whole Earth Household Store

●

Modern societies no longer can content themselves with the *selection of talent;* they must find the means for *developing talent.*

Any Child Can Write

For an excellent example of exactly the sort of teaching Bloom describes in **Human Characteristics and School Learning** *here is Harvey Wiener's* **Any Child Can Write**. *Every parent who has any hopes for raising literate children should read it. The sad truth is, schools are not teaching children to write, even the simplest forms of expression. In one high school I know, seniors are offered a special course in filling out job applications, as many of them lack the skills necessary for even so basic a task as answering standard application-form questions! One of the commitments of parenthood is to take responsiblity for our children's education, starting before school begins and continuing throughout the school years. No teacher has as much time, energy and interest to spare for a particular student as its own parent has, or should have. Wiener's book is an enjoyable, encouraging handbook for such a parent.*

One aspect of Bloom's theory that is clearly apparent in Wiener's practice is the importance of interaction between teacher (parent) and child. As Wiener points out, it is the parent's interest in details of the child's experience ("A frog? What color was it? Did it bite? What did it feel like?") that give the child a sense of the importance of his experience (and therefore himself) and the worth of communicating it. This is the basis for a child's future, at home, in school, in the great wide world — that he feel important and that his ideas and experiences are worth communicating. Yet so often from an early age children are denied this simple gift from the persons closest to them. In this respect the great value of Wiener's book goes beyond the teaching of writing. His activities and games all begin with the parent tuning in on the child's world, responding, appreciating, asking questions, offering related personal experiences, encouraging further description and narrative.

It's not a one-way street. Such a parent is bound to discover new and delightful insights and ideas in the child, and make the acquaintance of a unique and stimulating individual in a mere son or daughter.

Two suggestions:

If you are already at the difficult point where communication — interaction — between you and your child is awkward or nonexistent, you have to take a deliberately low-key initiative. Exploit an incident — any incident, even a potentially negative one — and communicate your interest by contributing an off-hand experience of your own: "Oh god, I left my jacket on the playground once, and when I finally found it a mouse had built her nest in the pocket." Offer enough detail to spark some interest, hopefully to inspire curiosity ("Really? She had babies in it? What did you do?"). It may take several or many efforts, but eventually the child comes to see you are interested enough in his experiences — good or bad — to relate them to your own.

One often neglected but most important element in communicating with children (or adults or any other animal, as Kipling well knew!) is eye contact. Even newborns respond to it. Your eyes are your most effective means of nonverbal communication: they can belie or reinforce anything you say. Even the most "difficult" and withdrawn child will respond to a conspiratorial twinkle or appreciative glance from a total stranger and seek out that person's eyes when they meet again. You can control what your eyes are saying as accurately as you can your voice, and often with far more impact. "Across a crowded room" you can communicate approval, disapproval, excitement, expectant interest, comfort, admiration, fear, etc. To the child, this is the beginning of meaningful exchange, a special language between you two alone — "We have a secret, you and I . . ." Eye contact is the cornerstone of trust, and the bridge from there to words and friendship is a short, happy one.

—Carol Van Strum

Any Child Can Write
(How to Improve Your Child's Writing Skills from Preschool through High School)
Harvey S. Wiener
1978; 255 pp.
$9.95 postpaid from:
McGraw-Hill
Book Company
Princeton Road
Hightstown, NJ 08520
or Whole Earth Household Store

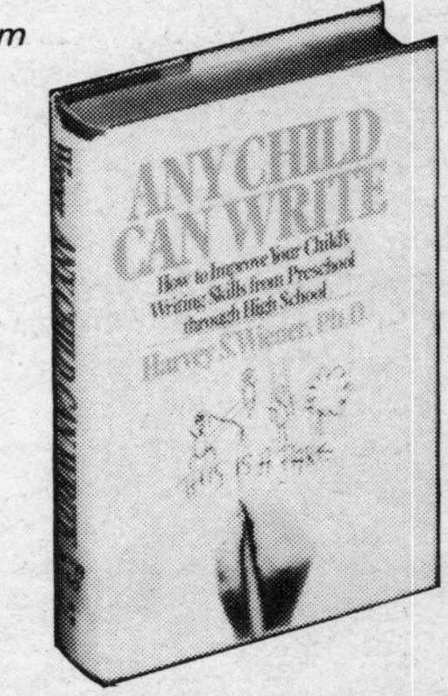

THE RISING SUN
NEIGHBORHOOD NEWSLETTER

Things about tidelands:

1. Loren Eiseley said that we are so absorbed in watching our own end games as a species that we aren't watching the tidelands closely enough to see the next adventurer leave the mud to start the next chain. *continued on next spread*

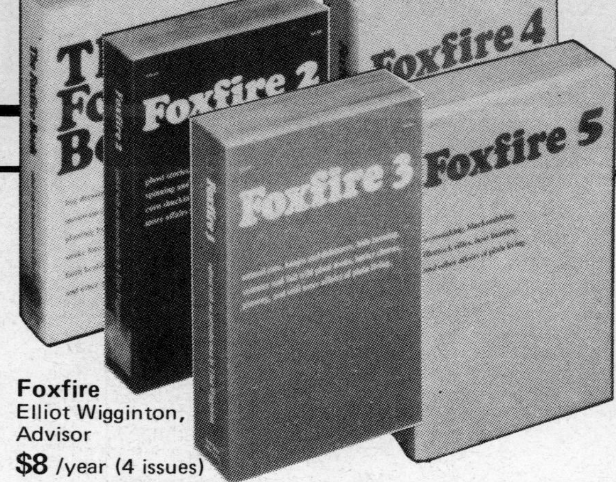

Foxfire

Foxfire is a quarterly publication concerned with researching, recording and preserving Appalachian folk art, crafts and traditions. A typical issue contains articles on quilting, chairmaking, soap making, home remedies, mountain recipes, feather beds and home-made hominy, plus regional poetry and book reviews. One issue was devoted entirely to log cabin building. These are not superficial "feature" articles, but definitive, detailed treatments of traditional skills and crafts that have come close to dying out of our culture.

***Foxfire** would be a credit to a group of professional folklorists. But when you consider that it is edited and published by high school kids at the Rabun Gap-Nacoochee School in Rabun Gap, Georgia, it becomes impressive indeed. The thing I like most about it is the way these kids are looking immediately around them for their inspiration, instead of taking cues from New York and California. In their own way, these people are as hip and sophisticated as any young people putting out a magazine on either coast. More so, even. They're cooler, more adult. **Foxfire**'s editors and writers (and some excellent photographers) seem to me as aware of what's wrong with the world as anyone. The thing that distinguishes them from their shrill counterparts in the cities is the absence of fad, slogan and cliche as they set out to improve the world. These kids in Georgia are living in a real world, studying real things, and in consequence they are creating a wonderfully real publication in **Foxfire**.*

—Gurney Norman

*Since Gurney wrote this review in 1969 **Foxfire** has grown and deepened with the years into a flat-out landmark of American education and folklore technique. It's been widely copied, always to good effect. Try it in your area. The old-timers tell things to youngsters they wouldn't say to anybody else.*

—SB

Foxfire
Elliot Wigginton, Advisor
$8 /year (4 issues)

The Foxfire Book — Hog dressing, log cabin building, mountain crafts and foods, planting by the signs, snake lore, hunting tales, faith healing, moonshining, and other affairs of plain living. 1972, $5.95 postpaid.

Foxfire 2 — Ghost stories, spring wild plant foods, spinning and weaving, midwifing, burial customs, corn shuckin's, wagon making and more affairs of plain living. 1973, $5.95 postpaid.

Foxfire 3 — Animal care, banjos and dulcimers, hide tanning, summer and fall wild plant foods, butter churns, ginseng, and still more affairs of plain living. 1975, $5.95 postpaid.

Foxfire 4 — Fiddle making, spring houses, horse trading, sassafras tea, berry buckets, gardening, and further affairs of plain living. 1977, $6.95 postpaid.

Foxfire 5 — Ironmaking, blacksmithing, flintlock rifles, bear hunting, and other affairs of plain living. 1979, $6.95 postpaid.

All from:
Foxfire Fund, Inc.
Rabun Gap, GA 30568

```
↓      ↓    ↑
Come butter come
↓      ↓    ↑
Come butter come
↓    ↑      ↓       ↓   ↑
Peter standing at the gate
↓      ↑     ↑      ↓    ↑
Waiting for a butter cake
↓      ↑    ↑
Come butter come.
```

→
The churner said the chant in time to the up and down movements of the dasher as indicated below. The arrows indicate the dasher movement.

Learning Magazine

For classroom teachers this is the trade journal. Anybody working with kids would pick up a lot from a year's worth. Strong, enjoyable stuff.

—SB

Learning
(The Magazine for Creative Teaching)
Morton Malkofsky, Editor
$14 /year (9 issues)
from:
Learning
Subscription Department
1255 Portland Place
Boulder, CO 80321

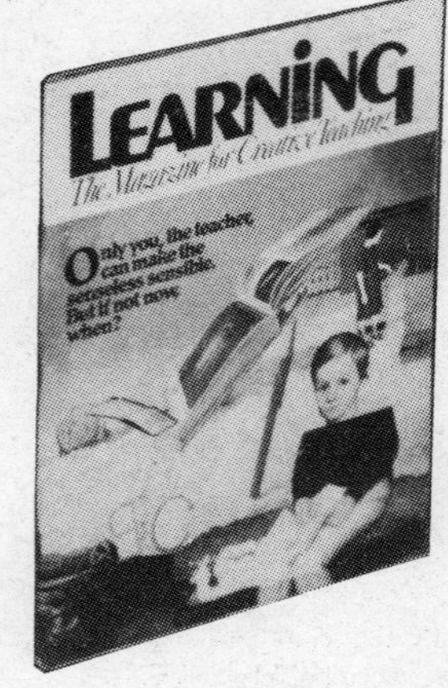

•

Resources for Teaching Citizenship

Background reading:

Ecotopia by Ernest Callenbach. From Bantam Books, Inc., $2.25.

Gaia: A New Look at Life on Earth by J.E. Lovelock. From Oxford University Press, $11.95.

Mankind and Mother Earth: A Narrative History of the World by Arnold Toynbee. From Oxford University Press, $25.

Muddling Toward Frugality by Warren Johnson. From Shambhala Publications (Box 271, 1123 Spruce Street, Boulder, CO 80306), $2.95.

Person/Planet: The Creative Disintegration of Industrial Society by Theodore Roszak. From Doubleday & Co., $5.95.

Publications and Teaching Materials

Energy and Education, a free monthly newsletter published by the National Science Teachers Association (1742 Connecticut Ave., N.W., Washington, DC 20009). The NSTA also has a series of instructional packets and fact sheets that deal with energy. Write for a list of publications.

Teachers and Writers Collaborative

The best way to teach reading is through writing. As a child comes into contact with his or her own voice, the idea of putting words on paper begins to make sense as does the idea that books contain other people's voices. The best material on developing a writing program that allows children's imagination to flow is produced by the Teachers and Writers Collaborative. This material comes out of work with children in school and is full of practical suggestions and examples of young people's writing. The Collaborative produces a newsletter that has features like how to make comic books, photonovellas, films and videotape scripts. It also features accounts of different ways of approaching poetry, fiction, fables, plays. I find the material helpful for my own writing as well as for children.

***The Whole Word Catalogs I & II** are useful collections of different things that can be done with writing. Karen Hubert's book **Teaching and Writing Popular Fiction: Horror, Adventure, Mystery and Romance in the American Classroom** is simply marvelous. She has all the formulas for popular writing down cold. I've thought of using her ideas to turn out a few pulps myself.*

—Herb Kohl

*(See **Any Child Can Write**, p. 569.)*

Teaching and Writing Popular Fiction
(Horror, Adventure, Mystery and Romance in the American Classroom)
Karen M. Hubert
1976; 235 pp.
$4 postpaid

The Whole Word Catalog
Rosellen Brown, Marvin Hoffman, Martin Kushner, Phillip Lopate and Sheila Murphy, Editors
1972; 72 pp.
$4 postpaid

The Whole Word Catalog 2
Bill Zavatsky and Ron Padgett
1977; 351 pp.
$6.95 postpaid

Teachers and Writers Magazine
Miguel A. Ortiz, Editor
$5 /year (3 issues)
all from:
Teachers and Writers Collaborative
84 Fifth Avenue
New York, NY 10011

•

You have been caught! Knocked unconscious by your enemies, you wake up in a dark cell with no windows. There is no way out: you cannot even find a door. You wonder where you are. Start recalling all the events that led to your capture. (Tell the story as it happens or as a flashback.)

—**Teaching and Writing Popular Fiction**

Filmmaking for kids

Break the hold of the TV cartoon monster. Help kids make their own animated films. And never mind that there's no Bolex in the budget. There are other ways. Like drawing on clear leader, or scratching on unprocessed film. I taught a class in animation using 3 by 5 cards as flipbooks. (Put a rubber band in the middle of a stack of 25 or so. Make a sequence of simple drawings on both ends. Flip with thumb.) Any super 8 camera with a single framing button can make wonderful pixilations (animation of real objects or people). You can put a lot of animation on one roll of film. Here are some resources.

***Animation Pie**, a film by Robert Bloomberg, is a wonderful, zany and inspiring film showing high school kids learning to make several kinds of animated movies: simple flipbooks, three-dimensional clay, and stop-action of the kids themselves (pixilation). It's won many awards. 26 minutes, color, sound, live and animated. Lease $375. Rent $37.50 per day from FilmWright, 4530 18th Street, San Francisco, CA 94114.*

***Making It Move** is a student text as well as a teacher's manual, well organized and covering all kinds of animation including many that don't require a camera. One unit includes the construction of a zoetrope, one of the pioneer motion picture machines.*

Making It Move
John Trojanski and Louis Rockwood
1973; 151 pp.
$5.40 postpaid from:
National Textbook Company
8259 Niles Center Road
Skokie, IL 60077
or Whole Earth Household Store

Moviemaking Illustrated — *Understanding how films are made has a lot to do with understanding how comic books are made. This book takes our familiarity with comics and neatly weaves it into a study of film. Not just for kids!*

—Tom Schneider

Moviemaking Illustrated
(The Comicbook Filmbook)
James Morrow and Murray Suid
1973; 150 pp.
$6.45 postpaid from:
Hayden Book Company
50 Essex Street
Rochelle Park, NJ 07662

The New Hooked on Books

*If you've wrestled with ways to teach a non-reader as a teacher, if you've wondered what you could do as a businessman to help an obviously weak reading program in your schools, or if you're the worried parent of a Book Avoider, then you'll tear through **Hooked on Books** with a firelike fervor fed on rekindled hopes.*

Fader's program involves the saturation of students' surroundings with newspapers, magazines and paperbound books chosen because they are written on subjects relevant to the world outside a classroom. Diffusion of such materials among teachers of all subjects and the use of writing, writing and more writing as the primary ways in which to teach English is another important tenet of this program.

It is a detailed report on an exciting and practical way to teach reading, and it's laced with such well written anecdotes about the inmates of Maxey Boys Training School where this program was first tried that Big Bill, Superduck, Hogman, and Lester the Poet seem as real and as teachable as they were to the authors.

—Carol Guyton Goodell

The new 1976 edition brings the relevance up to date.

—SB

The New Hooked on Books
(How to Learn and How to Teach Reading and Writing With Pleasure)
Daniel Fader et al.
1968, 1976; 294 pp.
$2.25 postpaid from:
Berkeley Publishing Company
390 Murray Hill Parkway
East Rutherford, NJ 07073
or Whole Earth Household Store

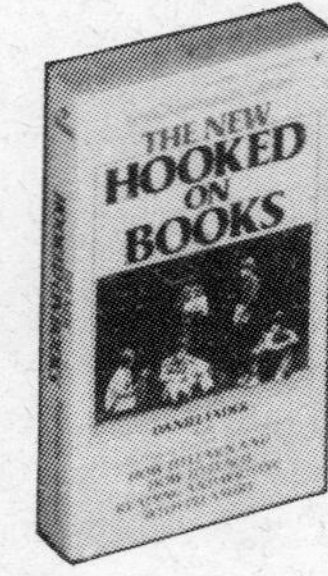

←
Relational Cutting

Relational cutting brings together people, places, and things that may never have had any connection in actuality. An example is a cut from the outside of a real submarine to a set that looks like a sub's interior. The cut gives the impression that we are now inside that particular sub.

—**Moviemaking Illustrated**

Nasco Science catalog

Once the **Next Catalog** *is finished I may get a couple of the weirdnesses in this amazing catalog for my very own. It blows Edmund Scientific (p. 562) clean out of the water. Here is every gizmo, instrument, chart, disgusting plastic organ, and lab critter you could possibly want. Happy birthday, sis, here's 3 live sea squirts ($4.50).*
—SB
[Suggested by Joyce Baron]

Nasco Science
Catalog
free from:
Nasco
901 Janesville Avenue
Fort Atkinson, WI 53538

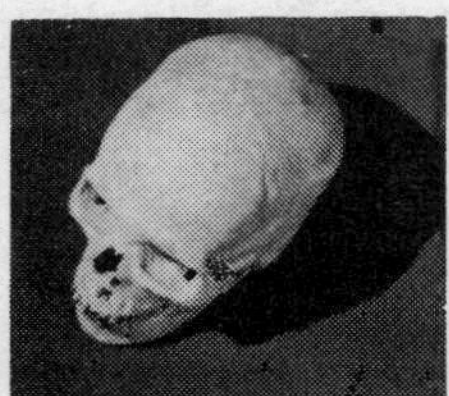

Human Skull
A good natural bone skull for general study and student use. Supplied in sturdy storage box. $92.30

Torso Model →
"Billy" accurately details over 100 intricate body structures. The outside shows superficial musculature, rib casing and other features. The torso opens to expose respiratory, circulatory, digestive, nervous and urinary systems. Lungs, heart and digestive organs (stomach, liver, intestines) are removable for examination. 56 page in-depth Lesson Plan includes detailed background information, identification of keyed features, and vocabulary. 28" x 12", $149.

← **Mean Machine — Skill Level 2**
Tallest rocket in the Estes fleet, over 6 feet long with giant 24" parachute — $7.20.
Single stage engine D.12-5 — 3 for $3.35.
Porta pad launcher — $5.40.

Mean Machine

The Complete Book of Fingermath

I first saw this form of calculation demonstrated by my brother-in-law in New York. It was more a magic show than a math lesson, and within minutes he had a growing audience of street kids trying it, demanding to be taught this new wizardry. Since the book found its way to our house, it's become a dining table attraction, irresistible to kids and adults alike.

Page by page, with clear diagrams and excellent sequential instructions, the book teaches you to use your fingers very much as an abacus; with ten fingers you have at your disposal 99 digits with which to perform innumerable calculations in addition, subtraction, multiplication, division. Very young children, as well as handicapped or "slow" kids, have little trouble with this finger game — in fact, they love it, and it gives them a great boost in confidence ("This isn't math, it couldn't be, it's too much fun!"). It is also a portable calculator for any purpose, requires no batteries, and short of mangling yourself with a skill saw, will last as long as you do. It's the best teaching "device" I've found, costs little, contains no plastic, and has no parts to lose under the couch.
—Carol Van Strum

The Complete Book of Fingermath
(Simple, Accurate, Scientific)
Edwin M. Lieberthal and Bernadette Lieberthal
1979; 342 pp.
$14 postpaid from:
McGraw-Hill Book Company
Princeton Road
Hightstown, NJ 08520
or Whole Earth Household Store

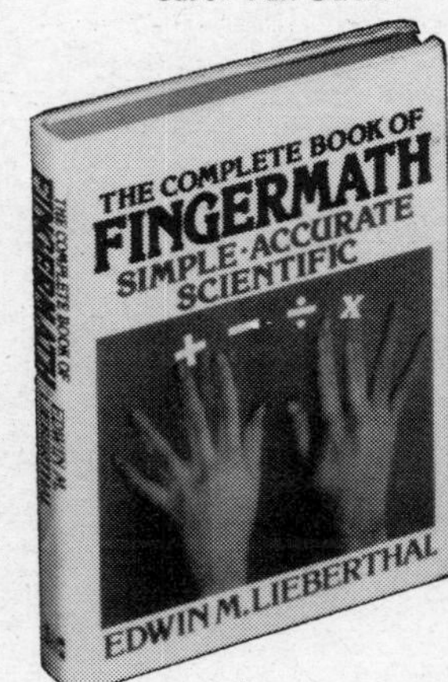

$$\begin{array}{r} 47 \\ \times 36 \\ \hline 1,692 \end{array}$$

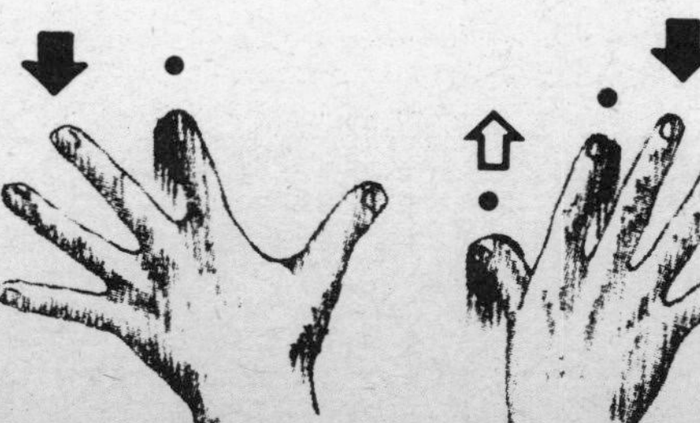

Workshop for Learning Things

An ever finer line of brilliant, cheap classroom and toy materials, featuring especially tri-wall cardboard. *—SB*

Workshop for Learning Things
Catalog

$1 from:
Workshop for Learning Things
5 Bridge Street
Watertown, MA 02172

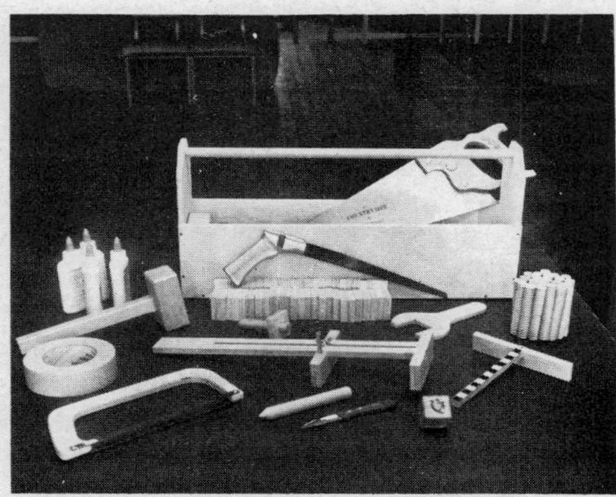

Kids' Classroom Cardboard Tool Kit, $82.

Optical Building Kit — A set of parts that go together in various ways, so you see the same parts making: microscopes, periscopes, slide viewers, kaleidoscopes, film strip viewers, cameras (several kinds) magnifiers, telescopes. $71.50.

Deschool Primer

A series of workbooks, play books, information books for children, each **Deschool Primer** *contains games, themes, lots of illustrations, and lots of information about almost everything you can think of. An enormous amount of territory is covered in these large size children's play and think manuals. Suitable for use in classrooms or at home, price for each primer is $3.*

Deschool Primer *No. 15 is about food. Did you ever play a game you could eat? Investigate a grocery store? Construct a solar hot dog cooker? Well now's your chance to do all those things and learn a lot more about that strange stuff we put into our bodies.*

Deschool Primer *No. 22 is a collection by Ron Jones of unusual world records set by children, senior citizens, and handicapped people. Activities in this book include world's tallest paper cup tower, fastest wheelchair, most inner tubes lifted by a group of people, world's largest human pin ball game and more.*
—Sylvia Jacobs and Ron Jones

(See "The Third Wave" by Ron Jones, pp. 374-377.)

Deschool Primer
Published by Zephyros, a non-profit collaborative of San Francisco Bay Area teachers, parents, toymakers, and friends.

$3 each postpaid from:
Zephyros
1201 Stanyan Street
San Francisco, CA 94117

Cuisenaire

Originators of the Renowned math-teaching "Cuisinaire Rods," the catalog now lists all manner of "problem solving with manipulatives." *—SB*

Cuisenaire Rods
Catalog
free from:
Cuisenaire Company of America
12 Church Street
New Rochelle, NY 10805

Starter sets for Cuisenaire rods include a set of 155 Cuisenaire rods in a self-sorting tray, idea book for Cuisenaire rods at the primary level, games and enrichment activities — a look at mathematics through models, and the Cuisenaire wall poster entitled "The Story of Cuisenaire Rods."

Starter set:	
plastic	**$22.50**
wood	**$24.50**

FACTORS

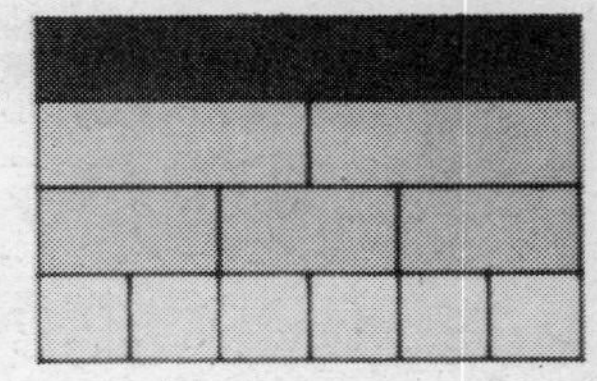

If ☐ = 1 then

1 × 6 = 6   3 × 2 = 6

2 × 3 = 6   6 × 1 = 6

Children's Book and Music Center

Music and dance instruments, records, and books for kids. Also history and contribution of black and Spanish-speaking Americans. *—SB*

(More records, pp. 480-482.)

Children's Book and Music Center
Parents' catalog
free

Teachers' catalog
$1
both from:
Children's Book and Music Center
2500 Santa Monica Blvd.
Santa Monica, CA 90404

Califone Phonograph ↓
A dependable phonograph for home and school use. Simple and durable enough to be operated by young children. Solid state 17 watt amplifier, 10" x 4" dual-cone speaker with clear, crisp sound. Among its many fine features are 4 speeds, 45 rpm twist-up adapter, diamond stylus, snap-on tonearm lock, and output jack for headset or listening center. Housed in rugged wooden carrying case, metal reinforced. $99.50

Outlook

The sort of teacher who is reminded of one child in the classroom even during the casual Saturday night movie will find much delight and support in this magazine. It contains thoughtful, philosophical enquiries into learning; reprints of classics that provide insights into the growth of children; open-ended, often surprising, examination of the subject matter of the arts and sciences; and pieces vividly recounting teachers' own experiences.
—Phylis and Philip Morrison

Outlook
Tony Kallet, Editor
$12.50/year (4 issues)

from:
The Mountain View Publishing Company
2929 6th Street
Boulder, CO 80302

•

John C *(third grader)* on salamanders: "Mrs. Easley has two salamanders."

Mr. A.: "She has three salamanders."

John C.: "Two salamanders and one shy one. I didn't count the shy one."

THE RISING SUN
NEIGHBORHOOD NEWSLETTER

continued from last spread

Things about tidelands:

2. In Hong Kong, they leave the waterfront alone. It's rough and strange and exciting and they figure if you want rough strange excitement you can go there and if not, not.

continued on next spread

The Technology of Teaching

This book focuses on classroom teaching, one of the more abysmal failures in modern civilization, but its principles — the behavioral principles of operant conditioning — apply to the teaching of anything, from tying shoelaces to controlling tempers to playing music or solving differential calculus problems. Many people have been conditioned to respond negatively to the very name of B.F. Skinner. If such persons consider themselves to be responsible, effective parents, teachers or citizens, they would do well to suspend an ill-formed judgment and read this book. Whether we like it or not, behavioral techniques work, on humans as effectively as on any other organisms. They not only work, they are and will be used upon us and our children by media, industry, government, religion, and cult. That such techniques can be used destructively no more condemns the techniques than a hammer used as a weapon by the wrong hands condemns the hammer. If we don't learn to control ourselves, someone else will do it for us, and not necessarily for our benefit. Behaviorism is a vital tool for teaching that control; the goal of a technology of teaching is a well-informed student who has learned to control himself, to take careful and thoughtful responsibility for the effects of his behavior on his world.

A personal observation of a phenomenon Dr. Skinner does not quite touch upon: children taught from an early age by behavioral techniques tend to have an unusual, exuberant approach to the unknown. A new word, an unread book, an unsolved problem, a strange engine, mysterious chemical reaction, or untried song are occasions for intense excitement and delight. Around every corner something new and wonderful awaits them. For such children the world will always be "so full of a number of things" — and the knowledge they have learned so happily to pursue will give them, like kings, considerable mastery over their own fate. —Carol Van Strum

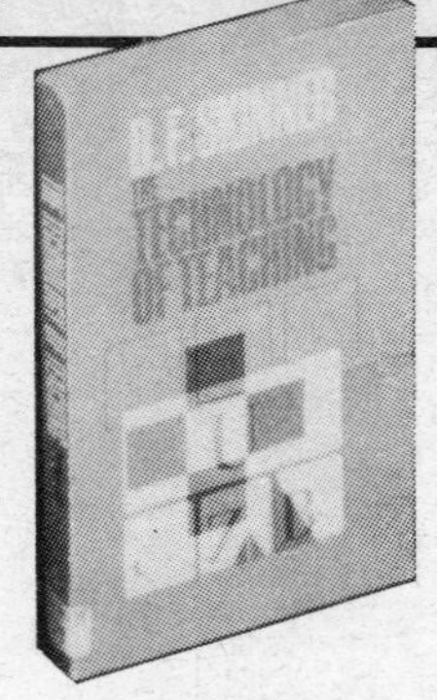

The Technology of Teaching
B.F. Skinner
1968; 271 pp.

$8.95 postpaid from:
Prentice-Hall
Box 500
Englewood Cliffs, NJ 07632

or Whole Earth Household Store

•

If you do not demand much change at each step, you will reinforce often, but your subject will progress slowly. If you demand too much, no response may satisfy, and the behavior generated up to that point will be extinguished. In deciding what behavior to reinforce at any given time, the basic rule is "Don't lose your pigeon!"

•

A dedicated person is one who remains active for long periods of time without reinforcement. He does so because, either in the hands of a skillful teacher or by accident, he has been exposed to a gradually lengthening variable-ratio schedule.

Increasing the enjoyment of other people is one of the most effective means of recreating socially constructive behavior in troubling youngsters.

How to Live With Your Special Child

No sweet romance here. Written mainly for teachers and mainly about children suffering from various forms of weirdness, it speaks to us all. Peculiar and powerful. Refreshingly skipping the theory in this book, von Hilsheimer tells you what to do to make kids act better. Simple. Good. Offensive! I'm not sure why, but I do think everyone should read it; in fact I downright ache for revolution in our schools, he makes it seem so possible, and because, as Richard Brautigan wrote in **Rommel Drives on Deep Into Egypt**:

I remember all those thousands of hours that I spent in grade school watching the clock, waiting for recess or lunch or to go home.

Waiting: for anything but school.

My teachers could eaily have ridden with Jesse James for all the time they stole from me. —*Diana Barich*

How to Live With Your Special Child
George von Hilsheimer
1970; 272 pp.

$7.50 postpaid from:
Acropolis Books
2400 17th Street N.W.
Washington, DC 20009

or Whole Earth Household Store

•

We believe that touching is so important that we actually run a "love-up" rota of staff in our elementary residential programs. Even the most wooden staff member is received with delight. Each child is tickled, rubbed, fondled, patted and kissed goodnight with special words of affection and joy. I am always impressed at the willingness of otherwise tough and aloof teenage criminals to accept this "baby" treatment. Our experience is sufficiently convincing that we persist in touching those teenagers who strongly reject touching. The weaker staff is not encouraged to take on these kids but strong staff members will tease and ridicule the aloofness and pursue and persist in touching.

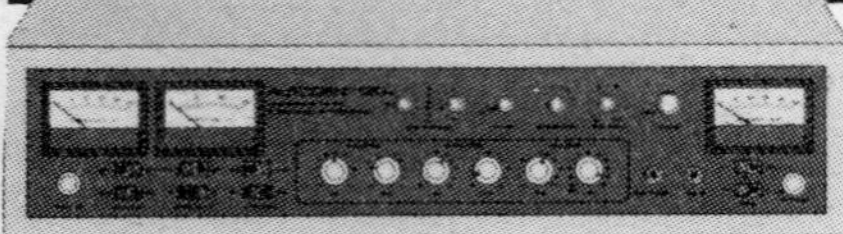

← Autogen 120 a $1700

Feedback, Bio and Otherwise

by George von Hilsheimer

In 1966 I read an article by Basmajian on letting kids hear amplified noise from the muscle activity over their larynxes as a way to suppress their subvocalizing whilst reading. We cobbled together a device to do the same thing, and Lo!, it did work. Almost as much fun as after reading Shagass (how could you forget that reference?) on conditioning brainwaves a decade earlier.

I thought I had a nice corner on this stuff when all of a sudden even humanistic psychologists were doing "biofeedback," and now a brainwave analyzer is almost a holy icon of something called "holistic medicine." It does puzzle me why biofeedback, a high technology method, is so popular among low technology addicts. Same thing with "right brainedness," which seems to be very popular among people who can't balance their checkbooks, but had to be figured out by people who passed their calculus. Oh well.

I do confess that I find the term "biofeedback" a clumsy neologism, and I always use the stuff whilst practicising Ericksonian hypnosis, old fashioned feedback with mirrors, mimicry, talk, and after painting the toes with Gentian Violet. I am not eclectic, merely thorough.

Well, back in 1970 in the **Last Whole Earth Catalog** I touted to you Autogenic Systems and their marvelous brain wave analyzer and feedback system. In 1980 the Winner and still Champion is Autogenic Systems.

First class operators will want to buy, for a mere $1700, the Autogenic 120A analyzer which reads the percentage of pulse rate activity in two bands (amplitude in one only), averages the pulse rate within two bands (amplitude in one), and sends you back a nice shushaby white noise or a mosquito-like tone. An alarm will screech at you if you go too slow, and silence greets going too fast. You can plug the signal into recorders if that is your desire, and the whole device fits nicely on a desk top. Mine has even survived a bounce to the floor when one agitated client tangoed too lustily.

I have had some bizarre experiences with a couple of devices from Autogenic Systems, but I figure the best test of a company is the way they respond to harsh words and trouble (shooting you or it). I have had a hilarious sequence of proofs of Murphy's laws, including at least 80 corollaries, in my transactions with Autogenic Systems and have unfailingly been met with cheerful and often useful responses. This is very rare in any business using computer technology, so Autogenic gets the palm.

Autogenic sells a number of devices. You can track your muscle tension, your skin conductance and your temperature at all sorts of interesting locations. The manuals are, God Bless Them, written in standard American English. My friends in possession of Autogenic equipment have all reacted with enthusiasm when queried regarding their beasties and I do use my 120A every day. Information is free from Autogenic Systems, 809 Allston Way, Berkeley, CA 94710.

Barbara B. Brown's **Stress and the Art of Biofeedback** (1977; $2.95 postpaid from Bantam Books, 414 East Golf Road, Des Plaines, IL 60016), is the middlebrow book everyone has read. It is a readable, creative, and useful introduction. Also see George D. Fuller, **Biofeedback: Methods and Procedures in Clinical Practice** (1980; $18 postpaid from Biofeedback Press, 3428 Sacramento Street, San Francisco, CA 94118). Readable. Useful. If you do not have the kind of gold the Autogenic Buicks cost (Grass makes the Cadillacs and Rolls Royces), then look on pages 68 - 71 of the Edmund Scientific catalog (our p. 562). Autogenic devices run from about $650 on up and are tools. Edmund's stuff runs from $40 for a kit to $200 and are toys. Edmund does sell some very nice tool quality devices for making very peaceful sound. ■

Super-Learning

A gee-whiz tour through some of the most innovative methods for accelerated learning becoming available, including suggestology. The data supports the author's contention that it is possible for normal people to learn mental and physical skills five to ten times faster, with better retention and with less effort using the techniques described.

Lots of exercises, lots of cheery confidence. Feels like one of the steps to overcoming our determination to maintain an educational system geared to work as slowly as possible. Read it and up-grade the schools in your town. —*Jim Fadiman*

•

As the class members shuffled through pages of material, the teacher started reading French phrases in different intonations. Then, stately classical music began in the background. The fifteen men and women leaned back, closed their eyes, and embarked on developing hypermnesia, more easily called supermemory. The teacher kept reciting. Sometimes her voice was businesslike as if ordering work to be done, sometimes it sounded soft, whispering, then unexpectedly hard and commanding.

Shadows began to darken in the room, it was sunset, yet the teacher kept on, repeating in a special rhythm French words, idioms, translations. Finally, she stopped. They weren't through yet; they still had to take a test. At least the class members weren't as keyed up. Somehow during the session their anxiety had been smoothed, the usual kinks relaxed. But they still didn't hold much hope for decent test scores.

Finally the teacher told them. "The class average is ninety-seven percent. You learned one thousand words in a day!"

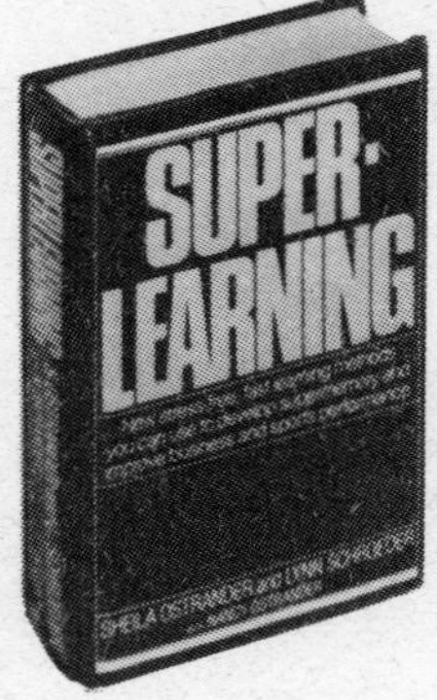

Super-Learning
(New Stress-free, Fast Learning Methods You Can Use to Develop Supermemory and Improve Business and Sports Performance)
Sheila Ostrander, Lynn Schroeder and Nancy Ostrander
1979; 342 pp.

$9.95 postpaid from:
Delacorte Press
1 Dag Hammarskjold Plaza
245 East 47th Street
New York, NY 10017

or Whole Earth Household Store

Suggestology and Outlines of Suggestopedy

The basic book by the originator of a different approach to education. Suggestology is the science of suggestion. The theory is presented in great detail, footnoted to death with both western and non-western sources. It is nothing short of an attempt to re-cognise the fundamental methods used in any teaching situation. Instead of manipulating, constraining, and conditioning the mind, Lozanov suggests that it is possible to teach more, hold the knowledge more usefully and flexibly as well as to transfer the knowledge to unfamiliar situations.

At the heart of the applications discussed here is the use of the human voice in teaching. We learn differently through our ears than through our eyes. We all know that learning with a teacher is different than working from a text (even the most stylish of behaviorist offerings) yet the rationale for this is not mentioned nor taught in western psychology.

After the theory, the book is filled with studies based on the theory, followed by sample materials that were really used. It all looks like straight scientific thinking, but it is far better and more valuable than that. The first uses in this country have been in the teaching of languages at 10 times the Berlitz speed and improving various subjects at the high school level. —*Jim Fadiman*

Suggestology and Outlines of Suggestopedy
Georgi Lozanov
1971, 1978; 377 pp.

$17.50 postpaid from:
Gordon and Breach Science Publishers
One Park Avenue
New York, NY 10016

Movements of the eyeballs of a subject at the hypnotically suggested age of two days.

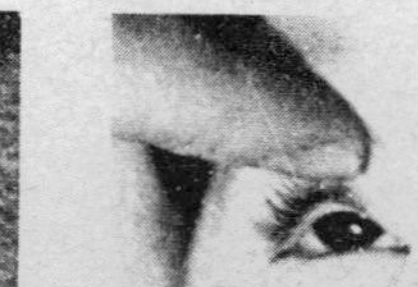

Movements of the eyeballs in a child during sleep.

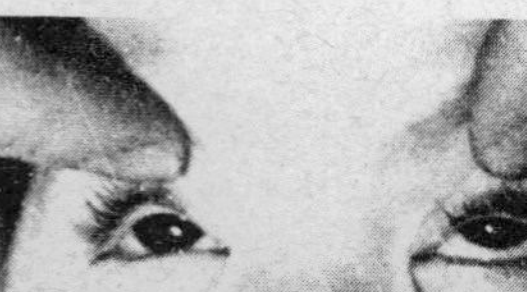

EDUCATION BY MAIL

by John Bear

John Bear, whose Ph.D. comes from Michigan State University, is President of Degree Consulting Services, which is probably the only inexpensive ($30) personal counseling service in the country for people seeking non-traditional degrees. They are located at Drawer HW, Littleriver, CA 95456. [Self-description]

The most important thing to say is, yes, it is honestly possible to earn a fully-accredited, unquestionably legal, universally-accepted degree, from major universities, without ever setting foot on a college campus. Even starting from scratch, right out of high school, a Bachelor's degree can easily be completed in less than two years, at a cost well under $1000. Master's degrees, doctorates, and even law degrees are also possible through non-resident study.

The way it works is this: First you are given academic credit for all learning experiences, whether or not they took place in a classroom. For instance, if you learned to speak a second language from your grandmother, you would be given the same number of units as if you had learned it in a college classroom. The same goes for flying an airplane, programming a computer, and hundreds of other learning experiences.

If you fall short of the units necessary for a degree, you can make up the deficit in three ways: taking equivalency examinations (given all over North America every month); taking correspondence courses (68 universities offer more than 2000 courses, both on paper and on videotape); or completing independent study projects. Master's and doctorates almost always require the writing of a thesis as well.

One major caution: while there are hundreds of excellent schools offering non-resident or short-residency degrees, there are also more degree mills than ever before, some really well disguised. Hardly a day passes in my degree consulting service that someone doesn't come to me, having already wasted $2000, $3000, even $5000 on a worthless degree. Some phonies use almost-real names (Cormell, Darthmouth); others are less coy and simply copy real school names. The basic rule is to check out any school you've never heard of. If it has a phone, use it to find out the credentials of the officers, and the names of a few graduates who live near you. No legitimate school will refuse these requests.

Here, then, are some outstanding sources in each of the above categories:

NON-RESIDENT BACHELOR'S DEGREES

University of the State of New York, Regents External Degree Program, Cultural Education Center, Albany, NY 11230. *The oldest chartered state university in America, dormant for nearly 200 years, was reactivated in the '70s, as a non-resident degree-granting school. They have no campus, no faculty, no library, no courses — but have awarded tens of thousands of fully-accredited B.A. and B.S. degrees. Outstanding catalog.*

Thomas A. Edison College, 101 W. State Street, Trenton, NJ 08608. *Virtually the same as the New York program. Counseling centers throughout New Jersey, but the degree may be earned while living anywhere in the world.*

Western Illinois University, Non-Traditional Programs, Macomb, IL 61455. *Unlike New York and Edison, Western Illinois requires students to complete fifteen units of their own courses — but these may be done entirely by correspondence. As with all the Bachelor's degree programs, the degree work can be in virtually any field of study.*

Columbia Union College, Flower Avenue, Takoma Park, MD 20012. *A traditional church-owned (Seventh Day Adventist) school, but one in which all the required courses can be done by correspondence.*

Connecticut Board for State Academic Awards, 340 Capitol Avenue, Hartford, CT 06115. *A program similar to that of New York and Edison, originally for Connecticut residents only, but now accepting students from anywhere.*

NON-RESIDENT OR VERY SHORT RESIDENCY MASTER'S DEGREES

California State University, External Degree Program, 1000 E. Victoria Street, Dominguez Hills, CA 90747. *The only totally non-resident Master's offered by any state university. The degree is in humanities, which can include philosophy, literature, music, art, history, etc. There is also a short-residency Master's in business administration.*

Syracuse University, 610 E. Fayette Street, Syracuse, NY 13202. *Short-residency Master's programs in business administration (24 days on campus), fine arts (four weeks on campus), and social science (24 days on campus). The residential periods normally take place during summer vacation, when dormitory space is available.*

University of Oklahoma, Norman, OK 73069. *The Master's program is in the general area of liberal arts, and was specifically designed for people with a highly specialized Bachelor's, who wish to become more generalized in their life and their credentials. Up to seven weeks on campus may be necessary.*

Beacon College, 2025 I Street N.W., Washington, DC 20006. *Totally non-resident degrees in virtually any field in which a monitor and a counselor are available. The catalog is excellent, and offers detailed examples of the kinds of learning contracts or agreements students prepare. Beacon is a candidate for accreditation.*

Goddard College, Plainfield, VT 05667. *Master of Arts degrees in education, humanities, the social sciences, creative writing, art therapy, social ecology, and learning disabilities. Students meet one or two weeks a year at seminars held in Vermont and sometimes in California, or other locations where clusters of ten students can assemble.*

NON-RESIDENT OR VERY SHORT RESIDENCY DOCTORATES

Nova University, College Avenue, Ft. Lauderdale, FL 33314. *The only fully-accredited short-residency doctorates available in the areas of education, public administration, and business administration. Students meet at various locations around the U.S., usually one day a month, and spend two weeks on the home campus.*

Union Graduate School, 2331 Victory Parkway, Cincinnati, OH 45206. *They are the Ph.D.-granting "arm" of the Union for Experimenting Colleges and Universities — a consortium including many major state universities. The work may be done in any field of study in which faculty advisors are available, or may be found. Roughly seven weeks of residency is required, at centers located in Cincinnati, Washington, DC, New Orleans, and San Francisco. Union is a candidate for accreditation.*

Walden University, 801 Anchor Rode Drive, Naples, FL 33940. *Most of Walden's students are professional educators, earning their Ph.D. or Doctor of Education degree, with four weeks of summer residency (Florida or California), and independent guided study at home. Walden is not accredited but is chartered in Florida and has an outstanding array of faculty and tutors.*

Columbia Pacific University, 150 Shoreline Highway, Mill Valley, CA 94941. *Founded by a medical doctor (who is also a psychiatrist and a homeopathic physician), Columbia Pacific offers totally non-resident doctorates in areas of holistic health, nutrition, and the health sciences, as well as many other fields (business, engineering, psychology, architecture, physical education administration, etc.). The students live in more than forty different countries, and most will never see the "home campus." The school is not accredited but is authorized by the state to grant degrees.*

Clayton University, P.O. Box 16150, St. Louis, MO 63105. *Non-resident doctoral programs in a wide variety of fields, including business, art, behavioral sciences (Carl Rogers is an advisor), nutrition (Linus Pauling is an advisor), chemistry, and music. Clayton is not accredited but has begun initial dialogue with its accrediting asssociation.*

LAW DEGREES BY CORRESPONDENCE

University of San Gabriel Valley, 222 East Glenarm, Pasadena, CA 91106.

Southland Law School, 69 North Catalina, Pasadena, CA 91106. *The two schools are almost identical in approach. Each offers the 3,456 hours of home study needed to take the California Bar and a much faster law degree for those who want basic legal knowledge without planning to practice.*

EQUIVALENCY EXAMINATIONS

College Level Examination Program, P.O. Box 1824, Princeton, NJ 08540.

Proficiency Examination Program, P.O. Box 168, Iowa City, IA 52240.

CORRESPONDENCE COURSES

University of Nebraska, Extension Division, Lincoln, NE 68508. *Nebraska also offers a high school diploma through correspondence study which is accepted nationwide. It is usually much less expensive than dealing with the schools found on matchbooks.*

University of Alaska, 101 Eielson, Fairbanks, AK 99701. *Because of the sparse and isolated population of the state, the University offers a huge array of courses (available to people in all states and nations), both academic and practical (from typing to radio repair to aviation ground school).*

University of California, University Extension, 2223 Fulton Street, Berkeley, CA 94720.

University of Tennessee, Center for Extended Learning, Knoxville, TN 37916. *California and Tennessee offer a huge menu of academic courses, covering many aspects of business, education, and the social sciences, among much else.*

Oklahoma State University, Independent and Correspondence Study, Stillwater, OK 74074. *O.S.U. offers a great deal in the hands-on practical studies in engineering, with courses in the mechanical, civil, electrical, industrial, and petroleum aspects of the field.*

TRADE SCHOOLS

There are literally thousands of non-degree-granting schools offering correspondence or residential instruction in non-academic subjects ranging from meat cutting to locksmithing to television repair to typewriting. Private, proprietary schools tend to be more expensive than universities per hour of study. Since many universities also offer home study in these "trade school" subjects, dealing with them can often be much more economical. A complete directory of which universities offer which courses is available from Peterson's Guides, Box 2123, Princeton, New Jersey 08540. It is called **Guide to Independent Study through Correspondence Instruction**, *and it sells for $4.50.*

Although most non-university-type trade schools give good value for money, there are some fly-by-night fast-buck operators as well. The two best ways to check out any school with which you are not familiar are: (1) Ask the National Home Study Council, 1601 18th St. N.W., Washington, DC 20009; and (2) Ask the school for the names of at least three graduates in your area, and talk to them. If three out of three are satisfied, you stand a good chance of being so yourself. ■

Bear's Guide to Non-traditional College Degrees

As sex and love are becoming separable subjects, so are accreditation and education. That may or may not be good, but it is so. This intelligent, practical book by the author of the survey above, responds accurately to the situation in American education today. For job opportunity, get some easy degrees. For an interesting life, get some hard education. I can see good argument for getting them separately — you don't cross your purposes or narrow your possibilities so much. —SB
[Suggested by J. Garwood]

Bear's Guide to Non-traditional College Degrees
John Bear
1980; 256 pp.
$20 postpaid from:
Dr. John Bear
P.O. Box 646
Mendocino, CA 95460
or Whole Earth Household Store

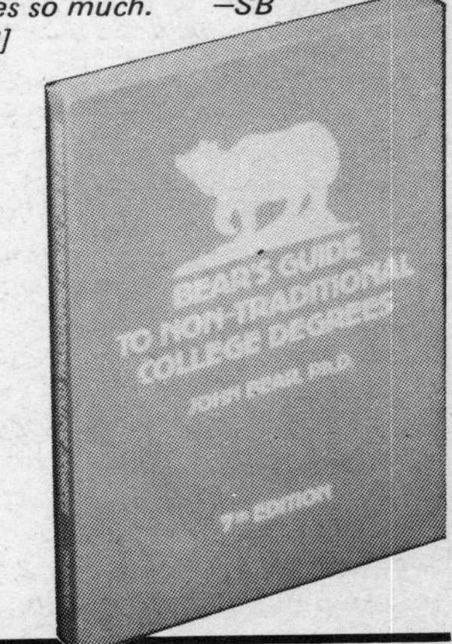

Private Independent Schools

I've been to a liberal grade school, an Archie and Veronica high school, a prestigious prep school (Exeter), a glossy college (Stanford), and the Army (Infantry). The most education happened at the prep school and the Army. This book describes private schools throughout the U.S., Canada, and overseas. If I had a kid and the money, I'd use it. If I were a kid with parents with the money, I'd use it. —SB

Private Independent Schools
Annual
$35 postpaid from:
Bunting and Lyon, Inc.
238 North Main Street
Wallingford, CT 06492

THE RISING SUN NEIGHBORHOOD NEWSLETTER

continued from last spread

Things about tidelands:

3. Creatures who live in tidal mud get to have two big changes a day — light and dark and air and water.

continued on next spread

> **P**ut yourself near the ragged edge, because that is where things are moving the fastest. If you're learning how to ski, the optimum learning rate is where you're not standing up all the way down the hill but neither are you wiping out every time — where you're right on the edge of being out of control.
> —Rusty Schweickart, Apollo 9 astronaut

Six Nonlectures

e.e. cummings distilling his own life into finest, headiest liquor. The man tells more news in less words, and more heart with less throb, than anyone else writing.

Life is a high calling, proves this book. —SB
[Suggested by Russell Troutman]

i: six nonlectures
e.e. cummings
1953, 1974; 114 pp.
$2.95 postpaid from:
Harvard University Press
79 Garden Street
Cambridge, MA 02138
or Whole Earth
Household Store

(Sensational listening — the original cummings nonlectures on Caedmon Records, 515 8th Avenue, New York, NY 10018.)

•

By way of describing my father, let me quote a letter . . .

I wot not how to answer your query about my father. He was a New Hampshire man, 6 foot 2, a crack shot & a famous fly-fisherman & a firstrate sailor (his sloop was named The Actress) & a woodsman who could find his way through forests primeval without a compass & a canoeist who'd stillpaddle you up to a deer without ruffling the surface of a pond & an ornithologist & taxidermist & (when he gave up hunting) an expert photographer (the best I've ever seen) & an actor who portrayed Julius Caesar in Sanders Theatre & a painter (both in oils & watercolours) & a better carpenter than any professional & an architect who designed his own houses before building them & (when he liked) a plumber who just for the fun of it installed all his own waterworks & (while at Harvard) a teacher with small use for professors — by whom (Royce, Lanman, Taussig, etc.) we were literally surrounded (but not defeated) — & later (at Doctor Hale's socalled South Congregational really Unitarian church) a preacher who announced, during the last war, that the Gott Mit Uns boys were in error since the only thing which mattered was for man to be on God's side (& one beautiful Sunday in Spring remarked from the pulpit that he couldn't understand why anyone had come to hear him on such a day) & horribly shocked his pewholders by crying "the Kingdom of Heaven is no spiritual roofgarden: it's inside you" & my father had the first telephone in Cambridge & (long before any Model T Ford) he piloted an Orient Buckboard with Friction Drive produced by the Waltham watch company & my father sent me to a certain public school because its principal was a gentle immense coal-black negress & when he became a diplomat (for World Peace) he gave me & my friends a tremendous party up in a tree at Sceaux Robinson & my father was a servant of the people who fought Boston's biggest & crookedest politician fiercely all day & a few evenings later sat down with him cheerfully at the Rotary Club & my father's voice was so magnificent that he was called on to impersonate God speaking from Beacon Hill (he was heard all over the common) & my father gave me Plato's metaphor of the cave with my mother's milk.

•

One ever memorable day, our ex-substantialist (deep in structural meditation) met head-on professor Royce; who was rolling peacefully home from a lecture. "Estlin" his courteous and gentle voice hazarded "I understand that you write poetry." I blushed. "Are you perhaps" he inquired, regarding a particular leaf of a particular tree "acquainted with the sonnets of Dante Gabriel Rossetti?" I blushed a different blush and shook an ignorant head. "Have you a moment?" he shyly suggested, less than half looking at me; and just perceptibly appended "I rather imagine you might enjoy them." Shortly thereafter, sage and ignoramus were sitting opposite each other in a diminutive study (marvellously smelling of tobacco and cluttered with student notebooks of a menacing bluish shade) — the ignoramus listening, enthralled; the sage intoning, lovingly and beautifully, his favorite poems. And very possibly (although I don't, as usual, know) that is the reason — or more likely the unreason — I've been writing sonnets ever since.

•

Back in the days of dog-eat-dog — my first anecdote begins — there lived a playboy; whose father could easily have owned the original superskyscraper-de-luxe: a self-styled Cathedral Of Commerce, endowed with every impetus to relaxation; not excluding ultraelevators which (on the laudable assumption that even machinery occasionally makes mistakes) were regularly tested. Testing an ultraelevator meant that its car was brought clean up, deprived of safety devices, and dropped. As the car hurtled downward, a column of air confined by the elevator shaft became more and more compressed; until (assuming that nothing untoward happened) it broke the car's fall completely — or so I was told by somebody who should know. At any rate, young Mr X was in the habit not only of attending these salubrious ceremonies, but of entering each about-to-be-dropped car, and of dropping with it as far and as long as the laws of a pre-Einsteinian universe permitted. Eventually, of course, somebody who shouldn't know telephoned a newspaper; which sent a reporter: who (after scarcely believing his senses) asked the transcender of Adam point-blank why he fell so often. Our playful protagonist shrugged his well-tailored shoulders — "for fun" he said simply; adding (in a strictly confidential undertone) "and it's wonderful for a hangover."

Here, I feel, we have the male American stance of my adolescence; or (if you prefer) the adolescent American male stance of what some wit once nicknamed a "lost generation": whereof — let me hastily append — the present speaker considers himself no worthy specimen. My point, however, isn't that many of us were even slightly heroic; and is that few of us declined a gamble. I don't think we enjoyed courting disaster. I do feel we liked being born.

I Never Promised You a Rose Garden

This must be one of the least reviewed and most persistent best sellers in history. It is the true account, lightly fictionalized, of a young girl's three years in an insane asylum, stone mad. I've read it twice. College students devour it. I don't know exactly why. It cuts through a world of bullshit. "Dr. Fried," the therapist in the story, was Frieda Fromm-Reichmann no less. Two heroines, these women. —SB

I Never Promised You a Rose Garden
Joanne Greenberg
(Hannah Green)
1964; 255 pp.
$1.95 postpaid from:
New American Library
P.O. Box 120
120 Woodbine
Bergenfield, NJ 07621
or Whole Earth
Household Store

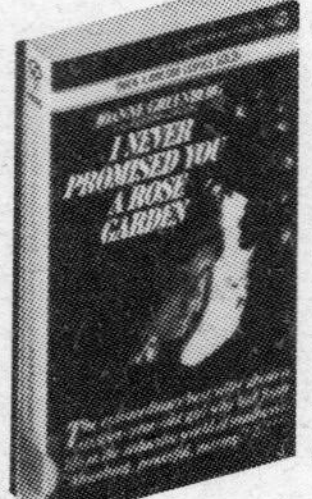

•

She began to thrash again, even though she was exhausted. "I'm all stopped and closed . . . like it was before I came here . . . only the volcano is burning hotter and hotter while the surface doesn't even know if it is alive or not!"

The doctor moved closer. "It is one of these times," she said quietly, "when what you say is most important."

Deborah pushed her head hard into the bed. "I can't even sort them out — the words."

"Well then, just let it come to us."

"Are you that strong?"

"We are both that strong."

Deborah took a breath. "I am poisonous and I hate it. I am going to be destroyed in shame and degradation and I hate it. I hate myself and the deceivers. I hate my life and my death. For my truth the world gives only lies; I tried with Royson time after time, but I saw that all he wanted was to be right. He might as well have said, 'Come to your senses and stop the silliness' — what they said for the years and years when I was disappointing them on the surface and lying to them with the inmost part of Yr and me and the enemy soldier. God curse me! God curse me!"

A soft scraping sound, a breathed rasp, came after, as she tried to cry, but the sound of it was so ridiculous and ugly that she soon stopped.

"Maybe when I leave," Furii said, "you can learn to cry. For now, let me say this: measure the hate you feel now, and the shame. That quantity is your capacity also to love and to feel joy and to have compassion. Also, I will see you tomorrow."

•

When her vision cleared, it was only enough to see and hear as if through a keyhole. She was aware that she was shouting and that attendants were in the room and that the walls of the room were covered with Yri words and sentences. Ranged around here were all the outpourings of hatred and anger and bitterness in a language whose metaphors used "broken" to mean "consenting" and "third rail" to mean "complying." All the words were extreme. *Uguru*, which was "dog-howling" and meant loneliness, was written in its superlative form in letters a foot high the length of one wall: U G U R U S U. The words were written in pencil and in blood, and in some places scratched with a broken button.

There was a look of horror and surprise even on the faces of a hardened D-ward staff, and it was that look which brought the full fire from her. The world's fear and hatred were like the sun, common and pervading, daily and accepted — a law of nature. Now its rays were focused in their look, waking fire. The words Deborah spoke were not loud, but they were full of hatred and they were Yri.

"Where is what you used to scratch this, Miss Blau?"

"Recreat," Deborah said. *"Recreat xangoarn, temr e xangoranan. Naza e fango xangoranan. Inai dum. Ageai dum."*

("Remember me. Remember me in anger, fear me in bitter anger. Heat-craze my teeth in bitterest anger. The signal glance drops. The Game" — Ageai meant the tearing of flesh with teeth as torture — "is over.")

The Lifetime Reading Plan

Will reading the best works of Plato, Marcus Aurelius, Chaucer, Shaw, Dickens, Voltaire, Thoreau, Freud, Nabokov, Borges, etc., make you a better person?

Yes.

Will this book, revised in 1978 for the first time since it appeared in 1960, help you DO IT? Also yes. The selection is fine, the 1-page introductions to each author by Fadiman are inviting, not daunting. —SB

The Lifetime Reading Plan
Clifton Fadiman
1960, 1978; 256 pp.
$10.95 postpaid from:
T.Y. Crowell and Co.
Harper and Row
Keystone Industrial Park
Scranton, PA 18512
or Whole Earth
Household Store

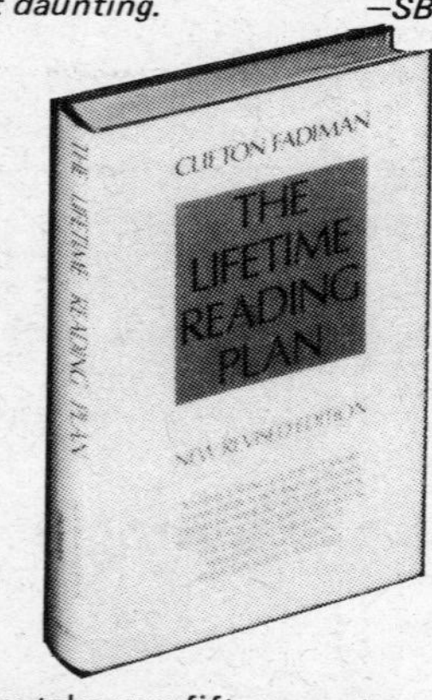

•

The books here discussed may take you fifty years to finish. They can of course be read in a much shorter time. The point is that they are intended to occupy an important part of a whole life, no matter what your present age may be. Many of them happen to be more entertaining than the latest best-seller. Still, it is not on the entertainment level that they are most profitably read. What they offer is of larger dimensions. It is rather like what is offered by loving and marrying, having and rearing children, carving out a career, creating a home. They can be a major experience, a source of continuous internal growth. Hence the word Lifetime. These authors are life companions. Once part of you, they work in and on and with you until you die. They should not be read in a hurry, any more than friends are made in a hurry.

•

William Blake (1757 - 1827) — Selected Works

Once, William Blake tells us, he walked to the end of the heath and touched the sky with his finger. At four he screamed upon perceiving God's head at the window. He saw angels in boughs and the prophet Ezekiel under a tree. His wife once remarked, quite placidly, "I have very little of Mr. Blake's company. He is always in Paradise." Perhaps an exaggeration, but there is no doubt that Blake felt himself on familiar terms with spirits. He is the supreme type, at least in modern times, of the visionary poet.

Toward this strange, baffling man of streaky genius one has a choice of attitudes. You may put him down as a faker, though the sweetness and honesty of his whole life belie it. Some of his contemporaries, quite celebrated then, quite forgotten now, called him a harmless lunatic. A psychologist will talk of Blake's "eidetic vision," which is simply a specialized ability to project into the external world images we usually hold in our minds. Many children have this power, Joan of Arc may have had it, and rationalists cite it when trying to explain the visions of saints and even Jesus. Finally you can ponder Blake's sly and, from the viewpoint of the professional artist and poet, quite practical advice to his friends: "Work up imagination to the state of vision."

It doesn't matter. By the pragmatic test (see William James, 80, and Dewey, 81) Blake is a success. His paintings, drawings, and engravings, though not of the highest order, are beautiful and moving. His finest verse, of which there is not a great deal, is original and unforgettable. His ideas, long mocked or neglected, appeal with increasing force to those who have lost faith in materialism's ability to bring happiness to the race.

Blake was that odd thing, a completely spontaneous human being. "A man without a mask," a friend called him. Living and dying in poverty, he was probably one of the most energetically joyful men of his time. He had some secret of ecstasy denied to most of us, and at times it stimulated odd behavior: he and his wife were once discovered in their little arbor, stark naked, reading **Paradise Lost** aloud.

In his rejection of most of the institutions of his time (as well as in his crankiness) he resembles other figures we have met, such as Thoreau, Nietzsche, and Lawrence. His romanticism is a far deeper thing than that of the Romantic poets who followed him — Wordsworth, Keats, Shelley. "Man is all imagination," he tells us. "God is man and exists in us and we in him." And again: "We are led to believe a lie when we see *with*, not *through*, the eye."

His scorn of what is called common sense led him to champion freedoms of all kinds, in the religious, political, and sexual spheres. Calmly, in a memorable sentence, he anticipates Freud: "Sooner murder an infant in its cradle than nurse unacted desires." For him "Exuberance is Beauty." Nonconformists of all stripes love to quote "Damn braces. Bless relaxes." He hated all those virtues arising out of measure and calculation: "The tigers of wrath are wiser than the horses of instruction."

Guide to Alternative Colleges and Universities

If you think you might be cut out for a life of taking the road less travelled by, these institutions can help, and this book will definitely help you decide. Of the 250 programs listed I'm familiar with a surprising number — UC Santa Cruz, College of the Atlantic, Deep Springs, Evergreen, Earlham, Goddard, San Francisco Art Institute — and I can vouch unreservedly for their excellence and difference. A common use of such places is to do two years at one and then two years elsewhere, usually a biggie like Harvard or UC Berkeley to get the advantages of both. Too long at any school is narrowing.

Another good idea is taking a year off between high school and college to travel, work, loaf, do military service, anything to get off the treadmill for a spell.

—SB

Guide to Alternative Colleges and Universities
(A Comprehensive Listing of Over 250 Innovative Programs)
Wayne Blaze, Bill Hertzberg, Roy Krantz and Al Lehrke
1974; 141 pp.

$4.25 postpaid from:
Beacon Press
Harper and Row
Keystone Industrial Park
Scranton, PA 18512

or Whole Earth Household Store

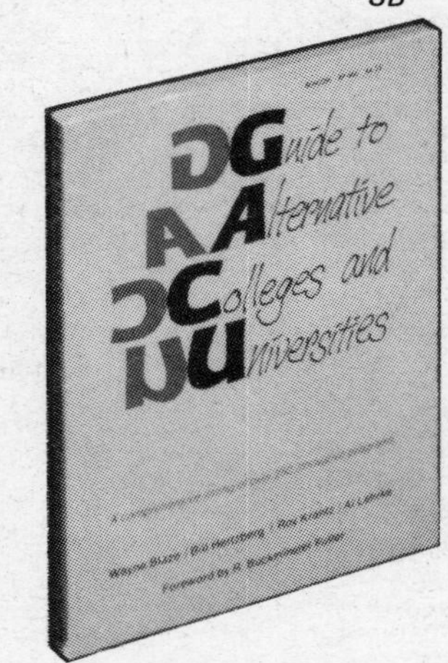

•

Deep Springs College, Deep Springs, California, Via: Dyer, Nevada 89010. Affiliation: Independent. Calendar: Semester. Yearly Fees: None. Enrollment: 22 men.

Deep Springs was founded in 1917 by Lucien L. Lunn, a successful lawyer and industrial entrepreneur who wanted to build a college modeled on his own philosophy. Mr. Lunn conceived, financed, and guided the College during its first years. Believing that the student should understand the value of manual work, and that the school must be free of the distraction of large communities, he purchased the Swinging T Ranch in isolated Deep Springs Valley, California. Here, in a dry 5,200-foot desert environment, 28 miles from Big Pine and 43 miles from Bishop (the nearest towns), students study, work the ranch, and involve themselves in the College's community affairs.

The academic program at Deep Springs has no majors. It is the school's belief that because this is the beginning of a young man's college career, a broad liberal arts education is most beneficial to him. On the other hand, because Deep Springs is composed of only 20 or so male students, and the largest class is 12 (with many being just two — a student and his instructor), the students can learn as fast as they wish. The only required courses are English Composition and Public Speaking. Grading is on the regular A,B,C,D,F scale. Independent work is plentiful, and students are expected to read beyond their courses. During his stay at Deep Springs a student earns the 60 credits necessary for transfer into another college or university at the junior level. Deep Springs students can usually get into any college they choose.

The school accepts only those high school juniors and seniors who show promise of making the fullest use of their two or more years here. It seeks those who display high academic achievement, creativity, and superior college board scores.

After classes in the morning, students tackle their daily ranch chores. About four hours of work is required of each student daily. The school believes there is educational value in blending practical work with academic pursuits. Mr. Lunn intended the work program to be a means of developing self-discipline and self-reliance. Each student takes individual responsibility for his job — a job on which every member of the community depends. The students milk the cows; make the butter; cut and bale the hay; feed the horses, pigs, and chickens; collect the eggs; slaughter and dress the beef and pork for ranch consumption; operate the bookstore; run the irrigation system; grow food; shovel snow; and so on.

The entire Deep Springs community numbers approximately 40. Everyone is on a first-name basis. The only women on the ranch are the faculty wives and a few of the staff. All the community live together and eat together. Except for vacations, special leaves, and official College business, students are restricted to the Deep Springs Valley — 12 miles long and 4 miles wide. Though one might think this isolated life would be boring, accord- to those at the College it isn't.

Studying and working the ranch occupy most of a student's time. Organized hiking trips, horseback riding, roundups, guest lecturers, debates, plays, movies, sports, public speaking, and community meetings account for all the rest.

Students not only work the ranch but have a great say in the workings of the College. Through the "Deed of the Trust," Lucien Lunn, when he founded the school, arranged that students in attendance at Deep Springs are to be the sole beneficiaries of the Trust, and the true owners of the College. They have authority to manage whatever they prove they can manage well.

All those accepted to Deep Springs receive a full room/board/tuition scholarship. It costs the students nothing. All applicants must be interviewed. One enters in the summer term, attends the fall and spring semester, takes a summer off, and, subject to reinvitation, returns for three more semesters. There is a four-week vacation each Christmas and from one to two weeks off between terms.

Homesteading learning centers and apprenticeships

Many of us dream of returning to the land; few of us know how to get started without taking unreasonable risks. Luckily there are several learning centers across the country and abroad that let you test your commitment and learn basic homesteading skills before you jump in over your head. Mary Jurinko at **Organic Gardening** *magazine keeps an updated list of these schools and will send it to you if you provide a self-addressed, stamped ($.15) envelope (SASE). The list includes organic gardening demonstration communities, owner-built housing learning centers, and other appropriate technology/self-sufficiency courses and workshops. Some are relatively new and others have been around for a surprisingly long time.*

—Mimi Abrams

Homesteading Learning Centers and Apprenticeships List

free (with business-size SASE) from:
Organic Gardening
Rodale Press
33 East Minor Street
Emmaus, PA 18049
Attn: Homesteader's List

•

Deep Run School of Homesteading (a School of Living Center), RD No. 7, Box 388A, York, PA 17402. (717) 757-4174. *A one-year program open to people of all ages interested in learning the skills of self-sufficiency and cooperative living. They also accept people at any time of the year for shorter periods from a week to several months.*

•

Working Weekends on Organic Farms (WWOOF), c/o Don Pynches, 19. Bradford Road, Lewes, Sussex, England BN7 1RB. *Puts town dwellers wishing to work on organic farms in touch with farmers needing help. Enclose SASE.*

•

Nature et Progres, Chateau de Chamarande, 91730 Chamarande, France. *Offers a list of farmers, horticulturalists, and country craftsmen willing to take young people for training in organic methods. To help cover costs, those writing from abroad should send 4 international reply coupons, or from France 8 F.*

Tutorial Study Program

So sensible you wonder what's taken it so long to reappear. A system of apprenticeship, internship, to an international guild of tutors. For a period of time like eight months you live near and work with a master the likes of Buckminster Fuller, Anna Halprin, Elisabeth Mann Borghese, George Leonard, Gary Snyder, Marshall McLuhan, Kenneth Rexroth, Yehudi Menuhin, Vine Deloria. Eight months tuition is $3600.

—SB

[Suggested by Gregory Bateson]

Marshall McLuhan

Tutorial Study Program
Catalog
$1

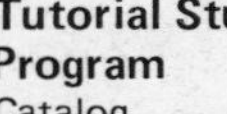

Information
free

Information on Guild of Tutors
free

all from:
International College
1019 Gayley Avenue
Suite 105
Los Angeles, CA 90024

Ravi Shankar

Paolo Soleri

Getting Skilled
Handbook of Trade and Technical Careers

One of the encouraging signs I see in our society these days is that there are many young people NOT going to college, nor planning to. Having made that decision, many just diddle around waiting for something to happen, which it often doesn't. There is a hunger to be good at something. A so-called "trade school" can be a good answer, and it fortunately is an answer that is rapidly losing a second-best reputation. OK. How do you find out about trade schools? This book is the best I've seen on the subject by far. My only reservation is that some of the people who need it most will not read it because their public "education" didn't prepare them to read. If you counsel students, this book will help you a lot. It also lists many schools in a huge appendix. The authors are well in tune with coming trends too; this isn't a rehashed 1938 text.

—J. Baldwin

For reasons obscure to us this book is no longer on the market, but in paperback form it is being furnished to libraries and high school counselors, where you may find it.

A very useful **Handbook of Trade and Technical Careers and Training** *indicates the range of skills that trade schools teach, which schools, and how to reach them. The price is right: free.*

—SB

•

Skilled people are in demand. Look in tonight's paper. There will be columns and columns of help wanted ads for skilled people — not college people, *skilled* people.

•

Because most private schools are small, with a low student-teacher ratio, students can expect to be close to their instructors. Teachers often give "extra-instructional assistance," that is, counseling and/or tutoring. Mr. Hilbig, a truck driving student at Ryder, told us: "We got some real fine instructors. I had some trouble down-shifting. They took me aside and gave me some special time." A classmate of his, Jim Tinch, agreed: "If you're having trouble, they just tell you to get down from the rig and cool off. They really want you to learn."

—Getting Skilled

Getting Skilled
(A Guide to Private Trade and Technical Schools)
Tom Hebert and John Coyne
1976, 1980; 262 pp.

Published by National Association of Trade and Technical Schools

Not available for sale; check your library or high school guidance office.

Handbook of Trade and Technical Careers and Training
National Association of Trade and Technical Schools
1980; 48 pp.

free from:
NATTS
Publication Department
2021 K Street NW
Suite 315
Washington, DC 20006

SKILL

Acting
Air Conditioning
Art, Commercial
Art, Fine
Appliance Repair
Architectural Engineering Technology
Automotive Mechanics
Aviation Mechanics
Baker
Barber/Hairstylist
Blueprint Reading
Brickmasonry
Broadcaster
Broadcasting Technician
Building Maintenance
Camera Service and Repair
Carpentry
Civil Engineering Technology
Coin Operated Machine Repair
Computer Service Technician
Construction Technology
Dance Instructor
Data Processing
Dental Assisting
Dental Laboratory Technician
Diamond Cutting and Grading
Diesel Mechanics
Dietetics
Diving
Drafting
Dress Making & Design
Electricity
Electrology
Electronics
Emergency Medical Technician
Engraving
Fashion Design
Fashion Illustration
Fashion Merchandising
Floral Design
Food Service
Gemologist
Gunsmithing
Heating
Heavy Equipment Operator
Horsemanship
Horticulture
Hotel-Motel Training
Illustration
Industrial Management
Inhalation Therapy Technician
Instrument Maker/Repairer
Instrumentation
Interior Design
Jewelry Design
Legal Secretarial/Asst.
Locksmith
Loss Prevention/Security
Machine Shop
Makeup Artist
Mechanical Engineering Technology
Medical Assistant
Medical/Dental Receptionist
Medical Lab Technician
Medical Office Manager
Medical Secretary
Motion Pictures
Motorcycle Mechanics
Musician
Nurse's Aide
Office Machine Repair
Operating Room Technician
Optometric Assisting
Painting
Paperhanger
PBX Switchboard
Pet Grooming
Photography
Pilot, Commercial
Plumbing
Printing
Real Estate Brokerage
Recording
Skin Care
Surveying
Tailor
Tool & Die
Travel Personnel
Truck Driving
Veterinarian Assisting
Vocational Nursing
Watchmaking & Repairing
Water & Wastewater Technology
Welding
X-Ray

—Handbook of Trade and Technical Careers and Training

THE RISING SUN
NEIGHBORHOOD NEWSLETTER

continued from last spread

Things about tidelands:

4. The mud left at low tide that was covered with ocean at high tide smells bad to highly evolved land noses.

continued on next spread

O.R.E.S. barquentine Regina Maris off New Zealand

Sail-Training Programs and Schoolships Throughout the World

by Mary T. Crowley, Ocean Voyages Institute

EXPLORING THE OCEAN world provides a superb opportunity for learning and adventure. Growing numbers of people wish to learn about sailing and the seas, and there is an ever-increasing need for an expanded range of seafaring programs. Schoolship and sail-training opportunities go beyond the limits of the traditional classroom and allow first-hand experience with the dynamic real world of the sea.

Sailing on the ocean brings one into immediate contact with the elements: powerful winds, dramatic sunrises and sunsets, torrential rains, star-filled skies, and sun-swept horizons. Ocean sailing introduces a broad spectrum of personal learning experiences as well.

At sea, a natural order is born of work responsibility; the captain's word is law. However, there is a definite discipline structure fostered by the necessity for order and safety in seafaring, rather than by the imposition of one individual's authority over another. This discipline is based on respect for knowledge and skill, and it generates a mutual appreciation of each person's individuality, gusto, humor, and spirit. Simultaneously, a strong sense of community develops on board. The realities of working together within a small group require that one learns to communicate and get along with others. The ship is a small island, a mini-community, which nourishes diversity and uniqueness within its borders. The vital and immediate world of the ocean enhances both our humanity and our appreciation of nature.

The experience of sailing has a substantial character-building effect. Young people today grow up quickly; by age 15 many are in fact quite adult and certainly ready for responsibility. But our society does not give them many chances to really assume responsibility, and this can cause a variety of problems. Seafaring requires responsibility. The real work of standing watches and being responsible for the ship can allow important growth experiences.

It is difficult to express the magnitude of what sailing and the ocean world have meant to me. I can only say that I feel that I am a better person for the time I have spent at sea, and I would love to see everyone who wishes to explore this world have an opportunity to do so.

Below is a list of organizations reflecting a wide range of educational and seafaring philosophies. The list is divided into categories both by subject matter (such as sail training, oceanography, academic school programs, etc.) and by geographic locations. The various programs do not necessarily share my personal sentiments about sailing; this is a reference of various vessels currently in operation.

I am interested in receiving comments on the programs from former participants and teachers. I also welcome additions to this list to keep my information current. My interest is in developing a wider range of schoolship opportunities, so I place great value on feedback from those with personal background in this area. Also, I'd enjoy hearing from anyone who has schoolship and/or sail-training programs in planning phases, or who would like to be involved in the variety of projects in planning by Ocean Voyages Institute, including a San Francisco Bay schoolship.

Refer any correspondence to Mary T. Crowley, Ocean Voyages Institute (address below).

(See seagoing section, pp. 437 - 439.)

UNITED STATES ORGANIZATIONS

***Ocean Voyages Institute,** 1709 Bridgeway, Sausalito, CA 94965.

O.V.I. is currently involved in operating a variety of sail-training and educational programs for both adults and young people on such vessels as the 94' brigantine Taiyo, the 65' schooner Sir Cloudesley Shovell, and many others, totaling a network of 40 worldwide sailing vessels. In planning for 1981 is an extensive sail-training program in the San Francisco Bay area, and in 1982 a high school program sailing throughout the Pacific basin. O.V.I. also operates a clearinghouse for information on worldwide sailing opportunities. O.V.I. coordinates vessels for ocean research, film, and special interest projects.

***Sea Education Association, Inc.,** P.O. Box 6, Church Street, Woods Hole, MA 02543.

The Sea Education Association offers a semester length program structured to provide college undergraduates with a thorough theoretical and practical introduction to the sea. Sea Semester is designed to form a regular part of college undergraduate education. Sea Semester is a year-round, 12-week program for liberal arts students involving six weeks academic training ashore in oceanography, seamanship, and marine policy, and six weeks at sea as a student on the 100' staysail schooner r/v Westward, engaged in oceanographic research. 16 credits.

***Ocean Research and Education Society,** 51 Commercial Wharf No. 6, Boston, MA 02110.

O.R.E.S. combines important cetacean research with college credit in marine biology on a series of 5- to 7-week expeditions on board r/v Regina Maris, a 144' barquentine. The scientific staff conducts courses in marine mammology and equips participants with skills basic to ocean research. Sail training and the operation of a "tall ship" are included in the program.

The Oceanics School of New York, 145 E. 74th Street, New York, NY 10021.

The Oceanics operates two 5-month semester sessions both on vessels and in land-based programs.

The Schooner Project, Schooner, Inc., 60 South Water Street, New Haven, CT 06519

Field trips, research and workshops in marine biology, island biogeography, bird ethology, salt marsh ecology, navigation and seamanship. 57' schooner Trade Wind.

Tabor Academy, Marion, MA 02738.

Summer: 7-week "Sea Ranger" program in oceanography and seamanship employing the 95' topsail schooner Tabor Boy, 50' ketch Diogenes, and 36' sloop Theme. Winter: 4-year regular boy's boarding school with sailing/oceanography optional program.

Tradition in Sail, P.O. Box 6098, San Diego, CA 92106; or P.O. Box 8314, Fort Lauderdale, FL 33310

Coeducational camp for youth 13 - 18, based on Big French Cay, Roatan, Bay Islands, Honduras, Central America, sailing aboard 112' ketch Heddy.

Unicorn Maritime Institute, 3105 W. Waters Avenue, Tampa, FL 33614

Conducts two-week sail-training programs on 125' brig Unicorn.

S.E.A. schooner Westward

The Flint School, P.O. Box 5809, Sarasota, FL 33579

The Flint School travels to foreign ports in Europe and the Mediterranean aboard 156' Te Vega and 176' Te Quest. The program is an intense academic experience with students attending classes eight hours a day. Students are also the crew of the ship and maintain specific work responsibilities as well. Students are on board the ships from September through May. Flint School accepts boys and girls with positive attitudes, ages 11 to 18.

St. George's School, Newport, RI 02840.

Regular four-year boy's boarding school with special winter semester aboard 54' cutter r/v Geronimo; summer program open to outside students.

Hurricane Island Outward Bound School, P.O. Box 492, Rockland, ME 04841.

28-day program involving survival training and coastwise sailing in open whale boats.

Landmark School, Headmaster, Landmark Summer School Programs, Pride's Crossing, MA 01965

Six-week courses in seamanship: three weeks ashore, and three weeks at sea aboard When and If, 60' schooner.

Mystic Seaport, Mariner Program, Mystic, CT, 06355

One-week training session on the stationary 120' full-rigged ship Joseph Conrad, or on 65' schooner Brilliant, cruising on Long Island Sound.

***Sloop Clearwater,** Hudson River Sloop Restoration, Inc., 88 Market Street, Poughkeepsie, NY 12601

Youth Adventure, Inc., 5005 91st Avenue SE, Mercer Island, WA 98040

CANADA

Toronto Brigantine, Director, Toronto Brigantine, One Young Street, Suite 2106, Toronto, Ontario, Canada M5E 1E5

Two-week summer programs involving one week of training ashore and one week aboard 60' brigantines Playfair or Pathfinder on Lake Ontario, Canada. For boys and girls aged 14 - 18.

Toronto Brigantine Incorporated, 245 Queen's Quay West, Toronto, Ontario, Canada M5J 1A7

Two 60' brigantines, Pathfinder and Playfair.

Kingston Brigantine Incorporated, c/o Mr. Tony Case, 599 Victoria Street, Apt. 7, Kingston, Ontario, Canada K2K 4S4

O.R.E.S. barquentine Regina Maris, used to study ocean mammals

UNITED KINGDOM

***Ocean Youth Club,** 2 Stoke Gardens, Gosport, Hants P012 1PD, England

Anyone over 15 and under 21 who is reasonably fit can join a crew for a week or a fortnight of sea cruising on one of OYC's seven 71' ketches operating around the coast of the British Isles. Sail training and navigation instruction. Sailing season is mid-March to the end of October.

***Mariners International,** 58 Woodville Road, New Barnet, Herts, EN 5 5EG, London, England

MI is a volunteer and enthusiastic international organization of people who deeply believe in sail training and square riggers, and whose aim is to provide both youth and adults with the opportunity to participate in the running of the world's great square rigged ships.

Christian Sailing Centre, Dodner Creek, Newport, Isle of Wight, England

Has a plastic-rigger called Carillon of Wight. Young men and women.

Sea Schools of the Outward Bound Trust, 34 Broadway, London SW1, Egaland

Several small yachts and boats.

Offshore Command, Sea Cadet Corps, HMS Dolphin, Gosport, Hants, England

They operate the brig Royalist but only take Sea Cadets (ages 15 - 18) plus the occasional Sea Scouts, Girls' Nautical Training Corps, etc. The Royalist is, however, available on charter for a couple of short cruises each year, to members of the supporting club, the Square Rigger Club: SRC, c/o Lt. Cdr. Morin Scott, 3 Sudley Lodge, Bognor Regis, Sussex, England.

**These are programs I am personally familiar with and can recommend.*

EUROPE

Clipper-Deutsches Jugendwerk Zur See E.V., Bruchstrasse 28, 2807 Achim, West Germany

The German STA, operating mixed cruises on the Baltic ketch Seute Deern II, the three-masted schooner, Amphitrite and the three-masted topsail schooner Albatros.

Mariners-France, Guilde Europeenne du Raid, 11 Rue de Vaugirard, 75006 Paris, France

Either a large brigantine or a three-masted topsail schooner (to be eventually rerigged as a barquentine). Both sexes, all ages.

Polish STA, c/o Chris Baranowski, Swierczewskiego 113, 05-440 Wesota, Poland

Barquentine Pogoria (to be commissioned this spring). MI-style.

Sorlandet, P.O. Box 427, 4601 Kristiansand, Norway

Full-rigger. Both sexes, age 16+, "civilians."

Svanen, Norsk Sjøfartsmuseum, Bygdøy, Oslo, Norway

Three-masted topsail schooner. Does short training cruises; based at the maritime museum.

VIRGIN ISLANDS

Captain Horatio Sinbad, Brigantine, Meka II, Pirate School, P.O. Box 9997, St. Thomas, V.I. 00801

Summer and winter cruises. For boys from 13 - 19 years old. Summer cruises out of North Carolina. Winter cruises out of Port Royal, Roatan, Honduras. Meka II, 54' brigantine.

NEW ZEALAND

***Spirit of Adventure**, P.O. Box 2276, Marsden Wharf, Quay Street, Auckland 1, New Zealand

Spirit of Adventure is a 90' auxiliary ketch that accommodates 30 students on 12-day adventure and study cruises. Program includes instruction in seamanship, navigation, engineering, marine biology, and allied subjects. Program open primarily to secondary school students, but activities may be planned for other age groups.

AUSTRALIA

The Alma Doepel, 142 Old Eltham Road, Lower Plenty, Victoria 3093, Australia

Crew on rigging of Regina Maris

Humpback whale near O.R.E.S. barquentine Regina Maris

MARITIME MUSEUMS

Many maritime museums conduct periodic programs aboard stationary or operational school vessels. Some of these are restricted to special groups because of funding. Two maritime museums with working vessels are:

Philadelphia Maritime Museum, 427 Chestnut Street, Philadelphia, PA 19106.

135' barkentine Gazela Primeiro.

South Street Seaport, 16 Fulton Street, New York, NY 10038

60' schooner Pioneer. ■

ASSOCIATIONS OF VESSELS INVOLVED IN SAIL TRAINING AND OCEAN RESEARCH

American Sail Training Association (ASTA), Eisenhower House, Fort Adams State Park, Newport, RI 02840

ASTA is formally affiliated with the Sail Training Association (Great Britain). For a deep-water sail training experience, ASTA helps to place young people aboard sail training vessels and ocean research ships. They also organize and run, along with STA, the Biennial "Tall Ships" Races, and the Annual East Coast Sail Training Races.

The Sail Training Association, The Schooner Director, Bosham, Chichester, Sussex, England

The STA operates the schooners Sir Winston Churchill and Malcolm Miller on 1-, 2-, and 3-week sail training courses for young people. Trainees must be at least 16 and under 25. There are also a few adult courses available. These trips operate year round.

S.E.A. schooner Westward

Outward Bound

There's been so much wrongheaded press coverage of Outward Bound programs that it comes as a true pleasure to see this friendly account written by a man who attended all seven Outward Bound schools in the U.S. The story is told by the people involved, the author participating rather than merely observing. Readers not in need of the experience offered by Outward Bound will probably be bored by things they already know and cannot remember not always knowing. But readers whose lives may be enhanced by an unfamiliar and challenging outdoor adventure guided by a sympathetic instructor and supported by others like themselves will find the book inciting, informative and close to how it will be. Those who have been to one of the schools will likely get a kick out of reading about other graduates, now about 70,000. I personally know many who have received good things from Outward Bound, and can recommend this book as a worthy introduction to their program.

—J. Baldwin

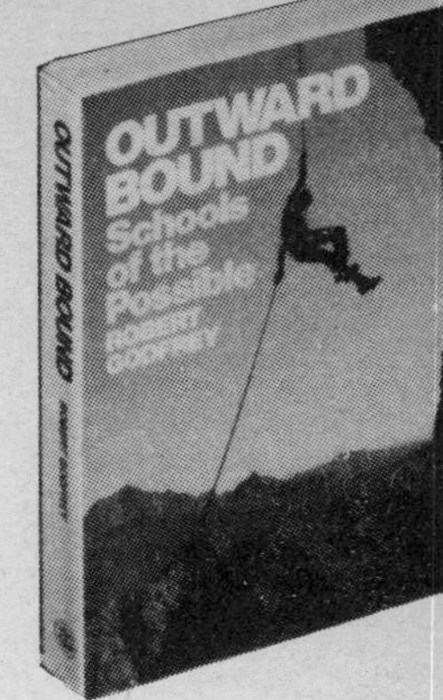

Outward Bound
(Schools of the Possible)
Robert Godfrey
1980; 273 pp.

$8.95 postpaid from:
Doubleday and Company
501 Franklin Avenue
Garden City, NY 11530
or Whole Earth Household Store

•

In her letter Suejee continues, "The washing and rebuilding of my self-image through this Outward Bound experience was just what I had needed. . . . The me that looked out at the world was friendlier, more relaxed, and also braver and less paranoid of life. I decided that bravery was not just a word we used to describe other people, the ones in the movies. Even *I* can do things that can be considered brave."

Solo: an island to yourself.

The lower slopes of Glacier Peak

The Wall, a traditional Outward Bound problem-solving exercise. The objective is to get the entire group over as quickly as possible; the dilemma is how to retrieve the last person. →

Clown College

Run away and join the circus. No kidding. Free tuition; you pay for room, board, and makeup. Eight week course begins every September.

—SB

Clown College
Information

free from:
Clown College
P.O. Box 1528
Venice, FL 33595

•

Q. What subjects are taught at clown college?

A. Clowning, Clown Makeup, Comedy Acrobatics, Fundamental Gymnastics, Acrobatableaux, Juggling, Equilibrium (unicycle riding, rolling cylinder, stilt walking), Mime, Comedic Movement, Pantomime, Arenaction, Yoga, Elephant Riding, Web-sitting, Clown Props Building, Clown Costuming (Design, Cutting and Draping). Lectures on: Trouper Nutrition; Famous Clowns of the Past; Origins of Clowning; The Mechanics of Visual Comedy; History of the Big Tops; Arena Circuses; Circus Jargon; Transportation and Logistics; Production Clowning; Engagement and Performance Direction; Circus Promotion, Publicity and Public Relations; Animal Training & Care; Circus Bands and Music; Thrill Acts; The Circus in Art and Literature.

THE RISING SUN
NEIGHBORHOOD NEWSLETTER

continued from last spread

Things about tidelands:

5. The mud flats at Emeryville on Highway 17 by the San Francisco Bay were going to be filled in and developed and then the Bay Conservation Development Committee stopped the development as part of its general effort to keep the Bay from being entirely filled in. The mud flats at Emeryville were used by duck hunters until duck hunting was outlawed in Emeryville. Now the mud flats at Emeryville are covered with surrealistic sculptures made out of driftwood (drift lumber usually) by kids and teenagers and grownup artists and who knows who all. The tide washes some away but new ones are always being built.

continued on next spread

Seasonal Jobs on Land and Sea

If you are young, restless, hungry, and not averse to hard work, this book is worth a look. The jobs here won't make you rich, but most will get you outside and away from home. Subjects covered include harvests of all kinds, fishing, logging, and teaching skiing and tennis. There is also information on working on an Israeli kibbutz and harvesting wine grapes in Germany and France.

Addresses of people with jobs or organizations that know about them are provided for each occupation. The author has little to say about pesticide exposure from working in orchards and vineyards, but he is honest about other negative aspects of hard or dangerous work.
—Richard Nilsen

Seasonal Jobs on Land and Sea
Max Steele
1979; 147 pp.
$4.50 postpaid from:
Harper and Row
Keystone Industrial Park
Scranton, PA 18512
or Whole Earth Household Store

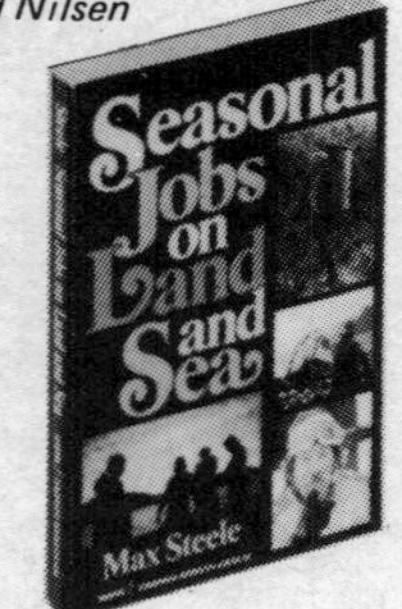

•

Try to make the rounds of all the boats two or even three times a day. Once in the early morning is a good practice, since it shows how sincere you are. As a rule, the professionals are suspicious of outsiders, and the more you show your face around the harbor the more willing they will be to help you. In a smaller town especially, let as many people as possible know you are looking for work on a fishing boat. A hotel clerk, a waitress, a supermarket cashier — any of these may prove valuable contacts. Ask them each time if they have heard of any shorthanded boats. In the evening go to local bars patronized by fishermen and strike up conversations with those around you. Keep your ears perked. Most fishing ports have a harbormaster who maintains the docks and keeps track of the comings and goings of boats. Get acquainted. Let him know why you're nosing around the harbor all the time. Check with him often; he probably knows more about the boats and fishermen than anyone else in town (it's his job). Some harbormaster offices have bulletin boards where you can put up a placard offering your services. A desperate skipper with a crew member too drunk to head out fishing may get in touch with you at the last moment. Have your most important belongings in a semipacked state so that you will be ready to leave at almost any time.

•

When Stephen worked for two months in 1977 on an above-average boat in southeastern Alaska, his gross earnings were about $4,100, after taxes. Food and fuel costs were deducted, and the "greenhorn" still ended up with $2,500 for two months' work.

How To Become A Seasonal Firefighter

by Randy Black

Select the region you want to work in and apply early! Federal, state, and other agencies have a surplus of applicants and they often make geographical limitations (i.e., the Forest Service allows you to choose just two forests). Your best bet is to consider, in December, a large, high fire risk area — one that will require many firefighters when summer comes.

The following agencies hire seasonal firefighters. However, your best chances are with the U.S. Forest Service, the Bureau of Land Management, the California Department of Forestry, and the departments of forestry for other states.

California Department of Forestry: *Open applications can be filed at any time for any season. You apply to the Ranger Unit near the area where you want to work. Write for the free Seasonal Firefighter Information Package from Department of Forestry Personnel Office, 1416 N Street, Sacramento, CA 95814.*

STEWART BRAND

←
Gradually women are infiltrating the fire crews. This is Stephanie Black at the California Division of Forestry Fire Academy's six-week engineer course. As engineer she will drive a truck and boss a crew.

United States Forest Service: *Information and addresses can be found in the "Federal Government Summer Job Announcement" (No. 414), which is available in early December at all U.S. Civil Service Commission Federal Job Information Centers. Application deadline — Feb. 15.*

There is also a requisition program (SSEP) that recruits students in forestry and related fields. Check college placement centers.

Bureau of Land Management: *As with the USFS, consult announcement No. 414. The BLM hires many firefighters to protect federal lands. Application deadline Feb. 1.*

State Departments of Forestry: *Write to capital cities, starting in December. Oregon and Washington in particular use a lot of seasonal crews.*

State Department of Parks and Recreation (California): *Send for information on "seasonal park aides" (not firefighters) to P.O. Box 2390, Sacramento, CA 95811.*

California Conservation Corps: *Now requires a one year commitment. Recruits mainly through high schools and employment offices. Write for free information to: CCC Recruitment Office, 1530 Capitol Avenue, Sacramento, CA 95814.*

Regional Park Districts: *Seasonal employment varies with the locality, but all expect early applications.*

Military facilities in rural areas: *A long shot, but they occasionally hire civilian firefighters. Contact individual bases.* ■

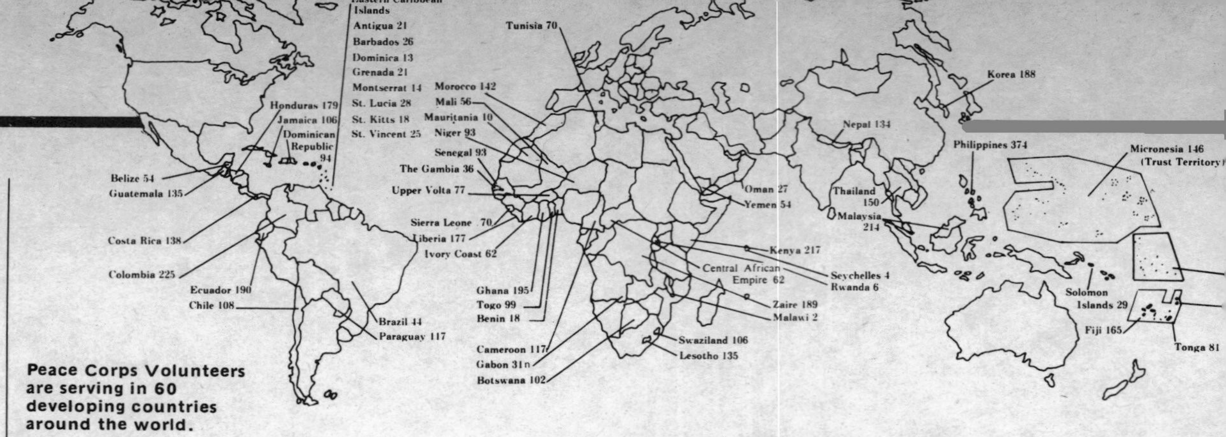

Peace Corps Volunteers are serving in 60 developing countries around the world.

Peace Corps

Visiting another country can be an eye-opening experience, but for many folks traveling abroad means ten cities in two weeks, tour buses, and strange hotels. If you have the time (two years minimum), a willingness to do without the standard comforts, and a desire to play an active role in the communities you visit, the Peace Corps may be your best travel bargain. The Peace Corps is not a playground, but there are benefits. They will teach you a new language, how to adapt to the culture you are about to be immersed in, and specific technical training in the projects you will be working on. During your stay your medical, dental, and basic living and moving expenses will be paid for. And you get 48 days paid vacation, plus local holidays, to travel on your own. When you return, you receive a lump-sum "readjustment allowance," $125 for each month in service, about $3300 for two years plus the training period. The Peace Corps veterans I've talked to all agree that the biggest benefit is the chance to learn more about yourself in ways that just aren't possible at home.

The rub is the association with your sponsor — good old Uncle Sam. However, since many projects are in remote areas of the world, you will be left pretty much on your own with an opportunity to bypass the bureaucracy and really communicate. The stated goals of the Peace Corps — "to provide technical assistance to the developing countries of the world which request it; to promote a better understanding overseas of American people; and to promote a better understanding of other people among Americans" — are a product of the visionary days of the early JFK administration. The modern Peace Corps has to deal with the urgent needs of a rapidly developing, overpopulated world that has been alienated by the heavy hand of U.S. economic and foreign policy. A few Peace Corps volunteers with skills and knowledge in alternative energy systems, resource management, reforestation, self-sustaining agriculture and aquaculture and biological pest control, as well as a healthy respect for the people and culture they are working for, have the potential to do more to promote international understanding and peace than an army of State Department minions in pin stripes and starched collars.

Travel, get your hands dirty, share your skills, make friends, and learn from them. Then bring it all back home.
—David Burnor

Peace Corps
Information

free from:
Peace Corps/VISTA
806 Connecticut Ave. NW
Washington, DC 20006

The Whole World Handbook

Where to find out about student discounts, work-study programs, "meeting-the-people" arrangements, independent study, work regulations, and just about anything else you might want to know. There are vast listings of opportunities that you may not have realized existed. All sorts of advice too, though not in as much detail as you'll find in a specialized area guidebook. Approximate fees are shown with suggestions for getting the most for your money.
—J. Baldwin

Whole World Handbook
(A Student Guide to Work, Study and Travel Abroad)
Marjorie Adoff Cohen
1972, 1978; 311 pp.
$2.95 postpaid from:
Simon and Schuster
Attn: Order Department
1230 Avenue of the Americas
New York, NY 10020

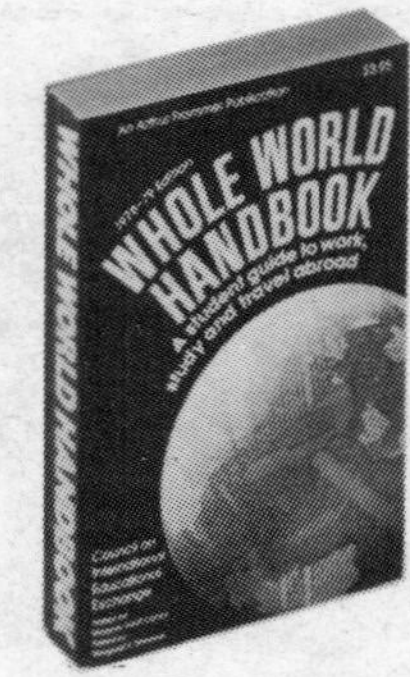

•

One travel writer we know thinks that the best way to find a job abroad is through what she calls "the blue-jean grapevine." She is convinced that word of mouth brings the best results without costing anything.

One book that may help you find a summer job overseas is the **Directory of Overseas Summer Jobs**, a paperback which is revised annually. It lists the names of employers, jobs available, and contact addresses; the reader takes over from there. The directory costs $6.95 and is distributed by the National Directory Service, 252 Ludlow Avenue, Cincinnati, OH 45220.

Transitions

A "guide to independent and educational travel" that consists almost entirely of articles and travel tips sent in by its travelling readers. It's usually about twenty pages long, printed on newsprint. The format and the writing are generally unpolished, but the articles are interesting, informative, and very timely. There are lots of specific addresses to help the traveller find work, classes, or any number of other situations all over the world. A number of inexpensive charter flights and other groups providing cheap transportation also advertise regularly. ***Transitions'*** *articles are often about Africa, Asia, and a lot of the less-touristed parts of the world as well as Europe and the more popular tourist spots.*
—Steve Dunnington

Transitions
(A periodical guide to travel, work, and study abroad)
William L. Gertz, Editor
$5 /year (4 issues)
from:
Prof. Clayton A. Hubbs
18 Hulst Road
Amherst, MA 01002

•

As with any seasonal work, the *vendange* always employs a fair number of people from outside the area. Where I picked, there were entire families of Italians, ski instructors waiting for the snow to fall in the Alps, French students on vacation, and itinerant agricultural workers who joined local housewives and the grower's own family in bringing in the harvest. Noontime brings this collection of people together at the grower's house for a lunch of a delicious Burgundian specialty served with the house wine. The effort expended in cutting grapes is at least equalled in the energy that fuels the conversation at the table.

•

Grapes are harvested all over Europe, but the bulk of commercial vineyards are in France, Switzerland, and Germany. The Burgundy region of France has probably the greatest concentration of grape-growing, so it's also one of the easiest places to find work. There is no special government permit necessary to work in the harvest; finding a job is mainly a question of talking to growers in a particular area until you find one who needs help. Working conditions can vary quite a bit from farm to farm, but it's common to include room and board along with a wage. A 10-hour work day is common for which one is paid between $10 and $25.

Licit & Illicit Drugs

The **Consumer Reports** *rundown on drugs — critical, intelligent, full of news. There's no better general book anywhere on all the brain drugs — including nicotine and alcohol. (See alcoholism, p. 328.)* —SB

Licit & Illicit Drugs
Edward M. Brecher and The Editors of Consumer Reports
1974; 623 pp.

$6.95 postpaid from:
Little, Brown and Company
200 West Street
Waltham, MA 02154
or Whole Earth Household Store

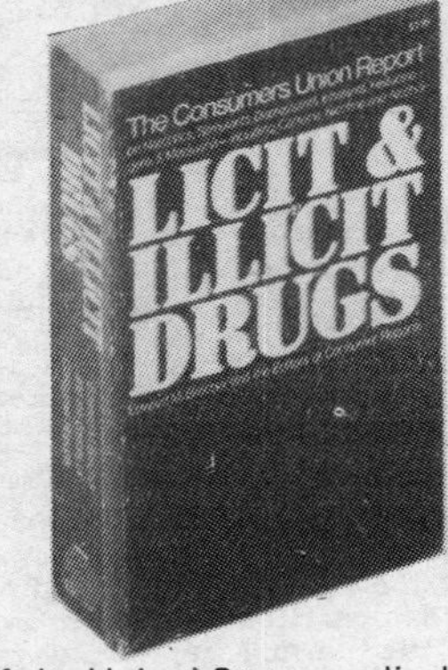

•

A conscientious search of the United States medical literature throughout recent decades has failed to turn up a single scientific paper reporting that heroin overdose, as established by these or any other reasonable methods of determining overdose, is in fact a cause of death among American heroin addicts. . . . But, beginning about 1943, a strange new kind of death began to make its appearance among heroin addicts. The cause of this new kind of death was not known, and remains unknown today — though it is now quite common.

A striking feature of this mysterious new mode of death is its suddenness. Instead of occurring after one or more hours of lethargy, stupor, and coma, as in true overdose cases, death occurs within a few minutes or less — perhaps only a few seconds after the drug is injected. Indeed, "collapse and death are so rapid," one authority reports, "that the syringe was found in the vein of the victim or on the floor after having dropped out of the vein, and the tourniquet was still in place on the arm." This explains in part why nalorphine and other narcotic antagonists, highly effective antidotes in true opiate overdose cases, are useless in the cases falsely labeled overdose.

An even more striking feature of these mysterious deaths is a sudden and massive flooding of the lungs with fluid: pulmonary edema. In many cases it is not even necessary to open the lungs or X-ray them to find the edema; "an abundance of partly dried frothy white edema fluid [is seen] oozing from the nostrils or mouth" when the body is first found. . . . Janis Joplin's death, of course, was popularly attributed to "heroin overdose." If the alcohol-barbiturate-heroin theory is correct, her fatal injection of heroin while drunk on alcohol was the prototype of many other deaths similarly mislabeled "overdose." . . .It might prove absurdly easy to confirm the alcohol-barbiturate hypothesis. All that might be necessary would be to addict a few monkeys or other primates to heroin, intoxicate them on alcohol or barbiturates, and then inject modest doses of heroin. If the monkeys drop dead of Syndrome X, a warning against shooting heroin while drunk on alcohol or barbiturates might save many hundreds of lives a year throughout the world.

Cocaine Consumer's Handbook

At the moment, the **Cocaine Consumer's Handbook** *will probably best prevent nose burn. There is, as yet, no good book on "cocaine base" — the alkaline form of cocaine that you smoke, don't snort or shoot. This is rapidly becoming the most common method of recreational intake for those who can afford it.*

—Peter Warshall

Cocaine Consumer's Handbook
David Lee
1976, 53 pp.

$5.45 postpaid from:
And/Or Press
P.O. Box 2246
Berkeley, CA 94702

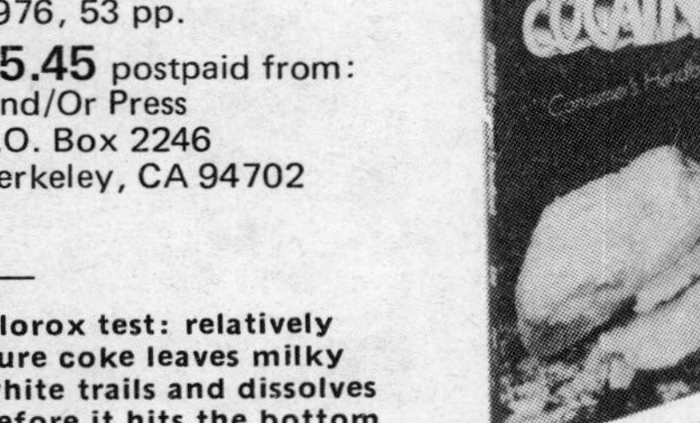

←

Clorox test: relatively pure coke leaves milky white trails and dissolves before it hits the bottom.

•

Most users of cocaine use inhalation as the method of ingestion. This is accomplished by chopping the cocaine thoroughly and sniffing it into the nasal passages, either from a small spoon or through a straw. The nasal membranes suffer greatly with extended use and should be protected. When cocaine sits on the surface of the membrane covering the interior nasal and sinus passages, it will cause burns and sores. Over a period of time this can lead to the degeneration of the membranes and can also eat through the cartilage itself. It is helpful in preventing this condition to wash the nasal passages out with warm water before retiring for the evening. A light spray of warm water, using a vaporizer, during the period cocaine is used will be helpful in preventing damage and helps cocaine enter the system.

•

If a large quantity is involved, the buyer should never make his purchase until after he has weighed and tested it. The seller should always expect such tests in large transactions. If the transaction is relatively small (one gram or less), the situation can become delicate. The clorox test is ideal for such a situation as the amount of cocaine used in the test is minute and the results are both quick and clear. A small, tightly-capped bottle of clorox should always be with you when a purchase is made.

If a test seems to annoy or offend the seller, the buyer could say he has violent allergic reactions to some substances used to adulterate cocaine and must be quite certain of these agents are not present in his purchase. An explanation of this type makes taking offense difficult and is sufficient to any seller who has confidence in his product.

PharmChem

For dopers this is a critical service. Accurate analysis for $10 of any drug you send them (whilst preserving your anonymity). And a monthly newsletter of what they're finding (misrepresentation, that's what).

—SB

PharmChem Newsletter
$25/year (10 issues)

from:
PharmChem Laboratories
3925 Bohannon Drive
Menlo Park, CA 94025

•

Analysis Anonymous is a drug analysis service that provides the public with unbiased, confidential information about the true content of illicit ("street") drugs. Particularly disturbing characteristics of the burgeoning street drug phenomenon are the continual appearance of new substances, widespread availability of dangerously adulterated and poorly synthesized drugs and intentional deception by illicit drug dealers. Test results on over a thousand drug samples submitted from throughout the United States have demonstrated the gross misrepresentation of drugs sold on the street. This flagrant discrepancy between the alleged and actual content of street drugs undoubtedly increases the number of overdoses and adverse reactions experienced by others; it also contributes to the dissemination of false and unreliable information about the effects of these drugs. Drug abuse professionals, educators, drug users and all others concerned with drug education are encouraged to support this service.

How to use Analysis Anonymous: Wrap the equivalent of one dose in plastic wrap; place the sample in an envelope along with $10 (cash or money order) to cover the cost of analysis; and assign the sample a code consisting of 5 random numbers followed by a letter of the alphabet. Please include information about the alleged content, street price, origin of sample (city and state), and note any undesirable side effects. If more than one sample, wrap each separately or mail in separate envelopes. Mark the envelope "Hand Cancel" and send it to PharmChem, 3925 Bohannon Drive, Menlo Park, CA 94025. The samples are qualitatively analyzed for approximately 350 drugs and related compounds. Quantitative analyses (reporting of percentages of sample ingredients) are available upon request only by a possessor of the proper Drug Enforcement Agency (DEA) license. Test results are obtained two days after the receipt of the sample by calling (415) 328-6200 and giving your number-letter code.

Analysis Anonymous does not accept food, herb, or vitamin samples, nor do we test for the presence of insecticides or herbicides (e.g., Paraquat). The analysis fee for aqueous solutions alleged to contain a drug is $20; any other liquid would have to be individually determined by prearrangement.

PharmChem's philosophy is that Analysis Anonymous should benefit as many people as possible. Reporting the test results of a particular drug only to the individual who submitted it is of limited value. Consequently, summaries of results are published in the **PharmChem Newsletter.**

The **PharmChem Newsletter** is a unique publication that features factual, timely information on licit and illicit drug use/abuse, drug legislation, and innovations in drug treatments, as well as result summaries of street drug samples analyzed by PharmChem's confidential drug testing program, Analysis Anonymous.

Laughing Gas

Definitive funky text on a form of dope which is so handy, reliable, and adaptive (proceed hit by hit and flash by flash) that enthusiasts have kept mum on the subject for years. Includes delightful history, practical manufacture, and safety precautions. —SB

Laughing Gas
(Nitrous Oxide)
M. Shedlin, D. Wallechinsky, S. Salyer, Editors
1973; 90 pp.

And/Or Press
P.O. Box 2246
Berkeley, CA 94702

Temporarily out of stock. Write for information.

•

It is impossible to convey an idea of the torrential character of the identification of opposites as it streams through the mind in this experience. I have sheet after sheet of phrases dictated or written during the intoxication, which to the sober reader seem meaningless drivel, but which at the moment of transcribing were fused in the fire of infinite rationality. God and devil, good and evil, life and death, I and thou, sober and drunk, matter and form, black and white, quantity and quality, shiver of ecstasy and shudder of horror, vomiting and swallowing, inspiration and expiration, fate and reason, great and small, extent and intent, joke and earnest, tragic and comic, and fifty other contrasts figure in these pages in the same monotonous way. The mind saw how each term belonged to its contrast through a knife-edge moment of transition which it effected, and which, perennial and eternal, was the nunc stans of life. The thought of mutual implication of the parts in the bare form of a judgment of oppositions as "nothing — but," "no more — than," "Only — if," etc. produced a perfect delirium of theoretic rapture. And at last, when definite ideas to work on come slowly, the mind went through the mere form of recognizing sameness in identity by contrasting the same word with itself, differently emphasized, or shorn of its initial letter. Let me transcribe a few sentences:

What's mistake but a kind of take?
What's nausea but a kind of -usea?
Sober, drunk, -unk, astonishment.
Everything can become the subject of criticism — how criticise without something to criticise?
Agreement — disagreement!!
Emotion — motion!!!
By God, how that hurts By God, how it doesn't hurt!
Reconciliation of two extremes.
By George, nothing but othing!
That sounds like nonsense, but it is pure onsense!
Thought deeper than speech. . . .!
Medical school; divinity school, school! SCHOOL!
Oh my God, oh God; oh God!

The most coherent and articulate sentence which came was this:
There are no differences of degree between different degrees of difference and no difference.

—William James, 1882

THE RISING SUN
NEIGHBORHOOD NEWSLETTER

continued from last spread

Things about tidelands:

There are two stories about who built the first sculpture on the mudflats. One is that some unknown folks did it, maybe inspired by the sight of all the abandoned duck blinds against the sky, thinking it would be even more interesting if the wood wasn't a rectangle but maybe a horse or a dragon. The other story is that some artists at the California College of Arts and Crafts were having a discussion about whether sculpture could and should be made of found materials and later, one of the discussers, to prove his point, went to Emeryville and built a sculpture out of duck blind parts. I find the second story unappealing and no fun to the point of being offensive but I realize that that's because I now find school as boring a notion as some people find mudflats. But art and school may be sometimes as messy and productive a combination as earth, air and water and just the place that some surprising new idea might crawl out of.

continued on next spread

Indians under Virola intoxication characteristically have faraway, dream-like expressions that are, of course, due to the active principles of the drug, but which the natives believe are associated with the temporary absence of the shamans' souls as they travel to distant places. The chants during the incessant dancing performed by shamans may at times reflect conversations with spirit forces. This transportation of the soul to other realms represents to the Waikā one of the most significant values of the effects of this hallucinogen.

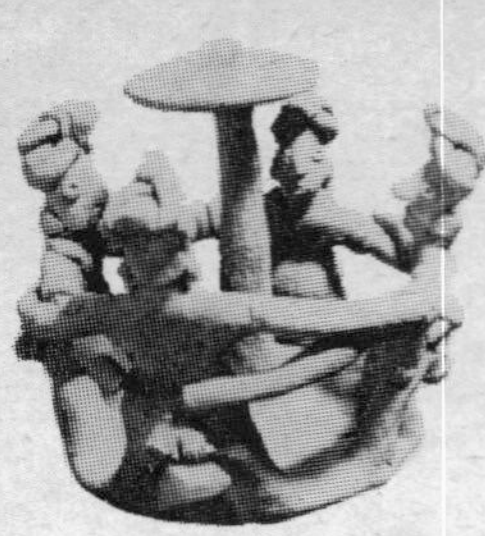

A faded Romanesque fresco in the late thirteenth-century Plaincourault Chapel depicts the Biblical temptation scene in the Garden of Eden. The Tree of Knowledge, entwined by a serpent, bears an uncanny resemblance to the Amanita muscaria mushroom. There has been considerable controversy concerning this fresco. Some feel that the figure represents the Fly Agaric.

Dated somewhere between 200 B.C. and A.D. 100, this beautiful ceramic artifact from Colima, Mexico, shows celebrants dancing around a mushroom effigy. From this artifact and the relative size and position of the fungus, it would appear that the mushroom represents something akin to the World Tree, the axis mundi. The mushroom, with its peaked cap, could well be Psilocybe mexicana or a close relative of this species.

Plants of the Gods

This is the coffee table version of the affordable Golden Press edition (also by Schultes). More detailed on the plants themselves, their preparations and uses, **Plants of the Gods** *gives precise and illuminating portraits of the many peoples on Earth who pay homage and gain insight with the aid of plants. The authors are* *__the__* *authorities on the subject.*
—Peter Warshall

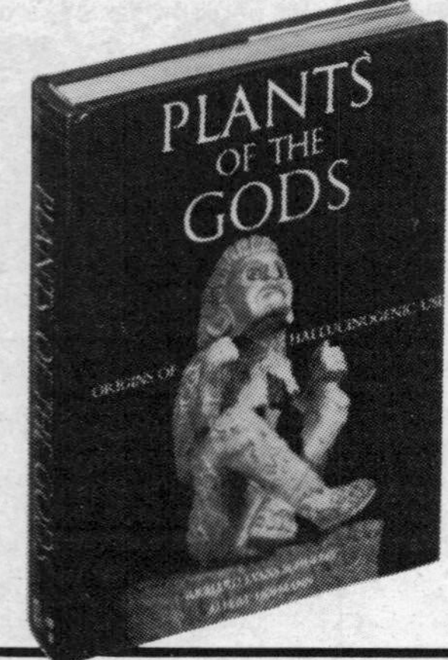

Plants of the Gods
(Origins of Hallucinogenic Use)
Richard Evans Schultes and Albert Hofmann
1979; 192 pp.

$34.95 postpaid from:
McGraw-Hill Book Company
Princeton Road
Hightstown, NJ 08520
or Whole Earth Household Store

Hallucinogenic Plants

Trust me folks. I've reviewed lots of your fad get-high books. Ingested as many in quest of verification. But never like this. No synthetics. No LSD. No STP. No DMT. This book is founded in a love of living plants — the "miraculous coincidence" that plant and human chemistries mix, create nourishment, life, death and visions. Writen by the U.S. Chief of Plant Power Research (Richard Evans Schultes) whose serene, plant-like soul treats our American pot cult in the same measured tones as the Fang Cult of Bwiti. This Golden Guide and **Wizard of the Upper Amazon** *are the two crucial grips on the vegetative reality of human spirit. Hey . . . out there . . . trust me. It's an old-fashioned sweet bargain.*
—Peter Warshall
[Suggested by Annie Hines]

Way back in the **Last Whole Earth Catalog** *I concluded a rave review of* **The Golden Book of Camping** *with the wise-ass remark, "I can hardly wait for the Golden Book of Dope." It's here. (For marijuana cultivation, see p. 103.)*
—SB

Hallucinogenic Plants
(A Golden Guide)
Richard Evans Schultes
1976; 160 pp.

$1.95 postpaid from:
Golden Press
Western Publishing Company
1220 Mound Avenue
Racine, WI 53404
or Whole Earth Household Store

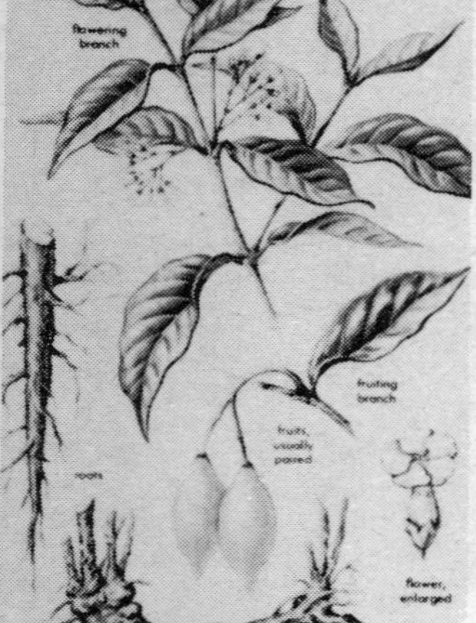

Old World Hallucinogens

Fly Agaric Mushroom; Agara, Ereriba;Kwashi, Galanga; Marihuana; Turkestan Mint; Syrian Rue; Kanna; Belladonna; Henbane; Mandrake; Dhatura; Iboga.

New World Hallucinogens

Puffballs; Mushrooms; Rapé dos Indios; Sweet Flag; Virolas; Masha-hari; Jurema; Yopo; Bilca; Genista; Mescal Bean; Colorines; Piule; Ayahuasca; Shanshi; Sinicuichi; San Pedro; Peyote; "False Peyotes"; Hierba Loca; Sacred Morning Glories; Hojas de la Pastora; Coleus, Borrachera, Arbol de los Brujos; Chiric-Caspi; Daturas; Tree Daturas; Culebra Borrachero; Shanin, Keule, Taique; Tupa, Zacatechichi.

Iboga *(Tabernanthe iboga)*, native to Gabon and the Congo, is the only member of the dogbane family, Apocynaceae, known to be used as an hallucinogen.

Wizard of the Upper Amazon

Plunged into the middle of a jungle foodweb, only visions, plant narcotics, hunting skills and an incredible intimacy with the natural world sustain Córdova-Rios. In no other book have I felt the mixing of human and animal and dream worlds to be so clear and direct.

I wrote the above paragraph in 1972 after reading the hardback. On re-reading the paper edition, I can only say that this book is far superior to anything Castaneda has attempted. The Huni Kui is not a destroyed tribe like the Yaqui. The Huni Kui have pleasant and important *__communal__* *visions much more astounding and connected-to-life than the individualistic "fearful" visions of Castaneda. To complete the praise: This is one of the three or four best books I have encountered while reviewing for the* **Whole Earth.**
—Peter Warshall

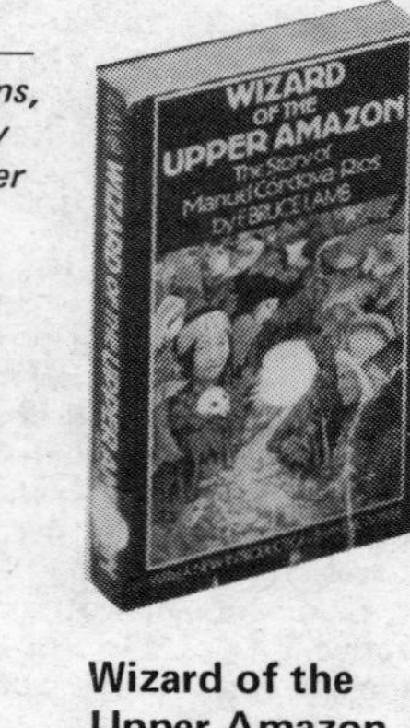

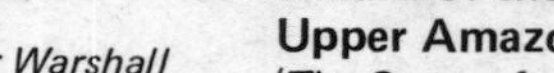

•

I was still kept on a strict diet, and it turned out that this was to be a period of intensive training for me. Once every eight days I would have a session of visions with the chief. These included examination of plants and their various uses both as food and as medicine, as well as further study of the animals. During the time between sessions I was taken often to the forest on both day and night trips with small groups of hunters. On these excursions I found to my delight that the intensified sense of perception and increased awareness of my surroundings originating in the sessions with the chief stayed with me. In the forest my companions would point out origins of sound and smell and continually test my progress in becoming completely one with the forest environment.

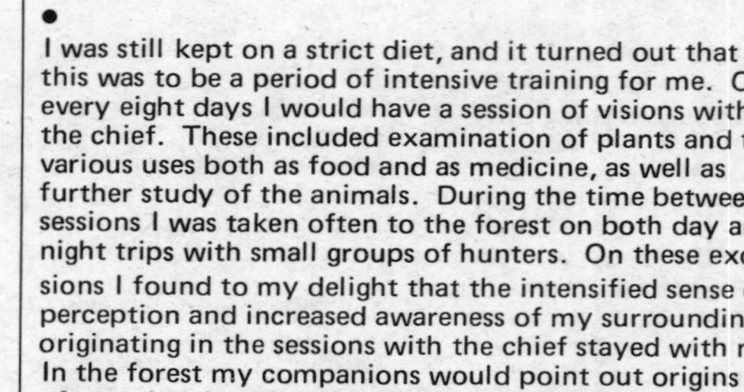

Wizard of the Upper Amazon
(The Story of Manuel Córdova-Rios)
F. Bruce Lamb
1971, 1974; 205 pp.

$3.95 postpaid from:
Houghton-Mifflin Company
Wayside Road
Burlington, MA 01803
or Whole Earth Household Store

Psychedelics Encyclopedia

As Allen Ginsberg says: "Peter Stafford has an elephant's memory for what happened to Public Consciousness . . ." This is a delightful Rabelaisian *__social history__* *of psychedelics in America (from the 1800s forward). My special favorite is the story of Harry J. Anslinger — the man who convinced the U.S. Government that marijuana was deathly.*
—Peter Warshall

Psychedelics Encyclopedia
Peter Stafford
1977; 384 pp.

$9.95 postpaid from:
And/Or Press
P.O. Box 2246
Berkeley, CA 94702
or Whole Earth Household Store

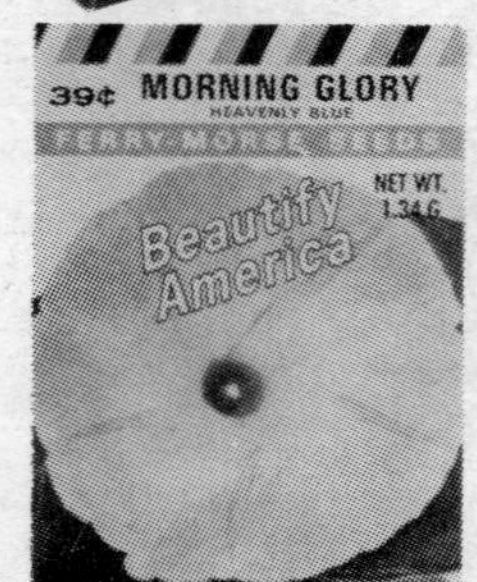

Varieties of *Ipomoea violacea* common in the U.S. containing d-lysergic acid amides are: Heavenly Blue, Pearly Gates, Flying Saucers, Blue Star, Summer Skies and Wedding Bells.

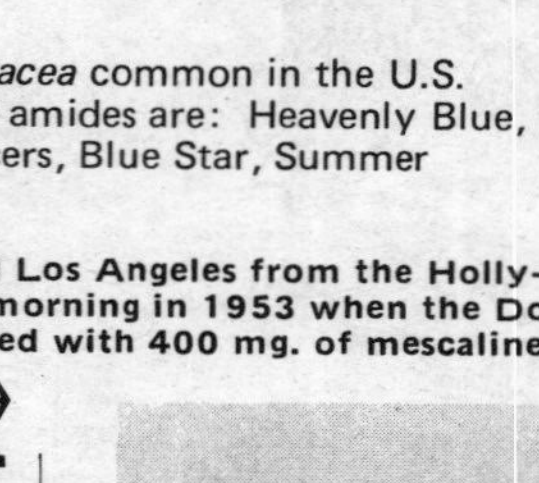

Aldous Huxley, surveying Los Angeles from the Hollywood Hills, on that May morning in 1953 when the Doors of Perception were cleansed with 400 mg. of mescaline.

The Beneficial Plant Research Association

The Beneficial Plant Research Association is a non-profit scientific and educational corporation that investigates and promotes plants that can improve human life. Currently, they are working on the Coca Project: an investigation of how the coca leaf (not cocaine) was used by native peoples of the Andes and how its leaf extract (not crystal) can be used for various medicinal preparations. They work closely with the native peoples who first "discovered" the plants. Another project helps the Cubeos (an Amazonian tribal people) market a special, smokey-flavored chile. Other projects include natural stimulants (guarana and yoco), sedatives (kava), dyes, sangre de grado, lulo, etc. An exciting group of the brainiest and most compassionate plant lovers on Earth.
—Peter Warshall

Beneficial Plant Research Association
Brochure

$1 from:
Beneficial Plant Research Association
Carmel Valley, CA 93924

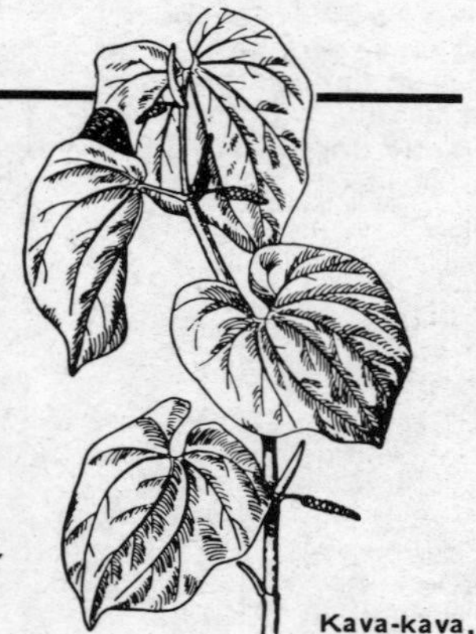

Kava-kava, Piper methysticum

We also plan to study natural sedatives that might serve as alternatives to the so-called "minor tranquilizers" that have become the most widely prescribed drugs in our society. Only recently has the public become aware that these powerful chemicals carry a variety of medical risk, including the possibility of severe dependence. The natural sedative that is receiving our first attention is kava *(Piper methysticum)*, which is used ceremonially in the islands of the South Seas. The beverage prepared from the fresh root produces a state of relaxation but does not dull the mind. Curiously, the dried root has little effect. We are working to determine how to preserve the desirable properties of fresh kava in a pharmaceutical preparation.

Brain/Mind Bulletin

Easily the handiest way to stay current with news and gossip on the soft psychology frontier. Despite success and a burgeoning of the subject matter, editor Marilyn Ferguson has admirably kept the bulletin's format to a terse, packed four pages. —SB

•

A false sense of self-control induced by bogus biofeedback reduced symptoms of cardiovascular disease in a recent experiment.

The clinical implications are straightforward, the researchers said. As few as three 10-minute sessions of bogus pulse-rate biofeedback can retard or reverse perceptions that one has little control over the body.

Gary Stern and his co-workers at the University of Colorado said that the illusion of slowing the pulse rate contributed to a sense of well-being.

•

Washoe, the chimpanzee that learned American sign language, had good reason to use it recently. She bit off the middle finger, right hand, of Stanford neuroscientist Karl Pribram — then made the sign for "Sorry, sorry, sorry."

Brain/Mind Bulletin
Marilyn Ferguson, Editor
$15/year (17 issues) from:
Interface Press
P.O. Box 42211
Los Angeles, CA 90042

Helplessness

This may be an important book. It offers a place to look for the problem when that hideous vague sense that "something's wrong" begins to grow. "Wrong" may very likely be that someone feels helpless, and the more they feel that way, the more they act that way, etc. on down. Positive feedback. Through experiments and anecdotes, Seligman shows how helplessness is learned, how it can be unlearned and even prevented. Not much gimmickry here. The book is about situations and their improvement. (See psychological self-care, pp. 327 - 329.) —SB

•

When the babysitter arrived for the first time, I introduced the babysitter to Amy; then when they were engrossed in playing, my wife and I sneaked off. Our fading away, we hoped, would avoid the traumatic separation, with Amy wailing and protesting, that we knew would otherwise occur. It certainly seemed like the path of least resistance, and it is a course many parents take.

After we did this several times, we noticed Amy's increased anxiety. Kerry then objected to our strategy: "The safety-signal theory has definite predictions about sneaking off."

"How so?" I asked.

"When we leave Amy with no clear warning signal, that's just like unpredictable shock," she said. "Amy is beginning to spend a lot of time in anxiety about separation, since she has learned that there is no predictor of leaving and therefore no predictor of our staying around. If, on the other hand, we go through an elaborate and explicit departure ritual, then Amy will learn that if the ritual hasn't occurred she doesn't have to worry."

This made a great deal of sense to me, so the next time, we told Amy at length that we were going out for a few hours, took her and the babysitter out to the car, waved bye-bye, exchanged hugs and kisses, and let them watch the car drive away. Amy understood enough of what we were doing to scream and protest, but we did go, and have followed this ritual ever since. Soon thereafter, Amy went back to being placid. Incidentally, Amy at age five is a calm child, who does not seem at all worried about her parents leaving her. The reader may ask where our experimental control is. Actually, since we now have another child of appropriate age, we could provide a "sneak off" control. But since the procedure appeared to work so well, I don't think we will.

Helplessness
(On Depression, Development, and Death)
Martin E.P. Seligman
1975; 250 pp.
$8.95 postpaid from:
W.H. Freeman and Company
660 Market Street
San Francisco, CA 94104
or Whole Earth Household Store

The Psychology of Consciousness

The idea of right-brain left-brain difference, whether it's a datum or a metaphor, is the dominant notion in experimental and theoretical psychology these days. This book of Robert Ornstein's, enjoyable as it is, is the one that reported the research and set loose the interpretations. —SB

•

If the left hemisphere is specialized for analysis, the right hemisphere (again, remember, connected to the left side of the body) seems specialized for holistic mentation. Its language ability is quite limited. This hemisphere is primarily responsible for our orientation in space, artistic endeavor, crafts, body image, recognition of faces. It processes information more diffusely than does the left hemisphere, and its responsibilities demand a ready integration of many inputs at once. If the left hemisphere can be termed predominantly analytic and sequential in its operation, then the right hemisphere is more holistic and relational, and more simultaneous in its mode of operation.

The Psychology of Consciousness
Robert E. Ornstein
1972; 247 pp.
$2.50 postpaid from:
Penguin Books
299 Murray Hill Parkway
East Rutherford, NJ 07073
or Whole Earth Household Store

Self Hypnotism   Self Hypnosis

One of the things that intrigues me most about hypnotism is that no one knows how it works — which accounts for some of its disrepute. No common factors, for example, have been found to pre-distinguish susceptibles from non-susceptibles. Black box business.

LeCron doesn't talk about any of this. He's concerned with how you can detect and desuggest old imprinted hang-ups and suggest in new ones you like better. (One subject suggested herself larger breasts, and got them.)

Sparks' book focusses less on use and more on technique. They supplement each other nicely.

Possibly the most general use of these books is their clear delineation of a simple avenue in — a meditative technique without much dogma. There are a lot of hypnosis books; these are the best we've seen for home uses.

Once when I was sky diving, a man jumping with me had a spiral fracture of his leg in mid-air (the parachute wrapped around his leg before opening) and then had to land on it. When I got to him he was green with agony and fully conscious with a long haul to the hospital ahead, and I taught him self-hypnosis for anesthesia on the spot. Needy as he was, it took effect immediately. —SB

Self Hypnotism
(The Technique and Its Use in Daily Living)
Leslie M. LeCron
1964; 208 pp.
$1.95 postpaid from:
New American Library
P.O. Box 120
120 Woodbine
Bergenfield, NJ 07621

Self Hypnosis
(A Conditioned-Reponse Technique)
Laurance Sparks
1962; 254 pp.
$4.50 postpaid from:
Wilshire Book Company
12015 Sherman Blvd.
North Hollywood, CA 91605
or Whole Earth Household Store

•

After she achieved a self-induced trance, I explained to her that she would see a movie that she had seen years ago, that it would be very clear and vivid and that she would see it upon a signal of snapping my fingers. I made a mistake, which had to do with the realization that I had neglected to give her certain instructions, and inadvertently snapped my fingers before explaining to her about the second signal. Imagine my surprise when she immediately woke up! I felt rather provoked with myself until I noticed her amazed expression, and she said, "Why, that's the most interesting thing that ever happened to me!"

"What happened?" I asked, not knowing quite what to expect.

"I just saw Gone With the Wind," she replied, laughing.

"How much of it did you see?"

"I saw the whole thing from beginning to end. It was even better than I remembered."

While I was still trying to figure out what had happened, she was telling me at great length about the picture. I found it hard to believe that she had really seen the whole picture, or even a small part of it, in such a short instant of time. But she convinced me by describing every detail of the opening scenes and dialogue, and continuing with vivid word-for-word reproduction as if she had just come from the theatre. Better, in fact, than if she had. It was clear that she had experienced imagery of the most vivid kind imaginable of a two-and-one-half hour picture in the time it took to snap my fingers — not between two signals; just during one snap!

—**Self Hypnosis**

The Esalen Catalog

Though you can't get a seminar at the Esalen Institute hot springs on the California Big Sur coast through the mail, you can get their catalog, survey the offerings along several dimensions of humanistic psychology, and go to Big Sur for one hell of a weekend. Since 1962 Esalen has been the stage where new acts and new actors try out for the Human Potential big time. —SB

The Esalen Catalog
$4/year (3 issues plus other mailings) from:
Esalen Institute
Big Sur, CA 93920

•

Weekend of June 20 - 22

The American Way of Birth and Death
Jessica Mitford, Bob Treuhaft, Suzanne Arms and Don Creevy

Jessica Mitford and Bob Treuhaft wrote **The American Way of Death** in 1963, giving us our first sustained look at what they called the funeral industry's "grotesque cloud-cuckooland where the trappings of Gracious Living are transformed, as in a nightmare, into the trappings of Gracious Dying." In 1975, Suzanne Arms wrote **Immaculate Deception**, an exposé of the "machine age of birth" based on invasive medical procedures and technological assumptions which "treat normal birth as a risky, dangerous, painful, and *abnormal* process in which pregnant women have no other choice than to submit graciously." Both of these best-sellers challenge the myth of expertise that has grown up around birth and dying. In cataloging the abuses of the funeral and hospital birth industries, both books have helped inspire alternatives to the control these monopolies have over dying and being born in America. The home birth movement, the proliferation of midwives, the development of community homes for birth and dying, and the regulation of the funeral industry, are among a number of reforms which figure prominently in the current revisioning of the American way(s) of birth and death. Author and long-time political activist Jessica Mitford and her husband Bob Treuhaft (appointed by Governor Jerry Brown to chair California's State Board of Funeral Directors) will join with Suzanne Arms and Don Creevy (co-founders of The Birth Place, a community birth home in Menlo Park), for a wide-ranging discussion of these and related issues. $170

Advanced Techniques of Hypnosis and Therapy

Gradually the sciences of the human mind are achieving levels of abstraction and rigor appropriate to the discussion of mental processes. But Milton Erickson has been ahead of the field in this respect for forty years. This big book is a collection of his papers with some commentary by Jay Haley, and it is a most extraordinary collection. Erickson's method, whether of therapy or research, is the precise use of hypnosis. Under this investigation, the human mind turns out to be as precise in its evolutions and timing as a minuet.
—*Gregory Bateson*

Advanced Techniques of Hypnosis and Therapy
(Selected Papers of Milton H. Erickson, M.D.)
Jay Haley, Editor
1967; 557 pp.
$48.25 postpaid from:
Grune and Stratton, Inc.
Harcourt Brace and Jovanovich
757 Third Avenue
New York, NY 10003
or Whole Earth Household Store

THE RISING SUN
NEIGHBORHOOD NEWSLETTER

continued from last spread

Things about tidelands:

But the mud flats are what they are not because of the first sculptors but because of the dozens since — people who would not call themselves artists but who can't resist a free zone and free wood and can-you-top-this anonymous competition and an expressway full of audience right next door.

continued on next spread

Zen and the Art of Motorcycle Maintenance

Philosophical practicality. Practical philosophy. Harsh realism. Lofty aspiring. With Pirsig on the motorcycle road with his disturbed son Chris, the apparent contradictions kick each other into robust life. A kickstart of a book for anyone. What the **Whole Earth Catalog** *may do to your fingers* **Zen and the Art of Motorcycle Maintenance** *does to viscera.*

(Some recent word on lives the book makes you interested in. Chris, getting steadily better at the Zen Center in San Francisco, was killed last year by muggers. Robert Pirsig is remarried and living on a Westsail 32 ketch in England — sailed capably in through the famous Fastnet storm — and is busy writing.) —SB

Zen and the Art of Motorcycle Maintenance
(An Inquiry into Values)
Robert Pirsig
1974; 412 pp.

$2.95 postpaid from:
Bantam Books
414 East Golf Road
Des Plaines, IL 60016
or Whole Earth Household Store

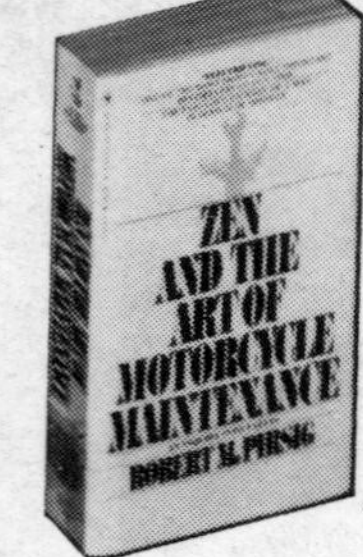

•

Care and quality are internal and external aspects of the same thing.

•

I like the word "gumption" because it's so homely and so forlorn and so out of style it looks as if it needs a friend and isn't likely to reject anyone who comes along. It's an old Scottish word, once used a lot by pioneers, but which, like "kin," seems to have all but dropped out of use. I like it also because it describes exactly what happens to someone who connects with Quality. He gets filled with gumption.

•

When he brought his motorcycle over I got my wrenches out but then noticed that no amount of tightening would stop the slippage, because the ends of the collars were pinched shut.

"You're going to have to shim those out," I said.

"What's shim?"

"It's a thin, flat strip of metal. You just slip it around the handlebar under the collar there and it will open up the collar to where you can tighten it again. You use shims like that to make adjustments in all kinds of machines."

"Oh," he said. He was getting interested. "Good. Where do you buy them?"

"I've got some right here," I said gleefully, holding up a can of beer in my hand.

He didn't understand for a moment. Then he said, *"What, the can?"*

"Sure," I said, "best shim stock in the world."

I thought this was pretty clever myself. Save him a trip to God knows where to get shim stock. Save him time. Save him money.

But to my surprise he didn't see the cleverness of this at all. In fact he got noticeably haughty about the whole thing. Pretty soon he was dodging and filling with all kinds of excuses and, before I realized what his real attitude was, we had decided not to fix the handlebars after all.

As far as I know those handlebars are still loose. And I believe now that he was actually offended at the time. I had had the *nerve* to propose repair of his new eighteen-hundred-dollar BMW, the pride of a half-century of German mechanical finesse, with a piece of old *beer* can!

Re-Visioning Psychology

What we consider the gods and goddesses of antiquity — those curious, lovely, and poetic myths — are truly the forces driving our lives — living our lives, trading off positions of power as need be between them. Learning to accept the rages of the soul is the work; to sacrifice to, not choose from, the possibilities. A complicated justification for the needs of diversity but an appealing one and one that goes far beyond the vain methodicalness of New Age men and women. My appetite for this book never ceases because it doesn't talk at me yet somehow reveals my rumors, dreams and visages to be more profound than I gave credit. An affirmation of the glorious spontaneity in spirit. —Terry Lawhead

Re-Visioning Psychology
James Hillman
1975; 266 pp.

$15 postpaid from
Harper and Row
Keystone Industrial Park
Scranton, PA 18512
or Whole Earth Household Store

•

This book is about soul-making. It is an attempt at a psychology of soul, an essay in re-visioning psychology from the point of view of soul. This book is therefore old-fashioned and radically novel because it harks back to the classical notions of soul and yet advances ideas that current psychology has not even begun to consider.

•

Finally, since ideas present archetypal visions, I do not ever truly have ideas; they have, hold, contain, govern me. Our wrestling with ideas is a sacred struggle, as with an angel; our attempts to formulate, a ritual activity to propitiate the angel. The emotions that ideas arouse are appropriate, and authentic, too, is our sense of being a victim of ideas, humiliated before their grand vision, our lifetime devotion to them, and the battles we must fight on their behalf.

•

If we look beyond Protagoras to the wider context of Greek culture, we see clearly that soul does not depend on personal life, nor do personal relationships provide any guarantee against psychological tragedy. The personal relationships in the family of Theseus, Phaedra, and Hippolytos, or the family of Alcestis, and even between Oedipus and Jocasta, are not lacking in the humanistic values of charity, dignity, concern, and humaneness. But tragedy comes, and it comes from the Gods.

The human in this Greek view of man depends not upon personal relationships but on relationships with archetypal powers which have their inhuman aspects. Greek humanism always "remained to some degree inhuman, not in the sense of barbarian, but in the sense of the Gods." They provide the inhuman perspective, so that the acute insights of the Greeks derive from a psyche, and a psychology, in which divine inhumanity has its place. A study of man can never give a sufficient perspective, for man is fundamentally limited; he is a frail *brotos, thnetos*, a poor mortal thing, not fully real. Gods are real. And these Gods are everywhere, in all aspects of existence, all aspects of human life. In this Greek view — and "Greece," as we have seen, refers to the polytheistic imagination — there is no place, no act, no moment where they are not. The Gods could not absent themselves from existence in a Protestant theological manner; they *were* existence.

The Act of Creation

Koestler takes his notion of bisociation to be the root of humor, discovery, and art. I take it to be one of the roots of learning, subject to applications of method (on yourself or whomever).

Koestler is a scientist of some reputation by now. He's made contributions beyond the work of others that he's generalized from. This is the book that gave him the reputation. —SB

The Act of Creation
Arthur Koestler
1964; 750 pp.

They may reprint this soon. Write for information.

OUT OF PRINT
Macmillan Publishing Company
866 Third Avenue
New York, NY 10022

•

When two independent matrices of perception or reasoning interact with each other the result (as I hope to show) is either a *collision* ending in laughter, or their *fusion* in a new intellectual synthesis, or their *confrontation* in an aesthetic experience. The bisociative patterns found in any domain of creative activity are tri-valent: that is to say, the same pair of matrices can produce comic, tragic, or intellectually challenging effects.

•

In the popular imagination men of science appear as ice-cold logicians, electronic brains mounted on dry sticks. But if one were shown an anthology of typical extracts from their letters and autobiographies with no names mentioned, and then asked to guess their profession, the likeliest answer would be: a bunch of poets or musicians of a rather romantically naive kind.

•

I have coined the term "bisociation" in order to make a distinction between the routine skills of thinking on a single "plane," as it were, and the creative act, which, as I shall try to show, always operates on more than one plane. The former may be called single-minded, the latter a double-minded, transitory state of unstable equilibrium where the balance of both emotion and thought is disturbed.

↓

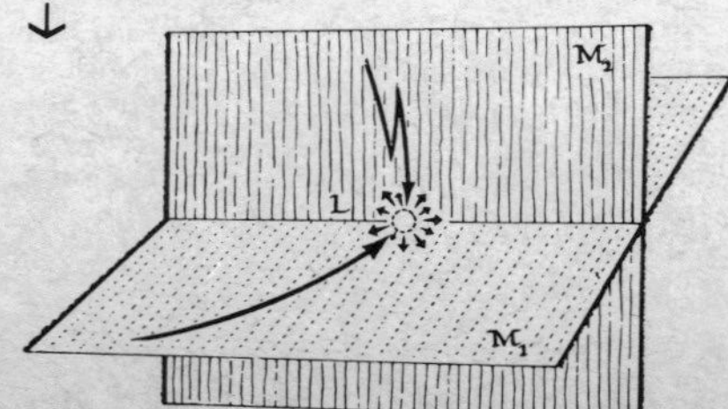

The Savage Mind

The formidable Levi-Strauss parses the worthy logic of totemism — native science based on deepest familiarity with fellow species and ritual celebration of mutual dependency. As with Hillman's re-visioning of the value to the shorn modern human soul of pantheons of deities, Levi-Strauss gestures in detail at the dramatic life awaiting lost souls willing to bear totemic relation to the life around them.

Poet Gary Snyder asked recently, "How can we readily measure if someone lives where they are? Well, we could ask them how many of the local plants they know by name. 250 would be a start." —SB

The Savage Mind
Claude Levi-Strauss
1962, 1966; 290 pp.

$5.50 postpaid from:
University of Chicago Press
Department PK
5801 Ellis Avenue
Chicago, IL 60637
or Whole Earth Household Store

The opposite of totemism: Naturalized Man. Sketch by Le Brun.

•

A native thinker makes the penetrating comment that "All sacred things must have their place." (Fletcher) It could even be said that being in their place is what makes them sacred for if they were taken out of their place, even in thought, the entire order of the universe would be destroyed. Sacred objects therefore contribute to the maintenance of order in the universe by occupying the places allocated to them. Examined superficially and from the outside, the refinements of ritual can appear pointless. They are explicable by a concern for what one might call "micro-adjustment" — the concern to assign every single creature, object or feature to a place within a class.

•

Several thousand Coahuila Indians never exhausted the natural resources of a desert region in South California, in which today only a handful of white families manage to subsist. They lived in a land of plenty, for in this apparently completely barren territory, they were familiar with no less than sixty kinds of edible plants and twenty-eight others of narcotic, stimulant or medicinal properties (Barrows). A single Seminole informant could identify two hundred and fifty species and varieties of plants (Sturtevant). Three hundred and fifty plants known to the Hopi Indians and more than five hundred to the Navaho have been recorded.

•

The natives themselves are sometimes acutely aware of the "concrete" nature of their science and contrast it sharply with that of the whites:

We know what the animals do, what are the needs of the beaver, the bear, the salmon, and other creatures, because long ago men married them and acquired this knowledge from their animal wives. Today the priests say we lie, but we know better. The white man has been only a short time in this country and knows very little about the animals; we have lived here thousands of years and were taught long ago by the animals themselves. The white man writes everything down in a book so that it will not be forgotten; but our ancestors married the animals, learned all their ways, and passed on the knowledge from one generation to another." (Jenness)

This disinterested, attentive, fond and affectionate lore acquired and transmitted through the attachments of marriage and upbringing is here described with such noble simplicity that it seems superfluous to conjure up the bizarre hypotheses suggested to philosophers by too theoretical a view of the development of human knowledge. Nothing here calls for the intervention of a so-called "principle of participation" or even for a mysticism embedded in metaphysics which we now perceive only through the distorting lens of the established religions.

The Structure of Scientific Revolutions

If you want to make a scientific revolution you might be interested in how it's done. This is the book that gave the word "paradigm" to the current podium crowd.
—SB

The Structure of Scientific Revolutions
Thomas S. Kuhn
1962, 1970; 210 pp.
$3.95 postpaid from:
University of Chicago Press
Department PK
5801 Ellis Avenue
Chicago, IL 60637
or Whole Earth Household Store

•

Normal science does not aim at novelties of fact or theory and, when successful, finds none. New and unsuspected phenomena are, however, repeatedly uncovered by scientific research, and radical new theories have again and again been invented by scientists. History even suggests that the scientific enterprise has developed a uniquely powerful technique for producing surprises of this sort. If this characteristic of science is to be reconciled with what has already been said, then research under a paradigm must be a particularly effective way of inducing paradigm change. That is what fundamental novelties of fact and theory do. Produced inadvertently by a game played under one set of rules, their assimilation requires the elaboration of another set. After they have become parts of science, the enterprise, at least of those specialists in whose particular field the novelties lie, is never quite the same again.

•

Aristotle's **Physica**, Ptolemy's **Almagest**, Newton's **Principia** and **Opticks**, Franklin's **Electricity**, Lavoisier's **Chemistry**, and Lyell's **Geology** — these and many other works served for a time implicitly to define the legitimate problems and methods of a research field for succeeding generations of practitioners. They were able to do so because they shared two essential characteristics. Their achievement was sufficiently unprecedented to attract an enduring group of adherents away from competing modes of scientific activity. Simultaneously, it was sufficiently open-ended to leave all sorts of problems for the redefined group of practitioners to resolve.

Achievements that share these two characteristics I shall henceforth refer to as "paradigms," a term that relates closely to "normal science."

Against Method

I have been curious for some time about the fact that so many people accept the truth of a variety of contradictory systems of knowledge and models of reality; science, astrology, Jungian psychology, magic, religion, mysticism, Zen, etc. **Against Method** *offers a philosophical background to such a pluralistic view of truth. Feyerabend argues that there is no singular method by which we are guaranteed to approach truth; that science is actually an ideology in disguise, and one that has taken command of our world view by force rather than by argument. Science is thus to be separated from the state and made to compete with other ideologies for our support. Truth is best served by a proliferation of theories, methods, and ideologies, and their free interaction; epistemological anarchy.*
—Kim Dovey

Against Method
(Outline of An Anarchistic Theory of Knowledge)
Paul Feyerabend
1975; 339 pp.
$7.95 postpaid from:
Schocken Books
200 Madison Avenue
New York, NY 10018
or Whole Earth Household Store

•

The only principle that does not inhibit progress is: anything goes.

•

The consistency condition which demands that new hypotheses agree with accepted theories is unreasonable because it preserves the older theory, and not the better theory. Hypotheses contradicting well-confirmed theories gives us evidence that cannot be obtained in any other way. Proliferation of theories is beneficial for science, while uniformity impairs its critical power.

•

There is no idea, however ancient and absurd, that is not capable of improving our knowledge.

Shiva Nataraja, Brahmanical bronze, South India, twelfth century.

The Tao of Physics
The Dancing Wu Li Masters

Two very agreeable excursions into farthest-out physics. **The Tao of Physics** *seeks to relate some of the profoundest insights of quantum physics with ditto from Oriental philosophy. Capra does not claim they are the same truths, fortunately, but they do illuminate one another brightly. For the reader familiar with either modern physics or Asian mysticism, the book is a quick secret staircase from the known field to the unknown one.*

The Dancing Wu Li Masters, *the more recent book, takes us via the improbable route of a conference at Esalen Institute into some of the most upsetting of current radical speculation in physics. A graceful book that has won surprising respect from the very physicists one would expect to scoff.*
—SB

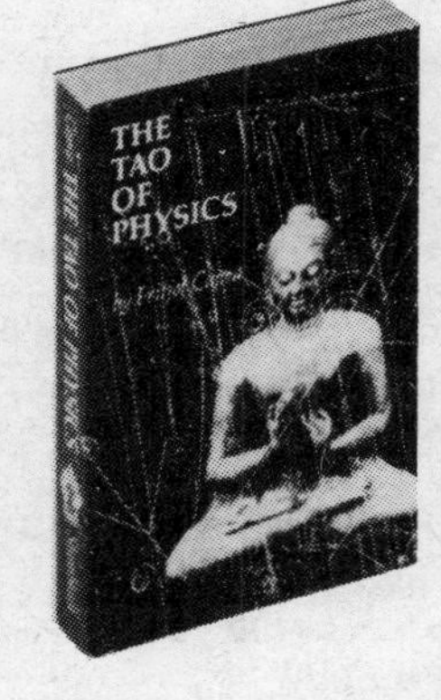

The Tao of Physics
(An Exploration of the Parallels Between Modern Physics and Eastern Mysticism)
Fritjof Capra
1975; 330 pp.
$6.95 postpaid from:
Shambhala Publications
1123 Spruce Street
Boulder, CO 80302
or Whole Earth Household Store

↑

The Dance of Shiva symbolizes not only the cosmic cycles of creation and destruction, but also the daily rhythm of birth and death which is seen in Indian mysticism as the basis of all existence. At the same time, Shiva reminds us that the manifold forms in the world are *maya* — not fundamental, but illusory and ever-changing — as he keeps creating and dissolving them in the ceaseless flow of his dance. As Heinrich Zimmer has put it:

"His gestures wild and full of grace, precipitate the cosmic illusion; his flying arms and legs and the swaying of his torso produce — indeed, they are — the continuous creation-destruction of the universe, death exactly balancing birth, annihilation the end of every coming-forth. . . ."

Modern physics has shown that the rhythm of creation and destruction is not only manifest in the turn of the seasons and in the birth and death of all living creatures, but is also the very essence of inorganic matter. According to quantum field theory, all interactions between the constituents of matter take place through the emission and absorption of virtual particles. More than that, the dance of creation and destruction is the basis of the very existence of matter, since all material particles "self-interact" by emitting and reabsorbing virtual particles. Modern physics has thus revealed that every sub-atomic particle not only performs an energy dance, but also *is* an energy dance; a pulsating process of creation and destruction.

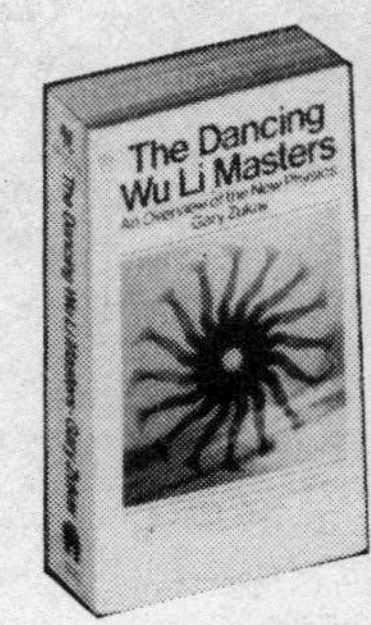

The Dancing Wu Li Masters
(An Overview of the New Physics)
Gary Zukav
1979; 341 pp.
$3.95 postpaid from:
Bantam Books
414 East Golf Road
Des Plaines, IL 60016
or Whole Earth Household Store

•

Bell's theorem has been reformulated in several ways since Bell published the original version in 1964. No matter how it is formulated, it projects the "irrational" aspects of subatomic phenomena squarely into the macroscopic domain. It says that not only do events in the realm of the very small behave in ways which are utterly different from our commonsense view of the world, but also that events in the world at large, the world of freeways and sports cars, behave in ways which are utterly different from our commonsense view of them. This incredible statement cannot be dismissed as fantasy because it is based upon the awesome and proven accuracy of the quantum theory itself.

Bell's theorem is based upon correlations between paired particles similar to the pair of hypothetical particles in the Einstein-Podolsky-Rosen thought experiment. For example, imagine a gas that emits light when it is electrically excited (think of a neon sign). The excited atoms in the gas emit photons in pairs. The photons in each pair fly off in opposite directions. Except for the difference in their direction of travel, the photons in each pair are identical twins. If one of them is polarized vertically, the other one also is polarized vertically. If one of the photons in the pair is polarized horizontally, the other photon also is polarized horizontally. No matter what the angle of polarization, both photons in every pair are polarized in the same plane. . . .

A light source in the center of the picture emits a pair of photons. On each side of the light source a polarizer is placed in the path of the emitted photon. Behind the polarizers are photomultiplier tubes which emit a click (or an inaudible electronic equivalent) whenever they detect a photon.

Whenever the photomultiplier tube in area A emits a click, the photomultiplier tube in area B also emits a click. . . .

Bell discovered that no matter what the settings of the polarizers, the clicks in area A are correlated too strongly to the number of clicks in area B to be explained by chance. They have to be connected somehow. However, if they are connected, then the principle of local causes (which says that what happens in one area does not depend upon variables subject to the control of an experimenter in a distant space-like area) is an illusion.

↓

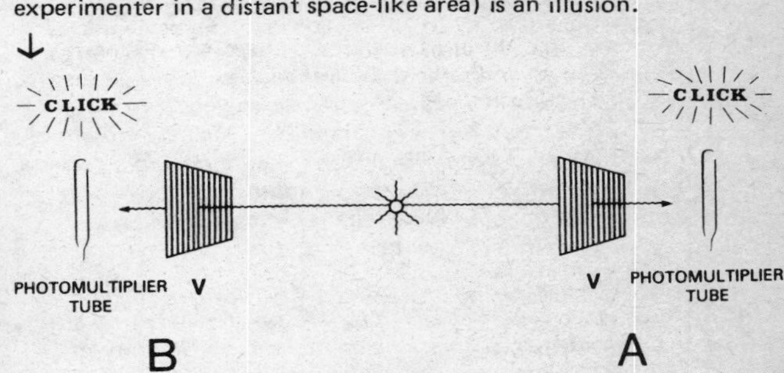

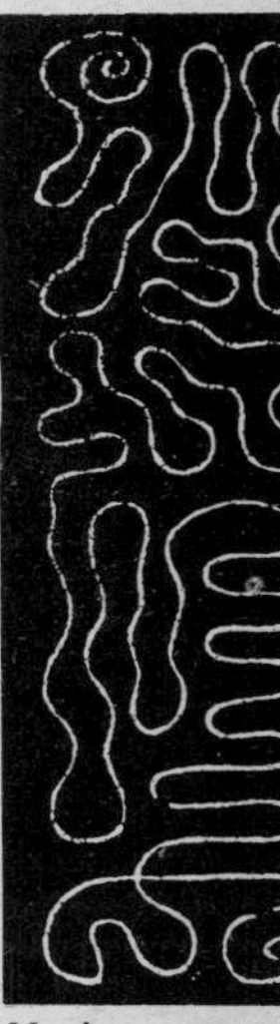

Magic diagram from the Taoist Canon, Sung dynasty
—Tao of Physics

The Logic of Scientific Discovery

It has been powerful magic, the scientific method. Here is an authoritative much quoted investigation of its philosophical core. When Popper takes you around an abstruse corner, you can trust him to show you something interesting that you can keep and use.
—SB

The Logic of Scientific Discovery
Karl R. Popper
1935, 1965; 480 pp.
$6.95 postpaid from:
Harper and Row
Keystone Industrial Park
Scranton, PA 18512
or Whole Earth Household Store

•

I shall certainly admit a system as empirical or scientific only if it is capable of being *tested* by experience. These considerations suggest that not the *verifiability* but the *falsifiability* of a system is to be taken as a criterion of demarcation. In other words: I shall not require of a scientific system that it shall be capable of being singled out, once and for all, in a positive sense; but I shall require that its logical form shall be such that it can be singled out, by means of empirical tests, in a negative sense: *it must be possible for an empirical scientific system to be refuted by experience.*

THE RISING SUN
NEIGHBORHOOD NEWSLETTER

continued from last spread

Things about tidelands:

6. In English common law, tidelands and marshlands belong to the King and cannot be owned by any other person. In modern law, the King translates into the state. American legal tradition is that English common law of all kinds is valid here unless it has been specifically denied by state or national government.

continued on next spread

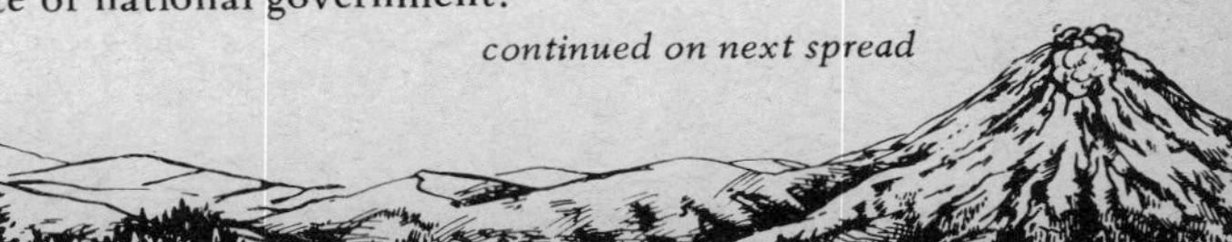

Continuing Buddhism

by Rick Fields

—From The Crystal Mirror

WHAT WE CALL BUDDHISM BEGAN with Siddhartha Gautama, a human being, prince of the realm, born in northern India around 500 B.D. Siddhartha had it all, as we might say today, prowess in arms, sages as tutors, dancing girls, a loving wife and son, a palace for every season — everything, but not quite enough. That "not quite" was like a shadow, a sliver of curiosity, that led him to look beyond the palace walls.

He found three things: a man hobbling along on a cane, a man lying in misery by the roadside, a man being carried to the burning grounds: old age, sickness, and death. And a fourth: a wandering sadhu, without caste, walking calmly down the road into the forest.

So he left the palace. The situation in Northern India at that time was not unlike our own during the last two decades. The forests and the marketplace were filled with seekers, teachers, and methods. Gautama mastered all the philosophies, attained the highest trances, and practiced austerities until his flesh shrank on his bones. Then he realized the body was not the enemy, he bathed and ate, and he sat beneath a tree on a mat of grass, legs folded, eyes half open, back straight, mindful of his breathing.

That sitting — not going anywhere but where you are — has formed the foundation of Buddhism ever since. In a sense, one might say that Buddhism is the path the Buddha cleared by sitting still. It is a path as up-to-date as the human mind, and the practice of it, though taken in the company of teacher and sangha (community), is always one's own. No one can eat, sleep, or breathe for you.

While there is no lack of Buddhist books, Buddhism has not been kept alive by referring to sacred texts. Instead, it has been practiced and transmitted from teacher to student. The survival of each school, or lineage, depends not on belief but on a kind of apprenticeship. Having to test and communicate your insight — or confusion for that matter — with another human being, whether master, guru, roshi, elder brother, or spiritual friend, can be difficult at times, but it also brings the whole journey down to Earth. (As the Buddha, when he finally won liberation, called the Earth to witness.)

It has taken about twenty-five hundred years for Buddhism to reach America. Thoreau, who translated and published possibly the first mahayana sutra in America (from the French, in **The Dial**, *1854), and who "realized what the Orientals mean by contemplation" as he sat in his sunny doorway one morning at Walden, is as good a place to start as any. D.T. Suzuki, the first patriarch of American Zen took an editing and translating job in LaSalle, Illinois in 1897, and there have been Zen Buddhists of some sort here ever since. In the sixties formal Zen practice became generally available, and in the seventies Americans trained in the forest monasteries of Southeast Asia returned home, while Tibetan exiles, having crossed the Himalayas on foot, arrived by jet.*

Now that Buddhism has taken root here — a process characterized by Zen pioneer Sokei-an as "holding the lotus to the rock" — those who have managed to survive their first enthusiasm are busy tending the new growth. The ground has been broken, and we are now in a period of cultivation and settlement. Buddhist groups have reinhabited abandoned seminaries, old age homes, state mental hospitals, and resorts — to give just a few examples.

It is dangerous to generalize, but safe to say that something we can call American Buddhism is hammering out its own shape: an emphasis on community in place of monastery, householder in place of monk, and hopefully all with a healthy sense of humor. But whatever the shape taken, the shining well-worn gold of the Buddha's teaching remains the same: the four noble truths — the fact of suffering, its origin, cessation, and the path through — and the sitting which puts it all into practice, again and again.

What follows is a selection of Buddhist training and practice centers in the U.S. (The books mentioned are best ordered from the centers, by the way.) Unlisted are the countless informal sitting groups, often unaffiliated, that have sprung up like mushrooms in the most unlikely places in recent years. The listings are organized into Theravadin, Mahayana, Vajrayana, the three traditional sub-divisions of Buddhist development. The Theravadin school is the earliest and is based on the Pali Canon; it now survives chiefly in Burma, Thailand, and Ceylon. Mahayana, a later development, based on the idea of the Bodhisattva, who postpones entry into Nirvana in order to work with others, is found in China, Japan, Korea, and Vietnam. Vajrayana, or Tantric Buddhism, developed in northern India. It was practiced in Tibet, Mongolia and Sikkim.

THERAVADIN CENTERS

Insight Meditation Society, Pleasant Street, Barre, MA 01005. *The central clearing house for vipassana (insight) meditation practice. IMS is a cooperative. Silence and a daily sitting schedule are maintained at all times. Retreats vary from one week to three months. Teachers include Joseph Goldstein, Jack Kornfield, Sharon Salberg, Ruth Denison. "The meditation practice is simple and direct: the systematic examination of the mind-body process through calm and focused awareness."*

Books: **The Experience of Insight** by Joseph Goldstein (1976; $4.95 postpaid) and **Living Buddhist Masters** by Jack Kornfield (1977; $6.95 postpaid), both from Unity Press, P.O. Box 1037, Santa Cruz, CA 95061.

Washington Vihara, 5017 16th Street, N.W., Washington, DC 20011. *A Theravadin center under the direction of the Ven. D. Piyananda Mahathera, and Gunaratna Mahathera — both bhikkus (monks) from Ceylon. Sattipatana (mindfulness) meditation is taught and practiced. A service is held every Sunday, occasional retreats.*

Publication: **The Washington Buddhist**, $3/year (4 issues).

MAHAYANA CENTERS

Zen Center of San Francisco, 300 Page Street, San Francisco, CA 94102. *A Soto Zen center founded by Shunryu Suzuki Roshi; his successor is Richard Baker Roshi. Zen Center includes Tassajara Zen Mountain Center, and Green Gulch Farm. Daily sittings at Page Street are open to the public.*

Publication: **Wind Bell**, $4/year (occasional publication).
Book: **Zen Mind, Beginners Mind**, by Shunryu Suzuki Roshi (1970; $3.50). The classic of American Zen. "When you do something, you should burn yourself completely, like a good bonfire, leaving no trace of yourself." (Also reviewed on p. 585.)

Genjo-Ji, 6367 Sonoma Mountain Road, Santa Rosa, CA 95404. *A lay Zen community under the direction of Jakusho Kwong, Sensei, who studied closely with Shunryu Suzuki Roshi for eleven years. There is a summer guest season, but guests are also welcome to visit at other times of the year.*

Minnesota Zen Meditation Center, 3343 East Calhoun Parkway, Minneapolis, MN 55408. *A zen community under the direction of Katigiri Roshi, who assisted Suzuki Roshi at San Francisco Zen Center and Tassajara.*

Bodhi, P.O. Box 638, Los Altos, CA 94022 and **Spring Mountain Sangha**, 11525 Mid Mountain Road, Potter Valley, CA 95469. *Bodhi comprises Zen practice communities in Los Altos and Santa Cruz. Spring Mountain is a rural Zen community, and family practice place. "People may practice as guest or resident. The residents work both on the farm to maintain it and in the city to maintain themselves." Under the direction of Kobun Chino, Sensei, who helped establish Tassajara with Suzuki Roshi.*

Zen Mission Society, Shasta Abbey, P.O. Box 478, Mt. Shasta, CA 96067. *A seminary and training monastery for the Reformed Soto Zen priesthood, which also offers a comprehensive lay program. Under the direction of Jiyu-Kennet Roshi, Abbess, an English woman who studied Ch'an (Zen) in Malaysia, received Dharma Transmission from the Chief Abbott of Sojiji Temple in Japan.*
Publication: **The Journal of Shasta Abbey**, $12/year (6 issues).
Book: **Zen Is Eternal Life**, formerly published as **Selling Water By The River** (1976; $10.95 postpaid).

New York Zen Center, 440 West End Avenue, New York, NY 10024. *Reverend Kando Nakajima, a Soto Zen priest, who has studied also in Ceylon. "Anyone wishing to sit regularly, listen to a lecture from a Zen priest, or come to sesshin once a month, may attend."*

Publication: **Zen Life.**

Zen Studies Society, 223 East 67th Street, New York, NY 10024. *Eido Shimano Roshi, a Rinzai Zen master, founder and teacher. International Dai Bosatsu Zendo in the New York Catskill Mountains is a country monastery, run in the traditional Japanese manner.*

Publication: **Dharma Seasons**, quarterly.

Book: **Golden Wind**, by Edo Shimano Roshi (1979; $6.95 postpaid).

Rinzai-ji, Cimmaron Zen Center, 2505 South Cimmaron Street, Los Angeles, CA 90018. *Rinzai Zen master Joshu Sasaki Roshi has adapted koan practice to American students. He is in Los Angeles for alternating three-month periods; the rest of the time he travels, giving sesshins — intensive meditation sessions — throughout North America. Affiliates include Mount Baldy, in California, where students can attend a three month winter retreat, Redondo Beach, California, Zen Center, Vancouver, and Jemez Bodhi Mandala, a rural Zen community in New Mexico.*

The Zen Center, 7 Arnold Park, Rochester, NY 14607. *Roshi Philip Kapleau trained in Japan for thirteen years. His teacher, Yasutani Roshi, taught an "integral" Zen grounded in both Rinzai and Soto. There are about twenty-five affiliate groups in different parts of the country.*

Publication: **Zen Bow**, subscription free.

Books: *Kapleau Roshi is the author of the classic* **Three Pillars of Zen** (1967, 1980; $5.95 postpaid), *which gives Yasutani Roshi's introductory talks on zazen, interviews with students during sesshin, and first-hand accounts of kensho, or satori. A new, revised edition has been published by Anchor/Doubleday. Kapleau Roshi is also the author of* **Zen Dawn In the West** (1979; $10.95 also from Doubleday).

Zen Center of Los Angeles, 905 South Normandie Avenue, Los Angeles, CA 90006. *An urban Zen community under the direction of Taizan Maezumi Roshi, a master in both Soto and Rinzai Zen. Four ninety-day training periods a year. The Institute for Transcultural Studies offers classes in Buddhist studies and related subjects. Affiliates include Black Mountain Zendo in San Diego, California.*

Publication: **The Ten Directions**, a quarterly newspaper.

Book: **The Hazy Moon of Enlightenment**, by Taizen Maezumi Roshi and Bernard Tetsugen Glassman (1978; $4.95 postpaid).

Zen Community of New York, P.O. Box 286 Riverdale Station, Riverdale, NY 10471. *Bernard Tetsugen Glassman, Sensei, Dharma Successor of Taizen Maezumi Roshi, has established ZCNY as a work, study and meditation community for Zen practice.*

Book: **Hazy Moon of Enlightenment** *(see above).*

Diamond Sangha Centers, Koko An Zendo, 2119 Kaloa Way, Honolulu, HI 96822.

Maui Zendo, R.R. 1, Box 220, Haiku, HI 96708. *Intensive practice periods at both centers. Under the direction of Robert Aitken Roshi, a master in the Sanbo Kyodan school of Zen Buddhism founded by Yasutani Roshi. The present Abbot of this school, Yamada Koun Roshi, visits Diamond Sangha occasionally. Aitken Roshi holds sesshin for Catholics once a year at Tacoma, WA. Contact Larry Ray-Keil, 331 17th Ave. East, Seattle, WA 98112.*

•

The poet Yang Wan Li wrote:

Standing by the stream waiting for the moon to rise;
But knowing how impatient I am, the moon takes its time.
Tired of waiting, I return to my study and close the door.
The moon leaps over a thousand peaks.

—**Wind Bell**, Winter '78-'79

Publication: **Kahawai**, a journal of women and Zen, published quarterly at Diamond Sangha. Contribution.

Book: **A Zen Wave, Basho's Haiku and Zen**, by Robert Aitken (1979; $7.95 postpaid).

Seattle Zen Center, 1517 34th, Seattle, WA 98122. *A Rinzai center under the direction of Takabayashi Genki Roshi.*

Sino-American Buddhist Association, Gold Mountain Monastery, 1731 15th Street, San Francisco, CA 94103.

City of Ten Thousand Buddhas, Box 217, Talmage, CA 95481. *Under the direction of the Venerable Master Hsuan Hua. Very intensive Ch'an (Chinese Zen) retreats; also Pure Land chanting of Amitabha's name. Classes in Chinese, Sanskrit. Some students have taken the full ordination of orthodox monks and nuns. Gold Wheel Temple is a branch in Los Angeles.*

Publication: **Vajra Bodhi Sea**, $22/year (12 issues).

Book: **Pure Land and Ch'an Dharma Talks**, Sino-American Buddhist Association (1974, $4 postpaid).

Providence Zen Center, RFD No. 5, Cumberland, RI 02864. *Headquarters of a nationwide network of centers under the direction of Seung Sahn Soen Sa Nim, a Korean master of the Chogye School. Each center has a daily schedule of morning and evening chanting and sitting Zen, a weekly lecture, and an intensive training period called Yong Maeng Jong Jin, "to leap like a tiger while sitting."*

Publication: **Newsletter**.

Book: **Dropping Ashes on the Buddha**, by Seung Sahn Soen Sa Nim (1976; $4.95 postpaid).

International Buddhist Meditation Center, 928 South New Hampshire Avenue, Los Angeles, CA 90006. *An interdenominational center under the direction of the Venerable Thich Thien-An, a Vietnamese Buddhist priest and Zen master.*

Publication: **Lotus in the West**.

Book: **Buddhism and Zen in Vietnam**, by Dr. Thich Tien-An (1975; $12.50).

VAJRAYANA

Vajradhatu, 1345 Spruce Street, Boulder, CO 80302. *A nationwide association of rural contemplative centers and urban centers, called Dharmadhatus, under the direction of the Venerable Chögyam Trungpa, Rinpoche, a master in the Kagyu and Nyingma lineages of Tibetan Buddhism. Dharmadhatus offer free meditation instruction, all day sittings, and study programs.*

Publication: **Vajradhatu Sun**.

Book: **Cutting Through Spiritual Materialism** by Chögyam Trungpa, Rinpoche (see below).

Karma Triyana Dharmachakra, Mountaintop Retreat Center, Mead Mountain Road, Woodstock, NY 12498.

Publication: **Vajradhatu Sun**.

Book: **Cutting Through Spiritual Materialism** by Chögyam Trungpa (see below).

Karma Triyana Dharmachakra, Mountaintop Retreat Center, Mead Mountain Road, Woodstock, NY 12498. *The North American seat of His Holiness the Gyalwa Karmapa, Head of the Kagyu lineage. The main purpose of the Retreat is to establish a traditional Tibetan monastery in America. There are twelve affiliated centers, all called Karma Thegsum Choling.*

Kagyu Droden Kunchab, 3746 21st Street, San Francisco, CA 94110. *A center for the teaching and practice of Tibetan Buddhism, under the direction of Kalu Rinpoche, a meditation master in the Kagyu school. Kagu Khunkhyab Chuling, a major center, is located at 725 West 14th Avenue, Vancouver, B.C. There are a number of affiliates nationwide.*

Book: **Writings of Kalu Rinpoche**, translated by Kenneth McLeod (1976; $5 postpaid).

Tibetan Nyingma Meditation Center, 2425 Hillside Avenue, Berkeley, CA 94704. *A center for the practice and study of the Nyingmapa lineage of Tibetan Buddhism, under the direction of Tarthang Tulku, Rinpoche. Classes in Tibetan language and culture. A rural community, Odiyan, is under construction.*

Publications: **Crystal Mirror** (annual), **Gesar** (quarterly).

Book: **Openness Mind** by Tarthang Tulku (1978; $5.95 postpaid).

Yeshe Nying Po, Orgyen Cho Dzong, 19 West 16th Street, New York, NY 10011. *The seat of His Holiness Dudjom Rinpoche, Head of the Nyingmapa lineage. Under the direction of Thinley Norbu, Rinpoche. Orgyen Cho Dhing, under the direction of Gyatrul Rinpoche is located in Berkeley, California.*

Maha Siddha Nyingmapa Center, Box 257, Conway, MA 03121. *Under the direction of Dodrup Chen, Rinpoche.*

Sakya Tegchen Choling Center, 4416 Burke Avenue North, Seattle, WA 98103. *A center for the practice and study of the Sakya lineage of Tibetan Buddhism. Under the direction of Sakya Jigdal Dagchen.*

Ewam Choden Tibetan Buddhist Center, 254 Cambridge Street, Kensington, CA 94708. *Under the direction of Kunga Thartse, Rinpoche of the Sakya school.*

Publication: **Virupa**.

Jetsun Sakya Center, 400 Riverside Drive, New York, NY 10025. *Under the direction of Deshung Rinpoche.*

Drayang Ling Buddhist Studies Center, 1382 Frank Street, Honolulu, HI 96816. *Under the direction of Nechung Rinpoche, a lama ordained in both Nyingma and Gelug lineages.*

Lamaist Buddhist Monastery of America, 140 East Third Street, Howell, NJ 07731. *Under the direction of Geshe Wangyal, of the Gelug school. There are also three other Geshes teaching at the Monastery. There is a Retreat House for more intensive study, as well as a translation center.* ■

Zen Mind, Beginner's Mind

Suzuki Roshi said he preferred to work with American students because they are such total earnest beginners, and that is an advantage in the Zen business. He was a remarkable person. During World War II in Japan he was a pacifist — unheard of. When the Americans came in the people in his town wanted to quickly tear down a war memorial statue they had; Roshi said don't do it, the Americans won't mind (they probably didn't even notice). Americans did notice during construction of the Tassajara Zen Center when the students found that their tiny Roshi could move as powerfully and gracefully with huge boulders as he could with obstacles to understanding. This book is a nicely edited transcription of words Suzuki Roshi spoke to a beginning Zen group in a Los Altos garage. It has become the classic beginning book for people interested in Zen. —SB

Zen Mind, Beginner's Mind
(Informal Talks on Zen Meditation and Practice)
Shunryu Suzuki Roshi
1970; 134 pp.

$3.95 postpaid from:
John Weatherhill, Inc.
Charles E. Tuttle Co.
Rutland, VT 05701
or Whole Earth Household Store

•

But perfect freedom is not found without some rules. People, especially young people, think that freedom is to do just what they want, that in Zen there is no need for rules. But it is absolutely necessary for us to have some rules. But this does not mean always to be under control. As long as you have rules, you have a chance for freedom. To try to obtain freedom without being aware of the rules means nothing. It is to acquire this perfect freedom that we practice zazen.

•

Zen mind is one of those enigmatic phrases used by Zen teachers to make you notice yourself, to go beyond the words and wonder what your own mind and being are. This is the purpose of all Zen teaching — to make you wonder and to answer that wondering with the deepest expression of your own nature. The calligraphy on the front of the binding reads *nyorai* in Japanese or *tathagata* in Sanskrit. This is a name for Buddha which means "he who has followed the path, who has returned from suchness, or is suchness, thusness, is-ness, emptiness, the fully completed one." It is the ground principle which makes the appearance of a Buddha possible. It is Zen mind. At the time Suzuki-roshi wrote this calligraphy — using for a brush the frayed end of one of the large swordlike leaves of the yucca plants that grow in the mountains around Zen Mountain Center — he said: "This means that Tathagata is the body of the whole earth."

—Richard Baker, introduction

•

I discovered that it is necessary, absolutely necessary, to believe in nothing. That is, we have to believe in something which has no form and no color — something which exists before all forms and colors appear. This is a very important point. No matter what god or doctrine you believe in, if you become attached to it, your belief will be based more or less on a self-centered idea. You strive for a perfect faith in order to save yourself. But it will take time to attain such a perfect faith. You will be involved in an idealistic practice. In constantly seeking to actualize your ideal, you will have no time for composure. But if you are always prepared for accepting everything we see as something appearing from nothing, knowing that there is some reason why a phenomenal existence of such and such form and color appears, then at that moment you will have perfect composure.

Cutting Through Spiritual Materialism

Gurus and religions are a dime a dozen. They supermarket comfort as a new bunch of rules and perceptions. In fact, the religions and gurus, once memorized, become huge burdens. Many of us try to avoid what's happening — internally, externally, wherever — by using Religion and Gurus as a comfortable crutch. This crutch is "spiritual materialism" and Trungpa will kick it out from your armpit. Thank goodness. Here's a spiritual companion — neither lofty nor pretentious — just startling, disarming and incessantly clear.

Trungpa (I've never met him) appears to be the most Whole Mind for the Whole Earth. From Tibet, a diamond clarity. From England, the tongue-in-cheek humor of Alice-in-Wonderland logicians. From France, existentialist sports car precision. From the USA, a peculiar impatience with Holden Caulfield, double-bind mind. So loosen up, have a drink, and meet the fusion of Whole Earth philosophical gentleness. (See Naropa Institute, p. 588.)

—Peter Warshall

Cutting Through Spiritual Materialism
Chögyam Trungpa
1973; 250 pp.

$6.50 postpaid from:
Shambhala Publications
P.O. Box 271
Boulder, CO 80306
or Whole Earth Household Store

•

We could say that compassion is the ultimate attitude of wealth: an anti-poverty attitude, a war on want. It contains all sorts of heroic, juicy, positive, visionary, expansive qualities. And it implies larger scale thinking, a freer and more expansive way of relating to yourself and the world. This is precisely why the second *yana* is called the "Mahayana," the "Great Vehicle." It is the attitude that one has been born fundamentally rich rather than that one must become rich. Without this kind of confidence meditation cannot be transferred into action at all.

Compassion automatically invites you to relate with people, because you no longer regard people as a drain on your energy. They recharge your energy, because in the process of relating with them you acknowledge your wealth, your richness.

•

Somehow you have to be right in no-man's land in order to see things as they are. Seeing things requires a leap, and one can only take this so-called leap without leaping from anywhere. If you see from somewhere, you will be conscious of the distance and conscious of the seer as well. So you can only see things as they are in the midst of nowhere. Like one cannot taste one's own tongue. Think about it.

•

Again it is said in the teachings: "Better not to begin. Once you begin, better to finish it." So you had better not step onto the spiritual path unless you must. Once you have stepped foot on the path, you have really done it; you cannot step back. There is no way of escaping.

THE RISING SUN
NEIGHBORHOOD NEWSLETTER

continued from last spread

Things about tidelands:

So — when the Sausalito houseboaters were trying to stop the developers by doing things like blocking bulldozers and getting arrested and challenging the arrests as illegal, Piro thought they should skip that and challenge the idea of someone owning the tidelands where the houseboats are as illegal. Say the developer didn't have the right to bring in bulldozers because the developer didn't have a right to lease the land from the guy who owns it because the guy who owns it doesn't really own it because nobody can own tidelands, because of common law never rescinded. Might not have worked but could have been a big enough legal battle to wear the developers down. But Piro got sick and went to New Zealand to visit friends and recover and when he got back some houseboaters had settled with the developers which was, from Piro's point of view, selling out, and the question of who owns the tide and its mud never went to court.

continued on next spread

19 ON ZEN

by anonymous

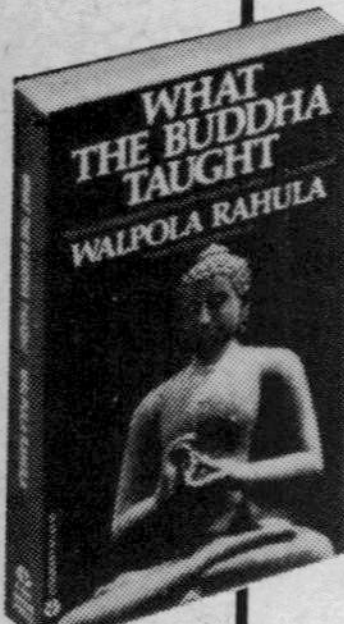

What the Buddha Taught

In detail and depth for beginners.

What the Buddha Taught
Walpola Rahula
1959, 1974; 151 pp.

$4.95 postpaid from:
Grove Press
G & S Books
1 Union Square
New York, NY 10003
or Whole Earth Household Store

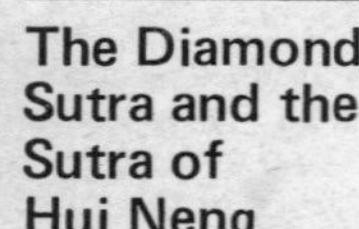

The Diamond Sutra and the Sutra of Hui Neng

Lightning strikes twice.

The Diamond Sutra and the Sutra of Hui Neng
A.F. Price and Wong Mou-Lam, Translators
1969; 114 pp.

$5.40 postpaid from:
Shambhala Publications
P.O. Box 271
Boulder, CO 80302
or Whole Earth Household Store

The Platform Sutra of the Sixth Patriarch (Hui Neng)

Liberating Chinese Zen. A contemporary study of this "so called" sixth patriarch.

The Platform Sutra of the Sixth Patriarch (Hui Neng)
Philip B. Yampolsky, Translator
1967; 212 pp.

$10 postpaid from:
Columbia University Press
Stock Department
136 South Broadway
New York, NY 10533
or Whole Earth Household Store

Zen Teaching of Huang Po

The poetry of insight, freedom.

Zen Teaching of Huang Po
(On the Transmission of Mind)
John Blofield, Translator
1958; 136 pp.

$3.95 postpaid from
Grove Press
G & S Books
1 Union Square
New York, NY 10003
or Whole Earth Household Store

Buddhist Wisdom Books

Necessary information. The great leap.

Buddhist Wisdom Books
(The Diamond Sutra and the Heart Sutra)
Edward Conze, Translator
1958, 1975; 110 pp.

$7.50 postpaid from
Allen and Unwin, Inc.
P.O. Box 978
Edison, NJ 08817
or Whole Earth Household Store

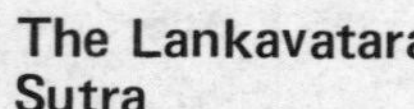

The Lankavatara Sutra

Wide Buddhist view of mind.

The Lankavatara Sutra
(A Mahayana Text)
Daisetz Teitaro Suzuki, Translator
1932; 295 pp.

$8.95 postpaid from:
Prajna Press
P.O. Box 271
Boulder, CO 80302
or Whole Earth Household Store

The Large Sutra on Perfect Wisdom

Emptiness. Now you are into it.

The Large Sutra on Perfect Wisdom
(With the Divisions of the Abhisamayalankara)
Edward Conze, Translator
1975; 679 pp.

$31.50 postpaid from:
University of California Press
2223 Fulton Street
Berkeley, CA 94720
or Whole Earth Household Store

The Buddhist Teaching of Totality

Wide Buddhist view of phenomenal and cosmic existence.

The Buddhist Teaching of Totality
(The Philosophy of Hwa Yen Buddhism)
Garma C.C. Chang
1971; 270 pp.

$8.95 postpaid from:
Pennsylvania State University Press
215 Wagner Building
University Park, PA 16802
or Whole Earth Household Store

Ch'an and Zen Teaching

Zen stories correctly expounded.

Ch'an and Zen Teaching
(Second Serires)
Lu K'uan Yu
1960

OUT OF PRINT from Shambhala Publications.

The Blue Cliff Record

This is it. Take a little at a time.

The Blue Cliff Record
Thomas Cleary and J.C. Cleary, Translators
1977; 3 volumes

$6.85 each (paperback) or
$21 together (hardbound)
all postpaid from:
Shambhala Publications
P.O. Box 271
Boulder, CO 80302
or Whole Earth Household Store

Zen Comments on the Mumonkan

Gateless Gate

Koans and excellent accompanying Zen lectures.

Zen Comments on the Mumonkan
Zenkei Shibayama

OUT OF PRINT from Harper and Row

Gateless Gate
(Mumonkan)
Koun Yamada
1979;

$7.50 postpaid from:
Center Publications
905 South Normandie St.
Los Angeles, CA 90006
or Whole Earth Household Store

Lucid Exposition of the Middle Way

Entry to the Buddhist philosopher, Nagarjuna. The ultimate dialectic.

Lucid Exposition of the Middle Way
(The Essential Chapters from the Prasannapada of Candrakirti)
Mervyn Sprung, Translator
1979; 283 pp.

$15 postpaid from
Prajna Press
P.O. Box 271
Boulder, CO 80302
or Whole Earth Household Store

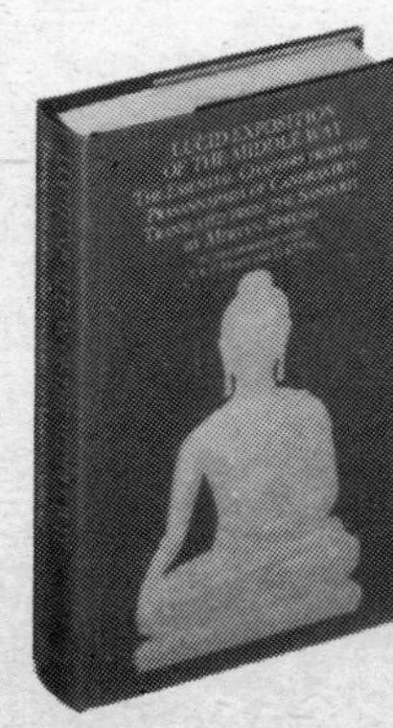

On Knowing Reality

Dharmas. Suchness (Especially the running translation.) An analysis of knowing reality.

On Knowing Reality
(The Tattvartha Chapter of Asanga's Bodhisattvabhumi)
Janice Dean Willis, Translator
1979; 202 pp.

$22.50 postpaid from:
Columbia University Press
Stock Department
136 South Broadway
Irvington-on-Hudson
NY 10533
or Whole Earth Household Store

Dogen's Formative Years in China

Teacher and Disciple. Useful history.

Dogen's Formative Years in China
(An Historical Study and Annotated Translation of the "Hokyo-ki")
Takashi James Kodera
1980; 258 pp.

$25 postpaid from:
Prajna Press
P.O. Box 271
Boulder, CO 80302
or Whole Earth Household Store

The Zen Master Hakuin

An extraordinary personality and teacher, brought together the koan study of Zen.

The Zen Master Hakuin
Philip B. Yampolsky, Translator
1971; 253 pp.

$17.50 postpaid from:
Columbia University Press
Stock Department
136 South Broadway
Irvington-on-Hudson
NY 10533
or Whole Earth Household Store

Timeless Spring

Lineage. The transmission of a teaching.

Timeless Spring
Thomas Cleary, Translator
1980; 173 pp.

$7.95 postpaid from:
John Weatherhill, Inc.
Charles E. Tuttle Co.
Rutland, VT 05701
or Whole Earth Household Store

One Robe, One Bowl

Ryokan: Zen Monk-Poet of Japan

Daily life.

One Robe, One Bowl
(The Zen Poetry of Ryokan)
John Stevens, Translator
1977; 85 pp.

$3.95 postpaid from:
John Weatherhill, Inc.
Charles E. Tuttle Co.
Rutland, VT 05701
or Whole Earth Household Store

Ryokan
(Zen Monk-Poet of Japan)
Burton Watson, Translator
1977

$12.50 postpaid from:
Columbia University Press
Stock Department
136 South Broadway
Irvington-on-Hudson
NY 10533
or Whole Earth Household Store ■

Alaya Stitchery

"Made by those who sit upon them" might be the best way to describe the products of Alaya Stitchery, which started 10 years ago as an in-house supplier of meditation cushions for the San Francisco Zen Center. They're now a storefront and mail order operation producing handmade meditation zafus, futons and cushions, as well as right livelihood for a half dozen happy Zennies.
—Dick Fugett

Alaya Stitchery
Catalog

free from:
Alaya Stitchery
848 Cole Street
San Francisco, CA 94117

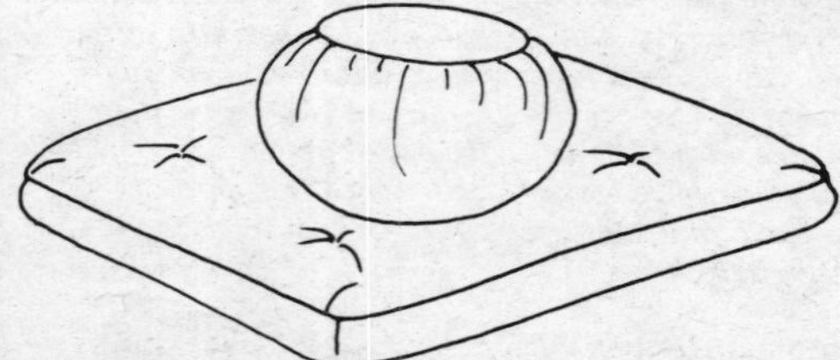

Zabuton — Flat floor cushion used under the zafu or by itself. Filled with 100% cotton batting in a choice of two thicknesses. Securely tacked with string ties. 31" x 34" $27.

Zafu — Traditional round cushion used for meditation and other floor sitting activities. Stuffed firmly with 100% kapok.
Standard 12" x 9" $17
Large 16" x 11" $22
Child's 9" x 7" $14

by Dick Fugett

Ask someone what yoga is all about and their most likely response will have to do with people doing headstands and other physical stuff. It's an interesting case of the tail wagging the dog, for way back when it all began the physical postures, or asanas, were only a small part of the main affair. Some 2 millennia ago Patanjali, whose work marks the first clear beginning of what is known today as yoga, produced the yogic sutras, a series of short aphorisms which formulate ashtanga, or eight limbed yoga. The asanas, or hatha yoga, are just one limb, and not one that received much of the founder's attention.

Patanjali's sparse aphorisms were intended to be memorized and handed down verbally by teachers who would then amplify with their own comments, thus in a book they are always accompanied by interpretation. The most available volume is **How to Know God** *by Christopher Isherwood and Swami Prabhavananda, and it's a good introduction to what yoga is all about, which is much more than headstands.*

How to Know God
(The Yoga Aphorisms of Patanjali)
Swami Prabhavananda and Christopher Isherwood
1953; 156 pp.

$1.50 postpaid from:
New American Library
P.O. Box 120
120 Woodbine
Bergenfield, NJ 07621
or Whole Earth Household Store

The word "yoga" comes from the same Sanskrit base that gives us our word "yoke," and implies a union or harnessing of energies, in this case a discipline or technique for investigating and developing the Self. A look at the literature reveals a fully developed philosophy, a way of explaining the world around us and why we're here. You might say it's similar to the Buddhist approach, but a bit less ethereal. Or it could be compared to some of the basic tenets of Hindu thinking, but since pinning down Hinduism with words and logic is like trying to put a puffy white cloud into a plain brown wrapper with a small plastic fork we are left with our curiosity, a few source documents like Patanjali, and whatever conclusions we reach on our own after going through the commentary and collating it with personal experience.

To be a yogi (or yogini, should you be both feminine and concerned with Sanskrit gender) would be to follow any of the paths that Patanjali outlined for us. Or the combinations/derivations/permutations thereof, and that covers a lot of ground. As Satprem wrote in Aurobindo's biography "the true system of yoga is to catch the thread of one's own consciousness . . . and to hold on to it and go to the very end." It's a loose definition for sure, and gives us room for both innovation and screwups. Think of a yogi as a Buddhist on an Independent Studies Program.

The orthodox form of yoga would be represented in **Autobiography of a Yogi**. *Yogananda came from a traditional Indian background in the last days before technology. As a young student he met his guru Sri Yukteswar, and then proceeded to go through the trials one expects to find on the path towards enlightenment.*

Yogananda went on to spend considerable time in the U.S., where he founded the Self Realization Fellowship. His student Swami Kriyananda became the energy behind Ananda Cooperative Village, one of the longest-lived and best known of the "new age" communities. The book is dedicated to Luther Burbank and includes chapters on Yogananda's meetings with the renowned horticulturist, as well as his visits with Mahatma Gandhi.

Autobiography of a Yogi
Paramahansa Yogananda
1946; 592 pp.

$2.50 postpaid from:
Self Realization Fellowship
3880 San Rafael Ave.
Los Angeles, CA 90065
or Whole Earth Household Store

Less orthodox would have been the life of Aurobindo, a contemporary of Gandhi who's best known today as the inspiration behind Auroville, the spiritual community in India that's dealing with such real life affairs as reforestation and desertification. Aurobindo's spiritual growth began when he was jailed by the British and put on trial for his life, accused of being the mad bomber of Calcutta. He used the time more constructively than many would, spending most of it in a very high state of meditation. After the trial he became a full time holy man, and one of India's principal writers and thinkers of this century. Satprem gives us an excellent summary of Aurobindo's thinking, along with a biography, in **Sri Aurobindo, or the Adventure of Consciousness.**

Sri Aurobindo
(Or the Adventure of Consciousness)
Satprem
1968; 381 pp.

$5.95 postpaid from:
Harper and Row
Keystone Industrial Park
Scranton, PA 18512

If Aurobindo was less than orthodox, then Richard Alpert's trip which began with Tim Leary and LSD, progressed to a guru in India and is now working on a dying center in New Mexico has to be described as thoroughly off the wall, but quite within yogic specs. (Remember that being a yogi is a more fluid status than many other spiritual positions, such as being the Pope.) Alpert became Ram Dass, and the story of the journey is the first chapter in a 3-chapter book called **Be Here Now**, *whose sales have reached 800,000 and make it possible that someday, after a rich hippie buys up the Hilton hotel chain, you will come upon a copy of* **Be Here Now** *in the dresser drawer, where always before you could count on Gideon's* **Bible.**

And where Exodus was you'll be face to face with the intensely illustrated Ram Dass amalgamation of Hinduism, Buddhism, Christianity and more. That's followed by **Cookbook for a Sacred Life**, *an excellent synopsis of methods and practices available to those who wish to work on themselves, to begin their own personal yoga.*

Be Here Now
Baba Ram Dass and the Lama Foundation
1971; 400 pp.

$4.83 postpaid from:
Crown Publishers
One Park Avenue South
New York, NY 10016
or Whole Earth Household Store

Interesting, you say, but since all three of the above books when laid end to end still say almost nothing about hatha yoga and you're hot to do headstands, then let's get on with it.

HATHA

The practice of hatha yoga acquaints us with our bodies in a slow, precise manner that no sport can offer. Diligent pursuit will reward us with a new physical well being, a clearer mind, and most importantly, an inner calm unknown before. Hatha is an invaluable tool for developing ourselves, one that we can take with us wherever we go, like meditation.

Because it can become more than just an exploration of the physical package, a teacher, especially at the beginning, can give insights that the purely self-taught person may miss. A few classes or a retreat can produce rewards that more than justify the money spent.

When it comes to books on the topic there's a bushel, but two could be said to be standards. **Integral Yoga Hatha** *has probably started more people than any other, it's simple, clear and well illustrated, and each asana, or posture, is also described in writing. If you'd like a closer look, there are numerous Integral Yoga Institutes around the country offering classes in hatha and related topics.*

Integral Yoga Hatha
Yogiraj Sri Swami Satchidananda
1970; 189 pp.

$6.95 postpaid from:
Holt Rinehart and Winston
383 Madison Avenue
New York, NY 10017
or Whole Earth Household Store

If you've reached advanced levels and enjoy new challenge (Beware of Egofeed — hey look, I did a Lotus!) then check out **Light on Yoga**. *Iyengar is a master of the art, and the pictures in the book illustrate his talent. They could also be discouraging for the beginner, so don't worry whether you'll ever be that loose, just appreciate the incredible possibilities inherent in the human structure, and wonder why the rest of us don't develop them. The book also has a superior introduction to the entire yogic philosophy.*

Light on Yoga
(Yoga Dipika)
B.K.S. Iyengar
1966, 1977; 544 pp.

$6.95 postpaid from:
Schocken Books
200 Madison Avenue
New York, NY 10016
or Whole Earth Household Store

Eagle Pose —A Child's Garden of Yoga

A Child's Garden of Yoga

To be presented with yoga when young is like being given a second language; it's a great gift that many of us old folks with crepitating joints and closed minds can easily envy. For kids, yoga can be a way of playing, as well as learning that awareness of the body which conscious use of the physical package can produce.

The book is for ages 3 to 12, and the postures range in difficulty from simple standing stretches to some fairly tough stuff, like the bound lotus, so no one will be overwhelmed or underchallenged. All the poses are illustrated by kids, not grownups, and text accompanies each photo.

A Child's Garden of Yoga
Baba Hari Dass
1980; 108 pp.

$5.95 postpaid from:
Sri Rama Publishing, Inc.
P.O. Box 1569
Santa Cruz, CA 95061

Easy Does It

Here's an illustrated book of yoga postures for older people and the handicapped who would like to improve their health and clarity of mind. It emphasizes basic hatha postures but also has sections on breathing, meditation, nutrition, and philosophy. Anyone who believes they are "over the hill," regardless of age, is creating a self-fulfilling prophecy. When the desire for change generates motivation many such limitations can fall away. The journey of a 1000 miles begins with the first step, which you must supply. Here's a road map when you're ready.

Easy Does It
(Yoga For Older People)
Alice Christensen and David Rankin
1975, 1979; 112 pp.

$5.95 postpaid from:
Harper and Row
Keystone Industrial Park
Scranton, PA 18512
or Whole Earth Household Store

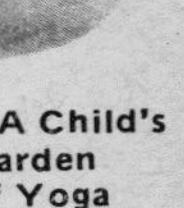

—A Child's Garden of Yoga

Yoga Journal

Yoga Journal *is a six-year old regional magazine that's becoming the reflection of the national movement, now that* **East West Journal** *has chosen to focus on the macrobiotic scene.* **YJ** *emphasizes hatha yoga, in particular the Iyengar methods, but has enough diversity to keep us reading as we observe the twists and turns that people go through these days on their way to getting holy.*

We watch in fascination as the inherent hedonism of middleclass America collides head on with the Spirit, and both lose ground. Thumbing through the pages provides flashes of everything from inside tips on a yoga vacation camp in the Bahamas and a $2395 charter flight tour of India with "5-star Michelin rated accomodations at some of India's finest hotels. . ." to worthwhile interviews with teachers and gurus, and a monthly feature analyzing a particular asana. Besides that there's ads for books, retreats and programs that might be the best part of all. How long **YJ** *will be able to straddle both hedonism and spiritual fulfillment without coming apart at the principles remains to be seen.*

Yoga Journal, Deena Brown, Editor, $9/year (6 issues) from California Yoga Teachers Association, 2054 University Avenue, Berkeley, CA 94704. ■

THE RISING SUN
NEIGHBORHOOD NEWSLETTER

continued from last spread

Things about tidelands:

7. You may think you're solid like a squishy rock but actually you're a donut like the earliest simplest sea creatures which were circles with sea water running through them that they grabbed nutrients from as it went by. The donut's gotten thicker as we've gotten away from the edge of the water, but the hole is still there from mouth to ass. And every cell in the dry-seeming body has got to have a tide of salt water washing over it constantly.

continued from last spread

Inner Development

A **Whole Earth Catalog** *(we don't say this very often) of spiritual books, including natives, Celts, astronomy, Christian Bibles, Baha'i, Cayce, fairy tales, Gurdjieff, humanistic psychology, Jewish mysticism, sufi, tarot, occult, Jung, Steiner, sacred geometry, etc., etc. It is a comprehensive gathering, up to date (1979), with capsule reviews of each book that do a remarkable job of summarizing the contents and remarking on their comparative value.*

Very nice work indeed by the Yes! Bookshop in Washington DC which I'll bet is worth a visit. —SB

Inner Development
(The Yes! Bookshop Guide)
Chris Popenoe
1979; 654 pp.

$9.95 postpaid from:
Random House
455 Hahn Road
Westminster, MD 21157
or Whole Earth Household Store

CALDER, NIGEL. **THE VIOLENT UNIVERSE—AN EYEWITNESS ACCOUNT OF THE NEW ASTRONOMY. 7"x9½", 160pp. Vik69/Fut, 4.95p.**
A superbly written, illustrated book which presents the current state of knowledge, investigation and speculation concerning quasars, pulsars, neutron stars, anti-matter, exploding galaxies, and gravity holes.

■ *WALEY, ARTHUR, tr.* **MONKEY. 306pp. Grv43/Pen, 4.95p.**
This classic combination of picaresque novel and folk epic, which mixes satire, allegory, and history, is one of the most popular books in China. It is the story of the roguish Monkey and his encounters with major and minor spirits, gods, demigods, demons, monsters, and fairies. Waley has given us a wonderful translation of Wu Ch'eng-en's novel.

■ *WATSON, BURTON, tr.* **CHUANG TZU, BASIC WRITINGS. 140pp. Col64, 3.90p.**
An excellent prose translation of the seven *inner chapters* which form the heart of Chuang Tzu's book, three of the *outer chapters*, and one other one. Watson does a wonderful job of recapturing Chuang Tzu's spirit and message. An illuminating, long introduction places Chuang Tzu in relation to Chinese history and thought.

WATSON, BURTON. **THE COMPLETE WORKS OF CHUANG TZU. 397pp. Col68, 24.75c.**
An excellent translation, probably the most scholarly and also most readable available. Watson also provides extensive annotations and an enlightening introduction.

GILES, HERBERT, tr. **CHUANG TZU: TAOIST PHILOSOPHER AND CHINESE MYSTIC. Introduction, notes, index, 335pp. A&U26, 13.75c/8.95c.**
This is a complete edition of Chuang Tzu's writings. Giles was an excellent scholar, but not the best translator for a writer like Chuang Tzu. His style is too stilted to recreate Chuang Tzu's flowing narrative. The translation combines prose and poetry, but it is mainly prose. The cheaper edition is from Taiwan.

Chuang Tzu (399-295 BC) lived 200 years after Lao Tzu. Using parables and anecdotes, allegory and paradox, he set forth the early ideas of what was to become Taoism. Central in these is the belief that only by understanding Tao (the Way of Nature) and dwelling in its unity can man achieve true happiness and be truly free, in both life and death. *To him, nature is not only spontaneity but nature is a state of constant flux and incessant transformation. This is the universal process that binds all things into one, equalizing all things and all opinions. The pure man makes this oneness his eternal abode, in which he becomes a "companion" of Nature and does not attempt to interfere with it by imposing the way of man on it. His goal is absolute spiritual emancipation and peace, to be achieved through knowing the capacity and limitations of one's own nature, nourishing it, and adapting to the universal process of transformation. He abandons selfishness of all descriptions, be it fame, wealth, bias or subjectivity. Having attained enlightenment through the light of Nature, he moves into the realm of "great knowledge" and "profound virtue."*

■ *BROWN, RAPHAEL, tr.* **THE LITTLE FLOWERS OF SAINT FRANCIS. 359pp. Dou58, 2.45p.**
This book was written 100 years after the death of St. Francis to try to capture the true spirit of his life and the Franciscan way for the followers of that time. It has come to us as the classic gospel of the great saint. This edition contains twenty chapters never published in English before, and is considered the definitive presentation of these legends. It also includes a long, enlightening introduction on the background of the book and its historical significance; a biography of St. Francis and biographical sketches of the principle characters in the book; and notes, appendices, and a bibliography. In addition, the texts of the following works are included: *The Five Considerations on the Holy Stigmata, The Life of Brother Juniper, The Life of Brother Giles,* and *The Sayings of Brother Giles.*

LEWIS, C.S. **TILL WE HAVE FACES. 313pp. Eer56, 2.95p.**
This was C.S. Lewis' last novel before his death in 1963, and the book he himself regarded as his best. Critics have said that the book has the stature of a religious classic, the intensity and eloquence of a powerful novel, and the provocative quality of a psychological drama.

GRIS, HENRY and WILLIAM DICK. **THE NEW SOVIET PSYCHIC DISCOVERIES: A FIRSTHAND REPORT ON THE LATEST BREAKTHROUGHS IN RUSSIAN PARAPSYCHOLOGY. Photographs, index, 324pp. PrH78, 10.95c.**
Not since **Psychic Discoveries Behind the Iron Curtain** was published in 1970 has there been such a comprehensive book on the Soviet Union's all out attempt to investigate and harness the powers of the human mind. In six separate visits to the USSR, the authors used special contacts in the Kremlin as well as the parapsychology underground to obtain unprecedented interviews with Russians involved in all related fields.

Living Together Alone

There are two good reasons and one bad one to read this clear account of life in nine quite various American monasteries (Trappist, Buddhist, Charismatic, etc.). Read it if you're thinking of becoming a monk for a while or ever. Read it to feel better about America's long-term prospects. Don't read it as an academic study please. —SB

Living Together Alone
(The New American Monasticism)
Charles A. Fracchia
1979; 186 pp.

$5.95 postpaid from:
Harper and Row
General Books
Keystone Industrial Park
Scranton, PA 18512
or Whole Earth Household Store

A Benedictine monk at Christ in the Desert Monastery in New Mexico plants flowers near the guest house.

"There is nothing wrong with arches and hoods and chant," Brother David answers. "Personally, these things are very much to my taste. But there is one decisive feature that makes an environment monastic: mindfulness. In fact, that's what a monastery is anywhere in the world, a place designed to foster mindfulness."

"Mindfulness in all its dimensions," Father John adds, "from the way we treat our garden tools, to responsible awareness of global issues, the arms race, exploitation, hunger." Gregory tells of Good Shepherd House of Hospitality in nearby Norwalk, an outreach of the Grange, of which he is in charge. Forty and more hungry people come there every day for a warm meal and for assurance that someone is mindful of them and cares. "Of course," he adds, "what we receive is so much more than what we can give. Often I'm overwhelmed by gratefulness."

Gratefulness, my three hosts agree, is inseparable from mindfulness. The problem, as they see it, is that our affluent society conditions us to take more and more things for granted. But what we take for granted does not make us happy; it means nothing to us. Thus, as gratefulness deteriorates, happiness is lost, and the meaning of life is lost. They see their monastic foundation as a school for grateful living. More and more people experience today a need to spend time in such a place.

Lucis Trust Library

Here's an unusual item — a mail library of 1600 magical books. You can borrow two books at a time for a month. Lucis is a nice service that subsists on contributions; it probably is fragile to exploitive use. —SB
[Suggested by Gerald Thatcher]

Lucis Trust Library
Catalog

$1 contribution from:
The Lucis Trust Library
866 United Nations Plaza
Suite 566 - 567
New York, NY 10017

•

Anacalypsis, An Attempt to Draw Aside the Veil — Godfrey Higgins
Apocalypse Unsealed, The — James Pryse
Appolonius of Tyana — G.R.S. Mead
Art of Seeing, The —Aldous Huxley
Art Spirit, The — Robert Henri
As Above, So Below — Alan Oken
Asian Journal of Thomas Merton, The — Thomas Merton
Astrologer's Manual, The — Landis Knight Green

Samuel Weiser

Weiser's is a huge mystical book store in Manhattan with a good mail order catalog. —SB

Samuel Weiser
Catalog

free from:
Samuel Weiser, Inc.
625 Broadway
New York, NY 10012

The Meaning of Witchcraft **by G.B. Gardner, $4.95—$7.95. The "old religion" in ancient, mediaeval and modern history.**

Naropa Institute

In Boulder, Colorado, a robust and innovative school has grown up around Chögyam Trungpa (author of **Cutting Through Spiritual Materialism** *— see p. 585). Theater, music, dance, science, martial arts, poetry, and psychology are some of the courses. Leading artists, philosophers, and spiritual teachers regularly hold forth. Impressive operation.* —SB

Naropa Institute
Information

free from:
Naropa Institute
1111 Pearl Street
Boulder, CO 80302

Mani Trading Company

Fine religious items (non-Christian). Meditation bells, drums, statuettes, incense, prayer flags, and sweet service. —SB

Mani Trading Company
Catalog

$2 from:
Mani Trading Company
Arnoldsberg Star Route
Box 57
Spencer, WV 25276

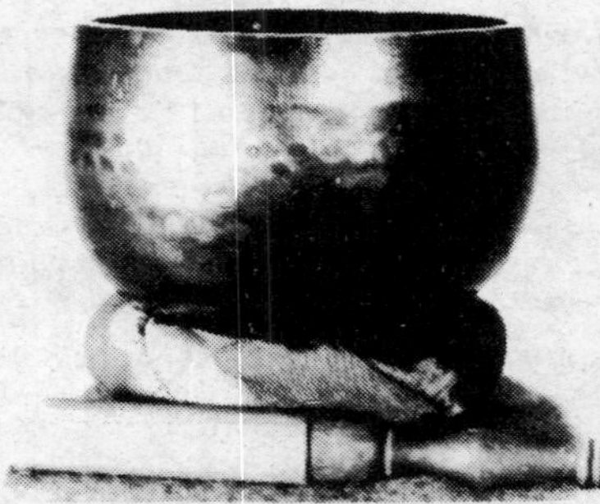

KEISU: These are the thicker beaten copper-alloy gongs with the low b'ong tone. Cushions included, strikers as available. The bigger the gong, the better the tone.

Smaller keisu gongs:	
AA(3½" gong)	Price: $19.
A (4¼")	Price: $21.
B (4½")	Price: $27.
C (4¾")	Price: $36.
D (5½")	Price: $48.
E (6")	Price: $64.
F (7¼", brass, more bell-like tone)	Price: $80.
Temple size keisu:	
8" gong, stand, cushion, and striker	Price: $250.
10" gong, stand, cushion, and striker	Price: $375.

Two steps in posture 19, Tao Nien-Hour, Yu **or step back and repulse monkey**

Clarity of vision has two aspects: awareness and concentration.

The principle of Leading Control applied from a static position

T'ai-Chi

Considered the best book on this most sophisticated of calisthenics, **T'ai-Chi** *is very well illustrated, as you might expect. But I can't imagine learning the art just from a book. To locate teachers near you try the yellow pages or write T'ai-Chi Chuan Association, 211 Canal Street, New York, NY 10013.*
—SB

T'ai-Chi
(The "Supreme Ultimate" Exercise for Health, Sport and Self-Defense)
Cheng Man-ch'ing
and Robert W. Smith
1966, 1967; 112 pp.

$15 postpaid from:
Charles E. Tuttle Company
Rutland, VT 05701
or Whole Earth
Household Store

•

How should a novice begin his training in T'ai-chi? He should relax completely. The aim is to throw every bone and muscle of the body wide open so that the *ch'i* may travel unobstructed. Once this is done, the chest must be further relaxed and the *ch'i* made to sink to the navel. After a time the *ch'i* will be felt accumulating for mass integration in the navel, from where it will begin to circulate throughout the body.

Aikido and the Dynamic Sphere

Aikido is the most recent and most brilliantly conceived of the Japanese martial arts. A superb fighting technique, it is scarcely interested in fighting — it doesn't even have matches, just training. You train to put your mind and body in the same place for once — the one-point at your center of gravity. You train to acquire and direct Ki — energy (not strength, but coherent energy: when it's flowing you don't have to move). You train to blend with your opponent and use his energy to unhinge his attack. I find this book by two Americans to be far more useful for learning aikido than the numerous texts by Japanese students of the original master Morihei Uyeshiba. The illustrations here are profoundly better than the usual photographs. They depict the mental image — which is the heart of aikido technique. An editor can use aikido, a general, an actor, a craftsman, a politician, a designer. What the body learns and practices becomes useful in any realm.
For teachers near you, get in touch with United States Aikido Federation, 142 West 18th Street, New York, NY 10011.
—SB

Aikido and the Dynamic Sphere
(An Illustrated Introduction)
A. Westbrook
and O. Ratti
1970; 375 pp.

$19.50 postpaid from:
Charles E. Tuttle Company
Rutland, VT 05701
or Whole Earth
Household Store

•

Your own Centre must become the center of your attacker's action as well. The Centre is not restricted in aikido, as we have indicated, to your personal dimension. If a man attacks you, he has lost his own point of independence and balance by the very irrationality of that act, and you must substitute your own Centre in an attempt to return the situation to normal. Thus he attacks, you evade; he plunges into a vacuum, you lead and guide him back around your own Centre and neutralize his attack.

•

A blow may be delivered to your head (attack no. 13, *shomen uchi*). You will pivot and kneel down, so that you are facing the same direction as your opponent. Your arm(s) will not "block" in the sense of stopping his motion, but will be extended so as to protect yourself. At the same time you will guide his motion (via his wrist or even sleeve) from the inside, lead him in full, circular extension forward and then down. This can be accomplished almost without touching him.

There is no pulling, no dragging; it is just a smooth, simple, circular lead, synchronized perfectly with your attacker's own movements. It is blended dynamically with them and, therefore, almost unnoticed until he is in flight. He falls, but yet does not know precisely how he came to fall.

Samadhi tank

Also called "sensory deprivation tank," it was developed by John Lilly of dolphin fame as a research tool. It is. In a shallow pool of epsom salts water you float silkily free of any surface, any sound, any light. Some use it for meditation, some for drug trips, some for comfort, some for curiosity.

Install one in your office. "I'm sorry, the director can't be disturbed right now. She's in the tank."
—SB

The Samadhi Deluxe Tank
$2,750 (approx.)

Information
free from:
Samadhi
23 First Street
Corte Madera, CA 94925

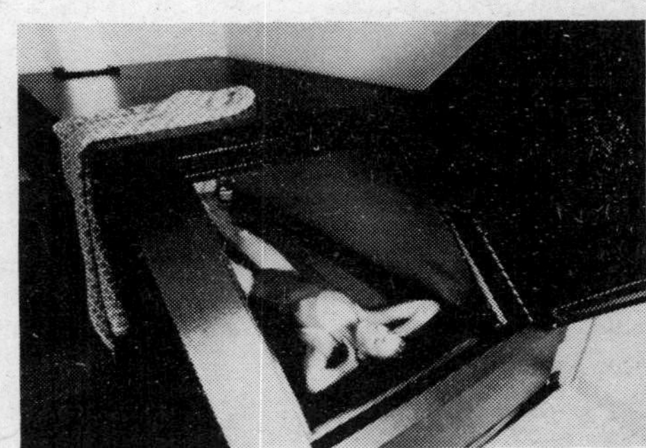

Martial arts supplies

Karate, aikido, kung-fu, judo uniforms, training aids, weapons, books, emblems.

Would the Vietnam War have been better if conducted strictly hand-to-hand? Why not do it that way next time?
—SB

[Suggested by Carl Harp]

Martial Arts Catalog
$1 from:
Martial Arts Supplies, Inc.
10711 Venice Blvd.
Los Angeles, CA 90034

BOUNCE BACK DUMMIES
Constructed out of laminated vinyl material on the outside with layered compressed foam core on the top. The bottom is constructed out of molded lead and encased in a special durable material to assure a reliable bounce back reaction.

S30-40 (50" tall) $225.00
S30-41 (60" tall) $275.00
Cannot be shipped to Canada.

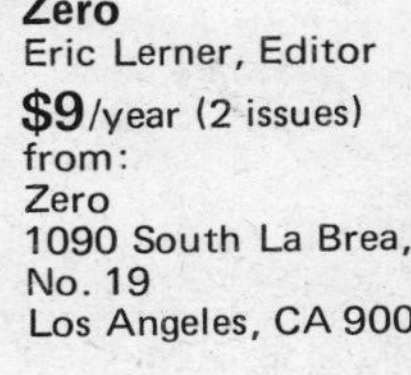

CURVED STRIKING PAD
Made of compressed foam covered with 18 oz. laminated vinyl. The holder will not feel the best punch you give.

S30-60 Vinyl $33.95
S30-65 Leather $53.95

Shikibo
STAFF DEFENSE
A twirling weapon made of hardwood. The leather loop enables the practitioner to twirl the weapon at tremendous speed . . . much faster than a Sai with more control. Will do anything a Sai does. Complete with instructions.

S61-36 (19½" Medium) .... $14.95 pair
S61-37 (22" Large) .... $16.95 pair

Zero

Why are magazines from religious groups so often classy? Because they can attract and keep good artists attentive to a higher calling than big bucks. (Political groups sometimes attract artists, but they can't keep them.) The premier issue of this magazine associated with Los Angeles Buddhists had an all-star cast — Leonard Cohen, Ram Dass, Joshu Sasaki Roshi, Kenneth Rexroth, Allen Ginsberg, John Ashbury, Gary Snyder, Robert Thurman.

All in all, a blockbuster of fine clarity, recalling two remarks. One from Ginsberg in **Zero**'s *promo — "Subtle understanding of glad emptiness our lives, American Earthly saves us from Apocalyptic pain, the 'Suffering of Suffering,' so a XXth Century Literature of Dharma Bums and Ladies & Gentlemen rises in Capitals & Provinces, exemplified herein* **Zero.**" *The other from Gregory Bateson in conversation, "The problem with Christianity is that it's a slave religion. Part of the attraction of Buddhism for me is that it was founded and sustained by aristocrats."*
—SB

Zero
Eric Lerner, Editor
$9/year (2 issues)
from:
Zero
1090 South La Brea,
No. 19
Los Angeles, CA 90019

•

Installation

The day after you graduate from college is a scary day. It's the day that the want ads in the paper become a threat instead of a throwaway. You're faced with making the machine you've been building all your life run. This is what might be called life's installation stage. Although our analogy may seem a bit weak, it's clear that now you must sink or swim as you are. Watch out!

•

Solitude

The one necessary thing is solitude, vast inner solitude. Going into yourself and for hours meeting no one — this you must be able to achieve. To be alone, the way you were alone as a child, when the grownups went around involved with things that seemed important and big because they themselves looked so busy and because you understood nothing of their activities.
—Ranier Maria Rilke

THE RISING SUN
NEIGHBORHOOD NEWSLETTER

continued from last spread

Things about tidelands:

8. I was just thinking how someone could try to create the Emeryville effect by writing a grant proposal to the Arts Commission or the Ford Foundation or something "to create a public performance and art creation space in which local citizens will be encouraged to create their own sculptures using found materials from the local area." The person who got the grant would have to rewrite the proposal three times and when it finally happened a year later, it would get 25 seconds on the local news and a story in the Sunday paper and the one sculpture that ever got built by 3 art school dropouts and two friendly kids would look like a technically limited imitation of the grant writer's work and they would have called that a success. But if you can keep the asphalt and guns out of the tidelands you'll get more new stuff than you could have imagined and better than you could've asked for without trying.

The King and the Corpse

I know of no better myth-telling than this, and no better myths. You've got Abu Kasem's Slippers, and then Conn-eda and John Golden-Mouth, and four romances from King Arthur that take deeper turns than T.H. White, and the prize: the ancient Hindu Romance of the Goddess, plumbing the involuntary creation. Collected by Heinrich Zimmer, edited by Joseph Campbell. There are few books with such a blend of extravagance and intelligence, and none that come so close to the heart of education.
—SB

The King and the Corpse
(Tales of the Soul's Conquest of Evil)
Heinrich Zimmer and Joseph Campbell
1948; 338 pp.

$4.95 postpaid from:
Princeton University Press
Princeton, NJ 08540
or Whole Earth Household Store

•

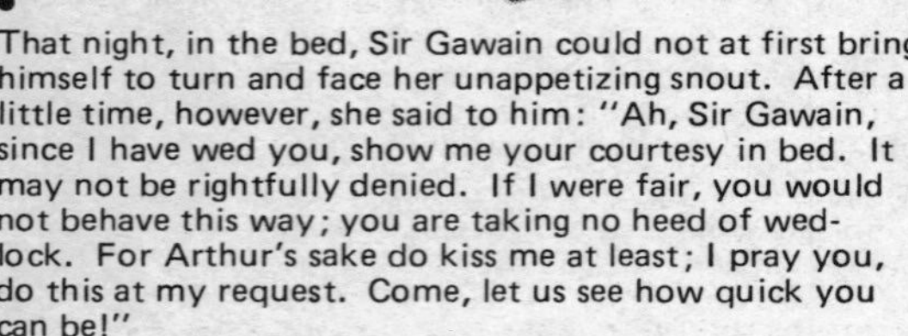

That night, in the bed, Sir Gawain could not at first bring himself to turn and face her unappetizing snout. After a little time, however, she said to him: "Ah, Sir Gawain, since I have wed you, show me your courtesy in bed. It may not be rightfully denied. If I were fair, you would not behave this way; you are taking no heed of wedlock. For Arthur's sake do kiss me at least; I pray you, do this at my request. Come, let us see how quick you can be!"

The knight and loyal nephew of the king collected every bit of his courage and kindness. "I will do more," he said in all gentleness, "I will do more than simply kiss, before God!" And he turned around to her. And he saw her to be the fairest creature that ever he had seen without measure.

She said: "What is your will?"

"Ah, Jesu!" he said, "what are ye?"

"Sir, I am your wife, securely; why are ye so unkind?"

"Ah, lady, I am to blame; I did not know. You are beautiful in my sight — whereas today you were the foulest wight my eye had ever seen! To have you thus, my lady, pleases me well." And he braced her in his arms and began kissing her, and they made great joy.

"Sir," she said, "my beauty will not hold. You may have me thus, but only for half the day. And so it is a question, and you must choose whether you would have me fair at night and foul by day before all men's eyes, or beautiful by day and foul at night."

"Alas," replied Gawain, "the choice is hard. To have you fair at night and no more, that would grieve my heart; but if I should decide to have you fair by day, then at night I should have a scabrous bed. Fain would I choose the best, yet know not what in this world I shall say. My dear lady, let it be as you would desire it; I rest the choice in your hand. My body and goods, my heart and all, is yours to buy and sell; that I avow before God."

"Ah, gramercy, courteous knight!" said the lady. "Mayst thou be blessed above all knights in the world, for now I am released from the enchantment and thou shalt have me fair and bright both night and day."

The Hero With A Thousand Faces

Myths and man's dreamworld have, for the past fifty years or so, been the objects of various alchemical attempts at synthesis. About the time I get convinced that screaming green weenies have some larger context than Madison Avenue, someone else denies the organic connection between them. The hero with a thousand faces is one of those syntheses. It's about the monomyth. Campbell traces his hero right out into the void.
—J.D. Smith

The Hero With A Thousand Faces
Joseph Campbell
1979; 416 pp.

$3.95 postpaid from:
Princeton University Press
Princeton, NJ 08540
or Whole Earth Household Store

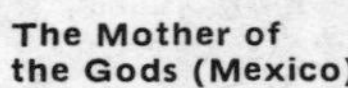

The Mother of the Gods (Mexico)

•

The passage of the mythological hero may be overground, incidentally; fundamentally it is inward — into depths where obscure resistances are overcome, and long lost, forgotten powers are revivified, to be made available for the transfiguration of the world. This deed accomplished, life no longer suffers hopelessly under the terrible mutilations of ubiquitous disaster, battered by time, hideous throughout space; but with its horror visible still, its cries of anguish still tumultuous, it becomes penetrated by an all-suffusing, all-sustaining love, and a knowledge of its own unconquered power. Something of the light that blazes invisible within the abysses of its normally opaque materiality breaks forth, with an increasing uproar. The dreadful mutilations are then seen as shadows, only, of an immanent, imperishable eternity; time yields to glory; and the world sings with the prodigious, angelic, but perhaps finally monotonous, siren music of the spheres. Like happy families, the myths and the worlds redeemed are all alike.

The Teachings of Don Juan
A Separate Reality

Astounding books exploring the methods of a Mexican Indian sorcerer, "Don Juan." Harsh, humorous, told with shocking adroitness, the truths here have been confirmed by others who have worked with native shamans or explored the nether reaches of sundry mystical paths. Unfortunately Castaneda's later books (there are now 5 total), though they are interesting, fictionalize ever farther away from his extraordinary field experience in the mountains of Mexico. The ideas in these two books have entered the American language to stay.
—SB

The Teachings of Don Juan
(A Yaqui Way of Knowledge)
Carlos Castaneda
1968; 276 pp.

$3.25 postpaid

A Separate Reality
(Further Conversations with Don Juan)
Carlos Castaneda
1971; 263 pp.

$3.95 postpaid
both from:
Pocket Books
Attn: Order Department
1230 Avenue of the Americas
New York, NY 10020
or Whole Earth Household Store

•

Once a man has vanquished fear, he is free from it for the rest of his life because instead of fear, he has acquired clarity of mind which erases fear. By then a man knows his desires; he knows how to satisfy those desires. He can anticipate the new steps of learning, and a sharp clarity surrounds everything. The man feels that nothing is concealed.

And thus he has encountered his second enemy: Clarity! That clarity of mind, which is so hard to obtain, dispels fear, but also blinds.

—The Teachings of Don Juan

•

"I say it is useless to waste your life on one path, especially if that path has no heart."

"But how do you know when a path has no heart, Don Juan?"

"Before you embark on it you ask the question Does this path have a heart? If the answer is no, you will know it, and then you must choose another path."

"But how will I know for sure whether a Path has a heart or not?"

"Anybody would know that. The trouble is nobody asks the question and when a man finally realizes that he has taken a path without a heart the path is ready to kill him. At that point very few men can stop to deliberate, and leave the path."

"How should I proceed to ask the question properly, Don Juan?"

"Just ask it."

"I mean, is there a proper method, so I would not lie to myself and believe the answer is yes when it really is no?"

"Why would you lie?"

"Perhaps because at the moment the path is pleasant and enjoyable."

"That is nonsense. A path without a heart is never enjoyable. You have to work hard even to take it. On the other hand, a path with a heart is easy; it does not make you work at liking it."

—The Teachings of Don Juan

The Way of the Shaman

An anthropologist who hangs out with shamans, Michael Harner tells some hairy adventure stories and proceeds to pass on some safe (if not sane) basics on how to enter the Shamanic State of Consciousness and make wholesome use of it.
—SB

The Way of the Shaman
(A Guide to Power and Healing)
Michael Harner
1980; 192 pp.

$9.95 postpaid from:
Harper and Row
Keystone Industrial Park
Scranton, PA 18512
or Whole Earth Household Store

•

Be careful, when you send power from your power animal to help another person, to send the power only to his animal. Do not send it directly to the person himself, because this might cause damage. Let the power safely filter through his own guardian, which is the only power animal that can be of direct help. *Also, avoid sending your own energy to help another person.* You will exhaust yourself and, importantly for the person you wish to help, you will find it hard to continue working. Instead, draw always on your guardian's power. If you do this, you will finish a healing session more energetic than ever, not tired.

Parabola

Underground rivers of juice flow in this new magazine of myth. The major players in the subject play here, with a graphic excitement never seen in academic publications.
—SB

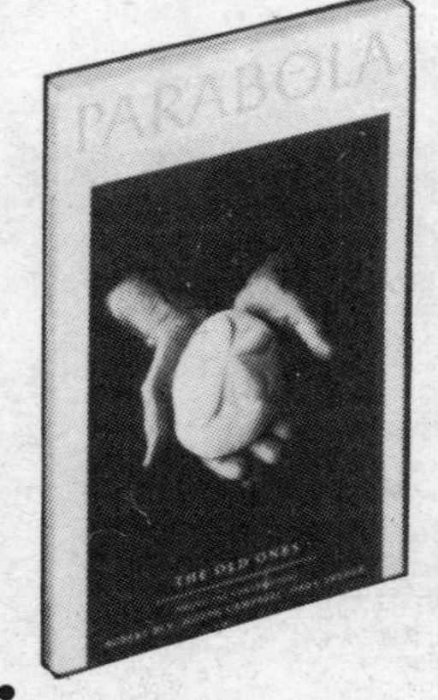

Parabola
(Myth and the Quest for Meaning)
D.M. Dooling, Editor

$14 /year (4 issues)
from:
Society for the Study of Myth and Tradition
G.P.O. Box 165
Brooklyn, NY 11202

→
Stone face
Prayer stone
Infused, active, seeing,
"Dark to the mind,
Radiant to the heart."

•

There are many people on the planet, now, who are not "inhabitants." Far from their home villages; removed from ancestral territories; moved into town from the farm; went to pan gold in California — work on the Pipeline — work for Bechtel in Iran. Actual inhabitants — peasants, paisanos, paysan, peoples of the land, have been sniffed at, laughed at, and overtaxed for centuries by the urban-based ruling elites. The intellectuals haven't the least notion of what kind of sophisticated, attentive, creative intelligence it takes to "grow food." Virtually all the plants in the gardens and the trees in the orchards, the sheep, cows, and goats in the pastures were domesticated in the Neolithic; before "civilization." The differing regions of the world have long had — each — their own precise subsistence pattern developed over millennia by people who had settled in there and learned what particular kinds of plants the ground would "say" at that spot.
—Gary Snyder

Good News Bible

*The **Bible** doesn't say what you think it says no matter what you think. It's older, stranger and longer than will fit into anyone's second hand summaries — and that's all most of us have of it since most editions preserve 16th century book design as well as language and are very hard for modern eyes to read.*

*This edition of the **Bible** is actually easy to read so you can get right to the strangeness of the stories. The things it has that most **Bibles** don't have are a clear typeface, well placed white space, lots of headings to tell you when a new story starts, lots of pictures integrated into the text, readable maps, and an easy-to-use index (done by page number, not chapter and verse).*

The translation itself is in clear conversational English. It was originally done by the American Bible Society for people in other countries who speak English as a second language. But once a few thousand were released in the United States people who saw it started ordering dozens of copies and it is now a perennial best seller, second only to the King James Version.

*It is also cheap and good quality. Everything the American Bible Society does is cheap and good quality. If you or anyone you know buys a **Bible**, the American Bible Society has a better selection at lower prices than any bookstore — King James, Revised Standard, and this translation are available in traditional formats, large print, illustrated, and in various portions, such as just the Psalms or just the New Testament. The Bible Society is one of those rare non-profit groups that passes its savings along to you.*

*If you've ever tried to read the **Bible** cover to cover, be advised it's a bad idea. The **Bible** was written by a lot of different people at a lot of different times, so it should be read more like a magazine than a book. Flip around, see what looks interesting, skip the boring parts. The individual stories are tightly written and short so it really isn't a big deal to read any one of them. And the way the **Good News Bible** is set up makes it easy to tell where one story stops and another begins. (Some good easy short stories to start on are Ruth, Esther, and Jonah.)*

—Anne Herbert

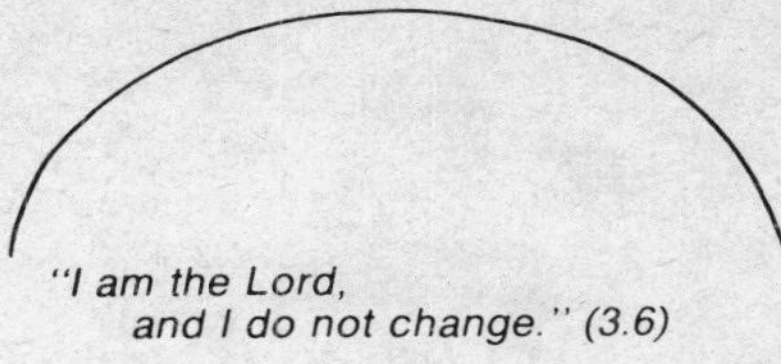

"I am the Lord,
and I do not change." (3.6)

Good News Bible
(Bible in Today's English Version)
American Bible Society
1966, 1976; 408 pp.
$4 postpaid
(hard cover)
$3.50 postpaid
(paperback)

American Bible Society Publications Catalog
free

all from:
American Bible Society
1865 Broadway
New York, NY 10023

•

Elijah and Elisha stopped by the river, and the fifty prophets stood a short distance away. Then Elijah took off his cloak, rolled it up, and struck the water with it; the water divided, and he and Elisha crossed to the other side on dry ground. There, Elijah said to Elisha, "Tell me what you want me to do for you before I am taken away."

"Let me receive the share of your power that will make me your successor," Elisha answered.

"That is a difficult request to grant," Elijah replied. "But you will receive it if you see me as I am being taken away from you; if you don't see me, you won't receive it."

They kept talking as they walked on; then suddenly a chariot of fire pulled by horses of fire came between them, and Elijah was taken up to heaven by a whirlwind. Elisha saw it and cried out to Elijah, "My father, my father! Mighty defender of Israel! You are gone!" And he never saw Elijah again.

Mysticism

The mystical event is to occupy ONE. Every time it happens it is a life enhancer and a history enhancer. Evelyn Underhill wrote this classic to gather and map the full range of Western mystical experience — Greek, Catholic, Protestant — and yours if you care to follow the steps. Each of those ONEs is unique. Each is the same. That seems pat, but this book approximately proves it.

—SB

Mysticism
(A Study in the Nature and Development of Man's Spiritual Consciousness)
Evelyn Underhill
1911, 1961; 519 pp.
$5.95 postpaid from:
E.P. Dutton and Co.
Two Park Avenue
New York, NY 10016
or Whole Earth Household Store

•

Where the philosopher guesses and argues, the mystic lives and looks; and speaks, consequently, the disconcerting language of first-hand experience, not the neat dialectic of the schools. Hence whilst the Absolute of the metaphysicians remains a diagram — impersonal and unattainable — the Absolute of the mystics is lovable, attainable, alive.

•

"All mystics," said Saint-Martin, "speak the same language, for they come from the same country." The deep undying life within us came from that country too: and it recognizes the accents of home, though it cannot always understand what they would say.

•

To go up alone into the mountain and come back as an ambassador to the world, has ever been the method of humanity's best friends.

A Guide for the Perplexed

*E.F. Schumacher, when confronted by a voracious bear, has a talent for reaching quickly down its throat, seizing its tiny tail, and jerking it inside out. He did that to economics in **Small Is Beautiful**. Now he's done it to philosophy in this final book which he regarded far more fondly than his previous work. He was right.* *—SB*

A Guide for the Perplexed
E.F. Schumacher
1977; 147 pp.
$3.95 postpaid from:
Harper and Row
Keystone Industrial Park
Scranton, PA 18512
or Whole Earth Household Store

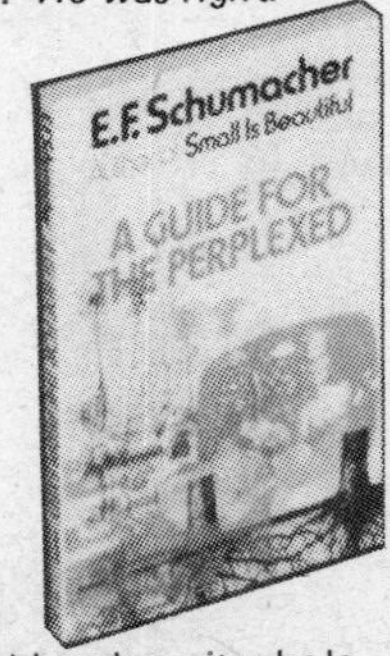

•

Our task is to look at the world and see it whole.

•

The modern experiment to live without religion has failed, and once we have understood this, we know what our "post modern" tasks really are.

A Hidden Wholeness

*No book has convinced me so directly that the life of active contemplation can be utterly wholesome. Here are indisputable photographs by Merton and by John Howard Griffin (remember **Black Like Me**? The white who dyed himself black so he could understand) . . . photographs and some calligraphy by Merton that attest something tough, pointed, and very healthy going on here that I don't understand.* *—SB*

A Hidden Wholeness
Thomas Merton,
John Howard Griffin
1970; 147 pp.
$7.95 postpaid from:
Houghton-Mifflin Co.
Wayside Road
Burlington, MA 01803
or Whole Earth Household Store

•

Merton maintained his monastic discipline in the hermitage. He got up at 3:00 a.m. In his private journals he speaks with great happiness of those hours before dawn. He relished them especially in times of snow or rain or storm, which gave him a deeper sense of isolation. In cold weather, he built up his fire and prepared coffee or strong black tea. He worked, prayed, studied, and especially he allowed himself to be saturated by an awareness of the reality of each moment, listening always for what it had to tell him.

"Think of it," he wrote one rainy night, "all that speech pouring down, selling nothing, judging nobody . . . What a thing it is to sit absolutely alone, in the forest, at night, cherished by this wonderful, unintelligible, perfectly innocent speech, the most comforting speech in the world, the talk that rain makes by itself all over the ridges . . . Nobody started it, nobody is going to stop it. It will talk as long as it wants, this rain. As long as it talks I am going to listen."

Inside Thomas Merton's hermitage ↓

The Way of a Pilgrim

*We do not know the Pilgrim's name. His world seems further removed from the world in which we live than most science fiction. The miracles he recounts seem less strange to us than the ordinary life of Russian villages and monasteries in the late 1850s, the setting of this autobiography. And yet seekers, whatever their path, will recognize both in the Pilgrim's travels and in his search the Way. All the elements are there: the guru (he calls him starets); the koan ("pray without ceasing"); the mantra (the Jesus Prayer, or Prayer of the Heart). Under the impact of Eastern Spirituality many Christians have rediscovered these realities in their own tradition. Salinger's **Franny and Zooey** sent the first big wave of readers to **The Way of a Pilgrim**. The Pilgrim, in turn, advertises on every other page the **Philokalia**. (**Writings from the Philokalia on Prayer of the Heart**, E. Kadloubovsky, translated by G.E. Palmer; 1951, 1962; $13.25, from Fernhill House Ltd., Humanities Press, Atlantic Highland, NJ 07716.) This is the book for anyone who seriously considers following this path. But the Prayer of the Heart is not for dabblers. I started on it before most **Whole Earth** readers were born. And I still have a long way to go. But it draws you. It's a Path with Heart, as Don Juan would say.*

—Brother David Steindl-Rast
Mount Saviour Monastery

The Way of a Pilgrim
(And The Pilgrim Continues His Way)
Translated from the Russian by R.M. French
1974; 180 pp.
$2.50 postpaid from:
Ballantine Books, Inc.
455 Hahn Road
Westminster, MD 21157
or Whole Earth Household Store

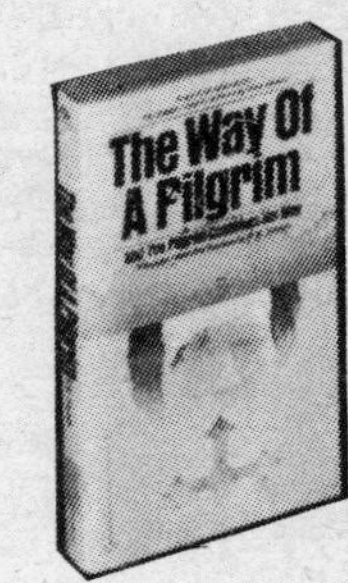

•

He opened the book, found the instruction by St. Simeon the New Theologian, and read: "Sit down alone and in silence. Lower your head, shut your eyes, breathe out gently and imagine yourself looking into your own heart. Carry your mind, *i.e.*, your thoughts from your head to your heart. As you breathe out, say 'Lord Jesus Christ, have mercy on me.' Say it moving your lips gently, or simply say it in your mind. Try to put all other thoughts aside. Be calm, be patient, and repeat the process very frequently."

THE RISING SUN
NEIGHBORHOOD NEWSLETTER

I keep hearing about more good cause organizations that take young people who want to do the right thing and subject them to low pay and intensely vicious office politics until they either start being vicious themselves or quit, swearing to never work for an environmental/political reform/hunger fighting/whatever organization again. It seems to me that strip mining idealism out of the young is as great a sin as strip mining the land and as likely to hurt us all as much in the long run.

Memories, Dreams, Reflections

I think there is no more remarkable autobiography in this century. Dream power and intellectual power collided in Jung's life, merged finally, and carried him pilot-and-passenger on a psychic Gulf Stream, far and strange. He took 20th Century science with him.

The recent editions of this book carry in full the **Seven Sermons to the Dead** *that Bateson reviews below. It was absent from earlier editions, from* **The Collected Works**, *and was published privately and anonymously when it was written (1916) — the rarest feather from a rare bird.* —SB

Memories, Dreams, Reflections
C.G. Jung
1961, 1965; 430 pp.

$3.95 postpaid from:
Vintage Books
455 Hahn Road
Westminster, MD 21157
or Whole Earth Household Store

•

At the beginning of 1944 I broke my foot, and this misadventure was followed by a heart attack. In a state of unconsciousness I experienced deliriums and visions which must have begun when I hung on the edge of death and was being given oxygen and camphor injections. The images were so tremendous that I myself concluded that I was close to death. My nurse afterward told me, "It was as if you were surrounded by a bright glow." That was a phenomenon she had sometimes observed in the dying, she added. I had reached the outermost limit, and do not know whether I was in a dream or an ecstasy. At any rate, extremely strange things began to happen to me.

It seemed to me that I was high up in space. Far below I saw the globe of the earth, bathed in a gloriously blue light. I saw the deep blue seas and the continents. Far below my feet lay Ceylon, and in the distance ahead of me the subcontinent of India. My field of vision did not include the whole earth, but its global shape was plainly distinguishable and its outlines shone with a silvery gleam through that wonderful blue light. In many places the globe seemed colored or spotted dark green like oxidized silver. Far away to the left lay a broad expanse — the reddish-yellow desert of Arabia; it was as though the silver of the earth had there assumed a reddish-gold hue. Then came the Red Sea, and far, far back — as if in the upper left of a map — I could just make out a bit of the Mediterranean. My gaze was directed chiefly toward that. Everything else appeared indistinct. I could also see the snow-covered Himalayas, but in that direction it was foggy or cloudy. I did not look to the right at all. I knew that I was on the point of departing from the earth.

Later I discovered how high in space one would have to be to have so extensive a view — approximately a thousand miles! The sight of the earth from this height was the most glorious thing I had ever seen.

Symbol of the sacred in a ring of flames floating above the world of war and technology. Painted in 1920, it was inspired by a dream Jung had had on 22 January 1914, anticipating the outbreak of war in August 1914.

C.G. Jung: Word and Image

If not nothing, then Jung is surely image. This collection by an old collaborator of his takes his lifelong caterpillar-crawl of thought and gives it colorful flight and new life. Jung's biography is visible, as well as the things he saw that moved him, the archetypal images he recognized, and his own bizarre beautiful paintings, carvings, buildings. He lived with beautiful care. The book is bright and clear and not the slightest bit slick. —SB

C.G. Jung: Word and Image
Aniela Jaffé, Editor
1979; 238 pp.

$25 postpaid from:
Princeton University Press
Princeton, NJ 08540
or Whole Earth Household Store

The Denial of Death

Psychoanalysis is not such a big favor, it says here. Successful analysis takes away your difficult-to-deal-with neurotic fears of fathers and elevators and mothers and crowds and high places and sex. And then you have to face the realistic and impossible-to-deal-with fear of death. Becker says that we will always be neurotic to some extent because neuroses are a necessary way of keeping ourselves from remembering how terrible life is, and how short. Most people can't stand facing the horrible truth, so they settle for an uncomfortable but bearable lie.

Creative people see more truth than most in Becker's view, and you notice that they go crazy a lot.

A good book to shake you up and remind you that not all ills are curable, some of the worst ones come with the human condition. (Becker's starting point is Freud. He disagrees with him and goes beyond him on many points but the book is probably Freudian enough to irritate people who totally reject Freud on feminist or general principles. I think it's worth it; some people might not.) —Anne Herbert

$2.95 postpaid from:
Macmillan
Publishing Company
Order Department
Front and Brown Streets
Riverside, NJ 08075
or Whole Earth Household Store

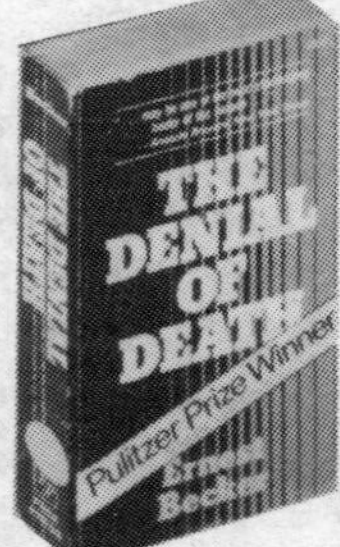

•

By pushing the problem of man to its limits, schizophrenia also reveals the nature of creativity. If you are physically unprogrammed in the culture *causa-sui* project, then you have to invent your own: you don't vibrate to anyone else's tune. You see that the fabrications of those around you are a lie, a denial of truth — a truth that usually takes the form of showing the terror of the human condition more fully than most men experience it. The creative person becomes, then, in art, literature, and religion the mediator of natural terror and the indicator of a new way to triumph over it. He reveals the darkness and the dread of the human condition and fabricates a new symbolic transcendence over it. This has been the function of the creative deviant from the shamans through Shakespeare.

C.G. Jung's Septem Sermones Ad Mortuos

by Gregory Bateson

This tiny book is for me the greatest achievement of Jung's life — the turning point in a long battle. He clearly recognizes in **Memories, Dreams, Reflections** that the days (in 1916) in which it was written were the beginning of all his later insights.

At that time he was coming out of a long period of slow recovery from the influence of Freud and from the break with Freud. It was the moment for a new (or return to a very old) natural history of Man-God-Cosmos.

The book is difficult to read. It is (of course) a sort of poetry, and therefore almost impossible to be reviewed and analysed in prose. And Jung's views clearly changed as he wrote, even in the three or four days of the writing. He was in a state of *transition*.

Man is a gateway, through which from the outer world of gods, daemons, and souls ye [the Dead] shall pass into the inner world; out of the greater into the smaller world. Small and transitory is man . . . At immeasurable distance standeth one single Star in the zenith.

The book then both *is* a progress from macrocosm to microcosm and is a description of the landscape at various stages of that progress.

It is not clear (does not matter) who is the novice and who the initiator in this strange catechism. Not only Jung but also the Dead are in transition. They came "back from Jerusalem, where they found not what they sought."

Excerpt from Jung's Septem Sermones ad Mortuos **(Seven Sermons to the Dead)** →

SERMO I

THE dead came back from Jerusalem, where they found not what they sought. They prayed me let them in and besought my word, and thus I began my teaching.

Harken: I begin with nothingness. Nothingness is the same as fullness. In infinity full is no better than empty. Nothingness is both empty and full. As well might ye say anything else of nothingness, as for instance, white is it, or black, or again, it is not, or it is. A thing that is infinite and eternal hath no qualities, since it hath all qualities.

This nothingness or fullness we name the PLEROMA. Therein both thinking and being cease, since the eternal and infinite possess no qualities. In it no being is, for he then would be distinct from the pleroma, and would possess qualities which would distinguish him as something distinct from the pleroma.

In the pleroma there is nothing and everything. It is quite fruitless to think about the pleroma, for this would mean self-dissolution.

CREATURA is not in the pleroma, but in itself. The pleroma is both beginning and end of created beings. It pervadeth them, as the light of the sun

From his state of transition, Jung sees three concepts to which he gives the Gnostic names: Pleroma, Creatura and Abraxas. There is also — man.

Abraxas is approximately, Shiva, the ultimate Creator-Destroyer. The most terrible and most beautiful of all the gods that man contains within his microcosmic self and that in turn is contained in the macrocosm. Within Abraxas, the more familiar figures (Helios, the Sun; and the Devil, darkness) are subsumed. But it is Abraxas that gets the poetry.

It is splendid as a lion in the instant he striketh down his victim.

It is beautiful as a day in Spring.

. . . .

To look upon it, is blindness.

To know it, is sickness.

To worship it, is death.

To fear it, is wisdom.

To resist it not, is redemption.

All this is within *creatura*, the realm where differences, distinctions, and ideas hold sway. The ground out of which creatura looms as figure (in the language of Gestalt theory) is *pleroma* — the totally unconceived and unstructured realm about which nothing can be said or thought because to say anything is to create distinction. Call it "void" or "fullness," it is still older and deeper than that first distinction by which creatura comes into recognition and therefore being.

The book is exasperating, profound and beautiful. ■

Altered States of Consciousness

Still the best anthology of recent explorations of internal terra incognita — Here Be Dragons, kiddo — dreams, drugs, hypnagogy, meditation. I complained to Mike Harner (shaman anthropologist, p. 590) recently that I felt like I hadn't had any really strong ideas in recent years. "Hm," says Harner. "How long has it been since you had any strong medicine?" "Over ten years . . ." I began. I don't remember the rest of what I said or he said. I remember his laughter. —SB

Altered States of Consciousness
(A Book of Readings)
Charles Tart, Editor
1969; 575 pp.

$5.95 postpaid from:
Doubleday and Company
501 Franklin Avenue
Garden City, NY 11530
or Whole Earth Household Store

•

When I have been flying in my dreams for two or three nights, then I know that a lucid dream is at hand. And the lucid dream itself is often initiated and accompanied all the time by the sensation of flying. Sometimes I feel myself floating swiftly through wide spaces; once I flew backwards, and once, dreaming that I was inside a cathedral, I flew upwards, with the immense building and all in it, at great speed.

Mount Analogue

The most compelling mystical journey in print. The more so because it is unfinished, interrupted in the middle of a sentence by the author's death. The story is of the theoretical proof of the existence of the impossibly difficult, seldom-glimpsed mystical mountain looming delicately above and beyond familiar ranges, the gathering of the expedition team, the finding, the preparation, the trek into and above the lower slopes. I can think of no better book to end with a comma. —SB

Mount Analogue
(A Novel of Symbolically Authentic Non-Euclidean Adventures in Mountain Climbing)
René Daumal
1952, 1960; 120 pp.
$2.50 postpaid from:
Penguin Books
299 Murray Hill Parkway
East Rutherford,
NJ 07073
or Whole Earth Household Store

•

"Pierre Sogol, Professor of Mountaineering. Lessons Thursday and Sunday, from 7 to 11 A.M. Means of access: Go out of the window, take a left turn, scale a chimney onto the cornice, climb a crumbling schist slope, follow the ridge from north to south, avoiding several gendarmes, and enter by the skylight on the east slope."

I willingly submitted to these fantasies, even though the stairs went on up to the sixth floor. The "turn" was a narrow ledge along the wall, the "chimney" a dark recess that needed only to be closed by the construction of an adjoining building to be called a court, the "schist slope" a dilapidated slate roof, and the "faults" some mitered and peaked chimneys. I entered through the skylight and found myself face to face with the man himself. Fairly tall, lean, and vigorous, with a heavy black moustache and wavy hair, he had the tranquility of a caged panther biding his time.

The Once and Future King

*One of the most popular story books around (***Camelot***, good play, so-so movie), this four-volumes-in-one tragedy of King Arthur is more about learning than any other fiction I can think of. Young Arthur learns the ways of the wide world by being magicked into the personae of various animals by Merlyn — a fish, a hawk, an ant, and grandest of all, a migrating goose. "Where did T.H. White get that?" Gregory Bateson kept asking, certain that it was borrowed from some tribe or other. Best of all, the learning doesn't stop with being crowned or being married, as most stories conveniently do. The hard lessons of full maturity, even of civilization itself growing up, are the simultaneous working and the burden of the tragedy.*

Twice in the reading of **The Once and Future King***, end of the first book and end of the fourth, I have dripped salt tears and been unable to go on reading aloud. No other book has managed that.* —SB

•

There is found here, rarely on the lower slopes and more frequently as one ascends, a clear and extremely hard stone, spherical and of variable size. It is a true crystal and — an extraordinary instance entirely unknown elsewhere on this planet — a curved crystal. In the French spoken in Port o' Monkeys, this stone is called *peradam*. Ivan Lapse is still puzzled by the formation and the root meaning of the word. It may mean, as he sees it, "harder than diamond," as is very much the case, or else "father of diamond." And some say that diamond is in reality the product of the disintegration of peradam by a sort of squaring of the circle or, more exactly, cubing of the sphere. Or else the word may mean "Adam's stone" and have had some secret and profound complicity with the original nature of man. This stone is so perfectly transparent and its index of refraction so close to that of air in spite of the crystal's great density that the inexperienced eye barely perceives it. But to any person who seeks it with sincerity and out of true need it reveals itself by a brilliant sparkle like that of a dewdrop. Peradam is the only substance, the only material thing, whose value is recognized by the guides of Mount Analogue. Therefore it remains the basis and standard of all currency, like gold in many countries.

The Once and Future King
T.H. White
1940; 639 pp.
$2.95 postpaid from:
Berkeley Publishing Company
390 Murray Hill Parkway
East Rutherford,
NJ 07073
or Whole Earth Household Store

•

"Come, sword," he said. "I must cry your mercy and take you for a better cause.

"This is extraordinary," said the Wart. "I feel strange when I have hold of this sword, and I notice everything much more clearly. Look at the beautiful gargoyles of the church, and of the monastery which it belongs to. See how splendidly all the famous banners in the aisle are waving. How nobly that yew holds up the red flakes of its timbers to worship God. How clean the snow is. I can smell something like fetherfew and sweet briar — and is it music that I hear?"

It was music, whether of pan-pipes or of recorders, and the light in the churchyard was so clear, without being dazzling, that one could have picked a pin out twenty yards away.

"There is something in this place," said the Wart. "There are people. Oh, people, what do you want?"

Nobody answered him, but the music was loud and the light beautiful.

"People," cried the Wart, "I must take this sword. It is not for me, but for Kay. I will bring it back."

There was still no answer, and Wart turned back to the anvil. He saw the golden letters, which he did not read, and the jewels on the pommel, flashing in the lovely light.

"Come, sword," said the Wart.

The I Ching

Gregory Bateson remarked once to his secretary, Judy Van Slooten, "I am going to build a church some day. It will have a holy of holies and a holy of holies of holies, and in that ultimate box will be a random number table." Check Bateson's **Mind and Nature** *(reviewed on p. 28). All originality, he says, whether in evolution or in human learning, comes from "raids on the random."*

The ancient Chinese Taoists who made this oracle may have had a similar idea, or they may have stumbled on it or co-evolved into it, but obviously it served them. And it serves us. It profoundly served the generation that emitted the original **Whole Earth Catalog***. Ending with this review is a piece of homage to that time and those people, both passing rapidly, both remembered too easily for superficial and dismissable things rather than for the real risks taken with real clarity in the face of overwhelming opposition.*

Everyone from then has **I Ching** *stories. Like the hippie who hid in his room for months, finally worked up the courage to go out, and asked the* **Ching** *how to proceed. "Retreat," said the* **Ching***. He threw it out the window.*

Clink clink go the tossed pennies. How about a statement for the end of **The Next Whole Earth Catalog***, ancient random number table . . . Hm, 8 (Holding Together) changing in the fourth place to 45 (Gathering Together).* —SB

The I Ching
(Or Book of Changes)
Richard Wilhelm and Cary F. Baynes, Translators
1950; 740 pp.
$12.50 postpaid from:
Princeton University Press
Princeton, NJ 08540
or Whole Earth Household Store

8. *Pi / Holding Together* [*Union*]

☵ *above* K'AN THE ABYSMAL, WATER
☷ *below* K'UN THE RECEPTIVE, EARTH

The waters on the surface of the earth flow together wherever they can, as for example in the ocean, where all the rivers come together. Symbolically this connotes holding together and the laws that regulate it. The same idea is suggested by the fact that all the lines of the hexagram except the fifth, the place of the ruler, are yielding. The yielding lines hold together because they are influenced by a man of strong will in the leading position, a man who is their center of union. Moreover, this strong and guiding personality in turn holds together with the others, finding in them the complement of his own nature.

THE JUDGMENT

HOLDING TOGETHER brings good fortune.
Inquire of the oracle once again
Whether you possess sublimity, constancy, and perseverance;
Then there is no blame.
Those who are uncertain gradually join.
Whoever comes too late
Meets with misfortune.

45. *Ts'ui / Gathering Together* [*Massing*]

☱ *above* TUI THE JOYOUS, LAKE
☷ *below* K'UN THE RECEPTIVE, EARTH

This hexagram is related in form and meaning to Pi, HOLDING TOGETHER (8). In the latter, water is over the earth; here a lake is over the earth. But since the lake is a place where water collects, the idea of gathering together is even more strongly expressed here than in the other hexagram. The same become so integrated in the spiritual life of the family that it cannot be dispersed or dissolved.

THE JUDGMENT

GATHERING TOGETHER. Success.
The king approaches his temple.
It furthers one to see the great man.
This brings success. Perseverance furthers.
To bring great offerings creates good fortune.
It furthers one to undertake something.

THE RISING SUN
NEIGHBORHOOD NEWSLETTER

When we get there we'll be able to look at the sun all day and never squint. The sun will be no dimmer but we'll be shining back.

IGH RISK, HIGH GAIN.

Point, the nonprofit foundation that publishes **CoEvolution, Whole Earth Catalog,** *and sundry other tools, is going over $80,000 in debt to get out the* **Next Catalog**. *From an anonymous angel came one $40,000 loan; the other came from me. No bank we could find would loan us any money whatever. (I had naively thought that's what banks are for.)*

As scrutiny of the figures below reveals, the first 100,000 **Next Catalogs** *sold won't quite make back our expenses. If the first printing doesn't sell out, we're in trouble. If we go into further printings, and they sell, we make $2.17 per book, assuming print costs stay the same, ho ho. (An additional 10,000 copies are going to Book-of-the-Month Club, with no significant income to us. Prior* **CoEvolution** *subscribers got 30,000 copies as their Fall 1980 issue, at some financial loss to us.) The cost of printing the books — $400,100 for the first 140,000 copies — is being fronted by Random House, bless them.*

If our luck holds (we got through production without a fire or earthquake, either of which could have demolished us permanently), a few hundred thousand copies will sell, and we'll get a few hundred thousand dollars to improve our magazine and other services, including new editions of **The Next Whole Earth Catalog**.

—SB

Next Whole Earth Catalog Expenses

PRODUCTION

*Salaries**	*$150,000*
Contributors	*19,000*
Rising Sun	*2,000*
Office supplies	*6,000*
Research (books & magazines)	*3,500*
Agent fee	*5,000*
Interest on loans	*5,500*
Rent	*2,000*
Production materials — film, stats, type, etc.	*22,500*
Phone	*6,500*
Index	*4,000*
Negatives	*4,000*
Total	*$230,000*

** Everyone gets $8.25/hour except old timers Andrea Sharp and Evelyn Eldridge-Diaz, who get $8.75/hour, and the editor, who gets a flat $20,000 a year (only it's withheld for 1980 until our ship comes in maybe in 1981). Hm, that's about 17,500 hours we put in.*

PRINTING *(first printing)*

100,000 copies for sale by Random House	*$287,000*
30,000 copies for 1980 **CoEvolution** *subscribers*	*86,100*
10,000 copies for Book-of-the-Month Club	*27,000*
Total	*$400,100*

Whole Earth Catalog Income

(What happens to your $12.50, thank you)

$ 6.00 to bookstore and jobbers
1.46 to Random House
2.87 to the printers
2.17 to us, Point

$12.50

On each 100,000 copies sold, Point gets

$217,000.

Plus whatever secondary business comes our way as **CoEvolution** *subscriptions, map and book orders, etc.*

Tree budget

Here's an estimate of the number of trees needed to produce **The Next Whole Earth Catalog**. *We're assuming a first printing of 140,000 copies, each weighing about 5½ lbs. First, we calculate the weight in paper: (140,000 copies) X (5.5 lbs.) = 770,000 lbs of paper. We can grossly estimate that an average pulpwood tree grown on a forest farm weighs about 250 lbs., and that, after processing, yields 125 lbs. of paper. This means the new edition of the catalog requires*

$$\frac{770{,}000 \text{ lbs.}}{125 \text{ lb./tree}} = 6{,}160 \text{ trees.}$$

Sounds like a lot of trees. But, let's change trees into forest. Most pulpwood trees are planted on anywhere from 6- to 10-foot centers. We'll be conservative and make the calculations easier by using 10-foot centers or 100 square feet per tree.

So, the 6,160 trees will occupy 616,000 square feet of land (6,160 X 100 sq. ft.). This all makes better sense in acres. An acre is roughly 44,000 square feet. The total acreage of watershed needed to grow the trees to produce the paper for the new catalog is 14 acres.

Supposedly well over 140,000 people will read a sold-out first printing of the **Next Catalog**. *If only 5% — 7,000 people — are inspired by our tree sermons to plant one tree each, there will be net tree gain. Otherwise, loss.*

Long live tree flesh and responsible tree people.

—Peter Warshall and Stewart Brand

Ordering books from the Whole Earth Household Store

Any book in this **Catalog** *that has underneath the access:*

or Whole Earth
Household Store

may be ordered by mail from:

Whole Earth Household Store
Building D, Fort Mason Center
San Francisco, CA 94123

(Do not order such books from **CoEvolution Quarterly**; *it leads to serious confusion.)*

Please follow these instructions:

1. *Print name and address to which you want the order shipped.*
2. *Print in the titles and quantities of the books you want, their* **Catalog** *page numbers and prices.*
3. *Total the prices of the books you are ordering.*
4. *For delivery in California add 6% tax (6½% for BART counties).*
5. *Add $2 to each order for packaging and delivery.*
6. *For rush orders UPS in the United States, add 40¢ for each book.*
7. *For foreign orders add 50¢ postage per book for each book over five. We also recommend International Registry Insurance, which costs an additional $3 per order.*
8. *Enclose payment in full with check or money order. VISA/Mastercharge customers print name from card, account no., interbank no., expiration date, and sign your name.*

**You can order by telephone using your VISA or Mastercharge. Dial direct (415) 441-7250 between 10:00 am and 4:30 pm Pacific Time.*

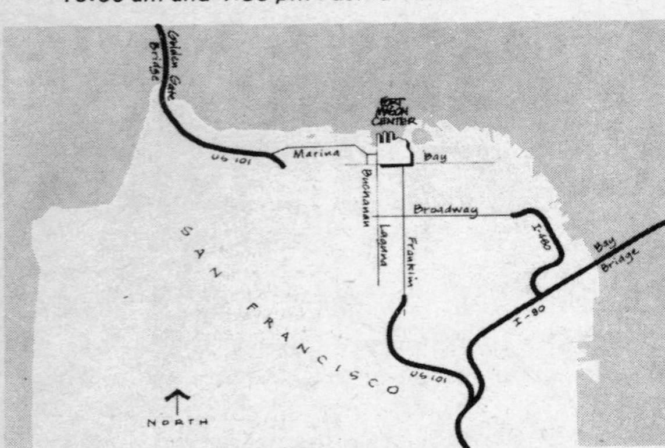

Ordering CoEvolution, additional Next Whole Earth Catalogs, and other items from CoEvolution Quarterly

Please note that we carry only the items listed here. Everything else should be ordered from the original suppliers or, if so indicated, from the Whole Earth Household Store.

CoEvolution Quarterly, *in business since 1973, is the on-going* **Whole Earth Catalog**. *Each issue has 144 pages, no ads, numerous book, periodical, catalog, and product reviews, and articles of "conceptual news." Our mailing address is:*

CoEvolution Quarterly
P.O. Box 428
Sausalito, CA 94966

$14	*One year (4 issues)* **CoEvolution Quarterly** *(foreign $16) (First class U.S. and Canada, add $5 per year. Air mail, for each year add: Mexico and Central America $6; South America $9; Europe $9; all others $12.)*
$12.50	**The Next Whole Earth Catalog**
$3.50	**World Biogeographical Provinces Map** *(See inside front cover.)*
$5	**One Million Galaxies Map** *(See inside back cover.) Sent UPS in continental U.S. Elsewhere $7.50.*
$4.50	**Space Colonies** *(Reviewed on p. 16.)*
$2	**Two Cybernetic Frontiers** *(Reviewed on p. 537.)*

$3	*Ten* **Whole Earth** *photo color postcards* ↑
$6	⟵ **CoEvolution T-shirt** *(Indicate: Extra Small, Small, Medium, Large, Extra Large.)*

All prices postpaid. Please send payment with order; we don't bill. Allow 5 - 6 weeks for delivery.

MIMI ABRAMS

To elaborate a bit on the credits on page 2, the index is illustrated with a few of the people and activities that made the book come together. All there is space for is a minute sampling. Normally we do one 144-page CoEvolution Quarterly every three months. In the summer of '80 the same people (plus help) and the same apparatus turned out the equivalent of 9½ CoEvolutions in five months. (One of the 9½ was a regular issue of the magazine.)

A major administrative shift that made this impossibility possible was that staff simply took over most of my boss functions. Scheduling, hiring and firing with compassionate ruthlessness, allocation and constant reallocation of duties, inspiring speeches, answering mail — all took place right at the point and time of need. Under sufficient duress sufficient talent makes anarchism work just fine. So I was freed to work strictly on coordinating the judgment in the book and trying to make the Catalog unified enough to meet the unity of the reader.

In this picture I'm manipulating our principal editorial tool, 3 x 5 cards which portray all the significant attributes of each Catalog item. Eliminating, grouping, and sequencing the groups of cards yields the rough page-edited spreading of the right amount of butter on the right amount of bread. —SB

INDEX

by Betty Berenson

PHOTOGRAPHS BY MIMI ABRAMS *et al.*

A

B

THE RISING SUN
NEIGHBORHOOD NEWSLETTER

What if they find out that sleeping causes old age and death and if you never go to sleep you can be schizophrenic and live forever?

—Kathleen

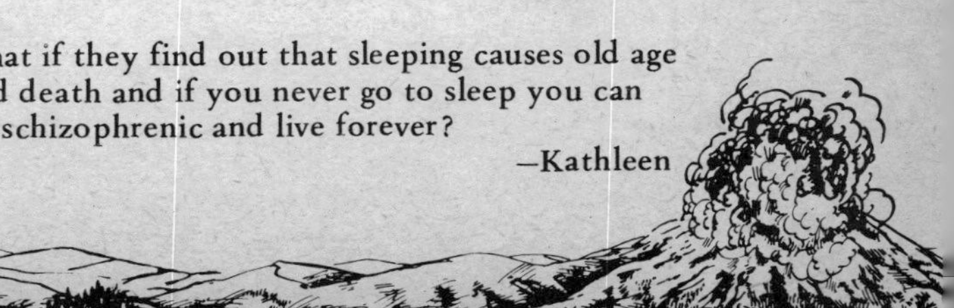

Art Kleiner and Mimi Abrams of research. Trying to nail down publishing information during a recession is like trying to take a particular ocean wave during a Force 8 gale and tack it to the wall. The Catalog that Art and Mimi and the others researched was twice or three times as large as what you're reading. The accurate information and experienced judgment they assembled is what made the winnowing possible. If tasks are monumental, theirs was a Statue of Liberty.

MIMI ABR

C

DONALD RYAN

MIMI ABRAMS

David Theis spent weeks calling potential review subjects and asking them to send their material today please, by express mail if possible. Through all possible responses from "You guys are great," through "I got so much frivolous response to my mention in the last Catalog that it almost put me out of business," to "What in the world is the Whole Earth Catalog?" he was unfailingly cheerful and, luckily, convincing.

D

THE RISING SUN
NEIGHBORHOOD NEWSLETTER

Another thing being a preachers kid taught me besides that somebody has to make the decisions is the truth about folding chairs which is that

1. God did not create this particular room in a state appropriate for this particular meeting. Someone had to set up the folding chairs.
2. God has not yet created a single person who is seized by sudden wild impulses to set up a few folding chairs, so whoever set up the folding chairs would rather be doing something else.
3. One fourth of all chairs unfolded at this particular church are unfolded by you.
4. No one thinks about the person who set up the folding chairs except the person who set up the folding chairs or someone who has set up folding chairs in their time.

E

Not your typical sensitive artist, Anne Herbert, author of The Rising Sun Neighborhood Newsletter, took on the most hard-nosed position of all — production editor, the multi-dimensional traffic light who moment by moment turns melee into flow. Her principle means of keeping everyone surpassing themselves was with 608 variations on, "You, __________, are doing an incredible job!" As with everyone else putting in 60 - 70 hours every week, the absence of private or social life led to sublimation-by-oddness while at work.

MIMI ABRAMS

F

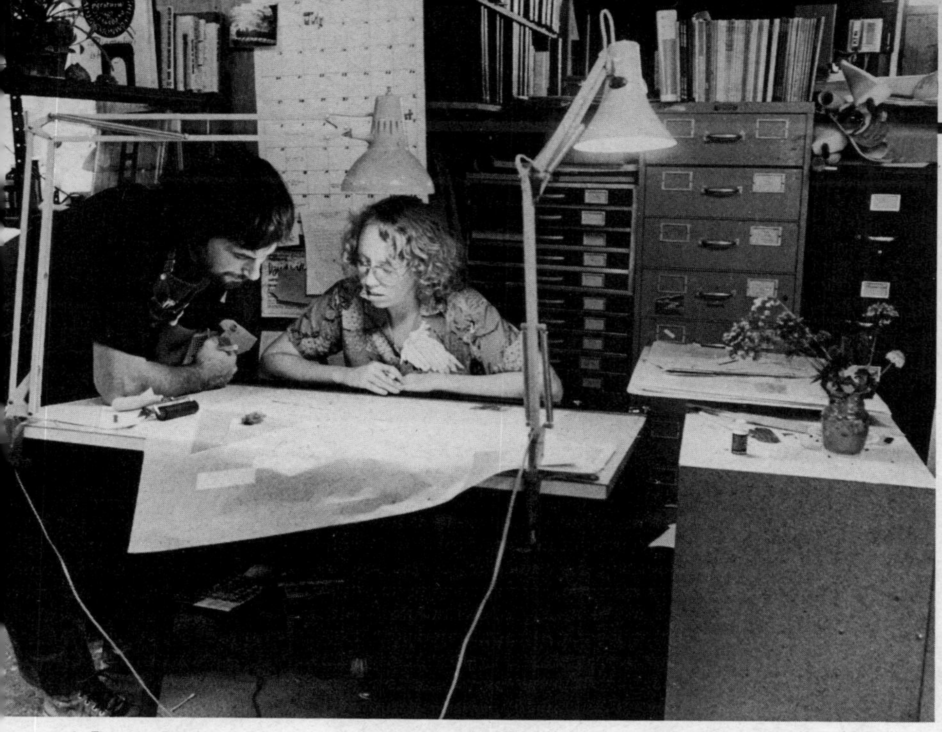

David Wills and Kathleen O'Neill are responsible for the Catalog having the visual sense and snap it does — qualities that most designers accomplish with adroit use of the white space on each page. David and Kathleen were given no white space at all. They are embodiments of grace under pressure.

G

THE RISING SUN
NEIGHBORHOOD NEWSLETTER

Carol Weber recently completed 18 years of schooling. She reports, "School teaches you to say things someone will agree with. Graduate school teaches you to say things someone has already agreed with."

H

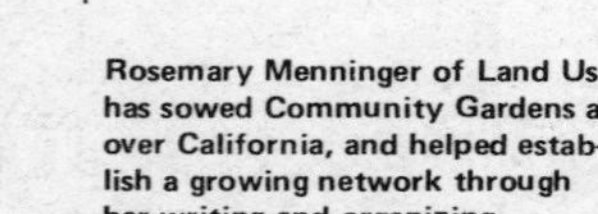

Rosemary Menninger of Land Use has sowed Community Gardens all over California, and helped establish a growing network through her writing and organizing.

Richard Nilsen of Land Use put in his long hours in April and May, before he departed his winter carpenter life in the Bay Area for his summer farmer life in Colorado.

MIMI ABRAMS

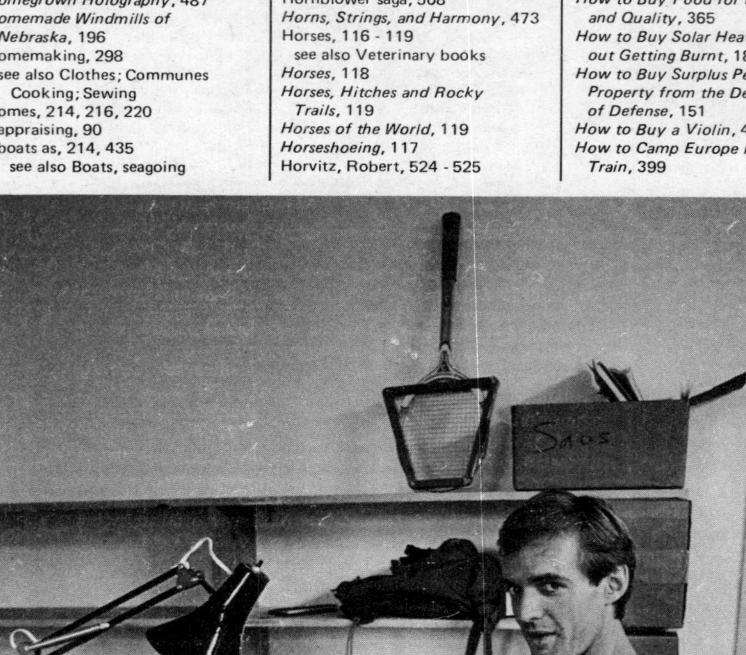

MIMI ABRAMS

I

J

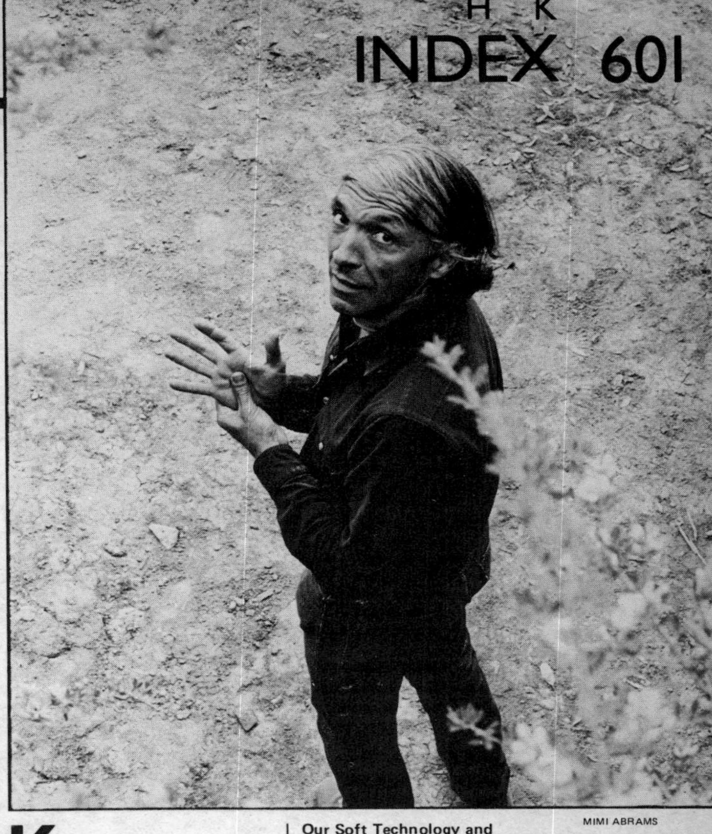

MIMI ABRAMS

Our Soft Technology and Nomadics editor since 1970, J. Baldwin is almost solely responsible for the authority we've acquired in those departments. His hands and head are quite a bit larger than most humans'.

K

MIMI ABRAMS

Who was minding the CoEvolution Quarterly store while most of the staff went Catalog crazy? Stephanie Mills, CQ's assistant editor, kept up with the mail, sent lots of "We'll get back to you in September" notes and generally kept the world outside at bay so the rest of us could concentrate on our internal crises. All this while doing superbly nit-picky proofing of the Catalog and coordinating the enormous task of proofreading the index as quickly as possible.

THE RISING SUN
NEIGHBORHOOD NEWSLETTER

I like what happens when people from different neighborhoods get together — Kara Adanalian and Angela Gennino compare Italian mothers in New York with Armenian mothers in Fresno, Evelyn Eldridge-Diaz tells stories about her father milling lumber in Montana and her husband growing up in El Paso, and we can all argue about the best way to wash dishes — sponge, rag or brush, standing or running water — based on a deep belief in the way our parents did it. But it's not just different pasts that make our neighborhoods different — even people standing in the same spot watching the same sunrise are in different neighborhoods — one mostly sees the clouds, another mostly hears the birds and a third is assessing land values in the gathering light. But if we talk and listen about each others' neighborhoods kindly, we will soon create another neighborhood — the one made of the noticing we have shared.

Isabella Kirkland, artist and former CQ subscription worker, came out of retirement to help with Catalog research.

DAVID WILLS

MIMI ABRA

Typesetter Evelyn Eldridge-Diaz from Montana is my idea of a pioneer woman. She types so fast she can destroy a machine that isn't tuned high enough. Not only does she have a remarkably low output of typos — typographical errors — she's the final finest filter for writer's "thinkos" — thought error. All while being 1 - 5 months pregnant.

MIMI ABRAMS

The biggest break of the day was lunch when everybody got to eat great food made by our many resident cooks. All the people in these pictures helped cook lunch pretty regularly to the benefit of those who only ate. Left to right above are Evelyn the typesetter, John Prestianni who did careful pasteup, Annette La Bette, leaning in the door, who did CQ mailing and shelved the books from the Catalog (she also manages the New Wave band The Contractions) and Stephanie Mills, CQ assistant editor and gourmet cook.

MIMI ABRAMS

Kara Adanalian, one of the two extra typesetters who saved the project. Both she and Dianna Rolfe were hired being told they would work 20 hours a week and were soon working forty and more at some strange hours — Dianna cheerfully worked from 5 p.m. to 1 a.m. for months. Kara and Angela Gennino, both in their early 20s became instant friends and brought an exuberance to lunch making and everything they did. In this picture, Kara is getting ready to have her picture taken for the WD 40 review on page 132.

MIMI ABRAMS

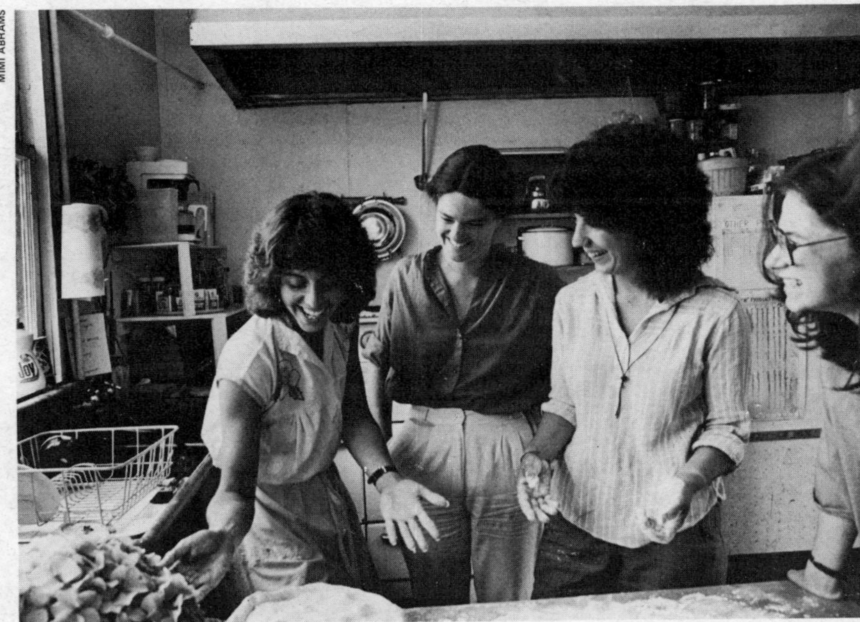

Kara Adanalian teaches Lorrie Gallagher, Angela Gennino and Nancy Dunn to make wonderful pies like hers. Kara did typesetting, Lorrie took care of the CQ subscription mail, Angela did proofreading, book shelving and whatever else was needed, and Nancy did proof reading and created the cross references as the book was made.

N

O

THE RISING SUN
NEIGHBORHOOD NEWSLETTER

Compare and contrast People and Man: The History of Man, The History of People. Man's Search for Meaning. People's Search for Meaning. Man Discovers the Wheel. People Discover the Wheel. The trouble with Man is not just that he's a man but that there's only one of him. One tall, jut-jawed, clear-eyed, well-hung male striding purposefully through the ages toward some goal both logical and grand. The History of People sounds casual and messy and it was.

P

Two games of volleyball a day help break whatever the tensions of the day are. We used to play at lunch; during the Catalog we played around 6 p.m. so the people who were working half the night could wake up a bit. Here Ben Campbell, who stayed up many nights ordering and organizing books for the Catalog, gets ready to serve.

Q

R

Ethelwyn Steese, long-time Sausalito resident, showed up almost every day to watch us play volleyball. It's nice to have an audience. SUSAN CRUTCHF

British punk-rocker Jonathan Evelegh (he manages bands these days) turned out to be a shockingly meticulous proofreader, rivalling Nancy Dunn and Stephanie Mills. As go-between with the various printers, he got to spend three weeks of his vacation in Hammond, Indiana, overseeing the printing of the Catalog. "Second prize," commented Rob Cowley, "four weeks in Hammond, Indiana."

S

SUSAN CRUTCHFIELD

A strong back line — Stephanie Mills, Kathleen O'Neill and Dick Fugett

THE RISING SUN
NEIGHBORHOOD NEWSLETTER

My village is a proud place
Such as it is.
We are at our best when dancing.
—Indian poem

The Catalog production was done on the Sausalito waterfront where there are interesting things all around. For example, Peter Bird launching his boat for his row to Australia (see the Rising Sun on pages 527 - 533 for more on that.)

The Butterfly has been around for years growing all the time with new additions of artfully used scrap.

This boat was built in about a week at the beginning of the summer out of scrap lumber and polyethylene.

This summer the developer who's trying to bring the spirit of condominiums to the waterfront destroyed the old ferry boat San Rafael and the paddle wheel is all that's left. But the developer isn't the only one moving in. This pyramid boat, at right, was built this summer as the Catalog was made.

T

MIMI ABRAMS

During the entire Catalog production summer the Sausalito waterfront community around us was under assault by developers with their bulldozers, tow trucks, security guards (screams in the night as they administered beatings), and cops. After several historic buildings were demolished with people in them during a dawn bulldozer attack, the Sausalito City Council and Mayor found themselves facing a counterassault by the people who elected them. The low-cost creative habitat of the Sausalito waterfront is what makes numerous activities such as this Catalog possible. If you want ducks, you gotta preserve wetlands.

THE RISING SUN
NEIGHBORHOOD NEWSLETTER

My neighborhood in this newsletter is partly made up and partly real (or what seems real to me.) Many of the people whose names recur are in the masthead of this book, so you can find their last names and faces if you'd like. (Some of the tricky parts of doing that reality check are that there are three Davids — Wills who talks about England and drawing and Burnor who talks about Golden Gate Park and acid trips and Theis who talks about making phone calls; that Kathy and Kathleen are the same person because K. O'Neill decided to change her name slightly; and the Susans are three or four different people — my sister and Susan Crutchfield who worked on the *Catalog* and a couple of my friends.)

The neighborhood that has been happening in the drawing underneath these words was created by Kathleen O'Neill of Mifflin Street in Madison and David Wills of Stonehenge Road in Amesbury. It includes a cottage in Wales, the Sausalito waterfront, some good places around San Francisco, an interesting mountain in Washington and a friendly pigeon.

—*Anne Herbert*

Dick Fugett has articles in the Catalog about aviation, yoga and beekeeping (pp. 458, 587, and 108) which is typical of his diverse knowledge. He does subscription work at the CQ and answers all the complaint mail, runs a small but beautiful farm in Sonoma County and does serious meditation. With him is his faithful companion and office mascot, DB.

one million galaxies

This map shows how the galaxies are distributed in our part of the universe – the local one-billion-light-year neighborhood.*

They are the one million brightest galaxies** visible by telescope from Earth's northern hemisphere and the northern hemisphere of our own Milky Way galaxy. Only galaxies are indicated here. Among the nearest is NGC 2403 – 6,000,000 light years away. The farthest are in the Serpens Virgo cloud (made up of ten galaxy clusters) – 1,000,000,000 light years away. Local debris such as Sun, Moon, planets, asteroids, and the 100,000,000,000 other stars of our galaxy are left out of the map.

The circle of the map shows a different perspective from what we are used to. It is the northern hemisphere *of our galaxy*. The rim of the circle is looking along the thick of our galaxy – not many other galaxies are visible through our dust. The center of the circle is looking straight out from the plane of our galaxy – with the clearer view of other galaxies you would expect.

The plane of the Earth's rotation is at a 60° angle to the plane of the galaxy, so the Earth's north pole points 60° away from the galactic north pole.

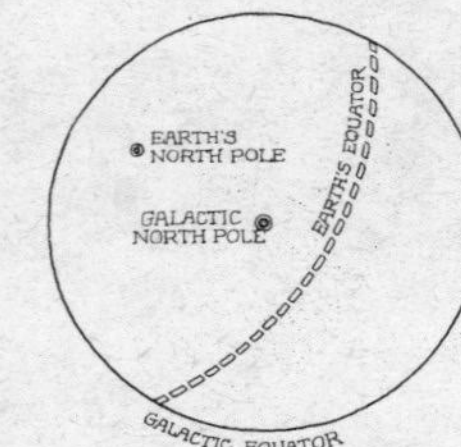

There is an unsurveyed crescent on the lower right of the map because the Earth's horizon limited the view from Lick Observatory, California (38° north latitude), where the survey was made. Study from an observatory closer to the Earth's equator could fill the gap – presumably the results would look like the rest of the map.

Galaxies vary considerably in size and structure. The diagrams at left show an edge-on view of a spiral galaxy like our own. Opposite are photographs of other typical galaxies.

The Lick Observatory-based survey was made by Donald Shane and Carl Wirtanen using a microscope on 1300 sky photographs, each one 17 inches square. It took them twelve years to complete the survey.

This map made from their data is divided into a million squares, each one representing a patch of sky 1/6° x 1/6°. (Horizon over to horizon is 180°.) The grey tone in each square represents the number of galaxies counted in that patch – black for none, dark grey for one, etc., up to white for 10 or more galaxies.

Only when this picture had been made could Shane and Wirtanen stand back and fully appreciate what they had been mapping. The complicated pattern of light and dark areas shows clearly that the galaxies are not smoothly distributed through space – they appear in tight clusters, in curious filaments, and broad clouds across the sky. This is the large-scale texture of the universe.

As galaxies tend to form clusters, the clusters tend to form super clusters, and so on up to an apparent limit of super-super cluster size at about 60,000,000 light years. (No one knows why that is the limit.) The best place to look for a galaxy, Shane and Wirtanen found, is right next to another galaxy.

Though it is more compehensive than anything tried before this map is still crude and local compared to what's possible. Take the 6° x 6° square indicated on the big map – it shows 1800 galaxies here. When Konrad Rucnicki and colleagues at the Jagellonian University in Poland took a deeper survey of that area – counting galaxies four times dimmer than shown here – they found 10,000 galaxies. If they did that for the entire area shown on our map, you might see 6,000,000 galaxies represented.

In that same 6° x 6° area the most powerful telescopes on Earth *could* locate 1,000,000 galaxies. The total number of galaxies visible from Earth in both galactic hemispheres may be over 1,100,000,000 – one billion one hundred million galaxies.

Telescopes in space will show us a great deal more than that. ■

–P. James E. Peebles and Stewart Brand

*A light year equals 5,878,000,000,000 miles.

**The faintest galaxies on the map – 19th magnitude – are 160,000 times dimmer than can be seen with the naked eye.

The map was made by Bernie Siebers, Mike Seldner and Ray Soneira, who were graduate students at Princeton University. They used a film scanner normally used in the graphic arts industry for making color separation negatives and modified by Paul Zucchino and John Lowrance as part of preliminary technical development for the Space Telescope. The diagrams are by Tom Parker, Alpine, New York.

For further reading see "The Clustering of Galaxies" by E.J. Groth, P.J.E. Peebles, M. Seldner and R.M. Soneira, *Scientific American*, Nov. 1977, p. 76; "A New Reduction of the Lick Catalog of Galaxies," by M. Seldner, B. Siebers, E.J. Groth and P.J.E. Peebles, *The Astronomical Journal*, Vol. 82, page 249, 1977; and "Two- and Three-Point Correlation Functions for the High Resolution Shane-Wirtanen Catalog of Galaxies," by E.J. Groth and P.J.E. Peebles, *The Astrophysical Journal*, Vol. 217, page 385, 1977.